Texas Corporation and Partnership Laws

2012 Edition

WITH TABLES AND INDEX

As Amended through the 2011 Regular and First Called Sessions of the 82nd Legislature

WEST®
A Thomson Reuters business

Mat #40952650

ISBN 978–0–314–92272–4

PREFACE

This Pamphlet contains the texts of the Business Organization Code and the Utilities Code. Also included in this pamphlet is Chapter 71 of the Business and Commerce Code, Assumed Business or Professional Name. The text is current through the 2011 Regular and First Called Sessions of the 82nd Legislature.

A detailed descriptive word Index is furnished at the end of this Pamphlet to facilitate the search for specific textual provisions. Tables of Sections Affected indicate sections of the Business Organizations Code and the Utilities Code affected through the 2011 Regular and First Called Sessions of the 82nd Legislature.

Comprehensive coverage of the judicial constructions and interpretations of these statutes, together with cross references, references to law review commentaries discussing particular provisions, and other editorial features, is provided in the volumes of Vernon's Texas Statutes and Codes Annotated.

For additional information or research assistance call the West reference attorneys at 1-800-REF-ATTY (1-800-733-2889). Contact West's editorial department directly with your questions and suggestions by e-mail at west.editor@thomson.com. Visit West's home page at west.thomson.com.

WEST

November, 2011

*

TABLE OF CONTENTS

	Page
Preface	III
Effective Dates	IX
Business Organization Code Disposition Table 1	XI
Business Organization Code Derivation Table 1	XIX
Business Organization Code Disposition Table 2	XXV
Business Organization Code Derivation Table 2	XLIII
Utilities Code Disposition Table	LVIII
Utilities Code Derivation Table	LXXI
Business Organization Code Table of Sections Affected by the 82nd Legislature, Regular and First Called Sessions	LXXXIII
Utilities Code Table of Sections Affected by the 82nd Legislature, Regular and First Called Sessions	LXXXVI

BUSINESS ORGANIZATIONS CODE

(Page 1)

TITLE 1. GENERAL PROVISIONS

Section Analysis, see beginning of each Chapter.

Chapter		
1.	Definitions and Other General Provisions	1
2.	Purposes and Power of Domestic Entity	11
3.	Formation and Governance	16
4.	Filings	27
5.	Names of Entities; Registered Agents and Registered Offices	34
6.	Meetings and Voting For Domestic Entities	44
7.	Liability	50
8.	Indemnification and Insurance	50
9.	Foreign Entities	56
10.	Mergers, Interest Exchanges, Conversions, and Sales of Assets	66
11.	Winding Up and Termination of Domestic Entity	90
12.	Administrative Powers	107

TITLE 2. CORPORATIONS

20.	General Provisions	110
21.	For-profit Corporations	111
22.	Nonprofit Corporations	168
23.	Special-Purpose Corporations	190

TITLE 3. LIMITED LIABILITY COMPANIES

101.	Limited Liability Companies	197

TABLE OF CONTENTS

TITLE 4. PARTNERSHIPS

Chapter		Page
151.	General Provisions	218
152.	General Partnerships	218
153.	Limited Partnerships	239
154.	Provisions Applicable to Both General and Limited Partnerships	257

TITLE 5. REAL ESTATE INVESTMENT TRUSTS

200.	Real Estate Investment Trusts	259

TITLE 6. ASSOCIATIONS

251.	Cooperative Associations	282
252.	Unincorporated Nonprofit Associations	291

TITLE 7. PROFESSIONAL ENTITIES

301.	Provisions Relating to Professional Entities	294
302.	Provisions Relating to Professional Associations	298
303.	Provisions Relating to Professional Corporations	299
304.	Provisions Relating to Professional Limited Liability Companies	300

TITLE 8. MISCELLANEOUS AND TRANSITION PROVISIONS

401.	General Provisions	300
402.	Miscellaneous and Transition Provisions	301

BUSINESS AND COMMERCE CODE

(Page 307)

TITLE 5. REGULATION OF BUSINESSES AND SERVICES

SUBTITLE A. GENERAL PRACTICES

Chapter		
71.	Assumed Business or Professional Name	307

UTILITIES CODE

(Page 313)

TITLE 1. GENERAL PROVISIONS

1.	General Provisions	314

TITLE 2. PUBLIC UTILITY REGULATORY ACT

SUBTITLE A. PROVISIONS APPLICABLE TO ALL UTILITIES

11.	General Provisions	314
12.	Organization of Commission	317
13.	Office of Public Utility Counsel	324
14.	Jurisdiction and Powers of Commission and Other Regulatory Authorities	329

TABLE OF CONTENTS

Chapter		Page
15.	Judicial Review, Enforcement, and Penalties	334
16.	Commission Financing	339
17.	Customer Protection	341

SUBTITLE B. ELECTRIC UTILITIES

31.	General Provisions	348
32.	Jurisdiction and Powers of Commission and Other Regulatory Authorities	352
33.	Jurisdiction and Powers of Municipality	354
34.	Electrical Planning [Repealed]	361
35.	Alternative Energy Providers	362
36.	Rates	368
37.	Certificates of Convenience and Necessity	385
38.	Regulation of Electric Services	391
39.	Restructuring of Electric Utility Industry	395
40.	Competition for Municipally Owned Utilities and River Authorities	463
41.	Electric Cooperatives and Competition	469
43.	Use of Electric Delivery System for Access to Broadband and Other Enhanced Services, Including Communications	475

SUBTITLE C. TELECOMMUNICATIONS UTILITIES

51.	General Provisions	478
52.	Commission Jurisdiction	482
53.	Rates	493
54.	Certificates	504
55.	Regulation of Telecommunications Services	516
56.	Telecommunications Assistance and Universal Service Fund	534
57.	Distance Learning and Other Advanced Services	548
58.	Incentive Regulation	550
59.	Infrastructure Plan	563
60.	Competitive Safeguards	569
61.	Information Technology Services [Repealed]	577
62.	Broadcaster Safeguards	577
63.	Electronic Publishing [Repealed]	578
64.	Customer Protection	579
65.	Deregulation of Certain Incumbent Local Exchange Company Markets	585
66.	State-Issued Cable and Video Franchise	592

TITLE 3. GAS REGULATION

SUBTITLE A. GAS UTILITY REGULATORY ACT

101.	General Provisions and Office of Public Utility Counsel	601
102.	Jurisdiction and Powers of Railroad Commission and Other Regulatory Authorities	604
103.	Jurisdiction and Powers of Municipality	609
104.	Rates and Services	611

TABLE OF CONTENTS

Chapter		Page
105.	Judicial Review; Enforcement and Penalties	622

SUBTITLE B. REGULATION OF TRANSPORTATION AND USE

121.	Gas Pipelines	623
122.	Gas Utility Pipeline Tax	637
123.	Use of Natural Gas for Agricultural Purposes	639
124.	Submetering to Mobile Home Parks and Apartment Houses	640

TITLE 4. DELIVERY OF UTILITY SERVICES

SUBTITLE A. UTILITY CORPORATIONS AND OTHER PROVIDERS

161.	Electric Cooperative Corporations	641
162.	Telephone Cooperative Corporations	649
163.	Joint Powers Agencies	661
164.	Joint Ownership of Electric Facilities by Public Entities	667

SUBTITLE B. PROVISIONS REGULATING DELIVERY OF SERVICES

181.	Miscellaneous Powers and Duties of Utilities	668
182.	Rights of Utility Customers	676
183.	Utility Deposits	678
184.	Electric and Water Metering	679
185.	Rating of Solar Energy Devices	683
186.	Provisions to Ensure the Reliability and Integrity of Utility Service	683

TITLE 5. PROVISIONS AFFECTING THE OPERATION OF UTILITY FACILITIES

251.	Underground Facility Damage Prevention and Safety	690

CONSOLIDATED INDEX

(Page I–1)

EFFECTIVE DATES

The following table shows the date of adjournment and the effective date of ninety day bills enacted at sessions of the legislature beginning with the year 1945:

Year	Leg.	Session	Adjournment Date	Effective Date
1945	49	Regular	June 5, 1945	September 4, 1945
1947	50	Regular	June 6, 1947	September 5, 1947
1949	51	Regular	June 6, 1949	September 5, 1949
1951	52	Regular	June 8, 1951	September 7, 1951
1953	53	Regular	May 27, 1953	August 26, 1953
1954	53	1st C.S.	May 13, 1954	August 12, 1954
1955	54	Regular	June 7, 1955	September 6, 1955
1957	55	Regular	May 23, 1957	August 22, 1957
1957	55	1st C.S.	November 12, 1957	February 11, 1958
1957	55	2nd C.S.	December 3, 1957	March 4, 1958
1959	56	Regular	May 12, 1959	August 11, 1959
1959	56	1st C.S.	June 16, 1959	September 15, 1959
1959	56	2nd C.S.	July 16, 1959	October 15, 1959
1959	56	3rd C.S.	August 6, 1959	November 5, 1959
1961	57	Regular	May 29, 1961	August 28, 1961
1961	57	1st C.S.	August 8, 1961	November 7, 1961
1961	57	2nd C.S.	August 14, 1961	November 13, 1961
1962	57	3rd C.S.	February 1, 1962	May 3, 1962
1963	58	Regular	May 24, 1963	August 23, 1963
1965	59	Regular	May 31, 1965	August 30, 1965
1966	59	1st C.S.	February 23, 1966	*
1967	60	Regular	May 29, 1967	August 28, 1967
1968	60	1st C.S.	July 3, 1968	*
1969	61	Regular	June 2, 1969	September 1, 1969
1969	61	1st C.S.	August 26, 1969	*
1969	61	2nd C.S.	September 9, 1969	December 9, 1969
1971	62	Regular	May 31, 1971	August 30, 1971
1971	62	1st C.S.	June 4, 1971	September 3, 1971
1972	62	2nd C.S.	March 30, 1972	June 29, 1972
1972	62	3rd C.S.	July 7, 1972	*
1972	62	4th C.S.	October 17, 1972	January 16, 1973
1973	63	Regular	May 28, 1973	August 27, 1973
1973	63	1st C.S.	December 20, 1973	*
1975	64	Regular	June 2, 1975	September 1, 1975
1977	65	Regular	May 30, 1977	August 29, 1977
1977	65	1st C.S.	July 21, 1977	*
1978	65	2nd C.S.	August 8, 1978	November 7, 1978
1979	66	Regular	May 28, 1979	August 27, 1979
1981	67	Regular	June 1, 1981	August 31, 1981

EFFECTIVE DATES

Year	Leg.	Session	Adjournment Date	Effective Date
1981	67	1st C.S.	August 11, 1981	November 10, 1981
1982	67	2nd C.S.	May 28, 1982	*
1982	67	3rd C.S.	September 9, 1982	*
1983	68	Regular	May 30, 1983	August 29, 1983
1983	68	1st C.S.	June 25, 1983	September 23, 1983
1984	68	2nd C.S.	July 3, 1984	October 2, 1984
1985	69	Regular	May 27, 1985	August 26, 1985
1985	69	1st C.S.	May 30, 1985	August 29, 1985
1986	69	2nd C.S.	September 4, 1986	December 4, 1986
1986	69	3rd C.S.	September 30, 1986	December 30, 1986
1987	70	Regular	June 1, 1987	August 31, 1987
1987	70	1st C.S.	June 3, 1987	September 2, 1987
1987	70	2nd C.S.	July 21, 1987	October 20, 1987
1989	71	Regular	May 29, 1989	August 28, 1989
1989	71	1st C.S.	July 19, 1989	October 18, 1989
1989	71	2nd C.S.	December 12, 1989	*
1990	71	3rd C.S.	March 28, 1990	*
1990	71	4th C.S.	May 1, 1990	*
1990	71	5th C.S.	May 30, 1990	*
1990	71	6th C.S.	June 7, 1990	September 6, 1990
1991	72	Regular	May 27, 1991	August 26, 1991
1991	72	1st C.S.	August 13, 1991	November 12, 1991
1991	72	2nd C.S.	August 25, 1991	November 24, 1991
1992	72	3rd C.S.	January 8, 1992	April 8, 1992
1992	72	4th C.S.	December 3, 1992	*
1993	73	Regular	May 31, 1993	August 30, 1993
1995	74	Regular	May 29, 1995	August 28, 1995
1997	75	Regular	June 2, 1997	September 1, 1997
1999	76	Regular	May 31, 1999	August 30, 1999
2001	77	Regular	May 28, 2001	September 1, 2001
2003	78	Regular	June 2, 2003	September 1, 2003
2003	78	1st C.S.	July 28, 2003	*
2003	78	2nd C.S.	August 26, 2003	*
2003	78	3rd C.S.	October 12, 2003	January 10, 2004
2004	78	4th C.S.	May 17, 2004	*
2005	79	Regular	May 30, 2005	August 29, 2005
2005	79	1st C.S.	July 20, 2005	October 19, 2005
2005	79	2nd C.S.	August 19, 2005	November 18, 2005
2006	79	3rd C.S.	May 16, 2006	August 15, 2006
2007	80	Regular	May 28, 2007	August 27, 2007
2009	81	Regular	June 1, 2009	August 31, 2009
2009	81	1st C.S.	July 2, 2009	*
2011	82	Regular	May 30, 2011	August 29, 2011
2011	82	1st C.S.	June 29, 2011	September 28, 2011

* No legislation for which the ninety day effective date is applicable.

DISPOSITION TABLE 1

Showing where the subject matter of articles and sections in the Business Corporation Act of 1955 are covered in the Business Organizations Code as originally enacted.

V.A.T.S., Bus.Corp. Act Article	Business Org. Code Section
1.01, § A	1.008
1.02, § A(2)	1.002(2)(D)
(3)	21.002
(4)	21.002
(5)	1.002(7)
(6)	1.005
(7)	21.002
(8)	1.002(10)(C)
(9)	1.002(11)
(10)	1.002(12)
(11)	1.002(14)
	1.002(17)
	1.002(18)
	1.101
	21.002
(12)	1.003
(13)	21.002
(14)	1.002(27)
	1.002(28)
	21.002
(15)	1.004
(16)	1.002(39)
(17)	21.002
(18)	1.002(55)(B)(iii)
(19)	21.002
(20)	1.002(56)
(21)	21.002
(22)	1.002(81)
(23)	1.002(80)
(24)	21.002
(25)	1.002(83)
(26)	1.002(84)
(27)	21.002
(28)	21.002
	21.171
(29)	1.002(87)(B)
§ C	1.052
2.01, § A	2.001
	2.008
§ B	2.003
	2.007
	2.105
§ C	2.006
2.02, § A	2.101
	3.003
§ B	2.113
§ C	2.113
2.02–1, § A	8.001
§ B	8.101
§ C	8.102
§ D	8.101
	8.102
§ E	8.102
§ F	8.103
§ G	8.101
	8.103
§ H	8.051
§ I	8.051
§ J	8.052
§ K	8.104
§ L	8.104
§ M	8.003
	8.004
§ N	8.106
§ O	8.105
§ P	8.001
	8.101
	8.102
	8.104
	8.105
§ Q	8.105
§ R	8.001
	8.151
§ S	8.152
§ T	8.001
	8.101
§ U	8.003
2.04	20.002
2.05, § A(1)	5.054
(2)	5.052
(3)	5.053
	5.102
(4)	5.061
§ B	5.051
§ C	5.001
2.06, § A	5.101
§ B	4.001
	4.002
	5.101
	5.102
	5.103
	5.104
§ C	4.001
	5.106
§ D	4.001
	5.104
2.07, § A	5.151
	5.153
§ B	4.001
	5.152
§ C	5.154
2.08	5.155
2.09	5.201
2.10, § A	5.202

V.A.T.S., Bus.Corp. Act Article	Business Org. Code Section
§ B	4.001
	4.002
	20.001
§ C	4.051
	5.202
§ D	4.002
	5.204
2.10–1, § A	5.203
§ B	4.001
	4.002
§ C	4.051
	5.203
2.11, § A	5.201
	5.255
§ B	5.251
	5.252
	5.253
§ C	5.254
§ D	5.257
2.12, § A	21.151
	21.152
	21.153
§ B	21.154
§ C(1)	21.651
	21.652
(2)	4.001
	21.653
(3)	4.001
	4.002
	20.001
(4)	4.051
	21.653
2.13, § A to C	21.155
§ D	4.001
	21.156
§ E	4.001
	4.002
	20.001
§ F	4.051
	21.156
2.14	21.165
§ D	21.166
2.14–1	21.168
	21.170
2.15, § A	21.160
	21.161
§ B	21.160
§ C	21.160
§ D to F	21.161
2.16, § A	21.157
	21.158
	21.159
§ B	21.162
2.18	21.172
2.19, § A	3.201
	3.202
	3.203
	3.204
§ B, C	3.202
§ D	3.205
§ G	3.202
2.20	21.163
	21.164
2.21, § A	21.223
§ B	21.224

V.A.T.S., Bus.Corp. Act Article	Business Org. Code Section
	21.225
§ C	21.217
§ D	21.226
§ E	21.226
2.22, § A	21.209
	21.801
§ B	21.210
§ C	21.213
§ D	21.211
§ E	21.212
(2)	4.001
	4.002
	20.001
§ F	4.051
	21.212
§ G	21.214
	21.216
2.22–1, § A	21.202
	21.204
§ B	21.204
§ C	21.206
§ D	21.207
2.23, § A	21.057
§ B	21.057
§ C	21.058
2.24, § A	6.001
§ B	21.351
§ C	21.352
§ D	21.655
2.25, § A	6.051
	21.353
§ B	6.053
2.26, § A	21.201
§ A(2)	21.215
§ B	6.101
	21.355
	21.357
§ C	6.102
	21.356
§ D	6.103
2.27, § A	21.354
	21.372
§ B	21.372
§ C	21.220
	21.221
2.28, § A	21.358
§ B	21.363
§ C	21.359
§ D	21.365
§ E	21.371
2.29, § A	21.366
§ B	6.152
§ C	21.367
	21.368
	21.369
	21.370
§ D	21.361
§ E	6.153
	9.204
§ F	6.154
§ G	6.155
§ H	6.156
2.30, § A	6.251
§ B	6.252
2.30–1, § A	21.101

V.A.T.S., Bus.Corp. Act Article	Business Org. Code Section
	21.104
§ B	21.101
	21.102
§ C	21.103
§ D	21.105
§ E	21.109
§ F	21.106
§ G	21.107
§ H	21.108
2.31	3.101
	21.401
	21.402
2.32, § A	21.403
	21.404
	21.405
	21.407
§ B	21.405
	21.406
	21.407
	21.408
§ C	21.409
§ D	21.654
2.33	21.408
2.34	21.410
2.35	21.413
	21.415
2.35–1	21.418
2.36	21.416
2.37, § A	6.001
§ B	6.051
	6.052
	21.411
	21.412
2.38, § A	21.302
	21.303
§ B	21.303
§ C	21.301
§ D	21.303
§ E	21.308
2.38–1, § A	21.310
§ B	21.311
§ C	21.312
	21.313
§ D	21.312
	21.313
§ E	21.311
2.38–2	21.002
2.38–3	21.314
2.38–4	21.315
2.41, § A(1)	21.316
§ A(3)	21.317
§ B	21.414
§ C	21.316
§ D	3.102
§ E	21.318
§ F	21.318
§ G	21.316
	21.318
2.42, § A	3.103
	21.417
§ B	3.103
§ C	3.105
2.43	3.104
2.44, § A	3.151
	21.173

V.A.T.S., Bus.Corp. Act Article	Business Org. Code Section
§ B	3.152
§ C	3.153
	21.218
§ D	21.222
§ E	21.218
§ F	21.219
§ G	21.218
3.01	3.004
	4.001
3.02, § A	3.005
	3.007
	3.008
§ B	2.112
3.03, § A	3.001
	4.001
	4.002
§ B	4.002
§ C	3.006
	4.001
	4.002
	4.051
3.04	3.001
§ A	4.051
§ B	3.006
	4.051
3.06	21.059
4.01, § A	3.051
	4.106
§ B	21.051
4.02, § A	21.052
	21.054
	21.055
	21.364
(1)	21.053
§ B	21.055
4.03	21.364
4.04, § A	3.054
§ B	3.053
	3.054
4.05	3.052
	4.002
§ A	4.001
4.06	3.056
§ A	4.051
4.07, § A	3.057
	3.058
	3.059
	4.106
	21.056
§ B	3.059
	3.060
§ C	3.059
	3.060
§ D	3.058
	4.001
	4.002
	21.056
§ E	4.002
§ F	3.063
	4.051
4.08, § A	21.304
	21.305
§ B	21.305
	21.306
	21.307

V.A.T.S., Bus.Corp. Act Article	Business Org. Code Section
4.10, § A	21.251
§ B	4.001
	20.001
§ C	4.001
	4.002
§ D	4.051
	21.251
4.11	21.252
§ B	4.001
	20.001
§ C	4.001
	4.002
§ D	4.051
4.12, § A	21.253
§ B	4.001
	20.001
§ C	4.001
	4.002
§ D	4.051
	21.253
§ E	21.254
4.13	21.309
4.14, § A	4.106
	10.301
§ B	4.001
	10.302
§ C	4.001
	10.303
(7)	4.051
§ D	10.304
§ E	10.305
§ F	10.306
5.01, § A	10.001
	21.457
§ B	10.002
	10.003
§ C	10.004
§ D	10.008
§ E	10.902
5.02, § A	10.051
	21.454
§ B	10.052
§ C	10.053
§ D	10.051
§ E	10.902
5.03, § A	10.001
	10.051
	21.452
§ B	21.452
	21.453
	21.454
§ C	21.452
	21.453
	21.454
§ D	10.355
	21.456
§ E	21.457
§ F	21.458
§ G	21.459
§ H	10.005
§ I	10.005
(3)	21.451
(4)	1.002(69)
(5)	21.451
(6)	21.451

V.A.T.S., Bus.Corp. Act Article	Business Org. Code Section
§ J	10.005
§ K	10.005
§ L	4.001
	4.002
	4.051
	10.201
	10.202
5.04, § A	4.001
	10.151
§ B	4.001
	10.153
§ C	4.002
	10.156
5.05	4.051
	10.007
	10.054
5.06, § A	10.008
§ B	10.055
§ C	10.008
5.08	10.251
	10.252
	10.253
5.09, § A	10.251
	10.252
	21.451
	21.455
	21.461
	21.462
§ B	21.451
5.10, § A	21.455
(3)	21.456
(4)	21.457
	21.458
§ B	10.254
5.11	10.354
§ A	21.460
5.12, § A	10.355
	10.356
	10.358
(1)	10.362
§ B	10.361
§ C	10.361
	10.363
§ D	10.363
	10.364
	10.365
§ E	10.366
§ G	10.356
	10.368
5.13, § A	10.366
§ B	10.356
	10.359
	10.360
§ C	10.357
	10.367
5.14, § A	21.551
	101.451
§ B	21.552
	101.452
§ C	21.553
	101.453
§ D(1)	21.555
	101.455
(2)	21.556
	101.456

V.A.T.S., Bus.Corp. Act Article	Business Org. Code Section
§ E	21.557
	101.457
§ F	21.558
	101.458
§ G	21.559
	101.459
§ H	21.554
	101.454
§ I	21.560
	101.460
§ J	21.561
	101.461
§ K	21.562
	101.462
§ L	21.563
	101.463
5.15	10.901
5.16, § A	10.006
§ B	4.001
	10.006
	10.008
	10.152
§ C	4.001
	10.006
	10.153
§ D	4.051
	10.006
	10.007
§ E	10.006
	10.354
	10.355
	10.356
	10.358
	10.361
	10.368
§ F	10.006
5.17, § A	10.101
	21.453
§ B	10.102
§ C	10.103
§ D	10.104
§ E	4.001
	4.002
	10.201
	10.202
5.18, § A	4.001
	10.154
§ B	4.001
	10.155
§ C	4.002
	10.156
5.19	4.051
	10.105
5.20, § A	10.106
	10.354
6.01	4.001
	4.002
	11.051
	21.501
	21.502
§ A(3)	4.051
	11.102
6.02	4.001
§ A	11.051
	21.502

V.A.T.S., Bus.Corp. Act Article	Business Org. Code Section
6.03,§ A	11.051
	21.364
	21.501
	21.502
	21.503
6.04	11.052
	11.053
	11.054
6.05, § A	11.151
	11.201
	21.364
	21.501
	21.502
	21.503
§ B	4.001
	11.202
§ C	4.002
	11.203
§ D	4.051
	11.151
	11.205
	11.206
6.06	11.101
6.07	11.101
§ A	4.001
	4.002
§ B	4.002
	4.051
	11.102
7.01, § A	11.051
	11.301
§ B	11.051
	11.251
§ C(1)	11.251
§ C(2)	11.252
§ D	4.051
	11.252
§ E	4.001
	4.002
	4.051
	11.253
§ F	11.051
	11.301
§ G	11.301
7.02, § A	9.152
	11.302
§ B	9.152
	11.302
§ C	9.153
	11.303
§ D	9.154
	11.304
§ E	9.155
	9.156
	11.305
	11.306
§ F	9.157
	11.307
7.03	9.158
	9.159
	9.160
	11.308
	11.309
	11.310
7.04	11.403

V.A.T.S., Bus.Corp. Act Article	Business Org. Code Section
§ A	11.402
7.05	11.404
§ A	11.402
7.06	11.405
§ A	11.402
7.07, § A	11.401
	11.406
§ B	11.406
§ C	11.407
§ D	11.408
§ E	11.408
§ F	11.409
	11.410
7.08	11.411
7.09	11.051
	11.313
	11.412
7.10	11.315
7.11, § A	11.352
	11.353
§ B	11.354
	11.355
7.12, § A	11.055
	11.356
§ B	11.357
§ C	11.351
	11.356
	11.359
§ D	11.358
	11.359
§ E	4.001
	11.051
	11.152
	11.311
§ F	11.001
(1)	11.254
8.01, § A	9.001
	9.004
	9.201
§ B	9.251
	9.252
8.02	1.002(43)(C)(ii)
	1.102
	1.104
	1.105
	9.055
	9.202
	9.203
8.03 § A(1)	5.054
(2)	5.051
	5.053
8.04	9.010
8.05, § A	9.004
	9.005
8.06, § A	4.001
	4.002
	9.004
§ B	4.002
8.07	4.051
	9.008
8.08	5.201
8.09, § A	4.001
	5.202
§ B	4.001
	4.002
§ C	4.051
	5.202
§ D	4.001
	4.002
	5.204
(2)	4.051
8.10, § A	5.201
	5.255
§ B	5.251
	5.252
	5.253
§ C	5.254
§ D	5.256
§ E	5.257
8.13, § A	4.001
	4.106
	9.009
§ B	4.001
	4.106
	9.009
§ D	4.001
	4.051
	4.106
	9.009
8.14	9.011
§ A	4.001
§ B	4.001
§ C	4.001
8.15	9.011
§ A	4.001
	4.002
§ B	4.051
8.16, § A	9.151
§ B	9.101
§ C(1)	9.101
§ D	4.002
	9.102
§ E	4.001
	4.002
	4.051
	9.103
	9.104
	9.105
§ F	9.151
§ G	9.151
8.17	9.161
8.18, § A	9.051
§ B	9.051
§ C	9.052
	9.054
9.01	12.002
9.02	12.003
9.03	12.001
9.04, § A	12.004
9.05	4.005
9.06	4.006
9.07, § A	4.004
§ B to F	21.802
9.09	6.052
9.10, § A(1)	6.201
	6.202
(2)	6.202
	6.203
(3)	1.007
(4)	6.202

V.A.T.S., Bus.Corp. Act Article	Business Org. Code Section
§ B	6.201
	21.415
	21.416
§ C	6.002
	6.003
§ D	6.204
9.11	1.053
9.12	1.054
9.14, § A	9.301
	23.001
§ C(4)	4.051
10.01, § A	4.151
	4.152
§ B	4.001
	4.002
10.02	4.008
10.03, § A	4.001
	4.052
	4.053
	4.055
	4.058
§ B	4.001
	4.002
§ C	4.059
§ D	4.054
	4.059
§ E	4.056
12.02, § A	21.701
(1)	1.002(8)
12.03	21.702
12.11	3.008
12.12	21.703
12.13, § A	4.106
	21.705
§ B	21.706
12.14	21.707
12.15	21.704
12.21	21.708
§ A	4.106
12.22, § A	21.709
§ B	4.001
	21.709
§ C	4.002
§ D	4.051
	21.709
§ E	21.709
12.23, § A to C	21.710
§ D	21.711
§ E	21.712
12.31	21.713
12.32	21.714

V.A.T.S., Bus.Corp. Act Article	Business Org. Code Section
12.33, § A	21.715
§ B	21.716
§ C	21.717
12.34, § A	21.718
§ B	4.001
	21.718
§ C	4.002
§ D	4.051
	21.718
12.35	21.719
12.36, § A	21.720
§ B	21.721
§ C	21.722
§ D	21.723
§ E	21.724
12.37, § A	21.725
§ B	21.726
§ C	21.727
§ D	21.728
§ E	21.729
§ F	21.730
12.38	21.731
12.39	21.732
12.51, § A	21.751
§ B	21.752
§ C	21.753
§ D	21.754
§ E	21.755
12.52, § A	21.756
§ B	21.757
12.53, § A	21.758
§ B	21.758
	21.759
	21.760
12.54, § A	21.761
§ B	21.761
	21.762
	21.763
13.02, § A(1)	1.002(1)
(2)	21.602
(3)	21.603
(4)	21.604
(5)	21.605
(6) to (10)	21.601
13.03	21.606
13.04	21.607
§ A	4.106
13.05	21.608
13.06	21.401
13.07, § A	21.609
§ B	21.610

DERIVATION TABLE 1

Showing where sections of the Business Organizations Code, as originally enacted, were covered in the Business Corporation Act of 1955.

Business Org. Code Section	V.A.T.S., Bus.Corp. Act Article
1.002(1)	13.02, § A(1)
1.002(2)(D)	1.02, § A(2)
1.002(7)	1.02, § A(5)
1.002(8)	12.02, § A(1)
1.002(10)(C)	1.02, § A(8)
1.002(11)	1.02, § A(9)
1.002(12)	1.02, § A(10)
1.002(14)	1.02, § A(11)
1.002(17)	1.02, § A(11)
1.002(18)	1.02, § A(11)
1.002(27)	1.02, § A(14)
1.002(28)	1.02, § A(14)
1.002(39)	1.02, § A(16)
1.002(43)(C)(ii)	8.02
1.002(55)(B)(iii)	1.02, § A(18)
1.002(56)	1.02, § A(20)
1.002(69)	5.03, § I(4)
1.002(80)	1.02, § A(23)
1.002(81)	1.02, § A(22)
1.002(83)	1.02, § A(25)
1.002(84)	1.02, § A(26)
1.002(87)(B)	1.02, § A(29)
1.003	1.02, § A(12)
1.004	1.02, § A(15)
1.005	1.02, § A(6)
1.007	9.10, § A(3)
1.008	1.01, § A
1.052	1.02, § C
1.053	9.11
1.054	9.12
1.101	1.02, § A(11)
1.102	8.02
1.104	8.02
1.105	8.02
2.001	2.01, § A
2.003	2.01, § B
2.006	2.01, § C
2.007	2.01, § B
2.008	2.01, § A
2.101	2.02, § A
2.105	2.01, § B
2.112	3.02, § B
2.113	2.02, § B, C
3.001	3.03, § A
	3.04
3.003	2.02, § A
3.004	3.01
3.005	3.02, § A
3.006	3.03, § C
	3.04, § B
3.007	3.02, § A
3.008	3.02, § A
	12.11
3.051	4.01, § A
3.052	4.05
3.053	4.04, § B
3.054	4.04, § A, B
3.056	4.06
3.057	4.07, § A
3.058	4.07, § A, D
3.059	4.07, § A to C
3.060	4.07, § B, C
3.063	4.07, § F
3.101	2.31
3.102	2.41, § D
3.103	2.42, § A, B
3.104	2.43
3.105	2.42, § C
3.151	2.44, § A
3.152	2.44, § B
3.153	2.44, § C
3.201	2.19, § A
3.202	2.19, § A to C, G
3.203	2.19, § A
3.204	2.19, § A
3.205	2.19, § D
4.001	2.06, § B to D
	2.07, § B
	2.10, § B
	2.10–1, § B
	2.12, § C(2), (3)
	2.13, § D, E
	2.22, § E(2)
	3.01
	3.03, § A, C
	4.05, § A
	4.07, § D
	4.10, § B, C
	4.11, § B, C
	4.12, § B, C
	4.14, § B, C
	5.03, § L
	5.04, § A, B
	5.16, § B, C
	5.17, § E
	5.18, § A, B
	6.01
	6.02
	6.05, § B
	6.07, § A
	7.01, § E
	7.12, § E
	8.06, § A
	8.09, § A, B, D

DERIVATION TABLE 1

Business Org. Code Section	V.A.T.S., Bus.Corp. Act Article
	8.13, § A, B, D
	8.14, § A to C
	8.15, § A
	8.16, § E
	10.01, § B
	10.03, § A, B
	12.22, § B
	12.34, § B
4.002	2.06, § B
	2.10, § B, D
	2.10–1, § B
	2.12, § C(3)
	2.13, § E
	2.22, § E(2)
	3.03, § A to C
	4.05
	4.07, § D, E
	4.10, § C
	4.11, § C
	4.12, § C
	5.03, § L
	5.04, § C
	5.17, § E
	5.18, § C
	6.01
	6.05, § C
	6.07, § A, B
	7.01, § E
	8.06, § A, B
	8.09, § B, D
	8.15, § A
	8.16, § D, E
	10.01, § B
	10.03, § B
	12.22, § C
	12.34, § C
4.004	9.07, § A
4.005	9.05
4.006	9.06
4.008	10.02
4.051	2.10, § C
	2.10–1, § C
	2.12, § C(4)
	2.13, § F
	2.22, § F
	3.03, § C
	3.04, § A, B
	4.06, § A
	4.07, § F
	4.10, § D
	4.11, § D
	4.12, § D
	4.14, § C(7)
	5.03, § L
	5.05
	5.16, § D
	5.19
	6.01, § A(3)
	6.05, § D
	6.07, § B
	7.01, § D, E
	8.07
	8.09, § C, D(2)
	8.13, § D
	8.15, § B

Business Org. Code Section	V.A.T.S., Bus.Corp. Act Article
	8.16, § E
	9.14, § C(4)
	12.22, § D
	12.34, § D
4.052	10.03, § A
4.053	10.03, § A
4.054	10.03, § D
4.055	10.03, § A
4.056	10.03, § E
4.058	10.03, § A
4.059	10.03, § C, D
4.106	4.01, § A
	4.07, § A
	4.14, § A
	8.13, § A, B, D
	12.13, § A
	12.21, § A
	13.04, § A
4.151	10.01, § A
4.152	10.01, § A
5.001	2.05, § C
5.051	2.05, § B
	8.03, § A(2)
5.052	2.05, § A(2)
5.053	2.05, § A(3)
	8.03, § A(2)
5.054	2.05, § A(1)
	8.03, § A(1)
5.061	2.05, § A(4)
5.101	2.06, § A, B
5.102	2.05, § A(3)
	2.06, § B
5.103	2.06, § B
5.104	2.06, § B, D
5.106	2.06, § C
5.151	2.07, § A
5.152	2.07, § B
5.153	2.07, § A
5.154	2.07, § C
5.155	2.08
5.201	2.09
	2.11, § A
	8.08
	8.10, § A
5.202	2.10, § A, C
	8.09, § A, C
5.203	2.10–1, § A, C
5.204	2.10, § D
	8.09, § D
5.251	2.11, § B
	8.10, § B
5.252	2.11, § B
	8.10, § B
5.253	2.11, § B
	8.10, § B
5.254	2.11, § C
	8.10, § C
5.255	2.11, § A
	8.10, § A
5.256	8.10, § D
5.257	2.11, § D
	8.10, § E
6.001	2.24, § A
	2.37, § A
6.002	9.10, § C

DERIVATION TABLE 1

Business Org. Code Section	V.A.T.S., Bus.Corp. Act Article
6.003	9.10, § C
6.051	2.25, § A
	2.37, § B
6.052	2.37, § B
	9.09
6.053	2.25, § B
6.101	2.26, § B
6.102	2.26, § C
6.103	2.26, § D
6.152	2.29, § B
6.153	2.29, § E
6.154	2.29, § F
6.155	2.29, § G
6.156	2.29, § H
6.201	9.10, § A(1), B
6.202	9.10, § A(1), (2), (4)
6.203	9.10, § A(2)
6.204	9.10, § D
6.251	2.30, § A
6.252	2.30, § B
8.001	2.02–1, § A, P, R, T
8.003	2.02–1, § M, U
8.004	2.02–1, § M
8.051	2.02–1, § H, I
8.052	2.02–1, § J
8.101	2.02–1, § B, D, G, P, T
8.102	2.02–1, § C, D, E, P
8.103	2.02–1, § F, G
8.104	2.02–1, § K, L, P
8.105	2.02–1, § O, P, Q
8.106	2.02–1, § N
8.151	2.02–1, § R
8.152	2.02–1, § S
9.001	8.01, § A
9.004	8.01, § A
	8.05, § A
	8.06, § A
9.005	8.05, § A
9.008	8.07
9.009	8.13, § A, B, D
9.010	8.04
9.011	8.14
	8.15
9.051	8.18, § A, B
9.052	8.18, § C
9.054	8.18, § C
9.055	8.02
9.101	8.16, § B, C(1)
9.102	8.16, § D
9.103	8.16, § E
9.104	8.16, § E
9.105	8.16, § E
9.151	8.16, § A, F, G
9.152	7.02, § A, B
9.153	7.02, § C
9.154	7.02, § D
9.155	7.02, § E
9.156	7.02, § E
9.157	7.02, § F
9.158	7.03
9.159	7.03
9.160	7.03
9.161	8.17
9.201	8.01, § A
9.202	8.02
9.203	8.02
9.204	2.29, § E
9.251	8.01, § B
9.252	8.01, § B
9.301	9.14, § A
10.001	5.01, § A
	5.03, § A
10.002	5.01, § B
10.003	5.01, § B
10.004	5.01, § C
10.005	5.03, § H to K
10.006	5.16, § A to F
10.007	5.05
	5.16, § D
10.008	5.01, § D
	5.06, § A, C
	5.16, § B
10.051	5.02, § A, D
	5.03, § A
10.052	5.02, § B
10.053	5.02, § C
10.054	5.05
10.055	5.06, § B
10.101	5.17, § A
10.102	5.17, § B
10.103	5.17, § C
10.104	5.17, § D
10.105	5.19
10.106	5.20, § A
10.151	5.04, § A
10.152	5.16, § B
10.153	5.04, § B
	5.16, § C
10.154	5.18, § A
10.155	5.18, § B
10.156	5.04, § C
	5.18, § C
10.201	5.03, § L
	5.17, § E
10.202	5.03, § L
	5.17, § E
10.251	5.08
	5.09, § A
10.252	5.08
	5.09, § A
10.253	5.08
10.254	5.10, § B
10.301	4.14, § A
10.302	4.14, § B
10.303	4.14, § C
10.304	4.14, § D
10.305	4.14, § E
10.306	4.14, § F
10.354	5.11
	5.16, § E
	5.20, § A
10.355	5.03, § D
	5.12, § A
	5.16, § E
10.356	5.12, § A, G
	5.13, § B
	5.16, § E
10.357	5.13, § C
10.358	5.12, § A
	5.16, § E

DERIVATION TABLE 1

Business Org. Code Section	V.A.T.S., Bus.Corp. Act Article
10.359	5.13, § B
10.360	5.13, § B
10.361	5.12, § B, C
	5.16, § E
10.362	5.12, § A(1)
10.363	5.12, § C, D
10.364	5.12, § D
10.365	5.12, § D
10.366	5.12, § E
	5.13, § A
10.367	5.13, § C
10.368	5.12, § G
	5.16, § E
10.901	5.15
10.902	5.01, § E
	5.02, § E
11.001	7.12, § F
11.051	6.01
	6.02, § A
	6.03, § A
	7.01, § A, B, F
	7.09
	7.12, § E
11.052	6.04
11.053	6.04
11.054	6.04
11.055	7.12, § A
11.101	6.06
	6.07
11.102	6.01, § A(3)
	6.07, § B
11.151	6.05, § A, D
11.152	7.12, § E
11.201	6.05, § A
11.202	6.05, § B
11.203	6.05, § C
11.205	6.05, § D
11.206	6.05, § D
11.251	7.01, § B, C(1)
11.252	7.01, § C(2), D
11.253	7.01, § E
11.254	7.12, § F(1)
11.301	7.01, § A, F, G
11.302	7.02, § A, B
11.303	7.02, § C
11.304	7.02, § D
11.305	7.02, § E
11.306	7.02, § E
11.307	7.02, § F
11.308	7.03
11.309	7.03
11.310	7.03
11.311	7.12, § E
11.313	7.09
11.315	7.10
11.351	7.12, § C
11.352	7.11, § A
11.353	7.11, § A
11.354	7.11, § B
11.355	7.11, § B
11.356	7.12, § A, C
11.357	7.12, § B
11.358	7.12, § D
11.359	7.12, § C, D
11.401	7.07, § A

Business Org. Code Section	V.A.T.S., Bus.Corp. Act Article
11.402	7.04, § A
	7.05, § A
	7.06, § A
11.403	7.04
11.404	7.05
11.405	7.06
11.406	7.07, § A, B
11.407	7.07, § C
11.408	7.07, § D, E
11.409	7.07, § F
11.410	7.07, § F
11.411	7.08
11.412	7.09
12.001	9.03
12.002	9.01
12.003	9.02
12.004	9.04, § A
20.001	2.10, § B
	2.12, § C(3)
	2.13, § E
	2.22, § E(2)
	4.10, § B
	4.11, § B
	4.12, § B
20.002	2.04
21.002	1.02, § A(3), (4), (7), (11), (13), (14), (17), (19), (21), (24), (27), (28)
	2.38–2
21.051	4.01, § B
21.052	4.02, § A
21.053	4.02, § A(1)
21.054	4.02, § A
21.055	4.02, § A, B
21.056	4.07, § A, D
21.057	2.23, § A, B
21.058	2.23, § C
21.059	3.06
21.101	2.30–1, § A, B
21.102	2.30–1, § B
21.103	2.30–1, § C
21.104	2.30–1, § A
21.105	2.30–1, § D
21.106	2.30–1, § F
21.107	2.30–1, § G
21.108	2.30–1, § H
21.109	2.30–1, § E
21.151	2.12, § A
21.152	2.12, § A
21.153	2.12, § A
21.154	2.12, § B
21.155	2.13, § A to C
21.156	2.13, § D, F
21.157	2.16, § A
21.158	2.16, § A
21.159	2.16, § A
21.160	2.15, § A to C
21.161	2.15, § A, D to F
21.162	2.16, § B
21.163	2.20
21.164	2.20
21.165	2.14
21.166	2.14, § D
21.168	2.14–1
21.170	2.14–1
21.171	1.02, § A(28)

DERIVATION TABLE 1

Business Org. Code Section	V.A.T.S., Bus.Corp. Act Article
21.172	2.18
21.173	2.44, § A
21.201	2.26, § A
21.202	2.22–1, § A
21.204	2.22–1, § A, B
21.206	2.22–1, § C
21.207	2.22–1, § D
21.209	2.22, § A
21.210	2.22, § B
21.211	2.22, § D
21.212	2.22, § E, F
21.213	2.22, § C
21.214	2.22, § G
21.215	2.26, § A(2)
21.216	2.22, § G
21.217	2.21, § C
21.218	2.44, § C, E, G
21.219	2.44, § F
21.220	2.27, § C
21.221	2.27, § C
21.222	2.44, § D
21.223	2.21, § A
21.224	2.21, § B
21.225	2.21, § B
21.226	2.21, § D, E
21.251	4.10, § A, D
21.252	4.11
21.253	4.12, § A, D
21.254	4.12, § E
21.301	2.38, § C
21.302	2.38, § A
21.303	2.38, § A, B, D
21.304	4.08, § A
21.305	4.08, § A, B
21.306	4.08, § B
21.307	4.08, § B
21.308	2.38, § E
21.309	4.13
21.310	2.38–1, § A
21.311	2.38–1, § B, E
21.312	2.38–1, § C, D
21.313	2.38–1, § C, D
21.314	2.38–3
21.315	2.38–4
21.316	2.41, § A(1), C, G
21.317	2.41, § A(3)
21.318	2.41, § E to G
21.351	2.24, § B
21.352	2.24, § C
21.353	2.25, § A
21.354	2.27, § A
21.355	2.26, § B
21.356	2.26, § C
21.357	2.26, § B
21.358	2.28, § A
21.359	2.28, § C
21.361	2.29, § D
21.363	2.28, § B
21.364	4.02, § A
	4.03
	6.03, § A
	6.05, § A
21.365	2.28, § D
21.366	2.29, § A
21.367	2.29, § C
21.368	2.29, § C
21.369	2.29, § C
21.370	2.29, § C
21.371	2.28, § E
21.372	2.27, § A, B
21.401	2.31
	13.06
21.402	2.31
21.403	2.32, § A
21.404	2.32, § A
21.405	2.32, § A, B
21.406	2.32, § B
21.407	2.32, § A, B
21.408	2.32, § B
	2.33
21.409	2.32, § C
21.410	2.34
21.411	2.37, § B
21.412	2.37, § B
21.413	2.35
21.414	2.41, § B
21.415	2.35
	9.10, § B
21.416	2.36
	9.10, § B
21.417	2.42, § A
21.418	2.35–1
21.451	5.03, § I(3), (5), (6)
	5.09, § A, B
21.452	5.03, § A to C
21.453	5.03, § B, C
	5.17, § A
21.454	5.02, § A
	5.03, § B, C
21.455	5.09, § A
	5.10, § A
21.456	5.03, § D
	5.10, § A(3)
21.457	5.01, § A
	5.03, § E
	5.10, § A(4)
21.458	5.03, § F
	5.10, § A(4)
21.459	5.03, § G
21.460	5.11, § A
21.461	5.09, § A
21.462	5.09, § A
21.501	6.01
	6.03, § A
	6.05, § A
21.502	6.01
	6.02, § A
	6.03, § A
	6.05, § A
21.503	6.03, § A
	6.05, § A
21.551	5.14, § A
21.552	5.14, § B
21.553	5.14, § C
21.554	5.14, § H
21.555	5.14, § D(1)
21.556	5.14, § D(2)
21.557	5.14, § E
21.558	5.14, § F
21.559	5.14, § G

DERIVATION TABLE 1

Business Org. Code Section	V.A.T.S., Bus.Corp. Act Article
21.560	5.14, § I
21.561	5.14, § J
21.562	5.14, § K
21.563	5.14, § L
21.601	13.02, § A(6) to (10)
21.602	13.02, § A(2)
21.603	13.02, § A(3)
21.604	13.02, § A(4)
21.605	13.02, § A(5)
21.606	13.03
21.607	13.04
21.608	13.05
21.609	13.07, § A
21.610	13.07, § B
21.651	2.12, § C(1)
21.652	2.12, § C(1)
21.653	2.12, § C(2), (4)
21.654	2.32, § D
21.655	2.24, § D
21.701	12.02, § A
21.702	12.03
21.703	12.12
21.704	12.15
21.705	12.13, § A
21.706	12.13, § B
21.707	12.14
21.708	12.21
21.709	12.22, § A, B, D, E
21.710	12.23, § A to C
21.711	12.23, § D
21.712	12.23, § E
21.713	12.31
21.714	12.32
21.715	12.33, § A
21.716	12.33, § B
21.717	12.33, § C
21.718	12.34, § A, B, D
21.719	12.35
21.720	12.36, § A
21.721	12.36, § B
21.722	12.36, § C
21.723	12.36, § D
21.724	12.36, § E
21.725	12.37, § A
21.726	12.37, § B
21.727	12.37, § C
21.728	12.37, § D
21.729	12.37, § E
21.730	12.37, § F
21.731	12.38
21.732	12.39
21.751	12.51, § A
21.752	12.51, § B
21.753	12.51, § C
21.754	12.51, § D
21.755	12.51, § E
21.756	12.52, § A
21.757	12.52, § B
21.758	12.53, § A, B
21.759	12.53, § B
21.760	12.53, § B
21.761	12.54, § A, B
21.762	12.54, § B
21.763	12.54, § B
21.801	2.22, § A
21.802	9.07, § B to F
23.001	9.14, § A
101.451	5.14, § A
101.452	5.14, § B
101.453	5.14, § C
101.454	5.14, § H
101.455	5.14, § D(1)
101.456	5.14, § D(2)
101.457	5.14, § E
101.458	5.14, § F
101.459	5.14, § G
101.460	5.14, § I
101.461	5.14, § J
101.462	5.14, § K
101.463	5.14, § L

DISPOSITION TABLE 2

Showing where previous provisions of articles of Vernon's Annotated Civil Statutes are now covered in the Business Organizations Code as originally enacted. The Business Organizations Code, as originally enacted, also contains the subject matter of certain former Business and Commerce Code and Government Code provisions.

Vernon's Ann. Civ.St. Article	Business Org. Code Section
1302–1.02	1.006
1302–1.03	9.301
	23.001
	251.003
§ A	1.002(25)
	23.102
1302–2.05	2.114
1302–2.06, § A	2.103
§ B	2.104
§ C	1.002(65)(B)
	1.002(85)
	2.104
§ D	2.104
1302–3.01	5.062
1302–3.05	2.006
1302–5.01	12.151
1302–5.02	12.152
1302–5.03	12.152
	12.153
1302–5.04	12.154
1302–5.05, § A	12.155
§ B	12.156
1302–5.06	12.261
1302–5.07	12.201
1302–5.08	12.201
1302–5.09	12.260
1302–5.10	12.251
1302–5.11	12.201
	12.259
1302–5.12	12.252
	12.254
1302–5.13	12.261
1302–5.14	12.253
1302–5.15	12.254
	12.258
1302–5.16	12.257
1302–5.17	12.255
1302–5.18	12.256
1302–5.19	12.261
1302–7.01	4.001
	4.101
1302–7.02	4.103
1302–7.03	4.002
	4.104
§ A	4.001
1302–7.04	4.105
1302–7.05	4.151
1302–7.06	7.001
1302–7.07	4.003

Vernon's Ann. Civ.St. Article	Business Org. Code Section
§ A	12.001
§ B	1.007
§ C	1.002(82)
	1.007
1302–7.08	4.002
1396–1.01, § A	1.008
1396–1.02, § A (1)	1.002(14)
	1.101
	22.001
(2)	1.002(27)
	1.002(28)
	22.001
(3)	1.002(59)
	22.001
(5)	22.001
(6)	1.002(53)(E)
(7)	22.001
(8)	1.002(70)(B)
(9)	1.002(88)(B)
(10)	1.002(79)(B)
(11)	1.002(86)(B)
(12)	1.002(39)
(14)	1.002(16)
(15)	22.001
1396–2.01, § A	2.001
	2.002
	2.009
	22.051
	22.052
§ B	2.003
	2.010
§ C, D	22.056
1396–2.02, § A	2.101
	2.102
	3.003
	22.055
§ B, C	2.113
1396–2.03	20.002
1396–2.04	5.052
	5.053
§ A (2)	5.102
(3)	5.061
1396–2.04A	5.101
1396–2.04A, § B	4.001
	5.103
	5.104
	5.106
1396–2.05	5.201
1396–2.06, § A	4.051

DISPOSITION TABLE 2

Vernon's Ann. Civ.St. Article		Business Org. Code Section
		5.202
	§ B	4.002
	§ C	4.051
		5.202
	§ D	4.001
		4.002
		5.204
	§ D (2)	4.051
1396–2.06A,	§ A	4.001
		5.203
	§ B	4.001
		4.002
	§ C	5.203
1396–2.07,	§ A	5.201
		5.255
	§ B	5.251
		5.252
		5.253
	§ C	5.254
	§ D	5.257
1396–2.08,	§ A, B, D	22.151
	§ E	22.152
1396–2.09		22.102
1396–2.10,	§ A	6.001
	§ A (2)	22.153
		22.154
	(3)	22.155
1396–2.11,	§ A	6.051
		22.156
	§ B	22.156
	§ C, D	22.157
1396–2.11A		6.101
	§ A to C, E	22.163
1396–2.11B		22.158
1396–2.12		22.159
1396–2.13,	§ A, B	22.160
	§ C	22.161
1396–2.14,	§ A	3.101
		22.201
		22.203
	§ B	22.207
	§ C	22.202
	§ D	22.201
	§ E	22.207
	§ F	22.210
1396–2.15,	§ A	22.204
	§ B	22.205
		22.206
		22.208
	§ C	22.208
		22.209
	§ D	22.211
1396–2.16		22.212
1396–2.17,	§ A, B	22.213
	§ C	22.214
	§ D	22.215
		22.216
1396–2.18,	§ A	22.218
	§ B	22.219
1396–2.19,	§ A	6.001
	§ B	6.051
		6.052
		22.217
1396–2.20,	§ A	3.103
		22.231
		22.232
	§ B	3.103
		22.231
	§ C	22.233
	§ D	3.105
		22.234
	§ E	3.105
1396–2.21		3.104
1396–2.22		22.235
1396–2.22A,	§ A	8.001
	§ B	8.101
	§ C	8.102
	§ D	8.101
		8.102
	§ E	8.102
	§ F	8.103
	§ G	8.101
		8.103
	§ H, I	8.051
	§ J	8.052
	§ K, L	8.104
	§ M	8.003
		8.004
	§ N	8.106
	§ O	8.105
	§ P	8.001
		8.101
		8.102
		8.104
		8.105
	§ Q	8.105
	§ R	8.151
	§ R (1)	8.001
	§ S	8.152
	§ T	8.001
		8.101
	§ U	8.003
1396–2.23,	§ A	3.151
	§ B	3.153
		22.351
1396–2.23A,	§ A, B	22.352
	§ C	22.353
	§ D	22.354
	§ E	22.355
1396–2.23B		22.356
1396–2.24		22.053
		22.054
1396–2.25		22.225
1396–2.26,	§ A	22.226
	§ B	22.227
	§ C	3.102
		22.226
	§ D	22.228
	§ E	22.229
1396–2.27,	§ A, B	2.107
1396–2.28,	§ A	22.221
	§ B	3.102
		22.222
	§ C	3.102
	§ D	22.221
	§ E	22.223
1396–2.29		22.224
1396–2.30		22.230

DISPOSITION TABLE 2

Vernon's Ann. Civ.St. Article	Business Org. Code Section
1396–2.31	2.106
1396–3.01, § A	3.004
§ B	22.101
1396–3.02, § A	3.005
	3.009
§ C	2.112
§ D	22.103
1396–3.03, § A	3.001
	4.001
	4.002
§ B	4.002
1396–3.04	3.001
	4.051
1396–3.05	22.104
1396–4.01	3.051
	4.106
1396–4.02, § A	22.164
§ A (1)	22.105
(2)	22.107
(3)	22.106
(4)	22.107
§ B	22.108
1396–4.03	3.053
	20.001
§ A	4.001
1396–4.04	3.052
§ A	4.001
	4.002
§ B	4.002
1396–4.05	3.056
§ A	4.051
1396–4.06, § A	3.057
	3.058
	3.059
	4.106
§ B	3.059
	3.061
§ C	3.059
	3.061
§ D	3.058
	4.001
	4.002
	20.001
§ E	4.002
§ F	3.063
	4.051
1396–5.01	10.010
§ A	10.001
§ B	10.002
	10.004
1396–5.02	10.010
§ A	10.001
§ B	10.002
	10.004
1396–5.03, § A	22.164
	22.253
§ A (1) to (3)	22.251
§ B	10.201
1396–5.04, § A	4.001
	10.151
§ B	4.001
	4.002
	10.153
	10.156
§ C	4.002
1396–5.05	4.051
	10.007
1396–5.06	10.008
1396–5.07, § A	10.001
	10.010
§ B	10.007
	10.008
1396–5.08	10.251
	10.252
	10.253
	22.255
1396–5.09	10.252
	22.164
	22.252
	22.253
	22.254
1396–6.01, § A	11.051
	22.164
	22.302
	22.303
1396–6.02, § A (1)	11.053
(2)	22.304
(3)	11.054
	22.304
1396–6.03	22.164
	22.302
	22.303
	22.305
1396–6.04, § A	11.151
	22.164
	22.302
	22.303
§ B	11.151
1396–6.05	11.101
	11.105
	20.001
§ A	4.001
	251.402
1396–6.06, § A	4.001
	4.002
§ B	4.002
	4.051
	11.102
1396–7.01, § A	11.051
	11.301
§ B	11.051
	11.251
§ C (1)	11.251
(2)	11.252
§ D	11.252
§ E	4.001
	4.002
	4.051
	11.253
§ F	11.051
	11.301
§ G	11.301
1396–7.02, § A	9.152
	11.302
§ B	9.152
	11.302
§ C	9.153
	11.303

DISPOSITION TABLE 2

Vernon's Ann. Civ.St. Article		Business Org. Code Section
	§ D	9.154
		11.304
	§ E	9.155
		9.156
		11.305
		11.306
	§ F	9.157
		11.307
1396–7.03		9.158
		9.159
		9.160
		11.308
		11.309
		11.310
1396–7.04		11.403
1396–7.04	§ A	11.402
1396–7.05	§ A	11.402
		11.404
1396–7.06	§ A	11.402
		11.405
	§ B	11.413
	§ C	11.405
1396–7.07	§ A	11.401
		11.406
	§ B	11.406
	§ C	11.407
	§ D, E	11.408
	§ F	11.409
		11.410
1396–7.08		11.411
1396–7.09		11.051
		11.412
1396–7.10		11.315
1396–7.11,	§ A	11.352
		11.353
	§ B	11.354
		11.355
1396–7.12,	§ A	11.055
		11.356
	§ B	11.357
	§ C	11.351
		11.356
		11.359
	§ D, E	11.358
	§ F	11.359
	§ G	11.051
		11.152
		11.311
		22.306
	§ H	11.001
1396–8.01,	§ A	9.001
		9.004
		9.201
	§ B	9.251
		9.252
1396–8.02		1.002(43)(C)(ii)
		1.102
		1.104
		1.105
		9.055
		9.202
		9.203
1396–8.03,	§ A (2)	5.053
	§ B	9.010
1396–8.04,	§ A	5.051
		9.004
		9.006
1396–8.05,	§ A	4.001
		4.002
		9.004
	§ B	4.002
1396–8.06		4.051
		9.008
1396–8.07		5.201
1396–8.08,	§ A	4.001
	§ B	4.001
		4.002
	§ C	4.051
	§ D	4.001
		4.002
		5.204
	§ D (2)	4.051
1396–8.09	§ A	5.201
		5.255
	§ B	5.251
		5.252
		5.253
	§ C	5.254
1396–8.12,	§ A	4.001
		4.106
		9.009
	§ B	4.001
		4.106
		9.009
	§ D	4.001
		4.051
		4.106
		9.009
1396–8.13		9.011
1396–8.14,	§ A	4.001
		4.002
	§ B	4.002
		4.051
1396–8.15,	§ A	9.151
	§ B	9.101
	§ C (1)	9.101
	§ D	4.002
		9.102
	§ E	4.001
		4.002
		4.051
		4.153
		9.103
		9.104
		9.105
	§ F, G	9.151
1396–8.16		9.161
1396–8.17		9.051
1396–9.01,	§ A, B	22.357
	§ C	22.358
		22.359
	§ D	22.358
	§ E	4.002
		22.359
1396–9.02,	§ A	22.360
	§ B	22.360
		22.361
		22.362

DISPOSITION TABLE 2

Vernon's Ann. Civ.St. Article	Business Org. Code Section
§ C	4.153
	22.363
§ D	22.363
§ E	22.364
§ F	4.153
	22.365
§ G	4.002
	22.365
1396–9.03	4.153
§ A	4.151
1396–9.03A	4.008
1396–9.04	12.001
1396–9.05	12.004
1396–9.06	4.005
1396–9.07	4.006
1396–9.08	22.162
1396–9.09	6.052
1396–9.10, § A, B	6.201
§ C (1)	6.202
	22.220
(2)	6.202
	6.203
	22.220
(3)	6.202
	22.220
(5)	1.007
1396–9.11, § A	6.002
	22.002
1396–10.01	1.053
1396–10.02	1.054
1396–10.04, § A	9.301
	23.001
	251.003
§ C	23.001
	251.003
1396–10.07, § A	4.052
	4.058
§ B	4.001
	4.052
	4.053
	4.055
§ C	4.001
	4.002
§ D	4.059
§ E	4.054
	4.059
§ F	4.056
1396–50.01, § 1	1.008
§ 2 (1)	1.101
(2)	1.002(53)(E)
(3) to (9)	251.001
§ 3	251.002
§ 5	2.011
§ 6	2.003
	2.011
	2.110
§ 8 (b)	3.013
	5.057
§ 9 (a), (b)	3.001
(c)	251.051
§ 10	251.052
§ 11	251.053
§ 12	251.053
§ 13 (a)	251.251
(b)	6.001
§ 14	6.051
	251.252
§ 15	251.253
§ 16	251.254
§ 17	251.255
§ 18	251.256
§ 19	251.257
§ 20	251.257
§ 21 (a) to (c)	251.101
(d)	6.001
§ 22	3.103
	251.102
§ 23	251.103
§ 24	251.104
§ 25	251.301
§ 26 (a)	251.151
(b)	2.011
§ 27, as amended Acts 72nd Leg., R.S., Ch. 897	251.153
§ 28	251.201
§ 29	251.202
§ 30	251.203
§ 31	251.204
§ 32	251.154
§ 33	251.152
§ 34	251.302
§ 35 (a)	251.351
(b) to (d)	251.352
§ 36	251.353
§ 37	251.354
§ 38 (a)	251.401
	251.402
(b)	251.404
(c)	251.401
	251.403
§ 39	251.452
(a)	5.057
§ 40 (a)	2.111
§ 43	9.001
§ 44	251.451
§ 45	251.003
1396–70.01, § 1	1.008
§ 2	252.001
§ 2 (1)	1.002(53)(E)
(2)	1.002(58)
§ 3	252.002
§ 4	252.003
§ 5	252.004
§ 6	252.005
§ 7	252.006
§ 8	252.007
§ 9	252.008
§ 10	252.009
§ 11	252.010
§ 12	252.011
§ 12 (d)	4.159
§ 13	252.012
§ 14	252.013
§ 15	252.014
§ 16	252.015
§ 18	252.016
1399	23.101

DISPOSITION TABLE 2

Vernon's Ann. Civ.St. Article		Business Org. Code Section
1400		23.104
1401		23.105
		23.107
1402		23.108
1403		23.110
1404		23.109
1405		23.103
1407		23.106
1407a,	§ 1	22.401
	§ 2	22.402
	§ 3	22.403
	§ 4	22.404
		22.405
	§ 5	22.406
	§ 6	22.407
	§ 7	22.408
	§ 8	22.409
1528e,	§ 1	1.008
	§ 3 (a)	1.002(76)
		301.003
	(b)	1.002(72)
		301.003
	§ 4 (a)	2.004
		3.001
		3.005
		3.014
		4.001
	(b)	301.003
		301.012
	§ 5	2.109
		4.157
		301.002
		303.001
		303.002
	§ 6	1.101
		2.004
	§ 8	5.054
		5.060
	§ 9	301.007
	§ 10	301.007
	§ 12	1.002(80)
		301.003
		301.004
		301.007
		301.009
		303.003
	§ 13	303.004
	§ 14	301.008
	§ 15	301.003
		301.004
		301.006
	§ 16	301.001
		301.010
	§ 17	3.003
		303.005
		303.006
	§ 19	301.011
	§ 19A	9.004
	(a)	4.001
		4.002
		9.001
		301.005
		301.006
	(b)	4.002

Vernon's Ann. Civ.St. Article		Business Org. Code Section
		301.005
1528f,	§ 1	1.008
	§ 2, as amended Acts 77th Leg., R.S., Chs. 508 and 883	301.003
	§ 2 (A)	1.101
	§ 2(A), as amended Acts 77th Leg., R.S., Chs. 508 and 883	1.002(71)
		302.011
	(B)	301.012
	(B)(1)	301.006
		301.007
	§ 3	1.002(76)
		301.003
	§ 4	5.058
		5.060
	§ 5	2.101
	§ 7	301.001
	§ 8 (A)	3.005
		3.014
		3.015
	(B)	3.015
		11.051
		302.002
		302.013
	(C), (D)	3.015
	(E)	3.015
		4.001
	§ 9 (A)	302.005
		302.007
	(B)	302.010
	(C)	301.007
		302.008
	(D)	302.004
	(E)	302.006
	(F)	302.009
	(G)	3.103
	§ 10	1.002(80)
		301.004
		301.007
		301.009
	§ 12 (A)	3.001
		4.001
		4.002
	(B)	4.002
	§ 13	3.001
		4.051
	§ 14	4.106
		302.003
	(A)	3.051
	§ 15	3.053
		4.001
	§ 16	3.052
	(A)	4.001
		4.002
	(B)	4.002
	§ 17	3.056
	(A)	4.051
	§ 18	4.001
		11.101
		302.013
	§ 19 (A)	4.001
		4.002

DISPOSITION TABLE 2

Vernon's Ann. Civ.St. Article			Business Org. Code Section
		(B)	4.002
	§ 20		4.051
	§ 21		4.001
			4.006
			302.012
	§ 22		4.156
	§ 24		301.010
	§ 25		2.108
			301.002
			302.001
	§ 26		4.008
1528g,	§ 1		23.051
	§ 2	(a)	23.052
		(b)	23.053
		(c)	23.053
			23.056
	§ 3	(a)	23.054
		(b)	23.055
	§ 4		23.061
	§ 5		23.062
	§ 6	(a)	23.066
		(b)	23.068
		(c)	23.067
		(d), (e)	23.068
		(f)	23.066
	§ 7		23.063
	§ 8	(a)	23.064
		(b)	23.065
	§ 9	(a), (b)	23.057
		(c)	23.060
		(d), (e)	23.058
		(f), (g)	23.059
	§ 10		23.069
	§ 11		23.070
	§ 12		23.071
1528n,	Art. 1.01,	§ A	1.008
	Art. 1.02,	§ A(3)	1.002(46)
			1.101
			101.001
		§ A(9)	9.003
			101.001
		§ A(10)	1.002(55)(B)(iii)
		§ A(11)	1.002(10)(C)
		§ A(12)	1.002(11)
		§ A(13)	1.002(12)
	Art. 2.01,	§ A	2.001
			2.005
		§ B	2.003
	Art. 2.02,	§ A	2.101
			3.003
			101.402
		§ B, C	2.113
		§ D	2.105
	Art. 2.03,	§ A	5.056
		§ A(2)	5.052
		§ A(3)	5.053
			5.102
		§ B	5.051
		§ C	5.001
	Art. 2.04,	§ A	5.101
		§ B	4.001
			4.002
			5.101
			5.102
			5.103
			5.104
		§ C	5.106
		§ D	5.104
	Art. 2.05		5.201
	Art. 2.06,	§ A	5.202
		§ B	4.001
			4.002
		§ C	4.051
			5.202
		§ D	4.001
			5.204
		§ D(2)	4.051
	Art. 2.07,	§ A	5.203
		§ B	4.001
			4.002
		§ C	4.051
			5.203
	Art. 2.08,	§ A	5.201
			5.255
		§ B	5.251
			5.252
			5.253
		§ C	5.254
		§ D	5.256
	Art. 2.09,	§ A	101.051
			101.052
		§ B	101.053
	Art. 2.11		2.101
			10.253
			101.254
	Art. 2.12		1.002(51)
			3.101
			101.251
			101.252
			101.253
			101.302
		§ A	101.255
			101.351
			101.352
	Art. 2.13		101.302
			101.303
			101.304
			101.306
	Art. 2.14		101.307
	Art. 2.15,	§ A, B	101.305
		§ C	101.306
	Art. 2.17		101.255
	Art. 2.18,	§ A	101.253
		§ C	101.253
	Art. 2.19,	§ A	6.001
		§ B	6.001
			6.051
			101.352
		§ C, D	101.352
		§ E	6.051
		§ F	6.052
	Art. 2.20,	§ A	8.002
			101.402
		§ B	101.401
	Art. 2.21,	§ A	3.103
		§ B	3.103
		§ C, D	101.254
	Art. 2.22,	§ A	3.151

DISPOSITION TABLE 2

Vernon's Ann. Civ.St. Article	Business Org. Code Section
	101.501
§ B	3.151
§ C	101.501
§ D	3.153
	101.502
§ E	3.153
	101.502
Art. 2.23, § A	101.353
	101.355
	101.357
§ B(1)	6.201
	6.202
	101.358
§ B(2)	1.007
§ C	6.002
	6.003
§ D	101.105
	101.356
§ E	101.356
§ F	101.354
	101.355
§ G, H	101.356
Art. 3.01	3.001
	3.004
	4.001
Art. 3.02, § A	3.005
	3.010
	101.051
§ B	2.112
Art. 3.03	4.002
§ A	3.001
	4.001
§ C	3.006
	4.001
	4.051
Art. 3.04	3.001
§ A	4.051
§ B	3.006
	4.051
Art. 3.05, § A	3.051
	4.106
Art. 3.06, § A	4.001
§ B	3.053
Art. 3.07	4.002
§ A	3.052
	4.001
Art. 3.08	3.056
§ A	4.051
Art. 3.09, § A	3.057
	3.058
	3.059
	4.106
§ B, C	3.059
§ D	3.058
	4.001
	4.002
§ E	4.002
§ F	3.063
	4.051
Art. 4.01, § A	1.002(53)(E)
	101.101
	101.103
§ B	101.103
§ C	101.102
Art. 4.02	101.104
§ A	101.105
Art. 4.03, § A	101.114
§ C	101.113
Art. 4.04	1.002(54)
	101.106
Art. 4.05, § A	1.002(54)
	101.108
	101.109
	101.111
§ B	3.201
§ C	101.109
Art. 4.06	101.112
Art. 4.07, § A	101.109
§ B	101.110
§ C	101.111
Art. 5.01	1.002(9)(B)
Art. 5.02, § A	101.151
§ B	101.152
	101.153
§ C	101.153
§ D	101.154
	101.155
	101.156
Art. 5.02–1	101.201
Art. 5.03	101.203
Art. 5.04	101.204
Art. 5.05	101.107
Art. 5.06	101.205
Art. 5.07	101.202
Art. 5.08	101.207
Art. 5.09	101.206
Art. 6.01	101.552
§ A	11.051
	11.056
§ B	11.152
Art. 6.02	11.314
Art. 6.03	11.052
	101.551
Art. 6.04	11.053
Art. 6.05	11.052
	11.053
	11.054
Art. 6.06	11.151
	101.552
Art. 6.07	11.101
Art. 6.08, § A	4.001
	4.002
	11.101
§ B	4.002
	4.051
	11.055
	11.102
Art. 7.01, § A	9.001
	9.004
	9.201
§ B	9.251
	9.252
Art. 7.02	1.002(43)(C)(ii)
	1.102
	1.104
	1.105
	9.055
	9.202

DISPOSITION TABLE 2

Vernon's Ann. Civ.St. Article	Business Org. Code Section
	9.203
Art. 7.03	5.052
	5.053
	5.056
Art. 7.04	9.010
Art. 7.05, § A	9.004
Art. 7.06, § A	4.001
	4.002
	9.004
§ B	4.002
Art. 7.07	4.051
	9.008
Art. 7.08, § A	4.001
	4.106
	9.009
§ B	4.001
	4.106
	9.009
§ D	4.001
	4.051
	4.106
	9.009
Art. 7.09	9.011
§ A, B	4.001
Art. 7.10	4.002
	9.011
§ A	4.001
§ B	4.051
Art. 7.11, § A	9.151
§ B	9.101
§ C(1)	9.101
§ D	4.002
	4.051
	9.102
§ E	4.001
	4.051
	4.154
	9.103
	9.104
	9.105
§ F	9.151
Art. 7.12	9.161
Art. 7.13, § A, B	9.051
§ C	9.052
	9.054
Art. 8.01	12.002
Art. 8.02	12.003
Art. 8.03	12.001
Art. 8.04	12.004
Art. 8.05	4.005
Art. 8.06	4.006
Art. 8.07	4.004
Art. 8.08	6.052
Art. 8.09	1.053
Art. 8.10	1.054
Art. 8.12, § A	4.001
	4.002
	5.151
	5.153
	5.154
	9.152 to 9.160
	10.301
	11.001
	11.152
	11.251 to 11.254
	11.301
	11.306 to 11.311
	11.315
	11.351 to 11.359
	11.401 to 11.412
	101.451 to 101.463
§ B	2.103
	2.104
	2.114
	4.001 to 4.003
	4.101
	4.103 to 4.105
	4.151
§ C	101.451 to 101.463
Art. 9.01, § A	4.151
	4.154
§ B	4.001
Art. 9.02	4.008
Art. 9.03, § A(1)	4.052
	4.058
§ A(2)	4.052
	4.053
§ A(3)	4.053
§ A(4)	4.055
§ B	4.001
§ C	4.059
§ D(1)	4.054
	4.059
§ D(2)	4.059
§ E	4.056
§ F	4.051
	4.057
	10.202
Art. 10.01	10.001
Art. 10.02, § A	10.002
	10.003
§ B	10.004
Art. 10.03, § A	4.001
	10.151
§ B	4.001
	4.002
	10.151
	10.153
	10.156
§ C	4.051
	10.007
Art. 10.04	10.008
Art. 10.05, § A	10.006
§ B	4.001
	10.006
	10.152
§ C	4.001
	4.051
	10.006
Art. 10.06, § A	10.051
	10.151
§ B	10.054
	10.055
	10.151
Art. 10.07	1.002(56)
Art. 10.08, § A	10.101
§ B	10.102
§ C	10.103

DISPOSITION TABLE 2

Vernon's Ann. Civ.St. Article			Business Org. Code Section
		§ D	10.104
	Art. 10.09,	§ A	10.154
		§ B	4.001
			10.155
		§ C	4.002
			10.156
	Art. 10.10		4.051
			10.105
	Art. 10.11		10.106
	Art. 11.01,	§ A	4.001
		§ A(1)	3.001
			3.005
			3.014
		§ A(2)	2.004
		§ A(3)	301.003
			301.012
		§ A(4)	301.012
		§ B	301.003
		§ B(1)	1.002(76)
		§ B(2)	1.002(75)
			301.004
			304.001
		§ B(3)	1.002(74)
			301.004
		§ B(4)	1.002(73)
	Art. 11.02		5.059
			5.060
	Art. 11.03,	§ A	301.007
			301.009
		§ B, C	301.008
	Art. 11.04		301.006
	Art. 11.05		301.001
			301.010
	Art. 11.06		301.011
	Art. 11.07,	§ A	4.001
			4.002
			301.005
			301.006
		§ B	4.002
6132a-1,	§ 1.01		1.008
	§ 1.02	(1)	151.001
		(2)	1.002(9)(B)
		(3)	151.001
		(4)	1.002(33)(B)
		(5)	1.002(49)(B)
			1.101
		(6)	1.002(50)
			1.101
		(7)	151.001
		(8)	1.002(55)(B)(iii)
		(9)	1.002(66)
		(10)	151.001
		(11)	1.002(68)
		(13)	153.208
	§ 1.03		5.052
			5.053
			5.055
			5.102
	§ 1.04	(a)	5.101
		(b)	5.101 to 5.106
	§ 1.05	(a)	4.001
			5.151
		(b)	4.001
			5.152
		(c)	4.051
			5.154
		(d)	4.001
			5.155
	§ 1.06	(a)	5.201
		(b)	4.001
			5.202
		(c)	4.001
			4.002
		(d)	4.051
			5.202
		(e)	4.051
			5.202
		(f)	4.001
			5.204
		(g)	4.002
			4.051
			5.204
		(h)	4.001
			5.203
		(i)	4.001
			4.002
			4.051
			5.203
	§ 1.07	(a), (b)	3.151
			153.551
		(c)	153.551
		(d), (e)	153.552
	§ 1.08	(a)	5.201
			5.255
		(b)	5.251
			5.252
			5.253
		(c)	5.254
	§ 1.09	(a)	2.001
			2.005
		(b)	2.003
		(c)	2.105
	§ 1.10		154.201
	§ 2.01	(a)	3.001
			3.004
			3.005
			3.011
			4.001
		(b)	3.001
			3.006
			4.051
			10.009
			10.107
	§ 2.02	(a)	3.051
			3.052
			3.053
			4.001
			4.106
		(b)	4.106
			153.051
		(c)	4.106
			153.051
		(d)	4.106
			153.052
		(e)	3.056
			4.051
			153.051
		(f)	4.001

DISPOSITION TABLE 2

Vernon's Ann. Civ.St. Article		Business Org. Code Section
		153.052
§ 2.03	(a)	4.001
		11.101
		11.102
		153.451
	(b)	11.101
		153.452
	(c)	4.051
		153.451
§ 2.04		153.553
	(a), (b)	4.001
§ 2.05		153.554
§ 2.06	(a)	4.106
		10.301
	(b)	10.302
	(c)	4.001
		10.303
	(d)	4.051
		10.303
	(e)	10.305
	(f)	10.306
§ 2.07	(a)	4.001
		4.002
	(b)	4.051
		9.008
	(c)	4.002
§ 2.08		4.007
§ 2.09		3.011
§ 2.10	(a)	3.057
		4.106
	(b)	3.058
		3.059
		4.001
	(c)	3.059
	(d)	3.063
		4.051
	(e)	3.057
§ 2.11	(a)	10.001
		10.009
	(b)	10.002
		10.003
	(c)	10.004
	(d)	4.001
		10.151
	(e)	3.006
		4.001
		4.002
		10.151
		10.153
		10.156
	(f)	4.051
		10.007
	(g)	10.008
		10.009
	(h)	10.051
		10.054
		10.055
		10.056
		10.151
§ 2.12	subsec. A	4.052
		4.053
		4.055
	subsec. B	4.001
	subsec. C	4.059
	subsec. D	4.054
		4.059
	subsec. E	4.056
	subsec. F	4.057
		10.202
§ 2.13	(a)	4.101
	(b)	4.103
	(c)	4.105
§ 2.14	(a)	153.351
	(b)	4.001
		153.352
	(c)	153.353
§ 2.15	(a)	10.101
		10.107
	(b)	10.102
	(c)	3.006
		10.103
	(d)	10.104
	(e)	4.001
		10.154
	(f)	4.051
		10.105
		10.155
	(g)	10.106
	(h)(1)	1.002(10)(C)
	(h)(2)	1.002(11)
	(h)(3)	1.002(12)
	(h)(4)	1.002(56)
§ 3.01		153.101
§ 3.02	(a)	154.101
	(b)	154.102
	(c), (d)	154.103
§ 3.03	(a)	153.101
	(b)	153.103
	(c)	153.104
	(d)	153.101
	(e)	153.105
§ 3.04	(a)	153.106
		153.107
	(b)	153.107
		153.108
	(c)	153.109
	(d)	153.108
	(e)	153.107
§ 4.01		153.151
§ 4.02	(a)	153.155
	(b)	153.156
§ 4.03		153.152
	(a)	3.101
§ 4.04		153.153
		153.154
§ 4.05	(a)	154.101
	(b)	154.102
§ 5.01		153.201
§ 5.02	(a) to (c)	153.202
	(d)	153.203
		153.204
		153.205
§ 5.03		153.206
§ 5.04		153.208
§ 6.01		153.209
§ 6.02	(a)	153.155
		153.157
		153.162

DISPOSITION TABLE 2

Vernon's Ann. Civ.St. Article		Business Org. Code Section
	(b)	153.158
	(c)	153.159
		153.160
	(d)	153.161
	(e)	153.158
§ 6.03		153.110
§ 6.04		153.111
§ 6.05		154.203
§ 6.06		153.207
§ 6.07	(a)	153.210
	(b)	153.112
§ 7.01		154.001
		154.002
§ 7.02	(a)	153.251
		153.252
	(b)	153.254
	(c)	3.201
§ 7.03	(a) to (c)	153.256
	(d)	153.257
§ 7.04	(a)	153.253
	(b)	153.253
		153.254
	(c)	153.255
§ 7.05		153.113
§ 7.06		153.555
§ 8.01		11.051
		11.058
		11.151
		11.152
		153.501
§ 8.02		11.051
		11.314
§ 8.04	(a)	11.052
		11.054
		153.502
	(b)	11.052
		11.053
		11.055
		153.503
	(c)	153.503
§ 8.05		11.053
		153.504
§ 9.01	(a)	1.002(43)(C)(ii)
		1.102
		1.104
		1.105
	(b)	9.004
	(c)	9.055
		9.202
§ 9.02	(a)	4.001
		4.003
		9.001
		9.004
	(b)	9.251
		9.252
§ 9.03	(a)	4.002
	(b)	5.051
§ 9.04		5.201
§ 9.05		4.007
		4.101
		4.106
		9.009
§ 9.06		4.001
		9.011
§ 9.07	(a) to (c)	9.051
	(d)	9.052
		9.054
§ 9.08		9.051
§ 9.09		4.001
		4.002
		4.051
§ 9.10	(a)	5.255
	(b)	5.251
		5.252
		5.253
	(c)	5.254
	(d)	5.256
§ 10.01		153.401
§ 10.02		153.402
§ 10.03		153.403
§ 10.04		153.404
§ 10.05		153.405
§ 11.01		8.001
§ 11.02		8.101
§ 11.03		8.102
§ 11.04		8.101
		8.102
§ 11.05		8.102
§ 11.06		8.103
§ 11.07		8.101
		8.103
§ 11.08		8.051
§ 11.09		8.051
§ 11.10		8.052
§ 11.11		8.104
§ 11.12		8.104
§ 11.13		8.003
		8.004
§ 11.14		8.106
§ 11.15		8.105
§ 11.16		8.001
		8.102
		8.104
		8.105
§ 11.17		8.105
§ 11.18		8.001
		8.151
§ 11.19		8.152
§ 11.20		8.001
		8.101
§ 11.21		8.003
§ 12.01		4.151
		4.155
§ 13.01		153.002
§ 13.02	(c)	4.051
§ 13.03	(a)	153.003
§ 13.04		4.003
	(b)	1.002(82)
		1.007
	(c)	4.002
§ 13.05	(a)	4.001
		153.301
		153.302
	(b)	4.001
		4.006
		4.155
		153.302
		153.303

DISPOSITION TABLE 2

Vernon's Ann. Civ.St. Article			Business Org. Code Section
	(c)		153.304
			153.305
	(d)		4.002
			4.006
			153.305
			153.306
	(e)		153.306
§ 13.06	(a)		9.101
			11.251
			153.307
	(b)		9.101
			11.251
			11.252
			153.307
			153.308
	(c), (d)		153.309
§ 13.07			153.310
	(a)		4.001
			4.155
	(b)		4.002
			4.051
§ 13.08			153.311
	(a)		4.002
			11.251
			11.252
	(b)		4.051
§ 13.09			153.312
	(a)		4.001
			4.155
			11.253
	(b)		4.002
			9.105
			11.253
6132b–1.01	(1)		1.002(5)
	(2)		151.001
	(4)		1.002(15)(B)(ii)
	(6) to (7)		152.001
	(8)		151.001
			152.001
	(9)		152.001
	(10)		151.001
			152.001
	(11)		1.002(34)
			1.002(67)
			1.101
			152.001
	(12)		151.001
			152.001
	(13)		1.002(68)
			152.001
	(14)		152.001
	(15)		1.002(77)
			152.001
	(16)		1.002(48)
			152.001
	(17) to (19)		152.001
6132b–1.02	(a)		151.002
	(b) to (e)		151.003
6132b–1.03			152.002
	(a)		8.002
6132b–1.04	(a)		152.003
	(b)		152.004
	(c)		152.005
6132b–1.05	(a)		1.002(43)(C)(ii)
			1.101
			1.103
	(b)		1.104
6132b–1.06			1.054
6132b–2.01			152.056
6132b–2.02	(a), (b)		152.051
	(c)		152.053
	(d)		10.009
			10.107
	(e)		152.055
6132b–2.03			152.052
	(c)		152.053
6132b–2.04			152.101
6132b–2.05			152.102
6132b–2.06	(a)		152.502
	(b)		152.701
	(c)		154.202
6132b–3.01			2.101
			2.105
6132b–3.02	(a)		152.301
			152.302
	(b), (c)		152.302
6132b–3.03			152.303
6132b–3.04			152.304
6132b–3.05	(a)		2.101
	(b)		152.305
	(c) to (f)		152.306
6132b–3.06	(a), (b)		152.054
	(c), (d)		152.307
6132b–3.07			152.304
6132b–3.08	(a)		152.801
	(a)	(12)	1.007
	(b)		4.001
	(b)	(1), (2)	152.802
		(3)	4.158
		(4)	4.051
			4.052
			152.802
		(5)	152.802
		(6)	4.051
			152.802
		(7)	4.051
			4.158
			152.802
		(8)	4.002
			152.802
		(9)	4.002
		(10)	4.006
		(11)	4.106
			4.158
			152.802
		(12)	1.002(82)
			4.003
		(13)	4.008
		(14)	152.802
		(15)	12.001
		(16)	4.002
			4.003
		(17)	4.003
		(18)	4.002
			4.003
	(c)		5.055
			5.063
			152.803

DISPOSITION TABLE 2

Vernon's Ann. Civ.St. Article		Business Org. Code Section
	(d)	152.804
	(e)	4.001
		152.805
6132b–4.01	(a), (b)	152.202
	(c)	152.203
	(d)	3.101
		152.203
	(e), (f)	152.203
	(g)	152.201
	(h)	152.209
	(i)	152.208
	(j)	152.214
	(k)	154.201
	(*l*)	154.101
	(m)	154.102
	(n)	154.103
6132b–4.02		154.203
6132b–4.03	(a), (b)	152.212
	(c)	152.213
6132b–4.04	(a)	152.204
	(b)	152.205
	(c)	152.206
	(d) to (f)	152.204
	(g)	152.207
6132b–4.05		152.210
6132b–4.06		152.211
6132b–4.07		152.709
	(a)	11.152
6132b–5.01		154.001
		154.002
6132b–5.02	(a)	154.001
	(b)	3.201
6132b–5.03	(a)	152.401
		152.402
	(b)	152.403
		152.404
	(c), (d)	152.404
	(e)	152.405
6132b–5.04		152.406
6132b–6.01		152.501
6132b–6.02		152.503
6132b–7.01	(a)	152.601
	(b)	152.602
	(c)	152.603
	(d)	152.604
	(e)	152.605
	(f)	152.606
	(g) to (j)	152.607
	(k)	152.608
	(*l*)	152.609
	(m)	152.610
	(n) to (q)	152.611
	(r), (s)	152.612
6132b–7.02		152.504
6132b–7.03	(a) to (d)	152.505
	(e)	152.506
6132b–8.01	(a) to (d)	11.051
		11.057
	(e)	11.051
		11.054
		11.314
	(f)	11.057
	(g)	11.057
		11.151

Vernon's Ann. Civ.St. Article		Business Org. Code Section
		152.709
6132b–8.02		11.103
		152.701
6132b–8.03	(a)	11.052
		11.054
		152.702
	(b)	11.052
		11.053
		152.703
	(c)	11.053
6132b–8.04		152.705
6132b–8.05		152.704
6132b–8.06	(a)	11.053
		152.706
	(b)	152.707
	(c) to (e)	152.708
6132b–9.01	(a)	4.001
		10.101
	(b)	4.001
		10.101
	(c)	10.009
	(f)	4.051
6132b–9.02	(a)	10.001
		10.009
	(b)	10.002
		10.003
	(c)	10.004
	(d)	4.001
		10.151
	(e)	4.001
		4.002
		10.153
		10.156
	(f)	4.051
		10.007
	(g)	10.008
		10.009
6132b–9.03	(a)	10.051
		10.056
	(b)	10.054
		10.055
		10.151
6132b–9.05	(a)	10.101
		10.107
	(b)	10.102
	(c)	10.103
	(d)	10.104
	(e)	4.001
		10.154
		10.155
	(f)	4.002
		10.156
	(g)	4.051
		10.105
	(h)	10.106
	(i) (1)	1.002(10)(C)
	(2)	1.002(11)
	(3)	1.002(12)
	(4)	1.002(17)
		1.002(18)
	(5)	1.002(27)
	(6)	1.002(56)
6132b–9.06		4.052
		4.054

DISPOSITION TABLE 2

Vernon's Ann. Civ.St. Article			Business Org. Code Section
			4.055
6132b–10.01		(a)	1.002(43)(C)(ii)
			1.103
			1.104
		(b), (c)	152.901
6132b–10.02		(a)	4.001
			9.004
			9.007
			152.902
			152.905
		(b)	4.001
			152.905
		(c)	4.001
			4.158
		(d)	4.051
			4.052
			152.905
		(e)	152.905
		(f)	4.001
			4.051
			152.906
			152.907
		(g)	4.001
			4.051
			4.158
			152.908
		(h)	4.002
			152.909
		(i)	4.002
			9.101
		(j)	4.006
		(k)	4.001
			4.158
			152.911
			152.912
		(*l*)	4.003
		(m)	4.008
		(n)	12.001
6132b–10.03			9.051
			152.910
		(c)	152.913
6132b–10.04			9.251
			9.252
			152.903
6132b–10.05			152.904
		(a)	5.201
		(b)	4.001
			5.202
		(c)	4.001
			4.002
		(d)	4.051
		(e)	4.002
			4.051
		(f)	4.001
			4.051
			5.204
		(g)	4.002
			5.204
		(h)	4.001
			5.203
		(i)	4.001
			4.002
			4.051
			5.203
		(j)	5.201
			5.255
		(k)	5.251
		(*l*)	5.252
			5.253
		(m)	5.254
		(n)	5.256
6132b–11.01			1.008
6138A,	§ 1.10		1.008
	§ 2.10		1.002(78)
			1.101
			200.001
	§ 3.10	(A)	2.012
			3.004
			3.005
			3.012
			4.001
			11.051
			200.101
		(A)(7)	1.002(80)
		(B)	3.001
			4.001
			4.009
			4.051
		(C)	200.060
	§ 3.20		200.004
	§ 3.30	(A)	200.102
			200.103
			200.152
		(B)	200.103
	§ 4.10	(A)	200.301
			200.302
			200.303
		(B)	200.304
			200.306
		(C)	200.307
		(D)	200.308
		(E)	200.310
		(F)	3.103
			3.104
			200.316
		(G)	200.351
		(H)	200.305
		(I)	200.503
	§ 4.20		200.317
	§ 4.30		200.311
	§ 5.10	(A)	5.201
		(B)	4.001
			5.202
		(C)	4.001
			5.204
		(D)	5.204
		(E)	4.051
			5.204
		(F)	4.001
			5.203
	§ 5.20	(A)	5.201
			5.255
		(B)	5.251
			5.252
			5.253
		(C)	5.254
		(D)	5.252
	§ 6.10	(A)	2.101

Vernon's Ann. Civ.St. Article		Business Org. Code Section
		200.005
	(B)	2.113
		200.005
	(C)	2.113
§ 7.10	(A), (C)	200.110
	(D)	200.111
§ 7.20	(A)	3.201
		3.202
		3.203
		3.204
	(B), (C)	3.202
	(D)	3.205
	(F), (G)	3.202
§ 7.30	(A)	200.104
		200.106
		200.107
	(B)	200.104
		200.105
	(C)	200.108
§ 7.40	(A)	200.153
	(B)	200.154
	(C), (D)	200.157
	(E)	200.155
	(F)	4.001
	(F)(1)	200.156
	(F)(2)	200.156
	(F)(4)	4.051
		200.156
	(G)	200.156
	(H)	200.158
		200.160
§ 8.10	(A)	200.161
	(B)	200.162
		200.163
	(C)	200.109
	(D), (E)	200.164
§ 9.10	(A), (B)	200.058
	(C)	200.059
§ 9.20	(A)	8.001
	(B)	8.101
	(C)	8.102
	(D)	8.101
		8.102
	(E)	8.102
	(F)	8.103
	(G)	8.101
		8.103
	(H), (I)	8.051
	(J)	8.052
	(K), (L)	8.104
	(M)	8.003
		8.004
	(N)	8.106
	(O)	8.105
	(P)	8.001
		8.101
		8.102
		8.104
		8.105
	(Q)	8.105
	(R)	8.001
		8.151
	(S)	8.152
	(T)	8.001
		8.101
	(U)	8.003
§ 10.10	(A)	6.001
	(B)	200.251
	(C)	200.252
§ 10.20	(A)	6.001
	(B)	200.309
§ 10.30	(A), (B)	6.201
	(C)	6.002
		6.003
	(D)	6.204
§ 11.10	(A)	200.253
	(B), (C)	6.053
§ 11.20	(A)	200.151
	(B)	200.159
	(C)	6.101
		200.254
		200.256
	(D)	6.102
		200.255
	(E)	6.103
§ 12.10	(A), (B)	200.257
	(C)	200.260
	(D)	200.258
	(E)	200.262
	(F)	200.268
§ 13.10	(A)	200.263
	(B)	6.152
	(C)	200.264
		200.265
		200.266
	(D)	200.267
	(E)(1)	200.258
	(E)(2)	200.259
	(F)	6.153
		9.204
	(G)	6.154
	(H)	6.155
	(I)	6.156
§ 13.20	(A)	6.251
	(B)	6.252
§ 14.10	(A)	200.201
	(B), (C)	200.202
	(D)	200.203
§ 14.20	(A)	200.205
	(B)	200.206
	(C)	200.207
		200.208
	(D)	200.207
		200.208
	(E)	200.206
§ 14.30		200.211
§ 14.40		200.209
§ 14.50		200.210
§ 14.60		200.204
§ 15.10	(A), (B)	200.312
	(C), (D)	3.102
	(E)	200.314
	(F)	200.315
	(G)	200.313
§ 17.10		200.502
§ 18.10	(A)	3.151
		200.113
	(B)	3.153

DISPOSITION TABLE 2

Vernon's Ann. Civ.St. Article		Business Org. Code Section
		200.501
	(C)	200.501
§ 19.10		11.051
		11.052
		11.053
		200.261
		200.451
		200.453
§ 19.20	(A)	4.001
		11.101
	(B)	4.001
		4.009
		11.101
	(C)	4.051
		11.102
§ 21.10		6.052
§ 22.10	(A)	3.051
		4.106
	(B)	200.052
§ 22.20		200.053
	(A)	200.054
		200.055
		200.056
		200.261
	(B)	200.056
§ 22.30		200.261
§ 22.40	(A)	3.055
		4.001
		200.006
	(B)	3.053
		3.055
§ 22.50		3.052
		4.001
		4.009
§ 22.60		3.056
	(A)	4.051
§ 22.70	(A)	3.057
		3.058
		3.059
		4.106
		200.057
	(B)	3.059
		3.062
	(C)	3.059
		3.062
	(D)	4.001
		200.006
		200.057
	(E)	3.063
		4.051
§ 23.10	(A)	10.001
	(B)	10.002
		10.003
	(C)	10.004
	(D)	10.008
	(E)	10.902
§ 23.20	(A)	10.051
	(B)	10.052
	(C)	10.053
	(D)	10.051
	(E)	10.902
§ 23.30	(A) to (C)	200.402
		200.404
	(D)	10.355
		200.406
	(E)	200.407
	(F)	200.408
	(G)	200.409
	(H)	200.401
	(I)	10.201
		10.202
§ 23.40	(A)	4.001
		10.151
		200.006
	(B)	4.001
		10.153
§ 23.50		4.051
		10.007
		10.054
§ 23.60	(A)	10.008
	(B)	10.055
	(C)	10.008
§ 24.10		200.405
	(A)	10.251
		10.252
		200.401
	(B)	200.401
	(C)	10.251
		10.253
§ 24.20	(A)	200.401
		200.405 to 200.408
	(B)	10.254
§ 25.10		10.354
		200.410
§ 25.20		200.410
	(A)	10.355
		10.356
		10.358
	(B)	10.361
	(C)	10.361
		10.363
	(D)	10.363
		10.364
		10.365
	(E)	10.366
	(G)	10.356
		10.368
§ 25.30		200.410
	(A)	10.366
	(B)	10.356
		10.359
		10.360
	(C)	10.357
		10.367
§ 26.10	(A)	4.106
		10.301
	(B)	10.301
	(C)	4.001
		10.302
	(D)	4.001
		10.302
		10.303
	(D)(6)	4.051
	(E)	10.304
	(F)	10.305
	(G)	10.306
§ 27.10	(A)	4.001
		4.052

DISPOSITION TABLE 2

Vernon's Ann. Civ.St. Article		Business Org. Code Section
		4.053
		4.055
	(B)	4.001
	(D)	4.054
	(E)	4.056
	(F)	4.052
§ 28.10	(A)	4.009
		200.002
		200.003
	(B)	200.002

Texas Bus & C. Section	Business Org. Code Section
1.201(46)	1.002(89)
43.002(8)	1.002(82)
43.002(12)	1.002(89)
43.007	1.002(89)
43.008(a)	1.002(89)

Texas Gov. Code Section	Business Org. Code Section
311.005(6)	1.002(82)
312.011(17)	1.002(89)
2054.060(e)(1)	1.002(82)

DERIVATION TABLE 2

Showing where sections of the Business Organizations Code, as originally enacted, were formerly covered in Vernon's Annotated Civil Statutes or elsewhere in Vernon's Texas Statutes. The Business Organizations Code, as originally enacted, also contains the subject matter of certain former Business and Commerce Code and Government Code provisions.

Business Org. Code Section	Vernon's Ann. Civ.St. Article
1.002(5)	6132b–1.01(1)
1.002(9)(B)	1528n, Art. 5.01
	6132a–1, § 1.02(2)
1.002(10)(C)	1528n, Art. 1.02, § A(11)
	6132a–1, § 2.15(h)(1)
	6132b–9.05(i)(1)
1.002(11)	1528n, Art. 1.02, § A(12)
	6132a–1, § 2.15(h)(2)
	6132b–9.05(i)(2)
1.002(12)	1528n, Art. 1.02, § A(13)
	6132a–1, § 2.15(h)(3)
	6132b–9.05(i)(3)
1.002(14)	1396–1.02, § A(1)
1.002(15)(B)(ii)	6132b–1.01(4)
1.002(16)	1396–1.02, § A(14)
1.002(17)	6132b–9.05(i)(4)
1.002(18)	6132b–9.05(i)(4)
1.002(25)	1302–1.03, § A
1.002(27)	1396–1.02, § A(2)
	6132b–9.05(i)(5)
1.002(28)	1396–1.02, § A(2)
1.002(33)(B)	6132a–1, § 1.02(4)
1.002(34)	6132b–1.01(11)
1.002(39)	1396–1.02, § A(12)
1.002(43)(C)(ii)	1396–8.02
	1528n, Art. 7.02
	6132a–1, § 9.01(a)
	6132b–1.05(a)
	6132b–10.01(a)
1.002(46)	1528n, Art 1.02, § A(3)
1.002(48)	6132b–1.01(16)
1.002(49)(B)	6132a–1, § 1.02(5)
1.002(50)	6132a–1, § 1.02(6)
1.002(51)	1528n, Art. 2.12
1.002(53)(E)	1396–1.02, § A(6)
	1396–50.01, § 2(2)
	1396–70.01, § 2(1)
	1528n, Art. 4.01, § A
1.002(54)	1528n, Art. 4.04
	1528n, Art. 4.05, § A
1.002(55)(B)(iii)	1528n, Art. 1.02, § A(10)
	6132a–1, § 1.02(8)
1.002(56)	1528n, Art. 10.07
	6132a–1, § 2.15(h)(4)
	6132b–9.05(i)(6)
1.002(58)	1396–70.01, § 2(2)
1.002(59)	1396–1.02, § A(3)
1.002(65)(B)	1302–2.06, § C
1.002(66)	6132a–1, § 1.02(9)
1.002(67)	6132b–1.01(11)
1.002(68)	6132a–1, § 1.02(11)
	6132b–1.01(13)
1.002(70)(B)	1396–1.02, § A(8)
1.002(71)	1528f, § 2(A), as amended Acts 77th Leg., R.S., Chs. 508 and 883
1.002(72)	1528e, § 3(b)
1.002(73)	1528n, Art. 11.01, § B(4)
1.002(74)	1528n, Art. 11.01, § B(3)
1.002(75)	1528n, Art. 11.01, § B(2)
1.002(76)	1528e, § 3(a)
	1528f, § 3
	1528n, Art. 11.01, § B(1)
1.002(77)	6132b–1.01(15)
1.002(78)	6138A, § 2.10
1.002(79)(B)	1396–1.02, § A(10)
1.002(80)	1528e, § 12
	1528f, § 10
	6138A, § 3.10(A)(7)
1.002(82)	1302–7.07, § C
	6132a–1, § 13.04(b)
	6132b–3.08(b)(12)
1.002(85)(B)	1302–2.06, § C
1.002(86)(B)	1396–1.02, § A(11)
1.002(88)(B)	1396–1.02, § A(9)
1.006	1302–1.02
1.007	1302–7.07, § B, C
	1396–9.10, § C(5)
	1528n, Art. 2.23, § B(2)
	6132a–1, § 13.04(b)
	6132b–3.08(a)(12)
1.008	1396–1.01, § A
	1396–50.01, § 1
	1396–70.01, § 1
	1528e, § 1
	1528f, § 1
	1528n, Art. 1.01, § A
	6132a–1, § 1.01
	6132b–11.01
	6138A, § 1.10
1.053	1396–10.01
	1528n, Art. 8.09
1.054	1396–10.02
	1528n, Art. 8.10
	6132b–1.06
1.101	1396–1.02, § A(1)
	1396–50.01, § 2(1)
	1528e, § 6
	1528f, § 2(A)

DERIVATION TABLE 2

Business Org. Code Section	Vernon's Ann. Civ.St. Article
	1528n, Art. 1.02, § A(3)
	6132a–1, § 1.02(5)
	6132a–1, § 1.02(6)
	6132b–1.01(11)
	6132b–1.05(a)
	6138A, § 2.10
1.102	1396–8.02
	1528n, Art. 7.02
	6132a–1, § 9.01(a)
1.103	6132b–1.05(a)
	6132b–10.01(a)
1.104	1396–8.02
	1528n, Art. 7.02
	6132a–1, § 9.01(a)
	6132b–1.05(b)
	6132b–10.01(a)
1.105	1396–8.02
	1528n, Art. 7.02
	6132a–1, § 9.01(a)
2.001	1396–2.01, § A
	1528n, Art. 2.01, § A
	6132a–1, § 1.09(a)
2.002	1396–2.01, § A
2.003	1396–2.01, § B
	1396–50.01, § 6
	1528n, Art. 2.01, § B
	6132a–1, § 1.09(b)
2.004	1528e, § 4(a)
	1528e, § 6
	1528n, Art. 11.01, § A(2)
2.005	1528n, Art. 2.01, § A
	6132a–1, § 1.09(a)
2.006	1302–3.05
2.009	1396–2.01, § A
2.010	1396–2.01, § B
2.011	1396–50.01, § 5
	1396–50.01, § 6
	1396–50.01, § 26(b)
2.012	6138A, § 3.10(A)
2.101	1396–2.02, § A
	1528f, § 5
	1528n, Art. 2.02, § A
	1528n, Art. 2.11
	6132b–3.01
	6132b–3.05(a)
	6138A, § 6.10(A)
2.102	1396–2.02, § A
2.103	1302–2.06, § A
	1528n, Art. 8.12, § B
2.104	1302–2.06, § B to D
	1528n, Art. 8.12, § B
2.105	1528n, Art. 2.02, § D
	6132a–1, § 1.09(c)
	6132b–3.01
2.106	1396–2.31
2.107	1396–2.27, § A, B
2.108	1528f, § 25
2.109	1528e, § 5
2.110	1396–50.01, § 6
2.111	1396–50.01, § 40(a)
2.112	1396–3.02, § C
	1528n, Art. 3.02, § B
2.113	1396–2.02, § B, C
	1528n, Art. 2.02, § B, C
	6138A, § 6.10(B), (C)
2.114	1302–2.05
	1528n, Art. 8.12, § B
3.001	1396–3.03, § A
	1396–3.04
	1396–50.01, § 9(a), (b)
	1528e, § 4(a)
	1528f, § 12(A)
	1528f, § 13
	1528n, Art. 3.01
	1528n, Art. 3.03, § A
	1528n, Art. 3.04
	1528n, Art. 11.01, § A(1)
	6132a–1, § 2.01(a), (b)
	6138A, § 3.10(B)
3.003	1396–2.02, § A
	1528e § 17
	1528n, Art. 2.02, § A
3.004	1396–3.01, § A
	1528n, Art. 3.01
	6132a–1, § 2.01(a)
	6138A, § 3.10(A)
3.005	1396–3.02, § A
	1528e, § 4(a)
	1528f, § 8(A)
	1528n, Art. 3.02, § A
	1528n, Art. 11.01, § A(1)
	6132a–1, § 2.01(a)
	6138A, § 3.10(A)
3.006	1528n, Art. 3.03, § C
	1528n, Art. 3.04, § B
	6132a–1, § 2.01(b)
	6132a–1, § 2.11(e)
	6132a–1, § 2.15(c)
3.009	1396–3.02, § A
3.010	1528n, Art. 3.02, § A
3.011	6132a–1, § 2.01(a)
	6132a–1, § 2.09
3.012	6138A, § 3.10(A)
3.013	1396–50.01, § 8(b)
3.014	1528e, § 4(a)
	1528f, § 8(A)
	1528n, Art. 11.01, § A(1)
3.015	1528f, § 8(A) to (E)
3.051	1396–4.01
	1528f, § 14(A)
	1528n, Art. 3.05, § A
	6132a–1, § 2.02(a)
	6138A, § 22.10(A)
3.052	1396–4.04
	1528f, § 16
	1528n, Art. 3.07, § A
	6132a–1, § 2.02(a)
	6138A, § 22.50
3.053	1396–4.03
	1528f, § 15
	1528n, Art. 3.06, § B
	6132a–1, § 2.02(a)
	6138A, § 22.40(B)
3.055	6138A, § 22.40(A), (B)
3.056	1396–4.05
	1528f, § 17
	1528n, Art. 3.08
	6132a–1, § 2.02(e)

DERIVATION TABLE 2

Business Org. Code Section	Vernon's Ann. Civ.St. Article
	6138A, § 22.60
3.057	1396–4.06, § A
	1528n, Art. 3.09, § A
	6132a–1, § 2.10(a), (e)
	6138A, § 22.70(A)
3.058	1396–4.06, § A, D
	1528n, Art. 3.09, § A, D
	6132a–1, § 2.10(b)
	6138A, § 22.70(A)
3.059	1396–4.06, § A to C
	1528n, Art. 3.09, § A to C
	6132a–1, § 2.10(b), (c)
	6138A, § 22.70(A) to (C)
3.061	1396–4.06, § B, C
3.062	6138A, § 22.70(B), (C)
3.063	1396–4.06, § F
	1528n, Art. 3.09, § F
	6132a–1, § 2.10(d)
	6138A, § 22.70(E)
3.101	1396–2.14, § A
	1528n, Art. 2.12
	6132a–1, § 4.03(a)
	6132b–4.01(d)
3.102	1396–2.26, § C
	1396–2.28, § B, C
	6138A, § 15.10(C), (D)
3.103	1396–2.20, § A, B
	1396–50.01, § 22
	1528f, § 9(G)
	1528n, Art. 2.21, § A, B
	6138A, § 4.10(F)
3.104	1396–2.21
	6138A, § 4.10(F)
3.105	1396–2.20, § D, E
3.151	1396–2.23, § A
	1528n, Art. 2.22, § A, B
	6132a–1, § 1.07(a), (b)
	6138A, § 18.10(A)
3.153	1396–2.23, § B
	1528n, Art. 2.22, § D, E
	6138A, § 18.10(B)
3.201	1528n, Art. 4.05, § B
	6132a–1, § 7.02(c)
	6132b–5.02(b)
	6138A, § 7.20(A)
3.202	6138A, § 7.20(A) to (C), (F), (G)
3.203	6138A, § 7.20(A)
3.204	6138A, § 7.20(A)
3.205	6138A, § 7.20(D)
4.001	1302–7.01
	1302–7.03, § A
	1396–2.04A, § B
	1396–2.06, § D
	1396–2.06A, § A, B
	1396–3.03, § A
	1396–4.03, § A
	1396–4.04, § A
	1396–4.06, § D
	1396–5.04, § A, B
	1396–6.05, § A
	1396–6.06, § A
	1396–7.01, § E
	1396–8.05, § A
	1396–8.08, § A, B, D
	1396–8.12, § A, B, D
	1396–8.14, § A
	1396–8.15, § E
	1396–10.07, § B, C
	1528e, § 4(a)
	1528e, § 19A(a)
	1528f, § 8(E)
	1528f, § 12(A)
	1528f, § 15
	1528f, § 16(A)
	1528f, § 18
	1528f, § 19(A)
	1528f, § 21
	1528n, Art. 2.04, § B
	1528n, Art. 2.06, § B, D
	1528n, Art. 2.07, § B
	1528n, Art. 3.01
	1528n, Art. 3.03, § A, C
	1528n, Art. 3.06, § A
	1528n, Art. 3.07 § A
	1528n, Art. 3.09, § D
	1528n, Art. 6.08, § A
	1528n, Art. 7.06, § A
	1528n, Art. 7.08, § A, B, D
	1528n, Art. 7.09, § A, B
	1528n, Art. 7.10, § A
	1528n, Art. 7.11, § E
	1528n, Art. 8.12, § A, B
	1528n, Art. 9.01, § B
	1528n, Art. 9.03, § B
	1528n, Art. 10.03, § A, B
	1528n, Art. 10.05, § B, C
	1528n, Art. 10.09, § B
	1528n, Art. 11.01, § A
	1528n, Art. 11.07, § A
	6132a–1, § 1.05(a), (b), (d)
	6132a–1, § 1.06(b), (c), (f), (h), (i)
	6132a–1, § 2.01(a)
	6132a–1, § 2.02(a), (f)
	6132a–1, § 2.03(a)
	6132a–1, § 2.04(a), (b)
	6132a–1, § 2.06(c)
	6132a–1, § 2.07(a)
	6132a–1, § 2.10(b)
	6132a–1, § 2.11(d), (e)
	6132a–1, § 2.12, subsec. B
	6132a–1, § 2.14(b)
	6132a–1, § 2.15(e)
	6132a–1, § 9.02(a)
	6132a–1, § 9.06
	6132a–1, § 9.09
	6132a–1, § 13.05(a), (b)
	6132a–1, § 13.07(a)
	6132a–1, § 13.09(a)
	6132b–3.08(b), (e)
	6132b–9.01(a), (b)
	6132b–9.02(d), (e)
	6132b–9.05(e)
	6132b–10.02(a) to (c), (f), (g), (k)
	6132b–10.05(b), (c), (f), (h), (i)
	6138A, § 3.10(A), (B)
	6138A, § 5.10(B), (C), (F)
	6138A, § 7.40(F)
	6138A, § 19.20(A), (B)

Business Org. Code Section	Vernon's Ann. Civ.St. Article
	6138A, § 22.40(A)
	6138A, § 22.50
	6138A, § 22.70(D)
	6138A, § 23.40(A), (B)
	6138A, § 26.10(C), (D)
	6138A, § 27.10(A), (B)
4.002	1302–7.03
	1302–7.08
	1396–2.06, § B, D
	1396–2.06A, § B
	1396–3.03, § A, B
	1396–4.04, § A, B
	1396–4.06, § D, E
	1396–5.04, § B, C
	1396–6.06, § A, B
	1396–7.01, § E
	1396–8.05, § A, B
	1396–8.08, § B, D
	1396–8.14, § A, B
	1396–8.15, § D, E
	1396–9.01, § E
	1396–9.02, § G
	1396–10.07, § C
	1528e, § 19A(a), (b)
	1528f, § 12(A), (B)
	1528f, § 16(A), (B)
	1528f, § 19(A), (B)
	1528n, Art. 2.04, § B
	1528n, Art. 2.06, § B
	1528n, Art. 2.07, § B
	1528n, Art. 3.03
	1528n, Art. 3.07
	1528n, Art. 3.09, § D, E
	1528n, Art. 6.08, § A, B
	1528n, Art. 7.06, § A, B
	1528n, Art. 7.10
	1528n, Art. 7.11, § D
	1528n, Art. 8.12, § A, B
	1528n, Art. 10.03, § B
	1528n, Art. 10.09, § C
	1528n, Art. 11.07, § A, B
	6132a–1, § 1.06(c), (g), (i)
	6132a–1, § 2.07(a), (c)
	6132a–1, § 2.11(e)
	6132a–1, § 9.03(a)
	6132a–1, § 9.09
	6132a–1, § 13.04(c)
	6132a–1, § 13.05(d)
	6132a–1, § 13.07(b)
	6132a–1, § 13.08(a)
	6132a–1, § 13.09(b)
	6132b–3.08(b)(8), (9), (16), (18)
	6132b–9.02(e)
	6132b–9.05(f)
	6132b–10.02(h), (i)
	6132b–10.05(c), (e), (g), (i)
4.003	1302–7.07
	1528n, Art. 8.12, § B
	6132a–1, § 9.02(a)
	6132a–1, § 13.04
	6132b–3.08(b)(12), (16) to (18)
	6132b–10.02(*l*)
4.004	1528n, Art. 8.07
4.005	1396–9.06
	1528n, Art. 8.05
4.006	1396–9.07
	1528f, § 21
	1528n, Art. 8.06
	6132a–1, § 13.05(b), (d)
	6132b–3.08(b)(10)
	6132b–10.02(j)
4.007	6132a–1, § 2.08
	6132a–1, § 9.05
4.008	1396–9.03A
	1528f, § 26
	1528n, Art. 9.02
	6132b–3.08(b)(13)
	6132b–10.02(m)
4.009	6138A, § 3.10(B)
	6138A, § 19.20(B)
	6138A, § 22.50
	6138A, § 28.10(A)
4.051	1396–2.06, § A, C, D(2)
	1396–3.04
	1396–4.05, § A
	1396–4.06, § F
	1396–5.05
	1396–6.06, § B
	1396–7.01, § E
	1396–8.06
	1396–8.08, § C, D(2)
	1396–8.12, § D
	1396–8.14, § B
	1396–8.15, § E
	1528f, § 13
	1528f, § 17(A)
	1528f, § 20
	1528n, Art. 2.06, § C, D(2)
	5128n, Art. 2.07, § C
	5128n, Art. 3.03, § C
	5128n, Art. 3.04, § A, B
	5128n, Art. 3.08, § A
	5128n, Art. 3.09, § F
	5128n, Art. 6.08, § B
	5128n, Art. 7.07
	5128n, Art. 7.08, § D
	5128n, Art. 7.10, § B
	5128n, Art. 7.11, § D, E
	5128n, Art. 9.03, § F
	5128n, Art. 10.03, § C
	5128n, Art. 10.05, § C
	5128n, Art. 10.10
	6132a–1, § 1.05(c)
	6132a–1, § 1.06(d), (e), (g), (i)
	6132a–1, § 2.01(b)
	6132a–1, § 2.02(e)
	6132a–1, § 2.03(c)
	6132a–1, § 2.06(d)
	6132a–1, § 2.07(b)
	6132a–1, § 2.10(d)
	6132a–1, § 2.11(f)
	6132a–1, § 2.15(f)
	6132a–1, § 9.09
	6132a–1, § 13.02(c)
	6132a–1, § 13.07(b)
	6132a–1, § 13.08(b)
	6132b–3.08(b)(4), (6), (7)
	6132b–9.01(f)

DERIVATION TABLE 2

Business Org. Code Section	Vernon's Ann. Civ.St. Article
	6132b–9.02(f)
	6132b–9.05(g)
	6132b–10.02(d), (f), (g)
	6132b–10.05(d) to (f), (i)
	6138A, § 3.10(B)
	6138A, § 5.10(E)
	6138A, § 7.40(F)(4)
	6138A, § 19.20(C)
	6138A, § 22.60(A)
	6138A, § 22.70(E)
	6138A, § 23.50
	6138A, § 26.10(D)(6)
4.052	1396–10.07, § A, B
	1528n, Art. 9.03, § A(1), (2)
	6132a–1, § 2.12, subsec. A
	6132b–3.08(b)(4)
	6132b–9.06
	6132b–10.02(d)
	6138A, § 27.10(A), (F)
4.053	1396–10.07, § B
	1528n, Art. 9.03, § A(2), (3)
	6132a–1, § 2.12, subsec. A
	6138A, § 27.10(A)
4.054	1396–10.07, § E
	1528n, Art. 9.03, § D(1)
	6132a–1, § 2.12, subsec. D
	6132b–9.06
	6138A, § 27.10(D)
4.055	1396–10.07, § B
	1528n, Art. 9.03, § A(4)
	6132a–1, § 2.12, subsec. A
	6132b–9.06
	6138A, § 27.10(A)
4.056	1396–10.07, § F
	1528n, Art. 9.03, § E
	6132a–1, § 2.12, subsec. E
	6138A, § 27.10(E)
4.057	1528n, Art. 9.03, § F
	6132a–1, § 2.12, subsec. F
4.058	1396–10.07, § A
	1528n, Art. 9.03, § A(1)
4.059	1396–10.07, § D, E
	1528n, Art. 9.03, § C, D(1), (2)
	6132a–1, § 2.12, subsecs. C, D
4.101	1302–7.01
	1528n, Art. 8.12, § B
	6132a–1, § 2.13(a)
	6132a–1, § 9.05
4.103	1302–7.02
	1528n, Art. 8.12, § B
	6132a–1, § 2.13(b)
4.104	1302–7.03
	1528n, Art. 8.12, § B
4.105	1302–7.04
	1528n, Art. 8.12, § B
	6132a–1, § 2.13(c)
4.106	1396–4.01
	1396–4.06, § A
	1396–8.12, § A, B, D
	1528f, § 14
	1528n, Art. 3.05, § A
	1528n, Art. 3.09, § A
	1528n, Art. 7.08, § A, B, D
	6132a–1, § 2.02(a) to (d)
	6132a–1, § 2.06(a)
	6132a–1, § 2.10(a)
	6132a–1, § 9.05
	6132b–3.08(b)(11)
	6138A, § 22.10(A)
	6138A, § 22.70(A)
	6138A, § 26.10(A)
4.151	1302–7.05
	1396–9.03, § A
	1528n, Art. 8.12, § B
	1528n, Art. 9.01, § A
	6132a–1, § 12.01
4.153	1396–8.15, § E
	1396–9.02, § C, F
	1396–9.03
4.154	1528n, Art. 7.11, § E
	1528n, Art. 9.01, § A
4.155	6132a–1, § 12.01
	6132a–1, § 13.05(b)
	6132a–1, § 13.07(a)
	6132a–1, § 13.09(a)
4.156	1528f, § 22
4.157	1528e, § 5
4.158	6132b–3.08(b)(3), (7), (11)
	6132b–10.02(c), (g), (k)
4.159	1396–70.01, § 12(d)
5.001	1528n, Art. 2.03, § C
5.051	1396–8.04, § A
	1528n, Art. 2.03, § B
	6132a–1, § 9.03(b)
5.052	1396–2.04
	1528n, Art. 2.03, § A(2)
	1528n, Art. 7.03
	6132a–1, § 1.03
5.053	1396–2.04
	1396–8.03, § A(2)
	1528n, Art. 2.03, § A(3)
	1528n, Art. 7.03
	6132a–1, § 1.03
5.054	1528e, § 8
5.055	6132a–1, § 1.03
	6132b–3.08(c)
5.056	1528n, Art. 2.03, § A
	1528n, Art. 7.03
5.057	1396–50.01, § 8(b)
	1396–50.01, § 39(a)
5.058	1528f, § 4
5.059	1528n, Art. 11.02
5.060	1528e, § 8
	1528f, § 4
	1528n, Art. 11.02
5.061	1396–2.04, § A(3)
5.062	1302–3.01
5.063	6132b–3.08(c)
5.101	1396–2.04A
	1528n, Art. 2.04, § A, B
	6132a–1, § 1.04(a), (b)
5.102	1396–2.04, § A(2)
	1528n, Art. 2.03, § A(3)
	1528n, Art. 2.04, § B
	6132a–1, § 1.03
	6132a–1, § 1.04(b)
5.103	1396–2.04A, § B
	1528n, Art. 2.04, § B

DERIVATION TABLE 2

Business Org. Code Section	Vernon's Ann. Civ.St. Article
	6132a–1, § 1.04(b)
5.104	1396–2.04A, § B
	1528n, Art. 2.04, § B, D
	6132a–1, § 1.04(b)
5.105	6132a–1, § 1.04(b)
5.106	1396–2.04A, § B
	1528n, Art. 2.04, § C
	6132a–1, § 1.04(b)
5.151	1528n, Art. 8.12, § A
	6132a–1, § 1.05(a)
5.152	6132a–1, § 1.05(b)
5.153	1528n, Art. 8.12, § A
5.154	1528n, Art. 8.12, § A
	6132a–1, § 1.05(c)
5.155	6132a–1, § 1.05(d)
5.201	1396–2.05
	1396–2.07, § A
	1396–8.07
	1396–8.09, § A
	1528n, Art. 2.05
	1528n, Art. 2.08, § A
	6132a–1, § 1.06(a)
	6132a–1, § 1.08(a)
	6132a–1, § 9.04
	6132b–10.05(a), (j)
	6138A, § 5.10(A)
	6138A, § 5.20(A)
5.202	1396–2.06, § A, C
	1528n, Art. 2.06, § A, C
	6132a–1, § 1.06(b), (d), (e)
	6132b–10.05(b)
	6138A, § 5.10(B)
5.203	1396–2.06A, § A, C
	1528n, Art. 2.07, § A, C
	6132a–1, § 1.06(h), (i)
	6132b–10.05(h), (i)
	6138A, § 5.10(F)
5.204	1396–2.06, § D
	1396–8.08, § D
	1528n, Art. 2.06, § D
	6132a–1, § 1.06(f), (g)
	6132b–10.05(f), (g)
	6138A, § 5.10(C) to (E)
5.251	1396–2.07, § B
	1396–8.09, § B
	1528n, Art. 2.08, § B
	6132a–1, § 1.08(b)
	6132a–1, § 9.10(b)
	6132b–10.05(k)
	6138A, § 5.20(B)
5.252	1396–2.07, § B
	1396–8.09, § B
	1528n, Art. 2.08, § B
	6132a–1, § 1.08(b)
	6132a–1, § 9.10(b)
	6132b–10.05(*l*)
	6138A, § 5.20(B), (D)
5.253	1396–2.07, § B
	1396–8.09, § B
	1528n, Art. 2.08, § B
	6132a–1, § 1.08(b)
	6132a–1, § 9.10(b)
	6132b–10.05(*l*)
	6138A, § 5.20(B)
5.254	1396–2.07, § C
	1396–8.09, § C
	1528n, Art. 2.08, § C
	6132a–1, § 1.08(c)
	6132a–1, § 9.10(c)
	6132b–10.05(m)
	6138A, § 5.20(C)
5.255	1396–2.07, § A
	1396–8.09, § A
	1528n, Art. 2.08, § A
	6132a–1, § 1.08(a)
	6132a–1, § 9.10(a)
	6132b–10.05(j)
	6138A, § 5.20(A)
5.256	1528n, Art. 2.08, § D
	6132a–1, § 9.10(d)
	6132b–10.05(n)
5.257	1396–2.07, § D
6.001	1396–2.10, § A
	1396–2.19, § A
	1396–50.01, § 13(b)
	1396–50.01, § 21(d)
	1528n, Art. 2.19, § A, B
	6138A, § 10.10(A)
	6138A, § 10.20(A)
6.002	1396–9.11, § A
	1528n, Art. 2.23, § C
	6138A, § 10.30(C)
6.003	1528n, Art. 2.23, § C
	6138A, § 10.30(C)
6.051	1396–2.11, § A
	1396–2.19, § B
	1396–50.01, § 14
	1528n, Art. 2.19, § B, E
6.052	1396–2.19, § B
	1396–9.09
	1528n, Art. 2.19, § F
	1528n, Art. 8.08
	6138A, § 21.10
6.053	6138A, § 11.10(B), (C)
6.101	1396–2.11A
	6138A, § 11.20(C)
6.102	6138A, § 11.20(D)
6.103	6138A, § 11.20(E)
6.152	6138A, § 13.10(B)
6.153	6138A, § 13.10(F)
6.154	6138A, § 13.10(G)
6.155	6138A, § 13.10(H)
6.156	6138A, § 13.10(I)
6.201	1396–9.10, § A, B
	1528n, Art. 2.23, § B(1)
	6138A, § 10.30(A), (B)
6.202	1396–9.10, § C(1) to (3)
	1528n, Art. 2.23, § B(1)
6.203	1396–9.10, § C(2)
6.204	6138A, § 10.30(D)
6.251	6138A, § 13.20(A)
6.252	6138A, § 13.20(B)
7.001	1302–7.06
8.001	1396–2.22A, § A, P, R(1), T
	6132a–1, § 11.01
	6132a–1, § 11.16
	6132a–1, § 11.18
	6132a–1, § 11.20

DERIVATION TABLE 2

Business Org. Code Section	Vernon's Ann. Civ.St. Article
	6138A, § 9.20(A), (P), (R), (T)
8.002	1528n, Art. 2.20, § A
	6132b–1.03(a)
8.003	1396–2.22A, § M, U
	6132a–1, § 11.13
	6132a–1, § 11.21
	6138A, § 9.20(M), (U)
8.004	1396–2.22A, § M
	6132a–1, § 11.13
	6138A, § 9.20(M)
8.051	1396–2.22A, § H, I
	6132a–1, § 11.08
	6132a–1, § 11.09
	6138A, § 9.20(H), (I)
8.052	1396–2.22A, § J
	6132a–1, § 11.10
	6138A, § 9.20(J)
8.101	1396–2.22A, § B, D, G, P, T
	6132a–1, § 11.02
	6132a–1, § 11.04
	6132a–1, § 11.07
	6132a–1, § 11.20
	6138A, § 9.20(B), (D), (G), (P), (T)
8.102	1396–2.22A, § C, D, E, P
	6132a–1, § 11.03
	6132a–1, § 11.04
	6132a–1, § 11.05
	6132a–1, § 11.16
	6138A, § 9.20(C) to (E), (P)
8.103	1396–2.22A, § F, G
	6132a–1, § 11.06
	6132a–1, § 11.07
	6138A, § 9.20(F), (G)
8.104	1396–2.22A, § K, L, P
	6132a–1, § 11.11
	6132a–1, § 11.12
	6132a–1, § 11.16
	6138A, § 9.20(K), (L), (P)
8.105	1396–2.22A, § O to Q
	6132a–1, § 11.15
	6132a–1, § 11.16
	6132a–1, § 11.17
	6138A, § 9.20(O) to (Q)
8.106	1396–2.22A, § N
	6132a–1, § 11.14
	6138A, § 9.20(N)
8.151	1396–2.22A, § R
	6132a–1, § 11.18
	6138A, § 9.20(R)
8.152	1396–2.22A, § S
	6132a–1, § 11.19
	6138A, § 9.20(S)
9.001	1396–8.01, § A
	1396–50.01, § 43
	1528e, § 19A(a)
	1528n, Art. 7.01, § A
	6132a–1, § 9.02(a)
9.003	1528n, Art. 1.02, § A(9)
9.004	1396–8.01, § A
	1396–8.04, § A
	1396–8.05, § A
	1528e, § 19A
	1528n, Art. 7.01, § A
	1528n, Art. 7.05, § A
	1528n, Art. 7.06, § A
	6132a–1, § 9.01(b)
	6132a–1, § 9.02(a)
	6132b–10.02(a)
9.006	1396–8.04, § A
9.007	6132b–10.02(a)
9.008	1396–8.06
	1528n, Art. 7.07
	6132a–1, § 2.07(b)
9.009	1396–8.12, § A, B, D
	1528n, Art. 7.08, § A, B, D
	6132a–1, § 9.05
9.010	1396–8.03, § B
	1528n, Art. 7.04
9.011	1396–8.13
	1528n, Art. 7.09
	1528n, Art. 7.10
	6132a–1, § 9.06
9.051	1396–8.17
	1528n, Art. 7.13, § A, B
	6132a–1, § 9.07(a) to (c)
	6132a–1, § 9.08
	6132b–10.03
9.052	1528n, Art. 7.13, § C
	6132a–1, § 9.07(d)
9.054	1528n, Art. 7.13, § C
	6132a–1, § 9.07(d)
9.055	1396–8.02
	1528n, Art. 7.02
	6132a–1, § 9.01(c)
9.101	1396–8.15, § B, C(1)
	1528n, Art. 7.11, § B, C(1)
	6132a–1, § 13.06(a), (b)
	6132b–10.02(i)
9.102	1396–8.15, § D
	1528n, Art. 7.11, § D
9.103	1396–8.15, § E
	1528n, Art. 7.11, § E
9.104	1396–8.15, § E
	1528n, Art. 7.11, § E
9.105	1396–8.15, § E
	1528n, Art. 7.11, § E
	6132a–1, § 13.09(b)
9.151	1396–8.15, § A, F, G
	1528n, Art. 7.11, § A, F
9.152	1396–7.02, § A, B
	1528n, Art. 8.12, § A
9.153	1396–7.02, § C
	1528n, Art. 8.12, § A
9.154	1396–7.02, § D
	1528n, Art. 8.12, § A
9.155	1396–7.02, § E
	1528n, Art. 8.12, § A
9.156	1396–7.02, § E
	1528n, Art. 8.12, § A
9.157	1396–7.02, § F
	1528n, Art. 8.12, § A
9.158	1396–7.03
	1528n, Art. 8.12, § A
9.159	1396–7.03
	1528n, Art. 8.12, § A
9.160	1396–7.03
	1528n, Art. 8.12, § A
9.161	1396–8.16

DERIVATION TABLE 2

Business Org. Code Section	Vernon's Ann. Civ.St. Article
	1528n, Art. 7.12
9.201	1396–8.01, § A
	1528n, Art. 7.01, § A
9.202	1396–8.02
	1528n, Art. 7.02
	6132a–1, § 9.01(c)
9.203	1396–8.02
	1528n, Art. 7.02
9.204	6138A, § 13.10(F)
9.251	1396–8.01, § B
	1528n, Art. 7.01, § B
	6132a–1, § 9.02(b)
	6132b–10.04
9.252	1396–8.01, § B
	1528n, Art. 7.01, § B
	6132a–1, § 9.02(b)
	6132b–10.04
9.301	1302–1.03
	1396–10.04, § A
10.001	1396–5.01, § A
	1396–5.02, § A
	1396–5.07, § A
	1528n, Art. 10.01
	6132a–1, § 2.11(a)
	6132b–9.02(a)
	6138A, § 23.10(A)
10.002	1396–5.01, § B
	1396–5.02, § B
	1528n, Art. 10.02, § A
	6132a–1, § 2.11(b)
	6132b–9.02(b)
	6138A, § 23.10(B)
10.003	1528n, Art. 10.02, § A
	6132a–1, § 2.11(b)
	6132b–9.02(b)
	6138A, § 23.10(B)
10.004	1396–5.01, § B
	1396–5.02, § B
	1528n, Art. 10.02, § B
	6132a–1, § 2.11(c)
	6132b–9.02(c)
	6138A, § 23.10(C)
10.006	1528n, Art. 10.05, § A to C
10.007	1396–5.05
	1396–5.07, § B
	1528n, Art. 10.03, § C
	6132a–1, § 2.11(f)
	6132b–9.02(f)
	6138A, § 23.50
10.008	1396–5.06
	1396–5.07, § B
	1528n, Art. 10.04
	6132a–1, § 2.11(g)
	6132b–9.02(g)
	6138A, § 23.10(D)
	6138A, § 23.60(A), (C)
10.009	6132a–1, § 2.01(b)
	6132a–1, § 2.11(a), (g)
	6132b–2.02(d)
	6132b–9.01(c)
	6132b–9.02(a), (g)
10.010	1396–5.01
	1396–5.02
	1396–5.07, § A
10.051	1528n, Art. 10.06, § A
	6132a–1, § 2.11(h)
	6132b–9.03(a)
	6138A, § 23.20(A), (D)
10.052	6138A, § 23.20(B)
10.053	6138A, § 23.20(C)
10.054	1528n, Art. 10.06, § B
	6132a–1, § 2.11(h)
	6132b–9.03(b)
	6138A, § 23.50
10.055	1528n, Art. 10.06, § B
	6132a–1, § 2.11(h)
	6132b–9.03(b)
	6138A, § 23.60(B)
10.056	6132a–1, § 2.11(h)
	6132b–9.03(a)
10.101	1528n, Art. 10.08, § A
	6132a–1, § 2.15(a)
	6132b–9.01(a), (b)
	6132b–9.05(a)
10.102	1528n, Art. 10.08, § B
	6132a–1, § 2.15(b)
	6132b–9.05(b)
10.103	1528n, Art. 10.08, § C
	6132a–1, § 2.15(c)
	6132b–9.05(c)
10.104	1528n, Art. 10.08, § D
	6132a–1, § 2.15(d)
	6132b–9.05(d)
10.105	1528n, Art. 10.10
	6132a–1, § 2.15(f)
	6132b–9.05(g)
10.106	1528n, Art. 10.11
	6132a–1, § 2.15(g)
	6132b–9.05(h)
10.107	6132a–1, § 2.01(b)
	6132a–1, § 2.15(a)
	6132b–2.02(d)
	6132b–9.05(a)
10.151	1396–5.04, § A
	1528n, Art. 10.03, § A, B
	1528n, Art. 10.06, § A, B
	6132a–1, § 2.11(d), (e), (h)
	6132b–9.02(d)
	6132b–9.03(b)
	6138A, § 23.40(A)
10.152	1528n, Art. 10.05, § B
10.153	1396–5.04, § B
	1528n, Art. 10.03, § B
	6132a–1, § 2.11(e)
	6132b–9.02(e)
	6138A, § 23.40(B)
10.154	1528n, Art. 10.09, § A
	6132a–1, § 2.15(e)
	6132b–9.05(e)
10.155	1528n, Art. 10.09, § B
	6132a–1, § 2.15(f)
	6132b–9.05(e)
10.156	1396–5.04, § B
	1528n, Art. 10.03, § B
	1528n, Art. 10.09, § C
	6132a–1, § 2.11(e)
	6132b–9.02(e)
	6132b–9.05(f)

DERIVATION TABLE 2

Business Org. Code Section	Vernon's Ann. Civ.St. Article
10.201	1396–5.03, § B
	6138A, § 23.30(I)
10.202	1528n, Art. 9.03, § F
	6132a–1, § 2.12, subsec. F
	6138A, § 23.30(I)
10.251	1396–5.08
	6138A, § 24.10(A), (C)
10.252	1396–5.08
	1396–5.09
	6138A, § 24.10(A)
10.253	1396–5.08
	1528n, Art. 2.11
	6138A, § 24.10(C)
10.254	6138A, § 24.20(B)
10.301	1528n, Art. 8.12, § A
	6132a–1, § 2.06(a)
	6138A, § 26.10(A), (B)
10.302	6132a–1, § 2.06(b)
	6138A, § 26.10(C), (D)
10.303	6132a–1, § 2.06(c), (d)
	6138A, § 26.10(D)
10.304	6138A, § 26.10(E)
10.305	6132a–1, § 2.06(e)
	6138A, § 26.10(F)
10.306	6132a–1, § 2.06(f)
	6138A, § 26.10(G)
10.354	6138A, § 25.10
10.355	6138A, § 23.30(D)
	6138A, § 25.20(A)
10.356	6138A, § 25.20(A), (G)
	6138A, § 25.30(B)
10.357	6138A, § 25.30(C)
10.358	6138A, § 25.20(A)
10.359	6138A, § 25.30(B)
10.360	6138A, § 25.30(B)
10.361	6138A, § 25.20(B), (C)
10.363	6138A, § 25.20(C), (D)
10.364	6138A, § 25.20(D)
10.365	6138A, § 25.20(D)
10.366	6138A, § 25.20(E)
	6138A, § 25.30(A)
10.367	6138A, § 25.30(C)
10.368	6138A, § 25.20(G)
10.902	6138A, § 23.10(E)
	6138A, § 23.20(E)
11.001	1396–7.12, § H
	1528n, Art. 8.12, § A
11.051	1396–6.01, § A
	1396–7.01, § A, B, F
	1396–7.09
	1396–7.12, § G
	1528f, § 8(B)
	1528n, Art. 6.01, § A
	6132a–1, § 8.01
	6132a–1, § 8.02
	6132b–8.01(a) to (e)
	6138A, § 3.10(A)
	6138A, § 19.10
11.052	1528n, Art. 6.03
	1528n, Art. 6.05
	6132a–1, § 8.04(a), (b)
	6132b–8.03(a), (b)
	6138A, § 19.10
11.053	1396–6.02, § A(1)
	1528n, Art. 6.04
	1528n, Art. 6.05
	6132a–1, § 8.04(b)
	6132a–1, § 8.05
	6132b–8.03(b), (c)
	6132b–8.06(a)
	6138A, § 19.10
11.054	1396–6.02, § A(3)
	1528n, Art. 6.05
	6132a–1, § 8.04(a)
	6132b–8.01(e)
	6132b–8.03(a)
11.055	1396–7.12, § A
	1528n, Art. 6.08, § B
	6132a–1, § 8.04(b)
11.056	1528n, Art. 6.01, § A
11.057	6132b–8.01(a) to (d), (f), (g)
11.058	6132a–8.01
11.101	1396–6.05
	1528f, § 18
	1528n, Art. 6.07
	1528n, Art. 6.08, § A
	6132a–1, § 2.03(a), (b)
	6138A, § 19.20(A), (B)
11.102	1396–6.06, § B
	1528n, Art. 6.08, § B
	6132a–1, § 2.03(a)
	6138A, § 19.20(C)
11.103	6132b–8.02
11.105	1396–6.05
11.151	1396–6.04, § A, B
	1528n, Art. 6.06
	6132a–1, § 8.01
	6132b–8.01(g)
11.152	1396–7.12, § G
	1528n, Art. 6.01, § B
	1528n, Art. 8.12, § A
	6132a–1, § 8.01
	6132b–4.07(a)
11.251	1396–7.01, § (B), (C)(1)
	1528n, Art. 8.12, § A
	6132a–1, § 13.06(a), (b)
	6132a–1, § 13.08(a)
11.252	1396–7.01, § (C)(2), (D)
	1528n, Art. 8.12, § A
	6132a–1, § 13.06(b)
	6132a–1, § 13.08(a)
11.253	1396–7.01, § (E)
	1528n, Art. 8.12, § A
	6132a–1, § 13.09(a), (b)
11.254	1528n, Art. 8.12, § A
11.301	1396–7.01, § A, F, G
	1528n, Art. 8.12, § A
11.302	1396–7.02, § A, B
11.303	1396–7.02, § C
11.304	1396–7.02, § D
11.305	1396–7.02, § E
11.306	1396–7.02, § E
	1528n, Art. 8.12, § A
11.307	1396–7.02, § F
	1528n, Art. 8.12, § A
11.308	1396–7.03
	1528n, Art. 8.12, § A
11.309	1396–7.03

DERIVATION TABLE 2

Business Org. Code Section	Vernon's Ann. Civ.St. Article
	1528n, Art. 8.12, § A
11.310	1396–7.03
	1528n, Art. 8.12, § A
11.311	1396–7.12, § G
	1528n, Art. 8.12, § A
11.314	1528n, Art. 6.02
	6132a–1, § 8.02
	6132b–8.01(e)
11.315	1396–7.10
	1528n, Art. 8.12, § A
11.351	1396–7.12, § C
	1528n, Art. 8.12, § A
11.352	1396–7.11, § A
	1528n, Art. 8.12, § A
11.353	1396–7.11, § A
	1528n, Art. 8.12, § A
11.354	1396–7.11, § B
	1528n, Art. 8.12, § A
11.355	1396–7.11, § B
	1528n, Art. 8.12, § A
11.356	1396–7.12, § A, C
	1528n, Art. 8.12, § A
11.357	1396–7.12, § B
	1528n, Art. 8.12, § A
11.358	1396–7.12, § D, E
	1528n, Art. 8.12, § A
11.359	1396–7.12, § C, F
	1528n, Art. 8.12, § A
11.401	1396–7.07, § A
	1528n, Art. 8.12, § A
11.402	1396–7.04, § A
	1396–7.05, § A
	1396–7.06, § A
	1528n, Art. 8.12, § A
11.403	1396–7.04
	1528n, Art. 8.12, § A
11.404	1396–7.05
	1528n, Art. 8.12, § A
11.405	1396–7.06, § A, C
	1528n, Art. 8.12, § A
11.406	1396–7.07, § A, B
	1528n, Art. 8.12, § A
11.407	1396–7.07, § C
	1528n, Art. 8.12, § A
11.408	1396–7.07, § D, E
	1528n, Art. 8.12, § A
11.409	1396–7.07, § F
	1528n, Art. 8.12, § A
11.410	1396–7.07, § F
	1528n, Art. 8.12, § A
11.411	1396–7.08
	1528n, Art. 8.12, § A
11.412	1396–7.09
	1528n, Art. 8.12, § A
11.413	1396–7.06, § B
12.001	1302–7.07, § A
	1396–9.04
	1528n, Art. 8.03
	6132b–3.08(b)(15)
	6132b–10.02(n)
12.002	1528n, Art. 8.01
12.003	1528n, Art. 8.02
12.004	1396–9.05
	1528n, Art. 8.04

Business Org. Code Section	Vernon's Ann. Civ.St. Article
12.151	1302–5.01
12.152	1302–5.02
	1302–5.03
12.153	1302–5.03
12.154	1302–5.04
12.155	1302–5.05, § A
12.156	1302–5.05, § B
12.201	1302–5.07
	1302–5.08
	1302–5.11
12.251	1302–5.10
12.252	1302–5.12
12.253	1302–5.14
12.254	1302–5.12
	1302–5.15
12.255	1302–5.17
12.256	1302–5.18
12.257	1302–5.16
12.258	1302–5.15
12.259	1302–5.11
12.260	1302–5.09
12.261	1302–5.06
	1302–5.13
	1302–5.19
20.001	1396–4.03
	1396–4.06, § D
	1396–6.05
20.002	1396–2.03
22.001	1396–1.02, § A(1) to (3), (5), (7), (15)
22.002	1396–9.11, § A
22.051	1396–2.01, § A
22.052	1396–2.01, § A
22.053	1396–2.24
22.054	1396–2.24
22.055	1396–2.02, § A
22.056	1396–2.01, § C, D
22.101	1396–3.01, § B
22.102	1396–2.09
22.103	1396–3.02, § D
22.104	1396–3.05
22.105	1396–4.02, § A(1)
22.106	1396–4.02, § A(3)
22.107	1396–4.02, § A(2), (4)
22.108	1396–4.02, § B
22.151	1396–2.08, § A, B, D
22.152	1396–2.08, § E
22.153	1396–2.10, § A(2)
22.154	1396–2.10, § A(2)
22.155	1396–2.10, § A(3)
22.156	1396–2.11, § A, B
22.157	1396–2.11, § C, D
22.158	1396–2.11B
22.159	1396–2.12
22.160	1396–2.13, § A, B
22.161	1396–2.13, § C
22.162	1396–9.08
22.163	1396–2.11A, § A to C, E
22.164	1396–4.02, § A
	1396–5.03, § A
	1396–5.09
	1396–6.01, § A
	1396–6.03
	1396–6.04, § A
22.201	1396–2.14, § A, D

DERIVATION TABLE 2

Business Org. Code Section	Vernon's Ann. Civ.St. Article
22.202	1396–2.14, § C
22.203	1396–2.14, § A
22.204	1396–2.15, § A
22.205	1396–2.15, § B
22.206	1396–2.15, § B
22.207	1396–2.14, § B, E
22.208	1396–2.15, § B, C
22.209	1396–2.15, § C
22.210	1396–2.14, § F
22.211	1396–2.15, § D
22.212	1396–2.16
22.213	1396–2.17, § A, B
22.214	1396–2.17, § C
22.215	1396–2.17, § D
22.216	1396–2.17, § D
22.217	1396–2.19, § B
22.218	1396–2.18, § A
22.219	1396–2.18, § B
22.220	1396–9.10, § C(1) to (3)
22.221	1396–2.28, § A, D
22.222	1396–2.28, § B
22.223	1396–2.28, § E
22.224	1396–2.29
22.225	1396–2.25
22.226	1396–2.26, § A, C
22.227	1396–2.26, § B
22.228	1396–2.26, § D
22.229	1396–2.26, § E
22.230	1396–2.30
22.231	1396–2.20, § A, B
22.232	1396–2.20, § A
22.233	1396–2.20, § C
22.234	1396–2.20, § D
22.235	1396–2.22
22.251	1396–5.03, § A(1) to (3)
22.252	1396–5.09
22.253	1396–5.03, § A
	1396–5.09
22.254	1396–5.09
22.255	1396–5.08
22.302	1396–6.01, § A
	1396–6.03
	1396–6.04, § A
22.303	1396–6.01, § A
	1396–6.03
	1396–6.04, § A
22.304	1396–6.02, § A(2), (3)
22.305	1396–6.03
22.306	1396–7.12, § G
22.351	1396–2.23, § B
22.352	1396–2.23A, § A, B
22.353	1396–2.23A, § C
22.354	1396–2.23A, § D
22.355	1396–2.23A, § E
22.356	1396–2.23B
22.357	1396–9.01, § A, B
22.358	1396–9.01, § C, D
22.359	1396–9.01, § C, E
22.360	1396–9.02, § A, B
22.361	1396–9.02, § B
22.362	1396–9.02, § B
22.363	1396–9.02, § C, D
22.364	1396–9.02, § E
22.365	1396–9.02, § F, G

Business Org. Code Section	Vernon's Ann. Civ.St. Article
22.401	1407a, § 1
22.402	1407a, § 2
22.403	1407a, § 3
22.404	1407a, § 4
22.405	1407a, § 4
22.406	1407a, § 5
22.407	1407a, § 6
22.408	1407a, § 7
22.409	1407a, § 8
23.001	1302–1.03
	1396–10.04, § A, C
23.051	1528g, § 1
23.052	1528g, § 2(a)
23.053	1528g, § 2(b), (c)
23.054	1528g, § 3(a)
23.055	1528g, § 3(b)
23.056	1528g, § 2(c)
23.057	1528g, § 9(a), (b)
23.058	1528g, § 9(d), (e)
23.059	1528g, § 9(f), (g)
23.060	1528g, § 9(c)
23.061	1528g, § 4
23.062	1528g, § 5
23.063	1528g, § 7
23.064	1528g, § 8(a)
23.065	1528g, § 8(b)
23.066	1528g, § 6(a), (f)
23.067	1528g, § 6(c)
23.068	1528g, § 6(b), (d), (e)
23.069	1528g, § 10
23.070	1528g, § 11
23.071	1528g, § 12
23.101	1399
23.102	1302–1.03, § A
23.103	1405
23.104	1400
23.105	1401
23.106	1407
23.107	1401
23.108	1402
23.109	1404
23.110	1403
101.001	1528n, Art. 1.02, § A(3), (9)
101.051	1528n, Art. 2.09, § A
	1528n, Art. 3.02, § A
101.052	1528n, Art. 2.09, § A
101.053	1528n, Art. 2.09, § B
101.101	1528n, Art. 4.01, § A
101.102	1528n, Art. 4.01, § C
101.103	1528n, Art. 4.01, § A, B
101.104	1528n, Art. 4.02
101.105	1528n, Art. 2.23, § D
	1528n, Art. 4.02, § A
101.106	1528n, Art. 4.04
101.107	1528n, Art. 5.05
101.108	1528n, Art. 4.05, § A
101.109	1528n, Art. 4.05, § A, C
	1528n, Art. 4.07, § A
101.110	1528n, Art. 4.07, § B
101.111	1528n, Art. 4.05, § A
	1528n, Art. 4.07, § C
101.112	1528n, Art. 4.06
101.113	1528n, Art. 4.03, § C
101.114	1528n, Art. 4.03, § A

DERIVATION TABLE 2

Business Org. Code Section	Vernon's Ann. Civ.St. Article
101.151	1528n, Art. 5.02, § A
101.152	1528n, Art. 5.02, § B
101.153	1528n, Art. 5.02, § B, C
101.154	1528n, Art. 5.02, § D
101.155	1528n, Art. 5.02, § D
101.156	1528n, Art. 5.02, § D
101.201	1528n, Art. 5.02–1
101.202	1528n, Art. 5.07
101.203	1528n, Art. 5.03
101.204	1528n, Art. 5.04
101.205	1528n, Art. 5.06
101.206	1528n, Art. 5.09
101.207	1528n, Art. 5.08
101.251	1528n, Art. 2.12
101.252	1528n, Art. 2.12
101.253	1528n, Art. 2.12
	1528n, Art. 2.18, § A, C
101.254	1528n, Art. 2.11
	1528n, Art. 2.21, § C, D
101.255	1528n, Art. 2.12, § A
	1528n, Art. 2.17
101.302	1528n, Art. 2.12
	1528n, Art. 2.13
101.303	1528n, Art. 2.13
101.304	1528n, Art. 2.13
101.305	1528n, Art. 2.15, § A, B
101.306	1528n, Art. 2.13
	1528n, Art. 2.15, § C
101.307	1528n, Art. 2.14
101.351	1528n, Art. 2.12, § A
101.352	1528n, Art. 2.12, § A
	1528n, Art. 2.19, § B to D
101.353	1528n, Art. 2.23, § A
101.354	1528n, Art. 2.23, § F
101.355	1528n, Art. 2.23, § A, F
101.356	1528n, Art. 2.23, § D, E, G, H
101.357	1528n, Art. 2.23, § A
101.358	1528n, Art. 2.23, § B(1)
101.401	1528n, Art. 2.20, § B
101.402	1528n, Art. 2.02, § A
	1528n, Art. 2.20, § A
101.451	1528n, Art. 8.12, § A, C
101.452	1528n, Art. 8.12, § A, C
101.453	1528n, Art. 8.12, § A, C
101.454	1528n, Art. 8.12, § A, C
101.455	1528n, Art. 8.12, § A, C
101.456	1528n, Art. 8.12, § A, C
101.457	1528n, Art. 8.12, § A, C
101.458	1528n, Art. 8.12, § A, C
101.459	1528n, Art. 8.12, § A, C
101.460	1528n, Art. 8.12, § A, C
101.461	1528n, Art. 8.12, § A, C
101.462	1528n, Art. 8.12, § A, C
101.463	1528n, Art. 8.12, § A, C
101.501	1528n, Art. 2.22, § A, C
101.502	1528n, Art. 2.22, § D, E
101.551	1528n, Art. 6.03
101.552	1528n, Art. 6.01
	1528n, Art. 6.06
151.001	6132a–1, § 1.02(1), (3), (7), (10)
	6132b–1.01(2), (8), (10), (12)
151.002	6132b–1.02(a)
151.003	6132b–1.02(b) to (e)
152.001	6132b–1.01(6) to (19)
152.002	6132b–1.03
152.003	6132b–1.04(a)
152.004	6132b–1.04(b)
152.005	6132b–1.04(c)
152.051	6132b–2.02(a), (b)
152.052	6132b–2.03
152.053	6132b–2.02(c)
	6132b–2.03(c)
152.054	6132b–3.06(a), (b)
152.055	6132b–2.02(e)
152.056	6132b–2.01
152.101	6132b–2.04
152.102	6132b–2.05
152.201	6132b–4.01(g)
152.202	6132b–4.01(a), (b)
152.203	6132b–4.01(c) to (f)
152.204	6132b–4.04(a), (d) to (f)
152.205	6132b–4.04(b)
152.206	6132b–4.04(c)
152.207	6132b–4.04(g)
152.208	6132b–4.01(i)
152.209	6132b–4.01(h)
152.210	6132b–4.05
152.211	6132b–4.06
152.212	6132b–4.03(a), (b)
152.213	6132b–4.03(c)
152.214	6132b–4.01(j)
152.301	6132b–3.02(a)
152.302	6132b–3.02(a) to (c)
152.303	6132b–3.03
152.304	6132b–3.04
	6132b–3.07
152.305	6132b–3.05(b)
152.306	6132b–3.05(c) to (f)
152.307	6132b–3.06(c), (d)
152.401	6132b–5.03(a)
152.402	6132b–5.03(a)
152.403	6132b–5.03(b)
152.404	6132b–5.03(b) to (d)
152.405	6132b–5.03(e)
152.406	6132b–5.04
152.501	6132b–6.01
152.502	6132b–2.06(a)
152.503	6132b–6.02
152.504	6132b–7.02
152.505	6132b–7.03(a) to (d)
152.506	6132b–7.03(e)
152.601	6132b–7.01(a)
152.602	6132b–7.01(b)
152.603	6132b–7.01(c)
152.604	6132b–7.01(d)
152.605	6132b–7.01(e)
152.606	6132b–7.01(f)
152.607	6132b–7.01(g) to (j)
152.608	6132b–7.01(k)
152.609	6132b–7.01(*l*)
152.610	6132b–7.01(m)
152.611	6132b–7.01(n) to (q)
152.612	6132b–7.01(r), (s)
152.701	6132b–2.06(b)
	6132b–8.02
152.702	6132b–8.03(a)
152.703	6132b–8.03(b)
152.704	6132b–8.05

DERIVATION TABLE 2

Business Org. Code Section	Vernon's Ann. Civ.St. Article
152.705	6132b–8.04
152.706	6132b–8.06(a)
152.707	6132b–8.06(b)
152.708	6132b–8.06(c) to (e)
152.709	6132b–4.07
	6132b–8.01(g)
152.801	6132b–3.08(a)
152.802	6132b–3.08(b)(1), (2), (4) to (8), (11), (14)
152.803	6132b–3.08(c)
152.804	6132b–3.08(d)
152.805	6132b–3.08(e)
152.901	6132b–10.01(b), (c)
152.902	6132b–10.02(a)
152.903	6132b–10.04
152.904	6132b–10.05
152.905	6132b–10.02(a), (b), (d), (e)
152.906	6132b–10.02(f)
152.907	6132b–10.02(f)
152.908	6132b–10.02(g)
152.909	6132b–10.02(h)
152.910	6132b–10.03
152.911	6132b–10.02(k)
152.912	6132b–10.02(k)
152.913	6132b–10.03(c)
153.002	6132a–1, § 13.01
153.003	6132a–1, § 13.03(a)
153.051	6132a–1, § 2.02(b), (c), (e)
153.052	6132a–1, § 2.02(d), (f)
153.101	6132a–1, § 3.01
153.102	6132a–1, § 3.03(a), (d)
153.103	6132a–1, § 3.03(b)
153.104	6132a–1, § 3.03(c)
153.105	6132a–1, § 3.03(e)
153.106	6132a–1, § 3.04(a)
153.107	6132a–1, § 3.04(a), (b), (e)
153.108	6132a–1, § 3.04(b), (d)
153.109	6132a–1, § 3.04(c)
153.110	6132a–1, § 6.03
153.111	6132a–1, § 6.04
153.112	6132a–1, § 6.07(b)
153.113	6132a–1, § 7.05
153.151	6132a–1, § 4.01
153.152	6132a–1, § 4.03
153.153	6132a–1, § 4.04
153.154	6132a–1, § 4.04
153.155	6132a–1, § 4.02(a)
	6132a–1, § 6.02(a)
153.156	6132a–1, § 4.02(b)
153.157	6132a–1, § 6.02(a)
153.158	6132a–1, § 6.02(b), (e)
153.159	6132a–1, § 6.02(c)
153.160	6132a–1, § 6.02(c)
153.161	6132a–1, § 6.02(d)
153.162	6132a–1, § 6.02(a)
153.201	6132a–1, § 5.01
153.202	6132a–1, § 5.02(a) to (c)
153.203	6132a–1, § 5.02(d)
153.204	6132a–1, § 5.02(d)
153.205	6132a–1, § 5.02(d)
153.206	6132a–1, § 5.03
153.207	6132a–1, § 6.06
153.208	6132a–1, § 1.02(13)
	6132a–1, § 5.04
153.209	6132a–1, § 6.01
153.210	6132a–1, § 6.07(a)
153.251	6132a–1, § 7.02(a)
153.252	6132a–1, § 7.02(a)
153.253	6132a–1, § 7.04(a), (b)
153.254	6132a–1, § 7.02(b)
	6132a–1, § 7.04(b)
153.255	6132a–1, § 7.04(c)
153.256	6132a–1, § 7.03(a) to (c)
153.257	6132a–1, § 7.03(d)
153.301	6132a–1, § 13.05(a)
153.302	6132a–1, § 13.05(a), (b)
153.303	6132a–1, § 13.05(b)
153.304	6132a–1, § 13.05(c)
153.305	6132a–1, § 13.05(c), (d)
153.306	6132a–1, § 13.05(d), (e)
153.307	6132a–1, § 13.06(a), (b)
153.308	6132a–1, § 13.06(b)
153.309	6132a–1, § 13.06(c), (d)
153.310	6132a–1, § 13.07
153.311	6132a–1, § 13.08
153.312	6132a–1, § 13.09
153.351	6132a–1, § 2.14(a)
153.352	6132a–1, § 2.14(b)
153.353	6132a–1, § 2.14(c)
153.401	6132a–1, § 10.01
153.402	6132a–1, § 10.02
153.403	6132a–1, § 10.03
153.404	6132a–1, § 10.04
153.405	6132a–1, § 10.05
153.451	6132a–1, § 2.03(a), (c)
153.452	6132a–1, § 2.03(b)
153.501	6132a–1, § 8.01
153.502	6132a–1, § 8.04(a)
153.503	6132a–1, § 8.04(b), (c)
153.504	6132a–1, § 8.05
153.551	6132a–1, § 1.07(a) to (c)
153.552	6132a–1, § 1.07(d), (e)
153.553	6132a–1, § 2.04
153.554	6132a–1, § 2.05
153.555	6132a–1, § 7.06
154.001	6132a–1, § 7.01
	6132b–5.01
	6132b–5.02(a)
154.002	6132a–1, § 7.01
	6132b–5.01
154.101	6132a–1, § 3.02(a)
	6132a–1, § 4.05(a)
	6132b–4.01(*l*)
154.102	6132a–1, § 3.02(b)
	6132a–1, § 4.05(b)
	6132b–4.01(m)
154.103	6132a–1, § 3.02(c), (d)
	6132b–4.01(n)
154.201	6132a–1, § 1.10
	6132b–4.01(k)
154.202	6132b–2.06(c)
154.203	6132a–1, § 6.05
	6132b–4.02
200.001	6138A, § 2.10
200.002	6138A, § 28.10(A), (B)
200.003	6138A, § 28.10(A)
200.004	6138A, § 3.20
200.005	6138A, § 6.10(A), (B)
200.006	6138A, § 22.40(A)

DERIVATION TABLE 2

Business Org. Code Section	Vernon's Ann. Civ.St. Article
	6138A, § 22.70(D)
	6138A, § 23.40(A)
200.052	6138A, § 22.10(B)
200.053	6138A, § 22.20
200.054	6138A, § 22.20(A)
200.055	6138A, § 22.20(A)
200.056	6138A, § 22.20(A), (B)
200.057	6138A, § 22.70(A), (D)
200.058	6138A, § 9.10(A), (B)
200.059	6138A, § 9.10(C)
200.060	6138A, § 3.10(C)
200.101	6138A, § 3.10(A)
200.102	6138A, § 3.30(A)
200.103	6138A, § 3.30(A), (B)
200.104	6138A, § 7.30(A), (B)
200.105	6138A, § 7.30(B)
200.106	6138A, § 7.30(A)
200.107	6138A, § 7.30(A)
200.108	6138A, § 7.30(C)
200.109	6138A, § 8.10(C)
200.110	6138A, § 7.10(A), (C)
200.111	6138A, § 7.10(D)
200.113	6138A, § 18.10(A)
200.151	6138A, § 11.20(A)
200.152	6138A, § 3.30(A)
200.153	6138A, § 7.40(A)
200.154	6138A, § 7.40(B)
200.155	6138A, § 7.40(E)
200.156	6138A, § 7.40(F)(1), (2), (4), (G)
200.157	6138A, § 7.40(C), (D)
200.158	6138A, § 7.40(H)
200.159	6138A, § 11.20(B)
200.160	6138A, § 7.40(H)
200.161	6138A, § 8.10(A)
200.162	6138A, § 8.10(B)
200.163	6138A, § 8.10(B)
200.164	6138A, § 8.10(D), (E)
200.201	6138A, § 14.10(A)
200.202	6138A, § 14.10(B), (C)
200.203	6138A, § 14.10(D)
200.204	6138A, § 14.60
200.205	6138A, § 14.20(A)
200.206	6138A, § 14.20(B), (E)
200.207	6138A, § 14.20(C), (D)
200.208	6138A, § 14.20(C), (D)
200.209	6138A, § 14.40
200.210	6138A, § 14.50
200.211	6138A, § 14.30
200.251	6138A, § 10.10(B)
200.252	6138A, § 10.10(C)
200.253	6138A, § 11.10(A)
200.254	6138A, § 11.20(C)
200.255	6138A, § 11.20(D)
200.256	6138A, § 11.20(C)
200.257	6138A, § 12.10(A), (B)
200.258	6138A, § 12.10(D)
	6138A, § 13.10(E)(1)
200.259	6138A, § 13.10(E)(2)
200.260	6138A, § 12.10(C)
200.261	6138A, § 19.10
	6138A, § 22.20(A)
	6138A, § 22.30
200.262	6138A, § 12.10(E)
200.263	6138A, § 13.10(A)

Business Org. Code Section	Vernon's Ann. Civ.St. Article
200.264	6138A, § 13.10(C)
200.265	6138A, § 13.10(C)
200.266	6138A, § 13.10(C)
200.267	6138A, § 13.10(D)
200.268	6138A, § 12.10(F)
200.301	6138A, § 4.10(A)
200.302	6138A, § 4.10(A)
200.303	6138A, § 4.10(A)
200.304	6138A, § 4.10(B)
200.305	6138A, § 4.10(H)
200.306	6138A, § 4.10(B)
200.307	6138A, § 4.10(C)
200.308	6138A, § 4.10(D)
200.309	6138A, § 10.20(B)
200.310	6138A, § 4.10(E)
200.311	6138A, § 4.30
200.312	6138A, § 15.10(A), (B)
200.313	6138A, § 15.10(G)
200.314	6138A, § 15.10(E)
200.315	6138A, § 15.10(F)
200.316	6138A, § 4.10(F)
200.317	6138A, § 4.20
200.351	6138A, § 4.10(G)
200.401	6138A, § 23.30(H)
	6138A, § 24.10(A), (B)
	6138A, § 24.20(A)
200.402	6138A, § 23.30(A) to (C)
200.404	6138A, § 23.30(A) to (C)
200.405	6138A, § 24.10
	6138A, § 24.20(A)
200.406	6138A, § 23.30(D)
	6138A, § 24.20(A)
200.407	6138A, § 23.30(E)
	6138A, § 24.20(A)
200.408	6138A, § 23.30(F)
	6138A, § 24.20(A)
200.409	6138A, § 23.30(G)
200.410	6138A, § 25.10
	6138A, § 25.20
	6138A, § 25.30
200.451	6138A, § 19.10
200.453	6138A, § 19.10
200.501	6138A, § 18.10(B), (C)
200.502	6138A, § 17.10
200.503	6138A, § 4.10(I)
251.001	1396–50.01, § 2(3) to (9)
251.002	1396–50.01, § 3
251.003	1302–1.03
	1396–10.04, § A, C
	1396–50.01, § 45
251.051	1396–50.01, § 9(c)
251.052	1396–50.01, § 10
251.053	1396–50.01, § 11
	1396–50.01, § 12
251.101	1396–50.01, § 21(a) to (c)
251.102	1396–50.01, § 22
251.103	1396–50.01, § 23
251.104	1396–50.01, § 24
251.151	1396–50.01, § 26(a)
251.152	1396–50.01, § 33
251.153	1396–50.01, § 27, as amended Acts 72nd Leg., R.S., Ch. 897
251.154	1396–50.01, § 32
251.201	1396–50.01, § 28

DERIVATION TABLE 2

Business Org. Code Section	Vernon's Ann. Civ.St. Article
251.202	1396–50.01, § 29
251.203	1396–50.01, § 30
251.204	1396–50.01, § 31
251.251	1396–50.01, § 13(a)
251.252	1396–50.01, § 14
251.253	1396–50.01, § 15
251.254	1396–50.01, § 16
251.255	1396–50.01, § 17
251.256	1396–50.01, § 18
251.257	1396–50.01, § 19
	1396–50.01, § 20
251.301	1396–50.01, § 25
251.302	1396–50.01, § 34
251.351	1396–50.01, § 35(a)
251.352	1396–50.01, § 35(b) to (d)
251.353	1396–50.01, § 36
251.354	1396–50.01, § 37
251.401	1396–50.01, § 38(a), (c)
251.402	1396–6.05, § A
	1396–50.01, § 38(a)
251.403	1396–50.01, § 38(c)
251.404	1396–50.01, § 38(b)
251.451	1396–50.01, § 44
251.452	1396–50.01, § 39
252.001	1396–70.01, § 2
252.002	1396–70.01, § 3
252.003	1396–70.01, § 4
252.004	1396–70.01, § 5
252.005	1396–70.01, § 6
252.006	1396–70.01, § 7
252.007	1396–70.01, § 8
252.008	1396–70.01, § 9
252.009	1396–70.01, § 10
252.010	1396–70.01, § 11
252.011	1396–70.01, § 12
252.012	1396–70.01, § 13
252.013	1396–70.01, § 14
252.014	1396–70.01, § 15
252.015	1396–70.01, § 16
252.016	1396–70.01, § 18
301.001	1528e, § 16
	1528f, § 7
	1528n, Art. 11.05
301.002	1528e, § 5
	1528f, § 25
301.003	1528e, § 3(a), (b)
	1528e, § 4(b)
	1528e, § 12
	1528e, § 15
	1528f, § 2, as amended Acts 77th Leg., R.S., Chs. 508 and 883
	1528f, § 3
	1528n, Art. 11.01, § A(3)
	1528n, Art. 11.01, § B
301.004	1528e, § 12
	1528e, § 15
	1528f, § 10
	1528n, Art. 11.01, § B(2), (3)
301.005	1528e, § 19A(a), (b)
	1528n, Art. 11.07, § A
301.006	1528e, § 15
	1528e, § 19A(a)
	1528f, § 2(B)(1)
	1528n, Art. 11.04
	1528n, Art. 11.07, § A
301.007	1528e, § 9
	1528e, § 10
	1528e, § 12
	1528f, § 2(B)(1)
	1528f, § 9(C)
	1528f, § 10
	1528n, Art. 11.03, § A
301.008	1528e, § 14
	1528n, Art. 11.03, § B, C
301.009	1528e, § 12
	1528f, § 10
	1528n, Art. 11.03, § A
301.010	1528e, § 16
	1528f, § 24
	1528n, Art. 11.05
301.011	1528e, § 19
	1528n, Art. 11.06
301.012	1528e, § 4(b)
	1528f, § 2(B)
	1528n, Art. 11.01, § A(3), (4)
302.001	1528f, § 25
302.002	1528f, § 8(B)
302.003	1528f, § 14
302.004	1528f, § 9(D)
302.005	1528f, § 9(A)
302.006	1528f, § 9(E)
302.007	1528f, § 9(A)
302.008	1528f, § 9(C)
302.009	1528f, § 9(F)
302.010	1528f, § 9(B)
302.011	1528f, § 2(A), as amended Acts 77th Leg., R.S., Chs. 508 and 883
302.012	1528f, § 21
302.013	1528f, § 8(B)
	1528f, § 18
303.001	1528e, § 5
303.002	1528e, § 5
303.003	1528e, § 12
303.004	1528e, § 13
303.005	1528e, § 17
303.006	1528e, § 17
304.001	1528n, Art. 11.01, § B(2)

Business Org. Code Section	Texas Bus & C. Section
1.002(82)	43.002(8)
1.002(89)(B)	1.201(46)
	43.002(12)
	43.007
	43.008(a)

Business Org. Code Section	Texas Gov. Code Section
1.002(82)	311.005(6)
1.002(82)	2054.060(e)(1)
1.002(89)(B)	312.011(17)

DISPOSITION TABLE

Showing where provisions of former articles of Vernon's Annotated Civil Statutes are covered in the Utilities Code.

Vernon's Civ.St. Article	Utilities Code Section
1120	181.901
	181.902
1124a, § 1	182.101
	182.102
	182.103
§§ 2, 3	182.101
§ 4	182.102
§ 5	182.104
1416	181.081
	181.082
1417	181.081
	181.083
	181.084
1418	181.085
1419	181.086
1420	181.087
1421	181.088
1422	181.081
	181.089
1428	181.061
	181.062
1429	181.063
1430	181.064
1431	181.065
1432	181.066
1432a, § 1	186.042
§ 2	186.043
§ 3	186.041
§ 4	186.044
	186.045
1432b	186.021
1435	181.001
	181.007
	181.008
	181.009
1435a, § 1	163.011
	163.012
	163.013
§ 2	163.001
§ 3	163.012
	163.013
§ 4(1)	163.013
(2)	163.013
	163.014
(3)	163.015
(4)	163.016
§ 4a(a)	163.054
	163.056
	163.058
	163.060
(b)	163.054
	163.055
	163.058
(c)	163.051
	163.057
(d)	163.057
	163.059
(e)	163.057
	163.059
(f)	163.059
	163.060
	163.062
(g)	163.062
	163.063
(h)	163.063
(i)	163.064
(j)	163.051
	163.064
(k)	163.064
(*l*)	163.066
(m)	163.065
(n)	163.064
(*o*)	163.060
	163.061
	163.062
(p)	163.060
(q)	163.066
(r)	163.066
	163.067
	163.068
(s)	163.052
	163.053
§ 4b	163.101
	163.102
§ 4c(a)	163.121
(b)	163.123
(c)	163.122
(d)	163.124
§ 5	163.011
1435b, § 1	164.001
	164.003
	164.004
§ 2	164.005
§ 3	164.002
	164.006
1436	181.004
	181.005
	181.006
1436a, § 1	181.041
	181.042
	181.043
	181.044

DISPOSITION TABLE

Vernon's Civ.St. Article	Utilities Code Section
	181.045
	181.046
	181.047
§ 1a	181.041
	181.042
	181.043
	181.044
	181.045
	181.046
	181.047
1436b, § 1	181.021
	181.022
	181.023
	181.024
	181.025
§ 2	181.021
	181.026
1437	181.002
	181.003
1438	181.009
1440	183.001
	183.002
	183.003
	183.004
	183.005
1440a	183.001
	183.002
	183.003
	183.004
	183.005
	183.006
1446a, § 1	186.002
§ 2	186.001
§ 3	186.004
§ 4	186.005
§ 6	186.003
§ 7	186.006
1446b, § 1	186.031
§ 2	186.032
§ 3	186.033
§ 4	186.032
1446c–0, § 1.001	11.001
§ 1.002	11.002
§ 1.003	11.003
(2)	11.006
§ 1.004	11.004
§ 1.005(a)	11.007
§ 1.006	11.005
§ 1.021(a)	12.001
	12.051
(c)	12.052
(d)	12.051
§ 1.022	12.005
	13.002
§ 1.023(a), (c)	12.053
(d)	12.151
	13.022
(e)	12.152
(f)	12.152
(g)	12.153
(h)	12.153
§ 1.024(a) to (e)	12.154
(f)	12.055
§ 1.025(a), (b)	12.155

Vernon's Civ.St. Article	Utilities Code Section
(c)	12.156
§ 1.026(a) to (c)	12.054
(d), (e)	12.059
§ 1.028(a)	12.101
	12.102
(b)	12.103
(c), (d)	12.104
§ 1.029(a)	12.105
(b) to (d)	12.106
§ 1.030	12.057
§ 1.031(a)	12.002
	12.058
(b)	12.202
§ 1.032	12.003
§ 1.033	12.056
§ 1.034	14.057
§ 1.035	12.203
§ 1.036(a), (b)	12.201
(c)	12.202
§ 1.037	12.004
§ 1.051(a)	13.001
(b)	13.021
(c) to (e)	13.022
(f)	13.042
(g)	13.022
§ 1.0511	13.023
§ 1.0512	13.043
§ 1.0513(a)	13.063
(b)	13.061
(c)	13.062
§ 1.052	13.024
§ 1.053(a)	13.041
(b)	13.044
(c), (d)	13.045
(e)	13.046
§ 1.054	13.003
§ 1.101(a)	14.001
(b)	14.002
	14.052
(c)	14.052
(d)	14.051
(e)	14.053
§ 1.102	14.202
§ 1.103	14.008
§ 1.104	14.054
§ 1.201(a) to (e)	14.151
(d)	14.203
(e)	14.203
§ 1.202(a)	14.003
(b)	14.007
§ 1.203(a)	14.204
	14.205
	14.207
(b)	14.206
(c)	14.201
§ 1.204	14.152
§ 1.205	14.153
§ 1.206	14.006
§ 1.251	14.101
§ 1.252	14.102
§ 1.253	14.103
§ 1.271	14.154
§ 1.272	14.004
§ 1.301	12.004

DISPOSITION TABLE

Vernon's Civ.St. Article	Utilities Code Section
	15.001
	15.002
§ 1.302	15.003
§ 1.321	15.021
§ 1.3215(a) to (c)	15.023
(d) to (i)	15.024
(j) to (m)	15.025
(n) to (p)	15.026
(q) to (s)	15.027
§ 1.322	15.028
§ 1.323	15.029
§ 1.325(a)	15.030
(b)	15.032
§ 1.326	15.022
§ 1.327	15.033
§ 1.328	15.031
§ 1.351(a), (c)	16.001
§ 1.352(a)	16.002
(b)	16.003
§ 1.353	16.0031
§ 1.354(a)	16.004
(b)	16.041
§ 1.355(a)	16.021
§ 1.356	16.042
	16.043
§ 1.357	16.044
§ 1.401(a), (b)	15.051
(c)	15.052
§ 1.402	14.055
	14.056
§ 1.403	15.004
§ 1.404	11.008
	11.009
§ 1.405	14.005
§ 1.407(a)	12.252
(b)	12.253
(c)	12.251
(d)	12.254
(e)	12.255
§ 2.001(a)	31.001
(b) to (d)	36.007
	36.207
§ 2.0011	31.002
§ 2.0012(a)	31.002
	32.051
	32.053
	37.001
(b)	32.052
(c)	32.053
(d), (e)	32.054
§ 2.002	31.004
§ 2.003	31.003
§ 2.051(a)	34.003
(aa)	34.001
(b)	34.004
(bb)	34.152
(c)	34.004
(cc)	34.172
(d)	34.003
(dd)	34.153
(e)	34.021
(ee)	34.173
(f)	34.022
(g)	34.002

Vernon's Civ.St. Article	Utilities Code Section
(h)	34.023
(i), (j)	34.024
(k)	34.051
(*l*)	34.052
(m)	34.053
(n)	34.055
	34.056
(*o*)	34.101
(p)	34.102
(q)	34.103
(r)	34.104
(s)	34.105
(t)	34.103
(u)	34.151
(v)	34.005
(w)	34.006
	34.171
	36.008
	36.204
(x)	34.151
(y)	34.151
(z)	34.054
§ 2.052(a)	35.061
(b), (c)	36.007
§ 2.053(a)	35.031
(b), (c)	35.032
§ 2.054(a)	35.033
(b)	35.034
(c)	35.035
§ 2.056(a)	35.005
§ 2.057(a)	35.004
	35.006
	35.007
(b)	35.006
(c)	35.004
(d)	35.008
(e)	35.0081
(f)	35.002
	35.003
(g)	35.001
§ 2.101(a)	33.001
(b)	33.002
(c)	33.003
(d), (e)	32.001
§ 2.102	32.002
§ 2.103	33.007
§ 2.104(a)	33.002
(b)	33.004
(c)	32.003
	33.022
(d)	33.005
(e)	33.006
§ 2.105(a), (b)	33.021
(c)	33.024
§ 2.106(a)	33.023
(b)	33.025
	33.026
§ 2.107	32.004
§ 2.108(a)	33.051
(b)	33.052
(c)(1)	33.101
(c)(2)	33.102
(c)(3)	33.103
(c)(4)	33.104

DISPOSITION TABLE

Vernon's Civ.St. Article	Utilities Code Section
(d)	33.121
	33.122
(e)	33.121
	33.123
(f)	33.053
(g)	33.054
	33.055
§ 2.151(a)	32.102
	36.056
(b)	32.103
	36.063
(c)	36.059
(d)	32.102
	32.103
	36.056
	36.059
	36.063
§ 2.1511	36.206
§ 2.152(a)	32.104
(b) to (e)	36.061
§ 2.153	36.002
	38.003
§ 2.154	32.101
§ 2.155(a)	38.001
(b)	38.002
(c)	38.003
(d)	38.004
§ 2.156(a)	14.206
	38.051
(b)	38.052
§ 2.201	36.001
§ 2.2011(a)	36.251
	36.252
	36.255
	36.301
(b)	36.253
(c)	36.302
(d)	36.303
(e)	36.304
(f)	36.305
(g) to (i)	36.307
(j)	36.308
(k), (*l*)	36.309
(m)	36.255
(n)	36.254
(*o*)	36.307
(p)	36.301
	36.306
§ 2.202	36.003
§ 2.203(a)	36.051
(b)	36.052
§ 2.204	36.006
§ 2.206(a)	36.053
	36.054
(b)	36.054
(c)	36.053
§ 2.207	36.055
§ 2.208(a)	36.057
(b)	36.058
(c)	36.060
(d)	36.062
(e)	36.057
§ 2.209(b)	35.062
	35.064
(c)	35.064
	35.065
	35.066
(d)	35.063
	35.065
(e)	36.208
§ 2.210	36.064
§ 2.211(a)	36.151
(b)	36.152
(c)	36.153
	36.154
(d)	36.155
(e)	36.156
§ 2.212(a)	36.102
	36.103
(b)	36.101
	36.104
(c)	36.105
	36.106
(d)	36.107
	36.108
	36.109
(e)	36.110
(f)	36.111
(g)(1)	36.201
(g)(2)	36.203
(g)(3)	36.205
(h)	36.202
§ 2.213	36.005
§ 2.214	36.003
	38.021
§ 2.2141	36.351
§ 2.215(a), (b)	36.004
(c)	36.352
§ 2.216	38.022
§ 2.217	36.353
§ 2.251	37.001
§ 2.252	37.051
§ 2.253	37.052
§ 2.254(a)	37.053
(b)	37.157
(c)	37.053
§ 2.255(a)	37.054
(b), (c)	37.056
(d)	37.058
(e)	37.057
§ 2.256(a) to (c)	37.101
(d)	37.102
§ 2.257	37.155
§ 2.258	37.055
§ 2.259(a)	37.151
(b), (c)	37.152
§ 2.260	37.153
§ 2.261	37.154
§ 2.262	37.156
§ 2.263	38.071
§ 2.264	37.059
§ 3.001	51.001
§ 3.002(1)	51.002
(2)	51.002
	52.004
(3), (5) to (7)	51.002
(8)	51.002
	51.004

DISPOSITION TABLE

Vernon's Civ.St. Article	Utilities Code Section
(9)	51.002
	51.003
	52.002
(10) to (12)	51.002
§ 3.051(a)	52.001
(b)	52.002
	52.003
(c)	52.101
	52.102
	52.104
	52.105
	52.106
(d)	52.103
(e)(1)	52.054
(e)(2)	52.055
(e)(3)	52.056
	52.057
(f)	52.058
(g)	52.051
	52.053
(h)	52.059
(i)	52.060
(j)	52.052
	52.057
(k)	52.006
(*l*)	52.107
(m)	51.004
	52.108
(n)	52.110
(*o*)	52.109
(p)	52.111
(q)	52.005
	52.006
	52.108
	52.109
	52.110
	52.111
(r)	52.151
	52.153
(s)(1)	52.151
	52.152
(s)(2)	52.151
	52.154
§ 3.052(a)	55.081
(b)	55.085
(c)	55.084
(d)	55.086
(e)	55.087
(f)	55.083
(g)	55.089
(h)	55.082
	55.083
(i)	55.088
§ 3.053	51.010
§ 3.101(a)	51.006
(b)	51.007
	51.008
§ 3.1015	51.009
§ 3.102	51.005
§ 3.151(a)	52.252
	53.056
(b)	52.253
	53.063
(c)	53.059

Vernon's Civ.St. Article	Utilities Code Section
§ 3.152(a)	52.254
(b) to (d)	53.061
§ 3.153	53.002
	55.003
§ 3.154	52.251
§ 3.1545	52.255
§ 3.155(a)	55.001
(b)	55.002
(c)	55.003
§ 3.1555(a) to (c)	55.007
§ 3.1556	53.007
§ 3.201	53.001
§ 3.202	53.003
§ 3.203(a)	53.051
(b)	53.052
§ 3.204	53.006
§ 3.206(a)	53.053
	53.054
(b)	53.054
(c)	53.053
§ 3.207	53.055
§ 3.208(a)	53.057
(b)	53.058
(c)	53.060
(d)	53.062
(e)	53.057
§ 3.209	53.064
§ 3.210(a)	53.151
(b)	53.152
(c)	53.151
§ 3.211(a)	53.102
	53.103
(b)	53.101
	53.104
(c)	53.105
	53.106
(d)	53.107
	53.108
	53.109
(e)	53.110
(f)	53.111
(g)	51.009
	53.201
(h)	53.112
(i)	53.202
(j)	53.113
§ 3.212	55.004
§ 3.213(a)	53.251
(b), (c)	53.304
(d)	53.305
(e), (f)	53.306
(g)	53.303
(h)	53.301
(i)	53.307
(j)	53.252
(k)	53.308
(*l*)	53.302
§ 3.2135(a), (b)	53.352
(c)	53.354
(d)	53.355
(e)	53.356
(f)	53.357
(g)	53.358
(h)	53.359

DISPOSITION TABLE

Vernon's Civ.St. Article	Utilities Code Section
(i)	53.353
(j), (k)	53.351
§ 3.214	53.005
§ 3.215	53.003
	55.005
§ 3.216	53.004
§ 3.217	55.006
§ 3.218	55.010
§ 3.219	55.009
§ 3.251(a), (b)	54.052
(c)	54.001
(d)	54.201
	54.202
§ 3.252(a)	54.002
	54.003
(b)	54.002
§ 3.253(a)	54.053
(b)	54.258
(c)	54.053
§ 3.2531(a)	54.102
(b)	54.005
(c)	54.102
	54.104
	54.106
	54.107
(d)	54.104
	54.105
(e)	54.103
(f)	54.103
	54.108
(g), (h)	54.103
(i)	54.109
(j)	54.110
(k)	54.111
§ 3.2532(a)	54.154
(b)	54.153
	54.155
(c)	54.154
(d)	54.156
	54.157
(e)	54.004
	54.152
(f)	54.159
(g)	54.158
(h)	54.153
§ 3.254(a)	54.005
(b), (c)	54.054
§ 3.255	54.203
§ 3.2555(a)	54.102
	54.154
	54.204
(b)	54.204
(c)	54.259
(d)	54.260
(e)	54.204
	54.259
	54.260
(f)	54.205
(g)	54.259
(h)	54.206
(i)	54.261
§ 3.256	54.256
§ 3.257	54.006
§ 3.2571	54.007
§ 3.2572(a)	52.201
	52.202
	52.204
(b), (c)	52.203
(d)	52.206
(e), (f)	52.205
(g)	52.207
§ 3.258(a)	54.251
(b), (c)	54.252
§ 3.259	54.254
§ 3.2595	54.253
§ 3.260	54.255
§ 3.261	54.257
§ 3.2615	55.201
§ 3.262(a)	55.008
	55.021
	55.022
	55.023
(b)	55.023
§ 3.2625(a)	55.172
(b)	55.174
(c)	55.175
(d)	55.176
(e)	55.177
(f)	55.173
(g)	55.180
(h)	55.179
(i)	55.171
§ 3.263	54.008
§ 3.302(a)	55.102
(b)	55.103
(c)	55.105
(d)	55.106
(e)	55.107
(f)	55.104
(g)	55.102
(h)(1)	55.101
(h)(2)	55.101
(h)(3), (4)	55.101
	55.103
(i)	55.103
§ 3.3025(a)	55.106
	55.110
(b)	55.108
	55.109
(c)	55.108
(d)	55.108
	55.110
(e)	55.108
§ 3.303	53.065
§ 3.304(a)	55.045
	55.046
	55.047
	55.048
(b)(1)	55.044
(b)(2)	55.041
	55.042
	55.043
(c)	55.044
§ 3.305	55.178
§ 3.306	55.251
§ 3.307	55.252
§ 3.308	55.024
§ 3.309	55.203

DISPOSITION TABLE

Vernon's Civ.St. Article	Utilities Code Section
§ 3.310	55.202
§ 3.311	55.025
§ 3.351	58.001
§ 3.352(a)	58.021
	58.054
(b)(1)	58.002
	58.023
(b)(2)	58.024
(c)	58.022
(d)	58.025
	58.026
	58.027
	58.062
§ 3.353(a)	58.051
(b)	58.053
	58.061
(b), (c)(1)	58.055
(c)(2)	58.056
(c)(3)	58.057
(c)(4)	58.058
(d)	58.052
(e)	58.054
	58.060
§ 3.354	58.059
§ 3.355(a), (b)	58.101
(c)	58.024
(d)	58.102
	58.103
	58.104
§ 3.356(a)	58.151
	58.152
(b)	58.024
(c)	58.152
(d)	58.028
§ 3.357	58.024
§ 3.358(a)	58.201
(b)	58.053
	58.202
(c)	58.203
(d)	58.204
(e)	58.205
(f)	58.206
§ 3.359(a)	58.251
(b)(1)(I)	58.264
(b)(1)(A)	58.252
	58.253
(b)(1)(B), (C)	58.255
(b)(1)(D)	58.259
(b)(1)(E)	58.260
(b)(1)(F)	58.261
(b)(1)(G)	58.262
(b)(1)(H)	58.256
(b)(2)	58.258
(b)(3)	58.257
(b)(4)	58.258
(b)(5)	58.263
(b)(6)	58.254
(c)	58.265
(d)	58.266
(e)	58.252
(f)	58.255
(g)	58.267
§ 3.401	59.001
§ 3.402(a)	59.021
(b), (c)	59.024
(d)	59.026
	59.027
	59.028
	59.029
(e)	59.022
(f)	59.023
(g)	59.024
	59.025
(h)	59.002
§ 3.403(a)	59.051
(b)(1) to (5)	59.052
(b)(6)	59.029
(c)(1)	59.072
(c)(2)	59.073
(c)(3) to (5)	59.074
(c)(6)	59.075
(c)(7)	59.079
(c)(8)	59.077
(c)(9)	59.076
(c)(10)	59.077
(c)(11)	59.078
(c)(12)	59.072
(c)(13)	59.080
(c)(14)	59.081
(d)	59.053
(e)	59.055
	59.082
(f)(1)	59.071
	59.072
(f)(2)	59.071
(g)	59.054
§ 3.451(a)	60.001
(b), (c)	60.002
§ 3.452(a)	60.021
(b), (c)	60.022
(d)	60.023
§ 3.453(a) to (c)	60.041
(d)	60.042
(e)	60.043
(f)	60.044
(g)	60.045
§ 3.454(a) to (c)	60.061
(d)	60.062
(e)	60.063
(f), (g)	60.061
(h)	60.064
(i)	60.065
§ 3.455(a)	60.082
(b)	60.081
(c)	60.083
	60.084
§ 3.456(a)	60.141
§ 3.457(a)(1), (b)	60.101
(c)	60.102
§ 3.458(a)	60.121
	60.123
(b)	60.124
	60.125
	60.126
(c), (d)	60.125
(e)	60.127
(f)	60.124
(g)	60.128

DISPOSITION TABLE

Vernon's Civ.St. Article	Utilities Code Section
(h)	60.122
§ 3.459(a)	60.161
(b)	60.162
(c)	60.006
§ 3.460	60.003
§ 3.461	60.004
	60.0041
§ 3.462	60.005
§ 3.463	60.163
§ 3.501(a)	62.021
(b)	62.022
(c), (d)	62.023
§ 3.502(a)	62.002
(b)	62.072
(c)	62.073
(d)	62.074
(e)	62.075
(f)	62.076
(g)	62.078
(h)	62.071
(i)	62.077
§ 3.503(a)	62.041
(b)	62.043
(c)	62.044
(d)	62.045
(e)	62.046
(f)	62.042
(g)	62.047
§ 3.504(a)	62.102
	62.103
(b)	62.103
(c)	62.104
(d)	62.104
	62.105
(e)	62.101
(f)	62.106
(g)	62.107
(h)	62.108
§ 3.505(a)	62.132
(b)	62.132
	62.133
(c)	62.131
(d)	62.134
(e)	62.135
(f)	62.136
§ 3.506	62.001
§ 3.551(1) to (4)	63.001
(5)	63.002
(6) to (10)	63.001
(11)	63.003
§ 3.552(a)	63.031
(b), (c)	63.004
§ 3.553	63.032
	63.034
§ 3.554(a)	63.033
	63.034
(b) to (e)	63.035
(f)	63.036
(g), (h)	63.033
§ 3.555	63.037
§ 3.556	63.006
§ 3.557	63.005
	63.063
§ 3.558	63.038

Vernon's Civ.St. Article	Utilities Code Section
§ 3.559(a)	63.039
(b)	63.040
(c)	63.041
§ 3.560	63.061
§ 3.561	63.062
§ 3.562	63.042
§ 3.563(a)	63.007
	63.009
(b)	63.007
	63.008
§ 3.564	63.010
§ 3.566	63.011
§ 3.581	61.001
§ 3.582(a)	61.021
(b), (c)	61.022
§ 3.583(a)	61.023
(b)	61.024
(c)	61.025
(d)	61.026
§ 3.584(a)	61.041
(b)	61.042
(c)	61.043
§ 3.601	56.071
§ 3.602(a)	56.072
(b)	56.073
	56.074
§ 3.603(a)	56.071
	56.075
(b)	56.076
	56.077
(c)	56.071
§ 3.604(a)	56.101
	56.102
(b)	56.102
	56.103
	56.104
	56.105
(c)	56.107
(d)	56.106
(e)	56.108
(f)	56.109
(g)	56.110
(h)	56.110
	56.111
	56.112
§ 3.605(a), (b)	57.022
(c)	57.024
(d)	57.023
(e)	57.022
(f), (g)	57.025
(h)	57.021
§ 3.606(a)(1) to (5), (7) to (9)	57.042
(b)	57.041
(c)	57.044
	57.045
(d), (e)	57.044
(f)	57.051
(g) to (i)	57.045
(j)	57.043
(k)	57.043
(*l*), (m)	57.048
(n)	57.043
	57.048

DISPOSITION TABLE

Vernon's Civ.St. Article	Utilities Code Section
(*o*)	57.049
(p)	57.045
(q)	57.046
(r) to (t)	57.047
(u)	57.050
(v)	57.047
§ 3.607	56.078
§ 3.608(a)	56.021
(b)(1) to (5)	56.025
(b)(6)	56.026
(c)	56.022
(d), (e)	56.023
(f)	56.023
	56.024
§ 3.609(a)	57.072
(b)	57.071
§ 3.610	56.002
	57.001
§ 3.651(1)	55.121
§ 3.652	55.122
§ 3.653(a)	55.123
	55.124
	55.125
	55.126
	55.127
	55.128
	55.129
(b), (c)	55.127
§ 3.654(a)	55.134
(b)	55.136
(c)	55.136
§ 3.655(a)	55.130
	55.131
(b)	55.130
	55.132
(c)	55.130
(d)	55.133
(e)	55.134
§ 3.656(a) to (d)	55.137
§ 3.657(a)	55.135
(b)	55.138
§ 3.659	55.151
§ 3.660	55.152
1446c–1, § 1	185.001
§ 2	185.003
§ 3	185.005
§ 4	185.004
§ 5	185.002
1446c–2, § 1	182.001
§ 2(a)	182.002
(b)	182.003
(c)	182.004
(d)	182.002
(e)	182.005
1446d, § 1	184.011
§ 2(a), (b)	184.012
(c)	184.013
§ 3	184.013
	184.014
§ 4	184.013
1446d–2, § 1	184.031
§ 2	184.032
	184.033
	184.034

Vernon's Civ.St. Article	Utilities Code Section
	184.035
1446e, § 1.01	101.001
§ 1.02	101.002
§ 1.03(1), (3), (4), (6), (7)	101.003
(8)	101.003
	101.004
(9) to (17)	101.003
§ 1.04	101.005
§ 2.01(a)	103.001
(b)	102.001
(c)	101.006
§ 2.02	102.002
§ 3.01	103.002
§ 3.02	103.021
§ 3.03(a)	103.022
(b)	103.023
	103.024
§ 3.04	102.005
§ 3.05(a)	103.051
(b)	103.052
(c)	103.053
(d)	103.054
(e)	103.055
	103.056
§ 4.01(a)	102.101
(b)	102.152
	104.054
(c)	102.153
	104.058
(d)	102.101
	102.202
(e)	104.056
(f)	102.101
	102.152
	102.153
	102.202
	104.054
	104.056
	104.058
§ 4.02	102.003
§ 4.03(a)	102.203
	102.204
	102.206
(b)	102.205
(c)	102.201
§ 4.04	102.154
	104.057
§ 4.05	104.002
§ 4.06	102.151
§ 4.07	102.102
§ 4.08	102.103
§ 4.09(a)	104.251
(b)	104.252
(c)	104.253
(d)	104.254
§ 4.10(a)	102.205
	104.256
(b)	104.257
§ 5.01	104.001
§ 5.02(a), (b)	104.003
(c)	104.201
(d)	104.003
(e)	104.111

DISPOSITION TABLE

Vernon's Civ.St. Article	Utilities Code Section
(f)	104.003
§ 5.03	104.051
(b)	104.111
§ 5.04(a)	104.052
(b)	104.008
§ 5.05	104.053
§ 5.06	104.055
§ 5.061	104.202
§ 5.07(a)	104.151
(b)	104.152
§ 5.08(a)	104.102
	104.103
(b)	104.101
	104.104
(c)	104.105
(d)	104.106
	104.107
	104.108
(e)	104.109
(f)	104.110
§ 5.09	104.006
§ 5.10	104.004
§ 5.11	104.005
§ 5.12	104.007
§ 5.13	104.203
§ 6.01	102.051
§ 6.02	102.052
§ 6.03	102.053
§ 6.04	102.054
§ 7.01	102.104
§ 7.02	102.004
§ 8.01	105.001
§ 9.01	105.021
§ 9.02	105.023
§ 9.03(a)	105.024
(b)	105.026
§ 9.04	105.022
§ 9.05	105.027
§ 9.06	105.025
§ 9.07(a)	101.051
(c)	101.054
(e)	101.053
(f) to (h)	101.052
§ 10.01	105.051
§ 10.02	102.251
	102.252
§ 10.03	105.002
§ 10.04	101.007
	101.008
§§ 10.05, 10.06	104.255
1446f, § 1	184.051
§ 2	184.052
1446g	184.071
1446h, § 1	182.051
§ 2	182.052
§ 3	182.053
§ 4	182.052
§ 5	182.054
§ 6	182.055
1528b, § 1	161.001
§ 2(1) to (3), (6) to (8)	161.002
§ 3	161.002
	161.122
§ 4	161.052

Vernon's Civ.St. Article	Utilities Code Section
	161.064
	161.076
	161.121
	161.123
	161.125
§ 4A	161.124
§ 5	161.051
§ 6(a)	161.052
	161.053
	161.054
	161.071
	161.072
(b)	161.054
§ 7	161.004
§ 8	161.055
§ 9	161.056
§ 10	161.057
§ 11	161.064
§ 12	161.065
§ 13	161.067
§ 14	161.068
§ 15	161.070
§ 16	161.060
	161.065
	161.066
§ 17	161.069
§ 18	161.071
§ 19	161.071
	161.072
	161.073
§ 19A	161.078
§ 20	161.072
§ 21	161.074
§ 22	161.075
§ 23	161.076
§ 24	161.077
§ 25	161.059
§ 26	161.151
	161.152
§ 27(a)	161.201
	161.202
(b)	161.202
§ 28(a)	161.251
(b)	161.252
	161.253
(c)	161.254
§ 29	161.055
	161.152
	161.202
	161.251
§ 30	161.061
	161.062
§ 31	161.063
§ 32	161.058
§ 33	161.079
§ 34	161.003
§ 36	161.005
1528c, § 1	162.001
§ 2(1) to (3), (6), (8)	162.003
§ 3	162.002
§ 4	162.052
	162.121
	162.122
	162.124

DISPOSITION TABLE

Vernon's Civ.St. Article	Utilities Code Section
§ 4A	162.079
§ 5	162.051
§ 6(a)	162.004
	162.052
	162.053
	162.054
	162.071
	162.072
(b)	162.054
§ 7	162.055
§ 8	162.056
§ 9	162.057
§ 10	162.064
§ 11(a)	162.065
(b)	162.066
§ 12(a), (b)	162.067
(c)	162.068
(d), (e)	162.070
§ 13	162.069
§ 14(a)	162.071
	162.072
	162.073
	162.074
	162.075
(b), (c)	162.072
(d)	162.075
(e)	162.071
§ 15	162.076
§ 16	162.077
§ 17	162.078
§ 18	162.151
	162.152
	162.153
	162.154
§ 19	162.080
§ 20(a)	162.201
	162.202
(b)	162.201
	162.202
§ 20A(a), (b)	162.203
(c)	162.203
	162.204
(d) to (f)	162.204
§ 20B	162.205
§ 20C(a), (b)	162.251
(c)	162.251
	162.252
(d) to (f)	162.252
§ 20D(a), (b)	162.253
(c), (d)	162.254
§ 21(a)	162.301
(b)	162.302
	162.303
(c)	162.304
§ 22	162.059
§ 23(a)	162.125
(b)	162.126
§ 24	162.060
§ 25	162.005
§ 26	162.006
§ 27	162.081
§ 28	162.055
	162.080
	162.154

Vernon's Civ.St. Article	Utilities Code Section
	162.202
	162.204
	162.252
	162.254
	162.301
§ 29	162.061
	162.062
§ 30	162.123
§ 31	162.063
§ 32	162.058
§ 33	162.082
6050, § 1(a), (b)	121.001
§ 1(c)	121.001
	121.051
(d)	121.002
(e)	121.051
§§ 2, 3	121.003
§ 4(a)	121.004
	121.005
(b)	121.005
§ 5	121.006
6051	121.052
6052	121.101
6053, § 1(a)	121.151
	121.152
(c)	121.103
§ 1a(a)	124.001
(b)	124.002
§ 2	121.251
	121.252
	121.253
6053–1, Subsecs. (A), (B)	121.201
Subsec. (C)	121.203
	121.204
	121.205
Subsec. (D)	121.202
6053–2, §§ (a) to (c)	121.206
(d) to (i)	121.207
(j)	121.208
(k)	121.209
(m)	121.210
6054	121.153
6055	121.154
6056	121.102
6057	121.104
6057a	121.104
6057b	121.310
6058	121.155
6059	121.401
	121.402
	121.403
6060, § 1(a)	122.001
	122.051
(b)	122.051
(c)	122.001
	122.052
§ 2(a)	122.101
	122.102
	122.103
(b)	122.102
§ 3(a)	122.151
(b)	122.104
(c)	122.152
§ 4(a)	122.201
	122.202
	122.203
	122.204

DISPOSITION TABLE

Vernon's Civ.St. Article	Utilities Code Section
6061	121.156
6062	121.302
(b)	122.205
	121.303
6062A, §§ (a) to (c)	121.304
(d) to (i)	121.305
(j)	121.306
(k)	121.308
(m)	121.309
(n)	121.307
6063	121.301
6064	121.157
6065	121.157
6066	121.158
6066f	123.001
	123.002
6066g, § 1	123.021
§ 2	123.022
§ 3	123.023
§ 4	123.024
9021, § 1	181.101
§§ 2, 3	181.102
§ 4(a), (b)	181.103
(c)	181.104

DERIVATION TABLE

Showing where provisions of the Utilities Code were formerly covered in Vernon's Annotated Civil Statutes.

Utilities Code Section	Vernon's Civ.St. Article
1.001	—
1.002	—
1.003	—
11.001	1446c–0, § 1.001
11.002	1446c–0, § 1.002
11.003	1446c–0, § 1.003
11.004	1446c–0, § 1.004
11.005	1446c–0, § 1.006
11.006	1446c–0, § 1.003(2)
11.007	1446c–0, § 1.005(a)
11.008	1446c–0, § 1.404
11.009	1446c–0, § 1.404
12.001	1446c–0, § 1.021(a)
12.002	1446c–0, § 1.031(a)
12.003	1446c–0, § 1.032
12.004	1446c–0, § 1.037
	1446c–0, § 1.301
12.005	1446c–0, § 1.022
12.051	1446c–0, § 1.021(a)
	1446c–0, § 1.021(d)
12.052	1446c–0, § 1.021(c)
12.053	1446c–0, § 1.023(a), (c)
12.054	1446c–0, § 1.026(a) to (c)
12.055	1446c–0, § 1.024(f)
12.056	1446c–0, § 1.033
12.057	1446c–0, § 1.030
12.058	1446c–0, § 1.031(a)
12.059	1446c–0, § 1.026(d), (e)
12.101	1446c–0, § 1.028(a)
12.102	1446c–0, § 1.028(a)
12.103	1446c–0, § 1.028(b)
12.104	1446c–0, § 1.028(c), (d)
12.105	1446c–0, § 1.029(a)
12.106	1446c–0, § 1.029(b) to (d)
12.151	1446c–0, § 1.023(d)
12.152	1446c–0, § 1.023(e)
	1446c–0, § 1.023(f)
12.153	1446c–0, § 1.023(g)
	1446c–0, § 1.023(h)
12.154	1446c–0, § 1.024(a) to (e)
12.155	1446c–0, § 1.025(a), (b)
12.156	1446c–0, § 1.025(c)
12.201	1446c–0, § 1.036(a), (b)
12.202	1446c–0, § 1.031(b)
	1446c–0, § 1.036(c)
12.203	1446c–0, § 1.035

Utilities Code Section	Vernon's Civ.St. Article
12.251	1446c–0, § 1.407(c)
12.252	1446c–0, § 1.407(a)
12.253	1446c–0, § 1.407(b)
12.254	1446c–0, § 1.407(d)
12.255	1446c–0, § 1.407(e)
13.001	1446c–0, § 1.051(a)
13.002	1446c–0, § 1.022
13.003	1446c–0, § 1.054
13.021	1446c–0, § 1.051(b)
13.022	1446c–0, §§ 1.023(d), 1.051(c) to (e), (g)
13.023	1446c–0, § 1.0511
13.024	1446c–0, § 1.052
13.041	1446c–0, § 1.053(a)
13.042	1446c–0, § 1.051(f)
13.043	1446c–0, § 1.0512
13.044	1446c–0, § 1.053(b)
13.045	1446c–0, § 1.053(c), (d)
13.046	1446c–0, § 1.053(e)
13.061	1446c–0, § 1.0513(b)
13.062	1446c–0, § 1.0513(c)
13.063	1446c–0, § 1.0513(a)
14.001	1446c–0, § 1.101(a)
14.002	1446c–0, § 1.101(b)
14.003	1446c–0, § 1.202(a)
14.004	1446c–0, § 1.272
14.005	1446c–0, § 1.405
14.006	1446c–0, § 1.206
14.007	1446c–0, § 1.202(b)
14.008	1446c–0, § 1.103
14.051	1446c–0, § 1.101(d)
14.052	1446c–0, § 1.101(b), (c)
14.053	1446c–0, § 1.101(e)
14.054	1446c–0, § 1.104
14.055	1446c–0, § 1.402
14.056	1446c–0, § 1.402
14.057	1446c–0, § 1.034
14.101	1446c–0, § 1.251
14.102	1446c–0, § 1.252
14.103	1446c–0, § 1.253
14.151	1446c–0, § 1.201(a) to (e)
14.152	1446c–0, § 1.204
14.153	1446c–0, § 1.205
14.154	1446c–0, § 1.271
14.201	1446c–0, § 1.203(c)
14.202	1446c–0, § 1.102

Utilities Code Section	Vernon's Civ.St. Article
14.203	1446c–0, § 1.201(d)
	1446c–0, § 1.201(e)
14.204	1446c–0, § 1.203(a)
14.205	1446c–0, § 1.203(a)
14.206	1446c–0, § 1.203(b)
	1446c–0, § 2.156(a)
14.207	1446c–0, § 1.203(a)
15.001	1446c–0, § 1.301
15.002	1446c–0, § 1.301
15.003	1446c–0, § 1.302
15.004	1446c–0, § 1.403
15.021	1446c–0, § 1.321
15.022	1446c–0, § 1.326
15.023	1446c–0, § 1.3215(a) to (c)
15.024	1446c–0, § 1.3215(d) to (i)
15.025	1446c–0, § 1.3215(j) to (m)
15.026	1446c–0, § 1.3215(n) to (p)
15.027	1446c–0, § 1.3215(q) to (s)
15.028	1446c–0, § 1.322
15.029	1446c–0, § 1.323
15.030	1446c–0, § 1.325(a)
15.031	1446c–0, § 1.328
15.032	1446c–0, § 1.325(b)
15.033	1446c–0, § 1.327
15.051	1446c–0, § 1.401(a), (b)
15.052	1446c–0, § 1.401(c)
16.001	1446c–0, § 1.351(a), (c)
16.002	1446c–0, § 1.352(a)
16.003	1446c–0, § 1.352(b)
16.0031	1446c–0, § 1.353
16.004	1446c–0, § 1.354(a)
16.021	1446c–0, § 1.355(a)
16.041	1446c–0, § 1.354(b)
16.042	1446c–0, § 1.356
16.043	1446c–0, § 1.356
16.044	1446c–0, § 1.357
31.001	1446c–0, § 2.001(a)
31.002	1446c–0, § 2.0011
	1446c–0, § 2.0012(a)
31.003	1446c–0, § 2.003
31.004	1446c–0, § 2.002
32.001	1446c–0, § 2.101(d), (e)
32.002	1446c–0, § 2.102
32.003	1446c–0, § 2.104(c)
32.004	1446c–0, § 2.107
32.051	1446c–0, § 2.0012(a)
32.052	1446c–0, § 2.0012(b)
32.053	1446c–0, § 2.0012(a)
	1446c–0, § 2.0012(c)
32.054	1446c–0, § 2.0012(d), (e)
32.101	1446c–0, § 2.154
32.102	1446c–0, § 2.151(a)
	1446c–0, § 2.151(d)
32.103	1446c–0, § 2.151(b)
	1446c–0, § 2.151(d)
32.104	1446c–0, § 2.152(a)
33.001	1446c–0, § 2.101(a)
33.002	1446c–0, § 2.101(b)
	1446c–0, § 2.104(a)
33.003	1446c–0, § 2.101(c)
33.004	1446c–0, § 2.104(b)
33.005	1446c–0, § 2.104(d)
33.006	1446c–0, § 2.104(e)
33.007	1446c–0, § 2.103
33.021	1446c–0, § 2.105(a), (b)
33.022	1446c–0, § 2.104(c)
33.023	1446c–0, § 2.106(a)
33.024	1446c–0, § 2.105(c)
33.025	1446c–0, § 2.106(b)
33.026	1446c–0, § 2.106(b)
33.051	1446c–0, § 2.108(a)
33.052	1446c–0, § 2.108(b)
33.053	1446c–0, § 2.108(f)
33.054	1446c–0, § 2.108(g)
33.055	1446c–0, § 2.108(g)
33.101	1446c–0, § 2.108(c)(1)
33.102	1446c–0, § 2.108(c)(2)
33.103	1446c–0, § 2.108(c)(3)
33.104	1446c–0, § 2.108(c)(4)
33.121	1446c–0, § 2.108(d), (e)
33.122	1446c–0, § 2.108(d)
33.123	1446c–0, § 2.108(e)
34.001	1446c–0, § 2.051(aa)
34.002	1446c–0, § 2.051(g)
34.003	1446c–0, § 2.051(a)
	1446c–0, § 2.051(d)
34.004	1446c–0, § 2.051(b)
	1446c–0, § 2.051(c)
34.005	1446c–0, § 2.051(v)
34.006	1446c–0, § 2.051(w)
34.021	1446c–0, § 2.051(e)
34.022	1446c–0, § 2.051(f)
34.023	1446c–0, § 2.051(h)
34.024	1446c–0, § 2.051(i), (j)
34.051	1446c–0, § 2.051(k)
34.052	1446c–0, § 2.051(*l*)
34.053	1446c–0, § 2.051(m)
34.054	1446c–0, § 2.051(z)
34.055	1446c–0, § 2.051(n)
34.056	1446c–0, § 2.051(n)
34.101	1446c–0, § 2.051(*o*)
34.102	1446c–0, § 2.051(p)
34.103	1446c–0, § 2.051(q)
	1446c–0, § 2.051(t)
34.104	1446c–0, § 2.051(r)
34.105	1446c–0, § 2.051(s)
34.151	1446c–0, § 2.051(u)
	1446c–0, § 2.051(x)
	1446c–0, § 2.051(y)
34.152	1446c–0, § 2.051(bb)
34.153	1446c–0, § 2.051(dd)
34.171	1446c–0, § 2.051(w)
34.172	1446c–0, § 2.051(cc)
34.173	1446c–0, § 2.051(ee)

DERIVATION TABLE

Utilities Code Section	Vernon's Civ.St. Article
35.001	1446c–0, § 2.057(g)
35.002	1446c–0, § 2.057(f)
35.003	1446c–0, § 2.057(f)
35.004	1446c–0, § 2.057(a)
	1446c–0, § 2.057(c)
35.005	1446c–0, § 2.056(a)
35.006	1446c–0, § 2.057(a)
	1446c–0, § 2.057(b)
35.007	1446c–0, § 2.057(a)
35.008	1446c–0, § 2.057(d)
35.0081	1446c–0, § 2.057(e)
35.031	1446c–0, § 2.053(a)
35.032	1446c–0, § 2.053(b), (c)
35.033	1446c–0, § 2.054(a)
35.034	1446c–0, § 2.054(b)
35.035	1446c–0, § 2.054(c)
35.061	1446c–0, § 2.052(a)
35.062	1446c–0, § 2.209(b)
35.063	1446c–0, § 2.209(d)
35.064	1446c–0, § 2.209(b)
	1446c–0, § 2.209(c)
35.065	1446c–0, § 2.209(c)
	1446c–0, § 2.209(d)
35.066	1446c–0, § 2.209(c)
36.001	1446c–0, § 2.201
36.002	1446c–0, § 2.153
36.003	1446c–0, § 2.202
	1446c–0, § 2.214
36.004	1446c–0, § 2.215(a), (b)
36.005	1446c–0, § 2.213
36.006	1446c–0, § 2.204
36.007	1446c–0, §§ 2.001(b) to (d), 2.052(b), (c)
36.008	1446c–0, § 2.051(w)
36.051	1446c–0, § 2.203(a)
36.052	1446c–0, § 2.203(b)
36.053	1446c–0, § 2.206(a)
	1446c–0, § 2.206(c)
36.054	1446c–0, § 2.206(a)
	1446c–0, § 2.206(b)
36.055	1446c–0, § 2.207
36.056	1446c–0, § 2.151(a)
	1446c–0, § 2.151(d)
36.057	1446c–0, § 2.208(a)
	1446c–0, § 2.208(e)
36.058	1446c–0, § 2.208(b)
36.059	1446c–0, § 2.151(c)
	1446c–0, § 2.151(d)
36.060	1446c–0, § 2.208(c)
36.061	1446c–0, § 2.152(b) to (e)
36.062	1446c–0, § 2.208(d)
36.063	1446c–0, § 2.151(b)
	1446c–0, § 2.151(d)
36.064	1446c–0, § 2.210
36.101	1446c–0, § 2.212(b)
36.102	1446c–0, § 2.212(a)
36.103	1446c–0, § 2.212(a)
36.104	1446c–0, § 2.212(b)
36.105	1446c–0, § 2.212(c)
36.106	1446c–0, § 2.212(c)
36.107	1446c–0, § 2.212(d)
36.108	1446c–0, § 2.212(d)
36.109	1446c–0, § 2.212(d)
36.110	1446c–0, § 2.212(e)
36.111	1446c–0, § 2.212(f)
36.151	1446c–0, § 2.211(a)
36.152	1446c–0, § 2.211(b)
36.153	1446c–0, § 2.211(c)
36.154	1446c–0, § 2.211(c)
36.155	1446c–0, § 2.211(d)
36.156	1446c–0, § 2.211(e)
36.201	1446c–0, § 2.212(g)(1)
36.202	1446c–0, § 2.212(h)
36.203	1446c–0, § 2.212(g)(2)
36.204	1446c–0, § 2.051(w)
36.205	1446c–0, § 2.212(g)(3)
36.206	1446c–0, § 2.1511
36.207	1446c–0, § 2.001(d)
36.208	1446c–0, § 2.209(e)
36.251	1446c–0, § 2.2011(a)
36.252	1446c–0, § 2.2011(a)
36.253	1446c–0, § 2.2011(b)
36.254	1446c–0, § 2.2011(n)
36.255	1446c–0, § 2.2011(a)
	1446c–0, § 2.2011(m)
36.301	1446c–0, § 2.2011(a)
	1446c–0, § 2.2011(p)
36.302	1446c–0, § 2.2011(c)
36.303	1446c–0, § 2.2011(d)
36.304	1446c–0, § 2.2011(e)
36.305	1446c–0, § 2.2011(f)
36.306	1446c–0, § 2.2011(p)
36.307	1446c–0, § 2.2011(g) to (i)
	1446c–0, § 2.2011(*o*)
36.308	1446c–0, § 2.2011(j)
36.309	1446c–0, § 2.2011(k), (*l*)
36.351	1446c–0, § 2.2141
36.352	1446c–0, § 2.215(c)
36.353	1446c–0, § 2.217
37.001	1446c–0, § 2.0012(a)
	1446c–0, § 2.251
37.051	1446c–0, § 2.252
37.052	1446c–0, § 2.253
37.053	1446c–0, § 2.254(a)
	1446c–0, § 2.254(c)
37.054	1446c–0, § 2.255(a)
37.055	1446c–0, § 2.258
37.056	1446c–0, § 2.255(b), (c)
37.057	1446c–0, § 2.255(e)
37.058	1446c–0, § 2.255(d)
37.059	1446c–0, § 2.264
37.101	1446c–0, § 2.256(a) to (c)
37.102	1446c–0, § 2.256(d)
37.151	1446c–0, § 2.259(a)

DERIVATION TABLE

Utilities Code Section	Vernon's Civ.St. Article
37.152	1446c–0, § 2.259(b), (c)
37.153	1446c–0, § 2.260
37.154	1446c–0, § 2.261
37.155	1446c–0, § 2.257
37.156	1446c–0, § 2.262
37.157	1446c–0, § 2.254(b)
38.001	1446c–0, § 2.155(a)
38.002	1446c–0, § 2.155(b)
38.003	1446c–0, § 2.153
	1446c–0, § 2.155(c)
38.004	1446c–0, § 2.155(d)
38.021	1446c–0, § 2.214
38.022	1446c–0, § 2.216
38.051	1446c–0, § 2.156(a)
38.052	1446c–0, § 2.156(b)
38.071	1446c–0, § 2.263
51.001	1446c–0, § 3.001
51.002	1446c–0, § 3.002(1) to (3), (5) to (12)
51.003	1446c–0, § 3.002(9)
51.004	1446c–0, § 3.002(8)
	1446c–0, § 3.051(m)
51.005	1446c–0, § 3.102
51.006	1446c–0, § 3.101(a)
51.007	1446c–0, § 3.101(b)
51.008	1446c–0, § 3.101(b)
51.009	1446c–0, § 3.1015
	1446c–0, § 3.211(g)
51.010	1446c–0, § 3.053
52.001	1446c–0, § 3.051(a)
52.002	1446c–0, § 3.002(9)
	1446c–0, § 3.051(b)
52.003	1446c–0, § 3.051(b)
52.004	1446c–0, § 3.002(2)
52.005	1446c–0, § 3.051(q)
52.006	1446c–0, § 3.051(k)
	1446c–0, § 3.051(q)
52.051	1446c–0, § 3.051(g)
52.052	1446c–0, § 3.051(j)
52.053	1446c–0, § 3.051(g)
52.054	1446c–0, § 3.051(e)(1)
52.055	1446c–0, § 3.051(e)(2)
52.056	1446c–0, § 3.051(e)(3)
52.057	1446c–0, § 3.051(e)(3)
	1446c–0, § 3.051(j)
52.058	1446c–0, § 3.051(f)
52.059	1446c–0, § 3.051(h)
52.060	1446c–0, § 3.051(i)
52.101	1446c–0, § 3.051(c)
52.102	1446c–0, § 3.051(c)
52.103	1446c–0, § 3.051(d)
52.104	1446c–0, § 3.051(c)
52.105	1446c–0, § 3.051(c)
52.106	1446c–0, § 3.051(c)
52.107	1446c–0, § 3.051(*l*)
52.108	1446c–0, § 3.051(m)
	1446c–0, § 3.051(q)
52.109	1446c–0, § 3.051(*o*)
	1446c–0, § 3.051(q)
52.110	1446c–0, § 3.051(n)
	1446c–0, § 3.051(q)
52.111	1446c–0, § 3.051(p)
	1446c–0, § 3.051(q)
52.151	1446c–0, § 3.051(r)
	1446c–0, § 3.051(s)(1)
	1446c–0, § 3.051(s)(2)
52.152	1446c–0, § 3.051(s)(1)
52.153	1446c–0, § 3.051(r)
52.154	1446c–0, § 3.051(s)(2)
52.201	1446c–0, § 3.2572(a)
52.202	1446c–0, § 3.2572(a)
52.203	1446c–0, § 3.2572(b), (c)
52.204	1446c–0, § 3.2572(a)
52.205	1446c–0, § 3.2572(e), (f)
52.206	1446c–0, § 3.2572(d)
52.207	1446c–0, § 3.2572(g)
52.251	1446c–0, § 3.154
52.252	1446c–0, § 3.151(a)
52.253	1446c–0, § 3.151(b)
52.254	1446c–0, § 3.152(a)
52.255	1446c–0, § 3.1545
53.001	1446c–0, § 3.201
53.002	1446c–0, § 3.153
53.003	1446c–0, § 3.202
	1446c–0, § 3.215
53.004	1446c–0, § 3.216
53.005	1446c–0, § 3.214
53.006	1446c–0, § 3.204
53.007	1446c–0, § 3.1556
53.051	1446c–0, § 3.203(a)
53.052	1446c–0, § 3.203(b)
53.053	1446c–0, § 3.206(a)
	1446c–0, § 3.206(c)
53.054	1446c–0, § 3.206(a)
	1446c–0, § 3.206(b)
53.055	1446c–0, § 3.207
53.056	1446c–0, § 3.151(a)
53.057	1446c–0, § 3.208(a)
	1446c–0, § 3.208(e)
53.058	1446c–0, § 3.208(b)
53.059	1446c–0, § 3.151(c)
53.060	1446c–0, § 3.208(c)
53.061	1446c–0, § 3.152(b) to (d)
53.062	1446c–0, § 3.208(d)
53.063	1446c–0, § 3.151(b)
53.064	1446c–0, § 3.209
53.065	1446c–0, § 3.303
53.101	1446c–0, § 3.211(b)
53.102	1446c–0, § 3.211(a)
53.103	1446c–0, § 3.211(a)
53.104	1446c–0, § 3.211(b)
53.105	1446c–0, § 3.211(c)
53.106	1446c–0, § 3.211(c)
53.107	1446c–0, § 3.211(d)

DERIVATION TABLE

Utilities Code Section	Vernon's Civ.St. Article
53.108	1446c–0, § 3.211(d)
53.109	1446c–0, § 3.211(d)
53.110	1446c–0, § 3.211(e)
53.111	1446c–0, § 3.211(f)
53.112	1446c–0, § 3.211(h)
53.113	1446c–0, § 3.211(j)
53.151	1446c–0, § 3.210(a)
	1446c–0, § 3.210(c)
53.152	1446c–0, § 3.210(b)
53.201	1446c–0, § 3.211(g)
53.202	1446c–0, § 3.211(i)
53.251	1446c–0, § 3.213(a)
53.252	1446c–0, § 3.213(j)
53.301	1446c–0, § 3.213(h)
53.302	1446c–0, § 3.213(*l*)
53.303	1446c–0, § 3.213(g)
53.304	1446c–0, § 3.213(b), (c)
53.305	1446c–0, § 3.213(d)
53.306	1446c–0, § 3.213(e), (f)
53.307	1446c–0, § 3.213(i)
53.308	1446c–0, § 3.213(k)
53.351	1446c–0, § 3.2135(j), (k)
53.352	1446c–0, § 3.2135(a), (b)
53.353	1446c–0, § 3.2135(i)
53.354	1446c–0, § 3.2135(c)
53.355	1446c–0, § 3.2135(d)
53.356	1446c–0, § 3.2135(e)
53.357	1446c–0, § 3.2135(f)
53.358	1446c–0, § 3.2135(g)
53.359	1446c–0, § 3.2135(h)
54.001	1446c–0, § 3.251(c)
54.002	1446c–0, § 3.252(a)
	1446c–0, § 3.252(b)
54.003	1446c–0, § 3.252(a)
54.004	1446c–0, § 3.2532(e)
54.005	1446c–0, § 3.2531(b)
	1446c–0, § 3.254(a)
54.006	1446c–0, § 3.257
54.007	1446c–0, § 3.2571
54.008	1446c–0, § 3.263
54.051	—
54.052	1446c–0, § 3.251(a), (b)
54.053	1446c–0, § 3.253(a)
	1446c–0, § 3.253(c)
54.054	1446c–0, § 3.254(b), (c)
54.101	—
54.102	1446c–0, § 3.2531(a)
	1446c–0, § 3.2531(c)
	1446c–0, § 3.2555(a)
54.103	1446c–0, § 3.2531(e) to (h)
54.104	1446c–0, § 3.2531(c)
	1446c–0, § 3.2531(d)
54.105	1446c–0, § 3.2531(d)
54.106	1446c–0, § 3.2531(c)
54.107	1446c–0, § 3.2531(c)
54.108	1446c–0, § 3.2531(f)
54.109	1446c–0, § 3.2531(i)
54.110	1446c–0, § 3.2531(j)
54.111	1446c–0, § 3.2531(k)
54.151	—
54.152	1446c–0, § 3.2532(e)
54.153	1446c–0, § 3.2532(b)
	1446c–0, § 3.2532(h)
54.154	1446c–0, § 3.2532(a)
	1446c–0, § 3.2532(c)
	1446c–0, § 3.2555(a)
54.155	1446c–0, § 3.2532(b)
54.156	1446c–0, § 3.2532(d)
54.157	1446c–0, § 3.2532(d)
54.158	1446c–0, § 3.2532(g)
54.159	1446c–0, § 3.2532(f)
54.201	1446c–0, § 3.251(d)
54.202	1446c–0, § 3.251(d)
54.203	1446c–0, § 3.255
54.204	1446c–0, § 3.2555(a)
	1446c–0, § 3.2555(b)
	1446c–0, § 3.2555(e)
54.205	1446c–0, § 3.2555(f)
54.206	1446c–0, § 3.2555(h)
54.251	1446c–0, § 3.258(a)
54.252	1446c–0, § 3.258(b), (c)
54.253	1446c–0, § 3.2595
54.254	1446c–0, § 3.259
54.255	1446c–0, § 3.260
54.256	1446c–0, § 3.256
54.257	1446c–0, § 3.261
54.258	1446c–0, § 3.253(b)
54.259	1446c–0, § 3.2555(c), (e), (g)
54.260	1446c–0, § 3.2555(d)
	1446c–0, § 3.2555(e)
54.261	1446c–0, § 3.2555(i)
55.001	1446c–0, § 3.155(a)
55.002	1446c–0, § 3.155(b)
55.003	1446c–0, §§ 3.153, 3.155(c)
55.004	1446c–0, § 3.212
55.005	1446c–0, § 3.215
55.006	1446c–0, § 3.217
55.007	1446c–0, § 3.1555(a) to (c)
55.008	1446c–0, § 3.262(a)
55.009	1446c–0, § 3.219
55.010	1446c–0, § 3.218
55.021	1446c–0, § 3.262(a)
55.022	1446c–0, § 3.262(a)
55.023	1446c–0, § 3.262(a), (b)
55.024	1446c–0, § 3.308
55.025	1446c–0, § 3.311
55.041	1446c–0, § 3.304(b)(2)
55.042	1446c–0, § 3.304(b)(2)
55.043	1446c–0, § 3.304(b)(2)
55.044	1446c–0, § 3.304(b)(1), (c)
55.045	1446c–0, § 3.304(a)
55.046	1446c–0, § 3.304(a)
55.047	1446c–0, § 3.304(a)
55.048	1446c–0, § 3.304(a)

Utilities Code Section	Vernon's Civ.St. Article
55.081	1446c–0, § 3.052(a)
55.082	1446c–0, § 3.052(h)
55.083	1446c–0, § 3.052(f), (h)
55.084	1446c–0, § 3.052(c)
55.085	1446c–0, § 3.052(b)
55.086	1446c–0, § 3.052(d)
55.087	1446c–0, § 3.052(e)
55.088	1446c–0, § 3.052(i)
55.089	1446c–0, § 3.052(g)
55.101	1446c–0, § 3.302(h)(1) to (4)
55.102	1446c–0, § 3.302(a), (g)
55.103	1446c–0, § 3.302(b), (h)(2), (i)
55.104	1446c–0, § 3.302(f)
55.105	1446c–0, § 3.302(c)
55.106	1446c–0, §§ 3.302(d), 3.3025(a)
55.107	1446c–0, § 3.302(e)
55.108	1446c–0, § 3.3025(b) to (e)
55.109	1446c–0, § 3.3025(b)
55.110	1446c–0, § 3.3025(a), (d)
55.121	1446c–0, § 3.651(1)
55.122	1446c–0, § 3.652
55.123	1446c–0, § 3.653(a)
55.124	1446c–0, § 3.653(a)
55.125	1446c–0, § 3.653(a)
55.126	1446c–0, § 3.653(a)
55.127	1446c–0, § 3.653(a) to (c)
55.128	1446c–0, § 3.653(a)
55.129	1446c–0, § 3.653(a)
55.130	1446c–0, § 3.655(a) to (c)
55.131	1446c–0, § 3.655(a)
55.132	1446c–0, § 3.655(b)
55.133	1446c–0, § 3.655(d)
55.134	1446c–0, §§ 3.654(a), 3.655(e)
55.135	1446c–0, § 3.657(a)
55.136	1446c–0, § 3.654(b), (c)
55.137	1446c–0, § 3.656(a) to (d)
55.138	1446c–0, § 3.657(b)
55.151	1446c–0, § 3.659
55.152	1446c–0, § 3.660
55.171	1446c–0, § 3.2625(i)
55.172	1446c–0, § 3.2625(a)
55.173	1446c–0, § 3.2625(f)
55.174	1446c–0, § 3.2625(b)
55.175	1446c–0, § 3.2625(c)
55.176	1446c–0, § 3.2625(d)
55.177	1446c–0, § 3.2625(e)
55.178	1446c–0, § 3.305
55.179	1446c–0, § 3.2625(h)
55.180	1446c–0, § 3.2625(g)
55.201	1446c–0, § 3.2615
55.202	1446c–0, § 3.310
55.203	1446c–0, § 3.309
55.251	1446c–0, § 3.306
55.252	1446c–0, § 3.307
56.001	—
56.002	1446c–0, § 3.610
56.021	1446c–0, § 3.608(a)
56.022	1446c–0, § 3.608(c)
56.023	1446c–0, § 3.608(d) to (f)
56.024	1446c–0, § 3.608(f)
56.025	1446c–0, § 3.608(b)(1) to (5)
56.026	1446c–0, § 3.608(b)(6)
56.071	1446c–0, §§ 3.601, 3.603(a) to (c)
56.072	1446c–0, § 3.602(a)
56.073	1446c–0, § 3.602(b)
56.074	1446c–0, § 3.602(b)
56.075	1446c–0, § 3.603(a)
56.076	1446c–0, § 3.603(b)
56.077	1446c–0, § 3.603(b)
56.078	1446c–0, § 3.607
56.101	1446c–0, § 3.604(a)
56.102	1446c–0, § 3.604(a), (b)
56.103	1446c–0, § 3.604(b)
56.104	1446c–0, § 3.604(b)
56.105	1446c–0, § 3.604(b)
56.106	1446c–0, § 3.604(d)
56.107	1446c–0, § 3.604(c)
56.108	1446c–0, § 3.604(e)
56.109	1446c–0, § 3.604(f)
56.110	1446c–0, § 3.604(g), (h)
56.111	1446c–0, § 3.604(h)
56.112	1446c–0, § 3.604(h)
57.001	1446c–0, § 3.610
57.021	1446c–0, § 3.605(h)
57.022	1446c–0, § 3.605(a), (b), (e)
57.023	1446c–0, § 3.605(d)
57.024	1446c–0, § 3.605(c)
57.025	1446c–0, § 3.605(f), (g)
57.041	1446c–0, § 3.606(b)
57.042	1446c–0, § 3.606(a)(1) to (5), (7) to (9)
57.043	1446c–0, § 3.606(j), (k), (n)
57.044	1446c–0, § 3.606(c) to (e)
57.045	1446c–0, § 3.606(c), (g) to (i), (p)
57.046	1446c–0, § 3.606(q)
57.047	1446c–0, § 3.606(r) to (t), (v)
57.048	1446c–0, § 3.606(*l*) to (n)
57.049	1446c–0, § 3.606(*o*)
57.050	1446c–0, § 3.606(u)
57.051	1446c–0, § 3.606(f)
57.071	1446c–0, § 3.609(b)
57.072	1446c–0, § 3.609(a)
58.001	1446c–0, § 3.351
58.002	1446c–0, § 3.352(b)(1)
58.021	1446c–0, § 3.352(a)
58.022	1446c–0, § 3.352(c)
58.023	1446c–0, § 3.352(b)(1)
58.024	1446c–0, §§ 3.352(b)(2), 3.355(c), 3.356(b), 3.357
58.025	1446c–0, § 3.352(d)

DERIVATION TABLE

Utilities Code Section	Vernon's Civ.St. Article
58.026	1446c–0, § 3.352(d)
58.027	1446c–0, § 3.352(d)
58.028	1446c–0, § 3.356(d)
58.051	1446c–0, § 3.353(a)
58.052	1446c–0, § 3.353(d)
58.053	1446c–0, §§ 3.353(b), 3.358(b)
58.054	1446c–0, §§ 3.352(a), 3.353(e)
58.055	1446c–0, § 3.353(b), (c)(1)
58.056	1446c–0, § 3.353(c)(2)
58.057	1446c–0, § 3.353(c)(3)
58.058	1446c–0, § 3.353(c)(4)
58.059	1446c–0, § 3.354
58.060	1446c–0, § 3.353(e)
58.061	1446c–0, § 3.353(b)
58.062	1446c–0, § 3.352(d)
58.101	1446c–0, § 3.355(a), (b)
58.102	1446c–0, § 3.355(d)
58.103	1446c–0, § 3.355(d)
58.104	1446c–0, § 3.355(d)
58.151	1446c–0, § 3.356(a)
58.152	1446c–0, § 3.356(a), (c)
58.201	1446c–0, § 3.358(a)
58.202	1446c–0, § 3.358(b)
58.203	1446c–0, § 3.358(c)
58.204	1446c–0, § 3.358(d)
58.205	1446c–0, § 3.358(e)
58.206	1446c–0, § 3.358(f)
58.251	1446c–0, § 3.359(a)
58.252	1446c–0, § 3.359(b)(1)(A), (e)
58.253	1446c–0, § 3.359(b)(1)(A)
58.254	1446c–0, § 3.359(b)(6)
58.255	1446c–0, § 3.359(b)(1)(B), (C), (f)
58.256	1446c–0, § 3.359(b)(1)(H)
58.257	1446c–0, § 3.359(b)(3)
58.258	1446c–0, § 3.359(b)(2), (4)
58.259	1446c–0, § 3.359(b)(1)(D)
58.260	1446c–0, § 3.359(b)(1)(E)
58.261	1446c–0, § 3.359(b)(1)(F)
58.262	1446c–0, § 3.359(b)(1)(G)
58.263	1446c–0, § 3.359(b)(5)
58.264	1446c–0, § 3.359(b)(1)(I)
58.265	1446c–0, § 3.359(c)
58.266	1446c–0, § 3.359(d)
58.267	1446c–0, § 3.359(g)
59.001	1446c–0, § 3.401
59.002	1446c–0, § 3.402(h)
59.021	1446c–0, § 3.402(a)
59.022	1446c–0, § 3.402(e)
59.023	1446c–0, § 3.402(f)
59.024	1446c–0, § 3.402(b), (c), (g)
59.025	1446c–0, § 3.402(g)
59.026	1446c–0, § 3.402(d)
59.027	1446c–0, § 3.402(d)
59.028	1446c–0, § 3.402(d)
59.029	1446c–0, §§ 3.402(d), 3.403(b)(6)
59.051	1446c–0, § 3.403(a)
59.052	1446c–0, §§ 3.403(b)(1) to (5)

Utilities Code Section	Vernon's Civ.St. Article
59.053	1446c–0, § 3.403(d)
59.054	1446c–0, § 3.403(g)
59.055	1446c–0, § 3.403(e)
59.071	1446c–0, § 3.403(f)(1), (2)
59.072	1446c–0, § 3.403(c)(1), (12), (f)(1)
59.073	1446c–0, § 3.403(c)(2)
59.074	1446c–0, § 3.403(c)(3) to (5)
59.075	1446c–0, § 3.403(c)(6)
59.076	1446c–0, § 3.403(c)(9)
59.077	1446c–0, § 3.403(c)(8), (10)
59.078	1446c–0, § 3.403(c)(11)
59.079	1446c–0, § 3.403(c)(7)
59.080	1446c–0, § 3.403(c)(13)
59.081	1446c–0, § 3.403(c)(14)
59.082	1446c–0, § 3.403(e)
60.001	1446c–0, § 3.451(a)
60.002	1446c–0, § 3.451(b), (c)
60.003	1446c–0, § 3.460
60.004	1446c–0, § 3.461
60.0041	1446c–0, § 3.461
60.005	1446c–0, § 3.462
60.006	1446c–0, § 3.459(c)
60.021	1446c–0, § 3.452(a)
60.022	1446c–0, § 3.452(b), (c)
60.023	1446c–0, § 3.452(d)
60.041	1446c–0, § 3.453(a) to (c)
60.042	1446c–0, § 3.453(d)
60.043	1446c–0, § 3.453(e)
60.044	1446c–0, § 3.453(f)
60.045	1446c–0, § 3.453(g)
60.061	1446c–0, §§ 3.454(a) to (c), (f), (g)
60.062	1446c–0, § 3.454(d)
60.063	1446c–0, § 3.454(e)
60.064	1446c–0, § 3.454(h)
60.065	1446c–0, § 3.454(i)
60.081	1446c–0, § 3.455(b)
60.082	1446c–0, § 3.455(a)
60.083	1446c–0, § 3.455(c)
60.084	1446c–0, § 3.455(c)
60.101	1446c–0, § 3.457(a)(1), (b)
60.102	1446c–0, § 3.457(c)
60.121	1446c–0, § 3.458(a)
60.122	1446c–0, § 3.458(h)
60.123	1446c–0, § 3.458(a)
60.124	1446c–0, § 3.458(b), (f)
60.125	1446c–0, § 3.458(b) to (d)
60.126	1446c–0, § 3.458(b)
60.127	1446c–0, § 3.458(e)
60.128	1446c–0, § 3.458(g)
60.141	1446c–0, § 3.456(a)
60.161	1446c–0, § 3.459(a)
60.162	1446c–0, § 3.459(b)
60.163	1446c–0, § 3.463
61.001	1446c–0, § 3.581
61.021	1446c–0, § 3.582(a)
61.022	1446c–0, § 3.582(b), (c)
61.023	1446c–0, § 3.583(a)

Utilities Code Section	Vernon's Civ.St. Article
61.024	1446c–0, § 3.583(b)
61.025	1446c–0, § 3.583(c)
61.026	1446c–0, § 3.583(d)
61.041	1446c–0, § 3.584(a)
61.042	1446c–0, § 3.584(b)
61.043	1446c–0, § 3.584(c)
62.001	1446c–0, § 3.506
62.002	1446c–0, § 3.502(a)
62.021	1446c–0, § 3.501(a)
62.022	1446c–0, § 3.501(b)
62.023	1446c–0, § 3.501(c), (d)
62.041	1446c–0, § 3.503(a)
62.042	1446c–0, § 3.503(f)
62.043	1446c–0, § 3.503(b)
62.044	1446c–0, § 3.503(c)
62.045	1446c–0, § 3.503(d)
62.046	1446c–0, § 3.503(e)
62.047	1446c–0, § 3.503(g)
62.071	1446c–0, § 3.502(h)
62.072	1446c–0, § 3.502(b)
62.073	1446c–0, § 3.502(c)
62.074	1446c–0, § 3.502(d)
62.075	1446c–0, § 3.502(e)
62.076	1446c–0, § 3.502(f)
62.077	1446c–0, § 3.502(i)
62.078	1446c–0, § 3.502(g)
62.101	1446c–0, § 3.504(e)
62.102	1446c–0, § 3.504(a)
62.103	1446c–0, § 3.504(a), (b)
62.104	1446c–0, § 3.504(c), (d)
62.105	1446c–0, § 3.504(d)
62.106	1446c–0, § 3.504(f)
62.107	1446c–0, § 3.504(g)
62.108	1446c–0, § 3.504(h)
62.131	1446c–0, § 3.505(c)
62.132	1446c–0, § 3.505(a), (b)
62.133	1446c–0, § 3.505(b)
62.134	1446c–0, § 3.505(d)
62.135	1446c–0, § 3.505(e)
62.136	1446c–0, § 3.505(f)
63.001	1446c–0, § 3.551(1) to (4), (6) to (10)
63.002	1446c–0, § 3.551(5)
63.003	1446c–0, § 3.551(11)
63.004	1446c–0, §§ 3.552(b), (c)
63.005	1446c–0, § 3.557
63.006	1446c–0, § 3.556
63.007	1446c–0, § 3.563(a), (b)
63.008	1446c–0, § 3.563(b)
63.009	1446c–0, § 3.563(a)
63.010	1446c–0, § 3.564
63.011	1446c–0, § 3.566
63.031	1446c–0, § 3.552(a)
63.032	1446c–0, § 3.553
63.033	1446c–0, § 3.554(a), (g), (h)
63.034	1446c–0, §§ 3.553, 3.554(a)
63.035	1446c–0, § 3.554(b) to (e)
63.036	1446c–0, § 3.554(f)
63.037	1446c–0, § 3.555
63.038	1446c–0, § 3.558
63.039	1446c–0, § 3.559(a)
63.040	1446c–0, § 3.559(b)
63.041	1446c–0, § 3.559(c)
63.042	1446c–0, § 3.562
63.061	1446c–0, § 3.560
63.062	1446c–0, § 3.561
63.063	1446c–0, § 3.557
101.001	1446e, § 1.01
101.002	1446e, § 1.02
101.003	1446e, § 1.03(1), (3), (4), (6) to (17)
101.004	1446e, § 1.03(8)
101.005	1446e, § 1.04
101.006	1446e, § 2.01(c)
101.007	1446e, § 10.04
101.008	1446e, § 10.04
101.051	1446e, § 9.07(a)
101.052	1446e, § 9.07(f) to (h)
101.053	1446e, § 9.07(e)
101.054	1446e, § 9.07(c)
102.001	1446e, § 2.01(b)
102.002	1446e, § 2.02
102.003	1446e, § 4.02
102.004	1446e, § 7.02
102.005	1446e, § 3.04
102.051	1446e, § 6.01
102.052	1446e, § 6.02
102.053	1446e, § 6.03
102.054	1446e, § 6.04
102.101	1446e, § 4.01(a)
	1446e, § 4.01(d)
	1446e, § 4.01(f)
102.102	1446e, § 4.07
102.103	1446e, § 4.08
102.104	1446e, § 7.01
102.151	1446e, § 4.06
102.152	1446e, § 4.01(b)
	1446e, § 4.01(f)
102.153	1446e, § 4.01(c)
	1446e, § 4.01(f)
102.154	1446e, § 4.04
102.201	1446e, § 4.03(c)
102.202	1446e, § 4.01(d)
	1446e, § 4.01(f)
102.203	1446e, § 4.03(a)
102.204	1446e, § 4.03(a)
102.205	1446e, § 4.03(b)
	1446e, § 4.10(a)
102.206	1446e, § 4.03(a)
102.251	1446e, § 10.02
102.252	1446e, § 10.02
103.001	1446e, § 2.01(a)
103.002	1446e, § 3.01
103.021	1446e, § 3.02

DERIVATION TABLE

Utilities Code Section	Vernon's Civ.St. Article
103.022	1446e, § 3.03(a)
103.023	1446e, § 3.03(b)
103.024	1446e, § 3.03(b)
103.051	1446e, § 3.05(a)
103.052	1446e, § 3.05(b)
103.053	1446e, § 3.05(c)
103.054	1446e, § 3.05(d)
103.055	1446e, § 3.05(e)
103.056	1446e, § 3.05(e)
104.001	1446e, § 5.01
104.002	1446e, § 4.05
104.003	1446e, §§ 5.02(a), (b), (d), (f)
104.004	1446e, § 5.10
104.005	1446e, § 5.11
104.006	1446e, § 5.09
104.007	1446e, § 5.12
104.008	1446e, § 5.04(b)
104.051	1446e, § 5.03
104.052	1446e, § 5.04(a)
104.053	1446e, § 5.05
104.054	1446e, § 4.01(b), (f)
104.055	1446e, § 5.06
104.056	1446e, § 4.01(e), (f)
104.057	1446e, § 4.04
104.058	1446e, § 4.01(c), (f)
104.101	1446e, § 5.08(b)
104.102	1446e, § 5.08(a)
104.103	1446e, § 5.08(a)
104.104	1446e, § 5.08(b)
104.105	1446e, § 5.08(c)
104.106	1446e, § 5.08(d)
104.107	1446e, § 5.08(d)
104.108	1446e, § 5.08(d)
104.109	1446e, § 5.08(e)
104.110	1446e, § 5.08(f)
104.111	1446e, §§ 5.02(e), 5.03(b)
104.151	1446e, § 5.07(a)
104.152	1446e, § 5.07(b)
104.201	1446e, § 5.02(c)
104.202	1446e, § 5.061
104.203	1446e, § 5.13
104.251	1446e, § 4.09(a)
104.252	1446e, § 4.09(b)
104.253	1446e, § 4.09(c)
104.254	1446e, § 4.09(d)
104.255	1446e, § 10.05, 10.06
104.256	1446e, § 4.10(a)
104.257	1446e, § 4.10(b)
105.001	1446e, § 8.01
105.002	1446e, § 10.03
105.021	1446e, § 9.01
105.022	1446e, § 9.04
105.023	1446e, § 9.02
105.024	1446e, § 9.03(a)
105.025	1446e, § 9.06
105.026	1446e, § 9.03(b)
105.027	1446e, § 9.05
105.051	1446e, § 10.01
121.001	6050, § 1(a) to (c)
121.002	6050, § 1(d)
121.003	6050, § 2, 3
121.004	6050, § 4(a)
121.005	6050, § 4(a), (b)
121.006	6050, § 5
121.051	6050, § 1(c), (e)
121.052	6051
121.101	6052
121.102	6056
121.103	6053, § 1(c)
121.104	6057, 6057a
121.151	6053, § 1(a)
121.152	6053, § 1(a)
121.153	6054
121.154	6055
121.155	6058
121.156	6061
121.157	6064, 6065
121.158	6066
121.201	6053–1, Subsecs. (A), (B)
121.202	6053–1, Subsec. (D)
121.203	6053–1, Subsec. (C)
121.204	6053–1, Subsec. (C)
121.205	6053–1, Subsec. (C)
121.206	6053–2(a) to (c)
121.207	6053–2(d) to (i)
121.208	6053–2, § (j)
121.209	6053–2, § (k)
121.210	6053–2, § (m)
121.251	6053, § 2
121.252	6053, § 2
121.253	6053, § 2
121.301	6063
121.302	6062
121.303	6062
121.304	6062A, §§ (a) to (c)
121.305	6062A, §§ (d) to (i)
121.306	6062A, § (j)
121.307	6062A, § (n)
121.308	6062A, § (k)
121.309	6062A, § (m)
121.310	6057b
121.401	6059
121.402	6059
121.403	6059
122.001	6060, § 1(a), (c)
122.051	6060, § 1(a), (b)
122.052	6060, § 1(c)
122.101	6060, § 2(a)
122.102	6060, § 2(a), (b)
122.103	6060, § 2(a)
122.104	6060, § 3(b)
122.151	6060, § 3(a)
122.152	6060, § 3(c)
122.201	6060, § 4(a)

DERIVATION TABLE

Utilities Code Section	Vernon's Civ.St. Article
122.202	6060, § 4(a)
122.203	6060, § 4(a)
122.204	6060, § 4(a)
122.205	6060, § 4(b)
123.001	6066f
123.002	6066f
123.021	6066g, § 1
123.022	6066g, § 2
123.023	6066g, § 3
123.024	6066g, § 4
124.001	6053, § 1a(a)
124.002	6053, § 1a(b)
161.001	1528b, § 1
161.002	1528b, §§ 2(1) to (3), (6) to (8), 3
161.003	1528b, § 34
161.004	1528b, § 7
161.005	1528b, § 36
161.051	1528b, § 5
161.052	1528b, §§ 4, 6(a)
161.053	1528b, § 6(a)
161.054	1528b, § 6(a), (b)
161.055	1528b, §§ 8, 29
161.056	1528b, § 9
161.057	1528b, § 10
161.058	1528b, § 32
161.059	1528b, § 25
161.060	1528b, § 16
161.061	1528b, § 30
161.062	1528b, § 30
161.063	1528b, § 31
161.064	1528b, §§ 4, 11
161.065	1528b, §§ 12, 16
161.066	1528b, § 16
161.067	1528b, § 13
161.068	1528b, § 14
161.069	1528b, § 17
161.070	1528b, § 15
161.071	1528b, §§ 6(a), 18, 19
161.072	1528b, §§ 6(a), 19, 20
161.073	1528b, § 19
161.074	1528b, § 21
161.075	1528b, § 22
161.076	1528b, §§ 4, 23
161.077	1528b, § 24
161.078	1528b, § 19A
161.079	1528b, § 33
161.121	1528b, § 4
161.122	1528b, § 3
161.123	1528b, § 4
161.124	1528b, § 4A
161.125	1528b, § 4
161.151	1528b, § 26
161.152	1528b, §§ 26, 29
161.201	1528b, § 27(a)
161.202	1528b, §§ 27(a), (b), 29
161.251	1528b, §§ 28(a), 29
161.252	1528b, § 28(b)
161.253	1528b, § 28(b)
161.254	1528b, § 28(c)
162.001	1528c, § 1
162.002	1528c, § 3
162.003	1528c, § 2(1) to (3), (6), (8)
162.004	1528c, § 6(a)
162.005	1528c, § 25
162.006	1528c, § 26
162.051	1528c, § 5
162.052	1528c, § 4
	1528c, § 6(a)
162.053	1528c, § 6(a)
162.054	1528c, § 6(a)
	1528c, § 6(b)
162.055	1528c, § 7
	1528c, § 28
162.056	1528c, § 8
162.057	1528c, § 9
162.058	1528c, § 32
162.059	1528c, § 22
162.060	1528c, § 24
162.061	1528c, § 29
162.062	1528c, § 29
162.063	1528c, § 31
162.064	1528c, § 10
162.065	1528c, § 11(a)
162.066	1528c, § 11(b)
162.067	1528c, §§ 12(a), (b)
162.068	1528c, § 12(c)
162.069	1528c, § 13
162.070	1528c, §§ 12(d), (e)
162.071	1528c, §§ 6(a), 14(a), (e)
162.072	1528c, §§ 6(a), 14(a) to (c)
162.073	1528c, § 14(a)
162.074	1528c, § 14(a)
162.075	1528c, § 14(a), (d)
162.076	1528c, § 15
162.077	1528c, § 16
162.078	1528c, § 17
162.079	1528c, § 4A
162.080	1528c, §§ 19, 28
162.081	1528c, § 27
162.082	1528c, § 33
162.121	1528c, § 4
162.122	1528c, § 4
162.123	1528c, § 30
162.124	1528c, § 4
162.125	1528c, § 23(a)
162.126	1528c, § 23(b)
162.151	1528c, § 18
162.152	1528c, § 18
162.153	1528c, § 18
162.154	1528c, §§ 18, 28
162.201	1528c, § 20(a), (b)
162.202	1528c, §§ 20(a), (b), 28
162.203	1528c, §§ 20A(a) to (c)
162.204	1528c, §§ 20A(c) to (f), 28

DERIVATION TABLE

Utilities Code Section	Vernon's Civ.St. Article
162.205	1528c, § 20B
162.251	1528c, §§ 20C(a) to (c)
162.252	1528c, §§ 20C(c) to (f), 28
162.253	1528c, §§ 20D(a), (b)
162.254	1528c, §§ 20D(c), (d), 28
162.301	1528c, §§ 21(a), 28
162.302	1528c, § 21(b)
162.303	1528c, § 21(b)
162.304	1528c, § 21(c)
163.001	1435a, § 2
163.011	1435a, §§ 1, 5
163.012	1435a, §§ 1, 3
163.013	1435a, §§ 1, 3, 4(1), (2)
163.014	1435a, § 4(2)
163.015	1435a, § 4(3)
163.016	1435a, § 4(4)
163.051	1435a, § 4a(c), (j)
163.052	1435a, § 4a(s)
163.053	1435a, § 4a(s)
163.054	1435a, § 4a(a), (b)
163.055	1435a, § 4a(b)
163.056	1435a, § 4a(a)
163.057	1435a, § 4a(c) to (e)
163.058	1435a, § 4a(a), (b)
163.059	1435a, § 4a(d) to (f)
163.060	1435a, § 4a(a), (f), (*o*), (p)
163.061	1435a, § 4a(*o*)
163.062	1435a, § 4a(f), (g), (*o*)
163.063	1435a, § 4a(g), (h)
163.064	1435a, § 4a(i) to (k), (n)
163.065	1435a, § 4a(m)
163.066	1435a, § 4a(*l*), (q), (r)
163.067	1435a, § 4a(r)
163.068	1435a, § 4a(r)
163.101	1435a, § 4b
163.102	1435a, § 4b
163.121	1435a, § 4c(a)
163.122	1435a, § 4c(c)
163.123	1435a, § 4c(b)
163.124	1435a, § 4c(d)
164.001	1435b, § 1
164.002	1435b, § 3
164.003	1435b, § 1
164.004	1435b, § 1
164.005	1435b, § 2
164.006	1435b, § 3
181.001	1435
181.002	1437
181.003	1437
181.004	1436
181.005	1436
181.006	1436
181.007	1435
181.008	1435
181.009	1435
	1438
181.021	1436b, § 1
	1436b, § 2
181.022	1436b, § 1
181.023	1436b, § 1
181.024	1436b, § 1
181.025	1436b, § 1
181.026	1436b, § 2
181.041	1436a, §§ 1, 1a
181.042	1436a, §§ 1, 1a
181.043	1436a, §§ 1, 1a
181.044	1436a, §§ 1, 1a
181.045	1436a, §§ 1, 1a
181.046	1436a, §§ 1, 1a
181.047	1436a, §§ 1, 1a
181.061	1428
181.062	1428
181.063	1429
181.064	1430
181.065	1431
181.066	1432
181.081	1416
	1417
	1422
181.082	1416
181.083	1417
181.084	1417
181.085	1418
181.086	1419
181.087	1420
181.088	1421
181.089	1422
181.101	9021, § 1
181.102	9021, §§ 2, 3
181.103	9021, § 4(a), (b)
181.104	9021, § 4(c)
181.901	1120
181.902	1120
182.001	1446c–2, § 1
182.002	1446c–2, § 2(a), (d)
182.003	1446c–2, § 2(b)
182.004	1446c–2, § 2(c)
182.005	1446c–2, § 2(e)
182.051	1446h, § 1
182.052	1446h, §§ 2, 4
182.053	1446h, § 3
182.054	1446h, § 5
182.055	1446h, § 6
182.101	1124a, §§ 1 to 3
182.102	1124a, §§ 1, 4
182.103	1124a, § 1
182.104	1124a, § 5
183.001	1440
	1440a
183.002	1440
	1440a
183.003	1440
	1440a
183.004	1440
	1440a

DERIVATION TABLE

Utilities Code Section	Vernon's Civ.St. Article
183.005	1440
	1440a
183.006	1440a
184.001	—
184.011	1446d, § 1
184.012	1446d, §§ 2(a), (b)
184.013	1446d, §§ 2(c), 3, 4
184.014	1446d, § 3
184.031	1446d–2, § 1
184.032	1446d–2, § 2
184.033	1446d–2, § 2
184.034	1446d–2, § 2
184.035	1446d–2, § 2
184.051	1446f, § 1
184.052	1446f, § 2
184.071	1446g
185.001	1446c–1, § 1
185.002	1446c–1, § 5
185.003	1446c–1, § 2
185.004	1446c–1, § 4
185.005	1446c–1, § 3
186.001	1446a, § 2
186.002	1446a, § 1
186.003	1446a, § 6
186.004	1446a, § 3
186.005	1446a, § 4
186.006	1446a, § 7
186.021	1432b
186.031	1446b, § 1
186.032	1446b, §§ 2, 4
186.033	1446b, § 3
186.041	1432a, § 3
186.042	1432a, § 1
186.043	1432a, § 2
186.044	1432a, § 4
186.045	1432a, § 4

BUSINESS ORGANIZATION CODE TABLE OF SECTIONS AFFECTED BY THE 82nd LEGISLATURE REGULAR SESSION

		Acts 2011	
Sec.	**Effect**	**Ch.**	**Sec.**
1.002(55–a)	Added	139	1
1.002(69–b)	Amended	139	1
1.002(69–c)	Added	139	1
1.002(69–d)	Added	139	1
1.002(69–e)	Added	139	1
1.002 note	—	139	65(a) 65(b)
5.201(d)	Added	1151	1
5.201 note	—	1151	2
5.257	Amended	7	1
5.257 note	—	7	3
6.101(b)	Amended	139	2
6.205(a)	Amended	139	3
8.001(1)	Amended	139	4
8.001(2)	Amended	139	4
8.103(d)	Amended	139	5
8.104(d)	Amended	139	6
8.105(d)	Amended	139	7
8.151(c–1)	Added	139	8
9.007(b)	Amended	139	9
10.002	Amended	139	10
10.008(a)	Amended	139	11
10.052(a)	Amended	139	12
10.103(a)	Amended	139	13
10.354(b)	Amended	139	14
10.355(c)	Amended	139	15
10.355(e)	Amended	139	15
10.356(b)	Amended	139	16
10.356(c)	Amended	139	16
10.356(d)	Amended	139	16
10.358(a)	Amended	139	17
10.358(d)	Amended	139	17
10.358(e)	Amended	139	17
11.057(f)	Added	139	18
11.402	Amended	139	19
11.404(b)	Amended	139	20
21.001	Repealed	139	66
21.109(a)	Amended	139	21
21.110	Added	139	22
21.203(c)	Added	139	23
21.206(a)	Amended	139	24
21.222(b)	Amended	139	25
21.357	Amended	139	26
21.415(a)	Amended	139	27
21.418(a)	Amended	139	28
21.418(b)	Amended	139	28
21.418(d)	Added	139	28
21.418(e)	Added	139	28
21.453(f)	Added	139	29
21.453(g)	Added	139	29
21.552	Amended	93	1
21.601(1)	Amended	139	30
21.603	Amended	139	31

TABLE OF SECTIONS AFFECTED

Sec.	Effect	Acts 2011 Ch.	Sec.
21.701(1)	Amended	139	32
22.0561	Added	782	1
22.0561 note	—	782	6
22.230(a)	Amended	139	33
22.230(b)	Amended	139	33
22.230(d)	Added	139	33
22.230(e)	Added	139	33
101.002	Added	25	1
101.054(a)	Amended	139	34
101.054(e)	Added	139	34
101.106(a–1)	Added	139	35
101.106(a–2)	Added	139	35
101.1115	Added	139	36
101.254(a)	Amended	139	37
101.255(a)	Amended	139	38
101.255(b)	Amended	139	38
101.255(d)	Added	139	38
101.255(e)	Added	139	38
101.357(b)	Amended	139	39
101.611(b)	Amended	139	40
151.003(d)	Amended	139	41
152.0551	Added	782	2
152.0551 note	—	782	6
152.304(a)	Amended	139	42
152.308	Added	139	43
152.406(a)	Amended	139	44
152.406(c)	Amended	139	44
152.707(b)	Amended	139	45
152.801	Amended	139	46
152.802(a)	Amended	139	47
152.802(f)	Amended	139	47
152.802(i)	Repealed	139	66
152.802(j)	Amended	139	47
152.804	Repealed	139	66
152.906(b)	Amended	139	48
152.910(b)	Amended	139	49
152.911(b)	Amended	139	50
153.004(a)	Amended	139	51
153.103	Amended	139	52
153.158(b)	Amended	139	53
153.501(b)	Amended	139	54
153.504	Amended	139	55
153.551(a)	Amended	139	56
200.317(a)	Amended	139	57
200.317(b)	Amended	139	57
200.317(d)	Added	139	57
200.317(e)	Added	139	57
252.011(b)	Amended	139	58
252.011(f)	Amended	139	58
301.012(a–1)	Added	782	3
301.012(a–2)	Added	782	3
301.012(a–3)	Added	782	3
301.012(a–4)	Added	782	3
301.012(a–5)	Added	782	3
301.012(a–6)	Added	782	3
301.012(a–7)	Added	782	3
301.012 note	—	782	6
401.001 note	—	139	65(a)
402.003	Amended	139	59
402.003 note	—	139	65(c)
402.004	Amended	139	60

		Acts 2011	
Sec.	Effect	Ch.	Sec.
402.005(c)	Added	139	61
402.0051	Added	139	62
402.013 heading	Amended	139	63
402.013(b–1)	Added	139	64
402.013(b–2)	Added	139	64

UTILITIES CODE
TABLE OF SECTIONS AFFECTED BY THE 82nd LEGISLATURE REGULAR SESSION

Sec.	Effect	Acts 2011 Ch.	Sec.
12.005	Amended	1232	1.08
13.002	Amended	1232	6.02
13.003(a)	Amended	416	1
13.063(a)	Repealed	1083	25(161)
14.101(a)	Amended	129	1
14.101 note	—	129	2
15.023 heading	Amended	996	1
15.023(e)	Added	996	2
15.023(f)	Added	996	2
15.023(g)	Added	996	2
15.023 note	—	996	8
15.024 heading	Amended	996	3
15.024(c)	Amended	91	25.001
15.024(f)	Amended	996	4
15.025(e)	Added	996	5
15.025(f)	Added	996	5
15.026(a)	Amended	996	6
15.026(b)	Amended	996	6
31.002(4–a)	Added	890	1
31.002(10)	Amended	890	1
		1069	1
31.002 note	—	1069	3
Ch. 35			
Subch. B heading	Amended	890	2
35.036	Added	890	3
35.151	Added	1069	2
35.152	Added	1069	2
36.009	Added	150	1
36.009 note	—	150	2
36.210	Added	196	1
37.053(c)	Added	949	1
37.053(d)	Added	949	1
37.053 note	—	949	2(b)
			3
			4
37.054(a)	Amended	416	2
37.054 note	—	416	3
37.056(d)	Added	949	2(a)
37.102(a)	Amended	1163	179
38.072	Added	640	1
39.151(n)	Added	1232	1.09
39.151(n–1)	Added	1232	1.09
39.157(a)	Amended	996	7
39.351(c)	Amended	890	4
39.402(a)	Amended	182	1
39.4525	Added	100	1
39.551	Added	1113	1
39.552	Added	1113	1
39.553	Added	1113	1
39.554	Added	1113	1
39.555	Added	1113	1
39.902(b)	Repealed	1083	25(162)
39.905(a)	Amended	180	1
39.905(b)	Amended	180	1
39.905(b–2)	Repealed	180	3
39.905(d)	Amended	180	1

UTILITIES CODE

Sec.	Effect	Acts 2011 Ch.	Sec.
39.905(f)	Amended	1346	1
39.905(h)	Added	180	1
39.905(i)	Added	180	1
39.905(j)	Added	180	1
39.905(k)	Added	180	1
39.9051(f)	Amended	1068	1
39.9051(g)	Added	1068	1
39.9051(h)	Added	1068	1
39.9052(b)	Amended	1068	2
39.9052(c)	Added	1068	2
39.9052(d)	Added	1068	2
39.9054	Added	180	2
39.907	Repealed	905	1
39.916(a)(2)	Amended	1070	1
39.916(k)	Added	1070	2
51.001(a)	Amended	98	1
51.001(g)	Amended	98	1
51.002(3–a)	Added	98	2
51.002(13)	Added	98	2
52.002(c)	Added	98	3
52.002(d)	Added	98	3
52.007	Added	98	4
52.056	Amended	21	1
		98	5
52.057	Repealed	21	4
		98	21
53.065(b)	Repealed	21	4
		98	21
53.301	Amended	118	1
53.301 note	—	118	4
53.304	Amended	118	2
53.305(b)	Amended	118	3
54.251(b)	Amended	98	6
54.3015	Amended	98	7
55.026	Added	98	8
55.049	Added	98	9
55.203(a)	Amended	973	32
55.204	Added	1180	4
56.021	Amended	314	1
56.023(d)	Amended	98	10
56.031	Amended	535	1
		3	
56.032	Added	98	11
		535	2
58.252(1–a)	Added	903	1
58.253(a)	Amended	903	2
58.255(b)	Amended	903	3
58.255(c)	Amended	21	2
		98	12
58.258(a)	Amended	903	4
58.259(b)	Amended	903	5
58.260(c)	Amended	903	6
58.261(b)	Amended	903	7
58.268	Amended	903	8
59.074(c)	Amended	21	3
		98	13
59.077(a)	Amended	903	9
59.083	Amended	903	10
65.051	Amended	98	14
65.052(a)	Amended	98	15
65.052(b)	Amended	98	15
65.052(c)	Amended	98	15

Sec.	Effect	Acts 2011 Ch.	Sec.
65.052(d)	Repealed	98	21
65.052(e)	Repealed	98	21
65.052(f)	Repealed	98	21
65.054	Repealed	98	21
65.055	Repealed	98	21
65.102	Amended	98	16
65.151	Amended	98	17
65.152	Amended	98	18
65.153(c)	Amended	98	19
65.153(c–1)	Added	98	19
65.154	Added	98	20
65.155	Added	98	20
65.251	Repealed	905	1
65.252	Repealed	905	1
66.003(a)	Amended	1077	1
66.004(a)	Amended	1077	2
66.004(b–1)	Added	1077	2
66.004(b–2)	Added	1077	2
66.004(b–3)	Added	1077	2
66.004(c)	Amended	1077	2
66.004(f)	Amended	1077	2
66.005(b)	Amended	1077	3
66.006	Amended	1077	4
66.006 note	—	1077	6
66.009(c)	Amended	1077	5
66.009(h)	Amended	1077	5
101.003(7)	Amended	4	1
104.059	Added	172	1
104.059(b)	Added	172	2
104.059(c)	Added	172	2
104.059(d)	Added	172	2
104.059(e)	Added	172	2
121.008	Added	4	2
121.201(d)	Amended	91	25.002
163.002	Repealed	1083	25(163)
181.005(a)	Amended	313	1
186.007	Added	1335	1
251.155	Amended	184	1
251.155 note	—	184	5
251.201(a–1)	Added	184	2
251.201(b)	Amended	184	2
251.201(b–1)	Added	184	2
251.201(c)	Amended	184	2
251.201(c–1)	Added	184	2
251.203 heading	Amended	184	3
251.203(a–1)	Added	184	4

UTILITIES CODE TABLE OF SECTIONS AFFECTED BY THE 82nd LEGISLATURE FIRST CALLED SESSION

Sec.	Effect	Acts 2011 Ch.	Sec.
121.211 heading	Amended	4	19.25
121.211(a)	Amended	4	19.26
121.211(b)	Amended	4	19.26
121.211(c)	Amended	4	19.26
121.211(d)	Amended	4	19.26
121.211(e)	Amended	4	19.26
121.211(h)	Amended	4	19.26

BUSINESS ORGANIZATIONS CODE

TITLE 1. GENERAL PROVISIONS

Chapter
1. Definitions and Other General Provisions.
2. Purposes and Power of Domestic Entity.
3. Formation and Governance.
4. Filings.
5. Names of Entities; Registered Agents and Registered Offices.
6. Meetings and Voting for Domestic Entities.
7. Liability.
8. Indemnification and Insurance.
9. Foreign Entities.
10. Mergers, Interest Exchanges, Conversions, and Sales of Assets.
11. Winding Up and Termination of Domestic Entity.
12. Administrative Powers.

TITLE 2. CORPORATIONS

20. General Provisions.
21. For–Profit Corporations.
22. Nonprofit Corporations.
23. Special–Purpose Corporations.

TITLE 3. LIMITED LIABILITY COMPANIES

101. Limited Liability Companies.

TITLE 4. PARTNERSHIPS

151. General Provisions.
152. General Partnerships.
153. Limited Partnerships.
154. Provisions Applicable to Both General and Limited Partnerships.

TITLE 5. REAL ESTATE INVESTMENT TRUSTS

200. Real Estate Investment Trusts.

TITLE 6. ASSOCIATIONS

251. Cooperative Associations.
252. Unincorporated Nonprofit Associations.

TITLE 7. PROFESSIONAL ENTITIES

301. Provisions Relating to Professional Entities.
302. Provisions Relating to Professional Associations.
303. Provisions Relating to Professional Corporations.
304. Provisions Relating to Professional Limited Liability Companies.

TITLE 8. MISCELLANEOUS AND TRANSITION PROVISIONS

401. General Provisions.
402. Miscellaneous and Transition Provisions.

TITLE 1. GENERAL PROVISIONS

CHAPTER 1. DEFINITIONS AND OTHER GENERAL PROVISIONS

SUBCHAPTER A. DEFINITIONS AND PURPOSE

Section
1.001. Purpose.
1.002. Definitions.
1.003. Disinterested Person.
1.004. Independent Person.
1.005. Conspicuous Information.
1.006. Synonymous Terms.
1.007. Signing of Document or Other Writing.
1.008. Short Titles.
1.009. Dollars as Monetary Units.

SUBCHAPTER B. CODE CONSTRUCTION

1.051. Construction of Code.
1.052. Reference in Law to Statute Revised by Code.
1.053. Applicability to Foreign and Interstate Affairs.
1.054. Reservation of Power.

SUBCHAPTER C. DETERMINATION OF APPLICABLE LAW

1.101. Domestic Filing Entities.
1.102. Foreign Filing Entities.
1.103. Entities Not Formed by Filing Instrument.
1.104. Law Applicable to Liability.
1.105. Internal Affairs.
1.106. Order of Precedence.

SUBCHAPTER A. DEFINITIONS AND PURPOSE

§ 1.001. Purpose

The purpose of this code is to make the law encompassed by this code more accessible and understandable by:

(1) rearranging the statutes into a more logical order;

(2) employing a format and numbering system designed to facilitate citation of the law and to accommodate future expansion of the law;

(3) eliminating repealed, duplicative, expired, executed, and other ineffective provisions; and

(4) restating the law in modern American English to the greatest extent possible.

Acts 2003, 78th Leg., ch. 182, § 1, eff. Jan. 1, 2006.

§ 1.002. Definitions

In this code:

(1) "Affiliate" means a person who controls, is controlled by, or is under common control with another person.

(2) "Associate," when used to indicate a relationship with a person, means:

(A) a domestic or foreign entity or organization for which the person:

(i) is an officer or governing person; or

(ii) beneficially owns, directly or indirectly, either individually or through an affiliate, 10 percent or more of a class of voting ownership interests or similar securities of the entity or organization;

(B) a trust or estate in which the person has a substantial beneficial interest or for which the person serves as trustee or in a similar fiduciary capacity;

(C) the person's spouse or a relative of the person related by consanguinity or affinity who resides with the person; or

(D) a governing person or an affiliate or officer of the person.

(3) "Association" means an entity governed as an association under Title 6 or 7. The term includes a cooperative association, nonprofit association, and professional association.

(4) "Assumed name" means a name adopted for use by a person. The term includes an assumed name filed under Chapter 71, Business & Commerce Code.

(5) "Business" means a trade, occupation, profession, or other commercial activity.

(6) "Certificate of formation" means:

(A) the document required to be filed with the filing officer under Chapter 3 to form a filing entity; and

(B) if appropriate, a restated certificate of formation and all amendments of an original or restated certificate of formation.

(7) "Certificated ownership interest" means an ownership interest of a domestic entity represented by a certificate issued in bearer or registered form.

(8) "Close corporation" means a for-profit corporation that elects to be governed as a close corporation in accordance with Subchapter O, Chapter 21.

(9) "Contribution" means a tangible or intangible benefit that a person transfers to an entity in consideration for an ownership interest in the entity or otherwise in the person's capacity as an owner or a member. The benefit includes cash, services rendered, a contract for services to be performed, a promissory note or other obligation of a person to pay cash or transfer property to the entity, or securities or other interests in or obligations of an entity, but does not include cash or property received by the entity:

(A) with respect to a promissory note or other obligation to the extent that the agreed value of the note or obligation has previously been included as a contribution; or

(B) that the person intends to be a loan to the entity.

(10) "Conversion" means:

(A) the continuance of a domestic entity as a non-code organization of any type;

(B) the continuance of a non-code organization as a domestic entity of any type;

(C) the continuance of a domestic entity of one type as a domestic entity of another type;

(D) the continuance of a domestic entity of one type as a foreign entity of the same type that may be treated as a domestication, continuance, or transfer transaction under the laws of the jurisdiction of formation of the foreign entity; or

(E) the continuance of a foreign entity of one type as a domestic entity of the same type that may be treated as a domestication, continuance, or transfer transaction under the laws of the jurisdiction of formation of the foreign entity.

(11) "Converted entity" means an organization resulting from a conversion.

(12) "Converting entity" means an organization as the organization existed before the organization's conversion.

(13) "Cooperative" or "cooperative association" means an association governed as a cooperative association under Chapter 251.

(14) "Corporation" means an entity governed as a corporation under Title 2 or 7. The term includes a for-profit corporation, nonprofit corporation, and professional corporation.

(15) "Debtor in bankruptcy" means a person who is the subject of:

(A) an order for relief under the United States bankruptcy laws (Title 11, United States Code); or

(B) a comparable order under a:

(i) successor statute of general applicability; or

(ii) federal or state law governing insolvency.

(16) "Director" means an individual who serves on the board of directors of a foreign or domestic corporation.

(17) "Domestic" means, with respect to an entity, that the entity is formed under this code or the entity's internal affairs are governed by this code.

(18) "Domestic entity" means an organization formed under or he internal affairs of which are governed by this code.

(19) "Domestic entity subject to dissenters' rights" means a domestic entity the owners of which have rights of dissent and appraisal under this code or the governing documents of the entity.

(20) "Effective date of this code" means January 1, 2006. The applicability of this code is governed by Title 8.

(20–a) "Electronic transmission" means a form of communication that:

(A) does not directly involve the physical transmission of paper;

(B) creates a record that may be retained, retrieved, and reviewed by the recipient; and

(C) may be directly reproduced in paper form by the recipient through an automated process.

(21) "Entity" means a domestic entity or foreign entity.

(22) "Filing entity" means a domestic entity that is a corporation, limited partnership, limited liability company, professional association, cooperative, or real estate investment trust.

(23) "Filing instrument" means an instrument, document, or statement that is required or authorized by this code to be filed by or for an entity with the filing officer in accordance with Chapter 4.

(24) "Filing officer" means:

(A) with respect to an entity other than a domestic real estate investment trust, the secretary of state; or

(B) with respect to a domestic real estate investment trust, the county clerk of the county in which the real estate investment trust's principal office is located in this state.

(25) "For–profit corporation" means a corporation governed as a for-profit corporation under Chapter 21.

(26) "For–profit entity" means an entity other than a nonprofit entity.

(27) "Foreign" means, with respect to an entity, that the entity is formed under, and the entity's internal affairs are governed by, the laws of a jurisdiction other than this state.

(28) "Foreign entity" means an organization formed under, and the internal affairs of which are governed by, the laws of a jurisdiction other than this state.

(29) "Foreign filing entity" means a foreign entity, other than a foreign limited liability partnership, that registers or is required to register as a foreign entity under Chapter 9.

(30) "Foreign governmental authority" means a governmental official, agency, or instrumentality of a jurisdiction other than this state.

(31) "Foreign nonfiling entity" means a foreign entity that is not a foreign filing entity.

(32) "Fundamental business transaction" means a merger, interest exchange, conversion, or sale of all or substantially all of an entity's assets.

(33) "General partner" means:

(A) each partner in a general partnership; or

(B) a person who is admitted to a limited partnership as a general partner in accordance with the governing documents of the limited partnership.

(34) "General partnership" means a partnership governed as a general partnership under Chapter 152. The term includes a general partnership registered as a limited liability partnership.

(35)(A) "Governing authority" means a person or group of persons who are entitled to manage and direct the affairs of an entity under this code and the governing documents of the entity, except that if the governing documents of the entity or this code divide the authority to manage and direct the affairs of the entity among different persons or groups of persons according to different matters, "governing authority" means the person or group of persons entitled to manage and direct the affairs of the entity with respect to a matter under the governing documents of the entity or this code. The term includes:

(i) the board of directors of a corporation or other persons authorized to perform the functions of the board of directors of a corporation;

(ii) the general partners of a general partnership or limited partnership;

(iii) the managers of a limited liability company that is managed by managers;

(iv) the members of a limited liability company that is managed by members who are entitled to manage the company;

(v) the board of directors of a cooperative association; and

(vi) the trust managers of a real estate investment trust.

(B) The term does not include an officer who is acting in the capacity of an officer.

(36) "Governing documents" means:

(A) in the case of a domestic entity:

(i) the certificate of formation for a domestic filing entity or the document or agreement under which a domestic nonfiling entity is formed; and

(ii) the other documents or agreements adopted by the entity under this code to govern the formation or the internal affairs of the entity; or

(B) in the case of a foreign entity, the instruments, documents, or agreements adopted under the law of its jurisdiction of formation to govern the formation or the internal affairs of the entity.

(37) "Governing person" means a person serving as part of the governing authority of an entity.

(38) "Individual" means a natural person.

(39) "Insolvency" means the inability of a person to pay the person's debts as they become due in the usual course of business or affairs.

(40) "Insolvent" means a person who is unable to pay the person's debts as they become due in the usual course of business or affairs.

(41) "Interest exchange" means the acquisition of an ownership or membership interest in a domestic entity as provided by Subchapter B, Chapter 10. The term does not include a merger or conversion.

(42) "Internal Revenue Code" means the Internal Revenue Code of 1986, as amended. The term includes corresponding provisions of subsequent federal tax laws.

(43) "Jurisdiction of formation" means:

(A) in the case of a domestic filing entity, this state;

(B) in the case of a foreign entity for which a certificate of formation or similar organizational instrument is filed in connection with its formation, the jurisdiction in which the entity's certificate of formation or similar organizational instrument is filed; or

(C) in the case of a domestic nonfiling entity or a foreign entity for which a certificate of formation or similar organizational instrument is not filed in connection with its formation:

(i) the jurisdiction the laws of which are chosen in the entity's governing documents to govern its internal affairs if that jurisdiction bears a reasonable relation to the owners or members or to the entity's business and affairs under the principles of this state that otherwise would apply to a contract among the owners or members; or

(ii) if Subparagraph (i) does not apply, the jurisdiction in which the entity has its chief executive office.

(44) "Law" means, unless the context requires otherwise, both statutory and common law.

(45) "License" means a license, certificate of registration, or other legal authorization.

(46) "Limited liability company" means an entity governed as a limited liability company under Title 3 or 7. The term includes a professional limited liability company.

(47) "Limited liability limited partnership" means a partnership governed as a limited liability partnership and a limited partnership under Title 4.

(48) "Limited liability partnership" means a partnership governed as a limited liability partnership under Title 4.

(49) "Limited partner" means a person who has been admitted to a limited partnership as a limited partner as provided by:

(A) in the case of a domestic limited partnership, Chapter 153; or

(B) in the case of a foreign limited partnership, the laws of its jurisdiction of formation.

(50) "Limited partnership" means a partnership that is governed as a limited partnership under Title 4 and that has one or more general partners and one or more limited partners. The term includes a limited partnership registered as a limited liability limited partnership.

(51) "Manager" means a person designated as a manager of a limited liability company that is not managed by members of the company.

(52) "Managerial official" means an officer or a governing person.

(53) "Member" means:

(A) in the case of a limited liability company, a person who is a member or has been admitted as a member in the limited liability company under its governing documents;

(B) in the case of a nonprofit corporation, a person who has membership rights in the nonprofit corporation under its governing documents;

(C) in the case of a cooperative association, a member of a nonshare or share association;

(D) in the case of a nonprofit association, a person who has membership rights in the nonprofit association under its governing documents; or

(E) in the case of a professional association, a person who has membership rights in the professional association under its governing documents.

(54) "Membership interest" means a member's interest in an entity. With respect to a limited liability company, the term includes a member's share of profits and losses or similar items and the right to receive distributions, but does not include a member's right to participate in management.

(55) "Merger" means:

(A) the division of a domestic entity into two or more new domestic entities or other organizations or into a surviving domestic entity and one or more new domestic or foreign entities or non-code organizations; or

(B) the combination of one or more domestic entities with one or more domestic entities or non-code organizations resulting in:

(i) one or more surviving domestic entities or non-code organizations;

(ii) the creation of one or more new domestic entities or non-code organizations; or

(iii) one or more surviving domestic entities or non-code organizations and the creation of one or more new domestic entities or non-code organizations.

(55–a) "National securities exchange" means an exchange registered as a national securities exchange under Section 6, Securities Exchange Act of 1934 (15 U.S.C. Section 78f).

(56) "Non–code organization" means an organization other than a domestic entity.

(56–a) "Non–United States entity" means a foreign entity formed under, and the internal affairs of which are governed by, the laws of a non-United States jurisdiction.

(56–b) "Non–United States jurisdiction" means a foreign country or other foreign jurisdiction that is not the United States or a state of the United States.

(57) "Nonfiling entity" means a domestic entity that is not a filing entity. The term includes a domestic general partnership and nonprofit association.

(58) "Nonprofit association" means an association governed as a nonprofit association under Chapter 252.

(59) "Nonprofit corporation" means a corporation governed as a nonprofit corporation under Chapter 22.

(60) "Nonprofit entity" means an entity that is a nonprofit corporation, nonprofit association, or other entity that is organized solely for one or more of the purposes specified by Section 2.002.

(61) "Officer" means an individual elected, appointed, or designated as an officer of an entity by the entity's governing authority or under the entity's governing documents.

(62) "Organization" means a corporation, limited or general partnership, limited liability company, business trust, real estate investment trust, joint venture, joint stock company, cooperative, association, bank, insurance company, credit union, savings and loan association, or other organization, regardless of whether the organization is for-profit, nonprofit, domestic, or foreign.

(63) "Owner," for purposes of Title 1, 7, or 8, means:

(A) with respect to a foreign or domestic for-profit corporation or real estate investment trust, a shareholder;

(B) with respect to a foreign or domestic partnership, a partner;

(C) with respect to a foreign or domestic limited liability company or professional association, a member; or

(D) with respect to another foreign or domestic entity, an owner of an equity interest in that entity.

(64) "Ownership interest" means an owner's interest in an entity. The term includes the owner's share of profits and losses or similar items and the right to receive distributions. The term does not include an owner's right to participate in management.

(65) "Parent" means an organization that, directly or indirectly through or with one or more of its subsidiaries:

(A) owns at least 50 percent of the outstanding ownership or membership interests of another organization; or

(B) possesses at least 50 percent of the voting power of the owners or members of another organization.

(66) "Partner" means a limited partner or general partner.

(67) "Partnership" means an entity governed as a partnership under Title 4.

(68) "Partnership interest" means a partner's interest in a partnership. The term includes the partner's share of profits and losses or similar items and the right to receive distributions. The term does not include a partner's right to participate in management.

(69) "Party to the merger" means a domestic entity or non-code organization that under a plan of merger is divided or combined by a merger. The term does not include a domestic entity or non-code organization that is not to be divided or combined into or with one or more domestic entities or non-code organizations, regardless of whether ownership interest of the entity are to be issued under the plan of merger.

(69–a) "Period of duration," in reference to when a domestic entity is required to wind up its business and affairs:

(A) means:

(i) a specified term or period of time, such as a specified number of months or years; or

(ii) a period that expires as of a specified time or date; and

(B) does not include:

(i) a period that expires or whose expiration is made contingent on the occurrence of a future event or fact, other than the passage of time or the occurrence of a specified time or date; or

(ii) a period specified to be perpetual.

(69–b) "Person" means an individual or a corporation, partnership, limited liability company, business trust, trust, association, or other organization, estate, government or governmental subdivision or agency, or other legal entity .

(69–c) "Plan of conversion" means a document that conforms with the requirements of Section 10.103.

(69–d) "Plan of exchange" means a document that conforms with the requirements of Section 10.052.

(69–e) "Plan of merger" means a document that conforms with the requirements of Sections 10.002 and 10.003.

(70) "President" means the:

(A) individual designated as president of an entity under the entity's governing documents; or

(B) officer or committee of persons authorized to perform the functions of the principal executive officer of an entity without regard to the designated name of the officer or committee.

(71) "Professional association" has the meaning assigned by Section 301.003.

(72) "Professional corporation" has the meaning assigned by Section 301.003.

(73) "Professional entity" has the meaning assigned by Section 301.003.

(74) "Professional individual" has the meaning assigned by Section 301.003.

(75) "Professional limited liability company" has the meaning assigned by Section 301.003.

(76) "Professional service" has the meaning assigned by Section 301.003.

(77) "Property" includes tangible and intangible property and an interest in that property.

(78) "Real estate investment trust" means an entity governed as a real estate investment trust under Title 5.

(79) "Secretary" means the:

(A) individual designated as secretary of an entity under the entity's governing documents; or

(B) officer or committee of persons authorized to perform the functions of secretary of an entity without regard to the designated name of the officer or committee.

(80) "Share" means a unit into which the ownership interest in a for-profit corporation, professional corporation, real estate investment trust, or professional association is divided, regardless of whether the share is certificated or uncertificated.

(81) "Shareholder" or "holder of shares" means:

(A) the person in whose name shares issued by a for-profit corporation, professional corporation, or real estate investment trust are registered in the share transfer records maintained by the for-profit corporation, professional corporation, or real estate investment trust; or

(B) the beneficial owner of shares issued by a for-profit corporation, whose shares are held in a voting trust or by a nominee on the beneficial owner's behalf, to the extent of the rights granted by a nominee statement on file with the for-profit corporation in accordance with Sections 21.201(b) and (c).

(82) "Signature" means any symbol executed or adopted by a person with present intention to authenticate a writing. Unless the context requires

otherwise, the term includes a digital signature, an electronic signature, and a facsimile of a signature.

(83) "Subscriber" means a person who agrees with or makes an offer to an entity to purchase by subscription an ownership interest in the entity.

(84) "Subscription" means an agreement between a subscriber and an entity, or a written offer made by a subscriber to an entity before or after the entity's formation, in which the subscriber agrees or offers to purchase a specified ownership interest in the entity.

(85) "Subsidiary" means an organization for which another organization, either directly or indirectly through or with one or more of its other subsidiaries:

(A) owns at least 50 percent of the outstanding ownership or membership interests of the organization; or

(B) possesses at least 50 percent of the voting power of the owners or members of the organization.

(86) "Treasurer" means the:

(A) individual designated as treasurer of an entity under the entity's governing documents; or

(B) officer or committee of persons authorized to perform the functions of treasurer of an entity without regard to the designated name of the officer or committee.

(87) "Uncertificated ownership interest" means an ownership interest in a domestic entity that is not represented by an instrument and is transferred by:

(A) amendment of the governing documents of the entity; or

(B) registration on books maintained by or on behalf of the entity for the purpose of registering transfers of ownership interests.

(88) "Vice president" means the:

(A) individual designated as vice president of an entity under the governing documents of the entity; or

(B) officer or committee of persons authorized to perform the functions of the president of the entity on the death, absence, or resignation of the president or on the inability of the president to perform the functions of office without regard to the designated name of the officer or committee.

(89) "Writing" or "written" means an expression of words, letters, characters, numbers, symbols, figures, or other textual information that is inscribed on a tangible medium or that is stored in an electronic or other medium that is retrievable in a perceivable form. Unless the context requires otherwise, the term:

(A) includes stored or transmitted electronic data, electronic transmissions, and reproductions of writings; and

(B) does not include sound or video recordings of speech other than transcriptions that are otherwise writings.

Acts 2003, 78th Leg., ch. 182, § 1, eff. Jan. 1, 2006. Amended by Acts 2005, 79th Leg., ch. 64, § 1, eff. Jan. 1, 2006; Acts 2007, 80th Leg., ch. 688, § 1, eff. Sept. 1, 2007; Acts 2007, 80th Leg., ch. 885, § 2.07, eff. April 1, 2009; Acts 2009, 81st Leg., ch. 84, § 1, eff. Sept. 1, 2009; Acts 2011, 82nd Leg., ch. 139 (S.B. 748), § 1, eff. Sept. 1, 2011.

§ 1.003. Disinterested Person

(a) For purposes of this code, a person is disinterested with respect to the approval of a contract, transaction, or other matter, or to the consideration of the disposition of a claim or challenge relating to a contract, transaction, or particular conduct, if the person or the person's associate:

(1) is not a party to the contract or transaction or materially involved in the conduct that is the subject of the claim or challenge; and

(2) does not have a material financial interest in the outcome of the contract or transaction or the disposition of the claim or challenge.

(b) For purposes of Subsection (a), a person is not materially involved in a contract or transaction that is the subject of a claim or challenge and does not have a material financial interest in the outcome of a contract or transaction or the disposition of a claim or challenge solely because:

(1) the person was nominated or elected as a governing person by a person who is:

(A) interested in the contract or transaction; or

(B) alleged to have engaged in the conduct that is the subject of the claim or challenge;

(2) the person receives normal fees or customary compensation, reimbursement for expenses, or benefits as a governing person of the entity;

(3) the person has a direct or indirect equity interest in the entity;

(4) the entity has, or its subsidiaries have, an interest in the contract or transaction or was affected by the alleged conduct;

(5) the person or an associate of the person receives ordinary and reasonable compensation for

reviewing, making recommendations regarding, or deciding on the disposition of the claim or challenge; or

(6) in the case of a review by the person of the alleged conduct that is the subject of the claim or challenge:

(A) the person is named as a defendant in the derivative proceeding regarding the matter or as a person who engaged in the alleged conduct; or

(B) the person, acting as a governing person, approved, voted for, or acquiesced in the act being challenged if the act did not result in a material personal or financial benefit to the person and the challenging party fails to allege particular facts that, if true, raise a significant prospect that the governing person would be held liable to the entity or its owners or members as a result of the conduct.

Acts 2003, 78th Leg., ch. 182, § 1, eff. Jan. 1, 2006.

§ 1.004. Independent Person

(a) For purposes of this code, a person is independent with respect to considering the disposition of a claim or challenge regarding a contract or transaction, or particular or alleged conduct, if the person:

(1) is disinterested;

(2) either:

(A) is not an associate, or member of the immediate family, of a party to the contract or transaction or of a person who is alleged to have engaged in the conduct that is the subject of the claim or challenge; or

(B) is an associate to a party or person described by Paragraph (A) that is an entity if the person is an associate solely because the person is a governing person of the entity or of the entity's subsidiaries or associates;

(3) does not have a business, financial, or familial relationship with a party to the contract or transaction, or with another person who is alleged to have engaged in the conduct, that is the subject of the claim or challenge that could reasonably be expected to materially and adversely affect the judgment of the person in favor of the party or other person with respect to the consideration of the matter; and

(4) is not shown, by a preponderance of the evidence, to be under the controlling influence of a party to the contract or transaction that is the subject of the claim or challenge or of a person who is alleged to have engaged in the conduct that is the subject of the claim or challenge.

(b) For purposes of Subsection (a), a person does not have a relationship that could reasonably be expected to materially and adversely affect the judgment of the person regarding the disposition of a matter that is the subject of a claim or challenge and is not otherwise under the controlling influence of a party to a contract or transaction that is the subject of a claim or challenge or that is alleged to have engaged in the conduct that is the subject of a claim or challenge solely because:

(1) the person has been nominated or elected as a governing person by a person who is interested in the contract or transaction or alleged to be engaged in the conduct that is the subject of the claim or challenge;

(2) the person receives normal fees or similar customary compensation, reimbursement for expenses, or benefits as a governing person of the entity;

(3) the person has a direct or indirect equity interest in the entity;

(4) the entity has, or its subsidiaries have, an interest in the contract or transaction or was affected by the alleged conduct;

(5) the person or an associate of the person receives ordinary and reasonable compensation for reviewing, making recommendations regarding, or deciding on the disposition of the claim or challenge; or

(6) the person, an associate of the person, other than the entity or its associates, or an immediate family member has a continuing business relationship with the entity that is not material to the person, associate, or family member.

Acts 2003, 78th Leg., ch. 182, § 1, eff. Jan. 1, 2006.

§ 1.005. Conspicuous Information

In this code, required information is conspicuous if the information is placed in a manner or displayed using a font that provides or should provide notice to a reasonable person affected by the information. Required information in a document is conspicuous if the font used for the information is capitalized, boldfaced, italicized, or underlined or is larger or of a different color than the remainder of the document.

Acts 2003, 78th Leg., ch. 182, § 1, eff. Jan. 1, 2006.

§ 1.006. Synonymous Terms

To the extent not inconsistent with the provisions of the constitution, other statutes or codes, and governing documents wherein such terms may be found, and as the context requires, in this code, any other statute or code of this state, or any governing documents:

(1) a reference to "articles of incorporation," "articles of organization," "articles of association," "certificate of limited partnership," and "charter" includes a "certificate of formation";

(2) a reference to "authorized capital stock" includes "authorized shares";

(3) a reference to "capital stock" includes "authorized and issued shares," "issued share," and "stated capital";

(4) a reference to a "certificate of registration," "certificate of authority," and "permit to do business" includes "registration";

(5) a reference to "stock" and "shares of stock" includes "shares";

(6) a reference to "stockholder" includes "shareholder";

(7) a reference to "no par stock" includes "shares without par value";

(8) a reference to "paid-up capital" includes "stated capital";

(9) a reference to "articles of merger" includes a "certificate of merger";

(10) a reference to "articles of exchange" includes a "certificate of exchange";

(11) a reference to "articles of conversion" includes a "certificate of conversion";

(12) a reference to "articles of amendment" includes a "certificate of amendment";

(13) a reference to "articles of dissolution" or "certificate of cancellation" includes a "certificate of termination";

(14) a reference to "incorporator" includes an "organizer";

(15) a reference to "certificate of authority to transact business" includes a "registration to transact business";

(16) a reference to "regulations" in connection with a limited liability company includes a "company agreement"; and

(17) a reference to "business corporation" includes a "for-profit corporation."

Acts 2003, 78th Leg., ch. 182, § 1, eff. Jan. 1, 2006. Amended by Acts 2005, 79th Leg., ch. 64, § 2, eff. Jan. 1, 2006; Acts 2007, 80th Leg., ch. 688, § 2, eff. Sept. 1, 2007.

§ 1.007. Signing of Document or Other Writing

For purposes of this code, a writing has been signed by a person when the writing includes, bears, or incorporates the person's signature. A transmission or reproduction of a writing signed by a person is considered signed by that person for purposes of this code.

Acts 2003, 78th Leg., ch. 182, § 1, eff. Jan. 1, 2006. Amended by Acts 2005, 79th Leg., ch. 64, § 3, eff. Jan. 1, 2006.

§ 1.008. Short Titles

(a) The provisions of this code as described by this section may be cited as provided by this section.

(b) The provisions of Title 2 and the provisions of Title 1 to the extent applicable to corporations may be cited as the "Texas Corporation Law."

(c) The provisions of Chapters 20 and 21 and the provisions of Title 1 to the extent applicable to for-profit corporations may be cited as the "Texas For–Profit Corporation Law."

(d) The provisions of Chapters 20 and 22 and the provisions of Title 1 to the extent applicable to nonprofit corporations may be cited as the "Texas Nonprofit Corporation Law."

(e) The provisions of Title 3 and the provisions of Title 1 to the extent applicable to limited liability companies may be cited as the "Texas Limited Liability Company Law."

(f) The provisions of Chapters 151, 152, and 154 and the provisions of Title 1 to the extent applicable to general partnerships may be cited as the "Texas General Partnership Law."

(g) The provisions of Chapters 151, 153, and 154 and the provisions of Title 1 and Chapter 152 to the extent applicable to limited partnerships may be cited as the "Texas Limited Partnership Law."

(h) The provisions of Title 5 and the provisions of Title 1 and Chapters 20 and 21 to the extent applicable to real estate investment trusts may be cited as the "Texas Real Estate Investment Trust Law."

(i) The provisions of Chapter 251 and the provisions of Title 1 and Chapters 20 and 22 to the extent applicable to cooperative associations may be cited as the "Texas Cooperative Association Law."

(j) The provisions of Title 7 and the provisions of Titles 1, 2, and 3 to the extent applicable to professional entities may be cited as the "Texas Professional Entities Law."

(k) The provisions of Chapter 252 may be cited as the "Uniform Unincorporated Nonprofit Association Act."

(*l*) The provisions of Chapters 301 and 302 and the provisions of Chapters 20 and 21 and Title 1 to the extent applicable to professional associations may be cited as the "Texas Professional Association Law."

(m) The provisions of Chapters 301 and 303 and the provisions of Chapters 20 and 21 and Title 1 to the extent applicable to professional corporations may be cited as the "Texas Professional Corporation Law."

(n) The provisions of Chapters 301 and 304 and the provisions of Titles 1 and 3 to the extent applicable to professional limited liability companies may be cited as the "Texas Professional Limited Liability Company Law."

Acts 2003, 78th Leg., ch. 182, § 1, eff. Jan. 1, 2006. Amended by Acts 2007, 80th Leg., ch. 688, § 3, eff. Sept. 1, 2007.

§ 1.009. Dollars as Monetary Units

Unless the context requires otherwise, a value or amount that is required by this code to be stated in monetary terms must be stated in United States dollars. Currency that is not specified is considered to be in United States dollars.

Acts 2003, 78th Leg., ch. 182, § 1, eff. Jan. 1, 2006.

SUBCHAPTER B. CODE CONSTRUCTION

§ 1.051. Construction of Code

Chapter 311, Government Code (Code Construction Act), applies to the construction of each provision in this code except as otherwise expressly provided by this code.

Acts 2003, 78th Leg., ch. 182, § 1, eff. Jan. 1, 2006.

§ 1.052. Reference in Law to Statute Revised by Code

A reference in a law to a statute or a part of a statute revised by this code is considered to be a reference to the part of this code that revises that statute or part of that statute.

Acts 2003, 78th Leg., ch. 182, § 1, eff. Jan. 1, 2006.

§ 1.053. Applicability to Foreign and Interstate Affairs

This code applies to the conduct of affairs with foreign countries and the other states of the United States only to the extent permitted under the United States Constitution.

Acts 2003, 78th Leg., ch. 182, § 1, eff. Jan. 1, 2006.

§ 1.054. Reservation of Power

The legislature at all times has the power to amend, repeal, or modify this code and to prescribe regulations, provisions, and limitations as the legislature considers advisable. The regulations, provisions, and limitations are binding on any entity subject to this code.

Acts 2003, 78th Leg., ch. 182, § 1, eff. Jan. 1, 2006.

SUBCHAPTER C. DETERMINATION OF APPLICABLE LAW

§ 1.101. Domestic Filing Entities

The law of this state governs the formation and internal affairs of an entity if the entity's formation occurs when a certificate of formation filed in accordance with Chapter 4 takes effect.

Acts 2003, 78th Leg., ch. 182, § 1, eff. Jan. 1, 2006.

§ 1.102. Foreign Filing Entities

If the formation of an entity occurs when a certificate of formation or similar instrument filed with a foreign governmental authority takes effect, the law of the state or other jurisdiction in which that foreign governmental authority is located governs the formation and internal affairs of the entity.

Acts 2003, 78th Leg., ch. 182, § 1, eff. Jan. 1, 2006.

§ 1.103. Entities Not Formed by Filing Instrument

If the formation of an entity does not occur when a certificate of formation or similar instrument filed with the secretary of state or with a foreign governmental authority takes effect, the law governing the entity's formation and internal affairs is the law of the entity's jurisdiction of formation.

Acts 2003, 78th Leg., ch. 182, § 1, eff. Jan. 1, 2006.

§ 1.104. Law Applicable to Liability

The law of the jurisdiction that governs an entity as determined under Sections 1.101–1.103 applies to the liability of an owner, a member, or a managerial official of the entity in the capacity as an owner, a member, or a managerial official for an obligation, including a debt or other liability, of the entity for which the owner, member, or managerial official is not otherwise liable by contract or under provisions of law other than this code.

Acts 2003, 78th Leg., ch. 182, § 1, eff. Jan. 1, 2006.

§ 1.105. Internal Affairs

For purposes of this code, the internal affairs of an entity include:

(1) the rights, powers, and duties of its governing authority, governing persons, officers, owners, and members; and

(2) matters relating to its membership or ownership interests.

Acts 2003, 78th Leg., ch. 182, § 1, eff. Jan. 1, 2006.

§ 1.106. Order of Precedence

(a) This title applies to all domestic entities and foreign entities to the extent provided by this title.

(b) Each title of this code, other than this title, applies to a different type of entity to the extent provided by that title.

(c) If a provision of this title conflicts with a provision in another title of this code, the provision of the other title supersedes the provision of this title.

Acts 2003, 78th Leg., ch. 182, § 1, eff. Jan. 1, 2006.

CHAPTER 2. PURPOSES AND POWER OF DOMESTIC ENTITY

SUBCHAPTER A. PURPOSES OF DOMESTIC ENTITY

Section
2.001. General Scope of Permissible Purposes.
2.002. Purposes of Nonprofit Entity.
2.003 General Prohibited Purposes.
2.004. Limitation on Purposes of Professional Entity.
2.005. Limitation in Governing Documents.
2.006. Repealed.
2.007. Additional Prohibited Activities of For–Profit Corporation.
2.008. Nonprofit Corporations.
2.009. Permissible Purpose of Nonprofit Corporation Related to Organized Labor.
2.010. Prohibited Activities of Nonprofit Corporation.
2.011. Purposes of Cooperative Association.
2.012. Limitation on Purposes of Real Estate Investment Trust.

SUBCHAPTER B. POWERS OF DOMESTIC ENTITY
2.101. General Powers.
2.102. Additional Powers of Nonprofit Entity or Institution.
2.103. Power to Incur Indebtedness.
2.104. Power to Make Guaranties.
2.105. Additional Powers of Certain Pipeline Businesses.
2.106. Power of Nonprofit Corporation to Serve as Trustee.
Section
2.107. Standard Tax Provisions for Certain Charitable Nonprofit Corporations; Power to Exclude.
2.108. Powers of Professional Association.
2.109. Powers of Professional Corporation.
2.110. Powers of Cooperative Association.
2.111. Limitation on Powers of Cooperative Association.
2.112. Stated Powers in Subchapter Sufficient.
2.113. Limitation on Powers.
2.114. Certificated Indebtedness; Manner of Issuance; Signature and Seal.

SUBCHAPTER A. PURPOSES OF DOMESTIC ENTITY

§ 2.001. General Scope of Permissible Purposes

A domestic entity has any lawful purpose or purposes, unless otherwise provided by this code.

Acts 2003, 78th Leg., ch. 182, § 1, eff. Jan. 1, 2006.

§ 2.002. Purposes of Nonprofit Entity

The purpose or purposes of a domestic nonprofit entity may include one or more of the following purposes:

(1) serving charitable, benevolent, religious, eleemosynary, patriotic, civic, missionary, educational, scientific, social, fraternal, athletic, aesthetic, agricultural, and horticultural purposes;

(2) operating or managing a professional, commercial, or trade association or labor union;

(3) providing animal husbandry; or

(4) operating on a nonprofit cooperative basis for the benefit of its members.

Acts 2003, 78th Leg., ch. 182, § 1, eff. Jan. 1, 2006.

§ 2.003 General Prohibited Purposes

A domestic entity may not:

(1) engage in a business or activity that:

(A) is expressly unlawful or prohibited by a law of this state; or

(B) cannot lawfully be engaged in by that entity under state law; or

(2) operate as a:

(A) bank;

(B) trust company;

(C) savings association;

(D) insurance company;

(E) cemetery organization, except as authorized by Chapter 711, 712, or 715, Health and Safety Code; or

(F) abstract or title company governed by Title 11, Insurance Code.

Acts 2003, 78th Leg., ch. 182, § 1, eff. Jan. 1, 2006. Amended by Acts 2005, 79th Leg., ch. 728, § 11.103, eff. Jan. 1, 2006; Acts 2007, 80th Leg., ch. 688, § 4, eff. Sept. 1, 2007; Acts 2009, 81st Leg., ch. 84, § 2, eff. Sept. 1, 2009.

§ 2.004. Limitation on Purposes of Professional Entity

Except as provided in Title 7, a professional entity may engage in only:

(1) one type of professional service, unless the entity is expressly authorized to provide more than one type of professional service under state law regulating the professional services; and

(2) services ancillary to that type of professional service.

Acts 2003, 78th Leg., ch. 182, § 1, eff. Jan. 1, 2006.

§ 2.005. Limitation in Governing Documents

The governing documents of a domestic entity may contain limitations on the entity's purposes.

Acts 2003, 78th Leg., ch. 182, § 1, eff. Jan. 1, 2006.

§ 2.006. Repealed by Acts 2009, 81st Leg., ch. 84, § 74, eff. Sept. 1, 2009

§ 2.007. Additional Prohibited Activities of For–Profit Corporation

A for-profit corporation may not:

(1) operate a cooperative association, limited cooperative association, or labor union;

(2) transact a combination of the businesses of:

(A) raising cattle and owning land for the raising of cattle, other than operating and owning feedlots and feeding cattle; and

(B) operating stockyards and slaughtering, refrigerating, canning, curing, or packing meat;

(3) engage in a combination of:

(A) the petroleum oil producing business in this state; and

(B) the oil pipeline business in this state other than through stock ownership in a for-profit corporation engaged in the oil pipeline business and other than the ownership or operation of private pipelines in and about the corporation's refineries, fields, or stations; or

(4) engage in a business or activity that may not be engaged in by a for-profit corporation without first obtaining a license under the laws of this state and a license to engage in that business or activity cannot lawfully be granted to the corporation.

Acts 2003, 78th Leg., ch. 182, § 1, eff. Jan. 1, 2006. Amended by Acts 2007, 80th Leg., ch. 688, § 5, eff. Sept. 1, 2007.

§ 2.008. Nonprofit Corporations

A corporation formed for the purpose of operating a nonprofit institution, including an institution devoted to a charitable, benevolent, religious, patriotic, civic, cultural, missionary, educational, scientific, social, fraternal, athletic, or aesthetic purpose, may be formed and governed only as a nonprofit corporation under this code and not as a for-profit corporation under this code.

Acts 2003, 78th Leg., ch. 182, § 1, eff. Jan. 1, 2006.

§ 2.009. Permissible Purpose of Nonprofit Corporation Related to Organized Labor

Subject to Chapter 101, Labor Code, a nonprofit corporation may be formed to organize laborers, workers, or wage earners to protect themselves in their various pursuits.

Acts 2003, 78th Leg., ch. 182, § 1, eff. Jan. 1, 2006.

§ 2.010. Prohibited Activities of Nonprofit Corporation

A nonprofit corporation may not be organized or registered under this code to conduct its affairs in this state to:

(1) engage in or operate as a group hospital service, rural credit union, agricultural and livestock pool, mutual loan corporation, cooperative association under Chapter 251, cooperative credit association, farmers' cooperative society, Co-operative Marketing Act corporation, rural electric cooperative corporation, telephone cooperative corporation, or fraternal organization operating under the lodge system and incorporated under Subchapter C, Chapter 23;

(2) engage in water supply or sewer service except as an entity incorporated under Chapter 67, Water Code; or

(3) engage in a business or activity that may not be engaged in by a nonprofit corporation without first obtaining a license under the laws of this state and a license to engage in that business or activity cannot lawfully be granted to the corporation.

Acts 2003, 78th Leg., ch. 182, § 1, eff. Jan. 1, 2006. Amended by Acts 2005, 79th Leg., ch. 64, § 4, eff. Jan. 1, 2006; Acts 2007, 80th Leg., ch. 688, § 6, eff. Sept. 1, 2007.

§ 2.011. Purposes of Cooperative Association

(a) A person may organize a cooperative association under this code to acquire, produce, build, operate, manufacture, furnish, exchange, or distribute any type of property, commodities, goods, or services for the primary and mutual benefit of the members of the cooperative association.

(b) A cooperative association may not be organized to:

(1) serve or function as a health maintenance organization;

(2) furnish medical or health care; or

(3) employ or contract with a health care provider in a manner prohibited by the statute under which the provider is licensed.

(c) A cooperative association may not directly or indirectly engage in a health maintenance organization or a prepaid legal service corporation.

Acts 2003, 78th Leg., ch. 182, § 1, eff. Jan. 1, 2006.

§ 2.012. Limitation on Purposes of Real Estate Investment Trust

The purposes of a real estate investment trust are limited by Section 3.012.

Acts 2003, 78th Leg., ch. 182, § 1, eff. Jan. 1, 2006.

SUBCHAPTER B. POWERS OF DOMESTIC ENTITY

§ 2.101. General Powers

Except as otherwise provided by this code, a domestic entity has the same powers as an individual to take action necessary or convenient to carry out its business and affairs. Except as otherwise provided by this code, the powers of a domestic entity include the power to:

(1) sue, be sued, and defend suit in the entity's business name;

(2) have and alter a seal and use the seal or a facsimile of it by impressing, affixing, or reproducing it;

(3) acquire, receive, own, hold, improve, use, and deal in and with property or an interest in property;

(4) sell, convey, mortgage, pledge, lease, exchange, and otherwise dispose of property;

(5) make contracts and guarantees;

(6) incur liabilities, borrow money, issue notes, bonds, or other obligations, which may be convertible into, or include the option to purchase, other securities or ownership interests in the entity, and secure its obligations by mortgaging or pledging its property, franchises, or income;

(7) lend money, invest its funds, and receive and hold property as security for repayment;

(8) acquire its own bonds, debentures, or other evidences of indebtedness or obligations;

(9) acquire its own ownership interests, regardless of whether redeemable, and hold the ownership interests as treasury ownership interests or cancel or dispose of the ownership interests;

(10) be a promoter, organizer, owner, partner, member, associate, or manager of an organization;

(11) acquire, receive, own, hold, vote, use, pledge, and dispose of ownership interests in or securities issued by another person;

(12) conduct its business, locate its offices, and exercise the powers granted by this code to further its purposes, in or out of this state;

(13) lend money to, and otherwise assist, its managerial officials, owners, members, or employees as necessary or appropriate if the loan or assistance reasonably may be expected to benefit, directly or indirectly, the entity;

(14) elect or appoint officers and agents of the entity, establish the length of their terms, define their duties, and fix their compensation;

(15) pay pensions and establish pension plans, pension trusts, profit-sharing plans, bonus plans, and incentive plans for managerial officials, owners, members, or employees or former managerial officials, owners, members, or employees;

(16) indemnify and maintain liability insurance for managerial officials, owners, members, employees, and agents of the entity or the entity's affiliate;

(17) adopt and amend governing documents for managing the affairs of the entity subject to applicable law;

(18) make donations for the public welfare or for a charitable, scientific, or educational purpose;

(19) voluntarily wind up its business and activities and terminate its existence;

(20) transact business or take action that will aid governmental policy;

(21) renounce, in its certificate of formation or by action of its governing authority, an interest or expectancy of the entity in, or an interest or expectancy of the entity in being offered an opportunity to participate in, specified business opportunities or a specified class or category of business opportuni-

ties presented to the entity or one or more of its managerial officials or owners; and

(22) take other action necessary or appropriate to further the purposes of the entity.

Acts 2003, 78th Leg., ch. 182, § 1, eff. Jan. 1, 2006. Amended by Acts 2005, 79th Leg., ch. 64, § 5, eff. Jan. 1, 2006; Acts 2007, 80th Leg., ch. 688, § 7, eff. Sept. 1, 2007.

§ 2.102. Additional Powers of Nonprofit Entity or Institution

To effect its purposes, a domestic nonprofit entity or institution formed for a religious, charitable, educational, or eleemosynary purpose may acquire, own, hold, mortgage, and dispose of and invest its funds in property for the use and benefit of, under the discretion of, and in trust for a convention, conference, or association organized under the laws of this state or another state with which it is affiliated or by which it is controlled.

Acts 2003, 78th Leg., ch. 182, § 1, eff. Jan. 1, 2006.

§ 2.103. Power to Incur Indebtedness

(a) Unless otherwise provided by its governing documents or this code, a domestic entity may create indebtedness for any consideration the entity considers appropriate, including:

(1) cash;

(2) property;

(3) a contract to receive property;

(4) a debt or other obligation of the entity or of another person;

(5) services performed or a contract for services to be performed; or

(6) a direct or indirect benefit realized by the entity.

(b) In the absence of fraud in the transaction, the judgment of the governing authority of a domestic entity as to the value of the consideration received by the entity for indebtedness is conclusive.

(c) The consideration for the indebtedness may be received either directly or indirectly by the domestic entity, including by a domestic or foreign organization that is wholly or partially owned, directly or indirectly, by the domestic entity.

(d) This section does not apply to indebtedness created by a domestic entity that is incurred by reason of the authorization or payment of a distribution.

Acts 2003, 78th Leg., ch. 182, § 1, eff. Jan. 1, 2006.

§ 2.104. Power to Make Guaranties

(a) In this section, "guaranty" means a guaranty, mortgage, pledge, security agreement, or other agreement making the domestic entity or its assets liable for another person's contract, security, or other obligation.

(b) Unless otherwise provided by its governing documents or this code, a domestic entity may:

(1) make a guaranty on behalf of a parent, subsidiary, or affiliate of the entity; or

(2) make a guaranty of the indebtedness of another person if the guaranty may reasonably be expected directly or indirectly to benefit the entity.

(c) For purposes of Subsection (b)(2), a decision by the governing authority of the domestic entity that a guaranty may reasonably be expected to benefit the entity is conclusive and not subject to attack by any person, except:

(1) a guaranty may not be enforced by a person who participated in a fraud on the domestic entity resulting in the making of the guaranty or by a person who had notice of that fraud at the time the person acquired rights under the guaranty;

(2) a proposed guaranty may be enjoined at the request of an owner of the domestic entity on the ground that the guaranty cannot reasonably be expected to benefit the domestic entity; or

(3) the domestic entity, whether acting directly or through a receiver, trustee, or other legal representative, or through an owner on behalf of the domestic entity, may bring suit for damages against the managerial officials, owners, or members who authorized the guaranty on the ground that the guaranty could not reasonably be expected to benefit the domestic entity.

(d) This section does not:

(1) apply to a domestic entity governed by the Insurance Code; or

(2) authorize a domestic entity that is not governed by the Insurance Code to engage in a business or transaction regulated by the Insurance Code.

Acts 2003, 78th Leg., ch. 182, § 1, eff. Jan. 1, 2006. Amended by Acts 2007, 80th Leg., ch. 688, § 8, eff. Sept. 1, 2007.

§ 2.105. Additional Powers of Certain Pipeline Businesses

In addition to the powers provided by the other sections of this subchapter, a corporation, general partnership, limited partnership, limited liability company, or other combination of those entities engaged as a common carrier in the pipeline business for the purpose of transporting oil, oil products, gas, carbon dioxide, salt brine, fuller's earth, sand, clay, liquefied minerals, or other mineral solutions has all the rights and powers conferred on a common carrier by Sections 111.019–111.022, Natural Resources Code.

Acts 2003, 78th Leg., ch. 182, § 1, eff. Jan. 1, 2006.

§ 2.106. Power of Nonprofit Corporation to Serve as Trustee

(a) A nonprofit corporation that is described by Section 501(c)(3) or 170(c), Internal Revenue Code, or a corresponding provision of a subsequent federal tax law, or a nonprofit corporation listed by the Internal Revenue Service in the Cumulative List of Organizations Described in Section 170(c) of the Internal Revenue Code of 1986, I.R.S. Publication 78, or any successor I.R.S. publication, may serve as the trustee of a trust:

(1) of which the nonprofit corporation is a beneficiary; or

(2) benefiting another organization described by one of those sections of the Internal Revenue Code, or a corresponding provision of a subsequent federal tax law, or listed by the Internal Revenue Service in the Cumulative List of Organizations Described in Section 170(c) of the Internal Revenue Code of 1986, I.R.S. Publication 78, or any successor I.R.S. publication.

(b) Any corporation (or person or entity assisting such corporation) described in this section shall have immunity from suit (including both a defense to liability and the right not to bear the cost, burden, and risk of discovery and trial) as to any claim alleging that the corporation's role as trustee of a trust described in this section constitutes engaging in the trust business in a manner requiring a state charter as defined in Section 181.002(a)(9), Finance Code. An interlocutory appeal may be taken if a court denies or otherwise fails to grant a motion for summary judgment that is based on an assertion of the immunity provided in this subsection.

Acts 2003, 78th Leg., ch. 182, § 1, eff. Jan. 1, 2006.

§ 2.107. Standard Tax Provisions for Certain Charitable Nonprofit Corporations; Power to Exclude

(a) Notwithstanding any conflicting provision of this chapter, Chapter 3, or the certificate of formation and except as provided by Subsection (b), the certificate of formation of each corporation that is a private foundation as defined by Section 509, Internal Revenue Code, is considered to contain the following provisions: "The corporation shall make distributions at the time and in the manner as not to subject it to tax under Section 4942 of the Internal Revenue Code of 1986; the corporation shall not engage in any act of self-dealing which would be subject to tax under Section 4941 of the Code; the corporation shall not retain any excess business holdings which would subject it to tax under Section 4943 of the Code; the corporation shall not make any investments which would subject it to tax under Section 4944 of the Code; and the corporation shall not make any taxable expenditures which would subject it to tax under Section 4945 of the Code."

(b) A nonprofit corporation described by Subsection (a) may amend the certificate of formation of the corporation to expressly exclude the application of Subsection (a).

Acts 2003, 78th Leg., ch. 182, § 1, eff. Jan. 1, 2006.

§ 2.108. Powers of Professional Association

Except as provided by Title 7, a professional association has the same powers, privileges, duties, restrictions, and liabilities as a for-profit corporation.

Acts 2003, 78th Leg., ch. 182, § 1, eff. Jan. 1, 2006.

§ 2.109. Powers of Professional Corporation

Except as provided by Title 7, a professional corporation has the same powers, privileges, duties, restrictions, and liabilities as a for-profit corporation.

Acts 2003, 78th Leg., ch. 182, § 1, eff. Jan. 1, 2006.

§ 2.110. Powers of Cooperative Association

(a) Except as provided by Chapter 251, a cooperative association may exercise the same powers and privileges and is subject to the same duties, restrictions, and liabilities as a nonprofit corporation.

(b) A cooperative association may:

(1) own and hold membership in other associations or corporations;

(2) own and hold share capital of other associations or corporations;

(3) own and exercise ownership rights in bonds or other obligations;

(4) make agreements of mutual aid or federation with other associations, other groups organized on a cooperative basis, or other nonprofit groups; and

(5) deliver money to a scholarship fund for rural students.

Acts 2003, 78th Leg., ch. 182, § 1, eff. Jan. 1, 2006.

§ 2.111. Limitation on Powers of Cooperative Association

Except for the payment of necessary legal fees or promotion expenses, a cooperative association may not directly or indirectly use its funds, issue shares, or incur indebtedness for the payment of compensation for the organization of the cooperative association in excess of five percent of the amount paid for the shares or membership certificates involved in the promotion transaction.

Acts 2003, 78th Leg., ch. 182, § 1, eff. Jan. 1, 2006.

§ 2.112. Stated Powers in Subchapter Sufficient

A domestic entity is not required to state any of the powers provided to the entity by this subchapter in its governing documents.

Acts 2003, 78th Leg., ch. 182, § 1, eff. Jan. 1, 2006.

§ 2.113. Limitation on Powers

(a) This subchapter does not authorize a domestic entity or a managerial official of a domestic entity to exercise a power in a manner inconsistent with a limitation on the purposes or powers of the entity contained in its governing documents, this code, or other law of this state.

(b) This code does not authorize any action in violation of the antitrust laws of this state.

Acts 2003, 78th Leg., ch. 182, § 1, eff. Jan. 1, 2006.

§ 2.114. Certificated Indebtedness; Manner of Issuance; Signature and Seal

(a) Except as otherwise provided by the governing documents of the domestic entity, this code, or other law, on the issuance by a domestic entity of a bond, debenture, or other evidence of indebtedness in certificated form, the seal of the entity, if the entity has adopted a seal, may be a facsimile that may be engraved or printed on the certificate.

(b) Except as otherwise provided by the governing documents of the domestic entity, this code, or other law, if a security described by Subsection (a) is authenticated with the manual signature of an authorized officer of the domestic entity or an authorized officer or representative, to the extent permitted by law, of a transfer agent or trustee appointed or named by an indenture of trust or other agreement under which the security is issued, the signature of any officer of the domestic entity may be a facsimile signature.

(c) A security described by Subsection (a) that contains the manual or facsimile signature of a person who is no longer an officer when the security is delivered by the entity may be adopted, issued, and delivered by the entity in the same manner and to the same extent as if the person had remained an officer of the entity.

Acts 2003, 78th Leg., ch. 182, § 1, eff. Jan. 1, 2006.

CHAPTER 3. FORMATION AND GOVERNANCE

SUBCHAPTER A. FORMATION, EXISTENCE, AND CERTIFICATE OF FORMATION

Section
3.001. Formation and Existence of Filing Entities.
3.002. Formation and Existence of Nonfiling Entities.
3.003. Duration.
3.004. Organizers.
3.005. Certificate of Formation.
3.006. Filings in Case of Merger or Conversion.
3.007. Supplemental Provisions Required in Certificate of Formation of For–Profit or Professional Corporation.
3.008. Supplemental Provisions Required in Certificate of Formation of Close Corporation.
3.009. Supplemental Provisions Required in Certificate of Formation of Nonprofit Corporation.
3.010. Supplemental Provisions Required in Certificate of Formation of Limited Liability Company.
3.011. Supplemental Provisions Regarding Certificate of Formation of Limited Partnership.
3.012. Supplemental Provisions Required in Certificate of Formation of Real Estate Investment Trust.
3.013. Supplemental Provisions Required in Certificate of Formation of Cooperative Association.
3.014. Supplemental Provisions Required in Certificate of Formation of Professional Entity.
3.015. Supplemental Provisions Required in Certificate of Formation of Professional Association.

SUBCHAPTER B. AMENDMENTS AND RESTATEMENTS OF CERTIFICATE OF FORMATION

3.051. Right to Amend Certificate of Formation.
3.052. Procedures to Amend Certificate of Formation.
3.053. Certificate of Amendment.
3.054. Execution of Certificate of Amendment of For–Profit Corporation.
3.055. Supplemental Provisions for Certificate of Amendment of Real Estate Investment Trust.
3.056. Effect of Filing of Certificate of Amendment.
3.057. Right to Restate Certificate of Formation.
3.058. Procedures to Restate Certificate of Formation.
3.059. Restated Certificate of Formation.

Section
3.060. Supplemental Provisions for Restated Certificate of Formation for For-Profit Corporation or Professional Corporation.
3.061. Supplemental Provisions for Restated Certificate of Formation for Nonprofit Corporation.
3.0611. Supplemental Provisions for Restated Certificate of Formation for Limited Liability Company.
3.062. Supplemental Provisions for Restated Certificate of Formation for Real Estate Investment Trust.
3.063. Effect of Filing of Restated Certificate of Formation.

SUBCHAPTER C. GOVERNING PERSONS AND OFFICERS

3.101. Governing Authority.
3.102. Rights of Governing Persons in Certain Cases.
3.103. Officers.
3.104. Removal of Officers.
3.105. Rights of Officers in Certain Cases.

SUBCHAPTER D. RECORDKEEPING OF FILING ENTITIES

3.151. Books and Records for All Filing Entities.
3.152. Governing Person's Right of Inspection.
3.153. Right of Examination by Owner or Member.

SUBCHAPTER E. CERTIFICATES REPRESENTING OWNERSHIP INTEREST

3.201. Certificated or Uncertificated Ownership Interest; Applicability.
3.202. Form and Validity of Certificates; Enforcement of Entity's Rights.
3.203. Signature Requirement.
3.204. Delivery Requirement.
3.205. Notice for Uncertificated Ownership Interest.

SUBCHAPTER F. EMERGENCY GOVERNANCE

3.251 Emergency Defined.
3.252 Provisions in Governing Documents.
3.253 Effect of Emergency Provisions.
3.254 Effect of Other Provisions in Governing Documents During Emergency.
3.255 Effect of Action Taken.

SUBCHAPTER A. FORMATION, EXISTENCE, AND CERTIFICATE OF FORMATION

§ 3.001. Formation and Existence of Filing Entities

(a) Subject to the other provisions of this code, to form a filing entity, a certificate of formation complying with Sections 3.003, 3.004, and 3.005 must be filed in accordance with Chapter 4.

(b) The filing of a certificate of formation described by Subsection (a) may be included in a filing under Chapter 10.

(c) The existence of a filing entity commences when the filing of the certificate of formation takes effect as provided by Chapter 4.

(d) Except in a proceeding by the state to terminate the existence of a filing entity, an acknowledgment of the filing of a certificate of formation issued by the filing officer is conclusive evidence of:

(1) the formation and existence of the filing entity;

(2) the satisfaction of all conditions precedent to the formation of the filing entity; and

(3) the authority of the filing entity to transact business in this state.

Acts 2003, 78th Leg., ch. 182, § 1, eff. Jan. 1, 2006.

§ 3.002. Formation and Existence of Nonfiling Entities

The requirements for the formation of and the determination of the existence of a nonfiling entity are governed by the title of this code that applies to that entity.

Acts 2003, 78th Leg., ch. 182, § 1, eff. Jan. 1, 2006.

§ 3.003. Duration

A domestic entity exists perpetually unless otherwise provided in the governing documents of the entity. A domestic entity may be terminated in accordance with this code or the Tax Code.

Acts 2003, 78th Leg., ch. 182, § 1, eff. Jan. 1, 2006.

§ 3.004. Organizers

(a) Any person having the capacity to contract for the person or for another may be an organizer of a filing entity.

(b) Each organizer of a filing entity must sign the certificate of formation of the filing entity, except that:

(1) each general partner must sign the certificate of formation of a domestic limited partnership; and

(2) each trust manager must sign and acknowledge before an officer who is authorized by law to take acknowledgment of a deed the certificate of formation of a domestic real estate investment trust.

Acts 2003, 78th Leg., ch. 182, § 1, eff. Jan. 1, 2006.

§ 3.005. Certificate of Formation

(a) The certificate of formation must state:

(1) the name of the filing entity being formed;

(2) the type of filing entity being formed;

(3) for filing entities other than limited partnerships, the purpose or purposes for which the filing entity is formed, which may be stated to be or include any lawful purpose for that type of entity;

(4) for filing entities other than limited partnerships, the period of duration, if the entity is not formed to exist perpetually and is intended to have a specific period of duration;

(5) the street address of the initial registered office of the filing entity and the name of the initial registered agent of the filing entity at the office;

(6) the name and address of each:

(A) organizer for the filing entity, unless the entity is formed under a plan of conversion or merger;

(B) general partner, if the filing entity is a limited partnership; or

(C) trust manager, if the filing entity is a real estate investment trust;

(7) if the filing entity is formed under a plan of conversion or merger, a statement to that effect and, if formed under a plan of conversion, the name, address, date of formation, prior form of organization, and jurisdiction of formation of the converting entity; and

(8) any other information required by this code to be included in the certificate of formation for the filing entity.

(b) The certificate of formation may contain other provisions not inconsistent with law relating to the organization, ownership, governance, business, or affairs of the filing entity.

(c) Except as provided by Section 3.004, Chapter 4 governs the signing and filing of a certificate of formation for a domestic entity.

Acts 2003, 78th Leg., ch. 182, § 1, eff. Jan. 1, 2006. Amended by Acts 2007, 80th Leg., ch. 688, § 9, eff. Sept. 1, 2007.

§ 3.006. Filings in Case of Merger or Conversion

(a) If a new domestic filing entity is formed under a plan of conversion or merger, the certificate of formation of the entity must be filed with the certificate of conversion or merger under Section 10.155(a) or 10.153(a). The certificate of formation is not required to be filed separately under Section 3.001.

(b) The formation and existence of a domestic filing entity that is a converted entity in a conversion or that is to be created under a plan of merger takes effect and commences on the effectiveness of the conversion or merger, as appropriate.

Acts 2003, 78th Leg., ch. 182, § 1, eff. Jan. 1, 2006.

§ 3.007. Supplemental Provisions Required in Certificate of Formation of For-Profit or Professional Corporation

(a) In addition to the information required by Section 3.005, the certificate of formation of a for-profit or professional corporation must state:

(1) the aggregate number of shares the corporation is authorized to issue;

(2) if the shares the corporation is authorized to issue consist of one class of shares only, the par value of each share or a statement that each share is without par value;

(3) if the corporation is to be managed by a board of directors, the number of directors constituting the initial board of directors and the name and address of each person who will serve as director until the first annual meeting of shareholders and until a successor is elected and qualified; and

(4) if the corporation is to be managed pursuant to a shareholders' agreement in a manner other than by a board of directors, the name and address of each person who will perform the functions required by this code to be performed by the initial board of directors.

(b) If the shares a for-profit or professional corporation is authorized to issue consist of more than one class of shares, the certificate of formation of the corporation must, with respect to each class, state:

(1) the designation of the class;

(2) the aggregate number of shares in the class;

(3) the par value of each share or a statement that each share is without par value;

(4) the preferences, limitations, and relative rights of the shares; and

(5) if the shares in a class the corporation is authorized to issue consist of more than one series, the following with respect to each series:

(A) the designation of the series;

(B) the aggregate number of shares in the series;

(C) any preferences, limitations, and relative rights of the shares to the extent provided in the certificate of formation; and

(D) any authority vested in the board of directors to establish the series and set and determine the preferences, limitations, and relative rights of the series.

(c) If the shareholders of a for-profit or professional corporation are to have a preemptive right or cumulative voting right, the certificate of formation of the corporation must comply with Section 21. 203 or 21.360, as appropriate.

Acts 2003, 78th Leg., ch. 182, § 1, eff. Jan. 1, 2006. Amended by Acts 2007, 80th Leg., ch. 688, § 10, eff. Sept. 1, 2007.

§ 3.008. Supplemental Provisions Required in Certificate of Formation of Close Corporation

(a) In addition to a provision required or permitted to be stated in the certificate of formation of a for-profit or professional corporation under Section 3.007, the certificate of formation of a close corporation, whether original, amended, or restated, must include the sentence, "This corporation is a close corporation."

(b) The certificate of formation of the close corporation may contain:

(1) a provision contained or permitted to be contained in a shareholders' agreement conforming to Subchapter O, Chapter 21, that the organizers elect to include in the certificate of formation; or

(2) a copy of a shareholders' agreement that conforms to Subchapter O, Chapter 21, and that may be filed in the manner provided by Section 21.212.

(c) A provision contained in the certificate of formation under Subsection (b) must be preceded by a statement that the provision is subject to the corporation remaining a close corporation.

Acts 2003, 78th Leg., ch. 182, § 1, eff. Jan. 1, 2006. Amended by Acts 2007, 80th Leg., ch. 688, § 11, eff. Sept. 1, 2007.

§ 3.009. Supplemental Provisions Required in Certificate of Formation of Nonprofit Corporation

In addition to the information required by Section 3.005, the certificate of formation of a nonprofit corporation must include:

(1) if the nonprofit corporation is to have no members, a statement to that effect;

(2) if management of the nonprofit corporation's affairs is to be vested in the nonprofit corporation's members, a statement to that effect;

(3) the number of directors constituting the initial board of directors and the names and addresses of those directors or, if the management of the nonprofit corporation is vested solely in the nonprofit corporation's members, a statement to that effect; and

(4) if the nonprofit corporation is to be authorized on its winding up to distribute the nonprofit corporation's assets in a manner other than as provided by Section 22.304, a statement describing the manner of distribution.

Acts 2003, 78th Leg., ch. 182, § 1, eff. Jan. 1, 2006.

§ 3.010. Supplemental Provisions Required in Certificate of Formation of Limited Liability Company

In addition to the information required by Section 3.005, the certificate of formation of a limited liability company must state:

(1) whether the limited liability company will or will not have managers;

(2) if the limited liability company will have managers, the name and address of each initial manager of the limited liability company; and

(3) if the limited liability company will not have managers, the name and address of each initial member of the limited liability company.

Acts 2003, 78th Leg., ch. 182, § 1, eff. Jan. 1, 2006.

§ 3.011. Supplemental Provisions Regarding Certificate of Formation of Limited Partnership

(a) To form a limited partnership, the partners must enter into a partnership agreement and file a certificate of formation.

(b) The partners of a limited partnership formed under Section 10.001 or 10.101 may include the partnership agreement required under Subsection (a) in the plan of merger or conversion.

(c) A certificate of formation for a limited partnership must include the address of the principal office of the partnership in the United States where records are to be kept or made available under Section 153.551.

(d) The fact that a certificate of formation is on file with the secretary of state is notice that the partnership is a limited partnership and of all other facts contained in the certificate as required by Section 3.005.

Acts 2003, 78th Leg., ch. 182, § 1, eff. Jan. 1, 2006.

§ 3.012. Supplemental Provisions Required in Certificate of Formation of Real Estate Investment Trust

In addition to the information required by Section 3.005, the certificate of formation of a real estate investment trust must state:

(1) that an assumed name certificate stating the name of the real estate investment trust has been filed in the manner provided by law;

(2) that the purpose of the real estate investment trust is to:

(A) purchase, hold, lease, manage, sell, exchange, develop, subdivide, and improve real property and interests in real property, other than severed mineral, oil, or gas royalty interests, and carry on any other business and perform any other action in connection with a purpose described by this paragraph;

(B) exercise powers conferred by the laws of this state on a real estate investment trust; and

(C) perform any action described by Chapter 200 or Title 1 to the same extent as an individual;

(3) the post office address of the initial principal office and place of business of the real estate investment trust;

(4) the aggregate number of shares of beneficial interest the real estate investment trust is authorized to issue and the par value to be received by the real estate investment trust for the issuance of each share;

(5) if shares described by Subdivision (4) are divided into classes as authorized by Section 200.102 or 200.103, a description of each class of shares, including any preferences, conversion and other rights, voting powers, restrictions, limitations as to dividends, qualifications, and terms and conditions of redemption; and

(6) that the trust managers shall manage the money or property received for the issuance of shares for the benefit of the shareholders of the real estate investment trust.

Acts 2003, 78th Leg., ch. 182, § 1, eff. Jan. 1, 2006.

§ 3.013. Supplemental Provisions Required in Certificate of Formation of Cooperative Association

In addition to the information required by Section 3.005, the certificate of formation of a cooperative association must state:

(1) whether the cooperative association is organized with or without shares;

(2) the number of shares or memberships subscribed for the cooperative association;

(3) if the cooperative association is organized with shares:

(A) the amount of authorized capital;

(B) the number and type of shares;

(C) par value of the shares, if any; and

(D) the rights, preferences, and restrictions of each type of share;

(4) the method of distribution on winding up and termination of any surplus of the cooperative association in accordance with Section 251.403; and

(5) the names and street addresses of the directors who will manage the affairs of the cooperative association for the initial year, unless sooner changed by the members.

Acts 2003, 78th Leg., ch. 182, § 1, eff. Jan. 1, 2006.

§ 3.014. Supplemental Provisions Required in Certificate of Formation of Professional Entity

In addition to the information required by Section 3.005, the certificate of formation of a professional entity must state:

(1) the type of professional service to be provided by the professional entity as the purpose of the entity; and

(2) that the professional entity is a:

(A) professional association;

(B) professional corporation; or

(C) professional limited liability company.

Acts 2003, 78th Leg., ch. 182, § 1, eff. Jan. 1, 2006.

§ 3.015. Supplemental Provisions Required in Certificate of Formation of Professional Association

(a) In addition to containing the information required under Sections 3.005 and 3.014, the certificate of formation of a professional association must:

(1) be signed by each member of the association; and

(2) state:

(A) the name and address of each original member of the association;

(B) whether the association is to be governed by a board of directors or by an executive committee; and

(C) the name and address of each person serving as an initial member of the board of directors or executive committee of the association.

(b) The certificate of formation of a professional association may contain:

(1) provisions regarding shares or units of ownership in the association;

(2) provisions governing the winding up and termination of the association's business; and

(3) any other provision consistent with state law regulating the internal affairs of a professional association.

(c) If the certificate of formation of a professional association contains provisions regarding shares in the association, the certificate of formation must also comply with Section 3.007.

Acts 2003, 78th Leg., ch. 182, § 1, eff. Jan. 1, 2006. Amended by Acts 2007, 80th Leg., ch. 688, § 12, eff. Sept. 1, 2007.

SUBCHAPTER B. AMENDMENTS AND RESTATEMENTS OF CERTIFICATE OF FORMATION

§ 3.051. Right to Amend Certificate of Formation

(a) A filing entity may amend its certificate of formation.

(b) An amended certificate of formation may contain only provisions that:

(1) would be permitted at the time of the amendment if the amended certificate of formation were a newly filed original certificate of formation; or

(2) effect a change, exchange, reclassification, subdivision, combination, or cancellation in the membership or ownership interests or the rights of owners or members of the filing entity.

Acts 2003, 78th Leg., ch. 182, § 1, eff. Jan. 1, 2006. Amended by Acts 2005, 79th Leg., ch. 64, § 6, eff. Jan. 1, 2006.

§ 3.052. Procedures to Amend Certificate of Formation

(a) The procedure to adopt an amendment to the certificate of formation is as provided by the title of this code that applies to the entity.

(b) A filing entity that amends its certificate of formation shall sign and file, in the manner required by Chapter 4, a certificate of amendment complying with Section 3.053 or a restated certificate of formation complying with Section 3.059.

Acts 2003, 78th Leg., ch. 182, § 1, eff. Jan. 1, 2006.

§ 3.053. Certificate of Amendment

A certificate of amendment for a filing entity must state:

(1) the name of the filing entity;

(2) the type of the filing entity;

(3) for each provision of the certificate of formation that is added, altered, or deleted, an identification by reference or description of the added, altered, or deleted provision and, if the provision is added or altered, a statement of the text of the amended or added provision;

(4) that the amendment or amendments have been approved in the manner required by this code and the governing documents of the entity; and

(5) any other matter required by the provisions of this code applicable to the filing entity to be in the certificate of amendment.

Acts 2003, 78th Leg., ch. 182, § 1, eff. Jan. 1, 2006.

§ 3.054. Execution of Certificate of Amendment of For–Profit Corporation

An officer shall sign the certificate of amendment on behalf of the for-profit corporation. If shares of the for-profit corporation have not been issued and the certificate of amendment is adopted by the board of directors, a majority of the directors may sign the certificate of amendment on behalf of the for-profit corporation.

Acts 2003, 78th Leg., ch. 182, § 1, eff. Jan. 1, 2006. Amended by Acts 2005, 79th Leg., ch. 64, § 7, eff. Jan. 1, 2006.

§ 3.055. Supplemental Provisions for Certificate of Amendment of Real Estate Investment Trust

(a) In addition to the statements required by Section 3.053, a certificate of amendment for a real estate investment trust must state:

(1) if the amendment provides for an exchange, reclassification, or cancellation of issued shares, the manner in which the exchange, reclassification, or cancellation of the issued shares will be effected if the manner is not specified in the amendment; and

(2) if the amendment effects a change in the amount of stated capital, the manner in which the change in the amount of stated capital is effected

and the amount of stated capital expressed in dollar terms as changed by the amendment.

(b) If shares of the real estate investment trust have not been issued and the certificate of amendment is adopted by the trust managers, a majority of the trust managers may execute the certificate of amendment on behalf of the real estate investment trust.

Acts 2003, 78th Leg., ch. 182, § 1, eff. Jan. 1, 2006.

§ 3.056. Effect of Filing of Certificate of Amendment

(a) An amendment to a certificate of formation takes effect when the filing of the certificate of amendment takes effect as provided by Chapter 4.

(b) An amendment to a certificate of formation does not affect:

(1) an existing cause of action in favor of or against the entity for which the certificate of amendment is sought;

(2) a pending suit to which the entity is a party; or

(3) an existing right of a person other than an existing owner.

(c) If the name of an entity is changed by amendment, an action brought by or against the entity in the former name of the entity does not abate because of the name change.

Acts 2003, 78th Leg., ch. 182, § 1, eff. Jan. 1, 2006.

§ 3.057. Right to Restate Certificate of Formation

(a) A filing entity may restate its certificate of formation.

(b) An amendment effected by a restated certificate of formation must comply with Section 3.051(b).

Acts 2003, 78th Leg., ch. 182, § 1, eff. Jan. 1, 2006.

§ 3.058. Procedures to Restate Certificate of Formation

(a) The procedure to adopt a restated certificate of formation is governed by the title of this code that applies to the entity.

(b) A filing entity that restates its certificate of formation shall sign and file, in the manner required by Chapter 4, a restated certificate of formation and accompanying statements complying with Section 3.059.

Acts 2003, 78th Leg., ch. 182, § 1, eff. Jan. 1, 2006.

§ 3.059. Restated Certificate of Formation

(a) A restated certificate of formation must accurately state the text of the previous certificate of formation, regardless of whether the certificate of formation is an original, corrected, or restated certificate, and include:

(1) each previous amendment to the certificate being restated that is carried forward; and

(2) each new amendment to the certificate being restated.

(b) A restated certificate of formation may omit:

(1) the name and address of each organizer other than the name and address of each general partner of a limited partnership or trust manager of a real estate investment trust; and

(2) any other information that may be omitted under the provisions of this code applicable to the filing entity.

(c) A restated certificate of formation that does not make new amendments to the certificate of formation being restated must be accompanied by:

(1) a statement that the restated certificate of formation accurately states the text of the certificate of formation being restated, as amended, restated, and corrected, except for information omitted under Subsection (b); and

(2) any other information required by other provisions of this code applicable to the filing entity.

(d) A restated certificate of formation that makes new amendments to the certificate of formation being restated must:

(1) be accompanied by a statement that each new amendment has been made in accordance with this code;

(2) identify by reference or description each added, altered, or deleted provision;

(3) be accompanied by a statement that each amendment has been approved in the manner required by this code and the governing documents of the entity;

(4) be accompanied by a statement that the restated certificate of formation:

(A) accurately states the text of the certificate of formation being restated and each amendment to the certificate of formation being restated that is in effect, as further amended by the restated certificate of formation; and

(B) does not contain any other change in the certificate of formation being restated except for information omitted under Subsection (b); and

(5) include any other information required by the title of this code applicable to the entity.

Acts 2003, 78th Leg., ch. 182, § 1, eff. Jan. 1, 2006.

§ 3.060. Supplemental Provisions for Restated Certificate of Formation for For–Profit Corporation or Professional Corporation.

(a) In addition to the provisions authorized or required by Section 3.059, a restated certificate of formation for a for-profit corporation or professional corporation may update the current number of directors and the names and addresses of the persons serving as directors.

(b) An officer shall sign the restated certificate of formation on behalf of the corporation. If shares of the corporation have not been issued and the restated certificate of formation is adopted by the board of directors, the majority of the directors may sign the restated certificate of formation on behalf of the corporation.

Acts 2003, 78th Leg., ch. 182, § 1, eff. Jan. 1, 2006. Amended by Acts 2007, 80th Leg., ch. 688, §§ 13, 14, eff. Sept. 1, 2007.

§ 3.061. Supplemental Provisions for Restated Certificate of Formation for Nonprofit Corporation

(a) In addition to the provisions authorized or required by Section 3.059, a restated certificate of formation for a nonprofit corporation may update the current number of directors and the names and addresses of the persons serving as directors.

(b) If the nonprofit corporation is a church in which management is vested in the church's members under Section 22.202, and the original certificate of formation is not required to contain a statement to that effect, any restated certificate of formation for the church must contain a statement to that effect in addition to the information required by Section 3.059.

Acts 2003, 78th Leg., ch. 182, § 1, eff. Jan. 1, 2006.

§ 3.0611. Supplemental Provisions for Restated Certificate of Formation for Limited Liability Company

In addition to the provisions authorized or required by Section 3.059, a restated certificate of formation for a limited liability company may:

(1) if the company's certificate of formation states that the company will have one or more managers, update the names and addresses of the persons serving as managers; or

(2) if the certificate of formation states that the company will not have managers, update the names and addresses of the members of the company.

Added by Acts 2007, 80th Leg., ch. 688, § 15, eff. Sept. 1, 2007.

§ 3.062. Supplemental Provisions for Restated Certificate of Formation for Real Estate Investment Trust

In addition to the provisions authorized or required by Section 3.059, a restated certificate of formation for a real estate investment trust may update the current number of trust managers and the names and addresses of the persons serving as trust managers.

Acts 2003, 78th Leg., ch. 182, § 1, eff. Jan. 1, 2006.

§ 3.063. Effect of Filing of Restated Certificate of Formation

(a) A restated certificate of formation takes effect when the filing of the restated certificate of formation takes effect as provided by Chapter 4.

(b) On the date the restated certificate of formation takes effect, the original certificate of formation and each prior amendment or restatement of the certificate of formation is superseded and the restated certificate of formation is the effective certificate of formation.

(c) Sections 3.056(b) and (c) apply to an amendment effected by a restated certificate of formation.

Acts 2003, 78th Leg., ch. 182, § 1, eff. Jan. 1, 2006.

SUBCHAPTER C. GOVERNING PERSONS AND OFFICERS

§ 3.101. Governing Authority

Subject to the title of this code that governs the domestic entity and the governing documents of the domestic entity, the governing authority of a domestic entity manages and directs the business and affairs of the domestic entity.

Acts 2003, 78th Leg., ch. 182, § 1, eff. Jan. 1, 2006.

§ 3.102. Rights of Governing Persons in Certain Cases

(a) In discharging a duty or exercising a power, a governing person, including a governing person who is a member of a committee, may, in good faith and with ordinary care, rely on information, opinions, reports, or statements, including financial statements and other financial data, concerning a domestic entity or another person and prepared or presented by:

(1) an officer or employee of the entity;

(2) legal counsel;

(3) a certified public accountant;

(4) an investment banker;

(5) a person who the governing person reasonably believes possesses professional expertise in the matter; or

(6) a committee of the governing authority of which the governing person is not a member.

(b) A governing person may not in good faith rely on the information described by Subsection (a) if the governing person has knowledge of a matter that makes the reliance unwarranted.

Acts 2003, 78th Leg., ch. 182, § 1, eff. Jan. 1, 2006.

§ 3.103. Officers

(a) Officers of a domestic entity may be elected or appointed in accordance with the governing documents of the entity or by the governing authority of the entity unless prohibited by the governing documents.

(b) An officer of an entity shall perform the duties in the management of the entity and has the authority as provided by the governing documents of the entity or the governing authority that elects or appoints the officer.

(c) A person may simultaneously hold any two or more offices of an entity unless prohibited by this code or the governing documents of the entity.

Acts 2003, 78th Leg., ch. 182, § 1, eff. Jan. 1, 2006.

§ 3.104. Removal of Officers

(a) Unless otherwise provided by the governing documents of a domestic entity, an officer may be removed for or without cause by the governing authority or as provided by the governing documents of the entity. The removal of an officer does not prejudice any contract rights of the person removed.

(b) Election or appointment of an officer does not by itself create contract rights.

Acts 2003, 78th Leg., ch. 182, § 1, eff. Jan. 1, 2006.

§ 3.105. Rights of Officers in Certain Cases

(a) In discharging a duty or exercising a power, an officer of a domestic entity may, in good faith and ordinary care, rely on information, opinions, reports, or statements, including financial statements and other financial data, concerning the entity or another person and prepared or presented by:

(1) another officer or an employee of the entity;

(2) legal counsel;

(3) a certified public accountant;

(4) an investment banker; or

(5) a person who the officer reasonably believes possesses professional expertise in the matter.

(b) An officer may not in good faith rely on the information described by Subsection (a) if the officer has knowledge of a matter that makes the reliance unwarranted.

Acts 2003, 78th Leg., ch. 182, § 1, eff. Jan. 1, 2006.

SUBCHAPTER D. RECORDKEEPING OF FILING ENTITIES

§ 3.151. Books and Records for All Filing Entities

(a) Each filing entity shall keep:

(1) books and records of accounts;

(2) minutes of the proceedings of the owners or members or governing authority of the filing entity and committees of the owners or members or governing authority of the filing entity;

(3) at its registered office or principal place of business, or at the office of its transfer agent or registrar, a current record of the name and mailing address of each owner or member of the filing entity; and

(4) other books and records as required by the title of this code governing the entity.

(b) The books, records, minutes, and ownership or membership records of any filing entity, including those described in Subsection (a)(4), may be in written paper form or another form capable of being converted into written paper form within a reasonable time.

(c) The records required by Subsection (a)(2) need not be maintained by a limited partnership or a limited liability company except to the extent required by its governing documents.

Acts 2003, 78th Leg., ch. 182, § 1, eff. Jan. 1, 2006. Amended by Acts 2005, 79th Leg., ch. 64, § 8, eff. Jan. 1, 2006.

§ 3.152. Governing Person's Right of Inspection

(a) A governing person of a filing entity may examine the entity's books and records maintained under Section 3.151 and other books and records of the entity for a purpose reasonably related to the governing person's service as a governing person.

(b) A court may require a filing entity to open the books and records of the filing entity, including the books and records maintained under Section 3.151, to permit a governing person to inspect, make copies of, or take extracts from the books and records on a showing by the governing person that:

(1) the person is a governing person of the entity;

(2) the person demanded to inspect the entity's books and records;

(3) the person's purpose for inspecting the entity's books and records is reasonably related to the person's service as a governing person; and

(4) the entity refused the person's good faith demand to inspect the books and records.

(c) A court may award a governing person attorney's fees and any other proper relief in a suit to require a filing entity to open its books and records under Subsection (b).

(d) This section does not apply to limited partnerships. Section 153.552 applies to limited partnerships.

Acts 2003, 78th Leg., ch. 182, § 1, eff. Jan. 1, 2006.

§ 3.153. Right of Examination by Owner or Member

Each owner or member of a filing entity may examine the books and records of the filing entity maintained under Section 3.151 and other books and records of the filing entity to the extent provided by the governing documents of the entity and the title of this code governing the filing entity.

Acts 2003, 78th Leg., ch. 182, § 1, eff. Jan. 1, 2006.

SUBCHAPTER E. CERTIFICATES REPRESENTING OWNERSHIP INTEREST

§ 3.201. Certificated or Uncertificated Ownership Interest; Applicability

(a) Ownership interests in a domestic entity may be certificated or uncertificated.

(b) The ownership interests in a for-profit corporation, real estate investment trust, or professional corporation must be certificated unless the governing documents of the entity or a resolution adopted by the governing authority of the entity states that the ownership interests are uncertificated. If a domestic entity changes the form of its ownership interests from certificated to uncertificated, a certificated ownership interest subject to the change becomes an uncertificated ownership interest only after the certificate is surrendered to the domestic entity.

(c) Ownership interests in a domestic entity, other than a domestic entity described by Subsection (b), are uncertificated unless this code or the governing documents of the domestic entity state that the interests are certificated.

(d) Sections 3.202–3.205 do not apply to a partnership or a limited liability company except to the extent that the governing documents of the partnership or limited liability company specify.

(e) The governing documents of a partnership or a limited liability company may:

(1) provide that an owner's ownership interest may be evidenced by a certificate of ownership interest issued by the entity;

(2) provide for the assignment or transfer of ownership interests represented by certificates; and

(3) make other provisions with respect to the certificate.

Acts 2003, 78th Leg., ch. 182, § 1, eff. Jan. 1, 2006.

§ 3.202. Form and Validity of Certificates; Enforcement of Entity's Rights

(a) A certificate representing the ownership interest in a domestic entity may contain an impression of the seal of the entity, if any. A facsimile of the entity's seal may be printed or lithographed on the certificate.

(b) If a domestic entity is authorized to issue ownership interests of more than one class or series, each certificate representing ownership interests that is issued by the entity must conspicuously state on the front or back of the certificate:

(1) the designations, preferences, limitations, and relative rights of the ownership interests of each class or series to the extent they have been determined and the authority of the governing authority to make those determinations as to subsequent series; or

(2) that the information required by Subdivision (1) is stated in the domestic entity's governing

documents and that the domestic entity, on written request to the entity's principal place of business or registered office, will provide a free copy of that information to the record holder of the certificate.

(c) A certificate representing ownership interests must state on the front of the certificate:

(1) that the domestic entity is organized under the laws of this state;

(2) the name of the person to whom the certificate is issued;

(3) the number and class of ownership interests and the designation of the series, if any, represented by the certificate; and

(4) if the ownership interests are shares, the par value of each share represented by the certificate, or a statement that the shares are without par value.

(d) A certificate representing ownership interests that is subject to a restriction, placed by or agreed to by the domestic entity under this code, or otherwise contained in its governing documents, on the transfer or registration of the transfer of the ownership interests must:

(1) conspicuously state or provide a summary of the restriction on the front of the certificate;

(2) state the restriction on the back of the certificate and conspicuously refer to that statement on the front of the certificate; or

(3) conspicuously state on the front or back of the certificate that a restriction exists pursuant to a specified document and:

(A) that the domestic entity, on written request to the entity's principal place of business, will provide a free copy of the document to the certificate record holder; or

(B) if the document has been filed in accordance with this code, that the document:

(i) is on file with the secretary of state or, in the case of a real estate investment trust, with the county clerk of the county in which the real estate investment trust's principal place of business is located; and

(ii) contains a complete statement of the restriction.

(e) A domestic entity that fails to provide to the record holder of a certificate within a reasonable time a document as required by Subsection (d)(3)(A) may not enforce the entity's rights under the restriction imposed on the certificated ownership interests.

(f) A certificate representing ownership interests may not be issued in bearer form.

Acts 2003, 78th Leg., ch. 182, § 1, eff. Jan. 1, 2006. Amended by Acts 2009, 81st Leg., ch. 84, § 3, eff. Sept. 1, 2009.

§ 3.203. Signature Requirement

(a) The managerial official or officials of a domestic entity authorized by the governing documents of the entity to sign certificated ownership interests of the entity must sign any certificate representing an ownership interest in the entity.

(b) A certificated ownership interest that contains the manual or facsimile signature of a person who is no longer a managerial official of a domestic entity when the certificate is issued may be issued by the entity in the same manner and with the same effect as if the person had remained a managerial official.

Acts 2003, 78th Leg., ch. 182, § 1, eff. Jan. 1, 2006.

§ 3.204. Delivery Requirement

A domestic entity shall deliver a certificate representing a certificated ownership interest to which the owner is entitled.

Acts 2003, 78th Leg., ch. 182, § 1, eff. Jan. 1, 2006.

§ 3.205. Notice for Uncertificated Ownership Interest

(a) Except as provided by Subsection (c) and in accordance with Chapter 8, Business & Commerce Code, after issuing or transferring an uncertificated ownership interest, a domestic entity shall notify the owner of the ownership interest in writing of any information required under this subchapter to be stated on a certificate representing the ownership interest.

(b) Except as otherwise expressly provided by law, the rights and obligations of the owner of an uncertificated ownership interest are the same as the rights and obligations of the owner of a certificated ownership interest of the same class and series.

(c) A domestic entity is not required to send a notice under Subsection (a) if:

(1) the required information is included in the governing documents of the entity; and

(2) the owner of the uncertificated ownership interest is provided with a copy of the governing documents.

Acts 2003, 78th Leg., ch. 182, § 1, eff. Jan. 1, 2006.

SUBCHAPTER F. EMERGENCY GOVERNANCE

§ 3.251 Emergency Defined

For purposes of this subchapter, an emergency exists if a majority of a domestic entity's governing persons cannot readily participate in a meeting because of the occurrence of a catastrophic event.

Added by Acts 2009, 81st Leg., ch. 84, § 4, eff. Sept. 1, 2009.

§ 3.252 Provisions in Governing Documents

(a) Except as otherwise provided by the entity's governing documents, the governing persons, owners, or members of a domestic entity may adopt provisions in the entity's governing documents regarding the management of the entity during an emergency, including provisions:

(1) prescribing procedures for calling a meeting of the governing persons;

(2) establishing minimum requirements for participation at the meeting of the governing persons; and

(3) designating additional or substitute governing persons.

(b) The emergency provisions must be adopted in accordance with:

(1) the requirements of the governing documents; and

(2) the applicable provisions of this code.

Added by Acts 2009, 81st Leg., ch. 84, § 4, eff. Sept. 1, 2009.

§ 3.253 Effect of Emergency Provisions

The emergency provisions adopted under Section 3.252 take effect only in the event of an emergency. The emergency provisions will no longer be effective after the emergency ends.

Added by Acts 2009, 81st Leg., ch. 84, § 4, eff. Sept. 1, 2009.

§ 3.254 Effect of Other Provisions in Governing Documents During Emergency

A provision of an entity's governing documents that is consistent with the emergency provisions adopted under Section 3.252 remains in effect during an emergency.

Added by Acts 2009, 81st Leg., ch. 84, § 4, eff. Sept. 1, 2009.

§ 3.255 Effect of Action Taken

An action of a domestic entity taken in good faith in accordance with the emergency provisions:

(1) is binding on the entity; and

(2) may not be used to impose liability on a managerial official, employee, or agent of the entity.

Added by Acts 2009, 81st Leg., ch. 84, § 4, eff. Sept. 1, 2009.

CHAPTER 4. FILINGS

SUBCHAPTER A. GENERAL PROVISIONS

Section

4.001. Signature and Delivery.
4.002. Action by Secretary of State.
4.003. Filing or Issuance of Reproduction or Facsimile.
4.004. Time for Filing.
4.005. Certificates and Certified Copies.
4.006. Forms Adopted by Secretary of State.
4.007. Liability for False Filing Instruments.
4.008. Offense; Penalty.
4.009. Filings by Real Estate Investment Trust.

SUBCHAPTER B. WHEN FILINGS TAKE EFFECT

4.051. General Rule.
4.052. Delayed Effectiveness of Certain Filings.
4.053. Conditions for Delayed Effectiveness.
4.054. Delayed Effectiveness on Future Event or Fact.
4.055. Statement of Event or Fact.
4.056. Failure to File Statement.
4.057. Abandonment Before Effectiveness.
4.058. Delayed Effectiveness Not Permitted.
4.059. Acknowledgment of Filing with Delayed Effectiveness.

SUBCHAPTER C. CORRECTION AND AMENDMENT

4.101. Correction of Filings.
4.102. Limitation on Correction of Filings.
4.103. Certificate of Correction.
4.104. Filing Certificate of Correction.
4.105. Effect of Certificate of Correction.
4.106. Amendment of Filings.

SUBCHAPTER D. FILING FEES

4.151. Filing Fees: All Entities.
4.152. Filing Fees: For-Profit Corporations.
4.153. Filing Fees: Nonprofit Corporations.
4.154. Filing Fees: Limited Liability Companies.
4.155. Filing Fees: Limited Partnerships.
4.156. Filing Fees: Professional Associations.
4.157. Filing Fees: Professional Corporations.
4.158. Filing Fees: General Partnerships.
4.159. Filing Fees: Nonprofit Associations.
4.160. Filing Fees: Foreign Filing Entities.
4.161. Filing Fees: Cooperative Associations.

SUBCHAPTER A. GENERAL PROVISIONS

§ 4.001. Signature and Delivery

(a) A filing instrument must be:

(1) signed by a person authorized by this code to act on behalf of the entity in regard to the filing instrument; and

(2) delivered to the secretary of state in person or by mail, courier, facsimile or electronic transmission, or any other comparable form of delivery.

(b) A person authorized by this code to sign a filing instrument for an entity is not required to show evidence of the person's authority as a requirement for filing.

Acts 2003, 78th Leg., ch. 182, § 1, eff. Jan. 1, 2006.

§ 4.002. Action by Secretary of State

(a) If the secretary of state finds that a filing instrument delivered under Section 4.001 conforms to the provisions of this code that apply to the entity and to applicable rules adopted under Section 12.001 and that all required fees have been paid, the secretary of state shall:

(1) file the instrument by accepting it into the filing system adopted by the secretary of state and assigning the instrument a date of filing; and

(2) deliver a written acknowledgment of filing to the entity or its representative.

(b) If a duplicate copy of the filing instrument is delivered to the secretary of state, on accepting the filing instrument, the secretary of state shall return the duplicate copy, endorsed with the word "Filed" and the month, day, and year of filing, to the entity or its representative with the acknowledgment of filing.

Acts 2003, 78th Leg., ch. 182, § 1, eff. Jan. 1, 2006. Amended by Acts 2005, 79th Leg., ch. 64, § 9, eff. Jan. 1, 2006.

§ 4.003. Filing or Issuance of Reproduction or Facsimile

(a) A photographic, photostatic, facsimile, electronic, or similar reproduction of a filing instrument, signature, acknowledgment of filing, or communication may be filed or issued in place of:

(1) an original filing instrument;

(2) an original signature on a filing instrument; or

(3) an original acknowledgment of filing or other written communication from the secretary of state relating to a filing instrument.

(b) To the extent any filing or action on a filing conforms to this subchapter, a filing instrument or an acknowledgment of filing issued by the secretary of state is not required to be on paper or to be reduced to printed form.

Acts 2003, 78th Leg., ch. 182, § 1, eff. Jan. 1, 2006.

§ 4.004. Time for Filing

Unless this code prescribes a specific period for filing, an entity shall promptly file each filing instrument that this code requires the entity to file.

Acts 2003, 78th Leg., ch. 182, § 1, eff. Jan. 1, 2006.

§ 4.005. Certificates and Certified Copies

(a) A court, public office, or official body shall accept a certificate issued as provided by this code by the secretary of state or a copy of a filing instrument accepted by the secretary of state for filing as provided by this code that is certified by the secretary of state as prima facie evidence of the facts stated in the certificate or instrument.

(b) A court, public office, or official body may record a certificate or certified copy described by Subsection (a).

(c) A court, public office, or official body shall accept a certificate issued under an official seal by the secretary of state as to the existence or nonexistence of facts that relate to an entity that would not appear from a certified copy of a filing instrument as prima facie evidence of the existence or nonexistence of the facts stated in the certificate.

(d) Subject to any qualification stated in the certificate, a certificate issued by the secretary of state stating that a domestic filing entity is in existence may be relied on as conclusive evidence of the entity's existence.

(e) Subject to any qualification stated in the certificate, a certificate issued by the secretary of state stating that a foreign filing entity is in existence or registered may be relied on as conclusive evidence that the foreign filing entity is registered and authorized to transact business in this state.

Acts 2003, 78th Leg., ch. 182, § 1, eff. Jan. 1, 2006. Amended by Acts 2009, 81st Leg., ch. 84, § 5, eff. Sept. 1, 2009.

§ 4.006. Forms Adopted by Secretary of State

(a) The secretary of state may adopt forms for a filing instrument or a report authorized or required by this code to be filed with the secretary of state.

(b) A person is not required to use a form adopted by the secretary of state unless this code expressly requires use of that form.

Acts 2003, 78th Leg., ch. 182, § 1, eff. Jan. 1, 2006.

§ 4.007. Liability for False Filing Instruments

(a) A person may recover damages, court costs, and reasonable attorney's fees if the person incurs a loss and:

(1) the loss is caused by a:

(A) forged filing instrument; or

(B) filed filing instrument that constitutes an offense under Section 4.008; or

(2) the person reasonably relies on:

(A) a false statement of material fact in a filed filing instrument; or

(B) the omission in a filed filing instrument of a material fact required by this code to be included in the instrument.

(b) A person may recover under Subsection (a) from:

(1) each person who forged the forged filing instrument or signed the filing instrument and knew when the instrument was signed of the false statement or omission;

(2) any managerial official of the entity who directed the signing and filing of the filing instrument who knew or should have known when the instrument was signed or filed of the false statement or omission; or

(3) the entity that authorizes the filing of the filing instrument.

Acts 2003, 78th Leg., ch. 182, § 1, eff. Jan. 1, 2006.

§ 4.008. Offense; Penalty

(a) A person commits an offense if the person signs or directs the filing of a filing instrument that the person knows is materially false with intent that the filing instrument be delivered on behalf of an entity to the secretary of state for filing.

(b) An offense under this section is a Class A misdemeanor unless the actor's intent is to defraud or harm another, in which event the offense is a state jail felony.

Acts 2003, 78th Leg., ch. 182, § 1, eff. Jan. 1, 2006.

§ 4.009. Filings by Real Estate Investment Trust

(a) A filing instrument relating to a domestic real estate investment trust must be filed with the county clerk of the county in which the domestic real estate investment trust's principal place of business is located.

(b) Subject to other state law governing the requirements for filing instruments with a county clerk, this chapter applies to a filing by a domestic real estate investment trust, except that in relation to such a filing a reference in this chapter to the secretary of state is considered to be a reference to the county clerk of the county in which the domestic real estate investment trust's principal place of business is located.

(c) A filing instrument relating to a foreign real estate investment trust must be filed with the secretary of state and not a county clerk.

Acts 2003, 78th Leg., ch. 182, § 1, eff. Jan. 1, 2006.

SUBCHAPTER B. WHEN FILINGS TAKE EFFECT

§ 4.051. General Rule

A filing instrument submitted to the secretary of state takes effect on filing, except as permitted by Section 4.052 or as provided by the provisions of this code that apply to the entity making the filing or other law.

Acts 2003, 78th Leg., ch. 182, § 1, eff. Jan. 1, 2006.

§ 4.052. Delayed Effectiveness of Certain Filings

Except as provided by Section 4.058, a filing instrument may take effect after the time the instrument would otherwise take effect as provided by this code for the entity filing the instrument and:

(1) at a specified date and time; or

(2) on the occurrence of a future event or fact, including an act of any person.

Acts 2003, 78th Leg., ch. 182, § 1, eff. Jan. 1, 2006.

§ 4.053. Conditions for Delayed Effectiveness

(a) The date and time at which a filing instrument takes effect is delayed if the instrument clearly and expressly states, in addition to any other required statement or information:

(1) the specific date and time at which the instrument takes effect; or

(2) if the instrument takes effect on the occurrence of a future event or fact that may occur:

(A) the manner in which the event or fact will cause the instrument to take effect; and

(B) the date of the 90th day after the date the instrument is signed.

(b) If a filing instrument is to take effect on a specific date and time other than that provided by this code:

(1) the date may not be later than the 90th day after the date the instrument is signed; and

(2) the specific time at which the instrument is to take effect may not be specified as "12:00 a.m." or "12:00 p.m."

Acts 2003, 78th Leg., ch. 182, § 1, eff. Jan. 1, 2006.

§ 4.054. Delayed Effectiveness on Future Event or Fact

A filing instrument that is to take effect on the occurrence of a future event or fact, other than the passage of time, and for which the statement required by Section 4.055 is filed within the prescribed time, takes effect on the date and time at which the last specified event or fact occurs or the date and time at which a condition is satisfied or waived.

Acts 2003, 78th Leg., ch. 182, § 1, eff. Jan. 1, 2006.

§ 4.055. Statement of Event or Fact

An entity that files a filing instrument that takes effect on the occurrence of a future event or fact, other than the passage of time, must sign and file as provided by Subchapter A, not later than the 90th day after the date the filing instrument is filed, a statement that:

(1) confirms that each event or fact on which the effect of the instrument is conditioned has been satisfied or waived; and

(2) states the date and time on which the condition was satisfied or waived.

Acts 2003, 78th Leg., ch. 182, § 1, eff. Jan. 1, 2006.

§ 4.056. Failure to File Statement

(a) If the effect of a filing instrument is conditioned on the occurrence of a future event or fact, other than the passage of time, and the statement required by Section 4.055 is not filed before the expiration of the prescribed time, the filing instrument does not take effect. This section does not preclude the filing of a subsequent filing instrument required by this code to make the action or transaction evidenced by the original filing instrument effective.

(b) If the effect of a filing instrument is conditioned on the occurrence of a future event or fact, other than the passage of time, and the specified event or fact does not occur and is not waived, the parties to the filing instrument must sign and file a certificate of abandonment as provided by Section 4.057.

Acts 2003, 78th Leg., ch. 182, § 1, eff. Jan. 1, 2006. Amended by Acts 2007, 80th Leg., ch. 688, § 16, eff. Sept. 1, 2007.

§ 4.057. Abandonment Before Effectiveness

(a) The parties to a filing instrument may abandon the filing instrument if the instrument has not taken effect.

(b) To abandon a filing instrument the parties to the instrument must file with the filing officer a certificate of abandonment.

(c) A certificate of abandonment must:

(1) be signed on behalf of each entity that is a party to the action or transaction by the person authorized by this code to act on behalf of the entity;

(2) state the nature of the filing instrument to be abandoned, the date of the instrument, and the parties to the instrument; and

(3) state that the filing instrument has been abandoned in accordance with the agreement of the parties.

(d) On the filing of the certificate of abandonment, the action or transaction evidenced by the original filing instrument is abandoned and may not take effect.

(e) If in the interim before a certificate of abandonment is filed the name of an entity that is a party to the action or transaction becomes the same as or deceptively similar to the name of another entity already on file or reserved or registered under this code, the filing officer may not file the certificate of abandonment unless the entity by or for whom the certificate is filed changes its name in the manner provided by this code for that entity.

Acts 2003, 78th Leg., ch. 182, § 1, eff. Jan. 1, 2006.

§ 4.058. Delayed Effectiveness Not Permitted

The effect of the following filing instruments may not be delayed:

(1) a reservation of name as provided by Subchapter C, Chapter 5;

(2) a registration of name as provided by Subchapter D, Chapter 5;

(3) a statement of event or fact as provided by Section 4.055; or

(4) a certificate of abandonment as provided by Section 4.057.

Acts 2003, 78th Leg., ch. 182, § 1, eff. Jan. 1, 2006.

§ 4.059. Acknowledgment of Filing with Delayed Effectiveness

(a) An acknowledgment of filing issued or other action taken by the secretary of state affirming the filing of a filing instrument that has a specific delayed effective date must state the date and time at which the instrument takes effect.

(b) An acknowledgment of filing issued or other action taken by the secretary of state affirming the filing of a filing instrument the effect of which is delayed until the occurrence of a future event or fact must:

(1) state that the effective date and time of the filing instrument is conditioned on the occurrence of a future event or fact as described in the filing instrument; or

(2) otherwise indicate that the effective date and time of the instrument is conditioned on the occurrence of a future event or fact.

Acts 2003, 78th Leg., ch. 182, § 1, eff. Jan. 1, 2006.

SUBCHAPTER C. CORRECTION AND AMENDMENT

§ 4.101. Correction of Filings

(a) A filing instrument that has been filed with the secretary of state that is an inaccurate record of the event or transaction evidenced in the instrument, that contains an inaccurate or erroneous statement, or that was defectively or erroneously signed, sealed, acknowledged, or verified may be corrected by filing a certificate of correction.

(b) A certificate of correction must be signed by the person authorized by this code to sign the filing instrument to be corrected.

Acts 2003, 78th Leg., ch. 182, § 1, eff. Jan. 1, 2006. Amended by Acts 2009, 81st Leg., ch. 84, § 6, eff. Sept. 1, 2009.

§ 4.102. Limitation on Correction of Filings

A filing instrument may be corrected to contain only those statements that this code authorizes or requires to be included in the original instrument. A certificate of correction may not alter, add, or delete a statement that by its alteration, addition, or deletion would have caused the secretary of state to determine the filing instrument did not conform to this code at the time of filing.

Acts 2003, 78th Leg., ch. 182, § 1, eff. Jan. 1, 2006.

§ 4.103. Certificate of Correction

The certificate of correction must:

(1) state the name of the entity;

(2) identify the filing instrument to be corrected by description and date of filing with the secretary of state;

(3) identify the inaccuracy, error, or defect to be corrected; and

(4) state in corrected form the portion of the filing instrument to be corrected.

Acts 2003, 78th Leg., ch. 182, § 1, eff. Jan. 1, 2006.

§ 4.104. Filing Certificate of Correction

The certificate of correction shall be filed with and acted on by the secretary of state as provided by Subchapter A. On filing, the secretary of state shall deliver to the entity or its representative an acknowledgment of the filing.

Acts 2003, 78th Leg., ch. 182, § 1, eff. Jan. 1, 2006.

§ 4.105. Effect of Certificate of Correction

(a) After the secretary of state files the certificate of correction, the filing instrument is considered to have been corrected on the date the filing instrument was originally filed, except as provided by Subsection (b).

(b) As to a person who is adversely affected by the correction, the filing instrument is considered to have been corrected on the date the certificate of correction is filed.

(c) An acknowledgment of filing or a similar instrument issued by the secretary of state before a filing instrument is corrected, with respect to the effect of filing the original filing instrument, applies to the corrected filing instrument as of the date the corrected filing instrument is considered to have been filed under this section.

Acts 2003, 78th Leg., ch. 182, § 1, eff. Jan. 1, 2006.

§ 4.106. Amendment of Filings

A filing instrument that an entity files with the secretary of state may be amended or supplemented to the extent permitted by the provisions of this code that apply to that entity.

Acts 2003, 78th Leg., ch. 182, § 1, eff. Jan. 1, 2006.

SUBCHAPTER D. FILING FEES

§ 4.151. Filing Fees: All Entities

The secretary of state shall impose the following fees:

(1) for filing a certificate of correction, $15;

(2) for filing an application for reservation or registration of a name, $40;

(3) for filing a notice of transfer of a name reservation, $15;

(4) for filing an application for renewal of registration of a name, $40;

(5) for filing a certificate of merger or conversion, other than a filing on behalf of a nonprofit corporation, $300 plus, with respect to a merger, any fee imposed for filing a certificate of formation for each newly created filing entity or, with respect to a conversion, the fee imposed for filing a certificate of formation for the converted entity;

(6) for filing a certificate of exchange, $300; and

(7) for preclearance of a filing instrument, $50.

Acts 2003, 78th Leg., ch. 182, § 1, eff. Jan. 1, 2006. Amended by Acts 2007, 80th Leg., ch. 688, § 17, eff. Sept. 1, 2007.

§ 4.152. Filing Fees: For-Profit Corporations

For a filing by or for a for-profit corporation, the secretary of state shall impose the following fees:

(1) for filing a certificate of formation, $300;

(2) for filing a certificate of amendment, $150;

(3) for filing an application of a foreign corporation for registration to transact business in this state, $750;

(4) for filing an application of a foreign corporation for an amended registration to transact business in this state, $150;

(5) for filing a restated certificate of formation and accompanying statement, $300;

(6) for filing a statement of change of registered office, registered agent, or both, $15;

(7) for filing a statement of change of name or address of a registered agent, $15, except that the maximum fee for simultaneous filings by a registered agent for more than one corporation may not exceed $750;

(8) for filing a statement of resolution establishing one or more series of shares, $15;

(9) for filing a certificate of termination, $40;

(10) for filing a certificate of withdrawal of a foreign corporation, $15;

(11) for filing a certificate from the home state of a foreign corporation that the corporation no longer exists in that state, $15;

(12) for filing a bylaw or agreement restricting transfer of shares or securities other than as an amendment to the certificate of formation, $15;

(13) for filing an application for reinstatement of a certificate of formation or registration as a foreign corporation following forfeiture under the Tax Code, $75;

(14) for filing an application for reinstatement of a corporation or registration as a foreign corporation after involuntary termination or revocation, $75; and

(15) for filing any instrument as provided by this code for which this section does not expressly provide a fee, $15.

Acts 2003, 78th Leg., ch. 182, § 1, eff. Jan. 1, 2006. Amended by Acts 2005, 79th Leg., ch. 64, § 10, eff. Jan. 1, 2006; Acts 2007, 80th Leg., ch. 688, § 18, eff. Sept. 1, 2007.

§ 4.153. Filing Fees: Nonprofit Corporations

For a filing by or for a nonprofit corporation, the secretary of state shall impose the following fees:

(1) for filing a certificate of formation, $25;

(2) for filing a certificate of amendment, $25;

(3) for filing a certificate of merger, conversion, or consolidation, without regard to whether the surviving or new corporation is a domestic or foreign corporation, $50;

(4) for filing a statement of change of a registered office, registered agent, or both, $5;

(5) for filing a certificate of termination, $5;

(6) for filing an application of a foreign corporation for registration to conduct affairs in this state, $25;

(7) for filing an application of a foreign corporation for an amended registration to conduct affairs in this state, $25;

(8) for filing a certificate of withdrawal of a foreign corporation, $5;

(9) for filing a restated certificate of formation and accompanying statement, $50;

(10) for filing a statement of change of name or address of a registered agent, $15, except that the maximum fee for simultaneous filings by a registered agent for more than one corporation may not exceed $250;

(11) for filing a report under Chapter 22, $5;

(12) for filing a report under Chapter 22 to reinstate a corporation's right to conduct affairs in this state, $5, plus a late fee in the amount of $5 or in the amount of $1 for each month or part of a month that the report remains unfiled, whichever amount is greater, except that the late fee may not exceed $25;

(13) for filing a report under Chapter 22 to reinstate a corporation or registration following involuntary termination or revocation, $25; and

(14) for filing any instrument of a domestic or foreign corporation as provided by this code for which this section does not expressly provide a fee, $5.

Acts 2003, 78th Leg., ch. 182, § 1, eff. Jan. 1, 2006. Amended by Acts 2005, 79th Leg., ch. 64, § 11, eff. Jan. 1, 2006.

§ 4.154. Filing Fees: Limited Liability Companies

For a filing by or for a limited liability company, the secretary of state shall impose the same fee as the filing fee for a similar instrument under Section 4.152.

Acts 2003, 78th Leg., ch. 182, § 1, eff. Jan. 1, 2006.

§ 4.155. Filing Fees: Limited Partnerships

For a filing by or for a limited partnership, the secretary of state shall impose the following fees:

(1) for filing a certificate of formation or an application for registration as a foreign limited partnership, $750;

(2) for filing a certificate of amendment or an amendment of registration of a foreign limited partnership, $150;

(3) for filing a restated certificate of formation, $300;

(4) for filing a statement for change of registered office, registered agent, or both, $15;

(5) for filing a statement of change of name or address of a registered agent, $15, except that the maximum fee for simultaneous filings by a registered agent for more than one limited partnership may not exceed $750;

(6) for filing a certificate of termination, $40;

(7) for filing a certificate of withdrawal of a foreign limited partnership, $15;

(8) for filing a certificate of reinstatement of a limited partnership or registration as a foreign limited partnership after involuntary termination or revocation under Chapter 11 or Chapter 9, $75;

(9) for filing a periodic report required under Chapter 153, $50;

(10) for reviving a limited partnership's right to transact business under Chapter 153, $50 plus a late fee in an amount equal to the lesser of:

(A) $25 for each month or part of a month that elapses after the date of the notice of forfeiture; or

(B) $100;

(11) for reinstatement of a certificate of formation or registration under Chapter 153, $50 plus a late fee of $100 and a reinstatement fee of $75;

(12) for filing any document required or permitted to be filed for a limited liability partnership, the secretary of state shall impose the same fee as the filing fee for a general partnership under Section 4.158. For purposes of calculation of the filing fee, all references to partners in Section 4.158 as applied to limited partnerships mean general partners only; and

(13) for filing any instrument as provided by this code for which this section does not expressly provide a fee, $15.

Acts 2003, 78th Leg., ch. 182, § 1, eff. Jan. 1, 2006. Amended by Acts 2005, 79th Leg., ch. 64, § 12, eff. Jan. 1, 2006.

§ 4.156. Filing Fees: Professional Associations

For a filing by or for a professional association, the secretary of state shall impose the following fees:

(1) for filing a certificate of formation or an application for registration as a foreign professional association, $750;

(2) for filing an annual statement, $35; and

(3) for filing any other instrument, the fee provided for the filing of a similar instrument under Section 4.152.

Acts 2003, 78th Leg., ch. 182, § 1, eff. Jan. 1, 2006.

§ 4.157. Filing Fees: Professional Corporations

For a filing by or for a professional corporation, the secretary of state shall impose the same fee as the filing fee for a similar instrument under Section 4.152.

Acts 2003, 78th Leg., ch. 182, § 1, eff. Jan. 1, 2006.

§ 4.158. Filing Fees: General Partnerships

For a filing by or for a general partnership, the secretary of state shall impose the following fees:

(1) for filing a limited liability partnership application, $200 for each partner;

(2) for filing a limited liability partnership renewal application, $200 for each partner on the date of renewal;

(3) for filing an application for registration by a foreign limited liability partnership, $200 for each partner in this state, except that the maximum fee may not exceed $750;

(4) for filing a renewal of registration by a foreign limited liability partnership, $200 for each partner in this state, except that the maximum fee may not exceed $750;

(5) for filing a certificate of amendment for a domestic limited liability partnership, $10, plus $200 for each partner added by the amendment;

(6) for filing a certificate of amendment for a foreign limited liability partnership, $10, plus $200 for each partner in this state added by amendment not to exceed $750; and

(7) for filing any other filing instrument, the filing fee imposed for a similar instrument under Section 4.155.

Acts 2003, 78th Leg., ch. 182, § 1, eff. Jan. 1, 2006. Amended by Acts 2007, 80th Leg., ch. 688, § 19, eff. Sept. 1, 2007.

§ 4.159. Filing Fees: Nonprofit Associations

For a filing by or for a nonprofit association, the secretary of state shall impose the following fees:

(1) for filing a statement appointing an agent to receive service of process, $25;

(2) for filing an amendment of a statement appointing an agent, $5; and

(3) for filing a cancellation of a statement appointing an agent, $5.

Acts 2003, 78th Leg., ch. 182, § 1, eff. Jan. 1, 2006.

§ 4.160. Filing Fees: Foreign Filing Entities

For a filing by or for a foreign filing entity when no other fee has been provided, the secretary of state shall impose the same fee as the filing fee for a similar instrument under Section 4.151 or 4.152.

Acts 2003, 78th Leg., ch. 182, § 1, eff. Jan. 1, 2006.

§ 4.161. Filing Fees: Cooperative Associations

For a filing by or for a cooperative association, the secretary of state shall impose the same fee as the filing fee for a similar instrument under Section 4.153.

Added by Acts 2005, 79th Leg., ch. 64, § 13, eff. Jan. 1, 2006.

CHAPTER 5. NAMES OF ENTITIES; REGISTERED AGENTS AND REGISTERED OFFICES

SUBCHAPTER A. GENERAL PROVISIONS

Section

5.001. Effect on Rights Under Other Law.

SUBCHAPTER B. GENERAL PROVISIONS RELATING TO NAMES OF ENTITIES

Section

5.051. Assumed Name.
5.052. Unauthorized Purpose in Name Prohibited.
5.053. Identical and Deceptively Similar Names Prohibited.
5.054. Name of Corporation, Foreign Corporation, Professional Corporation, or Foreign Professional Corporation.
5.055. Name of Limited Partnership or Foreign Limited Partnership.
5.056. Name of Limited Liability Company or Foreign Limited Liability Company.
5.057. Name of Cooperative Association or Foreign Cooperative Association.
5.058. Name of Professional Association or Foreign Professional Association.
5.059. Name of Professional Limited Liability Company or Foreign Professional Limited Liability Company.
5.060. Name of Professional Entity or Foreign Professional Entity; Conflicts With Other Law or Ethical Rule.
5.061. Name Containing "Lotto" or "Lottery" Prohibited.
5.062. Veterans Organizations; Unauthorized Use of Name.
5.063. Name of Limited Liability Partnership.

SUBCHAPTER C. RESERVATION OF NAMES

5.101. Application for Reservation of Name.
5.102. Reservation of Certain Names Prohibited; Exceptions.
5.103. Action on Application.
5.104. Duration of Reservation of Name.
5.1041. Prohibition on Fee for Withdrawal of Reservation of Name.
5.105. Renewal of Reservation.
5.106. Transfer of Reservation of Name.

SUBCHAPTER D. REGISTRATION OF NAMES

5.151. Application by Certain Entities for Registration of Name.
5.152. Application for Registration of Name.
5.153. Certain Registrations Prohibited; Exceptions.
5.154. Duration of Registration of Name.
5.155. Renewal of Registration.

SUBCHAPTER E. REGISTERED AGENTS AND REGISTERED OFFICES

5.200. Definitions.
5.201. Designation and Maintenance of Registered Agent and Registered Office.
5.2011. Consent to Serve as Registered Agent.
5.202. Change by Entity to Registered Office or Registered Agent.
5.203. Change by Registered Agent to Name or Address of Registered Office.
5.204. Resignation of Registered Agent.
5.205. Rejection of Appointment.
5.206. Duties of Registered Agent.
5.207. Designation of Registered Agent Without Consent; Penalties and Liabilities.
5.208. Immunity From Liability.

SUBCHAPTER F. SERVICE OF PROCESS

Section
5.251. Failure to Designate Registered Agent.
5.252. Service on Secretary of State.
5.253. Action by Secretary of State.
5.254. Required Records of Secretary of State.
5.255. Agent for Service of Process, Notice, or Demand as Matter of Law.
5.256. Other Means of Service Not Precluded.
5.257. Service of Process by Political Subdivision.

SUBCHAPTER A. GENERAL PROVISIONS

§ 5.001. Effect on Rights Under Other Law

(a) The filing of a certificate of formation by a filing entity under this code, an application for registration by a foreign filing entity under this code, or an application for reservation or registration of a name under this chapter does not authorize the use of a name in this state in violation of a right of another under:

(1) the Trademark Act of 1946, as amended (15 U.S.C. Section 1051 et seq.);

(2) Chapter 16 or 71, Business & Commerce Code; or

(3) common law.

(b) The secretary of state shall deliver a notice that contains the substance of Subsection (a) to each of the following:

(1) a filing entity that files a certificate of formation under this code;

(2) a foreign filing entity that registers under this code;

(3) a person that reserves a name under Subchapter C; and

(4) a person that registers a name under Subchapter D.

Acts 2003, 78th Leg., ch. 182, § 1, eff. Jan. 1, 2006. Amended by Acts 2007, 80th Leg., ch. 885, § 2.08, eff. April 1, 2009.

SUBCHAPTER B. GENERAL PROVISIONS RELATING TO NAMES OF ENTITIES

§ 5.051. Assumed Name

A domestic entity or a foreign entity having authority to transact business in this state may transact business under an assumed name by filing an assumed name certificate in accordance with Chapter 71, Business & Commerce Code. The requirements of this subchapter do not apply to an assumed name set forth in an assumed name certificate filed under that chapter.

Acts 2003, 78th Leg., ch. 182, § 1, eff. Jan. 1, 2006. Amended by Acts 2007, 80th Leg., ch. 885, § 2.09, eff. April 1, 2009.

§ 5.052. Unauthorized Purpose in Name Prohibited

A filing entity or a foreign filing entity may not have a name that contains any word or phrase that indicates or implies that the entity is engaged in a business that the entity is not authorized by law to pursue.

Acts 2003, 78th Leg., ch. 182, § 1, eff. Jan. 1, 2006.

§ 5.053. Identical and Deceptively Similar Names Prohibited

(a) A filing entity may not have a name, and a foreign filing entity may not register to transact business in this state under a name, that is the same as, or that the secretary of state determines to be deceptively similar or similar to:

(1) the name of another existing filing entity;

(2) the name of a foreign filing entity that is registered under Chapter 9;

(3) a name that is reserved under Subchapter C; or

(4) a name that is registered under Subchapter D.

(b) Subsection (a) does not apply if the other entity or the person for whom the name is reserved or registered, as appropriate, consents in writing to the use of the similar name.

Acts 2003, 78th Leg., ch. 182, § 1, eff. Jan. 1, 2006.

§ 5.054. Name of Corporation, Foreign Corporation, Professional Corporation, or Foreign Professional Corporation

(a) The name of a corporation or foreign corporation must contain:

(1) the word "company," "corporation," "incorporated," or "limited"; or

(2) an abbreviation of one of those words.

(b) Subsection (a) does not apply to a nonprofit corporation or foreign nonprofit corporation.

(c) Instead of a word or abbreviation required by Subsection (a), the name of a professional corporation or foreign professional corporation may contain the phrase "professional corporation" or an abbreviation of the phrase.

Acts 2003, 78th Leg., ch. 182, § 1, eff. Jan. 1, 2006. Amended by Acts 2007, 80th Leg., ch. 688, §§ 20, 21, eff. Sept. 1, 2007.

§ 5.055. Name of Limited Partnership or Foreign Limited Partnership

(a) The name of a limited partnership or foreign limited partnership must contain:

(1) the word "limited";

(2) the phrase "limited partnership"; or

(3) an abbreviation of that word or phrase.

(b) The name of a domestic or foreign limited partnership that is a limited liability limited partnership must also contain the phrase "limited liability partnership" or an abbreviation of that phrase.

(c) The name of a domestic or foreign limited partnership that is a limited liability limited partnership complies with the requirements of Subsections (a) and (b) if the name of the limited partnership contains the phrase "limited liability limited partnership" or an abbreviation of that phrase.

Acts 2003, 78th Leg., ch. 182, § 1, eff. Jan. 1, 2006. Amended by Acts 2007, 80th Leg., ch. 688, § 22, eff. Sept. 1, 2007.

§ 5.056. Name of Limited Liability Company or Foreign Limited Liability Company

(a) The name of a limited liability company or a foreign limited liability company doing business in this state must contain:

(1) the phrase "limited liability company" or "limited company"; or

(2) an abbreviation of one of those phrases.

(b) A limited liability company formed before September 1, 1993, the name of which complied with the laws of this state on the date of formation but does not comply with this section is not required to change its name.

Acts 2003, 78th Leg., ch. 182, § 1, eff. Jan. 1, 2006.

§ 5.057. Name of Cooperative Association or Foreign Cooperative Association

(a) The name of a cooperative association or foreign cooperative association must contain:

(1) the word "cooperative"; or

(2) an abbreviation of that word.

(b) A domestic or foreign entity may use the word "cooperative" in its name to the extent permitted by Section 251.452.

Acts 2003, 78th Leg., ch. 182, § 1, eff. Jan. 1, 2006. Amended by Acts 2007, 80th Leg., ch. 688, §§ 23, 24, eff. Sept. 1, 2007.

§ 5.058. Name of Professional Association or Foreign Professional Association

The name of a professional association or foreign professional association must contain:

(1) the word "associated," "associates," or "association";

(2) the phrase "professional association"; or

(3) an abbreviation of one of those words or that phrase.

Acts 2003, 78th Leg., ch. 182, § 1, eff. Jan. 1, 2006. Amended by Acts 2007, 80th Leg., ch. 688, § 25, eff. Sept. 1, 2007.

§ 5.059. Name of Professional Limited Liability Company or Foreign Professional Limited Liability Company

(a) The name of a professional limited liability company or foreign professional limited liability company must contain:

(1) the phrase "professional limited liability company"; or

(2) an abbreviation of that phrase.

(b) A professional limited liability company or foreign professional limited liability company formed before September 1, 1993, the name of which complied with the laws of this state on the date of formation but does not comply with this section, is not required to change its name.

Acts 2003, 78th Leg., ch. 182, § 1, eff. Jan. 1, 2006. Amended by Acts 2007, 80th Leg., ch. 688, § 26, eff. Sept. 1, 2007.

§ 5.060. Name of Professional Entity or Foreign Professional Entity; Conflicts With Other Law or Ethical Rule

The name of a professional entity or foreign professional entity must not be contrary to a statute or regulation of this state that governs a person who provides a professional service through the professional entity or foreign professional entity, including a rule of professional ethics.

Acts 2003, 78th Leg., ch. 182, § 1, eff. Jan. 1, 2006. Amended by Acts 2007, 80th Leg., ch. 688, § 27, eff. Sept. 1, 2007.

§ 5.061. Name Containing "Lotto" or "Lottery" Prohibited

A filing entity or a foreign filing entity may not have a name that contains the word "lotto" or "lottery."

Acts 2003, 78th Leg., ch. 182, § 1, eff. Jan. 1, 2006.

§ 5.062. Veterans Organizations; Unauthorized Use of Name

(a) Subject to Subsection (b), a filing entity may not have a name that:

(1) reasonably implies that the entity is created by or for the benefit of war veterans or their families; and

(2) contains the word or phrase, or any variation or abbreviation of:

(A) "veteran";

(B) "legion";

(C) "foreign";

(D) "Spanish";

(E) "disabled";

(F) "war"; or

(G) "world war."

(b) The prohibition in Subsection (a) does not apply to a filing entity with a name approved in writing by:

(1) a congressionally recognized veterans organization with a name containing the same word or phrase, or variation or abbreviation, contained in the filing entity's name; or

(2) if a veterans organization described by Subdivision (1) does not exist, the state commander of the:

(A) American Legion;

(B) Disabled American Veterans of the World War;

(C) Veterans of Foreign Wars of the United States;

(D) United Spanish War Veterans; or

(E) Veterans of the Spanish–American War.

Acts 2003, 78th Leg., ch. 182, § 1, eff. Jan. 1, 2006.

§ 5.063. Name of Limited Liability Partnership

(a) The name of a domestic or foreign limited liability partnership must contain:

(1) the phrase "limited liability partnership"; or

(2) an abbreviation of the phrase.

(b) A domestic or foreign limited liability partnership is not subject to Section 5.053.

(c) A domestic or foreign limited liability partnership that is also a limited partnership must comply with Section 5.055 and not this section.

Acts 2003, 78th Leg., ch. 182, § 1, eff. Jan. 1, 2006. Amended by Acts 2005, 79th Leg., ch. 64, § 14, eff. Jan. 1, 2006.

SUBCHAPTER C. RESERVATION OF NAMES

§ 5.101. Application for Reservation of Name

(a) Any person may file an application with the secretary of state to reserve the exclusive use of a name under this chapter.

(b) The application must be:

(1) accompanied by any required filing fee; and

(2) signed by the applicant or by the agent or attorney of the applicant.

Acts 2003, 78th Leg., ch. 182, § 1, eff. Jan. 1, 2006.

§ 5.102. Reservation of Certain Names Prohibited; Exceptions

(a) The secretary of state may not reserve a name that is the same as, or that the secretary of state considers deceptively similar or similar to:

(1) the name of an existing filing entity;

(2) the name of a foreign filing entity that is registered under Chapter 9;

(3) a name that is reserved under this subchapter; or

(4) a name that is registered under Subchapter D.

(b) Subsection (a) does not apply if the other entity or the person for whom the name is reserved or registered, as appropriate, consents in writing to the subsequent reservation of the similar name.

Acts 2003, 78th Leg., ch. 182, § 1, eff. Jan. 1, 2006.

§ 5.103. Action on Application

If the secretary of state determines that the name specified in the application is eligible for reservation, the secretary shall reserve that name for the exclusive use of the applicant.

Acts 2003, 78th Leg., ch. 182, § 1, eff. Jan. 1, 2006.

§ 5.104. Duration of Reservation of Name

The secretary of state shall reserve the name for the applicant until the earlier of:

(1) the 121st day after the date the application is accepted for filing; or

(2) the date the applicant files with the secretary of state a written notice of withdrawal of the reservation.

Acts 2003, 78th Leg., ch. 182, § 1, eff. Jan. 1, 2006.

§ 5.1041. Prohibition on Fee for Withdrawal of Reservation of Name

The secretary of state may not impose a fee for the filing of a written notice of withdrawal of a reservation of name.

Added by Acts 2005, 79th Leg., ch. 64, § 15, eff. Jan. 1, 2006.

§ 5.105. Renewal of Reservation

A person may renew the person's reservation of a name under this subchapter for successive 120–day periods if, during the 30–day period preceding the expiration of that reservation, the person:

(1) files a new application to reserve the name; and

(2) pays the required filing fee.

Acts 2003, 78th Leg., ch. 182, § 1, eff. Jan. 1, 2006.

§ 5.106. Transfer of Reservation of Name

(a) A person may transfer the person's reservation of a name by filing with the secretary of state a notice of transfer.

(b) The notice of transfer must:

(1) be signed by the person for whom the name is reserved; and

(2) state the name and address of the person to whom the reservation is to be transferred.

Acts 2003, 78th Leg., ch. 182, § 1, eff. Jan. 1, 2006.

SUBCHAPTER D. REGISTRATION OF NAMES

§ 5.151. Application by Certain Entities for Registration of Name

An organization that is authorized to do business in this state as a bank, trust company, savings association, or insurance company, or that is a foreign filing entity not registered to do business in this state under this code, may apply to register its name under this subchapter.

Acts 2003, 78th Leg., ch. 182, § 1, eff. Jan. 1, 2006.

§ 5.152. Application for Registration of Name

(a) To register a name under this subchapter, an organization must file an application with the secretary of state.

(b) The application must:

(1) state that the organization validly exists and is doing business;

(2) contain a brief statement of the nature of the organization's business;

(3) set out:

(A) the name of the organization;

(B) the name of the jurisdiction under whose laws the organization is formed; and

(C) the date the organization was formed; and

(4) be accompanied by any required filing fee.

Acts 2003, 78th Leg., ch. 182, § 1, eff. Jan. 1, 2006.

§ 5.153. Certain Registrations Prohibited; Exceptions

(a) The secretary of state may not register a name that is the same as, or that the secretary of state determines to be deceptively similar or similar to:

(1) the name of an existing filing entity;

(2) the name of a foreign filing entity that is registered under Chapter 9;

(3) a name that is reserved under Subchapter C; or

(4) a name that is registered under this subchapter.

(b) Subsection (a) does not apply if:

(1) the other entity or the person for whom the name is reserved or registered, as appropriate, consents in writing to the registration of the similar name; or

(2) the applicant is a bank, trust company, savings association, or insurance company that has been in continuous existence from a date that precedes the date the conflicting name is filed with the secretary of state.

Acts 2003, 78th Leg., ch. 182, § 1, eff. Jan. 1, 2006.

§ 5.154. Duration of Registration of Name

The registration of a name under this subchapter is effective until the earlier of:

(1) the first anniversary of the date the application is accepted for filing; or

(2) the date the entity files with the secretary of state a written notice of withdrawal of the registration.

Acts 2003, 78th Leg., ch. 182, § 1, eff. Jan. 1, 2006.

§ 5.155. Renewal of Registration

A person may renew the person's registration of a name under this subchapter for successive one-year periods if, during the 90–day period preceding the expiration of that registration, the person:

(1) files an application to renew the registration of the name; and

(2) pays the required filing fee.

Acts 2003, 78th Leg., ch. 182, § 1, eff. Jan. 1, 2006.

SUBCHAPTER E. REGISTERED AGENTS AND REGISTERED OFFICES

§ 5.200. Definitions

In this subchapter:

(1) "Registered agent filing" means:

(A) the certificate of formation or similar organizational document of a domestic represented entity;

(B) the application for registration of a foreign represented entity;

(C) an appointment of agent by an unincorporated nonprofit association under Section 252.011;

(D) an appointment of agent by a Texas financial institution under Section 201.103, Finance Code;

(E) an appointment of agent by a defense base development authority under Section 379B.004(b), Local Government Code;

(F) a statement by a represented entity to change the entity's registered agent, registered office, or both;

(G) a certificate of merger or certificate of conversion;

(H) a certificate of amendment to the certificate of formation or similar organizational document or the registration of a represented entity;

(I) a restated certificate of formation or similar organizational document of a represented entity;

(J) any other instrument that is required or permitted by law to be filed by a represented entity that effects a change or correction to the instruments listed in Paragraphs (A)–(I); and

(K) a certificate of reinstatement filed under Chapter 9 or 11.

(2) "Represented domestic entity" means:

(A) a filing entity;

(B) an unincorporated nonprofit association for which an appointment of agent has been filed;

(C) a Texas financial institution for which an appointment of agent has been filed;

(D) a defense base development authority for which an appointment of agent has been filed; or

(E) any corporation, association, or other organization incorporated or organized under any special statute of this state, that is governed wholly or partly by this code, or to which the general corporate laws are applicable.

(3) "Represented entity" means a represented domestic entity or represented foreign entity.

(4) "Represented foreign entity" means:

(A) a foreign filing entity for which a registration has been filed;

(B) a foreign limited liability partnership for which a registration has been filed;

(C) a foreign financial institution for which a registration has been filed; or

(D) any corporation, association, or other organization incorporated or organized under the laws of a jurisdiction other than this state that is granted authority to conduct its affairs in this state under any special statute of this state, that is governed wholly or partly by this code, or to which the general corporate laws are applicable.

Added by Acts 2009, 81st Leg., ch. 1123, § 1, eff. Jan. 1, 2010.

Section 6 of Acts 2009, 81st Leg., ch. 1123 provides:

"The changes in law made by this Act apply only to the designation or appointment of a registered agent made on or after the effective date of this Act. The designation or appointment of a registered agent made before the effective date of this Act is governed by the law in effect on the date the designation or appointment was made, and the former law is continued in effect for that purpose."

§ 5.201. Designation and Maintenance of Registered Agent and Registered Office

(a) Each filing entity and each foreign filing entity shall designate and continuously maintain in this state:

(1) a registered agent; and

(2) a registered office.

(b) The registered agent:

(1) is an agent of the entity on whom may be served any process, notice, or demand required or permitted by law to be served on the entity;

(2) may be:

(A) an individual who:

(i) is a resident of this state; and

(ii) has consented in a written or electronic form to be developed by the office of the secretary of state to serve as the registered agent of the entity; or

(B) an organization, other than the filing entity or foreign filing entity to be represented, that:

(i) is registered or authorized to do business in this state; and

(ii) has consented in a written or electronic form to be developed by the office of the secretary of state to serve as the registered agent of the entity; and

(3) must maintain a business office at the same address as the entity's registered office.

(c) The registered office:

(1) must be located at a street address where process may be personally served on the entity's registered agent;

(2) is not required to be a place of business of the filing entity or foreign filing entity; and

(3) may not be solely a mailbox service or a telephone answering service.

(d) A registered agent that is an organization must have an employee available at the registered office during normal business hours to receive service of process, notice, or demand. Any employee of the organization may receive service at the registered office.

Acts 2003, 78th Leg., ch. 182, § 1, eff. Jan. 1, 2006. Amended by Acts 2007, 80th Leg., ch. 688, § 28, eff. Sept. 1, 2007; Acts 2009, 81st Leg., ch. 1123, § 2, eff. Jan. 1, 2010; Acts 2011, 82nd Leg., ch. 1151 (H.B. 2047), § 1, eff. Sept. 1, 2011.

Section 6 of Acts 2009, 81st Leg., ch. 1123 provides:

"The changes in law made by this Act apply only to the designation or appointment of a registered agent made on or after the effective date of this Act. The designation or appointment of a registered agent made before the effective date of this Act is governed by the law in effect on the date the designation or appointment was made, and the former law is continued in effect for that purpose."

Section 2 of Acts 2011, 82nd Leg., ch. 1151 (H.B. 2047) provides:

"Section 5.201(d), Business Organizations Code, as added by this Act, applies to all process served on or after the effective date [Sept. 1, 2011] of this Act, without regard to whether the process was issued before, on, or after that date."

§ 5.2011. Consent to Serve as Registered Agent

(a) The designation or appointment of a person as registered agent by an organizer or managerial official of an entity in a registered agent filing is an affirmation by the organizer or managerial official that the person named as registered agent has consented to serve in that capacity.

(b) If a person designated or appointed as registered agent in a registered agent filing before the sale, acquisition, or transfer of a majority-in-interest or majority interest of the outstanding ownership or membership interests of the represented entity continues to serve in that capacity after the sale, acquisition, or transfer, the person's continuation of service is an affirmation by the governing authority of the represented entity that the governing authority has verified that the person named as registered agent has consented to continue to serve in that capacity.

Added by Acts 2009, 81st Leg., ch. 1123, § 3, eff. Jan. 1, 2010.

Section 6 of Acts 2009, 81st Leg., ch. 1123 provides:

"The changes in law made by this Act apply only to the designation or appointment of a registered agent made on or after the effective date of this Act. The designation or appointment of a registered agent made before the effective date of this Act is governed by the law in effect on the date the designation or appointment was made, and the former law is continued in effect for that purpose."

§ 5.202. Change by Entity to Registered Office or Registered Agent

(a) A filing entity or foreign filing entity may change its registered office, its registered agent, or both by filing a statement of the change in accordance with Chapter 4.

(b) The statement must contain:

(1) the name of the entity;

(2) the name of the entity's registered agent;

(3) the street address of the entity's registered agent;

(4) if the change relates to the registered agent, the name of the entity's new registered agent;

(5) if the change relates to the registered office, the street address of the entity's new registered office;

(6) a recitation that the change specified in the statement is authorized by the entity; and

(7) a recitation that the street address of the registered office and the street address of the registered agent's business are the same.

(c) On acceptance of the statement by the filing officer, the statement is effective as an amendment to the appropriate provision of:

(1) the filing entity's certificate of formation; or

(2) the foreign filing entity's registration.

Acts 2003, 78th Leg., ch. 182, § 1, eff. Jan. 1, 2006.

§ 5.203. Change by Registered Agent to Name or Address of Registered Office

(a) The registered agent of a filing entity or a foreign filing entity may change its name, its address as the address of the entity's registered office, or both by filing a statement of the change in accordance with Chapter 4.

(b) The statement must be signed by the registered agent, or a person authorized to sign the statement on behalf of the registered agent, and must contain:

(1) the name of the entity represented by the registered agent;

(2) the name of the entity's registered agent and the address at which the registered agent maintained the entity's registered office;

(3) if the change relates to the name of the registered agent, the new name of that agent;

(4) if the change relates to the address of the registered office, the new address of that office; and

(5) a recitation that written notice of the change was given to the entity at least 10 days before the date the statement is filed.

(c) On acceptance of the statement by the filing officer, the statement is effective as an amendment to the appropriate provision of:

(1) the filing entity's certificate of formation; or

(2) the foreign filing entity's registration.

(d) A registered agent may file a statement under this section that applies to more than one entity.

Acts 2003, 78th Leg., ch. 182, § 1, eff. Jan. 1, 2006.

§ 5.204. Resignation of Registered Agent

(a) A registered agent of a filing entity or a foreign filing entity may resign as the registered agent by giving notice to that entity and to the appropriate filing officer.

(b) Notice to the entity must be given to the entity at the address of the entity most recently known by the agent.

(c) Notice to the filing officer must be given before the 11th day after the date notice under Subsection (b) is mailed or delivered and must include:

(1) the address of the entity most recently known by the agent;

(2) a statement that written notice of the resignation has been given to the entity; and

(3) the date on which that written notice of resignation was given.

(d) On compliance with Subsections (b) and (c), the appointment of the registered agent and the designation of the registered office terminate. The termination is effective on the 31st day after the date the secretary of state receives the notice.

(e) If the filing officer finds that a notice of resignation received by the filing officer conforms to Subsections (b) and (c), the filing officer shall:

(1) notify the entity of the registered agent's resignation; and

(2) file the resignation in accordance with Chapter 4, except that a fee is not required to file the resignation.

Acts 2003, 78th Leg., ch. 182, § 1, eff. Jan. 1, 2006. Amended by Acts 2009, 81st Leg., ch. 1123, § 4, eff. Jan. 1, 2010.

Section 6 of Acts 2009, 81st Leg., ch. 1123 provides:

"The changes in law made by this Act apply only to the designation or appointment of a registered agent made on or after the effective date of this Act. The designation or appointment of a registered agent made before the effective date of this Act is governed by the law in effect on the date the designation or appointment was made, and the former law is continued in effect for that purpose."

§ 5.205. Rejection of Appointment

(a) A person designated or appointed as an entity's registered agent in a registered agent filing without the person's consent may terminate the person's appointment or designation as registered agent by filing a statement of rejection of appointment with the filing officer.

(b) The statement of rejection of appointment must:

(1) be signed by the person named as registered agent;

(2) contain the name of the represented entity; and

(3) contain a statement certifying that the person did not consent to serve as the represented entity's registered agent on the date on which the registered agent filing on which the person is named as registered agent took effect.

(c) On acceptance of the statement of rejection of appointment by the filing officer, the designation or appointment of that person as registered agent and the designation of the registered office terminate.

(d) On termination of the designation or appointment of a registered agent and the designation of the registered office, the secretary of state shall send notice to the represented entity of the necessity to designate or appoint a new registered agent and registered office in accordance with Section 9.101 or 11.251, as applicable.

(e) The filing officer may not charge a fee for the filing of a statement of rejection of appointment.

Added by Acts 2009, 81st Leg., ch. 1123, § 5, eff. Jan. 1, 2010.

Section 6 of Acts 2009, 81st Leg., ch. 1123 provides:

"The changes in law made by this Act apply only to the designation or appointment of a registered agent made on or after the effective date of this Act. The designation or appointment of a registered agent made before the effective date of this Act is governed by the law in effect on the date the designation or appointment was made, and the former law is continued in effect for that purpose."

§ 5.206. Duties of Registered Agent

(a) The only duties of a registered agent are to:

(1) receive or accept, and forward to the represented entity at the address most recently provided to the registered agent by the represented entity, or otherwise notify the represented entity at that address regarding, any process, notice, or demand that is served on or received by the registered agent; and

(2) provide the notices required or permitted by law to be given to the represented entity to the address most recently provided to the registered agent by the represented entity.

(b) A person named as the registered agent for a represented entity in a registered agent filing without the person's consent is not required to perform the duties prescribed by this section.

Added by Acts 2009, 81st Leg., ch. 1123, § 5, eff. Jan. 1, 2010.

Section 6 of Acts 2009, 81st Leg., ch. 1123 provides:

"The changes in law made by this Act apply only to the designation or appointment of a registered agent made on or after the effective date of this Act. The designation or appointment of a registered agent made before the effective date of this Act is governed by the law in effect on the date the designation or appointment was made, and the former law is continued in effect for that purpose."

§ 5.207. Designation of Registered Agent Without Consent; Penalties and Liabilities

Sections 4.007 and 4.008 apply with respect to a false statement in a registered agent filing that names a person the registered agent of a represented entity without the person's consent.

Added by Acts 2009, 81st Leg., ch. 1123, § 5, eff. Jan. 1, 2010.

Section 6 of Acts 2009, 81st Leg., ch. 1123 provides:

"The changes in law made by this Act apply only to the designation or appointment of a registered agent made on or after the effective date of this Act. The designation or appointment of a registered agent made before the effective date of this Act is governed by the law in effect on the date the designation or appointment was made, and the former law is continued in effect for that purpose."

§ 5.208. Immunity From Liability

(a) A person designated or appointed as the registered agent of a represented entity is not liable solely because of the person's designation or appointment as registered agent for the debts, liabilities, or obligations of the represented entity.

(b) A person who has been designated or appointed as a registered agent in a registered agent filing but has not consented to serve as the represented entity's registered agent may not be held liable:

(1) under a judgment, decree, or order of a court, agency, or tribunal of any type, or in any other manner, in this or any other state, or on any other basis, for a debt, obligation, or liability of the represented entity, whether arising in contract, tort, or otherwise, solely because of the person's designation or appointment as registered agent; or

(2) to the represented entity or to a person who reasonably relied on the unauthorized designation or appointment solely because of the person's failure or refusal to perform the duties of a registered agent under Section 5.206.

Added by Acts 2009, 81st Leg., ch. 1123, § 5, eff. Jan. 1, 2010.

Section 6 of Acts 2009, 81st Leg., ch. 1123 provides:

"The changes in law made by this Act apply only to the designation or appointment of a registered agent made on or after the effective date of this Act. The designation or appointment of a registered agent made before the effective date of this Act is governed by the law in effect on the date the designation or appointment was made, and the former law is continued in effect for that purpose."

SUBCHAPTER F. SERVICE OF PROCESS

§ 5.251. Failure to Designate Registered Agent

The secretary of state is an agent of an entity for purposes of service of process, notice, or demand on the entity if:

(1) the entity is a filing entity or a foreign filing entity and:

(A) the entity fails to appoint or does not maintain a registered agent in this state; or

(B) the registered agent of the entity cannot with reasonable diligence be found at the registered office of the entity; or

(2) the entity is a foreign filing entity and:

(A) the entity's registration to do business under this code is revoked; or

(B) the entity transacts business in this state without being registered as required by Chapter 9.

Acts 2003, 78th Leg., ch. 182, § 1, eff. Jan. 1, 2006.

§ 5.252. Service on Secretary of State

(a) Service on the secretary of state under Section 5.251 is effected by:

(1) delivering to the secretary duplicate copies of the process, notice, or demand; and

(2) accompanying the copies with any fee required by law, including this code or the Government Code, for:

(A) maintenance by the secretary of a record of the service; and

(B) forwarding by the secretary of the process, notice, or demand.

(b) Notice on the secretary of state under Subsection (a) is returnable in not less than 30 days.

Acts 2003, 78th Leg., ch. 182, § 1, eff. Jan. 1, 2006.

§ 5.253. Action by Secretary of State

(a) After service in compliance with Section 5.252, the secretary of state shall immediately send one of the copies of the process, notice, or demand to the named entity.

(b) The notice must be:

(1) addressed to the most recent address of the entity on file with the secretary of state; and

(2) sent by certified mail, with return receipt requested.

Acts 2003, 78th Leg., ch. 182, § 1, eff. Jan. 1, 2006.

§ 5.254. Required Records of Secretary of State

The secretary of state shall keep a record of each process, notice, or demand served on the secretary under this subchapter and shall record:

(1) the time when each service on the secretary was made; and

(2) each subsequent action of the secretary taken in relation to that service.

Acts 2003, 78th Leg., ch. 182, § 1, eff. Jan. 1, 2006.

§ 5.255. Agent for Service of Process, Notice, or Demand as Matter of Law

For the purpose of service of process, notice, or demand:

(1) the president and each vice president of a domestic or foreign corporation is an agent of that corporation;

(2) each general partner of a domestic or foreign limited partnership and each partner of a domestic or foreign general partnership is an agent of that partnership;

(3) each manager of a manager-managed domestic or foreign limited liability company and each member of a member-managed domestic or foreign limited liability company is an agent of that limited liability company;

(4) each person who is a governing person of a domestic or foreign entity, other than an entity listed in Subdivisions (1)–(3), is an agent of that entity; and

(5) each member of a committee of a nonprofit corporation authorized to perform the chief executive function of the corporation is an agent of that corporation.

Acts 2003, 78th Leg., ch. 182, § 1, eff. Jan. 1, 2006.

§ 5.256. Other Means of Service Not Precluded

This chapter does not preclude other means of service of process, notice, or demand on a domestic or foreign entity as provided by other law.

Acts 2003, 78th Leg., ch. 182, § 1, eff. Jan. 1, 2006.

§ 5.257. Service of Process by Political Subdivision

(a) A process, notice, or demand required or permitted by law to be served by a political subdivision of this state or by a person, including another political subdivision or an attorney, acting on behalf of a political subdivision in connection with the collection of a delinquent ad valorem tax may be served on a domestic or foreign corporation whose corporate privileges are forfeited under Section 171.251, Tax Code, a domestic or foreign limited liability company whose right to transact business in this state is forfeited under Section 171.2515, Tax Code, or a corporation or limited liability company that is involuntarily terminated under Chapter 11 or whose registration is revoked under Chapter 9 by delivery of the process, notice, or demand to any officer or director of the corporation or manager or member of the limited liability company, as listed in the most recent records of the secretary of state.

(b) If the officers or directors of a corporation or the managers or members of the limited liability company are unknown or cannot be found, service on the corporation or limited liability company may be made in the same manner as service is made on unknown shareholders under law.

(c) Notwithstanding any disability or reinstatement of a corporation or limited liability company, service of process under this section is sufficient for a judgment against the corporation or limited liability company or a judgment in rem against any property to which the corporation or limited liability company holds title.

Acts 2003, 78th Leg., ch. 182, § 1, eff. Jan. 1, 2006. Amended by Acts 2011, 82nd Leg., ch. 7 (S.B. 582), § 1, eff. Sept. 1, 2011.

Section 3 of Acts 2011, 82nd Leg., ch. 7 (S.B. 582) provides:

"Section 5.257, Business Organizations Code, as amended by this Act, and Section 17.091, Civil Practice and Remedies Code, as amended by this Act, apply only to service of process issued on or after the effective date [Sept. 1, 2011] of this Act. Service of process issued before the effective date of this Act is governed by the law as it existed immediately before the effective date of this Act, and that law is continued in effect for that purpose."

CHAPTER 6. MEETINGS AND VOTING FOR DOMESTIC ENTITIES

SUBCHAPTER A. MEETINGS

Section
6.001. Location of Meetings.
6.002. Alternative Forms of Meetings.
6.003. Participation Constitutes Presence.

SUBCHAPTER B. NOTICE OF MEETINGS

6.051. General Notice Requirements.
6.052. Waiver of Notice.
6.053. Exception.

SUBCHAPTER C. RECORD DATES

6.101. Record Date for Purpose Other Than Written Consent to Action.
6.102. Record Date for Written Consent to Action.
6.103. Record Date for Suspended Distributions.

SUBCHAPTER D. VOTING OF OWNERSHIP INTERESTS

6.151. Manner of Voting of Interests.
6.152. Voting of Interests Owned by Entity.
6.153. Voting of Interests Owned by Another Entity.
6.154. Voting of Interests in an Estate or Trust.
6.155. Voting of Interests by Receiver.
6.156. Voting of Pledged Interests.

SUBCHAPTER E. ACTION BY WRITTEN CONSENT

6.201. Unanimous Written Consent to Action.
6.202. Action by Less Than Unanimous Written Consent.
6.203. Delivery of Less Than Unanimous Written Consent.
6.204. Advance Notice Not Required.
6.205 Reproduction or Electronic Transmission of Consent.

SUBCHAPTER F. VOTING TRUSTS AND VOTING AGREEMENTS

Section
6.251. Voting Trusts.
6.252. Voting Agreements.

SUBCHAPTER G. APPLICABILITY OF CHAPTER

6.301. Applicability of Chapter to Partnerships.
6.302. Applicability of Subchapters C and D to Limited Liability Companies.

Acts 2007, 80th Leg., ch. 688, § 29, amended Chapter 6, "Meetings and Voting", to read as now appearing.

SUBCHAPTER A. MEETINGS

§ 6.001. Location of Meetings

(a) Meetings of the owners or members of a domestic entity may be held at locations in or outside the state as:

(1) provided by or fixed in accordance with the governing documents of the domestic entity; or

(2) agreed to by all persons entitled to notice of the meeting.

(b) If the location of meetings of the owners or members of the entity is not established under Subsection (a), the owners or members may hold meetings only at the registered office of the entity in this state or the principal office of the entity.

(c) The governing persons of a domestic entity, or a committee of the governing persons, may hold meetings in or outside the state as:

(1) provided by or fixed in accordance with:

(A) the governing documents of the domestic entity; or

(B) the person calling the meeting; or

(2) agreed to by all persons entitled to notice of the meeting.

Acts 2003, 78th Leg., ch. 182, § 1, eff. Jan. 1, 2006.

§ 6.002. Alternative Forms of Meetings

(a) Subject to this code and the governing documents of a domestic entity, the owners, members, or governing persons of the entity, or a committee of the owners, members, or governing persons, may hold meetings by using a conference telephone or similar communications equipment, or another suitable electronic communications system, including videoconferencing technology or the Internet, or any combination, if the telephone or other equipment or system permits each person participating in the meeting to communicate with all other persons participating in the meeting.

(b) If voting is to take place at the meeting, the entity must:

(1) implement reasonable measures to verify that every person voting at the meeting by means of remote communications is sufficiently identified; and

(2) keep a record of any vote or other action taken.

Acts 2003, 78th Leg., ch. 182, § 1, eff. Jan. 1, 2006.

§ 6.003. Participation Constitutes Presence

A person participating in a meeting is considered present at the meeting, unless the participation is for the express purpose of objecting to the transaction of business at the meeting on the ground that the meeting has not been lawfully called or convened.

Acts 2003, 78th Leg., ch. 182, § 1, eff. Jan. 1, 2006.

SUBCHAPTER B. NOTICE OF MEETINGS

§ 6.051. General Notice Requirements

(a) Subject to this code and the governing documents of the entity, notice of a meeting of the owners, members, or governing persons of a domestic entity, or a committee of the owners, members, or governing persons, must:

(1) be given in the manner determined by the governing authority of the entity; and

(2) state the date and time of the meeting and:

(A) if the meeting is not held solely by using a conference telephone or other communications system authorized by Section 6.002, the location of the meeting; or

(B) if the meeting is held solely or in part by using a conference telephone or other communications system authorized by Section 6.002, the form of communications system to be used for the meeting and the means of accessing the communications system.

(b) Subject to this code and the governing documents of a domestic entity, notice of a meeting that is:

(1) mailed is considered to be given on the date notice is deposited in the United States mail with postage paid in an envelope addressed to the person at the person's address as it appears on the ownership or membership records of the entity; and

(2) transmitted by facsimile or electronic message is considered to be given when the facsimile or electronic message is transmitted to a facsimile number or an electronic message address provided by the person, or to which the person consents, for the purpose of receiving notice.

Acts 2003, 78th Leg., ch. 182, § 1, eff. Jan. 1, 2006. Amended by Acts 2005, 79th Leg., ch. 64, § 16, eff. Jan. 1, 2006; Acts 2007, 80th Leg., ch. 688, § 30, eff. Sept. 1, 2007.

§ 6.052. Waiver of Notice

(a) Notice of a meeting is not required to be given to an owner, member, or governing person of a domestic entity, or a member of a committee of the owners, members, or governing persons, entitled to notice under this code or the governing documents of the entity if the person entitled to notice signs a written waiver of notice of the meeting, regardless of whether the waiver is signed before or after the time of the meeting.

(b) If a person entitled to notice of a meeting participates in or attends the meeting, the person's participation or attendance constitutes a waiver of notice of the meeting unless the person participates in or attends the meeting solely to object to the transaction of business at the meeting on the ground that the meeting was not lawfully called or convened.

(c) Unless required by the certificate of formation or the governing documents, the business to be transacted at a meeting of the owners, members, or governing persons of a domestic entity, or the members of a committee of the governing persons, or the purpose of such a meeting, is not required to be specified in a written waiver of notice of the meeting.

(d) The participation or attendance at a meeting of a person entitled to notice of the meeting constitutes a waiver by the person of notice of a particular matter at the meeting that is not included in the purposes or business of the meeting described in the notice unless the person objects to considering the matter when it is presented.

Acts 2003, 78th Leg., ch. 182, § 1, eff. Jan. 1, 2006. Amended by Acts 2005, 79th Leg., ch. 64, § 17, eff. Jan. 1, 2006; Acts 2009, 81st Leg., ch. 84, § 7, eff. Sept. 1, 2009.

§ 6.053. Exception

(a) Notice of a meeting is not required to be given to an owner or member of a filing entity entitled to notice under this code or the governing documents of the entity if either of the following is mailed to the person entitled to notice of the meeting to the person's address as it appears on the ownership or membership transfer records of the entity and is returned undeliverable:

(1) notice of two consecutive annual meetings and notice of any meeting held during the period between the two annual meetings; or

(2) all, but in no event less than two, payments of distribution or interest on securities during a 12–month period if the payments are sent by first class mail.

(b) Notice of a meeting is not required to be given to an owner or member entitled to notice under this code or the governing documents of a filing entity the notice requirements of which are subject to the Securities Exchange Act of 1934, as amended (15 U.S.C. Section 78a et seq.), if the person entitled to notice of the meeting is considered a lost security holder under that Act and the regulations adopted under that Act.

(c) An action taken or a meeting held without giving notice to a person not entitled to notice under this section has the same force and effect as if notice had been given to the person.

(d) A certificate or other document filed with the filing officer as a result of a meeting held or an action taken by a filing entity without giving notice of the meeting or action to a person not entitled to notice under this section may state that notice of the meeting or action was given to each person entitled to notice.

(e) Notice of a meeting must be given to a person not entitled to notice of the meeting under this section if the person delivers to the filing entity a written notice of the person's address.

Acts 2003, 78th Leg., ch. 182, § 1, eff. Jan. 1, 2006. Amended by Acts 2007, 80th Leg., ch. 688, § 31, eff. Sept. 1, 2007.

SUBCHAPTER C. RECORD DATES

§ 6.101. Record Date for Purpose Other Than Written Consent to Action

(a) Subject to this code, the governing documents of a domestic entity may provide the record date, or the manner of determining the record date, for:

(1) determining the owners or members of the entity entitled to:

(A) receive notice of a meeting of the owners or members;

(B) vote at a meeting of the owners or members or at any adjournment of a meeting; or

(C) receive a distribution from the entity other than a distribution involving a purchase or redemption by the entity of the entity's own securities; or

(2) any other proper purpose other than for determining the owners or members entitled to consent to action without a meeting of the owners or members.

(b) Subject to this code and the governing documents of a domestic entity, the governing authority of the entity, in advance, may provide a record date for determining the owners or members of the entity, except that the date may not be earlier than the 60th day before the date the action requiring the determination of owners or members is originally to be taken.

(c) Subject to this code and the governing documents of a domestic entity, the governing authority of the entity may provide for the closing of the ownership or membership transfer records of the entity for a period of not longer than 60 days to determine the owners or members of the entity for a purpose described by Subsection (a).

(d) If the owners or members of a domestic entity are not otherwise determined under this section, the record date for determining the owners or members of a domestic entity is the date on which:

(1) notice of the meeting is given to the owners or members entitled to notice of the meeting; or

(2) with respect to a distribution, other than a distribution involving a purchase or redemption by the domestic entity of any of its own securities, the governing authority adopts the resolution declaring the distribution.

(e) The record date for a meeting applies to any adjournment of the meeting unless:

(1) the owners or members entitled to vote are determined under Subsection (c); and

(2) the period during which the transfer records are closed expires.

Acts 2003, 78th Leg., ch. 182, § 1, eff. Jan. 1, 2006. Amended by Acts 2007, 80th Leg., ch. 688, § 32, eff. Sept. 1, 2007; Acts 2011, 82nd Leg., ch. 139 (S.B. 748), § 2, eff. Sept. 1, 2011.

§ 6.102. Record Date for Written Consent to Action

(a) Subject to this code and the governing documents of a domestic entity, the governing authority of the domestic entity may provide the record date for determining the owners or members of the domestic entity entitled to written consent to action without a meeting of the owners or members unless a record date is provided under Section 6.101 for that action. The record date may not be earlier than the date the governing authority adopts the resolution providing for the record date.

(b) Subject to this code and the governing documents of a domestic entity, the record date for determining the owners or members of the domestic entity entitled to written consent to action without a meeting of the owners or members is the date a signed written consent to action stating the action taken or proposed to be taken is first delivered to the domestic entity if:

(1) the governing authority of the domestic entity does not provide a record date under Subsection (a); and

(2) prior action by the governing authority is not required under this code.

(c) Subject to this code or the governing documents of a domestic entity, the record date for determining the owners or members of the domestic entity entitled to written consent to action without a meeting of the owners or members is at the close of business on the date the governing authority of the domestic entity adopts a resolution taking prior action if:

(1) the governing authority does not provide a record date under Subsection (a); and

(2) prior action by the governing authority is required by this code.

Acts 2003, 78th Leg., ch. 182, § 1, eff. Jan. 1, 2006. Amended by Acts 2007, 80th Leg., ch. 688, § 33, eff. Sept. 1, 2007.

§ 6.103. Record Date for Suspended Distributions

(a) In this section, "distribution" includes a distribution that:

(1) was payable to an owner or member but not paid and was held in suspension by the entity making the distribution; or

(2) is paid or delivered by the entity making the distribution into an escrow account or to a trustee or custodian.

(b) A distribution made by a domestic entity shall be payable by the entity, or an escrow agent, trustee, or custodian of the distribution, to the owner or member determined on the record date for the distribution as provided by this subchapter.

(c) The right to a distribution under this section may be transferred by contract, by operation of law, or under the laws of descent and distribution.

Acts 2003, 78th Leg., ch. 182, § 1, eff. Jan. 1, 2006.

SUBCHAPTER D. VOTING OF OWNERSHIP INTERESTS

§ 6.151. Manner of Voting of Interests

Subject to the title governing the domestic entity, voting of interests of a domestic entity must be conducted in the manner provided by the governing documents of the entity.

Acts 2003, 78th Leg., ch. 182, § 1, eff. Jan. 1, 2006.

§ 6.152. Voting of Interests Owned by Entity

(a) Except as provided by Subsection (b), an ownership interest owned by the domestic entity that is the issuer of the interest, or by its direct or indirect subsidiary, may not be:

(1) directly or indirectly voted at a meeting; or

(2) included in determining at any time the total number of outstanding ownership interests of the domestic entity.

(b) This section does not preclude a domestic or foreign entity from voting an ownership interest, including an interest in the entity, held or controlled by the entity in a fiduciary capacity or for which the entity otherwise exercises voting power in a fiduciary capacity.

Acts 2003, 78th Leg., ch. 182, § 1, eff. Jan. 1, 2006. Amended by Acts 2007, 80th Leg., ch. 688, § 34, eff. Sept. 1, 2007.

§ 6.153. Voting of Interests Owned by Another Entity

An ownership interest in a domestic entity owned by another entity, whether a domestic or foreign entity, may be voted by the officer, agent, or proxy as authorized by:

(1) the governing documents of the entity that owns the interest; or

(2) the governing authority of the entity that owns the interest, if the governing documents do not provide for the manner of voting.

Acts 2003, 78th Leg., ch. 182, § 1, eff. Jan. 1, 2006. Amended by Acts 2007, 80th Leg., ch. 688, § 35, eff. Sept. 1, 2007.

§ 6.154. Voting of Interests in an Estate or Trust

(a) An administrator, executor, guardian, or conservator of an estate who holds an ownership interest as part of the estate may vote the interest, in person or by proxy, without transferring the interest into the person's name.

(b) An ownership interest in the name of a trust may be voted in person or by proxy by:

(1) the trustee; or

(2) a person authorized to act on behalf of the trust by the trust agreement or the trustee.

Acts 2003, 78th Leg., ch. 182, § 1, eff. Jan. 1, 2006. Amended by Acts 2007, 80th Leg., ch. 688, § 36, eff. Sept. 1, 2007.

§ 6.155. Voting of Interests by Receiver

(a) A receiver may vote an ownership interest standing in the name of the receiver.

(b) A receiver may vote an ownership interest held by or under the control of the receiver without transferring the interest into the receiver's name if the court appointing the receiver authorizes the receiver to vote the interest.

Acts 2003, 78th Leg., ch. 182, § 1, eff. Jan. 1, 2006.

§ 6.156. Voting of Pledged Interests

A pledged ownership interest may be voted by:

(1) the owner of the pledged interest until the interest is transferred into the pledgee's name; and

(2) the pledgee after the pledged interest is transferred into the pledgee's name.

Acts 2003, 78th Leg., ch. 182, § 1, eff. Jan. 1, 2006.

SUBCHAPTER E. ACTION BY WRITTEN CONSENT

§ 6.201. Unanimous Written Consent to Action

(a) This section applies to any action required or authorized to be taken under this code or the governing documents of a filing entity at an annual or special meeting of the owners or members of the entity or at a regular, special, or other meeting of the governing authority of the entity or a committee of the governing authority.

(b) The owners or members or the governing authority of a filing entity, or a committee of the governing authority, may take action without holding a meeting, providing notice, or taking a vote if each person entitled to vote on the action signs a written consent or consents stating the action taken.

(c) A written consent described by Subsection (b) has the same effect as a unanimous vote at a meeting.

(d) A filing instrument filed with the filing officer may state that an action approved by written consent or consents has the effect of an approval by a unanimous vote at a meeting.

Acts 2003, 78th Leg., ch. 182, § 1, eff. Jan. 1, 2006.

§ 6.202. Action by Less Than Unanimous Written Consent

(a) This section applies to any action required or authorized to be taken under this code or the governing documents of a filing entity at an annual or special meeting of the owners or members of the entity.

(b) Except as provided by this code, the certificate of formation of a filing entity may authorize the owners or members of the entity to take action without holding a meeting, providing notice, or taking a vote if owners or members of the entity having at least the minimum number of votes that would be necessary to take the action that is the subject of the consent at a meeting, in which each owner or member entitled to vote on the action is present and votes, sign a written consent or consents stating the action taken.

(c) A written consent or consents described by Subsection (b) must include the date each owner or member signed the consent and is effective to take the action that is the subject of the consent only if the consent or consents are delivered to the entity not later than the 60th day after the date the earliest dated consent is delivered to the entity as required by Section 6.203.

(d) The entity shall promptly notify each owner or member who did not sign a consent described by Subsection (b) of the action that is the subject of the consent.

Acts 2003, 78th Leg., ch. 182, § 1, eff. Jan. 1, 2006.

§ 6.203. Delivery of Less Than Unanimous Written Consent

(a) A written consent signed by an owner or member of a filing entity as provided by Section 6.202, if the consent is not solicited on behalf of the entity or its governing authority, must be delivered by hand or certified or registered mail, return receipt requested, or by other means specified in the governing documents, to:

(1) the entity's registered office or principal executive office or place of business; or

(2) the managerial official or agent of the entity having custody of the entity's records of meetings of owners or members.

(b) A consent delivered to an entity's principal executive office or place of business under Subsection (a)(1) must be addressed to the chief managerial official of the entity or, if the entity does not have a chief managerial official, the governing authority of the entity.

Acts 2003, 78th Leg., ch. 182, § 1, eff. Jan. 1, 2006.

§ 6.204. Advance Notice Not Required

Any advance notice required by this code for an action to be taken at a meeting is not required to be given to take the action by written consent as provided by this subchapter.

Acts 2003, 78th Leg., ch. 182, § 1, eff. Jan. 1, 2006. Amended by Acts 2007, 80th Leg., ch. 688, § 37, eff. Sept. 1, 2007.

§ 6.205 Reproduction or Electronic Transmission of Consent

(a) Any photographic, photostatic, facsimile, or similarly reliable reproduction of a consent in writing signed by an owner, member, or governing person of a filing entity may be substituted or used instead of the original writing for any purpose for which the original writing could be used.

(b) Except as otherwise provided by an entity's governing documents, an electronic transmission of a consent by an owner, member, or governing person to the taking of an action by the entity is considered a signed writing if the transmission contains or is accompanied by information from which it can be determined:

(1) that the electronic transmission was transmitted by the owner, member, or governing person; and

(2) the date on which the owner, member, or governing person transmitted the electronic transmission.

(c) Unless the consent is otherwise dated, the date specified in Subsection (b)(2) is the date on which the consent is considered signed.

Added by Acts 2005, 79th Leg., ch. 64, § 18, eff. Jan. 1, 2006. Amended by Acts 2009, 81st Leg., ch. 84, § 8, eff. Sept. 1, 2009; Acts 2011, 82nd Leg., ch. 139 (S.B. 748), § 3, eff. Sept. 1, 2011.

SUBCHAPTER F. VOTING TRUSTS AND VOTING AGREEMENTS

§ 6.251. Voting Trusts

(a) Except as provided by this code or the governing documents, any number of owners of a domestic entity may enter into a written voting trust agreement to confer on a trustee the right to vote or otherwise represent ownership or membership interests of the domestic entity.

(b) An ownership or membership interest that is the subject of a voting trust agreement described by Subsection (a) shall be transferred to the trustee named in the agreement for purposes of the agreement.

(c) A copy of a voting trust agreement described by Subsection (a) shall be deposited with the domestic entity at the domestic entity's principal executive office or registered office and is subject to examination by:

(1) an owner, whether in person or by the owner's agent or attorney, in the same manner as the owner is entitled to examine the books and records of the domestic entity; and

(2) a holder of a beneficial interest in the voting trust, whether in person or by the holder's agent or attorney, at any reasonable time for any proper purpose.

Acts 2003, 78th Leg., ch. 182, § 1, eff. Jan. 1, 2006. Amended by Acts 2007, 80th Leg., ch. 688, § 38, eff. Sept. 1, 2007.

§ 6.252. Voting Agreements

(a) Except as provided by this code or the governing documents, any number of owners of a domestic entity, or any number of owners of the domestic entity and the domestic entity itself, may enter into a written voting agreement to provide the manner of voting of the ownership interests of the domestic entity. A voting agreement entered into under this subsection is not part of the governing documents of the domestic entity.

(b) A copy of a voting agreement entered into under Subsection (a):

(1) shall be deposited with the domestic entity at the domestic entity's principal executive office or registered office; and

(2) is subject to examination by an owner, whether in person or by the owner's agent or attorney, in the same manner as the owner is entitled to examine the books and records of the domestic entity.

(c) A voting agreement entered into under Subsection (a) is specifically enforceable against the holder of an ownership interest that is the subject of the agreement, and any successor or transferee of the holder, if:

(1) the voting agreement is noted conspicuously on the certificate representing the ownership interests; or

(2) a notation of the voting agreement is contained in a notice sent by or on behalf of the

domestic entity in accordance with Section 3.205, if the ownership interest is not represented by a certificate.

(d) Except as provided by Subsection (e), a voting agreement entered into under Subsection (a) is specifically enforceable against any person, other than a transferee for value, after the time the person acquires actual knowledge of the existence of the agreement.

(e) An otherwise enforceable voting agreement entered into under Subsection (a) is not enforceable against a transferee for value without actual knowledge of the existence of the agreement at the time of the transfer, or any subsequent transferee, without regard to value, if the voting agreement is not noted as required by Subsection (c).

(f) Section 6.251 does not apply to a voting agreement entered into under Subsection (a).

Acts 2003, 78th Leg., ch. 182, § 1, eff. Jan. 1, 2006. Amended by Acts 2007, 80th Leg., ch. 688, § 39, eff. Sept. 1, 2007.

SUBCHAPTER G. APPLICABILITY OF CHAPTER

Acts 2005, 79th Leg., ch. 64, § 19 amended the Subchapter G heading.

§ 6.301. Applicability of Chapter to Partnerships

This chapter does not apply to a general partnership or a limited partnership except to the extent its governing documents specify.

Acts 2003, 78th Leg., ch. 182, § 1, eff. Jan. 1, 2006.

§ 6.302. Applicability of Subchapters C and D to Limited Liability Companies

Subchapters C and D do not apply to a limited liability company except to the extent its governing documents specify.

Acts 2003, 78th Leg., ch. 182, § 1, eff. Jan. 1, 2006.

CHAPTER 7. LIABILITY

Section
7.001. Limitation of Liability of Governing Person.

§ 7.001. Limitation of Liability of Governing Person

(a) Subsections (b) and (c) apply to:

(1) a domestic entity other than a partnership or limited liability company;

(2) another organization incorporated or organized under another law of this state; and

(3) to the extent permitted by federal law, a federally chartered bank, savings and loan association, or credit union.

(b) The certificate of formation or similar instrument of an organization to which this section applies may provide that a governing person of the organization is not liable, or is liable only to the extent provided by the certificate of formation or similar instrument, to the organization or its owners or members for monetary damages for an act or omission by the person in the person's capacity as a governing person.

(c) Subsection (b) does not authorize the elimination or limitation of the liability of a governing person to the extent the person is found liable under applicable law for:

(1) a breach of the person's duty of loyalty, if any, to the organization or its owners or members;

(2) an act or omission not in good faith that:

(A) constitutes a breach of duty of the person to the organization; or

(B) involves intentional misconduct or a knowing violation of law;

(3) a transaction from which the person received an improper benefit, regardless of whether the benefit resulted from an action taken within the scope of the person's duties; or

(4) an act or omission for which the liability of a governing person is expressly provided by an applicable statute.

(d) The liability of a governing person may be limited or restricted:

(1) in a general partnership to the extent permitted under Chapter 152;

(2) in a limited partnership to the extent permitted under Chapter 153 and, to the extent applicable to limited partnerships, Chapter 152; and

(3) in a limited liability company to the extent permitted under Section 101.401.

Acts 2003, 78th Leg., ch. 182, § 1, eff. Jan. 1, 2006.

CHAPTER 8. INDEMNIFICATION AND INSURANCE

SUBCHAPTER A. GENERAL PROVISIONS

Section
8.001. Definitions.

Section
8.002. Application of Chapter.
8.003. Limitations in Governing Documents.
8.004. Limitations in Chapter.

SUBCHAPTER B. MANDATORY AND COURT–ORDERED INDEMNIFICATION
8.051. Mandatory Indemnification.
8.052. Court–Ordered Indemnification.

SUBCHAPTER C. PERMISSIVE INDEMNIFICATION AND ADVANCEMENT OF EXPENSES
8.101. Permissive Indemnification.
8.102. General Scope of Permissive Indemnification.
8.103. Manner for Determining Permissive Indemnification.
8.104. Advancement of Expenses to Present Governing Persons or Delegates.
8.105. Indemnification of and Advancement of Expenses to Persons Other Than Governing Persons.
8.106. Permissive Indemnification of and Reimbursement of Expenses to Witnesses.

SUBCHAPTER D. LIABILITY INSURANCE; REPORTING REQUIREMENTS
8.151. Insurance and Other Arrangements.
8.152. Reports of Indemnification and Advances.

SUBCHAPTER A. GENERAL PROVISIONS

§ 8.001. Definitions

In this chapter:

(1) "Delegate" means a person who, while serving as a governing person of an enterprise, is or was serving at the request of that enterprise as a representative of another enterprise, another organization, or an employee benefit plan. A person is a delegate to an employee benefit plan if the performance of the person's official duties to the enterprise also imposes duties on or otherwise involves service by the person to the plan or participants in or beneficiaries of the plan.

(2) "Enterprise" means a domestic entity or an organization subject to this chapter. The term includes a predecessor enterprise .

(3) "Expenses" includes:

(A) court costs, a judgment, a penalty, a settlement, a fine, and an excise or similar tax, including an excise tax assessed against the person with respect to an employee benefit plan; and

(B) reasonable attorney's fees.

(4) "Former governing person" means a person who was a governing person of an enterprise.

(5) "Judgment" includes an arbitration award.

(6) "Official capacity" means:

(A) with respect to a governing person, the office of the governing person in the enterprise or the exercise of authority by or on behalf of the governing person under this code or the governing documents of the enterprise; and

(B) with respect to a person other than a governing person, the elective or appointive office, if any, in the enterprise held by the person or the relationship undertaken by the person on behalf of the enterprise.

(7) "Predecessor enterprise" means a sole proprietorship or organization that is a predecessor to an enterprise in:

(A) a merger, conversion, consolidation, or other transaction in which the liabilities of the predecessor enterprise are transferred or allocated to the enterprise by operation of law; or

(B) any other transaction in which the enterprise assumes the liabilities of the predecessor enterprise and the liabilities that are the subject matter of this chapter are not specifically excluded.

(8) "Proceeding" means:

(A) a threatened, pending, or completed action or other proceeding, whether civil, criminal, administrative, arbitrative, or investigative;

(B) an appeal of an action or proceeding described by Paragraph (A); and

(C) an inquiry or investigation that could lead to an action or proceeding described by Paragraph (A).

(9) "Representative" means a person who is:

(A) serving as a partner, director, officer, venturer, proprietor, trustee, employee, administrator, or agent of an enterprise or other organization or of an employee benefit plan; or

(B) serving a similar function for an enterprise or other organization or for an employee benefit plan.

(10) "Respondent" means a person named as a respondent or defendant in a proceeding.

Acts 2003, 78th Leg., ch. 182, § 1, eff. Jan. 1, 2006. Amended by Acts 2005, 79th Leg., ch. 64, § 20, eff. Jan. 1, 2006; Acts 2011, 82nd Leg., ch. 139 (S.B. 748), § 4, eff. Sept. 1, 2011.

§ 8.002. Application of Chapter

(a) Except as provided by Subsection (b), this chapter does not apply to a:

(1) general partnership; or

(2) limited liability company.

(b) The governing documents of a general partnership or limited liability company may adopt provisions of this chapter or may contain other provisions, which will be enforceable, relating to:

(1) indemnification;

(2) advancement of expenses; or

(3) insurance or another arrangement to indemnify or hold harmless a governing person.

Acts 2003, 78th Leg., ch. 182, § 1, eff. Jan. 1, 2006. Amended by Acts 2007, 80th Leg., ch. 688, § 40, eff. Sept. 1, 2007.

§ 8.003. Limitations in Governing Documents

(a) The certificate of formation of an enterprise may restrict the circumstances under which the enterprise must or may indemnify or may advance expenses to a person under this chapter.

(b) The written partnership agreement of a limited partnership may restrict the circumstances in the same manner as the certificate of formation under Subsection (a).

Acts 2003, 78th Leg., ch. 182, § 1, eff. Jan. 1, 2006.

§ 8.004. Limitations in Chapter

Except as provided in Section 8.151, a provision for an enterprise to indemnify or advance expenses to a governing person is valid only to the extent it is consistent with this chapter.

Acts 2003, 78th Leg., ch. 182, § 1, eff. Jan. 1, 2006.

SUBCHAPTER B. MANDATORY AND COURT-ORDERED INDEMNIFICATION

§ 8.051. Mandatory Indemnification

(a) An enterprise shall indemnify a governing person, former governing person, or delegate against reasonable expenses actually incurred by the person in connection with a proceeding in which the person is a respondent because the person is or was a governing person or delegate if the person is wholly successful, on the merits or otherwise, in the defense of the proceeding.

(b) A court that determines, in a suit for indemnification, that a governing person, former governing person, or delegate is entitled to indemnification under this section shall order indemnification and award to the person the expenses incurred in securing the indemnification.

Acts 2003, 78th Leg., ch. 182, § 1, eff. Jan. 1, 2006. Amended by Acts 2005, 79th Leg., ch. 64, § 21, eff. Jan. 1, 2006.

§ 8.052. Court–Ordered Indemnification

(a) On application of a governing person, former governing person, or delegate and after notice is provided as required by the court, a court may order an enterprise to indemnify the person to the extent the court determines that the person is fairly and reasonably entitled to indemnification in view of all the relevant circumstances.

(b) This section applies without regard to whether the governing person, former governing person, or delegate applying to the court satisfies the requirements of Section 8.101 or has been found liable:

(1) to the enterprise; or

(2) because the person improperly received a personal benefit, without regard to whether the benefit resulted from an action taken in the person's official capacity.

(c) The indemnification ordered by the court under this section is limited to reasonable expenses if the governing person, former governing person, or delegate is found liable:

(1) to the enterprise; or

(2) because the person improperly received a personal benefit, without regard to whether the benefit resulted from an action taken in the person's official capacity.

Acts 2003, 78th Leg., ch. 182, § 1, eff. Jan. 1, 2006.

SUBCHAPTER C. PERMISSIVE INDEMNIFICATION AND ADVANCEMENT OF EXPENSES

§ 8.101. Permissive Indemnification

(a) An enterprise may indemnify a governing person, former governing person, or delegate who was, is, or is threatened to be made a respondent in a proceeding to the extent permitted by Section 8.102 if it is determined in accordance with Section 8.103 that:

(1) the person:

(A) acted in good faith;

(B) reasonably believed:

(i) in the case of conduct in the person's official capacity, that the person's conduct was in the enterprise's best interests; and

(ii) in any other case, that the person's conduct was not opposed to the enterprise's best interests; and

(C) in the case of a criminal proceeding, did not have a reasonable cause to believe the person's conduct was unlawful;

(2) with respect to expenses, the amount of expenses other than a judgment is reasonable; and

(3) indemnification should be paid.

(b) Action taken or omitted by a governing person or delegate with respect to an employee benefit plan in the performance of the person's duties for a purpose reasonably believed by the person to be in the interest of the participants and beneficiaries of the plan is for a purpose that is not opposed to the best interests of the enterprise.

(c) Action taken or omitted by a delegate to another enterprise for a purpose reasonably believed by the delegate to be in the interest of the other enterprise or its owners or members is for a purpose that is not opposed to the best interests of the enterprise.

(d) A person does not fail to meet the standard under Subsection (a)(1) solely because of the termination of a proceeding by:

(1) judgment;

(2) order;

(3) settlement;

(4) conviction; or

(5) a plea of nolo contendere or its equivalent.

Acts 2003, 78th Leg., ch. 182, § 1, eff. Jan. 1, 2006.

§ 8.102. General Scope of Permissive Indemnification

(a) Subject to Subsection (b), an enterprise may indemnify a governing person, former governing person, or delegate against:

(1) a judgment; and

(2) expenses, other than a judgment, that are reasonable and actually incurred by the person in connection with a proceeding.

(b) Indemnification under this subchapter of a person who is found liable to the enterprise or is found liable because the person improperly received a personal benefit:

(1) is limited to reasonable expenses actually incurred by the person in connection with the proceeding;

(2) does not include a judgment, a penalty, a fine, and an excise or similar tax, including an excise tax assessed against the person with respect to an employee benefit plan; and

(3) may not be made in relation to a proceeding in which the person has been found liable for:

(A) wilful or intentional misconduct in the performance of the person's duty to the enterprise;

(B) breach of the person's duty of loyalty owed to the enterprise; or

(C) an act or omission not committed in good faith that constitutes a breach of a duty owed by the person to the enterprise.

(c) A governing person, former governing person, or delegate is considered to have been found liable in relation to a claim, issue, or matter only if the liability is established by an order, including a judgment or decree of a court, and all appeals of the order are exhausted or foreclosed by law.

Acts 2003, 78th Leg., ch. 182, § 1, eff. Jan. 1, 2006.

§ 8.103. Manner for Determining Permissive Indemnification

(a) Except as provided by Subsections (b) and (c), the determinations required under Section 8.101(a) must be made by:

(1) a majority vote of the governing persons who at the time of the vote are disinterested and independent, regardless of whether the governing persons who are disinterested and independent constitute a quorum;

(2) a majority vote of a committee of the governing authority of the enterprise if the committee:

(A) is designated by a majority vote of the governing persons who at the time of the vote are disinterested and independent, regardless of whether the governing persons who are disinterested and independent constitute a quorum; and

(B) is composed solely of one or more governing persons who are disinterested and independent;

(3) special legal counsel selected by the governing authority of the enterprise, or selected by a committee of the governing authority, by vote in accordance with Subdivision (1) or (2);

(4) the owners or members of the enterprise in a vote that excludes the ownership or membership interests held by each governing person who is not disinterested and independent; or

(5) a unanimous vote of the owners or members of the enterprise.

(b) If special legal counsel determines under Subsection (a)(3) that a person meets the standard under Section 8.101(a)(1), the special legal counsel shall determine whether the amount of expenses other than a judgment is reasonable under Section 8.101(a)(2) but may not determine whether indemnification should be paid under Section 8.101(a)(3). The determination whether indemnification should be paid must be made in a manner specified by Subsection (a)(1), (2), (4), or (5).

(c) A provision contained in the governing documents of the enterprise, a resolution of the owners, members, or governing authority, or an agreement that requires the indemnification of a person who meets the standard under Section 8.101(a)(1) constitutes a determination under Section 8.101(a)(3) that indemnification should be paid even though the provision may not have been adopted or authorized in the same manner as the determinations required under Section 8.101(a). The determinations required under Sections 8.101(a)(1) and (2) must be made in a manner provided by Subsection (a).

(d) With respect to a limited partnership, a vote of a majority-in-interest of the limited partners in a vote that excludes the interest held by each general partner who is not disinterested and independent constitutes a determination under Subsection (a)(4). For purposes of this subsection, "majority-in-interest" means, with respect to limited partners, limited partners who own more than 50 percent of the current percentage or other interest in the profits of the partnership that is owned by all of the limited partners.

Acts 2003, 78th Leg., ch. 182, § 1, eff. Jan. 1, 2006. Amended by Acts 2005, 79th Leg., ch. 64, § 22, eff. Jan. 1, 2006; Acts 2007, 80th Leg., ch. 688, § 41, eff. Sept. 1, 2007; Acts 2011, 82nd Leg., ch. 139 (S.B. 748), § 5, eff. Sept. 1, 2011.

§ 8.104. Advancement of Expenses to Present Governing Persons or Delegates

(a) An enterprise may pay or reimburse reasonable expenses incurred by a present governing person or delegate who was, is, or is threatened to be made a respondent in a proceeding in advance of the final disposition of the proceeding without making the determinations required under Section 8.101(a) after the enterprise receives:

(1) a written affirmation by the person of the person's good faith belief that the person has met the standard of conduct necessary for indemnification under this chapter; and

(2) a written undertaking by or on behalf of the person to repay the amount paid or reimbursed if the final determination is that the person has not met that standard or that indemnification is prohibited by Section 8.102.

(b) A provision in the governing documents of the enterprise, a resolution of the owners, members, or governing authority, or an agreement that requires the payment or reimbursement permitted under this section authorizes that payment or reimbursement after the enterprise receives an affirmation and undertaking described by Subsection (a).

(c) The written undertaking required by Subsection (a)(2) must be an unlimited general obligation of the person but need not be secured and may be accepted by the enterprise without regard to the person's ability to make repayment.

(d) With respect to a limited partnership, a vote of a majority-in-interest of the limited partners in a vote that excludes the interest held by each general partner who is not disinterested and independent constitutes an authorization under Subsection (b). For purposes of this subsection, "majority-in-interest" means, with respect to limited partners, limited partners who own more than 50 percent of the current percentage or other interest in the profits of the partnership that is owned by all of the limited partners.

Acts 2003, 78th Leg., ch. 182, § 1, eff. Jan. 1, 2006. Amended by Acts 2005, 79th Leg., ch. 64, §§ 23, 24, eff. Jan. 1, 2006; Acts 2007, 80th Leg., ch. 688, § 42, eff. Sept. 1, 2007; Acts 2011, 82nd Leg., ch. 139 (S.B. 748), § 6, eff. Sept. 1, 2011.

§ 8.105. Indemnification of and Advancement of Expenses to Persons Other Than Governing Persons

(a) Notwithstanding any other provision of this chapter but subject to Section 8.003 and to the extent consistent with other law, an enterprise may indemnify and advance expenses to a person who is not a governing person, including an officer, employee, or agent, as provided by:

(1) the enterprise's governing documents;

(2) general or specific action of the enterprise's governing authority;

(3) resolution of the enterprise's owners or members;

(4) contract; or

(5) common law.

(b) An enterprise shall indemnify an officer to the same extent that indemnification is required under this chapter for a governing person.

(c) A person described by Subsection (a) may seek indemnification or advancement of expenses from an enterprise to the same extent that a governing person may seek indemnification or advancement of expenses under this chapter.

(d) Notwithstanding any authorization or determination specified in this chapter, an enterprise may pay or reimburse, in advance of the final disposition of a proceeding and on terms the enterprise considers appropriate, reasonable expenses incurred by:

(1) a former governing person or delegate who was, is, or is threatened to be made a respondent in the proceeding; or

(2) a present or former employee, agent, or officer who is not a governing person of the enterprise and who was, is, or is threatened to be made a respondent in the proceeding.

(e) A determination of indemnification for a person who is not a governing person of an enterprise, including an officer, employee, or agent, is not required to be made in accordance with Section 8.103.

Acts 2003, 78th Leg., ch. 182, § 1, eff. Jan. 1, 2006. Amended by Acts 2005, 79th Leg., ch. 64, § 25, eff. Jan. 1, 2006; Acts 2007, 80th Leg., ch. 688, § 43, eff. Sept. 1, 2007; Acts 2011, 82nd Leg., ch. 139 (S.B. 748), § 7, eff. Sept. 1, 2011.

§ 8.106. Permissive Indemnification of and Reimbursement of Expenses to Witnesses

Notwithstanding any other provision of this chapter, an enterprise may pay or reimburse reasonable expenses incurred by a governing person, officer, employee, agent, delegate, or other person in connection with that person's appearance as a witness or other participation in a proceeding at a time when the person is not a respondent in the proceeding.

Acts 2003, 78th Leg., ch. 182, § 1, eff. Jan. 1, 2006.

SUBCHAPTER D. LIABILITY INSURANCE; REPORTING REQUIREMENTS

§ 8.151. Insurance and Other Arrangements

(a) Notwithstanding any other provision of this chapter, an enterprise may purchase or procure or establish and maintain insurance or another arrangement to indemnify or hold harmless an existing or former governing person, delegate, officer, employee, or agent against any liability:

(1) asserted against and incurred by the person in that capacity; or

(2) arising out of the person's status in that capacity.

(b) The insurance or other arrangement established under Subsection (a) may insure or indemnify against the liability described by Subsection (a) without regard to whether the enterprise otherwise would have had the power to indemnify the person against that liability under this chapter.

(c) Insurance or another arrangement that involves self-insurance or an agreement to indemnify made with the enterprise or a person that is not regularly engaged in the business of providing insurance coverage may provide for payment of a liability with respect to which the enterprise does not otherwise have the power to provide indemnification only if the insurance or arrangement is approved by the owners or members of the enterprise.

(c–1) With respect to a limited partnership, a vote of a majority-in-interest of the limited partners constitutes approval of the owners for purposes of Subsection (c).

(d) For the benefit of persons to be indemnified by the enterprise, an enterprise may, in addition to purchasing or procuring or establishing and maintaining insurance or another arrangement:

(1) create a trust fund;

(2) establish any form of self-insurance, including a contract to indemnify;

(3) secure the enterprise's indemnity obligation by grant of a security interest or other lien on the assets of the enterprise; or

(4) establish a letter of credit, guaranty, or surety arrangement.

(e) Insurance or another arrangement established under this section may be purchased or procured or established and maintained:

(1) within the enterprise; or

(2) with any insurer or other person considered appropriate by the governing authority, regardless of whether all or part of the stock, securities, or other ownership interest in the insurer or other person is owned in whole or in part by the enterprise.

(f) The governing authority's decision as to the terms of the insurance or other arrangement and the selection of the insurer or other person participating in an arrangement is conclusive. The insurance or arrangement is not voidable and does not subject the governing persons approving the insurance or arrangement to liability, on any ground, regardless of whether the governing persons participating in approving the insurance or other arrangement are beneficiaries of the insurance or arrangement. This subsection does not apply in case of actual fraud.

Acts 2003, 78th Leg., ch. 182, § 1, eff. Jan. 1, 2006. Amended by Acts 2011, 82nd Leg., ch. 139 (S.B. 748), § 8, eff. Sept. 1, 2011.

§ 8.152. Reports of Indemnification and Advances

(a) An enterprise shall report in writing to the owners or members of the enterprise an indemnification of or advance of expenses to a governing person.

(b) Subject to Subsection (c), the report must be made with or before:

(1) the notice or waiver of notice of the next meeting of the owners or members of the enterprise; or

(2) the next submission to the owners or members of a consent to action without a meeting.

(c) The report must be made not later than the first anniversary of the date of the indemnification or advance.

Acts 2003, 78th Leg., ch. 182, § 1, eff. Jan. 1, 2006. Amended by Acts 2007, 80th Leg., ch. 688, § 44, eff. Sept. 1, 2007.

CHAPTER 9. FOREIGN ENTITIES

SUBCHAPTER A. REGISTRATION

Section
9.001. Foreign Entities Required to Register.
9.002. Foreign Entities Not Required to Register.
9.003. Permissive Registration.
9.004. Registration Procedure.
9.005 Supplemental Information Required in Application for Registration of Foreign Limited Liability Company.
9.006. Supplemental Information Required in Application for Registration of Foreign Nonprofit Corporation.
9.007. Application for Registration of Foreign Limited Liability Partnership.
9.008. Effect of Registration.
9.009. Amendments to Registration.
9.010. Name Change of Foreign Filing Entity.
9.011. Voluntary Withdrawal of Registration.
9.012 Automatic Withdrawal on Conversion to Domestic Filing Entity.

SUBCHAPTER B. FAILURE TO REGISTER

9.051. Transacting Business or Maintaining Court Proceeding Without Registration.
9.052. Civil Penalty.
9.053. Venue.
9.054. Late Filing Fee.
9.055. Requirements of Other Law.

SUBCHAPTER C. REVOCATION OF REGISTRATION BY SECRETARY OF STATE

9.101. Revocation of Registration by Secretary of State.

Section
9.102. Certificate of Revocation.
9.103. Reinstatement by Secretary of State After Revocation.
9.104. Procedures for Reinstatement.
9.105. Use of Name Similar to Previously Registered Name.
9.106. Reinstatement of Registration Following Tax Forfeiture.

SUBCHAPTER D. JUDICIAL REVOCATION OF REGISTRATION

9.151. Revocation of Registration by Court Action.
9.152. Notification of Cause by Secretary of State.
9.153. Filing of Action by Attorney General.
9.154. Cure Before Final Judgment.
9.155. Judgment Requiring Revocation.
9.156. Stay of Judgment.
9.157. Opportunity for Cure After Affirmation of Findings by Appeals Court.
9.158. Jurisdiction and Venue.
9.159. Process in State Action.
9.160. Publication of Notice.
9.161. Filing of Decree of Revocation Against Foreign Filing Entity.
9.162. Applicability of Subchapter to Foreign Limited Liability Partnerships.

SUBCHAPTER E. BUSINESS, RIGHTS, AND OBLIGATIONS

9.201. Business of Foreign Entity.
9.202. Rights and Privileges.
9.203. Obligations and Liabilities.
9.204. Right of Foreign Entity to Participate in Business of Certain Domestic Entities.

SUBCHAPTER F. DETERMINATION OF TRANSACTING BUSINESS IN THIS STATE

9.251 Activities Not Constituting Transacting Business in This State.
9.252. Other Activities.

SUBCHAPTER G. MISCELLANEOUS PROVISIONS

9.301. Applicability of Code to Certain Foreign Entities.

SUBCHAPTER A. REGISTRATION

§ 9.001. Foreign Entities Required to Register

(a) To transact business in this state, a foreign entity must register under this chapter if the entity:

(1) is a foreign corporation, foreign limited partnership, foreign limited liability company, foreign business trust, foreign real estate investment trust, foreign cooperative, foreign public or private limited company, or another foreign entity, the formation of which, if formed in this state, would require the filing under Chapter 3 of a certificate of formation; or

(2) affords limited liability under the law of its jurisdiction of formation for any owner or member.

(b) A foreign entity described by Subsection (a) must maintain the entity's registration while transacting business in this state.

Acts 2003, 78th Leg., ch. 182, § 1, eff. Jan. 1, 2006.

§ 9.002. Foreign Entities Not Required to Register

(a) A foreign entity not described by Section 9.001(a) may transact business in this state without registering under this chapter.

(b) Subsection (a) does not relieve a foreign entity from the duty to comply with applicable requirements under other law to file or register.

(c) A foreign entity is not required to register under this chapter if other state law authorizes the entity to transact business in this state.

(d) A foreign unincorporated nonprofit association is not required to register under this chapter.

Acts 2003, 78th Leg., ch. 182, § 1, eff. Jan. 1, 2006.

§ 9.003. Permissive Registration

A foreign entity that is eligible under other law of this state to register to transact business in this state, but that is not registered under that law, may register under this chapter unless that registration is prohibited by the other law. The registration under this chapter confers only the authority provided by this chapter.

Acts 2003, 78th Leg., ch. 182, § 1, eff. Jan. 1, 2006.

§ 9.004. Registration Procedure

(a) A foreign filing entity registers by filing an application for registration as provided by Chapter 4.

(b) The application must state:

(1) the entity's name and, if that name would not comply with Chapter 5, a name that complies with Chapter 5 under which the entity will transact business in this state;

(2) the entity's type;

(3) the entity's jurisdiction of formation;

(4) the date of the entity's formation;

(5) that the entity exists as a valid foreign filing entity of the stated type under the laws of the entity's jurisdiction of formation;

(6) for a foreign entity other than a foreign limited partnership:

(A) each business or activity that the entity proposes to pursue in this state, which may be stated to be any lawful business or activity under the law of this state; and

(B) that the entity is authorized to pursue the same business or activity under the laws of the entity's jurisdiction of formation;

(7) the date the foreign entity began or will begin to transact business in this state;

(8) the address of the principal office of the foreign filing entity;

(9) the address of the initial registered office and the name and the address of the initial registered agent for service of process that Chapter 5 requires to be maintained;

(10) the name and address of each of the entity's governing persons; and

(11) that the secretary of state is appointed the agent of the foreign filing entity for service of process under the circumstances provided by Section 5.251.

(c) A foreign filing entity may register regardless of any differences between the law of the entity's jurisdiction of formation and of this state applicable to the governing of the internal affairs or to the liability of an owner, member, or managerial official.

Acts 2003, 78th Leg., ch. 182, § 1, eff. Jan. 1, 2006.

§ 9.005 Supplemental Information Required in Application for Registration of Foreign Limited Liability Company

(a) This section applies only to a foreign limited liability company governed by a company agreement that establishes or provides for the establishment of a designated series of members, managers, membership interests, or assets that has any of the characteristics described by Subsection (b).

(b) A foreign limited liability company must state in its application for registration as a foreign limited liability company whether:

(1) the series has:

(A) separate rights, powers, or duties with respect to specified property or obligations of the foreign limited liability company; or

(B) separate profits and losses associated with specified property or obligations of the foreign limited liability company;

(2) any debts, liabilities, obligations, and expenses incurred, contracted for, or otherwise existing with respect to a particular series shall be enforceable

against the assets of that series only, and not against the assets of the company generally or the assets of any other series; and

(3) any debts, liabilities, obligations, and expenses incurred, contracted for, or otherwise existing with respect to the company generally or any other series shall be enforceable against the assets of that series.

Added by Acts 2009, 81st Leg., ch. 84, § 9, eff. Sept. 1, 2009.

§ 9.006. Supplemental Information Required in Application for Registration of Foreign Nonprofit Corporation

In addition to the information required by Section 9.004, a foreign nonprofit corporation's application for registration must state:

(1) the names and addresses of the nonprofit corporation's directors and officers;

(2) whether or not the nonprofit corporation has members; and

(3) any additional information as necessary or appropriate to enable the secretary of state to determine whether the nonprofit corporation is entitled to register to conduct affairs in this state.

Acts 2003, 78th Leg., ch. 182, § 1, eff. Jan. 1, 2006.

§ 9.007. Application for Registration of Foreign Limited Liability Partnership

(a) A foreign limited liability partnership registers by filing an application for registration under this section as provided by Chapter 4.

(b) The application for registration must state:

(1) the partnership's name;

(2) the federal taxpayer identification number of the partnership;

(3) the partnership's jurisdiction of formation;

(4) the date of initial registration as a limited liability partnership under the laws of the jurisdiction of formation;

(5) the date the foreign entity began or will begin to transact business in this state;

(6) that the partnership exists as a valid limited liability partnership under the laws of the jurisdiction of its formation;

(7) the number of partners at the date of the statement;

(8) each business or activity that the partnership proposes to pursue in this state, which may be stated to be any lawful business or activity under the laws of this state;

(9) the address of the principal office of the partnership;

(10) the address of the initial registered office and the name and address of the initial registered agent for service of process required to be maintained under Section 152.904; and

(11) that the secretary of state is appointed the agent of the partnership for service of process under the same circumstances as set forth by Section 5.251 for a foreign filing entity.

(c) Subchapter K, Chapter 152, governs the registration of a foreign limited liability partnership to transact business in this state.

Acts 2003, 78th Leg., ch. 182, § 1, eff. Jan. 1, 2006. Amended by Acts 2005, 79th Leg., ch. 64, § 26, eff. Jan. 1, 2006; Acts 2011, 82nd Leg., ch. 139 (S.B. 748), § 9, eff. Sept. 1, 2011.

§ 9.008. Effect of Registration

(a) The registration of a foreign entity other than a foreign limited liability partnership is effective when the application filed under Chapter 4 takes effect. The registration remains in effect until the registration terminates, is withdrawn, or is revoked.

(b) Except in a proceeding to revoke the registration, the secretary of state's issuance of an acknowledgment that the entity has filed an application is conclusive evidence of the authority of the foreign filing entity to transact business in this state under the entity's name or under another name stated in the application, in accordance with Section 9.004(b)(1).

(c) Subchapter K, Chapter 152, governs the effect of registration of a foreign limited liability partnership to transact business in this state.

Acts 2003, 78th Leg., ch. 182, § 1, eff. Jan. 1, 2006. Amended by Acts 2005, 79th Leg., ch. 64, § 27, eff. Jan. 1, 2006.

§ 9.009. Amendments to Registration

(a) A foreign filing entity must amend its registration to reflect:

(1) a change to its name;

(2) a change in the business or activity stated in its application for registration; and

(3) if the foreign filing entity is a limited partnership:

(A) the admission of a new general partner;

(B) the withdrawal of a general partner; and

(C) a change in the name of the general partner stated in its application for registration.

(a–1) A foreign filing entity may amend the entity's application for registration to disclose a change that results from:

(1) a conversion from one type of foreign filing entity to another type of foreign filing entity with the foreign filing entity making the amendment succeeding to the registration of the original foreign filing entity; or

(2) a merger into another foreign filing entity with the foreign filing entity making the amendment succeeding to the registration of the original foreign filing entity.

(b) A foreign filing entity may amend its application for registration by filing an application for amendment of registration in the manner required by Chapter 4.

(c) The application for amendment must be filed on or before the 91st day following the date of the change.

Acts 2003, 78th Leg., ch. 182, § 1, eff. Jan. 1, 2006. Amended by Acts 2005, 79th Leg., ch. 64, § 28, eff. Jan. 1, 2006; Acts 2009, 81st Leg., ch. 84, § 10, eff. Sept. 1, 2009.

§ 9.010. Name Change of Foreign Filing Entity

If a foreign filing entity authorized to transact business in this state changes its name to a name that would cause the entity to be denied an application for registration under this subchapter, the entity's registration must be suspended. An entity the registration of which has been suspended under this section may transact business in this state only after the entity:

(1) changes its name to a name that is available to it under the laws of this state; or

(2) otherwise complies with this chapter.

Acts 2003, 78th Leg., ch. 182, § 1, eff. Jan. 1, 2006. Amended by Acts 2005, 79th Leg., ch. 64, § 29, eff. Jan. 1, 2006; Acts 2007, 80th Leg., ch. 688, § 45, eff. Sept. 1, 2007.

§ 9.011. Voluntary Withdrawal of Registration

(a) A foreign filing entity or foreign limited liability partnership registered in this state may withdraw the entity's or partnership's registration at any time by filing a certificate of withdrawal in the manner required by Chapter 4.

(b) A certificate of withdrawal must state:

(1) the name of the foreign filing entity or foreign limited liability partnership as registered in this state;

(2) the type of foreign filing entity and the entity's or partnership's jurisdiction of formation;

(3) the address of the principal office of the foreign filing entity or foreign limited liability partnership;

(4) that the foreign filing entity or foreign limited liability partnership no longer is transacting business in this state;

(5) that the foreign filing entity or foreign limited liability partnership:

(A) revokes the authority of the entity's or partnership's registered agent in this state to accept service of process; and

(B) consents that service of process in any action, suit, or proceeding stating a cause of action arising in this state during the time the foreign filing entity or foreign limited liability partnership was authorized to transact business in this state may be made on the foreign filing entity or foreign limited liability partnership by serving the secretary of state;

(6) an address to which the secretary of state may mail a copy of any process against the foreign filing entity or foreign limited liability partnership served on the secretary of state; and

(7) that any money due or accrued to the state has been paid or that adequate provision has been made for the payment of that money.

(c) A certificate from the comptroller stating that all taxes administered by the comptroller under Title 2, Tax Code, have been paid must be filed with the certificate of withdrawal in accordance with Chapter 4 if the foreign filing entity is a taxable entity under Chapter 171, Tax Code, other than a foreign nonprofit corporation.

(d) If the existence or separate existence of a foreign filing entity or foreign limited liability partnership registered in this state terminates because of dissolution, termination, merger, conversion, or other circumstances, a certificate by an authorized governmental official of the entity's jurisdiction of formation that evidences the termination shall be filed with the secretary of state.

(e) The registration of the foreign filing entity in this state terminates when a certificate of withdrawal under this section or a certificate evidencing termination under Subsection (d) is filed.

(f) If the address stated in a certificate of withdrawal under Subsection (b)(6) changes, the foreign filing entity or foreign limited liability partnership must promptly amend the certificate of withdrawal to update the address.

(g) A certificate of withdrawal does not terminate the authority of the secretary of state to accept service of process on the foreign filing entity or foreign limited liability partnership with respect to a cause of action arising out of business or activity in this state.

Acts 2003, 78th Leg., ch. 182, § 1, eff. Jan. 1, 2006. Amended by Acts 2005, 79th Leg., ch. 64, § 30, eff. Jan. 1, 2006; Acts 2009, 81st Leg., ch. 84, § 11, eff. Sept. 1, 2009.

§ 9.012 Automatic Withdrawal on Conversion to Domestic Filing Entity

A foreign filing entity or foreign limited liability partnership registered in this state that converts to a domestic filing entity is considered to have withdrawn its registration on the effective date of the conversion. This section also applies to a conversion and continuance under Section 10.1025.

Added by Acts 2009, 81st Leg., ch. 84, § 12, eff. Sept. 1, 2009.

SUBCHAPTER B. FAILURE TO REGISTER

§ 9.051. Transacting Business or Maintaining Court Proceeding Without Registration

(a) On application by the attorney general, a court may enjoin a foreign filing entity or the entity's agent from transacting business in this state if:

(1) the entity is not registered in this state; or

(2) the entity's registration is obtained on the basis of a false or misleading representation.

(b) A foreign filing entity or the entity's legal representative may not maintain an action, suit, or proceeding in a court of this state, brought either directly by the entity or in the form of a derivative action in the entity's name, on a cause of action that arises out of the transaction of business in this state unless the foreign filing entity is registered in accordance with this chapter. This subsection does not affect the rights of an assignee of the foreign filing entity as:

(1) the holder in due course of a negotiable instrument; or

(2) the bona fide purchaser for value of a warehouse receipt, security, or other instrument made negotiable by law.

(c) The failure of a foreign filing entity to register does not:

(1) affect the validity of any contract or act of the foreign filing entity;

(2) prevent the entity from defending an action, suit, or proceeding in a court in this state; or

(3) except as provided by Subsection (d), cause any owner, member, or managerial official of the foreign filing entity to become liable for the debts, obligations, or liabilities of the foreign filing entity.

(d) Subsection (c)(3) does not apply to a general partner of a foreign limited partnership.

Acts 2003, 78th Leg., ch. 182, § 1, eff. Jan. 1, 2006.

§ 9.052. Civil Penalty

(a) A foreign filing entity that transacts business in this state and is not registered under this chapter is liable to this state for a civil penalty in an amount equal to all:

(1) fees and taxes that would have been imposed by law on the entity had the entity registered when first required and filed all reports required by law; and

(2) penalties and interest imposed by law for failure to pay those fees and taxes.

(b) The attorney general may bring suit to recover amounts due to this state under this section.

Acts 2003, 78th Leg., ch. 182, § 1, eff. Jan. 1, 2006.

§ 9.053. Venue

In addition to any other venue authorized by law, a suit under Section 9.051 or 9.052 may be brought in Travis County.

Acts 2003, 78th Leg., ch. 182, § 1, eff. Jan. 1, 2006.

§ 9.054. Late Filing Fee

(a) The secretary of state may collect from a foreign filing entity a late filing fee if the entity has transacted business in this state for more than 90 days without registering under this chapter. The secretary may condition the effectiveness of a registration after the 90–day period on the payment of the late filing fee.

(b) The amount of the late filing fee is an amount equal to the product of the amount of the registration fee for the foreign filing entity multiplied by the number of calendar years that the entity transacted business in this state without being registered. For purposes of computing the fee, a partial calendar year is counted as a full calendar year.

Acts 2003, 78th Leg., ch. 182, § 1, eff. Jan. 1, 2006. Amended by Acts 2007, 80th Leg., ch. 688, § 46, eff. Sept. 1, 2007.

§ 9.055. Requirements of Other Law

This chapter does not excuse a foreign entity from complying with duties imposed under other law, including other chapters of this code, relating to filing or registration requirements.

Acts 2003, 78th Leg., ch. 182, § 1, eff. Jan. 1, 2006.

SUBCHAPTER C. REVOCATION OF REGISTRATION BY SECRETARY OF STATE

§ 9.101. Revocation of Registration by Secretary of State

(a) If it appears to the secretary of state that, with respect to a foreign filing entity, a circumstance described by Subsection (b) exists, the secretary of state may notify the entity of the circumstance by mail or certified mail addressed to the foreign filing entity at the entity's registered office or principal place of business as shown on the records of the secretary of state.

(b) The secretary of state may revoke a foreign filing entity's registration if the secretary of state finds that:

(1) the entity has failed to, and, before the 91st day after the date notice was mailed, has not corrected the entity's failure to:

(A) file a report within the period required by law or pay a fee or penalty prescribed by law when due and payable;

(B) maintain a registered agent or registered office in this state as required by law; or

(C) amend its registration when required by law; or

(2) the entity has failed to, and, before the 16th day after the date notice was mailed, has not corrected the entity's failure to pay a fee required in connection with the application for registration, or payment of the fee was dishonored when presented by the state for payment.

Acts 2003, 78th Leg., ch. 182, § 1, eff. Jan. 1, 2006. Amended by Acts 2007, 80th Leg., ch. 688, § 47, eff. Sept. 1, 2007.

§ 9.102. Certificate of Revocation

(a) If revocation of a registration is required, the secretary of state shall:

(1) file a certificate of revocation; and

(2) deliver a certificate of revocation by regular or certified mail to the foreign filing entity at its registered office or principal place of business.

(b) The certificate of revocation must state:

(1) that the foreign filing entity's registration has been revoked; and

(2) the date and cause of the revocation.

(c) Except as otherwise provided by this chapter, the revocation of a foreign filing entity's registration under this subchapter takes effect on the date the certificate of revocation is filed.

Acts 2003, 78th Leg., ch. 182, § 1, eff. Jan. 1, 2006.

§ 9.103. Reinstatement by Secretary of State After Revocation

(a) The secretary of state shall reinstate the registration of an entity that has been revoked under this subchapter if the entity files an application for reinstatement in accordance with Section 9.104, accompanied by each amendment to the entity's registration that is required by intervening events, including circumstances requiring an amendment to the name of the entity or the name under which the entity is registered to transact business in this state as described in Section 9.105, and:

(1) the entity has corrected the circumstances that led to the revocation and any other circumstances that may exist of the types described by Section 9.101(b), including the payment of fees, interest, or penalties; or

(2) the secretary of state finds that the circumstances that led to the revocation did not exist at the time of revocation.

(b) If a foreign filing entity's registration is reinstated before the third anniversary of the revocation, the entity is considered to have been registered or in existence at all times during the period of revocation.

Acts 2003, 78th Leg., ch. 182, § 1, eff. Jan. 1, 2006.

§ 9.104. Procedures for Reinstatement

(a) A foreign filing entity, to have its registration reinstated, must complete the requirements of this section not later than the third anniversary of the date the revocation of the entity's registration took effect.

(b) The foreign filing entity shall file a certificate of reinstatement in accordance with Chapter 4.

(c) The certificate of reinstatement must contain:

(1) the name of the foreign filing entity;

(2) the filing number assigned by the filing officer to the entity;

(3) the effective date of the revocation of the entity's registration; and

(4) the name of the entity's registered agent and the address of the entity's registered office.

(d) A tax clearance letter from the comptroller stating that the foreign filing entity has satisfied all franchise tax liabilities and its registration may be reinstated must be filed with the certificate of reinstatement if the foreign filing entity is a taxable entity under Chapter 171, Tax Code, other than a foreign nonprofit corporation.

(e) The registration of a foreign filing entity may not be reinstated under this section if the termination occurred as a result of:

(1) an order of a court; or

(2) forfeiture under the Tax Code.

Acts 2003, 78th Leg., ch. 182, § 1, eff. Jan. 1, 2006. Amended by Acts 2009, 81st Leg., ch. 84, § 13, eff. Sept. 1, 2009.

§ 9.105. Use of Name Similar to Previously Registered Name

If the secretary of state determines that a foreign filing entity's name or the name under which it is registered to transact business in this state is the same as, deceptively similar to, or similar to a name of a filing entity or foreign filing entity as provided by or reserved or registered under this code, the secretary of state may not accept for filing the certificate of reinstatement unless the foreign filing entity amends its registration to change its name or obtains consent for the use of the similar name.

Acts 2003, 78th Leg., ch. 182, § 1, eff. Jan. 1, 2006.

§ 9.106. Reinstatement of Registration Following Tax Forfeiture

A foreign filing entity whose registration has been revoked under the provisions of the Tax Code must follow the procedures in the Tax Code to reinstate its registration.

Acts 2003, 78th Leg., ch. 182, § 1, eff. Jan. 1, 2006.

SUBCHAPTER D. JUDICIAL REVOCATION OF REGISTRATION

§ 9.151. Revocation of Registration by Court Action

(a) A court may revoke the registration of a foreign filing entity if, as a result of an action brought under Section 9.153, the court finds that one or more of the following problems exist:

(1) the entity did not comply with a condition precedent to the issuance of the entity's registration or an amendment to the registration;

(2) the entity's registration or any amendment to the entity's registration was fraudulently filed;

(3) a misrepresentation of a material matter was made in an application, report, affidavit, or other document the entity submitted under this code;

(4) the entity has continued to transact business beyond the scope of the purpose or purposes expressed in the entity's registration; or

(5) public interest requires revocation because:

(A) the entity has been convicted of a felony or a high managerial agent of the entity has been convicted of a felony committed in the conduct of the entity's affairs;

(B) the entity or the high managerial agent has engaged in a persistent course of felonious conduct; and

(C) revocation is necessary to prevent future felonious conduct of the same character.

(b) Sections 9.152–9.157 do not apply to Subsection (a)(5).

Acts 2003, 78th Leg., ch. 182, § 1, eff. Jan. 1, 2006.

§ 9.152. Notification of Cause by Secretary of State

(a) The secretary of state shall provide to the attorney general:

(1) the name of a foreign filing entity that has given cause under Section 9.151 for revocation of its registration; and

(2) the facts relating to the cause for revocation.

(b) When notice is provided under Subsection (a), the secretary of state shall send written notice of the circumstances to the foreign filing entity at its registered office in this state. The notice must state that the secretary of state has given notice under Subsection (a) and the grounds for the notification. The secretary of state must record the date a notice required by this subsection is sent.

(c) A court shall accept a certificate issued by the secretary of state as to the facts relating to the cause for judicial revocation of a foreign filing entity's registration and the sending of a notice under Subsection (b) as prima facie evidence of the facts stated in the certificate and the sending of the notice.

Acts 2003, 78th Leg., ch. 182, § 1, eff. Jan. 1, 2006.

§ 9.153. Filing of Action by Attorney General

The attorney general shall file an action against a foreign filing entity in the name of the state seeking the revocation of the entity's registration if:

(1) the entity has not cured the problems for which revocation is sought before the 31st day after the date the notice under Section 9.152(b) is mailed; and

(2) the attorney general determines that cause exists for judicial revocation of the entity's registration under Section 9.151.

Acts 2003, 78th Leg., ch. 182, § 1, eff. Jan. 1, 2006.

§ 9.154. Cure Before Final Judgment

An action filed by the attorney general under Section 9.153 shall be abated if, before a district court renders judgment on the action, the foreign filing entity:

(1) cures the problems for which revocation is sought; and

(2) pays the costs of the action.

Acts 2003, 78th Leg., ch. 182, § 1, eff. Jan. 1, 2006.

§ 9.155. Judgment Requiring Revocation

If a district court finds in an action brought under this subchapter that proper grounds exist under Section 9.151(a) for revocation of the foreign filing entity's registration, the court shall:

(1) make findings to that effect; and

(2) subject to Section 9.156, enter a judgment not earlier than the fifth day after the date the court makes its findings.

Acts 2003, 78th Leg., ch. 182, § 1, eff. Jan. 1, 2006.

§ 9.156. Stay of Judgment

(a) If, in an action brought under this subchapter, a foreign filing entity has proved by a preponderance of the evidence and obtained a finding that the problems for which the foreign filing entity has been found guilty were not wilful or the result of a failure to take reasonable precautions, the entity may make a sworn application to the court for a stay of entry of the judgment to allow the foreign filing entity a reasonable opportunity to cure the problems for which it has been found guilty. An application made under this subsection must be made not later than the fifth day after the date the court makes its findings under Section 9.155.

(b) After a foreign filing entity has made an application under Subsection (a), a court shall stay the entry of the judgment if the court is reasonably satisfied after considering the application and evidence offered for or against the application that the foreign filing entity:

(1) is able and intends in good faith to cure the problems for which it has been found guilty; and

(2) has not applied for the stay without just cause.

(c) A court shall stay an entry of judgment under Subsection (b) for the period the court determines is reasonably necessary to afford the foreign filing entity the opportunity to cure its problems if the entity acts with reasonable diligence. The court may not stay the entry of the judgment for longer than 60 days after the date the court's findings are made.

(d) The court shall dismiss an action against a foreign filing entity that, during the period the action is stayed by the court under this section, cures the problems for which revocation is sought and pays all costs accrued in the action.

(e) If a court finds that a foreign filing entity has not cured the problems for which revocation is sought within the period prescribed by Subsection (c), the court shall enter final judgment requiring revocation of the foreign filing entity's registration.

Acts 2003, 78th Leg., ch. 182, § 1, eff. Jan. 1, 2006.

§ 9.157. Opportunity for Cure After Affirmation of Findings by Appeals Court

(a) An appellate court that affirms a trial court's findings against a foreign filing entity under this subchapter shall remand the case to the trial court with instructions to grant the foreign filing entity an opportunity to cure the problems for which the entity has been found guilty if:

(1) the foreign filing entity did not make an application to the trial court for stay of the entry of the judgment;

(2) the appellate court is satisfied that the appeal was taken in good faith and not for purpose of delay or with no sufficient cause;

(3) the appellate court finds that the problems for which the foreign filing entity has been found guilty are capable of being cured; and

(4) the foreign filing entity has prayed for the opportunity to cure its problems in the appeal.

(b) The appellate court shall determine the period, which may not be longer than 60 days after the date the case is remanded to the trial court, to be afforded to a foreign filing entity to enable the foreign filing entity to cure its problems under Subsection (a).

(c) The trial court to which an action against a foreign filing entity has been remanded under this section shall dismiss the action if, during the period prescribed by the appellate court for that conduct, the foreign filing entity cures the problems for which revocation is sought and pays all costs accrued in the action.

(d) If a foreign filing entity has not cured the problems for which revocation is sought within the period prescribed by the appellate court under Subsection (b), the judgment requiring revocation shall become final.

Acts 2003, 78th Leg., ch. 182, § 1, eff. Jan. 1, 2006.

§ 9.158. Jurisdiction and Venue

(a) The attorney general shall bring an action for the revocation of the registration of a foreign filing entity under this subchapter in:

(1) a district court of the county in which the registered office or principal place of business of the filing entity in this state is located; or

(2) a district court of Travis County.

(b) A district court described by Subsection (a) has jurisdiction of the action for revocation of the registration of the foreign filing entity.

Acts 2003, 78th Leg., ch. 182, § 1, eff. Jan. 1, 2006.

§ 9.159. Process in State Action

Citation in an action for the involuntary revocation of a foreign filing entity's registration under this subchapter shall be issued and served as provided by law.

Acts 2003, 78th Leg., ch. 182, § 1, eff. Jan. 1, 2006.

§ 9.160. Publication of Notice

(a) If process in an action under this subchapter is returned not found, the attorney general shall publish notice in a newspaper in the county in which the registered office of the foreign filing entity in this state is located. The notice must contain:

(1) a statement of the pendency of the action;

(2) the title of the court;

(3) the title of the action; and

(4) the earliest date on which default judgment may be entered by the court.

(b) Notice under this section must be published at least once a week for two consecutive weeks beginning at any time after the citation has been returned.

(c) The attorney general may include in one published notice the name of each foreign filing entity against which an action for involuntary revocation is pending in the same court.

(d) Not later than the 10th day after the date notice under this section is first published, the attorney general shall send a copy of the notice to the appropriate foreign filing entity at the foreign filing entity's registered office in this state. A certificate from the attorney general regarding the sending of the notice is prima facie evidence that notice was sent under this section.

(e) Unless a foreign filing entity has been served with citation, a default judgment may not be taken against the entity before the 31st day after the date the notice is first published.

Acts 2003, 78th Leg., ch. 182, § 1, eff. Jan. 1, 2006.

§ 9.161. Filing of Decree of Revocation Against Foreign Filing Entity

(a) The clerk of a court that enters a decree revoking the registration of a foreign filing entity shall file a certified copy of the decree in accordance with Chapter 4.

(b) A fee may not be charged for the filing of a decree under this section.

Acts 2003, 78th Leg., ch. 182, § 1, eff. Jan. 1, 2006.

§ 9.162. Applicability of Subchapter to Foreign Limited Liability Partnerships

This subchapter applies to a partnership registered as a foreign limited liability partnership to the same extent as it applies to a foreign filing entity.

Added by Acts 2005, 79th Leg., ch. 64, § 31, eff. Jan. 1, 2006.

SUBCHAPTER E. BUSINESS, RIGHTS, AND OBLIGATIONS

§ 9.201. Business of Foreign Entity

(a) Except as provided by Subsection (b), a foreign entity may not conduct in this state a business or activity that is not permitted by this code to be transacted by the domestic entity to which it most closely corresponds, unless other law of this state authorizes the entity to conduct the business or activity.

(b) A foreign business trust may engage in a business or activity permitted by this code to be transacted by a limited liability company.

Acts 2003, 78th Leg., ch. 182, § 1, eff. Jan. 1, 2006. Amended by Acts 2007, 80th Leg., ch. 688, § 48, eff. Sept. 1, 2007.

§ 9.202. Rights and Privileges

A foreign nonfiling entity or a foreign filing entity registered under this chapter enjoys the same but no greater rights and privileges as the domestic entity to which it most closely corresponds.

Acts 2003, 78th Leg., ch. 182, § 1, eff. Jan. 1, 2006.

§ 9.203. Obligations and Liabilities

Subject to this code and other laws of this state and except as provided by Subchapter C, Chapter 1, in any matter that affects the transaction of intrastate business in this state, a foreign entity and each member, owner, or managerial official of the entity is subject to the same duties, restrictions, penalties, and liabilities imposed on a domestic entity to which it most closely corresponds or on a member, owner, or managerial official of that domestic entity.

Acts 2003, 78th Leg., ch. 182, § 1, eff. Jan. 1, 2006.

§ 9.204. Right of Foreign Entity to Participate in Business of Certain Domestic Entities

A vote cast or consent provided by a foreign entity with respect to its ownership or membership interest in a domestic entity of which the foreign entity is a lawful owner or member, and the foreign entity's participation in the management and control of the business and affairs of the domestic entity to the extent of the participation of other owners or members, are not invalidated if the foreign entity does not register to transact business in this state in accordance with this chapter, subject to all law governing a domestic entity, including the antitrust law of this state.

Acts 2003, 78th Leg., ch. 182, § 1, eff. Jan. 1, 2006. Amended by Acts 2005, 79th Leg., ch. 64, § 32, eff. Jan. 1, 2006.

SUBCHAPTER F. DETERMINATION OF TRANSACTING BUSINESS IN THIS STATE

§ 9.251 Activities Not Constituting Transacting Business in This State

For purposes of this chapter, activities that do not constitute transaction of business in this state include:

(1) maintaining or defending an action or suit or an administrative or arbitration proceeding, or effecting the settlement of:

(A) such an action, suit, or proceeding; or

(B) a claim or dispute to which the entity is a party;

(2) holding a meeting of the entity's managerial officials, owners, or members or carrying on another activity concerning the entity's internal affairs;

(3) maintaining a bank account;

(4) maintaining an office or agency for:

(A) transferring, exchanging, or registering securities the entity issues; or

(B) appointing or maintaining a trustee or depositary related to the entity's securities;

(5) voting the interest of an entity the foreign entity has acquired;

(6) effecting a sale through an independent contractor;

(7) creating, as borrower or lender, or acquiring indebtedness or a mortgage or other security interest in real or personal property;

(8) securing or collecting a debt due the entity or enforcing a right in property that secures a debt due the entity;

(9) transacting business in interstate commerce;

(10) conducting an isolated transaction that:

(A) is completed within a period of 30 days; and

(B) is not in the course of a number of repeated, similar transactions;

(11) in a case that does not involve an activity that would constitute the transaction of business in this state if the activity were one of a foreign entity acting in its own right:

(A) exercising a power of executor or administrator of the estate of a nonresident decedent under ancillary letters issued by a court of this state; or

(B) exercising a power of a trustee under the will of a nonresident decedent, or under a trust created by one or more nonresidents of this state, or by one or more foreign entities;

(12) regarding a debt secured by a mortgage or lien on real or personal property in this state:

(A) acquiring the debt in a transaction outside this state or in interstate commerce;

(B) collecting or adjusting a principal or interest payment on the debt;

(C) enforcing or adjusting a right or property securing the debt;

(D) taking an action necessary to preserve and protect the interest of the mortgagee in the security; or

(E) engaging in any combination of transactions described by this subdivision;

(13) investing in or acquiring, in a transaction outside of this state, a royalty or other nonoperating mineral interest;

(14) executing a division order, contract of sale, or other instrument incidental to ownership of a nonoperating mineral interest; or

(15) owning, without more, real or personal property in this state.

Acts 2003, 78th Leg., ch. 182, § 1, eff. Jan. 1, 2006. Amended by Acts 2009, 81st Leg., ch. 84, § 14, eff. Sept. 1, 2009.

§ 9.252. Other Activities

The list provided by Section 9.251 is not exclusive of activities that do not constitute transacting business in this state for the purposes of this code.

Acts 2003, 78th Leg., ch. 182, § 1, eff. Jan. 1, 2006.

SUBCHAPTER G. MISCELLANEOUS PROVISIONS

§ 9.301. Applicability of Code to Certain Foreign Entities

(a) Except as provided by a statute described by this subsection, the provisions of this code governing a foreign entity apply to a foreign entity registered or granted authority to transact business in this state under:

(1) a special statute that does not contain a provision regarding a matter provided for by this code with respect to a foreign entity; or

(2) another statute that specifically provides that the general law for the granting of a registration or certificate of authority to the foreign entity to transact business in this state supplements the special statute.

(b) Except as provided by a special statute described by Subsection (a), a document required to be filed with the secretary of state under the special statute must be signed and filed in accordance with Chapter 4.

Acts 2003, 78th Leg., ch. 182, § 1, eff. Jan. 1, 2006.

CHAPTER 10. MERGERS, INTEREST EXCHANGES, CONVERSIONS, AND SALES OF ASSETS

SUBCHAPTER A. MERGERS

Section
10.001. Adoption of Plan of Merger.
10.002. Plan of Merger: Required Provisions.
10.003. Contents of Plan of Merger: More Than One Successor.
10.004. Plan of Merger: Permissive Provisions.
10.005. Creation of Holding Company by Merger.
10.006. Short Form Merger.
10.007. Effectiveness of Merger.
10.008. Effect of Merger.
10.009. Special Provisions Applying to Partnership Mergers.
10.010. Special Provisions Applying to Nonprofit Corporation Mergers.

SUBCHAPTER B. EXCHANGES OF INTERESTS

10.051. Interest Exchanges.
10.052. Plan of Exchange: Required Provisions.
10.053. Plan of Exchange: Permissive Provisions.
10.054. Effectiveness of Exchange.
10.055. General Effect of Interest Exchange.
10.056. Special Provisions Applying to Partnerships.

SUBCHAPTER C. CONVERSIONS

10.101. Conversion of Domestic Entities.
10.102. Conversion of Non–Code Organizations.
10.1025 Conversion and Continuance.
10.103. Plan of Conversion: Required Provisions.
10.104. Plan of Conversion: Permissive Provisions.
10.105. Effectiveness of Conversion.
10.106. General Effect of Conversion.
10.107. Special Provisions Applying to Partnership Conversions.
10.108. Special Provisions Applying to Nonprofit Corporation Conversions.
10.109 Special Provisions Applying to Conversion and Continuance.

SUBCHAPTER D. CERTIFICATE OF MERGER, EXCHANGE, OR CONVERSION

10.151. Certificate of Merger and Exchange.
10.152. Certificate of Merger: Short Form Merger.
10.153. Filing of Certificate of Merger or Exchange.
10.154. Certificate of Conversion.
10.155. Filing of Certificate of Conversion.
10.156. Acceptance of Certificate for Filing.

SUBCHAPTER E. ABANDONMENT OF MERGER, EXCHANGE, OR CONVERSION

10.201. Abandonment of Plan of Merger, Exchange, or Conversion.
10.202. Abandonment After Filing.
10.203. Abandonment if No Filing Required.

SUBCHAPTER F. PROPERTY TRANSFERS AND DISPOSITIONS

Section
10.251. General Power of Domestic Entity to Sell, Lease, or Convey Property.
10.252. No Approval Required for Certain Dispositions of Property.
10.253. Recording Instrument Conveying Real Property of Domestic Entity.
10.254. Disposition of Property Not a Merger or Conversion; Liability.

SUBCHAPTER G. BANKRUPTCY REORGANIZATION
10.301. Reorganization Under Bankruptcy and Similar Laws.
10.302. Signing of Documents.
10.303. Reorganization With Other Entities.
10.304. Right of Dissent and Appraisal Excluded.
10.305. After Final Decree.
10.306. Chapter Cumulative of Other Changes.

SUBCHAPTER H. RIGHTS OF DISSENTING OWNERS
10.351. Applicability of Subchapter.
10.352. Definitions.
10.353. Form and Validity of Notice.
10.354. Rights of Dissent and Appraisal.
10.355. Notice of Right of Dissent and Appraisal.
10.356. Procedure for Dissent by Owners as to Actions; Perfection of Right of Dissent and Appraisal.
10.357. Withdrawal of Demand for Fair Value of Ownership Interest.
10.358. Response by Organization to Notice of Dissent and Demand for Fair Value by Dissenting Owner.
10.359. Record of Demand for Fair Value of Ownership Interest.
10.360. Rights of Transferee of Certain Ownership Interest.
10.361. Proceeding to Determine Fair Value of Ownership Interest and Owners Entitled to Payment; Appointment of Appraisers.
10.362. Computation and Determination of Fair Value of Ownership Interest.
10.363. Powers and Duties of Appraiser; Appraisal Procedures.
10.364. Objection to Appraisal; Hearing.
10.365. Court Costs; Compensation for Appraiser.
10.366. Status of Ownership Interest Held or Formerly Held by Dissenting Owner.
10.367. Rights of Owners Following Termination of Right of Dissent.
10.368. Exclusivity of Remedy of Dissent and Appraisal.

SUBCHAPTER Z. MISCELLANEOUS PROVISIONS
10.901. Creditors; Antitrust.
10.902. Nonexclusivity.

SUBCHAPTER A. MERGERS

§ 10.001. Adoption of Plan of Merger

(a) A domestic entity may effect a merger by complying with the applicable provisions of this code. A merger must be set forth in a plan of merger.

(b) To effect a merger, each domestic entity that is a party to the merger must act on and approve the plan of merger in the manner prescribed by this code for the approval of mergers by the domestic entity.

(c) A domestic entity subject to dissenters' rights must provide the notice required by Section 10.355.

(d) If one or more non-code organizations is a party to the merger or is to be created by the plan of merger:

(1) to effect the merger each non-code organization must take all action required by this code and its governing documents;

(2) the merger must be permitted by:

(A) the law of the state or country under whose law each non-code organization is incorporated or organized; or

(B) the governing documents of each non-code organization if the documents are not inconsistent with the law under which the non-code organization is incorporated or organized; and

(3) in effecting the merger each non-code organization that is a party to the merger must comply with:

(A) the applicable laws under which it is incorporated or organized; and

(B) the governing documents of the non-code organization.

(e) A domestic entity may not merge under this subchapter if an owner or member of that entity that is a party to the merger will, as a result of the merger, become personally liable, without that owner's or member's consent, for a liability or other obligation of any other person.

Acts 2003, 78th Leg., ch. 182, § 1, eff. Jan. 1, 2006.

§ 10.002. Plan of Merger: Required Provisions

(a) A plan of merger must be in writing and must include:

(1) the name of each organization that is a party to the merger;

(2) the name of each organization that will survive the merger;

(3) the name of each new organization that is to be created by the plan of merger;

(4) a description of the organizational form of each organization that is a party to the merger or that is to be created by the plan of merger and its jurisdiction of formation;

(5) the manner and basis of converting or exchanging any of the ownership or membership interests of each organization that is a party to the merger into:

(A) ownership interests, membership interests, obligations, rights to purchase securities, or other securities of one or more of the surviving or new organizations;

(B) cash;

(C) other property, including ownership interests, membership interests, obligations, rights to purchase securities, or other securities of any other person or entity; or

(D) any combination of the items described by Paragraphs (A)–(C);

(6) the identification of any of the ownership or membership interests of an organization that is a party to the merger that are to be canceled rather than converted or exchanged;

(7) the certificate of formation of each new domestic filing entity to be created by the plan of merger;

(8) the governing documents of each new domestic nonfiling entity to be created by the plan of merger; and

(9) the governing documents of each non-code organization that:

(A) is to survive the merger or to be created by the plan of merger; and

(B) is an entity that is not:

(i) organized under the laws of any state or the United States; or

(ii) required to file its certificate of formation or similar document under which the entity is organized with the appropriate governmental authority.

(b) An item required by Subsections (a)(7)–(9) may be included in the plan of merger by an attachment or exhibit to the plan.

(c) If the plan of merger provides for a manner and basis of converting or exchanging an ownership or membership interest that may be converted or exchanged in a manner or basis different than any other ownership or membership interest of the same class or series of the ownership or membership interest, the manner and basis of conversion or exchange must be included in the plan of merger in the same manner as provided by Subsection (a)(5). A plan of merger may provide for cancellation of an ownership or membership interest while providing for the conversion or exchange of other ownership or membership interests of the same class or series as the ownership or membership interest to be canceled.

Acts 2003, 78th Leg., ch. 182, § 1, eff. Jan. 1, 2006. Amended by Acts 2011, 82nd Leg., ch. 139 (S.B. 748), § 10, eff. Sept. 1, 2011.

§ 10.003. Contents of Plan of Merger: More Than One Successor

If more than one organization is to survive or to be created by the plan of merger, the plan of merger must include:

(1) the manner and basis of allocating and vesting the property of each organization that is a party to the merger among one or more of the surviving or new organizations;

(2) the name of each surviving or new organization that is primarily obligated for the payment of the fair value of an ownership or membership interest of an owner or member of a domestic entity subject to dissenters' rights that is a party to the merger and who complies with the requirements for dissent and appraisal under this code applicable to the domestic entity; and

(3) the manner and basis of allocating each liability and obligation of each organization that is a party to the merger, or adequate provisions for the payment and discharge of each liability and obligation, among one or more of the surviving or new organizations.

Acts 2003, 78th Leg., ch. 182, § 1, eff. Jan. 1, 2006.

§ 10.004. Plan of Merger: Permissive Provisions

A plan of merger may include:

(1) amendments to the governing documents of any surviving organization;

(2) provisions relating to an interest exchange, including a plan of exchange; and

(3) any other provisions relating to the merger that are not required by this chapter.

Acts 2003, 78th Leg., ch. 182, § 1, eff. Jan. 1, 2006.

§ 10.005. Creation of Holding Company by Merger

(a) In this section:

(1) "Direct or indirect wholly owned subsidiary" means, with respect to a domestic entity, another domestic entity, all of the outstanding voting ownership or membership interests of which are owned by the domestic entity or by one or more other domestic entities or non-code organizations, all of the outstanding voting ownership or membership inter-

ests of which are owned by the domestic entity or one or more other wholly owned domestic entities or non-code organizations.

(2) "Holding company" means a domestic entity that, from its organization until a merger takes effect, was at all times a direct or indirect wholly owned subsidiary of the merging domestic entity and the ownership or membership interests of which are issued to the members or owners of the merging domestic entity in the merger.

(3) "Merging domestic entity" means the original domestic entity that is a party to a merger that is intended to create a holding company structure under a plan of merger that satisfies the requirements of this section and whose members or owners are not required to approve the plan of merger under Subsection (b).

(4) "Surviving entity subsidiary" means the surviving entity in a merger of a merging domestic entity and a direct or indirect wholly owned subsidiary of the merging domestic entity, which immediately following the merger is a direct or indirect wholly owned subsidiary of the holding company.

(b) A domestic entity may, without owner or member approval and pursuant to a plan of merger, restructure the ownership or membership structure of that entity to create a holding company structure under this chapter and the provisions of this code under which the entity was formed. The approval of the owners or members of a merging domestic entity that is a party to a merger under a plan of merger that creates a holding company is not required if:

(1) the holding company is a domestic entity of the same organizational form as the merging domestic entity;

(2) approval is not otherwise required by the governing documents of the merging domestic entity;

(3) the merging domestic entity merges with a direct or indirect wholly owned subsidiary;

(4) after the merger the merging domestic entity or its successor is a direct or indirect wholly owned subsidiary of a holding company;

(5) the merging domestic entity and the direct or indirect wholly owned subsidiary are the only parties to the merger;

(6) each ownership or membership interest of the merging domestic entity that is outstanding preceding the merger is converted in the merger into an ownership or membership interest of the holding company having the same designations, preferences, limitations, and relative rights and corresponding obligations in respect of the ownership or membership interest as the ownership or membership interest held by the owner or member in the merging domestic entity;

(7) except as provided by Subsection (c), the governing documents of the holding company immediately following the merger contain provisions substantively identical to the governing documents of the merging domestic entity immediately preceding the merger;

(8) except as provided by Subsections (c) and (d), the governing documents of the surviving entity subsidiary immediately following the merger contain provisions substantively identical to the governing documents of the merging domestic entity immediately preceding the merger;

(9) the governing persons of the merging domestic entity become or remain the governing persons of the holding company when the merger takes effect;

(10) the owners or members of the merging domestic entity will not recognize gain or loss for United States federal income tax purposes, the United States federal tax classification of the holding company will be the same as that of the merging domestic entity, and the merger will not result in the loss of any tax benefit or attribute of the merging domestic entity, each as determined by the governing authority of the merging domestic entity; and

(11) the governing authority of the merging domestic entity adopts a resolution approving the plan of merger.

(c) Subsections (b)(7) and (8) do not require identical provisions regarding the organizer or organizers, the entity name, the registered office and agent, the initial governing persons, and the initial subscribers of ownership or membership interests and provisions contained in any amendment to the governing documents as were necessary to effect a change, exchange, reclassification, or cancellation of ownership or membership interests, if the change, exchange, reclassification, or cancellation was in effect preceding the merger.

(d) Notwithstanding Subsection (b)(8):

(1) the governing documents of the surviving entity subsidiary must require that an act or transaction by or involving the surviving entity subsidiary, other than the election or removal of the governing persons of the surviving entity subsidiary, that re-

quires for its approval under this code or the governing documents of the surviving entity subsidiary the approval of the owners or members of the surviving entity subsidiary must, by specific reference to this section, require the approval of the owners or members of the holding company, or any successor by merger, by the same vote as is required by this code and the governing documents of the surviving entity subsidiary;

(2) if the surviving entity subsidiary is not of the same organizational form as the merging domestic entity, the governing documents of the surviving entity subsidiary may differ from the governing documents of the merging domestic entity to the minimum extent necessary to make a change that takes into account the differences between the types of entities, including a change in reference to the types of owners, members, ownership interests, membership interests, governing persons, or governing authority, each as determined by the governing authority of the merging domestic entity;

(3) if the surviving entity subsidiary is not of the same organizational form as the merging domestic entity, the governing documents of the surviving entity subsidiary must require that:

(A) the surviving entity subsidiary obtain the approval of the owners or members of the holding company for any act or transaction by or involving the surviving entity subsidiary, other than the election or removal of the governing persons of the surviving entity subsidiary, that would require the approval of the owners or members of the surviving entity subsidiary if the surviving entity subsidiary were of the same organizational form as the merging domestic entity;

(B) any amendment to the governing documents of the surviving entity subsidiary that would, if adopted by an entity of the same organizational form as the merging domestic entity, be required to be included in the certificate of formation of the entity also require, by specific reference to this section, the approval of the owners or members of the holding company, or any successor by merger, by the same vote as is required by this code or by the governing documents of the surviving entity subsidiary; and

(C) the business affairs of the surviving entity subsidiary be managed by or under the direction of governing persons who are:

(i) subject to the same fiduciary duties applicable to the governing persons of an entity of the same organizational form as the merging domestic entity subject to this code; and

(ii) liable for the breach of any duties to the same extent as governing persons of that form of entity;

(4) the governing documents of the surviving entity subsidiary may change the classes and series of ownership or membership interests and the number of ownership or membership interests that the surviving entity subsidiary is authorized to issue; and

(5) this subsection or a provision of a surviving entity subsidiary's governing documents required by this subsection may not be construed as requiring the approval of the owners or members of the holding company to elect or remove governing persons of the surviving entity subsidiary.

(e) To the extent the provisions contained in Section 21.606 apply to a merging domestic entity and its owners or members when a merger takes effect under this section, those provisions continue to apply to the holding company and its owners or members immediately after the merger takes effect as though the holding company were the merging domestic entity. All ownership or membership interests of the holding company acquired in the merger, for purposes of Section 21.606, are considered to have been acquired at the time the ownership or membership interest of the merging domestic entity converted in the merger was acquired. Any owner or member who, preceding the merger, was not an affiliated owner or member as described by Section 21.606 does not solely by reason of the merger become an affiliated owner or member of the holding company.

(f) If the name of a holding company immediately following the effectiveness of a merger under this section is the same as the name of the merging domestic entity preceding the merger, the ownership or membership interests of the holding company into which the ownership or membership interests of the merging domestic entity are converted pursuant to the merger will be represented by the certificates, if any, that previously represented the ownership or membership interests in the merging domestic entity.

(g) This section shall not apply to a merger of a partnership with or into a domestic entity without the approval of the owners or members of the partnership and domestic entity as provided by this code.

Acts 2003, 78th Leg., ch. 182, § 1, eff. Jan. 1, 2006. Amended by Acts 2005, 79th Leg., ch. 64, § 33, eff. Jan. 1, 2006; Acts 2007, 80th Leg., ch. 688, § 49, eff. Sept. 1, 2007.

§ 10.006. Short Form Merger

(a) A parent organization that owns at least 90 percent of the outstanding ownership or membership interests of each class and series of each of one or more subsidiary organizations may merge with one or more of the subsidiary organizations as provided by this section if:

(1) at least one of the parties to the merger is a domestic entity and each other party is a domestic entity or another non-code organization organized under the laws of a jurisdiction that permits a merger of the type authorized by this chapter; and

(2) the resulting organization or organizations are the parent organization, one or more existing subsidiary organizations, or one or more new organizations.

(b) No action by any subsidiary organization that is a domestic entity is required to approve the merger.

(c) If the parent organization will not survive the merger, a plan of merger must be adopted by action of the parent organization in the same manner as a plan of merger not governed by this section or Section 10.005.

(d) If the parent organization will survive the merger, the merger is required to be approved only by a resolution adopted by the governing authority of the parent organization.

(e) Sections 10.001(c)–(e), 10.002(c), 10.003, and 10.007–10.010 apply to a merger approved under Subsection (d), except that the resolution approving the merger should be considered the plan of merger for purposes of those sections.

(f) The resolution approving the merger under Subsection (d) must describe:

(1) the basic terms of the merger;

(2) the organizations that are party to the merger; and

(3) the organizations that survive the merger.

(g) If the parent organization does not own all of the outstanding ownership or membership interests of each class or series of ownership or membership interests of each subsidiary organization that is a party to the merger, the resolution of the parent organization required by Subsection (d) must describe the terms of the merger, including the cash or other property, including ownership or membership interests, obligations, rights to purchase securities, or other securities of any person or organization or any combination of the ownership or membership interests, obligations, rights, or other securities, to be used, paid, or delivered by the parent organization on surrender of each ownership or membership interest of the subsidiary organizations not owned by the parent organization.

(h) An entity is not disqualified from effecting a merger under any other provision of this chapter because it qualifies for a merger under this section.

(i) This section shall not apply if a subsidiary organization that is a party to the merger is:

(1) a partnership; or

(2) a domestic entity that has in its governing documents the provision required by Section 10.005(d)(1) and of which there are outstanding ownership or membership interests that would be entitled to vote on the merger absent this section.

Acts 2003, 78th Leg., ch. 182, § 1, eff. Jan. 1, 2006. Amended by Acts 2005, 79th Leg., ch. 64, § 34, eff. Jan. 1, 2006.

§ 10.007. Effectiveness of Merger

Except as otherwise provided by Subchapter B, Chapter 4, a merger takes effect at the time provided by the plan of merger, except that a merger that requires a filing under Subchapter D takes effect on the acceptance of the filing of the certificate of merger by the secretary of state or county clerk, as appropriate.

Acts 2003, 78th Leg., ch. 182, § 1, eff. Jan. 1, 2006.

§ 10.008. Effect of Merger

(a) When a merger takes effect:

(1) the separate existence of each domestic entity that is a party to the merger, other than a surviving or new domestic entity, ceases;

(2) all rights, title, and interests to all real estate and other property owned by each organization that is a party to the merger is allocated to and vested, subject to any existing liens or other encumbrances on the property, in one or more of the surviving or new organizations as provided in the plan of merger without:

(A) reversion or impairment;

(B) any further act or deed; or

(C) any transfer or assignment having occurred;

(3) all liabilities and obligations of each organization that is a party to the merger are allocated to one or more of the surviving or new organizations in the manner provided by the plan of merger;

(4) each surviving or new domestic organization to which a liability or obligation is allocated under the plan of merger is the primary obligor for the liability or obligation, and, except as otherwise provided by the plan of merger or by law or contract, no other party to the merger, other than a surviving domestic entity or non-code organization liable or otherwise obligated at the time of the merger, and no other new domestic entity or non-code organization created under the plan of merger is liable for the debt or other obligation;

(5) any proceeding pending by or against any domestic entity or by or against any non-code organization that is a party to the merger may be continued as if the merger did not occur, or the surviving or new domestic entity or entities or the surviving or new non-code organization or non-code organizations to which the liability, obligation, asset, or right associated with that proceeding is allocated to and vested in under the plan of merger may be substituted in the proceeding;

(6) the governing documents of each surviving domestic entity are amended to the extent provided by the plan of merger;

(7) each new filing entity whose certificate of formation is included in the plan of merger under this chapter, on meeting any additional requirements, if any, of this code for its formation, is formed as a domestic entity under this code as provided by the plan of merger;

(8) the ownership or membership interests of each organization that is a party to the merger and that are to be converted or exchanged, in whole or part, into ownership or membership interests, obligations, rights to purchase securities, or other securities of one or more of the surviving or new organizations, into cash or other property, including ownership or membership interests, obligations, rights to purchase securities, or other securities of any organization, or into any combination of these, or that are to be canceled, are converted, exchanged, or canceled as provided in the plan of merger, and the former owners or members who held ownership or membership interests of each domestic entity that is a party to the merger are entitled only to the rights provided by the plan of merger or, if applicable, any rights to receive the fair value for the ownership interests provided under Subchapter H; and

(9) notwithstanding Subdivision (4), the surviving or new organization named in the plan of merger as primarily obligated to pay the fair value of an ownership or membership interest under Section 10.003(2) is the primary obligor for that payment and all other surviving or new organizations are secondarily liable for that payment.

(b) If the plan of merger does not provide for the allocation and vesting of the right, title, and interest in any particular real estate or other property or for the allocation of any liability or obligation of any party to the merger, the unallocated property is owned in undivided interest by, or the liability or obligation is the joint and several liability and obligation of, each of the surviving and new organizations, pro rata to the total number of surviving and new organizations resulting from the merger.

(c) If a surviving organization in a merger is not a domestic entity, the surviving organization is considered to have:

(1) appointed the secretary of state in this state as the organization's agent for service of process in a proceeding to enforce any obligation of a domestic entity that is a party to the merger; and

(2) agreed to promptly pay to the dissenting owners or members of each domestic entity that is a party to the merger who have the right of dissent and appraisal under this code the amount, if any, to which they are entitled under this code.

(d) If the surviving organization in a merger is not a domestic entity, the organization shall register to transact business in this state if the entity is required to register for that purpose by another provision of this code.

Acts 2003, 78th Leg., ch. 182, § 1, eff. Jan. 1, 2006. Amended by Acts 2005, 79th Leg., ch. 64, § 35, eff. Jan. 1, 2006; Acts 2007, 80th Leg., ch. 688, § 50, eff. Sept. 1, 2007; Acts 2011, 82nd Leg., ch. 139 (S.B. 748), § 11, eff. Sept. 1, 2011.

§ 10.009. Special Provisions Applying to Partnership Mergers

(a) A partner of a domestic partnership that is a party to a merger does not become liable as a result of the merger for the liability or obligation of another person that is a party to the merger unless the partner consents to becoming personally liable by action taken in connection with the specific plan of merger approved by the partner.

(b) A partner of a domestic partnership that is a party to a merger who remains in or enters a partnership is treated as an incoming partner in the partnership when the merger takes effect for purposes of determining the partner's liability for a debt or obligation of the partnership or partnerships that are parties to the merger or to be created in the merger and in which the partner was not a partner.

(c) If a partnership merges with an organization and, because of the merger, no longer exists, a former partner who becomes an owner or member of the surviving organization may, until the first anniversary of the effective date of the merger, bind the surviving organization to a transaction for which the owner or member no longer has authority to bind the organization if the transaction is one in which the actions by the owner or member as a partner would have bound the partnership before the effective date of the merger, and the other party to the transaction:

(1) does not have actual or constructive notice of the merger;

(2) had done business with the terminated partnership within one year preceding the effective date of the merger; and

(3) reasonably believes that the partner who was previously an owner or member of the partnership that was merged into the surviving organization and is now an owner or member of the surviving organization has the authority to bind the surviving organization to the transaction at the time of the transaction.

(d) If a partnership is formed under a plan of merger, the existence of the partnership as a partnership begins when the merger takes effect, and the persons to be partners become partners at that time.

(e) A partner in a domestic partnership that is a party to the merger but does not survive shall be treated as a partner who withdrew from the nonsurviving domestic partnership as of the effective date of the merger.

(f) The partnership agreement of each domestic partnership that is a party to the merger must contain provisions that authorize the merger provided for in the plan of merger adopted by the partnership.

(g) Each domestic partnership that is a party to the merger must approve the plan of merger in the manner prescribed in its partnership agreement.

Acts 2003, 78th Leg., ch. 182, § 1, eff. Jan. 1, 2006.

§ 10.010. Special Provisions Applying to Nonprofit Corporation Mergers

(a) A domestic nonprofit corporation may not merge into another entity if the domestic nonprofit corporation would, because of the merger, lose or impair its charitable status.

(b) One or more domestic or foreign for-profit entities or non-code organizations may merge into one or more domestic nonprofit corporations that continue as the surviving entity or entities.

(c) A domestic nonprofit corporation may not merge with a foreign for-profit entity if the domestic nonprofit corporation does not continue as the surviving entity.

(d) One or more domestic nonprofit corporations and non-code organizations may merge into one or more foreign nonprofit entities that continue as the surviving entity or entities.

Acts 2003, 78th Leg., ch. 182, § 1, eff. Jan. 1, 2006.

SUBCHAPTER B. EXCHANGES OF INTERESTS

§ 10.051. Interest Exchanges

(a) For the purpose of acquiring all of the outstanding ownership or membership interests of one or more classes or series of one or more domestic entities, one or more domestic entities or non-code organizations may adopt a plan of exchange.

(b) To make an interest exchange under this section:

(1) the governing authority of each domestic entity the ownership or membership interests of which are to be acquired in the interest exchange must act on a plan of exchange and, if otherwise required by this code, the owners or members of the domestic entity must approve the plan of exchange in the manner provided by this code; and

(2) each acquiring domestic entity must take all action that may otherwise be required by this code and its governing documents to effect the exchange.

(c) A domestic entity subject to dissenters' rights must provide the notice required by Section 10.355.

(d) If a non-code organization is to acquire ownership or membership interests in the exchange, each non-code organization must take all action that is required under the laws of the organization's jurisdiction of formation and the organization's governing documents to effect the exchange.

(e) If one or more non-code organizations as part of the plan of exchange are to issue ownership or membership interests, the issuance of the ownership or membership interests must be permitted by the laws under which the non-code organizations are incorporated or organized or not inconsistent with those laws.

(f) A plan of exchange may not be effected if any owner or member of a domestic entity that is a party to the interest exchange will, as a result of the interest exchange, become personally liable, without the consent of the owner or member, for the liabilities or obligations of any other person or organization.

Acts 2003, 78th Leg., ch. 182, § 1, eff. Jan. 1, 2006.

§ 10.052. Plan of Exchange: Required Provisions

(a) A plan of exchange must be in writing and must include:

(1) the name of each domestic entity the ownership or membership interests of which are to be acquired;

(2) the name of each acquiring organization;

(3) if there is more than one acquiring organization, the ownership or membership interests to be acquired by each organization;

(4) the terms and conditions of the exchange; and

(5) the manner and basis of exchanging the ownership or membership interests to be acquired for:

(A) ownership or membership interests, obligations, rights to purchase securities, or other securities of one or more of the acquiring organizations that is a party to the plan of exchange;

(B) cash;

(C) other property, including ownership or membership interests, obligations, rights to purchase securities, or other securities of any other person or entity; or

(D) any combination of those items.

(b) The manner and basis of exchanging an ownership or membership interest of an owner or member that is exchanged in a manner or basis different from any other owner or member having ownership or membership interests of the same class or series must be included in the plan of exchange in the same manner as provided by Subsection (a)(5).

Acts 2003, 78th Leg., ch. 182, § 1, eff. Jan. 1, 2006. Amended by Acts 2011, 82nd Leg., ch. 139 (S.B. 748), § 12, eff. Sept. 1, 2011.

§ 10.053. Plan of Exchange: Permissive Provisions

A plan of exchange may include any other provisions not required by Section 10.052 relating to the interest exchange.

Acts 2003, 78th Leg., ch. 182, § 1, eff. Jan. 1, 2006.

§ 10.054. Effectiveness of Exchange

Except as otherwise provided by Subchapter B, Chapter 4, an interest exchange takes effect at the time provided in the plan of exchange or otherwise agreed to by the parties, except that an interest exchange that requires a filing under Subchapter D takes effect on the acceptance of the filing of the certificate of exchange by the secretary of state or county clerk, as appropriate.

Acts 2003, 78th Leg., ch. 182, § 1, eff. Jan. 1, 2006.

§ 10.055. General Effect of Interest Exchange

When an interest exchange takes effect:

(1) the ownership or membership interest of each acquired organization is exchanged as provided in the plan of exchange, and the former owners or members whose interests are exchanged under the plan of exchange are entitled only to the rights provided in the plan of exchange or, if applicable, a right to receive the fair value for the ownership interests provided under Subchapter H; and

(2) the acquiring organization has all rights, title, and interests with respect to the ownership or membership interest to be acquired by it subject to the provisions of the plan of exchange.

Acts 2003, 78th Leg., ch. 182, § 1, eff. Jan. 1, 2006. Amended by Acts 2007, 80th Leg., ch. 688, § 51, eff. Sept. 1, 2007.

§ 10.056. Special Provisions Applying to Partnerships

To effect an interest exchange:

(1) the partnership agreement of each domestic partnership whose partnership interests are to be acquired pursuant to the plan of exchange must authorize the partnership interest exchange adopted by the partnership;

(2) each domestic partnership whose partnership interests are to be acquired under the plan of exchange must approve the plan of exchange in the manner prescribed by its partnership agreement; and

(3) each acquiring domestic partnership must take all actions that may be required by its partnership agreement in order to effect the exchange.

Acts 2003, 78th Leg., ch. 182, § 1, eff. Jan. 1, 2006.

SUBCHAPTER C. CONVERSIONS

§ 10.101. Conversion of Domestic Entities

(a) A domestic entity may convert into a different type of domestic entity or a non-code organization by adopting a plan of conversion.

(b) To effect a conversion, the converting entity must act on and the owners or members of the domestic entity must approve a plan of conversion in the manner prescribed by this code for the approval of conversions by the domestic entity or, if not prescribed by this code, in the same manner as prescribed by this code for the adoption and approval of a plan of merger by the domestic entity when the domestic entity does not survive the merger.

(c) A domestic entity subject to dissenters' rights must provide the notice required by Section 10.355.

(d) A conversion may not take effect if the conversion is prohibited by or inconsistent with the laws of the converted entity's jurisdiction of formation, and the formation, incorporation, or organization of the converted entity under the plan of conversion must be effected in compliance with those laws pursuant to the plan of conversion.

(e) At the time a conversion takes effect, each owner or member of the converting entity, other than those who receive payment of their ownership or membership interest under any applicable provisions of this code relating to dissent and appraisal, has, unless otherwise agreed to by that owner or member, an ownership or membership interest in, and is the owner or member of, the converted entity.

(f) A domestic entity may not convert under this section if an owner or member of the domestic entity, as a result of the conversion, becomes personally liable, without the consent of the owner or member, for a liability or other obligation of the converted entity.

Acts 2003, 78th Leg., ch. 182, § 1, eff. Jan. 1, 2006. Amended by Acts 2007, 80th Leg., ch. 688, § 52, eff. Sept. 1, 2007.

§ 10.102. Conversion of Non-Code Organizations

(a) A non-code organization may convert into a domestic entity by adopting a plan of conversion as provided by this section.

(b) To effect a conversion, the non-code organization must take any action that may be required for a conversion under the laws of the organization's jurisdiction of formation and the organization's governing documents.

(c) The conversion must be permitted by the laws under which the non-code organization is incorporated or organized or by its governing documents, which may not be inconsistent with the laws of the jurisdiction in which the non-code organization is incorporated or organized.

Acts 2003, 78th Leg., ch. 182, § 1, eff. Jan. 1, 2006.

§ 10.1025 Conversion and Continuance

(a) A converting entity may elect to continue its existence in its current organizational form and jurisdiction of formation in connection with the entity's:

(1) conversion under Section 10.101 as a domestic entity of one organizational form into a non-United States entity of the same organizational form; or

(2) conversion under Section 10.102 as a non-United States entity of one organizational form into a domestic entity of the same organizational form.

(b) The election permitted by Subsection (a) for the converting entity to continue its existence in its current organizational form and jurisdiction of formation must be:

(1) adopted and approved as part of the plan of conversion for the converting entity as required by Section 10.101(b) or 10.102(b), as applicable; and

(2) permitted by, or not prohibited by and inconsistent with, the laws of the applicable non-United States jurisdiction.

(c) Section 10.156(2) does not apply in connection with the filing of the certificate of conversion if the converting entity is a domestic filing entity that elects to continue its existence in accordance with this section.

(d) Chapter 9 does not apply to a non-United States entity that also exists as a domestic filing entity because of a conversion and election to continue its existence in accordance with this section.

Added by Acts 2009, 81st Leg., ch. 84, § 15, eff. Sept. 1, 2009.

§ 10.103. Plan of Conversion: Required Provisions

(a) A plan of conversion must be in writing and must include:

(1) the name of the converting entity;

(2) the name of the converted entity;

(3) a statement that the converting entity is continuing its existence in the organizational form of the converted entity;

(4) a statement of the type of entity that the converted entity is to be and the converted entity's jurisdiction of formation;

(5) if Sections 10.1025 and 10.109 do not apply, the manner and basis of converting the ownership

or membership interests of the converting entity into ownership or membership interests of the converted entity;

(6) any certificate of formation required to be filed under this code if the converted entity is a filing entity;

(7) the certificate of formation or similar organizational document of the converted entity if the converted entity is not a filing entity; and

(8) if Sections 10.1025 and 10.109 apply, a statement that the converting entity is electing to continue its existence in its current organizational form and jurisdiction of formation after the conversion takes effect.

(b) An item required by Subsection (a)(6) or (7) may be included in the plan of conversion by an attachment or exhibit to the plan.

Acts 2003, 78th Leg., ch. 182, § 1, eff. Jan. 1, 2006. Amended by Acts 2009, 81st Leg., ch. 84, § 16, eff. Sept. 1, 2009; Acts 2011, 82nd Leg., ch. 139 (S.B. 748), § 13, eff. Sept. 1, 2011.

§ 10.104. Plan of Conversion: Permissive Provisions

A plan of conversion may include other provisions relating to the conversion that are not inconsistent with law.

Acts 2003, 78th Leg., ch. 182, § 1, eff. Jan. 1, 2006.

§ 10.105. Effectiveness of Conversion

Except as otherwise provided by Subchapter B, Chapter 4, a conversion takes effect at the time provided by the plan of conversion, except that a conversion that requires a filing under Subchapter D takes effect on the acceptance of the filing of the certificate of conversion by the filing officer.

Acts 2003, 78th Leg., ch. 182, § 1, eff. Jan. 1, 2006.

§ 10.106. General Effect of Conversion

When a conversion takes effect:

(1) the converting entity continues to exist without interruption in the organizational form of the converted entity rather than in the organizational form of the converting entity;

(2) all rights, title, and interests to all property owned by the converting entity continues to be owned, subject to any existing liens or other encumbrances on the property, by the converted entity in the new organizational form without:

(A) reversion or impairment;

(B) further act or deed; or

(C) any transfer or assignment having occurred;

(3) all liabilities and obligations of the converting entity continue to be liabilities and obligations of the converted entity in the new organizational form without impairment or diminution because of the conversion;

(4) the rights of creditors or other parties with respect to or against the previous owners or members of the converting entity in their capacities as owners or members in existence when the conversion takes effect continue to exist as to those liabilities and obligations and may be enforced by the creditors and obligees as if a conversion had not occurred;

(5) a proceeding pending by or against the converting entity or by or against any of the converting entity's owners or members in their capacities as owners or members may be continued by or against the converted entity in the new organizational form and by or against the previous owners or members without a need for substituting a party;

(6) the ownership or membership interests of the converting entity that are to be converted into ownership or membership interests of the converted entity as provided in the plan of conversion are converted as provided by the plan, and if the converting entity is a domestic entity, the former owners or members of the domestic entity are entitled only to the rights provided in the plan of conversion or a right of dissent and appraisal under this code;

(7) if, after the conversion takes effect, an owner or member of the converted entity as an owner or member is liable for the liabilities or obligations of the converted entity, the owner or member is liable for the liabilities and obligations of the converting entity that existed before the conversion took effect only to the extent that the owner or member:

(A) agrees in writing to be liable for the liabilities or obligations;

(B) was liable, before the conversion took effect, for the liabilities or obligations; or

(C) by becoming an owner or member of the converted entity, becomes liable under other applicable law for the existing liabilities and obligations of the converted entity; and

(8) if the converted entity is a non-code organization, the converted entity is considered to have:

(A) appointed the secretary of state in this state as its agent for service of process in a proceeding to enforce any obligation or the rights of dissenting owners or members of the converting domestic entity; and

(B) agreed that the converted entity will promptly pay the dissenting owners or members of the converting domestic entity the amount, if any, to which they are entitled under this code.

Acts 2003, 78th Leg., ch. 182, § 1, eff. Jan. 1, 2006.

§ 10.107. Special Provisions Applying to Partnership Conversions

(a) If a partnership is formed under a plan of conversion under this code, the existence of the partnership as a partnership begins when the conversion takes effect, and the owners or members designated to become the partners under the plan of conversion become the partners at that time.

(b) The partnership agreement of a domestic partnership that is converting must contain provisions that authorize the conversion provided for in the plan of conversion adopted by the partnership.

(c) A domestic partnership that is converting must approve the plan of conversion in the manner provided in its partnership agreement.

Acts 2003, 78th Leg., ch. 182, § 1, eff. Jan. 1, 2006. Amended by Acts 2005, 79th Leg., ch. 64, § 36, eff. Jan. 1, 2006.

§ 10.108. Special Provisions Applying to Nonprofit Corporation Conversions

A domestic nonprofit corporation may not convert into a for-profit entity.

Acts 2003, 78th Leg., ch. 182, § 1, eff. Jan. 1, 2006.

§ 10.109 Special Provisions Applying to Conversion and Continuance

(a) This section applies only to a converting entity that elects to continue its existence in accordance with Section 10.1025.

(b) When the conversion of a converting entity to which this section applies takes effect:

(1) notwithstanding Section 10.106(1), the converting entity continues to exist both in its current organizational form and jurisdiction of formation and, as the converted entity, in the same organizational form in the new jurisdiction of formation;

(2) the converting entity and the converted entity, for purposes of the laws of this state, constitute a single entity formed, incorporated, created, or otherwise having come into being, as applicable, and existing under the laws of this state and the laws of the applicable non-United States jurisdiction, so long as the entity continues to exist as a domestic entity under the laws of this state following the conversion;

(3) if the converting entity is a domestic entity, this code and the other laws of this state apply to the converted entity to the same extent as the laws applied to the entity before the conversion;

(4) if the converting entity is a non-United States entity, the laws of the applicable non-United States jurisdiction apply to the converted entity to the same extent as the laws applied to the entity before the conversion;

(5) notwithstanding Section 10.106(2), all rights, title, and interests in all property owned by the converting entity continue to be owned by the converted entity, subject to any existing liens or other encumbrances on the property, in both the organizational form of the converting entity and the organizational form of the converted entity without:

(A) reversion or impairment;

(B) further act or deed; or

(C) the occurrence of a transfer or assignment; and

(6) notwithstanding Section 10.106(3), all liabilities and obligations of the converting entity remain the liabilities and obligations of the converted entity in both the organizational form of the converting entity and the organizational form of the converted entity without impairment or diminution because of the conversion.

Added by Acts 2009, 81st Leg., ch. 84, § 17, eff. Sept. 1, 2009.

SUBCHAPTER D. CERTIFICATE OF MERGER, EXCHANGE, OR CONVERSION

§ 10.151. Certificate of Merger and Exchange

(a) After approval of a plan of merger or a plan of exchange as provided by this code, a certificate of merger, which may also include an exchange, or a certificate of exchange, as applicable, must be filed for a merger or interest exchange to become effective if:

(1) for a merger:

(A) any domestic entity that is a party to the merger is a filing entity; or

(B) any domestic entity to be created under the plan of merger is a filing entity; or

(2) for an exchange, an ownership or membership interest in any filing entity is to be acquired in the interest exchange.

(b) If a certificate of merger or exchange is required to be filed in connection with an interest exchange or a merger, other than a merger under Section 10.006, the certificate must be signed on behalf of each domestic entity and non-code organization that is a party to the merger or exchange by an officer or other authorized representative and must include:

(1) the plan of merger or exchange or a statement certifying:

(A) the name and organizational form of each domestic entity or non-code organization that is a party to the merger or exchange;

(B) for a merger, the name and organizational form of each domestic entity or non-code organization that is to be created by the plan of merger;

(C) the name of the jurisdiction in which each domestic entity or non-code organization named under Paragraph (A) or (B) is incorporated or organized;

(D) for a merger, the amendments or changes to the certificate of formation of each filing entity that is a party to the merger, or if no amendments are desired to be effected by the merger, a statement to that effect;

(E) for a merger, that the certificate of formation of each new filing entity to be created under the plan of merger is being filed with the certificate of merger;

(F) that a signed plan of merger or exchange is on file at the principal place of business of each surviving, acquiring, or new domestic entity or non-code organization, and the address of each principal place of business; and

(G) that a copy of the plan of merger or exchange will be on written request furnished without cost by each surviving, acquiring, or new domestic entity or non-code organization to any owner or member of any domestic entity that is a party to or created by the plan of merger or exchange and, for a merger with multiple surviving domestic entities or non-code organizations, to any creditor or obligee of the parties to the merger at the time of the merger if a liability or obligation is then outstanding;

(2) if approval of the owners or members of any domestic entity that was a party to the plan of merger or exchange is not required by this code, a statement to that effect; and

(3) a statement that the plan of merger or exchange has been approved as required by the laws of the jurisdiction of formation of each organization that is a party to the merger or exchange and by the governing documents of those organizations.

(c) A certificate of merger may also constitute a certificate of exchange if it contains the information required for a certificate of exchange.

Acts 2003, 78th Leg., ch. 182, § 1, eff. Jan. 1, 2006. Amended by Acts 2007, 80th Leg., ch. 688, § 53, eff. Sept. 1, 2007.

§ 10.152. Certificate of Merger: Short Form Merger

(a) The certificate of merger for a merger under Section 10.006 is required to be signed only by an officer or other authorized representative of the parent organization described by that section.

(b) Except as provided by Subsection (c), the certificate of merger must include:

(1) the name of the parent organization, the name of each subsidiary organization that is a party to the merger, and the jurisdiction of formation of each named organization;

(2) the number of outstanding ownership interests of each class or series of each subsidiary organization and the number and percentage of ownership interests of each class or series owned by the parent organization;

(3) a copy of the resolution of merger adopted by the governing authority of the parent organization authorizing the merger and the date of the adoption of the resolution;

(4) a statement that the resolution has been approved as required by the laws of the jurisdiction of formation of the parent organization and by its governing documents; and

(5) if any surviving organization is not a domestic entity, the address, including street number, if any, of its registered or principal office in the organization's jurisdiction of formation.

(c) If a plan of merger is required to be adopted by action of the parent organization under Section 10.006(c), the certificate of merger must include the information required by Section 10.151(b).

Acts 2003, 78th Leg., ch. 182, § 1, eff. Jan. 1, 2006.

§ 10.153. Filing of Certificate of Merger or Exchange

(a) If a certificate of merger or exchange is required to be filed, the certificate of merger or exchange must be filed in accordance with Chapter 4. The certificate of formation of each filing entity that is to be formed under a plan of merger must also be filed with the certificate of merger in accordance with Chapter 4. Except as provided by this section, the certificate must be filed with the secretary of state.

(b) If a domestic real estate investment trust is a party to the merger or if an ownership interest in a domestic real estate investment trust is to be acquired in the interest exchange, the certificate of merger or exchange must be filed in accordance with Chapter 4 with the county clerk of the county in which the domestic real estate investment trust's principal place of business in this state is located.

(c) If a domestic real estate investment trust is to be created under the plan of merger, the certificate of formation of the domestic real estate investment trust must also be filed with the certificate of merger in accordance with Chapter 4 with the county clerk of the county in which the domestic real estate investment trust's principal place of business in this state is located.

Acts 2003, 78th Leg., ch. 182, § 1, eff. Jan. 1, 2006.

§ 10.154. Certificate of Conversion

(a) After approval of a plan of conversion as provided by this code, a certificate of conversion must be filed for the conversion to become effective if:

(1) any domestic entity that is a party to the conversion is a filing entity; or

(2) any domestic entity to be created under the plan of conversion is a filing entity.

(b) If a certificate of conversion is required to be filed in connection with a conversion, the certificate must be signed on behalf of the converting entity and must include:

(1) the plan of conversion or a statement certifying the following:

(A) the name, organizational form, and jurisdiction of formation of the converting entity;

(B) the name, organizational form, and jurisdiction of formation of the converted entity;

(C) that a signed plan of conversion is on file at the principal place of business of the converting entity, and the address of the principal place of business;

(D) that a signed plan of conversion will be on file after the conversion at the principal place of business of the converted entity, and the address of the principal place of business; and

(E) that a copy of the plan of conversion will be on written request furnished without cost by the converting entity before the conversion or by the converted entity after the conversion to any owner or member of the converting entity or the converted entity; and

(2) a statement that the plan of conversion has been approved as required by the laws of the jurisdiction of formation and the governing documents of the converting entity.

(c) In addition to complying with the requirements of Subsections (a) and (b), if Sections 10.1025 and 10.109 apply to the conversion, the certificate of conversion required by this section must:

(1) be titled "Certificate of Conversion and Continuance"; and

(2) include a statement certifying that the converting entity is electing to continue its existence in its current organizational form and jurisdiction of formation.

Acts 2003, 78th Leg., ch. 182, § 1, eff. Jan. 1, 2006. Amended by Acts 2007, 80th Leg., ch. 688, § 54, eff. Sept. 1, 2007; Acts 2009, 81st Leg., ch. 84, § 18, eff. Sept. 1, 2009.

§ 10.155. Filing of Certificate of Conversion

(a) If a certificate of conversion is required to be filed, the certificate of conversion must be filed in accordance with Chapter 4. If the converted entity is a filing entity, the certificate of formation of the filing entity must also be filed with the certificate of conversion in accordance with Chapter 4. Except as provided by this section, the certificate must be filed with the secretary of state.

(b) If the converting entity is a domestic real estate investment trust, the certificate of conversion must be filed in accordance with Chapter 4 with the county clerk of the county in which the converting entity's principal place of business in this state is located.

(c) If the converted entity is a domestic real estate investment trust, the certificate of formation of the converted entity must also be filed with the certificate of conversion in accordance with Chapter 4 with the county clerk of the county in which the converted entity's principal place of business in this state is located.

Acts 2003, 78th Leg., ch. 182, § 1, eff. Jan. 1, 2006.

§ 10.156. Acceptance of Certificate for Filing

The filing officer may not accept a certificate of merger, exchange, or conversion for filing if:

(1) the filing officer finds that the certificate of merger, exchange, or conversion does not conform to law; or

(2) the required franchise taxes have not been paid or the certificate of merger, exchange, or conversion does not provide that one or more of the surviving, new, or acquiring organizations or the converted entity is liable for the payment of the required franchise taxes.

Acts 2003, 78th Leg., ch. 182, § 1, eff. Jan. 1, 2006.

SUBCHAPTER E. ABANDONMENT OF MERGER, EXCHANGE, OR CONVERSION

§ 10.201. Abandonment of Plan of Merger, Exchange, or Conversion

After a merger, interest exchange, or conversion is approved as provided by this code, and at any time before the merger, interest exchange, or conversion takes effect, the plan of merger, interest exchange, or conversion may be abandoned, subject to any contractual rights, by any of the domestic entities that are a party to the merger, interest exchange, or conversion, without action by the owners or members, under the procedures provided by the plan of merger, exchange, or conversion or, if no abandonment procedures are provided, in the manner determined by the governing authority.

Acts 2003, 78th Leg., ch. 182, § 1, eff. Jan. 1, 2006.

§ 10.202. Abandonment After Filing

If a certificate of merger, exchange, or conversion has been filed, the merger, interest exchange, or conversion may be abandoned before its effectiveness in accordance with Sections 4.057 and 10.201.

Acts 2003, 78th Leg., ch. 182, § 1, eff. Jan. 1, 2006. Amended by Acts 2005, 79th Leg., ch. 64, § 37, eff. Jan. 1, 2006.

§ 10.203. Abandonment if No Filing Required

(a) If no filing is required by this chapter for the abandonment of a merger, interest exchange, or conversion, the merger, interest exchange, or conversion is abandoned:

(1) as provided by the procedures in the plan of merger, exchange, or conversion; or

(2) if no abandonment procedures are provided by the plan, in the manner determined by the governing authority of the abandoning entity.

(b) A filing of a certificate of abandonment under Section 4.057 is not required for the abandonment of a merger, interest exchange, or conversion if no filing is required under Subchapter D to make the merger, interest exchange, or conversion effective.

Added by Acts 2005, 79th Leg., ch. 64, § 38, eff. Jan. 1, 2006.

SUBCHAPTER F. PROPERTY TRANSFERS AND DISPOSITIONS

§ 10.251. General Power of Domestic Entity to Sell, Lease, or Convey Property

(a) Subject to any approval required by this code or the governing documents of the domestic entity, a domestic entity may transfer and convey by sale, lease, assignment, or another method an interest in property of the entity, including real property. The transfer and conveyance may:

(1) be made with or without the goodwill of the entity;

(2) be made on any terms and conditions and for any consideration, which may consist wholly or partly of money or other property, including an ownership interest in a domestic entity or non-code organization; and

(3) be evidenced by a deed, assignment, or other instrument of transfer or conveyance, with or without the seal of the entity.

(b) Subject to any approval required by this code or the governing documents of the domestic entity, a domestic entity may grant a pledge, mortgage, deed of trust, or trust indenture with respect to an interest in property of the entity, including real property, with or without the seal of the entity.

Acts 2003, 78th Leg., ch. 182, § 1, eff. Jan. 1, 2006.

§ 10.252. No Approval Required for Certain Dispositions of Property

Except as otherwise provided by this code, the governing documents of the domestic entity, or specific limitations established by the governing authority, a sale, lease, assignment, conveyance, pledge, mortgage, deed of trust, trust indenture, or other transfer of an interest in real property or other property made by a domestic entity does not require the approval of the members or owners of the entity.

Acts 2003, 78th Leg., ch. 182, § 1, eff. Jan. 1, 2006.

§ 10.253. Recording Instrument Conveying Real Property of Domestic Entity

(a) A deed or other instrument executed by a domestic entity that conveys an interest in real property may be recorded in the same manner and with the same effect as other similar instruments if the instrument is signed and acknowledged by:

(1) an officer, authorized attorney-in-fact, or other authorized person of the entity; or

(2) in the case of a partnership or limited liability company, a governing person of the entity.

(b) A deed or other instrument executed by a domestic entity that conveys an interest in real property and that is recorded and signed by an officer, authorized attorney-in-fact, or other authorized person of the entity constitutes prima facie evidence that the sale or conveyance that is the subject of the instrument was authorized under this code and the governing documents of the entity.

Acts 2003, 78th Leg., ch. 182, § 1, eff. Jan. 1, 2006.

§ 10.254. Disposition of Property Not a Merger or Conversion; Liability

(a) A disposition of all or part of the property of a domestic entity, regardless of whether the disposition requires the approval of the entity's owners or members, is not a merger or conversion for any purpose.

(b) Except as otherwise expressly provided by another statute, a person acquiring property described by this section may not be held responsible or liable for a liability or obligation of the transferring domestic entity that is not expressly assumed by the person.

Acts 2003, 78th Leg., ch. 182, § 1, eff. Jan. 1, 2006. Amended by Acts 2007, 80th Leg., ch. 688, § 55, eff. Sept. 1, 2007.

SUBCHAPTER G. BANKRUPTCY REORGANIZATION

§ 10.301. Reorganization Under Bankruptcy and Similar Laws

(a) A trustee appointed for a domestic entity that is being reorganized under a federal statute, the designated officers of a domestic entity being reorganized under a federal statute, or any other individual designated by a court having jurisdiction of a domestic entity being reorganized under a federal statute to act on behalf of the domestic entity may, without action by or notice to the domestic entity's governing authority, owners, or members, in order to carry out a plan of reorganization ordered by a court under the federal statute:

(1) amend or restate the domestic entity's certificate of formation if the certificate of formation after amendment or restatement contains only provisions required or permitted to be contained in the certificate of formation;

(2) merge or exchange an interest with one or more domestic entities or non-code organizations under a plan of merger or exchange having any provision required or permitted by Sections 10.002, 10.003, 10.004, 10.005, 10.052, and 10.053;

(3) change the location of the domestic entity's registered office, change its registered agent, and remove or appoint any agent to receive service of process;

(4) alter, amend, or repeal the domestic entity's governing documents other than filing instruments;

(5) constitute or reconstitute and classify or reclassify the domestic entity's governing authority and name, constitute, or appoint managerial officials in place of or in addition to all or some of the managerial officials;

(6) sell, lease, exchange, or otherwise dispose of all, or substantially all, of the domestic entity's property and assets;

(7) authorize and fix the terms, manner, and conditions of the issuance of bonds, debentures, or other obligations, regardless of whether the obligation is convertible into ownership interests of any class or bearing warrants or other evidences of optional rights to purchase or subscribe for any ownership interests of any class;

(8) wind up and terminate the entity's existence; or

(9) effect a conversion.

(b) An action taken under Subsection (a)(4) or (5) takes effect on entry of the order approving the plan of reorganization or on another effective date as may be specified, without further action of the domestic entity, as and to the extent provided by the plan of reorganization or the order approving the plan of reorganization.

Acts 2003, 78th Leg., ch. 182, § 1, eff. Jan. 1, 2006.

§ 10.302. Signing of Documents

A trustee appointed for a domestic entity being reorganized under a federal statute, the designated officers of a domestic entity being reorganized under a federal statute, or any other individual designated by a court having jurisdiction of a domestic entity being reorganized under a federal statute may sign on behalf of a domestic entity that is being reorganized:

(1) a certificate of amendment or restated certificate of formation containing:

(A) the name of the domestic entity;

(B) each amendment or the restatement approved by the court;

(C) the date of the court's order approving the certificate of amendment or the restatement;

(D) the name of the court having jurisdiction, file name, and case number of the reorganization case in which the order was entered; and

(E) a statement that the court had jurisdiction of the case under a federal statute;

(2) a certificate of merger or exchange containing:

(A) the name of the domestic entity;

(B) the part of the plan of reorganization that contains the plan of merger or exchange approved by the court, which must include the information required by Section 10.151(b) or 10.152, as applicable, but which is not required to include the resolution of the governing authority referred to in Section 10.152;

(C) the date of the court's order approving the plan of merger or consolidation;

(D) the name of the court having jurisdiction, file name, and case number of the reorganization case in which the order or decree was entered; and

(E) a statement that the court had jurisdiction of the case under a federal statute;

(3) a certificate of termination containing:

(A) the name of the domestic entity;

(B) the information required by Sections 11.101(c)(1)–(4);

(C) the date of the court's order approving the certificate of termination;

(D) a statement that the obligations of the domestic entity, including debts and liabilities, have been paid or discharged as provided by the plan of reorganization and the remaining property and assets of the domestic entity have been distributed as provided by the plan of reorganization;

(E) the name of the court having jurisdiction, file name, and case number of the reorganization case in which the order or decree was entered; and

(F) a statement that the court had jurisdiction of the case under a federal statute;

(4) a statement of change of registered office or registered agent, or both, containing:

(A) the name of the domestic entity;

(B) the information required by Section 5.202(b), as applicable, but not the information included in the statement referred to in Section 5.202(b)(6);

(C) the date of the court's order approving the statement of change of registered office or registered agent, or both;

(D) the name of the court having jurisdiction, file name, and case number of the reorganization case in which the order or decree was entered; and

(E) a statement that the court had jurisdiction of the case under a federal statute; or

(5) a certificate of conversion containing:

(A) the name of the domestic entity;

(B) the part of the plan of reorganization that contains the plan of conversion approved by the court, which must include the information required by Section 10.103;

(C) the date of the court's order or decree approving the plan of conversion;

(D) the name of the court having jurisdiction, file name, and case number of the reorganization case in which the order was entered; and

(E) a statement that the court had jurisdiction of the case under a federal statute.

Acts 2003, 78th Leg., ch. 182, § 1, eff. Jan. 1, 2006.

§ 10.303. Reorganization With Other Entities

If a domestic entity or non-code organization that is not being reorganized under a federal statute merges or exchanges an interest with a domestic entity that is being reorganized under a plan of reorganization under a federal statute:

(1) Subchapters A, B, D, E, and H apply to the domestic entity or non-code organization that is not being reorganized to the same extent those subchapters would apply if the domestic entity or non-code organization were merging or engaging in an interest exchange with a domestic entity that is not being reorganized, except as otherwise provided by the plan of reorganization ordered by a court under the federal statute;

(2) Subchapter H applies to a subsidiary organization that is not being reorganized to the same extent that subchapter would apply if the subsidiary organization were merging with a parent organization that is not being reorganized;

(3) on the receipt of all required authorization for all action required by this code for each domestic entity that is a party to the plan of merger or exchange that is not being reorganized and all

action by each domestic entity or non-code organization that is a party to the plan of merger or exchange required by the laws of the entity's or organization's jurisdiction of formation and governing documents, a certificate of merger or exchange shall be signed by each domestic entity or non-code organization that is a party to the merger or exchange other than the domestic entity that is being reorganized as provided by Section 10.151 and on behalf of the domestic entity that is being reorganized by the persons specified in Section 10.302;

(4) the certificate of merger or exchange must contain the information required by Section 10.302(2);

(5) the certificate of merger or exchange must be filed in the manner provided by Section 10.153; and

(6) on the acceptance for filing of the certificate of merger or exchange in accordance with Subchapter D, the merger or interest exchange, when effective, has the same effect as if it had been adopted by unanimous action of the governing authority and owners or members of the domestic entity being reorganized, and the effectiveness of the merger or interest exchange is determined as provided by Section 10.007 or 10.054.

Acts 2003, 78th Leg., ch. 182, § 1, eff. Jan. 1, 2006.

§ 10.304. Right of Dissent and Appraisal Excluded

An owner or member of a domestic entity subject to dissenters' rights being reorganized under a federal statute does not have a right to dissent and appraisal under this code except as provided by the plan of reorganization.

Acts 2003, 78th Leg., ch. 182, § 1, eff. Jan. 1, 2006.

§ 10.305. After Final Decree

This subchapter does not apply after the entry of a final decree in a reorganization case under a federal statute even though the court that renders the decree may retain jurisdiction of the case for limited purposes unrelated to consummation of the plan of reorganization.

Acts 2003, 78th Leg., ch. 182, § 1, eff. Jan. 1, 2006.

§ 10.306. Chapter Cumulative of Other Changes

This chapter does not preclude other changes in a domestic entity or its ownership or membership interests or securities by a plan of reorganization ordered by a court under a federal statute.

Acts 2003, 78th Leg., ch. 182, § 1, eff. Jan. 1, 2006.

SUBCHAPTER H. RIGHTS OF DISSENTING OWNERS

§ 10.351. Applicability of Subchapter

(a) This subchapter does not apply to a fundamental business transaction of a domestic entity if, immediately before the effective date of the fundamental business transaction, all of the ownership interests of the entity otherwise entitled to rights to dissent and appraisal under this code are held by one owner or only by the owners who approved the fundamental business transaction.

(b) This subchapter applies only to a "domestic entity subject to dissenters' rights," as defined in Section 1.002. That term includes a domestic for-profit corporation, professional corporation, professional association, and real estate investment trust. Except as provided in Subsection (c), that term does not include a partnership or limited liability company.

(c) The governing documents of a partnership or a limited liability company may provide that its owners are entitled to the rights of dissent and appraisal provided by this subchapter, subject to any modification to those rights as provided by the entity's governing documents.

Acts 2003, 78th Leg., ch. 182, § 1, eff. Jan. 1, 2006. Amended by Acts 2007, 80th Leg., ch. 688, § 56, eff. Sept. 1, 2007.

§ 10.352. Definitions

In this subchapter:

(1) "Dissenting owner" means an owner of an ownership interest in a domestic entity subject to dissenters' rights who:

(A) provides notice under Section 10.356; and

(B) complies with the requirements for perfecting that owner's right to dissent under this subchapter.

(2) "Responsible organization" means:

(A) the organization responsible for:

(i) the provision of notices under this subchapter; and

(ii) the primary obligation of paying the fair value for an ownership interest held by a dissenting owner;

(B) with respect to a merger or conversion:

(i) for matters occurring before the merger or conversion, the organization that is merging or converting; and

(ii) for matters occurring after the merger or conversion, the surviving or new organization that is primarily obligated for the payment of the fair value of the dissenting owner's ownership interest in the merger or conversion;

(C) with respect to an interest exchange, the organization the ownership interests of which are being acquired in the interest exchange; and

(D) with respect to the sale of all or substantially all of the assets of an organization, the organization the assets of which are to be transferred by sale or in another manner.

Acts 2003, 78th Leg., ch. 182, § 1, eff. Jan. 1, 2006.

§ 10.353. Form and Validity of Notice

(a) Notice required under this subchapter:

(1) must be in writing; and

(2) may be mailed, hand-delivered, or delivered by courier or electronic transmission.

(b) Failure to provide notice as required by this subchapter does not invalidate any action taken.

Acts 2003, 78th Leg., ch. 182, § 1, eff. Jan. 1, 2006.

§ 10.354. Rights of Dissent and Appraisal

(a) Subject to Subsection (b), an owner of an ownership interest in a domestic entity subject to dissenters' rights is entitled to:

(1) dissent from:

(A) a plan of merger to which the domestic entity is a party if owner approval is required by this code and the owner owns in the domestic entity an ownership interest that was entitled to vote on the plan of merger;

(B) a sale of all or substantially all of the assets of the domestic entity if owner approval is required by this code and the owner owns in the domestic entity an ownership interest that was entitled to vote on the sale;

(C) a plan of exchange in which the ownership interest of the owner is to be acquired;

(D) a plan of conversion in which the domestic entity is the converting entity if owner approval is required by this code and the owner owns in the domestic entity an ownership interest that was entitled to vote on the plan of conversion; or

(E) a merger effected under Section 10.006 in which:

(i) the owner is entitled to vote on the merger; or

(ii) the ownership interest of the owner is converted or exchanged; and

(2) subject to compliance with the procedures set forth in this subchapter, obtain the fair value of that ownership interest through an appraisal.

(b) Notwithstanding Subsection (a), subject to Subsection (c), an owner may not dissent from a plan of merger or conversion in which there is a single surviving or new domestic entity or non-code organization, or from a plan of exchange, if:

(1) the ownership interest, or a depository receipt in respect of the ownership interest, held by the owner is part of a class or series of ownership interests, or depository receipts in respect of ownership interests, that are, on the record date set for purposes of determining which owners are entitled to vote on the plan of merger, conversion, or exchange, as appropriate:

(A) listed on a national securities exchange ; or

(B) held of record by at least 2,000 owners;

(2) the owner is not required by the terms of the plan of merger, conversion, or exchange, as appropriate, to accept for the owner's ownership interest any consideration that is different from the consideration to be provided to any other holder of an ownership interest of the same class or series as the ownership interest held by the owner, other than cash instead of fractional shares or interests the owner would otherwise be entitled to receive; and

(3) the owner is not required by the terms of the plan of merger, conversion, or exchange, as appropriate, to accept for the owner's ownership interest any consideration other than:

(A) ownership interests, or depository receipts in respect of ownership interests, of a domestic entity or non-code organization of the same general organizational type that, immediately after the effective date of the merger, conversion, or exchange, as appropriate, will be part of a class or series of ownership interests, or depository receipts in respect of ownership interests, that are:

(i) listed on a national securities exchange or authorized for listing on the exchange on official notice of issuance; or

(ii) held of record by at least 2,000 owners;

(B) cash instead of fractional ownership interests the owner would otherwise be entitled to receive; or

(C) any combination of the ownership interests and cash described by Paragraphs (A) and (B).

(c) Subsection (b) shall not apply to a domestic entity that is a subsidiary with respect to a merger under Section 10.006.

Acts 2003, 78th Leg., ch. 182, § 1, eff. Jan. 1, 2006. Amended by Acts 2005, 79th Leg., ch. 64, § 39, eff. Jan. 1, 2006; Acts 2011, 82nd Leg., ch. 139 (S.B. 748), § 14, eff. Sept. 1, 2011.

§ 10.355. Notice of Right of Dissent and Appraisal

(a) A domestic entity subject to dissenters' rights that takes or proposes to take an action regarding which an owner has a right to dissent and obtain an appraisal under Section 10.354 shall notify each affected owner of the owner's rights under that section if:

(1) the action or proposed action is submitted to a vote of the owners at a meeting; or

(2) approval of the action or proposed action is obtained by written consent of the owners instead of being submitted to a vote of the owners.

(b) If a parent organization effects a merger under Section 10.006 and a subsidiary organization that is a party to the merger is a domestic entity subject to dissenters' rights, the responsible organization shall notify the owners of that subsidiary organization who have a right to dissent to the merger under Section 10.354 of their rights under this subchapter not later than the 10th day after the effective date of the merger. The notice must also include a copy of the certificate of merger and a statement that the merger has become effective.

(c) A notice required to be provided under Subsection (a) or (b) must:

(1) be accompanied by a copy of this subchapter; and

(2) advise the owner of the location of the responsible organization's principal executive offices to which a notice required under Section 10.356(b)(1) or (3) may be provided.

(d) In addition to the requirements prescribed by Subsection (c), a notice required to be provided under Subsection (a)(1) must accompany the notice of the meeting to consider the action, and a notice required under Subsection (a)(2) must be provided to:

(1) each owner who consents in writing to the action before the owner delivers the written consent; and

(2) each owner who is entitled to vote on the action and does not consent in writing to the action before the 11th day after the date the action takes effect.

(e) Not later than the 10th day after the date an action described by Subsection (a)(1) takes effect, the responsible organization shall give notice that the action has been effected to each owner who voted against the action and sent notice under Section 10.356(b)(1) .

Acts 2003, 78th Leg., ch. 182, § 1, eff. Jan. 1, 2006. Amended by Acts 2011, 82nd Leg., ch. 139 (S.B. 748), § 15, eff. Sept. 1, 2011.

§ 10.356. Procedure for Dissent by Owners as to Actions; Perfection of Right of Dissent and Appraisal

(a) An owner of an ownership interest of a domestic entity subject to dissenters' rights who has the right to dissent and appraisal from any of the actions referred to in Section 10.354 may exercise that right to dissent and appraisal only by complying with the procedures specified in this subchapter. An owner's right of dissent and appraisal under Section 10.354 may be exercised by an owner only with respect to an ownership interest that is not voted in favor of the action.

(b) To perfect the owner's rights of dissent and appraisal under Section 10.354, an owner:

(1) if the proposed action is to be submitted to a vote of the owners at a meeting, must give to the domestic entity a written notice of objection to the action that:

(A) is addressed to the entity's president and secretary;

(B) states that the owner's right to dissent will be exercised if the action takes effect;

(C) provides an address to which notice of effectiveness of the action should be delivered or mailed; and

(D) is delivered to the entity's principal executive offices before the meeting;

(2) with respect to the ownership interest for which the rights of dissent and appraisal are sought:

(A) must vote against the action if the owner is entitled to vote on the action and the action is approved at a meeting of the owners; and

(B) may not consent to the action if the action is approved by written consent; and

(3) must give to the responsible organization a demand in writing that:

(A) is addressed to the president and secretary of the responsible organization;

(B) demands payment of the fair value of the ownership interests for which the rights of dissent and appraisal are sought;

(C) provides to the responsible organization an address to which a notice relating to the dissent and appraisal procedures under this subchapter may be sent;

(D) states the number and class of the ownership interests of the domestic entity owned by the owner and the fair value of the ownership interests as estimated by the owner; and

(E) is delivered to the responsible organization at its principal executive offices at the following time:

(i) not later than the 20th day after the date the responsible organization sends to the owner the notice required by Section 10.355(e) that the action has taken effect , if the action was approved by a vote of the owners at a meeting;

(ii) not later than the 20th day after the date the responsible organization sends to the owner the notice required by Section 10.355(d)(2) that the action has taken effect , if the action was approved by the written consent of the owners; or

(iii) not later than the 20th day after the date the responsible organization sends to the owner a notice that the merger was effected, if the action is a merger effected under Section 10.006.

(c) An owner who does not make a demand within the period required by Subsection (b)(3)(E) or, if Subsection (b)(1) is applicable, does not give the notice of objection before the meeting of the owners is bound by the action and is not entitled to exercise the rights of dissent and appraisal under Section 10.354.

(d) Not later than the 20th day after the date an owner makes a demand under Subsection (b)(3) , the owner must submit to the responsible organization any certificates representing the ownership interest to which the demand relates for purposes of making a notation on the certificates that a demand for the payment of the fair value of an ownership interest has been made under this section. An owner's failure to submit the certificates within the required period has the effect of terminating, at the option of the responsible organization, the owner's rights to dissent and appraisal under Section 10.354 unless a court, for good cause shown, directs otherwise.

(e) If a domestic entity and responsible organization satisfy the requirements of this subchapter relating to the rights of owners of ownership interests in the entity to dissent to an action and seek appraisal of those ownership interests, an owner of an ownership interest who fails to perfect that owner's right of dissent in accordance with this subchapter may not bring suit to recover the value of the ownership interest or money damages relating to the action.

Acts 2003, 78th Leg., ch. 182, § 1, eff. Jan. 1, 2006. Amended by Acts 2011, 82nd Leg., ch. 139 (S.B. 748), § 16, eff. Sept. 1, 2011.

§ 10.357. Withdrawal of Demand for Fair Value of Ownership Interest

(a) An owner may withdraw a demand for the payment of the fair value of an ownership interest made under Section 10.356 before:

(1) payment for the ownership interest has been made under Sections 10.358 and 10.361; or

(2) a petition has been filed under Section 10.361.

(b) Unless the responsible organization consents to the withdrawal of the demand, an owner may not withdraw a demand for payment under Subsection (a) after either of the events specified in Subsections (a)(1) and (2).

Acts 2003, 78th Leg., ch. 182, § 1, eff. Jan. 1, 2006.

§ 10.358. Response by Organization to Notice of Dissent and Demand for Fair Value by Dissenting Owner

(a) Not later than the 20th day after the date a responsible organization receives a demand for payment made by a dissenting owner in accordance with Section 10.356(b)(3) , the responsible organization shall respond to the dissenting owner in writing by:

(1) accepting the amount claimed in the demand as the fair value of the ownership interests specified in the notice; or

(2) rejecting the demand and including in the response the requirements prescribed by Subsection (c).

(b) If the responsible organization accepts the amount claimed in the demand, the responsible organization shall pay the amount not later than the 90th day after the date the action that is the subject of the demand was effected if the owner delivers to the responsible organization:

(1) endorsed certificates representing the ownership interests if the ownership interests are certificated; or

(2) signed assignments of the ownership interests if the ownership interests are uncertificated.

(c) If the responsible organization rejects the amount claimed in the demand, the responsible organization shall provide to the owner:

(1) an estimate by the responsible organization of the fair value of the ownership interests; and

(2) an offer to pay the amount of the estimate provided under Subdivision (1).

(d) If the dissenting owner decides to accept the offer made by the responsible organization under Subsection (c)(2), the owner must provide to the responsible organization notice of the acceptance of the offer not later than the 90th day after the date the action that is the subject of the demand took effect .

(e) If, not later than the 90th day after the date the action that is the subject of the demand took effect, a dissenting owner accepts an offer made by a responsible organization under Subsection (c)(2) or a dissenting owner and a responsible organization reach an agreement on the fair value of the ownership interests, the responsible organization shall pay the agreed amount not later than the 120th day after the date the action that is the subject of the demand took effect , if the dissenting owner delivers to the responsible organization:

(1) endorsed certificates representing the ownership interests if the ownership interests are certificated; or

(2) signed assignments of the ownership interests if the ownership interests are uncertificated.

Acts 2003, 78th Leg., ch. 182, § 1, eff. Jan. 1, 2006. Amended by Acts 2011, 82nd Leg., ch. 139 (S.B. 748), § 17, eff. Sept. 1, 2011.

§ 10.359. Record of Demand for Fair Value of Ownership Interest

(a) A responsible organization shall note in the organization's ownership interest records maintained under Section 3.151 the receipt of a demand for payment from any dissenting owner made under Section 10.356.

(b) If an ownership interest that is the subject of a demand for payment made under Section 10.356 is transferred, a new certificate representing that ownership interest must contain:

(1) a reference to the demand; and

(2) the name of the original dissenting owner of the ownership interest.

Acts 2003, 78th Leg., ch. 182, § 1, eff. Jan. 1, 2006.

§ 10.360. Rights of Transferee of Certain Ownership Interest

A transferee of an ownership interest that is the subject of a demand for payment made under Section 10.356 does not acquire additional rights with respect to the responsible organization following the transfer. The transferee has only the rights the original dissenting owner had with respect to the responsible organization after making the demand.

Acts 2003, 78th Leg., ch. 182, § 1, eff. Jan. 1, 2006.

§ 10.361. Proceeding to Determine Fair Value of Ownership Interest and Owners Entitled to Payment; Appointment of Appraisers

(a) If a responsible organization rejects the amount demanded by a dissenting owner under Section 10.358 and the dissenting owner and responsible organization are unable to reach an agreement relating to the fair value of the ownership interests within the period prescribed by Section 10.358(d), the dissenting owner or responsible organization may file a petition requesting a finding and determination of the fair value of the owner's ownership interests in a court in:

(1) the county in which the organization's principal office is located in this state; or

(2) the county in which the organization's registered office is located in this state, if the organization does not have a business office in this state.

(b) A petition described by Subsection (a) must be filed not later than the 60th day after the expiration of the period required by Section 10.358(d).

(c) On the filing of a petition by an owner under Subsection (a), service of a copy of the petition shall be made to the responsible organization. Not later than the 10th day after the date a responsible organization receives service under this subsection, the responsible organization shall file with the clerk of the court in which the petition was filed a list containing the names and addresses of each owner of the organization who has demanded payment for ownership interests under Section 10.356 and with whom agreement as to the value of the ownership interests has not been reached with the responsible organization. If the responsible organization files a petition under Subsection (a), the petition must be accompanied by this list.

(d) The clerk of the court in which a petition is filed under this section shall provide by registered mail notice of the time and place set for the hearing to:

(1) the responsible organization; and

(2) each owner named on the list described by Subsection (c) at the address shown for the owner on the list.

(e) The court shall:

(1) determine which owners have:

(A) perfected their rights by complying with this subchapter; and

(B) become subsequently entitled to receive payment for the fair value of their ownership interests; and

(2) appoint one or more qualified appraisers to determine the fair value of the ownership interests of the owners described by Subdivision (1).

(f) The court shall approve the form of a notice required to be provided under this section. The judgment of the court is final and binding on the responsible organization, any other organization obligated to make payment under this subchapter for an ownership interest, and each owner who is notified as required by this section.

(g) The beneficial owner of an ownership interest subject to dissenters' rights held in a voting trust or by a nominee on the beneficial owner's behalf may file a petition described by Subsection (a) if no agreement between the dissenting owner of the ownership interest and the responsible organization has been reached within the period prescribed by Section 10.358(d). When the beneficial owner files a petition described by Subsection (a):

(1) the beneficial owner shall at that time be considered, for purposes of this subchapter, the owner, the dissenting owner, and the holder of the ownership interest subject to the petition; and

(2) the dissenting owner who demanded payment under Section 10.356 has no further rights regarding the ownership interest subject to the petition.

Acts 2003, 78th Leg., ch. 182, § 1, eff. Jan. 1, 2006. Amended by Acts 2009, 81st Leg., ch. 84, § 19, eff. Sept. 1, 2009.

§ 10.362. Computation and Determination of Fair Value of Ownership Interest

(a) For purposes of this subchapter, the fair value of an ownership interest of a domestic entity subject to dissenters' rights is the value of the ownership interest on the date preceding the date of the action that is the subject of the appraisal. Any appreciation or depreciation in the value of the ownership interest occurring in anticipation of the proposed action or as a result of the action must be specifically excluded from the computation of the fair value of the ownership interest.

(b) In computing the fair value of an ownership interest under this subchapter, consideration must be given to the value of the domestic entity as a going concern without including in the computation of value any control premium, any minority ownership discount, or any discount for lack of marketability. If the domestic entity has different classes or series of ownership interests, the relative rights and preferences of and limitations placed on the class or series of ownership interests, other than relative voting rights, held by the dissenting owner must be taken into account in the computation of value.

(c) The determination of the fair value of an ownership interest made for purposes of this subchapter may not be used for purposes of making a determination of the fair value of that ownership interest for another purpose or of the fair value of another ownership interest, including for purposes of determining any minority or liquidity discount that might apply to a sale of an ownership interest.

Acts 2003, 78th Leg., ch. 182, § 1, eff. Jan. 1, 2006. Amended by Acts 2007, 80th Leg., ch. 688, § 57, eff. Sept. 1, 2007.

§ 10.363. Powers and Duties of Appraiser; Appraisal Procedures

(a) An appraiser appointed under Section 10.361 has the power and authority that:

(1) is granted by the court in the order appointing the appraiser; and

(2) may be conferred by a court to a master in chancery as provided by Rule 171, Texas Rules of Civil Procedure.

(b) The appraiser shall:

(1) determine the fair value of an ownership interest of an owner adjudged by the court to be entitled to payment for the ownership interest; and

(2) file with the court a report of that determination.

(c) The appraiser is entitled to examine the books and records of a responsible organization and may conduct investigations as the appraiser considers appropriate. A dissenting owner or responsible organization may submit to an appraiser evidence or other information relevant to the determination of the fair value of the ownership interest required by Subsection (b)(1).

(d) The clerk of the court appointing the appraiser shall provide notice of the filing of the report under

Subsection (b) to each dissenting owner named in the list filed under Section 10.361 and the responsible organization.

Acts 2003, 78th Leg., ch. 182, § 1, eff. Jan. 1, 2006.

§ 10.364. Objection to Appraisal; Hearing

(a) A dissenting owner or responsible organization may object, based on the law or the facts, to all or part of an appraisal report containing the fair value of an ownership interest determined under Section 10.363(b).

(b) If an objection to a report is raised under Subsection (a), the court shall hold a hearing to determine the fair value of the ownership interest that is the subject of the report. After the hearing, the court shall require the responsible organization to pay to the holders of the ownership interest the amount of the determined value with interest, accruing from the 91st day after the date the applicable action for which the owner elected to dissent was effected until the date of the judgment.

(c) Interest under Subsection (b) accrues at the same rate as is provided for the accrual of prejudgment interest in civil cases.

(d) The responsible organization shall:

(1) immediately pay the amount of the judgment to a holder of an uncertificated ownership interest; and

(2) pay the amount of the judgment to a holder of a certificated ownership interest immediately after the certificate holder surrenders to the responsible organization an endorsed certificate representing the ownership interest.

(e) On payment of the judgment, the dissenting owner does not have an interest in the:

(1) ownership interest for which the payment is made; or

(2) responsible organization with respect to that ownership interest.

Acts 2003, 78th Leg., ch. 182, § 1, eff. Jan. 1, 2006.

§ 10.365. Court Costs; Compensation for Appraiser

(a) An appraiser appointed under Section 10.361 is entitled to a reasonable fee payable from court costs.

(b) All court costs shall be allocated between the responsible organization and the dissenting owners in the manner that the court determines to be fair and equitable.

Acts 2003, 78th Leg., ch. 182, § 1, eff. Jan. 1, 2006.

§ 10.366. Status of Ownership Interest Held or Formerly Held by Dissenting Owner

(a) An ownership interest of an organization acquired by a responsible organization under this subchapter:

(1) in the case of a merger, conversion, or interest exchange, shall be held or disposed of as provided in the plan of merger, conversion, or interest exchange; and

(2) in any other case, may be held or disposed of by the responsible organization in the same manner as other ownership interests acquired by the organization or held in its treasury.

(b) An owner who has demanded payment for the owner's ownership interest under Section 10.356 is not entitled to vote or exercise any other rights of an owner with respect to the ownership interest except the right to:

(1) receive payment for the ownership interest under this subchapter; and

(2) bring an appropriate action to obtain relief on the ground that the action to which the demand relates would be or was fraudulent.

(c) An ownership interest for which payment has been demanded under Section 10.356 may not be considered outstanding for purposes of any subsequent vote or action.

Acts 2003, 78th Leg., ch. 182, § 1, eff. Jan. 1, 2006. Amended by Acts 2009, 81st Leg., ch. 84, § 20, eff. Sept. 1, 2009.

§ 10.367. Rights of Owners Following Termination of Right of Dissent

(a) The rights of a dissenting owner terminate if:

(1) the owner withdraws the demand under Section 10.356;

(2) the owner's right of dissent is terminated under Section 10.356;

(3) a petition is not filed within the period required by Section 10.361; or

(4) after a hearing held under Section 10.361, the court adjudges that the owner is not entitled to elect to dissent from an action under this subchapter.

(b) On termination of the right of dissent under this section:

(1) the dissenting owner and all persons claiming a right under the owner are conclusively presumed to have approved and ratified the action to which the owner dissented and are bound by that action;

(2) the owner's right to be paid the fair value of the owner's ownership interests ceases;

(3) the owner's status as an owner of those ownership interests is restored, as if the owner's demand for payment of the fair value of the ownership interests had not been made under Section 10.356, if the owner's ownership interests were not canceled, converted, or exchanged as a result of the action or a subsequent action;

(4) the dissenting owner is entitled to receive the same cash, property, rights, and other consideration received by owners of the same class and series of ownership interests held by the owner, as if the owner's demand for payment of the fair value of the ownership interests had not been made under Section 10.356, if the owner's ownership interests were canceled, converted, or exchanged as a result of the action or a subsequent action;

(5) any action of the domestic entity taken after the date of the demand for payment by the owner under Section 10.356 will not be considered ineffective or invalid because of the restoration of the owner's ownership interests or the other rights or entitlements of the owner under this subsection; and

(6) the dissenting owner is entitled to receive dividends or other distributions made after the date of the owner's payment demand under Section 10.356, to owners of the same class and series of ownership interests held by the owner as if the demand had not been made, subject to any change in or adjustment to the ownership interests because of an action taken by the domestic entity after the date of the demand.

Acts 2003, 78th Leg., ch. 182, § 1, eff. Jan. 1, 2006. Amended by Acts 2007, 80th Leg., ch. 688, § 58, eff. Sept. 1, 2007; Acts 2009, 81st Leg., ch. 84, § 21, eff. Sept. 1, 2009.

§ 10.368. Exclusivity of Remedy of Dissent and Appraisal

In the absence of fraud in the transaction, any right of an owner of an ownership interest to dissent from an action and obtain the fair value of the ownership interest under this subchapter is the exclusive remedy for recovery of:

(1) the value of the ownership interest; or

(2) money damages to the owner with respect to the action.

Acts 2003, 78th Leg., ch. 182, § 1, eff. Jan. 1, 2006. Amended by Acts 2007, 80th Leg., ch. 688, § 59, eff. Sept. 1, 2007.

SUBCHAPTER Z. MISCELLANEOUS PROVISIONS

§ 10.901. Creditors; Antitrust

This code does not affect, nullify, or repeal the antitrust laws or abridge any right or rights of any creditor under existing laws.

Acts 2003, 78th Leg., ch. 182, § 1, eff. Jan. 1, 2006.

§ 10.902. Nonexclusivity

This chapter does not limit the power of a domestic entity or non-code organization to acquire all or part of the ownership or membership interests of one or more classes or series of a domestic entity through a voluntary exchange or otherwise.

Acts 2003, 78th Leg., ch. 182, § 1, eff. Jan. 1, 2006.

CHAPTER 11. WINDING UP AND TERMINATION OF DOMESTIC ENTITY

SUBCHAPTER A. GENERAL PROVISIONS

Section
11.001. Definitions.

SUBCHAPTER B. WINDING UP OF DOMESTIC ENTITY

11.051. Event Requiring Winding Up of Domestic Entity.
11.052. Winding Up Procedures.
11.053. Property Applied to Discharge Liabilities and Obligations.
11.054. Court Supervision of Winding Up Process.
11.055. Court Action or Proceeding During Winding Up.
11.056. Supplemental Provisions for Limited Liability Company.
11.057. Supplemental Provisions for Domestic General Partnership.
11.058. Supplemental Provision for Limited Partnership.
11.059. Supplemental Provisions for Corporations.

SUBCHAPTER C. TERMINATION OF DOMESTIC ENTITY

11.101. Certificate of Termination for Filing Entity.
11.102. Effectiveness of Termination of Filing Entity.
11.103. Effectiveness of Termination of Nonfiling Entity.
11.104. Action by Secretary of State.
11.105. Supplemental Information Required by Certificate of Termination of Nonprofit Corporation.

SUBCHAPTER D. REVOCATION AND CONTINUATION

Section
11.151. Revocation of Voluntary Winding Up.
11.152. Continuation of Business Without Winding Up.
11.153. Court Revocation of Fraudulent Termination.

SUBCHAPTER E. REINSTATEMENT OF TERMINATED ENTITY

11.201. Conditions for Reinstatement.
11.202. Procedures for Reinstatement.
11.203. Use of Name Similar to Previously Registered Name.
11.204. Effectiveness of Reinstatement of Nonfiling Entity.
11.205. Effectiveness of Reinstatement of Filing Entity.
11.206. Effect of Reinstatement.

SUBCHAPTER F. INVOLUNTARY TERMINATION OF FILING ENTITY BY SECRETARY OF STATE

11.251. Termination of Filing Entity by Secretary of State.
11.252. Certificate of Termination.
11.253. Reinstatement by Secretary of State After Involuntary Termination.
11.254. Reinstatement of Certificate of Formation Following Tax Forfeiture.

SUBCHAPTER G. JUDICIAL WINDING UP AND TERMINATION

11.301. Involuntary Winding Up and Termination of Filing Entity by Court Action.
11.302. Notification of Cause by Secretary of State.
11.303. Filing of Action by Attorney General.
11.304. Cure Before Final Judgment.
11.305. Judgment Requiring Winding Up and Termination.
11.306. Stay of Judgment.
11.307. Opportunity for Cure After Affirmation of Findings by Appeals Court.
11.308. Jurisdiction and Venue.
11.309. Process in State Action.
11.310. Publication of Notice.
11.311. Action Allowed After Expiration of Filing Entity's Duration.
11.312. Compliance by Terminated Entity.
11.313. Timing of Termination.
11.314 Involuntary Winding Up and Termination of Partnership or Limited Liability Company.
11.315. Filing of Decree of Termination Against Filing Entity.

SUBCHAPTER H. CLAIMS RESOLUTION ON TERMINATION

11.351. Liability of Terminated Filing Entity.
11.352. Deposit with Comptroller of Amount Due Owners and Creditors Who Are Unknown or Cannot Be Located.
11.353. Discharge of Liability of Person Responsible for Liquidation.
11.354. Payment From Account by Comptroller.
11.355. Notice of Escheat; Escheat.
11.356. Limited Survival After Termination.

Section
11.357. Governing Persons of Entity During Limited Survival.
11.358. Accelerated Procedure for Existing Claim Resolution.
11.359. Extinguishment of Existing Claim.

SUBCHAPTER I. RECEIVERSHIP

11.401. Code Governs.
11.402. Jurisdiction to Appoint Receiver.
11.403. Appointment of Receiver for Specific Property.
11.404. Appointment of Receiver to Rehabilitate Domestic Entity.
11.405. Appointment of Receiver to Liquidate Domestic Entity; Liquidation.
11.406. Receivers: Qualifications, Powers, and Duties.
11.407. Court–Ordered Filing of Claims.
11.408. Supervising Court; Jurisdiction; Authority.
11.409. Ancillary Receiverships of Foreign Entities.
11.410. Receivership for All Property and Business of Foreign Entity.
11.411. Governing Persons and Owners Not Necessary Parties Defendant.
11.412. Decree of Involuntary Termination.
11.413. Supplemental Provisions for Application of Proceeds From Liquidation of Nonprofit Corporation.
11.414. Filing of Decree of Involuntary Termination Against Filing Entity.

SUBCHAPTER A. GENERAL PROVISIONS

§ 11.001. Definitions

In this chapter:

(1) "Claim" means a right to payment, damages, or property, whether liquidated or unliquidated, accrued or contingent, matured or unmatured.

(2) "Event requiring a winding up" or "event requiring winding up" means an event specified by Section 11.051.

(3) "Existing claim" with respect to an entity means:

(A) a claim against the entity that existed before the entity's termination and is not barred by limitations; or

(B) a contractual obligation incurred after termination.

(4) "Terminated entity" means a domestic entity the existence of which has been:

(A) terminated in a manner authorized or required by this code, unless the entity has been reinstated in the manner provided by this code; or

(B) forfeited pursuant to the Tax Code, unless the forfeiture has been set aside.

(5) "Terminated filing entity" means a terminated entity that is a filing entity.

(6) "Voluntary decision to wind up" means the determination to wind up a domestic entity made by the domestic entity or the owners, members, or governing authority of the domestic entity in the manner specified by:

(A) the title of this code governing the domestic entity; or

(B) if applicable to the domestic entity, Section 11.057(a) or (b) or 11.058(a).

(7) "Voluntary winding up" means winding up as a result of a voluntary decision to wind up.

(8) "Winding up" means the process of winding up the business and affairs of a domestic entity as a result of the occurrence of an event requiring winding up.

Acts 2003, 78th Leg., ch. 182, § 1, eff. Jan. 1, 2006. Amended by Acts 2007, 80th Leg., ch. 688, § 60, eff. Sept. 1, 2007.

SUBCHAPTER B. WINDING UP OF DOMESTIC ENTITY

§ 11.051. Event Requiring Winding Up of Domestic Entity

Winding up of a domestic entity is required on:

(1) the expiration of any period of duration specified in the domestic entity's governing documents;

(2) a voluntary decision to wind up the domestic entity;

(3) an event specified in the governing documents of the domestic entity requiring the winding up, dissolution, or termination of the domestic entity, other than an event specified in another subdivision of this section;

(4) an event specified in other sections of this code requiring the winding up or termination of the domestic entity, other than an event specified in another subdivision of this section; or

(5) a decree by a court requiring the winding up, dissolution, or termination of the domestic entity, rendered under this code or other law.

Acts 2003, 78th Leg., ch. 182, § 1, eff. Jan. 1, 2006. Amended by Acts 2007, 80th Leg., ch. 688, § 61, eff. Sept. 1, 2007.

§ 11.052. Winding Up Procedures

(a) Except as provided by the title of this code governing the domestic entity, on the occurrence of an event requiring winding up of a domestic entity, unless the event requiring winding up is revoked under Section 11.151 or canceled under Section 11.152, the owners, members, managerial officials, or other persons specified in the title of this code governing the domestic entity shall, as soon as reasonably practicable, wind up the business and affairs of the domestic entity. The domestic entity shall:

(1) cease to carry on its business, except to the extent necessary to wind up its business;

(2) if the domestic entity is not a partnership, send a written notice of the winding up to each known claimant against the domestic entity;

(3) collect and sell its property to the extent the property is not to be distributed in kind to the domestic entity's owners or members; and

(4) perform any other act required to wind up its business and affairs.

(b) During the winding up process, the domestic entity may prosecute or defend a civil, criminal, or administrative action.

Acts 2003, 78th Leg., ch. 182, § 1, eff. Jan. 1, 2006.

§ 11.053. Property Applied to Discharge Liabilities and Obligations

(a) Except as provided by Subsection (b) and the title of this code governing the domestic entity, a domestic entity in the process of winding up shall apply and distribute its property to discharge, or make adequate provision for the discharge of, all of the domestic entity's liabilities and obligations.

(b) Except as provided by the title of this code governing the domestic entity, if the property of a domestic entity is not sufficient to discharge all of the domestic entity's liabilities and obligations, the domestic entity shall:

(1) apply its property, to the extent possible, to the just and equitable discharge of its liabilities and obligations, including liabilities and obligations owed to owners or members, other than for distributions; or

(2) make adequate provision for the application of the property described by Subdivision (1).

(c) Except as provided by the title of this code governing the domestic entity, after a domestic entity has discharged, or made adequate provision for the discharge of, all of its liabilities and obligations, the domestic entity shall distribute the remainder of its property, in cash or in kind, to the domestic entity's owners according to their respective rights and interests.

(d) A domestic entity may continue its business wholly or partly, including delaying the disposition of property of the domestic entity, for the limited period necessary to avoid unreasonable loss of the entity's property or business.

Acts 2003, 78th Leg., ch. 182, § 1, eff. Jan. 1, 2006.

§ 11.054. Court Supervision of Winding Up Process

Subject to the other provisions of this code, on application of a domestic entity or an owner or member of a domestic entity, a court may:

(1) supervise the winding up of the domestic entity;

(2) appoint a person to carry out the winding up of the domestic entity; and

(3) make any other order, direction, or inquiry that the circumstances may require.

Acts 2003, 78th Leg., ch. 182, § 1, eff. Jan. 1, 2006.

§ 11.055. Court Action or Proceeding During Winding Up

During the winding up process, a domestic entity may continue prosecuting or defending a court action or proceeding by or against the domestic entity.

Acts 2003, 78th Leg., ch. 182, § 1, eff. Jan. 1, 2006.

§ 11.056. Supplemental Provisions for Limited Liability Company

(a) The termination of the continued membership of the last remaining member of a domestic limited liability company is an event requiring winding up under Section 11.051(4) unless, not later than the 90th day after the date of the termination, the legal representative or successor of the last remaining member agrees:

(1) to continue the company; and

(2) to become a member of the company effective as of the date of the termination or to designate another person who agrees to become a member of the company effective as of the date of the termination.

(b) The event requiring winding up specified in Subsection (a) may be canceled in accordance with Sections 11.152(a) and 101.552(c).

Acts 2003, 78th Leg., ch. 182, § 1, eff. Jan. 1, 2006. Amended by Acts 2007, 80th Leg., ch. 688, § 62, eff. Sept. 1, 2007.

§ 11.057. Supplemental Provisions for Domestic General Partnership

(a) Unless otherwise provided by the partnership agreement, a voluntary decision to wind up a domestic general partnership, other than a partnership described by Subsection (b), requires the express will of a majority-in-interest of the partners who have not assigned their interests. A voluntary decision to wind up a partnership under this subsection may be revoked in accordance with Sections 11.151 and 152.709(e).

(b) Unless otherwise provided by the partnership agreement, a voluntary decision to wind up a domestic general partnership that has a period of duration or is for a particular undertaking, or in which the partnership agreement provides for the winding up of the partnership on occurrence of a specified event, requires the express will of all of the partners. A voluntary decision to wind up a partnership under this subsection may be revoked in accordance with Sections 11.151 and 152.709(d).

(c) An event requiring the winding up of a domestic general partnership under Section 11.051(4) includes the following:

(1) in a general partnership for a particular undertaking, the completion of the undertaking, unless otherwise provided by the partnership agreement;

(2) an event that makes it illegal for all or substantially all of the partnership business to be continued, but a cure of illegality before the 91st day after the date of notice to the general partnership of the event is effective retroactively to the date of the event for purposes of this subsection; and

(3) the sale of all or substantially all of the property of the general partnership outside the ordinary course of business, unless otherwise provided by the partnership agreement.

(d) In addition to the events specified by Subsection (c), unless otherwise provided by the partnership agreement, if a domestic general partnership does not have a period of duration, is not for a particular undertaking, and is not required under its partnership agreement to wind up the partnership on occurrence of a specified event, an event requiring winding up of the partnership under Section 11.051(4) occurs on the 60th day after the date on which the partnership receives notice of a request for winding up the partnership from a partner, other than a partner who has agreed not to withdraw, or a later date as specified by the request, unless a majority-in-interest of the partners deny the request for winding up or agree to continue the partnership. The continuation of the business by the other partners or by those who habitually acted in the business before the request, other than the partner making the request, without any settlement or liquidation of the partnership business, is prima facie evidence of an agreement to continue the partnership under this subsection.

(e) An event requiring winding up specified in Subsection (c)(1), (c)(3), or (d) may be canceled in accordance with Sections 11.152 and 152.709.

(f) "Majority-in-interest" means, with respect to all or a specified group of partners, partners who own more than 50 percent of the current percentage or other interest in the profits of the partnership that is owned by all of the partners or by the partners in the specified group, as appropriate.

Acts 2003, 78th Leg., ch. 182, § 1, eff. Jan. 1, 2006. Amended by Acts 2007, 80th Leg., ch. 688, § 63, eff. Sept. 1, 2007; Acts 2011, 82nd Leg., ch. 139 (S.B. 748), § 18, eff. Sept. 1, 2011.

§ 11.058. Supplemental Provision for Limited Partnership

(a) A voluntary decision to wind up a domestic limited partnership requires the written consent of all partners in the limited partnership unless otherwise provided by the partnership agreement. The voluntary decision to wind up may be revoked in accordance with Sections 11.151 and 153.501(d).

(b) An event of withdrawal of a general partner of a domestic limited partnership is an event requiring winding up under Section 11.051(4) unless otherwise provided by the partnership agreement. The event requiring winding up specified in this subsection may be canceled in accordance with Sections 11.152(a) and 153.501(b).

(c) An event requiring winding up of a limited partnership under Section 11.051(4) includes when there are no limited partners in the limited partnership. The event requiring winding up specified in this subsection may be canceled in accordance with Sections 11.152(a) and 153.501(e).

Acts 2003, 78th Leg., ch. 182, § 1, eff. Jan. 1, 2006. Amended by Acts 2007, 80th Leg., ch. 688, § 64, eff. Sept. 1, 2007.

§ 11.059. Supplemental Provisions for Corporations

For purposes of Section 11.051(3), the event requiring the winding up, dissolution, or termination of a domestic corporation must be specified in:

(1) the certificate of formation of the corporation; or

(2) a bylaw of the corporation adopted by the owners or members of the corporation in the same manner as an amendment to the certificate of formation of the corporation.

Acts 2003, 78th Leg., ch. 182, § 1, eff. Jan. 1, 2006. Amended by Acts 2007, 80th Leg., ch. 688, § 65, eff. Sept. 1, 2007.

SUBCHAPTER C. TERMINATION OF DOMESTIC ENTITY

§ 11.101. Certificate of Termination for Filing Entity

(a) On completion of the winding up process under Subchapter B, a filing entity must file a certificate of termination in accordance with Chapter 4.

(b) A certificate from the comptroller that all taxes administered by the comptroller under Title 2, Tax Code, have been paid must be filed with the certificate of termination if the filing entity is a taxable entity under Chapter 171, Tax Code, other than a nonprofit corporation.

(c) The certificate of termination must contain:

(1) the name of the filing entity;

(2) the name and address of each of the filing entity's governing persons;

(3) the entity's file number assigned by the secretary of state, unless the entity is a real estate investment trust;

(4) the nature of the event requiring winding up;

(5) a statement that the filing entity has complied with the provisions of this code governing its winding up; and

(6) any other information required by this code to be included in the certificate of termination for the filing entity.

Acts 2003, 78th Leg., ch. 182, § 1, eff. Jan. 1, 2006. Amended by Acts 2009, 81st Leg., ch. 84, § 22, eff. Sept. 1, 2009.

§ 11.102. Effectiveness of Termination of Filing Entity

Except as otherwise provided by this chapter, the existence of a filing entity terminates on the filing of a certificate of termination with the filing officer.

Acts 2003, 78th Leg., ch. 182, § 1, eff. Jan. 1, 2006.

§ 11.103. Effectiveness of Termination of Nonfiling Entity

Except as otherwise provided by this chapter, the existence of a nonfiling entity terminates on the completion of the winding up of its business and affairs. Notice of the termination must be provided by the nonfiling entity in the manner provided in the governing documents of the nonfiling entity if notice of termination is required under the governing documents.

Acts 2003, 78th Leg., ch. 182, § 1, eff. Jan. 1, 2006.

§ 11.104. Action by Secretary of State

The secretary of state shall remove from its active records a domestic filing entity whose period of duration specified in its certificate of formation has expired when the secretary of state determines that:

(1) the entity has failed to file a certificate of termination in accordance with Section 11.101; and

(2) the entity has failed to file an amendment to extend its period of duration in accordance with Section 11.152.

Acts 2003, 78th Leg., ch. 182, § 1, eff. Jan. 1, 2006. Amended by Acts 2007, 80th Leg., ch. 688, § 66, eff. Sept. 1, 2007.

§ 11.105. Supplemental Information Required by Certificate of Termination of Nonprofit Corporation

(a) In addition to the information required by Section 11.101, the certificate of termination filed by a nonprofit corporation that has completed its winding up process must contain a statement that:

(1) any property of the nonprofit corporation has been transferred, conveyed, applied, or distributed in accordance with this chapter and Chapter 22; and

(2) there is no suit pending against the nonprofit corporation or adequate provision has been made for the satisfaction of any judgment, order, or decree that may be entered against the nonprofit corporation in a pending suit.

(b) In addition to the statements required by Subsection (a), if the nonprofit corporation received and held property permitted to be used only for charitable, religious, eleemosynary, benevolent, educational, or similar purposes, but the nonprofit corporation did not hold the property on a condition requiring return, transfer, or conveyance because of the winding up and termination, the certificate of termination must include a statement that distribution of that property has been effected in accordance with a plan of distribution adopted in compliance with this code for the distribution of that property.

Acts 2003, 78th Leg., ch. 182, § 1, eff. Jan. 1, 2006.

SUBCHAPTER D. REVOCATION AND CONTINUATION

§ 11.151. Revocation of Voluntary Winding Up

(a) Before the termination of the existence of a domestic entity takes effect, the domestic entity may revoke a voluntary decision to wind up the entity by approval of the revocation in the manner specified in the title of this code governing the entity.

(b) A domestic entity may continue its business following the revocation of a voluntary decision to wind up under Subsection (a).

Acts 2003, 78th Leg., ch. 182, § 1, eff. Jan. 1, 2006.

§ 11.152. Continuation of Business Without Winding Up

(a) Subject to Subsections (c) and (d), a domestic entity to which an event requiring the winding up of the entity occurs as specified by Section 11.051(3) or (4) may cancel the event requiring winding up in the manner specified in the title of this code governing the domestic entity not later than the first anniversary of the date of the event requiring winding up or an earlier period prescribed by the title of this code governing the domestic entity.

(b) A domestic entity whose specified period of duration has expired may cancel that event requiring winding up by amending its governing documents in the manner provided by this code, not later than the third anniversary of the date the period expired or an earlier date prescribed by the title of this code governing the domestic entity, to extend its period of duration. The expiration of its period of duration does not by itself create a vested right on the part of an owner, member, or creditor of the entity to prevent the extension of that period. An act undertaken or a contract entered into by the domestic entity during a period in which the entity could have extended its period of duration as provided by this subsection is not invalidated by the expiration of that period, regardless of whether the entity has taken any action to extend its period of duration.

(c) A domestic entity may not cancel an event requiring winding up specified in Section 11.051(3) and continue its business if the action is prohibited by the entity's governing documents or the title of this code governing the entity.

(d) A domestic entity may cancel an event requiring winding up specified in Section 11.051(4) and continue its business only if the action:

(1) is not prohibited by the entity's governing documents; and

(2) is expressly authorized by the title of this code governing the entity.

(e) On cancellation of an event requiring winding up under this section, the domestic entity may continue its business.

Acts 2003, 78th Leg., ch. 182, § 1, eff. Jan. 1, 2006. Amended by Acts 2007, 80th Leg., ch. 688, § 67, eff. Sept. 1, 2007.

§ 11.153. Court Revocation of Fraudulent Termination

Notwithstanding any provision of this code to the contrary, a court may order the revocation of termination of an entity's existence that was terminated as a result of actual or constructive fraud. In an action under this section, any limitation period provided by law is tolled in accordance with the discovery rule. The secretary of state shall take any action necessary to implement an order under this section.

Added by Acts 2005, 79th Leg., ch. 64, § 40, eff. Jan. 1, 2006.

SUBCHAPTER E. REINSTATEMENT OF TERMINATED ENTITY

§ 11.201. Conditions for Reinstatement

(a) A terminated entity may be reinstated under this subchapter if:

(1) the termination was by mistake or inadvertent;

(2) the termination occurred without the approval of the entity's governing persons when their approval is required by the title of this code governing the terminated entity;

(3) the process of winding up before termination had not been completed by the entity; or

(4) the legal existence of the entity is necessary to:

(A) convey or assign property;

(B) settle or release a claim or liability;

(C) take an action; or

(D) sign an instrument or agreement.

(b) A terminated entity may not be reinstated under this section if the termination occurred as a result of:

(1) an order of a court or the secretary of state;

(2) an event requiring winding up that is specified in the title of this code governing the terminated entity, if that title prohibits reinstatement; or

(3) forfeiture under the Tax Code.

Acts 2003, 78th Leg., ch. 182, § 1, eff. Jan. 1, 2006.

§ 11.202. Procedures for Reinstatement

(a) To the extent applicable, a terminated entity, to be reinstated, must complete the requirements of this section not later than the third anniversary of the date the termination of the terminated entity's existence took effect.

(b) The owners, members, governing persons, or other persons must approve the reinstatement of the domestic entity in the manner provided by the title of this code governing the domestic entity.

(c) After approval of the reinstatement of a filing entity that was terminated, and not later than the third anniversary of the date of the filing of the entity's certificate of termination, the filing entity shall file a certificate of reinstatement in accordance with Chapter 4.

(d) A certificate of reinstatement filed under Subsection (c) must contain:

(1) the name of the filing entity;

(2) the filing number the filing officer assigned to the entity;

(3) the effective date of the entity's termination;

(4) a statement that the reinstatement of the filing entity has been approved in the manner required by this code; and

(5) the name of the entity's registered agent and the address of the entity's registered office.

(e) A tax clearance letter from the comptroller stating that the filing entity has satisfied all franchise tax liabilities and may be reinstated must be filed with the certificate of reinstatement if the filing entity is a taxable entity under Chapter 171, Tax Code, other than a nonprofit corporation.

Acts 2003, 78th Leg., ch. 182, § 1, eff. Jan. 1, 2006. Amended by Acts 2009, 81st Leg., ch. 84, § 23, eff. Sept. 1, 2009.

§ 11.203. Use of Name Similar to Previously Registered Name

If the secretary of state determines that a filing entity's name contained in a certificate of reinstatement filed under Section 11.202 is the same as, deceptively similar to, or similar to a name of a filing entity or foreign entity on file as provided by or reserved or registered under this code, the secretary of state may not accept for filing the certificate of reinstatement unless the filing entity contemporaneously amends its certificate of formation to change its name or obtains consent for the use of the similar name.

Acts 2003, 78th Leg., ch. 182, § 1, eff. Jan. 1, 2006.

§ 11.204. Effectiveness of Reinstatement of Nonfiling Entity

The reinstatement of a terminated nonfiling entity takes effect on the approval required by Section 11.202(b).

Acts 2003, 78th Leg., ch. 182, § 1, eff. Jan. 1, 2006.

§ 11.205. Effectiveness of Reinstatement of Filing Entity

The reinstatement of a terminated filing entity that previously filed a certificate of termination takes effect on the filing of the entity's certificate of reinstatement.

Acts 2003, 78th Leg., ch. 182, § 1, eff. Jan. 1, 2006.

§ 11.206. Effect of Reinstatement

When the reinstatement of a terminated entity takes effect:

(1) the existence of the terminated entity is considered to have continued without interruption from the date of termination; and

(2) the terminated entity may carry on its business as if the termination of its existence had not occurred.

Acts 2003, 78th Leg., ch. 182, § 1, eff. Jan. 1, 2006.

SUBCHAPTER F. INVOLUNTARY TERMINATION OF FILING ENTITY BY SECRETARY OF STATE

§ 11.251. Termination of Filing Entity by Secretary of State

(a) If it appears to the secretary of state that, with respect to a filing entity, a circumstance described by Subsection (b) exists, the secretary of state may notify the entity of the circumstance by regular or certified mail addressed to the entity at the entity's registered office or principal place of business as shown on the records of the secretary of state.

(b) The secretary of state may terminate a filing entity's existence if the secretary finds that:

(1) the entity has failed to, and, before the 91st day after the date notice was mailed has not corrected the entity's failure to:

(A) file a report within the period required by law or pay a fee or penalty prescribed by law when due and payable; or

(B) maintain a registered agent or registered office in this state as required by law; or

(2) the entity has failed to, and, before the 16th day after the date notice was mailed has not corrected the entity's failure to, pay a fee required in connection with the filing of its certificate of formation, or payment of the fee was dishonored when presented by the state for payment.

(c) This subchapter shall not apply to real estate investment trusts.

Acts 2003, 78th Leg., ch. 182, § 1, eff. Jan. 1, 2006. Amended by Acts 2007, 80th Leg., ch. 688, § 68, eff. Sept. 1, 2007.

§ 11.252. Certificate of Termination

(a) If termination of a filing entity's existence is required, the secretary of state shall:

(1) issue a certificate of termination; and

(2) deliver a certificate of termination by regular or certified mail to the filing entity at its registered office or principal place of business.

(b) The certificate of termination must state:

(1) that the filing entity has been involuntarily terminated; and

(2) the date and cause of the termination.

(c) Except as otherwise provided by this chapter, the existence of the filing entity is terminated on the issuance of the certificate of termination by the secretary of state.

Acts 2003, 78th Leg., ch. 182, § 1, eff. Jan. 1, 2006.

§ 11.253. Reinstatement by Secretary of State After Involuntary Termination

(a) The secretary of state shall reinstate a filing entity that has been involuntarily terminated under this subchapter if the entity files a certificate of reinstatement in accordance with Chapter 4 and:

(1) the entity has corrected the circumstances that led to the involuntary termination and any other circumstances that may exist of the types described by Section 11.251(b), including the payment of fees, interest, or penalties; or

(2) the secretary of state finds that the circumstances that led to the involuntary termination did not exist at the time of termination.

(b) A certificate of reinstatement filed under Subsection (a) must contain:

(1) the name of the filing entity;

(2) the filing number assigned by the filing officer to the entity;

(3) the effective date of the involuntary termination;

(4) a statement that the circumstances giving rise to the involuntary termination have been corrected; and

(5) the name of the entity's registered agent and the address of the entity's registered office.

(c) A certificate of reinstatement must be accompanied by:

(1) each amendment to the entity's certificate of formation that is required by intervening events, including circumstances requiring an amendment to the filing entity's name as described in Section 11.203; and

(2) a tax clearance letter from the comptroller stating that the filing entity has satisfied all franchise tax liabilities and may be reinstated, if the filing entity is a taxable entity under Chapter 171, Tax Code, other than a nonprofit corporation.

(d) If a filing entity is reinstated before the third anniversary of the date of its involuntary termination, the entity is considered to have continued in existence without interruption from the date of termination. The reinstatement shall have no effect on any issue of personal liability of the governing persons, officers, or agents of the filing entity during the period between termination and reinstatement.

Acts 2003, 78th Leg., ch. 182, § 1, eff. Jan. 1, 2006. Amended by Acts 2009, 81st Leg., ch. 84, § 24, eff. Sept. 1, 2009.

§ 11.254. Reinstatement of Certificate of Formation Following Tax Forfeiture

A filing entity whose certificate of formation has been forfeited under the provisions of the Tax Code must follow the procedures in the Tax Code to reinstate its certificate of formation.

Acts 2003, 78th Leg., ch. 182, § 1, eff. Jan. 1, 2006.

SUBCHAPTER G. JUDICIAL WINDING UP AND TERMINATION

§ 11.301. Involuntary Winding Up and Termination of Filing Entity by Court Action

(a) A court may enter a decree requiring winding up of a filing entity's business and termination of the filing entity's existence if, as the result of an action brought under Section 11.303, the court finds that one or more of the following problems exist:

(1) the filing entity or its organizers did not comply with a condition precedent to its formation;

(2) the certificate of formation of the filing entity or any amendment to the certificate of formation was fraudulently filed;

(3) a misrepresentation of a material matter has been made in an application, report, affidavit, or other document submitted by the filing entity under this code;

(4) the filing entity has continued to transact business beyond the scope of the purpose of the filing entity as expressed in its certificate of formation; or

(5) public interest requires winding up and termination of the filing entity because:

(A) the filing entity has been convicted of a felony or a high managerial agent of the filing entity has been convicted of a felony committed in the conduct of the filing entity's affairs;

(B) the filing entity or high managerial agent has engaged in a persistent course of felonious conduct; and

(C) termination is necessary to prevent future felonious conduct of the same character.

(b) Sections 11.302–11.307 do not apply to Subsection (a)(5).

Acts 2003, 78th Leg., ch. 182, § 1, eff. Jan. 1, 2006.

§ 11.302. Notification of Cause by Secretary of State

(a) The secretary of state shall provide to the attorney general:

(1) the name of a filing entity that has given cause under Section 11.301 for involuntary winding up of the entity's business and termination of the entity's existence; and

(2) the facts relating to the cause for the winding up and termination.

(b) When notice is provided under Subsection (a), the secretary of state shall notify the filing entity of the circumstances by writing sent to the entity at its registered office in this state. The notice must state that the secretary of state has given notice under Subsection (a) and the grounds for the notification. The secretary of state must record the date a notice required by this subsection is sent.

(c) A court shall accept a certificate issued by the secretary of state as to the facts relating to the cause for the winding up and termination and the sending of a notice under Subsection (b) as prima facie evidence of the facts stated in the certificate and the sending of the notice.

Acts 2003, 78th Leg., ch. 182, § 1, eff. Jan. 1, 2006.

§ 11.303. Filing of Action by Attorney General

The attorney general shall file an action against a filing entity in the name of the state seeking termination of the entity's existence if:

(1) the filing entity has not cured the problems for which winding up and termination is sought before the 31st day after the date the notice under Section 11.302(b) is mailed; and

(2) the attorney general determines that cause exists for the involuntary winding up of a filing entity's business and termination of the entity's existence under Section 11.301.

Acts 2003, 78th Leg., ch. 182, § 1, eff. Jan. 1, 2006.

§ 11.304. Cure Before Final Judgment

An action filed by the attorney general under Section 11.303 shall be abated if, before a district court renders judgment on the action, the filing entity:

(1) cures the problems for which winding up and termination is sought; and

(2) pays the costs of the action.

Acts 2003, 78th Leg., ch. 182, § 1, eff. Jan. 1, 2006.

§ 11.305. Judgment Requiring Winding Up and Termination

If a district court finds in an action brought under this subchapter that proper grounds exist under Section 11.301(a) for a winding up of a filing entity's business and termination of the filing entity's existence, the court shall:

(1) make findings to that effect; and

(2) subject to Section 11.306, enter a judgment not earlier than the fifth day after the date the court makes its findings.

Acts 2003, 78th Leg., ch. 182, § 1, eff. Jan. 1, 2006.

§ 11.306. Stay of Judgment

(a) If, in an action brought under this subchapter, a filing entity has proved by a preponderance of the evidence and obtained a finding that the problems for which the filing entity has been found guilty were not wilful or the result of a failure to take reasonable precautions, the entity may make a sworn application to the court for a stay of entry of the judgment to allow the filing entity a reasonable opportunity to cure the problems for which it has been found guilty. An application made under this subsection must be made not later than the fifth day after the date the court makes its findings under Section 11.305.

(b) After a filing entity has made an application under Subsection (a), a court shall stay the entry of the judgment if the court is reasonably satisfied after considering the application and evidence offered with respect to the application that the filing entity:

(1) is able and intends in good faith to cure the problems for which it has been found guilty; and

(2) has not applied for the stay without just cause.

(c) A court shall stay an entry of judgment under Subsection (b) for the period the court determines is reasonably necessary to afford the filing entity the opportunity to cure its problems if the entity acts with reasonable diligence. The court may not stay the entry of the judgment for longer than 60 days after the date the court's findings are made.

(d) The court shall dismiss an action against a filing entity that, during the period the action is stayed by the court under this section, cures the problems for which winding up and termination is sought and pays all costs accrued in the action.

(e) If a court finds that a filing entity has not cured the problems for which winding up and termination is sought within the period prescribed by Subsection (c), the court shall enter final judgment requiring a winding up of the filing entity's business.

Acts 2003, 78th Leg., ch. 182, § 1, eff. Jan. 1, 2006.

§ 11.307. Opportunity for Cure After Affirmation of Findings by Appeals Court

(a) An appellate court that affirms a trial court's findings against a filing entity under this subchapter shall remand the case to the trial court with instructions to grant the filing entity an opportunity to cure the problems for which the entity has been found guilty if:

(1) the filing entity did not make an application to the trial court for stay of the entry of the judgment;

(2) the appellate court is satisfied that the appeal was taken in good faith and not for purpose of delay or with no sufficient cause;

(3) the appellate court finds that the problems for which the filing entity has been found guilty are capable of being cured; and

(4) the filing entity has prayed for the opportunity to cure its problems in the appeal.

(b) The appellate court shall determine the period, which may not be longer than 60 days after the date the case is remanded to the trial court, to be afforded to a filing entity to enable the filing entity to cure its problems under Subsection (a).

(c) The trial court to which an action against a filing entity has been remanded under this section shall dismiss the action if, during the period prescribed by the appellate court for that conduct, the filing entity cures the problems for which winding up and termination is sought and pays all costs accrued in the action.

(d) If a filing entity has not cured the problems for which winding up and termination is sought within the period prescribed by the appellate court under Subsection (b), the judgment requiring winding up and termination shall become final.

Acts 2003, 78th Leg., ch. 182, § 1, eff. Jan. 1, 2006.

§ 11.308. Jurisdiction and Venue

(a) The attorney general shall bring an action for the involuntary winding up and termination of a filing entity under this subchapter in:

(1) a district court of the county in which the registered office or principal place of business of the filing entity in this state is located; or

(2) a district court of Travis County.

(b) A district court described by Subsection (a) has jurisdiction of the action for involuntary winding up and termination.

Acts 2003, 78th Leg., ch. 182, § 1, eff. Jan. 1, 2006.

§ 11.309. Process in State Action

Citation in an action for the involuntary winding up and termination of a filing entity under this subchapter shall be issued and served as provided by law.

Acts 2003, 78th Leg., ch. 182, § 1, eff. Jan. 1, 2006.

§ 11.310. Publication of Notice

(a) If process in an action under this subchapter is returned not found, the attorney general shall publish notice in a newspaper in the county in which the registered office of the filing entity in this state is located. The notice must contain:

(1) a statement of the pendency of the action;

(2) the title of the court;

(3) the title of the action; and

(4) the earliest date on which default judgment may be entered by the court.

(b) Notice under this section must be published at least once a week for two consecutive weeks beginning at any time after the citation has been returned.

(c) The attorney general may include in one published notice the name of each filing entity against which an action for involuntary winding up and termination is pending in the same court.

(d) Not later than the 10th day after the date notice under this section is first published, the attorney general shall send a copy of the notice to the filing entity at the filing entity's registered office in this state. A certificate from the attorney general regarding the sending of the notice is prima facie evidence that notice was sent under this section.

(e) Unless a filing entity has been served with citation, a default judgment may not be taken against the entity before the 31st day after the date the notice is first published.

Acts 2003, 78th Leg., ch. 182, § 1, eff. Jan. 1, 2006.

§ 11.311. Action Allowed After Expiration of Filing Entity's Duration

The expiration of a filing entity's period of duration does not, by itself, create a vested right on the part of an owner or creditor of the filing entity to prevent an action by the attorney general for the involuntary winding up of the filing entity's business and termination of the filing entity's existence.

Acts 2003, 78th Leg., ch. 182, § 1, eff. Jan. 1, 2006.

§ 11.312. Compliance by Terminated Entity

On the decree of a court requiring winding up of a filing entity's business, the filing entity shall comply with:

(1) the requirements of the decree concerning the winding up process; and

(2) Subchapter B to the extent it does not conflict with the decree.

Acts 2003, 78th Leg., ch. 182, § 1, eff. Jan. 1, 2006.

§ 11.313. Timing of Termination

A court may enter a decree under Section 11.301 terminating the existence of a filing entity:

(1) when the court considers it necessary or advisable; or

(2) on completion of the winding up process.

Acts 2003, 78th Leg., ch. 182, § 1, eff. Jan. 1, 2006.

§ 11.314 Involuntary Winding Up and Termination of Partnership or Limited Liability Company

A district court in the county in which the registered office or principal place of business in this state of a domestic partnership or limited liability company is located has jurisdiction to order the winding up and termination of the domestic partnership or limited liability company on application by:

(1) a partner in the partnership if the court determines that:

(A) the economic purpose of the partnership is likely to be unreasonably frustrated; or

(B) another partner has engaged in conduct relating to the partnership's business that makes it not reasonably practicable to carry on the business in partnership with that partner; or

(2) an owner of the partnership or limited liability company if the court determines that it is not reasonably practicable to carry on the entity's business in conformity with its governing documents.

Acts 2003, 78th Leg., ch. 182, § 1, eff. Jan. 1, 2006. Amended by Acts 2009, 81st Leg., ch. 84, § 25, eff. Sept. 1, 2009.

§ 11.315. Filing of Decree of Termination Against Filing Entity

(a) The clerk of a court that enters a decree terminating the existence of a filing entity shall file a certified copy of the decree in accordance with Chapter 4.

(b) A fee may not be charged for the filing of a decree under this section.

(c) Subject to Section 11.356, the existence of the filing entity ceases when the certified copy of the decree is filed in accordance with Chapter 4.

Acts 2003, 78th Leg., ch. 182, § 1, eff. Jan. 1, 2006. Amended by Acts 2005, 79th Leg., ch. 64, § 41, eff. Jan. 1, 2006.

SUBCHAPTER H. CLAIMS RESOLUTION ON TERMINATION

§ 11.351. Liability of Terminated Filing Entity

A terminated filing entity is liable only for an existing claim.

Acts 2003, 78th Leg., ch. 182, § 1, eff. Jan. 1, 2006.

§ 11.352. Deposit with Comptroller of Amount Due Owners and Creditors Who Are Unknown or Cannot Be Located

(a) On the voluntary or involuntary termination of a domestic filing entity, the portion of the entity's assets distributable to creditors or owners who are unknown or cannot be found after the exercise of reasonable diligence by a person responsible for the distribution in liquidation of the domestic filing entity's assets must be reduced to cash and deposited as provided by Subsection (b).

(b) Money from assets liquidated under Subsection (a) shall be deposited with the comptroller in a special account to be maintained by the comptroller. The money must be accompanied by a statement to the comptroller containing:

(1) the name and last known address of each person who is known to be entitled to all or part of the account;

(2) the amount of each entitled person's distributive portion of the money; and

(3) other information about each person who is entitled to all or part of the money as the comptroller may reasonably require.

(c) The comptroller shall issue a receipt for money received under this section.

Acts 2003, 78th Leg., ch. 182, § 1, eff. Jan. 1, 2006.

§ 11.353. Discharge of Liability of Person Responsible for Liquidation

A person responsible for the distribution in liquidation of a filing entity's assets will be released and discharged from further liability with respect to money received from the liquidation when the person deposits the money with the comptroller under Section 11.352.

Acts 2003, 78th Leg., ch. 182, § 1, eff. Jan. 1, 2006.

§ 11.354. Payment From Account by Comptroller

(a) To claim money deposited in an account under Section 11.352, a person must submit to the comptroller satisfactory written proof of the person's right to the money not later than the seventh anniversary of the date the money was deposited with the comptroller.

(b) The comptroller shall issue a warrant drawn on the account created under Section 11.352 in favor of a person who meets the requirements for making a claim under Subsection (a) and in the amount to which the person is entitled.

Acts 2003, 78th Leg., ch. 182, § 1, eff. Jan. 1, 2006.

§ 11.355. Notice of Escheat; Escheat

(a) If no claimant has made satisfactory proof of a right to the money within the period prescribed by Section 11.354(a), the comptroller shall publish in one issue of a newspaper of general circulation in Travis County a notice of the proposed escheat of the money.

(b) A notice published under Subsection (a) must contain:

(1) the name and last known address of any known creditor or owner entitled to the money;

(2) the amount of money deposited with the comptroller; and

(3) the name of the terminated filing entity from whose assets the money was derived.

(c) If no claimant makes satisfactory proof to the comptroller of a right to the money before the 61st day after the date notice under this section is published, the money automatically escheats to and becomes the property of the state and shall be deposited in the general revenue fund.

Acts 2003, 78th Leg., ch. 182, § 1, eff. Jan. 1, 2006.

§ 11.356. Limited Survival After Termination

(a) Notwithstanding the termination of a domestic filing entity under this chapter, the terminated filing entity continues in existence until the third anniversary of the effective date of the entity's termination only for purposes of:

(1) prosecuting or defending in the terminated filing entity's name an action or proceeding brought by or against the terminated entity;

(2) permitting the survival of an existing claim by or against the terminated filing entity;

(3) holding title to and liquidating property that remained with the terminated filing entity at the time of termination or property that is collected by the terminated filing entity after termination;

(4) applying or distributing property, or its proceeds, as provided by Section 11.053; and

(5) settling affairs not completed before termination.

(b) A terminated filing entity may not continue its existence for the purpose of continuing the business or affairs for which the terminated filing entity was formed unless the terminated filing entity is reinstated under Subchapter E.

(c) If an action on an existing claim by or against a terminated filing entity has been brought before the expiration of the three-year period after the date of the entity's termination and the claim was not extinguished under Section 11.359, the terminated filing entity continues to survive for purposes of:

(1) the action until all judgments, orders, and decrees have been fully executed; and

(2) the application or distribution of any property of the terminated filing entity as provided by Section 11.053 until the property has been applied or distributed.

Acts 2003, 78th Leg., ch. 182, § 1, eff. Jan. 1, 2006.

§ 11.357. Governing Persons of Entity During Limited Survival

(a) Subject to the provisions of the title governing the terminated filing entity, during the three-year period that a terminated filing entity's existence is continued under Section 11.356, the governing persons of the terminated filing entity serving at the time of termination shall continue to manage the affairs of the terminated filing entity for the limited purposes specified by Section 11.356 and have the powers necessary to accomplish those purposes. The number of governing persons:

(1) may be reduced because of the death of a governing person; and

(2) may include successors to governing persons chosen by the other governing persons.

(b) In exercising powers prescribed under Subsection (a), a governing person:

(1) has the same duties to the terminated filing entity that the person had immediately before the termination; and

(2) is liable to the terminated filing entity for the person's actions taken after the entity's termination to the same extent that the person would have been liable had the person taken those actions before the termination.

Acts 2003, 78th Leg., ch. 182, § 1, eff. Jan. 1, 2006.

§ 11.358. Accelerated Procedure for Existing Claim Resolution

(a) A terminated filing entity may shorten the period for resolving a person's existing claim against the entity by giving notice by registered or certified mail, return receipt requested, to the claimant at the claimant's last known address that the claim must be resolved under this section.

(b) The notice required under Subsection (a) must:

(1) state the requirements of Subsections (c) and (d) for presenting a claim;

(2) provide the mailing address to which the person's claim against the terminated filing entity must be sent;

(3) state that the claim will be extinguished if written presentation of the claim is not received at the address given on or before the date specified in the notice, which may not be earlier than the 120th day after the date the notice is mailed to the person by the terminated filing entity; and

(4) be accompanied by a copy of this section.

(c) To assert a claim, a person who is notified by a terminated filing entity that the person's claim must be resolved under this section must present the claim in writing to the terminated filing entity at the address given by the entity in the notice.

(d) A claim presented under Subsection (c) must:

(1) contain the:

(A) identity of the claimant; and

(B) nature and amount of the claim; and

(2) be received by the terminated filing entity not later than the date specified in the notice under Subsection (b)(3).

(e) If a person presents a claim that meets the requirements of this section, the terminated filing entity to whom the claim is presented may give written notice to the person that the claim is rejected by the terminated entity.

(f) Notice under Subsection (e) must:

(1) be sent by registered or certified mail, return receipt requested, and addressed to the last known address of the person presenting the claim;

(2) state that the claim has been rejected by the terminated entity;

(3) state that the claim will be extinguished unless an action on the claim is brought:

(A) not later than the 180th day after the date the notice of rejection of the claim was mailed to the person; and

(B) not later than the third anniversary of the effective date of the entity's termination; and

(4) state the date on which notice of the claim's rejection was mailed and the effective date of the entity's termination.

Acts 2003, 78th Leg., ch. 182, § 1, eff. Jan. 1, 2006.

§ 11.359. Extinguishment of Existing Claim

(a) Except as provided by Subsection (b), an existing claim by or against a terminated filing entity is extinguished unless an action or proceeding is brought on the claim not later than the third anniversary of the date of termination of the entity.

(b) A person's claim against a terminated filing entity may be extinguished before the period prescribed by Subsection (a) if the person is notified under Section 11.358(a) that the claim will be resolved under Section 11.358 and the person:

(1) fails to properly present the claim in writing under Sections 11.358(c) and (d); or

(2) fails to bring an action on a claim rejected under Section 11.358(e) before:

(A) the 180th day after the date the notice rejecting the claim was mailed to the person; and

(B) the third anniversary of the effective date of the entity's termination.

Acts 2003, 78th Leg., ch. 182, § 1, eff. Jan. 1, 2006.

SUBCHAPTER I. RECEIVERSHIP

§ 11.401. Code Governs

A receiver may be appointed for a domestic entity or for a domestic entity's property or business only as provided for and on the conditions set forth in this code.

Acts 2003, 78th Leg., ch. 182, § 1, eff. Jan. 1, 2006.

§ 11.402. Jurisdiction to Appoint Receiver

(a) A court that has subject matter jurisdiction over specific property of a domestic or foreign entity that is located in this state and is involved in litigation has jurisdiction to appoint a receiver for that property as provided by Section 11.403.

(b) A district court in the county in which the registered office or principal place of business of a domestic entity is located has jurisdiction to:

(1) appoint a receiver for the property and business of a domestic entity for the purpose of rehabilitating the entity as provided by Section 11.404; or

(2) order the liquidation of the property and business of a domestic entity and appoint a receiver to effect that liquidation as provided by Section 11.405.

Acts 2003, 78th Leg., ch. 182, § 1, eff. Jan. 1, 2006. Amended by Acts 2011, 82nd Leg., ch. 139 (S.B. 748), § 19, eff. Sept. 1, 2011.

§ 11.403. Appointment of Receiver for Specific Property

(a) Subject to Subsection (b), and on the application of a person whose right to or interest in any property or fund or the proceeds from the property or fund is probable, a court that has jurisdiction over specific property of a domestic or foreign entity may appoint a receiver in an action:

(1) by a vendor to vacate a fraudulent purchase of the property;

(2) by a creditor to subject the property or fund to the creditor's claim;

(3) between partners or others jointly owning or interested in the property or fund;

(4) by a mortgagee of the property for the foreclosure of the mortgage and sale of the property, when:

(A) it appears that the mortgaged property is in danger of being lost, removed, or materially injured; or

(B) it appears that the mortgage is in default and that the property is probably insufficient to discharge the mortgage debt; or

(5) in which receivers for specific property have been previously appointed by courts of equity.

(b) A court may appoint a receiver for the property or fund under Subsection (a) only if:

(1) with respect to an action brought under Subsection (a)(1), (2), or (3), it is shown that the property or fund is in danger of being lost, removed, or materially injured;

(2) circumstances exist that are considered by the court to necessitate the appointment of a receiver to conserve the property or fund and avoid damage to interested parties;

(3) all other requirements of law are complied with; and

(4) the court determines that other available legal and equitable remedies are inadequate.

(c) The court appointing a receiver under this section has and shall retain exclusive jurisdiction over the specific property placed in receivership. The court shall determine the rights of the parties in the property or its proceeds.

(d) If the condition necessitating the appointment of a receiver under this section is remedied, the receivership shall be terminated immediately, and the receiver shall redeliver to the domestic entity all of the property remaining in receivership.

Acts 2003, 78th Leg., ch. 182, § 1, eff. Jan. 1, 2006.

§ 11.404. Appointment of Receiver to Rehabilitate Domestic Entity

(a) Subject to Subsection (b), a court that has jurisdiction over the property and business of a domestic entity under Section 11.402(b) may appoint a receiver for the entity's property and business if:

(1) in an action by an owner or member of the domestic entity, it is established that:

(A) the entity is insolvent or in imminent danger of insolvency;

(B) the governing persons of the entity are deadlocked in the management of the entity's affairs, the owners or members of the entity are unable to break the deadlock, and irreparable injury to the entity is being suffered or is threatened because of the deadlock;

(C) the actions of the governing persons of the entity are illegal, oppressive, or fraudulent;

(D) the property of the entity is being misapplied or wasted; or

(E) with respect to a for-profit corporation, the shareholders of the entity are deadlocked in voting power and have failed, for a period of at least two years, to elect successors to the governing persons of the entity whose terms have expired or would have expired on the election and qualification of their successors;

(2) in an action by a creditor of the domestic entity, it is established that:

(A) the entity is insolvent, the claim of the creditor has been reduced to judgment, and an execution on the judgment was returned unsatisfied; or

(B) the entity is insolvent and has admitted in writing that the claim of the creditor is due and owing; or

(3) in an action other than an action described by Subdivision (1) or (2), courts of equity have traditionally appointed a receiver.

(b) A court may appoint a receiver under Subsection (a) only if:

(1) circumstances exist that are considered by the court to necessitate the appointment of a receiver to conserve the property and business of the domestic entity and avoid damage to interested parties;

(2) all other requirements of law are complied with; and

(3) the court determines that all other available legal and equitable remedies, including the appointment of a receiver for specific property of the domestic entity under Section 11.402(a) , are inadequate.

(c) If the condition necessitating the appointment of a receiver under this section is remedied, the receivership shall be terminated immediately, the management of the domestic entity shall be restored to its managerial officials, and the receiver shall redeliver to the domestic entity all of its property remaining in receivership.

Acts 2003, 78th Leg., ch. 182, § 1, eff. Jan. 1, 2006. Amended by Acts 2011, 82nd Leg., ch. 139 (S.B. 748), § 20, eff. Sept. 1, 2011.

§ 11.405. Appointment of Receiver to Liquidate Domestic Entity; Liquidation

(a) Subject to Subsection (b), a court that has jurisdiction over the property and business of a domestic entity under Section 11.402(b) may order the liquidation of the property and business of the domestic entity and may appoint a receiver to effect the liquidation:

(1) when an action has been filed by the attorney general under this chapter to terminate the existence of the entity and it is established that liquidation of the entity's business and affairs should precede the entry of a decree of termination;

(2) on application of the entity to have its liquidation continued under the supervision of the court;

(3) if the entity is in receivership and the court does not find that any plan presented before the first anniversary of the date the receiver was appointed is feasible for remedying the condition requiring appointment of the receiver;

(4) on application of a creditor of the entity if it is established that irreparable damage will ensue to the unsecured creditors of the domestic entity as a class, generally, unless there is an immediate liquidation of the property of the domestic entity; or

(5) on application of a member or director of a nonprofit corporation or cooperative association and it appears the entity is unable to carry out its purposes.

(b) A court may order a liquidation and appoint a receiver under Subsection (a) only if:

(1) the circumstances demand liquidation to avoid damage to interested persons;

(2) all other requirements of law are complied with; and

(3) the court determines that all other available legal and equitable remedies, including the appointment of a receiver for specific property of the domestic entity and appointment of a receiver to rehabilitate the domestic entity, are inadequate.

(c) If the condition necessitating the appointment of a receiver under this section is remedied, the receivership shall be terminated immediately, the management of the domestic entity shall be restored to its managerial officials, and the receiver shall redeliver to the domestic entity all of its property remaining in receivership.

Acts 2003, 78th Leg., ch. 182, § 1, eff. Jan. 1, 2006.

§ 11.406. Receivers: Qualifications, Powers, and Duties

(a) A receiver appointed under this chapter:

(1) must be an individual citizen of the United States or an entity authorized to act as receiver;

(2) shall give a bond in the amount required by the court and with any sureties as may be required by the court;

(3) may sue and be sued in the receiver's name in any court;

(4) has the powers and duties provided by other laws applicable to receivers; and

(5) has the powers and duties that are stated in the order appointing the receiver or that the appointing court:

(A) considers appropriate to accomplish the objectives for which the receiver was appointed; and

(B) may increase or diminish at any time during the proceedings.

(b) To be appointed a receiver under this chapter, a foreign entity must be registered to transact business in this state.

Acts 2003, 78th Leg., ch. 182, § 1, eff. Jan. 1, 2006.

§ 11.407. Court-Ordered Filing of Claims

(a) In a proceeding involving a receivership of the property or business of a domestic entity, the court may require all claimants of the domestic entity to file with the clerk of the court or the receiver, in the form provided by the court, proof of their respective claims under oath.

(b) A court that orders the filing of claims under Subsection (a) shall:

(1) set a date, which may not be earlier than four months after the date of the order, as the last day for the filing of those claims; and

(2) prescribe the notice that shall be given to claimants of the date set under Subdivision (1).

(c) Before the expiration of the period under Subsection (b) for the filing of claims, a court may extend the period for the filing of claims to a later date.

(d) A court may bar a claimant who fails to file a proof of claim during the period authorized by the court from participating in the distribution of the property of the domestic entity unless the claimant presents to the court a justifiable excuse for its delay in filing. A court may not order or effect a discharge of a claim of the claimant described by this subsection.

Acts 2003, 78th Leg., ch. 182, § 1, eff. Jan. 1, 2006.

§ 11.408. Supervising Court; Jurisdiction; Authority

(a) A court supervising a receivership under this subchapter may, from time to time:

(1) make allowances to a receiver or attorney in the proceeding; and

(2) direct the payment of a receiver or attorney from the property of the domestic entity that is within the scope of the receivership or the proceeds of any sale or disposition of that property.

(b) A court that appoints a receiver under this subchapter for the property or business of a domestic entity has exclusive jurisdiction over the domestic entity and all of its property, regardless of where the property is located.

Acts 2003, 78th Leg., ch. 182, § 1, eff. Jan. 1, 2006.

§ 11.409. Ancillary Receiverships of Foreign Entities

(a) Notwithstanding any provision of this code to the contrary, a district court in the county in which the registered office of a foreign entity doing business in this state is located has jurisdiction to appoint an ancillary receiver for the property and business of that entity when the court determines that circumstances exist to require the appointment of an ancillary receiver.

(b) A receiver appointed under Subsection (a) serves ancillary to a receiver acting under orders of an out-of-state court that has jurisdiction to appoint a receiver for the entity.

Acts 2003, 78th Leg., ch. 182, § 1, eff. Jan. 1, 2006.

§ 11.410. Receivership for All Property and Business of Foreign Entity

(a) A district court may appoint a receiver for all of the property, in and outside this state, of a foreign entity doing business in this state and its business if the court determines, in accordance with the ordinary usages of equity, that circumstances exist that necessitate the appointment of a receiver even if a receiver has not been appointed by another court.

(b) The appointing court shall convert a receivership created under Subsection (a) into an ancillary receivership if the appointing court determines an ancillary receivership is appropriate because a court in another state has ordered a receivership of all property and business of the entity.

Acts 2003, 78th Leg., ch. 182, § 1, eff. Jan. 1, 2006.

§ 11.411. Governing Persons and Owners Not Necessary Parties Defendant

Governing persons and owners or members of a domestic entity are not necessary parties to an action for a receivership or liquidation of the property and business of a domestic entity unless relief is sought against those persons individually.

Acts 2003, 78th Leg., ch. 182, § 1, eff. Jan. 1, 2006.

§ 11.412. Decree of Involuntary Termination

In an action in which the court has ordered the liquidation of the property and business of a domestic entity in accordance with other provisions of this code, the court shall enter a decree terminating the existence of the entity:

(1) when the costs and expenses of the action and all obligations and liabilities of the domestic entity have been paid and discharged or adequately provided for and all of the entity's remaining property has been distributed to its owners and members; or

(2) if the entity's property is not sufficient to discharge the costs and other expenses of the action and all obligations and liabilities of the entity, when all the property of the entity has been applied toward their payment.

Acts 2003, 78th Leg., ch. 182, § 1, eff. Jan. 1, 2006. Amended by Acts 2007, 80th Leg., ch. 688, § 69, eff. Sept. 1, 2007.

§ 11.413. Supplemental Provisions for Application of Proceeds From Liquidation of Nonprofit Corporation

(a) In proceedings under Section 11.405, the property of a nonprofit corporation or the proceeds resulting from a sale, conveyance, or other disposition of its property shall be applied to:

(1) pay, satisfy, and discharge all costs and expenses of the court proceedings and all liabilities and obligations of the nonprofit corporation; or

(2) make adequate provision for the payment, satisfaction, and discharge of the costs, expenses, liabilities, or obligations described by Subdivision (1).

(b) Any property remaining after application is made under this section must be applied and distributed in the manner provided by Section 22.304.

Acts 2003, 78th Leg., ch. 182, § 1, eff. Jan. 1, 2006.

§ 11.414. Filing of Decree of Involuntary Termination Against Filing Entity

(a) The clerk of a court that enters a decree terminating the existence of a filing entity under this subchapter shall file a certified copy of the decree in accordance with Chapter 4.

(b) A fee may not be charged for the filing of a decree under this section.

(c) Subject to Section 11.356, the existence of the filing entity ceases when the certified copy of the decree is filed in accordance with Chapter 4.

Added by Acts 2005, 79th Leg., ch. 64, § 42, eff. Jan. 1, 2006.

CHAPTER 12. ADMINISTRATIVE POWERS

SUBCHAPTER A. SECRETARY OF STATE

Section
12.001. Authority of Secretary of State.
12.002. Interrogatories by Secretary of State.
12.003. Information Disclosed by Interrogatories.
12.004. Appeals From Secretary of State.

SUBCHAPTER B. ATTORNEY GENERAL

12.151. Authority of Attorney General to Examine Books and Records.
12.152. Request to Examine.
12.153. Authority to Examine Management of Entity.
12.154. Authority to Disclose Information.
12.155. Forfeiture of Business Privileges.
12.156. Criminal Penalty.

SUBCHAPTER C. ENFORCEMENT LIEN

12.201. Lien for Law Violations.

SUBCHAPTER D. ENFORCEMENT PROCEEDINGS

Section
12.251. Receiver.
12.252. Foreclosure.
12.253. Action Against Insolvent Entity.
12.254. Suits by District or County Attorney.
12.255. Permission to Sue.
12.256. Examination and Notice.
12.257. Dismissal of Action.
12.258. Liquidation of Insolvent Entity.
12.259. Extraordinary Remedies; Bond.
12.260. Abatement of Suit.
12.261. Provisions Cumulative.

SUBCHAPTER A. SECRETARY OF STATE

§ 12.001. Authority of Secretary of State

(a) The secretary of state may adopt procedural rules for the filing of instruments, including the filing of instruments by electronic or other means, authorized to be filed with the secretary of state under this code.

(b) The secretary of state has the power and authority reasonably necessary to enable the secretary to perform the duties imposed on the secretary under this code.

(c) The secretary of state, on acceptance of the filing of an instrument authorized to be filed with the secretary of state under this code, may issue:

(1) a certificate that evidences the filing of the instrument;

(2) a letter that acknowledges the filing of the instrument; or

(3) a certificate that evidences the filing of the instrument and a letter that acknowledges the filing of the instrument.

(d) This section and Sections 12.003 and 12.004 do not apply to a domestic real estate investment trust.

Acts 2003, 78th Leg., ch. 182, § 1, eff. Jan. 1, 2006. Amended by Acts 2009, 81st Leg., ch. 84, § 26, eff. Sept. 1, 2009.

§ 12.002. Interrogatories by Secretary of State

(a) As necessary and proper for the secretary of state to determine whether a filing entity or a foreign filing entity has complied with this code, the secretary of state may serve by mail interrogatories on the entity or a managerial official.

(b) An entity or individual to whom an interrogatory is sent by the secretary of state shall answer the interrogatory before the later of the 31st day after the date the interrogatory is mailed or a date set by the secretary of state. Each answer to an interrogatory must be complete, in writing, and under oath. An interrogatory directed to an individual shall be answered by the individual, and an interrogatory directed to an entity shall be answered by a managerial official.

(c) The secretary of state is not required to file any instrument to which an interrogatory relates until the interrogatory is answered as provided by this section and only if the instrument conforms to the requirements of this code. The secretary of state shall certify to the attorney general for action as the attorney general may consider appropriate an interrogatory and answer to the interrogatory that disclose a violation of this code.

(d) This section and Sections 12.003 and 12.004 do not apply to domestic real estate investment trusts.

Acts 2003, 78th Leg., ch. 182, § 1, eff. Jan. 1, 2006.

§ 12.003. Information Disclosed by Interrogatories

An interrogatory sent by the secretary of state and the answer to the interrogatory are subject to Chapter 552, Government Code.

Acts 2003, 78th Leg., ch. 182, § 1, eff. Jan. 1, 2006.

§ 12.004. Appeals From Secretary of State

(a) If the secretary of state does not approve the filing of a filing instrument, the secretary of state shall, before the 11th day after the date of the delivery of the filing instrument to the secretary of state, notify the person delivering the filing instrument of the disapproval and specifying each reason for the disapproval. The disapproval of a filing instrument by the secretary of state may be appealed only to a district court of Travis County by filing with the court clerk a petition, a copy of the filing instrument sought to be filed, and a copy of any written disapproval by the secretary of state of the filing instrument. The court shall try the appeal de novo and shall sustain the action of the secretary of state or direct the secretary to take any action the court considers to be proper.

(b) A final order or judgment entered by the district court under this section in review of any ruling or decision of the secretary of state may be appealed as in other civil actions.

Acts 2003, 78th Leg., ch. 182, § 1, eff. Jan. 1, 2006.

SUBCHAPTER B. ATTORNEY GENERAL

§ 12.151. Authority of Attorney General to Examine Books and Records

Each filing entity and foreign filing entity shall permit the attorney general to inspect, examine, and make copies, as the attorney general considers necessary in the performance of a power or duty of the attorney general, of any record of the entity. A record of the entity includes minutes and a book, account, letter, memorandum, document, check, voucher, telegram, constitution, and bylaw.

Acts 2003, 78th Leg., ch. 182, § 1, eff. Jan. 1, 2006.

§ 12.152. Request to Examine

To examine the business of a filing entity or foreign filing entity, the attorney general shall make a written request to a managerial official, who shall immediately permit the attorney general to inspect, examine, and make copies of the records of the entity.

Acts 2003, 78th Leg., ch. 182, § 1, eff. Jan. 1, 2006.

§ 12.153. Authority to Examine Management of Entity

The attorney general may investigate the organization, conduct, and management of a filing entity or foreign filing entity and determine if the entity has been or is engaged in acts or conduct in violation of:

(1) its governing documents; or

(2) any law of this state.

Acts 2003, 78th Leg., ch. 182, § 1, eff. Jan. 1, 2006.

§ 12.154. Authority to Disclose Information

Information held by the attorney general and derived in the course of an examination of an entity's records or documents is not public information, is not subject to Chapter 552, Government Code, and may not be disclosed except:

(1) in the course of an administrative or judicial proceeding in which the state is a party;

(2) in a suit by the state to:

(A) revoke the registration of the foreign filing entity or terminate the certificate of formation of the filing entity; or

(B) collect penalties for a violation of the law of this state; or

(3) to provide information to any officer of this state charged with the enforcement of its laws.

Acts 2003, 78th Leg., ch. 182, § 1, eff. Jan. 1, 2006.

§ 12.155. Forfeiture of Business Privileges

A foreign filing entity or a filing entity that fails or refuses to permit the attorney general to examine or make copies of a record, without regard to whether the record is located in this or another state, forfeits the right of the entity to do business in this state, and the entity's registration or certificate of formation shall be revoked or terminated.

Acts 2003, 78th Leg., ch. 182, § 1, eff. Jan. 1, 2006.

§ 12.156. Criminal Penalty

(a) A managerial official or other individual having the authority to manage the affairs of a filing entity or foreign filing entity commits an offense if the official or individual fails or refuses to permit the attorney general to make an investigation of the entity or to examine or to make copies of a record of the entity.

(b) An offense under this section is a Class B misdemeanor.

Acts 2003, 78th Leg., ch. 182, § 1, eff. Jan. 1, 2006.

SUBCHAPTER C. ENFORCEMENT LIEN

§ 12.201. Lien for Law Violations

(a) If a filing entity or foreign filing entity violates a law of this state, including the law against trusts, monopolies, and conspiracies, or combinations or contracts in restraint of trade, for the violation of which a fine, penalties, or forfeiture is provided, all of the entity's property in this state at the time of the violation or that after the violation comes into this state is, because of the violation, liable for any fine or penalty under this chapter and for costs of suit and costs of collection.

(b) The state has a lien on all property of a filing entity or foreign filing entity in this state on the date a suit is instituted by or under the direction of the attorney general in a court of this state for the purpose of forfeiting the certificate of formation or revoking the registration of the entity or for the collection of a fine or penalty due to the state.

(c) The filing of a suit for a fine, penalties, or forfeiture is notice of the lien.

(d) In addition to the property subjected to the lien under Subsection (b), the lien applies to any property that comes into the possession of a receiver appointed under Subchapter D.

Acts 2003, 78th Leg., ch. 182, § 1, eff. Jan. 1, 2006.

SUBCHAPTER D. ENFORCEMENT PROCEEDINGS

§ 12.251. Receiver

In a suit filed by this state against a filing entity or foreign filing entity for the termination of the entity's certificate of formation or registration or for a fine or penalty, the court in this state in which the suit is pending:

(1) shall appoint a receiver for the property and business of the entity in this state or that subsequently comes into this state during the receivership if the filing entity or foreign filing entity commences the process of winding up its business in this or another state or a judgment is rendered against it in this or another state for the termination of the entity's certificate of formation or registration; and

(2) may appoint a receiver for the entity if the interest of the state requires the appointment.

Acts 2003, 78th Leg., ch. 182, § 1, eff. Jan. 1, 2006.

§ 12.252. Foreclosure

(a) The attorney general may bring suit to foreclose a lien created by this chapter.

(b) If a filing entity or a foreign filing entity subject to this code has commenced the winding up process or has had the entity's certificate of formation or registration terminated by a judgment, citation in a suit for foreclosure may be served on any person in this state who acted and was acting as agent of the entity in this state when the entity commenced the winding up process or the entity's certificate of formation or registration was terminated.

Acts 2003, 78th Leg., ch. 182, § 1, eff. Jan. 1, 2006.

§ 12.253. Action Against Insolvent Entity

When the attorney general is convinced that a filing entity or foreign filing entity is insolvent, the attorney general shall institute quo warranto or other appropriate proceedings to terminate the certificate of formation or registration of the filing entity or foreign filing entity that is insolvent.

Acts 2003, 78th Leg., ch. 182, § 1, eff. Jan. 1, 2006.

§ 12.254. Suits by District or County Attorney

A district or county attorney shall bring and prosecute a proceeding under Section 12.252 or 12.253 when directed to do so by the attorney general.

Acts 2003, 78th Leg., ch. 182, § 1, eff. Jan. 1, 2006.

§ 12.255. Permission to Sue

Before a petition may be filed by the attorney general or by a district or county attorney in a suit authorized by Section 12.252 or 12.253, leave must be granted by the judge of the court in which the proceeding is to be filed.

Acts 2003, 78th Leg., ch. 182, § 1, eff. Jan. 1, 2006.

§ 12.256. Examination and Notice

(a) The judge of a court in which a proceeding under Section 12.252 or 12.253 is to be filed shall carefully examine the petition before granting leave to sue. The judge may also require an examination into the facts. If it appears with reasonable certainty from the petition or from the petition and facts that there is a prima facie showing for the relief sought, the judge may grant leave to file.

(b) On an application for the appointment of a receiver, the entity proceeded against is entitled to 10 days' notice before the day set for the hearing.

Acts 2003, 78th Leg., ch. 182, § 1, eff. Jan. 1, 2006.

§ 12.257. Dismissal of Action

(a) A suit authorized by Section 12.253 or 12.258 may not be filed or, if filed, shall be dismissed if the entity, through its owners or members, reduces its indebtedness so that it is not insolvent.

(b) The respondent shall pay the costs of a dismissed suit under this section.

Acts 2003, 78th Leg., ch. 182, § 1, eff. Jan. 1, 2006.

§ 12.258. Liquidation of Insolvent Entity

(a) A court hearing a proceeding under Section 12.253 against an insolvent entity may, after the entity has been shown to be insolvent, appoint one or more receivers for the entity and its property. The receiver may settle the affairs of the entity, collect outstanding debts, and divide the money and property belonging to the entity among its owners after paying the debts of the entity and all expenses incidental to the judicial proceedings and receivership.

(b) The court may continue the existence of the entity for three years and for additional reasonable time as necessary to accomplish the purposes of this subchapter.

Acts 2003, 78th Leg., ch. 182, § 1, eff. Jan. 1, 2006.

§ 12.259. Extraordinary Remedies; Bond

The state has a right to a writ of attachment, garnishment, sequestration, or injunction, without bond, to aid in the enforcement of the state's rights created by this chapter.

Acts 2003, 78th Leg., ch. 182, § 1, eff. Jan. 1, 2006.

§ 12.260. Abatement of Suit

An action or cause of action for a fine, penalty, or forfeiture that this state has or may have against a filing entity or foreign filing entity does not abate because the entity winds up, voluntarily or otherwise, or the entity's certificate of formation is terminated or the entity's registration is revoked.

Acts 2003, 78th Leg., ch. 182, § 1, eff. Jan. 1, 2006. Amended by Acts 2007, 80th Leg., ch. 688, § 70, eff. Sept. 1, 2007.

§ 12.261. Provisions Cumulative

Each right or remedy provided by this chapter is cumulative and does not affect any other right or remedy for the enforcement, payment, or collection of a fine, forfeiture, or penalty or any other means provided by law for securing or preserving testimony or inquiring into the rights or privileges of an entity.

Acts 2003, 78th Leg., ch. 182, § 1, eff. Jan. 1, 2006.

TITLE 2. CORPORATIONS

CHAPTER 20. GENERAL PROVISIONS

Section

20.001. Requirement That Filing Instrument Be Signed by Officer.
20.002. Ultra Vires Acts.

§ 20.001. Requirement That Filing Instrument Be Signed by Officer

Unless otherwise provided by this title, a filing instrument of a corporation must be signed by an officer of the corporation.

Acts 2003, 78th Leg., ch. 182, § 1, eff. Jan. 1, 2006.

§ 20.002. Ultra Vires Acts

(a) Lack of capacity of a corporation may not be the basis of any claim or defense at law or in equity.

(b) An act of a corporation or a transfer of property by or to a corporation is not invalid because the act or transfer was:

(1) beyond the scope of the purpose or purposes of the corporation as expressed in the corporation's certificate of formation; or

(2) inconsistent with a limitation on the authority of an officer or director to exercise a statutory power of the corporation, as that limitation is expressed in the corporation's certificate of formation.

(c) The fact that an act or transfer is beyond the scope of the expressed purpose or purposes of the corporation or is inconsistent with an expressed limitation on the authority of an officer or director may be asserted in a proceeding:

(1) by a shareholder or member against the corporation to enjoin the performance of an act or the transfer of property by or to the corporation;

(2) by the corporation, acting directly or through a receiver, trustee, or other legal representative, or through members in a representative suit, against an officer or director or former officer or director of the corporation for exceeding that person's authority; or

(3) by the attorney general to:

(A) terminate the corporation;

(B) enjoin the corporation from performing an unauthorized act; or

(C) enforce divestment of real property acquired or held contrary to the laws of this state.

(d) If the unauthorized act or transfer sought to be enjoined under Subsection (c)(1) is being or is to be performed or made under a contract to which the corporation is a party and if each party to the contract is a party to the proceeding, the court may set aside and enjoin the performance of the contract. The court may award to the corporation or to another party to the contract, as appropriate, compensation for loss or damage resulting from the action of the court in setting aside and enjoining the performance of the contract, excluding loss of anticipated profits.

Acts 2003, 78th Leg., ch. 182, § 1, eff. Jan. 1, 2006.

CHAPTER 21. FOR–PROFIT CORPORATIONS

SUBCHAPTER A. GENERAL PROVISIONS

Section

21.001. Repealed.
21.002. Definitions.

SUBCHAPTER B. FORMATION AND GOVERNING DOCUMENTS

21.051. No Property Right in Certificate of Formation.
21.052. Procedures to Adopt Amendment to Certificate of Formation.
21.053. Adoption of Amendment by Board of Directors.
21.054. Adoption of Amendment by Shareholders.
21.055. Notice of and Meeting to Consider Proposed Amendment.
21.056. Restated Certificate of Formation.
21.057. Bylaws.
21.058. Dual Authority.
21.059. Organization Meeting.

SUBCHAPTER C. SHAREHOLDERS' AGREEMENTS

21.101. Shareholders' Agreement.
21.102. Term of Agreement.

Section

21.103. Disclosure of Agreement; Recall of Certain Certificates.
21.104. Effect of Shareholders' Agreement.
21.105. Right of Rescission; Knowledge of Purchaser of Shares.
21.106. Agreement Limiting Authority of and Supplanting Board of Directors; Liability.
21.107. Liability of Shareholder.
21.108. Persons Acting in Place of Shareholders.
21.109. Agreement Not Effective.
21.110. Other Shareholder Agreements Permitted.

SUBCHAPTER D. SHARES, OPTIONS, AND CONVERTIBLE SECURITIES

21.151. Number of Authorized Shares.
21.152. Classes and Series of Shares.
21.153. Designations, Preferences, Limitations, and Rights of a Class or Series.
21.154. Certain Optional Characteristics of Shares.
21.155. Series of Shares Established by Board of Directors.
21.156. Actions with Respect to Series of Shares.
21.157. Issuance of Shares.
21.158. Issuance of Shares Under Plan of Merger or Conversion.
21.159. Types of Consideration for Shares.
21.160. Determination of Consideration for Shares.
21.161. Amount of Consideration for Issuance of Certain Shares.
21.162. Value and Sufficiency of Consideration.
21.163. Issuance and Disposition of Fractional Shares or Scrip.
21.164. Rights of Holders of Fractional Shares or Scrip.
21.165. Subscriptions.
21.166. Preformation Subscription.
21.167. Commitment to Purchase Shares.
21.168. Stock Rights, Options, and Convertible Indebtedness.
21.169. Terms and Conditions of Rights and Options.
21.170. Consideration for Rights, Options, and Convertible Indebtedness.
21.171 Outstanding or Treasury Shares.
21.172. Expenses of Organization, Reorganization, and Financing of Corporation.
21.173. Supplemental Required Records.

SUBCHAPTER E. SHAREHOLDER RIGHTS AND RESTRICTIONS

21.201 Registered Holders as Owners; Shares Held by Nominees.
21.202. Definition of Shares.
21.203. No Statutory Preemptive Right Unless Provided by Certificate of Formation.
21.204. Statutory Preemptive Rights.
21.205. Waiver of Preemptive Right.
21.206. Limitation on Action to Enforce Preemptive Right.
21.207. Disposition of Shares Having Preemptive Rights.
21.208. Preemptive Right in Existing Corporation.
21.209. Transfer of Shares and Other Securities.
21.210. Restriction on Transfer of Shares and Other Securities.
21.211. Valid Restrictions on Transfer.

Section
21.212. Bylaw or Agreement Restricting Transfer of Shares or Other Securities.
21.213. Enforceability of Restriction on Transfer of Certain Securities.
21.214. Joint Ownership of Shares.
21.215. Liability for Designating Owner of Shares.
21.216. Liability Regarding Joint Ownership of Shares.
21.217. Liability of Assignee or Transferee.
21.218. Examination of Records.
21.219. Annual and Interim Statements of Corporation.
21.220. Penalty for Failure to Prepare Voting List.
21.221. Penalty for Failure to Provide Notice of Meeting.
21.222. Penalty for Refusal to Permit Examination of Certain Records.
21.223. Limitation of Liability for Obligations.
21.224 Preemption of Liability.
21.225. Exceptions to Limitations.
21.226. Pledgees and Trust Administrators.

SUBCHAPTER F. REDUCTIONS IN STATED CAPITAL; CANCELLATION OF TREASURY SHARES

21.251. Reduction of Stated Capital by Redemption or Purchase of Redeemable Shares.
21.252. Cancellation of Treasury Shares.
21.253. Procedures for Reduction of Stated Capital by Board of Directors.
21.254. Restriction on Reduction of Stated Capital.

SUBCHAPTER G. DISTRIBUTIONS AND SHARE DIVIDENDS

21.301. Definitions.
21.302. Authority for Distributions.
21.303. Limitations on Distributions.
21.304. Redemptions.
21.305. Notice of Redemption.
21.306. Deposit of Money for Redemption.
21.307. Payment of Redeemed Shares.
21.308. Priority of Distributions.
21.309. Reserves, Designations, and Allocations from Surplus.
21.310. Authority for Share Dividends.
21.311. Limitations on Share Dividends.
21.312. Value of Shares Issued as Share Dividends.
21.313. Transfer of Surplus for Share Dividends.
21.314. Determination of Solvency, Net Assets, Stated Capital, and Surplus.
21.315. Date of Determination of Solvency, Net Assets, Stated Capital, and Surplus.
21.316. Liability of Directors for Wrongful Distributions.
21.317. Statute of Limitations on Action for Wrongful Distribution.
21.318. Contribution from Certain Shareholders and Directors.

SUBCHAPTER H. SHAREHOLDERS' MEETINGS; NOTICE TO SHAREHOLDERS; VOTING AND QUORUM

21.351. Annual Meeting.
21.352. Special Meetings.
21.353. Notice of Meeting.
21.3531. Notice by Electronic Transmission.

Section
21.354. Inspection of Voting List.
21.355. Closing of Share Transfer Records.
21.356. Record Date for Written Consent to Action.
21.357. Record Date for Purpose of Shareholders' Meeting .
21.358. Quorum.
21.359. Voting in Election of Directors.
21.360. No Cumulative Voting Right Unless Authorized.
21.361. Cumulative Voting in Election of Directors.
21.362. Cumulative Voting Right in Certain Corporations.
21.363. Voting on Matters Other Than Election of Directors.
21.364. Vote Required to Approve Fundamental Action.
21.365. Changes in Vote Required for Certain Matters.
21.366. Number of Votes Per Share.
21.367. Voting in Person or by Proxy.
21.368. Term of Proxy.
21.369. Revocability of Proxy.
21.370. Enforceability of Proxy.
21.371. Procedures in Bylaws Relating to Proxies.
21.372. Shareholder Meeting List.

SUBCHAPTER I. BOARD OF DIRECTORS

21.401. Management by Board of Directors.
21.402. Board Member Eligibility Requirements.
21.403. Number of Directors.
21.404. Designation of Initial Board of Directors.
21.405. Election of Board of Directors.
21.406. Special Voting Rights of Directors.
21.407. Term of Office.
21.408. Special Terms of Office.
21.409. Removal of Directors.
21.4091. Resignation of Directors.
21.410. Vacancy.
21.411. Notice of Meeting.
21.412. Waiver of Notice.
21.413. Quorum.
21.414. Dissent to Action.
21.415. Action by Directors.
21.416. Committees of Board of Directors.
21.417. Election of Officers.
21.418. Contracts or Transactions Involving Interested Directors and Officers.

SUBCHAPTER J. FUNDAMENTAL BUSINESS TRANSACTIONS

21.451. Definitions.
21.452. Approval of Merger.
21.453. Approval of Conversion.
21.454. Approval of Exchange.
21.455. Approval of Sale of All or Substantially All of Assets.
21.456. General Procedure for Submission to Shareholders of Fundamental Business Transaction.
21.457. General Vote Requirement for Approval of Fundamental Business Transaction.
21.458. Class Voting Requirements for Certain Fundamental Business Transactions.
21.459. No Shareholder Vote Requirement for Certain Fundamental Business Transactions.
21.460. Rights of Dissent and Appraisal.
21.461. Pledge, Mortgage, Deed of Trust, or Trust Indenture.

Section
21.462. Conveyance by Corporation.

SUBCHAPTER K. WINDING UP AND TERMINATION
21.501. Approval of Voluntary Winding Up, Reinstatement, or Revocation of Voluntary Winding Up.
21.502. Certain Procedures Relating to Winding Up.
21.503. Meeting of Shareholders; Notice.
21.504. Responsibility for Winding Up.

SUBCHAPTER L. DERIVATIVE PROCEEDINGS
21.551. Definitions.
21.552. Standing to Bring Proceeding.
21.553. Demand.
21.554. Determination by Directors or Independent Persons.
21.555. Stay of Proceeding.
21.556. Discovery.
21.557. Tolling of Statute of Limitations.
21.558. Dismissal of Derivative Proceeding.
21.559. Proceeding Instituted After Demand Rejected.
21.560. Discontinuance or Settlement.
21.561. Payment of Expenses.
21.562. Application to Foreign Corporations.
21.563. Closely Held Corporation.

SUBCHAPTER M. AFFILIATED BUSINESS COMBINATIONS
21.601. Definitions.
21.602. Affiliated Shareholder.
21.603. Beneficial Owner of Shares or Other Securities.
21.604. Business Combination.
21.605. Control.
21.606. Three–Year Moratorium on Certain Business Combinations.
21.607. Application of Moratorium.
21.608. Effect on Other Actions.
21.609. Conflicting Provisions.
21.610. Change in Voting Requirements.

SUBCHAPTER N. PROVISIONS RELATING TO INVESTMENT COMPANIES
21.651. Definition.
21.652. Establishing Class or Series of Shares; Change in Number of Shares.
21.653. Required Statement Relating to Shares.
21.654. Term of Office of Directors.
21.655. Meetings of Shareholders.

SUBCHAPTER O. CLOSE CORPORATION
21.701. Definitions.
21.702. Applicability of Subchapter.
21.703. Formation of Close Corporation.
21.704. Bylaws of Close Corporation.
21.705. Adoption of Amendment for Close Corporation Status.
21.706. Adoption of Close Corporation Status Through Merger, Exchange, or Conversion.
21.707. Existing Close Corporation.
21.708. Termination of Close Corporation Status.
21.709. Statement Terminating Close Corporation Status; Filing; Notice.

Section
21.710. Effect of Termination of Close Corporation Status.
21.711. Shareholders' Meeting to Elect Directors.
21.712. Term of Office of Directors.
21.713. Management.
21.714. Shareholders' Agreement.
21.715. Execution of Shareholders' Agreement.
21.716. Adoption of Amendment of Shareholders' Agreement.
21.717. Delivery of Shareholders' Agreement.
21.718. Statement of Operation as Close Corporation.
21.719. Validity and Enforceability of Shareholders' Agreement.
21.720. Persons Bound by Shareholders' Agreement.
21.721. Delivery of Copy of Shareholders' Agreement to Transferee.
21.722. Effect of Required Statement on Share Certificate and Delivery of Shareholders' Agreement.
21.723. Party Not Bound by Shareholders' Agreement on Cessation; Liability.
21.724. Termination of Shareholders' Agreement.
21.725. Consequences of Management by Persons Other Than Board of Directors.
21.726. Shareholders Considered Directors.
21.727. Liability of Shareholders.
21.728. Mode and Effect of Taking Action by Shareholders and Others.
21.729. Limitation of Shareholder's Liability.
21.730. Lack of Formalities; Treatment as Partnership.
21.731. Other Agreements Among Shareholders Permitted.
21.732. Close Corporation Share Certificates.

SUBCHAPTER P. JUDICIAL PROCEEDINGS RELATING TO CLOSE CORPORATION
21.751. Definitions.
21.752. Proceedings Authorized.
21.753. Notice; Intervention.
21.754. Proceeding Nonexclusive.
21.755. Unavailability of Judicial Proceeding.
21.756. Judicial Proceeding to Enforce Close Corporation Provision.
21.757. Liquidation; Involuntary Winding Up and Termination; Receivership.
21.758. Appointment of Provisional Director.
21.759. Rights and Powers of Provisional Director.
21.760. Compensation of Provisional Director.
21.761. Appointment of Custodian.
21.762. Powers and Duties of Custodian.
21.763. Termination of Custodianship.

SUBCHAPTER Q. MISCELLANEOUS PROVISIONS
21.801. Shares and Other Securities Are Personal Property.
21.802. Penalties for Late Filing of Certain Instruments.

SUBCHAPTER A. GENERAL PROVISIONS

§ 21.001. Repealed by Acts 2011, 82nd Leg., ch. (S.B. 748), § 66, eff. Sept. 1, 2011

§ 21.002. Definitions

In this chapter:

(1) "Authorized share" means a share of any class the corporation is authorized to issue.

(2) "Board of directors" includes each person who is authorized to perform the functions of the board of directors under a shareholders' agreement as authorized by this chapter.

(3) "Cancel," with respect to an authorized share of a corporation, means the restoration of an issued share to the status of an authorized but unissued share.

(4) "Consuming assets corporation" means a corporation that:

(A) is engaged in the business of exploiting assets subject to depletion or amortization;

(B) states in its certificate of formation that it is a consuming assets corporation;

(C) includes the phrase "a consuming assets corporation" as part of its official corporate name and gives the phrase equal prominence with the rest of the corporate name on the financial statements and certificates of ownership of the corporation; and

(D) includes in each of the certificates of ownership of the corporation the sentence, "This corporation is permitted by law to pay dividends out of reserves that may impair its stated capital."

(5) "Corporation" or "domestic corporation" means a domestic for-profit corporation subject to this chapter.

(6)(A) "Distribution" means a transfer of property, including cash, or issuance of debt, by a corporation to its shareholders in the form of:

(i) a dividend on any class or series of its outstanding shares;

(ii) a purchase or redemption, directly or indirectly, of any of its own shares; or

(iii) a payment by the corporation in liquidation of all or a portion of its assets.

(B) The term does not include:

(i) a split-up or division of the issued shares of a class of a corporation into a larger number of shares within the same class that does not increase the stated capital of the corporation; or

(ii) a transfer of the corporation's own shares or rights to acquire its own shares.

(7) "Foreign corporation" means a for-profit corporation formed under the laws of a jurisdiction other than this state.

(8) "Investment Company Act" means the Investment Company Act of 1940 (15 U.S.C. Section 80a–1 et seq.), as amended.

(9) "Net assets" means the amount by which the total assets of a corporation exceed the total debts of the corporation.

(10) "Share dividend" means a dividend by a corporation that is payable in authorized but unissued shares or treasury shares of the corporation. The term does not include:

(A) an amendment to the corporation's certificate of formation to change the shares of a class or series, with or without par value, into the same or a different number of shares of the same or a different class or series, with or without par value; or

(B) a split-up or division of the issued shares of a class of a corporation into a larger number of shares within the same class that does not increase the stated capital of the corporation.

(11) "Stated capital" means the sum of:

(A) the par value of all shares of the corporation with par value that have been issued;

(B) the consideration, as expressed in terms of United States dollars, determined by the corporation in the manner provided by Section 21.160 for all shares of the corporation without par value that have been issued, except that part, but not all, of the consideration that:

(i) has been actually received; and

(ii) the board, by resolution adopted not later than the 60th day after the date of issuance of those shares, has allocated to surplus; and

(C) an amount not included in Paragraphs (A) and (B) that has been transferred to stated capital of the corporation, on the payment of a share dividend or on adoption by the board of directors of a resolution directing that all or part of surplus be transferred to stated capital, minus each reduction made as permitted by law.

(12) "Surplus" means the amount by which the net assets of a corporation exceed the stated capital of the corporation.

(13) "Treasury shares" means shares of a corporation that have been issued, and subsequently acquired by the corporation, that belong to the corporation and that have not been canceled. The term does not include shares held by a corporation in a fiduciary capacity, whether directly or through a trust or similar arrangement.

Acts 2003, 78th Leg., ch. 182, § 1, eff. Jan. 1, 2006.

SUBCHAPTER B. FORMATION AND GOVERNING DOCUMENTS

§ 21.051. No Property Right in Certificate of Formation

A shareholder of a corporation does not have a vested property right resulting from the certificate of formation, including a provision in the certificate of formation relating to the management, control, capital structure, dividend entitlement, purpose, or duration of the corporation.

Acts 2003, 78th Leg., ch. 182, § 1, eff. Jan. 1, 2006.

§ 21.052. Procedures to Adopt Amendment to Certificate of Formation

(a) To adopt an amendment to the certificate of formation of a corporation as provided by Subchapter B, Chapter 3, the board of directors of the corporation shall:

(1) adopt a resolution stating the proposed amendment; and

(2) follow the procedures prescribed by Sections 21.053–21.055.

(b) The resolution may incorporate the proposed amendment in a restated certificate of formation that complies with Section 3.059.

(b–1) The resolution may provide that at any time before the filing of a certificate of amendment takes effect as provided by Subchapter B, Chapter 3, the board of directors may abandon the proposed amendment to the certificate of formation without further action by the shareholders of the corporation, notwithstanding authorization of the proposed amendment by the shareholders.

(c) The certificate of amendment must be filed in accordance with Chapter 4 and takes effect as provided by Subchapter B, Chapter 3.

Acts 2003, 78th Leg., ch. 182, § 1, eff. Jan. 1, 2006. Amended by Acts 2005, 79th Leg., ch. 64, § 43, eff. Jan. 1, 2006.

§ 21.053. Adoption of Amendment by Board of Directors

(a) If a corporation does not have any issued and outstanding shares, the board of directors may adopt a proposed amendment to the corporation's certificate of formation by resolution without shareholder approval.

(b) Notwithstanding Section 21.054, the board of directors may adopt a proposed amendment without shareholder approval in the manner provided by Section 21.155 if the amendment to the corporation's certificate of formation relates to a series of shares established by the board under authority granted to the board in the certificate of formation as provided by Section 21.155.

Acts 2003, 78th Leg., ch. 182, § 1, eff. Jan. 1, 2006. Amended by Acts 2005, 79th Leg., ch. 64, § 44, eff. Jan. 1, 2006.

§ 21.054. Adoption of Amendment by Shareholders

If a corporation has issued and outstanding shares:

(1) a resolution described by Section 21.052 must also direct that the proposed amendment be submitted to a vote of the shareholders at a meeting; and

(2) the shareholders must approve the proposed amendment in the manner provided by Section 21.055.

Acts 2003, 78th Leg., ch. 182, § 1, eff. Jan. 1, 2006.

§ 21.055. Notice of and Meeting to Consider Proposed Amendment

(a) Each shareholder of record entitled to vote shall be given written notice containing the proposed amendment or a summary of the changes to be effected within the time and in the manner provided by this code for giving notice of meetings to shareholders. The proposed amendment or summary may be included in the notice required to be provided for an annual meeting.

(b) At the meeting, the proposed amendment shall be adopted only on receiving the affirmative vote of shareholders entitled to vote required by Section 21.364.

(c) An unlimited number of amendments may be submitted for adoption by the shareholders at a meeting.

Acts 2003, 78th Leg., ch. 182, § 1, eff. Jan. 1, 2006.

§ 21.056. Restated Certificate of Formation

(a) A corporation may adopt a restated certificate of formation as provided by Subchapter B, Chapter 3, by following the same procedures to amend its certificate of formation under Sections 21.052–21.055, except that shareholder approval is not required if an amendment is not adopted.

(b) The restated certificate of formation shall be filed in accordance with Chapter 4 and takes effect as provided by Subchapter B, Chapter 3.

Acts 2003, 78th Leg., ch. 182, § 1, eff. Jan. 1, 2006.

§ 21.057. Bylaws

(a) The board of directors of a corporation shall adopt initial bylaws.

(b) The bylaws may contain provisions for the regulation and management of the affairs of the corporation that are consistent with law and the corporation's certificate of formation.

(c) A corporation's board of directors may amend or repeal bylaws or adopt new bylaws unless:

(1) the corporation's certificate of formation or this code wholly or partly reserves the power exclusively to the corporation's shareholders; or

(2) in amending, repealing, or adopting a bylaw, the shareholders expressly provide that the board of directors may not amend, repeal, or readopt that bylaw.

Acts 2003, 78th Leg., ch. 182, § 1, eff. Jan. 1, 2006.

§ 21.058. Dual Authority

Unless the certificate of formation or a bylaw adopted by the shareholders provides otherwise as to all or a part of a corporation's bylaws, a corporation's shareholders may amend, repeal, or adopt the corporation's bylaws regardless of whether the bylaws may also be amended, repealed, or adopted by the corporation's board of directors.

Acts 2003, 78th Leg., ch. 182, § 1, eff. Jan. 1, 2006.

§ 21.059. Organization Meeting

(a) This section does not apply to a corporation created as a result of a conversion or merger the plan of which states the bylaws and names the officers of the corporation.

(b) After the filing of a certificate of formation takes effect, an organization meeting shall be held at the call of the majority of the initial board of directors or the persons named in the certificate of formation under Section 3.007(a)(4) for the purpose of adopting bylaws, electing officers, and transacting other business.

(c) Not later than the third day before the date of the meeting, the directors or other persons calling the meeting shall send notice of the time and place of the meeting to each other director or person named in the certificate of formation.

Acts 2003, 78th Leg., ch. 182, § 1, eff. Jan. 1, 2006.

SUBCHAPTER C. SHAREHOLDERS' AGREEMENTS

§ 21.101. Shareholders' Agreement

(a) The shareholders of a corporation may enter into an agreement that:

(1) restricts the discretion or powers of the board of directors;

(2) eliminates the board of directors and authorizes the business and affairs of the corporation to be managed, wholly or partly, by one or more of its shareholders or other persons;

(3) establishes the individuals who shall serve as directors or officers of the corporation;

(4) determines the term of office, manner of selection or removal, or terms or conditions of employment of a director, officer, or other employee of the corporation, regardless of the length of employment;

(5) governs the authorization or making of distributions whether in proportion to ownership of shares, subject to Section 21.303;

(6) determines the manner in which profits and losses will be apportioned;

(7) governs, in general or with regard to specific matters, the exercise or division of voting power by and between the shareholders, directors, or other persons, including use of disproportionate voting rights or director proxies;

(8) establishes the terms of an agreement for the transfer or use of property or for the provision of services between the corporation and another person, including a shareholder, director, officer, or employee of the corporation;

(9) authorizes arbitration or grants authority to a shareholder or other person to resolve any issue about which there is a deadlock among the directors, shareholders, or other persons authorized to manage the corporation;

(10) requires winding up and termination of the corporation at the request of one or more shareholders or on the occurrence of a specified event or contingency, in which case the winding up and termination of the corporation will proceed as if all of the shareholders had consented in writing to the winding up and termination as provided by Subchapter K; or

(11) otherwise governs the exercise of corporate powers, the management of the business and affairs of the corporation, or the relationship among the

shareholders, the directors, and the corporation as if the corporation were a partnership or in a manner that would otherwise be appropriate only among partners and not contrary to public policy.

(b) A shareholders' agreement authorized by this section must be:

(1) contained in:

(A) the certificate of formation or bylaws if approved by all of the shareholders at the time of the agreement; or

(B) a written agreement that is:

(i) signed by all of the shareholders at the time of the agreement; and

(ii) made known to the corporation; and

(2) amended only by all of the shareholders at the time of the amendment, unless the agreement provides otherwise.

Acts 2003, 78th Leg., ch. 182, § 1, eff. Jan. 1, 2006.

§ 21.102. Term of Agreement

A shareholders' agreement under this subchapter is valid for 10 years, unless the agreement provides otherwise.

Acts 2003, 78th Leg., ch. 182, § 1, eff. Jan. 1, 2006.

§ 21.103. Disclosure of Agreement; Recall of Certain Certificates

(a) The existence of an agreement authorized by this subchapter shall be noted conspicuously on the front or back of each certificate for outstanding shares or on the information statement required for uncertificated shares by Section 3.205.

(b) The disclosure required by this section must include the sentence, "These shares are subject to the provisions of a shareholders' agreement that may provide for management of the corporation in a manner different than in other corporations and may subject a shareholder to certain obligations or liabilities not otherwise imposed on shareholders in other corporations."

(c) A corporation that has outstanding shares represented by certificates at the time the shareholders of the corporation enter into an agreement under this subchapter shall recall the outstanding certificates and issue substitute certificates that comply with this subchapter.

(d) The failure to note the existence of the agreement on the certificate or information statement does not affect the validity of the agreement or an action taken pursuant to the agreement.

Acts 2003, 78th Leg., ch. 182, § 1, eff. Jan. 1, 2006.

§ 21.104. Effect of Shareholders' Agreement

A shareholders' agreement that complies with this subchapter is effective among the shareholders and between the shareholders and the corporation even if the terms of the agreement are inconsistent with this code.

Acts 2003, 78th Leg., ch. 182, § 1, eff. Jan. 1, 2006.

§ 21.105. Right of Rescission; Knowledge of Purchaser of Shares

(a) A purchaser of shares who does not have knowledge at the time of purchase of the existence of a shareholders' agreement authorized by this subchapter is entitled to rescind the purchase.

(b) A purchaser is considered to have knowledge of the existence of the shareholders' agreement for purposes of this section if:

(1) the existence of the agreement is noted on the certificate or information statement for the shares as required by Section 21.103; and

(2) with respect to shares that are not represented by a certificate, the information statement noting existence of the agreement is delivered to the purchaser not later than the time the shares are purchased.

(c) An action to enforce the right of rescission authorized by this section must be commenced not later than the earlier of:

(1) the 90th day after the date the existence of the shareholder agreement is discovered; or

(2) the second anniversary of the purchase date of the shares.

Acts 2003, 78th Leg., ch. 182, § 1, eff. Jan. 1, 2006.

§ 21.106. Agreement Limiting Authority of and Supplanting Board of Directors; Liability

(a) A shareholders' agreement authorized by this subchapter that limits the discretion or powers of the board of directors or supplants the board of directors relieves the directors of, and imposes on a person in whom the discretion or powers of the board of directors or the management of the business and affairs of the corporation is vested, liability for an act or omission of the person in accordance with Subsection (b).

(b) A person on whom liability for an act or omission is imposed under this section is liable in the same manner and to the same extent as a director on whom liability for an act or omission is imposed by this code or other law.

Acts 2003, 78th Leg., ch. 182, § 1, eff. Jan. 1, 2006.

§ 21.107. Liability of Shareholder

The existence of or a performance under a shareholders' agreement authorized by this subchapter is not a ground for imposing personal liability on a shareholder for an act or obligation of the corporation by disregarding the separate existence of the corporation or otherwise, even if the agreement or a performance under the agreement:

(1) treats the corporation as if the corporation were a partnership or in a manner that otherwise is appropriate only among partners;

(2) results in the corporation being considered a partnership for purposes of taxation; or

(3) results in failure to observe the corporate formalities otherwise applicable to the matters governed by the agreement.

Acts 2003, 78th Leg., ch. 182, § 1, eff. Jan. 1, 2006.

§ 21.108. Persons Acting in Place of Shareholders

An organizer or a subscriber for shares may act as a shareholder with respect to a shareholders' agreement authorized by this subchapter if no shares have been issued when the agreement is signed.

Acts 2003, 78th Leg., ch. 182, § 1, eff. Jan. 1, 2006.

§ 21.109. Agreement Not Effective

(a) A shareholders' agreement authorized by this subchapter ceases to be effective when shares of the corporation are:

(1) listed on a national securities exchange ; or

(2) regularly traded in a market maintained by one or more members of a national or affiliated securities association.

(b) If a corporation does not have a board of directors and an agreement of the shareholders of the corporation entered into under this subchapter ceases to be effective, a board of directors shall be instituted or reinstated to govern the corporation in the manner provided by Section 21.710(c).

(c) If a shareholders' agreement that ceases to be effective is contained in or referred to by the certificate of formation or bylaws of a corporation, the board of directors of the corporation may adopt an amendment to the certificate of formation or bylaws, without shareholder action, to delete the agreement and any references to the agreement.

Acts 2003, 78th Leg., ch. 182, § 1, eff. Jan. 1, 2006. Amended by Acts 2011, 82nd Leg., ch. 139 (S.B. 748), § 21, eff. Sept. 1, 2011.

§ 21.110. Other Shareholder Agreements Permitted

This subchapter does not prohibit or impair any agreement between two or more shareholders, or between the corporation and one or more of the corporation's shareholders, permitted by Title 1, this chapter, or other law.

Added by Acts 2011, 82nd Leg., ch. 139 (S.B. 748), § 22, eff. Sept. 1, 2011.

SUBCHAPTER D. SHARES, OPTIONS, AND CONVERTIBLE SECURITIES

§ 21.151. Number of Authorized Shares

A corporation may issue the number of authorized shares stated in the corporation's certificate of formation.

Acts 2003, 78th Leg., ch. 182, § 1, eff. Jan. 1, 2006.

§ 21.152. Classes and Series of Shares

(a) A corporation's certificate of formation may divide the corporation's authorized shares into one or more classes and may divide one or more classes into one or more series. If more than one class or series of shares is authorized, the certificate of formation must designate each class and series of authorized shares to distinguish that class and series from any other class or series.

(b) Shares of the same class must be of the same par value or be without par value, as stated in the certificate of formation.

(c) Shares of the same class must be identical in all respects unless the shares have been divided into one or more series. If the shares of a class have been divided into one or more series, the shares may vary between series, but all shares of the same series must be identical in all respects.

(d) A corporation's certificate of formation must authorize:

(1) one or more classes or series of shares that together have unlimited voting rights; and

(2) one or more classes or series of shares, which may be the same class or series of shares as those

with voting rights, that together are entitled to receive the net assets of the corporation on winding up and termination.

Acts 2003, 78th Leg., ch. 182, § 1, eff. Jan. 1, 2006. Amended by Acts 2009, 81st Leg., ch. 84, § 27, eff. Sept. 1, 2009.

§ 21.153. Designations, Preferences, Limitations, and Rights of a Class or Series

(a) If more than one class or series of shares is authorized under Section 21.152(d), the certificate of formation must state the designations, preferences, limitations, and relative rights, including voting rights, of each class or series.

(b) The certificate of formation may limit or deny the voting rights of, or provide special voting rights for, the shares of a class or series or the shares of a class or series held by a person or class of persons to the extent the limitation, denial, or provision is not inconsistent with this code.

(c) A designation, preference, limitation, or relative right, including a voting right, of a class or series of shares of a corporation may be made dependent on facts not contained in the certificate of formation, including future acts of the corporation, if the manner in which those facts will operate on the designation, preference, limitation, or right is clearly and expressly stated in the certificate of formation.

Acts 2003, 78th Leg., ch. 182, § 1, eff. Jan. 1, 2006. Amended by Acts 2009, 81st Leg., ch. 84, § 28, eff. Sept. 1, 2009.

§ 21.154. Certain Optional Characteristics of Shares

(a) Subject to Sections 21.152 and 21.153, if authorized by the corporation's certificate of formation, a corporation may issue shares that:

(1) are redeemable, at the option of the corporation, shareholder, or other person or on the occurrence of a designated event, subject to Sections 21.303 and 21.304;

(2) entitle the holders of the shares to cumulative, noncumulative, or partially cumulative distributions;

(3) have preferences over any or all other classes or series of shares with respect to payment of distributions;

(4) have preferences over any or all other classes or series of shares with respect to the assets of the corporation on the voluntary or involuntary winding up and termination of the corporation;

(5) are exchangeable, at the option of the corporation, shareholder, or other person or on the occurrence of a designated event, for shares, obligations, indebtedness, evidence of ownership, rights to purchase securities of the corporation or one or more other entities, or other property or for a combination of those rights, assets, or obligations, subject to Section 21.303; and

(6) are convertible into shares of any other class or series, at the option of the corporation, shareholder, or other person or on the occurrence of a designated event.

(b) Shares without par value may not be converted into shares with par value unless:

(1) at the time of conversion, the part of the corporation's stated capital represented by the shares without par value is at least equal to the aggregate par value of the shares to be converted; or

(2) the amount of any deficiency computed under Subdivision (1) is transferred from surplus to stated capital.

Acts 2003, 78th Leg., ch. 182, § 1, eff. Jan. 1, 2006. Amended by Acts 2009, 81st Leg., ch. 84, § 29, eff. Sept. 1, 2009.

§ 21.155. Series of Shares Established by Board of Directors

(a) If expressly authorized by the corporation's certificate of formation and subject to the certificate of formation, the board of directors of a corporation may establish series of unissued shares of any class by setting and determining the designations, preferences, limitations, and relative rights, including voting rights, of the shares of the series to be established to the same extent that the designations, preferences, limitations, or relative rights could be stated if fully specified in the certificate of formation.

(b) To establish a series if authorized by the certificate of formation, the board of directors must adopt a resolution specifying the designations, preferences, limitations, and relative rights, including voting rights, of the series to be established or specifying any designation, preference, limitation, or relative right that is not set and determined by the certificate of formation.

(c) If the certificate of formation does not expressly restrict the board of directors from increasing or decreasing the number of unissued shares of a series to be established under Subsection (a), the board of directors may increase or decrease the number of shares in each series to be established, except that the board of directors may not decrease the number of shares in a particular series to a number that is less than the number of shares in that series that are issued at the time of the decrease.

(d) To increase or decrease the number of shares of a series under Subsection (c), the board of directors must adopt a resolution setting and determining the new number of shares of each series in which the number of shares is increased or decreased. If the number of shares of a series is decreased, the shares by which the series is decreased will resume the status of authorized but unissued shares of the class of shares from which the series was established, unless otherwise provided by the certificate of formation or the terms of the class or series.

(e) If no shares of a series established by board resolution under Subsection (b) are outstanding because no shares of that series have been issued or no issued shares of that series remain outstanding, the board of directors by resolution may delete the series from the certificate of formation and delete any reference to the series contained in the certificate of formation. Unless otherwise provided by the certificate of formation, the shares of any series deleted from the certificate of formation under this section shall resume the status of authorized but unissued shares of the class of shares from which the series was established.

(f) If no shares of a series established by resolution of the board of directors under Subsection (b) are outstanding because no shares of that series have been issued, the board of directors may amend the designations, preferences, limitations, and relative rights, including voting rights, of the series or amend any designation, preference, limitation, or relative right that is not set and determined by the certificate of formation.

Acts 2003, 78th Leg., ch. 182, § 1, eff. Jan. 1, 2006.

§ 21.156. Actions with Respect to Series of Shares

(a) To effect an action authorized under Section 21.155, the corporation must file with the secretary of state a statement that contains:

(1) the name of the corporation;

(2) if the statement relates to the establishment of a series of shares, a copy of the resolution establishing and designating the series and setting and determining the designations, preferences, limitations, and relative rights of the series;

(3) if the statement relates to an increase or decrease in the number of shares of a series, a copy of the resolution setting and determining the new number of shares of each series in which the number of shares is increased or decreased;

(4) if the statement relates to the deletion of a series of shares and all references to the series from the certificate of formation, a copy of the resolution deleting the series and all references to the series from the certificate of formation;

(5) if the statement relates to the amendment of designations, preferences, limitations, or relative rights of shares of a series that was previously established by resolution of the board of directors, a copy of the resolution in which the amendment is specified;

(6) the date of the adoption of the resolution; and

(7) a statement that the resolution was adopted by all necessary action on the part of the corporation.

(b) On the filing of a statement described by Subsection (a), the following resolutions will become an amendment of the certificate of formation, as appropriate:

(1) the resolution establishing and designating the series and setting and determining the designations, preferences, limitations, and relative rights of the series;

(2) the resolution setting the new number of shares of each series in which the number of shares is increased or decreased;

(3) the resolution deleting a series and all references to the series from the certificate of formation; or

(4) the resolution amending the designations, preferences, limitations, and relative rights of a series.

(c) An amendment of the certificate of formation under this section is not subject to the procedure to amend the certificate of formation contained in Subchapter B.

Acts 2003, 78th Leg., ch. 182, § 1, eff. Jan. 1, 2006.

§ 21.157. Issuance of Shares

(a) Except as provided by Section 21.158, a corporation may issue shares for consideration if authorized by the board of directors of the corporation.

(b) Shares may not be issued until the consideration, determined in accordance with this subchapter, has been paid or delivered as required in connection with the authorization of the shares. When the consideration is paid or delivered:

(1) the shares are considered to be issued;

(2) the subscriber or other person entitled to receive the shares is a shareholder with respect to the shares; and

(3) the shares are considered fully paid and nonassessable.

(c) This subsection applies only to shares issued in accordance with Subsections (a) and (b) and Sections 21.160 and 21.161 for consideration consisting, wholly or partly, of a contract for future services or benefits or a promissory note. A corporation may place the shares, although fully paid and nonassessable, in escrow, or make other arrangements to restrict the transfer of the shares, and may credit distributions made with respect to the shares against their purchase price, until the services are performed, the note is paid, or the benefits are received. If the services are not performed, the note is not paid, or the benefits are not received, the corporation may pursue remedies provided or afforded under law or in the contract or note, including causing the shares that are placed in escrow or restricted to be forfeited or returned to or reacquired by the corporation and the distributions that have been credited to be wholly or partly returned to the corporation.

Acts 2003, 78th Leg., ch. 182, § 1, eff. Jan. 1, 2006. Amended by Acts 2009, 81st Leg., ch. 84, § 30, eff. Sept. 1, 2009.

§ 21.158. Issuance of Shares Under Plan of Merger or Conversion

(a) A converted corporation under a plan of conversion or a corporation created by a plan of merger may issue shares for consideration if authorized by the plan of conversion or plan of merger, as appropriate.

(b) A corporation may issue shares in the manner provided by and for consideration specified under a plan of merger or plan of conversion.

Acts 2003, 78th Leg., ch. 182, § 1, eff. Jan. 1, 2006.

§ 21.159. Types of Consideration for Shares

Shares with or without par value may be issued for the following types of consideration:

(1) a tangible or intangible benefit to the corporation;

(2) cash;

(3) a promissory note;

(4) services performed or a contract for services to be performed;

(5) a security of the corporation or any other organization; and

(6) any other property of any kind or nature.

Acts 2003, 78th Leg., ch. 182, § 1, eff. Jan. 1, 2006.

§ 21.160. Determination of Consideration for Shares

(a) Subject to Subsection (b), consideration to be received for shares must be determined:

(1) by the board of directors;

(2) by a plan of conversion, if the shares are to be issued by a converted corporation under the plan; or

(3) by a plan of merger, if the shares are to be issued under the plan by a corporation created under the plan.

(b) If the corporation's certificate of formation reserves to the shareholders the right to determine the consideration to be received for shares without par value, the shareholders shall determine the consideration for those shares before the shares are issued. The board of directors may not determine the consideration for shares under this subsection.

(c) A corporation may dispose of treasury shares for consideration that may be determined by the board of directors.

Acts 2003, 78th Leg., ch. 182, § 1, eff. Jan. 1, 2006.

§ 21.161. Amount of Consideration for Issuance of Certain Shares

(a) Consideration to be received by a corporation for the issuance of shares with par value may not be less than the par value of the shares.

(b) The part of the surplus of a corporation that is transferred to stated capital on the issuance of shares as a share distribution is considered to be the consideration for the issuance of those shares.

(c) The consideration received by a corporation for the issuance of shares on the conversion or exchange of its indebtedness or shares is:

(1) the principal of, and accrued interest on, the indebtedness exchanged or converted, or the stated capital on the issuance of the shares;

(2) the part of surplus, if any, transferred to stated capital on the issuance of the shares; and

(3) any additional consideration paid to the corporation on the issuance of the shares.

(d) The consideration received by a corporation for the issuance of shares on the exercise of rights or options is:

(1) any consideration received by the corporation for the rights or options; and

(2) any consideration received by the corporation for the issuance of shares on the exercise of the rights or options.

Acts 2003, 78th Leg., ch. 182, § 1, eff. Jan. 1, 2006.

§ 21.162. Value and Sufficiency of Consideration

In the absence of fraud in the transaction, the judgment of the board of directors, the shareholders, or the party approving the plan of conversion or the plan of merger, as appropriate, is conclusive in determining the value and sufficiency of the consideration received for the shares.

Acts 2003, 78th Leg., ch. 182, § 1, eff. Jan. 1, 2006.

§ 21.163. Issuance and Disposition of Fractional Shares or Scrip

(a) A corporation may:

(1) issue fractions of a share, either certificated or uncertificated;

(2) arrange for the disposition of fractional interests by persons entitled to the interests;

(3) pay cash for the fair value of fractions of a share determined when the shareholders entitled to receive the fractions are determined; or

(4) subject to Subsection (b), issue scrip in registered form that entitles the holder to receive a certificate for a full share or an uncertificated full share on the surrender of the scrip aggregating a full share.

(b) The board of directors may issue scrip:

(1) on the condition that the scrip will become void if not exchanged for certificated or uncertificated full shares before a specified date;

(2) on the condition that the shares for which the scrip is exchangeable may be sold by the corporation and the proceeds from the sale of the shares may be distributed to the holders of scrip; or

(3) subject to any other condition the board of directors may determine advisable.

Acts 2003, 78th Leg., ch. 182, § 1, eff. Jan. 1, 2006. Amended by Acts 2009, 81st Leg., ch. 84, § 31, eff. Sept. 1, 2009.

§ 21.164. Rights of Holders of Fractional Shares or Scrip

(a) A holder of a certificated or uncertificated fractional share is entitled to exercise voting rights, receive distributions, and make a claim with respect to the assets of the corporation in the event of winding up and termination.

(b) A holder of a certificate for scrip is not entitled to exercise voting rights, receive distributions, or make a claim with respect to the assets of the corporation in the event of winding up and termination unless the scrip provides for those rights.

Acts 2003, 78th Leg., ch. 182, § 1, eff. Jan. 1, 2006.

§ 21.165. Subscriptions

(a) A corporation may accept a subscription by notifying the subscriber in writing.

(b) A subscription to purchase shares in a corporation in the process of being formed is irrevocable for six months if the subscription is in writing and signed by the subscriber, unless the subscription provides for a longer or shorter period or all of the other subscribers agree to the revocation of the subscription.

(c) A written subscription entered into after the corporation is formed is a contract between the subscriber and the corporation.

Acts 2003, 78th Leg., ch. 182, § 1, eff. Jan. 1, 2006.

§ 21.166. Preformation Subscription

(a) The corporation may determine the payment terms of a preformation subscription unless the payment terms are specified by the subscription. The payment terms may authorize payment in full on acceptance or by installments.

(b) Unless the subscription provides otherwise, a corporation shall make calls placed to all subscribers of similar interests for payment on preformation subscriptions uniform as far as practicable.

(c) After the corporation is formed, if a subscriber fails to pay any installment or call when due, a corporation may:

(1) collect in the same manner as any other debt the amount due on any unpaid preformation subscription; or

(2) forfeit the subscription if the installment or call remains unpaid for 20 days after written notice to the subscriber.

(d) Although the forfeiture of a subscription terminates all the rights and obligations of the subscriber, the corporation may retain any amount previously paid on the subscription.

Acts 2003, 78th Leg., ch. 182, § 1, eff. Jan. 1, 2006.

§ 21.167. Commitment to Purchase Shares

(a) A person who contemplates the acquisition of shares in a corporation may commit to act in a specified manner with respect to the shares after the acquisition, including the voting of the shares or the retention or disposition of the shares. To be binding, the commitment must be in writing and be signed by the person acquiring the shares.

(b) A written commitment entered into under Subsection (a) is a contract between the shareholder and the corporation.

Acts 2003, 78th Leg., ch. 182, § 1, eff. Jan. 1, 2006.

§ 21.168. Stock Rights, Options, and Convertible Indebtedness

(a) Except as provided by the corporation's certificate of formation and regardless of whether done in connection with the issuance and sale of any other share or security of the corporation, a corporation may create and issue:

(1) rights or options that entitle the holders to purchase or receive from the corporation shares of any class or series or other securities; and

(2) indebtedness convertible into shares of any class or series of the corporation or other securities of the corporation.

(b) A right, option, or indebtedness described by this section shall be evidenced in the manner approved by the board of directors.

(c) Subject to the certificate of formation, a right or option described by this section must state the terms on which, the time within which, and any consideration, including a formula by which the consideration may be determined, for which the shares may be purchased or received from the corporation on the exercise of the right or option.

(d) Subject to the certificate of formation, convertible indebtedness described by this section must state the terms and conditions on which, the time within which, and the conversion ratio at which the indebtedness may be converted into shares.

Acts 2003, 78th Leg., ch. 182, § 1, eff. Jan. 1, 2006. Amended by Acts 2005, 79th Leg., ch. 64, § 45, eff. Jan. 1, 2006.

§ 21.169. Terms and Conditions of Rights and Options

(a) The terms and conditions of rights or options may include restrictions or conditions that:

(1) prohibit or limit the exercise, transfer, or receipt of the rights or options by certain persons or classes of persons, including:

(A) a person who beneficially owns or offers to acquire a specified number or percentage of the outstanding common shares, voting power, or other securities of the corporation; or

(B) a transferee of a person described by Paragraph (A); or

(2) invalidate or void the rights or options held by a person or transferee described by Subdivision (1).

(b) Rights or options created or issued before the effective date of this code that comply with this section and are not in conflict with other provisions of this code are ratified.

(c) Unless otherwise provided under the terms of rights or options or the agreement or plan under which the rights or options are issued, the authority to grant, amend, redeem, extend, or replace the rights or options on behalf of a corporation is vested exclusively in the board of directors of the corporation. A bylaw may not require the board to grant, amend, redeem, extend, or replace the rights or options.

(d) The terms of rights or options or the agreement or plan under which the rights or options are issued may provide that the board of directors by resolution may authorize one or more officers of the corporation to:

(1) designate officers and employees of the corporation or of any subsidiary of the corporation to receive rights or options created by the corporation; or

(2) determine the number of rights or options to be received under Subdivision (1).

(e) A resolution adopted under Subsection (d)(1) must specify the total number of rights or options the authorized officer or officers may award. An officer may not be designated as a recipient of any rights or options that the officer is authorized to award under Subsection (d)(1).

Acts 2003, 78th Leg., ch. 182, § 1, eff. Jan. 1, 2006. Amended by Acts 2005, 79th Leg., ch. 64, § 46, eff. Jan. 1, 2006.

§ 21.170. Consideration for Rights, Options, and Convertible Indebtedness

(a) In the absence of fraud in the transaction, the judgment of the board of directors of a corporation as to the adequacy of the consideration received for rights, options, or convertible indebtedness is conclusive.

(b) A corporation may issue rights or options to its shareholders, officers, consultants, independent contractors, employees, or directors without consideration if, in the judgment of the board of directors, the issuance of the rights or options is in the interests of the corporation.

(c) The consideration for shares having a par value, other than treasury shares, and issued on the exercise of the rights or options may not be less than the par value of the shares.

(d) A privilege of conversion may not be conferred on, or altered with respect to, any indebtedness that would result in the corporation receiving less than the minimum consideration required to be received on issuance of the shares.

(e) The consideration for shares issued on the exercise of rights, options, or convertible indebtedness shall be determined as provided by Section 21.161.

Acts 2003, 78th Leg., ch. 182, § 1, eff. Jan. 1, 2006.

§ 21.171 Outstanding or Treasury Shares

(a) Shares that are issued are outstanding shares unless the shares are treasury shares or are canceled.

(b) If there are outstanding shares, one or more shares that together have unlimited voting rights and one or more shares that together are entitled to receive the net assets of the corporation on the winding up and termination of the corporation must be outstanding shares.

(c) Treasury shares are considered to be issued shares and not outstanding shares.

(d) Treasury shares may not be included in the total assets of a corporation for purposes of determining the net assets of a corporation.

Acts 2003, 78th Leg., ch. 182, § 1, eff. Jan. 1, 2006. Amended by Acts 2009, 81st Leg., ch. 84, § 32, eff. Sept. 1, 2009.

§ 21.172. Expenses of Organization, Reorganization, and Financing of Corporation

A corporation may pay or authorize to be paid from the consideration received by the corporation as payment for the corporation's shares the reasonable charges and expenses of the organization or reorganization of the corporation and the sale or underwriting of the shares without rendering the shares not fully paid and nonassessable.

Acts 2003, 78th Leg., ch. 182, § 1, eff. Jan. 1, 2006.

§ 21.173. Supplemental Required Records

In addition to the books and records required to be kept under Section 3.151, a corporation shall keep at its registered office or principal place of business, or at the office of its transfer agent or registrar, a record of:

(1) the original issuance of shares issued by the corporation;

(2) each transfer of those shares that have been presented to the corporation for registration of transfer;

(3) the names and addresses of all past shareholders of the corporation; and

(4) the number and class or series of shares issued by the corporation held by each current and past shareholder.

Acts 2003, 78th Leg., ch. 182, § 1, eff. Jan. 1, 2006.

SUBCHAPTER E. SHAREHOLDER RIGHTS AND RESTRICTIONS

§ 21.201 Registered Holders as Owners; Shares Held by Nominees

(a) Except as otherwise provided by this code and subject to Chapter 8, Business & Commerce Code, a corporation may consider the person registered as the owner of a share in the share transfer records of the corporation at a particular time, including a record date set under Section 6.101 or 6.102 or Subchapter H, as the owner of that share at that time for purposes of:

(1) voting the share;

(2) receiving distributions on the share;

(3) transferring the share;

(4) receiving notice, exercising rights of dissent, exercising or waiving a preemptive right, or giving proxies with respect to that share;

(5) entering into agreements with respect to that share in accordance with Section 6.251, 6.252, or 21.210; or

(6) any other shareholder action.

(b) A corporation may establish a procedure by which the corporation recognizes as a shareholder the beneficial owner of shares registered in the name of a nominee.

(c) A procedure established under Subsection (b) must:

(1) determine the extent of the corporation's recognition of the beneficial owner as a shareholder; and

(2) include the nominee's filing of a statement with the corporation that contains information regarding the beneficial owner.

(d) A procedure established under Subsection (b) may set forth:

(1) the types of nominees to which the procedure applies;

(2) the rights or privileges that the corporation will recognize in a beneficial owner, to the extent that the rights or privileges are not inconsistent with Section 10.361(g);

(3) the manner in which the procedure is selected by the nominee;

(4) the information that must be provided when the procedure is selected;

(5) the period for which the selection of the procedure is effective; and

(6) any other aspect of the rights and duties to be established under the procedure.

Acts 2003, 78th Leg., ch. 182, § 1, eff. Jan. 1, 2006. Amended by Acts 2009, 81st Leg., ch. 84, § 33, eff. Sept. 1, 2009.

§ 21.202. Definition of Shares

In Sections 21.203–21.208, "shares" includes a security:

(1) that is convertible into shares; or

(2) that carries a right to subscribe for or acquire shares.

Acts 2003, 78th Leg., ch. 182, § 1, eff. Jan. 1, 2006.

§ 21.203. No Statutory Preemptive Right Unless Provided by Certificate of Formation

(a) Except as provided by Section 21.208, a shareholder of a corporation does not have a preemptive right under this subchapter to acquire the corporation's unissued or treasury shares except to the extent provided by the corporation's certificate of formation.

(b) If the certificate of formation includes a statement that the corporation "elects to have a preemptive right" or a similar statement, Section 21.204 applies to a shareholder except to the extent the certificate of formation expressly provides otherwise.

(c) This section and Sections 21.204 through 21.208 do not invalidate or impair a corporation's right or power to grant an enforceable nonstatutory preemptive right in:

(1) a contract between the corporation and a shareholder or other person; or

(2) the governing documents of the corporation.

Acts 2003, 78th Leg., ch. 182, § 1, eff. Jan. 1, 2006. Amended by Acts 2011, 82nd Leg., ch. 139 (S.B. 748), § 23, eff. Sept. 1, 2011.

§ 21.204. Statutory Preemptive Rights

(a) If the shareholders of a corporation have a preemptive right under this subchapter, the shareholders have a preemptive right to acquire proportional amounts of the corporation's unissued or treasury shares on the decision of the corporation's board of directors to issue the shares. The preemptive right granted under this subsection is subject to uniform terms and conditions prescribed by the board of directors to provide a fair and reasonable opportunity to exercise the preemptive right.

(b) No preemptive right exists with respect to:

(1) shares issued or granted as compensation to a director, officer, agent, or employee of the corporation or a subsidiary or affiliate of the corporation;

(2) shares issued or granted to satisfy conversion or option rights created to provide compensation to a director, officer, agent, or employee of the corporation or a subsidiary or affiliate of the corporation;

(3) shares authorized in the corporation's certificate of formation that are issued not later than the 180th day after the effective date of the corporation's formation; or

(4) shares sold, issued, or granted by the corporation for consideration other than money.

(c) A holder of a share of a class without general voting rights but with a preferential right to distributions of profits, income, or assets does not have a preemptive right with respect to shares of any class.

(d) A holder of a share of a class with general voting rights but without preferential rights to distributions of profits, income, or assets does not have a preemptive right with respect to shares of any class with preferential rights to distributions of profits, income, or assets unless the shares with preferential rights are convertible into or carry a right to subscribe for or acquire shares without preferential rights.

(e) For a one-year period after the date the shares have been offered to shareholders, shares subject to preemptive rights that are not acquired by a shareholder may be issued to a person at a consideration set by the corporation's board of directors that is not lower than the consideration set for the exercise of preemptive rights. An offer at a lower consideration or after the expiration of the period prescribed by this subsection is subject to the shareholder's preemptive rights.

Acts 2003, 78th Leg., ch. 182, § 1, eff. Jan. 1, 2006.

§ 21.205. Waiver of Preemptive Right

(a) A shareholder may waive a preemptive right granted to the shareholder.

(b) A written waiver of a preemptive right is irrevocable regardless of whether the waiver is supported by consideration.

Acts 2003, 78th Leg., ch. 182, § 1, eff. Jan. 1, 2006.

§ 21.206. Limitation on Action to Enforce Preemptive Right

(a) An action brought against a corporation, the board of directors or an officer, shareholder, or agent of the corporation, or an owner of a beneficial interest in shares of the corporation for the violation of a preemptive right of a shareholder under Sections 21.203 and 21.204 must be brought not later than the earlier of:

(1) the first anniversary of the date written notice is given to each shareholder whose preemptive right was violated; or

(2) the fourth anniversary of the latest of:

(A) the date the corporation issued the shares, securities, or rights;

(B) the date the corporation sold the shares, securities, or rights; or

(C) the date the corporation otherwise distributed the shares, securities, or rights.

(b) The notice required by Subsection (a)(1) must:

(1) be sent to the holder at the address for the holder as shown on the appropriate records of the corporation; and

(2) inform the holder that the issuance, sale, or other distribution of shares, securities, or rights violated the holder's preemptive right.

Acts 2003, 78th Leg., ch. 182, § 1, eff. Jan. 1, 2006. Amended by Acts 2011, 82nd Leg., ch. 139 (S.B. 748), § 24, eff. Sept. 1, 2011.

§ 21.207. Disposition of Shares Having Preemptive Rights

The transferee or successor of a share that has been transferred or otherwise disposed of by a shareholder of a corporation whose preemptive right to acquire shares in the corporation has been violated does not acquire the preemptive right, or any right or claim based on the violation, unless the previous shareholder has assigned the preemptive right to the transferee or successor.

Acts 2003, 78th Leg., ch. 182, § 1, eff. Jan. 1, 2006.

§ 21.208. Preemptive Right in Existing Corporation

Subject to the certificate of formation, a shareholder of a corporation incorporated before September 1, 2003, has a preemptive right to acquire unissued or treasury shares of the corporation to the extent provided by Sections 21.204, 21.206, and 21.207. After September 1, 2003, a corporation may limit or deny the preemptive right of the shareholders of the corporation by amending the corporation's certificate of formation.

Acts 2003, 78th Leg., ch. 182, § 1, eff. Jan. 1, 2006. Amended by Acts 2005, 79th Leg., ch. 64, § 47, eff. Jan. 1, 2006.

§ 21.209. Transfer of Shares and Other Securities

Except as otherwise provided by this code, the shares and other securities of a corporation are transferable in accordance with Chapter 8, Business & Commerce Code.

Acts 2003, 78th Leg., ch. 182, § 1, eff. Jan. 1, 2006.

§ 21.210. Restriction on Transfer of Shares and Other Securities

(a) A restriction on the transfer or registration of transfer of a security, or on the amount of a corporation's securities that may be owned by a person or group of persons, may be imposed by:

(1) the corporation's certificate of formation;

(2) the corporation's bylaws;

(3) a written agreement among two or more holders of the securities; or

(4) a written agreement among one or more holders of the securities and the corporation if:

(A) the corporation files a copy of the agreement at the principal place of business or registered office of the corporation; and

(B) the copy of the agreement is subject to the same right of examination by a shareholder of the corporation, in person or by agent, attorney, or accountant, as the books and records of the corporation.

(b) A restriction imposed under Subsection (a) is not valid with respect to a security issued before the restriction has been adopted, unless the holder of the security voted in favor of the restriction or is a party to the agreement imposing the restriction.

Acts 2003, 78th Leg., ch. 182, § 1, eff. Jan. 1, 2006. Amended by Acts 2005, 79th Leg., ch. 64, § 48, eff. Jan. 1, 2006.

§ 21.211. Valid Restrictions on Transfer

(a) Without limiting the general powers granted by Sections 21.210 and 21.213 to impose and enforce reasonable restrictions, a restriction placed on the transfer or registration of transfer of a security of a corporation is valid if the restriction reasonably:

(1) obligates the holder of the restricted security to offer a person, including the corporation or other holders of securities of the corporation, an opportunity to acquire the restricted security within a reasonable time before the transfer;

(2) obligates the corporation, to the extent provided by this code, or another person to purchase securities that are the subject of an agreement relating to the purchase and sale of the restricted security;

(3) requires the corporation or the holders of a class of the corporation's securities to consent to a proposed transfer of the restricted security or to approve the proposed transferee of the restricted security for the purpose of preventing a violation of law;

(4) prohibits the transfer of the restricted security to a designated person or group of persons and the designation is not manifestly unreasonable;

(5) maintains the status of the corporation as an electing small business corporation under Subchapter S of the Internal Revenue Code;

(6) maintains a tax advantage to the corporation;

(7) maintains the status of the corporation as a close corporation under Subchapter O;

(8) obligates the holder of the restricted securities to sell or transfer an amount of restricted securities to a person or group of persons, including the corporation or other holders of securities of the corporation; or

(9) causes or results in the automatic sale or transfer of an amount of restricted securities to a person or group of persons, including the corporation or other holders of securities of the corporation.

(b) A restriction placed on the transfer or registration of transfer of a security of a corporation, on the amount of the corporation's securities, or on the amount of the corporation's securities that may be owned by a person or group of persons is conclusively presumed to be for a reasonable purpose if the restriction:

(1) maintains a local, state, federal, or foreign tax advantage to the corporation or its shareholders, including:

(A) maintaining the corporation's status as an electing small business corporation under Subchapter S of the Internal Revenue Code;

(B) maintaining or preserving any tax attribute, including net operating losses; or

(C) qualifying or maintaining the qualification of the corporation as a real estate investment trust under the Internal Revenue Code or regulations adopted under the Internal Revenue Code; or

(2) maintains a statutory or regulatory advantage or complies with a statutory or regulatory requirement under applicable local, state, federal, or foreign law.

Acts 2003, 78th Leg., ch. 182, § 1, eff. Jan. 1, 2006. Amended by Acts 2005, 79th Leg., ch. 64, § 49, eff. Jan. 1, 2006; Acts 2007, 80th Leg., ch. 688, § 71, eff. Sept. 1, 2007.

§ 21.212. Bylaw or Agreement Restricting Transfer of Shares or Other Securities

(a) A corporation that has adopted a bylaw or is a party to an agreement that restricts the transfer of the shares or other securities of the corporation may file with the secretary of state, in accordance with Chapter 4, a copy of the bylaw or agreement and a statement attached to the copy that:

(1) contains the name of the corporation;

(2) states that the attached copy of the bylaw or agreement is a true and correct copy of the bylaw or agreement; and

(3) states that the filing has been authorized by the board of directors or, in the case of a corporation that is managed in some other manner under a shareholders' agreement, by the person empowered by the agreement to manage the corporation's business and affairs.

(b) After a statement described by Subsection (a) is filed with the secretary of state, the bylaws or agreement restricting the transfer of shares or other securities is a public record, and the fact that the statement has been filed may be stated on a certificate representing the restricted shares or securities if required by Section 3.202.

(c) A corporation that is a party to an agreement restricting the transfer of the shares or other securities of the corporation may make the agreement part of the corporation's certificate of formation without restating the provisions of the agreement in the certificate of formation by amending the certificate of formation. If the agreement alters any provision of the certificate of formation, the certificate of amendment shall identify the altered provision by reference or description. If the agreement is an addition to the certificate of formation, the certificate of amendment must state that fact.

(d) The certificate of amendment must:

(1) include a copy of the agreement restricting the transfer of shares or other securities;

(2) state that the attached copy of the agreement is a true and correct copy of the agreement; and

(3) state that inclusion of the certificate of amendment as part of the certificate of formation has been authorized in the manner required by this code to amend the certificate of formation.

Acts 2003, 78th Leg., ch. 182, § 1, eff. Jan. 1, 2006.

§ 21.213. Enforceability of Restriction on Transfer of Certain Securities

(a) A restriction placed on the transfer or registration of the transfer of a security of a corporation is specifically enforceable against the holder, or a successor or transferee of the holder, if:

(1) the restriction is reasonable and noted conspicuously on the certificate or other instrument representing the security; or

(2) with respect to an uncertificated security, the restriction is reasonable and a notation of the restriction is contained in the notice sent with respect to the security under Section 3.205.

(b) Unless noted in the manner specified by Subsection (a) with respect to a certificate or other instrument or an uncertificated security, an otherwise enforceable restriction is ineffective against a transferee for value without actual knowledge of the restriction at the time of the transfer or against a subsequent transferee, regardless of whether the transfer is for value. A restriction is specifically enforceable against a person other than a transferee for value from the time the person acquires actual knowledge of the restriction's existence.

Acts 2003, 78th Leg., ch. 182, § 1, eff. Jan. 1, 2006.

§ 21.214. Joint Ownership of Shares

(a) If shares are registered on the books of a corporation in the names of two or more persons as joint owners with the right of survivorship and one of the owners dies, the corporation may record on its books and effect the transfer of the shares to a person, including the surviving joint owner, and pay any distributions made with respect to the shares, as if the surviving joint owner was the absolute owner of the shares. The recording and distribution authorized by this subsection must be made after the death of a joint owner and before the corporation receives actual written notice that a party other than a surviving joint owner is claiming an interest in the shares or distribution.

(b) The discharge of a corporation from liability under Section 21.216 and the transfer of full legal and equitable title of the shares does not affect, reduce, or limit any cause of action existing in favor of an owner of an interest in the shares or distributions against the surviving owner.

Acts 2003, 78th Leg., ch. 182, § 1, eff. Jan. 1, 2006.

§ 21.215. Liability for Designating Owner of Shares

A corporation or an officer, director, employee, or agent of the corporation may not be held liable for considering the person who is registered as the owner of a share in the share transfer records of the corporation at a particular time to be the owner of the share at that time for a purpose described by Section 21.201, regardless of whether the person possesses a certificate for that share.

Acts 2003, 78th Leg., ch. 182, § 1, eff. Jan. 1, 2006.

§ 21.216. Liability Regarding Joint Ownership of Shares

A corporation that transfers shares or makes a distribution to a surviving joint owner under Section 21.214 before the corporation has received a written claim for the shares or distribution from another person is discharged from liability for the transfer or payment.

Acts 2003, 78th Leg., ch. 182, § 1, eff. Jan. 1, 2006.

§ 21.217. Liability of Assignee or Transferee

An assignee or transferee of certificated shares, uncertificated shares, or a subscription for shares in good faith and without knowledge that full consideration for the shares or subscription has not been paid may not be held personally liable to the corporation or a creditor of the corporation for an unpaid portion of the consideration.

Acts 2003, 78th Leg., ch. 182, § 1, eff. Jan. 1, 2006.

§ 21.218. Examination of Records

(a) In this section, a holder of a beneficial interest in a voting trust entered into under Section 6.251 is a holder of the shares represented by the beneficial interest.

(b) Subject to the governing documents and on written demand stating a proper purpose, a holder of shares of a corporation for at least six months immediately preceding the holder's demand, or a holder of at least five percent of all of the outstanding shares of a corporation, is entitled to examine and copy, at a reasonable time, the corporation's relevant books, records of account, minutes, and share transfer records. The examination may be conducted in person or through an agent, accountant, or attorney.

(c) This section does not impair the power of a court, on the presentation of proof of proper purpose by a beneficial or record holder of shares, to compel the production for examination by the holder of the books and records of accounts, minutes, and share transfer records of a corporation, regardless of the period during which the holder was a beneficial holder or record holder and regardless of the number of shares held by the person.

Acts 2003, 78th Leg., ch. 182, § 1, eff. Jan. 1, 2006.

§ 21.219. Annual and Interim Statements of Corporation

(a) On written request of a shareholder of the corporation, a corporation shall mail to the shareholder:

(1) the annual statements of the corporation for the last fiscal year that contain in reasonable detail the corporation's assets and liabilities and the results of the corporation's operations; and

(2) the most recent interim statements, if any, that have been filed in a public record or other publication.

(b) The corporation shall be allowed a reasonable time to prepare the annual statements.

Acts 2003, 78th Leg., ch. 182, § 1, eff. Jan. 1, 2006.

§ 21.220. Penalty for Failure to Prepare Voting List

An officer or agent of a corporation who is in charge of the corporation's share transfer records and who does not prepare the list of shareholders, keep the list on file for a 10–day period, or produce and keep the list available for inspection at the annual meeting as required by Sections 21.354 and 21.372 is liable to a shareholder who suffers damages because of the failure for the damage caused by the failure.

Acts 2003, 78th Leg., ch. 182, § 1, eff. Jan. 1, 2006. Amended by Acts 2007, 80th Leg., ch. 688, § 72, eff. Sept. 1, 2007.

§ 21.221. Penalty for Failure to Provide Notice of Meeting

If an officer or agent of a corporation is unable to comply with the duties prescribed by Sections 21.354 and 21.372 because the officer or agent did not receive notice of a meeting of shareholders within a sufficient time before the date of the meeting, the corporation, rather than the officer or agent, is liable to a shareholder who suffers damages because of the failure for the extent of the damage caused by the failure.

Acts 2003, 78th Leg., ch. 182, § 1, eff. Jan. 1, 2006. Amended by Acts 2007, 80th Leg., ch. 688, § 73, eff. Sept. 1, 2007.

§ 21.222. Penalty for Refusal to Permit Examination of Certain Records

(a) A corporation that refuses to allow a person to examine and make copies of account records, minutes, and share transfer records under Section 21.218 is liable to the shareholder for any cost or expense, including attorney's fees, incurred in enforcing the shareholder's rights under Section 21.218. The liability imposed on a corporation under this subsection is in addition to any other damages or remedy afforded to the shareholder by law.

(b) It is a defense to an action brought under this section that the person suing:

(1) has, within the two years preceding the date the action is brought, sold or offered for sale a list of shareholders or of holders of voting trust certificates for shares of the corporation or any other corporation;

(2) has aided or abetted a person in procuring a list of shareholders or of holders of voting trust certificates for the purpose described by Subdivision (1);

(3) has improperly used information obtained through a prior examination of the books and account records, minutes, or share transfer records of the corporation or any other corporation; or

(4) was not acting in good faith or for a proper purpose in making the person's request for examination.

Acts 2003, 78th Leg., ch. 182, § 1, eff. Jan. 1, 2006. Amended by Acts 2011, 82nd Leg., ch. 139 (S.B. 748), § 25, eff. Sept. 1, 2011.

§ 21.223. Limitation of Liability for Obligations

(a) A holder of shares, an owner of any beneficial interest in shares, or a subscriber for shares whose subscription has been accepted, or any affiliate of such a holder, owner, or subscriber or of the corporation, may not be held liable to the corporation or its obligees with respect to:

(1) the shares, other than the obligation to pay to the corporation the full amount of consideration, fixed in compliance with Sections 21.157–21.162, for which the shares were or are to be issued;

(2) any contractual obligation of the corporation or any matter relating to or arising from the obligation on the basis that the holder, beneficial owner, subscriber, or affiliate is or was the alter ego of the corporation or on the basis of actual or constructive fraud, a sham to perpetrate a fraud, or other similar theory; or

(3) any obligation of the corporation on the basis of the failure of the corporation to observe any corporate formality, including the failure to:

(A) comply with this code or the certificate of formation or bylaws of the corporation; or

(B) observe any requirement prescribed by this code or the certificate of formation or bylaws of the corporation for acts to be taken by the corporation or its directors or shareholders.

(b) Subsection (a)(2) does not prevent or limit the liability of a holder, beneficial owner, subscriber, or affiliate if the obligee demonstrates that the holder, beneficial owner, subscriber, or affiliate caused the corporation to be used for the purpose of perpetrating and did perpetrate an actual fraud on the obligee primarily for the direct personal benefit of the holder, beneficial owner, subscriber, or affiliate.

Acts 2003, 78th Leg., ch. 182, § 1, eff. Jan. 1, 2006. Amended by Acts 2007, 80th Leg., ch. 688, § 74, eff. Sept. 1, 2007.

§ 21.224 Preemption of Liability

The liability of a holder, beneficial owner, or subscriber of shares of a corporation, or any affiliate of such a holder, owner, or subscriber or of the corporation, for an obligation that is limited by Section 21.223 is exclusive and preempts any other liability imposed for that obligation under common law or otherwise.

Acts 2003, 78th Leg., ch. 182, § 1, eff. Jan. 1, 2006. Amended by Acts 2009, 81st Leg., ch. 84, § 34, eff. Sept. 1, 2009.

§ 21.225. Exceptions to Limitations

Section 21.223 or 21.224 does not limit the obligation of a holder, beneficial owner, subscriber, or affiliate to the obligee of the corporation if that person:

(1) expressly assumes, guarantees, or agrees to be personally liable to the obligee for the obligation; or

(2) is otherwise liable to the obligee for the obligation under this code or other applicable statute.

Acts 2003, 78th Leg., ch. 182, § 1, eff. Jan. 1, 2006.

§ 21.226. Pledgees and Trust Administrators

(a) A pledgee or other holder of shares as collateral security is not personally liable as a shareholder.

(b) An executor, administrator, conservator, guardian, trustee, assignee for the benefit of creditors, or receiver is not personally liable as a holder of or subscriber to shares of a corporation.

(c) The estate and funds administered by an executor, administrator, conservator, guardian, trustee, assignee for the benefit of creditors, or receiver are liable for the full amount of the consideration for which the shares were or are to be issued.

Acts 2003, 78th Leg., ch. 182, § 1, eff. Jan. 1, 2006.

SUBCHAPTER F. REDUCTIONS IN STATED CAPITAL; CANCELLATION OF TREASURY SHARES

§ 21.251. Reduction of Stated Capital by Redemption or Purchase of Redeemable Shares

(a) At the time a corporation redeems or purchases the redeemable shares of the corporation, the redemption or purchase has the effect of:

(1) canceling the shares; and

(2) restoring the shares to the status of authorized but unissued shares, unless the corporation's certificate of formation provides that shares may not be reissued after the shares are redeemed or purchased by the corporation.

(b) If the corporation is prohibited from reissuing the shares by the certificate of formation following a redemption or purchase under Subsection (a), the number of shares of the class that the corporation is authorized to issue is reduced by the number of shares canceled.

(c) If shares redeemed or purchased by a corporation under Subsection (a) constitute all of the outstanding shares of a particular class of shares and the certificate of formation provides that the shares of the class, when redeemed and repurchased, may not be reissued, the corporation may not issue any additional shares of the class of shares.

(d) Upon the redemption or purchase of redeemable shares under this section, the stated capital of the corporation shall be reduced by that part of the stated capital that was, at the time of the redemption or purchase, represented by those redeemable shares.

Acts 2003, 78th Leg., ch. 182, § 1, eff. Jan. 1, 2006.

§ 21.252. Cancellation of Treasury Shares

(a) A corporation, by resolution of the board of directors of the corporation, may cancel all or part of the corporation's treasury shares at any time.

(b) Upon the cancellation of treasury shares, the stated capital of the corporation shall be reduced by that part of the stated capital that was, at the time of the cancellation, represented by the canceled shares, and the canceled shares shall be restored to the status of authorized but unissued shares.

(c) This section does not prohibit a cancellation of shares or a reduction of stated capital in any other manner permitted by law.

Acts 2003, 78th Leg., ch. 182, § 1, eff. Jan. 1, 2006.

§ 21.253. Procedures for Reduction of Stated Capital by Board of Directors

(a) If all or part of the stated capital of a corporation is represented by shares without par value, the stated capital of the corporation may be reduced in the manner provided by this section.

(b) The board of directors shall adopt a resolution that:

(1) states the amount of the proposed reduction of the stated capital and the manner in which the reduction will be effected; and

(2) directs that the proposed reduction be submitted to a vote of the shareholders at an annual or special meeting.

(c) Each shareholder of record entitled to vote on the reduction of stated capital shall be given written notice stating that the purpose or one of the purposes of the meeting is to consider the matter of reducing the stated capital of the corporation in the amount and manner proposed by the board of directors. The notice shall be given in the time and manner provided by this code for giving notice of shareholders' meetings.

(d) The affirmative vote of the holders of at least the majority of the shares entitled to vote on the matter is required for approval of the resolution proposing the reduction of stated capital.

(e) Upon the approval of the resolution by the shareholders, the stated capital of the corporation shall be reduced as provided in the resolution.

Acts 2003, 78th Leg., ch. 182, § 1, eff. Jan. 1, 2006.

§ 21.254. Restriction on Reduction of Stated Capital

The stated capital of a corporation may not be reduced under this subchapter if the amount of the aggregate stated capital of the corporation would be reduced to an amount equal to or less than the sum of the:

(1) aggregate preferential amounts payable on all issued shares with a preferential right to the assets of the corporation in the event of voluntary winding up and termination; and

(2) aggregate par value of all issued shares with par value but no preferential right to the assets of the corporation in the event of voluntary winding up and termination.

Acts 2003, 78th Leg., ch. 182, § 1, eff. Jan. 1, 2006.

SUBCHAPTER G. DISTRIBUTIONS AND SHARE DIVIDENDS

§ 21.301. Definitions

In this subchapter:

(1) "Distribution limit," with respect to a distribution made by a corporation, other than a distribution described by Subdivision (2), means:

(A) the net assets of the corporation if the distribution:

(i) is a purchase or redemption of its own shares by a corporation that:

(a) is eliminating fractional shares;

(b) is collecting or compromising indebtedness owed by or to the corporation; or

(c) is paying dissenting shareholders entitled to payment for their shares under this code; or

(ii) is not the purchase or redemption of its own shares by a consuming assets corporation; or

(B) the surplus of the corporation for a distribution not described by Paragraph (A).

(2) "Distribution limit," with respect to a distribution that is a purchase or redemption of its own

shares by an investment company the certificate of formation of which provides that the company may purchase the company's own shares out of stated capital, means the net assets of the investment company rather than the surplus of the investment company.

(3) "Investment company" means a corporation registered as an open-end company under the Investment Company Act.

Acts 2003, 78th Leg., ch. 182, § 1, eff. Jan. 1, 2006.

§ 21.302. Authority for Distributions

The board of directors of a corporation may authorize a distribution and the corporation may make a distribution, subject to Section 21.303.

Acts 2003, 78th Leg., ch. 182, § 1, eff. Jan. 1, 2006.

§ 21.303. Limitations on Distributions

(a) A corporation may not make a distribution that violates the corporation's certificate of formation.

(b) Unless the distribution is made in compliance with Chapter 11, a corporation may not make a distribution:

(1) if the corporation would be insolvent after the distribution; or

(2) that exceeds the distribution limit.

Acts 2003, 78th Leg., ch. 182, § 1, eff. Jan. 1, 2006.

§ 21.304. Redemptions

(a) A distribution by a corporation that involves a redemption of outstanding redeemable shares of the corporation subject to redemption may be related to any or all of those shares.

(b) If less than all of the outstanding redeemable shares of a corporation subject to redemption are to be redeemed, the shares to be redeemed shall be selected for redemption:

(1) in accordance with the corporation's certificate of formation; or

(2) ratably or by lot in the manner prescribed by resolution of the corporation's board of directors, if the certificate of formation does not specify how shares are to be selected for redemption.

(c) A redemption of redeemable shares takes effect by call and written notice of the redemption of the shares.

Acts 2003, 78th Leg., ch. 182, § 1, eff. Jan. 1, 2006.

§ 21.305. Notice of Redemption

(a) A notice of redemption of redeemable shares of a corporation must state:

(1) the class or series of shares or part of the class or series of shares to be redeemed;

(2) the date set for redemption;

(3) the redemptive price; and

(4) the place at which the shareholders may obtain payment of the redemptive price.

(b) The notice of redemption shall be sent to each holder of redeemable shares being called not later than the 21st day or earlier than the 60th day before the date set for redemption.

(c) A notice that is mailed is considered to have been sent when the notice is deposited in the United States mail, with postage prepaid, addressed to the shareholder at the shareholder's address as it appears on the share transfer records of the corporation.

(d) A corporation may give the transfer agent described by Section 21.306 irrevocable instructions to send or complete the notice of redemption.

Acts 2003, 78th Leg., ch. 182, § 1, eff. Jan. 1, 2006.

§ 21.306. Deposit of Money for Redemption

(a) After the date the notice of redemption required by Section 21.305 is sent and before the day after the date set for redemption of redeemable shares of the corporation, a corporation may deposit with a bank or trust company in this or another state of the United States appointed and acting as transfer agent for the corporation an amount sufficient to redeem the shares called for redemption. The amount must be deposited as a trust fund.

(b) Unless the corporation's certificate of formation provides otherwise, if a corporation deposits money and gives payment instructions in accordance with Subsection (a) and Section 21.307(b):

(1) the shares called for redemption are considered redeemed, and distributions on those shares cease to accrue on and after the date set for redemption; and

(2) the deposit constitutes full payment of the shares called for redemption to the holders of the shares on and after the date set for redemption.

(c) Unless the certificate of formation provides otherwise, after the date a deposit is made and instructions are given under this section and Section 21.307(b), the shares called for redemption are not considered outstanding, and the holders of the shares cease to be shareholders of the shares and have no right with respect to the shares other than:

(1) the right to receive payment of the redemptive price of the shares without interest from the bank or trust company; and

(2) any right to convert those shares.

(d) Unless the certificate of formation provides otherwise, a bank or trust company receiving a deposit under this section shall pay to the corporation on demand the balance of the amount deposited if one or more holders of the shares called for redemption do not claim for redemption the amount deposited on or before the sixth anniversary of the date of the deposit. After making a payment under this subsection, the bank or trust company is relieved of all responsibility to the holders with respect to the amount deposited.

Acts 2003, 78th Leg., ch. 182, § 1, eff. Jan. 1, 2006.

§ 21.307. Payment of Redeemed Shares

(a) Payment of a certificated share shall be made only on the surrender of the respective share certificate.

(b) A corporation may give a transfer agent described by Section 21.306 irrevocable instructions to pay, on or after the date set for redemption of redeemable shares, the redemptive price to the respective holders of the shares as evidenced by a list of shareholders certified by an officer of the corporation.

Acts 2003, 78th Leg., ch. 182, § 1, eff. Jan. 1, 2006.

§ 21.308. Priority of Distributions

(a) Except as provided by Subsection (b) or (c), a corporation's indebtedness that arises as a result of the declaration of a distribution and a corporation's indebtedness issued in a distribution are at parity with the corporation's indebtedness to its general, unsecured creditors.

(b) The indebtedness described by Subsection (a) shall be subordinated to the extent required by an agreement binding on the corporation on the date the indebtedness arises or if agreed to by the person to whom the indebtedness is owed or, with respect to indebtedness issued in a distribution, as provided by the corporation.

(c) The indebtedness described by Subsection (a) shall be secured to the extent required by an agreement binding on the corporation.

Acts 2003, 78th Leg., ch. 182, § 1, eff. Jan. 1, 2006.

§ 21.309. Reserves, Designations, and Allocations from Surplus

(a) A corporation, by resolution of the board of directors of the corporation, may:

(1) create a reserve out of the surplus of the corporation; or

(2) designate or allocate in any manner a part or all of the corporation's surplus for a proper purpose.

(b) A corporation may increase, decrease, or abolish a reserve, designation, or allocation in the manner provided by Subsection (a).

Acts 2003, 78th Leg., ch. 182, § 1, eff. Jan. 1, 2006.

§ 21.310. Authority for Share Dividends

The board of directors of a corporation may authorize a share dividend and the corporation may pay a share dividend subject to Section 21.311 and any restriction in its certificate of formation.

Acts 2003, 78th Leg., ch. 182, § 1, eff. Jan. 1, 2006.

§ 21.311. Limitations on Share Dividends

A corporation may not pay a share dividend in authorized but unissued shares of any class if:

(1) the surplus of the corporation is less than the amount required by Section 21.313 to be transferred to stated capital at the time the share dividend is made; or

(2) the share dividend will be made to a holder of shares of any other class or series, unless:

(A) the corporation's certificate of formation provides for the dividend; or

(B) the share dividend is authorized by the holders of at least a majority of the outstanding shares of the class or series in which the share dividend is to be made.

Acts 2003, 78th Leg., ch. 182, § 1, eff. Jan. 1, 2006.

§ 21.312. Value of Shares Issued as Share Dividends

(a) A share dividend payable in authorized but unissued shares with par value shall be issued at the par value of the respective share.

(b) A share dividend payable in authorized but unissued shares without par value shall be issued at the value set by the board of directors when the share dividend is authorized.

Acts 2003, 78th Leg., ch. 182, § 1, eff. Jan. 1, 2006.

§ 21.313. Transfer of Surplus for Share Dividends

(a) When a share dividend payable in authorized but unissued shares with par value is made by a corporation, an amount of surplus designated by the corporation's board of directors that is not less than the aggregate par value of the shares issued as a share dividend shall be transferred to stated capital.

(b) When a share dividend payable in authorized but unissued shares without par value is made by a corporation, an amount of surplus equal to the aggregate value set by the corporation's board of directors with respect to shares under Section 21.312(b) shall be transferred to stated capital.

Acts 2003, 78th Leg., ch. 182, § 1, eff. Jan. 1, 2006.

§ 21.314. Determination of Solvency, Net Assets, Stated Capital, and Surplus

(a) For purposes of this subchapter, the determination of whether a corporation is or would be insolvent and the determination of the value of a corporation's net assets, stated capital, or surplus and each of the components of net assets, stated capital, or surplus may be based on:

(1) financial statements of the corporation, including financial statements that:

(A) include subsidiary corporations or other corporations accounted for on a consolidated basis or on the equity method of accounting; or

(B) present the financial condition of the corporation in accordance with generally accepted accounting principles;

(2) financial statements prepared using the method of accounting used to file the corporation's federal income tax return or using any other accounting practices and principles that are reasonable under the circumstances;

(3) financial information, including condensed or summary financial statements, that is prepared on the same basis as financial statements described by Subdivision (1) or (2);

(4) projection, forecast, or other forward-looking information relating to the future economic performance, financial condition, or liquidity of the corporation that is reasonable under the circumstances;

(5) a fair valuation or information from any other method that is reasonable under the circumstances; or

(6) a combination of a statement, valuation, or information authorized by this section.

(b) Subsection (a) does not apply to the computation of the Texas franchise tax or any other tax imposed on a corporation under the laws of this state.

Acts 2003, 78th Leg., ch. 182, § 1, eff. Jan. 1, 2006.

§ 21.315. Date of Determination of Solvency, Net Assets, Stated Capital, and Surplus

(a) For purposes of this subchapter, a determination of whether a corporation is or would be insolvent after a distribution or share dividend or a determination of the value of a corporation's net assets, stated capital, or surplus, or each component of net assets, stated capital, or surplus, shall be made:

(1) on the date the distribution or share dividend is authorized by the corporation's board of directors if the distribution or share dividend is made not later than the 120th day after the date of authorization; or

(2) if the distribution or share dividend is made more than 120 days after the date of authorization:

(A) on the date designated by the corporation's board of directors if the date so designated is not earlier than 120 days before the date the distribution or share dividend is made; or

(B) on the date the distribution or share dividend is made if the corporation's board of directors does not designate a date as described in Paragraph (A).

(b) For purposes of this section, a distribution that involves:

(1) the incurrence by a corporation of indebtedness or a deferred payment obligation is considered to have been made on the date the indebtedness or obligation is incurred; or

(2) a requirement in the corporation's certificate of formation or other contract of the corporation to redeem, exchange, or otherwise acquire any of its own shares is considered to have been made either on the date when the provision or other contract is made or takes effect or on the date when the shares to be redeemed, exchanged, or acquired are redeemed, exchanged, or acquired, at the option of the corporation.

Acts 2003, 78th Leg., ch. 182, § 1, eff. Jan. 1, 2006.

§ 21.316. Liability of Directors for Wrongful Distributions

(a) Subject to Subsection (c), the directors of a corporation who vote for or assent to a distribution by the corporation that is prohibited by Section 21. 303 are jointly and severally liable to the corporation for the amount by which the distribution exceeds the amount permitted by that section to be distributed.

(b) A director is not liable for all or part of the excess amount if a distribution of that amount would have been permitted by Section 21.303 after the date the director authorized the distribution.

(c) A director is not jointly and severally liable under Subsection (a) if, in voting for or assenting to the distribution, the director:

(1) relies in good faith and with ordinary care on:

(A) the statements, valuations, or information described by Section 21.314; or

(B) other information, opinions, reports, or statements, including financial statements and other financial data, concerning the corporation or another person that are prepared or presented by:

(i) one or more officers or employees of the corporation;

(ii) a legal counsel, public accountant, investment banker, or other person relating to a matter the director reasonably believes is within the person's professional or expert competence; or

(iii) a committee of the board of directors of which the director is not a member;

(2) acting in good faith and with ordinary care, considers the assets of the corporation to be valued at least at their book value; or

(3) in determining whether the corporation made adequate provision for payment, satisfaction, or discharge of all of the corporation's liabilities and obligations, as provided by Sections 11.053 and 11.356, relies in good faith and with ordinary care on financial statements of, or other information concerning, a person who was or became contractually obligated to pay, satisfy, or discharge some or all of the corporation's liabilities or obligations.

(d) The liability imposed under Subsection (a) is the only liability of a director to the corporation or its creditors for authorizing a distribution that is prohibited by Section 21.303.

(e) This section and Sections 21.317 and 21.318 do not limit any liability imposed under Chapter 24, Business & Commerce Code, or the United States Bankruptcy Code.

Acts 2003, 78th Leg., ch. 182, § 1, eff. Jan. 1, 2006.

§ 21.317. Statute of Limitations on Action for Wrongful Distribution

An action may not be brought against a director of a corporation under Section 21.316 after the second anniversary of the date the alleged act giving rise to the liability occurred.

Acts 2003, 78th Leg., ch. 182, § 1, eff. Jan. 1, 2006.

§ 21.318. Contribution from Certain Shareholders and Directors

(a) A director who is held liable for a claim asserted under Section 21.316 is entitled to receive contributions from shareholders who accepted or received the wrongful distribution knowing that it was prohibited by Section 21.303 in proportion to the amounts received by the shareholders.

(b) A director who is liable for a claim asserted under Section 21.316 is entitled to receive contributions from each of the other directors who are liable with respect to that claim in an amount appropriate to achieve equity.

(c) The liability provided by Subsection (a) is the only liability of a shareholder to the corporation or a creditor of the corporation for accepting or receiving a distribution by the corporation that is prohibited by Section 21.303, except for any liability under Chapter 24, Business & Commerce Code, or the United States Bankruptcy Code.

Acts 2003, 78th Leg., ch. 182, § 1, eff. Jan. 1, 2006.

SUBCHAPTER H. SHAREHOLDERS' MEETINGS; NOTICE TO SHAREHOLDERS; VOTING AND QUORUM

Acts 2005, 79th Leg., ch. 64, § 50 amended the Subchapter H heading.

§ 21.351. Annual Meeting

(a) An annual meeting of the shareholders of a corporation shall be held at a time that is stated in or set in accordance with the corporation's bylaws.

(b) On the application of a shareholder who has previously submitted a written request to the corporation that an annual meeting be held, a court in the county in which the principal executive office of the corporation is located may order a meeting to be held if the annual meeting is not held or written consent instead of the annual meeting is not executed within any 13-month period, unless the meeting is not required to be held under Section 21.655.

(c) The failure to hold an annual meeting at the designated time does not result in the winding up or termination of the corporation.

Acts 2003, 78th Leg., ch. 182, § 1, eff. Jan. 1, 2006.

§ 21.352. Special Meetings

(a) A special meeting of the shareholders of a corporation may be called by:

(1) the president, the board of directors, or any other person authorized to call special meetings by the certificate of formation or bylaws of the corporation; or

(2) the holders of the percentage of shares specified in the certificate of formation, not to exceed 50 percent of the shares entitled to vote or, if no percentage is specified, at least 10 percent of all of the shares of the corporation entitled to vote at the proposed special meeting.

(b) Unless stated in or set in accordance with the bylaws, the record date for determining which shareholders of the corporation are entitled to call a special meeting is the date the first shareholder signs the notice of that meeting.

(c) Other than procedural matters, the only business that may be conducted at a special meeting of the shareholders is business that is within the purposes described in the notice required by Section 21.353.

Acts 2003, 78th Leg., ch. 182, § 1, eff. Jan. 1, 2006.

§ 21.353. Notice of Meeting

(a) Except as provided by Section 21.456 and subject to Section 21.3531, written notice of a meeting in accordance with Section 6.051 shall be given to each shareholder entitled to vote at the meeting not later than the 10th day and not earlier than the 60th day before the date of the meeting. Notice shall be given at the direction of the president, secretary, or other person calling the meeting.

(b) The notice of a special meeting must contain a statement regarding the purpose or purposes of the meeting.

(c) If a meeting is held by means of remote communication, the notice of the meeting must include information on how to access the list of shareholders entitled to vote at the meeting required by Section 21.372.

Acts 2003, 78th Leg., ch. 182, § 1, eff. Jan. 1, 2006. Amended by Acts 2005, 79th Leg., ch. 64, § 51, eff. Jan. 1, 2006.

§ 21.3531. Notice by Electronic Transmission

(a) On consent of a shareholder, notice from a corporation under this code, the certificate of formation, or the bylaws may be provided to the shareholder by electronic transmission. The shareholder may specify the form of electronic transmission to be used to communicate notice.

(b) Notice is considered provided under this section when the notice is:

(1) transmitted to a facsimile number provided by the shareholder for the purpose of receiving notice;

(2) transmitted to an electronic mail address provided by the shareholder for the purpose of receiving notice;

(3) posted on an electronic network and a message is sent to the shareholder at the address provided by the shareholder for the purpose of alerting the shareholder of a posting; or

(4) communicated to the shareholder by any other form of electronic transmission consented to by the shareholder.

(c) A shareholder may revoke the shareholder's consent to receive notice by electronic transmission by providing written notice to the corporation. The shareholder's consent is considered revoked for purposes of Subsection (a) if the corporation is unable to deliver by electronic transmission two consecutive notices, and the secretary, assistant secretary, or transfer agent of the corporation, or another person responsible for delivering notice on behalf of the corporation, knows that delivery of those two electronic transmissions was unsuccessful. Inadvertent failure to treat the unsuccessful transmissions as a revocation of the shareholder's consent does not affect the validity of a meeting or other action.

(d) An affidavit of the secretary, assistant secretary, transfer agent, or other agent of a corporation stating that notice has been provided to a shareholder of the corporation by electronic transmission is, in the absence of fraud, prima facie evidence that the notice was provided under this section.

Added by Acts 2005, 79th Leg., ch. 64, § 52, eff. Jan. 1, 2006.

§ 21.354. Inspection of Voting List

(a) The list of shareholders entitled to vote at the meeting prepared under Section 21.372 shall be:

(1) subject to inspection by a shareholder during regular business hours; and

(2) produced and kept open at the meeting.

(a–1) If a meeting of the shareholders is held by means of remote communication, the list must be open to inspection by a shareholder during the meeting on a reasonably accessible electronic network.

(b) The original share transfer records are prima facie evidence of which shareholders are entitled to inspect the list.

Acts 2003, 78th Leg., ch. 182, § 1, eff. Jan. 1, 2006. Amended by Acts 2005, 79th Leg., ch. 64, § 53, eff. Jan. 1, 2006.

§ 21.355. Closing of Share Transfer Records

Share transfer records that are closed in accordance with Section 6.101 for the purpose of determining which shareholders are entitled to receive notice of a meeting of shareholders shall remain closed for at least 10 days immediately preceding the date of the meeting.

Acts 2003, 78th Leg., ch. 182, § 1, eff. Jan. 1, 2006.

§ 21.356. Record Date for Written Consent to Action

The record date provided in accordance with Section 6.102(a) may not be more than 10 days after the date on which the board of directors adopts the resolution setting the record date.

Acts 2003, 78th Leg., ch. 182, § 1, eff. Jan. 1, 2006.

§ 21.357. Record Date for Purpose of Shareholders' Meeting

The record date for the purpose of determining shareholders entitled to notice of or to vote at a shareholders' meeting or any adjournment of the meeting, as provided by the directors in accordance with Section 6.101, must be at least 10 days before the date of the shareholders' meeting .

Acts 2003, 78th Leg., ch. 182, § 1, eff. Jan. 1, 2006. Amended by Acts 2011, 82nd Leg., ch. 139 (S.B. 748), § 26, eff. Sept. 1, 2011.

§ 21.358. Quorum

(a) Subject to Subsection (b), the holders of the majority of the shares entitled to vote at a meeting of the shareholders of a corporation that are present or represented by proxy at the meeting are a quorum for the consideration of a matter to be presented at that meeting.

(b) The certificate of formation of a corporation may provide that a quorum is present only if:

(1) the holders of a specified portion of the shares that is greater than the majority of the shares entitled to vote are represented at the meeting in person or by proxy; or

(2) the holders of a specified portion of the shares that is less than the majority but not less than one-third of the shares entitled to vote are represented at the meeting in person or by proxy.

(c) Unless provided by the certificate of formation or bylaws of the corporation, after a quorum is present at a meeting of shareholders, the shareholders may conduct business properly brought before the meeting until the meeting is adjourned. The subsequent withdrawal from the meeting of a shareholder or the refusal of a shareholder present at or represented by proxy at the meeting to vote does not negate the presence of a quorum at the meeting.

(d) Unless provided by the certificate of formation or bylaws, the shareholders of the corporation at a meeting at which a quorum is not present may adjourn the meeting until the time and to the place as may be determined by a vote of the holders of the majority of the shares who are present or represented by proxy at the meeting.

Acts 2003, 78th Leg., ch. 182, § 1, eff. Jan. 1, 2006.

§ 21.359. Voting in Election of Directors

(a) Subject to Subsection (b), directors of a corporation shall be elected by a plurality of the votes cast by the holders of shares entitled to vote in the election of directors at a meeting of shareholders at which a quorum is present.

(b) The certificate of formation or bylaws of a corporation may provide that a director of a corporation shall be elected only if the director receives:

(1) the vote of the holders of a specified portion, but not less than the majority, of the shares entitled to vote in the election of directors;

(2) the vote of the holders of a specified portion, but not less than the majority, of the shares entitled to vote in the election of directors and represented in person or by proxy at a meeting of shareholders at which a quorum is present; or

(3) the vote of the holders of a specified portion, but not less than the majority, of the votes cast by the holders of shares entitled to vote in the election of directors at a meeting of shareholders at which a quorum is present.

Acts 2003, 78th Leg., ch. 182, § 1, eff. Jan. 1, 2006.

§ 21.360. No Cumulative Voting Right Unless Authorized

Except as provided by Section 21.361 or 21.362, a shareholder does not have the right to cumulate the shareholder's vote in the election of directors.

Acts 2003, 78th Leg., ch. 182, § 1, eff. Jan. 1, 2006.

§ 21.361. Cumulative Voting in Election of Directors

(a) At each election of directors of the corporation, each shareholder entitled to vote at the election is entitled to:

(1) vote the number of shares owned by the shareholder for as many candidates as there are directors to be elected and for whose election the shareholder is entitled to vote; or

(2) if expressly authorized by a corporation's certificate of formation in general or with respect to a specified class or series of shares or group of classes or series of shares and subject to Subsections (b) and (c), cumulate votes by:

(A) giving one candidate as many votes as the total of the number of the directors to be elected multiplied by the shareholder's shares; or

(B) distributing the votes among one or more candidates using the same principle.

(b) Cumulative voting permitted by the certificate of formation is permitted only in an election of directors in which a shareholder who intends to cumulate votes has given written notice of that intention to the secretary of the corporation on or before the day preceding the date of the election at which the shareholder intends to cumulate votes.

(c) All shareholders entitled to vote cumulatively may cumulate their votes if a shareholder gives the notice required by Subsection (b).

Acts 2003, 78th Leg., ch. 182, § 1, eff. Jan. 1, 2006. Amended by Acts 2009, 81st Leg., ch. 84, § 35, eff. Sept. 1, 2009.

§ 21.362. Cumulative Voting Right in Certain Corporations

Except as provided by the corporation's certificate of formation, a shareholder of a corporation incorporated before September 1, 2003, has the right to cumulatively vote the number of shares the shareholder owns in the election of directors to the extent permitted and in the manner provided by Section 21.361. A corporation may limit or deny a shareholder's right to cumulatively vote shares at any time after September 1, 2003, by amending its certificate of formation.

Acts 2003, 78th Leg., ch. 182, § 1, eff. Jan. 1, 2006. Amended by Acts 2005, 79th Leg., ch. 64, § 54, eff. Jan. 1, 2006.

§ 21.363. Voting on Matters Other Than Election of Directors

(a) Subject to Subsection (b), with respect to a matter other than the election of directors or a matter for which the affirmative vote of the holders of a specified portion of the shares entitled to vote is required by this code, the affirmative vote of the holders of the majority of the shares entitled to vote on, and who voted for, against, or expressly abstained with respect to, the matter at a shareholders' meeting of a corporation at which a quorum is present is the act of the shareholders.

(b) With respect to a matter other than the election of directors or a matter for which the affirmative vote of the holders of a specified portion of the shares entitled to vote is required by this code, the certificate of formation or bylaws of a corporation may provide that the act of the shareholders of the corporation is:

(1) the affirmative vote of the holders of a specified portion, but not less than the majority, of the shares entitled to vote on that matter;

(2) the affirmative vote of the holders of a specified portion, but not less than the majority, of the shares entitled to vote on that matter and represented in person or by proxy at a shareholders' meeting at which a quorum is present;

(3) the affirmative vote of the holders of a specified portion, but not less than the majority, of the shares entitled to vote on, and who voted for or against, the matter at a shareholders' meeting at which a quorum is present; or

(4) the affirmative vote of the holders of a specified portion, but not less than the majority, of the shares entitled to vote on, and who voted for, against, or expressly abstained with respect to, the matter at a shareholders' meeting at which a quorum is present.

Acts 2003, 78th Leg., ch. 182, § 1, eff. Jan. 1, 2006.

§ 21.364. Vote Required to Approve Fundamental Action

(a) In this section, a "fundamental action" means:

(1) an amendment of a certificate of formation, including an amendment required for cancellation of

an event requiring winding up in accordance with Section 11.152(b);

(2) a voluntary winding up under Chapter 11;

(3) a revocation of a voluntary decision to wind up under Section 11.151;

(4) a cancellation of an event requiring winding up under Section 11.152(a); or

(5) a reinstatement under Section 11.202.

(b) Except as otherwise provided by this code or the certificate of formation of a corporation in accordance with Section 21.365, the vote required for approval of a fundamental action by the shareholders is the affirmative vote of the holders of at least two-thirds of the outstanding shares entitled to vote on the fundamental action.

(c) If a class or series of shares is entitled to vote as a class or series on a fundamental action, the vote required for approval of the action by the shareholders is the affirmative vote of the holders of at least two-thirds of the outstanding shares in each class or series of shares entitled to vote on the action as a class or series and at least two-thirds of the outstanding shares otherwise entitled to vote on the action. Shares entitled to vote as a class or series shall be entitled to vote only as a class or series unless otherwise entitled to vote on each matter submitted to the shareholders generally or otherwise provided by the certificate of formation.

(d) Unless an amendment to the certificate of formation is undertaken by the board of directors under Section 21.155, separate voting by a class or series of shares of a corporation is required for approval of an amendment to the certificate of formation that would result in:

(1) the increase or decrease of the aggregate number of authorized shares of the class or series;

(2) the increase or decrease of the par value of the shares of the class or series, including changing shares with par value into shares without par value or changing shares without par value into shares with par value;

(3) effecting an exchange, reclassification, or cancellation of all or part of the shares of the class or series;

(4) effecting an exchange or creating a right of exchange of all or part of the shares of another class or series into the shares of the class or series;

(5) the change of the designations, preferences, limitations, or relative rights of the shares of the class or series;

(6) the change of the shares of the class or series, with or without par value, into the same or a different number of shares, with or without par value, of the same class or series or another class or series;

(7) the creation of a new class or series of shares with rights and preferences equal, prior, or superior to the shares of the class or series;

(8) increasing the rights and preferences of a class or series with rights and preferences equal, prior, or superior to the shares of the class or series;

(9) increasing the rights and preferences of a class or series with rights or preferences later or inferior to the shares of the class or series in such a manner that the rights or preferences will be equal, prior, or superior to the shares of the class or series;

(10) dividing the shares of the class into series and setting and determining the designation of the series and the variations in the relative rights and preferences between the shares of the series;

(11) the limitation or denial of existing preemptive rights or cumulative voting rights of the shares of the class or series;

(12) canceling or otherwise affecting the dividends on the shares of the class or series that have accrued but have not been declared; or

(13) the inclusion or deletion from the certificate of formation of provisions required or permitted to be included in the certificate of formation of a close corporation under Subchapter O.

(e) The vote required under Subsection (d) by a class or series of shares of a corporation is required notwithstanding that shares of that class or series do not otherwise have a right to vote under the certificate of formation.

(f) Unless otherwise provided by the certificate of formation, if the holders of the outstanding shares of a class that is divided into series are entitled to vote as a class on a proposed amendment that would affect equally all series of the class, other than a series in which no shares are outstanding or a series that is not affected by the amendment, the holders of the separate series are not entitled to separate class votes.

(g) Unless otherwise provided by the certificate of formation, a proposed amendment to the certificate of formation that would solely effect changes in the designations, preferences, limitations, or relative rights, including voting rights, of one or more series of shares of the corporation that have been established under the authority granted to the board of directors in the certificate of formation in accordance with Section 21.155 does not require the approval of the holders of the outstanding shares of a class or series other than the affected series if, after giving effect to the amendment:

(1) the preferences, limitations, or relative rights of the affected series may be set and determined by the board of directors with respect to the establishment of a new series of shares under the authority granted to the board of directors in the certificate of formation in accordance with Section 21.155; or

(2) any new series established as a result of a reclassification of the affected series are within the preferences, limitations, and relative rights that are described by Subdivision (1).

Acts 2003, 78th Leg., ch. 182, § 1, eff. Jan. 1, 2006. Amended by Acts 2007, 80th Leg., ch. 688, § 75, eff. Sept. 1, 2007.

§ 21.365. Changes in Vote Required for Certain Matters

(a) With respect to a matter for which the affirmative vote of the holders of a specified portion of the shares entitled to vote is required by this code, the certificate of formation of a corporation may provide that the affirmative vote of the holders of a specified portion, but not less than the majority, of the shares entitled to vote on that matter is required for shareholder action on that matter.

(b) With respect to a matter for which the affirmative vote of the holders of a specified portion of the shares of a class or series is required by this code, the certificate of formation may provide that the affirmative vote of the holders of a specified portion, but not less than the majority, of the shares of that class or series is required for action of the holders of shares of that class or series on that matter.

(c) If a provision of the certificate of formation provides that the affirmative vote of the holders of a specified portion that is greater than the majority of the shares entitled to vote on a matter is required for shareholder action on that matter, the provision may not be amended, directly or indirectly, without the same affirmative vote unless otherwise provided by the certificate of formation.

(d) If a provision of the certificate of formation provides that the affirmative vote of the holders of a specified portion that is greater than the majority of the shares of a class or series is required for shareholder action on a matter, the provision may not be amended, directly or indirectly, without the same affirmative vote unless otherwise provided by the certificate of formation.

Acts 2003, 78th Leg., ch. 182, § 1, eff. Jan. 1, 2006.

§ 21.366. Number of Votes Per Share

(a) Except as provided by the certificate of formation of a corporation or this code, each outstanding share, regardless of class, shall be entitled to one vote on each matter submitted to a vote at a shareholders' meeting.

(b) If the certificate of formation provides for more or less than one vote per share on a matter for all of the outstanding shares or for the shares of a class or series, each reference in this code or in the certificate of formation or bylaws, unless expressly stated otherwise, to a specified portion of the shares with respect to that matter refers to the portion of the votes entitled to be cast with respect to those shares under the certificate of formation.

Acts 2003, 78th Leg., ch. 182, § 1, eff. Jan. 1, 2006.

§ 21.367. Voting in Person or by Proxy

(a) A shareholder may vote in person or by proxy executed in writing by the shareholder.

(b) A telegram, telex, cablegram, or other form of electronic transmission, including telephonic transmission, by the shareholder, or a photographic, photostatic, facsimile, or similar reproduction of a writing executed by the shareholder, is considered an execution in writing for purposes of this section. Any electronic transmission must contain or be accompanied by information from which it can be determined that the transmission was authorized by the shareholder.

Acts 2003, 78th Leg., ch. 182, § 1, eff. Jan. 1, 2006.

§ 21.368. Term of Proxy

A proxy is not valid after 11 months after the date the proxy is executed unless otherwise provided by the proxy.

Acts 2003, 78th Leg., ch. 182, § 1, eff. Jan. 1, 2006.

§ 21.369. Revocability of Proxy

(a) In this section, a "proxy coupled with an interest" includes the appointment as proxy of:

(1) a pledgee;

(2) a person who purchased or agreed to purchase the shares subject to the proxy;

(3) a person who owns or holds an option to purchase the shares subject to the proxy;

(4) a creditor of the corporation who extended the corporation credit under terms requiring the appointment;

(5) an employee of the corporation whose employment contract requires the appointment; or

(6) a party to a voting agreement created under Section 6.252 or a shareholders' agreement created under Section 21.101.

(b) A proxy is revocable unless:

(1) the proxy form conspicuously states that the proxy is irrevocable; and

(2) the proxy is coupled with an interest.

Acts 2003, 78th Leg., ch. 182, § 1, eff. Jan. 1, 2006.

§ 21.370. Enforceability of Proxy

(a) An irrevocable proxy is specifically enforceable against the holder of shares or any successor or transferee of the holder if:

(1) the proxy is noted conspicuously on the certificate representing the shares subject to the proxy; or

(2) in the case of uncertificated shares, notation of the proxy is contained in the notice sent under Section 3.205 with respect to the shares subject to the proxy.

(b) An irrevocable proxy that is otherwise enforceable is ineffective against a transferee for value without actual knowledge of the existence of the irrevocable proxy at the time of the transfer or against a subsequent transferee, regardless of whether the transfer is for value, unless the proxy is:

(1) noted conspicuously on the certificate representing the shares subject to the proxy; or

(2) in the case of uncertificated shares, notation of the proxy is contained in the notice sent under Section 3.205 with respect to the shares subject to the proxy.

(c) An irrevocable proxy shall be specifically enforceable against a person who is not a transferee for value from the time the person acquires actual knowledge of the existence of the irrevocable proxy.

Acts 2003, 78th Leg., ch. 182, § 1, eff. Jan. 1, 2006.

§ 21.371. Procedures in Bylaws Relating to Proxies

A corporation may establish in the corporation's bylaws procedures consistent with this code for determining the validity of proxies and determining whether shares that are held of record by a bank, broker, or other nominee are represented at a meeting of shareholders. The procedures may incorporate rules of and determinations made by a stock exchange or self-regulatory organization regulating the corporation or that bank, broker, or other nominee.

Acts 2003, 78th Leg., ch. 182, § 1, eff. Jan. 1, 2006.

§ 21.372. Shareholder Meeting List

(a) Not later than the 11th day before the date of each meeting of the shareholders of a corporation, an officer or agent of the corporation who is in charge of the corporation's share transfer records shall prepare an alphabetical list of the shareholders entitled to vote at the meeting or at any adjournment of the meeting. The list of shareholders must:

(1) state:

(A) the address of each shareholder;

(B) the type of shares held by each shareholder;

(C) the number of shares held by each shareholder; and

(D) the number of votes that each shareholder is entitled to if the number of votes is different from the number of shares stated under Paragraph (C); and

(2) be kept on file at the registered office or principal executive office of the corporation for at least 10 days before the date of the meeting.

(a–1) Instead of being kept on file, the list required by Subsection (a) may be kept on a reasonably accessible electronic network if the information required to gain access to the list is provided with notice of the meeting. Section 21.353(c), Section 21.354(a–1), and this subsection may not be construed to require a corporation to include any electronic contact information of a shareholder on the list. A corporation that elects to make the list available on an electronic network must take reasonable measures to ensure the information is available only to shareholders of the corporation.

(b) The original share transfer records of the corporation are prima facie evidence of the shareholders of the corporation entitled to vote at the meeting.

(c) Failure to comply with this section does not affect the validity of any action taken at a meeting of the shareholders of the corporation.

Acts 2003, 78th Leg., ch. 182, § 1, eff. Jan. 1, 2006. Amended by Acts 2005, 79th Leg., ch. 64, § 55, eff. Jan. 1, 2006; Acts 2007, 80th Leg., ch. 688, § 76, eff. Sept. 1, 2007.

SUBCHAPTER I. BOARD OF DIRECTORS

§ 21.401. Management by Board of Directors

(a) Except as provided by Section 21.101 or Subchapter O, the board of directors of a corporation shall:

(1) exercise or authorize the exercise of the powers of the corporation; and

(2) direct the management of the business and affairs of the corporation.

(b) In discharging the duties of director under this code or otherwise and in considering the best interests of the corporation, a director may consider the long-term and short-term interests of the corporation and the shareholders of the corporation, including the possibility that those interests may be best served by the continued independence of the corporation.

Acts 2003, 78th Leg., ch. 182, § 1, eff. Jan. 1, 2006.

§ 21.402. Board Member Eligibility Requirements

Unless the certificate of formation or bylaws of a corporation provide otherwise, a person is not required to be a resident of this state or a shareholder of the corporation to serve as a director. The certificate of formation or bylaws may prescribe other qualifications for directors.

Acts 2003, 78th Leg., ch. 182, § 1, eff. Jan. 1, 2006.

§ 21.403. Number of Directors

(a) The board of directors of a corporation may consist of one or more directors.

(b) If the corporation is to be managed by a board of directors, the number of directors shall be set by, or in the manner provided by, the certificate of formation or bylaws of the corporation, except that the number of directors on the initial board of directors must be set by the certificate of formation.

(c) The number of directors may be increased or decreased by amendment to, or as provided by, the certificate of formation or bylaws. A decrease in the number of directors may not shorten the term of an incumbent director.

(d) If the certificate of formation or bylaws do not set the number constituting the board of directors or provide for the manner in which the number of directors must be determined, the number of directors is the same as the number constituting the initial board of directors as set by the certificate of formation.

Acts 2003, 78th Leg., ch. 182, § 1, eff. Jan. 1, 2006.

§ 21.404. Designation of Initial Board of Directors

If the corporation is to be managed by a board of directors, the certificate of formation of a corporation must state the names and addresses of the persons constituting the initial board of directors of the corporation.

Acts 2003, 78th Leg., ch. 182, § 1, eff. Jan. 1, 2006.

§ 21.405. Election of Board of Directors

(a) At the first annual meeting of shareholders of a corporation and at each subsequent annual meeting of shareholders, the holders of shares entitled to vote in the election of directors shall elect directors for the term provided under Section 21.407, except as provided by Section 21.408.

(b) A corporation's certificate of formation may provide that the holders of a class or series of shares or a group of classes or series of shares are entitled to elect one or more directors of the corporation.

Acts 2003, 78th Leg., ch. 182, § 1, eff. Jan. 1, 2006.

§ 21.406. Special Voting Rights of Directors

(a) The certificate of formation of a corporation may provide that directors, regardless of whether elected by the holders of a class or series of shares or by a group of classes or series of shares, as provided by Section 21.405, are entitled to cast more or less than one vote on all matters or on specified matters. Such a provision also applies to directors voting in any committee or subcommittee regarding all matters or the specified matters, as applicable, unless otherwise provided by the certificate of formation.

(b) Unless expressly stated otherwise, each reference in this code or in a corporation's certificate of formation or bylaws to a specified portion of the directors means the portion of the votes entitled to be cast by the directors to which the reference applies.

Acts 2003, 78th Leg., ch. 182, § 1, eff. Jan. 1, 2006. Amended by Acts 2009, 81st Leg., ch. 84, § 36, eff. Sept. 1, 2009.

§ 21.407. Term of Office

Except as otherwise provided by this subchapter, the term of office of a director extends from the date the director is elected and qualified or named in the corporation's certificate of formation until the next annual meeting of shareholders and until the director's successor is elected and qualified.

Acts 2003, 78th Leg., ch. 182, § 1, eff. Jan. 1, 2006. Amended by Acts 2005, 79th Leg., ch. 64, § 56, eff. Jan. 1, 2006.

§ 21.408. Special Terms of Office

(a) The certificate of formation or bylaws of a corporation may provide that all or some of the board of directors may be divided into two or three classes that shall include the same or a similar number of directors as each other class and that have staggered terms of office.

(b) The terms of office of the initial directors constituting the first class expire at the first annual meeting of shareholders after the election of those directors. The terms of office of the initial directors constituting the second class expire at the second annual meeting of shareholders after election of those directors. The terms of office of the initial directors constituting the third class, if any, expire at the third annual meeting of shareholders after election of those directors. In each case, the term of office of an initial director is extended until the director's successor is elected and has qualified.

(c) If the certificate of formation or bylaws provide for staggered terms of directors, the shareholders, at each annual meeting, shall elect a number of directors equal to the number of the class of directors whose terms expire at the time of the meeting. The directors elected at an annual meeting shall hold office until the second succeeding annual meeting, if there are two classes, or until the third succeeding annual meeting, if there are three classes.

(d) Unless provided by the certificate of formation or a bylaw adopted by the shareholders, staggered terms for directors must be effected at a meeting of shareholders at which directors are elected. Staggered terms for directors may not be effected if any shareholder has the right to cumulate votes for the election of directors and the board of directors consists of fewer than nine members.

(e) Directors elected by the holders of a class or series of shares or a group of classes or series of shares in accordance with the certificate of formation shall hold office for the terms specified by the certificate of formation.

Acts 2003, 78th Leg., ch. 182, § 1, eff. Jan. 1, 2006. Amended by Acts 2007, 80th Leg., ch. 688, § 77, eff. Sept. 1, 2007.

§ 21.409. Removal of Directors

(a) Except as otherwise provided by the certificate of formation or bylaws of a corporation or this subchapter, the shareholders of the corporation may remove a director or the entire board of directors of the corporation, with or without cause, at a meeting called for that purpose, by a vote of the holders of a majority of the shares entitled to vote at an election of the director or directors.

(b) If the certificate of formation entitles the holders of a class or series of shares or a group of classes or series of shares to elect one or more directors, only the holders of shares of that class, series, or group may vote on the removal of a director elected by the holders of shares of that class, series, or group.

(c) If the certificate of formation permits cumulative voting and less than the entire board is to be removed, a director may not be removed if the votes cast against the removal would be sufficient to elect the director if cumulatively voted at an election of the entire board of directors, or if there are classes of directors, at an election of the class of directors of which the director is a part.

(d) In the case of a corporation the directors of which serve staggered terms, a director may not be removed except for cause unless the certificate of formation provides otherwise.

Acts 2003, 78th Leg., ch. 182, § 1, eff. Jan. 1, 2006. Amended by Acts 2005, 79th Leg., ch. 64, § 57, eff. Jan. 1, 2006.

§ 21.4091. Resignation of Directors

(a) Except as otherwise provided by the certificate of formation or bylaws, a director of a corporation may resign at any time by providing written notice to the corporation.

(b) The director's resignation takes effect on the date the notice is received by the corporation, unless the notice prescribes a later effective date or states that the resignation takes effect on the occurrence of a future event, such as the director's failure to receive a specified vote for reelection as a director.

(c) If the director's resignation is to take effect on a later date or on the occurrence of a future event, the resignation takes effect on the later date or when the event occurs.

(d) The director's resignation is irrevocable when it takes effect. The director's resignation is revocable before it takes effect unless the notice of resignation expressly states it is irrevocable.

Added by Acts 2005, 79th Leg., ch. 64, § 58, eff. Jan. 1, 2006. Amended by Acts 2007, 80th Leg., ch. 688, § 78, eff. Sept. 1, 2007.

§ 21.410. Vacancy

(a) A vacancy occurring in the initial board of directors before the issuance of shares may be filled by the affirmative vote or written consent of the majority of the organizers or by the affirmative vote of the majority of the remaining directors, even if the remaining directors constitute less than a quorum of the board of directors.

(b) Except as provided by Subsection (e), a vacancy occurring in the board of directors after the issuance of shares may be filled by election at an annual or special meeting of shareholders called for that purpose or by the affirmative vote of the majority of the remaining directors, even if the remaining directors constitute less than a quorum of the board of directors.

(c) The term of a director elected to fill a vacancy occurring in the board of directors, including the initial directors, is the unexpired term of the director's predecessor in office.

(d) Except as provided by Subsection (e), a vacancy to be filled because of an increase in the number of directors may be filled by election at an annual or special meeting of shareholders called for that purpose or by the board of directors for a term of office continuing only until the next election of one or more directors by the shareholders. During a period between two successive annual meetings of shareholders, the board of directors may not fill more than two vacancies created by an increase in the number of directors.

(e) Unless otherwise authorized by a corporation's certificate of formation, a vacancy or a newly created vacancy in a director position that the certificate of formation entitles the holders of a class or series of shares or group of classes or series of shares to elect may be filled only:

(1) by the affirmative vote of the majority of the directors then in office elected by the class, series, or group;

(2) by the sole remaining director elected in that manner; or

(3) by the affirmative vote of the holders of the outstanding shares of the class, series, or group.

Acts 2003, 78th Leg., ch. 182, § 1, eff. Jan. 1, 2006. Amended by Acts 2007, 80th Leg., ch. 688, § 79, eff. Sept. 1, 2007.

§ 21.411. Notice of Meeting

(a) Regular meetings of the board of directors of a corporation may be held with or without notice as prescribed by the corporation's bylaws.

(b) Special meetings of the board of directors shall be held with notice as prescribed by the bylaws.

(c) A notice of a board meeting is not required to specify the business to be transacted at the meeting or the purpose of the meeting, unless required by the bylaws.

(d) Notice of the date, time, place, or purpose of a regular or special meeting of the board of directors may be provided to a director by electronic transmission on consent of the director. The director may specify the form of electronic transmission to be used to communicate notice.

(e) Notice is considered provided under Subsection (d) when the notice is:

(1) transmitted to a facsimile number provided by the director for the purpose of receiving notice;

(2) transmitted to an electronic mail address provided by the director for the purpose of receiving notice;

(3) posted on an electronic network and a message is sent to the director at the address provided by the director for the purpose of alerting the director of a posting; or

(4) communicated to the director by any other form of electronic transmission consented to by the director.

(f) A director may revoke the director's consent to receive notice by electronic transmission by providing written notice to the corporation. The director's consent is considered revoked for purposes of Subsection (d) if the corporation is unable to deliver by electronic transmission two consecutive notices, and the secretary, assistant secretary, or transfer agent of the corporation, or another person responsible for delivering notice on behalf of the corporation, knows that delivery of those two electronic transmissions was unsuccessful. Inadvertent failure to treat the unsuccessful transmissions as a revocation of the director's consent does not affect the validity of a meeting or other action.

(g) An affidavit of the secretary, assistant secretary, transfer agent, or other agent of a corporation stating that notice has been provided to a director of the corporation by electronic transmission is, in the absence of fraud, prima facie evidence that notice was provided under Subsections (d) and (e).

Acts 2003, 78th Leg., ch. 182, § 1, eff. Jan. 1, 2006. Amended by Acts 2005, 79th Leg., ch. 64, § 59, eff. Jan. 1, 2006.

§ 21.412. Waiver of Notice

(a) If the bylaws of a corporation require notice of a meeting to be given to a director, a written waiver of the notice signed by the director entitled to the notice, before or after the meeting, is equivalent to the giving of the notice.

(b) The attendance of a director at a board meeting constitutes a waiver of notice of the meeting, unless the director attends the meeting for the express purpose of objecting to the transaction of business at the meeting because the meeting has not been lawfully called or convened.

(c) A waiver of notice of a board meeting is not required to specify the business to be transacted at the meeting or the purpose of the meeting, unless required by the bylaws.

Acts 2003, 78th Leg., ch. 182, § 1, eff. Jan. 1, 2006.

§ 21.413. Quorum

(a) A quorum of the board of directors is the majority of the number of directors set or established in the manner provided by the certificate of formation or bylaws of a corporation unless the laws of this state, the certificate of formation, or the bylaws require a different number or portion.

(b) Neither the certificate of formation nor the bylaws may provide that less than one-third of the number of directors constitutes a quorum.

Acts 2003, 78th Leg., ch. 182, § 1, eff. Jan. 1, 2006.

§ 21.414. Dissent to Action

(a) A director of a corporation who is present at a meeting of the board of directors at which action has been taken is presumed to have assented to the action taken unless:

(1) the director's dissent has been entered in the minutes of the meeting;

(2) the director has filed a written dissent to the action with the person acting as the secretary of the meeting before the meeting is adjourned; or

(3) the director has sent a written dissent by registered mail to the secretary of the corporation immediately after the meeting has been adjourned.

(b) A director who voted in favor of an action may not dissent to the action.

Acts 2003, 78th Leg., ch. 182, § 1, eff. Jan. 1, 2006.

§ 21.415. Action by Directors

(a) The act of a majority of the directors present at a meeting at which a quorum is present at the time of the act is the act of the board of directors of a corporation, unless the act of a greater number is required by the certificate of formation or bylaws of the corporation or by this code.

(b) Unless otherwise provided by the certificate of formation or bylaws, a written consent stating the action taken and signed by all members of the board of directors is also an act of the board of directors.

Acts 2003, 78th Leg., ch. 182, § 1, eff. Jan. 1, 2006. Amended by Acts 2011, 82nd Leg., ch. 139 (S.B. 748), § 27, eff. Sept. 1, 2011.

§ 21.416. Committees of Board of Directors

(a) If authorized by the certificate of formation or bylaws of a corporation, the board of directors of the corporation may designate:

(1) committees composed of one or more directors; or

(2) directors as alternate members of committees to replace absent or disqualified committee members at a committee meeting, subject to any limitations imposed by the board of directors.

(b) To the extent provided by a resolution of the board of directors designating a committee or by the certificate of formation or bylaws and subject to Subsection (c), the committee has the authority of the board of directors.

(c) A committee of the board of directors may not:

(1) amend the certificate of formation, except to:

(A) establish series of shares;

(B) increase or decrease the number of shares in a series; or

(C) eliminate a series of shares as authorized by Section 21.155;

(2) propose a reduction of stated capital under Sections 21.253 and 21.254;

(3) approve a plan of merger, share exchange, or conversion of the corporation;

(4) recommend to shareholders the sale, lease, or exchange of all or substantially all of the property and assets of the corporation not made in the usual and regular course of its business;

(5) recommend to the shareholders a voluntary winding up and termination or a revocation of a voluntary winding up and termination;

(6) amend, alter, or repeal the bylaws or adopt new bylaws;

(7) fill vacancies on the board of directors;

(8) fill vacancies on or designate alternate members of a committee of the board of directors;

(9) fill a vacancy to be filled because of an increase in the number of directors;

(10) elect or remove officers of the corporation or members or alternate members of a committee of the board of directors;

(11) set the compensation of the members or alternate members of a committee of the board of directors; or

(12) alter or repeal a resolution of the board of directors that states that it may not be amended or repealed by a committee of the board of directors.

(d) A committee of the board of directors may authorize a distribution or the issuance of shares if authorized by the resolution designating the committee or the certificate of formation or bylaws.

(e) The board of directors may remove a member of a committee appointed by the board if the board determines the removal is in the best interests of the corporation. The removal of the member is without prejudice to any contract rights of the person removed. Appointment of a member of a committee does not create contract rights.

(f) The designation and delegation of authority to a committee of the board of directors does not relieve the board of directors or a director of responsibility imposed by law.

Acts 2003, 78th Leg., ch. 182, § 1, eff. Jan. 1, 2006. Amended by Acts 2005, 79th Leg., ch. 64, § 60, eff. Jan. 1, 2006.

§ 21.417. Election of Officers

The board of directors of a corporation shall elect a president and a secretary at the time and in the manner prescribed by the corporation's bylaws. Other officers, including assistant officers and agents as deemed necessary, may be elected in accordance with Section 3.103.

Acts 2003, 78th Leg., ch. 182, § 1, eff. Jan. 1, 2006.

§ 21.418. Contracts or Transactions Involving Interested Directors and Officers

(a) This section applies to a contract or transaction between a corporation and:

(1) one or more directors or officers, or one or more affiliates or associates of one or more directors or officers, of the corporation; or

(2) an entity or other organization in which one or more directors or officers, or one or more affiliates or associates of one or more directors or officers, of the corporation:

(A) is a managerial official; or

(B) has a financial interest.

(b) An otherwise valid and enforceable contract or transaction described by Subsection (a) is valid and enforceable, and is not void or voidable, notwithstanding any relationship or interest described by Subsection (a), if any one of the following conditions is satisfied :

(1) the material facts as to the relationship or interest described by Subsection (a) and as to the contract or transaction are disclosed to or known by:

(A) the corporation's board of directors or a committee of the board of directors, and the board of directors or committee in good faith authorizes the contract or transaction by the approval of the majority of the disinterested directors or committee members, regardless of whether the disinterested directors or committee members constitute a quorum; or

(B) the shareholders entitled to vote on the authorization of the contract or transaction, and the contract or transaction is specifically approved in good faith by a vote of the shareholders; or

(2) the contract or transaction is fair to the corporation when the contract or transaction is authorized, approved, or ratified by the board of directors, a committee of the board of directors, or the shareholders.

(c) Common or interested directors of a corporation may be included in determining the presence of a quorum at a meeting of the corporation's board of directors, or a committee of the board of directors, that authorizes the contract or transaction.

(d) A person who has the relationship or interest described by Subsection (a) may:

(1) be present at or participate in and, if the person is a director or committee member, may vote

at a meeting of the board of directors or of a committee of the board that authorizes the contract or transaction; or

(2) sign, in the person's capacity as a director or committee member, a unanimous written consent of the directors or committee members to authorize the contract or transaction.

(e) If at least one of the conditions of Subsection (b) is satisfied, neither the corporation nor any of the corporation's shareholders will have a cause of action against any of the persons described by Subsection (a) for breach of duty with respect to the making, authorization, or performance of the contract or transaction because the person had the relationship or interest described by Subsection (a) or took any of the actions authorized by Subsection (d).

Acts 2003, 78th Leg., ch. 182, § 1, eff. Jan. 1, 2006. Amended by Acts 2009, 81st Leg., ch. 84, § 37, eff. Sept. 1, 2009; Acts 2011, 82nd Leg., ch. 139 (S.B. 748), § 28, eff. Sept. 1, 2011.

SUBCHAPTER J. FUNDAMENTAL BUSINESS TRANSACTIONS

§ 21.451. Definitions

In this subchapter:

(1) "Participating shares" means shares that entitle the holders of the shares to participate without limitation in distributions.

(2) "Sale of all or substantially all of the assets" means the sale, lease, exchange, or other disposition, other than a pledge, mortgage, deed of trust, or trust indenture unless otherwise provided by the certificate of formation, of all or substantially all of the property and assets of a domestic corporation that is not made in the usual and regular course of the corporation's business without regard to whether the disposition is made with the goodwill of the business. The term does not include a transaction that results in the corporation directly or indirectly:

(A) continuing to engage in one or more businesses; or

(B) applying a portion of the consideration received in connection with the transaction to the conduct of a business that the corporation engages in after the transaction.

(3) "Shares" includes a receipt or other instrument issued by a depository representing an interest in one or more shares or fractions of shares of a domestic or foreign corporation that are deposited with the depository.

(4) "Voting shares" means shares that entitle the holders of the shares to vote unconditionally in elections of directors.

Acts 2003, 78th Leg., ch. 182, § 1, eff. Jan. 1, 2006.

§ 21.452. Approval of Merger

(a) A corporation that is a party to the merger under Chapter 10 must approve the merger by complying with this section.

(b) The board of directors of the corporation shall adopt a resolution that:

(1) approves the plan of merger; and

(2) if shareholder approval of the merger is required by this subchapter:

(A) recommends that the plan of merger be approved by the shareholders of the corporation; or

(B) directs that the plan of merger be submitted to the shareholders for approval without recommendation if the board of directors determines for any reason not to recommend approval of the plan of merger.

(c) Except as otherwise provided by this subchapter or Chapter 10, the plan of merger shall be submitted to the shareholders of the corporation for approval as provided by this subchapter. The board of directors may place conditions on the submission of the plan of merger to the shareholders.

(d) If the board of directors approves a plan of merger required to be approved by the shareholders of the corporation but does not adopt a resolution recommending that the plan of merger be approved by the shareholders, the board of directors shall communicate to the shareholders the reason for the board's determination to submit the plan of merger without a recommendation.

(e) Except as provided by Chapter 10 or Sections 21.457 and 21.459, the shareholders of the corporation shall approve the plan of merger as provided by this subchapter.

(f) If after adoption of a resolution under Subsection (b)(2) the board of directors of the corporation determines that the plan of merger is not advisable, the plan of merger may be submitted to the shareholders of the corporation with a recommendation that the shareholders not approve the plan of merger.

(g) A plan of merger for a corporation may include a provision requiring that the plan of merger be submitted to the shareholders of the corporation regardless of whether the board of directors determines, after adopting a resolution or making a determination under this section, that the plan of merger is not advisable and recommends that the shareholders not approve the plan of merger.

Acts 2003, 78th Leg., ch. 182, § 1, eff. Jan. 1, 2006. Amended by Acts 2005, 79th Leg., ch. 64, § 61, eff. Jan. 1, 2006; Acts 2007, 80th Leg., ch. 688, § 80, eff. Sept. 1, 2007.

§ 21.453. Approval of Conversion

(a) A corporation must approve a conversion under Chapter 10 by complying with this section.

(b) The board of directors of the corporation shall adopt a resolution that approves the plan of conversion and:

(1) recommends that the plan of conversion be approved by the shareholders of the corporation; or

(2) directs that the plan of conversion be submitted to the shareholders for approval without recommendation if the board of directors determines for any reason not to recommend approval of the plan of conversion.

(c) The plan of conversion shall be submitted to the shareholders of the corporation for approval as provided by this subchapter. The board of directors may place conditions on the submission of the plan of conversion to the shareholders.

(d) If the board of directors approves a plan of conversion but does not adopt a resolution recommending that the plan of conversion be approved by the shareholders of the corporation, the board of directors shall communicate to the shareholders the reason for the board's determination to submit the plan of conversion without a recommendation.

(e) Except as provided by Section 21.457, the shareholders of the corporation shall approve the plan of conversion as provided by this subchapter.

(f) If after the adoption of a resolution under Subsection (b) the board of directors of the corporation determines that the plan of conversion is not advisable, the plan of conversion may be submitted to the shareholders of the corporation with a recommendation that the shareholders not approve the plan of conversion.

(g) A plan of conversion for a corporation may include a provision requiring that the plan of conversion be submitted to the shareholders of the corporation, regardless of whether the board of directors determines, after adopting a resolution or making a determination under this section, that the plan of conversion is not advisable and recommends that the shareholders not approve the plan of conversion.

Acts 2003, 78th Leg., ch. 182, § 1, eff. Jan. 1, 2006. Amended by Acts 2007, 80th Leg., ch. 688, § 81, eff. Sept. 1, 2007; Acts 2011, 82nd Leg., ch. 139 (S.B. 748), § 29, eff. Sept. 1, 2011.

§ 21.454. Approval of Exchange

(a) A corporation the shares of which are to be acquired in an exchange under Chapter 10 must approve the exchange by complying with this section.

(b) The board of directors shall adopt a resolution that approves the plan of exchange and:

(1) recommends that the plan of exchange be approved by the shareholders of the corporation; or

(2) directs that the plan of exchange be submitted to the shareholders for approval without recommendation if the board of directors determines for any reason not to recommend approval of the plan of exchange.

(c) The plan of exchange shall be submitted to the shareholders of the corporation for approval as provided by this subchapter. The board of directors may place conditions on the submission of the plan of exchange to the shareholders.

(d) If the board of directors approves a plan of exchange but does not adopt a resolution recommending that the plan of exchange be approved by the shareholders of the corporation, the board of directors shall communicate to the shareholders the reason for the board's determination to submit the plan of exchange to shareholders without a recommendation.

(e) Except as provided by Section 21.457, the shareholders of the corporation shall approve the plan of exchange as provided by this subchapter.

(f) If after the adoption of a resolution under Subsection (b)(2) the board of directors of the corporation determines that the plan of exchange is not advisable, the plan of exchange may be submitted to the shareholders of the corporation with a recommendation that the shareholders not approve the plan of exchange.

(g) A plan of exchange for a corporation may include a provision requiring that the plan of exchange be submitted to the shareholders of the corporation regardless of whether the board of directors determines, after adopting a resolution or making a determination under this section, that the plan of exchange is not advisable and recommends that the shareholders not approve the plan of exchange.

Acts 2003, 78th Leg., ch. 182, § 1, eff. Jan. 1, 2006. Amended by Acts 2005, 79th Leg., ch. 64, § 62, eff. Jan. 1, 2006; Acts 2007, 80th Leg., ch. 688, § 82, eff. Sept. 1, 2007.

§ 21.455. Approval of Sale of All or Substantially All of Assets

(a) Except as provided by the certificate of formation of a domestic corporation, a sale, lease, pledge, mortgage, assignment, transfer, or other conveyance of an interest in real property or other assets of the corporation does not require the approval or consent of the shareholders of the corporation unless the transaction constitutes a sale of all or substantially all of the assets of the corporation.

(b) A corporation must approve the sale of all or substantially all of its assets by complying with this section.

(c) The board of directors of the corporation shall adopt a resolution that approves the sale of all or substantially all of the assets of the corporation and:

(1) recommends that the sale of all or substantially all of the assets of the corporation be approved by the shareholders of the corporation; or

(2) directs that the sale of all or substantially all of the assets of the corporation be submitted to the shareholders for approval without recommendation if the board of directors determines for any reason not to recommend approval of the sale.

(d) The resolution proposing the sale of all or substantially all of the assets of the corporation shall be submitted to the shareholders of the corporation for approval as provided by this subchapter. The board of directors may place conditions on the submission of the proposed sale to the shareholders.

(e) If the board of directors approves the sale of all or substantially all of the assets of the corporation but does not adopt a resolution recommending that the proposed sale be approved by the shareholders of the corporation, the board of directors shall communicate to the shareholders the reason for the board's determination to submit the proposed sale to shareholders without a recommendation.

(f) The shareholders of the corporation shall approve the sale of all or substantially all of the assets of the corporation as provided by this subchapter. After the approval of the sale by the shareholders, the board of directors may abandon the sale of all or substantially all of the assets of the corporation, subject to the rights of a third party under a contract relating to the assets, without further action or approval by the shareholders.

Acts 2003, 78th Leg., ch. 182, § 1, eff. Jan. 1, 2006.

§ 21.456. General Procedure for Submission to Shareholders of Fundamental Business Transaction

(a) If a fundamental business transaction involving a corporation is required to be submitted to the shareholders of the corporation under this subchapter, the corporation shall notify each shareholder of the corporation that the fundamental business transaction is being submitted to the shareholders for approval at a meeting of shareholders as required by this subchapter, regardless of whether the shareholder is entitled to vote on the matter.

(b) If the fundamental business transaction is a merger, conversion, or interest exchange, the notice required by Subsection (a) shall contain or be accompanied by a copy or summary of the plan of merger, conversion, or interest exchange, as appropriate, and the notice required by Section 10.355.

(c) The notice of the meeting must:

(1) be given not later than the 21st day before the date of the meeting; and

(2) state that the purpose, or one of the purposes, of the meeting is to consider the fundamental business transaction.

Acts 2003, 78th Leg., ch. 182, § 1, eff. Jan. 1, 2006.

§ 21.457. General Vote Requirement for Approval of Fundamental Business Transaction

(a) Except as provided by this code or the certificate of formation of a corporation in accordance with Section 21.365, the affirmative vote of the holders of at least two-thirds of the outstanding shares of the corporation entitled to vote on a fundamental business transaction is required to approve the transaction.

(b) Unless provided by the certificate of formation or Section 21.458, shares of a class or series that are not otherwise entitled to vote on matters submitted to shareholders generally are not entitled to vote for the approval of a fundamental business transaction.

(c) Except as provided by this code, if a class or series of shares of a corporation is entitled to vote on a fundamental business transaction as a class or series, in addition to the vote required under Subsection (a), the affirmative vote of the holders of at least two-thirds of the outstanding shares in each class or series of shares entitled to vote on the fundamental business transaction as a class or series is required to approve the transaction. Shares entitled to vote as a class or series shall only be entitled to vote as a class or series on the fundamental business transaction unless that class or series is otherwise entitled to vote on each matter submitted to the shareholders generally or is otherwise entitled to vote under the certificate of formation.

(d) Unless required by the certificate of formation, approval of a merger by shareholders is not required under this code for a corporation that is a party to the plan of merger unless that corporation is also a party to the merger.

Acts 2003, 78th Leg., ch. 182, § 1, eff. Jan. 1, 2006.

§ 21.458. Class Voting Requirements for Certain Fundamental Business Transactions

(a) Separate voting by a class or series of shares of a corporation is required for approval of a plan of merger or conversion if:

(1) the plan of merger or conversion contains a provision that would require approval by that class or series of shares under Section 21.364 if the provision was contained in a proposed amendment to the corporation's certificate of formation; or

(2) that class or series of shares is entitled under the certificate of formation to vote as a class or series on the plan of merger or conversion.

(b) Separate voting by a class or series of shares of a corporation is required for approval of a plan of exchange if:

(1) shares of that class or series are to be exchanged under the terms of the plan of exchange; or

(2) that class or series is entitled under the certificate of formation to vote as a class or series on the plan of exchange.

(c) Separate voting by a class or series of shares of a corporation is required for approval of a sale of all or substantially all of the assets of a corporation if that class or series of shares is entitled under the certificate of formation to vote as a class or series on the sale of the corporation's assets.

Acts 2003, 78th Leg., ch. 182, § 1, eff. Jan. 1, 2006.

§ 21.459. No Shareholder Vote Requirement for Certain Fundamental Business Transactions

(a) Unless required by the corporation's certificate of formation, a plan of merger is not required to be approved by the shareholders of a corporation if:

(1) the corporation is the sole surviving corporation in the merger;

(2) the certificate of formation of the corporation following the merger will not differ from the corporation's certificate of formation before the merger;

(3) immediately after the effective date of the merger, each shareholder of the corporation whose shares were outstanding immediately before the effective date of the merger will hold the same number of shares, with identical designations, preferences, limitations, and relative rights;

(4) the sum of the voting power of the number of voting shares outstanding immediately after the merger and the voting power of securities that may be acquired on the conversion or exercise of securities issued under the merger does not exceed by more than 20 percent the voting power of the total number of voting shares of the corporation that are outstanding immediately before the merger; and

(5) the sum of the number of participating shares that are outstanding immediately after the merger and the number of participating shares that may be acquired on the conversion or exercise of securities issued under the merger does not exceed by more than 20 percent the total number of participating shares of the corporation that are outstanding immediately before the merger.

(b) Unless required by the certificate of formation, a plan of merger effected under Section 10.005 or 10.006 does not require the approval of the shareholders of the corporation.

Acts 2003, 78th Leg., ch. 182, § 1, eff. Jan. 1, 2006.

§ 21.460. Rights of Dissent and Appraisal

A shareholder of a domestic corporation has the rights of dissent and appraisal under Subchapter H, Chapter 10, with respect to a fundamental business transaction.

Acts 2003, 78th Leg., ch. 182, § 1, eff. Jan. 1, 2006.

§ 21.461. Pledge, Mortgage, Deed of Trust, or Trust Indenture

Except as provided by the corporation's certificate of formation:

(1) the board of directors of a corporation may authorize a pledge, mortgage, deed of trust, or trust indenture; and

(2) an authorization or consent of shareholders is not required for the validity of the transaction or for any sale under the terms of the transaction.

Acts 2003, 78th Leg., ch. 182, § 1, eff. Jan. 1, 2006.

§ 21.462. Conveyance by Corporation

A corporation may convey real property of the corporation when authorized by appropriate resolution of the board of directors.

Acts 2003, 78th Leg., ch. 182, § 1, eff. Jan. 1, 2006.

SUBCHAPTER K. WINDING UP AND TERMINATION

§ 21.501. Approval of Voluntary Winding Up, Reinstatement, or Revocation of Voluntary Winding Up

A corporation must approve a voluntary winding up in accordance with Chapter 11, a reinstatement in accordance with Section 11.202, a cancellation of an event requiring winding up under Section 11.152(a), or revocation of a voluntary decision to wind up in accordance with Section 11.151 by complying with one of the procedures prescribed by this subchapter.

Acts 2003, 78th Leg., ch. 182, § 1, eff. Jan. 1, 2006. Amended by Acts 2007, 80th Leg., ch. 688, § 83, eff. Sept. 1, 2007.

§ 21.502. Certain Procedures Relating to Winding Up

To approve a voluntary winding up, a reinstatement, a cancellation of an event requiring winding up, or a revocation of a voluntary decision to wind up, a corporation must follow one of the following procedures:

(1) all shareholders of the corporation must consent in writing to the winding up, the reinstatement, the cancellation of an event requiring winding up, or the revocation of a voluntary decision to wind up the corporation;

(2) if the corporation has not commenced business and has not issued any shares, a majority of the organizers or the board of directors of the corporation must adopt a resolution to wind up, to reinstate, to cancel an event requiring winding up, or to revoke a voluntary decision to wind up; or

(3)(A) the board of directors of the corporation must adopt a resolution:

(i) recommending the winding up, reinstatement, cancellation of an event requiring winding up, or revocation of a voluntary decision to wind up the corporation; and

(ii) directing that the winding up, reinstatement, cancellation of an event requiring winding up, or revocation of a voluntary decision to wind up the corporation be submitted to the shareholders for approval at an annual or special meeting of shareholders; and

(B) the shareholders must approve the action described by Paragraph (A) in accordance with Section 21.503.

Acts 2003, 78th Leg., ch. 182, § 1, eff. Jan. 1, 2006.

§ 21.503. Meeting of Shareholders; Notice

(a) Each shareholder of record entitled to vote at a meeting described by Section 21.502(3)(A)(ii) must be given written notice stating that the purpose or one of the purposes of the meeting is to consider the winding up, reinstatement, cancellation of the event requiring winding up, or revocation of the voluntary decision to wind up the corporation. The notice must be given in the time and manner provided by Chapter 6 and this chapter for the giving of notice of shareholders' meetings.

(b) A vote of shareholders entitled to vote at the meeting shall be taken on the resolution to wind up, reinstate, cancel the event requiring winding up, or revoke the voluntary decision to wind up the corporation. The shareholders must approve the resolution by the affirmative vote required by Section 21.364.

Acts 2003, 78th Leg., ch. 182, § 1, eff. Jan. 1, 2006.

§ 21.504. Responsibility for Winding Up

If a corporation determines or is required to wind up, the directors of the corporation shall manage the process of winding up the business or affairs of the corporation.

Acts 2003, 78th Leg., ch. 182, § 1, eff. Jan. 1, 2006.

SUBCHAPTER L. DERIVATIVE PROCEEDINGS

§ 21.551. Definitions

In this subchapter:

(1) "Derivative proceeding" means a civil suit in the right of a domestic corporation or, to the extent provided by Section 21.562, in the right of a foreign corporation.

(2) "Shareholder" includes a beneficial owner whose shares are held in a voting trust or by a nominee on the beneficial owner's behalf.

Acts 2003, 78th Leg., ch. 182, § 1, eff. Jan. 1, 2006.

§ 21.552. Standing to Bring Proceeding

A shareholder may not institute or maintain a derivative proceeding unless:

(1) the shareholder:

(A) was a shareholder of the corporation at the time of the act or omission complained of; or

(B) became a shareholder by operation of law from a person that was a shareholder at the time of the act or omission complained of; and

(2) the shareholder fairly and adequately represents the interests of the corporation in enforcing the right of the corporation.

Acts 2003, 78th Leg., ch. 182, § 1, eff. Jan. 1, 2006. Amended by Acts 2005, 79th Leg., ch. 64, § 63, eff. Jan. 1, 2006; Acts 2011, 82nd Leg., ch. 93 (S.B. 1568), § 1, eff. Sept. 1, 2011.

§ 21.553. Demand

(a) A shareholder may not institute a derivative proceeding until the 91st day after the date a written demand is filed with the corporation stating with particularity the act, omission, or other matter that is the subject of the claim or challenge and requesting that the corporation take suitable action.

(b) The waiting period required by Subsection (a) before a derivative proceeding may be instituted is not required if:

(1) the shareholder has been previously notified that the demand has been rejected by the corporation;

(2) the corporation is suffering irreparable injury; or

(3) irreparable injury to the corporation would result by waiting for the expiration of the 90–day period.

Acts 2003, 78th Leg., ch. 182, § 1, eff. Jan. 1, 2006.

§ 21.554. Determination by Directors or Independent Persons

(a) A determination of how to proceed on allegations made in a demand or petition relating to a derivative proceeding must be made by an affirmative vote of the majority of:

(1) the independent and disinterested directors of the corporation present at a meeting of the board of directors of the corporation at which interested directors are not present at the time of the vote if the independent and disinterested directors constitute a quorum of the board of directors;

(2) a committee consisting of two or more independent and disinterested directors appointed by an affirmative vote of the majority of one or more independent and disinterested directors present at a meeting of the board of directors, regardless of whether the independent and disinterested directors constitute a quorum of the board of directors; or

(3) a panel of one or more independent and disinterested persons appointed by the court on a motion by the corporation listing the names of the persons to be appointed and stating that, to the best of the corporation's knowledge, the persons to be appointed are disinterested and qualified to make the determinations contemplated by Section 21.558.

(b) The court shall appoint a panel under Subsection (a)(3) if the court finds that the persons recommended by the corporation are independent and disinterested and are otherwise qualified with respect to expertise, experience, independent judgment, and other factors considered appropriate by the court under the circumstances to make the determinations. A person appointed by the court to a panel under this section may not be held liable to the corporation or the corporation's shareholders for an action taken or omission made by the person in that capacity, except for an act or omission constituting fraud or wilful misconduct.

Acts 2003, 78th Leg., ch. 182, § 1, eff. Jan. 1, 2006.

§ 21.555. Stay of Proceeding

(a) If the domestic or foreign corporation that is the subject of a derivative proceeding commences an inquiry into the allegations made in a demand or petition and the person or group of persons described by Section 21.554 is conducting an active review of the allegations in good faith, the court shall stay a derivative proceeding until the review is completed and a determination is made by the person or group regarding what further action, if any, should be taken.

(b) To obtain a stay, the domestic or foreign corporation shall provide the court with a written statement agreeing to advise the court and the shareholder making the demand of the determination promptly on the completion of the review of the matter. A stay, on application, may be reviewed every 60 days for the continued necessity of the stay.

(c) If the review and determination made by the person or group is not completed before the 61st day after the stay is ordered by the court, the stay may be renewed for one or more additional 60–day periods if the domestic or foreign corporation provides the court and the shareholder with a written statement of the status of the review and the reasons why a continued extension of the stay is necessary.

Acts 2003, 78th Leg., ch. 182, § 1, eff. Jan. 1, 2006.

§ 21.556. Discovery

(a) If a domestic or foreign corporation proposes to dismiss a derivative proceeding under Section 21.558, discovery by a shareholder after the filing of the derivative proceeding in accordance with this subchapter shall be limited to:

(1) facts relating to whether the person or group of persons described by Section 21.558 is independent and disinterested;

(2) the good faith of the inquiry and review by the person or group; and

(3) the reasonableness of the procedures followed by the person or group in conducting the review.

(b) Discovery described by Subsection (a) may not be expanded to include a fact or substantive matter regarding the act, omission, or other matter that is the subject matter of the derivative proceeding. The scope of discovery may be expanded if the court determines after notice and hearing that a good faith review of the allegations for purposes of Section 21.558 has not been made by an independent and disinterested person or group in accordance with that section.

Acts 2003, 78th Leg., ch. 182, § 1, eff. Jan. 1, 2006.

§ 21.557. Tolling of Statute of Limitations

A written demand filed with the corporation under Section 21.553 tolls the statute of limitations on the claim on which demand is made until the earlier of:

(1) the 91st day after the date of the demand; or

(2) the 31st day after the date the corporation advises the shareholder that the demand has been rejected or the review has been completed.

Acts 2003, 78th Leg., ch. 182, § 1, eff. Jan. 1, 2006.

§ 21.558. Dismissal of Derivative Proceeding

(a) A court shall dismiss a derivative proceeding on a motion by the corporation if the person or group of persons described by Section 21.554 determines in good faith, after conducting a reasonable inquiry and based on factors the person or group considers appropriate under the circumstances, that continuation of the derivative proceeding is not in the best interests of the corporation.

(b) In determining whether the requirements of Subsection (a) have been met, the burden of proof shall be on:

(1) the plaintiff shareholder if:

(A) the majority of the board of directors consists of independent and disinterested directors at the time the determination is made;

(B) the determination is made by a panel of one or more independent and disinterested persons appointed under Section 21.554(a)(3); or

(C) the corporation presents prima facie evidence that demonstrates that the directors appointed under Section 21.554(a)(2) are independent and disinterested; or

(2) the corporation in any other circumstance.

Acts 2003, 78th Leg., ch. 182, § 1, eff. Jan. 1, 2006.

§ 21.559. Proceeding Instituted After Demand Rejected

If a derivative proceeding is instituted after a demand is rejected, the petition must allege with particularity facts that establish that the rejection was not made in accordance with the requirements of Sections 21.554 and 21.558.

Acts 2003, 78th Leg., ch. 182, § 1, eff. Jan. 1, 2006.

§ 21.560. Discontinuance or Settlement

(a) A derivative proceeding may not be discontinued or settled without court approval.

(b) The court shall direct that notice be given to the affected shareholders if the court determines that a proposed discontinuance or settlement may substantially affect the interests of other shareholders.

Acts 2003, 78th Leg., ch. 182, § 1, eff. Jan. 1, 2006.

§ 21.561. Payment of Expenses

(a) In this section, "expenses" means reasonable expenses incurred by a party in a derivative proceeding, including:

(1) attorney's fees;

(2) costs in pursuing an investigation of the matter that was the subject of the derivative proceeding; or

(3) expenses for which the domestic or foreign corporation or a corporate defendant may be required to indemnify another person.

(b) On termination of a derivative proceeding, the court may order:

(1) the domestic or foreign corporation to pay the expenses the plaintiff incurred in the proceeding if the court finds the proceeding has resulted in a substantial benefit to the domestic or foreign corporation;

(2) the plaintiff to pay the expenses the domestic or foreign corporation or other defendant incurred in investigating and defending the proceeding if the court finds the proceeding has been instituted or maintained without reasonable cause or for an improper purpose; or

(3) a party to pay the expenses incurred by another party relating to the filing of a pleading, motion, or other paper if the court finds the pleading, motion, or other paper:

(A) was not well grounded in fact after reasonable inquiry;

(B) was not warranted by existing law or a good faith argument for the extension, modification, or reversal of existing law; or

(C) was interposed for an improper purpose, such as to harass, cause unnecessary delay, or cause a needless increase in the cost of litigation.

Acts 2003, 78th Leg., ch. 182, § 1, eff. Jan. 1, 2006.

§ 21.562. Application to Foreign Corporations

(a) In a derivative proceeding brought in the right of a foreign corporation, the matters covered by this subchapter are governed by the laws of the jurisdiction of incorporation of the foreign corporation, except for Sections 21.555, 21.560, and 21.561, which are procedural provisions and do not relate to the internal affairs of the foreign corporation.

(b) In the case of matters relating to a foreign corporation under Section 21.554, a reference to a person or group of persons described by that section refers to a person or group entitled under the laws of the jurisdiction of incorporation of the foreign corporation to review and dispose of a derivative proceeding. The standard of review of a decision made by the person or group to dismiss the derivative proceeding shall be governed by the laws of the jurisdiction of incorporation of the foreign corporation.

Acts 2003, 78th Leg., ch. 182, § 1, eff. Jan. 1, 2006.

§ 21.563. Closely Held Corporation

(a) In this section, "closely held corporation" means a corporation that has:

(1) fewer than 35 shareholders; and

(2) no shares listed on a national securities exchange or regularly quoted in an over-the-counter market by one or more members of a national securities association.

(b) Sections 21.552–21.559 do not apply to a closely held corporation.

(c) If justice requires:

(1) a derivative proceeding brought by a shareholder of a closely held corporation may be treated by a court as a direct action brought by the shareholder for the shareholder's own benefit; and

(2) a recovery in a direct or derivative proceeding by a shareholder may be paid directly to the plaintiff or to the corporation if necessary to protect the interests of creditors or other shareholders of the corporation.

Acts 2003, 78th Leg., ch. 182, § 1, eff. Jan. 1, 2006. Amended by Acts 2007, 80th Leg., ch. 688, § 84, eff. Sept. 1, 2007.

SUBCHAPTER M. AFFILIATED BUSINESS COMBINATIONS

§ 21.601. Definitions

In this subchapter:

(1) "Issuing public corporation" means a domestic corporation that has:

(A) 100 or more shareholders of record as shown by the share transfer records of the corporation;

(B) a class or series of the corporation's voting shares registered under the Securities Exchange Act of 1934 (15 U.S.C. Section 77b et seq.), as amended; or

(C) a class or series of the corporation's voting shares qualified for trading on a national securities exchange .

(2) "Person" includes two or more persons acting as a partnership, limited partnership, syndicate, or other group under an agreement, arrangement, or understanding, regardless of whether in writing, to acquire, hold, vote, or dispose of a corporation's shares.

(3) "Share acquisition date" means the date a person initially becomes an affiliated shareholder of an issuing public corporation.

(4) "Subsidiary" means a domestic or foreign corporation or other entity of which a majority of the outstanding voting shares are owned, directly or indirectly, by an issuing public corporation.

(5) "Voting share" means a share of capital stock of a corporation that entitles the holder of the share to vote generally in the election of directors.

Acts 2003, 78th Leg., ch. 182, § 1, eff. Jan. 1, 2006. Amended by Acts 2011, 82nd Leg., ch. 139 (S.B. 748), § 30, eff. Sept. 1, 2011.

§ 21.602. Affiliated Shareholder

(a) For purposes of this subchapter, a person, other than the issuing public corporation or a wholly owned subsidiary of the issuing public corporation, is an affiliated shareholder if the person:

(1) is the beneficial owner of 20 percent or more of the outstanding voting shares of the issuing public corporation; or

(2) during the preceding three-year period, was the beneficial owner of 20 percent or more of the outstanding voting shares of the issuing public corporation.

(b) To determine whether a person is an affiliated shareholder, the number of voting shares of the issuing public corporation considered outstanding includes shares considered beneficially owned by that person under Section 21.603, but does not include other unissued voting shares of the issuing public corporation that may be issuable under an agreement, arrangement, or understanding, or on exercise of conversion rights, warrants, or options.

Acts 2003, 78th Leg., ch. 182, § 1, eff. Jan. 1, 2006.

§ 21.603. Beneficial Owner of Shares or Other Securities

(a) For purposes of this subchapter , a person is a beneficial owner of shares or other securities if the person individually, or through an affiliate or associate, directly or indirectly beneficially owns the shares or other securities or has the right to:

(1) acquire the shares or other securities immediately or after the passage of time according to an oral or written agreement, arrangement, or understanding, or on the exercise of conversion rights, exchange rights, warrants, or options;

(2) vote the shares or other securities according to an oral or written agreement, arrangement, or understanding; or

(3) acquire, hold or dispose of, or vote the shares or other securities with another person who individually, or through an affiliate or associate, beneficially owns, directly or indirectly, the shares or other securities.

(b) A person, however, is not considered a beneficial owner of shares or other securities for purposes of this subchapter if:

(1) the shares or other securities are:

(A) tendered under a tender or exchange offer made by the person or an affiliate or associate of the person before the tendered shares or securities are accepted for purchase or exchange; or

(B) subject to an agreement, arrangement, or understanding that expressly conditions the acquisition or purchase of shares or securities on the approval of the acquisition or purchase under Section 21.606 if the person has no direct or indirect rights of ownership or voting with respect to the shares or other securities until the time the approval is obtained; or

(2) the agreement, arrangement, or understanding to vote the shares:

(A) arises solely from an immediately revocable proxy that authorizes the person named in the proxy to vote at a meeting of the shareholders that has been called when the proxy is delivered or at an adjournment of the meeting; and

(B) would not be reportable on a Schedule 13D under the Securities Exchange Act of 1934 (15 U.S.C. Section 77b et seq.), as amended, or a comparable or successor report.

Acts 2003, 78th Leg., ch. 182, § 1, eff. Jan. 1, 2006. Amended by Acts 2011, 82nd Leg., ch. 139 (S.B. 748), § 31, eff. Sept. 1, 2011.

§ 21.604. Business Combination

A business combination is:

(1) a merger, share exchange, or conversion of an issuing public corporation or a subsidiary with:

(A) an affiliated shareholder;

(B) a foreign or domestic corporation or other entity that is, or after the merger, share exchange, or conversion would be, an affiliate or associate of the affiliated shareholder; or

(C) another domestic or foreign corporation or other entity, if the merger, share exchange, or conversion is caused by an affiliated shareholder, or an affiliate or associate of an affiliated shareholder, and as a result of the merger, share exchange, or conversion this subchapter does not apply to the surviving corporation or other entity;

(2) a sale, lease, exchange, mortgage, pledge, transfer, or other disposition, in one transaction or a series of transactions, including an allocation of

assets under a merger, to or with the affiliated shareholder, or an affiliate or associate of the affiliated shareholder, of assets of the issuing public corporation or a subsidiary that:

(A) has an aggregate market value equal to 10 percent or more of the aggregate market value of all of the assets, determined on a consolidated basis, of the issuing public corporation;

(B) has an aggregate market value equal to 10 percent or more of the aggregate market value of all of the outstanding voting shares of the issuing public corporation; or

(C) represents 10 percent or more of the earning power or net income, determined on a consolidated basis, of the issuing public corporation;

(3) the issuance or transfer by an issuing public corporation or a subsidiary to an affiliated shareholder or an affiliate or associate of the affiliated shareholder, in one transaction or a series of transactions, of shares of the issuing public corporation or a subsidiary, except by the exercise of warrants or rights to purchase shares of the issuing public corporation offered, or a share dividend paid, pro rata to all shareholders of the issuing public corporation after the affiliated shareholder's share acquisition date;

(4) the adoption of a plan or proposal for the liquidation, winding up, or dissolution of an issuing public corporation proposed by or under any agreement, arrangement, or understanding, regardless of whether in writing, with an affiliated shareholder or an affiliate or associate of the affiliated shareholder;

(5) a reclassification of securities, including a reverse share split or a share split-up, share dividend, or other distribution of shares, a recapitalization of the issuing public corporation, a merger of the issuing public corporation with a subsidiary or pursuant to which the assets and liabilities of the issuing public corporation are allocated among two or more surviving or new domestic or foreign corporations or other entities, or any other transaction proposed by or under an agreement, arrangement, or understanding, regardless of whether in writing, with an affiliated shareholder or an affiliate or associate of the affiliated shareholder that has the effect, directly or indirectly, of increasing the proportionate ownership percentage of the outstanding shares of a class or series of voting shares or securities convertible into voting shares of the issuing public corporation that is beneficially owned by the affiliated shareholder or an affiliate or associate of the affiliated shareholder, except as a result of immaterial changes due to fractional share adjustments; or

(6) the direct or indirect receipt by an affiliated shareholder or an affiliate or associate of the affiliated shareholder of the benefit of a loan, advance, guarantee, pledge, or other financial assistance or a tax credit or other tax advantage provided by or through the issuing public corporation, except proportionately as a shareholder of the issuing public corporation.

Acts 2003, 78th Leg., ch. 182, § 1, eff. Jan. 1, 2006. Amended by Acts 2005, 79th Leg., ch. 64, § 64, eff. Jan. 1, 2006; Acts 2007, 80th Leg., ch. 688, § 85, eff. Sept. 1, 2007.

§ 21.605. Control

(a) For purposes of this subchapter, a person has control of another person if the person has possession, directly or indirectly, of the power to direct or cause the direction of the management and policies of the other person, through the ownership of equity securities, by contract, or in another manner.

(b) A person's beneficial ownership of 10 percent or more of a person's outstanding voting shares or similar interests creates a presumption that the person has control of the other person, but a person is not considered to have control of another person who holds the voting shares or similar interests in good faith and not to circumvent this part, as an agent, bank, broker, nominee, custodian, or trustee for one or more beneficial owners who do not individually or as a group have control of the person.

Acts 2003, 78th Leg., ch. 182, § 1, eff. Jan. 1, 2006.

§ 21.606. Three-Year Moratorium on Certain Business Combinations

An issuing public corporation may not, directly or indirectly, enter into or engage in a business combination with an affiliated shareholder, or any affiliate or associate of the affiliated shareholder, during the three-year period immediately following the affiliated shareholder's share acquisition date unless:

(1) the business combination or the purchase or acquisition of shares made by the affiliated shareholder on the affiliated shareholder's share acquisition date is approved by the board of directors of the issuing public corporation before the affiliated shareholder's share acquisition date; or

(2) the business combination is approved, by the affirmative vote of the holders of at least two-thirds of the outstanding voting shares of the issuing

public corporation not beneficially owned by the affiliated shareholder or an affiliate or associate of the affiliated shareholder, at a meeting of shareholders called for that purpose not less than six months after the affiliated shareholder's share acquisition date. Approval may not be by written consent.

Acts 2003, 78th Leg., ch. 182, § 1, eff. Jan. 1, 2006.

§ 21.607. Application of Moratorium

Section 21.606 does not apply to:

(1) a business combination of an issuing public corporation if:

(A) the original articles of incorporation or original bylaws of the corporation contain a provision expressly electing not to be governed by this subchapter;

(B) before December 31, 1997, the corporation adopted an amendment to the articles of incorporation or bylaws of the corporation expressly electing not to be governed by this subchapter; or

(C) after December 31, 1997, the corporation adopts an amendment to the articles of incorporation or bylaws of the corporation, approved by the affirmative vote of the holders, other than an affiliated shareholder or an affiliate or associate of the affiliated shareholder, of at least two-thirds of the outstanding voting shares of the issuing public corporation, expressly electing not to be governed by this subchapter, except that the amendment to the articles of incorporation or bylaws takes effect 18 months after the date of the vote and does not apply to a business combination of the issuing public corporation with an affiliated shareholder whose share acquisition date is on or before the effective date of the amendment;

(2) a business combination of an issuing public corporation with an affiliated shareholder who became an affiliated shareholder inadvertently, if the affiliated shareholder:

(A) as soon as practicable divests itself of a sufficient number of the voting shares of the issuing public corporation so that the affiliated shareholder no longer is the beneficial owner, directly or indirectly, of 20 percent or more of the outstanding voting shares of the issuing public corporation; and

(B) would not at any time within the three-year period preceding the announcement date of the business combination have been an affiliated shareholder except for the inadvertent acquisition;

(3) a business combination with an affiliated shareholder who was the beneficial owner of 20 percent or more of the outstanding voting shares of the issuing public corporation on December 31, 1996, and continuously until the announcement date of the business combination;

(4) a business combination with an affiliated shareholder who became an affiliated shareholder through a transfer of shares of the issuing public corporation by will or intestate succession and continuously was an affiliated shareholder until the announcement date of the business combination; or

(5) a business combination of an issuing public corporation with a domestic wholly owned subsidiary if the domestic subsidiary is not an affiliate or associate of the affiliated shareholder for a reason other than the affiliated shareholder's beneficial ownership of voting shares in the issuing public corporation.

Acts 2003, 78th Leg., ch. 182, § 1, eff. Jan. 1, 2006.

§ 21.608. Effect on Other Actions

(a) This subchapter does not affect, directly or indirectly, the validity of another action by the board of directors of an issuing public corporation.

(b) This subchapter does not preclude the board of directors of an issuing public corporation from taking other action in accordance with law.

(c) The board of directors of an issuing public corporation does not incur liability for an election made or not made under this subchapter.

Acts 2003, 78th Leg., ch. 182, § 1, eff. Jan. 1, 2006.

§ 21.609. Conflicting Provisions

If this subchapter conflicts with another provision of this code, this subchapter controls.

Acts 2003, 78th Leg., ch. 182, § 1, eff. Jan. 1, 2006.

§ 21.610. Change in Voting Requirements

The affirmative vote or concurrence of shareholders required for approval of an action that is required to be submitted to a vote of the shareholders under this subchapter may be increased but not decreased under Section 21.365.

Acts 2003, 78th Leg., ch. 182, § 1, eff. Jan. 1, 2006.

SUBCHAPTER N. PROVISIONS RELATING TO INVESTMENT COMPANIES

§ 21.651. Definition

In this subchapter, "investment company" means a corporation registered as an open-end company under the Investment Company Act.

Acts 2003, 78th Leg., ch. 182, § 1, eff. Jan. 1, 2006.

§ 21.652. Establishing Class or Series of Shares; Change in Number of Shares

(a) In addition to the actions the board may undertake under Subchapters D, E, and F, the board of directors of an investment company may:

(1) establish classes of shares and series of unissued shares of a class by setting and determining the designations, preferences, limitations, and relative rights, including voting rights, of the shares of the class or series established under this subdivision to the same extent that the designations, preferences, limitations, and relative rights could be stated if fully stated in the certificate of formation; and

(2) increase or decrease the aggregate number of shares or the number of shares of, or delete from the investment company's certificate of formation, a class or series of shares the corporation has authority to issue, unless a provision has been included in the certificate of formation of the corporation after September 1, 1993, expressly prohibiting those actions by the board of directors.

(b) The board of directors of an investment company may not:

(1) decrease the number of shares in a class or series to a number that is less than the number of shares of that class or series that are outstanding at the time; or

(2) delete from the certificate of formation a reference to a class or series that has shares outstanding at the time.

(c) To establish a class or series under this section, the board of directors must adopt a resolution stating the designation of the class or series and setting and determining the designations, preferences, limitations, and relative rights, including voting rights, of the class or series.

(d) To increase or decrease the number of shares of a class or series of shares or to delete from the certificate of formation a reference to a class or series of shares, the board of directors of an investment company must adopt a resolution setting and determining the new number of shares of each class or series in which the number of shares is increased or decreased or deleting the class or series and any reference to the class or series from the certificate of formation. The shares of a series removed from the certificate of formation shall resume the status of authorized but unissued shares of the class of shares from which the series was established unless otherwise provided by the resolution or the certificate of formation of the investment company.

Acts 2003, 78th Leg., ch. 182, § 1, eff. Jan. 1, 2006.

§ 21.653. Required Statement Relating to Shares

(a) Before the first issuance of shares of a class or series established or increased or decreased by resolution adopted by the board of directors of an investment company under Section 21.652, and to delete from the investment company's certificate of formation a class or series of shares and all references to the class or series contained in the certificate of formation, the investment company shall file with the secretary of state a statement that contains:

(1) the name of the investment company;

(2) if the statement relates to the establishment of a class or series of shares, a copy of the resolution establishing and designating the class or series or establishing and designating the class or series and setting and determining the preferences, limitations, and relative rights of the class or series;

(3) if the statement relates to an increase or decrease in the number of shares of a class or series, a copy of the resolution setting and determining the new number of shares of each class or series in which the number of shares is increased or decreased;

(4) if the statement relates to the deletion of a class or series of shares and all references to the class or series from the certificate of formation, a copy of the resolution deleting the class or series and all references to the class or series from the certificate of formation;

(5) the date of adoption of the resolution; and

(6) a statement that the resolution was adopted by all necessary action on the part of the investment company.

(b) After the statement described by Subsection (a) is filed, a resolution adopted under Section 21.652 becomes an amendment of the certificate of formation. An amendment of the certificate of formation described under this section is not subject to the procedure to amend the certificate of formation contained in Subchapter B.

Acts 2003, 78th Leg., ch. 182, § 1, eff. Jan. 1, 2006.

§ 21.654. Term of Office of Directors

Unless the director resigns or is removed in accordance with the certificate of formation or bylaws of the investment company, a director of an investment company shall serve as director for the term for which the director is elected and holds office until a successor is elected and qualifies.

Acts 2003, 78th Leg., ch. 182, § 1, eff. Jan. 1, 2006. Amended by Acts 2005, 79th Leg., ch. 64, § 65, eff. Jan. 1, 2006.

§ 21.655. Meetings of Shareholders

(a) If provided by the certificate of formation or bylaws of an investment company, the investment company is not required to hold an annual meeting of shareholders or elect directors in a year in which an election of directors is not required under the Investment Company Act.

(b) If an investment company is required to hold a meeting of shareholders to elect directors under the Investment Company Act, the meeting shall be designated as the annual meeting of shareholders for that year.

Acts 2003, 78th Leg., ch. 182, § 1, eff. Jan. 1, 2006.

SUBCHAPTER O. CLOSE CORPORATION

§ 21.701. Definitions

In this subchapter:

(1) "Close corporation" means a domestic corporation formed under this subchapter or governed by this subchapter because of Section 21.705, 21.706, or 21.707.

(2) "Close corporation provision" means a provision in the certificate of formation of a close corporation or in a shareholders' agreement of a close corporation.

(3) "Ordinary corporation" means a domestic corporation that is not a close corporation.

(4) "Shareholders' agreement" means a written agreement regulating an aspect of the business and affairs of or the relationship among the shareholders of a close corporation that has been executed under this subchapter.

Acts 2003, 78th Leg., ch. 182, § 1, eff. Jan. 1, 2006. Amended by Acts 2011, 82nd Leg., ch. 139 (S.B. 748), § 32, eff. Sept. 1, 2011.

§ 21.702. Applicability of Subchapter

(a) This subchapter applies only to a close corporation.

(b) This chapter applies to a close corporation to the extent not inconsistent with this subchapter.

Acts 2003, 78th Leg., ch. 182, § 1, eff. Jan. 1, 2006.

§ 21.703. Formation of Close Corporation

A close corporation shall be formed in accordance with Chapter 3.

Acts 2003, 78th Leg., ch. 182, § 1, eff. Jan. 1, 2006.

§ 21.704. Bylaws of Close Corporation

(a) A close corporation does not need to adopt bylaws if provisions required by law to be contained in the bylaws are contained in the certificate of formation or a shareholders' agreement.

(b) A close corporation that does not have bylaws when it terminates its status as a close corporation under Section 21.708 shall immediately adopt bylaws that comply with Section 21.057.

Acts 2003, 78th Leg., ch. 182, § 1, eff. Jan. 1, 2006.

§ 21.705. Adoption of Amendment for Close Corporation Status

(a) An ordinary corporation may become a close corporation by amending its certificate of formation in accordance with Chapter 3 to conform with Section 3.008.

(b) An amendment adopting close corporation status must be approved by the affirmative vote of the holders of all of the outstanding shares of each class established by the close corporation, regardless of whether a class is entitled to vote on the amendment by the certificate of formation of the ordinary corporation.

Acts 2003, 78th Leg., ch. 182, § 1, eff. Jan. 1, 2006.

§ 21.706. Adoption of Close Corporation Status Through Merger, Exchange, or Conversion

(a) A surviving or new corporation resulting from a merger or conversion or a corporation that acquires a corporation under an exchange under Chapter 10 may become a close corporation if, as part of the plan of merger, exchange, or conversion, the certificate of formation conforms with Section 3.008.

(b) A plan of merger, exchange, or conversion adopting close corporation status must be approved by the affirmative vote of the holders of all of the outstanding ownership or membership interests, and of each class or series of ownership or membership interests, of each entity or non-code organization that is party to the merger, exchange, or conversion, regardless of whether a class or series of ownership or membership interests is entitled to vote on the plan by the certificate of formation of the corporation.

Acts 2003, 78th Leg., ch. 182, § 1, eff. Jan. 1, 2006.

§ 21.707. Existing Close Corporation

(a) This section applies to an existing corporation that elected to become a close corporation before the mandatory application date of this code and has not terminated that status.

(b) A close corporation existing before the mandatory application date of this code is considered to be a close corporation under this code.

(c) A provision in the articles of incorporation of a close corporation authorized under former law is valid and enforceable if the corporation's status as a close corporation has not been terminated.

(d) An agreement among the shareholders of a close corporation in conformance with former law and Sections 21.714–21.725 before the mandatory application date of this code is considered to be a shareholders' agreement.

(e) A certificate representing the shares issued or delivered by the close corporation after the mandatory application date of this code, whether in connection with the original issue of shares or a transfer of shares, must conform with Section 21.732.

(f) In this section, "mandatory application date" has the meaning assigned by Section 401.001.

Acts 2003, 78th Leg., ch. 182, § 1, eff. Jan. 1, 2006. Amended by Acts 2007, 80th Leg., ch. 688, § 86, eff. Sept. 1, 2007.

§ 21.708. Termination of Close Corporation Status

A close corporation may terminate its status as a close corporation by:

(1) filing a statement terminating close corporation status under Section 21.709;

(2) amending the close corporation's certificate of formation under Chapter 3 by deleting from the certificate of formation the statement that it is a close corporation;

(3) engaging in a merger, interest exchange, or conversion under Chapter 10, unless the plan of merger, exchange, or conversion provides that the surviving or new corporation will continue as or become a close corporation and the plan has been approved by the affirmative vote or consent of the holders of all of the outstanding shares, and of each class and series of shares, of the close corporation, regardless of whether a class or series of shares is entitled to vote on the plan by the certificate of formation; or

(4) instituting a judicial proceeding to enforce a close corporation provision providing for the termination.

Acts 2003, 78th Leg., ch. 182, § 1, eff. Jan. 1, 2006.

§ 21.709. Statement Terminating Close Corporation Status; Filing; Notice

(a) If a close corporation provision specifies a time or event requiring the termination of close corporation status, regardless of whether the provision is identifiable by a person dealing with the close corporation, the termination of the close corporation status takes effect on the occurrence of the specified time or event and the filing of a statement terminating close corporation status under this section.

(b) Promptly after the time or occurrence of an event requiring termination of close corporation status, a statement terminating close corporation status shall be signed by an officer on behalf of the close corporation. A copy of the applicable close corporation provision must be included in or attached to the statement. The statement and any attachment shall be filed with the secretary of state in accordance with Chapter 4.

(c) The statement terminating close corporation status must contain:

(1) the name of the corporation;

(2) a statement that the corporation has terminated its status as a close corporation in accordance with the included or attached close corporation provision; and

(3) the time or event that caused the termination and, in the case of an event, the approximate date of the event.

(d) After a statement terminating close corporation status has been filed under this section, the certificate of formation of the close corporation is considered to be amended to delete from the certificate the statement that the corporation is a close corporation, and the corporation's status as a close corporation is terminated.

(e) The corporation shall personally deliver or mail a copy of the statement to each shareholder of the corporation. A copy of the statement is considered to have been delivered by mail under this section when the copy is deposited in the United States mail, with postage prepaid, addressed to the shareholder at the shareholder's address as it appears on the share transfer records of the corporation. The failure to deliver the copy of the statement does not affect the validity of the termination.

Acts 2003, 78th Leg., ch. 182, § 1, eff. Jan. 1, 2006.

§ 21.710. Effect of Termination of Close Corporation Status

(a) A close corporation that terminates its status as a close corporation and becomes an ordinary corporation is subject to this chapter as if the corporation had not elected close corporation status under this subchapter.

(b) The effect of termination of close corporation status on a shareholders' agreement is governed by Section 21.724.

(c) When the termination of close corporation status takes effect, if the close corporation's business and affairs have been managed by an entity other than a board of directors as provided by Section 21.725, governance by a board of directors is instituted or reinstated:

(1) if provided by a shareholders' agreement, in the manner stated in the agreement or by the persons named in the agreement to serve as the interim board of directors; or

(2) if each party to a shareholders' agreement agrees to elect a board of directors at a shareholders' meeting.

Acts 2003, 78th Leg., ch. 182, § 1, eff. Jan. 1, 2006.

§ 21.711. Shareholders' Meeting to Elect Directors

A shareholders' meeting required by Section 21.710(c)(2) shall be promptly called after the termination of close corporation status takes effect. If a meeting is not called before the 31st day after the date the termination takes effect, a shareholder may call a shareholders' meeting on the provision of notice required by Section 21.353, regardless of whether the shareholder is entitled to call a shareholders' meeting or vote at the meeting. At the meeting, the shareholders shall elect the number of directors specified in the certificate of formation or bylaws of the corporation or, in the absence of any specification, three directors.

Acts 2003, 78th Leg., ch. 182, § 1, eff. Jan. 1, 2006.

§ 21.712. Term of Office of Directors

A director succeeding to the management of the corporation under Section 21.710(c) shall have a term of office as set forth in Section 21.408. Until a board of directors is elected, the shareholders of the corporation shall act as the corporation's board of directors, and the business and affairs of the corporation shall be conducted under Section 21.726.

Acts 2003, 78th Leg., ch. 182, § 1, eff. Jan. 1, 2006.

§ 21.713. Management

A close corporation shall be managed:

(1) by a board of directors in the same manner an ordinary corporation would be managed under this chapter; or

(2) in the manner provided by the close corporation's certificate of formation or by a shareholders' agreement of the close corporation.

Acts 2003, 78th Leg., ch. 182, § 1, eff. Jan. 1, 2006.

§ 21.714. Shareholders' Agreement

(a) The shareholders of a close corporation may enter into one or more shareholders' agreements.

(b) The business and affairs of a close corporation or the relationships among the shareholders that may be regulated by a shareholders' agreement include:

(1) the management of the business and affairs of the close corporation by its shareholders, with or without a board of directors;

(2) the management of the business and affairs of the close corporation wholly or partly by one or more of its shareholders or other persons;

(3) buy–sell, first option, first refusal, or similar arrangements with respect to the close corporation's shares or other securities, and restrictions on the transfer of the shares or other securities, including more restrictions than those permitted by Section 21.211;

(4) the declaration and payment of dividends or other distributions in amounts authorized by Subchapter G, regardless of whether the distribution is in proportion to ownership of shares;

(5) the manner in which profits or losses shall be apportioned;

(6) restrictions placed on the rights of a transferee or assignee of shares to participate in the management or administration of the close corporation's business and affairs during the term of the shareholders' agreement;

(7) the right of one or more shareholders to cause the winding up and termination of the close corporation at will or on the occurrence of a specified event or contingency, in which case the winding up and termination of the close corporation shall proceed as if all of the shareholders of the close corporation had consented in writing to winding up and termination as provided by Chapter 11;

(8) the exercise or division of voting power either in general or with regard to specified matters by or among the shareholders of the close corporation or other persons, including:

(A) voting agreements and voting trusts that do not conform with Section 6.251 or 6.252;

(B) requiring the vote or consent of the holders of a larger or smaller number of shares than is otherwise required by this chapter or other law, including an action for termination of close corporation status;

(C) granting one or some other specified number of votes for each shareholder; and

(D) permitting an action for which this chapter requires approval by the vote of the board of directors or the shareholders of an ordinary corporation, or both, to be taken without a vote, in the manner provided by the shareholders' agreement;

(9) the terms and conditions of employment of a shareholder, director, officer, or other employee of the close corporation, regardless of the length of the period of employment;

(10) the individuals who will serve as directors, if any, and officers of the close corporation;

(11) the arbitration or mediation of issues about which the shareholders may become deadlocked in voting or about which the directors or those empowered to manage the close corporation may become deadlocked and the shareholders are unable to break the deadlock;

(12) the termination of close corporation status, including a right of dissent or other rights that may be granted to shareholders who object to the termination;

(13) qualifications of persons who are or are not entitled to be shareholders of the close corporation;

(14) amendments to or termination of the shareholders' agreement; and

(15) any provision required or permitted to be contained in the bylaws by this chapter.

Acts 2003, 78th Leg., ch. 182, § 1, eff. Jan. 1, 2006.

§ 21.715. Execution of Shareholders' Agreement

A shareholders' agreement shall be executed:

(1) in the case of an existing close corporation, by each shareholder at the time of execution, regardless of whether the shareholder has voting power;

(2) in the case of an existing ordinary corporation that will adopt close corporation status under Section 21.705, by each shareholder at the time of execution, regardless of whether the shareholder has voting power; or

(3) in the case of a close corporation that is being formed under Section 21.703, by each person who is a subscriber to the corporation's shares or agrees to become a holder of the corporation's shares under the shareholders' agreement of the close corporation.

Acts 2003, 78th Leg., ch. 182, § 1, eff. Jan. 1, 2006.

§ 21.716. Adoption of Amendment of Shareholders' Agreement

Unless otherwise provided by a shareholders' agreement, an amendment to the shareholders' agreement of a close corporation may be adopted only by the written consent of each person who would be required to execute the shareholders' agreement if it were being executed originally at the time of adoption of the amendment, regardless of whether the person has voting power in the close corporation.

Acts 2003, 78th Leg., ch. 182, § 1, eff. Jan. 1, 2006.

§ 21.717. Delivery of Shareholders' Agreement

(a) The close corporation shall deliver a complete copy of a shareholders' agreement to:

(1) each person who is bound by the shareholders' agreement;

(2) each person who is or will become a shareholder in the close corporation as provided by Section 21.715 when a certificate representing shares in the close corporation is delivered to the person; and

(3) each person to whom a certificate representing shares is issued and who has not received a complete copy of the agreement.

(b) The failure to deliver a complete copy of a shareholders' agreement as required by this section does not affect the validity or enforceability of the shareholders' agreement.

Acts 2003, 78th Leg., ch. 182, § 1, eff. Jan. 1, 2006.

§ 21.718. Statement of Operation as Close Corporation

(a) On or after the formation of a close corporation or adoption of close corporation status, a close corporation that begins to conduct its business and affairs under a shareholders' agreement that has become effective shall promptly execute and file with the secretary of state a statement of operation as a close corporation in accordance with Chapter 4.

(b) The statement required by Subsection (a) must:

(1) contain the name of the close corporation;

(2) state that the close corporation is being operated and its business and affairs are being conducted under the terms of a shareholders' agreement under this subchapter; and

(3) contain the date the operation of the corporation began.

(c) A statement of operation as a close corporation shall be executed by an officer on behalf of the corporation.

(d) On the filing of the statement of operation as a close corporation, the fact that the close corporation is being operated and its business and affairs are being conducted under the terms of a shareholders' agreement becomes a matter of public record.

Acts 2003, 78th Leg., ch. 182, § 1, eff. Jan. 1, 2006.

§ 21.719. Validity and Enforceability of Shareholders' Agreement

(a) A shareholders' agreement executed in accordance with Section 21.715 is valid and enforceable notwithstanding:

(1) the elimination of a board of directors;

(2) any restriction imposed on the discretion or powers of the board of directors or other person empowered to manage the close corporation; and

(3) that the effect of the shareholders' agreement is to treat the business and affairs of the close corporation as if the close corporation were a partnership or in a manner that would otherwise be appropriate only among partners.

(b) A close corporation, a shareholder of the close corporation, or a party to a shareholders' agreement may initiate a proceeding to enforce the shareholders' agreement in accordance with Section 21.756.

Acts 2003, 78th Leg., ch. 182, § 1, eff. Jan. 1, 2006.

§ 21.720. Persons Bound by Shareholders' Agreement

(a) A shareholders' agreement executed in accordance with Section 21.715 is:

(1) considered to be an agreement among all of the shareholders of the close corporation; and

(2) binding on and enforceable against each shareholder of the close corporation, regardless of whether:

(A) a particular shareholder acquired shares in the close corporation by purchase, gift, bequest, or otherwise; or

(B) the shareholder had actual knowledge of the existence of the shareholders' agreement at the time of acquiring shares.

(b) A transferee or assignee of shares of a close corporation in which there is a shareholders' agreement is bound by the agreement for all purposes, regardless of whether the transferee or assignee executed or was aware of the agreement.

Acts 2003, 78th Leg., ch. 182, § 1, eff. Jan. 1, 2006.

§ 21.721. Delivery of Copy of Shareholders' Agreement to Transferee

(a) Before the transfer of shares of a close corporation in which there is a shareholders' agreement, the transferor shall deliver a complete copy of the shareholders' agreement to the transferee.

(b) If the transferor fails to deliver a complete copy of the shareholders' agreement:

(1) the validity and enforceability of the shareholders' agreement against each shareholder of the corporation, including the transferee, is not affected;

(2) the right, title, or interest of the transferee in the transferred shares is not adversely affected; and

(3) the transferee is entitled to obtain on demand from the transferor or from the close corporation a complete copy of the shareholders' agreement at the transferor's expense.

Acts 2003, 78th Leg., ch. 182, § 1, eff. Jan. 1, 2006.

§ 21.722. Effect of Required Statement on Share Certificate and Delivery of Shareholders' Agreement

If a certificate representing shares of a close corporation contains the statement required by Section 21.732, and a complete copy of each shareholders' agreement has been delivered as required by Section 21.717, each holder, transferee, or other person claiming an interest in the shares of the close corporation is conclusively presumed to have knowledge of a close corporation provision in effect at the time of the transfer.

Acts 2003, 78th Leg., ch. 182, § 1, eff. Jan. 1, 2006.

§ 21.723. Party Not Bound by Shareholders' Agreement on Cessation; Liability

(a) Notwithstanding the person's signature, a person ceases to be a party to, and bound by, a shareholders' agreement when the person ceases to be a shareholder of the close corporation unless:

(1) the person's attempted cessation was in violation of Section 21.721 or the shareholders' agreement; or

(2) the shareholders' agreement provides to the contrary.

(b) Cessation as a party to a shareholders' agreement or as a shareholder does not relieve a person of liability the person may have incurred for breach of the shareholders' agreement.

Acts 2003, 78th Leg., ch. 182, § 1, eff. Jan. 1, 2006.

§ 21.724. Termination of Shareholders' Agreement

(a) Except as provided by Subsection (b), a shareholders' agreement terminates when the close corporation terminates its status as a close corporation.

(b) If provided by the shareholders' agreement, all or part of the agreement is valid and enforceable to the extent permitted for an ordinary corporation by this chapter or other law.

Acts 2003, 78th Leg., ch. 182, § 1, eff. Jan. 1, 2006.

§ 21.725. Consequences of Management by Persons Other Than Board of Directors

Sections 21.726–21.729 apply only to a close corporation the business and affairs of which are managed wholly or partly by the shareholders of the close corporation or any other person as provided by a shareholders' agreement rather than solely by a board of directors.

Acts 2003, 78th Leg., ch. 182, § 1, eff. Jan. 1, 2006.

§ 21.726. Shareholders Considered Directors

(a) When required by the context of this chapter, the shareholders of a close corporation described by Section 21.725 are considered to be directors of the close corporation for purposes of applying a provision of this chapter, other than a provision relating to the election and removal of directors.

(b) A requirement that an instrument filed with a governmental agency contain a statement that a specified action has been taken by the board of directors is satisfied by a statement that:

(1) the corporation is a close corporation with no board of directors; and

(2) the action was approved by the shareholders of the close corporation or the persons empowered to manage the business and affairs of the close corporation under a shareholders' agreement.

Acts 2003, 78th Leg., ch. 182, § 1, eff. Jan. 1, 2006.

§ 21.727. Liability of Shareholders

The shareholders of a close corporation described by Section 21.725 are subject to any liability imposed on a director of a corporation by this chapter or other law for a managerial act of or omission made by the shareholders or any other person empowered to manage the business and affairs of the close corporation under a shareholders' agreement and relating to the business and affairs of the close corporation, if the action is required by law to be undertaken by the board of directors.

Acts 2003, 78th Leg., ch. 182, § 1, eff. Jan. 1, 2006.

§ 21.728. Mode and Effect of Taking Action by Shareholders and Others

(a) An action that shall or may be taken by the board of directors of an ordinary corporation as required or authorized by this chapter shall or may be taken by action of the shareholders of a close corporation described by Section 21.725 at a meeting of the shareholders or, in the manner permitted by a shareholders' agreement, this subchapter, or this chapter, without a meeting.

(b) Unless otherwise provided by the certificate of formation of the close corporation or a shareholders' agreement of the close corporation, an action is binding on a close corporation if the action is taken after:

(1) the affirmative vote of the holders of the majority of all outstanding shares entitled to vote on the action; or

(2) the consent of all of the shareholders of the close corporation, which may be proven by:

(A) the full knowledge of the action by all of the shareholders and the shareholders' failure to object to the action in a timely manner;

(B) written consent to the action in accordance with Section 6.201 or this chapter or any other writing executed by or on behalf of all of the shareholders reasonably evidencing the consent; or

(C) any other means reasonably evidencing the consent.

Acts 2003, 78th Leg., ch. 182, § 1, eff. Jan. 1, 2006.

§ 21.729. Limitation of Shareholder's Liability

(a) A shareholder of a close corporation described by Section 21.725 is not liable because of a shareholders' vote or shareholder action without a vote unless the shareholder had the right to vote or consent to the action.

(b) A shareholder of a close corporation, without regard to the right to vote or consent, may not be held liable for an action taken by the shareholders or a person empowered to manage the business and affairs of the close corporation under a shareholders' agreement if the shareholder dissents from and has not voted for or consented to the action.

(c) The dissent of a shareholder may be proven by:

(1) an entry in the minutes of the meeting of shareholders;

(2) a written dissent filed with the secretary of the meeting before the adjournment of the meeting;

(3) a written dissent sent by registered mail to the secretary of the close corporation promptly after the meeting or after a written consent was obtained from the other shareholders; or

(4) any other means reasonably evidencing the dissent.

Acts 2003, 78th Leg., ch. 182, § 1, eff. Jan. 1, 2006.

§ 21.730. Lack of Formalities; Treatment as Partnership

The failure of a close corporation under this subchapter to observe a usual formality or requirement prescribed for an ordinary corporation by this chapter relating to the exercise of corporate powers or the management of a corporation's business and affairs and the performance of a shareholders' agreement that treats the close corporation as if the corporation were a partnership or in a manner that otherwise is appropriate only among partners may not:

(1) be a factor in determining whether to impose personal liability on the shareholders for the close corporation's obligations by disregarding the separate entity of the close corporation or otherwise;

(2) be grounds for invalidating an otherwise valid shareholders' agreement; or

(3) affect the status of the close corporation as a corporation under this chapter or other law.

Acts 2003, 78th Leg., ch. 182, § 1, eff. Jan. 1, 2006.

§ 21.731. Other Agreements Among Shareholders Permitted

Sections 21.713–21.730 do not prohibit or impair any other agreement between two or more shareholders of an ordinary corporation permitted by this chapter or other law.

Acts 2003, 78th Leg., ch. 182, § 1, eff. Jan. 1, 2006.

§ 21.732. Close Corporation Share Certificates

(a) In addition to a matter required or authorized by law to be stated on a certificate representing shares, each certificate representing shares issued by a close corporation must conspicuously state on the front or back of the certificate: "These shares are issued by a close corporation as defined by the Texas Business Organizations Code. Under Chapter 21 of that code, a shareholders' agreement may provide for management of a close corporation by the shareholders or in other ways different from an ordinary corporation. This may subject the holder of this certificate to certain obligations and liabilities not otherwise imposed on shareholders of an ordinary corporation. On a sale or transfer of these shares, the transferor is required to deliver to the transferee a complete copy of any shareholders' agreement."

(b) Notwithstanding this chapter and Section 3.202, the status of a corporation as a close corporation is not affected by the failure of a share certificate to contain the statement required by Subsection (a).

Acts 2003, 78th Leg., ch. 182, § 1, eff. Jan. 1, 2006.

SUBCHAPTER P. JUDICIAL PROCEEDINGS RELATING TO CLOSE CORPORATION

§ 21.751. Definitions

In this subchapter:

(1) "Court" means a district court in the county in which the principal office of the close corporation is located.

(2) "Custodian" means a person appointed by a court under Section 21.761.

(3) "Provisional director" means a person appointed by a court under Section 21.758.

(4) "Shareholder" means a record or beneficial owner of shares in a close corporation, including:

(A) a person holding a beneficial interest in the shares under an inter vivos, testamentary, or voting trust; or

(B) the personal representative, as defined by the Texas Probate Code, of a record or beneficial owner.

Acts 2003, 78th Leg., ch. 182, § 1, eff. Jan. 1, 2006.

§ 21.752. Proceedings Authorized

In addition to any other judicial proceeding pertaining to an ordinary corporation provided for by this chapter or other law, a close corporation or shareholder may institute a proceeding in a district court in the county in which the principal office of the close corporation is located to:

(1) enforce a close corporation provision;

(2) appoint a provisional director; or

(3) appoint a custodian.

Acts 2003, 78th Leg., ch. 182, § 1, eff. Jan. 1, 2006.

§ 21.753. Notice; Intervention

(a) Notice of the institution of a proceeding shall be given to the close corporation, if the corporation is not a plaintiff, and to each shareholder who is not a plaintiff in the manner prescribed by law and consistent with due process of law as directed by the court.

(b) The close corporation or a shareholder of the close corporation may intervene in the proceeding.

Acts 2003, 78th Leg., ch. 182, § 1, eff. Jan. 1, 2006.

§ 21.754. Proceeding Nonexclusive

Except as provided by Section 21.755, the right of a close corporation or a shareholder to institute a proceeding under Section 21.752 is in addition to another right or remedy the plaintiff is entitled to under law.

Acts 2003, 78th Leg., ch. 182, § 1, eff. Jan. 1, 2006.

§ 21.755. Unavailability of Judicial Proceeding

(a) A shareholder may not institute a proceeding before exhausting any nonjudicial remedy contained in a close corporation provision for resolution of an issue that is in dispute unless the shareholder proves that the close corporation, the shareholders as a whole, or the shareholder will suffer irreparable harm before the nonjudicial remedy is exhausted.

(b) A shareholder may not institute a proceeding to seek damages or other monetary relief if the shareholder is entitled to dissent from a proposed action and receive the fair value of the shareholder's shares under this code or a shareholders' agreement.

Acts 2003, 78th Leg., ch. 182, § 1, eff. Jan. 1, 2006.

§ 21.756. Judicial Proceeding to Enforce Close Corporation Provision

(a) In a judicial proceeding under this section, a court shall enforce a close corporation provision without regard to whether there is an adequate remedy at law.

(b) The court may enforce a close corporation provision by injunction, specific performance, or other relief the court determines to be fair and equitable under the circumstances, including:

(1) damages instead of or in addition to specific enforcement;

(2) the appointment of a provisional director or custodian;

(3) the appointment of a receiver for specific assets of the close corporation in accordance with Section 11.403;

(4) the appointment of a receiver to rehabilitate the close corporation in accordance with Section 11.404;

(5) subject to Section 21.757, the liquidation of the assets and business and involuntary termination of the close corporation and appointment of a receiver to effect the liquidation in accordance with Section 11.405; and

(6) the termination of close corporation status.

(c) The court may not order termination of close corporation status under Subsection (b)(6) unless the court determines that:

(1) any other remedy in law or equity, including appointment of a provisional director, custodian, or other type of receiver, is inadequate; and

(2) the size, the nature of the business, or the number of shareholders of the close corporation, or their relationship to one another or other similar factors, make it wholly impractical to continue close corporation status.

Acts 2003, 78th Leg., ch. 182, § 1, eff. Jan. 1, 2006.

§ 21.757. Liquidation; Involuntary Winding Up and Termination; Receivership

Except as provided by Section 21.756, in a case in which a shareholder is entitled to wind up and terminate a close corporation under a shareholders' agreement, a court may not order liquidation, involuntary termination, or receivership under that section unless the court determines that any other remedy in law or equity, including appointment of a provisional director, custodian, or other type of receiver, is inadequate.

Acts 2003, 78th Leg., ch. 182, § 1, eff. Jan. 1, 2006.

§ 21.758. Appointment of Provisional Director

(a) In a judicial proceeding under this section, a court shall appoint a provisional director for a close corporation on presentation of proof that the directors or the persons empowered to manage the business and affairs of the close corporation under a shareholders' agreement are so divided with respect to the management of the business and affairs of the close corporation that the required votes or consent to take action on behalf of the close corporation cannot be obtained, resulting in the business and affairs being conducted in a manner that is not to the general advantage of the shareholders.

(b) The provisional director must be an impartial person who is not a shareholder, a party to a shareholders' agreement, a person empowered to manage the close corporation under a shareholders' agreement, or a creditor of the close corporation or of a subsidiary or affiliate of the close corporation. The court shall determine any further qualifications.

(c) A provisional director shall serve until removed by court order or by a vote of the majority of the directors or the holders of the majority of the shares with voting power, or by a vote of a different number, not fewer than the majority, of shareholders or directors if a close corporation provision requires the concurrence of a larger or different majority for action by the directors or shareholders.

Acts 2003, 78th Leg., ch. 182, § 1, eff. Jan. 1, 2006.

§ 21.759. Rights and Powers of Provisional Director

A provisional director has all the rights and powers of an elected director of the close corporation, or the rights of vote or consent of a shareholder and other rights and powers of shareholders or other persons who have been empowered to manage the business and affairs of the close corporation under a shareholders' agreement with the voting power provided by court order, including the right to notice of, and to vote at, meetings of directors or shareholders.

Acts 2003, 78th Leg., ch. 182, § 1, eff. Jan. 1, 2006.

§ 21.760. Compensation of Provisional Director

(a) The compensation of a provisional director shall be determined by an agreement between the provisional director and the close corporation, subject to court approval.

(b) The court may set the compensation in the absence of an agreement or in the event of a disagreement between the provisional director and the close corporation.

Acts 2003, 78th Leg., ch. 182, § 1, eff. Jan. 1, 2006.

§ 21.761. Appointment of Custodian

(a) In a judicial proceeding under this section, a court shall appoint a custodian for a close corporation on presentation of proof that:

(1) at a meeting held for the election of directors, the shareholders are so divided that the shareholders have failed to elect successors to directors whose terms have expired or would have expired on qualification of a successor;

(2) the business of the close corporation is suffering or is threatened with irreparable injury because the directors, or the shareholders or the persons empowered to manage the business and affairs of the close corporation under a shareholders' agreement, are so divided with respect to the management of the business and affairs of the close corporation that the required vote or consent to take action on behalf of the close corporation cannot be obtained and a remedy with respect to the deadlock in a close corporation provision has failed; or

(3) the plaintiff or intervenor has the right to wind up and terminate the close corporation under a shareholders' agreement as provided by Section 21.714.

(b) To be eligible to serve as a custodian, a person must comply with all the qualifications required to serve as a receiver under Section 11.406.

Acts 2003, 78th Leg., ch. 182, § 1, eff. Jan. 1, 2006.

§ 21.762. Powers and Duties of Custodian

A person who qualifies as a custodian has all of the powers and duties and the title of a receiver appointed under Sections 11.404–11.406. The custodian shall continue the business of the close corporation and may not liquidate the affairs or distribute the assets of the close corporation, except as provided by court order or Section 21.761(a)(3).

Acts 2003, 78th Leg., ch. 182, § 1, eff. Jan. 1, 2006.

§ 21.763. Termination of Custodianship

If the condition requiring the appointment of a custodian is remedied other than by liquidation or winding up and termination, the court shall terminate the custodianship immediately and management of the close corporation shall be restored to the directors or shareholders of the close corporation or to the persons empowered to manage the business and affairs of the close corporation under a shareholders' agreement.

Acts 2003, 78th Leg., ch. 182, § 1, eff. Jan. 1, 2006.

SUBCHAPTER Q. MISCELLANEOUS PROVISIONS

§ 21.801. Shares and Other Securities Are Personal Property

Except as otherwise provided by this code, the shares and other securities of a corporation are personal property.

Acts 2003, 78th Leg., ch. 182, § 1, eff. Jan. 1, 2006.

§ 21.802. Penalties for Late Filing of Certain Instruments

(a) A person required under Title 1 or this title to file a change of registered office or agent, a certificate of voluntary withdrawal, or a certificate of termination for a corporation commits an offense if the person does not file the required filing with the secretary of state before the earlier of:

(1) the 30th day after the date of the change, withdrawal, or termination; or

(2) the date the filing is otherwise required by law.

(b) A person who violates Subsection (a) is liable to the state for a civil penalty in an amount not to exceed $2,500 for each violation. In determining the amount of a penalty under this subsection, the court shall consider all the circumstances giving rise to the offense. The attorney general or the prosecuting attorney in the county in which the violation occurs may bring suit to recover the civil penalty imposed under this section.

(c) The attorney general may bring an action in the name of the state to restrain or enjoin a person from violating this section.

(d) In an action or proceeding brought against a person who has not complied with this section, the plaintiff or other party bringing the suit or proceeding may recover, at the court's discretion, reasonable costs and attorney's fees incurred by locating and effecting service of process on the person. Any damages recovered must be in conjunction with a pending action or proceeding and shall be awarded as costs under the Texas Rules of Civil Procedure. This section does not create a private independent cause of action for failure to comply with this section.

(e) A person who is entitled to recover damages under Subsection (d) may request from the attorney general nonconfidential information on the other person for the purpose of effecting service of process. The attorney general shall comply with a request made under this subsection to the extent practicable.

Acts 2003, 78th Leg., ch. 182, § 1, eff. Jan. 1, 2006.

CHAPTER 22. NONPROFIT CORPORATIONS

SUBCHAPTER A. GENERAL PROVISIONS

Section
22.001. Definitions.
22.002. Meetings by Remote Communications Technology.

SUBCHAPTER B. PURPOSES AND POWERS

22.051. General Purposes.
22.052. Dental Health Service Corporation.
22.053. Dividends Prohibited.
22.054. Authorized Benefits and Distributions.
22.055. Power to Assist Employee or Officer.
22.056. Health Organization Corporation.
22.0561. Corporations Formed by Physicians and Physician Assistants.

SUBCHAPTER C. FORMATION AND GOVERNING DOCUMENTS

22.101. Incorporation of Certain Organizations.
22.102. Bylaws.
22.103. Inconsistency Between Certificate of Formation and Bylaw.
22.104. Organization Meeting.
22.105. Procedures to Adopt Amendment to Certificate of Formation by Members Having Voting Rights.
22.106. Procedures to Adopt Amendment to Certificate of Formation by Managing Members.
22.107. Procedures to Adopt Amendment to Certificate of Formation by Board of Directors.
22.108. Number of Amendments Subject to Vote at Meeting.
22.109. Restated Certificate of Formation.

SUBCHAPTER D. MEMBERS

22.151. Members.
22.152. Immunity From Liability.
22.153. Annual Meeting.
22.154. Failure to Call Annual Meeting.
22.155. Special Meetings of Members.
22.156. Notice of Meeting.
22.157. Special Bylaws Affecting Notice.
22.158. Preparation and Inspection of List of Voting Members.

Section
22.159. Quorum of Members.
22.160. Voting of Members.
22.161. Election of Directors.
22.162. Greater Voting Requirements Under Certificate of Formation.
22.163. Record Date for Determination of Members.
22.164. Vote Required to Approve Fundamental Action.

SUBCHAPTER E. MANAGEMENT
22.201. Management by Board of Directors.
22.202. Management by Members.
22.203. Board Member Eligibility Requirements.
22.204. Number of Directors.
22.205. Designation of Initial Board of Directors.
22.206. Election or Appointment of Board of Directors.
22.207. Election and Control by Certain Entities.
22.208. Term of Office.
22.209. Classification of Directors.
22.210. Ex Officio Member of Board.
22.211. Removal of Director.
22.2111. Resignation of Director.
22.212. Vacancy.
22.213. Quorum.
22.214. Action by Directors.
22.215. Voting in Person or by Proxy.
22.216. Term and Revocability of Proxy.
22.217. Notice of Meeting; Waiver of Notice.
22.218. Management Committee.
22.219. Other Committees.
22.220. Action Without Meeting of Directors or Committee.
22.221. General Standards for Directors.
22.222. Religious Corporation Director's Good Faith Reliance on Certain Information.
22.223. Not a Trustee.
22.224. Delegation of Investment Authority.
22.225. Loan to Director Prohibited.
22.226. Director Liability for Certain Distributions of Assets.
22.227. Dissent to Action.
22.228. Reliance on Written Opinion of Attorney.
22.229. Right to Contribution.
22.230. Contracts or Transactions Involving Interested Directors, Officers, and Members.
22.231. Officers.
22.232. Election or Appointment of Officers.
22.233. Application to Church.
22.234. Religious Corporation Officer's Good Faith Reliance on Certain Information.
22.235. Officer Liability.

SUBCHAPTER F. FUNDAMENTAL BUSINESS TRANSACTIONS
22.251. Approval of Merger.
22.252. Approval of Sale of All or Substantially All of Assets.
22.253. Meeting of Members; Notice.
22.254. Pledge, Mortgage, Deed of Trust, or Trust Indenture.
22.255. Conveyance by Corporation.
22.256. Approval of Conversion.
22.257. Approval of Exchange.

SUBCHAPTER G. WINDING UP AND TERMINATION
Section
22.301. Approval of Voluntary Winding Up, Reinstatement, Revocation of Voluntary Winding Up, or Distribution Plan.
22.302. Certain Procedures for Approval.
22.303. Meeting of Members; Notice.
22.304. Application and Distribution of Property.
22.305. Distribution Plan.
22.306. Repealed.
22.307. Responsibility for Winding Up.

SUBCHAPTER H. RECORDS AND REPORTS
22.351. Member's Right to Inspect Books and Records.
22.352. Financial Records and Annual Reports.
22.353. Availability of Financial Information for Public Inspection.
22.354. Failure to Maintain Financial Record or Prepare Annual Report; Offense.
22.355. Exemptions from Certain Requirements Relating to Financial Records and Annual Reports.
22.356. Corporations Assisting State Agencies.
22.357. Report of Domestic and Foreign Corporations.
22.358. Notice Regarding Report.
22.359. Filing of Report.
22.360. Failure to File Report.
22.361. Notice of Forfeiture.
22.362. Effect of Forfeiture.
22.363. Revival of Right to Conduct Affairs.
22.364. Failure to Revive; Termination or Revocation.
22.365. Reinstatement.

SUBCHAPTER I. CHURCH BENEFITS BOARDS
22.401. Definition.
22.402. Pensions and Benefits.
22.403. Contributions.
22.404. Power to Act as Trustee.
22.405. Documents and Agreements.
22.406. Indemnification.
22.407. Protection of Benefits.
22.408. Assignment of Benefits.
22.409. Insurance Code Not Applicable.

SUBCHAPTER A. GENERAL PROVISIONS

§ 22.001. Definitions

In this chapter:

(1) "Board of directors" means the group of persons vested with the management of the affairs of the corporation, regardless of the name used to designate the group.

(2) "Bylaws" means the rules adopted to regulate or manage the corporation, regardless of the name used to designate the rules.

(3) "Corporation" or "domestic corporation" means a domestic nonprofit corporation subject to this chapter.

(4) "Foreign corporation" means a foreign nonprofit corporation.

(5) "Nonprofit corporation" means a corporation no part of the income of which is distributable to a member, director, or officer of the corporation.

(6) "Ordinary care" means the care that an ordinarily prudent person in a similar position would exercise under similar circumstances.

Acts 2003, 78th Leg., ch. 182, § 1, eff. Jan. 1, 2006.

§ 22.002. Meetings by Remote Communications Technology

Subject to the provisions of this code and the certificate of formation and bylaws of a corporation, a meeting of the members of a corporation, the board of directors of a corporation, or any committee designated by the board of directors of a corporation may be held by means of a remote electronic communications system, including videoconferencing technology or the Internet, only if:

(1) each person entitled to participate in the meeting consents to the meeting being held by means of that system; and

(2) the system provides access to the meeting in a manner or using a method by which each person participating in the meeting can communicate concurrently with each other participant.

Acts 2003, 78th Leg., ch. 182, § 1, eff. Jan. 1, 2006.

SUBCHAPTER B. PURPOSES AND POWERS

§ 22.051. General Purposes

A nonprofit corporation may be formed for any lawful purpose or purposes not expressly prohibited under this chapter or Chapter 2, including any purpose described by Section 2.002.

Acts 2003, 78th Leg., ch. 182, § 1, eff. Jan. 1, 2006.

§ 22.052. Dental Health Service Corporation

(a) A charitable corporation may be formed to operate a dental health service corporation that manages and coordinates the relationship between a dentist who contracts to perform dental services and a patient who will receive the services as a member of a group that contracted with the dental health service corporation to provide dental care to group members.

(b) The certificate of formation for a charitable corporation formed under this section must have attached as an exhibit:

(1) an affidavit of the organizer or organizers stating:

(A) that not less than 30 percent of the dentists legally engaged in the practice of dentistry in this state have signed a contract to perform the required dental services for a period of at least one year after incorporation; and

(B) the names and addresses of those dentists; and

(2) a certification by the State Board of Dental Examiners that:

(A) the applicants are reputable residents of this state of good moral character; and

(B) the corporation will be in the best interest of the public health.

(c) A corporation formed under this section must have at least 12 directors, including 9 directors who are licensed to practice dentistry in this state and are actively engaged in the practice of dentistry in this state.

(d) A corporation formed under this section shall maintain as participating or contracting dentists at least 30 percent of the number of dentists actually engaged in the practice of dentistry in this state. The corporation shall file annually in September with the State Board of Dental Examiners the name and address of each participating or contracting dentist.

(e) A corporation formed under this section may not:

(1) prevent a patient from selecting the licensed dentist of the patient's choice to provide dental services to the patient;

(2) deny a licensed dentist the right to participate as a contracting dentist to perform the dental services contracted for by the patient;

(3) discriminate among patients or licensed dentists regarding payment or reimbursement for the cost of performing dental services; or

(4) authorize any person to regulate, interfere with, or intervene in any manner in the diagnosis or treatment provided by a licensed dentist to a patient.

(f) A corporation formed under this section may require the attending dentist to provide a narrative oral or written description of the dental services provided to determine benefits or provide proof of treatment. The corporation may request but may not require diagnostic aids used in the course of treatment.

Acts 2003, 78th Leg., ch. 182, § 1, eff. Jan. 1, 2006.

§ 22.053. Dividends Prohibited

A dividend may not be paid to, and no part of the income of a corporation may be distributed to, the corporation's members, directors, or officers.

Acts 2003, 78th Leg., ch. 182, § 1, eff. Jan. 1, 2006.

§ 22.054. Authorized Benefits and Distributions

A corporation may:

(1) pay compensation in a reasonable amount to the members, directors, or officers of the corporation for services provided;

(2) confer benefits on the corporation's members in conformity with the corporation's purposes; and

(3) make distributions to the corporation's members on winding up and termination to the extent authorized by this chapter.

Acts 2003, 78th Leg., ch. 182, § 1, eff. Jan. 1, 2006.

§ 22.055. Power to Assist Employee or Officer

(a) A corporation may lend money to or otherwise assist an employee or officer of the corporation, but not a director, if the loan or assistance may reasonably be expected to directly or indirectly benefit the corporation.

(b) A loan made to an officer must be:

(1) made for the purpose of financing the officer's principal residence; or

(2) set in an original principal amount that does not exceed:

(A) 100 percent of the officer's annual salary, if the loan is made before the first anniversary of the officer's employment; or

(B) 50 percent of the officer's annual salary, if the loan is made in any subsequent year.

Acts 2003, 78th Leg., ch. 182, § 1, eff. Jan. 1, 2006.

§ 22.056. Health Organization Corporation

(a) Doctors of medicine and osteopathy licensed by the Texas State Board of Medical Examiners and podiatrists licensed by the Texas State Board of Podiatric Medical Examiners may form a corporation that is jointly owned, managed, and controlled by those practitioners to perform a professional service that falls within the scope of practice of those practitioners and consists of:

(1) carrying out research in the public interest in medical science, medical economics, public health, sociology, or a related field;

(2) supporting medical education in medical schools through grants or scholarships;

(3) developing the capabilities of individuals or institutions studying, teaching, or practicing medicine, including podiatric medicine;

(4) delivering health care to the public; or

(5) instructing the public regarding medical science, public health, hygiene, or a related matter.

(b) When doctors of medicine, osteopathy, and podiatry form a corporation that is jointly owned by those practitioners, the authority of each of the practitioners is limited by the scope of practice of the respective practitioners and none can exercise control over the other's clinical authority granted by their respective licenses, either through agreements, the certificate of formation or bylaws of the corporation, directives, financial incentives, or other arrangements that would assert control over treatment decisions made by the practitioner. The Texas State Board of Medical Examiners and the Texas State Board of Podiatric Medical Examiners continue to exercise regulatory authority over their respective licenses.

Acts 2003, 78th Leg., ch. 182, § 1, eff. Jan. 1, 2006.

§ 22.0561. Corporations Formed by Physicians and Physician Assistants

(a) Physicians licensed under Subtitle B, Title 3, Occupations Code, and physician assistants licensed under Chapter 204, Occupations Code, may form a corporation to perform a professional service that falls within the scope of practice of those practitioners and consists of:

(1) carrying out research in the public interest in medical science, medical economics, public health, sociology, or a related field;

(2) supporting medical education in medical schools through grants or scholarships;

(3) developing the capabilities of individuals or institutions studying, teaching, or practicing medicine or acting as a physician assistant;

(4) delivering health care to the public; or

(5) instructing the public regarding medical science, public health, hygiene, or a related matter.

(b) A physician assistant may not be an officer of the corporation.

(c) A physician assistant may not contract with or employ a physician to be a supervising physician of the physician assistant or of any physician in the corporation.

(d) The authority of each practitioner is limited by the scope of practice of the respective practitioner. An organizer of the entity must be a physician and ensure that a physician or physicians control and manage the entity.

(e) Nothing in this section may be construed to allow the practice of medicine by someone not licensed as a physician under Subtitle B, Title 3, Occupations Code, or to allow a person not licensed as a physician to direct the activities of a physician in the practice of medicine.

(f) A physician assistant or combination of physician assistants may have only a minority ownership interest in an entity created under this section. The ownership interest of an individual physician assistant may not equal or exceed the ownership interest of any individual physician owner. A physician assistant or combination of physician assistants may not interfere with the practice of medicine by a physician owner or the supervision of physician assistants by a physician owner.

(g) The Texas Medical Board and the Texas Physician Assistant Board continue to exercise regulatory authority over their respective license holders according to applicable law. To the extent of a conflict between Subtitle B, Title 3, Occupations Code, and Chapter 204, Occupations Code, or any rules adopted under those statutes, Subtitle B, Title 3, or a rule adopted under that subtitle controls.

Added by Acts 2011, 82nd Leg., ch. 782 (H.B. 2098), § 1, eff. June 17, 2011.

Section 6 of Acts 2011, 82nd Leg., ch. 782 (H.B. 2098) provides:

"The restrictions on ownership interests in Sections 22.0561, 152.0551, and 301.012, Business Organizations Code, apply to an ownership interest acquired on or after the effective date [June 17, 2011] of this Act. An ownership interest acquired before the effective date of this Act is governed by the law in effect at the time the interest was acquired, and the former law is continued in effect for that purpose."

SUBCHAPTER C. FORMATION AND GOVERNING DOCUMENTS

§ 22.101. Incorporation of Certain Organizations

A religious society, a charitable, benevolent, literary, or social association, or a church may incorporate as a corporation governed by this chapter with the consent of a majority of its members. Those members shall authorize the organizers to execute the certificate of formation.

Acts 2003, 78th Leg., ch. 182, § 1, eff. Jan. 1, 2006.

§ 22.102. Bylaws

(a) The initial bylaws of a corporation shall be adopted by the corporation's board of directors or, if the management of the corporation is vested in the corporation's members, by the members.

(b) The bylaws may contain provisions for the regulation and management of the affairs of the corporation that are consistent with law and the certificate of formation.

(c) The board of directors may amend or repeal the bylaws, or adopt new bylaws, unless:

(1) this chapter or the corporation's certificate of formation wholly or partly reserves the power exclusively to the corporation's members;

(2) the management of the corporation is vested in the corporation's members; or

(3) in amending, repealing, or adopting a bylaw, the members expressly provide that the board of directors may not amend or repeal the bylaw.

Acts 2003, 78th Leg., ch. 182, § 1, eff. Jan. 1, 2006.

§ 22.103. Inconsistency Between Certificate of Formation and Bylaw

(a) A provision of a certificate of formation of a corporation that is inconsistent with a bylaw controls over the bylaw, except as provided by Subsection (b).

(b) A change in the number of directors by amendment to the bylaws controls over the number stated in the certificate of formation, unless the certificate of formation provides that a change in the number of directors may be made only by amendment to the certificate.

Acts 2003, 78th Leg., ch. 182, § 1, eff. Jan. 1, 2006.

§ 22.104. Organization Meeting

(a) After the certificate of formation is filed, the board of directors named in the certificate of formation of a corporation shall hold an organization meeting of the board, either in or out of this state, at the call of the organizers or a majority of the directors to adopt bylaws and elect officers and for other purposes determined by the board at the meeting. The organizers or directors calling the meeting shall send notice of the time and place of the meeting to each director named in the certificate of formation not later than the third day before the date of the meeting.

(b) A first meeting of the members may be held at the call of the majority of the directors on notice provided not later than the third day before the date of the meeting. The notice must state the purposes of the meeting.

(c) If the management of a corporation is vested in the corporation's members, the members shall hold the organization meeting on the call of an organizer. An organizer who calls the meeting shall:

(1) send notice of the time and place of the meeting to each member not later than the third day before the date of the meeting;

(2) if the corporation is a church, make an oral announcement of the time and place of the meeting at a regularly scheduled worship service before the meeting; or

(3) send notice of the meeting in the manner provided by the certificate of formation.

Acts 2003, 78th Leg., ch. 182, § 1, eff. Jan. 1, 2006. Amended by Acts 2005, 79th Leg., ch. 64, § 66, eff. Jan. 1, 2006.

§ 22.105. Procedures to Adopt Amendment to Certificate of Formation by Members Having Voting Rights

(a) Except as provided by Section 22.107(b), to amend the certificate of formation of a corporation with members having voting rights, the board of directors of the corporation must adopt a resolution specifying the proposed amendment and directing that the amendment be submitted to a vote at an annual or special meeting of the members having voting rights.

(b) Written notice containing the proposed amendment or a summary of the changes to be effected by the amendment shall be given to each member entitled to vote at the meeting within the time and in the manner provided by this chapter for giving notice of a meeting of members.

(c) The proposed amendment shall be adopted on receiving the vote required by Section 22.164.

Acts 2003, 78th Leg., ch. 182, § 1, eff. Jan. 1, 2006.

§ 22.106. Procedures to Adopt Amendment to Certificate of Formation by Managing Members

(a) To be approved, a proposed amendment to the certificate of formation of a corporation the management of the affairs of which is vested in the corporation's members under Section 22.202 must be submitted to a vote at an annual, regular, or special meeting of the members.

(b) Except as otherwise provided by the certificate of formation or bylaws, notice containing the proposed amendment or a summary of the changes to be effected by the amendment shall be given to the members within the time and in the manner provided by this chapter for giving notice of a meeting of members.

(c) The proposed amendment shall be adopted on receiving the vote required by Section 22.164.

Acts 2003, 78th Leg., ch. 182, § 1, eff. Jan. 1, 2006.

§ 22.107. Procedures to Adopt Amendment to Certificate of Formation by Board of Directors

(a) If a corporation has no members or has no members with voting rights, or in the case of an amendment under Subsection (b), an amendment to the corporation's certificate of formation shall be adopted at a meeting of the board of directors on receiving the vote of directors required by Section 22.164.

(b) Except as otherwise provided by the certificate of formation, the board of directors of a corporation with members having voting rights may, without member approval, adopt amendments to the certificate of formation to:

(1) extend the duration of the corporation if the corporation was incorporated when limited duration was required by law;

(2) delete the names and addresses of the initial directors;

(3) delete the name and address of the initial registered agent or registered office, if a statement of change is on file with the secretary of state; or

(4) change the corporate name by:

(A) substituting the word "corporation," "incorporated," "company," or "limited," or the abbreviation "corp.," "inc.," "co.," or "ltd.," for a similar word or abbreviation in the name; or

(B) adding, deleting, or changing a geographical attribution to the name.

Acts 2003, 78th Leg., ch. 182, § 1, eff. Jan. 1, 2006.

§ 22.108. Number of Amendments Subject to Vote at Meeting

Any number of amendments to the corporation's certificate of formation may be submitted to and voted on by a corporation's members at any one meeting of the members.

Acts 2003, 78th Leg., ch. 182, § 1, eff. Jan. 1, 2006.

§ 22.109. Restated Certificate of Formation

(a) The board of directors of a corporation may adopt a restated certificate of formation as provided by Subchapter B, Chapter 3, by following the same procedure to amend the corporation's certificate of formation provided by Sections 22.104–22.107, except that member approval is required only if the restated certificate of formation contains an amendment.

(b) A person shall file a restated certificate of formation as provided by Chapter 4, and the restated certificate of formation takes effect as provided by Subchapter B, Chapter 3.

Added by Acts 2005, 79th Leg., ch. 64, § 67, eff. Jan. 1, 2006.

SUBCHAPTER D. MEMBERS

§ 22.151. Members

(a) A corporation may have one or more classes of members or may have no members.

(b) If the corporation has one or more classes of members, the corporation's certificate of formation or bylaws must include:

(1) a designation of each class;

(2) the manner of the election or appointment of the members of each class; and

(3) the qualifications and rights of the members of each class.

(c) A corporation may issue a certificate, card, or other instrument evidencing membership rights, voting rights, or ownership rights as authorized by the certificate of formation or bylaws.

Acts 2003, 78th Leg., ch. 182, § 1, eff. Jan. 1, 2006.

§ 22.152. Immunity From Liability

The members of a corporation are not personally liable for a debt, liability, or obligation of the corporation.

Acts 2003, 78th Leg., ch. 182, § 1, eff. Jan. 1, 2006.

§ 22.153. Annual Meeting

(a) Except as provided by Subsection (b), a corporation shall hold an annual meeting of the members at a time that is stated in or determined in accordance with the corporation's bylaws.

(b) If the bylaws provide for more than one regular meeting of members each year, an annual meeting is not required. If an annual meeting is not required, directors may be elected at a meeting as provided by the bylaws.

Acts 2003, 78th Leg., ch. 182, § 1, eff. Jan. 1, 2006.

§ 22.154. Failure to Call Annual Meeting

(a) If the board of directors of a corporation fails to call the annual meeting of members when required, a member of the corporation may demand that the meeting be held within a reasonable time. The demand must be made in writing and sent to an officer of the corporation by registered mail.

(b) If a required annual meeting is not called before the 61st day after the date of demand, a member of the corporation may compel the holding of the meeting by legal action directed against the board of directors, and each of the extraordinary writs of common law and of courts of equity are available to the member to compel the holding of the meeting. Each member has a justiciable interest sufficient to enable the member to institute and prosecute the legal proceedings.

(c) Failure to hold a required annual meeting at the designated time does not result in the winding up and termination of the corporation.

Acts 2003, 78th Leg., ch. 182, § 1, eff. Jan. 1, 2006. Amended by Acts 2007, 80th Leg., ch. 688, § 87, eff. Sept. 1, 2007.

§ 22.155. Special Meetings of Members

A special meeting of the members of a corporation may be called by:

(1) the president;

(2) the board of directors;

(3) members having not less than one-tenth of the votes entitled to be cast at the meeting; or

(4) other officers or persons as provided by the certificate of formation or bylaws of the corporation.

Acts 2003, 78th Leg., ch. 182, § 1, eff. Jan. 1, 2006.

§ 22.156. Notice of Meeting

(a) A corporation other than a church shall provide written notice of the place, date, and time of a meeting of the members of the corporation and, if the meeting is a special meeting, the purpose or purposes for which the meeting is called. The notice shall be delivered to each member entitled to vote at the meeting not later than the 10th day and not earlier than the 60th day before the date of the meeting. Notice may be delivered personally or in accordance with Section 6.051(b).

(b) Notice of a meeting of the members of a corporation that is a church is sufficient if given by oral announcement at a regularly scheduled worship service before the meeting or as otherwise provided by the certificate of formation or bylaws of the corporation.

Acts 2003, 78th Leg., ch. 182, § 1, eff. Jan. 1, 2006.

§ 22.157. Special Bylaws Affecting Notice

(a) A corporation may provide in the corporation's bylaws that notice of an annual or regular meeting is not required.

(b) A corporation having more than 1,000 members at the time a meeting is scheduled or called may provide notice of a meeting by publication in a newspaper of general circulation in the community in which the principal office of the corporation is located, if the corporation provides for that notice in its bylaws.

Acts 2003, 78th Leg., ch. 182, § 1, eff. Jan. 1, 2006.

§ 22.158. Preparation and Inspection of List of Voting Members

(a) After setting a record date for the notice of a meeting, a corporation shall prepare an alphabetical list of the names of all its voting members. The list must identify:

(1) the members who are entitled to notice and the members who are not entitled to notice of the meeting;

(2) the address of each voting member; and

(3) the number of votes each voting member is entitled to cast at the meeting.

(b) Not later than the second business day after the date notice is given of a meeting for which a list was prepared in accordance with Subsection (a), and continuing through the meeting, the list of voting members must be available at the corporation's principal office or at a reasonable place in the municipality in which the meeting will be held, as identified in the notice of the meeting, for inspection by members entitled to vote at the meeting for the purpose of communication with other members concerning the meeting.

(c) A voting member or voting member's agent or attorney is entitled on written demand to inspect and, at the member's expense and subject to Section 22.351, copy the list at a reasonable time during the period the list is available for inspection.

(d) The corporation shall make the list of voting members available at the meeting. A voting member or voting member's agent or attorney is entitled to inspect the list at any time during the meeting or an adjournment of the meeting.

Acts 2003, 78th Leg., ch. 182, § 1, eff. Jan. 1, 2006.

§ 22.159. Quorum of Members

(a) Unless otherwise provided by the certificate of formation or bylaws of a corporation, members of the corporation holding one-tenth of the votes entitled to be cast, in person or by proxy, constitute a quorum.

(b) The vote of the majority of the votes entitled to be cast by the members present or represented by proxy at a meeting at which a quorum is present is the act of the members meeting, unless the vote of a greater number is required by law or the certificate of formation or bylaws.

(c) Unless otherwise provided by the certificate of formation or bylaws, a church incorporated before May 12, 1959, is considered to have provided in the certificate of formation or bylaws that members present at a meeting for which notice has been given constitute a quorum.

Acts 2003, 78th Leg., ch. 182, § 1, eff. Jan. 1, 2006.

§ 22.160. Voting of Members

(a) Each member of a corporation, regardless of class, is entitled to one vote on each matter submitted to a vote of the corporation's members, except to the extent that the voting rights of members of a class are limited, enlarged, or denied by the certificate of formation or bylaws of the corporation.

(b) A member may vote in person or, unless otherwise provided by the certificate of formation or bylaws, by proxy executed in writing by the member or the member's attorney-in-fact.

(c) Unless otherwise provided by the proxy, a proxy is revocable and expires 11 months after the date of its execution. A proxy may not be irrevocable for longer than 11 months.

(d) If authorized by the certificate of formation or bylaws of the corporation, a member vote on any matter may be conducted by mail, by facsimile transmission, by electronic message, or by any combination of those methods.

Acts 2003, 78th Leg., ch. 182, § 1, eff. Jan. 1, 2006.

§ 22.161. Election of Directors

(a) A member entitled to vote at an election of directors is entitled to vote, in person or by proxy, for as many persons as there are directors to be elected and for whose election the member has a right to vote.

(b) If expressly authorized by the corporation's certificate of formation, the member may cumulate the member's vote by:

(1) giving one candidate a number of votes equal to the number of the directors to be elected multiplied by the member's vote; or

(2) distributing the votes on the same principle among any number of the candidates.

(c) A member who intends to cumulate votes under Subsection (b) shall give written notice of the member's intention to the secretary of the corporation not later than the day preceding the date of the election.

Acts 2003, 78th Leg., ch. 182, § 1, eff. Jan. 1, 2006.

§ 22.162. Greater Voting Requirements Under Certificate of Formation

If the corporation's certificate of formation requires the vote or concurrence of a greater proportion of the members of a corporation than is required by this chapter with respect to an action to be taken by the members, the certificate of formation controls.

Acts 2003, 78th Leg., ch. 182, § 1, eff. Jan. 1, 2006.

§ 22.163. Record Date for Determination of Members

(a) The record date for determining members of a corporation may be set as provided by Section 6.101.

(b) If a record date is not set under Section 6.101:

(1) members on the date of the meeting who are otherwise eligible to vote are entitled to vote at the meeting;

(2) members at the close of business on the business day preceding the date notice is given, or if notice is waived, at the close of business on the business day preceding the date of the meeting, are entitled to notice of a meeting of members; and

(3) members at the close of business on the later of the day the board of directors adopts the resolution relating to the action or the 60th day before the date of the action are entitled to exercise any rights regarding any other lawful action.

(c) The record date for the determination of members entitled to notice of or to vote at a meeting is effective for an adjournment of the meeting unless the board of directors of a corporation sets a new date for determining the right to notice of or to vote at the adjournment.

Acts 2003, 78th Leg., ch. 182, § 1, eff. Jan. 1, 2006. Amended by Acts 2007, 80th Leg., ch. 688, § 88, eff. Sept. 1, 2007.

§ 22.164. Vote Required to Approve Fundamental Action

(a) In this section, "fundamental action" means:

(1) an amendment of a certificate of formation, including an amendment required for the cancellation of an event requiring winding up in accordance with Section 11.152(b);

(2) a voluntary winding up under Chapter 11;

(3) a revocation of a voluntary decision to wind up under Section 11.151;

(4) a cancellation of an event requiring winding up under Section 11.152(a);

(5) a reinstatement under Section 11.202;

(6) a distribution plan under Section 22.305;

(7) a plan of merger under Subchapter F;

(8) a sale of all or substantially all of the assets of a corporation under Subchapter F;

(9) a plan of conversion under Subchapter F; or

(10) a plan of exchange under Subchapter F.

(b) Except as otherwise provided by Subsection (c) or the certificate of formation in accordance with Section 22.162, the vote required for approval of a fundamental action is:

(1) at least two-thirds of the votes that members present in person or by proxy are entitled to cast at the meeting at which the action is submitted for a vote, if the corporation has members with voting rights;

(2) at least two-thirds of the votes of members present at the meeting at which the action is submitted for a vote, if the management of the affairs of the corporation is vested in the corporation's members under Section 22.202; or

(3) the affirmative vote of the majority of the directors in office, if the corporation has no members or has no members with voting rights.

(c) If any class of members is entitled to vote on the fundamental action as a class by the terms of the certificate of formation or the bylaws, the vote required for the approval of the fundamental action is the vote required by Subsection (b)(1) and at least two-thirds of the votes that the members of each class in person or by proxy are entitled to cast at the meeting at which the action is submitted for a vote.

Acts 2003, 78th Leg., ch. 182, § 1, eff. Jan. 1, 2006. Amended by Acts 2007, 80th Leg., ch. 688, § 89, eff. Sept. 1, 2007.

SUBCHAPTER E. MANAGEMENT

§ 22.201. Management by Board of Directors

Except as provided by Section 22.202, the affairs of a corporation are managed by a board of directors. The board of directors may be designated by any name appropriate to the customs, usages, or tenets of the corporation.

Acts 2003, 78th Leg., ch. 182, § 1, eff. Jan. 1, 2006.

§ 22.202. Management by Members

(a) The certificate of formation of a corporation may vest the management of the affairs of the corporation in the members of the corporation. If the corporation has a board of directors, the corporation may limit the authority of the board to the extent provided by the certificate of formation or bylaws.

(b) A corporation is considered to have vested the management of the corporation's affairs in the board of directors of the corporation in the absence of a provision to the contrary in the certificate of formation, unless the corporation is a church organized and operating under a congregational system that:

(1) was incorporated before January 1, 1994; and

(2) has the management of its affairs vested in the corporation's members.

Acts 2003, 78th Leg., ch. 182, § 1, eff. Jan. 1, 2006.

§ 22.203. Board Member Eligibility Requirements

A director of a corporation is not required to be a resident of this state or a member of the corporation unless the certificate of formation or a bylaw of the corporation imposes that requirement. The certificate of formation or bylaws may prescribe other qualifications for directors.

Acts 2003, 78th Leg., ch. 182, § 1, eff. Jan. 1, 2006.

§ 22.204. Number of Directors

(a) If the corporation has a board of directors, a corporation may not have fewer than three directors. The number of directors shall be set by, or in the manner provided by, the certificate of formation or bylaws of the corporation, except that the number of directors on the initial board of directors must be set by the certificate of formation.

(b) The number of directors may be increased or decreased by amendment to, or in the manner provided by, the certificate of formation or bylaws. A decrease in the number of directors may not shorten the term of an incumbent director.

(c) In the absence of a provision of the certificate of formation or a bylaw setting the number of directors or providing for the manner in which the number of directors shall be determined, the number of directors is the same as the number constituting the initial board of directors.

Acts 2003, 78th Leg., ch. 182, § 1, eff. Jan. 1, 2006.

§ 22.205. Designation of Initial Board of Directors

If the corporation is to be managed by a board of directors, the certificate of formation of a corporation must state the names of the members of the initial board of directors of the corporation.

Acts 2003, 78th Leg., ch. 182, § 1, eff. Jan. 1, 2006.

§ 22.206. Election or Appointment of Board of Directors

Directors other than the initial directors are elected, appointed, or designated in the manner provided by the certificate of formation or bylaws. If the method of election, designation, or appointment is not provided by the certificate of formation or bylaws, directors other than the initial directors are elected by the board of directors.

Acts 2003, 78th Leg., ch. 182, § 1, eff. Jan. 1, 2006.

§ 22.207. Election and Control by Certain Entities

(a) The board of directors of a religious, charitable, educational, or eleemosynary corporation may be affiliated with, elected, and controlled by an incorporated or unincorporated convention, conference, or association organized under the laws of this or another state, the membership of which is composed of representatives, delegates, or messengers from a church or other religious association.

(b) The board of directors of a corporation may be wholly or partly elected by one or more associations or corporations organized under the laws of this or another state if:

(1) the certificate of formation or bylaws of the corporation provide for that election; and

(2) the corporation has no members with voting rights.

Acts 2003, 78th Leg., ch. 182, § 1, eff. Jan. 1, 2006.

§ 22.208. Term of Office

(a) Unless the director resigns or is removed, a director on the initial board of directors of a corporation holds office until the first annual election of directors or for the period specified in the certificate of formation or bylaws of the corporation. Directors other than the initial directors are elected, appointed, or designated for the terms provided by the certificate of formation or bylaws.

(b) In the absence of a provision in the certificate of formation or bylaws setting the term of office for directors, a director holds office until the next annual election of directors and until a successor is elected, appointed, or designated and qualified.

(c) A director may be removed from office as provided in Section 22.211.

Acts 2003, 78th Leg., ch. 182, § 1, eff. Jan. 1, 2006. Amended by Acts 2005, 79th Leg., ch. 64, § 68, eff. Jan. 1, 2006.

§ 22.209. Classification of Directors

Directors may be divided into classes. The terms of office of the several classes are not required to be uniform.

Acts 2003, 78th Leg., ch. 182, § 1, eff. Jan. 1, 2006.

§ 22.210. Ex Officio Member of Board

(a) The certificate of formation or bylaws of a corporation may provide that a person may be an ex officio member of the board of directors of the corporation.

(b) A person designated as an ex officio member of the board is entitled to receive notice of and to attend board meetings.

(c) An ex officio member is not entitled to vote unless the certificate of formation or bylaws authorize the member to vote. An ex officio member of the board who is not entitled to vote does not have the duties or liabilities of a director provided by this chapter.

Acts 2003, 78th Leg., ch. 182, § 1, eff. Jan. 1, 2006.

§ 22.211. Removal of Director

(a) A director of a corporation may be removed from office under any procedure provided by the certificate of formation or bylaws of the corporation.

(b) In the absence of a provision for removal in the certificate of formation or bylaws, a director may be removed from office, with or without cause, by the persons entitled to elect, designate, or appoint the director. If the director was elected to office, removal requires an affirmative vote equal to the vote necessary to elect the director.

Acts 2003, 78th Leg., ch. 182, § 1, eff. Jan. 1, 2006.

§ 22.2111. Resignation of Director

Except as provided by the certificate of formation or bylaws, a director of a corporation may resign at any time by providing written notice to the corporation.

Added by Acts 2005, 79th Leg., ch. 64, § 69, eff. Jan. 1, 2006.

§ 22.212. Vacancy

(a) Unless otherwise provided by the certificate of formation or bylaws of the corporation, a vacancy in the board of directors of a corporation shall be filled by the affirmative vote of the majority of the remaining directors, regardless of whether that majority is less than a quorum. A director elected to fill a vacancy is elected for the unexpired term of the member's predecessor in office.

(b) A vacancy in the board occurring because of an increase in the number of directors shall be filled by election at an annual meeting or at a special meeting of members called for that purpose. If a corporation has no members or has no members with the right to vote on the vacancy, the vacancy shall be filled as provided by the certificate of formation or bylaws.

Acts 2003, 78th Leg., ch. 182, § 1, eff. Jan. 1, 2006.

§ 22.213. Quorum

(a) A quorum for the transaction of business by the board of directors of a corporation is the lesser of:

(1) the majority of the number of directors set by the corporation's bylaws or, in the absence of a bylaw setting the number of directors, a majority of the number of directors stated in the corporation's certificate of formation; or

(2) any number, not less than three, set as a quorum by the certificate of formation or bylaws.

(b) A director present by proxy at a meeting may not be counted toward a quorum.

Acts 2003, 78th Leg., ch. 182, § 1, eff. Jan. 1, 2006.

§ 22.214. Action by Directors

The act of a majority of the directors present in person or by proxy at a meeting at which a quorum is present is the act of the board of directors of a corporation, unless the act of a greater number is required by the certificate of formation or bylaws of the corporation.

Acts 2003, 78th Leg., ch. 182, § 1, eff. Jan. 1, 2006.

§ 22.215. Voting in Person or by Proxy

A director of a corporation may vote in person or, if authorized by the certificate of formation or bylaws of the corporation, by proxy executed in writing by the director.

Acts 2003, 78th Leg., ch. 182, § 1, eff. Jan. 1, 2006.

§ 22.216. Term and Revocability of Proxy

(a) A proxy expires three months after the date the proxy is executed.

(b) A proxy is revocable unless otherwise provided by the proxy or made irrevocable by law.

Acts 2003, 78th Leg., ch. 182, § 1, eff. Jan. 1, 2006.

§ 22.217. Notice of Meeting; Waiver of Notice

(a) Regular meetings of the board of directors of a corporation may be held with or without notice as prescribed by the corporation's bylaws.

(b) Special meetings of the board of directors shall be held with notice as prescribed by the bylaws. Attendance of a director at a meeting constitutes a waiver of notice, unless the director attends a meeting for the express purpose of objecting to the transaction of any business on the ground that the meeting is not lawfully called or convened.

(c) Unless required by the bylaws, the business to be transacted at, or the purpose of, a regular or special meeting of the board of directors is not required to be specified in the notice or waiver of notice of the meeting.

(d) Notice may be delivered personally or in accordance with Section 6.051(b).

Acts 2003, 78th Leg., ch. 182, § 1, eff. Jan. 1, 2006.

§ 22.218. Management Committee

(a) If authorized by the certificate of formation or bylaws of the corporation, the board of directors of a corporation, by resolution adopted by the majority of the directors in office, may designate one or more committees to have and exercise the authority of the board in the management of the corporation to the extent provided by:

(1) the resolution;

(2) the certificate of formation; or

(3) the bylaws.

(b) A committee designated under this section must consist of at least two persons. Except as provided by Subsection (b–1), the majority of the persons on the committee must be directors. If provided by the certificate of formation or bylaws, the remaining persons on the committee are not required to be directors.

(b–1) If a corporation is a religious institution and if provided by the corporation's certificate of formation or bylaws, a committee designated under this section may be composed entirely of persons who are not directors of the corporation.

(c) The designation of a committee and the delegation of authority to the committee does not operate to relieve the board of directors, or an individual director, of any responsibility imposed on the board or director by law. A committee member who is not a director has the same responsibility with respect to the committee as a committee member who is a director.

Acts 2003, 78th Leg., ch. 182, § 1, eff. Jan. 1, 2006. Amended by Acts 2009, 81st Leg., ch. 1007, § 1, eff. Sept. 1, 2009.

§ 22.219. Other Committees

(a) The board of directors of a corporation, by resolution adopted by the majority of the directors at a meeting at which a quorum is present, or the president, if authorized by a similar resolution of the board of directors or by the certificate of formation or bylaws of the corporation, may designate and appoint one or more committees that do not have the authority of the board of directors in the management of the corporation.

(b) The membership on a committee designated under this section may be limited to directors.

Acts 2003, 78th Leg., ch. 182, § 1, eff. Jan. 1, 2006.

§ 22.220. Action Without Meeting of Directors or Committee

(a) The certificate of formation or bylaws of a corporation may provide that an action required by this chapter to be taken at a meeting of the corporation's directors or an action that may be taken at a meeting of the directors or a committee may be taken without a meeting if a written consent, stating the action to be taken, is signed by the number of directors or committee members necessary to take that action at a meeting at which all of the directors or committee members are present and voting. The consent must state the date of each director's or committee member's signature.

(b) Prompt notice of the taking of an action by directors or a committee without a meeting by less than unanimous written consent shall be given to each director or committee member who did not consent in writing to the action.

Acts 2003, 78th Leg., ch. 182, § 1, eff. Jan. 1, 2006. Amended by Acts 2007, 80th Leg., ch. 688, § 90, eff. Sept. 1, 2007.

§ 22.221. General Standards for Directors

(a) A director shall discharge the director's duties, including duties as a committee member, in good faith, with ordinary care, and in a manner the director reasonably believes to be in the best interest of the corporation.

(b) A director is not liable to the corporation, a member, or another person for an action taken or not taken as a director if the director acted in compliance with this section. A person seeking to establish liability of a director must prove that the director did not act:

(1) in good faith;

(2) with ordinary care; and

(3) in a manner the director reasonably believed to be in the best interest of the corporation.

Acts 2003, 78th Leg., ch. 182, § 1, eff. Jan. 1, 2006.

§ 22.222. Religious Corporation Director's Good Faith Reliance on Certain Information

A director of a religious corporation, in the discharge of a duty imposed or power conferred on the director, including a duty imposed or power conferred as a committee member, may rely in good faith on information or on an opinion, report, or statement, including a financial statement or other financial data, concerning the corporation or another person that was prepared or presented by:

(1) a religious authority; or

(2) a minister, priest, rabbi, or other person whose position or duties in the religious organization the director believes justify reliance and confidence and whom the director believes to be reliable and competent in the matters presented.

Acts 2003, 78th Leg., ch. 182, § 1, eff. Jan. 1, 2006. Amended by Acts 2007, 80th Leg., ch. 688, § 91, eff. Sept. 1, 2007.

§ 22.223. Not a Trustee

A director of a corporation is not considered to have the duties of a trustee of a trust with respect to the corporation or with respect to property held or administered by the corporation, including property subject to restrictions imposed by the donor or transferor of the property.

Acts 2003, 78th Leg., ch. 182, § 1, eff. Jan. 1, 2006.

§ 22.224. Delegation of Investment Authority

(a) The board of directors of a corporation may:

(1) contract with an advisor who is an investment counsel or a trust company, bank, investment advisor, or investment manager; and

(2) confer on that advisor the authority to:

(A) purchase or otherwise acquire a stock, bond, security, or other investment on behalf of the corporation; and

(B) sell, transfer, or otherwise dispose of an asset or property of the corporation at a time and for a consideration the advisor considers appropriate.

(b) The board of directors may:

(1) confer on an advisor described by Subsection (a) other powers regarding the corporation's investments as the board considers appropriate; and

(2) authorize the advisor to hold title to an asset or property of the corporation, in the advisor's own name or in the name of a nominee, for the benefit of the corporation.

(c) The board of directors is not liable for an action taken or not taken by an advisor under this section if the board acted in good faith and with ordinary care in selecting the advisor. The board of directors may remove or replace the advisor, with or without cause, if the board considers that action appropriate or necessary.

Acts 2003, 78th Leg., ch. 182, § 1, eff. Jan. 1, 2006.

§ 22.225. Loan to Director Prohibited

(a) A corporation may not make a loan to a director.

(b) The directors of a corporation who vote for or assent to the making of a loan to a director, and any officer who participates in making the loan, are jointly and severally liable to the corporation for the amount of the loan until the loan is repaid.

Acts 2003, 78th Leg., ch. 182, § 1, eff. Jan. 1, 2006.

§ 22.226. Director Liability for Certain Distributions of Assets

(a) In addition to any other liability imposed by law on the directors of a corporation, the directors who vote for or assent to a distribution of assets other than in payment of the corporation's debts, when the corporation is insolvent or when distribution would render the corporation insolvent, or during the liquidation of the corporation, without the payment and discharge of or making adequate provisions for any known debt, obligation, or liability of the corporation, are jointly and severally liable to the corporation for the value of the assets distributed, to the extent that the debt, obligation, or liability is not paid and discharged.

(b) A director is not liable under this section if, in voting for or assenting to a distribution, the director:

(1) relied in good faith and with ordinary care on information or an opinion, report, or statement in accordance with Section 3.102;

(2) acting in good faith and with ordinary care, considered the assets of the corporation to be at least equal to their book value; or

(3) in determining whether the corporation made adequate provision for the discharge of all of its liabilities and obligations as provided in Section 11.053, relied in good faith and with ordinary care on financial statements of, or other information concerning, a person who was or became contractually obligated to discharge some or all of those liabilities or obligations.

Acts 2003, 78th Leg., ch. 182, § 1, eff. Jan. 1, 2006.

§ 22.227. Dissent to Action

(a) A director of a corporation who is present at a meeting of the board of directors at which action is taken on a corporate matter described by Section 22.226(a) is presumed to have assented to the action unless:

(1) the director's dissent has been entered in the minutes of the meeting;

(2) the director has filed a written dissent to the action with the person acting as the secretary of the meeting before the meeting is adjourned; or

(3) the director has sent a written dissent by registered mail to the secretary of the corporation immediately after the meeting has been adjourned.

(b) The right to dissent under this section does not apply to a director who voted in favor of the action.

Acts 2003, 78th Leg., ch. 182, § 1, eff. Jan. 1, 2006.

§ 22.228. Reliance on Written Opinion of Attorney

A director is not liable under Section 22.226 or 22.227 if, in the exercise of ordinary care, the director acted in good faith and in reliance on the written opinion of an attorney for the corporation.

Acts 2003, 78th Leg., ch. 182, § 1, eff. Jan. 1, 2006.

§ 22.229. Right to Contribution

A director against whom a claim is asserted under Section 22.226 or 22.227 and who is held liable on the claim is entitled to contribution from persons who accepted or received the distribution knowing the distribution to have been made in violation of that section, in proportion to the amounts received by those persons.

Acts 2003, 78th Leg., ch. 182, § 1, eff. Jan. 1, 2006.

§ 22.230. Contracts or Transactions Involving Interested Directors, Officers, and Members

(a) This section applies to a contract or transaction between a corporation and:

(1) one or more directors, officers, or members, or one or more affiliates or associates of one or more directors, officers, or members, of the corporation; or

(2) an entity or other organization in which one or more directors, officers, or members, or one or more affiliates or associates of one or more directors, officers, or members, of the corporation:

(A) is a managerial official or a member; or

(B) has a financial interest.

(b) An otherwise valid and enforceable contract or transaction is valid and enforceable, and is not void or voidable, notwithstanding any relationship or interest described by Subsection (a), if any one of the following conditions is satisfied :

(1) the material facts as to the relationship or interest and as to the contract or transaction are disclosed to or known by:

(A) the corporation's board of directors, a committee of the board of directors, or the members, and the board, the committee, or the members in good faith and with ordinary care authorize the contract or transaction by the affirmative vote of the majority of the disinterested directors, committee members or members, regardless of whether the disinterested directors, committee members or members constitute a quorum; or

(B) the members entitled to vote on the authorization of the contract or transaction, and the contract or transaction is specifically approved in good faith and with ordinary care by a vote of the members; or

(2) the contract or transaction is fair to the corporation when the contract or transaction is authorized, approved, or ratified by the board of directors, a committee of the board of directors, or the members.

(c) Common or interested directors or members of a corporation may be included in determining the presence of a quorum at a meeting of the board, a committee of the board, or members that authorizes the contract or transaction.

(d) A person who has the relationship or interest described by Subsection (a) may:

(1) be present at or participate in and, if the person is a director, member, or committee member, may vote at a meeting of the board of directors, of the members, or of a committee of the board that authorizes the contract or transaction; or

(2) sign, in the person's capacity as a director, member, or committee member, a written consent of the directors, members, or committee members to authorize the contract or transaction.

(e) If at least one of the conditions of Subsection (b) is satisfied, neither the corporation nor any of the corporation's shareholders will have a cause of action against any of the persons described by Subsection (a) for breach of duty with respect to the making, authorization, or performance of the contract or transaction because the person had the relationship or interest described by Subsection (a) or took any of the actions authorized by Subsection (d).

Acts 2003, 78th Leg., ch. 182, § 1, eff. Jan. 1, 2006. Amended by Acts 2011, 82nd Leg., ch. 139 (S.B. 748), § 33, eff. Sept. 1, 2011.

§ 22.231. Officers

(a) The officers of a corporation shall include a president and a secretary and may include one or more vice presidents, a treasurer, and other officers and assistant officers as considered necessary. Any two or more offices, other than the offices of president and secretary, may be held by the same person.

(b) A properly designated committee may perform the functions of an officer. A single committee may perform the functions of any two or more officers, including the functions of president and secretary.

(c) The officers of a corporation may be designated by other or additional titles as provided by the certificate of formation or bylaws of the corporation.

Acts 2003, 78th Leg., ch. 182, § 1, eff. Jan. 1, 2006.

§ 22.232. Election or Appointment of Officers

(a) An officer of a corporation shall be elected or appointed at the time, in the manner, and for the terms prescribed by the certificate of formation or bylaws of the corporation. The term of an officer may not exceed three years.

(b) If the certificate of formation or bylaws do not include provisions for the election or appointment of officers, the officers shall be elected or appointed annually by the board of directors or, if the management of the corporation is vested in the corporation's members, by the members.

Acts 2003, 78th Leg., ch. 182, § 1, eff. Jan. 1, 2006.

§ 22.233. Application to Church

A corporation that is a church is not required to have officers as provided by this subchapter. The duties and responsibilities of the officers may be vested in the corporation's board of directors or other designated body in any manner provided for by the certificate of formation or bylaws of the corporation.

Acts 2003, 78th Leg., ch. 182, § 1, eff. Jan. 1, 2006.

§ 22.234. Religious Corporation Officer's Good Faith Reliance on Certain Information

An officer of a religious corporation, in the discharge of a duty imposed or power conferred on the officer, may rely in good faith and with ordinary care on information or on an opinion, report, or statement, including a financial statement or other financial data, concerning the corporation or another person that was prepared or presented by:

(1) a religious authority; or

(2) a minister, priest, rabbi, or other person whose position or duties in the religious organization the officer believes justify reliance and confidence and whom the officer believes to be reliable and competent in the matters presented.

Acts 2003, 78th Leg., ch. 182, § 1, eff. Jan. 1, 2006. Amended by Acts 2007, 80th Leg., ch. 688, § 92, eff. Sept. 1, 2007.

§ 22.235. Officer Liability

(a) An officer is not liable to the corporation or any other person for an action taken or omission made by the officer in the person's capacity as an officer unless the officer's conduct was not exercised:

(1) in good faith;

(2) with ordinary care; and

(3) in a manner the officer reasonably believes to be in the best interest of the corporation.

(b) This section shall not affect the liability of the corporation for an act or omission of the officer.

Acts 2003, 78th Leg., ch. 182, § 1, eff. Jan. 1, 2006.

SUBCHAPTER F. FUNDAMENTAL BUSINESS TRANSACTIONS

§ 22.251. Approval of Merger

(a) A domestic corporation that is a party to a merger under Chapter 10 must approve the merger by complying with this section.

(b) If the corporation that is a party to the merger has no members or has no members with voting rights, the plan of merger must be approved by the vote of directors required by Section 22.164.

(c) If the management of the affairs of the corporation that is a party to the merger is vested in its members under Section 22.202, the plan of merger:

(1) must be submitted to a vote at an annual, regular, or special meeting of the members; and

(2) must be approved by the members by the vote required by Section 22.164.

(d) If the corporation that is a party to the merger has members with voting rights:

(1) the board of directors must adopt a resolution that:

(A) approves the plan of merger; and

(B) directs that the plan be submitted to a vote at an annual or special meeting of the members having voting rights; and

(2) the members must approve the plan of merger by the vote required by Section 22.164.

Acts 2003, 78th Leg., ch. 182, § 1, eff. Jan. 1, 2006.

§ 22.252. Approval of Sale of All or Substantially All of Assets

(a) A corporation must approve the sale of all or substantially all of its assets by complying with this section.

(b) If the corporation has no members or has no members with voting rights, the sale of all or substantially all of the assets of the corporation must be authorized by the vote of directors required by Section 22.164.

(c) If the management of the affairs of the corporation is vested in its members under Section 22.202, a resolution authorizing a sale of all or substantially all of the assets of the corporation:

(1) must be submitted to a vote at an annual, regular, or special meeting of the members; and

(2) must be approved by the members by the vote required by Section 22.164.

(d) If the corporation has members with voting rights:

(1) the board of directors of the corporation must adopt a resolution that:

(A) recommends the sale; and

(B) directs that the resolution be submitted to a vote at an annual or special meeting of the members having voting rights; and

(2) the members must approve the resolution by the vote required by Section 22.164.

(e) At the meeting required by Subsection (c) or (d), in addition to approving the resolution authorizing the sale, the members may set, or authorize the board of directors to set, the terms and conditions of the sale and the consideration to be received by the corporation for the sale by the same vote of members.

(f) After the members authorize a sale under Subsection (d), the board of directors may abandon the sale, subject to the rights of third parties under any contracts relating to the sale, without further action or approval by members.

(g) Notwithstanding Subsection (d), if a corporation is insolvent, a sale of all or substantially all of the assets of the corporation may be authorized on receiving the affirmative vote of the majority of the directors in office.

(h) The phrase "sale of all or substantially all of the assets" means the sale, lease, exchange, or other disposition, other than a pledge, mortgage, deed of trust, or trust indenture unless otherwise provided by the certificate of formation, of all or substantially all of the property and assets of a domestic corporation that is not made in the usual and regular course of the corporation's activities without regard to whether the disposition is made with the goodwill of the corporation's activities. The term does not include a transaction that results in the corporation directly or indirectly:

(1) continuing to engage in one or more activities; or

(2) applying a portion of the consideration received in connection with the transaction to the conduct of an activity that the corporation engages in after the transaction.

Acts 2003, 78th Leg., ch. 182, § 1, eff. Jan. 1, 2006.

§ 22.253. Meeting of Members; Notice

(a) The corporation must give to each member entitled to vote at a meeting described by Section 22.251(c) or (d) or Section 22.252(c) or (d) a written notice stating that the purpose or one of the purposes of the meeting is to consider the plan of merger or the sale of all or substantially all of the assets of the corporation. The notice must be given in the time and manner provided by Chapter 6 and this chapter for giving notice of a meeting to members.

(b) A vote of members entitled to vote at the meeting shall be taken on the plan of merger or the resolution authorizing the sale of all or substantially all of the assets of the corporation. The members must approve the plan or resolution by the vote required by Section 22.164.

(c) For a meeting to vote on a plan of merger, the notice of the meeting must contain the plan of merger or a summary of the plan of merger.

(d) For a corporation the management of the affairs of which is vested in its members under Section 22.202, the notice of the meeting is subject to the provisions of the certificate of formation or bylaws of the corporation.

Acts 2003, 78th Leg., ch. 182, § 1, eff. Jan. 1, 2006.

§ 22.254. Pledge, Mortgage, Deed of Trust, or Trust Indenture

(a) Except as otherwise provided by Subsection (b) or by the corporation's certificate of formation:

(1) the board of directors of a corporation may authorize a pledge, mortgage, deed of trust, or trust indenture; and

(2) an authorization or consent of members is not required for the validity of the transaction or for any sale under the terms of the transaction.

(b) If the management of the affairs of a corporation is vested in the corporation's members under Section 22.202:

(1) the members may authorize a pledge, mortgage, deed of trust, or trust indenture in the manner provided by Section 22.252(c) for a sale of all or substantially all of the assets of a corporation; and

(2) an authorization by the board of directors is not required for the validity of the transaction or for any sale under the terms of the transaction.

Acts 2003, 78th Leg., ch. 182, § 1, eff. Jan. 1, 2006.

§ 22.255. Conveyance by Corporation

A corporation may convey real property of the corporation when authorized by appropriate resolution of the board of directors or members.

Acts 2003, 78th Leg., ch. 182, § 1, eff. Jan. 1, 2006.

§ 22.256. Approval of Conversion

(a) A domestic corporation must approve a conversion under Chapter 10 by complying with this section.

(b) If the corporation has no members or has no members with voting rights, the plan of conversion must be approved by the vote of directors required by Section 22.164.

(c) If the management of the affairs of the corporation is vested in its members under Section 22.202, the plan of conversion:

(1) must be submitted to a vote at an annual, regular, or special meeting of the members; and

(2) must be approved by the members by the vote required by Section 22.164.

(d) If the corporation has members with voting rights:

(1) the board of directors must adopt a resolution that:

(A) approves the plan of conversion; and

(B) directs that the plan be submitted to a vote at an annual or special meeting of the members having voting rights; and

(2) the members must approve the plan of conversion by the vote required by Section 22.164.

Acts 2003, 78th Leg., ch. 182, § 1, eff. Jan. 1, 2006.

§ 22.257. Approval of Exchange

(a) A domestic corporation must approve an exchange under Chapter 10 by complying with this section.

(b) If the corporation has no members or has no members with voting rights, the plan of exchange must be approved by the vote of directors required by Section 22.164.

(c) If the management of the affairs of the corporation is vested in its members under Section 22.202, the plan of exchange:

(1) must be submitted to a vote at an annual, regular, or special meeting of the members; and

(2) must be approved by the members by the vote required by Section 22.164.

(d) If the corporation has members with voting rights:

(1) the board of directors must adopt a resolution that:

(A) approves the plan of exchange; and

(B) directs that the plan be submitted to a vote at an annual or special meeting of the members having voting rights; and

(2) the members must approve the plan of exchange by the vote required by Section 22.164.

Acts 2003, 78th Leg., ch. 182, § 1, eff. Jan. 1, 2006.

SUBCHAPTER G. WINDING UP AND TERMINATION

§ 22.301. Approval of Voluntary Winding Up, Reinstatement, Revocation of Voluntary Winding Up, or Distribution Plan

A corporation must approve a voluntary winding up in accordance with Chapter 11, a reinstatement in accordance with Section 11.202, a cancellation of an event requiring winding up under Section 11.152(a), a revocation of a voluntary decision to wind up in accordance with Section 11.151, or a distribution plan in accordance with Section 22.305 by complying with the procedures prescribed by this subchapter.

Acts 2003, 78th Leg., ch. 182, § 1, eff. Jan. 1, 2006. Amended by Acts 2007, 80th Leg., ch. 688, § 93, eff. Sept. 1, 2007.

§ 22.302. Certain Procedures for Approval

To approve a voluntary winding up, a reinstatement, a cancellation of an event requiring winding up, a revocation of a voluntary decision to wind up, or a distribution plan, a corporation must follow the following procedures:

(1) if the corporation has no members or has no members with voting rights, the corporation's board of directors must adopt a resolution to wind up, to reinstate, to cancel the event requiring winding up, to revoke a voluntary decision to wind up, or to effect the distribution plan by the vote of directors required by Section 22.164;

(2) if the management of the affairs of the corporation is vested in the corporation's members under Section 22.202, the winding up, reinstatement, cancellation of event requiring winding up, revocation of voluntary decision to wind up, or distribution plan:

(A) must be submitted to a vote at an annual, regular, or special meeting of members; and

(B) must be approved by the members by the vote required by Section 22.164; or

(3) if the corporation has members with voting rights:

(A) the corporation's board of directors must approve a resolution:

(i) recommending the winding up, reinstatement, cancellation of event requiring winding up, revocation of a voluntary decision to wind up, or distribution plan; and

(ii) directing that the winding up, reinstatement, cancellation of event requiring winding up, revocation of a voluntary decision to wind up, or distribution plan of the corporation be submitted to a vote at an annual or special meeting of members; and

(B) the members must approve the action described by Paragraph (A) in accordance with Section 22.303.

Acts 2003, 78th Leg., ch. 182, § 1, eff. Jan. 1, 2006.

§ 22.303. Meeting of Members; Notice

(a) The corporation must give to each member entitled to vote at a meeting described by Section 22.302(2) or (3) a written notice stating that the purpose or one of the purposes of the meeting is to consider the winding up, reinstatement, cancellation of event requiring winding up, revocation of the voluntary decision to wind up, or distribution plan of the corporation. The notice must be given in the time and manner provided by Chapter 6 and this chapter for the giving of notice of a meeting to members.

(b) A vote of members entitled to vote at the meeting shall be taken on the resolution to wind up, reinstate, cancel the event requiring winding up, revoke the voluntary decision to wind up, or effect the distribution plan of the corporation. The members must approve the resolution by the vote required under Section 22.164.

(c) For a meeting to vote on a distribution plan, the notice of the meeting must contain the proposed plan of distribution or a summary of the plan.

(d) For a corporation the management of the affairs of which is vested in its members under Section 22.202, the notice of the meeting is subject to the provisions of the certificate of formation or bylaws of the corporation.

Acts 2003, 78th Leg., ch. 182, § 1, eff. Jan. 1, 2006.

§ 22.304. Application and Distribution of Property

(a) After all liabilities and obligations of a corporation in the process of winding up are paid, satisfied, and discharged in accordance with Section 11.053, the property of the corporation shall be applied and distributed as follows:

(1) property held by the corporation on a condition requiring return, transfer, or conveyance because of the winding up or termination shall be returned, transferred, or conveyed in accordance with that requirement; and

(2) unless otherwise provided by the corporation's certificate of formation, the remaining property of the corporation shall be distributed only for tax-exempt purposes to one or more organizations that are exempt under Section 501(c)(3), Internal Revenue Code, or described by Section 170(c)(1) or (2), Internal Revenue Code, under a plan of distribution adopted under this chapter.

(b) A district court of the county in which the corporation's principal office is located shall distribute to one or more organizations exempt under Section 501(c)(3), Internal Revenue Code, or described by Section 170(c)(1) or (2), Internal Revenue Code, the property of the corporation remaining after a distribution of property under the plan of distribution. The court shall make the distribution in the manner the court determines will best accomplish the general purposes for which the corporation was organized.

Acts 2003, 78th Leg., ch. 182, § 1, eff. Jan. 1, 2006.

§ 22.305. Distribution Plan

A plan providing for the distribution of property may be adopted by a corporation in the process of winding up, and shall be adopted by a corporation to authorize a transfer or conveyance of assets for which this chapter requires a plan of distribution, in the manner provided by this subchapter.

Acts 2003, 78th Leg., ch. 182, § 1, eff. Jan. 1, 2006.

§ 22.306. Repealed by Acts 2007, 80th Leg., ch. 688, § 144(1), eff. Sept. 1, 2007

§ 22.307. Responsibility for Winding Up

If a corporation determines or is required to wind up, the winding up of the corporation's affairs shall be managed by:

(1) the directors, if management of the affairs is not vested in the corporation's members under Section 22.202; or

(2) the members, if management of the affairs is vested in the corporation's members under Section 22.202.

Acts 2003, 78th Leg., ch. 182, § 1, eff. Jan. 1, 2006.

SUBCHAPTER H. RECORDS AND REPORTS

§ 22.351. Member's Right to Inspect Books and Records

A member of a corporation, on written demand stating the purpose of the demand, is entitled to examine and copy at the member's expense, in person or by agent, accountant, or attorney, at any reasonable time and for a proper purpose, the books and records of the corporation relevant to that purpose.

Acts 2003, 78th Leg., ch. 182, § 1, eff. Jan. 1, 2006.

§ 22.352. Financial Records and Annual Reports

(a) A corporation shall maintain current and accurate financial records with complete entries as to each financial transaction of the corporation, including income and expenditures, in accordance with generally accepted accounting principles.

(b) Based on the records maintained under Subsection (a), the board of directors of the corporation shall annually prepare or approve a financial report for the corporation for the preceding year. The report must conform to accounting standards as adopted by the American Institute of Certified Public Accountants and must include:

(1) a statement of support, revenue, and expenses;

(2) a statement of changes in fund balances;

(3) a statement of functional expenses; and

(4) a balance sheet for each fund.

Acts 2003, 78th Leg., ch. 182, § 1, eff. Jan. 1, 2006.

§ 22.353. Availability of Financial Information for Public Inspection

(a) A corporation shall keep records, books, and annual reports of the corporation's financial activity at the corporation's registered or principal office in this state for at least three years after the close of the fiscal year.

(b) The corporation shall make the records, books, and reports available to the public for inspection and copying at the corporation's registered or principal office during regular business hours. The corporation may charge a reasonable fee for preparing a copy of a record or report.

Acts 2003, 78th Leg., ch. 182, § 1, eff. Jan. 1, 2006.

§ 22.354. Failure to Maintain Financial Record or Prepare Annual Report; Offense

(a) A corporation commits an offense if the corporation fails to maintain a financial record, prepare an annual report, or make the record or report available to the public in the manner required by Section 22.353.

(b) An offense under this section is a Class B misdemeanor.

Acts 2003, 78th Leg., ch. 182, § 1, eff. Jan. 1, 2006.

§ 22.355. Exemptions from Certain Requirements Relating to Financial Records and Annual Reports

Sections 22.352, 22.353, and 22.354 do not apply to:

(1) a corporation that solicits funds only from members of the corporation;

(2) a corporation that does not intend to solicit and receive and does not actually raise or receive during a fiscal year contributions in an amount exceeding $10,000 from a source other than its own membership;

(3) a private or independent institution of higher education described by Section 61.003, Education Code, accredited by a recognized accrediting agency as defined by Section 61.003, Education Code, a postsecondary educational institution authorized to grant degrees under a certificate of authority issued by the Texas Higher Education Coordinating Board or a foundation chartered for the benefit of the institution or any component part of the institution, a career school or college that has received a certificate of approval from the Texas Workforce Commission, a public institution of higher education or a foundation chartered for the benefit of the institution or any component part of the institution, or an elementary or secondary school;

(4) a religious institution that is a church, an ecclesiastical or denominational organization, or another established physical place for worship at which religious services are the primary activity and are regularly conducted;

(5) a trade association or professional society the income of which is principally derived from membership dues and assessments, sales, or services;

(6) an insurer licensed and regulated by the Texas Department of Insurance; or

(7) an alumni association of a public or private institution of higher education in this state that is recognized and acknowledged as the official alumni association by the institution.

Acts 2003, 78th Leg., ch. 182, § 1, eff. Jan. 1, 2006. Amended by Acts 2005, 79th Leg., ch. 64, § 70, eff. Jan. 1, 2006.

§ 22.356. Corporations Assisting State Agencies

(a) In this section, "state agency" means:

(1) a board, commission, department, office, or other entity that is in the executive branch of state government and that was created by the constitution or a statute of this state, including an institution of higher education as defined by Section 61.003, Education Code;

(2) the legislature or a legislative agency; or

(3) the supreme court, the court of criminal appeals, a court of appeals, the state bar, or another state judicial agency.

(b) The books and records of a corporation other than a bona fide alumni association are subject to audit at the discretion of the state auditor if:

(1) the corporation's charter specifically dedicates the corporation's activities to the benefit of a particular state agency; and

(2) a board member, officer, or employee of that state agency sits on the board of directors of the corporation in other than an ex officio capacity.

(c) If the corporation's charter specifically dedicates the corporation's activities to the benefit of a particular state agency but the conditions described by Subsection (b)(2) do not exist, a corporation shall file with the secretary of state a copy of the report required by Section 22.352(b) for the preceding fiscal year not later than the 89th day after the last day of the corporation's fiscal year.

Acts 2003, 78th Leg., ch. 182, § 1, eff. Jan. 1, 2006.

§ 22.357. Report of Domestic and Foreign Corporations

(a) The secretary of state may require a domestic corporation or a foreign corporation registered to conduct affairs in this state to file a report in accordance with Chapter 4 not more than once every four years as required by this subchapter. The report must state:

(1) the name of the corporation;

(2) the state or country under the laws of which the corporation is incorporated;

(3) the address of the registered office of the corporation in this state and the name of the registered agent at that address;

(4) if the corporation is a foreign corporation, the address of the principal office of the corporation in the state or country under the laws of which the corporation is incorporated; and

(5) the names and addresses of the directors and officers of the corporation.

(b) A corporation required to prepare a report under this section shall prepare the report on a form adopted by the secretary of state for that purpose and shall include in the report information that is accurate as of the date the report is executed. An officer or, if the corporation is in the hands of a receiver or trustee, the receiver or trustee shall sign the report on behalf of the corporation.

Acts 2003, 78th Leg., ch. 182, § 1, eff. Jan. 1, 2006.

§ 22.358. Notice Regarding Report

(a) The secretary of state shall send written notice that the report required by Section 22.357 is due. The notice must be:

(1) addressed to the corporation; and

(2) mailed to the corporation's registered agent or to the corporation at:

(A) the last known address of the corporation as it appears on record in the office of the secretary of state; or

(B) any other known place of business of the corporation.

(b) The secretary of state shall include with the notice a report form to be prepared and filed as provided by this subchapter.

Acts 2003, 78th Leg., ch. 182, § 1, eff. Jan. 1, 2006.

§ 22.359. Filing of Report

A copy of the report must be filed with the secretary of state in accordance with Chapter 4 not later than the 30th day after the date notice is mailed under Section 22.358.

Acts 2003, 78th Leg., ch. 182, § 1, eff. Jan. 1, 2006.

§ 22.360. Failure to File Report

(a) A domestic or foreign corporation that fails to file a report under Sections 22.357 and 22.359 when the report is due forfeits the corporation's right to conduct affairs in this state.

(b) The forfeiture takes effect, without judicial action, when the secretary of state enters on the record of the corporation kept in the office of the secretary of state:

(1) the words "right to conduct affairs forfeited"; and

(2) the date of forfeiture.

Acts 2003, 78th Leg., ch. 182, § 1, eff. Jan. 1, 2006.

§ 22.361. Notice of Forfeiture

Notice of forfeiture under Section 22. 360 shall be mailed to the corporation's registered agent at the registered office or to the corporation at:

(1) the address of the principal place of business of the corporation as it appears in the certificate of formation;

(2) the last known address of the corporation as it appears on record in the office of the secretary of state; or

(3) any other known place of business of the corporation.

Acts 2003, 78th Leg., ch. 182, § 1, eff. Jan. 1, 2006.

§ 22.362. Effect of Forfeiture

(a) Unless the right of the corporation to conduct affairs in this state is revived under Section 22.363:

(1) the corporation may not maintain an action, suit, or proceeding in a court of this state; and

(2) a successor or assignee of the corporation may not maintain an action, suit, or proceeding in a court of this state on a right, claim, or demand arising from the conduct of affairs by the corporation in this state.

(b) This section does not affect the right of an assignee of the corporation as:

(1) the holder in due course of a negotiable promissory note, check, or bill of exchange; or

(2) the bona fide purchaser for value of a warehouse receipt, stock certificate, or other instrument negotiable by law.

(c) The forfeiture of the right to conduct affairs in this state does not:

(1) impair the validity of a contract or act of the corporation; or

(2) prevent the corporation from defending an action, suit, or proceeding in a court of this state.

Acts 2003, 78th Leg., ch. 182, § 1, eff. Jan. 1, 2006.

§ 22.363. Revival of Right to Conduct Affairs

(a) A corporation may be relieved from a forfeiture under Section 22.360 by filing the required report, accompanied by the revival fee, not later than the 120th day after the date of mailing of the notice of forfeiture under Section 22.361.

(b) If a corporation complies with Subsection (a), the secretary of state shall:

(1) revive the right of the corporation to conduct affairs in this state;

(2) cancel the words regarding the forfeiture on the record of the corporation; and

(3) endorse on that record the word "revived" and the date of revival.

Acts 2003, 78th Leg., ch. 182, § 1, eff. Jan. 1, 2006.

§ 22.364. Failure to Revive; Termination or Revocation

(a) The failure of a corporation that has forfeited its right to conduct affairs in this state to revive that right under Section 22.363 is grounds for:

(1) the involuntary termination of the domestic corporation; or

(2) the revocation of the foreign corporation's registration to transact business in this state.

(b) The termination or revocation takes effect, without judicial action, when the secretary of state enters on the record of the corporation filed in the office of the secretary of state the word "forfeited" and the date of forfeiture and cites this chapter as authority for that forfeiture.

Acts 2003, 78th Leg., ch. 182, § 1, eff. Jan. 1, 2006.

§ 22.365. Reinstatement

(a) A corporation that is terminated or the registration of which has been revoked as provided by Section 22.364 may be relieved of the termination or revocation by filing the report required by Section 22.357, accompanied by the filing fee for the report, if the corporation has paid:

(1) all fees, taxes, penalties, and interest due and accruing before the termination or revocation; and

(2) an amount equal to the total taxes from the date of termination or revocation to the date of reinstatement that would have been payable if the corporation had not been terminated or had its registration revoked.

(b) When the report is filed and the filing fee is paid to the secretary of state, the secretary of state shall:

(1) reinstate the certificate of formation or registration without judicial action;

(2) cancel the word "forfeited" on the record; and

(3) endorse on the record kept in the secretary's office relating to the corporation the words "set aside" and the date of the reinstatement.

(c) If a termination or revocation is set aside under this section, the corporation shall determine from the secretary of state whether the name of the corporation is available. If the name of the corporation is not available at the time of reinstatement, the corporation shall amend its corporate name under this code.

Acts 2003, 78th Leg., ch. 182, § 1, eff. Jan. 1, 2006.

SUBCHAPTER I. CHURCH BENEFITS BOARDS

§ 22.401. Definition

In this chapter, "church benefits board" means an organization described by Section 414(e)(3)(A), Internal Revenue Code, that:

(1) has the principal purpose or function of administering or funding a plan or program to provide retirement benefits, welfare benefits, or both for the ministers or employees of a church or a conference, convention, or association of churches; and

(2) is controlled by or affiliated with a church or a conference, convention, or association of churches.

Acts 2003, 78th Leg., ch. 182, § 1, eff. Jan. 1, 2006.

§ 22.402. Pensions and Benefits

When authorized by the corporation's members or as otherwise provided by law, a domestic or foreign nonprofit corporation formed for a religious purpose may provide, directly or through a separate church benefits board, for the support and payment of benefits and pensions to:

(1) the ministers, teachers, employees, trustees, directors, or other functionaries of the corporation;

(2) the ministers, teachers, employees, trustees, directors, or other functionaries of organizations

controlled by or affiliated with a church or a conference, convention, or association of churches under the jurisdiction and control of the corporation; and

(3) the spouse, children, dependents, or other beneficiaries of the persons described by Subdivisions (1) and (2).

Acts 2003, 78th Leg., ch. 182, § 1, eff. Jan. 1, 2006.

§ 22.403. Contributions

(a) A church benefits board may provide for:

(1) the collection of contributions and other payments to assist in providing pensions and benefits under this subchapter; and

(2) the creation, maintenance, investment, management, and disbursement of necessary annuities, endowments, reserves, or other funds for a purpose under Subdivision (1).

(b) A church benefits board may receive payments from a trust fund or corporation that funds a church plan as defined by Section 414(e), Internal Revenue Code.

Acts 2003, 78th Leg., ch. 182, § 1, eff. Jan. 1, 2006.

§ 22.404. Power to Act as Trustee

A church benefits board may act as:

(1) a trustee under a lawful trust committed to the board by contract, will, or otherwise; and

(2) an agent for the performance of a lawful act relating to the purposes of the trust.

Acts 2003, 78th Leg., ch. 182, § 1, eff. Jan. 1, 2006.

§ 22.405. Documents and Agreements

A church benefits board may provide to a program participant a certificate or agreement of participation, a debenture, or an indemnification agreement, as appropriate to accomplish the purposes of the board.

Acts 2003, 78th Leg., ch. 182, § 1, eff. Jan. 1, 2006.

§ 22.406. Indemnification

A church benefits board, or an affiliate wholly owned by the board, may agree to indemnify against damage or risk of loss:

(1) a minister, teacher, employee, trustee, functionary, or director affiliated with the board or a family member, dependent, or beneficiary of one of those persons;

(2) a church or a convention, conference, or association of churches; or

(3) an organization that is controlled by or affiliated with the board or with a church or a convention, conference, or association of churches.

Acts 2003, 78th Leg., ch. 182, § 1, eff. Jan. 1, 2006.

§ 22.407. Protection of Benefits

(a) Money or other benefits that have been or will be provided to a participant or a beneficiary under a plan or program provided by or through a church benefits board under this subchapter are not subject to execution, attachment, garnishment, or other process and may not be appropriated or applied as part of a judicial, legal, or equitable process or operation of a law other than a constitution to pay a debt or liability of the participant or beneficiary.

(b) This section does not apply to a qualified domestic relations order or an amount required by the church benefits board to recover costs or expenses incurred in the plan or program.

Acts 2003, 78th Leg., ch. 182, § 1, eff. Jan. 1, 2006.

§ 22.408. Assignment of Benefits

An assignment or transfer or an attempt to make an assignment or transfer by a beneficiary of money, benefits, or other rights under a plan or program under this subchapter is void if:

(1) the plan or program contains a provision prohibiting the assignment or other transfer without the written consent of the church benefits board; and

(2) the beneficiary assigns or transfers or attempts to make an assignment or transfer without that consent.

Acts 2003, 78th Leg., ch. 182, § 1, eff. Jan. 1, 2006.

§ 22.409. Insurance Code Not Applicable

The Insurance Code does not apply to a church benefits board or a program, plan, benefit, or activity of the board or a person affiliated with the board.

Acts 2003, 78th Leg., ch. 182, § 1, eff. Jan. 1, 2006.

CHAPTER 23. SPECIAL–PURPOSE CORPORATIONS

SUBCHAPTER A. GENERAL PROVISIONS

Section
23.001. Determination of Applicable Law.
23.002. Applicability of Filing Requirements.
23.003. Domestic Corporation Organized Under Special Statute.

SUBCHAPTER B. BUSINESS DEVELOPMENT CORPORATIONS

Section
23.051. Definitions.
23.052. Organizers.
23.053. Purposes.
23.054. Powers.
23.055. Statewide Operation.
23.056. Certificate of Formation.
23.057. Management by Board of Directors; Number of Directors.
23.058. Election or Appointment of Directors.
23.059. Term of Office; Vacancy.
23.060. Officers.
23.061. Participation as Owner.
23.062. Financial Institution as Member of Corporation.
23.063. Withdrawal of Member.
23.064. Powers of Shareholders and Members.
23.065. Voting by Shareholder or Member.
23.066. Loan to Corporation.
23.067. Prohibited Loan.
23.068. Loan Limits.
23.069. Surplus.
23.070. Depository.
23.071. Annual Report; Provision of Required Information.

SUBCHAPTER C. GRAND LODGES

23.101. Formation.
23.102. Applicability of Chapter 22.
23.103. Duration.
23.104. Subordinate Lodges.
23.105. Trustees and Directors.
23.106. Franchise Taxes.
23.107. General Powers.
23.108. Authority Regarding Property.
23.109. Authority Regarding Loans.
23.110. Winding Up and Termination of Subordinate Body.

SUBCHAPTER A. GENERAL PROVISIONS

§ 23.001. Determination of Applicable Law

(a) A corporation created under this chapter or under a special statute outside this code, to the extent not inconsistent with a special statute regarding a particular corporation, is governed by:

(1) Title 1 and Chapter 21, if the corporation is organized for profit; and

(2) Title 1 and Chapter 22, if the corporation is organized not for profit.

(b) If a special statute does not contain any provision regarding a matter provided for in Title 1 or Chapter 21 or 22, or if the special statute specifically provides that the general laws for corporations supplement the statute, to the extent consistent with the special statute:

(1) Title 1 and Chapter 21 apply to a corporation organized for profit; and

(2) Title 1 and Chapter 22 apply to a corporation organized not for profit.

Acts 2003, 78th Leg., ch. 182, § 1, eff. Jan. 1, 2006.

§ 23.002. Applicability of Filing Requirements

Except as otherwise provided by the special statute, a document to be filed with the secretary of state under a special statute shall be executed and filed in accordance with Chapter 4.

Acts 2003, 78th Leg., ch. 182, § 1, eff. Jan. 1, 2006.

§ 23.003. Domestic Corporation Organized Under Special Statute

A corporation organized under a special statute other than this code is not considered a "domestic corporation" formed under this code, although this code may apply to the corporation.

Acts 2003, 78th Leg., ch. 182, § 1, eff. Jan. 1, 2006.

SUBCHAPTER B. BUSINESS DEVELOPMENT CORPORATIONS

§ 23.051. Definitions

In this subchapter:

(1) "Corporation" means a business development corporation organized under this subchapter.

(2) "Financial institution" means a banking corporation or trust company, savings and loan association, governmental agency, insurance company, or related corporation, partnership, foundation, or other institution engaged primarily in lending or investing funds.

(3) "Loan limit" means the maximum amount permitted to be outstanding at one time on loans made by a member to a corporation.

(4) "Member" means a financial institution authorized to do business in this state that undertakes to lend money to a corporation.

Acts 2003, 78th Leg., ch. 182, § 1, eff. Jan. 1, 2006.

§ 23.052. Organizers

Subject to The Securities Act (Article 581–1 et seq., Vernon's Texas Civil Statutes), 25 or more persons, the majority of whom must be residents of this state, may form a business development corporation to promote, develop, and advance the prosperity and economic welfare of this state.

Acts 2003, 78th Leg., ch. 182, § 1, eff. Jan. 1, 2006.

§ 23.053. Purposes

(a) A business development corporation may be organized as a:

(1) for-profit corporation under Chapter 21; or

(2) nonprofit corporation under Chapter 22.

(b) In accordance with Section 3.005(a)(3), the certificate of formation of a business development corporation must state that the purposes of the corporation are to:

(1) promote, stimulate, develop, and advance the business prosperity and economic welfare of this state and the residents of this state;

(2) encourage and assist, through loans, investments, or other business transactions, new business and industry in this state;

(3) rehabilitate and assist existing industry in this state;

(4) stimulate and assist in the expansion of business activity that will tend to promote the business development and maintain the economic stability of this state, provide maximum opportunities for employment, encourage thrift, and improve the standard of living of the residents of this state;

(5) cooperate and act in conjunction with other public or private organizations in the promotion and advancement of industrial, commercial, agricultural, and recreational developments in this state; and

(6) provide financing for the promotion, development, and conduct of business activity in this state.

Acts 2003, 78th Leg., ch. 182, § 1, eff. Jan. 1, 2006. Amended by Acts 2007, 80th Leg., ch. 688, § 94, eff. Sept. 1, 2007.

§ 23.054. Powers

(a) The powers of a corporation include, in addition to the powers conferred on the corporation by Chapters 2 and 21 or 22, as applicable, the power to:

(1) elect, appoint, and employ officers, agents, and employees;

(2) make contracts and incur liabilities for a purpose of the corporation;

(3) borrow money on a secured or unsecured basis to carry out a purpose of the corporation;

(4) issue for the purpose of borrowing money a bond, debenture, note, or other evidence of indebtedness, whether secured or unsecured;

(5) secure an evidence of indebtedness by mortgage, pledge, deed of trust, or other lien on a property, franchise, right, or privilege of the corporation, or any part of or interest in those items, without securing shareholder or member approval;

(6) make a secured or unsecured loan and establish and regulate the terms and conditions of that loan and the charges for interest or service connected with that loan;

(7) purchase, receive, hold, lease, or otherwise acquire, and sell, convey, transfer, lease, or otherwise dispose of, property and exercise those rights and privileges incidental and appurtenant to the acquisition or disposal of the property and to the use of the property, including any property acquired by the corporation periodically in the satisfaction of a debt or enforcement of an obligation;

(8) acquire improved or unimproved real property to construct an industrial plant or other business establishment on the property or dispose of the real property for the construction of an industrial plant or other business establishment;

(9) acquire, construct or reconstruct, alter, repair, maintain, operate, sell, convey, transfer, lease, or otherwise dispose of an industrial plant or business establishment;

(10) protect the corporation's position as creditor by acquiring the goodwill, business, rights, property, including a share, bond, debenture, note, other evidence of indebtedness, other asset, or any part of an asset or interest in an asset, of a person to whom the corporation loaned money and assume, undertake, or pay an obligation, debt, or liability of the person;

(11) mortgage, pledge, or otherwise encumber any property, right, or thing of value, acquired under Subdivision (7), (8), (9), or (10), as security for the payment of a part of the purchase price;

(12) promote the establishment of local development corporations in the various communities of this state, enter into agreements with those local development corporations, and cooperate with, assist, or otherwise encourage the local foundations; and

(13) participate with a properly authorized federal lending agency in the making of loans.

(b) A corporation may approve an application for a loan under Subsection (a)(6) only if the applicant demonstrates that:

(1) the applicant applied for the loan through ordinary banking channels; and

(2) the loan has been refused by at least two banks or other financial institutions.

Acts 2003, 78th Leg., ch. 182, § 1, eff. Jan. 1, 2006.

§ 23.055. Statewide Operation

A corporation organized under this subchapter is a state development company as defined by Section 103, Small Business Investment Act of 1958 (15 U.S.C. Section 662), as amended, or similar federal legislation, and may operate on a statewide basis.

Acts 2003, 78th Leg., ch. 182, § 1, eff. Jan. 1, 2006.

§ 23.056. Certificate of Formation

(a) The certificate of formation of a corporation must state:

(1) the name of the corporation;

(2) the purpose or purposes for which the corporation is organized as required by Section 23.053; and

(3) any other information required by:

(A) Chapter 4; and

(B) Chapter 21 or 22, as applicable.

(b) The name of a corporation must include the words "Business Development Corporation."

Acts 2003, 78th Leg., ch. 182, § 1, eff. Jan. 1, 2006.

§ 23.057. Management by Board of Directors; Number of Directors

(a) The organization, control, and management of a corporation are vested in a board of directors. The board must consist of not fewer than 15 and not more than 21 directors.

(b) The board of directors may exercise any power of the corporation not conferred on the shareholders or members by law or by the corporation's bylaws.

Acts 2003, 78th Leg., ch. 182, § 1, eff. Jan. 1, 2006.

§ 23.058. Election or Appointment of Directors

(a) The organizers of a corporation shall name the directors constituting the initial board of directors of the corporation. Directors other than the initial directors shall be elected at each annual meeting of the corporation. If an annual meeting is not held at the time designated by the bylaws of the corporation, the directors shall be elected at a special meeting held in lieu of the annual meeting.

(b) At an annual meeting or special meeting held in lieu of the annual meeting, the members of the corporation shall elect two-thirds of the directors, and the shareholders of the corporation shall elect the remaining directors.

Acts 2003, 78th Leg., ch. 182, § 1, eff. Jan. 1, 2006. Amended by Acts 2007, 80th Leg., ch. 688, § 95, eff. Sept. 1, 2007.

§ 23.059. Term of Office; Vacancy

(a) A director of a corporation holds office until the next annual election of directors and until a successor is elected and qualified, unless the director is removed at an earlier date in accordance with the corporation's bylaws.

(b) A vacancy in the office of a director elected by the members shall be filled by the directors elected by the members, and a vacancy in the office of a director elected by the shareholders shall be filled by the directors elected by the shareholders.

Acts 2003, 78th Leg., ch. 182, § 1, eff. Jan. 1, 2006.

§ 23.060. Officers

The board of directors of a corporation shall appoint a president, a treasurer, and any other agent or officer of the corporation and shall fill each vacancy other than a vacancy on the board.

Acts 2003, 78th Leg., ch. 182, § 1, eff. Jan. 1, 2006.

§ 23.061. Participation as Owner

(a) An individual, corporation, or other organization authorized to conduct business in this state, including a public utility company, insurance and casualty company, or foreign corporation licensed to do business in this state, or a trust may acquire, purchase, hold, sell, assign, transfer, mortgage, pledge, or otherwise dispose of a bond, security, or other evidence of indebtedness created by, or shares of, the corporation.

(b) An owner of shares of the corporation may exercise any right, power, or privilege of that ownership, including the right to vote.

Acts 2003, 78th Leg., ch. 182, § 1, eff. Jan. 1, 2006.

§ 23.062. Financial Institution as Member of Corporation

(a) A financial institution may become a member of a corporation and may make loans to the corporation as provided by this chapter.

(b) A financial institution may request membership in the corporation by applying to the corporation's board of directors in the manner prescribed by the board. Membership in the corporation takes effect on the board's acceptance of the application.

(c) A financial institution that is a member of a corporation may acquire, purchase, hold, sell, assign, transfer, mortgage, pledge, or otherwise dispose of a bond, security, or other evidence of indebtedness created by, or a share of, the corporation. As owner of shares of the corporation, a financial institution may exercise any right, power, or privilege of that ownership, including the right to vote. A member of a corporation may not acquire shares of the corporation in an amount greater than 10 percent of the member's loan limit. The amount of shares of the corporation that a member may acquire is in addition to the amount of shares of corporations that the member may otherwise acquire.

(d) A financial institution that is not a member of the corporation may not acquire any shares of the corporation.

Acts 2003, 78th Leg., ch. 182, § 1, eff. Jan. 1, 2006.

§ 23.063. Withdrawal of Member

(a) On written notice to the corporation's board of directors, a member may withdraw from a corporation on the date stated in the notice. The date of a member's withdrawal must be at least six months after the date notice is given under this subsection.

(b) A member is not obligated to make a loan to the corporation pursuant to a call made after the date of the member's withdrawal from the corporation, but a member shall fulfill any obligation that has accrued or for which a commitment has been made before the withdrawal date.

Acts 2003, 78th Leg., ch. 182, § 1, eff. Jan. 1, 2006.

§ 23.064. Powers of Shareholders and Members

The shareholders and members of a corporation may:

(1) determine the number of directors and elect the directors as provided by Section 23.058;

(2) make, amend, and repeal bylaws of the corporation; or

(3) exercise any other power of the corporation that is conferred on the shareholders and members by the bylaws.

Acts 2003, 78th Leg., ch. 182, § 1, eff. Jan. 1, 2006.

§ 23.065. Voting by Shareholder or Member

(a) Each shareholder of a corporation has one vote, in person or by proxy, for each share held by the shareholder.

(b) Each member of a corporation has one vote in person or by proxy.

(c) A member with a loan limit that exceeds $1,000 has one additional vote, in person or by proxy, for each additional $1,000 the member may have outstanding on loans to the corporation at any one time as determined under Section 23.068.

Acts 2003, 78th Leg., ch. 182, § 1, eff. Jan. 1, 2006.

§ 23.066. Loan to Corporation

(a) When called on by a corporation to make a loan to the corporation, a member of the corporation shall make the loan on those terms and conditions periodically approved by the board of directors.

(b) A loan made to the corporation by a member shall be evidenced by a bond, debenture, note, or other evidence of indebtedness of the corporation that:

(1) is freely transferable at any time; and

(2) accrues interest at a rate of not less than one-fourth of one percent more than the rate of interest determined by the board of directors to be the prime rate prevailing on the date of issuance on unsecured commercial loans.

Acts 2003, 78th Leg., ch. 182, § 1, eff. Jan. 1, 2006.

§ 23.067. Prohibited Loan

(a) A member may not make a loan to a corporation if, immediately after the loan would be made, the total amount of the obligations of the corporation would exceed 50 times the capital of the corporation.

(b) For purposes of this section, the capital of the corporation includes the amount of the outstanding shares of the corporation, whether common or preferred, and the earned or paid-in surplus of the corporation.

Acts 2003, 78th Leg., ch. 182, § 1, eff. Jan. 1, 2006.

§ 23.068. Loan Limits

(a) A loan limit shall be established at the $1,000 amount nearest to the amount computed in accordance with this section.

(b) The total amount outstanding on loans made to a corporation by a member at any one time, when added to the amount of the investment in the shares of the corporation then held by the member, may not exceed:

(1) 20 percent of the total amount then outstanding on loans to the corporation by all members,

including outstanding amounts validly called for a loan but not yet loaned; or

(2) the following limit, to be determined as of the time the member becomes a member of the corporation, or at any time requested by a member on the basis of the audited balance sheet of the member at the close of its fiscal year immediately preceding its application for membership or, in the case of an insurance company, its last annual statement to the Texas Department of Insurance:

(A) an amount equal to the lesser of $750,000 or two percent of the capital and surplus of a commercial bank or trust company;

(B) an amount equal to one percent of the total outstanding loans made by a savings and loan association;

(C) an amount equal to one percent of the capital and unassigned surplus of a stock insurance company other than a fire insurance company;

(D) an amount equal to one percent of the unassigned surplus of a mutual insurance company other than a fire insurance company;

(E) an amount equal to one-tenth of one percent of the assets of a fire insurance company; or

(F) the limits approved by the board of directors of the corporation for a government pension fund or other financial institution.

(c) Subject to Subsection (b), each call made by the corporation shall be prorated among the members of the corporation in substantially the same proportion that the adjusted loan limit of each member bears to the aggregate of the adjusted loan limits of all members.

(d) For purposes of Subsection (c), the adjusted loan limit of a member is the amount of the member's loan limit, reduced by the balance of outstanding loans made by the member to the corporation and the investment in shares of the corporation held by the member at the time of the call.

Acts 2003, 78th Leg., ch. 182, § 1, eff. Jan. 1, 2006.

§ 23.069. Surplus

(a) A corporation shall set apart as earned surplus not less than 10 percent of the corporation's net earnings each year until the surplus, with any unimpaired surplus paid in, is equal to one-half of the amount paid in on the shares then outstanding. The surplus shall be kept to secure against losses and contingencies. If the surplus becomes impaired, the surplus shall be reimbursed in the manner provided for its accumulation.

(b) Net earnings and surplus shall be determined by the board of directors after providing for the required reserves as the directors consider advisable. A good faith determination of net earnings and surplus by the directors under this subsection is conclusive.

Acts 2003, 78th Leg., ch. 182, § 1, eff. Jan. 1, 2006.

§ 23.070. Depository

(a) A corporation may deposit the corporation's funds in a banking institution that has been designated as a depository by a vote of the majority of the directors present at an authorized meeting of the board of directors of the corporation, excluding a director who is an officer or director of the designated depository.

(b) The corporation may not receive money on deposit.

Acts 2003, 78th Leg., ch. 182, § 1, eff. Jan. 1, 2006.

§ 23.071. Annual Report; Provision of Required Information

(a) A corporation shall annually make a report of its condition to the banking commissioner and the Texas Department of Insurance.

(b) A corporation shall provide any information that is required by the secretary of state.

Acts 2003, 78th Leg., ch. 182, § 1, eff. Jan. 1, 2006.

SUBCHAPTER C. GRAND LODGES

§ 23.101. Formation

(a) An institution or order, by resolution or other consent of its members, may incorporate under this subchapter if the institution or order is:

(1) the grand lodge of Texas, Ancient, Free and Accepted Masons;

(2) the Grand Royal Arch Chapter of Texas;

(3) the Grand Commandery of Knights Templars of Texas;

(4) the grand lodge of the Independent Order of Odd Fellows of Texas; or

(5) another similar institution or order organized for charitable or benevolent purposes.

(b) A corporation formed under this subchapter shall file a certificate of formation in accordance with Chapter 4 that complies with this subchapter.

Acts 2003, 78th Leg., ch. 182, § 1, eff. Jan. 1, 2006.

§ 23.102. Applicability of Chapter 22

If this subchapter does not contain any provision regarding a matter provided for in Chapter 22, to the extent consistent with this subchapter, Chapter 22 applies to a corporation formed under this subchapter.

Acts 2003, 78th Leg., ch. 182, § 1, eff. Jan. 1, 2006.

§ 23.103. Duration

A grand body that incorporates under this subchapter may provide in the grand body's certificate of formation for the expiration of its corporate powers at the end of a stated number of years. If the certificate of formation does not provide for the duration of the grand body, the grand body has perpetual existence. The grand body may by its corporate name have perpetual succession of its officers and members.

Acts 2003, 78th Leg., ch. 182, § 1, eff. Jan. 1, 2006.

§ 23.104. Subordinate Lodges

(a) The incorporation of a grand body includes each of its subordinate lodges or bodies holding a warrant or charter under the grand body.

(b) A subordinate body has all of the rights of other corporations under and by the name given to the grand body in the warrant or charter issued to the grand body to which it is attached. Those rights shall be provided for in the charter of the grand body.

(c) A subordinate body is subject to the jurisdiction and control of its respective grand body, and the warrant or charter of the subordinate body may be revoked by the grand body.

Acts 2003, 78th Leg., ch. 182, § 1, eff. Jan. 1, 2006.

§ 23.105. Trustees and Directors

A grand body and a subordinate of the grand body may elect trustees and directors or may appoint trustees or directors from among their officers.

Acts 2003, 78th Leg., ch. 182, § 1, eff. Jan. 1, 2006.

§ 23.106. Franchise Taxes

A corporation formed under this subchapter is not subject to or required to pay a franchise tax, except that a corporation is exempt from the franchise tax imposed by Chapter 171, Tax Code, only if the corporation is exempted by that chapter.

Acts 2003, 78th Leg., ch. 182, § 1, eff. Jan. 1, 2006.

§ 23.107. General Powers

A grand body and a subordinate of the grand body may take action as directed or provided by law in the case of other corporations and may make constitutions and bylaws to govern their affairs.

Acts 2003, 78th Leg., ch. 182, § 1, eff. Jan. 1, 2006.

§ 23.108. Authority Regarding Property

(a) A grand body or subordinate body may acquire and hold property as necessary or convenient for a site on which to erect a building for the use and occupancy of the body and to erect homes and schools for members' widows or orphans or elderly, disabled, or indigent members and may sell or mortgage the property.

(b) A conveyance must be executed by the presiding officer and attested to by the secretary with the seal.

(c) The authority of a subordinate body to sell or to mortgage property is subject to the conditions periodically prescribed or established by the grand body to which the subordinate is attached.

Acts 2003, 78th Leg., ch. 182, § 1, eff. Jan. 1, 2006.

§ 23.109. Authority Regarding Loans

(a) A grand body incorporated under this subchapter may:

(1) loan money held and owned by the grand body for charitable purposes, for the endowment of any of the institutions of the grand body, or otherwise; and

(2) secure loans by taking and receiving liens on real property or by another method elected by the grand body.

(b) On sale of real property secured by a lien, a grand body may become the purchaser of the real property and hold title to the property.

Acts 2003, 78th Leg., ch. 182, § 1, eff. Jan. 1, 2006.

§ 23.110. Winding Up and Termination of Subordinate Body

(a) On the winding up and termination of a subordinate body attached to a grand body, all property and rights existing in the subordinate body pass to and vest in the grand body to which it was attached, subject to the payment of any debt owed by the subordinate body.

(b) Notwithstanding a grand body's liability for the debt of a subordinate body under Subsection (a), the grand body is not liable for an amount greater than the actual cash value of the subordinate body's effects or authority.

Acts 2003, 78th Leg., ch. 182, § 1, eff. Jan. 1, 2006.

TITLE 3. LIMITED LIABILITY COMPANIES

CHAPTER 101. LIMITED LIABILITY COMPANIES

SUBCHAPTER A. GENERAL PROVISIONS

Section
101.001. Definitions.
101.002. Applicability of Other Laws.

SUBCHAPTER B. FORMATION AND GOVERNING DOCUMENTS

101.051. Certain Provisions Contained in Certificate of Formation.
101.0515. Execution of Filings.
101.052. Company Agreement.
101.053. Amendment of Company Agreement.
101.054. Waiver or Modification of Certain Statutory Provisions Prohibited; Exceptions.

SUBCHAPTER C. MEMBERSHIP

101.101. Members Required.
101.102. Qualification for Membership.
101.103. Effective Date of Membership.
101.104. Classes or Groups of Members or Membership Interests.
101.105. Issuance of Membership Interests After Formation of Company.
101.106. Nature of Membership Interest.
101.107. Withdrawal or Expulsion of Member Prohibited.
101.108. Assignment of Membership Interest.
101.109. Rights and Duties of Assignee of Membership Interest Before Membership.
101.110. Rights and Liabilities of Assignee of Membership Interest After Becoming Member.
101.111. Rights and Duties of Assignor of Membership Interest.
101.1115. Effect of Death or Divorce on Membership Interest.
101.112. Member's Membership Interest Subject to Charging Order.
101.113. Parties to Actions.
101.114. Liability for Obligations.

SUBCHAPTER D. CONTRIBUTIONS

101.151. Requirements for Enforceable Promise.
101.152. Enforceable Promise Not Affected by Change in Circumstances.

Section
101.153. Failure to Perform Enforceable Promise; Consequences.
101.154. Consent Required to Release Enforceable Obligation.
101.155. Creditor's Right to Enforce Certain Obligations.
101.156. Requirements to Enforce Conditional Obligation.

SUBCHAPTER E. ALLOCATIONS AND DISTRIBUTIONS

101.201. Allocation of Profits and Losses.
101.202. Distribution in Kind.
101.203. Sharing of Distributions.
101.204. Interim Distributions.
101.205. Distribution on Withdrawal.
101.206. Prohibited Distribution; Duty to Return.
101.207. Creditor Status With Respect to Distribution.
101.208 Record Date.

SUBCHAPTER F. MANAGEMENT

101.251. Governing Authority.
101.252. Management by Governing Authority.
101.253. Designation of Committees; Delegation of Authority.
101.254. Designation of Agents; Binding Acts.
101.255. Contracts or Transactions Involving Interested Governing Persons or Officers.

SUBCHAPTER G. MANAGERS

101.301. Applicability of Subchapter.
101.302. Number and Qualifications.
101.303. Term.
101.304. Removal.
101.305. Manager Vacancy.
101.306. Removal and Replacement of Manager Elected by Class or Group.
101.307. Methods of Classifying Managers.

SUBCHAPTER H. MEETINGS AND VOTING

101.351. Applicability of Subchapter.
101.352. General Notice Requirements.
101.353. Quorum.
101.354. Equal Voting Rights.
101.355. Act of Governing Authority, Members, or Committee.
101.356. Votes Required to Approve Certain Actions.
101.357. Manner of Voting.
101.358. Action by Less Than Unanimous Written Consent.
101.359. Effective Action by Members or Managers With or Without Meeting.

SUBCHAPTER I. MODIFICATION OF DUTIES; INDEMNIFICATION

101.401. Expansion or Restriction of Duties and Liabilities.
101.402. Permissive Indemnification, Advancement of Expenses, and Insurance or Other Arrangements.

SUBCHAPTER J. DERIVATIVE PROCEEDINGS

101.451. Definitions.
101.452. Standing to Bring Proceeding.
101.453. Demand.

Section
101.454. Determination by Governing or Independent Persons.
101.455. Stay of Proceeding.
101.456. Discovery.
101.457. Tolling of Statute of Limitations.
101.458. Dismissal of Derivative Proceeding.
101.459. Allegations if Demand Rejected.
101.460. Discontinuance or Settlement.
101.461. Payment of Expenses.
101.462. Application to Foreign Limited Liability Companies.
101.463. Closely Held Limited Liability Company.

SUBCHAPTER K. SUPPLEMENTAL RECORDKEEPING REQUIREMENTS
101.501. Supplemental Records Required for Limited Liability Companies.
101.502. Right to Examine Records and Certain Other Information.

SUBCHAPTER L. SUPPLEMENTAL WINDING UP AND TERMINATION PROVISIONS
101.551. Persons Eligible to Wind Up Company.
101.552. Approval of Voluntary Winding Up, Revocation, Cancellation, or Reinstatement.

SUBCHAPTER M. SERIES LIMITED LIABILITY COMPANY
101.601 Series of Members, Managers, Membership Interests, or Assets.
101.602 Enforceability of Obligations and Expenses of Series Against Assets.
101.603 Assets of Series.
101.604 Notice of Limitation on Liabilities of Series.
101.605 General Powers of Series.
101.606 Liability of Member or Manager for Obligations; Duties.
101.607 Class or Group of Members or Managers.
101.608 Governing Authority.
101.609 Applicability of Other Provisions of Chapter; Synonymous Terms.
101.610 Effect of Certain Event on Manager or Member.
101.611 Member Status with Respect to Distribution.
101.612 Record Date for Allocations and Distributions.
101.613 Distributions.
101.614 Authority to Wind Up and Terminate Series.
101.615 Termination of Series.
101.616 Event Requiring Winding Up.
101.617 Procedures for Winding Up and Termination of Series.
101.618 Revocation of Voluntary Winding Up.
101.619 Cancellation of Event Requiring Winding Up.
101.620 Continuation of Business.
101.621 Winding Up by Court Order.

SUBCHAPTER A. GENERAL PROVISIONS

§ 101.001. Definitions

In this title:

(1) "Company agreement" means any agreement, written or oral, of the members concerning the affairs or the conduct of the business of a limited liability company. A company agreement of a limited liability company having only one member is not unenforceable because only one person is a party to the company agreement.

(2) "Foreign limited liability company" or "foreign company" means a limited liability company formed under the laws of a jurisdiction other than this state.

(3) "Limited liability company" or "company" means a domestic limited liability company subject to this title.

Acts 2003, 78th Leg., ch. 182, § 1, eff. Jan. 1, 2006.

§ 101.002. Applicability of Other Laws

(a) Subject to Section 101.114, Sections 21.223, 21.224, 21.225, and 21.226 apply to a limited liability company and the company's members, owners, assignees, affiliates, and subscribers.

(b) For purposes of the application of Subsection (a):

(1) a reference to "shares" includes "membership interests";

(2) a reference to "holder," "owner," or "shareholder" includes a "member" and an "assignee";

(3) a reference to "corporation" or "corporate" includes a "limited liability company";

(4) a reference to "directors" includes "managers" of a manager-managed limited liability company and "members" of a member-managed limited liability company;

(5) a reference to "bylaws" includes "company agreement"; and

(6) the reference to "Sections 21.157–21.162" in Section 21.223(a)(1) refers to the provisions of Subchapter D of this chapter.

Added by Acts 2011, 82nd Leg., ch. 25 (S.B. 323), § 1, eff. Sept. 1, 2011.

SUBCHAPTER B. FORMATION AND GOVERNING DOCUMENTS

§ 101.051. Certain Provisions Contained in Certificate of Formation

(a) A provision that may be contained in the company agreement of a limited liability company may alternatively be included in the certificate of formation of the company as provided by Section 3.005(b).

(b) A reference in this title to the company agreement of a limited liability company includes any provision contained in the company's certificate of formation instead of the company agreement as provided by Subsection (a).

Acts 2003, 78th Leg., ch. 182, § 1, eff. Jan. 1, 2006.

§ 101.0515. Execution of Filings

Unless otherwise provided by this title, a filing instrument of a limited liability company must be signed by an authorized officer, manager, or member of the limited liability company.

Added by Acts 2007, 80th Leg., ch. 688, § 96, eff. Sept. 1, 2007.

§ 101.052. Company Agreement

(a) Except as provided by Section 101.054, the company agreement of a limited liability company governs:

(1) the relations among members, managers, and officers of the company, assignees of membership interests in the company, and the company itself; and

(2) other internal affairs of the company.

(b) To the extent that the company agreement of a limited liability company does not otherwise provide, this title and the provisions of Title 1 applicable to a limited liability company govern the internal affairs of the company.

(c) Except as provided by Section 101.054, a provision of this title or Title 1 that is applicable to a limited liability company may be waived or modified in the company agreement of a limited liability company.

(d) The company agreement may contain any provisions for the regulation and management of the affairs of the limited liability company not inconsistent with law or the certificate of formation.

Acts 2003, 78th Leg., ch. 182, § 1, eff. Jan. 1, 2006.

§ 101.053. Amendment of Company Agreement

The company agreement of a limited liability company may be amended only if each member of the company consents to the amendment.

Acts 2003, 78th Leg., ch. 182, § 1, eff. Jan. 1, 2006.

§ 101.054. Waiver or Modification of Certain Statutory Provisions Prohibited; Exceptions

(a) Except as provided by this section, the following provisions may not be waived or modified in the company agreement of a limited liability company:

(1) this section;

(2) Section 101.101, 101.151, 101.206, 101.501, 101.602(b), or 101. 613 ;

(3) Chapter 1, if the provision is used to interpret a provision or define a word or phrase contained in a section listed in this subsection;

(4) Chapter 2, except that Section 2.104(c)(2), 2.104(c)(3), or 2.113 may be waived or modified in the company agreement;

(5) Chapter 3, except that Subchapters C and E may be waived or modified in the company agreement; or

(6) Chapter 4, 5, 7, 10, 11, or 12, other than Section 11.056.

(b) A provision listed in Subsection (a) may be waived or modified in the company agreement if the provision that is waived or modified authorizes the limited liability company to waive or modify the provision in the company's governing documents.

(c) A provision listed in Subsection (a) may be modified in the company agreement if the provision that is modified specifies:

(1) the person or group of persons entitled to approve a modification; or

(2) the vote or other method by which a modification is required to be approved.

(d) A provision in this title or in that part of Title 1 applicable to a limited liability company that grants a right to a person, other than a member, manager, officer, or assignee of a membership interest in a limited liability company, may be waived or modified in the company agreement of the company only if the person consents to the waiver or modification.

(e) The company agreement may not unreasonably restrict a person's right of access to records and information under Section 101.502.

Acts 2003, 78th Leg., ch. 182, § 1, eff. Jan. 1, 2006. Amended by Acts 2007, 80th Leg., ch. 688, § 97, eff. Sept. 1, 2007; Acts 2009, 81st Leg., ch. 84, § 38, eff. Sept. 1, 2009; Acts 2011, 82nd Leg., ch. 139 (S.B. 748), § 34, eff. Sept. 1, 2011.

SUBCHAPTER C. MEMBERSHIP

§ 101.101. Members Required

(a) A limited liability company may have one or more members. Except as provided by this section, a limited liability company must have at least one member.

(b) A limited liability company that has managers is not required to have any members during a reasonable period between the date the company is formed and the date the first member is admitted to the company.

(c) A limited liability company is not required to have any members during the period between the date the continued membership of the last remaining member of the company is terminated and the date the agreement to continue the company described by Section 11.056 is executed.

Acts 2003, 78th Leg., ch. 182, § 1, eff. Jan. 1, 2006.

§ 101.102. Qualification for Membership

(a) A person may be a member of or acquire a membership interest in a limited liability company unless the person lacks capacity apart from this code.

(b) A person is not required, as a condition to becoming a member of or acquiring a membership interest in a limited liability company, to:

(1) make a contribution to the company;

(2) otherwise pay cash or transfer property to the company; or

(3) assume an obligation to make a contribution or otherwise pay cash or transfer property to the company.

(c) If one or more persons own a membership interest in a limited liability company, the company agreement may provide for a person to be admitted to the company as a member without acquiring a membership interest in the company.

Acts 2003, 78th Leg., ch. 182, § 1, eff. Jan. 1, 2006. Amended by Acts 2005, 79th Leg., ch. 64, § 71, eff. Jan. 1, 2006.

§ 101.103. Effective Date of Membership

(a) In connection with the formation of a company, a person becomes a member of the company on the date the company is formed if the person is named as an initial member in the company's certificate of formation.

(b) In connection with the formation of a company, a person being admitted as a member of the company but not named as an initial member in the company's certificate of formation becomes a member of the company on the latest of:

(1) the date the company is formed;

(2) the date stated in the company's records as the date the person becomes a member of the company; or

(3) if the company's records do not state a date described by Subdivision (2), the date the person's admission to the company is first reflected in the company's records.

(c) A person who, after the formation of a limited liability company, acquires directly or is assigned a membership interest in the company or is admitted as a member of the company without acquiring a membership interest becomes a member of the company on approval or consent of all of the company's members.

Acts 2003, 78th Leg., ch. 182, § 1, eff. Jan. 1, 2006. Amended by Acts 2005, 79th Leg., ch. 64, § 72, eff. Jan. 1, 2006.

§ 101.104. Classes or Groups of Members or Membership Interests

(a) The company agreement of a limited liability company may:

(1) establish within the company classes or groups of one or more members or membership interests each of which has certain expressed relative rights, powers, and duties, including voting rights; and

(2) provide for the manner of establishing within the company additional classes or groups of one or more members or membership interests each of which has certain expressed relative rights, powers, and duties, including voting rights.

(b) The rights, powers, and duties of a class or group of members or membership interests described by Subsection (a)(2) may be stated in the company agreement or stated at the time the class or group is established.

(c) If the company agreement of a limited liability company does not provide for the manner of establishing classes or groups of members or membership interests under Subsection (a)(2), additional classes or groups of members or membership interests may be established only by the adoption of an amendment to the company agreement.

(d) The rights, powers, or duties of any class or group of members or membership interests of a limited liability company may be senior to the rights, powers, or duties of any other class or group of members or membership interests in the company, including a previously established class or group.

Acts 2003, 78th Leg., ch. 182, § 1, eff. Jan. 1, 2006.

§ 101.105. Issuance of Membership Interests After Formation of Company

A limited liability company, after the formation of the company, may:

(1) issue membership interests in the company to any person with the approval of all of the members of the company; and

(2) if the issuance of a membership interest requires the establishment of a new class or group of members or membership interests, establish a new class or group as provided by Sections 101.104(a)(2), (b), and (c).

Acts 2003, 78th Leg., ch. 182, § 1, eff. Jan. 1, 2006.

§ 101.106. Nature of Membership Interest

(a) A membership interest in a limited liability company is personal property.

(a–1) A membership interest may be community property under applicable law.

(a–2) A member's right to participate in the management and conduct of the business of the limited liability company is not community property.

(b) A member of a limited liability company or an assignee of a membership interest in a limited liability company does not have an interest in any specific property of the company.

(c) Sections 9.406 and 9.408, Business & Commerce Code, do not apply to a membership interest in a limited liability company, including the rights, powers, and interests arising under the company's certificate of formation or company agreement or under this code. To the extent of any conflict between this subsection and Section 9.406 or 9.408, Business & Commerce Code, this subsection controls. It is the express intent of this subsection to permit the enforcement, as a contract among the members of a limited liability company, of any provision of a company agreement that would otherwise be ineffective under Section 9.406 or 9.408, Business & Commerce Code.

Acts 2003, 78th Leg., ch. 182, § 1, eff. Jan. 1, 2006. Amended by Acts 2009, 81st Leg., ch. 84, § 39, eff. Sept. 1, 2009; Acts 2011, 82nd Leg., ch. 139 (S.B. 748), § 35, eff. Sept. 1, 2011.

§ 101.107. Withdrawal or Expulsion of Member Prohibited

A member of a limited liability company may not withdraw or be expelled from the company.

Acts 2003, 78th Leg., ch. 182, § 1, eff. Jan. 1, 2006.

§ 101.108. Assignment of Membership Interest

(a) A membership interest in a limited liability company may be wholly or partly assigned.

(b) An assignment of a membership interest in a limited liability company:

(1) is not an event requiring the winding up of the company; and

(2) does not entitle the assignee to:

(A) participate in the management and affairs of the company;

(B) become a member of the company; or

(C) exercise any rights of a member of the company.

Acts 2003, 78th Leg., ch. 182, § 1, eff. Jan. 1, 2006.

§ 101.109. Rights and Duties of Assignee of Membership Interest Before Membership

(a) A person who is assigned a membership interest in a limited liability company is entitled to:

(1) receive any allocation of income, gain, loss, deduction, credit, or a similar item that the assignor is entitled to receive to the extent the allocation of the item is assigned;

(2) receive any distribution the assignor is entitled to receive to the extent the distribution is assigned;

(3) require, for any proper purpose, reasonable information or a reasonable account of the transactions of the company; and

(4) make, for any proper purpose, reasonable inspections of the books and records of the company.

(b) An assignee of a membership interest in a limited liability company is entitled to become a member of the company on the approval of all of the company's members.

(c) An assignee of a membership interest in a limited liability company is not liable as a member of the company until the assignee becomes a member of the company.

Acts 2003, 78th Leg., ch. 182, § 1, eff. Jan. 1, 2006.

§ 101.110. Rights and Liabilities of Assignee of Membership Interest After Becoming Member

(a) An assignee of a membership interest in a limited liability company, after becoming a member of the company, is:

(1) entitled, to the extent assigned, to the same rights and powers granted or provided to a member of the company by the company agreement or this code;

(2) subject to the same restrictions and liabilities placed or imposed on a member of the company by the company agreement or this code; and

(3) except as provided by Subsection (b), liable for the assignor's obligation to make contributions to the company.

(b) An assignee of a membership interest in a limited liability company, after becoming a member of the company, is not obligated for a liability of the assignor that:

(1) the assignee did not have knowledge of on the date the assignee became a member of the company; and

(2) could not be ascertained from the company agreement.

Acts 2003, 78th Leg., ch. 182, § 1, eff. Jan. 1, 2006.

§ 101.111. Rights and Duties of Assignor of Membership Interest

(a) An assignor of a membership interest in a limited liability company continues to be a member of the company and is entitled to exercise any unassigned rights or powers of a member of the company until the assignee becomes a member of the company.

(b) An assignor of a membership interest in a limited liability company is not released from the assignor's liability to the company, regardless of whether the assignee of the membership interest becomes a member of the company.

Acts 2003, 78th Leg., ch. 182, § 1, eff. Jan. 1, 2006.

§ 101.1115. Effect of Death or Divorce on Membership Interest

(a) For purposes of this code:

(1) on the divorce of a member, the member's spouse, to the extent of the spouse's membership interest, if any, is an assignee of the membership interest;

(2) on the death of a member, the member's surviving spouse, if any, and an heir, devisee, personal representative, or other successor of the member, to the extent of their respective membership interest, are assignees of the membership interest; and

(3) on the death of a member's spouse, an heir, devisee, personal representative, or other successor of the spouse, other than the member, to the extent of their respective membership interest, if any, is an assignee of the membership interest.

(b) This chapter does not impair an agreement for the purchase or sale of a membership interest at any time, including on the death or divorce of an owner of the membership interest.

Added by Acts 2011, 82nd Leg., ch. 139 (S.B. 748), § 36, eff. Sept. 1, 2011.

§ 101.112. Member's Membership Interest Subject to Charging Order

(a) On application by a judgment creditor of a member of a limited liability company or of any other owner of a membership interest in a limited liability company, a court having jurisdiction may charge the membership interest of the judgment debtor to satisfy the judgment.

(b) If a court charges a membership interest with payment of a judgment as provided by Subsection (a), the judgment creditor has only the right to receive any distribution to which the judgment debtor would otherwise be entitled in respect of the membership interest.

(c) A charging order constitutes a lien on the judgment debtor's membership interest. The charging order lien may not be foreclosed on under this code or any other law.

(d) The entry of a charging order is the exclusive remedy by which a judgment creditor of a member or of any other owner of a membership interest may satisfy a judgment out of the judgment debtor's membership interest.

(e) This section may not be construed to deprive a member of a limited liability company or any other owner of a membership interest in a limited liability company of the benefit of any exemption laws applicable to the membership interest of the member or owner.

(f) A creditor of a member or of any other owner of a membership interest does not have the right to obtain possession of, or otherwise exercise legal or equitable remedies with respect to, the property of the limited liability company.

Acts 2003, 78th Leg., ch. 182, § 1, eff. Jan. 1, 2006. Amended by Acts 2007, 80th Leg., ch. 688, § 98, eff. Sept. 1, 2007; Acts 2009, 81st Leg., ch. 84, § 40, eff. Sept. 1, 2009.

§ 101.113. Parties to Actions

A member of a limited liability company may be named as a party in an action by or against the limited liability company only if the action is brought to enforce the member's right against or liability to the company.

Acts 2003, 78th Leg., ch. 182, § 1, eff. Jan. 1, 2006.

§ 101.114. Liability for Obligations

Except as and to the extent the company agreement specifically provides otherwise, a member or manager is not liable for a debt, obligation, or liability of a limited liability company, including a debt, obligation, or liability under a judgment, decree, or order of a court.

Acts 2003, 78th Leg., ch. 182, § 1, eff. Jan. 1, 2006.

SUBCHAPTER D. CONTRIBUTIONS

§ 101.151. Requirements for Enforceable Promise

A promise to make a contribution or otherwise pay cash or transfer property to a limited liability company is enforceable only if the promise is:

(1) in writing; and

(2) signed by the person making the promise.

Acts 2003, 78th Leg., ch. 182, § 1, eff. Jan. 1, 2006.

§ 101.152. Enforceable Promise Not Affected by Change in Circumstances

A member of a limited liability company is obligated to perform an enforceable promise to make a contribution or otherwise pay cash or transfer property to the company without regard to the death, disability, or other change in circumstances of the member.

Acts 2003, 78th Leg., ch. 182, § 1, eff. Jan. 1, 2006.

§ 101.153. Failure to Perform Enforceable Promise; Consequences

(a) A member of a limited liability company, or the member's legal representative or successor, who does not perform an enforceable promise to make a contribution, including a previously made contribution, or to otherwise pay cash or transfer property to the company, is obligated, at the request of the company, to pay in cash the agreed value of the contribution, as stated in the company agreement or the company's records required under Sections 3.151 and 101.501, less:

(1) any amount already paid for the contribution; and

(2) the value of any property already transferred.

(b) The company agreement of a limited liability company may provide that the membership interest of a member who fails to perform an enforceable promise to make a payment of cash or transfer property to the company, whether as a contribution or in connection with a contribution already made, may be:

(1) reduced;

(2) subordinated to other membership interests of nondefaulting members;

(3) redeemed or sold at a value determined by appraisal or other formula; or

(4) made the subject of:

(A) a forced sale;

(B) forfeiture;

(C) a loan from other members of the company in an amount necessary to satisfy the enforceable promise; or

(D) another penalty or consequence.

Acts 2003, 78th Leg., ch. 182, § 1, eff. Jan. 1, 2006.

§ 101.154. Consent Required to Release Enforceable Obligation

The obligation of a member of a limited liability company, or of the member's legal representative or successor, to make a contribution or otherwise pay cash or transfer property to the company, or to return cash or property to the company paid or distributed to the member in violation of this code or the company agreement, may be released or settled only by consent of each member of the company.

Acts 2003, 78th Leg., ch. 182, § 1, eff. Jan. 1, 2006.

§ 101.155. Creditor's Right to Enforce Certain Obligations

A creditor of a limited liability company who extends credit or otherwise acts in reasonable reliance on an enforceable obligation of a member of the company that is released or settled as provided by Section 101.154 may enforce the original obligation if the obligation is stated in a document that is:

(1) signed by the member; and

(2) not amended or canceled to evidence the release or settlement of the obligation.

Acts 2003, 78th Leg., ch. 182, § 1, eff. Jan. 1, 2006.

§ 101.156. Requirements to Enforce Conditional Obligation

(a) An obligation of a member of a limited liability company that is subject to a condition may be enforced by the company or a creditor described by Section 101.155 only if the condition is satisfied or waived by or with respect to the member.

(b) A conditional obligation of a member of a limited liability company under this section includes a contribution payable on a discretionary call of the limited liability company before the time the call occurs.

Acts 2003, 78th Leg., ch. 182, § 1, eff. Jan. 1, 2006.

SUBCHAPTER E. ALLOCATIONS AND DISTRIBUTIONS

§ 101.201. Allocation of Profits and Losses

The profits and losses of a limited liability company shall be allocated to each member of the company on the basis of the agreed value of the contributions made by each member, as stated in the company's records required under Section 101.501.

Acts 2003, 78th Leg., ch. 182, § 1, eff. Jan. 1, 2006. Amended by Acts 2005, 79th Leg., ch. 64, § 73, eff. Jan. 1, 2006.

§ 101.202. Distribution in Kind

A member of a limited liability company is entitled to receive or demand a distribution from the company only in the form of cash, regardless of the form of the member's contribution to the company.

Acts 2003, 78th Leg., ch. 182, § 1, eff. Jan. 1, 2006.

§ 101.203. Sharing of Distributions

Distributions of cash and other assets of a limited liability company shall be made to each member of the company according to the agreed value of the member's contribution to the company as stated in the company's records required under Sections 3.151 and 101.501.

Acts 2003, 78th Leg., ch. 182, § 1, eff. Jan. 1, 2006.

§ 101.204. Interim Distributions

A member of a limited liability company, before the winding up of the company, is not entitled to receive and may not demand a distribution from the company until the company's governing authority declares a distribution to:

(1) each member of the company; or

(2) a class or group of members that includes the member.

Acts 2003, 78th Leg., ch. 182, § 1, eff. Jan. 1, 2006.

§ 101.205. Distribution on Withdrawal

A member of a limited liability company who validly exercises the member's right to withdraw from the company granted under the company agreement is entitled to receive, within a reasonable time after the date of withdrawal, the fair value of the member's interest in the company as determined as of the date of withdrawal.

Acts 2003, 78th Leg., ch. 182, § 1, eff. Jan. 1, 2006.

§ 101.206. Prohibited Distribution; Duty to Return

(a) Unless the distribution is made in compliance with Chapter 11, a limited liability company may not make a distribution to a member of the company if, immediately after making the distribution, the company's total liabilities, other than liabilities described by Subsection (b), exceed the fair value of the company's total assets.

(b) For purposes of Subsection (a), the liabilities of a limited liability company do not include:

(1) a liability related to the member's membership interest; or

(2) except as provided by Subsection (c), a liability for which the recourse of creditors is limited to specified property of the company.

(c) For purposes of Subsection (a), the assets of a limited liability company include the fair value of property subject to a liability for which recourse of creditors is limited to specified property of the company only if the fair value of that property exceeds the liability.

(d) A member of a limited liability company who receives a distribution from the company in violation of this section is not required to return the distribution to the company unless the member had knowledge of the violation.

(e) This section may not be construed to affect the obligation of a member of a limited liability company to return a distribution to the company under the company agreement or other state or federal law.

(f) For purposes of this section, "distribution" does not include an amount constituting reasonable compensation for present or past services or a reasonable payment made in the ordinary course of business under a bona fide retirement plan or other benefits program.

Acts 2003, 78th Leg., ch. 182, § 1, eff. Jan. 1, 2006. Amended by Acts 2009, 81st Leg., ch. 84, § 41, eff. Sept. 1, 2009.

§ 101.207. Creditor Status With Respect to Distribution

Subject to Sections 11.053 and 101.206, when a member of a limited liability company is entitled to receive a distribution from the company, the member, with respect to the distribution, has the same status as a creditor of the company and is entitled to any remedy available to a creditor of the company.

Acts 2003, 78th Leg., ch. 182, § 1, eff. Jan. 1, 2006.

§ 101.208 Record Date

A company agreement may establish or provide for the establishment of a record date with respect to allocations and distributions.

Added by Acts 2009, 81st Leg., ch. 84, § 42, eff. Sept. 1, 2009.

SUBCHAPTER F. MANAGEMENT

§ 101.251. Governing Authority

The governing authority of a limited liability company consists of:

(1) the managers of the company, if the company's certificate of formation states that the company will have one or more managers; or

(2) the members of the company, if the company's certificate of formation states that the company will not have managers.

Acts 2003, 78th Leg., ch. 182, § 1, eff. Jan. 1, 2006. Amended by Acts 2009, 81st Leg., ch. 84, § 43, eff. Sept. 1, 2009.

§ 101.252. Management by Governing Authority

The governing authority of a limited liability company shall manage the business and affairs of the company as provided by:

(1) the company agreement; and

(2) this title and the provisions of Title 1 applicable to a limited liability company to the extent that the company agreement does not provide for the management of the company.

Acts 2003, 78th Leg., ch. 182, § 1, eff. Jan. 1, 2006.

§ 101.253. Designation of Committees; Delegation of Authority

(a) The governing authority of a limited liability company by resolution may designate:

(1) one or more committees of the governing authority consisting of one or more governing persons of the company; and

(2) subject to any limitation imposed by the governing authority, a governing person to serve as an alternate member of a committee designated under Subdivision (1) at a committee meeting from which a member of the committee is absent or disqualified.

(b) A committee of the governing authority of a limited liability company may exercise the authority of the governing authority as provided by the resolution designating the committee.

(c) The designation of a committee under this section does not relieve the governing authority of any responsibility imposed by law.

Acts 2003, 78th Leg., ch. 182, § 1, eff. Jan. 1, 2006.

§ 101.254. Designation of Agents; Binding Acts

(a) Except as provided by this title and Title 1, each governing person of a limited liability company and each officer of a limited liability company vested with actual or apparent authority by the governing authority of the company is an agent of the company for purposes of carrying out the company's business.

(b) An act committed by an agent of a limited liability company described by Subsection (a) for the purpose of apparently carrying out the ordinary course of business of the company, including the execution of an instrument, document, mortgage, or conveyance in the name of the company, binds the company unless:

(1) the agent does not have actual authority to act for the company; and

(2) the person with whom the agent is dealing has knowledge of the agent's lack of actual authority.

(c) An act committed by an agent of a limited liability company described by Subsection (a) that is not apparently for carrying out the ordinary course of business of the company binds the company only if the act is authorized in accordance with this title.

Acts 2003, 78th Leg., ch. 182, § 1, eff. Jan. 1, 2006. Amended by Acts 2011, 82nd Leg., ch. 139 (S.B. 748), § 37, eff. Sept. 1, 2011.

§ 101.255. Contracts or Transactions Involving Interested Governing Persons or Officers

(a) This section applies to a contract or transaction between a limited liability company and:

(1) one or more governing persons or officers, or one or more affiliates or associates of one or more governing persons or officers, of the company; or

(2) an entity or other organization in which one or more governing persons or officers, or one or more affiliates or associates of one or more governing persons or officers, of the company:

(A) is a managerial official; or

(B) has a financial interest.

(b) An otherwise valid and enforceable contract or transaction described by Subsection (a) is valid and enforceable, and is not void or voidable, notwithstanding any relationship or interest described by Subsection (a), if any one of the following conditions is satisfied :

(1) the material facts as to the relationship or interest described by Subsection (a) and as to the contract or transaction are disclosed to or known by:

(A) the company's governing authority or a committee of the governing authority and the governing authority or committee in good faith authorizes the contract or transaction by the approval of the majority of the disinterested governing persons or committee members, regardless of whether the disinterested governing persons or committee members constitute a quorum; or

(B) the members of the company, and the members in good faith approve the contract or transaction by vote of the members; or

(2) the contract or transaction is fair to the company when the contract or transaction is authorized, approved, or ratified by the governing authority, a committee of the governing authority, or the members of the company.

(c) Common or interested governing persons of a limited liability company may be included in determining the presence of a quorum at a meeting of the company's governing authority or of a committee of the governing authority that authorizes the contract or transaction.

(d) A person who has the relationship or interest described by Subsection (a) may:

(1) be present at or participate in and, if the person is a governing person or committee member, may vote at a meeting of the governing authority or of a committee of the governing authority that authorizes the contract or transaction; or

(2) sign, in the person's capacity as a governing person or committee member, a written consent of the governing persons or committee members to authorize the contract or transaction.

(e) If at least one of the conditions of Subsection (b) is satisfied, neither the company nor any of the company's members will have a cause of action against any of the persons described by Subsection (a) for breach of duty with respect to the making, authorization, or performance of the contract or transaction because the person had the relationship or interest described by Subsection (a) or took any of the actions authorized by Subsection (d).

Acts 2003, 78th Leg., ch. 182, § 1, eff. Jan. 1, 2006. Amended by Acts 2009, 81st Leg., ch. 84, § 44, eff. Sept. 1, 2009; Acts 2011, 82nd Leg., ch. 139 (S.B. 748), § 38, eff. Sept. 1, 2011.

SUBCHAPTER G. MANAGERS

§ 101.301. Applicability of Subchapter

This subchapter applies only to a limited liability company that has one or more managers.

Acts 2003, 78th Leg., ch. 182, § 1, eff. Jan. 1, 2006.

§ 101.302. Number and Qualifications

(a) The managers of a limited liability company may consist of one or more persons.

(b) Except as provided by Subsection (c), the number of managers of a limited liability company consists of the number of initial managers listed in the company's certificate of formation.

(c) The number of managers of a limited liability company may be increased or decreased by amendment to, or as provided by, the company agreement, except that a decrease in the number of managers may not shorten the term of an incumbent manager.

(d) A manager of a limited liability company is not required to be a:

(1) resident of this state; or

(2) member of the company.

Acts 2003, 78th Leg., ch. 182, § 1, eff. Jan. 1, 2006.

§ 101.303. Term

A manager of a limited liability company serves:

(1) for the term, if any, for which the manager is elected and until the manager's successor is elected; or

(2) until the earlier resignation, removal, or death of the manager.

Acts 2003, 78th Leg., ch. 182, § 1, eff. Jan. 1, 2006.

§ 101.304. Removal

Subject to Section 101.306(a), a manager of a limited liability company may be removed, with or without cause, at a meeting of the company's members called for that purpose.

Acts 2003, 78th Leg., ch. 182, § 1, eff. Jan. 1, 2006.

§ 101.305. Manager Vacancy

(a) Subject to Section 101.306(b), a vacancy in the position of a manager of a limited liability company may be filled by:

(1) the affirmative vote of the majority of the remaining managers of the company, without regard to whether the remaining managers constitute a quorum; or

(2) if the vacancy is a result of an increase in the number of managers, an election at an annual or special meeting of the company's members called for that purpose.

(b) A person elected to fill a vacancy in the position of a manager serves for the unexpired term of the person's predecessor.

Acts 2003, 78th Leg., ch. 182, § 1, eff. Jan. 1, 2006.

§ 101.306. Removal and Replacement of Manager Elected by Class or Group

(a) If a class or group of the members of a limited liability company is entitled by the company agreement of the company to elect one or more managers of the company, a manager may be removed from office only by the class or group that elected the manager.

(b) A vacancy in the position of a manager elected as provided by Subsection (a) may be filled only by:

(1) a majority vote of the managers serving on the date the vacancy occurs who were elected by the class or group of members; or

(2) a majority vote of the members of the class or group.

Acts 2003, 78th Leg., ch. 182, § 1, eff. Jan. 1, 2006.

§ 101.307. Methods of Classifying Managers

Other methods of classifying managers of a limited liability company, including providing for managers who serve for staggered terms of office or terms that are not uniform, may be established in the company agreement.

Acts 2003, 78th Leg., ch. 182, § 1, eff. Jan. 1, 2006.

SUBCHAPTER H. MEETINGS AND VOTING

§ 101.351. Applicability of Subchapter

This subchapter applies only to a meeting of and voting by:

(1) the governing authority of a limited liability company;

(2) the members of a limited liability company if the members do not constitute the governing authority of the company; and

(3) a committee of the governing authority of a limited liability company.

Acts 2003, 78th Leg., ch. 182, § 1, eff. Jan. 1, 2006.

§ 101.352. General Notice Requirements

(a) Except as provided by Subsection (b), notice of a regular or special meeting of the governing authority or members of a limited liability company, or a committee of the company's governing authority, shall be given in writing to each governing person, member, or committee member, as appropriate, and as provided by Section 6.051.

(b) If the members of a limited liability company do not constitute the governing authority of the company, notice of a meeting of members required by Subsection (a) shall be given by or at the direction of the governing authority not later than the 10th day or earlier than the 60th day before the date of the meeting. Notice of a meeting required under this subsection must state the business to be transacted at the meeting or the purpose of the meeting if:

(1) the meeting is a special meeting; or

(2) a purpose of the meeting is to consider a matter described by Section 101.356.

Acts 2003, 78th Leg., ch. 182, § 1, eff. Jan. 1, 2006. Amended by Acts 2007, 80th Leg., ch. 688, § 99, eff. Sept. 1, 2007.

§ 101.353. Quorum

A majority of all of the governing persons, members, or committee members of a limited liability company constitutes a quorum for the purpose of transacting business at a meeting of the governing authority, members, or committee of the company, as appropriate.

Acts 2003, 78th Leg., ch. 182, § 1, eff. Jan. 1, 2006.

§ 101.354. Equal Voting Rights

Each governing person, member, or committee member of a limited liability company has an equal vote at a meeting of the governing authority, members, or committee of the company, as appropriate.

Acts 2003, 78th Leg., ch. 182, § 1, eff. Jan. 1, 2006.

§ 101.355. Act of Governing Authority, Members, or Committee

Except as provided by this title or Title 1, the affirmative vote of the majority of the governing persons, members, or committee members of a limited liability company present at a meeting at which a quorum is present constitutes an act of the governing authority, members, or committee of the company, as appropriate.

Acts 2003, 78th Leg., ch. 182, § 1, eff. Jan. 1, 2006.

§ 101.356. Votes Required to Approve Certain Actions

(a) Except as provided in this section or any other section in this title, an action of a limited liability company may be approved by the company's governing authority as provided by Section 101.355.

(b) Except as provided by Subsection (c), (d), or (e) or any other section in this title, an action of a limited liability company not apparently for carrying out the ordinary course of business of the company must be approved by the affirmative vote of the majority of all of the company's governing persons.

(c) Except as provided by Subsection (d) or (e) or any other section in this title, a fundamental business transaction of a limited liability company, or an action that would make it impossible for a limited liability company to carry out the ordinary business of the company, must be approved by the affirmative vote of the majority of all of the company's members.

(d) Except as provided by Subsection (e) or any other section of this title, the company's members must approve by an affirmative vote of all the members:

(1) an amendment to the certificate of formation of a limited liability company; or

(2) a restated certificate of formation that contains an amendment to the certificate of formation of a limited liability company.

(e) A requirement that an action of a limited liability company must be approved by the company's members does not apply during the period prescribed by Section 101.101(b).

(f) Approval of a restated certificate of formation by a limited liability company's members is required only if the restated certificate contains an amendment.

Acts 2003, 78th Leg., ch. 182, § 1, eff. Jan. 1, 2006. Amended by Acts 2005, 79th Leg., ch. 64, § 74, eff. Jan. 1, 2006.

§ 101.357. Manner of Voting

(a) A member of a limited liability company may vote:

(1) in person; or

(2) by a proxy executed in writing by the member.

(b) A manager or committee member of a limited liability company may vote:

(1) in person; or

(2) if authorized by the company agreement, by a proxy executed in writing by the manager or committee member, as appropriate.

Acts 2003, 78th Leg., ch. 182, § 1, eff. Jan. 1, 2006. Amended by Acts 2011, 82nd Leg., ch. 139 (S.B. 748), § 39, eff. Sept. 1, 2011.

§ 101.358. Action by Less Than Unanimous Written Consent

(a) This section applies only to an action required or authorized to be taken at an annual or special meeting of the governing authority, the members, or a committee of the governing authority of a limited liability company under this title, Title 1, or the governing documents of the company.

(b) Notwithstanding Sections 6.201 and 6.202, an action may be taken without holding a meeting, providing notice, or taking a vote if a written consent or consents stating the action to be taken is signed by the number of governing persons, members, or committee members of a limited liability company, as appropriate, necessary to have at least the minimum number of votes that would be necessary to take the action at a meeting at which each governing person, member, or committee member, as appropriate, entitled to vote on the action is present and votes.

Acts 2003, 78th Leg., ch. 182, § 1, eff. Jan. 1, 2006.

§ 101.359. Effective Action by Members or Managers With or Without Meeting

Members or managers of a limited liability company may take action at a meeting of the members or managers or without a meeting in any manner permitted by this title, Title 1, or the governing documents of the company. Unless otherwise provided by the governing documents, an action is effective if it is taken:

(1) by an affirmative vote of those persons having at least the minimum number of votes that would be necessary to take the action at a meeting at which each member or manager, as appropriate, entitled to vote on the action is present and votes; or

(2) with the consent of each member of the limited liability company, which may be established by:

(A) the member's failure to object to the action in a timely manner, if the member has full knowledge of the action;

(B) consent to the action in writing signed by the member; or

(C) any other means reasonably evidencing consent.

Added by Acts 2005, 79th Leg., ch. 64, § 75, eff. Jan. 1, 2006.

SUBCHAPTER I. MODIFICATION OF DUTIES; INDEMNIFICATION

§ 101.401. Expansion or Restriction of Duties and Liabilities

The company agreement of a limited liability company may expand or restrict any duties, including fiduciary duties, and related liabilities that a member, manager, officer, or other person has to the company or to a member or manager of the company.

Acts 2003, 78th Leg., ch. 182, § 1, eff. Jan. 1, 2006.

§ 101.402. Permissive Indemnification, Advancement of Expenses, and Insurance or Other Arrangements

(a) A limited liability company may:

(1) indemnify a person;

(2) pay in advance or reimburse expenses incurred by a person; and

(3) purchase or procure or establish and maintain insurance or another arrangement to indemnify or hold harmless a person.

(b) In this section, "person" includes a member, manager, or officer of a limited liability company or an assignee of a membership interest in the company.

Acts 2003, 78th Leg., ch. 182, § 1, eff. Jan. 1, 2006.

SUBCHAPTER J. DERIVATIVE PROCEEDINGS

§ 101.451. Definitions

In this subchapter:

(1) "Derivative proceeding" means a civil suit in the right of a domestic limited liability company or, to the extent provided by Section 101.462, in the right of a foreign limited liability company.

(2) "Member" includes a person who beneficially owns a membership interest through a voting trust or a nominee on the person's behalf.

Acts 2003, 78th Leg., ch. 182, § 1, eff. Jan. 1, 2006.

§ 101.452. Standing to Bring Proceeding

A member may not institute or maintain a derivative proceeding unless:

(1) the member:

(A) was a member of the limited liability company at the time of the act or omission complained of; or

(B) became a member by operation of law from a person that was a member at the time of the act or omission complained of; and

(2) the member fairly and adequately represents the interests of the limited liability company in enforcing the right of the limited liability company.

Acts 2003, 78th Leg., ch. 182, § 1, eff. Jan. 1, 2006.

§ 101.453. Demand

(a) A member may not institute a derivative proceeding until the 91st day after the date a written demand is filed with the limited liability company stating with particularity the act, omission, or other matter that is the subject of the claim or challenge and requesting that the limited liability company take suitable action.

(b) The waiting period required by Subsection (a) before a derivative proceeding may be instituted is not required if:

(1) the member has been previously notified that the demand has been rejected by the limited liability company;

(2) the limited liability company is suffering irreparable injury; or

(3) irreparable injury to the limited liability company would result by waiting for the expiration of the 90–day period.

Acts 2003, 78th Leg., ch. 182, § 1, eff. Jan. 1, 2006.

§ 101.454. Determination by Governing or Independent Persons

(a) The determination of how to proceed on allegations made in a demand or petition relating to a derivative proceeding must be made by an affirmative vote of the majority of:

(1) the independent and disinterested governing persons present at a meeting of the governing authority at which interested governing persons are not present at the time of the vote if the independent and disinterested governing persons constitute a quorum of the governing authority;

(2) a committee consisting of two or more independent and disinterested governing persons appointed by the majority of one or more independent and disinterested governing persons present at a meeting of the governing authority, regardless of whether the independent and disinterested governing persons constitute a quorum of the governing authority; or

(3) a panel of one or more independent and disinterested persons appointed by the court on a motion by the limited liability company listing the names of the persons to be appointed and stating that, to the best of the limited liability company's knowledge, the persons to be appointed are disinterested and qualified to make the determinations contemplated by Section 101.458.

(b) The court shall appoint a panel under Subsection (a)(3) if the court finds that the persons recommended by the limited liability company are independent and disinterested and are otherwise qualified with respect to expertise, experience, independent judgment, and other factors considered appropriate by the court under the circumstances to make the determinations. A person appointed by the court to a panel under this section may not be held liable to the limited liability company or the limited liability company's members for an action taken or omission made by the person in that capacity, except for acts or omissions constituting fraud or wilful misconduct.

Acts 2003, 78th Leg., ch. 182, § 1, eff. Jan. 1, 2006.

§ 101.455. Stay of Proceeding

(a) If the domestic or foreign limited liability company that is the subject of a derivative proceeding commences an inquiry into the allegations made in a demand or petition and the person or group of persons described by Section 101.454 is conducting an active review of the allegations in good faith, the court shall stay a derivative proceeding until the review is completed and a determination is made by the person or group regarding what further action, if any, should be taken.

(b) To obtain a stay, the domestic or foreign limited liability company shall provide the court with a written statement agreeing to advise the court and the member making the demand of the determination promptly on the completion of the review of the matter. A stay, on motion, may be reviewed every 60 days for the continued necessity of the stay.

(c) If the review and determination made by the person or group is not completed before the 61st day after the date on which the court orders the stay, the stay may be renewed for one or more additional 60–day periods if the domestic or foreign limited liability company provides the court and the member with a written statement of the status of the review and the reasons why a continued extension of the stay is necessary.

Acts 2003, 78th Leg., ch. 182, § 1, eff. Jan. 1, 2006.

§ 101.456. Discovery

(a) If a domestic or foreign limited liability company proposes to dismiss a derivative proceeding under Section 101.458, discovery by a member after the filing of the derivative proceeding in accordance with this subchapter shall be limited to:

(1) facts relating to whether the person or group of persons described by Section 101.458 is independent and disinterested;

(2) the good faith of the inquiry and review by the person or group; and

(3) the reasonableness of the procedures followed by the person or group in conducting the review.

(b) Discovery described by Subsection (a) may not be expanded to include a fact or substantive matter regarding the act, omission, or other matter that is the subject matter of the derivative proceeding. The scope of discovery may be expanded if the court determines after notice and hearing that a good faith review of the allegations for purposes of Section 101.458 has not been made by an independent and disinterested person or group in accordance with that section.

Acts 2003, 78th Leg., ch. 182, § 1, eff. Jan. 1, 2006.

§ 101.457. Tolling of Statute of Limitations

A written demand filed with the limited liability company under Section 101.453 tolls the statute of limitations on the claim on which demand is made until the earlier of:

(1) the 91st day after the date of the demand; or

(2) the 31st day after the date the limited liability company advises the member that the demand has been rejected or the review has been completed.

Acts 2003, 78th Leg., ch. 182, § 1, eff. Jan. 1, 2006.

§ 101.458. Dismissal of Derivative Proceeding

(a) A court shall dismiss a derivative proceeding on a motion by the limited liability company if the person or group of persons described by Section 101.454 determines in good faith, after conducting a reasonable inquiry and based on factors the person or group considers appropriate under the circumstances, that continuation of the derivative proceeding is not in the best interests of the limited liability company.

(b) In determining whether the requirements of Subsection (a) have been met, the burden of proof shall be on:

(1) the plaintiff member if:

(A) the majority of the governing authority consists of independent and disinterested persons at the time the determination is made;

(B) the determination is made by a panel of one or more independent and disinterested persons appointed under Section 101.454(a)(3); or

(C) the limited liability company presents prima facie evidence that demonstrates that the persons appointed under Section 101.454(a)(2) are independent and disinterested; or

(2) the limited liability company in any other circumstance.

Acts 2003, 78th Leg., ch. 182, § 1, eff. Jan. 1, 2006.

§ 101.459. Allegations if Demand Rejected

If a derivative proceeding is instituted after a demand is rejected, the petition must allege with particularity facts that establish that the rejection was not made in accordance with the requirements of Sections 101.454 and 101.458.

Acts 2003, 78th Leg., ch. 182, § 1, eff. Jan. 1, 2006.

§ 101.460. Discontinuance or Settlement

(a) A derivative proceeding may not be discontinued or settled without court approval.

(b) The court shall direct that notice be given to the affected members if the court determines that a proposed discontinuance or settlement may substantially affect the interests of other members.

Acts 2003, 78th Leg., ch. 182, § 1, eff. Jan. 1, 2006.

§ 101.461. Payment of Expenses

(a) In this section, "expenses" means reasonable expenses incurred by a party in a derivative proceeding, including:

(1) attorney's fees;

(2) costs of pursuing an investigation of the matter that was the subject of the derivative proceeding; or

(3) expenses for which the domestic or foreign limited liability company may be required to indemnify another person.

(b) On termination of a derivative proceeding, the court may order:

(1) the domestic or foreign limited liability company to pay the expenses the plaintiff incurred in the proceeding if the court finds the proceeding has resulted in a substantial benefit to the domestic or foreign limited liability company;

(2) the plaintiff to pay the expenses the domestic or foreign limited liability company or other defendant incurred in investigating and defending the proceeding if the court finds the proceeding has been instituted or maintained without reasonable cause or for an improper purpose; or

(3) a party to pay the expenses incurred by another party relating to the filing of a pleading, motion, or other paper if the court finds the pleading, motion, or other paper:

(A) was not well grounded in fact after reasonable inquiry;

(B) was not warranted by existing law or a good faith argument for the extension, modification, or reversal of existing law; or

(C) was interposed for an improper purpose, such as to harass, cause unnecessary delay, or cause a needless increase in the cost of litigation.

Acts 2003, 78th Leg., ch. 182, § 1, eff. Jan. 1, 2006.

§ 101.462. Application to Foreign Limited Liability Companies

(a) In a derivative proceeding brought in the right of a foreign limited liability company, the matters covered by this subchapter are governed by the laws of the jurisdiction of organization of the foreign limited liability company, except for Sections 101.455, 101.460, and 101.461, which are procedural provisions and do not relate to the internal affairs of the foreign limited liability company.

(b) In the case of matters relating to a foreign limited liability company under Section 101.454, a reference to a person or group of persons described by that section refers to a person or group entitled under the laws of the jurisdiction of organization of the foreign limited liability company to review and dispose of a derivative proceeding. The standard of review of a decision made by the person or group to dismiss the derivative proceeding shall be governed by the laws of the jurisdiction of organization of the foreign limited liability company.

Acts 2003, 78th Leg., ch. 182, § 1, eff. Jan. 1, 2006.

§ 101.463. Closely Held Limited Liability Company

(a) In this section, "closely held limited liability company" means a limited liability company that has:

(1) fewer than 35 members; and

(2) no membership interests listed on a national securities exchange or regularly quoted in an over-the-counter market by one or more members of a national securities association.

(b) Sections 101.452–101.459 do not apply to a closely held limited liability company.

(c) If justice requires:

(1) a derivative proceeding brought by a member of a closely held limited liability company may be treated by a court as a direct action brought by the member for the member's own benefit; and

(2) a recovery in a direct or derivative proceeding by a member may be paid directly to the plaintiff or to the limited liability company if necessary to protect the interests of creditors or other members of the limited liability company.

Acts 2003, 78th Leg., ch. 182, § 1, eff. Jan. 1, 2006. Amended by Acts 2007, 80th Leg., ch. 688, § 100, eff. Sept. 1, 2007.

SUBCHAPTER K. SUPPLEMENTAL RECORDKEEPING REQUIREMENTS

§ 101.501. Supplemental Records Required for Limited Liability Companies

(a) In addition to the books and records required to be kept under Section 3.151, a limited liability company shall keep at its principal office in the United States, or make available to a person at its principal office in the United States not later than the fifth day after the date the person submits a written request to examine the books and records of the company under Section 3.152(a) or 101.502:

(1) a current list that states:

(A) the percentage or other interest in the limited liability company owned by each member; and

(B) if one or more classes or groups of membership interests are established in or under the certificate of formation or company agreement, the names of the members of each specified class or group;

(2) a copy of the company's federal, state, and local tax information or income tax returns for each of the six preceding tax years;

(3) a copy of the company's certificate of formation, including any amendments to or restatements of the certificate of formation;

(4) if the company agreement is in writing, a copy of the company agreement, including any amendments to or restatements of the company agreement;

(5) an executed copy of any powers of attorney;

(6) a copy of any document that establishes a class or group of members of the company as provided by the company agreement; and

(7) except as provided by Subsection (b), a written statement of:

(A) the amount of a cash contribution and a description and statement of the agreed value of any other contribution made or agreed to be made by each member;

(B) the dates any additional contributions are to be made by a member;

(C) any event the occurrence of which requires a member to make additional contributions;

(D) any event the occurrence of which requires the winding up of the company; and

(E) the date each member became a member of the company.

(b) A limited liability company is not required to keep or make available at its principal office in the United States a written statement of the information required by Subsection (a)(7) if that information is stated in a written company agreement.

(c) A limited liability company shall keep at its registered office located in this state and make available to a member of the company on reasonable request the street address of the company's principal office in the United States in which the records required by this section and Section 3.151 are maintained or made available.

Acts 2003, 78th Leg., ch. 182, § 1, eff. Jan. 1, 2006. Amended by Acts 2007, 80th Leg., ch. 688, § 101, eff. Sept. 1, 2007.

§ 101.502. Right to Examine Records and Certain Other Information

(a) A member of a limited liability company or an assignee of a membership interest in a limited liability company, or a representative of the member or assignee, on written request and for a proper purpose, may examine and copy at any reasonable time and at the member's or assignee's expense:

(1) records required under Sections 3.151 and 101.501; and

(2) other information regarding the business, affairs, and financial condition of the company that is reasonable for the person to examine and copy.

(b) A limited liability company shall provide to a member of the company or an assignee of a membership interest in the company, on written request by the member or assignee sent to the company's principal office in the United States or, if different, the person and address designated in the company agreement, a free copy of:

(1) the company's certificate of formation, including any amendments to or restatements of the certificate of formation;

(2) if in writing, the company agreement, including any amendments to or restatements of the company agreement; and

(3) any tax returns described by Section 101.501(a)(2).

Acts 2003, 78th Leg., ch. 182, § 1, eff. Jan. 1, 2006.

SUBCHAPTER L. SUPPLEMENTAL WINDING UP AND TERMINATION PROVISIONS

§ 101.551. Persons Eligible to Wind Up Company

After an event requiring the winding up of a limited liability company unless a revocation as provided by Section 11.151 or a cancellation as provided by Section 11.152 occurs, the winding up of the company must be carried out by:

(1) the company's governing authority or one or more persons, including a governing person, designated by the governing authority, the members, or the governing documents;

(2) if the event requiring the winding up of the company is the termination of the continued membership of the last remaining member of the company, the legal representative or successor of the last remaining member or one or more persons designated by the legal representative or successor; or

(3) a person appointed by the court to carry out the winding up of the company under Section 11.054, 11.405, 11.409, or 11.410.

Acts 2003, 78th Leg., ch. 182, § 1, eff. Jan. 1, 2006.

§ 101.552. Approval of Voluntary Winding Up, Revocation, Cancellation, or Reinstatement

(a) A majority vote of all of the members of a limited liability company or, if the limited liability company has no members, a majority vote of all of the managers of the company is required to approve:

(1) a voluntary winding up of the company under Chapter 11;

(2) a revocation of a voluntary decision to wind up the company under Section 11.151; or

(3) a reinstatement of a terminated company under Section 11.202.

(b) The consent of all of the members of the limited liability company is required to approve a cancellation under Section 11.152 of an event requiring winding up specified in Section 11.051(1) or (3).

(c) An event requiring winding up specified in Section 11.056 may be canceled in accordance with Section 11.152(a) if the legal representative or successor of the last remaining member of the domestic limited liability company agrees to:

(1) cancel the event requiring winding up and continue the company; and

(2) become a member of the company effective as of the date of termination of the membership of the last remaining member of the company, or designate another person who agrees to become a member of the company effective as of the date of the termination.

Acts 2003, 78th Leg., ch. 182, § 1, eff. Jan. 1, 2006. Amended by Acts 2007, 80th Leg., ch. 688, § 102, eff. Sept. 1, 2007.

SUBCHAPTER M. SERIES LIMITED LIABILITY COMPANY

§ 101.601 Series of Members, Managers, Membership Interests, or Assets

(a) A company agreement may establish or provide for the establishment of one or more designated series of members, managers, membership interests, or assets that:

(1) has separate rights, powers, or duties with respect to specified property or obligations of the limited liability company or profits and losses associated with specified property or obligations; or

(2) has a separate business purpose or investment objective.

(b) A series established in accordance with Subsection (a) may carry on any business, purpose, or activity, whether or not for profit, that is not prohibited by Section 2.003.

Added by Acts 2009, 81st Leg., ch. 84, § 45, eff. Sept. 1, 2009.

§ 101.602 Enforceability of Obligations and Expenses of Series Against Assets

(a) Notwithstanding any other provision of this chapter or any other law, but subject to Subsection (b) and any other provision of this subchapter:

(1) the debts, liabilities, obligations, and expenses incurred, contracted for, or otherwise existing with respect to a particular series shall be enforceable against the assets of that series only, and shall not be enforceable against the assets of the limited liability company generally or any other series; and

(2) none of the debts, liabilities, obligations, and expenses incurred, contracted for, or otherwise existing with respect to the limited liability company generally or any other series shall be enforceable against the assets of a particular series.

(b) Subsection (a) applies only if:

(1) the records maintained for that particular series account for the assets associated with that series separately from the other assets of the company or any other series;

(2) the company agreement contains a statement to the effect of the limitations provided in Subsection (a); and

(3) the company's certificate of formation contains a notice of the limitations provided in Subsection (a).

Added by Acts 2009, 81st Leg., ch. 84, § 45, eff. Sept. 1, 2009.

§ 101.603 Assets of Series

(a) Assets associated with a series may be held directly or indirectly, including being held in the name of the series, in the name of the limited liability company, through a nominee, or otherwise.

(b) If the records of a series are maintained in a manner so that the assets of the series can be reasonably identified by specific listing, category, type, quantity, or computational or allocational formula or procedure, including a percentage or share of any assets, or by any other method in which the identity of the assets can be objectively determined, the records are considered to satisfy the requirements of Section 101.602(b)(1).

Added by Acts 2009, 81st Leg., ch. 84, § 45, eff. Sept. 1, 2009.

§ 101.604 Notice of Limitation on Liabilities of Series

Notice of the limitation on liabilities of a series required by Section 101.602 that is contained in a certificate of formation filed with the secretary of state satisfies the requirements of Section 101.602(b)(3), regardless of whether:

(1) the limited liability company has established any series under this subchapter when the notice is contained in the certificate of formation; and

(2) the notice makes a reference to a specific series of the limited liability company.

Added by Acts 2009, 81st Leg., ch. 84, § 45, eff. Sept. 1, 2009.

§ 101.605 General Powers of Series

A series established under this subchapter has the power and capacity, in the series' own name, to:

(1) sue and be sued;

(2) contract;

(3) hold title to assets of the series, including real property, personal property, and intangible property; and

(4) grant liens and security interests in assets of the series.

Added by Acts 2009, 81st Leg., ch. 84, § 45, eff. Sept. 1, 2009.

§ 101.606 Liability of Member or Manager for Obligations; Duties

(a) Except as and to the extent the company agreement specifically provides otherwise, a member or manager associated with a series or a member or manager of the company is not liable for a debt, obligation, or liability of a series, including a debt, obligation, or liability under a judgment, decree, or court order.

(b) The company agreement may expand or restrict any duties, including fiduciary duties, and related liabilities that a member, manager, officer, or other person associated with a series has to:

(1) the series or the company;

(2) a member or manager associated with the series; or

(3) a member or manager of the company.

Added by Acts 2009, 81st Leg., ch. 84, § 45, eff. Sept. 1, 2009.

§ 101.607 Class or Group of Members or Managers

(a) The company agreement may:

(1) establish classes or groups of one or more members or managers associated with a series each of which has certain express relative rights, powers, and duties, including voting rights; and

(2) provide for the manner of establishing additional classes or groups of one or more members or managers associated with the series each of which has certain express rights, powers, and duties, including providing for voting rights and rights, powers, and duties senior to existing classes and groups of members or managers associated with the series.

(b) The company agreement may provide for the taking of an action, including the amendment of the company agreement, without the vote or approval of any member or manager or class or group of members or managers, to create under the provisions of the company agreement a class or group of the series of membership interests that was not previously outstanding.

(c) The company agreement may provide that:

(1) all or certain identified members or managers or a specified class or group of the members or managers associated with a series have the right to vote on any matter separately or with all or any class or group of the members or managers associated with the series;

(2) any member or class or group of members associated with a series has no voting rights; and

(3) voting by members or managers associated with a series is on a per capita, number, financial interest, class, group, or any other basis.

Added by Acts 2009, 81st Leg., ch. 84, § 45, eff. Sept. 1, 2009.

§ 101.608 Governing Authority

(a) Notwithstanding any conflicting provision of the certificate of formation of a limited liability company, the governing authority of a series consists of the managers or members associated with the series as provided in the company agreement.

(b) If the company agreement does not provide for the governing authority of the series, the governing authority of the series consists of:

(1) the managers associated with the series, if the company's certificate of formation states that the company will have one or more managers; or

(2) the members associated with the series, if the company's certificate of formation states that the company will not have managers.

Added by Acts 2009, 81st Leg., ch. 84, § 45, eff. Sept. 1, 2009.

§ 101.609 Applicability of Other Provisions of Chapter; Synonymous Terms

(a) To the extent not inconsistent with this subchapter, this chapter applies to a series and its associated members and managers.

(b) For purposes of the application of any other provision of this chapter to a provision of this subchapter, and as the context requires:

(1) a reference to "limited liability company" or "company" means the "series";

(2) a reference to "member" means "member associated with the series"; and

(3) a reference to "manager" means "manager associated with the series."

Added by Acts 2009, 81st Leg., ch. 84, § 45, eff. Sept. 1, 2009.

§ 101.610 Effect of Certain Event on Manager or Member

(a) An event that under this chapter or the company agreement causes a manager to cease to be a manager with respect to a series does not, in and of itself, cause the manager to cease to be a manager of the limited liability company or with respect to any other series of the company.

(b) An event that under this chapter or the company agreement causes a member to cease to be associated with a series does not, in and of itself, cause the member to cease to be associated with any other series or terminate the continued membership of a member in the limited liability company or require the winding up of the series, regardless of whether the member was the last remaining member associated with the series.

Added by Acts 2009, 81st Leg., ch. 84, § 45, eff. Sept. 1, 2009.

§ 101.611 Member Status with Respect to Distribution

(a) Subject to Sections 101.613, 101.617, 101.618, 101.619, and 101.620, when a member associated with a series established under this subchapter is entitled to receive a distribution with respect to the series, the member, with respect to the distribution, has the same status as a creditor of the series and is entitled to any remedy available to a creditor of the series.

(b) Section 101.206 does not apply to a distribution with respect to the series.

Added by Acts 2009, 81st Leg., ch. 84, § 45, eff. Sept. 1, 2009. Amended by Acts 2011, 82nd Leg., ch. 139 (S.B. 748), § 40, eff. Sept. 1, 2011.

§ 101.612 Record Date for Allocations and Distributions

A company agreement may establish or provide for the establishment of a record date for allocations and distributions with respect to a series.

Added by Acts 2009, 81st Leg., ch. 84, § 45, eff. Sept. 1, 2009.

§ 101.613 Distributions

(a) A limited liability company may make a distribution with respect to a series.

(b) A limited liability company may not make a distribution with respect to a series to a member if, immediately after making the distribution, the total amount of the liabilities of the series, other than liabilities described by Subsection (c), exceeds the fair value of the assets associated with the series.

(c) For purposes of Subsection (b), the liabilities of a series do not include:

(1) a liability related to the member's membership interest; or

(2) except as provided by Subsection (e), a liability of the series for which the recourse of creditors is limited to specified property of the series.

(d) For purposes of Subsection (b), the assets associated with a series include the fair value of property of the series subject to a liability for which recourse of creditors is limited to specified property of the series only if the fair value of that property exceeds the liability.

(e) A member who receives a distribution from a series in violation of this section is not required to return the distribution to the series unless the member had knowledge of the violation.

(f) This section may not be construed to affect the obligation of a member to return a distribution to the series under the company agreement or other state or federal law.

(g) Section 101.206 does not apply to a distribution with respect to a series.

(h) For purposes of this section, "distribution" does not include an amount constituting reasonable compensation for present or past services or a reasonable payment made in the ordinary course of business under a bona fide retirement plan or other benefits program.

Added by Acts 2009, 81st Leg., ch. 84, § 45, eff. Sept. 1, 2009.

§ 101.614 Authority to Wind Up and Terminate Series

Except to the extent otherwise provided in the company agreement and subject to Sections 101.617, 101.618, 101.619, and 101.620, a series and its business and affairs may be wound up and terminated without causing the winding up of the limited liability company.

Added by Acts 2009, 81st Leg., ch. 84, § 45, eff. Sept. 1, 2009.

§ 101.615 Termination of Series

(a) Except as otherwise provided by Sections 101.617, 101.618, 101.619, and 101.620, the series terminates on the completion of the winding up of the business and affairs of the series in accordance with Sections 101.617, 101.618, 101.619, and 101.620.

(b) The limited liability company shall provide notice of the termination of a series in the manner provided in the company agreement for notice of termination, if any.

(c) The termination of the series does not affect the limitation on liabilities of the series provided by Section 101.602.

Added by Acts 2009, 81st Leg., ch. 84, § 45, eff. Sept. 1, 2009.

§ 101.616 Event Requiring Winding Up

Subject to Sections 101.617, 101.618, 101.619, and 101.620, the business and affairs of a series are required to be wound up:

(1) if the winding up of the limited liability company is required under Section 101.552(a) or Chapter 11; or

(2) on the earlier of:

(A) the time specified for winding up the series in the company agreement;

(B) the occurrence of an event specified with respect to the series in the company agreement;

(C) the occurrence of a majority vote of all of the members associated with the series approving the winding up of the series or, if there is more than one class or group of members associated with the series, a majority vote of the members of each class or group of members associated with the series approving the winding up of the series;

(D) if the series has no members, the occurrence of a majority vote of all of the managers associated with the series approving the winding up of the series or, if there is more than one class or group of managers associated with the series, a majority vote of the managers of each class or group of managers associated with the series approving the winding up of the series; or

(E) a determination by a court in accordance with Section 101.621.

Added by Acts 2009, 81st Leg., ch. 84, § 45, eff. Sept. 1, 2009.

§ 101.617 Procedures for Winding Up and Termination of Series

(a) The following provisions apply to a series and the associated members and managers of the series:

(1) Subchapters A, G, H, and I, Chapter 11; and

(2) Subchapter B, Chapter 11, other than Sections 11.051, 11.056, 11.057, 11.058, and 11.059.

(b) For purposes of the application of Chapter 11 to a series and as the context requires:

(1) a reference to "domestic entity," "filing entity," or "entity" means the "series";

(2) a reference to an "owner" means a "member associated with the series";

(3) a reference to the "governing authority" or a "governing person" means the "governing authority associated with the series" or a "governing person associated with the series"; and

(4) a reference to "business," "property," "obligations," or "liabilities" means the "business associated with the series," "property associated with the series," "obligations associated with the series," or "liabilities associated with the series."

(c) After the occurrence of an event requiring winding up of a series under Section 101.616, unless a revocation as provided by Section 101.618 or a cancellation as provided by Section 101.619 occurs, the winding up of the series must be carried out by:

(1) the governing authority of the series or one or more persons, including a governing person, designated by:

(A) the governing authority of the series;

(B) the members associated with the series; or

(C) the company agreement; or

(2) a person appointed by the court to carry out the winding up of the series under Section 11.054, 11.405, 11.409, or 11.410.

(d) An action taken in accordance with this section does not affect the limitation on liability of members and managers provided by Section 101.606.

Added by Acts 2009, 81st Leg., ch. 84, § 45, eff. Sept. 1, 2009.

§ 101.618 Revocation of Voluntary Winding Up

Before the termination of the series takes effect, a voluntary decision to wind up the series under Section 101.616(2)(C) or (D) may be revoked by:

(1) a majority vote of all of the members associated with the series approving the revocation or, if there is more than one class or group of members associated with the series, a majority vote of the members of each class or group of members associated with the series approving the revocation; or

(2) if the series has no members, a majority vote of all the managers associated with the series approving the revocation or, if there is more than one class or group of managers associated with the series, a majority vote of the managers of each class or group of managers associated with the series approving the revocation.

Added by Acts 2009, 81st Leg., ch. 84, § 45, eff. Sept. 1, 2009.

§ 101.619 Cancellation of Event Requiring Winding Up

(a) Unless the cancellation is prohibited by the company agreement, an event requiring winding up of the series under Section 101.616(1) or (2) may be canceled by the consent of all of the members of the series before the termination of the series takes effect.

(b) In connection with the cancellation, the members must amend the company agreement to:

(1) eliminate or extend the time specified for the series if the event requiring winding up of the series occurred under Section 101.616(1); or

(2) eliminate or revise the event specified with respect to the series if the event requiring winding up of the series occurred under Section 101.616(2).

Added by Acts 2009, 81st Leg., ch. 84, § 45, eff. Sept. 1, 2009.

§ 101.620 Continuation of Business

The series may continue its business following the revocation under Section 101.618 or the cancellation under Section 101.619.

Added by Acts 2009, 81st Leg., ch. 84, § 45, eff. Sept. 1, 2009.

§ 101.621 Winding Up by Court Order

A district court in the county in which the registered office or principal place of business in this state of a domestic limited liability company is located, on application by or for a member associated with the series, has jurisdiction to order the winding up and termination of a series if the court determines that it is not reasonably practicable to carry on the business of the series in conformity with the company agreement.

Added by Acts 2009, 81st Leg., ch. 84, § 45, eff. Sept. 1, 2009.

TITLE 4. PARTNERSHIPS

CHAPTER 151. GENERAL PROVISIONS

Section
151.001. Definitions.
151.002. Knowledge of Fact.
151.003. Notice of Fact.
151.004 Officers.

§ 151.001. Definitions

In this title:

(1) "Capital account" means the amount computed by:

(A) adding the amount of a partner's original and additional contributions of cash to a partnership, the agreed value of any other property that that partner originally or additionally contributed to the partnership, and allocations of partnership profits to that partner; and

(B) subtracting the amount of distributions to that partner and allocations of partnership losses to that partner.

(2) "Distribution" means a transfer of property, including cash, from a partnership to a partner in the partner's capacity as a partner or the partner's transferee.

(3) "Foreign limited partnership" means a partnership formed under the laws of another state that has one or more general partners and one or more limited partners.

(4) "Majority-in-interest," with respect to all or a specified group of partners, means partners who own more than 50 percent of the current percentage or other interest in the profits of the partnership that is owned by all of the partners or by the partners in the specified group, as appropriate.

(5) "Partnership agreement" means any agreement, written or oral, of the partners concerning a partnership.

Acts 2003, 78th Leg., ch. 182, § 1, eff. Jan. 1, 2006. Amended by Acts 2005, 79th Leg., ch. 64, § 76, eff. Jan. 1, 2006; Acts 2007, 80th Leg., ch. 688, § 103, eff. Sept. 1, 2007.

§ 151.002. Knowledge of Fact

For purposes of this title, a person has knowledge of a fact only if the person has actual knowledge of the fact.

Acts 2003, 78th Leg., ch. 182, § 1, eff. Jan. 1, 2006.

§ 151.003. Notice of Fact

(a) For purposes of this title, a person has notice of a fact if the person:

(1) has knowledge of the fact;

(2) has received a communication of the fact as provided by Subsection (c); or

(3) reasonably should have concluded, from all facts then known to that person, that the fact exists.

(b) A person notifies or gives notice to another person of a fact by taking actions reasonably required to inform the other person of the fact in the ordinary course of business, regardless of whether the other person actually has knowledge of the fact.

(c) A person is notified or receives notice of a fact when the fact is communicated to:

(1) the person;

(2) the person's place of business; or

(3) another place held out by the person as the place for receipt of communications.

(d) Receipt of notice by a general partner of a fact relating to the partnership is effective immediately as notice to the partnership unless fraud against the partnership is committed by or with the consent of the partner receiving the notice.

Acts 2003, 78th Leg., ch. 182, § 1, eff. Jan. 1, 2006. Amended by Acts 2011, 82nd Leg., ch. 139 (S.B. 748), § 41, eff. Sept. 1, 2011.

§ 151.004 Officers

A partnership may have elected or appointed officers in accordance with Section 3.103.

Added by Acts 2009, 81st Leg., ch. 84, § 46, eff. Sept. 1, 2009.

CHAPTER 152. GENERAL PARTNERSHIPS

SUBCHAPTER A. GENERAL PROVISIONS

Section
152.001. Definitions.
152.002. Effect of Partnership Agreement; Nonwaivable and Variable Provisions.
152.003. Supplemental Principles of Law.
152.004. Rule of Statutory Construction Not Applicable.
152.005. Applicable Interest Rate.

SUBCHAPTER B. NATURE AND CREATION OF PARTNERSHIP

152.051. Partnership Defined.
152.052. Rules for Determining if Partnership is Created.
152.053. Qualifications to be Partner; Nonpartner's Liability to Third Person.
152.054. False Representation of Partnership or Partner.

PARTNERSHIPS

Section
152.055. Authority of Certain Professionals to Create Partnership.
152.0551. Partnerships Formed by Physicians and Physician Assistants.
152.056. Partnership as Entity.

SUBCHAPTER C. PARTNERSHIP PROPERTY
152.101. Nature of Partnership Property.
152.102. Classification as Partnership Property.

SUBCHAPTER D. RELATIONSHIP BETWEEN PARTNERS AND BETWEEN PARTNERS AND PARTNERSHIPS
152.201. Admission as Partner.
152.202. Credits of and Charges to Partner.
152.203. Rights and Duties of Partner.
152.204. General Standards of Partner's Conduct.
152.205. Partner's Duty of Loyalty.
152.206. Partner's Duty of Care.
152.207. Standards of Conduct Applicable to Person Winding up Partnership Business.
152.208. Amendment to Partnership Agreement.
152.209. Decision–Making Requirement.
152.210. Partner's Liability to Partnership and Other Partners.
152.211. Remedies of Partnership and Partners.
152.212. Books and Records of Partnership.
152.213. Information Regarding Partnership.
152.214. Certain Third–Party Obligations Not Affected.

SUBCHAPTER E. RELATIONSHIP BETWEEN PARTNERS AND OTHER PERSONS
152.301. Partner as Agent.
152.302. Binding Effect of Partner's Action.
152.303. Liability of Partnership for Conduct of Partner.
152.304. Nature of Partner's Liability.
152.305. Remedy.
152.306. Enforcement of Remedy.
152.307. Extension of Credit in Reliance on False Representation.
152.308. Partner's Partnership Interest Subject to Charging Order.

SUBCHAPTER F. TRANSFER OF PARTNERSHIP INTERESTS
152.401. Transfer of Partnership Interest.
152.402. General Effect of Transfer.
152.403. Effect of Transfer on Transferor.
152.404. Rights and Duties of Transferee.
152.405. Power to Effect Transfer or Grant of Security Interest.
152.406. Effect of Death or Divorce on Partnership Interest.

SUBCHAPTER G. WITHDRAWAL OF PARTNER
152.501. Events of Withdrawal.
152.502. Effect of Event of Withdrawal on Partnership and Other Partners.
152.503. Wrongful Withdrawal; Liability.
152.504. Withdrawn Partner's Power to Bind Partnership.
152.505. Effect of Withdrawal on Partner's Existing Liability.

Section
152.506. Liability of Withdrawn Partner to Third Party.

SUBCHAPTER H. REDEMPTION OF WITHDRAWING PARTNER'S OR TRANSFEREE'S INTEREST
152.601. Redemption if Partnership Not Wound Up.
152.602. Redemption Price.
152.603. Contribution Obligation.
152.604. Setoff for Certain Damages.
152.605. Accrual of Interest.
152.606. Indemnification for Certain Liability.
152.607. Demand or Payment of Estimated Redemption.
152.608. Deferred Payment on Wrongful Withdrawal.
152.609. Action to Determine Terms of Redemption.
152.610. Deferred Payment on Winding Up Partnership.
152.611. Redemption of Transferee's Partnership Interest.
152.612. Action to Determine Transferee's Redemption Price.

SUBCHAPTER I. SUPPLEMENTAL WINDING UP AND TERMINATION PROVISIONS
152.701. Effect of Event Requiring Winding Up.
152.702. Persons Eligible to Wind Up Partnership Business.
152.703. Rights and Duties of Person Winding Up Partnership Business.
152.704. Binding Effect of Partner's Action After Event Requiring Winding Up.
152.705. Partner's Liability to Other Partners After Event Requiring Winding Up.
152.706. Disposition of Assets.
152.707. Settlement of Accounts.
152.708. Contributions to Discharge Obligations.
152.709. Cancellation or Revocation of Event Requiring Winding Up; Continuation of Partnership.
152.710. Reinstatement.

SUBCHAPTER J. LIMITED LIABILITY PARTNERSHIPS
152.801. Liability of Partner.
152.802. Registration.
152.803. Name.
152.804. Repealed.
152.805. Limited Partnership.

SUBCHAPTER K. FOREIGN LIMITED LIABILITY PARTNERSHIPS
152.901. General.
152.902. Name.
152.903. Activities Not Constituting Transacting Business.
152.904. Registered Agent and Registered Office.
152.905. Registration Procedure.
152.906. Withdrawal of Registration.
152.907. Effect of Certificate of Withdrawal.
152.908. Renewal of Registration.
152.909. Action by Secretary of State.
152.910. Effect of Failure to Register.
152.911. Amendment.
152.912. Execution of Application for Amendment.
152.913. Execution of Statement of Change of Registered Office or Registered Agent.
152.914. Revocation of Registration by Secretary of State.

SUBCHAPTER A. GENERAL PROVISIONS

§ 152.001. Definitions

In this chapter:

(1) "Event of withdrawal" or "withdrawal" means an event specified by Section 152.501(b).

(2) "Event requiring a winding up" means an event specified by Section 11.051 or 11.057.

(3) "Foreign limited liability partnership" means a partnership that:

(A) is foreign; and

(B) has the status of a limited liability partnership pursuant to the laws of the jurisdiction of formation.

(4) "Other partnership provisions" means the provisions of Chapters 151 and 154 and Title 1 to the extent applicable to partnerships.

(5) "Transfer" includes:

(A) an assignment;

(B) a conveyance;

(C) a lease;

(D) a mortgage;

(E) a deed;

(F) an encumbrance; and

(G) the creation of a security interest.

(6) "Withdrawn partner" means a partner with respect to whom an event of withdrawal has occurred.

Acts 2003, 78th Leg., ch. 182, § 1, eff. Jan. 1, 2006.

§ 152.002. Effect of Partnership Agreement; Nonwaivable and Variable Provisions

(a) Except as provided by Subsection (b), a partnership agreement governs the relations of the partners and between the partners and the partnership. To the extent that the partnership agreement does not otherwise provide, this chapter and the other partnership provisions govern the relationship of the partners and between the partners and the partnership.

(b) A partnership agreement or the partners may not:

(1) unreasonably restrict a partner's right of access to books and records under Section 152.212;

(2) eliminate the duty of loyalty under Section 152.205, except that the partners by agreement may identify specific types of activities or categories of activities that do not violate the duty of loyalty if the types or categories are not manifestly unreasonable;

(3) eliminate the duty of care under Section 152.206, except that the partners by agreement may determine the standards by which the performance of the obligation is to be measured if the standards are not manifestly unreasonable;

(4) eliminate the obligation of good faith under Section 152.204(b), except that the partners by agreement may determine the standards by which the performance of the obligation is to be measured if the standards are not manifestly unreasonable;

(5) vary the power to withdraw as a partner under Section 152.501(b)(1), (7), or (8), except for the requirement that notice be in writing;

(6) vary the right to expel a partner by a court in an event specified by Section 152.501(b)(5);

(7) restrict rights of a third party under this chapter or the other partnership provisions, except for a limitation on an individual partner's liability in a limited liability partnership as provided by this chapter;

(8) select a governing law not permitted under Sections 1.103 and 1.002(43)(C); or

(9) except as provided in Subsections (c) and (d), waive or modify the following provisions of Title 1:

(A) Chapter 1, if the provision is used to interpret a provision or to define a word or phrase contained in a section listed in this subsection;

(B) Chapter 2, other than Sections 2.104(c)(2), 2.104(c)(3), and 2.113;

(C) Chapter 3, other than Subchapters C and E of that chapter; or

(D) Chapters 4, 5, 10, 11, and 12, other than Sections 11.057(a), (b), (c)(1), (c)(3), and (d).

(c) A provision listed in Subsection (b)(9) may be waived or modified in a partnership agreement if the provision that is waived or modified authorizes the partnership to waive or modify the provision in the partnership's governing documents.

(d) A provision listed in Subsection (b)(9) may be waived or modified in a partnership agreement if the provision that is modified specifies:

(1) the person or group of persons entitled to approve a modification; or

(2) the vote or other method by which a modification is required to be approved.

Acts 2003, 78th Leg., ch. 182, § 1, eff. Jan. 1, 2006. Amended by Acts 2007, 80th Leg., ch. 688, § 104, eff. Sept. 1, 2007.

§ 152.003. Supplemental Principles of Law

The principles of law and equity and the other partnership provisions supplement this chapter unless otherwise provided by this chapter or the other partnership provisions.

Acts 2003, 78th Leg., ch. 182, § 1, eff. Jan. 1, 2006.

§ 152.004. Rule of Statutory Construction Not Applicable

The rule that a statute in derogation of the common law is to be strictly construed does not apply to this chapter or the other partnership provisions.

Acts 2003, 78th Leg., ch. 182, § 1, eff. Jan. 1, 2006.

§ 152.005. Applicable Interest Rate

If an obligation to pay interest arises under this chapter and the rate is not specified, the interest rate is the rate specified by Section 302.002, Finance Code.

Acts 2003, 78th Leg., ch. 182, § 1, eff. Jan. 1, 2006.

SUBCHAPTER B. NATURE AND CREATION OF PARTNERSHIP

§ 152.051. Partnership Defined

(a) In this section, "association" does not have the meaning of the term "association" under Section 1.002.

(b) Except as provided by Subsection (c) and Section 152.053(a), an association of two or more persons to carry on a business for profit as owners creates a partnership, regardless of whether:

(1) the persons intend to create a partnership; or

(2) the association is called a "partnership," "joint venture," or other name.

(c) An association or organization is not a partnership if it was created under a statute other than:

(1) this title and the provisions of Title 1 applicable to partnerships and limited partnerships;

(2) a predecessor to a statute referred to in Subdivision (1); or

(3) a comparable statute of another jurisdiction.

(d) The provisions of this chapter govern limited partnerships only to the extent provided by Sections 153.003 and 153.152 and Subchapter H, Chapter 153.

Acts 2003, 78th Leg., ch. 182, § 1, eff. Jan. 1, 2006.

§ 152.052. Rules for Determining if Partnership is Created

(a) Factors indicating that persons have created a partnership include the persons':

(1) receipt or right to receive a share of profits of the business;

(2) expression of an intent to be partners in the business;

(3) participation or right to participate in control of the business;

(4) agreement to share or sharing:

(A) losses of the business; or

(B) liability for claims by third parties against the business; and

(5) agreement to contribute or contributing money or property to the business.

(b) One of the following circumstances, by itself, does not indicate that a person is a partner in the business:

(1) the receipt or right to receive a share of profits as payment:

(A) of a debt, including repayment by installments;

(B) of wages or other compensation to an employee or independent contractor;

(C) of rent;

(D) to a former partner, surviving spouse or representative of a deceased or disabled partner, or transferee of a partnership interest;

(E) of interest or other charge on a loan, regardless of whether the amount varies with the profits of the business, including a direct or indirect present or future ownership interest in collateral or rights to income, proceeds, or increase in value derived from collateral; or

(F) of consideration for the sale of a business or other property, including payment by installments;

(2) co-ownership of property, regardless of whether the co-ownership:

(A) is a joint tenancy, tenancy in common, tenancy by the entirety, joint property, community property, or part ownership; or

(B) is combined with sharing of profits from the property;

(3) the right to share or sharing gross returns or revenues, regardless of whether the persons sharing the gross returns or revenues have a common or joint interest in the property from which the returns or revenues are derived; or

(4) ownership of mineral property under a joint operating agreement.

(c) An agreement by the owners of a business to share losses is not necessary to create a partnership.

Acts 2003, 78th Leg., ch. 182, § 1, eff. Jan. 1, 2006.

§ 152.053. Qualifications to be Partner; Nonpartner's Liability to Third Person

(a) A person may be a partner unless the person lacks capacity apart from this chapter.

(b) Except as provided by Section 152.307, a person who is not a partner in a partnership under Section 152.051 is not a partner as to a third person and is not liable to a third person under this chapter.

Acts 2003, 78th Leg., ch. 182, § 1, eff. Jan. 1, 2006.

§ 152.054. False Representation of Partnership or Partner

(a) A false representation or other conduct falsely indicating that a person is a partner with another person does not of itself create a partnership.

(b) A representation or other conduct indicating that a person is a partner in an existing partnership, if that is not the case, does not of itself make that person a partner in the partnership.

Acts 2003, 78th Leg., ch. 182, § 1, eff. Jan. 1, 2006.

§ 152.055. Authority of Certain Professionals to Create Partnership

(a) Persons licensed as doctors of medicine and persons licensed as doctors of osteopathy by the Texas State Board of Medical Examiners and persons licensed as podiatrists by the Texas State Board of Podiatric Medical Examiners may create a partnership that is jointly owned by those practitioners to perform a professional service that falls within the scope of practice of those practitioners.

(b) When doctors of medicine, osteopathy, and podiatry create a partnership that is jointly owned by those practitioners, the authority of each of the practitioners is limited by the scope of practice of the respective practitioners and none can exercise control over the other's clinical authority granted by their respective licenses, either through agreements, bylaws, directives, financial incentives, or other arrangements that would assert control over treatment decisions made by the practitioner.

(c) The Texas State Board of Medical Examiners and the Texas State Board of Podiatric Medical Examiners continue to exercise regulatory authority over their respective licenses.

Acts 2003, 78th Leg., ch. 182, § 1, eff. Jan. 1, 2006.

§ 152.0551. Partnerships Formed by Physicians and Physician Assistants

(a) Physicians licensed under Subtitle B, Title 3, Occupations Code, and physician assistants licensed under Chapter 204, Occupations Code, may create a partnership to perform a professional service that falls within the scope of practice of those practitioners.

(b) A physician assistant may not be a general partner or participate in the management of the partnership.

(c) A physician assistant may not contract with or employ a physician to be a supervising physician of the physician assistant or of any physician in the partnership.

(d) The authority of each practitioner is limited by the scope of practice of the respective practitioner. An organizer of the entity must be a physician and ensure that a physician or physicians control and manage the entity.

(e) Nothing in this section may be construed to allow the practice of medicine by someone not licensed as a physician under Subtitle B, Title 3, Occupations Code, or to allow a person not licensed as a physician to direct the activities of a physician in the practice of medicine.

(f) A physician assistant or combination of physician assistants may have only a minority ownership interest in an entity created under this section. The ownership interest of an individual physician assistant may not equal or exceed the ownership interest of any individual physician owner. A physician assistant or combination of physician assistants may not interfere with the practice of medicine by a physician owner or the supervision of physician assistants by a physician owner.

(g) The Texas Medical Board and the Texas Physician Assistant Board continue to exercise regulatory authority over their respective license holders according to applicable law. To the extent of a conflict between Subtitle B, Title 3, Occupations Code, and Chapter 204, Occupations Code, or any rules adopted under those statutes, Subtitle B, Title 3, or a rule adopted under that subtitle controls.

Added by Acts 2011, 82nd Leg., ch. 782 (H.B. 2098), § 2, eff. June 17, 2011.

Section 6 of Acts 2011, 82nd Leg., ch. 782 (H.B. 2098) provides:

"The restrictions on ownership interests in Sections 22.0561, 152.0551, and 301.012, Business Organizations Code, apply to an ownership interest acquired on or after the effective date [June 17, 2011] of this Act. An ownership interest acquired before the effective date of this Act is governed by the law in effect at the time the interest was acquired, and the former law is continued in effect for that purpose."

§ 152.056. Partnership as Entity

A partnership is an entity distinct from its partners.

Acts 2003, 78th Leg., ch. 182, § 1, eff. Jan. 1, 2006.

SUBCHAPTER C. PARTNERSHIP PROPERTY

§ 152.101. Nature of Partnership Property

Partnership property is not property of the partners. A partner or a partner's spouse does not have an interest in partnership property.

Acts 2003, 78th Leg., ch. 182, § 1, eff. Jan. 1, 2006.

§ 152.102. Classification as Partnership Property

(a) Property is partnership property if acquired in the name of:

(1) the partnership; or

(2) one or more partners, regardless of whether the name of the partnership is indicated, if the instrument transferring title to the property indicates:

(A) the person's capacity as a partner; or

(B) the existence of a partnership.

(b) Property is presumed to be partnership property if acquired with partnership property, regardless of whether the property is acquired as provided by Subsection (a).

(c) Property acquired in the name of one or more partners is presumed to be the partner's property, regardless of whether the property is used for partnership purposes, if the instrument transferring title to the property does not indicate the person's capacity as a partner or the existence of a partnership, and if the property is not acquired with partnership property.

(d) For purposes of this section, property is acquired in the name of the partnership by a transfer to:

(1) the partnership in its name; or

(2) one or more partners in the partners' capacity as partners in the partnership, if the name of the partnership is indicated in the instrument transferring title to the property.

Acts 2003, 78th Leg., ch. 182, § 1, eff. Jan. 1, 2006.

SUBCHAPTER D. RELATIONSHIP BETWEEN PARTNERS AND BETWEEN PARTNERS AND PARTNERSHIPS

§ 152.201. Admission as Partner

A person may become a partner only with the consent of all partners.

Acts 2003, 78th Leg., ch. 182, § 1, eff. Jan. 1, 2006.

§ 152.202. Credits of and Charges to Partner

(a) Each partner is credited with an amount equal to:

(1) the cash and the value of property the partner contributes to a partnership; and

(2) the partner's share of the partnership's profits.

(b) Each partner is charged with an amount equal to:

(1) the cash and the value of other property distributed by the partnership to the partner; and

(2) the partner's share of the partnership's losses.

(c) Each partner is entitled to be credited with an equal share of the partnership's profits and is chargeable with a share of the partnership's capital or operating losses in proportion to the partner's share of the profits.

Acts 2003, 78th Leg., ch. 182, § 1, eff. Jan. 1, 2006.

§ 152.203. Rights and Duties of Partner

(a) Each partner has equal rights in the management and conduct of the business of a partnership. A partner's right to participate in the management and conduct of the business is not community property.

(b) A partner may use or possess partnership property only on behalf of the partnership.

(c) A partner is not entitled to receive compensation for services performed for a partnership other than reasonable compensation for services rendered in winding up the business of the partnership.

(d) A partner who, in the proper conduct of the business of the partnership or for the preservation of its business or property, reasonably makes a payment or advance beyond the amount the partner agreed to contribute, or who reasonably incurs a liability, is entitled to be repaid and to receive interest from the date of the:

(1) payment or advance; or

(2) incurrence of the liability.

Acts 2003, 78th Leg., ch. 182, § 1, eff. Jan. 1, 2006.

§ 152.204. General Standards of Partner's Conduct

(a) A partner owes to the partnership, the other partners, and a transferee of a deceased partner's partnership interest as designated in Section 152.406(a)(2):

(1) a duty of loyalty; and

(2) a duty of care.

(b) A partner shall discharge the partner's duties to the partnership and the other partners under this code or under the partnership agreement and exercise any rights and powers in the conduct or winding up of the partnership business:

(1) in good faith; and

(2) in a manner the partner reasonably believes to be in the best interest of the partnership.

(c) A partner does not violate a duty or obligation under this chapter or under the partnership agreement merely because the partner's conduct furthers the partner's own interest.

(d) A partner, in the partner's capacity as partner, is not a trustee and is not held to the standards of a trustee.

Acts 2003, 78th Leg., ch. 182, § 1, eff. Jan. 1, 2006. Amended by Acts 2005, 79th Leg., ch. 64, § 77, eff. Jan. 1, 2006.

§ 152.205. Partner's Duty of Loyalty

A partner's duty of loyalty includes:

(1) accounting to and holding for the partnership property, profit, or benefit derived by the partner:

(A) in the conduct and winding up of the partnership business; or

(B) from use by the partner of partnership property;

(2) refraining from dealing with the partnership on behalf of a person who has an interest adverse to the partnership; and

(3) refraining from competing or dealing with the partnership in a manner adverse to the partnership.

Acts 2003, 78th Leg., ch. 182, § 1, eff. Jan. 1, 2006.

§ 152.206. Partner's Duty of Care

(a) A partner's duty of care to the partnership and the other partners is to act in the conduct and winding up of the partnership business with the care an ordinarily prudent person would exercise in similar circumstances.

(b) An error in judgment does not by itself constitute a breach of the duty of care.

(c) A partner is presumed to satisfy the duty of care if the partner acts on an informed basis and in compliance with Section 152.204(b).

Acts 2003, 78th Leg., ch. 182, § 1, eff. Jan. 1, 2006.

§ 152.207. Standards of Conduct Applicable to Person Winding up Partnership Business

Sections 152.204–152.206 apply to a person winding up the partnership business as the personal or legal representative of the last surviving partner to the same extent that those sections apply to a partner.

Acts 2003, 78th Leg., ch. 182, § 1, eff. Jan. 1, 2006.

§ 152.208. Amendment to Partnership Agreement

A partnership agreement may be amended only with the consent of all partners.

Acts 2003, 78th Leg., ch. 182, § 1, eff. Jan. 1, 2006.

§ 152.209. Decision–Making Requirement

(a) A difference arising in a matter in the ordinary course of the partnership business may be decided by a majority-in-interest of the partners.

(b) An act outside the ordinary course of business of a partnership may be undertaken only with the consent of all partners.

Acts 2003, 78th Leg., ch. 182, § 1, eff. Jan. 1, 2006.

§ 152.210. Partner's Liability to Partnership and Other Partners

A partner is liable to a partnership and the other partners for:

(1) a breach of the partnership agreement; or

(2) a violation of a duty to the partnership or other partners under this chapter that causes harm to the partnership or the other partners.

Acts 2003, 78th Leg., ch. 182, § 1, eff. Jan. 1, 2006.

§ 152.211. Remedies of Partnership and Partners

(a) A partnership may maintain an action against a partner for a breach of the partnership agreement or for the violation of a duty to the partnership causing harm to the partnership.

(b) A partner may maintain an action against the partnership or another partner for legal or equitable relief, including an accounting of partnership business, to:

(1) enforce a right under the partnership agreement;

(2) enforce a right under this chapter, including:

(A) the partner's rights under Sections 152.201–152.209, 152.212, and 152.213;

(B) the partner's right on withdrawal to have the partner's interest in the partnership redeemed under Subchapter H or to enforce any other right under Subchapters G and H; and

(C) the partner's rights under Subchapter I;

(3) enforce the rights and otherwise protect the interests of the partner, including rights and interests arising independently of the partnership relationship; or

(4) enforce a right under Chapter 11.

(c) The accrual of and a time limitation on a right of action for a remedy under this section is governed by other applicable law.

(d) A right to an accounting does not revive a claim barred by law.

Acts 2003, 78th Leg., ch. 182, § 1, eff. Jan. 1, 2006.

§ 152.212. Books and Records of Partnership

(a) In this section, "access" includes the opportunity to inspect and copy books and records during ordinary business hours.

(b) A partnership shall keep its books and records, if any, at its chief executive office.

(c) A partnership shall provide access to its books and records to a partner or an agent or attorney of a partner.

(d) The partnership shall provide a former partner or an agent or attorney of a former partner access to books and records pertaining to the period during which the former partner was a partner or for any other proper purpose with respect to another period.

(e) A partnership may impose a reasonable charge, covering the costs of labor and material, for copies of documents furnished under this section.

Acts 2003, 78th Leg., ch. 182, § 1, eff. Jan. 1, 2006.

§ 152.213. Information Regarding Partnership

(a) On request and to the extent just and reasonable, each partner and the partnership shall furnish complete and accurate information concerning the partnership to:

(1) a partner;

(2) the legal representative of a deceased partner or a partner who has a legal disability; or

(3) an assignee.

(b) A legal representative of a deceased partner or a partner who has a legal disability and an assignee are subject to the duties of a partner with respect to information made available.

Acts 2003, 78th Leg., ch. 182, § 1, eff. Jan. 1, 2006.

§ 152.214. Certain Third–Party Obligations Not Affected

Sections 152. 203, 152.208, and 152.209 do not limit a partnership's obligations to another person under Sections 152.301 and 152.302.

Acts 2003, 78th Leg., ch. 182, § 1, eff. Jan. 1, 2006.

SUBCHAPTER E. RELATIONSHIP BETWEEN PARTNERS AND OTHER PERSONS

§ 152.301. Partner as Agent

Each partner is an agent of the partnership for the purpose of its business.

Acts 2003, 78th Leg., ch. 182, § 1, eff. Jan. 1, 2006.

§ 152.302. Binding Effect of Partner's Action

(a) Unless a partner does not have authority to act for the partnership in a particular matter and the person with whom the partner is dealing knows that the partner lacks authority, an act of a partner, including the execution of an instrument in the partnership name, binds the partnership if the act is apparently for carrying on in the ordinary course:

(1) the partnership business; or

(2) business of the kind carried on by the partnership.

(b) An act of a partner that is not apparently for carrying on in the ordinary course a business described by Subsection (a) binds the partnership only if authorized by the other partners.

(c) A conveyance of real property by a partner on behalf of the partnership not otherwise binding on the partnership binds the partnership if the property has been conveyed by the grantee or a person claiming through the grantee to a holder for value without knowledge that the partner exceeded that partner's authority in making the conveyance.

Acts 2003, 78th Leg., ch. 182, § 1, eff. Jan. 1, 2006. Amended by Acts 2007, 80th Leg., ch. 688, § 105, eff. Sept. 1, 2007.

§ 152.303. Liability of Partnership for Conduct of Partner

(a) A partnership is liable for loss or injury to a person, including a partner, or for a penalty caused by or incurred as a result of a wrongful act or omission or other actionable conduct of a partner acting:

(1) in the ordinary course of business of the partnership; or

(2) with the authority of the partnership.

(b) A partnership is liable for the loss of money or property of a person who is not a partner that is:

(1) received in the course of the partnership's business; and

(2) misapplied by a partner while in the custody of the partnership.

Acts 2003, 78th Leg., ch. 182, § 1, eff. Jan. 1, 2006.

§ 152.304. Nature of Partner's Liability

(a) Except as provided by Subsection (b) or Section 152.801(a), all partners are jointly and severally liable for all obligations of the partnership unless otherwise:

(1) agreed by the claimant; or

(2) provided by law.

(b) A person who is admitted as a partner into an existing partnership does not have personal liability under Subsection (a) for an obligation of the partnership that:

(1) arises before the partner's admission to the partnership;

(2) relates to an action taken or omission occurring before the partner's admission to the partnership; or

(3) arises before or after the partner's admission to the partnership under a contract or commitment entered into before the partner's admission.

Acts 2003, 78th Leg., ch. 182, § 1, eff. Jan. 1, 2006. Amended by Acts 2007, 80th Leg., ch. 688, § 106, eff. Sept. 1, 2007; Acts 2011, 82nd Leg., ch. 139 (S.B. 748), § 42, eff. Sept. 1, 2011.

§ 152.305. Remedy

An action may be brought against a partnership and any or all of the partners in the same action or in separate actions.

Acts 2003, 78th Leg., ch. 182, § 1, eff. Jan. 1, 2006.

§ 152.306. Enforcement of Remedy

(a) A judgment against a partnership is not by itself a judgment against a partner. A judgment may be entered against a partner who has been served with process in a suit against the partnership.

(b) Except as provided by Subsection (c), a creditor may proceed against one or more partners or the property of the partners to satisfy a judgment based on a claim against the partnership only if a judgment:

(1) is also obtained against the partner; and

(2) based on the same claim:

(A) is obtained against the partnership;

(B) has not been reversed or vacated; and

(C) remains unsatisfied for 90 days after:

(i) the date on which the judgment is entered; or

(ii) the date on which the stay expires, if the judgment is contested by appropriate proceedings and execution on the judgment is stayed.

(c) Subsection (b) does not prohibit a creditor from proceeding directly against one or more partners or the property of the partners without first seeking satisfaction from partnership property if:

(1) the partnership is a debtor in bankruptcy;

(2) the creditor and the partnership agreed that the creditor is not required to comply with Subsection (b);

(3) a court orders otherwise, based on a finding that partnership property subject to execution in the state is clearly insufficient to satisfy the judgment or that compliance with Subsection (b) is excessively burdensome; or

(4) liability is imposed on the partner by law independently of the person's status as a partner.

(d) This section does not limit the effect of Section 152.801 with respect to a limited liability partnership.

Acts 2003, 78th Leg., ch. 182, § 1, eff. Jan. 1, 2006.

§ 152.307. Extension of Credit in Reliance on False Representation

(a) The rights of a person extending credit in reliance on a representation described by Section 152.054 are determined by applicable law other than this chapter and the other partnership provisions, including the law of estoppel, agency, negligence, fraud, and unjust enrichment.

(b) The rights and duties of a person held liable under Subsection (a) are also determined by law other than the law described by Subsection (a).

Acts 2003, 78th Leg., ch. 182, § 1, eff. Jan. 1, 2006.

§ 152.308. Partner's Partnership Interest Subject to Charging Order

(a) On application by a judgment creditor of a partner or of any other owner of a partnership interest, a court having jurisdiction may charge the partnership interest of the judgment debtor to satisfy the judgment.

(b) To the extent that the partnership interest is charged in the manner provided by Subsection (a), the judgment creditor has only the right to receive any distribution to which the judgment debtor would otherwise be entitled in respect of the partnership interest.

(c) A charging order constitutes a lien on the judgment debtor's partnership interest. The charging order lien may not be foreclosed on under this code or any other law.

(d) The entry of a charging order is the exclusive remedy by which a judgment creditor of a partner or of any other owner of a partnership interest may satisfy a judgment out of the judgment debtor's partnership interest.

(e) This section does not deprive a partner or other owner of a partnership interest of a right under exemption laws with respect to the judgment debtor's partnership interest.

(f) A creditor of a partner or of any other owner of a partnership interest does not have the right to obtain possession of, or otherwise exercise legal or equitable remedies with respect to, the property of the partnership.

Added by Acts 2011, 82nd Leg., ch. 139 (S.B. 748), § 43, eff. Sept. 1, 2011.

SUBCHAPTER F. TRANSFER OF PARTNERSHIP INTERESTS

§ 152.401. Transfer of Partnership Interest

A partner may transfer all or part of the partner's partnership interest.

Acts 2003, 78th Leg., ch. 182, § 1, eff. Jan. 1, 2006.

§ 152.402. General Effect of Transfer

A transfer of all or part of a partner's partnership interest:

(1) is not an event of withdrawal;

(2) does not by itself cause a winding up of the partnership business; and

(3) against the other partners or the partnership, does not entitle the transferee, during the continuance of the partnership, to participate in the management or conduct of the partnership business.

Acts 2003, 78th Leg., ch. 182, § 1, eff. Jan. 1, 2006.

§ 152.403. Effect of Transfer on Transferor

After transfer, the transferor continues to have the rights and duties of a partner other than the interest transferred.

Acts 2003, 78th Leg., ch. 182, § 1, eff. Jan. 1, 2006.

§ 152.404. Rights and Duties of Transferee

(a) A transferee of a partner's partnership interest is entitled to receive, to the extent transferred, distributions to which the transferor otherwise would be entitled.

(b) If an event requires a winding up of partnership business under Subchapter I, a transferee is entitled to receive, to the extent transferred, the net amount otherwise distributable to the transferor.

(c) Until a transferee becomes a partner, the transferee does not have liability as a partner solely as a result of the transfer.

(d) For a proper purpose the transferee may require reasonable information or an account of a partnership transaction and make reasonable inspection of the partnership books. In a winding up of partnership business, a transferee may require an accounting only from the date of the latest account agreed to by all of the partners.

(e) Until receipt of notice of a transfer, a partnership is not required to give effect to a transferee's rights under this section and Sections 152.401–152.403.

Acts 2003, 78th Leg., ch. 182, § 1, eff. Jan. 1, 2006.

§ 152.405. Power to Effect Transfer or Grant of Security Interest

A partnership is not required to give effect to a transfer prohibited by a partnership agreement.

Acts 2003, 78th Leg., ch. 182, § 1, eff. Jan. 1, 2006.

§ 152.406. Effect of Death or Divorce on Partnership Interest

(a) For purposes of this code:

(1) on the divorce of a partner, the partner's spouse, to the extent of the spouse's partnership interest, if any, is a transferee of the partnership interest ;

(2) on the death of a partner:

(A) if the partnership interest of the deceased partner is subject to redemption under Subchapter H, the partner's surviving spouse, if any, and an heir, devisee, personal representative, or other successor of the partner, to the extent of their respective right to the redemption price, are creditors of the partnership until the redemption price is paid; or

(B) if the partnership interest of the deceased partner is not subject to redemption under Subchapter H, the partner's surviving spouse, if any, and an heir, devisee, personal representative, or other successor of the partner, to the extent of their respective partnership interest, are transferees of the partnership interest; and

(3) on the death of a partner's spouse, an heir, devisee , personal representative, or other successor of the spouse, other than the partner, to the extent of their respective partnership interest, if any, is a transferee of the partnership interest .

(b) An event of the type described by Section 152.501 occurring with respect to a partner's spouse is not an event of withdrawal.

(c) This chapter does not impair an agreement for the purchase or sale of a partnership interest at any time, including on the death or divorce of an owner of the partnership interest.

Acts 2003, 78th Leg., ch. 182, § 1, eff. Jan. 1, 2006. Amended by Acts 2011, 82nd Leg., ch. 139 (S.B. 748), § 44, eff. Sept. 1, 2011.

SUBCHAPTER G. WITHDRAWAL OF PARTNER

§ 152.501. Events of Withdrawal

(a) A person ceases to be a partner on the occurrence of an event of withdrawal.

(b) An event of withdrawal of a partner occurs on:

(1) receipt by the partnership of notice of the partner's express will to withdraw as a partner on:

(A) the date on which the notice is received; or

(B) a later date specified by the notice;

(2) an event specified in the partnership agreement as causing the partner's withdrawal;

(3) the partner's expulsion as provided by the partnership agreement;

(4) the partner's expulsion by vote of a majority-in-interest of the other partners if:

(A) it is unlawful to carry on the partnership business with that partner;

(B) there has been a transfer of all or substantially all of that partner's partnership interest, other than:

(i) a transfer for security purposes that has not been foreclosed; or

(ii) the substitution of a successor trustee or successor personal representative;

(C) not later than the 90th day after the date on which the partnership notifies an entity partner, other than a nonfiling entity or foreign nonfiling entity partner, that it will be expelled because it has filed a certificate of termination or the equivalent, its existence has been involuntarily terminated or its charter has been revoked, or its right to conduct business has been terminated or suspended by the jurisdiction of its formation, if the certificate of termination or the equivalent is not revoked or its existence, charter, or right to conduct business is not reinstated; or

(D) an event requiring a winding up has occurred with respect to a nonfiling entity or foreign nonfiling entity that is a partner;

(5) the partner's expulsion by judicial decree, on application by the partnership or another partner, if the judicial decree determines that the partner:

(A) engaged in wrongful conduct that adversely and materially affected the partnership business;

(B) wilfully or persistently committed a material breach of:

(i) the partnership agreement; or

(ii) a duty owed to the partnership or the other partners under Sections 152.204–152.206; or

(C) engaged in conduct relating to the partnership business that made it not reasonably practicable to carry on the business in partnership with that partner;

(6) the partner's:

(A) becoming a debtor in bankruptcy;

(B) executing an assignment for the benefit of a creditor;

(C) seeking, consenting to, or acquiescing in the appointment of a trustee, receiver, or liquidator of that partner or of all or substantially all of that partner's property; or

(D) failing, not later than the 90th day after the appointment, to have vacated or stayed the appointment of a trustee, receiver, or liquidator of the partner or of all or substantially all of the partner's property obtained without the partner's consent or acquiescence, or not later than the 90th day after the date of expiration of a stay, failing to have the appointment vacated;

(7) if a partner is an individual:

(A) the partner's death;

(B) the appointment of a guardian or general conservator for the partner; or

(C) a judicial determination that the partner has otherwise become incapable of performing the partner's duties under the partnership agreement;

(8) termination of a partner's existence;

(9) if a partner has transferred all of the partner's partnership interest, redemption of the transferee's interest under Section 152.611; or

(10) an agreement to continue the partnership under Section 11.057(d) if the partnership has received a notice from the partner under Section 11.057(d) requesting that the partnership be wound up.

(c) Repealed by Acts 2007, 80th Leg., ch. 688, § 144(2).

Acts 2003, 78th Leg., ch. 182, § 1, eff. Jan. 1, 2006. Amended by Acts 2005, 79th Leg., ch. 64, § 78, eff. Jan. 1, 2006; Acts 2007, 80th Leg., ch. 688, §§ 107, 144(2), eff. Sept. 1, 2007.

§ 152.502. Effect of Event of Withdrawal on Partnership and Other Partners

A partnership continues after an event of withdrawal. The event of withdrawal affects the relationships among the withdrawn partner, the partnership, and the continuing partners as provided by Sections 152.503–152.506 and Subchapter H.

Acts 2003, 78th Leg., ch. 182, § 1, eff. Jan. 1, 2006.

§ 152.503. Wrongful Withdrawal; Liability

(a) At any time before the occurrence of an event requiring a winding up of partnership business, a partner may withdraw from the partnership and cease to be a partner as provided by Section 152.501.

(b) A partner's withdrawal is wrongful only if:

(1) the withdrawal breaches an express provision of the partnership agreement;

(2) in the case of a partnership that has a period of duration, is for a particular undertaking, or is required under its partnership agreement to wind up the partnership on occurrence of a specified event, before the expiration of the period of duration, the completion of the undertaking, or the occurrence of the event, as appropriate:

(A) the partner withdraws by express will;

(B) the partner withdraws by becoming a debtor in bankruptcy; or

(C) in the case of a partner that is not an individual, a trust other than a business trust, or an estate, the partner is expelled or otherwise withdraws because the partner wilfully dissolved or terminated; or

(3) the partner is expelled by judicial decree under Section 152.501(b)(5).

(c) In addition to other liability of the partner to the partnership or to the other partners, a wrongfully withdrawing partner is liable to the partnership and to the other partners for damages caused by the withdrawal.

Acts 2003, 78th Leg., ch. 182, § 1, eff. Jan. 1, 2006. Amended by Acts 2007, 80th Leg., ch. 688, § 108, eff. Sept. 1, 2007.

§ 152.504. Withdrawn Partner's Power to Bind Partnership

(a) The action of a withdrawn partner occurring not later than the first anniversary of the date of the person's withdrawal binds the partnership if the transaction would bind the partnership before the person's withdrawal and the other party to the transaction:

(1) does not have notice of the person's withdrawal as a partner;

(2) had done business with the partnership within one year preceding the date of withdrawal; and

(3) reasonably believed that the withdrawn partner was a partner at the time of the transaction.

(b) A withdrawn partner is liable to the partnership for loss caused to the partnership arising from an obligation incurred by the withdrawn partner after the withdrawal date and for which the partnership is liable under Subsection (a).

Acts 2003, 78th Leg., ch. 182, § 1, eff. Jan. 1, 2006.

§ 152.505. Effect of Withdrawal on Partner's Existing Liability

(a) Withdrawal of a partner does not by itself discharge the partner's liability for an obligation of the partnership incurred before the date of withdrawal.

(b) The estate of a deceased partner is liable for an obligation of the partnership incurred while the deceased was a partner to the same extent that a withdrawn partner is liable for an obligation of the partnership incurred before the date of withdrawal.

(c) A withdrawn partner is discharged from liability incurred before the date of withdrawal by an agreement to that effect between the partner and a partnership creditor.

(d) If a creditor of a partnership has notice of a partner's withdrawal and without the consent of the withdrawn partner agrees to a material alteration in the nature or time of payment of an obligation of the partnership incurred before the date of withdrawal, the withdrawn partner is discharged from the obligation.

Acts 2003, 78th Leg., ch. 182, § 1, eff. Jan. 1, 2006.

§ 152.506. Liability of Withdrawn Partner to Third Party

A person who withdraws as a partner in a circumstance that is not an event requiring a winding up of partnership business under Section 11.051 or 11.057 is liable to another party as a partner in a transaction entered into by the partnership or a surviving partnership under Section 10.001 not later than the second anniversary of the date of the partner's withdrawal only if the other party to the transaction:

(1) does not have notice of the partner's withdrawal; and

(2) reasonably believed that the withdrawn partner was a partner at the time of the transaction.

Acts 2003, 78th Leg., ch. 182, § 1, eff. Jan. 1, 2006.

SUBCHAPTER H. REDEMPTION OF WITHDRAWING PARTNER'S OR TRANSFEREE'S INTEREST

§ 152.601. Redemption if Partnership Not Wound Up

The partnership interest of a withdrawn partner automatically is redeemed by the partnership as of the date of withdrawal in accordance with this subchapter if:

(1) the event of withdrawal occurs under Sections 152.501(b)(1)–(9) and an event requiring a winding up of partnership business does not occur before the 61st day after the date of the withdrawal; or

(2) the event of a withdrawal occurs under Section 152.501(b)(10).

Acts 2003, 78th Leg., ch. 182, § 1, eff. Jan. 1, 2006.

§ 152.602. Redemption Price

(a) Except as provided by Subsection (b), the redemption price of a withdrawn partner's partnership interest is the fair value of the interest on the date of withdrawal.

(b) The redemption price of the partnership interest of a partner who wrongfully withdraws before the expiration of the partnership's period of duration, the completion of a particular undertaking, or the occurrence of a specified event requiring a winding up of partnership business is the lesser of:

(1) the fair value of the withdrawn partner's partnership interest on the date of withdrawal; or

(2) the amount that the withdrawn partner would have received if an event requiring a winding up of partnership business had occurred at the time of the partner's withdrawal.

(c) Interest is payable on the amount owed under this section.

Acts 2003, 78th Leg., ch. 182, § 1, eff. Jan. 1, 2006. Amended by Acts 2007, 80th Leg., ch. 688, § 109, eff. Sept. 1, 2007.

§ 152.603. Contribution Obligation

If a wrongfully withdrawing partner would have been required to make contributions to the partnership under Section 152.707 or 152.708 if an event requiring winding up of the partnership business had occurred at the time of withdrawal, the withdrawn partner is liable to the partnership to make contributions to the partnership in that amount and pay interest on the amount owed.

Acts 2003, 78th Leg., ch. 182, § 1, eff. Jan. 1, 2006.

§ 152.604. Setoff for Certain Damages

The partnership may set off against the redemption price payable to the withdrawn partner the damages for wrongful withdrawal under Section 152.503(b) and all other amounts owed by the withdrawn partner to the partnership, whether currently due, including interest.

Acts 2003, 78th Leg., ch. 182, § 1, eff. Jan. 1, 2006.

§ 152.605. Accrual of Interest

Interest payable under Sections 152.602–152.604 accrues from the date of the withdrawal to the date of payment.

Acts 2003, 78th Leg., ch. 182, § 1, eff. Jan. 1, 2006.

§ 152.606. Indemnification for Certain Liability

(a) A partnership shall indemnify a withdrawn partner against a partnership liability incurred before the date of withdrawal, except for a liability:

(1) that is unknown to the partnership at the time; or

(2) incurred by an act of the withdrawn partner under Section 152.504.

(b) For purposes of this section, a liability is unknown to the partnership if it is not known to a partner other than the withdrawn partner.

Acts 2003, 78th Leg., ch. 182, § 1, eff. Jan. 1, 2006.

§ 152.607. Demand or Payment of Estimated Redemption

(a) If a deferred payment is not authorized under Section 152.608 and an agreement on the redemption price of a withdrawn partner's interest is not reached before the 121st day after the date a written demand for payment is made by either party, not later than the 30th day after the expiration of the period, the partnership shall:

(1) pay to the withdrawn partner in cash the amount the partnership estimates to be the redemption price and any accrued interest, reduced by any setoffs and accrued interest under Section 152.604; or

(2) make written demand for payment of its estimate of the amount owed by the withdrawn partner to the partnership, minus any amount owed to the withdrawn partner by the partnership.

(b) If a deferred payment is authorized under Section 152.608 or a contribution or other amount is owed by the withdrawn partner to the partnership, the partnership may offer in writing to pay, or deliver a written statement of demand for, the amount it estimates to be the net amount owed, stating the amount and other terms of the obligation.

(c) On request of the other party, the payment, tender, offer, or demand required or allowed by Subsection (a) or (b) must be accompanied or followed promptly by:

(1) if payment, tender, offer, or demand is made or delivered by the partnership, a statement of partnership property and liabilities from the date of the partner's withdrawal and the most recent available partnership balance sheet and income statement, if any; and

(2) an explanation of the computation of the estimated payment obligation.

(d) The terms of a payment, tender, offer, or demand under Subsection (a) or (b) govern a redemption if:

(1) accompanied by written notice that:

(A) the payment or tendered amount, if made, fully satisfies a party's obligations relating to the redemption of the withdrawn partner's partnership interest; and

(B) an action to determine the redemption price, a contribution obligation or setoff under Section 152.603 or 152.604, or other terms of the redemption obligation must be commenced not later than the first anniversary of the later of:

(i) the date on which the written notice is given; or

(ii) the date on which the information required by Subsection (c) is delivered; and

(2) the party receiving the payment, tender, offer, or demand does not commence an action in the period described by Subdivision (1)(B).

Acts 2003, 78th Leg., ch. 182, § 1, eff. Jan. 1, 2006.

§ 152.608. Deferred Payment on Wrongful Withdrawal

(a) A partner who wrongfully withdraws before the expiration of the partnership's period of duration, the completion of a particular undertaking, or the occurrence of a specified event requiring a winding up of partnership business is not entitled to receive any portion of the redemption price until the expiration of the period, the completion of the undertaking, or the occurrence of the specified event, as appropriate, unless the partner establishes to the satisfaction of a court that earlier payment will not cause undue hardship to the partnership.

(b) A deferred payment accrues interest.

(c) The withdrawn partner may seek to demonstrate to the satisfaction of the court that security for a deferred payment is appropriate.

Acts 2003, 78th Leg., ch. 182, § 1, eff. Jan. 1, 2006. Amended by Acts 2007, 80th Leg., ch. 688, § 110, eff. Sept. 1, 2007.

§ 152.609. Action to Determine Terms of Redemption

(a) A withdrawn partner or the partnership may maintain an action against the other party under Section 152.211 to determine:

(1) the terms of redemption of that partner's interest, including a contribution obligation or setoff under Section 152.603 or 152.604; or

(2) other terms of the redemption obligations of either party.

(b) The action must be commenced not later than the first anniversary of the later of:

(1) the date of delivery of information required by Section 152.607(c); or

(2) the date written notice is given under Section 152.607(d).

(c) The court shall determine the terms of the redemption of the withdrawn partner's interest, any contribution obligation or setoff due under Section 152.603 or 152.604, and accrued interest and shall enter judgment for an additional payment or refund.

(d) If deferred payment is authorized under Section 152.608, the court shall also determine the security for payment if requested to consider whether security is appropriate.

(e) If the court finds that a party failed to tender payment or make an offer to pay or to comply with the requirements of Section 152.607(c) or otherwise acted arbitrarily, vexatiously, or not in good faith, the court may assess damages against the party, including, if appropriate, in an amount the court finds equitable:

(1) a share of the profits of the continuing business;

(2) reasonable attorney's fees; and

(3) fees and expenses of appraisers or other experts for a party to the action.

Acts 2003, 78th Leg., ch. 182, § 1, eff. Jan. 1, 2006.

§ 152.610. Deferred Payment on Winding Up Partnership

If a partner withdraws under Section 152.501 and not later than the 60th day after the date of withdrawal an event requiring winding up occurs under Section 11.051 or 11.057:

(1) the partnership may defer paying the redemption price to the withdrawn partner until the partnership makes a winding up distribution to the remaining partners; and

(2) the redemption price or contribution obligation is the amount the withdrawn partner would have received or contributed if the event requiring winding up had occurred at the time of the partner's withdrawal.

Acts 2003, 78th Leg., ch. 182, § 1, eff. Jan. 1, 2006.

§ 152.611. Redemption of Transferee's Partnership Interest

(a) A partnership must redeem the partnership interest of a transferee for its fair value if:

(1) the interest was transferred when:

(A) the partnership had a period of duration that had not yet expired;

(B) the partnership was for a particular undertaking not yet completed; or

(C) the partnership agreement provided for winding up of the partnership business on a specified event that had not yet occurred;

(2) the partnership's period of duration has expired, the particular undertaking has been completed, or the specified event has occurred; and

(3) the transferee makes a written demand for redemption.

(b) If an agreement for the redemption price of a transferee's interest is not reached before the 121st day after the date a written demand for redemption is made, the partnership must pay to the transferee in cash the amount the partnership estimates to be the redemption price and any accrued interest from the date of demand not later than the 30th day after the expiration of the period.

(c) On request of the transferee, the payment required by Subsection (b) must be accompanied or followed by:

(1) a statement of partnership property and liabilities from the date of the demand for redemption;

(2) the most recent available partnership balance sheet and income statement, if any; and

(3) an explanation of the computation of the estimated payment obligation.

(d) If the payment required by Subsection (b) is accompanied by written notice that the payment is in full satisfaction of the partnership's obligations relating to the redemption of the transferee's interest, the payment, less interest, is the redemption price unless the transferee, not later than the first anniversary of the written notice, commences an action to determine the redemption price.

Acts 2003, 78th Leg., ch. 182, § 1, eff. Jan. 1, 2006. Amended by Acts 2007, 80th Leg., ch. 688, § 111, eff. Sept. 1, 2007.

§ 152.612. Action to Determine Transferee's Redemption Price

(a) A transferee may maintain an action against a partnership to determine the redemption price of the transferee's interest.

(b) The court shall determine the redemption price of the transferee's interest and accrued interest and enter judgment for payment or refund.

(c) If the court finds that the partnership failed to make payment or otherwise acted arbitrarily, vexatiously, or not in good faith, the court may assess against the partnership in an amount the court finds equitable:

(1) reasonable attorney's fees; and

(2) fees and expenses of appraisers or other experts for a party to the action.

(d) The redemption of a transferee's interest under Sections 152.611(a) and (b) may be deferred as determined by the court if the partnership establishes to the satisfaction of the court that failure to defer redemption will cause undue hardship to the partnership business.

Acts 2003, 78th Leg., ch. 182, § 1, eff. Jan. 1, 2006.

SUBCHAPTER I. SUPPLEMENTAL WINDING UP AND TERMINATION PROVISIONS

§ 152.701. Effect of Event Requiring Winding Up

On the occurrence of an event requiring winding up of a partnership business under Section 11.051 or 11.057:

(1) the partnership continues until the winding up of its business is completed, at which time the partnership is terminated; and

(2) the relationship among the partners is changed as provided by this subchapter.

Acts 2003, 78th Leg., ch. 182, § 1, eff. Jan. 1, 2006.

§ 152.702. Persons Eligible to Wind Up Partnership Business

(a) After the occurrence of an event requiring a winding up of a partnership business, the partnership business may be wound up by:

(1) the partners who have not withdrawn;

(2) the legal representative of the last surviving partner; or

(3) a person appointed by the court to carry out the winding up under Subsection (b).

(b) On application of a partner, a partner's legal representative or transferee, or a withdrawn partner whose interest is not redeemed under Section 152.608, a court, for good cause, may appoint a person to carry out the winding up and may make an order, direction, or inquiry that the circumstances require.

Acts 2003, 78th Leg., ch. 182, § 1, eff. Jan. 1, 2006.

§ 152.703. Rights and Duties of Person Winding Up Partnership Business

(a) To the extent appropriate for winding up, as soon as reasonably practicable, and in the name of and for and on behalf of the partnership, a person winding up a partnership's business may take the actions specified in Sections 11.052, 11.053, and 11.055.

(b) Section 11.052(a)(2) shall not be applicable to a partnership.

Acts 2003, 78th Leg., ch. 182, § 1, eff. Jan. 1, 2006.

§ 152.704. Binding Effect of Partner's Action After Event Requiring Winding Up

After the occurrence of an event requiring winding up of the partnership business, a partnership is bound by a partner's act that:

(1) is appropriate for winding up; or

(2) would bind the partnership under Sections 152.301 and 152.302 before the occurrence of the event requiring winding up, if the other party to the transaction does not have notice that an event requiring winding up has occurred.

Acts 2003, 78th Leg., ch. 182, § 1, eff. Jan. 1, 2006.

§ 152.705. Partner's Liability to Other Partners After Event Requiring Winding Up

(a) Except as provided by Subsection (b), after the occurrence of an event requiring winding up of the partnership business, the losses with respect to which a partner must contribute under Section 152.708(a) include losses from a liability incurred under Section 152.704.

(b) A partner who incurs, with notice that an event requiring a winding up of the partnership business has occurred, a partnership liability under Section 152.704(2) by an act that is not appropriate for winding up is liable to the partnership for a loss caused to the partnership arising from that liability.

Acts 2003, 78th Leg., ch. 182, § 1, eff. Jan. 1, 2006.

§ 152.706. Disposition of Assets

(a) In winding up the partnership business, the property of the partnership, including any required contributions of the partners under Sections 152.707 and 152.708, shall be applied to discharge its obligations to creditors, including partners who are creditors other than in the partners' capacities as partners.

(b) A surplus shall be applied to pay in cash the net amount distributable to partners in accordance with their right to distributions under Section 152.707.

Acts 2003, 78th Leg., ch. 182, § 1, eff. Jan. 1, 2006.

§ 152.707. Settlement of Accounts

(a) Each partner is entitled to a settlement of all partnership accounts on winding up the partnership business.

(b) In settling accounts among the partners, the partnership interest of a withdrawn partner that is redeemed under Section 152.610 is credited with a share of any profits for the period after the partner's withdrawal but is charged with a share of losses for that period only to the extent of profits credited for that period.

(c) The profits and losses that result from the liquidation of the partnership property must be credited and charged to the partners' capital accounts.

(d) The partnership shall make a distribution to a partner in an amount equal to that partner's positive balance in the partner's capital account. Except as provided by Section 152.304(b) or 152.801, a partner shall contribute to the partnership an amount equal to that partner's negative balance in the partner's capital account.

Acts 2003, 78th Leg., ch. 182, § 1, eff. Jan. 1, 2006. Amended by Acts 2011, 82nd Leg., ch. 139 (S.B. 748), § 45, eff. Sept. 1, 2011.

§ 152.708. Contributions to Discharge Obligations

(a) Except as provided by Sections 152.304(b) and 152.801, to the extent not taken into account in settling the accounts among partners under Section 152.707:

(1) each partner shall contribute, in the proportion in which the partner shares partnership losses, the amount necessary to satisfy partnership obligations, excluding liabilities that creditors have agreed may be satisfied only with partnership property without recourse to individual partners;

(2) if a partner fails to contribute, the other partners shall contribute the additional amount necessary to satisfy the partnership obligations in the proportions in which the partners share partnership losses; and

(3) a partner or partner's legal representative may enforce or recover from the other partners, or from the estate of a deceased partner, contributions the partner or estate makes to the extent the amount contributed exceeds that partner's or the estate's share of the partnership obligations.

(b) The estate of a deceased partner is liable for the partner's obligation to contribute to the partnership.

(c) The following persons may enforce the obligation of a partner or the estate of a deceased partner to contribute to a partnership:

(1) the partnership;

(2) an assignee for the benefit of creditors of a partnership or a partner; or

(3) a person appointed by a court to represent creditors of a partnership or a partner.

Acts 2003, 78th Leg., ch. 182, § 1, eff. Jan. 1, 2006.

§ 152.709. Cancellation or Revocation of Event Requiring Winding Up; Continuation of Partnership

(a) If a partnership has a period of duration, is for a particular undertaking, or is required under its partnership agreement to wind up the partnership on occurrence of a specified event, all of the partners in the partnership may cancel under Section 11.152 an event requiring a winding up specified in Section 11.051(1) or (3), or Section 11.057(c)(1), by agreeing to continue the partnership business notwithstanding the expiration of the partnership's period of duration, the completion of the undertaking, or the occurrence of the event, as appropriate, other than the withdrawal of a partner. On reaching that agreement, the event requiring a winding up is canceled, the partnership is continued, and the partnership agreement is considered amended to provide that the expiration, the completion, or the occurrence of the event did not result in an event requiring winding up of the partnership.

(b) A continuation of the business for 90 days by the partners or those who habitually acted in the business during the partnership's period of duration or the undertaking or preceding the event, without a settlement or liquidation of the partnership business and without objection from a partner, is prima facie evidence of agreement by all partners to continue the business under Subsection (a).

(c) All of the partners of a partnership, by agreeing to continue the partnership, may cancel under Section 11.152 an event requiring winding up specified in Section 11.057(d) that arises from a request to wind up from a partner.

(d) To approve a revocation under Section 11.151 by a partnership of a voluntary decision to wind up pursuant to the express will of all the partners as specified in Section 11.057(b), prior to completion of the winding up process, all the partners must agree in writing to revoke the voluntary decision to wind up and to continue the business of the partnership.

(e) To approve a revocation under Section 11.151 by a partnership of a voluntary decision to wind up pursuant to the express will of a majority-in-interest of the partners as specified in Section 11.057(a), prior to completion of the winding up process, a majority-in-interest of the partners must agree in writing to revoke the voluntary decision to wind up and to continue the business of the partnership.

(f) All of the partners of a partnership, by agreeing to continue the partnership, may cancel under Section 11.152 an event requiring winding up specified in Section 11.057(c)(3) that arises from the sale of all or substantially all of the property of the partnership.

Acts 2003, 78th Leg., ch. 182, § 1, eff. Jan. 1, 2006. Amended by Acts 2007, 80th Leg., ch. 688, § 112, eff. Sept. 1, 2007.

§ 152.710. Reinstatement

To approve a reinstatement of a partnership under Section 11.202, all remaining partners, or another group or percentage of partners as specified by the partnership agreement, must agree in writing to reinstate and continue the business of the partnership.

Acts 2003, 78th Leg., ch. 182, § 1, eff. Jan. 1, 2006.

SUBCHAPTER J. LIMITED LIABILITY PARTNERSHIPS

§ 152.801. Liability of Partner

(a) Except as provided by the partnership agreement, a partner is not personally liable to any person, including a partner, directly or indirectly, by contribution, indemnity, or otherwise, for any obligation of the partnership incurred while the partnership is a limited liability partnership.

(b) Sections 2.101(1), 152.305, and 152.306 do not limit the effect of Subsection (a) in a limited liability partnership.

(c) For purposes of this section, an obligation is incurred while a partnership is a limited liability partnership if:

(1) the obligation relates to an action or omission occurring while the partnership is a limited liability partnership; or

(2) the obligation arises under a contract or commitment entered into while the partnership is a limited liability partnership.

(d) Subsection (a) does not affect:

(1) the liability of a partnership to pay its obligations from partnership property;

(2) the liability of a partner, if any, imposed by law or contract independently of the partner's status as a partner; or

(3) the manner in which service of citation or other civil process may be served in an action against a partnership.

(e) This section controls over the other parts of this chapter and the other partnership provisions regarding the liability of partners of a limited liability partnership, the chargeability of the partners for the obligations of the partnership, and the obligations of the partners regarding contributions and indemnity.

Acts 2003, 78th Leg., ch. 182, § 1, eff. Jan. 1, 2006. Amended by Acts 2009, 81st Leg., ch. 84, § 47, eff. Sept. 1, 2009; Acts 2011, 82nd Leg., ch. 139 (S.B. 748), § 46, eff. Sept. 1, 2011.

§ 152.802. Registration

(a) In addition to complying with Section 152.803 , a partnership, to become a limited liability partnership, must file an application with the secretary of state in accordance with Chapter 4 and this section. The application must:

(1) set out:

(A) the name of the partnership;

(B) the federal taxpayer identification number of the partnership;

(C) the street address of the partnership's principal office in this state or outside of this state, as applicable; and

(D) the number of partners at the date of application; and

(2) contain a brief statement of the partnership's business.

(b) The application must be signed by:

(1) a majority-in-interest of the partners; or

(2) one or more partners authorized by a majority-in-interest of the partners.

(c) A partnership is registered as a limited liability partnership by the secretary of state on:

(1) the date on which a completed initial or renewal application is filed in accordance with Chapter 4; or

(2) a later date specified in the application.

(d) A registration is not affected by subsequent changes in the partners of the partnership.

(e) The registration of a limited liability partnership is effective until the first anniversary of the date of registration or a later effective date, unless the application is:

(1) withdrawn or revoked at an earlier time; or

(2) renewed in accordance with Subsection (g).

(f) A registration may be withdrawn by filing a withdrawal notice with the secretary of state in accordance with Chapter 4. A certificate from the comptroller stating that all taxes administered by the comptroller under Title 2, Tax Code, have been paid must be filed with the notice of withdrawal. A withdrawal notice terminates the status of the partnership as a limited liability partnership from the date on which the notice is filed or a later date specified in the notice, but not later than the expiration date under Subsection (e). A withdrawal notice must:

(1) contain:

(A) the name of the partnership;

(B) the federal taxpayer identification number of the partnership;

(C) the date of registration of the partnership's last application under this subchapter; and

(D) the current street address of the partnership's principal office in this state and outside this state, if applicable; and

(2) be signed by:

(A) a majority-in-interest of the partners; or

(B) one or more partners authorized by a majority-in-interest of the partners.

(g) An effective registration may be renewed before its expiration by filing an application with the secretary of state in accordance with Chapter 4. A renewal application filed under this subsection continues an effective registration for one year after the date the registration would otherwise expire. The renewal application must contain:

(1) current information required for an initial application; and

(2) the most recent date of registration of the partnership.

(h) The secretary of state may remove from its active records the registration of a partnership the registration of which has:

(1) been withdrawn or revoked; or

(2) expired and not been renewed.

(i) Repealed by Acts 2011, 82nd Leg., ch. 139 (S.B. 748), § 66(2).

(j) A document filed under this subchapter may be amended by filing an application for amendment of registration with the secretary of state in accordance with Chapter 4 and this subsection. The application for amendment must:

(1) contain:

(A) the name of the partnership;

(B) the taxpayer identification number of the partnership;

(C) the identity of the document being amended;

(D) the date on which the document being amended was filed;

(E) a reference to the part of the document being amended; and

(F) the amendment or correction; and

(2) be signed by:

(A) a majority-in-interest of the partners; or

(B) one or more partners authorized by a majority-in-interest of the partners.

Acts 2003, 78th Leg., ch. 182, § 1, eff. Jan. 1, 2006. Amended by Acts 2009, 81st Leg., ch. 84, § 48, eff. Sept. 1, 2009; Acts 2011, 82nd Leg., ch. 139 (S.B. 748), §§ 47, 66(2), eff. Sept. 1, 2011.

§ 152.803. Name

The name of a limited liability partnership must comply with Section 5.063.

Acts 2003, 78th Leg., ch. 182, § 1, eff. Jan. 1, 2006.

§ 152.804. Repealed by Acts 2011, 82nd Leg., ch. (S.B. 748), § 66, eff. Sept. 1, 2011

§ 152.805. Limited Partnership

A limited partnership may become a limited liability partnership by complying with applicable provisions of Chapter 153.

Acts 2003, 78th Leg., ch. 182, § 1, eff. Jan. 1, 2006.

SUBCHAPTER K. FOREIGN LIMITED LIABILITY PARTNERSHIPS

§ 152.901. General

(a) A foreign limited liability partnership is subject to Section 2.101 with respect to its activities in this state to the same extent as a domestic limited liability partnership.

(b) A foreign limited liability partnership may not be denied registration because of a difference between the laws of the jurisdiction under which the partnership is formed and the laws of this state.

Acts 2003, 78th Leg., ch. 182, § 1, eff. Jan. 1, 2006. Amended by Acts 2007, 80th Leg., ch. 688, § 113, eff. Sept. 1, 2007.

§ 152.902. Name

The name of a foreign limited liability partnership must:

(1) satisfy the requirements of the jurisdiction of formation; and

(2) comply with Section 5.063.

Acts 2003, 78th Leg., ch. 182, § 1, eff. Jan. 1, 2006. Amended by Acts 2007, 80th Leg., ch. 688, § 114, eff. Sept. 1, 2007.

§ 152.903. Activities Not Constituting Transacting Business

Without excluding other activities that do not constitute transacting business in this state, a foreign limited liability partnership is not considered to be transacting business in this state for purposes of this code because it carries on in this state one or more of the activities listed by Section 9.251.

Acts 2003, 78th Leg., ch. 182, § 1, eff. Jan. 1, 2006.

§ 152.904. Registered Agent and Registered Office

A foreign limited liability partnership subject to this chapter shall maintain a registered office and registered agent in this state in the same manner and to the same extent as if the partnership were a foreign filing entity. Subchapters E and F, Chapter 5, apply to a foreign limited liability partnership to the same extent those subchapters apply to a foreign filing entity.

Acts 2003, 78th Leg., ch. 182, § 1, eff. Jan. 1, 2006. Amended by Acts 2005, 79th Leg., ch. 64, § 79, eff. Jan. 1, 2006.

§ 152.905. Registration Procedure

(a) Before transacting business in this state, a foreign limited liability partnership must file an application for registration in accordance with this section and Chapters 4 and 9.

(b) The application must be signed by:

(1) a majority-in-interest of the partners; or

(2) one or more partners authorized by a majority-in-interest of the partners.

(c) A partnership is registered as a foreign limited liability partnership on:

(1) the date on which a completed initial or renewal application for registration is filed with the secretary of state in accordance with Chapter 4; or

(2) a later date specified in the application.

(d) A registration is not affected by subsequent changes in the partners of the partnership.

(e) The registration of a foreign limited liability partnership is effective until the first anniversary of the date after the date of registration or a later effective date, unless the registration is:

(1) withdrawn or revoked at an earlier time; or

(2) renewed in accordance with Section 152.908.

Acts 2003, 78th Leg., ch. 182, § 1, eff. Jan. 1, 2006. Amended by Acts 2007, 80th Leg., ch. 688, §§ 115, 116, eff. Sept. 1, 2007.

§ 152.906. Withdrawal of Registration

(a) A registration may be voluntarily withdrawn by filing a certificate of withdrawal in accordance with this section and Section 9.011.

(b) In addition to the information required by Section 9.011, the certificate of withdrawal must:

(1) contain:

(A) the federal taxpayer identification number of the partnership; and

(B) the date of effectiveness of the partnership's last application for registration under this subchapter; and

(2) be signed by:

(A) a majority-in-interest of the partners; or

(B) one or more partners authorized by a majority-in-interest of the partners.

(c) A certificate from the comptroller stating that all taxes administered by the comptroller under Title 2, Tax Code, have been paid must be filed with the withdrawal of registration.

Acts 2003, 78th Leg., ch. 182, § 1, eff. Jan. 1, 2006. Amended by Acts 2005, 79th Leg., ch. 64, § 80, eff. Jan. 1, 2006; Acts 2009, 81st Leg., ch. 84, § 49, eff. Sept. 1, 2009; Acts 2011, 82nd Leg., ch. 139 (S.B. 748), § 48, eff. Sept. 1, 2011.

§ 152.907. Effect of Certificate of Withdrawal

A certificate of withdrawal terminates the registration of the partnership as a foreign limited liability partnership as of the date on which the notice is filed or a later date specified in the notice, but not later than the expiration date under Section 152.905(e).

Acts 2003, 78th Leg., ch. 182, § 1, eff. Jan. 1, 2006. Amended by Acts 2005, 79th Leg., ch. 64, § 81, eff. Jan. 1, 2006.

§ 152.908. Renewal of Registration

(a) An effective registration may be renewed before its expiration by filing a renewal application for registration with the secretary of state in accordance with Chapter 4.

(b) The renewal application must contain:

(1) current information required for an initial application for registration; and

(2) the most recent date of registration of the partnership.

(c) An application for registration filed under this section continues an effective registration for one year after the date the registration would otherwise expire.

Acts 2003, 78th Leg., ch. 182, § 1, eff. Jan. 1, 2006. Amended by Acts 2007, 80th Leg., ch. 688, § 117, eff. Sept. 1, 2007.

§ 152.909. Action by Secretary of State

The secretary of state may remove from its active records the registration of a foreign limited liability partnership the registration of which has:

(1) been withdrawn or revoked; or

(2) expired and not been renewed.

Acts 2003, 78th Leg., ch. 182, § 1, eff. Jan. 1, 2006.

§ 152.910. Effect of Failure to Register

(a) A foreign limited liability partnership that transacts business in this state without being registered is subject to Subchapter B, Chapter 9, to the same extent as a foreign filing entity.

(b) A partner of a foreign limited liability partnership is not liable for an obligation of the partnership solely because the partnership transacted business in this state without being registered.

Acts 2003, 78th Leg., ch. 182, § 1, eff. Jan. 1, 2006. Amended by Acts 2005, 79th Leg., ch. 64, § 82, eff. Jan. 1, 2006; Acts 2007, 80th Leg., ch. 688, § 118, eff. Sept. 1, 2007; Acts 2011, 82nd Leg., ch. 139 (S.B. 748), § 49, eff. Sept. 1, 2011.

§ 152.911. Amendment

(a) A document filed under this subchapter or an application for registration filed under Section 9.007 may be amended by filing with the secretary of state an application for amendment of registration in accordance with Chapter 4.

(b) The application for amendment must contain:

(1) the name of the partnership;

(2) the taxpayer identification number of the partnership;

(3) the identity of the document being amended;

(4) a reference to the date on which the document being amended was filed;

(5) the part of the document being amended; and

(6) the amendment or correction.

Acts 2003, 78th Leg., ch. 182, § 1, eff. Jan. 1, 2006. Amended by Acts 2005, 79th Leg., ch. 64, § 83, eff. Jan. 1, 2006; Acts 2011, 82nd Leg., ch. 139 (S.B. 748), § 50, eff. Sept. 1, 2011.

§ 152.912. Execution of Application for Amendment

The application for amendment must be signed by:

(1) a majority-in-interest of the partners; or

(2) one or more partners authorized by a majority-in-interest of the partners.

Acts 2003, 78th Leg., ch. 182, § 1, eff. Jan. 1, 2006.

§ 152.913. Execution of Statement of Change of Registered Office or Registered Agent

A statement filed by a foreign limited liability partnership in accordance with Section 5.202 must be signed by:

(1) a majority-in-interest of the partners; or

(2) one or more partners authorized by a majority-in-interest of the partners.

Acts 2003, 78th Leg., ch. 182, § 1, eff. Jan. 1, 2006.

§ 152.914. Revocation of Registration by Secretary of State

(a) The secretary of state may revoke the registration of a foreign limited liability partnership for the partnership's failure to:

(1) file a report within the period required by law or pay a fee or penalty prescribed by law when due and payable;

(2) maintain a registered agent or registered office address in this state as required by law; or

(3) pay a fee required in connection with a filing, or payment of the fee was dishonored when presented by the state for payment.

(b) If it appears to the secretary of state that, with respect to a foreign limited liability partnership, a circumstance described by Subsection (a) exists, the secretary of state shall provide notice to the partnership in the same manner and to the same extent as notice is required to be provided to a foreign filing entity under Sections 9.101 and 9.102.

(c) The secretary of state shall reinstate the registration of a foreign limited liability partnership if the partnership files an application for reinstatement in accordance with Subsection (e), accompanied by each amendment of the partnership's registration that is required by intervening events, and:

(1) the foreign limited liability partnership has corrected the circumstances that led to the revocation and any other circumstances described by Subsection (a) that may exist, including the payment of fees, interest, or penalties; or

(2) the secretary of state finds that the circumstances that led to the revocation did not exist at the time of revocation.

(d) A foreign limited liability partnership, to have its registration reinstated, must comply with the requirements of this section not later than the date the registration would have expired under Section 152.905(e) had the registration not been revoked under this section.

(e) The foreign limited liability partnership shall file a certificate of reinstatement in accordance with Chapter 4. The certificate of reinstatement must contain:

(1) the name of the partnership;

(2) the filing number assigned by the filing officer to the partnership;

(3) the effective date of the revocation of the partnership's registration; and

(4) the name of the partnership's registered agent and the address of the partnership's registered office.

(f) A tax clearance letter from the comptroller stating that a foreign limited liability partnership has satisfied all franchise tax liabilities and may be reinstated must be filed with the certificate of reinstatement if the foreign limited liability partnership is a taxable entity under Chapter 171, Tax Code.

Added by Acts 2005, 79th Leg., ch. 64, § 84, eff. Jan. 1, 2006. Amended by Acts 2007, 80th Leg., ch. 688, § 119, eff. Sept. 1, 2007; Acts 2009, 81st Leg., ch. 84, § 50, eff. Sept. 1, 2009.

CHAPTER 153. LIMITED PARTNERSHIPS

SUBCHAPTER A. GENERAL PROVISIONS

Section
153.001. Definition.
153.002. Construction.
153.003. Applicability of Other Laws.
153.004. Nonwaivable Title 1 Provisions.
153.005. Waiver or Modification of Rights of Third Parties.

SUBCHAPTER B. SUPPLEMENTAL PROVISIONS REGARDING AMENDMENT TO CERTIFICATE OF FORMATION

153.051. Required Amendment to Certificate of Formation.
153.052. Discretionary Amendment to Certificate of Formation.
153.053. Restated Certificate of Formation.

SUBCHAPTER C. LIMITED PARTNERS

153.101. Admission of Limited Partners.
153.102. Liability to Third Parties.
153.103. Actions Not Constituting Participation in Business for Liability Purposes.
153.104. Enumeration of Actions Not Exclusive.
153.105. Creation of Rights.
153.106. Erroneous Belief of Contributor Being Limited Partner.
153.107. Statement Required for Liability Protection.
153.108. Requirements for Liability Protection Following Expiration of Statement.
153.109. Liability of Erroneous Contributor.
153.110. Withdrawal of Limited Partner.
153.111. Distribution on Withdrawal.
153.112. Receipt of Wrongful Distribution.
153.113. Powers of Estate of Limited Partner Who is Deceased or Incapacitated.

SUBCHAPTER D. GENERAL PARTNERS

153.151. Admission of General Partners.
153.152. General Powers and Liabilities of General Partner.
153.153. Powers and Liabilities of Person Who is Both General Partner and Limited Partner.
153.154. Contributions by and Distributions to General Partner.
153.155. Withdrawal of General Partner.
153.156. Notice of Event of Withdrawal.
153.157. Withdrawal of General Partner in Violation of Partnership Agreement.
153.158. Effect of Withdrawal.
153.159. Conversion of Partnership Interest After Withdrawal.
153.160. Effect of Conversion of Partnership Interest.
153.161. Liability of General Partner for Debt Incurred After Event of Withdrawal.
153.162. Liability for Wrongful Withdrawal.

SUBCHAPTER E. FINANCES

153.201. Form of Contribution.
153.202. Enforceability of Promise to Make Contribution.
153.203. Release of Obligation to Partnership.
153.204. Enforceability of Obligation.
153.205. Requirements to Enforce Conditional Obligation.

Section
153.206. Allocation of Profits and Losses.
153.207. Right to Distribution.
153.208. Sharing of Distributions.
153.209. Interim Distributions.
153.210 Limitation on Distribution.

SUBCHAPTER F. PARTNERSHIP INTEREST

153.251. Assignment of Partnership Interest.
153.252. Rights of Assignor.
153.253. Rights of Assignee.
153.254. Liability of Assignee.
153.255. Liability of Assignor.
153.256. Partner's Partnership Interest Subject to Charging Order.
153.257. Exemption Laws Applicable to Partnership Interest Not Affected.

SUBCHAPTER G. REPORTS

153.301. Periodic Report.
153.302. Form and Contents of Report.
153.303. Filing Fee.
153.304. Delivery of Report.
153.305. Action by Secretary of State.
153.306. Effect of Filing Report.
153.307. Effect of Failure to File Report.
153.308. Notice of Forfeiture of Right to Transact Business.
153.309. Effect of Forfeiture of Right to Transact Business.
153.310. Revival of Right to Transact Business.
153.311 Termination of Certificate or Revocation of Registration After Forfeiture.
153.312. Reinstatement of Certificate of Formation or Registration.

SUBCHAPTER H. LIMITED PARTNERSHIP AS LIMITED LIABILITY PARTNERSHIP

153.351. Requirements.
153.352. Applicability of Other Requirements.
153.353. Law Applicable to Partners.

SUBCHAPTER I. DERIVATIVE ACTIONS

153.401. Right to Bring Action.
153.402. Proper Plaintiff.
153.403. Pleading.
153.404. Security for Expenses of Defendants.
153.405. Expenses of Plaintiff.

SUBCHAPTER J. CANCELLATION OF CERTIFICATE OF FORMATION [REPEALED]

153.451, 153.452. Repealed.

SUBCHAPTER K. SUPPLEMENTAL WINDING UP AND TERMINATION PROVISIONS

153.501. Cancellation or Revocation of Event Requiring Winding Up; Continuation of Business.
153.502. Winding Up Procedures.
153.503. Powers of Person Conducting Wind Up.
153.504. Disposition of Assets.
153.505. Approval of Reinstatement.

SUBCHAPTER L. MISCELLANEOUS PROVISIONS

Section
153.551. Records.
153.552. Examination of Records and Information.
153.553. Execution of Filings.
153.554. Execution, Amendment, or Cancellation by Judicial Order.
153.555. Permitted Transfer in Connection With Racetrack License.

SUBCHAPTER A. GENERAL PROVISIONS

§ 153.001. Definition

In this chapter, "other limited partnership provisions" means the provisions of Title 1 and Chapters 151 and 154, to the extent applicable to limited partnerships.

Acts 2003, 78th Leg., ch. 182, § 1, eff. Jan. 1, 2006.

§ 153.002. Construction

(a) This chapter and the other limited partnership provisions shall be applied and construed to effect its general purpose to make uniform the law with respect to limited partnerships among states that have similar laws.

(b) The rule that a statute in derogation of the common law is to be strictly construed does not apply to this chapter and the other limited partnership provisions.

Acts 2003, 78th Leg., ch. 182, § 1, eff. Jan. 1, 2006.

§ 153.003. Applicability of Other Laws

(a) Except as provided by Subsection (b), in a case not provided for by this chapter and the other limited partnership provisions, the provisions of Chapter 152 governing partnerships that are not limited partnerships and the rules of law and equity govern.

(b) The powers and duties of a limited partner shall not be governed by a provision of Chapter 152 that would be inconsistent with the nature and role of a limited partner as contemplated by this chapter.

(c) A limited partner shall not have any obligation or duty of a general partner solely by reason of being a limited partner.

Acts 2003, 78th Leg., ch. 182, § 1, eff. Jan. 1, 2006.

§ 153.004. Nonwaivable Title 1 Provisions

(a) Except as provided by this section, the following provisions of Title 1 may not be waived or modified in the partnership agreement of a limited partnership:

(1) Chapter 1, if the provision is used to interpret a provision or define a word or phrase contained in a section listed in this subsection;

(2) Chapter 2, other than Section 2.104(c)(2), 2.104(c)(3), or 2.113;

(3) Chapter 3, other than Subchapters C and E of that chapter and Section 3.151 (provided, that in all events a partnership agreement may not validly waive or modify Section 153.551 or unreasonably restrict a partner's right of access to books and records under Section 153.552); or

(4) Chapter 4, 5, 10, 11, or 12, other than Section 11.058.

(b) A provision listed in Subsection (a) may be waived or modified in the partnership agreement if the provision that is waived or modified authorizes the limited partnership to waive or modify the provision in the limited partnership's governing documents.

(c) A provision listed in Subsection (a) may be modified in the partnership agreement if the provision that is modified specifies:

(1) the person or group of persons who are entitled to approve a modification; or

(2) the vote or other method by which a modification is required to be approved.

Acts 2003, 78th Leg., ch. 182, § 1, eff. Jan. 1, 2006. Amended by Acts 2011, 82nd Leg., ch. 139 (S.B. 748), § 51, eff. Sept. 1, 2011.

§ 153.005. Waiver or Modification of Rights of Third Parties

A provision in this title or in that part of Title 1 applicable to a limited partnership that grants a right to a person, other than a general partner, a limited partner, or assignee of a partnership interest in a limited partnership, may be waived or modified in the partnership agreement of the limited partnership only if the person consents to the waiver or modification.

Acts 2003, 78th Leg., ch. 182, § 1, eff. Jan. 1, 2006.

SUBCHAPTER B. SUPPLEMENTAL PROVISIONS REGARDING AMENDMENT TO CERTIFICATE OF FORMATION

§ 153.051. Required Amendment to Certificate of Formation

(a) A general partner shall file a certificate of amendment reflecting the occurrence of one or more of the following events not later than the 30th day after the date on which the event occurred:

(1) the admission of a new general partner;

(2) the withdrawal of a general partner;

(3) a change in the name of the limited partnership; or

(4) except as provided by Section 5.202, a change in:

(A) the address of the registered office; or

(B) the name or address of the registered agent of the limited partnership.

(b) A general partner who becomes aware that a statement in a certificate of formation was false when made or that a matter described in the certificate has changed, making the certificate false in any material respect, shall promptly amend the certificate to make it accurate.

Acts 2003, 78th Leg., ch. 182, § 1, eff. Jan. 1, 2006.

§ 153.052. Discretionary Amendment to Certificate of Formation

(a) A certificate of formation may be amended at any time for a proper purpose as determined by the general partners.

(b) A certificate of formation may be amended to state the name, mailing address, and street address of the business or residence of each person winding up the limited partnership's affairs if, after an event requiring the winding up of a limited partnership but before the limited partnership is reconstituted or a certificate of termination is filed as provided by Section 11.101:

(1) the certificate of formation has been amended to reflect the withdrawal of all general partners; or

(2) a person who is not shown on the certificate of formation as a general partner is carrying out the winding up of a limited partnership's affairs.

(c) If the certificate of formation is amended under Subsection (b), each person winding up the limited partnership's affairs shall execute and file the certificate of amendment. A person winding up the partnership's affairs is not subject to liability as a general partner because of the filing of the certificate of amendment.

(d) A general partner who is not winding up the limited partnership's affairs is not required to execute and file a certificate of amendment as provided by this section.

Acts 2003, 78th Leg., ch. 182, § 1, eff. Jan. 1, 2006. Amended by Acts 2005, 79th Leg., ch. 64, § 85, eff. Jan. 1, 2006; Acts 2007, 80th Leg., ch. 688, § 120, eff. Sept. 1, 2007.

§ 153.053. Restated Certificate of Formation

(a) The general partners may adopt at any time a restated certificate of formation that does not contain an amendment to the certificate of formation.

(b) A restated certificate of formation that contains an amendment to the certificate of formation may be adopted at any time for a proper purpose as determined by the general partners.

Added by Acts 2005, 79th Leg., ch. 64, § 86, eff. Jan. 1, 2006.

SUBCHAPTER C. LIMITED PARTNERS

§ 153.101. Admission of Limited Partners

(a) In connection with the formation of a limited partnership, a person acquiring a limited partnership interest becomes a limited partner on the later of:

(1) the date on which the limited partnership is formed; or

(2) the date stated in the records of the limited partnership as the date on which the person becomes a limited partner or, if that date is not stated in those records, the date on which the person's admission is first reflected in the records of the limited partnership.

(b) After a limited partnership is formed, a person who acquires a partnership interest directly from the limited partnership becomes a new limited partner on:

(1) compliance with the provisions of the partnership agreement governing admission of new limited partners; or

(2) if the partnership agreement does not contain relevant admission provisions, the written consent of all partners.

(c) After formation of a limited partnership, an assignee of a partnership interest becomes a new limited partner as provided by Section 153.253(a).

(d) A person may be a limited partner unless the person lacks capacity apart from this chapter and the other limited partnership provisions.

Acts 2003, 78th Leg., ch. 182, § 1, eff. Jan. 1, 2006.

§ 153.102. Liability to Third Parties

(a) A limited partner is not liable for the obligations of a limited partnership unless:

(1) the limited partner is also a general partner; or

(2) in addition to the exercise of the limited partner's rights and powers as a limited partner, the limited partner participates in the control of the business.

(b) If the limited partner participates in the control of the business, the limited partner is liable only to a person who transacts business with the limited partnership reasonably believing, based on the limited partner's conduct, that the limited partner is a general partner.

Acts 2003, 78th Leg., ch. 182, § 1, eff. Jan. 1, 2006.

§ 153.103. Actions Not Constituting Participation in Business for Liability Purposes

For purposes of this section and Sections 153.102, 153.104, and 153.105, a limited partner does not participate in the control of the business because the limited partner has or has acted in one or more of the following capacities or possesses or exercises one or more of the following powers:

(1) acting as:

(A) a contractor for or an officer or other agent or employee of the limited partnership;

(B) a contractor for or an agent or employee of a general partner;

(C) an officer, director, or stockholder of a corporate general partner;

(D) a partner of a partnership that is a general partner of the limited partnership; or

(E) a member or manager of a limited liability company that is a general partner of the limited partnership;

(2) acting in a capacity similar to that described in Subdivision (1) with any other person that is a general partner of the limited partnership;

(3) consulting with or advising a general partner on any matter, including the business of the limited partnership;

(4) acting as surety, guarantor, or endorser for the limited partnership, guaranteeing or assuming one or more specific obligations of the limited partnership, or providing collateral for borrowings of the limited partnership;

(5) calling, requesting, attending, or participating in a meeting of the partners or the limited partners;

(6) winding up the business of a limited partnership under Chapter 11 and Subchapter K of this chapter;

(7) taking an action required or permitted by law to bring, pursue, settle, or otherwise terminate a derivative action in the right of the limited partnership;

(8) serving on a committee of the limited partnership or the limited partners; or

(9) proposing, approving, or disapproving, by vote or otherwise, one or more of the following matters:

(A) the winding up or termination of the limited partnership;

(B) an election to reconstitute the limited partnership or continue the business of the limited partnership;

(C) the sale, exchange, lease, mortgage, assignment, pledge, or other transfer of, or granting of a security interest in, an asset of the limited partnership;

(D) the incurring, renewal, refinancing, or payment or other discharge of indebtedness by the limited partnership;

(E) a change in the nature of the business of the limited partnership;

(F) the admission, removal, or retention of a general partner;

(G) the admission, removal, or retention of a limited partner;

(H) a transaction or other matter involving an actual or potential conflict of interest;

(I) an amendment to the partnership agreement or certificate of formation;

(J) if the limited partnership is qualified as an investment company under the federal Investment Company Act of 1940 (15 U.S.C. Section 80a-1 et seq.), as amended, any matter required by that Act or the rules and regulations of the Securities and Exchange Commission under that Act, to be approved by the holders of beneficial interests in an investment company, including:

(i) electing directors or trustees of the investment company;

(ii) approving or terminating an investment advisory or underwriting contract;

(iii) approving an auditor; and

(iv) acting on another matter that that Act requires to be approved by the holders of beneficial interests in the investment company;

(K) indemnification of a general partner under Chapter 8 or otherwise;

(L) any other matter stated in the partnership agreement;

(M) the exercising of a right or power granted or permitted to limited partners under this code and not specifically enumerated in this section; or

(N) the merger, conversion, or interest exchange with respect to a limited partnership.

Acts 2003, 78th Leg., ch. 182, § 1, eff. Jan. 1, 2006. Amended by Acts 2007, 80th Leg., ch. 688, § 121, eff. Sept. 1, 2007; Acts 2009, 81st Leg., ch. 84, § 51, eff. Sept. 1, 2009; Acts 2011, 82nd Leg., ch. 139 (S.B. 748), § 52, eff. Sept. 1, 2011.

§ 153.104. Enumeration of Actions Not Exclusive

The enumeration in Section 153.103 does not mean that a limited partner who has acted or acts in another capacity or possesses or exercises another power constitutes participation by that limited partner in the control of the business of the limited partnership.

Acts 2003, 78th Leg., ch. 182, § 1, eff. Jan. 1, 2006.

§ 153.105. Creation of Rights

Sections 153.103 and 153.104 do not create rights of limited partners. Rights of limited partners may be created only by:

(1) the certificate of formation;

(2) the partnership agreement;

(3) other sections of this chapter; or

(4) the other limited partnership provisions.

Acts 2003, 78th Leg., ch. 182, § 1, eff. Jan. 1, 2006.

§ 153.106. Erroneous Belief of Contributor Being Limited Partner

Except as provided by Section 153.109, a person who erroneously but in good faith believes that the person has made a contribution to and has become a limited partner in a limited partnership is not liable as a general partner or otherwise obligated because of making or attempting to make the contribution, receiving distributions from the partnership, or exercising the rights of a limited partner if, within a reasonable time after ascertaining the mistake, the person:

(1) causes an appropriate certificate of formation or certificate of amendment to be signed and filed;

(2) files or causes to be filed with the secretary of state a written statement in accordance with Section 153.107; or

(3) withdraws from participation in future profits of the enterprise by executing and filing with the secretary of state a certificate declaring the person's withdrawal under this section.

Acts 2003, 78th Leg., ch. 182, § 1, eff. Jan. 1, 2006.

§ 153.107. Statement Required for Liability Protection

(a) A written statement filed under Section 153.106(2) must be entitled "Filing under Section 153.106(2), Business Organizations Code," and contain:

(1) the name of the partnership;

(2) the name and mailing address of the person signing the written statement; and

(3) a statement that:

(A) the person signing the written statement acquired a limited partnership interest in the partnership;

(B) the person signing the written statement has made an effort to cause a general partner of the partnership to file an accurate certificate of formation required by the code and the general partner has failed or refused to file the certificate; and

(C) the statement is being filed under Section 153.106(2) and the person signing the written statement is claiming status as a limited partner of the partnership named in the document.

(b) The statement is effective for 180 days.

(c) A statement filed under Section 153.106(2) may be signed by more than one person claiming limited partnership status under this section and Sections 153.106, 153.108, and 153.109.

Acts 2003, 78th Leg., ch. 182, § 1, eff. Jan. 1, 2006.

§ 153.108. Requirements for Liability Protection Following Expiration of Statement

(a) If a certificate described by Section 153.106(1) has not been filed before the expiration of the 180–day period described by Section 153.107(b), the person filing the statement has no further protection from liability under Section 153.106(2) unless the person complies with this section. To be protected under Section 153.106 the person must, not later than the 10th day after the date of expiration of the 180–day period:

(1) withdraw under Section 153.106(3); or

(2) bring an action under Section 153.554 to compel the execution and filing of a certificate of formation or amendment.

(b) If an action is brought within the applicable period and is diligently prosecuted to conclusion, the person bringing the action continues to be protected from liability under Section 153.106(2) until the action is finally decided adversely to that person.

(c) This section and Sections 153.106, 153.107, and 153.109 do not protect a person from liability that arises under Sections 153.102–153.105.

Acts 2003, 78th Leg., ch. 182, § 1, eff. Jan. 1, 2006.

§ 153.109. Liability of Erroneous Contributor

Regardless of whether Sections 153.106, 153.107, and 153.108 apply, a person who makes a contribution in the circumstances described by Section 153.106 is liable as a general partner to a third party who transacts business with the partnership before an action taken under Section 153.106 if:

(1) the contributor has knowledge or notice that no certificate has been filed or that the certificate inaccurately referred to the contributor as a general partner; and

(2) the third party reasonably believed, based on the contributor's conduct, that the contributor was a general partner at the time of the transaction and extended credit to the partnership in reasonable reliance on the credit of the contributor.

Acts 2003, 78th Leg., ch. 182, § 1, eff. Jan. 1, 2006.

§ 153.110. Withdrawal of Limited Partner

A limited partner may withdraw from a limited partnership only at the time or on the occurrence of an event specified in a written partnership agreement. The withdrawal of the partner must be made in accordance with that agreement.

Acts 2003, 78th Leg., ch. 182, § 1, eff. Jan. 1, 2006.

§ 153.111. Distribution on Withdrawal

Except as otherwise provided by Section 153.210 or the partnership agreement, on withdrawal a withdrawing limited partner is entitled to receive, not later than a reasonable time after withdrawal, the fair value of that limited partner's interest in the limited partnership as of the date of withdrawal.

Acts 2003, 78th Leg., ch. 182, § 1, eff. Jan. 1, 2006.

§ 153.112. Receipt of Wrongful Distribution

A limited partner who receives a distribution that is not permitted under Section 153.210 is not required to return the distribution unless the limited partner knew that the distribution violated the prohibition of Section 153.210. This section does not affect an obligation of the limited partner under the partnership agreement or other applicable law to return the distribution.

Acts 2003, 78th Leg., ch. 182, § 1, eff. Jan. 1, 2006.

§ 153.113. Powers of Estate of Limited Partner Who is Deceased or Incapacitated

If a limited partner who is an individual dies or a court adjudges the limited partner to be incapacitated in managing the limited partner's person or property, the limited partner's executor, administrator, guardian, conservator, or other legal representative may exercise all of the limited partner's rights and powers to settle the limited partner's estate or administer the limited partner's property, including the power of an assignee to become a limited partner under the partnership agreement.

Acts 2003, 78th Leg., ch. 182, § 1, eff. Jan. 1, 2006.

SUBCHAPTER D. GENERAL PARTNERS

§ 153.151. Admission of General Partners

(a) After a limited partnership is formed, additional general partners may be admitted:

(1) in the manner provided by a written partnership agreement; or

(2) if a written partnership agreement does not provide for the admission of additional general partners, with the written consent of all partners.

(b) A person may be a general partner unless the person lacks capacity apart from this chapter.

(c) A written partnership agreement may provide that a person may be admitted as a general partner in a limited partnership, including as a sole general partner, and may acquire a partnership interest in the limited partnership without:

(1) making a contribution to the limited partnership; or

(2) assuming an obligation to make a contribution to the limited partnership.

(d) A written partnership agreement may provide that a person may be admitted as a general partner in a limited partnership, including as the sole general partner, without acquiring a partnership interest in the limited partnership.

(e) This section is not a limitation of or does not otherwise affect Section 153.152.

Acts 2003, 78th Leg., ch. 182, § 1, eff. Jan. 1, 2006. Amended by Acts 2005, 79th Leg., ch. 64, §§ 87, 88, eff. Jan. 1, 2006.

§ 153.152. General Powers and Liabilities of General Partner

(a) Except as provided by this chapter, the other limited partnership provisions, or a partnership agreement, a general partner of a limited partnership:

(1) has the rights and powers and is subject to the restrictions of a partner in a partnership without limited partners; and

(2) has the liabilities of a partner in a partnership without limited partners to the partnership and to the other partners.

(b) Except as provided by this chapter or the other limited partnership provisions, a general partner of a limited partnership has the liabilities of a partner in a partnership without limited partners to a person other than the partnership and the other partners.

Acts 2003, 78th Leg., ch. 182, § 1, eff. Jan. 1, 2006.

§ 153.153. Powers and Liabilities of Person Who is Both General Partner and Limited Partner

A person who is both a general partner and a limited partner:

(1) has the rights and powers and is subject to the restrictions and liabilities of a general partner; and

(2) except as otherwise provided by the partnership agreement, this chapter, or the other limited partnership provisions, has the rights and powers and is subject to the restrictions and liabilities, if any, of a limited partner to the extent of the general partner's participation in the partnership as a limited partner.

Acts 2003, 78th Leg., ch. 182, § 1, eff. Jan. 1, 2006.

§ 153.154. Contributions by and Distributions to General Partner

A general partner of a limited partnership may make a contribution to, be allocated profits and losses of, and receive a distribution from the limited partnership as a general partner, a limited partner, or both.

Acts 2003, 78th Leg., ch. 182, § 1, eff. Jan. 1, 2006.

§ 153.155. Withdrawal of General Partner

(a) A person ceases to be a general partner of a limited partnership on the occurrence of one or more of the following events of withdrawal:

(1) the general partner withdraws as a general partner from the limited partnership as provided by Subsection (b);

(2) the general partner ceases to be a general partner of the limited partnership as provided by Section 153.252(b);

(3) the general partner is removed as a general partner in accordance with the partnership agreement;

(4) unless otherwise provided by a written partnership agreement, or with the written consent of all partners, the general partner:

(A) makes a general assignment for the benefit of creditors;

(B) files a voluntary bankruptcy petition;

(C) becomes the subject of an order for relief or is declared insolvent in a federal or state bankruptcy or insolvency proceeding;

(D) files a petition or answer seeking for the general partner a reorganization, arrangement, composition, readjustment, liquidation, winding up, termination, dissolution, or similar relief under law;

(E) files a pleading admitting or failing to contest the material allegations of a petition filed against the general partner in a proceeding of the type described by Paragraphs (A)–(D); or

(F) seeks, consents to, or acquiesces in the appointment of a trustee, receiver, or liquidator of the general partner or of all or a substantial part of the general partner's properties;

(5) unless otherwise provided by a written partnership agreement or with the written consent of all partners, the expiration of:

(A) 120 days after the date of the commencement of a proceeding against the general partner seeking reorganization, arrangement, composition, readjustment, liquidation, dissolution, or similar relief under law if the proceeding has not been previously dismissed;

(B) 90 days after the date of the appointment, without the general partner's consent, of a trustee, receiver, or liquidator of the general partner or of all or a substantial part of the general partner's properties if the appointment has not previously been vacated or stayed; or

(C) 90 days after the date of expiration of a stay, if the appointment has not previously been vacated;

(6) the death of a general partner;

(7) a court adjudicating a general partner who is an individual mentally incompetent to manage the general partner's person or property;

(8) unless otherwise provided by a written partnership agreement or with the written consent of all partners, the commencement of winding up activities intended to conclude in the termination of a trust that is a general partner, but not merely the substitution of a new trustee;

(9) unless otherwise provided by a written partnership agreement or with the written consent of all partners, the commencement of winding up activities of a separate partnership that is a general partner;

(10) unless otherwise provided by a written partnership agreement or with the written consent of all partners, the:

(A) filing of a certificate of termination or its equivalent for an entity, other than a nonfiling entity or a foreign nonfiling entity, that is a general partner; or

(B) termination or revocation of the certificate of formation or its equivalent of an entity, other than a nonfiling entity or a foreign nonfiling entity, that is a general partner and the expiration of 90 days after the date of notice to the entity of termination or revocation without a reinstatement of its certificate of formation or its equivalent; or

(11) the distribution by the fiduciary of an estate that is a general partner of the estate's entire interest in the limited partnership.

(b) A general partner may withdraw at any time from a limited partnership and cease to be a general partner under Subsection (a) by giving written notice to the other partners.

Acts 2003, 78th Leg., ch. 182, § 1, eff. Jan. 1, 2006. Amended by Acts 2007, 80th Leg., ch. 688, § 122, eff. Sept. 1, 2007.

§ 153.156. Notice of Event of Withdrawal

A general partner who is subject to an event that with the passage of the specified period becomes an event of withdrawal under Section 153.155(a)(4) or (5) shall notify the other partners of the event not later than the 30th day after the date on which the event occurred.

Acts 2003, 78th Leg., ch. 182, § 1, eff. Jan. 1, 2006.

§ 153.157. Withdrawal of General Partner in Violation of Partnership Agreement

Unless otherwise provided by the partnership agreement, a withdrawal by a general partner of a partnership having a period of duration or for a particular undertaking before the expiration of that period or completion of that undertaking is a breach of the partnership agreement.

Acts 2003, 78th Leg., ch. 182, § 1, eff. Jan. 1, 2006. Amended by Acts 2007, 80th Leg., ch. 688, § 123, eff. Sept. 1, 2007.

§ 153.158. Effect of Withdrawal

(a) Unless otherwise provided by a written partnership agreement and subject to the liability created under Section 153.162, if a general partner ceases to be a general partner under Section 153.155, the remaining general partner or partners, or, if there are no remaining general partners, a majority-in-interest of the limited partners in a vote that excludes any limited partnership interest held by the withdrawing general partner, may:

(1) convert that general partner's partnership interest to that of a limited partner; or

(2) pay to the withdrawn general partner in cash, or secure by bond approved by a court of competent jurisdiction, the value of that partner's partnership interest minus the damages caused if the withdrawal constituted a breach of the partnership agreement.

(b) Until an action described by Subsection (a) is taken, the owner of the partnership interest of the withdrawn general partner has the status of an assignee under Subchapter F.

(c) If there are no remaining general partners following the withdrawal of a general partner, the partnership may be reconstituted.

Acts 2003, 78th Leg., ch. 182, § 1, eff. Jan. 1, 2006. Amended by Acts 2011, 82nd Leg., ch. 139 (S.B. 748), § 53, eff. Sept. 1, 2011.

§ 153.159. Conversion of Partnership Interest After Withdrawal

If the partners convert the partnership interest under Section 153.158(a)(1), the limited partnership interest may be reduced pro rata with all other partners to provide compensation, an interest in the partnership, or both, to a replacement general partner.

Acts 2003, 78th Leg., ch. 182, § 1, eff. Jan. 1, 2006.

§ 153.160. Effect of Conversion of Partnership Interest

(a) After an amendment to the certificate of formation reflecting the general partner's withdrawal as a general partner is filed under Section 153.051, the withdrawing general partner:

(1) may vote as a limited partner in all matters, to the same extent as the members of the class of limited partners having the least voting rights with respect to the matter on which the vote is taken; and

(2) may not vote on the admission and compensation of a general partner who replaces the withdrawing general partner.

(b) If the general partner's withdrawal violates the partnership agreement, the general partner does not have voting rights.

Acts 2003, 78th Leg., ch. 182, § 1, eff. Jan. 1, 2006.

§ 153.161. Liability of General Partner for Debt Incurred After Event of Withdrawal

(a) Unless otherwise provided by a written partnership agreement and subject to the liability created under Section 153.162, a general partner who ceases to be a general partner under Section 153.155 is not personally liable in the partner's capacity as a general partner for partnership debt incurred after that partner ceases to be a general partner unless the applicable creditor at the time the debt was incurred reasonably believed that the partner remained a general partner.

(b) A creditor of the partnership has reason to believe that a partner remains a general partner if:

(1) the creditor had no knowledge or notice of the general partner's withdrawal and:

(A) was a creditor of the partnership at the time of the general partner's withdrawal; or

(B) had extended credit to the partnership within two years before the date of withdrawal; or

(2) the creditor had known that the partner was a general partner in the partnership before the general partner's withdrawal and had no knowledge or notice of the withdrawal and the general partner's withdrawal had not been advertised in a newspaper of general circulation in each place at which the partnership business was regularly conducted.

Acts 2003, 78th Leg., ch. 182, § 1, eff. Jan. 1, 2006.

§ 153.162. Liability for Wrongful Withdrawal

(a) If a general partner's withdrawal from a limited partnership violates the partnership agreement, the partnership may recover damages from the withdrawing general partner for breach of the partnership agreement, including the reasonable cost of obtaining replacement of the services the withdrawn partner was obligated to perform.

(b) In addition to pursuing any remedy available under applicable law, the partnership may effect the recovery of damages under Subsection (a) by offsetting those damages against the amount otherwise distributable to the withdrawing general partner, reducing the limited partner interest into which the withdrawing general partner's interest may be converted under Section 153.158(a)(1), or both.

Acts 2003, 78th Leg., ch. 182, § 1, eff. Jan. 1, 2006.

SUBCHAPTER E. FINANCES

§ 153.201. Form of Contribution

The contribution of a partner may consist of a tangible or intangible benefit to the limited partnership or other property of any kind or nature, including:

(1) cash;

(2) a promissory note;

(3) services performed;

(4) a contract for services to be performed; and

(5) another interest in or security of the limited partnership, another domestic or foreign limited partnership, or other entity.

Acts 2003, 78th Leg., ch. 182, § 1, eff. Jan. 1, 2006. Amended by Acts 2005, 79th Leg., ch. 64, § 89, eff. Jan. 1, 2006.

§ 153.202. Enforceability of Promise to Make Contribution

(a) A promise by a limited partner to make a contribution to, or pay cash or transfer other property to, a limited partnership is not enforceable unless the promise is in writing and signed by the limited partner.

(b) Except as otherwise provided by the partnership agreement, a partner or the partner's legal representative or successor is obligated to the limited partnership to perform an enforceable promise to make a contribution to or pay cash or transfer other property to a limited partnership, notwithstanding the partner's death, disability, or other change in circumstances.

(c) If a partner or a partner's legal representative or successor does not make a contribution or other payment of cash or transfer of other property required by the enforceable promise, whether as a contribution or with respect to a contribution previously made, that partner or the partner's legal representative or successor is obligated, at the option of the limited partnership, to pay to the partnership an amount of cash equal to the portion of the agreed value, as stated in the partnership agreement or in the partnership records required to be kept under Sections 153.551 and 153.552, of the contribution represented by the amount of cash that has not been paid or the value of the property that has not been transferred.

(d) A partnership agreement may provide that the partnership interest of a partner who fails to make a payment of cash or transfer of other property to the partnership, whether as a contribution or with respect to a contribution previously made, required by an enforceable promise is subject to specified consequences, which may include:

(1) a reduction of the defaulting partner's percentage or other interest in the limited partnership;

(2) subordination of the partner's partnership interest to the interest of nondefaulting partners;

(3) a forced sale of the partner's partnership interest;

(4) forfeiture of the partner's partnership interest;

(5) the lending of money to the defaulting partner by other partners of the amount necessary to meet the defaulting partner's commitment;

(6) a determination of the value of the defaulting partner's partnership interest by appraisal or by formula and redemption or sale of the partnership interest at that value; or

(7) another penalty or consequence.

Acts 2003, 78th Leg., ch. 182, § 1, eff. Jan. 1, 2006.

§ 153.203. Release of Obligation to Partnership

Unless otherwise provided by the partnership agreement, the obligation of a partner or the legal representative or successor of a partner to make a contribution, pay cash, transfer other property, or return cash or property paid or distributed to the partner in violation of this chapter or the partnership agreement may be compromised or released only by consent of all of the partners.

Acts 2003, 78th Leg., ch. 182, § 1, eff. Jan. 1, 2006.

§ 153.204. Enforceability of Obligation

(a) Notwithstanding a compromise or release under Section 153.203, a creditor of a limited partnership who extends credit or otherwise acts in reasonable reliance on an obligation described by Section 153.203 may enforce the original obligation if:

(1) the obligation is reflected in a document signed by the partner; and

(2) the document is not amended or canceled to reflect the compromise or release.

(b) Notwithstanding the compromise or release, a general partner remains liable to persons other than the partnership and the other partners, as provided by Sections 153.152(a)(2) and (b).

Acts 2003, 78th Leg., ch. 182, § 1, eff. Jan. 1, 2006.

§ 153.205. Requirements to Enforce Conditional Obligation

(a) An obligation of a limited partner of a limited partnership that is subject to a condition may be enforced by the partnership creditor described by Section 153.204 only if the condition is satisfied or waived by or with respect to the limited partner.

(b) A conditional obligation of a limited partner of a limited partnership includes a contribution payable on a discretionary call of the limited partnership before the time the call occurs.

Acts 2003, 78th Leg., ch. 182, § 1, eff. Jan. 1, 2006.

§ 153.206. Allocation of Profits and Losses

(a) The profits and losses of a limited partnership shall be allocated among the partners in the manner provided by a written partnership agreement.

(b) If a written partnership agreement does not provide for the allocation of profits and losses, the profits and losses shall be allocated:

(1) in accordance with the current percentage or other interest in the partnership stated in partnership records of the kind described by Section 153.551(a); or

(2) if the allocation of profits and losses is not provided for in partnership records of the kind described by Section 153.551(a), in proportion to capital accounts.

Acts 2003, 78th Leg., ch. 182, § 1, eff. Jan. 1, 2006.

§ 153.207. Right to Distribution

Subject to Section 153.210, when a partner becomes entitled to receive a distribution, the partner has with respect to the distribution the status of and is entitled to all remedies available to a creditor of the limited partnership.

Acts 2003, 78th Leg., ch. 182, § 1, eff. Jan. 1, 2006.

§ 153.208. Sharing of Distributions

(a) A distribution of cash or another asset of a limited partnership shall be made to a partner in the manner provided by a written partnership agreement.

(b) If a written partnership agreement does not provide otherwise, a distribution that is a return of capital shall be made on the basis of the agreed value, as stated in the partnership records required to be maintained under Section 153.551(a), of the contribution made by each partner to the extent that the contribution has not been returned. A distribution that is not a return of capital shall be made in proportion to the allocation of profits as determined under Section 153.206.

(c) Unless otherwise defined by a written partnership agreement, in this section, "return of capital" means a distribution to a partner to the extent that the partner's capital account, immediately after the distribution, is less than the amount of that partner's contribution to the partnership as reduced by a prior distribution that was a return of capital.

Acts 2003, 78th Leg., ch. 182, § 1, eff. Jan. 1, 2006.

§ 153.209. Interim Distributions

Except as otherwise provided by this section and Section 153.210, a partner is entitled to receive a distribution from a limited partnership to the extent and at the time or on the occurrence of an event specified in the partnership agreement before:

(1) the partner withdraws from the partnership; and

(2) the winding up of the partnership business.

Acts 2003, 78th Leg., ch. 182, § 1, eff. Jan. 1, 2006.

§ 153.210 Limitation on Distribution

(a) Unless the distribution is made in compliance with Chapter 11, a limited partnership may not make a distribution to a partner if, immediately after giving effect to the distribution and despite any compromise of a claim referred to by Sections 153.203 and 153.204, all liabilities of the limited partnership, other than liabilities to partners with respect to their partnership interests and liabilities for which the recourse of creditors is limited to specified property of the limited partnership, exceed the fair value of the partnership assets. The fair value of property that is subject to a liability for which recourse of creditors is limited shall be included in the partnership assets for purposes of this subsection only to the extent that the fair value of that property exceeds that liability.

(b) For purposes of this section, "distribution" does not include an amount constituting reasonable compensation for present or past services or a reasonable payment made in the ordinary course of business under a bona fide retirement plan or other benefits program.

Acts 2003, 78th Leg., ch. 182, § 1, eff. Jan. 1, 2006. Amended by Acts 2009, 81st Leg., ch. 84, § 52, eff. Sept. 1, 2009.

SUBCHAPTER F. PARTNERSHIP INTEREST

§ 153.251. Assignment of Partnership Interest

(a) Except as otherwise provided by the partnership agreement, a partnership interest is assignable wholly or partly.

(b) Except as otherwise provided by the partnership agreement, an assignment of a partnership interest:

(1) does not require the winding up of a limited partnership;

(2) does not entitle the assignee to become, or to exercise rights or powers of, a partner; and

(3) entitles the assignee to be allocated income, gain, loss, deduction, credit, or similar items and to receive distributions to which the assignor was entitled to the extent those items are assigned.

Acts 2003, 78th Leg., ch. 182, § 1, eff. Jan. 1, 2006. Amended by Acts 2007, 80th Leg., ch. 688, § 124, eff. Sept. 1, 2007.

§ 153.252. Rights of Assignor

(a) Except as otherwise provided by the partnership agreement, until the assignee becomes a partner, the assignor partner continues to be a partner in the limited partnership. The assignor partner may exercise any rights or powers of a partner, except to the extent those rights or powers are assigned.

(b) Except as otherwise provided by the partnership agreement, on the assignment by a general partner of all of the general partner's rights as a general partner, the general partner's status as a general partner may be terminated by the affirmative vote of a majority-in-interest of the limited partners.

Acts 2003, 78th Leg., ch. 182, § 1, eff. Jan. 1, 2006.

§ 153.253. Rights of Assignee

(a) An assignee of a partnership interest, including the partnership interest of a general partner, may become a limited partner if and to the extent that:

(1) the partnership agreement provides; or

(2) all partners consent.

(b) An assignee who becomes a limited partner, to the extent of the rights and powers assigned, has the rights and powers and is subject to the restrictions and liabilities of a limited partner under a partnership agreement and this code.

Acts 2003, 78th Leg., ch. 182, § 1, eff. Jan. 1, 2006.

§ 153.254. Liability of Assignee

(a) Until an assignee of the partnership interest in a limited partnership becomes a partner, the assignee does not have liability as a partner solely as a result of the assignment.

(b) Unless otherwise provided by a written partnership agreement, an assignee who becomes a limited partner:

(1) is liable for the obligations of the assignor to make contributions as provided by Sections 153.202–153.204;

(2) is not obligated for liabilities unknown to the assignee at the time the assignee became a limited partner and that could not be ascertained from a written partnership agreement; and

(3) is not liable for the obligations of the assignor under Sections 153.105, 153.112, and 153.162.

Acts 2003, 78th Leg., ch. 182, § 1, eff. Jan. 1, 2006.

§ 153.255. Liability of Assignor

Regardless of whether an assignee of a partnership interest becomes a limited partner, the assignor is not released from the assignor's liability to the limited partnership under Subchapter E and Sections 153.105, 153.112, and 153.162.

Acts 2003, 78th Leg., ch. 182, § 1, eff. Jan. 1, 2006.

§ 153.256. Partner's Partnership Interest Subject to Charging Order

(a) On application by a judgment creditor of a partner or of any other owner of a partnership interest, a court having jurisdiction may charge the partnership interest of the judgment debtor to satisfy the judgment.

(b) To the extent that the partnership interest is charged in the manner provided by Subsection (a), the judgment creditor has only the right to receive any distribution to which the judgment debtor would otherwise be entitled in respect of the partnership interest.

(c) A charging order constitutes a lien on the judgment debtor's partnership interest. The charging order lien may not be foreclosed on under this code or any other law.

(d) The entry of a charging order is the exclusive remedy by which a judgment creditor of a partner or of any other owner of a partnership interest may satisfy a judgment out of the judgment debtor's partnership interest.

(e) This section does not deprive a partner or other owner of a partnership interest of a right under exemption laws with respect to the judgment debtor's partnership interest.

(f) A creditor of a partner or of any other owner of a partnership interest does not have the right to obtain possession of, or otherwise exercise legal or equitable remedies with respect to, the property of the limited partnership.

Acts 2003, 78th Leg., ch. 182, § 1, eff. Jan. 1, 2006. Amended by Acts 2007, 80th Leg., ch. 688, § 125, eff. Sept. 1, 2007; Acts 2009, 81st Leg., ch. 84, § 53, eff. Sept. 1, 2009.

§ 153.257. Exemption Laws Applicable to Partnership Interest Not Affected

Section 153.256 does not deprive a partner of the benefit of an exemption law applicable to that partner's partnership interest.

Acts 2003, 78th Leg., ch. 182, § 1, eff. Jan. 1, 2006.

SUBCHAPTER G. REPORTS

§ 153.301. Periodic Report

The secretary of state may require a domestic limited partnership or a foreign limited partnership registered to transact business in this state to file a report not more than once every four years as required by this subchapter.

Acts 2003, 78th Leg., ch. 182, § 1, eff. Jan. 1, 2006.

§ 153.302. Form and Contents of Report

(a) The report must:

(1) include:

(A) the name of the limited partnership;

(B) the state or territory under the laws of which the limited partnership is formed;

(C) the address of the registered office of the limited partnership in this state and the name of the registered agent at that address;

(D) the address of the principal office in the United States where records are to be kept or made available under Sections 153.551 and 153.552; and

(E) the name, mailing address, and street address of the business or residence of each general partner;

(2) be made on a form adopted by the secretary of state for that purpose; and

(3) be signed on behalf of the limited partnership by at least one general partner.

(b) The information contained in the report must be given as of the date of the execution of the report.

Acts 2003, 78th Leg., ch. 182, § 1, eff. Jan. 1, 2006.

§ 153.303. Filing Fee

The filing fee for the report is as provided by Chapter 4.

Acts 2003, 78th Leg., ch. 182, § 1, eff. Jan. 1, 2006.

§ 153.304. Delivery of Report

The report must be delivered to the secretary of state not later than the 30th day after the date on which notice is mailed under Section 153.305.

Acts 2003, 78th Leg., ch. 182, § 1, eff. Jan. 1, 2006.

§ 153.305. Action by Secretary of State

(a) The secretary of state shall send a notice that the report required by Section 153.301 is due.

(b) The notice must be:

(1) addressed to the limited partnership; and

(2) mailed to:

(A) the registered office of the limited partnership;

(B) the last known address of the limited partnership as it appears on record in the office of the secretary of state; or

(C) any other known place of business of the limited partnership.

(c) The secretary of state shall include with the notice a copy of a report form to be prepared and filed as provided by this subchapter.

Acts 2003, 78th Leg., ch. 182, § 1, eff. Jan. 1, 2006.

§ 153.306. Effect of Filing Report

(a) If the secretary of state finds that the report complies with this subchapter, the secretary shall:

(1) accept the report for filing;

(2) acknowledge to the limited partnership the filing of the report; and

(3) update the records of the secretary of state's office to reflect:

(A) a reported change in the address of the registered office or principal office, or in the business or residence address of a general partner; and

(B) a reported change in the name of the registered agent.

(b) The filing of a report under Section 153.301 does not relieve the limited partnership of the requirement to file an amendment to the certificate of formation required under Section 153.051 or 153.052, except that the limited partnership is not required to file an amendment to change the information specified in Subsection (a)(3).

Acts 2003, 78th Leg., ch. 182, § 1, eff. Jan. 1, 2006.

§ 153.307. Effect of Failure to File Report

(a) A domestic or foreign limited partnership that fails to file a report under Section 153.301 when the report is due forfeits the limited partnership's right to transact business in this state. A forfeiture under this section takes effect without judicial ascertainment.

(b) When the right to transact business has been forfeited under this section, the secretary of state shall note that the right to transact business has been forfeited and the date of forfeiture on the record kept in the secretary's office relating to the limited partnership.

Acts 2003, 78th Leg., ch. 182, § 1, eff. Jan. 1, 2006.

§ 153.308. Notice of Forfeiture of Right to Transact Business

Notice of the forfeiture under Section 153.307 shall be mailed to the limited partnership at:

(1) the registered office of the limited partnership;

(2) the last known address of the limited partnership; or

(3) any other place of business of the limited partnership.

Acts 2003, 78th Leg., ch. 182, § 1, eff. Jan. 1, 2006.

§ 153.309. Effect of Forfeiture of Right to Transact Business

(a) Unless the right of the limited partnership to transact business is revived in accordance with Section 153.310:

(1) the limited partnership may not maintain an action, suit, or proceeding in a court of this state; and

(2) a successor or assignee of the limited partnership may not maintain an action, suit, or proceeding in a court of this state on a right, claim, or demand arising from the transaction of business by the limited partnership in this state.

(b) The forfeiture of the right to transact business in this state does not:

(1) impair the validity of a contract or act of the limited partnership; or

(2) prevent the limited partnership from defending an action, suit, or proceeding in a court of this state.

(c) This section and Sections 153.307 and 153.308 do not affect the liability of a limited partner.

Acts 2003, 78th Leg., ch. 182, § 1, eff. Jan. 1, 2006. Amended by Acts 2009, 81st Leg., ch. 84, § 54, eff. Sept. 1, 2009.

§ 153.310. Revival of Right to Transact Business

(a) A limited partnership that forfeits the right to transact business in this state as provided by Section 153.309 may be relieved from the forfeiture by filing the required report not later than the 120th day after the date of mailing of the notice of forfeiture under Section 153.308, accompanied by the filing fees as provided by Chapter 4.

(b) If a limited partnership complies with Subsection (a), the secretary of state shall:

(1) revive the right of the limited partnership to transact business in this state;

(2) cancel the note regarding the forfeiture; and

(3) note the revival and the date of revival on the record kept in the secretary's office relating to the limited partnership.

Acts 2003, 78th Leg., ch. 182, § 1, eff. Jan. 1, 2006.

§ 153.311 Termination of Certificate or Revocation of Registration After Forfeiture

(a) The secretary of state may terminate the certificate of formation of a domestic limited partnership, or revoke the registration of a foreign limited partnership, if the limited partnership:

(1) forfeits its right to transact business in this state under Section 153.307; and

(2) fails to revive that right under Section 153.310.

(b) Termination of the certificate or revocation of registration takes effect without judicial ascertainment.

(c) The secretary of state shall note the termination or revocation and the date on the record kept in the secretary's office relating to the limited partnership.

(d) On termination or revocation, the status of the limited partnership is changed to inactive according to the records of the secretary of state. The change to inactive status does not affect the liability of a limited partner.

Acts 2003, 78th Leg., ch. 182, § 1, eff. Jan. 1, 2006. Amended by Acts 2009, 81st Leg., ch. 84, § 55, eff. Sept. 1, 2009.

§ 153.312. Reinstatement of Certificate of Formation or Registration

(a) A limited partnership the certificate of formation or registration of which has been terminated or revoked as provided by Section 153.311 may be relieved of the termination or revocation by filing the report required by Section 153.301, accompanied by the filing fees provided by Chapter 4.

(b) If the limited partnership pays the fees required by Subsection (a) and all taxes, penalties, and interest due and accruing before termination or revocation, the secretary of state shall:

(1) reinstate the certificate or registration of the limited partnership without judicial ascertainment;

(2) change the status of the limited partnership to active; and

(3) note the reinstatement on the record kept in the secretary's office relating to the limited partnership.

(c) If the name of the limited partnership is not available at the time of reinstatement, the secretary of state shall require the limited partnership as a precondition to reinstatement to:

(1) file an amendment to the partnership's certificate of formation; or

(2) in the case of a foreign limited partnership, amend its application for registration to adopt an assumed name for use in this state.

Acts 2003, 78th Leg., ch. 182, § 1, eff. Jan. 1, 2006. Amended by Acts 2009, 81st Leg., ch. 84, § 56, eff. Sept. 1, 2009.

SUBCHAPTER H. LIMITED PARTNERSHIP AS LIMITED LIABILITY PARTNERSHIP

§ 153.351. Requirements

A limited partnership is a limited liability partnership and a limited partnership if the partnership:

(1) registers as a limited liability partnership:

(A) as permitted by its partnership agreement; or

(B) if its partnership agreement does not include a provision for becoming a limited liability partnership, with the consent of partners required to amend its partnership agreement;

(2) complies with Subchapter J, Chapter 152; and

(3) complies with Chapter 5.

Acts 2003, 78th Leg., ch. 182, § 1, eff. Jan. 1, 2006.

§ 153.352. Applicability of Other Requirements

For purposes of applying Section 152.802 to a limited partnership:

(1) an application to become a limited liability partnership or to withdraw a registration must be signed by at least one general partner; and

(2) other references to a partner mean a general partner only.

Acts 2003, 78th Leg., ch. 182, § 1, eff. Jan. 1, 2006.

§ 153.353. Law Applicable to Partners

If a limited partnership is a limited liability partnership, Section 152.801 applies to a general partner and to a limited partner who is liable under other provisions of this chapter for the debts or obligations of the limited partnership.

Acts 2003, 78th Leg., ch. 182, § 1, eff. Jan. 1, 2006.

SUBCHAPTER I. DERIVATIVE ACTIONS

§ 153.401. Right to Bring Action

A limited partner may bring an action in a court on behalf of the limited partnership to recover a judgment in the limited partnership's favor if:

(1) all general partners with authority to bring the action have refused to bring the action; or

(2) an effort to cause those general partners to bring the action is not likely to succeed.

Acts 2003, 78th Leg., ch. 182, § 1, eff. Jan. 1, 2006.

§ 153.402. Proper Plaintiff

In a derivative action, the plaintiff must be a limited partner when the action is brought and:

(1) the person must have been a limited partner at the time of the transaction that is the subject of the action; or

(2) the person's status as a limited partner must have arisen by operation of law or under the terms of the partnership agreement from a person who was a limited partner at the time of the transaction.

Acts 2003, 78th Leg., ch. 182, § 1, eff. Jan. 1, 2006.

§ 153.403. Pleading

In a derivative action, the complaint must contain with particularity:

(1) the effort, if any, of the plaintiff to secure initiation of the action by a general partner; or

(2) the reasons for not making the effort.

Acts 2003, 78th Leg., ch. 182, § 1, eff. Jan. 1, 2006.

§ 153.404. Security for Expenses of Defendants

(a) In a derivative action, the court may require the plaintiff to give security for the reasonable expenses incurred or expected to be incurred by a defendant in the action, including reasonable attorney's fees.

(b) The court may increase or decrease at any time the amount of the security on a showing that the security provided is inadequate or excessive.

(c) If a plaintiff is unable to give security, the plaintiff may file an affidavit in accordance with the Texas Rules of Civil Procedure.

(d) Except as provided by Subsection (c), if a plaintiff fails to give the security within a reasonable time set by the court, the court shall dismiss the suit without prejudice.

(e) The court, on final judgment for a defendant and on a finding that suit was brought without reasonable cause against the defendant, may require the plaintiff to pay reasonable expenses, including reasonable attorney's fees, to the defendant, regardless of whether security has been required.

Acts 2003, 78th Leg., ch. 182, § 1, eff. Jan. 1, 2006.

§ 153.405. Expenses of Plaintiff

If a derivative action is successful, wholly or partly, or if anything is received by the plaintiff because of a judgment, compromise, or settlement of the action or claim constituting a part of the action, the court may award the plaintiff reasonable expenses, including reasonable attorney's fees, and shall direct the plaintiff to remit to a party identified by the court the remainder of the proceeds received by the plaintiff.

Acts 2003, 78th Leg., ch. 182, § 1, eff. Jan. 1, 2006.

SUBCHAPTER J. CANCELLATION OF CERTIFICATE OF FORMATION [REPEALED]

§§ 153.451, 153.452. Repealed by Acts 2007, 80th Leg., ch. 688, § 144(3), eff. Sept. 1, 2007

SUBCHAPTER K. SUPPLEMENTAL WINDING UP AND TERMINATION PROVISIONS

§ 153.501. Cancellation or Revocation of Event Requiring Winding Up; Continuation of Business

(a) The limited partnership may cancel under Section 11.152 an event requiring winding up arising from the expiration of its period of duration as specified in Section 11.051(1) or from the occurrence of an event specified in its governing documents as specified in Section 11.051(3) if, not later than the 90th day after the event, all remaining partners, or another group or percentage of partners as specified by the partnership agreement, agree in writing to continue the business of the limited partnership.

(b) The limited partnership may cancel under Section 11.152 an event requiring winding up arising from an event of withdrawal of a general partner as specified in Section 11.058(b) if:

(1) there remains at least one general partner and the partnership agreement permits the business of the limited partnership to be carried on by the remaining general partners and those remaining general partners carry on the business; or

(2) not later than one year after the event, all remaining partners, or another group or percentage of partners specified in the partnership agreement:

(A) agree in writing to continue the business of the limited partnership ; and

(B) to the extent that they desire or if there are no remaining general partners, agree to the appointment of one or more new general partners.

(c) The appointment of one or more new general partners under Subsection (b)(2)(B) is effective from the date of withdrawal.

(d) To approve a revocation under Section 11.151 by a limited partnership of a voluntary decision to wind up as specified in Section 11.058(a), prior to filing the certificate of termination required by Section 11.101, all remaining partners, or another group or percentage of partners as specified by the partnership agreement, must agree in writing to revoke the voluntary decision to wind up and continue the business of the limited partnership.

(e) The limited partnership may cancel under Section 11.152 an event requiring winding up arising when there are no limited partners in the limited partnership, as specified in Section 11.058(c), if, not later than the first anniversary of the date of the event requiring winding up:

(1) the legal representative or successor of the last remaining limited partner and all of the general partners agree to:

(A) continue the business of the limited partnership; and

(B) admit the legal representative or successor of the last remaining limited partner, or the person's nominee or designee, to the limited partnership as a limited partner, effective as of the date the event that caused the last remaining limited partner to cease to be a limited partner occurred; or

(2) a limited partner is admitted to the limited partnership in the manner provided by the partnership agreement, effective as of the date the event that caused the last remaining limited partner to cease to be a limited partner occurred.

Acts 2003, 78th Leg., ch. 182, § 1, eff. Jan. 1, 2006. Amended by Acts 2005, 79th Leg., ch. 64, § 93, eff. Jan. 1, 2006; Acts 2007, 80th Leg., ch. 688, § 126, eff. Sept. 1, 2007; Acts 2011, 82nd Leg., ch. 139 (S.B. 748), § 54, eff. Sept. 1, 2011.

§ 153.502. Winding Up Procedures

(a) Except as provided by the partnership agreement, the winding up of the partnership's affairs shall be accomplished by:

(1) the general partners;

(2) if there are no general partners, the limited partners or a person chosen by the limited partners; or

(3) a person appointed by the court to carry out the winding up under Subsection (b).

(b) On application of a partner or a partner's legal representative or transferee, a court, on cause shown, may wind up the limited partnership's affairs and, in connection with the winding up, may appoint a person to carry out the liquidation and may make all other orders, directions, and inquiries that the circumstances require.

(c) Section 11.052(a)(2) shall not be applicable to a limited partnership.

Acts 2003, 78th Leg., ch. 182, § 1, eff. Jan. 1, 2006.

§ 153.503. Powers of Person Conducting Wind Up

(a) After the occurrence of an event requiring winding up of a limited partnership and until the filing of a certificate of termination as provided by Section 11.101, unless a written partnership agreement provides otherwise, a person winding up the limited partnership's business in the name of and on behalf of the limited partnership may take the actions specified in Sections 11.052 and 11.053.

(b) The acts described by Subsection (a) do not create a liability for a limited partner that did not exist before an action to wind up the business of the partnership was taken.

Acts 2003, 78th Leg., ch. 182, § 1, eff. Jan. 1, 2006. Amended by Acts 2005, 79th Leg., ch. 64, § 94, eff. Jan. 1, 2006; Acts 2007, 80th Leg., ch. 688, § 127, eff. Sept. 1, 2007.

§ 153.504. Disposition of Assets

On the winding up of a limited partnership, its assets shall be paid or transferred as follows:

(1) to the extent otherwise permitted by law, to creditors, including partners who are creditors other than solely because of the application of Section 153.207, for the payment or the making of reasonable provision for payment to satisfy the liabilities of the limited partnership;

(2) unless otherwise provided by the partnership agreement, to partners and former partners to satisfy the partnership's liability for distributions under Section 153.111 or 153.209; and

(3) unless otherwise provided by the partnership agreement, to partners first for the return of their capital and second with respect to their partnership interests, in the proportions provided by Sections 153.208(a) and (b).

Acts 2003, 78th Leg., ch. 182, § 1, eff. Jan. 1, 2006. Amended by Acts 2011, 82nd Leg., ch. 139 (S.B. 748), § 55, eff. Sept. 1, 2011.

§ 153.505. Approval of Reinstatement

To approve a reinstatement of a limited partnership under Section 11.202, all of the remaining partners, or another group or percentage of partners as specified by the partnership agreement, must agree in writing to reinstate and continue the business of the limited partnership.

Added by Acts 2007, 80th Leg., ch. 688, § 128, eff. Sept. 1, 2007.

SUBCHAPTER L. MISCELLANEOUS PROVISIONS

§ 153.551. Records

(a) A domestic limited partnership shall maintain the following records in its principal office in the United States or make the records available in that office not later than the fifth day after the date on which a written request under Section 153.552(a) is received:

(1) a current list that states:

(A) the name and mailing address of each partner, separately identifying in alphabetical order the general partners and the limited partners;

(B) the last known street address of the business or residence of each general partner;

(C) the percentage or other interest in the partnership owned by each partner; and

(D) if one or more classes or groups are established under the partnership agreement, the names of the partners who are members of each specified class or group;

(2) a copy of:

(A) the limited partnership's federal, state, and local information or income tax returns for each of the partnership's six most recent tax years;

(B) the partnership agreement and certificate of formation; and

(C) all amendments or restatements;

(3) copies of any document that creates, in the manner provided by the partnership agreement, classes or groups of partners;

(4) an executed copy of any powers of attorney under which the partnership agreement, certificate of formation, and all amendments or restatements to the agreement and certificate have been executed;

(5) unless contained in the written partnership agreement, a written statement of:

(A) the amount of the cash contribution and a description and statement of the agreed value of any other contribution made by each partner;

(B) the amount of the cash contribution and a description and statement of the agreed value of any other contribution that the partner has agreed to make in the future as an additional contribution;

(C) the events requiring additional contributions to be made or the date on which additional contributions are to be made;

(D) the events requiring the winding up of the limited partnership; and

(E) the date on which each partner in the limited partnership became a partner; and

(6) books and records of the accounts of the limited partnership.

(b) A limited partnership shall maintain its records in written form or in another form capable of being converted to written form in a reasonable time.

(c) A limited partnership shall keep in its registered office in this state and make available to a partner on reasonable request the street address of its principal office in the United States in which the records required by this section are maintained.

Acts 2003, 78th Leg., ch. 182, § 1, eff. Jan. 1, 2006. Amended by Acts 2007, 80th Leg., ch. 688, § 129, eff. Sept. 1, 2007; Acts 2011, 82nd Leg., ch. 139 (S.B. 748), § 56, eff. Sept. 1, 2011.

§ 153.552. Examination of Records and Information

(a) On written request stating a proper purpose, a partner or an assignee of a partnership interest may examine and copy, in person or through a representative, records required to be kept under Section 153.551 and other information regarding the business, affairs, and financial condition of the limited partnership as is just and reasonable for the person to examine and copy.

(b) The records requested under Subsection (a) may be examined and copied at a reasonable time and at the partner's sole expense.

(c) On written request by a partner or an assignee of a partnership interest, the partnership shall provide to the requesting partner or assignee without charge copies of:

(1) the partnership agreement and certificate of formation and all amendments or restatements; and

(2) any tax return described by Section 153.551(a)(2).

(d) A request made under Subsection (c) must be made to:

(1) the person who is designated to receive the request in the partnership agreement at the address designated in the partnership agreement; or

(2) if there is no designation, a general partner at the partnership's principal office in the United States.

Acts 2003, 78th Leg., ch. 182, § 1, eff. Jan. 1, 2006.

§ 153.553. Execution of Filings.

(a) Except as provided by Subsection (a–1), a filing instrument required by this code to be filed by a limited partnership with the secretary of state must be signed by at least one general partner.

(a–1) The following certificates shall be executed as follows:

(1) an initial certificate of formation must be signed as provided in Section 3.004(b)(1);

(2) a certificate of amendment or restated certificate of formation must be signed by at least one general partner and by each other general partner designated in the certificate of amendment as a new general partner, unless signed and filed by a person under Section 153.052(b) or (c), but the certificate of amendment need not be signed by a withdrawing general partner;

(3) a certificate of termination must be signed by all general partners participating in the winding up of the limited partnership's business or, if no general partners are winding up the limited partnership's business, by all nonpartner liquidators or, if the limited partners are winding up the limited partnership's business, by a majority-in-interest of the limited partners;

(4) a certificate of merger, conversion, or exchange filed on behalf of a domestic limited partnership must be signed as provided by Chapter 10; and

(5) a certificate filed under Subchapter G, Chapter 10, must be signed by the person designated by the court.

(b) Any person may sign a certificate or partnership agreement or amendment or restated certificate by an attorney in fact. A power of attorney relating to the signing of a certificate or partnership agreement or amendment or restated certificate by an attorney in fact:

(1) is not required to be sworn to, verified, or acknowledged;

(2) is not required to be filed with the secretary of state; and

(3) shall be retained with the partnership records under Sections 153.551 and 153.552.

(c) The execution of a certificate by a general partner or the execution of a written statement by a person under Section 153.106(2) is an oath or affirmation, under a penalty of perjury, that, to the best of the executing party's knowledge and belief, the facts stated in the certificate or statement are true.

Acts 2003, 78th Leg., ch. 182, § 1, eff. Jan. 1, 2006. Amended by Acts 2005, 79th Leg., ch. 64, § 95, eff. Jan. 1, 2006; Acts 2007, 80th Leg., ch. 688, §§ 130, 131, eff. Sept. 1, 2007.

§ 153.554. Execution, Amendment, or Cancellation by Judicial Order

(a) If a person fails or refuses to execute or file a certificate as required by this chapter or Title 1 or to execute a partnership agreement, another person adversely affected by the failure or refusal may petition a court to direct the execution or filing of the certificate or the execution of the partnership agreement, as appropriate.

(b) If the court finds that the execution or filing of the certificate is proper and that a person required to execute or file the certificate has failed or refused to execute or file the certificate, the court shall order the secretary of state to record an appropriate certificate.

(c) The judicial remedy described by Subsection (b) is not a limit on the rights of a person to file a written statement under Section 153.106(2).

(d) If the court finds that the partnership agreement should be executed and that a person required to execute the partnership agreement has failed or refused to execute the agreement, the court shall enter an order granting appropriate relief.

(e) If a court enters an order in favor of the adversely affected person requesting relief under this section, the court shall award to that person reasonable expenses, including reasonable attorney's fees.

Acts 2003, 78th Leg., ch. 182, § 1, eff. Jan. 1, 2006.

§ 153.555. Permitted Transfer in Connection With Racetrack License

The following transfer relating to a limited partnership is not a prohibited transfer that violates Section 6.12(a), Texas Racing Act (Article 179e, Vernon's Texas Civil Statutes):

(1) a transfer by a general partnership of its assets to a limited partnership, the corporate general partner of which is controlled by the partners of the general partnership; or

(2) a transfer by a limited partnership of the beneficial use of or interest in any of its rights, privileges, or assets to a local development corporation incorporated before January 31, 1993, under Subchapter D, Chapter 431, Transportation Code.

Acts 2003, 78th Leg., ch. 182, § 1, eff. Jan. 1, 2006.

CHAPTER 154. PROVISIONS APPLICABLE TO BOTH GENERAL AND LIMITED PARTNERSHIPS

SUBCHAPTER A. PARTNERSHIP INTERESTS

Section
154.001. Nature of Partner's Partnership Interest.

Section
154.002. Transfer of Interest in Partnership Property Prohibited.

SUBCHAPTER B. PARTNERSHIP AGREEMENT
154.101. Class or Group of Partners.
154.102. Provisions Relating to Voting.
154.103. Notice of Action by Consent Without a Meeting.

SUBCHAPTER C. PARTNERSHIP TRANSACTIONS AND RELATIONSHIPS
154.201. Business Transactions Between Partner and Partnership.
154.202. Effect of Partner Change on Relationship Between Partnership and Creditors.
154.203. Distributions in Kind.

SUBCHAPTER A. PARTNERSHIP INTERESTS

§ 154.001. Nature of Partner's Partnership Interest

(a) A partner's partnership interest is personal property for all purposes.

(b) A partner's partnership interest may be community property under applicable law.

(c) A partner is not a co-owner of partnership property.

(d) Sections 9.406 and 9.408, Business & Commerce Code, do not apply to a partnership interest in a partnership, including the rights, powers, and interests arising under the governing documents of the partnership or under this code. To the extent of any conflict between this subsection and Section 9.406 or 9.408, Business & Commerce Code, this subsection controls. It is the express intent of this subsection to permit the enforcement, as a contract among the partners of a partnership, of any provision of a partnership agreement that would otherwise be ineffective under Section 9.406 or 9.408, Business & Commerce Code.

Acts 2003, 78th Leg., ch. 182, § 1, eff. Jan. 1, 2006. Amended by Acts 2009, 81st Leg., ch. 84, § 57, eff. Sept. 1, 2009.

§ 154.002. Transfer of Interest in Partnership Property Prohibited

A partner does not have an interest that can be transferred, voluntarily or involuntarily, in partnership property.

Acts 2003, 78th Leg., ch. 182, § 1, eff. Jan. 1, 2006.

SUBCHAPTER B. PARTNERSHIP AGREEMENT

§ 154.101. Class or Group of Partners

(a) A written partnership agreement may establish or provide for the future creation of additional classes or groups of one or more partners that have certain express relative rights, powers, and duties, including voting rights. The future creation of additional classes or groups may be expressed in the partnership agreement or at the time of creation of the class or group.

(b) The rights, powers, or duties of a class or group of partners may be senior to those partners of an existing class or group.

Acts 2003, 78th Leg., ch. 182, § 1, eff. Jan. 1, 2006.

§ 154.102. Provisions Relating to Voting

A written partnership agreement that grants or provides for granting a right to vote to a partner may contain a provision relating to:

(1) giving notice of the time, place, or purpose of a meeting at which a matter is to be voted on by the partners;

(2) waiver of notice;

(3) action by consent without a meeting;

(4) the establishment of a record date;

(5) quorum requirements;

(6) voting in person or by proxy; or

(7) other matters relating to the exercise of the right to vote.

Acts 2003, 78th Leg., ch. 182, § 1, eff. Jan. 1, 2006.

§ 154.103. Notice of Action by Consent Without a Meeting

(a) Prompt notice of the taking of an action under a partnership agreement that may be taken without a meeting by consent of fewer than all of the partners shall be given to a partner who has not given written consent to the action.

(b) For purposes of this section, the "taking of an action" includes:

(1) amending the partnership agreement; or

(2) creating under the partnership agreement a class of partners that did not previously exist.

Acts 2003, 78th Leg., ch. 182, § 1, eff. Jan. 1, 2006.

SUBCHAPTER C. PARTNERSHIP TRANSACTIONS AND RELATIONSHIPS

§ 154.201. Business Transactions Between Partner and Partnership

Except as otherwise provided by the partnership agreement, a partner may lend money to and transact other business with the partnership. Subject to other applicable law, a partner has the same rights and obligations with respect to those matters as a person who is not a partner.

Acts 2003, 78th Leg., ch. 182, § 1, eff. Jan. 1, 2006.

§ 154.202. Effect of Partner Change on Relationship Between Partnership and Creditors

The relationships between a partnership and its creditors are not affected by the:

(1) withdrawal of a partner; or

(2) addition of a new partner.

Acts 2003, 78th Leg., ch. 182, § 1, eff. Jan. 1, 2006.

§ 154.203. Distributions in Kind

(a) Except as provided by the partnership agreement, a partner, regardless of the nature of the partner's contribution, is not entitled to demand or receive from a partnership a distribution in any form other than cash.

(b) Except as provided by the partnership agreement, a partner may not be compelled to accept a disproportionate distribution of an asset in kind from a partnership to the extent that the percentage portion of assets distributed to the partner exceeds the percentage of those assets that equals the percentage in which the partner shares in distributions from the partnership.

Acts 2003, 78th Leg., ch. 182, § 1, eff. Jan. 1, 2006.

TITLE 5. REAL ESTATE INVESTMENT TRUSTS

CHAPTER 200. REAL ESTATE INVESTMENT TRUSTS

SUBCHAPTER A. GENERAL PROVISIONS

Section
200.001. Definition.
200.002. Applicability of Chapter.
200.003. Conflict with Other Law.
200.004. Ultra Vires Acts.

Section
200.005. Supplementary Powers of Real Estate Investment Trust.
200.006. Requirement That Filing Instrument be Signed by Officer.

SUBCHAPTER B. FORMATION AND GOVERNING DOCUMENTS

200.051. Declaration of Trust.
200.052. No Property Right in Certificate of Formation.
200.053. Procedures to Adopt Amendment to Certificate of Formation.
200.054. Adoption of Amendment by Trust Managers.
200.055. Adoption of Amendment by Shareholders.
200.056. Notice of and Meeting to Consider Proposed Amendment.
200.057. Adoption of Restated Certificate of Formation.
200.058. Bylaws.
200.059. Dual Authority.
200.060. Organization Meeting.

SUBCHAPTER C. SHARES

200.101. Number.
200.102. Classification of Shares.
200.103. Classes of Shares Established by Trust Managers.
200.104. Issuance of Shares.
200.105. Types of Consideration for Issuance of Shares.
200.106. Determination of Consideration for Shares.
200.107. Amount of Consideration for Issuance of Shares With Par Value.
200.108. Value of Consideration.
200.109. Liability of Assignee or Transferee.
200.110. Subscriptions.
200.111. Preformation Subscription.
200.112. Commitment in Connection With Purchase of Shares.
200.113. Supplemental Required Records.

SUBCHAPTER D. SHAREHOLDER RIGHTS AND RESTRICTIONS

200.151. Registered Holders as Owners.
200.152. No Statutory Preemptive Right Unless Specifically Provided by Certificate of Formation.
200.153. Characterization and Transfer of Shares and Other Securities.
200.154. Restriction on Transfer of Shares and Other Securities.
200.155. Valid Restriction on Transfer.
200.156. Bylaw or Agreement Restricting Transfer of Shares or Other Securities.
200.157. Enforceability of Restriction on Transfer of Certain Securities.
200.158. Joint Ownership of Shares.
200.159. Liability for Designating Owner of Shares.
200.160. Liability Regarding Joint Ownership of Shares.
200.161. Limitation of Liability for Obligations.
200.162. Preemption of Liability.
200.163. Exceptions to Limitations.
200.164. Pledgees and Trust Administrators.

SUBCHAPTER E. DISTRIBUTIONS AND SHARE DIVIDENDS

200.201. Authority for Distributions.

Section
200.202. Limitations on Distributions.
200.203. Priority of Distributions.
200.204. Reserves, Designations, and Allocations From Surplus.
200.205. Authority for Share Dividends.
200.206. Limitations on Share Dividends.
200.207. Value of Shares Issued as Share Dividends.
200.208. Transfer of Surplus for Share Dividends.
200.209. Determination of Solvency, Net Assets, Stated Capital, and Surplus.
200.210. Date of Determination of Surplus.
200.211. Split-up or Division of Shares.

SUBCHAPTER F. SHAREHOLDERS' MEETINGS; VOTING AND QUORUM

200.251. Annual Meeting.
200.252. Special Meetings.
200.253. Notice of Meeting.
200.254. Closing of Share Transfer Records.
200.255. Record Date for Written Consent to Action.
200.256. Record Date for Purpose Other Than Written Consent to Action.
200.257. Quorum.
200.258. Voting in Election of Trust Managers.
200.259. Cumulative Voting in Election of Trust Managers.
200.260. Voting on Matters Other Than Election of Trust Managers.
200.261. Vote Required to Approve Fundamental Action.
200.262. Changes in Vote Required for Certain Matters.
200.263. Number of Votes Per Share.
200.264. Voting in Person or by Proxy.
200.265. Term of Proxy.
200.266. Revocability of Proxy.
200.267. Enforceability of Proxy.
200.268. Procedures in Bylaws Relating to Proxies.

SUBCHAPTER G. TRUST MANAGERS

200.301. Management by Trust Managers.
200.302. Designation of Trust Managers.
200.303. Trust Manager Eligibility Requirements.
200.304. Number of Trust Managers.
200.305. Compensation.
200.306. Term of Trust Manager.
200.307. Staggered Terms of Trust Managers.
200.308. Vacancy.
200.309. Notice of Meeting.
200.310. Quorum.
200.311. Committees of Trust Managers.
200.312. Liability of Trust Managers.
200.313. Statute of Limitations on Certain Action Against Trust Managers.
200.314. Immunity From Liability for Performance of Duty.
200.315. Right of Contribution.
200.316. Officers.
200.317. Contracts or Transactions Involving Interested Trust Managers and Officers.

SUBCHAPTER H. INVESTMENTS

200.351. Investments.

SUBCHAPTER I. FUNDAMENTAL BUSINESS TRANSACTIONS

Section
200.401. Definitions.
200.402. Approval of Merger.
200.403. Approval of Conversion.
200.404. Approval of Exchange.
200.405. Approval of Sale of All or Substantially All of Assets.
200.406. General Procedure for Submission to Shareholders of Fundamental Business Transaction.
200.407. General Vote Requirement for Approval of Fundamental Business Transaction.
200.408. Class Voting Requirements for Certain Fundamental Business Transactions.
200.409. No Shareholder Vote Requirement for Certain Fundamental Business Transactions.
200.410. Rights of Dissent and Appraisal.

SUBCHAPTER J. SUPPLEMENTAL WINDING UP AND TERMINATION PROVISIONS

200.451. Approval of Voluntary Winding Up.
200.452. Approval of Reinstatement, Cancellation, or Revocation of Voluntary Winding Up.
200.453. Responsibility for Winding Up.

SUBCHAPTER K. MISCELLANEOUS PROVISIONS

200.501. Examination of Records.
200.502. Joinder of Shareholders Not Required.
200.503. Tax Law Requirements.

SUBCHAPTER A. GENERAL PROVISIONS

§ 200.001. Definition

In this chapter, "real estate investment trust" means an unincorporated trust:

(1) formed by one or more trust managers under this chapter and Chapter 3; and

(2) managed under this chapter.

Acts 2003, 78th Leg., ch. 182, § 1, eff. Jan. 1, 2006.

§ 200.002. Applicability of Chapter

(a) The provisions of Chapters 20 and 21 govern a matter to the extent that this chapter or Title 1 does not govern the matter.

(b) An unincorporated trust that does not meet the requirements of this chapter is an unincorporated association.

Acts 2003, 78th Leg., ch. 182, § 1, eff. Jan. 1, 2006.

§ 200.003. Conflict with Other Law

In case of conflict between this chapter and Chapters 20 and 21, this chapter controls. Chapters 20 and 21 do not control over this chapter merely because a provision of Chapter 20 or 21 is more or less extensive, restrictive, or detailed than a similar provision of this chapter.

Acts 2003, 78th Leg., ch. 182, § 1, eff. Jan. 1, 2006.

§ 200.004. Ultra Vires Acts

(a) Lack of capacity of a real estate investment trust may not be the basis of any claim or defense at law or in equity.

(b) An act of a real estate investment trust or a transfer of property by or to a real estate investment trust is not invalid because the act or transfer was:

(1) beyond the scope of the purpose or purposes of the real estate investment trust as expressed in the real estate investment trust's certificate of formation; or

(2) inconsistent with a limitation on the authority of an officer or trust manager to exercise a statutory power of the real estate investment trust, as that limitation is expressed in the real estate investment trust's certificate of formation.

(c) The fact that an act or transfer is beyond the scope of the expressed purpose or purposes of the real estate investment trust or is inconsistent with an expressed limitation on the authority of an officer or trust manager may be asserted in a proceeding:

(1) by a shareholder against the real estate investment trust to enjoin the performance of an act or the transfer of property by or to the real estate investment trust; or

(2) by the real estate investment trust, acting directly or through a receiver, trustee, or other legal representative, or through shareholders in a representative suit, against an officer or trust manager or former officer or trust manager of the real estate investment trust for exceeding that person's authority.

(d) If the unauthorized act or transfer sought to be enjoined under Subsection (c)(1) is being or is to be performed or made under a contract to which the real estate investment trust is a party and if each party to the contract is a party to the proceeding, the court may set aside and enjoin the performance of the contract. The court may award to the real estate investment trust or to another party to the contract, as appropriate, compensation for loss or damage resulting from the action of the court in setting aside and enjoining the performance of the contract, excluding loss of anticipated profits.

Acts 2003, 78th Leg., ch. 182, § 1, eff. Jan. 1, 2006.

§ 200.005. Supplementary Powers of Real Estate Investment Trust

(a) Subject to Section 2.113(a) and in addition to the powers specified in Section 2.101, a real estate investment trust may engage in activities mandated or authorized by:

(1) provisions of the Internal Revenue Code that are related to or govern real estate investment trusts; and

(2) regulations adopted under the Internal Revenue Code.

(b) This section does not authorize a real estate investment trust or an officer or trust manager of a real estate investment trust to exercise a power in a manner inconsistent with a limitation on the purposes or powers of the real estate investment trust contained in:

(1) the trust's certificate of formation;

(2) this code; or

(3) another law of this state.

Acts 2003, 78th Leg., ch. 182, § 1, eff. Jan. 1, 2006.

§ 200.006. Requirement That Filing Instrument be Signed by Officer

Unless otherwise provided by this chapter, a filing instrument of a real estate investment trust may be signed by an officer of the real estate investment trust.

Acts 2003, 78th Leg., ch. 182, § 1, eff. Jan. 1, 2006.

SUBCHAPTER B. FORMATION AND GOVERNING DOCUMENTS

§ 200.051. Declaration of Trust

For purposes of this code, the certificate of formation of a real estate investment trust is a declaration of trust. The certificate of formation may be titled "declaration of trust" or "certificate of formation."

Acts 2003, 78th Leg., ch. 182, § 1, eff. Jan. 1, 2006.

§ 200.052. No Property Right in Certificate of Formation

A shareholder of a real estate investment trust does not have a vested property right resulting from the certificate of formation, including a provision in the certificate of formation relating to the management, control, capital structure, dividend entitlement, purpose, or duration of the real estate investment trust.

Acts 2003, 78th Leg., ch. 182, § 1, eff. Jan. 1, 2006.

§ 200.053. Procedures to Adopt Amendment to Certificate of Formation

(a) To adopt an amendment to the certificate of formation of a real estate investment trust as provided by Subchapter B, Chapter 3, the trust managers shall:

(1) adopt a resolution stating the proposed amendment; and

(2) follow the procedures prescribed by Sections 200.054–200.056.

(b) The resolution may incorporate the proposed amendment in a restated certificate of formation that complies with Section 3.059.

Acts 2003, 78th Leg., ch. 182, § 1, eff. Jan. 1, 2006.

§ 200.054. Adoption of Amendment by Trust Managers

If a real estate investment trust does not have any issued and outstanding shares, the trust managers may adopt a proposed amendment to the real estate investment trust's certificate of formation by resolution without shareholder approval.

Acts 2003, 78th Leg., ch. 182, § 1, eff. Jan. 1, 2006.

§ 200.055. Adoption of Amendment by Shareholders

If a real estate investment trust has issued and outstanding shares:

(1) a resolution described by Section 200.053 must also direct that the proposed amendment be submitted to a vote of the shareholders at a meeting; and

(2) the shareholders must approve the proposed amendment in the manner provided by Section 200.056.

Acts 2003, 78th Leg., ch. 182, § 1, eff. Jan. 1, 2006.

§ 200.056. Notice of and Meeting to Consider Proposed Amendment

(a) Each shareholder of record entitled to vote shall be given written notice containing the proposed amendment or a summary of the changes to be effected within the time and in the manner provided by this code for giving notice of meetings to shareholders. If the proposed amendment is to be considered at an annual meeting, the proposed amendment or summary may be included in the notice required to be provided for an annual meeting.

(b) At the meeting, the proposed amendment shall be adopted only on receiving the affirmative vote of shareholders entitled to vote required by Section 200.261.

(c) An unlimited number of amendments may be submitted for adoption by the shareholders at a meeting.

Acts 2003, 78th Leg., ch. 182, § 1, eff. Jan. 1, 2006.

§ 200.057. Adoption of Restated Certificate of Formation

(a) A real estate investment trust may adopt a restated certificate of formation as provided by Subchapter B, Chapter 3, by following the same procedures to amend its certificate of formation under Sections 200.053–200.056, except that shareholder approval is not required if an amendment is not adopted.

(b) If shares of the real estate investment trust have not been issued and the restated certificate of formation is adopted by the trust managers, the majority of the trust managers may sign the restated certificate of formation on behalf of the real estate investment trust.

Acts 2003, 78th Leg., ch. 182, § 1, eff. Jan. 1, 2006.

§ 200.058. Bylaws

(a) The trust managers of a real estate investment trust shall adopt initial bylaws.

(b) The bylaws may contain provisions for the regulation and management of the affairs of the real estate investment trust that are consistent with law and the real estate investment trust's certificate of formation.

(c) The trust managers of a real estate investment trust may amend or repeal bylaws or adopt new bylaws unless:

(1) the real estate investment trust's certificate of formation or this chapter wholly or partly reserves the power exclusively to the real estate investment trust's shareholders; or

(2) in amending, repealing, or adopting a bylaw, the shareholders expressly provide that the trust managers may not amend, repeal, or readopt that bylaw.

Acts 2003, 78th Leg., ch. 182, § 1, eff. Jan. 1, 2006.

§ 200.059. Dual Authority

Unless the certificate of formation or a bylaw adopted by the shareholders provides otherwise as to all or a part of a real estate investment trust's bylaws, the shareholders of a real estate investment trust may amend, repeal, or adopt the bylaws of the real estate investment trust even if the bylaws may also be amended, repealed, or adopted by the trust managers of the real estate investment trust.

Acts 2003, 78th Leg., ch. 182, § 1, eff. Jan. 1, 2006.

§ 200.060. Organization Meeting

(a) After the real estate investment trust has been formed, the initial trust managers of the real estate investment trust shall hold an organization meeting, at the call of a majority of those trust managers, for the purpose of adopting bylaws, electing officers, and transacting other business.

(b) Not later than the third day before the date of the meeting, the initial trust managers calling the meeting shall send notice of the time and place of the meeting to the other initial trust managers named in the certificate of formation.

Acts 2003, 78th Leg., ch. 182, § 1, eff. Jan. 1, 2006.

SUBCHAPTER C. SHARES

§ 200.101. Number

A real estate investment trust may issue the number of shares stated in the real estate investment trust's certificate of formation.

Acts 2003, 78th Leg., ch. 182, § 1, eff. Jan. 1, 2006.

§ 200.102. Classification of Shares

A real estate investment trust may provide in the real estate investment trust's certificate of formation:

(1) that a specified class of shares is preferred over another class of shares as to its distributive share of the assets on voluntary or involuntary liquidation of the real estate investment trust;

(2) the amount of a preference described by Subdivision (1);

(3) that a specified class of shares may be redeemed at the option of the real estate investment trust or of the holders of the shares;

(4) the terms and conditions of a redemption of shares described by Subdivision (3), including the time and price of redemption;

(5) that a specified class of shares may be converted into shares of one or more other classes;

(6) the terms and conditions of a conversion described by Subdivision (5);

(7) that a holder of a specified security issued or to be issued by the real estate investment trust has voting or other rights authorized by law; and

(8) for other preferences, rights, restrictions, including restrictions on transferability, and qualifications consistent with law.

Acts 2003, 78th Leg., ch. 182, § 1, eff. Jan. 1, 2006.

§ 200.103. Classes of Shares Established by Trust Managers

(a) A real estate investment trust may provide in the real estate investment trust's certificate of formation that the trust managers may classify or reclassify any unissued shares by setting or changing the preferences, conversion or other rights, voting powers, restrictions, limitations as to dividends, qualifications, or terms or conditions of redemption of the shares.

(b) Before issuing shares, the trust managers who perform as authorized by the certificate of formation an action described by Subsection (a) must file with the county clerk of the county of the principal place of business of the real estate investment trust a statement of designation that contains:

(1) a description of the shares, including the preferences, conversion and other rights, voting powers, restrictions, limitations as to dividends, qualifications, and terms and conditions of redemption, as set or changed by the trust managers; and

(2) a statement that the shares have been classified or reclassified by the trust managers as authorized by the certificate of formation.

Acts 2003, 78th Leg., ch. 182, § 1, eff. Jan. 1, 2006.

§ 200.104. Issuance of Shares

(a) A real estate investment trust may issue shares for consideration if authorized by the trust managers.

(b) Shares may not be issued until the consideration, determined in accordance with this subchapter, has been paid to the real estate investment trust or to another entity of which all of the outstanding ownership interests are directly or indirectly owned by the real estate investment trust. When the consideration is paid:

(1) the shares are considered to be issued;

(2) the shareholder entitled to receive the shares is a shareholder with respect to the shares; and

(3) the shares are considered fully paid and nonassessable.

Acts 2003, 78th Leg., ch. 182, § 1, eff. Jan. 1, 2006.

§ 200.105. Types of Consideration for Issuance of Shares

Shares with or without par value may be issued by a real estate investment trust for the following types of consideration:

(1) a tangible or intangible benefit to the real estate investment trust;

(2) cash;

(3) a promissory note;

(4) services performed or a contract for services to be performed;

(5) a security of the real estate investment trust or any other organization; and

(6) any other property of any kind or nature.

Acts 2003, 78th Leg., ch. 182, § 1, eff. Jan. 1, 2006.

§ 200.106. Determination of Consideration for Shares

Consideration to be received by a real estate investment trust for shares shall be determined by the trust managers.

Acts 2003, 78th Leg., ch. 182, § 1, eff. Jan. 1, 2006.

§ 200.107. Amount of Consideration for Issuance of Shares With Par Value

Consideration to be received by a real estate investment trust for the issuance of shares with par value may not be less than the par value of the shares.

Acts 2003, 78th Leg., ch. 182, § 1, eff. Jan. 1, 2006.

§ 200.108. Value of Consideration

In the absence of fraud in the transaction, the judgment of the trust managers is conclusive in determining the value of the consideration received for the shares.

Acts 2003, 78th Leg., ch. 182, § 1, eff. Jan. 1, 2006.

§ 200.109. Liability of Assignee or Transferee

An assignee or transferee of certificated shares, uncertificated shares, or a subscription for shares in good faith and without knowledge that full consideration for the shares or subscription has not been paid may not be held personally liable to the real estate investment trust or a creditor of the real estate investment trust for an unpaid portion of the consideration.

Acts 2003, 78th Leg., ch. 182, § 1, eff. Jan. 1, 2006.

§ 200.110. Subscriptions

(a) A real estate investment trust may accept a subscription by notifying the subscriber in writing.

(b) A subscription to purchase shares in a real estate investment trust that is in the process of being formed is irrevocable for six months if the subscription is in writing and signed by the subscriber unless the subscription provides for a longer or shorter period or all of the other subscribers agree to the revocation of the subscription.

(c) A written subscription entered into after the real estate investment trust is formed is a contract between the subscriber and the real estate investment trust.

Acts 2003, 78th Leg., ch. 182, § 1, eff. Jan. 1, 2006.

§ 200.111. Preformation Subscription

(a) A real estate investment trust may determine the payment terms of a preformation subscription unless the payment terms are specified by the subscription. The payment terms may authorize payment in full on acceptance or by installments.

(b) Unless the subscription provides otherwise, a real estate investment trust shall make calls placed to all subscribers of similar interests for payment on preformation subscriptions uniform as far as practicable.

(c) After the real estate investment trust is formed, if a subscriber fails to pay any installment or call when due, the real estate investment trust may:

(1) collect in the same manner as any other debt the amount due on any unpaid preformation subscription; or

(2) forfeit the subscription if the installment or call remains unpaid for 20 days after written notice to the subscriber.

(d) Although the forfeiture of a subscription terminates all the rights and obligations of the subscriber, the real estate investment trust may retain any amount previously paid on the subscription.

Acts 2003, 78th Leg., ch. 182, § 1, eff. Jan. 1, 2006.

§ 200.112. Commitment in Connection With Purchase of Shares

(a) A person who contemplates the acquisition of shares in a real estate investment trust may commit to act in a specified manner with respect to the shares after the acquisition, including the voting of the shares or the retention or disposition of the shares. To be binding, the commitment must be in writing and be signed by the person acquiring the shares.

(b) A written commitment entered into under Subsection (a) is a contract between the shareholder and the real estate investment trust.

Acts 2003, 78th Leg., ch. 182, § 1, eff. Jan. 1, 2006.

§ 200.113. Supplemental Required Records

In addition to the books and records required to be kept under Section 3.151, a real estate investment trust must keep at its principal office or place of business, or at the office of its transfer agent or registrar, a record of the number of shares held by each shareholder.

Acts 2003, 78th Leg., ch. 182, § 1, eff. Jan. 1, 2006.

SUBCHAPTER D. SHAREHOLDER RIGHTS AND RESTRICTIONS

§ 200.151. Registered Holders as Owners

Except as otherwise provided by this code and subject to Chapter 8, Business & Commerce Code, a real estate investment trust may consider the person registered as the owner of a share in the share transfer records of the real estate investment trust at a particular time, including a record date set under Section 6.102, as the owner of that share at that time for purposes of:

(1) voting the share;

(2) receiving distributions on the share;

(3) transferring the share;

(4) receiving notice, exercising rights of dissent and appraisal, exercising or waiving a preemptive right, or giving proxies with respect to that share; or

(5) entering into agreements with respect to that share in accordance with Section 6.251 or 6.252 or with this subchapter.

Acts 2003, 78th Leg., ch. 182, § 1, eff. Jan. 1, 2006.

§ 200.152. No Statutory Preemptive Right Unless Specifically Provided by Certificate of Formation

A shareholder of a real estate investment trust does not have a preemptive right to acquire securities except to the extent specifically provided by the certificate of formation.

Acts 2003, 78th Leg., ch. 182, § 1, eff. Jan. 1, 2006.

§ 200.153. Characterization and Transfer of Shares and Other Securities

Except as otherwise provided by this code, the shares and other securities of a real estate investment trust are:

(1) personal property for all purposes; and

(2) transferable in accordance with Chapter 8, Business & Commerce Code.

Acts 2003, 78th Leg., ch. 182, § 1, eff. Jan. 1, 2006.

§ 200.154. Restriction on Transfer of Shares and Other Securities

(a) A restriction on the transfer or registration of transfer of a security may be imposed by:

(1) the real estate investment trust's certificate of formation;

(2) the real estate investment trust's bylaws;

(3) a written agreement among two or more holders of the securities; or

(4) a written agreement among one or more holders of the securities and the real estate investment trust if:

(A) the real estate investment trust files a copy of the agreement at the principal place of business or registered office of the real estate investment trust; and

(B) the copy of the agreement is subject to the same right of examination by a shareholder of the real estate investment trust, in person or by agent, attorney, or accountant, as the books and records of the real estate investment trust.

(b) A restriction imposed under Subsection (a) is not valid with respect to a security issued before the restriction has been adopted, unless the holder of the security voted in favor of the restriction or is a party to the agreement imposing the restriction.

Acts 2003, 78th Leg., ch. 182, § 1, eff. Jan. 1, 2006.

§ 200.155. Valid Restriction on Transfer

Notwithstanding Sections 200.154 and 200.157, a restriction placed on the transfer or registration of transfer of a security of a real estate investment trust is valid if the restriction reasonably:

(1) obligates the holder of the restricted security to offer a person, including the real estate investment trust or other holders of securities of the real estate investment trust, an opportunity to acquire the restricted security within a reasonable time before the transfer;

(2) obligates the real estate investment trust, to the extent provided by this code, or another person to purchase a security that is the subject of an agreement relating to the purchase and sale of the restricted security;

(3) requires the real estate investment trust or the holders of a class of the real estate investment trust's securities to consent to a proposed transfer of the restricted security or to approve the proposed transferee of the restricted security for the purpose of preventing a violation of law;

(4) prohibits the transfer of the restricted security to a designated person or group of persons and the designation is not manifestly unreasonable; or

(5) maintains a tax advantage to the real estate investment trust, including maintaining its status as a real estate investment trust under the relevant provisions of the Internal Revenue Code and regulations adopted under the Internal Revenue Code.

Acts 2003, 78th Leg., ch. 182, § 1, eff. Jan. 1, 2006.

§ 200.156. Bylaw or Agreement Restricting Transfer of Shares or Other Securities

(a) A real estate investment trust that has adopted a bylaw or is a party to an agreement that restricts the transfer of the shares or other securities of the real estate investment trust may file with the county clerk of the county of the principal place of business of the real estate investment trust a copy of the bylaw or agreement and a statement attached to the copy that:

(1) contains the name of the real estate investment trust;

(2) states that the attached copy of the bylaw or agreement is a true and correct copy of the bylaw or agreement; and

(3) states that the filing has been authorized by the trust managers or shareholders, as appropriate.

(b) After the statement is filed with the county clerk, the bylaws or agreement restricting the transfer of shares or other securities is a public record, and the fact that the statement has been filed must be stated on a certificate representing the restricted shares or securities if required by Section 3.202.

(c) A real estate investment trust that is a party to an agreement restricting the transfer of the shares or other securities of the real estate investment trust may make the agreement part of the real estate investment trust's certificate of formation without restating the provisions of the agreement in the certificate of formation by complying with this code or amending the certificate of formation. If the agreement alters the original or amended certificate of formation, the altered provision must be identified by reference or description in the certificate of amendment. If the agreement is an addition to the original or amended certificate of formation, the certificate of amendment must state that fact.

(d) The certificate of amendment must:

(1) include a copy of the agreement restricting the transfer of shares or other securities;

(2) state that the attached copy of the agreement is a true and correct copy of the agreement; and

(3) state that inclusion of the certificate of amendment as part of the certificate of formation has been authorized in the manner required by this code to amend the certificate of formation.

Acts 2003, 78th Leg., ch. 182, § 1, eff. Jan. 1, 2006.

§ 200.157. Enforceability of Restriction on Transfer of Certain Securities

(a) A restriction placed on the transfer or registration of the transfer of a security of a real estate investment trust is specifically enforceable against the holder, or a successor or transferee of the holder, if:

(1) the restriction is reasonable and noted conspicuously on the certificate or other instrument representing the security; or

(2) with respect to an uncertificated security, the restriction is reasonable and a notation of the restriction is contained in the notice sent with respect to the security under Section 3.205.

(b) Unless noted in the manner specified by Subsection (a) with respect to a certificate or other instrument or an uncertificated security, an otherwise enforceable restriction is ineffective against a transferee for value without actual knowledge of the restriction at the time of the transfer or against a subsequent transferee, regardless of whether the transfer is for value. A restriction is specifically enforceable against a person other than a transferee for value from the time the person acquires actual knowledge of the restriction's existence.

Acts 2003, 78th Leg., ch. 182, § 1, eff. Jan. 1, 2006.

§ 200.158. Joint Ownership of Shares

(a) If shares are registered on the books of a real estate investment trust in the names of two or more persons as joint owners with the right of survivorship and one of the owners dies, the real estate investment trust may record on its books and effect the transfer of the shares to a person, including the surviving joint owner, and pay any distributions made with respect to the shares, as if the surviving joint owner was the sole owner of the shares. The recording and distribution authorized by this subsection must be made after the death of a joint owner and before the real estate investment trust receives actual written notice that a party other than a surviving joint owner is claiming an interest in the shares or distribution.

(b) The discharge of a real estate investment trust from liability under Section 200.160 and the transfer of full legal and equitable title of the shares does not affect, reduce, or limit any cause of action existing in favor of an owner of an interest in the shares or distribution against the surviving owner.

Acts 2003, 78th Leg., ch. 182, § 1, eff. Jan. 1, 2006.

§ 200.159. Liability for Designating Owner of Shares

A real estate investment trust or an officer, trust manager, employee, or agent of the real estate investment trust may not be held liable for considering a person to be the owner of a share for a purpose described by Section 200.151, regardless of whether the person possesses a certificate for those shares.

Acts 2003, 78th Leg., ch. 182, § 1, eff. Jan. 1, 2006.

§ 200.160. Liability Regarding Joint Ownership of Shares

A real estate investment trust that transfers shares or makes a distribution to a surviving joint owner under Section 200.158 before the real estate investment trust has received a written claim for the shares or distribution from another person is discharged from liability for the transfer or payment.

Acts 2003, 78th Leg., ch. 182, § 1, eff. Jan. 1, 2006.

§ 200.161. Limitation of Liability for Obligations

(a) A holder of shares, an owner of any beneficial interest in shares, or a subscriber for shares whose subscription has been accepted is not under an obligation to the real estate investment trust or its obligees with respect to:

(1) the shares, other than the obligation to pay to the real estate investment trust the full amount of consideration, fixed in compliance with Sections 200.104–200.108, for which the shares were or are to be issued;

(2) any contractual obligation of the real estate investment trust on the basis that the holder, beneficial owner, or subscriber is or was the alter ego of the real estate investment trust or on the basis of actual or constructive fraud, a sham to perpetrate a fraud, or other similar theory; or

(3) any obligation of the real estate investment trust on the basis of the failure of the real estate investment trust to observe any formality, including the failure to:

(A) comply with this code or the declaration of trust or bylaws of the real estate investment trust; or

(B) observe any requirement prescribed by this code or the declaration of trust or bylaws of the real estate investment trust for acts to be taken by the real estate investment trust or its trust managers or shareholders.

(b) Subsection (a)(2) does not prevent or limit the liability of a holder, beneficial owner, or subscriber if the obligee demonstrates that the holder, beneficial owner, or subscriber caused the real estate investment trust to be used for the purpose of perpetrating and did perpetrate an actual fraud on the obligee primarily for the direct personal benefit of the holder, beneficial owner, or subscriber.

Acts 2003, 78th Leg., ch. 182, § 1, eff. Jan. 1, 2006.

§ 200.162. Preemption of Liability

The liability of a holder, beneficial owner, or subscriber of shares of a real estate investment trust for an obligation that is limited by Section 200.161 is exclusive and preempts any other liability imposed for that obligation under common law or otherwise.

Acts 2003, 78th Leg., ch. 182, § 1, eff. Jan. 1, 2006.

§ 200.163. Exceptions to Limitations

Section 200.161 or 200.162 does not limit the obligation of a holder, beneficial owner, or subscriber to the obligee of the real estate investment trust if that person:

(1) expressly assumes, guarantees, or agrees to be personally liable to the obligee for the obligation; or

(2) is otherwise liable to the obligee for the obligation under this code or other applicable statute.

Acts 2003, 78th Leg., ch. 182, § 1, eff. Jan. 1, 2006.

§ 200.164. Pledgees and Trust Administrators

(a) A pledgee or other holder of shares as collateral security is not personally liable as a shareholder.

(b) An executor, administrator, conservator, guardian, trustee, assignee for the benefit of creditors, or receiver is not personally liable as a holder of or subscriber to shares of a real estate investment trust.

(c) The estate and funds administered by an executor, administrator, conservator, guardian, trustee, assignee for the benefit of creditors, or receiver are liable for the full amount of the consideration for which the shares were or are to be issued.

Acts 2003, 78th Leg., ch. 182, § 1, eff. Jan. 1, 2006.

SUBCHAPTER E. DISTRIBUTIONS AND SHARE DIVIDENDS

§ 200.201. Authority for Distributions

The trust managers of a real estate investment trust may authorize a distribution and the real estate investment trust may make a distribution, subject to Section 200.202 and any restriction in the certificate of formation.

Acts 2003, 78th Leg., ch. 182, § 1, eff. Jan. 1, 2006.

§ 200.202. Limitations on Distributions

(a) A real estate investment trust may not make a distribution:

(1) if the real estate investment trust would be insolvent after the distribution; or

(2) that is more than the surplus of the real estate investment trust.

(b) Notwithstanding Subsection (a)(2), if the net assets of a real estate investment trust are not less than the amount of the proposed distribution, the real estate investment trust may make a distribution involving a purchase or redemption of its own shares if the purchase or redemption is made by the real estate investment trust to:

(1) eliminate fractional shares;

(2) collect or settle indebtedness owed by or to the real estate investment trust;

(3) pay dissenting shareholders entitled to receive payment for their shares under this chapter; or

(4) effect the purchase or redemption of redeemable shares in accordance with this code.

Acts 2003, 78th Leg., ch. 182, § 1, eff. Jan. 1, 2006.

§ 200.203. Priority of Distributions

A real estate investment trust's indebtedness that arises as a result of the declaration of a distribution and a real estate investment trust's indebtedness issued in a distribution are at parity with the real estate investment trust's indebtedness to its general, unsecured creditors, except to the extent the indebtedness is subordinated, or payment of that indebtedness is secured, by agreement.

Acts 2003, 78th Leg., ch. 182, § 1, eff. Jan. 1, 2006.

§ 200.204. Reserves, Designations, and Allocations From Surplus

(a) A real estate investment trust, by resolution of the trust managers of the real estate investment trust, may:

(1) create a reserve out of the surplus of the real estate investment trust; or

(2) designate or allocate in any manner a part or all of the real estate investment trust's surplus for a proper purpose.

(b) A real estate investment trust may increase, decrease, or abolish a reserve, designation, or allocation in the manner provided by Subsection (a).

Acts 2003, 78th Leg., ch. 182, § 1, eff. Jan. 1, 2006.

§ 200.205. Authority for Share Dividends

The trust managers of a real estate investment trust may authorize a share dividend, and the real estate investment trust may pay a share dividend subject to Section 200.206 and any restriction in the certificate of formation.

Acts 2003, 78th Leg., ch. 182, § 1, eff. Jan. 1, 2006.

§ 200.206. Limitations on Share Dividends

(a) A real estate investment trust may not pay a share dividend in authorized but unissued shares of any class if the surplus of the real estate investment trust is less than the amount required by Section 200.208 to be transferred to stated capital at the time the share dividend is made.

(b) A share dividend in shares of any class may not be made to a holder of shares of any other class unless:

(1) the real estate investment trust's certificate of formation provides for the dividend; or

(2) the share dividend is authorized by the affirmative vote or the written consent of the holders of at least a majority of the outstanding shares of the class in which the share dividend is to be made.

Acts 2003, 78th Leg., ch. 182, § 1, eff. Jan. 1, 2006.

§ 200.207. Value of Shares Issued as Share Dividends

(a) A share dividend payable in authorized but unissued shares with par value shall be issued at the par value of the shares.

(b) A share dividend payable in authorized but unissued shares without par value shall be issued at the value set by the trust managers when the share dividend is authorized.

Acts 2003, 78th Leg., ch. 182, § 1, eff. Jan. 1, 2006.

§ 200.208. Transfer of Surplus for Share Dividends

(a) When a share dividend payable in authorized but unissued shares with par value is made by a real estate investment trust, an amount of surplus designated by the trust managers that is not less than the aggregate par value of the shares issued as a share dividend shall be transferred to stated capital.

(b) When a share dividend payable in authorized but unissued shares without par value is made by a real estate investment trust, an amount of surplus equal to the aggregate value set by the trust managers with respect to the shares under Section 200.207(b) shall be transferred to stated capital.

Acts 2003, 78th Leg., ch. 182, § 1, eff. Jan. 1, 2006.

§ 200.209. Determination of Solvency, Net Assets, Stated Capital, and Surplus

(a) The determination of whether a real estate investment trust is or would be insolvent and the determination of the value of a real estate investment trust's net assets, stated capital, or surplus and each of the components of net assets, stated capital, or surplus may be based on:

(1) financial statements of the real estate investment trust that present the financial condition of the real estate investment trust in accordance with generally accepted accounting principles, including financial statements that include subsidiary entities or other entities accounted for on a consolidated basis or on the equity method of accounting;

(2) financial statements prepared using the method of accounting used to file the real estate investment trust's federal income tax return or using any other accounting practices and principles that are reasonable under the circumstances;

(3) financial information, including condensed or summary financial statements, that is prepared on the same basis as financial statements described by Subdivision (1) or (2);

(4) a projection, a forecast, or other forward-looking information relating to the future economic performance, financial condition, or liquidity of the real estate investment trust that is reasonable under the circumstances;

(5) a fair valuation or information from any other method that is reasonable under the circumstances; or

(6) a combination of a statement, a valuation, or information authorized by this section.

(b) Subsection (a) does not apply to the computation of any tax imposed under the laws of this state.

Acts 2003, 78th Leg., ch. 182, § 1, eff. Jan. 1, 2006.

§ 200.210. Date of Determination of Surplus

(a) For purposes of this subchapter, a determination of whether a real estate investment trust is or would be made insolvent by a distribution or share dividend or a determination of the value of a real estate investment trust's surplus shall be made:

(1) on the date the distribution or share dividend is authorized by the trust managers of the real estate investment trust if the distribution or the share dividend is made not later than the 120th day after the date of authorization; or

(2) if the distribution or the share dividend is made more than 120 days after the date of authorization:

(A) on the date designated by the trust managers if the date so designated is not earlier than 120 days before the date the distribution or the share dividend is made; or

(B) on the date the distribution or the share dividend is made if the trust managers do not designate a date as described in Paragraph (A).

(b) For purposes of this section, a distribution that involves:

(1) the incurrence by a real estate investment trust of indebtedness or a deferred payment obligation is considered to have been made on the date the indebtedness or obligation is incurred; or

(2) a contract by the real estate investment trust to acquire any of its own shares is considered to have been made on the date when the contract is made or takes effect or on the date the shares are

acquired, at the option of the real estate investment trust.

Acts 2003, 78th Leg., ch. 182, § 1, eff. Jan. 1, 2006.

§ 200.211. Split-up or Division of Shares

The trust managers of a real estate investment trust may authorize the real estate investment trust to carry out any split-up or division of the issued shares of a class of the real estate investment trust into a larger number of shares within the same class that does not increase the stated capital of the real estate investment trust because the split-up or division of issued shares is not a share dividend or a distribution.

Acts 2003, 78th Leg., ch. 182, § 1, eff. Jan. 1, 2006.

SUBCHAPTER F. SHAREHOLDERS' MEETINGS; VOTING AND QUORUM

§ 200.251. Annual Meeting

(a) An annual meeting of the shareholders of a real estate investment trust shall be held at a time that is stated in or set in accordance with the bylaws of the real estate investment trust.

(b) If the annual meeting is not held at the designated time, a shareholder may by certified or registered mail make a written request to an officer or trust manager of the real estate investment trust that the meeting be held within a reasonable time. If the annual meeting is not called before the 61st day after the date the request calling for a meeting is made, any shareholder may bring suit at law or in equity to compel the meeting to be held.

(c) Each shareholder has a justifiable interest sufficient to enable the shareholder to institute and prosecute a legal proceeding described by this section.

(d) The failure to hold an annual meeting at the designated time does not result in the winding up or termination of the real estate investment trust.

Acts 2003, 78th Leg., ch. 182, § 1, eff. Jan. 1, 2006.

§ 200.252. Special Meetings

A special meeting of the shareholders of a real estate investment trust may be called by:

(1) a trust manager, an officer of the real estate investment trust, or any other person authorized to call special meetings by the certificate of formation or bylaws of the real estate investment trust; or

(2) the holders of at least 10 percent of all of the shares of the real estate investment trust entitled to vote at the proposed special meeting unless a greater or lesser percentage of shares is specified in the certificate of formation, not to exceed 50 percent of the shares entitled to vote.

Acts 2003, 78th Leg., ch. 182, § 1, eff. Jan. 1, 2006.

§ 200.253. Notice of Meeting

(a) Written notice of a meeting in accordance with Section 6.051 shall be given to each shareholder entitled to vote at the meeting not later than the 10th day and not earlier than the 60th day before the date of the meeting. Notice shall be given in person or by mail by or at the direction of a trust manager, officer, or other person calling the meeting.

(b) The notice of a special meeting must contain a statement regarding the purpose or purposes of the meeting.

Acts 2003, 78th Leg., ch. 182, § 1, eff. Jan. 1, 2006.

§ 200.254. Closing of Share Transfer Records

Share transfer records that are closed in accordance with Section 6.101 for the purpose of determining which shareholders are entitled to receive notice of a meeting of shareholders shall remain closed for at least 10 days immediately preceding the date of the meeting.

Acts 2003, 78th Leg., ch. 182, § 1, eff. Jan. 1, 2006.

§ 200.255. Record Date for Written Consent to Action

The record date provided in accordance with Section 6.102(a) may not be more than 10 days after the date on which the trust managers adopt the resolution setting the record date.

Acts 2003, 78th Leg., ch. 182, § 1, eff. Jan. 1, 2006.

§ 200.256. Record Date for Purpose Other Than Written Consent to Action

The record date provided by the trust managers in accordance with Section 6.101 must be at least 10 days before the date on which the particular action requiring the determination of shareholders is to be taken.

Acts 2003, 78th Leg., ch. 182, § 1, eff. Jan. 1, 2006.

§ 200.257. Quorum

(a) Subject to Subsection (b), the holders of the majority of the shares entitled to vote at a meeting of the shareholders of a real estate investment trust that are present or represented by proxy at the meeting are a quorum for the consideration of a matter to be presented at that meeting.

(b) The certificate of formation of a real estate investment trust may provide that a quorum is present only if:

(1) the holders of a specified portion of the shares that is greater than the majority of the shares entitled to vote are represented at the meeting in person or by proxy; or

(2) the holders of a specified portion of the shares that is less than the majority but not less than one-third of the shares entitled to vote are represented at the meeting in person or by proxy.

(c) Unless provided by the certificate of formation or bylaws of the real estate investment trust, after a quorum is present at a meeting of shareholders, the shareholders may conduct business properly brought before the meeting until the meeting is adjourned. The subsequent withdrawal from the meeting of a shareholder or the refusal of a shareholder present at or represented by proxy at the meeting to vote does not negate the presence of a quorum at the meeting.

(d) Unless provided by the certificate of formation or bylaws, the shareholders of the real estate investment trust at a meeting at which a quorum is not present may adjourn the meeting until the time and to the place as may be determined by a vote of the holders of the majority of the shares who are present or represented by proxy at the meeting.

Acts 2003, 78th Leg., ch. 182, § 1, eff. Jan. 1, 2006.

§ 200.258. Voting in Election of Trust Managers

(a) Subject to Subsection (b), trust managers of a real estate investment trust shall be elected by two-thirds of the votes cast by the holders of shares entitled to vote in the election of trust managers at a meeting of shareholders at which a quorum is present.

(b) The certificate of formation or bylaws of a real estate investment trust may provide that a trust manager of the real estate investment trust shall be elected only if the trust manager receives:

(1) the vote of the holders of a specified portion, but not less than the majority, of the shares entitled to vote in the election of trust managers;

(2) the vote of the holders of a specified portion, but not less than the majority, of the shares entitled to vote in the election of trust managers and represented in person or by proxy at a meeting of shareholders at which a quorum is present; or

(3) the vote of the holders of a specified portion, but not less than the majority, of the votes cast by the holders of shares entitled to vote in the election of trust managers at a meeting of shareholders at which a quorum is present.

(c) Subject to Section 200.259, at each election of trust managers of a real estate investment trust, each shareholder entitled to vote at the election is entitled to vote, in person or by proxy, the number of shares owned by the shareholder for as many candidates as there are trust managers to be elected and for whose election the shareholder is entitled to vote.

Acts 2003, 78th Leg., ch. 182, § 1, eff. Jan. 1, 2006.

§ 200.259. Cumulative Voting in Election of Trust Managers

(a) Cumulative voting is allowed only if specifically authorized by the certificate of formation of a real estate investment trust.

(b) Cumulative voting occurs when a shareholder:

(1) gives one candidate as many votes as the total of the number of the trust managers to be elected multiplied by the shareholder's shares; or

(2) distributes the votes among one or more candidates using the same principle.

(c) If cumulative voting is specifically authorized by the certificate of formation, a shareholder who intends to cumulate votes must give written notice of that intention to the trust managers on or before the day preceding the date of the election at which the shareholder intends to cumulate votes.

Acts 2003, 78th Leg., ch. 182, § 1, eff. Jan. 1, 2006.

§ 200.260. Voting on Matters Other Than Election of Trust Managers

(a) Subject to Subsection (b), with respect to a matter other than the election of trust managers or a matter for which the affirmative vote of the holders of a specified portion of the shares entitled to vote is required by this code, the affirmative vote of the holders of the majority of the shares entitled to vote on, and who voted for, against, or expressly abstained with respect to, the matter at a shareholders' meeting of a real estate investment trust at which a quorum is present is the act of the shareholders.

(b) With respect to a matter other than the election of trust managers or a matter for which the affirmative vote of the holders of a specified portion of the shares entitled to vote is required by this code, the certificate of formation or bylaws of a real estate investment trust may provide that the act of the shareholders of the real estate investment trust is:

(1) the affirmative vote of the holders of a specified portion, but not less than the majority, of the shares entitled to vote on that matter;

(2) the affirmative vote of the holders of a specified portion, but not less than the majority, of the shares entitled to vote on that matter and represented in person or by proxy at a shareholders' meeting at which a quorum is present;

(3) the affirmative vote of the holders of a specified portion, but not less than the majority, of the shares entitled to vote on, and who voted for or against, the matter at a shareholders' meeting at which a quorum is present; or

(4) the affirmative vote of the holders of a specified portion, but not less than the majority, of the shares entitled to vote on, and who voted for, against, or expressly abstained with respect to, the matter at a shareholders' meeting at which a quorum is present.

Acts 2003, 78th Leg., ch. 182, § 1, eff. Jan. 1, 2006.

§ 200.261. Vote Required to Approve Fundamental Action

(a) In this section, a "fundamental action" means:

(1) an amendment of a certificate of formation, including an amendment required for cancellation of an event requiring winding up in accordance with Section 11.152(b);

(2) a voluntary winding up under Chapter 11;

(3) a revocation of a voluntary decision to wind up under Section 11.151;

(4) a cancellation of an event requiring winding up under Section 11.152(a); or

(5) a reinstatement under Section 11.202.

(b) Except as otherwise provided by this code or the certificate of formation or bylaws of a real estate investment trust in accordance with Section 200.260, the vote required for approval of a fundamental action by the shareholders is the affirmative vote of the holders of at least two-thirds of the outstanding shares entitled to vote on the fundamental action.

(c) If a class or series of shares is entitled to vote as a class or series on a fundamental action, the vote required for approval of the action by the shareholders is the affirmative vote of the holders of at least two-thirds of the outstanding shares in each class or series of shares entitled to vote on the action as a class and at least two-thirds of the outstanding shares otherwise entitled to vote on the action. Shares entitled to vote as a class or series shall be entitled to vote only as a class or series unless otherwise entitled to vote on each matter generally or otherwise provided by the certificate of formation.

(d) Unless an amendment to the certificate of formation is undertaken by the trust managers under Section 200.103, separate voting by a class or series of shares of a real estate investment trust is required for approval of an amendment to the certificate of formation that would result in:

(1) the increase or decrease of the aggregate number of authorized shares of the class or series;

(2) the increase or decrease of the par value of the shares of the class, including changing shares with par value into shares without par value or changing shares without par value into shares with par value;

(3) effecting an exchange, reclassification, or cancellation of all or part of the shares of the class or series;

(4) effecting an exchange or creating a right of exchange of all or part of the shares of another class or series into the shares of the class or series;

(5) the change of the designations, preferences, limitations, or relative rights of the shares of the class or series;

(6) the change of the shares of the class or series, with or without par value, into the same or a different number of shares, with or without par value, of the same class or series or another class or series;

(7) the creation of a new class or series of shares with rights and preferences equal, prior, or superior to the shares of the class or series;

(8) increasing the rights and preferences of a class or series with rights and preferences equal, prior, or superior to the shares of the class or series;

(9) increasing the rights and preferences of a class or series with rights or preferences later or inferior to the shares of the class or series in such a manner that the rights or preferences will be equal, prior, or superior to the shares of the class or series;

(10) dividing the shares of the class into series and setting and determining the designation of the series and the variations in the relative rights and preferences between the shares of the series;

(11) the limitation or denial of existing preemptive rights or cumulative voting rights of the shares of the class or series; or

(12) canceling or otherwise affecting the dividends on the shares of the class or series that have accrued but have not been declared.

(e) Unless otherwise provided by the certificate of formation, if the holders of the outstanding shares of a class that is divided into series are entitled to vote as a class on a proposed amendment that would affect equally all series of the class, other than a series in which no shares are outstanding or a series that is not affected by the amendment, the holders of the separate series are not entitled to separate class votes.

(f) Unless otherwise provided by the certificate of formation, a proposed amendment to the certificate of formation that would solely effect changes in the designations, preferences, limitations, or relative rights, including voting rights, of one or more series of shares of the real estate investment trust that have been established under the authority granted to the trust managers in the certificate of formation in accordance with Section 200.103 does not require the approval of the holders of the outstanding shares of a class or series other than the affected series if, after giving effect to the amendment:

(1) the preferences, limitations, or relative rights of the affected series may be set and determined by the trust managers with respect to the establishment of a new series of shares under the authority granted to the trust managers in the certificate of formation in accordance with Section 200.103; or

(2) any new series established as a result of a reclassification of the affected series are within the preferences, limitations, and relative rights that are described by Subdivision (1).

Acts 2003, 78th Leg., ch. 182, § 1, eff. Jan. 1, 2006. Amended by Acts 2007, 80th Leg., ch. 688, § 132, eff. Sept. 1, 2007.

§ 200.262. Changes in Vote Required for Certain Matters

(a) With respect to a matter for which the affirmative vote of the holders of a specified portion of the shares entitled to vote is required by this code, the certificate of formation of a real estate investment trust may provide that the affirmative vote of the holders of a specified portion, but not less than the majority, of the shares entitled to vote on that matter is required for shareholder action on that matter.

(b) With respect to a matter for which the affirmative vote of the holders of a specified portion of the shares of a class or series is required by this code, the certificate of formation may provide that the affirmative vote of the holders of a specified portion, but not less than the majority, of the shares of that class or series is required for action of the holders of shares of that class or series on that matter.

(c) If a provision of the certificate of formation provides that the affirmative vote of the holders of a specified portion that is greater than the majority of the shares entitled to vote on a matter is required for shareholder action on that matter, the provision may not be amended, directly or indirectly, without the same affirmative vote unless otherwise provided by the certificate of formation.

(d) If a provision of the certificate of formation provides that the affirmative vote of the holders of a specified portion that is greater than the majority of the shares of a class or series is required for shareholder action on a matter, the provision may not be amended, directly or indirectly, without the same affirmative vote unless otherwise provided by the certificate of formation.

Acts 2003, 78th Leg., ch. 182, § 1, eff. Jan. 1, 2006.

§ 200.263. Number of Votes Per Share

(a) Except as provided by the certificate of formation of a real estate investment trust or this title or Title 1, each outstanding share, regardless of class, is entitled to one vote on each matter submitted to a vote at a shareholders' meeting.

(b) If the certificate of formation provides for more or less than one vote per share on a matter for all of the outstanding shares or for the shares of a class or series, each reference in this code or in the certificate of formation or bylaws, unless expressly stated otherwise, to a specified portion of the shares with respect to that matter refers to the portion of the votes entitled to be cast with respect to those shares under the certificate of formation.

Acts 2003, 78th Leg., ch. 182, § 1, eff. Jan. 1, 2006.

§ 200.264. Voting in Person or by Proxy

(a) A shareholder may vote in person or by proxy executed in writing by the shareholder.

(b) A telegram, telex, cablegram, or other form of electronic transmission, including telephonic transmission, by the shareholder, or a photographic, photostatic, facsimile, or similar reproduction of a writing executed by the shareholder, is considered an execution in writing for purposes of this section. Any electronic transmission must contain or be accompanied by information from which it can be determined that the transmission was authorized by the shareholder.

Acts 2003, 78th Leg., ch. 182, § 1, eff. Jan. 1, 2006.

§ 200.265. Term of Proxy

A proxy is not valid after 11 months after the date the proxy is executed unless otherwise provided by the proxy.

Acts 2003, 78th Leg., ch. 182, § 1, eff. Jan. 1, 2006.

§ 200.266. Revocability of Proxy

(a) In this section, a "proxy coupled with an interest" includes the appointment as proxy of:

(1) a pledgee;

(2) a person who purchased or agreed to purchase the shares subject to the proxy;

(3) a person who owns or holds an option to purchase the shares subject to the proxy;

(4) a creditor of the real estate investment trust who extended the real estate investment trust credit under terms requiring the appointment;

(5) an employee of the real estate investment trust whose employment contract requires the appointment; or

(6) a party to a voting agreement created under Section 6.252.

(b) A proxy is revocable unless:

(1) the proxy form conspicuously states that the proxy is irrevocable; and

(2) the proxy is coupled with an interest.

Acts 2003, 78th Leg., ch. 182, § 1, eff. Jan. 1, 2006.

§ 200.267. Enforceability of Proxy

(a) An irrevocable proxy is specifically enforceable against the holder of shares or any successor or transferee of the holder if:

(1) the proxy is noted conspicuously on the certificate representing the shares subject to the proxy; or

(2) in the case of uncertificated shares, notation of the proxy is contained in the notice sent under Section 3.205 with respect to the shares subject to the proxy.

(b) An irrevocable proxy that is otherwise enforceable is ineffective against a transferee for value without actual knowledge of the existence of the irrevocable proxy at the time of the transfer or against a subsequent transferee, regardless of whether the transfer is for value, unless:

(1) the proxy is noted conspicuously on the certificate representing the shares subject to the proxy; or

(2) in the case of uncertificated shares, notation of the proxy is contained in the notice sent under Section 3.205 with respect to the shares subject to the proxy.

(c) An irrevocable proxy shall be specifically enforceable against a person who is not a transferee for value from the time the person acquires actual knowledge of the existence of the irrevocable proxy.

Acts 2003, 78th Leg., ch. 182, § 1, eff. Jan. 1, 2006.

§ 200.268. Procedures in Bylaws Relating to Proxies

A real estate investment trust may establish in the bylaws of the real estate investment trust procedures consistent with this code for determining the validity of proxies and determining whether shares held of record by a bank, broker, or other nominee are represented at a meeting of shareholders. The procedures may incorporate rules of and determinations made by a self-regulatory organization regulating that bank, broker, or other nominee.

Acts 2003, 78th Leg., ch. 182, § 1, eff. Jan. 1, 2006.

SUBCHAPTER G. TRUST MANAGERS

§ 200.301. Management by Trust Managers

The control, operation, disposition, investment, and management of the trust estate and the powers necessary or appropriate to effect any purpose for which a real estate investment trust is organized are vested in one or more trust managers.

Acts 2003, 78th Leg., ch. 182, § 1, eff. Jan. 1, 2006.

§ 200.302. Designation of Trust Managers

(a) The certificate of formation of a real estate investment trust must contain the name of each trust manager.

(b) A successor trust manager must be selected in accordance with the certificate of formation. The selection of a successor trust manager is considered an amendment to the certificate of formation of a real estate investment trust.

Acts 2003, 78th Leg., ch. 182, § 1, eff. Jan. 1, 2006.

§ 200.303. Trust Manager Eligibility Requirements

A trust manager of a real estate investment trust must be an individual. Unless the certificate of formation or bylaws of a real estate investment trust provide otherwise, a person is not required to be a resident of this state or a shareholder of the real estate investment trust to serve as a trust manager. The certificate of formation or bylaws may prescribe other qualifications for trust managers.

Acts 2003, 78th Leg., ch. 182, § 1, eff. Jan. 1, 2006.

§ 200.304. Number of Trust Managers

(a) The certificate of formation or bylaws of the real estate investment trust shall set the number of trust managers or provide for the manner of determining the number of trust managers, except that the certificate of formation shall set the number constituting the initial trust managers.

(b) The number of trust managers may be increased or decreased by amendment to, or as provided by, the certificate of formation or bylaws. A decrease in the number of trust managers may not shorten the term of an incumbent trust manager.

Acts 2003, 78th Leg., ch. 182, § 1, eff. Jan. 1, 2006.

§ 200.305. Compensation

A trust manager or officer of a real estate investment trust is entitled to receive compensation set by or in the manner provided by the certificate of formation or bylaws of the real estate investment trust. If the certificate of formation or bylaws do not provide for compensation to trust managers and officers, the trust managers of the real estate investment trust must determine the compensation by vote at a meeting or by written consent.

Acts 2003, 78th Leg., ch. 182, § 1, eff. Jan. 1, 2006.

§ 200.306. Term of Trust Manager

(a) Except as provided by the certificate of formation or bylaws of a real estate investment trust, a trust manager of the real estate investment trust serves until the trust manager's successor is elected.

(b) A trust manager may succeed himself or herself in office.

(c) If a successor trust manager is not elected, the trust manager in office continues to serve as trust manager until the trust manager's successor is elected.

Acts 2003, 78th Leg., ch. 182, § 1, eff. Jan. 1, 2006.

§ 200.307. Staggered Terms of Trust Managers

(a) A governing document of a real estate investment trust may provide that all or some of the board of trust managers may be divided into two or three classes. Each class must include the same or a similar number of trust managers as each other class.

(b) The terms of office of trust managers constituting the first class expire on the election of successors at the first annual meeting of shareholders after the election of those trust managers. The terms of office of trust managers constituting the second class expire on the election of successors at the second annual meeting of shareholders after election of those trust managers. The terms of office of trust managers constituting the third class, if any, expire on the election of successors at the third annual meeting of shareholders after election of those trust managers.

(c) If a governing document of the real estate investment trust provides for the classification of trust managers, an annual election for trust managers as a whole is not necessary. At each annual meeting held after the classification of trust managers, an election shall be held to elect the number of trust managers equal to the number of trust managers in the class the term of which expires on the date of the meeting, and those trust managers serve until:

(1) the second succeeding annual meeting if there are two classes; or

(2) the third succeeding annual meeting if there are three classes.

(d) Unless provided by the certificate of formation or a bylaw adopted by shareholders, staggered terms for trust managers do not take effect until the next annual meeting of shareholders at which trust managers are elected. Staggered terms for trust managers may not be effected if any shareholder has the right to cumulate votes for the election of trust managers and the number of trust managers is fewer than nine trust managers.

Acts 2003, 78th Leg., ch. 182, § 1, eff. Jan. 1, 2006.

§ 200.308. Vacancy

(a) Except as provided by Subsection (b), a vacancy occurring in the office of a trust manager of a real estate investment trust may be filled by the affirmative vote of the majority of the remaining trust managers, even if the majority of trust managers constitutes less than a quorum of the trust managers.

(b) The certificate of formation or bylaws of the real estate investment trust may provide an alternative procedure for filling a vacancy occurring in the office of a trust manager, including filling vacancies by simple majority or super majority votes of the shareholders.

(c) The term of a trust manager elected to fill a vacancy occurring in the office of a trust manager is the unexpired term of the trust manager's predecessor in office and until the trust manager's successor is elected and has qualified.

Acts 2003, 78th Leg., ch. 182, § 1, eff. Jan. 1, 2006.

§ 200.309. Notice of Meeting

(a) Regular meetings of the trust managers of a real estate investment trust may be held with or without notice as prescribed by the real estate investment trust's bylaws.

(b) Special meetings of the trust managers shall be held with notice as prescribed by the bylaws.

(c) A notice of a board meeting is not required to specify the business to be transacted at the meeting or the purpose of the meeting, unless required by the bylaws.

Acts 2003, 78th Leg., ch. 182, § 1, eff. Jan. 1, 2006.

§ 200.310. Quorum

A quorum of the board of trust managers of a real estate investment trust is the majority of the number of trust managers unless the certificate of formation or bylaws require a greater number.

Acts 2003, 78th Leg., ch. 182, § 1, eff. Jan. 1, 2006.

§ 200.311. Committees of Trust Managers

(a) If authorized by the certificate of formation or bylaws, the trust managers of a real estate investment trust, by resolution adopted by a majority of the trust managers, may designate:

(1) committees composed of one or more trust managers; or

(2) trust managers as alternate committee members to replace absent or disqualified committee members at a committee meeting, subject to any limitations imposed by the trust managers.

(b) To the extent provided by the resolution designating a committee or the certificate of formation or bylaws and subject to Subsection (c), the committee has the authority of the trust managers.

(c) A committee of the trust managers may not:

(1) amend the certificate of formation, except to classify or reclassify shares in accordance with Section 200.103 if authorized by the resolution designating the committee, certificate of formation, or bylaws;

(2) propose a reduction of stated capital of the real estate investment trust;

(3) approve a plan of merger or share exchange of the real estate investment trust;

(4) recommend to shareholders the sale, lease, or exchange of all or substantially all of the property and assets of the real estate investment trust not made in the usual and regular course of its business;

(5) recommend to the shareholders a voluntary winding up and termination or a revocation of the real estate investment trust;

(6) amend, alter, or repeal the bylaws or adopt new bylaws;

(7) fill vacancies in the offices of the trust managers;

(8) fill vacancies in or designate alternate members of a committee of the trust managers;

(9) fill a vacancy to be filled because of an increase in the number of trust managers;

(10) elect or remove officers of the real estate investment trust or members or alternate members of a committee of the trust managers;

(11) set the compensation of the members or alternate members of a committee of the trust managers; or

(12) alter or repeal a resolution of the trust managers that states that it may not be amended or repealed.

(d) A committee of the trust managers may authorize a distribution or the issuance of shares if authorized by the resolution designating the committee or by the certificate of formation or bylaws.

(e) The designation of and delegation of authority to a committee of the trust managers does not relieve a trust manager of responsibility imposed by law.

Acts 2003, 78th Leg., ch. 182, § 1, eff. Jan. 1, 2006.

§ 200.312. Liability of Trust Managers

(a) A trust manager of a real estate investment trust who votes for or assents to a distribution of assets made by the real estate investment trust to its shareholders during the liquidation of the real estate investment trust without the payment and discharge of or the making of adequate provision for the payment of all of the known debts, liabilities, and other obligations of the real estate investment trust is jointly and severally liable to the real estate investment trust for the value of the distributed assets to the extent the debts, liabilities, and other obligations are not paid and discharged.

(b) A trust manager of a real estate investment trust who votes for or assents to the making of a loan to another trust manager or officer of the real estate investment trust or to the making of a loan secured by shares of the real estate investment trust is jointly and severally liable to the real estate investment trust for the loan amount until the loan is repaid.

(c) A trust manager is not jointly and severally liable under Subsection (a) if, in determining the amount available for the distribution, the trust manager, acting in good faith and with ordinary care:

(1) relied on information, opinions, reports, or statements in accordance with Section 3.102; or

(2) considered the assets of the real estate investment trust to be valued at least at book value.

Acts 2003, 78th Leg., ch. 182, § 1, eff. Jan. 1, 2006.

§ 200.313. Statute of Limitations on Certain Action Against Trust Managers

An action may not be brought against a trust manager of a real estate investment trust under Section 200.312 after the second anniversary of the date the alleged act giving rise to the liability occurred.

Acts 2003, 78th Leg., ch. 182, § 1, eff. Jan. 1, 2006.

§ 200.314. Immunity From Liability for Performance of Duty

A trust manager of a real estate investment trust may not be held liable to the real estate investment trust for an act, omission, loss, damage, or expense arising from the performance of the trust manager's duties under the trust, except for liability arising from the wilful misfeasance, wilful malfeasance, or gross negligence of the trust manager.

Acts 2003, 78th Leg., ch. 182, § 1, eff. Jan. 1, 2006.

§ 200.315. Right of Contribution

A trust manager who is liable for a claim asserted under Section 200.312 is entitled to receive contribution from each of the other trust managers who are liable with respect to that claim in an amount appropriate to achieve equity.

Acts 2003, 78th Leg., ch. 182, § 1, eff. Jan. 1, 2006.

§ 200.316. Officers

(a) An officer of a real estate investment trust designated by the trust managers under Section 3.103 may exercise all of the powers of a trust manager relating to the business and affairs of the real estate investment trust, unless action by the trust managers is specified by this code or another applicable law.

(b) A designation of or delegation of authority to an officer of a real estate investment trust described by this section does not relieve a trust manager of responsibility imposed by law.

Acts 2003, 78th Leg., ch. 182, § 1, eff. Jan. 1, 2006.

§ 200.317. Contracts or Transactions Involving Interested Trust Managers and Officers

(a) This section applies to a contract or transaction between a real estate investment trust and:

(1) one or more trust managers or officers, or one or more affiliates or associates of one or more directors or officers, of the trust; or

(2) an entity or other organization in which one or more trust managers or officers, or one or more affiliates or associates of one or more directors or officers, of the trust:

(A) is a managerial official; or

(B) has a financial interest.

(b) An otherwise valid and enforceable contract or transaction described by Subsection (a) is valid and enforceable, and is not void or voidable, notwithstanding any relationship or interest described by Subsection (a), if any one of the following conditions is satisfied :

(1) the material facts as to the relationship or interest described by Subsection (a) and as to the contract or transaction are disclosed to or known by:

(A) the trust managers or a committee of the trust managers, and the trust managers or committee of the trust managers in good faith authorize the contract or transaction by the approval of the majority of disinterested trust managers or committee members, regardless of whether the disinterested trust managers or committee members constitute a quorum; or

(B) the shareholders entitled to vote on the authorization of the contract or transaction, and the contract or transaction is specifically approved in good faith by a vote of the shareholders; or

(2) the contract or transaction is fair to the real estate investment trust when the contract or transaction is authorized, approved, or ratified by the trust managers, a committee of the trust managers, or the shareholders.

(c) Common or interested trust managers may be included in determining the presence of a quorum at a meeting of the trust managers, or a committee of the trust managers, that authorizes the contract or transaction.

(d) A person who has the relationship or interest described by Subsection (a) may:

(1) be present at or participate in and, if the person is a trust manager or committee member, may vote at a meeting of the trust managers, or of a committee of the trust managers, that authorizes the contract or transaction; or

(2) sign, in the person's capacity as a trust manager or committee member, a unanimous written consent of the trust managers or committee members to authorize the contract or transaction.

(e) If at least one of the conditions of Subsection (b) is satisfied, neither the trust nor any of the trust's shareholders will have a cause of action against any of the persons described by Subsection (a) for breach of duty with respect to the making, authorization, or performance of the contract or transaction because the person had the relationship or interest described by Subsection (a) or took any of the actions authorized by Subsection (d).

Acts 2003, 78th Leg., ch. 182, § 1, eff. Jan. 1, 2006. Amended by Acts 2009, 81st Leg., ch. 84, § 58, eff. Sept. 1, 2009; Acts 2011, 82nd Leg., ch. 139 (S.B. 748), § 57, eff. Sept. 1, 2011.

SUBCHAPTER H. INVESTMENTS

§ 200.351. Investments

A trust manager or officer of a real estate investment trust has complete discretion with respect to the investment of the trust estate unless the investment is contrary to or inconsistent with:

(1) this chapter;

(2) a provision of the Internal Revenue Code relating to or governing real estate investment trusts; or

(3) regulations adopted under a provision of the Internal Revenue Code relating to or governing real estate investment trusts.

Acts 2003, 78th Leg., ch. 182, § 1, eff. Jan. 1, 2006.

SUBCHAPTER I. FUNDAMENTAL BUSINESS TRANSACTIONS

§ 200.401. Definitions

In this subchapter:

(1) "Participating shares" means shares that entitle the holders of the shares to participate without limitation in distributions.

(2) "Sale of all or substantially all of the assets" means the sale, lease, exchange, or other disposition, other than a pledge, mortgage, deed of trust, or trust indenture unless otherwise provided by the certificate of formation, of all or substantially all of the property and assets of a domestic real estate investment trust that is not made in the usual and regular course of the trust's business without regard to whether the disposition is made with the goodwill of the business. The term does not include a transaction that results in the real estate investment trust directly or indirectly:

(A) continuing to engage in one or more businesses; or

(B) applying a portion of the consideration received in connection with the transaction to the conduct of a business that the real estate investment trust engages in after the transaction.

(3) "Shares" includes a receipt or other instrument issued by a depository representing an interest in one or more shares or fractions of shares of a domestic or foreign real estate investment trust that are deposited with the depository.

(4) "Voting shares" means shares that entitle the holders of the shares to vote unconditionally in elections of trust managers.

Acts 2003, 78th Leg., ch. 182, § 1, eff. Jan. 1, 2006.

§ 200.402. Approval of Merger

(a) A real estate investment trust that is a party to the merger under Chapter 10 must approve the merger by complying with this section.

(b) The trust managers of the real estate investment trust shall adopt a resolution that:

(1) approves the plan of merger; and

(2) if shareholder approval of the merger is required by this subchapter:

(A) recommends that the plan of merger be approved by the shareholders of the real estate investment trust; or

(B) directs that the plan of merger be submitted to the shareholders for approval without recommendation if the trust managers determine for any reason not to recommend approval of the plan of merger.

(c) Except as provided by this subchapter or Chapter 10, the plan of merger shall be submitted to the shareholders of the real estate investment trust for approval as provided by this subchapter. The trust managers may place conditions on the submission of the plan of merger to the shareholders.

(d) If the trust managers approve a plan of merger required to be approved by the shareholders of the real estate investment trust but do not adopt a resolution recommending that the plan of merger be approved by the shareholders, the trust managers shall communicate to the shareholders the reason for the trust managers' determination to submit the plan of merger without a recommendation.

(e) Except as provided by Chapter 10 or Sections 200.407–200.409, the shareholders of the real estate investment trust shall approve the plan of merger as provided by this subchapter.

Acts 2003, 78th Leg., ch. 182, § 1, eff. Jan. 1, 2006.

§ 200.403. Approval of Conversion

(a) A real estate investment trust must approve a conversion under Chapter 10 by complying with this section.

(b) The trust managers of the real estate investment trust shall adopt a resolution that approves the plan of conversion and:

(1) recommends that the plan of conversion be approved by the shareholders of the real estate investment trust; or

(2) directs that the plan of conversion be submitted to the shareholders for approval without recommendation if the trust managers determine for any reason not to recommend approval of the plan of conversion.

(c) The plan of conversion shall be submitted to the shareholders of the real estate investment trust for approval as provided by this subchapter. The trust managers may place conditions on the submission of the plan of conversion to the shareholders.

(d) If the trust managers approve a plan of conversion but do not adopt a resolution recommending that the plan of conversion be approved by the shareholders of the real estate investment trust, the trust managers shall communicate to the shareholders the reason for the trust managers' determination to submit the plan of conversion without a recommendation.

(e) Except as provided by Sections 200.407–200.409, the shareholders of the real estate investment trust must approve the plan of conversion as provided by this subchapter.

Acts 2003, 78th Leg., ch. 182, § 1, eff. Jan. 1, 2006.

§ 200.404. Approval of Exchange

(a) A real estate investment trust the shares of which are to be acquired in an exchange under Chapter 10 must approve the exchange by complying with this section.

(b) The trust managers shall adopt a resolution that approves the plan of exchange and:

(1) recommends that the plan of exchange be approved by the shareholders of the real estate investment trust; or

(2) directs that the plan of exchange be submitted to the shareholders for approval without recommendation if the trust managers determine for any reason not to recommend approval of the plan of exchange.

(c) The plan of exchange shall be submitted to the shareholders of the real estate investment trust for approval as provided by this subchapter. The trust managers may place conditions on the submission of the plan of exchange to the shareholders.

(d) If the trust managers approve a plan of exchange but do not adopt a resolution recommending that the plan of exchange be approved by the shareholders of the real estate investment trust, the trust managers shall communicate to the shareholders the reason for the trust managers' determination to submit the plan of exchange to shareholders without a recommendation.

(e) Except as provided by Sections 200.407–200.409, the shareholders of the real estate investment trust shall approve the plan of exchange as provided by this subchapter.

Acts 2003, 78th Leg., ch. 182, § 1, eff. Jan. 1, 2006.

§ 200.405. Approval of Sale of All or Substantially All of Assets

(a) Except as provided by the certificate of formation of a domestic real estate investment trust, a sale, lease, pledge, mortgage, assignment, transfer, or other conveyance of an interest in real property or other assets of the real estate investment trust does not require the approval or consent of the shareholders of the real estate investment trust unless the transaction constitutes a sale of all or substantially all of the assets of the real estate investment trust.

(b) A real estate investment trust must approve the sale of all or substantially all of its assets by complying with this section.

(c) The trust managers of the real estate investment trust shall adopt a resolution that approves the sale of all or substantially all of the assets of the real estate investment trust and:

(1) recommends that the sale of all or substantially all of the assets of the real estate investment trust be approved by the shareholders of the real estate investment trust; or

(2) directs that the sale of all or substantially all of the assets of the real estate investment trust be submitted to the shareholders for approval without recommendation if the trust managers determine for any reason not to recommend approval of the sale.

(d) The sale of all or substantially all of the assets of the real estate investment trust shall be submitted to the shareholders of the real estate investment trust for approval as provided by this subchapter. The trust managers may place conditions on the submission of the proposed sale to the shareholders.

(e) If the trust managers approve the sale of all or substantially all of the assets of the real estate investment trust but do not adopt a resolution recommending that the proposed sale be approved by the shareholders of the real estate investment trust, the trust managers shall communicate to the shareholders the reason for the trust managers' determination to submit the proposed sale to shareholders without a recommendation.

(f) The shareholders of the real estate investment trust shall approve the sale of all or substantially all of the assets of the real estate investment trust as provided by this subchapter.

(g) After the approval of the sale by the shareholders, the trust managers may abandon the sale of all or substantially all of the assets of the real estate investment trust, subject to the rights of a third party under a contract relating to the assets, without further action or approval by the shareholders.

Acts 2003, 78th Leg., ch. 182, § 1, eff. Jan. 1, 2006.

§ 200.406. General Procedure for Submission to Shareholders of Fundamental Business Transaction

(a) If a fundamental business transaction involving a real estate investment trust is required to be submitted to the shareholders of the real estate investment trust under this subchapter, the real estate investment trust shall notify each shareholder of the real estate investment trust that the fundamental business transaction is being submitted to the shareholders for approval at a meeting of shareholders as required by this subchapter, regardless of whether the shareholder is entitled to vote on the matter.

(b) If the fundamental business transaction is a merger, conversion, or interest exchange, the notice required by Subsection (a) shall contain or be accompanied by a copy or summary of the plan of merger, conversion, or interest exchange, as appropriate, and the notice required by Section 10.355.

(c) The notice of the meeting must:

(1) be given not later than the 21st day before the date of the meeting; and

(2) state that the purpose, or one of the purposes, of the meeting is to consider the fundamental business transaction.

Acts 2003, 78th Leg., ch. 182, § 1, eff. Jan. 1, 2006.

§ 200.407. General Vote Requirement for Approval of Fundamental Business Transaction

(a) Except as provided by this code or the certificate of formation or bylaws of a real estate investment trust in accordance with Section 200.261, the affirmative vote of the holders of at least two-thirds of the outstanding shares of the real estate investment trust entitled to vote on a fundamental business transaction is required to approve the transaction.

(b) Unless provided by the certificate of formation or Section 200.408, shares of a class or series that are not otherwise entitled to vote on matters submitted to shareholders generally will not be entitled to vote for the approval of a fundamental business transaction.

(c) Except as provided by this code, if a class or series of shares of a real estate investment trust is entitled to vote on a fundamental business transaction as a class or series, in addition to the vote required under Subsection (a), the affirmative vote of the holders of at least two-thirds of the outstanding shares in each class or series of shares entitled to vote on the fundamental business transaction as a class or series is required to approve the transaction.

(d) Unless required by the certificate of formation, approval of a merger by shareholders is not required under this code for a real estate investment trust that is a party to the plan of merger unless that real estate investment trust is also a party to the merger.

Acts 2003, 78th Leg., ch. 182, § 1, eff. Jan. 1, 2006.

§ 200.408. Class Voting Requirements for Certain Fundamental Business Transactions

(a) Separate voting by a class or series of shares of a real estate investment trust is required for approval of a plan of merger or conversion if:

(1) the plan of merger or conversion contains a provision that would require approval by that class or series of shares under Section 200.262 if the provision was contained in a proposed amendment to the real estate investment trust's certificate of formation; or

(2) that class or series of shares is entitled under the certificate of formation to vote as a class or series on the plan of merger or conversion.

(b) Separate voting by a class or series of shares of a real estate investment trust is required for approval of a plan of exchange if:

(1) shares of that class or series are to be exchanged under the terms of the plan of exchange; or

(2) that class or series is entitled under the certificate of formation to vote as a class or series on the plan of exchange.

(c) Separate voting by a class or series of shares of a real estate investment trust is required for approval of a sale of all or substantially all of the assets of the real estate investment trust if that class or series of shares is entitled under the certificate of formation to vote as a class or series on the sale of the real estate investment trust's assets.

Acts 2003, 78th Leg., ch. 182, § 1, eff. Jan. 1, 2006.

§ 200.409. No Shareholder Vote Requirement for Certain Fundamental Business Transactions

(a) Unless required by the real estate investment trust's certificate of formation, a plan of merger is not required to be approved by the shareholders of a real estate investment trust if:

(1) the real estate investment trust is the sole surviving real estate investment trust in the merger;

(2) the certificate of formation of the real estate investment trust following the merger will not differ from the real estate investment trust's certificate of formation before the merger;

(3) immediately after the effective date of the merger, each shareholder of the real estate investment trust whose shares were outstanding immediately before the effective date of the merger will hold the same number of shares, with identical designations, preferences, limitations, and relative rights;

(4) the sum of the voting power of the number of voting shares outstanding immediately after the merger and the voting power of securities that may be acquired on the conversion or exercise of securities issued under the merger does not exceed by more than 20 percent the voting power of the total number of voting shares of the real estate investment trust that are outstanding immediately before the merger; and

(5) the sum of the number of participating shares that are outstanding immediately after the merger and the number of participating shares that may be acquired on the conversion or exercise of securities issued under the merger does not exceed by more than 20 percent the total number of participating shares of the real estate investment trust that are outstanding immediately before the merger.

(b) Unless required by the certificate of formation, a plan of merger effected under Section 10.005 or 10.006 does not require the approval of the shareholders of the real estate investment trust.

Acts 2003, 78th Leg., ch. 182, § 1, eff. Jan. 1, 2006.

§ 200.410. Rights of Dissent and Appraisal

A shareholder of a domestic real estate investment trust has the rights of dissent and appraisal under Subchapter H, Chapter 10, with respect to a fundamental business transaction.

Acts 2003, 78th Leg., ch. 182, § 1, eff. Jan. 1, 2006.

SUBCHAPTER J. SUPPLEMENTAL WINDING UP AND TERMINATION PROVISIONS

§ 200.451. Approval of Voluntary Winding Up

A real estate investment trust must approve a voluntary winding up under Chapter 11 by the affirmative vote of the shareholders in accordance with Section 200.261.

Acts 2003, 78th Leg., ch. 182, § 1, eff. Jan. 1, 2006.

§ 200.452. Approval of Reinstatement, Cancellation, or Revocation of Voluntary Winding Up

A real estate investment trust may reinstate its existence under Section 11.202, revoke a voluntary decision to wind up under Section 11.151, or cancel an event requiring winding up under Section 11.152 by the affirmative vote of the shareholders in accordance with Section 200.261.

Acts 2003, 78th Leg., ch. 182, § 1, eff. Jan. 1, 2006.

§ 200.453. Responsibility for Winding Up

If a real estate investment trust determines or is required to wind up, the trust managers shall manage the winding up of the business or affairs of the real estate investment trust.

Acts 2003, 78th Leg., ch. 182, § 1, eff. Jan. 1, 2006.

SUBCHAPTER K. MISCELLANEOUS PROVISIONS

§ 200.501. Examination of Records

(a) On written demand stating a proper purpose, a shareholder of record of a real estate investment trust for at least six months immediately preceding the shareholder's demand, or a holder of record of at least five percent of all of the outstanding shares of a real estate investment trust, is entitled to examine and copy, at a reasonable time, the real estate investment trust's relevant books and records of account, minutes, and share transfer records. The examination may be conducted in person or through an agent or attorney.

(b) This section does not impair the power of a court, on the presentation of proof of proper purpose by a shareholder, to compel the production for examination by the shareholder of the books and records of account, minutes, and share transfer records of a real estate investment trust, regardless of the period during which the shareholder was a record holder and regardless of the number of shares held by the person.

Acts 2003, 78th Leg., ch. 182, § 1, eff. Jan. 1, 2006.

§ 200.502. Joinder of Shareholders Not Required

The joinder of shareholders of a real estate investment trust is not required for any sale, lease, mortgage, or other disposition of all or part of the assets of the real estate investment trust.

Acts 2003, 78th Leg., ch. 182, § 1, eff. Jan. 1, 2006.

§ 200.503. Tax Law Requirements

In connection with a real estate investment trust qualifying or attempting to qualify as a real estate investment trust under the Internal Revenue Code and the regulations adopted under the Internal Revenue Code, a provision of this chapter is subject to the provisions of the Internal Revenue Code or the regulations relating to or governing real estate investment trusts adopted under those provisions if:

(1) the provision of this chapter is contrary to or inconsistent with the federal provisions or regulations;

(2) the federal provisions or regulations require a real estate investment trust to take any action required to secure or maintain its status as a real estate investment trust under the federal provisions or regulations; or

(3) the federal provisions or regulations prohibit the real estate investment trust from taking any action required to secure or maintain its status as a real estate investment trust under the federal provision or regulation.

Acts 2003, 78th Leg., ch. 182, § 1, eff. Jan. 1, 2006.

TITLE 6. ASSOCIATIONS

CHAPTER 251. COOPERATIVE ASSOCIATIONS

SUBCHAPTER A. GENERAL PROVISIONS

Section
251.001. Definitions.
251.002. Applicability of Nonprofit Corporation Provisions.
251.003. Exemption.

SUBCHAPTER B. FORMATION AND GOVERNING DOCUMENTS

251.051. Organization Meeting.
251.052. Amendment of Certificate of Formation.
251.053. Bylaws.
251.054. Restated Certificate of Formation.

SUBCHAPTER C. MANAGEMENT

251.101. Board of Directors.
251.102. Officers.
251.103. Removal of Directors and Officers.
251.104. Referendum.

SUBCHAPTER D. MEMBERSHIP

251.151. Eligibility and Admission.
251.152. Expulsion.
251.153. Subscribers.
251.154. Liability.

SUBCHAPTER E. SHARES

251.201. Share and Membership Certificates: Issuance and Contents.
251.202. Transfer of Shares and Membership; Withdrawal.
251.203. Share and Membership Certificates; Recall.
251.204. Certificates; Attachment.

SUBCHAPTER F. MEETINGS AND VOTING

251.251. Meetings.

Section
251.252. Notice of Special Meeting.
251.253. Meetings by Units of Membership.
251.254. One Member—One Vote.
251.255. No Proxy.
251.256. Voting by Mail.
251.257. Voting by Mail or by Delegates.

SUBCHAPTER G. CAPITAL AND NET SAVINGS
251.301. Limitations on Return on Capital.
251.302. Allocation and Distribution of Net Savings.

SUBCHAPTER H. REPORTS AND RECORDS
251.351. Recordkeeping.
251.352. Reports to Members.
251.353. Annual Report of Financial Condition.
251.354. Failure to File Report.

SUBCHAPTER I. WINDING UP AND TERMINATION
251.401. Voluntary Winding Up and Termination.
251.402. Execution of Certificate of Termination.
251.403. Distribution of Assets.
251.404. Involuntary Termination.

SUBCHAPTER J. MISCELLANEOUS PROVISIONS
251.451. Exemption From Taxes.
251.452. Use of Name "Cooperative".

SUBCHAPTER A. GENERAL PROVISIONS

§ 251.001. Definitions

In this chapter:

(1) "Cooperative basis" means that net savings, after payment of any investment dividends or after provision for separate funds has been made as required or authorized by law, the certificate of formation, or bylaws, are:

(A) allocated or distributed to a member patron or to each patron in proportion to patronage; or

(B) retained by the entity for:

(i) actual or potential expansion of the entity's services;

(ii) the reduction of charges to patrons; or

(iii) any other purpose consistent with the entity's nonprofit character.

(2) "Invested capital" means funds invested in a cooperative association by an investor with the expectation of receiving an investment dividend.

(3) "Investment dividend" means the return on invested capital or on membership capital derived from the net savings of the cooperative association.

(4) "Membership capital" means the funds of a cooperative association derived from members of the cooperative association generally as a requirement of membership or in lieu of patronage dividends. The term does not include deposits or loans from members.

(5) "Net savings" means the total income of a cooperative association less the costs of operation.

(6) "Patronage dividend" means a share of the net savings distributed among members of the cooperative association on the basis of patronage, as provided by the certificate of formation.

(7) "Savings returns" means the amount returned by a cooperative association to patrons of a cooperative association in proportion to patronage or otherwise.

Acts 2003, 78th Leg., ch. 182, § 1, eff. Jan. 1, 2006.

§ 251.002. Applicability of Nonprofit Corporation Provisions

(a) A provision of Title 1 and Chapters 20 and 22 governing nonprofit corporations applies to a cooperative association.

(b) Notwithstanding Subsection (a), this chapter controls over any conflicting provision of Title 1 and Chapters 20 and 22 governing nonprofit corporations.

Acts 2003, 78th Leg., ch. 182, § 1, eff. Jan. 1, 2006.

§ 251.003. Exemption

This chapter does not apply to a corporation or association organized on a cooperative basis under a statute of this state other than this chapter unless that other statute specifically states that this chapter does apply.

Acts 2003, 78th Leg., ch. 182, § 1, eff. Jan. 1, 2006.

SUBCHAPTER B. FORMATION AND GOVERNING DOCUMENTS

§ 251.051. Organization Meeting

After a cooperative association's certificate of formation is filed, the cooperative association shall hold an organization meeting in accordance with Section 22.104.

Acts 2003, 78th Leg., ch. 182, § 1, eff. Jan. 1, 2006.

§ 251.052. Amendment of Certificate of Formation

(a) The board of directors of a cooperative association may propose an amendment to the cooperative association's certificate of formation by a two-thirds vote of the board members. The members of a cooperative association may petition to amend the certificate of formation as provided by the bylaws.

(b) Not later than the 31st day before the date of the meeting, the secretary shall:

(1) send notice of a meeting to consider a proposed amendment to each member of the cooperative association at the member's last known address; or

(2) post notice of a meeting to consider a proposed amendment in a conspicuous place in all principal places of activity of the cooperative association.

(c) The notice required by Subsection (b) must include the full text of the proposed amendment and the text of the part of the certificate of formation to be amended.

(d) To be approved, an amendment must be adopted by the affirmative vote of two-thirds of the members voting on the amendment.

(e) Not later than the 30th day after the date an amendment is adopted by the members of a cooperative association, the cooperative association shall file a certificate of amendment with the secretary of state in accordance with Chapter 4. The certificate of amendment must be:

(1) signed by an authorized officer of the cooperative association; and

(2) in the form required by Section 3.052.

Acts 2003, 78th Leg., ch. 182, § 1, eff. Jan. 1, 2006.

§ 251.053. Bylaws

(a) Unless the certificate of formation or bylaws of a cooperative association require a greater majority, the bylaws may be adopted, amended, or repealed by a majority vote of the cooperative association's members voting on the matter.

(b) Except as provided by this code, the bylaws may contain:

(1) requirements for admission to membership;

(2) requirements for disposal of a member's interest on cessation of membership;

(3) the time, place, and manner of calling and conducting meetings;

(4) the number or percentage of the members constituting a quorum;

(5) the number, qualifications, powers, duties, and term of directors and officers;

(6) the method of electing, removing, and filling a vacancy of directors and officers;

(7) the division or classification, if any, of directors to provide for staggered terms;

(8) the compensation, if any, of the directors;

(9) the number of directors necessary to constitute a quorum;

(10) the method for distributing the net savings;

(11) a requirement that each officer or employee of the cooperative association who handles funds or securities be bonded;

(12) other discretionary provisions of this chapter, Title 1, and Chapters 20 and 22; and

(13) any other provision incident to a purpose or activity of the cooperative association.

Acts 2003, 78th Leg., ch. 182, § 1, eff. Jan. 1, 2006.

§ 251.054. Restated Certificate of Formation

(a) The board of directors of a cooperative association may adopt a restated certificate of formation as provided by Subchapter B, Chapter 3, by following the procedure to amend the association's certificate of formation provided by Section 251.052, except that member approval is required if the restated certificate of formation contains an amendment.

(b) A person shall file a restated certificate of formation as provided by Chapter 4, and the restated certificate of formation takes effect as provided by Subchapter B, Chapter 3.

Added by Acts 2005, 79th Leg., ch. 64, § 96, eff. Jan. 1, 2006.

SUBCHAPTER C. MANAGEMENT

§ 251.101. Board of Directors

(a) Except as provided by Subsections (b) and (c), a cooperative association is managed by a board of directors in accordance with Chapter 22.

(b) The board shall contain at least five directors elected by and from the cooperative association's members. A director:

(1) serves a term not to exceed three years as provided by the bylaws; and

(2) holds office until the director is removed or the director's successor is elected.

(c) The bylaws of a cooperative association may:

(1) apportion the number of directors among the units into which the cooperative association may be divided; and

(2) provide for the election of the directors by the respective units to which the directors are apportioned.

(d) An executive committee of the board of directors may be elected in the manner and with the powers and duties specified by the certificate of formation or bylaws.

Acts 2003, 78th Leg., ch. 182, § 1, eff. Jan. 1, 2006.

§ 251.102. Officers

(a) The directors of a cooperative association shall annually elect, unless otherwise provided by the bylaws, the following officers for the cooperative association:

(1) a president;

(2) one or more vice presidents; and

(3) a secretary and treasurer or a secretary-treasurer.

(b) Any two or more offices, other than the offices of president and secretary, may be held by the same person.

(c) The officers of a cooperative association may be designated by other titles as provided by the certificate of formation or the bylaws of the cooperative association.

(d) A committee duly designated by the board of directors may perform the functions of any office, and the functions of any two or more officers may be performed by a single committee, including the functions of both president and secretary.

Acts 2003, 78th Leg., ch. 182, § 1, eff. Jan. 1, 2006.

§ 251.103. Removal of Directors and Officers

(a) A director or officer of a cooperative association may be removed from office in the manner provided by the certificate of formation or bylaws of the cooperative association.

(b) If the certificate of formation or bylaws do not provide for the person's removal, a director or officer may be removed with cause by a vote of a majority of the members voting at a regular or special meeting. The director or officer who is to be removed is entitled to be heard at the meeting.

(c) Except as provided by the certificate of formation or bylaws, a vacancy on the board of directors caused by removal shall be filled by a director elected in the same manner provided by the bylaws for the election of directors.

Acts 2003, 78th Leg., ch. 182, § 1, eff. Jan. 1, 2006.

§ 251.104. Referendum

(a) The certificate of formation or bylaws of a cooperative association may provide for a referendum on any action undertaken by the cooperative association's board of directors if the referendum is:

(1) requested by petition of 10 percent or more of all of the members of the cooperative association; or

(2) requested and approved by the vote of at least a majority of the directors of the cooperative association.

(b) The proposition to be voted on in a referendum authorized under Subsection (a) must be submitted to the members of the cooperative association for consideration within the time specified in the document authorizing the referendum.

(c) A right of a third party that has vested between the time of the action and the time of the referendum is not impaired by the referendum results.

Acts 2003, 78th Leg., ch. 182, § 1, eff. Jan. 1, 2006.

SUBCHAPTER D. MEMBERSHIP

§ 251.151. Eligibility and Admission

A person, an unincorporated group or other person organized on a cooperative basis, or a nonprofit group may be admitted to membership in a cooperative association only if the person meets the qualifications for eligibility stated in the certificate of formation or bylaws of the cooperative association.

Acts 2003, 78th Leg., ch. 182, § 1, eff. Jan. 1, 2006.

§ 251.152. Expulsion

(a) A member of a cooperative association may be expelled by the vote of a majority of the cooperative association's members voting at a regular or special meeting.

(b) Not later than the 11th day before the date of the meeting, the cooperative association shall give the member written notice of the charges. The member is entitled to be heard at the meeting in person or by counsel.

(c) If the cooperative association votes to expel a member, the cooperative association's board of directors shall cause the cooperative association to purchase the member's capital holdings at par value if the purchase does not jeopardize the cooperative association's solvency.

Acts 2003, 78th Leg., ch. 182, § 1, eff. Jan. 1, 2006.

§ 251.153. Subscribers

(a) A person is a subscriber of a cooperative association only if the person is:

(1) eligible for membership in the cooperative association under Section 251.151; and

(2) legally obligated to purchase a share or membership in the cooperative association.

(b) The certificate of formation or bylaws of a cooperative association may state whether and the conditions under which voting rights or other membership rights are granted to a subscriber of the cooperative association.

Acts 2003, 78th Leg., ch. 182, § 1, eff. Jan. 1, 2006.

§ 251.154. Liability

(a) Except as provided by Subsection (b), a member or subscriber of a cooperative association is not jointly or severally liable for a debt of the cooperative association. A subscriber is liable for any unpaid amount on the subscriber's membership certificates or invested capital certificates.

(b) A subscriber who assigns the subscriber's interest in membership certificates or invested capital certificates is jointly and severally liable with the assignee until the appropriate certificates are fully paid.

Acts 2003, 78th Leg., ch. 182, § 1, eff. Jan. 1, 2006.

SUBCHAPTER E. SHARES

§ 251.201. Share and Membership Certificates: Issuance and Contents

(a) A cooperative association may not issue a certificate for membership capital or for invested capital until any par value of the certificate has been paid in full.

(b) Each certificate for membership capital issued by a cooperative association must contain a statement of the requirements of Sections 251.202(a) and (b), 251.254, and 251.255.

(c) Each certificate for invested capital issued by a cooperative association must contain a statement of the restrictions on transferability as provided by the cooperative association's bylaws.

Acts 2003, 78th Leg., ch. 182, § 1, eff. Jan. 1, 2006.

§ 251.202. Transfer of Shares and Membership; Withdrawal

(a) A member who decides to withdraw from a cooperative association shall make a written offer to sell the member's membership certificates to the cooperative association's board of directors.

(b) Not later than the 90th day after the date the directors receive an offer under Subsection (a), the directors may cause the cooperative association to purchase the holdings by paying the member the par value of the certificates and the directors shall cause the cooperative association to reissue or cancel the shares after purchasing the holdings. The directors shall cause the cooperative association to purchase the shares if a majority of the cooperative association's members voting at a regular or special meeting vote to require the purchase.

(c) An investor owning investor certificates must sell, assign, or convey the certificates in accordance with the cooperative association's bylaws. If an investor fails to sell, assign, or convey investor certificates in accordance with the bylaws, the cooperative association on written notice to its directors shall repurchase the certificates by paying the investor the par value of the certificate plus all accrued investment dividends. The certificates must be repurchased not later than the 90th day after the date the cooperative association receives notice of the failure.

Acts 2003, 78th Leg., ch. 182, § 1, eff. Jan. 1, 2006.

§ 251.203. Share and Membership Certificates; Recall

(a) The bylaws of a cooperative association may authorize the cooperative association's board of directors to recall during a specified time and in accordance with the bylaws the membership certificates of a member who fails to patronize the cooperative association. The board may use the reserve funds to recall, at par value, the membership certificates of any member in excess of the amount required for membership.

(b) After the board of directors of a cooperative association recalls a membership certificate under Subsection (a), membership in the cooperative association is terminated and the board shall cause the cooperative association to reissue or cancel the certificate. The board of directors may not recall membership certificates if recalling the certificates would jeopardize the cooperative association's solvency.

(c) The board of directors may use the reserve funds to recall and repurchase the investment certificates of an investor at par value plus any investment dividends due.

(d) The bylaws of a cooperative association may establish specific procedures, terms, and conditions for recalls and repurchases of investment certificates.

Acts 2003, 78th Leg., ch. 182, § 1, eff. Jan. 1, 2006.

§ 251.204. Certificates; Attachment

The minimum amount necessary for membership in a cooperative association, not to exceed $50, is exempt from attachment, execution, or garnishment for the debts of a member of a cooperative association. If a member's holdings are subject to attachment, execution, or garnishment, the directors of the cooperative association may admit the purchaser to membership or may purchase the holdings at par value.

Acts 2003, 78th Leg., ch. 182, § 1, eff. Jan. 1, 2006.

SUBCHAPTER F. MEETINGS AND VOTING

§ 251.251. Meetings

(a) Regular meetings of members of a cooperative association shall be held at least once a year as prescribed by the cooperative association's bylaws.

(b) A special meeting of the members of a cooperative association may be requested by a majority vote of the directors or by written petition of at least one-tenth of the membership of the cooperative association. The secretary shall call a special meeting to be held 30 days after receipt of the request for a special meeting.

Acts 2003, 78th Leg., ch. 182, § 1, eff. Jan. 1, 2006.

§ 251.252. Notice of Special Meeting

The notice of a special meeting of the members of a cooperative association shall state the purpose of the meeting.

Acts 2003, 78th Leg., ch. 182, § 1, eff. Jan. 1, 2006.

§ 251.253. Meetings by Units of Membership

(a) The certificate of formation or bylaws of a cooperative association may provide for the holding of meetings by units of the membership of the cooperative association and may provide for:

(1) a method of transmitting the votes cast at unit meetings to the central meeting;

(2) a method of representation of units of the membership by the election of delegates to the central meeting; or

(3) a combination of both methods.

(b) Except as otherwise provided by the certificate of formation or bylaws, a meeting by a unit of the membership shall be called and held in the same manner as a regular meeting of the members.

Acts 2003, 78th Leg., ch. 182, § 1, eff. Jan. 1, 2006.

§ 251.254. One Member—One Vote

(a) Except as provided by Subsection (b), a member of a cooperative association has one vote.

(b) If a cooperative association includes among its membership another cooperative association or a group that is organized on a cooperative basis, the voting rights of the cooperative association member or group member may be prescribed by the certificate of formation or bylaws of the cooperative association.

(c) Any voting agreement or other device that is made to evade the one-member-one-vote rule is not enforceable.

Acts 2003, 78th Leg., ch. 182, § 1, eff. Jan. 1, 2006.

§ 251.255. No Proxy

A member is not entitled to vote by proxy.

Acts 2003, 78th Leg., ch. 182, § 1, eff. Jan. 1, 2006.

§ 251.256. Voting by Mail

(a) The certificate of formation or bylaws of a cooperative association may contain the procedures in Subsection (b) or (c), or both, for voting by mail.

(b) With notice of a meeting sent to members of the cooperative association, the secretary may include a copy of a proposal to be offered at the meeting. If a mail vote is returned to the cooperative association within the specified number of days, the mail vote shall be counted with the votes cast at the meeting.

(c) The secretary may send to a member of the cooperative association who is absent from a meeting an exact copy of the proposal considered at the meeting. If the vote is returned to the cooperative association within the specified number of days, the mail vote is counted with the votes cast at the meeting.

(d) The certificate of formation or bylaws may state whether and to what extent mail votes are counted in computing a quorum.

Acts 2003, 78th Leg., ch. 182, § 1, eff. Jan. 1, 2006.

§ 251.257. Voting by Mail or by Delegates

(a) If a cooperative association has provided for voting by mail or by delegates, a provision of this chapter referring to votes cast by members of the cooperative association applies to votes cast by mail or by delegates.

(b) A delegate may not vote by mail.

Acts 2003, 78th Leg., ch. 182, § 1, eff. Jan. 1, 2006.

SUBCHAPTER G. CAPITAL AND NET SAVINGS

§ 251.301. Limitations on Return on Capital

(a) Except as otherwise provided by the cooperative association's bylaws, an investment dividend of a cooperative association may not be cumulative and may not exceed eight percent of investment capital.

(b) Total investment dividends distributed for a fiscal year may not exceed 50 percent of the net savings for the period.

Acts 2003, 78th Leg., ch. 182, § 1, eff. Jan. 1, 2006.

§ 251.302. Allocation and Distribution of Net Savings

(a) At least once each year the members or directors of a cooperative association, as provided by the certificate of formation or bylaws of the cooperative association, shall apportion the net savings of the cooperative association in the following order:

(1) subject to Section 251.301, investment dividends payable from the surplus of the total assets over total liabilities may be paid on invested capital or, if authorized by the bylaws, may be paid on the membership certificates;

(2) a portion of the remainder, as determined by the certificate of formation or bylaws, may be allocated to an educational fund to be used in teaching cooperation;

(3) a portion of the remainder may be allocated to funds for the general welfare of the members of the cooperative association;

(4) a portion of the remainder may be allocated to retained earnings; and

(5) the remainder shall be allocated at the same uniform rate to each patron of the cooperative association in proportion to individual patronage as follows:

(A) for a member patron, the proportionate amount of savings return distributed to the member may be any combination of cash, property, membership certificates, or investment certificates; and

(B) for a subscriber patron, the patron's proportionate amount of savings returns as provided by the certificate of formation or bylaws may be distributed to the subscriber patron or credited to the subscriber patron's account until the amount of capital subscribed for has been fully paid.

(b) This section does not prevent a cooperative association engaged in rendering services from disposing of the net savings from the rendering of services in a manner that lowers the fees charged for services or furthers the common benefit of the members.

(c) A cooperative association may adopt a system in which:

(1) the payment of savings returns that would otherwise be distributed are deferred for a fixed period; or

(2) the savings returns distributed are partly in cash or partly in shares, to be retired at a fixed future date, in the order of the shares' serial numbers or issuance dates.

Acts 2003, 78th Leg., ch. 182, § 1, eff. Jan. 1, 2006.

SUBCHAPTER H. REPORTS AND RECORDS

§ 251.351. Recordkeeping

A cooperative association shall keep books and records relating to the cooperative association's business operation in accordance with standard accounting practices.

Acts 2003, 78th Leg., ch. 182, § 1, eff. Jan. 1, 2006.

§ 251.352. Reports to Members

(a) A cooperative association shall submit a written report to its members at the annual meeting of the cooperative association. The annual report must contain:

(1) a balance sheet;

(2) an income and expense statement;

(3) the amount and nature of the cooperative association's authorized, subscribed, and paid-in capital;

(4) the total number of shareholders;

(5) the number of shareholders who were admitted to or withdrew from the association during the year;

(6) the par value of the association's shares;

(7) the rate at which any investment dividends have been paid; and

(8) if the cooperative association does not issue shares:

(A) the total number of members;

(B) the number of members who were admitted to or withdrew from the association during the year; and

(C) the amount of membership fees received.

(b) The directors shall appoint a committee composed of members who are not principal bookkeepers, accountants, or employees of the cooperative association to review the cooperative association.

(c) The committee appointed under Subsection (b) shall report on the quality of the annual report required by this section and the bookkeeping system of the cooperative association at the annual meeting.

Acts 2003, 78th Leg., ch. 182, § 1, eff. Jan. 1, 2006.

§ 251.353. Annual Report of Financial Condition

(a) This section applies only to a cooperative association that has at least 100 members or at least $20,000 in annual business.

(b) Not later than the 120th day after the date on which the association closes its business each year, a cooperative association shall file in the association's registered office a report of the association's financial condition stating:

(1) the name of the association;

(2) the address of the association's principal office;

(3) the name, address, occupation, and date of expiration of the term of office of each officer and director;

(4) any compensation paid by the association to each officer or director of the association;

(5) the amount and nature of the authorized, subscribed, and paid-in capital;

(6) the total number of shareholders;

(7) the number of shareholders who were admitted to or withdrew from the association during the year;

(8) the par value of the association's shares;

(9) the rate at which any investment dividends have been paid; and

(10) if the association has no shares:

(A) the total number of members;

(B) the number of members who were admitted to or withdrew from the association during the year; and

(C) the amount of membership fees received.

(c) The report required by Subsection (b) must:

(1) include a balance sheet and income and expense statement of the cooperative association; and

(2) be signed by the president and secretary.

(d) A cooperative association that has at least 3,000 members or at least $750,000 in annual business shall file a copy of the report required by this section with the secretary of state.

(e) A person commits an offense if the person signs a report that is required by this section and contains a materially false statement that the person knows is false. An offense under this subsection is a misdemeanor punishable by:

(1) a fine of not less than $25 or more than $200;

(2) confinement in county jail for a term of not less than 30 days or more than one year; or

(3) both the fine and confinement.

Acts 2003, 78th Leg., ch. 182, § 1, eff. Jan. 1, 2006.

§ 251.354. Failure to File Report

(a) If a cooperative association required by Section 251.353 to file a copy of a report with the secretary of state does not file the report within the prescribed time, the secretary of state shall send written notice of the requirement by registered mail to the cooperative association. The notice must be sent to the cooperative association's principal office not later than the 60th day after the date the report becomes due.

(b) If a cooperative association is required by Section 251.353 to file a report at its registered office but not with the secretary of state and fails to file the report within the prescribed time, the secretary of state or any member of the cooperative association may send written notice of the requirement by registered mail to the cooperative association's principal office.

(c) If the cooperative association does not file the report before the 61st day after the date notice is sent under Subsection (a) or (b), a member of the cooperative association or the attorney general may seek a writ of mandamus against the cooperative association and the appropriate officer or officers to compel the filing of the report. The court shall require the cooperative association or the officer who is determined to be at fault to pay the expenses of the proceeding, including attorney's fees.

Acts 2003, 78th Leg., ch. 182, § 1, eff. Jan. 1, 2006.

SUBCHAPTER I. WINDING UP AND TERMINATION

§ 251.401. Voluntary Winding Up and Termination

(a) A cooperative association may wind up and terminate its affairs in accordance with Chapter 11 and Sections 22.301–22.303.

(b) If a cooperative association is directed to wind up and liquidate its affairs, three members of the cooperative association elected by a vote of at least a majority of the members voting shall be designated as trustees on behalf of the cooperative association to:

(1) pay debts;

(2) liquidate the cooperative association's assets within the time set in the trustees' designation or any extension of time; and

(3) distribute the cooperative association's assets in the manner provided by Section 251.403.

Acts 2003, 78th Leg., ch. 182, § 1, eff. Jan. 1, 2006.

§ 251.402. Execution of Certificate of Termination

An officer of a cooperative association or one or more of the persons designated as a liquidating trustee under Section 251.401 shall execute the certificate of termination on behalf of the cooperative association.

Acts 2003, 78th Leg., ch. 182, § 1, eff. Jan. 1, 2006.

§ 251.403. Distribution of Assets

Subject to Sections 11.052 and 11.053(a), the trustees designated under Section 251.401 shall distribute the cooperative association's assets in the following order:

(1) by returning the par value of the investors' capital to investors;

(2) by returning the amounts paid on subscriptions to subscribers for invested capital;

(3) by returning the amount of patronage dividends credited to patrons' accounts to the patrons;

(4) by returning to members their membership capital; and

(5) by distributing any surplus in the manner provided by the certificate of formation:

(A) among the patrons who have been members or subscribers of the cooperative association during the six years preceding the date of termination, on the basis of patronage during that period;

(B) as a gift to any cooperative association or other nonprofit enterprise designated in the certificate of formation; or

(C) by a combination of both methods of distribution.

Acts 2003, 78th Leg., ch. 182, § 1, eff. Jan. 1, 2006. Amended by Acts 2007, 80th Leg., ch. 688, § 133, eff. Sept. 1, 2007.

§ 251.404. Involuntary Termination

A suit for involuntary termination of a cooperative association organized under this chapter may be instituted for the causes and prosecuted in the manner provided by Chapter 11. The assets of a cooperative association that is involuntarily terminated shall be distributed in accordance with Section 251.403.

Acts 2003, 78th Leg., ch. 182, § 1, eff. Jan. 1, 2006.

SUBCHAPTER J. MISCELLANEOUS PROVISIONS

§ 251.451. Exemption From Taxes

A cooperative association organized under this chapter is exempt from the franchise tax and license fees imposed by the state or a political subdivision of the state, except that a cooperative association is exempt from the franchise tax imposed by Chapter 171, Tax Code, only if the cooperative association is exempt under that chapter.

Acts 2003, 78th Leg., ch. 182, § 1, eff. Jan. 1, 2006.

§ 251.452. Use of Name "Cooperative"

(a) Only a cooperative association governed by this chapter, a group organized on a cooperative basis under another law of this state, or a foreign entity operating on a cooperative basis and authorized to do business in this state may use the term "cooperative" or any abbreviation or derivation of the term "cooperative" as part of its business name or represent itself, in advertising or otherwise, as conducting business on a cooperative basis.

(b) A person commits an offense if the person violates Subsection (a). An offense under this subsection is a misdemeanor punishable by:

(1) a fine of not less than $25 or more than $200 for the first month in which the violation occurs;

(2) a fine of not more than $200 for each month during which a violation occurs after the first month;

(3) confinement in the county jail for not less than 30 days or more than one year; or

(4) a combination of those punishments.

(c) The attorney general may sue to enjoin a violation of this section.

(d) If a court renders a judgment that a person who used the term "cooperative" before September 1, 1975, is not organized on a cooperative basis but is authorized to continue to use the term, the business shall place immediately after its name the words "does not comply with the cooperative association law of Texas" in the same kind of type and in letters not less than two-thirds the size of the letters used in the word "cooperative."

(e) Notwithstanding this section, The University Cooperative Society, a domestic nonprofit corporation related to The University of Texas, may continue to use the word "cooperative" in its name.

Acts 2003, 78th Leg., ch. 182, § 1, eff. Jan. 1, 2006.

CHAPTER 252. UNINCORPORATED NONPROFIT ASSOCIATIONS

Section

252.001. Definitions.
252.002. Supplementary General Principles of Law and Equity.
252.003. Territorial Application.
252.004. Real and Personal Property; Nonprofit Association as Beneficiary.
252.005. Statement of Authority as to Real Property.
252.006. Liability in Tort and Contract.
252.007. Capacity to Assert and Defend; Standing.
252.008. Effect of Judgment or Order.
252.009. Disposition of Personal Property of Inactive Nonprofit Association.
252.010. Books and Records.
252.011. Appointment of Agent to Receive Service of Process.
252.012. Claim Not Abated by Change.
252.013. Summons and Complaint; Service.
252.014. Uniformity of Application and Construction.
252.015. Transition Concerning Real and Personal Property.
252.016. Effect on Other Law.
252.017. Chapter Controlling.

§ 252.001. Definitions

In this chapter:

(1) "Member" means a person who, under the rules or practices of a nonprofit association, may participate in the selection of persons authorized to manage the affairs of the nonprofit association or in the development of policy of the nonprofit association.

(2) "Nonprofit association" means an unincorporated organization, other than one created by a trust, consisting of three or more members joined by mutual consent for a common, nonprofit purpose. A form of joint tenancy, tenancy in common, or tenancy by the entirety does not by itself establish a nonprofit association, regardless of whether the co-owners share use of the property for a nonprofit purpose.

Acts 2003, 78th Leg., ch. 182, § 1, eff. Jan. 1, 2006.

§ 252.002. Supplementary General Principles of Law and Equity

Principles of law and equity supplement this chapter unless displaced by a particular provision of this chapter.

Acts 2003, 78th Leg., ch. 182, § 1, eff. Jan. 1, 2006.

§ 252.003. Territorial Application

Real and personal property in this state may be acquired, held, encumbered, and transferred by a nonprofit association, regardless of whether the nonprofit association or a member has any other relationship to this state.

Acts 2003, 78th Leg., ch. 182, § 1, eff. Jan. 1, 2006.

§ 252.004. Real and Personal Property; Nonprofit Association as Beneficiary

(a) A nonprofit association in its name may acquire, hold, encumber, or transfer an estate or interest in real or personal property.

(b) A nonprofit association may be a beneficiary of a trust, contract, or will.

Acts 2003, 78th Leg., ch. 182, § 1, eff. Jan. 1, 2006.

§ 252.005. Statement of Authority as to Real Property

(a) A nonprofit association may execute and record a statement of authority to transfer an estate or interest in real property in the name of the nonprofit association.

(b) An estate or interest in real property in the name of a nonprofit association may be transferred by a person so authorized in a statement of authority recorded in the county clerk's office in the county in which a transfer of the property would be recorded.

(c) A statement of authority must contain:

(1) the name of the nonprofit association;

(2) the address in this state, including the street address, if any, of the nonprofit association, or, if

the nonprofit association does not have an address in this state, its address out of state; and

(3) the name or title of a person authorized to transfer an estate or interest in real property held in the name of the nonprofit association.

(d) A statement of authority must be executed in the same manner as a deed by a person who is not the person authorized to transfer the estate or interest.

(e) The county clerk may collect a fee for recording a statement of authority in the amount authorized for recording a transfer of real property.

(f) An amendment, including a cancellation, of a statement of authority must meet the requirements for execution and recording of an original statement. Unless canceled earlier, a recorded statement of authority or its most recent amendment is canceled by operation of law on the fifth anniversary of the date of the most recent recording.

(g) If the record title to real property is in the name of a nonprofit association and the statement of authority is recorded in the county clerk's office of the county in which a transfer of real property would be recorded, the authority of the person named in a statement of authority is conclusive in favor of a person who gives value without notice that the person lacks authority.

Acts 2003, 78th Leg., ch. 182, § 1, eff. Jan. 1, 2006.

§ 252.006. Liability in Tort and Contract

(a) A nonprofit association is a legal entity separate from its members for the purposes of determining and enforcing rights, duties, and liabilities in contract and tort.

(b) A person is not liable for a breach of a nonprofit association's contract or for a tortious act or omission for which a nonprofit association is liable merely because the person is a member, is authorized to participate in the management of the affairs of the nonprofit association, or is a person considered as a member by the nonprofit association.

(c) A tortious act or omission of a member or other person for which a nonprofit association is liable is not imputed to a person merely because the person is a member of the nonprofit association, is authorized to participate in the management of the affairs of the nonprofit association, or is a person considered as a member by the nonprofit association.

(d) A member of, or a person considered as a member by, a nonprofit association may assert a claim against the nonprofit association. A nonprofit association may assert a claim against a member or a person considered as a member by the nonprofit association.

Acts 2003, 78th Leg., ch. 182, § 1, eff. Jan. 1, 2006.

§ 252.007. Capacity to Assert and Defend; Standing

(a) A nonprofit association, in its name, may institute, defend, intervene, or participate in a judicial, administrative, or other governmental proceeding or in an arbitration, mediation, or any other form of alternative dispute resolution.

(b) A nonprofit association may assert a claim in its name on behalf of members of the nonprofit association if:

(1) one or more of the nonprofit association's members have standing to assert a claim in their own right;

(2) the interests the nonprofit association seeks to protect are germane to its purposes; and

(3) neither the claim asserted nor the relief requested requires the participation of a member.

Acts 2003, 78th Leg., ch. 182, § 1, eff. Jan. 1, 2006.

§ 252.008. Effect of Judgment or Order

A judgment or order against a nonprofit association is not by itself a judgment or order against a member or a person considered as a member by the nonprofit association.

Acts 2003, 78th Leg., ch. 182, § 1, eff. Jan. 1, 2006.

§ 252.009. Disposition of Personal Property of Inactive Nonprofit Association

(a) If a nonprofit association has been inactive for three years or longer, or a shorter period as specified in a document of the nonprofit association, a person in possession or control of personal property of the nonprofit association may transfer the custody of the property:

(1) if a document of a nonprofit association specifies a person to whom transfer is to be made under these circumstances, to that person; or

(2) if no person is specified, to a nonprofit association or nonprofit corporation pursuing broadly similar purposes, or to a government or governmental subdivision, agency, or instrumentality.

(b) Notwithstanding the above, if a nonprofit association is classified under the Internal Revenue Code as a 501(c)(3) organization or is or holds itself out to be established or operating for a charitable, religious, or educational purpose, as defined by Section 501(c)(3),

Internal Revenue Code, then any distribution must be made to another nonprofit association or nonprofit corporation with similar charitable, religious, or educational purposes.

Acts 2003, 78th Leg., ch. 182, § 1, eff. Jan. 1, 2006.

§ 252.010. Books and Records

(a) A nonprofit association shall keep correct and complete books and records of account for at least three years after the end of each fiscal year and shall make the books and records available on request to members of the association for inspection and copying.

(b) The attorney general may inspect, examine, and make copies of the books, records, and other documents the attorney general considers necessary and may investigate the association to determine if a violation of any law of this state has occurred.

Acts 2003, 78th Leg., ch. 182, § 1, eff. Jan. 1, 2006.

§ 252.011. Appointment of Agent to Receive Service of Process

(a) A nonprofit association may file in the office of the secretary of state a statement appointing an agent authorized to receive service of process.

(b) A statement appointing an agent must contain:

(1) the name of the nonprofit association;

(2) the federal taxpayer identification number of the nonprofit association, if applicable;

(3) the address in this state, including the street address, if any, of the nonprofit association or, if the nonprofit association does not have an address in this state, its address out of state; and

(4) the name of the person in this state authorized to receive service of process and the person's address, including the street address, in this state.

(c) A statement appointing an agent must be signed by a person authorized to manage the affairs of the nonprofit association. The statement must also be signed by the person appointed agent, who by signing accepts the appointment. The appointed agent may resign by filing a resignation in the office of the secretary of state and giving notice to the nonprofit association.

(d) The secretary of state may collect a fee for filing a statement appointing an agent to receive service of process, an amendment, a cancellation, or a resignation in the amount charged for filing similar documents.

(e) An amendment to a statement appointing an agent to receive service of process must meet the requirements for execution of an original statement.

(f) A statement appointing an agent may be canceled by filing with the secretary of state a written notice of cancellation executed by a person authorized to manage the affairs of the nonprofit association. A notice of cancellation must contain:

(1) the name of the nonprofit association;

(2) the federal taxpayer identification number of the nonprofit association, if applicable;

(3) the date of filing of the nonprofit association's statement appointing the agent; and

(4) a current street address, if any, of the nonprofit association in this state or, if the nonprofit association does not have an address in this state, its address out of state.

(g) The secretary of state may adopt forms and procedural rules for filing documents under this section.

Acts 2003, 78th Leg., ch. 182, § 1, eff. Jan. 1, 2006. Amended by Acts 2011, 82nd Leg., ch. 139 (S.B. 748), § 58, eff. Sept. 1, 2011.

§ 252.012. Claim Not Abated by Change

A claim for relief against a nonprofit association does not abate merely because of a change in the members or persons authorized to manage the affairs of the nonprofit association.

Acts 2003, 78th Leg., ch. 182, § 1, eff. Jan. 1, 2006.

§ 252.013. Summons and Complaint; Service

(a) In an action or proceeding against a nonprofit association, a summons and complaint must be served on an agent authorized by appointment to receive service of process, an officer, a managing or general agent, or a person authorized to participate in the management of its affairs, in accordance with the Civil Practice and Remedies Code.

(b) Not later than the 10th day after the date of a request by the attorney general to an officer or board member of a nonprofit association or to the nonprofit association, the nonprofit association shall provide to the attorney general the names, current addresses, and telephone numbers of:

(1) each agent authorized to receive service of process on behalf of the nonprofit association; and

(2) each officer, managing or general agent, and other person authorized to participate in the management of the affairs of the nonprofit association.

Acts 2003, 78th Leg., ch. 182, § 1, eff. Jan. 1, 2006.

§ 252.014. Uniformity of Application and Construction

This chapter shall be applied and construed to make uniform the law with respect to the subject of this chapter among states enacting it.

Acts 2003, 78th Leg., ch. 182, § 1, eff. Jan. 1, 2006.

§ 252.015. Transition Concerning Real and Personal Property

If, before September 1, 1995, an estate or interest in real or personal property was by the terms of the transfer purportedly transferred to a nonprofit association, but under the law the estate or interest was vested in a fiduciary such as officers of the nonprofit association to hold the estate or interest for members of the nonprofit association, on or after September 1, 1995, the fiduciary may transfer the estate or interest to the nonprofit association in its name, or the nonprofit association, by appropriate proceedings, may require that the estate or interest be transferred to it in its name.

Acts 2003, 78th Leg., ch. 182, § 1, eff. Jan. 1, 2006.

§ 252.016. Effect on Other Law

This chapter replaces existing law with respect to matters covered by this chapter but does not affect other law covering unincorporated nonprofit associations.

Acts 2003, 78th Leg., ch. 182, § 1, eff. Jan. 1, 2006.

§ 252.017. Chapter Controlling

(a) Except as provided by Subsection (b), the only provisions of this code that apply to or govern a nonprofit association are the provisions of this chapter.

(b) Chapters 1 and 4 and, if a nonprofit association designates an agent for service of process, Subchapter E, Chapter 5, apply to a nonprofit association.

Acts 2003, 78th Leg., ch. 182, § 1, eff. Jan. 1, 2006.

TITLE 7. PROFESSIONAL ENTITIES

CHAPTER 301. PROVISIONS RELATING TO PROFESSIONAL ENTITIES

Section

301.001. Applicability of Title.
301.002. Conflicts of Law.
301.003. Definitions.
301.004. Authorized Person.
301.005. Application for Registration of Foreign Professional Entity.
301.006. License Required to Provide Professional Service.
301.007. Certain Requirements to be Owner, Governing Person, or Officer.
301.008. Duties and Powers of Owner or Managerial Official Who Ceases to be Licensed; Purchase of Ownership Interest.
301.009. Transfer of Ownership Interest.
301.010. Liability.
301.011. Exemption From Securities Laws.
301.012. Joint Practice by Certain Professionals.

§ 301.001. Applicability of Title

(a) This title applies only to a professional entity or foreign professional entity.

(b) This title does not affect:

(1) the professional or confidential relationship between a person who provides a professional service and the recipient of that service; or

(2) a person's legal remedies against another person who commits an error, omission, negligent or incompetent act, or malfeasance while providing a professional service.

(c) This title does not apply to a partnership, including a limited liability partnership.

Acts 2003, 78th Leg., ch. 182, § 1, eff. Jan. 1, 2006. Amended by Acts 2007, 80th Leg., ch. 688, § 134, eff. Sept. 1, 2007.

§ 301.002. Conflicts of Law

This title prevails over a conflicting provision of Title 1, 2, or 3.

Acts 2003, 78th Leg., ch. 182, § 1, eff. Jan. 1, 2006.

§ 301.003. Definitions

In this title:

(1) "Licensed mental health professional" means a person, other than a physician, who is licensed by the state to engage in the practice of psychology or psychiatric nursing or to provide professional therapy or counseling services.

(2) "Professional association" means an association, as distinguished from either a partnership or a corporation, that is:

(A) formed for the purpose of providing the professional service rendered by a doctor of medicine, doctor of osteopathy, doctor of podiatry, dentist, chiropractor, optometrist, therapeutic optometrist, veterinarian, or licensed mental health professional; and

(B) governed as a professional entity under this title.

(3) "Professional corporation" means a corporation that is:

(A) formed for the purpose of providing a professional service, other than the practice of medicine by physicians, surgeons, or other doctors of medicine, that by law a corporation governed by Title 2 is prohibited from rendering; and

(B) governed as a professional entity under this title.

(4) "Professional entity" means a professional association, professional corporation, or professional limited liability company.

(5) "Professional individual," with respect to a professional entity, means an individual who is licensed to provide in this state or another jurisdiction the same professional service as is rendered by that professional entity.

(6) "Professional limited liability company" means a limited liability company formed for the purpose of providing a professional service and governed as a professional entity under this title.

(7) "Professional organization," with respect to a professional corporation or a professional limited liability company, means a person other than an individual, whether nonprofit, for-profit, domestic, or foreign and including a nonprofit corporation or nonprofit association, that renders the same professional service as the professional corporation or professional limited liability company only through owners, members, managerial officials, employees, or agents, each of whom is a professional individual or professional organization.

(8) "Professional service" means any type of service that requires, as a condition precedent to the rendering of the service, the obtaining of a license in this state, including the personal service rendered by an architect, attorney, certified public accountant, dentist, physician, public accountant, or veterinarian.

Acts 2003, 78th Leg., ch. 182, § 1, eff. Jan. 1, 2006. Amended by Acts 2005, 79th Leg., ch. 64, § 97, eff. Jan. 1, 2006; Acts 2007, 80th Leg., ch. 688, § 135, eff. Sept. 1, 2007.

§ 301.004. Authorized Person

For purposes of this title, a person is an authorized person with respect to:

(1) a professional association if the person is a professional individual; and

(2) a professional corporation or a professional limited liability company if the person is a professional individual or professional organization.

Acts 2003, 78th Leg., ch. 182, § 1, eff. Jan. 1, 2006.

§ 301.005. Application for Registration of Foreign Professional Entity

(a) When required by Chapter 9, a foreign professional entity must file an application for registration to transact business in this state.

(b) The secretary of state may accept an application filed under Subsection (a) only if:

(1) the name and purpose of the foreign professional entity stated in the application comply with this title and Chapters 2 and 5; and

(2) the application states that the jurisdiction of formation of the foreign professional entity permits reciprocal admission of an entity formed under this code.

Acts 2003, 78th Leg., ch. 182, § 1, eff. Jan. 1, 2006.

§ 301.006. License Required to Provide Professional Service

(a) A professional association or foreign professional association may provide a professional service in this state only through owners, managerial officials, employees, or agents, each of whom:

(1) is a professional individual; and

(2) is licensed in this state to provide the same professional service provided by the entity.

(b) A professional entity or foreign professional entity, other than a professional association or foreign professional association, may provide a professional service in this state only through owners, managerial officials, employees, or agents, each of whom is an authorized person.

(c) An individual may not, under the guise of employment, provide a professional service in this state unless the individual is licensed to provide the professional service under the laws of this state.

(d) This section may not be construed to prohibit a professional entity or foreign professional entity from employing nurses or from employing individuals who do not, according to general custom and practice, ordinarily provide a professional service, including clerks, secretaries, bookkeepers, technicians, or assistants. To the extent this subsection conflicts with any other law, this subsection controls.

Acts 2003, 78th Leg., ch. 182, § 1, eff. Jan. 1, 2006. Amended by Acts 2005, 79th Leg., ch. 64, § 98, eff. Jan. 1, 2006; Acts 2007, 80th Leg., ch. 688, § 136, eff. Sept. 1, 2007.

§ 301.007. Certain Requirements to be Owner, Governing Person, or Officer

(a) A person may be an owner of a professional entity or a governing person of a professional limited liability company only if the person is an authorized person.

(b) An individual may be an officer of a professional entity or a governing person of a professional association or professional corporation only if the individual is a professional individual.

Acts 2003, 78th Leg., ch. 182, § 1, eff. Jan. 1, 2006.

§ 301.008. Duties and Powers of Owner or Managerial Official Who Ceases to be Licensed; Purchase of Ownership Interest

(a) A managerial official of a professional entity who ceases to satisfy the requirements of Section 301.007 shall promptly resign the person's position and employment with the entity.

(b) An owner of a professional entity who ceases to be an authorized person as required by Section 301.007 shall promptly relinquish the person's ownership interest in the entity.

(c) A person who succeeds to the ownership interest of an owner shall promptly relinquish the person's financial interest in the entity if the person is not an authorized person as required by Section 301.007.

(d) A professional entity shall purchase or cause to be purchased the ownership interest in the entity of a person who is required to relinquish the person's financial interest in the entity under this section. The price and terms of a purchase of an ownership interest required under this subsection may be provided by the governing documents of the entity or an applicable agreement.

(e) A person who owns all of the outstanding ownership interests in a professional entity but is required under this section to relinquish the person's financial interest in the entity may act as a managerial official or owner of the entity only for the purpose of winding up the affairs of the entity, including selling the outstanding ownership interests and other assets of the entity.

Acts 2003, 78th Leg., ch. 182, § 1, eff. Jan. 1, 2006.

§ 301.009. Transfer of Ownership Interest

Except as limited by the governing documents of the professional entity or an applicable agreement, an ownership interest in a professional entity may be transferred only to:

(1) an owner of the entity;

(2) the entity itself; or

(3) an authorized person.

Acts 2003, 78th Leg., ch. 182, § 1, eff. Jan. 1, 2006.

§ 301.010. Liability

(a) A professional entity is jointly and severally liable for an error, omission, negligent or incompetent act, or malfeasance committed by a person who:

(1) is an owner, managerial official, employee, or agent of the entity; and

(2) while providing a professional service for the entity or during the course of the person's employment, commits the error, omission, negligent or incompetent act, or malfeasance.

(b) An owner, managerial official, employee, or agent of a professional entity other than an owner, managerial official, employee, or agent liable under Subsection (a) is not subject to the same liability imposed on the professional entity under this section.

(c) If a person described by Subsection (a) is a professional organization, the professional organization and the professional entity are jointly and severally liable for the error, omission, negligent or incompetent act, or malfeasance committed by the person, or the person's owner, member, managerial official, employee, or agent, while providing a professional service for the professional entity.

Acts 2003, 78th Leg., ch. 182, § 1, eff. Jan. 1, 2006.

§ 301.011. Exemption From Securities Laws

(a) A sale, issuance, or offer for sale of an ownership interest in a professional entity to a person authorized under this title to own an ownership interest in the professional entity is exempt from any state law, other than this code, that regulates the sale, issuance, or offer for sale of securities.

(b) A transaction described by Subsection (a) does not require the approval of or other action by a state official or regulatory agency authorized to regulate the sale, issuance, or offer for sale of securities.

Acts 2003, 78th Leg., ch. 182, § 1, eff. Jan. 1, 2006.

§ 301.012. Joint Practice by Certain Professionals

(a) Persons licensed as doctors of medicine and persons licensed as doctors of osteopathy by the Texas State Board of Medical Examiners and persons licensed as podiatrists by the Texas State Board of Podiatric Medical Examiners may jointly form and own a professional association or a professional limited liability company to perform professional services that fall within the scope of practice of those practitioners.

(a-1) Persons licensed as physicians under Subtitle B, Title 3, Occupations Code, and persons licensed as physician assistants under Chapter 204, Occupations Code, may form and own a professional association or a professional limited liability company to perform professional services that fall within the scope of practice of those practitioners.

(a-2) A physician assistant may not be an officer in the professional association or limited liability company.

(a-3) A physician assistant may not contract with or employ a physician to be a supervising physician of the physician assistant or of any physician in the professional association or limited liability company.

(a-4) The authority of each practitioner is limited by the scope of practice of the respective practitioner. An organizer of the entity must be a physician and ensure that a physician or physicians control and manage the entity.

(a-5) Nothing in this section may be construed to allow the practice of medicine by someone not licensed as a physician under Subtitle B, Title 3, Occupations Code, or to allow a person not licensed as a physician to direct the activities of a physician in the practice of medicine.

(a-6) A physician assistant or combination of physician assistants may have only a minority ownership interest in an entity created under this section. The ownership interest of an individual physician assistant may not equal or exceed the ownership interest of any individual physician owner. A physician assistant or combination of physician assistants may not interfere with the practice of medicine by a physician owner or the supervision of physician assistants by a physician owner.

(a-7) The Texas Medical Board and the Texas Physician Assistant Board continue to exercise regulatory authority over their respective license holders according to applicable law. To the extent of a conflict between Subtitle B, Title 3, Occupations Code, and Chapter 204, Occupations Code, or any rules adopted under those statutes, Subtitle B, Title 3, or a rule adopted under that subtitle controls.

(b) Professionals, other than physicians, engaged in related mental health fields such as psychology, clinical social work, licensed professional counseling, and licensed marriage and family therapy may form a professional entity that is jointly owned by those practitioners to perform professional services that fall within the scope of practice of those practitioners.

(c) Persons licensed as doctors of medicine and persons licensed as doctors of osteopathy by the Texas State Board of Medical Examiners and persons licensed as optometrists or therapeutic optometrists by the Texas Optometry Board may, subject to the provisions regulating those professionals, jointly form and own a professional association or a professional limited liability company to perform professional services that fall within the scope of practice of those practitioners.

(d) Only a physician, optometrist, or therapeutic optometrist may have an ownership interest in a professional association or professional limited liability company formed under Subsection (c).

(e) An entity formed under Subsection (c) is not prohibited from making one or more payments to an owner's estate following the owner's death under an agreement with the owner or as otherwise authorized or required by law.

(f) When doctors of medicine, osteopathy, and podiatry, or doctors of medicine, osteopathy, and optometry or therapeutic optometry, or mental health professionals form a professional entity as provided by Subsections (a), (b), and (c), the authority of each of the practitioners is limited by the scope of practice of the respective practitioners and none can exercise control over the other's clinical authority granted by their respective licenses, either through agreements, bylaws, directives, financial incentives, or other arrangements that would assert control over treatment decisions made by the practitioner.

(g) The state agencies exercising regulatory control over professions to which this section applies continue to exercise regulatory authority over their respective licenses.

Acts 2003, 78th Leg., ch. 182, § 1, eff. Jan. 1, 2006. Amended by Acts 2011, 82nd Leg., ch. 782 (H.B. 2098), § 3, eff. June 17, 2011.

Section 6 of Acts 2011, 82nd Leg., ch. 782 (H.B. 2098) provides:

"The restrictions on ownership interests in Sections 22.0561, 152.0551, and 301.012, Business Organizations Code, apply to an ownership interest acquired on or after the effective date [June 17, 2011] of this Act. An ownership interest acquired before the effective date of this Act is governed by the law in effect at the time the interest was acquired, and the former law is continued in effect for that purpose."

CHAPTER 302. PROVISIONS RELATING TO PROFESSIONAL ASSOCIATIONS

Section

302.001. Applicability of Certain Provisions Governing For-Profit Corporations.
302.002. Duration of Professional Association.
302.003. Amendment of Certificate of Formation.
302.004. Adoption of Bylaws; Delegation of Authority.
302.005. Governing Authority.
302.006. Members' Voting Rights.
302.007. Election of Officers.
302.008. Officer and Governing Person Eligibility Requirements.
302.009. Employment of Agents and Employees.
302.010. Limitation on Member's Power to Bind Association.
302.011. Division of Profits.
302.012. Annual Statement Required.
302.013. Winding Up and Termination; Certificate of Termination.

§ 302.001. Applicability of Certain Provisions Governing For-Profit Corporations

The provisions of Chapters 20 and 21 governing a for-profit corporation apply to a professional association, unless there is a conflict with this title.

Acts 2003, 78th Leg., ch. 182, § 1, eff. Jan. 1, 2006.

§ 302.002. Duration of Professional Association

A professional association continues:

(1) for all purposes as a separate entity independent of the association's members until:

(A) the expiration of the period of duration stated in the certificate of formation; or

(B) the association is wound up and terminated in the manner provided by the certificate of formation or, if the certificate of formation does not provide a manner for winding up and termination, by a two-thirds vote of the association's members; and

(2) in existence notwithstanding:

(A) the death, insanity, incompetency, felony conviction, resignation, withdrawal, transfer of ownership interest, or expulsion of a member other than the last surviving member of the association;

(B) the admission of a new member or the transfer of ownership interest to a new or existing member; or

(C) the occurrence of an event that would require the winding up of a partnership under state law or similar circumstances.

Acts 2003, 78th Leg., ch. 182, § 1, eff. Jan. 1, 2006.

§ 302.003. Amendment of Certificate of Formation

(a) A professional association may amend the association's certificate of formation as provided by Chapter 3 and:

(1) by the procedure for amendment stated in the certificate of formation; or

(2) if the certificate of formation does not provide a procedure for amending the certificate, by a two-thirds vote of the association's members.

(b) A professional association is not required to amend the association's certificate of formation to reflect a change in membership or a transfer of ownership interests in the association.

Acts 2003, 78th Leg., ch. 182, § 1, eff. Jan. 1, 2006. Amended by Acts 2005, 79th Leg., ch. 64, § 99, eff. Jan. 1, 2006.

§ 302.004. Adoption of Bylaws; Delegation of Authority

(a) The members of a professional association may adopt bylaws for the association.

(b) The authority to adopt bylaws for a professional association granted under Subsection (a) may be delegated under the certificate of formation to the governing authority of the association.

Acts 2003, 78th Leg., ch. 182, § 1, eff. Jan. 1, 2006.

§ 302.005. Governing Authority

(a) A professional association shall be governed by:

(1) a board of directors; or

(2) an executive committee.

(b) The governing authority of a professional association shall be elected by the members of the association.

Acts 2003, 78th Leg., ch. 182, § 1, eff. Jan. 1, 2006.

§ 302.006. Members' Voting Rights

A member of a professional association is entitled to cast a vote at a meeting of the members as provided by the certificate of formation of the association.

Acts 2003, 78th Leg., ch. 182, § 1, eff. Jan. 1, 2006.

§ 302.007. Election of Officers

The governing authority of a professional association shall elect the officers of the association.

Acts 2003, 78th Leg., ch. 182, § 1, eff. Jan. 1, 2006.

§ 302.008. Officer and Governing Person Eligibility Requirements

(a) Only a member of the professional association is eligible to serve as an officer or governing person of a professional association.

(b) Except as provided by Subsection (c), a person is not required to be a governing person of a professional association to serve as an officer of the association.

(c) Only a governing person of a professional association is eligible to serve as the president of the professional association.

Acts 2003, 78th Leg., ch. 182, § 1, eff. Jan. 1, 2006.

§ 302.009. Employment of Agents and Employees

The officers of a professional association may employ agents or employees for the association as the officers consider advisable.

Acts 2003, 78th Leg., ch. 182, § 1, eff. Jan. 1, 2006.

§ 302.010. Limitation on Member's Power to Bind Association

A member of a professional association is not entitled to bind the association within the scope of the association's business or profession merely by virtue of being a member of the professional association.

Acts 2003, 78th Leg., ch. 182, § 1, eff. Jan. 1, 2006.

§ 302.011. Division of Profits

The members of a professional association shall divide the profits derived from the association in the manner provided by the governing documents of the association.

Acts 2003, 78th Leg., ch. 182, § 1, eff. Jan. 1, 2006.

§ 302.012. Annual Statement Required

(a) In June of each year, a professional association shall file with the secretary of state a statement that:

(1) lists:

(A) the name and address of each member of the association; and

(B) the name of each officer and governing person of the association; and

(2) states that each member of the association is licensed to provide the same type of professional service provided by the association.

(b) The statement required by this section must be executed by an officer of the association on behalf of the association.

Acts 2003, 78th Leg., ch. 182, § 1, eff. Jan. 1, 2006.

§ 302.013. Winding Up and Termination; Certificate of Termination

(a) A professional association may wind up and terminate the association's business as provided by:

(1) the association's certificate of formation; or

(2) if the certificate of formation does not provide for the winding up and termination of the association, a two-thirds vote of the association's members.

(b) Except as provided by Subsection (c), a certificate of termination filed in accordance with Chapter 11 must be executed by an officer of the professional association on behalf of the association.

(c) If a professional association does not have any living officer, the certificate of termination must be executed by the legal representative of the last surviving officer of the association.

Acts 2003, 78th Leg., ch. 182, § 1, eff. Jan. 1, 2006.

CHAPTER 303. PROVISIONS RELATING TO PROFESSIONAL CORPORATIONS

Section
303.001. Applicability of Certain Provisions Governing For–Profit Corporations.
303.002. Authority and Liability of Shareholder.
303.003. Notice of Restriction on Transfer of Shares.
303.004. Redemption of Shares; Price and Terms.
303.005. Existence of Professional Corporation Before Winding Up and Termination.
303.006. Execution of Certificate of Termination.

§ 303.001. Applicability of Certain Provisions Governing For–Profit Corporations

The provisions of Chapters 20 and 21 governing a for-profit corporation apply to a professional corporation, unless there is a conflict with this title.

Acts 2003, 78th Leg., ch. 182, § 1, eff. Jan. 1, 2006.

§ 303.002. Authority and Liability of Shareholder

(a) A shareholder of a professional corporation is not required to supervise the performance of duties by an officer or employee of the corporation.

(b) A shareholder of a professional corporation is subject to no greater liability than a shareholder of a for-profit corporation.

Acts 2003, 78th Leg., ch. 182, § 1, eff. Jan. 1, 2006.

§ 303.003. Notice of Restriction on Transfer of Shares

Any restriction on the transfer of shares in a professional corporation that is imposed by the governing documents of the corporation or an applicable agreement must be:

(1) noted on each certificate representing the shares; or

(2) incorporated by reference in the manner provided by Chapter 21.

Acts 2003, 78th Leg., ch. 182, § 1, eff. Jan. 1, 2006.

§ 303.004. Redemption of Shares; Price and Terms

(a) A professional corporation may redeem shares of a shareholder, including a deceased shareholder.

(b) The price and other terms of a redemption of shares may be:

(1) agreed to between the board of directors of the professional corporation and the shareholder or the shareholder's personal representative; or

(2) specified in the governing documents of the professional corporation or an applicable agreement.

Acts 2003, 78th Leg., ch. 182, § 1, eff. Jan. 1, 2006.

§ 303.005. Existence of Professional Corporation Before Winding Up and Termination

A professional corporation continues to exist until the winding up and termination of the corporation as provided by Chapter 11 without regard to:

(1) the death, incompetency, bankruptcy, resignation, withdrawal, retirement, or expulsion of any shareholder of the corporation;

(2) the transfer of shares to a new shareholder; or

(3) the occurrence of an event requiring the winding up of a partnership.

Acts 2003, 78th Leg., ch. 182, § 1, eff. Jan. 1, 2006.

§ 303.006. Execution of Certificate of Termination

(a) Except as provided by Subsection (b), a certificate of termination filed in accordance with Chapter 11 must be executed by an officer of the professional corporation on behalf of the corporation.

(b) If a professional corporation does not have any living officer, the certificate of termination must be executed by a director of the corporation. If the professional corporation does not have any living director, the certificate of termination must be executed by the legal representative of the last living director of the corporation.

Acts 2003, 78th Leg., ch. 182, § 1, eff. Jan. 1, 2006. Amended by Acts 2007, 80th Leg., ch. 688, § 137, eff. Sept. 1, 2007.

CHAPTER 304. PROVISIONS RELATING TO PROFESSIONAL LIMITED LIABILITY COMPANIES

Section
304.001. Applicability of Certain Provisions Governing Limited Liability Companies.

§ 304.001. Applicability of Certain Provisions Governing Limited Liability Companies

Title 3 applies to a professional limited liability company, unless there is a conflict with this title.

Acts 2003, 78th Leg., ch. 182, § 1, eff. Jan. 1, 2006.

TITLE 8. MISCELLANEOUS AND TRANSITION PROVISIONS

CHAPTER 401. GENERAL PROVISIONS

Section
401.001. Definitions.

§ 401.001. Definitions

In this title:

(1) "Mandatory application date" means:

(A) for an entity subject to this code under Section 402.001, January 1, 2006;

(B) for an entity subject to this code under Section 402.003 or 402.004, the date of completion of the action required by that section but no earlier than January 1, 2006; and

(C) for any other entity, January 1, 2010.

(2) "Prior law" means the applicable law in effect before January 1, 2006.

Acts 2003, 78th Leg., ch. 182, § 1, eff. Jan. 1, 2006.

CHAPTER 402. MISCELLANEOUS AND TRANSITION PROVISIONS

Section
402.001. Applicability Upon Effective Date.
402.002. Early Effectiveness of Fees.
402.003. Early Adoption of Code by Existing Domestic Entity.
402.004. Early Adoption of Code by Registered Foreign Filing Entity.
402.005. Applicability to Existing Entities.
402.0051. Effect of References to Prior Law and Use of Synonymous Terms.
402.006. Applicability to Certain Acts, Contracts, and Transactions.
402.007. Indemnification.
402.008. Meetings of Owners and Members; Consents; Voting of Interests.
402.009. Meetings of Governing Authority and Committees; Consents.
402.010. Sale of Assets, Mergers, Reorganizations, Conversions.
402.011. Winding Up and Termination.
402.012. Registration of Certain Foreign Entities.
402.013. Reinstatement of Entities Canceled, Revoked, Dissolved, Involuntarily Dissolved, Suspended, or Forfeited Under Prior Law.
402.014. Maintenance of Prior Action.

§ 402.001. Applicability Upon Effective Date

(a) On or after the effective date of this code, this code applies to:

(1) a domestic entity formed on or after the effective date of this code;

(2) a domestic entity that is a converted entity resulting from a conversion that takes effect on or after the effective date of this code;

(3) a foreign filing entity, or other foreign entity, that is not registered with the secretary of state to transact business in this state before the effective date of this code; and

(4) a foreign nonfiling entity, including a foreign limited liability partnership.

(b) The registration of a domestic limited liability partnership or foreign limited liability partnership under prior law and in effect on the effective date of this code continues to be governed by the prior law until expiration of the current term of registration, unless earlier withdrawn or revoked.

(c) Notwithstanding Subsections (a) and (b), after the effective date of this code, Sections 152.802 and 152.803, instead of prior law, govern a renewal of registration or other filing with the secretary of state made on behalf of a domestic limited liability partnership registered under prior law.

(d) Notwithstanding Subsection (a), a domestic partnership that files an initial application for registration as a limited liability partnership after the effective date of this code is governed by Subchapter J, Chapter 152.

(e) Except as provided by Subsection (b), on or after the effective date of this code, Subchapter K, Chapter 152, applies to the registration of a foreign limited liability partnership registered under prior law.

Acts 2003, 78th Leg., ch. 182, § 1, eff. Jan. 1, 2006. Amended by Acts 2005, 79th Leg., ch. 64, § 100, eff. Jan. 1, 2006; Acts 2007, 80th Leg., ch. 688, § 138, eff. Sept. 1, 2007.

§ 402.002. Early Effectiveness of Fees

On or after the effective date of this code, the fees required by Chapter 4 apply to all filings made with the secretary of state, including comparable filings under prior law, regardless of whether an entity is subject to or has adopted this code. The intent of this section is to:

(1) require a filing fee for all documents filed under either this code or the prior law without regard to the difference in designation of the document; and

(2) make the filing fees described by Subdivision (1) uniform from the effective date of this code.

Acts 2003, 78th Leg., ch. 182, § 1, eff. Jan. 1, 2006.

§ 402.003. Early Adoption of Code by Existing Domestic Entity

(a) A domestic entity formed before the effective date of this code may voluntarily elect to adopt and become subject to this code by:

(1) adopting the code by complying with the procedures for approval, under prior law and its governing documents, of an amendment to:

(A) its articles of incorporation, with respect to a corporation or cooperative association;

(B) its regulations, with respect to a limited liability company;

(C) its articles of association, with respect to a professional association;

(D) its declaration of trust, with respect to a real estate investment trust;

(E) its partnership agreement, with respect to a partnership; or

(F) its primary governing document, with respect to another type of domestic entity;

(2) if any of its governing documents, including its certificate of formation, do not comply with this code, complying with the procedures, under prior law and its governing documents, to amend the noncomplying governing documents to comply with this code, including filing with the filing officer in accordance with Chapter 4 a certificate of amendment to cause its certificate of formation to comply with this code; and

(3) if the domestic entity is a filing entity, filing with the filing officer in accordance with Chapter 4 a statement that the filing entity is electing to adopt this code.

(b) A domestic entity that elected to adopt and become subject to this code as provided by Subsection (a) is not considered to have failed to comply with Subsection (a)(2) because:

(1) the entity's governing documents do not state the type of entity formed; or

(2) a circumstance described by Section 402.0051 applies.

Acts 2003, 78th Leg., ch. 182, § 1, eff. Jan. 1, 2006. Amended by Acts 2007, 80th Leg., ch. 688, § 139, eff. Sept. 1, 2007; Acts 2011, 82nd Leg., ch. 139 (S.B. 748), § 59, eff. Sept. 1, 2011.

§ 402.004. Early Adoption of Code by Registered Foreign Filing Entity

(a) A foreign filing entity registered with the secretary of state to transact business in this state before the effective date of this code may voluntarily elect to adopt and become subject to this code by filing with the secretary of state in accordance with Chapter 4:

(1) a statement that the foreign filing entity is electing to adopt this code; and

(2) an amendment to its application for registration that would cause its application for registration to comply with this code.

(b) A foreign filing entity that elected to adopt and become subject to this code as provided by Subsection (a) is not considered to have failed to comply with Subsection (a)(2) because:

(1) the application for registration or any amendment to the registration:

(A) does not state the entity's type; or

(B) does not include the appointment of the secretary of state as agent for service of process under the circumstances provided by Section 5.251; or

(2) a circumstance described by Section 402.0051 applies.

Acts 2003, 78th Leg., ch. 182, § 1, eff. Jan. 1, 2006. Amended by Acts 2005, 79th Leg., ch. 64, § 101, eff. Jan. 1, 2006; Acts 2011, 82nd Leg., ch. 139 (S.B. 748), § 60, eff. Sept. 1, 2011.

§ 402.005. Applicability to Existing Entities

(a) On or after January 1, 2010, if a domestic entity formed before January 1, 2006, or a foreign filing entity registered with the secretary of state to transact business in this state before January 1, 2006, has not taken the actions specified by Section 402.003 or 402.004 to elect to adopt this code:

(1) this code applies to the entity and all actions taken by the managerial officials, owners, or members of the entity, except as otherwise expressly provided by this title;

(2) if the entity is a domestic or foreign filing entity, the entity is not considered to have failed to comply with this code if the entity's certificate of formation or application for registration, as appropriate, does not comply with this code;

(3) if the entity is a domestic filing entity, the entity shall conform its certificate of formation to the requirements of this code when it next files an amendment to its certificate of formation; and

(4) if the entity is a foreign filing entity, the entity shall conform its application for registration to the requirements of this code when it next files an amendment to its application for registration.

(b) On or after January 1, 2010, and to the extent provided in Subchapter A, Chapter 23, this code applies to a corporation created under a special statute of this state outside this code before January 1, 2006. The corporation, if its certificate of formation, or equivalent governing document, is filed with the secretary of state, may elect for this code to apply to the corporation at any time on or after January 1, 2006, and prior to January 1, 2010, to the extent provided in Subchapter A, Chapter 23, by filing a statement and taking other actions in a manner similar to a domestic filing entity under Section 402.003.

(c) A domestic or foreign filing entity is not considered to have failed to comply with Subsection (a)(3) or (4) because:

(1) the certificate of formation does not state the type of entity formed;

(2) the application for registration or any amendment to the registration:

(A) does not state the entity's type; or

(B) does not include the appointment of the secretary of state as agent for service of process, notice, or demand under the circumstances provided by Section 5.251; or

(3) a circumstance described by Section 402.0051 applies.

Acts 2003, 78th Leg., ch. 182, § 1, eff. Jan. 1, 2006. Amended by Acts 2005, 79th Leg., ch. 64, § 102, eff. Jan. 1, 2006; Acts 2009, 81st Leg., ch. 84, § 59, eff. Sept. 1, 2009; Acts 2011, 82nd Leg., ch. 139 (S.B. 748), § 61, eff. Sept. 1, 2011.

§ 402.0051. Effect of References to Prior Law and Use of Synonymous Terms

(a) A governing document or a filing instrument, including a certificate of formation or application for registration, is not considered to have failed to conform to this code if the governing document or filing instrument:

(1) contains a reference to prior law that was applicable at the time of its filing or adoption;

(2) contains a provision that was authorized by prior law at the time of its filing or adoption;

(3) includes a term or phrase described by Section 1.006; or

(4) includes a term or phrase from prior law that is different from the corresponding term or phrase used in this code.

(b) A reference in a governing document or filing instrument to a statute or provision of a statute in effect before January 1, 2010, that was repealed by this code is considered to be a reference to the provision or provisions of this code that correspond to the repealed statute or provision unless the governing document or filing instrument expressly provides otherwise.

(c) An entity is not considered to have failed to comply with this code if a governing document or filing instrument makes a reference to prior law rather than to the corresponding provisions of the prior law in this code.

(d) For purposes of this section, prior law includes a predecessor statute to the prior law.

Added by Acts 2011, 82nd Leg., ch. 139 (S.B. 748), § 62, eff. Sept. 1, 2011.

§ 402.006. Applicability to Certain Acts, Contracts, and Transactions

Except as otherwise expressly provided by this title, all of the provisions of this code govern acts, contracts, or other transactions by an entity subject to this code or its managerial officials, owners, or members that occur on or after the mandatory application date. The prior law governs the acts, contracts, or transactions of the entity or its managerial officials, owners, or members that occur before the mandatory application date.

Acts 2003, 78th Leg., ch. 182, § 1, eff. Jan. 1, 2006. Amended by Acts 2005, 79th Leg., ch. 64, § 103, eff. Jan. 1, 2006.

§ 402.007. Indemnification

Chapter 8 governs any proposed indemnification by a domestic entity after the mandatory application date, regardless of whether the events on which the indemnification is based occurred before or after the mandatory application date. In a case in which indemnification is permitted but not required under Chapter 8, a provision relating to indemnification contained in the governing documents of a domestic entity on the mandatory application date that would otherwise have the effect of limiting the nature or type of indemnification permitted by Chapter 8 may not be construed after the mandatory application date as limiting the indemnification authorized by Chapter 8 unless the provision is intended to limit or restrict permissive indemnification under applicable law.

Acts 2003, 78th Leg., ch. 182, § 1, eff. Jan. 1, 2006. Amended by Acts 2005, 79th Leg., ch. 64, § 104, eff. Jan. 1, 2006.

§ 402.008. Meetings of Owners and Members; Consents; Voting of Interests

(a) Except as provided by Subsection (b) and regardless of whether a proxy or consent was executed by an owner or member before the mandatory application date, Chapter 6 and any other applicable provision of this code apply to:

(1) a meeting of owners or members held on or after the mandatory application date;

(2) an action undertaken by owners or members under a written consent that takes effect on or after the mandatory application date;

(3) a vote cast at a meeting described by Subdivision (1); and

(4) consent given for an action described by Subdivision (2).

(b) Prior law applies to a meeting of owners or members and to any vote cast at a meeting described by this section if the meeting was initially called for a date before the mandatory application date and notice of the meeting was given to owners or members entitled to vote at the meeting.

Acts 2003, 78th Leg., ch. 182, § 1, eff. Jan. 1, 2006.

§ 402.009. Meetings of Governing Authority and Committees; Consents

(a) Except as provided by Subsection (b), Chapter 6 and any other applicable provision of this code apply to:

(1) a meeting of the governing authority or a committee of the governing authority held on or after the mandatory application date;

(2) an action undertaken by the governing authority or a committee of the governing authority under a written consent that takes effect on or after the mandatory application date;

(3) a vote cast at a meeting described by Subdivision (1); and

(4) consent given for an action described by Subdivision (2).

(b) Prior law applies to a meeting of the governing authority or a committee of the governing authority and to any vote cast at a meeting described by this section if the meeting was initially called for a date before the mandatory application date and notice of the meeting was given to governing persons entitled to vote at the meeting.

Acts 2003, 78th Leg., ch. 182, § 1, eff. Jan. 1, 2006.

§ 402.010. Sale of Assets, Mergers, Reorganizations, Conversions

Chapter 10 and any other applicable provisions of this code apply to a transaction consummated by an entity after the mandatory application date, except that if a required approval of the owners or members of the entity has been given before the mandatory application date or has been given after the mandatory application date but at a meeting of owners or members initially called for a date before the mandatory application date, the transaction shall be governed by the prior law.

Acts 2003, 78th Leg., ch. 182, § 1, eff. Jan. 1, 2006.

§ 402.011. Winding Up and Termination

(a) Chapter 11 applies to:

(1) an action for involuntary or judicial winding up and termination commenced after the mandatory application date; or

(2) a voluntary winding up and termination proceeding initiated after the mandatory application date by:

(A) the governing authority;

(B) the terms of the governing documents; or

(C) applicable law.

(b) The prior law governs:

(1) an action described by Subsection (a)(1) that is pending on the mandatory application date; or

(2) a proceeding described by Subsection (a)(2) initiated before the mandatory application date.

Acts 2003, 78th Leg., ch. 182, § 1, eff. Jan. 1, 2006.

§ 402.012. Registration of Certain Foreign Entities

A foreign entity that has transacted intrastate business in this state before the mandatory application date and that is required by Chapter 9 to register to transact business is not subject to a direct or indirect penalty as a result of failure to register under Chapter 9 if the application for registration is filed not later than the 30th day after the mandatory application date.

Acts 2003, 78th Leg., ch. 182, § 1, eff. Jan. 1, 2006.

§ 402.013. Reinstatement of Entities Canceled, Revoked, Dissolved, Involuntarily Dissolved, Suspended, or Forfeited Under Prior Law

(a) On or after January 1, 2006, and before January 1, 2010, a domestic filing entity whose certificate of formation or equivalent governing document has been canceled, revoked, involuntarily dissolved, suspended, or forfeited under prior law may reinstate its certificate of formation or equivalent governing document in accordance with:

(1) prior law; or

(2) this code if it also complies with Section 402.003.

(b) On or after January 1, 2006, and before January 1, 2010, a foreign filing entity whose registration to do business has been canceled, revoked, involuntarily dissolved, suspended, or forfeited under prior law may reinstate its registration in accordance with:

(1) prior law; or

(2) this code if it also complies with Section 402.004.

(b–1) On or after January 1, 2010, a domestic filing entity whose existence has been voluntarily dissolved or involuntarily dissolved under prior law or whose certificate of formation or equivalent governing document has been canceled, revoked, suspended, or forfeited under prior law may reinstate the entity in accordance with this code.

(b–2) On or after January 1, 2010, a foreign filing entity whose registration to do business has been canceled, revoked, suspended, or forfeited under prior law may reinstate its registration in accordance with this code.

(c) If the certificate of formation of a domestic filing entity or the registration to do business of a foreign filing entity is forfeited under the Tax Code, the entity must revive the certificate of formation or registration in accordance with that code.

Acts 2003, 78th Leg., ch. 182, § 1, eff. Jan. 1, 2006. Amended by Acts 2005, 79th Leg., ch. 64, § 105, eff. Jan. 1, 2006; Acts 2011, 82nd Leg., ch. 139 (S.B. 748), § 64, eff. Sept. 1, 2011.

§ 402.014. Maintenance of Prior Action

Except as expressly provided by this title, this code does not apply to an action or proceeding commenced before the mandatory application date. Prior law applies to the action or proceeding.

Acts 2003, 78th Leg., ch. 182, § 1, eff. Jan. 1, 2006.

BUSINESS AND COMMERCE CODE

TITLE 5. REGULATION OF BUSINESSES AND SERVICES

SUBTITLE A. GENERAL PRACTICES

CHAPTER 71. ASSUMED BUSINESS OR PROFESSIONAL NAME

SUBCHAPTER A. GENERAL PROVISIONS

Section

71.001. Short Title.
71.002. Definitions.
71.003. Applicability of Chapter.

SUBCHAPTER B. REQUIREMENTS APPLICABLE TO CERTAIN UNINCORPORATED PERSONS

71.051 Certificate for Certain Unincorporated Persons.
71.052 Contents of Certificate.
71.053. Execution of Certificate.
71.054. Place of Filing.

SUBCHAPTER C. REQUIREMENTS APPLICABLE TO INCORPORATED BUSINESS OR PROFESSION AND CERTAIN OTHER ENTITIES

71.101 Certificate for Incorporated Business or Profession, Limited Partnership, Limited Liability Partnership, Limited Liability Company, or Foreign Filing Entity.
71.102 Contents of Certificate.
71.103 Place of Filing.
71.104. Execution of Certificate.

SUBCHAPTER D. GENERAL PROVISIONS REGARDING ASSUMED NAME CERTIFICATE

71.151. Duration and Renewal of Certificate.
71.152. Material Change in Information; New Certificate.
71.153. Abandonment of Use of Business or Professional Name.
71.154. Index of Certificates.
71.155. Filing Fees.
71.156. Prescribed Forms.
71.157. Effect of Filing.
71.158. Filing of Reproduction.

SUBCHAPTER E. PENALTIES

71.201. Civil Action; Sanction.
71.202. Criminal Penalty: General Violation.
71.203. Criminal Penalty: Fraudulent Filing.

SUBCHAPTER A. GENERAL PROVISIONS

§ 71.001. Short Title

This chapter may be cited as the Assumed Business or Professional Name Act.

Added by Acts 2007, 80th Leg., ch. 885, § 2.01, eff. April 1, 2009.

§ 71.002. Definitions

In this chapter:

(1) "Address" means:

(A) a post office address; and

(B) a street address, if the street address is not the same as the post office address.

(2) "Assumed name" means:

(A) for an individual, a name that does not include the surname of the individual;

(B) for a partnership, a name that does not include the surname or other legal name of each joint venturer or general partner;

(C) for an individual or a partnership, a name, including a surname, that suggests the existence of additional owners by including words such as "Company," "& Company," "& Son," "& Sons," "& Associates," "Brothers," and similar words, but not words that merely describe the business being conducted or the professional service being rendered;

(D) for a limited partnership, a name other than the name stated in its certificate of formation;

(E) for a company, a name used by the company;

(F) for a corporation, a name other than the name stated in its certificate of formation or a comparable document;

(G) for a limited liability partnership, a name other than the name stated in its application filed with the office of the secretary of state or a comparable document; and

(H) for a limited liability company, a name other than the name stated in its certificate of formation or a comparable document.

(3) "Certificate" means an assumed name certificate.

(4) "Company" means a real estate investment trust, a joint-stock company, or any other business, professional, or other association or legal entity that is not incorporated, other than a partnership, limited partnership, limited liability company, limited liability partnership, or foreign filing entity.

(5) "Corporation" means:

(A) a domestic or foreign corporation, professional corporation, professional association, or other corporation; or

(B) any other business, professional, or other association or legal entity that is incorporated.

(6) "Estate" means a person's property that is administered by a representative.

(6–a) "Foreign filing entity" means an entity formed under the laws of a jurisdiction other than this state that registers or is required by law to register with the secretary of state to conduct business or render professional services in this state under Chapter 9, Business Organizations Code.

(7) "Office" means:

(A) for a person that is not an individual or that is a corporation that is not required to or does not maintain a registered office in this state, the person's:

(i) principal office; and

(ii) principal place of business if not the same as the person's principal office; and

(B) for a corporation, limited partnership, limited liability partnership, limited liability company, or foreign filing entity that is required to maintain a registered office in this state, the entity's:

(i) registered office; and

(ii) principal office if not the same as the entity's registered office.

(8) "Partnership" means a joint venture or general partnership other than a limited partnership or a limited liability partnership.

(9) "Person" includes an individual, partnership, limited partnership, limited liability company, limited liability partnership, company, corporation, or foreign filing entity.

(10) "Registrant" means a person who has filed, or on whose behalf there has been filed, a certificate under this chapter or other law.

(11) "Representative" means a trustee, administrator, executor, independent executor, guardian, conservator, trustee in bankruptcy, receiver, or other person appointed by a court or by trust or will to have custody of, take possession of, have title to, or otherwise be empowered to control the person or property of any person.

Added by Acts 2007, 80th Leg., ch. 885, § 2.01, eff. April 1, 2009. Amended by Acts 2009, 81st Leg., ch. 84, § 62, eff. Sept. 1, 2009.

§ 71.003. Applicability of Chapter

(a) This chapter does not apply to an insurer authorized to engage in business in this state and described in Subchapter A, Chapter 805, Insurance Code, except as specifically provided by the Insurance Code.

(b) This chapter does not require a corporation, limited partnership, limited liability partnership, limited liability company, or foreign filing entity or its shareholders, associates, partners, or members to file a certificate to conduct business or render a professional service in this state under the name of the entity as stated in the certificate of formation, application filed with the office of the secretary of state, or other comparable document of the entity.

Added by Acts 2007, 80th Leg., ch. 885, § 2.01, eff. April 1, 2009. Amended by Acts 2009, 81st Leg., ch. 84, § 63, eff. Sept. 1, 2009.

SUBCHAPTER B. REQUIREMENTS APPLICABLE TO CERTAIN UNINCORPORATED PERSONS

§ 71.051 Certificate for Certain Unincorporated Persons

A person must file a certificate under this subchapter if the person regularly conducts business or renders a professional service in this state under an assumed name other than as a corporation, limited partnership, limited liability partnership, limited liability company, or foreign filing entity.

Added by Acts 2007, 80th Leg., ch. 885, § 2.01, eff. April 1, 2009. Amended by Acts 2009, 81st Leg., ch. 84, § 64, eff. Sept. 1, 2009.

§ 71.052 Contents of Certificate

The certificate must state:

(1) the assumed name under which the business is or is to be conducted or the professional service is or is to be rendered;

(2) if the registrant is:

(A) an individual, the individual's full name and residence address;

(B) a partnership:

(i) the venture or partnership name;

(ii) the venture or partnership office address;

(iii) the full name of each joint venturer or general partner; and

(iv) each joint venturer's or general partner's residence address if the venturer or partner is an individual or the joint venturer's or general partner's office address if the venturer or partner is not an individual;

(C) an estate:

(i) the name of the estate;

(ii) the estate's office address, if any;

(iii) the full name of each representative of the estate; and

(iv) each representative's residence address if the representative is an individual or the representative's office address if the representative is not an individual;

(D) a real estate investment trust:

(i) the name of the trust;

(ii) the address of the trust;

(iii) the full name of each trustee manager; and

(iv) each trustee manager's residence address if the trustee manager is an individual or the trustee manager's office address if the trustee manager is not an individual; or

(E) a company, other than a real estate investment trust:

(i) the name of the company;

(ii) the state, country, or other jurisdiction under the laws of which the company was organized; and

(iii) the company's office address;

(3) the period, not to exceed 10 years, during which the registrant will use the assumed name; and

(4) a statement specifying that the business that is or will be conducted or the professional service that is or will be rendered in the county under the assumed name is being or will be conducted or rendered as a proprietorship, sole practitioner, partnership, real estate investment trust, joint—stock company, or other form of unincorporated business or professional association or entity other than a limited partnership, limited liability company, limited liability partnership, or foreign filing entity.

Added by Acts 2007, 80th Leg., ch. 885, § 2.01, eff. April 1, 2009. Amended by Acts 2009, 81st Leg., ch. 84, § 65, eff. Sept. 1, 2009.

§ 71.053. Execution of Certificate

(a) The certificate must be executed and acknowledged:

(1) by each individual whose name is required to be stated in the certificate or the individual's representative or attorney-in-fact; and

(2) under oath on behalf of each person whose name is required to be stated in the certificate and who is not an individual, by:

(A) the person's representative or attorney-in-fact; or

(B) a joint venturer, general partner, trustee manager, officer, or other person having authority regarding the person comparable to the person's representative or attorney-in-fact.

(b) A certificate executed and acknowledged by an attorney-in-fact must include a statement that the attorney has been authorized in writing by the attorney's principal to execute and acknowledge the certificate.

Added by Acts 2007, 80th Leg., ch. 885, § 2.01, eff. April 1, 2009.

§ 71.054. Place of Filing

A person shall file the certificate in the office of the county clerk in each county in which the person:

(1) has or will maintain business or professional premises; or

(2) conducts business or renders a professional service, if the person does not or will not maintain business or professional premises in any county.

Added by Acts 2007, 80th Leg., ch. 885, § 2.01, eff. April 1, 2009.

SUBCHAPTER C. REQUIREMENTS APPLICABLE TO INCORPORATED BUSINESS OR PROFESSION AND CERTAIN OTHER ENTITIES

§ 71.101 Certificate for Incorporated Business or Profession, Limited Partnership, Limited Liability Partnership, Limited Liability Company, or Foreign Filing Entity

A corporation, limited partnership, limited liability partnership, limited liability company, or foreign filing entity must file a certificate under this subchapter if the entity:

(1) regularly conducts business or renders professional services in this state under an assumed name; or

(2) is required by law to use an assumed name in this state to conduct business or render professional services.

Added by Acts 2007, 80th Leg., ch. 885, § 2.01, eff. April 1, 2009. Amended by Acts 2009, 81st Leg., ch. 84, § 66, eff. Sept. 1, 2009.

§ 71.102 Contents of Certificate

The certificate must state:

(1) the assumed name under which the business is or is to be conducted or the professional service is or is to be rendered;

(2) the registrant's name as stated in the registrant's certificate of formation or application filed with the office of the secretary of state or other comparable document;

(3) the state, country, or other jurisdiction under the laws of which the registrant was incorporated or organized and the registrant's registered or similar office address in that state, country, or jurisdiction;

(4) the period, not to exceed 10 years, during which the registrant will use the assumed name;

(5) a statement specifying that the registrant is:

(A) a for-profit corporation, nonprofit corporation, professional corporation, professional association, or other type of corporation;

(B) a limited partnership, limited liability partnership, or limited liability company; or

(C) another type of incorporated business, professional or other association, or legal entity, foreign or domestic;

(6) the address of:

(A) the registrant's principal office; or

(B) if the registrant is not required to or does not maintain a registered office in this state:

(i) the registrant's office in this state; and

(ii) the registrant's place of business in this state and any office of the registrant outside this state, if the registrant is not incorporated or organized under the laws of this state; and

(7) the county or counties in this state where the registrant is or will be conducting business or rendering professional services under the assumed name.

Added by Acts 2007, 80th Leg., ch. 885, § 2.01, eff. April 1, 2009. Amended by Acts 2009, 81st Leg., ch. 84, § 67, eff. Sept. 1, 2009.

§ 71.103 Place of Filing

(a) The corporation, limited partnership, limited liability partnership, limited liability company, or foreign filing entity shall file the certificate in the office of the secretary of state and in the office or offices of each county clerk as specified by Subsection (b) or (c).

(b) An entity that maintains a registered office in this state shall file the certificate in the office of the county clerk of the county in which the entity's:

(1) registered office is located, if the entity's principal office is not located in this state; or

(2) principal office is located, if the entity's principal office is located in this state.

(c) An entity that does not maintain a registered office in this state shall file the certificate:

(1) in the office of the county clerk of the county in which the entity's office in this state is located; or

(2) in the office of the county clerk of the county in which the entity's principal place of business in this state is located, if:

(A) the entity is not incorporated or organized under the laws of this state; and

(B) the county in which the entity's principal place of business in this state is located is not the same county where the entity's office is located.

Added by Acts 2007, 80th Leg., ch. 885, § 2.01, eff. April 1, 2009. Amended by Acts 2009, 81st Leg., ch. 84, § 68, eff. Sept. 1, 2009.

§ 71.104. Execution of Certificate

(a) A certificate filed in the secretary of state's office must be executed by an officer, general partner, member, manager, or representative of or attorney-in-fact for the registrant.

(b) A certificate filed in a county clerk's office must be executed and acknowledged in the manner provided by Section 71.053 for a certificate filed under that section.

(c) A certificate executed by an attorney-in-fact must include a statement that the attorney has been authorized in writing by the attorney's principal to execute the certificate.

Added by Acts 2007, 80th Leg., ch. 885, § 2.01, eff. April 1, 2009.

SUBCHAPTER D. GENERAL PROVISIONS REGARDING ASSUMED NAME CERTIFICATE

§ 71.151. Duration and Renewal of Certificate

(a) A certificate is effective for a term not to exceed 10 years from the date the certificate is filed.

(b) A certificate is void at the end of the certificate's stated term, unless within six months preceding the certificate's expiration date the registrant files in the office of a county clerk and the secretary of state, if applicable, a renewal certificate complying with the requirements of this chapter for an original certificate.

(c) A registrant may renew a certificate under this section for any number of successive terms, but each term may not exceed 10 years.

Added by Acts 2007, 80th Leg., ch. 885, § 2.01, eff. April 1, 2009.

§ 71.152. Material Change in Information; New Certificate

(a) Not later than the 60th day after an event occurs that causes the information in a certificate to become materially misleading, a registrant must file a new certificate complying with this chapter in the office in which the original or renewal certificate was filed.

(b) An event that causes the information in a certificate to become materially misleading includes:

(1) a change in the name, identity, entity, form of business or professional organization, or location of a registrant;

(2) for a proprietorship or sole practitioner, a change in ownership; or

(3) for a partnership:

(A) the admission of a new partner or joint venturer; or

(B) the end of a general partner's or joint venturer's association with the partnership.

(c) A new certificate filed under this section is effective for a term not to exceed 10 years from the date the certificate is filed.

Added by Acts 2007, 80th Leg., ch. 885, § 2.01, eff. April 1, 2009. Amended by Acts 2009, 81st Leg., ch. 84, § 69, eff. Sept. 1, 2009.

§ 71.153. Abandonment of Use of Business or Professional Name

(a) A registrant who has filed a certificate under this chapter and who ceases to conduct business or render professional services in this state under the assumed name stated in the certificate may file a statement of abandonment of use of the assumed name in the office in which the registrant's certificate was filed.

(b) The statement of abandonment of use of an assumed name must state:

(1) the assumed name being abandoned;

(2) the date on which the certificate was filed in the office in which the statement of abandonment is being filed and in any other office in which the certificate was filed; and

(3) the registrant's name and residence or office address as required for a certificate filed under this chapter.

(c) A statement of abandonment must be executed and acknowledged in the same manner as if the registrant were filing a certificate under this chapter.

Added by Acts 2007, 80th Leg., ch. 885, § 2.01, eff. April 1, 2009.

§ 71.154. Index of Certificates

(a) The secretary of state and each county clerk shall keep an alphabetical index of:

(1) all assumed names that have been filed in the office of the respective officer; and

(2) the persons filing the certificates.

(b) A copy of a certificate or statement is presumptive evidence in any court in this state of the facts contained in the copy if the copy is certified to by:

(1) the county clerk in whose office the certificate or statement was filed; or

(2) the secretary of state.

Added by Acts 2007, 80th Leg., ch. 885, § 2.01, eff. April 1, 2009.

§ 71.155. Filing Fees

(a) The county clerk shall collect a fee of:

(1) $2 for filing each certificate or statement required or permitted to be filed under this chapter; and

(2) 50 cents for each name to be indexed.

(b) The secretary of state shall collect for the use of this state a fee of:

(1) $25 for indexing and filing each certificate or statement required or permitted to be filed under this chapter; and

(2) $10 for filing each statement of abandonment of use of an assumed name.

Added by Acts 2007, 80th Leg., ch. 885, § 2.01, eff. April 1, 2009.

§ 71.156. Prescribed Forms

(a) The secretary of state may prescribe a form to be used for filing a certificate or statement that complies with this chapter in the secretary's office or in the office of any county clerk in this state.

(b) Unless otherwise specifically provided by law, the use of a form prescribed under this section is not mandatory.

Added by Acts 2007, 80th Leg., ch. 885, § 2.01, eff. April 1, 2009.

§ 71.157. Effect of Filing

(a) This chapter does not give a registrant a right to use the assumed name in violation of the common or statutory law of unfair competition or unfair trade practices, common law copyright, or similar law.

(b) The filing of a certificate under this chapter does not in itself constitute actual use of the assumed name stated in the certificate for purposes of determining priority of rights.

Added by Acts 2007, 80th Leg., ch. 885, § 2.01, eff. April 1, 2009.

§ 71.158. Filing of Reproduction

(a) The secretary of state may accept for filing a photographic, photostatic, or similar reproduction of a signed original document required or authorized to be filed in the secretary's office under this chapter.

(b) A signature on a document required or authorized to be filed in the secretary of state's office under this chapter may be a facsimile.

Added by Acts 2007, 80th Leg., ch. 885, § 2.01, eff. April 1, 2009.

SUBCHAPTER E. PENALTIES

§ 71.201. Civil Action; Sanction

(a) A person's failure to comply with this chapter does not impair the validity of any contract or act by the person or prevent the person from defending any action or proceeding in any court of this state, but the person may not maintain in a court of this state an action or proceeding arising out of a contract or act in which an assumed name was used until an original, new, or renewed certificate has been filed as required by this chapter.

(b) In an action or proceeding brought against a person who has not complied with this chapter, the court may award the plaintiff or other party bringing the action or proceeding expenses incurred, including attorney's fees, in locating and effecting service of process on the defendant.

Added by Acts 2007, 80th Leg., ch. 885, § 2.01, eff. April 1, 2009.

§ 71.202. Criminal Penalty: General Violation

(a) A person commits an offense if the person:

(1) conducts business or renders a professional service in this state under an assumed name; and

(2) intentionally violates this chapter.

(b) An offense under this section is a Class A misdemeanor.

Added by Acts 2007, 80th Leg., ch. 885, § 2.01, eff. April 1, 2009.

§ 71.203. Criminal Penalty: Fraudulent Filing

(a) A person may not knowingly or intentionally sign and present for filing or cause to be presented for filing a document authorized or required to be filed under this chapter that:

(1) indicates that the person signing the document has the authority to act on behalf of the entity for which the document is presented and the person does not have that authority;

(2) contains a material false statement; or

(3) is forged.

(b) A person commits an offense if the person violates Subsection (a). An offense under this subsection is punishable as if it were an offense under Section 37.10, Penal Code.

Added by Acts 2007, 80th Leg., ch. 885, § 2.01, eff. April 1, 2009.

UTILITIES CODE

TITLE 1. GENERAL PROVISIONS

Chapter
1. General Provisions.

TITLE 2. PUBLIC UTILITY REGULATORY ACT

SUBTITLE A. PROVISIONS APPLICABLE TO ALL UTILITIES

11. General Provisions.
12. Organization of Commission.
13. Office of Public Utility Council.
14. Jurisdiction and Powers of Commission and Other Regulatory Authorities.
15. Judicial Review, Enforcement, and Penalties.
16. Commission Financing.
17. Customer Protection.

SUBTITLE B. ELECTRIC UTILITIES

31. General Provisions.
32. Jurisdiction and Powers of Commission and Other Regulatory Authorities.
33. Jurisdiction and Powers of Municipality.
34. Electrical Planning [Repealed].
35. Alternative Energy Providers.
36. Rates.
37. Certificates of Convenience and Necessity.
38. Regulation of Electric Services.
39. Restructuring of Electric Utility Industry.
40. Competition for Municipally Owned Utilities and River Authorities.
41. Electric Cooperatives and Competition.
43. Use of Electric Delivery System for Access to Broadband and Other Enhanced Services, Including Communications.

SUBTITLE C. TELECOMMUNICATIONS UTILITIES

51. General Provisions.
52. Commission Jurisdiction.
53. Rates.
54. Certificates.
55. Regulation of Telecommunications Services.
56. Telecommunications Assistance and Universal Service Fund.
57. Distance Learning and Other Advanced Services.
58. Incentive Regulation.
59. Infrastructure Plan.
60. Competitive Safeguards.
61. Information Technology Services [Repealed].
62. Broadcaster Safeguards.
63. Electronic Publishing [Repealed].
64. Customer Protection.
65. Deregulation of Certain Incumbent Local Exchange Company Markets.
66. State–Issued Cable and Video Franchise.

TITLE 3. GAS REGULATION

SUBTITLE A. GAS UTILITY REGULATORY ACT

Section
101. General Provisions and Office of Public Utility Counsel.
102. Jurisdiction and Powers of Railroad Commission and Other Regulatory Authorities.
103. Jurisdiction and Powers of Municipality.
104. Rates and Services.
105. Judicial Review; Enforcement and Penalties.

SUBTITLE B. REGULATION OF TRANSPORTATION AND USE

121. Gas Pipelines.
122. Gas Utility Pipeline Tax.
123. Use of Natural Gas For Agricultural Purposes.
124. Submetering to Mobile Home Parks and Apartment Houses.

TITLE 4. DELIVERY OF UTILITY SERVICES

SUBTITLE A. UTILITY CORPORATIONS AND OTHER PROVIDERS

161. Electric Cooperative Corporations.
162. Telephone Cooperative Corporations.
163. Joint Powers Agencies.
164. Joint Ownership of Electric Facilities by Public Entities.

SUBTITLE B. PROVISIONS REGULATING DELIVERY OF SERVICES

181. Miscellaneous Powers and Duties of Utilities.
182. Rights of Utility Customers.
183. Utility Deposits.
184. Electric and Water Metering.
185. Rating of Solar Energy Devices.
186. Provisions to Ensure the Reliability and Integrity of Utility Service.

TITLE 5. PROVISIONS AFFECTING THE OPERATION OF UTILITY FACILITIES

251. Underground Facility Damage Prevention and Safety.

Enactment

The Utilities Code was enacted by Acts 1997, 75th Leg., ch. 166, § 1, effective September 1, 1997, as a separate and distinct code. Sections 2 to 8 were amendatory provisions and § 9 was a repealer. Section 10 of the Act provides:

"Legislative Intent of No Substantive Change. This Act is enacted under Section 43, Article III, Texas Constitution. This Act

is intended as a recodification only, and no substantive change in law is intended by this Act."

TITLE 1. GENERAL PROVISIONS

CHAPTER 1. GENERAL PROVISIONS

Section
1.001. Purpose of Code.
1.002. Construction of Code.
1.003. Reference in Law to Statute Revised by Code.

§ 1.001. Purpose of Code

(a) This code is enacted as a part of the state's continuing statutory revision program, begun by the Texas Legislative Council in 1963 as directed by the legislature in the law codified as Section 323.007, Government Code. The program contemplates a topic-by-topic revision of the state's general and permanent statute law without substantive change.

(b) Consistent with the objectives of the statutory revision program, the purpose of this code is to make the law encompassed by this code more accessible and understandable by:

(1) rearranging the statutes into a more logical order;

(2) employing a format and numbering system designed to facilitate citation of the law and to accommodate future expansion of the law;

(3) eliminating repealed, duplicative, unconstitutional, expired, executed, and other ineffective provisions; and

(4) restating the law in modern American English to the greatest extent possible.

Acts 1997, 75th Leg., ch. 166, § 1, eff. Sept. 1, 1997.

§ 1.002. Construction of Code

Chapter 311, Government Code (Code Construction Act), applies to the construction of each provision in this code except as otherwise expressly provided by this code.

Acts 1997, 75th Leg., ch. 166, § 1, eff. Sept. 1, 1997.

§ 1.003. Reference in Law to Statute Revised by Code

A reference in a law to a statute or a part of a statute revised by this code is considered to be a reference to the part of this code that revises that statute or part of that statute.

Acts 1997, 75th Leg., ch. 166, § 1, eff. Sept. 1, 1997.

TITLE 2. PUBLIC UTILITY REGULATORY ACT

SUBTITLE A. PROVISIONS APPLICABLE TO ALL UTILITIES

CHAPTER 11. GENERAL PROVISIONS

Section
11.001. Short Title.
11.002. Purpose and Findings.
11.003. Definitions.
11.004. Definition of Utility.
11.0042. Definition of Affiliate.
11.005. Entity, Competitor, or Supplier Affected in Manner Other Than by Setting of Rates.
11.006. Person Determined to be Affiliate.
11.007. Administrative Procedure.
11.008. Liberal Construction.
11.009. Construction With Federal Authority.

§ 11.001. Short Title

This title may be cited as the Public Utility Regulatory Act.

Acts 1997, 75th Leg., ch. 166, § 1, eff. Sept. 1, 1997.

§ 11.002. Purpose and Findings

(a) This title is enacted to protect the public interest inherent in the rates and services of public utilities. The purpose of this title is to establish a comprehensive and adequate regulatory system for public utilities to assure rates, operations, and services that are just and reasonable to the consumers and to the utilities.

(b) Public utilities traditionally are by definition monopolies in the areas they serve. As a result, the normal forces of competition that regulate prices in a free enterprise society do not operate. Public agencies regulate utility rates, operations, and services as a substitute for competition.

(c) Significant changes have occurred in the telecommunications and electric power industries since the Public Utility Regulatory Act was originally adopted. Changes in technology and market structure have increased the need for minimum standards of service quality, customer service, and fair business practices to ensure high-quality service to customers and a healthy marketplace where competition is permitted by law. It is the purpose of this title to grant the Public Utility Commission of Texas authority to make and enforce rules necessary to protect customers of telecommunications and electric services consistent with the public interest.

Acts 1997, 75th Leg., ch. 166, § 1, eff. Sept. 1, 1997. Amended by Acts 1999, 76th Leg., ch. 1579, § 1, eff. Aug. 30, 1999.

§ 11.003. Definitions

In this title:

(1) "Affected person" means:

(A) a public utility or electric cooperative affected by an action of a regulatory authority;

(B) a person whose utility service or rates are affected by a proceeding before a regulatory authority; or

(C) a person who:

(i) is a competitor of a public utility with respect to a service performed by the utility; or

(ii) wants to enter into competition with a public utility.

(2) "Affiliate" means:

(A) a person who directly or indirectly owns or holds at least five percent of the voting securities of a public utility;

(B) a person in a chain of successive ownership of at least five percent of the voting securities of a public utility;

(C) a corporation that has at least five percent of its voting securities owned or controlled, directly or indirectly, by a public utility;

(D) a corporation that has at least five percent of its voting securities owned or controlled, directly or indirectly, by:

(i) a person who directly or indirectly owns or controls at least five percent of the voting securities of a public utility; or

(ii) a person in a chain of successive ownership of at least five percent of the voting securities of a public utility;

(E) a person who is an officer or director of a public utility or of a corporation in a chain of successive ownership of at least five percent of the voting securities of a public utility; or

(F) a person determined to be an affiliate under Section 11.006.

(3) "Allocation" means the division among municipalities or among municipalities and unincorporated areas of the plant, revenues, expenses, taxes, and reserves of a utility used to provide public utility service in a municipality or for a municipality and unincorporated areas.

(4) "Commission" means the Public Utility Commission of Texas.

(5) "Commissioner" means a member of the Public Utility Commission of Texas.

(6) "Cooperative corporation" means:

(A) an electric cooperative; or

(B) a telephone cooperative corporation organized under Chapter 162 or a predecessor statute to Chapter 162 and operating under that chapter.

(7) "Corporation" means a domestic or foreign corporation, joint-stock company, or association, and each lessee, assignee, trustee, receiver, or other successor in interest of the corporation, company, or association, that has any of the powers or privileges of a corporation not possessed by an individual or partnership. The term does not include a municipal corporation or electric cooperative, except as expressly provided by this title.

(8) "Counsellor" means the public utility counsel.

(9) "Electric cooperative" means:

(A) a corporation organized under Chapter 161 or a predecessor statute to Chapter 161 and operating under that chapter; or

(B) a corporation organized as an electric cooperative in a state other than Texas that has obtained a certificate of authority to conduct affairs in the State of Texas

(C) Deleted by Acts 2003, 78th Leg., ch. 1327, § 1.

(10) "Facilities" means all of the plant and equipment of a public utility, and includes the tangible and intangible property, without limitation, owned, operated, leased, licensed, used, controlled, or supplied for, by, or in connection with the business of the public utility.

(11) "Municipally owned utility" means a utility owned, operated, and controlled by a municipality or by a nonprofit corporation the directors of which are appointed by one or more municipalities.

(12) "Office" means the Office of Public Utility Counsel.

(13) "Order" means all or a part of a final disposition by a regulatory authority in a matter other than rulemaking, without regard to whether the disposition is affirmative or negative or injunctive or declaratory. The term includes:

(A) the issuance of a certificate of convenience and necessity; and

(B) the setting of a rate.

(14) "Person" includes an individual, a partnership of two or more persons having a joint or common interest, a mutual or cooperative association, and a corporation, but does not include an electric cooperative.

(15) "Proceeding" means a hearing, investigation, inquiry, or other procedure for finding facts or making a decision under this title. The term includes a denial of relief or dismissal of a complaint.

(16) "Rate" includes:

(A) any compensation, tariff, charge, fare, toll, rental, or classification that is directly or indirectly demanded, observed, charged, or collected by a public utility for a service, product, or commodity described in the definition of utility in Section 31.002 or 51.002; and

(B) a rule, practice, or contract affecting the compensation, tariff, charge, fare, toll, rental, or classification.

(17) "Ratemaking proceeding" means a proceeding in which a rate is changed.

(18) "Regulatory authority" means either the commission or the governing body of a municipality, in accordance with the context.

(19) "Service" has its broadest and most inclusive meaning. The term includes any act performed, anything supplied, and any facilities used or supplied by a public utility in the performance of the utility's duties under this title to its patrons, employees, other public utilities, an electric cooperative, and the public. The term also includes the interchange of facilities between two or more public utilities. The term does not include the printing, distribution, or sale of advertising in a telephone directory.

(20) "Test year" means the most recent 12 months, beginning on the first day of a calendar or fiscal year quarter, for which operating data for a public utility are available.

(21) "Trade association" means a nonprofit, cooperative, and voluntarily joined association of business or professional persons who are employed by public utilities or utility competitors to assist the public utility industry, a utility competitor, or the industry's or competitor's employees in dealing with mutual business or professional problems and in promoting their common interest.

Acts 1997, 75th Leg., ch. 166, § 1, eff. Sept. 1, 1997. Amended by Acts 1999, 76th Leg., ch. 405, § 1, eff. Sept. 1, 1999; Acts 2003, 78th Leg., ch. 1327, § 1, eff. Sept. 1, 2003.

§ 11.004. Definition of Utility

In Subtitle A,[1] "public utility" or "utility" means:

(1) an electric utility, as that term is defined by Section 31.002; or

(2) a public utility or utility, as those terms are defined by Section 51.002.

Acts 1997, 75th Leg., ch. 166, § 1, eff. Sept. 1, 1997.

[1] V.T.C.A., Utilities Code § 11.001.

§ 11.0042. Definition of Affiliate

(a) The term "person" or "corporation" as used in the definition of "affiliate" provided by Section 11.003(2) does not include:

(1) a broker or dealer registered under the Securities Exchange Act of 1934 (15 U.S.C. Section 78a et seq.), as amended;

(2) a bank or insurance company as defined under the Securities Exchange Act of 1934 (15 U.S.C. Section 78a et seq.), as amended;

(3) an investment adviser registered under state law or the Investment Advisers Act of 1940 (15 U.S.C. Section 80b–1 et seq.); or

(4) an investment company registered under the Investment Company Act of 1940 (15 U.S.C. Section 80a–1 et seq.); or

(5) an employee benefit plan, pension fund, endowment fund, or other similar entity that may, directly or indirectly, own, hold, or control five percent or more of the voting securities of a public utility or the parent corporation of a public utility if the entity did not acquire the voting securities:

(A) for the purpose of or with the effect of changing or influencing the control of the issuer of the securities; or

(B) in connection with or as a participant in any transaction that changes or influences the control of the issuer of the securities.

(b) For the purpose of determining whether a person is an affiliate under Section 11.006(a)(3), the term "person" does not include an entity that may, directly or indirectly, own, hold, or control the voting securities of a public utility or the parent corporation of a public utility if the entity did not acquire the voting securities:

(1) for the purpose of or with the effect of changing or influencing the control of the issuer of the securities; or

(2) in connection with or as a participant in any transaction that changes or influences the control of the issuer of the securities.

(c) A report filed by an entity described by Subsection (a)(5) or (b) with the Securities and Exchange Commission is conclusive evidence of the entity's intent if the report confirms that the voting securities were not acquired:

(1) for the purpose of or with the effect of changing or influencing the control of the issuer of the securities; or

(2) in connection with or as a participant in any transaction that changes or influences the control of the issuer of the securities.

Added by Acts 2005, 79th Leg., ch. 413, § 2, eff. June 17, 2005.

§ 11.005. Entity, Competitor, or Supplier Affected in Manner Other Than by Setting of Rates

In this title, an entity, including a utility competitor or utility supplier, is considered to be affected in a manner other than by the setting of rates for that class of customer if during a relevant calendar year the entity provides fuel, utility-related goods, utility-related products, or utility-related services to a regulated or unregulated provider of telecommunications or electric services or to an affiliate in an amount equal to the greater of $10,000 or 10 percent of the person's business.

Acts 1997, 75th Leg., ch. 166, § 1, eff. Sept. 1, 1997.

§ 11.006. Person Determined to be Affiliate

(a) The commission may determine that a person is an affiliate for purposes of this title if the commission after notice and hearing finds that the person:

(1) actually exercises substantial influence or control over the policies and actions of a public utility;

(2) is a person over which a public utility exercises the control described by Subdivision (1);

(3) is under common control with a public utility; or

(4) together with one or more persons with whom the person is related by ownership or blood relationship, or by action in concert, actually exercises substantial influence over the policies and actions of a public utility even though neither person may qualify as an affiliate individually.

(b) For purposes of Subsection (a)(3), "common control with a public utility" means the direct or indirect possession of the power to direct or cause the direction of the management and policies of another, without regard to whether that power is established through ownership or voting of securities or by any other direct or indirect means.

Acts 1997, 75th Leg., ch. 166, § 1, eff. Sept. 1, 1997.

§ 11.007. Administrative Procedure

(a) Chapter 2001, Government Code, applies to a proceeding under this title except to the extent inconsistent with this title.

(b) A communication of a member or employee of the commission with any person, including a party or a party's representative, is governed by Section 2001.061, Government Code.

Acts 1997, 75th Leg., ch. 166, § 1, eff. Sept. 1, 1997.

§ 11.008. Liberal Construction

This title shall be construed liberally to promote the effectiveness and efficiency of regulation of public utilities to the extent that this construction preserves the validity of this title and its provisions.

Acts 1997, 75th Leg., ch. 166, § 1, eff. Sept. 1, 1997.

§ 11.009. Construction With Federal Authority

This title shall be construed to apply so as not to conflict with any authority of the United States.

Acts 1997, 75th Leg., ch. 166, § 1, eff. Sept. 1, 1997.

CHAPTER 12. ORGANIZATION OF COMMISSION

SUBCHAPTER A. GENERAL PROVISIONS

Section
12.001. Public Utility Commission of Texas.
12.002. Office.
12.003. Seal.
12.004. Representation by the Attorney General.
12.005. Application of Sunset Act.

SUBCHAPTER B. COMMISSION APPOINTMENT AND FUNCTIONS

12.051. Appointment; Term.
12.052. Presiding Officer.
12.053. Membership Qualifications.
12.054. Removal of Commissioner.
12.055. Prohibition on Seeking Another Office.
12.056. Effect of Vacancy.
12.057. Compensation.
12.058. Meetings.
12.059. Training Program for Commissioners.

SUBCHAPTER C. COMMISSION PERSONNEL

12.101. Commission Employees.

Section
12.102. Duties of Employees.
12.103. Duties of Executive Director.
12.104. Repealed.
12.105. Career Ladder Program; Performance Evaluations; Merit Pay.
12.106. Equal Employment Opportunity Policy Statement.

SUBCHAPTER D. PROHIBITED RELATIONSHIPS AND ACTIVITIES
12.151. Registered Lobbyist.
12.152. Conflict of Interest.
12.153. Relationship With Trade Association.
12.154. Prohibited Activities.
12.155. Prohibition on Employment or Representation.
12.156. Qualifications and Standards of Conduct Information.

SUBCHAPTER E. PUBLIC INTEREST INFORMATION AND REPORTS
12.201. Public Interest Information.
12.202. Public Participation.
12.203. Annual Report.
12.204. Internet for Hearings and Meetings.

SUBCHAPTER F. HISTORICALLY UNDERUTILIZED BUSINESSES
12.251. Definition.
12.252. Commission Authority.
12.253. Report Required.
12.254. Discrimination Prohibited.
12.255. Cause of Action Not Created.

SUBCHAPTER A. GENERAL PROVISIONS

§ 12.001. Public Utility Commission of Texas

The Public Utility Commission of Texas exercises the jurisdiction and powers conferred by this title.

Acts 1997, 75th Leg., ch. 166, § 1, eff. Sept. 1, 1997.

§ 12.002. Office

(a) The principal office of the commission is in Austin.

(b) The office shall be open daily during usual business hours. The office is not required to be open on Saturday, Sunday, or a legal holiday.

Acts 1997, 75th Leg., ch. 166, § 1, eff. Sept. 1, 1997.

§ 12.003. Seal

(a) The commission has a seal bearing the inscription: "Public Utility Commission of Texas."

(b) The seal shall be affixed to each record and to an authentication of a copy of a record. The commission may require the seal to be affixed to other instruments.

(c) A court of this state shall take judicial notice of the seal.

Acts 1997, 75th Leg., ch. 166, § 1, eff. Sept. 1, 1997.

§ 12.004. Representation by the Attorney General

The attorney general shall represent the commission in a matter before a state court, a court of the United States, or a federal public utility regulatory commission.

Acts 1997, 75th Leg., ch. 166, § 1, eff. Sept. 1, 1997.

§ 12.005. Application of Sunset Act

The Public Utility Commission of Texas is subject to Chapter 325, Government Code (Texas Sunset Act). Unless continued in existence as provided by that chapter or by Chapter 39, the commission is abolished and this title expires September 1, 2013 .

Acts 1997, 75th Leg., ch. 166, § 1, eff. Sept. 1, 1997. Amended by Acts 1999, 76th Leg., ch. 405, § 2, eff. Sept. 1, 1999; Acts 1999, 76th Leg., ch. 1212, § 1, eff. Sept. 1, 1999; Acts 2005, 79th Leg., ch. 797, § 1, eff. Sept. 1, 2005; Acts 2005, 79th Leg., ch. 1227, § 3.06(a), eff. Sept. 1, 2005; Acts 2011, 82nd Leg., ch. 1232 (S.B. 652), § 1.08, eff. June 17, 2011.

SUBCHAPTER B. COMMISSION APPOINTMENT AND FUNCTIONS

§ 12.051. Appointment; Term

(a) The commission is composed of three commissioners appointed by the governor with the advice and consent of the senate.

(b) An appointment to the commission shall be made without regard to the race, color, disability, sex, religion, age, or national origin of the appointee.

(c) Commissioners serve staggered, six-year terms.

Acts 1997, 75th Leg., ch. 166, § 1, eff. Sept. 1, 1997.

§ 12.052. Presiding Officer

(a) The governor shall designate a commissioner as the presiding officer.

(b) The presiding officer serves in that capacity at the pleasure of the governor.

Acts 1997, 75th Leg., ch. 166, § 1, eff. Sept. 1, 1997.

§ 12.053. Membership Qualifications

(a) To be eligible for appointment, a commissioner must be:

(1) a qualified voter;

(2) a citizen of the United States; and

(3) a representative of the general public.

(b) A person is not eligible for appointment as a commissioner if the person:

(1) at any time during the two years preceding appointment:

(A) personally served as an officer, director, owner, employee, partner, or legal representative of a public utility, affiliate, or direct competitor of a public utility; or

(B) owned or controlled, directly or indirectly, stocks or bonds of any class with a value of $10,000 or more in a public utility, affiliate, or direct competitor of a public utility; or

(2) is not qualified to serve under Section 12.151, 12.152, or 12.153.

Acts 1997, 75th Leg., ch. 166, § 1, eff. Sept. 1, 1997.

§ 12.054. Removal of Commissioner

(a) It is a ground for removal from the commission if a commissioner:

(1) does not have at the time of appointment or maintain during service on the commission the qualifications required by Section 12.053;

(2) violates a prohibition provided by Section 12.053 or by Subchapter D; [1]

(3) cannot discharge the commissioner's duties for a substantial part of the term for which the commissioner is appointed because of illness or disability; or

(4) is absent from more than half of the regularly scheduled commission meetings that the commissioner is eligible to attend during a calendar year unless the absence is excused by majority vote of the commission.

(b) The validity of an action of the commission is not affected by the fact that the action is taken when a ground for removal of a commissioner exists.

(c) If the executive director has knowledge that a potential ground for removal exists, the executive director shall notify the presiding officer of the commission of the potential ground. The presiding officer shall then notify the governor and the attorney general that a potential ground for removal exists. If the potential ground for removal involves the presiding officer, the executive director shall notify the next highest officer of the commission, who shall notify the governor and the attorney general that a potential ground for removal exists.

Acts 1997, 75th Leg., ch. 166, § 1, eff. Sept. 1, 1997.

[1] V.T.C.A., Utilities Code § 12.151 et seq.

§ 12.055. Prohibition on Seeking Another Office

A person may not seek nomination or election to another civil office of this state or of the United States while serving as a commissioner. If a commissioner files for nomination or election to another civil office of this state or of the United States, the person's office as commissioner immediately becomes vacant, and the governor shall appoint a successor.

Acts 1997, 75th Leg., ch. 166, § 1, eff. Sept. 1, 1997.

§ 12.056. Effect of Vacancy

A vacancy or disqualification does not prevent the remaining commissioner or commissioners from exercising the powers of the commission.

Acts 1997, 75th Leg., ch. 166, § 1, eff. Sept. 1, 1997.

§ 12.057. Compensation

The annual salary of the commissioners is determined by the legislature.

Acts 1997, 75th Leg., ch. 166, § 1, eff. Sept. 1, 1997.

§ 12.058. Meetings

The commission shall hold meetings at its office and at other convenient places in this state as expedient and necessary for the proper performance of the commission's duties.

Acts 1997, 75th Leg., ch. 166, § 1, eff. Sept. 1, 1997.

§ 12.059. Training Program for Commissioners

(a) Before a commissioner may assume the commissioner's duties and before the commissioner may be confirmed by the senate, the commissioner must complete at least one course of the training program established under this section.

(b) A training program established under this section shall provide information to the commissioner regarding:

(1) the enabling legislation that created the commission and its policymaking body to which the commissioner is appointed to serve;

(2) the programs operated by the commission;

(3) the role and functions of the commission;

(4) the rules of the commission with an emphasis on the rules that relate to disciplinary and investigatory authority;

(5) the current budget for the commission;

(6) the results of the most recent formal audit of the commission;

(7) the requirements of Chapters 551, 552, and 2001, Government Code;

(8) the requirements of the conflict of interest laws and other laws relating to public officials; and

(9) any applicable ethics policies adopted by the commission or the Texas Ethics Commission.

(c) A person who is appointed to the commission is entitled to reimbursement, as provided by the General Appropriations Act, for the travel expenses incurred in attending the training program regardless of whether the attendance at the program occurs before or after the person qualifies for office.

Acts 1997, 75th Leg., ch. 166, § 1, eff. Sept. 1, 1997. Amended by Acts 2005, 79th Leg., ch. 797, § 2, eff. Sept. 1, 2005.

SUBCHAPTER C. COMMISSION PERSONNEL

§ 12.101. Commission Employees

The commission shall employ:

(1) an executive director; and

(2) officers and other employees the commission considers necessary to administer this title.

Acts 1997, 75th Leg., ch. 166, § 1, eff. Sept. 1, 1997. Amended by Acts 1999, 76th Leg., ch. 405, § 3, eff. Sept. 1, 1999.

§ 12.102. Duties of Employees

The commission shall develop and implement policies that clearly separate the policymaking responsibilities of the commission and the management responsibilities of the commission employees.

Acts 1997, 75th Leg., ch. 166, § 1, eff. Sept. 1, 1997. Amended by Acts 2005, 79th Leg., ch. 797, § 3, eff. Sept. 1, 2005.

§ 12.103. Duties of Executive Director

The executive director is responsible for the daily operations of the commission and shall coordinate the activities of commission employees.

Acts 1997, 75th Leg., ch. 166, § 1, eff. Sept. 1, 1997.

§ 12.104. Repealed by Acts 1999, 76th Leg., ch. 405, § 61(1), eff. Sept. 1, 1999

§ 12.105. Career Ladder Program; Performance Evaluations; Merit Pay

(a) The executive director or the executive director's designee shall develop an intra-agency career ladder program that addresses opportunities for mobility and advancement for commission employees. The program shall require intra-agency posting of each position concurrently with any public posting.

(b) The executive director or the executive director's designee shall develop a system of annual performance evaluations that are based on documented employee performance. Merit pay for commission employees must be based on the system established under this subsection.

Acts 1997, 75th Leg., ch. 166, § 1, eff. Sept. 1, 1997.

§ 12.106. Equal Employment Opportunity Policy Statement

(a) The executive director or the executive director's designee shall prepare and maintain a written policy statement to ensure implementation of a program of equal employment opportunity under which all personnel transactions are made without regard to race, color, disability, sex, religion, age, or national origin.

(b) The policy statement under Subsection (a) must include:

(1) personnel policies, including policies related to recruitment, evaluation, selection, appointment, training, and promotion of personnel, that are in compliance with the requirements of Chapter 21, Labor Code;

(2) a comprehensive analysis of the commission workforce that meets federal and state guidelines;

(3) procedures by which a determination can be made about the extent of underuse in the commission workforce of all persons for whom federal or state guidelines encourage a more equitable balance; and

(4) reasonable methods to appropriately address the underuse.

(c) A policy statement prepared under Subsection (b) must:

(1) cover an annual period;

(2) be updated at least annually;

(3) be reviewed by the Commission on Human Rights for compliance with Subsection (b)(1); and

(4) be filed with the governor's office.

(d) The governor's office shall deliver a biennial report to the legislature based on the information received under Subsection (c). The report may be made separately or as a part of other biennial reports to the legislature.

Acts 1997, 75th Leg., ch. 166, § 1, eff. Sept. 1, 1997.

SUBCHAPTER D. PROHIBITED RELATIONSHIPS AND ACTIVITIES

§ 12.151. Registered Lobbyist

A person required to register as a lobbyist under Chapter 305, Government Code, because of the person's activities for compensation on behalf of a profession related to the operation of the commission may not serve as a commissioner.

Acts 1997, 75th Leg., ch. 166, § 1, eff. Sept. 1, 1997. Amended by Acts 1999, 76th Leg., ch. 405, § 4, eff. Sept. 1, 1999.

§ 12.152. Conflict of Interest

(a) A person is not eligible for appointment as a commissioner or executive director of the commission if:

(1) the person serves on the board of directors of a company that supplies fuel, utility-related services, or utility-related products to regulated or unregulated electric or telecommunications utilities; or

(2) the person or the person's spouse:

(A) is employed by or participates in the management of a business entity or other organization that is regulated by or receives funds from the commission;

(B) directly or indirectly owns or controls more than a 10 percent interest or a pecuniary interest with a value exceeding $10,000 in:

(i) a business entity or other organization that is regulated by or receives funds from the commission; or

(ii) a utility competitor, utility supplier, or other entity affected by a commission decision in a manner other than by the setting of rates for that class of customer;

(C) uses or receives a substantial amount of tangible goods, services, or funds from the commission, other than compensation or reimbursement authorized by law for commission membership, attendance, or expenses; or

(D) notwithstanding Paragraph (B), has an interest in a mutual fund or retirement fund in which more than 10 percent of the fund's holdings at the time of appointment is in a single utility, utility competitor, or utility supplier in this state and the person does not disclose this information to the governor, senate, commission, or other entity, as appropriate.

(b) A person otherwise ineligible because of Subsection (a)(2)(B) may be appointed to the commission and serve as a commissioner or may be employed as executive director if the person:

(1) notifies the attorney general and commission that the person is ineligible because of Subsection (a)(2)(B); and

(2) divests the person or the person's spouse of the ownership or control:

(A) before beginning service or employment; or

(B) if the person is already serving or employed, within a reasonable time.

Acts 1997, 75th Leg., ch. 166, § 1, eff. Sept. 1, 1997. Amended by Acts 1999, 76th Leg., ch. 405, § 4, eff. Sept. 1, 1999.

§ 12.153. Relationship With Trade Association

A person may not serve as a commissioner or be a commission employee who is employed in a "bona fide executive, administrative, or professional capacity," as that phrase is used for purposes of establishing an exemption to the overtime provisions of the federal Fair Labor Standards Act of 1938 (29 U.S.C. Section 201 et seq.), if the person is:

(1) an officer, employee, or paid consultant of a trade association; or

(2) the spouse of an officer, manager, or paid consultant of a trade association.

Acts 1997, 75th Leg., ch. 166, § 1, eff. Sept. 1, 1997. Amended by Acts 2005, 79th Leg., ch. 797, § 4, eff. Sept. 1, 2005.

§ 12.154. Prohibited Activities

(a) During the period of service with the commission, a commissioner or commission employee may not:

(1) have a pecuniary interest, including an interest as an officer, director, partner, owner, employee, attorney, or consultant, in:

(A) a public utility or affiliate; or

(B) a person a significant portion of whose business consists of furnishing goods or services to public utilities or affiliates;

(2) directly or indirectly own or control securities in a public utility, affiliate, or direct competitor of a public utility; or

(3) accept a gift, gratuity, or entertainment from:

(A) a public utility, affiliate, or direct competitor of a public utility;

(B) a person a significant portion of whose business consists of furnishing goods or services to public utilities, affiliates, or direct competitors of public utilities; or

(C) an agent, representative, attorney, employee, officer, owner, director, or partner of a person described by Paragraph (A) or (B).

(b) A commissioner or a commission employee may not directly or indirectly solicit, request from, or suggest or recommend to a public utility or an agent, representative, attorney, employee, officer, owner, director, or partner of a public utility the appointment to a position or the employment of a person by the public utility or affiliate.

(c) A person may not give or offer to give a gift, gratuity, employment, or entertainment to a commissioner or commission employee if that person is:

(1) a public utility, affiliate, or direct competitor of a public utility;

(2) a person who furnishes goods or services to a public utility, affiliate, or direct competitor of a public utility; or

(3) an agent, representative, attorney, employee, officer, owner, director, or partner of a person described by Subdivision (1) or (2).

(d) A public utility, affiliate, or direct competitor of a public utility or a person furnishing goods or services to a public utility, affiliate, or direct competitor of a public utility may not aid, abet, or participate with a commissioner, commission employee, or former commission employee in conduct that violates Subsection (a)(3) or (c).

(e) Subsection (a)(1) does not apply to an interest in a nonprofit group or association, other than a trade association, that is solely supported by gratuitous contributions of money, property, or services.

(f) It is not a violation of this section if a commissioner or commission employee, on becoming the owner of stocks, bonds, or another pecuniary interest in a public utility, affiliate, or direct competitor of a public utility otherwise than voluntarily, informs the commission and the attorney general of the ownership and divests the ownership or interest within a reasonable time.

(g) It is not a violation of this section if a pecuniary interest is held indirectly by ownership of an interest in a retirement system, institution, or fund that in the normal course of business invests in diverse securities independently of the control of the commissioner or commission employee.

(h) This section does not apply to a contract for a public utility product or service or equipment for use of a public utility product when a commissioner or commission employee is acting as a consumer.

(i) In this section, a "pecuniary interest" includes income, compensation, and payment of any kind, in addition to an ownership interest.

Acts 1997, 75th Leg., ch. 166, § 1, eff. Sept. 1, 1997.

§ 12.155. Prohibition on Employment or Representation

(a) A commissioner, a commission employee, or an employee of the State Office of Administrative Hearings involved in hearing utility cases may not:

(1) be employed by a public utility that was in the scope of the commissioner's or employee's official responsibility while the commissioner or employee was associated with the commission or the State Office of Administrative Hearings; or

(2) represent a person before the commission or State Office of Administrative Hearings or a court in a matter:

(A) in which the commissioner or employee was personally involved while associated with the commission or State Office of Administrative Hearings; or

(B) that was within the commissioner's or employee's official responsibility while the commissioner or employee was associated with the commission or State Office of Administrative Hearings.

(b) The prohibition of Subsection (a)(1) applies until the:

(1) second anniversary of the date the commissioner ceases to serve as a commissioner; and

(2) first anniversary of the date the employee's employment with the commission or State Office of Administrative Hearings ceases.

(c) The prohibition of Subsection (a)(2) applies while a commissioner, commission employee, or employee of the State Office of Administrative Hearings involved in hearing utility cases is associated with the commission or State Office of Administrative Hearings and at any time after.

Acts 1997, 75th Leg., ch. 166, § 1, eff. Sept. 1, 1997.

§ 12.156. Qualifications and Standards of Conduct Information

The executive director or the executive director's designee shall provide to commissioners and commission employees as often as necessary information regarding their:

(1) qualifications for office or employment under this title; and

(2) responsibilities under applicable laws relating to standards of conduct for state officers and employees.

Acts 1997, 75th Leg., ch. 166, § 1, eff. Sept. 1, 1997.

SUBCHAPTER E. PUBLIC INTEREST INFORMATION AND REPORTS

§ 12.201. Public Interest Information

(a) The commission shall prepare information of public interest describing the functions of the commission and the commission's procedures by which a complaint is filed with and resolved by the commission. The commission shall make the information available to the public and appropriate state agencies.

(b) The commission by rule shall establish methods by which consumers and service recipients are notified of the name, mailing address, and telephone number of the commission for the purpose of directing complaints to the commission.

Acts 1997, 75th Leg., ch. 166, § 1, eff. Sept. 1, 1997.

§ 12.202. Public Participation

(a) The commission shall develop and implement policies that provide the public with a reasonable opportunity to appear before the commission and to speak on any issue under the jurisdiction of the commission.

(b) The commission shall comply with federal and state laws related to program and facility accessibility.

(c) The commission shall prepare and maintain a written plan that describes how a person who does not speak English may be provided reasonable access to the commission's programs and services.

Acts 1997, 75th Leg., ch. 166, § 1, eff. Sept. 1, 1997.

§ 12.203. Annual Report

(a) The commission shall prepare annually a complete and detailed written report accounting for all funds received and disbursed by the commission during the preceding fiscal year. The annual report must meet the reporting requirements applicable to financial reporting in the General Appropriations Act.

(b) In the annual report issued in the year preceding the convening of each regular session of the legislature, the commission shall make suggestions regarding modification and improvement of the commission's statutory authority and for the improvement of utility regulation in general that the commission considers appropriate for protecting and furthering the interest of the public.

Acts 1997, 75th Leg., ch. 166, § 1, eff. Sept. 1, 1997.

§ 12.204. Internet for Hearings and Meetings

The commission shall make publicly accessible without charge live Internet video of all public hearings and meetings the commission holds for viewing from the Internet website found at http://www.puc.state.tx.us. The commission may recover the costs of administering this section by imposing an assessment against a:

(1) public utility;

(2) corporation described by Section 32.053;

(3) retail electric provider that serves more than 250,000 customers; or

(4) power generation company that owns more than 5,000 megawatts of installed capacity in this state.

Added by Acts 2009, 81st Leg., ch. 400, § 1, eff. Sept. 1, 2009.

Section 3 of Acts 2009, 81st Leg., ch. 400 provides:

"Sec. 3. The change in law made by this Act applies to a hearing or meeting held on or after the effective date [Sept. 1, 2009] of this Act. A hearing or meeting held before the effective date of this Act is governed by the law as it existed immediately before that date, and that law is continued in effect for that purpose."

SUBCHAPTER F. HISTORICALLY UNDERUTILIZED BUSINESSES

§ 12.251. Definition

In this subchapter, "historically underutilized business" has the meaning assigned by Section 481.101, Government Code.

Acts 1997, 75th Leg., ch. 166, § 1, eff. Sept. 1, 1997.

§ 12.252. Commission Authority

The commission, after notice and hearing, may require each utility subject to regulation under this title to make an effort to overcome the underuse of historically underutilized businesses.

Acts 1997, 75th Leg., ch. 166, § 1, eff. Sept. 1, 1997.

§ 12.253. Report Required

The commission shall require each utility subject to regulation under this title to prepare and submit to the commission a comprehensive annual report detailing its use of historically underutilized businesses.

Acts 1997, 75th Leg., ch. 166, § 1, eff. Sept. 1, 1997.

§ 12.254. Discrimination Prohibited

The rules adopted under this subchapter may not be used to discriminate against a citizen on the basis of sex, race, color, creed, or national origin.

Acts 1997, 75th Leg., ch. 166, § 1, eff. Sept. 1, 1997.

§ 12.255. Cause of Action Not Created

This subchapter does not create a public or private cause of action.

Acts 1997, 75th Leg., ch. 166, § 1, eff. Sept. 1, 1997.

CHAPTER 13. OFFICE OF PUBLIC UTILITY COUNSEL

SUBCHAPTER A. GENERAL PROVISIONS; POWERS AND DUTIES

Section
13.001. Office of Public Utility Counsel.
13.002. Application of Sunset Act.
13.003. Office Powers and Duties.
13.004. Alternative Dispute Resolution Procedures.
13.005. Complaints.
13.006. Technology Policy.
13.007. Expired.

SUBCHAPTER B. PUBLIC UTILITY COUNSEL

13.021. Appointment; Term.
13.022. Qualifications.
13.023. Grounds for Removal.
13.024. Prohibited Acts.

SUBCHAPTER C. OFFICE PERSONNEL

13.041. Personnel.
13.042. Conflict of Interest.
13.043. Prohibition on Employment or Representation.
13.044. Career Ladder Program; Performance Evaluations; Merit Pay.
13.045. Equal Employment Opportunity Policy Statement.
13.046. Qualifications and Standards of Conduct Information.

SUBCHAPTER D. PUBLIC INTEREST INFORMATION AND REPORTS

Section
13.061. Public Interest Information.
13.062. Public Participation.
13.063. Annual Reports.
13.064. Public Hearing.

SUBCHAPTER A. GENERAL PROVISIONS; POWERS AND DUTIES

§ 13.001. Office of Public Utility Counsel

The independent office of public utility counsel represents the interests of residential and small commercial consumers.

Acts 1997, 75th Leg., ch. 166, § 1, eff. Sept. 1, 1997.

§ 13.002. Application of Sunset Act

The Office of Public Utility Counsel is subject to Chapter 325, Government Code (Texas Sunset Act). Unless continued in existence as provided by that chapter, the office is abolished and this chapter expires September 1, 2023 .

Acts 1997, 75th Leg., ch. 166, § 1, eff. Sept. 1, 1997. Amended by Acts 1999, 76th Leg., ch. 405, § 5, eff. Sept. 1, 1999; Acts 1999, 76th Leg., ch. 1212, § 2, eff. Sept. 1, 1999; Acts 2005, 79th Leg., ch. 300, § 1, eff. Sept. 1, 2005; Acts 2005, 79th Leg., ch. 1227, § 3.07(a), eff. Sept. 1, 2005; Acts 2011, 82nd Leg., ch. 1232 (S.B. 652), § 6.02, eff. June 17, 2011.

§ 13.003. Office Powers and Duties

(a) The office:

(1) shall assess the effect of utility rate changes and other regulatory actions on residential consumers in this state;

(2) shall advocate in the office's own name a position determined by the counsellor to be most advantageous to a substantial number of residential consumers;

(3) may appear or intervene, as a party or otherwise, as a matter of right on behalf of:

(A) residential consumers, as a class, in any proceeding before the commission, including an alternative dispute resolution proceeding; and

(B) small commercial consumers, as a class, in any proceeding in which the counsellor determines that small commercial consumers are in need of representation, including an alternative dispute resolution proceeding;

(4) may initiate or intervene as a matter of right or otherwise appear in a judicial proceeding:

(A) that involves an action taken by an administrative agency in a proceeding, including an alternative dispute resolution proceeding, in which the counsellor is authorized to appear; or

(B) in which the counsellor determines that residential electricity consumers or small commercial electricity consumers are in need of representation;

(5) is entitled to the same access as a party, other than commission staff, to records gathered by the commission under Section 14.204;

(6) is entitled to discovery of any nonprivileged matter that is relevant to the subject matter of a proceeding or petition before the commission;

(7) may represent an individual residential or small commercial consumer with respect to the consumer's disputed complaint concerning utility services that is unresolved before the commission;

(8) may recommend legislation to the legislature that the office determines would positively affect the interests of residential and small commercial consumers; and

(9) may advise persons who are interested parties for purposes of Section 37.054 on procedural matters related to proceedings before the commission on an application for a certificate of convenience and necessity filed under Section 37.053.

(b) This section does not limit the authority of the commission to represent residential or small commercial consumers.

(c) The appearance of the counsellor in a proceeding does not preclude the appearance of other parties on behalf of residential or small commercial consumers. The counsellor may not be grouped with any other party.

Acts 1997, 75th Leg., ch. 166, § 1, eff. Sept. 1, 1997. Amended by Acts 1999, 76th Leg., ch. 405, § 6, eff. Sept. 1, 1999; Acts 2011, 82nd Leg., ch. 416 (S.B. 855), § 1, eff. June 17, 2011.

§ 13.004. Alternative Dispute Resolution Procedures

(a) The counsellor shall develop and implement a policy to encourage the use of appropriate alternative dispute resolution procedures under Chapter 2009, Government Code, to assist in the resolution of internal disputes under the office's jurisdiction.

(b) The office's procedures relating to alternative dispute resolution must conform, to the extent possible, to any model guidelines issued by the State Office of Administrative Hearings for the use of alternative dispute resolution by state agencies.

(c) The counsellor shall designate a trained person to:

(1) coordinate the implementation of the policy adopted under Subsection (a);

(2) serve as a resource for any training needed to implement the procedures for alternative dispute resolution; and

(3) collect data concerning the effectiveness of those procedures, as implemented by the office.

Added by Acts 2005, 79th Leg., ch. 300, § 2, eff. Sept. 1, 2005.

§ 13.005. Complaints

(a) The office shall maintain a system to promptly and efficiently act on complaints filed with the office that the office has the authority to resolve. The office shall maintain information about parties to the complaint, the subject matter of the complaint, a summary of the results of the review or investigation of the complaint, and its disposition.

(b) The office shall make information available describing its procedures for complaint investigation and resolution.

(c) The office shall periodically notify the complaint parties of the status of the complaint until final disposition.

Added by Acts 2005, 79th Leg., ch. 300, § 2, eff. Sept. 1, 2005.

§ 13.006. Technology Policy

The counsellor shall implement a policy requiring the office to use appropriate technological solutions to improve the office's ability to perform its functions. The policy must ensure that the public is able to interact with the office on the Internet.

Added by Acts 2005, 79th Leg., ch. 300, § 2, eff. Sept. 1, 2005.

§ 13.007. Expired

SUBCHAPTER B. PUBLIC UTILITY COUNSEL

§ 13.021. Appointment; Term

(a) The chief executive of the office is the counsellor.

(b) The counsellor is appointed by the governor with the advice and consent of the senate.

(c) The appointment of the counsellor shall be made without regard to the race, color, disability, sex, religion, age, or national origin of the appointee.

(d) The counsellor serves a two-year term that expires on February 1 of the final year of the term.

Acts 1997, 75th Leg., ch. 166, § 1, eff. Sept. 1, 1997.

§ 13.022. Qualifications

(a) The counsellor must:

(1) be licensed to practice law in this state;

(2) have demonstrated a strong commitment to and involvement in efforts to safeguard the rights of the public; and

(3) possess the knowledge and experience necessary to practice effectively in utility proceedings.

(b) A person is not eligible for appointment as counsellor if:

(1) the person or the person's spouse:

(A) is employed by or participates in the management of a business entity or other organization that is regulated by or receives funds from the commission;

(B) directly or indirectly owns or controls more than a 10 percent interest or a pecuniary interest with a value exceeding $10,000 in:

(i) a business entity or other organization that is regulated by or receives funds from the commission or the office; or

(ii) a utility competitor, utility supplier, or other entity affected by a commission decision in a manner other than by the setting of rates for that class of customer;

(C) uses or receives a substantial amount of tangible goods, services, or funds from the commission or the office, other than compensation or reimbursement authorized by law for service as counsellor or for commission membership, attendance, or expenses; or

(D) notwithstanding Paragraph (B), has an interest in a mutual fund or retirement fund in which more than 10 percent of the fund's holdings is in a single utility, utility competitor, or utility supplier in this state and the person does not disclose this information to the governor, senate, or other entity, as appropriate; or

(2) the person is not qualified to serve under Section 13.042.

(c) Repealed by Acts 2005, 79th Leg., ch. 300, § 7.

(d) A person otherwise ineligible because of Subsection (b)(1)(B) may be appointed and serve as counsellor if the person:

(1) notifies the attorney general and commission that the person is ineligible because of Subsection (b)(1)(B); and

(2) divests the person or the person's spouse of the ownership or control:

(A) before beginning service; or

(B) if the person is already serving, within a reasonable time.

Acts 1997, 75th Leg., ch. 166, § 1, eff. Sept. 1, 1997. Amended by Acts 2005, 79th Leg., ch. 300, § 7, eff. Sept. 1, 2005.

§ 13.023. Grounds for Removal

(a) It is a ground for removal from office if the counsellor:

(1) does not have at the time of taking office or maintain during service as counsellor the qualifications required by Section 13.022;

(2) is ineligible for service as counsellor under Section 13.022, 13.042, or 13.043; or

(3) cannot discharge the counsellor's duties for a substantial part of the term for which the counsellor is appointed because of illness or disability.

(b) The validity of an action of the office is not affected by the fact that the action is taken when a ground for removal of the counsellor exists.

(c) If an employee has knowledge that a potential ground for removal of the counsellor exists, the employee shall notify the next highest ranking employee of the office, other than the counsellor, who shall then notify the governor and the attorney general that a potential ground for removal exists.

Acts 1997, 75th Leg., ch. 166, § 1, eff. Sept. 1, 1997. Amended by Acts 2005, 79th Leg., ch. 300, § 3, eff. Sept. 1, 2005.

§ 13.024. Prohibited Acts

(a) The counsellor may not have a direct or indirect interest in a utility company regulated under this title, its parent, or its subsidiary companies, corporations, or cooperatives or a utility competitor, utility supplier, or other entity affected in a manner other than by the setting of rates for that class of customer.

(b) The prohibition under Subsection (a) applies during the period of the counsellor's service.

Acts 1997, 75th Leg., ch. 166, § 1, eff. Sept. 1, 1997. Amended by Acts 1999, 76th Leg., ch. 405, § 7, eff. Sept. 1, 1999.

SUBCHAPTER C. OFFICE PERSONNEL

§ 13.041. Personnel

(a) The counsellor may employ lawyers, economists, engineers, consultants, statisticians, accountants, clerical staff, and other employees as the counsellor considers necessary to carry out this chapter.

(b) An employee receives compensation as prescribed by the legislature from the assessment imposed by Subchapter A, Chapter 16.[1]

Acts 1997, 75th Leg., ch. 166, § 1, eff. Sept. 1, 1997.

[1] V.T.C.A., Utilities Code § 16.001.

§ 13.042. Conflict of Interest

(a) In this section, "Texas trade association" means a cooperative and voluntarily joined statewide association of business or professional competitors in this state designed to assist its members and its industry or profession in dealing with mutual business or professional problems and in promoting their common interest.

(b) A person may not serve as counsellor or be an employee of the office employed in a "bona fide executive, administrative, or professional capacity," as that phrase is used for purposes of establishing an exemption to the overtime provisions of the federal Fair Labor Standards Act of 1938 (29 U.S.C. Section 201 et seq.) if the person is:

(1) an officer, employee, or paid consultant of a Texas trade association in the field of utilities; or

(2) the spouse of an officer, manager, or paid consultant of a Texas trade association in the field of utilities.

(c) A person may not serve as counsellor or act as the general counsel to the office if the person is required to register as a lobbyist under Chapter 305, Government Code, because of the person's activities for compensation on behalf of a profession related to the operation of the office.

Acts 1997, 75th Leg., ch. 166, § 1, eff. Sept. 1, 1997. Amended by Acts 2005, 79th Leg., ch. 300, § 4, eff. Sept. 1, 2005.

§ 13.043. Prohibition on Employment or Representation

(a) A former counsel may not make any communication to or appearance before the commission or an officer or employee of the commission before the second anniversary of the date the person ceases to serve as counsel if the communication or appearance is made:

(1) on behalf of another person in connection with any matter on which the person seeks official action; or

(2) with the intent to influence a commission decision or action, unless acting on his or her own behalf and without remuneration.

(b) A former counsel may not represent any person or receive compensation for services rendered on behalf of any person regarding a matter before the commission before the second anniversary of the date the person ceases to serve as counsel.

(c) A person commits an offense if the person violates this section. An offense under this subsection is a Class A misdemeanor.

(d) An employee of the office may not:

(1) be employed by a public utility that was in the scope of the employee's official responsibility while the employee was associated with the office; or

(2) represent a person before the commission or a court in a matter:

(A) in which the employee was personally involved while associated with the office; or

(B) that was within the employee's official responsibility while the employee was associated with the office.

(e) The prohibition of Subsection (d)(1) applies until the first anniversary of the date the employee's employment with the office ceases.

(f) The prohibition of Subsection (d)(2) applies while an employee of the office is associated with the office and at any time after.

(g) For purposes of this section, "person" includes an electric cooperative.

Acts 1997, 75th Leg., ch. 166, § 1, eff. Sept. 1, 1997. Amended by Acts 1999, 76th Leg., ch. 405, § 8, eff. Sept. 1, 1999.

§ 13.044. Career Ladder Program; Performance Evaluations; Merit Pay

(a) The counsellor or the counsellor's designee shall develop an intra-agency career ladder program that addresses opportunities for mobility and advancement for office employees. The program shall require intra-agency postings of each position concurrently with any public posting.

(b) The counsellor or the counsellor's designee shall develop a system of annual performance evaluations that are based on documented employee performance.

Merit pay for office employees must be based on the system established under this subsection.

Acts 1997, 75th Leg., ch. 166, § 1, eff. Sept. 1, 1997.

§ 13.045. Equal Employment Opportunity Policy Statement

(a) The counsellor or the counsellor's designee shall prepare and maintain a written policy statement to ensure implementation of a program of equal employment opportunity under which all personnel transactions are made without regard to race, color, disability, sex, religion, age, or national origin.

(b) The policy statement under Subsection (a) must include:

(1) personnel policies, including policies related to recruitment, evaluation, selection, appointment, training, and promotion of personnel, that are in compliance with the requirements of Chapter 21, Labor Code;

(2) a comprehensive analysis of the office workforce that meets federal and state guidelines;

(3) procedures by which a determination can be made about the extent of underuse in the office workforce of all persons for whom federal or state guidelines encourage a more equitable balance; and

(4) reasonable methods to appropriately address the underuse.

(c) A policy statement prepared under Subsection (b) must:

(1) cover an annual period;

(2) be updated at least annually;

(3) be reviewed by the Commission on Human Rights for compliance with Subsection (b)(1); and

(4) be filed with the governor's office.

(d) The governor's office shall deliver a biennial report to the legislature based on the information received under Subsection (c). The report may be made separately or as a part of other biennial reports to the legislature.

Acts 1997, 75th Leg., ch. 166, § 1, eff. Sept. 1, 1997.

§ 13.046. Qualifications and Standards of Conduct Information

The office shall provide to office employees as often as necessary information regarding their:

(1) qualifications for employment under this title; and

(2) responsibilities under applicable laws relating to standards of conduct for employees.

Acts 1997, 75th Leg., ch. 166, § 1, eff. Sept. 1, 1997.

SUBCHAPTER D. PUBLIC INTEREST INFORMATION AND REPORTS

§ 13.061. Public Interest Information

The office shall prepare information of public interest describing the functions of the office. The office shall make the information available to the public and appropriate state agencies.

Acts 1997, 75th Leg., ch. 166, § 1, eff. Sept. 1, 1997.

§ 13.062. Public Participation

(a) The office shall comply with federal and state laws related to program and facility accessibility.

(b) The office shall prepare and maintain a written plan that describes how a person who does not speak English may be provided reasonable access to the office's programs and services.

Acts 1997, 75th Leg., ch. 166, § 1, eff. Sept. 1, 1997.

§ 13.063. Annual Reports

(a) Repealed by Acts 2011, 82nd Leg., ch. 1083 (S.B. 1179), § 25(161).

(b) The office shall prepare annually a report on the office's activities during the preceding year and submit the report to the standing legislative committees that have jurisdiction over the office, the house appropriations committee, the senate finance committee, and the Sunset Advisory Commission. At a minimum, the report must include:

(1) a list of the types of activities conducted by the office and the time spent by the office on each activity;

(2) the number of hours billed by the office for representing residential or small commercial consumers in proceedings;

(3) the number of staff positions and the type of work performed by each position; and

(4) the office's rate of success in representing residential or small commercial consumers in appealing commission decisions.

Acts 1997, 75th Leg., ch. 166, § 1, eff. Sept. 1, 1997. Amended by Acts 2005, 79th Leg., ch. 300, § 5, eff. Sept. 1, 2005; Acts 2011, 82nd Leg., ch. 1083 (S.B. 1179), § 25(161), eff. June 17, 2011.

§ 13.064. Public Hearing

(a) The office annually shall conduct a public hearing to assist the office in developing a plan of priorities and to give the public, including residential and small commercial consumers, an opportunity to comment on the office's functions and effectiveness.

(b) A public hearing held under this section is not subject to Chapter 551, Government Code.

(c) The office shall file notice of a public hearing held under this section with the secretary of state for publication in the Texas Register.

Added by Acts 2005, 79th Leg., ch. 300, § 6, eff. Sept. 1, 2005.

CHAPTER 14. JURISDICTION AND POWERS OF COMMISSION AND OTHER REGULATORY AUTHORITIES

SUBCHAPTER A. GENERAL POWERS OF COMMISSION

Section
14.001. Power to Regulate and Supervise.
14.002. Rules.
14.0025. Negotiated Rulemaking and Alternative Dispute Resolution.
14.003. Commission Powers Relating to Reports.
14.004. Report of Substantial Interest.
14.005. Criteria and Guidelines Governing Termination of Services to Elderly and Disabled.
14.006. Interference With Terms or Conditions of Employment; Presumption of Reasonableness.
14.007. Assistance to Municipality.
14.008. Municipal Franchises.

SUBCHAPTER B. PRACTICE AND PROCEDURE
14.051. Procedural Powers.
14.052. Rules.
14.053. Powers and Duties of State Office of Administrative Hearings.
14.054. Settlements.
14.055. Record of Proceedings.
14.056. Right to be Heard.
14.057. Orders of Commission; Transcripts and Exhibits; Public Records.
14.058. Fees for Electronic Access to Information.
14.059. Technology Policy.

SUBCHAPTER C. RESTRICTIONS ON CERTAIN TRANSACTIONS
14.101. Report of Certain Transactions; Commission Consideration.
14.102. Report of Purchase of Voting Stock in Public Utility.
14.103. Report of Loan to Stockholders.

SUBCHAPTER D. RECORDS
14.151. Records of Public Utility.

Section
14.152. Maintenance of Office and Records in This State.
14.153. Communications With Regulatory Authority.
14.154. Jurisdiction Over Affiliate.

SUBCHAPTER E. AUDITS AND INSPECTIONS
14.201. Inquiry Into Management and Affairs.
14.202. Management Audits by Commission.
14.203. Audit of Accounts.
14.204. Inspection.
14.205. Examinations Under Oath.
14.206. Entering Premises of Public Utility.
14.207. Production of Out-Of-State Records.

SUBCHAPTER A. GENERAL POWERS OF COMMISSION

§ 14.001. Power to Regulate and Supervise

The commission has the general power to regulate and supervise the business of each public utility within its jurisdiction and to do anything specifically designated or implied by this title that is necessary and convenient to the exercise of that power and jurisdiction.

Acts 1997, 75th Leg., ch. 166, § 1, eff. Sept. 1, 1997.

§ 14.002. Rules

The commission shall adopt and enforce rules reasonably required in the exercise of its powers and jurisdiction.

Acts 1997, 75th Leg., ch. 166, § 1, eff. Sept. 1, 1997.

§ 14.0025. Negotiated Rulemaking and Alternative Dispute Resolution

(a) The commission shall develop and implement a policy to encourage the use of:

(1) negotiated rulemaking procedures under Chapter 2008, Government Code, for the adoption of commission rules; and

(2) appropriate alternative dispute resolution procedures under Chapter 2009, Government Code, to assist in the resolution of internal and external disputes under the commission's jurisdiction.

(b) The commission's procedures relating to alternative dispute resolution must conform, to the extent possible, to any model guidelines issued by the State Office of Administrative Hearings for the use of alternative dispute resolution by state agencies.

(c) The commission shall designate a trained person to:

(1) coordinate the implementation of the policy adopted under Subsection (a);

(2) serve as a resource for any training needed to implement the procedures for negotiated rulemaking or alternative dispute resolution; and

(3) collect data concerning the effectiveness of those procedures, as implemented by the commission.

Added by Acts 2005, 79th Leg., ch. 797, § 5, eff. Sept. 1, 2005.

§ 14.003. Commission Powers Relating to Reports

The commission may:

(1) require a public utility to report to the commission information relating to:

(A) the utility; and

(B) a transaction between the utility and an affiliate inside or outside this state, to the extent that the transaction is subject to the commission's jurisdiction;

(2) establish the form for a report;

(3) determine the time for a report and the frequency with which the report is to be made;

(4) require that a report be made under oath;

(5) require the filing with the commission of a copy of:

(A) a contract or arrangement between a public utility and an affiliate;

(B) a report filed with a federal agency or a governmental agency or body of another state; and

(C) an annual report that shows each payment of compensation, other than salary or wages subject to federal income tax withholding:

(i) to residents of this state;

(ii) with respect to legal, administrative, or legislative matters in this state; or

(iii) for representation before the legislature of this state or any governmental agency or body; and

(6) require that a contract or arrangement described by Subdivision (5)(A) that is not in writing be reduced to writing and filed with the commission.

Acts 1997, 75th Leg., ch. 166, § 1, eff. Sept. 1, 1997.

§ 14.004. Report of Substantial Interest

The commission may require disclosure of the identity and respective interests of each owner of at least one percent of the voting securities of a public utility or its affiliate.

Acts 1997, 75th Leg., ch. 166, § 1, eff. Sept. 1, 1997.

§ 14.005. Criteria and Guidelines Governing Termination of Services to Elderly and Disabled

The commission may establish criteria and guidelines with the utility industry relating to industry procedures used in terminating services to the elderly and disabled.

Acts 1997, 75th Leg., ch. 166, § 1, eff. Sept. 1, 1997.

§ 14.006. Interference With Terms or Conditions of Employment; Presumption of Reasonableness

The commission may not interfere with employee wages and benefits, working conditions, or other terms or conditions of employment that are the product of a collective bargaining agreement recognized under federal law. An employee wage rate or benefit that is the product of the collective bargaining is presumed to be reasonable.

Acts 1997, 75th Leg., ch. 166, § 1, eff. Sept. 1, 1997.

§ 14.007. Assistance to Municipality

On request by the governing body of a municipality, the commission may provide commission employees as necessary to advise and consult with the municipality on a pending matter.

Acts 1997, 75th Leg., ch. 166, § 1, eff. Sept. 1, 1997.

§ 14.008. Municipal Franchises

(a) This title does not restrict the rights and powers of a municipality to grant or refuse a franchise to use the streets and alleys in the municipality or to make a statutory charge for that use.

(b) A franchise agreement may not limit or interfere with a power conferred on the commission by this title.

Acts 1997, 75th Leg., ch. 166, § 1, eff. Sept. 1, 1997.

SUBCHAPTER B. PRACTICE AND PROCEDURE

§ 14.051. Procedural Powers

The commission may:

(1) call and hold a hearing;

(2) administer an oath;

(3) receive evidence at a hearing;

(4) issue a subpoena to compel the attendance of a witness or the production of a document; and

(5) make findings of fact and decisions to administer this title or a rule, order, or other action of the commission.

Acts 1997, 75th Leg., ch. 166, § 1, eff. Sept. 1, 1997.

§ 14.052. Rules

(a) The commission shall adopt and enforce rules governing practice and procedure before the commission and, as applicable, practice and procedure before the utility division of the State Office of Administrative Hearings.

(b) The commission shall adopt rules that authorize an administrative law judge to:

(1) limit the amount of time that a party may have to present its case;

(2) limit the number of requests for information that a party may make in a contested case;

(3) require a party to a contested case to identify contested issues and facts before the hearing begins;

(4) limit cross-examination to only those issues and facts identified before the hearing and to any new issues that may arise as a result of the discovery process; and

(5) group parties, other than the office, that have the same position on an issue to facilitate cross-examination on that issue.

(c) A rule adopted under Subsection (b)(5) must permit each party in a group to present that party's witnesses for cross-examination during the hearing.

(d) A rule adopted under this section must ensure that each party receives due process.

Acts 1997, 75th Leg., ch. 166, § 1, eff. Sept. 1, 1997.

§ 14.053. Powers and Duties of State Office of Administrative Hearings

(a) The utility division of the State Office of Administrative Hearings shall conduct each hearing in a contested case that is not conducted by one or more commissioners.

(b) The commission may delegate to the utility division of the State Office of Administrative Hearings the authority to make a final decision and to issue findings of fact, conclusions of law, and other necessary orders in a proceeding in which there is not a contested issue of fact or law.

(c) The commission by rule shall define the procedures by which it delegates final decision-making authority under Subsection (b).

(d) For review purposes an administrative law judge's final decision under Subsection (b) has the same effect as a final decision of the commission unless a commissioner requests formal review of the decision.

Acts 1997, 75th Leg., ch. 166, § 1, eff. Sept. 1, 1997.

§ 14.054. Settlements

(a) The commission by rule shall adopt procedures governing the use of settlements to resolve contested cases.

(b) Rules adopted under this section must ensure that:

(1) each party retains the right to:

(A) a full hearing before the commission on issues that remain in dispute; and

(B) judicial review of issues that remain in dispute;

(2) an issue of fact raised by a nonsettling party may not be waived by a settlement or stipulation of the other parties; and

(3) a nonsettling party may use an issue of fact raised by that party as the basis for judicial review.

Acts 1997, 75th Leg., ch. 166, § 1, eff. Sept. 1, 1997.

§ 14.055. Record of Proceedings

The regulatory authority shall keep a record of each proceeding before the authority.

Acts 1997, 75th Leg., ch. 166, § 1, eff. Sept. 1, 1997.

§ 14.056. Right to be Heard

Each party to a proceeding before a regulatory authority is entitled to be heard by attorney or in person.

Acts 1997, 75th Leg., ch. 166, § 1, eff. Sept. 1, 1997.

§ 14.057. Orders of Commission; Transcripts and Exhibits; Public Records

(a) A commission order must be in writing and contain detailed findings of the facts on which it is passed.

(b) The commission shall retain a copy of the transcript and the exhibits in any matter in which the commission issues an order.

(c) Subject to Chapter 552, Government Code, each file pertaining to a matter that was at any time pending before the commission or to a record, report, or inspection required by Section 14.003, 14.151,

14.152, 14.153, 14.201, or 14.203–14.207 or by Subtitle B or C [1] is public information.

Acts 1997, 75th Leg., ch. 166, § 1, eff. Sept. 1, 1997.

[1] V.T.C.A., Utilities Code § 31.001 et seq., or 51.001 et seq.

§ 14.058. Fees for Electronic Access to Information

The fees charged by the commission for electronic access to information that is stored in the system established by the commission using funds from the Texas Public Finance Authority and approved by the Department of Information Resources shall be established:

(1) by the commission in consultation with the comptroller; and

(2) in an amount reasonable and necessary to retire the debt to the Texas Public Finance Authority associated with establishing the electronic access system.

Added by Acts 1999, 76th Leg., ch. 62, § 18.01(a), eff. Sept. 1, 1999. Amended by Acts 2007, 80th Leg., ch. 937, § 1.115, eff. Sept. 1, 2007.

§ 14.059. Technology Policy

The commission shall implement a policy requiring the commission to use appropriate technological solutions to improve the commission's ability to perform its functions. The policy must ensure that the public is able to interact with the commission on the Internet.

Added by Acts 2005, 79th Leg., ch. 797, § 6, eff. Sept. 1, 2005.

SUBCHAPTER C. RESTRICTIONS ON CERTAIN TRANSACTIONS

§ 14.101. Report of Certain Transactions; Commission Consideration

(a) Unless a public utility reports the transaction to the commission within a reasonable time, the public utility may not:

(1) sell, acquire, or lease a plant as an operating unit or system in this state for a total consideration of more than $10 million ; or

(2) merge or consolidate with another public utility operating in this state.

(b) A public utility shall report to the commission within a reasonable time each transaction that involves the sale of at least 50 percent of the stock of the utility. On the filing of a report with the commission, the commission shall investigate the transaction, with or without a public hearing, to determine whether the action is consistent with the public interest. In reaching its determination, the commission shall consider:

(1) the reasonable value of the property, facilities, or securities to be acquired, disposed of, merged, transferred, or consolidated;

(2) whether the transaction will:

(A) adversely affect the health or safety of customers or employees;

(B) result in the transfer of jobs of citizens of this state to workers domiciled outside this state; or

(C) result in the decline of service;

(3) whether the public utility will receive consideration equal to the reasonable value of the assets when it sells, leases, or transfers assets; and

(4) whether the transaction is consistent with the public interest.

(c) If the commission finds that a transaction is not in the public interest, the commission shall take the effect of the transaction into consideration in ratemaking proceedings and disallow the effect of the transaction if the transaction will unreasonably affect rates or service.

(d) This section does not apply to:

(1) the purchase of a unit of property for replacement;

(2) an addition to the facilities of a public utility by construction; or

(3) transactions that facilitate unbundling, asset valuation, minimization of ownership or control of generation assets, or other purposes consistent with Chapter 39.

Acts 1997, 75th Leg., ch. 166, § 1, eff. Sept. 1, 1997. Amended by Acts 1999, 76th Leg., ch. 405, § 9, eff. Sept. 1, 1999; Acts 2011, 82nd Leg., ch. 129 (H.B. 1753), § 1, eff. Sept. 1, 2011.

Section 2 of Acts 2011, 82nd Leg., ch. 129 (H.B. 1753) provides:

"The change in law made by this Act applies only to an agreement for the sale, acquisition, or lease of a plant that is entered into on or after the effective date [Sept. 1, 2011] of this Act. An agreement for the sale, acquisition, or lease of a plant that is entered into before the effective date of this Act is governed by the law applicable to the agreement immediately before the effective date of this Act, and that law is continued in effect for that purpose."

§ 14.102. Report of Purchase of Voting Stock in Public Utility

A public utility may not purchase voting stock in another public utility doing business in this state unless the utility reports the purchase to the commission.

Acts 1997, 75th Leg., ch. 166, § 1, eff. Sept. 1, 1997.

§ 14.103. Report of Loan to Stockholders

A public utility may not loan money, stocks, bonds, notes, or other evidence of indebtedness to a person who directly or indirectly owns or holds any stock of the public utility unless the public utility reports the transaction to the commission within a reasonable time.

Acts 1997, 75th Leg., ch. 166, § 1, eff. Sept. 1, 1997.

SUBCHAPTER D. RECORDS

§ 14.151. Records of Public Utility

(a) Each public utility shall keep and provide to the regulatory authority, in the manner and form prescribed by the commission, uniform accounts of all business transacted by the utility.

(b) The commission may prescribe the form of books, accounts, records, and memoranda to be kept by a public utility, including:

(1) the books, accounts, records, and memoranda of:

(A) the provision of and capacity for service; and

(B) the receipt and expenditure of money; and

(2) any other form, record, and memorandum that the commission considers necessary to carry out this title.

(c) For a public utility subject to regulation by a federal regulatory agency, compliance with the system of accounts prescribed for the particular class of utilities by the federal agency may be considered sufficient compliance with the system prescribed by the commission. The commission may prescribe the form of books, accounts, records, and memoranda covering information in addition to that required by the federal agency. The system of accounts and the form of books, accounts, records, and memoranda prescribed by the commission for a public utility or class of utilities may not be inconsistent with the systems and forms established by a federal agency for that public utility or class of utilities.

(d) Each public utility shall:

(1) keep and provide its books, accounts, records, and memoranda accurately in the manner and form prescribed by the commission; and

(2) comply with the directions of the regulatory authority relating to the books, accounts, records, and memoranda.

(e) In this section, "public utility" includes a municipally owned utility.

Acts 1997, 75th Leg., ch. 166, § 1, eff. Sept. 1, 1997.

§ 14.152. Maintenance of Office and Records in This State

(a) Each public utility shall maintain an office in this state in a county in which some part of the utility's property is located. The utility shall keep in this office all books, accounts, records, and memoranda required by the commission to be kept in this state.

(b) A book, account, record, or memorandum required by the regulatory authority to be kept in this state may not be removed from this state, except as:

(1) provided by Section 52.255; and

(2) prescribed by the commission.

Acts 1997, 75th Leg., ch. 166, § 1, eff. Sept. 1, 1997.

§ 14.153. Communications With Regulatory Authority

(a) The regulatory authority shall adopt rules governing communications with the regulatory authority or a member or employee of the regulatory authority by:

(1) a public utility;

(2) an affiliate; or

(3) a representative of a public utility or affiliate.

(b) A record of a communication must contain:

(1) the name of the person contacting the regulatory authority or member or employee of the regulatory authority;

(2) the name of the business entity represented;

(3) a brief description of the subject matter of the communication; and

(4) the action, if any, requested by the public utility, affiliate, or representative.

(c) Records compiled under Subsection (b) shall be available to the public monthly.

Acts 1997, 75th Leg., ch. 166, § 1, eff. Sept. 1, 1997.

§ 14.154. Jurisdiction Over Affiliate

(a) The commission has jurisdiction over an affiliate that has a transaction with a public utility under the commission's jurisdiction to the extent of access to a record of the affiliate relating to the transaction, including a record of joint or general expenses, any portion of which may be applicable to the transaction.

(b) A record obtained by the commission relating to sale of electrical energy at wholesale by an affiliate to the public utility is confidential and is not subject to disclosure under Chapter 552, Government Code.

Acts 1997, 75th Leg., ch. 166, § 1, eff. Sept. 1, 1997.

SUBCHAPTER E. AUDITS AND INSPECTIONS

§ 14.201. Inquiry Into Management and Affairs

A regulatory authority may inquire into the management and affairs of each public utility and shall keep itself informed as to the manner and method in which each public utility is managed and its affairs are conducted.

Acts 1997, 75th Leg., ch. 166, § 1, eff. Sept. 1, 1997.

§ 14.202. Management Audits by Commission

(a) The commission shall:

(1) inquire into the management of the business of each public utility under its jurisdiction;

(2) keep itself informed as to the manner and method in which the utility's business is managed; and

(3) obtain from the public utility any information necessary to enable the commission to perform a management audit.

(b) The commission may audit a utility under its jurisdiction as frequently as needed. Six months after an audit, the utility shall report to the commission on the status of the implementation of the recommendations of the audit and shall file subsequent reports at times the commission considers appropriate.

Acts 1997, 75th Leg., ch. 166, § 1, eff. Sept. 1, 1997.

§ 14.203. Audit of Accounts

A regulatory authority may require the examination and audit of the accounts of a public or municipally owned utility.

Acts 1997, 75th Leg., ch. 166, § 1, eff. Sept. 1, 1997.

§ 14.204. Inspection

(a) A regulatory authority and, to the extent authorized by the regulatory authority, its counsel, agent, or employee, may:

(1) inspect and obtain copies of the papers, books, accounts, documents, and other business records of a public utility within its jurisdiction; and

(2) inspect the plant, equipment, and other property of a public utility within its jurisdiction.

(b) An action under this section must be conducted at a reasonable time for a reasonable purpose.

Acts 1997, 75th Leg., ch. 166, § 1, eff. Sept. 1, 1997.

§ 14.205. Examinations Under Oath

In connection with an action taken under Section 14.204, the regulatory authority may:

(1) examine under oath an officer, agent, or employee of a public utility; or

(2) authorize the person conducting the action to make the examination under oath.

Acts 1997, 75th Leg., ch. 166, § 1, eff. Sept. 1, 1997.

§ 14.206. Entering Premises of Public Utility

(a) A member, agent, or employee of a regulatory authority may enter the premises occupied by a public utility to conduct an inspection, examination, or test or to exercise any other authority provided by this title.

(b) A member, agent, or employee of the regulatory authority may act under this section only during reasonable hours and after reasonable notice to the public utility.

(c) A public utility is entitled to be represented when an inspection, examination, or test is conducted on its premises. The utility is entitled to a reasonable time to secure a representative before the inspection, examination, or test begins.

Acts 1997, 75th Leg., ch. 166, § 1, eff. Sept. 1, 1997.

§ 14.207. Production of Out-Of-State Records

(a) A regulatory authority may require, by order or subpoena served on a public utility, the production, at the time and place in this state that the regulatory authority designates, of any books, accounts, papers, or records kept by that public utility outside this state or, if ordered by the commission, verified copies of the books, accounts, papers, or records.

(b) A public utility that fails or refuses to comply with an order or subpoena under this section violates this title.

Acts 1997, 75th Leg., ch. 166, § 1, eff. Sept. 1, 1997.

CHAPTER 15. JUDICIAL REVIEW, ENFORCEMENT, AND PENALTIES

SUBCHAPTER A. JUDICIAL REVIEW

Section
15.001. Right to Judicial Review.

Section
15.002. Commission as Defendant.
15.003. Costs and Attorney's Fees.
15.004. Judicial Stay or Suspension.

SUBCHAPTER B. ENFORCEMENT AND PENALTIES
15.021. Action to Enjoin or Require Compliance.
15.022. Contempt.
15.023. Administrative Penalty, Disgorgement Order, or Mitigation Plan.
15.024. Administrative Penalty Assessment or Disgorgement Order Procedure.
15.025. Payment of Administrative Penalty.
15.026. Judicial Review of Administrative Penalty.
15.027. Administrative Penalty Collection; General Provisions.
15.028. Civil Penalty Against Public Utility, Pay Telephone Service Provider, or Affiliate.
15.029. Civil Penalty for Violating Section 12.055 or 12.154.
15.030. Offense.
15.031. Place for Suit.
15.032. Penalties Cumulative.
15.033. Disposition of Fines and Penalties.

SUBCHAPTER C. COMPLAINTS
15.051. Complaint by Affected Person.
15.052. Complaint Regarding Recreational Vehicle Park Owner.

SUBCHAPTER A. JUDICIAL REVIEW

§ 15.001. Right to Judicial Review

Any party to a proceeding before the commission is entitled to judicial review under the substantial evidence rule.

Acts 1997, 75th Leg., ch. 166, § 1, eff. Sept. 1, 1997.

§ 15.002. Commission as Defendant

The commission must be a defendant in a proceeding for judicial review.

Acts 1997, 75th Leg., ch. 166, § 1, eff. Sept. 1, 1997.

§ 15.003. Costs and Attorney's Fees

(a) A party represented by counsel who alleges that existing rates are excessive or that rates prescribed by the commission are excessive and who prevails in a proceeding for review of a commission order or decision is entitled in the same action to recover against the regulation fund reasonable fees for attorneys and expert witnesses and other costs for the party's efforts before the commission and the court.

(b) The court shall set the amount of attorney's fees awarded under Subsection (a).

(c) If a court finds that an action under Section 15.001 or this section was groundless and brought in bad faith and for the purpose of harassment, the court may award reasonable attorney's fees to the defendant public utility.

Acts 1997, 75th Leg., ch. 166, § 1, eff. Sept. 1, 1997.

§ 15.004. Judicial Stay or Suspension

While an appeal of an order, ruling, or decision of a regulatory authority is pending, the district court, court of appeals, or supreme court, as appropriate, may stay or suspend all or part of the operation of the order, ruling, or decision. In granting or refusing a stay or suspension, the court shall act in accordance with the practice of a court exercising equity jurisdiction.

Acts 1997, 75th Leg., ch. 166, § 1, eff. Sept. 1, 1997.

SUBCHAPTER B. ENFORCEMENT AND PENALTIES

§ 15.021. Action to Enjoin or Require Compliance

(a) The attorney general, on the request of the commission, shall apply in the name of the commission for a court order under Subsection (b) if the commission determines that a public utility or other person is:

(1) engaging in or about to engage in an act that violates this title or an order or rule of the commission entered or adopted under this title; or

(2) failing to comply with the requirements of this title or a rule or order of the commission.

(b) A court, in an action under this section, may:

(1) prohibit the commencement or continuation of an act that violates this title or an order or rule of the commission entered or adopted under this title; or

(2) require compliance with a provision of this title or an order or rule of the commission.

(c) The remedy under this section is in addition to any other remedy provided under this title.

Acts 1997, 75th Leg., ch. 166, § 1, eff. Sept. 1, 1997.

§ 15.022. Contempt

The commission may file a court action for contempt against a person who:

(1) fails to comply with a lawful order of the commission;

(2) fails to comply with a subpoena or subpoena duces tecum; or

(3) refuses to testify about a matter on which the person may be lawfully interrogated.

Acts 1997, 75th Leg., ch. 166, § 1, eff. Sept. 1, 1997.

§ 15.023. Administrative Penalty, Disgorgement Order, or Mitigation Plan

(a) The commission may impose an administrative penalty against a person regulated under this title who violates this title or a rule or order adopted under this title.

(b) The penalty for a violation may be in an amount not to exceed $25,000. Each day a violation continues or occurs is a separate violation for purposes of imposing a penalty.

(c) The commission by rule shall establish a classification system for violations that includes a range of administrative penalties that may be assessed for each class of violation based on:

(1) the seriousness of the violation, including:

(A) the nature, circumstances, extent, and gravity of a prohibited act; and

(B) the hazard or potential hazard created to the health, safety, or economic welfare of the public;

(2) the economic harm to property or the environment caused by the violation;

(3) the history of previous violations;

(4) the amount necessary to deter future violations;

(5) efforts to correct the violation; and

(6) any other matter that justice may require.

(d) The classification system established under Subsection (c) shall provide that a penalty in an amount that exceeds $5,000 may be assessed only if the violation is included in the highest class of violations in the classification system.

(e) For a violation of Section 39.157, the commission shall, in addition to the assessment of a penalty, order disgorgement of all excess revenue resulting from the violation. For any other violation of the statutes, rules, or protocols relating to wholesale electric markets, the commission may, in addition to the assessment of a penalty, order disgorgement of all excess revenue resulting from the violation.

(f) The commission and a person may develop and enter into a voluntary mitigation plan relating to a violation of Section 39.157 or rules adopted by the commission under that section. If the commission and a person enter into a voluntary mitigation plan, adherence to the plan constitutes an absolute defense against an alleged violation with respect to activities covered by the plan.

(g) In this subchapter, "excess revenue" means revenue in excess of revenue that would have occurred absent a violation.

Acts 1997, 75th Leg., ch. 166, § 1, eff. Sept. 1, 1997. Amended by Acts 2005, 79th Leg., ch. 797, § 7, eff. Sept. 1, 2005; Acts 2011, 82nd Leg., ch. 996 (H.B. 2133), §§ 1, 2, eff. Sept. 1, 2011.

Section 8 of Acts 2011, 82nd Leg., ch. 996 (H.B. 2133) provides:

"The changes in law made by this Act apply only to a violation that occurs on or after the effective date of this Act. A violation that occurs before the effective date of this Act is covered by the law in effect at the time the violation occurred, and the former law is continued in effect for that purpose."

§ 15.024. Administrative Penalty Assessment or Disgorgement Order Procedure

(a) If the executive director determines that a violation has occurred, the executive director may issue to the commission a report that states the facts on which the determination is based and the executive director's recommendation on the imposition of an administrative penalty, including a recommendation on the amount of the penalty.

(b) Not later than the 14th day after the date the report is issued, the executive director shall give written notice of the report to the person against whom the penalty may be assessed. The notice may be given by certified mail. The notice must:

(1) include a brief summary of the alleged violation;

(2) state the amount of the recommended penalty; and

(3) inform the person that the person has a right to a hearing on the occurrence of the violation, the amount of the penalty, or both the occurrence of the violation and the amount of the penalty.

(c) A penalty may not be assessed under this section if the person against whom the penalty may be assessed remedies the violation before the 31st day after the date the person receives the notice under Subsection (b). A person who claims to have remedied an alleged violation has the burden of proving to the commission that the alleged violation was remedied and was accidental or inadvertent. This subsection does not apply to a violation of Chapter 17, 55, or 64.

(d) Not later than the 20th day after the date the person receives the notice, the person may accept the determination and recommended penalty of the executive director in writing or may make a written request for a hearing on the occurrence of the violation, the amount of the penalty, or both the occurrence of the violation and the amount of the penalty.

(e) If the person accepts the executive director's determination and recommended penalty, the commission by order shall approve the determination and impose the recommended penalty.

(f) If the person requests a hearing or fails to timely respond to the notice, the executive director shall set a hearing and give notice of the hearing to the person. The parties to a proceeding under this subchapter shall be limited to the person and the commission, including the independent market monitor. The hearing shall be held by an administrative law judge of the State Office of Administrative Hearings. The administrative law judge shall make findings of fact and conclusions of law and promptly issue to the commission a proposal for a decision about the occurrence of the violation and the amount of a proposed penalty. Based on the findings of fact, conclusions of law, and proposal for a decision, the commission by order may find that a violation has occurred and impose a penalty or disgorgement order or may find that no violation occurred.

(g) The notice of the commission's order shall be given to the person as provided by Chapter 2001, Government Code, and must include a statement of the right of the person to judicial review of the order.

Acts 1997, 75th Leg., ch. 166, § 1, eff. Sept. 1, 1997. Amended by Acts 1999, 76th Leg., ch. 1212, § 3, eff. Sept. 1, 1999; Acts 1999, 76th Leg., ch. 1579, § 2, eff. Aug. 30, 1999; Acts 2011, 82nd Leg., ch. 91 (S.B. 1303), § 25.001, eff. Sept. 1, 2011; Acts 2011, 82nd Leg., ch. 996 (H.B. 2133), §§ 3, 4, eff. Sept. 1, 2011.

§ 15.025. Payment of Administrative Penalty

(a) Not later than the 30th day after the date the commission's order imposing an administrative penalty is final as provided by Section 2001.144, Government Code, the person shall:

(1) pay the amount of the penalty;

(2) pay the amount of the penalty and file a petition for judicial review contesting:

(A) the occurrence of the violation;

(B) the amount of the penalty; or

(C) both the occurrence of the violation and the amount of the penalty; or

(3) without paying the amount of the penalty, file a petition for judicial review contesting:

(A) the occurrence of the violation;

(B) the amount of the penalty; or

(C) both the occurrence of the violation and the amount of the penalty.

(b) Not later than the 30th day after the date the commission's order is final as provided by Section 2001.144, Government Code, a person who acts under Subsection (a)(3) may:

(1) stay enforcement of the penalty by:

(A) paying the amount of the penalty to the court for placement in an escrow account; or

(B) giving to the court a supersedeas bond that is approved by the court for the amount of the penalty and that is effective until all judicial review of the commission's order is final; or

(2) request the court to stay enforcement of the penalty by:

(A) filing with the court a sworn affidavit of the person stating that the person is financially unable to pay the amount of the penalty and is financially unable to give the supersedeas bond; and

(B) giving a copy of the affidavit to the executive director by certified mail.

(c) The executive director, on receipt of a copy of an affidavit under Subsection (b)(2), may file with the court, not later than the fifth day after the date the copy is received, a contest to the affidavit. The court shall hold a hearing on the facts alleged in the affidavit as soon as practicable and shall stay the enforcement of the penalty on finding that the alleged facts are true. The person who files an affidavit has the burden of proving that the person is financially unable to pay the amount of the penalty and to give a supersedeas bond.

(d) If the person does not pay the amount of the penalty and the enforcement of the penalty is not stayed, the executive director may refer the matter to the attorney general for collection of the amount of the penalty.

(e) Any excess revenue ordered disgorged under this section for a violation of the statutes, rules, or protocols relating to wholesale electric markets shall be returned to the affected wholesale electric market participants to be used to reduce costs or fees incurred by retail electric customers. The commission shall adopt rules to prescribe how revenue shall be returned to the affected wholesale electric market participants under this subsection.

(f) For purposes of this section and Section 15.026, a reference to a penalty shall be construed to include disgorgement.

Acts 1997, 75th Leg., ch. 166, § 1, eff. Sept. 1, 1997. Amended by Acts 2011, 82nd Leg., ch. 996 (H.B. 2133), § 5, eff. Sept. 1, 2011.

§ 15.026. Judicial Review of Administrative Penalty

(a) Judicial review of a commission order imposing an administrative penalty or disgorgement is:

(1) instituted by filing a petition as provided by Subchapter G, Chapter 2001, Government Code;[1] and

(2) under the substantial evidence rule.

(b) If the court sustains the occurrence of the violation, the court may uphold or reduce the amount of the penalty or disgorgement and order the person to pay the full or reduced amount of the penalty or disgorgement. If the court does not sustain the occurrence of the violation, the court shall order that no penalty or disgorgement is owed.

(c) When the judgment of the court becomes final, the court shall proceed under this subsection. If the person paid the amount of the penalty and that amount is reduced or is not upheld by the court, the court shall order that the appropriate amount plus accrued interest be remitted to the person. The rate of the interest is the rate charged on loans to depository institutions by the New York Federal Reserve Bank, and the interest shall be paid for the period beginning on the date the penalty was paid and ending on the date the penalty is remitted. If the person gave a supersedeas bond and the amount of the penalty is not upheld by the court, the court shall order the release of the bond. If the person gave a supersedeas bond and the amount of the penalty is reduced, the court shall order the release of the bond after the person pays the amount.

Acts 1997, 75th Leg., ch. 166, § 1, eff. Sept. 1, 1997. Amended by Acts 2011, 82nd Leg., ch. 996 (H.B. 2133), § 6, eff. Sept. 1, 2011.

[1] V.T.C.A., Government Code § 2001.171 et seq.

§ 15.027. Administrative Penalty Collection; General Provisions

(a) An administrative penalty collected under this subchapter shall be sent to the comptroller.

(b) A proceeding relating to an administrative penalty under this subchapter is subject to Chapter 2001, Government Code.

(c) The executive director may delegate any power or duty relating to an administrative penalty given the executive director by this subchapter to a person designated by the executive director.

Acts 1997, 75th Leg., ch. 166, § 1, eff. Sept. 1, 1997.

§ 15.028. Civil Penalty Against Public Utility, Pay Telephone Service Provider, or Affiliate

(a) A public utility, customer-owned pay telephone service provider under Section 55.178, or affiliate is subject to a civil penalty if the utility, provider, or affiliate knowingly violates this title, fails to perform a duty imposed on it, or fails or refuses to obey an order, rule, direction, or requirement of the commission or a decree or judgment of a court.

(b) A civil penalty under this section shall be in an amount of not less than $1,000 and not more than $5,000 for each violation.

(c) A public utility or affiliate commits a separate violation each day it continues to violate Subsection (a).

(d) The attorney general shall file in the name of the commission a suit on the attorney general's own initiative or at the request of the commission to recover the civil penalty under this section.

Acts 1997, 75th Leg., ch. 166, § 1, eff. Sept. 1, 1997.

§ 15.029. Civil Penalty for Violating Section 12.055 or 12.154

(a) A member of the commission or an officer or director of a public utility or affiliate who knowingly violates Section 12.055 or 12.154 is subject to a civil penalty of $1,000 for each violation.

(b) A person other than a person subject to Subsection (a) who knowingly violates Section 12.154 is subject to a civil penalty of $500 for each violation.

(c) A member, officer, or employee of the commission who in any action is found by a preponderance of the evidence to have violated a provision of Section 12.055 or 12.154 shall be removed from the person's office or employment.

(d) A civil penalty under this section is recoverable in a suit filed in the name of the commission by the attorney general on the attorney general's own initiative or at the request of the commission.

Acts 1997, 75th Leg., ch. 166, § 1, eff. Sept. 1, 1997.

§ 15.030. Offense

(a) A person commits an offense if the person wilfully and knowingly violates this title.

(b) This section does not apply to an offense described by Section 55.138.

(c) An offense under this section is a felony of the third degree.

Acts 1997, 75th Leg., ch. 166, § 1, eff. Sept. 1, 1997.

§ 15.031. Place for Suit

A suit for an injunction or a penalty under this title may be brought in:

(1) Travis County;

(2) a county in which the violation is alleged to have occurred; or

(3) a county in which a defendant resides.

Acts 1997, 75th Leg., ch. 166, § 1, eff. Sept. 1, 1997.

§ 15.032. Penalties Cumulative

(a) A penalty that accrues under this title is cumulative of any other penalty.

(b) A suit for the recovery of a penalty does not bar or affect the recovery of any other penalty or bar a criminal prosecution against any person.

Acts 1997, 75th Leg., ch. 166, § 1, eff. Sept. 1, 1997.

§ 15.033. Disposition of Fines and Penalties

A fine or penalty collected under this title, other than a fine or penalty collected in a criminal proceeding or a penalty collected under Section 15.027(a), shall be paid to the commission.

Acts 1997, 75th Leg., ch. 166, § 1, eff. Sept. 1, 1997.

SUBCHAPTER C. COMPLAINTS

§ 15.051. Complaint by Affected Person

(a) An affected person may complain to the regulatory authority in writing setting forth an act or omission by a public utility in violation or claimed violation of a law that the regulatory authority has jurisdiction to administer or of an order, ordinance, or rule of the regulatory authority.

(b) The commission shall keep for a reasonable period information about each complaint filed with the commission that the commission has authority to resolve. The information shall include:

(1) the date the complaint is received;

(2) the name of the complainant;

(3) the subject matter of the complaint;

(4) a record of each person contacted in relation to the complaint;

(5) a summary of the results of the review or investigation of the complaint; and

(6) if the commission took no action on the complaint, an explanation of the reason the complaint was closed without action.

(c) The commission shall keep a file about each written complaint filed with the commission that the commission has authority to resolve. The commission shall provide to the person filing the complaint and to each person or entity complained about information concerning the commission's policies and procedures on complaint investigation and resolution. The commission, at least quarterly and until final disposition of the complaint, shall notify the person filing the complaint and each person or entity complained about of the status of the complaint unless the notice would jeopardize an undercover investigation.

Acts 1997, 75th Leg., ch. 166, § 1, eff. Sept. 1, 1997. Amended by Acts 2005, 79th Leg., ch. 797, § 8, eff. Sept. 1, 2005.

§ 15.052. Complaint Regarding Recreational Vehicle Park Owner

(a) An affected person may complain to the regulatory authority in writing setting forth an act or omission by a recreational vehicle park owner who provides metered electric service under Subchapter C, Chapter 184,[1] in violation or claimed violation of a law that the regulatory authority has jurisdiction to administer or of an order, ordinance, or rule of the regulatory authority.

(b) The commission shall keep for a reasonable period an information file about each complaint filed with the commission relating to a recreational vehicle park owner.

(c) The commission, at least quarterly and until final disposition of the written complaint, shall notify the parties to the complaint of the status of the complaint unless the notice would jeopardize an undercover investigation.

Acts 1997, 75th Leg., ch. 166, § 1, eff. Sept. 1, 1997.

[1] V.T.C.A., Utilities Code § 184.031 et seq.

CHAPTER 16. COMMISSION FINANCING

SUBCHAPTER A. ASSESSMENT ON PUBLIC UTILITIES

Section
16.001. Assessment on Public Utilities.

Section
16.002. Payment Dates.
16.003. Late Payment Penalty.
16.0031. Expired.
16.004. Collection by Comptroller.

SUBCHAPTER B. GRANTS AND OTHER FINANCIAL ASSISTANCE

16.021. Grants of Federal Funds.

SUBCHAPTER C. MONEY DISPOSITION, ACCOUNTING, AND BUDGET

16.041. Application of State Funds Reform Act.
16.042. Accounting Records.
16.043. Audit.
16.044. Approval of Budget.

SUBCHAPTER A. ASSESSMENT ON PUBLIC UTILITIES

§ 16.001. Assessment on Public Utilities

(a) To defray the expenses incurred in the administration of this title, an assessment is imposed on each public utility, retail electric provider, and electric cooperative within the jurisdiction of the commission that serves the ultimate consumer, including each interexchange telecommunications carrier.

(b) An assessment under this section is equal to one-sixth of one percent of the public utility's, retail electric provider's, or electric cooperative's gross receipts from rates charged to the ultimate consumer in this state.

(c) An interexchange telecommunications carrier that does not provide local exchange telephone service may collect the fee imposed under this section as an additional item separately stated on the customer bill as "utility gross receipts assessment."

Acts 1997, 75th Leg., ch. 166, § 1, eff. Sept. 1, 1997. Amended by Acts 1999, 76th Leg., ch. 405, § 10, eff. Sept. 1, 1999.

§ 16.002. Payment Dates

(a) The assessment is due August 15.

(b) A public utility may instead make quarterly payments due August 15, November 15, February 15, and May 15.

Acts 1997, 75th Leg., ch. 166, § 1, eff. Sept. 1, 1997.

§ 16.003. Late Payment Penalty

(a) An additional fee equal to 10 percent of the amount due shall be assessed for any late payment of an assessment required under this subchapter.

(b) An assessment delinquent for more than 30 days accrues interest at an annual rate of 12 percent on the amount of the assessment and penalty due.

Acts 1997, 75th Leg., ch. 166, § 1, eff. Sept. 1, 1997.

§ 16.0031. Expired

§ 16.004. Collection by Comptroller

The comptroller shall collect the assessment and any penalty or interest due under this subchapter.

Acts 1997, 75th Leg., ch. 166, § 1, eff. Sept. 1, 1997.

SUBCHAPTER B. GRANTS AND OTHER FINANCIAL ASSISTANCE

§ 16.021. Grants of Federal Funds

(a) The commission may apply to an appropriate agency or officer of the United States to receive and spend federal funds available by grant or other similar form of financial assistance.

(b) This section does not impair the ability of the commission to contract with or receive assistance from a state, local, or other authorized source of funds.

Acts 1997, 75th Leg., ch. 166, § 1, eff. Sept. 1, 1997.

SUBCHAPTER C. MONEY DISPOSITION, ACCOUNTING, AND BUDGET

§ 16.041. Application of State Funds Reform Act

Money paid to the commission or to the office under this title is subject to Subchapter F, Chapter 404, Government Code.[1]

Acts 1997, 75th Leg., ch. 166, § 1, eff. Sept. 1, 1997.

[1] V.T.C.A., Government Code § 404.091 et seq.

§ 16.042. Accounting Records

The commission shall keep the accounting records required by the comptroller.

Acts 1997, 75th Leg., ch. 166, § 1, eff. Sept. 1, 1997.

§ 16.043. Audit

The financial transactions of the commission are subject to audit by the state auditor under Chapter 321, Government Code.

Acts 1997, 75th Leg., ch. 166, § 1, eff. Sept. 1, 1997.

§ 16.044. Approval of Budget

The commission budget is subject to legislative approval as part of the General Appropriations Act.

Acts 1997, 75th Leg., ch. 166, § 1, eff. Sept. 1, 1997.

CHAPTER 17. CUSTOMER PROTECTION

SUBCHAPTER A. GENERAL PROVISIONS

Section
17.001. Customer Protection Policy.
17.002. Definitions.
17.003. Customer Awareness.
17.004. Customer Protection Standards.
17.005. Protections for Customers of Municipally Owned Utilities.
17.006. Protections for Customers of Electric Cooperatives.
17.007. Eligibility Process for Customer Service Discounts.
17.008. Protection of Residential Electric Service Applicants and Customers.
17.009. Protection of Residential Telephone Service Applicants and Customers.

SUBCHAPTER B. CERTIFICATION, REGISTRATION, AND REPORTING REQUIREMENTS
17.051. Adoption of Rules.
17.052. Scope of Rules.
17.053. Reports.

SUBCHAPTER C. CUSTOMER'S RIGHT TO CHOICE
17.101. Policy.
17.102. Rules Relating to Choice.

SUBCHAPTER D. PROTECTION AGAINST UNAUTHORIZED CHARGES
17.151. Requirements for Submitting Charges.
17.152. Responsibilities of Billing Utility.
17.153. Records of Disputed Charges.
17.154. Notice.
17.155. Providing Copy of Records.
17.156. Violations.
17.157. Disputes.
17.158. Consistency With Federal Law.

SUBCHAPTER A. GENERAL PROVISIONS

§ 17.001. Customer Protection Policy

(a) The legislature finds that new developments in telecommunications services and the production and delivery of electricity, as well as changes in market structure, marketing techniques, and technology, make it essential that customers have safeguards against fraudulent, unfair, misleading, deceptive, or anticompetitive business practices and against businesses that do not have the technical and financial resources to provide adequate service.

(b) The purpose of this chapter is to establish retail customer protection standards and confer on the commission authority to adopt and enforce rules to protect retail customers from fraudulent, unfair, misleading, deceptive, or anticompetitive practices.

(c) Nothing in this section shall be construed to abridge customer rights set forth in commission rules in effect at the time of the enactment of this chapter.

(d) This chapter does not limit the constitutional, statutory, and common law authority of the office of the attorney general.

(e) Nothing in this chapter authorizes a customer to receive retail electric service from a person other than a certificated retail electric utility.

Added by Acts 1999, 76th Leg., ch. 1579, § 3, eff. Aug. 30, 1999.

§ 17.002. Definitions

In this chapter:

(1) "Billing agent" means any entity that submits charges to the billing utility on behalf of itself or any provider of a product or service.

(2) "Billing utility" means any telecommunications provider, as defined by Section 51.002, retail electric provider, or electric utility that issues a bill directly to a customer for any telecommunications or electric product or service.

(3) "Certificated telecommunications utility" means a telecommunications utility that has been granted either a certificate of convenience and necessity, a certificate of operating authority, or a service provider certificate of operating authority.

(4) "Customer" means any person in whose name telephone or retail electric service is billed, including individuals, governmental units at all levels of government, corporate entities, and any other entity with legal capacity to be billed for telephone or retail electric service.

(5) "Electric utility" has the meaning assigned by Section 31.002.

(6) "Retail electric provider" means a person that sells electric energy to retail customers in this state after the legislature authorizes a customer to receive retail electric service from a person other than a certificated retail electric utility.

(7) "Service provider" means any entity that offers a product or service to a customer and that directly or indirectly charges to or collects from a customer's bill an amount for the product or service on a customer's bill received from a billing utility.

(8) "Telecommunications utility" has the meaning assigned by Section 51.002.

Added by Acts 1999, 76th Leg., ch. 1579, § 3, eff. Aug. 30, 1999.

§ 17.003. Customer Awareness

(a) The commission shall promote public awareness of changes in the electric and telecommunications markets, provide customers with information necessary to make informed choices about available options, and ensure that customers have an adequate understanding of their rights.

(b) The commission shall compile a report on customer service at least once each year showing the comparative customer information from reports given to the commission it deems necessary.

(c) The commission shall adopt and enforce rules to require a certificated telecommunications utility, a retail electric provider, or an electric utility to give clear, uniform, and understandable information to customers about rates, terms, services, customer rights, and other necessary information as determined by the commission. The rules must include a list of defined terms common to the telecommunications and electricity industries and require that applicable terms be labeled uniformly on each retail bill sent to a customer by a certificated telecommunications utility, retail electric provider, or electric utility to facilitate consumer understanding of relevant billing elements.

(d) Customer awareness efforts by the commission shall be conducted in English and Spanish and any other language as necessary.

Added by Acts 1999, 76th Leg., ch. 1579, § 3, eff. Aug. 30, 1999. Amended by Acts 2009, 81st Leg., ch. 648, § 1, eff. Sept. 1, 2009.

§ 17.004. Customer Protection Standards

(a) All buyers of telecommunications and retail electric services are entitled to:

(1) protection from fraudulent, unfair, misleading, deceptive, or anticompetitive practices, including protection from being billed for services that were not authorized or provided;

(2) choice of a telecommunications service provider, a retail electric provider, or an electric utility, where that choice is permitted by law, and to have that choice honored;

(3) information in English and Spanish and any other language as the commission deems necessary concerning rates, key terms and conditions, and the basis for any claim of environmental benefits of certain production facilities;

(4) protection from discrimination on the basis of race, color, sex, nationality, religion, marital status, income level, or source of income and from unreasonable discrimination on the basis of geographic location;

(5) impartial and prompt resolution of disputes with a certificated telecommunications utility, a retail electric provider, or an electric utility and disputes with a telecommunications service provider related to unauthorized charges and switching of service;

(6) privacy of customer consumption and credit information;

(7) accuracy of metering and billing;

(8) bills presented in a clear, readable format and easy-to-understand language that uses defined terms as required by commission rules adopted under Section 17.003;

(9) information in English and Spanish and any other language as the commission deems necessary concerning low-income assistance programs and deferred payment plans;

(10) all consumer protections and disclosures established by the Fair Credit Reporting Act (15 U.S.C. Section 1681 et seq.) and the Truth in Lending Act (15 U.S.C. Section 1601 et seq.); and

(11) after retail competition begins as authorized by the legislature, programs provided by retail electric providers that offer eligible low-income customers energy efficiency programs, an affordable rate package, and bill payment assistance programs designed to reduce uncollectible accounts.

(b) The commission may adopt and enforce rules as necessary or appropriate to carry out this section, including rules for minimum service standards for a certificated telecommunications utility, a retail electric provider, or an electric utility relating to customer deposits and the extension of credit, switching fees, levelized billing programs, and termination of service and to energy efficiency programs, an affordable rate package, and bill payment assistance programs for low-income customers. The commission may waive language requirements for good cause.

(c) The commission shall request the comments of the office of the attorney general in developing the rules that may be necessary or appropriate to carry out this section.

(d) The commission shall coordinate its enforcement efforts regarding the prosecution of fraudulent, misleading, deceptive, and anticompetitive business practices with the office of the attorney general in order to ensure consistent treatment of specific alleged violations.

(e) Nothing in this section shall be construed to abridge customer rights set forth in commission rules or to abridge the rights of low-income customers to receive benefits through pending or operating programs in effect at the time of the enactment of this chapter.

(f) The commission shall adopt rules to provide automatic enrollment of eligible utility customers for lifeline telephone service and reduced electric rates available to low-income households. Each state agency, on the request of the commission, shall assist in the adoption and implementation of those rules.

(g) Notwithstanding any other provision of this title, the rules adopted under Subsection (b) shall provide full, concurrent reimbursement for the costs of any programs provided under Subsection (a)(11) and for reimbursement for the difference between any affordable rate package provided under Subsection (a)(11) and any rates otherwise applicable.

Added by Acts 1999, 76th Leg., ch. 1579, § 3, eff. Aug. 30, 1999. Amended by Acts 2009, 81st Leg., ch. 648, § 2, eff. Sept. 1, 2009.

§ 17.005. Protections for Customers of Municipally Owned Utilities

A municipally owned utility may not be deemed to be a "service provider" or "billing agent" for purposes of Sections 17.156(b) and (e). The governing body of a municipally owned utility shall adopt, implement, and enforce rules that shall have the effect of accomplishing the objectives set out in Sections 17.004(a) and (b) and 17.102, as to the municipally owned utility within its certificated service area. The governing body of a municipally owned utility or its designee shall perform the dispute resolution function provided for by Section 17.157 for disputes arising from services provided by the municipally owned utility to electric customers served within the municipally owned utility's certificated service area. With respect to electric customers served by a municipally owned utility outside its certificated service area or otherwise served through others' distribution facilities, after retail competition begins as authorized by the legislature, the provisions of this chapter as administered by the commission apply. Nothing in this chapter shall be deemed to apply to a wholesale customer of a municipally owned utility.

Added by Acts 1999, 76th Leg., ch. 1579, § 3, eff. Aug. 30, 1999.

§ 17.006. Protections for Customers of Electric Cooperatives

An electric cooperative shall not be deemed to be a "service provider" or "billing agent" for purposes of Sections 17.156(b) and (e). The electric cooperative shall adopt, implement, and enforce rules that shall have the effect of accomplishing the objectives set out in Sections 17.004(a) and (b) and 17.102. The board of directors of the electric cooperative or its designee shall perform the dispute resolution function provided for by Section 17.157 for electric customers served by the electric cooperative within its certificated service area. With respect to electric customers served by an electric cooperative outside its certificated service area or otherwise served through others' distribution facilities, after the legislature authorizes retail competition, the provisions of this chapter as administered by the commission shall apply. Nothing in this chapter shall be deemed to apply to a wholesale customer of an electric cooperative.

Added by Acts 1999, 76th Leg., ch. 1579, § 3, eff. Aug. 30, 1999.

§ 17.007. Eligibility Process for Customer Service Discounts

The commission by rule shall provide for an integrated eligibility process for customer service discounts, including discounts under Sections 39.903 and 55. 015.

Added by Acts 2001, 77th Leg., ch. 1451, § 1, eff. Sept. 1, 2001.

§ 17.008. Protection of Residential Electric Service Applicants and Customers

(a) In this section and in Section 17.009:

(1) "Credit history":

(A) means information regarding an individual's past history of:

(i) financial responsibility;

(ii) payment habits; or

(iii) creditworthiness; and

(B) does not include an individual's outstanding balance for retail electric or telecommunications service.

(2) "Credit score" means a score, grade, or value that is derived by a consumer reporting agency, as defined under Section 603(f) of the Fair Credit Reporting Act (15 U.S.C. Section 1681a(f)), using data from a credit history in any type of model, method, or program for the purpose of grading or

ranking credit report data, whether derived electronically, from an algorithm, through a computer software application model or program, or through any other analogous process.

(3) "Utility payment data" means a measure that is derived by a consumer reporting agency, as defined under Section 603(f) of the Fair Credit Reporting Act (15 U.S.C. Section 1681a(f)), from a model specifically designed to correlate to utility payment histories.

(b) A retail electric provider may not deny an applicant's request to become a residential electric service customer on the basis of the applicant's credit history or credit score, but may use the applicant's utility payment data until the later of January 1, 2007, or the date on which the price to beat is no longer in effect in the geographic area in which the customer is located.

(c) Notwithstanding Subsection (b), while a retail electric provider is required to provide service to a geographic area as the affiliated retail electric provider, the provider may not deny an applicant's request to become a residential electric service customer within that geographic area on the basis of the applicant's credit history, credit score, or utility payment data.

(d) After the date described in Subsection (b), a retail electric provider, including an affiliated retail electric provider, may not deny an applicant's request to become a residential electric service customer on the basis of the applicant's credit history, credit score, or utility payment data but may use the applicant's electric bill payment history.

(e) A retail electric provider may not use a credit score, a credit history, or utility payment data as the basis for determining the price for month-to-month electric service or electric service that includes a fixed price commitment of 12 months or less:

(1) for an existing residential customer; or

(2) in response to an applicant's request to become a residential electric service customer.

(f) After the date described in Subsection (b), on request by a customer or former customer in this state, a retail electric provider or electric utility shall timely provide to the customer or former customer bill payment history information with the retail electric provider or electric utility during the preceding 12-month period. Bill payment history information may be obtained by the customer or former customer once during each 12-month period without charge. If additional copies of bill payment history information are requested during a 12-month period, the electric service provider may charge the customer or former customer a reasonable fee for each copy.

(g) On request by a retail electric provider, another retail electric provider or electric utility shall timely verify information that purports to show a customer's service and bill payment history with the retail electric provider or electric utility.

(h) This section does not limit a retail electric provider's authority to require a deposit or advance payment as a condition of service.

(i) Notwithstanding Subsection (e), a retail electric provider may provide rewards, benefits, or credits to residential electric service customers on the basis of the customer's payment history for retail electric service to that provider.

Added by Acts 2005, 79th Leg., ch. 926, § 1, eff. Sept. 1, 2005.

§ 17.009. Protection of Residential Telephone Service Applicants and Customers

(a) A provider of basic local telecommunications services and nonbasic network services may not deny an applicant's request to become a residential customer on the basis of the applicant's credit history or credit score.

(b) A provider of basic local telecommunications services and nonbasic network services may not use a credit score or credit history as the basis for determining price for service:

(1) for an existing residential customer; or

(2) in response to an applicant's request to become a residential customer.

(c) This section does not limit the authority of a provider of basic local telecommunications services and nonbasic network services to require a deposit, advance payment, or credit limit as a condition of service.

Added by Acts 2005, 79th Leg., ch. 926, § 1, eff. Sept. 1, 2005.

SUBCHAPTER B. CERTIFICATION, REGISTRATION, AND REPORTING REQUIREMENTS

§ 17.051. Adoption of Rules

(a) The commission shall adopt rules relating to certification, registration, and reporting requirements for a certificated telecommunications utility, a retail electric provider, or an electric utility, as well as all telecommunications utilities that are not dominant carriers, pay telephone providers, qualifying facilities that are selling capacity into the wholesale or retail market, exempt wholesale generators, and power marketers.

(b) The rules adopted under Subsections (a) and (c) shall be consistent with and no less effective than federal law and may not require the disclosure of highly sensitive competitive or trade secret information.

(c) The commission shall adopt rules governing the local registration of retail electric providers under Section 39.358.

Added by Acts 1999, 76th Leg., ch. 1579, § 3, eff. Aug. 30, 1999. Amended by Acts 2003, 78th Leg., ch. 48, § 1, eff. Sept. 1, 2003.

§ 17.052. Scope of Rules

The commission may adopt and enforce rules to:

(1) require certification or registration with the commission as a condition of doing business in this state, except that this requirement does not apply to municipally owned utilities;

(2) amend certificates or registrations to reflect changed ownership and control;

(3) establish rules for customer service and protection;

(4) suspend or revoke certificates or registrations for repeated violations of this chapter or commission rules, except that the commission may not revoke a certificate of convenience and necessity of an electric utility except as provided by Section 37.059 or a certificate of convenience and necessity of a telecommunications utility except as provided by Section 54.008; and

(5) order disconnection of a pay telephone service provider's pay telephones or revocation of certification or registration for repeated violations of this chapter or commission rules.

Added by Acts 1999, 76th Leg., ch. 1579, § 3, eff. Aug. 30, 1999.

§ 17.053. Reports

The commission may require a telecommunications service provider, a retail electric provider, or an electric utility to submit reports to the commission concerning any matter over which it has authority under this chapter.

Added by Acts 1999, 76th Leg., ch. 1579, § 3, eff. Aug. 30, 1999.

SUBCHAPTER C. CUSTOMER'S RIGHT TO CHOICE

§ 17.101. Policy

It is the policy of this state that all customers be protected from the unauthorized switching of a telecommunications service provider, a retail electric provider, or an electric utility selected by the customer to provide service, where choice is permitted by law.

Added by Acts 1999, 76th Leg., ch. 1579, § 3, eff. Aug. 30, 1999.

§ 17.102. Rules Relating to Choice

The commission shall adopt and enforce rules that:

(1) ensure that customers are protected from deceptive practices employed in obtaining authorizations of service and in the verification of change orders, including negative option marketing, sweepstakes, and contests that cause customers to unknowingly change their telecommunications service provider, retail electric provider, or electric utility, where choice is permitted by law;

(2) provide for clear, easily understandable identification, in each bill sent to a customer, of all telecommunications service providers, retail electric providers, or electric utilities submitting charges on the bill;

(3) ensure that every service provider submitting charges on the bill is clearly and easily identified on the bill along with its services, products, and charges, using defined terms as required by commission rules adopted under Section 17.003;

(4) provide that unauthorized changes in service be remedied at no cost to the customer within a period established by the commission;

(5) require refunds or credits to the customer in the event of an unauthorized change; and

(6) provide for penalties for violations of commission rules adopted under this section, including fines and revocation of certificates or registrations, by this action denying the certificated telecommunications utility, the retail electric provider, or the electric utility the right to provide service in this state, except that the commission may not revoke a certificate of convenience and necessity of an electric utility except as provided by Section 37.059 or a certificate of convenience and necessity of a tele-

communications utility except as provided by Section 54.008.

Added by Acts 1999, 76th Leg., ch. 1579, § 3, eff. Aug. 30, 1999. Amended by Acts 2009, 81st Leg., ch. 648, § 3, eff. Sept. 1, 2009.

SUBCHAPTER D. PROTECTION AGAINST UNAUTHORIZED CHARGES

§ 17.151. Requirements for Submitting Charges

(a) A service provider, retail electric provider, or billing agent may submit charges for a new product or service to be billed on a customer's telephone or retail electric bill on or after the effective date of this section only if:

(1) the service provider offering the product or service has thoroughly informed the customer of the product or service being offered, including all associated charges, and has explicitly informed the customer that the associated charges for the product or service will appear on the customer's telephone or electric bill;

(2) the customer has clearly and explicitly consented to obtain the product or service offered and to have the associated charges appear on the customer's telephone or electric bill and the consent has been verified as provided by Subsection (b);

(3) the service provider offering the product or service and any billing agent for the service provider:

(A) has provided the customer with a toll-free telephone number the customer may call and an address to which the customer may write to resolve any billing dispute and to answer questions; and

(B) has contracted with the billing utility to bill for products and services on the billing utility's bill as provided by Subsection (c); and

(4) the service provider, retail electric provider, or billing agent uses defined terms on the bill as required by commission rules adopted under Section 17.003.

(b) The customer consent required by Subsection (a)(2) must be verified by the service provider offering the product or service by authorization from the customer. A record of the customer consent, including verification, must be maintained by the service provider offering the product or service for a period of at least 24 months immediately after the consent and verification have been obtained. The method of obtaining customer consent and verification must include one or more of the following:

(1) written authorization from the customer;

(2) toll-free electronic authorization placed from the telephone number that is the subject of the product or service;

(3) oral authorization obtained by an independent third party; or

(4) any other method of authorization approved by the commission or the Federal Communications Commission.

(c) The contract required by Subsection (a)(3)(B) must include the service provider's name, business address, and business telephone number and shall be maintained by the billing utility for as long as the billing for the products and services continues and for the 24 months immediately following the permanent discontinuation of the billing.

(d) A service provider offering a product or service to be charged on a customer's telephone or electric bill and any billing agent for the service provider may not use any fraudulent, unfair, misleading, deceptive, or anticompetitive marketing practice to obtain customers, including the use of negative option marketing, sweepstakes, and contests.

(e) Unless verification is required by federal law or rules implementing federal law, Subsection (b) does not apply to customer-initiated transactions with a certificated telecommunications provider or an electric utility for which the service provider has the appropriate documentation.

(f) If a service provider is notified by a billing utility that a customer has reported to the billing utility that a charge made by the service provider is unauthorized, the service provider shall cease to charge the customer for the unauthorized product or service.

(g) This section does not apply to message telecommunications services charges that are initiated by dialing 1+, 0+, 0–, 1010XXX, or collect calls and charges for video services if the service provider has the necessary call detail record to establish the billing for the call or service.

Added by Acts 1999, 76th Leg., ch. 1579, § 3, eff. Aug. 30, 1999. Amended by Acts 2009, 81st Leg., ch. 648, § 4, eff. Sept. 1, 2009.

§ 17.152. Responsibilities of Billing Utility

(a) If a customer's telephone or retail electric bill is charged for any product or service without proper customer consent or verification, the billing utility, on its knowledge or notification of any unauthorized charge, shall promptly, not later than 45 days after the date of knowledge or notification of the charge:

(1) notify the service provider to cease charging the customer for the unauthorized product or service;

(2) remove any unauthorized charge from the customer's bill;

(3) refund or credit to the customer all money that has been paid by the customer for any unauthorized charge, and if the unauthorized charge is not adjusted within three billing cycles, shall pay interest on the amount of the unauthorized charge;

(4) on the customer's request, provide the customer with all billing records under its control related to any unauthorized charge within 15 business days after the date of the removal of the unauthorized charge from the customer's bill; and

(5) maintain for at least 24 months a record of every customer who has experienced any unauthorized charge for a product or service on the customer's telephone or electric bill and who has notified the billing utility of the unauthorized charge.

(b) A record required by Subsection (a)(5) shall contain for each unauthorized charge:

(1) the name of the service provider that offered the product or service;

(2) any affected telephone numbers or addresses;

(3) the date the customer requested that the billing utility remove the unauthorized charge;

(4) the date the unauthorized charge was removed from the customer's telephone or electric bill; and

(5) the date any money that the customer paid for the unauthorized charges was refunded or credited to the customer.

(c) A billing utility may not:

(1) disconnect or terminate telecommunications or electric service to any customer for nonpayment of an unauthorized charge; or

(2) file an unfavorable credit report against a customer who has not paid charges the customer has alleged were unauthorized unless the dispute regarding the unauthorized charge is ultimately resolved against the customer, except that the customer shall remain obligated to pay any charges that are not in dispute, and this subsection does not apply to those undisputed charges.

Added by Acts 1999, 76th Leg., ch. 1579, § 3, eff. Aug. 30, 1999.

§ 17.153. Records of Disputed Charges

(a) Every service provider shall maintain a record of every disputed charge for a product or service placed on a customer's bill.

(b) The record required under Subsection (a) shall contain for every disputed charge:

(1) any affected telephone numbers or addresses;

(2) the date the customer requested that the billing utility remove the unauthorized charge;

(3) the date the unauthorized charge was removed from the customer's telephone or retail electric bill; and

(4) the date action was taken to refund or credit to the customer any money that the customer paid for the unauthorized charges.

(c) The record required by Subsection (a) shall be maintained for at least 24 months following the completion of all steps required by Section 17.152(a).

Added by Acts 1999, 76th Leg., ch. 1579, § 3, eff. Aug. 30, 1999.

§ 17.154. Notice

(a) A billing utility shall provide notice of a customer's rights under this section in the manner prescribed by the commission.

(b) Notice of a customer's rights must be provided by mail to each residential and retail business customer within 60 days of the effective date of this section or by inclusion in the publication of the telephone directory next following the effective date of this section. In addition, each billing utility shall send the notice to new customers at the time service is initiated or to any customer at that customer's request.

Added by Acts 1999, 76th Leg., ch. 1579, § 3, eff. Aug. 30, 1999.

§ 17.155. Providing Copy of Records

A billing utility shall provide a copy of records maintained under Sections 17.151(c), 17.152, and 17.154 to the commission staff on request. A service provider shall provide a copy of records maintained under Sections 17.151(b) and 17.153 to the commission on request.

Added by Acts 1999, 76th Leg., ch. 1579, § 3, eff. Aug. 30, 1999.

§ 17.156. Violations

(a) If the commission finds that a billing utility violated this subchapter, the commission may implement penalties and other enforcement actions under Chapter 15.

(b) If the commission finds that any other service provider or billing agent subject to this subchapter has violated this subchapter or has knowingly provided false information to the commission on matters subject to this subchapter, the commission may enforce the provisions of Chapter 15 against the service provider or billing agent as if it were regulated by the commission.

(c) Neither the authority granted under this section nor any other provision of this subchapter shall be construed to grant the commission jurisdiction to regulate service providers or billing agents who are not otherwise subject to commission regulation, other than as specifically provided by this chapter.

(d) If the commission finds that a billing utility or service provider repeatedly violates this subchapter, the commission may, if the action is consistent with the public interest, suspend, restrict, or revoke the registration or certificate of the telecommunications service provider, retail electric provider, or electric utility, by this action denying the telecommunications service provider, retail electric provider, or electric utility the right to provide service in this state, except that the commission may not revoke a certificate of convenience and necessity of an electric utility except as provided by Section 37.059 or a certificate of convenience and necessity of a telecommunications utility except as provided by Section 54.008.

(e) If the commission finds that a service provider or billing agent has repeatedly violated any provision of this subchapter, the commission may order the billing utility to terminate billing and collection services for that service provider or billing agent.

(f) Nothing in this subchapter shall be construed to preclude a billing utility from taking action on its own to terminate or restrict its billing and collection services.

Added by Acts 1999, 76th Leg., ch. 1579, § 3, eff. Aug. 30, 1999.

§ 17.157. Disputes

(a) The commission may resolve disputes between a retail customer and a billing utility, service provider, telecommunications utility, retail electric provider, or electric utility.

(b) In exercising its authority under Subsection (a), the commission may:

(1) order a billing utility, service provider, retail electric provider, or electric utility to produce information or records;

(2) require that all contracts, bills, and other communications from a billing utility, service provider, retail electric provider, or electric utility display a working toll-free telephone number that customers may call with complaints and inquiries;

(3) require a billing utility, service provider, retail electric provider, or electric utility to refund or credit overcharges or unauthorized charges with interest if the billing utility, service provider, retail electric provider, or electric utility has failed to comply with commission rules or a contract with the customer;

(4) order appropriate relief to ensure that a customer's choice of a telecommunications service provider, a retail electric provider, or an electric utility that encompasses a geographic area in which more than one provider has been certificated is honored;

(5) require the continuation of service to a residential or small commercial customer while a dispute is pending regarding charges the customer has alleged were unauthorized; and

(6) investigate an alleged violation.

(c) The commission shall adopt procedures for the resolution of disputes in a timely manner, which in no event shall exceed 60 days.

Added by Acts 1999, 76th Leg., ch. 1579, § 3, eff. Aug. 30, 1999.

§ 17.158. Consistency With Federal Law

Rules adopted by the commission under this subchapter shall be consistent with and not more burdensome than applicable federal laws and rules.

Added by Acts 1999, 76th Leg., ch. 1579, § 3, eff. Aug. 30, 1999.

SUBTITLE B. ELECTRIC UTILITIES

CHAPTER 31. GENERAL PROVISIONS

Section

31.001. Legislative Findings; Purpose of Subtitle.
31.002. Definitions.
31.003. Report on Scope of Competition.
31.004. Energy-Efficient School Facilities.
31.005. Customer–option Programs.

§ 31.001. Legislative Findings; Purpose of Subtitle

(a) This subtitle is enacted to protect the public interest inherent in the rates and services of electric utilities. The purpose of this subtitle is to establish a comprehensive and adequate regulatory system for electric utilities to assure rates, operations, and services that are just and reasonable to the consumers and to the electric utilities.

(b) Electric utilities are by definition monopolies in many of the services provided and areas they serve. As a result, the normal forces of competition that regulate prices in a free enterprise society do not always operate. Public agencies regulate electric utility rates, operations, and services, except as otherwise provided by this subtitle.

(c) The wholesale electric industry, through federal legislative, judicial, and administrative actions, is becoming a more competitive industry that does not lend itself to traditional electric utility regulatory rules, policies, and principles. As a result, the public interest requires that rules, policies, and principles be formulated and applied to protect the public interest in a more competitive marketplace. The development of a competitive wholesale electric market that allows for increased participation by electric utilities and certain nonutilities is in the public interest.

Acts 1997, 75th Leg., ch. 166, § 1, eff. Sept. 1, 1997.

§ 31.002. Definitions

In this subtitle:

(1) "Affiliated power generation company" means a power generation company that is affiliated with or the successor in interest of an electric utility certificated to serve an area.

(2) "Affiliated retail electric provider" means a retail electric provider that is affiliated with or the successor in interest of an electric utility certificated to serve an area.

(3) "Aggregation" includes the following:

(A) the purchase of electricity from a retail electric provider, a municipally owned utility, or an electric cooperative by an electricity customer for its own use in multiple locations, provided that an electricity customer may not avoid any nonbypassable charges or fees as a result of aggregating its load; or

(B) the purchase of electricity by an electricity customer as part of a voluntary association of electricity customers, provided that an electricity customer may not avoid any nonbypassable charges or fees as a result of aggregating its load.

(4) "Customer choice" means the freedom of a retail customer to purchase electric services, either individually or through voluntary aggregation with other retail customers, from the provider or providers of the customer's choice and to choose among various fuel types, energy efficiency programs, and renewable power suppliers.

(4–a) "Distributed natural gas generation facility" means a facility installed on the customer's side of the meter that uses natural gas to generate not more than 2,000 kilowatts of electricity.

(5) "Electric Reliability Council of Texas" or "ERCOT" means the area in Texas served by electric utilities, municipally owned utilities, and electric cooperatives that is not synchronously interconnected with electric utilities outside the state.

(6) "Electric utility" means a person or river authority that owns or operates for compensation in this state equipment or facilities to produce, generate, transmit, distribute, sell, or furnish electricity in this state. The term includes a lessee, trustee, or receiver of an electric utility and a recreational vehicle park owner who does not comply with Subchapter C, Chapter 184,[1] with regard to the metered sale of electricity at the recreational vehicle park. The term does not include:

(A) a municipal corporation;

(B) a qualifying facility;

(C) a power generation company;

(D) an exempt wholesale generator;

(E) a power marketer;

(F) a corporation described by Section 32.053 to the extent the corporation sells electricity exclusively at wholesale and not to the ultimate consumer;

(G) an electric cooperative;

(H) a retail electric provider;

(I) this state or an agency of this state; or

(J) a person not otherwise an electric utility who:

(i) furnishes an electric service or commodity only to itself, its employees, or its tenants as an incident of employment or tenancy, if that service or commodity is not resold to or used by others;

(ii) owns or operates in this state equipment or facilities to produce, generate, transmit, distribute, sell, or furnish electric energy to an electric utility, if the equipment or facilities are used primarily to produce and generate electric energy for consumption by that person; or

(iii) owns or operates in this state a recreational vehicle park that provides metered electric service in accordance with Subchapter C, Chapter 184.

(7) "Exempt wholesale generator" means a person who is engaged directly or indirectly through one or more affiliates exclusively in the business of owning or operating all or part of a facility for generating electric energy and selling electric energy at wholesale and who:

(A) does not own a facility for the transmission of electricity, other than an essential interconnecting transmission facility necessary to effect a sale of electric energy at wholesale; and

(B) has:

(i) applied to the Federal Energy Regulatory Commission for a determination under 15 U.S.C. Section 79z–5a; or

(ii) registered as an exempt wholesale generator as required by Section 35.032.

(8) "Freeze period" means the period beginning on January 1, 1999, and ending on December 31, 2001.

(9) "Independent system operator" means an entity supervising the collective transmission facilities of a power region that is charged with nondiscriminatory coordination of market transactions, systemwide transmission planning, and network reliability.

(10) "Power generation company" means a person, including a person who owns or operates a distributed natural gas generation facility, that:

(A) generates electricity that is intended to be sold at wholesale, including the owner or operator of electric energy storage equipment or facilities to which Subchapter E, Chapter 35, applies;

(B) does not own a transmission or distribution facility in this state other than an essential interconnecting facility, a facility not dedicated to public use, or a facility otherwise excluded from the definition of "electric utility" under this section; and

(C) does not have a certificated service area, although its affiliated electric utility or transmission and distribution utility may have a certificated service area.

(11) "Power marketer" means a person who:

(A) becomes an owner of electric energy in this state for the purpose of selling the electric energy at wholesale;

(B) does not own generation, transmission, or distribution facilities in this state;

(C) does not have a certificated service area; and

(D) has:

(i) been granted authority by the Federal Energy Regulatory Commission to sell electric energy at market-based rates; or

(ii) registered as a power marketer under Section 35.032.

(12) "Power region" means a contiguous geographical area which is a distinct region of the North American Electric Reliability Council.

(13) "Qualifying cogenerator" and "qualifying small power producer" have the meanings assigned those terms by 16 U.S.C. Sections 796(18)(C) and 796(17)(D). A qualifying cogenerator that provides electricity to the purchaser of the cogenerator's thermal output is not for that reason considered to be a retail electric provider or a power generation company.

(14) "Qualifying facility" means a qualifying cogenerator or qualifying small power producer.

(15) "Rate" includes a compensation, tariff, charge, fare, toll, rental, or classification that is directly or indirectly demanded, observed, charged, or collected by an electric utility for a service, product, or commodity described in the definition of electric utility in this section and a rule, practice, or contract affecting the compensation, tariff, charge, fare, toll, rental, or classification that must be approved by a regulatory authority.

(16) "Retail customer" means the separately metered end-use customer who purchases and ultimately consumes electricity.

(17) "Retail electric provider" means a person that sells electric energy to retail customers in this state. A retail electric provider may not own or operate generation assets.

(18) "Separately metered" means metered by an individual meter that is used to measure electric energy consumption by a retail customer and for which the customer is directly billed by a utility, retail electric provider, electric cooperative, or municipally owned utility.

(19) "Transmission and distribution utility" means a person or river authority that owns or operates for compensation in this state equipment or facilities to transmit or distribute electricity, except for facilities necessary to interconnect a generation facility with the transmission or distribution network, a facility not dedicated to public use, or a facility otherwise excluded from the definition of "electric utility" under this section, in a qualifying power region certified under Section 39.152, but

does not include a municipally owned utility or an electric cooperative.

(20) "Transmission service" includes construction or enlargement of facilities, transmission over distribution facilities, control area services, scheduling resources, regulation services, reactive power support, voltage control, provision of operating reserves, and any other associated electrical service the commission determines appropriate, except that, on and after the implementation of customer choice, control area services, scheduling resources, regulation services, provision of operating reserves, and reactive power support, voltage control, and other services provided by generation resources are not "transmission service."

Acts 1997, 75th Leg., ch. 166, § 1, eff. Sept. 1, 1997. Amended by Acts 1999, 76th Leg., ch. 405, § 11, eff. Sept. 1, 1999; Acts 2011, 82nd Leg., ch. 890 (S.B. 365), § 1, eff. Sept. 1, 2011; Acts 2011, 82nd Leg., ch. 1069 (S.B. 943), § 1, eff. Sept. 1, 2011.

[1] V.T.C.A., Utilities Code § 184.031 et seq.

Section 3 of Acts 2011, 82nd Leg., ch. 1069 (S.B. 943) provides:

"Subdivision (10), Section 31.002, Utilities Code, as amended by this Act, and Subchapter E, Chapter 35, Utilities Code, as added by this Act, may not be construed to determine the regulatory treatment of electricity acquired to charge electric energy storage equipment or facilities and used solely for the purpose of later sale as energy or ancillary services."

§ 31.003. Report on Scope of Competition

(a) Before January 15 of each odd-numbered year, the commission shall report to the legislature on the scope of competition in electric markets and the effect of competition and industry restructuring on customers in both competitive and noncompetitive markets.

(b) The report under this section must include:

(1) an assessment of the effect of competition on the rates and availability of electric services for residential and small commercial customers;

(2) a summary of commission action over the preceding two years that reflects changes in the scope of competition in regulated electric markets; and

(3) recommendations to the legislature for legislation that the commission finds appropriate to promote the public interest in the context of a partially competitive electric market.

Acts 1997, 75th Leg., ch. 166, § 1, eff. Sept. 1, 1997.

§ 31.004. Energy-Efficient School Facilities

(a) The commission may serve as a resource center to assist school districts in developing energy-efficient facilities.

(b) As a resource center under this section, the commission may:

(1) present programs to school districts relating to managing energy, training school-plant operators, and designing energy-efficient buildings;

(2) provide school districts with technical assistance in managing energy;

(3) collect and distribute information relating to energy management in school facilities; and

(4) offer energy resource workshops to educators and make available to educators a film library on energy-related matters and energy education lesson packages.

(c) The commission shall provide information to school districts regarding how a school district may finance the installation of solar electric generation panels for school district buildings.

Acts 1997, 75th Leg., ch. 166, § 1, eff. Sept. 1, 1997. Amended by Acts 2007, 80th Leg., ch. 939, § 18, eff. Sept. 1, 2007.

§ 31.005. Customer–option Programs

(a) This section applies to:

(1) a municipally owned electric utility;

(2) an electric cooperative;

(3) an electric utility;

(4) a power marketer;

(5) a retail electric provider; and

(6) a transmission and distribution utility.

(b) An entity to which this section applies shall consider establishing customer-option programs that encourage the reduction of air contaminant emissions, such as:

(1) an appliance retirement and recycling program;

(2) a solar water heating market transformation program;

(3) an air conditioning tune-up program;

(4) a program that allows the use of on-site energy storage as an eligible efficiency measure in existing programs;

(5) a program that encourages the deployment of advanced electricity meters;

(6) a program that encourages the installation of cool roofing materials;

(7) a program that establishes lighting limits;

(8) a distributed energy generation technology program; and

(9) a program that encourages the use of high-efficiency building distribution transformers and variable air volume fan controls.

Added by Acts 2005, 79th Leg., ch. 1095, § 6, eff. Sept. 1, 2005.

CHAPTER 32. JURISDICTION AND POWERS OF COMMISSION AND OTHER REGULATORY AUTHORITIES

SUBCHAPTER A. COMMISSION JURISDICTION

Section

32.001. Commission Jurisdiction.
32.0015. Regulation of Successor Electric Utility or Electric Cooperative.
32.002. Limitation on Commission Jurisdiction.
32.003. Exempt Area Jurisdiction.
32.004. Assistance to Municipality.

SUBCHAPTER B. EXEMPTIONS FROM COMMISSION JURISDICTION

32.051. Exemption of River Authority From Wholesale Rate Regulation.
32.052. Ability of Certain River Authorities to Construct Improvements.
32.053. Ability of Certain River Authority Affiliates to Construct Improvements.
32.054. Restrictions on Authority of Corporations or River Authority.

SUBCHAPTER C. REQUIRED REPORTS AND FILINGS

32.101. Tariff Filings.
32.102. Depreciation Account.
32.103. Accounts of Profits and Losses.
32.104. Report of Certain Expenses.

SUBCHAPTER A. COMMISSION JURISDICTION

§ 32.001. Commission Jurisdiction

(a) Except as provided by Section 32.002, the commission has exclusive original jurisdiction over the rates, operations, and services of an electric utility in:

(1) areas outside a municipality; and

(2) areas inside a municipality that surrenders its jurisdiction to the commission under Section 33.002.

(b) The commission has exclusive appellate jurisdiction to review an order or ordinance of a municipality exercising exclusive original jurisdiction under this subtitle.

Acts 1997, 75th Leg., ch. 166, § 1, eff. Sept. 1, 1997.

§ 32.0015. Regulation of Successor Electric Utility or Electric Cooperative

If an electric utility purchases, acquires, merges, or consolidates with or acquires 50 percent or more of the stock of an electric utility or electric cooperative, the commission shall regulate the successor electric utility or electric cooperative in the same manner that the commission would regulate the entity that was subject to the stricter regulation before the purchase, acquisition, merger, or consolidation.

Added by Acts 1999, 76th Leg., ch. 405, § 12, eff. Sept. 1, 1999.

§ 32.002. Limitation on Commission Jurisdiction

Except as otherwise provided by this title, this subtitle does not authorize the commission to:

(1) regulate or supervise a rate or service of a municipally owned utility; or

(2) affect the jurisdiction, power, or duty of a municipality exercising exclusive original jurisdiction in that municipality's regulation and supervision of an electric utility in the municipality.

Acts 1997, 75th Leg., ch. 166, § 1, eff. Sept. 1, 1997.

§ 32.003. Exempt Area Jurisdiction

Notwithstanding an election under Subchapter A, Chapter 33, by a municipality on the issue of surrendering its jurisdiction, the commission may:

(1) consider an electric utility's revenues and return on investment in an area exempt from commission regulation in establishing rates and charges in an area that is not exempt from commission regulation; and

(2) exercise necessary powers to give effect to an order under this title for the benefit of an area that is not exempt from commission regulation.

Acts 1997, 75th Leg., ch. 166, § 1, eff. Sept. 1, 1997.

§ 32.004. Assistance to Municipality

On request of a municipality, the commission may advise and assist the municipality with respect to a question or proceeding arising under this title. Assistance provided by the commission may include aid to a municipality on a matter pending before the commission, a court, or the municipality's governing body, such as making a staff member available as a witness or otherwise providing evidence to the municipality.

Acts 1997, 75th Leg., ch. 166, § 1, eff. Sept. 1, 1997.

SUBCHAPTER B. EXEMPTIONS FROM COMMISSION JURISDICTION

§ 32.051. Exemption of River Authority From Wholesale Rate Regulation

Notwithstanding any other provision of this title, the commission may not directly or indirectly regulate revenue requirements, rates, fuel costs, fuel charges, or fuel acquisitions that are related to the generation and sale of electricity at wholesale, and not to ultimate consumers, by a river authority operating a steam generating plant on or before January 1, 1999.

Acts 1997, 75th Leg., ch. 166, § 1, eff. Sept. 1, 1997. Amended by Acts 1999, 76th Leg., ch. 405, § 13, eff. Sept. 1, 1999.

§ 32.052. Ability of Certain River Authorities to Construct Improvements

A river authority operating a steam generating plant on or before January 1, 1999, may acquire, finance, construct, rebuild, repower, and use new or existing power plants, equipment, transmission lines, or other assets to sell electricity exclusively at wholesale to:

(1) a purchaser in San Saba, Llano, Burnet, Travis, Bastrop, Blanco, Colorado, or Fayette County; or

(2) a purchaser in an area served by the river authority on January 1, 1975.

Acts 1997, 75th Leg., ch. 166, § 1, eff. Sept. 1, 1997. Amended by Acts 1999, 76th Leg., ch. 405, § 13, eff. Sept. 1, 1999.

§ 32.053. Ability of Certain River Authority Affiliates to Construct Improvements

(a) This section applies only to a corporation that:

(1) sells electricity exclusively at wholesale, and not to ultimate consumers;

(2) is authorized by Chapter 152, Water Code; and

(3) acts on behalf of a river authority.

(b) Notwithstanding a river authority's enabling legislation or Chapter 152, Water Code, a corporation may:

(1) acquire, finance, construct, rebuild, repower, operate, or sell a facility directly related to the generation of electricity;

(2) sell, at wholesale only, the output of the facility to a purchaser, other than an ultimate consumer, at any location in this state; and

(3) purchase and sell electricity, at wholesale only, to a purchaser, other than an ultimate consumer, at any location in this state.

(c) This subchapter does not prevent a corporation from purchasing transmission and related services from a river authority.

(d) Except as provided by this section, the development, financing, ownership, and operation of a facility by a corporation is subject to all other applicable laws.

(e) The property, gross receipts, and income of a corporation acting on behalf of a river authority under this section are subject to, and the corporation shall pay, taxes and assessments of the federal government, this state, a political subdivision of this state, or a taxing district of this state on the same basis as an exempt wholesale generator.

(f) The proceeds from the sale of bonds or other obligations the interest on which is exempt from taxation and that are issued by a corporation or river authority subject to this section, other than a bond or obligation available to an investor-owned utility or exempt wholesale generator, may not be used by the corporation to finance the construction or acquisition of or the rebuilding or repowering of a facility for the generation of electricity by the corporation.

(g) Notwithstanding any other law, the board of directors of a river authority may sell, lease, loan, or otherwise transfer some, all, or substantially all of the electric generation property of the river authority to a nonprofit corporation authorized under this section or Chapter 152, Water Code. The property transfer shall be made under terms and conditions approved by the board of directors of the river authority.

(h) Subsections (a)–(f) do not apply to a corporation created under Chapter 152, Water Code, to serve an area described in Section 32.052.

Acts 1997, 75th Leg., ch. 166, § 1, eff. Sept. 1, 1997. Amended by Acts 1999, 76th Leg., ch. 405, § 14, eff. Sept. 1, 1999; Acts 2001, 77th Leg., ch. 1420, § 8.400, eff. Sept. 1, 2001.

§ 32.054. Restrictions on Authority of Corporations or River Authority

(a) This subchapter does not authorize a river authority to acquire, install, construct, make additions to, or operate steam generating plants having an aggregate capacity greater than 5,000 megawatts to serve a purchaser in the area served by the river authority on January 1, 1975.

(b) A river authority or a corporation acting on behalf of a river authority under this subchapter may provide retail service only to a retail customer served by the river authority or corporation on September 1, 1995.

(c) Except as provided by this subchapter, this subchapter does not limit a power granted a river authority in its enabling legislation or other applicable law.

Acts 1997, 75th Leg., ch. 166, § 1, eff. Sept. 1, 1997.

SUBCHAPTER C. REQUIRED REPORTS AND FILINGS

§ 32.101. Tariff Filings

(a) An electric utility shall file with each regulatory authority a tariff showing each rate that is:

(1) subject to the regulatory authority's original or appellate jurisdiction; and

(2) in effect for a utility service, product, or commodity offered by the utility.

(b) The electric utility shall file as a part of the tariff required under Subsection (a) each rule that relates to or affects:

(1) a rate of the utility; or

(2) a utility service, product, or commodity furnished by the electric utility.

(c) The commission shall consider customer names and addresses, prices, individual customer contracts, and expected load and usage data as highly sensitive trade secrets. That information is not subject to disclosure under Chapter 552, Government Code.

Acts 1997, 75th Leg., ch. 166, § 1, eff. Sept. 1, 1997.

§ 32.102. Depreciation Account

The commission shall require each electric or municipally owned utility to carry a proper and adequate depreciation account in accordance with:

(1) the rates and methods prescribed by the commission under Section 36.056; and

(2) any other rule the commission adopts.

Acts 1997, 75th Leg., ch. 166, § 1, eff. Sept. 1, 1997.

§ 32.103. Accounts of Profits and Losses

An electric or municipally owned utility shall keep separate accounts showing profits or losses from the sale or lease of merchandise, including an appliance, a fixture, or equipment.

Acts 1997, 75th Leg., ch. 166, § 1, eff. Sept. 1, 1997.

§ 32.104. Report of Certain Expenses

A regulatory authority may require an electric utility to annually report the utility's expenditures for:

(1) business gifts and entertainment; and

(2) advertising or public relations, including expenditures for institutional and consumption-inducing purposes.

Acts 1997, 75th Leg., ch. 166, § 1, eff. Sept. 1, 1997.

CHAPTER 33. JURISDICTION AND POWERS OF MUNICIPALITY

SUBCHAPTER A. GENERAL PROVISIONS

Section
33.001. Municipal Jurisdiction.
33.002. Surrender of Municipal Jurisdiction to Commission.
33.003. Reinstatement of Municipal Jurisdiction.
33.004. Area Exempt From Commission Regulation.
33.005. Exempt Area Reporting.
33.006. Commission Powers in Nonexempt Areas.
33.007. Allowable Charges.
33.008. Franchise Charges.

SUBCHAPTER B. RATE DETERMINATION

33.021. Rate Determination.
33.022. Consideration of Revenues and Return From Nonexempt Area.
33.023. Ratemaking Proceedings.
33.024. Statement of Intent.
33.025. Municipal Standing.
33.026. Judicial Review.

SUBCHAPTER C. APPEAL OF MUNICIPAL ORDER

33.051. Appeal by Party.
33.052. Appeal by Residents.
33.053. Filing of Appeal.
33.054. Hearing and Order.
33.055. Applicability of Rates.

SUBCHAPTER D. PROVISIONS APPLICABLE TO APPEAL BY RATEPAYERS OUTSIDE MUNICIPALITY

33.101. Appeal by Ratepayers Outside Municipality.
33.102. Identification of Ratepayers Outside Municipality.
33.103. Filing of Appeal.
33.104. Rate Application.

SUBCHAPTER E. RATE DETERMINATION AND APPEAL OF ORDERS OF CERTAIN MUNICIPAL UTILITIES

33.121. Application of Commission Review.
33.122. Review of Certain Rate Decisions.

Section
33.123. Review of Certain Decisions for Rates Charged Outside Municipality.

SUBCHAPTER A. GENERAL PROVISIONS

§ 33.001. Municipal Jurisdiction

(a) To provide fair, just, and reasonable rates and adequate and efficient services, the governing body of a municipality has exclusive original jurisdiction over the rates, operations, and services of an electric utility in areas in the municipality, subject to the limitations imposed by this title.

(b) Notwithstanding Subsection (a), the governing body of a municipality shall not have jurisdiction over the BPL system, BPL services, telecommunications using BPL services, or the rates, operations, or services of the electric utility or transmission and distribution utility to the extent that such rates, operations, or services are related, wholly or partly, to the construction, maintenance, or operation of a BPL system used to provide BPL services to affiliated or unaffiliated entities.

Acts 1997, 75th Leg., ch. 166, § 1, eff. Sept. 1, 1997. Amended by Acts 2005, 79th Leg., 2nd C.S., ch. 2, § 1, eff. Sept. 1, 2005.

§ 33.002. Surrender of Municipal Jurisdiction to Commission

(a) A municipality shall regulate all local utility service in the municipality until the commission assumes jurisdiction over a local utility under this subtitle.

(b) A municipality may elect to have the commission exercise exclusive original jurisdiction over electric utility rates, operations, and services in the municipality by ordinance or by submitting the question of the surrender of its jurisdiction to the voters at a municipal election.

(c) The governing body of a municipality shall submit at a municipal election the question of surrendering its jurisdiction to the commission if the governing body receives a petition signed by a number of qualified voters of the municipality equal to at least the lesser of 20,000 or 10 percent of the number of voters voting in the last preceding general election in the municipality.

Acts 1997, 75th Leg., ch. 166, § 1, eff. Sept. 1, 1997.

§ 33.003. Reinstatement of Municipal Jurisdiction

(a) A municipality that surrenders its jurisdiction to the commission may at any time reinstate its jurisdiction by a vote of the electorate.

(b) A municipality that reinstates its jurisdiction under Subsection (a) may not surrender that jurisdiction before the fifth anniversary of the date of the election in which the municipality elected to reinstate its jurisdiction.

(c) A municipality may not, by a vote of the electorate, reinstate the jurisdiction of the governing body during the time a case involving the municipality is pending before the commission.

Acts 1997, 75th Leg., ch. 166, § 1, eff. Sept. 1, 1997.

§ 33.004. Area Exempt From Commission Regulation

(a) If a municipality does not surrender its jurisdiction, local utility service in the municipality is exempt from regulation by the commission under this subtitle to the extent that this subtitle applies to local service.

(b) The municipality may exercise in the exempt area the same regulatory powers under the same standards and rules as the commission or under other consistent standards and rules.

Acts 1997, 75th Leg., ch. 166, § 1, eff. Sept. 1, 1997.

§ 33.005. Exempt Area Reporting

(a) An electric utility serving an area exempt from commission regulation is subject to the reporting requirements of this title.

(b) A report must be filed with:

(1) the governing body of the municipality; and

(2) the commission.

Acts 1997, 75th Leg., ch. 166, § 1, eff. Sept. 1, 1997.

§ 33.006. Commission Powers in Nonexempt Areas

This subchapter does not limit the duty and power of the commission to regulate the service and rates of a municipally regulated electric utility for service provided to another area in this state.

Acts 1997, 75th Leg., ch. 166, § 1, eff. Sept. 1, 1997.

§ 33.007. Allowable Charges

A municipality that performs a regulatory function under this title may make each charge that is authorized by:

(1) this title; or

(2) the applicable franchise agreement.

Acts 1997, 75th Leg., ch. 166, § 1, eff. Sept. 1, 1997.

§ 33.008. Franchise Charges

(a) Following the end of the freeze period for a municipality that has been served by an electric utility, and following the date a municipally owned utility or an electric cooperative has implemented customer choice for a municipality that has been served by that municipally owned utility or electric cooperative, a municipality may impose on an electric utility, transmission and distribution utility, municipally owned utility, or electric cooperative, as appropriate, that provides distribution service within the municipality a reasonable charge as specified in Subsection (b) for the use of a municipal street, alley, or public way to deliver electricity to a retail customer. A municipality may not impose a charge on:

(1) an electric utility, or transmission and distribution utility, municipally owned utility, or electric cooperative for electric service provided outside the municipality;

(2) a qualifying facility;

(3) an exempt wholesale generator;

(4) a power marketer;

(5) a retail electric provider;

(6) a power generation company;

(7) a person that generates electricity on and after January 1, 2002; or

(8) an aggregator, as that term is defined by Section 39.353.

(b) If a municipality collected a charge or fee for a franchise to use a municipal street, alley, or public way from an electric utility, a municipally owned utility, or an electric cooperative before the end of the freeze period, the municipality, after the end of the freeze period or after implementation of customer choice by the municipally owned utility or electric cooperative, as appropriate, is entitled to collect from each electric utility, transmission and distribution utility, municipally owned utility, or electric cooperative that uses the municipality's streets, alleys, or public ways to provide distribution service a charge based on each kilowatt hour of electricity delivered by the utility to each retail customer whose consuming facility's point of delivery is located within the municipality's boundaries. The charge imposed shall be equal to the total electric franchise fee revenue due the municipality from electric utilities, municipally owned utilities, or electric cooperatives, as appropriate, for calendar year 1998 divided by the total kilowatt hours delivered during 1998 by the applicable electric utility, municipally owned utility, or electric cooperative to retail customers whose consuming facilities' points of delivery were located within the municipality's boundaries. The compensation a municipality may collect from each electric utility, transmission and distribution utility, municipally owned utility, or electric cooperative providing distribution service shall be equal to the charge per kilowatt hour determined for 1998 multiplied times the number of kilowatt hours delivered within the municipality's boundaries.

(c) The municipal franchise charges authorized by this section shall be considered a reasonable and necessary operating expense of each electric utility, transmission and distribution utility, municipally owned utility, or electric cooperative that is subject to a charge under this section. The charge shall be included in the nonbypassable delivery charges that a customer's retail electric provider must pay under Section 39.107 to the utility serving the customer.

(d) The municipal franchise charges authorized by this section are in lieu of any franchise charges or fees payable under a franchise agreement in effect before the expiration of the freeze period or, as appropriate, before the implementation of customer choice by a municipally owned utility or electric cooperative. Except as otherwise provided by this section, this section does not affect a provision of a franchise agreement in effect before the end of the freeze period or, as appropriate, before the implementation of customer choice by a municipally owned utility or electric cooperative.

(e) A municipality may conduct an audit or other inquiry or may pursue any cause of action in relation to an electric utility's, transmission and distribution utility's, municipally owned utility's, or electric cooperative's payment of charges authorized by this section only if such audit, inquiry, or pursuit of a cause of action concerns a payment made less than two years before commencement of such audit, inquiry, or pursuit of a cause of action; provided, however, that this subsection does not apply to an audit, inquiry, or cause of action commenced before September 1, 1999. An electric utility, transmission and distribution utility, municipally owned utility, or electric cooperative shall, on request of the municipality in connection with a municipal audit, identify the service provider and the type of service delivered for any service in addition to electricity delivered directly to retail customers through the utility's electricity-conducting facilities that are located in the municipality's streets, alleys, or public ways and for which the utility receives compensation.

(f) Notwithstanding any other provision of this section, on the expiration of a franchise agreement existing on September 1, 1999, an electric utility, transmission and distribution utility, municipally owned utility, or electric cooperative and a municipality may mutually agree to a different level of compensation or to a different method for determining the amount the municipality may charge for the use of a municipal street, alley, or public way in connection with the delivery of electricity at retail within the municipality.

(g) After the end of the freeze period or after implementation of customer choice by the municipally owned utility or electric cooperative, as appropriate, a newly incorporated municipality or a municipality that has not previously collected compensation for the delivery of electricity at retail within the municipality may adopt and collect compensation based on the same rate per kilowatt hour that is collected by any other municipality in the same county that is served by the same electric utility, transmission and distribution utility, municipally owned utility, or electric cooperative.

(h) In this section, "distribution service" means the delivery of electricity to all retail customers.

Added by Acts 1999, 76th Leg., ch. 405, § 15, eff. Sept. 1, 1999.

SUBCHAPTER B. RATE DETERMINATION

§ 33.021. Rate Determination

(a) A municipality regulating an electric utility under this subtitle shall require the utility to submit information as necessary to make a reasonable determination of rate base, expenses, investment, and rate of return in the municipality.

(b) A municipality shall make a determination under Subsection (a) using the procedures and requirements prescribed by this title.

(c) A municipality shall retain personnel necessary to make the determination of reasonable rates.

Acts 1997, 75th Leg., ch. 166, § 1, eff. Sept. 1, 1997.

§ 33.022. Consideration of Revenues and Return From Nonexempt Area

In establishing rates and charges in an area exempt from commission regulation, the governing body may consider an electric utility's revenues and return on investment in an area that is not exempt from commission regulation.

Acts 1997, 75th Leg., ch. 166, § 1, eff. Sept. 1, 1997.

§ 33.023. Ratemaking Proceedings

(a) The governing body of a municipality participating in or conducting a ratemaking proceeding may engage rate consultants, accountants, auditors, attorneys, and engineers to:

(1) conduct investigations, present evidence, and advise and represent the governing body; and

(2) assist the governing body with litigation in an electric utility ratemaking proceeding before the governing body, a regulatory authority, or a court.

(b) The electric utility in the ratemaking proceeding shall reimburse the governing body of the municipality for the reasonable cost of the services of a person engaged under Subsection (a) to the extent the applicable regulatory authority determines is reasonable.

Acts 1997, 75th Leg., ch. 166, § 1, eff. Sept. 1, 1997.

§ 33.024. Statement of Intent

(a) Not later than the 31st day before the date an electric utility files a statement of intent under Section 36.102, the electric utility shall provide notice of intent to file the statement to each municipality having original jurisdiction.

(b) Not later than the 30th day after the date a municipality receives notice under Subsection (a), the municipality may request that the electric utility file with the municipality a statement of intent in accordance with Section 36.102.

(c) If requested by a municipality under Subsection (b), the electric utility shall file the statement of intent with the municipality at the same time the statement is filed with the commission.

Acts 1997, 75th Leg., ch. 166, § 1, eff. Sept. 1, 1997.

§ 33.025. Municipal Standing

(a) A municipality has standing in each case before the commission that relates to an electric utility providing service in the municipality.

(b) A municipality's standing is subject to the right of the commission to:

(1) determine standing in a case involving a retail service area dispute that involves two or more electric utilities; and

(2) consolidate municipalities on an issue of common interest.

Acts 1997, 75th Leg., ch. 166, § 1, eff. Sept. 1, 1997.

§ 33.026. Judicial Review

A municipality is entitled to judicial review of a commission order relating to an electric utility providing services in the municipality as provided by Section 15.001.

Acts 1997, 75th Leg., ch. 166, § 1, eff. Sept. 1, 1997.

SUBCHAPTER C. APPEAL OF MUNICIPAL ORDER

§ 33.051. Appeal by Party

A party to a rate proceeding before a municipality's governing body may appeal the governing body's decision to the commission.

Acts 1997, 75th Leg., ch. 166, § 1, eff. Sept. 1, 1997.

§ 33.052. Appeal by Residents

The residents of a municipality may appeal to the commission the decision of the municipality's governing body in a rate proceeding by filing with the commission a petition for review signed by a number of qualified voters of the municipality equal to at least the lesser of 20,000 or 10 percent of the qualified voters of the municipality.

Acts 1997, 75th Leg., ch. 166, § 1, eff. Sept. 1, 1997.

§ 33.053. Filing of Appeal

(a) An appeal under this subchapter is initiated by filing a petition for review with the commission and serving a copy of the petition on each party to the original rate proceeding.

(b) The appeal must be initiated not later than the 30th day after the date of the final decision by the governing body of the municipality.

Acts 1997, 75th Leg., ch. 166, § 1, eff. Sept. 1, 1997.

§ 33.054. Hearing and Order

(a) An appeal under this subchapter, Subchapter D, or Subchapter E[1] is de novo and based on the test year presented to the municipality.

(b) The commission shall enter a final order establishing the rates the commission determines the municipality should have set in the ordinance to which the appeal applies.

(c) In a proceeding involving the rates of a municipally owned utility, the commission must enter a final order on or before the 185th day after the date the appeal is perfected or the utility files a rate application as prescribed by Section 33.104.

(d) In a proceeding in which a rate change is concurrently sought from the commission under the commission's original jurisdiction, the commission must enter a final order on or before the later of the 120th day after the date the appeal is perfected or the date final action must be taken in the proceeding filed with the commission.

(e) In a proceeding not governed by Subsection (c) or (d), the commission must enter a final order on or before the 185th day after the date the appeal is perfected.

(f) If the commission fails to enter a final order before the expiration of the applicable period prescribed by Subsections (c)–(e), the rates proposed by the utility are considered to be approved by the commission and take effect on the expiration of that period.

Acts 1997, 75th Leg., ch. 166, § 1, eff. Sept. 1, 1997.

[1] V.T.C.A., Utilities Code § 33.101 et seq., or § 33.121 et seq.

§ 33.055. Applicability of Rates

(a) Temporary or permanent rates set by the commission are prospective and observed from the date of the applicable commission order, except an interim rate order necessary to effect uniform system-wide rates or to provide an electric utility the opportunity to avoid confiscation during the period beginning on the date a petition for review is filed with the commission and ending on the date of a final order establishing rates.

(b) The commission shall order interim rates on a prima facie showing by the electric utility that it has experienced confiscation during that period. The electric utility shall refund or credit against future bills:

(1) money collected under the interim rates in excess of the rate finally ordered; and

(2) interest on that money, at the current rate as determined by the commission.

(c) In this section, "confiscation" includes negative cash flow experienced by an electric utility at any time a rate case proceeding is pending.

Acts 1997, 75th Leg., ch. 166, § 1, eff. Sept. 1, 1997.

SUBCHAPTER D. PROVISIONS APPLICABLE TO APPEAL BY RATEPAYERS OUTSIDE MUNICIPALITY

§ 33.101. Appeal by Ratepayers Outside Municipality

(a) The ratepayers of a municipally owned utility who are outside the municipality may appeal to the commission an action of the governing body of the municipality affecting the municipally owned utility's rates by filing with the commission a petition for review signed by a number of ratepayers served by the utility outside the municipality equal to at least the lesser of 10,000 or five percent of those ratepayers.

(b) A petition for review is properly signed if signed by a person or the spouse of a person in whose name residential utility service is carried.

(c) For purposes of this section, each person who receives a separate bill is a ratepayer. A person who receives more than one bill may not be counted as more than one ratepayer.

Acts 1997, 75th Leg., ch. 166, § 1, eff. Sept. 1, 1997.

§ 33.102. Identification of Ratepayers Outside Municipality

(a) A municipality that owns a utility shall:

(1) disclose to any person, on request, the number of ratepayers who reside outside the municipality; and

(2) provide to any person, on request, a list of the names and addresses of the ratepayers who reside outside the municipality.

(b) The municipality may not charge a fee for disclosing the information under Subsection (a)(1). The municipality may charge a reasonable fee for providing information under Subsection (a)(2).

(c) The municipality shall provide information requested under Subsection (a)(1) by telephone or in writing, as preferred by the person making the request.

Acts 1997, 75th Leg., ch. 166, § 1, eff. Sept. 1, 1997.

§ 33.103. Filing of Appeal

(a) Not later than the 14th day after the date a governing body of a municipality makes a final decision, the municipality shall issue a written report stating the effect of the decision on each class of ratepayer.

(b) An appeal under this subchapter is initiated by filing a petition for review with the commission and serving a copy of the petition on each party to the original rate proceeding.

(c) The appeal must be initiated not later than the 45th day after the date the municipality issues the written report required by Subsection (a).

Acts 1997, 75th Leg., ch. 166, § 1, eff. Sept. 1, 1997.

§ 33.104. Rate Application

Not later than the 90th day after the date a petition for review is filed that complies with Section 33.103, the municipality shall file with the commission a rate application that complies in all material respects with the rules and forms prescribed by the commission. The commission may, for good cause shown, extend the period for filing a rate application.

Acts 1997, 75th Leg., ch. 166, § 1, eff. Sept. 1, 1997.

SUBCHAPTER E. RATE DETERMINATION AND APPEAL OF ORDERS OF CERTAIN MUNICIPAL UTILITIES

§ 33.121. Application of Commission Review

A municipally owned utility is subject to this subchapter if the utility is a utility:

(1) whose rates are appealed under Subchapter D; [1]

(2) for which the commission orders a decrease in annual nonfuel base revenues that exceeds the greater of $25,000,000 or 10 percent of the utility's nonfuel base revenues, as computed on a total system basis without regard to the utility's municipal boundaries and established in the appealed rate ordinance; and

(3) for which the commission finds that the rates paid by the combined residential or other major customer class, other than a class in which the municipality is the customer of the municipally owned utility, are removed from cost-of-service levels to the extent that, under the nonfuel base revenue requirement adopted by the commission as computed on a total system basis without regard to the municipality's boundaries, a change in nonfuel base rate revenues in excess of 50 percent from adjusted test year levels would be required to move that class to a relative rate of return of unity (1.00 or 100 percent) under the cost-of-service methodolo-

gy adopted by the commission in an appeal under Subchapter D.

Acts 1997, 75th Leg., ch. 166, § 1, eff. Sept. 1, 1997.

[1] V.T.C.A., Utilities Code § 33.101 et seq.

§ 33.122. Review of Certain Rate Decisions

(a) Except as provided by Subsections (b)–(f), for a period of 10 years beginning on the later of August 28, 1989, or the effective date of the rate ordinance that is the subject of the commission's final order invoking the application of this section, the commission has appellate jurisdiction over the rates charged by the municipally owned utility, both inside and outside the municipality, in the same manner and subject to the same commission powers and authority provided by this subtitle for an electric utility.

(b) The commission has jurisdiction to review the cost allocation and rate design methodologies adopted by the governing body of a municipally owned utility subject to this section. If the commission finds that the cost-of-service methodologies result in rates that are unjust, unreasonable, or unreasonably discriminatory, or unduly preferential to a customer class, the commission may order the implementation of ratesetting methodologies the commission finds reasonable.

(c) The commission shall ensure that a customer class, other than a class in which the municipality is the customer of the municipally owned utility, does not pay rates that result in a relative rate of return of more than 115 percent under the cost-of-service methodology found reasonable by the commission. A customer class may not experience a percentage base rate increase that is greater than 1½ times the system average base increase. In moving an above-cost class toward cost-of-service levels, each class farthest above cost shall be moved sequentially toward cost so that no above-cost class moves toward cost until no other class is further removed from cost.

(d) A municipality subject to this section may design residential rates, as a matter of intra-class rate design, to accomplish reasonable energy conservation goals, notwithstanding any other provision of this title.

(e) The commission's jurisdiction under this section may be invoked by any party to a local rate proceeding required by this section in the same manner as an appeal of the rates of an electric utility under Section 33.051.

(f) The commission's jurisdiction under this section does not extend to a municipally owned utility's:

(1) revenue requirements, whether base rate or fuel revenues;

(2) invested capital;

(3) return on invested capital;

(4) debt service coverage ratio; or

(5) level of transfer of revenues from the utility to the municipality's general fund.

(g) The governing body of a municipally owned utility subject to this section shall establish procedures similar to the procedures of a municipality that retains original jurisdiction under Section 33.001 to regulate an electric utility operating in the municipality. The procedures must include a public hearing process in which an affected ratepayer is granted party status on request and is grouped for purposes of participation in accordance with common or divergent interests, including the particular interests of all-electric residential ratepayers and residential ratepayers outside the municipality.

(h) This section does not require the governing body of a municipality or the governing board of a municipally owned utility subject to this section to adopt procedures that require the use of the Texas Rules of Evidence, the Texas Rules of Civil Procedure, or the presentation of sworn testimony or any other form of sworn evidence.

(i) The governing body of a municipally owned utility subject to this section shall appoint a consumer advocate to represent the interests of residential and small commercial ratepayers in the municipality's local rate proceedings. The consumer advocate's reasonable costs of participating in a proceeding, including the reasonable costs of ratemaking consultants and expert witnesses, shall be funded by and recovered from residential and small commercial ratepayers.

(j) The commission shall adopt rules applicable to a party to an appeal under Subchapter D[1] that provide for the public disclosure of financial and in-kind contributions and expenditures related to preparing and filing an appeal petition and preparing expert testimony or legal representation for an appeal. A party or customer who is a member of a party who makes a financial contribution or in-kind contribution to assist in an appeal by another party or customer class under Subchapter D shall be required, on a finding of the commission to that effect, to pay the municipally owned utility a penalty equivalent in amount to two times the amount of the contribution.

(k) This section does not limit the right of a party or customer to spend money to represent its own interests following the filing of a petition with the commission under Subchapter D.

Acts 1997, 75th Leg., ch. 166, § 1, eff. Sept. 1, 1997.

[1] V.T.C.A., Utilities Code § 33.101 et seq.

§ 33.123. Review of Certain Decisions for Rates Charged Outside Municipality

(a) For a period of 10 years beginning on the later of August 28, 1989, or the effective date of the rate ordinance that is the subject of the commission's final order invoking the application of this section, the commission has appellate jurisdiction over the rates charged by the municipally owned utility, outside the municipality, as provided by this section.

(b) Except as otherwise provided by this section, a ratepayer of a municipally owned utility subject to this section who resides outside the municipality may appeal any action of the governing body of a municipality affecting the rates charged by the municipally owned utility outside the municipality by filing a petition for review with the commission in the manner provided for an appeal under Subchapter D.[1] The petition must plainly disclose that the cost of the appeal will be funded by a surcharge on the monthly electric bills of ratepayers outside the municipality as prescribed by the commission.

(c) After the commission approves the sufficiency of a petition, the appellants shall submit to the office for approval a budget itemizing the scope and expected cost of consultant services to be purchased by the appellants in the appeal.

(d) Not later than the 120th day after the date the commission enters its final order, the municipality shall assess a onetime surcharge on a per capita basis among residential ratepayers who reside outside the municipality to pay the reasonable consultant and legal costs approved by the counsellor. The municipality shall reimburse the appellants for incurred costs not later than the 90th day after the date the commission enters its final order.

(e) A municipality may not:

(1) include the costs associated with its defense of an appeal under this section in the rates charged a ratepayer outside the municipality; or

(2) if the municipality appeals an order entered by the commission under this section, include the costs associated with its appeal in the rates charged a ratepayer outside the municipality.

(f) A ratepayer who brings an appeal under this section may not receive funding for rate case expenses except from a residential ratepayer who resides outside the municipality or from another municipality inside whose boundaries the municipally owned utility provides service. The commission shall adopt rules for reporting financial and in-kind contributions in support of an appeal under this section. If the commission finds that an appellant has received contributions from a source other than from a ratepayer who resides outside the municipality or from another municipality, the appeal and each commission order entered in the appeal are void.

(g) The commission has jurisdiction in an appeal under this section to review and ensure that the revenue requirements of a municipally owned utility subject to this section are reasonable. The jurisdiction under this subsection does not extend to regulating the use and level of a transfer of the utility's revenues to the municipality's general fund.

(h) The commission has jurisdiction to review the cost allocation and rate design methodologies adopted by the governing body of a municipally owned utility subject to this section. If the commission finds that the cost-of-service methodologies result in rates that are unjust, unreasonable, or unreasonably discriminatory or unduly preferential to a customer class, the commission may order the implementation of ratesetting methodologies the commission finds reasonable. The commission's jurisdiction under this subsection does not include intra-class residential rate design.

(i) An intervenor in an appeal under this section is limited to presenting evidence on cost allocation and rate design methodologies, except that an intervenor may present evidence in support of the municipality on an issue related to utility revenues.

(j) A ratepayer of a municipally owned utility subject to this section who resides outside the municipality may elect to petition for review under either this section or Subchapter D when appealing a rate ordinance or other ratesetting action of the governing body of a municipality.

Acts 1997, 75th Leg., ch. 166, § 1, eff. Sept. 1, 1997.

[1] V.T.C.A., Utilities Code § 33.101 et seq.

CHAPTER 34. ELECTRICAL PLANNING [REPEALED]

SUBCHAPTER A. GENERAL PROVISIONS [REPEALED]

§§ 34.001 to 34.006. Repealed by Acts 1999, 76th Leg., ch. 405, § 61(2), eff. Sept. 1, 1999

SUBCHAPTER B. PRELIMINARY INTEGRATED RESOURCE PLAN [REPEALED]

§§ 34.021 to 34.024. Repealed by Acts 1999, 76th Leg., ch. 405, § 61(2), eff. Sept. 1, 1999

SUBCHAPTER C. RESOURCE SOLICITATION [REPEALED]

§§ 34.051 to 34.056. Repealed by Acts 1999, 76th Leg., ch. 405, § 61(2), eff. Sept. 1, 1999

SUBCHAPTER D. FINAL INTEGRATED RESOURCE PLAN [REPEALED]

§§ 34.101 to 34.105. Repealed by Acts 1999, 76th Leg., ch. 405, § 61(2), eff. Sept. 1, 1999

SUBCHAPTER E. ACQUISITION OF RESOURCES OUTSIDE THE INTEGRATED RESOURCE PLANNING PROCESS [REPEALED]

§§ 34.151 to 34.153. Repealed by Acts 1999, 76th Leg., ch. 405, § 61(2), eff. Sept. 1, 1999

SUBCHAPTER F. MISCELLANEOUS PROVISIONS [REPEALED]

§§ 34.171 to 34.173. Repealed by Acts 1999, 76th Leg., ch. 405, § 61(2), eff. Sept. 1, 1999

CHAPTER 35. ALTERNATIVE ENERGY PROVIDERS

SUBCHAPTER A. COMPETITION AND TRANSMISSION ACCESS IN THE WHOLESALE MARKET

Section

35.001. Definition.
35.002. Right to Compete at Wholesale.
35.003. Purchase From Affiliate; Undue Preference Prohibited.
35.004. Provision of Transmission Service.
35.005. Authority to Order Transmission Service.
35.006. Rules Related to Wholesale Transmission Service, Rates, and Access.
35.007. Tariffs Required.
35.008. Alternative Dispute Resolution.
35.0081. Expired.

SUBCHAPTER B. EXEMPT WHOLESALE GENERATORS, DISTRIBUTED NATURAL GAS GENERATION FACILITIES, AND POWER MARKETERS

35.031. Authority to Operate.
35.032. Commission Registration and Required Reports.

Section

35.033. Affiliate Wholesale Provider.
35.034. Transfer of Assets.
35.035. Valuation and Accounting of Transferred Assets.
35.036. Distributed Natural Gas Generation Facilities.

SUBCHAPTER C. QUALIFYING FACILITIES

35.061. Encouragement of Economical Production.
35.062. Application for Certification.
35.063. Hearing.
35.064. Certification Standards.
35.065. Deadlines for Commission Action.
35.066. Term of Certification.

SUBCHAPTER D. STATE AUTHORITY TO SELL OR CONVEY POWER

35.101. Definitions.
35.102. State Authority to Sell or Convey Power or Natural Gas.
35.103. Access to Transmission and Distribution Systems; Rates.
35.104. Limit in Certain Areas.
35.105. Wholesale Customers.
35.106. Access to Power Generation.

SUBCHAPTER E. ELECTRIC ENERGY STORAGE

35.151. Electric Energy Storage.
35.152. Generation Assets.

SUBCHAPTER A. COMPETITION AND TRANSMISSION ACCESS IN THE WHOLESALE MARKET

§ 35.001. Definition

In this subchapter, "electric utility" includes a municipally owned utility and an electric cooperative.

Acts 1997, 75th Leg., ch. 166, § 1, eff. Sept. 1, 1997. Amended by Acts 1999, 76th Leg., ch. 405, § 16, eff. Sept. 1, 1999.

§ 35.002. Right to Compete at Wholesale

A provider of generation, including an electric utility affiliate, exempt wholesale generator, and qualifying facility, may compete for the business of selling power.

Acts 1997, 75th Leg., ch. 166, § 1, eff. Sept. 1, 1997.

§ 35.003. Purchase From Affiliate; Undue Preference Prohibited

(a) An electric utility may purchase power from an affiliate in accordance with this title.

(b) An electric utility may not grant an undue preference to a person in connection with the utility's purchase or sale of electric energy at wholesale or other utility service.

Acts 1997, 75th Leg., ch. 166, § 1, eff. Sept. 1, 1997.

§ 35.004. Provision of Transmission Service

(a) An electric utility or transmission and distribution utility that owns or operates transmission facilities shall provide wholesale transmission service at rates and terms, including terms of access, that are comparable to the rates and terms of the utility's own use of its system.

(b) The commission shall ensure that an electric utility or transmission and distribution utility provides nondiscriminatory access to wholesale transmission service for qualifying facilities, exempt wholesale generators, power marketers, power generation companies, retail electric providers, and other electric utilities or transmission and distribution utilities.

(c) When an electric utility, electric cooperative, or transmission and distribution utility provides wholesale transmission service within ERCOT at the request of a third party, the commission shall ensure that the utility recovers the utility's reasonable costs in providing wholesale transmission services necessary for the transaction from the entity for which the transmission is provided so that the utility's other customers do not bear the costs of the service.

(d) The commission shall price wholesale transmission services within ERCOT based on the postage stamp method of pricing under which a transmission-owning utility's rate is based on the ERCOT utilities' combined annual costs of transmission divided by the total demand placed on the combined transmission systems of all such transmission-owning utilities within a power region. An electric utility subject to the freeze period imposed by Section 39.052 may treat transmission costs in excess of transmission revenues during the freeze period as an expense for purposes of determining annual costs in the annual report filed under Section 39.257. Notwithstanding Section 36.201, the commission may approve wholesale rates that may be periodically adjusted to ensure timely recovery of transmission investment. Notwithstanding Section 36.054(a), if the commission determines that conditions warrant the action, the commission may authorize the inclusion of construction work in progress in the rate base for transmission investment required by the commission under Section 39.203(e).

(e) The commission shall ensure that ancillary services necessary to facilitate the transmission of electric energy are available at reasonable prices with terms and conditions that are not unreasonably preferential, prejudicial, discriminatory, predatory, or anticompetitive. In this subsection, "ancillary services" means services necessary to facilitate the transmission of electric energy including load following, standby power, backup power, reactive power, and any other services as the commission may determine by rule. On the introduction of customer choice in the ERCOT power region, acquisition of generation-related ancillary services on a nondiscriminatory basis by the independent organization in ERCOT on behalf of entities selling electricity at retail shall be deemed to meet the requirements of this subsection.

Acts 1997, 75th Leg., ch. 166, § 1, eff. Sept. 1, 1997. Amended by Acts 1999, 76th Leg., ch. 405, § 17, eff. Sept. 1, 1999; Acts 2003, 78th Leg., ch. 295, § 1, eff. June 18, 2003.

§ 35.005. Authority to Order Transmission Service

(a) The commission may require an electric utility to provide transmission service at wholesale to another electric utility, a qualifying facility, an exempt wholesale generator, or a power marketer and may determine whether terms for the transmission service are reasonable.

(b) The commission may require transmission service at wholesale, including the construction or enlargement of a facility.

(c) The commission may not issue a decision or rule relating to transmission service that is contrary to an applicable decision, rule, or policy statement of a federal regulatory agency having jurisdiction.

Acts 1997, 75th Leg., ch. 166, § 1, eff. Sept. 1, 1997. Amended by Acts 1999, 76th Leg., ch. 405, § 18, eff. Sept. 1, 1999.

§ 35.006. Rules Related to Wholesale Transmission Service, Rates, and Access

(a) The commission shall adopt rules relating to wholesale transmission service, rates, and access. The rules:

(1) must be consistent with the standards in this subchapter;

(2) may not be contrary to federal law, including any applicable decision, rule, or policy statement of a federal regulatory agency having jurisdiction;

(3) must require transmission services that are not less than the transmission services the Federal Energy Regulatory Commission may require in similar circumstances;

(4) must require that an electric utility provide all ancillary services associated with the utility's discounted wholesale sales at the same prices and under the same terms as the services are provided to a third person; and

(5) must require that an electric utility provide all ancillary services associated with the utility's dis-

counted wholesale sales to a third person on request.

(b) The commission shall adopt rules relating to the registration and reporting requirements of a qualifying facility, exempt wholesale generator, and power marketer.

Acts 1997, 75th Leg., ch. 166, § 1, eff. Sept. 1, 1997.

§ 35.007. Tariffs Required

(a) Except as provided by Subsection (b), an electric utility that owns or operates a transmission facility shall file a tariff in compliance with commission rules adopted under Section 35.006.

(b) An electric utility is not required to file a tariff under this section if the utility's terms for access and pricing for wholesale transmission service are included in another electric utility's tariff.

(c) An electric utility shall file a tariff required by this section with the appropriate state or federal regulatory agency having jurisdiction over the utility's transmission service.

Acts 1997, 75th Leg., ch. 166, § 1, eff. Sept. 1, 1997.

§ 35.008. Alternative Dispute Resolution

The commission may require that each party to a dispute concerning prices or terms of wholesale transmission service engage in a nonbinding alternative dispute resolution process before seeking resolution of the dispute by the commission.

Acts 1997, 75th Leg., ch. 166, § 1, eff. Sept. 1, 1997.

§ 35.0081. Expired

SUBCHAPTER B. EXEMPT WHOLESALE GENERATORS, DISTRIBUTED NATURAL GAS GENERATION FACILITIES, AND POWER MARKETERS

§ 35.031. Authority to Operate

An exempt wholesale generator or power marketer may sell electric energy only at wholesale.

Acts 1997, 75th Leg., ch. 166, § 1, eff. Sept. 1, 1997.

§ 35.032. Commission Registration and Required Reports

(a) An exempt wholesale generator or power marketer that sells electric energy in this state shall, not later than the 30th day after the date it becomes subject to this section:

(1) register with the commission; or

(2) provide to the commission proof that it has registered with the Federal Energy Regulatory Commission or has been authorized by the Federal Energy Regulatory Commission to sell electric energy at market-based rates.

(b) The exempt wholesale generator or power marketer may register by filing with the commission:

(1) a description of the location of any facility used to provide service;

(2) a description of the type of service provided;

(3) a copy of any information filed with the Federal Energy Regulatory Commission in connection with registration with that commission; and

(4) other information required by commission rule.

(c) An exempt wholesale generator or power marketer required to register under Subsection (a) shall file any report required by commission rule.

Acts 1997, 75th Leg., ch. 166, § 1, eff. Sept. 1, 1997.

§ 35.033. Affiliate Wholesale Provider

An affiliate of an electric utility may be an exempt wholesale generator or power marketer and may sell electric energy to its affiliated electric utility in accordance with laws governing wholesale sales of electric energy.

Acts 1997, 75th Leg., ch. 166, § 1, eff. Sept. 1, 1997. Amended by Acts 1999, 76th Leg., ch. 405, § 19, eff. Sept. 1, 1999.

§ 35.034. Transfer of Assets

(a) Unless an electric utility receives commission approval under Subsection (b), the utility may not sell or transfer a facility to an affiliate or otherwise consider the facility to be an eligible facility as defined by federal law if on May 27, 1995, the utility had a rate or charge in effect:

(1) for or in connection with the construction of the facility;

(2) for electric energy produced by the construction of the facility; or

(3) for electric energy produced by the facility other than a portion of a rate or charge that represents recovery of the cost of a wholesale rate or charge.

(b) The commission, after notice and hearing, may allow an electric utility to sell or transfer a facility governed by Subsection (a) to an affiliate or otherwise allow the facility to become an eligible facility only if the transaction:

(1) will benefit ratepayers of the utility making the sale or transfer;

(2) is in the public interest; and

(3) otherwise complies with state law.

(c) For purposes of this section, "electric utility" does not include a river authority.

Acts 1997, 75th Leg., ch. 166, § 1, eff. Sept. 1, 1997. Amended by Acts 1999, 76th Leg., ch. 405, § 20, eff. Sept. 1, 1999.

§ 35.035. Valuation and Accounting of Transferred Assets

(a) A transfer of assets from an electric utility to an affiliated exempt wholesale generator or power marketer shall be valued at the greater of net book cost or fair market value.

(b) A transfer of assets from an exempt wholesale generator or power marketer to an affiliated electric utility shall be valued at the lesser of net book cost or fair market value.

(c) At the time that a transfer of assets between an electric utility and an affiliated exempt wholesale generator or power marketer is approved, the commission shall order the utility to adjust its rates so that the utility's tariffs reflect benefits from the proceeds of the sale and exclude any costs associated with the transferred facility.

(d) For purposes of this section, "electric utility" does not include a river authority.

Acts 1997, 75th Leg., ch. 166, § 1, eff. Sept. 1, 1997. Amended by Acts 1999, 76th Leg., ch. 405, § 21, eff. Sept. 1, 1999.

§ 35.036. Distributed Natural Gas Generation Facilities

(a) A person who owns or operates a distributed natural gas generation facility may sell electric power generated by the facility. The electric utility, electric cooperative, or retail electric provider that provides retail electricity service to the facility may purchase electric power tendered to it by the owner or operator of the facility at a value agreed to by the electric utility, electric cooperative, or retail electric provider and the owner or operator of the facility. The value of the electric power may be based wholly or partly on the clearing price of energy at the time of day and at the location at which the electric power is made available to the electric grid.

(b) At the request of the owner or operator of the distributed natural gas generation facility, the electric utility or electric cooperative shall allow the owner or operator of the facility to use transmission and distribution facilities to transmit the electric power to another entity that is acceptable to the owner or operator in accordance with commission rules or a tariff approved by the Federal Energy Regulatory Commission.

(c) Subject to Subsections (e) and (f), if the owner or operator of a distributed natural gas generation facility requests to be interconnected to an electric utility or electric cooperative that does not have a transmission tariff approved by the Federal Energy Regulatory Commission, the electric utility or electric cooperative may recover from the owner or operator of the facility the reasonable costs of interconnecting the facility with the electric utility or electric cooperative that are necessary for and directly attributable to the interconnection of the facility.

(d) Subject to Subsections (e) and (f), an electric utility or electric cooperative may recover from the owner or operator of a distributed natural gas generation facility the reasonable costs of electric facility upgrades and improvements if:

(1) the rated capacity of the distributed natural gas generation facility is greater than the rated capacity of the electric utility or electric cooperative; and

(2) the costs are necessary for and directly attributable to accommodating the distributed natural gas generation facility's capacity.

(e) An electric utility or electric cooperative may recover costs under Subsection (c) or (d) only if:

(1) the electric utility or electric cooperative provides a written good faith cost estimate to the owner or operator of the distributed natural gas generation facility; and

(2) the owner or operator of the distributed natural gas generation facility agrees in writing to pay the reasonable and necessary costs of interconnection or capacity accommodation requested by the owner or operator and described in the estimate before the electric utility or electric cooperative incurs the costs.

(f) If an electric utility or electric cooperative seeks to recover from the owner or operator of a distributed natural gas generation facility an amount that exceeds the amount in the estimate provided under Subsection (e) by more than five percent, the commission shall resolve the dispute at the request of the owner or operator of the facility.

(g) A distributed natural gas generation facility must comply with emissions limitations established by the Texas Commission on Environmental Quality for a standard emissions permit for an electric generation facility unit installed after January 1, 1995.

(h) This section does not require an electric cooperative to transmit electricity to a retail point of delivery in the certificated service area of the electric cooperative if the electric cooperative has not adopted customer choice.

Added by Acts 2011, 82nd Leg., ch. 890 (S.B. 365), § 3, eff. Sept. 1, 2011.

SUBCHAPTER C. QUALIFYING FACILITIES

§ 35.061. Encouragement of Economical Production

The commission shall adopt and enforce rules to encourage the economical production of electric energy by qualifying facilities.

Acts 1997, 75th Leg., ch. 166, § 1, eff. Sept. 1, 1997.

§ 35.062. Application for Certification

(a) An electric utility or a qualifying facility may submit to the commission for certification a copy of an agreement between the utility and facility for the purchase of capacity.

(b) An agreement submitted for certification under this section may provide that the agreement is contingent on certification by the commission.

Acts 1997, 75th Leg., ch. 166, § 1, eff. Sept. 1, 1997.

§ 35.063. Hearing

(a) The commission, on its own motion or on the request of a party to the agreement or another affected person, may conduct a hearing on an agreement for which certification is sought under Section 35.062.

(b) A request for a hearing or a commission decision to hold a hearing must be made not later than the 90th day after the date the agreement is submitted to the commission.

Acts 1997, 75th Leg., ch. 166, § 1, eff. Sept. 1, 1997.

§ 35.064. Certification Standards

The commission shall certify an agreement submitted under Section 35.062 if the agreement:

(1) provides for payments over the contract term that are equal to or less than the electric utility's avoided costs, as established by the commission and in effect at the time the agreement was signed; and

(2) provides the electric utility the opportunity to acquire the cogeneration or small-power production installation before the installation is offered to another purchaser or provides other sufficient assurance that the electric utility will be provided with a comparable supply of electricity, if the qualifying facility ceases to operate the installation.

Acts 1997, 75th Leg., ch. 166, § 1, eff. Sept. 1, 1997.

§ 35.065. Deadlines for Commission Action

(a) Except as provided by Subsection (b), the commission shall make its determination regarding whether a certification should be granted under Section 35.064 not later than the 90th day after the date the agreement is submitted.

(b) If a hearing is held under Section 35.063, the commission shall make its determination regarding whether a certification should be granted not later than the 120th day after the date the agreement is submitted, except that this deadline is extended by two days for each day in excess of five days on which the commission conducts a hearing on the merits of the certification.

(c) If the commission does not make a determination by the date provided by Subsection (a) or (b), as applicable, the agreement is considered to meet the requirements of Section 35.064 and the certification is considered granted.

Acts 1997, 75th Leg., ch. 166, § 1, eff. Sept. 1, 1997.

§ 35.066. Term of Certification

A certification of an agreement granted under this subchapter is effective until the earlier of:

(1) the expiration date of the agreement; or

(2) the 15th anniversary of the date of the certification.

Acts 1997, 75th Leg., ch. 166, § 1, eff. Sept. 1, 1997.

SUBCHAPTER D. STATE AUTHORITY TO SELL OR CONVEY POWER

§ 35.101. Definitions

In this subchapter:

(1) "Commissioner" means the Commissioner of the General Land Office.

(2) "Public retail customer" means a retail customer that is an agency of this state, a state institution of higher education, a public school district, a political subdivision of this state, a military installa-

tion of the United States, or a United States Department of Veterans Affairs facility.

Added by Acts 1999, 76th Leg., ch. 405, § 22, eff. Sept. 1, 1999. Amended by Acts 2003, 78th Leg., ch. 149, § 19, eff. May 27, 2003.

§ 35.102. State Authority to Sell or Convey Power or Natural Gas

(a) The commissioner, acting on behalf of the state, may sell or otherwise convey power or natural gas generated from royalties taken in kind as provided by Sections 52.133(f), 53.026, and 53.077, Natural Resources Code, directly to a public retail customer regardless of whether the public retail customer is also classified as a wholesale customer under other provisions of this title.

(b) To ensure that the state receives the maximum benefit from the sale of power or natural gas generated from royalties taken in kind, the commissioner shall use all feasible means to sell that power or natural gas first to public retail customers that are military installations of the United States, agencies of this state, institutions of higher education, or public school districts. The remainder of the power or natural gas, if any, may be sold to public retail customers that are political subdivisions of this state or to a United States Department of Veterans Affairs facility.

Added by Acts 1999, 76th Leg., ch. 405, § 22, eff. Sept. 1, 1999. Amended by Acts 2003, 78th Leg., ch. 149, § 20, eff. May 27, 2003.

§ 35.103. Access to Transmission and Distribution Systems; Rates

(a) Except as provided in Section 35.104, the state is entitled to have access to all transmission and distribution systems of all electric utilities, transmission and distribution utilities, municipally owned utilities, and electric cooperatives that serve public retail customers.

(b) An entity described by Subsection (a) shall provide any utility service, including transmission, distribution, and other services, which must include any stranded costs associated with providing service, to the state at the lowest applicable rate charged for similar service to other customers.

Added by Acts 1999, 76th Leg., ch. 405, § 22, eff. Sept. 1, 1999.

§ 35.104. Limit in Certain Areas

Sections 35.102 and 35.103 do not apply to the rates, retail service area, facilities, or public retail customers of a municipally owned electric utility that has not adopted customer choice or an electric cooperative that has not adopted customer choice. In a certificated service area of an electric utility in which customer choice has not been introduced, the state may not engage in retail transactions that exceed 2.5 percent of a retail electric utility's total retail load.

Added by Acts 1999, 76th Leg., ch. 405, § 22, eff. Sept. 1, 1999.

§ 35.105. Wholesale Customers

This subchapter does not prevent the commissioner, acting on behalf of this state, from registering as a power marketer.

Added by Acts 1999, 76th Leg., ch. 405, § 22, eff. Sept. 1, 1999.

§ 35.106. Access to Power Generation

If pipeline capacity is available on an existing facility of a gas utility or municipally owned utility, a gas utility or a municipally owned utility may not refuse to provide gas service to an electric utility generating facility, if the purpose of the service is to generate power for public retail customers by the state or an agency of this state.

Added by Acts 1999, 76th Leg., ch. 405, § 22, eff. Sept. 1, 1999.

SUBCHAPTER E. ELECTRIC ENERGY STORAGE

Section 3 of Acts 2011, 82nd Leg., ch. 1069 (S.B. 943) provides:

"Subdivision (10), Section 31.002, Utilities Code, as amended by this Act, and Subchapter E, Chapter 35, Utilities Code, as added by this Act, may not be construed to determine the regulatory treatment of electricity acquired to charge electric energy storage equipment or facilities and used solely for the purpose of later sale as energy or ancillary services."

§ 35.151. Electric Energy Storage

This subchapter applies to electric energy storage equipment or facilities that are intended to provide energy or ancillary services at wholesale, including electric energy storage equipment or facilities listed on a power generation company's registration with the commission or, for an exempt wholesale generator, on the generator's registration with the Federal Energy Regulatory Commission.

Added by Acts 2011, 82nd Leg., ch. 1069 (S.B. 943), § 2, eff. Sept. 1, 2011.

Section 3 of Acts 2011, 82nd Leg., ch. 1069 (S.B. 943) provides:

"Subdivision (10), Section 31.002, Utilities Code, as amended by this Act, and Subchapter E, Chapter 35, Utilities Code, as added by this Act, may not be construed to determine the regulatory treatment of electricity acquired to charge electric energy storage equipment or facilities and used solely for the purpose of later sale as energy or ancillary services."

§ 35.152. Generation Assets

(a) Electric energy storage equipment or facilities that are intended to be used to sell energy or ancillary services at wholesale are generation assets.

(b) The owner or operator of electric energy storage equipment or facilities that are generation assets under Subsection (a) is a power generation company and is required to register under Section 39.351(a). The owner or operator of the equipment or facilities is entitled to:

(1) interconnect the equipment or facilities;

(2) obtain transmission service for the equipment or facilities; and

(3) use the equipment or facilities to sell electricity or ancillary services at wholesale in a manner consistent with the provisions of this title and commission rules applicable to a power generation company or an exempt wholesale generator.

(c) Notwithstanding Subsection (a), this section does not affect a determination made by the commission in a final order issued before December 31, 2010.

Added by Acts 2011, 82nd Leg., ch. 1069 (S.B. 943), § 2, eff. Sept. 1, 2011.

Section 3 of Acts 2011, 82nd Leg., ch. 1069 (S.B. 943) provides:

"Subdivision (10), Section 31.002, Utilities Code, as amended by this Act, and Subchapter E, Chapter 35, Utilities Code, as added by this Act, may not be construed to determine the regulatory treatment of electricity acquired to charge electric energy storage equipment or facilities and used solely for the purpose of later sale as energy or ancillary services."

CHAPTER 36. RATES

SUBCHAPTER A. GENERAL PROVISIONS

Section
36.001. Authorization to Establish and Regulate Rates.
36.002. Compliance With Title.
36.003. Just and Reasonable Rates.
36.004. Equality of Rates and Services.
36.005. Rates for Area Not in Municipality.
36.006. Burden of Proof.
36.007. Discounted Wholesale or Retail Rates.
36.008. State Transmission System.
36.009. Billing Demand for Certain Utility Customers.

SUBCHAPTER B. COMPUTATION OF RATES

36.051. Establishing Overall Revenues.
36.052. Establishing Reasonable Return.
36.053. Components of Invested Capital.
36.054. Construction Work in Progress.
36.055. Separations and Allocations.
36.056. Depreciation, Amortization, and Depletion.
Section
36.057. Net Income; Determination of Revenues and Expenses.
36.058. Consideration of Payment to Affiliate.
36.059. Treatment of Certain Tax Benefits.
36.060. Consolidated Income Tax Returns.
36.061. Allowance of Certain Expenses.
36.062. Consideration of Certain Expenses.
36.063. Consideration of Profit or Loss From Sale or Lease of Merchandise.
36.064. Self-Insurance.
36.065. Pension and Other Postemployment Benefits.

SUBCHAPTER C. GENERAL PROCEDURES FOR RATE CHANGES PROPOSED BY UTILITY

36.101. Definition.
36.102. Statement of Intent to Change Rates.
36.103. Notice of Intent to Change Rates.
36.104. Early Effective Date of Rate Change.
36.105. Determination of Propriety of Rate Change; Hearing.
36.106. Regional Hearing.
36.107. Preference to Hearing.
36.108. Rate Suspension; Deadline.
36.109. Temporary Rates.
36.110. Bonded Rates.
36.111. Establishment of Final Rates.

SUBCHAPTER D. RATE CHANGES PROPOSED BY REGULATORY AUTHORITY

36.151. Unreasonable or Violative Existing Rates.
36.152. Investigating Costs of Obtaining Service From Another Source.
36.153. Rate-Filing Package.
36.154. Deadline.
36.155. Interim Order Establishing Temporary Rates.
36.156. Automatic Temporary Rates.

SUBCHAPTER E. COST RECOVERY AND RATE ADJUSTMENT

36.201. Automatic Adjustment for Changes in Costs.
36.202. Adjustment for Change in Tax Liability.
36.203. Fuel Cost Recovery; Adjustment of Fuel Factor.
36.204. Cost Recovery and Incentives.
36.205. Purchased Power Cost Recovery.
36.206. Mark-Ups.
36.207. Use of Mark-Ups.
36.208. Payment to Qualifying Facility.
36.209. Recovery by Certain Non–ERCOT Utilities of Certain Transmission Costs.
36.210. Periodic Rate Adjustments.

SUBCHAPTER F. PARTIAL RATE DEREGULATION AVAILABLE TO CERTAIN COOPERATIVES [REPEALED]

36.251 to 36.255. Repealed.

SUBCHAPTER G. RATE CHANGES BY CERTAIN ELECTRIC COOPERATIVES [REPEALED]

36.301 to 36.309. Repealed.

SUBCHAPTER H. RATES FOR GOVERNMENTAL ENTITIES

Section
36.351. Discounted Rates for Certain Institutions of Higher Education.
36.352. Special Rate Class.
36.353. Payment in Lieu of Tax.
36.354. Discounted Rates for Military Bases.

SUBCHAPTER I. SECURITIZATION FOR RECOVERY OF SYSTEM RESTORATION COSTS

36.401. Securitization for Recovery of System Restoration Costs; Purpose.
36.402. System Restoration Costs; Standards and Definitions.
36.403. Standards and Procedures Governing Securitization and Recovery of System Restoration Costs.
36.404. Nonbypassable Charges.
36.405. Determination of System Restoration Costs.
36.406. Severability.

SUBCHAPTER A. GENERAL PROVISIONS

§ 36.001. Authorization to Establish and Regulate Rates

(a) The regulatory authority may establish and regulate rates of an electric utility and may adopt rules for determining:

(1) the classification of customers and services; and

(2) the applicability of rates.

(b) A rule or order of the regulatory authority may not conflict with a ruling of a federal regulatory body.

Acts 1997, 75th Leg., ch. 166, § 1, eff. Sept. 1, 1997.

§ 36.002. Compliance With Title

An electric utility may not charge or receive a rate for utility service except as provided by this title.

Acts 1997, 75th Leg., ch. 166, § 1, eff. Sept. 1, 1997.

§ 36.003. Just and Reasonable Rates

(a) The regulatory authority shall ensure that each rate an electric utility or two or more electric utilities jointly make, demand, or receive is just and reasonable.

(b) A rate may not be unreasonably preferential, prejudicial, or discriminatory but must be sufficient, equitable, and consistent in application to each class of consumer.

(c) An electric utility may not:

(1) grant an unreasonable preference or advantage concerning rates to a person in a classification;

(2) subject a person in a classification to an unreasonable prejudice or disadvantage concerning rates; or

(3) establish or maintain an unreasonable difference concerning rates between localities or between classes of service.

(d) In establishing an electric utility's rates, the commission may treat as a single class two or more municipalities that an electric utility serves if the commission considers that treatment to be appropriate.

(e) A charge to an individual customer for retail or wholesale electric service that is less than the rate approved by the regulatory authority does not constitute an impermissible difference, preference, or advantage.

Acts 1997, 75th Leg., ch. 166, § 1, eff. Sept. 1, 1997.

§ 36.004. Equality of Rates and Services

(a) An electric utility may not directly or indirectly charge, demand, or receive from a person a greater or lesser compensation for a service provided or to be provided by the utility than the compensation prescribed by the applicable tariff filed under Section 32.101.

(b) A person may not knowingly receive or accept a service from an electric utility for a compensation greater or less than the compensation prescribed by the tariff.

(c) Notwithstanding Subsections (a) and (b), an electric utility may charge an individual customer for wholesale or retail electric service in accordance with Section 36.007.

(d) This title does not prevent a cooperative corporation from returning to its members net earnings resulting from its operations in proportion to the members' purchases from or through the corporation.

Acts 1997, 75th Leg., ch. 166, § 1, eff. Sept. 1, 1997.

§ 36.005. Rates for Area Not in Municipality

Without the approval of the commission, an electric utility's rates for an area not in a municipality may not exceed 115 percent of the average of all rates for similar services for all municipalities served by the same utility in the same county as that area.

Acts 1997, 75th Leg., ch. 166, § 1, eff. Sept. 1, 1997.

§ 36.006. Burden of Proof

In a proceeding involving a proposed rate change, the electric utility has the burden of proving that:

(1) the rate change is just and reasonable, if the utility proposes the change; or

(2) an existing rate is just and reasonable, if the proposal is to reduce the rate.

Acts 1997, 75th Leg., ch. 166, § 1, eff. Sept. 1, 1997.

§ 36.007. Discounted Wholesale or Retail Rates

(a) On application by an electric utility, a regulatory authority may approve wholesale or retail tariffs or contracts containing charges that are less than rates approved by the regulatory authority but not less than the utility's marginal cost. The charges must be in accordance with the principles of this title and may not be unreasonably preferential, prejudicial, discriminatory, predatory, or anticompetitive.

(b) The method for computing the marginal cost of the electric utility consists of energy and capacity components. The energy component includes variable operation and maintenance expense and marginal fuel or the energy component of purchased power. The capacity component is based on the annual economic value of deferring, accelerating, or avoiding the next increment of needed capacity, without regard to whether the capacity is purchased or built.

(c) The commission shall ensure that the method for determining marginal cost is consistently applied among utilities but may recognize the individual load and resource requirements of the electric utility.

(d) Notwithstanding any other provision of this title, the commission shall ensure that the electric utility's allocable costs of serving customers paying discounted rates under this section are not borne by the utility's other customers.

Acts 1997, 75th Leg., ch. 166, § 1, eff. Sept. 1, 1997.

§ 36.008. State Transmission System

In establishing rates for an electric utility, the commission may review the state's transmission system and make recommendations to the utility on the need to build new power lines, upgrade power lines, and make other necessary improvements and additions.

Acts 1997, 75th Leg., ch. 166, § 1, eff. Sept. 1, 1997. Amended by Acts 1999, 76th Leg., ch. 405, § 23, eff. Sept. 1, 1999.

§ 36.009. Billing Demand for Certain Utility Customers

Notwithstanding any other provision of this code, the commission by rule shall require a transmission and distribution utility to:

(1) waive the application of demand ratchet provisions for each nonresidential secondary service customer that has a maximum load factor equal to or below a factor set by commission rule;

(2) implement procedures to verify annually whether each nonresidential secondary service customer has a maximum load factor that qualifies the customer for the waiver described by Subdivision (1);

(3) specify in the utility's tariff whether the utility's nonresidential secondary service customers that qualify for the waiver described by Subdivision (1) are to be billed for distribution service charges on the basis of:

(A) kilowatts;

(B) kilowatt-hours; or

(C) kilovolt-amperes; and

(4) modify the utility's tariff in the utility's next base rate case to implement the waiver described by Subdivision (1) and make the specification required by Subdivision (3).

Added by Acts 2011, 82nd Leg., ch. 150 (H.B. 1064), § 1, eff. May 28, 2011.

SUBCHAPTER B. COMPUTATION OF RATES

§ 36.051. Establishing Overall Revenues

In establishing an electric utility's rates, the regulatory authority shall establish the utility's overall revenues at an amount that will permit the utility a reasonable opportunity to earn a reasonable return on the utility's invested capital used and useful in providing service to the public in excess of the utility's reasonable and necessary operating expenses.

Acts 1997, 75th Leg., ch. 166, § 1, eff. Sept. 1, 1997.

§ 36.052. Establishing Reasonable Return

In establishing a reasonable return on invested capital, the regulatory authority shall consider applicable factors, including:

(1) the efforts and achievements of the utility in conserving resources;

(2) the quality of the utility's services;

(3) the efficiency of the utility's operations; and

(4) the quality of the utility's management.

Acts 1997, 75th Leg., ch. 166, § 1, eff. Sept. 1, 1997. Amended by Acts 1999, 76th Leg., ch. 405, § 24, eff. Sept. 1, 1999.

§ 36.053. Components of Invested Capital

(a) Electric utility rates shall be based on the original cost, less depreciation, of property used by and useful to the utility in providing service.

(b) The original cost of property shall be determined at the time the property is dedicated to public use, whether by the utility that is the present owner or by a predecessor.

(c) In this section, the term "original cost" means the actual money cost or the actual money value of consideration paid other than money.

(d) If the commission issues a certificate of convenience and necessity or, acting under Section 39.203(e), orders an electric utility or a transmission and distribution utility to construct or enlarge transmission or transmission-related facilities to facilitate meeting the goal for generating capacity from renewable energy technologies under Section 39.904(a), the commission shall find that the facilities are used and useful to the utility in providing service for purposes of this section and are prudent and includable in the rate base, regardless of the extent of the utility's actual use of the facilities.

Acts 1997, 75th Leg., ch. 166, § 1, eff. Sept. 1, 1997. Amended by Acts 2005, 79th Leg., 1st C.S., ch. 1, § 1, eff. Sept. 1, 2005.

§ 36.054. Construction Work in Progress

(a) Construction work in progress, at cost as recorded on the electric utility's books, may be included in the utility's rate base. The inclusion of construction work in progress is an exceptional form of rate relief that the regulatory authority may grant only if the utility demonstrates that inclusion is necessary to the utility's financial integrity.

(b) Construction work in progress may not be included in the rate base for a major project under construction to the extent that the project has been inefficiently or imprudently planned or managed.

Acts 1997, 75th Leg., ch. 166, § 1, eff. Sept. 1, 1997.

§ 36.055. Separations and Allocations

Costs of facilities, revenues, expenses, taxes, and reserves shall be separated or allocated as prescribed by the regulatory authority.

Acts 1997, 75th Leg., ch. 166, § 1, eff. Sept. 1, 1997.

§ 36.056. Depreciation, Amortization, and Depletion

(a) The commission shall establish proper and adequate rates and methods of depreciation, amortization, or depletion for each class of property of an electric or municipally owned utility.

(b) The rates and methods established under this section and the depreciation account required by Section 32.102 shall be used uniformly and consistently throughout rate-setting and appeal proceedings.

Acts 1997, 75th Leg., ch. 166, § 1, eff. Sept. 1, 1997.

§ 36.057. Net Income; Determination of Revenues and Expenses

(a) An electric utility's net income is the total revenues of the utility less all reasonable and necessary expenses as determined by the regulatory authority.

(b) The regulatory authority shall determine revenues and expenses in a manner consistent with this subchapter.

(c) The regulatory authority may adopt reasonable rules with respect to whether an expense is allowed for ratemaking purposes.

Acts 1997, 75th Leg., ch. 166, § 1, eff. Sept. 1, 1997.

§ 36.058. Consideration of Payment to Affiliate

(a) Except as provided by Subsection (b), the regulatory authority may not allow as capital cost or as expense a payment to an affiliate for:

(1) the cost of a service, property, right, or other item; or

(2) interest expense.

(b) The regulatory authority may allow a payment described by Subsection (a) only to the extent that the regulatory authority finds the payment is reasonable and necessary for each item or class of items as determined by the commission.

(c) A finding under Subsection (b) must include:

(1) a specific finding of the reasonableness and necessity of each item or class of items allowed; and

(2) a finding that the price to the electric utility is not higher than the prices charged by the supplying affiliate for the same item or class of items to:

(A) its other affiliates or divisions; or

(B) a nonaffiliated person within the same market area or having the same market conditions.

(d) In making a finding regarding an affiliate transaction, the regulatory authority shall:

(1) determine the extent to which the conditions and circumstances of that transaction are reasonably comparable relative to quantity, terms, date of contract, and place of delivery; and

(2) allow for appropriate differences based on that determination.

(e) This section does not require a finding to be made before payments made by an electric utility to an affiliate are included in the utility's charges to consumers if there is a mechanism for making the charges subject to refund pending the making of the finding.

(f) If the regulatory authority finds that an affiliate expense for the test period is unreasonable, the regulatory authority shall:

(1) determine the reasonable level of the expense; and

(2) include that expense in determining the electric utility's cost of service.

Acts 1997, 75th Leg., ch. 166, § 1, eff. Sept. 1, 1997. Amended by Acts 1999, 76th Leg., ch. 405, § 25, eff. Sept. 1, 1999; Acts 2005, 79th Leg., ch. 413, § 1, eff. June 17, 2005.

§ 36.059. Treatment of Certain Tax Benefits

(a) In determining the allocation of tax savings derived from liberalized depreciation and amortization, the investment tax credit, and the application of similar methods, the regulatory authority shall:

(1) balance equitably the interests of present and future customers; and

(2) apportion accordingly the benefits between consumers and the electric or municipally owned utility.

(b) If an electric utility or a municipally owned utility retains a portion of the investment tax credit, that portion shall be deducted from the original cost of the facilities or other addition to the rate base to which the credit applied to the extent allowed by the Internal Revenue Code.

Acts 1997, 75th Leg., ch. 166, § 1, eff. Sept. 1, 1997.

§ 36.060. Consolidated Income Tax Returns

(a) Unless it is shown to the satisfaction of the regulatory authority that it was reasonable to choose not to consolidate returns, an electric utility's income taxes shall be computed as though a consolidated return had been filed and the utility had realized its fair share of the savings resulting from that return, if:

(1) the utility is a member of an affiliated group eligible to file a consolidated income tax return; and

(2) it is advantageous to the utility to do so.

(b) The amount of income tax that a consolidated group of which an electric utility is a member saves, because the consolidated return eliminates the intercompany profit on purchases by the utility from an affiliate, shall be applied to reduce the cost of the property or service purchased from the affiliate.

(c) The investment tax credit allowed against federal income taxes, to the extent retained by the electric utility, shall be applied as a reduction in the rate-based contribution of the assets to which the credit applies, to the extent and at the rate allowed by the Internal Revenue Code.

Acts 1997, 75th Leg., ch. 166, § 1, eff. Sept. 1, 1997.

§ 36.061. Allowance of Certain Expenses

(a) The regulatory authority may not allow as a cost or expense for ratemaking purposes:

(1) an expenditure for legislative advocacy; or

(2) an expenditure described by Section 32.104 that the regulatory authority determines to be not in the public interest.

(b) The regulatory authority may allow as a cost or expense:

(1) reasonable charitable or civic contributions not to exceed the amount approved by the regulatory authority; and

(2) reasonable costs of participating in a proceeding under this title not to exceed the amount approved by the regulatory authority.

Acts 1997, 75th Leg., ch. 166, § 1, eff. Sept. 1, 1997.

§ 36.062. Consideration of Certain Expenses

The regulatory authority may not consider for ratemaking purposes:

(1) an expenditure for legislative advocacy, made directly or indirectly, including legislative advocacy expenses included in trade association dues;

(2) a payment made to cover costs of an accident, equipment failure, or negligence at a utility facility owned by a person or governmental entity not selling power in this state, other than a payment made under an insurance or risk-sharing arrangement executed before the date of loss;

(3) an expenditure for costs of processing a refund or credit under Section 36.110; or

(4) any other expenditure, including an executive salary, advertising expense, legal expense, or civil penalty or fine, the regulatory authority finds to be

unreasonable, unnecessary, or not in the public interest.

Acts 1997, 75th Leg., ch. 166, § 1, eff. Sept. 1, 1997.

§ 36.063. Consideration of Profit or Loss From Sale or Lease of Merchandise

In establishing an electric or municipally owned utility's rates, the regulatory authority may not consider any profit or loss that results from the sale or lease of merchandise, including appliances, fixtures, or equipment, to the extent that merchandise is not integral to providing utility service.

Acts 1997, 75th Leg., ch. 166, § 1, eff. Sept. 1, 1997.

§ 36.064. Self-Insurance

(a) An electric utility may self-insure all or part of the utility's potential liability or catastrophic property loss, including windstorm, fire, and explosion losses, that could not have been reasonably anticipated and included under operating and maintenance expenses.

(b) The commission shall approve a self-insurance plan under this section if the commission finds that:

(1) the coverage is in the public interest;

(2) the plan, considering all costs, is a lower cost alternative to purchasing commercial insurance; and

(3) ratepayers will receive the benefits of the savings.

(c) In computing an electric utility's reasonable and necessary expenses under this subchapter, the regulatory authority, to the extent the regulatory authority finds is in the public interest, shall allow as a necessary expense the money credited to a reserve account for self-insurance. The regulatory authority shall determine reasonableness under this subsection:

(1) from information provided at the time the self-insurance plan and reserve account are established; and

(2) on the filing of a rate case by an electric utility that has a reserve account.

(d) After a reserve account for self-insurance is established, the regulatory authority shall:

(1) determine whether the reserve account has a surplus or shortage under Subsection (e); and

(2) subtract any surplus from or add any shortage to the utility's rate base.

(e) A surplus in the reserve account exists if the charges against the account are less than the money credited to the account. A shortage in the reserve account exists if the charges against the account are greater than the money credited to the account.

(f) The allowance for self-insurance under this title for ratemaking purposes is not applicable to nuclear plant investment.

(g) The commission shall adopt rules governing self-insurance under this section.

Acts 1997, 75th Leg., ch. 166, § 1, eff. Sept. 1, 1997.

§ 36.065. Pension and Other Postemployment Benefits

(a) The regulatory authority shall include in the rates of an electric utility expenses for pension and other postemployment benefits, as determined by actuarial or other similar studies in accordance with generally accepted accounting principles, in an amount the regulatory authority finds reasonable. Expenses for pension and other postemployment benefits include, in an amount found reasonable by the regulatory authority, the benefits attributable to the service of employees who were employed by the predecessor integrated electric utility of an electric utility before the utility's unbundling under Chapter 39 irrespective of the business activity performed by the employee or the affiliate to which the employee was transferred on or after the unbundling.

(b) Effective January 1, 2005, an electric utility may establish one or more reserve accounts for expenses for pension and other postemployment benefits. An electric utility shall periodically record in the reserve account any difference between:

(1) the annual amount of pension and other postemployment benefits approved as an operating expense in the electric utility's last general rate proceeding or, if that amount cannot be determined from the regulatory authority's order, the amount recorded for pension and other postemployment benefits under generally accepted accounting principles during the first year that rates from the electric utility's last general rate proceeding are in effect; and

(2) the annual amount of pension and other postemployment benefits as determined by actuarial or other similar studies that are chargeable to the electric utility's operating expense.

(c) A surplus in the reserve account exists if the amount of pension and other postemployment benefits under Subsection (b)(1) is greater than the amount determined under Subsection (b)(2). A shortage in the reserve account exists if the amount of pension and other postemployment benefits under Subsection (b)(1) is less than the amount determined under Subsection (b)(2).

(d) If a reserve account for pension and other postemployment benefits is established, the regulatory authority at a subsequent general rate proceeding shall:

(1) review the amounts recorded to the reserve account to determine whether the amounts are reasonable expenses;

(2) determine whether the reserve account has a surplus or shortage under Subsection (c); and

(3) subtract any surplus from or add any shortage to the electric utility's rate base with the surplus or shortage amortized over a reasonable time.

Added by Acts 2005, 79th Leg., ch. 385, § 1, eff. June 17, 2005.

SUBCHAPTER C. GENERAL PROCEDURES FOR RATE CHANGES PROPOSED BY UTILITY

§ 36.101. Definition

In this subchapter, "major change" means an increase in rates that would increase the aggregate revenues of the applicant more than the greater of $100,000 or 2½ percent. The term does not include an increase in rates that the regulatory authority allows to go into effect or the electric utility makes under an order of the regulatory authority after hearings held with public notice.

Acts 1997, 75th Leg., ch. 166, § 1, eff. Sept. 1, 1997.

§ 36.102. Statement of Intent to Change Rates

(a) Except as provided by Section 33.024, an electric utility may not change its rates unless the utility files a statement of its intent with the regulatory authority that has original jurisdiction over those rates at least 35 days before the effective date of the proposed change.

(b) The electric utility shall also mail or deliver a copy of the statement of intent to the appropriate officer of each affected municipality.

(c) The statement of intent must include:

(1) proposed revisions of tariffs; and

(2) a detailed statement of:

(A) each proposed change;

(B) the effect the proposed change is expected to have on the revenues of the utility;

(C) each class and number of utility consumers affected; and

(D) any other information required by the regulatory authority's rules.

Acts 1997, 75th Leg., ch. 166, § 1, eff. Sept. 1, 1997.

§ 36.103. Notice of Intent to Change Rates

(a) The electric utility shall:

(1) publish, in conspicuous form and place, notice to the public of the proposed change once each week for four successive weeks before the effective date of the proposed change in a newspaper having general circulation in each county containing territory affected by the proposed change; and

(2) mail notice of the proposed change to any other affected person as required by the regulatory authority's rules.

(b) The regulatory authority may waive the publication of notice requirement prescribed by Subsection (a) in a proceeding that involves only a rate reduction for each affected ratepayer. The applicant shall give notice of the proposed rate change by mail to each affected utility customer.

(c) The regulatory authority by rule shall define other proceedings for which the publication of notice requirement prescribed by Subsection (a) may be waived on a showing of good cause. A waiver may not be granted in a proceeding involving a rate increase to any class or category of ratepayer.

Acts 1997, 75th Leg., ch. 166, § 1, eff. Sept. 1, 1997.

§ 36.104. Early Effective Date of Rate Change

(a) For good cause shown, the regulatory authority may allow a rate change, other than a major change, to take effect:

(1) before the end of the 35-day period prescribed by Section 36.102; and

(2) under conditions the regulatory authority prescribes, subject to suspension as provided by this subchapter.

(b) The electric utility shall immediately revise its tariffs to include the change.

Acts 1997, 75th Leg., ch. 166, § 1, eff. Sept. 1, 1997.

§ 36.105. Determination of Propriety of Rate Change; Hearing

(a) If a tariff changing rates is filed with a regulatory authority, the regulatory authority shall, on complaint by an affected person, or may, on its own motion, not later than the 30th day after the effective date of the change, enter on a hearing to determine the propriety of the change.

(b) The regulatory authority shall hold a hearing in every case in which the change constitutes a major change. The regulatory authority may, however, use an informal proceeding if the regulatory authority does not receive a complaint before the 46th day after the date notice of the change is filed.

(c) The regulatory authority shall give reasonable notice of the hearing, including notice to the governing body of each affected municipality and county. The electric utility is not required to provide a formal answer or file any other formal pleading in response to the notice, and the absence of an answer does not affect an order for a hearing.

Acts 1997, 75th Leg., ch. 166, § 1, eff. Sept. 1, 1997.

§ 36.106. Regional Hearing

The commission shall hold a regional hearing at an appropriate location in a case in which the commission determines it is in the public interest to hear testimony at a regional hearing for inclusion in the record.

Acts 1997, 75th Leg., ch. 166, § 1, eff. Sept. 1, 1997.

§ 36.107. Preference to Hearing

The regulatory authority shall:

(1) give preference to a hearing under this subchapter and to deciding questions arising under this subchapter and Subchapter E [1] over any other question pending before it; and

(2) decide the questions as quickly as possible.

Acts 1997, 75th Leg., ch. 166, § 1, eff. Sept. 1, 1997.

[1] V.T.C.A., Utilities Code § 36.201 et seq.

§ 36.108. Rate Suspension; Deadline

(a) Pending the hearing and a decision:

(1) the local regulatory authority, after delivering to the electric utility a written statement of the regulatory authority's reasons, may suspend the rate change for not longer than 90 days after the date the rate change would otherwise be effective; and

(2) the commission may suspend the rate change for not longer than 150 days after the date the rate change would otherwise be effective.

(b) The 150-day period prescribed by Subsection (a)(2) shall be extended two days for each day the actual hearing on the merits of the case exceeds 15 days.

(c) If the regulatory authority does not make a final determination concerning a rate change before expiration of the applicable suspension period, the regulatory authority is considered to have approved the change. This approval is subject to the authority of the regulatory authority thereafter to continue a hearing in progress.

Acts 1997, 75th Leg., ch. 166, § 1, eff. Sept. 1, 1997.

§ 36.109. Temporary Rates

(a) The regulatory authority may establish temporary rates to be in effect during the applicable suspension period under Section 36.108.

(b) If the regulatory authority does not establish temporary rates, the rates in effect when the suspended tariff was filed continue in effect during the suspension period.

Acts 1997, 75th Leg., ch. 166, § 1, eff. Sept. 1, 1997.

§ 36.110. Bonded Rates

(a) An electric utility may put a changed rate into effect throughout the area in which the utility sought to change its rates, including an area over which the commission is exercising appellate or original jurisdiction, by filing a bond with the commission if:

(1) the 150-day suspension period has been extended under Section 36.108(b); and

(2) the commission fails to make a final determination before the 151st day after the date the rate change would otherwise be effective.

(b) The bonded rate may not exceed the proposed rate.

(c) The bond must be:

(1) payable to the commission in an amount, in a form, and with a surety approved by the commission; and

(2) conditioned on refund.

(d) The electric utility shall refund or credit against future bills:

(1) money collected under the bonded rates in excess of the rate finally ordered; and

(2) interest on that money, at the current interest rate as determined by the commission.

Acts 1997, 75th Leg., ch. 166, § 1, eff. Sept. 1, 1997.

§ 36.111. Establishment of Final Rates

(a) If, after hearing, the regulatory authority finds the rates are unreasonable or in violation of law, the regulatory authority shall:

(1) enter an order establishing the rates the electric utility shall charge or apply for the service in question; and

(2) serve a copy of the order on the electric utility.

(b) The rates established in the order shall be observed thereafter until changed as provided by this title.

Acts 1997, 75th Leg., ch. 166, § 1, eff. Sept. 1, 1997.

SUBCHAPTER D. RATE CHANGES PROPOSED BY REGULATORY AUTHORITY

§ 36.151. Unreasonable or Violative Existing Rates

(a) If the regulatory authority, on its own motion or on complaint by an affected person, after reasonable notice and hearing, finds that the existing rates of an electric utility for a service are unreasonable or in violation of law, the regulatory authority shall:

(1) enter an order establishing the just and reasonable rates to be observed thereafter, including maximum or minimum rates; and

(2) serve a copy of the order on the electric utility.

(b) The rates established under Subsection (a) constitute the legal rates of the electric utility until changed as provided by this title.

Acts 1997, 75th Leg., ch. 166, § 1, eff. Sept. 1, 1997.

§ 36.152. Investigating Costs of Obtaining Service From Another Source

If an electric utility does not produce or generate the service that it distributes, transmits, or furnishes to the public for compensation but obtains the service from another source, the regulatory authority may investigate the cost of that production or generation in an investigation of the reasonableness of the electric utility's rates.

Acts 1997, 75th Leg., ch. 166, § 1, eff. Sept. 1, 1997.

§ 36.153. Rate-Filing Package

(a) An electric utility shall file a rate-filing package with the regulatory authority not later than the 120th day after the date the authority notifies the utility that the authority will proceed with an inquiry under Section 36.151.

(b) The regulatory authority may grant an extension of the 120-day period prescribed by Subsection (a) or waive the rate-filing package requirement on agreement of the parties.

Acts 1997, 75th Leg., ch. 166, § 1, eff. Sept. 1, 1997.

§ 36.154. Deadline

(a) The regulatory authority shall make a final determination not later than the 185th day after the date the electric utility files the rate-filing package required by Section 36.153.

(b) The deadline prescribed by Subsection (a) is extended two days for each day the actual hearing on the merits of the case exceeds 15 days.

Acts 1997, 75th Leg., ch. 166, § 1, eff. Sept. 1, 1997.

§ 36.155. Interim Order Establishing Temporary Rates

(a) At any time after an initial complaint is filed under Section 36.151, the regulatory authority may issue an interim order establishing temporary rates for the electric utility to be in effect until a final determination is made.

(b) On issuance of a final order, the regulatory authority:

(1) may require the electric utility to refund to customers or to credit against future bills:

(A) money collected under the temporary rates in excess of the rate finally ordered; and

(B) interest on that money, at the current interest rate as determined by the commission; or

(2) shall authorize the electric utility to surcharge bills to recover:

(A) the amount by which the money collected under the temporary rates is less than the money that would have been collected under the rate finally ordered; and

(B) interest on that amount, at the current interest rate as determined by the commission.

Acts 1997, 75th Leg., ch. 166, § 1, eff. Sept. 1, 1997.

§ 36.156. Automatic Temporary Rates

(a) The rates charged by the electric utility on the 185th day after the date the utility files the rate-filing package required by Section 36.153 automatically become temporary rates if:

(1) the 185-day period has been extended under Section 36.154(b); and

(2) the regulatory authority has not issued a final order or established temporary rates for the electric utility on or before the 185th day.

(b) On issuance of a final order, the regulatory authority:

(1) shall require the electric utility to refund to customers or to credit against future bills:

(A) money collected under the temporary rates in excess of the rate finally ordered; and

(B) interest on that money, at the current interest rate as determined by the commission; or

(2) shall authorize the electric utility to surcharge bills to recover:

(A) the amount by which the money collected under the temporary rates is less than the money that would have been collected under the rate finally ordered; and

(B) interest on that amount, at the current interest rate as determined by the commission.

Acts 1997, 75th Leg., ch. 166, § 1, eff. Sept. 1, 1997.

SUBCHAPTER E. COST RECOVERY AND RATE ADJUSTMENT

§ 36.201. Automatic Adjustment for Changes in Costs

Except as permitted by Section 36.204, the commission may not establish a rate or tariff that authorizes an electric utility to automatically adjust and pass through to the utility's customers a change in the utility's fuel or other costs.

Acts 1997, 75th Leg., ch. 166, § 1, eff. Sept. 1, 1997. Amended by Acts 1999, 76th Leg., ch. 405, § 26, eff. Sept. 1, 1999.

§ 36.202. Adjustment for Change in Tax Liability

(a) The commission, on its own motion or on the petition of an electric utility, shall provide for the adjustment of the utility's billing to reflect an increase or decrease in the utility's tax liability to this state if the increase or decrease:

(1) results from Chapter 5, Acts of the 72nd Legislature, 1st Called Session, 1991; and

(2) is attributable to an activity subject to the commission's jurisdiction.

(b) The commission shall apportion pro rata to each type and class of service provided by the utility any billing adjustment under this section. The adjustment:

(1) shall be made effective at the same time as the increase or decrease of tax liability described by Subsection (a)(1) or as soon after that increase or decrease as is reasonably practical; and

(2) remains effective only until the commission alters the adjustment as provided by this section or enters an order for the utility under Subchapter C or D.[1]

(c) Each year after an original adjustment, the commission shall:

(1) review the utility's increase or decrease of tax liability described by Subsection (a)(1); and

(2) alter the adjustment as necessary to reflect the increase or decrease.

(d) A proceeding under this section is not a rate case under Subchapter C.

Acts 1997, 75th Leg., ch. 166, § 1, eff. Sept. 1, 1997.

[1] V.T.C.A., Utilities Code § 36.101 et seq., or § 36.151 et seq.

§ 36.203. Fuel Cost Recovery; Adjustment of Fuel Factor

(a) Section 36.201 does not prohibit the commission from reviewing and providing for adjustments of a utility's fuel factor.

(b) The commission by rule shall implement procedures that provide for the timely adjustment of a utility's fuel factor, with or without a hearing. The procedures must require that:

(1) the findings required by Section 36.058 regarding fuel transactions with affiliated interests are made in a fuel reconciliation proceeding or in a rate case filed under Subchapter C or D;[1] and

(2) an affected party receive notice and have the opportunity to request a hearing before the commission.

(c) The commission may adjust a utility's fuel factor without a hearing if the commission determines that a hearing is not necessary. If the commission holds a hearing, the commission may consider at the hearing any evidence that is appropriate and in the public interest.

(d) The commission shall render a timely decision approving, disapproving, or modifying the adjustment to the utility's fuel factor.

(e) The commission by rule shall provide for the reconciliation of a utility's fuel costs on a timely basis.

(f) A proceeding under this section is not a rate case under Subchapter C.[1]

Acts 1997, 75th Leg., ch. 166, § 1, eff. Sept. 1, 1997.

[1] V.T.C.A., Utilities Code § 36.101 et seq., or § 36.151 et seq.

§ 36.204. Cost Recovery and Incentives

In establishing rates for an electric utility, the commission may:

(1) allow timely recovery of the reasonable costs of conservation, load management, and purchased power, notwithstanding Section 36.201; and

(2) authorize additional incentives for conservation, load management, purchased power, and renewable resources.

Acts 1997, 75th Leg., ch. 166, § 1, eff. Sept. 1, 1997. Amended by Acts 1999, 76th Leg., ch. 405, § 27, eff. Sept. 1, 1999.

§ 36.205. Purchased Power Cost Recovery

(a) This section applies only to an increase or decrease in the cost of purchased electricity that has been:

(1) accepted by a federal regulatory authority; or

(2) approved after a hearing by the commission.

(b) The commission may use any appropriate method to provide for the adjustment of the cost of purchased electricity on terms determined by the commission.

(c) Purchased electricity costs may be recovered:

(1) concurrently with the effective date of the changed costs to the purchasing electric utility; or

(2) as soon after the effective date as reasonably practical.

(d) The commission may provide a mechanism to allow an electric utility that has a noncontiguous geographical service area and that purchases power for resale for that noncontiguous service area from electric utilities that are not members of the Electric Reliability Council of Texas to recover purchased power costs for the area in a manner that reflects the purchased power cost for that specific geographical noncontiguous area. The commission may not require an electric cooperative corporation to use the mechanism provided under this section unless the electric cooperative corporation requests its use.

Acts 1997, 75th Leg., ch. 166, § 1, eff. Sept. 1, 1997.

§ 36.206. Mark-Ups

(a) A cost recovery factor established for the recovery of purchased power costs may include:

(1) the cost the electric utility incurs in purchasing capacity and energy;

(2) a mark-up added to the cost or another mechanism the commission determines will reasonably compensate the utility for any financial risk associated with purchased power obligations; and

(3) the value added by the utility in making the purchased power available to customers.

(b) The mark-ups and cost recovery factors, if allowed, may be those necessary to encourage the electric utility to include economical purchased power as part of the utility's energy and capacity resource supply plan.

Acts 1997, 75th Leg., ch. 166, § 1, eff. Sept. 1, 1997.

§ 36.207. Use of Mark-Ups

Any mark-ups approved under Section 36.206 are an exceptional form of rate relief that the electric utility may recover from ratepayers only on a finding by the commission that the relief is necessary to maintain the utility's financial integrity.

Acts 1997, 75th Leg., ch. 166, § 1, eff. Sept. 1, 1997. Amended by Acts 1999, 76th Leg., ch. 405, § 28, eff. Sept. 1, 1999.

§ 36.208. Payment to Qualifying Facility

In establishing an electric utility's rates, the regulatory authority shall:

(1) consider a payment made to a qualifying facility under an agreement certified under Subchapter C, Chapter 35,[1] to be a reasonable and necessary operating expense of the electric utility during the period for which the certification is effective; and

(2) allow full, concurrent, and monthly recovery of the amount of the payment.

Acts 1997, 75th Leg., ch. 166, § 1, eff. Sept. 1, 1997.

[1] V.T.C.A., Utilities Code § 35.061 et seq.

§ 36.209. Recovery by Certain Non–ERCOT Utilities of Certain Transmission Costs

(a) This section applies only to an electric utility that operates solely outside of ERCOT in areas of this state included in the Southeastern Electric Reliability Council, the Southwest Power Pool, or the Western Electricity Coordinating Council and that owns or operates transmission facilities.

(b) The commission, after notice and hearing, may allow an electric utility to recover on an annual basis its reasonable and necessary expenditures for transmission infrastructure improvement costs and changes in wholesale transmission charges to the electric utility under a tariff approved by a federal regulatory authority to the extent that the costs or charges have not otherwise been recovered. The commission may allow the electric utility to recover only the costs allocable to retail customers in the state and may not allow the electric utility to over-recover costs.

Added by Acts 2005, 79th Leg., ch. 1024, § 1, eff. June 18, 2005. Amended by Acts 2009, 81st Leg., ch. 1226, § 1, eff. June 19, 2009.

§ 36.210. Periodic Rate Adjustments

Text of section effective until January 1, 2017

(a) The commission or a regulatory authority, on the petition of an electric utility, may approve a tariff or rate schedule in which a nonfuel rate may be periodically adjusted upward or downward, based on changes in the parts of the utility's invested capital, as described by Section 36.053, that are categorized as distribution plant, distribution-related intangible plant, and distribution-related communication equipment and networks in accordance with commission rules adopted after consideration of the uniform system of accounts prescribed by the Federal Energy Regulatory Commission. A periodic rate adjustment must:

(1) be approved or denied in accordance with an expedited procedure that:

(A) provides for appropriate updates of information;

(B) allows for participation by the office and affected parties; and

(C) extends for not less than 60 days;

(2) take into account changes in the number of an electric utility's customers and the effects, on a weather-normalized basis, that energy consumption and energy demand have on the amount of revenue recovered through the electric utility's base rates;

(3) be consistent with the manner in which costs for invested capital described by this subsection were allocated to each rate class, as approved by the commission, in an electric utility's most recent base rate statement of intent proceeding with changes to residential and commercial class rates reflected in volumetric charges to the extent that residential and commercial class rates are collected in that manner based on the electric utility's most recent base rate statement of intent proceeding;

(4) not diminish the ability of the commission or a regulatory authority, on its own motion or on complaint by an affected person as provided by Subchapter D, after reasonable notice and hearing, to change the existing rates of an electric utility for a service after finding that the rates are unreasonable or in violation of law;

(5) be applied by an electric utility on a system-wide basis; and

(6) be supported by the sworn statement of an appropriate employee of the electric utility that affirms that:

(A) the filing is in compliance with the provisions of the tariff or rate schedule; and

(B) the filing is true and correct to the best of the employee's knowledge, information, and belief.

(b) An electric utility in the ERCOT power region, or an unbundled electric utility outside the ERCOT power region in whose service area retail competition is available, that requests a periodic rate adjustment under this section shall:

(1) except as provided by Subsection (f)(3) and to the extent possible, implement simultaneously all nonfuel rates to be adjusted in a 12-month period that are charged by the utility to retail electric providers; and

(2) provide notice to retail electric providers of the approved rates not later than the 45th day before the date the rates take effect.

(c) A periodic rate adjustment approved under this section may not be used to adjust the portion of a nonfuel rate relating to the generation of electricity.

(d) An electric utility may adjust the utility's rates under this section not more than once per year and not more than four times between comprehensive base rate proceedings.

(e) A periodic rate adjustment approved under this section may not include indirect corporate costs or capitalized operations and maintenance expenses.

(f) Nothing in this section is intended to:

(1) conflict with a provision contained in a financing order issued under Subchapter I of this chapter or Subchapter G or J, Chapter 39;

(2) affect the limitation on the commission's jurisdiction under Section 32.002;

(3) include in a periodic rate adjustment authorized by this section costs adjusted under a transmission cost-of-service adjustment approved under Section 35.004(d);

(4) limit the jurisdiction of a municipality over the rates, operations, and services of an electric utility as provided by Section 33.001;

(5) limit the ability of a municipality to obtain a reimbursement under Section 33.023 for the reasonable cost of services of a person engaged in an activity described by that section; or

(6) prevent the commission from:

(A) reviewing the investment costs included in a periodic rate adjustment or in the following comprehensive base rate proceeding to determine whether the costs were prudent, reasonable, and necessary; or

(B) refunding to customers any amount improperly recovered through the periodic rate adjustments, with appropriate carrying costs.

(g) The commission shall adopt rules necessary to implement this section. The rules must provide for:

(1) a procedure by which a tariff or rate schedule is to be reviewed and approved;

(2) filing requirements and discovery consistent with the expedited procedure described by Subsection (a)(1);

(3) an earnings monitoring report that allows the commission or regulatory authority to reasonably determine whether a utility is earning in excess of the utility's allowed return on investment as normalized for weather;

(4) denial of the electric utility's filing if the electric utility is earning more than the utility's authorized rate of return on investment, on a weather-normalized basis, at the time the periodic rate adjustment request is filed; and

(5) a mechanism by which the commission may refund customers any amounts determined to be improperly recovered through a periodic rate adjustment, including any interest on the amounts.

(h) The commission shall undertake a study and conduct a report analyzing any periodic rate adjustment established under this section. The study shall be available for the legislature's review by January 31, 2017, so that the legislature may properly be informed as to the need to continue the commission's authority to allow periodic rate adjustments. The report shall contain but shall not be limited to:

(1) an analysis of all periodic rate adjustments approved by the commission;

(2) an analysis of the amounts in real dollars and percentages of the approved amounts by the commission and the effects on all classes of ratepayers;

(3) the costs savings, if any, realized by all parties by utilizing periodic rate adjustment as opposed to ratemaking proceedings;

(4) an analysis on distribution costs included in periodic rate adjustments, and their appropriateness for inclusion in periodic rate adjustments; and

(5) an analysis submitted by the office on the effects of periodic rate adjustments.

(i) This section expires January 1, 2017.

Added by Acts 2011, 82nd Leg., ch. 196 (S.B. 1693), § 1, eff. May 28, 2011.

SUBCHAPTER F. PARTIAL RATE DEREGULATION AVAILABLE TO CERTAIN COOPERATIVES [REPEALED]

§§ 36.251 to 36.255. Repealed by Acts 1999, 76th Leg., ch. 405, § 61(3), eff. Sept. 1, 1999

SUBCHAPTER G. RATE CHANGES BY CERTAIN ELECTRIC COOPERATIVES [REPEALED]

§§ 36.301 to 36.309. Repealed by Acts 1999, 76th Leg., ch. 405, § 61(3), eff. Sept. 1, 1999

SUBCHAPTER H. RATES FOR GOVERNMENTAL ENTITIES

§ 36.351. Discounted Rates for Certain Institutions of Higher Education

(a) Notwithstanding any other provision of this title, each electric utility and municipally owned utility shall discount charges for electric service provided to a facility of a four-year state university, upper-level institution, Texas State Technical College, or college.

(b) The discount is a 20-percent reduction of the utility's base rates that would otherwise be paid under the applicable tariffed rate.

(c) An electric or municipally owned utility is exempt from this section if the 20-percent discount results in a reduction equal to more than one percent of the utility's total annual revenues.

(d) A municipally owned utility is exempt from this section if the municipally owned utility, on September 1, 1995, discounted base commercial rates for electric service provided to all four-year state universities or colleges in its service area by 20 percent or more.

(e) This section does not apply to a rate charged to an institution of higher education by a municipally owned utility that provides a discounted rate to the state for electric services below rates in effect on January 1, 1995, if the discounted rate provides a greater financial discount to the state than is provided to the institution of higher education through the discount provided by this section.

(f) An investor-owned electric utility may not recover from residential customers or any other customer class the assigned and allocated costs of serving a state university or college that receives a discount under this section.

(g) Each electric utility shall file tariffs with the commission reflecting the discount required under this section. The initial tariff filing is not a rate change for purposes of Subchapter C.[1]

Acts 1997, 75th Leg., ch. 166, § 1, eff. Sept. 1, 1997.

[1] V.T.C.A., Utilities Code § 36.101 et seq.

§ 36.352. Special Rate Class

Notwithstanding any other provision of this title, if the commission, on or before September 1, 1995, approved the establishment of a separate rate class for electric service for a university and grouped public schools in a separate rate class, the commission shall include community colleges in the rate class with public school customers.

Acts 1997, 75th Leg., ch. 166, § 1, eff. Sept. 1, 1997.

§ 36.353. Payment in Lieu of Tax

(a) A payment made in lieu of a tax by a municipally owned utility to the municipality by which the utility is owned may not be considered an expense of operation in establishing the utility's rate for providing utility service to a school district or hospital district.

(b) A rate a municipally owned utility receives from a school district or hospital district may not be used to make or to cover the cost of making payments in lieu of taxes to the municipality that owns the utility.

Acts 1997, 75th Leg., ch. 166, § 1, eff. Sept. 1, 1997.

§ 36.354. Discounted Rates for Military Bases

(a) Notwithstanding any other provision of this title, each municipally owned utility, electric cooperative, or electric utility in an area where customer choice is not available or the commission has delayed the implementation of full customer choice in accordance with Section 39.103 shall discount charges for electric service provided to a military base.

(b) The discount under Subsection (a) is a 20 percent reduction of the base commercial rate that the municipally owned utility, electric cooperative, or electric utility would otherwise charge the military installation.

(c) An electric utility, municipally owned utility, or electric cooperative may assess a surcharge to all of the utility's retail customers in the state to recover the difference in revenue between the revenues from the discounted rate for military bases provided under Subsection (a) and the base commercial rate. This subsection does not apply to an electric utility, municipally owned utility, or electric cooperative that was providing electric service to a military base on December 31, 2002, at a rate constituting a discount of 20 percent or more from the utility's base commercial rate that the utility would otherwise charge the military base.

(d) Each electric utility shall file a tariff with the commission reflecting the discount required by Subsection (a) and may file a tariff reflecting the surcharge provided by Subsection (c). Not later than the 30th day after the date the commission receives the electric utility's tariff reflecting the surcharge, the commission shall approve the tariff. A proceeding under this subsection is not a rate change for purposes of Subchapter C.

(e) An electric utility, municipally owned utility, or electric cooperative is exempt from the requirements of Subsection (a) if:

(1) the 20 percent discount would result in a reduction of revenue in an amount that is greater than one percent of the utility's total annual revenues; or

(2) the utility:

(A) was providing electric service to a military base on December 31, 2002, at a rate constituting a discount of 20 percent or more from the utility's base commercial rate that the utility would otherwise charge the military base; and

(B) continues to provide electric service to the military base at a rate constituting a discount of 20 percent or more from the utility's base commercial rate that the utility would otherwise charge the military base.

(f) Each electric utility shall provide the Texas Military Preparedness Commission with the base commercial rate that the utility would otherwise charge the military base and the rate the utility is charging the military base.

(g) For the purposes of this section, the term "military base" does not include a military base:

(1) that has been closed or realigned under the Defense Base Closure and Realignment Act of 1990 (10 U.S.C. Section 2687) and its subsequent amendments;

(2) that is administered by an authority established by a municipality under Chapter 378, Local Government Code, as added by Chapter 1221, Acts of the 76th Legislature, Regular Session, 1999;

(3) that is operated by or for the benefit of the Texas National Guard, as defined by Section 431.001, Government Code, unless the base is served by a municipally owned utility owned by a city with a population of 650,000 or more; or

(4) for which a municipally owned utility has acquired the electric distribution system under 10 U.S.C. Section 2688.

Added by Acts 2003, 78th Leg., ch. 149, § 21, eff. May 27, 2003.

SUBCHAPTER I. SECURITIZATION FOR RECOVERY OF SYSTEM RESTORATION COSTS

§ 36.401. Securitization for Recovery of System Restoration Costs; Purpose

(a) The purpose of this subchapter is to enable an electric utility to obtain timely recovery of system restoration costs and to use securitization financing to recover these costs, because that type of debt will lower the carrying costs associated with the recovery of these costs, relative to the costs that would be incurred using conventional financing methods. The proceeds of the transition bonds may be used only for the purposes of reducing the amount of recoverable system restoration costs, as determined by the commission in accordance with this subchapter, including the refinancing or retirement of utility debt or equity.

(b) It is the intent of the legislature that:

(1) securitization of system restoration costs will be accomplished using the same procedures, standards, and protections for securitization authorized under Subchapter G, Chapter 39, as in effect on the effective date of this section, except as provided by this subchapter; and

(2) the commission will ensure that securitization of system restoration costs provides greater tangible and quantifiable benefits to ratepayers than would have been achieved without the issuance of transition bonds.

Added by Acts 2009, 81st Leg., ch. 1, § 1, eff. April 16, 2009.

§ 36.402. System Restoration Costs; Standards and Definitions

(a) In this subchapter, "system restoration costs" means reasonable and necessary costs, including costs expensed, charged to self-insurance reserves, deferred, capitalized, or otherwise financed, that are incurred by an electric utility due to any activity or activities conducted by or on behalf of the electric utility in connection with the restoration of service and infrastructure associated with electric power outages affecting customers of the electric utility as the result of any tropical storm or hurricane, ice or snow storm, flood, or other weather-related event or natural disaster that occurred in calendar year 2008 or thereafter. System restoration costs include mobilization, staging, and construction, reconstruction, replacement, or repair of electric generation, transmission, distribution, or general plant facilities. System restoration costs shall include reasonable estimates of the costs of an activity or activities conducted or expected to be conducted by or on behalf of the electric utility in connection with the restoration of service or infrastructure associated with electric power outages, but such estimates shall be subject to true-up and reconciliation after the actual costs are known.

(b) System restoration costs shall include carrying costs at the electric utility's weighted average cost of capital as last approved by the commission in a general rate proceeding from the date on which the system restoration costs were incurred until the date that transition bonds are issued or until system restoration costs are otherwise recovered pursuant to the provisions of this subchapter.

(c) To the extent a utility subject to this subchapter receives insurance proceeds, governmental grants, or any other source of funding that compensate it for system restoration costs, those amounts shall be used to reduce the utility's system restoration costs recoverable from customers. If the timing of a utility's receipt of those amounts prevents their inclusion as a reduction to the system restoration costs that are securitized, or the commission later determines as a result of the true-up and reconciliation provided for in Subsection (a) that the actual costs incurred are less than estimated costs included in the determination of system restoration costs, the commission shall take those amounts into account in:

(1) the utility's next base rate proceeding; or

(2) any subsequent proceeding, other than a true-up proceeding under Section 39.307, in which the commission considers system restoration costs.

(d) If the commission determines that the insurance proceeds, governmental grants, or other sources of funding that compensate the electric utility for system restoration costs, or the amount resulting from a true-up of estimated system restoration costs are of a magnitude to justify a separate tariff rider, the commission may establish a tariff rider to credit such amounts against charges, other than transition charges or system restoration charges as defined in Section 36.403, being collected from customers.

(e) To the extent that the electric utility receives insurance proceeds, governmental grants, or any other source of funding that is used to reduce system restoration costs, the commission shall impute interest on those amounts at the same cost of capital included in the utility's system restoration costs until the date that those amounts are used to reduce the amount of system restoration costs that are securitized or otherwise reflected in the rates of the utility.

Added by Acts 2009, 81st Leg., ch. 1, § 1, eff. April 16, 2009.

§ 36.403. Standards and Procedures Governing Securitization and Recovery of System Restoration Costs

(a) The procedures and standards of this subchapter and the provisions of Subchapter G, Chapter 39,[1] govern an electric utility's application for, and the commission's issuance of, a financing order to provide for the securitization of system restoration costs, or to otherwise provide for the recovery of system restoration costs.

(b) Subject to the standards, procedures, and tests contained in this subchapter and Subchapter G, Chapter 39, the commission shall adopt a financing order on the application of the electric utility to recover its system restoration costs. If on its own motion or complaint by an affected person, the commission determines that it is likely that securitization of system restoration costs would meet the tests contained in Section 36.401(b), the commission shall require the utility to file an application for a financing order. On the commission's issuance of a financing order allowing for recovery and securitization of system restoration costs, the provisions of this subchapter and Subchapter G, Chapter 39, continue to govern the financing order and the rights and interests established in the order, and this subchapter and Subchapter G, Chapter 39, continue to govern any transition bonds issued pursuant to the financing order. To the extent any conflict exists between the provisions of this subchapter and Subchapter G, Chapter 39, in cases involving the securitization of system restoration costs, the provisions of this subchapter control.

(c) For purposes of this subchapter, "financing order," as defined by Section 39.302 and as used in Subchapter G, Chapter 39, includes a financing order authorizing the securitization of system restoration costs.

(d) For purposes of this subchapter, "qualified costs," as defined by Section 39.302 and as used in Subchapter G, Chapter 39, includes 100 percent of the electric utility's system restoration costs, net of any insurance proceeds, governmental grants, or other source of funding that compensate the utility for system restoration costs, received by the utility at the time it files an application for a financing order. Qualified costs also include the costs of issuing, supporting, and servicing transition bonds and any costs of retiring and refunding existing debt and equity securities of an electric utility subject to this subchapter in connection with the issuance of transition bonds. For purposes of this subchapter, the term qualified costs also includes:

(1) the costs to the commission of acquiring professional services for the purpose of evaluating proposed transactions under this subchapter; and

(2) costs associated with ancillary agreements such as any bond insurance policy, letter of credit, reserve account, surety bond, swap arrangement, hedging arrangement, liquidity or credit support arrangement, or other financial arrangement entered into in connection with the issuance or payment of transition bonds.

(e) For purposes of this subchapter, "transition bonds," as defined by Section 39.302 and as used in Subchapter G, Chapter 39, includes transition bonds issued in association with the recovery of system restoration costs. Transition bonds issued to securitize system restoration costs may be called "system restoration bonds" or may be called by any other name acceptable to the issuer and the underwriters of the transition bonds.

(f) For purposes of this subchapter, "transition charges," as defined by Section 39.302 and as used in Subchapter G, Chapter 39, includes nonbypassable amounts to be charged for the use of electric services, approved by the commission under a financing order to recover system restoration costs, that shall be collected by an electric utility, its successors, an assignee, or other collection agents as provided for in the financing order. Transition charges approved by the commission under a financing order to recover system restoration costs may be called "system restoration charges" or may be called by any other name acceptable to the issuer and the underwriters of the transition bonds.

(g) Notwithstanding Section 39.303(c), system restoration costs shall be functionalized and allocated to customers in the same manner as the corresponding facilities and related expenses are functionalized and allocated in the electric utility's current base rates. For an electric utility operating within the Electric Reliability Council of Texas, system restoration costs that are properly includable in the transmission cost of service mechanism adopted under Section 35.004 and associated deferred costs not included under Section 35.004 shall be recovered under the method of pricing provided for in that section and commission rules promulgated under that section; provided, however, that an electric utility operating under a rate freeze or other limitation on its ability to pass through wholesale costs to its customers may defer such costs and accrue carrying costs at its weighted average cost of capital as last approved by the commission in a general rate proceeding until such time as the freeze or limitation expires.

(h) The amount of any accumulated deferred federal income taxes offset, used to determine the securitization total, may not be considered in future rate proceedings. Any tax obligation of the electric utility arising from its receipt of securitization bond proceeds, or from the collection and remittance of transition charges, shall be recovered by the electric utility through the commission's implementation of this subchapter.

(i) Notwithstanding a rate freeze or limitations on an electric utility's ability to change rates authorized or imposed by any other provision of this title or by a regulatory authority, an electric utility is entitled to recover system restoration costs consistent with the provisions of this subchapter.

(j) If in the course of a proceeding to adopt a financing order the commission determines that the recovery of all or any portion of an electric utility's system restoration costs, using securitization, is not beneficial to ratepayers of the electric utility, under one or more of the tests applied to determine those benefits, the commission shall nonetheless use the proceeding to issue an order permitting the electric utility to recover the remainder of its system restoration costs through an appropriate customer surcharge mechanism, including carrying costs at the electric utility's weighted average cost of capital as last approved by the commission in a general rate proceeding, to the extent that the electric utility has not securitized those costs. A rate proceeding under Subchapter C or D shall not be required to determine and implement this surcharge mechanism. On the final implementation of rates resulting from the filing of a rate proceeding under Subchapter C or D that provides for the recovery of all remaining system restoration costs, a rider or surcharge mechanism adopted under this subsection shall expire. This subsection is limited to instances in which an electric utility has incurred system restoration costs of $100 million or more in any calendar year after January 1, 2008.

Added by Acts 2009, 81st Leg., ch. 1, § 1, eff. April 16, 2009.

[1] V.T.C.A., Utilities Code § 39.301 et seq.

§ 36.404. Nonbypassable Charges

The commission shall include terms in the financing order to ensure that the imposition and collection of transition charges associated with the recovery of system restoration costs are nonbypassable by imposing restrictions on bypassability of the type provided for in Chapter 39 or by alternative means of ensuring nonbypassability, as the commission considers appropriate, consistent with the purposes of securitization.

Added by Acts 2009, 81st Leg., ch. 1, § 1, eff. April 16, 2009.

§ 36.405. Determination of System Restoration Costs

(a) An electric utility is entitled to recover system restoration costs consistent with the provisions of this subchapter and is entitled to seek recovery of amounts not recovered under this subchapter, including system restoration costs not yet incurred at the time an application is filed under Subsection (b), in its next base rate proceeding or through any other proceeding authorized by Subchapter C or D.

(b) An electric utility may file an application with the commission seeking a determination of the amount of system restoration costs eligible for recovery and securitization. The commission may by rule prescribe the form of the application and the information reasonably needed to support the application; provided, however, that if such a rule is not in effect, the electric utility shall not be precluded from filing its application and such application cannot be rejected as being incomplete.

(c) The commission shall issue an order determining the amount of system restoration costs eligible for recovery and securitization not later than the 150th day after the date an electric utility files its application. The 150-day period begins on the date the electric utility files the application, even if the filing occurs before the effective date of this section.

(d) An electric utility may file an application for a financing order prior to the expiration of the 150-day period provided for in Subsection (c). The commission shall issue a financing order not later than 90 days after the utility files its request for a financing order; provided, however, that the commission need not issue the financing order until it has determined the amount of system restoration costs eligible for recovery and securitization.

(e) To the extent the commission has made a determination of the eligible system restoration costs of an electric utility before the effective date of this section, that determination may provide the basis for the utility's application for a financing order pursuant to this subchapter and Subchapter G, Chapter 39. A previous commission determination does not preclude the utility from requesting recovery of additional system restoration costs eligible for recovery under this subchapter, but not previously authorized by the commission.

(f) A rate proceeding under Subchapter C or D shall not be required to determine the amount of recoverable system restoration costs, as provided by this section, or for the issuance of a financing order.

(g) A commission order under this subchapter is not subject to rehearing. A commission order may be reviewed by appeal only to a Travis County district court by a party to the proceeding filed within 15 days after the order is signed by the commission. The judgment of the district court may be reviewed only by direct appeal to the Supreme Court of Texas filed within 15 days after entry of judgment. All appeals shall be heard and determined by the district court and the Supreme Court of Texas as expeditiously as possible with lawful precedence over other matters. Review on appeal shall be based solely on the record before the commission and briefs to the court and shall be limited to whether the order conforms to the constitution and laws of this state and the United States and is within the authority of the commission under this chapter.

Added by Acts 2009, 81st Leg., ch. 1, § 1, eff. April 16, 2009.

§ 36.406. Severability

Effective on the date the first utility transition bonds associated with system restoration costs are issued under this subchapter, if any provision in this title or portion of this title is held to be invalid or is invalidated, superseded, replaced, repealed, or expires for any reason, that occurrence does not affect the validity or continuation of this subchapter, Subchapter G, Chapter 39[1], as it applies to this subchapter, or any part of those provisions, or any other provision of this title that is relevant to the issuance, administration, payment, retirement, or refunding of transition bonds or to any actions of the electric utility, its successors, an assignee, a collection agent, or a financing party, and those provisions shall remain in full force and effect.

Added by Acts 2009, 81st Leg., ch. 1, § 1, eff. April 16, 2009.

[1] V.T.C.A., Utilities Code § 39.301 et seq.

CHAPTER 37. CERTIFICATES OF CONVENIENCE AND NECESSITY

SUBCHAPTER A. DEFINITIONS

Section
37.001. Definitions.

SUBCHAPTER B. CERTIFICATE OF CONVENIENCE AND NECESSITY

37.051. Certificate Required.
37.052. Exceptions to Certificate Requirement for Service Extension.
37.053. Application for Certificate.
37.054. Notice and Hearing on Application.
37.0541. Consolidation of Certain Proceedings.
37.055. Request for Preliminary Order.
37.056. Grant or Denial of Certificate.
37.057. Deadline for Application for New Transmission Facility.
37.058. Repealed.
37.059. Revocation or Amendment of Certificate.
37.060. Division of Multiply Certificated Service Areas.
37.061. Existing Service Area Agreements.

SUBCHAPTER C. MUNICIPALITIES

37.101. Service in Annexed or Incorporated Area.
37.102. Grant of Certificate for Certain Municipalities.

SUBCHAPTER D. REGULATION OF SERVICES, AREAS, AND FACILITIES

37.151. Provision of Service.
37.152. Grounds for Reduction of Service.
37.153. Required Refusal of Service.
37.154. Transfer of Certificate.
37.155. Application of Contracts.
37.156. Interference With Another Utility.
37.157. Maps.

SUBCHAPTER A. DEFINITIONS

§ 37.001. Definitions

In this chapter:

(1) "Certificate" means a certificate of convenience and necessity.

(2) "Electric utility" includes an electric cooperative.

(3) "Retail electric utility" means a person, political subdivision, electric cooperative, or agency that operates, maintains, or controls in this state a facility to provide retail electric utility service. The term does not include a corporation described by Section 32.053 to the extent that the corporation sells electricity exclusively at wholesale and not to the ultimate consumer. A qualifying cogenerator that sells electric energy at retail to the sole purchaser of the cogenerator's thermal output under Sections 35.061 and 36.007 is not for that reason considered to be a retail electric utility. The owner or operator of a qualifying cogeneration facility who was issued the necessary environmental permits from the Texas Natural Resource Conservation Commission after January 1, 1998, and who commenced construction of such qualifying facility before July 1, 1998, may provide electricity to the purchasers of the thermal output of that qualifying facility and shall not for that reason be considered an electric utility or a retail electric utility, provided that the purchasers of the thermal output are owners of manufacturing or process operation facilities that are located on a site entirely owned before September, 1987, by one owner who retained ownership after September, 1987, of some portion of the facilities and that those facilities now share some integrated operations, such as the provision of services and raw materials.

Acts 1997, 75th Leg., ch. 166, § 1, eff. Sept. 1, 1997. Amended by Acts 1999, 76th Leg., ch. 405, § 29, eff. Sept. 1, 1999.

SUBCHAPTER B. CERTIFICATE OF CONVENIENCE AND NECESSITY

§ 37.051. Certificate Required

(a) An electric utility or other person may not directly or indirectly provide service to the public under a franchise or permit unless the utility or other person first obtains from the commission a certificate that states that the public convenience and necessity requires or will require the installation, operation, or extension of the service.

(b) Except as otherwise provided by this chapter, a retail electric utility may not furnish or make available retail electric utility service to an area in which retail electric utility service is being lawfully furnished by another retail electric utility unless the utility first obtains a certificate that includes the area in which the consuming facility is located.

(c) Notwithstanding any other provision of this chapter, including Subsection (a), an electric cooperative is not required to obtain a certificate of public convenience and necessity for the construction, installation, operation, or extension of any generating facilities or necessary interconnection facilities.

(d) A certificate may be granted to an electric utility or other person under this section for a facility used as part of the transmission system serving the ERCOT power region solely for the transmission of electricity.

(e) The commission may consider an application filed by a person not currently certificated as an electric utility for a certificate of convenience and necessity to construct transmission capacity that serves the ERCOT power region. Before granting a certificate under this section, the commission must find, after notice and hearing, that:

(1) the applicant has the technical ability, financial ability, and sufficient resources in this state to own, operate, and maintain reliable transmission facilities;

(2) the applicant has the resources and ability to comply with commission rules, requirements of the independent organization certified under Section 39.151 for the ERCOT power region, and requirements of the National Electric Reliability Council applicable to the provisions of transmission service; and

(3) for an application filed by a person that is not an electric utility, granting the application will not adversely affect wholesale transmission rates, as compared to the rates projected to be charged if an existing electric utility were to build the transmission facility.

(f) The commission shall consider the requirements of Subsection (e) to have been met by an electric utility or other person that:

(1) is selected by the commission as a transmission provider under a plan adopted by the commis-

sion under Section 39.904 not later than September 1, 2009; and

(2) before the certificate is issued, provides to the commission a detailed plan regarding the offices, personnel, and other resources the electric utility or other person will have in this state to ensure provision of continuous and adequate transmission service.

Acts 1997, 75th Leg., ch. 166, § 1, eff. Sept. 1, 1997. Amended by Acts 1999, 76th Leg., ch. 405, § 30, eff. Sept. 1, 1999; Acts 2009, 81st Leg., ch. 1170, § 2, eff. June 19, 2009.

§ 37.052. Exceptions to Certificate Requirement for Service Extension

(a) An electric utility is not required to obtain a certificate for an:

(1) extension into territory that is:

(A) contiguous to the territory the electric utility serves;

(B) not receiving similar service from another electric utility; and

(C) not in another electric utility's certificated area;

(2) extension in or to territory the utility serves or is authorized to serve under a certificate; or

(3) operation, extension, or service in progress on September 1, 1975.

(b) An extension allowed under Subsection (a) is limited to a device used:

(1) to interconnect existing facilities; or

(2) solely to transmit electric utility services from an existing facility to a customer of retail electric utility service.

Acts 1997, 75th Leg., ch. 166, § 1, eff. Sept. 1, 1997.

§ 37.053. Application for Certificate

(a) An electric utility or other person that wants to obtain or amend a certificate must submit an application to the commission.

(b) The applicant shall file with the commission evidence the commission requires to show the applicant has received the consent, franchise, or permit required by the proper municipal or other public authority.

(c) The commission may not require the applicant to designate a preferred route for a proposed transmission line facility.

(d) For transmission facilities ordered or approved by the commission under Chapter 37 or 39, the rights extended to an electric corporation under Section 181.004 include all public land, except land owned by the state, on which the commission has approved the construction of the line. This subsection does not limit a municipality's rights or an electric utility's obligations under Chapter 33. Nothing in this subsection shall be interpreted to prevent a public entity from expressing a route preference in a proceeding under this chapter.

Acts 1997, 75th Leg., ch. 166, § 1, eff. Sept. 1, 1997. Amended by Acts 2009, 81st Leg., ch. 1170, § 3, eff. June 19, 2009; Acts 2011, 82nd Leg., ch. 949 (H.B. 971), § 1, eff. June 17, 2011.

Section 4 of Acts 2011, 82nd Leg., ch. 949 (H.B. 971) provides:

"The change in law made by this Act to Section 37.053(c), Utilities Code, applies only to an application for a certificate of convenience and necessity that is filed with the Public Utility Commission of Texas on or after the effective date [June 17, 2011] of this Act. An application for a certificate of convenience and necessity that was filed with the commission before the effective date of this Act is governed by the law in effect on the date the application was filed, and that law is continued in effect for that purpose."

§ 37.054. Notice and Hearing on Application

(a) When an application for a certificate is filed, the commission shall:

(1) give notice of the application to interested parties and to the office; and

(2) if requested:

(A) set a time and place for a hearing; and

(B) give notice of the hearing.

(b) A person or electric cooperative interested in the application may intervene at the hearing.

Acts 1997, 75th Leg., ch. 166, § 1, eff. Sept. 1, 1997. Amended by Acts 1999, 76th Leg., ch. 405, § 31, eff. Sept. 1, 1999; Acts 2011, 82nd Leg., ch. 416 (S.B. 855), § 2, eff. June 17, 2011.

Section 3 of Acts 2011, 82nd Leg., ch. 416 (S.B. 855) provides:

"Sec. 3. The change in law made by this Act to Section 37.054, Utilities Code, applies only to an application for a certificate of convenience and necessity filed on or after the effective date of this Act. An application for a certificate of convenience and necessity filed before the effective date of this Act is governed by the law in effect at the time the application was filed, and the former law is continued in effect for that purpose."

§ 37.0541. Consolidation of Certain Proceedings

The commission shall consolidate the proceeding on an application to obtain or amend a certificate of convenience and necessity for the construction of a transmission line with the proceeding on another application to obtain or amend a certificate of convenience and necessity for the construction of a transmission line if it is apparent from the applications or a motion to intervene in either proceeding that the transmission lines that are the subject of the separate proceedings share a common point of interconnection. This section does not apply to a proceeding on an application for a certificate of convenience and necessity for a transmission line to serve a competitive renewable energy zone as part of a plan developed by the commission under Section 39.904(g)(2).

Added by Acts 2009, 81st Leg., ch. 1170, § 1, eff. June 19, 2009.

§ 37.055. Request for Preliminary Order

(a) An electric utility or other person that wants to exercise a right or privilege under a franchise or permit that the utility or other person anticipates obtaining but has not been granted may apply to the commission for a preliminary order under this section.

(b) The commission may issue a preliminary order declaring that the commission, on application and under commission rules, will grant the requested certificate on terms the commission designates, after the electric utility or other person obtains the franchise or permit.

(c) The commission shall grant the certificate on presentation of evidence satisfactory to the commission that the electric utility or other person has obtained the franchise or permit.

Acts 1997, 75th Leg., ch. 166, § 1, eff. Sept. 1, 1997. Amended by Acts 2009, 81st Leg., ch. 1170, § 4, eff. June 19, 2009.

§ 37.056. Grant or Denial of Certificate

(a) The commission may approve an application and grant a certificate only if the commission finds that the certificate is necessary for the service, accommodation, convenience, or safety of the public.

(b) The commission may:

(1) grant the certificate as requested;

(2) grant the certificate for the construction of a portion of the requested system, facility, or extension or the partial exercise of the requested right or privilege; or

(3) refuse to grant the certificate.

(c) The commission shall grant each certificate on a nondiscriminatory basis after considering:

(1) the adequacy of existing service;

(2) the need for additional service;

(3) the effect of granting the certificate on the recipient of the certificate and any electric utility serving the proximate area; and

(4) other factors, such as:

(A) community values;

(B) recreational and park areas;

(C) historical and aesthetic values;

(D) environmental integrity;

(E) the probable improvement of service or lowering of cost to consumers in the area if the certificate is granted; and

(F) to the extent applicable, the effect of granting the certificate on the ability of this state to meet the goal established by Section 39.904(a) of this title.

(d) The commission by rule shall establish criteria, in addition to the criteria described by Subsection (c), for granting a certificate for a transmission project that serves the ERCOT power region, that is not necessary to meet state or federal reliability standards, and that does not serve a competitive renewable energy zone. The criteria must include a comparison of the estimated cost of the transmission project and the estimated cost savings that may result from the transmission project. The commission shall include with its decision on an application for a certificate to which this subsection applies findings on the criteria.

Acts 1997, 75th Leg., ch. 166, § 1, eff. Sept. 1, 1997. Amended by Acts 2003, 78th Leg., ch. 295, § 2, eff. June 18, 2003; Acts 2011, 82nd Leg., ch. 949 (H.B. 971), § 2(a), eff. June 17, 2011.

Section 2(b) of Acts 2011, 82nd Leg., ch. 949 (H.B. 971) provides:

"(b) The change in law made by this section applies only to a certificate application filed with the Public Utility Commission of Texas on or after the effective date [June 17, 2011] of this Act and to a certificate application pending on the effective date of this Act. A certificate application filed with the Public Utility Commission of Texas before the effective date of this Act and not pending on the effective date of this Act is subject to the law in effect on the date the application is filed, and that law is continued in effect for that purpose."

§ 37.057. Deadline for Application for New Transmission Facility

The commission may grant a certificate for a new transmission facility to a qualified applicant that meets the requirements of this subchapter. The commission must approve or deny an application for a certificate for a new transmission facility not later than the first anniversary of the date the application is filed. If the commission does not approve or deny the application on or before that date, a party may seek a writ of mandamus in a district court of Travis County to compel the commission to decide on the application.

Acts 1997, 75th Leg., ch. 166, § 1, eff. Sept. 1, 1997. Amended by Acts 2009, 81st Leg., ch. 1170, § 4, eff. June 19, 2009.

§ 37.058. Repealed by Acts 1999, 76th Leg., ch. 405, § 61(4), eff. Sept. 1, 1999

§ 37.059. Revocation or Amendment of Certificate

(a) The commission may revoke or amend a certificate after notice and hearing if the commission finds that the certificate holder has never provided or is no longer providing service in all or any part of the certificated area.

(b) The commission may require one or more electric utilities to provide service in an area affected by the revocation or amendment of a certificate.

Acts 1997, 75th Leg., ch. 166, § 1, eff. Sept. 1, 1997.

§ 37.060. Division of Multiply Certificated Service Areas

(a) This subsection and Subsections (b)–(g) apply only to areas in which each retail electric utility that is authorized to provide retail electric utility service to the area is providing customer choice. For purposes of this subsection, an electric cooperative or a municipally owned electric utility shall be deemed to be providing customer choice if it has approved a resolution adopting customer choice that is effective on January 1, 2002, or effective within 24 months after the date of the resolution adopting customer choice. All other retail electric utilities shall be deemed to be providing customer choice if customer choice will be allowed for customers of the retail electric utility on January 1, 2002. In areas in which each certificated retail electric utility is providing customer choice, the commission, if requested by a retail electric utility, shall examine all areas within the service area of the retail electric utility making the request that are also certificated to one or more other retail electric utilities and, after notice and hearing, shall amend the retail electric utilities' certificates so that only one retail electric utility is certificated to provide distribution services in any such area. Only retail electric utilities certificated to serve an area on June 1, 1999, may continue to serve the area or portion of the area under an amended certificate issued under this subsection.

(b) This section does not apply in any area in which a municipally owned utility is certificated to provide retail electric utility service if the municipally owned utility serving the area files with the commission by October 1, 2001, a request that areas within the certificated service area of the municipally owned utility remain as presently certificated.

(c) The commission shall enter its order dividing multiply certificated areas within one year of the date a request is received.

(d) In amending certificates under this section, the commission shall take into consideration the factors prescribed by Section 37.056.

(e) Notwithstanding Section 37.059, the commission shall revoke certificates to the extent necessary to achieve the division of retail electric service areas as provided by this section.

(f) Unless otherwise agreed by the affected retail electric utilities, each retail electric utility shall be allowed to continue to provide service to the location of electricity-consuming facilities it is serving on the date an application for division of the affected multiply certificated service areas is filed. No customer located within the affected multiply certificated service areas shall be permitted to switch from one retail electric utility to another while an application for division of the affected multiply certificated service areas is pending.

(g) If on June 1, 1999, retail service is being provided in an area by another retail electric utility with the written consent of the retail electric utility certificated to serve the area, that consent shall be filed with the commission. On notification of that consent and a request by an affected retail electric utility to amend the relevant certificates, the commission may grant an exception or amend a retail electric utility's certificate. This provision shall not be construed to limit the commission's authority to grant exceptions or to amend a retail electric utility's certificate, upon request and notification, for areas to which retail service is being provided pursuant to written consent granted after June 1, 1999.

(h) The commission may not grant an additional retail electric utility certificate to serve an area if the effect of the grant would cause the area to be multiply certificated unless the commission finds that the certificate holders are not providing service to any part of the area for which a certificate is sought and are not capable of providing adequate service to the area in accordance with applicable standards. However, neither this subsection nor the deadline of June 1, 1999, provided by Subsection (a) shall apply to any application for multiple certification filed with the commission on or before February 1, 1999, and those applications may be processed in accordance with applicable law in effect on the date the application was filed. Applications for multiple certification filed with the commission on or before February 1, 1999, may not be amended to expand the area for which a certificate is sought except for contiguous areas within municipalities that provide consent, as required by Section 37.053(b), not later than June 1, 1999.

(i) Notwithstanding any other provision of this section, if requested by a municipally owned utility, the commission shall examine all areas within the municipally owned utility's service area that are also certificated to one or more other retail electric utilities and, after notice and hearing, may amend the retail electric utilities' certificates so that only one retail electric utility is certificated to provide distribution services in the area, provided that:

(1) the application is filed with the commission within 12 months of the effective date of this provision and is limited to single certification of the area within the municipality's boundaries as of February 1, 1999;

(2) the commission preserves the right of an electric utility or an electric cooperative to serve its existing customers, including any property owned or leased by any customer; and

(3) the municipality is a member city of a municipal power agency, as that term is used in Section 40.059.

Added by Acts 1999, 76th Leg., ch. 405, § 32, eff. Sept. 1, 1999. Amended by Acts 2001, 77th Leg., ch. 796, § 1, eff. June 14, 2001.

§ 37.061. Existing Service Area Agreements

(a) Notwithstanding any other provision of this title, the commission shall allow a municipally owned utility to amend the service area boundaries of its certificate if:

(1) the municipally owned utility was the holder of a certificate as of January 1, 1999;

(2) the municipally owned utility has an agreement existing before January 1, 1999, with a public utility serving the area that the public utility will not contest an application to amend the certificate to add municipal territory; and

(3) the area for which a certificate is requested is not certificated to a retail electric utility that is not a party to the agreement and that has not consented in writing to certification of the area to the municipality.

(b) The commission may not amend the certificate of the public utility serving the affected area based on the granting of a certificate to the municipally owned utility.

Added by Acts 1999, 76th Leg., ch. 405, § 32, eff. Sept. 1, 1999.

SUBCHAPTER C. MUNICIPALITIES

§ 37.101. Service in Annexed or Incorporated Area

(a) If an area is or will be included within a municipality as the result of annexation, incorporation, or another reason, each electric utility and each electric cooperative that holds or is entitled to hold a certificate under this title to provide service or operate a facility in the area before the inclusion has the right to continue to provide the service or operate the facility and extend service within the utility's or cooperative's certificated area in the annexed or incorporated area under the rights granted by the certificate and this title.

(b) Notwithstanding any other law, an electric utility has the right to:

(1) continue and extend service within the utility's certificated area; and

(2) use roads, streets, highways, alleys, and public property to furnish retail electric utility service.

(c) The governing body of a municipality may require an electric utility to relocate the utility's facility at the utility's expense to permit the widening or straightening of a street by:

(1) giving the electric utility 30 days' notice; and

(2) specifying the new location for the facility along the right-of-way of the street.

(d) This section does not:

(1) limit the power of a city, town, or village to incorporate or of a municipality to extend its boundaries by annexation; or

(2) prohibit a municipality from levying a tax or other special charge for the use of the streets as authorized by Section 182.025, Tax Code.

Acts 1997, 75th Leg., ch. 166, § 1, eff. Sept. 1, 1997. Amended by Acts 1999, 76th Leg., ch. 405, § 33, eff. Sept. 1, 1999.

§ 37.102. Grant of Certificate for Certain Municipalities

(a) If a municipal corporation offers retail electric utility service in a municipality having a population of more than 145,000 that is located in a county having a population of more than 2 million , the commission shall singly certificate areas in the municipality's boundaries in which more than one electric utility provides electric utility service.

(b) In singly certificating an area under Subsection (a), the commission shall preserve the right of an electric utility to serve the customers the electric utility was serving on June 17, 1983. This subsection does not apply to a customer at least partially served by a nominal 69,000 volts system who gave notice of termination to the utility servicing that customer before June 17, 1983.

Acts 1997, 75th Leg., ch. 166, § 1, eff. Sept. 1, 1997. Amended by Acts 2011, 82nd Leg., ch. 1163 (H.B. 2702), § 179, eff. Sept. 1, 2011.

Section 201 of Acts 2011, 82nd Leg., ch. 1163 (H.B. 2702) provides:

"(a) This Act is not intended to revive a law that was impliedly repealed by a law enacted by the 81st Legislature or a previous legislature.

"(b) To the extent that a law enacted by the 82nd Legislature, Regular Session, 2011, conflicts with this Act, the other law prevails, regardless of the relative dates of enactment or the relative effective dates."

SUBCHAPTER D. REGULATION OF SERVICES, AREAS, AND FACILITIES

§ 37.151. Provision of Service

Except as provided by this section, Section 37.152, and Section 37.153, a certificate holder, other than one granted a certificate under Section 37.051(d), shall:

(1) serve every consumer in the utility's certificated area; and

(2) provide continuous and adequate service in that area.

Acts 1997, 75th Leg., ch. 166, § 1, eff. Sept. 1, 1997. Amended by Acts 2009, 81st Leg., ch. 1170, § 4, eff. June 19, 2009.

§ 37.152. Grounds for Reduction of Service

(a) Unless the commission issues a certificate that the present and future convenience and necessity will not be adversely affected, a certificate holder may not discontinue, reduce, or impair service to any part of the holder's certificated service area except for:

(1) nonpayment of charges;

(2) nonuse; or

(3) another similar reason that occurs in the usual course of business.

(b) A discontinuance, reduction, or impairment of service must be in compliance with and subject to any condition or restriction the commission prescribes.

Acts 1997, 75th Leg., ch. 166, § 1, eff. Sept. 1, 1997.

§ 37.153. Required Refusal of Service

A certificate holder shall refuse to serve a customer in the holder's certificated area if the holder is prohibited from providing the service under Section 212.012, 232.029, or 232.0291, Local Government Code.

Acts 1997, 75th Leg., ch. 166, § 1, eff. Sept. 1, 1997. Amended by Acts 2005, 79th Leg., ch. 708, § 13, eff. Sept. 1, 2005.

§ 37.154. Transfer of Certificate

(a) An electric utility may sell, assign, or lease a certificate or a right obtained under a certificate if the commission determines that the purchaser, assignee, or lessee can provide adequate service.

(b) A sale, assignment, or lease of a certificate or a right is subject to conditions the commission prescribes.

Acts 1997, 75th Leg., ch. 166, § 1, eff. Sept. 1, 1997.

§ 37.155. Application of Contracts

A contract approved by the commission between retail electric utilities that designates areas and customers to be served by the utilities:

(1) is valid and enforceable; and

(2) shall be incorporated into the appropriate areas of certification.

Acts 1997, 75th Leg., ch. 166, § 1, eff. Sept. 1, 1997.

§ 37.156. Interference With Another Utility

If an electric utility constructing or extending the utility's lines, plant, or system interferes or attempts to interfere with the operation of a line, plant, or system of another utility, the commission by order may:

(1) prohibit the construction or extension; or

(2) prescribe terms for locating the affected lines, plants, or systems.

Acts 1997, 75th Leg., ch. 166, § 1, eff. Sept. 1, 1997.

§ 37.157. Maps

An electric utility shall file with the commission one or more maps that show each utility facility and that separately illustrate each utility facility for the generation, transmission, or distribution of the utility's services on a date the commission orders.

Acts 1997, 75th Leg., ch. 166, § 1, eff. Sept. 1, 1997.

CHAPTER 38. REGULATION OF ELECTRIC SERVICES

SUBCHAPTER A. STANDARDS

Section
38.001. General Standard.

Section
38.002. Authority of Regulatory Authority Concerning Standards.
38.003. Rule or Standard.
38.004. Minimum Clearance Standard.
38.005. Electric Service Reliability Measures.

SUBCHAPTER B. PROHIBITIONS ON PREFERENCES AND DISCRIMINATION
38.021. Unreasonable Preference or Prejudice Concerning Service Prohibited.
38.022. Discrimination and Restriction on Competition.

SUBCHAPTER C. EXAMINATIONS, TESTS, AND INSPECTIONS
38.051. Examination and Test of Instrument or Equipment; Inspection.
38.052. Inspection for Consumer.

SUBCHAPTER D. IMPROVEMENTS IN SERVICE
38.071. Improvements in Service; Interconnecting Service.
38.072. Priorities for Power Restoration to Certain Medical Facilities.
38.073. Authority of Commission During an Emergency.

SUBCHAPTER E. INFRASTRUCTURE IMPROVEMENT AND MAINTENANCE REPORT
38.101. Report on Infrastructure Improvement and Maintenance.

SUBCHAPTER A. STANDARDS

§ 38.001. General Standard

An electric utility and an electric cooperative shall furnish service, instrumentalities, and facilities that are safe, adequate, efficient, and reasonable.

Acts 1997, 75th Leg., ch. 166, § 1, eff. Sept. 1, 1997. Amended by Acts 1999, 76th Leg., ch. 405, § 34, eff. Sept. 1, 1999.

§ 38.002. Authority of Regulatory Authority Concerning Standards

A regulatory authority, on its own motion or on complaint and after reasonable notice and hearing, may:

(1) adopt just and reasonable standards, classifications, rules, or practices an electric utility must follow in furnishing a service;

(2) adopt adequate and reasonable standards for measuring a condition, including quantity, quality, pressure, and initial voltage, relating to the furnishing of a service;

(3) adopt reasonable rules for examining, testing, and measuring a service; and

(4) adopt or approve reasonable rules, specifications, and standards to ensure the accuracy of equipment, including meters and instruments, used to measure a service.

Acts 1997, 75th Leg., ch. 166, § 1, eff. Sept. 1, 1997.

§ 38.003. Rule or Standard

(a) An electric utility may not impose a rule except as provided by this title.

(b) An electric utility may file with the regulatory authority a standard, classification, rule, or practice the utility follows.

(c) The standard, classification, rule, or practice continues in force until:

(1) amended by the utility; or

(2) changed by the regulatory authority as provided by this title.

Acts 1997, 75th Leg., ch. 166, § 1, eff. Sept. 1, 1997.

§ 38.004. Minimum Clearance Standard

Notwithstanding any other law, a transmission or distribution line owned by an electric utility or an electric cooperative must be constructed, operated, and maintained, as to clearances, in the manner described by the National Electrical Safety Code Standard ANSI (c)(2), as adopted by the American National Safety Institute and in effect at the time of construction.

Acts 1997, 75th Leg., ch. 166, § 1, eff. Sept. 1, 1997. Amended by Acts 1999, 76th Leg., ch. 405, § 35, eff. Sept. 1, 1999.

§ 38.005. Electric Service Reliability Measures

(a) The commission shall implement service quality and reliability standards relating to the delivery of electricity to retail customers by electric utilities and transmission and distribution utilities. The commission by rule shall develop reliability standards, including:

(1) the system-average interruption frequency index (SAIFI);

(2) the system-average interruption duration index (SAIDI);

(3) achievement of average response time for customer service requests or inquiries; or

(4) other standards that the commission finds reasonable and appropriate.

(b) The commission may take appropriate enforcement action under this section, including action against a utility, if any of the utility's feeders with 10 or more customers has had a SAIDI or SAIFI average that is more than 300 percent greater than the system average of all feeders during any two-year period, beginning in the year 2000. In determining the appropriate enforcement action, the commission shall consider:

(1) the feeder's operating and maintenance history;

(2) the cause of each interruption in the feeder's service;

(3) any action taken by a utility to address the feeder's performance;

(4) the estimated cost and benefit of remediating a feeder's performance; and

(5) any other relevant factor as determined by the commission.

(c) The standards implemented under Subsection (a) shall require each electric utility and transmission and distribution utility subject to this section to maintain adequately trained and experienced personnel throughout the utility's service area so that the utility is able to fully and adequately comply with the appropriate service quality and reliability standards.

(d) The standards shall ensure that electric utilities do not neglect any local neighborhood or geographic area, including rural areas, communities of less than 1,000 persons, and low-income areas, with regard to system reliability.

(e) The commission may require each electric utility and transmission and distribution utility to supply data to assist the commission in developing the reliability standards.

(f) Each electric utility, transmission and distribution utility, electric cooperative, municipally owned utility, and generation provider shall be obligated to comply with any operational criteria duly established by the independent organization as defined by Section 39.151 or adopted by the commission.

Added by Acts 1999, 76th Leg., ch. 405, § 36, eff. Sept. 1, 1999. Amended by Acts 2009, 81st Leg., ch. 424, § 1, eff. June 19, 2009.

SUBCHAPTER B. PROHIBITIONS ON PREFERENCES AND DISCRIMINATION

§ 38.021. Unreasonable Preference or Prejudice Concerning Service Prohibited

In providing a service to persons in a classification, an electric utility may not:

(1) grant an unreasonable preference or advantage to a person in the classification; or

(2) subject a person in the classification to an unreasonable prejudice or disadvantage.

Acts 1997, 75th Leg., ch. 166, § 1, eff. Sept. 1, 1997.

§ 38.022. Discrimination and Restriction on Competition

An electric utility may not:

(1) discriminate against a person or electric cooperative who sells or leases equipment or performs services in competition with the electric utility; or

(2) engage in a practice that tends to restrict or impair that competition.

Acts 1997, 75th Leg., ch. 166, § 1, eff. Sept. 1, 1997. Amended by Acts 1999, 76th Leg., ch. 405, § 37, eff. Sept. 1, 1999.

SUBCHAPTER C. EXAMINATIONS, TESTS, AND INSPECTIONS

§ 38.051. Examination and Test of Instrument or Equipment; Inspection

(a) A regulatory authority may:

(1) examine and test equipment, including meters and instruments, used to measure service of an electric utility; and

(2) set up and use on the premises occupied by an electric utility an apparatus or appliance necessary for the examination or test.

(b) The electric utility is entitled to be represented at an examination, test, or inspection made under this section.

(c) The electric utility and its officers and employees shall facilitate the examination, test, or inspection by giving reasonable aid to the regulatory authority and to any person designated by the regulatory authority for the performance of those duties.

Acts 1997, 75th Leg., ch. 166, § 1, eff. Sept. 1, 1997.

§ 38.052. Inspection for Consumer

(a) A consumer may have a meter or other measuring device tested by an electric utility:

(1) once without charge, after a reasonable period of presumed accuracy the regulatory authority establishes by rule; and

(2) at a shorter interval on payment of a reasonable fee established by the regulatory authority.

(b) The regulatory authority shall establish reasonable fees to be paid for other examining or testing of a measuring device on the request of a consumer.

(c) If the consumer requests the test under Subsection (a)(2) and the measuring device is found unreasonably defective or incorrect to the substantial disadvantage of the consumer, the fee the consumer paid at the time of the request shall be refunded.

Acts 1997, 75th Leg., ch. 166, § 1, eff. Sept. 1, 1997.

SUBCHAPTER D. IMPROVEMENTS IN SERVICE

§ 38.071. Improvements in Service; Interconnecting Service

The commission, after notice and hearing, may:

(1) order an electric utility to provide specified improvements in its service in a specified area if:

(A) service in the area is inadequate or substantially inferior to service in a comparable area; and

(B) requiring the company to provide the improved service is reasonable; or

(2) order two or more electric utilities or electric cooperatives to establish specified facilities for interconnecting service.

Acts 1997, 75th Leg., ch. 166, § 1, eff. Sept. 1, 1997. Amended by Acts 1999, 76th Leg., ch. 405, § 38, eff. Sept. 1, 1999.

§ 38.072. Priorities for Power Restoration to Certain Medical Facilities

(a) In this section:

(1) "Assisted living facility" has the meaning assigned by Section 247.002, Health and Safety Code.

(2) "Extended power outage" has the meaning assigned by Section 13.1395, Water Code.

(3) "Hospice services" has the meaning assigned by Section 142.001, Health and Safety Code.

(4) "Nursing facility" has the meaning assigned by Section 242.301, Health and Safety Code.

(b) The commission by rule shall require an electric utility to give to the following the same priority that it gives to a hospital in the utility's emergency operations plan for restoring power after an extended power outage:

(1) a nursing facility;

(2) an assisted living facility; and

(3) a facility that provides hospice services.

(c) The rules adopted by the commission under Subsection (b) must allow an electric utility to exercise the electric utility's discretion to prioritize power restoration for a facility after an extended power outage in accordance with the facility's needs and with the characteristics of the geographic area in which power must be restored.

(d) A municipally owned utility shall report the emergency operations plan for restoring power to a facility listed in Subsection (b) to the municipality's governing body or the body vested with the power to manage and operate the municipally owned utility.

(e) An electric cooperative shall report the emergency operations plan for restoring power to a facility listed in Subsection (b) to the board of directors of the electric cooperative.

Added by Acts 2011, 82nd Leg., ch. 640 (S.B. 937), § 1, eff. Sept. 1, 2011.

§ 38.073. Authority of Commission During an Emergency

(a) On a declaration of a natural disaster or other emergency by the governor, the commission may require an electric utility, municipally owned utility, electric cooperative, qualifying facility, power generation company, exempt wholesale generator, or power marketer to sell electricity to an electric utility, municipally owned utility, or electric cooperative that is unable to supply power to meet customer demand due to the natural disaster or other emergency. Any plant, property, equipment, or other items used to receive or deliver electricity under this subsection are used and useful in delivering service to the public, and the commission shall allow timely recovery for the costs of those items. The commission may order an electric utility, municipally owned utility, or electric cooperative to provide interconnection service to another electric utility, municipally owned utility, or electric cooperative to facilitate a sale of electricity under this section. If the commission does not order the sale of electricity during a declared emergency as described by this subsection, the commission shall promptly submit to the legislature a report describing the reasons why the commission did not make that order.

(b) If an entity receives electricity under Subsection (a), the receiving entity shall reimburse the supplying entity for the actual cost of providing the electricity. The entity receiving the electricity is responsible for any transmission and distribution service charges specifically incurred in relation to providing the electricity.

(c) An entity that pays for electricity received under Subsection (b) and that is regulated by the commission may fully recover the cost of the electricity in a timely manner by:

(1) including the cost in the entity's fuel cost under Section 36.203; or

(2) notwithstanding Section 36.201, imposing a different surcharge.

Added by Acts 2009, 81st Leg., ch. 1226, § 2, eff. June 19, 2009; Acts 2009, 81st Leg., ch. 1280, § 2.02, eff. Sept. 1, 2009.

SUBCHAPTER E. INFRASTRUCTURE IMPROVEMENT AND MAINTENANCE REPORT

§ 38.101. Report on Infrastructure Improvement and Maintenance

(a) Not later than May 1 of each year, each electric utility shall submit to the commission a report describing the utility's activities related to:

(1) identifying areas that are susceptible to damage during severe weather and hardening transmission and distribution facilities in those areas;

(2) vegetation management; and

(3) inspecting distribution poles.

(b) Each electric utility shall include in a report required under Subsection (a) a summary of the utility's activities related to preparing for emergency operations.

Added by Acts 2009, 81st Leg., ch. 1280, § 2.03, eff. Sept. 1, 2009.

CHAPTER 39. RESTRUCTURING OF ELECTRIC UTILITY INDUSTRY

SUBCHAPTER A. GENERAL PROVISIONS

Section

39.001. Legislative Policy and Purpose.
39.002. Applicability.
39.003. Contested Cases.

SUBCHAPTER B. TRANSITION TO COMPETITIVE RETAIL ELECTRIC MARKET

39.051. Unbundling.
39.052. Freeze on Existing Retail Base Rate Tariffs.
39.053. Cost Recovery Adjustments.
39.054. Retail Electric Service During Freeze Period.
39.055. Force Majeure.

SUBCHAPTER C. RETAIL COMPETITION

39.101. Customer Safeguards.
39.102. Retail Customer Choice.
39.1025. Limitations on Telephone Solicitation.

Section

39.103. Commission Authority to Delay Competition and Set New Rates.
39.104. Customer Choice Pilot Projects.
39.105. Limitation on Sale of Electricity.
39.106. Provider of Last Resort.
39.107. Metering and Billing Services.
39.108. Contractual Obligations.
39.109. New Owner or Successor.
39.112. Notice of Expiration and Price Change.
39.116. Expired.

SUBCHAPTER D. MARKET STRUCTURE

39.151. Essential Organizations.
39.1511. Public Meetings of the Governing Body of an Independent Organization.
39.1512. Disclosure of Interest in Matter Before Independent Organization's Governing Body; Participation in Decision.
39.1515. Wholesale Electric Market Monitor.
39.152. Qualifying Power Regions.
39.153. Capacity Auction.
39.154. Limitation of Ownership of Installed Capacity.
39.155. Commission Assessment of Market Power.
39.156. Market Power Mitigation Plan.
39.157. Commission Authority to Address Market Power.
39.158. Mergers and Consolidations.

SUBCHAPTER E. PRICE REGULATION AFTER COMPETITION

39.201. Cost of Service Tariffs and Charges.
39.202. Price to Beat.
39.203. Transmission and Distribution Service.
39.204. Tariffs for Open Access.
39.205. Regulation of Costs Following Freeze Period.
39.206. Nuclear Generating Unit Decommissioning Cost Plan.

SUBCHAPTER F. RECOVERY OF STRANDED COSTS THROUGH COMPETITION TRANSITION CHARGE

39.251. Definitions.
39.252. Right to Recover Stranded Costs.
39.253. Allocation of Stranded Costs.
39.254. Use of Revenues for Utilities With Stranded Costs.
39.255. Use of Revenues for Utilities With No Stranded Costs.
39.256. Option to Redirect Depreciation.
39.257. Annual Report.
39.258. Annual Report: Determination of Annual Costs.
39.259. Annual Report: Determination of Invested Capital.
39.260. Use of Generally Accepted Accounting Principles.
39.261. Review of Annual Report.
39.262. True-Up Proceeding.
39.263. Stranded Cost Recovery of Environmental Cleanup Costs.
39.264. Emissions Reductions of "Grandfathered Facilities".
39.265. Rights Not Affected.

SUBCHAPTER G. SECURITIZATION

39.301. Purpose.

Section
39.302. Definitions.
39.303. Financing Orders; Terms.
39.304. Property Rights.
39.305. No Setoff.
39.306. No Bypass.
39.307. True-Up.
39.308. True Sale.
39.309. Security Interests; Assignment; Commingling; Default.
39.310. Pledge of State.
39.311. Tax Exemption.
39.312. Not Public Utility.
39.313. Severability.

SUBCHAPTER H. CERTIFICATION AND REGISTRATION; PENALTIES

39.351. Registration of Power Generation Companies.
39.352. Certification of Retail Electric Providers.
39.353. Registration of Aggregators.
39.3535. Military Bases Aggregators.
39.354. Registration of Municipal Aggregators.
39.3545. Registration of Political Subdivision Aggregators.
39.355. Registration of Power Marketers.
39.356. Revocation of Certification.
39.357. Administrative Penalty.
39.358. Local Registration of Retail Electric Provider.

SUBCHAPTER I. PROVISIONS FOR CERTAIN NON-ERCOT UTILITIES

39.401. Applicability.
39.402. Regulation of Utility And Transition to Competition.
39.403 to 39.406. Repealed.
39.407. Customer Choice And Relevant Market and Related Matters.
39.408. Repealed.
39.409. Recoupment of Transition to Competition Costs.
39.410. Contractual Obligations.

SUBCHAPTER J. TRANSITION TO COMPETITION IN CERTAIN NON-ERCOT AREAS

39.451. Applicability.
39.452. Regulation of Utility and Transition to Competition.
39.4525. Hiring Assistance for Federal Proceedings.
39.453. Customer Choice and Relevant Market and Related Matters.
39.454. Recoupment of Transition to Competition Costs.
39.455. Recovery of Incremental Capacity Costs.
39.456. Franchise Agreements.
39.457. Contractual Rights.
39.458. Recovery and Securitization of Hurricane Reconstruction Costs; Purpose.
39.459. Hurricane Reconstruction Costs.
39.460. Standards and Procedures Governing Securitization of Hurricane Reconstruction Costs.
39.461. Nonbypassable Charges.
39.462. Determination of Hurricane Reconstruction Costs.
39.463. Severability.

SUBCHAPTER K. TRANSITION TO COMPETITION FOR CERTAIN AREAS OUTSIDE OF ERCOT

Section
39.501. Applicability.
39.502. Cost-of-service Regulation.
39.503. Transition to Competition.

SUBCHAPTER L. TRANSITION TO COMPETITION AND OTHER PROVISIONS FOR CERTAIN AREAS OUTSIDE OF ERCOT

39.551. Applicability.
39.552. Cost-of-Service Regulation.
39.553. Transition to Competition.
39.554. Interconnection of Distributed Renewable Generation.
39.555. Marketing of Energy Efficiency and Renewable Energy Programs.

SUBCHAPTER Z. MISCELLANEOUS PROVISIONS

39.901. Repealed.
39.9011. Expired.
39.9015. Expired.
39.9016. Nuclear Safety Fee.
39.902. Customer Education.
39.9025. Home Electric Energy Reports.
39.903. System Benefit Fund.
39.904. Goal for Renewable Energy.
39.9044. Goal for Natural Gas.
39.9048. Natural Gas Fuel.
39.905. Goal for Energy Efficiency.
39.9051. Energy Efficiency for Municipally Owned Utilities.
39.9052. Energy Efficiency for Electric Cooperatives.
39.9053. Expired.
39.9054. Energy Efficiency Plans and Reports; Public Information.
39.906. Displaced Workers.
39.907. Repealed.
39.908. Effect of Sunset Provision.
39.909. Plan and Report of Workforce Diversity and Other Business Practices.
39.910. Incentive Program and Goal for Energy Efficiency for Military Bases.
39.911. Alternative Funding for Energy Efficiency and Renewable Energy Systems.
39.912. Report on Combined Heating and Power Technology.
39.913. Combining Certain Reports.
39.914. Credit for Surplus Solar Generation by Public Schools.
39.915. Consideration and Approval of Certain Transactions.
39.916. Interconnection of Distributed Renewable Generation.

SUBCHAPTER A. GENERAL PROVISIONS

§ 39.001. Legislative Policy and Purpose

(a) The legislature finds that the production and sale of electricity is not a monopoly warranting regulation of rates, operations, and services and that the public interest in competitive electric markets requires that, except for transmission and distribution services and for the recovery of stranded costs, electric services and their prices should be determined by customer choices and the normal forces of competition. As a result, this chapter is enacted to protect the public interest during the transition to and in the establishment of a fully competitive electric power industry.

(b) The legislature finds that it is in the public interest to:

(1) implement on January 1, 2002, a competitive retail electric market that allows each retail customer to choose the customer's provider of electricity and that encourages full and fair competition among all providers of electricity;

(2) allow utilities with uneconomic generation-related assets and purchased power contracts to recover the reasonable excess costs over market of those assets and purchased power contracts;

(3) educate utility customers about anticipated changes in the provision of retail electric service to ensure that the benefits of the competitive market reach all customers; and

(4) protect the competitive process in a manner that ensures the confidentiality of competitively sensitive information during the transition to a competitive market and after the commencement of customer choice.

(c) Regulatory authorities, excluding the governing body of a municipally owned electric utility that has not opted for customer choice or the body vested with power to manage and operate a municipally owned electric utility that has not opted for customer choice, may not make rules or issue orders regulating competitive electric services, prices, or competitors or restricting or conditioning competition except as authorized in this title and may not discriminate against any participant or type of participant during the transition to a competitive market and in the competitive market.

(d) Regulatory authorities, excluding the governing body of a municipally owned electric utility that has not opted for customer choice or the body vested with power to manage and operate a municipally owned electric utility that has not opted for customer choice, shall authorize or order competitive rather than regulatory methods to achieve the goals of this chapter to the greatest extent feasible and shall adopt rules and issue orders that are both practical and limited so as to impose the least impact on competition.

(e) Judicial review of competition rules adopted by the commission shall be conducted under Chapter 2001, Government Code, except as otherwise provided by this chapter. Judicial review of the validity of competition rules shall be commenced in the Court of Appeals for the Third Court of Appeals District and shall be limited to the commission's rulemaking record. The rulemaking record consists of:

(1) the notice of the proposed rule;

(2) the comments of all interested persons;

(3) all studies, reports, memoranda, or other materials on which the commission relied in adopting the rule; and

(4) the order adopting the rule.

(f) A person who challenges the validity of a competition rule must file a notice of appeal with the court of appeals and serve the notice on the commission not later than the 15th day after the date on which the rule as adopted is published in the Texas Register. The notice of appeal shall designate the person challenging the rule as the appellant and the commission as the appellee. The commission shall prepare the rulemaking record and file it with the court of appeals not later than the 30th day after the date the notice of appeal is served on the commission. The court of appeals shall hear and determine each appeal as expeditiously as possible with lawful precedence over other matters. The appellant, and any person who is permitted by the court to intervene in support of the appellant's claims, shall file and serve briefs not later than the 30th day after the date the commission files the rulemaking record. The commission, and any person who is permitted by the court to intervene in support of the rule, shall file and serve briefs not later than the 60th day after the date the appellant files the appellant's brief. The court of appeals may, on its own motion or on motion of any person for good cause, modify the filing deadlines prescribed by this subsection. The court of appeals shall render judgment affirming the rule or reversing and, if appropriate on reversal, remanding the rule to the commission for further proceedings, consistent with the court's opinion and judgment. The Texas Rules of Appellate Procedure apply to an appeal brought under this section to the extent not inconsistent with this section.

Added by Acts 1999, 76th Leg., ch. 405, § 39, eff. Sept. 1, 1999.

§ 39.002. Applicability

This chapter, other than Sections 39.155, 39. 157(e), 39.203, 39.903, 39.904, 39.9051, 39.9052, and 39.914(e), does not apply to a municipally owned utility or an electric cooperative. Sections 39.157(e), 39.203, and 39.904, however, apply only to a municipally owned utility or an electric cooperative that is offering customer choice. If there is a conflict between the specific provisions of this chapter and any other provisions of this title, except for Chapters 40 and 41, the provisions of this chapter control.

Added by Acts 1999, 76th Leg., ch. 405, § 39, eff. Sept. 1, 1999. Amended by Acts 2007, 80th Leg., ch. 939, § 19, eff. Sept. 1, 2007.

§ 39.003. Contested Cases

Unless specifically provided otherwise, each commission proceeding under this chapter, other than a rulemaking proceeding, report, notification, or registration, shall be conducted as a contested case and the burden of proof is on the incumbent electric utility.

Added by Acts 1999, 76th Leg., ch. 405, § 39, eff. Sept. 1, 1999.

SUBCHAPTER B. TRANSITION TO COMPETITIVE RETAIL ELECTRIC MARKET

§ 39.051. Unbundling

(a) On or before September 1, 2000, each electric utility shall separate from its regulated utility activities its customer energy services business activities that are otherwise also already widely available in the competitive market.

(b) Not later than January 1, 2002, each electric utility shall separate its business activities from one another into the following units:

(1) a power generation company;

(2) a retail electric provider; and

(3) a transmission and distribution utility.

(c) An electric utility may accomplish the separation required by Subsection (b) either through the creation of separate nonaffiliated companies or separate affiliated companies owned by a common holding company or through the sale of assets to a third party. An electric utility may create separate transmission and distribution utilities. Notwithstanding any other provision of this chapter, an electric utility that does not have stranded costs described by Section 39.254 and that on September 1, 2005, has not finalized unbundling pursuant to a commission order approving an unbundling plan may also meet the requirements of Subsection (b) for generation facilities existing on September 1, 2005, in the Electric Reliability Council of Texas if it meets and maintains compliance with the following requirements:

(1) the electric utility has no more than 400 megawatts of Texas jurisdictional capacity from generating units within the Electric Reliability Council of Texas that have not been mothballed or retired;

(2) the electric utility has a contract or contracts with separate nonaffiliated companies or separate affiliated companies for the sale of all of the output from its generating units that have not been mothballed or retired with a contract term that is no shorter than 20 years or the life of the generating units, whichever is shorter; and

(3) the electric utility has a separate division within the electric utility for its generation business activities.

(c–1) A separate division described by Subsection (c)(3) is subject to Subsection (d) and, for the purposes of this chapter, is considered a separate affiliated power generation company and a competitive affiliate.

(d) Each electric utility shall unbundle under this section in a manner that provides for a separation of personnel, information flow, functions, and operations, consistent with Section 39.157(d).

(e) Each electric utility shall file with the commission a plan to implement this section by January 10, 2000.

(f) The commission shall adopt the utility's plan for business separation required by Subsection (b), adopt the plan with changes, or reject the plan and require the utility to file a new plan.

(g) Transactions by electric utilities involving sales, transfers, or other disposition of assets to accomplish the purposes of this section are not subject to Section 14.101, 35.034, or 35.035.

Added by Acts 1999, 76th Leg., ch. 405, § 39, eff. Sept. 1, 1999. Amended by Acts 2005, 79th Leg., ch. 413, § 3, eff. June 17, 2005.

§ 39.052. Freeze on Existing Retail Base Rate Tariffs

(a) Until January 1, 2002, an electric utility shall provide retail electric service within its certificated service area in accordance with the electric utility's retail base rate tariffs in effect on September 1, 1999, including its purchased power cost recovery factor.

(b) During the freeze period, an electric utility may not increase its retail base rates above the rates provided by this section except for losses caused by force majeure as provided by Section 39.055.

(c) Notwithstanding any other provision of this title, during the freeze period the regulatory authority may not reduce the retail base rates of an electric utility, except as may be ordered as stipulated to by an electric utility in a proceeding for which a final order had not been issued by January 1, 1999.

(d) During the freeze period, the retail base rates, overall revenues, return on invested capital, and net income of an electric utility are not subject to complaint, hearing, or determination as to reasonableness.

(e) An electric utility that has a rate proceeding pending before the commission as of January 2, 1999, shall provide service in accordance with the tariffs approved in that proceeding from the date of approval until the end of the freeze period.

(f) Nothing in this section affects the authority of the commission to fulfill its obligations under Section 39.262.

(g) Nothing in this section shall deny a utility its right to have the commission conduct proceedings and issue a final order pertaining to any matter that may be remanded to the commission by a court having jurisdiction, except that the final order may not affect the rates charged to customers during the freeze period but shall be taken into account during the utility's true-up proceeding under Section 39.262.

(h) Nothing in this title shall be construed to prevent an electric utility or a transmission and distribution utility from filing, and the commission from approving, a change in wholesale transmission service rates during the freeze period.

Added by Acts 1999, 76th Leg., ch. 405, § 39, eff. Sept. 1, 1999.

§ 39.053. Cost Recovery Adjustments

This subchapter does not limit or alter the ability of an electric utility during the freeze period to revise its fuel factor or to reconcile fuel expenses and to either refund fuel overcollections or surcharge fuel undercollections to customers, as authorized by its tariffs and Sections 36.203 and 36.205.

Added by Acts 1999, 76th Leg., ch. 405, § 39, eff. Sept. 1, 1999.

§ 39.054. Retail Electric Service During Freeze Period

(a) An electric utility shall provide retail electric service during the freeze period in accordance with any contract terms applicable to a particular retail customer approved by the regulatory authority and in effect on December 31, 1998.

(b) Nothing in Sections 39.052(c) and (d) shall be construed to restrict any customer's right to complain during the freeze period to the regulatory authority regarding the quality of retail electric service provided by the electric utility or the applicability of an electric utility's particular tariff to the customer.

(c) Nothing in this title shall be construed to restrict an electric utility, voluntarily and at its sole discretion, from offering new services or new tariff options to its customers during the freeze period, consistent with Section 39.051(a).

(d) Any offering of new services or tariff options under this section shall be equal to or greater than an electric utility's long-run marginal cost and may not be unreasonably preferential, prejudicial, discriminatory, predatory, or anticompetitive.

(e) Revenue from any new offering under this section shall be accounted for in a manner consistent with Section 36.007.

Added by Acts 1999, 76th Leg., ch. 405, § 39, eff. Sept. 1, 1999.

§ 39.055. Force Majeure

(a) An electric utility may recover losses resulting from force majeure through an increase in its retail base rates during the freeze period.

(b) Notwithstanding Subchapter C, Chapter 36,[1] the regulatory authority, after a hearing to determine the electric utility's losses from force majeure, shall permit the utility to fully collect any approved force majeure increase through an appropriate customer surcharge mechanism.

(c) For purposes of this section, "force majeure" means a major event or combination of major events, including new or expanded state or federal statutory or regulatory requirements; hurricanes, tornadoes, ice storms, or other natural disasters; or acts of war, terrorism, or civil disturbance, beyond the control of an electric utility that the regulatory authority finds increases the utility's total reasonable and necessary nonfuel costs or decreases the utility's total nonfuel revenues related to the generation and delivery of electricity by more than 10 percent for any calendar year during the freeze period. The term does not include any changes in general economic conditions such as inflation, interest rates, or other factors of general application.

Added by Acts 1999, 76th Leg., ch. 405, § 39, eff. Sept. 1, 1999.

[1] V.T.C.A., Utilities Code § 36.101.

SUBCHAPTER C. RETAIL COMPETITION

§ 39.101. Customer Safeguards

(a) Before customer choice begins on January 1, 2002, the commission shall ensure that retail customer protections are established that entitle a customer:

(1) to safe, reliable, and reasonably priced electricity, including protection against service disconnections in an extreme weather emergency as provided by Subsection (h) or in cases of medical emergency or nonpayment for unrelated services;

(2) to privacy of customer consumption and credit information;

(3) to bills presented in a clear format and in language readily understandable by customers;

(4) to the option to have all electric services on a single bill, except in those instances where multiple bills are allowed under Chapters 40 and 41;

(5) to protection from discrimination on the basis of race, color, sex, nationality, religion, or marital status;

(6) to accuracy of metering and billing;

(7) to information in English and Spanish and any other language as necessary concerning rates, key terms and conditions, in a standard format that will permit comparisons between price and service offerings, and the environmental impact of certain production facilities;

(8) to information in English and Spanish and any other language as necessary concerning low-income assistance programs and deferred payment plans; and

(9) to other information or protections necessary to ensure high-quality service to customers.

(b) A customer is entitled:

(1) to be informed about rights and opportunities in the transition to a competitive electric industry;

(2) to choose the customer's retail electric provider consistent with this chapter, to have that choice honored, and to assume that the customer's chosen provider will not be changed without the customer's informed consent;

(3) to have access to providers of energy efficiency services, to on-site distributed generation, and to providers of energy generated by renewable energy resources;

(4) to be served by a provider of last resort that offers a commission-approved standard service package;

(5) to receive sufficient information to make an informed choice of service provider;

(6) to be protected from unfair, misleading, or deceptive practices, including protection from being billed for services that were not authorized or provided; and

(7) to have an impartial and prompt resolution of disputes with its chosen retail electric provider and transmission and distribution utility.

(c) A retail electric provider, power generation company, aggregator, or other entity that provides retail electric service may not refuse to provide retail electric or electric generation service or otherwise discriminate in the provision of electric service to any customer because of race, creed, color, national origin, ancestry, sex, marital status, lawful source of income, disability, or familial status. A retail electric provider, power generation company, aggregator, or other entity that provides retail electric service may not refuse to provide retail electric or electric generation service to a customer because the customer is located in an economically distressed geographic area or qualifies for low-income affordability or energy efficiency services. The commission shall require a provider to comply with this subsection as a condition of certification or registration.

(d) A retail electric provider, power generation company, aggregator, or other entity that provides retail electric service shall submit reports to the commission and the office annually and on request relating to the person's compliance with this section. The commission by rule shall specify the form in which a report must be submitted. A report must include:

(1) information regarding the extent of the person's coverage;

(2) information regarding the service provided, compiled by zip code and census tract; and

(3) any other information the commission or the office considers relevant to determine compliance.

(e) The commission has the authority to adopt and enforce such rules as may be necessary or appropriate to carry out Subsections (a)–(d), including rules for minimum service standards for a retail electric provider relating to customer deposits and the extension of credit, switching fees, levelized billing programs, interconnection and use of on-site generation, termination of service, and quality of service. The commission has jurisdiction over all providers of electric service in enforcing Subsections (a)–(d) and may assess civil and administrative penalties under Section 15.023 and seek civil penalties under Section 15.028.

(f) On or before June 30, 2001, the commission shall modify its current rules regarding customer protections to ensure that at least the same level of customer protection against potential abuses and the same quality of service that exists on December 31, 1999, is maintained in a restructured electric industry.

(g) Compliance with Subsections (a)–(e) by a provider of electric service which is a municipally owned utility shall be administered solely by the governing body of the municipally owned utility, which shall adopt, implement, and enforce, as to the municipally owned utility, rules having the effect of accomplishing the objectives of Subsections (a)–(e). Reports containing the information required by Subsection (d) shall be filed by the municipally owned utility with the governing body.

(h) A retail electric provider, power generation company, aggregator, or other entity that provides retail electric service may not disconnect service to a residential customer during an extreme weather emergency or on a weekend day. The entity providing service shall defer collection of the full payment of bills that are due during an extreme weather emergency until after the emergency is over and shall work with customers to establish a pay schedule for deferred bills. For purposes of this subsection, "extreme weather emergency" means a period when:

(1) the previous day's highest temperature did not exceed 32 degrees Fahrenheit and the temperature is predicted to remain at or below that level for the next 24 hours according to the nearest National Weather Service reports; or

(2) the National Weather Service issues a heat advisory for any county in the relevant service territory, or when such an advisory has been issued on any one of the previous two calendar days.

Added by Acts 1999, 76th Leg., ch. 405, § 39, eff. Sept. 1, 1999.

§ 39.102. Retail Customer Choice

(a) Each retail customer in this state, except retail customers of electric cooperatives and municipally owned utilities that have not opted for customer choice, shall have customer choice on and after January 1, 2002.

(b) The affiliated retail electric provider of the electric utility serving a retail customer on December 31, 2001, may continue to serve that customer until the customer chooses service from a different retail electric provider, an electric cooperative offering customer choice, or a municipally owned utility offering customer choice.

(c) An electric utility that has in effect a system-wide freeze for residential and commercial customers in effect September 1, 1997, extending beyond December 31, 2001, that has been found by a regulatory authority to be in the public interest is not subject to this chapter. At the expiration of the utility's freeze period, the utility shall be subject to this chapter and, at that time, has no claim for stranded cost recovery.

(d) The commission shall oversee the compliance with this chapter by electric utilities that were not subject to this chapter before September 1, 2003, and in so doing shall establish schedules and procedures and require commission approvals as it deems necessary to achieve the objectives of this chapter. This subsection does not apply to an electric utility to which Subsection (c) applies.

(e) In establishing a schedule under Subsection (d), the commission shall consider:

(1) the effect of customer choice on the reliability of service provided by the electric utility;

(2) whether the electric utility's service area is located in more than one power region;

(3) whether any applicable power region has been certified as a qualifying power region under Section 39.152(a);

(4) whether other electric utilities in the power region offer retail customer choice; and

(5) any other relevant factor.

Added by Acts 1999, 76th Leg., ch. 405, § 39, eff. Sept. 1, 1999. Amended by Acts 2003, 78th Leg., ch. 1327, § 2, eff. Sept. 1, 2003.

§ 39.1025. Limitations on Telephone Solicitation

(a) A person may not make or cause to be made a telephone solicitation to a nonresidential electric customer who has given notice to the commission of the customer's objection to receiving telephone solicitations relating to the customer's choice of retail electric providers.

(b) The commission shall establish and provide for the operation of a database to compile a list of nonresidential electric customers who object to receiving telephone solicitations. The commission may operate the database or contract with another entity to operate the database.

(c) A customer shall pay a fee of not more than $5 for inclusion in the database. The commission shall prescribe the amount of the fee.

Added by Acts 1999, 76th Leg., ch. 405, § 39, eff. Sept. 1, 1999. Amended by Acts 2005, 79th Leg., ch. 171, § 3, eff. May 27, 2005.

§ 39.103. Commission Authority to Delay Competition and Set New Rates

If the commission determines under Section 39.104 that a power region is unable to offer fair competition and reliable service to all retail customer classes on January 1, 2002, the commission shall delay customer choice for the power region and may on or after January 1, 2002, establish new rates for all electric utilities in the power region as provided by Chapter 36.

Added by Acts 1999, 76th Leg., ch. 405, § 39, eff. Sept. 1, 1999.

§ 39.104. Customer Choice Pilot Projects

(a) Customer choice pilot projects may be used to allow the commission to evaluate the ability of each power region and electric utility to implement customer choice. However, in a multiply certificated area, an electric utility may not include customers that were served by an electric cooperative or a municipally owned utility on May 1, 1999.

(b) The commission shall require each electric utility to offer customer choice in its service area within this state amounting to five percent of the utility's combined load of all customer classes within this state beginning on June 1, 2001.

(c) The load designated for customer choice under this section shall be distributed among all customer classes of a utility consistent with the purpose of this section and subject to commission approval.

(d) Customers participating in a pilot project under this section may buy electric energy from any retail electric provider certified by the commission under Section 39.352, including an affiliated retail electric provider; provided, however, that a retail electric provider may not participate in a pilot project in the certificated service area served by the electric utility with which it is affiliated.

(e) Each utility operating a pilot project under this section shall charge residential and small commercial customers in accordance with Section 39.052.

(f) The commission may prescribe reporting requirements it considers necessary to evaluate a pilot project consistent with the purpose of this section.

(g) Customers having customer choice under this section shall be billed as provided by Section 39.107.

(h) The commission may prescribe terms and conditions it considers necessary to prohibit anticompetitive practices and to encourage customer choice offered under this section.

(i) Notwithstanding any other provision of this title, a retail electric provider participating in a pilot project under this section is not an electric utility or a retail electric utility.

(j) Twenty percent of the load designated for customer choice under this section shall be initially set aside for aggregated loads.

Added by Acts 1999, 76th Leg., ch. 405, § 39, eff. Sept. 1, 1999.

§ 39.105. Limitation on Sale of Electricity

(a) After January 1, 2002, a transmission and distribution utility may not sell electricity or otherwise participate in the market for electricity except for the purpose of buying electricity to serve its own needs.

(b) A person or retail electric utility may not provide, furnish, or make available electric service at retail within the certificated service area of an electric cooperative that has not adopted customer choice or a municipally owned utility that has not adopted customer choice. However, this subsection does not prohibit the provision of electric service in multiply certificated service areas to customers of any other retail electric utility.

Added by Acts 1999, 76th Leg., ch. 405, § 39, eff. Sept. 1, 1999.

§ 39.106. Provider of Last Resort

(a) The commission shall designate retail electric providers in areas of the state in which customer choice is in effect to serve as providers of last resort.

(b) A provider of last resort shall offer a standard retail service package for each class of customers designated by the commission at a fixed, nondiscountable rate approved by the commission.

(c) A provider of last resort shall provide the standard retail service package to any requesting customer in the territory for which it is the provider of last resort.

(d) The commission shall designate the provider or providers of last resort not later than June 1, 2001.

(e) The commission shall determine the procedures and criteria, which may include the solicitation of bids, for designating a provider or providers of last resort. The commission may redesignate the provider of last resort according to a schedule it considers appropriate.

(f) In the event that no retail electric provider applies to be the provider of last resort for a given area of the state on reasonable terms and conditions, the commission may require a retail electric provider to become the provider of last resort as a condition of receiving or maintaining a certificate under Section 39.352.

(g) In the event that a retail electric provider fails to serve any or all of its customers, the provider of last resort shall offer that customer the standard retail service package for that customer class with no interruption of service to any customer.

Added by Acts 1999, 76th Leg., ch. 405, § 39, eff. Sept. 1, 1999.

§ 39.107. Metering and Billing Services

(a) On introduction of customer choice in a service area, metering services for the area shall continue to be provided by the transmission and distribution utility affiliate of the electric utility that was serving the area before the introduction of customer choice. Metering services provided to commercial and industrial customers that are required by the independent system operator to have an interval data recorder meter may be provided on a competitive basis.

(b) Metering services provided to residential customers and to nonresidential customers other than those required by the independent system operator to have an interval data recorder meter shall continue to be provided by the transmission and distribution utility affiliate of the electric utility that was serving the area before the introduction of customer choice. Retail electric providers serving residential and nonresidential customers other than those required by the independent system operator to have an interval data recorder meter may request that the transmission and distribution utility provide specialized meters, meter features, or add-on accessories so long as they are technically feasible and generally available in the market and provided that the retail electric provider pays the differential cost of such a meter or accessory. Metering and billing services provided to residential customers shall be governed by the customer safeguards adopted by the commission under Section 39.101. All meter data, including all data generated, provided, or otherwise made available, by advanced meters and meter information networks, shall belong to a customer, including data used to calculate charges for service, historical load data, and any other proprietary customer information. A customer may authorize its data to be provided to one or more retail electric providers under rules and charges established by the commission.

(c) Beginning on the date of introduction of customer choice in a service area, tenants of leased or rented property that is separately metered shall have the right to choose a retail electric provider, an electric cooperative offering customer choice, or a municipally owned utility offering customer choice, and the owner of the property must grant reasonable and nondiscriminatory access to transmission and distribution utilities, retail electric providers, electric cooperatives, and municipally owned utilities for metering purposes.

(d) Beginning on the date of introduction of customer choice in a service area, a transmission and distribution utility, or an electric cooperative or municipally owned utility providing the customer's energy requirements shall bill a customer's retail electric provider for nonbypassable delivery charges as determined under Section 39.201. The retail electric provider or the electric cooperative or municipally owned utility, as appropriate, must pay these charges.

(e) A transmission and distribution utility may bill retail customers at the request of a retail electric provider or, if an electric cooperative or municipally owned utility is providing the customer's energy requirements, at the request of the electric cooperative or municipally owned utility. A transmission and distribution utility that provides billing service on such request shall offer billing service on comparable terms and conditions to those of any such requesting retail electric provider or, as applicable, the electric cooperative or municipally owned utility providing energy requirements to a customer served by the transmission and distribution utility.

(f) Beginning on the date of introduction of customer choice in a service area, any charges for metering and billing services shall comply with rules adopted by the commission relating to nondiscriminatory rates of service.

(g) Metered electric service sold to residential customers on a prepaid basis may not be sold at a price that is higher than the price charged by the provider of last resort.

(h) The commission shall establish a nonbypassable surcharge for an electric utility or transmission and distribution utility to use to recover reasonable and necessary costs incurred in deploying advanced metering and meter information networks to residential customers and nonresidential customers other than those required by the independent system operator to have an interval data recorder meter. The commission shall ensure that the nonbypassable surcharge reflects a deployment of advanced meters that is no more than one-third of the utility's total meters over each calendar year and shall ensure that the nonbypassable surcharge does not result in the utility recovering more than its actual, fully allocated meter and meter information network costs. The expenses must be allocated to the customer classes receiving the services, based on the electric utility's most recently approved tariffs.

(i) Subject to the restrictions in Subsection (h), it is the intent of the legislature that net metering and advanced meter information networks be deployed as rapidly as possible to allow customers to better manage energy use and control costs, and to facilitate demand response initiatives.

(j) Notwithstanding Subsection (b), a nonresidential customer may have a meter installed and metering services provided on a competitive basis as part of an energy savings performance contract.

Added by Acts 1999, 76th Leg., ch. 405, § 39, eff. Sept. 1, 1999. Amended by Acts 2005, 79th Leg., ch. 1095, § 7, eff. Sept. 1, 2005; Acts 2007, 80th Leg., ch. 527, § 10, eff. June 16, 2007; Acts 2007, 80th Leg., ch. 939, § 20, eff. Sept. 1, 2007; Acts 2009, 81st Leg., ch. 87, § 27.001(110), eff. Sept. 1, 2009.

§ 39.108. Contractual Obligations

This chapter may not:

(1) interfere with or abrogate the rights or obligations of any party, including a retail or wholesale customer, to a contract with an investor-owned electric utility, river authority, municipally owned utility, or electric cooperative;

(2) interfere with or abrogate the rights or obligations of a party under a contract or agreement concerning certificated utility service areas; or

(3) result in a change in wholesale power costs to wholesale customers in Texas purchasing electricity under wholesale power contracts the pricing provisions of which are based on formulary rates, fuel adjustments, or average system costs.

Added by Acts 1999, 76th Leg., ch. 405, § 39, eff. Sept. 1, 1999.

§ 39.109. New Owner or Successor

(a) To ensure the continued safe and reliable operation of electric generating facilities, the commission shall require a generating facility that is transferred to a new owner or successor in interest between June 1, 1999, and January 1, 2002, to continue to be operated and maintained by the same operating personnel for not less than two years, except that the personnel may be dismissed for cause.

(b) This section shall apply only if the facility is actually operated during the two-year period after the sale.

(c) This section shall not require that the purchaser cause the facility to be operated in whole or in part, nor shall it preclude a temporary closure of the facility during the two-year period.

(d) This section shall not create any obligation extending after the two-year period following the sale.

Added by Acts 1999, 76th Leg., ch. 405, § 39, eff. Sept. 1, 1999.

§ 39.112. Notice of Expiration and Price Change

(a) In this section, "fixed rate product" means a retail electric product with a term of at least three months for which the price for each billing period, including recurring charges, does not change throughout the term of the contract, except that the price may vary to reflect actual changes in transmission and distribution utility charges, changes to ERCOT or Texas Regional Entity administrative fees charged to loads, or changes to federal, state, or local laws that result in new or modified fees or costs that are not within the retail electric provider's control.

(b) A retail electric provider shall provide a residential customer who has a fixed rate product with at least one written notice of the date the fixed rate product will expire. The notice must:

(1) be sent to the customer's billing address by mail at least 30, but not more than 60, days preceding the date the contract will expire;

(2) be sent to the customer's e-mail address, if available to the provider and if the customer has agreed to receive notices electronically, at least 30, but not more than 60, days preceding the date the contract will expire;

(3) include on the outside of the envelope in which the notice is sent, a statement that reads: "Contract Expiration Notice. See Enclosed.";

(4) if included with a customer's bill, be printed on a separate page; and

(5) include a description of any fees or charges associated with the early termination of the customer's fixed rate product.

(c) A retail electric provider shall include on each billing statement the end date of the fixed rate product.

(d) No provision in this section shall be construed to prohibit the commission from adopting rules that would provide a greater degree of customer protection.

Added by Acts 2009, 81st Leg., ch. 648, § 5, eff. Sept. 1, 2009.

§ 39.116. Expired

SUBCHAPTER D. MARKET STRUCTURE

§ 39.151. Essential Organizations

(a) A power region must establish one or more independent organizations to perform the following functions:

(1) ensure access to the transmission and distribution systems for all buyers and sellers of electricity on nondiscriminatory terms;

(2) ensure the reliability and adequacy of the regional electrical network;

(3) ensure that information relating to a customer's choice of retail electric provider is conveyed in a timely manner to the persons who need that information; and

(4) ensure that electricity production and delivery are accurately accounted for among the generators and wholesale buyers and sellers in the region.

(b) "Independent organization" means an independent system operator or other person that is sufficiently independent of any producer or seller of electricity that its decisions will not be unduly influenced by any producer or seller.

(c) The commission shall certify an independent organization or organizations to perform the functions prescribed by this section. The commission shall apply the provisions of this section and Sections 39.1511, 39.1512, and 39.1515 so as to avoid conflict with a ruling of a federal regulatory body.

(d) The commission shall adopt and enforce rules relating to the reliability of the regional electrical network and accounting for the production and delivery of electricity among generators and all other market participants, or may delegate to an independent organization responsibilities for establishing or enforcing such rules. Any such rules adopted by an independent organization and any enforcement actions taken by the organization are subject to commission oversight and review. An independent organization certified by the commission is directly responsible and accountable to the commission. The commission has complete authority to oversee and investigate the organization's finances, budget, and operations as necessary to ensure the organization's accountability and to ensure that the organization adequately performs the organization's functions and duties. The organization shall fully cooperate with the commission in the commission's oversight and investigatory functions. The commission may take appropriate action against an organization that does not adequately perform the organization's functions or duties or does not comply with this section, including decertifying the organization or assessing an administrative penalty against the organization. The commission by rule shall adopt procedures governing decertification of an independent organization, selecting and certifying a successor organization, and transferring assets to the successor organization to ensure continuity of operations in the region. The commission may not implement, by order or by rule, a requirement that is contrary to an applicable federal law or rule.

(d–1) The commission may:

(1) require an independent organization to provide reports and information relating to the independent organization's performance of the functions prescribed by this section and relating to the organization's revenues, expenses, and other financial matters;

(2) prescribe a system of accounts for an independent organization;

(3) conduct audits of an independent organization's performance of the functions prescribed by this section or relating to its revenues, expenses, and other financial matters and may require an independent organization to conduct such an audit;

(4) inspect an independent organization's facilities, records, and accounts during reasonable hours and after reasonable notice to the independent organization;

(5) assess administrative penalties against an independent organization that violates this title or a rule or order adopted by the commission and, at the

request of the commission, the attorney general may apply for a court order to require an independent organization to comply with commission rules and orders in the manner provided by Chapter 15; and

(6) resolve disputes between an affected person and an independent organization and adopt procedures for the efficient resolution of such disputes.

(e) The commission may authorize an independent organization that is certified under this section to charge a reasonable and competitively neutral rate to wholesale buyers and sellers to cover the independent organization's costs. The commission shall investigate the organization's cost efficiencies, salaries and benefits, and use of debt financing and may require the organization to provide any information needed to effectively evaluate the organization's budget and the reasonableness and neutrality of a rate or proposed rate or to evaluate the effectiveness or efficiency of the organization. The commission shall work with the organization to establish the detail of information, both current and historical, and the time frames the commission needs to effectively evaluate a rate or a rate request.

(f) In implementing this section, the commission may cooperate with the utility regulatory commission of another state or the federal government and may hold a joint hearing or make a joint investigation with that commission.

(g) To maintain certification as an independent organization under this section, an organization's governing body must be composed of persons specified by this section and selected in accordance with formal bylaws or protocols of the organization. The bylaws or protocols must be approved by the commission and must reflect the input of the commission. The bylaws must specify the process by which appropriate stakeholders elect members and, for unaffiliated members, prescribe professional qualifications for selection as a member. The bylaws must require the use of a professional search firm to identify candidates for membership of unaffiliated members. The process must allow for commission input in identifying candidates. The governing body must be composed of:

(1) the chairman of the commission as an ex officio nonvoting member;

(2) the counsellor as an ex officio voting member representing residential and small commercial consumer interests;

(3) the chief executive officer of the independent organization as an ex officio voting member;

(4) six market participants elected by their respective market segments to serve one-year terms, with:

(A) one representing independent generators;

(B) one representing investor-owned utilities;

(C) one representing power marketers;

(D) one representing retail electric providers;

(E) one representing municipally owned utilities; and

(F) one representing electric cooperatives;

(5) one member representing industrial consumer interests and elected by the industrial consumer market segment to serve a one-year term;

(6) one member representing large commercial consumer interests selected in accordance with the bylaws to serve a one-year term; and

(7) five members unaffiliated with any market segment and selected by the other members of the governing body to serve three-year terms.

(g–1) The presiding officer of the governing body must be one of the members described by Subsection (g)(7).

(h) The ERCOT independent system operator may meet the criteria relating to the other functions of an independent organization provided by Subsection (a) by adopting procedures and acquiring resources needed to carry out those functions, consistent with any rules or orders of the commission.

(i) The commission may delegate authority to the existing independent system operator in ERCOT to enforce operating standards within the ERCOT regional electrical network and to establish and oversee transaction settlement procedures. The commission may establish the terms and conditions for the ERCOT independent system operator's authority to oversee utility dispatch functions after the introduction of customer choice.

(j) A retail electric provider, municipally owned utility, electric cooperative, power marketer, transmission and distribution utility, or power generation company shall observe all scheduling, operating, planning, reliability, and settlement policies, rules, guidelines, and procedures established by the independent system operator in ERCOT. Failure to comply with this subsection may result in the revocation, suspension, or amendment of a certificate as provided by Section 39.356 or in the imposition of an administrative penalty as provided by Section 39.357.

(k) To the extent the commission has authority over an independent organization outside of ERCOT, the commission may delegate authority to the independent organization consistent with Subsection (i).

(*l*) No operational criteria, protocols, or other requirement established by an independent organization, including the ERCOT independent system operator, may adversely affect or impede any manufacturing or other internal process operation associated with an industrial generation facility, except to the minimum extent necessary to assure reliability of the transmission network.

(m) A power region outside of ERCOT shall be deemed to have met the requirement to establish an independent organization to perform the transmission functions specified in Subsection (a) if the Federal Energy Regulatory Commission has approved a regional transmission organization for the region and found that the regional transmission organization meets the requirements of Subsection (a).

(n) An independent organization certified by the commission under this section is subject to review under Chapter 325, Government Code (Texas Sunset Act), but is not abolished under that chapter.The independent organization shall be reviewed during the periods in which the Public Utility Commission of Texas is reviewed.

Text of subsec. (n–1) effective until Sept. 1, 2013.

(n–1) Notwithstanding Subsection (n), an independent organization certified by the commission under this section is not subject to review in preparation for the work of the 83rd Legislature in Regular Session. This subsection expires September 1, 2013.

Added by Acts 1999, 76th Leg., ch. 405, § 39, eff. Sept. 1, 1999. Amended by Acts 2005, 79th Leg., ch. 797, § 9, eff. Sept. 1, 2005; Acts 2011, 82nd Leg., ch. 1232 (S.B. 652), § 1.09, eff. June 17, 2011.

§ 39.1511. Public Meetings of the Governing Body of an Independent Organization

(a) Meetings of the governing body of an independent organization certified under Section 39.151 and meetings of a subcommittee that includes a member of the governing body must be open to the public. The bylaws of the independent organization and the rules of the commission may provide for the governing body or subcommittee to enter into executive session closed to the public to address sensitive matters such as confidential personnel information, contracts, lawsuits, competitively sensitive information, or other information related to the security of the regional electrical network.

(b) The bylaws of the independent organization and rules of the commission must ensure that a person interested in the activities of the independent organization has an opportunity to obtain at least seven days' advance notice of meetings and the planned agendas of the meetings and an opportunity to comment on matters under discussion at the meetings. The bylaws and commission rules governing meetings of the governing body may provide for a shorter period of advance notice and for meetings by teleconference technology for governing body meetings to take action on urgent matters. The bylaws and rules must require actions taken on short notice or at teleconference meetings to be ratified at the governing body's next regular meeting. The notice requirements may be met by a timely electronic posting on the Internet.

(c) The commission shall ensure that an independent organization certified under Section 39.151 makes publicly accessible without charge live Internet video of all public meetings subject to this section for viewing from an Internet website.

Added by Acts 2005, 79th Leg., ch. 797, § 10, eff. Sept. 1, 2005. Amended by Acts 2009, 81st Leg., ch. 400, § 2, eff. Sept. 1, 2009.

Section 3 of Acts 2009, 81st Leg., ch. 400 provides:

"Sec. 3. The change in law made by this Act applies to a hearing or meeting held on or after the effective date [Sept. 1, 2009] of this Act. A hearing or meeting held before the effective date of this Act is governed by the law as it existed immediately before that date, and that law is continued in effect for that purpose."

§ 39.1512. Disclosure of Interest in Matter Before Independent Organization's Governing Body; Participation in Decision

(a) If a matter comes before the governing body of an independent organization certified under Section 39.151 and a member has a direct interest in that matter or is employed by or has a substantial financial interest in a person who has a direct interest in that matter, that member shall publicly disclose the fact of that interest to the governing body at a public meeting of the body. The member shall recuse himself or herself from the governing body's deliberations and actions on the matter and may not vote on the matter or otherwise participate in a governing body decision on the matter.

(b) A disclosure made under Subsection (a) shall be entered in the minutes of the meeting at which the disclosure is made.

(c) The fact that a member is recused from a vote or decision by application of this section does not affect the existence of a quorum.

Added by Acts 2005, 79th Leg., ch. 797, § 10, eff. Sept. 1, 2005.

§ 39.1515. Wholesale Electric Market Monitor

(a) An independent organization certified under Section 39.151 shall contract with an entity selected by the commission to act as the commission's wholesale electric market monitor to detect and prevent market manipulation strategies and recommend measures to enhance the efficiency of the wholesale market.

(b) The independent organization shall provide to the personnel of the market monitor:

(1) full access to the organization's main operations center and the organization's records that concern operations, settlement, and reliability; and

(2) other support and cooperation the commission determines is necessary for the market monitor to perform the market monitor's functions.

(c) The independent organization shall use money from the rate authorized by Section 39.151(e) to pay for the market monitor's activities.

(d) The commission is responsible for ensuring that the market monitor has the resources, expertise, and authority necessary to monitor the wholesale electric market effectively and shall adopt rules and perform oversight of the market monitor as necessary. The market monitor shall operate under the supervision and oversight of the commission. The commission shall retain all enforcement authority conferred under this title, and this section may not be construed to confer enforcement authority on the market monitor or to authorize the commission to delegate the commission's enforcement authority to the market monitor. The commission by rule shall define:

(1) the market monitor's monitoring responsibilities, including reporting obligations and limitations;

(2) the standards for funding the market monitor, including staffing requirements;

(3) qualifications for personnel of the market monitor; and

(4) ethical standards for the market monitor and the personnel of the market monitor.

(e) In adopting rules governing the standards for funding the market monitor, the commission shall consult with a subcommittee of the independent organization's governing body to receive information on how money is or should be spent for monitoring functions. Rules governing ethical standards must include provisions designed to ensure that the personnel of the market monitor are professionally and financially independent from market participants. The commission shall develop and implement policies that clearly separate the policymaking responsibilities of the commission and the monitoring, analysis, and reporting responsibilities of the market monitor.

(f) The market monitor immediately shall report directly to the commission any potential market manipulations and any discovered or potential violations of commission rules or rules of the independent organization.

(g) The personnel of the market monitor may communicate with commission staff on any matter without restriction.

(h) The market monitor annually shall submit to the commission and the independent organization a report that identifies market design flaws and recommends methods to correct the flaws. The commission and the independent organization shall review the report and evaluate whether changes to rules of the commission or the independent organization should be made.

Added by Acts 2005, 79th Leg., ch. 797, § 10, eff. Sept. 1, 2005.

§ 39.152. Qualifying Power Regions

(a) The commission shall certify a power region if:

(1) a sufficient number of interconnected utilities in the power region fall under the operational control of an independent organization as described by Section 39.151;

(2) the power region has a generally applicable tariff that guarantees open and nondiscriminatory access for all users to transmission and distribution facilities in the power region as provided by Section 39.203; and

(3) no person owns and controls more than 20 percent of the installed generation capacity located in or capable of delivering electricity to a power region, as determined according to Section 39.154.

(b) In determining whether a power region not entirely within the state meets the requirements of this section, the commission shall consider the extent to which the available transmission facilities limit the delivery of electricity from generators located outside the state to areas of the power region within the state.

(c) For a power region outside of ERCOT, the requirements of Subsection (a)(2) shall be deemed to have been met if power aggregating to approximately 50,000 megawatts can be delivered to the portion of the power region that is in this state through the payment of not more than one transmission tariff.

(d) For a power region outside of ERCOT, a power generation company that is affiliated with an electric utility may elect to demonstrate that it meets the requirements of Subsection (a)(3) by showing that it does not own and control more than 20 percent of the installed capacity in a geographic market that includes the power region, using the guidelines, standards, and methods adopted by the Federal Energy Regulatory Commission.

(e) In a power region outside of ERCOT, if customer choice is introduced before the requirements of Subsection (a) are met, an affiliated retail electric provider may not compete for retail customers in any area of the power region that is within this state and outside of the affiliated transmission and distribution utility's certificated service area unless the affiliated power generation company makes a commitment to maintain and does maintain rates that are based on cost of service for any electric cooperative or municipally owned utility that was a wholesale customer on January 1, 1999, and was purchasing power at rates that were based on cost of service. This subsection requires a power generation company to sell power at rates that are based on cost of service, notwithstanding the expiration of a contract for that service, until the requirements of Subsection (a) are met.

Added by Acts 1999, 76th Leg., ch. 405, § 39, eff. Sept. 1, 1999.

§ 39.153. Capacity Auction

(a) Each electric utility subject to this section shall sell at auction, at least 60 days before the date set for customer choice to begin, entitlements to at least 15 percent of the electric utility's Texas jurisdictional installed generation capacity. For the purposes of this section, the term "electric utility" includes any affiliated power generation company that is unbundled from the electric utility in accordance with Section 39.051, but does not include any entity owning less than 400 megawatts of installed generation capacity.

(b) The obligation to auction the entitlements shall continue until the earlier of 60 months after the date customer choice is introduced or the date the commission determines that 40 percent or more of the electric power consumed by residential and small commercial customers within the affiliated transmission and distribution utility's certificated service area before the onset of customer choice is provided by nonaffiliated retail electric providers.

(c) An affiliate of the electric utility selling entitlements in the auction required by this section may not purchase entitlements from the affiliated electric utility at the auction. Entitlements may only be purchased by entities lawfully able to sell electricity in Texas.

(d) An electric utility may choose to auction additional entitlements beyond those required by Subsection (a) or continue to auction entitlements after the period required by Subsection (b) in order to comply with Section 39.154.

(e) The commission shall adopt rules by December 31, 2000, that define the scope of the capacity entitlements to be auctioned. Entitlements may be auctioned in blocks of less than 15 percent. The rules shall state the minimum amount of capacity that can be sold at auction as an entitlement. At a minimum, the rules shall provide that the entitlements:

(1) may be sold and purchased in periods of not less than one month nor more than four years;

(2) may be resold to any lawful purchaser, except for a retail electric provider affiliated with the electric utility that originally auctioned the entitlement;

(3) include no possessory interest in the unit from which the power is produced;

(4) include no obligations of a possessory owner of an interest in the unit from which the power is produced; and

(5) give the purchaser the right to designate the dispatch of the entitlement, subject to planned outages, outages beyond the control of the utility operating the unit, and other considerations subject to the oversight of the applicable independent organization.

(f) The commission shall adopt rules by December 31, 2000, that prescribe the procedure for the auction of the entitlements. The rules shall include:

(1) a process for conducting the auction or auctions, including who shall conduct it, how often it shall be conducted, and how winning bidders shall be determined;

(2) a process for the electric utility to designate which generation units or combination of units are offered for auction;

(3) a provision for the utility to establish an opening bid price based on the electric utility's expected cost, with the commission prescribing the

means for determining the opening bid price, which may not include return on equity; and

(4) a provision that allows a bidder to specify the magnitude and term of the entitlement, subject to the conditions established in Subsection (e).

(g) In adopting the process under Subsection (f)(2), the commission shall consider the furtherance of the development of the competitive market, the cost of transmission, physical constraints of the transmission system, the proximity of the generation to load, economic efficiency, and any other factors the commission finds relevant. The process may provide for commission approval of the designation before auction. The commission may consult with the applicable independent organization to develop the process.

Added by Acts 1999, 76th Leg., ch. 405, § 39, eff. Sept. 1, 1999.

§ 39.154. Limitation of Ownership of Installed Capacity

(a) Beginning on the date of introduction of customer choice, a power generation company may not own and control more than 20 percent of the installed generation capacity located in, or capable of delivering electricity to, a power region.

(b) In a power region not entirely within the state, the commission may waive or modify the requirement in Subsection (a) on a finding of good cause.

(c) In determining the percentage shares of installed generation capacity under this section, the commission shall combine capacity owned and controlled by a power generation company and any entity that is affiliated with that power generation company within the power region, reduced by the installed generation capacity of those facilities that are made subject to capacity auctions under Sections 39.153(a) and (d).

(d) In this chapter, "installed generation capacity" means all potentially marketable electric generation capacity, including the capacity of:

(1) generating facilities that are connected with a transmission or distribution system;

(2) generating facilities used to generate electricity for consumption by the person owning or controlling the facility; and

(3) generating facilities that will be connected with a transmission or distribution system and operating within 12 months.

(e) In determining the percentage shares of installed generation capacity owned and controlled by a power generation company under this section and Section 39.156, the commission shall, for purposes of calculating the numerator, reduce the installed generation capacity owned and controlled by that power generation company by the installed generation capacity of any "grandfathered facility" within an ozone nonattainment area as of September 1, 1999, for which that power generation company has commenced complying or made a binding commitment to comply with Section 39.264. This subsection applies only to a power generation company that is affiliated with an electric utility that owned and controlled more than 27 percent of the installed generation capacity in the power region on January 1, 1999.

Added by Acts 1999, 76th Leg., ch. 405, § 39, eff. Sept. 1, 1999.

§ 39.155. Commission Assessment of Market Power

(a) Each person, municipally owned utility, electric cooperative, and river authority that owns generation facilities and offers electricity for sale in this state shall report to the commission its installed generation capacity, the total amount of capacity available for sale to others, the total amount of capacity under contract to others, the total amount of capacity dedicated to its own use, its annual wholesale power sales in the state, its annual retail power sales in the state, and any other information necessary for the commission to assess market power or the development of a competitive retail market in the state. The commission shall by rule prescribe the nature and detail of the reporting requirements and shall administer those reporting requirements in a manner that ensures the confidentiality of competitively sensitive information.

(b) The ERCOT independent system operator shall submit an annual report to the commission identifying existing and potential transmission and distribution constraints and system needs within ERCOT, alternatives for meeting system needs, and recommendations for meeting system needs. The first report shall be submitted on or before October 1, 1999. Subsequent reports shall be submitted by January 15 of each year or as determined necessary by the commission.

(c) Before the date of introduction of customer choice in a power region other than ERCOT, each electric utility owning transmission and distribution facilities in that region shall submit an annual report to the commission identifying existing and potential transmission and distribution constraints and system needs in the power region, alternatives for meeting system needs, and recommendations for meeting system needs as directed by the commission.

(d) In a qualifying power region, the reports required by Subsections (b) and (c) shall be submitted by the independent organization or organizations having authority over the power region or discrete areas thereof.

Added by Acts 1999, 76th Leg., ch. 405, § 39, eff. Sept. 1, 1999.

§ 39.156. Market Power Mitigation Plan

(a) In this section, "market power mitigation plan" or "plan" means a written proposal by an electric utility or a power generation company for reducing its ownership and control of installed generation capacity as required by Section 39.154.

(b) An electric utility or power generation company owning and controlling more than 20 percent of the generation capacity located in, or capable of delivering electricity to, a power region shall file a market power mitigation plan with the commission not later than December 1, 2000.

(c) The plan may provide for:

(1) the sale of generation assets to a nonaffiliated person;

(2) the exchange of generation assets with a nonaffiliated person located in a different power region;

(3) the auctioning of generation capacity entitlements as part of a capacity auction required by Section 39.153;

(4) the sale of the right to capacity to a nonaffiliated person for at least four years; or

(5) any reasonable method of mitigation.

(d) For the purposes of this section, generation capacity shall be net of the generation capacity subject to an auction under Section 39.153.

(e) The plan shall be in a form prescribed by the commission and shall provide information the commission finds reasonably necessary to evaluate the plan.

(f) The commission shall approve, modify, or reject a plan within 180 days after the date of a filing under Subsection (b). The commission may not modify a plan to require divestiture by the electric utility or the power generation company.

(g) In reaching its determination under Subsection (f), the commission shall consider:

(1) the degree to which the electric utility's or power generation company's stranded costs, if any, are minimized;

(2) whether on disposition of the generation assets the reasonable value is likely to be received;

(3) the effect of the plan on the electric utility's or power generation company's federal income taxes;

(4) the effect of the plan on current and potential competitors in the generation market; and

(5) whether the plan is consistent with the public interest.

(h) An electric utility or power generation company with an approved mitigation plan may request to amend or repeal its plan. On a showing of good cause, the commission shall modify or repeal an electric utility's or power generation company's mitigation plan.

(i) If an electric utility's or a power generation company's market power mitigation plan is not approved before January 1 of the year it is to take effect, the commission may order the electric utility or power generation company to auction generation capacity entitlements according to Section 39.153, subject to commission approval, of any capacity exceeding the maximum allowable capacity prescribed by Section 39.154 until the time a mitigation plan is approved.

(j) An auction under Subsection (i) shall be held not later than 60 days after the date the order is entered.

Added by Acts 1999, 76th Leg., ch. 405, § 39, eff. Sept. 1, 1999.

§ 39.157. Commission Authority to Address Market Power

(a) The commission shall monitor market power associated with the generation, transmission, distribution, and sale of electricity in this state. On a finding that market power abuses or other violations of this section are occurring, the commission shall require reasonable mitigation of the market power by ordering the construction of additional transmission or distribution facilities, by seeking an injunction or civil penalties as necessary to eliminate or to remedy the market power abuse or violation as authorized by Chapter 15, by imposing an administrative penalty as authorized by Chapter 15, by ordering the disgorgement of excess revenue as authorized by Chapter 15, or by suspending, revoking, or amending a certificate or registration as authorized by Section 39.356. Section 15.024(c) does not apply to an administrative penalty imposed under this section. For purposes of this subchapter, market power abuses are practices by persons possessing market power that are unreasonably discriminatory or tend to unreasonably restrict, impair, or reduce the level of competition, including practices that tie unregulated products or services to regulated products or services or unreasonably discriminate in the provision of regulated services. For purposes of this section, "market power abuses" include predatory pricing, withholding of production, precluding entry, and collusion. A violation of the code of conduct provided by Subsection (d) that materially impairs the ability of a person to compete in a competitive market shall be deemed to be an abuse of market power. The possession of a high market share in a market open to competition may not, of itself, be deemed to be an abuse of market power; however, this sentence shall not affect the application of state and federal antitrust laws.

(b) Beginning on the date of introduction of customer choice, a person that owns generation facilities may not own transmission or distribution facilities in this state except for those facilities necessary to interconnect a generation facility with the transmission or distribution network, a facility not dedicated to public use, or a facility otherwise excluded from the definition of "electric utility" under Section 31.002. However, nothing in this chapter shall prohibit a power generation company affiliated with a transmission and distribution utility from owning generation facilities.

(c) The commission shall monitor market shares of installed capacity to ensure that the limitations in Section 39.154 are not exceeded. If the commission finds that a person has violated a limitation in Section 39.154, the commission shall order the person to file, within 60 days of the date of the order, a market power mitigation plan consistent with the requirements in Section 39.156.

(d) Not later than January 10, 2000, the commission shall adopt rules and enforcement procedures to govern transactions or activities between a transmission and distribution utility and its competitive affiliates to avoid potential market power abuses and cross-subsidizations between regulated and competitive activities both during the transition to and after the introduction of competition. Nothing in this subsection is intended to affect or modify the obligations or duties relating to any rules or standards of conduct that may apply to a utility or the utility's affiliates under orders or regulations of the Federal Energy Regulatory Commission or the Securities and Exchange Commission. A utility that is subject to statutes or regulations in other states that conflict with a provision of this section may petition the commission for a waiver of the conflicting provision on a showing of good cause. The rules adopted under this section shall ensure that:

(1) a utility makes any products and services, other than corporate support services, that it provides to a competitive affiliate available, contemporaneously and in the same manner, to the competitive affiliate's competitors and applies its tariffs, prices, terms, conditions, and discounts for those products and services in the same manner to all similarly situated entities;

(2) a utility does not:

(A) give a competitive affiliate or a competitive affiliate's customers any preferential advantage, access, or treatment regarding services other than corporate support services; or

(B) act in a manner that is discriminatory or anticompetitive with respect to a nonaffiliated competitor of a competitive affiliate;

(3) a utility providing electric transmission or distribution services:

(A) provides those services on nondiscriminatory terms and conditions;

(B) does not establish as a condition for the provision of those services the purchase of other goods or services from the utility or the competitive affiliate; and

(C) does not provide competitive affiliates preferential access to the utility's transmission and distribution systems or to information about those systems;

(4) a utility does not release any proprietary customer information to a competitive affiliate or any other entity, other than an independent organization as defined by Section 39.151 or a provider of corporate support services for the purposes of providing the services, without obtaining prior verifiable authorization, as determined from the commission, from the customer;

(5) a utility does not:

(A) communicate with a current or potential customer about products or services offered by a competitive affiliate in a manner that favors a competitive affiliate; or

(B) allow a competitive affiliate, before September 1, 2005, to use the utility's corporate name, trademark, brand, or logo unless the competitive affiliate includes on employee business cards and in its advertisements of specific services to existing or potential residential or small commercial customers locating within the utility's certificated service area a disclaimer that states, "(Name of competitive affiliate) is not the same company as (name of utility) and is not regulated by the Public Utility Commission of Texas, and you do not have to buy (name of competitive affiliate)'s products to continue to receive quality regulated services from (name of utility).";

(6) a utility does not conduct joint advertising or promotional activities with a competitive affiliate in a manner that favors the competitive affiliate;

(7) a utility is a separate, independent entity from any competitive affiliates and, except as provided by Subdivisions (8) and (9), does not share employees, facilities, information, or other resources, other than permissible corporate support services, with those competitive affiliates unless the utility can prove to the commission that the sharing will not compromise the public interest;

(8) a utility's office space is physically separated from the office space of the utility's competitive affiliates by being located in separate buildings or, if within the same building, by a method such as having the offices on separate floors or with separate access, unless otherwise approved by the commission;

(9) a utility and a competitive affiliate:

(A) may, to the extent the utility implements adequate safeguards precluding employees of a competitive affiliate from gaining access to information in a manner inconsistent with Subsection (g) or (i), share common officers and directors, property, equipment, offices to the extent consistent with Subdivision (8), credit, investment, or financing arrangements to the extent consistent with Subdivision (17), computer systems, information systems, and corporate support services; and

(B) are not required to enter into prior written contracts or competitive solicitations for non-tariffed transactions between the utility and the competitive affiliate, except that the commission by rule may require the utility and the competitive affiliate to enter into prior written contracts or competitive solicitations for certain classes of transactions, other than corporate support services, that have a per unit value of more than $75,000 or that total more than $1 million;

(10) a utility does not temporarily assign, for less than one year, employees engaged in transmission or distribution system operations to a competitive affiliate unless the employee does not have knowledge of information that is intended to be protected under this section;

(11) a utility does not subsidize the business activities of an affiliate with revenues from a regulated service;

(12) a utility and its affiliates fully allocate costs for any shared services, corporate support services, and other items described by Subdivisions (8) and (9);

(13) a utility and its affiliates keep separate books of accounts and records and the commission may review records relating to a transaction between a utility and an affiliate;

(14) assets transferred or services provided between a utility and an affiliate, other than transfers that facilitate unbundling under Section 39.051 or asset valuation under Section 39.262, are priced at a level that is fair and reasonable to the customers of the utility and reflects the market value of the assets or services or the utility's fully allocated cost to provide those assets or services;

(15) regulated services that a utility provides on a routine or recurring basis are included in a tariff that is subject to commission approval;

(16) each transaction between a utility and a competitive affiliate is conducted at arm's length; and

(17) a utility does not allow an affiliate to obtain credit under an arrangement that would include a specific pledge of assets in the rate base of the utility or a pledge of cash reasonably necessary for utility operations.

(e) The commission shall by rule establish a code of conduct that must be observed by electric cooperatives and municipally owned utilities and their affiliates to protect against anticompetitive practices. The rules adopted by the commission under this subsection shall be consistent with Chapters 40 and 41 and may not be more restrictive than the rules adopted under Subsection (d).

(f) Following review of the annual reports submitted to it under Sections 39.155(b) and (c), the commission shall determine whether specific transmission or distribution constraints or bottlenecks within this state give rise to market power in specific geographic markets in the state. The commission, on a finding that specific transmission or distribution constraints or bottlenecks within this state give rise to market power, may order reasonable mitigation of that potential market power by ordering, under Section 39.203(e), one or more electric utilities or transmission and distribution utilities to construct additional transmission or distribution capacity, or both, subject to the certification provisions of this title.

(g) The sharing of corporate support services in accordance with this section may not allow or provide a means for the transfer of confidential information from a utility to an affiliate, create the opportunity for preferential treatment or an unfair competitive advantage, lead to customer confusion, or create significant opportunities for cross-subsidization of affiliates.

(h) A utility or competitive affiliate may not circumvent the provisions or the intent of the provisions of Subsection (d) by using any utility affiliate to provide information, services, or subsidies between the utility and a competitive affiliate.

(i) In this section:

(1) "Competitive affiliate" means an affiliate of a utility that provides services or sells products in a competitive energy-related market in this state, including telecommunications services, to the extent those services are energy related.

(2) "Corporate support services" means services shared by a utility, its parent holding company, or a separate affiliate created to perform corporate support services, with its affiliates of joint corporate oversight, governance, support systems, and personnel. Examples of services that may be shared, to the extent the services comply with the requirements prescribed by Subsections (d) and (g), include human resources, procurement, information technology, regulatory services, administrative services, real estate services, legal services, accounting, environmental services, research and development, internal audit, community relations, corporate communications, financial services, financial planning and management support, corporate services, corporate secretary, lobbying, and corporate planning. Examples of services that may not be shared include engineering, purchasing of electric transmission, transmission and distribution system operations, and marketing.

Added by Acts 1999, 76th Leg., ch. 405, § 39, eff. Sept. 1, 1999. Amended by Acts 2011, 82nd Leg., ch. 996 (H.B. 2133), § 7, eff. Sept. 1, 2011.

§ 39.158. Mergers and Consolidations

(a) An owner of electric generation facilities that offers electricity for sale in the state and proposes to merge, consolidate, or otherwise become affiliated with another owner of electric generation facilities that offers electricity for sale in this state shall obtain the approval of the commission before closing if the electricity offered for sale in the power region by the merged, consolidated, or affiliated entity will exceed one percent of the total electricity for sale in the power region. The approval shall be requested at least 120 days before the date of the proposed closing. The commission shall approve the transaction unless the commission finds that the transaction results in a violation of Section 39.154. If the commission finds that the transaction as proposed would violate Section 39.154, the commission may condition approval of the transaction on adoption of reasonable modifications to the transaction as prescribed by the commission to mitigate potential market power abuses.

(b) Nothing in this chapter shall be construed to confer immunity from state or federal antitrust laws. This chapter is intended to complement other state and federal antitrust provisions. Therefore, antitrust remedies may also be sought in state or federal court to remedy anticompetitive activities.

(c) This section may not be deemed to authorize commission review or approval of transactions entered into between or among municipally owned utilities, river authorities, special districts created by law, or other political subdivisions, whether or not those transactions may be characterized as mergers, consolidations, or other affiliations, when the transaction is authorized or structured under state law.

(d) Notwithstanding any other provision of this title, an electric utility which, before the effective date of this chapter, entered into a stipulation or agreement in support of approval of a merger which was approved by the commission on or after January 1, 1996, requiring the utility to pass through to ratepayers the savings resulting from the merger of that utility with another utility shall continue to be bound by the terms of that stipulation or agreement. The commission shall ensure that the pass-through of all merger savings required under any such stipulation or agreement shall be fully implemented during the freeze period and shall be reflected in setting the price to beat for that utility.

Added by Acts 1999, 76th Leg., ch. 405, § 39, eff. Sept. 1, 1999.

SUBCHAPTER E. PRICE REGULATION AFTER COMPETITION

§ 39.201. Cost of Service Tariffs and Charges

(a) Each electric utility shall, on or before April 1, 2000, file proposed tariffs for its proposed transmission and distribution utility.

(b) The filing under this section shall include supporting cost data for determination of nonbypassable delivery charges, which shall be the sum of:

(1) transmission and distribution utility charges by customer class based on a forecasted 2002 test year;

(2) a system benefit fund fee; and

(3) an expected competition transition charge, if any.

(c) Each electric utility shall also identify the unbundled generation and retail energy service costs by customer class.

(d) In accordance with a schedule and procedures it establishes, the commission shall hold a hearing and approve or modify and make effective as of January 1, 2002, the transmission and distribution utility's proposed tariffs for transmission and distribution services, the system benefit fund fee, and the expected competition transition charge as determined under Subsections (g) and (h) and as implemented under Subsections (i)–(*l*), if any.

(e) The system benefit fund fee shall be that established by the commission under Section 39.903.

(f) The expected competition transition charge shall be that as determined under Subsections (g) and (h) and as implemented under Subsections (i)–(*l*).

(g) The expected competition transition charge approved by the commission shall be calculated from the amount of stranded costs as defined in Subchapter F[1] that are reasonably projected to exist on the last day of the freeze period modified to reflect any adjustments determined appropriate by the commission under Section 39.261(c).

(h) The electric utility shall use the ECOM administrative model referenced in Section 39.262 to determine estimated stranded costs. The model must include updated company-specific inputs. Natural gas prices used in the model must be market-based natural gas forward prices, where available. Growth rates in generating plant operations and maintenance costs and allocated administrative and general costs shall be benchmarked by comparing those costs to the best available information on cost trends for comparable generating plants. Capital additions shall be benchmarked using the limitation in Section 39.259(b).

(i) An electric utility may:

(1) at any time after the start of the freeze period, securitize 100 percent of its regulatory assets as defined by Section 39.302 and up to 75 percent of its estimated stranded costs as defined by this section and recover those charges through a transition charge, in accordance with a financing order issued by the commission under Section 39.303;

(2) implement, under bond, a nonbypassable charge of up to 100 percent of its estimated stranded costs; or

(3) use a combination of the two methods under Subdivisions (1) and (2).

(j) Any competition transition charge shall be allocated among retail customer classes according to Section 39.253.

(k) In determining the length of time over which stranded costs under Subsection (h) may be recovered, the commission shall consider:

(1) the electric utility's rates as of the end of the freeze period;

(2) the sum of the transmission and distribution charges and the system benefit fund fees;

(3) the proportion of estimated stranded costs to the invested capital of the electric utility; and

(4) any other factor consistent with the public interest as expressed in this chapter.

(*l*) Two years after customer choice is introduced, the stranded cost estimate under this section shall be reviewed and, if necessary, adjusted to reflect a final, actual valuation in the true-up proceeding under Section 39.262. If, based on that proceeding, the competition transition charge is not sufficient, the commission may extend the collection period for the charge or, if necessary, increase the charge. Alternatively, if it is found in the true-up proceeding that the competition transition charge is larger than is needed to recover any remaining stranded costs, the commission may:

(1) reduce the competition transition charge, to the extent it has not been securitized;

(2) reverse, in whole or in part, the depreciation expense that has been redirected under Section 39.256;

(3) reduce the transmission and distribution utility's rates; or

(4) implement a combination of the elements in Subdivisions (1)–(3).

Added by Acts 1999, 76th Leg., ch. 405, § 39, eff. Sept. 1, 1999.

[1] V.T.C.A., Utilities Code § 39.251.

§ 39.202. Price to Beat

(a) From January 1, 2002, until January 1, 2007, an affiliated retail electric provider shall make available to residential and small commercial customers of its affiliated transmission and distribution utility rates that, on a bundled basis, are six percent less than the affiliated electric utility's corresponding average residential and small commercial rates, on a bundled basis, that were in effect on January 1, 1999, adjusted to reflect the fuel factor determined as provided by Subsection (b) and adjusted for any base rate reduction as stipulated to by an electric utility in a proceeding for which a final order had not been issued by January 1, 1999. These rates on a bundled basis shall be known as the "price to beat" for residential and small commercial customers, except that the "price to beat" for a utility is the rate in effect as a result of a settlement approved by the commission after January 1, 1999, if the commission determines that base rates for that utility have been reduced by more than 12 percent as a result of a final order issued by the commission after October 1, 1998.

(b) The commission shall determine the fuel factor for each electric utility as of December 31, 2001.

(c) After the date of customer choice, each affiliated power generation company shall file a final fuel reconciliation for the period ending the day before the date customer choice is introduced. The final fuel balance from that reconciliation shall be included in the true-up proceeding under Section 39.262.

(d) An affiliated retail electric provider shall make public its price to beat in a manner that provides adequate disclosure as determined by the commission.

(e) The affiliated retail electric provider may not charge rates for residential or small commercial customers that are different from the price to beat until the earlier of 36 months after the date customer choice is introduced or:

(1) for service to residential customers, the date the commission determines that 40 percent or more of the electric power consumed by residential customers within the affiliated transmission and distribution utility's certificated service area before the onset of customer choice is committed to be served by nonaffiliated retail electric providers; or

(2) for service to small commercial customers, the date the commission determines that 40 percent or more of the electric power consumed by small commercial customers within the affiliated transmission and distribution utility's certificated service area before the onset of customer choice is committed to be served by nonaffiliated retail electric providers.

(f) Notwithstanding Subsection (e), the affiliated retail electric provider may charge rates that are different from the price to beat for service to aggregated loads of nonresidential customers having an aggregated peak demand greater than 1,000 kilowatts, provided that all affected customers are:

(1) commonly owned; or

(2) franchisees of the same franchisor.

(g) The affiliated retail electric provider may not encourage or provide an incentive to a customer to switch to a nonaffiliated retail electric provider, promote any nonaffiliated retail electric provider, or exchange customers with any nonaffiliated retail electric provider to comply with the requirements of Subsection (e)(1) or (2).

(h) The following standards shall be used for measuring electric power consumption during the period before the onset of customer choice:

(1) the consumption of residential and small commercial customers with an annual peak demand less than or equal to 20 kilowatts shall be based on the average annual consumption of those respective groups during the year 2000;

(2) consumption for all small commercial customers with an annual peak demand larger than 20 kilowatts shall be based on each customer's usage during the year 2000; and

(3) for purposes of determining whether an affiliated retail electric provider has met the requirements of Subsection (e)(2), the aggregated loads of nonresidential customers having a peak demand greater than 1,000 kilowatts that are served by the affiliated retail electric provider at a rate different from the price to beat under Subsection (f) shall be deducted from the electric power consumption of small commercial customers during the period before the onset of customer choice.

(i) For purposes of Subsection (h)(2), if less than 12 months of consumption history exists for any such customer, the usage history shall be supplemented with the prior history of that customer's location. For service to a new location, the annual consumption shall be determined as the transmission and distribution utility's estimate of the maximum annual kilowatt demand used in sizing the electric service to that customer multiplied by 8,760 hours, and that product multiplied by the average annual customer load factor for small commercial customers with loads greater than 20 kilowatts for the year 2000.

(j) On determining that its affiliated retail electric provider has met the requirements of Subsection (e)(1) or (2), an electric utility or a transmission and distribution utility shall make a filing with the commission attesting to the fact that those requirements have been met and that the restrictions of Subsection (e)(1) or (2) and the true-up in Section 39.262(e) are no longer applicable. The commission shall adopt appropriate procedures to enable it to accept or reject the filing within 30 days.

(k) Following the true-up proceedings conducted under Section 39.262, the commission may adjust the price to beat.

(*l*) An affiliated retail electric provider may request that the commission adjust the fuel factor established under Subsection (b) not more than twice a year if the affiliated retail electric provider demonstrates that the existing fuel factor does not adequately reflect significant changes in the market price of natural gas and purchased energy used to serve retail customers.

(m) In a power region outside of ERCOT, if customer choice is introduced before the requirements of Section 39.152(a) are met, an affiliated retail electric provider shall charge rates to customers other than residential and small commercial customers that are no higher than the rates that, on a bundled basis, were in effect on January 1, 1999, adjusted to reflect the fuel factor as provided by Subsection (b) and adjusted for any base rate reduction as stipulated to by an electric utility in a proceeding for which a final order had not been issued by January 1, 1999.

(n) Notwithstanding Subsection (a), in a power region outside of ERCOT, if customer choice is introduced before the requirements of Section 39.152(a) are met, an affiliated retail electric provider shall continue to offer the price to beat to residential and small commercial customers, unless the price is changed by the commission in accordance with this chapter, until the later of 60 months after the date customer choice is introduced or the requirements of Section 39.152(a) are met.

(*o*) In this section, "small commercial customer" means a commercial customer having a peak demand of 1,000 kilowatts or less.

(p) On finding that a retail electric provider will be unable to maintain its financial integrity if it complies with Subsection (a), the commission shall set the retail electric provider's price to beat at the minimum level that will allow the retail electric provider to maintain its financial integrity. However, in no event shall the price to beat exceed the level of rates, on a bundled basis, charged by the affiliated electric utility on September 1, 1999, adjusted for fuel as provided by Subsection (b).

Added by Acts 1999, 76th Leg., ch. 405, § 39, eff. Sept. 1, 1999.

§ 39.203. Transmission and Distribution Service

(a) All transmission and distribution utilities shall provide transmission service at wholesale under Subchapter A, Chapter 35. In addition, on and after January 1, 2002, a transmission and distribution utility shall provide transmission or distribution service, or both, at retail to an electric utility, a retail electric provider, a municipally owned utility, an electric cooperative, or an end-use customer at rates, terms of access, and conditions that are comparable to those that apply to the transmission and distribution utility and its affiliates. A municipally owned utility offering customer choice or an electric cooperative offering customer choice shall likewise provide transmission or distribution service, or both, at retail to all such entities in accordance with the commission's rules applicable to terms and conditions of access and at rates adopted in accordance with Sections 40.055(a)(1) and 41.055(1), respectively.

(b) When necessary to serve a wholesale customer an electric utility, an electric cooperative that has not opted for customer choice, or a municipally owned utility that has not opted for customer choice shall provide wholesale transmission service at distribution voltage. A customer of a municipally owned utility that has not opted for customer choice or of an electric cooperative that has not opted for customer choice may not claim the status of a wholesale customer or be designated as a wholesale customer if the customer is being or has been served under a retail rate schedule of the municipally owned utility or electric cooperative.

(c) On or before January 1, 2002, the commission shall establish for all retail electric utilities offering customer choice reasonable and comparable terms and conditions, in accordance with Section 39.201, that comply with Subsection (a) for open access on distribution facilities and shall establish, for all retail electric utilities offering customer choice other than municipally owned utilities and electric cooperatives, reasonable and comparable rates for open access on distribution facilities.

(d) The terms of access, conditions, and rates established under Subsection (c) shall be comparable to the terms of access, conditions, and rates that the electric utility applies to itself or its affiliates. The rules shall also provide that all ancillary services provided by the utility to itself or its affiliates are also available to third parties on request on a nondiscriminatory basis.

(e) The commission may require an electric utility or a transmission and distribution utility to construct or enlarge facilities to ensure safe and reliable service for the state's electric markets and to reduce transmission constraints within ERCOT in a cost-effective manner where the constraints are such that they are not being resolved through Chapter 37 or the ERCOT transmission planning process. The commission shall require an electric utility or a transmission and distribution utility to construct or enlarge transmission or transmission-related facilities for the purpose of meeting the goal for generating capacity from renewable energy technologies under Section 39.904(a). In any proceeding brought under Chapter 37, an electric utility or transmission and distribution utility ordered to construct or enlarge facilities under this subchapter need not prove that the construction ordered is necessary for the service, accommodation, convenience, or safety of the public and need not address the factors listed in Sections 37.056(c)(1)–(3) and (4)(E). Notwithstanding any other law, including Section 37.057, in any proceeding brought under Chapter 37 by an electric utility or a transmission and distribution utility related to an application for a certificate of public convenience and necessity to construct or enlarge transmission or transmission-related facilities under this subsection, the commission shall issue a final order before the 181st day after the date the application is filed with the commission. If the commission does not issue a final order before that date, the application is approved.

(f) The commission's rules must be consistent with the standards of this title and may not be contrary to an applicable decision, rule, or policy statement of a federal regulatory agency having jurisdiction.

(g) Each power region shall have generally applicable tariffs approved by the commission or a federal regulatory agency having jurisdiction that guarantees open and nondiscriminatory access as required by Section 39.152. This subsection may not be deemed to vest in the commission power to set or approve distribution access rates of a municipally owned utility or an electric cooperative that has adopted customer choice.

(h) A customer in a multiply certificated service area may switch its retail distribution service provider among certificated retail electric utilities only by disconnecting from the facilities of one retail electric utility and connecting to the facilities of another retail electric utility.

Added by Acts 1999, 76th Leg., ch. 405, § 39, eff. Sept. 1, 1999. Amended by Acts 2003, 78th Leg., ch. 295, § 3, eff. June 18, 2003; Acts 2005, 79th Leg., 1st C.S., ch. 1, § 2, eff. Sept. 1, 2005.

§ 39.204. Tariffs for Open Access

Each transmission and distribution utility shall file a tariff implementing the open access rules with the commission or the federal regulatory authority having jurisdiction over the transmission and distribution service of the utility not later than the 90th day before the date customer choice is offered by that utility.

Added by Acts 1999, 76th Leg., ch. 405, § 39, eff. Sept. 1, 1999.

§ 39.205. Regulation of Costs Following Freeze Period

At the conclusion of the freeze period, any remaining costs associated with nuclear decommissioning obligations continue to be subject to cost of service rate regulation and shall be included as a nonbypassable charge to retail customers. The commission may adopt rules necessary to ensure that money for decommissioning is prudently collected, managed, and spent for its intended purpose and that money that remains unspent after decommissioning is completed is returned to retail customers.

Added by Acts 1999, 76th Leg., ch. 405, § 39, eff. Sept. 1, 1999. Amended by Acts 2005, 79th Leg., ch. 121, § 2, eff. Sept. 1, 2005.

§ 39.206. Nuclear Generating Unit Decommissioning Cost Plan

(a) For purposes of this section:

(1) "Decommissioning" includes decommissioning and decontamination of a nuclear generating unit consistent with federal Nuclear Regulatory Commission requirements.

(2) "Nuclear decommissioning trust" means an external and irrevocable trust created for the purpose of funding decommissioning obligations for a nuclear generating unit, consistent with federal Nuclear Regulatory Commission requirements.

(3) "Nuclear generating unit" means an electric generating facility that uses nuclear energy to generate electricity for sale and is licensed by the

Nuclear Regulatory Commission and was under construction in this state after January 1, 2007, but before January 1, 2015.

(4) "Power generation company" has the meaning assigned by Section 31.002.

(5) "Retail electric customer" means a retail electric customer:

(A) in a geographic area of this state in which retail customer choice has been implemented; or

(B) of a municipally owned utility or electric cooperative that has an agreement to purchase power from a nuclear generating unit.

(b) This section applies only to the first six nuclear generation units under construction by January 1, 2015, owned in whole or in part by a power generation company that elects to utilize the decommissioning mechanism set forth in this section.

(c) Nothing in this section shall be construed to require a power generation company to use a commission approved method to provide funds for decommissioning, if the power generation company can otherwise satisfy the decommissioning financial assurance requirements of the federal Nuclear Regulatory Commission.

(d) A power generation company that owns a nuclear generating unit shall fund out of operating revenues on an annual basis:

(1) the costs associated with funding the decommissioning obligations for the nuclear generating unit; or

(2) the power generation company's portion of the decommissioning costs for the nuclear generating unit in proportion to the company's ownership interest in the nuclear generating unit if the unit is owned by more than one person.

(e) The obligation to fund a nuclear decommissioning trust fund is not dischargeable in bankruptcy.

(f) A power generation company shall establish a nuclear decommissioning trust for a nuclear generating unit it owns or for the proportionate share of a nuclear generating unit of which it owns a part. The funding obligations for the trust must begin before the nuclear generating unit commences its initial fuel load and begins commercial operation to generate power for sale. The terms of the trust must be consistent with trust terms and conditions the federal Nuclear Regulatory Commission requires for providing financial assurance for decommissioning.

(g) The commission by order shall establish for a nuclear generating unit the amount of annual decommissioning funding necessary to meet the decommissioning obligations for the nuclear generating unit over the unit's operating license period as established by the federal Nuclear Regulatory Commission or over a shorter period of time at the election of the power generation company. The power generation company shall perform a study on the cost of decommissioning to establish the decommissioning obligations before the nuclear generating unit begins commercial operation to generate power for sale. The study shall be performed by the power generation company at least once in each three-year period during the unit's operating license period using the most current reasonably available information on the cost of decommissioning. The commission shall conduct a proceeding at least once in each three-year period to review the study and other current reasonably available information on the cost of decommissioning and determine the reasonableness of the study.

(h) A power generation company shall file an annual report to provide the status of the decommissioning trust fund and to update the commission as to its ability to fund the decommissioning trust fund. In determining the amount of the annual decommissioning funding under this subsection, at least once in each three-year period, the commission shall conduct a proceeding to review the balance of each nuclear decommissioning trust and the projected amount of annual decommissioning funding for the associated nuclear generating unit. On the conclusion of the review proceeding, the commission by order shall revise the amount of annual funding for the nuclear generating unit in order to ensure that the nuclear decommissioning trust fund is adequately funded.

(i) A power generation company shall remit the appropriate amount of annual decommissioning funding to the nuclear decommissioning trust created for its proportionate ownership position in a nuclear generating unit in accordance with the commission's funding order issued under Subsection (g) or (h). The commission shall take appropriate actions to ensure proper funding of the nuclear decommissioning trust, including possibly terminating the power generation company's registration to operate, if the company violates this subsection.

(j) A power generation company that owns a nuclear generating unit is the funds administrator of the nuclear decommissioning trust for the associated nuclear generating unit. The company, as funds administrator, shall invest the trust funds in accordance with guidelines established by commission rule and consistent with the federal Nuclear Regulatory Commission guidelines so that the decommissioning funds, plus the amounts earned from investment of the funds, will be available at the time of decommissioning. The commission shall adopt rules to define the company's specific duties as funds administrator and requirements regarding prudent management and investment of nuclear decommissioning trust funds.

(k) The commission shall adopt rules necessary to ensure that:

(1) a power generation company remits sufficient funds to a nuclear decommissioning trust on an annual basis, including projected earnings to approximate the amount remaining to be accumulated to cover the cost of decommissioning a nuclear generating unit at the end of its operating license period divided by the remaining years of the license and in accordance with applicable state and federal laws and regulations or over a shorter period of time at the election of the power generation company;

(2) the periodic cost studies and reviews described in Subsections (g) and (h) include all current reasonably available information as determined necessary and appropriate by the commission;

(3) all funds remitted to a nuclear decommissioning trust are prudently managed and spent for their intended purpose;

(4) the funds remitted to a nuclear decommissioning trust and the amounts earned from investing the funds, will be available for, and restricted to the purpose of decommissioning of the associated nuclear generating unit, including if the trust or nuclear generating unit is transferred to another person; and

(5) before a power generation company is allowed to take advantage of the mechanisms in this section, the company meets creditworthiness standards established by the commission to minimize the risk that retail electric customers will be responsible for funding any shortfall in the cost of decommissioning a nuclear generating unit.

(*l*) In addition to the nuclear decommissioning trust required by Subsection (f), for purposes of Subsection (k), the power generation company and its parent and affiliates shall provide financial assurances that funds will be available to satisfy up to 16 years of annual decommissioning funding in the event the power generation company defaults on its obligation to make annual funding to the decommissioning trust. Within 180 days after the effective date of this section, the commission by rule shall establish the acceptable forms of financial assurance, which shall include, but not be limited to, parent guarantees and support agreements, letters of credit, surety or insurance, and such other requirements necessary to ensure compliance with this section. In establishing the acceptable forms of assurance, and the eligibility requirements for each form of assurance, the commission shall consider the relative risk factors and creditworthiness attributes of potential applicant financial characteristics in order to minimize exposure of retail electric customers to default by power generation companies under this section. The power generation company may choose the manner of financial assurance for which it is eligible under the commission's rules.

(m) In the event the financial assurances provided by Subsection (k) are insufficient to meet the annual funding requirements of the decommissioning trust, the retail electric customers shall be responsible for funding any shortfall in the cost of decommissioning the nuclear generating unit.

(n) The commission shall determine the manner in which any shortfall in the cost of decommissioning a nuclear generating unit shall be recovered from retail electric customers in the state, consistent with law.

(*o*) For retail electric customers of a municipally owned utility or an electric cooperative that has an agreement to purchase power from a nuclear generating unit, the amount of the shortfall in the cost of decommissioning the nuclear generating unit that the customers are responsible for is limited to a portion of that shortfall that bears the same proportion to the total shortfall as the amount of electric power generated by the nuclear generating unit and purchased by the municipally owned utility or electric cooperative bears to the total amount of power the nuclear generating unit generated.

(p) If retail electric customers in this state become responsible for the costs of decommissioning a nuclear generating unit and incur costs under this section and the nuclear generating unit is operational, as a condition of operating the generating unit, the power generation company or any new owner shall repay the costs the electric customers incurred in the manner determined by the commission. The commission may authorize the repayment to occur over a period established by the commission.

(q) The commission shall, in conjunction with the Nuclear Regulatory Commission, investigate the development of a mechanism whereby the State of Texas could ensure that funds for decommissioning will be obtained when necessary in the same manner as if the State of Texas were the licensee under federal law. The commission shall file legislative recommendations regarding any changes in law that may be necessary to carry out the purposes of this subsection prior to January 15, 2009, which may be combined with the report required by Section 31.003.

(r) The commission by rule shall ensure that:

(1) money for decommissioning a nuclear generating unit is prudently collected, managed, and spent for its intended purposes; and

(2) decommissioning money that remains unspent after decommissioning of the nuclear generating unit is complete is returned to the power generation company and the retail electric customers based on the proportionate amount of money the power generation company and retail electric customers paid into the fund.

Added by Acts 2007, 80th Leg., ch. 1019, § 1, eff. Sept. 1, 2007.

SUBCHAPTER F. RECOVERY OF STRANDED COSTS THROUGH COMPETITION TRANSITION CHARGE

§ 39.251. Definitions

In this subchapter:

(1) "Above market purchased power costs" means wholesale demand and energy costs that a utility is obligated to pay under an existing purchased power contract to the extent the costs are greater than the purchased power market value.

(2) "Existing purchased power contract" means a purchased power contract in effect on January 1, 1999, including any amendments and revisions to that contract resulting from litigation initiated before January 1, 1999.

(3) "Generation assets" means all assets associated with the production of electricity, including generation plants, electrical interconnections of the generation plant to the transmission system, fuel contracts, fuel transportation contracts, water contracts, lands, surface or subsurface water rights, emissions-related allowances, and gas pipeline interconnections.

(4) "Market value" means, for nonnuclear assets and certain nuclear assets, the value the assets would have if bought and sold in a bona fide third-party transaction or transactions on the open market under Section 39.262(h) or, for certain nuclear assets, as described by Section 39.262(i), the value determined under the method provided by that subsection.

(5) "Purchased power market value" means the value of demand and energy bought and sold in a bona fide third-party transaction or transactions on the open market and determined by using the weighted average costs of the highest three offers from the market for purchase of the demand and energy available under the existing purchased power contracts.

(6) "Retail stranded costs" means that part of net stranded cost associated with the provision of retail service.

(7) "Stranded cost" means the positive excess of the net book value of generation assets over the market value of the assets, taking into account all of the electric utility's generation assets, any above market purchased power costs, and any deferred debit related to a utility's discontinuance of the application of Statement of Financial Accounting Standards No. 71 ("Accounting for the Effects of Certain Types of Regulation") for generation-related assets if required by the provisions of this chapter. For purposes of Section 39.262, book value shall be established as of December 31, 2001, or the date a market value is established through a market valuation method under Section 39.262(h), whichever is earlier, and shall include stranded costs incurred under Section 39.263.

Added by Acts 1999, 76th Leg., ch. 405, § 39, eff. Sept. 1, 1999.

§ 39.252. Right to Recover Stranded Costs

(a) An electric utility is allowed to recover all of its net, verifiable, nonmitigable stranded costs incurred in purchasing power and providing electric generation service.

(b)(1) Recovery of retail stranded costs by an electric utility shall be from all existing or future retail customers, including the facilities, premises, and loads of those retail customers, within the utility's geographical certificated service area as it existed on May 1, 1999. A retail customer may not avoid stranded cost recovery charges by switching to new on-site generation except as provided by Section 39.262(k). For purposes of this subchapter, "new on-site generation" means electric generation capacity greater than 10 megawatts capable of being lawfully delivered to the site without use of utility distribution or transmission facilities and which was not, on or before December 31, 1999, either:

(A) a fully operational facility; or

(B) a project supported by substantially complete filings for all necessary site-specific environmental permits under the rules of the Texas Natural Resource Conservation Commission in effect at the time of filing.

(2) If a customer commences taking energy from new on-site generation which materially reduces the customer's use of energy delivered through the utility's facilities, the customer shall pay an amount each month computed by multiplying the output of the on-site generation by the new sum of competition transition charges under Section 39.201 and transition charges under Subchapter G which are in effect during that month. Payment shall be made to the utility, its successors, an assignee, or other collection agent responsible for collecting the competition transition charges and transition charges and shall be collected in addition to the competition transition charges and transition charges applicable to energy actually delivered to the customer through the utility's facilities.

(c) In multiply certificated areas, a retail customer may not avoid stranded cost recovery charges by switching to another electric utility, electric cooperative, or municipally owned utility after May 1, 1999. A customer in a multiply certificated service area that requested to switch providers on or before May 1, 1999, or was not taking service from an electric utility on May 1, 1999, and does not do so after that date is not responsible for paying retail stranded costs of that utility.

(d) An electric utility shall pursue commercially reasonable means to reduce its potential stranded costs, including good faith attempts to renegotiate above-cost fuel and purchased power contracts or the exercise of normal business practices to protect the value of its assets. The commission shall consider the utility's efforts under this subsection when determining the amount of the utility's stranded costs; provided, however, that nothing in this section authorizes the commission to substitute its judgment for a market valuation of generation assets determined under Sections 39.262(h) and (i).

Added by Acts 1999, 76th Leg., ch. 405, § 39, eff. Sept. 1, 1999.

§ 39.253. Allocation of Stranded Costs

(a) Any capital costs incurred by an electric utility to improve air quality under Section 39.263 or 39.264 that are included in a utility's invested capital in accordance with those sections shall be allocated among customer classes as follows:

(1) 50 percent of those costs shall be allocated in accordance with the methodology used to allocate the costs of the underlying assets in the electric utility's most recent commission order addressing rate design; and

(2) the remainder shall be allocated on the basis of the energy consumption of the customer classes.

(b) All other retail stranded costs shall be allocated among retail customer classes in accordance with Subsections (c)–(i).

(c) The allocation to the residential class shall be determined by allocating to all customer classes 50 percent of the stranded costs in accordance with the methodology used to allocate the costs of the underlying assets in the electric utility's most recent commission order addressing rate design and allocating the remainder of the stranded costs on the basis of the energy consumption of the classes.

(d) After the allocation to the residential class required by Subsection (c) has been calculated, the remaining stranded costs shall be allocated to the remaining customer classes in accordance with the methodology used to allocate the costs of the underlying assets in the electric utility's most recent commission order addressing rate design. Non-firm industrial customers shall be allocated stranded costs equal to 150 percent of the amount allocated to that class.

(e) After the allocation to the residential class required by Subsection (c) and the allocation to the nonfirm industrial class required by Subsection (d) have been calculated, the remaining stranded costs shall be allocated to the remaining customer classes in accordance with the methodology used to allocate the costs of the underlying assets in the electric utility's most recent commission order addressing rate design.

(f) Notwithstanding any other provision of this section, to the extent that the total retail stranded costs, including regulatory assets, of investor-owned utilities exceed $5 billion on a statewide basis, any stranded costs in excess of $5 billion shall be allocated among retail customer classes in accordance with the methodology used to allocate the costs of the underlying assets in the electric utility's most recent commission order addressing rate design.

(g) The energy consumption of the customer classes used in Subsections (a)(2) and (c) shall be based on the relevant class characteristics as of May 1, 1999, adjusted for normal weather conditions.

(h) For purposes of this section, "stranded costs" includes regulatory assets.

(i) Except as provided by Section 39.262(k), no customer or customer class may avoid the obligation to pay the amount of stranded costs allocated to that customer class.

Added by Acts 1999, 76th Leg., ch. 405, § 39, eff. Sept. 1, 1999.

§ 39.254. Use of Revenues for Utilities With Stranded Costs

This subchapter provides a number of tools to an electric utility to mitigate stranded costs. Each electric utility that was reported by the commission to have positive "excess costs over market" (ECOM), denoted as the "base case" for the amount of stranded costs before full retail competition in 2002 with respect to its Texas jurisdiction, in the April 1998 Report to the Texas Senate Interim Committee on Electric Utility Restructuring entitled "Potentially Strandable Investment (ECOM) Report: 1998 Update," must use these tools to reduce the net book value of, otherwise referred to as "accelerate" the cost recovery of, its stranded costs each year. Any positive difference under the report required by Section 39.257(b) shall be applied to the net book value of generation assets.

Added by Acts 1999, 76th Leg., ch. 405, § 39, eff. Sept. 1, 1999.

§ 39.255. Use of Revenues for Utilities With No Stranded Costs

(a) An electric utility that does not have stranded costs described by Section 39.254 shall be permitted to use any positive difference under the report required by Section 39.257(b) on capital expenditures to improve or expand transmission or distribution facilities, or on capital expenditures to improve air quality, as approved by the commission. Any such capital expenditures shall be made in the calendar year immediately following the year for which the report required by Section 39.257 is calculated. The capital expenditures shall be reflected in any future proceeding under this chapter to set transmission or distribution rates as a reduction to the utility's transmission and distribution invested capital, as approved by the commission.

(b) To the extent that positive differences under the report required by Section 39.257(b) are not used for capital expenditures, the amounts shall be flowed back to the electric utility's Texas jurisdictional customers through the power cost recovery factor.

(c) This section applies only to the use of positive differences under the report required by Section 39.257(b) for each year during the freeze period.

Added by Acts 1999, 76th Leg., ch. 405, § 39, eff. Sept. 1, 1999.

§ 39.256. Option to Redirect Depreciation

(a) For the calendar years of 1998, 1999, 2000, and 2001, an electric utility described by Section 39.254 may redirect all or a part of the depreciation expense relating to transmission and distribution assets to its net generation plant assets.

(b) The electric utility shall report a decision under Subsection (a) to the commission and any other applicable regulatory authority.

(c) Any adjustments made to the book value of transmission and distribution assets or the creation of any related regulatory assets resulting from the redirection under this section shall be accepted and applied by the commission for establishing net invested capital and transmission and distribution rates for retail customers in all future proceedings.

(d) Notwithstanding Subsection (c), the design of post-freeze-period retail rates may not:

(1) shift the allocation of responsibility for stranded costs;

(2) include the adjusted costs in wholesale transmission and distribution rates; or

(3) apply the adjustments for the purpose of establishing net invested capital and transmission and distribution rates for wholesale customers.

Added by Acts 1999, 76th Leg., ch. 405, § 39, eff. Sept. 1, 1999.

§ 39.257. Annual Report

(a) Beginning with the 1999 calendar year, each electric utility shall file a report with the commission not later than 90 days after the end of each year during the freeze period under a schedule and a format determined by the commission.

(b) The report shall identify any positive difference between annual revenues, reduced by the amount of annual revenues under Sections 36.203 and 36.205, the revenues received under the interutility billing process as adopted by the commission to implement Sections

35.004, 35.006, and 35.007, revenues associated with transition charges as defined by Section 39.302, and annual costs.

Added by Acts 1999, 76th Leg., ch. 405, § 39, eff. Sept. 1, 1999.

§ 39.258. Annual Report: Determination of Annual Costs

For the purposes of determining the annual costs in each annual report, the following amounts shall be used:

(1) the lesser of:

(A) the utility's Texas jurisdictional operation and maintenance expense reflected in each utility's Federal Energy Regulatory Commission Form 1 of the report year, plus factoring expenses not included in operation and maintenance, adjusted for:

(i) costs under Sections 36.062, 36.203, and 36.205; and

(ii) revenues recorded under the interutility billing process adopted by the commission to implement Sections 35.004, 35.006, and 35.007; or

(B) the Texas jurisdictional operation and maintenance expense reflected in each utility's 1996 Federal Energy Regulatory Commission Form 1, plus factoring expenses not included in operation and maintenance, adjusted for:

(i) costs under Sections 36.062, 36.203, and 36.205, and not indexed for inflation;

(ii) any difference between the annual revenues and the expenses recorded under the interutility billing process adopted by the commission to implement Sections 35.004, 35.006, and 35.007; and

(iii) the annual percentage change in the average number of utility customers;

(2) the amount of nuclear decommissioning expense approved in the electric utility's last rate proceeding before the commission, as may be required to be adjusted to comply with applicable federal regulatory requirements;

(3) the depreciation rates approved in the electric utility's last rate proceeding before the commission;

(4) the amortization expense approved in the electric utility's last rate proceeding before the commission or in any other proceeding in which deferred costs and the amortization of those costs are established, except that if the items are fully amortized during the freeze period, the expense shall be adjusted accordingly;

(5) taxes and fees, including municipal franchise fees to the extent not included in Subdivision (1), other than federal income taxes, and assessments incurred that year;

(6) federal income tax expense, computed according to the stand-alone methodology and using the actual capital structure and actual cost of debt as of December 31 of the report year;

(7) return on invested capital, computed by multiplying invested capital as of December 31 of the report year, determined as provided by Section 39.259, by the cost of capital approved in the electric utility's most recent rate proceeding before the commission in which the cost of capital was specifically adopted, or, in the case of a range, the midpoint of the range, if the final rate order for the proceeding was issued on or after January 1, 1992, or if such an order does not exist, a cost of capital of 9.6 percent shall be used; and

(8) the amount resulting from any operation and maintenance expense savings tracker from a merger of two utilities and contained in a settlement agreement approved by the commission before January 1, 1999.

Added by Acts 1999, 76th Leg., ch. 405, § 39, eff. Sept. 1, 1999.

§ 39.259. Annual Report: Determination of Invested Capital

(a) For the purposes of determining invested capital in each annual report, the net plant in service, regulatory assets, and deferred federal income taxes shall be updated each year, and generation-related invested capital shall be reduced by the amount of securitization under Sections 39.201(i) and 39.262(c) to the extent otherwise included in invested capital.

(b) Capital additions to a plant in an amount less than 1½ percent of the electric utility's net plant in service on December 31, 1998, less plant items previously excluded by the commission, for each of the years 1999 through 2001 are presumed prudent.

(c) All other items in invested capital shall be as approved in the electric utility's last rate proceeding before the commission.

Added by Acts 1999, 76th Leg., ch. 405, § 39, eff. Sept. 1, 1999.

§ 39.260. Use of Generally Accepted Accounting Principles

(a) The definition and identification of invested capital and other terms used in this subchapter and

Subchapter G that affect the net book value of generation assets and the treatment of transactions performed under Section 35.035 and other transactions authorized by this title or approved by the regulatory authority that affect the net book value of generation assets during the freeze period shall be treated in accordance with generally accepted accounting principles as modified by regulatory accounting rules generally applicable to utilities.

(b) The principles and criteria described by Subsection (a), including the criteria for applicability of Statement of Financial Accounting Standards No. 71 ("Accounting for the Effects of Certain Types of Regulation"), shall be applied for purposes of this subchapter as they existed on January 1, 1999.

Added by Acts 1999, 76th Leg., ch. 405, § 39, eff. Sept. 1, 1999.

§ 39.261. Review of Annual Report

(a) The annual report filed under this subchapter is a public document and shall be reviewed by the staff of the commission and the office. Both staffs may review work papers and supporting documents and engage in discussions with the utility about the data underlying the reports.

(b) The staff of the commission and the office shall communicate in writing to an electric utility not later than the 180th day after the date the report is filed if they have any disagreements with the data or computations.

(c) The commission shall finalize and resolve any disagreements related to the annual report, consistent with the requirements of Section 39.258, as follows:

(1) for each calendar year, the commission shall finalize the annual report before establishing the competition transition charge under Section 39.201; and

(2) for each calendar year, the commission shall finalize the annual report and reflect the result as part of the true-up proceeding under Section 39.262.

Added by Acts 1999, 76th Leg., ch. 405, § 39, eff. Sept. 1, 1999.

§ 39.262. True-Up Proceeding

(a) An electric utility, together with its affiliated retail electric provider and its affiliated transmission and distribution utility, may not be permitted to overrecover stranded costs through the procedures established by this section or through the application of the measures provided by the other sections of this chapter.

(b) After the freeze period, an electric utility located in a power region that is not certified under Section 39.152 shall continue to file annual reports under Sections 39.257, 39.258, and 39.259 as if the freeze period remained in effect, until the time the power region qualifies as certified under Section 39.152. In addition, the commission staff and the office shall continue to review the annual reports as provided by Section 39.261.

(c) After January 10, 2004, at a schedule and under procedures to be determined by the commission, each transmission and distribution utility, its affiliated retail electric provider, and its affiliated power generation company shall jointly file to finalize stranded costs under Subsections (h) and (i) and reconcile those costs with the estimated stranded costs used to develop the competition transition charge in the proceeding held under Section 39.201. Any resulting difference shall be applied to the nonbypassable delivery rates of the transmission and distribution utility, except that at the utility's option, any or all of the amounts recovered under this section may be securitized under Subchapter G.

(d) The affiliated power generation company shall reconcile, and either credit or bill to the transmission and distribution utility, the net sum of:

(1) the former electric utility's final fuel balance determined under Section 39.202(c); and

(2) any difference between the price of power obtained through the capacity auctions under Sections 39.153 and 39.156 and the power cost projections that were employed for the same time period in the ECOM model to estimate stranded costs in the proceeding under Section 39.201.

(e) To the extent that the price to beat exceeded the market price of electricity, the affiliated retail electric provider shall reconcile and credit to the affiliated transmission and distribution utility any positive difference between the price to beat established under Section 39.202, reduced by the nonbypassable delivery charge established under Section 39.201, and the prevailing market price of electricity during the same time period. A reconciliation for the applicable customer class is not required under this subsection for an affiliated retail electric provider that satisfies the requirements of Section 39.202(e)(1) or (2) before the expiration of two years from the introduction of customer choice. If a reconciliation is required, in no event shall the amount credited exceed an amount equal to the number of residential or small commercial customers served by the affiliated transmission and distribution utility that are buying electricity from the affiliated retail electric provider at the price to beat on the second anniversary of the beginning of competition, minus the number of new customers obtained outside the service area, multiplied by $150.

(f) To the extent that any amount of regulatory assets included in a transition charge or competition transition charge exceeds the amount of regulatory assets approved in a rate order which became effective on or before September 1, 1999, the commission shall conduct a review during the true-up proceeding to determine whether such amounts were appropriately calculated and constituted reasonable and necessary costs pursuant to Subchapter B, Chapter 36.[2] If the commission finds that the amount of regulatory assets specified in Section 39.302(5) is subject to modification, a credit or other rate adjustment shall be made to the transmission and distribution utility's nonbypassable delivery rates; provided, however, that no adjustment may be made to a transition charge established under Subchapter G.[1]

(g) Based on the credits or bills received from its affiliates under Subsections (d), (e), and (f), the transmission and distribution utility shall make necessary adjustments to the nonbypassable delivery rates it charges to retail electric providers. If the commission determines that the nonbypassable delivery rates are not sufficient, the commission may extend the original collection period for the charge or, if necessary, increase the charge. Alternatively, if the commission determines that the nonbypassable delivery rates are larger than are needed to recover the transmission and distribution utility's costs, the commission shall correspondingly reduce:

(1) the competition transition charge, to the extent it has not been securitized;

(2) the depreciation expense that has been redirected under Section 39.256;

(3) the transmission and distribution utility's rates; or

(4) a combination of the elements in Subdivisions (1)–(3).

(h) Except as provided in Subsection (i), for the purpose of finalizing the stranded cost estimate used to establish the competition transition charge under Section 39.201, the affiliated power generation company shall quantify its stranded costs using one or more of the following methods:

(1) Sale of Assets. If, at any time after December 31, 1999, an electric utility or its affiliated power generation company has sold some or all of its generation assets, which sale shall include all generating assets associated with each generating plant that is sold, in a bona fide third-party transaction under a competitive offering, the total net value realized from the sale establishes the market value of the generation assets sold. If not all assets are sold, the market value of the remaining generation assets shall be established by one or more of the other methods in this section.

(2) Stock Valuation Method. If, at any time after December 31, 1999, an electric utility or its affiliated power generation company has transferred some or all of its generation assets, including, at the election of the electric utility or power generation company, any fuel and fuel transportation contracts related to those assets, to one or more separate affiliated or nonaffiliated corporations, not less than 51 percent of the common stock of each corporation is spun off and sold to public investors through a national stock exchange, and the common stock has been traded for not less than one year, the resulting average daily closing price of the common stock over 30 consecutive trading days chosen by the commission out of the last 120 consecutive trading days before the filing required under Subsection (c) establishes the market value of the common stock equity in each transferee corporation. The book value of each transferee corporation's debt and preferred stock securities shall be added to the market value of its assets. The market value of each transferee corporation's assets shall be reduced by the corresponding net book value of the assets acquired by each transferee corporation from any entity other than the affiliated electric utility or power generation company. The resulting market value of the assets establishes the market value of the generation assets transferred by the electric utility or power generation company to each separate corporation. If not all assets are disposed of in this manner, the market value of the remaining assets shall be established by one or more of the other methods in this section.

(3) Partial Stock Valuation Method. If, at any time after December 31, 1999, an electric utility or its affiliated power generation company has transferred some or all of its generation assets, including, at the election of the electric utility or power generation company, any fuel and fuel transportation contracts related to those assets, to one or more separate affiliated or nonaffiliated corporations, at least 19 percent, but less than 51 percent, of the

common stock of each corporation is spun off and sold to public investors through a national stock exchange, and the common stock has been traded for not less than one year, the resulting average daily closing price of the common stock over 30 consecutive trading days chosen by the commission out of the last 120 consecutive trading days before the filing required under Subsection (c) shall be presumed to establish the market value of the common stock equity in each transferee corporation. The commission may accept the market valuation to conclusively establish the value of the common stock equity in each transferee corporation or convene a valuation panel of three independent financial experts to determine whether the percentage of common stock sold is fairly representative of the total common stock equity or whether a control premium exists for the retained interest. The valuation panel must consist of financial experts, chosen from proposals submitted in response to commission requests, from the top 10 nationally recognized investment banks with demonstrated experience in the United States electric industry as indicated by the dollar amount of public offerings of long-term debt and equity of United States investor-owned electric companies over the immediately preceding three years as ranked by the publications "Securities Data" or "Institutional Investor." If the panel determines that a control premium exists for the retained interest, the panel shall determine the amount of the control premium, and the commission shall adopt the determination but may not increase the market value by a control premium greater than 10 percent. The costs and expenses of the panel, as approved by the commission, shall be paid by each transferee corporation. The determination of the commission based on the finding of the panel conclusively establishes the value of the common stock of each transferee corporation. The book value of each transferee corporation's debt and preferred stock securities shall be added to the market value of its assets. The market value of each transferee corporation's assets shall be reduced by the corresponding net book value of the assets acquired by each transferee corporation from any entity other than the affiliated electric utility or power generation company. The resulting market value of the assets establishes the market value of the generation assets transferred by the electric utility or power generation company to each separate corporation.

(4) Exchange of Assets. If, at any time after December 31, 1999, an electric utility or its affiliated power generation company has transferred some or all of its generation assets, including any fuel and fuel transportation contracts related to those assets, in a bona fide third-party exchange transaction, the stranded costs related to the transferred assets shall be the difference between the book value and the market value of the transferred assets at the time of the exchange, taking into account any other consideration received or given. The market value of the transferred assets may be determined through an appraisal by a nationally recognized independent appraisal firm, if the market value is subject to a market valuation by means of an offer of sale in accordance with this subdivision. To obtain a market valuation by means of an offer of sale, the owner of the asset shall offer it for sale to other parties under procedures that provide broad public notice of the offer and a reasonable opportunity for other parties to bid on the asset. The owner of the asset may establish a reserve price for any offer based on the sum of the appraised value of the asset and the tax impact of selling the asset, as determined by the commission.

(i) Unless an electric utility or its affiliated power generation company combines all of its remaining generation assets into one or more transferee corporations as described in Subsections (h)(2) and (3), the electric utility shall quantify its stranded costs for nuclear assets using the ECOM method. The ECOM method is the estimation model prepared for and described by the commission's April 1998 Report to the Texas Senate Interim Committee on Electric Restructuring entitled "Potentially Strandable Investment (ECOM) Report: 1998 Update." The methodology used in the model must be the same as that used in the 1998 report to determine the "base case." At the time of the proceeding under this section, the ECOM model shall be rerun using updated company-specific inputs required by the model, updating the market price of electricity, and using updated natural gas price forecasts and the capacity cost based on the long-run marginal cost of the most economic new generation technology then available. Natural gas price projections used in the model must be market-based natural gas forward prices, where available. Growth rates in generating plant operations and maintenance costs and allocated administrative and general costs shall be benchmarked by comparing those costs to the best available information on cost trends for comparable generating plants. Capital additions shall be benchmarked using the limitation in Section 39.259(b).

(j) The commission shall issue a final order not later than the 150th day after the date of the filing under this section by the transmission and distribution utility, its affiliated retail electric provider, and its affiliated power generation company, and the resulting order shall be subject to judicial review under Chapter 2001, Government Code.

(k) Notwithstanding Section 39.252, to the extent that a customer's actual load has been lawfully served by a fully operational qualifying facility before September 1, 2001, or by an on-site power production facility with a rated capacity of 10 megawatts or less, any charge for recovery of stranded costs under this section or Subchapter G[1] assessed on that customer after the facility becomes fully operational shall be included only in those tariffs or charges associated with the services actually provided by the transmission and distribution utility, if any, to the customer after the facility became fully operational and may not include any costs associated with the service provided to the customer by the electric utility or its affiliated transmission and distribution utility under their tariffs before the operation of that qualifying facility. To qualify under this subsection, a qualifying facility must have made substantially complete filings on or before December 31, 1999, for all necessary site-specific environmental permits under the rules of the Texas Natural Resource Conservation Commission in effect at the time of filing.

(*l*) To protect retail customers in this state, and ensure the appropriateness of the nonbypassable rates of electric utilities and transmission and distribution utilities, notwithstanding any other provision of this title, an electric utility or transmission and distribution utility must report to and obtain approval of the commission before closing any transaction in which:

(1) the electric utility or transmission and distribution utility will be merged or consolidated with another electric utility or transmission and distribution utility;

(2) at least 50 percent of the stock of the electric utility or transmission and distribution utility will be transferred or sold; or

(3) a controlling interest or operational control of the electric utility or transmission and distribution utility will be transferred.

(m) The commission shall approve a transaction under Subsection (*l*) if the commission finds that the transaction is in the public interest. In making its determination, the commission shall consider whether the transaction will adversely affect the reliability of service, availability of service, or cost of service of the electric utility or transmission and distribution utility. The commission shall make the determination concerning a transaction under this subsection not later than the 180th day after the date the commission receives the relevant report. If the commission has not made a determination before the 181st day after that date, the transaction is considered approved.

(n) Subsections (*l*) and (m) do not apply to a transaction described by Subsection (*l*) for which a definitive agreement was executed before April 1, 2007, if an electric utility or transmission and distribution utility or a person seeking to acquire or merge with an electric utility or transmission and distribution utility made a filing for review of the transaction under Section 14.101 before May 1, 2007, and the resulting proceeding was not withdrawn.

(*o*) If an electric utility or transmission and distribution utility or a person seeking to acquire or merge with an electric utility or transmission and distribution utility files with the commission a stipulation, representation, or commitment in advance of or as part of a filing under Subsection (*l*) or under Section 14.101, the commission may enforce the stipulation, representation, or commitment to the extent that the stipulation, representation, or commitment is consistent with the standards provided by this section and Section 14.101. The commission may reasonably interpret and enforce conditions adopted under this section.

Added by Acts 1999, 76th Leg., ch. 405, § 39, eff. Sept. 1, 1999. Amended by Acts 2007, 80th Leg., ch. 1186, § 1, eff. June 15, 2007.

[1] V.T.C.A., Utilities Code § 39.301.
[2] V.T.C.A., Utilities Code § 36.051.

§ 39.263. Stranded Cost Recovery of Environmental Cleanup Costs

(a) Subject to Subsection (c), capital costs incurred by an electric utility to improve air quality before January 1, 2002, are eligible for inclusion as net invested capital under Section 39.259, notwithstanding the limitations imposed under Sections 39.259(b) and (c).

(b) Subject to Subsection (c), capital costs incurred by an electric utility or an affiliated power generation company to improve air quality after January 1, 2002, and before May 1, 2003, are eligible for inclusion in the determination of invested capital in the true-up proceeding under Section 39.262.

(c) Reasonable costs incurred under Subsections (a) and (b) shall be included as invested capital and considered in an electric utility's stranded cost determination only to the extent that:

(1) the cost is applied to offset or reduce the emission of airborne contaminants from an electric generating facility, where:

(A) the reduction or offset is determined by the Texas Natural Resource Conservation Commission to be an essential component in achieving compliance with a national ambient air quality standard; or

(B) the reduction or offset is necessary in order for an unpermitted electric generating facility to obtain a permit in the manner provided by Section 39.264;

(2) the retrofit decision is determined to be the most cost-effective after consideration of alternative measures, including the retirement of the generating facility; and

(3) the amount and location of resulting emission reductions is consistent with the air quality goals and policies of the Texas Natural Resource Conservation Commission.

(d) If the retirement of a generating facility is the most cost-effective alternative, taking into account the cost of replacement generating capacity, the net book value, including retirement costs and offsetting salvage value, of the affected facility shall be included in the electric utility's stranded cost determination, notwithstanding Section 39.259(c).

Added by Acts 1999, 76th Leg., ch. 405, § 39, eff. Sept. 1, 1999.

§ 39.264. Emissions Reductions of "Grandfathered Facilities"

(a) In this section:

(1) "Conservation commission" means the Texas Natural Resource Conservation Commission.

(2) "Electric generating facility" means a facility that generates electric energy for compensation and is owned or operated by a person in this state, including a municipal corporation, electric cooperative, or river authority.

(b) This section applies only to an electric generating facility existing on January 1, 1999, that is not subject to the requirement to obtain a permit under Section 382.0518(g), Health and Safety Code.

(c) It is the intent of the legislature that, for the 12-month period beginning on May 1, 2003, and for each 12-month period after the end of that period, total annual emissions of nitrogen oxides from facilities subject to this section may not exceed levels equal to 50 percent of the total emissions of that pollutant during 1997, as reported to the conservation commission, and total annual emissions of sulphur dioxides from coal-fired facilities subject to this section may not exceed levels equal to 75 percent of the total emissions of that pollutant during 1997, as reported to the conservation commission. The limitations prescribed by this subsection may be met through an emissions allocation and allowance transfer system described by this section.

(d) A municipal corporation, electric cooperative, or river authority may exclude any electric generating facilities of 25 megawatts or less from the requirements prescribed by this section. Not later than January 1, 2000, a municipal corporation, electric cooperative, or river authority must inform the conservation commission of its intent to exclude those facilities.

(e) The owner or operator of an electric generating facility shall apply to the conservation commission for a permit for the emission of air contaminants on or before September 1, 2000. A permit issued by the conservation commission under this section shall require the facility to achieve emissions reductions or trading emissions allowances as provided by this section. If the facility uses coal as a fuel, the permit must also be conditioned on the facility's emissions meeting opacity limitations provided by conservation commission rules. Notwithstanding Section 382.0518(g), Health and Safety Code, a facility that does not obtain a permit as required by this subsection may not operate after May 1, 2003, unless the conservation commission finds good cause for an extension.

(f) The conservation commission shall develop rules for the permitting of electric generating facilities. The rules adopted under this subsection shall provide, by region, for the allocation of emissions allowances of sulphur dioxides and nitrogen oxides among electric generating facilities and for facilities to trade emissions allowances for those contaminants.

(g) The conservation commission by rule shall establish an East Texas Region, a West Texas Region, and an El Paso Region for allocation of air contaminants under the permitting program under Subsection (f). The East Texas Region must contain all counties traversed by or east of Interstate Highway 35 or Interstate Highway 37, including Bosque, Coryell,

Hood, Parker, Somervell, and Wise counties. The West Texas Region includes all of the state not contained in the East Texas Region or the El Paso Region. The El Paso Region includes El Paso County.

(h) Not later than January 1, 2000, the conservation commission shall allocate to each electric generating facility in each region a number of annual emissions allowances, with each allowance equal to one ton of sulphur dioxides or of nitrogen oxides emitted in a year, that permit emissions of the contaminants from the facility in that year. The conservation commission must allocate to each facility a number of emissions allowances equal to an emissions rate measured in pounds per million British thermal units divided by 2,000 and multiplied by the facility's total heat input in terms of million British thermal units during 1997. For the East Texas Region, the emissions rate shall be 0.14 pounds per million British thermal units for nitrogen oxides and 1.38 pounds per million British thermal units for sulphur dioxides. For the West Texas and El Paso regions, the emissions rate shall be 0.195 pounds per million British thermal units for nitrogen oxides. Allowances for sulphur dioxides may only be allocated among coal-fired facilities.

(i) A person, municipal corporation, electric cooperative, or river authority that owns and operates an electric generating facility not covered by this section may elect to designate that facility to become subject to the requirements of this section and to receive emissions allowances for the purpose of complying with the emissions limitations prescribed by Subsection (c). The conservation commission shall adopt rules governing this election that:

(1) require an owner or operator of an electric generating facility to designate to the conservation commission in its permit application under Subsection (e) any facilities that will become subject to this section;

(2) require the conservation commission, notwithstanding the allocation mechanism provided by Subsection (h), to allocate additional allowances to facilities governed by this subsection in an amount equal to each facility's actual emissions in tons in 1997;

(3) provide that any unit designated under this subsection may not transfer or bank allowances conserved as a result of reduced utilization or shutdown, except that the allowances may be transferred or carried forward for use in subsequent years to the extent that the reduced utilization or shutdown results from the replacement of thermal energy from the unit designated under this subsection with thermal energy generated by any other unit; and

(4) provide that emissions reductions from electing facilities designated in this subsection may only be used to satisfy the emissions reductions for grandfathered facilities defined in Subsection (c) to the extent that reductions used to satisfy the limitations in Subsection (c) are beyond the requirements of any other state or federal standard, or both.

(j) The conservation commission by rule shall permit a facility to trade emissions allocations with other electric generating facilities only in the same region.

(k) The conservation commission by rule shall provide methods for the conservation commission to determine whether a facility complies with the permit issued under this section. The rules must provide for:

(1) monitoring and reporting actual emissions of sulphur dioxides and nitrogen oxides from each facility;

(2) provisions for saving unused allowances for use in later years; and

(3) a system for tracking traded allowances.

(*l*) A facility may not trade an unused allowance for a contaminant for use as a credit for another contaminant.

(m) A person possessing market power shall not withhold emissions allowances from the market in a manner that is unreasonably discriminatory or tends to unreasonably restrict, impair, or reduce the level of competition.

(n) The conservation commission shall penalize a facility that emits an air contaminant that exceeds the facility's allowances for that contaminant by:

(1) enforcing an administrative penalty, in an amount determined by conservation commission rules, for each ton of air contaminant emissions by which the facility exceeds its allocated emissions allowances; and

(2) reducing the facility's emissions allowances for the next year by an amount of emissions equal to the excessive emissions in the year the facility emitted the excessive air contaminants.

(*o*) The conservation commission may penalize a facility that emits an air contaminant that exceeds the facility's allowances for that contaminant by:

(1) ordering the facility to cease operations; or

(2) taking other enforcement action provided by conservation commission rules.

(p) The conservation commission by rule shall provide for a facility in the El Paso Region to meet emissions allowances by using credits from emissions reductions achieved in Ciudad Juarez, United Mexican States.

(q) If the conservation commission or the United States Environmental Protection Agency determines that reductions in nitrogen oxides emissions in the El Paso Region otherwise required by this section would result in increased ambient ozone levels in El Paso County, facilities in the El Paso Region are exempt from the nitrogen oxides reduction requirements.

(r) An applicant for a permit under Subsection (e) shall publish notice of intent to obtain the permit in accordance with Section 382.056, Health and Safety Code. The conservation commission shall provide an opportunity for a public hearing and the submission of public comment and send notice of a decision on an application for a permit under Subsection (e) in the same manner as provided by Sections 382.0561 and 382.0562, Health and Safety Code. The conservation commission shall review and renew a permit issued under this section in accordance with Section 382.055, Health and Safety Code.

(s) This section does not limit the authority of the conservation commission to require further reductions of nitrogen oxides, sulphur dioxides, or any other pollutant from generating facilities subject to this section or Section 39.263.

Added by Acts 1999, 76th Leg., ch. 405, § 39, eff. Sept. 1, 1999.

§ 39.265. Rights Not Affected

This chapter is not intended to alter any rights of utilities to recover stranded costs from wholesale customers.

Added by Acts 1999, 76th Leg., ch. 405, § 39, eff. Sept. 1, 1999.

SUBCHAPTER G. SECURITIZATION

§ 39.301. Purpose

The purpose of this subchapter is to enable utilities to use securitization financing to recover regulatory assets, all other amounts determined under Section 39.262, and any amounts being recovered under a competition transition charge determined as a result of the proceedings under Sections 39.201 and 39.262. This type of debt will lower the carrying costs of the assets relative to the costs that would be incurred using conventional utility financing methods. The proceeds of the transition bonds shall be used solely for the purposes of reducing the amount of recoverable regulatory assets and other amounts, as determined by the commission in accordance with this chapter, through the refinancing or retirement of utility debt or equity. The commission shall ensure that securitization provides tangible and quantifiable benefits to ratepayers, greater than would have been achieved absent the issuance of transition bonds. The commission shall ensure that the structuring and pricing of the transition bonds result in the lowest transition bond charges consistent with market conditions and the terms of the financing order. The amount securitized may not exceed the present value of the revenue requirement over the life of the proposed transition bond associated with the regulatory assets or other amounts sought to be securitized. The present value calculation shall use a discount rate equal to the proposed interest rate on the transition bonds.

Added by Acts 1999, 76th Leg., ch. 405, § 39, eff. Sept. 1, 1999. Amended by Acts 2007, 80th Leg., ch. 1186, § 2, eff. June 15, 2007.

§ 39.302. Definitions

In this subchapter:

(1) "Assignee" means any individual, corporation, or other legally recognized entity to which an interest in transition property is transferred, other than as security, including any assignee of that party.

(2) "Financing order" means an order of the commission adopted under Section 39.201 or 39.262 approving the issuance of transition bonds and the creation of transition charges for the recovery of qualified costs.

(3) "Financing party" means a holder of transition bonds, including trustees, collateral agents, and other persons acting for the benefit of the holder.

(4) "Qualified costs" means 100 percent of an electric utility's regulatory assets and 75 percent of its recoverable costs determined by the commission under Section 39.201 and any remaining amounts determined under Section 39.262 together with the costs of issuing, supporting, and servicing transition bonds and any costs of retiring and refunding the electric utility's existing debt and equity securities in connection with the issuance of transition bonds. The term includes the costs to the commission of acquiring professional services for the purpose of evaluating proposed transactions under Section 39.201 and this subchapter.

(5) "Regulatory assets" means the generation-related portion of the Texas jurisdictional portion of the amount reported by the electric utility in its 1998 annual report on Securities and Exchange Commission Form 10-K as regulatory assets and liabilities, offset by the applicable portion of generation-related investment tax credits permitted under the Internal Revenue Code of 1986.

(6) "Transition bonds" means bonds, debentures, notes, certificates of participation or of beneficial interest, or other evidences of indebtedness or ownership that are issued by an electric utility, its successors, or an assignee under a financing order, that have a term not longer than 15 years, and that are secured by or payable from transition property. If certificates of participation, beneficial interest, or ownership are issued, references in this subchapter to principal, interest, or premium shall refer to comparable amounts under those certificates.

(7) "Transition charges" means nonbypassable amounts to be charged for the use or availability of electric services, approved by the commission under a financing order to recover qualified costs, that shall be collected by an electric utility, its successors, an assignee, or other collection agents as provided for in the financing order.

(8) "Transition property" means the property described in Section 39.304.

Added by Acts 1999, 76th Leg., ch. 405, § 39, eff. Sept. 1, 1999. Amended by Acts 2007, 80th Leg., ch. 1186, § 3, eff. June 15, 2007.

§ 39.303. Financing Orders; Terms

(a) The commission shall adopt a financing order, on application of a utility to recover the utility's regulatory assets and other amounts determined under Section 39.201 or 39.262, on making a finding that the total amount of revenues to be collected under the financing order is less than the revenue requirement that would be recovered over the remaining life of the regulatory assets or other amounts using conventional financing methods and that the financing order is consistent with the standards in Section 39.301.

(b) The financing order shall detail the amount of regulatory assets and other amounts to be recovered and the period over which the nonbypassable transition charges shall be recovered, which period may not exceed 15 years. If an amount determined under Section 39.262 is subject to judicial review at the time of the securitization proceeding, the financing order shall include an adjustment mechanism requiring the utility to adjust its rates, other than transition charges, or provide credits, other than credits to transition charges, in a manner that would refund over the remaining life of the transition bonds any overpayments resulting from securitization of amounts in excess of the amount resulting from a final determination after completion of all appellate reviews. The adjustment mechanism may not affect the stream of revenue available to service the transition bonds. An adjustment may not be made under this subsection until all appellate reviews, including, if applicable, appellate reviews following a commission decision on remand of its original orders, have been completed.

(c) Transition charges shall be collected and allocated among customers in the same manner as competition transition charges under Section 39.201.

(d) A financing order shall become effective in accordance with its terms, and the financing order, together with the transition charges authorized in the order, shall thereafter be irrevocable and not subject to reduction, impairment, or adjustment by further action of the commission, except as permitted by Section 39.307.

(e) The commission shall issue a financing order under Subsections (a) and (g) not later than 90 days after the utility files its request for the financing order.

(f) A financing order is not subject to rehearing by the commission. A financing order may be reviewed by appeal only to a Travis County district court by a party to the proceeding filed within 15 days after the financing order is signed by the commission. The judgment of the district court may be reviewed only by direct appeal to the Supreme Court of Texas filed within 15 days after entry of judgment. All appeals shall be heard and determined by the district court and the Supreme Court of Texas as expeditiously as possible with lawful precedence over other matters. Review on appeal shall be based solely on the record before the commission and briefs to the court and shall be limited to whether the financing order conforms to the constitution and laws of this state and the United States and is within the authority of the commission under this chapter.

(g) At the request of an electric utility, the commission may adopt a financing order providing for retiring and refunding transition bonds on making a finding that the future transition charges required to service the new transition bonds, including transaction costs, will be less than the future transition charges required to service the transition bonds being refunded. On the retirement of the refunded transition bonds, the commission shall adjust the related transition charges accordingly.

Added by Acts 1999, 76th Leg., ch. 405, § 39, eff. Sept. 1, 1999. Amended by Acts 2007, 80th Leg., ch. 1186, § 4, eff. June 15, 2007.

§ 39.304. Property Rights

(a) The rights and interests of an electric utility or successor under a financing order, including the right to impose, collect, and receive transition charges authorized in the order, shall be only contract rights until they are first transferred to an assignee or pledged in connection with the issuance of transition bonds, at which time they will become "transition property."

(b) Transition property shall constitute a present property right for purposes of contracts concerning the sale or pledge of property, even though the imposition and collection of transition charges depends on further acts of the utility or others that have not yet occurred. The financing order shall remain in effect and the property shall continue to exist for the same period as the pledge of the state described in Section 39.310.

(c) All revenues and collections resulting from transition charges shall constitute proceeds only of the transition property arising from the financing order.

Added by Acts 1999, 76th Leg., ch. 405, § 39, eff. Sept. 1, 1999.

§ 39.305. No Setoff

The interest of an assignee or pledgee in transition property and in the revenues and collections arising from that property are not subject to setoff, counterclaim, surcharge, or defense by the electric utility or any other person or in connection with the bankruptcy of the electric utility or any other entity. A financing order shall remain in effect and unabated notwithstanding the bankruptcy of the electric utility, its successors, or assignees.

Added by Acts 1999, 76th Leg., ch. 405, § 39, eff. Sept. 1, 1999.

§ 39.306. No Bypass

A financing order shall include terms ensuring that the imposition and collection of transition charges authorized in the order shall be nonbypassable.

Added by Acts 1999, 76th Leg., ch. 405, § 39, eff. Sept. 1, 1999.

§ 39.307. True-Up

A financing order shall include a mechanism requiring that transition charges be reviewed and adjusted at least annually, within 45 days of the anniversary date of the issuance of the transition bonds, to correct any overcollections or undercollections of the preceding 12 months and to ensure the expected recovery of amounts sufficient to timely provide all payments of debt service and other required amounts and charges in connection with the transition bonds.

Added by Acts 1999, 76th Leg., ch. 405, § 39, eff. Sept. 1, 1999.

§ 39.308. True Sale

An agreement by an electric utility or assignee to transfer transition property that expressly states that the transfer is a sale or other absolute transfer signifies that the transaction is a true sale and is not a secured transaction and that title, legal and equitable, has passed to the entity to which the transition property is transferred. This true sale shall apply regardless of whether the purchaser has any recourse against the seller, or any other term of the parties' agreement, including the seller's retention of an equity interest in the transition property, the fact that the electric utility acts as the collector of transition charges relating to the transition property, or the treatment of the transfer as a financing for tax, financial reporting, or other purposes.

Added by Acts 1999, 76th Leg., ch. 405, § 39, eff. Sept. 1, 1999.

§ 39.309. Security Interests; Assignment; Commingling; Default

(a) Transition property does not constitute an account or general intangible under Section 9.106, Business & Commerce Code. The creation, granting, perfection, and enforcement of liens and security interests in transition property are governed by this section and not by the Business & Commerce Code.

(b) A valid and enforceable lien and security interest in transition property may be created only by a financing order and the execution and delivery of a security agreement with a financing party in connection with the issuance of transition bonds. The lien and security interest shall attach automatically from the time that value is received for the bonds and, on perfection through the filing of notice with the secretary of state in accordance with the rules prescribed under Subsection (d), shall be a continuously perfected lien and security interest in the transition property and all proceeds of the property, whether accrued or not, shall have priority in the order of filing and take precedence over any subsequent judicial or other lien creditor. If notice is filed within 10 days after value is received for the transition bonds, the security interest shall be perfected retroactive to the date value was received, otherwise, the security interest shall be perfected as of the date of filing.

(c) Transfer of an interest in transition property to an assignee shall be perfected against all third parties, including subsequent judicial or other lien creditors, when the financing order becomes effective, transfer documents have been delivered to the assignee, and a notice of that transfer has been filed in accordance with the rules prescribed under Subsection (d); provided, however, that if notice of the transfer has not been filed in accordance with this subsection within 10 days after the delivery of transfer documentation, the transfer of the interest is not perfected against third parties until the notice is filed.

(d) The secretary of state shall implement this section by establishing and maintaining a separate system of records for the filing of notices under this section and prescribing the rules for those filings based on Chapter 9, Business & Commerce Code, adapted to this subchapter and using the terms defined in this subchapter.

(e) The priority of a lien and security interest perfected under this section is not impaired by any later modification of the financing order under Section 39.307 or by the commingling of funds arising from transition charges with other funds, and any other security interest that may apply to those funds shall be terminated when they are transferred to a segregated account for the assignee or a financing party. If transition property has been transferred to an assignee, any proceeds of that property shall be held in trust for the assignee.

(f) If a default or termination occurs under the transition bonds, the financing parties or their representatives may foreclose on or otherwise enforce their lien and security interest in any transition property as if they were secured parties under Chapter 9, Business & Commerce Code, and the commission may order that amounts arising from transition charges be transferred to a separate account for the financing parties' benefit, to which their lien and security interest shall apply. On application by or on behalf of the financing parties, a district court of Travis County shall order the sequestration and payment to them of revenues arising from the transition charges.

Added by Acts 1999, 76th Leg., ch. 405, § 39, eff. Sept. 1, 1999.

§ 39.310. Pledge of State

Transition bonds are not a debt or obligation of the state and are not a charge on its full faith and credit or taxing power. The state pledges, however, for the benefit and protection of financing parties and the electric utility, that it will not take or permit any action that would impair the value of transition property, or, except as permitted by Section 39.307, reduce, alter, or impair the transition charges to be imposed, collected, and remitted to financing parties, until the principal, interest and premium, and any other charges incurred and contracts to be performed in connection with the related transition bonds have been paid and performed in full. Any party issuing transition bonds is authorized to include this pledge in any documentation relating to those bonds.

Added by Acts 1999, 76th Leg., ch. 405, § 39, eff. Sept. 1, 1999.

§ 39.311. Tax Exemption

Transactions involving the transfer and ownership of transition property and the receipt of transition charges are exempt from state and local income, sales, franchise, gross receipts, and other taxes or similar charges.

Added by Acts 1999, 76th Leg., ch. 405, § 39, eff. Sept. 1, 1999.

§ 39.312. Not Public Utility

An assignee or financing party may not be considered to be a public utility or person providing electric service solely by virtue of the transactions described in this subchapter.

Added by Acts 1999, 76th Leg., ch. 405, § 39, eff. Sept. 1, 1999.

§ 39.313. Severability

Effective on the date the first utility transition bonds are issued under this subchapter, if any provision in this title or portion of this title is held to be invalid or is invalidated, superseded, replaced, repealed, or expires for any reason, that occurrence does not affect the validity or continuation of this subchapter, Section 39.201, 39.251, 39.252, or 39.262, or any part of those provisions, or any other provision of this title that is relevant to the issuance, administration, payment, retirement, or refunding of transition bonds or to any actions of the electric utility, its successors, an assignee, a collection agent, or a financing party, which shall remain in full force and effect.

Added by Acts 1999, 76th Leg., ch. 405, § 39, eff. Sept. 1, 1999.

SUBCHAPTER H. CERTIFICATION AND REGISTRATION; PENALTIES

§ 39.351. Registration of Power Generation Companies

(a) A person may not generate electricity unless the person is registered with the commission as a power generation company in accordance with this section. A person may register as a power generation company by filing the following information with the commission:

(1) a description of the location of any facility used to generate electricity;

(2) a description of the type of services provided;

(3) a copy of any information filed with the Federal Energy Regulatory Commission in connection with registration with that commission; and

(4) any other information required by commission rule, provided that in requiring that information the commission shall protect the competitive process in a manner that ensures the confidentiality of competitively sensitive information.

(b) A power generation company shall comply with the reliability standards adopted by an independent organization certified by the commission to ensure the reliability of the regional electrical network for a power region in which the power generation company is generating or selling electricity.

(c) The commission may establish simplified filing requirements for distributed natural gas generation facilities .

Added by Acts 1999, 76th Leg., ch. 405, § 39, eff. Sept. 1, 1999. Amended by Acts 2011, 82nd Leg., ch. 890 (S.B. 365), § 4, eff. Sept. 1, 2011.

§ 39.352. Certification of Retail Electric Providers

(a) After the date of customer choice, a person, including an affiliate of an electric utility, may not provide retail electric service in this state unless the person is certified by the commission as a retail electric provider, in accordance with this section.

(b) The commission shall issue a certificate to provide retail electric service to a person applying for certification who demonstrates:

(1) the financial and technical resources to provide continuous and reliable electric service to customers in the area for which the certification is sought;

(2) the managerial and technical ability to supply electricity at retail in accordance with customer contracts;

(3) the resources needed to meet the customer protection requirements of this title; and

(4) ownership or lease of an office located within this state for the purpose of providing customer service, accepting service of process, and making available in that office books and records sufficient to establish the retail electric provider's compliance with the requirements of this subchapter.

(c) A person applying for certification under this section shall comply with all applicable customer protection provisions, disclosure requirements, and marketing guidelines established by the commission and by this title.

(d) Notwithstanding Subsections (b)(1)–(3), if a retail electric provider files with the commission a signed, notarized affidavit from each retail customer with which it has contracted to provide one megawatt or more of capacity stating that the customer is satisfied that the retail electric provider meets the standards prescribed by Subsections (b)(1)–(3) and Subsection (c), the retail electric provider shall be certified for purposes of serving those customers only, so long as it demonstrates that it meets the requirements of Subsection (b)(4).

(e) A retail electric provider may apply for certification any time after September 1, 2000.

(f) The commission shall use any information required in this section in a manner that ensures the confidentiality of competitively sensitive information.

(g) If a retail electric provider serves an aggregate load in excess of 300 megawatts within this state, not less than five percent of the load in megawatt hours must consist of residential customers. This requirement applies to an affiliated retail electric provider only with respect to load served outside of the electric utility's service area, and, in relation to that load, the affiliated retail electric provider shall meet the requirements of this subsection by serving residential customers outside of the electric utility's service area. For the purpose of this subsection, the load served by retail electric providers that are under common ownership shall be combined. A retail electric provider may meet the requirements of this subsection by demonstrating on an annual basis that it serves residential load amounting to five percent of its total load, by demonstrating that another retail electric provider serves sufficient qualifying residential load on its behalf, or by paying an amount into the system benefit fund equal to $1 multiplied by a number equal to the difference between the number of megawatt hours it sold to residential customers and the number of megawatt hours it was required to sell to such customers, or in the case of an affiliated retail electric provider, $1 multiplied by a number equal to the difference between the number of megawatt hours sold to residential customers outside of the electric utility's service area and the number of megawatt hours it was required to sell to such customers outside of the electric utility's service area. Qualifying residential load may not include customers served by an affiliated retail electric provider in its own service area. Each retail electric provider shall file reports with the commission that are necessary to implement this subsection. This subsection applies for 36 months after retail competition begins. The commission shall adopt rules to implement this subsection.

Added by Acts 1999, 76th Leg., ch. 405, § 39, eff. Sept. 1, 1999.

§ 39.353. Registration of Aggregators

(a) A person may not provide aggregation services in the state unless the person is registered with the commission as an aggregator.

(b) In this subchapter, "aggregator" means a person joining two or more customers, other than municipalities and political subdivision corporations, into a single purchasing unit to negotiate the purchase of electricity from retail electric providers. Aggregators may not sell or take title to electricity. Retail electric providers are not aggregators.

(c) A person registering under this section shall comply with all customer protection provisions, all disclosure requirements, and all marketing guidelines established by the commission and by this title.

(d) The commission shall establish terms and conditions it determines necessary to regulate the reliability and integrity of aggregators in the state by June 1, 2000.

(e) An aggregator may register any time after September 1, 2000.

(f) The commission shall have up to 60 days to process applications for registration filed by aggregators.

(g) Registration is not required of a customer that is aggregating loads from its own location or facilities.

(h) The commission shall work with the Texas Department of Economic Development to communicate information about opportunities for operation as aggregators to potential new aggregators, including small and historically underutilized businesses.

Added by Acts 1999, 76th Leg., ch. 405, § 39, eff. Sept. 1, 1999.

§ 39.3535. Military Bases Aggregators

(a) In this section, "military bases aggregator" means a person joining two or more military bases that are located in areas of the state offering customer choice under this chapter into a single purchasing unit to negotiate electricity purchases from retail electric providers.

(b) It is the policy of this state to encourage military bases located in areas of the state offering customer choice under this chapter to aggregate their facilities into a single purchasing unit as a method to reduce costs of electricity consumed by those bases. The commission shall provide assistance to a military bases aggregator regarding the evaluation of offers from retail electric providers on the request of the military bases aggregator.

(c) An aggregator registered under another section of this subchapter may provide aggregation services to military bases.

(d) A person, including a state agency, may register as a military bases aggregator to provide aggregation services exclusively to military bases located in areas of the state offering customer choice under this chapter.

(e) A person registered as a military bases aggregator under Subsection (d) is not required to comply with customer protection provisions, disclosure requirements, or marketing guidelines prescribed by this title or established by the commission while providing aggregation services exclusively to military bases.

(f) The commission shall expedite consideration of an application submitted by an applicant for registration under Subsection (d).

Added by Acts 2003, 78th Leg., ch. 149, § 22, eff. May 27, 2003.

§ 39.354. Registration of Municipal Aggregators

(a) A municipal aggregator may not provide aggregation services in the state unless the municipal aggregator registers with the commission.

(b) In this section, "municipal aggregator" means a person authorized by two or more municipal governing bodies to join the bodies into a single purchasing unit to negotiate the purchase of electricity from retail electric providers or aggregation by a municipality under Chapter 304, Local Government Code.

(c) A municipal aggregator may register any time after September 1, 2000.

Added by Acts 1999, 76th Leg., ch. 405, § 39, eff. Sept. 1, 1999. Amended by Acts 2001, 77th Leg., ch. 1420, § 21.002(22), eff. Sept. 1, 2001.

§ 39.3545. Registration of Political Subdivision Aggregators

(a) A political subdivision aggregator may not provide aggregation services in the state unless the political subdivision aggregator registers with the commission.

(b) In this section, "political subdivision aggregator" means a person or political subdivision corporation authorized by two or more political subdivision governing bodies to join the bodies into a single purchasing unit or multiple purchasing units to negotiate the purchase of electricity from retail electric providers for the facilities of the aggregated political subdivisions or aggregation by a person or political subdivision under Chapter 304, Local Government Code.

(c) A political subdivision aggregator may register any time after September 1, 2000.

Added by Acts 1999, 76th Leg., ch. 405, § 39, eff. Sept. 1, 1999; Acts 2001, 77th Leg., ch. 1420, § 21.002(23), eff. Sept. 1, 2001.

§ 39.355. Registration of Power Marketers

A person may not sell electric energy at wholesale as a power marketer unless the person registers with the commission pursuant to Section 35.032.

Added by Acts 1999, 76th Leg., ch. 405, § 39, eff. Sept. 1, 1999.

§ 39.356. Revocation of Certification

(a) The commission may suspend, revoke, or amend a retail electric provider's certificate for significant violations of this title or the rules adopted under this title or of any reliability standard adopted by an independent organization certified by the commission to ensure the reliability of a power region's electrical network, including the failure to observe any scheduling, operating, planning, reliability, or settlement protocols established by the independent organization. The commission may also suspend or revoke a retail electric provider's certificate if the provider no longer has the financial or technical capability to provide continuous and reliable electric service.

(b) The commission may suspend or revoke a power generation company's registration for significant violations of this title or the rules adopted under this title or of the reliability standards adopted by an independent organization certified by the commission to ensure the reliability of a power region's electrical network, including the failure to observe any scheduling, operating, planning, reliability, or settlement protocols established by the independent organization.

(c) The commission may suspend or revoke an aggregator's registration for significant violations of this title or of the rules adopted under this title.

Added by Acts 1999, 76th Leg., ch. 405, § 39, eff. Sept. 1, 1999.

§ 39.357. Administrative Penalty

In addition to the suspension, revocation, or amendment of a certification, the commission may impose an administrative penalty, as provided by Section 15.023, for violations described by Section 39.356.

Added by Acts 1999, 76th Leg., ch. 405, § 39, eff. Sept. 1, 1999.

§ 39.358. Local Registration of Retail Electric Provider

(a) A municipality may require a retail electric provider to register with the municipality as a condition of serving residents of the municipality. The municipality may assess a reasonable administrative fee for this purpose.

(b) The municipality may suspend or revoke a retail electric provider's registration and operation in that municipality for significant violations of this chapter or the rules adopted under this chapter.

Added by Acts 1999, 76th Leg., ch. 405, § 39, eff. Sept. 1, 1999.

SUBCHAPTER I. PROVISIONS FOR CERTAIN NON-ERCOT UTILITIES

§ 39.401. Applicability

This subchapter shall apply to investor-owned electric utilities operating solely outside of ERCOT having fewer than six synchronous interconnections with voltage levels above 69 kilovolts systemwide on the effective date of this subchapter. The legislature finds that circumstances exist that require that areas served by such utilities be treated as competitive development areas in which it is not in the public interest to transition to full retail customer choice at this time.

Added by Acts 1999, 76th Leg., ch. 405, § 39, eff. Sept. 1, 1999. Amended by Acts 2001, 77th Leg., ch. 1041, § 1, eff. June 15, 2001.

§ 39.402. Regulation of Utility And Transition to Competition

(a) Until the date on which an electric utility subject to this subchapter is authorized by the commission to implement customer choice, the rates of the utility shall be regulated under traditional cost of service regulation and the utility is subject to all applicable regulatory authority prescribed by this subtitle and Subtitle A, including Chapters 14, 32, 33, 36, and 37. Until the date on which an electric utility subject to this subchapter implements customer choice, the provisions of this chapter, other than this subchapter, Sections 39.904 and 39.905, and the provisions relating to the duty to obtain a permit from the Texas Commission on Environmental Quality for an electric generating facility and to reduce emissions from an electric generating facility, shall not apply to that utility. That portion of any commission order entered before September 1, 2001, to comply with this subchapter shall be null and void.

(b) Until the date on which an electric utility subject to this subchapter implements customer choice, Section 33.008 does not apply and the utility shall pay franchise fees to a municipality as required by the utility's franchise agreement with the municipality. After the date on which an electric utility subject to this subchapter implements customer choice, Section 33.008 applies. However, for purposes of computing the franchise fees as provided by Section 33.008(b), the calendar year immediately preceding the implementation of customer choice shall be substituted for the year 1998.

(c) On or after January 1, 2007, an electric utility subject to this subchapter may choose to participate in customer choice. An electric utility that chooses to participate in customer choice shall file a transition to competition plan with the commission. This transition to competition plan shall identify how utilities subject to this subchapter intend to mitigate market power and achieve full customer choice, including specific alternatives for constructing additional transmission facilities, auctioning rights to generation capacity, divesting generation capacity, or any other measure that is consistent with the public interest. The utility shall also include in the transition to competition plan a provision to establish a price to beat for residential customers and commercial customers having a peak load of 1,000 kilowatts or less. The commission may prescribe additional information or provisions that must be included in the plan. The commission shall approve, modify, or reject a plan within 180 days after the date of a filing under this section; provided, however, that if a hearing is requested by any party to the proceeding, the 180-day deadline will be extended one day for each day of hearings. The transition to competition plan may be updated or amended annually, subject to commission approval until the applicable power region is certified as a qualifying power region under Section 39.152.

(d) On implementation of customer choice, an electric utility subject to this subchapter is subject to the provisions of this subtitle and Subtitle A to the same extent as other electric utilities, including the provisions of Chapter 37 concerning certificates of convenience and necessity.

Added by Acts 1999, 76th Leg., ch. 405, § 39, eff. Sept. 1, 1999. Amended by Acts 2001, 77th Leg., ch. 1041, § 1, eff. June 15, 2001; Acts 2011, 82nd Leg., ch. 182 (S.B. 1150), § 1, eff. May 28, 2011.

§§ 39.403 to 39.406. Repealed by Acts 2001, 77th Leg., ch. 1041, § 3, eff. June 15, 2001.

§ 39.407. Customer Choice And Relevant Market and Related Matters

(a) If an electric utility chooses on or after January 1, 2007, to participate in customer choice, the commission may not authorize customer choice until the applicable power region has been certified as a qualifying power region under Section 39.152(a). Except as otherwise provided by this subsection, the commission shall certify that the requirements of Section 39.152(a)(3) are met for electric utilities subject to this subchapter only upon a finding that the total capacity owned and controlled by each such electric utility and its affiliates does not exceed 20 percent of the total installed generation capacity within the constrained geographic region served by each such electric utility plus the total available transmission capacity capable of delivering firm power and energy to that constrained geographic region. Not later than May 1, 2002, each electric utility subject to this subchapter shall submit to the electric utility restructuring legislative oversight committee an analysis of the needed transmission facilities necessary to make the electric utility's service area transmission capability comparable to areas within the ERCOT power region. On or after September 1, 2003, each electric utility subject to this subchapter shall file the utility's plans to develop the utility's transmission interconnections with the utility's power region or other adjacent power regions. The commission shall review the plan and not later than the 180th day after the date the plan is filed, determine the additional transmission facilities necessary to provide access to power and energy that is comparable to the access provided in areas within the ERCOT power region; provided, however, that if a hearing is requested by any party to the proceeding, the 180-day deadline will be extended one day for each day of hearings. The commission shall, as a part of the commission's approval of the plan, approve a rate rider mechanism for the recovery of the incremental costs of those facilities after the facilities are completed and in-service. A finding of need under this subsection shall meet the requirements of Sections 37.056(c)(1), (2), and (4)(E). The commission may certify that the requirements of Section 39.152(a)(3) are met for electric utilities subject to this subchapter if the commission finds that:

(1) each such utility has sufficient transmission facilities to provide customers access to power and energy from capacity controlled by suppliers not affiliated with the incumbent utility that is comparable to the access to power and energy from capacity controlled by suppliers not affiliated with the incumbent utilities in areas of the ERCOT power region; and

(2) the total capacity owned and controlled by each such electric utility and its affiliates does not exceed 20 percent of the total installed generation capacity within the power region.

(b) In the area of a power region served by an electric utility subject to this subchapter, the electric utility may not choose to participate in customer choice unless the affiliated power generation company makes a commitment to maintain and does maintain rates that are based on cost of service for any electric cooperative or municipally owned utility that was a wholesale customer on the date the utility chooses to participate in customer choice and was purchasing power at rates that were based on cost of service. This subsection requires a power generation company to sell power at rates that are based on cost of service, notwithstanding the expiration of a contract for that service, until the requirements of Section 39.152(a) are met.

(c) If the requirements of Section 39.152(a) have not been met for an electric utility subject to this subchapter when the electric utility chooses to participate in customer choice, then any power generation company in the power region affiliated with an electric utility subject to this subchapter shall maintain adequate supply and facilities to provide electric service to persons who were retail customers of the electric utility on the date the utility chooses to participate in customer choice. The obligation provided by this subsection remains in effect until the commission determines that the requirements of Section 39.152(a) have been met for the region.

Added by Acts 1999, 76th Leg., ch. 405, § 39, eff. Sept. 1, 1999. Amended by Acts 2001, 77th Leg., ch. 1041, § 1, eff. June 15, 2001.

§ 39.408. Repealed by Acts 2001, 77th Leg., ch. 1041, § 3, eff. June 15, 2001.

§ 39.409. Recoupment of Transition to Competition Costs

An electric utility subject to this subchapter is entitled to recover, as provided by this section, all reasonable and necessary expenditures made or incurred before September 1, 2001, to comply with the provisions of this chapter. Not later than December 1, 2001, each electric utility subject to this subchapter may file with the commission an application for recovery detailing the amounts spent or incurred. After notice and hearing, the commission shall review the amounts and, if found to be reasonable and necessary, approve a transition to competition retail rate rider mechanism for the recovery of the approved transition to competition costs. A rate rider implemented to recover approved transition to competition costs shall expire not later than December 31, 2006.

Added by Acts 2001, 77th Leg., ch. 1041, § 2, eff. June 15, 2001.

§ 39.410. Contractual Obligations

This subchapter may not:

(1) interfere with or abrogate the rights or obligations of any party, including a retail or wholesale customer, to a contract with an investor-owned electric utility, river authority, municipally owned utility, or electric cooperative;

(2) interfere with or abrogate the rights or obligations of a party under a contract or agreement concerning certificated utility service areas; or

(3) result in a change in wholesale power costs to wholesale customers in Texas purchasing electricity under wholesale power contracts the pricing provisions of which are based on formulary rates, fuel adjustments, or average system costs.

Added by Acts 2001, 77th Leg., ch. 1041, § 2, eff. June 15, 2001.

SUBCHAPTER J. TRANSITION TO COMPETITION IN CERTAIN NON-ERCOT AREAS

§ 39.451. Applicability

This subchapter applies only to an investor-owned electric utility that is operating solely outside of ERCOT in areas of this state that were included in the Southeastern Electric Reliability Council on January 1, 2005.

Added by Acts 2005, 79th Leg., ch. 1072, § 1, eff. June 18, 2005.

§ 39.452. Regulation of Utility and Transition to Competition

(a) Until the date on which an electric utility subject to this subchapter is authorized by the commission to implement customer choice under Section 39.453, the rates of the electric utility shall be regulated under traditional cost-of-service regulation and the electric utility is subject to all applicable regulatory authority prescribed by this subtitle and Subtitle A, including Chapters 14, 32, 33, 36, and 37.

(b) An electric utility subject to this subchapter shall propose a competitive generation tariff to allow eligible customers the ability to contract for competitive generation. The commission shall approve, reject, or modify the proposed tariff not later than September 1, 2010. The tariffs subject to this subsection may not be considered to offer a discounted rate or rates under Section 36.007, and the utility's rates shall be set, in the proceeding in which the tariff is adopted, to recover any costs unrecovered as a result of the implementation of the tariff. The commission shall ensure that a competitive generation tariff shall not be implemented in a manner that harms the sustainability or competitiveness of manufacturers that choose not to take advantage of competitive generation. Pursuant to the competitive generation tariff, an electric utility subject to this subsection shall purchase competitive generation service, selected by the customer, and provide the generation at retail to the customer. An electric utility subject to this subsection shall provide and price retail transmission service, including necessary ancillary services, to retail customers who choose to take advantage of the competitive generation tariff at a rate that is unbundled from the utility's cost of service. Such customers shall not be considered wholesale transmission customers. Notwithstanding any other provision of this chapter, the commission may not issue a decision relating to a competitive generation tariff that is contrary to an applicable decision, rule, or policy statement of a federal regulatory agency having jurisdiction.

(c) That portion of any commission order issued before the effective date of this section requiring the electric utility to comply with a provision of this chapter is void.

(d) Until the date on which an electric utility subject to this subchapter implements customer choice:

(1) the provisions of this chapter do not apply to that electric utility, other than this subchapter, Sections 39.904 and 39.905, the provisions relating to the duty to obtain a permit from the Texas Commission on Environmental Quality for an electric generating facility and to reduce emissions from an electric generating facility, and the provisions of Subchapter G that pertain to the recovery and securitization of hurricane reconstruction costs authorized by Sections 39.458–39.463; and

(2) the electric utility is not subject to a rate freeze and, subject to the limitation provided by Subsection (b), may file for rate changes under Chapter 36 and for approval of one or more of the rate rider mechanisms authorized by Sections 39.454 and 39.455.

(e) An electric utility subject to this subchapter may proceed with and complete jurisdictional separation to establish two vertically integrated utilities, one of which is solely subject to the retail jurisdiction of the commission and one of which is solely subject to the retail jurisdiction of the Louisiana Public Service Commission.

(f) Not later than January 1, 2006, an electric utility subject to this subchapter shall file a plan with the commission for identifying the applicable power region or power regions, enumerating the steps to achieve the certification of a power region in accordance with Section 39.453, and specifying the schedule for achieving the certification of a power region. The utility may amend the plan as appropriate. The commission may, on its own motion or the motion of any affected person, initiate a proceeding to certify a qualified power region under Section 39.152 when the conditions supporting such a proceeding exist.

(g) Not later than the earlier of January 1, 2007, or the 90th day after the date the applicable power region is certified in accordance with Section 39.453, the electric utility shall file a transition to competition plan. The transition to competition plan must:

(1) identify how the electric utility intends to mitigate market power and to achieve full customer choice, including specific alternatives for constructing additional transmission facilities, auctioning rights to generation capacity, divesting generation capacity, or any other measure that is consistent with the public interest;

(2) include a provision to reinstate a customer choice pilot project and to establish a price to beat for residential customers and commercial customers having a peak load of 1,000 kilowatts or less; and

(3) include any other additional information or provisions that the commission may require.

(h) The commission shall approve, modify, or reject a plan filed under Subsection (g) not later than the 180th day after the date the plan is filed unless a hearing is requested by any party to the proceeding. A modification to the plan by the commission may not be in conflict with the jurisdiction or orders of the Federal Energy Regulatory Commission or result in significant additional cost without allowing for timely recovery for that cost. If a hearing is requested, the 180–day deadline is extended one day for each day of the hearing. The transition to competition plan shall be updated or amended annually, subject to commission approval, until the initiation of customer choice by an electric utility subject to this subchapter. Consistent with its jurisdiction, the commission shall have the authority in approving or modifying the transition to competition plan to require the electric utility to take reasonable steps to facilitate the development of a wholesale generation market within the boundaries of the electric utility's service territory.

(i) Notwithstanding any other provision of this chapter, if the commission has not approved the transition to competition plan under this section before January 1, 2009, an electric utility subject to this subchapter shall cease all activities relating to the transition to competition under this section. The commission may, on its own motion or the motion of any affected person, initiate a proceeding under Section 39.152 to certify a power region to which the utility belongs as a qualified power region when the conditions supporting such a proceeding exist. The commission may not approve a plan under Subsection (g) until the expiration of four years from the time that the commission certifies a power region under Subsection (f). If after the expiration of four years from the time the commission certifies a power region under Subsection (f), and after notice and a hearing, the commission determines consistent with the study required by Section 5, S.B. No. 1492, Acts of the 81st Legislature, Regular Session, 2009, that the electric utility cannot comply with Section 38.073, it shall consider approving a plan under Subsection (g).

(j) Notwithstanding any other provision of this subtitle, in awarding a certificate of convenience and necessity or allowing cost recovery for purchased power by an electric utility subject to this section, the commission shall ensure in its determination that the provisions of Sections 37.056(c)(4)(D) and (E) are met.

Added by Acts 2005, 79th Leg., ch. 1072, § 1, eff. June 18, 2005. Amended by Acts 2006, 79th Leg., 3rd C.S., ch. 11, § 1, eff. May 26, 2006; Acts 2009, 81st Leg., ch. 1226, § 3, eff. June 19, 2009.

§ 39.4525. Hiring Assistance for Federal Proceedings

(a) The commission may retain any consultant, accountant, auditor, engineer, or attorney the commission considers necessary to represent the commission in a proceeding before the Federal Energy Regulatory Commission, or before a court reviewing proceedings of that federal commission, related to:

(1) the relationship of an electric utility subject to this subchapter to a power region, regional transmission organization, or independent system operator; or

(2) the approval of an agreement among the electric utility and the electric utility's affiliates concerning the coordination of the operations of the electric utility and the electric utility's affiliates.

(b) Assistance for which a consultant, accountant, auditor, engineer, or attorney may be retained under Subsection (a) may include:

(1) conducting a study;

(2) conducting an investigation;

(3) presenting evidence;

(4) advising the commission; or

(5) representing the commission.

(c) The electric utility shall pay timely the reasonable costs of the services of a person retained under Subsection (a), as determined by the commission. The total costs an electric utility is required to pay under this subsection may not exceed $1.5 million in a 12–month period.

(d) The commission shall allow the electric utility to recover both the total costs the electric utility paid under Subsection (c) and the carrying charges for those costs through a rider established annually to recover the costs paid and carrying charges incurred during the preceding calendar year. The rider may not be implemented before the rider is reviewed and approved by the commission.

(e) The commission shall consult the attorney general before the commission retains a consultant, accountant, auditor, or engineer under Subsection (a). The retention of an attorney under Subsection (a) is subject to the approval of the attorney general under Section 402.0212, Government Code.

(f) The commission shall be precluded from engaging any individual who is required to register under Section 305.003, Government Code.

(g) This section expires December 31, 2017.

Added by Acts 2011, 82nd Leg., ch. 100 (S.B. 1153), § 1, eff. May 20, 2011.

§ 39.453. Customer Choice and Relevant Market and Related Matters

(a) The commission may not authorize customer choice until the commission certifies the applicable power region as a qualifying power region under Section 39.152(a). Sections 39.152(b)–(d) also apply to the electric utility and commission in determining whether to certify the applicable power region.

(b) The commission shall certify that the requirement of Section 39.152(a)(3) is met for an electric utility subject to this subchapter only if the commission finds that the total capacity owned and controlled by the electric utility and the utility's affiliates does not exceed 20 percent of the total installed generation capacity within the power region of that utility.

Added by Acts 2005, 79th Leg., ch. 1072, § 1, eff. June 18, 2005.

§ 39.454. Recoupment of Transition to Competition Costs

An electric utility subject to this subchapter is entitled to recover, as provided by this section, all reasonable and necessary expenditures made or incurred before the effective date of this section to comply with this chapter, to the extent the costs have not otherwise been recovered. The electric utility may file with the commission an application for recovery that gives details of the amounts spent or incurred. After notice and hearing, the commission shall review the amounts and, if the amounts are found to be reasonable and necessary and not otherwise previously recovered, approve a transition to competition retail rate rider mechanism for the recovery of the approved transition to competition costs. A rate proceeding under Chapter 36 is not required to implement the rider. A rate rider implemented to recover approved transition to competition costs shall provide for recovery of those costs over a period not to exceed 15 years, with appropriate carrying costs.

Added by Acts 2005, 79th Leg., ch. 1072, § 1, eff. June 18, 2005.

§ 39.455. Recovery of Incremental Capacity Costs

An electric utility subject to this subchapter is entitled to recover, through a rate rider mechanism, reasonable and necessary costs of incremental resources required to meet load requirements to the extent those costs result in the utility expending more for capacity costs under purchase power agreements than were included in the utility's last base rate case, adjusted for load growth. Any rider under this section shall be implemented after review and approval by the commission, after notice and opportunity for hearing. Following the initial implementation of the rider, an electric utility subject to this subchapter may request revisions semiannually, after notice and opportunity for hearing, on the dates provided in the commission's rules for filing petitions to revise the utility's fuel factor. In conjunction with the utility's fuel reconciliation proceedings, the commission shall reconcile the costs recovered under the rider and the actual incremental capacity costs eligible for recovery under this section. The rider shall expire on the introduction of customer choice or on the implementation of rates resulting from the filing of a Subchapter C, Chapter 36, rate proceeding. In no event may the amount recovered annually under the rider exceed five percent of the utility's annual base rate revenues.

Added by Acts 2005, 79th Leg., ch. 1072, § 1, eff. June 18, 2005.

§ 39.456. Franchise Agreements

A municipality, with the agreement of an electric utility, may accelerate the expiration date of a franchise agreement that was in existence on September 1, 1999. Any new franchise agreement must be approved by the governing body of the municipality. To the extent that a new franchise agreement would result in an increase in the payment of franchise fees to the municipality, and subject to the terms of the franchise agreement, either the electric utility or the municipality, without the need for a rate proceeding under Chapter 36, may file with the commission for approval of a rider for the electric utility's recovery of franchise payments resulting from the agreement, so long as such rider is collected only from customers of the electric utility that are located within the boundaries of the municipality.

Added by Acts 2005, 79th Leg., ch. 1072, § 1, eff. June 18, 2005.

§ 39.457. Contractual Rights

In the event that the electric utility subject to this subchapter either merges, consolidates, or otherwise becomes affiliated with another owner of electric generation, or completes the jurisdictional separation authorized by Section 39.452(e) and the resulting vertically integrated utility proposes to join a regional transmission organization, and either action adversely affects the rights or obligations of an electric cooperative under a wholesale generation or transmission agreement entered into before the effective date of this subchapter or otherwise adversely affects the electric cooperative's access to its existing generation resources under said agreements, then the utility shall submit a proposal agreeable to the cooperative and the utility for addressing such rights and obligations in the appropriate regulatory proceeding. Such proposal shall be consistent with applicable law regarding the rights and obligations of the electric cooperative and the utility under such existing generation or transmission agreements.

Added by Acts 2005, 79th Leg., ch. 1072, § 1, eff. June 18, 2005.

§ 39.458. Recovery and Securitization of Hurricane Reconstruction Costs; Purpose

(a) The purpose of this section and of Sections 39.459–39.463 is to enable an electric utility subject to this subchapter to obtain timely recovery of hurricane reconstruction costs and to use securitization financing to recover these costs, because that type of debt will lower the carrying costs associated with the recovery of hurricane reconstruction costs relative to the costs that would be incurred using conventional financing methods. The proceeds of the transition bonds may be used only for the purposes of reducing the amount of recoverable hurricane reconstruction costs, as determined by the commission in accordance with this subchapter, through the refinancing or retirement of utility debt or equity.

(b) It is the intent of the legislature that:

(1) securitization of hurricane reconstruction costs will be subject to the same procedures, standards, and protections for the securitization of stranded costs and regulatory assets under Subchapter G in effect on the effective date of this section, except as provided by this subchapter; and

(2) the commission will ensure that securitization of hurricane reconstruction costs provides greater tangible and quantifiable benefits to ratepayers than would have been achieved without the issuance of transition bonds.

Added by Acts 2006, 79th Leg., 3rd C.S., ch. 11, § 2, eff. May 26, 2006.

§ 39.459. Hurricane Reconstruction Costs

(a) In this subchapter:

(1) "Hurricane reconstruction costs" means reasonable and necessary costs, including costs expensed, charged to the storm reserve, or capitalized, that are incurred by an electric utility subject to this subchapter due to any activity or activities conducted by or on behalf of the electric utility in connection with the restoration of service associated with electric power outages affecting customers of the electric utility as the result of Hurricane Rita, including mobilization, staging, and construction, reconstruction, replacement, or repair of electric generation, transmission, distribution, or general plant facilities.

(2) "Hurricane Rita" means the hurricane of that name that struck the coastal region of this state in September 2005.

(b) If the commission determines it to be appropriate, hurricane reconstruction costs may include carrying costs from the date on which the hurricane reconstruction costs were incurred until the date that transition bonds are issued.

(c) To the extent a utility subject to this subchapter receives insurance proceeds, governmental grants, or any other source of funding that compensates it for hurricane reconstruction costs, those amounts shall be used to reduce the utility's hurricane reconstruction costs recoverable from customers. If the timing of a utility's receipt of those amounts prevents their inclusion as a reduction to the hurricane reconstruction costs that are securitized, the commission shall take those amounts into account in:

(1) the utility's next base rate proceeding; or

(2) any proceeding in which the commission considers hurricane reconstruction costs.

Added by Acts 2006, 79th Leg., 3rd C.S., ch. 11, § 2, eff. May 26, 2006.

§ 39.460. Standards and Procedures Governing Securitization of Hurricane Reconstruction Costs

(a) The procedures and standards of this subchapter and the provisions of Subchapter G govern the application for, and the commission's issuance of, a financing order to provide for the securitization of hurricane reconstruction costs by an electric utility subject to this subchapter.

(b) Subject to the standards, procedures, and tests contained in this subchapter and Subchapter G, the commission shall adopt a financing order on the application of the utility to recover its hurricane reconstruction costs. On the commission's issuance of a financing order allowing for recovery and securitization of hurricane reconstruction costs, the provisions of this subchapter and Subchapter G continue to govern the financing order and the rights and interests established in the order, and this subchapter and Subchapter G continue to govern any transition bonds issued pursuant to the financing order. To the extent any conflict exists between the provisions of this subchapter and Subchapter G in cases involving the securitization of hurricane reconstruction costs, the provisions of this subchapter control.

(c) For purposes of this subchapter, "financing order," as defined by Section 39.302 and as used in Subchapter G, includes a financing order authorizing the securitization of hurricane reconstruction costs.

(d) For purposes of this subchapter, "qualified costs," as defined by Section 39.302 and as used in Subchapter G, includes 100 percent of the electric utility's hurricane reconstruction costs together with the costs of issuing, supporting, and servicing transition bonds and any costs of retiring and refunding existing debt and equity securities of an electric utility subject to this subchapter in connection with the issuance of transition bonds. For purposes of this subchapter, the term also includes the costs to the commission of acquiring professional services for the purpose of evaluating proposed transactions under this subchapter.

(e) For purposes of this subchapter, "transition bonds," as defined by Section 39.302 and as used in Subchapter G, includes transition bonds issued in association with the recovery of hurricane reconstruction costs. Transition bonds issued to securitize hurricane reconstruction costs may be called "hurricane reconstruction bonds" or may be called by any other name acceptable to the issuer and the underwriters of the transition bonds.

(f) For purposes of this subchapter, "transition charges," as defined by Section 39.302 and as used in Subchapter G, includes nonbypassable amounts to be charged for the use of electric services, approved by the commission under a financing order to recover hurricane reconstruction costs, that shall be collected by an electric utility subject to this subchapter, its successors, an assignee, or other collection agents as provided for in the financing order.

(g) Notwithstanding Section 39.303(c), hurricane reconstruction costs shall be functionalized and allocated to customers in the same manner as the corresponding facilities and related expenses are functionalized and allocated in the utility's current base rates.

(h) The amount of any accumulated deferred federal income taxes offset, used to determine the securitization total, may not be considered in future rate proceedings. Any tax obligation of the electric utility arising from its receipt of securitization bond proceeds, or from the collection and remittance of transition charges, shall be recovered by the electric utility through the commission's implementation of Section 39.458, Section 39.459, this section, and Sections 39.461–39.463.

(i) If the commission determines that recovery of all or any portion of an electric utility's hurricane reconstruction costs using securitization is not beneficial to ratepayers of the electric utility, under one or more of the tests applied to determine those benefits, the commission shall permit the electric utility to recover the entirety of the hurricane reconstruction costs through an appropriate customer surcharge mechanism, including appropriate carrying costs, provided that the electric utility has not securitized any portion of its hurricane reconstruction costs. A rate proceeding under Chapter 36 may not be required to determine and implement this surcharge mechanism. A rider adopted under this subsection must expire on the implementation of rates resulting from the filing of a Subchapter C, Chapter 36, rate proceeding.

Added by Acts 2006, 79th Leg., 3rd C.S., ch. 11, § 2, eff. May 26, 2006.

§ 39.461. Nonbypassable Charges

The commission may include terms in the financing order to ensure that the imposition and collection of transition charges associated with the recovery of hurricane reconstruction costs are nonbypassable by imposing restrictions on bypassability of the type provided for in this chapter or by alternative means of ensuring nonbypassability, as the commission considers appropriate, consistent with the purposes of securitization.

Added by Acts 2006, 79th Leg., 3rd C.S., ch. 11, § 2, eff. May 26, 2006.

§ 39.462. Determination of Hurricane Reconstruction Costs

(a) An electric utility subject to this subchapter is entitled to recover hurricane reconstruction costs consistent with the provisions of this subchapter and is entitled to seek recovery of amounts not recovered under this subchapter, including hurricane reconstruction costs not yet incurred at the time an application is filed under Subsection (b), in its next base rate proceeding or through any other proceeding authorized by Subchapter C, Chapter 36.

(b) The commission shall issue an order determining the amount of hurricane reconstruction costs eligible for recovery and securitization not later than the 150th day after the date an electric utility subject to this subchapter files an application seeking that determination. The 150–day period begins on the date the electric utility files the application, even if the filing occurs before the effective date of this section.

(c) On issuance by the commission of an order determining the amount of eligible hurricane reconstruction costs, an electric utility subject to this subchapter may file an application for a financing order, which shall be governed by the procedures in Subchapter G.

(d) To the extent the commission has made a determination of the eligible hurricane reconstruction costs of an electric utility subject to this subchapter before the effective date of this section, that determination may provide the basis for the utility's application for a financing order pursuant to this subchapter and Subchapter G. A previous commission determination does not preclude the utility from requesting recovery of additional hurricane reconstruction costs eligible for recovery under this subchapter, but not previously authorized by the commission.

(e) A rate proceeding under Chapter 36 is not required to determine the amount of recoverable hurricane reconstruction costs as provided by this section.

Added by Acts 2006, 79th Leg., 3rd C.S., ch. 11, § 2, eff. May 26, 2006.

§ 39.463. Severability

Effective on the date the first utility transition bonds associated with hurricane reconstruction costs are issued under this subchapter, if any provision in this title or portion of this title is held to be invalid or is invalidated, superseded, replaced, repealed, or expires for any reason, that occurrence does not affect the validity or continuation of this subchapter, Subchapter G as it applies to an electric utility subject to this subchapter, or any part of those provisions, or any other provision of this title that is relevant to the issuance, administration, payment, retirement, or refunding of transition bonds or to any actions of the electric utility, its successors, an assignee, a collection agent, or a financing party, and those provisions shall remain in full force and effect.

Added by Acts 2006, 79th Leg., 3rd C.S., ch. 11, § 2, eff. May 26, 2006.

SUBCHAPTER K. TRANSITION TO COMPETITION FOR CERTAIN AREAS OUTSIDE OF ERCOT

§ 39.501. Applicability

(a) This subchapter applies to an investor-owned electric utility:

(1) that is operating solely outside of ERCOT in areas of this state that were included in the Southwest Power Pool on January 1, 2008;

(2) that was not affiliated with the Southeastern Electric Reliability Council on January 1, 2008; and

(3) to which Subchapter I[1] does not apply.

(b) The legislature finds that an electric utility subject to this subchapter is unable at this time to offer fair competition and reliable service to all retail customer classes in the area served by the utility. As a result, the introduction of retail competition for such an electric utility is delayed until fair competition and reliable service are available to all retail customer classes as determined under this subchapter.

Added by Acts 2009, 81st Leg., ch. 128, § 1, eff. Sept. 1, 2009.

[1] V.T.C.A., Utilities Code § 39.451 et seq.

§ 39.502. Cost-of-service Regulation

(a) Until the date on which an electric utility subject to this subchapter is authorized by the commission under Section 39.503(f) to implement retail customer choice, the rates of the utility are subject to regulation under Chapter 36.

(b) Until the date on which an electric utility subject to this subchapter implements customer choice, the provisions of this chapter, other than this subchapter and Sections 39.904 and 39.905, do not apply to that utility.

Added by Acts 2009, 81st Leg., ch. 128, § 1, eff. Sept. 1, 2009.

§ 39.503. Transition to Competition

(a) The events prescribed by Subsections (b)–(f) shall be followed to introduce retail competition in the service area of an electric utility subject to this subchapter. The commission may modify the sequence of events required by Subsections (b)–(e), but not the substance of the requirements. Full retail competition may not begin in the service area of an electric utility subject to this subchapter until all actions prescribed by those subsections are completed.

(b) The first stage for the transition to competition consists of the following activities:

(1) approval of a regional transmission organization by the Federal Energy Regulatory Commission for the power region that includes the electric utility's service area and commencement of independent operation of the transmission network under the approved regional transmission organization;

(2) development of retail market protocols to facilitate retail competition; and

(3) completion of an expedited proceeding to develop non-bypassable delivery rates for the customer choice pilot project to be implemented under Subsection (c)(1).

(c) The second stage for the transition to competition consists of the following activities:

(1) initiation of the customer choice pilot project in accordance with Section 39.104;

(2) development of a balancing energy market, a market for ancillary services, and a market-based congestion management system for the wholesale market in the power region in which the regional transmission organization operates; and

(3) implementation of a seams agreement with adjacent power regions to reduce barriers to entry and facilitate competition.

(d) The third stage for the transition to competition consists of the following activities:

(1) the electric utility filing with the commission:

(A) an application for business separation in accordance with Section 39.051;

(B) an application for unbundled transmission and distribution rates in accordance with Section 39.201;

(C) an application for certification of a qualified power region in accordance with Section 39.152; and

(D) an application for price-to-beat rates in accordance with Section 39.202;

(2) the commission:

(A) approving a business separation plan for the utility;

(B) setting unbundled transmission and distribution rates for the utility;

(C) certifying a qualified power region, which includes conducting a formal evaluation of wholesale market power in the region, in accordance with Section 39.152;

(D) setting price-to-beat rates for the utility; and

(E) determining which competitive energy services must be separated from regulated utility activities in accordance with Section 39.051; and

(3) completion of the testing of retail and wholesale systems, including those systems necessary for switching customers to the retail electric provider of their choice and for settlement of wholesale market transactions, by the regional transmission organization, the registration agent, and market participants.

(e) The fourth stage for the transition to competition consists of the following activities:

(1) commission evaluation of the results of the pilot project;

(2) initiation by the electric utility of a capacity auction in accordance with Section 39.153 at a time to be determined by the commission; and

(3) separation by the utility of competitive energy services from its regulated utility activities, in accordance with the commission order approving the separation of competitive energy services.

(f) The fifth stage for the transition to competition consists of the following activities:

(1) evaluation by the commission of whether the electric utility can offer fair competition and reliable service to all retail customer classes in the area served by the utility, and:

(A) if the commission concludes that the electric utility can offer fair competition and reliable service to all retail customer classes in the area served by the utility, the commission issuing an order initiating retail competition for the utility; and

(B) if the commission determines that the electric utility cannot offer fair competition and reliable service to all retail customer classes in the area served by the utility, the commission issuing an order further delaying retail competition for the utility; and

(2) on the issuance of an order from the commission initiating retail competition for the utility, completion by the utility of the business separation and unbundling in accordance with the commission order approving the unbundling.

Added by Acts 2009, 81st Leg., ch. 128, § 1, eff. Sept. 1, 2009.

SUBCHAPTER L. TRANSITION TO COMPETITION AND OTHER PROVISIONS FOR CERTAIN AREAS OUTSIDE OF ERCOT

§ 39.551. Applicability

(a) This subchapter applies only to an investor-owned electric utility:

(1) that is operating solely outside of ERCOT in areas of this state that were included in the Western Electricity Coordinating Council on January 1, 2011;

(2) that was not affiliated with ERCOT on January 1, 2011; and

(3) to which Subchapters I, J, and K do not apply.

(b) The legislature finds that an electric utility subject to this subchapter is unable at this time to offer fair competition and reliable service to all retail customer classes in the area served by the utility. As a result, the introduction of retail competition for such an electric utility is delayed until fair competition and reliable service are available to all retail customer classes as determined under this subchapter.

Added by Acts 2011, 82nd Leg., ch. 1113 (S.B. 1910), § 1, eff. June 17, 2011.

§ 39.552. Cost–of–Service Regulation

(a) Until the date on which an electric utility subject to this subchapter is authorized by the commission under Section 39.553(f) to implement retail customer choice, the rates of the utility are subject to regulation under Chapter 36.

(b) Until the date on which an electric utility subject to this subchapter implements customer choice, the provisions of this chapter, other than this subchapter and Sections 39.904 and 39.905, do not apply to that utility.

Added by Acts 2011, 82nd Leg., ch. 1113 (S.B. 1910), § 1, eff. June 17, 2011.

§ 39.553. Transition to Competition

(a) The events prescribed by Subsections (b)–(f) shall be followed to introduce retail competition in the service area of an electric utility subject to this subchapter. The commission shall ensure that the listed items in each stage are completed before the next stage is initiated. Unless stated otherwise, the commission shall conduct each activity with the electric utility and other interested parties. The commission may modify the sequence of events required by Subsections (b)–(e), but not the substance of the requirements, if the commission finds good cause to do so. Full retail competition may not begin in the service area of an electric utility subject to this subchapter until all actions prescribed by those subsections are completed.

(b) The first stage for the transition to competition consists of the following activities:

(1) approval of a regional transmission organization by the Federal Energy Regulatory Commission for the power region that includes the electric utility's service area and commencement of independent operation of the transmission network under the approved regional transmission organization;

(2) development of retail market protocols to facilitate retail competition; and

(3) completion of an expedited proceeding to develop nonbypassable delivery rates for the customer choice pilot project to be implemented under Subsection (c)(1).

(c) The second stage for the transition to competition consists of the following activities:

(1) initiation of the customer choice pilot project in accordance with Section 39.104;

(2) development of a balancing energy market, a market for ancillary services, and a market-based congestion management system for the wholesale market in the power region in which the regional transmission organization operates; and

(3) implementation of a seams agreement with adjacent power regions to reduce barriers to entry and facilitate competition.

(d) The third stage for the transition to competition consists of the following activities:

(1) the electric utility filing with the commission:

(A) an application for business separation in accordance with Section 39.051;

(B) an application for unbundled transmission and distribution rates in accordance with Section 39.201;

(C) an application for certification of a qualified power region in accordance with Section 39.152; and

(D) an application for price-to-beat rates in accordance with Section 39.202;

(2) the commission:

(A) approving a business separation plan for the utility;

(B) setting unbundled transmission and distribution rates for the utility;

(C) certifying a qualified power region, which includes conducting a formal evaluation of wholesale market power in the region, in accordance with Section 39.152;

(D) setting price-to-beat rates for the utility; and

(E) determining which competitive energy services must be separated from regulated utility activities in accordance with Section 39.051; and

(3) completion of the testing of retail and wholesale systems, including those systems necessary for switching customers to the retail electric provider of their choice and for settlement of wholesale market transactions, by the regional transmission organization, the registration agent, and market participants.

(e) The fourth stage for the transition to competition consists of the following activities:

(1) commission evaluation of the results of the pilot project;

(2) initiation by the electric utility of a capacity auction in accordance with Section 39.153 at a time to be determined by the commission; and

(3) separation by the utility of competitive energy services from its regulated utility activities, in accordance with the commission order approving the separation of competitive energy services.

(f) The fifth stage for the transition to competition consists of the following activities:

(1) evaluation by the commission of whether the electric utility can offer fair competition and reliable service to all retail customer classes in the area served by the utility, and:

(A) if the commission concludes that the electric utility can offer fair competition and reliable service to all retail customer classes in the area served by the utility, the commission issuing an order initiating retail competition for the utility; and

(B) if the commission determines that the electric utility cannot offer fair competition and reliable service to all retail customer classes in the area served by the utility, the commission issuing an order further delaying retail competition for the utility; and

(2) on the issuance of an order from the commission initiating retail competition for the utility, completion by the utility of the business separation and unbundling in accordance with the commission order approving the unbundling.

Added by Acts 2011, 82nd Leg., ch. 1113 (S.B. 1910), § 1, eff. June 17, 2011.

§ 39.554. Interconnection of Distributed Renewable Generation

(a) In this section:

(1) "Distributed renewable generation" has the meaning assigned by Section 39.916.

(2) "Distributed renewable generation owner" means an owner of distributed renewable generation that is a retail electric customer.

(3) "Interconnection" has the meaning assigned by Section 39.916.

(b) A distributed renewable generation owner in the service area of an electric utility subject to this subchapter may request interconnection by filing an application for interconnection with the utility. An application for interconnection is subject to the utility's safety and reliability requirements. The utility's procedures for the submission and processing of an application for interconnection shall be consistent with rules adopted by the commission regarding interconnection.

(c) An electric utility that approves an application of a distributed renewable generation owner under Subsection (b):

(1) shall install, maintain, and retain ownership of the meter and metering equipment; and

(2) may install load research metering equipment on the premises of the owner, at no expense to the owner.

(d) At the request of an electric utility that approves an application of a distributed renewable generation owner under Subsection (b), the owner shall:

(1) provide and install a meter socket, a metering cabinet, or both a socket and cabinet at a location

designated by the utility on the premises of the owner; and

(2) provide, at no expense to the utility, a suitable location for the utility to install meters and equipment associated with billing and load research.

(e) An electric utility that approves an application of a distributed renewable generation owner under Subsection (b) shall provide to the owner the metering options described by Section 39.916(f) and an option to interconnect with the utility through a single meter that runs forward and backward if:

(1) the owner:

(A) intends to interconnect the distributed renewable generation at an apartment house, as defined by Section 184.011, occupied by low-income elderly tenants that qualifies for master metering under Section 184.012(b) and the distributed renewable generation is reasonably expected to generate not less than 50 percent of the apartment house's annual electricity use; or

(B) has a qualifying facility with a design capacity of not more than 50 kilowatts; and

(2) the distributed renewable generation or qualifying facility that is the subject of the application is rated to produce an amount of electricity that is less than or equal to:

(A) the owner's estimated annual kilowatt hour consumption for a new apartment house or qualifying facility; or

(B) the amount of electricity the owner consumed in the year before installation of the distributed renewable generation or qualifying facility.

(f) For a distributed renewable generation owner that chooses interconnection through a single meter under Subsection (e):

(1) the amount of electricity the owner generates through distributed renewable generation or a qualifying facility for a given billing period offsets the owner's consumption for that billing period; and

(2) any electricity the owner generates through distributed renewable generation or a qualifying facility that exceeds the owner's consumption for a given billing period shall be credited to the owner under Subsection (g).

(g) An electric utility that purchases surplus electricity under Subsection (f)(2) shall purchase the electricity from the distributed renewable generation owner at the cost of the utility as determined by commission rule. The utility shall take reasonable steps to inform the owner of the amount of surplus electricity purchased from the owner in kilowatt hours during the owner's most recent billing cycle. A credit balance of not more than $50 on the owner's monthly bill may be carried forward onto the owner's next monthly bill. The utility shall refund to the owner a credit balance that is not carried forward or the portion of a credit balance that exceeds $50 if the credit balance is carried forward.

(h) In a base rate proceeding or fuel cost recovery proceeding conducted under Chapter 36, the commission shall ensure that any additional cost associated with the metering and payment options described by Subsections (e), (f), and (g) is allocated only to customer classes that include distributed renewable generation owners who have chosen those metering options.

Added by Acts 2011, 82nd Leg., ch. 1113 (S.B. 1910), § 1, eff. June 17, 2011.

§ 39.555. Marketing of Energy Efficiency and Renewable Energy Programs

An electric utility subject to this subchapter may market an energy efficiency or renewable energy program directly to a retail electric customer in its service territory and provide rebate or incentive funds directly to a customer to promote or facilitate the success of programs implemented under Section 39.905.

Added by Acts 2011, 82nd Leg., ch. 1113 (S.B. 1910), § 1, eff. June 17, 2011.

SUBCHAPTER Z. MISCELLANEOUS PROVISIONS

§ 39.901. Repealed by Acts 2005, 79th Leg., ch. 412, § 18(2), eff. September 1, 2005

§ 39.9011. Expired.

§ 39.9015. Expired

§ 39.9016. Nuclear Safety Fee

An electric utility that operates a nuclear asset located in a county on the coast of the Gulf of Mexico shall pay a nuclear safety fee for the year 2000 and the year 2001 to each taxing unit in which the nuclear asset is located, other than a school district, in an amount equal to the difference between the ad valorem taxes imposed by the taxing unit in 1999 and the amount of ad valorem taxes imposed by the unit in the year for which the fee is due, except that the amount of the fee may not exceed one-half the taxes imposed on the asset by the unit in 1999. The nuclear safety fee shall be considered a tax or fee under Section 39.258(5).

Added by Acts 1999, 76th Leg., ch. 405, § 39, eff. Sept. 1, 1999.

§ 39.902. Customer Education

(a) On or before January 1, 2001, the commission shall develop and implement an educational program to inform customers, including low-income and non-English-speaking customers, about changes in the provision of electric service resulting from the opening of the retail electric market and the customer choice pilot program under this chapter. The educational program shall be neutral and nonpromotional and shall provide customers with the information necessary to make informed decisions relating to the source and type of electric service available for purchase and other information the commission considers necessary. The educational program shall inform customers of their rights and of the protections available through the commission and the office. The educational program may not duplicate customer information efforts undertaken by retail electric providers or other private entities. The educational program may not be targeted to areas served by municipally owned utilities or electric cooperatives that have not adopted customer choice. In planning and implementing this program, the commission shall consult with the office, with the Texas Department of Housing and Community Affairs, and with customers of and providers of retail electric service. The commission may enter into contracts for professional services to carry out the customer education program.

(b) Repealed by Acts 2011, 82nd Leg., ch. 1083 (S.B. 1179), § 25(162).

(c) After the opening of the retail electric market, the commission shall conduct ongoing customer education designed to help customers make informed choices of electric services and retail electric providers. As part of ongoing education, the commission may provide customers information concerning specific retail electric providers, including instances of complaints against them and records relating to quality of customer service.

Added by Acts 1999, 76th Leg., ch. 405, § 39, eff. Sept. 1, 1999. Amended by Acts 2011, 82nd Leg., ch. 1083 (S.B. 1179), § 25(162), eff. June 17, 2011.

§ 39.9025. Home Electric Energy Reports

The commission may encourage retail electric providers to deliver individualized home electric energy reports to educate consumers about electric energy use and energy efficiency to assist consumers to use energy more efficiently.

Added by Acts 2007, 80th Leg., ch. 939, § 21, eff. Sept. 1, 2007.

§ 39.903. System Benefit Fund

(a) The system benefit fund is an account in the general revenue fund. Money in the account may be appropriated only for the purposes provided by this section or other law. Interest earned on the system benefit fund shall be credited to the fund. Section 403.095, Government Code, does not apply to the system benefit fund.

(b) The system benefit fund is financed by a nonbypassable fee set by the commission in an amount not to exceed 65 cents per megawatt hour. The system benefit fund fee is allocated to customers based on the amount of kilowatt hours used.

(c) The nonbypassable fee may not be imposed on the retail electric customers of a municipally owned utility or electric cooperative before the sixth month preceding the date on which the utility or cooperative implements customer choice. Money distributed from the system benefit fund to a municipally owned utility or an electric cooperative shall be proportional to the nonbypassable fee paid by the municipally owned utility or the electric cooperative, subject to the reimbursement provided by Subsection (i). On request by a municipally owned utility or electric cooperative, the commission shall reduce the nonbypassable fee imposed on retail electric customers served by the municipally owned utility or electric cooperative by an amount equal to the amount provided by the municipally owned utility or electric cooperative or its ratepayers for local low-income programs and local programs that educate customers about the retail electric market in a neutral and nonpromotional manner.

(d) The commission shall annually review and approve system benefit fund accounts, projected revenue requirements, and proposed nonbypassable fees. The commission shall report to the electric utility restructuring legislative oversight committee if the system benefit fund fee is insufficient to fund the purposes set forth in Subsection (e) to the extent required by this section.

(e) Money in the system benefit fund may be appropriated to provide funding solely for the following regulatory purposes, in the following order of priority:

(1) programs to:

(A) assist low-income electric customers by providing the 10 percent reduced rate prescribed by Subsection (h); and

(B) provide one-time bill payment assistance to electric customers who are or who have in their households one or more seriously ill or disabled low-income persons and who have been threatened with disconnection for nonpayment;

(2) customer education programs, administrative expenses incurred by the commission in implementing and administering this chapter, and expenses incurred by the office under this chapter;

(3) programs to assist low-income electric customers by providing the targeted energy efficiency programs described by Subsection (f)(2);

(4) programs to assist low-income electric customers by providing the 20 percent reduced rate prescribed by Subsection (h); and

(5) reimbursement to the commission and the Health and Human Services Commission for expenses incurred in the implementation and administration of an integrated eligibility process created under Section 17.007 for customer service discounts relating to retail electric service, including outreach expenses the commission determines are reasonable and necessary.

(f) Notwithstanding Section 39.106(b), the commission shall adopt rules regarding programs to assist low-income electric customers on the introduction of customer choice. The programs may not be targeted to areas served by municipally owned utilities or electric cooperatives that have not adopted customer choice. The programs shall include:

(1) reduced electric rates as provided by Subsections (h)–(*l*); and

(2) targeted energy efficiency programs to be administered by the Texas Department of Housing and Community Affairs in coordination with existing weatherization programs.

(g) Until customer choice is introduced in a power region, an electric utility may not reduce, in any manner, programs already offered to assist low-income electric customers.

(h) The commission shall adopt rules for a retail electric provider to determine a reduced rate for eligible customers to be discounted off the standard retail service package as approved by the commission under Section 39.106, or the price to beat established by Section 39.202, whichever is lower. Municipally owned utilities and electric cooperatives shall establish a reduced rate for eligible customers to be discounted off the standard retail service package established under Section 40.053 or 41.053, as appropriate. The reduced rate for a retail electric provider shall result in a total charge that is at least 10 percent and, if sufficient money in the system benefit fund is available, up to 20 percent, lower than the amount the customer would otherwise be charged. To the extent the system benefit fund is insufficient to fund the initial 10 percent rate reduction, the commission may increase the fee to an amount not more than 65 cents per megawatt hour, as provided by Subsection (b). If the fee is set at 65 cents per megawatt hour or if the commission determines that appropriations are insufficient to fund the 10 percent rate reduction, the commission may reduce the rate reduction to less than 10 percent. For a municipally owned utility or electric cooperative, the reduced rate shall be equal to an amount that can be fully funded by that portion of the nonbypassable fee proceeds paid by the municipally owned utility or electric cooperative that is allocated to the utility or cooperative by the commission under Subsection (e) for programs for low-income customers of the utility or cooperative. The reduced rate for municipally owned utilities and electric cooperatives under this section is in addition to any rate reduction that may result from local programs for low-income customers of the municipally owned utilities or electric cooperatives.

(i) A retail electric provider, municipally owned utility, or electric cooperative seeking reimbursement from the system benefit fund may not charge an eligible low-income customer a rate higher than the appropriate rate determined under Subsection (h). A retail electric provider not subject to the price to beat, or a municipally owned utility or electric cooperative subject to the nonbypassable fee under Subsection (c), shall be reimbursed from the system benefit fund for the difference between the reduced rate and the rate established under Section 39.106 or, as appropriate, the rate established under Section 40.053 or 41.053. A retail electric provider who is subject to the price to beat shall be reimbursed from the system benefit fund for the difference between the reduced rate and the price to beat. The commission shall adopt rules providing for the reimbursement.

(j) The commission shall adopt rules providing for methods of enrolling customers eligible to receive reduced rates under Subsection (h). The rules must provide for automatic enrollment as one enrollment option. The Texas Department of Human Services, on request of the commission, shall assist in the adoption and implementation of these rules. The commission and the Texas Department of Human Services shall enter into a memorandum of understanding establishing the respective duties of the commission and the department in relation to the automatic enrollment.

(j–1) The commission shall adopt rules governing the bill payment assistance program provided under Subsection (e)(1)(B). The rules must provide that a customer is eligible to receive the assistance only if the assistance is necessary to prevent the disconnection of service for nonpayment of bills and the electric customer is or has in the customer's household one or more seriously ill or disabled low-income persons whose health or safety may be injured by the disconnection. The commission may prescribe the documentation necessary to demonstrate eligibility for the assistance and may establish additional eligibility criteria. The Health and Human Services Commission, on request of the commission, shall assist in the adoption and implementation of these rules.

(k) A retail electric provider is prohibited from charging the customer a fee for participation in the reduced rate program.

(*l*) For the purposes of this section, a "low-income electric customer" is an electric customer:

(1) whose household income is not more than 125 percent of the federal poverty guidelines; or

(2) who receives food stamps from the Texas Department of Human Services or medical assistance from a state agency administering a part of the medical assistance program.

Added by Acts 1999, 76th Leg., ch. 405, § 39, eff. Sept. 1, 1999. Amended by Acts 2001, 77th Leg., ch. 1466, § 19(a), eff. June 15, 2001; Acts 2001, 77th Leg., ch. 1394, § 3, eff. Sept. 1, 2001; Acts 2001, 77th Leg., ch. 1451, § 3, eff. Sept. 1, 2001; Acts 2003, 78th Leg., ch. 211, § 2.02, eff. June 16, 2003; Acts 2003, 78th Leg., ch. 1296, § 4(a), eff. June 20, 2003; Acts 2005, 79th Leg., ch. 412, § 17, eff. Sept. 1, 2005; Acts 2005, 79th Leg., ch. 728, § 21.001, eff. Sept. 1, 2005; Acts 2005, 79th Leg., ch. 797, §§ 11, 12, eff. Sept. 1, 2005; Acts 2005, 79th Leg., ch. 899, § 14.01, eff. Aug. 29, 2005.

§ 39.904. Goal for Renewable Energy

(a) It is the intent of the legislature that by January 1, 2015, an additional 5,000 megawatts of generating capacity from renewable energy technologies will have been installed in this state. The cumulative installed renewable capacity in this state shall total 5,880 megawatts by January 1, 2015, and the commission shall establish a target of 10,000 megawatts of installed renewable capacity by January 1, 2025. The cumulative installed renewable capacity in this state shall total 2,280 megawatts by January 1, 2007, 3,272 megawatts by January 1, 2009, 4,264 megawatts by January 1, 2011, 5,256 megawatts by January 1, 2013, and 5,880 megawatts by January 1, 2015. Of the renewable energy technology generating capacity installed to meet the goal of this subsection after September 1, 2005, the commission shall establish a target of having at least 500 megawatts of capacity from a renewable energy technology other than a source using wind energy.

(b) The commission shall establish a renewable energy credits trading program. Any retail electric provider, municipally owned utility, or electric cooperative that does not satisfy the requirements of Subsection (a) by directly owning or purchasing capacity using renewable energy technologies shall purchase sufficient renewable energy credits to satisfy the requirements by holding renewable energy credits in lieu of capacity from renewable energy technologies.

(c) Not later than January 1, 2000, the commission shall adopt rules necessary to administer and enforce this section. At a minimum, the rules shall:

(1) establish the minimum annual renewable energy requirement for each retail electric provider, municipally owned utility, and electric cooperative operating in this state in a manner reasonably calculated by the commission to produce, on a statewide basis, compliance with the requirement prescribed by Subsection (a); and

(2) specify reasonable performance standards that all renewable capacity additions must meet to count against the requirement prescribed by Subsection (a) and that:

(A) are designed and operated so as to maximize the energy output from the capacity additions in accordance with then-current industry standards; and

(B) encourage the development, construction, and operation of new renewable energy projects at those sites in this state that have the greatest economic potential for capture and development of this state's environmentally beneficial renewable resources.

(d) In this section, "renewable energy technology" means any technology that exclusively relies on an energy source that is naturally regenerated over a short time and derived directly from the sun, indirectly from the sun, or from moving water or other natural movements and mechanisms of the environment. Renewable energy technologies include those that rely on energy derived directly from the sun, on wind, geothermal, hydroelectric, wave, or tidal energy, or on biomass or biomass-based waste products, including landfill gas. A renewable energy technology does not rely on energy resources derived from fossil fuels, waste products from fossil fuels, or waste products from inorganic sources.

(e) A municipally owned utility operating a gas distribution system may credit toward satisfaction of the requirements of this section any production or acquisition of landfill gas supplied to the gas distribution system, based on conversion to kilowatt hours of the thermal energy content in British thermal units of the renewable source and using for the conversion factor the annual heat rate of the most efficient gas-fired unit of the combined utility's electric system as measured in British thermal units per kilowatt hour and using the British thermal unit measurement based on the higher heating value measurement.

(f) A municipally owned utility operating a gas distribution system may credit toward satisfaction of the requirements of this section any production or acquisition of landfill gas supplied to the gas distribution system, based on conversion to kilowatt hours of the thermal energy content in British thermal units of the renewable source and using for the conversion factor the systemwide average heat rate of the gas-fired units of the combined utility's electric system as measured in British thermal units per kilowatt hour.

(g) The commission, after consultation with each appropriate independent organization, electric reliability council, or regional transmission organization:

(1) shall designate competitive renewable energy zones throughout this state in areas in which renewable energy resources and suitable land areas are sufficient to develop generating capacity from renewable energy technologies;

(2) shall develop a plan to construct transmission capacity necessary to deliver to electric customers, in a manner that is most beneficial and cost-effective to the customers, the electric output from renewable energy technologies in the competitive renewable energy zones; and

(3) shall consider the level of financial commitment by generators for each competitive renewable energy zone in determining whether to designate an area as a competitive renewable energy zone and whether to grant a certificate of convenience and necessity.

(h) In considering an application for a certificate of public convenience and necessity for a transmission project intended to serve a competitive renewable energy zone, the commission is not required to consider the factors provided by Sections 37.056(c)(1) and (2).

(i) Transmission service to a competitive renewable energy zone must be provided in a manner consistent with Subchapter A, Chapter 35.[1]

(j) The commission, after consultation with each appropriate independent organization, electric reliability council, or regional transmission organization, shall file a report with the legislature not later than December 31 of each even-numbered year. The report must include:

(1) an evaluation of the commission's implementation of competitive renewable energy zones;

(2) the estimated cost of transmission service improvements needed for each competitive renewable energy zone; and

(3) an evaluation of the effects that additional renewable generation has on system reliability and on the cost of alternatives to mitigate the effects.

(k) The commission and the independent organization certified for ERCOT shall study the need for increased transmission and generation capacity throughout this state and report to the legislature the results of the study and any recommendations for legislation. The report must be filed with the legislature not later than December 31 of each even-numbered year and may be filed as a part of the report required by Subsection (j).

(*l*) The commission may adopt rules requiring renewable power facilities to have reactive power control capabilities or any other feasible technology designed to reduce the facilities' effects on system reliability.

(m) A renewable energy credit retired for purposes other than to meet the requirements of Subsection (c)(1) may not affect the minimum annual renewable energy requirement under Subsection (c)(1) for a retail electric provider, municipally owned utility, or electric cooperative.

(m–1) As provided by this subsection, the commission shall reduce the requirement under Subsection (c)(1) for a retail electric provider, municipally owned utility, or electric cooperative that is subject to a renewable energy requirement under this section and that serves a customer receiving electric service at transmission-level voltage if, before any year for which the commission calculates renewable energy requirements under Subsection (c)(1), the customer notifies the commission in writing that the customer chooses not to support the goal for renewable energy generation under this section for that year. The commission shall exclude from the calculation of a retail electric provider's, municipally owned utility's, or electric cooperative's requirement under Subsection (c)(1) energy sold by the retail electric provider, municipally owned utility, or electric cooperative at transmission-level voltage to customers who have submitted the notice to the commission under this subsection for the applicable year.

(m–2) The commission shall determine the reporting requirements and schedule necessary to implement Subsections (m) and (m–1).

(m–3) Subsections (m), (m–1), and (m–2) do not alter the renewable energy goals or targets established in Subsection (a) or reduce the minimum statewide renewable energy requirements of Subsection (c)(1).

(n) Notwithstanding any other provision of law, the commission shall have the authority to cap the price of renewable energy credits and may suspend the goal contained in Subsection (a) if such suspension is necessary to protect the reliability and operation of the grid.

(*o*) The commission may establish an alternative compliance payment. An entity that has a renewable energy purchase requirement under this section may elect to pay the alternative compliance payment instead of applying renewable energy credits toward the satisfaction of the entity's obligation under this section. The commission may establish a separate alternative compliance payment for the goal of 500 megawatts of capacity from renewable energy technologies other than wind energy. The alternative compliance payment for a renewable energy purchase requirement that could be satisfied with a renewable energy credit from wind energy may not be less than $2.50 per credit or greater than $20 per credit. Prior to September 1, 2009, an alternative compliance payment under this subsection may not be set above $5 per credit. In implementing this subsection, the commission shall consider:

(1) the effect of renewable energy credit prices on retail competition;

(2) the effect of renewable energy credit prices on electric rates;

(3) the effect of the alternative compliance payment level on the renewable energy credit market; and

(4) any other factors necessary to ensure the continued development of the renewable energy industry in this state while protecting ratepayers from unnecessary rate increases.

Added by Acts 1999, 76th Leg., ch. 405, § 39, eff. Sept. 1, 1999. Amended by Acts 2005, 79th Leg., 1st C.S., ch. 1, § 3, eff. Sept. 1, 2005; Acts 2007, 80th Leg., ch. 1013, § 2, eff. Sept. 1, 2007.

[1] V.T.C.A., Utilities Code § 35.001.

§ 39.9044. Goal for Natural Gas

(a) It is the intent of the legislature that 50 percent of the megawatts of generating capacity installed in this state after January 1, 2000, use natural gas. To the extent permitted by law, the commission shall establish a program to encourage utilities to comply with this section by using natural gas produced in this state as the preferential fuel. This section does not apply to generating capacity for renewable energy technologies.

(b) The commission shall establish a natural gas energy credits trading program. Any power generation company, municipally owned utility, or electric cooperative that does not satisfy the requirements of Subsection (a) by directly owning or purchasing capacity using natural gas technologies shall purchase sufficient natural gas energy credits to satisfy the requirements by holding natural gas energy credits in lieu of capacity from natural gas energy technologies.

(c) Not later than January 1, 2000, the commission shall adopt rules necessary to administer and enforce this section and to perform any necessary studies in cooperation with the Railroad Commission of Texas. At a minimum, the rules shall:

(1) establish the minimum annual natural gas generation requirement for each power generation company, municipally owned utility, and electric cooperative operating in this state in a manner reasonably calculated by the commission to produce, on a statewide basis, compliance with the requirement prescribed by Subsection (a); and

(2) specify reasonable performance standards that all natural gas capacity additions must meet to count against the requirement prescribed by Subsection (a) and that:

(A) are designed and operated so as to maximize the energy output from the capacity additions in accordance with then-current industry standards and best industry standards; and

(B) encourage the development, construction, and operation of new natural gas energy projects at those sites in this state that have the greatest economic potential for capture and development of this state's environmentally beneficial natural gas resources.

(d) The commission, with the assistance of the Railroad Commission of Texas, shall adopt rules allowing and encouraging retail electric providers and municipally owned utilities and electric cooperatives that have adopted customer choice to market electricity generated using natural gas produced in this state as environmentally beneficial. The rules shall allow a provider, municipally owned utility, or cooperative to:

(1) emphasize that natural gas produced in this state is the cleanest-burning fossil fuel; and

(2) label the electricity generated using natural gas produced in this state as "green" electricity.

(e) In this section, "natural gas technology" means any technology that exclusively relies on natural gas as a primary fuel source.

Added by Acts 1999, 76th Leg., ch. 405, § 39, eff. Sept. 1, 1999.

§ 39.9048. Natural Gas Fuel

It is the intent of the legislature that:

(1) the cost of generating electricity remain as low as possible; and

(2) the state establish and publicize a program to keep the costs of fuel, such as natural gas, used for generating electricity low.

Added by Acts 1999, 76th Leg., ch. 405, § 39, eff. Sept. 1, 1999.

§ 39.905. Goal for Energy Efficiency

(a) It is the goal of the legislature that:

(1) electric utilities will administer energy efficiency incentive programs in a market-neutral, nondiscriminatory manner but will not offer underlying competitive services;

(2) all customers, in all customer classes, will have a choice of and access to energy efficiency alternatives and other choices from the market that allow each customer to reduce energy consumption, summer and winter peak demand, or energy costs;

(3) each electric utility annually will provide, through market-based standard offer programs or through targeted market-transformation programs, incentives sufficient for retail electric providers and competitive energy service providers to acquire additional cost-effective energy efficiency, subject to cost ceilings established by the commission, for the utility's residential and commercial customers equivalent to:

(A) not less than:

(i) 30 percent of the electric utility's annual growth in demand of residential and commercial customers by December 31 of each year beginning with the 2013 calendar year; and

(ii) the amount of energy efficiency to be acquired for the utility's residential and commercial customers for the most recent preceding year; and

(B) for an electric utility whose amount of energy efficiency to be acquired under this subsection is equivalent to at least four tenths of one percent of the electric utility's summer weather-adjusted peak demand for residential and commercial customers in the previous calendar year, not less than:

(i) four-tenths of one percent of the utility's summer weather-adjusted peak demand for residential and commercial customers by December 31 of each subsequent year; and

(ii) the amount of energy efficiency to be acquired for the utility's residential and commercial customers for the most recent preceding year;

(4) each electric utility in the ERCOT region shall use its best efforts to encourage and facilitate the involvement of the region's retail electric providers in the delivery of efficiency programs and demand response programs under this section, including programs for demand-side renewable energy systems that:

(A) use distributed renewable generation, as defined by Section 39.916; or

(B) reduce the need for energy consumption by using a renewable energy technology, a geothermal heat pump, a solar water heater, or another natural mechanism of the environment;

(5) retail electric providers in the ERCOT region, and electric utilities outside of the ERCOT region, shall provide customers with energy efficiency educational materials; and

(6) notwithstanding Subsection (a)(3), electric utilities shall continue to make available, at 2007 funding and participation levels, any load management standard offer programs developed for industrial customers and implemented prior to May 1, 2007.

(b) The commission shall provide oversight and adopt rules and procedures to ensure that the utilities can achieve the goal of this section, including:

(1) establishing an energy efficiency cost recovery factor for ensuring timely and reasonable cost

recovery for utility expenditures made to satisfy the goal of this section;

(2) establishing an incentive under Section 36.204 to reward utilities administering programs under this section that exceed the minimum goals established by this section;

(3) providing a utility that is unable to establish an energy efficiency cost recovery factor in a timely manner due to a rate freeze with a mechanism to enable the utility to:

(A) defer the costs of complying with this section; and

(B) recover the deferred costs through an energy efficiency cost recovery factor on the expiration of the rate freeze period;

(4) ensuring that the costs associated with programs provided under this section and any shareholder bonus awarded are borne by the customer classes that receive the services under the programs;

(5) ensuring the program rules encourage the value of the incentives to be passed on to the end-use customer;

(6) ensuring that programs are evaluated, measured, and verified using a framework established by the commission that promotes effective program design and consistent and streamlined reporting; and

(7) ensuring that an independent organization certified under Section 39.151 allows load participation in all energy markets for residential, commercial, and industrial customer classes, either directly or through aggregators of retail customers, to the extent that load participation by each of those customer classes complies with reasonable requirements adopted by the organization relating to the reliability and adequacy of the regional electric network and in a manner that will increase market efficiency, competition, and customer benefits.

(b–1) The energy efficiency cost recovery factor under Subsection (b)(1) may not result in an over-recovery of costs but may be adjusted each year to change rates to enable utilities to match revenues against energy efficiency costs and any incentives to which they are granted. The factor shall be adjusted to reflect any over-collection or under-collection of energy efficiency cost recovery revenues in previous years.

(b–2) Repealed by Acts 2011, 82nd Leg., ch. 180 (S.B. 1125), § 3.

(b–3) Beginning not later than January 1, 2008, the commission, in consultation with the State Energy Conservation Office, annually for a period of five years shall compute and report to ERCOT the projected energy savings and demand impacts for each entity in the ERCOT region that administers standard offer programs, market transformation programs, combined heating and power technology, demand response programs, solar incentive programs, appliance efficiency standards, energy efficiency programs in public buildings, and any other relevant programs that are reasonably anticipated to reduce electricity energy or peak demand or that serve as substitutes for electric supply.

(b–4) The commission and ERCOT shall develop a method to account for the projected efficiency impacts under Subsection (b–3) in ERCOT's annual forecasts of future capacity, demand, and reserves.

(c) A standard offer program provided under Subsection (a)(3) must be neutral with respect to technologies, equipment, and fuels, including thermal, chemical, mechanical, and electrical energy storage technologies.

(d) The commission shall establish a procedure for reviewing and evaluating market-transformation program options described by this subsection and other options. In evaluating program options, the commission may consider the ability of a program option to reduce costs to customers through reduced demand, energy savings, and relief of congestion. Utilities may choose to implement any program option approved by the commission after its evaluation in order to satisfy the goal in Subsection (a), including:

(1) energy-smart schools;

(2) appliance retirement and recycling;

(3) air conditioning system tune-ups;

(4) the installation of variable speed air conditioning systems, motors, and drives;

(5) the use of trees or other landscaping for energy efficiency;

(6) customer energy management and demand response programs;

(7) high performance residential and commercial buildings that will achieve the levels of energy efficiency sufficient to qualify those buildings for federal tax incentives;

(8) commissioning services for commercial and institutional buildings that result in operational and maintenance practices that reduce the buildings' energy consumption;

(9) programs for customers who rent or lease their residence or commercial space;

(10) programs providing energy monitoring equipment to customers that enable a customer to better understand the amount, price, and time of the customer's energy use;

(11) energy audit programs for owners and other residents of single-family or multifamily residences and for small commercial customers;

(12) net-zero energy new home programs;

(13) solar thermal or solar electric programs;

(14) programs for using windows and other glazing systems, glass doors, and skylights in residential and commercial buildings that reduce solar gain by at least 30 percent from the level established for the federal Energy Star windows program;

(15) data center efficiency programs; and

(16) energy use programs with measurable and verifiable results that reduce energy consumption through behavioral changes that lead to efficient use patterns and practices.

(e) An electric utility may use money approved by the commission for energy efficiency programs to perform necessary energy efficiency research and development to foster continuous improvement and innovation in the application of energy efficiency technology and energy efficiency program design and implementation. Money the utility uses under this subsection may not exceed 10 percent of the greater of:

(1) the amount the commission approved for energy efficiency programs in the utility's most recent full rate proceeding; or

(2) the commission-approved expenditures by the utility for energy efficiency in the previous year.

(f) Unless funding is provided under Section 39.903, each unbundled transmission and distribution utility shall include in its energy efficiency plan a targeted low-income energy efficiency program as described by Section 39.903(f)(2), and the savings achieved by the program shall count toward the transmission and distribution utility's energy efficiency goal. The commission shall determine the appropriate level of funding to be allocated to both targeted and standard offer low-income energy efficiency programs in each unbundled transmission and distribution utility service area. The level of funding for low-income energy efficiency programs shall be provided from money approved by the commission for the transmission and distribution utility's energy efficiency programs. The commission shall ensure that annual expenditures for the targeted low-income energy efficiency programs of each unbundled transmission and distribution utility are not less than 10 percent of the transmission and distribution utility's energy efficiency budget for the year. A targeted low-income energy efficiency program must comply with the same audit requirements that apply to federal weatherization subrecipients . In an energy efficiency cost recovery factor proceeding related to expenditures under this subsection, the commission shall make findings of fact regarding whether the utility meets requirements imposed under this subsection . The state agency that administers the federal weatherization assistance program shall provide reports as required by the commission to provide the most current information available on energy and peak demand savings achieved in each transmission and distribution utility service area. The agency shall participate in energy efficiency cost recovery factor proceedings related to expenditures under this subsection to ensure that targeted low-income weatherization programs are consistent with federal weatherization programs and adequately funded.

(g) The commission may provide for a good cause exemption to a utility's liability for an administrative penalty or other sanction if the utility fails to meet a goal for energy efficiency under this section and the utility's failure to meet the goal is caused by one or more factors outside of the utility's control, including:

(1) insufficient demand by retail electric providers and competitive energy service providers for program incentive funds made available by the utility through its programs;

(2) changes in building energy codes; and

(3) changes in government-imposed appliance or equipment efficiency standards.

(h) For an electric utility operating in an area not open to competition, the utility may achieve the goal of this section by:

(1) providing rebate or incentive funds directly to customers to promote or facilitate the success of programs implemented under this section; or

(2) developing, subject to commission approval, new programs other than standard offer programs and market transformation programs, to the extent that the new programs satisfy the same cost-effectiveness requirements as standard offer programs and market transformation programs.

(i) For an electric utility operating in an area open to competition, on demonstration to the commission, after a contested case hearing, that the requirements under Subsection (a) cannot be met in a rural area through retail electric providers or competitive energy service providers, the utility may achieve the goal of this section by providing rebate or incentive funds directly to customers in the rural area to promote or facilitate the success of programs implemented under this section.

(j) An electric utility may use energy audit programs to achieve the goal of this section if:

(1) the programs do not constitute more than three percent of total program costs under this section; and

(2) the addition of the programs does not cause a utility's portfolio of programs to no longer be cost-effective.

(k) To help a residential or nongovernmental non-profit customer make informed decisions regarding energy efficiency, the commission may consider program designs that ensure, to the extent practicable, the customer is provided with information using standardized forms and terms that allow the customer to compare offers for varying degrees of energy efficiency attainable using a measure the customer is considering by cost, estimated energy savings, and payback periods.

Added by Acts 1999, 76th Leg., ch. 405, § 39, eff. Sept. 1, 1999. Amended by Acts 2005, 79th Leg., ch. 328, § 1, eff. Sept. 1, 2005; Acts 2007, 80th Leg., ch. 939, § 22, eff. Sept. 1, 2007; Acts 2011, 82nd Leg., ch. 180 (S.B. 1125), §§ 1, 3, eff. Sept. 1, 2011; Acts 2011, 82nd Leg., ch. 1346 (S.B. 1434), § 1, eff. June 17, 2011.

§ 39.9051. Energy Efficiency for Municipally Owned Utilities

(a) In this section, "municipally owned utility" has the meaning assigned by Section 11.003.

(b) This section applies only to a municipally owned utility that had retail sales of more than 500,000 megawatt hours in 2005.

(c) It is the goal of the legislature that:

(1) municipally owned utilities will administer energy savings incentive programs;

(2) customers of a municipally owned utility will have a choice of and access to energy efficiency alternatives that allow customers to reduce energy consumption, peak demand, or energy costs; and

(3) each municipally owned utility will provide incentives sufficient for municipally owned utilities to acquire additional cost-effective energy efficiency.

(d) The governing body of a municipally owned utility shall provide oversight and adopt rules and procedures, as necessary, to ensure that the utility can achieve the goal of this section.

(e) If a municipally owned utility adopts customer choice by decision of the governing body under Chapter 40, the commission shall provide oversight and adopt rules and procedures, as necessary, to ensure that the municipally owned utility can achieve the goal in this section in a market-neutral, nondiscriminatory manner. The commission shall, to the extent possible, include existing energy efficiency programs already adopted by the municipally owned utility.

(f) Beginning April 1, 2012 , a municipally owned utility must report each year to the State Energy Conservation Office, on a standardized form developed by the office, information regarding the combined effects of the energy efficiency activities of the utility from the previous calendar year, including the utility's annual goals, programs enacted to achieve those goals, and any achieved energy demand or savings goals.

(g) The State Energy Conservation Office shall provide the reports made under Subsection (f) to the Energy Systems Laboratory at the Texas Engineering Experiment Station of The Texas A&M University System. The laboratory shall calculate the energy savings and estimated pollution reductions that resulted from the reported activities.

(h) The energy systems laboratory shall share the results of the analysis with the Public Utility Commission of Texas, ERCOT, the United States Environmental Protection Agency, and the Texas Commission on Environmental Quality.

Added by Acts 2007, 80th Leg., ch. 939, § 23, eff. Sept. 1, 2007. Amended by Acts 2011, 82nd Leg., ch. 1068 (S.B. 924), § 1, eff. June 17, 2011.

§ 39.9052. Energy Efficiency for Electric Cooperatives

(a) An electric cooperative shall consider adopting and implementing energy efficiency programs that reduce the cooperative's annual growth in demand in a manner consistent with standards established in the state for other utilities.

(b) Beginning April 1, 2012 , an electric cooperative that had retail sales of more than 500,000 megawatt hours in 2005 must report each year to the State Energy Conservation Office, on a standardized form developed by the office, information regarding the combined effects of the energy efficiency activities of the electric cooperative from the previous calendar year, including the electric cooperative's annual goals, programs enacted to achieve those goals, and any achieved energy demand or savings goals.

(c) The State Energy Conservation Office shall provide the reports made under Subsection (b) to the Energy Systems Laboratory at the Texas Engineering Experiment Station of The Texas A&M University System. The laboratory shall calculate the energy savings and estimated pollution reductions that resulted from the reported activities.

(d) The energy systems laboratory shall share the results of the analysis with the Public Utility Commission of Texas, ERCOT, the United States Environmental Protection Agency, and the Texas Commission on Environmental Quality.

Added by Acts 2007, 80th Leg., ch. 939, § 23, eff. Sept. 1, 2007. Amended by Acts 2011, 82nd Leg., ch. 1068 (S.B. 924), § 2, eff. June 17, 2011.

§ 39.9053. Expired

§ 39.9054. Energy Efficiency Plans and Reports; Public Information

(a) An electric utility shall submit electronically an energy efficiency plan and report in a searchable form prescribed by the commission on or before April 1 of each year. The commission by rule shall adopt a form that will permit the public to easily compare information submitted by different electric utilities. The plan and report must:

(1) provide information on the utility's performance in achieving energy efficiency goals for the previous five years;

(2) describe how the utility intends to achieve future goals; and

(3) provide any other information the commission considers relevant.

(b) On the Internet website found at http://www.puc.state.tx.us, the commission shall publish information on energy efficiency programs, including:

(1) an explanation of the goal for energy efficiency in this state;

(2) a description of the types of energy efficiency programs available to certain classes of eligible customers;

(3) a link to the plans and reports filed as prescribed by Subsection (a); and

(4) a list of persons who install or provide energy efficiency measures or services by area.

(c) This section does not require the commission to warrant that the list required to be displayed under Subsection (b) constitutes a complete or accurate list of all persons who install energy efficiency measures or services in the marketplace.

Added by Acts 2011, 82nd Leg., ch. 180 (S.B. 1125), § 2, eff. Sept. 1, 2011.

§ 39.906. Displaced Workers

In order to mitigate potential negative impacts on utility personnel directly affected by electric industry restructuring, the commission shall allow the recovery of reasonable employee-related transition costs incurred and projected for severance, retraining, early retirement, outplacement, and related expenses for the employees.

Added by Acts 1999, 76th Leg., ch. 405, § 39, eff. Sept. 1, 1999.

§ 39.907. Repealed by Acts 2011, 82nd Leg., ch. 905 (S.B. 781), § 1, eff. June 17, 2011

§ 39.908. Effect of Sunset Provision

(a) If the commission is abolished and the other provisions of this title expire as provided by Chapter 325, Government Code (Texas Sunset Act), this subchapter, including the provisions of this title referred to in this subchapter, continues in full force and effect and does not expire.

(b) The authorities, duties, and functions of the commission under this chapter shall be performed and carried out by a successor agency to be designated by the legislature before abolishment of the commission or, if the legislature does not designate the successor, by the secretary of state.

Added by Acts 1999, 76th Leg., ch. 405, § 39, eff. Sept. 1, 1999.

§ 39.909. Plan and Report of Workforce Diversity and Other Business Practices

(a) In this section, "small business" and "historically underutilized business" have the meanings assigned by Section 481.191, Government Code.

(b) Before January 1, 2000, each electric utility shall develop and submit to the commission a comprehensive five-year plan to enhance diversity of its workforce in all occupational categories and to increase contracting opportunities for small and historically underutilized businesses. The plan must consist of:

(1) the electric utility's historical and current performance with regard to workforce diversity and

contracting with small and historically underutilized businesses;

(2) initiatives that the electric utility will pursue in these areas over the period of the plan;

(3) a listing of programs and activities the electric utility will undertake to achieve each of those initiatives; and

(4) a listing of the business partnership initiatives the electric utility will undertake to facilitate small and historically underutilized business entry into the electric energy market as generators and retail energy providers taking into account opportunities for contracting and joint ventures.

(c) Each electric utility shall submit an annual report to the commission and the legislature relating to its efforts to improve workforce diversity and contracting opportunities for small and historically underutilized businesses. The report must be submitted on October 1 of each year or may be included as part of any other annual report submitted by the electric utility to the commission. The report must include:

(1) the diversity of the electric utility's workforce as of the time of the report;

(2) the electric utility's level of contracting with small and historically underutilized businesses;

(3) the specific progress made under the plan under Subsection (b);

(4) the specific initiatives, programs, and activities undertaken under the plan during the preceding year;

(5) an assessment of the success of each of those initiatives, programs, and activities;

(6) the extent to which the electric utility has carried out its initiatives to facilitate opportunities for contracts or joint ventures with small and historically underutilized businesses; and

(7) the initiatives, programs, and activities the electric utility will pursue during the next year to increase the diversity of its workforce and contracting opportunities for small and historically underutilized businesses.

Added by Acts 1999, 76th Leg., ch. 405, § 39, eff. Sept. 1, 1999.

§ 39.910. Incentive Program and Goal for Energy Efficiency for Military Bases

(a) The commission by rule shall establish an electric energy efficiency incentive program under which each electric utility in an area where customer choice is not available will provide incentives sufficient for military bases, retail electric providers, or competitive energy service providers to install energy efficiency devices or other alternatives at military bases. The commission shall design the program to provide military bases with a variety of choices for cost-effective energy efficiency devices and other alternatives from the market to reduce energy consumption and energy costs.

(b) The commission shall establish a goal for the program to reduce, before January 1, 2005, the consumption of electricity by military bases in this state by five percent as compared to consumption levels in 2002.

(c) The commission shall approve a nonbypassable surcharge or other rate mechanism to recover costs associated with the program established under this section.

(d) An electric utility shall administer the electric energy efficiency incentive program in a market-neutral, nondiscriminatory manner. An electric utility may not offer underlying competitive services.

Added by Acts 2003, 78th Leg., ch. 149, § 23, eff. May 27, 2003.

§ 39.911. Alternative Funding for Energy Efficiency and Renewable Energy Systems

The State Energy Conservation Office, in coordination with the governor, the Department of Agriculture, the Texas Commission on Environmental Quality, the Texas Education Agency, the commission, and other appropriate state agencies, shall solicit gifts, grants, and other financial resources available to fund energy efficiency improvements and renewable energy systems for public and private facilities in this state.

Added by Acts 2007, 80th Leg., ch. 939, § 23, eff. Sept. 1, 2007.

§ 39.912. Report on Combined Heating and Power Technology

The commission shall study the installation and use of combined heating and power technology in this state, and shall submit a report regarding the commission's findings to the 81st Legislature. The report shall include:

(1) an explanation describing combined heating and power technology and its use; and

(2) an explanation of how combined heating and power technology can be implemented in this state to meet energy efficiency goals.

Added by Acts 2007, 80th Leg., ch. 939, § 23, eff. Sept. 1, 2007.

§ 39.913. Combining Certain Reports

The commission may combine the reports required under Sections 39.905(b–2) and 39.912.

Added by Acts 2007, 80th Leg., ch. 939, § 23, eff. Sept. 1, 2007.

§ 39.914. Credit for Surplus Solar Generation by Public Schools

(a) An electric utility or retail electric provider shall provide for net metering and contract with an independent school district so that:

(1) surplus electricity produced by a school building's solar electric generation panels is made available for sale to the electric transmission grid and distribution system; and

(2) the net value of that surplus electricity is credited to the district.

(b) For areas of this state in which customer choice has not been introduced, the commission by rule shall require that credits for electricity produced by a school building's solar electric generation panels reflect the value of the electricity that is made available for sale to the electric utility in accordance with federal regulations.

(c) For independent school districts in areas in which customer choice has been introduced, the district must sell the school buildings' surplus electricity produced to the retail electric provider that serves the school district's load at a value agreed to between the district and the provider that serves the district's load. The agreed value may be based on the clearing price of energy at the time of day that the electricity is made available to the grid. The independent organization identified in Section 39.151 shall develop procedures so that the amount of electricity purchased from a district under this section is accounted for in settling the total load served by the provider that serves the district's load. A district requesting net metering services for purposes of this section must have metering devices capable of providing measurements consistent with the independent organization's settlement requirements.

(d) A transmission and distribution utility shall make available to an independent school district for purposes of this section metering required for services provided under this section, including separate meters that measure the load and generator output or a single meter capable of measuring separately in-flow and out-flow at the point of common coupling meter point. The district must pay the differential cost of the metering unless the meters are provided at no additional cost. Except as provided by this section, Section 39.107 applies to metering under this section.

(e) A municipally owned utility or electric cooperative shall consider and complete the determinations regarding net metering service as provided by the federal Public Utility Regulatory Policies Act of 1978 (16 U.S.C. Section 2601 et seq., as amended by the federal Energy Policy Act of 2005 (Pub. L. No. 109–58)) after proceedings conducted in accordance with that law. A municipally owned utility or electric cooperative shall report the determinations made under this subsection to the State Energy Conservation Office and include in that report information regarding metering electricity generated by solar panels on public school building rooftops.

Added by Acts 2007, 80th Leg., ch. 939, § 24, eff. Sept. 1, 2007.

§ 39.915. Consideration and Approval of Certain Transactions

(a) To protect retail customers in this state, and to ensure the continuation of cost-effective energy efficiency measures and delivery systems, notwithstanding any other provision of this title, an electric utility or transmission and distribution utility must report to and obtain approval of the commission before closing any transaction in which:

(1) the electric utility or transmission and distribution utility will be merged or consolidated with another electric utility or transmission and distribution utility;

(2) at least 50 percent of the stock of the electric utility or transmission and distribution utility will be transferred or sold; or

(3) a controlling interest or operational control of the electric utility or transmission and distribution utility will be transferred.

(b) The commission shall approve a transaction under Subsection (a) if the commission finds that the transaction is in the public interest. In making its determination, the commission shall consider whether the transaction will adversely affect the reliability of service, availability of service, or cost of service of the electric utility or transmission and distribution utility. The commission shall make the determination concerning a transaction under this subsection not later than the 180th day after the date the commission receives the relevant report. If the commission has not made a determination before the 181st day after that date, the transaction is considered approved.

(c) Subsections (a) and (b) do not apply to a transaction described by Subsection (a) for which a definitive agreement was executed before April 1, 2007, if an electric utility or transmission and distribution utility or a person seeking to acquire or merge with an electric utility or transmission and distribution utility made a filing for review of the transaction under Section 14.101 before May 1, 2007, and the resulting proceeding was not withdrawn.

(d) If an electric utility or transmission and distribution utility or a person seeking to acquire or merge with an electric utility or transmission and distribution utility files with the commission a stipulation, representation, or commitment in advance of or as part of a filing under this section or under Section 14.101, the commission may enforce the stipulation, representation, or commitment to the extent that the stipulation, representation, or commitment is consistent with the standards provided by this section and Section 14.101. The commission may reasonably interpret and enforce conditions adopted under this section.

Added by Acts 2007, 80th Leg., ch. 939, § 25, eff. Sept. 1, 2007.

§ 39.916. Interconnection of Distributed Renewable Generation

(a) In this section:

(1) "Distributed renewable generation" means electric generation with a capacity of not more than 2,000 kilowatts provided by a renewable energy technology, as defined by Section 39.904, that is installed on a retail electric customer's side of the meter.

(2) "Distributed renewable generation owner" means:

(A) an owner of distributed renewable generation;

(B) a retail electric customer on whose side of the meter distributed renewable generation is installed and operated, regardless of whether the customer takes ownership of the distributed renewable generation; or

(C) a person who by contract is assigned ownership rights to energy produced from distributed renewable generation located at the premises of the customer on the customer's side of the meter.

(3) "Interconnection" means the right of a distributed renewable generation owner to physically connect distributed renewable generation to an electricity distribution system, and the technical requirements, rules, or processes for the connection.

(b) A transmission and distribution utility or electric utility shall allow interconnection if:

(1) the distributed renewable generation to be interconnected has a five-year warranty against breakdown or undue degradation; and

(2) the rated capacity of the distributed renewable generation does not exceed the transmission and distribution utility or electric utility service capacity.

(c) A customer may request interconnection by filing an application for interconnection with the transmission and distribution utility or electric utility. Procedures of a transmission and distribution utility or electric utility for the submission and processing of a customer's application for interconnection shall be consistent with rules adopted by the commission regarding interconnection.

(d) The commission by rule shall establish safety, technical, and performance standards for distributed renewable generation that may be interconnected. In adopting the rules, the commission shall consider standards published by the Underwriters Laboratories, the National Electric Code, the National Electric Safety Code, and the Institute of Electrical and Electronics Engineers.

(e) A transmission and distribution utility, electric utility, or retail electric provider may not require a distributed renewable generation owner whose distributed renewable generation meets the standards established by rule under Subsection (d) to purchase an amount, type, or classification of liability insurance the distributed renewable generation owner would not have in the absence of the distributed renewable generation.

(f) A transmission and distribution utility or electric utility shall make available to a distributed renewable generation owner for purposes of this section metering required for services provided under this section, including separate meters that measure the load and generator output or a single meter capable of measuring in-flow and out-flow at the point of common coupling meter point. The distributed renewable generation owner must pay the differential cost of the metering unless the meters are provided at no additional cost. Except as provided by this section, Section 39.107 applies to metering under this section.

(g) A renewable energy credit that is earned by a distributed renewable generation owner through the interconnection of a renewable electric system is the sole property of the distributed renewable generation owner unless the distributed renewable generation owner engages in a transaction to sell or trade the credit under Section 39.904. For electric utilities, the commission shall address the ownership of renewable energy credits associated with power sold to the utility.

(h) An electric utility or retail electric provider may contract with a distributed renewable generation owner so that:

(1) surplus electricity produced by distributed renewable generation is made available for sale to the transmission grid and distribution system; and

(2) the net value of that surplus electricity is credited to the distributed renewable generation owner.

(j) For distributed renewable generation owners in areas in which customer choice has been introduced, the distributed renewable generation owner must sell the owner's surplus electricity produced to the retail electric provider that serves the distributed renewable generation owner's load at a value agreed to between the distributed renewable generation owner and the provider that serves the owner's load which may include, but is not limited to, an agreed value based on the clearing price of energy at the time of day that the electricity is made available to the grid or it may be a credit applied to an account during a billing period that may be carried over to subsequent billing periods until the credit has been redeemed. The independent organization identified in Section 39.151 shall develop procedures so that the amount of electricity purchased from a distributed renewable generation owner under this section is accounted for in settling the total load served by the provider that serves that owner's load by January 1, 2009. A distributed renewable generation owner requesting net metering services for purposes of this section must have metering devices capable of providing measurements consistent with the independent organization's settlement requirements.

(k) Neither a retail electric customer that uses distributed renewable generation nor the owner of the distributed renewable generation that the retail electric customer uses is an electric utility, power generation company, or retail electric provider for the purposes of this title and neither is required to register with or be certified by the commission if at the time distributed renewable generation is installed, the estimated annual amount of electricity to be produced by the distributed renewable generation is less than or equal to the retail electric customer's estimated annual electricity consumption.

Added by Acts 2007, 80th Leg., ch. 939, § 26, eff. Sept. 1, 2007. Amended by Acts 2011, 82nd Leg., ch. 1070 (S.B. 981), §§ 1 and 2, eff. Sept. 1, 2011.

CHAPTER 40. COMPETITION FOR MUNICIPALLY OWNED UTILITIES AND RIVER AUTHORITIES

SUBCHAPTER A. GENERAL PROVISIONS

Section

40.001. Applicable Law.
40.002. Definition.
40.003. Securitization.
40.004. Jurisdiction of Commission.

SUBCHAPTER B. MUNICIPALLY OWNED UTILITY CHOICE

40.051. Governing Body Decision.
40.052. Utility Not Offering Customer Choice.
40.053. Retail Customer's Right of Choice.
40.054. Service Outside Area.
40.055. Jurisdiction of Municipal Governing Body.
40.056. Anticompetitive Actions.
40.057. Billing.
40.058. Tariffs for Open Access.
40.059. Municipal Power Agency; Recovery of Stranded Costs.
40.060. No Power to Amend Certificates.

SUBCHAPTER C. RIGHTS NOT AFFECTED

40.101. Interference With Contract.
40.102. Access to Wholesale Market.
40.103. Protection of Bondholders.
40.104. Tax-Exempt Status.

SUBCHAPTER A. GENERAL PROVISIONS

§ 40.001. Applicable Law

(a) Notwithstanding any other provision of law, except Sections 39.155, 39.157(e), 39.203, 39.903, and 39.904, this chapter governs the transition to and the establishment of a fully competitive electric power industry for municipally owned utilities. With respect to the regulation of municipally owned utilities, this chapter controls over any other provision of this title, except for sections in which the term "municipally owned utility" is specifically used.

(b) Except as specifically provided in this subsection, Chapter 39 does not apply to a river authority operating a steam generating plant on or before January 1, 1999, or a corporation authorized by Chapter 152, Water Code, or Section 32.053. A river authority operating a steam generating plant on or before January 1, 1999, is subject to Sections 39.051(a)–(c), 39.108, 39.155, 39.157(e), and 39.203.

(c) For purposes of Section 39.051, hydroelectric assets may not be deemed to be generating assets, and the transfer of generating assets to a corporation authorized by Chapter 152, Water Code, satisfies the requirements of Section 39.051.

(d) Accommodation shall be made in the code of conduct established under Section 39.157(e) for the provisions of Chapter 152, Water Code, and the commission may not prohibit a river authority and any related corporation from sharing officers, directors, employees, equipment, and facilities or from providing goods or services to each other at cost without the need for a competitive bid.

Added by Acts 1999, 76th Leg., ch. 405, § 39, eff. Sept. 1, 1999. Amended by Acts 2001, 77th Leg., ch. 1420, § 8.401, eff. Sept. 1, 2001.

§ 40.002. Definition

For purposes of this chapter, "body vested with the power to manage and operate a municipally owned utility" means a body created in accordance with Section 1502.070, Government Code, or Subchapter G, Chapter 552, Local Government Code,[1] or by municipal charter.

Added by Acts 1999, 76th Leg., ch. 405, § 39, eff. Sept. 1, 1999. Amended by Acts 2001, 77th Leg., ch. 1420, § 8.402, eff. Sept. 1, 2001; Acts 2007, 80th Leg., ch. 885, § 3.77(29), eff. April 1, 2009.

[1] V.T.C.A., Local Government Code § 552.121 et seq.

§ 40.003. Securitization

(a) Municipally owned utilities and river authorities may adopt and use securitization provisions having the effect of the provisions provided by Subchapter G, Chapter 39,[1] to recover through appropriate charges their stranded costs, at a recovery level deemed appropriate by the municipally owned utility or river authority up to 100 percent, under rules and procedures that shall be established:

(1) in the case of a municipally owned utility, by the municipal governing body or a body vested with the power to manage and operate the municipally owned utility, including procedures providing for rate orders of the governing body having the effect of financing orders, providing for a separate nonbypassable charge approved by the governing body, in the nature of a transition charge, to be collected from all retail electric customers of the municipally owned utility, identified as of a date determined by the governing body, to fund the recovery of the stranded costs of the municipally owned utility and of all reasonable related expenses, as determined by the governing body, and providing for the issuance of bonds, having a term and other characteristics as determined by the governing body, as necessary to recover the amount deemed appropriate by the governing body through securitization financing; and

(2) in the case of a river authority, by the commission.

(b) In order to implement securitization financing under the rules and procedures established by and for a municipally owned utility under Subsection (a)(1), municipalities are expressly authorized and empowered to issue bonds, notes, or other obligations, including refunding bonds, payable from and secured by a lien on and pledge of the revenues collected under an order of the governing body of the municipality, and the bonds shall be issued, without an election or any requirement of giving notice of intent to issue the bonds, by ordinance adopted by the governing body of the municipality, in the form and manner and sold on a negotiated basis or on receipt of bids and on the terms and conditions as shall be determined by the governing body of the municipality.

(c) Bonds issued under the authority conferred by Subsections (a)(1) and (2) and Subsection (b) may be issued in the form and manner, with or without credit enhancement or liquidity enhancement and using the procedures as provided in Chapter 1201, Government Code, or other laws applicable to the issuance of bonds, including Subchapters A-C, Chapter 1207, Government Code,[2] and Chapter 1371, Government Code, as if those laws were fully restated in this section and made a part of this section for all purposes, and a municipality or river authority shall have the right and authority to use those other laws, notwithstanding any applicable restrictions contained in those laws, to the extent convenient or necessary to carry out any power or authority, express or implied, granted under this section, in the issuance of bonds by a municipality or river authority in connection with securitization financing. This section is wholly sufficient authority for the issuance of bonds, notes, or other obligations, including refunding bonds, and the performance of the other authorized acts and procedures, without reference to any other laws or any restrictions or limitations contained in those laws. To the extent of any conflict or inconsistency between the provisions of this authorization and any provisions of any other law or home-rule charter, the authorization and power to issue bonds conferred on municipalities or river authorities under this section shall prevail and control.

(d) The rules and procedures for securitization established by the commission under Subsection (a)(2) shall include procedures for the recovery of qualified costs under the terms of a financing order adopted by the governing body of the river authority.

(e) The rules and procedures for securitization established by the commission under Subsection (a)(2) shall include rules and procedures for the issuance of transition bonds. Findings made by the governing body of a river authority in a financing order issued under the rules and procedures described in this subsection shall be conclusive, and any transition charge incorporated in the rate order to recover the principal, interest, and all reasonable expenses associated with any transition bonds shall constitute property rights, as described in Subchapter G, Chapter 39,[1] and otherwise conform in all material respects to the transition charges provided by Subchapter G, Chapter 39.

(f) The rules and procedures established under this section shall be consistent with other law applicable to municipally owned utilities and river authorities and with the terms of any resolutions, orders, charter provisions, or ordinances authorizing outstanding bonds or other indebtedness of the municipalities or river authorities.

Added by Acts 1999, 76th Leg., ch. 405, § 39, eff. Sept. 1, 1999. Amended by Acts 2001, 77th Leg., ch. 1420, § 8.403, eff. Sept. 1, 2001.

[1] V.T.C.A., Utilities Code § 39.301.
[2] V.T.C.A., Government Code § 1207.001.

§ 40.004. Jurisdiction of Commission

Except as specifically otherwise provided in this chapter, the commission has jurisdiction over municipally owned utilities only for the following purposes:

(1) to regulate wholesale transmission rates and service, including terms of access, to the extent provided by Subchapter A, Chapter 35;[1]

(2) to regulate certification of retail service areas to the extent provided by Chapter 37;

(3) to regulate rates on appeal under Subchapters D and E, Chapter 33,[2] subject to Section 40.051(c);

(4) to establish a code of conduct as provided by Section 39.157(e) applicable to anticompetitive activities and to affiliate activities limited to structurally unbundled affiliates of municipally owned utilities, subject to Section 40.054;

(5) to establish terms and conditions for open access to transmission and distribution facilities for municipally owned utilities providing customer choice, as provided by Section 39.203;

(6) to require collection of the nonbypassable fee established under Section 39.903(b) and to administer the renewable energy credits program under Section 39.904(b) and the natural gas energy credits program under Section 39.9044(b); and

(7) to require reports of municipally owned utility operations only to the extent necessary to:

(A) enable the commission to determine the aggregate load and energy requirements of the state and the resources available to serve that load; or

(B) enable the commission to determine information relating to market power as provided by Section 39.155.

Added by Acts 1999, 76th Leg., ch. 405, § 39, eff. Sept. 1, 1999.

[1] V.T.C.A., Utilities Code § 35.101.
[2] V.T.C.A., Utilities Code § 33.101.

SUBCHAPTER B. MUNICIPALLY OWNED UTILITY CHOICE

§ 40.051. Governing Body Decision

(a) The municipal governing body or a body vested with the power to manage and operate a municipally owned utility has the discretion to decide when or if the municipally owned utility will provide customer choice.

(b) Municipally owned utilities may choose to participate in customer choice at any time on or after January 1, 2002, by adoption of an appropriate resolution of the municipal governing body or a body vested with power to manage and operate the municipally owned utility. The decision to participate in customer choice by the adoption of a resolution is irrevocable.

(c) After a decision to offer customer choice has been made, Subchapters D and E, Chapter 33,[1] do not apply to any action taken under this chapter.

Added by Acts 1999, 76th Leg., ch. 405, § 39, eff. Sept. 1, 1999.

[1] V.T.C.A., Utilities Code § 33.101.

§ 40.052. Utility Not Offering Customer Choice

(a) A municipally owned utility that has not chosen to participate in customer choice may not offer electric energy at unregulated prices directly to retail customers outside its certificated retail service area.

(b) A municipally owned utility under Subsection (a) retains the right to offer and provide a full range of customer service and pricing programs to the customers within its certificated area and to purchase and sell electric energy at wholesale without geographic restriction.

Added by Acts 1999, 76th Leg., ch. 405, § 39, eff. Sept. 1, 1999.

§ 40.053. Retail Customer's Right of Choice

(a) If a municipally owned utility chooses to participate in customer choice, after that choice all retail customers served by the municipally owned utility within the certificated retail service area of the municipally owned utility shall have the right of customer choice consistent with the provisions of this chapter, and the municipally owned utility shall provide open access for retail service.

(b) Notwithstanding Section 39.107, the metering function may not be deemed a competitive service for customers of the municipally owned utility within that service area and may, at the option of the municipally owned utility, continue to be offered by the municipally owned utility as sole provider.

(c) On its initiation of customer choice, a municipally owned utility shall designate itself or another entity as the provider of last resort for customers within the municipally owned utility's certificated service area as that area existed on the date of the utility's initiation of customer choice. The municipally owned utility shall fulfill the role of default provider of last resort in the event no other entity is available to act in that capacity.

(d) If a customer is unable to obtain service from a retail electric provider, on request by the customer, the provider of last resort shall offer the customer the standard retail service package for the appropriate customer class, with no interruption of service, at a fixed, nondiscountable rate that is at least sufficient to cover the reasonable costs of providing that service, as approved by the governing body of the municipally owned utility that has the authority to set rates.

(e) The governing body of a municipally owned utility may establish the procedures and criteria for designating the provider of last resort and may redesignate the provider of last resort according to a schedule it considers appropriate.

Added by Acts 1999, 76th Leg., ch. 405, § 39, eff. Sept. 1, 1999.

§ 40.054. Service Outside Area

(a) A municipally owned utility participating in customer choice shall have the right to offer electric energy and related services at unregulated prices directly to retail customers who have customer choice without regard to geographic location.

(b) In providing service under Subsection (a) to retail customers outside its certificated retail service area as that area exists on the date of adoption of customer choice, a municipally owned utility is subject to the commission's rules establishing a code of conduct regulating anticompetitive practices.

(c) For municipally owned utilities participating in customer choice, the commission shall have jurisdiction to establish terms and conditions, but not rates, for access by other retail electric providers to the municipally owned utility's distribution facilities.

(d) Accommodation shall be made in the commission's terms and conditions for access and in the code of conduct for specific legal requirements imposed by state or federal law applicable to municipally owned utilities.

(e) The commission does not have jurisdiction to require unbundling of services or functions of, or to regulate the recovery of stranded investment of, a municipally owned utility or, except as provided by this section, jurisdiction with respect to the rates, terms, and conditions of service for retail customers of a municipally owned utility within the utility's certificated service area.

(f) A municipally owned utility shall maintain separate books and records of its operations from those of the operations of any affiliate.

Added by Acts 1999, 76th Leg., ch. 405, § 39, eff. Sept. 1, 1999.

§ 40.055. Jurisdiction of Municipal Governing Body

(a) The municipal governing body or a body vested with the power to manage and operate a municipally owned utility has exclusive jurisdiction to:

(1) set all terms of access, conditions, and rates applicable to services provided by the municipally owned utility, subject to Sections 40.054 and 40.056, including nondiscriminatory and comparable rates for distribution but excluding wholesale transmission rates, terms of access, and conditions for wholesale transmission service set by the commission under this subtitle, provided that the rates for distribution access established by the municipal gov-

erning body shall be comparable to the distribution access rates that apply to the municipally owned utility and the municipally owned utility's affiliates;

(2) determine whether to unbundle any energy-related activities and, if the municipally owned utility chooses to unbundle, whether to do so structurally or functionally;

(3) reasonably determine the amount of the municipally owned utility's stranded investment;

(4) establish nondiscriminatory transition charges reasonably designed to recover the stranded investment over an appropriate period of time, provided that recovery of retail stranded costs shall be from all existing or future retail customers, including the facilities, premises, and loads of those retail customers, within the utility's geographical certificated service area as it existed on May 1, 1999;

(5) determine the extent to which the municipally owned utility will provide various customer services at the distribution level, including other services that the municipally owned utility is legally authorized to provide, or will accept the services from other providers;

(6) manage and operate the municipality's electric utility systems, including exercise of control over resource acquisition and any related expansion programs;

(7) establish and enforce service quality and reliability standards and consumer safeguards designed to protect retail electric customers, including safeguards that will accomplish the objectives of Sections 39.101(a) and (b), consistent with this chapter;

(8) determine whether a base rate reduction is appropriate for the municipally owned utility;

(9) determine any other utility matters that the municipal governing body or body vested with power to manage and operate the municipally owned utility believes should be included;

(10) make any other decisions affecting the municipally owned utility's participation in customer choice that are not inconsistent with this chapter; and

(11) determine the extent to which the municipally owned utility offers energy efficiency programs and how the programs are administered by the utility, except as provided by Section 39.9051(e).

(b) In multiply certificated areas, a retail customer, including a retail customer of an electric cooperative or a municipally owned utility, may not avoid stranded cost recovery charges by switching to another electric utility, electric cooperative, or municipally owned utility.

Added by Acts 1999, 76th Leg., ch. 405, § 39, eff. Sept. 1, 1999. Amended by Acts 2007, 80th Leg., ch. 939, § 27, eff. Sept. 1, 2007.

§ 40.056. Anticompetitive Actions

(a) If, on complaint by a retail electric provider, the commission finds that a municipal rule, action, or order relating to customer choice is anticompetitive or does not provide other retail electric providers with nondiscriminatory terms and conditions of access to distribution facilities or customers within the municipally owned utility's certificated retail service area that are comparable to the municipally owned utility's and its affiliates' terms and conditions of access to distribution facilities or customers, the commission shall notify the municipally owned utility.

(b) The municipally owned utility shall have three months to cure the anticompetitive or noncompliant behavior described in Subsection (a), following opportunity for hearing on the complaint. If the rule, action, or order is not fully remedied within that time, the commission may prohibit the municipally owned utility or affiliate from providing retail service outside its certificated retail service area until the rule, action, or order is remedied.

Added by Acts 1999, 76th Leg., ch. 405, § 39, eff. Sept. 1, 1999.

§ 40.057. Billing

(a) A municipally owned utility that opts for customer choice may continue to bill directly electric customers located in its certificated retail service area, as that area exists on the date of adoption of customer choice, for all transmission and distribution services. The municipally owned utility may also bill directly for generation services and customer services provided by the municipally owned utility to those customers.

(b) A municipally owned utility that opts for customer choice may not adopt anticompetitive billing practices that would discourage customers in its service area from choosing a retail electric provider.

(c) A customer that is being provided wires service by a municipally owned utility at distribution or transmission voltage and that is served by a retail electric provider for retail service has the option of being billed directly by each service provider or to receive a single bill for distribution, transmission, and generation services from the municipally owned utility.

Added by Acts 1999, 76th Leg., ch. 405, § 39, eff. Sept. 1, 1999.

§ 40.058. Tariffs for Open Access

A municipally owned utility that owns or operates transmission and distribution facilities shall file with the commission tariffs implementing the open access rules established by the commission under Section 39.203 and shall file with the commission the rates for open access on distribution facilities as set by the municipal regulatory authority, before the 90th day preceding the date the utility offers customer choice. The commission does not have authority to determine the rates for distribution access service for a municipally owned utility.

Added by Acts 1999, 76th Leg., ch. 405, § 39, eff. Sept. 1, 1999.

§ 40.059. Municipal Power Agency; Recovery of Stranded Costs

(a) In this section, "member city" means a municipality that participated in the creation of a municipal power agency formed under Chapter 163 by the adoption of a concurrent resolution by the municipality on or before August 1, 1975.

(b) After a member city adopts a resolution choosing to participate in customer choice under Section 40.051(b), a member city may include stranded costs described in Subsection (c) in its distribution costs and may recover those costs through a nonbypassable charge. The nonbypassable charge shall be as determined by the member city's governing body and may be spread over 16 years.

(c) The stranded costs that may be recovered under this section are those costs that were determined by the commission and stated in the commission's April 1998 Report to the Texas Senate Interim Committee on Electric Utility Restructuring entitled "Potentially Strandable Investment (ECOM) Report: 1998 Update" and specifically stated in the report at Appendix A (ECOM Estimates Including the Effects of Transition Plans) under the commission base case benchmark base market price for the year 2002.

(d) The stranded cost amounts described in this section may not be included in the generation costs used in setting rates by the member city's governing body.

(e) The provisions of this section are cumulative of all other provisions of this chapter, and nothing in this section shall be construed to limit or restrict the application of any provision of this chapter to the member cities.

(f) The municipal power agency shall extinguish the agency's indebtedness by sale of the electric facility to one or more purchasers, by way of a sale through the issuance of taxable or tax-exempt debt to the member cities, or by any other method. The agency shall set as an objective the extinguishment of the agency's debt by September 1, 2000. In the event this objective is not met, the agency shall provide detailed reasons to the electric utility restructuring legislative oversight committee by November 1, 2000, why the agency was not able to meet this objective.

(g) The municipal power agency or its successor in interest may, at its option, use the rate of return method for calculating its transmission cost of service. If the rate of return method is used, the return component for the transmission cost of service revenue requirement shall be sufficient to meet the transmission function's pro rata share of levelized debt service and debt service coverage ratio (1.50) and other annual debt obligations; provided, however, that the total levelized debt service may not exceed the total debt service under the current payment schedule. Any additional revenue generated by the methodology described in this subsection shall be applied to reduce the agency's outstanding indebtedness.

Added by Acts 1999, 76th Leg., ch. 405, § 39, eff. Sept. 1, 1999.

§ 40.060. No Power to Amend Certificates

Nothing in this chapter empowers a municipal governing body or a body vested with the power to manage and operate a municipally owned utility to issue, amend, or rescind a certificate of public convenience and necessity granted by the commission. This subsection does not affect the ability of a municipal governing body or a body vested with the power to manage and operate the municipally owned utility to pass a resolution under Section 40.051(b).

Added by Acts 1999, 76th Leg., ch. 405, § 39, eff. Sept. 1, 1999.

SUBCHAPTER C. RIGHTS NOT AFFECTED

§ 40.101. Interference With Contract

(a) This subtitle may not interfere with or abrogate the rights or obligations of parties, including a retail or wholesale customer, to a contract with a municipally owned utility or river authority.

(b) This subtitle may not interfere with or abrogate the rights or obligations of a party under a contract or agreement concerning certificated utility service areas.

Added by Acts 1999, 76th Leg., ch. 405, § 39, eff. Sept. 1, 1999.

§ 40.102. Access to Wholesale Market

Nothing in this subtitle shall limit the access of municipally owned utilities to the wholesale electric market.

Added by Acts 1999, 76th Leg., ch. 405, § 39, eff. Sept. 1, 1999.

§ 40.103. Protection of Bondholders

Nothing in this subtitle or any rule adopted under this subtitle shall impair contracts, covenants, or obligations between this state, river authorities, municipalities, and the bondholders of revenue bonds issued by the river authorities or municipalities.

Added by Acts 1999, 76th Leg., ch. 405, § 39, eff. Sept. 1, 1999.

§ 40.104. Tax-Exempt Status

Nothing in this subtitle may impair the tax-exempt status of municipalities, electric cooperatives, or river authorities, nor shall anything in this subtitle compel any municipality, electric cooperative, or river authority to use its facilities in a manner that violates any contractual provisions, bond covenants, or other restrictions applicable to facilities financed by tax-exempt debt. Notwithstanding any other provision of law, the decision to participate in customer choice by the adoption of a resolution in accordance with Section 40.051(b) is irrevocable.

Added by Acts 1999, 76th Leg., ch. 405, § 39, eff. Sept. 1, 1999.

CHAPTER 41. ELECTRIC COOPERATIVES AND COMPETITION

SUBCHAPTER A. GENERAL PROVISIONS

Section
41.001. Applicable Law.
41.002. Definitions.
41.003. Securitization.
41.004. Jurisdiction of Commission.
41.005. Limitation on Municipal Authority.

SUBCHAPTER B. ELECTRIC COOPERATIVE UTILITY CHOICE

41.051. Board Decision.

Section
41.052. Electric Cooperatives Not Offering Customer Choice.
41.053. Retail Customer Right of Choice.
41.054. Service Outside Certificated Area.
41.055. Jurisdiction of Board of Directors.
41.056. Anticompetitive Actions.
41.057. Billing.
41.058. Tariffs for Open Access.
41.059. No Power to Amend Certificates.
41.060. Customer Service Information.
41.061. Retail Rate Changes by Electric Cooperatives.
41.062. Allocation of Stranded Investment.
41.063. Repealed.

SUBCHAPTER C. RIGHTS NOT AFFECTED

41.101. Interference With Contract.
41.102. Access to Wholesale Market.
41.103. Protection of Bondholders.
41.104. Tax-Exempt Status.

SUBCHAPTER A. GENERAL PROVISIONS

§ 41.001. Applicable Law

Notwithstanding any other provision of law, except Sections 39.155, 39.157(e), 39.203, 39.903, and 39.904, this chapter governs the transition to and the establishment of a fully competitive electric power industry for electric cooperatives. Regarding the regulation of electric cooperatives, this chapter shall control over any other provision of this title, except for sections in which the term "electric cooperative" is specifically used.

Added by Acts 1999, 76th Leg., ch. 405, § 39, eff. Sept. 1, 1999.

§ 41.002. Definitions

In this chapter:

(1) "Board of directors" means the board of directors of an electric cooperative as described in Section 161.071.

(2) "Rate" includes any compensation, tariff, charge, fare, toll, rental, or classification that is directly or indirectly demanded, observed, charged, or collected by an electric cooperative for any service, product, or commodity and any rule, practice, or contract affecting the compensation, tariff, charge, fare, toll, rental, or classification.

(3) "Stranded investment" means:

(A) the excess, if any, of the net book value of generation assets over the market value of the generation assets; and

(B) any above market purchased power costs.

Added by Acts 1999, 76th Leg., ch. 405, § 39, eff. Sept. 1, 1999.

§ 41.003. Securitization

(a) Electric cooperatives may adopt and use securitization provisions having the effect of the provisions provided by Subchapter G, Chapter 39,[1] to recover through rates stranded costs at a recovery level deemed appropriate by the board of directors up to 100 percent, under rules and procedures that shall be established by the commission.

(b) The rules and procedures for securitization established under Subsection (a) shall include rules and procedures for the recovery of stranded costs under the terms of a rate order adopted by the board of directors of the electric cooperative, which rate order shall have the effect of a financing order.

(c) The rules and procedures established by the commission under Subsection (b) shall include rules and procedures for the issuance of transition bonds issued in a securitized financing transaction. The issuance of any transition bonds issued in a securitized financing transaction by an electric cooperative is expressly authorized and shall be governed by the laws governing the issuance of bonds or other obligations by the electric cooperative. Findings made by the board of directors of an electric cooperative in a rate order issued under the rules and procedures described by this subsection shall be conclusive, and any transition charges incorporated in the rate order to recover the principal, interest, and all reasonable expenses associated with any securitized financing transaction shall constitute property rights, as described in Subchapter G, Chapter 39,[1] and shall otherwise conform in all material respects to the transition charges provided by Subchapter G, Chapter 39.

Added by Acts 1999, 76th Leg., ch. 405, § 39, eff. Sept. 1, 1999.

[1] V.T.C.A., Utilities Code § 39.301.

§ 41.004. Jurisdiction of Commission

Except as specifically provided otherwise in this chapter, the commission has jurisdiction over electric cooperatives only as follows:

(1) to regulate wholesale transmission rates and service, including terms of access, to the extent provided in Subchapter A, Chapter 35;[1]

(2) to regulate certification to the extent provided in Chapter 37;

(3) to establish a code of conduct as provided in Section 39.157(e) subject to Section 41.054;

(4) to establish terms and conditions, but not rates, for open access to distribution facilities for electric cooperatives providing customer choice, as provided in Section 39.203; and

(5) to require reports of electric cooperative operations only to the extent necessary to:

(A) ensure the public safety;

(B) enable the commission to satisfy its responsibilities relating to electric cooperatives under this chapter;

(C) enable the commission to determine the aggregate electric load and energy requirements in the state and the resources available to serve that load; or

(D) enable the commission to determine information relating to market power as provided in Section 39.155.

Added by Acts 1999, 76th Leg., ch. 405, § 39, eff. Sept. 1, 1999.

[1] V.T.C.A., Utilities Code § 35.001.

§ 41.005. Limitation on Municipal Authority

Notwithstanding any other provision of this title, a municipality may not directly or indirectly regulate the rates, operations, and services of an electric cooperative, except, with respect to operations, to the extent necessary to protect the public health, safety, or welfare. This section does not prohibit a municipality from making a lawful charge for the use of public rights-of-way within the municipality as provided by Section 182.025, Tax Code, and Section 33.008. An electric cooperative shall be an electric utility for purposes of Section 182.025, Tax Code, and Section 33.008.

Added by Acts 1999, 76th Leg., ch. 405, § 39, eff. Sept. 1, 1999.

SUBCHAPTER B. ELECTRIC COOPERATIVE UTILITY CHOICE

§ 41.051. Board Decision

(a) The board of directors has the discretion to decide when or if the electric cooperative will provide customer choice.

(b) Electric cooperatives that choose to participate in customer choice may do so at any time on or after January 1, 2002, by adoption of an appropriate resolution of the board of directors. The decision to participate in customer choice by the adoption of a resolution may be revoked only if no customer has opted for choice within four years of the resolution's adoption. An electric cooperative may initiate a customer choice pilot project at any time.

Added by Acts 1999, 76th Leg., ch. 405, § 39, eff. Sept. 1, 1999.

§ 41.052. Electric Cooperatives Not Offering Customer Choice

(a) An electric cooperative that chooses not to participate in customer choice may not offer electric energy at unregulated prices directly to retail customers outside its certificated retail service area.

(b) An electric cooperative under Subsection (a) retains the right to offer and provide a full range of customer service and pricing programs to the customers within its certificated retail service area and to purchase and sell electric energy at wholesale without geographic restriction.

(c) A generation and transmission electric cooperative may offer electric energy at unregulated prices directly to retail customers outside of its parent electric cooperatives' certificated service areas only if a majority of the parent electric cooperatives of the generation and transmission electric cooperative have chosen to offer customer choice.

(d) A subsidiary of an electric cooperative may not provide electric energy at unregulated prices outside of its parent electric cooperative's certificated retail service area unless the electric cooperative offers customer choice inside its certificated retail service area.

Added by Acts 1999, 76th Leg., ch. 405, § 39, eff. Sept. 1, 1999.

§ 41.053. Retail Customer Right of Choice

(a) If an electric cooperative chooses to participate in customer choice, after that choice, all retail customers within the certificated service area of the electric cooperative shall have the right of customer choice, and the electric cooperative shall provide nondiscriminatory open access for retail service.

(b) Notwithstanding Section 39.107, the metering function may not be deemed a competitive service for customers of the electric cooperative within that service area and may, at the option of the electric cooperative, continue to be offered by the electric cooperative as sole provider.

(c) On its initiation of customer choice, an electric cooperative shall designate itself or another entity as the provider of last resort for retail customers within the electric cooperative's certificated service area and shall fulfill the role of default provider of last resort in the event no other entity is available to act in that capacity.

(d) If a retail electric provider fails to serve a customer described in Subsection (c), on request by the customer, the provider of last resort shall offer the customer the standard retail service package for the appropriate customer class, with no interruption of service, at a fixed, nondiscountable rate that is at least sufficient to cover the reasonable costs of providing that service, as approved by the board of directors.

(e) The board of directors may establish the procedures and criteria for designating the provider of last resort and may redesignate the provider of last resort according to a schedule it considers appropriate.

Added by Acts 1999, 76th Leg., ch. 405, § 39, eff. Sept. 1, 1999.

§ 41.054. Service Outside Certificated Area

(a) Notwithstanding any provisions of Chapter 161:

(1) an electric cooperative participating in customer choice shall have the right to offer electric energy and related services at unregulated prices directly to retail customers who have customer choice without regard to geographic location; and

(2) any person, without restriction, except as may be provided in the electric cooperative's articles of incorporation and bylaws, may be a member of an electric cooperative.

(b) In providing service under Subsection (a) to retail customers outside its certificated service area as that area exists on the date of adoption of customer choice, an electric cooperative becomes subject to commission jurisdiction as to the commission's rules establishing a code of conduct regulating anticompetitive practices under Section 39.157(e), except to the extent those rules conflict with this chapter.

(c) For electric cooperatives participating in customer choice, the commission shall have jurisdiction to establish terms and conditions, but not rates, for access by other electric providers to the electric cooperative's distribution facilities.

(d) Notwithstanding Subsections (b) and (c), the commission shall make accommodation in the code of conduct for specific legal requirements imposed by state or federal law applicable to electric cooperatives. The commission shall accommodate the organizational structures of electric cooperatives and may not prohibit an electric cooperative and any related entity from sharing officers, directors, or employees.

(e) The commission does not have jurisdiction to require the unbundling of services or functions of, or to regulate the recovery of stranded investment of, an electric cooperative or, except as provided by this section, jurisdiction with respect to the rates, terms, and conditions of service for retail customers of an electric cooperative within the electric cooperative's certificated service area.

(f) An electric cooperative shall maintain separate books and records of its operations and the operations of any subsidiary and shall ensure that the rates charged for provision of electric service do not include any costs of its subsidiary or any other costs not related to the provision of electric service.

Added by Acts 1999, 76th Leg., ch. 405, § 39, eff. Sept. 1, 1999.

§ 41.055. Jurisdiction of Board of Directors

A board of directors has exclusive jurisdiction to:

(1) set all terms of access, conditions, and rates applicable to services provided by the electric cooperative, except as provided by Sections 41.054 and 41.056, including nondiscriminatory and comparable rates for distribution but excluding wholesale transmission rates, terms of access, and conditions for wholesale transmission service set by the commission under Subchapter A, Chapter 35,[1] provided that the rates for distribution established by the electric cooperative shall be comparable to the distribution rates that apply to the electric cooperative and its subsidiaries;

(2) determine whether to unbundle any energy-related activities and, if the board of directors chooses to unbundle, whether to do so structurally or functionally;

(3) reasonably determine the amount of the electric cooperative's stranded investment;

(4) establish nondiscriminatory transition charges reasonably designed to recover the stranded investment over an appropriate period of time;

(5) determine the extent to which the electric cooperative will provide various customer services, including nonelectric services, or accept the services from other providers;

(6) manage and operate the electric cooperative's utility systems, including exercise of control over resource acquisition and any related expansion programs;

(7) establish and enforce service quality standards, reliability standards, and consumer safeguards designed to protect retail electric customers;

(8) determine whether a base rate reduction is appropriate for the electric cooperative;

(9) determine any other utility matters that the board of directors believes should be included;

(10) sell electric energy and capacity at wholesale, regardless of whether the electric cooperative participates in customer choice;

(11) determine the extent to which the electric cooperative offers energy efficiency programs and how the programs are administered by the electric cooperative; and

(12) make any other decisions affecting the electric cooperative's method of conducting business that are not inconsistent with the provisions of this chapter.

Added by Acts 1999, 76th Leg., ch. 405, § 39, eff. Sept. 1, 1999. Amended by Acts 2007, 80th Leg., ch. 939, § 28, eff. Sept. 1, 2007.

[1] V.T.C.A., Utilities Code § 35.001.

§ 41.056. Anticompetitive Actions

(a) If, after notice and hearing, the commission finds that an electric cooperative providing customer choice has engaged in anticompetitive behavior by not providing other retail electric providers with nondiscriminatory terms and conditions of access to distribution facilities or customers within the electric cooperative's certificated service area that are comparable to the electric cooperative's and its subsidiaries' terms and conditions of access to distribution facilities or customers, the commission shall notify the electric cooperative.

(b) The electric cooperative shall have three months to cure the anticompetitive or noncompliant behavior described in Subsection (a). If the behavior is not fully remedied within that time, the commission may prohibit the electric cooperative or its subsidiary from providing retail service outside its certificated retail service area until the behavior is remedied.

Added by Acts 1999, 76th Leg., ch. 405, § 39, eff. Sept. 1, 1999.

§ 41.057. Billing

(a) An electric cooperative that opts for customer choice may continue to bill directly electric customers located in its certificated service area for all transmission and distribution services. The electric cooperative may also bill directly for generation and customer services provided by the electric cooperative or its subsidiaries to those customers.

(b) A customer served by an electric cooperative for transmission and distribution services and by a retail electric provider for retail service has the option of being billed directly by each service provider or receiving a single bill for distribution, transmission, and generation services from the electric cooperative.

Added by Acts 1999, 76th Leg., ch. 405, § 39, eff. Sept. 1, 1999.

§ 41.058. Tariffs for Open Access

An electric cooperative that owns or operates transmission and distribution facilities shall file tariffs implementing the open access rules established by the commission under Section 39.203 with the appropriate regulatory authorities having jurisdiction over the transmission and distribution service of the electric cooperative before the 90th day preceding the date the electric cooperative offers customer choice.

Added by Acts 1999, 76th Leg., ch. 405, § 39, eff. Sept. 1, 1999.

§ 41.059. No Power to Amend Certificates

Nothing in this chapter empowers a board of directors to issue, amend, or rescind a certificate of public convenience and necessity granted by the commission.

Added by Acts 1999, 76th Leg., ch. 405, § 39, eff. Sept. 1, 1999.

§ 41.060. Customer Service Information

(a) The commission shall keep information submitted by customers and retail electric providers pertaining to the provision of electric service by electric cooperatives.

(b) The commission shall notify the appropriate electric cooperative of information submitted by a customer or retail electric provider, and the electric cooperative shall respond to the customer or retail electric provider. The electric cooperative shall notify the commission of its response.

(c) The commission shall prepare a report for the Sunset Advisory Commission that includes information submitted and responses by electric cooperatives in accordance with the Sunset Advisory Commission's schedule for reviewing the commission.

Added by Acts 1999, 76th Leg., ch. 405, § 39, eff. Sept. 1, 1999.

§ 41.061. Retail Rate Changes by Electric Cooperatives

(a) This section shall apply to retail rates of an electric cooperative that has not adopted customer choice and to the retail delivery rates of an electric cooperative that has adopted customer choice. This section may not apply to rates for:

(1) sales of electric energy by an electric cooperative that has adopted customer choice; or

(2) wholesale sales of electric energy.

(b) An electric cooperative may change its rates by:

(1) adopting a resolution approving the proposed change;

(2) mailing notice of the proposed change to each affected customer whose rate would be increased by the proposed change at least 30 days before implementation of the proposed change, which notice may be included in a monthly billing; and

(3) holding a meeting to discuss the proposed rate changes with affected customers, if any change is expected to increase total system annual revenues by more than $100,000 or one percent, whichever is greater.

(c) An electric cooperative may implement the proposed rates on completion of the requirements under Subsection (b), and those rates shall remain in effect until changed by the electric cooperative as provided by this section or, for rates other than retail delivery rates, until this section is no longer applicable because the electric cooperative adopts customer choice.

(d) The electric cooperative may reconsider a rate change at any time and adjust the rate by board resolution without additional notice or meeting of customers if the rate as adjusted is not expected to increase the revenues from a customer class. However, if notice is given to a customer class that would receive an increase as a result of the adjustment, then the rates for the customer class may be increased without additional meeting of the customers. A customer may petition to appeal within the time provided in Subsection (f).

(e) Retail rates set by an electric cooperative that has not adopted customer choice and retail delivery rates set by an electric cooperative that has adopted customer choice shall be just and reasonable, not unreasonably preferential, prejudicial, or discriminatory; provided, however, if the customer agrees, an electric cooperative may charge a market-based rate to customers who have energy supply options if rates are not increased for other customers as a result.

(f) A customer of the electric cooperative who is adversely affected by a rate setting resolution of the electric cooperative is entitled to judicial review. A person initiates judicial review by filing a petition in the district court of Travis County not later than the 90th day after the resolution is implemented.

(g) The resolution of the electric cooperative setting rates, as it may have been amended as described in Subsection (d), shall be presumed valid, and the burden of showing that the resolution is invalid rests on the persons challenging the resolution. A court reviewing a change of a rate or rates by an electric cooperative may consider any relevant factor including the cost of providing service.

(h) If the court finds that the electric cooperative's resolution setting rates violates the standards contained in Subsection (e), or that the electric cooperative's rate violates Subsection (e), the court shall enter an order:

(1) stating the specific basis for its determination that the rates set in the electric cooperative's resolution violate Subsection (e); and

(2) directing the electric cooperative to:

(A) set, within 60 days, revised retail rates that do not violate the standards of Subsection (e); and

(B) refund or credit against future bills, at the electric cooperative's option, revenues collected under the rate found to violate the standards of Subsection (e) that exceed the revenues that would have been collected under the revised rates. The refund or credit shall be made over a period of not more than 12 months, as determined by the court.

(i) The court may not enter an order delaying or prohibiting implementation of a rate change or set revised rates either for the period the challenged resolution was in effect or prospectively.

(j) A person having obtained an order of the court requiring an electric cooperative to set revised retail rates pursuant to Subsection (h)(2)(A) may, once the order is no longer subject to appeal, initiate an original proceeding in the district court of Travis County either to:

(1) seek enforcement of the court's order by writ of mandamus if the electric cooperative has failed to adopt a resolution approving revised rates within the time prescribed; or

(2) seek judicial review of the electric cooperative's most current resolution setting rates as provided in this section, if the electric cooperative has set revised rates pursuant to the order of the court within the time prescribed. In the event of such enforcement proceeding or judicial review the court may, in addition to the other remedies provided for in this section, award reasonable costs, including reasonable attorney's fees, to the party prevailing on the case as a whole. Additionally, if the court finds that either party has acted in bad faith solely for the purpose of perpetuating the rate dispute between the parties, the court may impose sanctions on the offending party in accordance with the provisions of Subsections (b), (c), and (e), Section 10.004, Civil Practice and Remedies Code.

(k) An electric cooperative that has not adopted customer choice and that has not changed each of its nonresidential rates since January 1, 1999, shall, on or before May 1, 2002, adopt a resolution setting rates. The resolution shall be subject to judicial review as provided in this section whether or not any rate is changed. In the event the electric cooperative fails to adopt a resolution setting rates pursuant to this subsection, a customer may petition for judicial review of the electric cooperative's rates. A person initiates judicial review by filing a petition in the district court of Travis County not later than November 1, 2002.

Added by Acts 1999, 76th Leg., ch. 405, § 39, eff. Sept. 1, 1999.

§ 41.062. Allocation of Stranded Investment

Any competition transition charge shall be allocated among retail customer classes based on the relevant customer class characteristics as of the end of the electric cooperative's most recent fiscal year before implementation of customer choice, in accordance with the methodology used to allocate the costs of the underlying assets or expenses in the electric cooperative's most recent cost of service study certified by a professional engineer or certified public accountant or approved by the commission. In multiply certificated areas, a retail customer may not avoid stranded cost recovery charges by switching to another electric cooperative, an electric utility, or a municipally owned utility.

Added by Acts 1999, 76th Leg., ch. 405, § 39, eff. Sept. 1, 1999.

§ 41.063. Repealed by Acts 2003, 78th Leg., ch. 1327, § 3, eff. Sept. 1, 2003

SUBCHAPTER C. RIGHTS NOT AFFECTED

§ 41.101. Interference With Contract

(a) This subtitle may not interfere with or abrogate the rights or obligations of parties, including a retail or wholesale customer, to a contract with an electric cooperative or its subsidiary.

(b) No provision of this subtitle may interfere with or be deemed to abrogate the rights or obligations of a party under a contract or an agreement concerning certificated service areas.

Added by Acts 1999, 76th Leg., ch. 405, § 39, eff. Sept. 1, 1999.

§ 41.102. Access to Wholesale Market

Nothing in this subtitle shall limit the access of an electric cooperative or its subsidiary, either on its own behalf or on behalf of its customers, to the wholesale electric market.

Added by Acts 1999, 76th Leg., ch. 405, § 39, eff. Sept. 1, 1999.

§ 41.103. Protection of Bondholders

Nothing in this subtitle or any rule adopted under this subtitle shall impair contracts, covenants, or obligations between an electric cooperative and its lenders and holders of bonds issued on behalf of or by the electric cooperative.

Added by Acts 1999, 76th Leg., ch. 405, § 39, eff. Sept. 1, 1999.

§ 41.104. Tax-Exempt Status

Nothing in this subtitle may impair the tax-exempt status of electric cooperatives, nor shall anything in this subtitle compel any electric cooperative to use its facilities in a manner that violates any contractual provisions, bond covenants, or other restrictions applicable to facilities financed by tax-exempt or federally insured or guaranteed debt.

Added by Acts 1999, 76th Leg., ch. 405, § 39, eff. Sept. 1, 1999.

CHAPTER 43. USE OF ELECTRIC DELIVERY SYSTEM FOR ACCESS TO BROADBAND AND OTHER ENHANCED SERVICES, INCLUDING COMMUNICATIONS

SUBCHAPTER A. GENERAL PROVISIONS

Section
43.001. Legislative Findings.
43.002. Applicability.
43.003. Definitions.

SUBCHAPTER B. DEVELOPMENT OF BPL SYSTEMS

43.051. Authorization for BPL System.
43.052. Ownership and Operation of BPL System.

Section
43.053. Fees and Charges.
43.054. No Additional Easements or Consideration Required.
43.055. Reliability of Electric Systems Maintained.

SUBCHAPTER C. IMPLEMENTATION OF BPL SYSTEM BY ELECTRIC UTILITY

43.101. Participation by Electric Utility.
43.102. Cost Recovery for Deployment of BPL and Utility Applications.

SUBCHAPTER D. MISCELLANEOUS PROVISIONS

43.151. Affiliates of Electric Utility.
43.152. Compliance With Federal Law.

SUBCHAPTER A. GENERAL PROVISIONS

§ 43.001. Legislative Findings

(a) The legislature finds that broadband over power lines, also known as BPL, is an emerging technology platform that offers a means of providing broadband services to reach homes and businesses. BPL services can also be used to enhance existing electric delivery systems, which can result in improved service and reliability for electric customers.

(b) The legislature finds that access to quality, high speed broadband services is important to this state. BPL deployment in Texas has the potential to extend broadband service to customers where broadband access is currently not available and may provide an additional option for existing broadband consumers in Texas, resulting in a more competitive market for broadband services. The legislature further finds that BPL development in Texas is fully dependent upon the participation of electric utilities in this state that own and operate power lines and related facilities that are necessary for the construction of BPL systems and the provision of BPL services.

(c) Consistent with the goal of increasing options for telecommunications in this state, the legislature finds that it is in the public interest to encourage the deployment of BPL by permitting affiliates of the electric utility, or permitting unaffiliated entities, to own or operate all or a portion of such BPL systems. The purpose of this chapter is to provide the appropriate framework to support the deployment of BPL.

(d) The legislature finds that an electric utility may choose to implement BPL under the procedures set forth in this chapter, but is not required to do so. The electric utility shall have the right to decide, in its sole discretion, whether to implement BPL and may not be penalized for deciding to implement or not to implement BPL.

Added by Acts 2005, 79th Leg., 2nd C.S., ch. 2, § 2, eff. Sept. 1, 2005.

§ 43.002. Applicability

(a) This chapter applies to an electric utility whether or not the electric utility is offering customer choice under Chapter 39.

(b) If there is a conflict between the specific provisions of this chapter and any other provisions of this title, the provisions of this chapter control.

(c) No provision of this title shall impose an obligation on an electric utility to implement BPL, to provide broadband services, or to allow others to install BPL facilities or use the electric utility's facilities for the provision of broadband services.

Added by Acts 2005, 79th Leg., 2nd C.S., ch. 2, § 2, eff. Sept. 1, 2005.

§ 43.003. Definitions

In this chapter:

(1) "BPL," "broadband over power lines," and "BPL services" mean the provision of broadband services over electric power lines and related facilities, whether above ground or in underground conduit.

(2) "BPL access" means the ability to access broadband services via a BPL operator or BPL Internet service provider.

(3) "BPL operator" means an entity that owns or operates a BPL system on the electric power lines and related facilities of an electric utility.

(4) "BPL Internet service provider" and "BPL ISP" mean an entity that provides Internet services to others on a wholesale basis or to end-use customers on a retail basis.

(5) "BPL system" means the materials, equipment, and other facilities installed on electric utility property to facilitate the provision of BPL services.

(6) "BPL electric utility applications" means services and technologies that are used and useful and designed to improve the operational performance and service reliability of an electric utility including, but not limited to, automated meter reading, real time system monitoring and meter control, remote service control, outage detection and restoration, predictive maintenance and diagnostics, and monitoring and enhancement of power quality.

(7) "Electric delivery system" means the power lines and related transmission and distribution facilities used by an electric utility to deliver electric energy.

(8) "Electric utility" shall include an electric utility and a transmission and distribution utility as defined in Section 31.002(6) or (19) .

Added by Acts 2005, 79th Leg., 2nd C.S., ch. 2, § 2, eff. Sept. 1, 2005.

SUBCHAPTER B. DEVELOPMENT OF BPL SYSTEMS

§ 43.051. Authorization for BPL System

An affiliate of an electric utility or a person unaffiliated with an electric utility may own, construct, maintain, and operate a BPL system and provide BPL services on an electric utility's electric delivery system consistent with the requirements of this chapter. Nothing in this chapter shall prohibit an entity defined in Section 11.003(9) from providing BPL service or owning and operating a BPL system. Nothing in this chapter shall prohibit an electric utility from providing construction or maintenance services to a BPL operator or BPL ISP provided that the costs of these services are properly accounted for between the electric utility and the BPL operator or BPL ISP.

Added by Acts 2005, 79th Leg., 2nd C.S., ch. 2, § 2, eff. Sept. 1, 2005.

§ 43.052. Ownership and Operation of BPL System

(a) An electric utility may elect to:

(1) allow an affiliate to own or operate a BPL system on the utility's electric delivery system;

(2) allow an unaffiliated entity to own or operate a BPL system on the electric utility's electric delivery system; or

(3) allow an affiliate or unaffiliated entity to provide Internet service over a BPL system.

(b) The BPL operator and the electric utility shall determine what BPL Internet service providers may have access to broadband capacity on the BPL system.

Added by Acts 2005, 79th Leg., 2nd C.S., ch. 2, § 2, eff. Sept. 1, 2005.

§ 43.053. Fees and Charges

(a) An electric utility that allows an affiliate or an unaffiliated entity to own a BPL system on the electric utility's electric delivery system shall charge the owner of the BPL system for the use of the electric utility's electric delivery system.

(b) An electric utility may pay a BPL owner, a BPL operator, or a BPL ISP for the use of the BPL system required to operate BPL utility applications.

(c) If all or part of a BPL system is installed on poles or other structures of a telecommunications utility as that term is defined in Section 51.002, the owner of the BPL system shall be required to pay the telecommunications utility an annual fee consistent with the usual and customary charges for access to the space occupied by that portion of the BPL system so installed.

(d) Notwithstanding Subsections (a)–(c):

(1) an electric utility may not charge an affiliate under this section an amount less than the electric utility would charge an unaffiliated entity for the same item or class of items;

(2) an electric utility may not pay an affiliate under this section an amount more than the affiliate would charge an unaffiliated entity for the same item or class of items; and

(3) an electric utility or an affiliate of an electric utility may not discriminate against a retail electric provider that is not affiliated with the utility in the terms or availability of BPL services.

Added by Acts 2005, 79th Leg., 2nd C.S., ch. 2, § 2, eff. Sept. 1, 2005.

§ 43.054. No Additional Easements or Consideration Required

Because BPL systems provide benefits to electric delivery systems, the installation of a BPL system on an electric delivery system shall not require the electric utility or the owner of the BPL system or an entity defined in Section 11.003(9) to obtain or expand easements or other rights-of-way for the BPL system or to give additional consideration as a result of the installation or the operation of a BPL system. For purposes of this section, installation of a BPL system shall be deemed to be consistent with installation of an electric delivery system.

Added by Acts 2005, 79th Leg., 2nd C.S., ch. 2, § 2, eff. Sept. 1, 2005.

§ 43.055. Reliability of Electric Systems Maintained

An electric utility that allows the installation and operation of a BPL system on its electric delivery system shall employ all reasonable measures to ensure that the operation of the BPL system does not interfere with or diminish the reliability of the utility's electric delivery system. Should a disruption in the provision of electric service occur, the electric utility shall be governed by the terms and conditions of the retail electric delivery service tariff. At all times, the provision of broadband services shall be secondary to the reliable provision of electric delivery services.

Added by Acts 2005, 79th Leg., 2nd C.S., ch. 2, § 2, eff. Sept. 1, 2005.

SUBCHAPTER C. IMPLEMENTATION OF BPL SYSTEM BY ELECTRIC UTILITY

§ 43.101. Participation by Electric Utility

(a) An electric utility, through an affiliate or through an unaffiliated entity, may elect to install and operate a BPL system on some or all of its electric delivery system in any part or all of its certificated service area.

(b) The installation, operation, and use of a BPL system and the provision of BPL services shall not be regulated by any state agency, a municipality, or local government other than as provided for in this chapter.

(c) The commission or a state or local government or a regulatory or quasi-governmental or a quasi-regulatory authority may not:

(1) require an electric utility, either through an affiliate or an unaffiliated entity, to install a BPL system on its power lines or offer BPL services in all or any part of the electric utility's certificated service area;

(2) require an electric utility to allow others to install a BPL system on the utility's electric delivery system in any part or all of the electric utility's certificated service area; or

(3) prohibit an electric utility from having an affiliate or unaffiliated entity install a BPL system or offering BPL services in any part or all of the electric utility's certificated service area.

(d) If a municipality or local government is already collecting a charge or fee from the electric utility for the use of the public rights-of-way for the delivery of electricity to retail electric customers, the municipality or local government is prohibited from requiring a franchise or an amendment to a franchise or from requiring a charge, fee, or tax from any entity for use of the public rights-of-way for a BPL system.

(e) The state or a municipality may impose a charge on the provision of BPL services, but the charge may not be greater than the lowest charge that the state or municipality imposes on other providers of broadband services for use of the public rights-of-way in its respective jurisdiction.

Added by Acts 2005, 79th Leg., 2nd C.S., ch. 2, § 2, eff. Sept. 1, 2005.

§ 43.102. Cost Recovery for Deployment of BPL and Utility Applications

(a) Where an electric utility permits the installation of a BPL system on its electric delivery system under Section 43.052(a), the electric utility's investment in that BPL system to directly support the BPL electric utility applications and other BPL services consumed by the electric utility that are used and useful in providing electric utility service shall be eligible for inclusion in the electric utility's invested capital, and any fees or operating expenses that are reasonable and necessary shall be eligible for inclusion as operating expenses for purposes of any proceeding under Chapter 36. The invested capital and expenses described in this section must be allocated to the customer classes directly receiving the services.

(b) In any proceeding under Chapter 36, just and reasonable charges for the use of the electric utility's electric delivery system by a BPL owner or operator shall be limited to the usual and customary pole attachment charges paid to the electric utility for comparable space by cable television operators.

(c) The revenues of an affiliated BPL operator or an affiliated BPL ISP shall not be deemed the revenues of an electric utility for purposes of setting rates under Chapter 36.

Added by Acts 2005, 79th Leg., 2nd C.S., ch. 2, § 2, eff. Sept. 1, 2005.

SUBCHAPTER D. MISCELLANEOUS PROVISIONS

§ 43.151. Affiliates of Electric Utility

(a) Subject to the limitations of this chapter, an electric utility may have a full or partial ownership interest in a BPL operator or a BPL ISP. Whether a BPL operator or a BPL ISP is an affiliate of the electric utility shall be determined under Section 11.003(2) or Section 11.006.

(b) Neither a BPL operator nor a BPL ISP shall be considered a "competitive affiliate" of an electric utility as that term is defined in Section 39.157.

Added by Acts 2005, 79th Leg., 2nd C.S., ch. 2, § 2, eff. Sept. 1, 2005.

§ 43.152. Compliance With Federal Law

BPL operators shall comply with all applicable federal laws, including those protecting licensed spectrum users from interference by BPL systems. The operator of a radio frequency device shall be required to cease operating the device upon notification by a Federal Communications Commission or Public Utilities Commission representative that the device is causing harmful interference. Operation shall not resume until the condition causing the harmful interference has been corrected.

Added by Acts 2005, 79th Leg., 2nd C.S., ch. 2, § 2, eff. Sept. 1, 2005.

SUBTITLE C. TELECOMMUNICATIONS UTILITIES

CHAPTER 51. GENERAL PROVISIONS

Section

51.001. Policy.
51.002. Definitions.
51.003. Applicability.
51.004. Pricing Flexibility.
51.005. Assistance to Municipality.
51.006. Municipal Participation in Ratemaking Proceedings.
51.007. Municipal Standing in Certain Cases.
51.008. Judicial Review.
51.009. Municipal Fees.
51.010. Commission Investigation of Sale, Merger, or Certain Other Actions.

§ 51.001. Policy

(a) Significant changes have occurred in telecommunications since the law from which this title is derived was originally adopted. Communications providers, including providers not subject to state regulation, such as wireless communications providers and Voice over Internet Protocol providers, have made investments in this state and broadened the range of communications choices available to consumers. To encourage and accelerate the development of a competitive and advanced telecommunications environment and infrastructure, rules, policies, and principles must be reformulated to reduce regulation of incumbent local exchange companies, ensure fair business practices, and protect the public interest.

(b) It is the policy of this state to:

(1) promote diversity of telecommunications providers and interconnectivity;

(2) encourage a fully competitive telecommunications marketplace; and

(3) maintain a wide availability of high quality, interoperable, standards-based telecommunications services at affordable rates.

(c) The policy goals described by Subsection (b) are best achieved by legislation that modernizes telecommunications regulation by:

(1) guaranteeing the affordability of basic telephone service in a competitively neutral manner; and

(2) fostering free market competition in the telecommunications industry.

(d) The technological advancements, advanced telecommunications infrastructure, and increased customer choices for telecommunications services generated by a truly competitive market play a critical role in Texas' economic future by raising living standards for Texans through:

(1) enhanced economic development; and

(2) improved delivery of education, health, and other public and private services.

(e) The strength of competitive forces varies widely between markets, products, and services. It is the policy of this state to require the commission to take action necessary to enhance competition by adjusting regulation to match the degree of competition in the marketplace to:

(1) reduce the cost and burden of regulation; and

(2) protect markets that are not competitive.

(f) It is the policy of this state to ensure that high quality telecommunications services are available, accessible, and usable by an individual with a disability, unless making the services available, accessible, or usable would:

(1) result in an undue burden, including unreasonable cost or technical infeasibility; or

(2) have an adverse competitive effect.

(g) It is the policy of this state to ensure that customers in all regions of this state, including low-income customers and customers in rural and high cost areas, have access to telecommunications and information services, including interexchange services, cable services, wireless services, and advanced telecommunications and information services, that are reasonably comparable to those services provided in urban areas and that are available at prices that are reasonably comparable to prices charged for similar services in urban areas.

Acts 1997, 75th Leg., ch. 166, § 1, eff. Sept. 1, 1997. Amended by Acts 1999, 76th Leg., ch. 1212, § 4, eff. Sept. 1, 1999; Acts 2011, 82nd Leg., ch. 98 (S.B. 980), § 1, eff. Sept. 1, 2011.

§ 51.002. Definitions

In this subtitle:

(1) "Basic local telecommunications service" means:

(A) flat rate residential and business local exchange telephone service, including primary directory listings;

(B) tone dialing service;

(C) access to operator services;

(D) access to directory assistance services;

(E) access to 911 service provided by a local authority or dual party relay service;

(F) the ability to report service problems seven days a week;

(G) lifeline and tel-assistance services; and

(H) any other service the commission determines after a hearing is a basic local telecommunications service.

(2) "Dominant carrier" means a provider of a communication service provided wholly or partly over a telephone system who the commission determines has sufficient market power in a telecommunications market to control prices for that service in that market in a manner adverse to the public interest. The term includes a provider who provided local exchange telephone service within a certificated exchange area on September 1, 1995, as to that service and as to any other service for which a competitive alternative is not available in a particular geographic market. In addition, with respect to:

(A) intraLATA long distance message telecommunications service originated by dialing the access code "1-plus," the term includes a provider of local exchange telephone service in a certificated exchange area for whom the use of that access code for the origination of "1-plus" intraLATA calls in the exchange area is exclusive; and

(B) interexchange services, the term does not include an interexchange carrier that is not a certificated local exchange company.

(3) "Incumbent local exchange company" means a local exchange company that has a certificate of convenience and necessity on September 1, 1995.

(3–a) "Internet Protocol enabled service" means a service, capability, functionality, or application that uses Internet Protocol or a successor protocol to allow an end user to send or receive a data, video, or voice communication in Internet Protocol or a successor protocol.

(4) "Local exchange company" means a telecommunications utility that has a certificate of convenience and necessity or a certificate of operating authority to provide in this state:

(A) local exchange telephone service;

(B) basic local telecommunications service; or

(C) switched access service.

(5) "Local exchange telephone service" means telecommunications service provided within an exchange to establish connections between customer premises within the exchange, including connections between a customer premises and a long distance provider serving the exchange. The term includes tone dialing service, service connection charges, and directory assistance services offered in connection with basic local telecommunications service and interconnection with other service providers. The term does not include the following services, whether offered on an intraexchange or interexchange basis:

(A) central office based PBX-type services for systems of 75 stations or more;

(B) billing and collection services;

(C) high-speed private line services of 1.544 megabits or greater;

(D) customized services;

(E) private line or virtual private line services;

(F) resold or shared local exchange telephone services if permitted by tariff;

(G) dark fiber services;

(H) non-voice data transmission service offered as a separate service and not as a component of basic local telecommunications service;

(I) dedicated or virtually dedicated access services; or

(J) any other service the commission determines is not a "local exchange telephone service."

(6) "Long run incremental cost" has the meaning assigned by 16 T.A.C. Section 23.91 or its successor.

(7) "Pricing flexibility" includes:

(A) customer specific contracts;

(B) packaging of services;

(C) volume, term, and discount pricing;

(D) zone density pricing, with a zone to be defined as an exchange; and

(E) other promotional pricing.

(8) "Public utility" or "utility" means a person or river authority that owns or operates for compensation in this state equipment or facilities to convey, transmit, or receive communications over a telephone system as a dominant carrier. The term includes a lessee, trustee, or receiver of any of those entities, or a combination of those entities. The term does not include a municipal corporation. A person is not a public utility solely because the person:

(A) furnishes or furnishes and maintains a private system;

(B) manufactures, distributes, installs, or maintains customer premise communications equipment and accessories; or

(C) furnishes a telecommunications service or commodity only to itself, its employees, or its tenants as an incident of employment or tenancy, if that service or commodity is not resold to or used by others.

(9) "Separation" means the division of plant, revenues, expenses, taxes, and reserves applicable to exchange or local service if these items are used in common to provide public utility service to both local exchange telephone service and other service, such as interstate or intrastate toll service.

(10) "Telecommunications provider":

(A) means:

(i) a certificated telecommunications utility;

(ii) a shared tenant service provider;

(iii) a nondominant carrier of telecommunications services;

(iv) a provider of commercial mobile service as defined by Section 332(d), Communications Act of 1934 (47 U.S.C. Section 151 et seq.), Federal Communications Commission rules, and the Omnibus Budget Reconciliation Act of 1993 (Public Law 103–66), except that the term does not include these entities for the purposes of Chapter 17, 55, or 64;

(v) a telecommunications entity that provides central office based PBX-type sharing or resale arrangements;

(vi) an interexchange telecommunications carrier;

(vii) a specialized common carrier;

(viii) a reseller of communications;

(ix) a provider of operator services;

(x) a provider of customer-owned pay telephone service; or

(xi) a person or entity determined by the commission to provide telecommunications services to customers in this state; and

(B) does not mean:

(i) a provider of enhanced or information services, or another user of telecommunications services, who does not also provide telecommunications services; or

(ii) a state agency or state institution of higher education, or a service provided by a state agency or state institution of higher education.

(11) "Telecommunications utility" means:

(A) a public utility;

(B) an interexchange telecommunications carrier, including a reseller of interexchange telecommunications services;

(C) a specialized communications common carrier;

(D) a reseller of communications;

(E) a communications carrier who conveys, transmits, or receives communications wholly or partly over a telephone system;

(F) a provider of operator services as defined by Section 55.081, unless the provider is a subscriber to customer-owned pay telephone service; and

(G) a separated affiliate or an electronic publishing joint venture as defined in Chapter 63.

(12) "Tier 1 local exchange company" has the meaning assigned by the Federal Communications Commission.

(13) "Voice over Internet Protocol service" means a service that:

(A) uses Internet Protocol or a successor protocol to enable a real-time, two-way voice communication that originates from or terminates to the user's location in Internet Protocol or a successor protocol;

(B) requires a broadband connection from the user's location; and

(C) permits a user generally to receive a call that originates on the public switched telephone network and to terminate a call to the public switched telephone network.

Acts 1997, 75th Leg., ch. 166, § 1, eff. Sept. 1, 1997. Amended by Acts 1999, 76th Leg., ch. 1212, § 5, eff. Sept. 1, 1999; Acts 1999, 76th Leg., ch. 1579, § 4, eff. Aug. 30, 1999; Acts 2001, 77th Leg., ch. 651, § 5, eff. Sept. 1, 2001; Acts 2011, 82nd Leg., ch. 98 (S.B. 980), § 2, eff. Sept. 1, 2011.

§ 51.003. Applicability

Except as otherwise expressly provided by this title, this title does not apply to:

(1) a company that as its only form of business:

(A) is a telecommunications manager; or

(B) administers central office based or customer based PBX-type sharing/resale arrangements;

(2) telegraph services;

(3) television or radio stations;

(4) community antenna television services; or

(5) a provider of commercial mobile service as defined by Section 332(d), Communications Act of 1934 (47 U.S.C. Section 151 et seq.), Federal Communications Commission rules, and the Omnibus Budget Reconciliation Act of 1993 (Public Law 103–66), other than conventional rural radio-telephone services provided by a wire-line telephone company under the Public Mobile Service rules of the Federal Communications Commission (47 C.F.R. Part 22).

Acts 1997, 75th Leg., ch. 166, § 1, eff. Sept. 1, 1997.

§ 51.004. Pricing Flexibility

(a) A discount or other form of pricing flexibility may not be:

(1) unreasonably preferential, prejudicial, or discriminatory; or

(2) predatory or anticompetitive.

(b) This title does not prohibit a volume discount or other discount based on a reasonable business purpose. A price that is set at or above the long run incremental cost of a service is presumed not to be a predatory price.

(c) This title allows an offer based on a reasonable business purpose, including an offer made at any time to a selected customer or a group of customers in response to a competitor's offer or a former customer's acceptance of a competitor's offer if the price of the offer meets the requirements of Section 52.0584, 58.063, or 59.031.

(d) An offer made under Subsection (c) must be made in compliance with Chapter 304, Business & Commerce Code.

Acts 1997, 75th Leg., ch. 166, § 1, eff. Sept. 1, 1997. Amended by Acts 1999, 76th Leg., ch. 1212, § 6, eff. Sept. 1, 1999; Acts 2003, 78th Leg., ch. 32, § 1, eff. Sept. 1, 2003; Acts 2007, 80th Leg., ch. 885, § 2.39, eff. April 1, 2009.

§ 51.005. Assistance to Municipality

On request of a municipality, the commission may advise and assist the municipality with respect to a question or proceeding arising under this title. Assistance provided by the commission may include aid to a municipality on a matter pending before the commission or a court, such as making a staff member available as a witness or otherwise providing evidence to the municipality.

Acts 1997, 75th Leg., ch. 166, § 1, eff. Sept. 1, 1997.

§ 51.006. Municipal Participation in Ratemaking Proceedings

(a) The governing body of a municipality participating in a ratemaking proceeding may engage rate consultants, accountants, auditors, attorneys, and engineers to:

(1) conduct investigations, present evidence, and advise and represent the governing body; and

(2) assist the governing body with litigation before the commission or a court.

(b) The public utility in the ratemaking proceeding shall reimburse the governing body of the municipality for the reasonable cost of the services of a person engaged under Subsection (a) to the extent the commission determines is reasonable.

Acts 1997, 75th Leg., ch. 166, § 1, eff. Sept. 1, 1997.

§ 51.007. Municipal Standing in Certain Cases

(a) A municipality has standing in each case before the commission that relates to a utility providing service in the municipality.

(b) A municipality's standing is subject to the right of the commission to:

(1) determine standing in a case involving a retail service area dispute that involves two or more utilities; and

(2) consolidate municipalities on an issue of common interest.

Acts 1997, 75th Leg., ch. 166, § 1, eff. Sept. 1, 1997.

§ 51.008. Judicial Review

A municipality is entitled to judicial review of a commission order relating to a utility providing services in the municipality as provided by Section 15.001.

Acts 1997, 75th Leg., ch. 166, § 1, eff. Sept. 1, 1997.

§ 51.009. Municipal Fees

(a) Nothing in this title, including Section 53.201, may be construed as in any way limiting the right of a public utility to pass through a municipal fee, including an increase in a municipal fee.

(b) A public utility that traditionally passes through municipal fees shall promptly pass through any municipal fee reduction.

Acts 1997, 75th Leg., ch. 166, § 1, eff. Sept. 1, 1997.

§ 51.010. Commission Investigation of Sale, Merger, or Certain Other Actions

(a) The commission, not later than the 180th day after the date a public utility reports to the commission under Section 14.101, shall complete an investigation under that section and enter a final order.

(b) If a final order is not entered as required by Subsection (a), the commission is considered to have determined that the action taken by the public utility is consistent with the public interest.

(c) Section 14.101 does not apply to:

(1) a company that receives a certificate of operating authority or a service provider certificate of operating authority under Chapter 54; or

(2) a company electing under Chapter 58.

Acts 1997, 75th Leg., ch. 166, § 1, eff. Sept. 1, 1997.

CHAPTER 52. COMMISSION JURISDICTION

SUBCHAPTER A. GENERAL POWERS AND DUTIES OF COMMISSION

Section
52.001. Policy.
52.002. Authority to Regulate.
52.003. Cooperation With Other Regulatory Authorities.
52.004. Commission May Establish Separate Markets.
52.005. Minimum Requirements for Dominant Carriers.
52.006. Commission to Report to Legislature.
52.007. Tariff Requirements Relating to Providers Not Subject to Rate of Return Regulation.

SUBCHAPTER B. INCUMBENT LOCAL EXCHANGE COMPANIES

52.051. Policy.
52.052. Applicability.
52.053. Certain Rates Prohibited.
52.054. Rules and Procedures for Incumbent Local Exchange Companies.
52.055. Hearing to Determine Level of Competition.
52.056. Specifically Authorized Regulatory Treatments.
52.057. Repealed.
52.058. General Provisions Relating To New or Experimental Services or Promotional Rates.

Section
52.0583. New Services.
52.0584. Pricing and Packaging Flexibility; Customer Promotional Offerings.
52.0585. Customer Promotional Offerings.
52.059. Rates to Cover Appropriate Costs.
52.060. Administrative Fee or Assessment.

SUBCHAPTER C. TELECOMMUNICATIONS UTILITIES THAT ARE NOT DOMINANT CARRIERS

52.101. Applicability.
52.102. Limited Regulatory Authority.
52.103. Registration Required.
52.104. Commission May Investigate.
52.105. Access to Certain Services Required.
52.106. Quality of Service Required.
52.107. Predatory Pricing.
52.108. Other Prohibited Practices.
52.109. Availability of Service.
52.110. Burden of Proof.
52.111. Commission May Exempt.
52.112. Reduction Pass-Through Required.

SUBCHAPTER D. CERTIFICATE HOLDERS

52.151. Applicability.
52.152. Limited Regulatory Authority.
52.153. Books and Records.
52.154. Commission May Not Overburden.
52.155. Prohibition of Excessive Access Charges.
52.156. Retail Rates, Terms, and Conditions.

SUBCHAPTER E. DEREGULATION OF SERVICE

52.201. Deregulation of Service.
52.202. Determination of Geographic Market.
52.203. Market Power Test.
52.204. Rate for Deregulated Service.
52.205. Investigation of Competition.
52.206. Reregulation of Market.
52.207. Reports; Confidential Information.

SUBCHAPTER F. REQUIRED REPORTS AND FILINGS; RECORDS

52.251. Tariff Filings.
52.252. Depreciation Account.
52.253. Accounts of Profits and Losses.
52.254. Repealed.
52.255. Availability of Records.
52.256. Plan and Report of Workforce Diversity and Other Business Practices.

SUBCHAPTER A. GENERAL POWERS AND DUTIES OF COMMISSION

§ 52.001. Policy

(a) It is the policy of this state to protect the public interest in having adequate and efficient telecommunications service available to each resident of this state at just, fair, and reasonable rates.

(b) The telecommunications industry, through technical advancements, federal legislative, judicial, and administrative actions, and the formulation of new telecommunications enterprises, has become and will continue to be in many and growing areas a competitive industry that does not lend itself to traditional public utility regulatory rules, policies, and principles. As a result, the public interest requires that rules, policies, and principles be formulated and applied to:

(1) protect the public interest; and

(2) provide equal opportunity to each telecommunications utility in a competitive marketplace.

Acts 1997, 75th Leg., ch. 166, § 1, eff. Sept. 1, 1997.

§ 52.002. Authority to Regulate

(a) To carry out the public policy stated by Section 52.001 and to regulate rates, operations, and services so that the rates are just, fair, and reasonable and the services are adequate and efficient, the commission has exclusive original jurisdiction over the business and property of a telecommunications utility in this state subject to the limitations imposed by this title.

(b) The commission's regulatory authority as to a telecommunications utility other than a public utility is only as prescribed by this title.

(c) The commission may not require a telecommunications utility that is not a public utility, including a deregulated or transitioning company, to comply with a requirement or standard that is more burdensome than a requirement or standard the commission imposes on a public utility.

(d) Notwithstanding any other law, a department, agency, or political subdivision of this state may not by rule, order, or other means directly or indirectly regulate rates charged for, service or contract terms for, conditions for, or requirements for entry into the market for Voice over Internet Protocol services or other Internet Protocol enabled services. This subsection does not:

(1) affect requirements pertaining to use of a right-of-way or payment of right-of-way fees applicable to Voice over Internet Protocol services under Chapter 283, Local Government Code;

(2) affect any person's obligation to provide video or cable service, as defined under applicable state or federal law, the applicability of Chapter 66, or a requirement to make a payment under Chapter 66;

(3) require or prohibit assessment of enhanced 9–1–1, relay access service, or universal service fund fees on Voice over Internet Protocol service;

(4) affect any entity's obligations under Sections 251 and 252, Communications Act of 1934 (47 U.S.C. Sections 251 and 252), or a right granted to an entity by those sections;

(5) affect any applicable wholesale tariff;

(6) grant, modify, or affect the authority of the commission to implement, carry out, or enforce the rights or obligations provided by Sections 251 and 252, Communications Act of 1934 (47 U.S.C. Sections 251 and 252), or of an applicable wholesale tariff through arbitration proceedings or other available mechanisms and procedures;

(7) require or prohibit payment of switched network access rates or other intercarrier compensation rates, as applicable;

(8) limit any commission authority over the subjects listed in Subdivisions (1)–(7) or grant the commission any authority over those subjects; or

(9) affect the assessment, administration, collection, or enforcement of any tax or fee over which the comptroller has authority.

Acts 1997, 75th Leg., ch. 166, § 1, eff. Sept. 1, 1997. Amended by Acts 2011, 82nd Leg., ch. 98 (S.B. 980), § 3, eff. Sept. 1, 2011.

§ 52.003. Cooperation With Other Regulatory Authorities

In regulating the rates, operations, and services of a telecommunications utility providing service in a municipality located on the state line adjacent to a municipality in an adjoining state, the commission may cooperate with the utility regulatory commission of the adjoining state or of the federal government and may hold a joint hearing or make a joint investigation with that commission.

Acts 1997, 75th Leg., ch. 166, § 1, eff. Sept. 1, 1997.

§ 52.004. Commission May Establish Separate Markets

(a) The commission may establish separate telecommunications markets in this state if the commission determines that the public interest will be served. The commission shall hold hearings and require evidence as necessary to:

(1) carry out the public purpose of this chapter; and

(2) determine the need and effect of establishing separate markets.

(b) A provider determined to be a dominant carrier as to a particular telecommunications service in a market may not be presumed to be a dominant carrier of a different telecommunications service in that market.

Acts 1997, 75th Leg., ch. 166, § 1, eff. Sept. 1, 1997.

§ 52.005. Minimum Requirements for Dominant Carriers

The commission shall impose as minimum requirements for a dominant carrier the same requirements imposed by Subchapter C,[1] except Section 52.107.

Acts 1997, 75th Leg., ch. 166, § 1, eff. Sept. 1, 1997.

[1] V.T.C.A, Utilities Code § 52.101 et seq.

§ 52.006. Commission to Report to Legislature

(a) Before January 15 of each odd-numbered year, the commission shall report to the legislature on:

(1) the scope of competition in regulated telecommunications markets; and

(2) the effect of competition on customers in both competitive and noncompetitive markets, with a specific focus on rural markets.

(b) The report shall include:

(1) an assessment of the effect of competition on the rates and availability of telecommunications services for residential and business customers;

(2) a summary of commission action over the preceding two years that reflects changes in the scope of competition in regulated telecommunications markets; and

(3) recommendations for legislation the commission determines is appropriate to promote the public interest in the context of a partially competitive telecommunications market.

(c) The commission, in its assessment under Subsection (b)(1), shall specifically address any effects on universal service.

(d) A telecommunications utility shall cooperate with the commission as necessary for the commission to satisfy the requirements of this section.

Acts 1997, 75th Leg., ch. 166, § 1, eff. Sept. 1, 1997.

§ 52.007. Tariff Requirements Relating to Providers Not Subject to Rate of Return Regulation

(a) This section applies only to a telecommunications provider that is not subject to rate of return regulation under Chapter 53.

(b) A telecommunications provider:

(1) may, but is not required to, maintain on file with the commission tariffs, price lists, or customer

service agreements governing the terms of providing service;

(2) may make changes in its tariffs, price lists, and customer service agreements in relation to services that are not subject to regulation without commission approval; and

(3) may cross-reference its federal tariff in its state tariff if the provider's intrastate switched access rates are the same as the provider's interstate switched access rates.

(c) A telecommunications provider may withdraw a tariff, price list, or customer service agreement not required to be filed or maintained with the commission under this section if the telecommunications provider:

(1) files written notice of the withdrawal with the commission; and

(2) notifies its customers of the withdrawal and posts the current tariffs, price lists, or generic customer service agreements on the telecommunications provider's Internet website.

(d) The commission may not require a telecommunications provider to withdraw a tariff, price list, or customer service agreement.

(e) This section does not affect the authority of the commission to regulate wholesale services, or administer or enforce Chapter 56 or any other applicable regulation permitted or required under this title.

Added by Acts 2011, 82nd Leg., ch. 98 (S.B. 980), § 4, eff. Sept. 1, 2011.

SUBCHAPTER B. INCUMBENT LOCAL EXCHANGE COMPANIES

§ 52.051. Policy

In adopting rules and establishing procedures under this subchapter, the commission shall:

(1) attempt to balance the public interest in a technologically advanced telecommunications system providing a wide range of new and innovative services with traditional regulatory concerns for:

(A) preserving universal service;

(B) prohibiting anticompetitive practices; and

(C) preventing the subsidization of competitive services with revenues from regulated monopoly services; and

(2) incorporate an appropriate mix of regulatory and market mechanisms reflecting the level and nature of competition in the marketplace.

Acts 1997, 75th Leg., ch. 166, § 1, eff. Sept. 1, 1997.

§ 52.052. Applicability

This subchapter does not apply to basic local telecommunications service, including local measured service.

Acts 1997, 75th Leg., ch. 166, § 1, eff. Sept. 1, 1997.

§ 52.053. Certain Rates Prohibited

A rate established under this subchapter may not be:

(1) unreasonably preferential, prejudicial, or discriminatory;

(2) subsidized either directly or indirectly by a regulated monopoly service; or

(3) predatory or anticompetitive.

Acts 1997, 75th Leg., ch. 166, § 1, eff. Sept. 1, 1997.

§ 52.054. Rules and Procedures for Incumbent Local Exchange Companies

(a) To carry out the public policy stated in Section 52.001, notwithstanding any other provision of this title, the commission may adopt rules and establish procedures applicable to incumbent local exchange companies to:

(1) determine the level of competition in a specific telecommunications market or submarket; and

(2) provide appropriate regulatory treatment to allow an incumbent local exchange company to respond to significant competitive challenges.

(b) This section does not change the burden of proof on an incumbent local exchange company under Sections 53.003, 53.006, 53.051, 53.052, 53.053, 53.054, 53.055, 53.057, 53.058, 53.060, and 53.062.

Acts 1997, 75th Leg., ch. 166, § 1, eff. Sept. 1, 1997.

§ 52.055. Hearing to Determine Level of Competition

In determining the level of competition in a specific market or submarket, the commission shall hold an evidentiary hearing to consider:

(1) the number and size of telecommunications utilities or other persons providing the same, equivalent, or substitutable service;

(2) the extent to which the same, equivalent, or substitutable service is available;

(3) the ability of a customer to obtain the same, equivalent, or substitutable service at comparable rates and terms;

(4) the ability of a telecommunications utility or other person to make the same, equivalent, or substitutable service readily available at comparable rates and terms;

(5) the existence of a significant barrier to the entry or exit of a provider of the service; and

(6) other relevant information the commission determines is appropriate.

Acts 1997, 75th Leg., ch. 166, § 1, eff. Sept. 1, 1997.

§ 52.056. Specifically Authorized Regulatory Treatments

The regulatory treatments the commission may implement under Section 52.054 include:

(1) approval of a range of rates for a specific service; and

(2) the detariffing of rates.

Acts 1997, 75th Leg., ch. 166, § 1, eff. Sept. 1, 1997. Amended by Acts 2011, 82nd Leg., ch. 21 (S.B. 983), § 1, eff. Sept. 1, 2011; Acts 2011, 82nd Leg., ch. 98 (S.B. 980), § 5, eff. Sept. 1, 2011.

§ 52.057. Repealed by Acts 2011, 82nd Leg., ch. 21 (S.B. 983), § 4, eff. Sept. 1, 2011; Acts 2011, 82nd Leg., ch. 98 (S.B. 980), § 21(1), eff. Sept. 1, 2011

§ 52.058. General Provisions Relating To New or Experimental Services or Promotional Rates

(a) To encourage the rapid introduction of new or experimental services or promotional rates, the commission shall adopt rules and establish procedures that allow:

(1) the expedited introduction of new or experimental services or promotional rates;

(2) the establishment and adjustment of rates; and

(3) the withdrawal of those services or promotional rates.

(b) The rules and procedures described by Subsection (a) must include rules and procedures to allow the governing body of a municipality served by an incumbent local exchange company having more than 500,000 access lines in this state to make requests to the commission for new or experimental services or promotional rates.

(c) A rate established or adjusted at the request of a municipality may not:

(1) result in higher rates for ratepayers outside the municipal boundaries; or

(2) include a rate for incumbent local exchange company interexchange service or interexchange carrier access service.

Acts 1997, 75th Leg., ch. 166, § 1, eff. Sept. 1, 1997. Amended by Acts 1999, 76th Leg., ch. 1212, § 7, eff. Sept. 1, 1999.

§ 52.0583. New Services

(a) An incumbent local exchange company may introduce a new service 10 days after providing an informational notice to the commission, to the office, and to any person who holds a certificate of operating authority in the incumbent local exchange company's certificated area or areas or who has an effective interconnection agreement with the incumbent local exchange company.

(b) An incumbent local exchange company shall price each new service at or above the service's long run incremental cost. The commission shall allow a company serving fewer than one million access lines in this state to establish a service's long run incremental cost by adopting, at that company's option, the cost studies of a larger company for that service that have been accepted by the commission.

(c) An affected person, the office on behalf of residential or small commercial customers, or the commission may file a complaint at the commission challenging whether the pricing by an incumbent local exchange company of a new service is in compliance with Subsection (b).

(d) If a complaint is filed under Subsection (c), the incumbent local exchange company has the burden of proving that the company set the price for the new service in accordance with the applicable provisions of this subchapter. If the complaint is finally resolved in favor of the complainant, the company:

(1) shall, not later than the 10th day after the date the complaint is finally resolved, amend the price of the service as necessary to comply with the final resolution; or

(2) may, at the company's option, discontinue the service.

(e) A company electing incentive regulation under Chapter 58 or 59 may introduce new services only in accordance with the applicable provisions of Chapter 58 or 59.

Added by Acts 1999, 76th Leg., ch. 1212, § 8, eff. Sept. 1, 1999.

§ 52.0584. Pricing and Packaging Flexibility; Customer Promotional Offerings

(a) Notwithstanding any other provision of this title, an incumbent local exchange company may exercise pricing flexibility in accordance with this section, including the packaging of any regulated service such as basic local telecommunications service with any other regulated or unregulated service or any service of an affiliate. The company may exercise pricing flexibility 10 days after providing an informational notice to the commission, to the office, and to any person who holds a certificate of operating authority in the incumbent local exchange company's certificated area or areas or who has an effective interconnection agreement with the incumbent local exchange company. Pricing flexibility includes all pricing arrangements included in the definition of "pricing flexibility" prescribed by Section 51.002 and includes packaging of any regulated service with any unregulated service or any service of an affiliate.

(b) An incumbent local exchange company, at the company's option, shall price each regulated service offered separately or as part of a package under Subsection (a) at either the service's tariffed rate or at a rate not lower than the service's long run incremental cost. The commission shall allow a company serving fewer than one million access lines in this state to establish a service's long run incremental cost by adopting, at that company's option, the cost studies of a larger company for that service that have been accepted by the commission.

(c) An affected person, the office on behalf of residential or small commercial customers, or the commission may file a complaint alleging that an incumbent local exchange company has priced a regulated service in a manner that does not meet the pricing standards of this subchapter. The complaint must be filed before the 31st day after the date the company implements the rate.

(d) A company electing incentive regulation under Chapter 58 or 59 may use pricing and packaging flexibility and introduce customer promotional offerings only in accordance with the applicable provisions of Chapter 58 or 59.

Added by Acts 1999, 76th Leg., ch. 1212, § 8, eff. Sept. 1, 1999.

§ 52.0585. Customer Promotional Offerings

(a) An incumbent local exchange company may offer a promotion for a regulated service for not more than 90 days in any 12-month period.

(b) The company shall file with the commission a promotional offering that consists of:

(1) waiver of installation charges or service order charges, or both, for not more than 90 days in a 12-month period; or

(2) a temporary discount of not more than 25 percent from the tariffed rate for not more than 60 days in a 12-month period.

(c) An incumbent local exchange company is not required to obtain commission approval to make a promotional offering described by Subsection (b).

(d) An incumbent local exchange company may offer a promotion of any regulated service as part of a package of services consisting of any regulated service with any other regulated or unregulated service or any service of an affiliate.

Added by Acts 1999, 76th Leg., ch. 1212, § 8, eff. Sept. 1, 1999.

§ 52.059. Rates to Cover Appropriate Costs

(a) The commission by rule shall adopt standards necessary to ensure that a rate established under this subchapter covers appropriate costs as determined by the commission.

(b) Until standards are set under Subsection (a), the commission shall use a costing methodology that is in the public interest to determine whether a rate established under this subchapter covers appropriate costs.

Acts 1997, 75th Leg., ch. 166, § 1, eff. Sept. 1, 1997.

§ 52.060. Administrative Fee or Assessment

The commission may prescribe and collect a fee or assessment from local exchange companies necessary to recover the cost to the commission and to the office of activities carried out and services provided under this subchapter and Section 52.006.

Acts 1997, 75th Leg., ch. 166, § 1, eff. Sept. 1, 1997.

SUBCHAPTER C. TELECOMMUNICATIONS UTILITIES THAT ARE NOT DOMINANT CARRIERS

§ 52.101. Applicability

This subchapter applies only to a telecommunications utility that is not:

(1) a dominant carrier; or

(2) the holder of a certificate of operating authority or a service provider certificate of operating authority.

Acts 1997, 75th Leg., ch. 166, § 1, eff. Sept. 1, 1997.

§ 52.102. Limited Regulatory Authority

(a) Except as otherwise provided by this subchapter, Subchapters D and K, Chapter 55,[1] and Section 55.011, the commission has only the following jurisdiction over a telecommunications utility subject to this subchapter:

(1) to require registration under Section 52.103;

(2) to conduct an investigation under Section 52.104;

(3) to require the filing of reports as the commission periodically directs;

(4) to require the maintenance of statewide average rates or prices of telecommunications service;

(5) to require a telecommunications utility that had more than six percent of the total intrastate access minutes of use as measured for the most recent 12-month period to pass switched access rate reductions under this title to customers as required by Section 52.112;

(6) to require access to telecommunications service under Section 52.105; and

(7) to require the quality of telecommunications service provided to be adequate under Section 52.106.

(b) The authority provided by Subsection (a)(5) expires on the date on which Section 52.112 expires.

Acts 1997, 75th Leg., ch. 166, § 1, eff. Sept. 1, 1997. Amended by Acts 1999, 76th Leg., ch. 62, § 18.04(a), eff. Sept. 1, 1999; Acts 1999, 76th Leg., ch. 1212, § 9, eff. Sept. 1, 1999.

[1] V.T.C.A., Utilities Code §§ 55.081 et seq. and 55.301 et seq.

§ 52.103. Registration Required

(a) A telecommunications utility shall register with the commission not later than the 30th day after the date the utility commences service to the public.

(b) A telecommunications utility that registers under Subsection (a) shall file with the commission a description of:

(1) the location and type of service provided;

(2) the price to the public of that service; and

(3) other registration information the commission directs.

(c) An interexchange telecommunications utility doing business in this state shall maintain on file with the commission tariffs or lists governing the terms of providing its services.

Acts 1997, 75th Leg., ch. 166, § 1, eff. Sept. 1, 1997.

§ 52.104. Commission May Investigate

(a) The commission may investigate as necessary to determine the effect and scope of competition in the telecommunications industry. The investigation may include:

(1) identifying dominant carriers in the local telecommunications and intraLATA interexchange telecommunications industry; and

(2) defining the telecommunications market or markets.

(b) In conducting an investigation under this section, the commission may:

(1) hold a hearing;

(2) issue a subpoena to compel the attendance of a witness or the production of a document; and

(3) make findings of fact and decisions to administer this title or a rule, order, or other action of the commission.

Acts 1997, 75th Leg., ch. 166, § 1, eff. Sept. 1, 1997.

§ 52.105. Access to Certain Services Required

(a) The commission may require that each local exchange area have access to local and interexchange telecommunications service, except as otherwise provided by this section.

(b) The commission shall allow a telecommunications utility to discontinue service to a local exchange area if:

(1) comparable service is available in the area; and

(2) discontinuing the service is not contrary to the public interest.

(c) This section does not authorize the commission to require a telecommunications utility to initiate service to a local exchange area to which the telecommunications utility:

(1) did not provide service during the preceding 12-month period; and

(2) has not provided service previously for a cumulative period of at least one year.

Acts 1997, 75th Leg., ch. 166, § 1, eff. Sept. 1, 1997.

§ 52.106. Quality of Service Required

The commission may require the quality of telecommunications service provided in a local exchange in which the commission determines that service has deteriorated and become unreliable to be adequate to protect the public interest and the interests of customers of that exchange.

Acts 1997, 75th Leg., ch. 166, § 1, eff. Sept. 1, 1997.

§ 52.107. Predatory Pricing

(a) The commission may enter an order necessary to protect the public interest if the commission finds by a preponderance of the evidence after notice and hearing that an interexchange telecommunications utility has:

(1) engaged in predatory pricing; or

(2) attempted to engage in predatory pricing.

(b) A hearing held by the commission under Subsection (a) must be based on a complaint from another interexchange telecommunications utility.

(c) An order entered under Subsection (a) may include the imposition on a specific service of the commission's full regulatory authority under:

(1) this chapter;

(2) Chapters 14, 15, 51, 53, and 54; and

(3) Subchapters A, D, and H, Chapter 55.[1]

(d) This section applies only to an interexchange telecommunications utility.

Acts 1997, 75th Leg., ch. 166, § 1, eff. Sept. 1, 1997.

[1] V.T.C.A., Utilities Code § 55.001 et seq., § 55.081 et seq., and § 55.171 et seq.

§ 52.108. Other Prohibited Practices

The commission may enter any order necessary to protect the public interest if the commission finds after notice and hearing that a telecommunications utility has:

(1) failed to maintain statewide average rates;

(2) abandoned interexchange message telecommunications service to a local exchange area in a manner contrary to the public interest;

(3) engaged in a pattern of preferential or discriminatory activities prohibited by Section 53.003, 55.005, or 55.006; or

(4) failed to pass switched access rate reductions to customers under Chapter 56 or other law, as required by Section 52.112.

Acts 1997, 75th Leg., ch. 166, § 1, eff. Sept. 1, 1997. Amended by Acts 1999, 76th Leg., ch. 1212, § 10, eff. Sept. 1, 1999.

§ 52.109. Availability of Service

(a) The commission may require a telecommunications utility that provides a service to make that service available in an exchange served by the telecommunications utility within a reasonable time after receipt of a bona fide request for the service in that exchange.

(b) A telecommunications utility may not be required to extend a service to an area if:

(1) the local exchange company is unable to provide the required access or other service; or

(2) extending the service would, after consideration of the public interest to be served, impose unreasonable costs on or require unreasonable investments by the telecommunications utility.

(c) The commission may require from a telecommunications utility or a local exchange company information necessary to enforce this section.

Acts 1997, 75th Leg., ch. 166, § 1, eff. Sept. 1, 1997.

§ 52.110. Burden of Proof

(a) In a proceeding before the commission in which it is alleged that a telecommunications utility engaged in conduct in violation of Section 52.107, 52.108, 52.109, or 52.112, the burden of proof is on:

(1) a telecommunications utility complaining of conduct committed against it in violation of this subchapter; or

(2) except as provided by Subsection (b), the responding telecommunications utility if the proceedings are:

(A) brought by a customer or customer representative who is not a telecommunications utility; or

(B) initiated by the commission.

(b) The commission may impose the burden of proof on the complaining party in a proceeding described by Subsection (a)(2) if the commission determines that placing the burden of proof on the complaining party is in the public interest.

Acts 1997, 75th Leg., ch. 166, § 1, eff. Sept. 1, 1997. Amended by Acts 1999, 76th Leg., ch. 1212, § 11, eff. Sept. 1, 1999.

§ 52.111. Commission May Exempt

The commission may exempt from a requirement of this subchapter a telecommunications utility that:

(1) does not have a significant effect on the public interest, as determined by the commission; or

(2) relies solely on the facilities of others to complete long distance calls, if the commission determines that the exemption is in the public interest.

Acts 1997, 75th Leg., ch. 166, § 1, eff. Sept. 1, 1997.

§ 52.112. Reduction Pass-Through Required

(a) Each telecommunications utility that had more than six percent of the total intrastate access minutes of use as measured for the most recent 12–month period shall pass through to customers switched access rate reductions under this title. The residential customer class shall receive not less than a proportionate share of the reductions.

(b) Within six months following each reduction in intrastate switched access rates under this title, each telecommunications utility subject to this section shall file with the commission a sworn affidavit confirming that the utility has reduced the per minute rates it charges under its basic rate schedule to reflect the per minute reduction in intrastate switched access rates.

(c) This section expires on the second anniversary of the date incumbent local exchange companies doing business in the state are no longer prohibited by federal law from offering interLATA and interstate long distance service.

Added by Acts 1999, 76th Leg., ch. 1212, § 12, eff. Sept. 1, 1999.

SUBCHAPTER D. CERTIFICATE HOLDERS

§ 52.151. Applicability

This subchapter applies only to a telecommunications utility that holds a certificate of operating authority or a service provider certificate of operating authority.

Acts 1997, 75th Leg., ch. 166, § 1, eff. Sept. 1, 1997.

§ 52.152. Limited Regulatory Authority

Except as otherwise specifically provided by this title, the commission has only the following authority over a telecommunications utility subject to this subchapter:

(1) to enforce this title under Subchapter B, Chapter 15; [1]

(2) to assert jurisdiction over a specific service under Subchapter E; [2]

(3) to require co-carriage reciprocity; and

(4) to regulate condemnation and building access.

Acts 1997, 75th Leg., ch. 166, § 1, eff. Sept. 1, 1997.

[1] V.T.C.A., Utilities Code § 15.051 et seq.

[2] V.T.C.A., Utilities Code § 52.201 et seq.

§ 52.153. Books and Records

The commission may prescribe forms of books, accounts, records, and memoranda to be kept by a telecommunications utility, but only as necessary to enforce the limited jurisdiction over those companies that this title provides to the commission.

Acts 1997, 75th Leg., ch. 166, § 1, eff. Sept. 1, 1997.

§ 52.154. Commission May Not Overburden

The commission may not, by a rule or regulatory practice adopted under this chapter, impose on a telecommunications utility a greater regulatory burden than is imposed on a holder of a certificate of convenience and necessity serving the same area.

Acts 1997, 75th Leg., ch. 166, § 1, eff. Sept. 1, 1997.

§ 52.155. Prohibition of Excessive Access Charges

(a) A telecommunications utility that holds a certificate of operating authority or a service provider certificate of operating authority may not charge a higher amount for originating or terminating intrastate switched access than the prevailing rates charged by the holder of the certificate of convenience and necessity or the holder of a certificate of operating authority issued under Chapter 65 in whose territory the call originated or terminated unless:

(1) the commission specifically approves the higher rate; or

(2) subject to commission review, the telecommunications utility establishes statewide average composite originating and terminating intrastate switched access rates based on a reasonable approximation of traffic originating and terminating between all holders of certificates of convenience and necessity in this state.

(b) Notwithstanding any other provision of this title, the commission has all jurisdiction necessary to enforce this section.

(c) Notwithstanding Subsection (a), Chapter 65 governs the switched access rates of a company that holds a certificate of operating authority issued under Chapter 65.

Added by Acts 1999, 76th Leg., ch. 1212, § 13, eff. Sept. 1, 1999. Amended by Acts 2005, 79th Leg., 2nd C.S., ch. 2, § 3, eff. Sept. 1, 2005.

§ 52.156. Retail Rates, Terms, and Conditions

A telecommunications utility may not:

(1) establish a retail rate, term, or condition that is anticompetitive or unreasonably preferential, prejudicial, or discriminatory; or

(2) engage in predatory pricing or attempt to engage in predatory pricing.

Added by Acts 2005, 79th Leg., 2nd C.S., ch. 2, § 4, eff. Sept. 1, 2005.

SUBCHAPTER E. DEREGULATION OF SERVICE

§ 52.201. Deregulation of Service

Notwithstanding any other provision of this title, the commission may deregulate the price of a service in a geographic market if, after notice and hearing, the commission determines that:

(1) the incumbent local exchange company is not dominant for the service in that geographic market; or

(2) the holder of a certificate of operating authority who is a dominant carrier is no longer dominant for the service in that geographic market.

Acts 1997, 75th Leg., ch. 166, § 1, eff. Sept. 1, 1997.

§ 52.202. Determination of Geographic Market

In determining the geographic market under Section 52.201, the commission shall consider the economic and technical conditions of the market.

Acts 1997, 75th Leg., ch. 166, § 1, eff. Sept. 1, 1997.

§ 52.203. Market Power Test

(a) To determine whether an incumbent local exchange company or holder of a certificate of operating authority who is a dominant carrier is no longer dominant for a service in a geographic market, the commission must find that:

(1) there is an effective competitive alternative; and

(2) the incumbent local exchange company or certificate holder does not have market power sufficient to control, in a manner that is adverse to the public interest, the price of the service in the geographic area.

(b) To determine whether the incumbent local exchange company or certificate holder is dominant for a service in the geographic area, the commission shall consider:

(1) the number and size of telecommunications utilities or other persons who provide the same, equivalent, or substitutable service in the relevant market;

(2) the extent to which the service is available in the relevant market;

(3) the ability of customers in the relevant market to obtain the same, equivalent, or substitutable service at comparable rates and on comparable terms;

(4) the ability of a telecommunications utility or other person to make the same, equivalent, or substitutable service readily available in the relevant market at comparable rates and on comparable terms;

(5) the proportion of the relevant market that is being provided the service by a telecommunications utility other than the incumbent local exchange company or holder of a certificate of operating authority who is a dominant carrier; and

(6) other relevant information the commission considers necessary.

Acts 1997, 75th Leg., ch. 166, § 1, eff. Sept. 1, 1997.

§ 52.204. Rate for Deregulated Service

If the price of a service in a geographic market is deregulated under this subchapter, the incumbent local exchange company or holder of a certificate of operating authority may set the rate for the service at any level higher than the service's long run incremental cost.

Acts 1997, 75th Leg., ch. 166, § 1, eff. Sept. 1, 1997.

§ 52.205. Investigation of Competition

(a) On request of an incumbent local exchange company or holder of a certificate of operating authority who is a dominant carrier made in conjunction with an application under this subchapter, the commission shall investigate to determine the effect and scope of competition in the geographic and service markets at issue.

(b) The commission has the power necessary and convenient to conduct the investigation. In conducting an investigation, the commission may:

(1) hold a hearing;

(2) issue a subpoena to compel the attendance of a witness and the production of a document; and

(3) make findings of fact and decisions with respect to the markets.

(c) A party to a proceeding may use, in an application for pricing flexibility, the results of an investigation conducted under this section.

Acts 1997, 75th Leg., ch. 166, § 1, eff. Sept. 1, 1997.

§ 52.206. Reregulation of Market

The commission, on its own motion or on a complaint that the commission considers to have merit, may assert regulation over a service in a geographic market if:

(1) the incumbent local exchange company or holder of a certificate of operating authority who was previously a dominant carrier is found to again be dominant for the service in that geographic market; or

(2) the provider of services under a certificate of operating authority or service provider certificate of operating authority is found to be dominant for the service in that geographic market.

Acts 1997, 75th Leg., ch. 166, § 1, eff. Sept. 1, 1997.

§ 52.207. Reports; Confidential Information

(a) In conjunction with the commission's authority to collect and compile information, the commission may collect a report from a holder of a:

(1) certificate of operating authority; or

(2) service provider certificate of operating authority.

(b) The commission shall maintain the confidentiality of information contained in a report collected under this section that is claimed to be confidential for competitive purposes. The confidential information is exempt from disclosure under Chapter 552, Government Code.

(c) To protect the confidential information, the commission shall aggregate the information to the maximum extent possible considering the purpose of the proceeding.

Acts 1997, 75th Leg., ch. 166, § 1, eff. Sept. 1, 1997.

SUBCHAPTER F. REQUIRED REPORTS AND FILINGS; RECORDS

§ 52.251. Tariff Filings

(a) A public utility shall file with the commission a tariff showing each rate that is:

(1) subject to the commission's jurisdiction; and

(2) in effect for a utility service, product, or commodity offered by the utility.

(b) The public utility shall file as a part of the tariff required under Subsection (a) each rule that relates to or affects:

(1) a rate of the utility; or

(2) a utility service, product, or commodity furnished by the utility.

Acts 1997, 75th Leg., ch. 166, § 1, eff. Sept. 1, 1997.

§ 52.252. Depreciation Account

The commission shall require each public utility to carry a proper and adequate depreciation account in accordance with:

(1) the rates and methods prescribed by the commission under Section 53.056; and

(2) any other rule the commission adopts.

Acts 1997, 75th Leg., ch. 166, § 1, eff. Sept. 1, 1997.

§ 52.253. Accounts of Profits and Losses

A public utility shall keep separate accounts showing profits or losses from the sale or lease of merchandise, including an appliance, a fixture, or equipment.

Acts 1997, 75th Leg., ch. 166, § 1, eff. Sept. 1, 1997.

§ 52.254. Repealed by Acts 2005, 79th Leg., ch. 797, § 14, eff. September 1, 2005

§ 52.255. Availability of Records

Notwithstanding Section 14.152, a book, account, record, or memorandum of a public utility may be removed from this state if the book, account, record, or memorandum is returned to this state for any commission inspection authorized by this title.

Acts 1997, 75th Leg., ch. 166, § 1, eff. Sept. 1, 1997.

§ 52.256. Plan and Report of Workforce Diversity and Other Business Practices

(a) In this section, "small business" and "historically underutilized business" have the meanings assigned by Section 481.191, Government Code.

(b) Before January 1, 2000, each telecommunications utility shall develop and submit to the commission a comprehensive five-year plan to enhance diversity of its workforce in all occupational categories and for increasing opportunities for small and historically underutilized businesses. The plan must consist of:

(1) the telecommunications utility's performance with regard to workforce diversity and contracting with small and historically underutilized businesses;

(2) initiatives that the telecommunications utility will pursue in these areas over the period of the plan;

(3) a listing of programs and activities the telecommunications utility will undertake to achieve each of these initiatives; and

(4) a listing of the business partnership initiatives the telecommunications utility will undertake to facilitate small and historically underutilized business entry into the telecommunications market, taking into account opportunities for contracting and joint ventures.

(c) Each telecommunications utility shall submit an annual report to the commission and the legislature relating to its efforts to improve workforce diversity and contracting opportunities for small and historically underutilized businesses. The report must include:

(1) the diversity of the telecommunications utility's workforce as of the time of the report;

(2) the telecommunications utility's level of contracting with small and historically underutilized businesses;

(3) the specific progress made under the plan under Subsection (b);

(4) the specific initiatives, programs, and activities undertaken under the plan during the preceding year;

(5) an assessment of the success of each of those initiatives, programs, and activities;

(6) the extent to which the telecommunications utility has carried out its initiatives to facilitate opportunities for contracts or joint ventures with small and historically underutilized businesses; and

(7) the initiatives, programs, and activities the telecommunications utility will pursue during the next year to increase the diversity of its workforce and contracting opportunities for small and historically underutilized businesses.

Added by Acts 1999, 76th Leg., ch. 1212, § 14, eff. Sept. 1, 1999.

CHAPTER 53. RATES

SUBCHAPTER A. GENERAL PROVISIONS

Section
53.001. Authorization to Establish and Regulate Rates.
53.002. Compliance With Title.

Section
53.003. Just and Reasonable Rates.
53.004. Equality of Rates and Services.
53.005. Rates for Area Not in Municipality.
53.006. Burden of Proof.
53.007. Limit on Reconnection Fee.

SUBCHAPTER B. COMPUTATION OF RATES

53.051. Establishing Overall Revenues.
53.052. Establishing Reasonable Return.
53.053. Components of Invested Capital.
53.054. Construction Work in Progress.
53.055. Separations and Allocations.
53.056. Depreciation, Amortization, and Depletion.
53.057. Net Income; Determination of Revenues and Expenses.
53.058. Consideration of Payment to Affiliate.
53.059. Treatment of Certain Tax Benefits.
53.060. Computation of Income Tax; Consolidated Return.
53.061. Allowance of Certain Expenses.
53.062. Consideration of Certain Expenses.
53.063. Consideration of Profit or Loss From Sale or Lease of Merchandise.
53.064. Self-Insurance.
53.065. Interexchange Services; Rates of Incumbent Local Exchange Company.

SUBCHAPTER C. GENERAL PROCEDURES FOR RATE CHANGE PROPOSED BY UTILITY

53.101. Definition.
53.102. Statement of Intent to Change Rates.
53.103. Notice of Intent to Change Rates.
53.104. Early Effective Date of Rate Change.
53.105. Determination of Propriety of Change; Hearing.
53.106. Regional Hearing.
53.107. Preference to Hearing.
53.108. Rate Suspension; Deadline.
53.109. Temporary Rates.
53.110. Bonded Rates.
53.111. Establishment of Final Rates.
53.112. Expiration of Suspension; Effect on Certain Rates.
53.113. FCC-Approved Tariffs for Switched-Access Service.

SUBCHAPTER D. RATE CHANGES PROPOSED BY COMMISSION

53.151. Unreasonable or Violative Existing Rates.
53.152. Investigating Costs of Obtaining Service From Another Source.

SUBCHAPTER E. COST RECOVERY AND RATE ADJUSTMENTS

53.201. Automatic Adjustment for Change in Costs Prohibited.
53.202. Repealed.

SUBCHAPTER F. REGULATORY POLICY FOR SMALL INCUMBENT LOCAL EXCHANGE COMPANIES AND COOPERATIVES

53.251. General Policy.
53.252. Adoption of Certain Policies.

SUBCHAPTER G. SPECIAL PROCEDURES FOR SMALL LOCAL EXCHANGE COMPANIES AND COOPERATIVES

Section
53.301. Definition.
53.302. Applicability.
53.303. Provisions Not Exclusive.
53.304. Procedure to Offer Certain Services or Make Minor Changes.
53.305. Notice to Affected Customers.
53.306. Commission Review of Proposed Change.
53.307. Compliance With Principles; Reduced Rates.
53.308. Fees and Assessments.

SUBCHAPTER H. PARTIAL DEREGULATION AVAILABLE TO CERTAIN COOPERATIVE CORPORATIONS

53.351. Provisions Not Exclusive.
53.352. Partial Deregulation by Ballot.
53.353. Voting Procedures.
53.354. Procedure to Offer Certain Services or Make Certain Changes.
53.355. Statement of Intent.
53.356. Notice to Affected Persons.
53.357. Filing of Affidavits Verifying Notice.
53.358. Commission Review of Proposed Action.
53.359. Reversal of Deregulation by Ballot.

SUBCHAPTER A. GENERAL PROVISIONS

§ 53.001. Authorization to Establish and Regulate Rates

(a) Except as otherwise provided by this title, the commission may establish and regulate rates of a public utility and may adopt rules for determining:

(1) the classification of customers and services; and

(2) the applicability of rates.

(b) A rule or order of the commission may not conflict with a ruling of a federal regulatory body.

Acts 1997, 75th Leg., ch. 166, § 1, eff. Sept. 1, 1997.

§ 53.002. Compliance With Title

A utility may not charge or receive a rate for utility service except as provided by this title.

Acts 1997, 75th Leg., ch. 166, § 1, eff. Sept. 1, 1997.

§ 53.003. Just and Reasonable Rates

(a) The commission shall ensure that each rate a public utility or two or more public utilities jointly make, demand, or receive is just and reasonable.

(b) A rate may not be unreasonably preferential, prejudicial, or discriminatory but must be sufficient, equitable, and consistent in application to each class of consumer.

(c) A public utility may not:

(1) grant an unreasonable preference or advantage concerning rates to a person in a classification;

(2) subject a person in a classification to an unreasonable prejudice or disadvantage concerning rates; or

(3) establish or maintain an unreasonable difference concerning rates between localities or between classes of service.

(d) In establishing a public utility's rates, the commission may treat as a single class two or more municipalities that a public utility serves if the commission considers that treatment to be appropriate.

Acts 1997, 75th Leg., ch. 166, § 1, eff. Sept. 1, 1997.

§ 53.004. Equality of Rates and Services

(a) A public utility may not directly or indirectly charge, demand, or receive from a person a greater or lesser compensation for a service provided or to be provided by the utility than the compensation prescribed by the applicable tariff filed under Section 52.251.

(b) A person may not knowingly receive or accept a service from a public utility for a compensation greater or less than the compensation prescribed by the tariff.

(c) This title does not prevent a cooperative corporation from returning to its members net earnings resulting from its operations in proportion to the members' purchases from or through the corporation.

Acts 1997, 75th Leg., ch. 166, § 1, eff. Sept. 1, 1997.

§ 53.005. Rates for Area Not in Municipality

Without the approval of the commission, a public utility's rates for an area not in a municipality may not exceed 115 percent of the average of all rates for similar services for all municipalities served by the same utility in the same county as that area.

Acts 1997, 75th Leg., ch. 166, § 1, eff. Sept. 1, 1997.

§ 53.006. Burden of Proof

(a) In a proceeding involving a proposed rate change, the public utility has the burden of proving that:

(1) the rate change is just and reasonable, if the utility proposes the change; or

(2) an existing rate is just and reasonable, if the proposal is to reduce the rate.

(b) In a proceeding in which the rate of an incumbent local exchange company is in issue, the incumbent local exchange company has the burden of proving that the rate is just and reasonable.

Acts 1997, 75th Leg., ch. 166, § 1, eff. Sept. 1, 1997.

§ 53.007. Limit on Reconnection Fee

The commission shall establish a reasonable limit on the amount that a local exchange company may charge a customer for changing the location at which the customer receives service.

Acts 1997, 75th Leg., ch. 166, § 1, eff. Sept. 1, 1997.

SUBCHAPTER B. COMPUTATION OF RATES

§ 53.051. Establishing Overall Revenues

In establishing a public utility's rates, the commission shall establish the utility's overall revenues at an amount that will permit the utility a reasonable opportunity to earn a reasonable return on the utility's invested capital used and useful in providing service to the public in excess of the utility's reasonable and necessary operating expenses.

Acts 1997, 75th Leg., ch. 166, § 1, eff. Sept. 1, 1997.

§ 53.052. Establishing Reasonable Return

In establishing a reasonable return on invested capital, the commission shall consider applicable factors, including:

(1) the quality of the utility's services;

(2) the efficiency of the utility's operations; and

(3) the quality of the utility's management.

Acts 1997, 75th Leg., ch. 166, § 1, eff. Sept. 1, 1997.

§ 53.053. Components of Invested Capital

(a) Public utility rates shall be based on the original cost, less depreciation, of property used by and useful to the utility in providing service.

(b) The original cost of property shall be determined at the time the property is dedicated to public use, whether by the utility that is the present owner or by a predecessor.

(c) In this section, "original cost" means the actual money cost or the actual money value of consideration paid other than money.

Acts 1997, 75th Leg., ch. 166, § 1, eff. Sept. 1, 1997.

§ 53.054. Construction Work in Progress

(a) Construction work in progress, at cost as recorded on the public utility's books, may be included in the utility's rate base. The inclusion of construction work in progress is an exceptional form of rate relief that the commission may grant only if the utility demonstrates that inclusion is necessary to the utility's financial integrity.

(b) Construction work in progress may not be included in the rate base for a major project under construction to the extent that the project has been inefficiently or imprudently planned or managed.

Acts 1997, 75th Leg., ch. 166, § 1, eff. Sept. 1, 1997.

§ 53.055. Separations and Allocations

Costs of facilities, revenues, expenses, taxes, and reserves shall be separated or allocated as prescribed by the commission.

Acts 1997, 75th Leg., ch. 166, § 1, eff. Sept. 1, 1997.

§ 53.056. Depreciation, Amortization, and Depletion

(a) The commission shall establish proper and adequate rates and methods of depreciation, amortization, or depletion for each class of property of a public utility.

(b) On application of a utility, the commission shall establish depreciation rates that promote the use of new technology and infrastructure. In establishing rates under this subsection, the commission shall consider depreciation practices of nonregulated telecommunications providers.

(c) The rates and methods established under this section and the depreciation account required by Section 52.252 shall be used uniformly and consistently throughout rate-setting and appeal proceedings.

(d) Notwithstanding this section, a company electing under Chapter 58 may determine its own depreciation rates and amortizations. The company shall notify the commission of any change in those rates or amortizations.

Acts 1997, 75th Leg., ch. 166, § 1, eff. Sept. 1, 1997.

§ 53.057. Net Income; Determination of Revenues and Expenses

(a) A public utility's net income is the total revenues of the utility less all reasonable and necessary expenses as determined by the commission.

(b) The commission shall determine revenues and expenses in a manner consistent with this subchapter.

(c) The commission may adopt reasonable rules with respect to whether an expense is allowed for ratemaking purposes.

Acts 1997, 75th Leg., ch. 166, § 1, eff. Sept. 1, 1997.

§ 53.058. Consideration of Payment to Affiliate

(a) Except as provided by Subsection (b), the commission may not allow as capital cost or as expense a payment to an affiliate for:

(1) cost of a service, property, right, or other item; or

(2) interest expense.

(b) The commission may allow a payment described by Subsection (a) only to the extent that the commission finds the payment is reasonable and necessary for each item or class of items as determined by the commission.

(c) A finding under Subsection (b) must include:

(1) a specific finding of the reasonableness and necessity of each item or class of items allowed; and

(2) except as provided by Subsection (d), a finding that the price to the utility is not higher than the prices charged by the supplying affiliate to:

(A) its other affiliates or divisions for the same item or class of items; or

(B) a nonaffiliated person within the same market area or having the same market conditions.

(d) A finding under this section is not required as to the prices charged by the supplying affiliate to its other affiliates or divisions if the supplying affiliate computed its charges to the utility in a manner consistent with Federal Communications Commission rules.

(e) If the commission finds that the affiliate expense for the test period is unreasonable, the commission shall:

(1) determine the reasonable level of the expense; and

(2) include that expense in determining the utility's cost of service.

Acts 1997, 75th Leg., ch. 166, § 1, eff. Sept. 1, 1997.

§ 53.059. Treatment of Certain Tax Benefits

(a) In determining the allocation of tax savings derived from liberalized depreciation and amortization, the investment tax credit, and the application of similar methods, the commission shall:

(1) balance equitably the interests of present and future customers; and

(2) apportion accordingly the benefits between consumers and the public utility.

(b) If a public utility retains a portion of the investment tax credit, that portion shall be deducted from the original cost of the facilities or other addition to the rate base to which the credit applied to the extent allowed by the Internal Revenue Code.

Acts 1997, 75th Leg., ch. 166, § 1, eff. Sept. 1, 1997.

§ 53.060. Computation of Income Tax; Consolidated Return

(a) Unless it is shown to the satisfaction of the commission that it was reasonable to choose not to consolidate returns, a public utility's income taxes shall be computed as though a consolidated return had been filed and the utility had realized its fair share of the savings resulting from that return, if:

(1) the utility is a member of an affiliated group eligible to file a consolidated income tax return; and

(2) it is advantageous to the utility to do so.

(b) The amount of income tax that a consolidated group of which a public utility is a member saves, because the consolidated return eliminates the intercompany profit on purchases by the utility from an affiliate, shall be applied to reduce the cost of the property or service purchased from the affiliate.

(c) The investment tax credit allowed against federal income taxes, to the extent retained by the utility, shall be applied as a reduction in the rate-based contribution of the assets to which the credit applies, to the extent and at the rate allowed by the Internal Revenue Code.

Acts 1997, 75th Leg., ch. 166, § 1, eff. Sept. 1, 1997.

§ 53.061. Allowance of Certain Expenses

(a) The commission may not allow as a cost or expense for ratemaking purposes:

(1) an expenditure for legislative advocacy; or

(2) an expenditure described by Section 52.254 that the commission determines to be not in the public interest.

(b) The commission may allow as a cost or expense reasonable charitable or civic contributions not to exceed the amount approved by the commission.

Acts 1997, 75th Leg., ch. 166, § 1, eff. Sept. 1, 1997.

§ 53.062. Consideration of Certain Expenses

The commission may not consider for ratemaking purposes:

(1) an expenditure for legislative advocacy, made directly or indirectly, including legislative advocacy expenses included in trade association dues;

(2) an expenditure for costs of processing a refund or credit under Section 53.110; or

(3) any other expenditure, including an executive salary, advertising expense, legal expense, or civil penalty or fine the commission finds to be unreasonable, unnecessary, or not in the public interest.

Acts 1997, 75th Leg., ch. 166, § 1, eff. Sept. 1, 1997.

§ 53.063. Consideration of Profit or Loss From Sale or Lease of Merchandise

In establishing a public utility's rates, the commission may not consider a profit or loss that results from the sale or lease of merchandise, including appliances, fixtures, or equipment, to the extent that merchandise is not integral to providing utility service.

Acts 1997, 75th Leg., ch. 166, § 1, eff. Sept. 1, 1997.

§ 53.064. Self-Insurance

(a) A public utility may self-insure all or part of the utility's potential liability or catastrophic property loss, including windstorm, fire, and explosion losses, that could not have been reasonably anticipated and included under operating and maintenance expenses.

(b) The commission shall approve a self-insurance plan under this section if the commission finds that:

(1) the coverage is in the public interest;

(2) the plan, considering all costs, is a lower cost alternative to purchasing commercial insurance; and

(3) ratepayers will receive the benefits of the savings.

(c) In computing a utility's reasonable and necessary expenses under this subchapter, the commission, to the extent the commission finds is in the public interest, shall allow as a necessary expense money credited to a reserve account for self-insurance. The commission shall determine reasonableness under this subsection:

(1) from information provided at the time the self-insurance plan and reserve account are established; and

(2) on the filing of a rate case by a utility that has a reserve account.

(d) After a reserve account for self-insurance is established, the commission shall:

(1) determine whether the account has a surplus or shortage under Subsection (e); and

(2) subtract any surplus from or add any shortage to the utility's rate base.

(e) A surplus in the reserve account exists if the charges against the account are less than the money credited to the account. A shortage in the reserve account exists if the charges against the account are greater than the money credited to the account.

(f) The commission shall adopt rules governing self-insurance under this section.

Acts 1997, 75th Leg., ch. 166, § 1, eff. Sept. 1, 1997.

§ 53.065. Interexchange Services; Rates of Incumbent Local Exchange Company

(a) An incumbent local exchange company's rates for interexchange telecommunications services must be statewide average rates except as ordered by the commission after application and hearing.

(b) Repealed by Acts 2011, 82nd Leg., ch. 21 (S.B. 983), § 4; Acts 2011, ch. 98 (S.B. 980), § 21(2).

Acts 1997, 75th Leg., ch. 166, § 1, eff. Sept. 1, 1997. Amended by Acts 2011, 82nd Leg., ch. 21 (S.B. 983), § 4, eff. Sept. 1, 2011; Acts 2011, 82nd Leg., ch. 98 (S.B. 980), § 21(2), eff. Sept. 1, 2011.

SUBCHAPTER C. GENERAL PROCEDURES FOR RATE CHANGE PROPOSED BY UTILITY

§ 53.101. Definition

In this subchapter, "major change" means an increase in rates that would increase the aggregate revenues of the applicant more than the greater of $100,000 or 2½ percent. The term does not include an increase in rates that the commission allows to go into effect or the utility makes under an order of the commission after hearings held with public notice.

Acts 1997, 75th Leg., ch. 166, § 1, eff. Sept. 1, 1997.

§ 53.102. Statement of Intent to Change Rates

(a) A utility may not change its rates unless the utility files a statement of its intent with the commission at least 35 days before the effective date of the proposed change.

(b) The utility shall also mail or deliver a copy of the statement of intent to the appropriate officer of each affected municipality.

(c) The statement of intent must include:

(1) proposed revisions of tariffs; and

(2) a detailed statement of:

(A) each proposed change;

(B) the effect the proposed change is expected to have on the revenues of the utility;

(C) each class and number of utility consumers affected; and

(D) any other information required by the commission's rules.

Acts 1997, 75th Leg., ch. 166, § 1, eff. Sept. 1, 1997.

§ 53.103. Notice of Intent to Change Rates

(a) The utility shall:

(1) publish, in conspicuous form and place, notice to the public of the proposed change once each week for four successive weeks before the effective date of the proposed change in a newspaper having general circulation in each county containing territory affected by the proposed change; and

(2) mail notice of the proposed change to any other affected person as required by the commission's rules.

(b) The commission may waive the publication of notice requirement prescribed by Subsection (a) in a proceeding that involves only a rate reduction for each affected ratepayer. The applicant shall give notice of the proposed rate change by mail to each affected utility customer.

(c) The commission by rule shall define other proceedings for which the publication of notice requirement prescribed by Subsection (a) may be waived on a showing of good cause. A waiver may not be granted in a proceeding involving a rate increase to any class or category of ratepayer.

Acts 1997, 75th Leg., ch. 166, § 1, eff. Sept. 1, 1997.

§ 53.104. Early Effective Date of Rate Change

(a) For good cause shown, the commission may allow a rate change, other than a major change, to take effect:

(1) before the end of the 35-day period prescribed by Section 53.102; and

(2) under conditions the commission prescribes, subject to suspension as provided by this subchapter.

(b) The utility shall immediately revise its tariffs to include the change.

Acts 1997, 75th Leg., ch. 166, § 1, eff. Sept. 1, 1997.

§ 53.105. Determination of Propriety of Change; Hearing

(a) If a tariff changing rates is filed with the commission, the commission shall, on complaint by an affected person, or may, on its own motion, not later than the 30th day after the effective date of the change, enter on a hearing to determine the propriety of the change.

(b) The commission shall hold a hearing in every case in which the change constitutes a major change. The commission may, however, use an informal proceeding if the commission does not receive a complaint before the 46th day after the date notice of the change is filed.

(c) The commission shall give reasonable notice of the hearing, including notice to the governing body of each affected municipality and county. The utility is not required to provide a formal answer or file any other formal pleading in response to the notice, and the absence of an answer does not affect an order for a hearing.

Acts 1997, 75th Leg., ch. 166, § 1, eff. Sept. 1, 1997.

§ 53.106. Regional Hearing

The commission shall hold a regional hearing at an appropriate location in a case in which the commission determines it is in the public interest to hear testimony at a regional hearing for inclusion in the record.

Acts 1997, 75th Leg., ch. 166, § 1, eff. Sept. 1, 1997.

§ 53.107. Preference to Hearing

The commission shall:

(1) give preference to a hearing under this subchapter and to deciding questions arising under this subchapter and Subchapter E [1] over any other question pending before it; and

(2) decide the questions as quickly as possible.

Acts 1997, 75th Leg., ch. 166, § 1, eff. Sept. 1, 1997.

[1] V.T.C.A., Utilities Code §§ 53.201, 53.202.

§ 53.108. Rate Suspension; Deadline

(a) Pending the hearing and a decision, the commission, after delivering to the utility a written statement of the commission's reasons, may suspend the rate change for not longer than 150 days after the date the rate change would otherwise be effective.

(b) The 150-day period prescribed by Subsection (a) shall be extended two days for each day the actual hearing on the merits of the case exceeds 15 days.

(c) If the commission does not make a final determination concerning a rate change before expiration of the suspension period, the commission is considered to have approved the change. This approval is subject to the authority of the commission thereafter to continue a hearing in progress.

Acts 1997, 75th Leg., ch. 166, § 1, eff. Sept. 1, 1997.

§ 53.109. Temporary Rates

(a) The commission may establish temporary rates to be in effect during the suspension period under Section 53.108.

(b) If the commission does not establish temporary rates, the rates in effect when the suspended tariff was filed continue in effect during the suspension period.

Acts 1997, 75th Leg., ch. 166, § 1, eff. Sept. 1, 1997.

§ 53.110. Bonded Rates

(a) A utility may put a changed rate into effect by filing a bond with the commission if:

(1) the 150-day suspension period has been extended under Section 53.108(b); and

(2) the commission fails to make a final determination before the 151st day after the date the rate change would otherwise be effective.

(b) The bonded rate may not exceed the proposed rate.

(c) The bond must be:

(1) payable to the commission in an amount, in a form, and with a surety approved by the commission; and

(2) conditioned on refund.

(d) The utility shall refund or credit against future bills:

(1) money collected under the bonded rates in excess of the rate finally ordered; and

(2) interest on that money, at the current interest rate as determined by the commission.

Acts 1997, 75th Leg., ch. 166, § 1, eff. Sept. 1, 1997.

§ 53.111. Establishment of Final Rates

(a) If, after hearing, the commission finds the rates are unreasonable or in violation of law, the commission shall:

(1) enter an order establishing the rates the utility shall charge or apply for the service in question; and

(2) serve a copy of the order on the utility.

(b) The rates established in the order shall be observed thereafter until changed as provided by this title.

(c) This section does not apply to a company electing under Chapter 58 or 59 except as otherwise provided by those chapters or by Chapter 60.

Acts 1997, 75th Leg., ch. 166, § 1, eff. Sept. 1, 1997.

§ 53.112. Expiration of Suspension; Effect on Certain Rates

(a) Notwithstanding Section 53.111(a), if the commission does not make a final determination concerning an incumbent local exchange company's rate change before expiration of the 150-day suspension period, the rates finally approved by the commission take effect on and the incumbent local exchange company is entitled to collect those rates from the date the 150-day suspension period expired.

(b) A surcharge or other charge necessary to effectuate this section may not be recovered over a period of less than 90 days from the date of the commission's final order.

Acts 1997, 75th Leg., ch. 166, § 1, eff. Sept. 1, 1997.

§ 53.113. FCC-Approved Tariffs for Switched-Access Service

(a) An incumbent local exchange company may file with the commission tariffs for switched-access service that have been approved by the Federal Communications Commission. The tariffs must include all rate elements in the company's interstate access tariff other than end-user charges.

(b) Not later than the 60th day after the date a company files tariffs under Subsection (a), the commission shall order the rates and terms to be the incumbent local exchange company's intrastate switched-access rates and terms if, on review, the tariffs contain the same rates and terms, excluding end-user charges, as approved by the Federal Communications Commission.

Acts 1997, 75th Leg., ch. 166, § 1, eff. Sept. 1, 1997.

SUBCHAPTER D. RATE CHANGES PROPOSED BY COMMISSION

§ 53.151. Unreasonable or Violative Existing Rates

(a) If the commission, on its own motion or on complaint by an affected person, after reasonable notice and hearing, finds that the existing rates of a public utility for a service are unreasonable or in violation of law, the commission shall:

(1) enter an order establishing the just and reasonable rates to be observed thereafter, including maximum or minimum rates; and

(2) serve a copy of the order on the utility.

(b) The rates established under Subsection (a) constitute the legal rates of the public utility until changed as provided by this title.

(c) This section does not apply to a company electing under Chapter 58 or Chapter 59 except as otherwise provided by those chapters.

Acts 1997, 75th Leg., ch. 166, § 1, eff. Sept. 1, 1997.

§ 53.152. Investigating Costs of Obtaining Service From Another Source

If a public utility does not produce or generate the service that it distributes, transmits, or furnishes to the public for compensation but obtains the service from another source, the commission may investigate the cost of that production or generation in an investigation of the reasonableness of the utility's rates.

Acts 1997, 75th Leg., ch. 166, § 1, eff. Sept. 1, 1997.

SUBCHAPTER E. COST RECOVERY AND RATE ADJUSTMENTS

§ 53.201. Automatic Adjustment for Change in Costs Prohibited

The commission may not establish a rate or tariff that authorizes a utility to automatically adjust and pass through to the utility's customers a change in the utility's costs.

Acts 1997, 75th Leg., ch. 166, § 1, eff. Sept. 1, 1997.

§ 53.202. Repealed by Acts 2009, 81st Leg., ch. 891, § 1, eff. Sept. 1, 2009

SUBCHAPTER F. REGULATORY POLICY FOR SMALL INCUMBENT LOCAL EXCHANGE COMPANIES AND COOPERATIVES

§ 53.251. General Policy

Regulatory policy should recognize that:

(1) there are differences between small and large incumbent local exchange companies;

(2) there are a large number of customer-owned telephone cooperatives and small, locally owned investor companies; and

(3) it is appropriate to provide incentives and flexibility to allow an incumbent local exchange company that serves a rural area to:

(A) provide existing services; and

(B) introduce new technology and new services in a prompt, efficient, and economical manner.

Acts 1997, 75th Leg., ch. 166, § 1, eff. Sept. 1, 1997.

§ 53.252. Adoption of Certain Policies

Notwithstanding any other provision of this title, the commission shall consider and may adopt policies to:

(1) provide for evaluation of the overall reasonableness of the rates of a rural or small incumbent local exchange company or cooperative not more frequently than once every three years;

(2) permit consideration of future construction plans and operational changes in evaluating the reasonableness of the rates of a rural or small incumbent local exchange company or cooperative; or

(3) allow a rural or small incumbent local exchange company or cooperative to:

(A) provide required information by report or by other means, as necessary, including a required rate filing package, in substantially less burdensome and complex form than is required of a larger incumbent local exchange company;

(B) change depreciation and amortization rates, if customer rates are not affected, after notice to the commission, subject to commission review in a proceeding under Subchapter C or Subchapter D;[1]

(C) adopt for a new service the rates for the same or a substantially similar service offered by a larger incumbent local exchange company, without additional cost justification; and

(D) submit to the commission, instead of a management audit otherwise required by law, policy, or rule, financial audits regularly performed by an independent auditor or required and performed as a result of the company's or cooperative's participation in a federal or state financing or revenue-sharing program.

Acts 1997, 75th Leg., ch. 166, § 1, eff. Sept. 1, 1997.

[1] V.T.C.A, Utilities Code § 53.101 et seq. or §§ 53.151, 53.152.

SUBCHAPTER G. SPECIAL PROCEDURES FOR SMALL LOCAL EXCHANGE COMPANIES AND COOPERATIVES

§ 53.301. Definition

(a) In this subchapter, "minor change" means a change, including the restructuring of rates of existing services, that:

(1) decreases the rates or revenues of an incumbent local exchange company; or

(2) together with any other rate change or approved tariff changes in the 12 months preceding the effective date of the proposed change, increases the company's total regulated intrastate gross annual revenues by not more than five percent.

(b) With regard to a change to a basic local access line rate, a "minor change" does not include a change that, together with any other change to the basic local access line rate that took effect during the 12 months preceding the effective date of the proposed change, results in an increase of more than 50 percent.

Acts 1997, 75th Leg., ch. 166, § 1, eff. Sept. 1, 1997. Amended by Acts 2011, 82nd Leg., ch. 118 (H.B. 2680), § 1, eff. Sept. 1, 2011.

Section 4 of Acts 2011, 82nd Leg., ch. 118 (H.B. 2680) provides:

"This Act applies only to a proposal to offer a service or to change a rate or tariff notice of which is filed on or after the effective date [Sept. 1, 2011] of this Act. A proposal to offer a service or to change a rate or tariff for which a statement of intent is filed before the effective date of this Act is governed by the law in effect on the date the statement was filed, and that law is continued in effect for that purpose."

§ 53.302. Applicability

This subchapter does not apply to an incumbent local exchange company that is a cooperative corporation partially deregulated under Subchapter H.[1]

Acts 1997, 75th Leg., ch. 166, § 1, eff. Sept. 1, 1997.

[1] V.T.C.A., Utilities Code § 53.351 et seq.

§ 53.303. Provisions Not Exclusive

This subchapter does not prohibit:

(1) an incumbent local exchange company from filing for a new service or rate change under another section of this title; or

(2) the commission from conducting a review under Subchapter D.[1]

Acts 1997, 75th Leg., ch. 166, § 1, eff. Sept. 1, 1997.

[1] V.T.C.A., Utilities Code §§ 53.151, 53.152.

§ 53.304. Procedure to Offer Certain Services or Make Minor Changes

(a) An incumbent local exchange company may offer an extended local calling service, a packaged service, or a new or promotional service on an optional basis or make a minor change in its rates or tariffs if the company:

(1) is a cooperative corporation or has, together with all affiliated incumbent local exchange companies, fewer than 31,000 access lines in service in this state;

(2) files with the commission and the office notice , as prescribed by Subsection (b), not later than the 10th day before the effective date of the proposed change;

(3) provides notice as prescribed by Section 53.305; and

(4) files with the commission affidavits verifying that notice as prescribed by Section 53.305 was provided.

(b) The notice must include:

(1) a copy of a resolution adopted by the incumbent local exchange company's board of directors approving the proposed change;

(2) a description of the services affected by the proposed change;

(3) a copy of the proposed tariff for the affected service;

(4) a copy of the customer notice required by Subsection (a)(3);

(5) the number of access lines the company and each affiliate have in service in this state; and

(6) the amount by which the company's total regulated intrastate gross annual revenues will increase or decrease as a result of the proposed change.

Acts 1997, 75th Leg., ch. 166, § 1, eff. Sept. 1, 1997. Amended by Acts 2011, 82nd Leg., ch. 118 (H.B. 2680), § 2, eff. Sept. 1, 2011.

§ 53.305. Notice to Affected Customers

(a) A company shall provide notice of a proposed change to affected customers in the manner prescribed by the commission.

(b) Notice must:

(1) be provided not later than the 10th day before the effective date of the proposed change; and

(2) include:

(A) a description of the services affected by the proposed change;

(B) the effective date of the proposed change;

(C) an explanation of the customer's right to petition the commission for a review under Section 53.306, including the number of persons required to petition before a commission review will occur;

(D) an explanation of the customer's right to information concerning how to obtain a copy of the proposed tariff from the company;

(E) the amount by which the company's total regulated intrastate gross annual revenues will increase or decrease as a result of the proposed change; and

(F) a list of rates that are affected by the proposed rate change.

Acts 1997, 75th Leg., ch. 166, § 1, eff. Sept. 1, 1997. Amended by Acts 2011, 82nd Leg., ch. 118 (H.B. 2680), § 3, eff. Sept. 1, 2011.

§ 53.306. Commission Review of Proposed Change

(a) The commission shall review a proposed change filed under this subchapter if:

(1) the commission receives complaints relating to the proposed change signed by a number of affected local service customers equal at least to the lesser of 1,500 or five percent of those customers;

(2) the commission receives a complaint relating to the proposed change from an affected intrastate access customer, or a group of affected intrastate access customers, that in the preceding 12 months accounted for more than 10 percent of the company's total intrastate gross access revenues;

(3) the proposed change is not a minor change;

(4) the company does not comply with the procedural requirements of this subchapter; or

(5) the proposed change is inconsistent with the commission's substantive policies as expressed in its rules.

(b) The commission may suspend a tariff proposed under this subchapter during the review.

Acts 1997, 75th Leg., ch. 166, § 1, eff. Sept. 1, 1997.

§ 53.307. Compliance With Principles; Reduced Rates

A rate established under this subchapter must be in accordance with the rate-setting principles of this chapter, except that a company may provide to its board members, officers, employees, or agents free or reduced rates for services.

Acts 1997, 75th Leg., ch. 166, § 1, eff. Sept. 1, 1997.

§ 53.308. Fees and Assessments

The commission may prescribe and collect a fee or assessment from incumbent local exchange companies necessary to recover the cost to the commission and to the office of activities carried out and services provided under:

(1) this subchapter;

(2) Section 53.112;

(3) Subchapter H; [1] and

(4) Section 55.004.

Acts 1997, 75th Leg., ch. 166, § 1, eff. Sept. 1, 1997.

[1] V.T.C.A., Utilities Code § 53.351 et seq.

SUBCHAPTER H. PARTIAL DEREGULATION AVAILABLE TO CERTAIN COOPERATIVE CORPORATIONS

§ 53.351. Provisions Not Exclusive

(a) This subchapter does not:

(1) prohibit a cooperative from filing for a new service or a rate change under another applicable provision of this title; or

(2) affect the application of a provision of this title not directly related to:

(A) establishing rates; or

(B) the authority of the commission to require a cooperative to file a report required under this title or the commission's rules.

(b) Notwithstanding any other provision of this subchapter, the commission may conduct a review under Subchapter D.[1]

Acts 1997, 75th Leg., ch. 166, § 1, eff. Sept. 1, 1997.

[1] V.T.C.A, Utilities Code §§ 53.151, 53.152.

§ 53.352. Partial Deregulation by Ballot

(a) An incumbent local exchange company that is a cooperative corporation may vote to partially deregulate the cooperative by sending a ballot to each cooperative member. The incumbent local exchange company may include the ballot in a bill or send the ballot separately. The ballot shall be printed to permit voting for or against the proposition: "Authorizing the partial deregulation of the (name of the cooperative)."

(b) The cooperative is partially deregulated if a majority of the ballots returned to the cooperative not later than the 45th day after the date the ballots are mailed favor deregulation.

Acts 1997, 75th Leg., ch. 166, § 1, eff. Sept. 1, 1997.

§ 53.353. Voting Procedures

The commission by rule shall prescribe the voting procedures a cooperative must use under this subchapter.

Acts 1997, 75th Leg., ch. 166, § 1, eff. Sept. 1, 1997.

§ 53.354. Procedure to Offer Certain Services or Make Certain Changes

After the initial balloting, a cooperative may offer extended local calling services, offer new services on an optional basis, or make changes in its rates or tariffs if the cooperative:

(1) files a statement of intent under Section 53.355;

(2) provides notice of the proposed action to each customer and municipality as prescribed by Section 53.356; and

(3) files with the commission affidavits verifying that notice was provided as prescribed by Section 53.357.

Acts 1997, 75th Leg., ch. 166, § 1, eff. Sept. 1, 1997.

§ 53.355. Statement of Intent

(a) A cooperative must file a statement of intent to use this subchapter with the commission and the office not later than the 61st day before the effective date of the proposed change.

(b) The statement must include:

(1) a copy of a resolution, signed by a majority of the members of the cooperative's board of directors, approving the proposed action and authorizing the filing of the statement of intent;

(2) a description of the services affected by the proposed action;

(3) a copy of the proposed tariff for the affected service; and

(4) a copy of the customer notice required by Section 53.356.

Acts 1997, 75th Leg., ch. 166, § 1, eff. Sept. 1, 1997.

§ 53.356. Notice to Affected Persons

(a) The cooperative shall provide to each affected customer or party, including a municipality, at least two notices of the proposed action by bill insert or by individual notice.

(b) The cooperative shall provide:

(1) the first notice not later than the 61st day before the effective date of the proposed action; and

(2) the last notice not later than the 31st day before the effective date of the proposed action.

(c) A notice prescribed by this section must include:

(1) a description of the services affected by the proposed action;

(2) the effective date of the proposed action;

(3) an explanation of the customer's right to:

(A) obtain a copy of the proposed tariff from the cooperative; and

(B) petition the commission for a review under Section 53.358;

(4) a statement of the amount by which the cooperative's total gross annual revenues will increase or decrease and a statement explaining the effect on the cooperative revenues as a result of the proposed action; and

(5) a list of rates that are affected by the proposed rate action, showing the effect of the proposed action on each of those rates.

Acts 1997, 75th Leg., ch. 166, § 1, eff. Sept. 1, 1997.

§ 53.357. Filing of Affidavits Verifying Notice

Not later than the 15th day before the effective date of a proposed action, the cooperative shall file with the commission affidavits that verify that the cooperative provided each notice required by Section 53.356.

Acts 1997, 75th Leg., ch. 166, § 1, eff. Sept. 1, 1997.

§ 53.358. Commission Review of Proposed Action

(a) The commission shall review a proposed action filed under this subchapter if:

(1) the commission receives, not later than the 45th day after the date the first notice is provided under Section 53.356, complaints relating to the proposed action:

(A) signed by at least five percent of the affected local service customers; or

(B) from an affected intrastate access customer, or group of affected intrastate access customers, that in the preceding 12 months accounted for more than 10 percent of the cooperative's total intrastate access revenues;

(2) the cooperative does not comply with the procedural requirements of this subchapter; or

(3) the proposed action is inconsistent with the commission's substantive policies as expressed in its rules.

(b) If the commission conducts a review of the proposed action under this section before the action's effective date, the commission may suspend the proposed action during the review.

Acts 1997, 75th Leg., ch. 166, § 1, eff. Sept. 1, 1997.

§ 53.359. Reversal of Deregulation by Ballot

(a) A cooperative that is partially deregulated under this subchapter may vote to reverse the deregulation by sending a ballot to each cooperative member.

(b) The cooperative's board of directors may order reballoting on its own motion. If the board receives a written request for that action from at least 10 percent of its members, the board shall reballot not later than the 60th day after the date the board receives that request.

(c) The cooperative may include the ballot in a bill or send the ballot separately. The ballot shall be printed to permit voting for or against the proposition: "Reversing the partial deregulation of the (name of the cooperative)."

(d) The partial deregulation is reversed if a majority of the ballots returned to the cooperative not later than the 45th day after the date the ballots are mailed favor reversal.

Acts 1997, 75th Leg., ch. 166, § 1, eff. Sept. 1, 1997.

CHAPTER 54. CERTIFICATES

SUBCHAPTER A. GENERAL PROVISIONS

Section
54.001. Certificate Required.
54.002. Exceptions to Certificate Requirement for Service Extension.
54.003. Exceptions to Certificate Requirement for Certain Services.
54.004. Relinquishment Plan.
54.005. Notice of and Hearing on Application.
54.006. Request for Preliminary Order.
54.007. Flexibility Plan.
54.008. Revocation or Amendment of Certificate.

SUBCHAPTER B. CERTIFICATE OF CONVENIENCE AND NECESSITY

54.051. Definition.
54.052. Certificate Required for Public Utility.
54.053. Application for Certificate.
54.054. Grant or Denial of Certificate.

SUBCHAPTER C. CERTIFICATE OF OPERATING AUTHORITY

54.101. Definition.
54.102. Application for Certificate.
54.103. Grant or Denial of Certificate.
54.104. Time of Service Requirements.
54.105. Penalty for Violation of Title.
54.106. Renumbered.
54.107 to 54.110. Deleted.
54.111. Renumbered.

SUBCHAPTER D. SERVICE PROVIDER CERTIFICATE OF OPERATING AUTHORITY

Section
54.151. Definition.
54.152. Limitation on Grant of Certificate.
54.153. Eligibility for Certificate.
54.154. Application for Certificate.
54.155. Grant or Denial of Certificate.
54.156. Resale of Services.
54.157. Optional Extended Area Service or Expanded Local Calling Service.
54.158. Interference With Resold Services Prohibited.
54.159. Retention of Access Service and IntraLATA Toll Service.

SUBCHAPTER E. MUNICIPALITIES

54.201. Certification Prohibited.
54.202. Prohibited Municipal Services.
54.2025. Lease of Fiber Optic Cable Facilities.
54.203. Service in Annexed or Incorporated Area.
54.204. Discrimination by Municipality Prohibited.
54.205. Municipality's Right to Control Access.
54.206. Recovery of Municipal Fee.

SUBCHAPTER F. REGULATION OF SERVICES, AREAS, AND FACILITIES

54.251. Provision of Service.
54.252. Grounds for Reduction of Service by Holder of Certificate of Convenience and Necessity.
54.253. Discontinuation of Service by Certain Certificate Holders.
54.254. Required Refusal of Service.
54.255. Transfer of Certain Certificates.
54.256. Application of Contracts.
54.257. Interference With Another Telecommunications Utility.
54.258. Maps.
54.259. Discrimination by Property Owner Prohibited.
54.260. Property Owner's Conditions.
54.261. Shared Tenant Services Contract.

SUBCHAPTER G. PROVIDER OF LAST RESORT

54.301. Definitions.
54.3015. Applicability of Subchapter.
54.302. Provider of Last Resort; Facilities-based Providers.
54.303. Successor Telecommunications Utility When no Sufficient Facilities Exist.
54.304. Abandonment or Cessation by Facilities-based Provider; Emergency Restoration.
54.305. Commission Participation in Bankruptcy Proceedings.

SUBCHAPTER A. GENERAL PROVISIONS

§ 54.001. Certificate Required

A person may not provide local exchange telephone service, basic local telecommunications service, or switched access service unless the person obtains a:

(1) certificate of convenience and necessity;

(2) certificate of operating authority; or

(3) service provider certificate of operating authority.

Acts 1997, 75th Leg., ch. 166, § 1, eff. Sept. 1, 1997.

§ 54.002. Exceptions to Certificate Requirement for Service Extension

(a) A telecommunications utility is not required to obtain a certificate of convenience and necessity, a certificate of operating authority, or a service provider certificate of operating authority for an:

(1) extension into territory that is:

(A) contiguous to the territory the telecommunications utility serves;

(B) not receiving similar service from another telecommunications utility; and

(C) not in another telecommunications utility's certificated area;

(2) extension in or to territory the telecommunications utility serves or is authorized to serve under a certificate of public convenience and necessity, a certificate of operating authority, or a service provider certificate of operating authority; or

(3) operation, extension, or service in progress on September 1, 1975.

(b) An extension allowed by Subsection (a) is limited to a device used:

(1) to interconnect existing facilities; or

(2) solely to transmit telecommunications utility services from an existing facility to a customer of retail utility service.

Acts 1997, 75th Leg., ch. 166, § 1, eff. Sept. 1, 1997.

§ 54.003. Exceptions to Certificate Requirement for Certain Services

A telecommunications utility is not required to obtain a certificate of convenience and necessity, a certificate of operating authority, or a service provider certificate of operating authority for:

(1) an interexchange telecommunications service;

(2) a nonswitched private line service;

(3) a shared tenant service;

(4) a specialized communications common carrier service;

(5) a commercial mobile service; or

(6) an operator service as defined by Section 55.081.

Acts 1997, 75th Leg., ch. 166, § 1, eff. Sept. 1, 1997.

§ 54.004. Relinquishment Plan

A holder of a service provider certificate of operating authority who applies for a certificate of operating authority or a certificate of convenience and necessity for the same territory must include with the application a plan to relinquish the service provider certificate of operating authority.

Acts 1997, 75th Leg., ch. 166, § 1, eff. Sept. 1, 1997.

§ 54.005. Notice of and Hearing on Application

(a) When an application for a certificate of convenience and necessity, a certificate of operating authority, or a service provider certificate of operating authority is filed, the commission shall:

(1) give notice of the application to interested parties; and

(2) if requested:

(A) set a time and place for a hearing; and

(B) give notice of the hearing.

(b) A person interested in the application may intervene at the hearing.

Acts 1997, 75th Leg., ch. 166, § 1, eff. Sept. 1, 1997.

§ 54.006. Request for Preliminary Order

(a) A telecommunications utility that wants to exercise a right or privilege under a franchise or permit that the utility anticipates obtaining but has not been granted may apply to the commission for a preliminary order under this section.

(b) The commission may issue a preliminary order declaring that the commission, on application and under commission rules, will grant the requested certificate of convenience and necessity, certificate of operating authority, or service provider certificate of operating authority, on terms the commission designates, after the telecommunications utility obtains the franchise or permit.

(c) The commission shall grant the certificate on presentation of evidence satisfactory to the commission that the telecommunications utility has obtained the franchise or permit.

Acts 1997, 75th Leg., ch. 166, § 1, eff. Sept. 1, 1997.

§ 54.007. Flexibility Plan

(a) After the commission grants an application for a certificate of convenience and necessity, a certificate of operating authority, or a service provider certificate of operating authority or determines that a certificate is not needed for the applicant to provide the relevant services, the commission shall conduct appropriate proceedings to establish a transitional flexibility plan for the incumbent local exchange company in the same area or areas as the new certificate holder.

(b) A basic local telecommunications service price of the incumbent local exchange company may not be increased before the fourth anniversary of the date the certificate is granted to the applicant except that the price may be increased as provided by this title.

Acts 1997, 75th Leg., ch. 166, § 1, eff. Sept. 1, 1997. Amended by Acts 1999, 76th Leg., ch. 1212, § 15, eff. Sept. 1, 1999.

§ 54.008. Revocation or Amendment of Certificate

(a) The commission may revoke or amend a certificate of convenience and necessity, a certificate of operating authority or a service provider certificate of operating authority after notice and hearing if the commission finds that the certificate holder has never provided or is no longer providing service in all or any part of the certificated area.

(b) The commission may require one or more public utilities to provide service in an area affected by the revocation or amendment of a certificate held by a public utility.

Acts 1997, 75th Leg., ch. 166, § 1, eff. Sept. 1, 1997.

SUBCHAPTER B. CERTIFICATE OF CONVENIENCE AND NECESSITY

§ 54.051. Definition

In this subchapter, "certificate" means a certificate of convenience and necessity.

Acts 1997, 75th Leg., ch. 166, § 1, eff. Sept. 1, 1997.

§ 54.052. Certificate Required for Public Utility

(a) A public utility may not directly or indirectly provide service to the public under a franchise or permit unless the utility first obtains from the commission a certificate that states that the public convenience and necessity requires or will require the installation, operation, or extension of the service.

(b) Except as otherwise provided by this chapter, a public utility may not furnish or make available retail public utility service to an area in which retail utility service is being lawfully furnished by another public utility unless the utility first obtains a certificate that includes the area in which the consuming facility is located.

Acts 1997, 75th Leg., ch. 166, § 1, eff. Sept. 1, 1997.

§ 54.053. Application for Certificate

(a) A public utility that wants to obtain or amend a certificate must submit an application to the commission.

(b) The applicant shall file with the commission evidence the commission requires to show the applicant has received the consent, franchise, or permit required by the proper municipal or other public authority.

Acts 1997, 75th Leg., ch. 166, § 1, eff. Sept. 1, 1997.

§ 54.054. Grant or Denial of Certificate

(a) The commission may approve an application and grant a certificate only if the commission finds that the certificate is necessary for the service, accommodation, convenience, or safety of the public.

(b) The commission may:

(1) grant the certificate as requested;

(2) grant the certificate for the construction of a portion of the requested system, facility, or extension or the partial exercise of the requested right or privilege; or

(3) refuse to grant the certificate.

(c) The commission shall grant each certificate on a nondiscriminatory basis after considering:

(1) the adequacy of existing service;

(2) the need for additional service;

(3) the effect of granting the certificate on the recipient of the certificate and any public utility of the same kind serving the proximate area; and

(4) other factors, such as:

(A) community values;

(B) recreational and park areas;

(C) historical and aesthetic values;

(D) environmental integrity; and

(E) the probable improvement of service or lowering of cost to consumers in the area if the certificate is granted.

Acts 1997, 75th Leg., ch. 166, § 1, eff. Sept. 1, 1997.

SUBCHAPTER C. CERTIFICATE OF OPERATING AUTHORITY

Acts 1999, 76th Leg., ch. 1212, § 16, amended Subchapter C.

§ 54.101. Definition

In this subchapter, "certificate" means a certificate of operating authority.

Acts 1997, 75th Leg., ch. 166, § 1, eff. Sept. 1, 1997. Amended by Acts 1999, 76th Leg., ch. 1212, § 16, eff. Sept. 1, 1999.

§ 54.102. Application for Certificate

(a) A person may apply for a certificate of operating authority.

(b) The applicant must file with the application a sworn statement that the applicant has applied for each municipal consent, franchise, or permit required for the type of services and facilities for which the applicant has applied.

(c) An affiliate of a person holding a certificate of convenience and necessity may hold a certificate of operating authority if the holder of the certificate of convenience and necessity is in compliance with federal law and Federal Communications Commission rules governing affiliates and structural separation. An affiliate of a person holding a certificate of convenience and necessity may not directly or indirectly sell to a non-affiliate any regulated product or service purchased from the person holding a certificate of convenience and necessity at any rate or price less than the price paid to the person holding a certificate of convenience and necessity.

(d) A person may hold a certificate for all or any portion of a service area for which one or more affiliates of the person holds a certificate of operating authority, a service provider certificate of operating authority, or a certificate of convenience and necessity.

(e) An affiliate of a company that holds a certificate of convenience and necessity and that serves more than five million access lines in this state may hold a certificate of operating authority or service provider certificate of operating authority to provide service in an area of this state in which its affiliated company is the incumbent local exchange company. However, the affiliate holding the certificate of operating authority or service provider certificate of operating authority may not provide in that area any service listed in Sections 58.051(a)(1)–(4) or Sections 58.151(1)–(4), or any subset of those services, in a manner that results in a customer-specific contract so long as the affiliated company that is the incumbent local exchange company may not provide those services or subsets of services in a manner that results in a customer-specific contract under Section 58.003 in that area. This subsection does not preclude an affiliate of a company holding a certificate of convenience and necessity from holding a certificate of operating authority in any area of this state to provide advanced services as defined by rules or orders of the Federal Communications Commission, or preclude such an advanced services affiliate from using any form of pricing flexibility, with regard to services other than those subject to the restrictions provided by this subsection. This subsection does not preclude a long distance affiliate from using any form of pricing flexibility with regard to services other than those services subject to the restrictions provided by this subsection. In addition, the affiliate holding the certificate of operating authority or service provider certificate of operating authority may not offer, in an area for which the affiliated incumbent local exchange company holds a certificate of convenience and necessity, a service listed in Sections 58.151(1)–(4) as a component of a package of services, as a promotional offering, or with a volume or term discount until the affiliated incumbent local exchange company may offer those services in pricing flexibility offerings in accordance with Section 58.004, unless the customer of one of these pricing flexibility offerings is a federal, state, or local governmental entity.

(f) The commission has the authority to enforce this section.

Acts 1997, 75th Leg., ch. 166, § 1, eff. Sept. 1, 1997. Amended by Acts 1999, 76th Leg., ch. 1212, § 16, eff. Sept. 1, 1999.

§ 54.103. Grant or Denial of Certificate

(a) The commission must grant or deny a certificate not later than the 60th day after the date the application for the certificate is filed. The commission may extend the deadline on good cause shown.

(b) The commission shall grant each certificate on a nondiscriminatory basis after considering factors such as:

(1) the technical and financial qualifications of the applicant; and

(2) the applicant's ability to meet the commission's quality of service requirements.

(c) In an exchange of an incumbent local exchange company that serves fewer than 31,000 access lines, in addition to the factors described by Subsection (b), the commission shall consider:

(1) the effect of granting the certificate on a public utility serving the area and on that utility's customers;

(2) the ability of that public utility to provide adequate service at reasonable rates;

(3) the effect of granting the certificate on the ability of that public utility to act as the provider of last resort; and

(4) the ability of the exchange, not the company, to support more than one provider of service.

(d) Except as provided by Subsections (e) and (f), the commission may grant an application for a certificate only for an area or areas that are contiguous and reasonably compact and cover an area of at least 27 square miles.

(e) In an exchange in a county that has a population of less than 500,000 and that is served by an incumbent local exchange company that has more than 31,000 access lines, an area covering less than 27 square miles may be approved if the area is contiguous and reasonably compact and has at least 20,000 access lines.

(f) In an exchange of a company that serves fewer than 31,000 access lines in this state, the commission may grant an application only for an area that has boundaries similar to the boundaries of the serving central office that is served by the incumbent local exchange company that holds the certificate of convenience and necessity for the area.

(g) Expired.

Acts 1997, 75th Leg., ch. 166, § 1, eff. Sept. 1, 1997. Amended by Acts 1999, 76th Leg., ch. 1212, § 16, eff. Sept. 1, 1999.

§ 54.104. Time of Service Requirements

(a) The commission by rule may prescribe the period within which a certificate holder must be able to serve customers.

(b) Notwithstanding Subsection (a), a certificate holder must serve a customer not later than the 30th day after the date the customer requests service.

Acts 1997, 75th Leg., ch. 166, § 1, Sept. 1, 1997. Renumbered from V.T.C.A., Utilities Code § 54.106 and amended by Acts 1999, 76th Leg., ch. 1212, § 16, eff. Sept. 1, 1999.

§ 54.105. Penalty for Violation of Title

If a certificate holder fails to comply with a requirement of this title, the commission may:

(1) revoke the holder's certificate;

(2) impose against the holder administrative penalties under Subchapter B, Chapter 15;[1] or

(3) take another action under Subchapter B, Chapter 15.[1]

Acts 1997, 75th Leg., ch. 166, § 1, eff. Sept. 1, 1997. Renumbered from V.T.C.A., Utilities Code § 54.111 by Acts 1999, 76th Leg., ch. 1212, § 16, eff. Sept. 1, 1999.

[1] V.T.C.A., Utilities Code § 15.021 et seq.

§ 54.106. Renumbered as V.T.C.A., Utilities Code § 54.104 by Acts 1999, 76th Leg., ch. 1212, § 16, eff. Sept. 1, 1999

§§ 54.107 to 54.110. Deleted by Acts 1999, 76th Leg., ch. 1212, § 16, eff. Sept. 1, 1999

§ 54.111. Renumbered as V.T.C.A., Utilities Code § 54.105 by Acts 1999, 76th Leg., ch. 1212, § 16, eff. Sept. 1, 1999

SUBCHAPTER D. SERVICE PROVIDER CERTIFICATE OF OPERATING AUTHORITY

§ 54.151. Definition

In this subchapter, "certificate" means a service provider certificate of operating authority.

Acts 1997, 75th Leg., ch. 166, § 1, eff. Sept. 1, 1997.

§ 54.152. Limitation on Grant of Certificate

The commission may not grant a certificate to a holder of a:

(1) certificate of convenience and necessity for the same territory; or

(2) certificate of operating authority for the same territory.

Acts 1997, 75th Leg., ch. 166, § 1, eff. Sept. 1, 1997.

§ 54.153. Eligibility for Certificate

(a) A company is not eligible to obtain a certificate under this subchapter if the company, together with affiliates, had more than six percent of the total intrastate switched access minutes of use as measured for the most recent 12-month period:

(1) that precedes the date the application is filed; and

(2) for which the access information is available.

(b) The commission shall obtain information necessary to determine eligibility from the incumbent local exchange telephone companies and the applicant.

(c) The commission shall certify eligibility not later than the 10th day after the date the application is filed.

(d) In this section:

(1) "Affiliate" means an entity that, directly or indirectly, owns or controls, is owned or controlled by, or is under common ownership or control with a company that applies for a certificate under this subchapter.

(2) "Control" means to exercise substantial influence over the policies and actions of another.

Acts 1997, 75th Leg., ch. 166, § 1, eff. Sept. 1, 1997.

§ 54.154. Application for Certificate

(a) The commission may grant a certificate to encourage an innovative, competitive, and entrepreneurial business to provide telecommunications services.

(b) An applicant for a certificate must:

(1) file with the application:

(A) a sworn statement that the applicant has applied for each municipal consent, franchise, or permit required for the type of services and facilities for which the applicant has applied; and

(B) a description of the services the applicant will provide;

(2) show the areas in which the applicant will provide the services;

(3) demonstrate that the applicant has the financial and technical ability to provide services; and

(4) demonstrate that the services will meet the requirements of this subchapter.

Acts 1997, 75th Leg., ch. 166, § 1, eff. Sept. 1, 1997.

§ 54.155. Grant or Denial of Certificate

(a) The commission must grant or deny a certificate not later than the 60th day after the date the application for the certificate is filed. The commission may extend the deadline on good cause shown.

(b) The commission shall grant each certificate on a nondiscriminatory basis after considering factors such as:

(1) the technical and financial qualifications of the applicant; and

(2) the applicant's ability to meet the commission's quality of service requirements.

Acts 1997, 75th Leg., ch. 166, § 1, eff. Sept. 1, 1997.

§ 54.156. Resale of Services

(a) A certificate holder may obtain services under the resale tariffs approved by the commission under Subchapter C, Chapter 60,[1] except in a certificated area of a company that serves fewer than 31,000 access lines.

(b) A certificate holder may obtain for resale the monthly recurring flat rate local exchange telephone service and associated nonrecurring charges, including any mandatory extended area service, of an incumbent local exchange company at a five percent discount to the tariffed rate.

(c) The incumbent local exchange company shall sell a feature service that may be provided to a customer in conjunction with local exchange service at a five percent discount to the tariffed rate, including any associated nonrecurring charge for those services, provided that the incumbent local exchange company shall make available to a certificate holder, at an additional five percent discount, any discounts made available to customers of the incumbent local exchange company who are similarly situated to the customers of the certificate holder. In this subsection "feature service" includes:

(1) toll restriction;

(2) call control options;

(3) tone dialing;

(4) custom calling; and

(5) caller identification.

(d) A certificate holder and an incumbent local exchange company may agree to a rate lower than the tariffed rate or discounted rate.

(e) The five percent discounts provided by this section do not apply in an exchange of a company that has fewer than 31,000 access lines in this state.

(f) If the tariffed rate for a resold service changes, the five percent discount prescribed by this section applies to the changed rate. The commission may not, for certificate holders, create a special class for purposes of resold services.

(g) A certificate holder:

(1) may not use a resold flat rate local exchange telephone service to avoid the rates and terms of an incumbent local exchange company's tariffs;

(2) may not terminate both flat rate local exchange telephone service and services obtained under the resale tariff approved under Section 60.041 on the same end user customer's premises;

(3) may not use resold flat rate local exchange telephone services to provide access services to another interexchange carrier, cellular carrier, competitive access provider, or retail telecommunications provider, but may permit customers to use resold local exchange telephone services to access such a carrier or provider;

(4) may sell the flat rate local exchange telephone service only to the same class of customers to which the incumbent local exchange company sells that service;

(5) may obtain services offered by or negotiated with a holder of a certificate of convenience and necessity or a certificate of operating authority; and

(6) may obtain for resale single or multiple line flat rate intraLATA calling service when provided by the local exchange company at the tariffed rate for online digital communications.

Acts 1997, 75th Leg., ch. 166, § 1, eff. Sept. 1, 1997.

[1] V.T.C.A., Utilities Code § 60.041 et seq.

§ 54.157. Optional Extended Area Service or Expanded Local Calling Service

(a) A certificate holder may purchase for resale:

(1) optional extended area service; and

(2) expanded local calling service.

(b) The purchase of optional extended area service and expanded local calling service may not be discounted.

Acts 1997, 75th Leg., ch. 166, § 1, eff. Sept. 1, 1997.

§ 54.158. Interference With Resold Services Prohibited

An incumbent local exchange company may not:

(1) delay providing or maintaining a service provided under this subchapter;

(2) degrade the quality of access the company provides to another provider;

(3) impair the speed, quality, or efficiency of a line used by another provider;

(4) fail to fully disclose in a timely manner after a request all available information necessary for a certificate holder to provide resale services; or

(5) refuse to take a reasonable action to allow a certificate holder efficient access to the company's ordering, billing, or repair management system.

Acts 1997, 75th Leg., ch. 166, § 1, eff. Sept. 1, 1997.

§ 54.159. Retention of Access Service and IntraLATA Toll Service

An incumbent local exchange company that sells flat rate local exchange telephone service to a certificate holder may retain all access service and "1-plus" intraLATA toll service that originates over the resold flat rate local exchange telephone service.

Acts 1997, 75th Leg., ch. 166, § 1, eff. Sept. 1, 1997.

SUBCHAPTER E. MUNICIPALITIES

§ 54.201. Certification Prohibited

The commission may not grant to a municipality a:

(1) certificate of convenience and necessity;

(2) certificate of operating authority; or

(3) service provider certificate of operating authority.

Acts 1997, 75th Leg., ch. 166, § 1, eff. Sept. 1, 1997.

§ 54.202. Prohibited Municipal Services

(a) A municipality or municipal electric system may not offer for sale to the public:

(1) a service for which a certificate of convenience and necessity, a certificate of operating authority, or a service provider certificate of operating authority is required; or

(2) a nonswitched telecommunications service used to connect a customer's premises with:

(A) another customer's premises within the exchange; or

(B) a long distance provider that serves the exchange.

(b) Subsection (a) applies to a service offered either directly or indirectly through a telecommunications provider.

(c) This section may not be construed to prevent a municipally owned utility from providing to its energy customers, either directly or indirectly, any energy related service involving the transfer or receipt of information or data concerning the use, measurement, monitoring, or management of energy utility services provided by the municipally owned utility, including services such as load management or automated meter reading.

Acts 1997, 75th Leg., ch. 166, § 1, eff. Sept. 1, 1997. Amended by Acts 2005, 79th Leg., 2nd C.S., ch. 2, § 5, eff. Sept. 1, 2005.

§ 54.2025. Lease of Fiber Optic Cable Facilities

Nothing in this subchapter shall prevent a municipality, or a municipal electric system that is a member of a municipal power agency formed under Chapter 163 by adoption of a concurrent resolution by the participating municipalities on or before August 1, 1975, from leasing any of the excess capacity of its fiber optic cable facilities (dark fiber), so long as the rental of the fiber facilities is done on a nondiscriminatory, nonpreferential basis.

Added by Acts 1999, 76th Leg., ch. 1212, § 17, eff. Sept. 1, 1999.

§ 54.203. Service in Annexed or Incorporated Area

(a) If an area is or will be included within a municipality as the result of annexation, incorporation, or another reason, each telecommunications utility that holds or is entitled to hold a certificate under this title to provide service or operate a facility in the area before the inclusion has the right to continue to provide the service or operate the facility and extend service in the utility's certificated area within the annexed or incorporated area under the rights granted by the certificate and this title.

(b) Notwithstanding any other law, a certificated telecommunications utility has the right to:

(1) continue and extend service within the utility's certificated area; and

(2) use roads, streets, highways, alleys, and public property to furnish retail utility service.

(c) The governing body of a municipality may require a certificated telecommunications utility to relocate the utility's facility at the utility's expense to permit the widening or straightening of a street by:

(1) giving the utility 30 days' notice; and

(2) specifying the new location for the facility along the right-of-way of the street.

(d) This section does not limit the power of a city, town, or village to incorporate or of a municipality to extend its boundaries by annexation.

Acts 1997, 75th Leg., ch. 166, § 1, eff. Sept. 1, 1997.

§ 54.204. Discrimination by Municipality Prohibited

(a) Notwithstanding Section 14.008, a municipality or a municipally owned utility may not discriminate against a certificated telecommunications provider regarding:

(1) the authorization or placement of a facility in a public right-of-way;

(2) access to a building; or

(3) a municipal utility pole attachment rate or term.

(b) In granting consent, a franchise, or a permit for the use of a public street, alley, or right-of-way within its municipal boundaries, a municipality or municipally owned utility may not discriminate in favor of or against a certificated telecommunications provider regarding:

(1) municipal utility pole attachment or underground conduit rates or terms; or

(2) the authorization, placement, replacement, or removal of a facility in a public right-of-way and the reasonable compensation for the authorization, placement, replacement, or removal regardless of whether the compensation is in the form of:

(A) money;

(B) services;

(C) use of facilities; or

(D) another kind of consideration.

(c) A municipality or a municipally owned utility may not charge any entity, regardless of the nature of the services provided by that entity, a pole attachment rate or underground conduit rate that exceeds the fee the municipality or municipally owned utility would be permitted to charge under rules adopted by the Federal Communications Commission under 47 U.S.C. Section 224(e) if the municipality's or municipally owned utility's rates were regulated under federal law and the rules of the Federal Communications Commission. In addition, not later than September 1, 2006, a municipality or municipally owned utility shall charge a single, uniform pole attachment or underground conduit rate to all entities that are not affiliated with the municipality or municipally owned utility regardless of the services carried over the networks attached to the poles or underground conduit.

(d) Notwithstanding any other law, the commission has the jurisdiction necessary to enforce this section.

Acts 1997, 75th Leg., ch. 166, § 1, eff. Sept. 1, 1997. Amended by Acts 2005, 79th Leg., 2nd C.S., ch. 2, § 6, eff. Sept. 1, 2005.

§ 54.205. Municipality's Right to Control Access

This title does not restrict a municipality's historical right to control and receive reasonable compensation for access to the municipality's public streets, alleys, or rights-of-way or to other public property.

Acts 1997, 75th Leg., ch. 166, § 1, eff. Sept. 1, 1997.

§ 54.206. Recovery of Municipal Fee

(a) A holder of a certificate of convenience and necessity, a certificate of operating authority, or a service provider certificate of operating authority has the right to collect a fee that a municipality imposes under Section 54.204 or 54.205 through a pro rata charge to the customers in the boundaries of the municipality.

(b) The charge may be shown on the customer's bill as a separate line item.

Acts 1997, 75th Leg., ch. 166, § 1, eff. Sept. 1, 1997.

SUBCHAPTER F. REGULATION OF SERVICES, AREAS, AND FACILITIES

§ 54.251. Provision of Service

(a) Except as provided by this section, Section 54.252, Section 54.253, and Section 54.254, a telecommunications utility that holds a certificate of convenience and necessity or a certificate of operating authority shall:

(1) offer all basic local telecommunications services to each customer in the utility's certificated area; and

(2) provide continuous and adequate service in that area.

(b) Except as specifically determined otherwise by the commission under this subchapter or Subchapter G of this chapter, and except as provided by Subchapters C and D, Chapter 65, the holder of a certificate of convenience and necessity for an area has the obligations of a provider of last resort regardless of whether another provider has a certificate of operating authority or service provider certificate of operating authority for that area.

(c) A certificate holder may meet the holder's provider of last resort obligations using any available technology. Notwithstanding any provision of Chapter 56, the commission may adjust disbursements from the universal service fund to companies using technologies other than traditional wireline or landline technologies to meet provider of last resort obligations. As determined by the commission, the certificate holder shall meet minimum quality of service standards, including standards for 911 service, comparable to those established for traditional wireline or landline technologies and shall offer services at a price comparable to the monthly service charge for comparable services in that exchange or the provider's nearest exchange.

Acts 1997, 75th Leg., ch. 166, § 1, eff. Sept. 1, 1997. Amended by Acts 2003, 78th Leg., ch. 76, § 1, eff. Sept. 1, 2003; Acts 2005, 79th Leg., 2nd C.S., ch. 2, § 7, eff. Sept. 1, 2005. Amended by Acts 2011, 82nd Leg., ch. 98 (S.B. 980), § 6, eff. Sept. 1, 2011.

§ 54.252. Grounds for Reduction of Service by Holder of Certificate of Convenience and Necessity

(a) Except to the extent otherwise ordered by the commission in accordance with this subchapter, the holder of a certificate of convenience and necessity may not discontinue, reduce, or impair service to any part of the holder's certificated service area except for:

(1) nonpayment of charges;

(2) nonuse; or

(3) another similar reason that occurs in the usual course of business.

(b) A discontinuance, reduction, or impairment of service must be in compliance with and is subject to any condition or restriction the commission prescribes.

Acts 1997, 75th Leg., ch. 166, § 1, eff. Sept. 1, 1997. Amended by Acts 2003, 78th Leg., ch. 76, § 2, eff. Sept. 1, 2003.

§ 54.253. Discontinuation of Service by Certain Certificate Holders

(a) A telecommunications utility that holds a certificate of operating authority or a service provider certificate of operating authority may:

(1) cease operations in the utility's certificated area; or

(2) discontinue an optional service that is not essential to providing basic local telecommunications service.

(b) Before the telecommunications utility ceases operations or discontinues an optional service, the utility, in the manner required by the commission, must give notice of the intended action to:

(1) the commission;

(2) each affected customer;

(3) the Commission on State Emergency Communications;

(4) the office; and

(5) each wholesale provider of telecommunications facilities or services from which the utility has purchased facilities or services.

(c) The telecommunications utility is entitled to discontinue an optional service on or after the 61st day after the date the utility gives the notice.

(d) The telecommunications utility may not cease operations in its certificated area unless the commission authorizes the utility to cease operations and:

(1) another provider of basic local telecommunications services has adequate facilities and capacity to serve the customers in the certificated area; or

(2) the utility is an "exiting utility," as that term is defined by Section 54.301, no other telecommunications utility has facilities sufficient to provide basic local telecommunications service in the defined geographic area, and the utility acts in good faith to provide for a transition of the utility's existing basic local telecommunications service customers to another holder of a certificate for that area.

(e) The commission may not authorize the telecommunications utility to cease operations under Subsection (d) before the 61st day after the date the utility gives the notice required by Subsection (b). Unless the commission receives a complaint from an affected person, the commission may enter an order under this subsection administratively.

Acts 1997, 75th Leg., ch. 166, § 1, eff. Sept. 1, 1997. Amended by Acts 2003, 78th Leg., ch. 76, § 3, eff. Sept. 1, 2003.

§ 54.254. Required Refusal of Service

A holder of a certificate of convenience and necessity, a certificate of operating authority, or a service provider certificate of operating authority shall refuse to serve a customer in the holder's certificated area if the holder is prohibited from providing the service under Section 212.012, 232.029, or 232.0291, Local Government Code.

Acts 1997, 75th Leg., ch. 166, § 1, eff. Sept. 1, 1997. Amended by Acts 2005, 79th Leg., ch. 708, § 14, eff. Sept. 1, 2005.

§ 54.255. Transfer of Certain Certificates

(a) A telecommunications utility may sell, assign, or lease a certificate of convenience and necessity or a certificate of operating authority or a right obtained under such a certificate if the commission determines that the purchaser, assignee, or lessee can provide adequate service.

(b) The sale, assignment, or lease of a certificate or a right is subject to conditions the commission prescribes.

Acts 1997, 75th Leg., ch. 166, § 1, eff. Sept. 1, 1997.

§ 54.256. Application of Contracts

A contract approved by the commission between telecommunications utilities that designates areas and customers to be served by the utilities:

(1) is valid and enforceable; and

(2) shall be incorporated into the appropriate areas of certification.

Acts 1997, 75th Leg., ch. 166, § 1, eff. Sept. 1, 1997.

§ 54.257. Interference With Another Telecommunications Utility

If a telecommunications utility constructing or extending the utility's lines, plant, or system interferes or attempts to interfere with the operation of a line, plant, or system of another utility, the commission by order may:

(1) prohibit the construction or extension; or

(2) prescribe terms for locating the affected lines, plants, or systems.

Acts 1997, 75th Leg., ch. 166, § 1, eff. Sept. 1, 1997.

§ 54.258. Maps

A public utility shall file with the commission one or more maps that show each utility facility and that separately illustrate each utility facility for transmission or distribution of the utility's services on a date the commission orders.

Acts 1997, 75th Leg., ch. 166, § 1, eff. Sept. 1, 1997.

§ 54.259. Discrimination by Property Owner Prohibited

(a) If a telecommunications utility holds a consent, franchise, or permit as determined to be the appropriate grants of authority by the municipality and holds a certificate if required by this title, a public or private property owner may not:

(1) prevent the utility from installing on the owner's property a telecommunications service facility a tenant requests;

(2) interfere with the utility's installation on the owner's property of a telecommunications service facility a tenant requests;

(3) discriminate against such a utility regarding installation, terms, or compensation of a telecommunications service facility to a tenant on the owner's property;

(4) demand or accept an unreasonable payment of any kind from a tenant or the utility for allowing the utility on or in the owner's property; or

(5) discriminate in favor of or against a tenant in any manner, including rental charge discrimination, because of the utility from which the tenant receives a telecommunications service.

(b) Subsection (a) does not apply to an institution of higher education. In this subsection, "institution of higher education" means:

(1) an institution of higher education as defined by Section 61.003, Education Code; or

(2) a private or independent institution of higher education as defined by Section 61.003, Education Code.

(c) Notwithstanding any other law, the commission has the jurisdiction to enforce this section.

Acts 1997, 75th Leg., ch. 166, § 1, eff. Sept. 1, 1997.

§ 54.260. Property Owner's Conditions

(a) Notwithstanding Section 54.259, if a telecommunications utility holds a municipal consent, franchise, or permit as determined to be the appropriate grant of authority by the municipality and holds a certificate if required by this title, a public or private property owner may:

(1) impose a condition on the utility that is reasonably necessary to protect:

(A) the safety, security, appearance, and condition of the property; and

(B) the safety and convenience of other persons;

(2) impose a reasonable limitation on the time at which the utility may have access to the property to install a telecommunications service facility;

(3) impose a reasonable limitation on the number of such utilities that have access to the owner's property, if the owner can demonstrate a space constraint that requires the limitation;

(4) require the utility to agree to indemnify the owner for damage caused installing, operating, or removing a facility;

(5) require the tenant or the utility to bear the entire cost of installing, operating, or removing a facility; and

(6) require the utility to pay compensation that is reasonable and nondiscriminatory among such telecommunications utilities.

(b) Notwithstanding any other law, the commission has the jurisdiction to enforce this section.

Acts 1997, 75th Leg., ch. 166, § 1, eff. Sept. 1, 1997.

§ 54.261. Shared Tenant Services Contract

Sections 54.259 and 54.260 do not require a public or private property owner to enter into a contract with a telecommunications utility to provide shared tenant services on a property.

Acts 1997, 75th Leg., ch. 166, § 1, eff. Sept. 1, 1997.

SUBCHAPTER G. PROVIDER OF LAST RESORT

§ 54.301. Definitions

In this subchapter:

(1) "Exiting utility" means a telecommunications utility that:

(A) holds a certificate of operating authority or a service provider certificate of operating authority;

(B) is the predominant provider of basic local telecommunications service in a defined geographic area and provides those services using the utility's own facilities; and

(C) ceases operations in all or part of the utility's certificated service area under Section 54.253 or 54.303.

(2) "Provider of last resort" means a certificated telecommunications utility that must offer basic local telecommunications service throughout a defined geographic area.

(3) "Successor utility" means a telecommunications utility that holds a certificate of convenience and necessity, certificate of operating authority, or service provider certificate of operating authority, and that is or is designated to become the provider of last resort for the defined geographic area previously served by an exiting utility.

Added by Acts 2003, 78th Leg., ch. 76, § 4, eff. Sept. 1, 2003.

§ 54.3015. Applicability of Subchapter

This subchapter applies to a transitioning company under Chapter 65 in relation to its regulated exchanges in the same manner and to the same extent this subchapter applies to a holder of a certificate of convenience and necessity.

Added by Acts 2005, 79th Leg., 2nd C.S., ch. 2, § 8, eff. Sept. 1, 2005. Amended by Acts 2011, 82nd Leg., ch. 98 (S.B. 980), § 7, eff. Sept. 1, 2011.

§ 54.302. Provider of Last Resort; Facilities–based Providers

(a) Notwithstanding any other provision of this title, if a telecommunications utility installs facilities to serve customers located in a defined geographic area to provide telecommunications services, including basic local telecommunications service, before the holder of the certificate of convenience and necessity installs facilities to serve customers located in that defined geographic area, the holder of the certificate of convenience and necessity may petition the commission for an order relieving the utility of the utility's designation as the provider of last resort in that defined geographic area.

(b) The commission shall relieve the holder of the certificate of convenience and necessity of the obligations of service as the provider of last resort for the defined geographic area, and the commission shall designate the facilities-based telecommunications utility as the provider of last resort if the commission determines that:

(1) the holder of the certificate of convenience and necessity does not have facilities in place to provide basic local telecommunications service to all customers within that defined geographic area;

(2) another certificated telecommunications utility has installed facilities adequate to provide that service throughout that area; and

(3) the public interest would be served by transferring the provider of last resort obligations for that area.

(c) The commission shall complete proceedings necessary to make the determinations prescribed by this section not later than the 91st day after the date the petition is filed under Subsection (a).

Added by Acts 2003, 78th Leg., ch. 76, § 4, eff. Sept. 1, 2003.

§ 54.303. Successor Telecommunications Utility When no Sufficient Facilities Exist

(a) When the commission obtains notice as required under Section 54.253 or otherwise that a utility intends to become an exiting utility and no other telecommunications utility has facilities sufficient to provide basic local telecommunications service in that defined geographic area, the commission shall open a contested case proceeding to determine:

(1) the identity of the successor utility under this section; and

(2) the amount of universal service funding under Subchapter G, Chapter 56,[1] to be made available to the successor utility.

(b) On designation as the successor utility under this section, the commission, if applicable, shall provide to the successor utility:

(1) a reasonable time, in accordance with industry practices and not subject to otherwise applicable commission service quality rules or standards, to modify, construct, or obtain facilities necessary to serve the customers of the exiting telecommunications utility; and

(2) an exemption on a transitional basis from any obligation to unbundle the utility's network elements or to provide service for resale within that defined geographic area for nine months or another reasonable period the commission may authorize as necessary to modify the utility's network to provide that unbundling or resale.

(c) A customer within the defined geographic area to be served by the successor utility is considered to have applied for service from the successor utility on the effective date of that designation by the commission. Each right, privilege, and obligation of being a customer of the successor utility applies to that customer and the customer is subject to the successor utility's applicable terms of service as specified in an applicable tariff or contract.

Added by Acts 2003, 78th Leg., ch. 76, § 4, eff. Sept. 1, 2003.

[1] V.T.C.A., Utilities Code § 56.251.

§ 54.304. Abandonment or Cessation by Facilities–based Provider; Emergency Restoration

(a) The commission, on its own motion or on the petition of an interested party, may institute an expedited proceeding under this section if the commission finds that:

(1) a holder of a certificate of operating authority or service provider certificate of operating authority is the predominant provider of basic local telecommunications service in a defined geographic area and the utility provides that service using the utility's own facilities;

(2) no other telecommunications utility has facilities sufficient to provide basic local telecommunications service in that defined geographic area; and

(3) the holder of the certificate of operating authority or service provider certificate of operating authority has:

(A) ceased providing basic local telecommunications service to the utility's customers in that defined geographic area; or

(B) abandoned the operation of the utility's facilities in the defined geographic area that are used to provide basic local telecommunications service.

(b) In a proceeding under this section, the commission may declare that an emergency exists and issue any order necessary to protect the health, safety, and welfare of affected customers of the utility and to expedite the restoration and continuation of basic local telecommunications service to those customers. An order issued by the commission under this subsection may include an order to:

(1) provide for a temporary arrangement for operation of the utility's facilities by an uncertificated entity that agrees to provide service;

(2) authorize one or more third parties to enter the premises of the abandoned facilities; or

(3) grant temporary waivers from quality of service requirements.

(c) The commission may designate a successor utility in accordance with Section 54.303 during a proceeding under this section.

Added by Acts 2003, 78th Leg., ch. 76, § 4, eff. Sept. 1, 2003.

§ 54.305. Commission Participation in Bankruptcy Proceedings

(a) The commission, on written notice that a certificated telecommunications utility has filed a petition in bankruptcy or is the subject of an involuntary petition in bankruptcy, may inform the appropriate court and parties of the commission's interest in obtaining notice of proceedings.

(b) Within the time prescribed by the applicable statutes, rules, and court orders, the commission may intervene and participate in any bankruptcy proceedings that affect customers or providers of telecommunications services in this state.

(c) The office may inform the appropriate court and parties of the office's interest in obtaining notice of the proceedings. Within the time prescribed by the applicable statutes, rules, and court orders, the office may intervene and participate in any bankruptcy proceeding on behalf of residential and small commercial customers.

Added by Acts 2003, 78th Leg., ch. 76, § 4, eff. Sept. 1, 2003.

CHAPTER 55. REGULATION OF TELECOMMUNICATIONS SERVICES

SUBCHAPTER A. GENERAL PROVISIONS

Section
55.001. General Standard.
55.002. Commission Authority Concerning Standards.
55.003. Rule or Standard.
55.004. Local Exchange Company Rule or Practice Change.
55.005. Unreasonable Preference or Prejudice Concerning Service Prohibited.
55.006. Discrimination and Restriction on Competition.
55.007. Minimum Services.
55.008. Improvements in Service; Interconnecting Service.
55.009. IntraLATA Calls.
55.010. Billing for Service to the State.
55.011. Notice of Identity of Interexchange Carrier.
55.012. Limitations on Discontinuance of Basic Local Telecommunications Service.
55.013. Limitations on Discontinuance of Basic Local Telecommunications Service.
55.014. Provision of Advanced Telecommunications Services.
55.015. Lifeline Service.
55.016. Telecommunications Billing.
55.017. Identification Required.

SUBCHAPTER B. EXTENDED AREA SERVICE

55.021. Extended Area Service.
55.022. Mandatory Service.
55.023. Optional Extended Area Service.
Section
55.024. Charge for Extended Area Service.
55.025. Hunting Service.
55.026. New Orders Prohibited After Certain Date.

SUBCHAPTER C. EXPANDED TOLL-FREE LOCAL CALLING AREAS

55.041. Definitions.
55.042. Contiguous Exchange.
55.043. Splitting Exchanges Prohibited.
55.044. Exemption.
55.045. Eligibility to Petition.
55.046. Petition Requirements.
55.047. Balloting and Consideration.
55.048. Charges.
55.049. Expansion Prohibited After Certain Date.

SUBCHAPTER D. OPERATOR SERVICE PROVIDERS

55.081. Definition.
55.082. Applicability.
55.083. Rules and Procedures.
55.084. Information Displayed on Public Use Telephone.
55.085. Connection Announcement.
55.086. Information Required on Access to Local Exchange Company Operator.
55.087. Access to Local Exchange Company and Other Utilities Required.
55.088. Access to Live Operator Required.
55.089. Commission May Investigate and Act on Violation.

SUBCHAPTER E. CALLER IDENTIFICATION SERVICE

55.101. Definitions.
55.102. Applicability.
55.103. Provision of Service.
55.104. Use of Information.
55.105. Per-Call Blocking.
55.106. Per-Line Blocking.
55.1065. Repealed.
55.107. Limitation on Commission Authority.
55.108. Expired.
55.109. Implementation of Panel Recommendations.
55.110. Report of Blocking Failure.

SUBCHAPTER F. AUTOMATIC DIAL ANNOUNCING DEVICES

55.121. Definition.
55.122. Exemptions.
55.123. Notice of Use of Device to Telecommunications Utility.
55.124. Random or Sequential Number Calling.
55.125. Hours When Use Prohibited.
55.126. Device Disconnection.
55.127. Contents of Recorded Message.
55.128. Duration of Recorded Message.
55.129. Permit Required.
55.130. Permit.
55.131. Permit Fee.
55.132. Notification of Change.
55.133. Notification of Local Exchange Company.
55.134. Complaints and Enforcement.
55.135. Revocation of Permit.
55.136. Disconnection of Service.

Section
55.137. Administrative Penalty.
55.138. Criminal Penalty.

SUBCHAPTER G. TELEPHONE SOLICITATION
55.151 to 55.153. Repealed.

SUBCHAPTER H. PAY TELEPHONES
55.171. Definition.
55.172. Limitation.
55.173. Registration.
55.1735. Charge for Pay Phone Access Line.
55.174. Prohibition on Charge for Certain Calls.
55.175. Charge for Local Calls.
55.176. Charge for 800-Type Calls.
55.177. Charge for Credit Card, Calling Card, or Operator-Assisted Calls.
55.178. Notice of Inability to Receive Calls.
55.179. Information Requirements.
55.180. Violations.

SUBCHAPTER I. DIRECTORY LISTINGS AND ASSISTANCE
55.201. Terms of Directory Listings and Assistance.
55.202. Directory Published by Telecommunications Utility.
55.203. Directory Published by Private Publisher.
55.204. Electronic Telephone Directory.

SUBCHAPTER J. TELECOMMUNICATIONS SERVICE BY CERTAIN PROVIDERS
55.251. Charge for Hotel or Motel Call.
55.252 900 Service Used By Probationers Or Parolees.
55.253. Telephone Prepaid Calling Services.

SUBCHAPTER K. SELECTION OF TELECOMMUNICATIONS UTILITIES
55.301. State Policy.
55.302. Commission Rules.
55.303. Verification of Change.
55.304. Unauthorized Change.
55.305. Corrective Action and Penalties.
55.306. Repeated and Reckless Violation.
55.307. Deceptive or Fraudulent Practice.
55.308. Consistency With Federal Law.

SUBCHAPTER A. GENERAL PROVISIONS

§ 55.001. General Standard

A public utility shall furnish service, instrumentalities, and facilities that are safe, adequate, efficient, and reasonable.

Acts 1997, 75th Leg., ch. 166, § 1, eff. Sept. 1, 1997.

§ 55.002. Commission Authority Concerning Standards

The commission, on its own motion or on complaint and after reasonable notice and hearing, may:

(1) adopt just and reasonable standards, classifications, rules, or practices a public utility must follow in furnishing a service;

(2) adopt adequate and reasonable standards for measuring a condition, including quantity and quality, relating to the furnishing of a service;

(3) adopt reasonable rules for examining, testing, and measuring a service; and

(4) adopt or approve reasonable rules, specifications, and standards to ensure the accuracy of equipment, including meters and instruments, used to measure a service.

Acts 1997, 75th Leg., ch. 166, § 1, eff. Sept. 1, 1997.

§ 55.003. Rule or Standard

(a) A public utility may not impose a rule except as provided by this title.

(b) A public utility may file with the commission a standard, classification, rule, or practice the utility follows.

(c) The standard, classification, rule, or practice continues in force until:

(1) amended by the utility; or

(2) changed by the commission as provided by this subtitle.

Acts 1997, 75th Leg., ch. 166, § 1, eff. Sept. 1, 1997.

§ 55.004. Local Exchange Company Rule or Practice Change

(a) To make a change in an incumbent local exchange company's tariffed rules or practices that does not affect the company's charges or rates, the company must file the proposed change with the commission at least 35 days before the effective date of the change. The commission may require the incumbent local exchange company to provide to ratepayers appropriate notice as determined by the commission.

(b) The commission, on complaint by an affected person or on its own motion and after reasonable notice, may hold a hearing to determine the propriety of a change proposed under this section. Pending the hearing and decision, the commission may suspend the change for not longer than 120 days after the date the change would otherwise be effective. The commission shall approve, deny, or modify the change before the period of suspension expires.

(c) In a proceeding under this section, the incumbent local exchange company has the burden of proving the proposed change:

(1) is in the public interest; and

(2) complies with this title.

Acts 1997, 75th Leg., ch. 166, § 1, eff. Sept. 1, 1997.

§ 55.005. Unreasonable Preference or Prejudice Concerning Service Prohibited

In providing a service to persons in a classification, a public utility may not:

(1) grant an unreasonable preference or advantage to a person in the classification; or

(2) subject a person in the classification to an unreasonable prejudice or disadvantage.

Acts 1997, 75th Leg., ch. 166, § 1, eff. Sept. 1, 1997.

§ 55.006. Discrimination and Restriction on Competition

A public utility may not:

(1) discriminate against a person who sells or leases equipment or performs services in competition with the public utility; or

(2) engage in a practice that tends to restrict or impair that competition.

Acts 1997, 75th Leg., ch. 166, § 1, eff. Sept. 1, 1997.

§ 55.007. Minimum Services

(a) The commission shall require a holder of a certificate of convenience and necessity or a certificate of operating authority to provide at the applicable tariff rate, if any, to each customer, regardless of race, national origin, income, or residence in an urban or rural area:

(1) single-party service;

(2) tone-dialing service;

(3) basic custom calling features;

(4) equal access for an interLATA interexchange carrier on a bona fide request; and

(5) digital switching capability in an exchange on customer request, provided by a digital switch in the exchange or by connection to a digital switch in another exchange.

(b) Notwithstanding Subsection (a), an electing incumbent local exchange company serving more than 175,000 but fewer than 1,500,000 access lines on January 1, 1995, shall install a digital switch in each central office that serves an exchange of fewer than 20,000 access lines.

(c) The commission may temporarily waive a requirement imposed by Subsection (a) or (b) on a showing of good cause.

(d) The commission may not consider the cost of implementing this section in determining whether an electing company is entitled to:

(1) a rate increase under Chapter 58 or 59; or

(2) increased universal service funds under Subchapter B, Chapter 56.[1]

(e) Expired.

Acts 1997, 75th Leg., ch. 166, § 1, eff. Sept. 1, 1997.

[1] V.T.C.A., Utilities Code § 56.021 et seq.

§ 55.008. Improvements in Service; Interconnecting Service

The commission, after notice and hearing, may:

(1) order a public utility to provide specified improvements in its service in a specified area if:

(A) service in the area is inadequate or substantially inferior to service in a comparable area; and

(B) requiring the company to provide the improved service is reasonable; or

(2) order two or more utilities to establish specified facilities for interconnecting service.

Acts 1997, 75th Leg., ch. 166, § 1, eff. Sept. 1, 1997.

§ 55.009. IntraLATA Calls

(a) If federal law prohibits a local exchange company in this state from providing interLATA telecommunications services, the local exchange companies in this state designated or de facto authorized to receive a "0-plus" or "1-plus" dialed intraLATA call are exclusively designated or authorized to receive such a call.

(b) A telecommunications utility operating under a certificate of operating authority or a service provider certificate of operating authority is de facto authorized to receive a "0-plus" or "1-plus" dialed intraLATA call on the date the utility receives its certificate, to the extent the utility is not restricted by Section 54.159.

(c) If federal law allows all local exchange companies to provide interLATA telecommunications services, the commission shall ensure that:

(1) a customer may designate a provider of the customer's choice to carry the customer's "0-plus" and "1-plus" dialed intraLATA calls; and

(2) equal access in the public network is implemented to allow the provider to carry those calls.

Acts 1997, 75th Leg., ch. 166, § 1, eff. Sept. 1, 1997.

§ 55.010. Billing for Service to the State

A telecommunications utility providing service to the state, including service to an agency in any branch of state government, may not impose a fee, a penalty, interest, or any other charge for delinquent payment of a bill for that service.

Acts 1997, 75th Leg., ch. 166, § 1, eff. Sept. 1, 1997.

§ 55.011. Notice of Identity of Interexchange Carrier

(a) A local exchange company shall print on the first page of each bill sent to a customer of the local exchange company the name of the customer's primary interexchange carrier if the company provides billing services for that carrier.

(b) The bill must contain instructions on how the customer can contact the commission if the customer believes that the named carrier is not the customer's primary interexchange carrier.

(c) The commission may, for good cause, waive the billing requirement prescribed by this section in exchanges served by local exchange companies serving not more than 31,000 access lines.

Added by Acts 1999, 76th Leg., ch. 62, § 18.04(b), eff. Sept. 1, 1999.

§ 55.012. Limitations on Discontinuance of Basic Local Telecommunications Service

(a) A provider of basic local telecommunications service may not discontinue that service because of nonpayment by a residential customer of charges for long distance service. Payment shall first be allocated to basic local telecommunications service.

(b) For purposes of allocating payment in this section, if the provider of basic local telecommunications service bundles its basic local telecommunications service with long distance service or any other service and provides a discount for the basic local telecommunications service because of that bundling, the rate of basic local telecommunications service shall be the rate the provider charges for stand-alone basic local telecommunications service.

(c) Notwithstanding Subsection (a), the commission shall adopt and implement rules, not later than January 1, 2000, to prevent customer abuse of the protections afforded by this section. The rules must include:

(1) provisions requiring a provider of basic local telecommunications service to offer and implement, at the request and expense of a long distance service provider, toll blocking capability to limit a customer's ability to incur additional charges for long distance services after nonpayment for long distance services; and

(2) provisions regarding fraudulent activity in response to which a provider may discontinue a residential customer's basic local telecommunications service.

(d) Notwithstanding any other provision of this title, the commission has all jurisdiction necessary to establish a maximum price that an incumbent local exchange company may charge a long distance service provider to initiate the toll blocking capability required to be offered under the rules adopted under Subsection (c). The maximum price established under this subsection shall be observed by all providers of basic local telecommunications service in the incumbent local exchange company's certificated service area. Notwithstanding Sections 52.102 and 52.152, the commission has all jurisdiction necessary to enforce this section.

Added by Acts 1999, 76th Leg., ch. 1579, § 5, eff. Aug. 30, 1999.

§ 55.013. Limitations on Discontinuance of Basic Local Telecommunications Service

(a) A provider of basic local telecommunications service may not discontinue that service because of nonpayment by a residential customer of charges for long distance service. Payment shall first be allocated to basic local telecommunications service.

(b) For purposes of allocating payment in this section, if the provider of basic local telecommunications service bundles its basic local telecommunications service with long distance service or any other service and provides a discount for the basic local telecommunications service because of that bundling, the rate of basic local telecommunications service shall be the rate the provider charges for stand-alone basic local telecommunications service.

(c) Notwithstanding Subsection (a), the commission shall adopt and implement rules, not later than January 1, 2000, to prevent customer abuse of the protections afforded by this section. The rules must include:

(1) provisions requiring a provider of basic local telecommunications service to offer and implement toll blocking capability to limit a customer's ability to incur additional charges for long distance services after nonpayment for long distance services; and

(2) provisions regarding fraudulent activity in response to which a provider may discontinue a residential customer's basic local telecommunications service.

(d) Notwithstanding any other provision of this title, the commission has all jurisdiction necessary to establish a maximum price that an incumbent local exchange company may charge a long distance service provider to initiate the toll blocking capability required to be offered under the rules adopted under Subsection (c). The maximum price established under this subsection shall be observed by all providers of basic local telecommunications service in the incumbent local exchange company's certificated service area. Notwithstanding Sections 52.102 and 52.152, the commission has all jurisdiction necessary to enforce this section.

(e) A provider of basic local exchange telecommunications service shall comply with the requirements of this section not later than March 1, 2000.

Added by Acts 1999, 76th Leg., ch. 1212, § 19, eff. Sept. 1, 1999.

§ 55.014. Provision of Advanced Telecommunications Services

(a) In this section, "advanced service" means any telecommunications service other than residential or business basic local exchange telephone service, caller identification service, and customer calling features.

(b) This section applies to a company electing under Chapter 58 or a company that holds a certificate of operating authority or service provider certificate of operating authority.

(c) Notwithstanding any other provision of this title, beginning September 1, 2001, a company to which this section applies that provides advanced telecommunications services within the company's urban service areas, shall, on a bona fide retail request for those services, provide in rural areas of this state served by the company advanced telecommunications services that are reasonably comparable to the advanced services provided in urban areas. The company shall offer the advanced telecommunications services:

(1) at prices, terms, and conditions that are reasonably comparable to the prices, terms, and conditions for similar advanced services provided by the company in urban areas; and

(2) within 15 months after the bona fide request for those advanced services.

(d) Notwithstanding any other provision of this title, a company to which this section applies shall, on a bona fide retail request for those services, offer caller identification service and custom calling features in rural areas served by the company. The company shall offer the services:

(1) at prices, terms, and conditions reasonably comparable to the company's prices, terms, and conditions for similar services in urban areas; and

(2) within 15 months after the bona fide request for those services.

(e) This section may not be construed to require a company to:

(1) begin providing services in a rural area in which the company does not provide local exchange telephone service; or

(2) provide a service in a rural area of this state unless the company provides the service in urban areas of this state.

(f) For purposes of this section, a company to which this section applies is considered to provide services in urban areas of this state if the company provides services in a municipality with a population of more than 190,000.

(g) Notwithstanding any other provision of this title, the commission has all jurisdiction necessary to enforce this section.

Added by Acts 1999, 76th Leg., ch. 1212, § 20, eff. Sept. 1, 1999.

§ 55.015. Lifeline Service

(a) The commission shall adopt rules prohibiting a certificated provider of local exchange telephone service from discontinuing basic network services listed in Section 58.051 to a consumer who receives lifeline service because of nonpayment by the consumer of charges for other services billed by the provider, including interexchange telecommunications service.

(b) The commission shall adopt rules providing for automatic enrollment to receive lifeline service for eligible consumers. The Texas Department of Human Services, on request of the commission, shall assist in the adoption and implementation of those rules. The commission and the Texas Department of Human Services shall enter into a memorandum of understanding establishing the respective duties of the commission and department in relation to the automatic enrollment.

(b–1) The commission shall adopt rules requiring certificated providers of local exchange telephone service to implement procedures to ensure that all consumers are clearly informed both orally and in writing of the existence of the lifeline service program when they request or initiate service or change service locations or providers. On or before June 1, 2006, the commission shall enter into a memorandum of understanding with the Health and Human Services Commission, and, to the maximum extent feasible, housing authorities in the principal cities of each metropolitan statistical area, to improve enrollment rates in the lifeline service program.

(c) A certificated provider of local exchange telephone service may block a lifeline service participant's access to all interexchange telecommunications service except toll-free numbers when the participant owes an outstanding amount for that service. The provider shall remove the block without additional cost to the participant on payment of the outstanding amount.

(d) A certificated provider of local exchange telephone service shall offer a consumer who applies for or receives lifeline service the option of blocking all toll calls or, if technically capable, placing a limit on the amount of toll calls. The provider may not charge the consumer an administrative charge or other additional amount for the blocking service.

(d–1) A certificated provider of local exchange telephone service shall provide access to lifeline service to a customer whose income is not more than 150 percent of the applicable income level established by the federal poverty guidelines or in whose household resides a person who receives or has a child who receives:

(1) Medicaid;

(2) food stamps;

(3) Supplemental Security Income;

(4) federal public housing assistance;

(5) Low Income Home Energy Assistance Program (LIHEAP) assistance; or

(6) health benefits coverage under the state child health plan under Chapter 62, Health and Safety Code.

(d–2) A certificated provider of local exchange telephone service shall provide consumers who apply for or receive lifeline service access to available vertical services or custom calling features, including caller ID, call waiting, and call blocking, at the same price as other consumers. Lifeline discounts shall only apply to that portion of the bill that is for basic network service.

(e) In this section, "lifeline service" means a retail local service offering described by 47 C.F.R. Section 54.401(a), as amended.

Added by Acts 1999, 76th Leg., ch. 1212, § 21, eff. Sept. 1, 1999. Amended by Acts 2005, 79th Leg., 2nd C.S., ch. 2, § 9, eff. Sept. 1, 2005.

§ 55.016. Telecommunications Billing

(a) The proliferation of charges for separate services, products, surcharges, fees, and taxes on a bill for telecommunications products or services has increased the complexity of those bills to such an extent that in some cases the bills have become difficult for customers to understand.

(b) A bill from a local exchange company for telecommunications products or services should be consistent with providing customers sufficient information about the charges included in the bill to understand the basis and source of the charges.

(c) To the extent permitted by law, a monthly bill from a local exchange company for local exchange telephone service shall clearly identify all charges including basic local service charges, fees, carrier's charges, assessments, surcharges, optional services, and taxes.

(d) Local exchange carriers shall annually file a copy of that portion of their bill that has not been previously approved by the commission for compliance review with this section.

(e) The commission shall have all necessary authority to enforce this section.

Added by Acts 1999, 76th Leg., ch. 1212, § 18, eff. Mar. 1, 2000. Amended by Acts 2001, 77th Leg., ch. 963, § 1, eff. June 14, 2001. Renumbered from V.T.C.A., Utilities Code § 55.012 by Acts 2001, 77th Leg., ch. 1420, § 21.001(110), eff. Sept. 1, 2001.

§ 55.017. Identification Required

(a) A representative of a telecommunications provider or a video or cable service provider that has an easement in or a right-of-way over or through real property must show proof of identification to the owner of the real property when entering the property if requested by the owner.

(b) This section does not apply to regularly scheduled service readings or examinations.

Added by Acts 2005, 79th Leg., 2nd C.S., ch. 2, § 10, eff. Sept. 1, 2005.

SUBCHAPTER B. EXTENDED AREA SERVICE

§ 55.021. Extended Area Service

After notice and a hearing, the commission may order one or more local exchange companies that are dominant carriers to provide:

(1) mandatory extended area service in accordance with Section 55.022; or

(2) optional extended area service in accordance with Section 55.023.

Acts 1997, 75th Leg., ch. 166, § 1, eff. Sept. 1, 1997.

§ 55.022. Mandatory Service

The commission may order mandatory extended area service in a specified metropolitan area if:

(1) there is a sufficient community of interest in the area; and

(2) the company can reasonably provide the service.

Acts 1997, 75th Leg., ch. 166, § 1, eff. Sept. 1, 1997.

§ 55.023. Optional Extended Area Service

(a) The commission may order optional extended area service in a specified calling area if:

(1) each affected company and the representatives of at least one political subdivision in the proposed calling area agree to the service; and

(2) the proposed common calling area has a single, continuous boundary.

(b) The commission may not adopt rules that diminish in any manner the ability of an affected company or a political subdivision to enter into joint agreements for optional extended area service under this section.

(c) In this section, "political subdivision" means:

(1) a county;

(2) a municipality; or

(3) an unincorporated town or village that has 275 or more access lines.

Acts 1997, 75th Leg., ch. 166, § 1, eff. Sept. 1, 1997.

§ 55.024. Charge for Extended Area Service

(a) An incumbent local exchange company that provides mandatory two-way extended area service to customers shall impose for that service a separately stated monthly charge of $3.50 a line for a residential customer and $7 a line for a business customer if, on September 1, 1995, the company:

(1) served more than 1,000,000 access lines in this state; and

(2) imposed a separately stated monthly charge for mandatory two-way extended area service of more than $3.50 a line for a residential customer and more than $7 a line for a business customer.

(b) The company shall recover all costs incurred and all loss of revenue that results from imposition of the rates prescribed by Subsection (a) in the manner prescribed by Section 55.048(c).

(c) The rate limitation prescribed by Subsection (a) does not apply to a separately stated monthly charge for:

(1) extended area service in or into a metropolitan exchange; or

(2) extended metropolitan service.

Acts 1997, 75th Leg., ch. 166, § 1, eff. Sept. 1, 1997.

§ 55.025. Hunting Service

(a) A local exchange company shall make available, at a reasonable tariffed rate, hunting service from local exchange lines to extended metropolitan service lines.

(b) The company may not require a customer to purchase additional extended metropolitan service to obtain the hunting service.

Acts 1997, 75th Leg., ch. 166, § 1, eff. Sept. 1, 1997.

§ 55.026. New Orders Prohibited After Certain Date

On or after September 1, 2011, the commission may not require a telecommunications provider to provide mandatory or optional extended area service to additional metropolitan areas or calling areas.

Added by Acts 2011, 82nd Leg., ch. 98 (S.B. 980), § 8, eff. Sept. 1, 2011.

SUBCHAPTER C. EXPANDED TOLL-FREE LOCAL CALLING AREAS

§ 55.041. Definitions

In this subchapter, "metropolitan exchange," "local calling area of a metropolitan exchange," and "exchange" have the meanings and boundaries assigned by the commission on September 1, 1993.

Acts 1997, 75th Leg., ch. 166, § 1, eff. Sept. 1, 1997.

§ 55.042. Contiguous Exchange

The commission may expand a toll-free local calling area into an exchange that is not in a metropolitan exchange but is in a local calling area that is contiguous to a metropolitan exchange that the commission determines has a community of interest with the exchange for which a petition is filed under this subchapter.

Acts 1997, 75th Leg., ch. 166, § 1, eff. Sept. 1, 1997.

§ 55.043. Splitting Exchanges Prohibited

Notwithstanding any other provision of this subchapter, the commission may not split a petitioning or requested exchange in establishing a toll-free local calling area.

Acts 1997, 75th Leg., ch. 166, § 1, eff. Sept. 1, 1997.

§ 55.044. Exemption

(a) The commission may not require an incumbent local exchange company serving the petitioning or requested exchange to expand the company's toll-free local calling area under this subchapter if:

(1) the incumbent local exchange company has fewer than 10,000 access lines;

(2) the petitioning or requested exchange is served by a telephone cooperative corporation;

(3) extended area service or extended metropolitan service is available between the exchanges;

(4) the petitioning or requested exchange is a metropolitan exchange; or

(5) the commission determines that the company has shown that to serve the area is not geographically or technologically feasible.

(b) To promote the wide dispersion of pay telephones, the commission may:

(1) exempt pay telephones from this subchapter; or

(2) change the rates charged for calls from pay telephones.

Acts 1997, 75th Leg., ch. 166, § 1, eff. Sept. 1, 1997.

§ 55.045. Eligibility to Petition

The telephone subscribers of an incumbent local exchange company exchange that serves not more than 10,000 access lines may petition the commission for expansion of the company's toll-free local calling area if:

(1) the petitioning exchange's central switching office is located within 22 miles, using vertical and horizontal geographic coordinates, of the central switching office of the exchange requested for expanded local calling service; or

(2) the petitioning exchange's central office is not more than 50 miles from the central office of the exchange requested for expanded local calling service and the exchanges share a community of interest.

Acts 1997, 75th Leg., ch. 166, § 1, eff. Sept. 1, 1997.

§ 55.046. Petition Requirements

(a) A petition under this subchapter must be signed by a number of the exchange's subscribers equal at least to the lesser of 100 of the exchange's subscribers or five percent of the exchange's subscribers.

(b) An exchange that petitions under Section 55.045(2) must demonstrate in the petition that the exchange shares a community of interest with the requested exchange.

(c) For purposes of this section, the relationships between exchanges that create a community of interest include:

(1) a relationship because of schools, hospitals, local governments, or business centers; or

(2) other relationships that would make the unavailability of expanded local calling service a hardship for the residents of the area.

Acts 1997, 75th Leg., ch. 166, § 1, eff. Sept. 1, 1997.

§ 55.047. Balloting and Consideration

(a) If the commission receives a petition that complies with this subchapter, the commission shall order the incumbent local exchange company to provide ballots to the subscribers in the petitioning exchange.

(b) The commission shall consider the request for expansion of the toll-free local calling area if at least 70 percent of the subscribers who vote do so in favor of the expansion.

(c) The commission by rule shall provide for an expedited hearing on the issue of expansion.

Acts 1997, 75th Leg., ch. 166, § 1, eff. Sept. 1, 1997.

§ 55.048. Charges

(a) The incumbent local exchange company shall recover all costs incurred and all loss of revenue from an expansion of a toll-free local calling area under this subchapter through a request other than a revenue requirement showing by imposing a monthly fee under Subsection (b) or (c), or both.

(b) The company may impose a monthly fee against each residential and business customer in the petitioning exchange. The fee may not exceed $3.50 a line for a residential customer and $7 a line for a business customer unless the customer's toll-free local calling area includes more than five exchanges. The company may impose an additional monthly fee of $1.50 for each exchange in excess of five. This subsection applies regardless of the number of petitions required to obtain access to the exchanges. A company may impose a fee under this subsection only until the company's next general rate case.

(c) The company may impose a monthly fee against each of the company's local exchange service customers in this state. This fee is in addition to the company's local exchange rates.

(d) The company may not recover regulatory case expenses under this subchapter by imposing a surcharge on the subscribers of the petitioning exchange.

Acts 1997, 75th Leg., ch. 166, § 1, eff. Sept. 1, 1997.

§ 55.049. Expansion Prohibited After Certain Date

On or after September 1, 2011, the commission may not order an expansion of a toll-free local calling area.

Added by Acts 2011, 82nd Leg., ch. 98 (S.B. 980), § 9, eff. Sept. 1, 2011.

SUBCHAPTER D. OPERATOR SERVICE PROVIDERS

§ 55.081. Definition

In this subchapter, "operator service" means a service using live operator or automated operator functions to handle telephone service such as toll calling using collect, third-number billing, and calling card services. The term does not include a call for which the called party has arranged to be billed (800 service).

Acts 1997, 75th Leg., ch. 166, § 1, eff. Sept. 1, 1997.

§ 55.082. Applicability

Except as provided by Section 55.088, this subchapter applies only to a telecommunications utility that is not a dominant carrier.

Acts 1997, 75th Leg., ch. 166, § 1, eff. Sept. 1, 1997.

§ 55.083. Rules and Procedures

(a) The commission may adopt rules and establish procedures to enforce and implement this subchapter.

(b) A rule adopted under this subchapter must be nondiscriminatory and designed to promote competition that facilitates consumer choice.

Acts 1997, 75th Leg., ch. 166, § 1, eff. Sept. 1, 1997.

§ 55.084. Information Displayed on Public Use Telephone

(a) An operator service provider shall furnish each entity with which it contracts to provide operator service a sticker, card, or other form of information approved by the commission for each telephone that:

(1) has access to the service; and

(2) is intended for use by the public.

(b) The commission may grant the owner of a telephone approval for an alternative form of information.

(c) The information must state:

(1) the provider's name;

(2) that the operator service provider will provide rate information on a caller's request;

(3) that a caller, on the caller's request, will be informed of the method of access to the local exchange carrier operator; and

(4) that a complaint about the service may be made to the provider or to the commission at the designated telephone number.

(d) The operator service provider shall by contract require an entity receiving information to display the information on or near each telephone for which the operator service provider is required to furnish the information.

Acts 1997, 75th Leg., ch. 166, § 1, eff. Sept. 1, 1997.

§ 55.085. Connection Announcement

Before connecting a call, the operator service provider shall:

(1) announce the provider's name; and

(2) at the caller's request, quote the rate and any other fee or surcharge that applies to the call and is charged by the provider.

Acts 1997, 75th Leg., ch. 166, § 1, eff. Sept. 1, 1997.

§ 55.086. Information Required on Access to Local Exchange Company Operator

(a) An operator service provider, on a caller's request, shall inform the caller of the method of access to the local exchange carrier operator serving the exchange from which the call is made.

(b) A charge may not be made for information provided under this section.

Acts 1997, 75th Leg., ch. 166, § 1, eff. Sept. 1, 1997.

§ 55.087. Access to Local Exchange Company and Other Utilities Required

(a) The commission by rule shall require an operator service provider to include in its contract with each entity through which it provides operator service a provision that requires each telephone subscribed to its service to allow access to:

(1) the local exchange carrier operator serving the exchange from which the call is made; and

(2) other telecommunications utilities.

(b) To prevent fraudulent use of its service, an operator service provider or an entity through which it provides operator service may block the access described by Subsection (a) by obtaining a waiver for this purpose from the commission or the Federal Communications Commission. The commission by rule shall establish the procedure and criteria for obtaining a waiver from the commission.

Acts 1997, 75th Leg., ch. 166, § 1, eff. Sept. 1, 1997.

§ 55.088. Access to Live Operator Required

(a) A dominant or nondominant telecommunications utility that provides operator service shall ensure that a caller has access to a live operator at the beginning of a live or mechanized operator-assisted call through a method designed to be easily and clearly understandable and accessible to the caller.

(b) A telecommunications utility described by Subsection (a) shall submit to the commission for review the method by which the utility will provide access to a live operator.

(c) This section applies regardless of the method by which the telecommunications utility provides operator service.

(d) This section does not apply to a telephone located in a prison or jail facility.

Acts 1997, 75th Leg., ch. 166, § 1, eff. Sept. 1, 1997.

§ 55.089. Commission May Investigate and Act on Violation

(a) If the commission determines that an operator service provider has violated or is about to violate this subchapter, the commission, after notice and evidentiary hearing, may take action to stop, correct, or prevent the violation.

(b) The commission may investigate a complaint that it receives concerning an operator service.

Acts 1997, 75th Leg., ch. 166, § 1, eff. Sept. 1, 1997.

SUBCHAPTER E. CALLER IDENTIFICATION SERVICE

§ 55.101. Definitions

In this subchapter:

(1) "Caller identification information" means any information that may be used to identify the specific originating number or originating location of a wire or electronic communication transmitted by a telephone, including the telephone listing number or the name of the customer from whose telephone a telephone number is dialed.

(2) "Caller identification service" means a service that provides caller identification information to a device that can display the information.

(3) "Per-call blocking" means a telecommunications service that prevents caller identification information from being transmitted to a called party on an individual call when the calling party affirmatively acts to prevent the transmission.

(4) "Per-line blocking" means a telecommunications service that prevents caller identification information from being transmitted to a called party on each call unless the calling party affirmatively acts to permit the transmission.

Acts 1997, 75th Leg., ch. 166, § 1, eff. Sept. 1, 1997.

§ 55.102. Applicability

(a) This subchapter applies only to the provision of caller identification service.

(b) This subchapter does not apply to:

(1) an identification service that is used in a limited system, including a central office based PBX-type system;

(2) information that is used on a public agency's emergency telephone line or on a line that receives the primary emergency telephone number (911);

(3) information exchanged between telecommunications utilities, enhanced service providers, or other entities that is necessary for the setting up, processing, transmission, or billing of telecommunications or related services;

(4) information provided in compliance with applicable law or legal process; or

(5) an identification service provided in connection with a 700, 800, or 900 access code telecommunications service.

Acts 1997, 75th Leg., ch. 166, § 1, eff. Sept. 1, 1997.

§ 55.103. Provision of Service

(a) A telecommunications utility may offer caller identification services under this subchapter only if the utility obtains written authorization from the commission.

(b) A commercial mobile service provider may offer caller identification services in accordance with Sections 55.104, 55.105, 55.106, 55.1065, and 55.107.

Acts 1997, 75th Leg., ch. 166, § 1, eff. Sept. 1, 1997. Amended by Acts 1999, 76th Leg., ch. 62, § 18.05(a), eff. Sept. 1, 1999.

§ 55.104. Use of Information

(a) A person may not use a caller identification service to compile and sell specific local call information without the affirmative approval of the originating telephone customer.

(b) This section does not prohibit a provider of caller identification service from:

(1) verifying network performance or testing the caller identification service;

(2) compiling, using, and disclosing aggregate caller identification information; or

(3) complying with applicable law or legal process.

Acts 1997, 75th Leg., ch. 166, § 1, eff. Sept. 1, 1997.

§ 55.105. Per-Call Blocking

Except as provided by Section 55.1065, the commission shall require that a provider of caller identification service offer free per-call blocking to each telephone subscriber in the specific area in which the service is offered.

Acts 1997, 75th Leg., ch. 166, § 1, eff. Sept. 1, 1997. Amended by Acts 1999, 76th Leg., ch. 62, § 18.05(b), eff. Sept. 1, 1999.

§ 55.106. Per-Line Blocking

(a) Except as provided by Section 55.1065, the commission shall require that a provider of caller identification service offer free per-line blocking to a particular customer if the commission receives from the customer written certification that the customer has a compelling need for per-line blocking.

(b) A provider who is ordered to offer per-line blocking under this section shall notify the customer by mail of the date the blocking will begin.

(c) If a customer removes and later reinstates the per-line block, the provider may assess a service order charge in an amount approved by the commission for the provider's administrative expenses relating to the reinstatement.

(d) The commission may impose a fee or assessment on a provider in an amount sufficient to cover the additional expenses the commission incurs in implementing the customer certification provisions of this section.

(e) Information received under this section by the commission or by a provider is confidential and may be used only to administer this section.

Acts 1997, 75th Leg., ch. 166, § 1, eff. Sept. 1, 1997. Amended by Acts 1999, 76th Leg., ch. 62, § 18.05(c), eff. Sept. 1, 1999.

§ 55.1065. Repealed by Acts 2001, 77th Leg., ch. 1429, § 3, eff. June 15, 2001

§ 55.107. Limitation on Commission Authority

The commission may prescribe in relation to blocking only a requirement authorized by Sections 55.105, 55.106, and 55.1065.

Acts 1997, 75th Leg., ch. 166, § 1, eff. Sept. 1, 1997. Amended by Acts 1999, 76th Leg., ch. 62, § 18.05(e), eff. Sept. 1, 1999.

§ 55.108. Expired

§ 55.109. Implementation of Panel Recommendations

The commission may implement the recommendations of the Caller ID Consumer Education Panel and interested parties to the extent consistent with the public interest.

Acts 1997, 75th Leg., ch. 166, § 1, eff. Sept. 1, 1997.

§ 55.110. Report of Blocking Failure

(a) A provider of caller ID services who becomes aware of the failure of per-call or per-line blocking to block identification of a customer shall report that failure to the commission, the Caller ID Consumer Education Panel, and the customer whose identification was not blocked.

(b) The provider shall make a reasonable effort to notify the customer within 24 hours after the provider becomes aware of the failure. The provider is not required to notify the customer if the customer reported the failure.

(c) In this section, "caller ID service" means a service that permits the called party to determine the identity, telephone number, or address of the calling party. The term does not include 911 services.

Acts 1997, 75th Leg., ch. 166, § 1, eff. Sept. 1, 1997.

SUBCHAPTER F. AUTOMATIC DIAL ANNOUNCING DEVICES

§ 55.121. Definition

In this subchapter, "automated dial announcing device" means automated equipment used for telephone solicitation or collection that can:

(1) store telephone numbers to be called or produce numbers to be called through use of a random or sequential number generator; and

(2) convey, alone or in conjunction with other equipment, a prerecorded or synthesized voice message to the number called without the use of a live operator.

Acts 1997, 75th Leg., ch. 166, § 1, eff. Sept. 1, 1997.

§ 55.122. Exemptions

This subchapter does not apply to the use of an automated dial announcing device:

(1) to make a call relating to an emergency or a public service under a program developed or approved by the emergency management coordinator of the county in which the call is received; or

(2) by a public or private primary or secondary school system to locate or account for a truant student.

Acts 1997, 75th Leg., ch. 166, § 1, eff. Sept. 1, 1997.

§ 55.123. Notice of Use of Device to Telecommunications Utility

A person may not use an automated dial announcing device to make a telephone call in which the device plays a recorded message when the connection is completed unless the person gives to each telecommunications utility over whose system the device is to be used written notice specifying the type of device to be used.

Acts 1997, 75th Leg., ch. 166, § 1, eff. Sept. 1, 1997.

§ 55.124. Random or Sequential Number Calling

A person may not use an automated dial announcing device for random number dialing or to dial numbers determined by successively increasing or decreasing integers if the person uses the device to make a telephone call in which the device plays a recorded message when the connection is completed.

Acts 1997, 75th Leg., ch. 166, § 1, eff. Sept. 1, 1997.

§ 55.125. Hours When Use Prohibited

(a) A person may not use an automated dial announcing device to make a telephone solicitation call terminating in this state in which the device plays a recorded message when the connection is completed if the call is made:

(1) before noon or after 9 p.m. on a Sunday; or

(2) before 9 a.m. or after 9 p.m. on a weekday or a Saturday.

(b) A person may not use an automated dial announcing device to make a telephone collection call terminating in this state in which the device plays a recorded message when the connection is completed if the call is made at an hour at which collection calls are prohibited under the federal Fair Debt Collection Practices Act (15 U.S.C. Section 1692 et seq.).

Acts 1997, 75th Leg., ch. 166, § 1, eff. Sept. 1, 1997.

§ 55.126. Device Disconnection

A person may not use an automated dial announcing device to make a telephone call in which the device plays a recorded message when the connection is completed unless the device disconnects from the called person's line not later than five seconds after the call is terminated by either party. If the device cannot disconnect during that period, a live operator must introduce the call and receive the called person's oral consent before beginning a prerecorded or synthesized voice message.

Acts 1997, 75th Leg., ch. 166, § 1, eff. Sept. 1, 1997. Amended by Acts 1999, 76th Leg., ch. 667, § 2, eff. Sept. 1, 1999.

§ 55.127. Contents of Recorded Message

(a) A person may not use an automated dial announcing device to make a telephone call in which the device plays a recorded message when the connection is completed unless the recorded message states during the first 30 seconds of the call:

(1) the nature of the call;

(2) the identity of the person, company, or organization making the call; and

(3) the telephone number from which the call is made.

(b) In addition to the requirements prescribed by Subsection (a), a call during which a cross-promotion or reference to a pay-per-call information service is made must include a statement of:

(1) the fact that a caller who makes a call to a pay-per-call information service's telephone number will be charged for that call;

(2) the amount of the flat-rate or cost-per-minute charge the caller will incur or the amount of both if both charges will be incurred; and

(3) the estimated amount of time required to receive all the information offered by the service during a call.

(c) Subsection (a) does not apply to the use of a device if the device is used:

(1) for debt collection purposes in compliance with applicable federal law and regulations; and

(2) by a live operator for automated dialing or hold announcement purposes.

(d) In this section, "pay-per-call information service" means a service that routinely delivers, for a predetermined and sometimes time-sensitive fee, a prerecorded or live message or interactive program after the caller dials a specified 900 or 976 number.

Acts 1997, 75th Leg., ch. 166, § 1, eff. Sept. 1, 1997.

§ 55.128. Duration of Recorded Message

A person may not use an automated dial announcing device to make for solicitation purposes a telephone call in which the device plays a recorded message when the connection is completed unless:

(1) the recorded message is shorter than 30 seconds; or

(2) the device has the technical capacity to:

(A) recognize a telephone answering device on the called person's line; and

(B) terminate the call within 30 seconds.

Acts 1997, 75th Leg., ch. 166, § 1, eff. Sept. 1, 1997. Amended by Acts 1999, 76th Leg., ch. 62, § 18.05(f), eff. Sept. 1, 1999.

§ 55.129. Permit Required

A person may not use an automated dial announcing device to make a telephone call in which the device plays a recorded message when the connection is completed unless the person has a permit under Section 55.130.

Acts 1997, 75th Leg., ch. 166, § 1, eff. Sept. 1, 1997.

§ 55.130. Permit

(a) A person may not use an automated dial announcing device without a permit issued by the commission.

(b) An applicant for an original permit must submit to the commission an application on a form that:

(1) is prescribed by the commission; and

(2) contains:

(A) the telephone number of each automated dial announcing device that the person will use; and

(B) the physical address from which each automated dial announcing device will operate.

(c) An original permit is valid for one year and may be renewed annually by filing with the commission the information required by Subsection (b)(2).

(d) An application for an original permit or a filing required for the renewal of the permit must be accompanied by the appropriate fee prescribed by Section 55.131.

(e) In determining whether to deny an application for an original permit or renewal of the permit, the commission shall consider the compliance record of the owner or operator of the automated dial announcing device and may deny the application based on that record.

Acts 1997, 75th Leg., ch. 166, § 1, eff. Sept. 1, 1997.

§ 55.131. Permit Fee

(a) The commission shall prescribe a fee for an original permit or renewal of a permit.

(b) The amount of the original permit fee must be reasonable and cover the enforcement cost to the commission but may not exceed $500.

(c) The fee for renewal of a permit may not exceed $100.

Acts 1997, 75th Leg., ch. 166, § 1, eff. Sept. 1, 1997.

§ 55.132. Notification of Change

(a) The owner or operator of an automated dial announcing device shall notify the commission if the telephone number of the device or the physical address from which the device operates changes.

(b) The owner or operator shall give the notice by certified mail not later than the 48th hour before the hour the device begins operating with the new telephone number or at the new address.

(c) If the owner or operator of a device fails to give notice as required by Subsection (b), the person's permit is invalid.

Acts 1997, 75th Leg., ch. 166, § 1, eff. Sept. 1, 1997.

§ 55.133. Notification of Local Exchange Company

The commission shall provide to a local exchange company on request a copy of a permit issued under this subchapter and of any change relating to the permit.

Acts 1997, 75th Leg., ch. 166, § 1, eff. Sept. 1, 1997.

§ 55.134. Complaints and Enforcement

(a) The commission shall:

(1) investigate complaints relating to the use of an automated dial announcing device; and

(2) enforce this subchapter.

(b) A local exchange company that receives a complaint relating to the use of an automated dial announcing device shall send the complaint to the commission. The commission by rule shall prescribe the procedures and requirements for sending a complaint to the commission.

Acts 1997, 75th Leg., ch. 166, § 1, eff. Sept. 1, 1997.

§ 55.135. Revocation of Permit

The commission may revoke a person's permit if the person fails to comply with this subchapter.

Acts 1997, 75th Leg., ch. 166, § 1, eff. Sept. 1, 1997.

§ 55.136. Disconnection of Service

(a) If the commission or a court determines that a person has violated this subchapter, the commission or court shall require a telecommunications utility to disconnect service to the person.

(b) The telecommunications utility may reconnect service to the person only on a determination by the commission that the person will comply with this subchapter.

(c) Not later than the third day before the date of the disconnection, the telecommunications utility shall give notice to the person using the device of its intent to disconnect service. However, if the device is causing network congestion or blockage, the notice may be given on the day before the date of disconnection.

(d) A telecommunications utility, without an order by the commission or a court, may disconnect or refuse to connect service to a person using or intending to use an automated dial announcing device if the utility determines that the device would cause or is causing network harm.

Acts 1997, 75th Leg., ch. 166, § 1, eff. Sept. 1, 1997.

§ 55.137. Administrative Penalty

(a) The commission may impose an administrative penalty against a person who owns or operates an automated dial announcing device in violation of this subchapter or a commission rule or order.

(b) The penalty for a violation may be in an amount not to exceed $1,000 for each day or portion of a day during which the device operates in violation of this subchapter or a commission rule or order.

(c) The administrative penalty is civil in nature and is in addition to any other penalty provided by law.

(d) The commission by rule shall prescribe the procedures for assessing an administrative penalty under this section. The procedures must require proper notice and hearing in accordance with Chapter 2001, Government Code.

(e) A person may appeal the final order of the commission under Chapter 2001, Government Code. The substantial evidence rule applies on appeal.

(f) The proceeds of administrative penalties collected under this section shall be deposited to the credit of the commission. The commission shall use the proceeds to enforce this subchapter.

Acts 1997, 75th Leg., ch. 166, § 1, eff. Sept. 1, 1997. Amended by Acts 1999, 76th Leg., ch. 62, § 18.05(g), eff. Sept. 1, 1999.

§ 55.138. Criminal Penalty

(a) A person commits an offense if the person owns or operates an automated dial announcing device that the person knows is operating in violation of this subchapter.

(b) An offense under this section is a Class A misdemeanor.

Acts 1997, 75th Leg., ch. 166, § 1, eff. Sept. 1, 1997.

SUBCHAPTER G. TELEPHONE SOLICITATION

§§ 55.151 to 55.153. Repealed by Acts 2001, 77th Leg., ch. 1429, § 3, eff. June 15, 2001.

SUBCHAPTER H. PAY TELEPHONES

§ 55.171. Definition

In this subchapter, "provider" means an entity that provides pay telephone service, including:

(1) an incumbent local exchange company; and

(2) a subscriber to a customer-owned pay telephone service.

Acts 1997, 75th Leg., ch. 166, § 1, eff. Sept. 1, 1997.

§ 55.172. Limitation

This subchapter prescribes the limits of:

(1) the right of a provider to set the provider's rates and charges for pay telephone services; and

(2) the commission's authority over the pay telephone service rates of an incumbent local exchange company.

Acts 1997, 75th Leg., ch. 166, § 1, eff. Sept. 1, 1997.

§ 55.173. Registration

(a) A person may not provide pay telephone service in this state unless the person is registered with the commission.

(b) This section does not apply to a provider who holds a certificate of convenience and necessity.

Acts 1997, 75th Leg., ch. 166, § 1, eff. Sept. 1, 1997.

§ 55.1735. Charge for Pay Phone Access Line

The charge or surcharge a local exchange company imposes for an access line used to provide pay telephone service in an exchange may not exceed the amount of the charge or surcharge the company imposes for an access line used for regular business purposes in that exchange.

Added by Acts 2005, 79th Leg., 2nd C.S., ch. 2, § 11, eff. Sept. 1, 2005.

§ 55.174. Prohibition on Charge for Certain Calls

A provider may not charge a person making a call on a pay telephone for:

(1) local directory assistance; or

(2) a call made under Chapter 771 or 772, Health and Safety Code.

Acts 1997, 75th Leg., ch. 166, § 1, eff. Sept. 1, 1997.

§ 55.175. Charge for Local Calls

(a) The commission shall establish the limit on the amount a provider may charge for a pay telephone coin sent-paid call in the local exchange company's toll-free calling area.

(b) The commission may establish a statewide ceiling on the amount a provider may charge for a local pay telephone call that is:

(1) collect;

(2) operator assisted; or

(3) paid by credit card or calling card.

(c) The commission may not establish the ceiling under Subsection (b) at an amount that is less than the applicable local rates for such a call imposed by any of the four largest interexchange telecommunications carriers operating in this state.

Acts 1997, 75th Leg., ch. 166, § 1, eff. Sept. 1, 1997.

§ 55.176. Charge for 800-Type Calls

(a) A provider may charge at a pay telephone a fee of not more than 25 cents for initiating an 800-type call.

(b) A provider may impose the fee only if:

(1) the pay telephone is registered with the commission; and

(2) the provider certifies that the pay telephone complies with commission rules regarding the provision of pay telephone service.

(c) Subsection (b) does not apply to a local exchange company pay telephone.

(d) A provider may not impose the fee if imposition is inconsistent with federal law.

(e) A provider may not impose the fee for a:

(1) local call;

(2) 911 call;

(3) local directory assistance call; or

(4) call that is covered by the Telephone Operator Consumer Services Improvement Act of 1990 (47 U.S.C. Section 226).

(f) A provider who imposes the fee must post on each pay telephone notice that the fee will be charged. The provider must post the notice:

(1) in plain sight of the user; and

(2) in a manner consistent with existing commission requirements for posting information.

(g) The commission may not impose on a local exchange company the duty or obligation to:

(1) record the use of pay telephone service;

(2) bill or collect for the use of the pay telephone; or

(3) remit to the provider the fee authorized by this section.

Acts 1997, 75th Leg., ch. 166, § 1, eff. Sept. 1, 1997.

§ 55.177. Charge for Credit Card, Calling Card, or Operator-Assisted Calls

(a) A provider may not impose for a credit card, calling card, or live or automated operator-assisted call a rate or charge that is greater than the authorized rates and charges published on March 18, 1995, in the eight newspapers having the largest circulation in this state.

(b) The published rates may not be changed.

(c) This section does not apply to a local exchange company. Chapter 58 governs the pay telephone rates of an incumbent local exchange company that elects incentive regulation under that chapter.

Acts 1997, 75th Leg., ch. 166, § 1, eff. Sept. 1, 1997.

§ 55.178. Notice of Inability to Receive Calls

(a) A provider may not display the telephone number of a pay telephone that cannot receive telephone calls.

(b) A provider shall place in a conspicuous location on each pay telephone that cannot receive telephone calls a notice stating in letters one-fourth inch high: "THIS TELEPHONE CANNOT RECEIVE TELEPHONE CALLS."

(c) A provider that violates this section or a rule or order adopted by the commission under this section is subject to a civil penalty as provided by Section 15.028 unless the provider takes corrective action to comply with this section or the rule or order not later than the 14th day after the date the provider receives written notice of the violation.

(d) The commission has jurisdiction over a provider to the extent necessary to enforce this section regardless of whether a provider is a telecommunications utility regulated under this title.

(e) The commission may establish procedures to enforce this section.

Acts 1997, 75th Leg., ch. 166, § 1, eff. Sept. 1, 1997.

§ 55.179. Information Requirements

(a) The commission by rule may prescribe the information that must be posted on a pay telephone.

(b) A commission rule may not require a provider or an affiliate of a provider to police compliance by another provider with the commission's rules.

Acts 1997, 75th Leg., ch. 166, § 1, eff. Sept. 1, 1997.

§ 55.180. Violations

The commission may order the disconnection of pay telephone service for not more than one year for repeat violations of commission rules.

Acts 1997, 75th Leg., ch. 166, § 1, eff. Sept. 1, 1997.

SUBCHAPTER I. DIRECTORY LISTINGS AND ASSISTANCE

§ 55.201. Terms of Directory Listings and Assistance

(a) Each company that provides local exchange telephone service in overlapping certificated areas shall negotiate the terms of printed directory listings and directory assistance in those areas.

(b) On complaint by the incumbent local exchange company or the holder of a certificate of convenience and necessity, a certificate of operating authority, or a service provider certificate of operating authority, the commission may:

(1) resolve a dispute between the parties; and

(2) issue an order setting the terms of the directory listings or directory assistance, if necessary.

(c) This section does not affect the authority of an incumbent local exchange company to voluntarily conduct negotiations with an applicant for a certificate of convenience and necessity, a certificate of operating authority, or a service provider certificate of operating authority.

Acts 1997, 75th Leg., ch. 166, § 1, eff. Sept. 1, 1997.

§ 55.202. Directory Published by Telecommunications Utility

A telecommunications utility or an affiliate of that utility that publishes a residential or business telephone directory that is distributed to the public shall publish in the directory the name of each state senator or representative who represents all or part of the geographical area for which the directory contains listings.

Acts 1997, 75th Leg., ch. 166, § 1, eff. Sept. 1, 1997.

§ 55.203. Directory Published by Private Publisher

(a) A private for-profit publisher of a residential telephone directory that is distributed to the public at minimal or no cost shall include in the directory:

(1) a listing of any toll-free and local telephone numbers of:

(A) state agencies;

(B) state public services; and

(C) each state elected official who represents all or part of the geographical area for which the directory contains listings; and

(2) the Internet address of the state electronic Internet portal and a statement that Internet sites for state agencies may be accessed through the state electronic Internet portal .

(b) The listing required by this section must be:

(1) clearly identified; and

(2) located or clearly referenced at the front of the directory before the main listing of residential and business telephone numbers.

(c) The commission by rule may specify:

(1) the format of the listing; and

(2) criteria for inclusion of agencies, services, and officials.

(d) The commission's rules must require a publisher to list:

(1) the telephone number for state government information; and

(2) telephone numbers alphabetically by:

(A) the subject matter of agency programs; and

(B) agency name.

(e) The commission, with the cooperation of other state agencies, shall:

(1) compile relevant information to ensure accuracy of information in the listing; and

(2) provide the information to a telecommunications utility or telephone directory publisher within a reasonable time after a request by the utility or publisher.

(f) The Department of Information Resources shall cooperate with the commission and with publishers to ensure that the subject matter listing of programs and telephone numbers in the telephone directories are consistent with the categorization developed by the Records Management Interagency Coordinating Council under Section 441. 203(j), Government Code.

(g) The rules adopted under Subsection (d) must provide that a telecommunications utility that publishes and distributes to the public a residential or business telephone directory shall list prominently in the directory the contact information for the specialized telecommunications assistance program established under Subchapter E, Chapter 56.[1]

Acts 1997, 75th Leg., ch. 166, § 1, eff. Sept. 1, 1997. Amended by Acts 1999, 76th Leg., ch. 62, § 18.06(a), eff. Sept. 1, 1999; Acts 2001, 77th Leg., ch. 424, § 5, eff. Sept. 1, 2001; Acts 2001, 77th Leg., ch. 1420, § 20.002, eff. Sept. 1, 2001; Acts 2003, 78th Leg., ch. 165, § 1, eff. Sept. 1, 2003; Acts 2007, 80th Leg., ch. 937, § 2.08, eff. Sept. 1, 2007; Acts 2011, 82nd Leg., ch. 973 (H.B. 1504), § 32, eff. June 17, 2011.

[1] V.T.C.A., Utilities Code § 56.151.

§ 55.204. Electronic Telephone Directory

(a) Notwithstanding any other law, a telecommunications provider or telecommunications utility, to further the recycling goals, may publish on the provider's or the utility's Internet website a telephone directory or directory listing instead of providing for general distribution to the public of printed directories or listings.

(b) A provider or utility that publishes a telephone directory or directory listing as described by Subsection (a) shall provide a print or digital copy of the directory or listing to a customer on request. If a provider or utility exercises this option, it shall notify its customers that the provider or utility shall provide the first print or digital copy requested by a customer in each calendar year at no charge to the customer.

Added by Acts 2011, 82nd Leg., ch. 1180 (H.B. 3395), § 4, eff. June 17, 2011.

SUBCHAPTER J. TELECOMMUNICATIONS SERVICE BY CERTAIN PROVIDERS

§ 55.251. Charge for Hotel or Motel Call

A hotel or motel may not charge more than 50 cents for:

(1) a local telephone call;

(2) a credit card telephone call;

(3) a collect telephone call; or

(4) any other local telephone call for which assistance from the hotel or motel operator is not required.

Acts 1997, 75th Leg., ch. 166, § 1, eff. Sept. 1, 1997.

§ 55.252 900 Service Used By Probationers Or Parolees

(a) This section applies only to a telecommunications utility that transports or provides an intrastate 900 service that is:

(1) covered by a contract authorized by Chapter 76 or 508, Government Code; and

(2) used by a defendant under the supervision of a community supervision and corrections department or the parole division of the Texas Department of Criminal Justice to:

(A) pay a fee or cost; or

(B) comply with telephone reporting requirements.

(b) A telecommunications utility may adjust or authorize the adjustment of an end-user's bill for 900 service described by Subsection (a) only with the consent of the contracting community supervision and corrections department or the contracting parole division of the Texas Department of Criminal Justice.

Acts 1997, 75th Leg., ch. 166, § 1, eff. Sept. 1, 1997. Amended by Acts 1999, 76th Leg., ch. 62, § 18.07(a), eff. Sept. 1, 1999; Acts 2009, 81st Leg., ch. 87, § 25.155, eff. Sept. 1, 2009.

§ 55.253. Telephone Prepaid Calling Services

(a) In this section:

(1) "Prepaid calling card company" means a company that provides a prepaid calling service to the public using its own network or resold services.

(2) "Prepaid calling service" means a prepaid telecommunications service that allows an end user to originate a call using an access number and authorization code.

(b) The commission by rule may prescribe standards regarding the information a prepaid calling card company shall disclose to customers in relation to the rates and terms of service for prepaid calling services offered in this state.

(c) The commission is granted all necessary jurisdiction to adopt rules under this section and to enforce those rules and this section.

(d) A violation of a rule adopted under this section is subject to enforcement under Subchapter B, Chapter 15.[1]

Added by Acts 1999, 76th Leg., ch. 411, § 1, eff. June 18, 1999.

[1] V.T.C.A., Utilities Code §§ 55.021 to 55.025.

SUBCHAPTER K. SELECTION OF TELECOMMUNICATIONS UTILITIES

§ 55.301. State Policy

It is the policy of this state to ensure that all customers are protected from the unauthorized switching of a telecommunications utility selected by the customer to provide telecommunications service.

Added by Acts 1999, 76th Leg., ch. 1212, § 22, eff. Sept. 1, 1999; Acts 1999, 76th Leg., ch. 1579, § 6, eff. Aug. 30, 1999.

§ 55.302. Commission Rules

(a) The commission shall adopt nondiscriminatory and competitively neutral rules to implement this subchapter, including rules that:

(1) ensure that customers are protected from deceptive practices in the obtaining of authorizations and verifications required by this subchapter;

(2) are applicable to all local exchange telephone services, interexchange telecommunications service, and other telecommunications service provided by telecommunications utilities in this state;

(3) are consistent with the rules and regulations prescribed by the Federal Communications Commission for the selection of telecommunications utilities;

(4) permit telecommunications utilities to select any method of verification of a change order authorized by Section 55.303;

(5) require the reversal of certain changes in the selection of a customer's telecommunications utility in accordance with Section 55.304(a);

(6) prescribe, in accordance with Section 55.304(b), the duties of a telecommunications utility that initiates an unauthorized customer change; and

(7) provide for corrective action and the imposition of penalties in accordance with Sections 55.305 and 55.306.

(b) The commission is granted all necessary jurisdiction to adopt rules required by this subchapter and to enforce those rules and this subchapter.

(c) The commission may notify customers of their rights under the rules.

Added by Acts 1999, 76th Leg., ch. 1212, § 22, eff. Sept. 1, 1999; Acts 1999, 76th Leg., ch. 1579, § 6, eff. Aug. 30, 1999.

§ 55.303. Verification of Change

A telecommunications utility may verify a change order by:

(1) obtaining written authorization from the customer;

(2) obtaining a toll-free electronic authorization placed from the telephone number that is the subject of the change order; or

(3) an oral authorization obtained by an independent third party.

Added by Acts 1999, 76th Leg., ch. 1212, § 22, eff. Sept. 1, 1999; Acts 1999, 76th Leg., ch. 1579, § 6, eff. Aug. 30, 1999.

§ 55.304. Unauthorized Change

(a) If a change in the selection of a customer's telecommunications utility is not made or verified in accordance with this subchapter, the change, on request by the customer, shall be reversed within a period established by commission ruling.

(b) A telecommunications utility that initiates an unauthorized customer change shall:

(1) pay all usual and customary charges associated with returning the customer to its original telecommunications utility;

(2) pay the telecommunications utility from which the customer was changed any amount paid by the customer that would have been paid to that telecommunications utility if the unauthorized change had not been made;

(3) return to the customer any amount paid by the customer that exceeds the charges that would have been imposed for identical services by the telecommunications utility from which the customer was changed if the unauthorized change had not been made; and

(4) provide to the original telecommunications utility from which the customer was changed all billing records to enable that telecommunications utility to comply with this subchapter.

(c) The telecommunications utility from which the customer was changed shall provide to the customer all benefits associated with the service on receipt of payment for service provided during the unauthorized change.

(d) A customer is not liable for charges incurred during the first 30 days after the date of an unauthorized carrier change.

Added by Acts 1999, 76th Leg., ch. 1212, § 22, eff. Sept. 1, 1999; Acts 1999, 76th Leg., ch. 1579, § 6, eff. Aug. 30, 1999.

§ 55.305. Corrective Action and Penalties

(a) If the commission finds that a telecommunications utility has repeatedly violated the commission's telecommunications utility selection rules, the commission shall order the utility to take corrective action as necessary. In addition, the utility may be subject to administrative penalties under Sections 15.023–15.027.

(b) An administrative penalty collected under this section shall be used to enforce this subchapter.

Added by Acts 1999, 76th Leg., ch. 1212, § 22, eff. Sept. 1, 1999; Acts 1999, 76th Leg., ch. 1579, § 6, eff. Aug. 30, 1999.

§ 55.306. Repeated and Reckless Violation

If the commission finds that a telecommunications utility has repeatedly and recklessly violated the commission's telecommunications utility selection rules, the commission may, if consistent with the public interest, suspend, restrict, deny, or revoke the registration or certificate, including an amended certificate, of the telecommunications utility and, by taking that action, deny the telecommunications utility the right to provide service in this state.

Added by Acts 1999, 76th Leg., ch. 1212, § 22, eff. Sept. 1, 1999; Acts 1999, 76th Leg., ch. 1579, § 6, eff. Aug. 30, 1999.

§ 55.307. Deceptive or Fraudulent Practice

The commission may prohibit a utility from engaging in a deceptive or fraudulent practice, including a marketing practice, involving the selection of a customer's telecommunications utility. The commission may define deceptive and fraudulent practices to which this section applies.

Added by Acts 1999, 76th Leg., ch. 1212, § 22, eff. Sept. 1, 1999; Acts 1999, 76th Leg., ch. 1579, § 6, eff. Aug. 30, 1999.

§ 55.308. Consistency With Federal Law

Notwithstanding any other provision of this subchapter, rules adopted by the commission under this subchapter shall be consistent with applicable federal laws and rules.

Added by Acts 1999, 76th Leg., ch. 1212, § 22, eff. Sept. 1, 1999.

CHAPTER 56. TELECOMMUNICATIONS ASSISTANCE AND UNIVERSAL SERVICE FUND

SUBCHAPTER A. GENERAL PROVISIONS

Section
56.001. Definitions.
56.002. Conflict of Provisions.

SUBCHAPTER B. UNIVERSAL SERVICE FUND

56.021. Universal Service Fund Established.
56.022. Uniform Charge.

Section
56.023. Commission Powers and Duties.
56.024. Reports; Confidentiality.
56.025. Maintenance of Rates and Expansion of Fund for Certain Companies.
56.026. Universal Service Fund Disbursements.
56.027. [Blank].
56.028. Universal Service Fund Reimbursement for Certain IntraLATA Service.
56.029. Expired.
56.030. Affidavits of Compliance.
56.031. Adjustments: Texas High Cost Universal Service Plan.
56.031. Adjustments.
56.032. Support Available to Deregulated Markets.
56.032. Adjustments: Small and Rural Incumbent Local Exchange Company Universal Service Plan.

SUBCHAPTER C. TEL–ASSISTANCE SERVICE PROGRAM [REPEALED]

56.071 to 56.079. Repealed.

SUBCHAPTER D. STATEWIDE TELECOMMUNICATIONS RELAY ACCESS SERVICE

56.101. Purpose.
56.102. Telecommunications Relay Access Service.
56.103. Telecommunications Relay Access Service Requirements.
56.104. Telecommunications Relay Access Service Charges.
56.105. Trial Service Costs and Design Information.
56.106. Telecommunications Relay Access Service Assessments.
56.107. Universal Service Fund Surcharge.
56.108. Selection of Telecommunications Relay Access Service Carrier.
56.1085. Special Features for Relay Access Service.
56.109. Compensation of Carrier.
56.110. Advisory Committee.
56.111. Advisory Committee Duties.
56.112. Advisory Committee Support and Costs.
56.113. Advisory Committee Compensation and Expenses.

SUBCHAPTER E. SPECIALIZED TELECOMMUNICATIONS ASSISTANCE PROGRAM

56.151. Specialized Telecommunications Assistance Program.
56.152. Eligibility.
56.153. Vouchers.
56.154. Commission Duties.
56.155. Recovery of Specialized Telecommunications Device Assistance Program Surcharge.
56.156. Promotion of Program.

SUBCHAPTER F. SERVICE TO UNCERTIFICATED AREA

56.201. Definition.
56.202. Designation of Provider.
56.203. Petition for Service.
56.204. Contents of Petition.
56.205. Hearing.
56.206. Denial of Petition.

Section
56.207. Order.
56.208. Designation of Provider.
56.209. Recovery of Costs.
56.210. Aid to Construction Charge; Contract for Services.
56.211. Permanent Premises Required.
56.212. Subsequent Related Petitions.
56.213. Preferred Provider.
56.214. Certificate Not Amended.

SUBCHAPTER G. FUNDING FOR CERTAIN TELECOMMUNICATIONS UTILITIES

56.251. Definition.
56.252. Telecommunications Utilities Eligible to Receive Funding Under This Subchapter.
56.253. Determination of Successor Utility's Costs to be Recovered.
56.254. Recovery of Costs.

SUBCHAPTER H. AUDIO NEWSPAPER PROGRAM

56.301. Audio Newspaper Assistance Program.

SUBCHAPTER A. GENERAL PROVISIONS

§ 56.001. Definitions

In this chapter:

(1) "Department" means the Texas Department of Human Services.

(2) "Designated provider" means a telecommunications provider designated by the commission to provide services to an uncertificated area under Subchapter F.[1]

Acts 1997, 75th Leg., ch. 166, § 1, eff. Sept. 1, 1997. Amended by Acts 2001, 77th Leg., ch. 651, § 1, eff. Sept. 1, 2001.

[1] V.T.C.A., Utilities Code § 56.201.

§ 56.002. Conflict of Provisions

If this chapter conflicts with another provision of this title, this chapter prevails.

Acts 1997, 75th Leg., ch. 166, § 1, eff. Sept. 1, 1997.

SUBCHAPTER B. UNIVERSAL SERVICE FUND

§ 56.021. Universal Service Fund Established

(1) assist telecommunications providers in providing basic local telecommunications service at reasonable rates in high cost rural areas under two plans:

(A) the Texas High Cost Universal Service Plan (16 T.A.C. Section 26.403); and

(B) the Small and Rural Incumbent Local Exchange Company Universal Service Plan (16 T.A.C. Section 26.404);

(2) reimburse the telecommunications carrier that provides the statewide telecommunications relay access service under Subchapter D;[1]

(3) finance the specialized telecommunications assistance program established under Subchapter E;[2]

(4) reimburse the department, the Texas Commission for the Deaf and Hard of Hearing, and the commission for costs incurred in implementing this chapter and Chapter 57;

(5) reimburse a telecommunications carrier providing lifeline service as provided by 47 C.F.R. Part 54, Subpart E, as amended;

(6) finance the implementation and administration of an integrated eligibility process created under Section 17.007 for customer service discounts relating to telecommunications services, including outreach expenses the commission determines are reasonable and necessary;

(7) reimburse a designated provider under Subchapter F;

(8) reimburse a successor utility under Subchapter G; and

(9) finance the program established under Subchapter H.

Acts 1997, 75th Leg., ch. 166, § 1, eff. Sept. 1, 1997. Amended by Acts 1999, 76th Leg., ch. 62, § 18.08(a), eff. Sept. 1, 1999; Acts 1999, 76th Leg., ch. 835, § 2, eff. Sept. 1, 1999; Acts 1999, 76th Leg., ch. 1212, § 23, eff. Sept. 1, 1999; Acts 1999, 76th Leg., ch. 1553, § 1, eff. Sept. 1, 1999; Acts 2001, 77th Leg., ch. 651, § 2, eff. Sept. 1, 2001; Acts 2001, 77th Leg., ch. 1451, § 2, eff. Sept. 1, 2001; Acts 2003, 78th Leg., ch. 76, § 5, eff. Sept. 1, 2003; Acts 2003, 78th Leg., ch. 1276, § 17.001, eff. Sept. 1, 2003; Acts 2005, 79th Leg., 2nd C.S., ch. 2, § 12, eff. Sept. 1, 2005; Acts 2011, 82nd Leg., ch. 314 (H.B. 2295), § 1, eff. June 17, 2011.

[1] V.T.C.A., Utilities Code § 56.101 et seq.

[2] V.T.C.A., Utilities Code § 56.151 et seq.

§ 56.022. Uniform Charge

(a) The universal service fund is funded by a statewide uniform charge payable by each telecommunications provider that has access to the customer base.

(b) A telecommunications provider shall pay the charge in accordance with procedures approved by the commission.

(c) The uniform charge is on services and at rates the commission determines. In establishing the charge and the services to which the charge will apply, the commission may not:

(1) grant an unreasonable preference or advantage to a telecommunications provider;

(2) assess the charge on pay telephone service; or

(3) subject a telecommunications provider to unreasonable prejudice or disadvantage.

Acts 1997, 75th Leg., ch. 166, § 1, eff. Sept. 1, 1997. Amended by Acts 2001, 77th Leg., ch. 404, § 1, eff. Sept. 1, 2001.

§ 56.023. Commission Powers and Duties

(a) The commission shall:

(1) in a manner that assures reasonable rates for basic local telecommunications service, adopt eligibility criteria and review procedures, including a method for administrative review, the commission finds necessary to fund the universal service fund and make distributions from that fund;

(2) determine which telecommunications providers meet the eligibility criteria;

(3) determine the amount of and approve a procedure for reimbursement to telecommunications providers of revenue lost in providing tel-assistance service under Subchapter C; [1]

(4) establish and collect fees from the universal service fund necessary to recover the costs the department and the commission incur in administering this chapter and Chapter 57; and

(5) approve procedures for the collection and disbursal of the revenue of the universal service fund.

(b) The eligibility criteria must require that a telecommunications provider, in compliance with the commission's quality of service requirements:

(1) offer service to each consumer within the company's certificated area and to any permanent residential or business premises to which the company is designated to provide services under Subchapter F; and

(2) render continuous and adequate service within the company's certificated area and to any permanent residential or business premises to which the company is designated to provide services under Subchapter F.

(c) A company designated under Subchapter F to provide services to permanent residential or business premises within an uncertificated area and that complies with Subsection (b) shall receive universal service fund distributions to assist the provider in providing those services. In addition, the commission shall designate the provider as an eligible telecommunications carrier under 47 U.S.C. Section 214(e)(2), as amended, for those permanent residential or business premises.

(d) The commission shall adopt rules for the administration of the universal service fund and this chapter and may act as necessary and convenient to administer the fund and this chapter. The rules must include procedures to ensure reasonable transparency and accountability in the administration of the universal service fund.

(e) A successor utility, as that term is defined by Section 54.301, that is or becomes an eligible telecommunications carrier under 47 U.S.C. Section 214(e)(2), as amended, is entitled to receive universal service fund distributions for costs in accordance with Subchapter G.

Acts 1997, 75th Leg., ch. 166, § 1, eff. Sept. 1, 1997. Amended by Acts 1999, 76th Leg., ch. 1212, § 24, eff. Sept. 1, 1999; Acts 2001, 77th Leg., ch. 651, § 3, eff. Sept. 1, 2001; Acts 2003, 78th Leg., ch. 76, § 6, eff. Sept. 1, 2003; Acts 2011, 82nd Leg., ch. 98 (S.B. 980), § 10, eff. Sept. 1, 2011.

[1] V.T.C.A., Utilities Code § 56.071 et seq.

§ 56.024. Reports; Confidentiality

(a) The commission may require a telecommunications provider to provide a report or information necessary to assess contributions and disbursements to the universal service fund.

(b) A report or information is confidential and not subject to disclosure under Chapter 552, Government Code.

Acts 1997, 75th Leg., ch. 166, § 1, eff. Sept. 1, 1997. Amended by Acts 1999, 76th Leg., ch. 1212, § 24, eff. Sept. 1, 1999.

§ 56.025. Maintenance of Rates and Expansion of Fund for Certain Companies

(a) In addition to the authority provided by Section 56.021, for each local exchange company that serves fewer than 31,000 access lines and each cooperative, the commission:

(1) may adopt a mechanism necessary to maintain reasonable rates for local exchange telephone service; and

(2) shall adopt rules to expand the universal service fund in the circumstances prescribed by this section.

(b) The commission shall implement a mechanism through the universal service fund to replace the reasonably projected reduction in high cost assistance revenue caused by a commission order, rule, or policy. This subsection does not apply to an order entered in a proceeding related to an individual company's revenue requirements.

(c) The commission shall implement a mechanism to replace the reasonably projected change in revenue caused by a Federal Communications Commission order, rule, or policy that changes:

(1) the federal universal service fund revenue of a local exchange company; or

(2) costs or revenue assigned to the intrastate jurisdiction.

(d) The commission shall implement a mechanism to replace the reasonably projected reduction in contribution caused by a change of commission policy regarding intraLATA "1-plus" dialing access. In this subsection, "contribution" means the average intraLATA long distance message telecommunications service revenue per minute, including intraLATA toll pooling and associated impacts, less the average message telecommunications service cost per minute less the average contribution from switched access multiplied by the projected change in intraLATA "1-plus" minutes of use.

(e) The commission shall implement a mechanism to replace the reasonably projected increase in costs or decrease in revenue of the intrastate jurisdiction caused by another governmental agency's order, rule, or policy.

(f) A mechanism implemented under Subsection (c), (d), or (e) must be through:

(1) an increase in rates, if the increase would not adversely affect universal service; or

(2) the universal service fund.

Acts 1997, 75th Leg., ch. 166, § 1, eff. Sept. 1, 1997. Amended by Acts 2005, 79th Leg., 2nd C.S., ch. 2, § 13, eff. Sept. 1, 2005.

§ 56.026. Universal Service Fund Disbursements

(a) A revenue requirement showing is not required for a disbursement from the universal service fund under this subchapter.

(b) The commission shall make each disbursement from the universal service fund promptly and efficiently so that a telecommunications provider does not experience an unnecessary cash-flow change as a result of a change in governmental policy.

(c) to (e) Expired.

Acts 1997, 75th Leg., ch. 166, § 1, eff. Sept. 1, 1997. Amended by Acts 1999, 76th Leg., ch. 1212, § 25, eff. Sept. 1, 1999; Acts 2005, 79th Leg., 2nd C.S., ch. 2, § 14, eff. Sept. 1, 2005.

§ 56.027. [Blank]

§ 56.028. Universal Service Fund Reimbursement for Certain IntraLATA Service

On request of an incumbent local exchange company that is not an electing company under Chapters 58 and 59, the commission shall provide reimbursement through the universal service fund for reduced rates for intraLATA interexchange high capacity (1.544 Mbps) service for entities described in Section 58.253(a). The amount of reimbursement shall be the difference between the company's tariffed rate for that service as of January 1, 1998, and the lowest rate offered for that service by any local exchange company electing incentive regulation under Chapter 58.

Added by Acts 1999, 76th Leg., ch. 1212, § 26, eff. Sept. 1, 1999.

§ 56.029. Expired

§ 56.030. Affidavits of Compliance

On or before September 1 of each year, a telecommunications provider that receives disbursements from the universal service fund shall file with the commission an affidavit certifying that the telecommunications provider is in compliance with the requirements for receiving money from the universal service fund and requirements regarding the use of money from each universal service fund program for which the telecommunications provider receives disbursements.

Added by Acts 2005, 79th Leg., 2nd C.S., ch. 2, § 15, eff. Sept. 1, 2005.

§ 56.031. Adjustments: Texas High Cost Universal Service Plan

Text of section effective until September 1, 2013. See, also, text of § 56.031 effective September 1, 2013.

The commission may revise the monthly per line support amounts to be made available from the Texas High Cost Universal Service Plan after notice and an opportunity for hearing. In determining appropriate monthly per line support amounts, the commission shall consider the adequacy of basic rates to support universal service.

Added by Acts 2005, 79th Leg., 2nd C.S., ch. 2, § 15, eff. Sept. 1, 2005. Amended by Acts 2011, 82nd Leg., ch. 535 (H.B. 2603), § 1, eff. Sept. 1, 2011.

§ 56.031. Adjustments

Text of section effective September 1, 2013. See, also, text of § 56.031 effective until September 1, 2013.

The commission may revise the monthly per line support amounts to be made available from the Texas High Cost Universal Service Plan and from the Small and Rural Incumbent Local Exchange Company Universal Service Plan at any time after September 1, 2007, after notice and an opportunity for hearing. In determining appropriate monthly per line support amounts, the commission shall consider the adequacy of basic rates to support universal service.

Added by Acts 2005, 79th Leg., 2nd C.S., ch. 2, § 15, eff. Sept. 1, 2005. Amended by Acts 2011, 82nd Leg., ch. 535 (H.B. 2603), § 1, eff. Sept. 1, 2011; Acts 2011, 82nd Leg., ch. 535 (H.B. 2603), § 3, eff. Sept. 1, 2013.

§ 56.032. Support Available to Deregulated Markets

Text of section as added by Acts 2011, 82nd Leg., ch. 98 (S.B. 980), § 11, effective January 2, 2012. See, also, section as added by Acts 2011, 82nd Leg., ch. 535 (H.B. 2603), § 2.

(a) An incumbent local exchange company may not receive support from the universal service fund for a deregulated market that has a population of at least 30,000.

(b) An incumbent local exchange company may receive support from the universal service fund for a deregulated market that has a population of less than 30,000 only if the company demonstrates to the commission that the company needs the support to provide basic local telecommunications service at reasonable rates in the affected market. A company may use evidence from outside the affected market to make the demonstration.

(c) An incumbent local exchange company may make the demonstration described by Subsection (b) in relation to a market before submitting a petition to deregulate the market.

Added by Acts 2011, 82nd Leg., ch. 98 (S.B. 980), § 11, eff. Jan. 2, 2012.

§ 56.032. Adjustments: Small and Rural Incumbent Local Exchange Company Universal Service Plan

Text of section as added by Acts 2011, 82nd Leg., ch. 535 (H.B. 2603), § 2. See, also, section as added by Acts 2011, 82nd Leg., ch. 98 (S.B. 980), § 11.

(a) For purposes of this section, "consumer price index" means the Consumer Price Index for All Urban Consumers, as published by the federal Bureau of Labor Statistics of the United States Department of Labor.

(b) Except as provided by Subsections (c), (d), (e), and (f), the commission may revise the monthly support amounts to be made available from the Small and Rural Incumbent Local Exchange Company Universal Service Plan by revising the monthly per line support amounts, after notice and an opportunity for hearing. In determining appropriate monthly per line support amounts, the commission shall consider the adequacy of basic rates to support universal service.

(c) On the written request of a small or rural incumbent local exchange company that receives monthly per line support amounts, the commission shall disburse funds to the company in fixed monthly amounts based on the company's annualized amount of recovery for the calendar year ending on December 31, 2010. A company may submit only one request under this subsection and must submit the request on or before December 31, 2011.

(d) On the written request of a small or rural incumbent local exchange company that is not an electing company under Chapter 58 or 59, the commission annually shall set the company's monthly support amounts for the following 12 months by dividing by 12 the annualized support amount calculated under this subsection. The commission shall calculate the annualized amount:

(1) for the initial 12-month period for which a company makes an election under this subsection, by:

(A) determining the annualized support amount calculated for the requestor in the final order issued by the commission in Docket No. 18516; and

(B) adjusting the support amount determined under Paragraph (A) at the beginning of each calendar year by a factor equal to the most recent consumer price index published at that time, beginning with the 1999 calendar year and ending in the year the company makes an election under this subsection; and

(2) for the 12-month period following the initial period for which a company made an election under this subsection and for subsequent 12-month periods, by adjusting the most recent annualized support amount calculated by the commission by a factor equal to the percentage change in the consumer price index for the most recent 12-month period.

(e) If a company elects to receive monthly support amounts under Subsection (d), the commission, on its own motion or on the written request of the company, may initiate a proceeding to recalculate the most recent annualized support amount to be used as the basis for adjustment for a subsequent 12-month period under Subsection (d)(2). If, based on the recalculation, the commission by order adjusts a company's most recent annualized support amount, the adjusted support amount supersedes the annualized support amount calculated in accordance with Subsection (d).

(f) The commission shall administratively review requests filed under Subsections (c) and (d). Except for good cause, the commission shall approve the request not later than the 60th day after the date the commission determines the company is eligible and has met all the procedural requirements under this subchapter.

(g) This section does not affect the commission's authority under Chapter 53 or this chapter.

(h) This section and any monthly support amount approved under this section expire on September 1, 2013.

Added by Acts 2011, 82nd Leg., ch. 535 (H.B. 2603), § 2, eff. Sept. 1, 2011.

SUBCHAPTER C. TEL–ASSISTANCE SERVICE PROGRAM [REPEALED]

§§ 56.071 to 56.079. Repealed by Acts 2001, 77th Leg., ch. 1451, § 4(a), eff. Sept. 1, 2001

SUBCHAPTER D. STATEWIDE TELECOMMUNICATIONS RELAY ACCESS SERVICE

§ 56.101. Purpose

The purpose of this subchapter is to provide for the uniform and coordinated provision by one telecommunications carrier of a statewide telecommunications relay access service for persons with an impairment of hearing or speech.

Acts 1997, 75th Leg., ch. 166, § 1, eff. Sept. 1, 1997.

§ 56.102. Telecommunications Relay Access Service

(a) The commission shall adopt and enforce rules establishing a statewide telecommunications relay access service for the use of a person with an impairment of hearing or speech.

(b) The commission rules shall provide that the service must:

(1) use specialized communications equipment, such as a telecommunications device for the deaf, and operator translations; and

(2) meet the criteria provided by Sections 56.103, 56.104, and 56.105.

Acts 1997, 75th Leg., ch. 166, § 1, eff. Sept. 1, 1997.

§ 56.103. Telecommunications Relay Access Service Requirements

(a) The telecommunications relay access service shall provide a person with an impairment of hearing or speech with access to the telecommunications network in this state equivalent to the access provided other customers.

(b) The service consists of:

(1) switching and transmission of the call;

(2) live or automated verbal and print translations of communications between a person with an impairment of hearing or speech who uses a telecommunications device for the deaf or a similar automated device and a person who does not have such equipment; and

(3) other service enhancements proposed by the carrier and approved by the commission.

Acts 1997, 75th Leg., ch. 166, § 1, eff. Sept. 1, 1997.

§ 56.104. Telecommunications Relay Access Service Charges

(a) For a call made using the telecommunications relay access service, the person calling or called:

(1) may not be charged for a call that originates and terminates in the same local calling area; and

(2) shall pay one-half of the total charges established by contract with the commission for intrastate interexchange calls.

(b) Charges related to providing the service that, under Subsection (a), are not charged to a person calling or called shall be funded from the universal service fund, as specified by the service provider's contract with the commission.

(c) A local exchange company may not impose an interexchange carrier access charge on a call using the service that originates and terminates in the same local calling area.

(d) A local exchange company shall provide billing and collection services for the service at just and reasonable rates.

Acts 1997, 75th Leg., ch. 166, § 1, eff. Sept. 1, 1997.

§ 56.105. Trial Service Costs and Design Information

If the commission orders a local exchange company to provide for a trial telecommunications relay access service for persons with an impairment of hearing or speech, all pertinent costs and design information from the trial must be made available to the public.

Acts 1997, 75th Leg., ch. 166, § 1, eff. Sept. 1, 1997.

§ 56.106. Telecommunications Relay Access Service Assessments

(a) The commission shall set appropriate assessments for all telecommunications utilities to fund the telecommunications relay access service.

(b) In setting an assessment, the commission shall consider:

(1) the aggregate calling pattern of service users; and

(2) any other factor the commission finds appropriate and in the public interest.

(c) The commission shall:

(1) review the assessments annually; and

(2) adjust the assessments as appropriate.

Acts 1997, 75th Leg., ch. 166, § 1, eff. Sept. 1, 1997.

§ 56.107. Universal Service Fund Surcharge

(a) A telecommunications utility may recover the utility's universal service fund assessment for the telecommunications relay access service through a surcharge added to the utility customers' bills.

(b) The commission shall specify how each telecommunications utility is to determine the amount of the surcharge.

(c) If a telecommunications utility imposes the surcharge, the bill shall list the surcharge as the "universal service fund surcharge."

Acts 1997, 75th Leg., ch. 166, § 1, eff. Sept. 1, 1997.

§ 56.108. Selection of Telecommunications Relay Access Service Carrier

(a) The commission shall select one telecommunications carrier to provide the statewide telecommunications relay access service.

(b) The commission shall make a written award of the contract to the telecommunications carrier whose proposal is the most advantageous to this state, considering:

(1) price;

(2) the interests of the community of persons with an impairment of hearing or speech in having access to a high quality and technologically advanced telecommunications system; and

(3) any other factor listed in the commission's request for proposals.

(c) The commission shall consider each proposal in a manner that does not disclose the contents of the proposal to a telecommunications carrier making a competing proposal.

(d) The commission's evaluation of a telecommunications carrier's proposal shall include the:

(1) charges for the service;

(2) service enhancements proposed by the carrier;

(3) technological sophistication of the network proposed by the carrier; and

(4) date proposed for beginning the service.

Acts 1997, 75th Leg., ch. 166, § 1, eff. Sept. 1, 1997.

§ 56.1085. Special Features for Relay Access Service

(a) The commission may contract for a special feature for the state's telecommunications relay access service if the commission determines:

(1) the feature will benefit the communication of persons with an impairment of hearing or speech;

(2) installation of the feature will be of benefit to the state; and

(3) the feature will make the relay access service available to a greater number of users.

(b) If the carrier selected to provide the telecommunications relay access service under Section 56.108 is unable to provide the special feature at the best value to the state, the commission may make a written award of a contract for a carrier to provide the special feature to the telecommunications carrier whose proposal is most advantageous to the state, considering:

(1) the factors provided by Section 56.108(b); and

(2) the past performance, demonstrated capability, and experience of the carrier.

(c) The commission shall consider each proposal in a manner that does not disclose the contents of the proposal to a telecommunications carrier making a competing proposal.

(d) The commission's evaluation of a telecommunications carrier's proposal shall include the considerations provided by Section 56.108(d).

Added by Acts 1999, 76th Leg., ch. 1553, § 2, eff. Sept. 1, 1999.

§ 56.109. Compensation of Carrier

(a) The telecommunications carrier selected to provide the telecommunications relay access service under Section 56.108 or the carrier selected to provide a special feature for the telecommunications relay access service under Section 56.1085 shall be compensated at rates and on terms provided by the carrier's contract with the commission.

(b) The compensation may include:

(1) a return on the investment required to provide the service; and

(2) compensation for unbillable or uncollectible calls placed through the service.

(c) Compensation for unbillable or uncollectible calls is subject to a reasonable limitation determined by the commission.

Acts 1997, 75th Leg., ch. 166, § 1, eff. Sept. 1, 1997. Amended by Acts 1999, 76th Leg., ch. 1553, § 3, eff. Sept. 1, 1999.

§ 56.110. Advisory Committee

(a) An advisory committee to assist the commission in administering this subchapter is composed of the following persons appointed by the commission:

(1) two persons with disabilities that impair the ability to effectively access the telephone network other than disabilities described by Subdivisions (2)–(7);

(2) one deaf person recommended by the Texas Deaf Caucus;

(3) one deaf person recommended by the Texas Association of the Deaf;

(4) one person with a hearing impairment recommended by Self-Help for the Hard of Hearing;

(5) one person with a hearing impairment recommended by the American Association of Retired Persons;

(6) one deaf and blind person recommended by the Texas Deaf/Blind Association;

(7) one person with a speech impairment and one person with a speech and hearing impairment recommended by the Coalition of Texans with Disabilities;

(8) two representatives of telecommunications utilities, one representing a nonlocal exchange utility and one representing a local exchange company, chosen from a list of candidates provided by the Texas Telephone Association;

(9) two persons, at least one of whom is deaf, with experience in providing relay services recommended by the Texas Commission for the Deaf and Hard of Hearing; and

(10) two public members recommended by organizations representing consumers of telecommunications services.

(b) Members of the advisory committee serve two-year terms. A member whose term has expired shall continue to serve until a qualified replacement is appointed.

Acts 1997, 75th Leg., ch. 166, § 1, eff. Sept. 1, 1997. Amended by Acts 1999, 76th Leg., ch. 62, § 18.08(b), eff. Sept. 1, 1999; Acts 1999, 76th Leg., ch. 1553, § 4, eff. Sept. 1, 1999.

§ 56.111. Advisory Committee Duties

The advisory committee shall:

(1) monitor the establishment, administration, and promotion of the statewide telecommunications relay access service;

(2) advise the commission in pursuing a service that meets the needs of persons with an impairment of hearing or speech in communicating with other telecommunications services users; and

(3) advise the commission and the Texas Commission for the Deaf and Hard of Hearing, at the request of either commission, regarding any issue related to the specialized telecommunications assistance program established under Subchapter E,[1] including:

(A) devices or services suitable to meet the needs of persons with disabilities in communicating with other users of telecommunications services; and

(B) oversight and administration of the program.

Acts 1997, 75th Leg., ch. 166, § 1, eff. Sept. 1, 1997. Amended by Acts 1999, 76th Leg., ch. 62, § 18.08(c), eff. Sept. 1, 1999; Acts 1999, 76th Leg., ch. 1553, § 5, eff. Sept. 1, 1999.

[1] V.T.C.A., Utilities Code § 56.151.

§ 56.112. Advisory Committee Support and Costs

(a) The commission shall provide to the advisory committee:

(1) clerical and staff support; and

(2) a secretary to record committee meetings.

(b) The costs associated with the advisory committee shall be reimbursed from the universal service fund.

Acts 1997, 75th Leg., ch. 166, § 1, eff. Sept. 1, 1997. Amended by Acts 1999, 76th Leg., ch. 62, § 18.08(d), eff. Sept. 1, 1999.

§ 56.113. Advisory Committee Compensation and Expenses

A member of the advisory committee serves without compensation but is entitled to reimbursement at rates established for state employees for travel and per diem incurred in the performance of the member's official duties.

Added by Acts 2001, 77th Leg., ch. 1158, § 93, eff. Sept. 1, 2001.

SUBCHAPTER E. SPECIALIZED TELECOMMUNICATIONS ASSISTANCE PROGRAM

Acts 1999, 76th Leg., ch. 1553, § 6 in the subchapter heading deleted "device" preceding "assistance".

§ 56.151. Specialized Telecommunications Assistance Program

The commission and the Texas Commission for the Deaf and Hard of Hearing by rule shall establish a specialized telecommunications assistance program to provide financial assistance to individuals with disabilities that impair the individuals' ability to effectively access the telephone network to assist the individuals with the purchase of basic specialized equipment or services to provide the individuals with telephone network access that is functionally equivalent to that enjoyed by individuals without disabilities. The agencies may adopt joint rules that identify devices and services eligible for vouchers under the program.

Added by Acts 1999, 76th Leg., ch. 62, § 18.08(e), eff. Sept. 1, 1999. Amended by Acts 1999, 76th Leg., ch. 1553, § 7, eff. Sept. 1, 1999; Acts 2001, 77th Leg., ch. 424, § 1, eff. Sept. 1, 2001.

§ 56.152. Eligibility

The Texas Commission for the Deaf and Hard of Hearing by rule shall prescribe eligibility standards for individuals, including deaf individuals and individuals who have an impairment of hearing or speech, to receive an assistance voucher under the program. To be eligible, an individual must be a resident of this state with a disability that impairs the individual's ability to effectively access the telephone network.

Added by Acts 1999, 76th Leg., ch. 62, § 18.08(e), eff. Sept. 1, 1999. Amended by Acts 1999, 76th Leg., ch. 1553, § 7, eff. Sept. 1, 1999; Acts 2001, 77th Leg., ch. 424, § 2, eff. Sept. 1, 2001.

§ 56.153. Vouchers

(a) The Texas Commission for the Deaf and Hard of Hearing shall determine a reasonable price for a basic specialized telecommunications device that permits, or basic specialized services that permit, telephone network access and distribute to each eligible applicant a voucher that guarantees payment of that amount to a distributor of new specialized telecommunications devices described by Section 56.151 or to a provider of services described by that section. The Texas Commission for the Deaf and Hard of Hearing may issue a voucher for a service only if the service is less expensive than a device eligible for a voucher under the program to meet the same need.

(b) A voucher must have the value printed on its face. The individual exchanging a voucher for the purchase of a specialized telecommunications device or service is responsible for payment of the difference between the voucher's value and the price of the device or service.

(c) The commission and the Texas Commission for the Deaf and Hard of Hearing by rule shall provide that a distributor of devices or a provider of services will receive not more than the full price of the device or service if the recipient of a voucher exchanges the voucher for a device or service that the distributor or provider sells for less than the voucher's value.

(d) An individual who has exchanged a voucher for a specialized telecommunications device is not eligible to receive another voucher before the fifth anniversary of the date the individual exchanged the previously issued voucher unless, before that date, the recipient develops a need for a different type of telecommunications device or service under the program because the recipient's disability changes or the recipient acquires another disability.

(e) Except as provided by rules adopted under this subsection, an individual is not eligible for a voucher if the Texas Commission for the Deaf and Hard of Hearing has issued a voucher for a device or service to another individual with the same type of disability in the individual's household. The Texas Commission for the Deaf and Hard of Hearing by rule may provide for financially independent individuals who reside in a congregate setting to be eligible for a voucher regardless of whether another individual living in that setting has received a voucher.

(f) The Texas Commission for the Deaf and Hard of Hearing shall determine eligibility of each person who files an application for a voucher and issue each eligible applicant an appropriate voucher.

(g) The Texas Commission for the Deaf and Hard of Hearing shall maintain a record regarding each individual who receives a voucher under the program.

(h) The Texas Commission for the Deaf and Hard of Hearing shall deposit money collected under the program to the credit of the universal service fund.

Acts 1999, 76th Leg., ch. 62, § 18.08(e), eff. Sept. 1, 1999. Amended by Acts 1999, 76th Leg., ch. 1553, § 7, eff. Sept. 1, 1999; Acts 2001, 77th Leg., ch. 424, § 3, eff. Sept. 1, 2001.

§ 56.154. Commission Duties

(a) Not later than the 45th day after the date the commission receives a voucher a telecommunications device distributor presents for payment or a voucher a telecommunications service provider presents for payment, the commission shall pay to the distributor or service provider the lesser of the value of a voucher properly exchanged for a specialized telecommunications device or service or the full price of the device or service for which a voucher recipient exchanges the voucher. The payments must be made from the universal service fund.

(b) The commission may investigate whether the presentation of a voucher for payment represents a valid transaction for a telecommunications device or service under the program. The Texas Commission for the Deaf and Hard of Hearing shall cooperate with and assist the commission in an investigation under this subsection.

(c) Notwithstanding Section 56.153(a), the commission may:

(1) delay payment of a voucher to a distributor of devices or a service provider if there is a dispute regarding the amount or propriety of the payment or whether the device or service is appropriate or adequate to meet the needs of the person to whom the Texas Commission for the Deaf and Hard of Hearing issued the voucher until the dispute is resolved;

(2) provide that payment of the voucher is conditioned on the return of the payment if the device is returned to the distributor or if the service is not

used by the person to whom the voucher was issued; and

(3) provide an alternative dispute resolution process for resolving a dispute regarding a subject described by Subdivision (1) or (2).

Added by Acts 1999, 76th Leg., ch. 62, § 18.08(e), eff. Sept. 1, 1999. Amended by Acts 1999, 76th Leg., ch. 1553, § 7, eff. Sept. 1, 1999.

§ 56.155. Recovery of Specialized Telecommunications Device Assistance Program Surcharge

(a) The commission shall allow a telecommunications utility to recover the universal service fund assessment related to the specialized telecommunications assistance program through a surcharge added to the utility's customers' bills.

(b) The commission shall specify how each utility must determine the amount of the surcharge and by rule shall prohibit a utility from recovering an aggregation of more than 12 months of assessments in a single surcharge. The rules must require a utility to apply for approval of a surcharge before the 91st day after the date the period during which the aggregated surcharges were assessed closes.

(c) If a utility chooses to impose the surcharge, the utility shall include the surcharge in the "universal service fund surcharge" listing as provided by Section 56.107.

Added by Acts 1999, 76th Leg., ch. 62, § 18.08(e), eff. Sept. 1, 1999. Amended by Acts 1999, 76th Leg., ch. 1553, § 8, eff. Sept. 1, 1999.

§ 56.156. Promotion of Program

The Texas Commission for the Deaf and Hard of Hearing may promote the program established under this subchapter by means of participation in events, advertisements, pamphlets, brochures, forms, pins, or other promotional items or efforts that provide contact information for persons interested in applying for a voucher under the program.

Added by Acts 2001, 77th Leg., ch. 424, § 4, eff. Sept. 1, 2001.

SUBCHAPTER F. SERVICE TO UNCERTIFICATED AREA

§ 56.201. Definition

In this subchapter, "permanent residential or business premises" means a premises that has permanent facilities for water, wastewater, and electricity.

Added by Acts 2001, 77th Leg., ch. 651, § 4, eff. Sept. 1, 2001.

§ 56.202. Designation of Provider

(a) Notwithstanding Section 54.001, the commission may designate a telecommunications provider under this section to provide voice-grade services to permanent residential or business premises that are not included within the certificated area of a holder of a certificate of convenience and necessity.

(b) The commission may designate a provider only if the provider is otherwise eligible to receive universal service funds under Section 56.023(b).

Added by Acts 2001, 77th Leg., ch. 651, § 4, eff. Sept. 1, 2001.

§ 56.203. Petition for Service

Persons residing in permanent residential premises or owners of permanent residential or business premises that are not included within the certificated area of a holder of a certificate of convenience and necessity may petition the commission to designate a telecommunications provider to provide to those premises voice-grade services supported by state and federal universal service support mechanisms.

Added by Acts 2001, 77th Leg., ch. 651, § 4, eff. Sept. 1, 2001.

§ 56.204. Contents of Petition

(a) A petition for designation of a service provider must:

(1) state with reasonable particularity the locations of the permanent residential or business premises for which the petitioners are requesting service;

(2) establish that those locations are within reasonable proximity to one another so that the petitioners possess a sufficient community of interest to warrant the designation of a provider and the expenditure of universal service funds necessary to establish service;

(3) except as provided by Subsection (b), be signed by at least five persons who:

(A) are not members of the same household;

(B) reside in the permanent residential premises or are the owners of the permanent residential or business premises for which service is sought and that are not located within a certificated area;

(C) want service to those premises; and

(D) commit to pay the aid to construction charges for service to those premises as determined by the commission;

(4) nominate as potential providers of service not more than five telecommunications providers serv-

ing territory that is contiguous to the location of the permanent residential or business premises using wireless or wireline facilities, resale, or unbundled network elements; and

(5) include as an attachment or an appendix documentation indicating the required residence or ownership, including a state-issued license or identification, tax records, deeds, or voter registration materials.

(b) The commission may accept a petition that is signed by fewer than five persons if a petitioner provides an affidavit stating that the petitioners have taken all reasonable steps to secure the signatures of the residents of permanent residential premises or the owners of permanent residential or business premises within reasonably close proximity to the petitioning premises who are not receiving telephone service when the petition is filed and who want telephone service initiated.

Added by Acts 2001, 77th Leg., ch. 651, § 4, eff. Sept. 1, 2001.

§ 56.205. Hearing

If the commission finds that the petition complies with Section 56.204, the commission shall hold an evidentiary hearing to determine if a telecommunications provider is willing to be designated to provide service to those premises or, if a provider is not willing to be designated, to determine the telecommunications provider that is best able to serve those premises under the criteria prescribed by this subchapter.

Added by Acts 2001, 77th Leg., ch. 651, § 4, eff. Sept. 1, 2001.

§ 56.206. Denial of Petition

The commission shall deny a petition if the commission determines that services cannot be extended to the petitioning premises at a reasonable cost. In making that determination, the commission shall consider all relevant factors, including:

(1) the original cost to be incurred by a designated provider to deploy service to the petitioning premises, and the effect of reimbursement of those costs on the state universal service fund;

(2) the number of access lines requested by the petitioners for the petitioning premises;

(3) the size of the geographic territory in which the petitioning premises are included;

(4) the proximity of existing facilities and the existence of a preferred designated provider under Section 56.213; and

(5) any technical barriers to the provision of service.

Added by Acts 2001, 77th Leg., ch. 651, § 4, eff. Sept. 1, 2001.

§ 56.207. Order

In any order granting a petition, the commission shall:

(1) approve the facilities to be deployed based on the estimated costs of deployment submitted in accordance with Section 56.208(a);

(2) approve the amount of original cost of deployment to be recovered from the state universal service fund and the terms of original cost recovery under Section 56.209; and

(3) approve the recurring cost recovery under Section 56.209, including the monthly rate for services and the monthly per line fee to be recovered from the state universal service fund under that section.

Added by Acts 2001, 77th Leg., ch. 651, § 4, eff. Sept. 1, 2001.

§ 56.208. Designation of Provider

(a) In determining which nominated telecommunications provider the commission will designate to provide service to the petitioning premises, the commission shall consider the relative estimated cost to be incurred by contiguous providers to serve the petitioning premises and give preference to the provider having the least cost technology that meets the quality of service standards prescribed by the commission applicable to that provider.

(b) The commission may not designate a telecommunications provider to serve the petitioning premises unless the premises are located in an area that is contiguous to an area in which the telecommunications provider has previously been designated eligible to receive universal service funding under Section 56.023(b). This subsection does not apply if the commission designates the provider after the provider voluntarily agrees to provide service to the petitioning premises.

Added by Acts 2001, 77th Leg., ch. 651, § 4, eff. Sept. 1, 2001.

§ 56.209. Recovery of Costs

(a) If, after a hearing, the commission designates a telecommunications provider to serve the petitioning premises, the commission shall permit the designated provider to recover from the state universal service fund the provider's actual costs of providing service to the premises, including the provider's original cost of deployment and actual recurring costs.

(b) The reimbursable original cost of deploying facilities to the petitioning premises is the original cost of the telecommunications provider's facilities installed in, or upgraded to permit the provision of service to, the petitioning premises as determined by the financial accounting standards applicable to the provider, including an amount for the recovery of all costs that are typically included as capital costs for accounting purposes, that are not recovered through an aid to construction charge assessed to the petitioners. The final order permitting or requiring the designated provider to provide service to the petitioning premises shall ensure that all the original cost of the provider shall be amortized and recovered from the state universal service fund, together with interest at the prevailing commercial lending rate:

(1) not later than the third anniversary of the date of the order, for a deployment with an original cost of $1 million or less;

(2) not later than the fifth anniversary of the date of the order, for a deployment with an original cost of more than $1 million, but not more than $2 million; and

(3) not later than the seventh anniversary of the date of the order, for a deployment with an original cost of more than $2 million.

(c) The designated provider shall recover the provider's actual recurring costs of service, including maintenance and the ongoing operational costs of providing service after deployment of the facilities to the petitioning premises and a reasonable operating margin, from:

(1) the monthly rate charged the customer; and

(2) a monthly per line state universal service fund payment in an amount equal to the unrecovered recurring costs incurred in providing service divided by the access lines served in the petitioning premises.

(d) The monthly per line fee established under Subsection (c) is in addition to the universal service funds associated with the recovery of the original cost of deployment and interest authorized by Subsection (b) and in addition to the universal service funds the designated provider receives to provide service in other areas of this state.

(e) The commission may not authorize or require any services to be provided to petitioning premises under this subchapter during a fiscal year if the total amount of required reimbursements of actual original cost of deployment to all approved petitioning premises under this section, together with interest, including obligations for reimbursements from preceding years, would equal an amount that exceeds 0.02 percent of the annual gross revenues reported to the state universal service fund during the preceding fiscal year.

Added by Acts 2001, 77th Leg., ch. 651, § 4, eff. Sept. 1, 2001.

§ 56.210. Aid to Construction Charge; Contract for Services

The commission shall establish a reasonable aid to construction charge, not to exceed $3,000, to be assessed each petitioner. The commission may not require a designated provider to begin construction until:

(1) each petitioner has paid or executed an agreement acceptable to the provider to pay the aid to construction charge; and

(2) each petitioner has executed an assignable agreement for subscription to basic local service to the petitioning premises from the designated provider for a period at least equal to the period during which the provider will receive reimbursement for the original cost of deployment under Section 56.209(b).

Added by Acts 2001, 77th Leg., ch. 651, § 4, eff. Sept. 1, 2001.

§ 56.211. Permanent Premises Required

A telecommunications provider may not under any circumstances be required to extend service to a location that is not a permanent residential or business premises or be required to provide service to the petitioning premises before the 180th day after the date the provider was designated to provide service to the petitioning premises.

Added by Acts 2001, 77th Leg., ch. 651, § 4, eff. Sept. 1, 2001.

§ 56.212. Subsequent Related Petitions

(a) If the commission approves a petition requesting service, residents of permanent residential premises or owners of permanent residential or business premises in reasonable proximity to the premises that were the subject of an approved petition who did not sign the prior petition requesting service are not entitled to receive service under this subchapter until the fifth anniversary of the date the prior petition was filed unless the residents or owners file a new petition under this subchapter and agree to pay aid to construction charges on the same terms as applicable to the prior petitioners.

(b) The designated provider shall receive reimbursement for the original cost of deployment and actual recurring costs of providing service to those additional residents in the same manner as the provider received reimbursement of those costs in relation to the prior petitioners. The provider may not receive reimbursement for the original cost of deployment under a subsequent petition if the provider previously received complete reimbursement for those costs from the state universal service fund. If the state universal service fund has completely reimbursed the original cost of deployment as provided by this subchapter, each subsequent petitioner must pay into the state universal service fund an amount equal to the aid to construction charge paid by each prior petitioner.

Added by Acts 2001, 77th Leg., ch. 651, § 4, eff. Sept. 1, 2001.

§ 56.213. Preferred Provider

(a) A provider who is designated to serve petitioning premises located within an uncertificated area under this subchapter is the preferred provider for any permanent residential or business premises in reasonable proximity to those petitioning premises for later petitions filed under Section 56.212.

(b) A preferred designated provider is entitled to an opportunity for a hearing under Section 56.205 on a petition filed under Section 56.203.

Added by Acts 2001, 77th Leg., ch. 651, § 4, eff. Sept. 1, 2001.

§ 56.214. Certificate Not Amended

The designation of a provider to serve permanent residential or business premises within an uncertificated area under this subchapter does not have the effect of:

(1) amending the boundaries of the provider's certificate to provide local exchange service; or

(2) imposing carrier of last resort responsibilities on the provider.

Added by Acts 2001, 77th Leg., ch. 651, § 4, eff. Sept. 1, 2001.

SUBCHAPTER G. FUNDING FOR CERTAIN TELECOMMUNICATIONS UTILITIES

§ 56.251. Definition

In this subchapter, "successor utility" has the meaning assigned by Section 54.301.

Added by Acts 2003, 78th Leg., ch. 76, § 7, eff. Sept. 1, 2003.

§ 56.252. Telecommunications Utilities Eligible to Receive Funding Under This Subchapter

A telecommunications utility may receive funding under this subchapter only if:

(1) the telecommunications utility is eligible to receive universal service funding under Section 56.023(b); and

(2) the telecommunications utility is designated as a successor utility under Section 54.303.

Added by Acts 2003, 78th Leg., ch. 76, § 7, eff. Sept. 1, 2003.

§ 56.253. Determination of Successor Utility's Costs to be Recovered

(a) At the time the commission designates the successor utility under Section 54.303, the commission shall determine the extent to which the utility should recover the costs the utility will incur in accepting and establishing service to the affected service area.

(b) In making the determination under Subsection (a), the commission shall consider relevant information, including the costs of acquiring and restoring or upgrading the utility's facilities in the geographic area as necessary to make those facilities compatible with the facilities in the utility's other certificated service areas and to comply with commission quality of service standards.

Added by Acts 2003, 78th Leg., ch. 76, § 7, eff. Sept. 1, 2003.

§ 56.254. Recovery of Costs

The commission order designating the successor utility under Section 54.303 shall authorize the utility to recover the costs determined under Section 56.253. The costs may be amortized and recovered from the state universal service fund, together with interest at the prevailing commercial lending rate:

(1) not later than the first anniversary of the date of the order if the costs are not more than $1 million;

(2) not later than the second anniversary of the date of the order if the costs are more than $1 million but no more than $2 million; and

(3) not later than the third anniversary of the date of the order if the costs are more than $2 million.

Added by Acts 2003, 78th Leg., ch. 76, § 7, eff. Sept. 1, 2003.

SUBCHAPTER H. AUDIO NEWSPAPER PROGRAM

§ 56.301. Audio Newspaper Assistance Program

The commission by rule shall establish a program to provide from the universal service fund financial assistance for a free telephone service for blind and visually impaired persons that offers the text of newspapers using synthetic speech. The commission may adopt rules to implement the program.

Added by Acts 2005, 79th Leg., 2nd C.S., ch. 2, § 17, eff. Sept. 1, 2005.

CHAPTER 57. DISTANCE LEARNING AND OTHER ADVANCED SERVICES

SUBCHAPTER A. GENERAL PROVISIONS

Section

57.001. Conflict of Provisions.

SUBCHAPTER B. DISTANCE LEARNING AND INFORMATION SHARING

57.021. Definitions.
57.022. Reduced Rates for Distance Learning or Information Sharing Services.
57.023. Service and Rate Requirements.
57.024. Tariff Filings.
57.025. Changes in Rate Program.

SUBCHAPTER C. TELECOMMUNICATIONS INFRASTRUCTURE FUND [REPEALED]

57.041, 57.042. Repealed.
57.043. Repealed.
57.044 to 57.051. Repealed.

SUBCHAPTER D. INTERACTIVE MULTIMEDIA COMMUNICATIONS

57.071. Definition.
57.072. Rates for Interactive Multimedia Communications.

SUBCHAPTER A. GENERAL PROVISIONS

§ 57.001. Conflict of Provisions

If this chapter conflicts with another provision of this title, this chapter prevails.

Acts 1997, 75th Leg., ch. 166, § 1, eff. Sept. 1, 1997.

SUBCHAPTER B. DISTANCE LEARNING AND INFORMATION SHARING

§ 57.021. Definitions

In this subchapter:

(1) "Distance learning" means an instruction, learning, or training resource, including video, data, voice, or electronic information, that is:

(A) used by an educational institution predominantly for instruction, learning, or training; and

(B) transmitted from a site to one or more other sites by a telecommunications service.

(2) "Educational institution" includes:

(A) an accredited primary or secondary school;

(B) an institution of higher education as defined by Section 61.003, Education Code;

(C) a private institution of higher education accredited by a recognized accrediting agency as defined by Section 61.003, Education Code;

(D) the Texas Education Agency and its successors and assigns;

(E) a regional education service center established and operated in accordance with Chapter 8, Education Code; or

(F) the Texas Higher Education Coordinating Board and its successors and assigns.

(3) "Library" means:

(A) a public library or regional library system as defined by Section 441.122, Government Code; or

(B) a library operated by an institution of higher education or a school district.

Acts 1997, 75th Leg., ch. 166, § 1, eff. Sept. 1, 1997.

§ 57.022. Reduced Rates for Distance Learning or Information Sharing Services

(a) The commission by rule shall require a dominant carrier to file a tariff that includes a reduced rate for a telecommunications service the commission finds is directly related to:

(1) a distance learning activity that is or could be conducted by an educational institution in this state; or

(2) an information sharing program that is or could be conducted by a library in this state.

(b) The commission rules shall specify:

(1) each telecommunications service to which Subsection (a) applies;

(2) the process for an educational institution or library to qualify for a reduced rate;

(3) the date by which a dominant carrier is required to file a tariff;

(4) guidelines and criteria that require the services and reduced rates to further the goals prescribed by Section 57.023; and

(5) any other requirement or term that the commission determines to be in the public interest.

(c) The commission is not required to determine the long run incremental cost of providing a service before approving a reduced rate for the service.

(d) Until cost determination rules are developed and the rates established under this section are changed as necessary to ensure proper cost recovery, the reduced rates established by the commission shall be equal to 75 percent of the otherwise applicable rate.

(e) After the commission develops cost determination rules for telecommunications services generally, the commission shall ensure that a reduced rate approved under this section:

(1) recovers service-specific long run incremental costs; and

(2) avoids subsidizing an educational institution or a library.

Acts 1997, 75th Leg., ch. 166, § 1, eff. Sept. 1, 1997.

§ 57.023. Service and Rate Requirements

The services and reduced rates must be designed to:

(1) encourage the development and offering of:

(A) distance learning activities by educational institutions; and

(B) information sharing programs of libraries;

(2) meet the:

(A) distance learning needs identified by the educational community; and

(B) information sharing needs identified by libraries; and

(3) recover the long run incremental costs of providing the services, to the extent those costs can be identified, to avoid subsidizing an educational institution or a library.

Acts 1997, 75th Leg., ch. 166, § 1, eff. Sept. 1, 1997.

§ 57.024. Tariff Filings

A tariff filed by a dominant carrier under Section 57.022:

(1) may concern the implementation of this subchapter only;

(2) is not a rate change under Subchapter C, Chapter 53; [1] and

(3) does not affect the carrier's other rates or services.

Acts 1997, 75th Leg., ch. 166, § 1, eff. Sept. 1, 1997.

[1] V.T.C.A., Utilities Code § 53.101 et seq.

§ 57.025. Changes in Rate Program

(a) An educational institution, library, or dominant carrier may request the commission to:

(1) provide for a reduced rate for a service that:

(A) is directly related to a distance learning activity or an information sharing program; and

(B) is not covered by commission rules;

(2) change a rate;

(3) amend a tariff; or

(4) amend a commission rule.

(b) The commission shall take the action requested under Subsection (a) if the commission determines the action is appropriate.

Acts 1997, 75th Leg., ch. 166, § 1, eff. Sept. 1, 1997.

SUBCHAPTER C. TELECOMMUNICATIONS INFRASTRUCTURE FUND [REPEALED]

§§ 57.041, 57.042. Repealed by Acts 2007, 80th Leg., ch. 831, § 1(b), eff. Oct. 1, 2007

§ 57.043. Repealed by Acts 2005, 79th Leg., ch. 899, § 9.04, eff. Sept. 1, 2005

§§ 57.044 to 57.051. Repealed by Acts 2007, 80th Leg., ch. 831, § 1(b), eff. Oct. 1, 2007

SUBCHAPTER D. INTERACTIVE MULTIMEDIA COMMUNICATIONS

§ 57.071. Definition

In this subchapter, "interactive multimedia communications" means real-time, two-way, interactive voice, video, and data communications conducted over networks that link geographically dispersed locations.

Acts 1997, 75th Leg., ch. 166, § 1, eff. Sept. 1, 1997.

§ 57.072. Rates for Interactive Multimedia Communications

(a) The commission shall permit a local exchange company that provides an interactive multimedia communications service to establish, using sound ratemaking principles, rates necessary to recover costs associated with providing the service.

(b) A local exchange company may not establish a rate under Subsection (a) that is less than the local exchange company's long run incremental costs of providing the interactive multimedia communications service, unless the commission determines it to be in the public interest to do so.

Acts 1997, 75th Leg., ch. 166, § 1, eff. Sept. 1, 1997.

CHAPTER 58. INCENTIVE REGULATION

SUBCHAPTER A. GENERAL PROVISIONS

Section
58.001. Policy.
58.002. Definition.
58.003. Customer-Specific Contracts.
58.004. Packaging, Term and Volume Discounts, and Promotional Offerings.

SUBCHAPTER B. ELECTION OF INCENTIVE REGULATION

58.021. Election.
58.022. Chapter Controls.
58.023. Service Classification.
58.024. Service Reclassification.
58.025. Complaint or Hearing.
58.026. Consumer Complaints Regarding Tariffs.
58.027. Consumer Complaints Regarding Services; Enforcement of Standards.
58.028. Expired.

SUBCHAPTER C. BASIC NETWORK SERVICES

58.051. Services Included.
58.052. Regulation of Services.
58.053. Investment Limitation on Service Standards.
58.054. Rates Capped.
58.055. Rate Adjustment by Company.
58.056. Rate Adjustment for Changes in FCC Separations.
58.057. Rate Adjustment for Certain Companies.
58.058. Rate Group Reclassification.
58.059. Commission Rate Adjustment Procedure.
58.060. Rate Adjustment After Cap Expiration.
58.061. Effect on Certain Charges.
58.062. Repealed.
58.063. Pricing and Packaging Flexibility.

SUBCHAPTER D. DISCRETIONARY SERVICES [REPEALED]

58.101 to 58.104. Repealed.

SUBCHAPTER E. NONBASIC SERVICES

Section
58.151. Services Included.
58.152. Prices.
58.153. New Services.
[Section 58.154 reserved for expansion]
58.155. Interconnection.

SUBCHAPTER F. GENERAL INFRASTRUCTURE COMMITMENT

58.201. Statement of State Goal.
58.202. Policy Goals for Implementation.
58.203. Infrastructure Goals of All Electing Companies.
58.204. Additional Infrastructure Commitment of Certain Companies.
58.205. Extension or Waiver of Infrastructure Requirements.
58.206. Implementation Costs; Increase in Rates and Universal Service Funds.

SUBCHAPTER G. INFRASTRUCTURE COMMITMENT TO CERTAIN ENTITIES

58.251. Intent and Goal of Subchapter.
58.252. Definitions.
58.253. Private Network Services for Certain Entities.
58.254. Priorities.
58.255. Contracts for Private Network Services.
58.256. Preferred Rate Treatment Warranted.
58.257. Election of Rate Treatment.
58.258. Private Network Services Rates and Tariffs.
58.259. Tariff Rate for Certain IntraLATA Service.
58.260. Point-To-Point 45 Megabits a Second IntraLATA Service.
58.261. Broadband Digital Special Access Service.
58.262. Expanded Interconnection.
58.263. Internet Access.
58.264. Complaints Limited.
58.265. Interconnection of Network Services.
58.266. Sharing or Resale of Network Services.
58.267. Implementation Costs; Increase in Rates and Universal Service Funds.
58.268. Continuation of Obligation.

SUBCHAPTER H. SWITCHED ACCESS SERVICES

58.301. Switched Access Rate Reduction.
58.302. Switched Access Rate Cap.
58.303. Expired.

SUBCHAPTER A. GENERAL PROVISIONS

§ 58.001. Policy

Considering the status of competition in the telecommunications industry, it is the policy of this state to:

(1) provide a framework for an orderly transition from the traditional regulation of return on invested capital to a fully competitive telecommunications marketplace in which all telecommunications providers compete on fair terms;

(2) preserve and enhance universal telecommunications service at affordable rates;

(3) upgrade the telecommunications infrastructure of this state;

(4) promote network interconnectivity; and

(5) promote diversity in the supply of telecommunications services and innovative products and services throughout the entire state, including urban and rural areas.

Acts 1997, 75th Leg., ch. 166, § 1, eff. Sept. 1, 1997.

§ 58.002. Definition

In this chapter, "electing company" means an incumbent local exchange company that elects to be subject to incentive regulation and to make the corresponding infrastructure commitment under this chapter.

Acts 1997, 75th Leg., ch. 166, § 1, eff. Sept. 1, 1997.

§ 58.003. Customer-Specific Contracts

(a) Notwithstanding any other provision of this chapter, but subject to Subsection (b), an electing company may not offer in an exchange a service, or an appropriate subset of a service, listed in Sections 58.051(a)(1)–(4) or Sections 58.151(1)–(4) in a manner that results in a customer-specific contract, unless the other party to the contract is a federal, state, or local governmental entity, until the earlier of September 1, 2003, or the date on which the commission finds that at least 40 percent of the total access lines for that service or appropriate subset of that service in that exchange are served by competitive alternative providers that are not affiliated with the electing company.

(b) The requirements prescribed by Subsection (a) do not apply to an electing company serving fewer than five million access lines after the date on which it completes the infrastructure improvements described in this subsection. The electing company must also notify the commission of the company's binding commitment to make the following infrastructure improvements not later than September 1, 2000:

(1) install Common Channel Signaling 7 capability in each central office; and

(2) connect all of the company's serving central offices to their respective LATA tandem central offices with optical fiber or equivalent facilities.

(c) The commission by rule shall prescribe appropriate subsets of services.

(d) An electing company may file with the commission a request for a finding under this section. The filing must include information sufficient for the commission to perform a review and evaluation in relation to the particular exchange and the particular service or appropriate subset of a service for which the electing company wants to offer customer-specific contracts. The commission must grant or deny the request not later than the 60th day after the date the electing company files the request.

(e) The commitments described by Subsection (b) do not apply to exchanges of the company sold or transferred before, or for which contracts for sale or transfer are pending on, September 1, 2001. In the case of exchanges for which contracts for sale or transfer are pending as of March 1, 2001, where the purchaser withdrew or defaulted before September 1, 2001, the company shall have one year from the date of withdrawal or default to comply with the commitments.

(f) This section does not preclude an electing company from offering a customer-specific contract to the extent allowed by this title as of August 31, 1999.

Added by Acts 1999, 76th Leg., ch. 1212, § 33, eff. Sept. 1, 1999.

§ 58.004. Packaging, Term and Volume Discounts, and Promotional Offerings

(a) Notwithstanding any other provision of this chapter, an electing company that has more than five million access lines in this state may not offer in an exchange a service listed in Sections 58.151(1)–(4) as a component of a package of services or as a promotional offering until the company makes the reduction in switched access service rates required by Section 58.301(2) unless the customer of one of the pricing flexibility offerings described in this subsection is a federal, state, or local governmental entity.

(b) Notwithstanding any other provision of this chapter, an electing company that has more than five million access lines in this state may not offer a volume or term discount on any service listed in Sections 58.151(1)–(4) until September 1, 2000, unless the customer of one of the pricing flexibility offerings described in this subsection is a federal, state, or local governmental entity.

(c) Notwithstanding any other provision of this chapter, an electing company that has more than five million access lines in this state may offer in an exchange a service listed in Sections 58.051(a)(1)–(4) as a component of a package of services, as a promotional offering, or with a volume or term discount on and after September 1, 1999.

Added by Acts 1999, 76th Leg., ch. 1212, § 34, eff. Sept. 1, 1999.

SUBCHAPTER B. ELECTION OF INCENTIVE REGULATION

§ 58.021. Election

(a) An incumbent local exchange company may elect to be subject to incentive regulation and to make the corresponding infrastructure commitment under this chapter by notifying the commission in writing of its election.

(b) The notice must include a statement that the company agrees to:

(1) limit until September 1, 2005, any increase in a rate the company charges for basic network services as prescribed by Subchapter C; [1] and

(2) fulfill the infrastructure commitment prescribed by Subchapters F and G.[2]

(c) Except as provided in Subsection (d), an election under this chapter remains in effect until the legislature eliminates the incentive regulation authorized by this chapter and Chapter 59.

(d) The commission may allow an electing company serving fewer than five million access lines to withdraw the company's election under this chapter:

(1) on application by the company; and

(2) only for good cause.

(e) In this section, "good cause" includes only matters beyond the control of the company.

Acts 1997, 75th Leg., ch. 166, § 1, eff. Sept. 1, 1997. Amended by Acts 1999, 76th Leg., ch. 1212, § 35, eff. Sept. 1, 1999.

[1] V.T.C.A., Utilities Code § 58.051 et seq.

[2] V.T.C.A., Utilities Code § 58.201 et seq. and § 58.251 et seq.

§ 58.022. Chapter Controls

This chapter governs the regulation of an electing company's telecommunications services regardless of whether the company is a dominant carrier.

Acts 1997, 75th Leg., ch. 166, § 1, eff. Sept. 1, 1997.

§ 58.023. Service Classification

On election, the services provided by an electing company are classified into two categories:

(1) basic network services governed by Subchapter C; [1] and

(2) nonbasic services governed by Subchapter E.[2]

(3) Renumbered (2) by Acts 1999, 76th Leg., ch. 1212, § 36, eff. Sept. 1, 1999

Acts 1997, 75th Leg., ch. 166, § 1, eff. Sept. 1, 1997. Amended by Acts 1999, 76th Leg., ch. 1212, § 36, eff. Sept. 1, 1999.

[1] V.T.C.A., Utilities Code § 58.051 et seq.

[2] V.T.C.A., Utilities Code § 58.151 et seq.

§ 58.024. Service Reclassification

(a) The commission may reclassify a basic network service as a nonbasic service.

(b) The commission shall establish criteria for determining whether a service should be reclassified. The criteria must include consideration of the:

(1) availability of the service from other providers;

(2) effect of the reclassification on service subscribers; and

(3) nature of the service.

(c) The commission may not reclassify a service until:

(1) each competitive safeguard prescribed by Subchapters B–H, Chapter 60,[1] is fully implemented; or

(2) for a company that serves more than five million access lines in this state, the date on which the Federal Communications Commission determines in accordance with 47 U.S.C. Section 271 that the company or any of its affiliates may enter the interLATA telecommunications market in this state.

(d) The commission may reclassify a service subject to the following conditions:

(1) the electing company must file a request for a service reclassification including information sufficient for the commission to perform a review and evaluation under Subsection (b);

(2) the commission must grant or deny the request not later than the 60th day after the date the electing company files the request for service reclassification; and

(3) there is a rebuttable presumption that the request for service reclassification by the electing company should be granted if the commission finds that there is a competitive alternative provider serving customers through means other than total service resale.

Acts 1997, 75th Leg., ch. 166, § 1, eff. Sept. 1, 1997. Amended by Acts 1999, 76th Leg., ch. 62, § 18.11, eff. Sept. 1, 1999; Acts 1999, 76th Leg., ch. 1212, § 37, eff. Sept. 1, 1999.

[1] V.T.C.A., Utilities Code § 60.021 et seq. to § 60.141.

§ 58.025. Complaint or Hearing

(a) An electing company is not, under any circumstances, subject to a complaint, hearing, or determination regarding the reasonableness of the company's:

(1) rates;

(2) overall revenues;

(3) return on invested capital; or

(4) net income.

(b) This section does not prohibit a complaint, hearing, or determination on an electing company's implementation and enforcement of a competitive safeguard required by Chapter 60.

Acts 1997, 75th Leg., ch. 166, § 1, eff. Sept. 1, 1997.

§ 58.026. Consumer Complaints Regarding Tariffs

(a) This chapter does not restrict:

(1) a consumer's right to complain to the commission about the application of an ambiguous tariff; or

(2) the commission's right to determine:

(A) the proper application of that tariff; or

(B) the proper rate if that tariff does not apply.

(b) This section does not permit the commission to:

(1) lower a tariff rate except as specifically provided by this title;

(2) change the commission's interpretation of a tariff; or

(3) extend the application of a tariff to a new class of customers.

Acts 1997, 75th Leg., ch. 166, § 1, eff. Sept. 1, 1997.

§ 58.027. Consumer Complaints Regarding Services; Enforcement of Standards

This chapter does not restrict:

(1) a consumer's right to complain to the commission about quality of service; or

(2) the commission's right to enforce a quality of service standard.

Acts 1997, 75th Leg., ch. 166, § 1, eff. Sept. 1, 1997.

§ 58.028. Expired

SUBCHAPTER C. BASIC NETWORK SERVICES

§ 58.051. Services Included

(a) Unless reclassified under Section 58.024, the following services are basic network services:

(1) flat rate residential local exchange telephone service, including primary directory listings and the receipt of a directory and any applicable mileage or zone charges;

(2) residential tone dialing service;

(3) lifeline and tel-assistance service;

(4) service connection for basic residential services;

(5) direct inward dialing service for basic residential services;

(6) private pay telephone access service;

(7) call trap and trace service;

(8) access for all residential and business end users to 911 service provided by a local authority and access to dual party relay service;

(9) mandatory residential extended area service arrangements; and

(10) mandatory residential extended metropolitan service or other mandatory residential toll-free calling arrangements.

(a–1) Notwithstanding Subsection (a) and Section 58.151, basic network services include residential caller identification services if the customer to whom the service is billed is at least 65 years of age.

(b) Electing companies shall offer each basic network service as a separately tariffed service in addition to any packages or other pricing flexibility offerings that include those basic network services.

(c) At the election of the affected incumbent local exchange company, the price for basic network service shall also include the fees and charges for any mandatory extended area service arrangements, mandatory expanded toll-free calling plans, and any other service included in the definition of basic network service.

(d) A nonpermanent expanded toll-free local calling service surcharge established by the commission to recover the costs of mandatory expanded toll-free local calling service:

(1) is considered a part of basic network service;

(2) may not be aggregated under Subsection (c); and

(3) continues to be transitioned in accordance with commission orders and substantive rules.

Acts 1997, 75th Leg., ch. 166, § 1, eff. Sept. 1, 1997. Amended by Acts 1999, 76th Leg., ch. 1212, § 39, eff. Sept. 1, 1999; Acts 2005, 79th Leg., 2nd C.S., ch. 2, § 18, eff. Sept. 1, 2005.

§ 58.052. Regulation of Services

(a) Except as provided by Subchapter E, Chapter 52,[1] basic network services of an electing company are regulated:

(1) in accordance with this chapter; and

(2) to the extent not inconsistent with this chapter, in accordance with:

(A) Subtitle A; [2]

(B) Chapters 51, 54, 60, 62, and 63;

(C) Chapter 52, except for Subchapter F; [3]

(D) Subchapters C, D, and E, Chapter 53; [4]

(E) Chapter 55, except for:

(i) Subchapters F and G; [5] and

(ii) Sections 55.001, 55.002, 55.003, and 55.004;

(F) Sections 53.001, 53.003, 53.004, 53.006, 53.065, 55.005, 55.006, 55.009, and 55.010; and

(G) commission rules and procedures.

(b) The commission must approve a change in the terms of the tariff offering of a basic network service.

Acts 1997, 75th Leg., ch. 166, § 1, eff. Sept. 1, 1997.

[1] V.T.C.A., Utilities Code § 52.201 et seq.
[2] V.T.C.A., Utilities Code § 11.001 et seq.
[3] V.T.C.A., Utilities Code § 52.251 et seq.
[4] V.T.C.A., Utilities Code § 53.101 et seq., §§ 53.151, 53.152; and §§ 53.201, 53.202.
[5] V.T.C.A., Utilities Code § 55.121 et seq. and §§ 55.151, 55.152.

§ 58.053. Investment Limitation on Service Standards

(a) The commission may not raise a service standard applicable to the provision of local exchange telephone service by an electing company if the increased investment required to comply with the raised standard in any year exceeds 10 percent of the company's average annual intrastate additions in capital investment for the most recent five-year period.

(b) In computing the average under Subsection (a), the company shall exclude:

(1) extraordinary investments made during the five-year period; and

(2) investments required by Section 58.203.

Acts 1997, 75th Leg., ch. 166, § 1, eff. Sept. 1, 1997.

§ 58.054. Rates Capped

(a) As a condition of election under this chapter, an electing company shall commit to not increasing a rate for a basic network service on or before the fourth anniversary of its election date.

(b) The rates an electing company may charge on or before that fourth anniversary are the rates charged by the company on June 1, 1995, or, for a company that elects under this chapter after September 1, 1999, the rates charged on the date of its election, without regard to a proceeding pending under:

(1) Section 15.001;

(2) Subchapter D, Chapter 53; [1] or

(3) Subchapter G, Chapter 2001, Government Code.[2]

(c) Notwithstanding Subsections (a) and (b), the cap on the rates for basic network services for a company electing under this chapter may not expire before September 1, 2005.

Acts 1997, 75th Leg., ch. 166, § 1, eff. Sept. 1, 1997. Amended by Acts 1999, 76th Leg., ch. 1212, § 40, eff. Sept. 1, 1999.

[1] V.T.C.A., Utilities Code §§ 53.151, 53.152.
[2] V.T.C.A., Government Code § 2001.171 et seq.

§ 58.055. Rate Adjustment by Company

(a) An electing company may increase a rate for a basic network service during the election period prescribed by Section 58.054 only:

(1) with commission approval that the proposed change is included in Section 58.056, 58.057, or 58.058; and

(2) as provided by Sections 58.056, 58.057, 58.058, and 58.059.

(b) Notwithstanding Subchapter F, Chapter 60,[1] an electing company may, on its own initiative, decrease a rate for a basic network service during the electing period.

(c) The company may decrease the rate for a basic local telecommunications service to an amount above the service's appropriate cost. If the company has been required to perform or has elected to perform a long run incremental cost study, the appropriate cost for the service is the service's long run incremental cost.

Acts 1997, 75th Leg., ch. 166, § 1, eff. Sept. 1, 1997. Amended by Acts 1999, 76th Leg., ch. 1212, § 40, eff. Sept. 1, 1999.

[1] V.T.C.A., Utilities Code §§ 60.101, 60.102.

§ 58.056. Rate Adjustment for Changes in FCC Separations

The commission, on motion of the electing company or on its own motion, shall proportionally adjust rates for services to reflect changes in Federal Communications Commission separations that affect intrastate net income by at least 10 percent.

Acts 1997, 75th Leg., ch. 166, § 1, eff. Sept. 1, 1997.

§ 58.057. Rate Adjustment for Certain Companies

(a) An electing company, after the 42nd month after the date the company elects incentive regulation under this chapter, may file an application for a commission review of the company's need for changes in the rates of its services if the company:

(1) has fewer than five million access lines in this state; and

(2) is complying with:

(A) the company's infrastructure commitment;

(B) each requirement relating to quality of service; and

(C) each commission rule adopted under Chapter 60.

(b) The company's application may request that the commission adjust rates, implement new pricing plans, restructure rates, or rebalance revenues between services to recognize changed market conditions and the effects of competitive entry.

(c) The commission may use an index and a productivity offset in determining the requested changes.

(d) The commission may not:

(1) order an increase in the rate for residential local exchange telephone service that would cause the rate to increase by more than the United States Consumer Price Index in any 12-month period; or

(2) set the monthly rate for residential local exchange telephone service in an amount that exceeds the nationwide average rates for similar local exchange telephone services.

Acts 1997, 75th Leg., ch. 166, § 1, eff. Sept. 1, 1997.

§ 58.058. Rate Group Reclassification

Notwithstanding Subchapter B,[1] the commission, on request of the electing company, shall allow a rate group reclassification that results from access line growth.

Acts 1997, 75th Leg., ch. 166, § 1, eff. Sept. 1, 1997.

[1] V.T.C.A., Utilities Code § 58.021 et seq.

§ 58.059. Commission Rate Adjustment Procedure

(a) In accordance with this section, an electing company may request and the commission may authorize a rate adjustment under Section 58.056, 58.057, or 58.058.

(b) The electing company must provide to the commission notice of its intent to adjust rates. The notice must be accompanied by sufficient documentary evidence to demonstrate that the rate adjustment is authorized under Section 58.056, 58.057, or 58.058. The commission by rule or order shall prescribe the documentation required under this subsection.

(c) The electing company must also provide notice to its customers after providing notice to the commission. The notice to the customers must:

(1) within a reasonable period after notice to the commission, be published once in a newspaper of general circulation in the affected service area;

(2) be included in or printed on each affected consumer's bill in the first billing that occurs after notice is filed with the commission;

(3) have a title that includes the name of the company and the words "NOTICE OF POSSIBLE RATE CHANGE"; and

(4) include:

(A) a statement that the consumer's rate may change;

(B) an estimate of the amount of the annual change for the typical residential, business, or access consumer if the commission approves the rate change;

(C) a statement that a consumer who wants to comment on the rate change or who wants additional information regarding the rate change may call or write the commission and that the information will be provided without cost to the consumer and at the expense of the electing company; and

(D) the commission's telephone number and address.

(d) The estimate of the amount of the annual change required by Subsection (c)(4)(B) must be printed in a type style and size that is distinct from and larger than the type style and size of the body of the notice.

(e) The commission shall review the proposed rates to determine if the rate adjustment is authorized under Section 58.056, 58.057, or 58.058.

(f) The rate adjustment takes effect on the 90th day after the date the electing company completes the notice required by this section unless the commission suspends the effective date under Subsection (g).

(g) At any time before a rate adjustment is scheduled to take effect, the commission, on its own motion or on complaint by an affected party, may suspend the effective date of the rate adjustment and conduct a hearing to review the proposed adjustment. After the hearing, the commission may issue an order approving the adjustment, or if it finds that the adjustment is not authorized under Section 58.056, 58.057, or 58.058, issue an order modifying or rejecting the adjustment. An order modifying or rejecting a rate adjustment must specify:

(1) each reason why the proposed adjustment was not authorized by Section 58.056, 58.057, or 58.058; and

(2) how the proposed adjustment may be changed so that it is authorized.

(h) Except as provided by this section, a request for a rate restructure must comply with the notice and hearing requirements prescribed by Sections 53.101–53.106.

(i) An electing company that has not more than five percent of the total access lines in this state may adopt as the cost for a service the cost for the same or substantially similar service offered by a larger incumbent local exchange company. The electing company may adopt the larger company's cost only if the cost was determined based on a long run incremental cost study. An electing company that adopts a cost under this subsection is not required to present its own long run incremental cost study to support the adopted cost.

Acts 1997, 75th Leg., ch. 166, § 1, eff. Sept. 1, 1997.

§ 58.060. Rate Adjustment After Cap Expiration

After the expiration of the period during which the rates for basic network services are capped as prescribed by Section 58.054, an electing company may increase a rate for a basic network service only:

(1) with commission approval subject to this title; and

(2) to the extent consistent with achieving universal affordable service.

Acts 1997, 75th Leg., ch. 166, § 1, eff. Sept. 1, 1997. Amended by Acts 1999, 76th Leg., ch. 1212, § 41, eff. Sept. 1, 1999.

§ 58.061. Effect on Certain Charges

This subchapter does not affect a charge permitted under:

(1) Section 55.024;

(2) Subchapter C, Chapter 55; [1] or

(3) Subchapter B, Chapter 56.[2]

Acts 1997, 75th Leg., ch. 166, § 1, eff. Sept. 1, 1997.

[1] V.T.C.A., Utilities Code § 55.041 et seq.

[2] V.T.C.A., Utilities Code § 56.021 et seq.

§ 58.062. Repealed by Acts 1999, 76th Leg., ch. 1212, § 57(1), eff. Sept. 1, 1999

§ 58.063. Pricing and Packaging Flexibility

(a) Notwithstanding Section 58.052(b) or Subchapter F, Chapter 60,[1] an electing company may exercise pricing flexibility for basic network services, including the packaging of basic network services with any other regulated or unregulated service or any service of an affiliate. The company may exercise pricing flexibility in accordance with this section 10 days after providing an informational notice to the commission, to the office, and to any person who holds a certificate of operating authority in the electing company's certificated area or areas or who has an effective interconnection agreement with the electing company.

(b) An electing company shall set the price of a package of services containing basic network services and nonbasic services at any level at or above the lesser of:

(1) the sum of the long run incremental costs of any basic network services and nonbasic services contained in the package; or

(2) the sum of the tariffed prices of any basic network services contained in the package and the long run incremental costs of nonbasic services contained in the package.

(c) Except as provided by Section 58.003, an electing company may flexibly price a package that includes a basic network service in any manner provided by Section 51.002(7).

Added by Acts 1999, 76th Leg., ch. 1212, § 42, eff. Sept. 1, 1999.

[1] V.T.C.A., Utilities Code §§ 60.101, 60.102.

SUBCHAPTER D. DISCRETIONARY SERVICES [REPEALED]

§§ 58.101 to 58.104. Repealed by Acts 1999, 76th Leg., ch. 1212, § 57(2), eff. Sept. 1, 1999

SUBCHAPTER E. NONBASIC SERVICES

Acts 1999, 76th Leg., ch. 1212, § 43, in the Subchapter E heading substituted "Nonbasic" for "Competitive".

§ 58.151. Services Included

The following services are classified as nonbasic services:

(1) flat rate business local exchange telephone service, including primary directory listings and the receipt of a directory, and any applicable mileage or zone charges, except that the prices for this service shall be capped until September 1, 2005, at the prices in effect on September 1, 1999;

(2) business tone dialing service, except that the prices for this service shall be capped until September 1, 2005, at the prices in effect on September 1, 1999;

(3) service connection for all business services, except that the prices for this service shall be capped until September 1, 2005, at the prices in effect on September 1, 1999;

(4) direct inward dialing for basic business services, except that the prices for this service shall be capped until September 1, 2005, at the prices in effect on September 1, 1999;

(5) "1–plus" intraLATA message toll services;

(6) 0+ and 0- operator services;

(7) call waiting, call forwarding, and custom calling, except that:

(A) residential call waiting service shall be classified as a basic network service until July 1, 2006; and

(B) for an electing company subject to Section 58.301, prices for residential call forwarding and other custom calling services shall be capped at the prices in effect on September 1, 1999, until the electing company implements the reduction in switched access rates described by Section 58.301(2);

(8) call return, caller identification, and call control options, except that, for an electing company subject to Section 58.301, prices for residential call return, caller identification, and call control options shall be capped at the prices in effect on September 1, 1999, until the electing company implements the reduction in switched access rates described by Section 58.301(2);

(9) central office based PBX–type services;

(10) billing and collection services, including installment billing and late payment charges for customers of the electing company;

(11) integrated services digital network (ISDN) services, except that prices for Basic Rate Interface (BRI) ISDN services, which comprise up to two 64 Kbps B–channels and one 16 Kbps D–channel, shall be capped until September 1, 2005, at the prices in effect on September 1, 1999;

(12) new services;

(13) directory assistance services, except that an electing company shall provide to a residential customer the first three directory assistance inquiries in a monthly billing cycle at no charge until July 1, 2006;

(14) services described in the WATS tariff as the tariff existed on January 1, 1995;

(15) 800 and foreign exchange services;

(16) private line service;

(17) special access service;

(18) services from public pay telephones;

(19) paging services and mobile services (IMTS);

(20) 911 services provided to a local authority that are available from another provider;

(21) speed dialing;

(22) three–way calling; and

(23) all other services subject to the commission's jurisdiction that are not specifically classified as basic network services in Section 58.051, except that nothing in this section shall preclude a customer from subscribing to a local flat rate residential or business line for a computer modem or a facsimile machine.

Acts 1997, 75th Leg., ch. 166, § 1, eff. Sept. 1, 1997. Amended by Acts 1999, 76th Leg., ch. 1212, § 43, eff. Sept. 1, 1999; Acts 2005, 79th Leg., 2nd C.S., ch. 2, § 19, eff. Sept. 1, 2005.

§ 58.152. Prices

(a) An electing company may set the price for any nonbasic service at any level above the lesser of the:

(1) service's long run incremental cost in accordance with the imputation rules prescribed by or under Subchapter D, Chapter 60;[1] or

(2) price for the service in effect on September 1, 1999.

(b) Subject to Section 51.004, an electing company may use pricing flexibility for a nonbasic service. Pricing flexibility includes all pricing arrangements included in the definition of "pricing flexibility" prescribed by Section 51.002 and includes packages that include basic network services.

Acts 1997, 75th Leg., ch. 166, § 1, eff. Sept. 1, 1997. Amended by Acts 1999, 76th Leg., ch. 1212, § 43, eff. Sept. 1, 1999.

[1] V.T.C.A., Utilities Code § 60.061 et seq.

§ 58.153. New Services

(a) Subject to the pricing conditions prescribed by Section 58.152(a), an electing company may introduce a new service 10 days after providing an informational notice to the commission, to the office, and to any person who holds a certificate of operating authority in the electing company's certificated area or areas or who has an effective interconnection agreement with the electing company.

(b) An electing company serving more than five million access lines in this state shall provide notice to any person who holds a certificate of operating authority in the electing company's certificated area or areas or who has an effective interconnection agreement with the electing company of any changes in the generally available prices and terms under which the electing company offers basic or nonbasic telecommunications services regulated by the commission at retail rates to subscribers that are not telecommunications providers. Changes requiring notice under this subsection include the introduction of any new nonbasic services, any new features or functions of basic or nonbasic services, promotional offerings of basic or nonbasic services, or the discontinuation of then-current features or services. The electing company shall provide the notice:

(1) if the electing company is required to give notice to the commission, at the same time the company provides that notice; or

(2) if the electing company is not required to give notice to the commission, at least 45 days before the effective date of a price change or 90 days before the effective date of a change other than a price change, unless the commission determines that the notice should not be given.

(c) An affected person, the office on behalf of residential or small commercial customers, or the commission may file a complaint at the commission challenging whether the pricing by an incumbent local exchange company of a new service is in compliance with Section 58.152(a). The commission shall allow the company to continue to provide the service while the complaint is pending.

(d) If a complaint is filed under Subsection (c), the electing company has the burden of proving that the company set the price for the new service in accordance with Section 58.152(a). If the complaint is finally resolved in favor of the complainant, the company:

(1) shall, not later than the 10th day after the date the complaint is finally resolved, amend the price of the service as necessary to comply with the final resolution; or

(2) may, at the company's option, discontinue the service.

(e) The notice requirement prescribed by Subsection (b) expires September 1, 2003.

Added by Acts 1999, 76th Leg., ch. 1212, § 43, eff. Sept. 1, 1999.

[Section 58.154 reserved for expansion]

§ 58.155. Interconnection

Because interconnection to competitive providers and interconnection for commercial mobile service providers are subject to the requirements of Sections 251 and 252, Communications Act of 1934 (47 U.S.C. Sections 251 and 252), as amended, and Federal Communications Commission rules, including the commission's authority to arbitrate issues, interconnection is not addressed in this subchapter or Subchapter B.[1]

Added by Acts 1999, 76th Leg., ch. 1212, § 44, eff. Sept. 1, 1999.

[1] V.T.C.A., Utilities Code § 58.021 et seq.

SUBCHAPTER F. GENERAL INFRASTRUCTURE COMMITMENT

§ 58.201. Statement of State Goal

(a) It is the goal of this state to facilitate and promote the deployment of an advanced telecommunications infrastructure to spur economic development throughout this state. This state should be among the leaders in achieving this objective.

(b) The primary means of achieving this goal is through encouraging private investment in this state's telecommunications infrastructure by creating incentives for that investment and promoting the development of competition.

(c) The best way to bring the benefits of an advanced telecommunications network infrastructure to communities in this state is through innovation and competition among all the state's communications providers. Competition will provide residents of this state with a choice of telecommunications providers and will drive technology deployment, innovation, service quality, and cost-based prices as competing firms try to satisfy customer needs.

Acts 1997, 75th Leg., ch. 166, § 1, eff. Sept. 1, 1997.

§ 58.202. Policy Goals for Implementation

In implementing this subchapter, the commission shall consider this state's policy goals to:

(1) ensure the availability of the widest possible range of competitive choices in the provision of telecommunications services and facilities;

(2) foster competition and rely on market forces where competition exists to determine the price, terms, and availability of service;

(3) ensure the universal availability of basic local telecommunications services at reasonable rates;

(4) encourage the continued development and deployment of advanced and reliable capabilities and services in telecommunications networks;

(5) ensure interconnection and interoperability, based on uniform technical standards, among telecommunications carriers;

(6) eliminate unnecessary administrative procedures that impose regulatory barriers to competition and ensure that competitive entry is fostered on an economically rational basis;

(7) ensure consumer protection and protection against anticompetitive conduct;

(8) regulate a provider of services only to the extent the provider has market power to control the price of services to customers;

(9) encourage cost-based pricing of telecommunications services so that consumers pay a fair price for services they use; and

(10) subject to Subchapter C,[1] develop appropriate quality of service standards for local exchange companies so as to place this state among the leaders in deployment of an advanced telecommunications infrastructure.

Acts 1997, 75th Leg., ch. 166, § 1, eff. Sept. 1, 1997.

[1] V.T.C.A., Utilities Code § 58.051 et seq.

§ 58.203. Infrastructure Goals of All Electing Companies

(a) Recognizing that it will take time for competition to develop in the local exchange market, the commission shall, in the absence of competition, ensure that each electing company achieves the infrastructure goals described by this section.

(b) Not later than December 31, 1996, an electing company shall make available to each customer in the company's territory access to end-to-end digital connectivity.

(c) Each new central office switch installed for an electing company after September 1, 1995, must be digital or technically equal to or superior to digital. In addition, a switch installed after September 1, 1997, must, at a minimum, be capable of providing integrated services digital network (ISDN) services in a manner consistent with generally accepted national standards.

(d) Not later than January 1, 2000, 50 percent of the local exchange access lines in each electing company's territory must be served by a digital central office switch.

(e) Not later than January 1, 2000, an electing company's public switched network backbone interoffice facilities must employ broadband facilities capable of 45 or more megabits a second. The company may employ facilities at a lower bandwidth if technology permits the delivery of video signal at the lower bandwidth at a quality level comparable to a television broadcast signal. The requirements of this subsection do not apply to local loop facilities.

Acts 1997, 75th Leg., ch. 166, § 1, eff. Sept. 1, 1997.

§ 58.204. Additional Infrastructure Commitment of Certain Companies

(a) Not later than December 31, 1998, an electing company serving more than one million but fewer than five million access lines shall provide digital switching central offices in all exchanges.

(b) Not later than January 1, 2000, an electing company serving more than five million access lines shall:

(1) install Common Channel Signaling 7 capability in each central office; and

(2) connect all of the company's serving central offices to their respective LATA tandem central offices with optical fiber or equivalent facilities.

Acts 1997, 75th Leg., ch. 166, § 1, eff. Sept. 1, 1997.

§ 58.205. Extension or Waiver of Infrastructure Requirements

(a) For an electing company that serves more than one million but fewer than two million access lines, the commission may temporarily extend a deadline prescribed by Section 58.203 if the company demonstrates that the extension is in the public interest.

(b) For an electing company that serves fewer than one million access lines, the commission may waive a requirement prescribed by Section 58.203 if the company demonstrates that the investment is not viable economically.

(c) Before granting a waiver under Subsection (b), the commission must consider the public benefits that would result from compliance with the requirement.

Acts 1997, 75th Leg., ch. 166, § 1, eff. Sept. 1, 1997.

§ 58.206. Implementation Costs; Increase in Rates and Universal Service Funds

The commission may not consider the cost of implementing Section 58.203 or 58.204 in determining whether an electing company is entitled to:

(1) a rate increase under this chapter; or

(2) increased universal service funds under Subchapter B, Chapter 56.[1]

Acts 1997, 75th Leg., ch. 166, § 1, eff. Sept. 1, 1997.

[1] V.T.C.A., Utilities Code § 56.021 et seq.

SUBCHAPTER G. INFRASTRUCTURE COMMITMENT TO CERTAIN ENTITIES

§ 58.251. Intent and Goal of Subchapter

(a) It is the intent of this subchapter to establish a telecommunications infrastructure that interconnects the public entities described in this subchapter. The interconnection of these entities requires ubiquitous, broadband, digital services for voice, video, and data in the local serving area. The ubiquitous nature of these connections must allow individual networks of these entities to interconnect and interoperate across the broadband digital service infrastructure. The delivery of these advanced telecommunications services requires collaborations and partnerships of public, private, and commercial telecommunications service network providers.

(b) The goal of this subchapter is to interconnect and aggregate the connections to every entity described in this subchapter, in the local serving area. It is further intended that the infrastructure implemented under this subchapter connect each entity that requests a service offered under this subchapter.

Acts 1997, 75th Leg., ch. 166, § 1, eff. Sept. 1, 1997.

§ 58.252. Definitions

In this subchapter:

(1) "Educational institution" has the meaning assigned by Section 57.021.

(1–a) "Health center" means a federally qualified health center service delivery site.

(2) "Library" means:

(A) a public library or regional library system as those terms are defined by Section 441.122, Government Code;

(B) a library operated by an institution of higher education or a school district; or

(C) a library operated by a nonprofit corporation as defined by Section 441.221(3), Government Code.

(3) "Private network services" means:

(A) broadband digital service that is capable of providing transmission speeds of 45 megabits a second or greater for customer applications; and

(B) other customized or packaged network services.

(4) "Telemedicine center" means a facility that is equipped to transmit, by video, data, or voice service, medical information for the diagnosis or treatment of illness or disease and that is:

(A) owned or operated by a public or not-for-profit hospital, including an academic health center; or

(B) owned by one or more state-licensed health care practitioners and operated on a nonprofit basis.

Acts 1997, 75th Leg., ch. 166, § 1, eff. Sept. 1, 1997. Amended by Acts 2007, 80th Leg., ch. 831, § 11, eff. Sept. 1, 2008; Acts 2011, 82nd Leg., ch. 903 (S.B. 773), § 1, eff. Sept. 1, 2011.

§ 58.253. Private Network Services for Certain Entities

(a) On customer request, an electing company shall provide private network services to:

(1) an educational institution;

(2) a library as defined in Section 57.021;

(3) a nonprofit telemedicine center;

(4) a public or not-for-profit hospital;

(5) a legally constituted consortium or group of entities listed in this subsection; or

(6) a health center.

(b) Except as provided by Section 58.266, the electing company shall provide the private network services for the private and sole use of the receiving entity.

Acts 1997, 75th Leg., ch. 166, § 1, eff. Sept. 1, 1997. Amended by Acts 2001, 77th Leg., ch. 959, § 9, eff. June 14, 2001; Acts 2001, 77th Leg., ch. 1220, § 4, eff. Sept. 1, 2001; Acts 2001, 77th Leg., ch. 1255, § 16, eff. June 15, 2001; Acts 2001, 77th Leg., ch. 1350, § 7, eff. Sept. 1, 2001; Acts 2007, 80th Leg., ch. 831, § 12, eff. Sept. 1, 2008; Acts 2011, 82nd Leg., ch. 903 (S.B. 773), § 2, eff. Sept. 1, 2011.

§ 58.254. Priorities

An electing company shall give priority to serving:

(1) rural areas;

(2) areas designated as critically underserved either medically or educationally; and

(3) educational institutions with high percentages of economically disadvantaged students.

Acts 1997, 75th Leg., ch. 166, § 1, eff. Sept. 1, 1997.

§ 58.255. Contracts for Private Network Services

(a) An electing company shall provide a private network service under a customer specific contract.

(b) An electing company shall offer private network service contracts under this subchapter at 110 percent of the long run incremental cost of providing the private network service, including installation.

(c) Commission approval of a contract is not required.

(d) Subtitle D, Title 10, Government Code,[1] does not apply to a contract entered into under this subchapter.

Acts 1997, 75th Leg., ch. 166, § 1, eff. Sept. 1, 1997. Amended by Acts 2011, 82nd Leg., ch. 21 (S.B. 983), § 2, eff. Sept. 1, 2011; Acts 2011, 82nd Leg., ch. 98 (S.B. 980), § 12, eff. Sept. 1, 2011; Acts 2011, 82nd Leg., ch. 903 (S.B. 773), § 3, eff. Sept. 1, 2011.

[1] V.T.C.A., Government Code § 2151.001 et seq.

§ 58.256. Preferred Rate Treatment Warranted

An entity described by Section 58.253(a) warrants preferred rate treatment. However, a rate charged for a service must cover the service's long run incremental cost.

Acts 1997, 75th Leg., ch. 166, § 1, eff. Sept. 1, 1997.

§ 58.257. Election of Rate Treatment

An educational institution or a library may elect the rate treatment provided by this subchapter or the discount provided by Subchapter B, Chapter 57.[1]

Acts 1997, 75th Leg., ch. 166, § 1, eff. Sept. 1, 1997.

[1] V.T.C.A., Utilities Code § 57.021 et seq.

§ 58.258. Private Network Services Rates and Tariffs

(a) Notwithstanding the pricing flexibility authorized by this subtitle, an electing company's rates for private network services may not be increased before January 1, 2016 . However, an electing company may increase a rate in accordance with the provisions of a customer specific contract.

(b) An electing company may not charge an entity described by Section 58.253(a) a special construction or installation charge.

Acts 1997, 75th Leg., ch. 166, § 1, eff. Sept. 1, 1997. Amended by Acts 2005, 79th Leg., 2nd C.S., 2nd C.S., ch. 2, § 20, eff. Sept. 1, 2005; Acts 2011, 82nd Leg., ch. 903 (S.B. 773), § 4, eff. Sept. 1, 2011.

§ 58.259. Tariff Rate for Certain IntraLATA Service

(a) An electing company shall file a flat monthly tariff rate for point-to-point intraLATA 1.544 megabits a second service for the entities described by Section 58.253(a).

(b) The tariff rate may not be:

(1) distance sensitive; or

(2) higher than 110 percent of the service's statewide average long run incremental cost, including installation.

Acts 1997, 75th Leg., ch. 166, § 1, eff. Sept. 1, 1997. Amended by Acts 2011, 82nd Leg., ch. 903 (S.B. 773), § 5, eff. Sept. 1, 2011.

§ 58.260. Point-To-Point 45 Megabits a Second IntraLATA Service

(a) On request of an entity described by Section 58.253(a), an electing company shall provide to the entity point-to-point 45 megabits a second intraLATA services.

(b) The service must be provided under a customer specific contract except that any interoffice portion of the service must be recovered on a statewide average basis that is not distance sensitive.

(c) The rate for the service may not be higher than 110 percent of the service's long run incremental cost, including installation.

Acts 1997, 75th Leg., ch. 166, § 1, eff. Sept. 1, 1997. Amended by Acts 2011, 82nd Leg., ch. 903 (S.B. 773), § 6, eff. Sept. 1, 2011.

§ 58.261. Broadband Digital Special Access Service

(a) An electing company shall provide to an entity described by Section 58.253(a) broadband digital special access service to interexchange carriers.

(b) The rate for the service may not be higher than 110 percent of the service's long run incremental cost, including installation.

Acts 1997, 75th Leg., ch. 166, § 1, eff. Sept. 1, 1997. Amended by Acts 2011, 82nd Leg., ch. 903 (S.B. 773), § 7, eff. Sept. 1, 2011.

§ 58.262. Expanded Interconnection

(a) On request of an entity described by Section 58.253(a), an electing company shall provide to the entity expanded interconnection (virtual colocation).

(b) The company shall provide expanded interconnection:

(1) in accordance with commission rules adopted under Subchapter H, Chapter 60;[1] and

(2) at 105 percent of long run incremental cost, including installation.

(c) An entity described by Section 58.253(a) is not required to qualify for expanded interconnection if expanded interconnection is ordered by the commission.

Acts 1997, 75th Leg., ch. 166, § 1, eff. Sept. 1, 1997.

[1] V.T.C.A., Utilities Code § 60.141.

§ 58.263. Internet Access

(a) This section applies only to an educational institution or library in an exchange of an electing company serving more than five million access lines in which toll-free access to the Internet is not available.

(b) On request of the educational institution or library, the electing company shall make available a toll-free connection or toll-free dialing arrangement that the institution or library may use to obtain access to the Internet in an exchange in which toll-free access to the Internet is available.

(c) The electing company shall provide the connection or dialing arrangement at no charge to the educational institution or library until Internet access becomes available in the exchange of the requesting educational institution or library.

(d) The electing company is not required to arrange for Internet access or to pay Internet charges for the requesting educational institution or library.

Acts 1997, 75th Leg., ch. 166, § 1, eff. Sept. 1, 1997.

§ 58.264. Complaints Limited

(a) Notwithstanding any other provision of this title, an electing company is subject to a complaint under this subchapter only by an entity described by Section 58.253(a).

(b) An entity may only complain that the company provided a private network service under this subchapter preferentially to a similarly situated customer.

Acts 1997, 75th Leg., ch. 166, § 1, eff. Sept. 1, 1997.

§ 58.265. Interconnection of Network Services

The private network services provided under this subchapter may be interconnected with other similar networks for distance learning, telemedicine, and information-sharing purposes.

Acts 1997, 75th Leg., ch. 166, § 1, eff. Sept. 1, 1997.

§ 58.266. Sharing or Resale of Network Services

(a) A private network service may be used by and shared among the entities described by Section 58.253(a) but may not be otherwise shared or resold to other customers.

(b) A service provided under this subchapter may not be required to be resold to another customer at a rate provided by this subchapter.

(c) This section does not prohibit an otherwise permitted resale of another service that an electing company may offer through the use of the same facilities used to provide a private network service offered under this subchapter.

Acts 1997, 75th Leg., ch. 166, § 1, eff. Sept. 1, 1997.

§ 58.267. Implementation Costs; Increase in Rates and Universal Service Funds

The commission may not consider the cost of implementing this subchapter in determining whether an electing company is entitled to:

(1) a rate increase under this chapter; or

(2) increased universal service funds under Subchapter B, Chapter 56.[1]

Acts 1997, 75th Leg., ch. 166, § 1, eff. Sept. 1, 1997.

[1] V.T.C.A., Utilities Code § 56.021 et seq.

§ 58.268. Continuation of Obligation

Notwithstanding any other provision of this title, an electing company shall continue to comply with this subchapter until January 1, 2016 , regardless of:

(1) the date the company elected under this chapter; or

(2) any action taken in relation to that company under Chapter 65.

Added by Acts 2005, 79th Leg., 2nd C.S., ch. 2, § 21, eff. Sept. 1, 2005. Amended by Acts 2011, 82nd Leg., ch. 903 (S.B. 773), § 8, eff. Sept. 1, 2011.

SUBCHAPTER H. SWITCHED ACCESS SERVICES

§ 58.301. Switched Access Rate Reduction

An electing company with greater than five million access lines in this state shall reduce its switched access rates on a combined originating and terminating basis as follows:

(1) the electing company shall reduce switched access rates on a combined originating and terminating basis in effect on September 1, 1999, by one cent a minute; and

(2) the electing company shall reduce switched access rates on a combined originating and terminating basis by an additional two cents a minute on the earlier of:

(A) July 1, 2000; or

(B) the date the electing company, or its affiliate formed in compliance with 47 U.S.C. Section 272, as amended, actually begins providing interLATA services in this state in accordance with the authorization required by 47 U.S.C. Section 271, as amended.

Added by Acts 1999, 76th Leg., ch. 1212, § 45, eff. Sept. 1, 1999.

§ 58.302. Switched Access Rate Cap

(a) An electing company may not increase the per minute rates for switched access services on a combined originating and terminating basis above the lesser of:

(1) the rates for switched access services charged by that electing company on September 1, 1999, as may be further reduced on implementation of the universal service fund under Chapter 56; or

(2) the applicable rate described by Section 58.301 as may be further reduced on implementation of the universal service fund under Chapter 56.

(b) Notwithstanding Subchapter F, Chapter 60,[1] but subject to Section 60.001, an electing company may, on its own initiative, decrease a rate charged for switched access service to any amount above the long run incremental cost of the service.

Added by Acts 1999, 76th Leg., ch. 1212, § 45, eff. Sept. 1, 1999.

[1] V.T.C.A., Utilities Code §§ 60.101, 60.102.

§ 58.303. Expired

CHAPTER 59. INFRASTRUCTURE PLAN

SUBCHAPTER A. GENERAL PROVISIONS

Section

59.001. Policy.
59.002. Definitions.

SUBCHAPTER B. INFRASTRUCTURE INCENTIVES

59.021. Election.
59.022. Withdrawal of Election.
59.023. Election Under Chapter 58.
59.024. Rate Changes.
59.025. Switched Access Rates.
59.026. Complaint or Hearing.
59.027. Consumer Complaints Regarding Tariffs.
59.028. Consumer Complaints Regarding Services; Enforcement of Standards.
59.029. Investment Limitation on Service Standards.
59.030. New Services.
59.031. Pricing and Packaging Flexibility.
59.032. Customer Promotional Offerings.

SUBCHAPTER C. INFRASTRUCTURE COMMITMENT AND GOALS

59.051. Infrastructure Commitment.
59.052. Infrastructure Goals.
59.053. Waiver of Infrastructure Requirements.
59.054. Progress Report.
59.055. Implementation Costs; Increase in Rates and Universal Service Funds.

SUBCHAPTER D. INFRASTRUCTURE COMMITMENT TO CERTAIN ENTITIES

59.071. Definitions.
59.072. Private Network Services for Certain Entities.
59.073. Investment Priorities.
59.074. Contracts for Private Network Services.
59.075. Preferred Rate Treatment Warranted.
59.076. Election of Rate Treatment.
59.077. Private Network Services Rates and Tariffs.
59.078. Private Line or Special Access Rates.
59.079. Complaints Limited.
59.080. Interconnection of Network Services.
59.081. Sharing or Resale of Network Services.
59.082. Implementation Costs; Increase in Rates and Universal Service Funds.
59.083. Continuation of Obligation.

SUBCHAPTER A. GENERAL PROVISIONS

§ 59.001. Policy

It is the policy of this state that an incumbent local exchange company that does not elect to be regulated under Chapter 58 should have incentives to deploy infrastructure that will benefit the residents of this state while maintaining reasonable local rates and universal service.

Acts 1997, 75th Leg., ch. 166, § 1, eff. Sept. 1, 1997.

§ 59.002. Definitions

In this chapter:

(1) "Electing company" means an incumbent local exchange company that elects for an infrastructure commitment and corresponding regulation under this chapter.

(2) "Election date" means the date on which the commission receives notice of election under Subchapter B.[1]

Acts 1997, 75th Leg., ch. 166, § 1, eff. Sept. 1, 1997.

[1] V.T.C.A., Utilities Code § 59.021 et seq.

SUBCHAPTER B. INFRASTRUCTURE INCENTIVES

§ 59.021. Election

(a) An incumbent local exchange company may elect to make an infrastructure commitment and to be subject to corresponding regulation under this chapter if the company:

(1) serves less than five percent of the access lines in this state; and

(2) has not elected incentive regulation under Chapter 58.

(b) A company makes the election by notifying the commission in writing of the company's election.

(c) A company electing under this chapter may renew the election for successive two-year periods. An election that is renewed under this subsection remains in effect until the earlier of the date that:

(1) the election expires because it was not renewed;

(2) the commission allows the company to withdraw its election under Section 59.022; or

(3) the legislature eliminates the incentive regulation authorized by this chapter and Chapter 58.

Acts 1997, 75th Leg., ch. 166, § 1, eff. Sept. 1, 1997. Amended by Acts 1999, 76th Leg., ch. 1212, § 46, eff. Sept. 1, 1999.

§ 59.022. Withdrawal of Election

(a) The commission may allow an electing company to withdraw the company's election under this chapter:

(1) on application by the company; and

(2) only for good cause.

(b) In this section, "good cause" includes only matters beyond the control of the company.

Acts 1997, 75th Leg., ch. 166, § 1, eff. Sept. 1, 1997.

§ 59.023. Election Under Chapter 58

(a) This chapter does not prohibit a company electing under this chapter from electing incentive regulation under Chapter 58.

(b) If a company makes an election under Chapter 58, the infrastructure commitment made under this chapter offsets the infrastructure commitment required in connection with the Chapter 58 election.

Acts 1997, 75th Leg., ch. 166, § 1, eff. Sept. 1, 1997.

§ 59.024. Rate Changes

(a) Except for the charges permitted under Subchapter C, Chapter 55,[1] Subchapter B, Chapter 56,[2] and Section 55.024, an electing company may not, before the end of the company's election period under this chapter, increase a rate previously established for that company under this title unless the commission approves the proposed change as authorized under Subsection (c) or (d).

(b) For purposes of Subsection (a), the company's previously established rates are the rates charged by the company on its election date without regard to a proceeding pending under:

(1) Section 15.001;

(2) Subchapter D, Chapter 53;[3] or

(3) Subchapter G, Chapter 2001, Government Code.[4]

(c) The commission, on motion of the electing company or on its own motion, shall adjust prices for services to reflect changes in Federal Communications Commission separations that affect intrastate net income by at least 10 percent.

(d) Notwithstanding Subsection (a), the commission, on request of the electing company, shall allow a rate group reclassification that results from access line growth.

(e) Section 58.059 applies to a rate change under this section.

Acts 1997, 75th Leg., ch. 166, § 1, eff. Sept. 1, 1997. Amended by Acts 1999, 76th Leg., ch. 1212, § 47, eff. Sept. 1, 1999.

[1] V.T.C.A., Utilities Code § 55.041 et seq.
[2] V.T.C.A., Utilities Code § 56.021 et seq.
[3] V.T.C.A., Utilities Code §§ 53.151, 53.152.
[4] V.T.C.A., Government Code § 2001.171 et seq.

§ 59.025. Switched Access Rates

Notwithstanding any other provision of this title, the commission may not, on the commission's own motion, reduce an electing company's rates for switched access services before the expiration of the election period prescribed by Section 59.024, but may approve a reduction proposed by the electing company.

Acts 1997, 75th Leg., ch. 166, § 1, eff. Sept. 1, 1997. Amended by Acts 1999, 76th Leg., ch. 1212, § 48, eff. Sept. 1, 1999.

§ 59.026. Complaint or Hearing

(a) On or before the end of the company's election period, an electing company is not, under any circumstances, subject to:

(1) a complaint or hearing regarding the reasonableness of the company's:

(A) rates;

(B) overall revenues;

(C) return on invested capital; or

(D) net income; or

(2) a complaint that a rate is excessive.

(b) Subsection (a) applies only to a company that is in compliance with the company's infrastructure commitment under this chapter.

(c) This section does not prohibit a complaint, hearing, or determination on an electing company's implementation of a competitive safeguard required by Chapter 60.

Acts 1997, 75th Leg., ch. 166, § 1, eff. Sept. 1, 1997. Amended by Acts 1999, 76th Leg., ch. 1212, § 49, eff. Sept. 1, 1999.

§ 59.027. Consumer Complaints Regarding Tariffs

(a) This chapter does not restrict:

(1) a consumer's right to complain to the commission about the application of an ambiguous tariff; or

(2) the commission's right to determine:

(A) the proper application of that tariff; or

(B) the proper tariff rate if that tariff does not apply.

(b) This section does not permit the commission to:

(1) lower a tariff rate except as specifically provided by this title;

(2) change the commission's interpretation of a tariff; or

(3) extend the application of a tariff to a new class of customers.

Acts 1997, 75th Leg., ch. 166, § 1, eff. Sept. 1, 1997.

§ 59.028. Consumer Complaints Regarding Services; Enforcement of Standards

This chapter does not restrict:

(1) a consumer's right to complain to the commission about quality of service; or

(2) the commission's right to enforce a quality of service standard.

Acts 1997, 75th Leg., ch. 166, § 1, eff. Sept. 1, 1997.

§ 59.029. Investment Limitation on Service Standards

(a) The commission may not raise a service standard applicable to the provision of local exchange telephone service by an electing company if the increased investment required to comply with the raised standard in any year exceeds 10 percent of the company's average annual intrastate additions in capital investment for the most recent five-year period.

(b) In computing the average under Subsection (a), the electing company shall exclude:

(1) extraordinary investments made during the five-year period; and

(2) investments required by Section 59.052.

Acts 1997, 75th Leg., ch. 166, § 1, eff. Sept. 1, 1997.

§ 59.030. New Services

(a) An electing company may introduce a new service 10 days after providing an informational notice to the commission, to the office, and to any person who holds a certificate of operating authority in the electing company's certificated area or areas or who has an effective interconnection agreement with the electing company.

(b) An electing company shall price each new service at or above the service's long run incremental cost. The commission shall allow a company serving fewer than one million access lines to establish a service's long run incremental cost by adopting, at that company's option, the cost studies of a larger company for that service that has been accepted by the commission.

(c) An affected person, the office on behalf of residential or small commercial customers, or the commission may file a complaint at the commission challenging whether the pricing by an electing company of a new service is in compliance with Subsection (b).

(d) If a complaint is filed under Subsection (c), the electing company has the burden of proving that the company set the price for the new service in accordance with the applicable provisions of this subchapter. If the complaint is finally resolved in favor of the complainant, the electing company:

(1) shall, not later than the 10th day after the date the complaint is finally resolved, amend the price of the service as necessary to comply with the final resolution; or

(2) may, at the company's option, discontinue the service.

Added by Acts 1999, 76th Leg., ch. 1212, § 50, eff. Sept. 1, 1999.

§ 59.031. Pricing and Packaging Flexibility

(a) Notwithstanding Section 59.027(b) or Subchapter F, Chapter 60,[1] an electing company may exercise pricing flexibility in accordance with this section, including the packaging of any regulated service such as basic local telecommunications service with any other regulated or unregulated service or any service of an affiliate. The electing company may exercise pricing flexibility 10 days after providing an informational notice to the commission, to the office, and to any person who holds a certificate of operating authority in the electing company's certificated area or areas or who has an effective interconnection agreement with the electing company. Pricing flexibility includes all pricing arrangements included in the definition of "pricing flexibility" prescribed by Section 51.002(7) and includes packaging of regulated services with unregulated services or any service of an affiliate.

(b) An electing company, at the company's option, shall price each regulated service offered separately or as part of a package under Subsection (a) at either the service's tariffed rate or at a rate not lower than the service's long run incremental cost. The commission shall allow a company serving fewer than one million access lines to establish a service's long run incremental cost by adopting, at that company's option, the cost studies of a larger company for that service that have been accepted by the commission.

(c) An affected person, the office on behalf of residential or small commercial customers, or the commission may file a complaint alleging that an electing company has priced a regulated service in a manner that does not meet the pricing standards of this subchapter. The complaint must be filed before the 31st day after the company implements the rate.

Added by Acts 1999, 76th Leg., ch. 1212, § 50, eff. Sept. 1, 1999.

[1] V.T.C.A., Utilities Code §§ 60.101, 60.102.

§ 59.032. Customer Promotional Offerings

(a) An electing company may offer a promotion for a regulated service for not more than 90 days in any 12-month period.

(b) The electing company shall file with the commission a promotional offering that consists of:

(1) waiver of installation charges or service order charges, or both, for not more than 90 days in a 12-month period; or

(2) a temporary discount of not more than 25 percent from the tariffed rate for not more than 60 days in a 12-month period.

(c) An electing company is not required to obtain commission approval to make a promotional offering described by Subsection (b).

(d) An electing company may offer a promotion of any regulated service as part of a package of services consisting of any regulated service with any other regulated or unregulated service or any service of an affiliate.

Added by Acts 1999, 76th Leg., ch. 1212, § 50, eff. Sept. 1, 1999.

SUBCHAPTER C. INFRASTRUCTURE COMMITMENT AND GOALS

§ 59.051. Infrastructure Commitment

(a) An electing company shall commit to make in this state, during the six years after the election date, the telecommunications infrastructure investment prescribed by this chapter.

(b) The company shall make the commitment to the governor and the commission in writing.

Acts 1997, 75th Leg., ch. 166, § 1, eff. Sept. 1, 1997.

§ 59.052. Infrastructure Goals

(a) The commission shall ensure that each electing company achieves the infrastructure goals described by this section.

(b) Each new central office switch installed for an electing company in this state after September 1, 1995, must be digital.

(c) An electing company shall make available to each customer in the company's territory access to end-to-end digital connectivity. In this subsection, "make available" has the meaning assigned by 16 T.A.C. Section 23.69.

(d) In each electing company's territory, 50 percent of the local exchange access lines must be served by a digital central office switch.

(e) An electing company's public switched network backbone interoffice facilities must employ broadband facilities that serve at least 50 percent of the local exchange access lines and are capable of 45 or more megabits a second. The company may employ facilities at a lower bandwidth if technology permits the delivery of video signal at the lower bandwidth at a quality level comparable to a television broadcast signal. The requirements of this subsection do not apply to local loop facilities.

(f) An electing company shall install Common Channel Signaling 7 capability in each access tandem office.

(g) The infrastructure goals specified by Subsections (c)–(f) must be achieved not later than January 1, 2000.

Acts 1997, 75th Leg., ch. 166, § 1, eff. Sept. 1, 1997.

§ 59.053. Waiver of Infrastructure Requirements

(a) For an electing company that serves fewer than one million lines, the commission may waive a requirement prescribed by Section 59.052 if the company demonstrates that the investment is not viable economically.

(b) Before granting a waiver under Subsection (a), the commission must consider the public benefits that would result from compliance with the requirement.

Acts 1997, 75th Leg., ch. 166, § 1, eff. Sept. 1, 1997.

§ 59.054. Progress Report

(a) On each anniversary of the company's election date, an electing company shall file with the commission a report on the company's progress on its infrastructure commitment.

(b) The report must include a statement of:

(1) the institutions requesting service under Subchapter D; [1]

(2) the institutions served under Subchapter D;

(3) the investments and expenses for the previous period and the total investments and expenses for all periods; and

(4) other information the commission considers necessary.

Acts 1997, 75th Leg., ch. 166, § 1, eff. Sept. 1, 1997.

[1] V.T.C.A., Utilities Code § 59.071 et seq.

§ 59.055. Implementation Costs; Increase in Rates and Universal Service Funds

The commission may not consider the cost of implementing Section 59.052 in determining whether an electing company is entitled to:

(1) a rate increase under this chapter; or

(2) increased universal service funds under Subchapter B, Chapter 56.[1]

Acts 1997, 75th Leg., ch. 166, § 1, eff. Sept. 1, 1997.

[1] V.T.C.A., Utilities Code § 56.021 et seq.

SUBCHAPTER D. INFRASTRUCTURE COMMITMENT TO CERTAIN ENTITIES

§ 59.071. Definitions

In this subchapter:

(1) "Educational institution" has the meaning assigned by Section 57.021.

(2) "Library" means:

(A) a public library or regional library system as those terms are defined by Section 441.122, Government Code;

(B) a library operated by an institution of higher education or a school district; or

(C) a library operated by a nonprofit corporation as defined by Section 441.221(3), Government Code.

(3) "Private network services" means telecommunications services provided to an entity described by Section 59.072(a), including broadband services, customized services, and packaged network services.

(4) "Telemedicine center" means a facility that is equipped to transmit, by video or data service, medical information for the diagnosis or treatment of illness or disease and that is:

(A) owned or operated by a public or not-for-profit hospital; or

(B) owned by a state-licensed health care practitioner and operated on a nonprofit basis.

Acts 1997, 75th Leg., ch. 166, § 1, eff. Sept. 1, 1997. Amended by Acts 2007, 80th Leg., ch. 831, § 13, eff. Sept. 1, 2008.

§ 59.072. Private Network Services for Certain Entities

(a) On customer request, an electing company shall provide private network services to:

(1) an educational institution;

(2) a library;

(3) a telemedicine center; or

(4) a legally constituted consortium or group of entities listed in this subsection.

(b) Except as provided by Section 59.081, the electing company shall provide the private network services for the private and sole use of the receiving entity. However, the company may provide the services with a facility that is used to provide another service to another customer.

(c) The customers listed in Subsection (a) are a special class of customers for purposes of the private network for distance learning, telemedicine, and information-sharing purposes.

Acts 1997, 75th Leg., ch. 166, § 1, eff. Sept. 1, 1997.

§ 59.073. Investment Priorities

An electing company shall give investment priority to serving:

(1) rural areas;

(2) areas designated as critically underserved medically or educationally; and

(3) educational institutions with high percentages of economically disadvantaged students.

Acts 1997, 75th Leg., ch. 166, § 1, eff. Sept. 1, 1997.

§ 59.074. Contracts for Private Network Services

(a) An electing company shall provide a private network service under a customer-specific contract.

(b) An electing company shall offer private network service contracts under this subchapter at 110 percent of the long run incremental cost of providing the private network service, including installation costs.

(c) Commission approval of a contract is not required.

Acts 1997, 75th Leg., ch. 166, § 1, eff. Sept. 1, 1997. Amended by Acts 2011, 82nd Leg., ch. 21 (S.B. 983), § 3, eff. Sept. 1, 2011; Acts 2011, 82nd Leg., ch. 98 (S.B. 980), § 13, eff. Sept. 1, 2011.

§ 59.075. Preferred Rate Treatment Warranted

The classes of customers described by Section 59.072(a) warrant preferred rate treatment. However, a rate charged for a service must cover the service's long run incremental cost.

Acts 1997, 75th Leg., ch. 166, § 1, eff. Sept. 1, 1997.

§ 59.076. Election of Rate Treatment

An educational institution or a library may elect the rate treatment provided by this subchapter or the discount provided by Subchapter B, Chapter 57.[1]

Acts 1997, 75th Leg., ch. 166, § 1, eff. Sept. 1, 1997.

[1] V.T.C.A., Utilities Code § 57.021 et seq.

§ 59.077. Private Network Services Rates and Tariffs

(a) Notwithstanding the pricing flexibility authorized by this subtitle, an electing company's rates for private network services may not be increased before January 1, 2016 .

(b) An electing company may not assess an entity described by Section 59.072(a) a tariffed special construction or installation charge unless the company and the entity agree on the assessment.

Acts 1997, 75th Leg., ch. 166, § 1, eff. Sept. 1, 1997. Amended by Acts 2005, 79th Leg., 2nd C.S., ch. 2, § 22, eff. Sept. 1, 2005; Acts 2011, 82nd Leg., ch. 903 (S.B. 773), § 9, eff. Sept. 1, 2011.

§ 59.078. Private Line or Special Access Rates

(a) On request by an educational institution or a library, an electing company shall provide 1.544 megabits a second private line or special access service at 110 percent of the service's long run incremental cost, including installation costs.

(b) The rate provided by Subsection (a) is in lieu of the discount provided by Subchapter B, Chapter 57.[1]

Acts 1997, 75th Leg., ch. 166, § 1, eff. Sept. 1, 1997.

[1] V.T.C.A., Utilities Code § 57.021 et seq.

§ 59.079. Complaints Limited

Notwithstanding any other provision of this title, an electing company is subject to a complaint under Subchapter C [1] or this subchapter only by an entity described by Section 59.072(a).

Acts 1997, 75th Leg., ch. 166, § 1, eff. Sept. 1, 1997.

[1] V.T.C.A., Utilities Code § 59.051 et seq.

§ 59.080. Interconnection of Network Services

The private network services provided under this subchapter may be interconnected with other similar networks for distance learning, telemedicine, and information-sharing purposes.

Acts 1997, 75th Leg., ch. 166, § 1, eff. Sept. 1, 1997.

§ 59.081. Sharing or Resale of Network Services

(a) A private network service may be used and shared among the entities described by Section 59.072(a) but may not be otherwise shared or resold to other customers.

(b) A service provided under this subchapter may not be required to be resold to other customers at a rate provided by this subchapter.

(c) This section does not prohibit an otherwise permitted resale of another service that an electing company may offer through the use of the same facilities used to provide a private network service offered under this subchapter.

Acts 1997, 75th Leg., ch. 166, § 1, eff. Sept. 1, 1997.

§ 59.082. Implementation Costs; Increase in Rates and Universal Service Funds

The commission may not consider the cost of implementing this subchapter in determining whether an electing company is entitled to:

(1) a rate increase under this chapter; or

(2) increased universal service funds under Subchapter B, Chapter 56.[1]

Acts 1997, 75th Leg., ch. 166, § 1, eff. Sept. 1, 1997.

[1] V.T.C.A., Utilities Code § 56.021 et seq.

§ 59.083. Continuation of Obligation

Notwithstanding any other provision of this title, an electing company shall continue to comply with this subchapter until January 1, 2016 , regardless of:

(1) the date the company elected under this chapter; or

(2) any action taken in relation to that company under Chapter 65.

Added by Acts 2005, 79th Leg., 2nd C.S., ch. 2, § 23, eff. Sept. 1, 2005. Amended by Acts 2011, 82nd Leg., ch. 903 (S.B. 773), § 10, eff. Sept. 1, 2011.

CHAPTER 60. COMPETITIVE SAFEGUARDS

SUBCHAPTER A. GENERAL PROVISIONS

Section
60.001. Fair Competition.
60.002. Exclusive Jurisdiction; Enforcement.
60.003. Commission Authority.
60.004. Applicability to Certain Smaller Incumbent Local Exchange Companies; Rules.
60.0041. Expired.
60.005. Applicability to Certain Larger Incumbent Local Exchange Companies; Rules.
60.006. Bulletin Board Systems Unaffected.

SUBCHAPTER B. UNBUNDLING

60.021. Minimum Unbundling Requirement.
60.022. Commission Unbundling Orders.
60.023. Assignment of Unbundled Component to Category of Service.

SUBCHAPTER C. RESALE

60.041. Loop Resale Tariff.
60.042. Prohibited Resale or Sharing.
60.043. Resale Obligation.

Section
60.044. Elimination of Resale Prohibitions.
60.045. Resale or Sharing Arrangements Unaffected.

SUBCHAPTER D. IMPUTATION

60.061. Rules.
60.062. Exception for Capped Price.
60.063. Imputation for Switched Access.
60.064. Recovery of Cost of Providing Service.
60.065. Waivers.

SUBCHAPTER E. TELECOMMUNICATIONS NUMBER PORTABILITY

60.081. Definition.
60.082. Portability Guidelines.
60.083. Interim Retention of Consumer Numbers.
60.084. Rates for Interim Portability Measures.

SUBCHAPTER F. PRICING

60.101. Pricing Rule.
60.102. Adoption of Cost Studies by Certain Companies.

SUBCHAPTER G. INTERCONNECTION

60.121. Definition.
60.122. Exclusive Jurisdiction.
60.123. Inapplicability of Subchapter.
60.124. Interoperable Networks Required.
60.125. Determination of Interconnection Rates.
60.126. Interconnectivity Negotiations; Dispute Resolution.
60.127. Adoption of Approved Interconnection Rates.
60.128. Use of Rates Restricted.

SUBCHAPTER H. EXPANDED INTERCONNECTION

60.141. Expanded Interconnection Rules.

SUBCHAPTER I. LOCAL EXCHANGE COMPANY REQUIREMENTS

60.161. Incumbent Local Exchange Company Requirements.
60.162. Expanded Interconnection.
60.163. Infrastructure Sharing.
60.164. Permissible Joint Marketing.
60.165. Affiliate Rule.

SUBCHAPTER J. WHOLESALE CODE OF CONDUCT

60.201. Statement of Policy.
60.202. Applicability of Subchapter.
60.203. Minimum Service Requirements.
60.204. Interconnection.
60.205. Number Portability.
60.206. Duty to Negotiate.
60.207. Dialing Parity.
60.208. Access to Rights–of–way.
60.209. Reciprocal Compensation.
60.210. Access to Services.

SUBCHAPTER A. GENERAL PROVISIONS

§ 60.001. Fair Competition

To the extent necessary to ensure that competition in telecommunications is fair to each participant and to accelerate the improvement of telecommunications in this state, the commission shall ensure that the rates and rules of an incumbent local exchange company:

(1) are not unreasonably preferential, prejudicial, or discriminatory; and

(2) are applied equitably and consistently.

Acts 1997, 75th Leg., ch. 166, § 1, eff. Sept. 1, 1997.

§ 60.002. Exclusive Jurisdiction; Enforcement

(a) The commission has exclusive jurisdiction to implement competitive safeguards.

(b) Section 58.025 does not prevent the commission from enforcing this chapter.

Acts 1997, 75th Leg., ch. 166, § 1, eff. Sept. 1, 1997.

§ 60.003. Commission Authority

(a) The commission may:

(1) establish procedures with respect to a policy stated in this subchapter or Subchapters B-H; [1] and

(2) resolve a dispute that arises under a policy described by Subdivision (1).

(b) The commission shall adopt procedures for a proceeding under Subchapters B and C.[2] A procedure may:

(1) limit discovery; and

(2) for purposes of cross-examination align any party, other than the office, with another party that has a similar position.

(c) In adopting a procedure under this section and in resolving a dispute, the commission shall consider the action's effect on:

(1) consumers;

(2) competitors; and

(3) the incumbent local exchange company.

(d) The commission, by order or rule, may not implement a requirement that is contrary to a federal law or rule.

Acts 1997, 75th Leg., ch. 166, § 1, eff. Sept. 1, 1997.

[1] V.T.C.A., Utilities Code § 60.021 et seq. to § 60.141.

[2] V.T.C.A., Utilities Code § 60.041 et seq.

§ 60.004. Applicability to Certain Smaller Incumbent Local Exchange Companies; Rules

(a) Subchapters B, C, and H [1] may be applied to an incumbent local exchange company that serves fewer than 31,000 access lines only on a bona fide request from a certificated telecommunications utility.

(b) In applying the rules adopted under Subchapters B, C, and H to a company described by Subsection (a), the commission may modify the rules in the public interest.

(c) This section takes effect September 1, 1998.

Acts 1997, 75th Leg., ch. 166, § 1, eff. Sept. 1, 1997.

[1] V.T.C.A., Utilities Code § 60.021 et seq., § 60.041 et seq., and § 60.141.

§ 60.0041. Expired

§ 60.005. Applicability to Certain Larger Incumbent Local Exchange Companies; Rules

(a) Subchapters B, D, and F [1] may be applied to an incumbent local exchange company that, as of September 1, 1995, has 31,000 or more access lines in this state but fewer than one million access lines in this state only on a bona fide request from a holder of a certificate of operating authority or a service provider certificate of operating authority.

(b) In applying the rules adopted under Subchapters B, D, and F to a company described by Subsection (a), the commission may modify the rules in the public interest.

Acts 1997, 75th Leg., ch. 166, § 1, eff. Sept. 1, 1997.

[1] V.T.C.A., Utilities Code § 60.021 et seq., § 60.061 et seq., and §§ 60.101, 60.102.

§ 60.006. Bulletin Board Systems Unaffected

This subtitle does not:

(1) require the commission to change the rate treatment established by the commission in Docket No. 8387 for a bulletin board system in a residence;

(2) regulate or tax a bulletin board system or Internet service provider that provides only enhanced or information services and that does not provide a telecommunications service; or

(3) require a change in a rate charged to an entity described by Subdivision (2) under a tariff in effect on September 1, 1995.

Acts 1997, 75th Leg., ch. 166, § 1, eff. Sept. 1, 1997.

SUBCHAPTER B. UNBUNDLING

§ 60.021. Minimum Unbundling Requirement

At a minimum, an incumbent local exchange company shall unbundle its network to the extent the Federal Communications Commission orders.

Acts 1997, 75th Leg., ch. 166, § 1, eff. Sept. 1, 1997.

§ 60.022. Commission Unbundling Orders

(a) The commission may adopt an order relating to the issue of unbundling of local exchange company services in addition to the unbundling required by Section 60.021.

(b) Before ordering further unbundling, the commission must consider the public interest and competitive merits of further unbundling.

(c) On the request of a party, the commission shall proceed by evidentiary hearing. If a request for a hearing is not made, the commission may proceed by rulemaking.

Acts 1997, 75th Leg., ch. 166, § 1, eff. Sept. 1, 1997.

§ 60.023. Assignment of Unbundled Component to Category of Service

The commission may assign an unbundled component to the appropriate category of services under Chapter 58 according to the purposes and intents of the categories.

Acts 1997, 75th Leg., ch. 166, § 1, eff. Sept. 1, 1997.

SUBCHAPTER C. RESALE

§ 60.041. Loop Resale Tariff

(a) An incumbent local exchange company that on September 1, 1995, serves one million or more access lines or that on or before September 1, 1995, elects regulation under Chapter 58 shall file a usage sensitive loop resale tariff.

(b) An incumbent local exchange company shall file a usage sensitive loop resale tariff not later than the 60th day after the date a certificate of operating authority or a service provider certificate of operating authority is granted under Chapter 54 if the company:

(1) serves fewer than one million access lines; and

(2) is not an electing company under Chapter 58.

(c) The commission shall conduct an appropriate proceeding to determine the rates and terms of the resale tariff not later than the 180th day after the date the tariff is filed.

(d) The commission may not approve a usage sensitive rate unless the rate recovers:

(1) the total long run incremental cost of the loop on an unseparated basis; and

(2) an appropriate contribution to joint and common costs.

(e) Except as provided by Section 60.044, a person may not purchase from the resale tariff unless the person is the holder of:

(1) a certificate of convenience and necessity;

(2) a certificate of operating authority; or

(3) a service provider certificate of operating authority.

(f) In this section, "loop resale" means the purchase of the local distribution channel or loop facility from the incumbent local exchange company to resell to end user customers.

Acts 1997, 75th Leg., ch. 166, § 1, eff. Sept. 1, 1997.

§ 60.042. Prohibited Resale or Sharing

(a) A provider of telecommunications service may not impose a restriction on the resale or sharing of a service:

(1) for which the provider is not a dominant provider; or

(2) entitled to regulatory treatment as a nonbasic service under Subchapter E, Chapter 58,[1] if the provider is a company electing regulation under Chapter 58.

(b) An incumbent local exchange company must comply with the resale provisions of 47 U.S.C. Section 251(c)(4), as amended, unless exempted under 47 U.S.C. Section 251(f), as amended.

(c) If a company electing under Chapter 58 offers basic or nonbasic services regulated by the commission to its retail customers as a promotional offering, the electing company shall make those services available for resale by a certificated telecommunications utility on terms that are no less favorable than the terms on which the services are made available to retail customers in accordance with this section. For a promotion with a duration of 90 days or less, the electing company's basic or nonbasic services shall be made available to the certificated telecommunications utility at the electing company's promotional rate, without an avoided-cost discount. For a promotion with a duration of more than 90 days, the electing company's basic or nonbasic services shall be made available to the certificated telecommunications utility at a rate reflecting the avoided-cost discount, if any, from the promotional rate.

Acts 1997, 75th Leg., ch. 166, § 1, eff. Sept. 1, 1997. Amended by Acts 1999, 76th Leg., ch. 1212, § 51, eff. Sept. 1, 1999.

[1] V.T.C.A., Utilities Code § 58.151 et seq.

§ 60.043. Resale Obligation

A holder of a certificate of operating authority or a service provider certificate of operating authority shall permit a local exchange company to resell the holder's loop facilities at the holder's regularly published rates if the local exchange company:

(1) does not have loop facilities; and

(2) has a request for service.

Acts 1997, 75th Leg., ch. 166, § 1, eff. Sept. 1, 1997.

§ 60.044. Elimination of Resale Prohibitions

(a) Except as provided by Subsections (c) and (d), the commission shall eliminate all resale prohibitions in the tariffs of an electing company on the:

(1) completion of the commission's costing and pricing rulemaking;

(2) completion of rate rebalancing of the incumbent local exchange company rates under Subchapter F;[1] and

(3) removal of all prohibitions on an incumbent local exchange company's provision of interLATA services.

(b) Except as provided by Subsections (c) and (d), the commission shall eliminate all resale prohibitions in the tariffs of an electing company that has one million access lines or more on removal of all prohibitions on the company's provision of interLATA service.

(c) After the resale prohibitions are eliminated under this section:

(1) the commission shall continue to prohibit the resale of local exchange or directory assistance flat rate services as a substitute for usage sensitive services; and

(2) residence service may not be resold to a business customer.

(d) A service or function may be offered for resale only to the same class of customer to which the incumbent local exchange company sells the service if the commission finds that:

(1) as a result of the costing and pricing proceeding the rate for the service or function will be less than the cost of providing the service or function; and

(2) the difference in rate and cost will not be recovered from the universal service fund.

Acts 1997, 75th Leg., ch. 166, § 1, eff. Sept. 1, 1997.

[1] V.T.C.A., Utilities Code §§ 60.101, 60.102.

§ 60.045. Resale or Sharing Arrangements Unaffected

This subchapter does not change a resale or sharing arrangement permitted in an incumbent local exchange company tariff that:

(1) existed on September 1, 1995; or

(2) was filed on or before May 1, 1995, by an incumbent local exchange company that serves more than five million access lines in this state.

Acts 1997, 75th Leg., ch. 166, § 1, eff. Sept. 1, 1997.

SUBCHAPTER D. IMPUTATION

§ 60.061. Rules

(a) The commission shall adopt rules governing imputation of the price of a service.

(b) Imputation is a regulatory policy the commission shall apply to prevent an incumbent local exchange company from selling a service or function to another telecommunications utility at a price that is higher than the rate the incumbent local exchange company implicitly includes in services it provides to the company's retail customers.

(c) The commission may require imputation only of the price of a service that is:

(1) not generally available from a source other than the incumbent local exchange company; and

(2) necessary for the competitor to provide a competing service.

(d) The commission may require imputation only on a service-by-service basis and may not require imputation on a rate-element-by-element basis.

(e) For a service for which the commission may require imputation under Subsection (c) and that is provided under a customer specific contract, the commission:

(1) may require imputation only on a service-by-service basis within the contract; and

(2) may not require imputation on a rate-element-by-element basis.

Acts 1997, 75th Leg., ch. 166, § 1, eff. Sept. 1, 1997.

§ 60.062. Exception for Capped Price

The commission may not require imputation of the price to a local exchange telephone service while the price is capped under Chapter 58 or 59.

Acts 1997, 75th Leg., ch. 166, § 1, eff. Sept. 1, 1997.

§ 60.063. Imputation for Switched Access

The commission shall impute the price of switched access service to the price of each service for which switched access service is a component until switched access service is competitively available.

Acts 1997, 75th Leg., ch. 166, § 1, eff. Sept. 1, 1997.

§ 60.064. Recovery of Cost of Providing Service

(a) An incumbent local exchange company shall demonstrate that the price it charges for retail service recovers the cost of providing the service.

(b) For purposes of this section, the cost of providing the service is the sum of:

(1) each specifically tariffed premium rate for each noncompetitive service or service function, or each element of a noncompetitive service or service function, or the functional equivalent, that is used to provide the service;

(2) the total service long run incremental cost of the competitive services or service functions that are used;

(3) each cost, not reflected in Subdivision (1) or (2), that is specifically associated with providing the service or group of services; and

(4) each cost or surcharge associated with an explicit subsidy applied to all providers of the service to promote universal service.

Acts 1997, 75th Leg., ch. 166, § 1, eff. Sept. 1, 1997.

§ 60.065. Waivers

If the commission determines that a waiver is in the public interest, the commission may waive an imputation requirement for a public interest service such as:

(1) 9–1–1 service; or

(2) dual party relay service.

Acts 1997, 75th Leg., ch. 166, § 1, eff. Sept. 1, 1997.

SUBCHAPTER E. TELECOMMUNICATIONS NUMBER PORTABILITY

§ 60.081. Definition

In this subchapter, "telecommunications number portability" means the ability of a telecommunications services user who is changing from one telecommunications service provider to another provider to retain a telephone number, to the extent technically feasible, without impairing the quality, reliability, or convenience of service.

Acts 1997, 75th Leg., ch. 166, § 1, eff. Sept. 1, 1997.

§ 60.082. Portability Guidelines

(a) Because a uniform national number plan is valuable and necessary to this state, the commission by rule shall adopt guidelines governing telecommunications number portability and the assignment of telephone numbers in a competitively neutral manner.

(b) The rules may not be inconsistent with the rules and regulations of the Federal Communications Commission regarding telecommunications number portability.

Acts 1997, 75th Leg., ch. 166, § 1, eff. Sept. 1, 1997.

§ 60.083. Interim Retention of Consumer Numbers

As an interim measure, the commission shall adopt reasonable mechanisms, including, at minimum, the use of call forwarding and direct inward dialing, to allow consumers to retain their telephone numbers.

Acts 1997, 75th Leg., ch. 166, § 1, eff. Sept. 1, 1997.

§ 60.084. Rates for Interim Portability Measures

(a) An incumbent local exchange company with one million or more access lines shall file tariffs, and the commission shall determine reasonable rates to be charged by the company for:

(1) call forwarding;

(2) direct inward dialing; and

(3) any other mechanism the commission determines should be used as an interim telecommunications number portability measure by a new entrant.

(b) An incumbent local exchange company with fewer than one million access lines that serves an area in which a certificate of operating authority or a service provider certificate of operating authority has been granted shall, not later than the 60th day after the date of a bona fide request, file tariffs in accordance with Subsection (a).

(c) Not later than the 60th day after the date a company files tariffs under Subsection (b), the commission shall determine reasonable rates in accordance with Subsection (a).

Acts 1997, 75th Leg., ch. 166, § 1, eff. Sept. 1, 1997.

SUBCHAPTER F. PRICING

§ 60.101. Pricing Rule

(a) The commission shall adopt a pricing rule.

(b) In adopting the pricing rule, the commission shall:

(1) ensure that each price for a monopoly service remains affordable;

(2) ensure that each price for competitive service is not:

(A) unreasonably preferential, prejudicial, or discriminatory;

(B) directly or indirectly subsidized by a noncompetitive service; or

(C) predatory or anticompetitive; and

(3) require that each service recover the appropriate costs, including joint and common costs, of each facility and function used to provide the service.

Acts 1997, 75th Leg., ch. 166, § 1, eff. Sept. 1, 1997.

§ 60.102. Adoption of Cost Studies by Certain Companies

The commission shall allow an incumbent local exchange company that is not a Tier 1 local exchange company on September 1, 1995, to adopt, at that company's option, the cost studies approved by the commission for a Tier 1 local exchange company.

Acts 1997, 75th Leg., ch. 166, § 1, eff. Sept. 1, 1997.

SUBCHAPTER G. INTERCONNECTION

§ 60.121. Definition

In this subchapter, "interconnection" means, for calls that originate and terminate in this state, the termination of local intraexchange traffic of another local exchange company or holder of a service provider certificate of operating authority within the local calling area of the terminating local exchange company or certificate holder.

Acts 1997, 75th Leg., ch. 166, § 1, eff. Sept. 1, 1997.

§ 60.122. Exclusive Jurisdiction

The commission has exclusive jurisdiction to determine rates and terms for interconnection for a holder of a certificate of convenience and necessity, a certificate of operating authority, or a service provider certificate of operating authority.

Acts 1997, 75th Leg., ch. 166, § 1, eff. Sept. 1, 1997.

§ 60.123. Inapplicability of Subchapter

This subchapter does not apply to a rate for the existing termination of cellular or interexchange traffic.

Acts 1997, 75th Leg., ch. 166, § 1, eff. Sept. 1, 1997.

§ 60.124. Interoperable Networks Required

(a) The commission shall require each telecommunications provider to maintain interoperable networks.

(b) The commission may:

(1) adopt rules, including generic rules that are responsive to changes in federal law or a development in the local exchange market; and

(2) set policies governing interconnection arrangements.

Acts 1997, 75th Leg., ch. 166, § 1, eff. Sept. 1, 1997.

§ 60.125. Determination of Interconnection Rates

(a) Telecommunications providers shall negotiate network interconnectivity, charges, and terms.

(b) If interconnectivity, charges, and terms are successfully negotiated, the commission shall approve the interconnection rates.

(c) If telecommunications providers do not enter into a mutually agreed compensation rate under this section, each provider shall reciprocally terminate the other provider's traffic at no charge for the first nine months after the date the first call is terminated between the providers.

(d) During the nine-month period prescribed by Subsection (c), the commission shall complete a proceeding to establish reciprocal interconnection rates and terms. The commission shall establish reciprocal interconnection rates and terms based solely on the commission proceeding.

(e) In establishing the initial interconnection rate, the commission may not require cost studies from the new entrant.

(f) On or after the third anniversary of the date the first call is terminated between the providers, the commission, on receipt of a complaint, may require cost studies by a new entrant to establish interconnection rates.

Acts 1997, 75th Leg., ch. 166, § 1, eff. Sept. 1, 1997.

§ 60.126. Interconnectivity Negotiations; Dispute Resolution

The commission may resolve a dispute filed by a party to a negotiation under Section 60.125(a).

Acts 1997, 75th Leg., ch. 166, § 1, eff. Sept. 1, 1997.

§ 60.127. Adoption of Approved Interconnection Rates

(a) An incumbent local exchange company may adopt the interconnection rates the commission approves for a larger incumbent local exchange company without additional cost justification.

(b) If an incumbent local exchange company does not adopt the interconnection rates of a larger company or negotiates under Section 60.125(a), the company is governed by Sections 60.125(c)–(f).

(c) If the incumbent local exchange company adopts the interconnection rates of another incumbent local exchange company, the new entrant may adopt those rates as the new entrant's interconnection rates.

(d) If the incumbent local exchange company elects to file its own tariff, the new entrant must also file its own interconnection tariff.

Acts 1997, 75th Leg., ch. 166, § 1, eff. Sept. 1, 1997.

§ 60.128. Use of Rates Restricted

The commission may not use interconnection rates under this subchapter as a basis to alter interconnection rates for other services.

Acts 1997, 75th Leg., ch. 166, § 1, eff. Sept. 1, 1997.

SUBCHAPTER H. EXPANDED INTERCONNECTION

§ 60.141. Expanded Interconnection Rules

The commission shall adopt rules for expanded interconnection that:

(1) are consistent with the rules and regulations of the Federal Communications Commission relating to expanded interconnection;

(2) treat intrastate private line services as special access service; and

(3) provide that if an incumbent local exchange company is required to provide expanded interconnection to another local exchange company, the second local exchange company shall in a similar manner provide expanded interconnection to the first company.

Acts 1997, 75th Leg., ch. 166, § 1, eff. Sept. 1, 1997.

SUBCHAPTER I. LOCAL EXCHANGE COMPANY REQUIREMENTS

§ 60.161. Incumbent Local Exchange Company Requirements

An incumbent local exchange company may not unreasonably:

(1) discriminate against another provider by refusing access to the local exchange;

(2) refuse or delay an interconnection to another provider;

(3) degrade the quality of access the company provides to another provider;

(4) impair the speed, quality, or efficiency of a line used by another provider;

(5) fail to fully disclose in a timely manner on request all available information necessary to design equipment that will meet the specifications of the local exchange network; or

(6) refuse or delay access by a person to another provider.

Acts 1997, 75th Leg., ch. 166, § 1, eff. Sept. 1, 1997.

§ 60.162. Expanded Interconnection

This subchapter does not require an incumbent local exchange company to provide expanded interconnection as that term is defined by the Federal Communications Commission.

Acts 1997, 75th Leg., ch. 166, § 1, eff. Sept. 1, 1997.

§ 60.163. Infrastructure Sharing

(a) The commission shall adopt rules that require a local exchange company to share public switched network infrastructure and technology with a requesting local exchange company that lacks economies of scale or scope, to enable the requesting company to provide telecommunications services in each geographic area for which the requesting company is designated as the sole carrier of last resort.

(b) The rules governing the sharing:

(1) may not require a local exchange company to make a decision that is uneconomic or adverse to the public;

(2) shall permit, but may not require, joint ownership and operation of public switched network infrastructure and services by or among the local exchange companies that share infrastructure; and

(3) shall establish conditions that promote cooperation between local exchange companies.

Acts 1997, 75th Leg., ch. 166, § 1, eff. Sept. 1, 1997.

§ 60.164. Permissible Joint Marketing

Except as prescribed in Chapters 61, 62, and 63, the commission may not adopt any rule or order that would prohibit a local exchange company from jointly marketing or selling its products and services with the products and services of any of its affiliates in any manner permitted by federal law or applicable rules or orders of the Federal Communications Commission.

Added by Acts 1999, 76th Leg., ch. 1212, § 52, eff. Sept. 1, 1999.

§ 60.165. Affiliate Rule

Except as prescribed in Chapters 61, 62, and 63, the commission may not adopt any rule or order that would prescribe for any local exchange company any affiliate rule, including any accounting rule, any cost allocation rule, or any structural separation rule, that is more burdensome than federal law or applicable rules or orders of the Federal Communications Commission. Notwithstanding any other provision in this title, the commission may not attribute or impute to a local exchange company a price discount offered by an affiliate of the local exchange company to the affiliate's customers. This section does not limit the authority of the commission to consider a complaint brought under Subchapter A, Chapter 52, Section 53.003, or this chapter.

Added by Acts 1999, 76th Leg., ch. 1212, § 52, eff. Sept. 1, 1999.

SUBCHAPTER J. WHOLESALE CODE OF CONDUCT

§ 60.201. Statement of Policy

It is the policy of this state that providers of telecommunications services operate in a manner that is consistent with minimum standards to provide customers with continued competitive choices.

Added by Acts 2005, 79th Leg., 2nd C.S., ch. 2, § 24, eff. Sept. 1, 2005.

§ 60.202. Applicability of Subchapter

A provision of this subchapter applies only to the extent the provision has not been preempted by federal law or a rule, regulation, or order of the Federal Communications Commission.

Added by Acts 2005, 79th Leg., 2nd C.S., ch. 2, § 24, eff. Sept. 1, 2005.

§ 60.203. Minimum Service Requirements

A telecommunications provider may not unreasonably:

(1) discriminate against another provider by refusing access to an exchange;

(2) refuse or delay an interconnection to another provider;

(3) degrade the quality of access the telecommunications provider provides to another provider;

(4) impair the speed, quality, or efficiency of a line used by another provider;

(5) fail to fully disclose in a timely manner on request all available information necessary to design equipment that will meet the specifications of the network; or

(6) refuse or delay access by a person to another provider.

Added by Acts 2005, 79th Leg., 2nd C.S., ch. 2, § 24, eff. Sept. 1, 2005.

§ 60.204. Interconnection

A telecommunications provider shall provide interconnection with other telecommunications providers' networks for the transmission and routing of telephone exchange service and exchange access.

Added by Acts 2005, 79th Leg., 2nd C.S., ch. 2, § 24, eff. Sept. 1, 2005.

§ 60.205. Number Portability

A telecommunications provider shall provide number portability in accordance with federal requirements.

Added by Acts 2005, 79th Leg., 2nd C.S., ch. 2, § 24, eff. Sept. 1, 2005.

§ 60.206. Duty to Negotiate

A telecommunications provider shall negotiate in good faith the terms and conditions of any agreement.

Added by Acts 2005, 79th Leg., 2nd C.S., ch. 2, § 24, eff. Sept. 1, 2005.

§ 60.207. Dialing Parity

(a) A telecommunications provider shall provide dialing parity to competing telecommunications providers of telephone exchange service and telephone toll service.

(b) A telecommunications provider shall provide nondiscriminatory access to telephone numbers, operator services, directory assistance, and directory listings and may not delay that access unreasonably.

Added by Acts 2005, 79th Leg., 2nd C.S., ch. 2, § 24, eff. Sept. 1, 2005.

§ 60.208. Access to Rights-of-way

A telecommunications provider shall provide access to poles, ducts, conduits, and rights-of-way to competing providers of telecommunications service on rates, terms, and conditions that are just, reasonable, and nondiscriminatory.

Added by Acts 2005, 79th Leg., 2nd C.S., ch. 2, § 24, eff. Sept. 1, 2005.

§ 60.209. Reciprocal Compensation

A telecommunications provider shall establish reciprocal compensation arrangements for the transport and termination of telecommunications.

Added by Acts 2005, 79th Leg., 2nd C.S., ch. 2, § 24, eff. Sept. 1, 2005.

§ 60.210. Access to Services

A telecommunications provider shall provide access to:

(1) 911 and E–911 service;

(2) directory assistance service to allow other telecommunications providers' customers to obtain telephone numbers; and

(3) operator call completion service.

Added by Acts 2005, 79th Leg., 2nd C.S., ch. 2, § 24, eff. Sept. 1, 2005.

CHAPTER 61. INFORMATION TECHNOLOGY SERVICES [REPEALED]

SUBCHAPTER A. GENERAL PROVISIONS [REPEALED]

§ 61.001. Repealed by Acts 2005, 79th Leg., 2nd C.S., ch. 2, § 29(2), eff. Sept. 1, 2005

SUBCHAPTER B. PROVISION OF INFORMATION TECHNOLOGY SERVICES [REPEALED]

§§ 61.021 to 61.026. Repealed by Acts 2005, 79th Leg., 2nd C.S., ch. 2, § 29(2), eff. Sept. 1, 2005

SUBCHAPTER C. ADDITIONAL COMPETITIVE SAFEGUARDS [REPEALED]

§§ 61.041 to 61.043. Repealed by Acts 2005, 79th Leg., 2nd C.S., ch. 2, § 29(2), eff. Sept. 1, 2005

CHAPTER 62. BROADCASTER SAFEGUARDS

SUBCHAPTER A. GENERAL PROVISIONS

Section
62.001. Applicability of Chapter.
62.002. Definitions.
62.003. Requirements Relating to Audio and Video Programming.

SUBCHAPTER B. CUSTOMER PROPRIETARY NETWORK INFORMATION [REPEALED]
62.021 to 62.023. Repealed.

SUBCHAPTER C. ADVERTISING [REPEALED]
62.041 to 62.047. Repealed.

SUBCHAPTER D. AUDIO AND VIDEO PROGRAMMING [REPEALED]
62.071 to 62.078. Repealed.

SUBCHAPTER E. VIDEO CARRIAGE [EXPIRED]
62.101 to 62.108. Expired.

SUBCHAPTER F. AUDIO CARRIAGE [EXPIRED]
62.131 to 62.136. Expired.

SUBCHAPTER A. GENERAL PROVISIONS

§ 62.001. Applicability of Chapter

This chapter does not apply to a cable company.

Acts 1997, 75th Leg., ch. 166, § 1, eff. Sept. 1, 1997.

§ 62.002. Definitions

In this chapter:

(1) "Audio programming":

(A) means programming:

(i) provided by an amplitude modulation or frequency modulation broadcast radio station; or

(ii) generally considered comparable to programming described by Subparagraph (i); and

(B) does not include an audio-related service offered by an incumbent local exchange company on September 1, 1995.

(2) "Video programming" means programming provided by or generally considered comparable to programming provided by a television broadcast station as defined by Section 602, Communications Act of 1934 (47 U.S.C. Section 522).

Acts 1997, 75th Leg., ch. 166, § 1, eff. Sept. 1, 1997.

§ 62.003. Requirements Relating to Audio and Video Programming

(a) This section applies only to a provider of advanced services or local exchange telephone service that has more than 500,000 access lines in service in this state and that delivers audio programming with localized content or video programming to its subscribers in those service areas where such provider is not regulated as a cable system under federal law.

(b) Notwithstanding any other provision of this title, a provider of advanced services or local exchange telephone service shall provide subscribers access to the signals of the local broadcast television and radio stations licensed by the Federal Communications Commission to serve those subscribers over the air; provided with respect to low power television stations, this section shall only apply to those low power television stations that are "qualified low power stations" as defined in 47 U.S.C. Section 534(h)(2).

(c) To facilitate access by subscribers of a provider of advanced services or local exchange telephone service to the signals of local broadcast stations, a station either shall be granted mandatory carriage or may request retransmission consent with the provider.

(d) This title does not require a provider of advanced services or local exchange telephone service to provide a television or radio station valuable consideration in exchange for carriage.

(e) A provider of advanced services or local exchange telephone service shall transmit without degradation the signals a local broadcast station delivers to the provider. The transmission quality offered a broadcast station may not be lower than the quality made available to another broadcast station or video or audio programming source.

(f) A provider of advanced services or local exchange telephone service that delivers audio or video programming to its subscribers may not:

(1) discriminate among broadcast stations or between broadcast stations on the one hand and programming providers on the other with respect to transmission of their signals, taking into account any consideration afforded a provider of advanced services or local exchange telephone service by any such programming provider or broadcast station; or

(2) delete, change, or alter a copyright identification transmitted as part of a broadcast station's signal.

(g) A provider of advanced services or local exchange telephone service that delivers audio or video programming shall be subject to any applicable network nonduplication or syndicated exclusivity rules promulgated by the Federal Communications Commission to the extent applicable to cable systems as defined by the commission.

(h) A provider of advanced services or local exchange telephone service that delivers audio or video programming to its subscribers shall include all programming providers in a subscriber programming guide, if any, that lists program schedules.

Added by Acts 2005, 79th Leg., 2nd C.S., ch. 2, § 25, eff. Sept. 1, 2005.

SUBCHAPTER B. CUSTOMER PROPRIETARY NETWORK INFORMATION [REPEALED]

§§ 62.021 to 62.023. Repealed by Acts 2005, 79th Leg., 2nd C.S., ch. 2, § 29(1), eff. Sept. 1, 2005

SUBCHAPTER C. ADVERTISING [REPEALED]

§§ 62.041 to 62.047. Repealed by Acts 2005, 79th Leg., 2nd C.S., ch. 2, § 29(1), eff. Sept. 1, 2005

SUBCHAPTER D. AUDIO AND VIDEO PROGRAMMING [REPEALED]

§§ 62.071 to 62.078. Repealed by Acts 2005, 79th Leg., 2nd C.S., ch. 2, § 29(1), eff. Sept. 1, 2005

SUBCHAPTER E. VIDEO CARRIAGE [EXPIRED]

§§ 62.101 to 62.108. Expired

SUBCHAPTER F. AUDIO CARRIAGE [EXPIRED]

§§ 62.131 to 62.136. Expired

CHAPTER 63. ELECTRONIC PUBLISHING [REPEALED]

SUBCHAPTER A. GENERAL PROVISIONS [REPEALED]

§§ 63.001 to 63.011. Repealed by Acts 2005, 79th Leg., 2nd C.S. ch. 2, § 29(2), eff. Sept. 1, 2005

SUBCHAPTER B. ELECTRONIC PUBLISHING SAFEGUARDS [REPEALED]

§§ 63.031 to 63.042. Repealed by Acts 2005, 79th Leg., 2nd C.S., ch. 2, § 29(2), eff. Sept. 1, 2005

SUBCHAPTER C. ELECTRONIC PUBLISHING TRANSACTIONS [REPEALED]

§§ 63.061 to 63.063. Repealed by Acts 2005, 79th Leg., 2nd C.S., ch. 2, § 29(2), eff. Sept. 1, 2005

CHAPTER 64. CUSTOMER PROTECTION

SUBCHAPTER A. GENERAL PROVISIONS

Section
64.001. Customer Protection Policy.
64.002. Definitions.
64.003. Customer Awareness.
64.004. Customer Protection Standards.

SUBCHAPTER B. CERTIFICATION, REGISTRATION, AND REPORTING REQUIREMENTS
64.051. Adoption of Rules.
64.052. Scope of Rules.
64.053. Reports.

SUBCHAPTER C. CUSTOMER'S RIGHT TO CHOICE
64.101. Policy.
64.102. Rules Relating to Choice.

SUBCHAPTER D. PROTECTION AGAINST UNAUTHORIZED CHARGES
64.151. Requirements for Submitting Charges.
64.152. Responsibilities of Billing Utility.
64.153. Records of Disputed Charges.
64.154. Notice.
64.155. Providing Copy of Records.
64.156. Violations.
64.157. Disputes.
64.158. Consistency With Federal Law.

SUBCHAPTER E. PUBLICATION OF MOBILE SERVICE CUSTOMER TELEPHONE NUMBERS
64.201. Definition.
64.202. Consent Required.
64.203. Violations.

SUBCHAPTER A. GENERAL PROVISIONS

§ 64.001. Customer Protection Policy

(a) The legislature finds that new developments in telecommunications services, as well as changes in market structure, marketing techniques, and technology, make it essential that customers have safeguards against fraudulent, unfair, misleading, deceptive, or anticompetitive business practices and against businesses that do not have the technical and financial resources to provide adequate service.

(b) The purpose of this chapter is to establish customer protection standards and confer on the commission authority to adopt and enforce rules to protect customers from fraudulent, unfair, misleading, deceptive, or anticompetitive practices.

(c) Nothing in this section shall be construed to abridge customer rights set forth in commission rules in effect at the time of the enactment of this chapter.

(d) This chapter does not limit the constitutional, statutory, and common law authority of the office of the attorney general.

Added by Acts 1999, 76th Leg., ch. 1212, § 55, eff. Sept. 1, 1999.

§ 64.002. Definitions

In this chapter:

(1) "Billing agent" means any entity that submits charges to the billing utility on behalf of itself or any provider of a product or service.

(2) "Billing utility" means any telecommunications provider, as defined by Section 51.002, that issues a bill directly to a customer for any telecommunications product or service.

(3) "Certificated telecommunications utility" means a telecommunications utility that has been granted either a certificate of convenience and necessity, a certificate of operating authority, or a service provider certificate of operating authority.

(4) "Customer" means any person in whose name telephone service is billed, including individuals, governmental units at all levels of government, corporate entities, and any other entity with legal capacity to be billed for telephone service.

(5) "Service provider" means any entity that offers a product or service to a customer and that directly or indirectly charges to or collects from a customer's bill an amount for the product or service on a customer's bill received from a billing utility.

(6) "Telecommunications utility" has the meaning assigned by Section 51.002.

Added by Acts 1999, 76th Leg., ch. 1212, § 55, eff. Sept. 1, 1999.

§ 64.003. Customer Awareness

(a) The commission shall promote public awareness of changes in telecommunications markets, provide customers with information necessary to make informed choices about available options, and ensure that customers have an adequate understanding of their rights.

(b) The commission shall compile a report on customer service at least once each year showing the comparative customer information from reports given to the commission it deems necessary.

(c) The commission shall adopt and enforce rules to require a certificated telecommunications utility to give clear, uniform, and understandable information to customers about rates, terms, services, customer rights, and other necessary information as determined by the commission.

(d) Customer awareness efforts by the commission shall be conducted in English and Spanish and any other language as necessary.

Added by Acts 1999, 76th Leg., ch. 1212, § 55, eff. Sept. 1, 1999.

§ 64.004. Customer Protection Standards

(a) All buyers of telecommunications services are entitled to:

(1) protection from fraudulent, unfair, misleading, deceptive, or anticompetitive practices, including protection from being billed for services that were not authorized or provided;

(2) choice of a telecommunications service provider and to have that choice honored;

(3) information in English and Spanish and any other language as the commission deems necessary concerning rates, key terms, and conditions;

(4) protection from discrimination on the basis of race, color, sex, nationality, religion, marital status, income level, or source of income and from unreasonable discrimination on the basis of geographic location;

(5) impartial and prompt resolution of disputes with a certificated telecommunications utility and disputes with a telecommunications service provider related to unauthorized charges and switching of service;

(6) privacy of customer consumption and credit information;

(7) accuracy of billing;

(8) bills presented in a clear, readable format and easy-to-understand language;

(9) information in English and Spanish and any other language as the commission deems necessary concerning low-income assistance programs and deferred payment plans;

(10) all consumer protections and disclosures established by the Fair Credit Reporting Act (15 U.S.C. Section 1681 et seq.) and the Truth in Lending Act (15 U.S.C. Section 1601 et seq.); and

(11) programs that offer eligible low-income customers an affordable rate package and bill payment assistance programs designed to reduce uncollectible accounts.

(b) The commission may adopt and enforce rules as necessary or appropriate to carry out this section, including rules for minimum service standards for a certificated telecommunications utility relating to customer deposits and the extension of credit, switching fees, termination of service, an affordable rate package, and bill payment assistance programs for low-income customers. The commission may waive language requirements for good cause.

(c) The commission shall request the comments of the office of the attorney general in developing the rules that may be necessary or appropriate to carry out this section.

(d) The commission shall coordinate its enforcement efforts regarding the prosecution of fraudulent, misleading, deceptive, and anticompetitive business practices with the office of the attorney general in order to ensure consistent treatment of specific alleged violations.

(e) Nothing in this section shall be construed to abridge customer rights set forth in commission rules in effect at the time of the enactment of this chapter.

Added by Acts 1999, 76th Leg., ch. 1212, § 55, eff. Sept. 1, 1999.

SUBCHAPTER B. CERTIFICATION, REGISTRATION, AND REPORTING REQUIREMENTS

§ 64.051. Adoption of Rules

(a) The commission shall adopt rules relating to certification, registration, and reporting requirements for a certificated telecommunications utility, all telecommunications utilities that are not dominant carriers, and pay telephone providers.

(b) The rules adopted under Subsection (a) shall be consistent with and no less effective than federal law and may not require the disclosure of highly sensitive competitive or trade secret information.

Added by Acts 1999, 76th Leg., ch. 1212, § 55, eff. Sept. 1, 1999.

§ 64.052. Scope of Rules

The commission may adopt and enforce rules to:

(1) require certification or registration with the commission as a condition of doing business in this state;

(2) amend certificates or registrations to reflect changed ownership and control;

(3) establish rules for customer service and protection;

(4) suspend or revoke certificates or registrations for repeated violations of this chapter or commission rules, except that the commission may not revoke a certificate of convenience and necessity of a telecommunications utility except as provided by Section 54.008; and

(5) order disconnection of a pay telephone service provider's pay telephones or revocation of certification or registration for repeated violations of this chapter or commission rules.

Added by Acts 1999, 76th Leg., ch. 1212, § 55, eff. Sept. 1, 1999.

§ 64.053. Reports

The commission may require a telecommunications service provider to submit reports to the commission concerning any matter over which it has authority under this chapter.

Added by Acts 1999, 76th Leg., ch. 1212, § 55, eff. Sept. 1, 1999.

SUBCHAPTER C. CUSTOMER'S RIGHT TO CHOICE

§ 64.101. Policy

It is the policy of this state that all customers be protected from the unauthorized switching of a telecommunications service provider selected by the customer to provide service.

Added by Acts 1999, 76th Leg., ch. 1212, § 55, eff. Sept. 1, 1999.

§ 64.102. Rules Relating to Choice

The commission shall adopt and enforce rules that:

(1) ensure that customers are protected from deceptive practices employed in obtaining authorizations of service and in the verification of change orders, including negative option marketing, sweepstakes, and contests that cause customers to unknowingly change their telecommunications service provider;

(2) provide for clear, easily understandable identification, in each bill sent to a customer, of all telecommunications service providers submitting charges on the bill;

(3) ensure that every service provider submitting charges on the bill is clearly and easily identified on the bill along with its services, products, and charges;

(4) provide that unauthorized changes in service be remedied at no cost to the customer within a period established by the commission;

(5) require refunds or credits to the customer in the event of an unauthorized change; and

(6) provide for penalties for violations of commission rules adopted under this section, including fines and revocation of certificates or registrations, by this action denying the certificated telecommunications utility the right to provide service in this state, except that the commission may not revoke a certificate of convenience and necessity of a telecommunications utility except as provided by Section 54.008.

Added by Acts 1999, 76th Leg., ch. 1212, § 55, eff. Sept. 1, 1999.

SUBCHAPTER D. PROTECTION AGAINST UNAUTHORIZED CHARGES

§ 64.151. Requirements for Submitting Charges

(a) A service provider or billing agent may submit charges for a new product or service to be billed on a customer's telephone bill on or after the effective date of this section only if:

(1) the service provider offering the product or service has thoroughly informed the customer of the product or service being offered, including all associated charges, and has explicitly informed the customer that the associated charges for the product or service will appear on the customer's telephone bill;

(2) the customer has clearly and explicitly consented to obtain the product or service offered and to have the associated charges appear on the customer's telephone bill and the consent has been verified as provided by Subsection (b); and

(3) the service provider offering the product or service and any billing agent for the service provider:

(A) has provided the customer with a toll-free telephone number the customer may call and an address to which the customer may write to resolve any billing dispute and to answer questions; and

(B) has contracted with the billing utility to bill for products and services on the billing utility's bill as provided by Subsection (c).

(b) The customer consent required by Subsection (a)(2) must be verified by the service provider offering the product or service by authorization from the customer. A record of the customer consent, including verification, must be maintained by the service provider offering the product or service for a period of at least 24 months immediately after the consent and verification have been obtained. The method of obtaining customer consent and verification must include one or more of the following:

(1) written authorization from the customer;

(2) toll-free electronic authorization placed from the telephone number that is the subject of the product or service;

(3) oral authorization obtained by an independent third party; or

(4) any other method of authorization approved by the commission or the Federal Communications Commission.

(c) The contract required by Subsection (a)(3)(B) must include the service provider's name, business address, and business telephone number and shall be maintained by the billing utility for as long as the billing for the products and services continues and for the 24 months immediately following the permanent discontinuation of the billing.

(d) A service provider offering a product or service to be charged on a customer's telephone bill and any billing agent for the service provider may not use any fraudulent, unfair, misleading, deceptive, or anticompetitive marketing practice to obtain customers, including the use of negative option marketing, sweepstakes, and contests.

(e) Unless verification is required by federal law or rules implementing federal law, Subsection (b) does not apply to customer-initiated transactions with a certificated telecommunications provider for which the service provider has the appropriate documentation.

(f) If a service provider is notified by a billing utility that a customer has reported to the billing utility that a charge made by the service provider is unauthorized, the service provider shall cease to charge the customer for the unauthorized product or service.

(g) This section does not apply to message telecommunications services charges that are initiated by dialing 1+, 0+, 0–, 1010XXX, or collect calls and charges for video services if the service provider has the necessary call detail record to establish the billing for the call or service.

Added by Acts 1999, 76th Leg., ch. 1212, § 55, eff. Sept. 1, 1999.

§ 64.152. Responsibilities of Billing Utility

(a) If a customer's telephone bill is charged for any product or service without proper customer consent or verification, the billing utility, on its knowledge or notification of any unauthorized charge, shall promptly, not later than 45 days after the date of knowledge or notification of the charge:

(1) notify the service provider to cease charging the customer for the unauthorized product or service;

(2) remove any unauthorized charge from the customer's bill;

(3) refund or credit to the customer all money that has been paid by the customer for any unauthorized charge, and if the unauthorized charge is not adjusted within three billing cycles, shall pay interest on the amount of the unauthorized charge;

(4) on the customer's request, provide the customer with all billing records under its control related to any unauthorized charge within 15 business days after the date of the removal of the unauthorized charge from the customer's bill; and

(5) maintain for at least 24 months a record of every customer who has experienced any unauthorized charge for a product or service on the customer's telephone bill and who has notified the billing utility of the unauthorized charge.

(b) A record required by Subsection (a)(5) shall contain for each unauthorized charge:

(1) the name of the service provider that offered the product or service;

(2) any affected telephone numbers or addresses;

(3) the date the customer requested that the billing utility remove the unauthorized charge;

(4) the date the unauthorized charge was removed from the customer's telephone bill; and

(5) the date any money that the customer paid for the unauthorized charges was refunded or credited to the customer.

(c) A billing utility may not:

(1) disconnect or terminate telecommunications service to any customer for nonpayment of an unauthorized charge; or

(2) file an unfavorable credit report against a customer who has not paid charges the customer has alleged were unauthorized unless the dispute regarding the unauthorized charge is ultimately resolved against the customer, except that the customer shall remain obligated to pay any charges that are not in dispute, and this subsection does not apply to those undisputed charges.

Added by Acts 1999, 76th Leg., ch. 1212, § 55, eff. Sept. 1, 1999.

§ 64.153. Records of Disputed Charges

(a) Every service provider shall maintain a record of every disputed charge for a product or service placed on a customer's bill.

(b) The record required under Subsection (a) shall contain for every disputed charge:

(1) any affected telephone numbers or addresses;

(2) the date the customer requested that the billing utility remove the unauthorized charge;

(3) the date the unauthorized charge was removed from the customer's telephone bill; and

(4) the date action was taken to refund or credit to the customer any money that the customer paid for the unauthorized charges.

(c) The record required by Subsection (a) shall be maintained for at least 24 months following the completion of all steps required by Section 64.152(a).

Added by Acts 1999, 76th Leg., ch. 1212, § 55, eff. Sept. 1, 1999.

§ 64.154. Notice

(a) A billing utility shall provide notice of a customer's rights under this section in the manner prescribed by the commission.

(b) Notice of a customer's rights must be provided by mail to each residential and retail business customer within 60 days of the effective date of this section or by inclusion in the publication of the telephone directory next following the effective date of this section. In addition, each billing utility shall send the notice to new customers at the time service is initiated or to any customer at that customer's request.

Added by Acts 1999, 76th Leg., ch. 1212, § 55, eff. Sept. 1, 1999.

§ 64.155. Providing Copy of Records

A billing utility shall provide a copy of records maintained under Sections 64.151(c), 64.152, and 64.154 to the commission staff on request. A service provider shall provide a copy of records maintained under Sections 64.151(b) and 64.153 to the commission on request.

Added by Acts 1999, 76th Leg., ch. 1212, § 55, eff. Sept. 1, 1999.

§ 64.156. Violations

(a) If the commission finds that a billing utility violated this subchapter, the commission may implement penalties and other enforcement actions under Chapter 15.

(b) If the commission finds that any other service provider or billing agent subject to this subchapter has violated this subchapter or has knowingly provided false information to the commission on matters subject to this subchapter, the commission may enforce the provisions of Chapter 15 against the service provider or billing agent as if it were regulated by the commission.

(c) Neither the authority granted under this section nor any other provision of this subchapter shall be construed to grant the commission jurisdiction to regulate service providers or billing agents who are not otherwise subject to commission regulation, other than as specifically provided by this chapter.

(d) If the commission finds that a billing utility or service provider repeatedly violates this subchapter, the commission may, if the action is consistent with the public interest, suspend, restrict, or revoke the registration or certificate of the telecommunications service provider, by this action denying the telecommunications service provider the right to provide service in this state, except that the commission may not revoke a certificate of convenience and necessity of a telecommunications utility except as provided by Section 54.008.

(e) If the commission finds that a service provider or billing agent has repeatedly violated any provision of this subchapter, the commission may order the billing utility to terminate billing and collection services for that service provider or billing agent.

(f) Nothing in this subchapter shall be construed to preclude a billing utility from taking action on its own to terminate or restrict its billing and collection services.

Added by Acts 1999, 76th Leg., ch. 1212, § 55, eff. Sept. 1, 1999.

§ 64.157. Disputes

(a) The commission may resolve disputes between a retail customer and a billing utility, service provider, or telecommunications utility.

(b) In exercising its authority under Subsection (a), the commission may:

(1) order a billing utility or service provider to produce information or records;

(2) require that all contracts, bills, and other communications from a billing utility or service provider display a working toll-free telephone number that customers may call with complaints and inquiries;

(3) require a billing utility or service provider to refund or credit overcharges or unauthorized charges with interest if the billing utility or service provider has failed to comply with commission rules or a contract with the customer;

(4) order appropriate relief to ensure that a customer's choice of a telecommunications service provider is honored;

(5) require the continuation of service to a residential or small commercial customer while a dispute is pending regarding charges the customer has alleged were unauthorized; and

(6) investigate an alleged violation.

(c) The commission shall adopt procedures for the resolution of disputes in a timely manner, which in no event shall exceed 60 days.

Added by Acts 1999, 76th Leg., ch. 1212, § 55, eff. Sept. 1, 1999.

§ 64.158. Consistency With Federal Law

Rules adopted by the commission under this subchapter shall be consistent with and not more burdensome than applicable federal laws and rules.

Added by Acts 1999, 76th Leg., ch. 1212, § 55, eff. Sept. 1, 1999.

SUBCHAPTER E. PUBLICATION OF MOBILE SERVICE CUSTOMER TELEPHONE NUMBERS

§ 64.201. Definition

In this subchapter, "commercial mobile service provider" means a provider of commercial mobile service as defined by Section 332(d), Communications Act of 1934 (47 U.S.C. Section 151 et seq.), Federal Communications Commission rules, and the Omnibus Budget Reconciliation Act of 1993 (Pub. L. No. 103–66).

Added by Acts 2005, 79th Leg., ch. 226, § 1, eff. Sept. 1, 2005.

§ 64.202. Consent Required

(a) A commercial mobile service provider doing business in this state may not publish in a directory or provide for publication in a directory the name and telephone number of a mobile service customer in this state without the express consent of the customer. The consent of a customer must be given:

(1) in writing on a separate document that includes the customer's signature and the date;

(2) verbally; or

(3) on a website maintained by the commercial mobile service provider.

(b) Before a customer consents under Subsection (a), a commercial mobile service provider must disclose to the customer in writing or verbally, as appropriate, that:

(1) by consenting the customer agrees to have the customer's telephone number sold or licensed as part of a list of customers and the customer's telephone number may be included in a publicly available directory; and

(2) if the customer's calling plan bills the customer for unsolicited calls or text messages from a telemarketer, by consenting to have the customer's telephone number sold or licensed as part of a list of customers or be included in a publicly available directory, the customer may incur additional charges for receiving unsolicited calls or text messages.

(c) A customer who consents under Subsection (a) may revoke that consent at any time. A commercial mobile service provider shall comply with the customer's request not later than the 60th day after the date the request is made.

(d) A commercial mobile service provider may not bill a mobile services customer for not consenting under Subsection (a).

Added by Acts 2005, 79th Leg., ch. 226, § 1, eff. Sept. 1, 2005.

§ 64.203. Violations

(a) The attorney general may investigate violations of this subchapter and file civil enforcement actions seeking injunctive relief, attorney's fees, and civil penalties in an amount not to exceed $1,000 for each violation. If the court finds the defendant wilfully or knowingly violated this subchapter, the court may increase the amount of the civil penalties to an amount not to exceed $3,000 for each violation.

(b) Chapter 15 does not apply to a violation of this subchapter.

Added by Acts 2005, 79th Leg., ch. 226, § 1, eff. Sept. 1, 2005.

CHAPTER 65. DEREGULATION OF CERTAIN INCUMBENT LOCAL EXCHANGE COMPANY MARKETS

SUBCHAPTER A. GENERAL PROVISIONS

Section
65.001. Statement of Policy.
65.002. Definitions.
65.003. Commission Authority.
65.004. Information.
65.005. Customer Protection.

SUBCHAPTER B. DETERMINATION OF WHETHER MARKET SHOULD BE REGULATED

65.051. Markets Deregulated.
65.052. Determination of Whether a Market Should Remain Regulated.
65.053. Incumbent Local Exchange Company Markets.
65.054. Repealed.
65.055. Repealed.

SUBCHAPTER C. DEREGULATED COMPANY

65.101. Issuance of Certificate of Operating Authority.
65.102. Requirements.

SUBCHAPTER D. TRANSITIONING COMPANY

65.151. Provisions Applicable to Transitioning Company.
65.152. General Requirements.
65.153. Rate Requirements.
65.154. Rate and Price Requirements Not Applicable.
65.155. Complaint by Affected Person.

SUBCHAPTER E. REDUCTION OF SWITCHED ACCESS RATES

65.201. Reduction of Switched Access Rates by Deregulated Company.
65.202. Reduction of Switched Access Rates by Transitioning Company With More Than Three Million Access Lines.
65.203. Reduction of Switched Access Rates by Certain Transitioning Companies With Not More Than Three Million Access Lines.
65.204. Reduction of Switched Access Rates by Newly Designated Transitioning Company.
65.205. Maintenance of Reduction or Parity.

SUBCHAPTER F. LEGISLATIVE OVERSIGHT COMMITTEE [REPEALED]

65.251, 65.252. Repealed.

SUBCHAPTER A. GENERAL PROVISIONS

§ 65.001. Statement of Policy

It is the policy of this state to provide for full rate and service competition in the telecommunications market of this state so that customers may benefit from innovations in service quality and market-based pricing.

Added by Acts 2005, 79th Leg., 2nd C.S., ch. 2, § 26, eff. Sept. 1, 2005.

§ 65.002. Definitions

In this chapter:

(1) "Deregulated company" means an incumbent local exchange company for which all of the company's markets have been deregulated.

(2) "Market" means an exchange in which an incumbent local exchange company provides residential local exchange telephone service.

(3) "Regulated company" means an incumbent local exchange company for which none of the company's markets have been deregulated.

(4) "Stand–alone residential local exchange voice service" means:

(A) residential tone dialing service;

(B) services and functionalities supported under the lifeline program;

(C) access for all residential end users to 911 service provided by a local authority and access to dual party relay service;

(D) at the election of the incumbent local exchange company, mandatory residential extended area service arrangements, mandatory residential extended metropolitan service or other mandatory residential toll-free calling arrangements, mandatory expanded local calling service arrangements, or another service that a company is required under a tariff to provide to a customer who subscribes or may subscribe to basic network services;

(E) flat rate residential local exchange telephone service delivered by landline, but only if the service is ordered and received independent of:

(i) a service classified as a nonbasic service under Section 58.151 or residential call waiting service;

(ii) a package of services that includes a service classified as a nonbasic service under Section 58.151; or

(iii) another flat rate residential local exchange service delivered by landline; and

(F) residential caller identification services if the customer to whom the service is billed is at least 65 years of age.

(5) "Transitioning company" means an incumbent local exchange company for which at least one, but not all, of the company's markets has been deregulated.

Added by Acts 2005, 79th Leg., 2nd C.S., ch. 2, § 26, eff. Sept. 1, 2005.

§ 65.003. Commission Authority

(a) Notwithstanding any other provisions of this title, the commission has authority to implement and enforce this chapter.

(b) The commission may adopt rules and conduct proceedings necessary to administer and enforce this chapter, including rules to determine whether a market should remain regulated, should be deregulated, or should be reregulated.

Added by Acts 2005, 79th Leg., 2nd C.S., ch. 2, § 26, eff. Sept. 1, 2005.

§ 65.004. Information

(a) The commission may collect and compile information from all telecommunications providers as necessary to implement and enforce this chapter.

(b) The commission shall maintain the confidentiality of information collected under this chapter that is claimed to be confidential for competitive purposes. Information that is claimed to be confidential is exempt from disclosure under Chapter 552, Government Code.

Added by Acts 2005, 79th Leg., 2nd C.S., ch. 2, § 26, eff. Sept. 1, 2005.

§ 65.005. Customer Protection

This chapter does not affect a customer's right to complain to the commission regarding a telecommunications provider.

Added by Acts 2005, 79th Leg., 2nd C.S., ch. 2, § 26, eff. Sept. 1, 2005.

SUBCHAPTER B. DETERMINATION OF WHETHER MARKET SHOULD BE REGULATED

§ 65.051. Markets Deregulated

A market that is deregulated as of September 1, 2011, shall remain deregulated. Notwithstanding any other provision of this title, the commission may not reregulate a market or company that has been deregulated .

Added by Acts 2005, 79th Leg., 2nd C.S., ch. 2, § 26, eff. Sept. 1, 2005. Amended by Acts 2011, 82nd Leg., ch. 98 (S.B. 980), § 14, eff. Sept. 1, 2011.

§ 65.052. Determination of Whether a Market Should Remain Regulated

(a) An incumbent local exchange company may petition the commission to deregulate a market of the company that the commission previously determined should remain regulated. Notwithstanding any other provision of this title, only the incumbent local exchange company may initiate a proceeding to deregulate one of the company's markets. Not later than the 90th day after the date the commission receives the petition, the commission shall:

(1) determine whether the regulated market should remain regulated ; and

(2) issue a final order classifying the market in accordance with this section .

(b) In making a determination under Subsection (a), the commission may not determine that a market should remain regulated if:

(1) the population in the area included in the market is at least 100,000; or

(2) the population in the area included in the market is less than 100,000 and, in addition to the incumbent local exchange company, there are at least two competitors operating in all or part of the market that :

(A) are unaffiliated with the incumbent local exchange company ; and

(B) provide voice communications service without regard to the delivery technology, including through:

(i) Internet Protocol or a successor protocol;

(ii) satellite; or

(iii) a technology used by a wireless provider or a commercial mobile service provider, as that term is defined by Section 64.201

(c) If the commission deregulates a market under this section and the deregulation results in a regulated or transitioning company no longer meeting the definition of a regulated or transitioning company, the commission shall issue an order reclassifying the company as a transitioning company or deregulated company, as those terms are defined by Section 65.002 .

(d) to (f) Repealed by Acts 2011, 82nd Leg., ch. 98 (S.B. 980), § 21(3).

Added by Acts 2005, 79th Leg., 2nd C.S., ch. 2, § 26, eff. Sept. 1, 2005. Amended by Acts 2011, 82nd Leg., ch. 98 (S.B. 980), §§ 15, 21(3), eff. Sept. 1, 2011.

§ 65.053. Incumbent Local Exchange Company Markets

(a) Notwithstanding Section 65.052, an incumbent local exchange company may elect to have all of the company's markets remain regulated on and after January 1, 2006.

(b) To make an election under Subsection (a), an incumbent local exchange company must file an affidavit with the commission making that election not later than December 1, 2005.

(c) If an incumbent local exchange company makes an election under this section, the commission shall issue an order classifying the company as a regulated company that is subject to the provisions of this title that applied to the company on September 1, 2005. This subsection does not affect the authority of a regulated company to elect under Chapter 58 or 59 after January 1, 2005, and to be regulated under the chapter under which the company elected.

Added by Acts 2005, 79th Leg., 2nd C.S., ch. 2, § 26, eff. Sept. 1, 2005.

§ 65.054. Repealed by Acts Acts 2011, 82nd Leg., ch. 98 (S.B. 980), § 21(4), eff. Sept. 1, 2011

§ 65.055. Repealed by Acts Acts 2011, 82nd Leg., ch. 98 (S.B. 980), § 21(5), eff. Sept. 1, 2011

SUBCHAPTER C. DEREGULATED COMPANY

§ 65.101. Issuance of Certificate of Operating Authority

(a) A deregulated company may petition the commission to relinquish the company's certificate of convenience and necessity and receive a certificate of operating authority.

(b) The commission shall issue the deregulated company a certificate of operating authority and rescind the deregulated company's certificate of convenience and necessity if the commission finds that all of the company's markets have been deregulated under Subchapter B.[1]

Added by Acts 2005, 79th Leg., 2nd C.S., ch. 2, § 26, eff. Sept. 1, 2005.

[1] V.T.C.A., Utilities Code § 65.051.

§ 65.102. Requirements

(a) A deregulated company that holds a certificate of operating authority issued under this subchapter:

(1) is a nondominant carrier governed in the same manner as a holder of a certificate of operating authority issued under Chapter 54;

(2) is not required to:

(A) fulfill the obligations of a provider of last resort;

(B) comply with retail quality of service standards or reporting requirements;

(C) file an earnings report with the commission unless the company is receiving support from the Texas High Cost Universal Service Plan; or

(D) comply with a pricing requirement other than a requirement prescribed by this subchapter; and

(3) is subject to the following provisions in the same manner as an incumbent local exchange company that is not deregulated:

(A) Sections 54.156, 54.158, and 54.159;

(B) Section 55.012; and

(C) Chapter 60 .

(b) Except as provided by Subsection (c), in each deregulated market, a deregulated company shall make available to all residential customers uniformly throughout that market the same price, terms, and conditions for all basic and non-basic services, consistent with any pricing flexibility available to such company .

(c) A deregulated company may offer to an individual residential customer a promotional offer that is not available uniformly throughout the market if the company makes the offer through a medium other than direct mail or mass electronic media and the offer is intended to retain or obtain a customer.

Added by Acts 2005, 79th Leg., 2nd C.S., ch. 2, § 26, eff. Sept. 1, 2005. Amended by Acts 2011, 82nd Leg., ch. 98 (S.B. 980), § 16, eff. Sept. 1, 2011.

SUBCHAPTER D. TRANSITIONING COMPANY

§ 65.151. Provisions Applicable to Transitioning Company

(a) Except as provided by Subsection (b), a transitioning company is governed by this subchapter and the provisions of this title that applied to the company immediately before the date the company was classified as a transitioning company. If there is a conflict between this subchapter and the other applicable provisions of this title, this subchapter controls.

(b) A transitioning company is not required to fulfill the obligations of a provider of last resort in a deregulated market.

Added by Acts 2005, 79th Leg., 2nd C.S., ch. 2, § 26, eff. Sept. 1, 2005. Amended by Acts 2011, 82nd Leg., ch. 98 (S.B. 980), § 17, eff. Sept. 1, 2011.

§ 65.152. General Requirements

(a) A transitioning company may:

(1) exercise pricing flexibility in a market subject only to the price and rate standards prescribed by Sections 65.153 and 65.154 ; and

(2) introduce a new service in a market subject only to the price and rate standards prescribed by Sections 65.153 and 65.154 .

(b) A transitioning company may not be required to:

(1) comply with retail quality of service standards or reporting requirements in a market that is deregulated; or

(2) file an earnings report with the commission unless the company is receiving support from the Texas High Cost Universal Service Plan.

Added by Acts 2005, 79th Leg., 2nd C.S., ch. 2, § 26, eff. Sept. 1, 2005. Amended by Acts 2011, 82nd Leg., ch. 98 (S.B. 980), § 18, eff. Sept. 1, 2011.

§ 65.153. Rate Requirements

(a) In a market that remains regulated, a transitioning company shall price the company's retail services in accordance with the provisions that applied to that company immediately before the date the company was classified as a transitioning company.

(b) In a market that is deregulated, a transitioning company shall price the company's retail services as follows:

(1) for all services, other than basic local telecommunications service, at any price higher than the service's long run incremental cost; and

(2) for basic local telecommunications service, at any price higher than the lesser of the service's long run incremental cost or the tariffed price on the date that market was deregulated, provided that the company may not increase the company's rates for stand-alone residential local exchange voice service before the date that the commission has the opportunity to revise the monthly per line support under the Texas High Cost Universal Service Plan pursuant to Section 56.031, regardless of whether the company is an electing company under Chapter 58.

(c) Except as provided by Subsection (c–1), in each deregulated market, a transitioning company shall make available to all residential customers uniformly throughout that market the same price, terms, and conditions for all basic and non-basic services, consistent with any pricing flexibility available to such company .

(c–1) A transitioning company may offer to an individual residential customer a promotional offer that is not available uniformly throughout the market if the company makes the offer through a medium other than direct mail or mass electronic media and the offer is intended to retain or obtain a customer.

(d) In any market, regardless of whether regulated or deregulated, the transitioning company may not:

(1) establish a retail rate, term, or condition that is anticompetitive or unreasonably preferential, prejudicial, or discriminatory;

(2) establish a retail rate for a basic or non-basic service in a deregulated market that is subsidized either directly or indirectly by a basic or non-basic service provided in an exchange that is not deregulated; or

(3) engage in predatory pricing or attempt to engage in predatory pricing.

(e) A rate that meets the pricing requirements in Subsection (b) shall be deemed compliant with Subsection (d)(2).

Added by Acts 2005, 79th Leg., 2nd C.S., ch. 2, § 26, eff. Sept. 1, 2005. Amended by Acts 2011, 82nd Leg., ch. 98 (S.B. 980), § 19, eff. Sept. 1, 2011.

§ 65.154. Rate and Price Requirements Not Applicable

Text of section effective Jan. 2, 2012

(a) A transitioning company is not required to comply with the following requirements prescribed by this title on submission of a written notice to the commission:

(1) a direct or indirect requirement to price a residential service at, above, or according to the long-run incremental cost of the service or to otherwise use long-run incremental cost in establishing prices for residential services; or

(2) a requirement to file with the commission a long-run incremental cost study for residential or business services.

(b) Notwithstanding Subsection (a), a transitioning company may not:

(1) establish a retail rate, price, term, or condition that is anticompetitive or unreasonably preferential, prejudicial, or discriminatory;

(2) establish a retail rate for a basic or non-basic service in a deregulated market that is subsidized either directly or indirectly by a basic or non-basic service provided in an exchange that is not deregulated; or

(3) engage in predatory pricing or attempt to engage in predatory pricing.

(c) A rate or price for a basic local telecommunications service is not anticompetitive, predatory, or unreasonably preferential, prejudicial, or discriminatory if the rate or price is equal to or greater than the rate or price in the transitioning company's tariff for that service in effect on the date the transitioning company submits notice to the commission under Subsection (a).

(d) This section, including Subsection (a)(1), does not affect:

(1) other law or legal standards governing predatory pricing or anticompetitive conduct; or

(2) an infrastructure commitment under Chapter 58 or 59.

Added by Acts 2011, 82nd Leg., ch. 98 (S.B. 980), § 20, eff. Jan. 2, 2012.

§ 65.155. Complaint by Affected Person

Text of section effective Jan. 2, 2012

(a) An affected person may file a complaint at the commission challenging whether a transitioning company is complying with Section 65.154(b).

(b) Notwithstanding Section 65.154(a)(2), the commission may require a transitioning company to submit a long-run incremental cost study for a business service that is the subject of a complaint submitted under Subsection (a).

Added by Acts 2011, 82nd Leg., ch. 98 (S.B. 980), § 20, eff. Jan. 2, 2012.

SUBCHAPTER E. REDUCTION OF SWITCHED ACCESS RATES

§ 65.201. Reduction of Switched Access Rates by Deregulated Company

(a) On the date the last market of an incumbent local exchange company is deregulated, the company shall reduce both the company's originating and terminating per minute of use switched access rates in each market to parity with the company's respective federal originating and terminating per minute of use switched access rates.

(b) After reducing the rates under Subsection (a), a deregulated company shall maintain parity with the company's federal originating and terminating per minute of use switched access rates. If the company's federal originating and terminating per minute of use switched access rates are changed, the company shall change the company's per minute of use switched access rates in each market as necessary to re-achieve parity with the company's federal originating and terminating per minute of use switched access rates.

Added by Acts 2005, 79th Leg., 2nd C.S., ch. 2, § 26, eff. Sept. 1, 2005.

§ 65.202. Reduction of Switched Access Rates by Transitioning Company With More Than Three Million Access Lines

(a) Notwithstanding any other provision of this title, a transitioning company that has more than three million access lines in service in this state on January 1, 2006, shall:

(1) on July 1, 2006, reduce both the company's originating and terminating per minute of use switched access rates in each market by an amount equal to 33 percent of the difference in the rates in effect on June 30, 2006, and the company's respective federal originating and terminating per minute of use switched access rates;

(2) on July 1, 2007, reduce both the company's originating and terminating per minute of use switched access rates in each market by an amount equal to 33 percent of the difference in the rates in effect on June 30, 2006, and the company's respective federal originating and terminating per minute of use switched access rates; and

(3) on July 1, 2008, reduce both the company's originating and terminating per minute of use switched access rates in each market to parity with the company's respective federal originating and terminating per minute of use switched access rates.

(b) After reducing the rates under Subsection (a), a transitioning company shall maintain parity with the company's federal originating and terminating per minute of use switched access rates. If the company's federal originating and terminating per minute of use switched access rates are changed, the company shall change the company's per minute of use switched access rates in each market as necessary to re-achieve parity with the company's federal originating and terminating per minute of use switched access rates.

Added by Acts 2005, 79th Leg., 2nd C.S., ch. 2, § 26, eff. Sept. 1, 2005.

§ 65.203. Reduction of Switched Access Rates by Certain Transitioning Companies With Not More Than Three Million Access Lines

(a) Notwithstanding any other provision of this title, a company that is classified as a transitioning company effective January 1, 2006, and that has not more than three million access lines in service in this state on that date shall reduce both the company's originating and terminating per minute of use switched access rates in each market in accordance with this section.

(b) On July 1, 2006, the transitioning company shall reduce both the company's originating and terminating per minute of use switched access rates in each market by an amount equal to the lesser of:

(1) 25 percent of the difference in the company's rates in effect on June 30, 2006, and the company's respective federal originating and terminating per minute of use switched access rates in effect on that date; or

(2) an amount derived by multiplying that difference by a percentage derived by dividing the number of the company's markets that are not regulated on July 1, 2006, by the total number of the company's markets on December 30, 2005.

(c) On July 1, 2007, the transitioning company shall reduce both the company's originating and terminating per minute of use switched access rates in each market by an amount equal to the lesser of:

(1) 25 percent of the difference in the company's rates in effect on June 30, 2006, and the company's respective federal originating and terminating per minute of use switched access rates in effect on that date; or

(2) an amount derived by multiplying that difference by a percentage derived by dividing the number of the company's markets that were deregulated in the prior 12 months by the total number of the company's markets on December 30, 2005.

(d) On July 1, 2008, the transitioning company shall reduce both the company's originating and terminating per minute of use switched access rates in each market by an amount equal to the lesser of:

(1) 25 percent of the difference in the company's rates in effect on June 30, 2006, and the company's respective federal originating and terminating per minute of use switched access rates in effect on that date; or

(2) an amount derived by multiplying that difference by a percentage derived by dividing the number of the company's markets that were deregulated in the prior 12 months by the total number of the company's markets on December 30, 2005.

(e) On July 1, 2009, and each succeeding year thereafter on July 1, the transitioning company shall reduce both the company's originating and terminating per minute of use switched access rates in each market by an amount derived by multiplying the difference in the company's rates in effect on June 30, 2006, and the company's respective federal originating and terminating per minute of use switched access rates in effect on that date by a percentage derived by dividing the number of the company's markets that were deregulated in the prior 12 months by the total number of the company's markets on December 30, 2005, except that a transitioning company shall be required to reduce both the company's originating and terminating per minute of use switched access charges to parity with the company's respective federal originating and terminating per minute of use switched access charges if more than 75 percent of the transitioning company's markets are not regulated on July 1 of 2009 or any succeeding year.

(f) After reducing the rates under Subsection (e), a transitioning company shall maintain parity with the company's federal originating and terminating per minute of use switched access rates. If the company's federal originating and terminating per minute of use switched access rates are changed, the company shall change the company's per minute of use switched access rates in each market as necessary to re-achieve parity with the company's federal originating and terminating per minute of use switched access rates.

Added by Acts 2005, 79th Leg., 2nd C.S., ch. 2, § 26, eff. Sept. 1, 2005.

§ 65.204. Reduction of Switched Access Rates by Newly Designated Transitioning Company

(a) Notwithstanding any other provision of this title, a company that is classified as a transitioning company after January 1, 2006, shall reduce both the company's originating and terminating per minute of use switched access rates in each market in accordance with this section.

(b) On the date the company is classified as a transitioning company, the company shall reduce both the company's originating and terminating per minute of use switched access rates in each market by an amount equal to the lesser of:

(1) 25 percent of the difference in the company's rates in effect on the day before the date the company was classified, and the company's respective federal originating and terminating per minute of use switched access rates in effect on that date; or

(2) an amount derived by multiplying that difference by a percentage derived by dividing the number of the company's markets that are not regulated on the date the company is classified as a transitioning company by the total number of the company's markets on December 30, 2005.

(c) On the first anniversary of the date the company is classified as a transitioning company, the company shall reduce both the company's originating and terminating per minute of use switched access rates in each market by an amount equal to the lesser of:

(1) 25 percent of the difference in the company's rates in effect on the day before the date the company was classified, and the company's respective federal originating and terminating per minute of use switched access rates in effect on that date; or

(2) an amount derived by multiplying that difference by a percentage derived by dividing the number of the company's markets that were deregulated in the prior 12 months by the total number of the company's markets on December 30, 2005.

(d) On the second anniversary of the date the company is classified as a transitioning company, the company shall reduce both the company's originating and terminating per minute of use switched access rates in each market by an amount equal to the lesser of:

(1) 25 percent of the difference in the company's rates in effect on the day before the date the company was classified, and the company's respective federal originating and terminating per minute of use switched access rates in effect on that date; or

(2) an amount derived by multiplying that difference by a percentage derived by dividing the number of the company's markets that were deregulated in the prior 12 months by the total number of the company's markets on December 30, 2005.

(e) On the third anniversary of the date the company is classified as a transitioning company and each anniversary thereafter, the company shall reduce both the company's originating and terminating per minute of use switched access rates in each market by an amount derived by multiplying the difference in the company's rates in effect on the day before the date the company was classified as a transitioning company, and the company's respective federal originating and terminating per minute of use switched access rates in effect on that date by a percentage derived by dividing the number of the company's markets that were deregulated in the prior 12 months by the total number of the company's markets on December 30, 2005, except that a transitioning company shall be required to reduce both the company's originating and terminating per minute of use switched access charges to parity with the company's respective federal originating and terminating per minute of use switched access charges if more than 75 percent of the transitioning company's markets are not regulated on July 1 of 2009 or any succeeding year.

(f) After reducing the rates under Subsection (e), a transitioning company shall maintain parity with the company's federal originating and terminating per minute of use switched access rates. If the company's federal originating and terminating per minute of use switched access rates are changed, the company shall change the company's per minute of use switched access rates in each market as necessary to re-achieve parity with the company's federal originating and terminating per minute of use switched access rates.

Added by Acts 2005, 79th Leg., 2nd C.S., ch. 2, § 26, eff. Sept. 1, 2005.

§ 65.205. Maintenance of Reduction or Parity

(a) After a deregulated or transitioning company reduces the company's rates under this subchapter, the company may not increase those rates above the applicable rates prescribed by this subchapter.

(b) If a transitioning company's federal per minute of use switched access rates are reduced, the company shall reduce the company's per minute of use switched access rates to not more than the applicable rates prescribed by this subchapter.

(c) Notwithstanding Subsections (a) and (b), a deregulated or transitioning company may decrease the company's per minute of use switched access rates to amounts that are less than the applicable rates prescribed by this subchapter.

Added by Acts 2005, 79th Leg., 2nd C.S., ch. 2, § 26, eff. Sept. 1, 2005.

SUBCHAPTER F. LEGISLATIVE OVERSIGHT COMMITTEE [REPEALED]

§§ 65.251, 65.252. Repealed by Acts 2011, 82nd Leg., ch. 905 (S.B. 781) § 1, eff. June 17, 2011

CHAPTER 66. STATE–ISSUED CABLE AND VIDEO FRANCHISE

Section
66.001. Franchising Authority.
66.002. Definitions.
66.003. State Authorization to Provide Cable Service or Video Service.
66.004. Eligibility for Commission–issued Franchise.
66.005. Franchise Fee.
66.006. In–kind Contributions to Municipality.
66.007. Build–out.
66.008. Customer Service Standards.
66.009. Public, Educational, and Governmental Access Channels.
66.010. Nondiscrimination by Municipality.
66.011. Municipal Police Power; Other Authority.
66.012. Indemnity in Connection With Right–of–way; Notice of Liability.
66.013. Municipal Authority.
66.014. Discrimination Prohibited.
66.015. Compliance.
66.016. Applicability of Other Laws.
66.017. Expired.

§ 66.001. Franchising Authority

The commission shall be designated as the franchising authority for a state-issued franchise for the provision of cable service or video service.

Added by Acts 2005, 79th Leg., 2nd C.S., ch. 2, § 27, eff. Sept. 1, 2005.

§ 66.002. Definitions

In this chapter:

(1) "Actual incremental cost" means only current out-of-pocket expenses for labor, equipment repair, equipment replacement, and tax expenses directly associated with the labor or the equipment of a service provider that is necessarily and directly used to provide what were, under a superseded franchise, in-kind services, exclusive of any profit or overhead such as depreciation, amortization, or administrative expense.

(2) "Cable service" is defined as set forth in 47 U.S.C. Section 522(6).

(3) "Cable service provider" means a person who provides cable service.

(4) "Communications network" means a component or facility that is, wholly or partly, physically located within a public right-of-way and that is used to provide video programming, cable, voice, or data services.

(5) "Franchise" means an initial authorization, or renewal of an authorization, issued by a franchising authority, regardless of whether the authorization is designated as a franchise, permit, license, resolution, contract, certificate, agreement, or otherwise, that authorizes the construction and operation of a cable or video services network in the public rights-of-way.

(6)(A) "Gross revenues" means all consideration of any kind or nature including without limitation cash, credits, property, and in-kind contributions (services or goods) derived by the holder of a state-issued certificate of franchise authority from the operation of the cable service provider's or the video service provider's network to provide cable service or video service within the municipality. Gross revenue shall include all consideration paid to the holder of a state-issued certificate of franchise authority and its affiliates (to the extent either is acting as a provider of a cable service or video service as authorized by this chapter), which shall include but not be limited to the following: (i) all fees charged to subscribers for any and all cable service or video service provided by the holder of a state-issued certificate of franchise authority; (ii) any fee imposed on the holder of a state-issued certificate of franchise authority by this chapter that is passed through and paid by subscribers (including without limitation the franchise fee set forth in this chapter); and (iii) compensation received by the holder of a state- issued certificate of franchise authority or its affiliates that is derived from the operation of the holder of a state-issued certificate of franchise authority's network to provide cable service or video service with respect to commissions that are paid to the holder of a state-issued certificate of franchise authority as compensation for promotion or exhibition of any products or services on the holder of a state-issued certificate of franchise authority's network, such as a "home shopping" or a similar channel, subject to Paragraph (B)(v). Gross revenue includes a pro rata portion of all revenue derived by the holder of a state-issued certificate of franchise authority or its affiliates pursuant to compensation arrangements for advertising derived from the operation of the holder of a state-issued certificate of franchise authority's network to provide cable service or the video service within a municipality, subject to Paragraph (B)(iii). The allocation shall be based on the number of subscribers in the municipality divided by the total number of subscribers in relation to the relevant regional or national compensation arrangement. Advertising commissions paid to third parties shall not be netted against advertising revenue included in gross revenue. Revenue of an affiliate derived from the affiliate's provision of cable service or the video service shall be gross revenue to the extent the treatment of such revenue as revenue of the affiliate and not of the holder of a state-issued certificate of franchise authority has the effect (whether intentional or unintentional) of evading the payment of fees which would otherwise be paid to the municipality. In no event shall revenue of an affiliate be gross revenue to the holder of a state-issued certificate of franchise authority if such revenue is otherwise subject to fees to be paid to the municipality.

(B) For purposes of this section, "gross revenues" does not include:

(i) any revenue not actually received, even if billed, such as bad debt;

(ii) non-cable services or non-video services revenues received by any affiliate or any other person in exchange for supplying goods or services used by the holder of a state-issued certificate of franchise authority to provide cable service or video service;

(iii) refunds, rebates, or discounts made to subscribers, leased access providers, advertisers, or a municipality;

(iv) any revenues from services classified as non-cable service or non-video service under federal law including without limitation revenue received from telecommunications services; revenue received from information services (but not excluding cable services or video services); and any other revenues attributed by the holder of a state-issued certificate of franchise authority to non-cable service or non-video service in accordance with Federal Communications Commission or commission rules, regulations, standards, or orders;

(v) any revenue paid by subscribers to home shopping programmers directly from the sale of merchandise through any home shopping channel offered as part of the cable services or video services, but not excluding any commissions that are paid to the holder of a state-issued certificate of franchise authority as compensation for promotion or exhibition of any products or services on the holder of a state-issued certificate of franchise authority's network, such as a "home shopping" or a similar channel;

(vi) the sale of cable services or video services for resale in which the purchaser is required to collect this chapter's fees from the purchaser's customer. Nothing under this chapter is intended to limit state's rights pursuant to 47 U.S.C. Section 542(h);

(vii) the provision of cable services or video services to customers at no charge, as required or allowed by this chapter, including without limitation the provision of cable services or video services to public institutions, as required or permitted in this chapter, including without limitation public schools or governmental entities, as required or permitted in this chapter;

(viii) any tax of general applicability imposed upon the holder of a state-issued certificate of franchise authority or upon subscribers by a city, state, federal, or any other governmental entity and required to be collected by the holder of a state-issued certificate of franchise authority and remitted to the taxing entity (including, but not limited to, sales and use tax, gross receipts tax, excise tax, utility users tax, public service tax, communication taxes, and fees not imposed by this chapter);

(ix) any forgone revenue from the holder of a state-issued certificate of franchise authority's provision of free or reduced cost cable services or video services to any person including without limitation employees of the holder of a state-issued certificate of franchise authority, to the municipality and other public institutions or other institutions as allowed in this chapter; provided, however, that any forgone revenue which the holder of a state-issued certificate of franchise authority chooses not to receive in exchange for trades, barters, services, or other items of value shall be included in gross revenue;

(x) sales of capital assets or sales of surplus equipment that is not used by the purchaser to receive cable services or video services from the holder of a state-issued certificate of franchise authority;

(xi) directory or Internet advertising revenue including, but not limited to, yellow pages, white pages, banner advertisement, and electronic publishing; and

(xii) reimbursement by programmers of marketing costs incurred by the holder of a state-issued franchise for the introduction of new programming that exceed the actual costs.

(C) For purposes of this definition, a provider's network consists solely of the optical spectrum wavelengths, bandwidth, or other current or future technological capacity used for the transmission of video programming over wireline directly to subscribers within the geographic area within the municipality as designated by the provider in its franchise.

(7) "Incumbent cable service provider" means the cable service provider serving the largest number of cable subscribers in a particular municipal franchise area on September 1, 2005.

(8) "Public right-of-way" means the area on, below, or above a public roadway, highway, street, public sidewalk, alley, waterway, or utility easement in which a municipality has an interest.

(9) "Video programming" means programming provided by, or generally considered comparable to programming provided by, a television broadcast station, as set forth in 47 U.S.C. Section 522(20).

(10) "Video service" means video programming services provided through wireline facilities located at least in part in the public right-of-way without regard to delivery technology, including Internet protocol technology. This definition does not include any video service provided by a commercial mobile service provider as defined in 47 U.S.C. Section 332(d).

(11) "Video service provider" means a video programming distributor that distributes video programming services through wireline facilities located at least in part in the public right-of-way without regard to delivery technology. This term does not include a cable service provider.

Added by Acts 2005, 79th Leg., 2nd C.S., ch. 2, § 27, eff. Sept. 1, 2005.

§ 66.003. State Authorization to Provide Cable Service or Video Service

(a) An entity or person seeking to provide cable service or video service in this state shall file an application for a state-issued certificate of franchise authority with the commission as required by this section. An entity providing cable service or video service under a franchise agreement with a municipality is not subject to this subsection with respect to such municipality until the franchise agreement is terminated under Section 66.004 or until the franchise agreement expires.

(a–1) The commission shall notify an applicant for a state-issued certificate of franchise authority whether the applicant's affidavit described by Subsection (b) is complete before the 15th business day after the applicant submits the affidavit.

(b) The commission shall issue a certificate of franchise authority to offer cable service or video service before the 17th business day after receipt of a completed affidavit submitted by the applicant and signed by an officer or general partner of the applicant affirming:

(1) that the applicant has filed or will timely file with the Federal Communications Commission all forms required by that agency in advance of offering cable service or video service in this state;

(2) that the applicant agrees to comply with all applicable federal and state statutes and regulations;

(3) that the applicant agrees to comply with all applicable municipal regulations regarding the use and occupation of public rights-of-way in the delivery of the cable service or video service, including the police powers of the municipalities in which the service is delivered;

(4) a description of the service area footprint to be served within the municipality, if applicable, otherwise the municipality to be served by the applicant, which may include certain designations of unincorporated areas, which description shall be updated by the applicant prior to the expansion of cable service or video service to a previously undesignated service area and, upon such expansion, notice to the commission of the service area to be served by the applicant; and

(5) the location of the applicant's principal place of business and the names of the applicant's principal executive officers.

(c) The certificate of franchise authority issued by the commission shall contain:

(1) a grant of authority to provide cable service or video service as requested in the application;

(2) a grant of authority to use and occupy the public rights-of-way in the delivery of that service, subject to the laws of this state, including the police powers of the municipalities in which the service is delivered; and

(3) a statement that the grant of authority is subject to lawful operation of the cable service or video service by the applicant or its successor in interest.

(d) The certificate of franchise authority issued by the commission is fully transferable to any successor in interest to the applicant to which it is initially granted. A notice of transfer shall be filed with the commission and the relevant municipality within 14 business days of the completion of such transfer.

(e) The certificate of franchise authority issued by the commission may be terminated by the cable service provider or video service provider by submitting notice to the commission.

Added by Acts 2005, 79th Leg., 2nd C.S., ch. 2, § 27, eff. Sept. 1, 2005. Amended by Acts 2011, 82nd Leg., ch. 1077 (S.B. 1087), § 1, eff. Sept. 1, 2011.

§ 66.004. Eligibility for Commission-issued Franchise

(a) A cable service provider or a video service provider that currently has or had previously received a franchise to provide cable service or video service with respect to such municipalities is not eligible to seek a state-issued certificate of franchise authority under this chapter as to those municipalities until the expiration date of the existing franchise agreement, except as provided by Subsections (b), (b–1), (b–2), (b–3), and (c).

(b) Beginning September 1, 2005, a cable service provider or video service provider that is not the incumbent cable service provider and serves fewer than 40 percent of the total cable customers in a particular municipal franchise area may elect to terminate that municipal franchise and seek a state-issued certificate of franchise authority by providing written notice to the commission and the affected municipality before January 1, 2006. The municipal franchise is terminated on the date the commission issues the state-issued certificate of franchise authority.

(b–1) Beginning September 1, 2011, a cable service provider or video service provider in a municipality with a population of less than 215,000 that was not allowed to or did not terminate a municipal franchise under Subsection (b) may elect to terminate not less than all unexpired franchises in municipalities with a population of less than 215,000 and seek a state-issued certificate of franchise authority for each area served under a terminated municipal franchise by providing written notice to the commission and each affected municipality before January 1, 2012. A municipal franchise is terminated on the date the commission issues a state-issued certificate of franchise authority to the provider for the area served under that terminated franchise.

(b–2) A cable service provider or video service provider in a municipality with a population of at least 215,000 may terminate a municipal franchise in that municipality in the manner described by Subsection (b–1) if:

(1) the cable service provider or video service provider is not the incumbent cable service provider in that municipality; and

(2) the incumbent cable service provider received a state-issued certificate of franchise authority from the commission before September 1, 2011.

(b–3) A municipality with a population of at least 215,000 may enter into an agreement with any cable service provider in the municipality to terminate a municipal cable franchise before the expiration of the franchise. To the extent that the mutually agreed on terms and conditions for early termination of the unexpired municipal cable franchise conflict with a provision of this chapter, the agreed on terms and conditions control.

(c) A cable service provider that elects under Subsection (b), (b–1), or (b–2) to terminate an existing municipal franchise is responsible for remitting to the affected municipality before the 91st day after the date the municipal franchise is terminated any accrued but unpaid franchise fees due under the terminated franchise. If the cable service provider has credit remaining from prepaid franchise fees, the provider may deduct the amount of the remaining credit from any future fees or taxes it must pay to the municipality, either directly or through the comptroller.

(d) For purposes of this section, a cable service provider or video service provider will be deemed to have or have had a franchise to provide cable service or video service in a specific municipality if any affiliates or successor entity of the cable or video provider has or had a franchise agreement granted by that specific municipality.

(e) The terms "affiliates or successor entity" in this section shall include but not be limited to any entity receiving, obtaining, or operating under a municipal cable or video franchise through merger, sale, assignment, restructuring, or any other type of transaction.

(f) Except as provided in this chapter, nothing in this chapter is intended to abrogate, nullify, or adversely affect in any way the contractual rights, duties, and obligations existing and incurred by a cable service provider or a video service provider before the date a franchise expires or the date a provider terminates a franchise under Subsection (b–1) or (b–2), as applicable, and owed or owing to any private person, firm, partnership, corporation, or other entity including without limitation those obligations measured by and related to the gross revenue hereafter received by the holder of a state-issued certificate of franchise authority for services provided in the geographic area to which such prior franchise or permit applies. All liens, security interests, royalties, and other contracts, rights, and interests in effect on September 1, 2005, or the date a franchise is terminated under Subsection (b–1) or (b–2) shall continue in full force and effect, without the necessity for renewal, extension, or continuance, and shall be paid and performed by the holder of a state-issued certificate of franchise authority, and shall apply as though the revenue generated by the holder of a state-issued certificate of franchise authority continued to be generated pursuant to the permit or franchise issued by the prior local franchising authority or municipality within the geographic area to which the prior permit or franchise applies. It shall be a condition to the issuance and continuance of a state-issued certificate of franchise authority that the private contractual rights and obligations herein described continue to be honored, paid, or performed to the same extent as though the cable service provider continued to operate under its prior franchise or permit, for the duration of such state-issued certificate of franchise authority and any renewals or extensions thereof, and that the applicant so agrees. Any person, firm, partnership, corporation, or other entity holding or claiming rights herein reserved may enforce same by an action brought in a court of competent jurisdiction.

Added by Acts 2005, 79th Leg., 2nd C.S., ch. 2, § 27, eff. Sept. 1, 2005. Amended by Acts 2011, 82nd Leg., ch. 1077 (S.B. 1087), § 2, eff. Sept. 1, 2011.

§ 66.005. Franchise Fee

(a) The holder of a state-issued certificate of franchise authority shall pay each municipality in which it provides cable service or video service a franchise fee of five percent based upon the definition of gross revenues as set forth in this chapter. That same franchise fee structure shall apply to any unincorporated areas that are annexed by a municipality after the effective date of the state-issued certificate of franchise authority.

(b) The franchise fee payable under this section is to be paid quarterly, within 45 days after the end of the quarter for the preceding calendar quarter. Each payment shall be accompanied by a summary explaining the basis for the calculation of the fee. A municipality may review the business records of the cable service provider or video service provider to the extent necessary to ensure compensation in accordance with Subsection (a), provided that the municipality may only review records that relate to the 48–month period preceding the date of the last franchise fee payment. Each party shall bear the party's own costs of the examination. A municipality may, in the event of a dispute concerning compensation under this section, bring an action in a court of competent jurisdiction.

(c) The holder of a state-issued certificate of franchise authority may recover from the provider's customers any fee imposed by this chapter.

Added by Acts 2005, 79th Leg., 2nd C.S., ch. 2, § 27, eff. Sept. 1, 2005. Amended by Acts 2011, 82nd Leg., ch. 1077 (S.B. 1087), § 3, eff. Sept. 1, 2011.

§ 66.006. In–kind Contributions to Municipality

(a) Until the expiration or termination of the incumbent cable service provider's agreement, the holder of a state-issued certificate of franchise authority shall pay a municipality in which it is offering cable service or video service the same cash payments on a per subscriber basis as required by the incumbent cable service provider's franchise agreement. All cable service providers and all video service providers shall report quarterly to the municipality the total number of subscribers served within the municipality. The amount paid by the holder of a state-issued certificate of franchise authority shall be calculated quarterly by the municipality by multiplying the amount of cash payment under the incumbent cable service provider's franchise agreement by a number derived by dividing the number of subscribers served by a video service provider or cable service provider by the total number of video or cable service subscribers in the municipality. Such pro rata payments are to be paid quarterly to the municipality within 45 days after the end of the quarter for the preceding calendar quarter.

(b) On the expiration or termination of the incumbent cable service provider's agreement, the holder of a state-issued certificate of franchise authority shall pay a municipality in which it is offering cable service or video service one percent of the provider's gross revenues, as defined by this chapter, or at the municipality's election, the per subscriber fee that was paid to the municipality under the expired or terminated incumbent cable service provider's agreement, in lieu of in-kind compensation and grants. Payments under this subsection shall be paid in the same manner as outlined in Section 66.005(b).

(c) All fees paid to municipalities under this section are paid in accordance with 47 U.S.C. Sections 531 and 541(a)(4)(B) and may be used by the municipality as allowed by federal law; further, these payments are not chargeable as a credit against the franchise fee payments authorized under this chapter.

(c–1) The holder of a state-issued certificate of franchise authority shall include with a fee paid to a municipality under this section a statement identifying the fee.

(c–2) A municipality that receives fees under this section:

(1) shall maintain revenue from the fees in a separate account established for that purpose;

(2) may not commingle revenue from the fees with any other money;

(3) shall maintain a record of each deposit to and disbursement from the separate account, including a record of the payee and purpose of each disbursement; and

(4) may not spend revenue from the fees except directly from the separate account.

(d) The following services shall continue to be provided by the cable provider that was furnishing services pursuant to its municipal cable franchise until the expiration or termination of the franchise and thereafter as provided in Subdivisions (1) and (2) below:

(1) institutional network capacity, however defined or referred to in the municipal cable franchise but generally referring to a private line data network capacity for use by the municipality for noncommercial purposes, shall continue to be provided at the same capacity as was provided to the municipality prior to the date of expiration or termination, provided that the municipality will compensate the provider for the actual incremental cost of the capacity; and

(2) cable services to community public buildings, such as municipal buildings and public schools, shall continue to be provided to the same extent provided immediately prior to the date of the termination. On the expiration or termination of the franchise agreement, a provider that provides the services may deduct from the franchise fee to be paid to the municipality an amount equal to the actual incremental cost of the services if the municipality requires the services after that date. Such cable service generally refers to the existing cable drop connections to such facilities and the tier of cable service provided pursuant to the franchise at the time of the expiration or termination.

Added by Acts 2005, 79th Leg., 2nd C.S., ch. 2, § 27, eff. Sept. 1, 2005. Amended by Acts 2011, 82nd Leg., ch. 1077 (S.B. 1087), § 4, eff. Sept. 1, 2011.

Section 6 of Acts 2011, 82nd Leg., ch. 1077 (S.B. 1087) provides:

"(a) A municipality that received fees described by Subsection (c), Section 66.006, Utilities Code, before September 1, 2011, shall, on September 1, 2011, transfer any fees that have not been disbursed to a separate account as required by Subsection (c–2), Section 66.006, Utilities Code, as added by this Act.

"(b) The change in law made by this Act in adding Subdivision (3), Subsection (c–2), Section 66.006, Utilities Code, applies only to transfers, deposits, and disbursements made on or after the effective date [Sept. 1, 2011] of this Act. A transfer, deposit, or disbursement made before the effective date of this Act is governed by the law in effect on the date the transfer, deposit, or disbursement was made, and the former law is continued in effect for that purpose."

§ 66.007. Build–out

The holder of a state-issued certificate of franchise authority shall not be required to comply with mandatory build-out provisions.

Added by Acts 2005, 79th Leg., 2nd C.S., ch. 2, § 27, eff. Sept. 1, 2005.

§ 66.008. Customer Service Standards

The holder of a state-issued certificate of franchise authority shall comply with customer service requirements consistent with 47 C.F.R. Section 76.309(c) until there are two or more providers offering service, excluding direct-to-home satellite service, in the relevant municipality.

Added by Acts 2005, 79th Leg., 2nd C.S., ch. 2, § 27, eff. Sept. 1, 2005.

§ 66.009. Public, Educational, and Governmental Access Channels

(a) Not later than 120 days after a request by a municipality, the holder of a state-issued certificate of franchise authority shall provide the municipality with capacity in its communications network to allow public, educational, and governmental (PEG) access channels for noncommercial programming.

(b) The holder of a state-issued certificate of franchise authority shall provide no fewer than the number of PEG access channels a municipality has activated under the incumbent cable service provider's franchise agreement as of September 1, 2005.

(c) If a municipality did not have the maximum number of PEG access channels as of September 1, 2005, as provided by Subdivisions (1) and (2) based on the municipality's population on that date, the cable service provider or video service provider shall furnish at the request of the municipality:

(1) up to three PEG channels for a municipality with a population of at least 50,000; and

(2) up to two PEG channels for a municipality with a population of less than 50,000.

(d) Any PEG channel provided pursuant to this section that is not utilized by the municipality for at least eight hours a day shall no longer be made available to the municipality, but may be programmed at the cable service provider's or video service provider's discretion. At such time as the municipality can certify to the cable service provider or video service provider a schedule for at least eight hours of daily programming, the cable service provider or video service provider shall restore the previously lost channel but shall be under no obligation to carry that channel on a basic or analog tier.

(e) In the event a municipality has not utilized the minimum number of access channels as permitted by Subsection (c), access to the additional channel capacity allowed in Subsection (c) shall be provided upon 90 days' written notice if the municipality meets the following standard: if a municipality has one active PEG channel and wishes to activate an additional PEG channel, the initial channel shall be considered to be substantially utilized when 12 hours are programmed on that channel each calendar day. In addition, at least 40 percent of the 12 hours of programming for each business day on average over each calendar quarter must be nonrepeat programming. Nonrepeat programming shall include the first three video-castings of a program. If a municipality is entitled to three PEG channels under Subsection (c) and has in service two active PEG channels, each of the two active channels shall be considered to be substantially utilized when 12 hours are programmed on each channel each calendar day and at least 50 percent of the 12 hours of programming for each business day on average over each calendar quarter is nonrepeat programming for three consecutive calendar quarters.

(f) The operation of any PEG access channel provided pursuant to this section shall be the responsibility of the municipality receiving the benefit of such channel, and the holder of a state-issued certificate of franchise authority bears only the responsibility for the transmission of such channel. The holder of a state-issued certificate of franchise authority shall be responsible for providing the connectivity to each PEG access channel distribution point up to the first 200 feet.

(g) The municipality must ensure that all transmissions, content, or programming to be transmitted over a channel or facility by a holder of a state-issued certificate of franchise authority are provided or submitted to the cable service provider or video service provider in a manner or form that is capable of being accepted and transmitted by a provider, without requirement for additional alteration or change in the content by the provider, over the particular network of the cable service provider or video service provider, which is compatible with the technology or protocol utilized by the cable service provider or video service provider to deliver services.

(h) Where technically feasible, the holder of a state-issued certificate of franchise authority that is not an incumbent cable service provider and an incumbent cable service provider, including an incumbent cable service provider that holds a state-issued certificate of franchise authority issued under Section 66.004(b–1), shall use reasonable efforts to interconnect their cable or video systems for the purpose of providing PEG programming. Interconnection may be accomplished by direct cable, microwave link, satellite, or other reasonable method of connection. The holder of a state-issued certificate of franchise authority and the incumbent cable service provider shall negotiate in good faith, and the incumbent cable service provider may not withhold interconnection of PEG channels.

(i) A court of competent jurisdiction shall have exclusive jurisdiction to enforce any requirement under this section.

Added by Acts 2005, 79th Leg., 2nd C.S., ch. 2, § 27, eff. Sept. 1, 2005. Amended by Acts 2011, 82nd Leg., ch. 1077 (S.B. 1087), § 5, eff. Sept. 1, 2011.

§ 66.010. Nondiscrimination by Municipality

(a) A municipality shall allow the holder of a state-issued certificate of franchise authority to install, construct, and maintain a communications network within a public right-of-way and shall provide the holder of a state-issued certificate of franchise authority with open, comparable, nondiscriminatory, and competitively neutral access to the public right-of-way. All use of a public right-of-way by the holder of a state-issued certificate of franchise authority is nonexclusive and subject to Section 66.011.

(b) A municipality may not discriminate against the holder of a state-issued certificate of franchise authority regarding:

(1) the authorization or placement of a communications network in a public right-of-way;

(2) access to a building; or

(3) a municipal utility pole attachment term.

Added by Acts 2005, 79th Leg., 2nd C.S., ch. 2, § 27, eff. Sept. 1, 2005.

§ 66.011. Municipal Police Power; Other Authority

(a) A municipality may enforce police power-based regulations in the management of a public right-of-way that apply to the holder of a state-issued certificate of franchise authority within the municipality. A municipality may enforce police power-based regulations in the management of the activities of the holder of a state-issued certificate of franchise authority to the extent that they are reasonably necessary to protect the health, safety, and welfare of the public. Police power-based regulation of the holder of a state-issued certificate of franchise authority's use of the public right-of-way must be competitively neutral and may not be unreasonable or discriminatory. A municipality may not impose on activities of the holder of a state-issued certificate of franchise authority a requirement:

(1) that particular business offices be located in the municipality;

(2) regarding the filing of reports and documents with the municipality that are not required by state or federal law and that are not related to the use of the public right-of-way except that a municipality may request maps and records maintained in the ordinary course of business for purposes of locating the portions of a communications network that occupy public rights-of-way. Any maps or records of the location of a communications network received by a municipality shall be confidential and exempt from disclosure under Chapter 552, Government Code, and may be used by a municipality only for the purpose of planning and managing construction activity in the public right-of-way. A municipality may not request information concerning the capacity or technical configuration of the holder of a state-issued certificate of franchise authority's facilities;

(3) for the inspection of the holder of a state-issued certificate of franchise authority's business records except to extent permitted under Section 66.005(b);

(4) for the approval of transfers of ownership or control of the holder of a state-issued certificate of franchise authority's business, except that a municipality may require that the holder of a state-issued certificate of franchise authority maintain a current point of contact and provide notice of a transfer within a reasonable time; or

(5) that the holder of a state-issued certificate of franchise authority that is self-insured under the provisions of state law obtain insurance or bonding for any activities within the municipality, except that a self-insured provider shall provide substantially the same defense and claims processing as an insured provider. A bond may not be required from a provider for any work consisting of aerial construction except that a reasonable bond may be required of a provider that cannot demonstrate a record of at least four years' performance of work in any municipal public right-of-way free of currently unsatisfied claims by a municipality for damage to the right-of-way.

(b) Notwithstanding any other law, a municipality may require the issuance of a construction permit, without cost, to the holder of a state-issued certificate of franchise authority that is locating facilities in or on a public right-of-way in the municipality. The terms of the permit shall be consistent with construction permits issued to other persons excavating in a public right-of-way.

(c) In the exercise of its lawful regulatory authority, a municipality shall promptly process all valid and administratively complete applications of the holder of a state-issued certificate of franchise authority for a permit, license, or consent to excavate, set poles, locate lines, construct facilities, make repairs, affect traffic flow, or obtain zoning or subdivision regulation approvals or other similar approvals. A municipality shall make every reasonable effort not to delay or unduly burden the provider in the timely conduct of the provider's business.

(d) If there is an emergency necessitating response work or repair, the holder of a state-issued certificate of franchise authority may begin the repair or emergency response work or take any action required under the circumstances without prior approval from the affected municipality, if the holder of a state-issued certificate of franchise authority notifies the municipality as promptly as possible after beginning the work and later obtains any approval required by a municipal ordinance applicable to emergency response work.

(e) The commission shall have no jurisdiction to review such police power-based regulations and ordinances adopted by a municipality to manage the public rights-of-way.

Added by Acts 2005, 79th Leg., 2nd C.S., ch. 2, § 27, eff. Sept. 1, 2005.

§ 66.012. Indemnity in Connection With Right-of-way; Notice of Liability

(a) The holder of a state-issued certificate of franchise authority shall indemnify and hold a municipality and its officers and employees harmless against any and all claims, lawsuits, judgments, costs, liens, losses, expenses, fees (including reasonable attorney's fees and costs of defense), proceedings, actions, demands, causes of action, liability, and suits of any kind and nature, including personal or bodily injury (including death), property damage, or other harm for which recovery of damages is sought, that is found by a court of competent jurisdiction to be caused solely by the negligent act, error, or omission of the holder of a state-issued certificate of franchise authority or any agent, officer, director, representative, employee, affiliate, or subcontractor of the holder of a state-issued certificate of franchise authority or their respective officers, agents, employees, directors, or representatives, while installing, repairing, or maintaining facilities in a public right-of-way. The indemnity provided by this subsection does not apply to any liability resulting from the negligence of the municipality or its officers, employees, contractors, or subcontractors. If the holder of a state-issued certificate of franchise authority and the municipality are found jointly liable by a court of competent jurisdiction, liability shall be apportioned comparatively in accordance with the laws of this state without, however, waiving any governmental immunity available to the municipality under state law and without waiving any defenses of the parties under state law. This subsection is solely for the benefit of the municipality and the holder of a state-issued certificate of franchise authority and does not create or grant any rights, contractual or otherwise, for or to any other person or entity.

(b) The holder of a state-issued certificate of franchise authority and a municipality shall promptly advise the other in writing of any known claim or demand against the holder of a state-issued certificate of franchise authority or the municipality related to or arising out of the holder of a state-issued certificate of franchise authority's activities in a public right-of-way.

(c) The commission shall have no jurisdiction to review such police power-based regulations and ordinances adopted by a municipality to manage the public rights-of-way.

Added by Acts 2005, 79th Leg., 2nd C.S., ch. 2, § 27, eff. Sept. 1, 2005.

§ 66.013. Municipal Authority

In addition to a municipality's authority to exercise its nondiscriminatory police power with respect to public rights-of-way under current law, a municipality's authority to regulate the holder of state-issued certificate of franchise authority is limited to:

(1) a requirement that the holder of a state-issued certificate of franchise authority who is providing cable service or video service within the municipality register with the municipality and maintain a point of contact;

(2) the establishment of reasonable guidelines regarding the use of public, educational, and governmental access channels; and

(3) submitting reports within 30 days on the customer service standards referenced in Section 66.008 if the provider is subject to those standards and has continued and unresolved customer service complaints indicating a clear failure on the part of the holder of a state-issued certificate of franchise authority to comply with the standards.

Added by Acts 2005, 79th Leg., 2nd C.S., ch. 2, § 27, eff. Sept. 1, 2005.

§ 66.014. Discrimination Prohibited

(a) The purpose of this section is to prevent discrimination among potential residential subscribers.

(b) A cable service provider or video service provider that has been granted a state-issued certificate of franchise authority may not deny access to service to any group of potential residential subscribers because of the income of the residents in the local area in which such group resides.

(c) An affected person may seek enforcement of the requirements described by Subsection (b) by initiating a proceeding with the commission. A municipality within which the potential residential cable service or video service subscribers referenced in Subsection (b) may be considered an affected person for purposes of this section.

(d) The holder of a state-issued certificate of franchise authority shall have a reasonable period of time to become capable of providing cable service or video service to all households within the designated franchise area as defined in Section 66.003(b)(4) and may satisfy the requirements of this section through the use of an alternative technology that provides comparable content, service, and functionality.

(e) Notwithstanding any provision of this chapter, the commission has the authority to make the determination regarding the comparability of the technology and the service provided. Notwithstanding any provision of this chapter, the commission has the authority to monitor the deployment of cable services, video services, or alternate technology.

Added by Acts 2005, 79th Leg., 2nd C.S., ch. 2, § 27, eff. Sept. 1, 2005.

§ 66.015. Compliance

(a) Should the holder of a state-issued certificate of franchise authority be found by a court of competent jurisdiction to be in noncompliance with the requirements of this chapter, the court shall order the holder a state-issued certificate of franchise authority, within a specified reasonable period of time, to cure such noncompliance. Failure to comply shall subject the holder of the state-issued franchise of franchise authority to penalties as the court shall reasonably impose, up to and including revocation of the state-issued certificate of franchise authority granted under this chapter.

(b) A municipality within which the provider offers cable service or video service shall be an appropriate party in any such litigation.

Added by Acts 2005, 79th Leg., ch. 2, § 27, eff. Sept. 1, 2005.

§ 66.016. Applicability of Other Laws

(a) Nothing in this chapter shall be interpreted to prevent a voice provider, cable service provider or video service provider, or municipality from seeking clarification of its rights and obligations under federal law or to exercise any right or authority under federal or state law.

(b) Nothing in this chapter shall limit the ability of a municipality under existing law to receive compensation for use of the public rights-of-way from entities determined not to be subject to all or part of this chapter, including but not limited to provider of Internet protocol cable or video services, unless such payments are expressly prohibited by federal law.

Added by Acts 2005, 79th Leg., 2nd C.S., ch. 2, § 27, eff. Sept. 1, 2005.

§ 66.017. Expired

TITLE 3. GAS REGULATION

SUBTITLE A. GAS UTILITY REGULATORY ACT

CHAPTER 101. GENERAL PROVISIONS AND OFFICE OF PUBLIC UTILITY COUNSEL

SUBCHAPTER A. GENERAL PROVISIONS

Section

101.001. Short Title.
101.002. Purpose and Findings.
101.003. Definitions.
101.004. Person Determined to be Affiliate.
101.005. Administrative Procedure.
101.006. Cumulative Effect; Application to Gas Utilities.
101.007. Liberal Construction.
101.008. Construction With Federal Authority.

SUBCHAPTER B. OFFICE OF PUBLIC UTILITY COUNSEL

101.051. Office of Public Utility Counsel.
101.052. Office Powers and Duties.
101.053. Prohibited Acts.
101.054. Personnel.

SUBCHAPTER A. GENERAL PROVISIONS

§ 101.001. Short Title

This subtitle may be cited as the Gas Utility Regulatory Act.

Acts 1997, 75th Leg., ch. 166, § 1, eff. Sept. 1, 1997.

§ 101.002. Purpose and Findings

(a) This subtitle is enacted to protect the public interest inherent in the rates and services of gas utilities. The purpose of this subtitle is to establish a comprehensive and adequate regulatory system for gas utilities to assure rates, operations, and services that are just and reasonable to the consumers and to the utilities.

(b) Gas utilities are by definition monopolies in the areas they serve. As a result, the normal forces of competition that regulate prices in a free enterprise society do not operate. Public agencies regulate utility rates, operations, and services as a substitute for competition.

Acts 1997, 75th Leg., ch. 166, § 1, eff. Sept. 1, 1997.

§ 101.003. Definitions

In this subtitle:

(1) "Affected person" means:

(A) a gas utility affected by an action of a regulatory authority;

(B) a person whose utility service or rates are affected by a proceeding before a regulatory authority; or

(C) a person who:

(i) is a competitor of a gas utility with respect to a service performed by the utility; or

(ii) wants to enter into competition with a gas utility.

(2) "Affiliate" means:

(A) a person who directly or indirectly owns or holds at least five percent of the voting securities of a gas utility;

(B) a person in a chain of successive ownership of at least five percent of the voting securities of a gas utility;

(C) a corporation that has at least five percent of its voting securities owned or controlled, directly or indirectly, by a gas utility;

(D) a corporation that has at least five percent of its voting securities owned or controlled, directly or indirectly, by:

(i) a person who directly or indirectly owns or controls at least five percent of the voting securities of a gas utility; or

(ii) a person in a chain of successive ownership of at least five percent of the voting securities of a gas utility;

(E) a person who is an officer or director of a gas utility or of a corporation in a chain of successive ownership of at least five percent of the voting securities of a gas utility; or

(F) a person determined to be an affiliate under Section 101.004.

(3) "Allocation" means the division among municipalities or among municipalities and unincorporated areas of the plant, revenues, expenses, taxes, and reserves of a gas utility used to provide gas utility service in a municipality or for a municipality and unincorporated areas.

(4) "Corporation" means a domestic or foreign corporation, joint-stock company, or association, and each lessee, assignee, trustee, receiver, or other successor in interest of the corporation, company, or association, that has any of the powers or privileges of a corporation not possessed by an individual or partnership. The term does not include a municipal corporation, except as expressly provided by this subtitle.

(5) "Counsellor" means the chief executive of the Office of Public Utility Counsel.

(6) "Facilities" means all of the plant and equipment of a gas utility and includes the tangible and intangible property, without limitation, owned, operated, leased, licensed, used, controlled, or supplied for, by, or in connection with the business of the gas utility.

(7) "Gas utility" includes a person or river authority that owns or operates for compensation in this state equipment or facilities to transmit or distribute combustible hydrocarbon natural gas or synthetic natural gas for sale or resale in a manner not subject to the jurisdiction of the Federal Energy Regulatory Commission under the Natural Gas Act (15 U.S.C. Section 717 et seq.). The term includes a lessee, trustee, or receiver of a gas utility. The term does not include:

(A) a municipal corporation;

(B) a person or river authority to the extent the person or river authority:

(i) produces, gathers, transports, or sells natural gas or synthetic natural gas under Section 121.004 or 121.005;

(ii) distributes or sells liquefied petroleum gas; or

(iii) transports, delivers, or sells natural gas for fuel for irrigation wells or any other direct agricultural use;

(C) a person to the extent the person:

(i) sells natural gas for use as vehicle fuel;

(ii) sells natural gas to a person who later sells the natural gas for use as vehicle fuel; or

(iii) owns or operates equipment or facilities to sell or transport natural gas for ultimate use as vehicle fuel;

(D) a person not otherwise a gas utility who furnishes gas or gas service only to itself, its employees, or its tenants as an incident of employment or tenancy, if the gas or gas service is not resold to or used by others;

(E) a person excluded from being considered a gas utility under Section 121.007; or

(F) an electric cooperative, as that term is defined by Section 11.003, or its subsidiary, that is excluded from regulation as a gas utility by Section 121.008.

(8) "Municipally owned utility" means a utility owned, operated, and controlled by a municipality or by a nonprofit corporation the directors of which are appointed by one or more municipalities.

(9) "Order" means all or a part of a final disposition by a regulatory authority in a matter other than rulemaking, without regard to whether the disposition is affirmative or negative or injunctive or declaratory. The term includes the setting of a rate.

(10) "Person" includes an individual, a partnership of two or more persons having a joint or common interest, a mutual or cooperative association, a limited liability company, and a corporation.

(11) "Proceeding" means a hearing, investigation, inquiry, or other procedure for finding facts or making a decision under this subtitle. The term includes a denial of relief or dismissal of a complaint.

(12) "Rate" means:

(A) any compensation, tariff, charge, fare, toll, rental, or classification that is directly or indirectly demanded, observed, charged, or collected by a gas utility for a service, product, or commodity described in the definition of gas utility in this section; and

(B) a rule, regulation, practice, or contract affecting the compensation, tariff, charge, fare, toll, rental, or classification.

(13) "Regulatory authority" means either the railroad commission or the governing body of a municipality, in accordance with the context.

(14) "Service" has its broadest and most inclusive meaning. The term includes any act performed, anything supplied, and any facilities used or supplied by a gas utility in the performance of the utility's duties under this subtitle to its patrons, employees, other gas utilities, and the public. The term also includes the interchange of facilities between two or more gas utilities.

(15) "State agency" has the meaning assigned by Section 572.002, Government Code, to the extent the state agency must obtain the approval described by Section 31.401(a), Natural Resources Code.

(16) "Test year" means the most recent 12 months, beginning on the first day of a calendar or fiscal year quarter, for which operating data for a gas utility are available.

Acts 1997, 75th Leg., ch. 166, § 1, eff. Sept. 1, 1997. Amended by Acts 1999, 76th Leg., ch. 11, § 1, eff. May 3, 1999; Acts 2007, 80th Leg., ch. 709, § 1, eff. June 15, 2007; Acts 2011, 82nd Leg., ch. 4 (S.B. 312), § 1, eff. April 21, 2011.

§ 101.004. Person Determined to be Affiliate

(a) The railroad commission may determine that a person is an affiliate for purposes of this subtitle if the railroad commission after notice and hearing finds that the person:

(1) actually exercises substantial influence or control over the policies and actions of a gas utility;

(2) is a person over which a gas utility exercises the control described by Subdivision (1);

(3) is under common control with a gas utility; or

(4) actually exercises substantial influence over the policies and actions of a gas utility in conjunction with one or more persons with whom the person is related by ownership or blood relationship, or by action in concert, that together they are affiliated with the gas utility within the meaning of this section even though neither person may qualify as an affiliate individually.

(b) For purposes of Subsection (a)(3), "common control with a gas utility" means the direct or indirect possession of the power to direct or cause the direction of the management and policies of another, without regard to whether that power is established through ownership or voting of securities or by any other direct or indirect means.

Acts 1997, 75th Leg., ch. 166, § 1, eff. Sept. 1, 1997.

§ 101.005. Administrative Procedure

Chapter 2001, Government Code, applies to a proceeding under this subtitle except to the extent inconsistent with this subtitle.

Acts 1997, 75th Leg., ch. 166, § 1, eff. Sept. 1, 1997.

§ 101.006. Cumulative Effect; Application to Gas Utilities

(a) This subtitle is cumulative of laws existing on September 1, 1983, relating to the jurisdiction, power, or authority of the railroad commission over a gas utility, and, except as specifically in conflict with this subtitle, that jurisdiction, power, and authority are not limited by this subtitle.

(b) This subtitle applies to all gas utilities, including a gas utility that is under the jurisdiction, power, or authority of the railroad commission in accordance with a law other than this subtitle.

Acts 1997, 75th Leg., ch. 166, § 1, eff. Sept. 1, 1997.

§ 101.007. Liberal Construction

This subtitle shall be construed liberally to promote the effectiveness and efficiency of regulation of gas utilities to the extent that this construction preserves the validity of this subtitle and its provisions.

Acts 1997, 75th Leg., ch. 166, § 1, eff. Sept. 1, 1997.

§ 101.008. Construction With Federal Authority

This subtitle shall be construed to apply so as not to conflict with any authority of the United States.

Acts 1997, 75th Leg., ch. 166, § 1, eff. Sept. 1, 1997.

SUBCHAPTER B. OFFICE OF PUBLIC UTILITY COUNSEL

§ 101.051. Office of Public Utility Counsel

The independent office of public utility counsel represents the interests of residential consumers.

Acts 1997, 75th Leg., ch. 166, § 1, eff. Sept. 1, 1997.

§ 101.052. Office Powers and Duties

(a) The office:

(1) may appear or intervene as a party or otherwise represent residential consumers, as a class, in appeals to the railroad commission only at the written request of an affected municipality's governing body;

(2) may initiate or intervene as a matter of right or otherwise appear in a judicial proceeding that involves an action taken by the railroad commission in a proceeding in which the office was a party;

(3) is entitled to the same access as a party, other than railroad commission staff, to records gathered by the railroad commission under Section 102.203;

(4) is entitled to discovery of any nonprivileged matter that is relevant to the subject matter of a proceeding or petition before the railroad commission;

(5) may represent an individual residential consumer with respect to the consumer's disputed complaint concerning utility services that is unresolved before the railroad commission; and

(6) may recommend legislation to the legislature that the office determines would positively affect the interests of residential consumers.

(b) The office may represent only as a class the residential consumers of a municipality that makes a request under Subsection (a)(1).

(c) This section does not limit the authority of the railroad commission to represent residential consumers.

(d) The appearance of the counsellor in a proceeding does not preclude the appearance of other parties on behalf of residential consumers. The counsellor may not be grouped with any other party.

Acts 1997, 75th Leg., ch. 166, § 1, eff. Sept. 1, 1997.

§ 101.053. Prohibited Acts

(a) The counsellor may not:

(1) have a direct or indirect interest in a gas utility company regulated under this subtitle; or

(2) provide legal services directly or indirectly to or be employed in any capacity by a gas utility company regulated under this subtitle, its parent, or its subsidiary companies, corporations, or cooperatives.

(b) The prohibition under Subsection (a) applies during the period of the counsellor's service and until the first anniversary of the date the counsellor ceases to serve as counsellor.

(c) This section does not prohibit a person from otherwise engaging in the private practice of law after the person ceases to serve as counsellor.

Acts 1997, 75th Leg., ch. 166, § 1, eff. Sept. 1, 1997.

§ 101.054. Personnel

(a) The counsellor may employ lawyers, economists, engineers, consultants, statisticians, accountants, clerical staff, and other employees as the counsellor determines necessary to carry out this subchapter.

(b) An employee receives compensation as prescribed by the legislature from the assessment imposed by Subchapter A, Chapter 16.

Acts 1997, 75th Leg., ch. 166, § 1, eff. Sept. 1, 1997.

CHAPTER 102. JURISDICTION AND POWERS OF RAILROAD COMMISSION AND OTHER REGULATORY AUTHORITIES

SUBCHAPTER A. GENERAL POWERS OF RAILROAD COMMISSION

Section

102.001. Railroad Commission Jurisdiction.
102.002. Limitation on Railroad Commission Jurisdiction.
102.003. Railroad Commission Powers Relating to Reports.
102.004. Report of Substantial Interest.
102.005. Assistance to Municipality.
102.006. Administrative Hearings in Contested Cases.

SUBCHAPTER B. RESTRICTIONS ON CERTAIN TRANSACTIONS

Section
102.051. Report of Certain Transactions; Railroad Commission Consideration.
102.052. Report of Purchase of Voting Stock in Gas Utility.
102.053. Report of Loan to Stockholders.
102.054. Repealed.

SUBCHAPTER C. RECORDS

102.101. Records of Gas Utility.
102.102. Maintenance of Office and Records in This State.
102.103. Communications With Regulatory Authority.
102.104. Jurisdiction Over Affiliate.

SUBCHAPTER D. REQUIRED REPORTS AND FILINGS

102.151. Schedule Filings.
102.152. Depreciation Account.
102.153. Accounts of Profits and Losses.
102.154. Report of Certain Expenses.

SUBCHAPTER E. AUDITS AND INSPECTIONS

102.201. Inquiry Into Management and Affairs.
102.202. Audit of Accounts.
102.203. Inspection.
102.204. Examinations Under Oath.
102.205. Entering Premises of Gas Utility.
102.206. Production of Out-Of-State Records.

SUBCHAPTER F. GENERAL PROVISIONS RELATING TO PROCEEDINGS BEFORE REGULATORY AUTHORITY

102.251. Record of Proceeding.
102.252. Right to be Heard.

SUBCHAPTER A. GENERAL POWERS OF RAILROAD COMMISSION

§ 102.001. Railroad Commission Jurisdiction

(a) The railroad commission has exclusive original jurisdiction over the rates and services of a gas utility:

(1) that distributes natural gas or synthetic natural gas in:

(A) areas outside a municipality; and

(B) areas inside a municipality that surrenders its jurisdiction to the railroad commission under Section 103.003; and

(2) that transmits, transports, delivers, or sells natural gas or synthetic natural gas to a gas utility that distributes the gas to the public.

(b) The railroad commission has exclusive appellate jurisdiction to review an order or ordinance of a municipality exercising exclusive original jurisdiction as provided by this subtitle.

Acts 1997, 75th Leg., ch. 166, § 1, eff. Sept. 1, 1997. Amended by Acts 2001, 77th Leg., ch. 1233, § 63, eff. Sept. 1, 2001.

§ 102.002. Limitation on Railroad Commission Jurisdiction

Except as otherwise provided by this subtitle, this subtitle does not authorize the railroad commission to:

(1) regulate or supervise a rate or service of a municipally owned utility; or

(2) affect the jurisdiction, power, or duty of a municipality that has elected to regulate and supervise a gas utility in the municipality.

Acts 1997, 75th Leg., ch. 166, § 1, eff. Sept. 1, 1997.

§ 102.003. Railroad Commission Powers Relating to Reports

The railroad commission may:

(1) require a gas utility to report to the railroad commission information relating to the gas utility and an affiliate inside or outside this state as useful in administering this subtitle;

(2) establish the form for a report;

(3) determine the time for a report and the frequency with which the report is to be made;

(4) require that a report be made under oath;

(5) require the filing with the railroad commission of a copy of:

(A) a contract or arrangement between a gas utility and an affiliate;

(B) a report filed with a federal agency or a governmental agency or body of another state; and

(C) an annual report that shows each payment of compensation, other than salary or wages subject to federal income tax withholding:

(i) to residents of this state;

(ii) with respect to legal, administrative, or legislative matters in this state; or

(iii) for representation before the legislature of this state or any governmental agency or body; and

(6) require that a contract or arrangement described by Subdivision (5)(A) that is not in writing be reduced to writing and filed with the railroad commission.

Acts 1997, 75th Leg., ch. 166, § 1, eff. Sept. 1, 1997.

§ 102.004. Report of Substantial Interest

The railroad commission may require disclosure of the identity and respective interests of each owner of at least one percent of the voting securities of a gas utility or its affiliate.

Acts 1997, 75th Leg., ch. 166, § 1, eff. Sept. 1, 1997.

§ 102.005. Assistance to Municipality

On request of a municipality, the railroad commission may advise and assist the municipality with respect to a question or proceeding arising under this subtitle. Assistance provided by the railroad commission may include aid to a municipality on a matter pending before the railroad commission, a court, or the municipality's governing body, such as making a staff member available as a witness or otherwise providing evidence.

Acts 1997, 75th Leg., ch. 166, § 1, eff. Sept. 1, 1997.

§ 102.006. Administrative Hearings in Contested Cases

(a) The railroad commission by rule shall provide for administrative hearings in contested cases to be conducted by one or more members of the railroad commission, by railroad commission hearings examiners, or by the utility division of the State Office of Administrative Hearings. The rules must provide for a railroad commission hearings examiner or the utility division of the State Office of Administrative Hearings to conduct each hearing in a contested case that is not conducted by one or more members of the railroad commission. A hearing must be conducted in accordance with the rules and procedures adopted by the railroad commission.

(b) The railroad commission may delegate to a railroad commission hearings examiner or to the utility division of the State Office of Administrative Hearings the authority to make a final decision and to issue findings of fact, conclusions of law, and other necessary orders in a proceeding in which there is not a contested issue of fact or law.

(c) The railroad commission by rule shall define the procedures by which it delegates final decision-making authority under Subsection (b) to a railroad commission hearings examiner or to the utility division of the State Office of Administrative Hearings.

(d) For purposes of judicial review, the final decision of a railroad commission hearings examiner or an administrative law judge of the State Office of Administrative Hearings in a matter delegated under Subsection (b) has the same effect as a final decision of the railroad commission unless a member of the commission requests formal review of the decision.

(e) The State Office of Administrative Hearings shall charge the railroad commission a fixed annual rate for hearings conducted by the office under this section only if the legislature appropriates money for that purpose. If the legislature does not appropriate money for the payment of a fixed annual rate under this section, the State Office of Administrative Hearings shall charge the railroad commission an hourly rate of not more than $90 per hour for hearings conducted by the office under this section.

Added by Acts 2001, 77th Leg., ch. 1233, § 64, eff. Sept. 1, 2001. Amended by Acts 2003, 78th Leg., ch. 200, § 3, eff. Sept. 1, 2003.

Repeal

Without reference to the amendment of this section by Acts 2003, 78th Leg., ch. 200, § 3, Acts 2003, 78th Leg., ch. 300, § 1 repealed this section effective June 18, 2003.

SUBCHAPTER B. RESTRICTIONS ON CERTAIN TRANSACTIONS

§ 102.051. Report of Certain Transactions; Railroad Commission Consideration

(a) Not later than the 60th day after the date the transaction takes effect, a gas utility shall report to the railroad commission:

(1) a sale, acquisition, or lease of a plant as an operating unit or system in this state for a total consideration of more than $1 million; or

(2) a merger or consolidation with another gas utility operating in this state.

(b) On the filing of a report with the railroad commission, the railroad commission shall investigate the transaction described by Subsection (a), with or without a public hearing, to determine whether the action is consistent with the public interest. In reaching its determination, the railroad commission shall consider the reasonable value of the property, facilities, or securities to be acquired, disposed of, merged, or consolidated.

(c) If the railroad commission finds that a transaction is not in the public interest, the railroad commission shall take the effect of the transaction into consideration in ratemaking proceedings and disallow the effect of the transaction if the transaction will unreasonably affect rates or service.

(d) This section does not apply to:

(1) the purchase of a unit of property for replacement; or

(2) an addition to the facilities of a gas utility by construction.

Acts 1997, 75th Leg., ch. 166, § 1, eff. Sept. 1, 1997. Amended by Acts 1999, 76th Leg., ch. 32, § 1, eff. Sept. 1, 1999; Acts 2005, 79th Leg., ch. 1000, § 1, eff. Sept. 1, 2005.

§ 102.052. Report of Purchase of Voting Stock in Gas Utility

A gas utility may not purchase voting stock in another gas utility doing business in this state unless the utility reports the purchase to the railroad commission.

Acts 1997, 75th Leg., ch. 166, § 1, eff. Sept. 1, 1997.

§ 102.053. Report of Loan to Stockholders

A gas utility may not loan money, stocks, bonds, notes, or other evidence of indebtedness to a person who directly or indirectly owns or holds any stock of the gas utility unless the gas utility reports the transaction to the railroad commission within a reasonable time.

Acts 1997, 75th Leg., ch. 166, § 1, eff. Sept. 1, 1997.

§ 102.054. Repealed by Acts 1999, 76th Leg., ch. 32, § 2, eff. Sept. 1, 1999

SUBCHAPTER C. RECORDS

§ 102.101. Records of Gas Utility

(a) Each gas utility shall keep and provide to the regulatory authority, in the manner and form prescribed by the railroad commission, uniform accounts of all business transacted by the gas utility.

(b) The railroad commission may prescribe the form of books, accounts, records, and memoranda to be kept by a gas utility, including:

(1) the books, accounts, records, and memoranda of:

(A) the provision of and capacity for service; and

(B) the receipt and expenditure of money; and

(2) any other form, record, and memorandum that the railroad commission considers necessary to carry out this subtitle.

(c) For a gas utility subject to regulation by a federal regulatory agency, compliance with the system of accounts prescribed for the particular class of utilities by the federal agency may be considered sufficient compliance with the system prescribed by the railroad commission. The railroad commission may prescribe the form of books, accounts, records, and memoranda covering information in addition to that required by the federal agency. The system of accounts and the form of books, accounts, records, and memoranda prescribed by the railroad commission for a gas utility or class of utilities may not be inconsistent with the systems and forms established by a federal agency for that gas utility or class of utilities.

(d) Each gas utility shall:

(1) keep and provide its books, accounts, records, and memoranda accurately and faithfully in the manner and form prescribed by the railroad commission; and

(2) comply with the directions of the regulatory authority relating to the books, accounts, records, and memoranda.

(e) In this section, "gas utility" includes a municipally owned utility.

Acts 1997, 75th Leg., ch. 166, § 1, eff. Sept. 1, 1997.

§ 102.102. Maintenance of Office and Records in This State

(a) Each gas utility shall maintain an office in this state in a county in which some part of the utility's property is located. The gas utility shall keep in this office all books, accounts, records, and memoranda required by the railroad commission to be kept in this state.

(b) A book, account, record, or memorandum required by the regulatory authority to be kept in this state may not be removed from this state except as prescribed by the railroad commission.

Acts 1997, 75th Leg., ch. 166, § 1, eff. Sept. 1, 1997.

§ 102.103. Communications With Regulatory Authority

(a) The regulatory authority shall adopt rules governing communications with the regulatory authority or a member or employee of the regulatory authority by:

(1) a gas utility;

(2) an affiliate; or

(3) a representative of a gas utility or affiliate.

(b) A record of a communication must contain:

(1) the name of the person contacting the regulatory authority or member or employee of the regulatory authority;

(2) the name of the business entity represented;

(3) a brief description of the subject matter of the communication; and

(4) the action, if any, requested by the gas utility, affiliate, or representative.

(c) Records compiled under Subsection (b) shall be available to the public monthly.

Acts 1997, 75th Leg., ch. 166, § 1, eff. Sept. 1, 1997.

§ 102.104. Jurisdiction Over Affiliate

The railroad commission has jurisdiction over an affiliate that has a transaction with a gas utility under the railroad commission's jurisdiction to the extent of access to an account or a record of the affiliate relating to the transaction, including an account or a record of joint or general expenses, any portion of which may be applicable to the transaction.

Acts 1997, 75th Leg., ch. 166, § 1, eff. Sept. 1, 1997.

SUBCHAPTER D. REQUIRED REPORTS AND FILINGS

§ 102.151. Schedule Filings

(a) A gas utility shall file with each regulatory authority schedules showing all rates that are:

(1) subject to the regulatory authority's original or appellate jurisdiction; and

(2) in effect for a gas utility service, product, or commodity offered by the gas utility.

(b) The gas utility shall file as a part of the schedules required under Subsection (a) each rule or regulation that relates to or affects:

(1) a rate of the gas utility; or

(2) a gas utility service, product, or commodity furnished by the gas utility.

Acts 1997, 75th Leg., ch. 166, § 1, eff. Sept. 1, 1997.

§ 102.152. Depreciation Account

The railroad commission shall require each gas utility or municipally owned utility to carry a proper and adequate depreciation account in accordance with:

(1) the rates and methods prescribed by the railroad commission under Section 104.054; and

(2) any other rule the railroad commission adopts.

Acts 1997, 75th Leg., ch. 166, § 1, eff. Sept. 1, 1997.

§ 102.153. Accounts of Profits and Losses

A gas utility or municipally owned utility shall keep separate accounts showing profits or losses from the sale or lease of merchandise, including an appliance, a fixture, or equipment.

Acts 1997, 75th Leg., ch. 166, § 1, eff. Sept. 1, 1997.

§ 102.154. Report of Certain Expenses

A regulatory authority may require a gas utility to annually report the utility's expenditures for:

(1) business gifts and entertainment; and

(2) advertising or public relations, including expenditures for institutional and consumption-inducing purposes.

Acts 1997, 75th Leg., ch. 166, § 1, eff. Sept. 1, 1997.

SUBCHAPTER E. AUDITS AND INSPECTIONS

§ 102.201. Inquiry Into Management and Affairs

A regulatory authority may inquire into the management and affairs of each gas utility and shall keep itself informed as to the manner and method in which each gas utility is managed and its affairs are conducted.

Acts 1997, 75th Leg., ch. 166, § 1, eff. Sept. 1, 1997.

§ 102.202. Audit of Accounts

A regulatory authority may require the examination and audit of the accounts of a gas or municipally owned utility.

Acts 1997, 75th Leg., ch. 166, § 1, eff. Sept. 1, 1997.

§ 102.203. Inspection

At a reasonable time for a reasonable purpose, a regulatory authority and, to the extent authorized by the regulatory authority, its counsel, agent, or employee may:

(1) inspect and obtain copies of the papers, books, accounts, documents, and other business records of a gas utility within its jurisdiction; and

(2) inspect the plant, equipment, and other property of a gas utility within its jurisdiction.

Acts 1997, 75th Leg., ch. 166, § 1, eff. Sept. 1, 1997.

§ 102.204. Examinations Under Oath

In connection with an investigation taken under Section 102.203, the regulatory authority may:

(1) examine under oath an officer, agent, or employee of a gas utility; or

(2) authorize the person conducting the action to make the examination under oath.

Acts 1997, 75th Leg., ch. 166, § 1, eff. Sept. 1, 1997.

§ 102.205. Entering Premises of Gas Utility

(a) A member, agent, or employee of a regulatory authority may enter the premises occupied by a gas utility to conduct an inspection, examination, or test or to exercise any other authority provided by this subtitle.

(b) A member, agent, or employee of the regulatory authority may act under this section only during reasonable hours and after reasonable notice to the gas utility.

(c) A gas utility is entitled to be represented when an inspection, examination, or test is conducted on its premises. The gas utility is entitled to a reasonable time to secure a representative before the inspection, examination, or test begins.

Acts 1997, 75th Leg., ch. 166, § 1, eff. Sept. 1, 1997.

§ 102.206. Production of Out-Of-State Records

(a) A regulatory authority may require, by order or subpoena served on a gas utility, the production, at the time and place in this state that the regulatory authority designates, of any books, accounts, papers, or records kept by that gas utility outside this state or, if ordered by the railroad commission, verified copies of the books, accounts, papers, or records.

(b) A gas utility that fails or refuses to comply with an order or subpoena under this section violates this subtitle.

Acts 1997, 75th Leg., ch. 166, § 1, eff. Sept. 1, 1997.

SUBCHAPTER F. GENERAL PROVISIONS RELATING TO PROCEEDINGS BEFORE REGULATORY AUTHORITY

§ 102.251. Record of Proceeding

The regulatory authority shall keep a record of each proceeding before the authority.

Acts 1997, 75th Leg., ch. 166, § 1, eff. Sept. 1, 1997.

§ 102.252. Right to be Heard

Each party to a proceeding before a regulatory authority is entitled to be heard by attorney or in person.

Acts 1997, 75th Leg., ch. 166, § 1, eff. Sept. 1, 1997.

CHAPTER 103. JURISDICTION AND POWERS OF MUNICIPALITY

SUBCHAPTER A. GENERAL PROVISIONS

Section

103.001. Municipal Jurisdiction.
103.002. Franchises.
103.003. Surrender of Municipal Jurisdiction to Railroad Commission; Reinstatement of Jurisdiction.

SUBCHAPTER B. RATE DETERMINATION

103.021. Municipal Proceedings.
103.022. Rate Assistance and Cost Reimbursement.
103.023. Municipal Standing.
103.024. Judicial Review.

SUBCHAPTER C. APPEAL OF MUNICIPAL ORDER

103.051. Appeal by Party.
103.052. Appeal by Residents.
103.053. Appeal by Ratepayers Outside Municipality.
103.054. Filing of Appeal.
103.055. Hearing and Order.
103.056. Applicability of Rates.

SUBCHAPTER A. GENERAL PROVISIONS

§ 103.001. Municipal Jurisdiction

To provide fair, just, and reasonable rates and adequate and efficient services, the governing body of a municipality has exclusive original jurisdiction over the rates, operations, and services of a gas utility within the municipality, subject to the limitations imposed by this subtitle, unless the municipality surrenders its jurisdiction to the railroad commission under Section 103.003.

Acts 1997, 75th Leg., ch. 166, § 1, eff. Sept. 1, 1997. Amended by Acts 2001, 77th Leg., ch. 1233, § 65, eff. Sept. 1, 2001.

§ 103.002. Franchises

(a) This subtitle does not restrict the rights and powers of a municipality to grant or refuse a franchise to use the streets and alleys in the municipality or to make a statutory charge for that use.

(b) A municipality that performs a regulatory function under this subtitle may make each charge that is authorized by:

(1) this subtitle; or

(2) the applicable franchise agreement.

(c) A franchise agreement may not limit or interfere with a power conferred on the railroad commission by this subtitle.

Acts 1997, 75th Leg., ch. 166, § 1, eff. Sept. 1, 1997.

§ 103.003. Surrender of Municipal Jurisdiction to Railroad Commission; Reinstatement of Jurisdiction

(a) A municipality may elect to have the railroad commission exercise exclusive original jurisdiction over gas utility rates, operations, and services in the municipality by ordinance or by submitting the question of the surrender of its jurisdiction to the voters at a municipal election.

(b) The governing body of a municipality shall submit at a municipal election the question of surrendering its jurisdiction to the railroad commission if the governing body receives a petition signed by a number of qualified voters of the municipality equal to at least the lesser of 20,000 or 10 percent of the number of voters voting in the last preceding general election in the municipality.

(c) A municipality may not elect to surrender its jurisdiction while a case involving the municipality is pending.

(d) A municipality that surrenders its jurisdiction to the railroad commission may reinstate its jurisdiction. The provisions of this section governing the surrender of jurisdiction apply to the reinstatement of jurisdiction.

Added by Acts 2001, 77th Leg., ch. 1233, § 66, eff. Sept. 1, 2001.

SUBCHAPTER B. RATE DETERMINATION

§ 103.021. Municipal Proceedings

(a) A municipality regulating a gas utility under this subtitle shall require the utility to submit information as necessary to make a reasonable determination of rate base, expenses, investment, and rate of return in the municipality.

(b) A municipality shall make a determination under Subsection (a) using the procedures and requirements prescribed by this subtitle.

(c) A municipality shall retain personnel necessary to make the determination of reasonable rates.

Acts 1997, 75th Leg., ch. 166, § 1, eff. Sept. 1, 1997.

§ 103.022. Rate Assistance and Cost Reimbursement

(a) The governing body of a municipality participating in or conducting a ratemaking proceeding may engage rate consultants, accountants, auditors, attorneys, and engineers to:

(1) conduct investigations, present evidence, and advise and represent the governing body; and

(2) assist the governing body with litigation or a gas utility ratemaking proceeding before a regulatory authority or court.

(b) The gas utility in the ratemaking proceeding shall reimburse the governing body of the municipality for the reasonable cost of the services of a person engaged under Subsection (a) to the extent the applicable regulatory authority determines reasonable.

Acts 1997, 75th Leg., ch. 166, § 1, eff. Sept. 1, 1997.

§ 103.023. Municipal Standing

(a) A municipality has standing in each case before the railroad commission that relates to a gas utility's rates and services in the municipality.

(b) A municipality's standing is subject to the right of the railroad commission to consolidate that municipality with another party on an issue of common interest.

Acts 1997, 75th Leg., ch. 166, § 1, eff. Sept. 1, 1997.

§ 103.024. Judicial Review

A municipality is entitled to judicial review of a railroad commission order relating to a gas utility's rates and services in a municipality as provided by Section 105.001.

Acts 1997, 75th Leg., ch. 166, § 1, eff. Sept. 1, 1997.

SUBCHAPTER C. APPEAL OF MUNICIPAL ORDER

§ 103.051. Appeal by Party

A party to a rate proceeding before a municipality's governing body may appeal the governing body's decision to the railroad commission.

Acts 1997, 75th Leg., ch. 166, § 1, eff. Sept. 1, 1997.

§ 103.052. Appeal by Residents

The residents of a municipality may appeal to the railroad commission the decision of the municipality's governing body in a rate proceeding by filing with the railroad commission a petition for review signed by a number of qualified voters of the municipality equal to at least the lesser of 20,000 or 10 percent of the qualified voters of the municipality.

Acts 1997, 75th Leg., ch. 166, § 1, eff. Sept. 1, 1997.

§ 103.053. Appeal by Ratepayers Outside Municipality

(a) The ratepayers of a municipally owned utility who are outside the municipality may appeal to the railroad commission an action of the municipality's governing body affecting the municipally owned utility's rates by filing with the railroad commission a petition for review signed by a number of ratepayers served by the utility outside the municipality equal to at least the lesser of 10,000 or five percent of those ratepayers.

(b) A petition for review is properly signed if signed by a person or the spouse of a person in whose name residential utility service is carried.

(c) For purposes of this section, each person who receives a separate bill is a ratepayer. A person who receives more than one bill may not be counted as more than one ratepayer.

Acts 1997, 75th Leg., ch. 166, § 1, eff. Sept. 1, 1997.

§ 103.054. Filing of Appeal

(a) An appeal under this subchapter is initiated by filing a petition for review with the railroad commission and serving a copy of the petition on each party to the original rate proceeding.

(b) The appeal must be initiated not later than the 30th day after the date of the final decision by the governing body of the municipality.

Acts 1997, 75th Leg., ch. 166, § 1, eff. Sept. 1, 1997.

§ 103.055. Hearing and Order

(a) An appeal under this subchapter is de novo and based on the test year presented to the municipality adjusted for known changes and conditions that are measurable with reasonable accuracy.

(b) The railroad commission shall enter a final order establishing the rates the railroad commission determines the municipality should have set in the ordinance to which the appeal applies.

(c) If the railroad commission fails to enter a final order within 185 days after the date the appeal is perfected, the rates proposed by the gas utility are considered to be approved by the railroad commission and take effect on the expiration of the 185-day period.

Acts 1997, 75th Leg., ch. 166, § 1, eff. Sept. 1, 1997.

§ 103.056. Applicability of Rates

Temporary or permanent rates set by the railroad commission are prospective and observed from the date of the applicable railroad commission order, except an interim rate order necessary to provide a gas utility the opportunity to avoid confiscation during the period beginning on the date a petition for review is filed with the railroad commission and ending on the date of a final order establishing rates.

Acts 1997, 75th Leg., ch. 166, § 1, eff. Sept. 1, 1997.

CHAPTER 104. RATES AND SERVICES

SUBCHAPTER A. GENERAL PROVISIONS

Section

104.001. Authorization to Establish and Regulate Rates.
104.002. Compliance With Subtitle.
104.003. Just and Reasonable Rates.
104.004. Unreasonable Preference or Prejudice Prohibited.
104.005. Equality of Rates and Services.
104.006. Rates for Area Not in Municipality.
104.007. Discrimination and Restriction on Competition.
104.008. Burden of Proof.

SUBCHAPTER B. COMPUTATION OF RATES

104.051. Establishing Overall Revenues.
104.052. Establishing Fair Rate of Return.
104.053. Components of Adjusted Value of Invested Capital.
104.054. Depreciation, Amortization, and Depletion.
104.055. Net Income; Allowable Expenses.
104.056. Treatment of Certain Tax Benefits.
104.057. Consideration of Certain Expenses.
104.058. Consideration of Profit or Loss From Sale or Lease of Merchandise.
104.059. Pension and Other Postemployment Benefits.

SUBCHAPTER C. RATE CHANGES PROPOSED BY UTILITY

104.101. Definition.
104.102. Statement of Intent to Increase Rates.
104.103. Notice of Intent to Increase Rates.
104.104. Early Effective Date of Rate Increase.
104.105. Determination of Propriety of Rate Change; Hearing.
104.106. Preference to Hearing.
104.107. Rate Suspension; Deadline.
104.108. Temporary Rates.
104.109. Bonded Rates.
104.110. Establishment of Final Rates.
104.111. Approval of Decrease in Rates.
104.112. Surcharge to Recover Relocation Costs.

SUBCHAPTER D. RATE CHANGES PROPOSED BY COMMISSION

104.151. Unreasonable or Violative Existing Rates.
104.152. Investigating Costs of Obtaining Service From Another Source.

SUBCHAPTER E. RATES FOR GOVERNMENTAL ENTITIES

Section
104.201. Transportation Rates Between Gas Utility or Municipally Owned Utility and State Agency.
104.202. Excluded Expenses.
104.203. Payment in Lieu of Tax.

SUBCHAPTER F. SERVICES

104.251. General Standard.
104.252. Authority of Regulatory Authority Concerning Standards.
104.253. Rule or Standard.
104.254. Service.
104.2545. Required Service to Public Retail Customer.
104.255. Billing.
104.2551. Electronic Billing.
104.256. Examination and Test of Instrument or Equipment; Inspection.
104.257. Inspection for Consumer.
104.258. Disconnection of Gas Service.

SUBCHAPTER G. INTERIM COST RECOVERY AND RATE ADJUSTMENT

104.301. Interim Adjustment for Changes in Investment.

SUBCHAPTER A. GENERAL PROVISIONS

§ 104.001. Authorization to Establish and Regulate Rates

(a) The railroad commission is vested with all the authority and power of this state to ensure compliance with the obligations of gas utilities in this subtitle.

(b) The regulatory authority may establish and regulate rates of a gas utility and may adopt rules for determining:

(1) the classification of customers and services; and

(2) the applicability of rates.

(c) A rule or order of the regulatory authority may not conflict with a ruling of a federal regulatory body.

Acts 1997, 75th Leg., ch. 166, § 1, eff. Sept. 1, 1997.

§ 104.002. Compliance With Subtitle

A gas utility may not:

(1) charge, collect, or receive a rate for utility service except as provided by this subtitle; or

(2) impose a rule or regulation except as provided by this subtitle.

Acts 1997, 75th Leg., ch. 166, § 1, eff. Sept. 1, 1997.

§ 104.003. Just and Reasonable Rates

(a) The regulatory authority shall ensure that each rate a gas utility or two or more gas utilities jointly make, demand, or receive is just and reasonable. A rate may not be unreasonably preferential, prejudicial, or discriminatory but must be sufficient, equitable, and consistent in application to each class of consumer. In establishing a gas utility's rates, the railroad commission may treat as a single class two or more municipalities that a gas utility serves if the commission considers that treatment to be appropriate.

(b) A rate for a pipeline-to-pipeline transaction or to a transportation, industrial, or similar large volume contract customer is considered to be just and reasonable and otherwise to comply with this section and shall be approved by the regulatory authority if:

(1) neither the gas utility nor the customer had an unfair advantage during the negotiations;

(2) the rate is substantially the same as the rate between the gas utility and at least two of those customers under the same or similar conditions of service; or

(3) competition does or did exist with another gas utility, another supplier of natural gas, or a supplier of an alternative form of energy.

(c) Subsection (b) does not apply:

(1) if a complaint is filed with the railroad commission by a transmission pipeline purchaser of gas sold or transported under the pipeline-to-pipeline or transportation rate; or

(2) to a direct sale for resale to a gas distribution utility at a city gate.

(d) The reasonableness of gas purchase costs included in a city gate rate proposed to be charged for a sale for resale to a gas distribution utility at a city gate may be reviewed at a city gate rate proceeding even though the costs have been previously approved as a rate for other parties under Subsection (b).

(e) Subsection (b)(1) does not apply to a rate charged or offered to be charged to an affiliated pipeline utility.

Acts 1997, 75th Leg., ch. 166, § 1, eff. Sept. 1, 1997.

§ 104.004. Unreasonable Preference or Prejudice Prohibited

A gas utility may not:

(1) grant an unreasonable preference or advantage concerning rates or services to a person in a classification;

(2) subject a person in a classification to an unreasonable prejudice or disadvantage concerning rates or services; or

(3) establish or maintain an unreasonable difference concerning rates of services between localities or between classes of service.

Acts 1997, 75th Leg., ch. 166, § 1, eff. Sept. 1, 1997.

§ 104.005. Equality of Rates and Services

(a) A gas utility may not directly or indirectly charge, demand, collect, or receive from a person a greater or lesser compensation for a service provided or to be provided by the utility than the compensation prescribed by the applicable schedule of rates filed under Section 102.151.

(b) A person may not knowingly receive or accept a service from a gas utility for a compensation greater or less than the compensation prescribed by the schedules. A rate charged and collected by a gas utility on September 1, 1983, may be continued until schedules are filed.

(c) After notice and hearing, the railroad commission may, in the public interest, order a gas utility to refund with interest compensation received in violation of this section.

(d) This subtitle does not prevent a cooperative corporation from returning to its members net earnings resulting from its operations in proportion to the members' purchases from or through the corporation.

Acts 1997, 75th Leg., ch. 166, § 1, eff. Sept. 1, 1997.

§ 104.006. Rates for Area Not in Municipality

Without the approval of the railroad commission, a gas utility's rates for an area not in a municipality may not exceed 115 percent of the average of all rates for similar services for all municipalities served by the same utility in the same county as that area.

Acts 1997, 75th Leg., ch. 166, § 1, eff. Sept. 1, 1997.

§ 104.007. Discrimination and Restriction on Competition

A gas utility may not:

(1) discriminate against a person who sells or leases equipment or performs services in competition with the gas utility; or

(2) engage in a practice that tends to restrict or impair that competition.

Acts 1997, 75th Leg., ch. 166, § 1, eff. Sept. 1, 1997.

§ 104.008. Burden of Proof

In a proceeding involving a proposed rate change, the gas utility has the burden of proving that:

(1) the rate change is just and reasonable, if the utility proposes the change; or

(2) an existing rate is just and reasonable, if the proposal is to reduce the rate.

Acts 1997, 75th Leg., ch. 166, § 1, eff. Sept. 1, 1997.

SUBCHAPTER B. COMPUTATION OF RATES

§ 104.051. Establishing Overall Revenues

In establishing a gas utility's rates, the regulatory authority shall establish the utility's overall revenues at an amount that will permit the utility a reasonable opportunity to earn a reasonable return on the utility's invested capital used and useful in providing service to the public in excess of its reasonable and necessary operating expenses.

Acts 1997, 75th Leg., ch. 166, § 1, eff. Sept. 1, 1997.

§ 104.052. Establishing Fair Rate of Return

The regulatory authority may not establish a rate that yields more than a fair return on the adjusted value of the invested capital used and useful in providing service to the public.

Acts 1997, 75th Leg., ch. 166, § 1, eff. Sept. 1, 1997.

§ 104.053. Components of Adjusted Value of Invested Capital

(a) Gas utility rates shall be based on the adjusted value of invested capital used and useful to the utility in providing service and that adjusted value shall be computed on the basis of a reasonable balance between:

(1) original cost, less depreciation; and

(2) current cost, less an adjustment for present age and condition.

(b) The regulatory authority may determine a reasonable balance that reflects:

(1) not less than 60 percent nor more than 75 percent of the original cost of the property at the time the property was dedicated to public use, whether by the gas utility that is the present owner or by a predecessor, less depreciation; and

(2) not less than 25 percent nor more than 40 percent of the current cost less an adjustment for present age and condition.

(c) In determining a reasonable balance, the regulatory authority may consider inflation, deflation, quality of service being provided, growth rate of the service area, and need for the gas utility to attract new capital.

(d) Construction work in progress, at cost as recorded on the gas utility's books, may be included as part of the adjusted value of invested capital used by and useful to the utility in providing service, as necessary to the financial integrity of the utility.

(e) Costs of facilities, revenues, expenses, taxes, and reserves shall be separated or allocated as prescribed by the regulatory authority.

(f) In this section, "original cost" means the actual money cost or the actual money value of consideration paid other than money.

Acts 1997, 75th Leg., ch. 166, § 1, eff. Sept. 1, 1997.

§ 104.054. Depreciation, Amortization, and Depletion

(a) The railroad commission shall establish proper and adequate rates and methods of depreciation, amortization, or depletion for each class of property of a gas utility or municipally owned utility.

(b) The rates and methods established under this section and the depreciation account required under Section 102.152 shall be used uniformly and consistently throughout rate-setting and appeal proceedings.

Acts 1997, 75th Leg., ch. 166, § 1, eff. Sept. 1, 1997.

§ 104.055. Net Income; Allowable Expenses

(a) Net income shall be used to establish just and reasonable rates. For that purpose, "net income" means the total revenues of the gas utility from gas utility service less all reasonable and necessary expenses related to that gas utility service. The regulatory authority shall determine those revenues and expenses in a manner consistent with this subchapter.

(b) In establishing a gas utility's rates, the regulatory authority may not allow a gas utility's payment to an affiliate for the cost of a service, property, right, or other item or for an interest expense to be included as capital cost or as expense related to gas utility service except to the extent that the regulatory authority finds the payment is reasonable and necessary for each item or class of items as determined by the regulatory authority. That finding must include:

(1) a specific finding of the reasonableness and necessity of each item or class of items allowed; and

(2) a finding that the price to the gas utility is not higher than the prices charged by the supplying affiliate to its other affiliates or divisions or to a nonaffiliated person for the same item or class of items.

(c) If an expense is allowed to be included in utility rates, or an investment is included in the utility rate base, the related income tax deduction or benefit shall be included in the computation of income tax expense to reduce the rates. If an expense is disallowed or not included in utility rates, or an investment is not included in the utility rate base, the related income tax deduction or benefit may not be included in the computation of income tax expense to reduce the rates. The income tax expense shall be computed using the statutory income tax rates.

(d) The regulatory authority may adopt reasonable rules complying with this section with respect to including and excluding certain expenses in computing the rates to be established.

(e) This section is not intended to increase gas utility rates to the customer not caused by utility service. Utility rates may include only expenses caused by utility service.

Acts 1997, 75th Leg., ch. 166, § 1, eff. Sept. 1, 1997.

§ 104.056. Treatment of Certain Tax Benefits

(a) In determining the allocation of tax savings derived from liberalized depreciation and amortization, the investment tax credit, and the application of similar methods, the regulatory authority shall:

(1) balance equitably the interests of present and future customers; and

(2) apportion accordingly the benefits between consumers and the gas utility or municipally owned utility.

(b) If a gas utility or municipally owned utility retains a portion of the investment tax credit, that portion shall be deducted from the original cost of the facilities or other addition to the rate base to which the credit applied to the extent allowed by the Internal Revenue Code.

Acts 1997, 75th Leg., ch. 166, § 1, eff. Sept. 1, 1997.

§ 104.057. Consideration of Certain Expenses

(a) In establishing a gas utility's rates, the regulatory authority may not allow as a cost or expense an expenditure:

(1) described by Section 102.154 that the regulatory authority determines to be not in the public interest; or

(2) for legislative advocacy.

(b) The regulatory authority may allow as a cost or expense reasonable charitable or civic contributions not to exceed the amount approved by the regulatory authority.

Acts 1997, 75th Leg., ch. 166, § 1, eff. Sept. 1, 1997.

§ 104.058. Consideration of Profit or Loss From Sale or Lease of Merchandise

In establishing a gas utility's or municipally owned utility's rates, the regulatory authority may not consider a profit or loss that results from the sale or lease of merchandise, including appliances, fixtures, or equipment, to the extent that merchandise is not integral to providing utility service.

Acts 1997, 75th Leg., ch. 166, § 1, eff. Sept. 1, 1997.

§ 104.059. Pension and Other Postemployment Benefits

(a) In establishing a gas utility's rates, the regulatory authority shall allow recovery of the gas utility's costs of pensions and other postemployment benefits, as determined by actuarial or other similar studies in accordance with generally accepted accounting principles, in amounts the regulatory authority finds reasonable and necessary.

(b) If a gas utility establishes one or more reserve accounts for the purpose of tracking changes in the costs of pensions and other postemployment benefits, the gas utility shall periodically record in a reserve account any difference between:

(1) the annual amount of pension and other postemployment benefits approved and included in the gas utility's then current rates or, if that annual amount cannot be determined from the regulatory authority's order, the amount recorded for pension and other postemployment benefits under generally accepted accounting principles during the first year that rates from the gas utility's last general rate proceeding were in effect; and

(2) the annual amount of costs of pensions and other postemployment benefits as determined by actuarial or other similar studies that would otherwise be recorded by the gas utility were this provision not applicable.

(c) The gas utility must:

(1) establish separate reserve accounts for pensions and for other postemployment benefits; and

(2) apply the same methodology to allocate pension and other postemployment benefits between capital and expense as in the gas utility's last rate case.

(d) A surplus in a reserve account exists if the amount of pension and other postemployment benefits under Subsection (b)(1) is greater than the amount determined under Subsection (b)(2). A shortage in a reserve account exists if the amount of pension and other postemployment benefits under Subsection (b)(1) is less than the amount determined under Subsection (b)(2).

(e) If the gas utility establishes reserve accounts for the costs of pensions and other postemployment benefits, the regulatory authority at a subsequent general rate proceeding shall:

(1) review the amounts recorded to each reserve account to determine whether the amounts are reasonable and necessary;

(2) determine in accordance with Subsection (d) whether each reserve account has a surplus or shortage; and

(3) subtract any surplus from or add any shortage to the gas utility's rate base, with the surplus or shortage amortized over a reasonable time.

Added by Acts 2011, 82nd Leg., ch. 172 (S.B. 403), § 1, eff. May 28, 2011.

Section 2 of Acts 2011, 82nd Leg., ch. 172 (S.B. 403) provides:

"Subsections (b) through (e), Section 104.059, Utilities Code, as added by this Act, apply only in relation to a reserve account established by a gas utility on or after January 1, 2012."

SUBCHAPTER C. RATE CHANGES PROPOSED BY UTILITY

§ 104.101. Definition

In this subchapter, "major change" means an increase in rates that would increase the aggregate revenues of the applicant more than the greater of $100,000 or 2½ percent. The term does not include an increase in rates that the regulatory authority allows to go into effect or the gas utility makes under an order of the regulatory authority after hearings held with public notice.

Acts 1997, 75th Leg., ch. 166, § 1, eff. Sept. 1, 1997.

§ 104.102. Statement of Intent to Increase Rates

(a) A gas utility may not increase its rates unless the utility files a statement of its intent with the regulatory authority that has original jurisdiction over those rates at least 35 days before the effective date of the proposed increase.

(b) The gas utility shall also mail or deliver a copy of the statement of intent to the appropriate officer of each affected municipality.

(c) The statement of intent must include:

(1) proposed revisions of tariffs and schedules; and

(2) a detailed statement of:

(A) each proposed increase;

(B) the effect the proposed increase is expected to have on the revenues of the utility;

(C) each class and number of utility consumers affected; and

(D) any other information required by the regulatory authority's rules and regulations.

Acts 1997, 75th Leg., ch. 166, § 1, eff. Sept. 1, 1997.

§ 104.103. Notice of Intent to Increase Rates

(a) The gas utility shall:

(1) publish, in conspicuous form, notice to the public of the proposed increase once each week for four successive weeks in a newspaper having general circulation in each county containing territory affected by the proposed increase; and

(2) provide notice of the proposed increase to any other affected person as required by the regulatory authority's rules.

(b) Instead of publishing newspaper notice, a gas utility may provide notice to the public in an area outside the affected municipality or in a municipality with a population of less than 2,500 by:

(1) mailing the notice by United States mail, postage prepaid, to the billing address of each directly affected customer; or

(2) including the notice, in conspicuous form, in the bill of each directly affected customer.

Acts 1997, 75th Leg., ch. 166, § 1, eff. Sept. 1, 1997.

§ 104.104. Early Effective Date of Rate Increase

(a) For good cause shown, the regulatory authority may allow a rate increase, other than a major change, to take effect:

(1) before the end of the 35-day period prescribed by Section 104.102; and

(2) under conditions the regulatory authority prescribes, subject to suspension as provided by this subchapter.

(b) The gas utility shall immediately revise its schedules to include the increase.

Acts 1997, 75th Leg., ch. 166, § 1, eff. Sept. 1, 1997.

§ 104.105. Determination of Propriety of Rate Change; Hearing

(a) If a schedule modifying or increasing rates is filed with a regulatory authority, the regulatory authority shall, on complaint by an affected person, or may, on its own motion, not later than the 30th day after the effective date of the increase, enter on a hearing to determine the propriety of the increase.

(b) The regulatory authority shall hold a hearing in every case in which the increase constitutes a major change. The regulatory authority may, however, use an informal proceeding if the regulatory authority does not receive a complaint before the expiration of 45 days after the date notice of the increase is filed.

(c) The regulatory authority shall give reasonable notice of the hearing, including notice to the governing body of each affected municipality and county. The gas utility is not required to provide a formal answer or file any other formal pleading in response to the notice, and the absence of an answer does not affect an order for a hearing.

Acts 1997, 75th Leg., ch. 166, § 1, eff. Sept. 1, 1997.

§ 104.106. Preference to Hearing

The regulatory authority shall:

(1) give preference to the hearing under this subchapter and to deciding questions arising under this subchapter over any other question pending before it; and

(2) decide the questions as quickly as possible.

Acts 1997, 75th Leg., ch. 166, § 1, eff. Sept. 1, 1997.

§ 104.107. Rate Suspension; Deadline

(a) Pending the hearing and a decision:

(1) the local regulatory authority, after delivering to the gas utility a written statement of the regulatory authority's reasons, may suspend the operation of the schedule for not longer than 90 days after the date the schedule would otherwise be effective; and

(2) the railroad commission may suspend the operation of the schedule for not longer than 150 days after the date the schedule would otherwise be effective.

(b) The 150-day period prescribed by Subsection (a)(2) shall be extended for two days for each day the actual hearing on the merits of the case exceeds 15 days.

(c) If the regulatory authority does not make a final determination concerning a schedule of rates before expiration of the applicable suspension period, the regulatory authority is considered to have approved the schedule. This approval is subject to the authority of the regulatory authority thereafter to continue a hearing in progress.

Acts 1997, 75th Leg., ch. 166, § 1, eff. Sept. 1, 1997. Amended by Acts 2001, 77th Leg., ch. 1233, § 67, eff. Sept. 1, 2001.

§ 104.108. Temporary Rates

(a) The regulatory authority may establish temporary rates to be in effect during the applicable suspension period under Section 104.107.

(b) If the regulatory authority does not establish temporary rates, the rates in effect when the suspended schedule was filed continue in effect during the suspension period.

Acts 1997, 75th Leg., ch. 166, § 1, eff. Sept. 1, 1997.

§ 104.109. Bonded Rates

(a) A gas utility may put a changed rate into effect by filing a bond with the regulatory authority if the regulatory authority fails to make a final determination within 90 days from the date the proposed increase would otherwise be effective.

(b) The bonded rate may not exceed the proposed rate.

(c) The bond must be:

(1) payable to the regulatory authority in an amount, in a form, and with a surety approved by the regulatory authority; and

(2) conditioned on refund.

(d) The gas utility shall refund or credit against future bills:

(1) money collected under the bonded rates in excess of the rate finally ordered; and

(2) interest on that money, at the current interest rate as determined by the regulatory authority.

Acts 1997, 75th Leg., ch. 166, § 1, eff. Sept. 1, 1997.

§ 104.110. Establishment of Final Rates

(a) If, after hearing, the regulatory authority finds the rates are unreasonable or in violation of law, the regulatory authority shall:

(1) enter an order establishing the rates the gas utility shall charge or apply for the service in question; and

(2) serve a copy of the order on the gas utility.

(b) The rates established in the order shall be observed thereafter until changed as provided by this subtitle.

Acts 1997, 75th Leg., ch. 166, § 1, eff. Sept. 1, 1997.

§ 104.111. Approval of Decrease in Rates

Notwithstanding any other provision in this subtitle, the regulatory authority may, without reference to the cost of service standard prescribed by Section 104.051, administratively approve a decrease in rates proposed by the applicant and agreed on by each party directly affected unless the regulatory authority determines that the proposed decrease is not in the public interest.

Acts 1997, 75th Leg., ch. 166, § 1, eff. Sept. 1, 1997.

§ 104.112. Surcharge to Recover Relocation Costs

(a) This section applies to a gas utility's costs of relocating a facility to accommodate construction or improvement of a highway, road, street, public way, or other public work by or on behalf of the United States, this state, a political subdivision of this state, or another entity having the power of eminent domain that are not reimbursed by a source other than as provided by this section.

(b) A gas utility may recover its relocation costs to which this section applies through a surcharge on gas volumes sold and transported to customers in the service area where the relocation occurred by applying to each appropriate regulatory authority for a new rate schedule or tariff. The gas utility is not required to file a statement of intent to increase rates to institute the surcharge, and the other provisions of this subchapter, other than appeal rights, do not apply to institution of the surcharge.

(c) An application under Subsection (b) must include sufficient documentation to demonstrate:

(1) the requirement for each relocation;

(2) the entity requiring the relocation;

(3) costs incurred for relocation of comparable facilities;

(4) surcharge computations; and

(5) that reasonable efforts have been made to receive reimbursement from the entity requiring the relocation, if applicable.

(d) Not later than the 35th day after the date an application under Subsection (b) is received, the regulatory authority shall administratively grant or deny the application. Denial of the application must be based on a finding that:

(1) the relocation was not necessary or required;

(2) the costs of the relocation were excessive or not supported;

(3) the utility did not pursue reimbursement from the entity requiring the relocation, if applicable;

(4) the surcharge is unduly discriminatory among customers or classes of customers located in the service area; or

(5) the period over which the relocation costs are designed to be recovered is less than one or more than three years.

(e) If the regulating authority does not make a decision before the deadline prescribed by Subsection (d), the application is approved.

Added by Acts 1999, 76th Leg., ch. 219, § 1, eff. Sept. 1, 1999. Amended by Acts 2001, 77th Leg., ch. 662, § 1, eff. Sept. 1, 2001.

SUBCHAPTER D. RATE CHANGES PROPOSED BY COMMISSION

§ 104.151. Unreasonable or Violative Existing Rates

(a) If the regulatory authority, on its own motion or on complaint by an affected person, after reasonable notice and hearing, finds that the existing rates of a gas utility for a service are unreasonable or in violation of law, the regulatory authority shall:

(1) enter an order establishing the just and reasonable rates to be observed thereafter, including maximum or minimum rates; and

(2) serve a copy of the order on the gas utility.

(b) The rates set under Subsection (a) constitute the legal rates of the gas utility until changed as provided by this subtitle.

Acts 1997, 75th Leg., ch. 166, § 1, eff. Sept. 1, 1997.

§ 104.152. Investigating Costs of Obtaining Service From Another Source

If a gas utility does not produce the service that it distributes, transmits, or furnishes to the public for compensation but obtains the service from another source, the regulatory authority may investigate the cost of that production in an investigation of the reasonableness of the gas utility's rates.

Acts 1997, 75th Leg., ch. 166, § 1, eff. Sept. 1, 1997.

SUBCHAPTER E. RATES FOR GOVERNMENTAL ENTITIES

§ 104.201. Transportation Rates Between Gas Utility or Municipally Owned Utility and State Agency

(a) Notwithstanding Section 104.003(b), absent a contract for transportation service between a state agency and a gas utility or municipally owned utility, the railroad commission, not later than the 210th day after the date either party files a request to set a transportation rate, shall establish the transportation rate for the state agency. The commission has exclusive original jurisdiction to establish a transportation rate for a state agency under this section.

(b) The railroad commission shall base its determination of the transportation rate under Subsection (a) on the cost of providing the transportation service for both the distribution system and the transmission system, as applicable, of the gas utility or municipally owned utility.

(c) The railroad commission may order temporary rates under Subsection (a) as provided for under the commission's appellate jurisdiction.

Acts 1997, 75th Leg., ch. 166, § 1, eff. Sept. 1, 1997.

§ 104.202. Excluded Expenses

(a) The rates that a gas utility or municipally owned utility charges a state agency may not include an amount representing a gross receipts assessment, regulatory assessment, or similar expense of the utility.

(b) An expense under Subsection (a) that is reasonable and is not recovered from a state agency under this section may be recovered from other customers of the gas utility or municipally owned utility.

(c) A gross receipts assessment, regulatory assessment, or similar expense of the utility does not include a payment to a municipality under a contract, franchise, or other agreement.

Acts 1997, 75th Leg., ch. 166, § 1, eff. Sept. 1, 1997. Amended by Acts 1999, 76th Leg., ch. 1326, § 1, eff. June 18, 1999.

§ 104.203. Payment in Lieu of Tax

(a) A payment made in lieu of a tax by a municipally owned utility to the municipality by which the utility is owned may not be considered an expense of operation in establishing the utility's rate for providing utility service to a school district or hospital district.

(b) A rate a municipally owned utility receives from a school district or hospital district may not be used to make or to cover the cost of making payments in lieu of taxes to the municipality that owns the utility.

Acts 1997, 75th Leg., ch. 166, § 1, eff. Sept. 1, 1997.

SUBCHAPTER F. SERVICES

§ 104.251. General Standard

A gas utility shall furnish service, instrumentalities, and facilities that are safe, adequate, efficient, and reasonable.

Acts 1997, 75th Leg., ch. 166, § 1, eff. Sept. 1, 1997.

§ 104.252. Authority of Regulatory Authority Concerning Standards

A regulatory authority, on its own motion or on complaint and after reasonable notice and hearing, may:

(1) adopt just and reasonable standards, classifications, regulations, or practices a gas utility must follow in furnishing a service;

(2) adopt adequate and reasonable standards for measuring a condition, including quantity, quality, and pressure relating to the furnishing of a service;

(3) adopt reasonable regulations for examining, testing, and measuring a service; and

(4) adopt or approve reasonable rules, regulations, specifications, and standards to ensure the accuracy of equipment, including meters and instruments, used to measure a service.

Acts 1997, 75th Leg., ch. 166, § 1, eff. Sept. 1, 1997.

§ 104.253. Rule or Standard

(a) A gas utility may file with the regulatory authority a standard, classification, regulation, or practice the utility follows.

(b) The standard, classification, regulation, or practice continues in force until:

(1) amended by the utility; or

(2) changed by the regulatory authority as provided by this subtitle.

Acts 1997, 75th Leg., ch. 166, § 1, eff. Sept. 1, 1997.

§ 104.254. Service

A gas utility or municipally owned utility may not refuse to provide service to a state agency if pipeline capacity is available on an existing facility of the utility.

Acts 1997, 75th Leg., ch. 166, § 1, eff. Sept. 1, 1997.

§ 104.2545. Required Service to Public Retail Customer

(a) In this section, "service site" means facilities or buildings operated by a public retail customer or a group of adjacent facilities or buildings operated by a public retail customer within one contiguous geographical area.

(b) Unless the utility is prohibited by other law from providing the service and if sufficient pipeline capacity is available on an existing facility of the utility to provide the service, a gas utility or municipally owned utility may not refuse to provide service to a public retail customer at a service site, at rates established as provided by Subsection (c), the following services:

(1) the sale of gas;

(2) the transportation of an annual average of 25 million British thermal units or more each day of gas that is:

(A) taken as a royalty in kind; and

(B) owned by the state or managed by a marketing program operated by the state or by a state agency; or

(3) a combination of the services described by Subdivisions (1) and (2).

(c) A utility shall provide a service described by Subsection (b) at rates provided by a written contract negotiated between the utility and the state or a state agency. If the utility and the state or state agency are not able to agree to a contract rate, a fair and reasonable rate may be determined for the public retail customer, as a rate for a separate class of service, by the railroad commission or, for municipally owned gas utilities, by the relevant regulatory body under this chapter.

(d) In this section, "public retail customer" has the meaning assigned by Section 35.101.

Added by Acts 1999, 76th Leg., ch. 300, § 1, eff. Sept. 1, 1999. Amended by Acts 2003, 78th Leg., ch. 563, § 1, eff. June 20, 2003.

§ 104.255. Billing

(a) A gas utility or municipally owned utility may not bill or otherwise require the state or a state agency or institution to pay for service before the service is provided.

(b) The railroad commission shall adopt rules concerning payment of bills by the state or a state agency to a gas utility or municipally owned utility. The rules must be consistent with Chapter 2251, Government Code.

(c) This subtitle does not prohibit a gas utility or municipally owned utility from entering into an agreement with the state or a state agency to establish a level or average monthly service billing plan. An agreement under this subsection must require reconciliation of the leveled or equalized bills quarterly.

Acts 1997, 75th Leg., ch. 166, § 1, eff. Sept. 1, 1997.

§ 104.2551. Electronic Billing

A gas utility or municipally owned utility may transmit the utility's bill for services through the Internet or by other electronic means instead of through the United States mail on the request of a customer of the gas utility or municipally owned utility.

Added by Acts 2001, 77th Leg., ch. 1233, § 68, eff. Sept. 1, 2001.

§ 104.256. Examination and Test of Instrument or Equipment; Inspection

(a) A regulatory authority may:

(1) examine and test equipment, including meters and instruments, used to measure service of a gas utility; and

(2) set up and use on the premises occupied by a gas utility an apparatus or appliance necessary for the examination or test.

(b) The gas utility is entitled to be represented at an examination, test, or inspection made under this section.

(c) The gas utility and its officers and employees shall facilitate the examination, test, or inspection by giving reasonable aid to the regulatory authority and to any person designated by the regulatory authority for the performance of those duties.

Acts 1997, 75th Leg., ch. 166, § 1, eff. Sept. 1, 1997.

§ 104.257. Inspection for Consumer

(a) A consumer may have a meter or other measuring device tested by a gas utility:

(1) once without charge, after a reasonable period of presumed accuracy that the regulatory authority establishes by rule; and

(2) at a shorter interval on payment of a reasonable fee established by the regulatory authority.

(b) The regulatory authority shall establish reasonable fees to be paid for other examining or testing of a measuring device on the request of a consumer.

(c) If the consumer requests the test under Subsection (a)(2) and the measuring device is found unreasonably defective or incorrect to the substantial disadvantage of the consumer, the fee the consumer paid at the time of the request shall be refunded.

Acts 1997, 75th Leg., ch. 166, § 1, eff. Sept. 1, 1997.

§ 104.258. Disconnection of Gas Service

(a) In this section:

(1) "Extreme weather emergency" means a period during which the previous day's highest temperature did not exceed 32 degrees Fahrenheit and the temperature is predicted to remain at or below that level for the next 24 hours according to the nearest National Weather Service reports.

(2) "Provider" means:

(A) a gas utility, as defined by Sections 101.003 and 121.001; and

(B) an owner, operator, or manager of a mobile home park or apartment who purchases natural gas through a master meter for delivery to a dwelling unit in a mobile home park or apartment house under Chapter 124.

(b) A provider may not disconnect natural gas service to a residential customer on a weekend day unless personnel of the provider are available on that day to take payments and reconnect service.

(c) A provider may not disconnect natural gas service to a residential customer during an extreme weather emergency. The provider shall defer collection of the full payment of bills that are due during an extreme weather emergency until after the emergency is over and shall work with customers to establish a pay schedule for deferred bills.

Added by Acts 2001, 77th Leg., ch. 1149, § 1, eff. Sept. 1, 2001.

SUBCHAPTER G. INTERIM COST RECOVERY AND RATE ADJUSTMENT

§ 104.301. Interim Adjustment for Changes in Investment

(a) A gas utility that has filed a rate case under Subchapter C[1] within the preceding two years may file with the regulatory authority a tariff or rate schedule that provides for an interim adjustment in the utility's monthly customer charge or initial block rate to recover the cost of changes in the investment in service for gas utility services. The adjustment shall be allocated among the gas utility's classes of customers in the same manner as the cost of service was allocated among classes of customers in the utility's latest effective rates for the area in which the tariff or rate schedule is implemented. The gas utility shall file the tariff or rate schedule, or the annual adjustment under Subsection (c), with the regulatory authority at least 60 days before the proposed implementation date of the tariff, rate schedule, or annual adjustment. The gas utility shall provide notice of the tariff, rate schedule, or annual adjustment to affected customers by bill insert or direct mail not later than the 45th day after the date the utility files the tariff, rate schedule, or annual adjustment with the regulatory authority. During the 60–day period, the regulatory authority may act to suspend the implementation of the tariff, rate schedule, or annual adjustment for up to 45 days. After the issuance of a final order or decision by a regulatory authority in a rate case that is filed after the implementation of a tariff or rate schedule under this section, any change in investment that has been included in an interim adjustment in accordance with the tariff or rate schedule under this section shall no longer be subject to subsequent review for reasonableness or prudence. Until the issuance of a final order or decision by a regulatory authority in a rate case that is filed after the implementation of a tariff or rate schedule under this section, all amounts collected under the tariff or rate schedule before the filing of the rate case are subject to refund.

(b) The amount the gas utility shall adjust the utility's rates upward or downward under the tariff or rate schedule each calendar year is based on the difference between the value of the invested capital for the preceding calendar year and the value of the invested capital for the calendar year preceding that calendar year. The value of the invested capital is equal to the original cost of the investment at the time the investment was first dedicated to public use minus the accumulated depreciation related to that investment.

(c) The interim adjustment shall be recalculated on an annual basis in accordance with the requirements of Subsection (b). The gas utility may file a request with the regulatory authority to suspend the operation of the tariff or rate schedule for any year. The request must be in writing and state the reasons why the suspension is justified. The regulatory authority may grant the suspension on a showing by the utility of reasonable justification.

(d) A gas utility may only adjust the utility's rates under the tariff or rate schedule for the return on investment, depreciation expense, ad valorem taxes, revenue related taxes, and incremental federal income taxes related to the difference in the value of the invested capital as determined under Subsection (b). The return on investment, depreciation, and incremental federal income tax factors used in the computation must be the same as the factors reflected in the final order issued by or settlement agreement approved by the regulatory authority establishing the gas utility's latest effective rates for the area in which the tariff or rate schedule is implemented.

(e) A gas utility that implements a tariff or rate schedule under this section shall file with the regulatory authority an annual report describing the investment projects completed and placed in service during the preceding calendar year and the investments retired or abandoned during the preceding calendar year. The annual report shall also state the cost, need, and customers benefited by the change in investment.

(f) In addition to the report required under Subsection (e), the gas utility shall file with the regulatory authority an annual earnings monitoring report demonstrating the utility's earnings during the preceding calendar year.

(g) If the gas utility is earning a return on invested capital, as demonstrated by the report filed under Subsection (f), of more than 75 basis points above the return established in the latest effective rates approved by a regulatory authority for the area in which the tariff or rate schedule is implemented under this section, the gas utility shall file a statement with that report stating the reasons why the rates are not unreasonable or in violation of law.

(h) If a gas utility that implements a tariff or rate schedule under this section does not file a rate case under Subchapter C[1] before the fifth anniversary of the date on which the tariff or rate schedule takes effect, the gas utility shall file a rate case under that subchapter not later than the 180th day after that anniversary in relation to any rates subject to the tariff or rate schedule.

(i) This section does not limit the power of a regulatory authority under Section 104.151.

(j) A gas utility implementing a tariff or rate schedule under this section shall reimburse the railroad commission the utility's proportionate share of the railroad commission's costs related to the administration of the interim rate adjustment mechanism provided by this section.

Added by Acts 2003, 78th Leg., ch. 938, § 1, eff. Sept. 1, 2003. Amended by Acts 2005, 79th Leg., ch. 948, § 1, eff. Sept. 1, 2005.

[1] V.T.C.A., Utilities Code § 104.101.

CHAPTER 105. JUDICIAL REVIEW; ENFORCEMENT AND PENALTIES

SUBCHAPTER A. JUDICIAL REVIEW

Section
105.001. Right to Judicial Review.
105.002. Judicial Stay or Suspension.

SUBCHAPTER B. ENFORCEMENT AND PENALTIES

105.021. Action to Enjoin or Require Compliance.
105.022. Contempt.
105.023. Civil Penalty Against Gas Utility or Affiliate.
105.024. Offense.
105.025. Place for Suit.
105.026. Penalties Cumulative.
105.027. Disposition of Fines and Penalties.

SUBCHAPTER C. COMPLAINTS

105.051. Complaint by Affected Person.

SUBCHAPTER A. JUDICIAL REVIEW

§ 105.001. Right to Judicial Review

(a) Any party to a proceeding before the railroad commission is entitled to judicial review under the substantial evidence rule.

(b) The issue of confiscation is determined by a preponderance of the evidence.

Acts 1997, 75th Leg., ch. 166, § 1, eff. Sept. 1, 1997.

§ 105.002. Judicial Stay or Suspension

While an appeal of an order, ruling, or decision of a regulatory authority is pending, the district court, court of appeals, or supreme court, as appropriate, may stay or suspend all or part of the operation of the order, ruling, or decision. In granting or refusing a stay or suspension, the court shall act in accordance with the practice of a court exercising equity jurisdiction.

Acts 1997, 75th Leg., ch. 166, § 1, eff. Sept. 1, 1997.

SUBCHAPTER B. ENFORCEMENT AND PENALTIES

§ 105.021. Action to Enjoin or Require Compliance

(a) The attorney general, on the request of the railroad commission, shall apply in the name of the commission for an order under Subsection (b) if the commission determines that a gas utility or other person is:

(1) engaging in or about to engage in an act that violates this subtitle or an order or rule of the commission entered or adopted under this subtitle; or

(2) failing to comply with the requirements of this subtitle or a rule or order of the commission.

(b) A court, in an action under this section, may:

(1) prohibit the commencement or continuation of an act that violates this subtitle or an order or rule of the commission entered or adopted under this subtitle; or

(2) require compliance with a provision of this subtitle or an order or rule of the commission.

(c) The remedy under this section is in addition to any other remedy provided under this subtitle.

Acts 1997, 75th Leg., ch. 166, § 1, eff. Sept. 1, 1997.

§ 105.022. Contempt

The railroad commission may file an action for contempt against a person who:

(1) fails to comply with a lawful order of the commission;

(2) fails to comply with a subpoena or subpoena duces tecum; or

(3) refuses to testify about a matter on which the person may be lawfully interrogated.

Acts 1997, 75th Leg., ch. 166, § 1, eff. Sept. 1, 1997.

§ 105.023. Civil Penalty Against Gas Utility or Affiliate

(a) A gas utility or affiliate is subject to a civil penalty if the gas utility or affiliate knowingly violates this subtitle, fails to perform a duty imposed on it, or fails, neglects, or refuses to obey an order, rule, direction, or requirement of the railroad commission or a decree or judgment of a court.

(b) A civil penalty under this section shall be in an amount of not less than $1,000 and not more than $5,000 for each violation.

(c) A gas utility or affiliate commits a separate violation each day it continues to violate Subsection (a).

(d) The attorney general shall file in the name of the railroad commission a suit on the attorney general's own initiative or at the request of the commission to recover the civil penalty under this section.

Acts 1997, 75th Leg., ch. 166, § 1, eff. Sept. 1, 1997.

§ 105.024. Offense

(a) A person commits an offense if the person knowingly violates this subtitle.

(b) An offense under this section is a felony of the third degree.

Acts 1997, 75th Leg., ch. 166, § 1, eff. Sept. 1, 1997.

§ 105.025. Place for Suit

A suit for an injunction or a penalty under this subtitle may be brought in:

(1) Travis County;

(2) a county in which the violation is alleged to have occurred; or

(3) a county in which a defendant resides.

Acts 1997, 75th Leg., ch. 166, § 1, eff. Sept. 1, 1997.

§ 105.026. Penalties Cumulative

(a) A penalty that accrues under this subtitle is cumulative of any other penalty.

(b) A suit for the recovery of a penalty does not bar or affect the recovery of any other penalty or bar a criminal prosecution against any person, including a gas utility or officer, director, agent, or employee of a gas utility.

Acts 1997, 75th Leg., ch. 166, § 1, eff. Sept. 1, 1997.

§ 105.027. Disposition of Fines and Penalties

A fine or penalty collected under this subtitle, other than a fine or penalty collected in a criminal proceeding, shall be paid to the railroad commission.

Acts 1997, 75th Leg., ch. 166, § 1, eff. Sept. 1, 1997.

SUBCHAPTER C. COMPLAINTS

§ 105.051. Complaint by Affected Person

An affected person may complain to the regulatory authority in writing setting forth an act or omission by a gas utility in violation or claimed violation of a law that the regulatory authority has jurisdiction to administer or of an order, ordinance, or rule of the regulatory authority.

Acts 1997, 75th Leg., ch. 166, § 1, eff. Sept. 1, 1997.

SUBTITLE B. REGULATION OF TRANSPORTATION AND USE

CHAPTER 121. GAS PIPELINES

SUBCHAPTER A. GAS UTILITY DEFINED

Section
121.001. Definition of Gas Utility.
121.002. Affiliate of Gas Utility Excluded.
121.003. Agricultural Service Excluded.
121.004. Transportation of Gas Solely for Interstate Commerce Excluded.
121.005. Transportation of Gas in Vicinity of Place of Production Excluded.
121.006. Vehicle Fuel Excluded.
121.007. Transportation of Gas to and From Liquefied Natural Gas Marine Terminal Excluded.
121.008. Certain Storage Facilities Owned by Electric Cooperatives Excluded.

SUBCHAPTER B. PUBLIC POLICY

121.051. Gas Utility: Public Interest and Jurisdiction of Railroad Commission.
121.052. Pipelines: Monopolies Subject to Railroad Commission.

SUBCHAPTER C. DUTIES OF GAS UTILITIES AND PIPELINES

121.101. Maintenance of Office and Records in This State.
121.102. Operator's Report.
121.103. Duty to Serve Certain Users Extinguished.
121.104. Discrimination in Service and Charges Prohibited.

SUBCHAPTER D. REGULATION BY RAILROAD COMMISSION

121.151. Railroad Commission Regulation of Gas Pipelines.
121.152. Initiation of Regulatory Proceeding.
121.153. Railroad Commission Review of Gas Pipeline Orders and Agreements.
121.154. Refund of Excess Charges.
121.155. Rate Reduction or Determination by Municipality and Appeal.
121.156. Repealed.
121.157. Railroad Commission Employees.
121.158. Payment From the General Revenue Fund.

SUBCHAPTER E. PIPELINE SAFETY

121.201. Safety Rules: Railroad Commission Power.
121.2015. Required Safety Rules.
121.202. Municipal and County Authority.
121.2025. Authority of Municipality to Assess Charges.
121.203. Enforcement: Injunction.
121.204. Civil Penalty.
121.205. Settlement by Attorney General.

Section

121.206. Administrative Penalty for Violation of Pipeline Safety Standard or Rule.
121.207. Pipeline Safety Administrative Penalty: Assessment Procedure.
121.208. Pipeline Safety Administrative Penalty: Payment of Penalty.
121.209. Pipeline Safety Administrative Penalty: Refund of Payment or Release of Bond.
121.210. Recovery by Attorney General.
121.211. Pipeline Safety and Regulatory Fees.

SUBCHAPTER F. GAS SAFETY

121.251. Railroad Commission to Investigate Use of Gas Malodorants.
121.252. Regulation of Use of Malodorants.
121.253. Interstate Transportation of Gas Excluded.

SUBCHAPTER G. ENFORCEMENT REMEDIES

121.301. Receivership.
121.302. Civil Penalty.
121.303. Penalty Recoverable by Victim of Discrimination.
121.304. Pollution or Public Safety Administrative Penalty.
121.305. Pollution or Public Safety Administrative Penalty: Assessment Procedure.
121.306. Pollution or Public Safety Administrative Penalty: Payment of Penalty.
121.307. Pollution or Public Safety Administrative Penalty: Appeals.
121.308. Pollution or Public Safety Administrative Penalty: Refund of Payment or Release of Bond.
121.309. Pollution or Public Safety Administrative Penalty: Recovery.
121.310. Criminal Penalty.

SUBCHAPTER H. APPEALS

121.401. Appeal to Court.
121.402. Appeal: Burden and Standard of Proof.
121.403. Appeal From Trial Court.

SUBCHAPTER I. SOUR GAS PIPELINE FACILITIES

121.451. Definitions.
121.452. Applicability.
121.453. Permit Application.
121.454. Railroad Commission Approval or Denial.

SUBCHAPTER J. TESTING OF NATURAL GAS PIPING SYSTEMS IN SCHOOL FACILITIES

121.5005. Applicability.
121.501. Definition.
121.502. Duty to Pressure Test.
121.503. Requirements of Test.
121.504. Notice of Test.
121.505. Termination of Service.
121.506. Report of Leakage.
121.507. Enforcement.

SUBCHAPTER A. GAS UTILITY DEFINED

§ 121.001. Definition of Gas Utility

(a) In this chapter, "gas utility" means a person who owns, manages, operates, leases, or controls in this state property or equipment or a pipeline, plant, facility, franchise, license, or permit for a business that:

(1) transports, conveys, distributes, or delivers natural gas:

(A) for public use or service for compensation;

(B) for sale to municipalities or persons engaged in distributing or selling natural gas to the public, in a situation described by Subdivision (3);

(C) for sale or delivery to a person operating under a franchise or contract with a political subdivision of this state; or

(D) for sale or delivery to the public for domestic or other use;

(2) owns, operates, or manages a pipeline:

(A) that is for transporting or carrying natural gas, whether for public hire or not; and

(B) for which the right-of-way has been or is hereafter acquired by exercising the right of eminent domain; or

(3) produces or purchases natural gas and transports or causes the transportation of natural gas by a pipeline to or near the limits of a municipality in which the gas is received and distributed or sold to the public by another gas utility or by the municipality in a situation in which the business is the only or practically the only agency of supply of natural gas to the gas utility or municipality.

(b) In this subchapter, "person" means an individual, company, limited liability company, or private corporation and includes a lessee, trustee, or receiver of an individual, company, limited liability company, or private corporation.

Acts 1997, 75th Leg., ch. 166, § 1, eff. Sept. 1, 1997. Amended by Acts 1999, 76th Leg., ch. 11, § 2, eff. May 3, 1999.

§ 121.002. Affiliate of Gas Utility Excluded

A person is not a gas utility solely because the person is an affiliate of a gas utility.

Acts 1997, 75th Leg., ch. 166, § 1, eff. Sept. 1, 1997.

§ 121.003. Agricultural Service Excluded

(a) The act or acts of transporting, delivering, selling, or otherwise making available natural gas for fuel, either directly or indirectly, to an owner of an irrigation well, or the sale, transportation, or delivery of natural gas for any other direct use in an agricultural activity, does not make a person a gas utility or make the person subject to the jurisdiction, control, and regulation of the railroad commission as a gas utility.

(b) In order for a person furnishing natural gas to qualify for the exemption under Subsection (a), the person to whom the gas was furnished under Subsection (a) shall use the gas exclusively to pump water for farm and other agricultural purposes.

Acts 1997, 75th Leg., ch. 166, § 1, eff. Sept. 1, 1997.

§ 121.004. Transportation of Gas Solely for Interstate Commerce Excluded

Except as provided by Section 121.001(a)(2), a person is not a gas utility if the person certifies to the railroad commission that the person transports natural or synthetic gas, for sale, for hire, or otherwise, solely in, or in the vicinity of, the field or fields where the gas is produced, to another person for transportation or sale in interstate commerce.

Acts 1997, 75th Leg., ch. 166, § 1, eff. Sept. 1, 1997.

§ 121.005. Transportation of Gas in Vicinity of Place of Production Excluded

(a) Except as provided by Section 121.001(a)(2), a person is not a gas utility if the person certifies to the railroad commission that the person transports natural or synthetic gas, for sale, for hire, or otherwise, solely:

(1) in, or in the vicinity of, the field or fields where the gas is produced to a gas processing plant or treating facility;

(2) from the outlet of a gas processing plant or treating facility described by Subdivision (1) to a person:

(A) at, or in the vicinity of, the plant or treating facility; or

(B) described by Subdivision (3) or Section 121.004; or

(3) to another person in, or in the vicinity of, the field or fields where the gas is produced for transportation or sale in intrastate commerce.

(b) A person is not a gas utility because the person delivers or sells gas:

(1) for lease use, compressor fuel, processing plant fuel, or a similar use;

(2) under a lease or right-of-way agreement;

(3) in, or in the vicinity of, the field where the gas is produced; or

(4) at a processing plant outlet.

(c) Subsection (b) does not exclude as a gas utility a pipeline that:

(1) transmits or distributes to end users of gas, other than:

(A) those described by Subsection (b); or

(B) a person who qualifies for the exemption provided by Section 121.003; or

(2) makes city-gate deliveries for local distribution.

(d) The railroad commission may review a certification made by a person under Subsection (a). The railroad commission shall invite a person whose certification is being reviewed to an informal meeting to resolve the person's status under this subsection. If the person's status remains unresolved after the informal meeting and there is sufficient reason to move forward, the railroad commission shall provide notice and an opportunity for a hearing. After notice and an opportunity for a hearing, the railroad commission may determine whether the person is eligible for an exemption under this subsection.

Acts 1997, 75th Leg., ch. 166, § 1, eff. Sept. 1, 1997. Amended by Acts 2009, 81st Leg., ch. 406, § 1, eff. Sept. 1, 2009.

§ 121.006. Vehicle Fuel Excluded

A person is not a gas utility to the extent that the person:

(1) sells natural gas for use as vehicle fuel;

(2) sells natural gas to a person who later sells the natural gas for use as vehicle fuel; or

(3) owns or operates equipment or facilities to sell or transport the natural gas for ultimate use as vehicle fuel.

Acts 1997, 75th Leg., ch. 166, § 1, eff. Sept. 1, 1997.

§ 121.007. Transportation of Gas to and From Liquefied Natural Gas Marine Terminal Excluded

(a) A person operating a natural gas pipeline, a liquefied natural gas pipeline, or an underground storage facility is not a gas utility if the person certifies to the railroad commission that the person uses the pipeline or underground storage facility solely to deliver natural gas or liquefied natural gas or the constituents of natural gas or liquefied natural gas:

(1) to a liquefied natural gas marine terminal;

(2) from a liquefied natural gas marine terminal to the owner of the gas or another person on behalf of the owner of the gas;

(3) that is acquired, liquefied, or sold by the person as necessary for the operation or mainte-

nance of its facility that is excluded as a gas utility under this section; or

(4) that has been stored for export.

(b) This section does not confer the power of eminent domain to a pipeline or underground storage facility excluded as a gas utility under this section.

Added by Acts 2007, 80th Leg., ch. 709, § 2, eff. June 15, 2007. Amended by Acts 2009, 81st Leg., ch. 406, § 2, eff. Sept. 1, 2009; Acts 2009, 81st Leg., ch. 556, § 1, eff. Sept. 1, 2009.

§ 121.008. Certain Storage Facilities Owned by Electric Cooperatives Excluded

An electric cooperative, as that term is defined by Section 11.003, or its subsidiary, that sells electricity at wholesale is not a gas utility or subject to regulation as a gas utility solely because it provides gas storage services for hire if the gas storage facility is predominantly operated to support the integration of renewable resources. Such a gas storage facility may not have a working gas capacity of greater than five billion cubic feet.

Added by Acts 2011, 82nd Leg., ch. 4 (S.B. 312), § 2, eff. April 21, 2011.

SUBCHAPTER B. PUBLIC POLICY

§ 121.051. Gas Utility: Public Interest and Jurisdiction of Railroad Commission

(a) A gas utility, including a business described by Section 121.001(a)(3), is affected with a public interest.

(b) A business described by Section 121.001(a)(3) is a virtual monopoly.

(c) A business described by Section 121.001(a)(3) and the property of the business used in this state is subject to the jurisdiction, control, and regulation of the railroad commission as provided by this chapter.

Acts 1997, 75th Leg., ch. 166, § 1, eff. Sept. 1, 1997.

§ 121.052. Pipelines: Monopolies Subject to Railroad Commission

(a) The operation of a pipeline for buying, selling, transporting, producing, or otherwise dealing in natural gas is a business which in its nature and according to the established method of conducting the business is a monopoly.

(b) A business described by this section may not be conducted unless the gas pipeline used in connection with the business is subject to the jurisdiction conferred by this chapter on the railroad commission.

(c) The attorney general shall enforce this section by injunction or other remedy.

Acts 1997, 75th Leg., ch. 166, § 1, eff. Sept. 1, 1997.

SUBCHAPTER C. DUTIES OF GAS UTILITIES AND PIPELINES

§ 121.101. Maintenance of Office and Records in This State

(a) A gas utility shall maintain an office in this state in a county in which some part of the gas utility's property is located. The gas utility shall keep in this office all books, accounts, papers, records, vouchers, and receipts that the railroad commission requires.

(b) A book, account, paper, record, receipt, voucher, or other item of information required by the railroad commission to be kept in this state may not be removed from this state except as prescribed by the railroad commission.

Acts 1997, 75th Leg., ch. 166, § 1, eff. Sept. 1, 1997.

§ 121.102. Operator's Report

The railroad commission may require a person or corporation that owns, controls, or operates a pipeline subject to this chapter to make to the commission a sworn report of any matter relating to the business of the person or corporation that the commission determines to be pertinent, including:

(1) the total quantity of gas distributed by the pipelines;

(2) the total quantity of gas held in storage;

(3) the source of supply of gas;

(4) the number of wells from which the person or corporation draws its supply;

(5) the amount of pipeline pressure maintained; and

(6) the amount and character and description of the equipment used.

Acts 1997, 75th Leg., ch. 166, § 1, eff. Sept. 1, 1997.

§ 121.103. Duty to Serve Certain Users Extinguished

(a) A gas utility that provides gas to a customer does not have an obligation to serve the customer or to maintain the gas supply or physical capacity to serve the customer if the customer:

(1) is a transportation, industrial, commercial, or other similar large-volume contract customer;

(2) is an end-use customer of the gas utility;

(3) reduces or ceases the purchase of natural gas or natural gas service from the gas utility; and

(4) purchases natural gas or natural gas service from another supplier or purchases an alternate form of energy.

(b) Subsection (a) does not apply to the extent that:

(1) the customer continues to purchase natural gas or natural gas service of any class from the gas utility; or

(2) the gas utility has a written contract to provide natural gas or natural gas service of any class to the customer.

(c) This section does not prevent the railroad commission from requiring a gas utility to comply with an order of the railroad commission in apportioning gas under a curtailment plan and order.

(d) Notwithstanding Subsection (a), a gas utility that has provided gas to a commercial customer is obligated to serve that customer if the gas utility has a sufficient gas supply and physical capacity to do so without reducing service to its other customers.

Acts 1997, 75th Leg., ch. 166, § 1, eff. Sept. 1, 1997. Amended by Acts 2001, 77th Leg., ch. 1233, § 69, eff. Sept. 1, 2001.

§ 121.104. Discrimination in Service and Charges Prohibited

(a) A pipeline gas utility may not:

(1) discriminate in favor of or against any person or place in:

(A) apportioning the supply of natural gas; or

(B) charging for natural gas; or

(2) directly or indirectly charge, demand, collect, or receive from anyone a greater or lesser compensation for a service provided than the compensation charged, demanded, or received from another for a similar and contemporaneous service.

(b) This section does not limit the right of the railroad commission to prescribe:

(1) different rates and rules for the use of natural gas for manufacturing and similar purposes; or

(2) rates and rules for service from or to other or different places.

Acts 1997, 75th Leg., ch. 166, § 1, eff. Sept. 1, 1997.

SUBCHAPTER D. REGULATION BY RAILROAD COMMISSION

§ 121.151. Railroad Commission Regulation of Gas Pipelines

The railroad commission shall:

(1) establish and enforce the adequate and reasonable price of gas and fair and reasonable rates of charges and rules for transporting, producing, distributing, buying, selling, and delivering gas by pipelines subject to this chapter in this state;

(2) establish fair and equitable rules for the full control and supervision of the pipelines subject to this chapter and all their holdings pertaining to the gas business in all their relations to the public, as the railroad commission determines to be proper;

(3) establish a fair and equitable division of the proceeds of the sale of gas between the companies transporting or producing the gas and the companies distributing or selling it;

(4) prescribe and enforce rules for the government and control of pipelines subject to this chapter in respect to their pipelines and producing, receiving, transporting, and distributing facilities;

(5) regulate and apportion the supply of gas between municipalities and between municipalities and corporations; and

(6) prescribe fair and reasonable rules requiring pipelines subject to this chapter to augment their supply of gas, when:

(A) the supply of gas controlled by any gas pipeline is inadequate; and

(B) the railroad commission determines that augmentation is practicable.

Acts 1997, 75th Leg., ch. 166, § 1, eff. Sept. 1, 1997.

§ 121.152. Initiation of Regulatory Proceeding

The railroad commission shall exercise power under Section 121.151:

(1) on:

(A) its own motion;

(B) the petition of a person or county commissioner's precinct showing a substantial interest in the subject;

(C) the petition of the attorney general; or

(D) the petition of a district or county attorney of a county in which any portion of a business subject to this chapter is conducted; and

(2) after notice has been given.

Acts 1997, 75th Leg., ch. 166, § 1, eff. Sept. 1, 1997.

§ 121.153. Railroad Commission Review of Gas Pipeline Orders and Agreements

The railroad commission, after notice to a person or corporation owning, controlling, or operating a pipeline subject to this chapter and after a hearing, may review, revise, and regulate an order or agreement that is made by the person or corporation and establishes a price, rate, rule, regulation, or condition of service.

Acts 1997, 75th Leg., ch. 166, § 1, eff. Sept. 1, 1997.

§ 121.154. Refund of Excess Charges

(a) On a complaint against a person or corporation owning or operating a pipeline business subject to this chapter filed by any person authorized by Section 121.152 to file a petition and complaint and sustained in whole or in part by the railroad commission, each customer of the pipeline is entitled to reparation for or reimbursement of a rate or charge made or adopted by the pipeline for a purpose relating to the operation of that business, including a rate or charge for gas, service, or meter rental, or in the event of an inadequate supply of gas or inadequate service in any respect.

(b) The amount recoverable under Subsection (a) is the amount paid after the filing of the complaint in excess of the proper rate or charge of the pipeline as finally determined by the railroad commission.

Acts 1997, 75th Leg., ch. 166, § 1, eff. Sept. 1, 1997.

§ 121.155. Rate Reduction or Determination by Municipality and Appeal

A gas utility the rates of which have been reduced by a municipality may appeal the municipal order, decision, regulation, or ordinance to the railroad commission. The appeal is initiated by filing with the railroad commission in the manner and on the conditions that the railroad commission may direct a petition for review and a bond. The appeal is de novo. The railroad commission shall set a hearing and may make any order or decision in relation to the matter appealed that the commission considers just and reasonable. To change a rate, rental, or charge, a gas utility that is a local distributing company or concern and the rates of which have been established by a municipality must submit an application to the municipality in which the utility is located. The municipality shall make a determination on an application not later than the 60th day after the date the application is filed. If the municipality rejects the application or fails or refuses to act on the application on or before the deadline prescribed by this section, the gas utility may appeal to the railroad commission as provided by this section. The railroad commission shall make a determination on the appeal not later than the 60th day after the date the appeal is filed unless the gas utility agrees in writing to a longer period. The rates established by the municipality remain in effect until changed by the railroad commission.

Acts 1997, 75th Leg., ch. 166, § 1, eff. Sept. 1, 1997.

§ 121.156. Repealed by Acts 2003, 78th Leg., ch. 519, § 1, eff. June 20, 2003

§ 121.157. Railroad Commission Employees

(a) The railroad commission may employ or appoint persons as necessary to:

(1) inspect and audit records or receipts, disbursements, vouchers, prices, payrolls, time cards, and books;

(2) inspect the property and records of a gas utility subject to this chapter; and

(3) perform other services as directed by, or under the authority of, the railroad commission.

(b) The railroad commission shall set the amount of compensation for persons employed by the railroad commission.

(c) The chief supervisor of the oil and gas division of the railroad commission shall assist the railroad commission in the performance of the railroad commission's duties under this chapter, as directed by, and under the rules of, the railroad commission.

Acts 1997, 75th Leg., ch. 166, § 1, eff. Sept. 1, 1997.

§ 121.158. Payment From the General Revenue Fund

All expenses, including witness fees and mileage, employee wages and fees, and the salary and expenses of the chief supervisor of the oil and gas division of the railroad commission incurred by or under authority of the railroad commission or a railroad commissioner in administering and enforcing, or exercising a power under, this chapter shall be paid from the general revenue fund.

Acts 1997, 75th Leg., ch. 166, § 1, eff. Sept. 1, 1997.

SUBCHAPTER E. PIPELINE SAFETY

§ 121.201. Safety Rules: Railroad Commission Power

(a) The railroad commission may:

(1) by rule prescribe or adopt safety standards for the transportation of gas and for gas pipeline facilities, including safety standards related to the prevention of damage to such a facility resulting

from the movement of earth by a person in the vicinity of the facility, other than movement by tillage that does not exceed a depth of 16 inches;

(2) by rule require an operator that does not file operator organization information under Section 91.142, Natural Resources Code, to provide the information to the commission in the form of an application;

(3) by rule require record maintenance and reports;

(4) inspect records and facilities to determine compliance with safety standards prescribed or adopted under Subdivision (1);

(5) make certifications and reports from time to time;

(6) seek designation by the United States secretary of transportation as an agent to conduct safety inspections of interstate gas pipeline facilities located in this state; and

(7) by rule take any other requisite action in accordance with 49 U.S.C. Section 60101 et seq., or a succeeding law.

(b) The power granted by Subsection (a):

(1) does not apply to the transportation of gas or to gas facilities subject to the exclusive control of the United States but applies to the transportation of gas and gas pipeline facilities in this state to the maximum degree permissible under 49 U.S.C. Section 60101 et seq., or a succeeding law; and

(2) is granted to provide exclusive state control over safety standards and practices applicable to the transportation of gas and gas pipeline facilities within the borders of this state to the maximum degree permissible under that law.

(c) A term that is used in this section and defined by Chapter 601, Title 49, United States Code (49 U.S.C. Section 60101 et seq.), or a succeeding law has the meaning assigned by that chapter or the succeeding law.

(d) In this subsection, "telecommunications service" and "information service" have the meanings assigned by 47 U.S.C. Section 153. Notwithstanding Subsection (a), this title does not grant the railroad commission jurisdiction or right-of-way management authority over a provider of telecommunications service or information service. A provider of telecommunications service or information service shall comply with all applicable safety standards, including those provided by Subchapter H , Chapter 756, Health and Safety Code.

(e) The power granted by Subsection (a) does not apply to:

(1) surface mining operations; or

(2) other entities or occupations if the railroad commission determines in its rulemaking process that exempting those entities or occupations from rules adopted under that subsection:

(A) is in the public interest; or

(B) is not likely to cause harm to the safety and welfare of the public.

(f) Expired.

Acts 1997, 75th Leg., ch. 166, § 1, eff. Sept. 1, 1997. Amended by Acts 1999, 76th Leg., ch. 62, § 18.12(a), eff. Sept. 1, 1999; Acts 1999, 76th Leg., ch. 1272, § 1, eff. June 18, 1999; Acts 2005, 79th Leg., ch. 267, § 13, eff. Sept. 1, 2005; Acts 2011, 82nd Leg., ch. 91 (S.B. 1303), § 25.002, eff. Sept. 1, 2011.

§ 121.2015. Required Safety Rules

(a) The railroad commission shall adopt rules regarding:

(1) public education and awareness relating to gas pipeline facilities; and

(2) community liaison for responding to an emergency relating to a gas pipeline facility.

(b) The railroad commission shall require operators or their designated representatives to communicate and conduct liaison activities with fire, police, and other appropriate public emergency response officials. The liaison activities must be conducted by meetings in person except as provided by this section. An operator or the operator's representative may conduct required community liaison activities as provided by Subsection (c) only if the operator or the operator's representative has made an effort to conduct a community liaison meeting in person with the officials by one of the following methods:

(1) mailing a written request for a meeting in person to the appropriate officials by certified mail, return receipt requested;

(2) sending a request for a meeting in person to the appropriate officials by facsimile transmission; or

(3) making one or more telephone calls or e-mail message transmissions to the appropriate officials to request a meeting in person.

(c) If the operator or operator's representative cannot arrange a meeting in person after complying with Subsection (b), the operator or the operator's representative shall conduct community liaison activities by one of the following methods:

(1) holding a telephone conference with the appropriate officials; or

(2) delivering the community liaison information required to be conveyed by certified mail, return receipt requested.

Added by Acts 1999, 76th Leg., ch. 62, § 18.12(b), eff. Sept. 1, 1999. Amended by Acts 2001, 77th Leg., ch. 1233, § 70, eff. Sept. 1, 2001; Acts 2009, 81st Leg., ch. 1197, § 1, eff. Sept. 1, 2009.

§ 121.202. Municipal and County Authority

(a) A municipality or a county may not adopt or enforce an ordinance that establishes a safety standard or practice applicable to a facility that is regulated under this subchapter, another state law, or a federal law.

(b) Except as provided by Subsection (a) and by Section 121.2025, this subchapter does not reduce, limit, or impair:

(1) a power vested by law in:

(A) a county in relation to a county road; or

(B) a municipality; or

(2) the ability of a municipality to:

(A) adopt an ordinance that establishes conditions for mapping, inventorying, locating, or relocating pipelines over, under, along, or across a public street or alley or private residential area in the boundaries of the municipality; or

(B) establish conditions for mapping or taking an inventory in an area in a municipality's extraterritorial jurisdiction.

Acts 1997, 75th Leg., ch. 166, § 1, eff. Sept. 1, 1997. Amended by Acts 2005, 79th Leg., ch. 530, § 5, eff. Sept. 1, 2005; Acts 2005, 79th Leg., ch. 720, § 3, eff. Sept. 1, 2005.

§ 121.2025. Authority of Municipality to Assess Charges

(a) Except as otherwise provided by this section or Section 182.025, Tax Code, a municipality may not assess a charge for the placement, construction, maintenance, repair, replacement, operation, use, relocation, or removal of a gas pipeline facility on, along, under, or across a public road, highway, street, alley, stream, canal, or other public way.

(b) A municipality may:

(1) assess a reasonable annual charge for the placement, construction, maintenance, repair, replacement, operation, use, relocation, or removal by an owner or operator of a gas pipeline facility on, along, or across the public roads, highways, streets, alleys, streams, canals, or other public ways located within the municipality and maintained by the municipality; and

(2) recover the reasonable cost of repairing damage to a public road, highway, street, alley, stream, canal, or other public way located within the municipality and maintained by the municipality that is caused by the placement, construction, maintenance, repair, replacement, operation, use, relocation, or removal of a gas pipeline facility if the owner or operator of the facility does not repair the damage in accordance with generally applicable paving standards or other applicable standards in the municipality.

(c) A charge authorized by Subsection (b)(1) may not exceed the cost to the municipality of administering, supervising, inspecting, and otherwise regulating the location of the gas pipeline facility, including maintaining records and maps of the location of the pipeline facility.

(d) The owner or operator of a gas pipeline facility may appeal the assessment of a charge under Subsection (b)(1) to the railroad commission. The railroad commission shall hear the appeal de novo. Unless the municipality that assessed the charge establishes that the charge is authorized by this section, the railroad commission shall declare the charge invalid or reduce the charge to an amount authorized by this section. The railroad commission has exclusive jurisdiction to determine whether a charge under Subsection (b)(1) is authorized by this section. The owner or operator of the gas pipeline facility and the municipality shall share equally the costs incurred by the railroad commission in connection with the appeal.

(e) A municipality must file suit to collect a charge authorized by Subsection (b)(1) not later than the fourth anniversary of the date the charge becomes due. The running of the limitations period under this subsection is tolled on the filing of an appeal of the charge under Subsection (d) and begins running again on the date the appeal is determined.

(f) This section may not be construed to prevent a municipality from:

(1) recovering the reasonable cost of repairing damage to a municipal facility, other than a public way, caused by acts of the owner or operator of a gas pipeline facility; or

(2) requiring the owner or operator of a gas pipeline facility to relocate the pipeline facility, at

the owner's or operator's expense, to permit the construction, maintenance, modification, or alteration of a municipal facility.

(g) Notwithstanding Subsection (f)(2), the municipality shall pay the cost of relocating a gas pipeline facility if the pipeline facility is authorized by a property right that has priority over the municipality's right to use the public way for the municipal facility.

Added by Acts 2005, 79th Leg., ch. 530, § 6, eff. Sept. 1, 2005; Acts 2005, 79th Leg., ch. 720, § 4, eff. Sept. 1, 2005. Amended by Acts 2009, 81st Leg., ch. 1311, § 1, eff. June 19, 2009.

§ 121.203. Enforcement: Injunction

The attorney general, on behalf of the railroad commission, is entitled to injunctive relief to restrain a violation of a safety standard adopted under this subchapter, including an injunction that restrains the transportation of gas or the operation of a pipeline facility.

Acts 1997, 75th Leg., ch. 166, § 1, eff. Sept. 1, 1997.

§ 121.204. Civil Penalty

Each day of each violation of a safety standard adopted under this subchapter is subject to a civil penalty of not more than $25,000, except that the maximum penalty that may be assessed for any related series of violations may not exceed $500,000. The penalty is payable to the state.

Acts 1997, 75th Leg., ch. 166, § 1, eff. Sept. 1, 1997.

§ 121.205. Settlement by Attorney General

A civil penalty under Section 121.204 may be compromised by the attorney general who in determining a compromise shall consider:

(1) the appropriateness of the penalty in relation to the size of the business of the person charged;

(2) the gravity of the violation; and

(3) the good faith of the person charged in attempting to achieve compliance after notification of the violation.

Acts 1997, 75th Leg., ch. 166, § 1, eff. Sept. 1, 1997.

§ 121.206. Administrative Penalty for Violation of Pipeline Safety Standard or Rule

(a) The railroad commission may assess an administrative penalty against a person who violates Section 121.201 or a safety standard or other rule prescribed or adopted under that section.

(b) The penalty for each violation may not exceed $10,000. Each day a violation continues may be considered a separate violation for the purpose of penalty assessment.

(c) In determining the amount of the penalty, the railroad commission shall consider the guidelines adopted under Subsection (d).

(d) The railroad commission by rule shall adopt guidelines to be used in determining the amount of a penalty under this subchapter. The guidelines shall include a penalty calculation worksheet that specifies the typical penalty for certain violations, circumstances justifying enhancement of a penalty and the amount of the enhancement, and circumstances justifying a reduction in a penalty and the amount of the reduction. The guidelines shall take into account:

(1) the person's history of previous violations of Section 121.201 or a safety standard or other rule prescribed or adopted under that section, including the number of previous violations;

(2) the seriousness of the violation and of any pollution resulting from the violation;

(3) any hazard to the health or safety of the public;

(4) the degree of culpability;

(5) the demonstrated good faith of the person charged; and

(6) any other factor the commission considers relevant.

Acts 1997, 75th Leg., ch. 166, § 1, eff. Sept. 1, 1997. Amended by Acts 1999, 76th Leg., ch. 62, § 18.13(b), eff. Sept. 1, 1999; Acts 2001, 77th Leg., ch. 1233, § 71, eff. Sept. 1, 2001; Acts 2005, 79th Leg., ch. 267, § 14, eff. Sept. 1, 2005.

§ 121.207. Pipeline Safety Administrative Penalty: Assessment Procedure

(a) An administrative penalty may be assessed only after a person charged under Section 121.206 has been given an opportunity for a public hearing.

(b) If a public hearing is held, the railroad commission shall make findings of fact and shall issue a written decision as to the occurrence of the violation and the penalty amount warranted by the violation, incorporating, if appropriate, an order requiring that the penalty be paid.

(c) If appropriate, the railroad commission shall consolidate the hearings with other proceedings under Section 121.206.

(d) If a person charged under Section 121.206 fails to take advantage of the opportunity for a public hearing, an administrative penalty may be assessed by the railroad commission after it has determined:

(1) that a violation occurred; and

(2) the penalty amount warranted by the violation.

(e) After assessing an administrative penalty, the railroad commission shall issue an order requiring the penalty to be paid.

(f) Not later than the 30th day after the date an order is issued finding that a violation described under Section 121.206 occurred, the railroad commission shall inform the person found in violation of the amount of the penalty.

Acts 1997, 75th Leg., ch. 166, § 1, eff. Sept. 1, 1997.

§ 121.208. Pipeline Safety Administrative Penalty: Payment of Penalty

Not later than the 30th day after the date the railroad commission's decision or order imposing an administrative penalty becomes final as provided by Section 2001.144, Government Code, the person charged with the violation shall:

(1) pay the penalty in full; or

(2) if the person seeks judicial review of either the amount of the penalty or the fact of the violation, or both:

(A) pay the penalty to the railroad commission for placement in an escrow account; or

(B) give to the railroad commission a supersedeas bond in a form approved by the railroad commission for the amount of the penalty that is effective until all judicial review of the order or decision is final.

Acts 1997, 75th Leg., ch. 166, § 1, eff. Sept. 1, 1997.

§ 121.209. Pipeline Safety Administrative Penalty: Refund of Payment or Release of Bond

If through judicial review of a decision or order regarding an administrative penalty it is determined that a violation did not occur or that the amount of the penalty should be reduced or not assessed, the railroad commission shall, not later than the 30th day after the date of that determination:

(1) remit the appropriate amount to the person, with accrued interest if the utility paid the penalty to the railroad commission; or

(2) execute a release of the bond if the utility posted a supersedeas bond.

Acts 1997, 75th Leg., ch. 166, § 1, eff. Sept. 1, 1997.

§ 121.210. Recovery by Attorney General

An administrative penalty owed under Sections 121.206–121.208 may be recovered in a civil action brought by the attorney general at the request of the railroad commission.

Acts 1997, 75th Leg., ch. 166, § 1, eff. Sept. 1, 1997.

§ 121.211. Pipeline Safety and Regulatory Fees

(a) The railroad commission by rule may adopt a fee to be assessed annually against operators of natural gas distribution pipelines and their pipeline facilities and natural gas master metered pipelines and their pipeline facilities subject to this title .

(b) The railroad commission by rule shall establish the method by which the fee will be calculated and assessed. In adopting a fee structure, the railroad commission may consider any factors necessary to provide for the equitable allocation among operators of the costs of administering the railroad commission's pipeline safety and regulatory program under this title .

(c) The total amount of fees estimated to be collected under rules adopted by the railroad commission under this section may not exceed the amount estimated by the railroad commission to be necessary to recover the costs of administering the railroad commission's pipeline safety and regulatory program under this title , excluding costs that are fully funded by federal sources.

(d) The commission may assess each operator of a natural gas distribution system subject to this title an annual fee not to exceed one dollar for each service line reported by the system on the Distribution Annual Report, Form RSPA F7100.1–1, due on March 15 of each year. The fee is due March 15 of each year.

(e) The railroad commission may assess each operator of a natural gas master metered system subject to this title an annual fee not to exceed $100 for each master metered system. The fee is due June 30 of each year.

(f) The railroad commission may assess a late payment penalty of 10 percent of the total assessment due under Subsection (d) or (e) that is not paid within 30 days after the annual due date established by the applicable subsection.

(g) Each operator of a natural gas distribution system and each natural gas master meter operator shall recover as a surcharge to its existing rates the amounts paid to the commission under this section. Amounts collected under this subsection by an investor-owned natural gas distribution system or a cooperatively owned natural gas distribution system shall not be included in the revenue or gross receipts of the company for the purpose of calculating municipal franchise fees or any tax imposed under Subchapter B, Chapter 182, Tax Code,[1] or under Chapter 122. Those amounts are not subject to a sales and use tax imposed by Chapter 151, Tax Code, or Subtitle C, Title 3, Tax Code.[2]

(h) A fee collected under this section shall be deposited to the credit of the general revenue fund to be used for the pipeline safety and regulatory program.

Added by Acts 2003, 78th Leg., ch. 200, § 12(a), eff. Sept. 1, 2003; Acts 2003, 78th Leg., ch. 520, § 1, eff. Sept. 1, 2003. Amended by Acts 2005, 79th Leg., ch. 728, § 21.003, eff. Sept. 1, 2005; Acts 2005, 79th Leg., ch. 948, § 2, eff. Sept. 1, 2005; Acts 2009, 81st Leg., ch. 62, § 1, eff. Sept. 1, 2009; Acts 2011, 82nd Leg., 1st C.S., ch. 4 (S.B. 1), §§ 19.25, 19.26, eff. Sept. 28, 2011.

[1] V.T.C.A., Tax Code § 182.021.

[2] V.T.C.A., Tax Code § 321.001.

Section 19.29 of Acts 2011, 82nd Leg., 1st C.S., ch. 4 (S.B. 1) provides:

"On the effective date [Sept. 28, 2011] of this article:

"(1) the oil-field cleanup fund is abolished;

"(2) any money remaining in the oil-field cleanup fund is transferred to the oil and gas regulation and cleanup fund;

"(3) any claim against the oil-field cleanup fund is transferred to the oil and gas regulation and cleanup fund; and

"(4) any amount required to be deposited to the credit of the oil-field cleanup fund shall be deposited to the credit of the oil and gas regulation and cleanup fund."

SUBCHAPTER F. GAS SAFETY

§ 121.251. Railroad Commission to Investigate Use of Gas Malodorants

The railroad commission shall investigate the use of malodorants by a person, firm, or corporation in the business of:

(1) handling, storing, selling, or distributing natural or liquefied petroleum gases, including butane and other odorless gases, for private or commercial uses; or

(2) supplying these products to a public building or the general public.

Acts 1997, 75th Leg., ch. 166, § 1, eff. Sept. 1, 1997.

§ 121.252. Regulation of Use of Malodorants

(a) The railroad commission, by rule as necessary to carry out the purposes of this section, may:

(1) require a person, firm, or corporation subject to Section 121.251 to odorize the gas by using a malodorant agent that indicates the presence of gas by a distinctive odor;

(2) regulate the method of the use of malodorants; and

(3) direct and approve the use of containers and other equipment used in connection with malodorants.

(b) A required malodorant agent must be:

(1) nontoxic and noncorrosive; and

(2) not harmful to leather diaphragms in gas equipment.

Acts 1997, 75th Leg., ch. 166, § 1, eff. Sept. 1, 1997.

§ 121.253. Interstate Transportation of Gas Excluded

This subchapter does not apply to gas transported out of this state.

Acts 1997, 75th Leg., ch. 166, § 1, eff. Sept. 1, 1997.

SUBCHAPTER G. ENFORCEMENT REMEDIES

§ 121.301. Receivership

(a) On application of the railroad commission, a court having jurisdiction to appoint a receiver may appoint a receiver to control and manage, under the direction of the court, the property of a pipeline subject to this chapter if the person or corporation owning, operating, or controlling the pipeline violates this chapter or a rule of the railroad commission.

(b) The railroad commission may apply for a receivership only if the railroad commission determines that the public interest requires a receivership.

(c) The grounds for the appointment of a receiver under this section are in addition to any other ground provided by law.

Acts 1997, 75th Leg., ch. 166, § 1, eff. Sept. 1, 1997.

§ 121.302. Civil Penalty

(a) A gas utility is subject to a civil penalty if the gas utility:

(1) violates this chapter;

(2) fails to perform a duty imposed by this chapter; or

(3) fails to comply with an order of the railroad commission if the order is not stayed or suspended by a court order. A penalty under this section is payable to the state and shall be not less than $100

and not more than $1,000 for each violation or failure.

(b) Each violation and each day that the failure continues is subject to a separate penalty.

Acts 1997, 75th Leg., ch. 166, § 1, eff. Sept. 1, 1997.

§ 121.303. Penalty Recoverable by Victim of Discrimination

(a) A penalty of not less than $100 and not more than $1,000 for each violation is recoverable by any person against whom discrimination prohibited by Section 121.104 is committed.

(b) A suit to collect a penalty under this section must be brought in the name of and for the benefit of the person aggrieved.

(c) A person who recovers a penalty under this section is also entitled to reasonable attorney's fees.

(d) The penalty under this section is in addition to a penalty under Section 121.302.

Acts 1997, 75th Leg., ch. 166, § 1, eff. Sept. 1, 1997.

§ 121.304. Pollution or Public Safety Administrative Penalty

(a) The railroad commission may assess an administrative penalty against a gas utility that violates this chapter, fails to perform a duty imposed by this chapter, or fails to comply with an order of the railroad commission issued under this chapter and applicable to the gas utility if the violation:

(1) results in pollution of the air or water of this state; or

(2) poses a threat to the public safety.

(b) The penalty for each violation or failure may not exceed $10,000 a day. Each day a violation continues may be considered a separate violation for purposes of penalty assessment.

(c) In determining the amount of the penalty, the railroad commission shall consider:

(1) the gas utility's history of previous violations of this chapter;

(2) the seriousness of the violation; and

(3) any hazard to the health or safety of the public.

Acts 1997, 75th Leg., ch. 166, § 1, eff. Sept. 1, 1997.

§ 121.305. Pollution or Public Safety Administrative Penalty: Assessment Procedure

(a) An administrative penalty may be assessed under Section 121.304 only after a gas utility charged under Section 121.304 has been given an opportunity for a public hearing.

(b) If a public hearing is held, the railroad commission shall make findings of fact and shall issue a written decision as to the occurrence of the violation and the penalty amount warranted by the violation, incorporating, if appropriate, an order requiring that the penalty be paid.

(c) If appropriate, the railroad commission shall consolidate the hearings with other proceedings under Section 121.304.

(d) If a gas utility charged under Section 121.304 fails to take advantage of the opportunity for a public hearing, an administrative penalty may be assessed by the railroad commission after it has determined:

(1) that a violation occurred; and

(2) the penalty amount warranted by the violation.

(e) After assessing an administrative penalty, the railroad commission shall issue an order requiring the penalty to be paid.

(f) Not later than the 30th day after the date an order is issued finding that a violation described under Section 121.304 occurred, the railroad commission shall inform the gas utility found in violation of the amount of the penalty.

Acts 1997, 75th Leg., ch. 166, § 1, eff. Sept. 1, 1997.

§ 121.306. Pollution or Public Safety Administrative Penalty: Payment of Penalty

(a) Not later than the 30th day after the date the railroad commission's decision or order imposing an administrative penalty becomes final as provided by Section 2001.144, Government Code, the gas utility charged with the violation shall:

(1) pay the penalty in full; or

(2) if the gas utility seeks judicial review of either the amount of the penalty or the fact of the violation, or both:

(A) pay the penalty to the railroad commission for placement in an escrow account; or

(B) except as provided by Subsection (b), give to the railroad commission a supersedeas bond, in the amount of the penalty and in the form approved by the railroad commission, to stay the collection of the penalty until all judicial review of the order or decision is final.

(b) If the gas utility is appealing a second or subsequent decision or order assessing an administrative penalty against the gas utility, regardless of the finality of judicial review of any previous decision or order, the railroad commission may, but is not required to, accept a supersedeas bond.

Acts 1997, 75th Leg., ch. 166, § 1, eff. Sept. 1, 1997.

§ 121.307. Pollution or Public Safety Administrative Penalty: Appeals

(a) The district courts of Travis County have exclusive jurisdiction of the appeal of an order or decision of the railroad commission assessing an administrative penalty under Section 121.304.

(b) Subchapter G, Chapter 2001, Government Code,[1] and the substantial evidence rule apply to an appeal under this section.

Acts 1997, 75th Leg., ch. 166, § 1, eff. Sept. 1, 1997.

[1] V.T.C.A., Government Code § 2001.171 et seq.

§ 121.308. Pollution or Public Safety Administrative Penalty: Refund of Payment or Release of Bond

If through judicial review of a decision or order regarding an administrative penalty it is determined that a violation did not occur or that the amount of the penalty should be reduced or not assessed, the railroad commission shall, not later than the 30th day after the date of that determination:

(1) remit the appropriate amount to the gas utility with accrued interest if the utility paid the penalty to the railroad commission; or

(2) execute a release of the bond if the utility posted a supersedeas bond.

Acts 1997, 75th Leg., ch. 166, § 1, eff. Sept. 1, 1997.

§ 121.309. Pollution or Public Safety Administrative Penalty: Recovery

An administrative penalty owed under Sections 121.304–121.308 may be recovered in a civil action brought by the attorney general at the request of the railroad commission.

Acts 1997, 75th Leg., ch. 166, § 1, eff. Sept. 1, 1997.

§ 121.310. Criminal Penalty

(a) A person commits an offense if:

(1) the person is an owner, officer, director, agent, or employee of a person or corporation owning, operating, or controlling a pipeline of a gas utility; and

(2) the person wilfully violates this chapter or Chapter 122.

(b) An offense under this section is punishable by a fine of not less than $50 and not more than $1,000. In addition to the fine, the offense may be punishable by confinement in jail for not less than 10 days nor more than six months.

Acts 1997, 75th Leg., ch. 166, § 1, eff. Sept. 1, 1997.

SUBCHAPTER H. APPEALS

§ 121.401. Appeal to Court

(a) A gas utility or other party at interest may appeal to a court a decision of any rate, classification, rule, charge, order, or act adopted by the railroad commission by filing a petition against the railroad commission as defendant and specifying each particular reason for objection.

(b) An action under this section is tried and determined as are other civil causes in the court except as provided by Section 121.402.

Acts 1997, 75th Leg., ch. 166, § 1, eff. Sept. 1, 1997.

§ 121.402. Appeal: Burden and Standard of Proof

In a trial under this subchapter, the burden of proof is on the plaintiff, who must show by clear and satisfactory evidence that the rate, rule, order, classification, act, or charge that is the subject of the complaint is unreasonable and unjust to the plaintiff.

Acts 1997, 75th Leg., ch. 166, § 1, eff. Sept. 1, 1997.

§ 121.403. Appeal From Trial Court

An appeal from an action under Section 121.402:

(1) is at once returnable to the appellate court; and

(2) has precedence in the appellate court over each other pending cause of a different character.

Acts 1997, 75th Leg., ch. 166, § 1, eff. Sept. 1, 1997.

SUBCHAPTER I. SOUR GAS PIPELINE FACILITIES

§ 121.451. Definitions

In this subchapter:

(1) "Affected party" means the owner or occupant of real property located in the radius of exposure, as computed in accordance with a methodolo-

gy approved by the railroad commission, of the proposed route of a sour gas pipeline facility.

(2) "Construction" includes any activity conducted during the initial construction of a pipeline, including the removal of earth, vegetation, or obstructions along the proposed pipeline right-of-way. The term does not include:

(A) surveying or acquiring the right-of-way; or

(B) clearing the right-of-way with the consent of the owner.

(3) "Low-pressure gathering system" means a pipeline that operates at a working pressure of less than 50 pounds per square inch.

(4) "Sour gas pipeline facility" means a pipeline facility that contains a concentration of 100 parts per million or more of hydrogen sulfide.

Added by Acts 1999, 76th Leg., ch. 62, § 18.13(a), eff. Sept. 1, 1999.

§ 121.452. Applicability

This subchapter does not apply to:

(1) an extension of an existing sour gas pipeline facility that is in compliance with the railroad commission's rules for oil, gas, or geothermal resource operation in a hydrogen sulfide area if:

(A) the extension is not longer than five miles;

(B) the nominal pipe size is not larger than six inches in diameter; and

(C) the railroad commission is given notice of the construction of the extension not later than 24 hours before the start of construction;

(2) a new or an extension of a low-pressure gathering system; or

(3) an interstate gas pipeline facility, as defined by 49 U.S.C. Section 60101, that is used for the transportation of sour gas.

Added by Acts 1999, 76th Leg., ch. 62, § 18.13(a), eff. Sept. 1, 1999.

§ 121.453. Permit Application

(a) A person may not begin construction of a sour gas pipeline facility before the person obtains from the railroad commission a permit to construct the facility.

(b) An applicant for a permit to construct a sour gas pipeline facility must:

(1) publish notice of the application in a form determined by the railroad commission in a newspaper of general circulation in each county that contains part of the proposed route of the sour gas pipeline facility; and

(2) provide a copy of the application to the county clerk of each county that contains part of the proposed route.

Added by Acts 1999, 76th Leg., ch. 62, § 18.13(a), eff. Sept. 1, 1999.

§ 121.454. Railroad Commission Approval or Denial

(a) The railroad commission by order may approve an application for a permit to construct a sour gas pipeline facility if the railroad commission finds that the materials to be used in and method of construction and operation of the facility comply with the rules and safety standards adopted by the railroad commission.

(b) The railroad commission may issue an order under this section without holding a hearing unless an affected party files a written protest with the railroad commission not later than the 30th day after the date notice is published under Section 121.453. If an affected party files a written protest, the railroad commission shall:

(1) hold a hearing not later than the 60th day after the date the protest is filed; and

(2) issue an order:

(A) approving the permit application; or

(B) denying the application and stating the reasons for the denial.

Added by Acts 1999, 76th Leg., ch. 62, § 18.13(a), eff. Sept. 1, 1999.

SUBCHAPTER J. TESTING OF NATURAL GAS PIPING SYSTEMS IN SCHOOL FACILITIES

§ 121.5005. Applicability

This subchapter applies to a facility of a public elementary or secondary school, including a charter school, or a private elementary or secondary school, but does not apply to a home school.

Added by Acts 2001, 77th Leg., ch. 1233, § 73, eff. Sept. 1, 2001.

§ 121.501. Definition

In this subchapter, "supplier" means an individual or company that sells and delivers natural gas to a school facility. If more than one individual or company sells and delivers natural gas to a school facility, each individual or company is a supplier for purposes of this subchapter.

Added by Acts 1999, 76th Leg., ch. 62, § 18.14(a), eff. Sept. 1, 1999. Amended by Acts 2001, 77th Leg., ch. 1233, § 74, eff. Sept. 1, 2001.

§ 121.502. Duty to Pressure Test

(a) A person responsible for a school facility shall perform biennial pressure tests on the natural gas piping system in the school facility. The tests must be performed before the beginning of the school year.

(b) A person responsible for more than one school facility may perform the tests on a two-year cycle under which the person pressure tests the natural gas piping system in approximately one-half of the facilities each year.

(c) If the person responsible for one or more school facilities operates the facilities on a year-round calendar, the pressure test in each of those facilities must be conducted and reported not later than July 1 of the year in which the pressure test is performed.

(d) A natural gas piping pressure test performed under a municipal code satisfies the pressure testing requirements prescribed by this section.

Added by Acts 1999, 76th Leg., ch. 62, § 18.14(a), eff. Sept. 1, 1999. Amended by Acts 2001, 77th Leg., ch. 1233, § 74, eff. Sept. 1, 2001.

§ 121.503. Requirements of Test

(a) The person responsible for a school facility shall perform the pressure test to determine whether the natural gas piping downstream of the school facility's meter holds at least normal operating pressure over a specified period determined by the railroad commission.

(b) During the pressure test, each system supply inlet and outlet in the school facility must be closed.

(c) At the request of a person responsible for a school facility, the railroad commission shall assist the person in developing a procedure for conducting the test.

Added by Acts 1999, 76th Leg., ch. 62, § 18.14(a), eff. Sept. 1, 1999. Amended by Acts 2001, 77th Leg., ch. 1233, § 74, eff. Sept. 1, 2001.

§ 121.504. Notice of Test

(a) A person responsible for a school facility shall provide written notice to the school's supplier specifying the date and result of each pressure test or other inspection.

(b) The supplier shall maintain a copy of the notice until at least the first anniversary of the date on which the supplier received the notice.

Added by Acts 1999, 76th Leg., ch. 62, § 18.14(a), eff. Sept. 1, 1999. Amended by Acts 2001, 77th Leg., ch. 1233, § 74, eff. Sept. 1, 2001.

§ 121.505. Termination of Service

(a) A supplier shall terminate service to a school facility if:

(1) the supplier receives official notification from the firm or individual conducting the test of a hazardous natural gas leakage in the facility piping system; or

(2) a test or other inspection at the facility is not performed as required by this subchapter.

(b) A supplier is not liable for any damages that result from a failure to terminate service as required by Subsection (a)(2) for a facility other than a school district facility.

Added by Acts 1999, 76th Leg., ch. 62, § 18.14(a), eff. Sept. 1, 1999. Amended by Acts 2001, 77th Leg., ch. 1233, § 74, eff. Sept. 1, 2001.

§ 121.506. Report of Leakage

An identified natural gas leakage in a school district facility must be reported to the board of trustees of the district in which the facility is located. An identified natural gas leakage in another school facility must be reported to the person responsible for the school facility.

Added by Acts 1999, 76th Leg., ch. 62, § 18.14(a), eff. Sept. 1, 1999. Amended by Acts 2001, 77th Leg., ch. 1233, § 74, eff. Sept. 1, 2001.

§ 121.507. Enforcement

The railroad commission shall enforce this subchapter.

Added by Acts 1999, 76th Leg., ch. 62, § 18.14(a), eff. Sept. 1, 1999.

CHAPTER 122. GAS UTILITY PIPELINE TAX

SUBCHAPTER A. DEFINITIONS

Section

122.001. Definitions.

SUBCHAPTER B. TAX IMPOSED

122.051. Tax Imposed; Rate.
122.052. Deduction of Certain Costs.

SUBCHAPTER C. PAYMENTS, REPORTS, AND RECORDS

Section
122.101. Tax Payment.
122.102. Report.
122.103. Payment and Report Deadline.
122.104. Records.

SUBCHAPTER D. ADMINISTRATION

122.151. Administration by Railroad Commission.
122.152. Examination of Records and Person Doing Business in This State.

SUBCHAPTER E. PENALTIES AND INTEREST

122.201. Penalty for Failure to Report Tax.
122.202. Penalty for Failure to Pay Tax.
122.203. Penalty for Failure to Report and Pay Tax.
122.204. Minimum Penalty.
122.205. Interest.

SUBCHAPTER A. DEFINITIONS

§ 122.001. Definitions

In this chapter:

(1) "Gas utility" has the meaning assigned by Section 121.001(a)(2) and includes a person without regard to whether the person acquired a part of the right-of-way for the pipeline by eminent domain.

(2) "Gross income" includes all gross receipts the gas utility received from activities described by Section 121.001(a)(2) that are performed in this state, other than an activity excluded by Chapter 121 from the activities that make a person a gas utility for purposes of that chapter, and excludes the amount of the deduction allowed by Section 122.052.

Acts 1997, 75th Leg., ch. 166, § 1, eff. Sept. 1, 1997.

SUBCHAPTER B. TAX IMPOSED

§ 122.051. Tax Imposed; Rate

(a) A tax is imposed on each gas utility.

(b) The gas utility tax is imposed at the rate of one-half of one percent of the gross income of the gas utility.

Acts 1997, 75th Leg., ch. 166, § 1, eff. Sept. 1, 1997.

§ 122.052. Deduction of Certain Costs

A gas utility is entitled to deduct from the utility's gross receipts the amount of the cost paid to another person by the utility for purchasing, treating, or storing natural gas or for gathering or transporting natural gas to the utility's facilities.

Acts 1997, 75th Leg., ch. 166, § 1, eff. Sept. 1, 1997.

SUBCHAPTER C. PAYMENTS, REPORTS, AND RECORDS

§ 122.101. Tax Payment

(a) A gas utility on whom a tax is imposed by this chapter during a calendar quarter shall pay the tax to the railroad commission.

(b) A gas utility shall make the tax payment payable to the comptroller.

Acts 1997, 75th Leg., ch. 166, § 1, eff. Sept. 1, 1997.

§ 122.102. Report

(a) A gas utility on whom a tax is imposed by this chapter during a calendar quarter shall include with the tax payment a report to the railroad commission that includes a statement of:

(1) all activity subject to the tax during the period covered by the report; and

(2) the gross income from that activity.

(b) The president, secretary, or general manager of a gas utility that is a corporation or an owner of a gas utility that is not a corporation must verify the truth and accuracy of the report.

Acts 1997, 75th Leg., ch. 166, § 1, eff. Sept. 1, 1997.

§ 122.103. Payment and Report Deadline

A tax payment and report under this chapter for a calendar quarter are due on or before the 20th day of the second month of the succeeding quarter.

Acts 1997, 75th Leg., ch. 166, § 1, eff. Sept. 1, 1997.

§ 122.104. Records

A person on whom a tax is imposed by this chapter shall maintain until the fourth anniversary of the date the tax report and payment for a calendar quarter are due records sufficient to:

(1) document the person's tax report; and

(2) establish the amount of the tax imposed.

Acts 1997, 75th Leg., ch. 166, § 1, eff. Sept. 1, 1997.

SUBCHAPTER D. ADMINISTRATION

§ 122.151. Administration by Railroad Commission

The railroad commission:

(1) shall administer and collect the taxes imposed by this chapter; and

(2) may adopt rules necessary to administer this chapter and to collect and enforce the taxes.

Acts 1997, 75th Leg., ch. 166, § 1, eff. Sept. 1, 1997.

§ 122.152. Examination of Records and Person Doing Business in This State

To enforce this chapter, the railroad commission may examine:

(1) a book, record, or paper of a person permitted to do business in this state, including an agent of the person, at an office of the person or agent in the United States; and

(2) an officer or employee of a person described by Subdivision (1) under oath.

Acts 1997, 75th Leg., ch. 166, § 1, eff. Sept. 1, 1997.

SUBCHAPTER E. PENALTIES AND INTEREST

§ 122.201. Penalty for Failure to Report Tax

A person who is required to report a tax imposed by this chapter and fails to report as required by Sections 122.102 and 122.103 shall pay:

(1) a penalty of five percent of the amount of the tax due with the report; and

(2) if the report is not made before the 31st day after the date the report is initially required to be made, an additional penalty of five percent of the amount of the tax due with the report.

Acts 1997, 75th Leg., ch. 166, § 1, eff. Sept. 1, 1997.

§ 122.202. Penalty for Failure to Pay Tax

A person who is required to pay a tax imposed by this chapter and fails to pay the tax as required by Sections 122.101 and 122.103 shall pay:

(1) a penalty of five percent of the amount of the tax due and unpaid; and

(2) if the tax is not paid before the 31st day after the date the tax payment is initially required to be made, an additional penalty of five percent of the amount of the tax due and unpaid.

Acts 1997, 75th Leg., ch. 166, § 1, eff. Sept. 1, 1997.

§ 122.203. Penalty for Failure to Report and Pay Tax

If a person fails to make the report and to pay the tax for a reporting period, only the penalty and additional penalty under Section 122.201, as applicable, for failure to make the report is imposed.

Acts 1997, 75th Leg., ch. 166, § 1, eff. Sept. 1, 1997.

§ 122.204. Minimum Penalty

If the amount of a penalty or additional penalty computed as provided by this subchapter is less than \$5, the amount of the penalty or additional penalty is \$5.

Acts 1997, 75th Leg., ch. 166, § 1, eff. Sept. 1, 1997.

§ 122.205. Interest

A tax imposed by this chapter that becomes delinquent draws interest at the rate of 12 percent a year beginning on the 60th day after the date the tax becomes delinquent and continues to draw interest until the date the tax is paid.

Acts 1997, 75th Leg., ch. 166, § 1, eff. Sept. 1, 1997.

CHAPTER 123. USE OF NATURAL GAS FOR AGRICULTURAL PURPOSES

SUBCHAPTER A. NATURAL GAS SUPPLY FOR AGRICULTURAL PURPOSES

Section
123.001. Natural Gas Supply for Agricultural Purposes.
123.002. Exception.

SUBCHAPTER B. AGRICULTURE GAS USERS ACT

123.021. Short Title.
123.022. Definitions.
123.023. Contract for Natural Gas.
123.024. Exception.

SUBCHAPTER A. NATURAL GAS SUPPLY FOR AGRICULTURAL PURPOSES

§ 123.001. Natural Gas Supply for Agricultural Purposes

A person, firm, corporation, partnership, association, or cooperative who sells natural gas for irrigation may not reduce the supply of natural gas for an agricultural purpose, including irrigation pumping or crop drying, if that person or entity:

(1) sells and distributes natural gas in a municipality; or

(2) delivers gas to the boundary of a municipality for resale in the municipality.

Acts 1997, 75th Leg., ch. 166, § 1, eff. Sept. 1, 1997.

§ 123.002. Exception

This subchapter does not apply to the extent that the supply of natural gas is required to maintain natural gas service for:

(1) use by residential users or hospitals; or

(2) an analogous use that is vital to public health and safety.

Acts 1997, 75th Leg., ch. 166, § 1, eff. Sept. 1, 1997.

SUBCHAPTER B. AGRICULTURE GAS USERS ACT

§ 123.021. Short Title

This subchapter may be cited as the Agriculture Gas Users Act.

Acts 1997, 75th Leg., ch. 166, § 1, eff. Sept. 1, 1997.

§ 123.022. Definitions

In this subchapter:

(1) "Agriculture energy user" means a person who purchases or uses natural gas for fuel for an irrigation well.

(2) "Corporation" means a domestic or foreign corporation or association, and each lessee, assignee, trustee, receiver, or other successor in interest of the corporation or association, that has any of the powers or privileges of a corporation not possessed by an individual or partnership.

(3) "Person" includes an individual, a partnership of two or more persons having a joint or common interest, a mutual or cooperative association, and a corporation.

(4) "Supplier" means a person who furnishes natural gas to an agriculture energy user.

Acts 1997, 75th Leg., ch. 166, § 1, eff. Sept. 1, 1997.

§ 123.023. Contract for Natural Gas

(a) A supplier and an agriculture energy user may by contract establish a price and other terms of service for the furnishing of natural gas.

(b) A contract under this section must be negotiated in good faith and the result of arm's-length bargaining between the parties.

(c) Each party shall provide information and maintain records as reasonably necessary for the contract.

(d) A price charged to an agriculture energy user under the contract may not exceed the price charged to a majority of the supplier's commercial users or other similar large-volume users.

Acts 1997, 75th Leg., ch. 166, § 1, eff. Sept. 1, 1997.

§ 123.024. Exception

This subchapter does not apply to a transaction between an agriculture energy user and a supplier who does not deliver gas to a municipality unless:

(1) the parties agree the subchapter applies to the transaction; and

(2) the contract states the subchapter applies to the transaction.

Acts 1997, 75th Leg., ch. 166, § 1, eff. Sept. 1, 1997.

CHAPTER 124. SUBMETERING TO MOBILE HOME PARKS AND APARTMENT HOUSES

Section

124.001. Definitions.
124.002. Submetering.

§ 124.001. Definitions

In this chapter:

(1) "Apartment house" means one or more buildings containing more than five dwelling units each of which is rented primarily for nontransient use with rent paid at intervals of one week or longer. The term includes a rented or owner-occupied residential condominium.

(2) "Dwelling unit" means:

(A) one or more rooms that are suitable for occupancy as a residence and that contain kitchen and bathroom facilities; or

(B) a mobile home in a mobile home park.

Acts 1997, 75th Leg., ch. 166, § 1, eff. Sept. 1, 1997.

§ 124.002. Submetering

(a) The railroad commission shall adopt rules under which an owner, operator, or manager of a mobile home park or apartment house may purchase natural gas through a master meter for delivery to a dwelling unit in the mobile home park or apartment house using individual submeters to allocate fairly the cost of the gas consumption of each dwelling unit.

(b) In addition to other appropriate safeguards for a resident of a mobile home park or apartment house, the rules must provide that the owner, operator, or manager of the mobile home park or apartment house:

(1) may not deliver natural gas for sale or resale for profit; and

(2) shall maintain adequate records relating to that submetering and make those records available for inspection by the resident during reasonable business hours.

Acts 1997, 75th Leg., ch. 166, § 1, eff. Sept. 1, 1997.

TITLE 4. DELIVERY OF UTILITY SERVICES

SUBTITLE A. UTILITY CORPORATIONS AND OTHER PROVIDERS

CHAPTER 161. ELECTRIC COOPERATIVE CORPORATIONS

SUBCHAPTER A. GENERAL PROVISIONS

Section
161.001. Short Title.
161.002. Definitions.
161.003. Construction of Chapter.
161.004. Certain Corporate Names Prohibited.
161.005. Chapter Complete and Controlling.

SUBCHAPTER B. CREATION AND OPERATION OF ELECTRIC COOPERATIVES

161.051. Incorporators.
161.052. Duration of Corporation.
161.053. Name of Electric Cooperative.
161.054. Articles of Incorporation.
161.055. Filing and Recording of Articles of Incorporation.
161.056. Revival of Articles of Incorporation.
161.057. Organizational Meeting.
161.058. Perfecting Defectively Organized Corporation.
161.059. Nonprofit Operation.
161.060. Members Not Liable for Debts of Electric Cooperative.
161.061. License Fee.
161.062. Exemption From Excise Taxes.
161.063. Exemption From Application of Securities Act.
161.064. Bylaws.
161.065. Membership.
161.066. Certificate of Membership.
161.067. Meetings of Members.
161.068. Notice of Members' Meeting.
161.069. Quorum of Members.
161.070. Voting by Members.
161.071. Board of Directors.
161.072. Election of Directors; Vacancies.
161.073. Compensation of Directors.
161.074. Quorum of Directors.
161.075. Board Meetings.
161.076. Officers, Agents, and Employees.
161.077. Executive Committee.
161.078. Indemnification.
161.079. Applicability of Chapter to Corporations Organized Under Other Law.

SUBCHAPTER C. POWERS OF ELECTRIC COOPERATIVE

Section
161.121. General Powers.
161.122. Provision of Rural Electrification.
161.123. Powers Relating to Provision of Electric Energy.
161.124. Provision of Electric Energy to Certain Nonmember Entities.
161.125. Eminent Domain.

SUBCHAPTER D. AMENDMENT OF ARTICLES OF INCORPORATION

161.151. Amendment of Articles of Incorporation.
161.152. Articles of Amendment.

SUBCHAPTER E. CONSOLIDATION OF ELECTRIC COOPERATIVES

161.201. Consolidation.
161.202. Articles of Consolidation.

SUBCHAPTER F. DISSOLUTION

161.251. Dissolution.
161.252. Existence Following Dissolution.
161.253. Distribution of Net Assets on Dissolution.
161.254. Dissolution of Defectively Incorporated Electric Cooperative.

SUBCHAPTER A. GENERAL PROVISIONS

§ 161.001. Short Title

This chapter may be cited as the Electric Cooperative Corporation Act.

Acts 1997, 75th Leg., ch. 166, § 1, eff. Sept. 1, 1997.

§ 161.002. Definitions

In this chapter:

(1) "Acquire" means and includes construct, acquire by purchase, lease, devise, or gift, or other mode of acquisition.

(2) "Board" means the board of directors of an electric cooperative.

(3) "Central station service" means electric service provided by a municipally owned electric system or by an electric corporation described by Subchapter A, Chapter 181.[1]

(4) "Electric cooperative" means a corporation that is organized under this chapter or that becomes subject to this chapter as provided by this chapter.

(5) "Member" means:

(A) an incorporator of an electric cooperative; or

(B) a person admitted to membership in the electric cooperative as provided by Section 161.065.

(6) "Obligation" includes a bond, note, debenture, interim certificate or receipt, or other evidence of indebtedness issued by an electric cooperative.

(7) "Rural area" means an area, including both farm and nonfarm population of the area, that is not located in:

(A) a municipality having a population greater than 1,500; or

(B) an unincorporated city, town, village, or borough having a population greater than 1,500.

Acts 1997, 75th Leg., ch. 166, § 1, eff. Sept. 1, 1997.

[1] V.T.C.A., Utilities Code § 181.001.

§ 161.003. Construction of Chapter

This chapter shall be liberally construed. The enumeration of a purpose, power, method, or thing does not exclude similar purposes, powers, methods, or things.

Acts 1997, 75th Leg., ch. 166, § 1, eff. Sept. 1, 1997.

§ 161.004. Certain Corporate Names Prohibited

A corporation organized under the laws of this state or authorized to do business in this state may not use the words "electric cooperative" in the corporation's name unless the corporation is organized under this chapter.

Acts 1997, 75th Leg., ch. 166, § 1, eff. Sept. 1, 1997.

§ 161.005. Chapter Complete and Controlling

This chapter is complete in itself and is controlling.

Acts 1997, 75th Leg., ch. 166, § 1, eff. Sept. 1, 1997.

SUBCHAPTER B. CREATION AND OPERATION OF ELECTRIC COOPERATIVES

§ 161.051. Incorporators

(a) Three or more individuals may act as incorporators of an electric cooperative by executing articles of incorporation as provided by this chapter.

(b) An incorporator must:

(1) be at least 21 years of age; and

(2) reside in this state.

Acts 1997, 75th Leg., ch. 166, § 1, eff. Sept. 1, 1997.

§ 161.052. Duration of Corporation

An electric cooperative may be created as a perpetual corporation.

Acts 1997, 75th Leg., ch. 166, § 1, eff. Sept. 1, 1997.

§ 161.053. Name of Electric Cooperative

The name of an electric cooperative must:

(1) include the words "Electric Cooperative";

(2) include the term "Corporation," "Incorporated," "Inc.," "Association," or "Company"; and

(3) be distinct from the name of any other corporation organized under the laws of this state.

Acts 1997, 75th Leg., ch. 166, § 1, eff. Sept. 1, 1997.

§ 161.054. Articles of Incorporation

(a) The articles of incorporation of an electric cooperative must state:

(1) the name of the cooperative;

(2) the purpose for which the cooperative is formed;

(3) the name and address of each incorporator;

(4) the number of directors;

(5) the address of the cooperative's principal office and the name and address of its agent on whom process may be served;

(6) the duration of the cooperative;

(7) the terms under which a person is admitted to membership and retains membership in the cooperative, unless the articles expressly state that the determination of membership matters is reserved to the directors by the bylaws; and

(8) any provisions that the incorporators include for the regulation of the business and the conduct of the affairs of the cooperative.

(b) The articles of incorporation do not need to state any of the corporate powers enumerated in this chapter.

Acts 1997, 75th Leg., ch. 166, § 1, eff. Sept. 1, 1997.

§ 161.055. Filing and Recording of Articles of Incorporation

(a) The secretary of state shall receive articles of incorporation of an electric cooperative if the incorporators of the cooperative:

(1) apply for filing the articles;

(2) furnish satisfactory evidence of compliance with this chapter to the secretary of state; and

(3) pay a fee of $10.

(b) The secretary of state shall:

(1) file the articles of incorporation in the secretary's office;

(2) record the articles at length in a book to be kept for that purpose;

(3) retain the original articles of incorporation on file in the secretary's office; and

(4) issue a certificate showing the recording of the articles of incorporation and the electric cooperative's authority to do business under the articles.

(c) A copy of the articles of incorporation or of the record of the articles, certified under the state seal, is evidence of the creation of the electric cooperative.

(d) The existence of the electric cooperative dates from the filing of the articles in the office of the secretary of state. The certificate of the secretary of state is evidence of that filing.

Acts 1997, 75th Leg., ch. 166, § 1, eff. Sept. 1, 1997.

§ 161.056. Revival of Articles of Incorporation

(a) If the articles of incorporation of an electric cooperative expire by limitation, the cooperative, with the consent of a majority of its members, may revive the articles by filing:

(1) new articles of incorporation under this chapter; and

(2) a certified copy of the expired original articles.

(b) An electric cooperative that revives its articles of incorporation has all the privileges, immunities, and rights of property exercised and held by the cooperative at the time the original articles expired.

(c) New articles of incorporation filed under this section must recite the privileges, immunities, and rights of property exercised and held by the cooperative at the time the original articles expired.

Acts 1997, 75th Leg., ch. 166, § 1, eff. Sept. 1, 1997.

§ 161.057. Organizational Meeting

(a) After the certificate of incorporation is issued, the incorporators of an electric cooperative shall meet to adopt bylaws, elect officers, and transact other business that properly comes before the meeting.

(b) A majority of the incorporators shall call the organizational meeting.

(c) The incorporators calling the organizational meeting shall give at least three days' notice of the meeting by mail to each incorporator. The notice must state the time and place of the meeting. The notice may be waived in writing.

Acts 1997, 75th Leg., ch. 166, § 1, eff. Sept. 1, 1997.

§ 161.058. Perfecting Defectively Organized Corporation

(a) An electric cooperative that files defective articles of incorporation or fails to take an action necessary to perfect its corporate organization may:

(1) file corrected articles of incorporation or amend the original articles; and

(2) take any action necessary to correct the defect.

(b) An action taken under this section is valid and binding on any person concerned.

Acts 1997, 75th Leg., ch. 166, § 1, eff. Sept. 1, 1997.

§ 161.059. Nonprofit Operation

(a) An electric cooperative shall operate without profit to its members.

(b) The rates, fees, rents, and other charges for electric energy and other facilities, supplies, equipment, or services furnished by the cooperative must be sufficient at all times to:

(1) pay all operating and maintenance expenses necessary or desirable for the prudent conduct of its business;

(2) pay the principal of and interest on the obligations issued or assumed by the cooperative in performing the purpose for which the cooperative was organized; and

(3) create reserves.

(c) The cooperative shall devote its revenues:

(1) first to the payment of operating and maintenance expenses and the principal and interest on outstanding obligations; and

(2) then to the reserves prescribed by the board for improvement, new construction, depreciation, and contingencies.

(d) The cooperative shall periodically return revenues not required for the purposes prescribed by Subsection (c) to the members in proportion to the amount of business done with each member during the applicable period. The cooperative may return revenues:

(1) in cash, by abatement of current charges for electric energy, or in another manner determined by the board; or

(2) through a general rate reduction to members.

Acts 1997, 75th Leg., ch. 166, § 1, eff. Sept. 1, 1997.

§ 161.060. Members Not Liable for Debts of Electric Cooperative

A member is not liable for a debt of an electric cooperative except for:

(1) a debt contracted between the member and the cooperative; or

(2) an amount not to exceed the unpaid amount of the member's membership fee.

Acts 1997, 75th Leg., ch. 166, § 1, eff. Sept. 1, 1997.

§ 161.061. License Fee

Not later than May 1 of each year, each electric cooperative shall pay to the secretary of state a license fee of $10.

Acts 1997, 75th Leg., ch. 166, § 1, eff. Sept. 1, 1997.

§ 161.062. Exemption From Excise Taxes

An electric cooperative is exempt from all excise taxes but is exempt from the franchise tax imposed by Chapter 171, Tax Code, only if the cooperative is exempted by that chapter.

Acts 1997, 75th Leg., ch. 166, § 1, eff. Sept. 1, 1997.

§ 161.063. Exemption From Application of Securities Act

The Securities Act (Article 581–1 et seq., Vernon's Texas Civil Statutes) does not apply to:

(1) an obligation issued to secure a debt of an electric cooperative to the United States; or

(2) the issuance of a membership certificate by an electric cooperative.

Acts 1997, 75th Leg., ch. 166, § 1, eff. Sept. 1, 1997.

§ 161.064. Bylaws

(a) The board may adopt, amend, or repeal the bylaws of the cooperative.

(b) The bylaws may contain any provision for the regulation and management of the affairs of the electric cooperative that is consistent with the articles of incorporation.

Acts 1997, 75th Leg., ch. 166, § 1, eff. Sept. 1, 1997.

§ 161.065. Membership

(a) A person is eligible to become a member of an electric cooperative if the person has a dwelling, structure, apparatus, or point of delivery at which the person does not receive central station service from another source and that is located in an area in which the cooperative is authorized to provide electric energy, and the person:

(1) uses or agrees to use electric energy or the facilities, supplies, equipment, or services furnished by the cooperative at the dwelling, structure, apparatus, or point of delivery; or

(2) is an incorporator of the cooperative.

(b) An electric cooperative may become a member of another electric cooperative and may fully use the facilities and services of that cooperative.

(c) Membership in an electric cooperative is not transferable.

Acts 1997, 75th Leg., ch. 166, § 1, eff. Sept. 1, 1997.

§ 161.066. Certificate of Membership

(a) An electric cooperative shall issue a certificate of membership to a member who pays the member's membership fee in full.

(b) A certificate of membership is not transferable.

(c) A certificate of membership shall be surrendered to the cooperative on the resignation, expulsion, or death of the member.

Acts 1997, 75th Leg., ch. 166, § 1, eff. Sept. 1, 1997.

§ 161.067. Meetings of Members

(a) An electric cooperative may hold a meeting of its members at a place provided in the bylaws. If the bylaws do not provide for a place for a meeting, the cooperative shall hold the meeting in the principal office of the cooperative in this state.

(b) An electric cooperative shall hold an annual meeting of its members at the time provided in the bylaws. Failure to hold the annual meeting at the designated time does not result in forfeiture or dissolution of the cooperative.

(c) A special meeting of the members may be called by:

(1) the president;

(2) the board;

(3) a majority of the directors;

(4) the members by a petition signed by at least 10 percent of the members; or

(5) an officer or other person as provided by the articles of incorporation or bylaws.

Acts 1997, 75th Leg., ch. 166, § 1, eff. Sept. 1, 1997.

§ 161.068. Notice of Members' Meeting

(a) Written notice of each meeting of the members shall be delivered to each member of record, either personally or by mail, not earlier than the 30th day or later than the 10th day before the date of the meeting. The notice must be delivered by or at the direction of the president, the secretary, or the officers or other persons calling the meeting.

(b) The notice must state the time and place of the meeting and, in the case of a special meeting, each purpose for which the meeting is called.

(c) A member may waive notice of meetings in writing.

(d) A notice that is mailed is considered to be delivered when the notice is deposited in the United States mail in a sealed envelope with postage prepaid addressed to the member at the member's address as it appears on the records of the electric cooperative.

Acts 1997, 75th Leg., ch. 166, § 1, eff. Sept. 1, 1997.

§ 161.069. Quorum of Members

Unless otherwise provided by the articles of incorporation, a quorum for the transaction of business at a meeting of the members of an electric cooperative is a majority of the members present in person or represented by proxy. If voting by mail is provided for in the bylaws, members voting by mail are counted as present for purposes of determining whether a quorum is present.

Acts 1997, 75th Leg., ch. 166, § 1, eff. Sept. 1, 1997.

§ 161.070. Voting by Members

Each member present at a meeting of the members is entitled to one vote on each matter submitted to a vote at the meeting. The bylaws may provide for voting by proxy or by mail.

Acts 1997, 75th Leg., ch. 166, § 1, eff. Sept. 1, 1997.

§ 161.071. Board of Directors

(a) The business and affairs of an electric cooperative shall be managed by a board of directors. The board consists of at least three directors. Each director must be a member of the cooperative. The bylaws may prescribe additional qualifications for directors.

(b) The board may exercise any power of an electric cooperative not conferred on the members by this chapter or by the cooperative's articles of incorporation or bylaws.

Acts 1997, 75th Leg., ch. 166, § 1, eff. Sept. 1, 1997.

§ 161.072. Election of Directors; Vacancies

(a) The incorporators of an electric cooperative named in the articles of incorporation shall serve as directors until the first annual meeting of the members, and until their successors are elected and qualify. Subsequently, the directors shall be elected by the members at each annual meeting or as otherwise provided by the bylaws.

(b) A vacancy on the board shall be filled as provided by the bylaws. A person selected to fill a vacancy serves until the next regular election of directors.

Acts 1997, 75th Leg., ch. 166, § 1, eff. Sept. 1, 1997.

§ 161.073. Compensation of Directors

A director of an electric cooperative is entitled to the compensation and reimbursement for expenses actually and necessarily incurred by the director as provided by the bylaws.

Acts 1997, 75th Leg., ch. 166, § 1, eff. Sept. 1, 1997.

§ 161.074. Quorum of Directors

(a) A majority of the directors is a quorum unless the articles of incorporation or the bylaws provide that a greater number of the directors is a quorum.

(b) A majority of the directors present at a meeting at which a quorum is present may exercise the board's authority unless the articles of incorporation or the bylaws require a greater number of directors to exercise the board's authority.

Acts 1997, 75th Leg., ch. 166, § 1, eff. Sept. 1, 1997.

§ 161.075. Board Meetings

(a) The board shall hold a regular or special board meeting at the place and on the notice prescribed by the bylaws.

(b) The attendance of a director at a board meeting constitutes a waiver of notice of the meeting unless the director attends the meeting for the express purpose of objecting to the transaction of business at the meeting because the meeting is not lawfully called or convened.

(c) A notice or waiver of notice of a board meeting is not required to specify the business to be transacted at the meeting or the purpose of the meeting.

Acts 1997, 75th Leg., ch. 166, § 1, eff. Sept. 1, 1997.

§ 161.076. Officers, Agents, and Employees

(a) The board shall elect from the board's membership a president, a vice president, a secretary, and a treasurer. The terms of office, powers, duties, and compensation of the officers elected under this subsection shall be provided for by the bylaws.

(b) The same person may hold the offices of secretary and of treasurer.

(c) The board may appoint other officers, agents, and employees as the board considers necessary and shall prescribe the powers, duties, and compensation of those persons.

(d) The board may remove an officer, agent, or employee elected or appointed by the board if the board determines that the removal will serve the best interests of the cooperative.

Acts 1997, 75th Leg., ch. 166, § 1, eff. Sept. 1, 1997.

§ 161.077. Executive Committee

(a) The bylaws of an electric cooperative may authorize the board to elect an executive committee from the board's membership.

(b) The board may delegate to the executive committee the management of the current and ordinary business of the cooperative and other duties as prescribed by the bylaws.

(c) The designation of an executive committee and the delegation of authority to the committee does not relieve the board or any director of a responsibility imposed on the board or the director by this chapter.

Acts 1997, 75th Leg., ch. 166, § 1, eff. Sept. 1, 1997.

§ 161.078. Indemnification

An electric cooperative may indemnify and provide indemnity insurance in the same manner and to the same extent as a nonprofit corporation under Article 2.22A, Texas Non-Profit Corporation Act (Article 1396–2.22A, Vernon's Texas Civil Statutes).

Acts 1997, 75th Leg., ch. 166, § 1, eff. Sept. 1, 1997.

§ 161.079. Applicability of Chapter to Corporations Organized Under Other Law

A cooperative or nonprofit corporation or association organized under any other law of this state for the purpose of engaging in rural electrification may, by a majority vote of the members present in person or represented by proxy at a meeting called for that purpose, amend its articles of incorporation to comply with this chapter.

Acts 1997, 75th Leg., ch. 166, § 1, eff. Sept. 1, 1997.

SUBCHAPTER C. POWERS OF ELECTRIC COOPERATIVE

§ 161.121. General Powers

An electric cooperative may:

(1) sue and be sued in its corporate name;

(2) adopt and alter a corporate seal and use the seal or a facsimile of the seal as required by law;

(3) acquire, own, hold, maintain, exchange, or use property or an interest in property, including plants, buildings, works, machinery, supplies, equipment, apparatus, and transmission and distribution lines or systems that are necessary, convenient, or useful;

(4) dispose of, mortgage, or lease as lessor any of its property or assets;

(5) borrow money and otherwise contract indebtedness, issue obligations for its indebtedness, and secure the payment of indebtedness by mortgage, pledge, or deed of trust on any or all of its property or revenue;

(6) accept gifts or grants of money, services, or property;

(7) make any contracts necessary or convenient for the exercise of the powers granted by this chapter;

(8) conduct its business and have offices inside or outside this state;

(9) adopt and amend bylaws not inconsistent with the articles of incorporation for the administration and regulation of the affairs of the cooperative; and

(10) perform any other acts for the cooperative or its members or for another electric cooperative or its members, and exercise any other power, that may be necessary, convenient, or appropriate to accomplish the purpose for which the cooperative is organized, including other or additional purposes that benefit members and nonmembers, either directly or through affiliates, described in Section A, Article 2.01, Texas Non-Profit Corporation Act (Article 1396–2.01, Vernon's Texas Civil Statutes).

Acts 1997, 75th Leg., ch. 166, § 1, eff. Sept. 1, 1997. Amended by Acts 1999, 76th Leg., ch. 62, § 18.15(a), eff. Sept. 1, 1999.

§ 161.122. Provision of Rural Electrification

An electric cooperative may engage in rural electrification by:

(1) furnishing electric energy to any person for delivery to a dwelling, structure, apparatus, or point of delivery that is:

(A) located in a rural area; and

(B) not receiving central station service, even if the person is receiving central station service at other points of delivery;

(2) furnishing electric energy to a person desiring that service in a municipality or unincorporated city or town, rural or nonrural, served by the cooperative and in which central station service was not available at the time the cooperative began furnishing electric energy to the residents of the municipality or unincorporated city or town;

(3) assisting in the wiring of the premises of persons in rural areas or the acquisition, supply, or installation of electrical or plumbing equipment in those premises; or

(4) furnishing electric energy, wiring facilities, or electrical or plumbing equipment or service to another electric cooperative or to the members of another electric cooperative.

Acts 1997, 75th Leg., ch. 166, § 1, eff. Sept. 1, 1997.

§ 161.123. Powers Relating to Provision of Electric Energy

An electric cooperative may:

(1) generate, acquire, and accumulate electric energy and transmit, distribute, sell, furnish, and dispose of that electric energy to its members only;

(2) assist its members only to wire their premises and install in those premises electrical and plumbing fixtures, machinery, supplies, apparatus, and equipment of any kind, and in connection with those activities:

(A) acquire, lease, sell, distribute, install, and repair electrical and plumbing fixtures, machinery, supplies, apparatus, and equipment of any kind; and

(B) receive, acquire, endorse, pledge, and dispose of notes, bonds, and other evidences of indebtedness;

(3) furnish to other electric cooperatives or their members electric energy, wiring facilities, electrical and plumbing equipment, and services that are convenient or useful; and

(4) establish, regulate, and collect rates, fees, rents, or other charges for electric energy or other facilities, supplies, equipment, or services furnished by the electric cooperative.

Acts 1997, 75th Leg., ch. 166, § 1, eff. Sept. 1, 1997.

§ 161.124. Provision of Electric Energy to Certain Nonmember Entities

An electric cooperative may generate, acquire, and accumulate electric energy and transmit, distribute, sell, furnish, and dispose of that electric energy to any of the following that is engaged in the generation, transmission, or distribution of electricity:

(1) a corporation, association, or firm;

(2) the United States;

(3) this state or a political subdivision of this state; or

(4) a municipal power agency or political subdivision of this state that is a co-owner with the electric cooperative of an electric generation facility.

Acts 1997, 75th Leg., ch. 166, § 1, eff. Sept. 1, 1997.

§ 161.125. Eminent Domain

An electric cooperative may exercise the power of eminent domain in the manner provided by state law for acquiring private property for public use. The power does not apply to state property or property of a political subdivision in this state.

Acts 1997, 75th Leg., ch. 166, § 1, eff. Sept. 1, 1997.

SUBCHAPTER D. AMENDMENT OF ARTICLES OF INCORPORATION

§ 161.151. Amendment of Articles of Incorporation

(a) An electric cooperative may amend its articles of incorporation by a majority vote of the members of the cooperative present in person or represented by proxy at a regular meeting or at a special meeting of its members called for that purpose as provided by the bylaws.

(b) Notice of the meeting to members must state the general nature of each proposed amendment to be presented and voted on at the meeting. Valid action may not be taken at the meeting unless at least five percent of the members of the electric cooperative either attend the meeting in person or are represented at the meeting by proxy.

(c) The power to amend the articles of incorporation includes the power to accomplish any desired change in the articles of incorporation and to include any purpose, power, or provision that is permitted to be included in original articles of incorporation executed at the time the amendment is made.

Acts 1997, 75th Leg., ch. 166, § 1, eff. Sept. 1, 1997.

§ 161.152. Articles of Amendment

(a) Articles of amendment of an electric cooperative must be:

(1) signed by the president or vice president and attested by the secretary, certifying to the amendment and its lawful adoption; and

(2) executed, acknowledged, filed, and recorded in the same manner as the original articles of incorporation.

(b) An amendment takes effect when the secretary of state accepts the articles of amendment for filing and recording and issues a certificate of amendment. The certificate of amendment is evidence of the filing of the amendment.

(c) The secretary of state shall charge and collect a fee of $2.50 for filing articles of amendment and issuing a certificate of amendment.

Acts 1997, 75th Leg., ch. 166, § 1, eff. Sept. 1, 1997.

SUBCHAPTER E. CONSOLIDATION OF ELECTRIC COOPERATIVES

§ 161.201. Consolidation

(a) Two or more electric cooperatives may enter into an agreement to consolidate the cooperatives. The agreement must state:

(1) the terms of the consolidation;

(2) the name of the proposed consolidated cooperative;

(3) the number of directors of the proposed consolidated cooperative;

(4) the time of the annual meeting and election; and

(5) the names of at least three persons to be directors until the first annual meeting.

(b) A consolidation agreement may be approved only on the votes of a majority of the members of each electric cooperative present in person or represented by proxy at a regular meeting or at a special meeting of its members called for that purpose.

Acts 1997, 75th Leg., ch. 166, § 1, eff. Sept. 1, 1997.

§ 161.202. Articles of Consolidation

(a) The articles of consolidation must:

(1) conform substantially to original articles of incorporation of an electric cooperative; and

(2) be executed, acknowledged, filed, and recorded in the same manner as original articles of incorporation.

(b) The directors named in the consolidation agreement shall as incorporators sign and acknowledge the articles of consolidation.

(c) The secretary of state shall charge and collect a fee of $10 for filing articles of consolidation and issuing a certificate of consolidation.

(d) When the secretary of state accepts the articles of consolidation for filing and recording and issues a certificate of consolidation, the proposed consolidated electric cooperative described in the articles under its designated name exists as a body corporate, with all the powers of an electric cooperative originally organized under this chapter.

Acts 1997, 75th Leg., ch. 166, § 1, eff. Sept. 1, 1997.

SUBCHAPTER F. DISSOLUTION

§ 161.251. Dissolution

(a) An electric cooperative may be dissolved by a majority vote of its members present in person or represented by proxy at a regular meeting or at a special meeting of its members called for that purpose.

(b) A certificate of dissolution must be:

(1) signed by the president or vice president and attested by the secretary, certifying to the dissolution and stating that the officers have been authorized by a vote of the members under Subsection (a) to execute and file the certificate; and

(2) executed, acknowledged, filed, and recorded in the same manner as original articles of incorporation of an electric cooperative.

(c) The cooperative is dissolved when the secretary of state accepts the certificate of dissolution for filing and recording and issues a certificate of dissolution.

(d) The secretary of state shall charge and collect a fee of $2.50 for filing articles of dissolution.

Acts 1997, 75th Leg., ch. 166, § 1, eff. Sept. 1, 1997.

§ 161.252. Existence Following Dissolution

(a) A dissolved electric cooperative continues to exist to:

(1) satisfy existing liabilities or obligations;

(2) collect or liquidate its assets; and

(3) take any other action required to adjust and wind up its business and affairs.

(b) A dissolved electric cooperative may sue and be sued in its corporate name.

Acts 1997, 75th Leg., ch. 166, § 1, eff. Sept. 1, 1997.

§ 161.253. Distribution of Net Assets on Dissolution

Assets of a dissolved electric cooperative that remain after all liabilities or obligations of the cooperative have been satisfied shall be distributed pro rata to the members of the cooperative who were members when the certificate of dissolution was filed.

Acts 1997, 75th Leg., ch. 166, § 1, eff. Sept. 1, 1997.

§ 161.254. Dissolution of Defectively Incorporated Electric Cooperative

(a) An electric cooperative that purports to have been incorporated or reincorporated under this chapter but that has not complied with a requirement for legal corporate existence may file a certificate of dissolution in the same manner as a validly incorporated electric cooperative.

(b) The certificate of dissolution may be authorized by a majority of the incorporators or directors at a meeting called by an incorporator and held at the principal office of the cooperative named in the articles of incorporation.

(c) The incorporator calling the meeting must give at least 10 days' notice of the meeting by mail to the last known post office address of each incorporator or director.

Acts 1997, 75th Leg., ch. 166, § 1, eff. Sept. 1, 1997.

CHAPTER 162. TELEPHONE COOPERATIVE CORPORATIONS

SUBCHAPTER A. GENERAL PROVISIONS

Section
162.001. Short Title.
162.002. Purpose.
162.003. Definitions.
162.004. Certain Corporate Names Prohibited.
162.005. Effect of Recording Certain Mortgages Executed by Telephone Cooperatives.
162.006. Construction Standards.

SUBCHAPTER B. CREATION AND OPERATION OF TELEPHONE COOPERATIVES

162.051. Incorporators.
162.052. Duration of Corporation.
162.053. Name of Telephone Cooperative.
162.054. Articles of Incorporation.
162.055. Filing and Recording of Articles of Incorporation.
162.056. Revival of Articles of Incorporation.
162.057. Organizational Meeting.
162.058. Perfecting Defectively Organized Corporations.
162.059. Nonprofit Operation.
162.060. Members Not Liable for Debts of Telephone Cooperative.
162.061. License Fee.
162.062. Exemption From Excise Taxes.
162.063. Exemption From Application of Securities Act.
162.064. Bylaws.
162.065. Membership.
162.066. Patrons.
162.067. Meetings of Members.
162.068. Notice of Members' Meeting.
162.069. Waiver of Notice.
162.070. Members' Meeting: Quorum and Voting.
162.071. Board of Directors.
162.072. Election of Directors; Terms.
162.073. Compensation of Directors.
162.074. Insurance for Directors.
162.075. Board Meetings; Quorum.
162.076. Districts.
162.077. Officers, Agents, and Employees.
162.078. Executive Committee.
162.079. Indemnification.
162.080. Change of Location of Principal Office.
162.081. Director, Officer, or Member Acting as Notary.
162.082. Applicability to Corporations Organized Under Other Law.

SUBCHAPTER C. POWERS OF TELEPHONE COOPERATIVE

162.121. General Powers.
162.122. Powers Relating to Provision of Communication Service.
162.123. Connection and Interconnection of Facilities.
162.124. Eminent Domain.
162.125. Encumbrance and Disposition of Property Without Members' Authorization.
162.126. Encumbrance, Lease, and Disposition of Property With Members' Authorization.

SUBCHAPTER D. AMENDMENT OF ARTICLES OF INCORPORATION

162.151. Amendment of Articles of Incorporation.
162.152. Presentation and Approval of Proposed Amendment.
162.153. Articles of Amendment.
162.154. Filing of Articles of Amendment.

SUBCHAPTER E. CONSOLIDATION OR MERGER OF TELEPHONE COOPERATIVES

162.201. Consolidation.

Section
162.202. Articles of Consolidation.
162.203. Merger.
162.204. Articles of Merger.
162.205. Effect of Consolidation or Merger.

SUBCHAPTER F. CONVERSION OF CORPORATION INTO TELEPHONE COOPERATIVE
162.251. Conversion of Corporation Into Telephone Cooperative.
162.252. Articles of Conversion.
162.253. Consolidation and Conversion of Corporations Into Telephone Cooperative.
162.254. Articles of Consolidation and Conversion.

SUBCHAPTER G. DISSOLUTION
162.301. Dissolution.
162.302. Existence Following Dissolution.
162.303. Distribution of Net Assets on Dissolution.
162.304. Dissolution of Defectively Incorporated Telephone Cooperative.

SUBCHAPTER A. GENERAL PROVISIONS

§ 162.001. Short Title

This chapter may be cited as the Telephone Cooperative Act.

Acts 1997, 75th Leg., ch. 166, § 1, eff. Sept. 1, 1997.

§ 162.002. Purpose

A cooperative, nonprofit corporation may be organized under this chapter to furnish communication service to the widest practicable number of users of that service.

Acts 1997, 75th Leg., ch. 166, § 1, eff. Sept. 1, 1997.

§ 162.003. Definitions

In this chapter:

(1) "Board" means the board of directors of a telephone cooperative.

(2) "Communication service" means:

(A) the transmission or reception of information, signals, or messages by any means, including by wire, radio, cellular radio, microwave, or fiber optics; and

(B) the provision of lines, facilities, and systems used in the transmission or reception described by Paragraph (A).

(3) "Member" means:

(A) an incorporator of a telephone cooperative; or

(B) a person admitted to membership in a telephone cooperative as provided by Section 162.065.

(4) "Patron" means a member who is eligible to receive patronage dividends or to earn capital credits as a result of purchasing certain services from a telephone cooperative as provided by Section 162.066.

(5) "Telephone cooperative" means a corporation that is organized under this chapter or that becomes subject to this chapter as provided by this chapter.

Acts 1997, 75th Leg., ch. 166, § 1, eff. Sept. 1, 1997.

§ 162.004. Certain Corporate Names Prohibited

A corporation organized under the laws of this state or authorized to do business in this state may not use the words "telephone cooperative" in the corporation's name unless the corporation is organized under this chapter.

Acts 1997, 75th Leg., ch. 166, § 1, eff. Sept. 1, 1997.

§ 162.005. Effect of Recording Certain Mortgages Executed by Telephone Cooperatives

(a) An instrument executed by a telephone cooperative or a foreign corporation doing business in this state under this chapter that affects real and personal property and that is recorded in the real property records of any county in which the property is located or is to be located has the same effect as if the instrument were also recorded as provided by law in the proper office in that county as a mortgage of personal property.

(b) All after-acquired property of a telephone cooperative or foreign corporation doing business in this state under this chapter described by or referred to as being pledged in an instrument to which Subsection (a) applies becomes subject to the lien described by the instrument immediately when the cooperative or corporation acquires the property, without regard to whether the property existed at the time the instrument was executed. The execution of the instrument constitutes notice and otherwise has the same effect with respect to after-acquired property to which this subsection applies as it has under the laws relating to recordation with respect to property that is owned by the cooperative or foreign corporation at the time the instrument is executed and that is described in the instrument as being pledged by the instrument.

(c) After a lien on personal property under an instrument to which Subsection (a) applies is recorded, the lien continues in existence and of record for the period specified in the instrument without:

(1) the refiling of the instrument; or

(2) the filing of any renewal certificate, affidavit, or other supplemental information required by a law relating to the renewal, maintenance, or extension of a lien on personal property.

Acts 1997, 75th Leg., ch. 166, § 1, eff. Sept. 1, 1997.

§ 162.006. Construction Standards

A telephone cooperative that constructs communication lines or facilities must at a minimum comply with the standards of the National Electrical Safety Code in effect at the time of construction.

Acts 1997, 75th Leg., ch. 166, § 1, eff. Sept. 1, 1997.

SUBCHAPTER B. CREATION AND OPERATION OF TELEPHONE COOPERATIVES

§ 162.051. Incorporators

(a) Three or more individuals may act as incorporators of a telephone cooperative by executing articles of incorporation as provided by this chapter.

(b) An incorporator must:

(1) be at least 21 years of age; and

(2) reside in this state.

Acts 1997, 75th Leg., ch. 166, § 1, eff. Sept. 1, 1997.

§ 162.052. Duration of Corporation

A telephone cooperative may be created as a perpetual corporation.

Acts 1997, 75th Leg., ch. 166, § 1, eff. Sept. 1, 1997.

§ 162.053. Name of Telephone Cooperative

The name of a telephone cooperative must:

(1) include the words "telephone" and "cooperative" and the abbreviation "Inc."; and

(2) be distinct from the name of any other corporation organized under the laws of or authorized to do business in this state.

Acts 1997, 75th Leg., ch. 166, § 1, eff. Sept. 1, 1997.

§ 162.054. Articles of Incorporation

(a) The articles of incorporation of a telephone cooperative must:

(1) state that the articles are executed under this chapter;

(2) be signed by each incorporator and acknowledged by at least two incorporators; and

(3) state:

(A) the name of the cooperative;

(B) the purpose for which the cooperative is formed;

(C) the name and address of each incorporator;

(D) the number of directors;

(E) the address of the cooperative's principal office and the name and address of its agent on whom process may be served;

(F) the duration of the cooperative;

(G) the terms under which a person is admitted to membership and retains membership in the cooperative, unless the articles expressly state that the determination of membership matters is reserved to the directors by the bylaws; and

(H) any provisions that the incorporators include for the regulation of the business and the conduct of the affairs of the cooperative.

(b) The articles of incorporation do not need to state any of the corporate powers enumerated in this chapter.

Acts 1997, 75th Leg., ch. 166, § 1, eff. Sept. 1, 1997.

§ 162.055. Filing and Recording of Articles of Incorporation

(a) The secretary of state shall receive articles of incorporation of a telephone cooperative if the incorporators of the cooperative:

(1) apply for filing the articles;

(2) furnish satisfactory evidence of compliance with this chapter to the secretary of state; and

(3) pay a fee of $25.

(b) The secretary of state shall:

(1) file the articles of incorporation in the secretary's office;

(2) record the articles at length in a book to be kept for that purpose;

(3) retain the original articles of incorporation on file in the secretary's office; and

(4) issue a certificate showing the recording of the articles of incorporation and the telephone cooperative's authority to do business under the articles.

(c) A copy of the articles of incorporation or of the record of the articles, certified under the state seal, is evidence of the creation of the telephone cooperative.

(d) The existence of the telephone cooperative dates from the filing of the articles in the office of the secretary of state. The certificate of the secretary of state is evidence of that filing.

Acts 1997, 75th Leg., ch. 166, § 1, eff. Sept. 1, 1997.

§ 162.056. Revival of Articles of Incorporation

(a) If the articles of incorporation of a telephone cooperative expire by limitation, the cooperative, with the consent of a majority of its members, may revive the articles by filing:

(1) new articles of incorporation under this chapter; and

(2) a certified copy of the expired original articles.

(b) A telephone cooperative that revives its articles of incorporation has all the privileges, immunities, and rights of property exercised and held by the cooperative at the time the original articles expired.

(c) New articles of incorporation filed under this section must recite the privileges, immunities, and rights of property exercised and held by the cooperative at the time the original articles expired.

Acts 1997, 75th Leg., ch. 166, § 1, eff. Sept. 1, 1997.

§ 162.057. Organizational Meeting

(a) After the certificate of incorporation is issued, the incorporators of a telephone cooperative shall meet to adopt bylaws, elect officers, and transact other business that properly comes before the meeting.

(b) A majority of the incorporators shall call the organizational meeting.

(c) The incorporators calling the organizational meeting shall give at least three days' notice of the meeting by mail to each incorporator. The notice must state the time and place of the meeting. The notice may be waived in writing.

Acts 1997, 75th Leg., ch. 166, § 1, eff. Sept. 1, 1997.

§ 162.058. Perfecting Defectively Organized Corporations

(a) A telephone cooperative that files defective articles of incorporation or fails to take an action necessary to perfect its corporate organization may:

(1) file corrected articles of incorporation or amend the original articles; and

(2) take any action necessary to correct the defect.

(b) An action taken under this section is valid and binding on any person concerned.

Acts 1997, 75th Leg., ch. 166, § 1, eff. Sept. 1, 1997.

§ 162.059. Nonprofit Operation

(a) A telephone cooperative shall be operated on a nonprofit basis for the mutual benefit of its members and patrons.

(b) A cooperative's bylaws and its contracts with members and patrons must contain appropriate provisions relating to the disposition of revenues and receipts to establish and maintain the cooperative's nonprofit and cooperative character.

Acts 1997, 75th Leg., ch. 166, § 1, eff. Sept. 1, 1997.

§ 162.060. Members Not Liable for Debts of Telephone Cooperative

A member is not liable for a debt of a telephone cooperative, and the member's property is not subject to execution for that debt.

Acts 1997, 75th Leg., ch. 166, § 1, eff. Sept. 1, 1997.

§ 162.061. License Fee

Not later than July 1 of each year, each telephone cooperative doing business in this state shall pay to the secretary of state a fee of $10.

Acts 1997, 75th Leg., ch. 166, § 1, eff. Sept. 1, 1997.

§ 162.062. Exemption From Excise Taxes

A telephone cooperative doing business in this state is exempt from all excise taxes but is exempt from the franchise tax imposed by Chapter 171, Tax Code, only if the cooperative is exempted by that chapter.

Acts 1997, 75th Leg., ch. 166, § 1, eff. Sept. 1, 1997.

§ 162.063. Exemption From Application of Securities Act

The Securities Act (Article 581–1 et seq., Vernon's Texas Civil Statutes) does not apply to:

(1) a note, bond, or other evidence of indebtedness issued by a telephone cooperative doing business in this state to the United States;

(2) an instrument executed to secure a debt of a telephone cooperative to the United States; or

(3) the issuance of a membership certificate by a telephone cooperative or a foreign corporation doing business in this state under this chapter.

Acts 1997, 75th Leg., ch. 166, § 1, eff. Sept. 1, 1997.

§ 162.064. Bylaws

(a) The board shall adopt the initial bylaws of a telephone cooperative to be adopted following:

(1) an incorporation;

(2) a consolidation; or

(3) an amendment by an existing cooperative, corporation, or association of its articles of incorporation as provided by Section 162.082.

(b) After the initial bylaws are adopted, the members may adopt, amend, or repeal the bylaws by the affirmative vote of a majority of those members voting on the question at a meeting of the members.

(c) The bylaws may contain any provision for the regulation and management of the affairs of the telephone cooperative that is consistent with the articles of incorporation.

Acts 1997, 75th Leg., ch. 166, § 1, eff. Sept. 1, 1997.

§ 162.065. Membership

(a) Each incorporator of a telephone cooperative is a member of the cooperative. A person other than an incorporator may become a member of a telephone cooperative only if the person agrees to use communication service furnished by the cooperative when that service is made available through the cooperative's facilities. The bylaws may prescribe additional qualifications and limitations with respect to membership.

(b) Membership in a telephone cooperative is evidenced by a certificate of membership. A membership certificate must contain the provisions, consistent with this chapter and the articles of incorporation, that are prescribed by the cooperative's bylaws. A certificate may be transferred only as provided by the bylaws.

(c) A telephone cooperative may become a member of another telephone cooperative and may fully use the facilities and services of that cooperative.

Acts 1997, 75th Leg., ch. 166, § 1, eff. Sept. 1, 1997.

§ 162.066. Patrons

(a) A member is a patron of a telephone cooperative if the member purchases local telecommunications service or toll telecommunications service or pays end user access charges in the ordinary course of business of the cooperative.

(b) The use of interexchange access, payment of interexchange access fees or settlements, or purchase of equipment does not qualify a member or other person as a patron.

Acts 1997, 75th Leg., ch. 166, § 1, eff. Sept. 1, 1997.

§ 162.067. Meetings of Members

(a) A telephone cooperative shall hold an annual meeting of members at the time and place provided by the bylaws. Failure to hold the annual meeting at the designated time does not result in forfeiture or dissolution of the cooperative.

(b) A special meeting of the members may be called by:

(1) the president;

(2) the board;

(3) any three directors; or

(4) the lesser of:

(A) 200 members; or

(B) 10 percent of all the members.

Acts 1997, 75th Leg., ch. 166, § 1, eff. Sept. 1, 1997.

§ 162.068. Notice of Members' Meeting

(a) Except as otherwise provided by this chapter, written notice of each meeting of the members shall be given to each member, either personally or by mail, not earlier than the 25th day or later than the 10th day before the date of the meeting.

(b) The notice must state the time and place of the meeting and, in the case of a special meeting, each purpose for which the meeting is called.

(c) A notice that is mailed is considered to have been given when the notice is deposited in the United States mail with postage prepaid addressed to the member at the member's address as it appears on the records of the telephone cooperative.

Acts 1997, 75th Leg., ch. 166, § 1, eff. Sept. 1, 1997.

§ 162.069. Waiver of Notice

A person entitled to notice of a meeting may waive notice in writing either before or after the meeting. If a person entitled to notice of a meeting attends the meeting, the person's attendance constitutes a waiver of notice of the meeting, unless the person participates in the meeting solely to object to the transaction of business because the meeting is not legally called or convened.

Acts 1997, 75th Leg., ch. 166, § 1, eff. Sept. 1, 1997.

§ 162.070. Members' Meeting: Quorum and Voting

(a) Unless the bylaws prescribe a greater percentage or number of members for a quorum, a quorum at a meeting of the members of a telephone cooperative is the personal presence of:

(1) 10 percent of all members, if the cooperative has 500 or fewer members; or

(2) the greater of 50 members or two percent of all members, if the cooperative has more than 500 members.

(b) If fewer than a quorum are present at a meeting, a majority of the members present in person may adjourn the meeting from time to time without further notice.

(c) Each member present at a meeting of the members is entitled to one vote on each matter submitted to a vote at the meeting. Voting must be in person unless the bylaws provide for voting by mail.

Acts 1997, 75th Leg., ch. 166, § 1, eff. Sept. 1, 1997.

§ 162.071. Board of Directors

(a) A board of at least five directors shall manage the business of a telephone cooperative. Each director must be a member of the cooperative. The bylaws must prescribe the number of directors and their qualifications other than those prescribed by this chapter.

(b) The board may exercise any power of a telephone cooperative not conferred on the members by this chapter or by the cooperative's articles of incorporation or bylaws.

Acts 1997, 75th Leg., ch. 166, § 1, eff. Sept. 1, 1997.

§ 162.072. Election of Directors; Terms

(a) The incorporators of a telephone cooperative named in the articles of incorporation shall serve as directors and hold office until the first annual meeting of the members and until their successors are elected and qualify.

(b) At each annual meeting or, in the case of failure to hold the annual meeting as specified in the bylaws, at a special meeting called for that purpose, the members shall elect directors to hold office until the next annual members' meeting, except as otherwise provided by this chapter. Except as provided by Subsection (e), each director holds office for the term for which the person is elected and until the person's successor is elected and qualifies.

(c) Instead of electing all the directors annually, the bylaws may provide that the directors, other than those named in the articles of incorporation to serve until the first annual meeting of the members, are elected by the members for a term of two years or three years. The terms must be set so that:

(1) one-half of the directors, as nearly as possible, are elected annually, if a two-year term is provided; or

(2) one-third of the directors, as nearly as possible, are elected annually, if a three-year term is provided.

(d) After the implementation of two-year or three-year terms for directors, as directors' terms expire, the members shall elect their successors to serve until the second or third succeeding annual meeting after their election, as appropriate.

(e) The bylaws must prescribe the manner of electing a successor to a director who resigns, dies, or otherwise becomes incapable of acting. The bylaws may provide for the removal of a director from office and for the election of the director's successor.

Acts 1997, 75th Leg., ch. 166, § 1, eff. Sept. 1, 1997.

§ 162.073. Compensation of Directors

(a) A director may not receive a salary for services as a director. Except in an emergency, a director may not receive a salary for services in a capacity other than director without the approval of the members.

(b) The bylaws may:

(1) prescribe a fixed fee for attendance at each board meeting, committee meeting, industry-related conference approved by the board, or training program; and

(2) provide for reimbursement of actual expenses of attendance or a reasonable per diem.

Acts 1997, 75th Leg., ch. 166, § 1, eff. Sept. 1, 1997.

§ 162.074. Insurance for Directors

A telephone cooperative may provide liability, accident, life, and health insurance coverage for a director who chooses to have that coverage.

Acts 1997, 75th Leg., ch. 166, § 1, eff. Sept. 1, 1997.

§ 162.075. Board Meetings; Quorum

(a) The bylaws shall prescribe the manner of holding board meetings.

(b) A majority of the directors is a quorum.

Acts 1997, 75th Leg., ch. 166, § 1, eff. Sept. 1, 1997.

§ 162.076. Districts

(a) The bylaws may provide for the territory served or to be served by a telephone cooperative to be divided into two or more districts for any purpose, including the nomination and election of directors and the election and functioning of district delegates.

(b) The bylaws must prescribe:

(1) the boundaries of each district or the manner of establishing a district's boundaries;

(2) the manner of changing a district's boundaries; and

(3) the manner in which each district functions.

(c) District delegates may nominate and elect directors. A district delegate must be a member.

(d) A member may not vote by proxy or by mail at a district meeting.

(e) A district delegate may not vote by proxy or by mail at any meeting.

Acts 1997, 75th Leg., ch. 166, § 1, eff. Sept. 1, 1997.

§ 162.077. Officers, Agents, and Employees

(a) The board of a telephone cooperative shall annually elect from the board's membership a president, a vice president, a secretary, and a treasurer.

(b) An officer who ceases to be a director ceases to hold office.

(c) The same person may hold the offices of secretary and of treasurer.

(d) The board may also elect or appoint other officers, agents, or employees as the board considers appropriate and shall prescribe the powers and duties of those persons.

(e) An officer may be removed from office and a successor elected in the manner prescribed by the bylaws.

Acts 1997, 75th Leg., ch. 166, § 1, eff. Sept. 1, 1997.

§ 162.078. Executive Committee

(a) The bylaws of a telephone cooperative may authorize the board to elect an executive committee from the board's membership.

(b) The board may delegate to the executive committee the management of the current and ordinary business of the cooperative and other duties as prescribed by the bylaws.

(c) The designation of an executive committee and the delegation of authority to the committee does not relieve the board or any director of a responsibility imposed on the board or the director by this chapter.

Acts 1997, 75th Leg., ch. 166, § 1, eff. Sept. 1, 1997.

§ 162.079. Indemnification

Article 2.22A, Texas Non-Profit Corporation Act (Article 1396–2.22A, Vernon's Texas Civil Statutes), applies to a telephone cooperative in the same manner as if the cooperative were formed under the Texas Non-Profit Corporation Act.

Acts 1997, 75th Leg., ch. 166, § 1, eff. Sept. 1, 1997.

§ 162.080. Change of Location of Principal Office

(a) A telephone cooperative may, with the authorization of the board or the members, change the location of its principal office by filing a certificate reciting the change of principal office with the secretary of state.

(b) The cooperative's president or vice president must execute and acknowledge the certificate under the cooperative's seal as attested by the secretary.

(c) The secretary of state shall charge and collect a fee of $5 for filing a certificate of change of principal office.

Acts 1997, 75th Leg., ch. 166, § 1, eff. Sept. 1, 1997.

§ 162.081. Director, Officer, or Member Acting as Notary

A person who is an officer, director, or member of a telephone cooperative and who is authorized to take acknowledgments under state law is not disqualified because of the person's association with the cooperative from taking an acknowledgment of an instrument executed in favor of the cooperative or to which the cooperative is a party.

Acts 1997, 75th Leg., ch. 166, § 1, eff. Sept. 1, 1997.

§ 162.082. Applicability to Corporations Organized Under Other Law

A cooperative or nonprofit corporation or association organized under any other law of this state for the purpose of furnishing communication service may, by a majority vote of the members present in person at a meeting called for that purpose, amend its articles of incorporation to comply with this chapter.

Acts 1997, 75th Leg., ch. 166, § 1, eff. Sept. 1, 1997.

SUBCHAPTER C. POWERS OF TELEPHONE COOPERATIVE

§ 162.121. General Powers

A telephone cooperative may:

(1) sue and be sued in its corporate name;

(2) adopt and alter a corporate seal and use the seal or a facsimile of the seal as required by law;

(3) construct, acquire, lease, improve, install, equip, maintain, and operate, and, subject to Sections 162.125 and 162.126, dispose of, lease, or encumber, communication lines, facilities or systems, lands, structures, plants and equipment, exchanges, and other property, considered appropriate to accomplish the purpose for which the cooperative is organized;

(4) issue membership certificates as provided by this chapter;

(5) borrow money and otherwise contract indebtedness, issue or guarantee notes, bonds, and other evidences of indebtedness, and secure the payment of indebtedness by pledge or other encumbrance on any or all of its property or revenue;

(6) conduct its business and exercise its powers inside or outside this state;

(7) adopt, amend, and repeal bylaws;

(8) make any contracts appropriate for the full exercise of the powers granted by this chapter; and

(9) perform any other acts and exercise any other power that may be appropriate to accomplish the purpose for which the cooperative is organized.

Acts 1997, 75th Leg., ch. 166, § 1, eff. Sept. 1, 1997.

§ 162.122. Powers Relating to Provision of Communication Service

(a) A telephone cooperative may:

(1) furnish and improve communication service to its members, to governmental agencies and political subdivisions, to any number of subscribers of other communication systems through interconnection of facilities, and to any number of users through pay stations;

(2) connect and interconnect its communication lines, facilities, or systems with other communication lines, facilities, or systems;

(3) make its facilities available to persons furnishing communication service inside or outside this state; and

(4) construct, maintain, and operate a communication line along, on, under, or across publicly owned land or a public thoroughfare, subject to the same restrictions and obligations that apply to an electric transmission cooperative under Subchapter C, Chapter 181.[1]

(b) A telephone cooperative that acquires communication facilities may continue to furnish service to a person who is already receiving service from those facilities without requiring the person to become a member, but the person may become a member on the terms prescribed by the bylaws.

Acts 1997, 75th Leg., ch. 166, § 1, eff. Sept. 1, 1997.

[1] V.T.C.A., Utilities Code § 181.041 et seq.

§ 162.123. Connection and Interconnection of Facilities

A telephone cooperative doing business in this state may require a person furnishing communication service to the public in this state to interconnect that person's lines, facilities, or systems with, or otherwise make available those lines, facilities, or systems to, the cooperative's communication lines, facilities, or systems to provide a continuous line of communication for the cooperative's subscribers.

Acts 1997, 75th Leg., ch. 166, § 1, eff. Sept. 1, 1997.

§ 162.124. Eminent Domain

A telephone cooperative may exercise the power of eminent domain in the manner provided by state law for the exercise of that power by other corporations constructing or operating communication lines, facilities, or systems.

Acts 1997, 75th Leg., ch. 166, § 1, eff. Sept. 1, 1997.

§ 162.125. Encumbrance and Disposition of Property Without Members' Authorization

(a) The board of a telephone cooperative may, without authorization of the members, authorize the execution and delivery of a mortgage or deed of trust of or the encumbering of any property of the cooperative, including property to be acquired and the revenues from property of the cooperative, to secure any indebtedness of the cooperative to the United States or any lending institution licensed by the United States or a state.

(b) A mortgage or deed of trust described by Subsection (a) is exempt from a tax for recording the instrument.

Acts 1997, 75th Leg., ch. 166, § 1, eff. Sept. 1, 1997.

§ 162.126. Encumbrance, Lease, and Disposition of Property With Members' Authorization

(a) Except as provided by Section 162.125, a telephone cooperative may not dispose of, lease, or encumber all or a major portion of its property unless the disposition, lease, or encumbrance is authorized by the affirmative vote of at least two-thirds of all the members of the cooperative.

(b) The board may, on the authorization of two-thirds of all the members of the cooperative at a members' meeting, dispose of or lease all or a major portion of its property to:

(1) another telephone cooperative;

(2) a foreign corporation doing business in this state under this chapter; or

(3) the holder of a note, bond, or other evidence of indebtedness issued to the United States or to a lending institution licensed by the United States or a state.

(c) The notice of a meeting at which a disposition or lease under Subsection (b) is to be considered must state the proposed action.

Acts 1997, 75th Leg., ch. 166, § 1, eff. Sept. 1, 1997.

SUBCHAPTER D. AMENDMENT OF ARTICLES OF INCORPORATION

§ 162.151. Amendment of Articles of Incorporation

A telephone cooperative may amend its articles of incorporation in accordance with this subchapter.

Acts 1997, 75th Leg., ch. 166, § 1, eff. Sept. 1, 1997.

§ 162.152. Presentation and Approval of Proposed Amendment

(a) A proposed amendment to the articles of incorporation must be presented to a meeting of the members. The notice of the meeting must state the proposed amendment or must have the proposed amendment attached to it.

(b) A proposed amendment, with any changes, may be approved only on the affirmative vote of at least two-thirds of the members voting on the question at the meeting.

Acts 1997, 75th Leg., ch. 166, § 1, eff. Sept. 1, 1997.

§ 162.153. Articles of Amendment

(a) The president or vice president, on behalf of the telephone cooperative, shall execute and acknowledge the approved articles of amendment. The cooperative's seal must be affixed to the articles of amendment and attested by its secretary.

(b) The articles of amendment must state:

(1) that the articles of amendment are executed under this chapter;

(2) the name of the telephone cooperative;

(3) the address of the cooperative's principal office; and

(4) the amendment to the articles of incorporation.

(c) The president or vice president executing the articles of amendment shall make and attach to the articles an affidavit stating that the cooperative complied with this subchapter with respect to the amendment set forth in the articles.

Acts 1997, 75th Leg., ch. 166, § 1, eff. Sept. 1, 1997.

§ 162.154. Filing of Articles of Amendment

(a) Articles of amendment shall be filed with the secretary of state in the same manner as the original articles of incorporation.

(b) The secretary of state shall charge and collect a fee of $25 for filing articles of amendment.

Acts 1997, 75th Leg., ch. 166, § 1, eff. Sept. 1, 1997.

SUBCHAPTER E. CONSOLIDATION OR MERGER OF TELEPHONE COOPERATIVES

§ 162.201. Consolidation

(a) Two or more telephone cooperatives may enter into an agreement to consolidate the cooperatives. The agreement must state:

(1) the terms of the consolidation;

(2) the name of the proposed consolidated cooperative;

(3) the number of directors of the proposed consolidated cooperative;

(4) the time of the annual meeting and election; and

(5) the names of at least five persons to be directors until the first annual meeting.

(b) A consolidation agreement may be approved only on the votes of a majority of the members of each telephone cooperative at a regular meeting or at a special meeting of its members called for that purpose.

(c) Telephone cooperatives may not consolidate for the purpose of duplicating the facilities of another communication company where the other communication company is giving or is willing to give reasonably adequate communication service.

Acts 1997, 75th Leg., ch. 166, § 1, eff. Sept. 1, 1997.

§ 162.202. Articles of Consolidation

(a) The articles of consolidation must:

(1) conform substantially to original articles of incorporation of a telephone cooperative; and

(2) be executed, acknowledged, filed, and recorded in the same manner as original articles of incorporation.

(b) The directors named in the consolidation agreement shall as incorporators sign and acknowledge the articles of consolidation.

(c) The secretary of state shall charge and collect a fee of $50 for filing articles of consolidation.

(d) When the secretary of state accepts the articles of consolidation for filing and recording and issues a certificate of consolidation, the proposed consolidated telephone cooperative described in the articles under its designated name exists as a body corporate, with all the powers of a telephone cooperative originally organized under this chapter.

Acts 1997, 75th Leg., ch. 166, § 1, eff. Sept. 1, 1997.

§ 162.203. Merger

(a) One or more telephone cooperatives may merge into another cooperative as provided by this section and Section 162.204.

(b) The proposition for the merger and proposed articles of merger must be submitted at a meeting of the members of each merging cooperative and the surviving cooperative. A copy of the proposed articles of merger must be attached to the notice of each meeting.

(c) A proposed merger and proposed articles of merger, with any amendments, may be approved only on the affirmative vote of at least two-thirds of the members of each cooperative voting on the proposed merger and articles.

Acts 1997, 75th Leg., ch. 166, § 1, eff. Sept. 1, 1997.

§ 162.204. Articles of Merger

(a) The president or vice president of each telephone cooperative, on behalf of the telephone cooperative, shall execute and acknowledge the approved articles of merger. The cooperative's seal must be affixed to the articles of merger and attested by its secretary.

(b) The articles of merger must state:

(1) that they are executed under this chapter;

(2) the name of each merging cooperative and the address of its principal office;

(3) the name of the surviving cooperative and the address of its principal office;

(4) that each merging cooperative and the surviving cooperative agree to the merger;

(5) the name and address of each director of the surviving cooperative;

(6) the terms of the merger and the manner in which the merger will be carried out, including the manner in which members of the merging cooperatives become or may become members of the surviving cooperative;

(7) the duration of the surviving cooperative; and

(8) the purpose for which the surviving cooperative is formed.

(c) The articles of merger may contain any provision consistent with this chapter considered appropriate for the conduct of the business of the surviving cooperative. The president or vice president of each cooperative executing the articles of merger shall make and attach to the articles an affidavit stating that the cooperative complied with this subchapter with respect to the articles.

(d) The original and a copy of the articles of merger shall be delivered to the secretary of state. If the secretary of state finds that the articles conform to law, the secretary of state, on payment of a fee of $50, shall:

(1) file and record the articles of merger;

(2) issue a certificate of merger; and

(3) attach to the certificate of merger the copy of the articles of merger and deliver the certificate and attached copy to the surviving cooperative or its representative.

Acts 1997, 75th Leg., ch. 166, § 1, eff. Sept. 1, 1997.

§ 162.205. Effect of Consolidation or Merger

(a) In a consolidation the existence of each telephone cooperative ceases and the articles of consolidation are considered to be the articles of incorporation of the new cooperative. In a merger the separate existence of each merging telephone cooperative ceases and the articles of incorporation of the surviving cooperative are considered to be amended to the extent, if any, that amendment is provided for in the articles of merger.

(b) All the rights, privileges, immunities, property, and applications for membership of each of the consolidating or merging cooperatives are transferred to and vested in the new or surviving cooperative, except that this chapter does not relieve a cooperative of the obligation to comply with the applicable provisions of Title 2.[1]

(c) The new or surviving cooperative is liable for all the liabilities and obligations of the consolidating or merging cooperatives. A claim existing or action or proceeding pending by or against a consolidating or merging cooperative may be prosecuted as if the consolidation or merger had not taken place, and the new or surviving cooperative may be substituted in the place of the consolidating or merging cooperative. The consolidation or merger does not impair the rights of creditors of or liens on the property of a consolidating or merging cooperative.

Acts 1997, 75th Leg., ch. 166, § 1, eff. Sept. 1, 1997.

[1] V.T.C.A., Utilities Code § 11.001 et seq.

SUBCHAPTER F. CONVERSION OF CORPORATION INTO TELEPHONE COOPERATIVE

§ 162.251. Conversion of Corporation Into Telephone Cooperative

(a) A corporation organized under the laws of this state that furnishes or is authorized to furnish communication service may be converted into a telephone cooperative in accordance with this subchapter. On conversion, the corporation is subject to this chapter as if it had been originally organized under this chapter.

(b) The proposition for the conversion and proposed articles of conversion must be submitted at a meeting of the members or stockholders of the corporation or, in the case of a corporation that does not have members or stockholders, at a meeting of the incorporators of the corporation. A copy of the proposed articles of conversion must be attached to the notice of the meeting.

(c) A proposed conversion and proposed articles of conversion, with any amendments, may be approved only on the affirmative vote of:

(1) at least two-thirds of the members of the corporation voting on the proposed conversion and articles;

(2) the holders of at least two-thirds of the shares of the capital stock of the corporation represented at the meeting and voting on the proposition and articles, if the corporation is a stock corporation; or

(3) at least two-thirds of the corporation's incorporators, if the corporation does not have members or outstanding shares of capital stock.

Acts 1997, 75th Leg., ch. 166, § 1, eff. Sept. 1, 1997.

§ 162.252. Articles of Conversion

(a) The president or vice president, on behalf of the corporation, shall execute and acknowledge the approved articles of conversion. The corporation's seal must be affixed to the articles and attested by its secretary.

(b) The articles of conversion must state:

(1) that they are executed under this chapter;

(2) the name of the corporation and the address of its principal office before its conversion into a telephone cooperative;

(3) the law under which the corporation was organized;

(4) that the corporation elects to become a cooperative, nonprofit corporation subject to this chapter;

(5) the corporation's name as a cooperative;

(6) the address of the principal office of the cooperative;

(7) the name and address of each director of the cooperative;

(8) the manner in which a member, stockholder, or incorporator of the corporation becomes or may become a member of the cooperative;

(9) the duration of the cooperative; and

(10) the purpose for which the cooperative is formed.

(c) The articles of conversion may contain any provision consistent with this chapter considered appropriate for the conduct of the business of the cooperative. The president or vice president executing the articles of conversion shall make and attach to the articles an affidavit stating that the corporation complied with this section with respect to the articles. The articles of conversion are considered to be the articles of incorporation of the cooperative.

(d) The original and a copy of the articles of conversion shall be delivered to the secretary of state. If the secretary of state finds that the articles conform to law, the secretary of state, on payment of a fee of $50, shall:

(1) file and record the articles of conversion;

(2) issue a certificate of conversion; and

(3) attach to the certificate of conversion the copy of the articles of conversion and deliver the certificate and attached copy to the cooperative or its representative.

Acts 1997, 75th Leg., ch. 166, § 1, eff. Sept. 1, 1997.

§ 162.253. Consolidation and Conversion of Corporations Into Telephone Cooperative

(a) Two or more corporations organized under the laws of this state that furnish or are authorized to furnish communication service may, if otherwise permitted to consolidate under state law, consolidate and convert into a telephone cooperative in accordance with this subchapter. On consolidation and conversion, the new cooperative is subject to this chapter as if it had been originally organized under this chapter.

(b) The proposition for the consolidation and conversion and the proposed articles of consolidation and conversion, with any amendments, must be approved by each corporation in accordance with:

(1) the law under which it was organized; and

(2) Sections 162.251 and 162.252.

Acts 1997, 75th Leg., ch. 166, § 1, eff. Sept. 1, 1997.

§ 162.254. Articles of Consolidation and Conversion

(a) The approved articles of consolidation and conversion:

(1) shall be executed, acknowledged, and sealed as prescribed by Section 162.252 and by the law under which the consolidating and converting corporations were organized;

(2) must:

(A) state that they are executed under this chapter and the law under which the corporations were organized and that each consolidating corporation elects that the new corporation be a cooperative; and

(B) contain all other information required by the law under which the corporations were organized; and

(3) may contain any provision consistent with this chapter considered appropriate for the conduct of the business of the cooperative.

(b) The president or vice president executing the articles of consolidation and conversion shall make and attach to the articles an affidavit stating that the corporations complied with this section and Section 162.253 and with the applicable provisions of the law under which the consolidating corporations were organized with respect to the articles. The articles of consolidation and conversion are considered to be the articles of incorporation of the cooperative and shall be filed in accordance with the provisions both of this chapter and of the law under which the consolidating corporations were organized.

(c) The original and a copy of the articles of consolidation and conversion shall be delivered to the secretary of state. If the secretary of state finds that the articles conform to law, the secretary of state, on payment of a fee of $50, shall:

(1) file and record the articles of consolidation and conversion;

(2) issue a certificate of consolidation and conversion; and

(3) attach to the certificate the copy of the articles and deliver the certificate and attached copy to the cooperative or its representative.

Acts 1997, 75th Leg., ch. 166, § 1, eff. Sept. 1, 1997.

SUBCHAPTER G. DISSOLUTION

§ 162.301. Dissolution

(a) A telephone cooperative may be dissolved by a two-thirds vote of all the members of the cooperative. The vote must be taken at a regular meeting or at a special meeting of its members called for that purpose. Votes must be cast in person.

(b) A certificate of dissolution must be:

(1) signed by the president or vice president and attested by the secretary, certifying to the dissolution and stating that the officers have been authorized by a vote of the members under Subsection (a) to execute and file the certificate; and

(2) executed, acknowledged, filed, and recorded in the same manner as original articles of incorporation of a telephone cooperative.

(c) The cooperative is dissolved when the secretary of state accepts the certificate of dissolution for filing and recording and issues a certificate of dissolution.

(d) The secretary of state shall charge and collect:

(1) a fee of $5 for filing a certificate of election to dissolve; and

(2) a fee of $5 for filing articles of dissolution.

Acts 1997, 75th Leg., ch. 166, § 1, eff. Sept. 1, 1997.

§ 162.302. Existence Following Dissolution

(a) A dissolved telephone cooperative continues to exist to:

(1) satisfy existing liabilities or obligations;

(2) collect or liquidate its assets; and

(3) take any other action required to adjust and wind up its business and affairs.

(b) A dissolved telephone cooperative may sue and be sued in its corporate name.

Acts 1997, 75th Leg., ch. 166, § 1, eff. Sept. 1, 1997.

§ 162.303. Distribution of Net Assets on Dissolution

Assets of a dissolved telephone cooperative that remain after all liabilities or obligations of the cooperative have been satisfied shall be distributed as follows:

(1) first, to patrons for the pro rata return of amounts standing to their credit because of their patronage; and

(2) second, to members for the pro rata repayment of membership fees.

Acts 1997, 75th Leg., ch. 166, § 1, eff. Sept. 1, 1997.

§ 162.304. Dissolution of Defectively Incorporated Telephone Cooperative

(a) A telephone cooperative that purports to have been incorporated or reincorporated under this chapter but that has not complied with a requirement for legal corporate existence may file a certificate of dissolution in the same manner as a validly incorporated telephone cooperative.

(b) The certificate of dissolution may be authorized by a majority of the incorporators or directors at a meeting called by an incorporator and held at the principal office of the cooperative named in the articles of incorporation.

(c) The incorporator calling the meeting must give at least ten days' notice of the meeting by mail to the last known post office address of each incorporator or director.

Acts 1997, 75th Leg., ch. 166, § 1, eff. Sept. 1, 1997.

CHAPTER 163. JOINT POWERS AGENCIES

SUBCHAPTER A. GENERAL PROVISIONS

Section
163.001. Definitions.
163.002. Repealed.

SUBCHAPTER B. COOPERATION BY PUBLIC AND PRIVATE ENTITIES

163.011. Effect of Subchapter.
163.012. Authority to Make Agreements.
163.013. General Rights, Powers, and Duties of Entities.
163.014. Use of Eminent Domain.
163.015. Taxation.
163.016. Insurance.

SUBCHAPTER C. MUNICIPAL POWER AGENCIES

163.051. Definitions.
163.052. Construction.
163.053. Conflicts With Other Law.
163.054. Creation of Agency.
163.055. Re-Creation of Agency.
163.056. Notice.
163.057. Contents of Concurrent Ordinance.
163.058. Election.
163.059. Board of Directors.
163.060. Powers.
163.061. Construction Contracts.
163.062. Sale or Exchange of Electric Energy.
163.063. Rates and Charges.
163.064. Revenue Bonds.
163.065. Refunding Bonds.
163.066. Issuance, Form, and Provisions of Bonds.
163.067. Nonnegotiable Purchase Money Notes.
163.068. Bond Anticipation Notes.

SUBCHAPTER D. AGENCY RECEIVING POWER THROUGH INTERSTATE SYSTEM

163.101. Creation.
163.102. Powers.

SUBCHAPTER E. ELECTRIC COOPERATIVE CORPORATIONS

163.121. Creation.
163.122. Application of Open Meetings Law.
163.123. Authority of Public Utility Commission.
163.124. Power to Issue Certain Bonds or Securities.

SUBCHAPTER A. GENERAL PROVISIONS

§ 163.001. Definitions

In this chapter:

(1) "Electric facility" means a facility necessary or incidental to generating or transmitting electric power and energy, including:

(A) a generating unit or plant or a plant site;

(B) transmission lines;

(C) a right-of-way or other right relating to a facility; and

(D) property and equipment.

(2) "Entity" means a person who engages in the authorized generation, transmission, or distribution of electric energy for sale to the public.

(3) "Private entity" means an entity that is not a public entity.

(4) "Public entity" means an entity that is an agency or political subdivision of this state.

Acts 1997, 75th Leg., ch. 166, § 1, eff. Sept. 1, 1997.

§ 163.002. Repealed by Acts 2011, 82nd Leg., ch. 1083 (S.B. 1179), § 25(163), eff. June 17, 2011

SUBCHAPTER B. COOPERATION BY PUBLIC AND PRIVATE ENTITIES

§ 163.011. Effect of Subchapter

This subchapter does not affect:

(1) the statutory purposes prescribed by state law relating to creating, establishing, or operating an entity that co-owns a facility;

(2) an entity's rights or powers in effect on August 27, 1973, relating to the generation, transmission, distribution, or sale of electric power and energy; or

(3) a contract in effect on August 27, 1973.

Acts 1997, 75th Leg., ch. 166, § 1, eff. Sept. 1, 1997.

§ 163.012. Authority to Make Agreements

Public and private entities may by agreement jointly plan, finance, acquire, construct, own, operate, and maintain electric facilities to:

(1) achieve economies of scale in providing electric energy to the public;

(2) promote the economic development of this state and its natural resources; and

(3) meet the state's future power needs.

Acts 1997, 75th Leg., ch. 166, § 1, eff. Sept. 1, 1997.

§ 163.013. General Rights, Powers, and Duties of Entities

(a) A participating entity may:

(1) use its means and assets to plan, acquire, construct, own, operate, and maintain its interest in an electric facility;

(2) issue bonds and other securities to raise money for a purpose described by Subdivision (1) in the same manner and to the same extent and subject to the same conditions as would be applicable if the entity had sole ownership of the electric facility;

(3) acquire, for the use and benefit of each participating entity, land, easements, and property for an electric facility by purchase or by exercising the power of eminent domain; and

(4) transfer or otherwise convey the acquired land, property, or property interest or otherwise cause the land, property, or interest to become vested in other participating entities to the extent to which and in the manner in which the participating entities agree.

(b) Each participating entity is a cotenant or co-owner of the electric facility and in relation to the entity's undivided interest in the facility has each right, privilege, exemption, power, duty, and liability the entity would have had if the entity had sole ownership.

Acts 1997, 75th Leg., ch. 166, § 1, eff. Sept. 1, 1997.

§ 163.014. Use of Eminent Domain

(a) A participating entity has the power of eminent domain to be exercised as provided by this section.

(b) The use of eminent domain authority by a participating entity is governed by the law relating to an eminent domain proceeding involving a municipality in this state.

(c) A participating entity may acquire a fee title to the condemned real property.

(d) A participating entity may not use eminent domain authority to acquire:

(1) an interest in an electric facility that belongs to another entity; or

(2) an interest in real property to drill, mine, or produce from that property oil, gas, geothermal resources, geothermal/geopressured resources, or lignite, coal, sulphur, uranium, plutonium, or other minerals that belong to another person regardless of whether the material is in place or is in the process of being drilled, mined, or produced.

(e) Subsection (d) does not affect the authority of a participating entity to acquire full title to real property for a plant site and any related surface installation or equipment, including a cooling reservoir.

Acts 1997, 75th Leg., ch. 166, § 1, eff. Sept. 1, 1997.

§ 163.015. Taxation

(a) A participating private entity shall render for ad valorem taxation its undivided fractional interest in a jointly owned electric facility. An ad valorem or similar tax shall be imposed separately against the undivided interest of the participating private entity.

(b) A tax or assessment, including an excise tax or sales and use tax, attributable to a property or service bought, sold, leased, or used to construct, maintain, repair, or operate a jointly owned electric facility shall be imposed separately against each participating entity in proportion to the entity's respective undivided interest in the facility.

(c) A participating entity is not liable for a tax or assessment attributable to another participating entity under Subsection (a) or (b).

(d) A participating entity is entitled to each constitutional or statutory ad valorem or other tax exemption attributable to the jointly owned electric facility or to a property or service bought, sold, leased, or used to construct, maintain, repair, or operate the facility to the extent the entity would have been exempt from the tax if the entity's undivided interest were an entire interest in the facility or in the property or service. The entity is entitled to any applicable exemption certificate or statement provided by law to claim or prove the exemption.

Acts 1997, 75th Leg., ch. 166, § 1, eff. Sept. 1, 1997.

§ 163.016. Insurance

A participating entity may:

(1) contract for insurance, including specialized insurance for property and risks relating to the ownership, operation, and maintenance of electric facilities;

(2) contract for insurance for the use and benefit of each of the other participating entities as though the insurance was for the sole benefit of the contracting entity; and

(3) cause the rights of the other participating entities to be protected under the contract in accordance with each entity's undivided interest or entitlement under any applicable agreement between the entities.

Acts 1997, 75th Leg., ch. 166, § 1, eff. Sept. 1, 1997.

SUBCHAPTER C. MUNICIPAL POWER AGENCIES

§ 163.051. Definitions

In this subchapter:

(1) "Agency" means a municipal power agency created under this subchapter.

(2) "Bond" includes a note, but does not include a nonnegotiable purchase money note issued under Section 163.067.

(3) "Concurrent ordinance" means an ordinance or order adopted under this subchapter by two or more public entities that relates to the creation or re-creation of a municipal power agency.

(4) "Obligations" means revenue bonds or notes.

Acts 1997, 75th Leg., ch. 166, § 1, eff. Sept. 1, 1997.

§ 163.052. Construction

This subchapter shall be liberally construed to carry out its purpose.

Acts 1997, 75th Leg., ch. 166, § 1, eff. Sept. 1, 1997.

§ 163.053. Conflicts With Other Law

This subchapter prevails to the extent of a conflict between this subchapter and any other law, including:

(1) a law regulating the affairs of a municipal corporation; or

(2) a home-rule charter provision.

Acts 1997, 75th Leg., ch. 166, § 1, eff. Sept. 1, 1997.

§ 163.054. Creation of Agency

(a) Public entities may create an agency by concurrent ordinances subject to voter approval.

(b) A public entity may join in the creation of an agency under this subchapter only if on May 8, 1975, and at the time the concurrent ordinance is adopted, the entity was engaged in the authorized generation of electric energy for sale to the public. This subsection does not prohibit a public entity from disposing of its electric generating capabilities after creation of the agency.

(c) An agency is a:

(1) separate municipal corporation;

(2) political subdivision of this state; and

(3) political entity and corporate body.

(d) An agency may not impose a tax but has all the other powers relating to municipally owned utilities and provided by law to a municipality that owns a public utility.

Acts 1997, 75th Leg., ch. 166, § 1, eff. Sept. 1, 1997.

§ 163.055. Re-Creation of Agency

(a) The public entities that create an agency may by concurrent ordinances re-create the agency by adding or deleting, or both, a public entity.

(b) The public entities may not re-create an agency if the re-creation will impair an agency obligation.

(c) Re-creation by adding a public entity is subject to voter approval in accordance with Section 163.058.

Acts 1997, 75th Leg., ch. 166, § 1, eff. Sept. 1, 1997.

§ 163.056. Notice

(a) The governing body of each public entity shall publish notice of its intention to create an agency once a week for two consecutive weeks.

(b) The first publication must appear before the 14th day before the date set for passage of the concurrent ordinance.

(c) The notice must state:

(1) the date, time, and location at which the governing body proposes to enact the concurrent ordinance; and

(2) that an agency will be created on the date on which the concurrent ordinances take effect.

Acts 1997, 75th Leg., ch. 166, § 1, eff. Sept. 1, 1997.

§ 163.057. Contents of Concurrent Ordinance

A concurrent ordinance creating an agency under Section 163.054 or re-creating an agency under Section 163.055 must, as adopted by each public entity:

(1) contain identical provisions;

(2) define the boundaries of the agency to include the territory within the boundaries of each participating public entity;

(3) designate the name of the agency; and

(4) designate the number, place, initial term, and manner of appointment of directors in accordance with Section 163.059.

Acts 1997, 75th Leg., ch. 166, § 1, eff. Sept. 1, 1997.

§ 163.058. Election

(a) An agency may not be created unless the creation is approved by a majority of the qualified voters of each public entity creating the agency at an election called and held for that purpose.

(b) An agency may not be re-created by addition of a public entity unless the re-creation is approved by a majority of the qualified voters of the additional public entity at an election called and held for that purpose.

(c) Notice of an election under this section shall be given in accordance with Section 1251.003, Government Code. The election shall be called and held in accordance with:

(1) the Election Code;

(2) Chapter 1251, Government Code; and

(3) this subchapter.

Acts 1997, 75th Leg., ch. 166, § 1, eff. Sept. 1, 1997. Amended by Acts 2001, 77th Leg., ch. 1420, § 8.404, eff. Sept. 1, 2001.

§ 163.059. Board of Directors

(a) The agency shall be governed by a board of directors. The board is responsible for the management, operation, and control of the property belonging to the agency.

(b) The board must include at least four directors. Each director must be appointed by place by the governing bodies of the participating public entities. Each participating public entity is entitled to appoint at least one director.

(c) Directors must serve staggered terms. Successor directors are appointed in the same manner as the original appointees.

(d) To qualify to serve as a director, a person must be a qualified voter and reside in the boundaries of the appointing public entity when the person takes the constitutional oath of office.

(e) An employee, officer, or member of the governing body of a public entity may serve as a director but may not have a personal interest in a contract executed by the agency other than as an employee, officer, or member of the governing body of the public entity.

(f) Directors serve without compensation.

Acts 1997, 75th Leg., ch. 166, § 1, eff. Sept. 1, 1997.

§ 163.060. Powers

(a) An agency may not engage in any utility business other than the generation, transmission, and sale or exchange of electric energy to:

(1) a participating public entity; or

(2) a private entity that owns jointly with the agency an electric generating facility in this state.

(b) The agency may:

(1) perform any act necessary to the full exercise of the agency's powers;

(2) enter into a contract, lease, or agreement with or accept a grant or loan from a:

(A) department or agency of the United States;

(B) department, agency, or political subdivision of this state; or

(C) public or private person;

(3) sell, lease, convey, or otherwise dispose of any right, interest, or property the agency considers to be unnecessary for the efficient maintenance or operation of its electric facilities;

(4) use the uniform system of accounts prescribed for utilities and licenses by the Federal Energy Regulatory Commission; and

(5) adopt rules to govern the operation of the agency and its employees, facilities, and service.

Acts 1997, 75th Leg., ch. 166, § 1, eff. Sept. 1, 1997.

§ 163.061. Construction Contracts

(a) Except as provided by Subsection (c), an agency may award a contract for construction of an improvement that involves the expenditure of more than $20,000 only on the basis of competitive bids.

(b) The agency shall publish notice of intent to receive bids once a week for two consecutive weeks in a newspaper of general circulation in this state. The first publication must appear before the 14th day before the date bids are to be received.

(c) An entity that has joint ownership of the improvement to be constructed or that is an agent of a joint owner shall award a contract using the entity's contracting procedures.

Acts 1997, 75th Leg., ch. 166, § 1, eff. Sept. 1, 1997.

§ 163.062. Sale or Exchange of Electric Energy

(a) An agency may participate through appropriate contracts in power pooling and power exchange agreements with other entities through direct or indirect system interconnections.

(b) An entity that participates with an agency under this section may:

(1) purchase electric energy from the agency;

(2) sell or dispose of electric energy to the agency; or

(3) exchange electric energy with the agency.

(c) An entity payment for electric energy purchased from the agency is an operating expense of the entity's electric system.

(d) An agency contract to sell or exchange electric energy may require the purchaser to pay for the electric energy regardless of whether the electric energy is produced or delivered.

Acts 1997, 75th Leg., ch. 166, § 1, eff. Sept. 1, 1997.

§ 163.063. Rates and Charges

(a) An agency may establish and maintain rates and charges for electric power and energy the agency delivers, transmits, or exchanges. The rates and charges must:

(1) be reasonable and in accordance with prudent utility practices;

(2) be based on periodic cost of service studies and subject to modification, unless such a basis for rates and charges is waived by the purchaser by contract; and

(3) be developed to recover the agency's cost of producing and transmitting the electric power and energy, as applicable, which cost must include the amortization of capital investment.

(b) Notwithstanding Subsection (a), this state reserves its power to regulate an agency's rates and charges for electric energy supplied by the agency's facilities.

(c) Until obligations issued under this subchapter have been paid and discharged, with all interest on the obligations, interest on unpaid interest installments on the obligations, and other connected and incurred costs or expenses, this state pledges to and agrees with the purchasers and successive holders of the obligations that it will not:

(1) limit or alter the power of an agency to establish and collect rates and charges under this section sufficient to pay:

(A) necessary operational and maintenance expenses;

(B) interest and principal on obligations issued by the agency;

(C) sinking funds and reserve fund payments; and

(D) other charges necessary to fulfill the terms of any agreement; or

(2) take any action that will impair the rights or remedies of the holders of the obligations.

Acts 1997, 75th Leg., ch. 166, § 1, eff. Sept. 1, 1997.

§ 163.064. Revenue Bonds

(a) The agency may issue revenue bonds to accomplish the purposes of the agency.

(b) The agency may pledge to the payment of the obligations the revenues of all or part of its electric facilities, including facilities acquired after the obligations are issued. However, operating and maintenance expenses, including salaries and labor, materials, and repairs of electric facilities necessary to render efficient service constitute a first lien on and charge against the pledged revenue.

(c) The agency may set aside from the proceeds from the sale of the obligations amounts for payment into the interest and sinking fund and reserve fund, and for interest and operating expenses during construction and development, as specified in the proceedings authorizing the obligations.

(d) Obligation proceeds may be invested, pending their use, in securities, interest-bearing certificates, or time deposits as specified in the authorizing proceedings.

(e) Agency obligations are authorized investments for:

(1) a bank;

(2) a savings bank;

(3) a trust company;

(4) a savings and loan association; and

(5) an insurance company.

(f) The obligations, when accompanied by all appurtenant, unmatured coupons and to the extent of the lesser of their face value or market value, are eligible to secure the deposit of public funds of this state, a political subdivision of this state, and any other political corporation of this state.

Acts 1997, 75th Leg., ch. 166, § 1, eff. Sept. 1, 1997.

§ 163.065. Refunding Bonds

The agency may issue refunding bonds.

Acts 1997, 75th Leg., ch. 166, § 1, eff. Sept. 1, 1997.

§ 163.066. Issuance, Form, and Provisions of Bonds

(a) Agency bonds that are payable from agency revenues or anticipated bond proceeds and the records relating to their issuance must be submitted to the attorney general for examination before delivery.

(b) The bonds:

(1) must mature serially or otherwise not more than 50 years after the date of issuance;

(2) may be made redeemable before maturity at the time and at the price or prices set by the agency; and

(3) may be sold at public or private sale under the terms and for the price the agency determines to be in the best interest of the agency.

(c) The bonds must be signed by the presiding officer or assistant presiding officer of the agency, be attested by the secretary, and bear the seal of the agency. The signatures may be printed on the bonds if authorized by the agency, and the seal may be impressed or printed on the bonds. The agency may adopt or use for any purpose the signature of an individual who has been an officer of the agency, regardless of whether the individual has ceased to be an officer at the time the bonds are delivered to the purchaser.

Acts 1997, 75th Leg., ch. 166, § 1, eff. Sept. 1, 1997.

§ 163.067. Nonnegotiable Purchase Money Notes

(a) The agency may issue nonnegotiable purchase money notes to acquire land or fuel resources.

(b) Nonnegotiable purchase money notes are:

(1) payable in installments;

(2) secured by the property acquired with the notes or other collateral the agency substitutes; and

(3) not a security or agency obligation.

(c) Nonnegotiable purchase money notes may be further secured by a promise to issue bonds or bond anticipation notes to pay the purchase money notes.

Acts 1997, 75th Leg., ch. 166, § 1, eff. Sept. 1, 1997.

§ 163.068. Bond Anticipation Notes

(a) The agency may issue bond anticipation notes:

(1) for any purpose for which the agency may issue bonds; or

(2) to refund previously issued bond anticipation notes or nonnegotiable purchase money notes.

(b) Bond anticipation notes are subject to the limitations and conditions prescribed by this subchapter for bonds.

(c) The agency may contract with purchasers of bond anticipation notes that the proceeds of one or more series of bonds will be used to pay or refund the notes.

Acts 1997, 75th Leg., ch. 166, § 1, eff. Sept. 1, 1997.

SUBCHAPTER D. AGENCY RECEIVING POWER THROUGH INTERSTATE SYSTEM

§ 163.101. Creation

(a) Notwithstanding Section 163.054, two or more public entities may create a municipal power agency governed by Subchapter C [1] if the entities:

(1) are municipalities;

(2) are engaged in the distribution and sale of electric energy to the public; and

(3) receive a major portion of their power through or from an interstate electric system.

(b) The entities must comply with the provisions of Subchapter C relating to the creation of a municipal power agency, including the concurrent ordinance and election provisions.

Acts 1997, 75th Leg., ch. 166, § 1, eff. Sept. 1, 1997.

[1] V.T.C.A., Utilities Code § 163.051 et seq.

§ 163.102. Powers

(a) An agency created under this subchapter may:

(1) generate and transmit electric power and energy inside and outside this state;

(2) sell, purchase, or exchange electric power and energy with entities inside or outside this state; and

(3) construct or acquire new steam electric generating facilities, but only if the facilities are owned jointly by the agency and one or more private entities.

(b) This section does not authorize an agency created under this subchapter to engage in the distribution and retail sale of electric power and energy.

Acts 1997, 75th Leg., ch. 166, § 1, eff. Sept. 1, 1997.

SUBCHAPTER E. ELECTRIC COOPERATIVE CORPORATIONS

§ 163.121. Creation

An electric cooperative corporation may join one or more public entities to create a joint powers agency as if the corporation were also a public entity.

Acts 1997, 75th Leg., ch. 166, § 1, eff. Sept. 1, 1997.

§ 163.122. Application of Open Meetings Law

A joint powers agency created under this subchapter is a governmental body subject to Chapter 551, Government Code.

Acts 1997, 75th Leg., ch. 166, § 1, eff. Sept. 1, 1997.

§ 163.123. Authority of Public Utility Commission

A joint powers agency created under this subchapter is:

(1) subject to all applicable provisions of Title 2; [1] and

(2) under the jurisdiction of the Public Utility Commission of Texas as provided by Title 2.

Acts 1997, 75th Leg., ch. 166, § 1, eff. Sept. 1, 1997.

[1] V.T.C.A., Utilities Code § 11.001 et seq.

§ 163.124. Power to Issue Certain Bonds or Securities

This subchapter does not authorize an electric cooperative corporation to issue bonds or other securities that are tax exempt under federal law.

Acts 1997, 75th Leg., ch. 166, § 1, eff. Sept. 1, 1997.

CHAPTER 164. JOINT OWNERSHIP OF ELECTRIC FACILITIES BY PUBLIC ENTITIES

Section

164.001. Joint Ownership of Electric Utility Facilities Authorized.
164.002. Public Purpose.
164.003. Approval of Agreement by Attorney General.
164.004. Increase in Ownership Shares.
164.005. Contractual Obligations as Lien on System Revenue.
164.006. Construction with Other Laws.

§ 164.001. Joint Ownership of Electric Utility Facilities Authorized

(a) Political subdivisions may join together to finance, construct, complete, acquire, or operate electric utility facilities so that the facilities or an undivided interest in the facilities is jointly owned by the political subdivisions as cotenants or co-owners.

(b) The ownership shares in the facilities are those approved by the governing bodies of the political subdivisions, as set forth in an agreement authorized by the governing bodies.

Acts 1997, 75th Leg., ch. 166, § 1, eff. Sept. 1, 1997.

§ 164.002. Public Purpose

The exercise by a political subdivision of the authority granted by this chapter, including the exercise of the power to issue bonds, notes, or other obligations to accomplish the purposes of this chapter, and the performance of an agreement entered into under this chapter are considered to be additional public purposes of the political subdivision, without regard to any express or implied limitation on the authority or purposes of the political subdivision under any other general or special law or charter provision.

Acts 1997, 75th Leg., ch. 166, § 1, eff. Sept. 1, 1997.

§ 164.003. Approval of Agreement by Attorney General

(a) An agreement between political subdivisions establishing an interest in electric utility facilities that is executed under this chapter shall be submitted to the attorney general in connection with any proceeding to finance the contractual obligation by the issuance of bonds.

(b) An agreement submitted under Subsection (a) is incontestable on approval as to legality by the attorney general.

Acts 1997, 75th Leg., ch. 166, § 1, eff. Sept. 1, 1997.

§ 164.004. Increase in Ownership Shares

(a) An agreement under this chapter may provide for a political subdivision to increase its present or future ownership share of the electric utility facilities by installment purchase payments and for another political subdivision that is a party to the agreement to transfer, in consideration of those payments, any portion of its present or future ownership share of the facilities to the purchasing political subdivision.

(b) A payment made by a political subdivision to acquire an ownership interest is not treated as a maintenance and operating expense but is treated as a capital cost as if the political subdivision had issued bonds to construct or acquire the ownership interest, unless otherwise specified in the agreement.

Acts 1997, 75th Leg., ch. 166, § 1, eff. Sept. 1, 1997.

§ 164.005. Contractual Obligations as Lien on System Revenue

(a) If the electric utility facilities financed, acquired, constructed, or completed are a part of a utility system of a political subdivision, the obligation to make the contract payments to acquire an ownership interest is a lien on the revenue of the system on a parity with the outstanding bonds of the system to the extent permitted in the ordinance or resolution authorizing or the deed of trust or indenture securing the payment of the outstanding bonds.

(b) If the ordinance or resolution authorizing or the deed of trust or trust indenture securing the revenue bonds of a utility system provides for the subsequent issuance of additional bonds or the creation of a contractual obligation described by Section 164.004 and provides that the payments to be made for the security or payment of the subsequent bonds or contractual obligation are to be on a parity with the previously issued bonds or bonds then to be issued, the political subdivision may, subject to any conditions contained in that ordinance, resolution, deed of trust, or trust indenture, authorize, issue, and sell additional bonds or incur the contractual obligation in a different series payable from the entire revenue of the utility system on a parity with the previously issued bonds or bonds then to be issued and secured by a lien on the revenue of the system on a parity with the lien securing the previously issued bonds or bonds then to be issued. This subsection applies without regard to whether the previously issued bonds:

(1) were issued before August 29, 1977; or

(2) are an original issue or a refunding issue.

(c) A political subdivision may pledge the revenue of a utility system to pay contract payments to acquire an ownership interest in an electric utility facility under this chapter.

(d) In this section, "utility system" includes a combined utility system.

Acts 1997, 75th Leg., ch. 166, § 1, eff. Sept. 1, 1997.

§ 164.006. Construction with Other Laws

To provide full authority for the execution of an agreement under this chapter, this chapter applies to a municipality as if this chapter were originally contained in Chapter 1501 or 1502, Government Code, or Chapter 552, Local Government Code. This chapter prevails over any charter provision or general or special law.

Acts 1997, 75th Leg., ch. 166, § 1, eff. Sept. 1, 1997. Amended by Acts 2001, 77th Leg., ch. 1420, § 8.405, eff. Sept. 1, 2001; Acts 2007, 80th Leg., ch. 885, § 3.77(30), eff. April 1, 2009.

SUBTITLE B. PROVISIONS REGULATING DELIVERY OF SERVICES

CHAPTER 181. MISCELLANEOUS POWERS AND DUTIES OF UTILITIES

SUBCHAPTER A. POWERS AND DUTIES OF GAS AND ELECTRIC CORPORATIONS

Section
181.001. Definitions.

Section
181.002. Corporate Powers.
181.003. Authority to Borrow Money, Issue Stock, or Mortgage Property.
181.004. Condemnation of Property.
181.005. Authority to Lay and Maintain Lines.
181.006. Consent Required in Municipality.
181.007. Authority to Hold Land or Other Property.
181.008. Authority Relating to Transport or Sale.
181.009. Discrimination Prohibited.

SUBCHAPTER B. PROVISIONS APPLYING TO GAS UTILITIES

181.021. Definitions.
181.022. Authority to Lay and Maintain Gas Facility.
181.023. Consent Required in Municipality.
181.024. Notice to State or County.
181.025. Relocation of Gas Facility to Allow Change to Traffic Lane.
181.026. Effect of Municipal Incorporation on Gas Facility Previously Laid.

SUBCHAPTER C. PROVISIONS APPLYING TO ELECTRIC UTILITIES

181.041. Definitions.
181.042. Authority to Construct, Maintain, and Operate Lines.
181.043. Consent Required in Municipality.
181.044. Notice to State or County.
181.045. Standards for Construction, Operation, and Maintenance of Lines.
181.046. Relocation of Line to Allow Road or Ditch Improvement.
181.047. Effect of Municipal Incorporation on Line Previously Constructed.

SUBCHAPTER D. PROVISIONS APPLYING TO TELEGRAPH COMPANIES

181.061. Definition.
181.062. Telegraph Connections.
181.063. Exceptions.
181.064. Hearing and Determination.
181.065. Penalty.
181.066. Appeal.

SUBCHAPTER E. PROVISIONS APPLYING TO TELEPHONE AND TELEGRAPH CORPORATIONS

181.081. Definitions.
181.082. Authority to Install Facility in Relation to Public Property.
181.083. Authority to Construct Line on Private Property.
181.084. Appropriation or Condemnation of Land.
181.085. Prohibition on Land Contract Excluding Another Telegraph Utility.
181.086. Lines In or Outside State.
181.087. Use of Another's Telegraph Line.
181.088. Consolidation of Utilities.
181.089. Municipal Regulation.

SUBCHAPTER F. PROVISIONS APPLYING TO COMMUNITY ANTENNA AND CABLE TELEVISION UTILITIES

Section
181.101. Definitions.
181.102. Authority to Install and Maintain Equipment.
181.103. Notice to State or County.
181.104. Relocation of Equipment to Allow Change to Traffic Lane.

SUBCHAPTER Z. MISCELLANEOUS PROVISIONS

181.901. Authority of General-Law Municipality to Protect Utility.
181.902. Authority of General-Law Municipality to Prevent Use or Waste of Utility Commodity or Service.

SUBCHAPTER A. POWERS AND DUTIES OF GAS AND ELECTRIC CORPORATIONS

§ 181.001. Definitions

In this chapter:

(1) "Corporation" includes:

(A) a partnership, limited partnership, or master limited partnership;

(B) a combination of business entities composed exclusively of corporations or in which a corporation is a general partner;

(C) a limited liability company; and

(D) a gas utility or electric utility regardless of form of organization, but not including a municipally owned utility.

(2) "Electric corporation" means an electric current and power corporation.

Acts 1997, 75th Leg., ch. 166, § 1, eff. Sept. 1, 1997. Amended by Acts 1999, 76th Leg., ch. 11, § 3, eff. May 3, 1999; Acts 2003, 78th Leg., ch. 559, § 1, eff. June 20, 2003.

§ 181.002. Corporate Powers

A gas or electric corporation has the powers and rights of a corporation organized for profit in this state whenever those powers and duties may be applicable.

Acts 1997, 75th Leg., ch. 166, § 1, eff. Sept. 1, 1997.

§ 181.003. Authority to Borrow Money, Issue Stock, or Mortgage Property

A gas or electric corporation has the right to:

(1) borrow money;

(2) issue stock, including preferred stock; or

(3) mortgage a franchise or other property of the corporation to secure a debt contracted for any purpose of the corporation.

Acts 1997, 75th Leg., ch. 166, § 1, eff. Sept. 1, 1997.

§ 181.004. Condemnation of Property

A gas or electric corporation has the right and power to enter on, condemn, and appropriate the land, right-of-way, easement, or other property of any person or corporation.

Acts 1997, 75th Leg., ch. 166, § 1, eff. Sept. 1, 1997.

§ 181.005. Authority to Lay and Maintain Lines

(a) A gas corporation has the right to lay and maintain lines over, along, under, and across a public road, an interurban railroad, a street railroad, a canal or stream, or a municipal street or alley and over, under, and across a railroad or a railroad right-of-way only if:

(1) the pipeline complies with:

(A) all safety regulations adopted by the Railroad Commission of Texas and all federal regulations relating to pipeline facilities and pipelines; and

(B) all rules adopted by the Texas Department of Transportation or the Railroad Commission of Texas and all federal regulations regarding the accommodation of utility facilities on a right-of-way, including regulations relating to the horizontal or vertical placement of the pipeline; and

(2) the owner or operator of the pipeline ensures that the public right-of-way and any associated facility are promptly restored to their former condition of usefulness after the installation or maintenance of the pipeline.

(b) The right granted by Subsection (a) relating to the use of a municipal street or alley is subject to the payment of charges in accordance with Section 121.2025 of this code and Sections 182.025 and 182.026, Tax Code.

(c) In determining the route of a pipeline within a municipality, a gas corporation shall consider using existing easements and public rights-of-way, including streets, roads, highways, and utility rights-of-way. In deciding whether to use a public easement or right-of-way, the gas corporation shall consider whether:

(1) the use is economically practicable;

(2) adequate space exists; and

(3) the use will violate, or cause the violation of any pipeline safety regulations.

(d) The Texas Department of Transportation may require the owner or operator of a pipeline to relocate the pipeline:

(1) at the expense of the owner or operator of the pipeline, if the pipeline is located on a right-of-way of the state highway system;

(2) at the expense of this state, if the pipeline is located on property in which the owner or operator of the pipeline has a private interest; or

(3) in accordance with Section 203.092, Transportation Code, at the expense of this state, if the pipeline is owned or operated by a gas utility as defined by Section 181.021 of this code or a common carrier as defined by Chapter 111, Natural Resources Code.

(e) Rules adopted by the Texas Department of Transportation regarding horizontal and vertical placement of pipelines must be reasonable and, for rights-of-way of the state highway system, must provide an appeals process through the Texas Department of Transportation.

Acts 1997, 75th Leg., ch. 166, § 1, eff. Sept. 1, 1997. Amended by Acts 2009, 81st Leg., ch. 1311, § 2, eff. June 19, 2009; Acts 2011, 82nd Leg., ch. 313 (H.B. 2289), § 1, eff. June 17, 2011.

§ 181.006. Consent Required in Municipality

A gas corporation may exercise authority under Section 181.005 in relation to a municipal street or alley with the consent of and subject to the direction of the governing body of the municipality.

Acts 1997, 75th Leg., ch. 166, § 1, eff. Sept. 1, 1997.

§ 181.007. Authority to Hold Land or Other Property

A gas or electric corporation has the power to own, hold, or use land, a right-of-way, an easement, a franchise, or a building or other structure as necessary for the purpose of the corporation.

Acts 1997, 75th Leg., ch. 166, § 1, eff. Sept. 1, 1997.

§ 181.008. Authority Relating to Transport or Sale

(a) A gas or electric corporation has the power to generate, make, manufacture, transport, and sell gas, electric current, and power to an individual, the public, or a municipality for any purpose.

(b) A gas or electric corporation may:

(1) impose reasonable charges for an action taken under Subsection (a); and

(2) construct, maintain, and operate power plants and substations and any machinery, apparatus, pipe, pole, wire, device, or arrangements as necessary to operate its lines in this state.

Acts 1997, 75th Leg., ch. 166, § 1, eff. Sept. 1, 1997.

§ 181.009. Discrimination Prohibited

A gas or electric corporation may not discriminate against a person, corporation, firm, association, or location in:

(1) charging for gas, electric current, or power; or

(2) providing service under similar circumstances.

Acts 1997, 75th Leg., ch. 166, § 1, eff. Sept. 1, 1997.

SUBCHAPTER B. PROVISIONS APPLYING TO GAS UTILITIES

§ 181.021. Definitions

In this subchapter:

(1) "Gas facility" means a pipe, main, conductor, or other facility or fixture used to carry gas.

(2) "Gas utility" means a person, firm, corporation, or municipality engaged in the business of transporting or distributing gas for public consumption.

Acts 1997, 75th Leg., ch. 166, § 1, eff. Sept. 1, 1997.

§ 181.022. Authority to Lay and Maintain Gas Facility

A gas utility has the right to lay and maintain a gas facility through, under, along, across, or over a public highway, a public road, a public street or alley, or public water.

Acts 1997, 75th Leg., ch. 166, § 1, eff. Sept. 1, 1997.

§ 181.023. Consent Required in Municipality

A gas utility may exercise authority under Section 181.022 in a municipality with the consent of and subject to the direction of the governing body of the municipality.

Acts 1997, 75th Leg., ch. 166, § 1, eff. Sept. 1, 1997.

§ 181.024. Notice to State or County

(a) A gas utility proposing under this subchapter to locate a gas facility in the right-of-way of a state highway or a county road not in a municipality shall give notice of the proposal to:

(1) the Texas Transportation Commission if the proposal relates to a state highway; or

(2) the commissioners court of the county if the proposal relates to a county road.

(b) On receipt of the notice, the Texas Transportation Commission or the commissioners court may designate the location in the right-of-way where the gas utility may place the gas facility.

Acts 1997, 75th Leg., ch. 166, § 1, eff. Sept. 1, 1997.

§ 181.025. Relocation of Gas Facility to Allow Change to Traffic Lane

(a) The authority of the Texas Transportation Commission under this section is limited to a gas facility on a state highway not in a municipality. The authority of the commissioners court under this section is limited to a gas facility on a county road not in a municipality.

(b) The Texas Transportation Commission or the commissioners court of a county may require a gas utility to relocate the utility's gas facility, at the utility's own expense, to allow the widening or other changing of a traffic lane.

(c) To impose a requirement under this section, the Texas Transportation Commission or the commissioners court, as appropriate, must give to the gas utility 30 days' written notice of the requirement. The notice must identify the gas facility to be relocated and indicate the location on the new right-of-way where the gas utility may place the facility.

(d) The gas utility shall replace the grade and surface of the highway or road at the utility's own expense.

Acts 1997, 75th Leg., ch. 166, § 1, eff. Sept. 1, 1997.

§ 181.026. Effect of Municipal Incorporation on Gas Facility Previously Laid

A gas utility having a gas facility located in an area that becomes incorporated after the facility is in place may continue to exercise in that area the authority granted by this subchapter until the 10th anniversary of the date of the incorporation without the consent of but subject to the direction of the governing body of the municipality.

Acts 1997, 75th Leg., ch. 166, § 1, eff. Sept. 1, 1997.

SUBCHAPTER C. PROVISIONS APPLYING TO ELECTRIC UTILITIES

§ 181.041. Definitions

In this subchapter:

(1) "Electric utility" means:

(A) an electric cooperative organized under Chapter 161;

(B) a corporation or river authority, if the river authority is created by a statute of this state:

(i) that generates, transmits, or distributes electric energy in this state; and

(ii) whose operations are subject to the judicial and legislative processes of this state; or

(C) a municipal electric utility.

(2) "Municipal electric utility" means a municipality in this state that owns and operates an electric generating plant or that operates electric transmission lines or an electric distribution system.

Acts 1997, 75th Leg., ch. 166, § 1, eff. Sept. 1, 1997.

§ 181.042. Authority to Construct, Maintain, and Operate Lines

An electric utility has the right to construct, maintain, and operate lines over, under, across, on, or along a state highway, a county road, a municipal street or alley, or other public property in a municipality.

Acts 1997, 75th Leg., ch. 166, § 1, eff. Sept. 1, 1997.

§ 181.043. Consent Required in Municipality

(a) An electric utility may exercise authority under Section 181.042 in a municipality with the consent of and subject to the direction of the governing body of the municipality.

(b) Subsection (a) does not apply to a municipal electric utility exercising authority under Section 181.042 in its municipal territory.

Acts 1997, 75th Leg., ch. 166, § 1, eff. Sept. 1, 1997.

§ 181.044. Notice to State or County

(a) An electric utility proposing under this subchapter to construct a line along the right-of-way of a state highway or a county road not in a municipality shall give notice of the proposal to:

(1) the Texas Transportation Commission if the proposal relates to a state highway; or

(2) the commissioners court of the county if the proposal relates to a county road.

(b) On receipt of the notice, the Texas Transportation Commission or the commissioners court may designate the location along the right-of-way where the electric utility may construct the line.

Acts 1997, 75th Leg., ch. 166, § 1, eff. Sept. 1, 1997.

§ 181.045. Standards for Construction, Operation, and Maintenance of Lines

(a) A municipal electric utility shall construct, operate, and maintain its lines for the transmission and distribution of electric energy along highways and at other places in accordance with the national electrical safety code. With regard to clearances, an electric utility that is not a municipal electric utility shall construct, operate, and maintain its lines for the transmission and distribution of electric energy along highways and at other places in accordance with the national electrical safety code.

(b) Regardless of Subsection (a), an electric utility shall:

(1) use single pole construction for a line along a highway or county road;

(2) construct a transmission line that crosses a highway or road so that the line is at least 22 feet above the surface of the traffic lane; and

(3) construct a line that is above a railroad track or railroad siding so that the line is at least 22 feet above the surface of the track or siding.

(c) Subsection (a) does not apply to a line in a municipality to the extent an ordinance or regulation applying in the municipality provides differently than the national electrical safety code.

(d) In this section, "national electrical safety code" means the National Electrical Safety Code, as published in March 1948 by the National Bureau of Standards, Handbook 30, as revised by Handbook 81, published by the National Bureau of Standards in November 1961.

Acts 1997, 75th Leg., ch. 166, § 1, eff. Sept. 1, 1997.

§ 181.046. Relocation of Line to Allow Road or Ditch Improvement

(a) The authority of the Texas Transportation Commission under this section is limited to a line on a state highway not in a municipality. The authority of the commissioners court under this section is limited to a line on a county road not in a municipality.

(b) The Texas Transportation Commission or the commissioners court of a county may require an electric utility to relocate a line of the utility, at the utility's own expense, to allow the:

(1) widening of a right-of-way;

(2) changing of a traffic lane;

(3) improving of a road bed; or

(4) improving of a drainage ditch located on a right-of-way.

(c) To impose a requirement under this section, the Texas Transportation Commission or the commissioners court, as appropriate, must give to the electric utility 30 days' written notice of the requirement. The notice must identify the line to be relocated and indicate the location on the new right-of-way where the electric utility may place the line.

Acts 1997, 75th Leg., ch. 166, § 1, eff. Sept. 1, 1997.

§ 181.047. Effect of Municipal Incorporation on Line Previously Constructed

(a) An electric utility that owns a line on a state highway or county road in a city or town that, at the time of the construction of the line, is unincorporated but that later incorporates as a municipality may continue to exercise in the municipality the authority granted by Section 181.042 until the 10th anniversary of the date of the incorporation.

(b) After that period, to continue to exercise the authority in the municipality the electric utility must have the consent of the governing body of the municipality.

(c) The governing body of the municipality may require the electric utility to relocate a pole or line, at the utility's own expense, to allow the widening or straightening of a street. To impose a requirement under this subsection, the governing body of the municipality must give to the electric utility 30 days' notice. The notice must indicate the new location for the pole or line along the right-of-way of the street.

(d) This section does not prohibit a municipality from imposing a tax or special charge for the use of a street as authorized by Subchapter B, Chapter 182, Tax Code.[1]

Acts 1997, 75th Leg., ch. 166, § 1, eff. Sept. 1, 1997.

[1] V.T.C.A., Tax Code § 182.021 et seq.

SUBCHAPTER D. PROVISIONS APPLYING TO TELEGRAPH COMPANIES

§ 181.061. Definition

In this subchapter, "telegraph company" includes a person, firm, corporation, or association engaged in the business of accepting and transmitting messages to and from different locations in this state through use of a telegraph.

Acts 1997, 75th Leg., ch. 166, § 1, eff. Sept. 1, 1997.

§ 181.062. Telegraph Connections

A telegraph company engaged in business at the same location or in the same municipality as another telegraph company shall provide:

(1) means through which a message may be transferred to the lines of the other telegraph company at common locations and transmitted to the message's final destination; and

(2) facilities to assure the transfer of a message in compliance with this section.

Acts 1997, 75th Leg., ch. 166, § 1, eff. Sept. 1, 1997.

§ 181.063. Exceptions

(a) A telegraph company is not required to transfer a message to another line if:

(1) the message originated on the company's line; and

(2) the company can deliver the message directly to its intended recipient on the company's lines.

(b) A telegraph company is not required to receive a message from another's line and transmit the message to its final destination if the message originated at a location on the company's lines.

Acts 1997, 75th Leg., ch. 166, § 1, eff. Sept. 1, 1997.

§ 181.064. Hearing and Determination

(a) The governing body of a municipality or, for an unincorporated area, the commissioners court of the county, shall on its own motion or on application of at least 100 residents:

(1) hear evidence as the governing body or commissioners court considers necessary; and

(2) determine whether a connection between different lines or other arrangements for transfer of messages is:

(A) necessary for public convenience; and

(B) just to the telegraph companies.

(b) After conducting a hearing and making the determinations required by Subsection (a), the governing body or commissioners court shall issue an order that:

(1) includes the findings of the governing body or commissioners court;

(2) specifies the conditions under which the arrangements for transfer of messages will be made; and

(3) specifies the proportion of expense to be paid by the owner or operator of each line.

Acts 1997, 75th Leg., ch. 166, § 1, eff. Sept. 1, 1997.

§ 181.065. Penalty

(a) A telegraph company shall comply with an order of a municipality's governing body or a commissioners court requiring the company to arrange for transfer of messages.

(b) A telegraph company that fails to comply with an order is subject to a penalty of $10 for each day of noncompliance, payable to the state. The county or district attorney may bring suit to recover the penalty.

(c) A penalty may not be imposed against a telegraph company for noncompliance with an order if:

(1) the company is prevented from making a connection through the fault or omission of another company; and

(2) the fault or omission causes the company's failure to connect.

Acts 1997, 75th Leg., ch. 166, § 1, eff. Sept. 1, 1997.

§ 181.066. Appeal

(a) A telegraph company ordered to transfer messages under this subchapter has the right to appeal to the court having jurisdiction over the matter.

(b) If the court finds that the telegraph company had reasonable grounds for bringing the appeal, the court shall suspend any penalty imposed under this subchapter until the appeal is finally determined.

Acts 1997, 75th Leg., ch. 166, § 1, eff. Sept. 1, 1997.

SUBCHAPTER E. PROVISIONS APPLYING TO TELEPHONE AND TELEGRAPH CORPORATIONS

§ 181.081. Definitions

In this subchapter:

(1) "Facility" means a pole, pier, abutment, wire, or other fixture related to a telephone or magnetic telegraph line.

(2) "Telegraph corporation" means a corporation created to construct and maintain magnetic telegraph lines.

(3) "Telephone corporation" means a corporation created to construct and maintain telephone lines.

Acts 1997, 75th Leg., ch. 166, § 1, eff. Sept. 1, 1997.

§ 181.082. Authority to Install Facility in Relation to Public Property

A telephone or telegraph corporation may install a facility of the corporation along, on, or across a public road, a public street, or public water in a manner that does not inconvenience the public in the use of the road, street, or water.

Acts 1997, 75th Leg., ch. 166, § 1, eff. Sept. 1, 1997.

§ 181.083. Authority to Construct Line on Private Property

A telephone or telegraph corporation may enter land in which a private person or a corporation owns a fee or lesser estate to:

(1) make a preliminary survey or examination to prepare for the construction of a telephone or telegraph line;

(2) change the location of a part of a telephone or telegraph line as necessary; or

(3) construct or repair a telephone or telegraph line.

Acts 1997, 75th Leg., ch. 166, § 1, eff. Sept. 1, 1997.

§ 181.084. Appropriation or Condemnation of Land

A telephone or telegraph corporation has the right to:

(1) appropriate as much land owned by a private person or a corporation as is necessary to construct a facility; or

(2) condemn land to acquire a right-of-way or other interest in the land for the use of the telephone or telegraph corporation.

Acts 1997, 75th Leg., ch. 166, § 1, eff. Sept. 1, 1997.

§ 181.085. Prohibition on Land Contract Excluding Another Telegraph Utility

A telegraph corporation may not contract with an owner of land for the right to construct and maintain a telegraph line over the land to the exclusion of the line of another telegraph corporation.

Acts 1997, 75th Leg., ch. 166, § 1, eff. Sept. 1, 1997.

§ 181.086. Lines In or Outside State

A telegraph corporation may construct, own, use, or maintain a telegraph line in or outside this state.

Acts 1997, 75th Leg., ch. 166, § 1, eff. Sept. 1, 1997.

§ 181.087. Use of Another's Telegraph Line

(a) A telegraph corporation may:

(1) lease the telegraph line of another telegraph corporation;

(2) as the result of a lease or purchase, attach to its telegraph line the telegraph line of another telegraph corporation; or

(3) join with any other corporation or association to construct, lease, own, use, or maintain a telegraph line.

(b) An action under Subsection (a)(3) must be taken in accordance with an agreement made by the directors or managers of the telegraph corporations.

Acts 1997, 75th Leg., ch. 166, § 1, eff. Sept. 1, 1997.

§ 181.088. Consolidation of Utilities

(a) A telephone or telegraph corporation organized under the law of this state may consolidate or otherwise unite with one or more other companies organized under the law of a state or the United States if the union or consolidation:

(1) is approved, at a regular meeting of the corporation's stockholders, by a vote of persons holding a majority of the shares of stock of the corporation; and

(2) is done with the consent of each other company.

(b) The company resulting from the consolidation or other union may hold, use, and enjoy the rights and privileges given by the law of this state to, and has the same liabilities of, a company separately organized under the law of this state relating to corporations.

Acts 1997, 75th Leg., ch. 166, § 1, eff. Sept. 1, 1997.

§ 181.089. Municipal Regulation

(a) The appropriate authorities of a municipality through which a line of a telephone or telegraph corporation is to pass may adopt, by ordinance or another method, regulations governing the corporation that specify the:

(1) location of the facilities of the corporation;

(2) kind of posts that must be used by the corporation; or

(3) height at which the wires of the corporation must be placed.

(b) After the construction of the telephone or telegraph line, the appropriate authorities of the municipality, after giving the corporation or its agents an opportunity to be heard, may direct any change in:

(1) the construction or location of the facilities; or

(2) the height at which the corporation must locate the wires.

Acts 1997, 75th Leg., ch. 166, § 1, eff. Sept. 1, 1997.

SUBCHAPTER F. PROVISIONS APPLYING TO COMMUNITY ANTENNA AND CABLE TELEVISION UTILITIES

§ 181.101. Definitions

In this subchapter:

(1) "Equipment" means a line, wire, cable, pipe, conduit, conductor, pole, or other facility for the transmission of community antenna or cable television service.

(2) "Person" means an individual, firm, or corporation.

Acts 1997, 75th Leg., ch. 166, § 1, eff. Sept. 1, 1997.

§ 181.102. Authority to Install and Maintain Equipment

(a) In an unincorporated area, a person in the business of providing community antenna or cable television service to the public may install and maintain equipment through, under, along, across, or over a utility easement, a public road, an alley, or a body of public water in accordance with this subchapter.

(b) The installation and maintenance of the equipment must be done in a way that does not unduly inconvenience the public using the affected property.

Acts 1997, 75th Leg., ch. 166, § 1, eff. Sept. 1, 1997.

§ 181.103. Notice to State or County

(a) A person proposing to install equipment under Section 181.102 in the right-of-way of a state highway or a county road shall give notice of the proposal to:

(1) the Texas Department of Transportation if the proposal relates to a state highway; or

(2) the commissioners court of the county if the proposal relates to a county road.

(b) On receipt of the notice, the Texas Department of Transportation or commissioners court may designate the location in the right-of-way where the person may install the equipment, if the equipment is not to be installed on an existing facility.

Acts 1997, 75th Leg., ch. 166, § 1, eff. Sept. 1, 1997.

§ 181.104. Relocation of Equipment to Allow Change to Traffic Lane

(a) The authority of the Texas Department of Transportation under this section is limited to equipment installed in connection with a state highway. The authority of the commissioners court under this section is limited to equipment installed in connection with a county road.

(b) The Texas Department of Transportation or the commissioners court of a county may require a person who has installed equipment in the right-of-way of a state highway or county road to relocate the person's equipment to allow the widening or other changing of a traffic lane.

(c) To impose a requirement under this section, the Texas Department of Transportation or the commissioners court, as appropriate, must give to the person written notice of the requirement not later than the 45th day before the date the relocation is to be made. The notice must identify the equipment to be relocated and indicate the location in the right-of-way where the person may reinstall the equipment.

(d) The person shall pay the cost of repairing a state highway or county road damaged by the relocation.

Acts 1997, 75th Leg., ch. 166, § 1, eff. Sept. 1, 1997.

SUBCHAPTER Z. MISCELLANEOUS PROVISIONS

§ 181.901. Authority of General-Law Municipality to Protect Utility

(a) The governing body of a general-law municipality may adopt an ordinance that applies to a utility using the streets and public grounds of the municipality and that protects the utility:

(1) in the free enjoyment of the utility's rights and privileges; and

(2) from interference with the utility's property and franchises.

(b) In this section, "utility" means a person, company, or corporation engaged in furnishing water, gas, telephone, light, power, or sewage service to the public.

Acts 1997, 75th Leg., ch. 166, § 1, eff. Sept. 1, 1997.

§ 181.902. Authority of General-Law Municipality to Prevent Use or Waste of Utility Commodity or Service

(a) The governing body of a general-law municipality may adopt an ordinance that prevents the free or unauthorized use or the waste of a commodity or service furnished by a utility that uses the streets and public grounds of the municipality.

(b) In this section, "utility" has the meaning assigned to the term by Section 181.901.

Acts 1997, 75th Leg., ch. 166, § 1, eff. Sept. 1, 1997.

CHAPTER 182. RIGHTS OF UTILITY CUSTOMERS

SUBCHAPTER A. PAYMENT DATE OF UTILITY BILL FOR ELDERLY INDIVIDUAL

Section

182.001. Definitions.
182.002. Delay of Bill Payment Date for Elderly Individual.
182.003. Request for Delay.
182.004. Proof of Age.
182.005. Certain Utilities Not Affected.

SUBCHAPTER B. CONFIDENTIALITY OF CUSTOMER INFORMATION

182.051. Definitions.
182.052. Confidentiality of Personal Information.
182.053. Fee.
182.054. Exceptions.
182.055. No Civil Liability From Violation.

SUBCHAPTER C. TESTING OF METERS

182.101. Definitions.
182.102. Testing of Meter.
182.103. Utility Representative; Notice.
182.104. Offense.

SUBCHAPTER A. PAYMENT DATE OF UTILITY BILL FOR ELDERLY INDIVIDUAL

§ 182.001. Definitions

In this subchapter:

(1) "Elderly individual" means an individual who is 60 years of age or older.

(2) "Utility" means an electric, gas, water, or telephone utility operated by a public or private entity.

Acts 1997, 75th Leg., ch. 166, § 1, eff. Sept. 1, 1997.

§ 182.002. Delay of Bill Payment Date for Elderly Individual

(a) On request by an elderly individual, a utility shall delay without penalty the payment date of a bill for providing utility service to that individual until the 25th day after the date the bill is issued.

(b) This subchapter applies only to an elderly individual who:

(1) is a residential customer; and

(2) occupies the entire premises for which a delay is requested.

Acts 1997, 75th Leg., ch. 166, § 1, eff. Sept. 1, 1997.

§ 182.003. Request for Delay

An elderly individual may request that the utility implement the delay under Section 182.002 for:

(1) the most recent utility bill; or

(2) the most recent utility bill and each subsequent utility bill.

Acts 1997, 75th Leg., ch. 166, § 1, eff. Sept. 1, 1997.

§ 182.004. Proof of Age

A utility may require an individual requesting a delay under this subchapter to present reasonable proof that the individual is 60 years of age or older.

Acts 1997, 75th Leg., ch. 166, § 1, eff. Sept. 1, 1997.

§ 182.005. Certain Utilities Not Affected

This subchapter does not apply to a utility that:

(1) does not assess a late payment charge on a residential customer;

(2) does not suspend service before the 26th day after the date of the bill for which collection action is taken; and

(3) is regulated under Title 2.[1]

Acts 1997, 75th Leg., ch. 166, § 1, eff. Sept. 1, 1997.

[1] V.T.C.A., Utilities Code § 11.001 et seq.

SUBCHAPTER B. CONFIDENTIALITY OF CUSTOMER INFORMATION

§ 182.051. Definitions

In this subchapter:

(1) "Consumer reporting agency" means a person who, for a monetary fee or payment of dues, or on a cooperative nonprofit basis, regularly engages in the practice of assembling or evaluating consumer credit information or other information relating to consumers in order to furnish a consumer report to a third party.

(2) "Governmental body" has the meaning assigned by Section 552.003, Government Code.

(3) "Government-operated utility" means a governmental body or an entity governed by a governmental body that, for compensation, provides water, wastewater, sewer, gas, garbage, electricity, or drainage service.

(4) "Personal information" means an individual's address, telephone number, or social security number.

Acts 1997, 75th Leg., ch. 166, § 1, eff. Sept. 1, 1997.

§ 182.052. Confidentiality of Personal Information

(a) Except as provided by Section 182.054, a government-operated utility may not disclose personal information in a customer's account record, or any information relating to the volume or units of utility usage or the amounts billed to or collected from the individual for utility usage, if the customer requests that the government-operated utility keep the information confidential. However, a government-operated utility may disclose information related to the customer's volume or units of utility usage or amounts billed to or collected from the individual for utility usage if the primary source of water for such utility was a sole-source designated aquifer.

(b) A customer may request confidentiality by delivering to the government-operated utility an appropriately marked form provided under Subsection (c)(3) or any other written request for confidentiality.

(c) A government-operated utility shall include with a bill sent to each customer:

(1) a notice of the customer's right to request confidentiality under this subchapter;

(2) a statement of the amount of any fee applicable to the request; and

(3) a form by which the customer may request confidentiality by marking an appropriate box on the form and returning it to the government-operated utility.

(d) A customer may rescind a request for confidentiality by providing the government-operated utility written permission to disclose personal information.

Acts 1997, 75th Leg., ch. 166, § 1, eff. Sept. 1, 1997. Amended by Acts 2001, 77th Leg., ch. 966, § 2.59, eff. Sept. 1, 2001.

§ 182.053. Fee

A government-operated utility may charge each customer who requests confidentiality under this subchapter a fee not to exceed the administrative cost of complying with the request of confidentiality.

Acts 1997, 75th Leg., ch. 166, § 1, eff. Sept. 1, 1997.

§ 182.054. Exceptions

This subchapter does not prohibit a government-operated utility from disclosing personal information in a customer's account record to:

(1) an official or employee of the state, a political subdivision of the state, or the United States acting in an official capacity;

(2) an employee of a utility acting in connection with the employee's duties;

(3) a consumer reporting agency;

(4) a contractor or subcontractor approved by and providing services to the utility, the state, a political subdivision of the state, or the United States;

(5) a person for whom the customer has contractually waived confidentiality for personal information; or

(6) another entity that provides water, wastewater, sewer, gas, garbage, electricity, or drainage service for compensation.

Acts 1997, 75th Leg., ch. 166, § 1, eff. Sept. 1, 1997.

§ 182.055. No Civil Liability From Violation

A government-operated utility or an officer or employee of a government-operated utility is immune from civil liability for a violation of this subchapter.

Acts 1997, 75th Leg., ch. 166, § 1, eff. Sept. 1, 1997.

SUBCHAPTER C. TESTING OF METERS

§ 182.101. Definitions

In this subchapter:

(1) "Consumer" means a person who obtains electricity or gas from a utility.

(2) "Gas" includes natural gas and artificial gas.

(3) "Meter" means an instrument or machine used to measure and record the use of electricity or gas.

(4) "Test" includes, in reference to the testing of a meter and as necessary to the reading and examination of a meter, the authority to break the seal.

(5) "Utility" means a person, other than a governmental entity, who provides for compensation electricity or gas for consumption in a municipality.

Acts 1997, 75th Leg., ch. 166, § 1, eff. Sept. 1, 1997.

§ 182.102. Testing of Meter

(a) On complaint by a consumer to the governing body of a municipality, an agent or employee of the municipality shall examine, read, and test a meter that is installed by the utility furnishing the electricity or gas.

(b) On demand by a consumer to the governing body of a municipality, the governing body shall provide the consumer with a detailed report stating the results of the examination, reading, and test, including:

(1) whether the meter is in good condition;

(2) whether the meter functions properly; and

(3) the amount of electricity or gas used during a period designated by the consumer in the demand, not to exceed one year.

Acts 1997, 75th Leg., ch. 166, § 1, eff. Sept. 1, 1997.

§ 182.103. Utility Representative; Notice

A utility representative may be present during a meter test. The municipality shall provide notice to a utility regarding the testing of a meter not later than the third day before the date the meter test is conducted.

Acts 1997, 75th Leg., ch. 166, § 1, eff. Sept. 1, 1997.

§ 182.104. Offense

(a) A utility or other person commits an offense if the utility or other person fails or refuses to allow an agent or employee of a municipality to examine a meter.

(b) An offense under this section is a misdemeanor punishable by a fine not to exceed $200.

(c) Each day a utility or other person refuses to allow an agent or employee of a municipality to examine a meter is a separate offense.

Acts 1997, 75th Leg., ch. 166, § 1, eff. Sept. 1, 1997.

CHAPTER 183. UTILITY DEPOSITS

Section
183.001. Definitions.
183.002. Interest on Deposit.
183.003. Rate of Interest.
183.004. Interest Payment to Depositor.
183.005. Return of Deposit.
183.006. Criminal Penalty.

§ 183.001. Definitions

In this chapter:

(1) "Commission" means the Public Utility Commission of Texas.

(2) "Utility" means a person, firm, company, corporation, receiver, or trustee who furnishes water, electric, gas, or telephone service.

Acts 1997, 75th Leg., ch. 166, § 1, eff. Sept. 1, 1997.

§ 183.002. Interest on Deposit

A utility that requires the user of a service to pay a money deposit as a condition to furnishing the service shall pay interest on the deposit from the time the deposit is made.

Acts 1997, 75th Leg., ch. 166, § 1, eff. Sept. 1, 1997.

§ 183.003. Rate of Interest

The commission each December 1, or the next regular workday if December 1 is a Saturday, Sunday, or legal holiday, shall set the annual interest rate for the next calendar year on deposits governed by this chapter at the average rate paid over the previous 12–month period on United States treasury bills with a 26–week maturity.

Acts 1997, 75th Leg., ch. 166, § 1, eff. Sept. 1, 1997. Amended by Acts 2005, 79th Leg., ch. 1320, § 1, eff. Sept. 1, 2005.

§ 183.004. Interest Payment to Depositor

A utility shall pay interest on the deposit to the depositor or the depositor's heirs or assigns annually on demand or sooner if the service is discontinued.

Acts 1997, 75th Leg., ch. 166, § 1, eff. Sept. 1, 1997.

§ 183.005. Return of Deposit

(a) When the service is discontinued, the utility shall return the deposit and any unpaid interest on the deposit to the depositor or the depositor's heirs or legal representatives.

(b) The utility company may deduct from the amount returned under Subsection (a) any payments due for the services.

Acts 1997, 75th Leg., ch. 166, § 1, eff. Sept. 1, 1997.

§ 183.006. Criminal Penalty

(a) A person commits an offense if the person violates this chapter.

(b) An offense under this section is punishable by:

(1) a fine of not less than $25 and not more than $200;

(2) confinement in jail for not less than six months and not more than one year; or

(3) both the fine and confinement.

Acts 1997, 75th Leg., ch. 166, § 1, eff. Sept. 1, 1997.

CHAPTER 184. ELECTRIC AND WATER METERING

SUBCHAPTER A. GENERAL PROVISIONS

Section

184.001. Definition.

SUBCHAPTER B. METERING IN APARTMENTS, CONDOMINIUMS, AND MOBILE HOME PARKS

184.011. Definitions.
184.012. New Construction or Conversion.
184.0125. Housing for Older Persons.
184.013. Submetering.
184.014. Rules.

SUBCHAPTER C. METERING IN RECREATIONAL VEHICLE PARKS

184.031. Definitions.
184.032. Metered Sale Under Commission Rules.
184.033. Metered Sale Under This Chapter.
184.034. Computation of Charges.
184.035. Refund of Surcharges.

SUBCHAPTER D. CENTRAL SYSTEM UTILITIES

184.051. Definitions.
184.052. Rules.

SUBCHAPTER E. LIABILITY FOR RULE VIOLATION

184.071. Liability.

SUBCHAPTER A. GENERAL PROVISIONS

§ 184.001. Definition

In this chapter, "commission" means the Public Utility Commission of Texas.

Acts 1997, 75th Leg., ch. 166, § 1, eff. Sept. 1, 1997.

SUBCHAPTER B. METERING IN APARTMENTS, CONDOMINIUMS, AND MOBILE HOME PARKS

§ 184.011. Definitions

In this subchapter:

(1) "Apartment house" means one or more buildings containing more than five dwelling units each of which is rented primarily for nontransient use with rent paid at intervals of one week or longer. The term includes a rented or owner-occupied residential condominium.

(2) "Dwelling unit" means:

(A) one or more rooms that are suitable for occupancy as a residence and that contain kitchen and bathroom facilities; or

(B) a mobile home in a mobile home park.

Acts 1997, 75th Leg., ch. 166, § 1, eff. Sept. 1, 1997.

§ 184.012. New Construction or Conversion

(a) A political subdivision may not authorize the construction or occupancy of a new apartment house, including the conversion of property to a condominium, unless the construction plan provides for the measurement of the quantity of electricity consumed by the occupants of each dwelling unit of the apartment house, either by individual metering by the utility company or by submetering by the owner.

(b) This section does not prohibit a political subdivision from issuing a permit to a nonprofit organization for construction of a new apartment house for occupancy by low-income elderly tenants if the nonprofit organization establishes, by submitting engineering and cost data and a sworn statement, that all cost savings will be passed on to the low-income elderly tenants.

Acts 1997, 75th Leg., ch. 166, § 1, eff. Sept. 1, 1997.

§ 184.0125. Housing for Older Persons

(a) Section 184.012 does not prohibit a political subdivision from issuing a permit for the construction of housing for older persons with 100 or more dwelling units.

(b) Before issuing a permit, certificate, or other authorization for the construction of housing for older persons, a political subdivision shall require that the construction plan provide for the requirements prescribed by this section.

(c) To qualify for the exemption provided by this section, the housing, at a minimum, must have:

(1) significant facilities and services specifically designed to meet the physical or social needs of older persons or, if the provision of those facilities and services is not practicable, the housing must be necessary to provide important housing opportunities for older persons;

(2) at least 80 percent of the dwelling units set aside for occupancy by at least one person 55 years of age or older in each dwelling unit; and

(3) policies and procedures that demonstrate an intent by the owner or manager to provide housing for persons 55 years of age or older.

(d) The owner or manager must adhere to the policies and procedures required by Subsection (c)(3).

(e) In this section, "housing for older persons" means housing:

(1) intended for and solely occupied by persons 62 years of age or older; or

(2) intended and operated for occupancy by at least one person 55 years of age or older in each dwelling unit.

Added by Acts 1999, 76th Leg., ch. 62, § 18.16(a), eff. Sept. 1, 1999.

§ 184.013. Submetering

(a) The owner of an apartment house or mobile home park may submeter each dwelling unit in the apartment house or mobile home park to measure the quantity of electricity consumed by the occupants of the dwelling unit.

(b) Electric submetering equipment is subject to:

(1) the same rules adopted by the commission for accuracy, testing, and recordkeeping of meters installed by electric utilities; and

(2) the meter testing requirements of Subchapter C, Chapter 38.[1]

(c) If not more than 90 days before the date an owner, operator, or manager of an apartment house installs individual meters or submeters in the apartment house the owner, operator, or manager increases rental rates and the increase in rental rates is attributable to the increased cost of utilities, the owner, operator, or manager, on installation of the meters or submeters, shall:

(1) immediately reduce the rental rate by the amount of the increase attributable to the increased cost of utilities; and

(2) refund the amount of the increased rent:

(A) collected in the 90-day period preceding the installation of the meters or submeters; and

(B) attributable to the cost of increased utilities.

Acts 1997, 75th Leg., ch. 166, § 1, eff. Sept. 1, 1997.

[1] V.T.C.A., Utilities Code §§ 38.051, 38.052.

§ 184.014. Rules

(a) The commission shall adopt rules under which an owner, operator, or manager of an apartment house or mobile home park for which electricity is not individually metered may install submetering equipment to allocate fairly the cost of the electrical consumption of each dwelling unit in the apartment house or mobile home park.

(b) In addition to other appropriate safeguards for a tenant of an apartment house or mobile home park, a rule adopted under Subsection (a) must provide that:

(1) the apartment house owner or a mobile home park owner may not charge a tenant more than the cost per kilowatt hour charged by the utility to the owner; and

(2) the apartment house owner shall maintain adequate records relating to submetering and make those records available for inspection by the tenant during reasonable business hours.

(c) A rule adopted under this section has the same effect as a rule adopted under Title 2,[1] and a utility company and the owner, operator, or manager of an apartment house subject to this subchapter is subject to enforcement under Sections 15.021, 15.022, 15.028, 15.029, 15.030, 15.031, 15.032, and 15.033.

Acts 1997, 75th Leg., ch. 166, § 1, eff. Sept. 1, 1997.

[1] V.T.C.A., Utilities Code § 11.001 et seq.

SUBCHAPTER C. METERING IN RECREATIONAL VEHICLE PARKS

§ 184.031. Definitions

In this subchapter:

(1) "Recreational vehicle" has the meaning assigned by Section 522.004(b), Transportation Code.

(2) "Supplying utility" means the electric utility from which a recreational vehicle park owner purchases electricity consumed at the recreational vehicle park.

Acts 1997, 75th Leg., ch. 166, § 1, eff. Sept. 1, 1997.

§ 184.032. Metered Sale Under Commission Rules

The metered sale of electricity by a recreational vehicle park owner in compliance with submetering rules adopted by the commission under Title 2[1] does not constitute the provision of electric service for compensation.

Acts 1997, 75th Leg., ch. 166, § 1, eff. Sept. 1, 1997.

[1] V.T.C.A., Utilities Code § 11.001 et seq.

§ 184.033. Metered Sale Under This Chapter

Notwithstanding any provision of Title 2,[1] the metered sale of electricity by a recreational vehicle park owner does not constitute the provision of electric service for compensation if:

(1) the electricity is consumed in a recreational vehicle that is located in a recreational vehicle park;

(2) the owner can show that the owner does not annually recover from recreational vehicle occupants through metered charges more than the supplying utility charges the owner for electricity that is submetered, taking into account fuel refunds;

(3) the owner establishes a fiscal year for the purposes of this subchapter and maintains for at least three years records of:

(A) bills received from the supplying utility;

(B) charges made to recreational vehicle occupants; and

(C) consumption records for each fiscal year;

(4) the owner charges for electricity using a fixed rate per kilowatt hour for each fiscal year computed at the beginning of the fiscal year in the manner provided by Section 184.034; and

(5) the owner complies with the refund requirements of Section 184.035.

Acts 1997, 75th Leg., ch. 166, § 1, eff. Sept. 1, 1997.

[1] V.T.C.A., Utilities Code § 11.001 et seq.

§ 184.034. Computation of Charges

(a) For the purposes of computing the charge for electricity under Section 184.033(4), the recreational vehicle park owner shall divide the amount charged the owner by the supplying utility for the preceding fiscal year by the total number of kilowatt hours consumed by occupants visiting the park in the preceding fiscal year and round the quotient to the nearest cent.

(b) If since or during the preceding fiscal year the supplying utility increases its rates, the owner may recompute the preceding fiscal year's charges by the utility using the current rates charged by the utility.

(c) If since or during the preceding fiscal year the supplying utility decreases its rates, the owner shall recompute the preceding fiscal year's charges by the utility using the current rates charged by the utility.

(d) An owner may not:

(1) include a charge by the supplying utility for electricity used in a common area or office of the recreational vehicle park in computing the amounts under Subsection (b) or (c); or

(2) recover that charge through a metered charge to a recreational vehicle occupant.

Acts 1997, 75th Leg., ch. 166, § 1, eff. Sept. 1, 1997.

§ 184.035. Refund of Surcharges

A recreational vehicle park owner who determines at the end of a fiscal year that the owner has collected more than the amount charged by the supplying utility shall refund the excess amount to occupants visiting the park in the succeeding fiscal year.

Acts 1997, 75th Leg., ch. 166, § 1, eff. Sept. 1, 1997.

SUBCHAPTER D. CENTRAL SYSTEM UTILITIES

§ 184.051. Definitions

In this subchapter:

(1) "Apartment house" means one or more buildings containing two or more dwelling units rented primarily for nontransient use with rent paid at intervals of one week or longer.

(2) "Apartment house owner" means the legal titleholder of an apartment house or an individual, firm, or corporation purporting to be the landlord of tenants in the apartment house.

(3) "Central system utilities" means electricity and water consumed by and wastewater services related to a central air conditioning system, central heating system, central hot water system, or central chilled water system in an apartment house. The term does not include utilities directly consumed in a dwelling unit.

(4) "Customer" means an individual, firm, or corporation in whose name a master meter is connected by a utility.

(5) "Dwelling unit" means one or more rooms that are suitable for occupancy as a residence and that contain kitchen and bathroom facilities.

(6) "Nonsubmetered master metered utility service" means an electric utility service that is master metered for an apartment house but is not submetered.

(7) "Tenant" means a person who is entitled to occupy a dwelling unit in an apartment house to the exclusion of others and who is obligated to pay for the occupancy under a written or oral rental agreement.

(8) "Utility" means a public, private, or member-owned utility that provides electricity, water, or wastewater service to an apartment house served by a master meter.

Acts 1997, 75th Leg., ch. 166, § 1, eff. Sept. 1, 1997.

§ 184.052. Rules

(a) The commission shall adopt rules governing billing systems or methods used by an apartment house owner to prorate or allocate among tenants central system utility costs or nonsubmetered master metered utility service costs.

(b) In addition to other appropriate safeguards for a tenant of an apartment house, a rule adopted under this section must require that:

(1) a rental agreement contain:

(A) a clear written description of the method of computing the allocation of central system utilities or nonsubmetered master metered utilities for the apartment house; and

(B) a statement of the average apartment unit monthly bill for all apartment units for any allocation of central system utilities' costs or nonsubmetered master metered utility service costs for the previous calendar year; and

(2) the apartment house owner:

(A) not impose a charge on a tenant in excess of the actual charge imposed on the owner for utility consumption by the apartment house; and

(B) maintain adequate records, including utility bills and records concerning the central system utility or nonsubmetered master metered utility service consumption of the apartment house, the charges assessed by the utility, and the allocation of central system utilities' costs or nonsubmetered master metered utility service costs to the tenants and make the records available for inspection by the tenants during normal business hours.

(c) A rule adopted under this section has the same effect as a rule adopted under Title 2,[1] and an owner, operator, or manager of an apartment house subject to this subchapter is subject to enforcement under Sections 15.021, 15.022, 15.028, 15.029, 15.030, 15.031, 15.032, and 15.033.

Acts 1997, 75th Leg., ch. 166, § 1, eff. Sept. 1, 1997.

[1] V.T.C.A., Utilities Code § 11.001 et seq.

SUBCHAPTER E. LIABILITY FOR RULE VIOLATION

§ 184.071. Liability

(a) A landlord who violates a commission rule relating to submetering of electric utilities consumed exclusively in a tenant's dwelling unit or a rule relating to the allocation of central system utility costs or nonsubmetered master metered electric utility costs is liable to the tenant for:

(1) three times the amount of any overcharge;

(2) a civil penalty equal to one month's rent;

(3) reasonable attorney's fees; and

(4) court costs.

(b) A landlord is not liable for the civil penalty provided by Subsection (a)(2) if the landlord proves that the landlord's violation of the rule was an unintentional mistake made in good faith.

Acts 1997, 75th Leg., ch. 166, § 1, eff. Sept. 1, 1997.

CHAPTER 185. RATING OF SOLAR ENERGY DEVICES

Section
185.001. Definitions.
185.002. Compliance.
185.003. Adoption of Standards.
185.004. Use of National Standards.
185.005. Review of Standards.

§ 185.001. Definitions

In this chapter:

(1) "Commission" means the Public Utility Commission of Texas.

(2) "Solar energy device" means a solar energy collector or solar energy system that provides for the collection of solar energy or the subsequent use of that energy as thermal, mechanical, or electrical energy.

Acts 1997, 75th Leg., ch. 166, § 1, eff. Sept. 1, 1997.

§ 185.002. Compliance

A person who rates, labels, or certifies the performance of a solar energy device in this state shall comply with the standards adopted by the commission under this chapter.

Acts 1997, 75th Leg., ch. 166, § 1, eff. Sept. 1, 1997.

§ 185.003. Adoption of Standards

(a) The commission shall study and adopt standards for rating solar energy devices. The standards shall be used in performance labeling and certification of solar energy devices in this state.

(b) The commission shall examine rating standards and certification programs used by other states and by industry in adopting standards under this section.

(c) The commission shall adopt the standards that the commission finds are the most widely used unless the commission finds that those standards are not suitable for use in this state. If the commission finds that a widely used standard is not suitable, the commission may amend the standard or adopt a standard that the commission finds suitable.

Acts 1997, 75th Leg., ch. 166, § 1, eff. Sept. 1, 1997.

§ 185.004. Use of National Standards

If national standards for rating and certifying solar energy devices are developed by a federal agency in conjunction with the states and industry, the commission shall adopt those national standards as the standards for use in this state.

Acts 1997, 75th Leg., ch. 166, § 1, eff. Sept. 1, 1997.

§ 185.005. Review of Standards

The commission shall periodically review the standards adopted under this chapter and shall amend those standards as necessary to ensure that the standards are:

(1) appropriate in view of current technology; and

(2) the same as or similar to the standards widely used by other states and by industry.

Acts 1997, 75th Leg., ch. 166, § 1, eff. Sept. 1, 1997.

CHAPTER 186. PROVISIONS TO ENSURE THE RELIABILITY AND INTEGRITY OF UTILITY SERVICE

SUBCHAPTER A. CONTINUITY OF UTILITY SERVICE

Section
186.001. Definition.
186.002. Policy.
186.003. Enforcement by Executive Department.
186.004. Unlawful Picketing, Threats, or Intimidation.
186.005. Restraining Order.
186.006. Employee Rights.
186.007. Weather Emergency Preparedness Report.

SUBCHAPTER B. MANIPULATION OF SERVICE FOR CERTAIN LAW ENFORCEMENT PURPOSES

186.021. Emergency Involving Hostage or Armed Suspect.

SUBCHAPTER C. FRAUDULENT OBTAINING OF SERVICE

186.031. Definitions.
186.032. Fraudulently Obtaining Telecommunications Services.
186.033. Disposition of Certain Equipment.

SUBCHAPTER D. AVAILABILITY OF EMERGENCY TELEPHONE SERVICE

Section
186.041. Definitions.
186.042. Obstruction of Emergency Telephone Call; Penalty.
186.043. Falsification of Emergency Telephone Call; Penalty.
186.044. Notice of Certain Offenses Required.
186.045. Failure to Provide Notice; Penalty.

SUBCHAPTER E. CONSTRUCTION AND MAINTENANCE OF FACILITIES ALONG, OVER, UNDER, OR ACROSS RAILROAD RIGHT–OF–WAY

186.051. Definitions.
186.052. Exemptions.
186.053. Applicability.
186.054. Construction and Maintenance of Utility, Common Carrier, Cable Operator, and Energy Transporter Facilities.
186.055. Documentation of Rights Acquired.
186.056. Valuation of Rights Acquired.
186.057. Right to Maintain Facilities.
186.058. License and Renewal.
186.059. Restrictions on Payment of Costs Awarded Against Railroad in Condemnation.
186.060. Cumulative Rights and Responsibilities.
186.061. Effect on Other Law.

SUBCHAPTER A. CONTINUITY OF UTILITY SERVICE

§ 186.001. Definition

In this subchapter, "public utility" means and includes a private corporation that does business in this state and has the right of eminent domain, a municipality, or a state agency, authority, or subdivision engaged in the business of:

(1) generating, transmitting, or distributing electric energy to the public;

(2) producing, transmitting, or distributing natural or artificial gas to the public; or

(3) furnishing water to the public.

Acts 1997, 75th Leg., ch. 166, § 1, eff. Sept. 1, 1997.

§ 186.002. Policy

(a) Continuous service by a public utility is essential to the life, health, and safety of the public. A person's wilful interruption of that service is a public calamity that cannot be endured.

(b) A public utility is dedicated to public service. The primary duty of a public utility, including its management and employees, is to maintain continuous and adequate service at all times to protect the safety and health of the public against the danger inherent in the interruption of service.

(c) Each court and administrative agency of this state shall:

(1) recognize the policy stated in this section; and

(2) interpret and apply this subchapter in accordance with that policy.

Acts 1997, 75th Leg., ch. 166, § 1, eff. Sept. 1, 1997.

§ 186.003. Enforcement by Executive Department

In accordance with Section 186.002, the governor, and the department of the executive branch of government under the governor's direction, shall exercise all power available under the constitution and laws of this state to protect the public from dangers incident to an interruption in water, electric, or gas utility service in this state that occurs because of a violation of this subchapter.

Acts 1997, 75th Leg., ch. 166, § 1, eff. Sept. 1, 1997.

§ 186.004. Unlawful Picketing, Threats, or Intimidation

(a) A person may not:

(1) picket the plant, premises, or other property of a public utility with intent to disrupt the service of that utility or to prevent the maintenance of that service; or

(2) engage in picketing that has the effect of disrupting the service of a public utility or preventing the maintenance of that service.

(b) A person may not:

(1) intimidate, threaten, or harass an employee of a public utility with intent to disrupt the service of the utility or prevent the maintenance of that service; or

(2) intimidate, threaten, or harass an employee of a public utility if that conduct has the effect of disrupting the service of the utility or preventing the maintenance of that service.

Acts 1997, 75th Leg., ch. 166, § 1, eff. Sept. 1, 1997.

§ 186.005. Restraining Order

(a) A district court shall immediately inquire into the matter if a public utility presents a verified petition to the court:

(1) alleging that in the judicial district of the court a person is violating or threatening to violate Section 186.004 and that the violation or threatened

violation will interfere with the maintenance of adequate water, electric, or gas service; and

(2) describing the acts committed in violation of Section 186.004, or the threatened acts that, if committed, will violate Section 186.004.

(b) If it appears that there is a violation or threatened violation of Section 186.004, the court shall immediately issue an order restraining the person, the person's agent, and any other person acting with them from committing an act prohibited by that section.

(c) A restraining order issued under this section is effective when the petitioner files with the clerk of the court a good and sufficient bond in an amount set by the court to cover court costs that may reasonably accrue in connection with the case. A judgment rendered in the case may not be superseded pending appeal.

(d) Venue for a suit under this section is in any judicial district in which the violation or threat to violate occurs.

Acts 1997, 75th Leg., ch. 166, § 1, eff. Sept. 1, 1997.

§ 186.006. Employee Rights

This subchapter does not limit the right of an employee of a public utility to:

(1) quit work and leave the employer's premises at any time the employee chooses; or

(2) refuse to report for work when the employee does not want to report.

Acts 1997, 75th Leg., ch. 166, § 1, eff. Sept. 1, 1997.

§ 186.007. Weather Emergency Preparedness Report

(a) In this section, "commission" means the Public Utility Commission of Texas.

(a–1) The commission shall analyze emergency operations plans developed by electric utilities as defined by Section 31.002, power generation companies, municipally owned utilities, and electric cooperatives that operate generation facilities in this state and prepare a weather emergency preparedness report on power generation weatherization preparedness. In preparing the report, the commission shall:

(1) review the emergency operations plans currently on file with the commission;

(2) analyze and determine the ability of the electric grid to withstand extreme weather events in the upcoming year;

(3) consider the anticipated weather patterns for the upcoming year as forecasted by the National Weather Service or any similar state or national agency; and

(4) make recommendations on improving emergency operations plans and procedures in order to ensure the continuity of electric service.

(b) The commission may require an electric generation entity subject to this section to file an updated emergency operations plan if it finds that an emergency operations plan on file does not contain adequate information to determine whether the electric generation entity can provide adequate electric generation services.

(c) The commission may adopt rules relating to the implementation of the report described by Subsection (a–1).

(d) The commission shall submit the report described by Subsection (a–1) to the lieutenant governor, the speaker of the house of representatives, and the members of the legislature not later than September 30, 2012.

(e) The commission may submit subsequent weather emergency preparedness reports if the commission finds that significant changes to weatherization techniques have occurred or are necessary to protect consumers or vital services, or if there have been changes to statutes or rules relating to weatherization requirements. A report under this subsection must be submitted not later than:

(1) March 1 for a summer weather emergency preparedness report; and

(2) September 1 for a winter weather emergency preparedness report.

(f) The emergency operations plans submitted for the report described by Subsection (a–1) and any subsequent plans submitted under Subsection (e) are public information except for the portions of the plan considered confidential under Chapter 552, Government Code, or other state or federal law. If portions of a plan are designated as confidential, the plan shall be provided to the commission in a redacted form for public inspection with the confidential portions removed. An electric generation entity within the ERCOT power region shall provide the entity's plan to ERCOT in its entirety.

Added by Acts 2011, 82nd Leg., ch. 1335 (S.B. 1133), § 1, eff. June 17, 2011.

SUBCHAPTER B. MANIPULATION OF SERVICE FOR CERTAIN LAW ENFORCEMENT PURPOSES

§ 186.021. Emergency Involving Hostage or Armed Suspect

(a) In an emergency in which the supervising law enforcement official having jurisdiction in the geographical area has probable cause to believe that an armed and barricaded suspect or a person holding a hostage is committing a crime, the supervising law enforcement official may order a designated telephone company security official to cut or otherwise control telephone lines to prevent telephone communication by the armed suspect or the hostage holder with a person other than a peace officer or person authorized by a peace officer.

(b) The serving telephone company in the geographical area of a law enforcement unit shall designate a telephone company security official and an alternate to provide all required assistance to law enforcement officials to carry out this section.

(c) Good faith reliance on an order given by a supervising law enforcement official under this section is a complete defense to a civil or criminal action brought against a telephone company or the company's director, officer, agent, or employee as a result of compliance with the order.

Acts 1997, 75th Leg., ch. 166, § 1, eff. Sept. 1, 1997.

SUBCHAPTER C. FRAUDULENT OBTAINING OF SERVICE

§ 186.031. Definitions

In this subchapter:

(1) "Publish" means to communicate information to another by any means.

(2) "Telecommunications service" means the transmission of a message or other information by a public utility, including a telephone or telegraph company.

Acts 1997, 75th Leg., ch. 166, § 1, eff. Sept. 1, 1997.

§ 186.032. Fraudulently Obtaining Telecommunications Services

(a) A person commits an offense if:

(1) knowing that another will use the published information to avoid payment of a charge for telecommunications service, the person publishes:

(A) an existing, cancelled, revoked, or nonexistent telephone number;

(B) a credit number or other credit device; or

(C) a method of numbering or coding that is used in issuing telephone numbers or credit devices, including credit numbers; or

(2) the person makes or possesses equipment specifically designed to be used fraudulently to avoid charges for telecommunications service.

(b) An offense under this section is a misdemeanor punishable by a fine of not more than $500, by confinement in jail for not more than 60 days, or by both, unless the person has been previously convicted of an offense under this section. A second or subsequent offense is a felony punishable by a fine of not more than $5,000, by imprisonment in the Texas Department of Criminal Justice for not less than two years and not more than five years, or by both.

(c) This section does not apply to an employee of a public utility who provides telecommunications service while acting in the course of employment.

Acts 1997, 75th Leg., ch. 166, § 1, eff. Sept. 1, 1997. Amended by Acts 2009, 81st Leg., ch. 87, § 25.156, eff. Sept. 1, 2009.

§ 186.033. Disposition of Certain Equipment

(a) A peace officer may seize equipment described by Section 186.032(a)(2) under a warrant or incident to a lawful arrest.

(b) If the person who possessed equipment seized under Subsection (a) is convicted under Section 186.032, the court entering the judgment of conviction shall order the sheriff to destroy the equipment.

Acts 1997, 75th Leg., ch. 166, § 1, eff. Sept. 1, 1997.

SUBCHAPTER D. AVAILABILITY OF EMERGENCY TELEPHONE SERVICE

§ 186.041. Definitions

In this subchapter:

(1) "Emergency" means a situation in which property or human life is in jeopardy and the prompt summoning of aid is essential.

(2) "Party line" means a subscriber's telephone circuit, consisting of two or more main telephone stations connected with the circuit, each station with a distinctive ring or telephone number.

Acts 1997, 75th Leg., ch. 166, § 1, eff. Sept. 1, 1997.

§ 186.042. Obstruction of Emergency Telephone Call; Penalty

(a) A person commits an offense if:

(1) the person wilfully refuses to relinquish a party line immediately on being informed that the line is needed for an emergency call described by Subdivision (2); and

(2) the party line is needed for an emergency call:

(A) to a fire or police department; or

(B) for medical aid or an ambulance service.

(b) An offense under this section is a misdemeanor punishable by:

(1) a fine of not less than $25 and not more than $500;

(2) confinement in the county jail for not more than one month; or

(3) both fine and confinement.

Acts 1997, 75th Leg., ch. 166, § 1, eff. Sept. 1, 1997.

§ 186.043. Falsification of Emergency Telephone Call; Penalty

(a) A person commits an offense if the person secures the use of a party line by falsely stating that the line is needed for an emergency call:

(1) to a fire or police department; or

(2) for medical aid or an ambulance service.

(b) An offense under this section is a misdemeanor punishable by:

(1) a fine of not less than $25 and not more than $500;

(2) confinement in the county jail for not more than one month; or

(3) both fine and confinement.

Acts 1997, 75th Leg., ch. 166, § 1, eff. Sept. 1, 1997.

§ 186.044. Notice of Certain Offenses Required

(a) A telephone directory distributed to the public in this state that lists the telephone numbers of an exchange located in this state must contain a notice explaining the offenses under Sections 186.042 and 186.043. The notice must be:

(1) printed in type not smaller than the smallest type on the same page; and

(2) preceded by the word "warning" printed in type at least as large as the largest type on the same page.

(b) At least once each year, a person providing telephone service shall enclose in the telephone bill mailed to each person who uses a party line telephone a notice of Sections 186.042 and 186.043.

(c) This section does not apply to a directory, commonly known as a classified directory, that is distributed solely for business advertising purposes.

Acts 1997, 75th Leg., ch. 166, § 1, eff. Sept. 1, 1997.

§ 186.045. Failure to Provide Notice; Penalty

(a) A person providing telephone service commits an offense if the person:

(1) distributes copies of a telephone directory subject to Section 186.044(a) from which the notice required by that section is wilfully omitted; or

(2) wilfully fails to enclose in telephone bills the notice required by Section 186.044(b).

(b) An offense under this section is a misdemeanor punishable by a fine of not less than $25 and not more than $500.

Acts 1997, 75th Leg., ch. 166, § 1, eff. Sept. 1, 1997.

SUBCHAPTER E. CONSTRUCTION AND MAINTENANCE OF FACILITIES ALONG, OVER, UNDER, OR ACROSS RAILROAD RIGHT–OF–WAY

§ 186.051. Definitions

In this subchapter:

(1) "Cable operator" means an entity that owns or operates a cable system, as that term is defined by 47 U.S.C. Section 522, as amended.

(2) "Common carrier" means a common carrier as described by Section 111.002, Natural Resources Code, or a person who submits to regulation by the state as a common carrier under Article 2.01, Texas Business Corporation Act.

(3) "Energy transporter" means a person who gathers or transports oil, gas, or oil and gas products by pipeline.

(4) "Railroad" means an entity that owns, operates, or controls a railroad or property or assets owned or previously owned by a railroad in this state, including agents, assignees, or parties that by contract own, control, or manage railroad rights-of-way, easements, or other real property rights belonging to a railroad. The term includes interurban and street railroads owned by a private entity but excludes a terminal railroad and a railroad or interurban and street railroad owned by a governmental

entity, including a navigation district or port authority, or a wharf.

(5) "Railroad right-of-way" means the real property rights owned or controlled by a railroad, including fee and easement interests used or previously used as a railroad operating corridor.

(6) "Utility" means:

(A) a gas, water, electric, or telecommunications entity that is defined as a utility under the laws of this state;

(B) an electric cooperative; or

(C) a municipally owned utility.

Added by Acts 2003, 78th Leg., ch. 1087, § 2, eff. Sept. 1, 2003.

§ 186.052. Exemptions

(a) The inclusion of an energy transporter or cable operator in this subchapter does not subject the transporter or operator to regulation as a utility or common carrier.

(b) The inclusion of a common carrier in this subchapter does not subject the carrier to regulation as a utility.

Added by Acts 2003, 78th Leg., ch. 1087, § 2, eff. Sept. 1, 2003.

§ 186.053. Applicability

(a) Except as provided by Section 186.058, this subchapter applies only to facilities along, over, under, or across a railroad or railroad right-of-way in place under a license, agreement, or nonperpetual easement.

(b) In relation to cable operators, this subchapter applies only to those lines over which the cable operator is offering or transporting high-speed Internet or broadband information services.

Added by Acts 2003, 78th Leg., ch. 1087, § 2, eff. Sept. 1, 2003.

§ 186.054. Construction and Maintenance of Utility, Common Carrier, Cable Operator, and Energy Transporter Facilities

(a) A utility, common carrier, cable operator, or energy transporter may acquire an easement by eminent domain along, over, under, or across a railroad or railroad right-of-way as provided by this subchapter to maintain, operate, or upgrade its facilities consistent with preexisting licenses or agreements.

(b) A utility, common carrier, cable operator, or energy transporter:

(1) shall provide notice to the railroad within a reasonable period of any proposed activity relating to the construction, maintenance, or operation of the facilities; and

(2) may not unreasonably interfere with railroad operations.

(c) Absent terms to the contrary in an easement acquired by condemnation under this subchapter, existing license, or agreement, a railroad may require a utility, common carrier, cable operator, or energy transporter to relocate any portion of a facility that is located in the railroad right-of-way that is not in the public right-of-way if:

(1) a reasonable alternate route is available;

(2) a reasonable amount of time is provided;

(3) substantial interference with the railroad operations is established; and

(4) the railroad reimburses the utility, common carrier, cable operator, or energy transporter for the reasonable cost of relocation.

Added by Acts 2003, 78th Leg., ch. 1087, § 2, eff. Sept. 1, 2003.

§ 186.055. Documentation of Rights Acquired

If a railroad requires a utility, common carrier, cable operator, or energy transporter to obtain from the railroad a right to use a railroad right-of-way, the railroad shall produce, if requested in writing, the readily available documentation from the railroad's records indicating the extent of the railroad's right, title, or interest in the property sought to be used by the utility, common carrier, cable operator, or energy transporter. The utility, common carrier, cable operator, or energy transporter shall reimburse the railroad for the reasonable cost of producing the documentation as required by this section. The reimbursable cost, including internal costs, may not exceed $500, unless the parties agree otherwise. A railroad that produces documentation as provided by this section is not limited or prevented from asserting a right, title, or interest in real property based on documentation that has not been produced under this section.

Added by Acts 2003, 78th Leg., ch. 1087, § 2, eff. Sept. 1, 2003.

§ 186.056. Valuation of Rights Acquired

(a) In the absence of an agreement to convey a permanent easement for the continued right to use a preexisting facility located in a railroad right-of-way, a utility, common carrier, cable operator, or energy transporter may obtain the right to continuously use the right-of-way through the exercise of eminent domain under Chapter 21, Property Code.

(b) The award of damages due the railroad under an eminent domain proceeding as provided by Subsection (a) is:

(1) the market value of the real property interest to be used; and

(2) if a portion of the railroad's right-of-way is taken, damages, if any, to the railroad's remaining property.

(c) The railroad may also recover:

(1) reasonable costs and expenses for interference with railroad operations, including internal costs for providing flagging services; and

(2) reasonable costs and expenses to repair any damage to its facilities caused by the maintenance, operation, or upgrade of the preexisting utility, common carrier, cable operator, or energy transporter facilities.

(d) The payment by the utility, common carrier, cable operator, or energy transporter determined under this section is the only compensation due to the railroad for the perpetual use of the interest obtained.

Added by Acts 2003, 78th Leg., ch. 1087, § 2, eff. Sept. 1, 2003.

§ 186.057. Right to Maintain Facilities

(a) A utility, common carrier, cable operator, or energy transporter may not be required to remove an existing facility for 180 days after the date the utility, common carrier, cable operator, or energy transporter receives a written notice from the railroad that an existing facility must be removed from the railroad's right-of-way if:

(1) the facility was located along, under, over, or across the railroad right-of-way with the written consent of the railroad; and

(2) the utility, common carrier, cable operator, or energy transporter is not in default under an agreement with the railroad.

(b) If a utility, common carrier, cable operator, or energy transporter requests documentation under Section 186.055, the 180–day period provided by Subsection (a) is tolled until the utility, common carrier, cable operator, or energy transporter receives a written response to its request from the railroad.

(c) If a utility, common carrier, cable operator, or energy transporter does not condemn or enter into an agreement regarding the disputed area involving the railroad's right-of-way within the 180–day period provided by Subsection (a) or any extended period provided by Subsection (b), the license or agreement between the utility, common carrier, cable operator, or energy transporter and the railroad is terminated.

(d) The possessory right provided by this section is in addition to any possessory right provided by Chapter 21, Property Code.

Added by Acts 2003, 78th Leg., ch. 1087, § 2, eff. Sept. 1, 2003.

§ 186.058. License and Renewal

(a) A utility, common carrier, cable operator, or energy transporter may obtain an original license or renew a license for the right to use a railroad right-of-way for a one-time fee paid based on:

(1) the agreement of the railroad and the utility, common carrier, cable operator, or energy transporter; or

(2) a mutually acceptable third-party determination of market value.

(b) A fee paid under this section is the only fee payment required. The license remains in effect without the requirement of additional fee payments for renewal of the license.

(c) The terms of the license or license renewal may provide that the railroad is not later subject to this subchapter, except the railroad continues to be subject to eminent domain authority granted by other law.

Added by Acts 2003, 78th Leg., ch. 1087, § 2, eff. Sept. 1, 2003.

§ 186.059. Restrictions on Payment of Costs Awarded Against Railroad in Condemnation

If the special commissioners or a court awards costs against a railroad under Section 21.047, Property Code, because the award of damages to the railroad is equal to or less than the amount the utility, common carrier, cable operator, or energy transporter exercising the right of eminent domain under this subchapter offered to pay, the costs awarded against the railroad must be paid by the railroad without reimbursement by or contribution from any agent or representative, including an agent or representative that handled or assisted in the condemnation proceedings.

Added by Acts 2003, 78th Leg., ch. 1087, § 2, eff. Sept. 1, 2003.

§ 186.060. Cumulative Rights and Responsibilities

The rights, privileges, and responsibilities provided by this subchapter are in addition to and not in diminution of or substitution for those rights granted by any other state or federal law.

Added by Acts 2003, 78th Leg., ch. 1087, § 2, eff. Sept. 1, 2003.

§ 186.061. Effect on Other Law

This subchapter does not affect the elements a condemnor must establish by law to acquire real property.

Added by Acts 2003, 78th Leg., ch. 1087, § 2, eff. Sept. 1, 2003.

TITLE 5. PROVISIONS AFFECTING THE OPERATION OF UTILITY FACILITIES

CHAPTER 251. UNDERGROUND FACILITY DAMAGE PREVENTION AND SAFETY

SUBCHAPTER A. GENERAL PROVISIONS

Section
251.001. Short Title.
251.002. Definitions.
251.003. Exemptions.
251.004. Application to Certain Contractors and State Employees.
251.005. Conversion of Facility or Operator.
251.006. Compliance by Permit Holders.
251.007. Facility on County or Municipal Road.
251.008. Effect on Civil Remedies.
251.009. Provision of General Information.

SUBCHAPTER B. TEXAS UNDERGROUND FACILITY NOTIFICATION CORPORATION

251.051. Purpose.
251.052. Nonprofit Corporation.
251.053. Application of Open Meetings and Open Records Laws.
251.054. Expenses and Liabilities of Corporation.
251.055. Board of Directors.
251.056. Terms.
251.057. Declaration of Board Vacancy.
251.058. Officers.
251.059. Entitlement to Vote.
251.060. Duties of Corporation.
251.061. Contract for Statewide Toll-Free Number and Call Router System.
251.062. Fees and Rates.

SUBCHAPTER C. NOTIFICATION CENTERS

251.101. Notification Center.
251.102. General Duties of Notification Center.
251.103. Records.
251.104. Insurance.

Section
251.105. Fees and Charges.
251.106. Payments to Corporation.
251.107. Duty to Participate in Notification Center.

SUBCHAPTER D. REQUIREMENTS RELATING TO EXCAVATION

251.151. Duty of an Excavator.
251.152. Information Included in Notice.
251.153. Duty of Notification Center.
251.154. Notification by an Excavator.
251.155. Exception in Case of Emergency; Offense.
251.156. Other Exceptions to Duty of Excavators.
251.157. Duty of Operator to Person Excavating.
251.158. Duty of Operator in Event of an Extraordinary Circumstance.
251.159. Excavation Damage.

SUBCHAPTER E. PENALTIES

251.201. Civil Penalty or Warning Letter.
251.2011. Warning Letter and Safety Training Course.
251.202. Allocation of Civil Penalty.
251.203. Criminal Penalty .

SUBCHAPTER A. GENERAL PROVISIONS

§ 251.001. Short Title

This chapter may be cited as the Underground Facility Damage Prevention and Safety Act.

Added by Acts 1999, 76th Leg., ch. 62, § 18.17(a), eff. Sept. 1, 1999.

§ 251.002. Definitions

In this chapter:

(1) "Class A underground facility" means an underground facility that is used to produce, store, convey, transmit, or distribute:

(A) electrical energy;

(B) natural or synthetic gas;

(C) petroleum or petroleum products;

(D) steam;

(E) any form of telecommunications service, including voice, data, video, or optical transmission, or cable television service; or

(F) any other liquid, material, or product not defined as a Class B underground facility.

(2) "Class B underground facility" means an underground facility that is used to produce, store, convey, transmit, or distribute:

(A) water;

(B) slurry; or

(C) sewage.

(3) "Corporation" means the Texas Underground Facility Notification Corporation.

(4) "Damage" means:

(A) the defacing, scraping, displacement, penetration, destruction, or partial or complete severance of an underground facility or of any protective coating, housing, or other protective device of an underground facility;

(B) the weakening of structural or lateral support of an underground facility; or

(C) the failure to properly replace the backfill covering an underground facility.

(5) "Excavate" means to use explosives or a motor, engine, hydraulic or pneumatically powered tool, or other mechanized equipment of any kind and includes auguring, backfilling, boring, compressing, digging, ditching, drilling, dragging, dredging, grading, mechanical probing, plowing-in, pulling-in, ripping, scraping, trenching, and tunneling to remove or otherwise disturb soil to a depth of 16 or more inches.

(6) "Excavator" means a person that excavates or intends to excavate in this state.

(7) "Exploration and production underground facility" means an underground facility used by a person producing gas or oil, or both, for the production of that gas or oil, including facilities used for field separation, treatment, gathering, or storage of gas or oil.

(8) "High speed data transmission" means a method of data transmission that does not include facsimile or voice transmission.

(9) "Legal holiday" means a holiday specified as a legal holiday by Subchapter B, Chapter 662, Government Code.[1]

(10) "Mechanized equipment" means equipment operated by mechanical power, including a trencher, bulldozer, power shovel, auger, backhoe, scraper, drill, cable or pipe plow, and other equipment used to plow in or pull in cable or pipe.

(11) "Operator" means a person that operates an underground facility.

(12) "Secured facility" means a parcel of land used for commercial or industrial purposes that is surrounded entirely by a fence or other means of preventing access, including a fence with one or more gates that are locked at all times or monitored by an individual who can prevent unauthorized access.

(13) "Underground facility" means a line, cable, pipeline system, conduit, or structure that is located partially or totally underground and that is used to produce, store, convey, transmit, or distribute telecommunications, electricity, gas, water, sewage, steam, or liquids such as petroleum, petroleum products, or hazardous liquids.

(14) "Saturday notification" means a notice of intent to excavate provided by an excavator to a notification center on a Saturday before 11:59 a.m.

(15) "Violation" means a violation of Section 251.151, 251.152, or 251.159.

Added by Acts 1999, 76th Leg., ch. 62, § 18.17(a), eff. Sept. 1, 1999.

[1] V.T.C.A., Government Code § 662.021.

§ 251.003. Exemptions

The following are not subject to this chapter as underground facilities:

(1) an aboveground or underground storage tank, sump, or impoundment or piping connected to an aboveground or underground storage tank, sump, or impoundment located in the same tract of land as the storage tank, sump, or impoundment;

(2) an underground facility operated by the owner of a secured facility and located entirely within the secured facility;

(3) an underground facility that serves only the owner of the underground facility or the owner's tenant and that is located solely on the owner's property;

(4) piping within a well bore;

(5) the portion of an exploration and production underground facility that is located within the boundaries of the oil or gas field from which the oil and gas is produced and that is not located in the boundaries of an established easement or right-of-way granted for the benefit of a governmental entity or a private entity if the easement or right-of-way is granted for a public purpose; or

(6) an underground facility that serves a cemetery and is located solely on the cemetery's property.

Added by Acts 1999, 76th Leg., ch. 62, § 18.17(a), eff. Sept. 1, 1999.

§ 251.004. Application to Certain Contractors and State Employees

(a) This chapter does not apply to a contractor working in the public right-of-way under a contract with the Texas Department of Transportation.

(b) Excavation by an employee of the Texas Department of Transportation on a segment of the state highway system is not subject to this chapter if the excavation is more than 10 feet from the right-of-way line.

Added by Acts 1999, 76th Leg., ch. 62, § 18.17(a), eff. Sept. 1, 1999. Amended by Acts 2003, 78th Leg., ch. 1276, § 17.004(a), eff. Sept. 1, 2003.

§ 251.005. Conversion of Facility or Operator

(a) An operator of an underground facility that is exempted under this subchapter may voluntarily convert that facility to a Class A underground facility by sending written communication from a competent authority of the operator to the corporation advising of the status change.

(b) An operator of a Class B underground facility may voluntarily convert to a Class A underground facility operator by sending written communication from a competent authority of the operator to the corporation advising of the status change.

Added by Acts 1999, 76th Leg., ch. 62, § 18.17(a), eff. Sept. 1, 1999.

§ 251.006. Compliance by Permit Holders

(a) The fact that a person has a legal permit, permission from the owner of the property or the owner's licensee, or an easement to conduct excavation operations does not affect the person's duty to comply with this chapter.

(b) Compliance with this chapter does not affect a person's responsibility to obtain a permit required by law.

Added by Acts 1999, 76th Leg., ch. 62, § 18.17(a), eff. Sept. 1, 1999.

§ 251.007. Facility on County or Municipal Road

This chapter does not affect a contractual or statutory right of a county or municipality to require an operator to relocate, replace, or repair its underground facility.

Added by Acts 1999, 76th Leg., ch. 62, § 18.17(a), eff. Sept. 1, 1999.

§ 251.008. Effect on Civil Remedies

Except as otherwise specifically provided by this chapter, this chapter, including Section 251.201, does not affect any civil remedy for personal injury or for property damage, including any damage to an underground facility.

Added by Acts 1999, 76th Leg., ch. 62, § 18.17(a), eff. Sept. 1, 1999.

§ 251.009. Provision of General Information

At least once each calendar year, at intervals not exceeding 15 months, each Class A underground facility operator who conveys, transmits, or distributes by means of its underground facilities service directly to more than one million residential customers within this state shall provide all of its residential customers in this state general information about excavation activities covered by this chapter and the statewide toll-free telephone number established by the corporation.

Added by Acts 1999, 76th Leg., ch. 62, § 18.17(a), eff. Sept. 1, 1999.

SUBCHAPTER B. TEXAS UNDERGROUND FACILITY NOTIFICATION CORPORATION

§ 251.051. Purpose

The Texas Underground Facility Notification Corporation provides statewide notification services under this chapter.

Added by Acts 1999, 76th Leg., ch. 62, § 18.17(a), eff. Sept. 1, 1999.

§ 251.052. Nonprofit Corporation

The corporation is a public nonprofit corporation and has all the powers and duties incident to a nonprofit corporation under the Texas Non-Profit Corporation Act (Article 1396–1.01 et seq., Vernon's Texas Civil Statutes), except that the corporation:

(1) may not make donations for the public welfare or for charitable, scientific, or educational purposes or in aid of war activities;

(2) may not merge or consolidate with another corporation;

(3) is not subject to voluntary or involuntary dissolution; and

(4) may not be placed in receivership.

Added by Acts 1999, 76th Leg., ch. 62, § 18.17(a), eff. Sept. 1, 1999.

§ 251.053. Application of Open Meetings and Open Records Laws

The corporation is subject to Chapters 551 and 552, Government Code, except that the corporation may not disseminate, make available, or otherwise distribute service area map data or information provided by an operator unless that action is necessary to perform the corporation's specific obligations under this chapter.

Added by Acts 1999, 76th Leg., ch. 62, § 18.17(a), eff. Sept. 1, 1999.

§ 251.054. Expenses and Liabilities of Corporation

(a) All expenses of the corporation shall be paid from income of the corporation.

(b) A liability created by the corporation is not a debt of this state, and the corporation may not secure a liability with funds or assets of this state.

Added by Acts 1999, 76th Leg., ch. 62, § 18.17(a), eff. Sept. 1, 1999.

§ 251.055. Board of Directors

(a) The board of directors of the corporation is composed of the following 12 members appointed by the governor:

(1) six representatives of the general public;

(2) one representative of the gas industry;

(3) one representative of the telecommunications industry;

(4) one representative of the electric industry;

(5) one representative of cable television companies;

(6) one representative of municipalities; and

(7) one representative of persons who engage in excavation operations who are not also facility operators.

(b) Board membership is voluntary and a director is not entitled to receive compensation for serving on the board.

Added by Acts 1999, 76th Leg., ch. 62, § 18.17(a), eff. Sept. 1, 1999.

§ 251.056. Terms

(a) Directors serve staggered three-year terms, with the terms of four directors expiring each August 31.

(b) A director serves until the director's successor is appointed by the governor and assumes office.

Added by Acts 1999, 76th Leg., ch. 62, § 18.17(a), eff. Sept. 1, 1999.

§ 251.057. Declaration of Board Vacancy

(a) The board may declare a director's office vacant if the director ceases to be associated with the industry or an operator the director represents.

(b) Not later than the 60th day after the date a vacancy on the board is declared, the governor shall appoint a person to fill the vacancy for the remainder of the unexpired term.

Added by Acts 1999, 76th Leg., ch. 62, § 18.17(a), eff. Sept. 1, 1999.

§ 251.058. Officers

(a) The board shall elect from among its directors a chair and vice chair.

(b) The chair and vice chair serve for a term of one year and may be reelected.

Added by Acts 1999, 76th Leg., ch. 62, § 18.17(a), eff. Sept. 1, 1999.

§ 251.059. Entitlement to Vote

The corporation's bylaws must provide that each director is entitled to one vote.

Added by Acts 1999, 76th Leg., ch. 62, § 18.17(a), eff. Sept. 1, 1999.

§ 251.060. Duties of Corporation

The corporation shall develop and implement processes to:

(1) maintain a registration of:

(A) notification centers as provided by Section 251.101(a)(3);

(B) operators who elect to convert facilities to Class A facilities under Section 251.005(a); or

(C) operators who elect to become Class A underground facility operators under Section 251.005(b);

(2) establish minimum technical standards used by notification centers;

(3) establish a statewide toll-free telephone number to be used by excavators that incorporates the use of a call router system that routes calls to the notification centers on a pro rata basis;

(4) oversee the bid process and select the vendor for the statewide toll-free telephone number;

(5) oversee the bid process and select the vendor for the call router system;

(6) determine before May 1 of each year the cost-sharing between the notification centers of:

(A) the toll-free telephone number; and

(B) the call router system prescribed by Section 251.102(4);

(7) develop public service announcements to educate the public about statewide one-call notification and its availability;

(8) establish a format for information transfer among notification centers other than high speed data transmission, if appropriate;

(9) on a complaint concerning charges, investigate and determine appropriate charges;

(10) recommend a civil penalty against a notification center that does not meet the requirements of this chapter of not less than $1,000 or more than $5,000 for each violation;

(11) refer the recommended penalty to the attorney general, who shall institute a suit in a court of competent jurisdiction to recover the penalty;

(12) assist in dispute resolution among notification centers or between a notification center and an operator;

(13) assist any operator who encounters difficulty in joining a notification center; and

(14) review and study design standards for the placement of underground facilities throughout this state.

Added by Acts 1999, 76th Leg., ch. 62, § 18.17(a), eff. Sept. 1, 1999.

§ 251.061. Contract for Statewide Toll-Free Number and Call Router System

(a) The corporation shall solicit proposals for the contract to establish and operate the statewide toll-free telephone number and the call router system by using a request for proposals process that includes specifications that have been approved by the board of directors in accordance with this chapter.

(b) The corporation is not required to award the contract to the lowest offeror if the terms of another proposal would result in a lower annual cost and are more advantageous to the corporation and its members. The corporation may reject all proposals if the corporation finds that none of the proposals is acceptable.

(c) After the proposals are opened, each document relating to the consideration of a proposal or the award of a contract and the text of the contract are considered books and records of the corporation for the purposes of Article 2.23, Texas Non-Profit Corporation Act (Article 1396–2.23, Vernon's Texas Civil Statutes).

Added by Acts 1999, 76th Leg., ch. 62, § 18.17(a), eff. Sept. 1, 1999.

§ 251.062. Fees and Rates

(a) Except as provided by this section, the corporation may not, for any reason, impose an assessment, fee, or other charge, including a charge for inputting data, against an operator.

(b) Before January 15 of each year, a Class A facility operator shall pay to the corporation a fee of $50 for services to be performed by the corporation during that calendar year. A fee for a part of a year may not be prorated.

Added by Acts 1999, 76th Leg., ch. 62, § 18.17(a), eff. Sept. 1, 1999.

SUBCHAPTER C. NOTIFICATION CENTERS

§ 251.101. Notification Center

(a) A notification center is a legal entity that:

(1) operates a notification system capable of serving excavators and operators statewide;

(2) is created to:

(A) receive notification of an intent to excavate and of damage to an underground facility and disseminate that information to member operators that may be affected by the excavation or damage and to other notification centers operating in this state; and

(B) receive notification of an extraordinary circumstance and disseminate that information to member operators and to other notification centers operating in this state; and

(3) registers the following information with the corporation:

(A) its name, address, and telephone number;

(B) the name of a contact person;

(C) a statement of compliance with Section 251.104; and

(D) a listing of the counties in which it operates.

(b) A notification center operating on September 1, 1997, may continue to operate if the notification center complies with this chapter.

Added by Acts 1999, 76th Leg., ch. 62, § 18.17(a), eff. Sept. 1, 1999.

§ 251.102. General Duties of Notification Center

A notification center shall:

(1) operate 24 hours a day every day of the year;

(2) have the capability to receive emergency information 24 hours a day from excavators and disseminate the information as soon as it is received to

the appropriate operators and to all registered and affected notification centers operating in this state;

(3) have the capacity to receive extraordinary circumstance information 24 hours a day from operators and disseminate the information as soon as it is received to all registered and affected notification centers;

(4) submit to the corporation, not later than May 15 of each year, a pro rata share of the expense, as established by the corporation, of the statewide toll-free telephone number and the call router;

(5) provide, on request of an excavator, a contact name and telephone number of a representative of the operator for special circumstances; and

(6) have personnel capable of assisting Spanish-speaking customers.

Added by Acts 1999, 76th Leg., ch. 62, § 18.17(a), eff. Sept. 1, 1999.

§ 251.103. Records

(a) A notification center shall maintain for not less than four years a record to document:

(1) the receipt of a notice of:

(A) intent to excavate;

(B) damage to an underground facility;

(C) an emergency excavation; and

(D) an extraordinary circumstance;

(2) the information the excavator is required to provide to the notification center under this chapter;

(3) contact with operators and other notification centers; and

(4) the information the notification center provided to the excavator.

(b) A notification center may not destroy records that relate to any matter that is involved in litigation if the notification center is placed on notice that the litigation has not been finally resolved.

Added by Acts 1999, 76th Leg., ch. 62, § 18.17(a), eff. Sept. 1, 1999.

§ 251.104. Insurance

A notification center shall, at all times, maintain a minimum of $5 million professional liability and errors and omissions insurance to cover duties prescribed by this chapter.

Added by Acts 1999, 76th Leg., ch. 62, § 18.17(a), eff. Sept. 1, 1999.

§ 251.105. Fees and Charges

(a) A notification center that notifies another notification center under Section 251.102(2) or (3) or Section 251.153(b) shall recover an amount not exceeding the actual cost of providing the notice from the notification center receiving the notice.

(b) The notification center shall charge a Class A underground facility operator not more than $1.25 for a call made to the system that affects the operator. The board may increase or decrease the maximum charge only on an affirmative vote of at least two-thirds of the total number of votes entitled to be cast. A notification center may petition the corporation for an increase in the maximum charge and is entitled to the increase on proof that costs exceed the maximum charge.

(c) The notification center may not charge an operator any additional fee such as an initiation fee, a membership fee, or a set-up fee.

Added by Acts 1999, 76th Leg., ch. 62, § 18.17(a), eff. Sept. 1, 1999.

§ 251.106. Payments to Corporation

Each time a notification center receives a call from an excavator under Section 251.151, the notification center shall pay the corporation five cents. The corporation shall waive this charge for the remainder of any year in which the corporation receives $250,000 under this section.

Added by Acts 1999, 76th Leg., ch. 62, § 18.17(a), eff. Sept. 1, 1999. Amended by Acts 2001, 77th Leg., ch. 652, § 1, eff. Sept. 1, 2001.

§ 251.107. Duty to Participate in Notification Center

(a) Each operator of a Class A underground facility, including a political subdivision of this state, shall participate in a notification center as a condition of doing business in this state.

(b) Each operator of a Class A underground facility shall provide to the notification center:

(1) maps or grid locations or other identifiers determined by the operator indicating the location of the operator's underground facilities;

(2) the name and telephone number of a contact person or persons; and

(3) at least quarterly but, if possible, as those changes occur, information relating to each change in the operator's maps or grid locations or other

identifiers or in the person or persons designated as the operator's contact person or persons.

(c) The notification center may not require an operator to conduct a survey of the operator's underground facilities or alter the operator's existing signage.

(d) A notification center may not disseminate, make available, or otherwise distribute maps or information provided by an operator unless that action is necessary to perform the notification center's specific obligations under this chapter.

Added by Acts 1999, 76th Leg., ch. 62, § 18.17(a), eff. Sept. 1, 1999.

SUBCHAPTER D. REQUIREMENTS RELATING TO EXCAVATION

§ 251.151. Duty of an Excavator

(a) Except as provided by Sections 251.155 and 251.156, a person who intends to excavate shall notify a notification center not earlier than the 14th day before the date the excavation is to begin or later than the 48th hour before the time the excavation is to begin, excluding Saturdays, Sundays, and legal holidays.

(b) Notwithstanding Subsection (a), if an excavator makes a Saturday notification, the excavator may begin the excavation the following Tuesday at 11:59 a.m. unless the intervening Monday is a holiday. If the intervening Monday is a holiday, the excavator may begin the excavation the following Wednesday at 11:59 a.m.

(c) To have a representative present during the excavation, the operator shall contact the excavator and advise the excavator of the operator's intent to be present during excavation and confirm the start time of the excavation. If the excavator wants to change the start time, the excavator shall notify the operator to set a mutually agreed-to time to begin the excavation.

Added by Acts 1999, 76th Leg., ch. 62, § 18.17(a), eff. Sept. 1, 1999.

§ 251.152. Information Included in Notice

The excavator shall include in the notice required under Section 251.151:

(1) the name of the person serving the notice;

(2) the location of the proposed area of excavation, including:

(A) the street address, if available, and the location of the excavation at the street address; or

(B) if there is no street address, an accurate description of the excavation area using any available designations such as the closest street, road, or intersection;

(3) the name, address, and telephone number of the excavator or the excavator's company;

(4) the excavator's field telephone number, if one is available;

(5) a telephone facsimile number, e-mail address, or another electronic number or address approved by the board to which an operator may send the notification required by Section 251.157(d);

(6) the starting date and time and the anticipated completion date of excavation; and

(7) a statement as to whether explosives will be used.

Added by Acts 1999, 76th Leg., ch. 62, § 18.17(a), eff. Sept. 1, 1999. Amended by Acts 2001, 77th Leg., ch. 858, § 1, eff. Nov. 1, 2001.

§ 251.153. Duty of Notification Center

(a) At the time an excavator provides a notification center with the excavator's intent to excavate, the notification center shall advise the excavator that water, slurry, and sewage underground facilities in the area of the proposed excavation may not receive information concerning the excavator's proposed excavation.

(b) Not later than two hours after the time the notification center receives a notice of intent to excavate from an excavator, the notification center shall provide to every other affected notification center operating in this state the information required by Section 251.152 and received from the excavator. The notification center shall provide the information by the use of high speed data transmission.

(c) Not later than two hours after the time the notification center receives a notice of intent to excavate from an excavator or from a different notification center, the notification center shall notify each member operator that may have an underground facility in the vicinity of the proposed excavation operation.

Added by Acts 1999, 76th Leg., ch. 62, § 18.17(a), eff. Sept. 1, 1999.

§ 251.154. Notification by an Excavator

(a) A person required to provide notice under this chapter is considered to have provided the notice when the person delivers the required information and a notification center receives that information within the time limits prescribed by this chapter.

(b) A person may deliver information required under this chapter by any appropriate method, including the use of any electronic means of data transfer.

Added by Acts 1999, 76th Leg., ch. 62, § 18.17(a), eff. Sept. 1, 1999.

§ 251.155. Exception in Case of Emergency; Offense

(a) Section 251.151 does not apply to an emergency excavation that is necessary to respond to a situation that endangers life, health, or property or a situation in which the public need for uninterrupted service and immediate reestablishment of service if service is interrupted compels immediate action.

(b) The excavator may begin emergency excavation under Subsection (a) immediately and shall take reasonable care to protect underground facilities.

(c) When an emergency exists, the excavator shall notify a notification center as promptly as practicably possible.

(d) An excavator may not misrepresent a fact or circumstance used in the determination of an emergency excavation under Subsection (a). A person that violates this subsection is subject to a penalty under:

(1) Section 251.201;

(2) Section 251.203; or

(3) both Section 251.201 and Section 251.203.

Added by Acts 1999, 76th Leg., ch. 62, § 18.17(a), eff. Sept. 1, 1999. Amended by Acts 2011, 82nd Leg., ch. 184 (S.B. 1217), § 1, eff. Sept. 1, 2011.

Section 5 of Acts 2011, 82nd Leg., ch. 184 (S.B. 1217) provides:

"The changes in law made by this Act apply only to conduct occurring on or after the effective date [Sept. 1, 2011] of this Act. Conduct occurring before the effective date of this Act is governed by the law in effect on the date the conduct occurred, and the former law is continued in effect for that purpose."

§ 251.156. Other Exceptions to Duty of Excavators

(a) Section 251.151 does not apply to:

(1) interment operations of a cemetery;

(2) operations at a secured facility if:

(A) the excavator operates each underground facility at the secured facility, other than those within a third-party underground facility easement or right-of-way; and

(B) the excavation activity is not within a third-party underground facility or right-of-way;

(3) routine railroad maintenance within 15 feet of either side of the midline of the track if the maintenance will not disturb the ground at a depth of more than 18 inches;

(4) activities performed on private property in connection with agricultural operations;

(5) operations associated with the exploration or production of oil or gas if the operations are not conducted within an underground facility easement or right-of-way;

(6) excavations by or for a person that:

(A) owns, leases, or owns a mineral leasehold interest in the real property on which the excavation occurs; and

(B) operates all underground facilities located at the excavation site; or

(7) routine maintenance by a county employee on a county road right-of-way to a depth of not more than 24 inches.

(b) If a person excepted under Subsection (a)(4) elects to comply with this chapter and the operator fails to comply with this chapter, the person is not liable to the underground facility owner for damages to the underground facility.

(c) In this section:

(1) "Agricultural operations" means activities performed on land and described by Section 23.51(2), Tax Code.

(2) "Routine maintenance" means operations, not to exceed 24 inches in depth, within a road or drainage ditch involving grading and removal or replacement of pavement and structures.

Added by Acts 1999, 76th Leg., ch. 62, § 18.17(a), eff. Sept. 1, 1999.

§ 251.157. Duty of Operator to Person Excavating

(a) Each Class A underground facility operator contacted by the notification system shall mark the approximate location of its underground facilities at or near the site of the proposed excavation if the operator believes that marking the location is necessary. The operator shall mark the location not later than:

(1) the 48th hour after the time the excavator gives to the notification system notice of intent to excavate, excluding Saturdays, Sundays, and legal holidays;

(2) 11:59 a.m. on the Tuesday following a Saturday notification unless the intervening Monday is a holiday;

(3) 11:59 a.m. on the Wednesday following a Saturday notification if the intervening Monday is a holiday; or

(4) a time agreed to by the operator and the excavator.

(b) An operator shall refer to the American Public Works Association color coding standards when marking.

(c) An excavator who has fully complied with this chapter may not be liable for damage to an underground facility that was not marked in accordance with this chapter.

(d) Not later than the 48th hour after the time the excavator gives to the notification center notice of intent to excavate, an operator contacted by the notification center shall notify the excavator of the operator's plans to not mark the proximate location of an underground facility at or near the site of the proposed excavation. The operator must provide the notification by e-mail or facsimile or by another verifiable electronic method approved by the board.

Added by Acts 1999, 76th Leg., ch. 62, § 18.17(a), eff. Sept. 1, 1999. Amended by Acts 2001, 77th Leg., ch. 858, § 2, eff. Nov. 1, 2001.

§ 251.158. Duty of Operator in Event of an Extraordinary Circumstance

(a) The deadline prescribed by Section 251.157(a) does not apply if the operator experiences an extraordinary circumstance due to an act of God, including a tornado, a hurricane, an ice storm, or a severe flood, or a war, riot, work stoppage, or strike that limits personnel or resources needed to fulfill the operator's obligations under this chapter.

(b) The operator shall notify a notification center of the extraordinary circumstance and shall include in the notification:

(1) the nature and location of the extraordinary circumstance;

(2) the expected duration of the situation and the approximate time at which the operator will be able to resume location request activities; and

(3) the name and telephone number of the individual that the notification system can contact if there is an emergency that requires the operator's immediate attention.

(c) In addition to the notification required by Subsection (b), the operator shall also notify each excavator that has a pending location request in the location where an extraordinary circumstance is being experienced and shall include in the notification:

(1) the fact that the operator is experiencing an extraordinary circumstance; and

(2) the approximate time at which the operator will mark the requested location.

(d) A notification center shall inform each excavator notifying the system under Section 251.151 that the operator's location request activities are suspended until the extraordinary circumstance has discontinued or has been corrected within the affected location.

(e) An excavator is relieved from all provisions of this chapter until the operator notifies the notification center that the operator has resumed location request activities within the affected location.

Added by Acts 1999, 76th Leg., ch. 62, § 18.17(a), eff. Sept. 1, 1999.

§ 251.159. Excavation Damage

(a) If an excavation operation results in damage to an underground facility, the excavator shall immediately contact the underground facility operator to report the damage.

(b) If the excavator is not certain of the operator's identity, the excavator shall contact a notification center to report the damage, and the notification center shall immediately notify all other affected notification centers. Immediately on receiving notification, each notification center shall contact each member operator that has underground facilities in or near the area in which the damage occurred.

(c) Only the operator or a person authorized by the operator may perform repairs, and the repairs must be made in an expeditious manner.

(d) An excavator shall delay backfilling in the immediate area of the damage until the damage is reported to the operator and a repair schedule is mutually agreed to by the excavator and the operator.

(e) If damage endangers life, health, or property because of the presence of flammable material, the excavator shall keep sources of ignition away.

Added by Acts 1999, 76th Leg., ch. 62, § 18.17(a), eff. Sept. 1, 1999.

SUBCHAPTER E. PENALTIES

§ 251.201. Civil Penalty or Warning Letter

(a) An excavator that violates Section 251.151, 251.152, or 251.159 is liable for a civil penalty of not less than $500 or more than $1,000. If a county attorney or district attorney decides not to bring an action to recover the civil penalty, the board of directors of the corporation may, in accordance with Section 251.2011, give the excavator a warning letter and require the excavator to attend a safety training course approved by the board. The county attorney or district attorney shall notify the board of its decision.

(a–1) An excavator that violates Section 251.155(d) is liable for a civil penalty of not less than $1,000 or more than $2,000. If a county attorney or district attorney decides not to bring an action to recover the civil penalty, the board of directors of the corporation may, in accordance with Section 251.2011, give the excavator a warning letter and require the excavator to attend a safety training course approved by the board. The county attorney or district attorney shall notify the board of its decision.

(b) Except as provided by Subsection (b–1), if it is found at the trial on a civil penalty that the excavator has violated this chapter and has been assessed a penalty under this section or has received a warning letter from the board one other time before the first anniversary of the date of the most recent violation, the excavator is liable for a civil penalty of not less than $1,000 or more than $2,000.

(b–1) If it is found at the trial on a civil penalty that the excavator has violated Section 251.155(d) and has been assessed a penalty under this section or has received a warning letter from the board one other time before the first anniversary of the date of the most recent violation, the excavator is liable for a civil penalty of not less than $2,000 or more than $5,000.

(c) Except as provided by Subsection (c–1), if it is found at the trial on a civil penalty that the excavator has violated this chapter and has been assessed a penalty under this section at least two other times before the first anniversary of the date of the most recent violation, or has been assessed a penalty at least one other time before the first anniversary of the date of the most recent violation and has received a warning letter from the board during that period, the excavator is liable for a civil penalty of not less than $2,000 or more than $5,000.

(c–1) If it is found at the trial on a civil penalty that the excavator has violated Section 251.155(d) and has been assessed a penalty under this section at least two other times before the first anniversary of the date of the most recent violation, or has been assessed a penalty at least one other time before the first anniversary of the date of the most recent violation and has received a warning letter from the board during that period, the excavator is liable for a civil penalty of not less than $5,000 or more than $10,000.

(d) In assessing the civil penalty the court shall consider the actual damage to the facility, the effect of the excavator's actions on the public health and safety, whether the violation was a wilful act, and any good faith of the excavator in attempting to achieve compliance.

(e) Venue for a proceeding to collect a civil penalty under this section is in the county in which:

(1) all or part of the alleged violation occurred;

(2) the defendant has its principal place of business in this state; or

(3) the defendant resides, if in this state.

(f) The appropriate county attorney or criminal district attorney shall bring the action to recover the civil penalty.

(g) This section does not apply to a residential property owner excavating on the property owner's own residential lot.

Added by Acts 1999, 76th Leg., ch. 62, § 18.17(a), eff. Sept. 1, 1999. Amended by Acts 2001, 77th Leg., ch. 652, § 2, eff. Sept. 1, 2001; Acts 2011, 82nd Leg., ch. 184 (S.B. 1217), § 2, eff. Sept. 1, 2011.

Section 5 of Acts 2011, 82nd Leg., ch. 184 (S.B. 1217) provides:

"The changes in law made by this Act apply only to conduct occurring on or after the effective date [Sept. 1, 2011] of this Act. Conduct occurring before the effective date of this Act is governed by the law in effect on the date the conduct occurred, and the former law is continued in effect for that purpose."

§ 251.2011. Warning Letter and Safety Training Course

(a) The board of directors of the corporation shall establish a procedure to ensure that the board verifies that an excavator has violated Section 251.151, 251.152, or 251.159 before giving the excavator a warning letter and requiring the excavator to attend a safety training course under Section 251. 201.

(b) The board shall solicit and consider advice and recommendations from excavators in establishing or approving a safety training course that an excavator may be required to attend under Section 251.201.

Added by Acts 2001, 77th Leg., ch. 652, § 3, eff. Sept. 1, 2001.

§ 251.202. Allocation of Civil Penalty

(a) Fifty percent of the civil penalty collected under Section 251.201 shall be transferred to the county treasurer of the county prosecuting the action and 50 percent of the civil penalty collected under Section 251.201 shall be transferred to the corporation.

(b) The county treasurer shall deposit all money received under this section in the county road and bridge fund.

(c) The corporation shall use the money received under this section to develop public service announcements to educate the public about the statewide one-call notification system and its availability as prescribed by Section 251.060(7).

Added by Acts 1999, 76th Leg., ch. 62, § 18.17(a), eff. Sept. 1, 1999.

§ 251.203. Criminal Penalty

(a) A person commits an offense if:

(1) the person without authorization from the owner or operator of the facility intentionally removes, damages, or conceals a marker or sign giving information about the location of a Class A underground facility; and

(2) the marker or sign gives notice of the penalty for intentional removal, damage, or concealment of the marker or sign.

(a–1) A person commits an offense if the person intentionally or recklessly violates Section 251.155(d).

(b) An offense under this section is a Class B misdemeanor.

Added by Acts 1999, 76th Leg., ch. 62, § 18.17(a), eff. Sept. 1, 1999. Amended by Acts 2011, 82nd Leg., ch. 184 (S.B. 1217), §§ 3, 4, eff. Sept. 1, 2011.

Section 5 of Acts 2011, 82nd Leg., ch. 184 (S.B. 1217) provides:

"The changes in law made by this Act apply only to conduct occurring on or after the effective date [Sept. 1, 2011] of this Act. Conduct occurring before the effective date of this Act is governed by the law in effect on the date the conduct occurred, and the former law is continued in effect for that purpose."

INDEX

Abbreviations

Bus & C .... Business and Commerce Code
Bus Org .... Business Organizations Code
Util .... Utilities Code

ABANDONED OR UNCLAIMED PROPERTY
Assumed or fictitious names, business and commerce, professions and occupations, **Bus & C 71.153**

ABANDONMENT
Cooperative associations, **Bus Org 10.201 et seq.**
  Filing, **Bus Org 4.057**
Corporations, this index
Foreign corporations, **Bus Org 10.201 et seq.**
  Filing, **Bus Org 4.057**
Limited Liability Companies, this index
Limited partnerships. Partnerships, this index
Nonprofit Corporations, this index
Partnerships, this index
Professional Associations and Societies, this index
Professional Corporations, this index
Telecommunications, successor utilities, termination of service, providers of last resort, **Util 54.304**

ABATEMENT OF ACTIONS AND PROCEEDINGS
Cooperative Associations, this index
Corporations, this index
Foreign Corporations, this index
Limited Liability Companies, this index
Limited partnerships. Partnerships, this index
Nonprofit Corporations, this index
Partnerships, this index
Professional Associations and Societies, this index
Professional Corporations, this index

ABOVE MARKET PURCHASED POWER COSTS
Definitions, electricity, competition, stranded costs, recovery, **Util 39.251**

ABSENCE AND ABSENTEES
Public utility commission, commissioners, removal, **Util 12.054**

ACCOUNTS AND ACCOUNTING
Corporations, this index

ACCOUNTS AND ACCOUNTING —Cont'd
Electricity, this index
Foreign Corporations, this index
Gas Utilities, this index
Limited Liability Companies, this index
Nonprofit Corporations, this index
Partnerships, this index
Public Utilities, this index
Public utility commission, **Util 16.042**
Real estate investment trusts, examinations and examiners, **Bus Org 200.501**
Telecommunications, this index

ACKNOWLEDGMENTS
Cooperative Associations, this index
Corporations, this index
Foreign Corporations, this index
Limited Liability Companies, this index
Limited partnerships. Partnerships, this index
Nonprofit Corporations, this index
Partnerships, this index
Professional Corporations, this index

ACTIONS AND PROCEEDINGS
Assumed or fictitious names, business and commerce, professions and occupations, **Bus & C 71.201**
Compromise and Settlement, generally, this index
Conflict of Laws, generally, this index
Cooperative Associations, this index
Corporations, this index
Costs, generally, this index
Damages, generally, this index
Definitions,
  Gas utilities, **Util 101.003**
  Public utilities, **Util 11.003**
Electric Cooperative Corporations, this index
Eminent Domain, generally, this index
Evidence, generally, this index
Executions, generally, this index
Foreign Corporations, this index
Garnishment, generally, this index
Gas Utilities, this index
Injunctions, generally, this index
Limited Liability Companies, this index

ACTIONS AND PROCEEDINGS —Cont'd
Limited partnerships. Partnerships, this index
Municipalities, this index
Nonprofit Corporations, this index
Partnerships, this index
Probate Proceedings, generally, this index
Professional Associations and Societies, this index
Professional Corporations, this index
Public Utilities, this index
Real estate investment trusts, ultra vires, **Bus Org 200.004**
Stay of proceedings. Supersedeas or Stay, generally, this index
Supersedeas or Stay, generally, this index
Telecommunications, this index
Telephone cooperative corporations, **Util 162.121**

ACTIVE TRUSTS
Trusts and Trustees, generally, this index

ACTS
Statutes, generally, this index

ADDRESS
Cooperative Associations, this index
Definitions, assumed or fictitious names, business and commerce, professions and occupations, **Bus & C 71.002**
Limited Liability Companies, this index
Limited partnerships. Partnerships, this index
Partnerships, this index

ADMINISTRATIVE HEARINGS OFFICE
Public utilities, contested cases, **Util 14.053**
Utilities, contested cases, **Util 14.053**

ADMINISTRATIVE LAW AND PROCEDURE
Contested cases,
  Electricity, competition, **Util 39.003**
  Public Utilities, this index
Electricity, contested cases, competition, **Util 39.003**
Gas Utilities, this index
Public Utilities, this index

ADMINISTRATOR DE BONIS NON
Probate Proceedings, generally, this index

ADMISSIBILITY OF EVIDENCE
Evidence, generally, this index

ADMISSIONS
Limited partnerships. Partnerships, this index
Partnerships, this index

ADVANCED SERVICES
Definitions, telecommunications, **Util 55.014**

ADVANCEMENTS
Nonprofit Corporations, this index
Partnerships, this index

ADVERSE OR PECUNIARY INTEREST
Conflict of Interest, generally, this index

ADVERTISEMENTS
Electricity,
Computation of rates, **Util 36.061**
Reports, **Util 32.104**
Gas Utilities, this index
Telecommunications, this index

ADVISORY COMMITTEES
Hearing Impaired Persons, this index
Speech impairment, telecommunications relay access service, **Util 56.110 et seq.**
Telecommunications, statewide relay access service, hearing and speech impaired persons, **Util 56.110 et seq.**

ADVOCATES
Electricity, municipally owned utilities, **Util 33.122**
Public utilities, consumers, **Util 13.001, 13.003**

AFFECTED PARTIES
Definitions, gas utilities, pipes and pipelines, sour gas, **Util 121.451**

AFFIDAVITS
Oaths and Affirmations, generally, this index
Telecommunications, universal service fund, **Util 56.030**
Telephone cooperative corporations, notice to customers, deregulation, **Util 53.357**

AFFILIATED CORPORATIONS
Corporations, business combinations, **Bus Org 21.601 et seq.**

AFFILIATED POWER GENERATION COMPANY
Definitions, **Util 31.002**

AFFILIATED RETAIL ELECTRIC PROVIDER
Definitions, **Util 31.002**

AFFILIATES
Definitions,
Business organizations, **Bus Org 1.002**
Gas utilities, **Util 101.003**
Public utilities, **Util 11.003**
Telecommunications, certificates of authority, **Util 54.153**
Electricity, this index
Gas Utilities, this index
Public Utilities, this index
River authorities, improvements, electricity, **Util 32.053**
Telecommunications, this index

AFFIRMATIONS
Oaths and Affirmations, generally, this index

AGED PERSONS
Apartment houses, construction, electricity, meters, exemptions, **Util 184.0125**
Assisted Living Facilities, generally, this index
Condominiums, construction, electricity, meters, exemptions, **Util 184.0125**
Electricity,
Payment, delay, **Util 182.001 et seq.**
Termination of service, **Util 14.005**
Gas utilities, payment, delay, **Util 182.001 et seq.**
Housing, electricity, meters, construction, exemptions, **Util 184.0125**
Nursing and Convalescent Homes, generally, this index
Public Utilities, this index
Telecommunications,
Lifeline service, **Util 55.015**
Payment, delay, **Util 182.001 et seq.**
Termination of service, **Util 14.005**
Water supply, payment, delay, **Util 182.001 et seq.**

AGENTS AND AGENCIES
Business development corporations, **Bus Org 23.054**
Churches, retirement and pensions, **Bus Org 22.404**
Cooperative Associations, this index
Corporations, this index
Definitions, municipal power agencies, **Util 163.051**
Foreign Corporations, this index
Limited Liability Companies, this index
Limited partnerships, changes, filing, fines and penalties, **Bus Org 21.802**
Managers and Management, generally, this index
Nonprofit Corporations, this index
Partnerships, this index
Professional Associations and Societies, this index
Professional Corporations, this index
Religious organizations and societies, retirement and pensions, **Bus Org 22.404**
State Agencies, generally, this index
Sunset Act, generally, this index

AGGREGATORS
Definitions, electricity, registration, **Util 39.353**

AGING AND DISABILITY SERVICES DEPARTMENT
Aged Persons, generally, this index
Nursing and Convalescent Homes, generally, this index

AGREEMENTS
Contracts, generally, this index

AGRICULTURE
Contracts, natural gas, **Util 123.023**
Definitions, oil and gas, use, **Util 123.021**
Exemptions, natural gas, **Util 123.024**
Gas utilities, **Util 123.001 et seq.**
Pipelines, exemptions, **Util 121.003**
Irrigation, generally, this index
Natural gas, **Util 123.021 et seq.**
Contracts, suppliers, **Util 123.023**
Definitions, **Util 123.022**
Exemptions, suppliers, **Util 123.024**
Gas utilities, **Util 123.001, 123.002**
Rates and charges, natural gas, **Util 123.023**
Records and recordation, natural gas, suppliers, **Util 123.023**
Sales, natural gas, **Util 123.021 et seq.**

AGRICULTURE GAS USERS ACT
Generally, **Util 123.021 et seq.**

AIR CONDITIONING
Apartment houses, central system utilities, **Util 184.051, 184.052**

AIR FORCE
Military Forces, generally, this index

AIR POLLUTION
Electricity, this index
Emissions, electricity, reductions, competition, **Util 39.264**
Gas utilities, pipes and pipelines, penalties, **Util 121.304 et seq.**

ALLEYS
Streets and Alleys, generally, this index

ALTERNATIVE DISPUTE RESOLUTION
Electricity, transmission, wholesalers, **Util 35.008**
Public utilities, commission, **Util 14.0025**
Telecommunications, this index

ALTERNATIVE ENERGY
Solar Energy, generally, this index

ALTERNATIVE FUELS
Gas utilities, application of law, **Util 101.003**

AMORTIZATION
Electricity, computation of rates, **Util 36.056**

AMORTIZATION—Cont'd
Gas utilities, computation of rates, **Util 104.054**
Telecommunications, computation of rates, **Util 53.056**

ANCILLARY PROCEEDINGS
Executions, generally, this index
Garnishment, generally, this index

ANCILLARY SERVICES
Definitions, electricity, transmission, **Util 35.004**

ANNEXATION
Municipalities, this index

ANNUAL REPORTS
Reports, generally, this index

ANNUITIES
Churches, retirement and pensions, contributions, **Bus Org 22.403**
Religious organizations and societies, retirement and pensions, contributions, **Bus Org 22.403**

ANTITRUST
Monopolies and Unfair Trade, generally, this index

APARTMENT HOUSES
Aged persons, construction, electricity, meters, exemptions, **Util 184.0125**
Air conditioning, central system utilities, **Util 184.051, 184.052**
Allocations, central heating and cooling, **Util 184.052**
Attorney fees, central system utilities, recovery, **Util 184.071**
Central system utilities, cooling and heating, **Util 184.051, 184.052**
Charges, central heating and cooling, **Util 184.052**
Condominiums, generally, this index
Construction, electricity, metering, **Util 184.012**
Costs, central system utilities, recovery, **Util 184.071**
Definitions,
  Central heating and cooling, **Util 184.051**
  Electricity, metering, **Util 184.011**
  Gas submetering, **Util 124.001**
Electricity, metering, **Util 184.001 et seq.**
Fines and penalties, central system utilities, **Util 184.071**
Gas meters,
  Submetering, **Util 124.001, 124.002**
  Termination, **Util 104.258**
Heating, central system utilities, **Util 184.051, 184.052**
Meters,
  Central heating and cooling, **Util 184.052**
  Electricity, **Util 184.001 et seq.**
Rates and charges, central heating and cooling, **Util 184.052**

APARTMENT HOUSES—Cont'd
Records and recordation,
  Central heating and cooling, **Util 184.052**
  Electricity, submetering, **Util 184.014**
  Gas submetering, **Util 124.002**
Submetering,
  Electricity, **Util 184.013, 184.014**
  Gas utilities, **Util 124.001, 124.002**

APPEAL AND REVIEW
Cooperative Associations, this index
Corporations, this index
Court of Criminal Appeals, generally, this index
Criminal cases. Court of Criminal Appeals, generally, this index
Electricity, this index
Foreign Corporations, this index
Gas Utilities, this index
Limited Liability Companies, this index
Limited partnerships. Partnerships, this index
Nonprofit Corporations, this index
Partnerships, this index
Professional Associations and Societies, this index
Professional Corporations, this index
Public Utilities, this index
Telecommunications, this index
Telephone cooperative corporations, deregulation, review, **Util 53.358**

APPEALS COURT
Courts of Appeals, generally, this index

APPEALS IN CRIMINAL PROSECUTIONS
Court of Criminal Appeals, generally, this index

APPRAISALS AND APPRAISERS
Real estate investment trusts, shares and shareholders, fundamental business transactions, **Bus Org 200.410**

AQUIFERS
Water Supply, this index

ARMED FORCES
Military Forces, generally, this index

ARMY
Military Forces, generally, this index

ARTICLES OF INCORPORATION
Electric Cooperative Corporations, this index
Telephone Cooperative Corporations, this index

ARTIFICIAL GAS
Gas Utilities, generally, this index

ASSEMBLY
Religious Organizations and Societies, generally, this index

ASSESSMENTS
Gas utilities, pipes and pipelines, **Util 121.2025**
Oil and Gas, this index
Pipes and pipelines, gas utilities, **Util 121.2025**
Public Utilities, this index
Sewers and Sewer Systems, this index
Telecommunications, this index
Water Supply, this index

ASSIGNEES
Definitions, electricity, securities, competition, **Util 39.302**

ASSIGNMENTS
Business development corporations, bonds, **Bus Org 23.061**
  Financial institutions, **Bus Org 23.062**
Churches, retirement and pensions, **Bus Org 22.408**
Cooperative Associations, this index
Corporations, this index
Electricity, this index
Foreign Corporations, this index
Limited Liability Companies, this index
Limited partnerships. Partnerships, this index
Partnerships, this index
Real Estate Investment Trusts, this index
Religious organizations and societies, retirement and pensions, **Bus Org 22.408**
Telecommunications, transfers of certificates, **Util 54.255**

ASSISTED LIVING FACILITIES
Definitions, electricity, priorities and preferences, **Util 38.072**
Electricity, priorities and preferences, **Util 38.072**
Priorities and preferences, electricity, **Util 38.072**

ASSOCIATE
Definitions, business organizations, **Bus Org 1.002**

ASSOCIATIONS AND SOCIETIES
Banks and Banking, generally, this index
Benevolent Societies, generally, this index
Charities, generally, this index
Cooperative Associations, generally, this index
Corporations, generally, this index
Definitions,
  Business organizations, **Bus Org 1.002**
  Partnerships, **Bus Org 152.051**
Independent Order of Odd Fellows, generally, this index
Lobbyists. Legislature, this index
Lodges, generally, this index
Masonic Societies, generally, this index
Monopolies and Unfair Trade, generally, this index
Nonprofit Corporations, generally, this index

ASSOCIATIONS AND SOCIETIES
—Cont'd
Professional Associations and Societies, generally, this index
Religious Organizations and Societies, generally, this index
Restraint of trade. Monopolies and Unfair Trade, generally, this index
Trade Associations, generally, this index
Trusts and monopolies. Monopolies and Unfair Trade, generally, this index
Unincorporated nonprofit associations. Nonprofit Corporations, this index

ASSUMED BUSINESS OR PROFESSIONAL NAME ACT
Generally, **Bus & C 71.001 et seq.**

ASSUMED OR FICTITIOUS NAMES
Generally, **Bus & C 71.001 et seq.**
Abandoned or unclaimed property, business and commerce, professions and occupations, **Bus & C 71.153**
Actions and proceedings, business and commerce, professions and occupations, **Bus & C 71.201**
Attorney fees, actions and proceedings, business and commerce, professions and occupations, **Bus & C 71.201**
Business and commerce, **Bus & C 71.001 et seq.**
Certificates and certification, business and commerce, professions and occupations, **Bus & C 71.051 et seq.**
Corporations, this index
Costs, actions and proceedings, business and commerce, professions and occupations, **Bus & C 71.201**
Crimes and offenses, business and commerce, professions and occupations, **Bus & C 71.202**
Fraud, **Bus & C 71.203**
Definitions,
Business and commerce, professions and occupations, **Bus & C 71.002**
Business organizations, **Bus Org 1.002**
Fees, certificates and certification, filing, business and commerce, **Bus & C 71.155**
Filing, certificates and certification, business and commerce, **Bus & C 71.155 et seq.**
Foreign corporations, **Bus & C 71.001 et seq.**
Forgery, filing, business and commerce, professions and occupations, **Bus & C 71.203**
Fraud, filing, business and commerce, professions and occupations, **Bus & C 71.203**
Indexes, certificates and certification, business and commerce, professions and occupations, **Bus & C 71.154**
Limited liability companies, **Bus & C 71.001 et seq.**
Partnerships, **Bus & C 71.001 et seq.**

ASSUMED OR FICTITIOUS NAMES
—Cont'd
Professional associations and societies, **Bus & C 71.001 et seq.**
Professional corporations, **Bus & C 71.001 et seq.**
Professions and occupations, **Bus & C 71.001 et seq.**
Real estate investment trusts, **Bus & C 71.001 et seq.**
Certificate of formation, **Bus Org 3.012**

ATHLETIC CORPORATIONS
Nonprofit Corporations, generally, this index

ATOMIC ENERGY
Electricity, decommissioning, costs, plans and specifications, **Util 39.206**
Nuclear Power Plants, generally, this index

ATTACHMENT
Churches, retirement and pensions, **Bus Org 22.407**
Cooperative Associations, this index
Religious organizations and societies, retirement and pensions, **Bus Org 22.407**

ATTORNEY FEES
Apartment houses, central system utilities, recovery, **Util 184.071**
Assumed or fictitious names, actions and proceedings, business and commerce, professions and occupations, **Bus & C 71.201**
Cooperative Associations, this index
Corporations, this index
Electric cooperative corporations, rates and charges, actions and proceedings, customer choice, **Util 41.061**
Foreign Corporations, this index
Gas utilities, pipes and pipelines, discrimination, fines and penalties, **Util 121.303**
Limited Liability Companies, this index
Limited partnerships. Partnerships, this index
Nonprofit Corporations, this index
Partnerships, this index
Professional Associations and Societies, this index
Professional Corporations, this index
Public utilities, appeal and review, rates, **Util 15.003**
Telecommunications, this index

ATTORNEY GENERAL
Electricity, joint ownership, public entities, approval, **Util 164.003**
Public utility commission, representation, **Util 12.004**

ATTORNEYS
Attorney Fees, generally, this index
Compensation and salaries. Attorney Fees, generally, this index

ATTORNEYS—Cont'd
Conversion, generally, this index
Electricity, this index
Fees. Attorney Fees, generally, this index
Gas Utilities, this index
Public Utilities, this index
State bar,
Audits and auditors, nonprofit corporations, **Bus Org 22.356**
Books and papers, nonprofit corporations, audits and auditors, **Bus Org 22.356**
Nonprofit corporations, audits and auditors, **Bus Org 22.356**
Records and recordation, nonprofit corporations, audits and auditors, **Bus Org 22.356**

ATTORNEYS FEES
Attorney Fees, generally, this index

AUCTIONS AND AUCTIONEERS
Electricity, customer choice, installed generation capacity, entitlements, **Util 39.153**

AUDITS AND AUDITORS
Boards and Commissions, this index
Colleges and Universities, this index
Cooperative associations, **Bus Org 251.352**
Court of Criminal Appeals, this index
Courts, this index
Courts of Appeals, this index
Electricity, municipalities, rates and charges, franchises, **Util 33.008**
Gas Utilities, this index
Legislature, this index
Public Utilities, this index
State, this index
State Agencies, this index
State Departments, this index
Supreme Court, this index
Telecommunications, this index

AUTHORITIES
River Authorities, generally, this index

AUTOMATED DIAL ANNOUNCING DEVICES
Telecommunications, this index

AWARDS
Grants, generally, this index

BALLOTS
Elections, this index

BANKING ACT
Banks and Banking, generally, this index

BANKRUPTCY
Atomic energy, electricity, decommissioning, trust funds, **Util 39.206**
Electricity,
Atomic energy, decommissioning, trust funds, **Util 39.206**

BANKRUPTCY—Cont'd
Electricity—Cont'd
Setoff and counterclaim, transition property, securities, competition, **Util 39.305**
Notice, telecommunications, providers of last resort, termination of service, **Util 54.305**
Telecommunications, providers of last resort, termination of service, notice, **Util 54.305**

BANKS AND BANKING
Conduct, damages, **Bus Org 7.001**
Credit Unions, generally, this index
Damages, officers and employees, **Bus Org 7.001**
Directors, damages, **Bus Org 7.001**
Franchise Taxes, generally, this index
Indemnity, damages, **Bus Org 7.001**
Misconduct, damages, **Bus Org 7.001**
Names, registration, **Bus Org 5.151 et seq.**
Officers and employees, damages, **Bus Org 7.001**
Registration, names, **Bus Org 5.151 et seq.**
Taxation. Franchise Taxes, generally, this index

BARGAINING
Collective bargaining. Labor Disputes, this index

BASIC LOCAL SERVICE
Telecommunications, this index

BENEVOLENT SOCIETIES
Generally, **Bus Org 1.001 et seq.**
Application of law, **Bus Org 23.102**
Bylaws, powers and duties, **Bus Org 23.107**
Certificate of formation, **Bus Org 23.101**
Time, **Bus Org 23.103**
Charities, generally, this index
Constitutions, powers and duties, **Bus Org 23.107**
Damages, **Bus Org 23.110**
Deeds and conveyances, **Bus Org 23.108**
Directors, elections, **Bus Org 23.105**
Elections, **Bus Org 23.105**
Filing, certificate of formation, **Bus Org 23.101**
Franchises, taxation, **Bus Org 23.106**
Liens and incumbrances, **Bus Org 23.109**
Loans, **Bus Org 23.109**
Mortgages, **Bus Org 23.108**
Nonprofit Corporations, generally, this index
Powers and duties, **Bus Org 23.107**
Property, **Bus Org 23.108**
Real estate, **Bus Org 23.109**
Revocation or suspension, subordinate lodges, **Bus Org 23.104**
Sales, property, **Bus Org 23.108**
Schools and school districts, **Bus Org 23.108**
Subordinate lodges, **Bus Org 23.104**
Winding up, **Bus Org 23.110**

BENEVOLENT SOCIETIES—Cont'd
Termination, subordinate, **Bus Org 23.110**
Time, certificate of formation, **Bus Org 23.103**
Trusts and trustee, elections, **Bus Org 23.105**
Winding up, subordinate lodges, **Bus Org 23.110**

BENZINE
Oil and Gas, generally, this index

BEQUESTS
Gifts, generally, this index

BIAS OR PREJUDICE
Discrimination, generally, this index

BIDS AND BIDDING
Electricity, municipal power agencies, construction contracts, **Util 163.061**
Telecommunications, statewide relay access service, hearing and speech impaired persons, **Util 56.108**

BILLING AGENTS
Definitions,
Electricity, deceptive trade practices and consumer protection, **Util 17.002**
Telecommunications, deceptive trade practices and consumer protection, **Util 17.002, 64.002**

BILLING UTILITY
Definitions,
Electricity, deceptive trade practices and consumer protection, **Util 17.002**
Telecommunications, deceptive trade practices and consumer protection, **Util 17.002, 64.002**

BILLS
Statutes, generally, this index

BILLS AND BILLING
Electricity, this index
Gas Utilities, this index
Sewers and Sewer Systems, this index
Telecommunications, local exchange service, **Util 55.016**

BILLS OF LADING
Corporations, **Bus Org 1.001 et seq.**

BLIND PERSONS
Audio newspapers, telecommunications, universal service fund, **Util 56.301**
Newspapers, audio newspapers, telecommunications, universal service fund, **Util 56.301**
Telecommunications, audio newspapers, universal service fund, **Util 56.301**

BLUE SKY LAW
Securities, generally, this index

BOARD OF DIRECTORS
Directors, generally, this index

BOARDS AND COMMISSIONS
Audits and auditors, nonprofit corporations, **Bus Org 22.356**
Books and papers, nonprofit corporations, audits and auditors, **Bus Org 22.356**
Definitions,
Electric cooperative corporations, **Util 161.002**
Electricity, state, sales, royalties, in kind, **Util 35.101**
Public utilities, **Util 11.003**
Customers deposits, **Util 183.001**
Multiple units, meters, **Util 184.001**
Solar energy, ratings, devices, **Util 185.001**
Telephone cooperative corporations, **Util 162.003**
Weather, emergencies, electricity, plans and specifications, reports, **Util 186.007**
Electricity, municipal power agencies, directors, **Util 163.059**
Nonprofit corporations, audits and auditors, **Bus Org 22.356**
Oaths and Affirmations, generally, this index
Railroad Commission, generally, this index
Records and recordation, nonprofit corporations, audits and auditors, **Bus Org 22.356**
Sunset Act, generally, this index

BOND ANTICIPATION NOTES
Electricity, municipal power agencies, **Util 163.068**

BONDS
Business development corporations, **Bus Org 23.054**
Sales, **Bus Org 23.061**
Corporations, this index
Definitions, municipal power agencies, **Util 163.051**
Electric Cooperative Corporations, this index
Electricity, this index
Nonprofit Corporations, this index
Partnerships, this index

BONDS (OFFICERS AND FIDUCIARIES)
Electricity, rate changes, pending final determination, **Util 36.110**
Gas Utilities, this index
Public utilities,
Interruption of service, restraining orders, **Util 186.005**
Judicial review, administrative penalties, **Util 15.025, 15.026**
Telecommunications, this index

BOOKS AND PAPERS
Boards and Commissions, this index
Colleges and Universities, this index

BOOKS AND PAPERS—Cont'd
Compelling production. Production of Books and Papers, generally, this index
Cooperative Associations, this index
Corporations, this index
Courts, this index
Evidence. Production of Books and Papers, generally, this index
Foreign Corporations, this index
Legislature, this index
Libraries, generally, this index
Limited Liability Companies, this index
Limited partnerships. Partnerships, this index
Nonprofit Corporations, this index
Partnerships, this index
Production of Books and Papers, generally, this index
Professional Associations and Societies, this index
Professional Corporations, this index
Real estate investment trusts, examinations and examiners, **Bus Org 200.501**
State, this index
State Agencies, this index
State Departments, this index

BORROWING
Loans, generally, this index

BOULEVARDS
Streets and Alleys, generally, this index

BOUNDARIES
Telephone cooperative corporations, districts, **Util 162.076**

BPL
Broadband over power lines, **Util 43.001 et seq.**

BRANDS, MARKS AND LABELS
Oil and Gas, this index
Public Utilities, this index

BROADBAND OVER POWER LINES
Generally, **Util 43.001 et seq.**

BROADCASTERS
Television and radio, safeguards, **Util 62.001 et seq.**

BROADCASTING
Television and Radio, generally, this index

BUDGET
Public utility commission, **Util 16.044**

BUILDINGS
Apartment Houses, generally, this index
Definitions, public utilities, **Util 11.003**
School Buildings and Grounds, generally, this index

BURDEN OF PROOF
Evidence, this index

BUSINESS AND COMMERCE
Assumed or fictitious names, **Bus & C 71.001 et seq.**
Business Development Corporations, generally, this index
Corporations, generally, this index
Definitions, organizations, **Bus Org 1.002**
Foreign commerce. Interstate Commerce, generally, this index
Gas utilities, large volume customers, termination, **Util 121.103**
Incorporation. Corporations, this index
Interstate Commerce, generally, this index
Lobbyists. Legislature, this index
Monopolies and Unfair Trade, generally, this index
Partnerships, generally, this index
Restraint of trade. Monopolies and Unfair Trade, generally, this index
Small Businesses, generally, this index
Trusts and monopolies. Monopolies and Unfair Trade, generally, this index

BUSINESS COMBINATIONS
Generally, **Bus Org 21.601 et seq.**

BUSINESS CORPORATIONS
Corporations, generally, this index

BUSINESS CORPORATIONS ACT
Corporations, generally, this index

BUSINESS DEVELOPMENT CORPORATIONS
Generally, **Bus Org 1.001 et seq., 23.051 et seq.**
Agents and agencies, **Bus Org 23.054**
Assignments, bonds, **Bus Org 23.061**
  Financial institutions, **Bus Org 23.062**
Bonds, **Bus Org 23.054**
  Sales, **Bus Org 23.061**
Certificate of formation, **Bus Org 23.056**
  Purposes, **Bus Org 23.053**
Contracts, **Bus Org 23.054**
Deeds and conveyances, **Bus Org 23.054**
Deeds of trust, **Bus Org 23.054**
Definitions, **Bus Org 23.051**
Deposits, funds, **Bus Org 23.070**
Directors, **Bus Org 23.057 et seq.**
Disclosure, information, **Bus Org 23.071**
Domicile and residence, organization, **Bus Org 23.052**
Duties. Powers and duties, generally, post
Elections, **Bus Org 23.054, 23.065**
  Directors, **Bus Org 23.058**
  Funds, deposits, **Bus Org 23.070**
Evidence, loans, **Bus Org 23.066**
Financial institutions, members, **Bus Org 23.062**
Franchises, **Bus Org 23.054**
Funds, deposits, **Bus Org 23.070**
Information, disclosure, **Bus Org 23.071**
Interest, loans, **Bus Org 23.066**
Leases, **Bus Org 23.054**
Liens and incumbrances, **Bus Org 23.054**
Limitations, loans, **Bus Org 23.067, 23.068**

BUSINESS DEVELOPMENT CORPORATIONS—Cont'd
Loans, **Bus Org 23.054, 23.066**
  Financial institutions, **Bus Org 23.062**
  Limitations, **Bus Org 23.067, 23.068**
Local development corporations, **Bus Org 23.054**
Managers and management, directors, **Bus Org 23.057 et seq.**
Meetings, directors, elections, **Bus Org 23.058**
Members,
  Elections, **Bus Org 23.065**
  Financial institutions, **Bus Org 23.062**
  Powers and duties, **Bus Org 23.064**
  Withdrawal, **Bus Org 23.063**
Mortgages, **Bus Org 23.054**
  Bonds, **Bus Org 23.061**
    Financial institutions, **Bus Org 23.062**
Names, certificate of formation, **Bus Org 23.056**
Notice, members, withdrawal, **Bus Org 23.063**
Numbers and numbering, directors, **Bus Org 23.057**
Officers and employees, **Bus Org 23.054, 23.060**
Organization, **Bus Org 23.052**
Pledges, **Bus Org 23.054**
  Bonds, **Bus Org 23.061**
    Financial institutions, **Bus Org 23.062**
Powers and duties, **Bus Org 23.054**
  Directors, **Bus Org 23.057**
  Financial institutions, **Bus Org 23.062**
  Shares and shareholders, **Bus Org 23.061**
President, **Bus Org 23.060**
Property, **Bus Org 23.054**
Purposes, **Bus Org 23.053**
Reports, **Bus Org 23.071**
Sales,
  Bonds, **Bus Org 23.061**
    Financial institutions, **Bus Org 23.062**
  Property, **Bus Org 23.054**
Shares and shareholders,
  Elections, **Bus Org 23.065**
  Financial institutions, **Bus Org 23.062**
  Powers and duties, **Bus Org 23.061, 23.064**
Surplus, **Bus Org 23.069**
Terms of office, directors, **Bus Org 23.059**
Time, members, withdrawal, **Bus Org 23.063**
Transfers,
  Bonds, **Bus Org 23.061**
    Financial institutions, **Bus Org 23.062**
  Property, **Bus Org 23.054**
Treasurers, **Bus Org 23.060**
Vacancies in office, directors, **Bus Org 23.059**
Withdrawal, members, **Bus Org 23.063**

BUSINESS ORGANIZATIONS CODE
Generally, **Bus Org 1.001 et seq.**

BUSINESS TRUST
Trusts and Trustees, this index

CABLE OPERATORS
Definitions, railroads, right of way, **Util 186.051**

CABLE TELEVISION
See, also, Public Utilities, generally, this index
Application of law,
Franchises, **Util 66.016**
Telecommunications, **Util 51.003**
Applications, franchises, certificate of authority, **Util 66.003 et seq.**
Assessments, underground facilities, notification corporation, excavations, **Util 251.062**
Brands, marks and labels, underground facilities,
Crimes and offenses, excavations, **Util 251.203**
Excavations, **Util 251.157, 251.158**
Broadcasters, safeguards, application of law, **Util 62.001**
Build out, franchises, exemptions, **Util 66.007**
Call router system, underground facilities, contracts, notification corporation, excavations, **Util 251.061**
Certificate of authority, franchises, applications, **Util 66.003 et seq.**
Compliance, orders of court, franchises, **Util 66.015**
Construction, easements, standards, **Util 181.102**
Contracts, underground facilities, toll free numbers, notification corporation, excavations, **Util 251.061**
Counties, highways and roads, easements, notice, **Util 181.103**
Crimes and offenses, underground facilities, brands, marks and labels, excavations, **Util 251.203**
Customer service, standards, franchises, **Util 66.008**
Damages, underground facilities, **Util 251.001 et seq.**
Directors, underground facilities, notification corporation, excavations, **Util 251.055 et seq.**
Discrimination, franchises, municipalities, **Util 66.010, 66.014**
Easements, **Util 181.101 et seq.**
Entry on property, identity and identification, **Util 55.017**
Railroads, right of way, eminent domain, **Util 186.051 et seq.**
Underground facilities, excavations, **Util 251.006**
Educational access channels, franchises, **Util 66.009**
Emergencies, underground facilities, notice, excavations, **Util 251.155**
Eminent domain, railroads, right of way, **Util 186.051 et seq.**
Entry on property, identity and identification, **Util 55.017**
Excavations, underground facilities, **Util 251.001 et seq.**

CABLE TELEVISION—Cont'd
Exemptions,
Franchises, build out, **Util 66.007**
Underground facilities, notice, excavations, **Util 251.156**
Expenses and expenditures, underground facilities, notification corporation, excavations, **Util 251.054**
Fees,
Franchises, **Util 66.005**
Municipalities, **Util 66.006**
Railroads, right of way, use, **Util 186.058**
Underground facilities, post
Fines and penalties, underground facilities, excavations, **Util 251.201 et seq.**
Franchises,
Municipalities, fees, **Util 66.006**
State, **Util 66.001 et seq.**
Fraud, underground facilities, emergencies, excavations, **Util 251.155**
Fines and penalties, **Util 251.201**
Governmental access channels, franchises, **Util 66.009**
Highways and roads,
Easements, **Util 181.101 et seq.**
Underground facilities, excavations, **Util 251.007**
Identity and identification, entry on property, **Util 55.017**
In kind contributions, franchises, municipalities, **Util 66.006**
Indemnity, franchises, municipalities, **Util 66.012**
Insurance, underground facilities, notification center, excavations, **Util 251.104**
Licenses and permits,
Railroads, right of way, use, **Util 186.058**
Underground facilities, excavations, **Util 251.006**
Municipalities, franchises, **Util 66.009 et seq.**
Fees, **Util 66.006**
Termination, **Util 66.004**
Notice,
Easements, highways and roads, **Util 181.103**
Railroads, right of way, easements, **Util 186.054**
Underground facilities, post
Notification center, underground facilities, excavations, **Util 251.101 et seq.**
Notification corporation, underground facilities, excavations, **Util 251.051 et seq.**
Officers and employees, underground facilities, notification corporation, excavations, **Util 251.058**
Open meetings, underground facilities, notification corporation, excavations, **Util 251.053**
Open records, underground facilities, notification corporation, excavations, **Util 251.053**

CABLE TELEVISION—Cont'd
Orders of court, compliance, franchises, **Util 66.015**
Payment, underground facilities, notification center, excavations, **Util 251.106**
PEG channels, franchises, municipalities, **Util 66.009**
Powers and duties. Underground facilities, post
Public access channels, franchises, **Util 66.009**
Railroads, right of way, easements, eminent domain, **Util 186.051 et seq.**
Rates and charges. Underground facilities, post
Records and recordation, underground facilities, notification center, excavations, **Util 251.103**
Relocation, machinery and equipment, easements, **Util 181.104**
Remedies, underground facilities, excavations, **Util 251.008**
Repairs, underground facilities, excavations, **Util 251.159**
Reports, underground facilities, damages, excavations, **Util 251.159**
Right of way, **Util 181.101 et seq.**
Franchises, municipalities, **Util 66.010 et seq.**
Safety, underground facilities, **Util 251.001 et seq.**
Standards, customer service, franchises, **Util 66.008**
State,
Franchises, **Util 66.001 et seq.**
Highways and roads, easements, notice, **Util 181.103**
Streets and alleys, easements, **Util 181.101 et seq.**
Termination, franchises, municipalities, **Util 66.004**
Toll free numbers, underground facilities, contracts, notification corporation, excavations, **Util 251.061**
Underground facilities,
Assessments, notification corporation, excavations, **Util 251.062**
Brands, marks and labels,
Crimes and offenses, excavations, **Util 251.203**
Excavations, **Util 251.157, 251.158**
Call router system, contracts, notification corporation, excavations, **Util 251.061**
Contracts, toll free numbers, notification corporation, excavations, **Util 251.061**
Conversion, **Util 251.005**
Crimes and offenses, brands, marks and labels, excavations, **Util 251.203**
Damages, **Util 251.001 et seq.**
Notification corporation, excavations, **Util 251.054**
Directors, notification corporation, excavations, **Util 251.055 et seq.**
Easements, excavations, **Util 251.006**

CABLE TELEVISION—Cont'd
Underground facilities—Cont'd
Emergencies, notice, excavations, **Util 251.155**
Excavations, **Util 251.001 et seq.**
Exemptions, notice, excavations, **Util 251.156**
Expenses and expenditures, notification corporation, excavations, **Util 251.054**
Fees,
Notification center, excavations, **Util 251.105**
Notification corporation, excavations, **Util 251.062**
Fines and penalties, excavations, **Util 251.201 et seq.**
Fraud, emergencies, excavations, **Util 251.155**
Fines and penalties, **Util 251.201**
Highways and roads, excavations, **Util 251.007**
Insurance, notification center, excavations, **Util 251.104**
Licenses and permits, excavations, **Util 251.006**
Notice, excavations, **Util 251.009, 251.151 et seq.**
Notification center, excavations, **Util 251.101 et seq.**
Notification corporation, excavations, **Util 251.051 et seq.**
Officers and employees, notification corporation, excavations, **Util 251.058**
Open meetings, notification corporation, excavations, **Util 251.053**
Open records, notification corporation, excavations, **Util 251.053**
Payment, notification center, excavations, **Util 251.106**
Powers and duties,
Notification center, excavations, **Util 251.102**
Notification corporation, excavations, **Util 251.060**
Rates and charges,
Notification center, excavations, **Util 251.105**
Notification corporation, excavations, **Util 251.062**
Records and recordation, notification center, excavations, **Util 251.103**
Remedies, excavations, **Util 251.008**
Repairs, excavations, **Util 251.159**
Reports, damages, excavations, **Util 251.159**
Safety, **Util 251.001 et seq.**
Toll free numbers, contracts, notification corporation, excavations, **Util 251.061**
Venue, fines and penalties, excavations, **Util 251.201**
Warnings, excavations, **Util 251.201, 251.2011**
Venue, underground facilities, fines and penalties, excavations, **Util 251.201**

CABLE TELEVISION—Cont'd
Warnings, underground facilities, excavations, **Util 251.201, 251.2011**

CALLER IDENTIFICATION SERVICE
Telecommunications, this index

CANALS
Corporations, **Bus Org 1.001 et seq.**
Drainage corporations, **Bus Org 1.001 et seq.**

CAPITAL
Cooperative associations, **Bus Org 251.301**

CARRIERS
Definitions, railroads, right of way, **Util 186.051**
Easements, railroads, right of way, eminent domain, **Util 186.051 et seq.**
Eminent domain, railroads, right of way, **Util 186.051 et seq.**
Fees, railroads, right of way, use, **Util 186.058**
Licenses and permits, railroads, right of way, use, **Util 186.058**
Notice, railroads, right of way, easements, **Util 186.054**
Pipes and pipelines, powers and duties, **Bus Org 2.105**
Railroads, generally, this index

CASH
Money, generally, this index

CERTIFICATE OF AUTHORITY
Cable television, franchises, applications, **Util 66.003 et seq.**
Television and radio, franchises, applications, **Util 66.003 et seq.**

CERTIFICATE OF FORMATION
Business development corporations, **Bus Org 23.056**
Purposes, **Bus Org 23.053**
Cooperative Associations, this index
Corporations, this index
Definitions, business organizations, **Bus Org 1.002**
Grand lodges, **Bus Org 23.101**
Time, **Bus Org 23.103**
Limited Liability Companies, this index
Lodges, **Bus Org 23.101**
Time, **Bus Org 23.103**
Nonprofit Corporations, this index
Partnerships, this index
Prior law, reference, **Bus Org 402.0051**
Professional Associations and Societies, this index
Professional Corporations, this index
Real Estate Investment Trusts, this index

CERTIFICATED TELECOMMUNICATIONS UTILITY
Definitions, deceptive trade practices and consumer protection, **Util 17.002, 64.002**

CERTIFICATES AND CERTIFICATION
Assumed or fictitious names, business and commerce, professions and occupations, **Bus & C 71.051 et seq.**
Certificate of Formation, generally, this index
Cogeneration, contracts, purchase of power, **Util 35.062 et seq.**
Cooperative Associations, this index
Corporations, this index
Definitions,
Assumed or fictitious names, business and commerce, professions and occupations, **Bus & C 71.002**
Electricity, convenience and necessity, **Util 37.001**
Telecommunications,
Certificates of operating authority, **Util 54.151**
Convenience and necessity, **Util 54.051**
Operating authority, **Util 54.101**
Electric Cooperative Corporations, this index
Electricity, this index
Foreign Corporations, this index
Formation. Certificate of Formation, generally, this index
Limited liability companies,
Evidence, existence, **Bus Org 4.005**
Filing, **Bus Org 12.001**
Limited partnerships. Partnerships, this index
Nonprofit Corporations, this index
Partnerships, this index
Professional Associations and Societies, this index
Professional Corporations, this index
Shares and shareholders. Corporations, this index
Telecommunications, this index
Telephone Cooperative Corporations, this index

CERTIFICATES OF CONVENIENCE AND NECESSITY
Electric Cooperative Corporations, this index
Electricity, this index
Telecommunications, this index

CERTIFICATES OF FORMATION
Certificate of Formation, generally, this index

CERTIFICATES OF OPERATING AUTHORITY
Telecommunications, this index

CERTIFICATION
Certificates and Certification, generally, this index

CERTIFIED COPIES
Corporations, this index
Limited Liability Companies, this index

CESTUI QUE TRUST
Trusts and Trustees, generally, this index

CHARGES
Rates and Charges, generally, this index

CHARITABLE ORGANIZATIONS AND SOCIETIES
Charities, generally, this index

CHARITIES
Certificate of formation, taxation, statements, **Bus Org 2.107**
Grand Lodges, generally, this index
Incorporation, lodges, **Bus Org 1.001 et seq., 23.101 et seq.**
Lodges, incorporation, **Bus Org 1.001 et seq., 23.101 et seq.**
Nonprofit Corporations, generally, this index
Statements, taxation, certificate of formation, **Bus Org 2.107**

CHARTER SCHOOLS
Schools and School Districts, this index

CHARTERS
Schools and School Districts, this index

CHILDREN AND MINORS
Guardian and Ward, generally, this index
Schools and School Districts, generally, this index

CHIROPODISTS
Podiatrists, generally, this index

CHIROPRACTORS
Associations and societies. Professional Associations and Societies, generally, this index
Professional Associations and Societies, generally, this index
Telemedicine, generally, this index

CHOICE OF LAW
Conflict of Laws, generally, this index

CHURCHES
See, also, Religious Organizations and Societies, generally, this index
Agents and agencies, retirement and pensions, **Bus Org 22.404**
Annuities, retirement and pensions, contributions, **Bus Org 22.403**
Application of law, retirement and pensions, insurance, **Bus Org 22.409**
Assignments, retirement and pensions, **Bus Org 22.408**
Attachment, retirement and pensions, **Bus Org 22.407**
Benefits, boards and commissions, retirement and pensions, **Bus Org 22.401 et seq.**
Boards and commissions, retirement and pensions, **Bus Org 22.401 et seq.**
Contributions, retirement and pensions, **Bus Org 22.403**

CHURCHES—Cont'd
Damages, retirement and pensions, indemnity, **Bus Org 22.406**
Definitions, officers and employees, retirement and pensions, **Bus Org 22.401**
Directors,
  Nonprofit corporations, **Bus Org 22.233**
  Retirement and pensions, **Bus Org 22.401 et seq.**
Domestic relations orders, retirement and pensions, **Bus Org 22.407**
Executions, retirement and pensions, **Bus Org 22.407**
Garnishment, retirement and pensions, **Bus Org 22.407**
Indemnity. Retirement and pensions, post
Insurance, retirement and pensions, application of law, **Bus Org 22.409**
Investments, retirement and pensions, contributions, **Bus Org 22.403**
Managers and management, nonprofit corporations, **Bus Org 22.233**
Nonprofit corporations, managers and management, **Bus Org 22.233**
Officers and employees, retirement and pensions, **Bus Org 22.401 et seq.**
Payment, retirement and pensions, contributions, **Bus Org 22.403**
Reserves, retirement and pensions, contributions, **Bus Org 22.403**
Retirement and pensions,
  Indemnity, **Bus Org 22.405, 22.406**
  Officers and employees, **Bus Org 22.401 et seq.**
Schoolteachers, retirement and pensions, **Bus Org 22.401 et seq.**
Teachers, retirement and pensions, **Bus Org 22.401 et seq.**
Transfers, retirement and pensions, **Bus Org 22.408**
Trusts and trustees, retirement and pensions, **Bus Org 22.401 et seq.**

CITIES, TOWNS AND VILLAGES
Municipalities, generally, this index

CITY
Municipalities, generally, this index

CITY COMMUNITY COLLEGE
Community colleges and districts. Colleges and Universities, this index

CIVIC CORPORATIONS
Nonprofit Corporations, generally, this index

CIVIL ACTIONS
Actions and Proceedings, generally, this index

CIVIL COURTS OF APPEALS
Courts of Appeals, generally, this index

CLASS A UNDERGROUND FACILITIES
Definitions, excavations, **Util 251.001**

CLASS B UNDERGROUND FACILITIES
Definitions, excavations, **Util 251.001**

CLERGY
Benefit boards, retirement and pensions, **Bus Org 22.401 et seq.**
Retirement and pensions, **Bus Org 22.401 et seq.**

CLOSE CORPORATIONS
Corporations, this index

COAST GUARD
Military Forces, generally, this index

CODE OF CONDUCT
Telecommunications, **Util 60.201 et seq.**

CODES
Business Organizations Code, **Bus Org 1.001 et seq.**

COGENERATION
  Generally, **Util 35.001 et seq., 35.061 et seq.**
Authority, sales, **Util 35.002**
Certificates and certification, contracts, purchase of power, **Util 35.062 et seq.**
Certificates of convenience and necessity, application of law, **Util 37.001**
Contracts, purchase of power, certification, **Util 35.062 et seq.**
Definitions, **Util 31.002**
Hearings, contracts, certificates and certification, **Util 35.063**
Public policy, **Util 35.061**
Rates and charges, payments, cost recovery, **Util 36.208**
Time, contracts, certificates and certification, purchase of power, **Util 35.065, 35.066**
Transmission, access to facilities, **Util 35.004 et seq.**

COLLECTIONS
Gas Utilities, this index
Public Utilities, this index
Sewers and Sewer Systems, this index
Telecommunications, this index

COLLECTIVE BARGAINING
Labor Disputes, this index

COLLEGES AND UNIVERSITIES
Audits and auditors, nonprofit corporations, **Bus Org 22.356**
Books and papers, nonprofit corporations, audits and auditors, **Bus Org 22.356**
Community colleges and districts, electricity, rates and charges, **Util 36.352**
Distance learning, telecommunications, **Util 57.021 et seq.**

COLLEGES AND UNIVERSITIES
—Cont'd
Electricity, rates and charges, **Util 36.351, 36.352**
Names, University Cooperative Society, **Bus Org 251.452**
Nonprofit corporations, audits and auditors, **Bus Org 22.356**
Records and recordation, nonprofit corporations, audits and auditors, **Bus Org 22.356**
Telecommunications,
Distance learning, **Util 57.021 et seq.**
Landlord and tenant, installations, exemptions, **Util 54.259**
Private network services, **Util 58.251 et seq., 59.071 et seq.**
University Cooperative Society, names, **Bus Org 251.452**

COLOR
Discrimination, generally, this index

COMBINATIONS IN RESTRAINT OF TRADE
Monopolies and Unfair Trade, generally, this index

COMMERCE
Business and Commerce, generally, this index

COMMERCIAL CODE
Sales, generally, this index

COMMISSIONERS
Boards and Commissions, generally, this index

COMMISSIONS
Boards and Commissions, generally, this index

COMMITTEES
Cooperative associations, directors, **Bus Org 251.102**
Nonprofit Corporations, this index
Real estate investment trusts, managers and management, **Bus Org 200.311**

COMMON CARRIERS
Carriers, generally, this index

COMMUNICATIONS
Electronic Communications, generally, this index
Telecommunications, generally, this index
Wire communications. Electronic Communications, generally, this index

COMMUNITY ANTENNA TELEVISION
Cable Television, generally, this index

COMMUNITY COLLEGES AND DISTRICTS
Colleges and Universities, this index

COMMUNITY PROPERTY
Limited liability companies, members, **Bus Org 101.106**

COMMUNITY SUPERVISION
Telecommunications, nine hundred (900) information service, charges, **Util 55.252**

COMPELLING PRODUCTION OF BOOKS AND PAPERS
Production of Books and Papers, generally, this index

COMPENSATION AND SALARIES
Attorney Fees, generally, this index
Corporations, this index
Electric cooperative corporations, directors, **Util 161.073**
Foreign Corporations, this index
Garnishment, generally, this index
Gas utilities, railroad commission, pipelines, **Util 121.157, 121.158**
Limited partnerships. Partnerships, this index
Lobbyists. Legislature, this index
Nonprofit Corporations, this index
Partnerships, this index
Public Utilities, this index
Public utility commission, commissioners, **Util 12.057**
Real estate investment trusts, numbers and numbering, managers and management, **Bus Org 200.305**
Telecommunications, this index
Telephone cooperative corporations, directors, **Util 162.073**

COMPETITIONS
Monopolies and Unfair Trade, generally, this index

COMPETITIVE AFFILIATE
Definitions, electricity, customer choice, **Util 39.157**

COMPLAINTS
Electricity, this index
Gas Utilities, this index
Public Utilities, this index
Telecommunications, this index
Telephone cooperative corporations, deregulation, **Util 53.358**

COMPROMISE AND SETTLEMENT
Gas utilities, pipes and pipelines, penalties, **Util 121.205**
Partnerships, winding up, **Bus Org 152.707**
Public utilities, contested cases, **Util 14.054**

COMPTROLLER OF PUBLIC ACCOUNTS
General revenue fund. State Treasury, this index

COMPUTERS
Electronic Communications, generally, this index
Internet, generally, this index
Schools and School Districts, this index

CONDEMNATION
Eminent Domain, generally, this index

CONDOMINIUMS
Aged Persons, this index
Construction, electricity, metering, **Util 184.012**
Conversion, electricity, metering, **Util 184.012**
Electricity, metering, **Util 184.001 et seq.**
Meters, electricity, **Util 184.001 et seq.**

CONDUCT
Banks and Banking, this index
Corporations, this index
Nonprofit Corporations, this index
Partnerships, this index

CONFIDENTIAL OR PRIVILEGED INFORMATION
See, also, Privileges and Immunities, generally, this index
Electricity, this index
Gas utilities, customers, **Util 182.051 et seq.**
Public Utilities, this index
Sewers and sewer systems, customers, **Util 182.051 et seq.**
Solid waste, customers, **Util 182.051 et seq.**
Telecommunications, this index
Water supply, customers, **Util 182.051 et seq.**

CONFISCATION
Electricity, municipalities, rate appeals, **Util 33.055**

CONFLICT OF INTEREST
Corporations, this index
Definitions, public utility commission, **Util 12.154**
Electricity, customer choice, independent organizations, **Util 39.1512**
Foreign Corporations, this index
Gas utilities, public utilities counsel office, **Util 101.053**
Nonprofit Corporations, this index
Partnerships, this index
Public Utilities, this index
Real estate investment trusts, contracts, **Bus Org 200.317**

CONFLICT OF LAWS
Broadband over power lines, **Util 43.002**
Business combinations, **Bus Org 21.609**
Electricity, this index
Foreign Corporations, this index
Gas Utilities, this index
Public utilities, federal law, **Util 11.009**
Real estate investment trusts, **Bus Org 200.003**

CONFLICT OF LAWS—Cont'd
River authorities, electricity, **Util 32.054**
Telecommunications, this index
Telephone cooperative corporations, amendments of articles, compliance, **Util 162.082**

CONSERVATION
Electricity, rates and charges, cost recovery, **Util 36.204**

CONSERVATORS AND CONSERVATORSHIP
Real estate investment trusts, shares and shareholders, privileges and immunities, **Bus Org 200.164**

CONSIDERATION
Shares and shareholders. Corporations, this index

CONSOLIDATION
Merger and Consolidation, generally, this index

CONSPIRACY
Monopolies and Unfair Trade, generally, this index

CONSTRUCTION
Apartment houses, electricity, metering, **Util 184.012**
Cable television, easements, standards, **Util 181.102**
Condominiums, electricity, metering, **Util 184.012**
Definitions, gas utilities, pipes and pipelines, sour gas, **Util 121.451**
Electricity, this index
Gas utilities, works in progress, valuation, computation of rates, **Util 104.053**
Telecommunications, this index
Telephone cooperative corporations, standards, **Util 162.006**

CONSTRUCTION OF LAWS
Statutes, this index

CONSUMER PRICE INDEX
Definitions, telecommunications, small and rural incumbent local exchange companies, universal service fund, **Util 56.032**

CONSUMER PROTECTION
Electric cooperative corporations, **Util 17.006**
Gas utilities, **Util 101.051 et seq.**

CONSUMERS
Electricity, municipally owned utilities, advocacy, **Util 33.122**
Public utilities, advocacy, **Util 13.001, 13.003**

CONTAINERS
Gas utilities, safety, **Util 121.252**

CONTEMPT
Gas utilities, **Util 105.022**
Public utilities, **Util 15.022**

CONTESTED CASES
Administrative Law and Procedure, this index

CONTRACTS
Adverse or pecuniary interest. Conflict of Interest, generally, this index
Agriculture, natural gas, **Util 123.023**
Business development corporations, **Bus Org 23.054**
Cogeneration, purchase of power, certification, **Util 35.062 et seq.**
Conflict of Interest, generally, this index
Cooperative Associations, this index
Corporations, this index
Deeds and Conveyances, generally, this index
Electric cooperative corporations, **Util 161.121**
  Consolidation, **Util 161.201**
Electricity, this index
Foreign Corporations, this index
Gas utilities, **Util 102.003**
Indemnity, generally, this index
Limited partnerships. Partnerships, this index
Monopolies and Unfair Trade, generally, this index
Nonprofit Corporations, this index
Oil and Gas, this index
Partnerships, this index
Professional Associations and Societies, this index
Public Utilities, this index
Real Estate Investment Trusts, this index
Restraint of trade. Monopolies and Unfair Trade, generally, this index
River Authorities, this index
Sewers and Sewer Systems, this index
Telecommunications, this index
Telephone cooperative corporations, **Util 162.121**
  Consolidation, **Util 162.201**
Trusts and monopolies. Monopolies and Unfair Trade, generally, this index
Water Supply, this index

CONTRIBUTIONS
Churches, retirement and pensions, **Bus Org 22.403**
Definitions,
  Business organizations, **Bus Org 1.002**
  Telecommunications, universal service fund, adjustments, **Util 56.025**
Limited Liability Companies, this index
Limited partnerships. Partnerships, this index
Partnerships, this index
Religious organizations and societies, retirement and pensions, **Bus Org 22.403**

CONVALESCENT HOMES
Nursing and Convalescent Homes, generally, this index

CONVERSION
Condominiums, this index
Cooperative Associations, this index
Corporations, this index
Definitions, business organizations, **Bus Org 1.002**
Foreign Corporations, this index
Limited Liability Companies, this index
Limited partnerships. Partnerships, this index
Nonprofit Corporations, this index
Partnerships, this index
Professional Associations and Societies, this index
Professional Corporations, this index
Real estate investment trusts, **Bus Org 200.403 et seq.**
Shares and shareholders. Corporations, this index
Telecommunications, incentives, elections, **Util 59.023**
Telephone cooperative corporations, **Util 162.251 et seq.**

CONVEYANCES
Deeds and Conveyances, generally, this index

COOPERATIVE ASSOCIATIONS
  Generally, **Bus Org 1.001 et seq., 251.001 et seq., 301.001 et seq.**
Abandonment, **Bus Org 10.201 et seq.**
  Filing, **Bus Org 4.057**
Abatement of actions and proceedings,
  State, **Bus Org 12.260**
  Termination, involuntary termination, **Bus Org 11.304**
Acceptance, certificates and certification, **Bus Org 10.156**
Accounts and accounting, **Bus Org 3.151 et seq.**
  Examinations and examiners, **Bus Org 12.151 et seq.**
Acknowledgments,
  Certificate of formation, **Bus Org 3.004**
    Evidence, **Bus Org 3.001**
  Filing, **Bus Org 4.002**
    Effective date, delay, **Bus Org 4.059**
Actions and proceedings,
  Business Organizations Code, prior law, **Bus Org 402.014**
  Certificate of formation, amendments, **Bus Org 3.056**
  Indemnity, **Bus Org 8.001 et seq.**
  Insolvency, **Bus Org 12.253 et seq.**
  Receivers and receivership, **Bus Org 11.406**
  Records and recordation, inspection and inspectors, **Bus Org 3.152**
  State, liens and incumbrances, **Bus Org 12.201 et seq.**
  Termination, **Bus Org 251.404**

COOPERATIVE ASSOCIATIONS —Cont'd
Actions and proceedings—Cont'd
Termination—Cont'd
Involuntary termination, **Bus Org 11.303**
Winding up, post
Address, certificate of formation, **Bus Org 3.005**
Directors, **Bus Org 3.013**
Admissions, members, **Bus Org 251.151**
Adoption, Business Organizations Code, **Bus Org 402.003**
Advancements, indemnity, expenses and expenditures, **Bus Org 8.104, 8.105**
Reports, **Bus Org 8.152**
Agent for service of process, **Bus Org 5.251 et seq.**
Agents and agencies,
Changes, filing, fines and penalties, **Bus Org 21.802**
Damages, **Bus Org 301.010**
Licenses and permits, **Bus Org 301.006**
Registered agent, generally, post
Allocations, **Bus Org 251.302**
Merger and consolidation, property, **Bus Org 10.003**
Alternatives, service of process, **Bus Org 5.256**
Amendments,
Business Organizations Code, statutes, **Bus Org 1.054**
Bylaws, **Bus Org 251.053**
Certificate of formation, **Bus Org 3.051 et seq.**
Filing, **Bus Org 4.106**
Ancillary receiverships, **Bus Org 11.409**
Answer, interrogatories, time, **Bus Org 12.002**
Antitrust, application of law, **Bus Org 10.901**
Appeal and review,
Filing, **Bus Org 12.004**
Termination, involuntary termination, **Bus Org 11.307**
Winding up, involuntary winding up, **Bus Org 11.307**
Application of law, **Bus Org 251.002, 301.001**
Antitrust, **Bus Org 10.901**
Business Organizations Code, **Bus Org 402.001 et seq.**
Foreign countries, foreign states, **Bus Org 1.053**
Certificate of formation, **Bus Org 1.101 et seq.**
Elections, **Bus Org 6.301, 6.302**
Exemptions, **Bus Org 251.003**
Indebtedness, **Bus Org 10.901**
Indemnity, **Bus Org 8.002**
Meetings, **Bus Org 6.301, 6.302**
Monopolies and unfair trade, **Bus Org 10.901**
Reorganization, **Bus Org 10.306**
Appointments, receivers and receivership, **Bus Org 11.401 et seq.**

COOPERATIVE ASSOCIATIONS —Cont'd
Appraisals and appraisers, reorganization, **Bus Org 10.304**
Assets,
Disposition, **Bus Org 10.251 et seq.**
Reorganization, **Bus Org 10.301**
Distribution and distributors, **Bus Org 251.403, 251.404**
Liens and incumbrances, state, **Bus Org 12.201**
Sales, Business Organizations Code, mandatory application date, **Bus Org 402.010**
Winding up, distribution and distributors, **Bus Org 11.053**
Assignments, **Bus Org 10.251 et seq.**
Shares and shareholders, certificates and certification, **Bus Org 3.201**
Assumed or fictitious names, names, **Bus Org 5.051 et seq.**
Attachment,
Certificates and certification, **Bus Org 251.204**
State, **Bus Org 12.259**
Attorney fees,
Filing,
Fines and penalties, **Bus Org 21.802**
Fraud, **Bus Org 4.007**
Records and recordation, inspection and inspectors, **Bus Org 3.152**
Reports, filing, **Bus Org 251.354**
Audits and auditors, **Bus Org 251.352**
Bankruptcy, **Bus Org 10.301 et seq.**
Bonds, **Bus Org 2.110**
Reorganization, **Bus Org 10.301**
Bonds (officers and fiduciaries), receivers and receivership, **Bus Org 11.406**
Books and papers, **Bus Org 3.151 et seq., 251.351**
Confidential or privileged information, **Bus Org 12.154**
Disclosure, **Bus Org 12.154**
Duplicates and copies, **Bus Org 12.151 et seq.**
Examinations and examiners, **Bus Org 3.153, 12.151 et seq.**
Inspection and inspectors, **Bus Org 3.152**
Powers and duties, limitations, **Bus Org 2.005**
Reorganization, **Bus Org 10.301**
Signatures, **Bus Org 1.007**
Bylaws, **Bus Org 251.053**
Recall, certificates and certification, **Bus Org 251.203**
Cancellation,
Reinstatement, **Bus Org 402.013**
Winding up, **Bus Org 11.152**
Capital, **Bus Org 251.301**
Certificate of formation, **Bus Org 3.001 et seq.**
Amendments, **Bus Org 3.051 et seq., 251.052**
Application of law, **Bus Org 1.101 et seq.**
Definitions, **Bus Org 1.002**

COOPERATIVE ASSOCIATIONS —Cont'd
Certificate of formation—Cont'd
Directors, post
Merger and consolidation, **Bus Org 10.002**
Names, **Bus Org 3.005**
Amendments, **Bus Org 3.053, 3.056**
Directors, **Bus Org 3.013**
Reinstatement, **Bus Org 402.013**
Reorganization, **Bus Org 10.301 et seq.**
Restatement, **Bus Org 3.057 et seq., 251.054**
Signatures, **Bus Org 3.004**
Amendments, **Bus Org 3.052, 3.054**
Restatement, **Bus Org 3.058, 3.060**
Time, **Bus Org 3.001, 3.003**
Amendments, **Bus Org 3.056, 251.052**
Restatement, **Bus Org 3.063**
Certificates and certification,
Acceptance, **Bus Org 10.156**
Certificate of formation, generally, ante
Conversion, **Bus Org 10.154 et seq.**
Exchange of property, **Bus Org 10.151 et seq.**
Existence, evidence, **Bus Org 4.005**
Filing, **Bus Org 12.001**
Corrections, **Bus Org 4.101 et seq.**
Fines and penalties, **Bus Org 21.802**
Members, **Bus Org 251.201 et seq.**
Merger and consolidation, **Bus Org 10.151 et seq.**
Shares and shareholders, **Bus Org 3.201 et seq.**
Termination, post
Certified copies,
Filing, **Bus Org 4.005**
Involuntary termination, judgments and decrees, **Bus Org 11.414**
Changes, registered offices, registered agent, **Bus Org 5.202, 5.203**
Citizens and citizenship, receivers and receivership, **Bus Org 11.406**
Claims,
Receivers and receivership, filing, **Bus Org 11.407**
Termination, **Bus Org 11.351 et seq.**
Committees, directors, **Bus Org 251.101, 251.102**
Compensation and salaries, receivers and receivership, **Bus Org 11.408**
Conduct,
Business Organizations Code, application of law, **Bus Org 402.006**
Damages, **Bus Org 7.001, 301.010**
Confidential or privileged information, interrogatories, **Bus Org 12.003**
Conflict of interest, elections, **Bus Org 6.152, 6.153**
Conflict of laws, **Bus Org 301.002**
Consent,
Meetings, duplicates and copies, action without meeting, **Bus Org 6.205**
Registered agents, **Bus Org 5.2011**
Consolidation. Merger and consolidation, generally, post

COOPERATIVE ASSOCIATIONS
—Cont'd
Construction of laws, Business Organizations Code, statutes, **Bus Org 1.006, 1.051 et seq.**
Contracts, **Bus Org 2.110**
Business Organizations Code, application of law, **Bus Org 402.006**
Elections, **Bus Org 6.252**
Winding up, **Bus Org 11.152**
Contributions, definitions, business organizations, **Bus Org 1.002**
Conversion, **Bus Org 10.101 et seq.**
Abandonment, **Bus Org 10.201 et seq.**
Acceptance, certificates and certification, **Bus Org 10.156**
Business Organizations Code, mandatory application date, **Bus Org 402.010**
Certificates and certification, **Bus Org 10.154 et seq.**
Dissenting shareholders, **Bus Org 10.351 et seq.**
Effective date, **Bus Org 10.105, 10.106**
Filing,
Certificates and certification, **Bus Org 10.155**
Fees, **Bus Org 4.151**
Foreign corporations, registration, withdrawal, **Bus Org 9.012**
Names, **Bus Org 10.103**
Notice, **Bus Org 10.101**
Plans and specifications, **Bus Org 10.101 et seq.**
Reorganization, **Bus Org 10.301 et seq.**
Copies. Duplicates and copies, generally, post
Corrections, filing, **Bus Org 4.101 et seq.**
Fees, **Bus Org 4.151**
Costs,
Filing,
Fines and penalties, **Bus Org 21.802**
Fraud, **Bus Org 4.007**
Insolvency, dismissal and nonsuit, **Bus Org 12.257**
Liens and incumbrances, foreclosure, dismissal and nonsuit, **Bus Org 12.257**
Reports, filing, **Bus Org 251.354**
Credit Unions, generally, this index
Crimes and offenses,
Books and papers, examinations and examiners, **Bus Org 12.156**
Damages, **Bus Org 7.001**
Filing, fraud, **Bus Org 4.008**
Fraud, generally, post
Names, **Bus Org 251.452**
Reports, **Bus Org 251.353**
Termination, involuntary termination, **Bus Org 11.301 et seq.**
Winding up, involuntary winding up, **Bus Org 11.301 et seq.**
Damages, **Bus Org 301.010**
Application of law, **Bus Org 1.104**
Filing, **Bus Org 21.802**
Fraud, **Bus Org 4.007**
Indemnity, generally, post

COOPERATIVE ASSOCIATIONS
—Cont'd
Damages—Cont'd
Members, **Bus Org 251.154**
Officers and employees, post
Deception, names, **Bus Org 5.052**
Deeds and conveyances, **Bus Org 10.251 et seq.**
Definitions, **Bus Org 1.002, 251.001, 301.003**
Business organizations, **Bus Org 1.002**
Indemnity, **Bus Org 8.001**
Mandatory application date, **Bus Org 401.001**
Prior law, **Bus Org 401.001**
Termination, **Bus Org 11.001**
Winding up, **Bus Org 11.001**
Delay, filing, effective date, **Bus Org 4.052 et seq.**
Delivery,
Filing, **Bus Org 4.001**
Meetings, action without meeting, **Bus Org 6.203**
Shares and shareholders, certificates and certification, **Bus Org 3.204**
Deposits, termination, claims, **Bus Org 11.352**
Directors, **Bus Org 251.101 et seq.**
Agent for service of process, **Bus Org 5.255**
Certificate of formation, **Bus Org 3.007, 3.013**
Amendments, **Bus Org 3.054**
Restatement, **Bus Org 3.060**
Committees, **Bus Org 251.102**
Damages, **Bus Org 7.001**
Indemnity, **Bus Org 7.001**
Discharge,
Receivers and receivership, **Bus Org 11.412**
Termination, claims, **Bus Org 11.353**
Winding up, indebtedness, **Bus Org 11.053**
Disclosure, interrogatories, **Bus Org 12.003**
Dismissal and nonsuit,
Insolvency, **Bus Org 12.257**
Liens and incumbrances, foreclosure, **Bus Org 12.257**
Disposition, **Bus Org 10.251 et seq.**
Reorganization, **Bus Org 10.301**
Dissenting shareholders. Shares and shareholders, post
Dissolution, involuntary dissolution, reinstatement, **Bus Org 402.013**
Distribution and distributors, **Bus Org 251.302**
Assets, **Bus Org 251.403, 251.404**
Dividends, **Bus Org 251.301**
Record date, **Bus Org 6.101 et seq.**
Winding up, assets, **Bus Org 11.053**
Dividends, **Bus Org 251.301**
Dual office holding, **Bus Org 251.102**
Officers and employees, **Bus Org 3.103**
Duplicates and copies,
Agent for service of process, **Bus Org 5.252**

COOPERATIVE ASSOCIATIONS
—Cont'd
Duplicates and copies—Cont'd
Books and papers, **Bus Org 12.151 et seq.**
Consent, meetings, action without meeting, **Bus Org 6.205**
Filing, **Bus Org 4.003**
Records and recordation, **Bus Org 3.152**
Shares and shareholders, certificates and certification, **Bus Org 3.202**
Duties. Powers and duties, generally, post
Effective date,
Business Organizations Code, **Bus Org 402.001**
Adoption, **Bus Org 402.005**
Conversion, **Bus Org 10.105, 10.106**
Exchange of property, **Bus Org 10.054, 10.055**
Filing, **Bus Org 4.051 et seq.**
Merger and consolidation, **Bus Org 10.007**
Termination, post
Elections, **Bus Org 6.151 et seq.**
Application of law, **Bus Org 6.301, 6.302**
Bylaws, **Bus Org 251.053**
Conflict of interest, **Bus Org 6.152, 6.153**
Contracts, **Bus Org 6.252**
Directors, **Bus Org 251.101**
Estates, **Bus Org 6.154**
Indemnity, **Bus Org 8.103**
Members, **Bus Org 251.254 et seq.**
Expulsion, **Bus Org 251.152**
Officers and employees, post
Pledges, **Bus Org 6.156**
Probate proceedings, **Bus Org 6.154**
Receivers and receivership, **Bus Org 6.155**
Trusts and trustees, **Bus Org 6.154, 6.251**
Electric Cooperative Corporations, generally, this index
Electronic communications, consent, meetings, **Bus Org 6.205**
Electronic filing, **Bus Org 12.001**
Emergencies, governance, **Bus Org 3.251 et seq.**
Employees. Officers and employees, generally, post
Errors,
Damages, **Bus Org 301.010**
Termination, reinstatement, **Bus Org 11.201 et seq.**
Escheat, termination, claims, **Bus Org 11.355**
Estates, elections, **Bus Org 6.154**
Evidence,
Certificate of formation, acknowledgments, **Bus Org 3.001**
Existence, certificates and certification, **Bus Org 4.005**
Filing, **Bus Org 4.001**

COOPERATIVE ASSOCIATIONS
—Cont'd
Evidence—Cont'd
Shares and shareholders, certificates and certification, **Bus Org 3.201**
Examinations and examiners,
Books and papers, **Bus Org 12.151 et seq.**
Elections, contracts, **Bus Org 6.252**
Records and recordation, **Bus Org 3.153**
Exchange of property, **Bus Org 10.051 et seq.**
Abandonment, **Bus Org 10.201 et seq.**
Acceptance, certificates and certification, **Bus Org 10.156**
Certificates and certification, **Bus Org 10.151 et seq.**
Dissenting shareholders, **Bus Org 10.351 et seq.**
Filing,
Certificates and certification, **Bus Org 10.153**
Fees, **Bus Org 4.151**
Reorganization, **Bus Org 10.301**
Shares and shareholders, post
Voluntary, **Bus Org 10.902**
Executions, certificates and certification, **Bus Org 251.204**
Exemptions,
Application of law, **Bus Org 251.003**
Interrogatories, **Bus Org 12.002**
Securities, sales, **Bus Org 301.011**
Tax exemptions, **Bus Org 251.451**
Termination, involuntary termination, **Bus Org 11.251**
Expenses and expenditures, indemnity, **Bus Org 8.001 et seq.**
Expulsion, members, **Bus Org 251.152**
Facsimile, **Bus Org 1.007**
Consent, meetings, action without meeting, **Bus Org 6.205**
Filing, **Bus Org 4.003**
Meetings, notice, **Bus Org 6.051**
Shares and shareholders, certificates and certification, **Bus Org 3.203**
Fees,
Business Organizations Code, effective date, **Bus Org 402.002**
Filing, **Bus Org 4.151 et seq.**
Names, reservation, **Bus Org 5.101**
Withdrawal, **Bus Org 5.1041**
Filing, **Bus Org 4.001 et seq., 12.001 et seq.**
Abandonment, **Bus Org 4.057**
Acknowledgments, **Bus Org 4.002**
Effective date, delay, **Bus Org 4.059**
Amendments, **Bus Org 4.106**
Appeal and review, **Bus Org 12.004**
Assumed or fictitious names, **Bus Org 5.051**
Attorney fees,
Fines and penalties, **Bus Org 21.802**
Fraud, **Bus Org 4.007**
Business Organizations Code, effective date, **Bus Org 402.002**

COOPERATIVE ASSOCIATIONS
—Cont'd
Filing—Cont'd
Certificate of formation, **Bus Org 3.001 et seq.**
Certificates and certification, ante
Certified copies, **Bus Org 4.005**
Conversion, certificates and certification, **Bus Org 10.155**
Corrections, **Bus Org 4.101 et seq.**
Fees, **Bus Org 4.151**
Costs,
Fines and penalties, **Bus Org 21.802**
Fraud, **Bus Org 4.007**
Damages, **Bus Org 21.802**
Fraud, **Bus Org 4.007**
Delay, effective date, **Bus Org 4.052 et seq.**
Delivery, **Bus Org 4.001**
Duplicates and copies, **Bus Org 4.003**
Effective date, **Bus Org 4.051 et seq.**
Electronic filing, **Bus Org 12.001**
Evidence, **Bus Org 4.001**
Facsimile, **Bus Org 4.003**
Fees, **Bus Org 4.151 et seq.**
Fines and penalties, **Bus Org 21.802**
Fraud, **Bus Org 4.008**
Forms, **Bus Org 4.006**
Fraud, **Bus Org 4.007, 4.008**
Interrogatories, **Bus Org 12.002, 12.003**
Jurisdiction, fines and penalties, **Bus Org 21.802**
Limitations,
Corrections, **Bus Org 4.102**
Effective date, delay, **Bus Org 4.058**
Names, registration, **Bus Org 5.152**
Real estate investment trusts, **Bus Org 4.009**
Receivers and receivership, claims, **Bus Org 11.407**
Registered agent, resignation, **Bus Org 5.204**
Reports, **Bus Org 251.354**
Service of process, **Bus Org 21.802**
Signatures, **Bus Org 4.001**
Corrections, certificates and certification, **Bus Org 4.101**
Termination, involuntary termination, **Bus Org 11.315**
Time, **Bus Org 4.004**
Corrections, **Bus Org 4.105**
Effective date, **Bus Org 4.051 et seq.**
Fines and penalties, **Bus Org 21.802**
Winding up, involuntary winding up, **Bus Org 11.315**
Financial statements and reports, **Bus Org 251.352 et seq.**
Officers and employees, good faith, **Bus Org 3.102, 3.105**
Fines and penalties,
Books and papers, examinations and examiners, **Bus Org 12.156**
Filing, **Bus Org 21.802**
Fraud, **Bus Org 4.008**
Names, **Bus Org 251.452**
Registered agents, consent, **Bus Org 5.207**

COOPERATIVE ASSOCIATIONS
—Cont'd
Fines and penalties—Cont'd
Reports, **Bus Org 251.353**
Foreclosure, liens and incumbrances, **Bus Org 12.252 et seq.**
Foreign corporations,
Acknowledgments, registration, **Bus Org 9.008**
Actions and proceedings,
Registration, **Bus Org 9.051 et seq.**
Transacting business in Texas, **Bus Org 9.251**
Amendments, registration, **Bus Org 9.009**
Application of law, Business Organizations Code, **Bus Org 9.301**
Banks and banking, transacting business in Texas, **Bus Org 9.251**
Certificates and certification, registration,
Reinstatement, **Bus Org 9.104**
Revocation or suspension, **Bus Org 9.102**
Certified copies, registration, revocation or suspension, **Bus Org 9.161**
Claims, transacting business in Texas, **Bus Org 9.251**
Conflict of laws, registration, **Bus Org 9.055**
Conversion, registration, withdrawal, **Bus Org 9.012**
Dismissal and nonsuit, registration, revocation or suspension, **Bus Org 9.156**
Elections, transacting business in Texas, **Bus Org 9.251**
Evidence, registration, acknowledgments, **Bus Org 9.008**
Exemptions, registration, **Bus Org 9.002**
Fees, registration, collection, **Bus Org 9.054**
Filing, registration, revocation or suspension, **Bus Org 9.161**
Fines and penalties, registration, **Bus Org 9.052**
Indebtedness, transacting business in Texas, **Bus Org 9.251**
Injunctions, registration, **Bus Org 9.051**
Investments, transacting business in Texas, **Bus Org 9.251**
Judgments and decrees, registration, revocation or suspension, **Bus Org 9.154 et seq.**
Jurisdiction, registration, revocation or suspension, **Bus Org 9.158**
Liens and incumbrances, transacting business in Texas, **Bus Org 9.251**
Lists, transacting business in Texas, **Bus Org 9.251, 9.252**
Loans, transacting business in Texas, **Bus Org 9.251**
Meetings, transacting business in Texas, **Bus Org 9.251**
Mines and minerals, transacting business in Texas, **Bus Org 9.251**

COOPERATIVE ASSOCIATIONS
—Cont'd
Foreign corporations—Cont'd
Mortgages, transacting business in Texas, **Bus Org 9.251**
Names, **Bus Org 5.057, 251.452**
Registration,
Change of name, **Bus Org 9.010**
Reinstatement, **Bus Org 9.105**
Notice, registration,
Revocation or suspension, **Bus Org 9.101, 9.152**
Service of process, revocation or suspension, **Bus Org 9.160**
Offices, transacting business in Texas, **Bus Org 9.251**
Probate proceedings, transacting business in Texas, **Bus Org 9.251**
Registration, **Bus Org 9.001 et seq.**
Acknowledgments, **Bus Org 9.008**
Actions and proceedings, **Bus Org 9.051 et seq.**
Amendments, **Bus Org 9.009**
Applications, **Bus Org 9.004**
Certificates and certification,
Reinstatement, **Bus Org 9.104**
Revocation or suspension, **Bus Org 9.102**
Certified copies, revocation or suspension, **Bus Org 9.161**
Conflict of laws, **Bus Org 9.055**
Dismissal and nonsuit, revocation or suspension, **Bus Org 9.156**
Evidence, acknowledgments, **Bus Org 9.008**
Exemptions, **Bus Org 9.002**
Fees, collection, **Bus Org 9.054**
Filing, revocation or suspension, **Bus Org 9.161**
Fines and penalties, **Bus Org 9.052**
Fraud, **Bus Org 9.051 et seq.**
Injunctions, **Bus Org 9.051**
Judgments and decrees, revocation or suspension, **Bus Org 9.154 et seq.**
Jurisdiction, revocation or suspension, **Bus Org 9.158**
Names,
Change of name, **Bus Org 9.010**
Reinstatement, **Bus Org 9.105**
Notice,
Revocation or suspension, **Bus Org 9.101, 9.152**
Service of process, revocation or suspension, **Bus Org 9.160**
Reinstatement, **Bus Org 9.103 et seq.**
Remand, revocation or suspension, **Bus Org 9.157**
Revocation or suspension, **Bus Org 9.101 et seq., 9.151 et seq.**
Same or similar names, reinstatement, **Bus Org 9.105**
Service of process,
Revocation or suspension, **Bus Org 9.159, 9.160**
Withdrawal, **Bus Org 9.011**

COOPERATIVE ASSOCIATIONS
—Cont'd
Foreign corporations—Cont'd
Registration—Cont'd
Supersedeas or stay, revocation or suspension, **Bus Org 9.156**
Taxation, forfeitures, reinstatement, **Bus Org 9.106**
Time, amendments, **Bus Org 9.009**
Venue, **Bus Org 9.053**
Revocation or suspension, **Bus Org 9.158**
Withdrawal, **Bus Org 9.011**
Reinstatement, registration, **Bus Org 9.103 et seq.**
Remand, registration, revocation or suspension, **Bus Org 9.157**
Revocation or suspension, registration, **Bus Org 9.101 et seq., 9.151 et seq.**
Sales, transacting business in Texas, **Bus Org 9.251**
Same or similar names, registration, reinstatement, **Bus Org 9.105**
Securities, transacting business in Texas, **Bus Org 9.251**
Service of process, registration,
Revocation or suspension, **Bus Org 9.159, 9.160**
Withdrawal, **Bus Org 9.011**
Supersedeas or stay, registration, revocation or suspension, **Bus Org 9.156**
Taxation, registration, forfeitures, reinstatement, **Bus Org 9.106**
Time, registration, amendments, **Bus Org 9.009**
Transacting business in Texas, **Bus Org 9.201 et seq.**
Lists, **Bus Org 9.251, 9.252**
Trusts and trustees, transacting business in Texas, **Bus Org 9.251**
Venue, registration, **Bus Org 9.053**
Revocation or suspension, **Bus Org 9.158**
Withdrawal, registration, **Bus Org 9.011**
Foreign countries,
Business Organizations Code, application of law, **Bus Org 1.053**
Certificate of formation, application of law, **Bus Org 1.102**
Foreign states,
Business Organizations Code, application of law, **Bus Org 1.053**
Certificate of formation, application of law, **Bus Org 1.102**
Meetings, location, **Bus Org 6.001**
Forfeitures,
Books and papers, examinations and examiners, **Bus Org 12.155**
Reinstatement, **Bus Org 402.013**
Formation. Certificate of formation, generally, ante
Forms,
Filing, **Bus Org 4.006**
Shares and shareholders, certificates and certification, **Bus Org 3.202**

COOPERATIVE ASSOCIATIONS
—Cont'd
Franchise taxes, exemptions, **Bus Org 251.451**
Fraud,
Filing, **Bus Org 4.007, 4.008**
Names, **Bus Org 5.052**
Receivers and receivership, **Bus Org 11.403**
Reports, **Bus Org 251.353**
Termination,
Involuntary termination, **Bus Org 11.301 et seq.**
Revocation or suspension, **Bus Org 11.153**
Winding up, involuntary winding up, **Bus Org 11.301 et seq.**
Funds, limitations, **Bus Org 2.111**
Garnishment,
Certificates and certification, **Bus Org 251.204**
State, **Bus Org 12.259**
Gas utilities, refunds to members, **Util 104.005**
Good faith,
Damages, **Bus Org 7.001**
Officers and employees, **Bus Org 3.102, 3.105**
Health maintenance organizations, limitations, **Bus Org 2.011**
Hold harmless. Indemnity, generally, post
Holding companies, merger and consolidation, **Bus Org 10.005**
Identity and identification, names, same or similar, **Bus Org 5.053**
Indebtedness,
Application of law, **Bus Org 10.901**
Members, **Bus Org 251.154**
Winding up, discharge, **Bus Org 11.053**
Indemnity,
Business Organizations Code, application of law, **Bus Org 402.007**
Insurance, **Bus Org 8.151**
Mandatory, **Bus Org 8.051**
Officers and employees, **Bus Org 7.001, 8.001 et seq.**
Orders of court, **Bus Org 8.052**
Permissive indemnification, **Bus Org 8.101 et seq.**
Reports, **Bus Org 8.152**
Initiative and referendum, directors, **Bus Org 251.104**
Injunctions,
Names, **Bus Org 251.452**
State, **Bus Org 12.259**
Insolvency, actions and proceedings, **Bus Org 12.253 et seq.**
Inspection and inspectors,
Books and papers, **Bus Org 12.151 et seq.**
Records and recordation, **Bus Org 3.152**
Insurance, indemnity, **Bus Org 8.151**
Internal affairs, **Bus Org 1.105**
Internet, meetings, **Bus Org 6.002**
Interrogatories, **Bus Org 12.002, 12.003**

COOPERATIVE ASSOCIATIONS—Cont'd
Involuntary termination, **Bus Org 11.251 et seq.**
Certified copies, judgments and decrees, **Bus Org 11.414**
Joint practices, **Bus Org 301.012**
Judgments and decrees,
Names, **Bus Org 251.452**
Receivers and receivership, termination, **Bus Org 11.412**
Reorganization, **Bus Org 10.305**
Termination, **Bus Org 11.301 et seq.**
Involuntary termination, certified copies, **Bus Org 11.414**
Winding up, **Bus Org 11.301 et seq.**
Jurisdiction,
Filing, fines and penalties, **Bus Org 21.802**
Insolvency, **Bus Org 12.253**
Liens and incumbrances, foreclosure, **Bus Org 12.253**
Receivers and receivership, **Bus Org 11.402 et seq.**
Reorganization, **Bus Org 10.302**
Termination, involuntary termination, **Bus Org 11.308**
Winding up, involuntary winding up, **Bus Org 11.308**
Leases, **Bus Org 10.251 et seq.**
Reorganization, **Bus Org 10.301**
Licenses and permits, **Bus Org 301.006**
Tax exemptions, **Bus Org 251.451**
Liens and incumbrances,
Foreclosure, **Bus Org 12.252 et seq.**
State, **Bus Org 12.201**
Limitation of actions, termination, claims, **Bus Org 11.359**
Limitations,
Capital, **Bus Org 251.301**
Filing,
Corrections, **Bus Org 4.102**
Effective date, delay, **Bus Org 4.058**
Indemnity, **Bus Org 8.003, 8.004**
Powers and duties, **Bus Org 2.111**
Purposes, **Bus Org 2.003 et seq.**
Liquidation, receivers and receivership, **Bus Org 12.258**
Orders of court, **Bus Org 11.405**
Location, meetings, **Bus Org 6.001**
Lottery, names, **Bus Org 5.061**
Mail and mailing,
Meetings, notice, **Bus Org 6.051**
Members, elections, **Bus Org 251.256, 251.257**
Managers and management,
Agent for service of process, **Bus Org 5.255**
Damages, **Bus Org 301.010**
Licenses and permits, **Bus Org 301.006**
Resignation, **Bus Org 301.008**
Mandamus, reports, filing, **Bus Org 251.354**
Mandatory application date, Business Organizations Code, **Bus Org 401.001 et seq.**

COOPERATIVE ASSOCIATIONS—Cont'd
Meetings, **Bus Org 6.001 et seq.**
Action without meeting, **Bus Org 6.102**
Consent, **Bus Org 6.201 et seq.**
Application of law, **Bus Org 6.301, 6.302**
Business Organizations Code, mandatory application date, **Bus Org 402.008, 402.009**
Consent, action without meeting, **Bus Org 6.102, 6.201 et seq.**
Delivery, action without meeting, **Bus Org 6.203**
Emergencies, **Bus Org 3.251 et seq.**
Facsimile, notice, **Bus Org 6.051**
Foreign states, location, **Bus Org 6.001**
Internet, **Bus Org 6.002**
Location, **Bus Org 6.001**
Mail and mailing, notice, **Bus Org 6.051**
Members, **Bus Org 251.251 et seq.**
Notice, **Bus Org 6.051 et seq.**
Action without meeting, **Bus Org 6.204**
Objections and exceptions, **Bus Org 6.003**
Notice, waiver, **Bus Org 6.053**
Organization, **Bus Org 251.051**
Record date, **Bus Org 6.101 et seq.**
Records and recordation, **Bus Org 6.002**
Shares and shareholders, post
Telecommunications, **Bus Org 6.002**
Video recordings, **Bus Org 6.002**
Waiver, notice, **Bus Org 6.052**
Objections and exceptions, **Bus Org 6.053**
Members and membership, **Bus Org 251.151 et seq.**
Certificates and certification, **Bus Org 251.201 et seq.**
Elections, **Bus Org 251.254 et seq.**
Mail and mailing, elections, **Bus Org 251.256, 251.257**
Meetings, **Bus Org 251.251 et seq.**
Numbers and numbering, elections, **Bus Org 251.254**
Proxies, **Bus Org 251.255**
Special meetings, **Bus Org 251.251, 251.252**
Transfers, **Bus Org 251.202**
Withdrawal, **Bus Org 251.202**
Merger and consolidation, **Bus Org 10.001 et seq.**
Abandonment, **Bus Org 10.201 et seq.**
Acceptance, certificates and certification, **Bus Org 10.156**
Allocations, property, **Bus Org 10.003**
Business Organizations Code, mandatory application date, **Bus Org 402.010**
Certificate of formation, **Bus Org 3.005, 3.006, 10.002**
Certificates and certification, **Bus Org 10.151 et seq.**
Dissenting shareholders, **Bus Org 10.351 et seq.**

COOPERATIVE ASSOCIATIONS—Cont'd
Merger and consolidation—Cont'd
Effect, **Bus Org 10.008**
Effective date, **Bus Org 10.007**
Filing,
Certificates and certification, **Bus Org 10.153**
Fees, **Bus Org 4.151**
Holding companies, **Bus Org 10.005**
Names, **Bus Org 10.002**
Plans and specifications, **Bus Org 10.001 et seq.**
Property, allocations, **Bus Org 10.003**
Reorganization, **Bus Org 10.301 et seq.**
Subsidiaries, **Bus Org 10.006**
Certificates and certification, **Bus Org 10.152**
Time, effective date, **Bus Org 10.007**
Misconduct, damages, **Bus Org 7.001**
Money, **Bus Org 1.009**
Monopolies and unfair trade, application of law, **Bus Org 10.901**
Mortgages, receivers and receivership, **Bus Org 11.403**
Names, **Bus Org 5.001 et seq., 251.452**
Assumed or fictitious names, **Bus Org 5.051 et seq.**
Certificate of formation, ante
Conversion, **Bus Org 10.103**
Deception, **Bus Org 5.052**
Exchange of property, plans and specifications, **Bus Org 10.052**
Fees, reservation, **Bus Org 5.101**
Withdrawal, **Bus Org 5.1041**
Filing,
Fees, **Bus Org 4.151**
Registration, **Bus Org 5.152**
Foreign corporations, ante
Fraud, **Bus Org 5.052**
Identity and identification, same or similar, **Bus Org 5.053**
Lottery, **Bus Org 5.061**
Merger and consolidation, **Bus Org 10.002**
Notice, **Bus Org 5.001**
Registration, **Bus Org 5.151 et seq.**
Renewal,
Registration, **Bus Org 5.155**
Reservation, **Bus Org 5.105**
Reservation, **Bus Org 5.101 et seq.**
Same or similar, **Bus Org 5.053**
Registration, **Bus Org 5.153**
Reservation, **Bus Org 5.102**
Termination, reinstatement, **Bus Org 11.203**
Time,
Registration, **Bus Org 5.154**
Reservation, **Bus Org 5.104**
Trademarks and trade names, **Bus Org 5.001**
Transfers, reservation, **Bus Org 5.106**
Veterans organizations, **Bus Org 5.062**
Words and phrases, **Bus Org 5.057**
Negligence, damages, **Bus Org 301.010**
Nonfiling, certificate of formation, **Bus Org 3.002**

COOPERATIVE ASSOCIATIONS —Cont'd

Notice,
  Agent for service of process, **Bus Org 5.252, 5.253**
  Conversion, **Bus Org 10.101**
  Indemnity, orders of court, **Bus Org 8.052**
  Insolvency, **Bus Org 12.256**
  Liens and incumbrances,
    Foreclosure, **Bus Org 12.256**
    State, **Bus Org 12.201**
  Meetings, **Bus Org 6.051 et seq.**
    Action without meeting, **Bus Org 6.204**
  Names, **Bus Org 5.001**
  Receivers and receivership, claims, **Bus Org 11.407**
  Registered agent, resignation, **Bus Org 5.204**
  Reorganization, **Bus Org 10.301**
  Sales, certificates and certification, **Bus Org 251.202**
  Shares and shareholders, post
  Special meetings, **Bus Org 251.252**
  Termination, post
  Winding up, post
Numbers and numbering,
  Directors, **Bus Org 251.101**
  Members, elections, **Bus Org 251.254**
Oaths and affirmations, interrogatories, answer, **Bus Org 12.002**
Objections and exceptions, meetings, **Bus Org 6.003**
  Notice, waiver, **Bus Org 6.053**
Offenses. Crimes and offenses, generally, ante
Officers and employees, **Bus Org 3.101 et seq., 251.102, 251.103**
  Agent for service of process, **Bus Org 5.255**
  Damages, **Bus Org 7.001, 301.010**
    Application of law, **Bus Org 1.104**
  Dual office holding, **Bus Org 3.103**
  Elections, **Bus Org 3.103**
    Removal, **Bus Org 251.103**
  Good faith, **Bus Org 3.105**
  Indemnity, **Bus Org 7.001, 8.001 et seq.**
  Licenses and permits, **Bus Org 301.006**
  Removal, **Bus Org 3.104**
Offices,
  Changes, filing, fines and penalties, **Bus Org 21.802**
  Registered offices, generally, post
  Reorganization, **Bus Org 10.301**
Omissions, certificate of formation, restatement, **Bus Org 3.059**
Open records, interrogatories, **Bus Org 12.003**
Orders of court, receivers and receivership, **Bus Org 11.402**
  Liquidation, **Bus Org 11.405**
Organization, meetings, **Bus Org 251.051**
Parties, receivers and receivership, **Bus Org 11.411**
Payment, termination,
  Claims, **Bus Org 11.354**

COOPERATIVE ASSOCIATIONS —Cont'd

Payment, termination—Cont'd
  Taxation, **Bus Org 11.101**
Penalties. Fines and penalties, generally, ante
Permissive indemnification, **Bus Org 8.101 et seq.**
Personal property,
  Disposition, **Bus Org 10.251 et seq.**
    Reorganization, **Bus Org 10.301**
  Shares and shareholders, **Bus Org 21.801**
Photography and pictures, consent, meetings, action without meeting, **Bus Org 6.205**
Plans and specifications,
  Conversion, **Bus Org 10.101 et seq.**
  Exchange of property, **Bus Org 10.051 et seq.**
  Merger and consolidation, **Bus Org 10.001 et seq.**
Pledges, elections, **Bus Org 6.156**
Political subdivisions, service of process, **Bus Org 5.257**
Powers and duties, **Bus Org 2.110**
  Limitations, **Bus Org 2.111**
  Receivers and receivership, **Bus Org 11.406**
Prepaid legal service, limitations, **Bus Org 2.011**
President, **Bus Org 251.102**
  Agent for service of process, **Bus Org 5.255**
Prior laws, Business Organizations Code, **Bus Org 401.001 et seq.**
Priorities and preferences,
  Business Organizations Code, application of law, **Bus Org 1.106**
  Certificate of formation, shares and shareholders, **Bus Org 3.007**
Privileges and immunities,
  Property, disposition, **Bus Org 10.254**
  Registered agents, **Bus Org 5.208**
Probate proceedings, elections, **Bus Org 6.154**
Proceedings. Actions and proceedings, generally, ante
Process. Service of process, generally, post
Property,
  Disposition, **Bus Org 10.251 et seq.**
    Reorganization, **Bus Org 10.301**
  Liens and incumbrances,
    Foreclosure, **Bus Org 12.252 et seq.**
    State, **Bus Org 12.201**
  Merger and consolidation, allocations, **Bus Org 10.003**
Proxies, members, **Bus Org 251.255**
Publication, termination, involuntary termination, **Bus Org 11.310**
Purchases and purchasing,
  Indemnity, insurance, **Bus Org 8.151**
  Title to property, **Bus Org 301.008**
Purposes, **Bus Org 2.001 et seq.**
  Certificate of formation, **Bus Org 3.005**

COOPERATIVE ASSOCIATIONS —Cont'd

Quo warranto, insolvency, **Bus Org 12.253 et seq.**
Recall, certificates and certification, **Bus Org 251.203**
Receipts, termination, claims, **Bus Org 11.352**
Receivers and receivership, **Bus Org 11.401 et seq.**
  Actions and proceedings, **Bus Org 11.406**
  Ancillary receiverships, **Bus Org 11.409**
  Appointments, **Bus Org 11.401 et seq.**
  Bonds (officers and fiduciaries), **Bus Org 11.406**
  Citizens and citizenship, **Bus Org 11.406**
  Claims, filing, **Bus Org 11.407**
  Compensation and salaries, **Bus Org 11.408**
  Discharge, **Bus Org 11.412**
  Elections, **Bus Org 6.155**
  Filing, claims, **Bus Org 11.407**
  Foreign entities, **Bus Org 11.409, 11.410**
  Fraud, **Bus Org 11.403**
  Judgments and decrees, termination, **Bus Org 11.412**
  Jurisdiction, **Bus Org 11.402 et seq.**
  Liens and incumbrances, state, **Bus Org 12.201**
  Liquidation, **Bus Org 12.258**
    Orders of court, **Bus Org 11.405**
  Mortgages, **Bus Org 11.403**
  Notice, claims, **Bus Org 11.407**
  Orders of court, **Bus Org 11.402**
    Liquidation, **Bus Org 11.405**
  Parties, **Bus Org 11.411**
  Powers and duties, **Bus Org 11.406**
  Registration, **Bus Org 11.406**
  Rehabilitation, **Bus Org 11.404**
  State, **Bus Org 12.251**
  Termination, **Bus Org 11.403**
    Judgments and decrees, **Bus Org 11.412**
Record date, **Bus Org 6.101 et seq.**
Records and recordation, **Bus Org 3.151 et seq., 251.351**
  Certified copies, filing, **Bus Org 4.005**
  Confidential or privileged information, **Bus Org 12.154**
  Deeds and conveyances, **Bus Org 10.253**
  Disclosure, **Bus Org 12.154**
  Examinations and examiners, **Bus Org 3.153, 12.151 et seq.**
  Inspection and inspectors, **Bus Org 3.152**
  Interrogatories, open records, **Bus Org 12.003**
  Meetings, **Bus Org 6.002**
  Record date, **Bus Org 6.101 et seq.**
  Reorganization, **Bus Org 10.301**
  Service of process, **Bus Org 5.254**
  Signatures, **Bus Org 1.007**
  Termination, removal, **Bus Org 11.104**

COOPERATIVE ASSOCIATIONS —Cont'd
Records and recordation—Cont'd
Time, record date, **Bus Org 6.101 et seq.**
Registered agent, **Bus Org 5.200 et seq.**
Changes, **Bus Org 5.202**
Filing, fines and penalties, **Bus Org 21.802**
Reorganization, **Bus Org 10.301**
Resignation, **Bus Org 5.204**
Registered offices, **Bus Org 5.200 et seq.**
Changes, **Bus Org 5.202**
Filing, fines and penalties, **Bus Org 21.802**
Registration,
Foreign corporations, ante
Names, **Bus Org 5.151 et seq.**
Receivers and receivership, **Bus Org 11.406**
Rehabilitation, receivers and receivership, **Bus Org 11.404**
Reinstatement. Termination, post
Rejection, registered agents, **Bus Org 5.205**
Remand, termination, involuntary termination, **Bus Org 11.307**
Removal,
Directors, **Bus Org 251.101**
Officers and employees, **Bus Org 3.104, 251.103**
Renewal, names,
Registration, **Bus Org 5.155**
Reservation, **Bus Org 5.105**
Reorganization, **Bus Org 10.301 et seq.**
Business Organizations Code, mandatory application date, **Bus Org 402.010**
Repeals,
Business Organizations Code, statutes, **Bus Org 1.054**
Bylaws, **Bus Org 251.053**
Reports, **Bus Org 251.352 et seq.**
Indemnity, **Bus Org 8.152**
Officers and employees, good faith, **Bus Org 3.102, 3.105**
Reservation, names, **Bus Org 5.101 et seq.**
Resignation,
Managers and management, **Bus Org 301.008**
Registered agent, **Bus Org 5.204**
Resolutions, indemnity, **Bus Org 8.103**
Restatement, certificate of formation, **Bus Org 3.057 et seq., 251.054**
Review. Appeal and review, generally, ante
Revocation or suspension,
Reinstatement, **Bus Org 402.013**
Termination, fraud, **Bus Org 11.153**
Winding up, **Bus Org 11.151**
Sales, **Bus Org 10.251 et seq.**
Certificates and certification, **Bus Org 251.202**
Reorganization, **Bus Org 10.301**
Securities, exemptions, **Bus Org 301.011**
Same or similar. Names, ante

COOPERATIVE ASSOCIATIONS —Cont'd
Scholarships, delivery, **Bus Org 2.110**
Seals, shares and shareholders, certificates and certification, **Bus Org 3.202**
Secretaries, **Bus Org 251.102**
Secretary of state, agent for service of process, **Bus Org 5.251 et seq.**
Securities, sales, exemptions, **Bus Org 301.011**
Sequestration, state, **Bus Org 12.259**
Service of process, **Bus Org 5.251 et seq.**
Reorganization, **Bus Org 10.301**
Termination, involuntary termination, **Bus Org 11.309**
Winding up, involuntary winding up, **Bus Org 11.309**
Shares and shareholders, **Bus Org 2.110**
Abandonment, exchange of property, **Bus Org 10.201 et seq.**
Acceptance, exchange of property, certificates and certification, **Bus Org 10.156**
Appointments, dissenting shareholders, appraisal and appraisers, **Bus Org 10.361**
Appraisals and appraisers, dissenting shareholders, **Bus Org 10.354 et seq.**
Assignments, certificates and certification, **Bus Org 3.201**
Books and papers, dissenting shareholders, fair market value, **Bus Org 10.363**
Certificate of formation, **Bus Org 3.013**
Numbers and numbering, **Bus Org 3.007**
Certificates and certification, **Bus Org 3.201 et seq.**
Exchange of property, **Bus Org 10.151 et seq.**
Compensation and salaries, dissenting shareholders, appraisals and appraisers, **Bus Org 10.365**
Computation, dissenting shareholders, fair market value, **Bus Org 10.362**
Contracts, elections, **Bus Org 6.252**
Costs, dissenting shareholders, appraisals and appraisers, **Bus Org 10.365**
Delivery,
Certificates and certification, **Bus Org 3.204**
Meetings, action without meeting, **Bus Org 6.203**
Demand, dissenting shareholders, fair market value, **Bus Org 10.357 et seq.**
Dissenting shareholders, **Bus Org 10.351 et seq.**
Appointments, appraisal and appraisers, **Bus Org 10.361**
Appraisals and appraisers, **Bus Org 10.354 et seq.**
Books and papers, fair market value, **Bus Org 10.363**

COOPERATIVE ASSOCIATIONS —Cont'd
Shares and shareholders—Cont'd
Dissenting shareholders—Cont'd
Compensation and salaries, appraisals and appraisers, **Bus Org 10.365**
Computation, fair market value, **Bus Org 10.362**
Costs, appraisals and appraisers, **Bus Org 10.365**
Definitions, **Bus Org 10.352**
Demand, fair market value, **Bus Org 10.357 et seq.**
Exclusive remedy, **Bus Org 10.368**
Fair market value, demand, **Bus Org 10.357 et seq.**
Forms, **Bus Org 10.353**
Hearings, fair market value, **Bus Org 10.361**
Investigations and investigators, fair market value, **Bus Org 10.363**
Notice, **Bus Org 10.353, 10.355**
Objections and exceptions, appraisals and appraisers, **Bus Org 10.364**
Perfection, **Bus Org 10.356**
Petitions, fair market value, **Bus Org 10.361**
Records and recordation, fair market value, **Bus Org 10.363**
Demand, **Bus Org 10.359**
Reorganization, **Bus Org 10.304**
Termination, **Bus Org 10.367**
Title to property, **Bus Org 10.366**
Withdrawal, **Bus Org 10.357**
Distribution and distributors, record date, **Bus Org 6.101 et seq.**
Duplicates and copies, certificates and certification, **Bus Org 3.202**
Elections,
Contracts, **Bus Org 6.252**
Trusts and trustees, **Bus Org 6.251**
Evidence, certificates and certification, **Bus Org 3.201**
Examinations and examiners, elections, contracts, **Bus Org 6.252**
Exchange of property, **Bus Org 10.051 et seq.**
Abandonment, **Bus Org 10.201 et seq.**
Acceptance, certificates and certification, **Bus Org 10.156**
Certificates and certification, **Bus Org 10.151 et seq.**
Filing, certificates and certification, **Bus Org 10.153**
Exclusive remedy, dissenting shareholders, **Bus Org 10.368**
Facsimile, certificates and certification, **Bus Org 3.203**
Fair market value, dissenting shareholders, demand, **Bus Org 10.357 et seq.**
Filing, exchange of property, certificates and certification, **Bus Org 10.153**

COOPERATIVE ASSOCIATIONS —Cont'd
Shares and shareholders—Cont'd
Forms,
Certificates and certification, **Bus Org 3.202**
Dissenting shareholders, **Bus Org 10.353**
Hearings, dissenting shareholders, fair market value, **Bus Org 10.361**
Investigations and investigators, dissenting shareholders, fair market value, **Bus Org 10.363**
Meetings,
Action without meeting, **Bus Org 6.102**
Consent, **Bus Org 6.201 et seq.**
Consent, action without meeting, **Bus Org 6.102, 6.201 et seq.**
Delivery, action without meeting, **Bus Org 6.203**
Notice, action without meeting, **Bus Org 6.204**
Notice,
Dissenting shareholders, **Bus Org 10.353, 10.355**
Meetings, action without meeting, **Bus Org 6.204**
Uncertificated shares, **Bus Org 3.205**
Objections and exceptions, dissenting shareholders, appraisals and appraisers, **Bus Org 10.364**
Perfection, dissenting shareholders, **Bus Org 10.356**
Personal property, **Bus Org 21.801**
Petitions, dissenting shareholders, fair market value, **Bus Org 10.361**
Record date, **Bus Org 6.101 et seq.**
Records and recordation, dissenting shareholders, fair market value, **Bus Org 10.363**
Demand, **Bus Org 10.359**
Reorganization, dissenting shareholders, **Bus Org 10.304**
Seals, certificates and certification, **Bus Org 3.202**
Signatures, certificates and certification, **Bus Org 3.203**
Termination, dissenting shareholders, **Bus Org 10.367**
Time, record date, **Bus Org 6.101 et seq.**
Title to property, dissenting shareholders, **Bus Org 10.366**
Transfers, certificates and certification, **Bus Org 3.201**
Trusts and trustees, elections, **Bus Org 6.251**
Uncertificated shares, **Bus Org 3.201**
Notice, **Bus Org 3.205**
Withdrawal, dissenting shareholders, **Bus Org 10.357**
Signatures, **Bus Org 1.007**
Certificate of formation, ante
Filing, **Bus Org 4.001**
Corrections, certificates and certification, **Bus Org 4.101**

COOPERATIVE ASSOCIATIONS —Cont'd
Signatures—Cont'd
Reorganization, **Bus Org 10.302**
Reports, **Bus Org 251.353**
Shares and shareholders, certificates and certification, **Bus Org 3.203**
Special meetings, members, **Bus Org 251.251, 251.252**
Specifications. Plans and specifications, generally, ante
State,
Liens and incumbrances, **Bus Org 12.201**
Receivers and receivership, **Bus Org 12.251**
Statements,
Certificate of formation,
Amendments, **Bus Org 3.053, 3.054**
Restatement, **Bus Org 3.059**
Officers and employees, good faith, **Bus Org 3.102, 3.105**
Termination, claims, **Bus Org 11.352**
Statutes, Business Organizations Code, construction of laws, **Bus Org 1.006, 1.051 et seq.**
Subscriptions, **Bus Org 251.153**
Damages, **Bus Org 251.154**
Subsidiaries, merger and consolidation, **Bus Org 10.006**
Certificates and certification, **Bus Org 10.152**
Supersedeas or stay, termination, involuntary termination, **Bus Org 11.306**
Supervision, winding up, **Bus Org 11.054**
Suspension. Revocation or suspension, generally, ante
Tax exemptions, **Bus Org 251.451**
Taxation,
Service of process, **Bus Org 5.257**
Termination,
Forfeitures, reinstatement, **Bus Org 11.254, 402.013**
Payment, **Bus Org 11.101**
Telecommunications, meetings, **Bus Org 6.002**
Telephone Cooperative Corporations, generally, this index
Termination, **Bus Org 11.001 et seq., 251.401 et seq.**
Abatement of actions and proceedings, involuntary termination, **Bus Org 11.304**
Actions and proceedings, involuntary termination, **Bus Org 11.303**
Appeal and review, involuntary termination, **Bus Org 11.307**
Business Organizations Code, mandatory application date, **Bus Org 402.011**
Certificates and certification, **Bus Org 11.101 et seq.**
Involuntary termination, **Bus Org 11.252**
Reinstatement, **Bus Org 11.202**

COOPERATIVE ASSOCIATIONS —Cont'd
Termination—Cont'd
Certified copies, involuntary termination, judgments and decrees, **Bus Org 11.414**
Claims, **Bus Org 11.351 et seq.**
Crimes and offenses, involuntary termination, **Bus Org 11.301 et seq.**
Deposits, claims, **Bus Org 11.352**
Discharge, claims, **Bus Org 11.353**
Effective date, **Bus Org 11.102, 11.103**
Claims, **Bus Org 11.356 et seq.**
Reinstatement, **Bus Org 11.204 et seq.**
Errors, reinstatement, **Bus Org 11.201 et seq.**
Escheat, claims, **Bus Org 11.355**
Exemptions, involuntary termination, **Bus Org 11.251**
Filing,
Fines and penalties, **Bus Org 21.802**
Involuntary termination, **Bus Org 11.315**
Fraud,
Involuntary termination, **Bus Org 11.301 et seq.**
Revocation or suspension, **Bus Org 11.153**
Involuntary termination, **Bus Org 11.251 et seq., 11.301 et seq.**
Certified copies, judgments and decrees, **Bus Org 11.414**
Judgments and decrees, **Bus Org 11.301 et seq.**
Involuntary termination, certified copies, **Bus Org 11.414**
Jurisdiction, involuntary termination, **Bus Org 11.308**
Limitation of actions, claims, **Bus Org 11.359**
Names, reinstatement, **Bus Org 11.203**
Notice,
Claims, **Bus Org 11.358**
Escheat, claims, **Bus Org 11.355**
Involuntary termination, **Bus Org 11.251, 11.302, 11.310**
Payment,
Claims, **Bus Org 11.354**
Taxation, **Bus Org 11.101**
Publication, involuntary termination, **Bus Org 11.310**
Receipts, claims, **Bus Org 11.352**
Receivers and receivership, **Bus Org 11.403**
Judgments and decrees, **Bus Org 11.412**
Records and recordation, removal, **Bus Org 11.104**
Reinstatement, **Bus Org 11.201 et seq.**
Involuntary termination, **Bus Org 11.253**
Taxation, forfeitures, **Bus Org 11.254**
Remand, involuntary termination, **Bus Org 11.307**
Revocation or suspension, fraud, **Bus Org 11.153**

COOPERATIVE ASSOCIATIONS
—Cont'd
Termination—Cont'd
Service of process, involuntary termination, **Bus Org 11.309**
Statements, claims, **Bus Org 11.352**
Supersedeas or stay, involuntary termination, **Bus Org 11.306**
Taxation,
Forfeitures, reinstatement, **Bus Org 11.254**
Payment, **Bus Org 11.101**
Time,
Involuntary termination, **Bus Org 11.305, 11.313**
Reinstatement, **Bus Org 11.202**
Venue, involuntary termination, **Bus Org 11.308**
Terms of office, directors, **Bus Org 251.101**
Time,
Business Organizations Code, effective date, **Bus Org 402.001**
Adoption, **Bus Org 402.005**
Certificate of formation, ante
Exchange of property, **Bus Org 10.054, 10.055**
Filing, ante
Interrogatories, answer, **Bus Org 12.002**
Members, expulsion, **Bus Org 251.152**
Merger and consolidation, effective date, **Bus Org 10.007**
Record date, **Bus Org 6.101 et seq.**
Reports, **Bus Org 251.353**
Filing, **Bus Org 251.354**
Service of process, **Bus Org 5.254**
Termination, ante
Winding up, post
Title to property, **Bus Org 301.007 et seq.**
Purchases and purchasing, **Bus Org 301.008**
Trademarks and trade names, names, **Bus Org 5.001**
Transfers,
Members, **Bus Org 251.202**
Names, reservation, **Bus Org 5.106**
Property, **Bus Org 10.251 et seq.**
Shares and shareholders, certificates and certification, **Bus Org 3.201**
Title to property, **Bus Org 301.009**
Transition, Business Organizations Code, **Bus Org 402.001 et seq.**
Treasurers, **Bus Org 251.102**
Trusts and trustees,
Elections, **Bus Org 6.154, 6.251**
Reorganization, **Bus Org 10.301 et seq.**
Uncertificated shares, **Bus Org 3.201**
Notice, **Bus Org 3.205**
Units, meetings, **Bus Org 251.253**
Venue,
Termination, involuntary termination, **Bus Org 11.308**
Winding up, involuntary winding up, **Bus Org 11.308**
Veterans organizations, names, **Bus Org 5.062**

COOPERATIVE ASSOCIATIONS
—Cont'd
Vice president, **Bus Org 251.102**
Agent for service of process, **Bus Org 5.255**
Video recordings, meetings, **Bus Org 6.002**
Waiver, meetings, notice, **Bus Org 6.052**
Objections and exceptions, **Bus Org 6.053**
Winding up, **Bus Org 11.001 et seq., 11.051 et seq., 251.401 et seq.**
Abatement of actions and proceedings, involuntary winding up, **Bus Org 11.304**
Actions and proceedings, **Bus Org 11.052, 11.055**
Involuntary winding up, **Bus Org 11.303**
Appeal and review, involuntary winding up, **Bus Org 11.307**
Assets, distribution and distributors, **Bus Org 11.053**
Business Organizations Code, mandatory application date, **Bus Org 402.011**
Cancellation, **Bus Org 11.152**
Contracts, **Bus Org 11.152**
Crimes and offenses, involuntary winding up, **Bus Org 11.301 et seq.**
Discharge, indebtedness, **Bus Org 11.053**
Distribution and distributors, assets, **Bus Org 11.053**
Filing, involuntary winding up, **Bus Org 11.315**
Fraud, involuntary winding up, **Bus Org 11.301 et seq.**
Indebtedness, discharge, **Bus Org 11.053**
Involuntary winding up, **Bus Org 11.301 et seq.**
Judgments and decrees, **Bus Org 11.301 et seq.**
Jurisdiction, involuntary winding up, **Bus Org 11.308**
Notice, **Bus Org 11.052**
Involuntary winding up, **Bus Org 11.302, 11.310**
Publication, involuntary winding up, **Bus Org 11.310**
Remand, involuntary winding up, **Bus Org 11.307**
Revocation or suspension, **Bus Org 11.151**
Service of process, involuntary winding up, **Bus Org 11.309**
Supersedeas or stay, involuntary winding up, **Bus Org 11.306**
Supervision, **Bus Org 11.054**
Time, **Bus Org 11.056**
Cancellation, **Bus Org 11.152**
Involuntary winding up, **Bus Org 11.305, 11.313**
Venue, involuntary winding up, **Bus Org 11.308**

COOPERATIVE ASSOCIATIONS
—Cont'd
Withdrawal,
Filing, fines and penalties, **Bus Org 21.802**
Members, **Bus Org 251.202**
Names, reservation, fees, **Bus Org 5.1041**
Witnesses, indemnity, expenses and expenditures, **Bus Org 8.106**
Writings, signatures, **Bus Org 1.007**

COOPERATIVES
Cooperative Associations, generally, this index
Definitions, business organizations, **Bus Org 1.002**

COPARTNERS
Partnerships, generally, this index

CORPORATE SUPPORT SERVICES
Definitions, electricity, customer choice, **Util 39.157**

CORPORATIONS
Generally, **Bus Org 1.001 et seq., 20.001 et seq., 301.001 et seq.**
Abandonment, **Bus Org 10.201 et seq.**
Filing, **Bus Org 4.057**
Abatement of actions and proceedings,
State, **Bus Org 12.260**
Termination, involuntary termination, **Bus Org 11.304**
Winding up, involuntary winding up, **Bus Org 11.304**
Acceptance, certificates and certification, **Bus Org 10.156**
Accounts and accounting, **Bus Org 3.151 et seq.**
Examinations and examiners, **Bus Org 12.151 et seq.**
Fines and penalties, **Bus Org 21.222**
Acknowledgments,
Certificate of formation, **Bus Org 3.004**
Evidence, **Bus Org 3.001**
Filing, **Bus Org 4.002**
Effective date, delay, **Bus Org 4.059**
Actions and proceedings, **Bus Org 2.101**
Business Organizations Code, prior law, **Bus Org 402.014**
Certificate of formation, amendments, **Bus Org 3.056**
Close corporations, post
Derivative actions, generally, post
Guaranty, **Bus Org 2.104**
Indemnity, **Bus Org 8.001 et seq.**
Insolvency, **Bus Org 12.253 et seq.**
Receivers and receivership, **Bus Org 11.406**
Records and recordation, inspection and inspectors, **Bus Org 3.152**
State, liens and incumbrances, **Bus Org 12.201 et seq.**
Termination, involuntary termination, **Bus Org 11.303**
Winding up, post

CORPORATIONS—Cont'd
Address,
Certificate of formation, **Bus Org 3.005**
Directors, **Bus Org 21.404**
Adoption, Business Organizations Code, **Bus Org 402.003**
Advancements, indemnity, expenses and expenditures, **Bus Org 8.104, 8.105**
Reports, **Bus Org 8.152**
Adverse or pecuniary interest. Conflict of interest, generally, post
Affiliated corporations, business combinations, **Bus Org 21.601 et seq.**
Agent for service of process, **Bus Org 5.251 et seq.**
Agents and agencies,
Changes, filing, fines and penalties, **Bus Org 21.802**
Damages, **Bus Org 301.010**
Elections, **Bus Org 21.417**
Licenses and permits, **Bus Org 301.006**
Registered agent, generally, post
Agreements. Contracts, generally, post
Allocations, merger and consolidation, property, **Bus Org 10.003**
Alternatives, service of process, **Bus Org 5.256**
Amendments,
Business Organizations Code, statutes, **Bus Org 1.054**
Bylaws, **Bus Org 21.057**
Certificate of formation, **Bus Org 3.051 et seq., 21.052 et seq.**
Close corporations, post
Directors, numbers and numbering, **Bus Org 21.403**
Filing, **Bus Org 4.106**
Fees, **Bus Org 4.152**
Shares and shareholders, post
Ancillary receiverships, **Bus Org 11.409**
Answer, interrogatories, time, **Bus Org 12.002**
Antitrust, application of law, **Bus Org 10.901**
Appeal and review,
Derivative actions, **Bus Org 21.555**
Filing, **Bus Org 12.004**
Termination, involuntary termination, **Bus Org 11.307**
Winding up, involuntary winding up, **Bus Org 11.307**
Application of law, **Bus Org 301.001**
Antitrust, **Bus Org 10.901**
Business Organizations Code, **Bus Org 402.001 et seq.**
Foreign countries, foreign states, **Bus Org 1.053**
Certificate of formation, **Bus Org 1.101 et seq.**
Close corporations, post
Derivative actions, **Bus Org 21.562**
Elections, **Bus Org 6.301, 6.302**
Indebtedness, **Bus Org 10.901**
Indemnity, **Bus Org 8.002**
Meetings, **Bus Org 6.301, 6.302**
Monopolies and unfair trade, **Bus Org 10.901**

CORPORATIONS—Cont'd
Application of law—Cont'd
Reorganization, **Bus Org 10.306**
Special purpose corporations, **Bus Org 23.001 et seq.**
Appointments, receivers and receivership, **Bus Org 11.401 et seq.**
Appraisals and appraisers,
Fundamental business transactions, **Bus Org 21.460**
Reorganization, **Bus Org 10.304**
Assets,
Disposition, **Bus Org 10.251 et seq.**
Reorganization, **Bus Org 10.301**
Insolvency, **Bus Org 21.314**
Time, **Bus Org 21.315**
Liens and incumbrances, state, **Bus Org 12.201**
Liquidation, generally, post
Sales,
Business combinations, **Bus Org 21.601 et seq.**
Business Organizations Code, mandatory application date, **Bus Org 402.010**
Consent, **Bus Org 21.455**
Winding up, distribution and distributors, **Bus Org 11.053**
Assignments, **Bus Org 10.251 et seq.**
Consent, **Bus Org 21.455**
Shares and shareholders, post
Assumed or fictitious names, **Bus & C 71.001 et seq.; Bus Org 5.051 et seq.**
Attachment, state, **Bus Org 12.259**
Attorney fees,
Derivative actions, payment, **Bus Org 21.561**
Filing,
Fines and penalties, **Bus Org 21.802**
Fraud, **Bus Org 4.007**
Records and recordation,
Examinations and examiners, fines and penalties, **Bus Org 21.222**
Inspection and inspectors, **Bus Org 3.152**
Bankruptcy, **Bus Org 10.301 et seq.**
Benevolent Societies, generally, this index
Board of directors. Directors, generally, post
Bonds, **Bus Org 2.101**
Reorganization, **Bus Org 10.301**
Bonds (officers and fiduciaries), receivers and receivership, **Bus Org 11.406**
Bonuses, officers and employees, **Bus Org 2.101**
Books and papers, **Bus Org 3.151 et seq.**
Confidential or privileged information, **Bus Org 12.154**
Disclosure, **Bus Org 12.154**
Duplicates and copies, **Bus Org 12.151 et seq.**
Examinations and examiners, **Bus Org 3.153, 12.151 et seq.**
Fines and penalties, **Bus Org 21.222**
Inspection and inspectors, **Bus Org 3.152**
Notice, **Bus Org 1.005**

CORPORATIONS—Cont'd
Books and papers—Cont'd
Powers and duties, limitations, **Bus Org 2.005**
Reorganization, **Bus Org 10.301**
Shares and shareholders, post
Signatures, **Bus Org 1.007, 20.001**
Business combinations, **Bus Org 21.601 et seq.**
Business Development Corporations, generally, this index
Bylaws, **Bus Org 2.101, 21.057**
Amendments, shareholders, **Bus Org 21.058**
Close corporations, **Bus Org 21.704**
Contracts, **Bus Org 21.101 et seq.**
Electronic communications, notice, shares and shareholders, **Bus Org 21.3531**
Filing, fees, **Bus Org 4.152**
Notice, electronic communications, shares and shareholders, **Bus Org 21.3531**
Shares and shareholders, post
Winding up, **Bus Org 11.059**
Cancellation,
Reinstatement, **Bus Org 402.013**
Winding up, **Bus Org 11.152, 21.501 et seq.**
Capital. Stated capital, generally, post
Certificate of formation, **Bus Org 3.001 et seq.**
Amendments, **Bus Org 3.051 et seq., 21.052 et seq.**
Application of law, **Bus Org 1.101 et seq.**
Contracts, **Bus Org 21.101 et seq.**
Definitions, **Bus Org 1.002**
Directors, post
Filing,
Fees, **Bus Org 4.152**
Restatement, **Bus Org 21.056**
Merger and consolidation, post
Names, post
Property, rights, **Bus Org 21.051**
Reinstatement, **Bus Org 402.013**
Reorganization, **Bus Org 10.301 et seq.**
Restatement, **Bus Org 3.057 et seq., 21.056**
Shares and shareholders, post
Signatures, **Bus Org 3.004, 20.001**
Amendments, **Bus Org 3.052, 3.054**
Restatement, **Bus Org 3.058, 3.060**
Statements,
Amendments, **Bus Org 3.053, 3.054**
Restatement, **Bus Org 3.059**
Time, **Bus Org 3.001, 3.003**
Amendments, **Bus Org 3.056**
Restatement, **Bus Org 3.063**
Winding up, **Bus Org 11.059**
Certificates and certification,
Acceptance, **Bus Org 10.156**
Certificate of formation, generally, ante
Close corporations, shares and shareholders, **Bus Org 21.732**
Conversion, **Bus Org 10.154 et seq.**

CORPORATIONS—Cont'd
Certificates and certification—Cont'd
Exchange of property, **Bus Org 10.151 et seq.**
Existence, evidence, **Bus Org 4.005**
Filing, **Bus Org 12.001**
Corrections, **Bus Org 4.101 et seq.**
Fines and penalties, **Bus Org 21.802**
Indebtedness, **Bus Org 2.114**
Merger and consolidation, **Bus Org 10.151 et seq.**
Shares and shareholders, post
Termination, post
Certified copies,
Filing, **Bus Org 4.005**
Involuntary termination, judgments and decrees, **Bus Org 11.414**
Changes,
Registered agent, post
Registered offices, **Bus Org 5.202, 5.203**
Charitable corporations. Charities, generally, this index
Citizens and citizenship, receivers and receivership, **Bus Org 11.406**
Claims,
Disinterested persons, conflict of interest, **Bus Org 1.003**
Independent persons, conflict of interest, **Bus Org 1.004**
Receivers and receivership, filing, **Bus Org 11.407**
Termination, **Bus Org 11.351 et seq.**
Classification. Shares and shareholders, post
Close corporations, **Bus Org 1.001 et seq., 21.701 et seq.**
Actions and proceedings, **Bus Org 21.751 et seq.**
Derivative actions, **Bus Org 21.563**
Shares and shareholders, contracts, **Bus Org 21.719**
Termination, **Bus Org 21.708**
Amendments,
Certificate of formation, **Bus Org 21.705**
Shares and shareholders, contracts, **Bus Org 21.716**
Application of law, **Bus Org 21.702**
Existing corporations, **Bus Org 21.707**
Termination, **Bus Org 21.710**
Appointments,
Custodian, **Bus Org 21.761**
Provisional directors, **Bus Org 21.758**
Arbitration and award, shares and shareholders, contracts, **Bus Org 21.714**
Assignments, shares and shareholders, contracts, **Bus Org 21.714, 21.720**
Bylaws, **Bus Org 21.704**
Shares and shareholders, contracts, **Bus Org 21.714**
Certificate of formation, **Bus Org 3.008**
Amendments, **Bus Org 21.705**
Certificates and certification, shares and shareholders, **Bus Org 21.732**

CORPORATIONS—Cont'd
Close corporations—Cont'd
Compensation and salaries, provisional directors, **Bus Org 21.760**
Conflict of interest, provisional directors, **Bus Org 21.758**
Consent, shares and shareholders, **Bus Org 21.728**
Contracts, consent, **Bus Org 22.230**
Conversion, **Bus Org 21.706**
Termination, **Bus Org 21.708**
Custodian, **Bus Org 21.761 et seq.**
Damages, **Bus Org 21.756**
Shares and shareholders, **Bus Org 21.727**
Contracts, **Bus Org 21.723**
Limitations, **Bus Org 21.729**
Definitions, **Bus Org 21.701**
Actions and proceedings, **Bus Org 21.751**
Business organizations, **Bus Org 1.002**
Delivery, shares and shareholders, contracts, **Bus Org 21.717, 21.721**
Derivative actions, **Bus Org 21.563**
Directors, **Bus Org 21.711 et seq.**
Provisional directors, **Bus Org 21.758 et seq.**
Shares and shareholders, **Bus Org 21.726**
Contracts, **Bus Org 21.714**
Dividends, shares and shareholders, contracts, **Bus Org 21.714**
Effective date, grandfather rights, **Bus Org 21.707**
Elections,
Directors, meetings, **Bus Org 21.711**
Shares and shareholders, contracts, **Bus Org 21.714**
Evidence, shares and shareholders, contracts, **Bus Org 21.722**
Exchange of property, **Bus Org 21.706**
Termination, **Bus Org 21.708**
Existing corporations, application of law, **Bus Org 21.707**
Filing, operations, statements, **Bus Org 21.718**
Formation, **Bus Org 21.703**
Grandfather rights, **Bus Org 21.707**
Intervention, actions and proceedings, **Bus Org 21.753**
Jurisdiction, actions and proceedings, **Bus Org 21.752**
Labor and employment, shares and shareholders, contracts, **Bus Org 21.714**
Liquidation, **Bus Org 21.757**
Mail and mailing, termination, statements, **Bus Org 21.709**
Managers and management, **Bus Org 21.713**
Shares and shareholders, contracts, **Bus Org 21.714, 21.725**
Mediation, shares and shareholders, contracts, **Bus Org 21.714**
Meetings,
Attendance, **Bus Org 22.230**

CORPORATIONS—Cont'd
Close corporations—Cont'd
Meetings—Cont'd
Directors, elections, **Bus Org 21.711**
Merger and consolidation, **Bus Org 21.706**
Termination, **Bus Org 21.708**
Notice,
Actions and proceedings, **Bus Org 21.753**
Termination, **Bus Org 21.709**
Operations, statements, **Bus Org 21.718**
Partnerships, treatment, **Bus Org 21.730**
Powers and duties,
Custodian, **Bus Org 21.762**
Provisional directors, **Bus Org 21.759**
Privileges and immunities, shares and shareholders, **Bus Org 21.729**
Provisional directors, **Bus Org 21.758 et seq.**
Purchases and purchasing, shares and shareholders, contracts, **Bus Org 21.714**
Receivers and receivership, **Bus Org 21.757**
Removal, provisional directors, **Bus Org 21.758**
Sales, shares and shareholders, contracts, **Bus Org 21.714**
Shares and shareholders,
Actions and proceedings, **Bus Org 21.751 et seq.**
Certificates and certification, **Bus Org 21.732**
Consent, **Bus Org 21.728**
Contracts, **Bus Org 21.714 et seq.**
Definitions, **Bus Org 21.701**
Damages, **Bus Org 21.727**
Limitations, **Bus Org 21.729**
Directors, **Bus Org 21.726**
Elections, meetings, **Bus Org 21.711**
Privileges and immunities, **Bus Org 21.729**
Signatures,
Shares and shareholders, contracts, **Bus Org 21.715**
Termination, statements, **Bus Org 21.709**
Statements,
Operations, **Bus Org 21.718**
Termination, **Bus Org 21.709**
Termination, **Bus Org 21.708 et seq., 21.757**
Bylaws, **Bus Org 21.704**
Custodian, **Bus Org 21.763**
Shares and shareholders, contracts, **Bus Org 21.714, 21.724**
Terms of office, directors, **Bus Org 21.712**
Time, termination, **Bus Org 21.709**
Transfers, shares and shareholders, contracts, **Bus Org 21.714, 21.720**
Delivery, **Bus Org 21.721**
Venue, actions and proceedings, **Bus Org 21.752**

CORPORATIONS—Cont'd
Close corporations—Cont'd
Winding up, **Bus Org 21.757**
Shares and shareholders, contracts, **Bus Org 21.714**
Closing, shares and shareholders, transfers, records and recordation, **Bus Org 21.355**
Combinations, **Bus Org 21.601 et seq.**
Compensation and salaries,
Close corporations, provisional directors, **Bus Org 21.760**
Disinterested persons, conflict of interest, **Bus Org 1.003**
Independent persons, conflict of interest, **Bus Org 1.004**
Officers and employees, **Bus Org 2.101**
Receivers and receivership, **Bus Org 11.408**
Compromise and settlement, derivative actions, **Bus Org 21.560**
Conduct,
Business Organizations Code, application of law, **Bus Org 402.006**
Damages, **Bus Org 7.001, 301.010**
Confidential or privileged information, interrogatories, **Bus Org 12.003**
Conflict of interest,
Close corporations, provisional directors, **Bus Org 21.758**
Directors, contracts, **Bus Org 21.418**
Disinterested persons, **Bus Org 1.003**
Elections, **Bus Org 6.152, 6.153**
Independent persons, **Bus Org 1.004**
Conflict of laws, **Bus Org 301.002**
Business combinations, **Bus Org 21.609**
Consent,
Close corporations, contracts, **Bus Org 22.230**
Duplicates and copies, meetings, action without meeting, **Bus Org 6.205**
Registered agents, **Bus Org 5.2011**
Shares and shareholders, post
Conservators and conservatorship, shares and shareholders, privileges and immunities, **Bus Org 21.226**
Consideration. Shares and shareholders, post
Consolidation. Merger and consolidation, generally, post
Construction of laws, Business Organizations Code, statutes, **Bus Org 1.006, 1.051 et seq.**
Contracts, **Bus Org 2.101**
Business Organizations Code, application of law, **Bus Org 402.006**
Close corporations, consent, **Bus Org 22.230**
Directors, conflict of interest, **Bus Org 21.418**
Disinterested persons, conflict of interest, **Bus Org 1.003**
Elections, **Bus Org 6.252**
Indebtedness, **Bus Org 2.103**
Independent persons, conflict of interest, **Bus Org 1.004**
Shares and shareholders, post

CORPORATIONS—Cont'd
Contracts—Cont'd
Ultra vires, **Bus Org 20.002**
Winding up, **Bus Org 11.152**
Contributions,
Definitions, business organizations, **Bus Org 1.002**
Distribution and distributors, damages, **Bus Org 21.318**
Conversion, **Bus Org 10.101 et seq.**
Abandonment, **Bus Org 10.201 et seq.**
Acceptance, certificates and certification, **Bus Org 10.156**
Appraisal and appraisers, **Bus Org 21.460**
Business combinations, **Bus Org 21.601 et seq.**
Business Organizations Code, mandatory application date, **Bus Org 402.010**
Certificates and certification, **Bus Org 10.154 et seq.**
Close corporations, **Bus Org 21.706**
Combinations, **Bus Org 21.601 et seq.**
Definitions, business organizations, **Bus Org 1.002**
Dissenting shareholders, **Bus Org 10.351 et seq.**
Effective date, **Bus Org 10.105, 10.106**
Elections, **Bus Org 21.457 et seq.**
Filing,
Certificates and certification, **Bus Org 10.155**
Fees, **Bus Org 4.151**
Names, **Bus Org 10.103**
Notice, **Bus Org 10.101**
Meetings, **Bus Org 21.456**
Objections and exceptions, **Bus Org 21.460**
Plans and specifications, **Bus Org 10.101 et seq., 21.451 et seq.**
Reorganization, **Bus Org 10.301 et seq.**
Shares and shareholders, post
Conveyances. Deeds and conveyances, generally, post
Cooperative Associations, generally, this index
Copies. Duplicates and copies, generally, post
Corrections, filing, **Bus Org 4.101 et seq.**
Fees, **Bus Org 4.151**
Costs,
Derivative actions, payment, **Bus Org 21.561**
Filing,
Fines and penalties, **Bus Org 21.802**
Fraud, **Bus Org 4.007**
Insolvency, dismissal and nonsuit, **Bus Org 12.257**
Liens and incumbrances, foreclosure, dismissal and nonsuit, **Bus Org 12.257**
Records and recordation, examinations and examiners, **Bus Org 21.222**
Crimes and offenses,
Books and papers, examinations and examiners, **Bus Org 12.156**

CORPORATIONS—Cont'd
Crimes and offenses—Cont'd
Damages, **Bus Org 7.001**
Filing, fraud, **Bus Org 4.008**
Fraud, generally, post
Termination, involuntary termination, **Bus Org 11.301 et seq.**
Winding up, involuntary winding up, **Bus Org 11.301 et seq.**
Custodian, close corporations, **Bus Org 21.761 et seq.**
Damages, **Bus Org 301.010**
Application of law, **Bus Org 1.104**
Close corporations, ante
Directors, **Bus Org 7.001**
Disinterested persons, conflict of interest, **Bus Org 1.003**
Distribution and distributors, directors, **Bus Org 21.316**
Filing, **Bus Org 21.802**
Fraud, **Bus Org 4.007**
Guaranty, **Bus Org 2.104**
Indemnity, generally, post
Officers and employees, post
Shares and shareholders, post
Ultra vires, **Bus Org 20.002**
Death, shares and shareholders, joint tenants, **Bus Org 21.214**
Debts. Indebtedness, generally, post
Deception, names, **Bus Org 5.052**
Deeds and conveyances, **Bus Org 10.251 et seq., 21.462**
Property, **Bus Org 2.101**
Records and recordation, **Bus Org 10.253**
Deeds of trust, consent, **Bus Org 21.461**
Defenses,
Records and recordation, examinations and examiners, fines and penalties, **Bus Org 21.222**
Ultra vires, **Bus Org 20.002**
Definitions, **Bus Org 1.002, 21.002, 301.003**
Actions and proceedings, close corporations, **Bus Org 21.751**
Agriculture gas users, **Util 123.022**
Assumed or fictitious names, **Bus & C 71.002**
Business combinations, **Bus Org 21.601**
Business development corporations, **Bus Org 23.051**
Close corporations, ante
Distribution and distributors, **Bus Org 21.301**
Fundamental business transactions, **Bus Org 21.451**
Gas and electrical corporations, **Util 181.001**
Gas utilities, **Util 101.003**
Indemnity, **Bus Org 8.001**
Mandatory application date, **Bus Org 401.001**
Nonprofit corporations, **Bus Org 22.001**
Prior law, **Bus Org 401.001**
Public utilities, **Util 11.003, 11.0042**
Termination, **Bus Org 11.001**

CORPORATIONS—Cont'd
Definitions—Cont'd
Underground facilities, excavations, **Util 251.001**
Winding up, **Bus Org 11.001**
Delay, filing, effective date, **Bus Org 4.052 et seq.**
Delivery,
Filing, **Bus Org 4.001**
Meetings, action without meeting, **Bus Org 6.203**
Shares and shareholders, certificates and certification, **Bus Org 3.204**
Demand,
Derivative actions, **Bus Org 21.553**
Shares and shareholders, post
Deposits, termination, claims, **Bus Org 11.352**
Derivative actions, **Bus Org 21.551 et seq.**
Appeal and review, **Bus Org 21.555**
Application of law, **Bus Org 21.562**
Attorney fees, payment, **Bus Org 21.561**
Close corporations, **Bus Org 21.563**
Compromise and settlement, **Bus Org 21.560**
Costs, payment, **Bus Org 21.561**
Definitions, **Bus Org 21.551**
Demand, **Bus Org 21.553**
Rejection, **Bus Org 21.559**
Discontinuance, **Bus Org 21.560**
Discovery, **Bus Org 21.556**
Disinterested persons, conflict of interest, **Bus Org 1.003**
Dismissal and nonsuit, **Bus Org 21.558**
Elections, **Bus Org 21.554**
Evidence,
Discovery, **Bus Org 21.556**
Dismissal and nonsuit, **Bus Org 21.558**
Expenses and expenditures, payment, **Bus Org 21.561**
Limitation of actions, tolling, **Bus Org 21.557**
Panel, **Bus Org 21.554**
Payment, expenses and expenditures, **Bus Org 21.561**
Rejection, demand, **Bus Org 21.559**
Standing, **Bus Org 21.552**
Supersedeas or stay, **Bus Org 21.555**
Termination, costs, payment, **Bus Org 21.561**
Tolling, limitation of actions, **Bus Org 21.557**
Directors, **Bus Org 21.401 et seq.**
Address, **Bus Org 21.404**
Adverse or pecuniary interest, contracts, **Bus Org 21.418**
Agent for service of process, **Bus Org 5.255**
Amendments, numbers and numbering, **Bus Org 21.403**
Certificate of formation, **Bus Org 3.007**
Amendments, **Bus Org 3.054, 21.053**
Restatement, **Bus Org 3.060**
Close corporations, ante
Committees, **Bus Org 21.416**

CORPORATIONS—Cont'd
Directors—Cont'd
Conflict of interest, contracts, **Bus Org 21.418**
Consent, meetings, notice, electronic communications, **Bus Org 21.411**
Contracts, **Bus Org 21.101 et seq.**
Conflict of interest, **Bus Org 21.418**
Contributions, distribution and distributors, damages, **Bus Org 21.318**
Damages, **Bus Org 7.001**
Definitions, business organizations, **Bus Org 21.002**
Distribution and distributors, damages, **Bus Org 21.316**
Elections, **Bus Org 21.405, 21.406**
Electronic communications, meetings, notice, **Bus Org 21.411**
Evidence, notice, electronic communications, **Bus Org 21.411**
Indemnity, **Bus Org 7.001**
Loans, **Bus Org 2.101**
Meetings, **Bus Org 21.411 et seq.**
Electronic communications, notice, **Bus Org 21.411**
Names, **Bus Org 21.404**
Notice,
Meetings, **Bus Org 21.411**
Waiver, **Bus Org 21.412**
Resignation, **Bus Org 21.4091**
Numbers and numbering, **Bus Org 21.403**
Objections and exceptions, meetings, **Bus Org 21.414**
Open end investment companies, terms of office, **Bus Org 21.654**
Organization, meetings, **Bus Org 21.059**
Powers and duties, **Bus Org 21.401**
Qualifications, **Bus Org 21.402**
Quorum, meetings, **Bus Org 21.413, 21.415**
Removal, **Bus Org 21.409**
Resignation, notice, **Bus Org 21.4091**
Shares and shareholders, post
Terms of office, **Bus Org 21.407, 21.408**
Close corporations, **Bus Org 21.712**
Open end investment companies, **Bus Org 21.654**
Ultra vires, **Bus Org 20.002**
Vacancies in office, **Bus Org 21.410**
Waiver, meetings, notice, **Bus Org 21.412**
Discharge,
Receivers and receivership, **Bus Org 11.412**
Termination, claims, **Bus Org 11.353**
Winding up, indebtedness, **Bus Org 11.053**
Disclosure, interrogatories, **Bus Org 12.003**
Discontinuance, derivative actions, **Bus Org 21.560**
Discovery, derivative actions, **Bus Org 21.556**
Disinterested persons, conflict of interest, **Bus Org 1.003**

CORPORATIONS—Cont'd
Dismissal and nonsuit,
Derivative actions, **Bus Org 21.558**
Insolvency, **Bus Org 12.257**
Liens and incumbrances, foreclosure, **Bus Org 12.257**
Disposition. Assets, ante
Dissenting shareholders. Shares and shareholders, post
Dissolution, **Bus Org 2.101**
Involuntary dissolution, reinstatement, **Bus Org 402.013**
Distribution and distributors, **Bus Org 21.301 et seq.**
Contracts, **Bus Org 21.101 et seq.**
Definitions, business organizations, **Bus Org 21.002**
Dividends, generally, post
Record date, **Bus Org 6.101 et seq.**
Shares and shareholders, post
Winding up, assets, **Bus Org 11.053**
Dividends, **Bus Org 21.310 et seq.**
Limitations, **Bus Org 21.311**
Par value, **Bus Org 21.312**
Payment, **Bus Org 21.310**
Surplus, transfers, **Bus Org 21.313**
Transfers, surplus, **Bus Org 21.313**
Drains and drainage, **Bus Org 1.001 et seq.**
Dual office holding, officers and employees, **Bus Org 3.103**
Duplicates and copies,
Agent for service of process, **Bus Org 5.252**
Books and papers, **Bus Org 12.151 et seq.**
Consent, meetings, action without meeting, **Bus Org 6.205**
Filing, **Bus Org 4.003**
Records and recordation, **Bus Org 3.152**
Shares and shareholders, certificates and certification, **Bus Org 3.202**
Duties. Powers and duties, generally, post
Educational corporations. Nonprofit Corporations, generally, this index
Effective date,
Business Organizations Code, **Bus Org 402.001**
Adoption, **Bus Org 402.005**
Close corporations, grandfather rights, **Bus Org 21.707**
Conversion, **Bus Org 10.105, 10.106**
Exchange of property, **Bus Org 10.054, 10.055**
Filing, **Bus Org 4.051 et seq.**
Merger and consolidation, **Bus Org 10.007**
Termination, post
Elections, **Bus Org 6.151 et seq.**
Application of law, **Bus Org 6.301, 6.302**
Business combinations, **Bus Org 21.610**
Conflict of interest, **Bus Org 6.152, 6.153**
Contracts, **Bus Org 6.252, 21.101 et seq.**

CORPORATIONS—Cont'd
Elections—Cont'd
Derivative actions, **Bus Org 21.554**
Directors, **Bus Org 21.405, 21.406**
Disinterested persons, conflict of interest, **Bus Org 1.003**
Estates, **Bus Org 6.154**
Indemnity, **Bus Org 8.103**
Officers and employees, post
Pledges, **Bus Org 6.156**
Probate proceedings, **Bus Org 6.154**
Receivers and receivership, **Bus Org 6.155**
Shares and shareholders, post
Trusts and trustees, **Bus Org 6.154, 6.251**
Electric Cooperative Corporations, generally, this index
Electronic communications,
Consent, meetings, **Bus Org 6.205**
Directors, meetings, notice, **Bus Org 21.411**
Shares and shareholders, notice, **Bus Org 21.3531**
Electronic filing, **Bus Org 12.001**
Emergencies, governance, **Bus Org 3.251 et seq.**
Employees. Officers and employees, generally, post
Errors,
Damages, **Bus Org 301.010**
Termination, reinstatement, **Bus Org 11.201 et seq.**
Escheat, termination, claims, **Bus Org 11.355**
Estates, elections, **Bus Org 6.154**
Evidence,
Certificate of formation, acknowledgments, **Bus Org 3.001**
Derivative actions, ante
Existence, certificates and certification, **Bus Org 4.005**
Filing, **Bus Org 4.001**
Indebtedness, fraud, **Bus Org 2.103**
Independent persons, conflict of interest, **Bus Org 1.004**
Shares and shareholders, post
Examinations and examiners,
Accounts and accounting, ante
Books and papers, ante
Elections, contracts, **Bus Org 6.252**
Records and recordation, post
Shares and shareholders, post
Exchange of property, **Bus Org 2.101, 10.051 et seq.**
Abandonment, **Bus Org 10.201 et seq.**
Acceptance, certificates and certification, **Bus Org 10.156**
Appraisal and appraisers, **Bus Org 21.460**
Business combinations, **Bus Org 21.601 et seq.**
Certificates and certification, **Bus Org 10.151 et seq.**
Close corporations, **Bus Org 21.706**
Combinations, **Bus Org 21.601 et seq.**

CORPORATIONS—Cont'd
Exchange of property—Cont'd
Dissenting shareholders, **Bus Org 10.351 et seq.**
Elections, **Bus Org 21.457 et seq.**
Filing,
Certificates and certification, **Bus Org 10.153**
Fees, **Bus Org 4.151**
Notice, meetings, **Bus Org 21.456**
Objections and exceptions, **Bus Org 21.460**
Plans and specifications, **Bus Org 21.451 et seq.**
Reorganization, **Bus Org 10.301**
Shares and shareholders, post
Voluntary, **Bus Org 10.902**
Exemptions,
Guaranty, powers and duties, **Bus Org 2.104**
Interrogatories, **Bus Org 12.002**
Securities, sales, **Bus Org 301.011**
Termination, involuntary termination, **Bus Org 11.251**
Expenses and expenditures,
Derivative actions, payment, **Bus Org 21.561**
Indemnity, **Bus Org 8.001 et seq.**
Shares and shareholders, post
Facsimile, **Bus Org 1.007**
Consent, meetings, action without meeting, **Bus Org 6.205**
Filing, **Bus Org 4.003**
Indebtedness, certificates and certification, **Bus Org 2.114**
Meetings, notice, **Bus Org 6.051**
Seals, **Bus Org 2.101**
Shares and shareholders,
Certificates and certification, **Bus Org 3.203**
Notice, **Bus Org 21.3531**
Fees,
Business Organizations Code, effective date, **Bus Org 402.002**
Disinterested persons, conflict of interest, **Bus Org 1.003**
Filing, **Bus Org 4.151 et seq.**
Independent persons, conflict of interest, **Bus Org 1.004**
Names, reservation, **Bus Org 5.101**
Withdrawal, **Bus Org 5.1041**
Filing, **Bus Org 4.001 et seq., 12.001 et seq.**
Abandonment, **Bus Org 4.057**
Acknowledgments, **Bus Org 4.002**
Effective date, delay, **Bus Org 4.059**
Amendments, **Bus Org 4.106**
Appeal and review, **Bus Org 12.004**
Assumed or fictitious names, **Bus Org 5.051**
Attorney fees, ante
Business Organizations Code, effective date, **Bus Org 402.002**
Certificate of formation, **Bus Org 3.001 et seq.**
Restatement, **Bus Org 21.056**
Certificates and certification, ante

CORPORATIONS—Cont'd
Filing—Cont'd
Certified copies, **Bus Org 4.005**
Close corporations, operations, statements, **Bus Org 21.718**
Conversion, certificates and certification, **Bus Org 10.155**
Corrections, **Bus Org 4.101 et seq.**
Fees, **Bus Org 4.151**
Costs, ante
Damages, ante
Delay, effective date, **Bus Org 4.052 et seq.**
Delivery, **Bus Org 4.001**
Duplicates and copies, **Bus Org 4.003**
Effective date, **Bus Org 4.051 et seq.**
Electronic filing, **Bus Org 12.001**
Evidence, **Bus Org 4.001**
Facsimile, **Bus Org 4.003**
Fees, **Bus Org 4.151 et seq.**
Fines and penalties, post
Forms, **Bus Org 4.006**
Fraud, **Bus Org 4.007, 4.008**
Interrogatories, **Bus Org 12.002, 12.003**
Jurisdiction, fines and penalties, **Bus Org 21.802**
Limitations,
Corrections, **Bus Org 4.102**
Effective date, delay, **Bus Org 4.058**
Names, post
Real estate investment trusts, **Bus Org 4.009**
Receivers and receivership, claims, **Bus Org 11.407**
Registered agent, resignation, **Bus Org 5.204**
Service of process, **Bus Org 21.802**
Signatures, post
Special purpose corporations, records and recordation, **Bus Org 23.002**
Termination, post
Time, **Bus Org 4.004**
Corrections, **Bus Org 4.105**
Effective date, **Bus Org 4.051 et seq.**
Fines and penalties, **Bus Org 21.802**
Winding up, involuntary winding up, **Bus Org 11.315**
Financial statements and reports,
Insolvency, **Bus Org 21.314**
Officers and employees, good faith, **Bus Org 3.102, 3.105**
Fines and penalties,
Books and papers, examinations and examiners, **Bus Org 12.156**
Filing, **Bus Org 21.802**
Fraud, **Bus Org 4.008**
Meetings, notice, **Bus Org 21.221**
Records and recordation, examinations and examiners, **Bus Org 21.222**
Registered agents, consent, **Bus Org 5.207**
Shares and shareholders, post
Foreclosure, liens and incumbrances, **Bus Org 12.252 et seq.**
Foreign Corporations, generally, this index

CORPORATIONS—Cont'd
Foreign countries,
Business Organizations Code, application of law, **Bus Org 1.053**
Certificate of formation, application of law, **Bus Org 1.102**
Foreign states,
Business Organizations Code, application of law, **Bus Org 1.053**
Certificate of formation, application of law, **Bus Org 1.102**
Meetings, location, **Bus Org 6.001**
Forfeitures,
Books and papers, examinations and examiners, **Bus Org 12.155**
Reinstatement, **Bus Org 402.013**
Formation. Certificate of formation, generally, ante
Forms,
Filing, **Bus Org 4.006**
Shares and shareholders, certificates and certification, **Bus Org 3.202**
Franchise Taxes, generally, this index
Fraud,
Filing, **Bus Org 4.007, 4.008**
Guaranty, **Bus Org 2.104**
Indebtedness, evidence, **Bus Org 2.103**
Names, **Bus Org 5.052**
Receivers and receivership, **Bus Org 11.403**
Shares and shareholders, post
Termination,
Involuntary termination, **Bus Org 11.301 et seq.**
Revocation or suspension, **Bus Org 11.153**
Winding up, involuntary winding up, **Bus Org 11.301 et seq.**
Frauds, statute of, powers and duties, **Bus Org 2.112**
Fundamental business transactions, **Bus Org 21.451 et seq.**
Garnishment, state, **Bus Org 12.259**
Gifts, **Bus Org 2.101**
Good faith,
Damages, **Bus Org 7.001**
Officers and employees, **Bus Org 3.102, 3.105**
Grand lodges, incorporation, **Bus Org 23.101 et seq.**
Grand Royal Arch, incorporation, **Bus Org 23.101 et seq.**
Grandfather rights, close corporations, **Bus Org 21.707**
Guaranty, **Bus Org 2.101**
Powers and duties, **Bus Org 2.104**
Hold harmless. Indemnity, generally, post
Identity and identification, names, same or similar, **Bus Org 5.053**
Incentives, officers and employees, **Bus Org 2.101**
Incorporation,
Grand lodges, **Bus Org 23.101 et seq.**
Lodges, **Bus Org 23.101 et seq.**
Indebtedness, **Bus Org 2.101, 2.103**
Application of law, **Bus Org 10.901**

CORPORATIONS—Cont'd
Indebtedness—Cont'd
Certificates and certification, **Bus Org 2.114**
Winding up, discharge, **Bus Org 11.053**
Indemnity,
Business Organizations Code, application of law, **Bus Org 402.007**
Insurance, **Bus Org 8.151**
Mandatory, **Bus Org 8.051**
Officers and employees, post
Orders of court, **Bus Org 8.052**
Permissive indemnification, **Bus Org 8.101 et seq.**
Reports, **Bus Org 8.152**
Independent persons, conflict of interest, **Bus Org 1.004**
Information, notice, **Bus Org 1.005**
Injunctions,
Guaranty, **Bus Org 2.104**
State, **Bus Org 12.259**
Ultra vires, **Bus Org 20.002**
Insolvency,
Actions and proceedings, **Bus Org 12.253 et seq.**
Definitions, **Bus Org 1.002**
Determination, **Bus Org 21.314**
Time, **Bus Org 21.315**
Inspection and inspectors,
Books and papers, **Bus Org 12.151 et seq.**
Records and recordation, **Bus Org 3.152**
Insurance, generally, this index
Internal affairs, **Bus Org 1.105**
International commerce development corporations, **Bus Org 1.001 et seq.**
Internet, meetings, **Bus Org 6.002**
Interrogatories, **Bus Org 12.002, 12.003**
Intervention, close corporations, actions and proceedings, **Bus Org 21.753**
Investments, **Bus Org 2.101**
Open end investment companies, **Bus Org 21.651 et seq.**
Involuntary dissolution, reinstatement, **Bus Org 402.013**
Involuntary termination, **Bus Org 11.251 et seq., 11.301 et seq.**
Certified copies, judgments and decrees, **Bus Org 11.414**
Irrigation, this index
Joint practices, **Bus Org 301.012**
Judgments and decrees,
Receivers and receivership, termination, **Bus Org 11.412**
Reorganization, **Bus Org 10.305**
Termination, **Bus Org 11.301 et seq.**
Involuntary termination, certified copies, **Bus Org 11.414**
Winding up, **Bus Org 11.301 et seq.**
Jurisdiction,
Close corporations, actions and proceedings, **Bus Org 21.752**
Filing, fines and penalties, **Bus Org 21.802**
Insolvency, **Bus Org 12.253**

CORPORATIONS—Cont'd
Jurisdiction—Cont'd
Liens and incumbrances, foreclosure, **Bus Org 12.253**
Receivers and receivership, **Bus Org 11.402 et seq.**
Reorganization, **Bus Org 10.302**
Termination, involuntary termination, **Bus Org 11.308**
Winding up, involuntary winding up, **Bus Org 11.308**
Knights Templar, incorporation, **Bus Org 23.101 et seq.**
Leases, **Bus Org 2.101, 10.251 et seq.**
Business combinations, **Bus Org 21.601 et seq.**
Consent, **Bus Org 21.455**
Reorganization, **Bus Org 10.301**
Licenses and permits, **Bus Org 301.006**
Liens and incumbrances,
Foreclosure, **Bus Org 12.252 et seq.**
State, **Bus Org 12.201**
Limitation of actions,
Derivative actions, tolling, **Bus Org 21.557**
Distribution and distributors, **Bus Org 21.317**
Shares and shareholders, post
Termination, claims, **Bus Org 11.359**
Limitations,
Distribution and distributors, **Bus Org 21.303**
Dividends, **Bus Org 21.311**
Filing, ante
Indemnity, **Bus Org 8.003, 8.004**
Powers and duties, **Bus Org 2.113**
Purposes, **Bus Org 2.003 et seq.**
Limited Liability Companies, generally, this index
Liquidation,
Close corporations, **Bus Org 21.757**
Receivers and receivership, **Bus Org 12.258**
Orders of court, **Bus Org 11.405**
Lists. Shares and shareholders, post
Loans, **Bus Org 2.101**
Officers and employees, **Bus Org 2.101**
Lobbyists. Legislature, this index
Location,
Meetings, **Bus Org 6.001**
Offices, **Bus Org 2.101**
Lodges, **Bus Org 1.001 et seq.**
Incorporation, **Bus Org 23.101 et seq.**
Losses, contracts, **Bus Org 21.101 et seq.**
Lottery, names, **Bus Org 5.061**
Mail and mailing, meetings, notice, **Bus Org 6.051**
Managers and management,
Agent for service of process, **Bus Org 5.255**
Close corporations, **Bus Org 21.713**
Damages, **Bus Org 301.010**
Directors, generally, ante
Licenses and permits, **Bus Org 301.006**
Resignation, **Bus Org 301.008**
Winding up, **Bus Org 21.504**

CORPORATIONS—Cont'd
Mandatory application date, Business Organizations Code, **Bus Org 401.001 et seq.**
Meetings, **Bus Org 6.001 et seq.**
  Action without meeting, **Bus Org 6.102**
    Consent, **Bus Org 6.201 et seq.**
  Application of law, **Bus Org 6.301, 6.302**
  Business Organizations Code, mandatory application date, **Bus Org 402.008, 402.009**
  Certificate of formation, amendments, **Bus Org 21.055**
  Close corporations, attendance, **Bus Org 22.230**
  Consent, action without meeting, **Bus Org 6.102, 6.201 et seq.**
  Delivery, action without meeting, **Bus Org 6.203**
  Directors, **Bus Org 21.411 et seq.**
  Emergencies, **Bus Org 3.251 et seq.**
  Facsimile, notice, **Bus Org 6.051**
  Foreign states, location, **Bus Org 6.001**
  Internet, **Bus Org 6.002**
  Location, **Bus Org 6.001**
  Mail and mailing, notice, **Bus Org 6.051**
  Notice, **Bus Org 6.051 et seq., 21.411**
    Action without meeting, **Bus Org 6.204**
    Fines and penalties, **Bus Org 21.221**
    Organization, **Bus Org 21.059**
    Waiver, **Bus Org 21.412**
  Objections and exceptions, **Bus Org 6.003, 21.414**
    Notice, waiver, **Bus Org 6.053**
  Open end investment companies, shares and shareholders, **Bus Org 21.655**
  Organization, **Bus Org 21.059**
  Quorum, **Bus Org 21.413, 21.415**
  Record date, **Bus Org 6.101 et seq.**
  Records and recordation, **Bus Org 6.002**
  Shares and shareholders, post
  Telecommunications, **Bus Org 6.002**
  Video recordings, **Bus Org 6.002**
  Waiver, notice, **Bus Org 6.052**
    Objections and exceptions, **Bus Org 6.053**
Merger and consolidation, **Bus Org 10.001 et seq.**
  Abandonment, **Bus Org 10.201 et seq.**
  Acceptance, certificates and certification, **Bus Org 10.156**
  Allocations, property, **Bus Org 10.003**
  Appraisal and appraisers, **Bus Org 21.460**
  Business combinations, **Bus Org 21.601 et seq.**
  Business Organizations Code, mandatory application date, **Bus Org 402.010**
  Certificate of formation, **Bus Org 3.005, 3.006, 10.002**
  Certificates and certification, **Bus Org 10.151 et seq.**

CORPORATIONS—Cont'd
Merger and consolidation—Cont'd
  Close corporations, **Bus Org 21.706**
  Combinations, **Bus Org 21.601 et seq.**
  Definitions, **Bus Org 1.002**
    Business organizations, **Bus Org 1.002**
  Dissenting shareholders, **Bus Org 10.351 et seq.**
  Effect, **Bus Org 10.008**
  Effective date, **Bus Org 10.007**
  Elections, **Bus Org 21.457 et seq.**
  Filing,
    Certificates and certification, **Bus Org 10.153**
    Fees, **Bus Org 4.151**
  Holding companies, **Bus Org 10.005**
  Names, **Bus Org 10.002**
  Notice, meetings, **Bus Org 21.456**
  Objections and exceptions, **Bus Org 21.460**
  Plans and specifications, **Bus Org 10.001 et seq., 21.451 et seq.**
  Property, allocations, **Bus Org 10.003**
  Reorganization, **Bus Org 10.301 et seq.**
  Shares and shareholders, post
  Subsidiaries, post
  Time, effective date, **Bus Org 10.007**
Misconduct, damages, **Bus Org 7.001**
Money, **Bus Org 1.009**
Monopolies and Unfair Trade, generally, this index
Moratoriums, business combinations, **Bus Org 21.606, 21.607**
Mortgages, **Bus Org 2.101**
  Business combinations, **Bus Org 21.601 et seq.**
  Consent, **Bus Org 21.455, 21.461**
  Powers and duties, **Bus Org 2.104**
  Receivers and receivership, **Bus Org 11.403**
Names, **Bus Org 5.001 et seq.**
  Certificate of formation, **Bus Org 3.005**
    Amendments, **Bus Org 3.053, 3.056**
  Conversion, **Bus Org 10.103**
  Deception, **Bus Org 5.052**
  Directors, **Bus Org 21.404**
  Exchange of property, plans and specifications, **Bus Org 10.052**
  Fees, reservation, **Bus Org 5.101**
    Withdrawal, **Bus Org 5.1041**
  Filing,
    Fees, **Bus Org 4.151, 4.152**
    Registration, **Bus Org 5.152**
  Fraud, **Bus Org 5.052**
  Identity and identification, same or similar, **Bus Org 5.053**
  Lottery, **Bus Org 5.061**
  Merger and consolidation, **Bus Org 10.002**
  Notice, **Bus Org 5.001**
  Registration, **Bus Org 5.151 et seq.**
  Renewal,
    Registration, **Bus Org 5.155**
    Reservation, **Bus Org 5.105**
  Reservation, **Bus Org 5.101 et seq.**
  Same or similar, **Bus Org 5.053**

CORPORATIONS—Cont'd
Names—Cont'd
  Same or similar—Cont'd
    Registration, **Bus Org 5.153**
    Reservation, **Bus Org 5.102**
  Termination, reinstatement, **Bus Org 11.203**
  Time,
    Registration, **Bus Org 5.154**
    Reservation, **Bus Org 5.104**
  Trademarks and trade names, **Bus Org 5.001**
  Transfers, reservation, **Bus Org 5.106**
  Veterans organizations, **Bus Org 5.062**
  Words and phrases, **Bus Org 5.054**
Negligence, damages, **Bus Org 301.010**
Nonfiling, certificate of formation, **Bus Org 3.002**
Nonprofit Corporations, generally, this index
Nonsuit. Dismissal and nonsuit, generally, ante
Notice,
  Agent for service of process, **Bus Org 5.252, 5.253**
  Certificate of formation, amendments, **Bus Org 21.055**
  Close corporations,
    Actions and proceedings, **Bus Org 21.753**
    Termination, **Bus Org 21.709**
  Conversion, **Bus Org 10.101**
  Directors, ante
  Fundamental business transactions, meetings, **Bus Org 21.456**
  Guaranty, fraud, **Bus Org 2.104**
  Indemnity, orders of court, **Bus Org 8.052**
  Information, **Bus Org 1.005**
  Insolvency, **Bus Org 12.256**
  Liens and incumbrances,
    Foreclosure, **Bus Org 12.256**
    State, **Bus Org 12.201**
  Meetings, ante
  Names, **Bus Org 5.001**
  Receivers and receivership, claims, **Bus Org 11.407**
  Registered agent, resignation, **Bus Org 5.204**
  Reorganization, **Bus Org 10.301**
  Shares and shareholders, post
  Termination, post
  Winding up, post
Numbers and numbering,
  Directors, **Bus Org 21.403**
  Shares and shareholders, post
Oaths and affirmations, interrogatories, answer, **Bus Org 12.002**
Objections and exceptions,
  Directors, meetings, **Bus Org 21.414**
  Meetings, **Bus Org 6.003**
    Notice, waiver, **Bus Org 6.053**
Offenses. Crimes and offenses, generally, ante

CORPORATIONS—Cont'd
Officers and employees, **Bus Org 3.101 et seq.**
  Agent for service of process, **Bus Org 5.255**
  Compensation and salaries, **Bus Org 2.101**
  Contracts, **Bus Org 21.101 et seq.**
  Damages, **Bus Org 7.001, 301.010**
    Application of law, **Bus Org 1.104**
  Directors, generally, ante
  Dual office holding, **Bus Org 3.103**
  Elections, **Bus Org 2.101, 3.103, 21.417**
  Good faith, **Bus Org 3.105**
  Indemnity, **Bus Org 2.101, 7.001, 8.001 et seq.**
  Licenses and permits, **Bus Org 301.006**
  Loans, **Bus Org 2.101**
  Removal, **Bus Org 3.104**
  Retirement and pensions, **Bus Org 2.101**
  Secretaries, elections, **Bus Org 21.417**
  Signatures, **Bus Org 20.001**
  Ultra vires, **Bus Org 20.002**
Offices, **Bus Org 2.101**
  Changes, filing, fines and penalties, **Bus Org 21.802**
  Registered offices, generally, post
  Reorganization, **Bus Org 10.301**
Omissions, certificate of formation, restatement, **Bus Org 3.059**
Open end investment companies, shares and shareholders, **Bus Org 21.651 et seq.**
Open records, interrogatories, **Bus Org 12.003**
Options, shares and shareholders, **Bus Org 21.168 et seq.**
Orders of court, receivers and receivership, **Bus Org 11.402**
  Liquidation, **Bus Org 11.405**
Organization, meetings, **Bus Org 21.059**
Outstanding shares, **Bus Org 21.171**
Panel, derivative actions, **Bus Org 21.554**
Papers. Books and papers, generally, ante
Par value, dividends, **Bus Org 21.312**
Par value shares, consideration, **Bus Org 21.161**
Parties, receivers and receivership, **Bus Org 11.411**
Payment,
  Derivative actions, expenses and expenditures, **Bus Org 21.561**
  Dividends, **Bus Org 21.310**
  Shares and shareholders, post
  Termination,
    Claims, **Bus Org 11.354**
    Taxation, **Bus Org 11.101**
Penalties. Fines and penalties, generally, ante
Permissive indemnification, **Bus Org 8.101 et seq.**
Personal property, **Bus Org 2.101**
  Disposition, **Bus Org 10.251 et seq.**
    Reorganization, **Bus Org 10.301**

CORPORATIONS—Cont'd
Personal property—Cont'd
  Shares and shareholders, **Bus Org 21.801**
Photography and pictures, consent, meetings, action without meeting, **Bus Org 6.205**
Plans and specifications,
  Conversion, **Bus Org 10.101 et seq.**
  Exchange of property, **Bus Org 10.051 et seq.**
  Merger and consolidation, **Bus Org 10.001 et seq.**
Pledges,
  Business combinations, **Bus Org 21.601 et seq.**
  Consent, **Bus Org 21.455, 21.461**
  Elections, **Bus Org 6.156**
Political subdivisions, service of process, **Bus Org 5.257**
Powers and duties, **Bus Org 2.101 et seq.**
  Close corporations,
    Custodian, **Bus Org 21.762**
    Directors, provisional directors, **Bus Org 21.759**
  Receivers and receivership, **Bus Org 11.406**
Preemption, shares and shareholders, damages, **Bus Org 21.224, 21.225**
Preemptive rights, shares and shareholders, **Bus Org 21.201 et seq.**
President,
  Agent for service of process, **Bus Org 5.255**
  Elections, **Bus Org 21.417**
Prior laws, Business Organizations Code, **Bus Org 401.001 et seq.**
Priorities and preferences,
  Business Organizations Code, application of law, **Bus Org 1.106**
  Certificate of formation, shares and shareholders, **Bus Org 3.007**
  Distribution and distributors, **Bus Org 21.308**
  Shares and shareholders, post
Privileges and immunities,
  Close corporations, shares and shareholders, **Bus Org 21.729**
  Property, disposition, **Bus Org 10.254**
  Registered agents, **Bus Org 5.208**
Probate Proceedings, this index
Proceedings. Actions and proceedings, generally, ante
Process. Service of process, generally, post
Professional Corporations, generally, this index
Profit sharing, officers and employees, **Bus Org 2.101**
Profits, contracts, **Bus Org 21.101 et seq.**
Property, **Bus Org 2.101**
  Certificate of formation, rights, **Bus Org 21.051**
  Definitions, **Bus Org 1.002**
  Exchange of property, generally, ante
  Liens and incumbrances,
    Foreclosure, **Bus Org 12.252 et seq.**

CORPORATIONS—Cont'd
Property—Cont'd
  Liens and incumbrances—Cont'd
    State, **Bus Org 12.201**
  Merger and consolidation, allocations, **Bus Org 10.003**
  Personal property, generally, ante
  Real estate, generally, post
Proxies, elections, **Bus Org 21.367 et seq.**
Publication, termination, involuntary termination, **Bus Org 11.310**
Purchases and purchasing,
  Indemnity, insurance, **Bus Org 8.151**
  Title to property, **Bus Org 301.008**
Purposes, **Bus Org 2.001 et seq.**
  Certificate of formation, **Bus Org 3.005**
Qualifications, directors, **Bus Org 21.402**
Quo warranto, insolvency, **Bus Org 12.253 et seq.**
Real estate, **Bus Org 2.101**
  Disposition, **Bus Org 10.251 et seq.**
    Reorganization, **Bus Org 10.301**
  Records and recordation, deeds and conveyances, **Bus Org 10.253**
  Sales, consent, **Bus Org 21.455**
Receipts, termination, claims, **Bus Org 11.352**
Receivers and receivership, **Bus Org 11.401 et seq.**
  Actions and proceedings, **Bus Org 11.406**
  Ancillary receiverships, **Bus Org 11.409**
  Appointments, **Bus Org 11.401 et seq.**
  Bonds (officers and fiduciaries), **Bus Org 11.406**
  Citizens and citizenship, **Bus Org 11.406**
  Claims, filing, **Bus Org 11.407**
  Close corporations, **Bus Org 21.757**
  Compensation and salaries, **Bus Org 11.408**
  Discharge, **Bus Org 11.412**
  Elections, **Bus Org 6.155**
  Filing, claims, **Bus Org 11.407**
  Foreign entities, **Bus Org 11.409, 11.410**
  Fraud, **Bus Org 11.403**
  Judgments and decrees, termination, **Bus Org 11.412**
  Jurisdiction, **Bus Org 11.402 et seq.**
  Liens and incumbrances, state, **Bus Org 12.201**
  Liquidation, **Bus Org 12.258**
    Orders of court, **Bus Org 11.405**
  Mortgages, **Bus Org 11.403**
  Notice, claims, **Bus Org 11.407**
  Orders of court, **Bus Org 11.402**
    Liquidation, **Bus Org 11.405**
  Parties, **Bus Org 11.411**
  Powers and duties, **Bus Org 11.406**
  Registration, **Bus Org 11.406**
  Rehabilitation, **Bus Org 11.404**
  State, **Bus Org 12.251**
  Termination, **Bus Org 11.403**
    Judgments and decrees, **Bus Org 11.412**
  Ultra vires, **Bus Org 20.002**

CORPORATIONS—Cont'd
Record date, **Bus Org 6.101 et seq.**
Shares and shareholders, meetings, notice, **Bus Org 21.357**
Records and recordation, **Bus Org 3.151 et seq.**
Attorney fees, ante
Certified copies, filing, **Bus Org 4.005**
Confidential or privileged information, **Bus Org 12.154**
Disclosure, **Bus Org 12.154**
Examinations and examiners, **Bus Org 3.153, 12.151 et seq.**
Fines and penalties, **Bus Org 21.222**
Fines and penalties, ante
Inspection and inspectors, **Bus Org 3.152**
Interrogatories, open records, **Bus Org 12.003**
Meetings, **Bus Org 6.002**
Notice, **Bus Org 1.005**
Real estate, deeds and conveyances, **Bus Org 10.253**
Record date, **Bus Org 6.101 et seq.**
Reorganization, **Bus Org 10.301**
Service of process, **Bus Org 5.254**
Shares and shareholders, post
Signatures, **Bus Org 1.007, 20.001**
Special purpose corporations, filing, **Bus Org 23.002**
Termination, removal, **Bus Org 11.104**
Time, record date, **Bus Org 6.101 et seq.**
Registered agent, **Bus Org 5.200 et seq.**
Changes, **Bus Org 5.202, 5.203**
Filing, fines and penalties, **Bus Org 21.802**
Reorganization, **Bus Org 10.301**
Resignation, **Bus Org 5.204**
Registered offices, **Bus Org 5.200 et seq.**
Changes, **Bus Org 5.202, 5.203**
Filing, fines and penalties, **Bus Org 21.802**
Registration,
Names, **Bus Org 5.151 et seq.**
Receivers and receivership, **Bus Org 11.406**
Rehabilitation, receivers and receivership, **Bus Org 11.404**
Reimbursement, disinterested persons, conflict of interest, **Bus Org 1.003**
Reinstatement,
Termination, post
Winding up, **Bus Org 21.501 et seq.**
Rejection, registered agents, **Bus Org 5.205**
Religious Organizations and Societies, generally, this index
Remand, termination, involuntary termination, **Bus Org 11.307**
Removal,
Close corporations, provisional directors, **Bus Org 21.758**
Directors, **Bus Org 21.409**
Officers and employees, **Bus Org 3.104**
Renewal, names,
Registration, **Bus Org 5.155**

CORPORATIONS—Cont'd
Renewal, names—Cont'd
Reservation, **Bus Org 5.105**
Reorganization, **Bus Org 10.301 et seq.**
Business Organizations Code, mandatory application date, **Bus Org 402.010**
Repeals,
Business Organizations Code, statutes, **Bus Org 1.054**
Bylaws, **Bus Org 21.057**
Shares and shareholders, **Bus Org 21.058**
Reports,
Financial statements and reports, generally, ante
Indemnity, **Bus Org 8.152**
Officers and employees, good faith, **Bus Org 3.102, 3.105**
Rescission, shares and shareholders, contracts, **Bus Org 21.105**
Reservation, names, **Bus Org 5.101 et seq.**
Reserves, surplus, **Bus Org 21.309**
Resignation,
Directors, notice, **Bus Org 21.4091**
Managers and management, **Bus Org 301.008**
Registered agent, **Bus Org 5.204**
Resolutions, indemnity, **Bus Org 8.103**
Restatement, certificate of formation, **Bus Org 3.057 et seq., 21.056**
Restraint of trade. Monopolies and Unfair Trade, generally, this index
Retirement and pensions, officers and employees, **Bus Org 2.101**
Review. Appeal and review, generally, ante
Revival. Abatement of actions and proceedings, generally, ante
Revocation or suspension,
Reinstatement, **Bus Org 402.013**
Termination, fraud, **Bus Org 11.153**
Winding up, **Bus Org 11.151, 21.501 et seq.**
Salaries. Compensation and salaries, generally, ante
Sales, **Bus Org 10.251 et seq.**
Assets, ante
Property, **Bus Org 2.101**
Reorganization, **Bus Org 10.301**
Securities, exemptions, **Bus Org 301.011**
Shares and shareholders, assets, **Bus Org 21.455**
Same or similar. Names, ante
Seals, **Bus Org 2.101**
Indebtedness, certificates and certification, **Bus Org 2.114**
Shares and shareholders, certificates and certification, **Bus Org 3.202**
Secretaries, elections, **Bus Org 21.417**
Secretary of state, agent for service of process, **Bus Org 5.251 et seq.**
Securities, **Bus Org 2.101**
Powers and duties, **Bus Org 2.104**
Sales, exemptions, **Bus Org 301.011**
Transfers, **Bus Org 21.209 et seq.**

CORPORATIONS—Cont'd
Sequestration, state, **Bus Org 12.259**
Series, shares and shareholders, **Bus Org 21.152 et seq.**
Service of process, **Bus Org 5.251 et seq.**
Reorganization, **Bus Org 10.301**
Termination, involuntary termination, **Bus Org 11.309**
Winding up, involuntary winding up, **Bus Org 11.309**
Shares and shareholders, **Bus Org 21.151 et seq.**
Abandonment, exchange of property, **Bus Org 10.201 et seq.**
Acceptance, exchange of property, certificates and certification, **Bus Org 10.156**
Actions and proceedings. Derivative actions, generally, ante
Amendments,
Bylaws, **Bus Org 21.058**
Certificate of formation, **Bus Org 21.054, 21.055**
Elections, **Bus Org 21.364**
Transfers, **Bus Org 21.212**
Appeal and review, derivative actions, **Bus Org 21.555**
Appointments, dissenting shareholders, appraisal and appraisers, **Bus Org 10.361**
Appraisals and appraisers,
Dissenting shareholders, **Bus Org 10.354 et seq.**
Fundamental business transactions, **Bus Org 21.460**
Assets, sales, **Bus Org 21.455**
Assignments,
Certificates and certification, **Bus Org 3.201**
Damages, **Bus Org 21.217**
Privileges and immunities, **Bus Org 21.226**
Attorney fees, derivative actions, payment, **Bus Org 21.561**
Beneficial owners, nominees, **Bus Org 21.201**
Books and papers, **Bus Org 21.173**
Dissenting shareholders, fair market value, **Bus Org 10.363**
Examinations and examiners, **Bus Org 21.218**
Business combinations, **Bus Org 21.601 et seq.**
Business Development Corporations, this index
Bylaws,
Amendments, **Bus Org 21.058**
Elections, proxies, **Bus Org 21.371**
Meetings,
Directors, elections, **Bus Org 21.359**
Quorum, **Bus Org 21.358**
Repeals, **Bus Org 21.058**
Transfers, **Bus Org 21.212**
Certificate of formation, **Bus Org 21.054 et seq., 21.055**

CORPORATIONS—Cont'd
Shares and shareholders—Cont'd
Certificate of formation—Cont'd
Amendments, elections, **Bus Org 21.364**
Elections, **Bus Org 21.363 et seq.**
Meetings,
Directors, elections, **Bus Org 21.359**
Quorum, **Bus Org 21.358**
Notice, electronic communications, **Bus Org 21.3531**
Numbers and numbering, **Bus Org 3.007**
Preemptive rights, **Bus Org 21.203**
Transfers, **Bus Org 21.212**
Certificates and certification, **Bus Org 3.201 et seq.**
Exchange of property, **Bus Org 10.151 et seq.**
Classification, **Bus Org 21.152**
Open end investment companies, **Bus Org 21.652, 21.653**
Priorities and preferences, **Bus Org 21.153**
Close corporations, ante
Closing, transfers, records and recordation, **Bus Org 21.355**
Combinations, **Bus Org 21.601 et seq.**
Commitment, **Bus Org 21.167**
Compensation and salaries, dissenting shareholders, appraisals and appraisers, **Bus Org 10.365**
Compromise and settlement, derivative actions, **Bus Org 21.560**
Computation, dissenting shareholders, fair market value, **Bus Org 10.362**
Consent,
Meetings, notice, electronic communications, **Bus Org 21.3531**
Record date, **Bus Org 21.356**
Conservators and conservatorship, privileges and immunities, **Bus Org 21.226**
Consideration, **Bus Org 21.157 et seq.**
Rights, options, **Bus Org 21.170**
Construction of laws, Business Organizations Code, statutes, **Bus Org 1.006**
Contracts, **Bus Org 21.101 et seq.**
Damages, **Bus Org 21.106, 21.107**
Disclosure, **Bus Org 21.103**
Effective date, **Bus Org 21.109**
Elections, **Bus Org 6.252**
Limitation of actions, rescission, **Bus Org 21.105**
Nonshareholders, **Bus Org 21.108**
Privileges and immunities, **Bus Org 21.223**
Rescission, **Bus Org 21.105**
Signatures, **Bus Org 21.101**
Time, **Bus Org 21.102, 21.109**
Transfers, **Bus Org 21.212**
Conversion, **Bus Org 21.154, 21.158 et seq.**
Appraisal and appraisers, **Bus Org 21.460**

CORPORATIONS—Cont'd
Shares and shareholders—Cont'd
Conversion—Cont'd
Elections, **Bus Org 21.457 et seq.**
Notice, meetings, **Bus Org 21.456**
Objections and exceptions, **Bus Org 21.460**
Plans and specifications, **Bus Org 21.451 et seq.**
Convertible, **Bus Org 21.154**
Indebtedness, **Bus Org 21.168 et seq.**
Costs, dissenting shareholders, appraisals and appraisers, **Bus Org 10.365**
Cumulative voting, **Bus Org 21.360 et seq.**
Damages,
Assignments, **Bus Org 21.217**
Contracts, **Bus Org 21.106, 21.107**
Joint tenants, death, **Bus Org 21.214**
Preemption, **Bus Org 21.224, 21.225**
Privileges and immunities, **Bus Org 21.223**
Title to property, **Bus Org 21.215**
Transfers, **Bus Org 21.217**
Death, joint tenants, **Bus Org 21.214**
Definitions, **Bus Org 1.002**
Preemptive rights, **Bus Org 21.202**
Delivery,
Certificates and certification, **Bus Org 3.204**
Meetings, action without meeting, **Bus Org 6.203**
Demand,
Derivative actions, **Bus Org 21.553**
Rejection, **Bus Org 21.559**
Dissenting shareholders, fair market value, **Bus Org 10.357 et seq.**
Deposits, redemption, **Bus Org 21.306**
Derivative actions, generally, ante
Directors,
Distribution and distributors, damages, **Bus Org 21.316**
Elections, **Bus Org 21.406**
Meetings, **Bus Org 21.359**
Meetings, elections, **Bus Org 21.359**
Disclosure, contracts, **Bus Org 21.103**
Discontinuance, derivative actions, **Bus Org 21.560**
Discovery, derivative actions, **Bus Org 21.556**
Dismissal and nonsuit, derivative actions, **Bus Org 21.558**
Disposition, preemptive rights, **Bus Org 21.207**
Dissenting shareholders, **Bus Org 10.351 et seq.**
Appointments, appraisal and appraisers, **Bus Org 10.361**
Appraisals and appraisers, **Bus Org 10.354 et seq.**
Books and papers, fair market value, **Bus Org 10.363**
Compensation and salaries, appraisals and appraisers, **Bus Org 10.365**
Computation, fair market value, **Bus Org 10.362**

CORPORATIONS—Cont'd
Shares and shareholders—Cont'd
Dissenting shareholders—Cont'd
Costs, appraisals and appraisers, **Bus Org 10.365**
Definitions, **Bus Org 10.352**
Demand, fair market value, **Bus Org 10.357 et seq.**
Exclusive remedy, **Bus Org 10.368**
Fair market value, demand, **Bus Org 10.357 et seq.**
Forms, **Bus Org 10.353**
Hearings, fair market value, **Bus Org 10.361**
Investigations and investigators, fair market value, **Bus Org 10.363**
Notice, **Bus Org 10.353, 10.355**
Objections and exceptions, appraisals and appraisers, **Bus Org 10.364**
Perfection, **Bus Org 10.356**
Petitions, fair market value, **Bus Org 10.361**
Records and recordation,
Demand, fair market value, **Bus Org 10.359**
Fair market value, **Bus Org 10.363**
Reorganization, **Bus Org 10.304**
Termination, **Bus Org 10.367**
Title to property, **Bus Org 10.366**
Withdrawal, **Bus Org 10.357**
Distribution and distributors, **Bus Org 21.301 et seq.**
Dividends, generally, ante
Record date, **Bus Org 6.101 et seq.**
Dividends, generally, ante
Duplicates and copies, certificates and certification, **Bus Org 3.202**
Effective date, contracts, **Bus Org 21.109**
Elections,
Amendments, certificate of formation, **Bus Org 21.364**
Bylaws, proxies, **Bus Org 21.371**
Certificate of formation, **Bus Org 21.363**
Amendments, **Bus Org 21.364**
Changes, **Bus Org 21.365**
Changes, **Bus Org 21.365**
Certificate of formation, **Bus Org 21.365**
Contracts, **Bus Org 6.252**
Cumulative voting, **Bus Org 21.360 et seq.**
Derivative actions, **Bus Org 21.554**
Directors, **Bus Org 21.405, 21.406**
Cumulative voting, **Bus Org 21.361**
Fundamental business transactions, **Bus Org 21.457 et seq.**
Grandfather rights, cumulative voting, **Bus Org 21.362**
Inspection and inspectors, lists, **Bus Org 21.354**
Irrevocable proxies, **Bus Org 21.370**
Limitations, **Bus Org 21.153**
Lists, **Bus Org 21.354**
Fines and penalties, **Bus Org 21.220**

CORPORATIONS—Cont'd
Shares and shareholders—Cont'd
Elections—Cont'd
Lists—Cont'd
Meetings, **Bus Org 21.372**
Meetings, **Bus Org 21.354 et seq.**
Numbers and numbering, **Bus Org 21.366**
Proxies, **Bus Org 21.367 et seq.**
Revocation or suspension, proxies, **Bus Org 21.369**
Termination, reinstatement, **Bus Org 21.364**
Time, proxies, **Bus Org 21.368**
Trusts and trustees, **Bus Org 6.251**
Winding up, **Bus Org 21.364**
Electricity, **Util 181.003**
Electronic communications, notice, **Bus Org 21.3531**
Evidence,
Certificates and certification, **Bus Org 3.201**
Derivative actions,
Discovery, **Bus Org 21.556**
Dismissal and nonsuit, **Bus Org 21.558**
Notice, electronic communications, **Bus Org 21.3531**
Examinations and examiners,
Books and papers, **Bus Org 21.218**
Elections, contracts, **Bus Org 6.252**
Records and recordation, fines and penalties, **Bus Org 21.222**
Exchange of property, **Bus Org 10.051 et seq., 21.154**
Abandonment, **Bus Org 10.201 et seq.**
Acceptance, certificates and certification, **Bus Org 10.156**
Appraisal and appraisers, **Bus Org 21.460**
Certificates and certification, **Bus Org 10.151 et seq.**
Elections, **Bus Org 21.457 et seq.**
Filing, certificates and certification, **Bus Org 10.153**
Notice, meetings, **Bus Org 21.456**
Objections and exceptions, **Bus Org 21.460**
Plans and specifications, **Bus Org 21.451 et seq.**
Exclusive remedy, dissenting shareholders, **Bus Org 10.368**
Expenses and expenditures,
Derivative actions, payment, **Bus Org 21.561**
Payment, **Bus Org 21.172**
Facsimile,
Certificates and certification, **Bus Org 3.203**
Notice, **Bus Org 21.3531**
Fair market value, dissenting shareholders, demand, **Bus Org 10.357 et seq.**

CORPORATIONS—Cont'd
Shares and shareholders—Cont'd
Filing,
Exchange of property, certificates and certification, **Bus Org 10.153**
Fees, **Bus Org 4.152**
Fines and penalties,
Elections, lists, **Bus Org 21.220**
Meetings, notice, **Bus Org 21.221**
Records and recordation, examinations and examiners, **Bus Org 21.222**
Foreign Corporations, this index
Forms,
Certificates and certification, **Bus Org 3.202**
Dissenting shareholders, **Bus Org 10.353**
Fractional shares, **Bus Org 21.163, 21.164**
Fraud, privileges and immunities, **Bus Org 21.223**
Fundamental business transactions, **Bus Org 21.451 et seq.**
Grandfather rights, elections, cumulative voting, **Bus Org 21.362**
Guardian and Ward, this index
Hearings, dissenting shareholders, fair market value, **Bus Org 10.361**
Indebtedness,
Convertible indebtedness, **Bus Org 21.168 et seq.**
Privileges and immunities, **Bus Org 21.223**
Inspection and inspectors, elections, lists, **Bus Org 21.354**
Investigations and investigators, dissenting shareholders, fair market value, **Bus Org 10.363**
Investments, open end investment companies, **Bus Org 21.651 et seq.**
Irrevocable proxies, elections, **Bus Org 21.370**
Joint tenants, **Bus Org 21.214**
Limitation of actions,
Contracts, rescission, **Bus Org 21.105**
Derivative actions, tolling, **Bus Org 21.557**
Distribution and distributors, **Bus Org 21.317**
Preemptive rights, **Bus Org 21.206**
Limitations,
Distribution and distributors, **Bus Org 21.303**
Transfers, **Bus Org 21.213**
Lists, elections, **Bus Org 21.354**
Meetings, **Bus Org 21.372**
Mail and mailing, statements, **Bus Org 21.219**
Managers and management, winding up, **Bus Org 21.504**
Meetings, **Bus Org 21.351 et seq.**
Action without meeting, **Bus Org 6.102**
Consent, **Bus Org 6.201 et seq.**

CORPORATIONS—Cont'd
Shares and shareholders—Cont'd
Meetings—Cont'd
Bylaws,
Directors, elections, **Bus Org 21.359**
Quorum, **Bus Org 21.358**
Certificate of formation,
Directors, elections, **Bus Org 21.359**
Quorum, **Bus Org 21.358**
Consent, action without meeting, **Bus Org 6.102, 6.201 et seq.**
Delivery, action without meeting, **Bus Org 6.203**
Directors, elections, **Bus Org 21.359, 21.405**
Elections, **Bus Org 21.354 et seq.**
Electronic communications, notice, **Bus Org 21.3531**
Lists, elections, **Bus Org 21.372**
Notice, **Bus Org 21.353**
Action without meeting, **Bus Org 6.204**
Electronic communications, **Bus Org 21.3531**
Fines and penalties, **Bus Org 21.221**
Record date, **Bus Org 21.357**
Open end investment companies, **Bus Org 21.655**
Quorum, **Bus Org 21.358**
Record date, notice, **Bus Org 21.357**
Special meetings, **Bus Org 21.352**
Time, **Bus Org 21.351**
Notice, **Bus Org 21.353**
Winding up, **Bus Org 21.502, 21.503**
Merger and consolidation, **Bus Org 21.158 et seq.**
Appraisal and appraisers, **Bus Org 21.460**
Elections, **Bus Org 21.457 et seq.**
Notice, meetings, **Bus Org 21.456**
Objections and exceptions, **Bus Org 21.460**
Plans and specifications, **Bus Org 21.451 et seq.**
Nominees, title to property, **Bus Org 21.201**
Notice,
Dissenting shareholders, **Bus Org 10.353, 10.355**
Electronic communications, **Bus Org 21.3531**
Facsimile, **Bus Org 21.3531**
Fundamental business transactions, meetings, **Bus Org 21.456**
Meetings, **Bus Org 21.353**
Action without meeting, **Bus Org 6.204**
Fines and penalties, **Bus Org 21.221**
Redemption, **Bus Org 21.305**
Subscriptions, **Bus Org 21.165**
Uncertificated shares, **Bus Org 3.205**
Winding up, meetings, **Bus Org 21.503**

CORPORATIONS—Cont'd
Shares and shareholders—Cont'd
Numbers and numbering, **Bus Org 21.151**
Elections, **Bus Org 21.366**
Open end investment companies, **Bus Org 21.652**
Objections and exceptions,
Dissenting shareholders, appraisals and appraisers, **Bus Org 10.364**
Fundamental business transactions, **Bus Org 21.460**
Open end investment companies, **Bus Org 21.651 et seq.**
Options, **Bus Org 21.168 et seq.**
Outstanding shares, **Bus Org 21.171**
Panel, derivative actions, **Bus Org 21.554**
Par value shares, consideration, **Bus Org 21.161**
Payment,
Derivative actions, expenses and expenditures, **Bus Org 21.561**
Expenses and expenditures, **Bus Org 21.172**
Redemption, **Bus Org 21.307**
Subscriptions, preformation, **Bus Org 21.166**
Perfection, dissenting shareholders, **Bus Org 10.356**
Personal property, **Bus Org 21.801**
Petitions, dissenting shareholders, fair market value, **Bus Org 10.361**
Pledges, privileges and immunities, **Bus Org 21.226**
Preemption, damages, **Bus Org 21.224, 21.225**
Preemptive rights, **Bus Org 21.201 et seq.**
Preformation, subscriptions, **Bus Org 21.166**
Priorities and preferences, **Bus Org 21.153, 21.154**
Distribution and distributors, **Bus Org 21.308**
Privileges and immunities, **Bus Org 21.223**
Probate Proceedings, this index
Proxies, elections, **Bus Org 21.367 et seq.**
Purchases and purchasing, contracts, rescission, **Bus Org 21.105**
Quorum, meetings, **Bus Org 21.358**
Real Estate Investment Trusts, this index
Record date, **Bus Org 6.101 et seq.**
Consent, **Bus Org 21.356**
Meetings, notice, **Bus Org 21.357**
Records and recordation, **Bus Org 21.173**
Dissenting shareholders, fair market value, **Bus Org 10.363**
Demand, **Bus Org 10.359**
Examinations and examiners, **Bus Org 21.218**
Fines and penalties, **Bus Org 21.222**

CORPORATIONS—Cont'd
Shares and shareholders—Cont'd
Records and recordation—Cont'd
Transfers, closing, **Bus Org 21.355**
Redemption, **Bus Org 21.154, 21.304 et seq.**
Registration, title to property, **Bus Org 21.201**
Reinstatement, termination, elections, **Bus Org 21.364**
Rejection, derivative actions, demand, **Bus Org 21.559**
Reorganization, dissenting shareholders, **Bus Org 10.304**
Repeals, bylaws, **Bus Org 21.058**
Rescission, contracts, **Bus Org 21.105**
Revocation or suspension, elections, proxies, **Bus Org 21.369**
Rights, **Bus Org 21.168 et seq.**
Preemptive rights, **Bus Org 21.201 et seq.**
Sales, assets, **Bus Org 21.455**
Scrip, **Bus Org 21.163, 21.164**
Seals, certificates and certification, **Bus Org 3.202**
Securities, generally, this index
Series, **Bus Org 21.152 et seq.**
Signatures,
Certificates and certification, **Bus Org 3.203**
Commitment, **Bus Org 21.167**
Contracts, **Bus Org 21.101**
Subscriptions, **Bus Org 21.165**
Special meetings, **Bus Org 21.352**
Standing, derivative actions, **Bus Org 21.552**
Statements,
Mail and mailing, **Bus Org 21.219**
Open end investment companies, **Bus Org 21.653**
Series, **Bus Org 21.156**
Statutes, Business Organizations Code, construction of laws, **Bus Org 1.006**
Subscriptions, **Bus Org 21.165**
Preformation, **Bus Org 21.166**
Privileges and immunities, **Bus Org 21.223**
Supersedeas or stay, derivative actions, **Bus Org 21.555**
Telecommunications, merger and consolidation, **Util 181.088**
Termination,
Derivative actions, costs, payment, **Bus Org 21.561**
Dissenting shareholders, **Bus Org 10.367**
Elections, reinstatement, **Bus Org 21.364**
Time,
Contracts, **Bus Org 21.102, 21.109**
Elections, proxies, **Bus Org 21.368**
Meetings, **Bus Org 21.351**
Notice, **Bus Org 21.353**
Record date, **Bus Org 6.101 et seq.**
Title to property,
Damages, **Bus Org 21.215**

CORPORATIONS—Cont'd
Shares and shareholders—Cont'd
Title to property—Cont'd
Dissenting shareholders, **Bus Org 10.366**
Registration, **Bus Org 21.201**
Tolling, derivative actions, limitation of actions, **Bus Org 21.557**
Transfers, **Bus Org 21.209 et seq.**
Certificates and certification, **Bus Org 3.201**
Records and recordation, closing, **Bus Org 21.355**
Treasury shares, **Bus Org 21.171**
Cancellation, **Bus Org 21.252**
Definitions, **Bus Org 21.002**
Disposition, **Bus Org 21.160**
Preemptive rights, **Bus Org 21.204, 21.208**
Trusts and trustees,
Elections, **Bus Org 6.251**
Privileges and immunities, **Bus Org 21.226**
Ultra vires, **Bus Org 20.002**
Uncertificated shares, **Bus Org 3.201**
Notice, **Bus Org 3.205**
Unissued shares, **Bus Org 21.155**
Preemptive rights, **Bus Org 21.204, 21.208**
Value, consideration, **Bus Org 21.162**
Waiver, preemptive rights, **Bus Org 21.205**
Winding up,
Elections, **Bus Org 21.364**
Meetings, **Bus Org 21.502, 21.503**
Withdrawal, dissenting shareholders, **Bus Org 10.357**
Signatures, **Bus Org 1.007**
Certificate of formation, ante
Close corporations, ante
Definitions, business organizations, **Bus Org 1.002**
Filing, **Bus Org 4.001, 20.001**
Corrections, certificates and certification, **Bus Org 4.101**
Indebtedness, certificates and certification, **Bus Org 2.114**
Reorganization, **Bus Org 10.302**
Shares and shareholders, ante
Small Businesses, generally, this index
Special purpose corporations, **Bus Org 23.001 et seq.**
Standing, derivative actions, **Bus Org 21.552**
State,
Liens and incumbrances, **Bus Org 12.201**
Receivers and receivership, **Bus Org 12.251**
Stated capital,
Computation, reduction, **Bus Org 21.254**
Definitions, **Bus Org 21.002**
Elections, reduction, **Bus Org 21.253**
Insolvency, **Bus Org 21.314**
Time, **Bus Org 21.315**
Reduction, **Bus Org 21.251 et seq.**

CORPORATIONS—Cont'd
Stated capital—Cont'd
Reduction—Cont'd
Computation, **Bus Org 21.254**
Elections, **Bus Org 21.253**
Treasury shares, cancellation, **Bus Org 21.252**
Statements,
Certificate of formation, ante
Close corporations, ante
Financial statements and reports, generally, ante
Officers and employees, good faith, **Bus Org 3.102, 3.105**
Open end investment companies, **Bus Org 21.653**
Shares and shareholders, ante
Termination, claims, **Bus Org 11.352**
Statute of limitations. Limitation of actions, generally, ante
Stock. Shares and shareholders, generally, ante
Subscriptions. Shares and shareholders, ante
Subsidiaries,
Business combinations, **Bus Org 21.601 et seq.**
Merger and consolidation, **Bus Org 10.006**
Certificates and certification, **Bus Org 10.152**
Supersedeas or stay,
Derivative actions, **Bus Org 21.555**
Termination, involuntary termination, **Bus Org 11.306**
Winding up, involuntary winding up, **Bus Org 11.306**
Supervision, winding up, **Bus Org 11.054**
Surplus,
Dividends, transfers, **Bus Org 21.313**
Insolvency, **Bus Org 21.314**
Time, **Bus Org 21.315**
Reserves, **Bus Org 21.309**
Suspension. Revocation or suspension, generally, ante
Taxation,
Service of process, **Bus Org 5.257**
Termination,
Forfeitures, reinstatement, **Bus Org 11.254, 402.013**
Payment, **Bus Org 11.101**
Telecommunications, meetings, **Bus Org 6.002**
Telephone Cooperative Corporations, generally, this index
Termination, **Bus Org 11.001 et seq.**
Abatement of actions and proceedings, involuntary termination, **Bus Org 11.304**
Actions and proceedings, involuntary termination, **Bus Org 11.303**
Appeal and review, involuntary termination, **Bus Org 11.307**
Business Organizations Code, mandatory application date, **Bus Org 402.011**

CORPORATIONS—Cont'd
Termination—Cont'd
Certificates and certification, **Bus Org 11.101 et seq.**
Involuntary termination, **Bus Org 11.252**
Reinstatement, **Bus Org 11.202**
Certified copies, involuntary termination, judgments and decrees, **Bus Org 11.414**
Claims, **Bus Org 11.351 et seq.**
Close corporations, ante
Contracts, **Bus Org 21.101 et seq.**
Crimes and offenses, involuntary termination, **Bus Org 11.301 et seq.**
Deposits, claims, **Bus Org 11.352**
Derivative actions, costs, payment, **Bus Org 21.561**
Discharge, claims, **Bus Org 11.353**
Effective date, **Bus Org 11.102, 11.103**
Claims, **Bus Org 11.356 et seq.**
Reinstatement, **Bus Org 11.204 et seq.**
Errors, reinstatement, **Bus Org 11.201 et seq.**
Escheat, claims, **Bus Org 11.355**
Exemptions, involuntary termination, **Bus Org 11.251**
Filing,
Fees, **Bus Org 4.152**
Fines and penalties, **Bus Org 21.802**
Involuntary termination, **Bus Org 11.315**
Fraud,
Involuntary termination, **Bus Org 11.301 et seq.**
Revocation or suspension, **Bus Org 11.153**
Involuntary termination, **Bus Org 11.251 et seq., 11.301 et seq.**
Certified copies, judgments and decrees, **Bus Org 11.414**
Judgments and decrees, **Bus Org 11.301 et seq.**
Involuntary termination, certified copies, **Bus Org 11.414**
Jurisdiction, involuntary termination, **Bus Org 11.308**
Limitation of actions, claims, **Bus Org 11.359**
Names, reinstatement, **Bus Org 11.203**
Notice,
Claims, **Bus Org 11.358**
Escheat, claims, **Bus Org 11.355**
Involuntary termination, **Bus Org 11.251, 11.302, 11.310**
Payment,
Claims, **Bus Org 11.354**
Taxation, **Bus Org 11.101**
Publication, involuntary termination, **Bus Org 11.310**
Receipts, claims, **Bus Org 11.352**
Receivers and receivership, **Bus Org 11.403**
Judgments and decrees, **Bus Org 11.412**

CORPORATIONS—Cont'd
Termination—Cont'd
Records and recordation, removal, **Bus Org 11.104**
Reinstatement, **Bus Org 11.201 et seq.**
Involuntary termination, **Bus Org 11.253**
Shares and shareholders, elections, **Bus Org 21.364**
Taxation, forfeitures, **Bus Org 11.254**
Remand, involuntary termination, **Bus Org 11.307**
Revocation or suspension, fraud, **Bus Org 11.153**
Service of process, involuntary termination, **Bus Org 11.309**
Shares and shareholders, ante
Statements, claims, **Bus Org 11.352**
Supersedeas or stay, involuntary termination, **Bus Org 11.306**
Taxation,
Forfeitures, reinstatement, **Bus Org 11.254**
Payment, **Bus Org 11.101**
Time,
Involuntary termination, **Bus Org 11.305, 11.313**
Reinstatement, **Bus Org 11.202**
Ultra vires, **Bus Org 20.002**
Venue, involuntary termination, **Bus Org 11.308**
Terms of office. Directors, ante
Time,
Business combinations, moratorium, **Bus Org 21.606, 21.607**
Business Organizations Code, effective date, **Bus Org 402.001**
Adoption, **Bus Org 402.005**
Certificate of formation, ante
Close corporations, termination, **Bus Org 21.709**
Exchange of property, **Bus Org 10.054, 10.055**
Filing, ante
Insolvency, determination, **Bus Org 21.315**
Interrogatories, answer, **Bus Org 12.002**
Meetings, organization, **Bus Org 21.059**
Merger and consolidation, effective date, **Bus Org 10.007**
Record date, **Bus Org 6.101 et seq.**
Service of process, **Bus Org 5.254**
Shares and shareholders, ante
Termination, ante
Winding up, post
Title to property, **Bus Org 301.007 et seq.**
Shares and shareholders, ante
Tolling, derivative actions, limitation of actions, **Bus Org 21.557**
Trademarks and trade names, **Bus Org 5.001**
Transfers,
Business combinations, **Bus Org 21.601 et seq.**
Close corporations, ante
Consent, **Bus Org 21.455**
Dividends, surplus, **Bus Org 21.313**

CORPORATIONS—Cont'd
Transfers—Cont'd
Names, reservation, **Bus Org 5.106**
Property, **Bus Org 10.251 et seq.**
Shares and shareholders, ante
Title to property, **Bus Org 301.009**
Transition, Business Organizations Code, **Bus Org 402.001 et seq.**
Treasury shares. Shares and shareholders, ante
Trusts and monopolies. Monopolies and Unfair Trade, generally, this index
Trusts and trustees,
Elections, **Bus Org 6.154, 6.251**
Reorganization, **Bus Org 10.301 et seq.**
Shares and shareholders, ante
Ultra vires, **Bus Org 20.002**
Ultra vires, **Bus Org 20.002**
Uncertificated shares. Shares and shareholders, ante
Underground facility notification corporation, **Util 251.051 et seq.**
Vacancies in office, directors, **Bus Org 21.410**
Venue,
Close corporations, actions and proceedings, **Bus Org 21.752**
Termination, involuntary termination, **Bus Org 11.308**
Winding up, involuntary winding up, **Bus Org 11.308**
Veterans organizations, names, **Bus Org 5.062**
Vice president, agent for service of process, **Bus Org 5.255**
Video recordings, meetings, **Bus Org 6.002**
Waiver,
Directors, meetings, notice, **Bus Org 21.412**
Meetings, notice, **Bus Org 6.052**
Objections and exceptions, **Bus Org 6.053**
Winding up, **Bus Org 11.001 et seq., 11.051 et seq., 21.501 et seq.**
Abatement of actions and proceedings, involuntary winding up, **Bus Org 11.304**
Actions and proceedings, **Bus Org 11.052, 11.055**
Involuntary winding up, **Bus Org 11.303**
Appeal and review, involuntary winding up, **Bus Org 11.307**
Assets, distribution and distributors, **Bus Org 11.053**
Business Organizations Code, mandatory application date, **Bus Org 402.011**
Bylaws, **Bus Org 11.059**
Cancellation, **Bus Org 11.152**
Certificate of formation, **Bus Org 11.059**
Close corporations, **Bus Org 21.757**
Contracts, **Bus Org 11.152, 21.101 et seq.**

CORPORATIONS—Cont'd
Winding up—Cont'd
Crimes and offenses, involuntary winding up, **Bus Org 11.301 et seq.**
Discharge, indebtedness, **Bus Org 11.053**
Distribution and distributors, assets, **Bus Org 11.053**
Filing, involuntary winding up, **Bus Org 11.315**
Fraud, involuntary winding up, **Bus Org 11.301 et seq.**
Indebtedness, discharge, **Bus Org 11.053**
Involuntary winding up, **Bus Org 11.301 et seq.**
Judgments and decrees, **Bus Org 11.301 et seq.**
Jurisdiction, involuntary winding up, **Bus Org 11.308**
Managers and management, **Bus Org 21.504**
Meetings, **Bus Org 21.502, 21.503**
Notice, **Bus Org 11.052**
Involuntary winding up, **Bus Org 11.302, 11.310**
Meetings, **Bus Org 21.503**
Publication, involuntary winding up, **Bus Org 11.310**
Remand, involuntary winding up, **Bus Org 11.307**
Revocation or suspension, **Bus Org 11.151**
Service of process, involuntary winding up, **Bus Org 11.309**
Shares and shareholders, ante
Supersedeas or stay, involuntary winding up, **Bus Org 11.306**
Supervision, **Bus Org 11.054**
Time, **Bus Org 11.056**
Cancellation, **Bus Org 11.152**
Involuntary winding up, **Bus Org 11.305, 11.313**
Venue, involuntary winding up, **Bus Org 11.308**
Withdrawal,
Filing, fines and penalties, **Bus Org 21.802**
Names, reservation, fees, **Bus Org 5.1041**
Witnesses, indemnity, expenses and expenditures, **Bus Org 8.106**
Writings,
Definitions, business organizations, **Bus Org 1.002**
Powers and duties, **Bus Org 2.112**
Signatures, **Bus Org 1.007**

COSTS
Apartment houses, central system utilities, recovery, **Util 184.071**
Assumed or fictitious names, actions and proceedings, business and commerce, professions and occupations, **Bus & C 71.201**
Attorney Fees, generally, this index
Cooperative Associations, this index

COSTS—Cont'd
Corporations, this index
Eminent Domain, this index
Foreign Corporations, this index
Limited Liability Companies, this index
Limited partnerships. Partnerships, this index
Nonprofit Corporations, this index
Partnerships, this index
Professional Associations and Societies, this index
Professional Corporations, this index
Public utilities, appeal and review, rates, **Util 15.003**
Railroads, this index

COUNSEL
Attorneys, generally, this index

COUNSELORS AND COUNSELING
Definitions,
Gas utilities, **Util 101.003**
Public utilities, **Util 11.003**

COUNTIES
Cable television, highways and roads, easements, notice, **Util 181.103**
Elections, generally, this index
Electricity, highways and roads, easements, notice, **Util 181.044**
Gas utilities, highways and roads, easements, notice, **Util 181.024**
Municipalities, generally, this index
Nine One One (911), generally, this index

COUNTY COMMUNITY COLLEGES
Community colleges and districts. Colleges and Universities, this index

COUNTY COURTS
Garnishment, generally, this index

COURT OF APPEAL
Courts of Appeals, generally, this index

COURT OF CRIMINAL APPEALS
Audits and auditors, nonprofit corporations, **Bus Org 22.356**
Books and papers, nonprofit corporations, audits and auditors, **Bus Org 22.356**
Nonprofit corporations, audits and auditors, **Bus Org 22.356**
Records and recordation, nonprofit corporations, audits and auditors, **Bus Org 22.356**

COURT ORDERS
Orders of Court, generally, this index

COURTS
Actions and Proceedings, generally, this index
Appeals. Courts of Appeals, generally, this index
Audits and auditors, nonprofit corporations, **Bus Org 22.356**
Books and papers, nonprofit corporations, audits and auditors, **Bus Org 22.356**
Costs, generally, this index

COURTS—Cont'd
Court of Criminal Appeals, generally, this index
Courts of Appeals, generally, this index
Definitions, close corporations, actions and proceedings, **Bus Org 21.751**
Nonprofit corporations, audits and auditors, **Bus Org 22.356**
Orders of Court, generally, this index
Records and recordation, nonprofit corporations, audits and auditors, **Bus Org 22.356**
Supreme Court, generally, this index

COURTS OF APPEALS
Audits and auditors, nonprofit corporations, **Bus Org 22.356**
Books and papers, nonprofit corporations, audits and auditors, **Bus Org 22.356**
Nonprofit corporations, audits and auditors, **Bus Org 22.356**
Records and recordation, nonprofit corporations, audits and auditors, **Bus Org 22.356**

CREDIT
Interest, generally, this index

CREDIT CARDS
Telecommunications, this index

CREDIT HISTORY
Definitions, public utilities, payment, **Util 17.008**

CREDIT REPORTS
Telecommunications, this index

CREDIT SCORE
Definitions, public utilities, payment, **Util 17.008**

CREDIT UNIONS
Conduct, damages, **Bus Org 7.001**
Damages, officers and employees, **Bus Org 7.001**
Directors, damages, **Bus Org 7.001**
Indemnity, damages, **Bus Org 7.001**
Misconduct, damages, **Bus Org 7.001**
Officers and employees, damages, **Bus Org 7.001**

CREDITORS
Indebtedness, generally, this index

CRIMES AND OFFENSES
Appeal and review. Court of Criminal Appeals, generally, this index
Assumed or Fictitious Names, this index
Conversion, generally, this index
Cooperative Associations, this index
Corporations, this index
Costs, generally, this index
Court of Criminal Appeals, generally, this index
Criminal appeals court. Court of Criminal Appeals, generally, this index
Discrimination, generally, this index
Electricity, this index

CRIMES AND OFFENSES—Cont'd
Foreign Corporations, this index
Gas Utilities, this index
Limited Liability Companies, this index
Limited partnerships. Partnerships, this index
Monopolies and Unfair Trade, generally, this index
Nonprofit Corporations, this index
Oil and Gas, this index
Partnerships, this index
Professional Associations and Societies, this index
Professional Corporations, this index
Public Utilities, this index
Restraint of trade. Monopolies and Unfair Trade, generally, this index
Sewers and Sewer Systems, this index
Stay of proceedings. Supersedeas or Stay, generally, this index
Supersedeas or Stay, generally, this index
Telecommunications, this index
Water Supply, this index

CRIMINAL APPEALS COURT
Court of Criminal Appeals, generally, this index

CULTURAL CORPORATIONS
Nonprofit Corporations, generally, this index

CURRENCY
Money, generally, this index

CUSTODIAL CARE HOMES
Nursing and Convalescent Homes, generally, this index

CUSTOMERS
Definitions,
  Electricity, deceptive trade practices and consumer protection, **Util 17.002**
  Telecommunications, deceptive trade practices and consumer protection, **Util 17.002, 64.002**

DAMAGES
Banks and Banking, this index
Churches, retirement and pensions, indemnity, **Bus Org 22.406**
Cooperative Associations, this index
Corporations, this index
Definitions, underground facilities, excavations, **Util 251.001**
Eminent Domain, this index
Foreign Corporations, this index
Limited Liability Companies, this index
Limited partnerships. Partnerships, this index
Nonprofit Corporations, this index
Oil and Gas, this index
Partnerships, this index
Professional Associations and Societies, this index
Professional Corporations, this index
Public Utilities, this index

DAMAGES—Cont'd
Railroads, this index
Real estate investment trusts, managers and management, **Bus Org 200.312 et seq.**
Religious organizations and societies, retirement and pensions, indemnity, **Bus Org 22.406**
Sewers and Sewer Systems, this index
Telecommunications, this index
Underground Natural Gas, this index
Water Supply, this index

DAMS AND RESERVOIRS
Water Supply, generally, this index

DEATH
Limited liability companies, members, **Bus Org 101.1115**
Limited partnerships. Partnerships, this index
Partnerships, this index
Real estate investment trusts, shares and shareholders, joint tenants, **Bus Org 200.158**

DEBENTURES
Bonds, generally, this index

DEBT
Indebtedness, generally, this index

DEBTORS AND CREDITORS
Bankruptcy, generally, this index
Indebtedness, generally, this index

DEBTS
Indebtedness, generally, this index

DECEDENTS ESTATES
Probate Proceedings, generally, this index

DECEPTIVE TRADE PRACTICES
Electricity, this index
Telecommunications, this index

DECOMMISSIONING
Definitions, atomic energy, costs, **Util 39.206**

DEEDS AND CONVEYANCES
Business development corporations, **Bus Org 23.054**
Corporations, this index
Deeds of Trust, generally, this index
Electricity, private and public entities, cooperation, **Util 163.013**
Foreign Corporations, this index
Limited Liability Companies, this index
Limited partnerships. Partnerships, this index
Nonprofit Corporations, this index
Partnerships, this index
Real estate investment trusts, **Bus Org 200.405 et seq.**
Trust deeds. Deeds of Trust, generally, this index

DEEDS OF TRUST
Business development corporations, **Bus Org 23.054**
Telephone cooperative corporations, **Util 162.125, 162.126**

DEFINITIONS
Words and Phrases, generally, this index

DENTISTS AND DENTISTRY
Associations and societies. Professional Associations and Societies, generally, this index
Certificate of formation, health service corporations, **Bus Org 22.052**
Charitable corporations, health service corporations, **Bus Org 22.052**
Directors, health service corporations, **Bus Org 22.052**
Filing, health service corporations, **Bus Org 22.052**
Health service corporations, nonprofit corporations, **Bus Org 22.052**
Nonprofit corporations, health service corporations, **Bus Org 22.052**
Numbers and numbering, health service corporations, directors, **Bus Org 22.052**
Professional Associations and Societies, generally, this index
Telemedicine, generally, this index

DEPARTMENT
Definitions, telecommunications, universal services, **Util 56.001**
State Departments, generally, this index

DEPLETION
Electricity, computation of rates, **Util 36.056**
Gas utilities, computation of rates, **Util 104.054**
Telecommunications, computation of rates, **Util 53.056**

DEPOSITS
Business development corporations, funds, **Bus Org 23.070**
Electricity, this index
Gas utilities, customers, **Util 183.001 et seq.**
Public utilities, customers, **Util 183.001 et seq.**
Telecommunications, this index
Water Supply, this index

DEPRECIATION
Electricity, this index
Gas Utilities, this index
Telecommunications, this index

DERIVATIVE ACTIONS
Corporations, this index
Foreign Corporations, this index
Limited Liability Companies, this index
Limited partnerships. Partnerships, this index

DESIGNS
Telecommunications, statewide relay access service, hearing and speech impaired persons, **Util 56.105**

DEVISES AND DEVISEES
Gifts, generally, this index

DIRECTORIES
Internet, telecommunications, **Util 55.204**
Telecommunications, this index

DIRECTORS
Banks and Banking, this index
Cooperative Associations, this index
Corporations, this index
Credit Unions, this index
Definitions,
  Business organizations, **Bus Org 1.002**
  Electric cooperative corporations, competition, **Util 41.002**
Electric Cooperative Corporations, this index
Electricity, municipal power agencies, **Util 163.059**
Foreign Corporations, this index
Limited Liability Companies, this index
Limited partnerships. Partnerships, this index
Nonprofit Corporations, this index
Partnerships, this index
Professional Associations and Societies, this index
Professional Corporations, this index
Public utilities, commission, adverse or pecuniary interest, commissioners and employees, **Util 12.152, 12.154**
Sewers and Sewer Systems, this index
Telephone Cooperative Corporations, this index
Water Supply, this index

DISADVANTAGED BUSINESSES
Historically Underutilized Businesses, generally, this index

DISASTERS
Electricity,
  Restoration, bonds, **Util 36.401 et seq.**
  Sales, **Util 38.073**

DISCHARGE
Cooperative Associations, this index
Corporations, this index
Foreign Corporations, this index
Limited Liability Companies, this index
Limited partnerships. Partnerships, this index
Nonprofit Corporations, this index
Partnerships, this index
Professional Associations and Societies, this index
Professional Corporations, this index

DISCLOSURE
Business development corporations, information, **Bus Org 23.071**
Electricity, this index

DISCLOSURE—Cont'd
Partnerships, this index
Telecommunications, this index

DISCOUNTS
Electricity, this index
Telecommunications, this index

DISCOVERY
Gas utilities, consumer representation, **Util 101.052**

DISCRIMINATION
Cable television, franchises, municipalities, **Util 66.010, 66.014**
Electric cooperative corporations, customer choice, **Util 41.056**
Electricity, this index
Gas Utilities, this index
Municipalities, this index
Public Utilities, this index
Telecommunications, this index
Television and radio, franchises, municipalities, **Util 66.010, 66.014**

DISMISSAL AND NONSUIT
Corporations, this index
Foreign Corporations, this index
Limited Liability Companies, this index
Limited partnerships. Partnerships, this index
Nonprofit Corporations, this index
Partnerships, this index

DISPUTES
Labor Disputes, generally, this index

DISSENTING SHAREHOLDERS
Shares and shareholders. Corporations, this index

DISSOLUTION
Corporations, this index
Electric cooperative corporations, **Util 161.251 et seq.**
Foreign Corporations, this index
Limited partnerships. Partnerships, this index
Nonprofit Corporations, this index
Partnerships, this index
Telephone cooperative corporations, **Util 162.301 et seq.**

DISSOLUTION OF MARRIAGE
Marriage, this index

DISTANCE LEARNING
Colleges and Universities, this index
Telecommunications, **Util 57.021 et seq.**

DISTRIBUTED NATURAL GAS GENERATION FACILITIES
Oil and gas. Electricity, this index

DISTRIBUTION SERVICE
Definitions, electricity, municipalities, rates and charges, franchises, **Util 33.008**

DISTRICT COURTS
Costs, generally, this index
Supersedeas or Stay, generally, this index

DISTRICTS
Entry On Property, generally, this index
Schools and School Districts, generally, this index
Telephone cooperative corporations, **Util 162.076**

DIVIDENDS
Corporations, this index
Foreign Corporations, this index

DIVORCE
Dissolution of marriage. Marriage, this index

DOCTORS
Physicians and Surgeons, generally, this index

DOG RACES
Licenses and permits, transfers, partnerships, limited partnerships, **Bus Org 153.555**
Partnerships, limited partnerships, licenses and permits, transfers, **Bus Org 153.555**
Transfers, licenses and permits, partnerships, limited partnerships, **Bus Org 153.555**

DOGS
Greyhound racing. Dog Races, generally, this index
Racing. Dog Races, generally, this index

DOMESTIC CORPORATIONS
Corporations, generally, this index

DOMESTIC RELATIONS ORDERS
Churches, retirement and pensions, **Bus Org 22.407**
Religious organizations and societies, retirement and pensions, **Bus Org 22.407**

DOMICILE AND RESIDENCE
Business development corporations, organization, **Bus Org 23.052**
Real estate investment trusts, managers and management, **Bus Org 200.303**

DOMINANT CARRIERS
Telecommunications, this index

DONATIONS
Gifts, generally, this index

DRAINS AND DRAINAGE
Corporations, **Bus Org 1.001 et seq.**

DRINKING WATER
Water Supply, generally, this index

DRUGS AND MEDICINE
Prescriptions. Telemedicine, generally, this index

DRUGS AND MEDICINE—Cont'd
Telemedicine, generally, this index

DUAL OFFICE HOLDING
Public utility commission, commissioners, **Util 12.055**

DUPLICATES AND COPIES
Cooperative Associations, this index
Corporations, this index
Foreign Corporations, this index
Limited Liability Companies, this index
Limited partnerships. Partnerships, this index
Nonprofit Corporations, this index
Partnerships, this index
Professional Associations and Societies, this index
Professional Corporations, this index

EARNINGS
Compensation and Salaries, generally, this index

EASEMENTS
Cable Television, this index
Electricity, this index
Gas Utilities, this index
Highways and Roads, this index
Interurban Railroads, this index
Oil and Gas Pipelines, this index
Public Utilities, this index
Streets and alleys, public utilities, municipal franchises, fees, **Util 14.008**
Telecommunications, this index
Water Supply, this index

ECONOMIC DEVELOPMENT
Business Development Corporations, generally, this index
Cogeneration, generally, this index

EDUCATION
Colleges and Universities, generally, this index
Distance learning, telecommunications, **Util 57.021 et seq.**
Electricity, competition, **Util 39.902**
Nonprofit Corporations, generally, this index
Schools and School Districts, generally, this index
Telecommunications, this index
Training, generally, this index

EDUCATIONAL CORPORATIONS
Nonprofit Corporations, generally, this index

ELDERLY PERSONS
Aged Persons, generally, this index

ELECTIONS
Ballots, telephone cooperative corporations, deregulation, **Util 53.352**
Business Development Corporations, this index
Cities, towns and villages. Municipal Elections, generally, this index

ELECTIONS—Cont'd
Cooperative Associations, this index
Corporations, this index
Electric cooperative corporations, directors, **Util 161.072**
Electricity, municipal power agencies, creation, **Util 163.054 et seq.**
Foreign Corporations, this index
Initiative and Referendum, generally, this index
Limited Liability Companies, this index
Limited partnerships. Partnerships, this index
Municipal Elections, generally, this index
Nonprofit Corporations, this index
Notice, municipal power agencies, **Util 163.058**
Partnerships, this index
Professional Associations and Societies, this index
Professional Corporations, this index
Real Estate Investment Trusts, this index
Referendum. Initiative and Referendum, generally, this index
Telecommunications,
- Conversion, incentive, **Util 59.023**
- Incentives, **Util 58.021 et seq., 59.021 et seq.**
- Private networks, education, **Util 58.257, 59.076**
- Toll free calls, **Util 55.047**

Telephone Cooperative Corporations, this index

ELECTRIC COOPERATIVE CORPORATIONS
- Generally, **Util 161.001 et seq.**

Actions and proceedings, **Util 161.121**
- Rates and charges, customer choice, **Util 41.061**

Air pollution, emissions, reduction, customer options, **Util 31.005**
Amendments,
- Articles of incorporation, post
- Bylaws, **Util 161.064**

Anticompetitive actions, customer choice, **Util 41.056**
Appeal and review. Rates and charges, post
Application of law, **Util 161.005**
- Rural areas, amendments of articles, **Util 161.079**
- Securities Act, **Util 161.063**

Articles of consolidation, **Util 161.202**
Articles of incorporation, **Util 161.054**
- Amendments, **Util 161.151, 161.152**
  - Defective articles, **Util 161.058**
  - Rural areas, compliance, **Util 161.079**
- Consolidation and merger, **Util 161.202**
- Defective articles, perfecting, **Util 161.058**
- Filing and recording, **Util 161.055**
- Incorporators, **Util 161.051**
- Meetings, amendments, **Util 161.151**
- Notice, meetings, amendments, **Util 161.151**

ELECTRIC COOPERATIVE CORPORATIONS—Cont'd
Articles of incorporation—Cont'd
Perfecting, defective articles, **Util 161.058**
Revival, **Util 161.056**
Attorney fees, rates and charges, actions and proceedings, customer choice, **Util 41.061**
Bills and billing, customer choice, **Util 41.057**
Boards and commissions. Directors, generally, post
Bonds, **Util 41.103, 161.123**
Joint powers agencies, tax exemptions, **Util 163.124**
Stranded costs, competition, **Util 41.003**
Bylaws, **Util 161.064, 161.121**
Certificates and certification,
Articles of incorporation, **Util 161.055**
Dissolution, **Util 161.251, 161.254**
Membership, **Util 161.066**
Certificates of convenience and necessity,
Customer choice, **Util 41.059**
Generation, **Util 37.051**
Interconnection facilities, **Util 37.051**
Renewable energy, zones, **Util 39.904**
Charges. Rates and charges, generally, post
Compensation and salaries, directors, **Util 161.073**
Competition, **Util 41.001 et seq.**
Customer choice, generally, post
Consolidation and merger, **Util 161.201, 161.202**
Construction of law, **Util 161.003**
Consumer protection, **Util 17.006**
Contracts, **Util 161.121**
Consolidation, **Util 161.201**
Interference, **Util 41.101**
Customer choice, **Util 41.051 et seq.**
Installed generation capacity, reports, **Util 39.155**
Reports, installed generation capacity, **Util 39.155**
Customer options, air pollution, emissions, reduction, **Util 31.005**
Deceptive trade practices and consumer protection, **Util 17.006**
Defects, incorporation, dissolution, **Util 161.254**
Definitions, **Util 161.002**
Directors, **Util 161.071 et seq.**
Compensation and salaries, **Util 161.073**
Customer choice, jurisdiction, **Util 41.055**
Elections, **Util 161.072**
Executive committees, **Util 161.077**
Indemnity, **Util 161.078**
Meetings, **Util 161.074, 161.075**
Notice, meetings, **Util 161.075**
Officers, **Util 161.076**
Powers and duties, **Util 161.071**
Quorum, **Util 161.074**
Discounts, military bases, rates and charges, **Util 36.354**

ELECTRIC COOPERATIVE CORPORATIONS—Cont'd
Discrimination, customer choice, **Util 41.056**
Dissolution, **Util 161.251 et seq.**
Distribution of assets, dissolution, **Util 161.253**
Duration, **Util 161.052**
Easements, railroads, right of way, eminent domain, **Util 186.051 et seq.**
Efficiency, **Util 39.9052**
Elections, directors, **Util 161.072**
Eligibility, members, **Util 161.065**
Eminent domain, **Util 161.125**
Railroads, right of way, **Util 186.051 et seq.**
Executive committees, directors, **Util 161.077**
Exemptions,
Gas utilities, **Util 101.003, 121.008**
Securities Act, **Util 161.063**
Taxation, **Util 161.062**
Expenses and expenditures,
Directors, reimbursement, **Util 161.073**
Payment, **Util 161.059**
Extension of service, rural electrification, **Util 161.122**
Fees,
Articles of amendment, filing, **Util 161.152**
Articles of consolidation, filing, **Util 161.202**
Articles of incorporation, filing, **Util 161.055**
Certificates of dissolution, **Util 161.251**
Licenses, **Util 161.061**
Railroads, right of way, use, **Util 186.058**
Rates and charges, generally, post
System benefit fund, **Util 39.303**
Foreign states, offices, **Util 161.121**
Forms,
Articles of amendment, **Util 161.152**
Articles of consolidation, **Util 161.202**
Articles of incorporation, **Util 161.054**
Certificates of dissolution, **Util 161.251**
Franchise taxes, **Util 161.062**
Funds, system benefit fund, **Util 39.903**
Gas utilities, exemptions, **Util 101.003, 121.008**
Generation, **Util 161.123**
Certificates of convenience and necessity, **Util 37.051**
Nonmembers, sales, **Util 161.124**
Oil and gas, **Util 39.9044, 39.9048**
Gifts, **Util 161.121**
Incorporation. Articles of incorporation, generally, ante
Incorporators, **Util 161.051**
Members and membership, **Util 161.065**
Organizational meetings, **Util 161.057**
Indebtedness, **Util 161.121**
Dissolution, payment, **Util 161.252**
Liability of members, **Util 161.060**
Services, **Util 161.123**
Indemnity, **Util 161.078**

ELECTRIC COOPERATIVE CORPORATIONS—Cont'd
Information, customer choice, **Util 41.060**
Installed generation capacity, customer choice, reports, **Util 39.155**
Interconnection facilities, certificates of convenience and necessity, **Util 37.051**
Investments, stranded investments, rates and charges, customer choice, **Util 41.062**
Joint powers agencies, **Util 163.121 et seq.**
Jurisdiction,
Competition, **Util 41.004**
Customer choice, directors, **Util 41.055**
Joint powers agencies, **Util 163.123**
Leases, **Util 161.121**
Liberal construction of law, **Util 161.003**
Licenses and permits,
Fees, **Util 161.061**
Railroads, right of way, use, **Util 186.058**
Liquidation, assets, dissolution, **Util 161.252**
Loans, **Util 161.121**
Low or moderate income persons, rates and charges, system benefit fund, **Util 39.903**
Machinery and equipment,
Assistance, **Util 161.123**
Rural electrification, **Util 161.122**
Managers and management, executive committees, directors, **Util 161.077**
Markets and marketing, wholesalers, **Util 41.102**
Meetings,
Articles of incorporation, amendments, **Util 161.151**
Directors, **Util 161.074, 161.075**
Members and membership, **Util 161.067**
Amendments, articles of incorporation, approval, **Util 161.151**
Dissolution, **Util 161.251, 161.254**
Election of directors, **Util 161.072**
Merger and consolidation, approval, **Util 161.201**
Notice, **Util 161.068**
Quorum, **Util 161.069**
Voting, **Util 161.070**
Organizational meetings, incorporators, **Util 161.057**
Members and membership, **Util 161.065**
Articles of incorporations, amendments, **Util 161.151**
Certificates, **Util 161.066**
Dissolution, **Util 161.251, 161.254**
Distribution of assets, dissolution, **Util 161.253**
Eligibility, **Util 161.065**
Indebtedness, liability, **Util 161.060**
Meetings, ante
Merger and consolidation, approval, **Util 161.201**
Notice, meetings, **Util 161.068**
Proxies, **Util 161.070**
Refunds, **Util 161.059**

ELECTRIC COOPERATIVE CORPORATIONS—Cont'd
Members and membership—Cont'd
Voting, **Util 161.070**
Merger and consolidation, **Util 161.201, 161.202**
Meters, net metering, **Util 39.914**
Military bases, rates and charges, **Util 36.354**
Municipalities, competition, **Util 41.005**
Names, **Util 161.004, 161.053**
Natural gas, generation, **Util 39.9044, 39.9048**
Nonmembers, sales, **Util 161.124**
Nonprofit corporations, status, **Util 161.059**
Notice,
Articles of incorporation, amendments, meetings, **Util 161.151**
Directors, meetings, **Util 161.075**
Meetings, members, **Util 161.068**
Organizational meetings, incorporators, **Util 161.057**
Railroads, right of way, easements, **Util 186.054**
Rates and charges, post
Officers and employees, **Util 161.076**
Indemnity, **Util 161.078**
Oil and gas, generation, **Util 39.9044, 39.9048**
Open meetings, joint powers agencies, **Util 163.122 et seq.**
Organizational meetings, incorporators, **Util 161.057**
Pilot programs, customer choice, **Util 41.051**
Powers and duties, **Util 161.121 et seq.**
Profits, **Util 161.059**
Property, **Util 161.121**
Eminent domain, **Util 161.125**
Proxies, members, **Util 161.070**
Public entities, joint powers agencies, **Util 163.121 et seq.**
Quorum,
Directors, **Util 161.074**
Members, meetings, **Util 161.069**
Railroads, right of way, easements, eminent domain, **Util 186.051 et seq.**
Rates and charges, **Util 161.123**
Actions and proceedings, customer choice, **Util 41.061**
Adjustments, purchased power, **Util 36.205 et seq.**
Appeal and review, customer choice, **Util 41.061**
Attorney fees, actions and proceedings, customer choice, **Util 41.061**
Changes, customer choice, **Util 41.061**
Customer choice, **Util 41.055, 41.061**
Discounts, military bases, **Util 36.354**
Investments, stranded investments, customer choice, **Util 41.062**
Low or moderate income persons, system benefit fund, **Util 39.903**
Military bases, **Util 36.354**
Notice, proposed changes, customer choice, **Util 41.061**

ELECTRIC COOPERATIVE CORPORATIONS—Cont'd
Rates and charges—Cont'd
Purchased power, adjustments, **Util 36.205 et seq.**
Refunds, earnings, **Util 36.004**
Stranded investments, customer choice, **Util 41.062**
Surcharges, military bases, **Util 36.354**
Records and recordation,
Articles of amendment, **Util 161.152**
Articles of consolidation, **Util 161.202**
Articles of incorporation, **Util 161.055**
Certificates of dissolution, **Util 161.251**
Refunds,
Members, **Util 161.059**
Rates and charges, **Util 36.004**
Renewable energy, **Util 39.904**
Reports,
Efficiency, **Util 39.9052**
Installed generation capacity, customer choice, **Util 39.155**
Renewable energy, zones, **Util 39.904**
Reserves, **Util 161.059**
Resolutions, customer choice, **Util 41.051**
Revival, articles of incorporation, **Util 161.056**
Rural areas,
Amendments of articles, compliance, **Util 161.079**
Electrification, **Util 161.122**
Sales, nonmembers, energy, **Util 161.124**
Seals, **Util 161.121**
Securities, stranded costs, competition, **Util 41.003**
Securities Act, exemptions, **Util 161.063**
Special meetings, members, **Util 161.067**
Standards, deceptive trade practices and consumer protection, **Util 17.006**
Stranded investments, rates and charges, customer choice, **Util 41.062**
Surcharges, military bases, rates and charges, **Util 36.354**
System benefit fund, **Util 39.903**
Tariffs,
Open access, customer choice, **Util 41.058**
Rates and charges, generally, ante
Tax exemptions, **Util 40.104, 41.104, 161.062**
Joint powers agencies, bonds and securities, **Util 163.124**
Telecommunications, generally, this index
Time,
Articles of amendment, effect, **Util 161.152**
Creation of corporations, **Util 161.055**
Duration of corporation, **Util 161.052**
Meetings, members, **Util 161.067**
Transition bonds, stranded costs, competition, **Util 41.003**
Transmission, **Util 161.123**
Nonmembers, sales, **Util 161.124**
Vacancies in office, directors, **Util 161.072**
Voting, members, meetings, **Util 161.070**
Wholesalers, markets and marketing, **Util 41.102**

ELECTRIC COOPERATIVE CORPORATIONS—Cont'd
Winding up affairs, dissolution, **Util 161.252, 161.253**
Zones, renewable energy, **Util 39.904**

ELECTRIC ENERGY
Electricity, generally, this index

ELECTRIC INTERURBAN RAILROADS
Interurban Railroads, generally, this index

ELECTRIC LIGHT AND POWER COMPANIES
Electricity, generally, this index

ELECTRICITY
See, also, Public Utilities, generally, this index
Generally, **Util 31.001 et seq.**
Accounts and accounting,
Depreciation, **Util 32.102**
Municipal power agencies, **Util 163.060**
Profits and losses, **Util 32.103**
Rates and charges, allocation of costs and expenses, **Util 36.055**
Retirement and pensions, reserves, **Util 36.065**
Self insurance, reserve accounts, **Util 36.064**
Actions and proceedings, true up proceedings, stranded costs, competition, recovery, **Util 39.262**
Adjustments, rates and charges,
Cost recovery, **Util 36.201 et seq.**
Periodic adjustments, **Util 36.210**
Administrative law and procedure, contested cases, competition, **Util 39.003**
Advertisements, expenses,
Computation of rates, **Util 36.061**
Reports, **Util 32.104**
Advocates, municipally owned utilities, **Util 33.122**
Affidavits, rates and charges, periodic adjustments, **Util 36.210**
Affiliates,
Alternative energy, **Util 35.002**
Authority, purchase of power, **Util 35.003**
Broadband over power lines, **Util 43.151**
Competition, unbundling, **Util 39.051**
Confidential or privileged information, sales, **Util 14.154**
Exempt wholesale generators, **Util 35.033 et seq.**
Hearings, transfer of assets, exemptions, **Util 35.034**
Income tax, consolidated returns, computation of rates, **Util 36.060**
Power marketers, **Util 35.033 et seq.**
Rates and charges, transfers,
Computation of rates, **Util 36.058**
Exemptions, **Util 35.035**
Transfers of assets, exemptions, **Util 35.035**
Wholesale generators and power marketers, **Util 35.034**

ELECTRICITY—Cont'd
Affiliates—Cont'd
Valuation, transfer of assets, exemptions, **Util 35.035**
Aged persons,
Payment, delay, **Util 182.001 et seq.**
Termination of service, **Util 14.005**
Aggregators,
Fines and penalties, **Util 39.357**
Military bases, **Util 39.3535**
Registration, **Util 39.353 et seq.**
Agreements. Contracts, generally, post
Air pollution,
Emissions, reductions,
Competition, **Util 39.264**
Customer options, **Util 31.005**
Stranded costs, competition, recovery, **Util 39.253, 39.263**
Allowances, air pollution, emissions, competition, **Util 39.264**
Alternative dispute resolution, transmission, wholesalers, **Util 35.008**
Alternative energy, **Util 35.001 et seq.**
Amendments. Certificates of convenience and necessity, post
Amortization, computation of rates, **Util 36.056**
Anticompetitive actions, municipalities, customer choice, **Util 40.056**
Anticompetitive practices. Deceptive trade practices and consumer protection, generally, post
Apartment houses, metering, **Util 184.001 et seq.**
Appeal and review,
Competition, rules and regulations, **Util 39.001**
Municipalities, post
Municipally owned utilities, **Util 33.121 et seq.**
Nonresidents, municipally owned utilities, rates, **Util 33.123**
Restoration, bonds, **Util 36.405**
Application of law,
Broadband over power lines, **Util 43.002**
Certificates of convenience and necessity, post
Cooperation, public and private entities, **Util 163.011**
Joint ownership, public entities, **Util 164.006**
Municipalities, **Util 33.006**
NonERCOT areas, **Util 39.451**
NonERCOT utilities, **Util 39.401, 39.551**
Rates and charges, **Util 36.002**
Assessments, underground facilities, notification corporation, excavations, **Util 251.062**
Assignments,
Certificates of convenience and necessity, **Util 37.154**
Transition property, securities, competition, **Util 39.309**
Assisted living facilities, priorities and preferences, **Util 38.072**

ELECTRICITY—Cont'd
Atomic energy. Nuclear Power Plants, generally, this index
Attorney general, joint ownership, approval, **Util 164.003**
Attorneys,
Municipally owned utilities, review of rates, **Util 33.122**
Nonresidents, municipally owned utilities, review of rates, **Util 33.123**
Auctions and auctioneers, customer choice, installed generation capacity, entitlements, **Util 39.153**
Audits and auditors, municipalities, rates and charges, franchises, **Util 33.008**
Bankruptcy,
Atomic energy, decommissioning, trust funds, **Util 39.206**
Setoff and counterclaim, transition property, securities, competition, **Util 39.305**
Bids and bidding, municipal power agencies, construction contracts, **Util 163.061**
Bills and billing,
Confidential or privileged information, customers, government operated utilities, **Util 182.052**
Customer choice, **Util 39.107**
Deceptive trade practices and consumer protection, **Util 17.001 et seq.**
Municipalities, customer choice, **Util 40.057**
Uniformity, **Util 17.003**
Boards and commissions, municipal power agencies, directors, **Util 163.059**
Bond anticipation notes, municipal power agencies, **Util 163.068**
Bonds,
Competition, **Util 39.301 et seq.**
Hurricanes, reconstruction costs, non-ERCOT areas, **Util 39.460**
Joint ownership, public entities, **Util 164.002, 164.005**
Municipal power agencies, post
Municipalities, post
Private and public entities, cooperation, **Util 163.013**
Restoration, **Util 36.401 et seq.**
Bonds (officers and fiduciaries), rate changes, pending final determination, **Util 36.110**
BPL, broadband over power lines, **Util 43.001 et seq.**
Brands, marks and labels, underground facilities,
Crimes and offenses, excavations, **Util 251.203**
Excavations, **Util 251.157, 251.158**
Broadband over power lines, **Util 43.001 et seq.**
Burden of proof, rates and charges, changes, **Util 36.006**
Business units, unbundling, competition, **Util 39.051**

ELECTRICITY—Cont'd
Call router system, underground facilities, contracts, notification corporation, excavations, **Util 251.061**
Certificates and certification,
Customer choice, post
Deceptive trade practices and consumer protection, **Util 17.051 et seq.**
Retail electric providers, **Util 39.352, 39.356**
Revocation or suspension,
Retail electric providers, **Util 39.356**
Unauthorized charges, **Util 17.156**
Small power producers, contracts, **Util 35.062 et seq.**
Certificates of convenience and necessity, **Util 37.001 et seq.**
Amendments, **Util 37.059**
Multiply certificated service areas, division, **Util 37.060**
Municipalities, service areas, boundaries, **Util 37.061**
Application of law, **Util 37.001**
Applications, **Util 37.053**
Assignments, **Util 37.154**
Boundaries, service areas, municipalities, amendments, **Util 37.061**
Consolidation, hearings, applications, **Util 37.0541**
Contracts, customers, **Util 37.155**
Criteria, **Util 37.056**
Customer choice, multiply certificated service areas, division, **Util 37.060**
Customer service, **Util 37.151 et seq.**
Denial, **Util 37.056**
Distribution and distributors, multiply certificated service areas, division, **Util 37.060**
Division, multiply certificated service areas, **Util 37.060**
Easements, municipalities, annexation of territory, **Util 37.101**
ERCOT, **Util 37.051**
Exclusive rights, **Util 37.051**
Exemptions, **Util 37.052**
Extensions of service, exemptions, **Util 37.052**
Hearings,
Applications, **Util 37.054**
Revocation or amendment, **Util 37.059**
Interference, other utilities, **Util 37.156**
Intervention, hearings, **Util 37.054**
Consolidation, **Util 37.0541**
Leases, certificates, **Util 37.154**
Mandamus, transmission, applications, **Util 37.057**
Maps, **Util 37.157**
Merger and consolidation, hearings, applications, **Util 37.0541**
Multiply certificated service areas, division, **Util 37.060**
Municipalities, **Util 37.101 et seq., 37.102**
Annexation of territory, **Util 37.101**
Competition, amendments, **Util 40.060**

ELECTRICITY—Cont'd
Certificates of convenience and necessity —Cont'd
Municipalities—Cont'd
Easements, annexation of territory, **Util 37.101**
Exclusive rights, **Util 37.102**
Multiply certificated service areas, division, **Util 37.060**
Service areas, boundaries, amendments, **Util 37.061**
Notice, applications, hearings, **Util 37.054**
Orders, preliminary orders, **Util 37.055**
Preliminary orders, **Util 37.055**
Reduction of service, **Util 37.152**
Refusal of service, **Util 37.153**
Renewable energy, zones, **Util 39.904**
Requirement, **Util 37.051**
Revocation or suspension, **Util 37.059**
Multiply certificated service areas, division, **Util 37.060**
Sales, certificates, **Util 37.154**
Service areas, municipalities, boundaries, amendments, **Util 37.061**
Services, **Util 37.151 et seq.**
Standards, **Util 37.056**
Termination of service, **Util 37.152**
Time, transmission, applications, **Util 37.057**
Transfers of certificates, **Util 37.154**
Transmission,
Applications, time for approval, **Util 37.057**
Extensions of service, exemptions, **Util 37.052**
Interference, **Util 37.156**
Changes. Rates and charges, post
Charges. Rates and charges, generally, post
Choice. Customer choice, generally, post
Cities. Municipalities, generally, post
Clearance, transmission lines, **Util 38.004**
Cogeneration, generally, this index
Collections, terminology, uniformity, **Util 17.003**
Colleges and Universities, this index
Community colleges and districts, rates and charges, **Util 36.352**
Compensation and salaries, municipal power agencies, directors, **Util 163.059**
Competition, **Util 39.001 et seq.**
Affiliates, unbundling, **Util 39.051**
Appeal and review, rules and regulations, **Util 39.001**
Assessments and reports, **Util 31.003**
Bonds, **Util 39.301 et seq.**
Business units, unbundling, **Util 39.051**
Contested cases, **Util 39.003**
Customer choice, generally, post
Debentures, **Util 39.301 et seq.**
Discrimination, **Util 38.022**
Displaced workers, costs, **Util 39.906**
Distribution and distributors, rates and charges, **Util 39.203**
Education, **Util 39.902**

ELECTRICITY—Cont'd
Competition—Cont'd
Financing orders, securities, **Util 39.303 et seq.**
Hearings, rates and charges, **Util 39.201**
Municipalities, **Util 40.001 et seq.**
NonERCOT utilities, **Util 39.401 et seq., 39.551 et seq.**
Notes, **Util 39.301 et seq.**
Open access, tariffs, **Util 39.204**
Plans and specifications, nonERCOT utilities, **Util 39.402**
Power generation companies, unbundling, **Util 39.051**
Rates and charges, **Util 39.001 et seq., 39.201 et seq.**
Stranded costs, recovery, **Util 39.251 et seq.**
Transition charges,
NonERCOT utilities, recovery, **Util 39.409**
Stranded costs, recovery, **Util 39.251 et seq.**
Reports, stranded costs, recovery, **Util 39.257 et seq.**
Retail electric providers, unbundling, **Util 39.051**
Securities, **Util 39.301 et seq.**
Stranded costs, recovery, **Util 39.251 et seq.**
Tariffs, open access, **Util 39.204**
Transition, southwest power pool, nonERCOT areas, **Util 39.501 et seq.**
Transition bonds, **Util 39.301 et seq.**
Transition charges,
NonERCOT utilities, recovery, **Util 39.409**
Stranded costs, recovery, **Util 39.251 et seq.**
Transmission,
Rates and charges, **Util 39.203**
Unbundling, **Util 39.051**
Unbundling, business units, **Util 39.051**
Complaints,
Meters, testing, **Util 182.102**
Rates and charges, changes, **Util 36.105**
Regulatory authorities, **Util 36.151**
Condominiums, metering, **Util 184.001 et seq.**
Confidential or privileged information,
Affiliates, sales, **Util 14.154**
Government operated utilities, customers, **Util 182.051 et seq.**
Tariffs, filing, **Util 32.101**
Conflict of interest, customer choice, independent organizations, **Util 39.1512**
Conflict of laws,
Broadband over power lines, **Util 43.002**
Joint ownership, public entities, **Util 164.006**
Municipal power agencies, **Util 163.053**
River authorities, **Util 32.054**
Connections, renewable energy, **Util 39.916**

ELECTRICITY—Cont'd
Conservation, rates and charges, cost recovery, **Util 36.204**
Construction,
Broadband over power lines, **Util 43.051, 43.101**
Hurricanes, expenses and expenditures, nonERCOT areas, **Util 39.458 et seq.**
Municipal power agencies, contracts, **Util 163.061**
Private and public entities, cooperation, **Util 163.012, 163.013**
Works in progress, computation of rates, **Util 36.054**
Consumer protection. Deceptive trade practices and consumer protection, generally, post
Consumers, municipally owned utilities, advocacy, **Util 33.122**
Contested cases, competition, **Util 39.003**
Continuity of service, **Util 186.001 et seq.**
Contracts,
Certificates of convenience and necessity, customers, **Util 37.155**
Cogeneration, purchase of power, certification, **Util 35.062 et seq.**
Customer choice, **Util 39.108**
Wholesalers, independent organizations, markets and marketing, monitors, **Util 39.1515**
Historically underutilized businesses, **Util 39.909**
Interference, nonERCOT utilities, **Util 39.410**
Joint ownership, public entities, **Util 164.001 et seq.**
Municipal power agencies, **Util 163.060, 163.061**
Energy, **Util 163.062**
Municipalities, post
NonERCOT areas, **Util 39.457**
Franchises, **Util 39.456**
Public and private entities, cooperation, **Util 163.012**
River authorities, interference, **Util 40.101**
Small businesses, **Util 39.909**
Small power producers, certification, **Util 35.062 et seq.**
Underground facilities, toll free numbers, notification corporation, excavations, **Util 251.061**
Convenience and necessity. Certificates of convenience and necessity, generally, ante
Cooperation, public and private entities, **Util 163.011 et seq.**
Cooperative associations. Electric Cooperative Corporations, generally, this index
Cooperatives. Electric Cooperative Corporations, generally, this index
Corporate powers, **Util 181.002**
Cost recovery. Recovery of costs, generally, post
Costs. Stranded costs, generally, post

ELECTRICITY—Cont'd
Counties, this index
Credit reports,
Deceptive trade practices and consumer protection, payment, **Util 17.008**
Unauthorized charges, nonpayment, **Util 17.152**
Credits, air pollution, emissions, competition, **Util 39.264**
Crimes and offenses,
Customers deposits, **Util 183.006**
Meters, testing, refusal, **Util 182.104**
Underground facilities, brands, marks and labels, excavations, **Util 251.203**
Customer choice, **Util 17.101, 17.102, 39.101 et seq.**
Air pollution, emissions, reduction, **Util 31.005**
Auctions and auctioneers, installed generation capacity, entitlements, **Util 39.153**
Bills and billing, **Util 39.107**
Certificates and certification,
Independent organizations, **Util 39.151**
Power regions, **Util 39.152**
NonERCOT utilities, **Util 39.407**
Certificates of convenience and necessity, multiply certificated service areas, division, **Util 37.060**
Conflict of interest, independent organizations, **Util 39.1512**
Contracts, **Util 39.108**
Wholesalers, independent organizations, markets and marketing, monitors, **Util 39.1515**
Disclosure, independent organizations, conflict of interest, **Util 39.1512**
Education, **Util 39.902**
Entitlements, installed generation capacity, auctions and auctioneers, **Util 39.153**
Fines and penalties, market power, **Util 39.157**
Generation,
Merger and consolidation, **Util 39.158**
Sales, officers and employees, **Util 39.109**
Independent organizations, **Util 39.151 et seq.**
Independent system operators, **Util 39.151**
Injunctions, market power, **Util 39.157**
Installed generation capacity,
Auctions and auctioneers, entitlements, **Util 39.153**
Limitation, **Util 39.154**
Plans and specifications, mitigation, **Util 39.156**
Reports, **Util 39.155**
Landlord and tenant, **Util 39.107**
Last resort providers, **Util 39.106**
Leases, **Util 39.107**
Markets and marketing, **Util 39.151 et seq.**

ELECTRICITY—Cont'd
Customer choice—Cont'd
Meetings, independent organizations, **Util 39.1511**
Merger and consolidation, **Util 39.158**
Meters, **Util 39.107**
Military bases,
Aggregators, **Util 39.3535**
Energy efficiency, incentives, **Util 39.910**
Monitors, markets and marketing, independent organizations, wholesalers, **Util 39.1515**
Municipalities, **Util 40.051 et seq.**
NonERCOT areas, **Util 39.453**
NonERCOT utilities, **Util 39.407**
Notice, independent organizations, meetings, **Util 39.1511**
Pilot programs, **Util 39.104**
Plans and specifications, mitigation, installed generation capacity, **Util 39.156**
Power regions, **Util 39.152**
NonERCOT utilities, **Util 39.407**
Rates and charges, **Util 39.201 et seq.**
Independent organizations, **Util 39.151**
Reports, installed generation capacity, **Util 39.155**
Sales,
Generation, officers and employees, **Util 39.109**
Installed generation capacity, entitlements, **Util 39.153**
Limitation, **Util 39.105**
Solicitations, telecommunications, **Util 39.1025**
Sunset Act, independent organizations, **Util 39.151**
Telecommunications, solicitations, **Util 39.1025**
Wholesalers, contracts, **Util 39.108**
Independent organizations, markets and marketing, monitors, **Util 39.1515**
Customer protection. Deceptive trade practices and consumer protection, generally, post
Customers, stranded costs, competition, recovery, **Util 39.251 et seq.**
Damages, underground facilities, **Util 251.001 et seq.**
Debentures, competition, **Util 39.301 et seq.**
Deceptive trade practices and consumer protection, **Util 17.001 et seq.**
Certificates and certification, **Util 17.051 et seq.**
Credit reports,
Payment, **Util 17.008**
Unauthorized charges, nonpayment, **Util 17.152**
Customer choice, **Util 17.101, 17.102**
Discounts, **Util 17.007**
Disputed charges, records and recordation, **Util 17.153**

ELECTRICITY—Cont'd
Deceptive trade practices and consumer protection—Cont'd
Fines and penalties, unauthorized charges, **Util 17.156**
Military bases, aggregators, application of law, **Util 39.3535**
New products or services, rates and charges, **Util 17.151 et seq.**
Notice, new products or services, rates and charges, **Util 17.151 et seq.**
Payment, credit reports, **Util 17.008**
Records and recordation,
Disputed charges, **Util 17.153**
Unauthorized charges, **Util 17.152**
Registration, **Util 17.051 et seq.**
Reports, **Util 17.051 et seq.**
Standards, **Util 17.004**
Switching providers, **Util 17.101, 17.102**
Termination of service, unauthorized charges, nonpayment, **Util 17.152**
Unauthorized charges, **Util 17.151 et seq.**
Deeds and conveyances,
Private and public entities, cooperation, **Util 163.013**
State, royalties, in kind, **Util 35.101 et seq.**
Default, liens and incumbrances, transition property, securities, competition, **Util 39.309**
Definitions, **Util 31.002**
Credit reports, payment, **Util 17.008**
Joint powers agencies, **Util 163.001**
Meters, testing, **Util 182.101**
Municipal power agencies, **Util 163.051**
Oil and gas, distributed natural gas generation facilities, **Util 31.002**
Priorities and preferences, health care facilities, **Util 38.072**
Depletion, computation of rates, **Util 36.056**
Deposits, customers, **Util 183.001 et seq.**
Depreciation,
Accounts, **Util 32.102**
Rates and charges, computation, **Util 36.053, 36.056**
Stranded costs, competition, recovery, **Util 39.256**
Deregulation. Competition, generally, ante
Directors,
Municipal power agencies, **Util 163.059**
Underground facilities, notification corporation, excavations, **Util 251.055 et seq.**
Disasters, this index
Disclosure,
Customer choice, independent organizations, conflict of interest, **Util 39.1512**
Military bases, aggregators, application of law, **Util 39.3535**
Municipally owned utilities, review of rates, contributions, **Util 33.122, 33.123**

ELECTRICITY—Cont'd
Disconnection. Termination of service, generally, post
Discounts,
Military bases, rates and charges, **Util 36.354**
Rates and charges, post
Discrimination, **Util 39.101, 181.009**
Competitors, service, **Util 38.022**
Municipalities, customer choice, **Util 40.056**
Rates and charges, **Util 36.003**
Transmission, access, **Util 35.006**
Wholesalers, **Util 35.004**
Services, **Util 38.021**
Displaced workers, costs, competition, **Util 39.906**
Dispute resolution, transmission, wholesalers, **Util 35.008**
Disputed charges. Rates and charges, post
Distributed natural gas generation facilities. Oil and gas, post
Distribution and distributors,
Certificates of convenience and necessity, multiply certificated service areas, division, **Util 37.060**
Competition, **Util 39.001 et seq.**
Rates and charges, **Util 39.203**
Municipalities, competition, **Util 40.001 et seq.**
Rates and charges, competition, **Util 39.203**
State, sales, royalties, in kind, **Util 35.103**
Easements, **Util 181.007, 181.041 et seq.**
Broadband over power lines, **Util 43.054**
Certificates of convenience and necessity, municipalities, annexation of territory, **Util 37.101**
Clearance, highways and roads, **Util 181.045**
Highways and roads, **Util 181.042 et seq.**
Incorporation of municipalities, effect, **Util 181.047**
Municipalities, streets and alleys, consent, **Util 181.043**
Notice, highways and roads, **Util 181.044**
Private and public entities, cooperation, **Util 163.013**
Railroads,
Right of way, eminent domain, **Util 186.051 et seq.**
Standards of construction, **Util 181.045**
Relocation of facilities, highways and roads, **Util 181.046**
Standards, construction of facilities, **Util 181.045**
Streets and alleys, **Util 181.042 et seq.**
Underground facilities, excavations, **Util 251.006**
Education, competition, **Util 39.902**

ELECTRICITY—Cont'd
Efficiency,
Incentives, **Util 39.905**
Military bases, **Util 39.910**
Plans and specifications, **Util 39.9054**
Reports, **Util 39.9054**
Elections, municipal power agencies, creation, **Util 163.054 et seq.**
Electric Cooperative Corporations, generally, this index
Emergencies,
Sales, **Util 38.073**
Termination of service, extreme weather emergencies, **Util 39.101**
Underground facilities, notice, excavations, **Util 251.155**
Weather, plans and specifications, reports, **Util 186.007**
Eminent domain, **Util 181.004**
Public and private entities, cooperation, **Util 163.014**
Railroads, right of way, **Util 186.051 et seq.**
Entitlements, installed generation capacity, customer choice, auctions and auctioneers, **Util 39.153**
Environmental protection, cleanup, stranded costs, competition, recovery, **Util 39.263**
Evidence, aged persons, delay in payment, proof of age, **Util 182.004**
Excavations, underground facilities, **Util 251.001 et seq.**
Exchange agreements, municipal power agencies, **Util 163.062**
Exclusive rights, certificates of convenience and necessity, **Util 37.051**
Exemptions, **Util 31.002**
Aged persons, delay in payment, **Util 182.005**
Certificates of convenience and necessity, **Util 37.052**
Colleges and universities, rates and charges, discounts, **Util 36.351**
Confidential or privileged information, government operated utilities, customers, **Util 182.054**
Municipalities, jurisdiction, **Util 32.002, 32.003, 33.004, 33.005**
River authorities, jurisdiction, **Util 32.051 et seq.**
Transmission, rates and charges, demand charges, **Util 36.009**
Underground facilities, notice, excavations, **Util 251.156**
Expenses and expenditures,
Atomic energy, decommissioning, plans and specifications, **Util 39.206**
Emergencies, recovery, **Util 38.073**
NonERCOT areas, recovery, **Util 39.455**
Recovery of costs, generally, post
Retirement and pensions, **Util 36.065**
Stranded costs, competition, recovery, **Util 39.251 et seq.**
Underground facilities, notification corporation, excavations, **Util 251.054**

ELECTRICITY—Cont'd
Extensions of service, certificates of convenience and necessity, exemptions, **Util 37.052**
Facilities, storage, **Util 35.151**
Registration, **Util 35.152**
Federal income tax. Income tax, generally, post
Fees,
Atomic energy, safety, fees, **Util 39.9016**
Broadband over power lines, **Util 43.053, 43.101**
Confidential or privileged information, government operated utilities, **Util 182.053**
Municipalities, post
Nuclear safety fees, **Util 39.9016**
Railroads, right of way, use, **Util 186.058**
Rates and charges, generally, post
Underground facilities, post
Filing,
Oil and gas, distributed natural gas generation facilities, **Util 39.351**
Rates and charges, **Util 32.101, 36.102**
Financing orders, securities, competition, **Util 39.303 et seq.**
Fines and penalties,
Aggregators, **Util 39.357**
Allowances, air pollution, emissions, competition, **Util 39.264**
Customer choice, market power, **Util 39.157**
Customers, safeguards, **Util 39.101**
Customers deposits, **Util 183.006**
Efficiency, **Util 39.905**
Meters, testing, refusal, **Util 182.104**
Municipally owned utilities, review of rates, contributions, **Util 33.122**
Power generation companies, **Util 39.357**
Retail electric providers, **Util 39.357**
Unauthorized charges, **Util 17.156**
Underground facilities, excavations, **Util 251.201 et seq.**
Fixed rate products, expiration, notice, **Util 39.112**
Floods and flood control, restoration, bonds, **Util 36.401 et seq.**
Force majeure, rates and charges, freeze period, **Util 39.055**
Foreign states, expenses and expenditures, computation of rates, **Util 36.062**
Forms,
Confidential or privileged information, government operated utilities, **Util 182.052**
Municipal power agencies,
Bonds, **Util 163.066**
Ordinances, **Util 163.057**
Statements of intent, rate changes, **Util 36.102**
Franchises,
Municipalities, rates and charges, **Util 33.008**

ELECTRICITY—Cont'd
Franchises—Cont'd
NonERCOT areas, contracts, **Util 39.456**
Fraud,
Deceptive trade practices and consumer protection, generally, ante
Underground facilities, emergencies, excavations, **Util 251.155**
Fines and penalties, **Util 251.201**
Freeze period, rates and charges, **Util 39.052 et seq.**
Fuel, rate adjustments, cost recovery, **Util 36.201, 36.203**
Funds, system benefit fund, **Util 39.903**
Gas. Oil and gas, generally, post
Generation, **Util 181.008**
Alternative energy, **Util 35.001 et seq.**
Certificates of convenience and necessity, generally, ante
Cogeneration, generally, this index
Cooperative corporations, **Util 161.123**
Customer choice,
Merger and consolidation, **Util 39.158**
Sales, officers and employees, **Util 39.109**
Exempt wholesale generators, **Util 35.031 et seq.**
Exemptions, **Util 31.002**
Merger and consolidation, customer choice, **Util 39.158**
Oil and gas, generally, post
Plans and specifications, generally, post
Power generation companies, generally, post
Registration, power generation companies, **Util 39.351, 39.356**
Small power producers, generally, post
Stranded costs, competition, recovery, **Util 39.251 et seq.**
Gifts, business expenses,
Computation of rates, expenses, **Util 36.061**
Reports, **Util 32.104**
Goals, military bases, energy efficiency, incentives, **Util 39.910**
Handicapped persons, termination of service, **Util 14.005**
Health care facilities and services, priorities and preferences, **Util 38.072**
Hearings,
Certificates of convenience and necessity, **Util 37.059**
Applications, **Util 37.054**
Improvements, service, **Util 38.071**
Municipalities, appeal and review, rates, **Util 33.054**
Municipally owned utilities, rates, **Util 33.122**
Rates and charges, post
Small power producers, contracts, certificates and certification, **Util 35.063**
Standards, **Util 38.002**

ELECTRICITY—Cont'd
Hearings—Cont'd
Tariffs, recovery of costs, nonERCOT utilities, transmission, improvements, **Util 36.209**
Heating, reports, **Util 39.912**
Highways and roads,
Easements, **Util 181.042 et seq.**
Underground facilities, excavations, **Util 251.007**
Historically underutilized businesses, contracts, **Util 39.909**
History, credit reports, payment, **Util 17.008**
Hospices, priorities and preferences, **Util 38.072**
Hurricanes, expenses and expenditures, nonERCOT areas, **Util 39.458 et seq.**
Identity and identification, municipalities, appeal and review, nonresidents, **Util 33.102**
Improvements,
Infrastructure, reports, **Util 38.101**
River authorities, **Util 32.052 et seq.**
Service, orders, **Util 38.071**
Transmission, nonERCOT utilities, recovery of costs, **Util 36.209**
Incentives,
Energy efficiency, **Util 39.905**
Military bases, **Util 39.910**
Rates and charges, cost recovery, conservation, **Util 36.204**
Income, computation of rates, **Util 36.057**
Income tax, **Util 36.059**
Adjustments, **Util 36.202**
Consolidated returns, **Util 36.060**
Indebtedness, **Util 181.003**
Independent organizations, customer choice, **Util 39.151 et seq.**
Independent system operators, customer choice, **Util 39.151**
Infrastructure, reports, improvements, maintenance, **Util 38.101**
Initiative and referendum,
Municipal power agencies, **Util 163.054, 163.055, 163.058**
Municipalities, surrender, jurisdiction, **Util 33.002, 33.003**
Injunctions, customer choice, market power, **Util 39.157**
Inspection and inspectors,
Equipment, **Util 38.051**
Meters, **Util 38.051, 38.052, 182.101 et seq.**
Installed generation capacity. Customer choice, ante
Installments, joint ownership, public entities, payment for shares, **Util 164.004**
Insurance,
Private and public entities, cooperation, **Util 163.016**
Self insurance, **Util 36.064**
Underground facilities, notification center, excavations, **Util 251.104**
Integrated resource plans. Plans and specifications, generally, post

ELECTRICITY—Cont'd
Interconnection, nonERCOT utilities, **Util 39.554**
Interest, customers deposits, **Util 183.002 et seq.**
Interference,
Broadband over power lines, **Util 43.152**
Certificates of convenience and necessity, other utilities, **Util 37.156**
Contracts, nonERCOT utilities, **Util 39.410**
Internet,
Customer choice, meetings, independent organizations, **Util 39.1511**
Efficiency, plans and specifications, reports, **Util 39.9054**
Interruption of service, prevention, **Util 186.001 et seq.**
Interstate commerce, municipal power agencies, distribution, **Util 163.101, 163.102**
Intervention, certificates of convenience and necessity, hearings, **Util 37.054**
Consolidation, **Util 37.0541**
Investigations and investigators, rates and charges, changes, **Util 36.152**
Investments,
Municipal power agencies, bonds, **Util 163.064**
Rates and charges, return on investments, **Util 36.051 et seq.**
Joint actions, private and public entities, cooperation, **Util 163.011 et seq.**
Joint ownership, public entities, **Util 164.001 et seq.**
Joint powers agencies, **Util 163.001 et seq.**
Definitions, **Util 163.001**
Electric cooperative corporations, **Util 163.121 et seq.**
Interstate electricity, distribution, **Util 163.101, 163.102**
Municipal power agencies, generally, post
Public and private entities, cooperation, **Util 163.011 et seq.**
Jurisdiction,
Joint powers agencies, electric cooperative corporations, **Util 163.123**
Municipal power agencies, rates and charges, **Util 163.063**
Municipalities, post
Nonresidents, municipally owned utilities, review of rates, **Util 33.123**
Public utility commission, **Util 32.001 et seq.**
Rates and charges, post
Landlord and Tenant, this index
Leases,
Certificates of convenience and necessity, **Util 37.154**
Customer choice, **Util 39.107**
Merchandise, computation of rates, **Util 36.063**
Municipal power agencies, **Util 163.060**

ELECTRICITY—Cont'd
Licenses and permits,
Air pollution, emissions, competition, **Util 39.264**
Railroads, right of way, use, **Util 186.058**
Underground facilities, excavations, **Util 251.006**
Liens and incumbrances,
Joint ownership, public entities, revenues, **Util 164.005**
Transition property, securities, competition, **Util 39.309**
Lines. Transmission, generally, post
Loans, **Util 181.003**
Municipal power agencies, **Util 163.060**
Losses, accounts, **Util 32.103**
Low or moderate income persons, rates and charges, system benefit fund, **Util 39.903**
Machinery and equipment,
Meters, generally, ante
Storage, **Util 35.151**
Registration, **Util 35.152**
Maintenance, infrastructure, reports, **Util 38.101**
Mandamus, certificates of convenience and necessity, transmission, applications, **Util 37.057**
Maps and plats, certificates of convenience and necessity, **Util 37.157**
Mark up, rates and charges, purchase of power, cost recovery, **Util 36.206, 36.207**
Markets and marketing,
Competition, **Util 39.001 et seq.**
Customer choice, **Util 39.151 et seq.**
Exemptions, **Util 31.002**
Military bases, aggregators, guidelines, application of law, **Util 39.3535**
Monitors, customer choice, independent organizations, wholesalers, **Util 39.1515**
Municipalities, competition, **Util 40.001 et seq.**
NonERCOT utilities, **Util 39.555**
Power marketers, **Util 31.002, 35.031 et seq.**
Relevant market, nonERCOT utilities, **Util 39.407**
Measures. Meters, generally, post
Meetings, customer choice, independent organizations, **Util 39.1511**
Merger and consolidation, **Util 39.915**
Certificates of convenience and necessity, hearings, applications, **Util 37.0541**
Customer choice, **Util 39.158**
Regulation, successors, **Util 32.0015**
Reports, **Util 39.262**
Meters,
Confidential or privileged information, customers, government operated utilities, **Util 182.052**
Customer choice, **Util 39.107**
Electric cooperative corporations, net metering, **Util 39.914**

ELECTRICITY—Cont'd
Meters—Cont'd
Inspection and inspectors, **Util 38.052**
Multiple unit complexes, **Util 184.001 et seq.**
Recreational vehicle parks, **Util 184.031 et seq.**
Standards, **Util 38.002**
Submetering, multiple unit complexes, **Util 184.013, 184.014**
Tests, **Util 182.101 et seq.**
Mineral rights, private and public entities, cooperation, eminent domain, **Util 163.014**
Misleading practices. Deceptive trade practices and consumer protection, generally, ante
Mitigation, plans and specifications, customer choice, installed generation capacity, **Util 39.156**
Mobile Homes and Mobile Home Parks, this index
Monitors, markets and marketing, customer choice, independent organizations, wholesalers, **Util 39.1515**
Monopolies and unfair trade,
Competition, generally, ante
NonERCOT areas, **Util 39.451 et seq.**
Multiply certificated service areas, certificates of convenience and necessity, division, **Util 37.060**
Municipal power agencies, **Util 163.051 et seq.**
Accounts and accounting, **Util 163.060**
Anticipation notes, bonds, **Util 163.068**
Bids and bidding, construction contracts, **Util 163.061**
Boards of directors, **Util 163.059**
Bonds, **Util 163.064**
Anticipation notes, **Util 163.068**
Forms, **Util 163.066**
Nonnegotiable notes, **Util 163.067**
Rates and charges, payment, **Util 163.063**
Refunding bonds, **Util 163.065**
Compensation and salaries, directors, **Util 163.059**
Conflict of laws, **Util 163.053**
Construction, contracts, **Util 163.061**
Construction of law, **Util 163.052**
Contracts, **Util 163.060, 163.061**
Energy, **Util 163.062**
Creation, **Util 163.054**
Definitions, **Util 163.051**
Deletions, public entities, **Util 163.055**
Directors, **Util 163.059**
Elections, creation, **Util 163.054, 163.055, 163.058**
Exchange agreements, **Util 163.062**
Fiber optics, leases, cable facilities, **Util 54.2025**
Forms,
Bonds, **Util 163.066**
Ordinances, **Util 163.057**
Initiative and referendum, **Util 163.054, 163.055, 163.058**

ELECTRICITY—Cont'd
Municipal power agencies—Cont'd
Interstate electric system, distributors, **Util 163.101, 163.102**
Investments, bonds, **Util 163.064**
Jurisdiction, rates and charges, **Util 163.063**
Leases, **Util 163.060**
Fiber optics, cable facilities, **Util 54.2025**
Loans, **Util 163.060**
Nonnegotiable notes, **Util 163.067**
Notice,
Construction contracts, bidding, **Util 163.061**
Creation, **Util 163.056**
Elections, **Util 163.058**
Ordinances, **Util 163.057**
Pooling agreements, **Util 163.062**
Powers and duties, **Util 163.060**
Interstate electricity, distribution, **Util 163.102**
Public entities, **Util 163.055**
Publication,
Construction contracts, bidding, **Util 163.061**
Creation, **Util 163.056**
Purchase money, **Util 163.067**
Rates and charges, **Util 163.063**
Recreation, **Util 163.055**
Refunding bonds, **Util 163.065**
Reserves, **Util 163.063, 163.064**
Revenue bonds, **Util 163.064**
Rules and regulations, **Util 163.060**
Sales, **Util 163.060, 163.062**
Bonds, **Util 163.066**
Interstate electricity, distribution, **Util 163.102**
Secured transactions, nonnegotiable notes, **Util 163.067**
Sinking funds, **Util 163.063, 163.064**
Stranded costs, recovery, customer choice, **Util 40.059**
Taxation, imposition, **Util 163.054**
Municipalities, **Util 33.001 et seq.**
Aggregators, registration, **Util 39.354, 39.356**
Air pollution, emissions, reduction, customer options, **Util 31.005**
Alternative energy, application of law, **Util 35.001**
Anticompetitive actions, customer choice, **Util 40.056**
Appeal and review,
Applications, compliance, nonresidents, **Util 33.104**
Boundaries, **Util 33.101 et seq.**
Confiscation, rates, **Util 33.055**
Filing,
Nonresidents, **Util 33.103**
Rates, **Util 33.053**
Hearings, rates, **Util 33.054**
Nonresidents, **Util 33.101 et seq.**
Orders, rates, **Util 33.054**
Prospective effect, rates, **Util 33.055**
Public utility commission, **Util 33.026**
Rates and charges, **Util 33.121 et seq.**

ELECTRICITY—Cont'd
Municipalities—Cont'd
Appeal and review—Cont'd
Rates and charges—Cont'd
Orders, **Util 33.051 et seq.**
Residents, rates, **Util 33.052**
Assistance, public utility commission, **Util 32.004**
Bills and billing, customer choice, **Util 40.057**
Bonds, **Util 40.103**
Competition, **Util 40.003**
Certificates of convenience and necessity, ante
Colleges and universities, rates and charges, discounts, **Util 36.351**
Competition, **Util 40.001 et seq.**
Confidential or privileged information, customers, **Util 182.051 et seq.**
Contracts, interference, **Util 40.101**
Cooperation, public and private entities, **Util 163.011 et seq.**
Customer choice, **Util 40.051 et seq.**
Installed generation capacity, reports, **Util 39.155**
Customer options, air pollution, emissions, reduction, **Util 31.005**
Deceptive trade practices and consumer protection, **Util 17.005**
Discounts, military bases, rates and charges, **Util 36.354**
Discrimination, customer choice, **Util 40.056**
Distribution and distributors, competition, **Util 40.001 et seq.**
Easements,
Railroads, right of way, **Util 186.051 et seq.**
Streets and alleys, consent, **Util 181.043**
Electric cooperative corporations, joint powers agencies, **Util 163.121 et seq.**
Eminent domain, railroads, right of way, **Util 186.051 et seq.**
Exemptions, jurisdiction, **Util 32.002, 32.003, 33.004, 33.005**
Exports and imports, jurisdiction, **Util 33.006**
Fees,
Railroads, right of way, **Util 186.058**
Regulation, **Util 33.007**
System benefit fund, **Util 39.303**
Franchises, rates and charges, **Util 33.008**
Funds, system benefit fund, **Util 39.903**
Generation, oil and gas, **Util 39.9044, 39.9048**
Hearings, appeal and review, rates, **Util 33.054**
Identity and identification, appeal and review, nonresidents, **Util 33.102**
Incorporation, easements, effect, **Util 181.047**
Initiative and referendum, surrender, jurisdiction, **Util 33.002, 33.003**

ELECTRICITY—Cont'd
Municipalities—Cont'd
Installed generation capacity, customer choice, reports, **Util 39.155**
Joint ownership, **Util 164.001 et seq.**
Joint powers agencies. Municipal power agencies, generally, ante
Jurisdiction, **Util 32.001 et seq., 33.001 et seq.**
Competition, **Util 40.004**
Customer choice, **Util 40.055**
Licenses and permits, railroads, right of way, **Util 186.058**
Low or moderate income persons, rates and charges, system benefit fund, **Util 39.903**
Markets and marketing, competition, **Util 40.001 et seq.**
Meters, testing, **Util 182.102**
Military bases, rates and charges, **Util 36.354**
Multiply certificated service areas, division, exemptions, **Util 37.060**
Natural gas, generation, **Util 39.9044, 39.9048**
Nonresidents, appeal and review, **Util 33.101 et seq.**
Notice, railroads, right of way, **Util 186.054**
Oil and gas, generation, **Util 39.9044, 39.9048**
Orders, appeal and review, rates, **Util 33.054**
Powers and duties, **Util 33.001 et seq.**
Public policy, jurisdiction, **Util 33.001**
Public utility commission, **Util 33.002 et seq.**
Railroads, right of way, eminent domain, **Util 186.051 et seq.**
Rates and charges, **Util 33.021 et seq.**
Appeal and review, municipal orders, **Util 33.051 et seq.**
Appeals, **Util 33.121 et seq.**
Boundaries, **Util 36.005**
Competition, **Util 40.001 et seq.**
Confiscation, appeals, interim rates, **Util 33.055**
Expenses and expenditures, proceedings, **Util 33.023**
Exports and imports, jurisdiction, **Util 33.006**
Filing, **Util 33.021**
Franchises, **Util 33.008**
Interim rates, appeals, **Util 33.055**
Low or moderate income persons, system benefit fund, **Util 39.903**
Military bases, **Util 36.354**
Municipally owned utilities, appeals, **Util 33.121 et seq.**
Nonregulated areas, returns, consideration, **Util 33.022**
Nonresidents, appeals, **Util 33.101 et seq.**
Notice, statements of intent, **Util 33.024**
Open access, **Util 40.058**

ELECTRICITY—Cont'd
Municipalities—Cont'd
Rates and charges—Cont'd
Payments in lieu of taxes, cost recovery, **Util 36.353**
Staff and employees, proceedings, **Util 33.023**
Standing, public utility commission, **Util 33.025**
Statement of intent, **Util 33.024**
Registration,
Aggregators, **Util 39.354, 39.356**
Retail electric providers, **Util 39.358**
Reinstatement, jurisdiction, **Util 33.003**
Renewable energy, **Util 39.904**
Reports,
Customer choice, installed generation capacity, **Util 39.155**
Regulated areas, **Util 33.005**
Retail electric providers, registration, **Util 39.358**
Securities, competition, **Util 40.003**
Service areas, boundaries, certificates of convenience and necessity, amendments, **Util 37.061**
Standards, deceptive trade practices and consumer protection, **Util 17.005**
Standing, public utility commission, **Util 33.025**
Stranded costs, securities, competition, **Util 40.003**
Surcharges, military bases, rates and charges, **Util 36.354**
System benefit fund, **Util 39.903**
Tariffs, open access, **Util 40.058**
Tax exemptions, **Util 40.104**
Taxation, payments in lieu of, cost recovery, **Util 36.353**
Telecommunications, **Util 54.202**
Time, appeal and review, rates, **Util 33.053**
Nonresidents, **Util 33.103, 33.104**
Orders, **Util 33.054**
Transition bonds, competition, **Util 40.003**
Wholesalers, markets and marketing, **Util 40.102**
Natural gas. Oil and gas, generally, post
Necessity. Certificates of convenience and necessity, generally, ante
New service, rates and charges, **Util 17.151 et seq.**
NonERCOT areas, **Util 39.451 et seq.**
NonERCOT utilities, **Util 39.401 et seq., 39.551 et seq.**
Nonresidents,
Municipalities, appeal and review, **Util 33.101 et seq.**
Municipally owned utilities, review of rates, **Util 33.123**
Notes, competition, **Util 39.301 et seq.**
Notice,
Certificates of convenience and necessity, applications, hearings, **Util 37.054**
Changes, rates and charges, **Util 36.103**

ELECTRICITY—Cont'd
Notice—Cont'd
Confidential or privileged information, government operated utilities, customers, **Util 182.052**
Customer choice, independent organizations, meetings, **Util 39.1511**
Easements, highways and roads, **Util 181.044**
Meters, testing, **Util 182.103**
Municipal power agencies, ante
Railroads, right of way, easements, **Util 186.054**
Rates and charges, post
Relocation of facilities, easements, highways and roads, **Util 181.046**
Tariffs, recovery of costs, nonERCOT utilities, transmission, improvements, **Util 36.209**
Underground facilities, post
Notification center, underground facilities, excavations, **Util 251.101 et seq.**
Notification corporation, underground facilities, excavations, **Util 251.051 et seq.**
Nuclear Power Plants, generally, this index
Nursing and convalescent homes, priorities and preferences, **Util 38.072**
Offenses. Crimes and offenses, generally, ante
Officers and employees,
Displacement, costs, competition, **Util 39.906**
Diversity, **Util 39.909**
Retirement and pensions, **Util 36.065**
Underground facilities, notification corporation, excavations, **Util 251.058**
Oil and gas, **Util 39.9044, 39.9048**
Definitions, distributed natural gas generation facilities, **Util 31.002**
Distributed natural gas generation facilities, **Util 35.036**
Definitions, **Util 31.002**
Filing, **Util 39.351**
Filing, distributed natural gas generation facilities, **Util 39.351**
Utilities, **Util 181.003**
Open access, tariffs, competition, **Util 39.204**
Open meetings,
Joint powers agencies, electric cooperative corporations, **Util 163.122 et seq.**
Underground facilities, notification corporation, excavations, **Util 251.053**
Open records, underground facilities, notification corporation, excavations, **Util 251.053**
Orders,
Certificates of convenience and necessity, ante
Improvements, service, **Util 38.071**
Municipalities, appeal and review, rates, **Util 33.054**
Rates and charges, post

ELECTRICITY—Cont'd
Orders—Cont'd
Transmission, access, wholesalers, **Util 35.005**
Wholesalers, access, **Util 35.005**
Ordinances, municipal power agencies, **Util 163.057**
Payment,
Aged persons, delay, **Util 182.001 et seq.**
Credit reports, deceptive trade practices and consumer protection, **Util 17.008**
Customers, deposits, interest, **Util 183.004**
Joint ownership, public entities, increases, **Util 164.004**
Underground facilities, notification center, excavations, **Util 251.106**
Penalties. Fines and penalties, generally, ante
Periodic adjustments, rates and charges, **Util 36.210**
Permits. Licenses and permits, generally, ante
Pilot programs, customer choice, **Util 39.104**
Planning. Plans and specifications, generally, post
Plans and specifications,
Atomic energy, decommissioning, costs, **Util 39.206**
Certificates of convenience and necessity, generally, ante
Competition, **Util 39.402**
Customer choice, mitigation, installed generation capacity, **Util 39.156**
Efficiency, **Util 39.9054**
Historically underutilized businesses, contracts, **Util 39.909**
Officers and employees, diversity, **Util 39.909**
Private and public entities, cooperation, **Util 163.012, 163.013**
Small businesses, contracts, **Util 39.909**
Weather, emergencies, reports, **Util 186.007**
Poles and wires. Transmission, generally, post
Political Subdivisions, this index
Pooling agreements, municipal power agencies, **Util 163.062**
Postemployment benefits, **Util 36.065**
Power agencies. Municipal power agencies, generally, ante
Power generation companies,
Competition, unbundling, **Util 39.051**
Fines and penalties, **Util 39.357**
Registration, **Util 39.351, 39.356**
Storage, machinery and equipment, registration, **Util 35.152**
Power marketers, **Util 35.031 et seq.**
Registration, **Util 39.355**
Power regions, customer choice, **Util 39.152**
Powers and duties, **Util 181.001 et seq.**
Municipalities, **Util 33.001 et seq.**

ELECTRICITY—Cont'd
Powers and duties—Cont'd
Underground facilities, post
Preferences. Priorities and preferences, generally, post
Priorities and preferences,
Health care facilities, **Util 38.072**
Purchases and purchasing, **Util 35.003**
Rates and charges, **Util 36.003**
Changes, hearings, **Util 36.107**
Services, **Util 38.021**
System benefit fund, **Util 39.303**
Private and public entities, cooperation, **Util 163.011 et seq.**
Privileged information. Confidential or privileged information, generally, ante
Privileges and immunities, confidential or privileged information, government operated utilities, **Util 182.055**
Profits, accounts, **Util 32.103**
Property, **Util 181.007**
Private and public entities, cooperation, **Util 163.013**
Eminent domain, **Util 163.014**
Providers. Customer choice, generally, ante
Public and private entities, cooperation, **Util 163.011 et seq.**
Public policy, **Util 31.001**
Cogeneration and small power production, **Util 35.061**
Joint ownership, public entities, **Util 164.002**
Military bases, aggregators, **Util 39.3535**
Municipal jurisdiction, **Util 33.001**
Public utility commission, jurisdiction, **Util 32.001 et seq.**
Publication,
Efficiency, plans and specifications, reports, **Util 39.9054**
Municipal power agencies, ante
Notice of intent, rate changes, **Util 36.103**
Purchased power, stranded costs, competition, recovery, **Util 39.251 et seq.**
Purchases and purchasing,
Aggregators, generally, ante
Municipalities, aggregators, registration, **Util 39.354, 39.356**
Political subdivisions, aggregators, registration, **Util 39.3545, 39.356**
Rates and charges, cost recovery, **Util 36.205 et seq.**
Regulation, successors, **Util 32.0015**
Railroads, this index
Rates and charges, **Util 36.001 et seq.**
Accounts and accounting, allocation of costs and expenses, **Util 36.055**
Adjustments,
Cost recovery, **Util 36.201 et seq.**
Periodic adjustments, **Util 36.210**
Advertisements, expenses, computation of rates, **Util 36.061**
Affidavits, periodic adjustments, **Util 36.210**

ELECTRICITY—Cont'd
Rates and charges—Cont'd
Affiliates, transfers,
Computation of rates, **Util 36.058**
Exemptions, **Util 35.035**
Amortization, computation of rates, **Util 36.056**
Application of law, **Util 36.002**
Atomic energy, decommissioning, costs, **Util 39.206**
Authority, regulation, **Util 36.001**
Automatic adjustments, cost recovery, **Util 36.201**
Automatic temporary rates, changes, **Util 36.156**
Basis, return on investments, computation of rates, **Util 36.053**
Bonds (officers and fiduciaries), pending final determination, **Util 36.110**
Broadband over power lines, **Util 43.053, 43.101**
Burden of proof, changes, **Util 36.006**
Changes, **Util 36.101 et seq.**
Adjustments, cost recovery, **Util 36.201 et seq.**
Automatic temporary rates, changes, **Util 36.155**
Burden of proof, **Util 36.006**
Complaints, **Util 36.105, 36.151**
Cost recovery, adjustments, **Util 36.201 et seq.**
Early effective dates, **Util 36.104**
Final determination, **Util 36.111, 36.154**
Freeze period, **Util 39.052 et seq.**
Fuel costs, recovery, adjustments, **Util 36.201, 36.203**
Hearings, **Util 36.105 et seq.**
Increases, **Util 36.101 et seq.**
Investigations, regulatory authorities, **Util 36.152**
Mark up, purchase of power, cost recovery, **Util 36.206, 36.207**
Notice of intent, **Util 36.103**
Orders, **Util 36.151**
Final determination, **Util 36.111**
Preferences, hearings, **Util 36.107**
Purchased power, cost recovery, **Util 36.205 et seq.**
Reductions, **Util 36.151 et seq.**
Regional hearings, **Util 36.106**
Regulatory authorities, proposals, **Util 36.151 et seq.**
Responses, changes, **Util 36.153**
Statements of intent, **Util 36.102**
Surcharges, temporary rates, pending final determination, **Util 36.155, 36.156**
Tax liability, adjustments, **Util 36.202**
Temporary rates, pending final determination, **Util 36.109, 36.155, 36.156**
Cogeneration, payments, cost recovery, **Util 36.208**
Colleges and universities, **Util 36.352**
Discounts, **Util 36.351**

ELECTRICITY—Cont'd
Rates and charges—Cont'd
Community colleges and districts, **Util 36.352**
Competition, ante
Complaints, changes, **Util 36.105**
Regulatory authorities, **Util 36.151**
Compliance with law, **Util 36.002**
Computation, **Util 36.051 et seq.**
Discounted rates, **Util 36.007**
Confidential or privileged information, filing, **Util 32.101**
Consent, new products or services, **Util 17.151 et seq.**
Conservation, cost recovery, **Util 36.204**
Construction, works in progress, computation of rates, **Util 36.054**
Credit reports,
Deceptive trade practices and consumer protection, **Util 17.008**
Unauthorized charges, nonpayment, **Util 17.152**
Criteria, municipally owned utilities, **Util 33.122**
Customer choice, **Util 39.201 et seq.**
Independent organizations, **Util 39.151**
Deceptive trade practices and consumer protection, **Util 17.001 et seq.**
Definitions, **Util 31.002**
Depletion, computation of rates, **Util 36.056**
Deposits, customers, interest, **Util 183.003**
Depreciation, computation of rates, **Util 36.053, 36.056**
Discounts, **Util 36.007**
Colleges and universities, **Util 36.351**
Deceptive trade practices and consumer protection, **Util 17.007**
Military bases, **Util 36.354**
Discrimination, **Util 36.003, 181.009**
Transmission, access, wholesalers, **Util 35.004, 35.006**
Disputed charges, **Util 17.157**
Records and recordation, **Util 17.153**
Distribution and distributors, competition, **Util 39.203**
Electric Cooperative Corporations, this index
Exceeding, **Util 36.004**
Expenses and expenditures, computation of rates, **Util 36.062**
Filing, **Util 32.101, 36.102**
Final determination, proposed changes, **Util 36.111**
Fines and penalties, unauthorized charges, **Util 17.156**
Fixed rate products, expiration, notice, **Util 39.112**
Force majeure, freeze period, **Util 39.055**
Foreign states, expenses and expenditures, computation of rates, **Util 36.062**
Franchises, municipalities, **Util 33.008**
Freeze period, **Util 39.052 et seq.**

ELECTRICITY—Cont'd
Rates and charges—Cont'd
Fuel costs, recovery, adjustments, **Util 36.201, 36.203**
Gifts, expenses, computation of rates, **Util 36.061**
Governmental entities, **Util 36.351 et seq.**
Hearings,
Adjustments, cost recovery, **Util 36.202, 36.203**
Changes, **Util 36.105 et seq.**
Competition, **Util 39.201**
Hurricanes, reconstruction costs, non-ERCOT areas, **Util 39.460, 39.461**
Incentives, cost recovery, conservation, **Util 36.204**
Income, computation of rates, **Util 36.057**
Income tax, computation of rates, **Util 36.059, 36.060**
Increases, proposed changes, **Util 36.101 et seq.**
Investigations and investigators, changes, **Util 36.152**
Investments, returns, computation of rates, **Util 36.051 et seq.**
Joint ownership, public entities, liens and incumbrances, **Util 164.005**
Jurisdiction, **Util 32.001 et seq.**
Municipal power agencies, **Util 163.063**
Municipally owned utilities, review, **Util 33.122**
Just and reasonable rates, **Util 36.003**
Leases, merchandise, computation of rates, **Util 36.063**
Legislative advocacy, expenses, computation of rates, **Util 36.061, 36.062**
Low or moderate income persons, system benefit fund, **Util 39.903**
Major changes, **Util 36.101**
Mark up, purchase of power, cost recovery, **Util 36.206, 36.207**
Military bases, **Util 36.354**
Aggregators, **Util 39.3535**
Energy efficiency, incentives, **Util 39.910**
Municipal power agencies, **Util 163.063**
Municipalities, ante
Net income, computation of rates, **Util 36.057**
New service, **Util 17.151 et seq.**
Nonallowable expenses, **Util 36.061, 36.062**
NonERCOT utilities, **Util 39.552**
Nonresidents, municipally owned utilities, review, **Util 33.123**
Notice,
Changes, **Util 36.103**
Hearings, **Util 36.105**
Fixed rate products, expiration, **Util 39.112**
New products or services, **Util 17.151 et seq.**
Periodic adjustments, **Util 36.210**

ELECTRICITY—Cont'd
Rates and charges—Cont'd
Orders,
Changes, final determination, **Util 36.111**
Reductions, **Util 36.151**
Original costs, computation of rates, **Util 36.053**
Payment, aged persons, delay, **Util 182.001 et seq.**
Periodic adjustments, **Util 36.210**
Priorities and preferences, **Util 36.003**
Changes, hearings, **Util 36.107**
Publication, notice of intent, rate changes, **Util 36.103**
Purchased power, cost recovery, adjustments, **Util 36.205 et seq.**
Records and recordation,
Disputed charges, **Util 17.153**
Unauthorized charges, **Util 17.152**
Reductions, proposed changes, **Util 36.151 et seq.**
Refunds,
Expenses and expenditures, computation of rates, **Util 36.062**
Proposed changes, bonds (officers and fiduciaries), **Util 36.110**
Temporary rates, pending final determination, **Util 36.155, 36.156**
Regional hearings, changes, **Util 36.106**
Reports, **Util 32.101**
Restoration, **Util 36.404**
Retirement and pensions, **Util 36.065**
Return on investments, computation of rates, **Util 36.051 et seq.**
Returns, municipally owned utilities, **Util 33.122**
Sales, merchandise, computation of rates, **Util 36.063**
Schools and school districts, **Util 36.352**
Self insurance, computation of rates, **Util 36.064**
Small power producers, payments, cost recovery, **Util 36.208**
State, sales, royalties, in kind, **Util 35.103**
Statements of intent, changes, **Util 36.102**
Stranded costs, competition, recovery, **Util 39.251 et seq.**
Surcharge, generally, post
Suspension, pending final determination, **Util 36.108**
Tax liability, adjustments, **Util 36.202**
Taxation, post
Temporary rates, changes, pending final determination, **Util 36.109, 36.155, 36.156**
Time,
Changes,
Early effective dates, **Util 36.104**
Notice of intent, **Util 36.103**
Statements of intent, **Util 36.102**
Final determination, changes, **Util 36.154**
Suspension, changes, pending final determination, **Util 36.108**

ELECTRICITY—Cont'd
Rates and charges—Cont'd
Trade associations, expenses, computation of rates, **Util 36.062**
Transition charges, stranded costs, competition, recovery, **Util 39.251 et seq.**
Transmission, post
Unauthorized charges, **Util 17.151 et seq.**
Underground facilities, post
Wholesalers, discounted rates, **Util 36.007**
Real estate. Property, generally, ante
Records and recordation,
Disputed charges, **Util 17.153**
Rates and charges, ante
Unauthorized charges, **Util 17.152**
Underground facilities, notification center, excavations, **Util 251.103**
Recoupment, nonERCOT areas, monopolies and unfair trade, **Util 39.454**
Recovery of costs,
Adjustments, **Util 36.201 et seq.**
Broadband over power lines, **Util 43.102**
Freeze period, **Util 39.053**
Hurricanes, nonERCOT areas, **Util 39.458 et seq.**
NonERCOT areas, **Util 39.455**
Hurricanes, **Util 39.458 et seq.**
NonERCOT utilities,
Competition, **Util 39.409**
Transmission, improvements, **Util 36.209**
Rates and charges, adjustments, **Util 36.201 et seq.**
Recreational vehicle parks, submetering, **Util 184.031 et seq.**
Reduction of service, certificates of convenience and necessity, **Util 37.152**
Refunds,
Customers deposits, **Util 183.005**
Rates and charges, generally, ante
Registration,
Aggregators, **Util 39.353 et seq.**
Deceptive trade practices and consumer protection, **Util 17.051 et seq.**
Exemptions, wholesale generators and power marketers, **Util 35.032**
Military bases, aggregators, **Util 39.3535**
Municipalities, ante
Political subdivisions, aggregators, **Util 39.3545, 39.356**
Power generation companies, **Util 39.351, 39.356**
Storage, machinery and equipment, **Util 35.152**
Power marketers, **Util 39.355**
Renewable energy, **Util 39.916**
Retail electric providers, municipalities, **Util 39.358**
Revocation or suspension,
Aggregators, **Util 39.356**
Power generation companies, **Util 39.356**

ELECTRICITY—Cont'd
Registration—Cont'd
Revocation or suspension—Cont'd
Unauthorized charges, **Util 17.156**
Storage, machinery and equipment, **Util 35.152**
Reliability standards, **Util 38.005**
Broadband over power lines, **Util 43.055**
Relocation of facilities, easements, highways and roads, **Util 181.046**
Remedies, underground facilities, excavations, **Util 251.008**
Renewable energy,
Energy, this index
Registration, **Util 39.916**
Repairs, underground facilities, excavations, **Util 251.159**
Reports,
Advertisements, **Util 32.104**
Atomic energy, decommissioning, trust funds, **Util 39.206**
Business and commerce, gifts, **Util 32.104**
Competition, **Util 31.003**
Consumers, energy efficiency, **Util 39.9025**
Customer choice, installed generation capacity, **Util 39.155**
Customers, safeguards, **Util 39.101**
Deceptive trade practices and consumer protection, **Util 17.051 et seq.**
Efficiency, **Util 39.9054**
Emergencies, sales, **Util 38.073**
Exempt wholesale generators, **Util 35.032**
Heating, **Util 39.912**
Historically underutilized businesses, contracts, **Util 39.909**
Infrastructure, improvements, maintenance, **Util 38.101**
Merger and consolidation, **Util 39.262**
Meters, testing, **Util 182.102**
Municipalities, ante
Officers and employees, diversity, **Util 39.909**
Power marketers, **Util 35.032**
Rates and charges, **Util 32.101**
Renewable energy, zones, **Util 39.904**
Small businesses, contracts, **Util 39.909**
Stranded costs, competition, recovery, **Util 39.257 et seq.**
Transmission, wholesalers, access, **Util 35.006**
Underground facilities, damages, excavations, **Util 251.159**
Weather, emergencies, plans and specifications, **Util 186.007**
Requests,
Aged persons, delay in payment, **Util 182.002, 182.003**
Confidential or privileged information, government operated utilities, **Util 182.052**
Reserves,
Municipal power agencies, **Util 163.063, 163.064**

ELECTRICITY—Cont'd
Reserves—Cont'd
  Retirement and pensions, **Util 36.065**
  Self insurance, **Util 36.064**
Restoration, bonds, **Util 36.401 et seq.**
Retail electric providers,
  Certificates and certification, **Util 39.352, 39.356**
  Competition, unbundling, **Util 39.051**
  Fines and penalties, **Util 39.357**
  Military bases, energy efficiency, incentives, **Util 39.910**
  Municipalities, registration, **Util 39.358**
  Registration, municipalities, **Util 39.358**
Retirement and pensions, **Util 36.065**
Review. Appeal and review, generally, ante
Revocation or suspension,
  Certificates of convenience and necessity, ante
  Rate changes, pending final determination, **Util 36.108**
  Registration, ante
Rewards, credit reports, payment, **Util 17.008**
River Authorities, this index
Rules and regulations,
  Competition, **Util 39.001 et seq.**
  Customers, safeguards, **Util 39.101**
  Municipal power agencies, **Util 163.060**
  Municipally owned utilities, rates, appeals, **Util 33.122**
  Rates and charges, periodic adjustments, **Util 36.210**
  Standards, **Util 38.002, 38.003**
  Submetering, multiple unit complexes, **Util 184.014**
  Transmission, access, wholesalers, **Util 35.006**
Safety,
  Standards, **Util 38.001**
  Underground facilities, **Util 251.001 et seq.**
Sales, **Util 181.008**
  Certificates of convenience and necessity, **Util 37.154**
  Customer choice, ante
  Disasters, **Util 38.073**
  Emergencies, **Util 38.073**
  Interstate electricity, distribution, municipal power agencies, **Util 163.102**
  Joint ownership, public entities, increases, **Util 164.004**
  Merchandise, computation of rates, **Util 36.063**
  Municipal power agencies, ante
  Power marketers, registration, **Util 39.355**
  Registration, power marketers, **Util 39.355**
  State, royalties, in kind, **Util 35.101 et seq.**
  Transition property, securities, competition, **Util 39.308**
School Buildings and Grounds, this index
Schools and school districts, rates and charges, **Util 36.352**
Scoring, credit reports, payment, **Util 17.008**
Secured transactions, municipal power agencies, nonnegotiable notes, **Util 163.067**
Securities,
  Competition, **Util 39.301 et seq.**
  Municipalities, competition, **Util 40.003**
Security interest, transition property, securities, competition, **Util 39.309**
Self consuming generators, exemptions, **Util 31.002**
Self insurance, **Util 36.064**
Service to customers,
  Customer choice, generally, ante
  Standards, **Util 38.005**
Services,
  Certificates of convenience and necessity, **Util 37.151 et seq.**
  Standards, **Util 38.001 et seq.**
Setoff and counterclaim, transition property, securities, competition, **Util 39.305**
Shares and shareholders, **Util 181.003**
Sinking funds, municipal power agencies, **Util 163.063, 163.064**
Small businesses, contracts, **Util 39.909**
Small power producers, **Util 35.001 et seq., 35.061 et seq.**
  Authority, sales, **Util 35.002**
  Contracts, certification, **Util 35.062 et seq.**
  Definitions, **Util 31.002**
  Hearings, contracts, certificates and certification, **Util 35.063**
  Public policy, **Util 35.061**
  Rates and charges, payments, cost recovery, **Util 36.208**
  Terms of contract, certification, **Util 35.064**
  Time, contracts, certificates and certification, **Util 35.065, 35.066**
  Transmission, access, **Util 35.004 et seq.**
Solar Energy, generally, this index
Solicitations, customer choice, telecommunications, **Util 39.1025**
Southwest power pool, competition, transition, nonERCOT areas, **Util 39.501 et seq.**
Specifications. Plans and specifications, generally, ante
Standards, **Util 38.001 et seq.**
  Certificates of convenience and necessity, **Util 37.056**
  Deceptive trade practices and consumer protection, **Util 17.004**
  Easements, construction of facilities, **Util 181.045**
State,
  Highways and roads, easements, notice, **Util 181.044**
  Sales, royalties, in kind, **Util 35.101 et seq.**
State agencies, military bases, aggregators, **Util 39.3535**
Statements of intent, rate changes, **Util 36.102**
Storage, machinery and equipment, **Util 35.151**
  Registration, **Util 35.152**
Stranded costs,
  Competition, recovery, **Util 39.251 et seq.**
  Municipal power agencies, recovery, customer choice, **Util 40.059**
  Municipalities, securities, competition, **Util 40.003**
  River authorities, securities, competition, **Util 40.003**
Streets and alleys, easements, **Util 181.042 et seq.**
Submetering,
  Multiple unit complexes, **Util 184.013, 184.014**
  Recreational vehicle parks, **Util 184.031 et seq.**
Sunset Act, customer choice, independent organizations, **Util 39.151**
Surcharge,
  Force majeure, freeze period, **Util 39.055**
  Military bases, **Util 36.354**
    Energy efficiency, **Util 39.910**
  Temporary rates, pending final determination, **Util 36.155, 36.156**
Suspension. Revocation or suspension, generally, ante
Switching providers, **Util 17.101, 17.102**
System benefit fund, **Util 39.903**
  Discounts, deceptive trade practices and consumer protection, **Util 17.007**
System restoration, bonds, **Util 36.401 et seq.**
Tariffs,
  Municipalities, open access, **Util 40.058**
  Open access, competition, **Util 39.204**
  Rates and charges, generally, ante
  Recovery of costs, nonERCOT utilities, transmission, improvements, **Util 36.209**
Tax exemptions,
  Joint powers agencies,
    Bonds and securities, **Util 163.124**
    Electric cooperative corporations, bonds and securities, **Util 163.124**
  Municipalities, **Util 40.104**
  Private and public entities, cooperation, **Util 163.015**
  Transition property, securities, competition, **Util 39.311**
Taxation,
  Municipal power agencies, imposition, **Util 163.054**
  Private and public entities, cooperation, **Util 163.015**
  Rates and charges,
    Adjustments, **Util 36.202**

ELECTRICITY—Cont'd
Taxation—Cont'd
Rates and charges—Cont'd
Computation,
Consolidated returns, **Util 36.060**
Tax benefits, **Util 36.059**
River authorities, affiliates, **Util 32.053**
Telecommunications, customer choice, solicitations, **Util 39.1025**
Termination of service,
Aged and handicapped persons, **Util 14.005**
Certificates of convenience and necessity, standards, **Util 37.152**
Emergencies, extreme weather emergencies, **Util 39.101**
Unauthorized charges, nonpayment, **Util 17.152**
Weather, extreme weather emergencies, **Util 39.101**
Weekends, **Util 39.101**
Tests, machinery and equipment, **Util 38.051, 38.052, 102.101 et seq.**
Time,
Aged persons, payment, **Util 182.002**
Certificates of convenience and necessity, transmission, applications, **Util 37.057**
Municipalities, ante
Notice of intent, rate changes, **Util 36.103**
Rates and charges, ante
Small power producers, contracts, certificates and certification, **Util 35.065, 35.066**
Statements of intent, rate changes, **Util 36.102**
Toll free numbers, underground facilities, contracts, notification corporation, excavations, **Util 251.061**
Trade associations, computation of rates, expenses, **Util 36.062**
Transition bonds,
Competition, **Util 39.301 et seq.**
Municipalities, competition, **Util 40.003**
Transition charges, stranded costs, competition, recovery, **Util 39.251 et seq.**
Transmission, **Util 31.002, 181.008**
Alternative providers, access, **Util 35.004 et seq.**
Certificates of convenience and necessity, ante
Clearance, **Util 38.004**
Competition,
Rates and charges, **Util 39.203**
Unbundling, **Util 39.051**
Cooperative corporations, **Util 161.123**
Dispute resolution, wholesalers, **Util 35.008**
Easements, generally, ante
Exemptions, rates and charges, demand charges, **Util 36.009**
Improvements,
NonERCOT utilities, recovery of costs, **Util 36.209**
Recommendations, **Util 36.008**
Minimum clearance, **Util 38.004**

ELECTRICITY—Cont'd
Transmission—Cont'd
Orders, access, wholesalers, **Util 35.005**
Rates and charges,
Access, wholesalers, **Util 35.004 et seq., 35.007**
Competition, **Util 39.203**
Exemptions, demand charges, **Util 36.009**
Renewable energy, connections, **Util 39.916**
Reports, wholesalers, access, **Util 35.006**
Rules and regulations, access, wholesalers, **Util 35.006**
State, sales, royalties, in kind, **Util 35.103**
Tariffs, access, wholesalers, **Util 35.007**
Wholesalers, **Util 35.004 et seq.**
True up proceedings, stranded costs, competition, recovery, **Util 39.262**
Trust funds, atomic energy, decommissioning, costs, **Util 39.206**
Trusts and trustees, decommissioning trusts, costs, **Util 39.206**
Unauthorized charges, **Util 17.151 et seq.**
Unbundling, business units, competition, **Util 39.051**
Underground facilities,
Assessments, notification corporation, excavations, **Util 251.062**
Brands, marks and labels,
Crimes and offenses, excavations, **Util 251.203**
Excavations, **Util 251.157, 251.158**
Call router system, contracts, notification corporation, excavations, **Util 251.061**
Contracts, toll free numbers, notification corporation, excavations, **Util 251.061**
Conversion, **Util 251.005**
Crimes and offenses, brands, marks and labels, excavations, **Util 251.203**
Damages, **Util 251.001 et seq.**
Notification corporation, excavations, **Util 251.054**
Directors, notification corporation, excavations, **Util 251.055 et seq.**
Easements, excavations, **Util 251.006**
Emergencies, notice, excavations, **Util 251.155**
Excavations, **Util 251.001 et seq.**
Exemptions, notice, excavations, **Util 251.156**
Expenses and expenditures, notification corporation, excavations, **Util 251.054**
Fees,
Notification center, excavations, **Util 251.105**
Notification corporation, excavations, **Util 251.062**
Fines and penalties, excavations, **Util 251.201 et seq.**
Fraud, emergencies, excavations, **Util 251.155**

ELECTRICITY—Cont'd
Underground facilities—Cont'd
Fraud, emergencies, excavations —Cont'd
Fines and penalties, **Util 251.201**
Highways and roads, excavations, **Util 251.007**
Insurance, notification center, excavations, **Util 251.104**
Licenses and permits, excavations, **Util 251.006**
Notice, excavations, **Util 251.009, 251.151 et seq.**
Notification center, excavations, **Util 251.101 et seq.**
Notification corporation, excavations, **Util 251.051 et seq.**
Officers and employees, notification corporation, excavations, **Util 251.058**
Open meetings, notification corporation, excavations, **Util 251.053**
Open records, notification corporation, excavations, **Util 251.053**
Payment, notification center, excavations, **Util 251.106**
Powers and duties,
Notification center, excavations, **Util 251.102**
Notification corporation, excavations, **Util 251.060**
Rates and charges,
Notification center, excavations, **Util 251.105**
Notification corporation, excavations, **Util 251.062**
Records and recordation, notification center, excavations, **Util 251.103**
Remedies, excavations, **Util 251.008**
Repairs, excavations, **Util 251.159**
Reports, damages, excavations, **Util 251.159**
Safety, **Util 251.001 et seq.**
Toll free numbers, contracts, notification corporation, excavations, **Util 251.061**
Venue, fines and penalties, excavations, **Util 251.201**
Warnings, excavations, **Util 251.201, 251.2011**
Unfair practices. Deceptive trade practices and consumer protection, generally, ante
Valuation, affiliates, transfers of assets, exemptions, **Util 35.035**
Venue, underground facilities, fines and penalties, excavations, **Util 251.201**
Warnings, underground facilities, excavations, **Util 251.201, 251.2011**
Weather,
Emergencies, plans and specifications, reports, **Util 186.007**
Termination of service, extreme weather emergencies, **Util 39.101**
Weekends, termination of service, **Util 39.101**

ELECTRICITY—Cont'd
Weights and measures. Meters, generally, ante
Wholesalers,
Alternative energy, **Util 35.001 et seq.**
Certificates of convenience and necessity, application of law, **Util 37.001**
Customer choice, contracts, **Util 39.108**
Independent organizations, markets and marketing, monitors, **Util 39.1515**
Exemptions, **Util 35.031 et seq.**
Generation, exemptions, **Util 31.002**
Municipalities, markets and marketing, **Util 40.102**
Orders, access, **Util 35.005**
Power marketers, **Util 35.031 et seq.**
Registration, **Util 39.355**
Priorities and preferences, **Util 35.003**
Rates and charges, discounts, **Util 36.007**
Registration, power marketers, **Util 39.355**
River authorities, jurisdiction, **Util 32.051 et seq.**
Transmission, **Util 35.004 et seq.**
Zones, renewable energy, **Util 39.904**

ELECTRONIC COMMUNICATIONS
See, also, Telecommunications, generally, this index
Cooperative associations, consent, meetings, **Bus Org 6.205**
Corporations, this index
Limited liability companies, consent, meetings, **Bus Org 6.205**
Nonprofit corporations, consent, meetings, **Bus Org 6.205**
Professional associations and societies, consent, meetings, **Bus Org 6.205**
Professional corporations, consent, meetings, **Bus Org 6.205**

ELECTRONIC TRANSACTIONS
Communications. Electronic Communications, generally, this index

ELEEMOSYNARY ORGANIZATIONS
Nonprofit Corporations, generally, this index

ELEMENTARY SCHOOLS
Schools and School Districts, generally, this index

EMERGENCIES
Cooperative associations, governance, **Bus Org 3.251 et seq.**
Corporations, governance, **Bus Org 3.251 et seq.**
Definitions,
Business organizations, governance, **Bus Org 3.251**
Telecommunications, **Util 186.041**
Electricity, this index
Firefighters and Fire Departments, this index

EMERGENCIES—Cont'd
Foreign corporations, governance, **Bus Org 3.251 et seq.**
Gas utilities, pipes and pipelines, liaison, **Util 121.2015**
Limited liability companies, governance, **Bus Org 3.251 et seq.**
Nonprofit corporations, governance, **Bus Org 3.251 et seq.**
Oil and Gas, this index
Partnerships, governance, **Bus Org 3.251 et seq.**
Plans and specifications, electricity, weather, reports, **Util 186.007**
Police, this index
Professional associations and societies, governance, **Bus Org 3.251 et seq.**
Professional corporations, governance, **Bus Org 3.251 et seq.**
Sewers and Sewer Systems, this index
Telecommunications, this index
Water Supply, this index
Weather, electricity, plans and specifications, reports, **Util 186.007**

EMINENT DOMAIN
Costs, railroads, public utilities, right of way, **Util 186.056, 186.059**
Damages, public utilities, **Util 186.056, 186.059**
Electric cooperative corporations, **Util 161.125**
Electricity, this index
Gas Utilities, this index
Interurban Railroads, this index
Oil and Gas Pipelines, this index
Public Utilities, this index
Railroads, this index
Telecommunications, this index
Telephone cooperative corporations, **Util 162.124**
Water Supply, this index

EMISSIONS
Air Pollution, this index

ENCUMBRANCES
Liens and Incumbrances, generally, this index

ENERGY
Alternative energy. Solar Energy, generally, this index
Electricity, generally, this index
Gifts, efficiency, **Util 39.911**
Grants, efficiency, **Util 39.911**
Oil and Gas, generally, this index
Renewable energy, **Util 39.904**
Connections, **Util 39.916**
Markets and marketing, nonERCOT utilities, **Util 39.555**
Reports,
Combining, **Util 39.913**
Heating, electricity, **Util 39.912**
Solar Energy, generally, this index

ENERGY TRANSPORTERS
Definitions, railroads, right of way, **Util 186.051**

ENTITY
Definitions, business organizations, **Bus Org 1.002**

ENTRY ON PROPERTY
Cable television, identity and identification, **Util 55.017**
Gas utilities, inspections, **Util 102.205**
Public utilities, inspection, **Util 14.206**
Telecommunications, this index

ENVIRONMENTAL PROTECTION
Electricity, cleanup, stranded costs, competition, recovery, **Util 39.263**
Solar Energy, generally, this index

ERCOT
Definitions, electricity, **Util 31.002**

ESTATES
Probate Proceedings, generally, this index

EVIDENCE
Burden of proof,
Electricity, rates and charges, changes, **Util 36.006**
Gas Utilities, this index
Telecommunications, this index
Business development corporations, loans, **Bus Org 23.066**
Confidential or Privileged Information, generally, this index
Cooperative Associations, this index
Corporations, this index
Foreign Corporations, this index
Gas Utilities, this index
Limited Liability Companies, this index
Limited partnerships. Partnerships, this index
Nonprofit Corporations, this index
Partnerships, this index
Presumptions. Partnerships, this index
Privileged communications. Confidential or Privileged Information, generally, this index
Production of Books and Papers, generally, this index
Professional Associations and Societies, this index
Professional Corporations, this index
Public utilities, aged persons, delay in payment, proof of age, **Util 182.004**
Telecommunications, this index

EXCAVATE
Definitions, underground facilities, **Util 251.001**

EXCAVATORS
Definitions, underground facilities, **Util 251.001**

EXCHANGE OF PROPERTY
Cooperative Associations, this index
Corporations, this index

EXCHANGE OF PROPERTY—Cont'd
Foreign Corporations, this index
Limited Liability Companies, this index
Limited partnerships. Partnerships, this index
Nonprofit Corporations, this index
Partnerships, this index
Professional Associations and Societies, this index
Professional Corporations, this index
Real estate investment trusts, **Bus Org 200.404 et seq.**
Shares and shareholders. Corporations, this index

EXCLUSIVE RIGHTS
Electricity, certificates of convenience and necessity, **Util 37.051**

EXECUTIONS
Churches, retirement and pensions, **Bus Org 22.407**
Cooperative associations, certificates and certification, **Bus Org 251.204**
Religious organizations and societies, retirement and pensions, **Bus Org 22.407**

EXECUTIVE COMMITTEES
County executive committees. Elections, generally, this index

EXECUTIVE DEPARTMENTS
Governor, generally, this index

EXECUTIVE DIRECTORS
Public utility commission, **Util 12.101, 12.103**

EXECUTIVE ORDERS
Governor, this index

EXEMPTIONS
Agriculture, this index
Cable Television, this index
Cooperative Associations, this index
Corporations, this index
Electric Cooperative Corporations, this index
Electricity, this index
Foreign Corporations, this index
Gas Utilities, this index
Limited Liability Companies, this index
Limited partnerships. Partnerships, this index
Nonprofit Corporations, this index
Oil and Gas, this index
Partnerships, this index
Professional Associations and Societies, this index
Professional Corporations, this index
Public Utilities, this index
Sewers and Sewer Systems, this index
Tax Exemptions, generally, this index
Telecommunications, this index
Telephone Cooperative Corporations, this index
Television and Radio, this index

EXEMPTIONS—Cont'd
Water Supply, this index

EXISTING PURCHASED POWER CONTRACT
Definitions, electricity, competition, stranded costs, recovery, **Util 39.251**

EXPLORATION AND PRODUCTION UNDERGROUND FACILITIES
Definitions, excavations, **Util 251.001**

EXPRESS TRUST
Trusts and Trustees, generally, this index

EXTREME WEATHER EMERGENCIES
Definitions,
  Electricity, termination of service, **Util 39.101**
  Gas utilities, termination, **Util 104.258**

FACSIMILE
Cooperative Associations, this index
Corporations, this index
Foreign Corporations, this index
Limited Liability Companies, this index
Limited partnerships. Partnerships, this index
Nonprofit Corporations, this index
Partnerships, this index
Professional Associations and Societies, this index
Professional Corporations, this index

FAITH BASED ORGANIZATIONS
Religious Organizations and Societies, generally, this index

FARES
Rates and Charges, generally, this index

FARMS AND FARMERS
Agriculture, generally, this index

FEDERAL AID
Public utilities, commission, **Util 16.021**

FEDERAL LAW
Gas utilities,
  Conflict of laws, **Util 101.008**
  Pipes and pipelines, safety, **Util 121.201**
Public utilities, conflict of laws, **Util 11.009**
Telecommunications, unbundling of services, **Util 60.021**

FIBER OPTICS
Telecommunications, this index

FICTITIOUS AND ASSUMED NAMES
Assumed or Fictitious Names, generally, this index

FIDELITY BONDS
Bonds (Officers and Fiduciaries), generally, this index

FIDUCIARIES
Bonds (Officers and Fiduciaries), generally, this index

FIDUCIARIES—Cont'd
Guardian and Ward, generally, this index
Trusts and Trustees, generally, this index

FINANCIAL ASSISTANCE
Telecommunications, hearing impaired persons, machinery and equipment, **Util 56.151 et seq.**

FINANCIAL INSTITUTIONS
Banks and Banking, generally, this index
Business development corporations, members, **Bus Org 23.062**
Credit Unions, generally, this index
Definitions, business development corporations, **Bus Org 23.051**

FINANCIAL INTEREST
Conflict of Interest, generally, this index

FINANCIAL STATEMENTS AND REPORTS
Corporations, this index

FINANCING ORDERS
Definitions, electricity, securities, competition, **Util 39.302**

FINANCING PARTIES
Definitions, electricity, securities, competition, **Util 39.302**

FINES AND PENALTIES
Apartment Houses, this index
Cooperative Associations, this index
Corporations, this index
Electricity, this index
Foreign Corporations, this index
Gas Utilities, this index
Limited Liability Companies, this index
Limited partnerships. Partnerships, this index
Nonprofit Corporations, this index
Oil and Gas, this index
Oil and Gas Pipelines, this index
Partnerships, this index
Professional Associations and Societies, this index
Professional Corporations, this index
Public Utilities, this index
Telecommunications, this index
Underground Natural Gas, this index
Water Supply, this index

FIREFIGHTERS AND FIRE DEPARTMENTS
Emergencies, gas utilities, pipes and pipelines, liaison, **Util 121.2015**

FLOODS AND FLOOD CONTROL
Electricity, restoration, bonds, **Util 36.401 et seq.**

FORCE MAJEURE
Definitions, electricity, rates and charges, freeze period, **Util 39.055**

FOREIGN ASSOCIATIONS
Professional Associations and Societies, this index

FOREIGN COMMERCE
Interstate Commerce, generally, this index

FOREIGN CORPORATIONS
Generally, **Bus Org 1.001 et seq., 301.001 et seq.**
Abandonment, **Bus Org 10.201 et seq.**
Filing, **Bus Org 4.057**
Abatement of actions and proceedings,
State, **Bus Org 12.260**
Termination, involuntary termination, **Bus Org 11.304**
Winding up, involuntary winding up, **Bus Org 11.304**
Acceptance, certificates and certification, **Bus Org 10.156**
Accounts and accounting, **Bus Org 3.151 et seq.**
Examinations and examiners, **Bus Org 12.151 et seq.**
Fines and penalties, **Bus Org 21.222**
Acknowledgments,
Certificate of formation, **Bus Org 3.004**
Evidence, **Bus Org 3.001**
Filing, **Bus Org 4.002**
Effective date, delay, **Bus Org 4.059**
Registration, **Bus Org 9.008**
Actions and proceedings, **Bus Org 2.101**
Abatement of actions and proceedings, generally, ante
Business Organizations Code, prior law, **Bus Org 402.014**
Certificate of formation, amendments, **Bus Org 3.056**
Derivative actions, generally, post
Guaranty, **Bus Org 2.104**
Indemnity, **Bus Org 8.001 et seq.**
Insolvency, **Bus Org 12.253 et seq.**
Receivers and receivership, **Bus Org 11.406**
Records and recordation, inspection and inspectors, **Bus Org 3.152**
Registration, **Bus Org 9.051 et seq.**
State, liens and incumbrances, **Bus Org 12.201 et seq.**
Termination, involuntary termination, **Bus Org 11.303**
Transacting business in Texas, **Bus Org 9.251**
Venue, generally, post
Winding up, post
Address,
Certificate of formation, **Bus Org 3.005**
Directors, **Bus Org 21.404**
Adoption, Business Organizations Code, **Bus Org 402.003**
Advancements, indemnity, expenses and expenditures, **Bus Org 8.104, 8.105**
Reports, **Bus Org 8.152**
Adverse or pecuniary interest. Conflict of interest, generally, post

FOREIGN CORPORATIONS—Cont'd
Affiliated corporations, business combinations, **Bus Org 21.601 et seq.**
Agent for service of process, **Bus Org 5.251 et seq.**
Agents and agencies,
Changes, filing, fines and penalties, **Bus Org 21.802**
Damages, **Bus Org 301.010**
Elections, **Bus Org 21.417**
Licenses and permits, **Bus Org 301.006**
Registered agent, generally, post
Agreements. Contracts, generally, post
Allocations, merger and consolidation, property, **Bus Org 10.003**
Alternatives, service of process, **Bus Org 5.256**
Amendments,
Business Organizations Code, statutes, **Bus Org 1.054**
Bylaws, **Bus Org 21.057**
Certificate of formation, **Bus Org 3.051 et seq., 21.052 et seq.**
Directors, numbers and numbering, **Bus Org 21.403**
Filing, **Bus Org 4.106**
Fees, **Bus Org 4.152**
Registration, **Bus Org 9.009**
Shares and shareholders, post
Ancillary receiverships, **Bus Org 11.409**
Answer, interrogatories, time, **Bus Org 12.002**
Antitrust, application of law, **Bus Org 10.901**
Appeal and review,
Derivative actions, **Bus Org 21.555**
Filing, **Bus Org 12.004**
Termination, involuntary termination, **Bus Org 11.307**
Winding up, involuntary winding up, **Bus Org 11.307**
Application of law, **Bus Org 301.001**
Antitrust, **Bus Org 10.901**
Business Organizations Code, **Bus Org 9.301, 402.001 et seq.**
Foreign countries, foreign states, **Bus Org 1.053**
Certificate of formation, **Bus Org 1.101 et seq.**
Derivative actions, **Bus Org 21.562**
Indebtedness, **Bus Org 10.901**
Indemnity, **Bus Org 8.002**
Monopolies and unfair trade, **Bus Org 10.901**
Reorganization, **Bus Org 10.306**
Appointments, receivers and receivership, **Bus Org 11.401 et seq.**
Appraisals and appraisers,
Fundamental business transactions, **Bus Org 21.460**
Reorganization, **Bus Org 10.304**
Assets,
Disposition, **Bus Org 10.251 et seq.**
Reorganization, **Bus Org 10.301**
Insolvency, **Bus Org 21.314**
Time, **Bus Org 21.315**

FOREIGN CORPORATIONS—Cont'd
Assets—Cont'd
Liens and incumbrances, state, **Bus Org 12.201**
Sales,
Business combinations, **Bus Org 21.601 et seq.**
Business Organizations Code, mandatory application date, **Bus Org 402.010**
Consent, **Bus Org 21.455**
Winding up, distribution and distributors, **Bus Org 11.053**
Assignments, **Bus Org 10.251 et seq.**
Consent, **Bus Org 21.455**
Shares and shareholders, post
Assumed or fictitious names, **Bus & C 71.001 et seq.; Bus Org 5.051 et seq.**
Attachment, state, **Bus Org 12.259**
Attorney fees,
Derivative actions, payment, **Bus Org 21.561**
Filing,
Fines and penalties, **Bus Org 21.802**
Fraud, **Bus Org 4.007**
Records and recordation,
Examinations and examiners, fines and penalties, **Bus Org 21.222**
Inspection and inspectors, **Bus Org 3.152**
Bankruptcy, **Bus Org 10.301 et seq.**
Banks and banking, transacting business in Texas, **Bus Org 9.251**
Bonds, **Bus Org 2.101**
Reorganization, **Bus Org 10.301**
Bonds (officers and fiduciaries), receivers and receivership, **Bus Org 11.406**
Bonuses, officers and employees, **Bus Org 2.101**
Books and papers, **Bus Org 3.151 et seq.**
Confidential or privileged information, **Bus Org 12.154**
Disclosure, **Bus Org 12.154**
Duplicates and copies, **Bus Org 12.151 et seq.**
Examinations and examiners, **Bus Org 3.153, 12.151 et seq.**
Fines and penalties, **Bus Org 21.222**
Inspection and inspectors, **Bus Org 3.152**
Notice, **Bus Org 1.005**
Powers and duties, limitations, **Bus Org 2.005**
Reorganization, **Bus Org 10.301**
Shares and shareholders, post
Signatures, **Bus Org 1.007**
Business combinations, **Bus Org 21.601 et seq.**
Bylaws, **Bus Org 2.101, 21.057**
Amendments, shares and shareholders, **Bus Org 21.058**
Contracts, **Bus Org 21.101 et seq.**
Electronic communications, notice, shares and shareholders, **Bus Org 21.3531**
Filing, fees, **Bus Org 4.152**

FOREIGN CORPORATIONS—Cont'd
Bylaws—Cont'd
Notice, electronic communications, shares and shareholders, **Bus Org 21.3531**
Shares and shareholders, post
Cancellation,
Reinstatement, **Bus Org 402.013**
Winding up, **Bus Org 11.152, 21.501 et seq.**
Certificate of formation, **Bus Org 3.001 et seq.**
Amendments, **Bus Org 3.051 et seq., 21.052 et seq.**
Application of law, **Bus Org 1.101 et seq.**
Contracts, **Bus Org 21.101 et seq.**
Definitions, **Bus Org 1.002**
Directors, post
Filing,
Fees, **Bus Org 4.152**
Restatement, **Bus Org 21.056**
Merger and consolidation, post
Names, post
Property, rights, **Bus Org 21.051**
Reinstatement, **Bus Org 402.013**
Reorganization, **Bus Org 10.301 et seq.**
Restatement, **Bus Org 3.057 et seq., 21.056**
Shares and shareholders, post
Signatures, **Bus Org 3.004**
Amendments, **Bus Org 3.052, 3.054**
Restatement, **Bus Org 3.058, 3.060**
Statements,
Amendments, **Bus Org 3.053, 3.054**
Restatement, **Bus Org 3.059**
Time, **Bus Org 3.001, 3.003**
Amendments, **Bus Org 3.056**
Restatement, **Bus Org 3.063**
Certificates and certification,
Acceptance, **Bus Org 10.156**
Certificate of formation, generally, ante
Conversion, **Bus Org 10.154 et seq.**
Evidence, existence, **Bus Org 4.005**
Exchange of property, **Bus Org 10.151 et seq.**
Filing, **Bus Org 12.001**
Corrections, **Bus Org 4.101 et seq.**
Fines and penalties, **Bus Org 21.802**
Indebtedness, **Bus Org 2.114**
Merger and consolidation, **Bus Org 10.151 et seq.**
Registration, post
Shares and shareholders, **Bus Org 3.201 et seq.**
Termination, post
Certified copies,
Filing, **Bus Org 4.005**
Involuntary termination, judgments and decrees, **Bus Org 11.414**
Registration, revocation or suspension, **Bus Org 9.161**
Changes,
Registered agent, post
Registered offices, post
Citizens and citizenship, receivers and receivership, **Bus Org 11.406**

FOREIGN CORPORATIONS—Cont'd
Claims,
Disinterested persons, conflict of interest, **Bus Org 1.003**
Independent persons, conflict of interest, **Bus Org 1.004**
Receivers and receivership, filing, **Bus Org 11.407**
Termination, **Bus Org 11.351 et seq.**
Transacting business in Texas, **Bus Org 9.251**
Closing, shares and shareholders, transfers, records and recordation, **Bus Org 21.355**
Combinations, **Bus Org 21.601 et seq.**
Compensation and salaries,
Disinterested persons, conflict of interest, **Bus Org 1.003**
Independent persons, conflict of interest, **Bus Org 1.004**
Officers and employees, **Bus Org 2.101**
Receivers and receivership, **Bus Org 11.408**
Compromise and settlement, derivative actions, **Bus Org 21.560**
Conduct,
Business Organizations Code, application of law, **Bus Org 402.006**
Damages, **Bus Org 7.001, 301.010**
Confidential or privileged information, interrogatories, **Bus Org 12.003**
Conflict of interest,
Directors, contracts, **Bus Org 21.418**
Disinterested persons, **Bus Org 1.003**
Independent persons, **Bus Org 1.004**
Conflict of laws, **Bus Org 301.002**
Business combinations, **Bus Org 21.609**
Registration, **Bus Org 9.055**
Consent, registered agents, **Bus Org 5.2011**
Conservators and conservatorship, shares and shareholders, privileges and immunities, **Bus Org 21.226**
Consolidation. Merger and consolidation, generally, post
Construction of laws, Business Organizations Code, statutes, **Bus Org 1.006, 1.051 et seq.**
Contracts, **Bus Org 2.101**
Business Organizations Code, application of law, **Bus Org 402.006**
Directors, conflict of interest, **Bus Org 21.418**
Disinterested persons, conflict of interest, **Bus Org 1.003**
Indebtedness, **Bus Org 2.103**
Independent persons, conflict of interest, **Bus Org 1.004**
Shares and shareholders, post
Winding up, **Bus Org 11.152**
Contributions,
Definitions, business organizations, **Bus Org 1.002**
Distribution and distributors, damages, **Bus Org 21.318**
Conversion, **Bus Org 10.101 et seq.**
Abandonment, **Bus Org 10.201 et seq.**

FOREIGN CORPORATIONS—Cont'd
Conversion—Cont'd
Acceptance, certificates and certification, **Bus Org 10.156**
Appraisal and appraisers, **Bus Org 21.460**
Business combinations, **Bus Org 21.601 et seq.**
Business Organizations Code, mandatory application date, **Bus Org 402.010**
Certificates and certification, **Bus Org 10.154 et seq.**
Combinations, **Bus Org 21.601 et seq.**
Definitions, business organizations, **Bus Org 1.002**
Dissenting shareholders, **Bus Org 10.351 et seq.**
Effective date, **Bus Org 10.105, 10.106**
Elections, **Bus Org 21.457 et seq.**
Filing,
Certificates and certification, **Bus Org 10.155**
Fees, **Bus Org 4.151**
Names, **Bus Org 10.103**
Notice, **Bus Org 10.101**
Meetings, **Bus Org 21.456**
Objections and exceptions, **Bus Org 21.460**
Plans and specifications, **Bus Org 10.101 et seq., 21.451 et seq.**
Registration, withdrawal, **Bus Org 9.012**
Reorganization, **Bus Org 10.301 et seq.**
Shares and shareholders, post
Conveyances. Deeds and conveyances, generally, post
Cooperative Associations, this index
Copies. Certified copies, generally, ante
Corrections, filing, **Bus Org 4.101 et seq.**
Fees, **Bus Org 4.151**
Costs,
Derivative actions, payment, **Bus Org 21.561**
Filing,
Fines and penalties, **Bus Org 21.802**
Fraud, **Bus Org 4.007**
Insolvency, dismissal and nonsuit, **Bus Org 12.257**
Liens and incumbrances, foreclosure, dismissal and nonsuit, **Bus Org 12.257**
Records and recordation, examinations and examiners, **Bus Org 21.222**
Crimes and offenses,
Books and papers, examinations and examiners, **Bus Org 12.156**
Damages, **Bus Org 7.001**
Fraud, generally, post
Termination, involuntary termination, **Bus Org 11.301 et seq.**
Winding up, involuntary winding up, **Bus Org 11.301 et seq.**
Damages, **Bus Org 301.010**
Application of law, **Bus Org 1.104**
Disinterested persons, conflict of interest, **Bus Org 1.003**

FOREIGN CORPORATIONS—Cont'd
Damages—Cont'd
Distribution and distributors, directors, **Bus Org 21.316**
Filing, **Bus Org 21.802**
Fraud, **Bus Org 4.007**
Guaranty, **Bus Org 2.104**
Indemnity, generally, post
Officers and employees, post
Shares and shareholders, post
Death, shares and shareholders, joint tenants, **Bus Org 21.214**
Debts. Indebtedness, generally, post
Deception, names, **Bus Org 5.052**
Deeds and conveyances, **Bus Org 10.251 et seq., 21.462**
Property, **Bus Org 2.101**
Records and recordation, **Bus Org 10.253**
Deeds of trust, consent, **Bus Org 21.461**
Defenses, records and recordation, examinations and examiners, fines and penalties, **Bus Org 21.222**
Definitions, **Bus Org 1.002, 21.002, 301.003**
Business combinations, **Bus Org 21.601**
Distribution and distributors, **Bus Org 21.301**
Fundamental business transactions, **Bus Org 21.451**
Indemnity, **Bus Org 8.001**
Mandatory application date, **Bus Org 401.001**
Nonprofit corporations, **Bus Org 22.001**
Prior law, **Bus Org 401.001**
Termination, **Bus Org 11.001**
Winding up, **Bus Org 11.001**
Delay, filing, effective date, **Bus Org 4.052 et seq.**
Delivery,
Filing, **Bus Org 4.001**
Shares and shareholders, certificates and certification, **Bus Org 3.204**
Demand,
Derivative actions, **Bus Org 21.553**
Shares and shareholders, post
Deposits, termination, claims, **Bus Org 11.352**
Derivative actions, **Bus Org 21.551 et seq.**
Appeal and review, **Bus Org 21.555**
Application of law, **Bus Org 21.562**
Attorney fees, payment, **Bus Org 21.561**
Compromise and settlement, **Bus Org 21.560**
Costs, payment, **Bus Org 21.561**
Definitions, **Bus Org 21.551**
Demand, **Bus Org 21.553**
Rejection, **Bus Org 21.559**
Discontinuance, **Bus Org 21.560**
Discovery, **Bus Org 21.556**
Disinterested persons, conflict of interest, **Bus Org 1.003**
Dismissal and nonsuit, **Bus Org 21.558**
Elections, **Bus Org 21.554**
Evidence,
Discovery, **Bus Org 21.556**

FOREIGN CORPORATIONS—Cont'd
Derivative actions—Cont'd
Evidence—Cont'd
Dismissal and nonsuit, **Bus Org 21.558**
Expenses and expenditures, payment, **Bus Org 21.561**
Limitation of actions, tolling, **Bus Org 21.557**
Panel, **Bus Org 21.554**
Payment, expenses and expenditures, **Bus Org 21.561**
Rejection, demand, **Bus Org 21.559**
Standing, **Bus Org 21.552**
Supersedeas or stay, **Bus Org 21.555**
Termination, costs, payment, **Bus Org 21.561**
Tolling, limitation of actions, **Bus Org 21.557**
Directors, **Bus Org 21.401 et seq.**
Address, **Bus Org 21.404**
Agent for service of process, **Bus Org 5.255**
Amendments, numbers and numbering, **Bus Org 21.403**
Certificate of formation, **Bus Org 3.007**
Amendments, **Bus Org 3.054, 21.053**
Restatement, **Bus Org 3.060**
Committees, **Bus Org 21.416**
Conflict of interest, contracts, **Bus Org 21.418**
Consent, meetings, notice, electronic communications, **Bus Org 21.411**
Contracts, **Bus Org 21.101 et seq.**
Conflict of interest, **Bus Org 21.418**
Contributions, distribution and distributors, damages, **Bus Org 21.318**
Damages, **Bus Org 7.001**
Definitions, business organizations, **Bus Org 21.002**
Distribution and distributors, damages, **Bus Org 21.316**
Elections, **Bus Org 21.405, 21.406**
Electronic communications, meetings, notice, **Bus Org 21.411**
Evidence, notice, electronic communications, **Bus Org 21.411**
Indemnity, **Bus Org 7.001**
Loans, **Bus Org 2.101**
Meetings, **Bus Org 21.411**
Electronic communications, notice, **Bus Org 21.411**
Notice, **Bus Org 21.411**
Waiver, **Bus Org 21.412**
Objections and exceptions, **Bus Org 21.414**
Organization, **Bus Org 21.059**
Quorum, **Bus Org 21.413, 21.415**
Names, **Bus Org 21.404**
Notice,
Meetings, **Bus Org 21.411**
Electronic communications, **Bus Org 21.411**
Waiver, **Bus Org 21.412**
Resignation, **Bus Org 21.4091**
Numbers and numbering, **Bus Org 21.403**

FOREIGN CORPORATIONS—Cont'd
Directors—Cont'd
Objections and exceptions, meetings, **Bus Org 21.414**
Organization, meetings, **Bus Org 21.059**
Powers and duties, **Bus Org 21.401**
Qualifications, **Bus Org 21.402**
Quorum, meetings, **Bus Org 21.413, 21.415**
Removal, **Bus Org 21.409**
Resignation, notice, **Bus Org 21.4091**
Shares and shareholders, post
Terms of office, **Bus Org 21.407, 21.408**
Vacancies in office, **Bus Org 21.410**
Waiver, meetings, notice, **Bus Org 21.412**
Discharge,
Receivers and receivership, **Bus Org 11.412**
Termination, claims, **Bus Org 11.353**
Winding up, indebtedness, **Bus Org 11.053**
Disclosure, interrogatories, **Bus Org 12.003**
Discontinuance, derivative actions, **Bus Org 21.560**
Discovery, derivative actions, **Bus Org 21.556**
Disinterested persons, conflict of interest, **Bus Org 1.003**
Dismissal and nonsuit,
Derivative actions, **Bus Org 21.558**
Insolvency, **Bus Org 12.257**
Liens and incumbrances, foreclosure, **Bus Org 12.257**
Registration, revocation or suspension, **Bus Org 9.156**
Dissenting shareholders. Shares and shareholders, post
Dissolution, **Bus Org 2.101**
Filing, fees, **Bus Org 4.152**
Involuntary dissolution, reinstatement, **Bus Org 402.013**
Distribution and distributors, **Bus Org 21.301 et seq.**
Contracts, **Bus Org 21.101 et seq.**
Winding up, assets, **Bus Org 11.053**
Dividends, **Bus Org 21.310 et seq.**
Limitations, **Bus Org 21.311**
Par value, **Bus Org 21.312**
Payment, **Bus Org 21.310**
Surplus, transfers, **Bus Org 21.313**
Transfers, surplus, **Bus Org 21.313**
Drains and drainage, **Bus Org 1.001 et seq.**
Dual office holding, officers and employees, **Bus Org 3.103**
Duplicates and copies,
Agent for service of process, **Bus Org 5.252**
Books and papers, **Bus Org 12.151 et seq.**
Filing, **Bus Org 4.003**
Records and recordation, **Bus Org 3.152**
Shares and shareholders, certificates and certification, **Bus Org 3.202**

FOREIGN CORPORATIONS—Cont'd
Effective date,
  Business Organizations Code, **Bus Org 402.001**
    Adoption, **Bus Org 402.005**
  Conversion, **Bus Org 10.105, 10.106**
  Exchange of property, **Bus Org 10.054, 10.055**
  Filing, **Bus Org 4.051 et seq.**
  Merger and consolidation, **Bus Org 10.007**
  Termination, post
Elections,
  Business combinations, **Bus Org 21.610**
  Contracts, **Bus Org 21.101 et seq.**
  Derivative actions, **Bus Org 21.554**
  Directors, **Bus Org 21.405, 21.406**
  Disinterested persons, conflict of interest, **Bus Org 1.003**
  Indemnity, **Bus Org 8.103**
  Officers and employees, post
  Shares and shareholders, post
  Transacting business in Texas, **Bus Org 9.251**
Electronic communications,
  Directors, meetings, notice, **Bus Org 21.411**
  Shares and shareholders, notice, **Bus Org 21.3531**
Electronic filing, **Bus Org 12.001**
Emergencies, governance, **Bus Org 3.251 et seq.**
Employees. Officers and employees, generally, post
Errors,
  Damages, **Bus Org 301.010**
  Termination, reinstatement, **Bus Org 11.201 et seq.**
Escheat, termination, claims, **Bus Org 11.355**
Evidence,
  Certificate of formation, acknowledgments, **Bus Org 3.001**
  Derivative actions,
    Discovery, **Bus Org 21.556**
    Dismissal and nonsuit, **Bus Org 21.558**
  Existence, certificates and certification, **Bus Org 4.005**
  Filing, **Bus Org 4.001**
  Indebtedness, fraud, **Bus Org 2.103**
  Independent persons, conflict of interest, **Bus Org 1.004**
  Registration, acknowledgments, **Bus Org 9.008**
  Shares and shareholders, post
Examinations and examiners,
  Books and papers, ante
  Records and recordation, post
Exchange of property, **Bus Org 2.101, 10.051 et seq.**
  Abandonment, **Bus Org 10.201 et seq.**
  Acceptance, certificates and certification, **Bus Org 10.156**
  Appraisal and appraisers, **Bus Org 21.460**

FOREIGN CORPORATIONS—Cont'd
Exchange of property—Cont'd
  Business combinations, **Bus Org 21.601 et seq.**
  Certificates and certification, **Bus Org 10.151 et seq.**
  Combinations, **Bus Org 21.601 et seq.**
  Dissenting shareholders, **Bus Org 10.351 et seq.**
  Elections, **Bus Org 21.457 et seq.**
  Filing,
    Certificates and certification, **Bus Org 10.153**
    Fees, **Bus Org 4.151**
  Notice, meetings, **Bus Org 21.456**
  Objections and exceptions, **Bus Org 21.460**
  Plans and specifications, **Bus Org 21.451 et seq.**
  Reorganization, **Bus Org 10.301**
  Shares and shareholders, post
  Voluntary, **Bus Org 10.902**
Exemptions,
  Guaranty, powers and duties, **Bus Org 2.104**
  Interrogatories, **Bus Org 12.002**
  Registration, **Bus Org 9.002**
  Securities, sales, **Bus Org 301.011**
  Termination, involuntary termination, **Bus Org 11.251**
Expenses and expenditures,
  Derivative actions, payment, **Bus Org 21.561**
  Indemnity, **Bus Org 8.001 et seq.**
Facsimile, **Bus Org 1.007**
  Filing, **Bus Org 4.003**
  Indebtedness, certificates and certification, **Bus Org 2.114**
  Seals, **Bus Org 2.101**
  Shares and shareholders,
    Certificates and certification, **Bus Org 3.203**
    Notice, **Bus Org 21.3531**
Fees,
  Business Organizations Code, effective date, **Bus Org 402.002**
  Disinterested persons, conflict of interest, **Bus Org 1.003**
  Filing, **Bus Org 4.151 et seq., 4.152, 4.160**
  Independent persons, conflict of interest, **Bus Org 1.004**
  Names, reservation, **Bus Org 5.101**
    Withdrawal, **Bus Org 5.1041**
  Registration, collection, **Bus Org 9.054**
Filing, **Bus Org 4.001 et seq., 12.001 et seq.**
  Abandonment, **Bus Org 4.057**
  Acknowledgments, **Bus Org 4.002**
    Effective date, delay, **Bus Org 4.059**
  Amendments, **Bus Org 4.106**
  Appeal and review, **Bus Org 12.004**
  Assumed or fictitious names, **Bus Org 5.051**
  Attorney fees,
    Fines and penalties, **Bus Org 21.802**
    Fraud, **Bus Org 4.007**

FOREIGN CORPORATIONS—Cont'd
Filing—Cont'd
  Business Organizations Code, effective date, **Bus Org 402.002**
  Certificate of formation, **Bus Org 3.001 et seq.**
    Restatement, **Bus Org 21.056**
  Certificates and certification, ante
  Certified copies, **Bus Org 4.005**
  Conversion, certificates and certification, **Bus Org 10.155**
  Corrections, **Bus Org 4.101 et seq.**
    Fees, **Bus Org 4.151**
  Costs,
    Fines and penalties, **Bus Org 21.802**
    Fraud, **Bus Org 4.007**
  Damages, **Bus Org 21.802**
    Fraud, **Bus Org 4.007**
  Delay, effective date, **Bus Org 4.052 et seq.**
  Delivery, **Bus Org 4.001**
  Duplicates and copies, **Bus Org 4.003**
  Effective date, **Bus Org 4.051 et seq.**
  Electronic filing, **Bus Org 12.001**
  Evidence, **Bus Org 4.001**
  Facsimile, **Bus Org 4.003**
  Fees, **Bus Org 4.151 et seq., 4.152, 4.160**
  Fines and penalties, **Bus Org 21.802**
    Fraud, **Bus Org 4.008**
  Forms, **Bus Org 4.006**
  Fraud, **Bus Org 4.007, 4.008**
  Interrogatories, **Bus Org 12.002, 12.003**
  Jurisdiction, fines and penalties, **Bus Org 21.802**
  Limitations,
    Corrections, **Bus Org 4.102**
    Effective date, delay, **Bus Org 4.058**
  Names, post
  Real estate investment trusts, **Bus Org 4.009**
  Receivers and receivership, claims, **Bus Org 11.407**
  Registered agents, resignation, **Bus Org 5.204**
  Registration, revocation or suspension, **Bus Org 9.161**
  Service of process, **Bus Org 21.802**
  Signatures, **Bus Org 4.001**
    Corrections, certificates and certification, **Bus Org 4.101**
  Termination, involuntary termination, **Bus Org 11.315**
  Time, **Bus Org 4.004**
    Corrections, **Bus Org 4.105**
    Effective date, **Bus Org 4.051 et seq.**
    Fines and penalties, **Bus Org 21.802**
  Winding up, involuntary winding up, **Bus Org 11.315**
  Withdrawal, post
Financial statements and reports,
  Insolvency, **Bus Org 21.314**
  Officers and employees, good faith, **Bus Org 3.102, 3.105**
Fines and penalties,
  Books and papers, examinations and examiners, **Bus Org 12.156**

FOREIGN CORPORATIONS—Cont'd
Fines and penalties—Cont'd
Filing, **Bus Org 21.802**
Fraud, **Bus Org 4.008**
Meetings, notice, **Bus Org 21.221**
Records and recordation, examinations and examiners, **Bus Org 21.222**
Registered agents, consent, **Bus Org 5.207**
Registration, **Bus Org 9.052**
Shares and shareholders, post
Foreclosure, liens and incumbrances, **Bus Org 12.252 et seq.**
Forfeitures,
Books and papers, examinations and examiners, **Bus Org 12.155**
Reinstatement, **Bus Org 402.013**
Formation. Certificate of formation, generally, ante
Forms,
Filing, **Bus Org 4.006**
Shares and shareholders, certificates and certification, **Bus Org 3.202**
Fraud,
Filing, **Bus Org 4.007, 4.008**
Guaranty, **Bus Org 2.104**
Indebtedness, evidence, **Bus Org 2.103**
Names, **Bus Org 5.052**
Receivers and receivership, **Bus Org 11.403**
Termination,
Involuntary termination, **Bus Org 11.301 et seq.**
Revocation or suspension, **Bus Org 11.153**
Winding up, involuntary winding up, **Bus Org 11.301 et seq.**
Frauds, statute of, powers and duties, **Bus Org 2.112**
Fundamental business transactions, **Bus Org 21.451 et seq.**
Garnishment, state, **Bus Org 12.259**
Gifts, **Bus Org 2.101**
Good faith,
Damages, **Bus Org 7.001**
Officers and employees, **Bus Org 3.102, 3.105**
Guaranty, **Bus Org 2.101**
Powers and duties, **Bus Org 2.104**
Hold harmless. Indemnity, generally, post
Holding companies, merger and consolidation, **Bus Org 10.005**
Identity and identification, names, same or similar, **Bus Org 5.053**
Incentives, officers and employees, **Bus Org 2.101**
Incumbrances. Liens and incumbrances, generally, post
Indebtedness, **Bus Org 2.101, 2.103**
Application of law, **Bus Org 10.901**
Certificates and certification, **Bus Org 2.114**
Transacting business in Texas, **Bus Org 9.251**
Winding up, discharge, **Bus Org 11.053**

FOREIGN CORPORATIONS—Cont'd
Indemnity,
Business Organizations Code, application of law, **Bus Org 402.007**
Insurance, **Bus Org 8.151**
Mandatory, **Bus Org 8.051**
Officers and employees, post
Orders of court, **Bus Org 8.052**
Permissive indemnification, **Bus Org 8.101 et seq.**
Reports, **Bus Org 8.152**
Independent persons, conflict of interest, **Bus Org 1.004**
Information, notice, **Bus Org 1.005**
Injunctions,
Guaranty, **Bus Org 2.104**
Registration, **Bus Org 9.051**
State, **Bus Org 12.259**
Insolvency,
Actions and proceedings, **Bus Org 12.253 et seq.**
Definitions, **Bus Org 1.002**
Determination, **Bus Org 21.314**
Time, **Bus Org 21.315**
Inspection and inspectors,
Books and papers, **Bus Org 12.151 et seq.**
Records and recordation, **Bus Org 3.152**
Insurance, indemnity, **Bus Org 2.101, 8.151**
Internal affairs, **Bus Org 1.105**
International commerce development corporations, **Bus Org 1.001 et seq.**
Interrogatories, **Bus Org 12.002, 12.003**
Investments, **Bus Org 2.101**
Transacting business in Texas, **Bus Org 9.251**
Involuntary termination, **Bus Org 11.251 et seq.**
Certified copies, judgments and decrees, **Bus Org 11.414**
Joint practices, **Bus Org 301.012**
Judgments and decrees,
Receivers and receivership, termination, **Bus Org 11.412**
Registration, revocation or suspension, **Bus Org 9.154 et seq.**
Reorganization, **Bus Org 10.305**
Termination, **Bus Org 11.301 et seq.**
Involuntary termination, certified copies, **Bus Org 11.414**
Winding up, **Bus Org 11.301 et seq.**
Jurisdiction,
Filing, fines and penalties, **Bus Org 21.802**
Insolvency, **Bus Org 12.253**
Liens and incumbrances, foreclosure, **Bus Org 12.253**
Receivers and receivership, **Bus Org 11.402 et seq.**
Registration, revocation or suspension, **Bus Org 9.158**
Reorganization, **Bus Org 10.302**
Termination, involuntary termination, **Bus Org 11.308**

FOREIGN CORPORATIONS—Cont'd
Jurisdiction—Cont'd
Winding up, involuntary winding up, **Bus Org 11.308**
Leases, **Bus Org 2.101, 10.251 et seq.**
Business combinations, **Bus Org 21.601 et seq.**
Consent, **Bus Org 21.455**
Reorganization, **Bus Org 10.301**
Licenses and permits, **Bus Org 301.006**
Liens and incumbrances,
Foreclosure, **Bus Org 12.252 et seq.**
Notice,
Foreclosure, **Bus Org 12.256**
State, **Bus Org 12.201**
State, **Bus Org 12.201**
Transacting business in Texas, **Bus Org 9.251**
Limitation of actions,
Derivative actions, tolling, **Bus Org 21.557**
Distribution and distributors, **Bus Org 21.317**
Shares and shareholders, post
Termination, claims, **Bus Org 11.359**
Limitations,
Distribution and distributors, **Bus Org 21.303**
Dividends, **Bus Org 21.311**
Filing, ante
Indemnity, **Bus Org 8.003, 8.004**
Powers and duties, **Bus Org 2.113**
Purposes, **Bus Org 2.003 et seq.**
Liquidation, receivers and receivership, **Bus Org 12.258**
Orders of court, **Bus Org 11.405**
Lists,
Shares and shareholders, post
Transacting business in Texas, **Bus Org 9.251, 9.252**
Loans, **Bus Org 2.101**
Transacting business in Texas, **Bus Org 9.251**
Location, offices, **Bus Org 2.101**
Lodges, **Bus Org 1.001 et seq.**
Losses, contracts, **Bus Org 21.101 et seq.**
Lottery, names, **Bus Org 5.061**
Managers and management,
Agent for service of process, **Bus Org 5.255**
Damages, **Bus Org 301.010**
Directors, generally, ante
Licenses and permits, **Bus Org 301.006**
Resignation, **Bus Org 301.008**
Winding up, **Bus Org 21.504**
Mandatory application date, Business Organizations Code, **Bus Org 401.001 et seq.**
Meetings,
Business Organizations Code, mandatory application date, **Bus Org 402.008, 402.009**
Certificate of formation, amendments, **Bus Org 21.055**
Directors, ante
Emergencies, **Bus Org 3.251 et seq.**

FOREIGN CORPORATIONS—Cont'd
Meetings—Cont'd
Notice,
Fines and penalties, **Bus Org 21.221**
Organization, **Bus Org 21.059**
Organization, **Bus Org 21.059**
Shares and shareholders, post
Transacting business in Texas, **Bus Org 9.251**
Merger and consolidation, **Bus Org 10.001 et seq.**
Abandonment, **Bus Org 10.201 et seq.**
Acceptance, certificates and certification, **Bus Org 10.156**
Allocations, property, **Bus Org 10.003**
Appraisal and appraisers, **Bus Org 21.460**
Business combinations, **Bus Org 21.601 et seq.**
Business Organizations Code, mandatory application date, **Bus Org 402.010**
Certificate of formation, **Bus Org 3.005, 3.006, 10.002**
Certificates and certification, **Bus Org 10.151 et seq.**
Combinations, **Bus Org 21.601 et seq.**
Definitions, **Bus Org 1.002**
Business organizations, **Bus Org 1.002**
Dissenting shareholders, **Bus Org 10.351 et seq.**
Effect, **Bus Org 10.008**
Effective date, **Bus Org 10.007**
Elections, **Bus Org 21.457 et seq.**
Filing,
Certificates and certification, **Bus Org 10.153**
Fees, **Bus Org 4.151**
Holding companies, **Bus Org 10.005**
Names, **Bus Org 10.002**
Notice, meetings, **Bus Org 21.456**
Objections and exceptions, **Bus Org 21.460**
Plans and specifications, **Bus Org 10.001 et seq., 21.451 et seq.**
Property, allocations, **Bus Org 10.003**
Reorganization, **Bus Org 10.301 et seq.**
Shares and shareholders, post
Subsidiaries, **Bus Org 10.006**
Certificates and certification, **Bus Org 10.152**
Time, effective date, **Bus Org 10.007**
Mines and minerals, transacting business in Texas, **Bus Org 9.251**
Misconduct, damages, **Bus Org 7.001**
Money, **Bus Org 1.009**
Monopolies and unfair trade, application of law, **Bus Org 10.901**
Moratoriums, business combinations, **Bus Org 21.606, 21.607**
Mortgages, **Bus Org 2.101**
Business combinations, **Bus Org 21.601 et seq.**
Consent, **Bus Org 21.455, 21.461**
Powers and duties, **Bus Org 2.104**

FOREIGN CORPORATIONS—Cont'd
Mortgages—Cont'd
Receivers and receivership, **Bus Org 11.403**
Transacting business in Texas, **Bus Org 9.251**
Names, **Bus Org 5.001 et seq.**
Assumed or fictitious names, **Bus Org 5.051 et seq.**
Certificate of formation, **Bus Org 3.005**
Amendments, **Bus Org 3.053, 3.056**
Conversion, **Bus Org 10.103**
Deception, **Bus Org 5.052**
Directors, **Bus Org 21.404**
Exchange of property, plans and specifications, **Bus Org 10.052**
Fees, reservation, **Bus Org 5.101**
Withdrawal, **Bus Org 5.1041**
Filing,
Fees, **Bus Org 4.151, 4.152**
Registration, **Bus Org 5.152**
Fraud, **Bus Org 5.052**
Identity and identification, same or similar, **Bus Org 5.053**
Lottery, **Bus Org 5.061**
Merger and consolidation, **Bus Org 10.002**
Notice, **Bus Org 5.001**
Registration, **Bus Org 5.151 et seq.**
Change of name, **Bus Org 9.010**
Reinstatement, **Bus Org 9.105**
Renewal,
Registration, **Bus Org 5.155**
Reservation, **Bus Org 5.105**
Reservation, **Bus Org 5.101 et seq.**
Same or similar, **Bus Org 5.053**
Registration, **Bus Org 5.153**
Reservation, **Bus Org 5.102**
Termination, reinstatement, **Bus Org 11.203**
Time,
Registration, **Bus Org 5.154**
Reservation, **Bus Org 5.104**
Trademarks and trade names, **Bus Org 5.001**
Transfers, reservation, **Bus Org 5.106**
Veterans organizations, **Bus Org 5.062**
Words and phrases, **Bus Org 5.054**
Negligence, damages, **Bus Org 301.010**
Nonfiling, certificate of formation, **Bus Org 3.002**
Nonprofit Corporations, this index
Notice,
Agent for service of process, **Bus Org 5.252, 5.253**
Certificate of formation, amendments, **Bus Org 21.055**
Conversion, **Bus Org 10.101**
Directors, ante
Fundamental business transactions, meetings, **Bus Org 21.456**
Guaranty, fraud, **Bus Org 2.104**
Indemnity, orders of court, **Bus Org 8.052**
Information, **Bus Org 1.005**
Insolvency, **Bus Org 12.256**
Liens and incumbrances, ante

FOREIGN CORPORATIONS—Cont'd
Notice—Cont'd
Meetings,
Fines and penalties, **Bus Org 21.221**
Organization, **Bus Org 21.059**
Names, **Bus Org 5.001**
Receivers and receivership, claims, **Bus Org 11.407**
Registered agent, resignation, **Bus Org 5.204**
Registration, post
Reorganization, **Bus Org 10.301**
Shares and shareholders, post
Termination, post
Winding up, post
Numbers and numbering,
Directors, **Bus Org 21.403**
Shares and shareholders, **Bus Org 21.151**
Elections, **Bus Org 21.366**
Oaths and affirmations, interrogatories, answer, **Bus Org 12.002**
Objections and exceptions, directors, meetings, **Bus Org 21.414**
Offenses. Crimes and offenses, generally, ante
Officers and employees, **Bus Org 3.101 et seq.**
Agent for service of process, **Bus Org 5.255**
Compensation and salaries, **Bus Org 2.101**
Contracts, **Bus Org 21.101 et seq.**
Damages, **Bus Org 7.001, 301.010**
Application of law, **Bus Org 1.104**
Directors, generally, ante
Dual office holding, **Bus Org 3.103**
Elections, **Bus Org 2.101, 3.103, 21.417**
Good faith, **Bus Org 3.105**
Indemnity, **Bus Org 2.101, 7.001, 8.001 et seq.**
Licenses and permits, **Bus Org 301.006**
Loans, **Bus Org 2.101**
Removal, **Bus Org 3.104**
Retirement and pensions, **Bus Org 2.101**
Offices, **Bus Org 2.101**
Changes, filing, fines and penalties, **Bus Org 21.802**
Registered offices, generally, post
Reorganization, **Bus Org 10.301**
Transacting business in Texas, **Bus Org 9.251**
Omissions, certificate of formation, restatement, **Bus Org 3.059**
Open records, interrogatories, **Bus Org 12.003**
Orders of court, receivers and receivership, **Bus Org 11.402**
Liquidation, **Bus Org 11.405**
Organization, meetings, **Bus Org 21.059**
Panel, derivative actions, **Bus Org 21.554**
Par value, dividends, **Bus Org 21.312**
Parties, receivers and receivership, **Bus Org 11.411**

FOREIGN CORPORATIONS—Cont'd
Payment,
  Derivative actions, expenses and expenditures, **Bus Org 21.561**
  Dividends, **Bus Org 21.310**
  Shares and shareholders, post
  Termination,
    Claims, **Bus Org 11.354**
    Taxation, **Bus Org 11.101**
Penalties. Fines and penalties, generally, ante
Permissive indemnification, **Bus Org 8.101 et seq.**
Personal property, **Bus Org 2.101**
  Disposition, **Bus Org 10.251 et seq.**
    Reorganization, **Bus Org 10.301**
  Shares and shareholders, **Bus Org 21.801**
Plans and specifications,
  Conversion, **Bus Org 10.101 et seq.**
  Exchange of property, **Bus Org 10.051 et seq.**
  Merger and consolidation, **Bus Org 10.001 et seq.**
Pledges,
  Business combinations, **Bus Org 21.601 et seq.**
  Consent, **Bus Org 21.455, 21.461**
Political subdivisions, service of process, **Bus Org 5.257**
Powers and duties, **Bus Org 2.101 et seq.**
  Receivers and receivership, **Bus Org 11.406**
Preemption, shares and shareholders, damages, **Bus Org 21.224, 21.225**
President,
  Agent for service of process, **Bus Org 5.255**
  Elections, **Bus Org 21.417**
Prior laws, Business Organizations Code, **Bus Org 401.001 et seq.**
Priorities and preferences,
  Business Organizations Code, application of law, **Bus Org 1.106**
  Certificate of formation, shares and shareholders, **Bus Org 3.007**
  Distribution and distributors, **Bus Org 21.308**
  Shares and shareholders, **Bus Org 21.153**
Privileges and immunities,
  Property, disposition, **Bus Org 10.254**
  Registered agents, **Bus Org 5.208**
Probate Proceedings, this index
Proceedings. Actions and proceedings, generally, ante
Process. Service of process, generally, post
Professional Corporations, this index
Profit sharing, officers and employees, **Bus Org 2.101**
Profits, contracts, **Bus Org 21.101 et seq.**
Property, **Bus Org 2.101**
  Certificate of formation, rights, **Bus Org 21.051**
  Definitions, **Bus Org 1.002**
  Exchange of property, generally, ante

FOREIGN CORPORATIONS—Cont'd
Property—Cont'd
  Liens and incumbrances,
    Foreclosure, **Bus Org 12.252 et seq.**
    State, **Bus Org 12.201**
  Merger and consolidation, allocations, **Bus Org 10.003**
  Real estate, generally, post
Publication,
  Termination, involuntary termination, **Bus Org 11.310**
  Winding up, involuntary winding up, **Bus Org 11.310**
Purchases and purchasing,
  Indemnity, insurance, **Bus Org 8.151**
  Title to property, **Bus Org 301.008**
Purposes, **Bus Org 2.001 et seq.**
  Certificate of formation, **Bus Org 3.005**
Qualifications, directors, **Bus Org 21.402**
Quo warranto, insolvency, **Bus Org 12.253 et seq.**
Real estate, **Bus Org 2.101**
  Disposition, **Bus Org 10.251 et seq.**
    Reorganization, **Bus Org 10.301**
  Records and recordation, deeds and conveyances, **Bus Org 10.253**
  Sales, consent, **Bus Org 21.455**
Receipts, termination, claims, **Bus Org 11.352**
Receivers and receivership, **Bus Org 11.401 et seq.**
  Actions and proceedings, **Bus Org 11.406**
  Ancillary receiverships, **Bus Org 11.409**
  Appointments, **Bus Org 11.401 et seq.**
  Bonds (officers and fiduciaries), **Bus Org 11.406**
  Citizens and citizenship, **Bus Org 11.406**
  Claims, filing, **Bus Org 11.407**
  Compensation and salaries, **Bus Org 11.408**
  Discharge, **Bus Org 11.412**
  Filing, claims, **Bus Org 11.407**
  Foreign entities, **Bus Org 11.409, 11.410**
  Fraud, **Bus Org 11.403**
  Judgments and decrees, termination, **Bus Org 11.412**
  Jurisdiction, **Bus Org 11.402 et seq.**
  Liens and incumbrances, state, **Bus Org 12.201**
  Liquidation, **Bus Org 12.258**
    Orders of court, **Bus Org 11.405**
  Mortgages, **Bus Org 11.403**
  Notice, claims, **Bus Org 11.407**
  Orders of court, **Bus Org 11.402**
    Liquidation, **Bus Org 11.405**
  Parties, **Bus Org 11.411**
  Powers and duties, **Bus Org 11.406**
  Registration, **Bus Org 11.406**
  Rehabilitation, **Bus Org 11.404**
  State, **Bus Org 12.251**
  Termination, **Bus Org 11.403**
    Judgments and decrees, **Bus Org 11.412**

FOREIGN CORPORATIONS—Cont'd
Record date, shares and shareholders, meetings, notice, **Bus Org 21.357**
Records and recordation, **Bus Org 3.151 et seq.**
  Certified copies, filing, **Bus Org 4.005**
  Confidential or privileged information, **Bus Org 12.154**
  Disclosure, **Bus Org 12.154**
  Examinations and examiners, **Bus Org 3.153, 12.151 et seq.**
    Fines and penalties, **Bus Org 21.222**
  Inspection and inspectors, **Bus Org 3.152**
  Interrogatories, open records, **Bus Org 12.003**
  Notice, **Bus Org 1.005**
  Real estate, deeds and conveyances, **Bus Org 10.253**
  Reorganization, **Bus Org 10.301**
  Service of process, **Bus Org 5.254**
  Shares and shareholders, post
  Signatures, **Bus Org 1.007**
  Termination, removal, **Bus Org 11.104**
Registered agent, **Bus Org 5.200 et seq.**
  Changes, **Bus Org 5.202**
    Filing, fines and penalties, **Bus Org 21.802**
    Registered agent, **Bus Org 5.202, 5.203**
  Reorganization, **Bus Org 10.301**
  Resignation, **Bus Org 5.204**
Registered offices, **Bus Org 5.200 et seq.**
  Changes, **Bus Org 5.202**
    Filing, fines and penalties, **Bus Org 21.802**
Registration, **Bus Org 9.001 et seq.**
  Acknowledgments, **Bus Org 9.008**
  Actions and proceedings, **Bus Org 9.051 et seq.**
  Amendments, **Bus Org 9.009**
  Applications, **Bus Org 9.004**
  Business Organizations Code,
    Adoption, **Bus Org 402.004**
    Mandatory application date, **Bus Org 402.012**
  Certificates and certification,
    Reinstatement, **Bus Org 9.104**
    Revocation or suspension, **Bus Org 9.102**
  Certified copies, revocation or suspension, **Bus Org 9.161**
  Conflict of laws, **Bus Org 9.055**
  Conversion, withdrawal, **Bus Org 9.012**
  Dismissal and nonsuit, revocation or suspension, **Bus Org 9.156**
  Evidence, acknowledgments, **Bus Org 9.008**
  Exemptions, **Bus Org 9.002**
  Fees, collection, **Bus Org 9.054**
  Filing, revocation or suspension, **Bus Org 9.161**
  Fines and penalties, **Bus Org 9.052**
  Fraud, **Bus Org 9.051 et seq.**
  Injunctions, **Bus Org 9.051**
  Judgments and decrees, revocation or suspension, **Bus Org 9.154 et seq.**

FOREIGN CORPORATIONS—Cont'd
Registration—Cont'd
Jurisdiction, revocation or suspension, **Bus Org 9.158**
Names, ante
Notice,
Revocation or suspension, **Bus Org 9.101, 9.152**
Service of process, revocation or suspension, **Bus Org 9.160**
Receivers and receivership, **Bus Org 11.406**
Reinstatement, **Bus Org 9.103 et seq.**
Remand, revocation or suspension, **Bus Org 9.157**
Revocation or suspension, **Bus Org 9.101 et seq., 9.151 et seq.**
Same or similar names, reinstatement, **Bus Org 9.105**
Service of process,
Revocation or suspension, **Bus Org 9.159, 9.160**
Withdrawal, **Bus Org 9.011**
Supersedeas or stay, revocation or suspension, **Bus Org 9.156**
Taxation, forfeitures, reinstatement, **Bus Org 9.106**
Time, amendments, **Bus Org 9.009**
Venue, **Bus Org 9.053**
Revocation or suspension, **Bus Org 9.158**
Withdrawal, **Bus Org 9.011**
Rehabilitation, receivers and receivership, **Bus Org 11.404**
Reimbursement, disinterested persons, conflict of interest, **Bus Org 1.003**
Reinstatement,
Registration, **Bus Org 9.103 et seq.**
Termination, post
Winding up, **Bus Org 21.501 et seq.**
Rejection, registered agents, **Bus Org 5.205**
Remand,
Registration, revocation or suspension, **Bus Org 9.157**
Termination, involuntary termination, **Bus Org 11.307**
Winding up, involuntary winding up, **Bus Org 11.307**
Removal,
Directors, **Bus Org 21.409**
Officers and employees, **Bus Org 3.104**
Renewal, names,
Registration, **Bus Org 5.155**
Reservation, **Bus Org 5.105**
Reorganization, **Bus Org 10.301 et seq.**
Business Organizations Code, mandatory application date, **Bus Org 402.010**
Repeals,
Business Organizations Code, statutes, **Bus Org 1.054**
Bylaws, **Bus Org 21.057**
Shares and shareholders, **Bus Org 21.058**
Reports,
Indemnity, **Bus Org 8.152**

FOREIGN CORPORATIONS—Cont'd
Reports—Cont'd
Officers and employees, good faith, **Bus Org 3.102, 3.105**
Rescission, shares and shareholders, contracts, **Bus Org 21.105**
Reservation, names, **Bus Org 5.101 et seq.**
Reserves, surplus, **Bus Org 21.309**
Resignation,
Directors, notice, **Bus Org 21.4091**
Managers and management, **Bus Org 301.008**
Registered agent, **Bus Org 5.204**
Resolutions, indemnity, **Bus Org 8.103**
Restatement, certificate of formation, **Bus Org 3.057 et seq., 21.056**
Retirement and pensions, officers and employees, **Bus Org 2.101**
Review. Appeal and review, generally, ante
Revocation or suspension,
Registration, **Bus Org 9.101 et seq., 9.151 et seq.**
Reinstatement, **Bus Org 402.013**
Termination, fraud, **Bus Org 11.153**
Winding up, **Bus Org 11.151, 21.501 et seq.**
Salaries. Compensation and salaries, generally, ante
Sales, **Bus Org 10.251 et seq.**
Assets, ante
Property, **Bus Org 2.101**
Reorganization, **Bus Org 10.301**
Securities, exemptions, **Bus Org 301.011**
Transacting business in Texas, **Bus Org 9.251**
Same or similar. Names, ante
Seals, **Bus Org 2.101**
Indebtedness, certificates and certification, **Bus Org 2.114**
Shares and shareholders, certificates and certification, **Bus Org 3.202**
Secretaries, elections, **Bus Org 21.417**
Secretary of state, agent for service of process, **Bus Org 5.251 et seq.**
Securities, **Bus Org 2.101**
Powers and duties, **Bus Org 2.104**
Sales, exemptions, **Bus Org 301.011**
Transacting business in Texas, **Bus Org 9.251**
Sequestration, state, **Bus Org 12.259**
Service of process, **Bus Org 5.251 et seq.**
Registration, ante
Reorganization, **Bus Org 10.301**
Termination, involuntary termination, **Bus Org 11.309**
Winding up, involuntary winding up, **Bus Org 11.309**
Shares and shareholders, **Bus Org 21.151 et seq.**
Abandonment, exchange of property, **Bus Org 10.201 et seq.**
Acceptance, exchange of property, certificates and certification, **Bus Org 10.156**

FOREIGN CORPORATIONS—Cont'd
Shares and shareholders—Cont'd
Actions and proceedings. Derivative actions, generally, ante
Amendments,
Bylaws, **Bus Org 21.058**
Certificate of formation, **Bus Org 21.054, 21.055**
Elections, **Bus Org 21.364**
Transfers, **Bus Org 21.212**
Appeal and review, derivative actions, **Bus Org 21.555**
Appointments, dissenting shareholders, appraisal and appraisers, **Bus Org 10.361**
Appraisals and appraisers,
Dissenting shareholders, **Bus Org 10.354 et seq.**
Fundamental business transactions, **Bus Org 21.460**
Assets, sales, **Bus Org 21.455**
Assignments,
Certificates and certification, **Bus Org 3.201**
Damages, **Bus Org 21.217**
Privileges and immunities, **Bus Org 21.226**
Attorney fees, derivative actions, payment, **Bus Org 21.561**
Books and papers, **Bus Org 21.173**
Dissenting shareholders, fair market value, **Bus Org 10.363**
Examinations and examiners, **Bus Org 21.218**
Business combinations, **Bus Org 21.601 et seq.**
Bylaws,
Amendments, **Bus Org 21.058**
Elections, proxies, **Bus Org 21.371**
Meetings,
Directors, elections, **Bus Org 21.359**
Quorum, **Bus Org 21.358**
Repeals, **Bus Org 21.058**
Transfers, **Bus Org 21.212**
Certificate of formation, **Bus Org 21.054 et seq.**
Amendments, elections, **Bus Org 21.364**
Elections, **Bus Org 21.363 et seq.**
Meetings,
Directors, elections, **Bus Org 21.359**
Quorum, **Bus Org 21.358**
Notice, electronic communications, **Bus Org 21.3531**
Numbers and numbering, **Bus Org 3.007**
Preemptive rights, **Bus Org 21.203**
Transfers, **Bus Org 21.212**
Certificates and certification, **Bus Org 3.201 et seq.**
Exchange of property, **Bus Org 10.151 et seq.**
Classification, **Bus Org 21.152**
Priorities and preferences, **Bus Org 21.153**

FOREIGN CORPORATIONS—Cont'd
Shares and shareholders—Cont'd
Closing, transfers, records and recordation, **Bus Org 21.355**
Combinations, **Bus Org 21.601 et seq.**
Commitment, **Bus Org 21.167**
Compensation and salaries, dissenting shareholders, appraisals and appraisers, **Bus Org 10.365**
Compromise and settlement, derivative actions, **Bus Org 21.560**
Computation, dissenting shareholders, fair market value, **Bus Org 10.362**
Consent,
Meetings, notice, electronic communications, **Bus Org 21.3531**
Record date, **Bus Org 21.356**
Conservators and conservatorship, privileges and immunities, **Bus Org 21.226**
Consideration, **Bus Org 21.157 et seq.**
Rights, options, **Bus Org 21.170**
Construction of laws, Business Organizations Code, statutes, **Bus Org 1.006**
Contracts, **Bus Org 21.101 et seq.**
Damages, **Bus Org 21.106, 21.107**
Disclosure, **Bus Org 21.103**
Effective date, **Bus Org 21.109**
Limitation of actions, rescission, **Bus Org 21.105**
Nonshareholders, **Bus Org 21.108**
Privileges and immunities, **Bus Org 21.223**
Rescission, **Bus Org 21.105**
Signatures, **Bus Org 21.101**
Time, **Bus Org 21.102, 21.109**
Transfers, **Bus Org 21.212**
Conversion, **Bus Org 21.154, 21.158 et seq.**
Appraisal and appraisers, **Bus Org 21.460**
Elections, **Bus Org 21.457 et seq.**
Notice, meetings, **Bus Org 21.456**
Objections and exceptions, **Bus Org 21.460**
Plans and specifications, **Bus Org 21.451 et seq.**
Convertible, **Bus Org 21.154**
Indebtedness, **Bus Org 21.168 et seq.**
Costs, dissenting shareholders, appraisals and appraisers, **Bus Org 10.365**
Cumulative voting, **Bus Org 21.360 et seq.**
Damages,
Assignments, **Bus Org 21.217**
Contracts, **Bus Org 21.106, 21.107**
Joint tenants, death, **Bus Org 21.214**
Preemption, **Bus Org 21.224, 21.225**
Privileges and immunities, **Bus Org 21.223**
Title to property, **Bus Org 21.215**
Transfers, **Bus Org 21.217**
Death, joint tenants, **Bus Org 21.214**
Definitions, **Bus Org 1.002**
Preemptive rights, **Bus Org 21.202**

FOREIGN CORPORATIONS—Cont'd
Shares and shareholders—Cont'd
Delivery, certificates and certification, **Bus Org 3.204**
Demand,
Derivative actions, **Bus Org 21.553**
Rejection, **Bus Org 21.559**
Dissenting shareholders, fair market value, **Bus Org 10.357 et seq.**
Deposits, redemption, **Bus Org 21.306**
Derivative actions, generally, ante
Directors,
Distribution and distributors, damages, **Bus Org 21.316**
Elections, **Bus Org 21.406**
Meetings, **Bus Org 21.359**
Meetings, elections, **Bus Org 21.359**
Disclosure, contracts, **Bus Org 21.103**
Discontinuance, derivative actions, **Bus Org 21.560**
Discovery, derivative actions, **Bus Org 21.556**
Dismissal and nonsuit, derivative actions, **Bus Org 21.558**
Disposition, preemptive rights, **Bus Org 21.207**
Dissenting shareholders, **Bus Org 10.351 et seq.**
Appointments, appraisal and appraisers, **Bus Org 10.361**
Appraisals and appraisers, **Bus Org 10.354 et seq.**
Books and papers, fair market value, **Bus Org 10.363**
Compensation and salaries, appraisals and appraisers, **Bus Org 10.365**
Computation, fair market value, **Bus Org 10.362**
Costs, appraisals and appraisers, **Bus Org 10.365**
Definitions, **Bus Org 10.352**
Demand, fair market value, **Bus Org 10.357 et seq.**
Exclusive remedy, **Bus Org 10.368**
Fair market value, demand, **Bus Org 10.357 et seq.**
Forms, **Bus Org 10.353**
Hearings, fair market value, **Bus Org 10.361**
Investigations and investigators, fair market value, **Bus Org 10.363**
Notice, **Bus Org 10.353, 10.355**
Objections and exceptions, appraisals and appraisers, **Bus Org 10.364**
Perfection, **Bus Org 10.356**
Petitions, fair market value, **Bus Org 10.361**
Records and recordation, fair market value, **Bus Org 10.363**
Demand, **Bus Org 10.359**
Reorganization, **Bus Org 10.304**
Termination, **Bus Org 10.367**
Title to property, **Bus Org 10.366**
Withdrawal, **Bus Org 10.357**
Distribution and distributors, **Bus Org 21.301 et seq.**

FOREIGN CORPORATIONS—Cont'd
Shares and shareholders—Cont'd
Dividends, definitions, **Bus Org 21.002**
Duplicates and copies, certificates and certification, **Bus Org 3.202**
Effective date, contracts, **Bus Org 21.109**
Elections,
Amendments, certificate of formation, **Bus Org 21.364**
Bylaws, proxies, **Bus Org 21.371**
Certificate of formation, **Bus Org 21.363**
Amendments, **Bus Org 21.364**
Changes, **Bus Org 21.365**
Changes, **Bus Org 21.365**
Certificate of formation, **Bus Org 21.365**
Cumulative voting, **Bus Org 21.360 et seq.**
Derivative actions, **Bus Org 21.554**
Directors, **Bus Org 21.405, 21.406**
Cumulative voting, **Bus Org 21.361**
Fundamental business transactions, **Bus Org 21.457 et seq.**
Grandfather rights, cumulative voting, **Bus Org 21.362**
Inspection and inspectors, lists, **Bus Org 21.354**
Irrevocable proxies, **Bus Org 21.370**
Limitations, **Bus Org 21.153**
Lists, **Bus Org 21.354**
Fines and penalties, **Bus Org 21.220**
Meetings, **Bus Org 21.372**
Meetings, **Bus Org 21.354 et seq.**
Numbers and numbering, **Bus Org 21.366**
Proxies, **Bus Org 21.367 et seq.**
Revocation or suspension, proxies, **Bus Org 21.369**
Termination, reinstatement, **Bus Org 21.364**
Time, proxies, **Bus Org 21.368**
Winding up, **Bus Org 21.364**
Electronic communications, notice, **Bus Org 21.3531**
Evidence,
Certificates and certification, **Bus Org 3.201**
Derivative actions,
Discovery, **Bus Org 21.556**
Dismissal and nonsuit, **Bus Org 21.558**
Notice, electronic communications, **Bus Org 21.3531**
Examinations and examiners,
Books and papers, **Bus Org 21.218**
Records and recordation, fines and penalties, **Bus Org 21.222**
Exchange of property, **Bus Org 10.051 et seq., 21.154**
Abandonment, **Bus Org 10.201 et seq.**
Acceptance, certificates and certification, **Bus Org 10.156**

FOREIGN CORPORATIONS—Cont'd
Shares and shareholders—Cont'd
Exchange of property—Cont'd
Appraisal and appraisers, **Bus Org 21.460**
Certificates and certification, **Bus Org 10.151 et seq.**
Elections, **Bus Org 21.457 et seq.**
Filing, certificates and certification, **Bus Org 10.153**
Notice, meetings, **Bus Org 21.456**
Objections and exceptions, **Bus Org 21.460**
Plans and specifications, **Bus Org 21.451 et seq.**
Exclusive remedy, dissenting shareholders, **Bus Org 10.368**
Expenses and expenditures,
Derivative actions, payment, **Bus Org 21.561**
Payment, **Bus Org 21.172**
Facsimile,
Certificates and certification, **Bus Org 3.203**
Notice, **Bus Org 21.3531**
Fair market value, dissenting shareholders, demand, **Bus Org 10.357 et seq.**
Filing,
Exchange of property, certificates and certification, **Bus Org 10.153**
Fees, **Bus Org 4.152**
Fines and penalties,
Elections, lists, **Bus Org 21.220**
Meetings, notice, **Bus Org 21.221**
Records and recordation, examinations and examiners, **Bus Org 21.222**
Forms,
Certificates and certification, **Bus Org 3.202**
Dissenting shareholders, **Bus Org 10.353**
Fractional shares, **Bus Org 21.163, 21.164**
Fraud, privileges and immunities, **Bus Org 21.223**
Fundamental business transactions, **Bus Org 21.451 et seq.**
Grandfather rights, elections, cumulative voting, **Bus Org 21.362**
Guardian and ward, privileges and immunities, **Bus Org 21.226**
Hearings, dissenting shareholders, fair market value, **Bus Org 10.361**
Indebtedness,
Convertible indebtedness, **Bus Org 21.168 et seq.**
Privileges and immunities, **Bus Org 21.223**
Inspection and inspectors, elections, lists, **Bus Org 21.354**
Investigations and investigators, dissenting shareholders, fair market value, **Bus Org 10.363**
Irrevocable proxies, elections, **Bus Org 21.370**
Joint tenants, **Bus Org 21.214**
Limitation of actions,
Contracts, rescission, **Bus Org 21.105**
Derivative actions, tolling, **Bus Org 21.557**
Distribution and distributors, **Bus Org 21.317**
Preemptive rights, **Bus Org 21.206**
Limitations,
Distribution and distributors, **Bus Org 21.303**
Transfers, **Bus Org 21.213**
Lists,
Elections, **Bus Org 21.354**
Meetings, **Bus Org 21.372**
Meetings, elections, **Bus Org 21.372**
Mail and mailing, statements, **Bus Org 21.219**
Managers and management, winding up, **Bus Org 21.504**
Meetings, **Bus Org 21.351 et seq.**
Bylaws,
Directors, elections, **Bus Org 21.359**
Quorum, **Bus Org 21.358**
Certificate of formation,
Directors, elections, **Bus Org 21.359**
Quorum, **Bus Org 21.358**
Directors, elections, **Bus Org 21.359, 21.405**
Elections, **Bus Org 21.354 et seq.**
Electronic communications, notice, **Bus Org 21.3531**
Lists, elections, **Bus Org 21.372**
Notice, **Bus Org 21.353**
Electronic communications, **Bus Org 21.3531**
Fines and penalties, **Bus Org 21.221**
Record date, **Bus Org 21.357**
Quorum, **Bus Org 21.358**
Record date, notice, **Bus Org 21.357**
Special meetings, **Bus Org 21.352**
Time, **Bus Org 21.351**
Notice, **Bus Org 21.353**
Winding up, **Bus Org 21.502, 21.503**
Merger and consolidation, **Bus Org 21.158 et seq.**
Appraisal and appraisers, **Bus Org 21.460**
Elections, **Bus Org 21.457 et seq.**
Notice, meetings, **Bus Org 21.456**
Objections and exceptions, **Bus Org 21.460**
Plans and specifications, **Bus Org 21.451 et seq.**
Notice,
Dissenting shareholders, **Bus Org 10.353, 10.355**
Electronic communications, **Bus Org 21.3531**
Facsimile, **Bus Org 21.3531**

FOREIGN CORPORATIONS—Cont'd
Shares and shareholders—Cont'd
Notice—Cont'd
Fundamental business transactions, meetings, **Bus Org 21.456**
Meetings, **Bus Org 21.353**
Fines and penalties, **Bus Org 21.221**
Redemption, **Bus Org 21.305**
Subscriptions, **Bus Org 21.165**
Uncertificated shares, **Bus Org 3.205**
Winding up, meetings, **Bus Org 21.503**
Numbers and numbering, **Bus Org 21.151**
Elections, **Bus Org 21.366**
Objections and exceptions,
Dissenting shareholders, appraisals and appraisers, **Bus Org 10.364**
Fundamental business transactions, **Bus Org 21.460**
Options, **Bus Org 21.168 et seq.**
Outstanding shares, **Bus Org 21.171**
Panel, derivative actions, **Bus Org 21.554**
Par value shares, consideration, **Bus Org 21.161**
Payment,
Derivative actions, expenses and expenditures, **Bus Org 21.561**
Expenses and expenditures, **Bus Org 21.172**
Redemption, **Bus Org 21.307**
Subscriptions, preformation, **Bus Org 21.166**
Perfection, dissenting shareholders, **Bus Org 10.356**
Personal property, **Bus Org 21.801**
Petitions, dissenting shareholders, fair market value, **Bus Org 10.361**
Pledges, privileges and immunities, **Bus Org 21.226**
Preemption, damages, **Bus Org 21.224, 21.225**
Preemptive rights, **Bus Org 21.201 et seq.**
Preformation, subscriptions, **Bus Org 21.166**
Priorities and preferences, **Bus Org 21.153, 21.154**
Distribution and distributors, **Bus Org 21.308**
Privileges and immunities, **Bus Org 21.223**
Probate proceedings, privileges and immunities, **Bus Org 21.226**
Proxies, elections, **Bus Org 21.367 et seq.**
Purchases and purchasing, contracts, rescission, **Bus Org 21.105**
Quorum, meetings, **Bus Org 21.358**
Record date,
Consent, **Bus Org 21.356**
Meetings, notice, **Bus Org 21.357**
Records and recordation, **Bus Org 21.173**

FOREIGN CORPORATIONS—Cont'd
Shares and shareholders—Cont'd
Records and recordation—Cont'd
Dissenting shareholders, fair market value, **Bus Org 10.363**
Demand, **Bus Org 10.359**
Examinations and examiners, **Bus Org 21.218**
Fines and penalties, **Bus Org 21.222**
Transfers, closing, **Bus Org 21.355**
Redemption, **Bus Org 21.154, 21.304 et seq.**
Registration, title to property, **Bus Org 21.201**
Reinstatement, termination, elections, **Bus Org 21.364**
Rejection, derivative actions, demand, **Bus Org 21.559**
Reorganization, dissenting shareholders, **Bus Org 10.304**
Repeals, bylaws, **Bus Org 21.058**
Rescission, contracts, **Bus Org 21.105**
Revocation or suspension, elections, proxies, **Bus Org 21.369**
Rights, **Bus Org 21.168 et seq.**
Preemptive rights, **Bus Org 21.201 et seq.**
Sales, assets, **Bus Org 21.455**
Scrip, **Bus Org 21.163, 21.164**
Seals, certificates and certification, **Bus Org 3.202**
Series, **Bus Org 21.152 et seq.**
Signatures,
Certificates and certification, **Bus Org 3.203**
Commitment, **Bus Org 21.167**
Contracts, **Bus Org 21.101**
Subscriptions, **Bus Org 21.165**
Special meetings, **Bus Org 21.352**
Standing, derivative actions, **Bus Org 21.552**
Statements,
Mail and mailing, **Bus Org 21.219**
Series, **Bus Org 21.156**
Statutes, Business Organizations Code, construction of laws, **Bus Org 1.006**
Subscriptions, **Bus Org 21.165**
Preformation, **Bus Org 21.166**
Privileges and immunities, **Bus Org 21.223**
Supersedeas or stay, derivative actions, **Bus Org 21.555**
Termination,
Derivative actions, costs, payment, **Bus Org 21.561**
Dissenting shareholders, **Bus Org 10.367**
Elections, reinstatement, **Bus Org 21.364**
Time,
Contracts, **Bus Org 21.102, 21.109**
Elections, proxies, **Bus Org 21.368**
Meetings, **Bus Org 21.351**
Notice, **Bus Org 21.353**

FOREIGN CORPORATIONS—Cont'd
Shares and shareholders—Cont'd
Title to property,
Damages, **Bus Org 21.215**
Dissenting shareholders, **Bus Org 10.366**
Registration, **Bus Org 21.201**
Tolling, derivative actions, limitation of actions, **Bus Org 21.557**
Transfers, **Bus Org 21.209 et seq.**
Certificates and certification, **Bus Org 3.201**
Records and recordation, closing, **Bus Org 21.355**
Treasury shares, **Bus Org 21.171**
Cancellation, **Bus Org 21.252**
Definitions, **Bus Org 21.002**
Disposition, **Bus Org 21.160**
Preemptive rights, **Bus Org 21.204, 21.208**
Trusts and trustees, privileges and immunities, **Bus Org 21.226**
Uncertificated shares, **Bus Org 3.201**
Notice, **Bus Org 3.205**
Unissued shares, **Bus Org 21.155**
Preemptive rights, **Bus Org 21.204, 21.208**
Value, consideration, **Bus Org 21.162**
Waiver, preemptive rights, **Bus Org 21.205**
Winding up,
Elections, **Bus Org 21.364**
Meetings, **Bus Org 21.502, 21.503**
Withdrawal, dissenting shareholders, **Bus Org 10.357**
Signatures, **Bus Org 1.007**
Certificate of formation, ante
Definitions, business organizations, **Bus Org 1.002**
Filing, **Bus Org 4.001**
Corrections, certificates and certification, **Bus Org 4.101**
Indebtedness, certificates and certification, **Bus Org 2.114**
Reorganization, **Bus Org 10.302**
Shares and shareholders, ante
Specifications. Plans and specifications, generally, ante
Standing, derivative actions, **Bus Org 21.552**
State,
Liens and incumbrances, **Bus Org 12.201**
Receivers and receivership, **Bus Org 12.251**
Stated capital,
Computation, reduction, **Bus Org 21.254**
Definitions, **Bus Org 21.002**
Elections, reduction, **Bus Org 21.253**
Insolvency, **Bus Org 21.314**
Time, **Bus Org 21.315**
Reduction, **Bus Org 21.251 et seq.**
Computation, **Bus Org 21.254**
Elections, **Bus Org 21.253**
Treasury shares, cancellation, **Bus Org 21.252**

FOREIGN CORPORATIONS—Cont'd
Statements,
Business Organizations Code, adoption, **Bus Org 402.004**
Certificate of formation, ante
Officers and employees, good faith, **Bus Org 3.102, 3.105**
Termination, claims, **Bus Org 11.352**
Statute of limitations. Limitation of actions, generally, ante
Stocks and stockholders. Shares and shareholders, generally, ante
Subscriptions. Shares and shareholders, ante
Subsidiaries,
Business combinations, **Bus Org 21.601 et seq.**
Merger and consolidation, **Bus Org 10.006**
Certificates and certification, **Bus Org 10.152**
Suits. Actions and proceedings, generally, ante
Supersedeas or stay,
Derivative actions, **Bus Org 21.555**
Registration, revocation or suspension, **Bus Org 9.156**
Termination, involuntary termination, **Bus Org 11.306**
Winding up, involuntary winding up, **Bus Org 11.306**
Supervision, winding up, **Bus Org 11.054**
Surplus,
Dividends, transfers, **Bus Org 21.313**
Insolvency, **Bus Org 21.314**
Time, **Bus Org 21.315**
Reserves, **Bus Org 21.309**
Suspension. Revocation or suspension, generally, ante
Taxation,
Registration, forfeitures, reinstatement, **Bus Org 9.106**
Service of process, **Bus Org 5.257**
Termination,
Forfeitures, reinstatement, **Bus Org 11.254, 402.013**
Payment, **Bus Org 11.101**
Termination, **Bus Org 11.001 et seq.**
Abatement of actions and proceedings, involuntary termination, **Bus Org 11.304**
Actions and proceedings, involuntary termination, **Bus Org 11.303**
Appeal and review, involuntary termination, **Bus Org 11.307**
Business Organizations Code, mandatory application date, **Bus Org 402.011**
Certificates and certification, **Bus Org 11.101 et seq.**
Involuntary termination, **Bus Org 11.252**
Reinstatement, **Bus Org 11.202**
Certified copies, involuntary termination, judgments and decrees, **Bus Org 11.414**
Claims, **Bus Org 11.351 et seq.**

FOREIGN CORPORATIONS—Cont'd
Termination—Cont'd
Contracts, **Bus Org 21.101 et seq.**
Crimes and offenses, involuntary termination, **Bus Org 11.301 et seq.**
Deposits, claims, **Bus Org 11.352**
Derivative actions, costs, payment, **Bus Org 21.561**
Discharge, claims, **Bus Org 11.353**
Effective date, **Bus Org 11.102, 11.103**
Claims, **Bus Org 11.356 et seq.**
Reinstatement, **Bus Org 11.204 et seq.**
Errors, reinstatement, **Bus Org 11.201 et seq.**
Escheat, claims, **Bus Org 11.355**
Exemptions, involuntary termination, **Bus Org 11.251**
Filing,
Fines and penalties, **Bus Org 21.802**
Involuntary termination, **Bus Org 11.315**
Fraud,
Involuntary termination, **Bus Org 11.301 et seq.**
Revocation or suspension, **Bus Org 11.153**
Involuntary termination, **Bus Org 11.251 et seq., 11.301 et seq.**
Certified copies, judgments and decrees, **Bus Org 11.414**
Judgments and decrees, **Bus Org 11.301 et seq.**
Involuntary termination, certified copies, **Bus Org 11.414**
Jurisdiction, involuntary termination, **Bus Org 11.308**
Limitation of actions, claims, **Bus Org 11.359**
Names, reinstatement, **Bus Org 11.203**
Notice,
Claims, **Bus Org 11.358**
Escheat, claims, **Bus Org 11.355**
Involuntary termination, **Bus Org 11.251, 11.302, 11.310**
Payment,
Claims, **Bus Org 11.354**
Taxation, **Bus Org 11.101**
Publication, involuntary termination, **Bus Org 11.310**
Receipts, claims, **Bus Org 11.352**
Receivers and receivership, **Bus Org 11.403**
Judgments and decrees, **Bus Org 11.412**
Records and recordation, removal, **Bus Org 11.104**
Reinstatement, **Bus Org 11.201 et seq.**
Involuntary termination, **Bus Org 11.253**
Shares and shareholders, elections, **Bus Org 21.364**
Taxation, forfeitures, **Bus Org 11.254**
Remand, involuntary termination, **Bus Org 11.307**
Revocation or suspension, fraud, **Bus Org 11.153**

FOREIGN CORPORATIONS—Cont'd
Termination—Cont'd
Service of process, involuntary termination, **Bus Org 11.309**
Shares and shareholders, ante
Statements, claims, **Bus Org 11.352**
Supersedeas or stay, involuntary termination, **Bus Org 11.306**
Taxation,
Forfeitures, reinstatement, **Bus Org 11.254**
Payment, **Bus Org 11.101**
Time,
Involuntary termination, **Bus Org 11.305, 11.313**
Reinstatement, **Bus Org 11.202**
Venue, involuntary termination, **Bus Org 11.308**
Terms of office, directors, **Bus Org 21.407, 21.408**
Time,
Business combinations, moratorium, **Bus Org 21.606, 21.607**
Business Organizations Code, effective date, **Bus Org 402.001**
Adoption, **Bus Org 402.005**
Certificate of formation, ante
Exchange of property, **Bus Org 10.054, 10.055**
Filing, ante
Insolvency, determination, **Bus Org 21.315**
Interrogatories, answer, **Bus Org 12.002**
Meetings, organization, **Bus Org 21.059**
Merger and consolidation, effective date, **Bus Org 10.007**
Registration, amendments, **Bus Org 9.009**
Service of process, **Bus Org 5.254**
Shares and shareholders, ante
Termination, ante
Winding up, post
Title to property, **Bus Org 301.007 et seq.**
Purchases and purchasing, **Bus Org 301.008**
Shares and shareholders, ante
Tolling, derivative actions, limitation of actions, **Bus Org 21.557**
Trademarks and trade names, **Bus Org 5.001**
Transacting business in Texas, **Bus Org 9.201 et seq.**
Lists, **Bus Org 9.251, 9.252**
Transfers,
Business combinations, **Bus Org 21.601 et seq.**
Consent, **Bus Org 21.455**
Dividends, surplus, **Bus Org 21.313**
Names, reservation, **Bus Org 5.106**
Property, **Bus Org 10.251 et seq.**
Shares and shareholders, ante
Title to property, **Bus Org 301.009**
Transition, Business Organizations Code, **Bus Org 402.001 et seq.**
Treasury shares. Shares and shareholders, ante

FOREIGN CORPORATIONS—Cont'd
Trusts and trustees,
Reorganization, **Bus Org 10.301 et seq.**
Transacting business in Texas, **Bus Org 9.251**
Uncertificated shares, **Bus Org 3.201**
Notice, **Bus Org 3.205**
Vacancies in office, directors, **Bus Org 21.410**
Venue,
Registration, **Bus Org 9.053**
Revocation or suspension, **Bus Org 9.158**
Termination, involuntary termination, **Bus Org 11.308**
Winding up, involuntary winding up, **Bus Org 11.308**
Veterans organizations, names, **Bus Org 5.062**
Vice president, agent for service of process, **Bus Org 5.255**
Waiver, directors, meetings, notice, **Bus Org 21.412**
Winding up, **Bus Org 11.001 et seq., 11.051 et seq., 21.501 et seq.**
Abatement of actions and proceedings, involuntary winding up, **Bus Org 11.304**
Actions and proceedings, **Bus Org 11.052, 11.055**
Involuntary winding up, **Bus Org 11.303**
Appeal and review, involuntary winding up, **Bus Org 11.307**
Assets, distribution and distributors, **Bus Org 11.053**
Business Organizations Code, mandatory application date, **Bus Org 402.011**
Cancellation, **Bus Org 11.152**
Contracts, **Bus Org 11.152, 21.101 et seq.**
Crimes and offenses, involuntary winding up, **Bus Org 11.301 et seq.**
Discharge, indebtedness, **Bus Org 11.053**
Distribution and distributors, assets, **Bus Org 11.053**
Filing, involuntary winding up, **Bus Org 11.315**
Fraud, involuntary winding up, **Bus Org 11.301 et seq.**
Indebtedness, discharge, **Bus Org 11.053**
Involuntary winding up, **Bus Org 11.301 et seq.**
Judgments and decrees, **Bus Org 11.301 et seq.**
Jurisdiction, involuntary winding up, **Bus Org 11.308**
Managers and management, **Bus Org 21.504**
Meetings, **Bus Org 21.502, 21.503**
Notice, **Bus Org 11.052**
Involuntary winding up, **Bus Org 11.302, 11.310**
Meetings, **Bus Org 21.503**

FOREIGN CORPORATIONS—Cont'd
Winding up—Cont'd
Publication, involuntary winding up, **Bus Org 11.310**
Remand, involuntary winding up, **Bus Org 11.307**
Revocation or suspension, **Bus Org 11.151**
Service of process, involuntary winding up, **Bus Org 11.309**
Shares and shareholders, ante
Supersedeas or stay, involuntary winding up, **Bus Org 11.306**
Supervision, **Bus Org 11.054**
Time, **Bus Org 11.056**
Cancellation, **Bus Org 11.152**
Involuntary winding up, **Bus Org 11.305, 11.313**
Venue, involuntary winding up, **Bus Org 11.308**
Withdrawal,
Filing,
Fees, **Bus Org 4.152**
Fines and penalties, **Bus Org 21.802**
Names, reservation, fees, **Bus Org 5.1041**
Registration, **Bus Org 9.011**
Witnesses, indemnity, expenses and expenditures, **Bus Org 8.106**
Writings,
Definitions, business organizations, **Bus Org 1.002**
Powers and duties, **Bus Org 2.112**
Signatures, **Bus Org 1.007**

FOREIGN COUNTRIES
Conflict of Laws, generally, this index

FOREIGN LIMITED LIABILITY COMPANIES
Generally, **Bus Org 301.001 et seq.**
Limited Liability Companies, this index

FOREIGN LIMITED PARTNERSHIPS
Partnerships, this index

FOREIGN REAL ESTATE INVESTMENT TRUSTS
Real Estate Investment Trusts, this index

FOREIGN STATES
Conflict of Laws, generally, this index
Cooperative Associations, this index
Corporations, this index
Electric cooperative corporations, offices, **Util 161.121**
Electricity, accidents, expenses and expenditures, rates and charges, **Util 36.062**
Foreign states, nonresidents. Interstate Commerce, generally, this index
Gas utilities, production of books and papers, **Util 102.206**
Limited Liability Companies, this index
Professional Corporations, this index
Public utilities, production of books and papers, **Util 14.207**

FOREIGN STATES—Cont'd
Telecommunications,
Cooperation, regulatory authorities, **Util 52.003**
Telegraph lines, **Util 181.086**

FORFEITURES
Corporations, this index
Foreign Corporations, this index
Limited partnerships. Partnerships, this index
Nonprofit Corporations, this index
Partnerships, this index

FORGERY
Assumed or fictitious names, filing, business and commerce, professions and occupations, **Bus & C 71.203**

FORMS
Corporations, this index
Electric Cooperative Corporations, this index
Electricity, this index
Foreign Corporations, this index
Gas Utilities, this index
Limited Liability Companies, this index
Limited partnerships. Partnerships, this index
Nonprofit Corporations, this index
Partnerships, this index
Public Utilities, this index
Telecommunications, this index
Telephone Cooperative Corporations, this index

FRANCHISE TAXES
Cooperative associations, tax exemptions, **Bus Org 251.451**
Electric cooperative corporations, **Util 161.062**
Telephone cooperative corporations, exemptions, **Util 162.062**

FRANCHISES
Business development corporations, **Bus Org 23.054**
Cable television, state, **Util 66.001 et seq.**
Electricity, this index
Franchise Taxes, generally, this index
State, television and radio, **Util 66.001 et seq.**
Taxes. Franchise Taxes, generally, this index
Telecommunications, discrimination, municipalities, **Util 54.204**
Television and Radio, this index

FRAUD
Assumed or fictitious names, filing, business and commerce, professions and occupations, **Bus & C 71.203**
Cooperative Associations, this index
Corporations, this index
Electricity, this index
Foreign Corporations, this index
Limited Liability Companies, this index

FRAUD—Cont'd
Limited partnerships. Partnerships, this index
Nine one one (911), party lines, **Util 186.043**
Nonprofit Corporations, this index
Oil and Gas, this index
Partnerships, this index
Professional Associations and Societies, this index
Professional Corporations, this index
Public Utilities, this index
Telecommunications, this index

FREEZE PERIOD
Definitions, electricity, **Util 31.002**

FUEL
Electricity, rate adjustments, cost recovery, **Util 36.201, 36.203**
Motor Vehicle Fuel, generally, this index

FUNDAMENTAL BUSINESS TRANSACTIONS
Real estate investment trusts, **Bus Org 200.401 et seq.**

FUNDS
Business development corporations, deposits, **Bus Org 23.070**
Electricity, system benefit fund, **Util 39.903**
Telecommunications, this index
Trusts and Trustees, generally, this index
Universal service fund, telecommunications, **Util 56.021 et seq.**

FURNITURE
Carriers, generally, this index
Transportation. Carriers, generally, this index

GARBAGE AND REFUSE
Solid Waste, generally, this index

GARNISHMENT
Churches, retirement and pensions, **Bus Org 22.407**
Cooperative Associations, this index
Corporations, state, **Bus Org 12.259**
Religious organizations and societies, retirement and pensions, **Bus Org 22.407**

GAS
Oil and Gas, generally, this index

GAS METERS
Apartment houses,
Submetering, **Util 124.001, 124.002**
Termination, **Util 104.258**
Confidential or privileged information, customers, government operated utilities, **Util 182.052**
Definitions, testing, **Util 182.101**
Inspection and inspectors, **Util 104.256, 182.101 et seq.**
Mobile homes and mobile home parks,
Submetering, **Util 124.001, 124.002**

GAS METERS—Cont'd
Mobile homes and mobile home parks —Cont'd
  Termination, **Util 104.258**
Standards, **Util 104.252**
Submetering, multiple unit complexes, **Util 124.001, 124.002**
Tests, **Util 104.256, 104.257, 182.101 et seq.**

GAS PLANTS OR SYSTEMS
Gas Utilities, generally, this index

GAS UTILITIES
  See, also,
    Oil and Gas, generally, this index
    Public Utilities, generally, this index
  Generally, **Util 101.001 et seq.**
Accounts and accounting, **Util 102.101**
  Advertisements, **Util 102.154**
  Affiliates, jurisdiction, **Util 102.104**
  Audits, **Util 102.202**
  Depreciation, **Util 102.152**
  Merchandise, sales and leases, **Util 102.153**
  Retirement and pensions, **Util 104.059**
Actions and proceedings,
  Consumer representation, **Util 101.052**
  Enforcement, **Util 105.021 et seq.**
  Municipalities, pipes and pipelines, rates and charges, **Util 121.2025**
  Pipes and pipelines, post
Administrative law and procedure, **Util 101.005**
  Hearings, generally, post
Adverse or pecuniary interest, public utility counsel office, **Util 101.053**
Advertisements,
  Accounts, **Util 102.154**
  Rates and charges, computation, **Util 104.057**
Affiliates, **Util 101.003**
  Accounts and accounting, jurisdiction, **Util 102.104**
  Determination, **Util 101.004**
  Hearings, determination, **Util 101.004**
  Jurisdiction, accounts and records, **Util 102.104**
  Ownership, reports, **Util 102.004**
  Pipes and pipelines, **Util 121.002**
  Rates and charges, pipes and pipelines, **Util 104.003**
  Records and recordation, jurisdiction, **Util 102.104**
Aged persons, payment, delay, **Util 182.001 et seq.**
Agriculture, **Util 123.001 et seq.**
  Pipes and pipelines, exemptions, **Util 121.003**
Air pollution, pipes and pipelines, penalties, **Util 121.304 et seq.**
Allocations, pipes and pipelines, **Util 121.151**
Amortization, computation of rates, **Util 104.054**

GAS UTILITIES—Cont'd
Appeal and review, **Util 105.001, 105.002**
  Consumer representation, **Util 101.052**
  Filing, municipal orders, petitions, **Util 103.054**
  Hearings, municipal orders, **Util 103.055**
  Municipalities,
    Municipal orders, **Util 103.051 et seq.**
    Railroad commission, **Util 103.024**
  Orders, **Util 105.001, 105.002**
    Railroad commission, **Util 103.055**
  Petitions, municipal orders, **Util 103.052 et seq.**
  Pipes and pipelines, post
  Railroad commission, orders, **Util 105.001, 105.002**
  Rates and charges, **Util 103.056**
  Substantial evidence rule, judicial review, **Util 105.001**
  Supersedeas or stay, pending appeals, **Util 105.002**
  Time, municipal orders, **Util 103.054**
Application of law, **Util 101.006**
  Administrative law and procedure, **Util 101.005**
Applications,
  Pipes and pipelines, sour gas, licenses and permits, **Util 121.453**
  Relocation, surcharge, **Util 104.112**
Assessments, pipes and pipelines, **Util 121.2025**
Attorney fees, pipes and pipelines, discrimination, fines and penalties, recovery, **Util 121.303**
Attorneys,
  Consumer representation, **Util 101.052**
  Inspection and inspectors, representation, **Util 102.205**
  Right to be heard, **Util 102.252**
Audits and auditors, **Util 102.201 et seq.**
  Accounts, **Util 102.202**
  Foreign states, production of books and papers, **Util 102.206**
  Inspections, **Util 102.203**
  Oaths, **Util 102.204**
  Pipes and pipelines, **Util 121.157**
    Taxation, **Util 122.152**
Bills and billing,
  Confidential or privileged information, customers, government operated utilities, **Util 182.052**
  Electronic billing, **Util 104.2551**
  Notice, rates and charges, changes, **Util 104.103**
  Rates and charges, adjustment, **Util 104.301**
  State agencies, **Util 104.255**
Boards and commissions. Railroad commission, generally, post
Bonds (officers and fiduciaries),
  Pipes and pipelines, penalties, **Util 121.208, 121.209, 121.306, 121.308**
  Rates and charges, changes, **Util 104.109**
Books and papers. Records and recordation, generally, post

GAS UTILITIES—Cont'd
Burden of proof,
  Pipes and pipelines, appeals, **Util 121.402**
  Rate changes, **Util 104.008**
Changes,
  Rates and charges, post
  Rules and regulations, standards of service, **Util 104.253**
Charges. Rates and charges, generally, post
Collections,
  Bills and billing, generally, ante
  Pipes and pipelines, taxation, **Util 122.151**
Communications, regulatory authorities, **Util 102.103**
Compensation and salaries, railroad commission, **Util 121.157, 121.158**
Competition, discrimination, **Util 104.007**
Complaints, **Util 105.051**
  Forms, **Util 105.051**
  Meters, testing, **Util 182.102**
  Pipes and pipelines, **Util 121.152**
  Rates and charges,
    Changes, hearings, **Util 104.105**
    Hearings, **Util 104.151**
  Standards, service, **Util 104.252**
Compromise and settlement, pipes and pipelines, penalties, **Util 121.205**
Confidential or privileged information, government operated utilities, customers, **Util 182.051 et seq.**
Conflict of laws, **Util 101.006**
  Federal law, **Util 101.008**
  Pipes and pipelines, safety, **Util 121.201, 121.202**
Construction, works in progress, valuation, computation of rates, **Util 104.053**
Construction of law, **Util 101.007**
Consumer protection, **Util 101.051 et seq.**
Containers, malodorants, safety, **Util 121.252**
Contempt, **Util 105.022**
Continuity of service, **Util 186.001 et seq.**
Contracts, **Util 102.003**
Cooperative associations, refunds to members, **Util 104.005**
Corporate powers, **Util 181.002**
Counties, highways and roads, easements, notice, **Util 181.024**
Crimes and offenses, **Util 105.024**
  Customers deposits, **Util 183.006**
  Meters, testing, refusal, **Util 182.104**
  Pipes and pipelines, **Util 121.310**
Definitions, **Util 101.003, 181.021**
  Pipelines, **Util 121.001**
  Pipes and pipelines, taxation, **Util 122.001**
  Records, **Util 102.101**
  Termination of service, **Util 104.258**
Depletion, computation of rates, **Util 104.054**
Deposits, customers, **Util 183.001 et seq.**
Depreciation,
  Accounts, **Util 102.152**

GAS UTILITIES—Cont'd
Depreciation—Cont'd
Investments, computation of rates, Util **104.053, 104.054**
Rates and charges, adjustment, Util **104.301**
Disconnection. Termination, generally, post
Discovery, consumer representation, Util **101.052**
Discrimination, Util **181.009**
Pipes and pipelines, Util **121.104**
Penalties, recovery, Util **121.303**
Rates and charges, post
Distribution and distributors,
Costs, investigations and investigators, Util **104.152**
Pipes and pipelines, generally, post
State agencies, rates charged, Util **104.201**
Easements, Util **181.007**
Highways and roads, Util **181.005, 181.022 et seq.**
Incorporation of municipalities, effect, Util **181.026**
Municipalities, streets and alleys, consent, Util **181.023**
Notice, highways and roads, Util **181.024**
Relocation, highways and roads, Util **181.025**
Streets and alleys, Util **103.002, 181.005, 181.006, 181.022 et seq.**
Electric cooperative corporations, exemptions, Util **101.003, 121.008**
Eminent domain, Util **181.004**
Employees. Officers and employees, generally, post
Enforcement,
Actions and proceedings, Util **105.021 et seq.**
Pipes and pipelines, Util **121.301 et seq.**
Entry on property, inspections, Util **102.205**
Equipment. Machinery and equipment, generally, post
Evidence,
Aged persons, delay in payment, proof of age, Util **182.004**
Consumer representation, discovery, Util **101.052**
Pipes and pipelines, penalty appeals, Util **121.307**
Examinations and examiners. Inspection and inspectors, generally, post
Exemptions, Util **101.003**
Aged persons, delay in payment, Util **182.005**
Agriculture, Util **123.024**
Priorities, Util **123.001, 123.002**
Confidential or privileged information, government operated utilities, customers, Util **182.054**
Interstate commerce, malodorants, Util **121.253**
Marine terminals, Util **121.007**
Pipes and pipelines, post

GAS UTILITIES—Cont'd
Expenses and expenditures,
Distribution and distributors, costs, investigations, Util **104.152**
Municipalities, rate determination, Util **103.022**
Net income, rate computation, Util **104.055**
Pipes and pipelines, taxation, deductions, Util **122.052**
Rates and charges, reimbursement, Util **104.301**
Relocation, recovery, Util **104.112**
Valuation of investments, computation of rates, Util **104.053**
Extreme weather emergencies, termination, Util **104.258**
Federal law,
Conflict of laws, Util **101.008**
Pipes and pipelines, safety, Util **121.201**
Fees,
Confidential or privileged information, government operated utilities, Util **182.053**
Inspection and inspectors, machinery and equipment, Util **104.257**
Pipes and pipelines, safety, Util **121.211**
Rates and charges, generally, post
Filing,
Appeal and review, municipal orders, petitions, Util **103.054**
Rates and charges, Util **102.151**
Municipalities, Util **103.021**
Fines and penalties, Util **105.023**
Civil penalties, Util **105.023**
Criminal penalties, Util **105.024**
Cumulative penalties, Util **105.026**
Customers deposits, Util **183.006**
Disposition of funds, Util **105.027**
Meters, testing, refusal, Util **182.104**
Pipes and pipelines, post
Foreign states, production of books and papers, Util **102.206**
Forms,
Bonds (officers and fiduciaries), rates and charges, changes, Util **104.109**
Communications, regulatory authorities, Util **102.103**
Complaints, Util **105.051**
Confidential or privileged information, government operated utilities, Util **182.052**
Notice of intent, rate changes, Util **104.103**
Records, Util **102.101**
Reports, Util **102.003**
Statements, rates and charges, changes, Util **104.102**
Gifts,
Business and commerce, accounts and accounting, Util **102.154**
Rates and charges, computation, Util **104.057**
Harbors and ports, exemptions, marine terminals, Util **121.007**
Hearings,
Affiliates, determination, Util **101.004**

GAS UTILITIES—Cont'd
Hearings—Cont'd
Appeal and review, municipal orders, Util **103.055**
Consumer representation, Util **101.052**
Major transactions, investigations, Util **102.051**
Municipalities, rates and charges, Util **103.021**
Pipes and pipelines, post
Rates and charges, post
Records and recordation, Util **102.251**
Right to be heard, Util **102.252**
Standards, service, Util **104.252**
Highways and Roads, this index
Hydrogen sulfide, pipes and pipelines, Util **121.451 et seq.**
Income, rate computation, Util **104.055**
Income tax, rates and charges, Util **104.055, 104.056**
Adjustment, Util **104.301**
Indebtedness, Util **181.003**
Injunctions, Util **105.021**
Pipes and pipelines, safety, Util **121.203**
Inspection and inspectors, Util **102.203**
Consumers, machinery and equipment, Util **104.257**
Entry on property, Util **102.205**
Machinery and equipment, Util **104.257**
Meters, Util **104.256, 182.101 et seq.**
Pipes and pipelines, Util **121.157**
Fees, safety, Util **121.211**
Taxation, books and records, Util **122.152**
Interest,
Customers deposits, Util **183.002 et seq.**
Pipes and pipelines, taxation, delinquency, Util **122.205**
Interruption of service, prevention, Util **186.001 et seq.**
Interstate commerce,
Malodorants, exemptions, Util **121.253**
Pipes and pipelines, exemptions, Util **121.004**
Investigations and investigators,
Major transactions, Util **102.051**
Malodorants, safety, Util **121.251**
Investments,
Rates and charges, adjustment, Util **104.301**
Returns, computation of rates, Util **104.051 et seq.**
Irrigation, Util **123.001, 123.002**
Jurisdiction, Util **102.001, 102.002, 103.003**
Affiliates, accounts and records, Util **102.104**
Municipalities, Util **103.001**
Surrender, Util **103.003**
Pipes and pipelines, Util **121.051, 121.052**
Rates and charges, Util **104.001**
State agencies, transportation rates, Util **104.201**
Large volume customers,
Rates, standards, Util **104.003**
Termination of service, Util **121.103**

GAS UTILITIES—Cont'd
Leases,
Merchandise, accounts and accounting, **Util 102.153**
Reports, investigations, **Util 102.051**
Liberal construction of law, **Util 101.007**
Licenses and permits, pipes and pipelines, sour gas, **Util 121.453, 121.454**
Limitation of actions, municipalities, pipes and pipelines, rates and charges, **Util 121.2025**
Liquefied petroleum gas, application of law, **Util 101.003**
Loans, **Util 181.003**
Shareholders, reports, **Util 102.053**
Lobbyists,
Rates and charges, computation, **Util 104.057**
Reports, **Util 102.003**
Machinery and equipment,
Consumers, inspection for, **Util 104.257**
Gas Meters, generally, this index
Inspection and inspectors, **Util 104.256, 104.257**
Merchandise, sales, accounts and accounting, **Util 102.153**
Pipes and pipelines, generally, post
Sales, rate computation, **Util 104.058**
Malodorants, safety, **Util 121.251 et seq.**
Managers and management, evaluation, **Util 102.201**
Marine terminals, exemptions, **Util 121.007**
Meetings, pipes and pipelines, liaison activities, **Util 121.2015**
Merger and consolidation, reports, investigations, **Util 102.051**
Meters. Gas Meters, generally, this index
Monopolies and unfair trade, pipes and pipelines, jurisdiction, **Util 121.051, 121.052**
Mortgages, **Util 181.003**
Motor vehicle fuel, pipes and pipelines, exemptions, **Util 121.006**
Municipalities, **Util 103.001 et seq.**
Agriculture, supplies, priorities and preferences, **Util 123.001, 123.002**
Appeal and review,
Municipal orders, **Util 103.051 et seq.**
Orders, **Util 103.024**
Application of law, **Util 101.003**
Assistance, technical assistance, **Util 102.005**
Bills and billing, electronic billing, **Util 104.2551**
Confidential or privileged information, customers, **Util 182.051 et seq.**
Easements,
Railroads, right of way, **Util 186.051 et seq.**
Streets and alleys, consent, **Util 181.023**
Eminent domain, railroads, right of way, **Util 186.051 et seq.**
Expenses and expenditures, rate determination, **Util 103.022**

GAS UTILITIES—Cont'd
Municipalities—Cont'd
Fees, railroads, right of way, **Util 186.058**
Franchises, streets and alleys, **Util 103.002**
Hearings, rates and charges, **Util 103.021**
Incorporation, easements, effect, **Util 181.026**
Jurisdiction, **Util 103.001**
Surrender, **Util 103.003**
Licenses and permits, railroads, right of way, **Util 186.058**
Meters, testing, **Util 182.102**
Nonresidents, appeals of orders, **Util 103.053**
Notice, railroads, right of way, **Util 186.054**
Officers and employees, rate determination, **Util 103.021, 103.022**
Orders, appeals, **Util 103.051 et seq.**
Pipes and pipelines,
Fees, safety, **Util 121.211**
Rates and charges, **Util 121.2025**
Safety, conflict of laws, **Util 121.202**
Railroad commission, jurisdiction, **Util 102.001, 102.002**
Railroads, right of way, eminent domain, **Util 186.051 et seq.**
Rates and charges, **Util 103.021 et seq.**
Boundaries, **Util 104.006**
In lieu of tax payments, computation, **Util 104.203**
Pipes and pipelines, appeals, **Util 121.155**
Residents, appeals of orders, **Util 103.052**
Standing, rate proceedings, **Util 103.023**
Streets and alleys, franchises, **Util 103.002**
Taxation, in lieu payments, rates and charges, **Util 104.203**
Technical assistance, **Util 102.005**
Net income, rate computation, **Util 104.055**
Nonresidents,
Municipalities, appeals of orders, **Util 103.053**
Rates and charges, municipalities, **Util 104.006**
Notice,
Changes, rates and charges, **Util 104.103**
Confidential or privileged information, government operated utilities, customers, **Util 182.052**
Easements, highways and roads, **Util 181.024**
Inspection and inspectors, **Util 102.205**
Meters, tests, **Util 182.103**
Municipalities, ante
Pipes and pipelines, post
Rates and charges, post
Relocation of facilities, easements, highways and roads, **Util 181.025**

GAS UTILITIES—Cont'd
Oaths and affirmations,
Examinations, **Util 102.204**
Reports, **Util 102.003**
Odors, malodorants, safety, **Util 121.251 et seq.**
Officers and employees,
Municipalities, rate determination, **Util 103.021, 103.022**
Oaths and affirmations, examinations, **Util 102.204**
Public utility counsel office, **Util 101.054**
Railroad commission, pipelines, **Util 121.157**
Offices, **Util 102.102**
Pipes and pipelines, **Util 121.101**
Oil and gas pipelines. Pipes and pipelines, generally, post
Orders,
Appeal and writs of error, **Util 105.001, 105.002**
Contempt, **Util 105.022**
Fines and penalties, **Util 105.023**
Injunctions, **Util 105.021**
Municipalities, appeals, **Util 103.051 et seq.**
Pipes and pipelines, post
Railroad commission, appeal and review, **Util 103.055**
Rates and charges, **Util 104.110, 104.151**
Ownership, reports, **Util 102.004**
Payment,
Aged persons, delay, **Util 182.001 et seq.**
Customers deposits, interest, **Util 183.004**
Pipes and pipelines, post
Penalties. Fines and penalties, generally, ante
Petitions, municipal orders, appeals, **Util 103.052 et seq.**
Pipes and pipelines, **Util 121.001 et seq.**
Actions and proceedings,
Discrimination, fines and penalties, recovery, **Util 121.303**
Recovery of penalties, **Util 121.210, 121.309**
Administrative penalties, **Util 121.206 et seq.**
Affiliates, **Util 121.002**
Agriculture, exemptions, **Util 121.003**
Air pollution, penalties, **Util 121.304 et seq.**
Allocations, **Util 121.151**
Appeal and review, **Util 121.401 et seq.**
Fines and penalties, **Util 121.307**
Railroad commission, **Util 121.153**
Rates, **Util 121.155**
Applications, sour gas, licenses and permits, **Util 121.453**
Assessments, **Util 121.2025**
Attorney fees, discrimination, fines and penalties, recovery, **Util 121.303**
Audits and auditors, **Util 121.157**

GAS UTILITIES—Cont'd
Pipes and pipelines—Cont'd
Bonds (officers and fiduciaries), penalties, **Util 121.208, 121.209, 121.306, 121.308**
Burden of proof, appeals, **Util 121.402**
Community liaisons, emergencies, **Util 121.2015**
Complaints, **Util 121.152**
Compromise and settlement, penalties, **Util 121.205**
Conflict of laws, safety, **Util 121.201, 121.202**
Crimes and offenses, **Util 121.310**
Discrimination, **Util 121.104**
Penalties, recovery, **Util 121.303**
Easements, railroads, right of way, **Util 186.051 et seq.**
Education, safety, **Util 121.2015**
Emergencies, community liaisons, **Util 121.2015**
Eminent domain, railroads, right of way, **Util 186.051 et seq.**
Enforcement, **Util 121.151, 121.301 et seq.**
Evidence, penalty appeals, **Util 121.307**
Exemptions,
Agriculture, **Util 121.003**
Interstate commerce, **Util 121.004**
Motor vehicle fuel, **Util 121.006**
Production, **Util 121.005**
Federal law, safety, **Util 121.201**
Fees,
Railroads, right of way, **Util 186.058**
Safety, **Util 121.211**
Fines and penalties, **Util 121.302 et seq.**
Safety, **Util 121.204 et seq.**
Fees, **Util 121.211**
Taxation, **Util 122.201 et seq.**
Hearings, **Util 121.153**
Exemptions, **Util 121.005**
Fines and penalties, **Util 121.207, 121.305**
Sour gas, licenses and permits, **Util 121.454**
Hydrogen sulfide, **Util 121.451 et seq.**
Injunctions, safety, **Util 121.203**
Inspection and inspectors, **Util 121.157, 121.201**
Safety, fees, **Util 121.211**
Interstate commerce, exemptions, **Util 121.004**
Judicial review, **Util 121.401 et seq.**
Jurisdiction, **Util 121.051, 121.052**
Large volume customers, termination of service, **Util 121.103**
Leaks, school buildings and grounds, reports, **Util 121.506**
Liaison activities, emergencies, **Util 121.2015**
Licenses and permits,
Railroads, right of way, **Util 186.058**
Sour gas, **Util 121.453, 121.454**
Local preemption, safety, **Util 121.202**
Location, exemptions, **Util 121.005**
Malodorants, safety, **Util 121.251 et seq.**

GAS UTILITIES—Cont'd
Pipes and pipelines—Cont'd
Monopolies and unfair trade, jurisdiction, **Util 121.051, 121.052**
Motor vehicle fuel, exemptions, **Util 121.006**
Municipalities, ante
Notice,
Exemptions, hearings, **Util 121.005**
Fines and penalties, **Util 121.207, 121.305**
Railroads, right of way, **Util 186.054**
Regulatory proceedings, **Util 121.152, 121.153**
School buildings and grounds, tests, **Util 121.504**
Sour gas, licenses and permits, applications, **Util 121.453**
Odors, malodorants, safety, **Util 121.251 et seq.**
Offices, **Util 121.101**
Orders,
Fines and penalties, **Util 121.207, 121.305**
Review, **Util 121.153**
Sour gas, licenses and permits, **Util 121.454**
Payment,
Penalties, **Util 121.208, 121.306**
Taxation, **Util 122.101**
Penalties, **Util 122.202, 122.203**
Pollution, penalties, **Util 121.304 et seq.**
Pressure tests, school buildings and grounds, **Util 121.5005 et seq.**
Priorities and preferences, appeal and review, **Util 121.403**
Public policy, **Util 121.051, 121.052**
Railroad commission, **Util 121.051, 121.052, 121.151 et seq.**
Railroads, right of way, eminent domain, **Util 186.051 et seq.**
Rates and charges,
Appeal and review, **Util 121.155, 121.401 et seq.**
Changes, **Util 121.155**
Discrimination, **Util 121.104**
Enforcement, **Util 121.151**
Refunds, **Util 121.154**
Safety, fees, **Util 121.211**
Receivers and receivership, violations, **Util 121.301**
Records and recordation, **Util 121.101**
Safety, **Util 121.201**
Refunds,
Penalty payments, **Util 121.209, 121.308**
Rates and charges, **Util 121.154**
Registration, operators, **Util 121.201**
Reports, **Util 121.102**
School buildings and grounds, leaks, **Util 121.506**
Taxation, **Util 122.102**
Penalties, **Util 122.201, 122.203**
Right of way, telecommunications, **Util 121.201**
Rules and regulations, **Util 121.151**
Safety standards, **Util 121.202**

GAS UTILITIES—Cont'd
Pipes and pipelines—Cont'd
Rules and regulations—Cont'd
Taxation, **Util 122.151**
Safety, **Util 121.201 et seq.**
Fees, **Util 121.211**
School buildings and grounds, tests, **Util 121.5005 et seq.**
Separate offenses, penalties, **Util 121.206, 121.302, 121.304**
Sour gas, **Util 121.451 et seq.**
Standards, safety, **Util 121.201, 121.202**
Taxation, **Util 122.001 et seq.**
Administration, **Util 122.151**
Audits and auditors, **Util 122.152**
Collections, **Util 122.151**
Deductions, **Util 122.052**
Definitions, **Util 122.001**
Fines and penalties, **Util 122.201 et seq.**
Imposition, **Util 122.051**
Inspection and inspectors, books and records, **Util 122.152**
Interest, delinquency, **Util 122.205**
Minimum penalty, **Util 122.204**
Payment, **Util 122.101**
Penalties, **Util 122.202, 122.203**
Rates, **Util 122.051**
Records and recordation, **Util 122.104**
Reports, **Util 122.102**
Penalties, **Util 122.201, 122.203**
Rules and regulations, **Util 122.151**
Time,
Delinquent payments, interest, **Util 122.205**
Payment, **Util 122.103**
Termination of service,
Large volume customers, **Util 121.103**
School buildings and grounds, tests, **Util 121.505**
Tests, school buildings and grounds, **Util 121.5005 et seq.**
Water pollution, penalties, **Util 121.304 et seq.**
Pollution, pipes and pipelines, penalties, **Util 121.304 et seq.**
Powers and duties, **Util 181.001 et seq.**
Preferences. Priorities and preferences, generally, post
Prices. Rates and charges, generally, post
Priorities and preferences,
Agriculture, **Util 123.001, 123.002**
Pipes and pipelines, appeal and review, **Util 121.403**
Rates and charges, **Util 104.003, 104.004**
Changes, hearings, **Util 104.106**
Privileges and immunities, confidential or privileged information, government operated utilities, **Util 182.055**
Proceedings. Actions and proceedings, generally, ante
Production of books and papers, foreign states, **Util 102.206**

GAS UTILITIES—Cont'd
Property, **Util 181.007**
Public buildings and works, relocation, surcharge, **Util 104.112**
Public policy, **Util 101.002**
  Pipes and pipelines, **Util 121.051, 121.052**
Public retail customers, service, **Util 104.2545**
Public utility counsel office, **Util 101.051 et seq.**
Publication, rates and charges, changes, **Util 104.103**
Railroad commission, **Util 102.001 et seq.**
  Appeal and review, orders, **Util 105.001, 105.002**
  Communications, **Util 102.103**
  Compensation and salaries, pipelines, **Util 121.157, 121.158**
  Consumer representation, **Util 101.052**
  Jurisdiction, **Util 102.001, 102.002**
  Municipal orders, appeals, **Util 103.051 et seq.**
  Officers and employees, pipelines, **Util 121.157**
  Orders, appeal and review, **Util 103.055**
  Pipes and pipelines, **Util 121.151 et seq.**
    Jurisdiction, **Util 121.051, 121.052**
    Taxation, administration, **Util 122.151**
  Proposed rates, **Util 104.151, 104.152**
  Rates and charges, authority, **Util 104.001**
  Regulatory authority, **Util 101.003**
  Reports, **Util 102.003, 102.004**
Railroads, easements, **Util 181.005**
Rates and charges, **Util 101.003, 104.001 et seq.**
  Administration of law, **Util 104.001**
  Amortization, computation of rates, **Util 104.054**
  Bonds (officers and fiduciaries), changes, **Util 104.109**
  Changes, **Util 104.101 et seq.**
    Adjustment, **Util 104.301**
    Boards and commissions, proposals, **Util 104.151, 104.152**
    Bonds (officers and fiduciaries), changes, **Util 104.109**
    Burden of proof, **Util 104.008**
    Decreases, **Util 104.111 et seq.**
    Hearings, **Util 104.105, 104.106, 104.151**
    Notice, intent to change, **Util 104.103**
    Orders, **Util 104.151**
      Final rates, **Util 104.110**
    Pipes and pipelines, **Util 121.155**
    Proposals, **Util 104.101 et seq.**
    Retirement and pensions, **Util 104.059**
    Statements of intent, **Util 104.102**
    Suspension, changes, **Util 104.107**
    Temporary rates, changes, **Util 104.108**
  Complaints, changes, hearings, **Util 104.105**
  Compliance, **Util 104.002, 104.005**

GAS UTILITIES—Cont'd
Rates and charges—Cont'd
  Computation, **Util 104.051 et seq.**
  Decreases, **Util 104.111 et seq.**
  Depletion, computation of rates, **Util 104.054**
  Deposits, customers, interest, **Util 183.003**
  Depreciation, valuation of investments, computation, **Util 104.053, 104.054**
  Discrimination, **Util 104.003, 104.004, 181.009**
    Competitors, **Util 104.007**
    Pipes and pipelines, **Util 121.104**
  Distribution and distributors, costs, investigations, **Util 104.152**
  Filing, **Util 102.151**
    Municipalities, **Util 103.021**
  Final rates, proposed changes, orders, **Util 104.110**
  Gifts, expenses and expenditures, **Util 104.057**
  Hearings,
    Changes, **Util 104.105, 104.106**
    Decreases, **Util 104.151**
    Municipalities, **Util 103.021**
  Imposition, authority, **Util 104.002**
  Income tax, computation, **Util 104.055, 104.056**
  Increases, **Util 104.101 et seq.**
    Time, **Util 104.102, 104.104**
  Investments, returns, **Util 104.051 et seq.**
  Jurisdiction, **Util 102.001, 102.002, 104.001**
    State agencies, transportation rates, **Util 104.201**
  Just and reasonable rates, standards, **Util 104.003**
  Large volume customers, standards, **Util 104.003**
  Major changes, **Util 104.101**
  Major transactions, effect, **Util 102.051**
  Municipalities, ante
  Net income, computation, **Util 104.055**
  Nonresidents, municipalities, **Util 104.006**
  Notice,
    Adjustment, **Util 104.301**
    Changes, **Util 104.103**
      Hearings, **Util 104.105**
    Decreases, hearings, **Util 104.151**
  Orders, **Util 104.151**
    Final rates, **Util 104.110**
  Original costs, valuation of investments, computation, **Util 104.053**
  Payment, aged persons, delay, **Util 182.001 et seq.**
  Pipes and pipelines, ante
  Priorities and preferences, **Util 104.003, 104.004**
    Changes, hearings, **Util 104.106**
  Prospective rates, orders, **Util 103.056**
  Public relations, expenses and expenditures, computation, **Util 104.057**
  Public retail customers, **Util 104.2545**
  Reductions, **Util 104.111 et seq.**

GAS UTILITIES—Cont'd
Rates and charges—Cont'd
  Refunds,
    Adjustment, **Util 104.301**
    Bonds (officers and fiduciaries), changes, **Util 104.109**
    Pipes and pipelines, **Util 121.154**
    Schedules, **Util 104.005**
  Retirement and pensions, **Util 104.059**
  Rules and regulations, **Util 104.001**
  Sales, merchandise, computation of rates, **Util 104.058**
  Schedules, filing, **Util 102.151**
  Standards, **Util 104.003**
    Return on investments, **Util 104.051, 104.052**
  State agencies, **Util 104.201, 104.202**
  Statements, changes, **Util 104.102**
  Surcharge,
    Pipes and pipelines, safety, **Util 121.211**
    Relocation of facilities, **Util 104.112**
  Suspension, changes, **Util 104.107**
  Taxation,
    Computation, **Util 104.055, 104.056**
    Pipes and pipelines, taxation, **Util 122.051**
  Temporary rates, changes, **Util 104.108**
  Time,
    Changes, **Util 104.102, 104.104, 104.107**
    Prospective rates, appeals or writs of error, **Util 103.056**
  Transportation rates, state agencies, **Util 104.201**
  Valuation, investments, returns, **Util 104.052, 104.053**
Real estate, **Util 181.007**
Receivers and receivership, pipes and pipelines, violations, **Util 121.301**
Records and recordation, **Util 102.101 et seq.**
  Affiliates, jurisdiction, **Util 102.104**
  Communications, regulatory authorities, **Util 102.103**
  Foreign states, production, **Util 102.206**
  Forms, **Util 102.101**
  Hearings, **Util 102.251**
  Inspections, **Util 102.203**
  Offices, maintenance of records, **Util 102.102**
  Pipes and pipelines, **Util 121.101**
    Safety, **Util 121.201**
    Taxation, **Util 122.104**
  Removal from state, **Util 102.102**
Refunds,
  Customers deposits, **Util 183.005**
  Pipes and pipelines, ante
  Rates and charges, ante
Relocation,
  Easements, highways and roads, **Util 181.025**
  Surcharge, **Util 104.112**
Reports, **Util 102.003, 102.151 et seq.**
  Advertisements, accounts, **Util 102.154**
  Forms, **Util 102.003**
  Loans, shareholders, **Util 102.053**

GAS UTILITIES—Cont'd
Reports—Cont'd
Major transactions, **Util 102.051**
Merger and consolidation, **Util 102.051**
Meters, testing, **Util 182.102**
Ownership, **Util 102.004**
Pipes and pipelines, ante
Railroad commission, **Util 102.003, 102.004**
Rates and charges, adjustment, **Util 104.301**
Shares and shareholders, purchases and purchasing, **Util 102.052**
Requests,
Aged persons, delay in payment, **Util 182.002, 182.003**
Confidential or privileged information, government operated utilities, **Util 182.052**
Required service, public retail customers, **Util 104.2545**
Reserve accounts, retirement and pensions, **Util 104.059**
Retirement and pensions, **Util 104.059**
Review. Appeal and review, generally, ante
Right of way, pipes and pipelines, telecommunications, **Util 121.201**
River authorities, **Util 101.003**
Rules and regulations,
Changes, **Util 104.253**
Pipes and pipelines, ante
Rates and charges, **Util 104.001**
Service, standards, **Util 104.252, 104.253**
Safety,
Pipes and pipelines, **Util 121.201 et seq.**
Fees, **Util 121.211**
Standards, **Util 104.251 et seq.**
Sales, **Util 181.008**
Merchandise,
Accounts and accounting, **Util 102.153**
Rate computation, **Util 104.058**
Reports, investigations, **Util 102.051**
Shares and shareholders, **Util 181.003**
Loans, shareholders, reports, **Util 102.053**
Purchases and purchasing, reports, **Util 102.052**
Sour gas, pipes and pipelines, **Util 121.451 et seq.**
Standards, **Util 104.251 et seq.**
Pipes and pipelines, safety, **Util 121.201, 121.202**
Rates and charges, **Util 104.003**
Return on investments, **Util 104.051, 104.052**
Standing, municipalities, rate proceedings, **Util 103.023**
State, highways and roads, easements, notice, **Util 181.024**
State agencies,
Bills and billing, **Util 104.255**
Rates, **Util 104.201, 104.202**
Refusal of service, **Util 104.254**

GAS UTILITIES—Cont'd
Stock and stockholders. Shares and shareholders, generally, ante
Streets and Alleys, this index
Submetering, multiple unit complexes, **Util 124.001, 124.002**
Subpoenas, contempt, **Util 105.022**
Supersedeas or stay, pending appeals, **Util 105.002**
Surcharge,
Pipes and pipelines, safety, fees, **Util 121.211**
Relocation of facilities, **Util 104.112**
Surplus, retirement and pensions, reserve accounts, **Util 104.059**
Suspension, rates and charges, changes, **Util 104.107**
Tariffs. Rates and charges, generally, ante
Taxation,
Municipally owned utilities, in lieu payments, rates and charges, computation, **Util 104.203**
Pipes and pipelines, ante
Rates and charges, **Util 104.055, 104.056**
Adjustment, **Util 104.301**
Telecommunications, pipes and pipelines, right of way, **Util 121.201**
Temporary rates, changes, **Util 104.108**
Termination, **Util 104.258**
Large volume customers, **Util 121.103**
Pipes and pipelines, school buildings and grounds, tests, **Util 121.505**
Tests, pipes and pipelines, school buildings and grounds, **Util 121.5005 et seq.**
Time,
Aged persons, payment, **Util 182.002**
Appeal and review, municipal orders, **Util 103.054**
Inspection and inspectors, **Util 102.205**
Pipes and pipelines, taxation,
Delinquent payments, interest, **Util 122.205**
Payment, **Util 122.103**
Public utility counsel office, labor and employment, **Util 101.053**
Rates and charges, ante
Transportation. Pipes and pipelines, generally, ante
Valuation, investments, computation of rates, **Util 104.052, 104.053**
Venue, enforcement actions, **Util 105.025**
Water pollution, pipes and pipelines, penalties, **Util 121.304 et seq.**
Weights and measures,
Gas Meters, generally, this index
Standards, **Util 104.252**
Writs of error. Appeal and review, generally, ante

GAS UTILITY REGULATORY ACT
Generally, **Util 101.001 et seq.**

GASOLINE
Motor Vehicle Fuel, generally, this index

GENERAL ASSEMBLY
Legislature, generally, this index

GENERAL ELECTIONS
Elections, generally, this index

GENERAL OBLIGATION BONDS
Bonds, generally, this index

GENERAL PARTNERS
Partnerships, this index

GENERAL REVENUE FUND
State Treasury, this index

GENERATION
Electricity, this index

GENERATION ASSETS
Definitions, electricity, competition, stranded costs, recovery, **Util 39.251**

GIFTS
Contributions, generally, this index
Electric cooperative corporations, **Util 161.121**
Electricity,
Business expenses, computation of rates, expenses, **Util 36.061**
Reports, **Util 32.104**
Energy, efficiency, **Util 39.911**
Gas utilities,
Business and commerce, accounts and accounting, **Util 102.154**
Rates and charges, computation, **Util 104.057**
Grants, generally, this index
Public utility commission, commissioners and employees, **Util 12.154**
Telecommunications, this index

GOOD CAUSE
Definitions, telecommunications, incentive regulation, elections, withdrawal, **Util 58.021**

GOOD FAITH
Limited Liability Companies, this index
Limited partnerships. Partnerships, this index
Nonprofit Corporations, this index
Partnerships, this index

GOODS, WARES AND MERCHANDISE
Carriers, generally, this index
Cooperative Associations, generally, this index
Sales, generally, this index
Transportation. Carriers, generally, this index

GOVERNING LAW
Conflict of Laws, generally, this index

GOVERNMENTAL ENTITIES
Political Subdivisions, generally, this index

GOVERNOR
Appointments,
Public utilities, counselors, **Util 13.021**

GOVERNOR—Cont'd
Appointments—Cont'd
Public utility commission, **Util 12.051**
Executive orders, public utilities, continuity of service, **Util 186.003**

GRAND LODGES
Generally, **Bus Org 1.001 et seq.**
Application of law, **Bus Org 23.102**
Bylaws, powers and duties, **Bus Org 23.107**
Certificate of formation, **Bus Org 3.001 et seq., 23.101**
Definitions, **Bus Org 1.002**
Time, **Bus Org 23.103**
Constitutions, powers and duties, **Bus Org 23.107**
Contributions, definitions, business organizations, **Bus Org 1.002**
Damages, **Bus Org 23.110**
Deeds and conveyances, **Bus Org 23.108**
Definitions, **Bus Org 1.002**
Directors, elections, **Bus Org 23.105**
Elections, **Bus Org 23.105**
Filing, certificate of formation, **Bus Org 23.101**
Franchises, taxation, **Bus Org 23.106**
Incorporation, **Bus Org 1.001 et seq., 23.101 et seq.**
Liens and incumbrances, **Bus Org 23.109**
Loans, **Bus Org 23.109**
Mortgages, **Bus Org 23.108**
Powers and duties, **Bus Org 23.107**
Property, **Bus Org 23.108**
Real estate, **Bus Org 23.109**
Revocation or suspension, subordinate lodges, **Bus Org 23.104**
Sales, property, **Bus Org 23.108**
Schools and school districts, **Bus Org 23.108**
Subordinate lodges, **Bus Org 23.104**
Winding up, **Bus Org 23.110**
Termination, subordinate, **Bus Org 23.110**
Time, certificate of formation, **Bus Org 23.103**
Trusts and trustee, elections, **Bus Org 23.105**
Winding up, subordinate lodges, **Bus Org 23.110**

GRAND ROYAL ARCH
Incorporation, **Bus Org 23.101 et seq.**

GRANTS
Deeds and Conveyances, generally, this index
Energy, efficiency, **Util 39.911**
Hospitals, this index
Medical Care and Treatment, this index
Physicians and Surgeons, this index
Public utilities, commission, federal aid, **Util 16.021**
School Funds, this index

GREYHOUND RACING
Dog Races, generally, this index

GRIEVANCES
Labor Disputes, generally, this index

GROSS RECEIPTS
Public utilities, assessments, financing, **Util 16.001**

GUARDIAN AND WARD
Partnerships, withdrawal, **Bus Org 152.501**
Probate Proceedings, generally, this index
Real estate investment trusts, shares and shareholders, privileges and immunities, **Bus Org 200.164**
Shares and shareholders, privileges and immunities, **Bus Org 21.226**

HANDICAPPED PERSONS
Blind Persons, generally, this index
Electricity, termination of service, **Util 14.005**
Public utilities, termination of service, **Util 14.005**
Telecommunications, this index

HARASSMENT
Public utilities, interruption of service, **Util 186.004**

HARBORS AND PORTS
Gas utilities, exemptions, marine terminals, **Util 121.007**

HEALTH AND SANITATION
Hospitals, generally, this index
Medical Care and Treatment, generally, this index

HEALTH CARE
Medical Care and Treatment, generally, this index

HEALTH CARE FACILITIES AND SERVICES
See, also, Medical Care and Treatment, generally, this index
Electricity, priorities and preferences, **Util 38.072**
Hospitals, generally, this index
Nursing and Convalescent Homes, generally, this index
Priorities and preferences, electricity, **Util 38.072**
Telemedicine, generally, this index

HEALTH CARE PROFESSIONALS
Dentists and Dentistry, generally, this index
Physician Assistants, generally, this index
Physicians and Surgeons, generally, this index
Podiatrists, generally, this index
Telemedicine, generally, this index

HEALTH MAINTENANCE ORGANIZATIONS
Cooperative associations, limitations, **Bus Org 2.011**

HEALTH ORGANIZATION CORPORATIONS
Nonprofit corporations, **Bus Org 22.056, 22.0561**

HEALTH SERVICE CORPORATIONS
Dentists and Dentistry, this index

HEARING IMPAIRED PERSONS
Advisory committees, telecommunications relay access service, **Util 56.110 et seq.**
Telecommunications, this index

HEATING
Apartment houses, central system utilities, **Util 184.051, 184.052**
Electricity, reports, **Util 39.912**
Reports, electricity, **Util 39.912**
Solar Energy, generally, this index

HEIRS
Probate Proceedings, generally, this index

HIGH SPEED DATA TRANSMISSION
Definitions, underground facilities, excavations, **Util 251.001**

HIGHER EDUCATION
Colleges and Universities, generally, this index

HIGHWAYS AND ROADS
See, also, Streets and Alleys, generally, this index
Cable Television, this index
Easements,
Cable television, **Util 181.101 et seq.**
Electricity, **Util 181.042 et seq.**
Gas utilities, **Util 181.022 et seq.**
Telecommunications, **Util 181.082**
Electricity, this index
Gas utilities,
Easements, **Util 181.005, 181.022 et seq.**
Relocation, surcharge, **Util 104.112**
Oil and Gas, this index
Oil and Gas Pipelines, this index
Public utilities, underground facilities, excavations, **Util 251.007**
Right of way,
Cable television, **Util 181.101 et seq.**
Telephone cooperative corporations, public lands, **Util 162.122**
Streets and Alleys, generally, this index
Telecommunications,
Easements, **Util 181.082**
Underground facilities, excavations, **Util 251.007**
Water Supply, this index

HISTORICALLY UNDERUTILIZED BUSINESSES
Definitions, public utilities, **Util 12.251**
Electricity, contracts, **Util 39.909**
Public utilities, assistance, **Util 12.251 et seq.**
Telecommunications, contracts, **Util 52.256**

HISTORY
Electricity, credit reports, payment, **Util 17.008**
Telecommunications, credit reports, payment, **Util 17.009**

HOLDING COMPANIES
Merger and consolidation, **Bus Org 10.005**

HORSE RACING
Licenses and permits, partnerships, limited partnerships, transfers, **Bus Org 153.555**
Partnerships, limited partnerships, transfers, licenses and permits, **Bus Org 153.555**
Transfers, licenses and permits, partnerships, limited partnerships, **Bus Org 153.555**

HORSES
Racing. Horse Racing, generally, this index

HOSPICES
Definitions, electricity, priorities and preferences, **Util 38.072**
Electricity, priorities and preferences, **Util 38.072**
Priorities and preferences, electricity, **Util 38.072**

HOSPITALS
Telecommunications, private network services, **Util 58.251 et seq., 59.071 et seq.**

HOTELS AND MOTELS
Telecommunications, rates and charges, **Util 55.251**

HOUSE TRAILERS
Mobile Homes and Mobile Home Parks, generally, this index

HOUSING
Aged Persons, this index
Apartment Houses, generally, this index
Condominiums, generally, this index
Deeds and Conveyances, generally, this index
Loans. Mortgages, generally, this index
Mortgages, generally, this index

HOUSING FOR OLDER PERSONS
Definitions, construction, electricity, meters, exemptions, **Util 184.0125**

HURRICANES
Electricity, expenses and expenditures, nonERCOT areas, **Util 39.458 et seq.**

HUSBAND AND WIFE
Dissolution of marriage. Marriage, this index
Partnerships, this index

ICE COMPANIES
Generally, **Bus Org 1.001 et seq.**

IDENTITY AND IDENTIFICATION
Cable television, entry on property, **Util 55.017**
Electricity, municipalities, appeals or writs of error, nonresidents, **Util 33.102**
Telecommunications, this index

ILLNESS
Hospices, generally, this index

IMMUNITIES
Privileges and Immunities, generally, this index

IMPROVEMENTS
See, also, Construction, generally, this index
Electricity, this index
River authorities, electricity, **Util 32.052 et seq.**
Telecommunications, orders, **Util 55.008**

INCAPACITATED PERSONS
Guardian and Ward, generally, this index

INCENTIVES
Electricity, this index

INCOME
Electricity, computation of rates, **Util 36.057**
Gas utilities, rate computation, **Util 104.055**
Telecommunications, computation of rates, **Util 53.057**

INCOME TAX
Electricity, this index
Gas utilities, rate computation, **Util 104.055, 104.056**
Telecommunications, this index

INCORPORATION
Municipalities, this index

INCUMBRANCES
Liens and Incumbrances, generally, this index

INDEBTEDNESS
Bankruptcy, generally, this index
Bonds, generally, this index
Cooperative Associations, this index
Corporations, this index
Electric Cooperative Corporations, this index
Electricity, **Util 181.003**
Foreign Corporations, this index
Garnishment, generally, this index
Gas utilities, **Util 181.003**
Limited Liability Companies, this index
Limited partnerships. Partnerships, this index
Loans, generally, this index
Mortgages, generally, this index
Nonprofit Corporations, this index

INDEBTEDNESS—Cont'd
Partnerships, this index
Real estate investment trusts, shares and shareholders, privileges and immunities, **Bus Org 200.161**
Telephone Cooperative Corporations, this index

INDEMNITY
Banks and Banking, this index
Cable television, franchises, municipalities, **Util 66.012**
Cooperative Associations, this index
Electric cooperative corporations, **Util 161.078**
Insurance, this index
Limited Liability Companies, this index
Limited partnerships. Partnerships, this index
Partnerships, this index
Professional Associations and Societies, this index
Telephone cooperative corporations, **Util 162.079**
Television and radio, franchises, municipalities, **Util 66.012**

INDEPENDENT ORDER OF ODD FELLOWS
Generally, **Bus Org 1.001 et seq.**
Application of law, **Bus Org 23.102**
Bylaws, powers and duties, **Bus Org 23.107**
Certificate of formation, **Bus Org 23.101**
Time, **Bus Org 23.103**
Constitutions, powers and duties, **Bus Org 23.107**
Damages, **Bus Org 23.110**
Deeds and conveyances, **Bus Org 23.108**
Directors, elections, **Bus Org 23.105**
Elections, **Bus Org 23.105**
Filing, certificate of formation, **Bus Org 23.101**
Franchises, taxation, **Bus Org 23.106**
Liens and incumbrances, **Bus Org 23.109**
Loans, **Bus Org 23.109**
Mortgages, **Bus Org 23.108**
Powers and duties, **Bus Org 23.107**
Property, **Bus Org 23.108**
Real estate, **Bus Org 23.109**
Revocation or suspension, subordinate lodges, **Bus Org 23.104**
Sales, property, **Bus Org 23.108**
Schools and school districts, **Bus Org 23.108**
Subordinate lodges, **Bus Org 23.104**
Winding up, **Bus Org 23.110**
Termination, subordinate, **Bus Org 23.110**
Time, certificate of formation, **Bus Org 23.103**
Trusts and trustees, elections, **Bus Org 23.105**
Winding up, subordinate lodges, **Bus Org 23.110**

INDEPENDENT ORGANIZATIONS
Definitions, electricity, customer choice, **Util 39.151**

INDEPENDENT SYSTEM OPERATORS
Definitions, electricity, **Util 31.002**

INDEXES
Assumed or fictitious names, certificates and certification, business and commerce, professions and occupations, **Bus & C 71.154**

INFORMATION
Public Utilities, this index

INFRASTRUCTURE
Telecommunications, this index

INITIATIVE AND REFERENDUM
Cooperative associations, directors, **Bus Org 251.104**
Electricity,
  Municipal power agencies, **Util 163.054, 163.055, 163.058**
  Municipalities, surrender, jurisdiction, **Util 33.002, 33.003**
Gas utilities, jurisdiction, **Util 103.003**
Municipal Elections, this index

INJUNCTIONS
Cooperative Associations, this index
Corporations, this index
Electricity, customer choice, market power, **Util 39.157**
Foreign Corporations, this index
Gas utilities, **Util 105.021**
  Pipes and pipelines, safety, **Util 121.203**
Limited partnerships. Partnerships, this index
Partnerships, this index
Public Utilities, this index
Real estate investment trusts, ultra vires, **Bus Org 200.004**
Telecommunications, this index

INSOLVENCY
See, also, Bankruptcy, generally, this index
Corporations, this index
Foreign Corporations, this index
Nonprofit corporations, actions and proceedings, **Bus Org 12.253 et seq.**

INSPECTION AND INSPECTORS
Corporations, this index
Electricity, this index
Gas meters, **Util 182.101 et seq.**
Gas Utilities, this index
Limited Liability Companies, this index
Limited partnerships. Partnerships, this index
Nonprofit Corporations, this index
Oil and gas pipelines, fees, safety, **Util 121.211**
Partnerships, this index
Public Utilities, this index

INSTALLED GENERATION CAPACITY
Definitions, electricity, customer choice, limitation, **Util 39.154**

INSTALLMENTS
Electricity, joint ownership, public entities, payment for shares, **Util 164.004**

INSTITUTIONS OF HIGHER EDUCATION
Colleges and Universities, generally, this index

INSURANCE
Churches, this index
Electricity, this index
Indemnity, **Bus Org 2.101, 8.151**
Limited partnerships, indemnity, **Bus Org 2.101, 8.151**
Names, registration, **Bus Org 5.151 et seq.**
Nonprofit Corporations, this index
Oil and Gas, this index
Partnerships, this index
Registration, names, **Bus Org 5.151 et seq.**
Religious Organizations and Societies, this index
Self insurance,
  Electricity, **Util 36.064**
  Telecommunications, computation of rates, **Util 53.064**
Telecommunications,
  Self insurance, computation of rates, **Util 53.064**
  Telephone cooperative corporations, directors, **Util 162.074**
  Underground facilities, notification center, excavations, **Util 251.104**

INTER VIVOS TRUST
Trusts and Trustees, generally, this index

INTERACTIVE MULTIMEDIA COMMUNICATIONS
Telecommunications, **Util 57.071, 57.072**

INTERCONNECTION SERVICE
Telecommunications, this index

INTEREST
Business development corporations, loans, **Bus Org 23.066**
Electricity,
  Customers deposits, **Util 183.002 et seq.**
  System benefit fund, **Util 39.303**
Gas utilities,
  Customers deposits, **Util 183.002 et seq.**
  Pipes and pipelines, taxation, delinquency, **Util 122.205**
Partnerships, this index
Public Utilities, this index
Telecommunications, customers deposits, **Util 183.002 et seq.**
Water Supply, this index

INTEREXCHANGE SERVICE
Telecommunications, this index

INTERFERENCE
Electricity, certificates of convenience and necessity, other utilities, **Util 37.156**
Public utilities, municipalities, **Util 181.901**
Telecommunications, this index

INTERMEDIATE CARE FACILITIES
Nursing and Convalescent Homes, generally, this index

INTERNAL REVENUE CODE
Definitions, business organizations, **Bus Org 1.002**

INTERNATIONAL COMMERCE DEVELOPMENT CORPORATIONS
Generally, **Bus Org 1.001 et seq.**

INTERNATIONAL TRADING CORPORATIONS
Generally, **Bus Org 1.001 et seq.**
Definitions, **Bus Org 1.002**

INTERNET
BPL, broadband over power lines, **Util 43.001 et seq.**
Broadband over power lines, **Util 43.001 et seq.**
Competition, safeguards, application of law, **Util 60.006**
Directories, telecommunications, **Util 55.204**
Electricity,
  Customer choice, meetings, independent organizations, **Util 39.1511**
  Efficiency, plans and specifications, reports, **Util 39.9054**
Gas utilities, bills and billing, **Util 104.2551**
Private network services, educational institutions, access, **Util 58.263**
Public utilities, commission, hearings, meetings, **Util 12.204**
Rates and charges, **Util 52.002**
Voice over Internet protocol services, rates and charges, **Util 52.002**

INTERROGATORIES
Limited Liability Companies, this index

INTERSTATE COMMERCE
Electricity, municipal power agencies, distribution, **Util 163.101, 163.102**
Gas utilities,
  Malodorants, exemptions, **Util 121.253**
  Pipes and pipelines, exemptions, **Util 121.004**

INTERURBAN RAILROADS
See, also, Railroads, generally, this index
Easements, eminent domain, public utilities, right of way, **Util 186.051 et seq.**
Eminent domain, public utilities, easements, right of way, **Util 186.051 et seq.**
Right of way, public utilities, easements, eminent domain, **Util 186.051 et seq.**

INTERVENTION
Electricity, certificates of convenience and necessity, hearings, **Util 37.054**
Consolidation, **Util 37.0541**

INVESTMENT CONTRACTS
Securities, generally, this index

INVESTMENTS
Churches, retirement and pensions, contributions, **Bus Org 22.403**
Corporations, this index
Electricity, this index
Foreign Corporations, this index
Gas Utilities, this index
Nonprofit Corporations, this index
Open End Investment Companies, generally, this index
Partnerships, this index
Public Utilities, this index
Real Estate Investment Trusts, generally, this index
Religious organizations and societies, retirement and pensions, contributions, **Bus Org 22.403**
Securities, generally, this index
Telecommunications, this index

IRRIGATION
Corporations, **Bus Org 1.001 et seq.**
Gas utilities, **Util 123.001, 123.002**

JOINT OWNERSHIP
Joint Tenants, generally, this index

JOINT POWERS AGENCIES
Electricity, this index

JOINT TENANTS
Electricity, public entities, **Util 164.001 et seq.**
Real estate investment trusts, shares and shareholders, **Bus Org 200.158**
Privileges and immunities, **Bus Org 200.160**

JUDGMENTS AND DECREES
Cooperative Associations, this index
Corporations, this index
Executions, generally, this index
Foreign Corporations, this index
Limited Liability Companies, this index
Limited partnerships. Partnerships, this index
Nonprofit Corporations, this index
Partnerships, this index
Professional Associations and Societies, this index
Professional Corporations, this index

JUDICIAL DEPARTMENT
State bar. Attorneys, this index

JUDICIAL NOTICE
Public utility commission, seals, **Util 12.003**

JUDICIAL SALES
Executions, generally, this index

JUDICIARY
Courts, generally, this index

JUNIOR COLLEGES AND UNIVERSITIES
Community colleges and districts. Colleges and Universities, this index

JURISDICTION
Cooperative Associations, this index
Corporations, this index
Electric Cooperative Corporations, this index
Electricity, this index
Foreign Corporations, this index
Gas Utilities, this index
Limited Liability Companies, this index
Limited partnerships. Partnerships, this index
Municipalities, this index
Nonprofit Corporations, this index
Partnerships, this index
Professional Associations and Societies, this index
Professional Corporations, this index
Public Utilities, this index
Telecommunications, this index

JUVENILE DELINQUENTS AND DEPENDENTS
Truancy. Schools and School Districts, this index

KEROSENE
Oil and Gas, generally, this index

KNIGHTS TEMPLAR
Generally, **Bus Org 1.001 et seq.**
Incorporation, **Bus Org 23.101 et seq.**

LABOR AND EMPLOYMENT
Collective bargaining. Labor Disputes, this index
Compensation and Salaries, generally, this index
Disputes. Labor Disputes, generally, this index
Grievances. Labor Disputes, generally, this index
Pay. Compensation and Salaries, generally, this index
Picketing. Labor Disputes, this index
Public utilities, commission, United States agencies, actions and proceedings, **Util 39.4525**
Salaries. Compensation and Salaries, generally, this index
Strikes. Labor Disputes, generally, this index
Telecommunications, this index
Wages. Compensation and Salaries, generally, this index

LABOR DISPUTES
Collective bargaining, public utilities, interference, commission, **Util 14.006**
Picketing, public utilities, interruption of service, **Util 186.004**

LABOR DISPUTES—Cont'd
Public utilities, interruption of service, **Util 186.004, 186.006**

LABOR ORGANIZATIONS
Generally, **Bus Org 2.009**
Lobbyists. Legislature, this index
Picketing. Labor Disputes, this index

LAKES AND PONDS
Water Supply, generally, this index

LANDLORD AND TENANT
See, also, Leases, generally, this index
Apartment Houses, generally, this index
Definitions, central heating and cooling, **Util 184.051**
Electricity, customer choice, **Util 39.107**
Public utilities, bills and billing, **Util 184.001 et seq.**
Telecommunications, installations, **Util 54.259 et seq.**

LAW
Statutes, generally, this index

LAW GOVERNING
Conflict of Laws, generally, this index

LAWS
Statutes, generally, this index

LAWSUITS
Actions and Proceedings, generally, this index

LAWYERS
Attorneys, generally, this index

LEASES
See, also, Landlord and Tenant, generally, this index
Business development corporations, **Bus Org 23.054**
Corporations, this index
Electric cooperative corporations, **Util 161.121**
Electricity, this index
Foreign Corporations, this index
Gas Utilities, this index
Limited Liability Companies, this index
Limited partnerships. Partnerships, this index
Monopolies and Unfair Trade, generally, this index
Municipalities, this index
Nonprofit Corporations, this index
Partnerships, this index
Public Utilities, this index
Real estate investment trusts, **Bus Org 200.405 et seq.**
Telecommunications, this index
Telephone cooperative corporations, **Util 162.121, 162.125, 162.126**

LEGACIES AND LEGATEES
Gifts, generally, this index

LEGAL ACTIONS
Actions and Proceedings, generally, this index

LEGAL COUNSEL
Attorneys, generally, this index

LEGAL HOLIDAYS
Definitions, underground facilities, excavations, **Util 251.001**

LEGISLATION
Statutes, generally, this index

LEGISLATURE
Audits and auditors, nonprofit corporations, **Bus Org 22.356**
Books and papers, nonprofit corporations, audits and auditors, **Bus Org 22.356**
Code construction. Statutes, this index
Laws. Statutes, generally, this index
Lobbyists,
  Gas utilities,
    Rates and charges, computation, **Util 104.057**
    Reports, **Util 102.003**
  Public utilities, office of public utility counsel, conflict of interest, **Util 13.042**
  Public utility commission, **Util 12.151**
Nonprofit corporations, audits and auditors, **Bus Org 22.356**
Records and recordation, nonprofit corporations, audits and auditors, **Bus Org 22.356**
Reports, telecommunications, competition, **Util 52.006**
Statutes, generally, this index
Telecommunications, directories, listing, **Util 55.202, 55.203**

LIBRARIES
Definitions,
  Distance learning, telecommunications, **Util 57.021**
  Telecommunications, private network services, **Util 58.252, 59.071**
Information sharing, telecommunications, **Util 57.021 et seq.**
Telecommunications,
  Distance learning, **Util 57.021 et seq.**
  Private network services, **Util 58.251 et seq., 59.071 et seq.**

LICENSES AND PERMITS
Contested cases. Administrative Law and Procedure, this index
Cooperative Associations, this index
Definitions, business organizations, **Bus Org 1.002**
Electric cooperative corporations, fees, **Util 161.061**
Electricity, this index
Foreign Corporations, this index
Gas utilities, pipes and pipelines, sour gas, **Util 121.453, 121.454**
Oil and Gas, this index
Oil and Gas Pipelines, this index

LICENSES AND PERMITS—Cont'd
Railroads, this index
Sewers and Sewer Systems, this index
Sour gas, pipes and pipelines, **Util 121.453, 121.454**
Telecommunications, this index
Telephone cooperative corporations, fees, **Util 162.061**
Water Supply, this index

LIENS AND INCUMBRANCES
Business development corporations, **Bus Org 23.054**
Corporations, this index
Electricity, this index
Foreign Corporations, this index
Limited Liability Companies, this index
Mortgages, generally, this index
Nonprofit Corporations, this index
Partnerships, this index
Telephone cooperative corporations, **Util 162.005, 162.125, 162.126**

LIFELINE SERVICE
Generally, **Util 55.015**

LIMITATION OF ACTIONS
Corporations, this index
Foreign Corporations, this index
Municipalities, this index
Nonprofit corporations, termination, claims, **Bus Org 11.359**
Partnerships, this index
Real estate investment trusts, managers and management, **Bus Org 200.313**

LIMITED LIABILITY COMPANIES
  Generally, **Bus Org 1.001 et seq., 101.001 et seq., 301.001 et seq.**
Abandonment, **Bus Org 10.201 et seq.**
  Filing, **Bus Org 4.057**
Abatement of actions and proceedings,
  State, **Bus Org 12.260**
  Termination, involuntary termination, **Bus Org 11.304**
  Winding up, involuntary winding up, **Bus Org 11.304**
Acceptance, certificates and certification, **Bus Org 10.156**
Accounts and accounting, **Bus Org 3.151 et seq.**
  Examinations and examiners, **Bus Org 12.151 et seq.**
  Series limited liability companies, **Bus Org 101.602**
Acknowledgments,
  Certificate of formation, **Bus Org 3.004**
    Evidence, **Bus Org 3.001**
  Filing, **Bus Org 4.002**
    Effective date, delay, **Bus Org 4.059**
Actions and proceedings, **Bus Org 2.101**
  Abatement of actions and proceedings, generally, ante
  Business Organizations Code, prior law, **Bus Org 402.014**
  Certificate of formation, amendments, **Bus Org 3.056**
  Guaranty, **Bus Org 2.104**

LIMITED LIABILITY COMPANIES—Cont'd
Actions and proceedings—Cont'd
  Indemnity, **Bus Org 8.001 et seq.**
  Insolvency, **Bus Org 12.253 et seq.**
  Receivers and receivership, **Bus Org 11.406**
  Records and recordation, inspection and inspectors, **Bus Org 3.152**
  Series limited liability companies, **Bus Org 101.605**
  State, liens and incumbrances, **Bus Org 12.201 et seq.**
  Termination, involuntary termination, **Bus Org 11.303**
  Winding up, post
Address,
  Certificate of formation, **Bus Org 3.005**
    Managers and management, **Bus Org 3.010**
  Records and recordation, **Bus Org 101.501**
Adoption, Business Organizations Code, **Bus Org 402.003**
Advances, **Bus Org 101.402**
  Indemnity, expenses and expenditures, **Bus Org 8.104, 8.105**
    Reports, **Bus Org 8.152**
Agent for service of process, **Bus Org 5.251 et seq.**
Agents and agencies, **Bus Org 101.254**
  Changes, filing, fines and penalties, **Bus Org 21.802**
  Damages, **Bus Org 301.010**
  Licenses and permits, **Bus Org 301.006**
  Registered agents, generally, post
Agreements. Contracts, generally, ante
Allocations,
  Merger and consolidation, property, **Bus Org 10.003**
  Profits, losses, **Bus Org 101.201**
  Record date, **Bus Org 101.208**
Alternatives, service of process, **Bus Org 5.256**
Amendments,
  Business Organizations Code, statutes, **Bus Org 1.054**
  Certificate of formation, **Bus Org 3.051 et seq.**
  Contracts, **Bus Org 101.053**
  Filing, **Bus Org 4.106**
Ancillary receiverships, **Bus Org 11.409**
Answer, interrogatories, time, **Bus Org 12.002**
Antitrust, application of law, **Bus Org 10.901**
Appeal and review,
  Derivative actions, **Bus Org 101.455**
  Filing, **Bus Org 12.004**
  Termination, involuntary termination, **Bus Org 11.307**
  Winding up, involuntary winding up, **Bus Org 11.307**
Application of law, **Bus Org 101.002, 301.001**
  Antitrust, **Bus Org 10.901**
  Business Organizations Code, post

LIMITED LIABILITY COMPANIES
—Cont'd
Application of law—Cont'd
Certificate of formation, **Bus Org 1.101 et seq.**
Elections, **Bus Org 6.302**
Meetings, **Bus Org 101.351**
Indebtedness, **Bus Org 10.901**
Indemnity, **Bus Org 8.002**
Managers and management, **Bus Org 101.301**
Meetings, **Bus Org 6.302, 101.351**
Monopolies and unfair trade, **Bus Org 10.901**
Professional limited liability companies, **Bus Org 304.001**
Reorganization, **Bus Org 10.306**
Series limited liability companies, **Bus Org 101.609**
Winding up, **Bus Org 101.617**
Appointments, receivers and receivership, **Bus Org 11.401 et seq.**
Appraisals and appraisers, reorganization, **Bus Org 10.304**
Assets,
Disposition, **Bus Org 10.251 et seq.**
Reorganization, **Bus Org 10.301**
Liens and incumbrances, state, **Bus Org 12.201**
Sales, Business Organizations Code, mandatory application date, **Bus Org 402.010**
Series limited liability companies, generally, post
Winding up, distribution and distributors, **Bus Org 11.053**
Assignments, **Bus Org 10.251 et seq.**
Indemnity, **Bus Org 101.402**
Members, **Bus Org 101.108 et seq.**
Shares and shareholders, certificates and certification, **Bus Org 3.201**
Assumed or fictitious names, **Bus & C 71.001 et seq.**
Names, **Bus Org 5.051 et seq.**
Attachment, state, **Bus Org 12.259**
Attorney fees,
Derivative actions, payment, **Bus Org 101.461**
Filing,
Fines and penalties, **Bus Org 21.802**
Fraud, **Bus Org 4.007**
Records and recordation, inspection and inspectors, **Bus Org 3.152**
Bankruptcy, **Bus Org 10.301 et seq.**
Bonds, **Bus Org 2.101**
Reorganization, **Bus Org 10.301**
Bonds (officers and fiduciaries), receivers and receivership, **Bus Org 11.406**
Bonuses, officers and employees, **Bus Org 2.101**
Books and papers, **Bus Org 3.151 et seq.**
Confidential or privileged information, **Bus Org 12.154**
Disclosure, **Bus Org 12.154**
Duplicates and copies, **Bus Org 12.151 et seq.**

LIMITED LIABILITY COMPANIES
—Cont'd
Books and papers—Cont'd
Examinations and examiners, **Bus Org 3.153, 12.151 et seq., 101.501, 101.502**
Inspection and inspectors, **Bus Org 3.152**
Powers and duties, limitations, **Bus Org 2.005**
Reorganization, **Bus Org 10.301**
Business Organizations Code, application of law, **Bus Org 402.001 et seq.**
Foreign countries, foreign states, **Bus Org 1.053**
Bylaws, **Bus Org 2.101**
Cancellation,
Reinstatement, **Bus Org 402.013**
Winding up, **Bus Org 11.152, 101.552**
Certificate of formation, **Bus Org 3.001 et seq., 101.051**
Amendments, **Bus Org 3.051 et seq.**
Application of law, **Bus Org 1.101 et seq.**
Contracts, **Bus Org 101.051**
Definitions, **Bus Org 1.002**
Duplicates and copies, **Bus Org 101.501**
Examinations and examiners, **Bus Org 101.502**
Merger and consolidation, **Bus Org 10.002**
Names, post
Reinstatement, **Bus Org 402.013**
Reorganization, **Bus Org 10.301 et seq.**
Restatement, **Bus Org 3.057 et seq.**
Signatures, **Bus Org 3.004**
Amendments, **Bus Org 3.052, 3.054**
Restatement, **Bus Org 3.058, 3.060**
Statements,
Amendments, **Bus Org 3.053, 3.054**
Restatement, **Bus Org 3.059**
Time, **Bus Org 3.001**
Amendments, **Bus Org 3.056**
Restatement, **Bus Org 3.063**
Certificates and certification,
Acceptance, **Bus Org 10.156**
Certificate of formation, generally, ante
Conversion, **Bus Org 10.154 et seq.**
Evidence, existence, **Bus Org 4.005**
Exchange of property, **Bus Org 10.151 et seq.**
Filing, **Bus Org 12.001**
Corrections, **Bus Org 4.101 et seq.**
Fines and penalties, **Bus Org 21.802**
Indebtedness, **Bus Org 2.114**
Merger and consolidation, **Bus Org 10.151 et seq.**
Shares and shareholders, **Bus Org 3.201 et seq.**
Termination, post
Certified copies,
Filing, **Bus Org 4.005**
Involuntary termination, judgments and decrees, **Bus Org 11.414**
Changes, registered offices, registered agent, **Bus Org 5.202, 5.203**

LIMITED LIABILITY COMPANIES
—Cont'd
Citizens and citizenship, receivers and receivership, **Bus Org 11.406**
Claims,
Receivers and receivership, filing, **Bus Org 11.407**
Termination, **Bus Org 11.351 et seq.**
Classification,
Managers and management, **Bus Org 101.307**
Members, **Bus Org 101.104, 101.105**
Series limited liability companies, **Bus Org 101.607**
Closely held limited liability companies, derivative actions, **Bus Org 101.463**
Committees, managers and management, **Bus Org 101.253**
Community property, members, **Bus Org 101.106**
Compensation and salaries,
Officers and employees, **Bus Org 2.101**
Receivers and receivership, **Bus Org 11.408**
Compromise and settlement,
Contributions, **Bus Org 101.154**
Derivative actions, **Bus Org 101.460**
Computations, distribution and distributors, **Bus Org 101.203**
Conduct,
Business Organizations Code, application of law, **Bus Org 402.006**
Damages, **Bus Org 7.001, 301.010**
Confidential or privileged information, interrogatories, **Bus Org 12.003**
Conflict of interest, contracts, **Bus Org 101.255**
Conflict of laws, **Bus Org 301.002**
Consent,
Contributions, release, **Bus Org 101.154**
Duplicates and copies, meetings, action without meeting, **Bus Org 6.205**
Registered agents, **Bus Org 5.2011**
Winding up, cancellation, **Bus Org 101.552**
Consolidation. Merger and consolidation, generally, post
Construction of laws, Business Organizations Code, statutes, **Bus Org 1.006, 1.051 et seq.**
Contracts, **Bus Org 2.101, 101.051 et seq.**
Amendments, **Bus Org 101.053**
Business Organizations Code, application of law, **Bus Org 402.006**
Certificate of formation, **Bus Org 101.051**
Conflict of interest, **Bus Org 101.255**
Duplicates and copies, **Bus Org 101.501**
Elections, **Bus Org 6.252**
Examinations and examiners, **Bus Org 101.502**
Indebtedness, **Bus Org 2.103**
Managers and management, post
Members, classification, **Bus Org 101.104**
Modification, **Bus Org 101.054**

LIMITED LIABILITY COMPANIES
—Cont'd
Contracts—Cont'd
Officers and employees, **Bus Org 101.255**
Powers and duties, modification, **Bus Org 101.401**
Series limited liability companies, **Bus Org 101.605**
Waiver, **Bus Org 101.054**
Winding up, **Bus Org 11.152**
Contributions,
Compromise and settlement, **Bus Org 101.154**
Consent, release, **Bus Org 101.154**
Death, **Bus Org 101.152**
Definitions, business organizations, **Bus Org 1.002**
Disability, **Bus Org 101.152**
Fines and penalties, **Bus Org 101.153**
Forced sales, **Bus Org 101.153**
Frauds, statute of, **Bus Org 101.151**
Indebtedness, **Bus Org 101.155, 101.156**
Loans, **Bus Org 101.153**
Members, post
Records and recordation, **Bus Org 101.501**
Release, **Bus Org 101.154**
Signatures, **Bus Org 101.151**
Conversion, **Bus Org 10.101 et seq.**
Abandonment, **Bus Org 10.201 et seq.**
Acceptance, certificates and certification, **Bus Org 10.156**
Business Organizations Code, mandatory application date, **Bus Org 402.010**
Certificates and certification, **Bus Org 10.154 et seq.**
Dissenting shareholders, **Bus Org 10.351 et seq.**
Effective date, **Bus Org 10.105, 10.106**
Filing,
Certificates and certification, **Bus Org 10.155**
Fees, **Bus Org 4.151**
Names, **Bus Org 10.103**
Notice, **Bus Org 10.101**
Plans and specifications, **Bus Org 10.101 et seq.**
Reorganization, **Bus Org 10.301 et seq.**
Conveyances. Deeds and conveyances, generally, post
Corrections, filing, **Bus Org 4.101 et seq.**
Fees, **Bus Org 4.151**
Costs,
Derivative actions, payment, **Bus Org 101.461**
Filing,
Fines and penalties, **Bus Org 21.802**
Fraud, **Bus Org 4.007**
Insolvency, dismissal and nonsuit, **Bus Org 12.257**
Liens and incumbrances, foreclosure, dismissal and nonsuit, **Bus Org 12.257**

LIMITED LIABILITY COMPANIES
—Cont'd
Crimes and offenses,
Books and papers, examinations and examiners, **Bus Org 12.156**
Damages, **Bus Org 7.001**
Fraud, generally, post
Termination, involuntary termination, **Bus Org 11.301 et seq.**
Winding up, involuntary winding up, **Bus Org 11.301 et seq.**
Damages, **Bus Org 301.010**
Application of law, **Bus Org 1.104**
Filing, **Bus Org 21.802**
Fraud, **Bus Org 4.007**
Guaranty, **Bus Org 2.104**
Indemnity, generally, post
Members, **Bus Org 101.110 et seq.**
Officers and employees, post
Death,
Contributions, **Bus Org 101.152**
Members, **Bus Org 101.1115**
Deception, names, **Bus Org 5.052**
Deductions, members, assignments, **Bus Org 101.109**
Deeds and conveyances, **Bus Org 10.251 et seq.**
Property, **Bus Org 2.101**
Records and recordation, **Bus Org 10.253**
Definitions, **Bus Org 1.002, 101.001, 301.003**
Business organizations, **Bus Org 1.002**
Closely held limited liability company, derivative actions, **Bus Org 101.463**
Indemnity, **Bus Org 8.001**
Mandatory application date, **Bus Org 401.001**
Prior law, **Bus Org 401.001**
Series limited liability companies,
Application of law, **Bus Org 101.609**
Winding up, **Bus Org 101.617**
Termination, **Bus Org 11.001**
Winding up, **Bus Org 11.001**
Delay, filing, effective date, **Bus Org 4.052 et seq.**
Delivery,
Filing, **Bus Org 4.001**
Meetings, action without meeting, **Bus Org 6.203**
Shares and shareholders, certificates and certification, **Bus Org 3.204**
Demand, derivative actions, **Bus Org 101.453**
Rejection, **Bus Org 101.459**
Deposits, termination, claims, **Bus Org 11.352**
Derivative actions, **Bus Org 101.451 et seq.**
Appeal and review, **Bus Org 101.455**
Attorney fees, payment, **Bus Org 101.461**
Closely held limited liability companies, **Bus Org 101.463**
Compromise and settlement, **Bus Org 101.460**
Costs, payment, **Bus Org 101.461**

LIMITED LIABILITY COMPANIES
—Cont'd
Derivative actions—Cont'd
Definitions, **Bus Org 101.451**
Closely held limited liability company, **Bus Org 101.463**
Demand, **Bus Org 101.453**
Rejection, **Bus Org 101.459**
Discovery, **Bus Org 101.456**
Dismissal and nonsuit, **Bus Org 101.456, 101.458**
Elections, **Bus Org 101.454**
Evidence, dismissal and nonsuit, **Bus Org 101.458**
Expenses and expenditures, payment, **Bus Org 101.461**
Fraud, privileges and immunities, **Bus Org 101.454**
Jurisdiction, foreign limited liability companies, **Bus Org 101.462**
Limitation of actions, **Bus Org 101.457**
Notice,
Compromise and settlement, **Bus Org 101.460**
Dismissal and nonsuit, **Bus Org 101.456**
Parties, **Bus Org 101.452**
Payment,
Closely held limited liability company, **Bus Org 101.463**
Costs, **Bus Org 101.461**
Privileges and immunities, **Bus Org 101.454**
Rejection, demand, **Bus Org 101.459**
Supersedeas or stay, **Bus Org 101.455**
Time, demand, **Bus Org 101.453**
Tolling, limitation of actions, **Bus Org 101.457**
Directors,
Agent for service of process, **Bus Org 5.255**
Certificate of formation,
Amendments, **Bus Org 3.054**
Restatement, **Bus Org 3.060**
Damages, **Bus Org 7.001**
Indemnity, **Bus Org 7.001**
Loans, **Bus Org 2.101**
Disability, contributions, **Bus Org 101.152**
Discharge,
Receivers and receivership, **Bus Org 11.412**
Termination, claims, **Bus Org 11.353**
Winding up, indebtedness, **Bus Org 11.053**
Disclosure, interrogatories, **Bus Org 12.003**
Discovery, derivative actions, **Bus Org 101.456**
Dismissal and nonsuit,
Derivative actions, **Bus Org 101.456, 101.458**
Insolvency, **Bus Org 12.257**
Liens and incumbrances, foreclosure, **Bus Org 12.257**
Dissenting shareholders. Shares and shareholders, post

LIMITED LIABILITY COMPANIES —Cont'd
Dissolution, **Bus Org 2.101**
  Involuntary dissolution, reinstatement, **Bus Org 402.013**
Dissolution of marriage, members, **Bus Org 101.1115**
Distributions, **Bus Org 101.202 et seq.**
  Computations, **Bus Org 101.203**
  Indebtedness, **Bus Org 101.207**
  Members, assignments, **Bus Org 101.109**
  Record date, **Bus Org 101.208**
    Series limited liability companies, **Bus Org 101.612**
  Returns, **Bus Org 101.206**
  Series limited liability companies, **Bus Org 101.611, 101.613**
    Record date, **Bus Org 101.612**
  Time, **Bus Org 101.204**
  Winding up, assets, **Bus Org 11.053**
  Withdrawal, **Bus Org 101.205**
Domicile and residence, managers and management, **Bus Org 101.302**
Dual office holding, officers and employees, **Bus Org 3.103**
Duplicates and copies,
  Agent for service of process, **Bus Org 5.252**
  Books and papers, **Bus Org 12.151 et seq.**
  Consent, meetings, action without meeting, **Bus Org 6.205**
  Filing, **Bus Org 4.003**
  Records and recordation, **Bus Org 3.152, 101.501**
  Shares and shareholders, certificates and certification, **Bus Org 3.202**
Duties. Powers and duties, generally, post
Effective date,
  Business Organizations Code, **Bus Org 402.001**
    Adoption, **Bus Org 402.005**
  Conversion, **Bus Org 10.105, 10.106**
  Exchange of property, **Bus Org 10.054, 10.055**
  Filing, **Bus Org 4.051 et seq.**
  Members, **Bus Org 101.103**
  Merger and consolidation, **Bus Org 10.007**
  Termination, post
Elections,
  Application of law, **Bus Org 6.302**
    Meetings, **Bus Org 101.351**
  Contracts, **Bus Org 6.252**
  Derivative actions, **Bus Org 101.454**
  Indemnity, **Bus Org 8.103**
  Managers and management, post
  Meetings, **Bus Org 101.351 et seq.**
  Officers and employees, **Bus Org 2.101, 3.103**
  Proxies, **Bus Org 101.357**
  Series limited liability companies, post
  Termination, reinstatement, **Bus Org 101.552**
  Trusts and trustees, **Bus Org 6.251**

LIMITED LIABILITY COMPANIES —Cont'd
Elections—Cont'd
  Winding up, revocation or suspension, **Bus Org 101.552**
Electronic communications, consent, meetings, **Bus Org 6.205**
Electronic filing, **Bus Org 12.001**
Emergencies, governance, **Bus Org 3.251 et seq.**
Employees. Officers and employees, generally, post
Errors,
  Damages, **Bus Org 301.010**
  Termination, reinstatement, **Bus Org 11.201 et seq.**
Escheat, termination, claims, **Bus Org 11.355**
Evidence,
  Certificate of formation, acknowledgments, **Bus Org 3.001**
  Derivative actions, dismissal and nonsuit, **Bus Org 101.458**
  Existence, certificates and certification, **Bus Org 4.005**
  Filing, **Bus Org 4.001**
  Indebtedness, fraud, **Bus Org 2.103**
  Shares and shareholders, certificates and certification, **Bus Org 3.201**
Examinations and examiners,
  Books and papers, ante
  Elections, contracts, **Bus Org 6.252**
  Records and recordation, post
Exchange of property, **Bus Org 2.101, 10.051 et seq.**
  Abandonment, **Bus Org 10.201 et seq.**
  Acceptance, certificates and certification, **Bus Org 10.156**
  Certificates and certification, **Bus Org 10.151 et seq.**
  Dissenting shareholders, **Bus Org 10.351 et seq.**
  Filing,
    Certificates and certification, **Bus Org 10.153**
    Fees, **Bus Org 4.151**
  Reorganization, **Bus Org 10.301**
  Shares and shareholders, post
  Voluntary, **Bus Org 10.902**
Exemptions,
  Guaranty, powers and duties, **Bus Org 2.104**
  Interrogatories, **Bus Org 12.002**
  Securities, sales, **Bus Org 301.011**
  Termination, involuntary termination, **Bus Org 11.251**
Expenses and expenditures, **Bus Org 101.402**
  Derivative actions, payment, **Bus Org 101.461**
  Examinations and examiners, **Bus Org 101.502**
  Indemnity, **Bus Org 8.001 et seq.**
  Series limited liability companies, **Bus Org 101.602**
Expulsion, members, **Bus Org 101.107**

LIMITED LIABILITY COMPANIES —Cont'd
Facsimile,
  Consent, meetings, action without meeting, **Bus Org 6.205**
  Filing, **Bus Org 4.003**
  Indebtedness, certificates and certification, **Bus Org 2.114**
  Meetings, notice, **Bus Org 6.051**
  Seals, **Bus Org 2.101**
  Shares and shareholders, certificates and certification, **Bus Org 3.203**
Fees,
  Business Organizations Code, effective date, **Bus Org 402.002**
  Filing, **Bus Org 4.154**
  Names, reservation, **Bus Org 5.101**
    Withdrawal, **Bus Org 5.1041**
Filing, **Bus Org 4.001 et seq., 12.001 et seq.**
  Abandonment, **Bus Org 4.057**
  Acknowledgments, ante
  Amendments, **Bus Org 4.106**
  Appeal and review, **Bus Org 12.004**
  Assumed or fictitious names, **Bus Org 5.051**
  Attorney fees,
    Fines and penalties, **Bus Org 21.802**
    Fraud, **Bus Org 4.007**
  Business Organizations Code, effective date, **Bus Org 402.002**
  Certificate of formation, **Bus Org 3.001 et seq.**
  Certificates and certification, **Bus Org 12.001**
    Abandonment, **Bus Org 4.057**
    Corrections, **Bus Org 4.101 et seq.**
  Certified copies, **Bus Org 4.005**
  Conversion, certificates and certification, **Bus Org 10.155**
  Corrections, **Bus Org 4.101 et seq.**
    Fees, **Bus Org 4.151**
  Costs,
    Fines and penalties, **Bus Org 21.802**
    Fraud, **Bus Org 4.007**
  Damages, **Bus Org 21.802**
    Fraud, **Bus Org 4.007**
  Delay, effective date, **Bus Org 4.052 et seq.**
  Delivery, **Bus Org 4.001**
  Duplicates and copies, **Bus Org 4.003**
  Effective date, **Bus Org 4.051 et seq.**
  Electronic filing, **Bus Org 12.001**
  Evidence, **Bus Org 4.001**
  Facsimile, **Bus Org 4.003**
  Fees, **Bus Org 4.154**
  Fines and penalties, **Bus Org 21.802**
    Fraud, **Bus Org 4.008**
  Forms, **Bus Org 4.006**
  Fraud, **Bus Org 4.007, 4.008**
  Interrogatories, **Bus Org 12.002, 12.003**
  Jurisdiction, fines and penalties, **Bus Org 21.802**
  Limitations,
    Corrections, **Bus Org 4.102**
    Effective date, delay, **Bus Org 4.058**
  Names, registration, **Bus Org 5.152**

LIMITED LIABILITY COMPANIES
—Cont'd
Filing—Cont'd
Real estate investment trusts, **Bus Org 4.009**
Receivers and receivership, claims, **Bus Org 11.407**
Registered agent, resignation, **Bus Org 5.204**
Service of process, **Bus Org 21.802**
Signatures, **Bus Org 4.001, 101.0515**
Corrections, certificates and certification, **Bus Org 4.101**
Termination, involuntary termination, **Bus Org 11.315**
Time, **Bus Org 4.004**
Corrections, **Bus Org 4.105**
Effective date, **Bus Org 4.051 et seq.**
Fines and penalties, **Bus Org 21.802**
Winding up, involuntary winding up, **Bus Org 11.315**
Financial statements and reports, officers and employees, good faith, **Bus Org 3.102, 3.105**
Fines and penalties,
Books and papers, examinations and examiners, **Bus Org 12.156**
Contributions, **Bus Org 101.153**
Filing, **Bus Org 21.802**
Fraud, **Bus Org 4.008**
Registered agents, consent, **Bus Org 5.207**
Forced sales, contributions, **Bus Org 101.153**
Foreclosure, liens and incumbrances, **Bus Org 12.252 et seq.**
Foreign countries,
Business Organizations Code, application of law, **Bus Org 1.053**
Certificate of formation, application of law, **Bus Org 1.102**
Foreign limited liability companies, **Bus Org 301.001 et seq.**
Acknowledgments, registration, **Bus Org 9.008**
Actions and proceedings,
Registration, **Bus Org 9.051 et seq.**
Transacting business in Texas, **Bus Org 9.251**
Amendments, registration, **Bus Org 9.009**
Application of law, Business Organizations Code, **Bus Org 9.301**
Banks and banking, transacting business in Texas, **Bus Org 9.251**
Certificates and certification, registration,
Reinstatement, **Bus Org 9.104**
Revocation or suspension, **Bus Org 9.102**
Certified copies, registration, revocation or suspension, **Bus Org 9.161**
Claims, transacting business in Texas, **Bus Org 9.251**
Conflict of laws, registration, **Bus Org 9.055**
Definitions, **Bus Org 101.001**

LIMITED LIABILITY COMPANIES
—Cont'd
Foreign limited liability companies
—Cont'd
Derivative actions, generally, ante
Dismissal and nonsuit, registration, revocation or suspension, **Bus Org 9.156**
Elections, transacting business in Texas, **Bus Org 9.251**
Evidence, registration, acknowledgments, **Bus Org 9.008**
Exemptions, registration, **Bus Org 9.002**
Fees, registration, collection, **Bus Org 9.054**
Filing, registration, revocation or suspension, **Bus Org 9.161**
Fines and penalties, registration, **Bus Org 9.052**
Indebtedness, transacting business in Texas, **Bus Org 9.251**
Injunctions, registration, **Bus Org 9.051**
Investments, transacting business in Texas, **Bus Org 9.251**
Judgments and decrees, registration, revocation or suspension, **Bus Org 9.154 et seq.**
Jurisdiction,
Derivative actions, **Bus Org 101.462**
Registration, revocation or suspension, **Bus Org 9.158**
Liens and incumbrances, transacting business in Texas, **Bus Org 9.251**
Lists, transacting business in Texas, **Bus Org 9.251, 9.252**
Loans, transacting business in Texas, **Bus Org 9.251**
Meetings, transacting business in Texas, **Bus Org 9.251**
Mines and minerals, transacting business in Texas, **Bus Org 9.251**
Mortgages, transacting business in Texas, **Bus Org 9.251**
Names, **Bus Org 5.059**
Registration,
Change of name, **Bus Org 9.010**
Reinstatement, **Bus Org 9.105**
Notice, registration,
Revocation or suspension, **Bus Org 9.101, 9.152**
Service of process, revocation or suspension, **Bus Org 9.160**
Offices, transacting business in Texas, **Bus Org 9.251**
Probate proceedings, transacting business in Texas, **Bus Org 9.251**
Registration, **Bus Org 9.001 et seq.**
Acknowledgments, **Bus Org 9.008**
Actions and proceedings, **Bus Org 9.051 et seq.**
Amendments, **Bus Org 9.009**
Applications, **Bus Org 9.004**
Separate interests, **Bus Org 9.005**
Certificates and certification,
Reinstatement, **Bus Org 9.104**

LIMITED LIABILITY COMPANIES
—Cont'd
Foreign limited liability companies
—Cont'd
Registration—Cont'd
Certificates and certification—Cont'd
Revocation or suspension, **Bus Org 9.102**
Certified copies, revocation or suspension, **Bus Org 9.161**
Conflict of laws, **Bus Org 9.055**
Dismissal and nonsuit, revocation or suspension, **Bus Org 9.156**
Evidence, acknowledgments, **Bus Org 9.008**
Exemptions, **Bus Org 9.002**
Fees, collection, **Bus Org 9.054**
Filing, revocation or suspension, **Bus Org 9.161**
Fines and penalties, **Bus Org 9.052**
Fraud, **Bus Org 9.051 et seq.**
Injunctions, **Bus Org 9.051**
Judgments and decrees, revocation or suspension, **Bus Org 9.154 et seq.**
Jurisdiction, revocation or suspension, **Bus Org 9.158**
Names,
Change of name, **Bus Org 9.010**
Reinstatement, **Bus Org 9.105**
Notice,
Revocation or suspension, **Bus Org 9.101, 9.152**
Service of process, revocation or suspension, **Bus Org 9.160**
Reinstatement, **Bus Org 9.103 et seq.**
Remand, revocation or suspension, **Bus Org 9.157**
Revocation or suspension, **Bus Org 9.101 et seq., 9.151 et seq.**
Same or similar names, reinstatement, **Bus Org 9.105**
Service of process,
Revocation or suspension, **Bus Org 9.159, 9.160**
Withdrawal, **Bus Org 9.011**
Supersedeas or stay, revocation or suspension, **Bus Org 9.156**
Taxation, forfeitures, reinstatement, **Bus Org 9.106**
Time, amendments, **Bus Org 9.009**
Venue, **Bus Org 9.053**
Revocation or suspension, **Bus Org 9.158**
Withdrawal, **Bus Org 9.011**
Reinstatement, registration, **Bus Org 9.103 et seq.**
Remand, registration, revocation or suspension, **Bus Org 9.157**
Revocation or suspension, registration, **Bus Org 9.101 et seq., 9.151 et seq.**
Sales, transacting business in Texas, **Bus Org 9.251**
Same or similar names, registration, reinstatement, **Bus Org 9.105**
Securities, transacting business in Texas, **Bus Org 9.251**

LIMITED LIABILITY COMPANIES
—Cont'd
Foreign limited liability companies
—Cont'd
Separate interests, registration, applications, **Bus Org 9.005**
Service of process, registration,
Revocation or suspension, **Bus Org 9.159, 9.160**
Withdrawal, **Bus Org 9.011**
Supersedeas or stay, registration, revocation or suspension, **Bus Org 9.156**
Taxation, registration, forfeitures, reinstatement, **Bus Org 9.106**
Time, registration, amendments, **Bus Org 9.009**
Transacting business in Texas, **Bus Org 9.201 et seq.**
Lists, **Bus Org 9.251, 9.252**
Trusts and trustees, transacting business in Texas, **Bus Org 9.251**
Venue, registration, **Bus Org 9.053**
Revocation or suspension, **Bus Org 9.158**
Withdrawal, registration, **Bus Org 9.011**
Foreign states,
Business Organizations Code, application of law, **Bus Org 1.053**
Certificate of formation, application of law, **Bus Org 1.102**
Meetings, location, **Bus Org 6.001**
Forfeitures,
Books and papers, examinations and examiners, **Bus Org 12.155**
Reinstatement, **Bus Org 402.013**
Forms,
Filing, **Bus Org 4.006**
Shares and shareholders, certificates and certification, **Bus Org 3.202**
Fraud,
Derivative actions, privileges and immunities, **Bus Org 101.454**
Filing, **Bus Org 4.007, 4.008**
Guaranty, **Bus Org 2.104**
Indebtedness, evidence, **Bus Org 2.103**
Names, **Bus Org 5.052**
Receivers and receivership, **Bus Org 11.403**
Termination,
Involuntary termination, **Bus Org 11.301 et seq.**
Revocation or suspension, **Bus Org 11.153**
Winding up, involuntary winding up, **Bus Org 11.301 et seq.**
Frauds, statute of,
Contributions, **Bus Org 101.151**
Powers and duties, **Bus Org 2.112**
Garnishment, state, **Bus Org 12.259**
Gifts, **Bus Org 2.101**
Good faith,
Damages, **Bus Org 7.001**
Officers and employees, **Bus Org 3.102, 3.105**
Governing authorities. Managers and management, generally, post

LIMITED LIABILITY COMPANIES
—Cont'd
Groups, members, **Bus Org 101.104, 101.105**
Guaranty, **Bus Org 2.101**
Powers and duties, **Bus Org 2.104**
Hold harmless. Indemnity, generally, post
Holding companies, merger and consolidation, **Bus Org 10.005**
Identity and identification, names, same or similar, **Bus Org 5.053**
Immunities. Privileges and immunities, generally, post
Incentives, officers and employees, **Bus Org 2.101**
Income, members, assignments, **Bus Org 101.109**
Incumbrances. Liens and incumbrances, generally, post
Indebtedness, **Bus Org 2.101, 2.103**
Application of law, **Bus Org 10.901**
Certificates and certification, **Bus Org 2.114**
Contributions, **Bus Org 101.155, 101.156**
Distribution and distributors, **Bus Org 101.207**
Members, **Bus Org 101.114**
Series limited liability companies, **Bus Org 101.602**
Winding up, discharge, **Bus Org 11.053**
Indemnity, **Bus Org 101.402**
Business Organizations Code, application of law, **Bus Org 402.007**
Insurance, **Bus Org 8.151**
Managers and management, post
Mandatory, **Bus Org 8.051**
Officers and employees, post
Orders of court, **Bus Org 8.052**
Permissive indemnification, **Bus Org 8.101 et seq.**
Reports, **Bus Org 8.152**
Injunctions,
Guaranty, **Bus Org 2.104**
State, **Bus Org 12.259**
Insolvency, actions and proceedings, **Bus Org 12.253 et seq.**
Inspection and inspectors,
Books and papers, **Bus Org 12.151 et seq.**
Records and recordation, **Bus Org 3.152**
Insurance, indemnity, **Bus Org 2.101, 8.151**
Internal affairs, **Bus Org 1.105**
Internet, meetings, **Bus Org 6.002**
Interrogatories, **Bus Org 12.002, 12.003**
Investments, **Bus Org 2.101**
Involuntary termination, **Bus Org 11.251 et seq.**
Certified copies, judgments and decrees, **Bus Org 11.414**
Joint practices, **Bus Org 301.012**
Judgments and decrees,
Members, post

LIMITED LIABILITY COMPANIES
—Cont'd
Judgments and decrees—Cont'd
Receivers and receivership, termination, **Bus Org 11.412**
Reorganization, **Bus Org 10.305**
Termination, **Bus Org 11.301 et seq.**
Involuntary termination, certified copies, **Bus Org 11.414**
Winding up, **Bus Org 11.301 et seq.**
Jurisdiction,
Filing, fines and penalties, **Bus Org 21.802**
Insolvency, **Bus Org 12.253**
Liens and incumbrances, foreclosure, **Bus Org 12.253**
Receivers and receivership, **Bus Org 11.402 et seq.**
Reorganization, **Bus Org 10.302**
Termination, involuntary termination, **Bus Org 11.308, 11.314**
Winding up, involuntary winding up, **Bus Org 11.308, 11.314**
Leases, **Bus Org 2.101, 10.251 et seq.**
Reorganization, **Bus Org 10.301**
Licenses and permits, **Bus Org 301.006**
Liens and incumbrances,
Foreclosure, **Bus Org 12.252 et seq.**
Members, judgments and decrees, **Bus Org 101.112**
Series limited liability companies, **Bus Org 101.605**
State, **Bus Org 12.201**
Limitation of actions,
Derivative actions, **Bus Org 101.457**
Termination, claims, **Bus Org 11.359**
Limitations,
Filing,
Corrections, **Bus Org 4.102**
Effective date, delay, **Bus Org 4.058**
Indemnity, **Bus Org 8.003, 8.004**
Powers and duties, **Bus Org 2.113**
Purposes, **Bus Org 2.003 et seq.**
Series limited liability companies, notice, **Bus Org 101.604**
Liquidation, receivers and receivership, **Bus Org 12.258**
Orders of court, **Bus Org 11.405**
Lists, members, **Bus Org 101.501**
Loans, **Bus Org 2.101**
Contributions, **Bus Org 101.153**
Location,
Meetings, **Bus Org 6.001**
Offices, **Bus Org 2.101**
Losses,
Allocations, **Bus Org 101.201**
Members, assignments, **Bus Org 101.109**
Lottery, names, **Bus Org 5.061**
Mail and mailing, meetings, notice, **Bus Org 6.051**
Managers and management, **Bus Org 101.251 et seq., 101.301 et seq.**
Agent for service of process, **Bus Org 5.255**
Application of law, **Bus Org 101.301**
Certificate of formation, **Bus Org 3.010**

LIMITED LIABILITY COMPANIES
—Cont'd
Managers and management—Cont'd
Classification, **Bus Org 101.307**
Committees, **Bus Org 101.253**
Contracts, **Bus Org 101.252**
Classification, **Bus Org 101.307**
Conflict of interest, **Bus Org 101.255**
Damages, **Bus Org 301.010**
Domicile and residence, **Bus Org 101.302**
Elections, vacancies in office, **Bus Org 101.305, 101.306**
Indemnity, **Bus Org 101.402**
Licenses and permits, **Bus Org 301.006**
Numbers and numbering, **Bus Org 101.302**
Qualifications, **Bus Org 101.302**
Removal, **Bus Org 101.304, 101.306**
Replacement, **Bus Org 101.306**
Resignation, **Bus Org 301.008**
Series limited liability companies, generally, post
Terms of office, **Bus Org 101.303**
Vacancies in office, **Bus Org 101.305, 101.306**
Mandatory application date, Business Organizations Code, **Bus Org 401.001 et seq.**
Meetings, **Bus Org 6.001 et seq., 101.351 et seq.**
Action without meeting, **Bus Org 101.358, 101.359**
Consent, **Bus Org 6.201 et seq.**
Application of law, **Bus Org 6.302, 101.351**
Business Organizations Code, mandatory application date, **Bus Org 402.008, 402.009**
Consent, action without meeting, **Bus Org 6.201 et seq.**
Delivery, action without meeting, **Bus Org 6.203**
Emergencies, **Bus Org 3.251 et seq.**
Facsimile, notice, **Bus Org 6.051**
Foreign states, location, **Bus Org 6.001**
Internet, **Bus Org 6.002**
Location, **Bus Org 6.001**
Mail and mailing, notice, **Bus Org 6.051**
Notice, **Bus Org 6.051 et seq., 101.352**
Action without meeting, **Bus Org 6.204, 101.358**
Objections and exceptions, **Bus Org 6.003**
Notice, waiver, **Bus Org 6.053**
Quorum, **Bus Org 101.353**
Records and recordation, **Bus Org 6.002**
Shares and shareholders, post
Telecommunications, **Bus Org 6.002**
Video recordings, **Bus Org 6.002**
Waiver, notice, **Bus Org 6.052**
Objections and exceptions, **Bus Org 6.053**
Members, **Bus Org 101.101 et seq.**
Assignments, **Bus Org 101.108 et seq.**

LIMITED LIABILITY COMPANIES
—Cont'd
Members—Cont'd
Classification, **Bus Org 101.104, 101.105**
Community property, **Bus Org 101.106**
Contributions, **Bus Org 101.151 et seq.**
Damages, **Bus Org 101.114**
Death, **Bus Org 101.1115**
Derivative actions, generally, ante
Dissolution of marriage, **Bus Org 101.1115**
Effective date, **Bus Org 101.103**
Expulsion, **Bus Org 101.107**
Groups, **Bus Org 101.104, 101.105**
Indebtedness, **Bus Org 101.114**
Indemnity, **Bus Org 101.402**
Judgments and decrees, **Bus Org 101.114**
Assignments, **Bus Org 101.112**
Lists, **Bus Org 101.501**
Numbers and numbering, **Bus Org 101.101**
Orders of court, **Bus Org 101.114**
Parties, **Bus Org 101.113**
Personal property, **Bus Org 101.106**
Powers and duties, assignments, **Bus Org 101.109 et seq.**
Qualifications, **Bus Org 101.102**
Series limited liability companies, generally, post
Time, **Bus Org 101.101, 101.103**
Withdrawal, **Bus Org 101.107**
Merger and consolidation, **Bus Org 10.001 et seq.**
Abandonment, **Bus Org 10.201 et seq.**
Acceptance, certificates and certification, **Bus Org 10.156**
Allocations, property, **Bus Org 10.003**
Business Organizations Code, mandatory application date, **Bus Org 402.010**
Certificate of formation, **Bus Org 3.005, 10.002**
Certificates and certification, **Bus Org 10.151 et seq.**
Dissenting shareholders, **Bus Org 10.351 et seq.**
Effect, **Bus Org 10.008**
Effective date, **Bus Org 10.007**
Filing,
Certificates and certification, **Bus Org 10.153**
Fees, **Bus Org 4.151**
Holding companies, **Bus Org 10.005**
Names, **Bus Org 10.002**
Plans and specifications, **Bus Org 10.001 et seq.**
Property, allocations, **Bus Org 10.003**
Reorganization, **Bus Org 10.301 et seq.**
Subsidiaries, **Bus Org 10.006**
Certificates and certification, **Bus Org 10.152**
Time, effective date, **Bus Org 10.007**
Misconduct, damages, **Bus Org 7.001**
Modification,
Contracts, **Bus Org 101.054**

LIMITED LIABILITY COMPANIES
—Cont'd
Modification—Cont'd
Powers and duties, **Bus Org 101.401**
Money, **Bus Org 1.009**
Monopolies and unfair trade, application of law, **Bus Org 10.901**
Mortgages, **Bus Org 2.101**
Powers and duties, **Bus Org 2.104**
Receivers and receivership, **Bus Org 11.403**
Names, **Bus Org 5.001 et seq.**
Assumed or fictitious names, **Bus Org 5.051 et seq.**
Certificate of formation, **Bus Org 3.005**
Amendments, **Bus Org 3.053, 3.056**
Managers and management, **Bus Org 3.010**
Conversion, **Bus Org 10.103**
Deception, **Bus Org 5.052**
Exchange of property, plans and specifications, **Bus Org 10.052**
Fees, reservation, **Bus Org 5.101**
Withdrawal, **Bus Org 5.1041**
Filing,
Fees, **Bus Org 4.151**
Registration, **Bus Org 5.152**
Foreign limited liability companies, ante
Fraud, **Bus Org 5.052**
Identity and identification, same or similar, **Bus Org 5.053**
Lottery, **Bus Org 5.061**
Merger and consolidation, **Bus Org 10.002**
Notice, **Bus Org 5.001**
Registration, **Bus Org 5.151 et seq.**
Renewal,
Registration, **Bus Org 5.155**
Reservation, **Bus Org 5.105**
Reservation, **Bus Org 5.101 et seq.**
Same or similar, **Bus Org 5.053**
Registration, **Bus Org 5.153**
Reservation, **Bus Org 5.102**
Termination, reinstatement, **Bus Org 11.203**
Time,
Registration, **Bus Org 5.154**
Reservation, **Bus Org 5.104**
Trademarks and trade names, **Bus Org 5.001**
Transfers, reservation, **Bus Org 5.106**
Veterans organizations, **Bus Org 5.062**
Words and phrases, **Bus Org 5.056, 5.059**
Negligence, damages, **Bus Org 301.010**
Nonfiling, certificate of formation, **Bus Org 3.002**
Nonsuit. Dismissal and nonsuit, generally, ante
Notice,
Agent for service of process, **Bus Org 5.252, 5.253**
Conversion, **Bus Org 10.101**
Derivative actions,
Compromise and settlement, **Bus Org 101.460**

LIMITED LIABILITY COMPANIES
—Cont'd
Notice—Cont'd
Derivative actions—Cont'd
Dismissal and nonsuit, **Bus Org 101.456**
Foreign limited liability companies, ante
Guaranty, fraud, **Bus Org 2.104**
Indemnity, orders of court, **Bus Org 8.052**
Insolvency, **Bus Org 12.256**
Liens and incumbrances,
Foreclosure, **Bus Org 12.256**
State, **Bus Org 12.201**
Meetings, ante
Names, **Bus Org 5.001**
Receivers and receivership, claims, **Bus Org 11.407**
Registered office or agent, resignation, **Bus Org 5.204**
Reorganization, **Bus Org 10.301**
Series limited liability companies, limitations, **Bus Org 101.604**
Shares and shareholders, post
Termination, post
Winding up, post
Numbers and numbering,
Managers and management, **Bus Org 101.302**
Members, **Bus Org 101.101**
Oaths and affirmations, interrogatories, answer, **Bus Org 12.002**
Objections and exceptions, meetings, **Bus Org 6.003**
Notice, waiver, **Bus Org 6.053**
Offenses. Crimes and offenses, generally, ante
Officers and employees, **Bus Org 3.101 et seq.**
Agent for service of process, **Bus Org 5.255**
Compensation and salaries, **Bus Org 2.101**
Contracts, conflict of interest, **Bus Org 101.255**
Damages, **Bus Org 7.001, 301.010**
Application of law, **Bus Org 1.104**
Dual office holding, **Bus Org 3.103**
Elections, **Bus Org 2.101, 3.103**
Good faith, **Bus Org 3.105**
Indemnity, **Bus Org 2.101, 7.001, 8.001 et seq., 101.402**
Licenses and permits, **Bus Org 301.006**
Loans, **Bus Org 2.101**
Removal, **Bus Org 3.104**
Retirement and pensions, **Bus Org 2.101**
Offices, **Bus Org 2.101**
Changes, filing, fines and penalties, **Bus Org 21.802**
Location, **Bus Org 101.501**
Registered offices, generally, post
Reorganization, **Bus Org 10.301**
Omissions, certificate of formation, restatement, **Bus Org 3.059**

LIMITED LIABILITY COMPANIES
—Cont'd
Open records, interrogatories, **Bus Org 12.003**
Orders of court,
Members, **Bus Org 101.114**
Receivers and receivership, **Bus Org 11.402**
Liquidation, **Bus Org 11.405**
Series limited liability companies, winding up, **Bus Org 101.621**
Termination, involuntary termination, **Bus Org 11.314**
Parties,
Derivative actions, **Bus Org 101.452**
Members, **Bus Org 101.113**
Receivers and receivership, **Bus Org 11.411**
Payment,
Derivative actions,
Closely held limited liability company, **Bus Org 101.463**
Costs, **Bus Org 101.461**
Termination,
Claims, **Bus Org 11.354**
Taxation, **Bus Org 11.101**
Penalties. Fines and penalties, generally, ante
Permissive indemnification, **Bus Org 8.101 et seq.**
Personal property, **Bus Org 2.101**
Disposition, **Bus Org 10.251 et seq.**
Reorganization, **Bus Org 10.301**
Members, **Bus Org 101.106**
Shares and shareholders, **Bus Org 21.801**
Photography and pictures, consent, meetings, action without meeting, **Bus Org 6.205**
Physicians and surgeons, professional limited liability companies, physician assistants, **Bus Org 301.012**
Plans and specifications,
Conversion, **Bus Org 10.101 et seq.**
Exchange of property, **Bus Org 10.051 et seq.**
Merger and consolidation, **Bus Org 10.001 et seq.**
Political subdivisions, service of process, **Bus Org 5.257**
Power of attorney, **Bus Org 101.501**
Powers and duties, **Bus Org 2.101 et seq.**
Modification, **Bus Org 101.401**
Receivers and receivership, **Bus Org 11.406**
Series limited liability companies, **Bus Org 101.605**
President, agent for service of process, **Bus Org 5.255**
Prior laws, Business Organizations Code, **Bus Org 401.001 et seq.**
Priorities and preferences,
Business Organizations Code, application of law, **Bus Org 1.106**
Certificate of formation, shares and shareholders, **Bus Org 3.007**

LIMITED LIABILITY COMPANIES
—Cont'd
Privileges and immunities,
Derivative actions, **Bus Org 101.454**
Property, disposition, **Bus Org 10.254**
Registered agents, **Bus Org 5.208**
Series limited liability companies, **Bus Org 101.606**
Proceedings. Actions and proceedings, generally, ante
Process. Service of process, generally, post
Professional limited liability companies, **Bus Org 301.001 et seq.**
Application of law, **Bus Org 304.001**
Physicians and surgeons, physician assistants, **Bus Org 301.012**
Profits,
Allocations, **Bus Org 101.201**
Officers and employees, sharing, **Bus Org 2.101**
Property, **Bus Org 2.101**
Disposition, **Bus Org 10.251 et seq.**
Reorganization, **Bus Org 10.301**
Liens and incumbrances,
Foreclosure, **Bus Org 12.252 et seq.**
State, **Bus Org 12.201**
Merger and consolidation, allocations, **Bus Org 10.003**
Title to property, generally, post
Proxies, elections, **Bus Org 101.357**
Publication,
Termination, involuntary termination, **Bus Org 11.310**
Winding up, involuntary winding up, **Bus Org 11.310**
Purchases and purchasing,
Indemnity, insurance, **Bus Org 8.151**
Title to property, **Bus Org 301.008**
Purposes, **Bus Org 2.001 et seq.**
Certificate of formation, **Bus Org 3.005**
Qualifications, members, **Bus Org 101.102**
Quo warranto, insolvency, **Bus Org 12.253 et seq.**
Quorum, meetings, **Bus Org 101.353**
Real estate, **Bus Org 2.101**
Disposition, **Bus Org 10.251 et seq.**
Reorganization, **Bus Org 10.301**
Records and recordation, deeds and conveyances, **Bus Org 10.253**
Receipts, termination, claims, **Bus Org 11.352**
Receivers and receivership, **Bus Org 11.401 et seq.**
Actions and proceedings, **Bus Org 11.406**
Ancillary receiverships, **Bus Org 11.409**
Appointments, **Bus Org 11.401 et seq.**
Bonds (officers and fiduciaries), **Bus Org 11.406**
Citizens and citizenship, **Bus Org 11.406**
Claims, filing, **Bus Org 11.407**
Compensation and salaries, **Bus Org 11.408**
Discharge, **Bus Org 11.412**
Filing, claims, **Bus Org 11.407**

LIMITED LIABILITY COMPANIES
—Cont'd
Receivers and receivership—Cont'd
Foreign entities, **Bus Org 11.409, 11.410**
Fraud, **Bus Org 11.403**
Judgments and decrees, termination, **Bus Org 11.412**
Jurisdiction, **Bus Org 11.402 et seq.**
Liens and incumbrances, state, **Bus Org 12.201**
Liquidation, **Bus Org 12.258**
Orders of court, **Bus Org 11.405**
Mortgages, **Bus Org 11.403**
Notice, claims, **Bus Org 11.407**
Orders of court, **Bus Org 11.402**
Liquidation, **Bus Org 11.405**
Parties, **Bus Org 11.411**
Powers and duties, **Bus Org 11.406**
Registration, **Bus Org 11.406**
Rehabilitation, **Bus Org 11.404**
State, **Bus Org 12.251**
Termination, **Bus Org 11.403**
Judgments and decrees, **Bus Org 11.412**
Record date, allocations, distributions, **Bus Org 101.208**
Series limited liability companies, **Bus Org 101.612**
Records and recordation, **Bus Org 3.151 et seq.**
Certified copies, filing, **Bus Org 4.005**
Confidential or privileged information, **Bus Org 12.154**
Disclosure, **Bus Org 12.154**
Examinations and examiners, **Bus Org 3.153, 12.151 et seq., 101.501, 101.502**
Inspection and inspectors, **Bus Org 3.152**
Interrogatories, open records, **Bus Org 12.003**
Meetings, **Bus Org 6.002**
Real estate, deeds and conveyances, **Bus Org 10.253**
Reorganization, **Bus Org 10.301**
Service of process, **Bus Org 5.254**
Termination, removal, **Bus Org 11.104**
Registered agents, **Bus Org 5.200 et seq.**
Changes, **Bus Org 5.202**
Filing, fines and penalties, **Bus Org 21.802**
Reorganization, **Bus Org 10.301**
Resignation, **Bus Org 5.204**
Registered offices, **Bus Org 5.200 et seq.**
Changes, **Bus Org 5.202**
Filing, fines and penalties, **Bus Org 21.802**
Registration,
Foreign limited liability companies, ante
Names, **Bus Org 5.151 et seq.**
Receivers and receivership, **Bus Org 11.406**
Rehabilitation, receivers and receivership, **Bus Org 11.404**

LIMITED LIABILITY COMPANIES
—Cont'd
Reimbursement, expenses and expenditures, **Bus Org 101.402**
Reinstatement,
Termination, post
Winding up, **Bus Org 101.552**
Rejection,
Derivative actions, demand, **Bus Org 101.459**
Registered agents, **Bus Org 5.205**
Release,
Contributions, **Bus Org 101.154**
Members, damages, assignments, **Bus Org 101.111**
Remand,
Termination, involuntary termination, **Bus Org 11.307**
Winding up, involuntary winding up, **Bus Org 11.307**
Removal,
Managers and management, **Bus Org 101.304, 101.306**
Officers and employees, **Bus Org 3.104**
Renewal, names,
Registration, **Bus Org 5.155**
Reservation, **Bus Org 5.105**
Reorganization, **Bus Org 10.301 et seq.**
Business Organizations Code, mandatory application date, **Bus Org 402.010**
Repeals, Business Organizations Code, statutes, **Bus Org 1.054**
Replacement, managers and management, **Bus Org 101.306**
Reports,
Indemnity, **Bus Org 8.152**
Officers and employees, good faith, **Bus Org 3.102, 3.105**
Reservation. Names, ante
Resignation,
Managers and management, **Bus Org 301.008**
Registered agent, **Bus Org 5.204**
Resolutions, indemnity, **Bus Org 8.103**
Restatement, certificate of formation, **Bus Org 3.057 et seq.**
Retirement and pensions, officers and employees, **Bus Org 2.101**
Returns,
Distribution and distributors, **Bus Org 101.206**
Tax returns, duplicates and copies, **Bus Org 101.501**
Review. Appeal and review, generally, ante
Revocation or suspension,
Foreign limited liability companies, ante
Reinstatement, **Bus Org 402.013**
Termination, fraud, **Bus Org 11.153**
Winding up, **Bus Org 11.151, 101.552**
Series limited liability companies, **Bus Org 101.618**
Sales, **Bus Org 10.251 et seq.**
Property, **Bus Org 2.101**
Reorganization, **Bus Org 10.301**

LIMITED LIABILITY COMPANIES
—Cont'd
Sales—Cont'd
Securities, exemptions, **Bus Org 301.011**
Same or similar. Names, post
Seals, **Bus Org 2.101**
Indebtedness, certificates and certification, **Bus Org 2.114**
Shares and shareholders, certificates and certification, **Bus Org 3.202**
Secretary of state, agent for service of process, **Bus Org 5.251 et seq.**
Securities, **Bus Org 2.101**
Powers and duties, **Bus Org 2.104**
Sales, exemptions, **Bus Org 301.011**
Sequestration, state, **Bus Org 12.259**
Series limited liability companies, **Bus Org 101.601 et seq.**
Accounts and accounting, **Bus Org 101.602**
Actions and proceedings, **Bus Org 101.605**
Allocations, record date, **Bus Org 101.612**
Application of law, **Bus Org 101.609**
Winding up, **Bus Org 101.617**
Classification, **Bus Org 101.607**
Contracts, **Bus Org 101.605**
Definitions,
Application of law, **Bus Org 101.609**
Winding up, **Bus Org 101.617**
Distributions, **Bus Org 101.611, 101.613**
Record date, **Bus Org 101.612**
Elections, **Bus Org 101.607**
Winding up, **Bus Org 101.616**
Revocation or suspension, **Bus Org 101.618**
Expenses and expenditures, **Bus Org 101.602**
Indebtedness, **Bus Org 101.602**
Liabilities, **Bus Org 101.606**
Liens and incumbrances, **Bus Org 101.605**
Limitations, notice, **Bus Org 101.604**
Notice, limitations, **Bus Org 101.604**
Orders of court, winding up, **Bus Org 101.621**
Powers and duties, **Bus Org 101.605**
Privileges and immunities, **Bus Org 101.606**
Record date, allocations, distributions, **Bus Org 101.612**
Revocation or suspension, winding up, **Bus Org 101.618**
Termination, **Bus Org 101.614, 101.615, 101.617**
Title to property, **Bus Org 101.605**
Winding up, **Bus Org 101.614 et seq.**
Service of process, **Bus Org 5.251 et seq.**
Foreign limited liability companies, ante
Reorganization, **Bus Org 10.301**
Termination, involuntary termination, **Bus Org 11.309**
Winding up, involuntary winding up, **Bus Org 11.309**

LIMITED LIABILITY COMPANIES
—Cont'd
Services, certificate of formation, **Bus Org 3.014**
Shares and shareholders,
Abandonment, exchange of property, **Bus Org 10.201 et seq.**
Acceptance, exchange of property, certificates and certification, **Bus Org 10.156**
Appointments, dissenting shareholders, appraisal and appraisers, **Bus Org 10.361**
Appraisals and appraisers, dissenting shareholders, **Bus Org 10.354 et seq.**
Assignments, certificates and certification, **Bus Org 3.201**
Books and papers, dissenting shareholders, fair market value, **Bus Org 10.363**
Certificate of formation, numbers and numbering, **Bus Org 3.007**
Certificates and certification, **Bus Org 3.201 et seq.**
Exchange of property, **Bus Org 10.151 et seq.**
Compensation and salaries, dissenting shareholders, appraisals and appraisers, **Bus Org 10.365**
Computation, dissenting shareholders, fair market value, **Bus Org 10.362**
Contracts, elections, **Bus Org 6.252**
Costs, dissenting shareholders, appraisals and appraisers, **Bus Org 10.365**
Delivery,
Certificates and certification, **Bus Org 3.204**
Meetings, action without meeting, **Bus Org 6.203**
Demand, dissenting shareholders, fair market value, **Bus Org 10.357 et seq.**
Dissenting shareholders, **Bus Org 10.351 et seq.**
Appointments, appraisal and appraisers, **Bus Org 10.361**
Appraisals and appraisers, **Bus Org 10.354 et seq.**
Books and papers, fair market value, **Bus Org 10.363**
Compensation and salaries, appraisals and appraisers, **Bus Org 10.365**
Computation, fair market value, **Bus Org 10.362**
Costs, appraisals and appraisers, **Bus Org 10.365**
Definitions, **Bus Org 10.352**
Demand, fair market value, **Bus Org 10.357 et seq.**
Exclusive remedy, **Bus Org 10.368**
Fair market value, demand, **Bus Org 10.357 et seq.**
Forms, **Bus Org 10.353**
Hearings, fair market value, **Bus Org 10.361**

LIMITED LIABILITY COMPANIES
—Cont'd
Shares and shareholders—Cont'd
Dissenting shareholders—Cont'd
Investigations and investigators, fair market value, **Bus Org 10.363**
Notice, **Bus Org 10.353, 10.355**
Objections and exceptions, appraisals and appraisers, **Bus Org 10.364**
Perfection, **Bus Org 10.356**
Petitions, fair market value, **Bus Org 10.361**
Records and recordation, fair market value, **Bus Org 10.363**
Demand, **Bus Org 10.359**
Reorganization, **Bus Org 10.304**
Termination, **Bus Org 10.367**
Title to property, **Bus Org 10.366**
Withdrawal, **Bus Org 10.357**
Distribution and distributors, record date, **Bus Org 6.101 et seq.**
Duplicates and copies, certificates and certification, **Bus Org 3.202**
Elections, trusts and trustees, **Bus Org 6.251**
Evidence, certificates and certification, **Bus Org 3.201**
Examinations and examiners, elections, contracts, **Bus Org 6.252**
Exchange of property, **Bus Org 10.051 et seq.**
Abandonment, **Bus Org 10.201 et seq.**
Acceptance, certificates and certification, **Bus Org 10.156**
Certificates and certification, **Bus Org 10.151 et seq.**
Filing, certificates and certification, **Bus Org 10.153**
Exclusive remedy, dissenting shareholders, **Bus Org 10.368**
Facsimile, certificates and certification, **Bus Org 3.203**
Fair market value, dissenting shareholders, demand, **Bus Org 10.357 et seq.**
Filing, exchange of property, certificates and certification, **Bus Org 10.153**
Forms,
Certificates and certification, **Bus Org 3.202**
Dissenting shareholders, **Bus Org 10.353**
Hearings, dissenting shareholders, fair market value, **Bus Org 10.361**
Investigations and investigators, dissenting shareholders, fair market value, **Bus Org 10.363**
Meetings,
Action without meeting, consent, **Bus Org 6.201 et seq.**
Consent, action without meeting, **Bus Org 6.201 et seq.**
Delivery, action without meeting, **Bus Org 6.203**

LIMITED LIABILITY COMPANIES
—Cont'd
Shares and shareholders—Cont'd
Meetings—Cont'd
Notice, action without meeting, **Bus Org 6.204**
Notice,
Dissenting shareholders, **Bus Org 10.353, 10.355**
Meetings, action without meeting, **Bus Org 6.204**
Uncertificated shares, **Bus Org 3.205**
Objections and exceptions, dissenting shareholders, appraisals and appraisers, **Bus Org 10.364**
Perfection, dissenting shareholders, **Bus Org 10.356**
Personal property, **Bus Org 21.801**
Petitions, dissenting shareholders, fair market value, **Bus Org 10.361**
Records and recordation, dissenting shareholders, fair market value, **Bus Org 10.363**
Demand, **Bus Org 10.359**
Reorganization, dissenting shareholders, **Bus Org 10.304**
Seals, certificates and certification, **Bus Org 3.202**
Signatures, certificates and certification, **Bus Org 3.203**
Termination, dissenting shareholders, **Bus Org 10.367**
Title to property, dissenting shareholders, **Bus Org 10.366**
Transfers, certificates and certification, **Bus Org 3.201**
Trusts and trustees, elections, **Bus Org 6.251**
Uncertificated shares, **Bus Org 3.201**
Notice, **Bus Org 3.205**
Withdrawal, dissenting shareholders, **Bus Org 10.357**
Signatures,
Certificate of formation, ante
Contributions, **Bus Org 101.151**
Filing, **Bus Org 4.001, 101.0515**
Corrections, certificates and certification, **Bus Org 4.101**
Indebtedness, certificates and certification, **Bus Org 2.114**
Reorganization, **Bus Org 10.302**
Shares and shareholders, certificates and certification, **Bus Org 3.203**
Specifications. Plans and specifications, generally, ante
State,
Liens and incumbrances, **Bus Org 12.201**
Receivers and receivership, **Bus Org 12.251**
Statements,
Certificate of formation, ante
Officers and employees, good faith, **Bus Org 3.102, 3.105**
Termination, claims, **Bus Org 11.352**

LIMITED LIABILITY COMPANIES —Cont'd
Statutes, Business Organizations Code, construction of laws, **Bus Org 1.006, 1.051 et seq.**
Subsidiaries, merger and consolidation, **Bus Org 10.006**
Certificates and certification, **Bus Org 10.152**
Supersedeas or stay,
Derivative actions, **Bus Org 101.455**
Termination, involuntary termination, **Bus Org 11.306**
Winding up, involuntary winding up, **Bus Org 11.306**
Supervision, winding up, **Bus Org 11.054**
Suspension. Revocation or suspension, generally, ante
Tax returns, duplicates and copies, **Bus Org 101.501**
Taxation,
Service of process, **Bus Org 5.257**
Termination,
Forfeitures, reinstatement, **Bus Org 11.254, 402.013**
Payment, **Bus Org 11.101**
Telecommunications, meetings, **Bus Org 6.002**
Termination, **Bus Org 11.001 et seq., 101.551, 101.552**
Abatement of actions and proceedings, involuntary termination, **Bus Org 11.304**
Actions and proceedings, involuntary termination, **Bus Org 11.303**
Appeal and review, involuntary termination, **Bus Org 11.307**
Business Organizations Code, mandatory application date, **Bus Org 402.011**
Certificates and certification, **Bus Org 11.101 et seq.**
Involuntary termination, **Bus Org 11.252**
Reinstatement, **Bus Org 11.202**
Certified copies, involuntary termination, judgments and decrees, **Bus Org 11.414**
Claims, **Bus Org 11.351 et seq.**
Crimes and offenses, involuntary termination, **Bus Org 11.301 et seq.**
Deposits, claims, **Bus Org 11.352**
Discharge, claims, **Bus Org 11.353**
Effective date, **Bus Org 11.102, 11.103**
Claims, **Bus Org 11.356 et seq.**
Reinstatement, **Bus Org 11.204 et seq.**
Errors, reinstatement, **Bus Org 11.201 et seq.**
Escheat, claims, **Bus Org 11.355**
Exemptions, involuntary termination, **Bus Org 11.251**
Filing,
Fines and penalties, **Bus Org 21.802**
Involuntary termination, **Bus Org 11.315**

LIMITED LIABILITY COMPANIES —Cont'd
Termination—Cont'd
Fraud,
Involuntary termination, **Bus Org 11.301 et seq.**
Revocation or suspension, **Bus Org 11.153**
Involuntary termination, **Bus Org 11.251 et seq., 11.301 et seq.**
Certified copies, judgments and decrees, **Bus Org 11.414**
Judgments and decrees, **Bus Org 11.301 et seq.**
Involuntary termination, certified copies, **Bus Org 11.414**
Jurisdiction, involuntary termination, **Bus Org 11.308, 11.314**
Limitation of actions, claims, **Bus Org 11.359**
Names, reinstatement, **Bus Org 11.203**
Notice,
Claims, **Bus Org 11.358**
Escheat, claims, **Bus Org 11.355**
Involuntary termination, **Bus Org 11.251, 11.302, 11.310**
Orders of court, involuntary termination, **Bus Org 11.314**
Payment,
Claims, **Bus Org 11.354**
Taxation, **Bus Org 11.101**
Publication, involuntary termination, **Bus Org 11.310**
Receipts, claims, **Bus Org 11.352**
Receivers and receivership, **Bus Org 11.403**
Judgments and decrees, **Bus Org 11.412**
Records and recordation, removal, **Bus Org 11.104**
Reinstatement, **Bus Org 11.201 et seq.**
Involuntary termination, **Bus Org 11.253**
Taxation, forfeitures, **Bus Org 11.254**
Remand, involuntary termination, **Bus Org 11.307**
Revocation or suspension, fraud, **Bus Org 11.153**
Series limited liability companies, **Bus Org 101.614, 101.615, 101.617**
Service of process, involuntary termination, **Bus Org 11.309**
Statements, claims, **Bus Org 11.352**
Supersedeas or stay, involuntary termination, **Bus Org 11.306**
Taxation,
Forfeitures, reinstatement, **Bus Org 11.254**
Payment, **Bus Org 11.101**
Time,
Involuntary termination, **Bus Org 11.305, 11.313**
Reinstatement, **Bus Org 11.202**
Venue, involuntary termination, **Bus Org 11.308**
Terms of office, managers and management, **Bus Org 101.303**

LIMITED LIABILITY COMPANIES —Cont'd
Time,
Business Organizations Code, effective date, **Bus Org 402.001**
Adoption, **Bus Org 402.005**
Certificate of formation, ante
Derivative actions, demand, **Bus Org 101.453**
Distribution and distributors, **Bus Org 101.204**
Effective date, generally, ante
Exchange of property, **Bus Org 10.054, 10.055**
Filing, ante
Interrogatories, answer, **Bus Org 12.002**
Members, **Bus Org 101.101, 101.103**
Merger and consolidation, effective date, **Bus Org 10.007**
Service of process, **Bus Org 5.254**
Termination, ante
Winding up, post
Title to property, **Bus Org 301.007 et seq.**
Purchases and purchasing, **Bus Org 301.008**
Series limited liability companies, **Bus Org 101.605**
Tolling, derivative actions, limitation of actions, **Bus Org 101.457**
Trademarks and trade names, names, **Bus Org 5.001**
Transfers,
Names, reservation, **Bus Org 5.106**
Property, **Bus Org 10.251 et seq.**
Shares and shareholders, certificates and certification, **Bus Org 3.201**
Title to property, **Bus Org 301.009**
Transition, Business Organizations Code, **Bus Org 402.001 et seq.**
Trusts and trustees,
Elections, **Bus Org 6.251**
Reorganization, **Bus Org 10.301 et seq.**
Uncertificated shares, **Bus Org 3.201**
Notice, **Bus Org 3.205**
Vacancies in office, managers and management, **Bus Org 101.305, 101.306**
Venue,
Termination, involuntary termination, **Bus Org 11.308**
Winding up, involuntary winding up, **Bus Org 11.308**
Veterans organizations, names, **Bus Org 5.062**
Vice president, agent for service of process, **Bus Org 5.255**
Video recordings, meetings, **Bus Org 6.002**
Waiver,
Contracts, **Bus Org 101.054**
Meetings, notice, **Bus Org 6.052**
Objections and exceptions, **Bus Org 6.053**
Winding up, **Bus Org 11.001 et seq., 11.051 et seq., 101.551, 101.552**
Abatement of actions and proceedings, involuntary winding up, **Bus Org 11.304**

LIMITED LIABILITY COMPANIES —Cont'd
Winding up—Cont'd
Actions and proceedings, **Bus Org 11.052, 11.055**
Involuntary winding up, **Bus Org 11.303**
Appeal and review, involuntary winding up, **Bus Org 11.307**
Assets, distribution and distributors, **Bus Org 11.053**
Business Organizations Code, mandatory application date, **Bus Org 402.011**
Cancellation, **Bus Org 11.152**
Contracts, **Bus Org 11.152**
Crimes and offenses, involuntary winding up, **Bus Org 11.301 et seq.**
Discharge, indebtedness, **Bus Org 11.053**
Distribution and distributors, assets, **Bus Org 11.053**
Filing, involuntary winding up, **Bus Org 11.315**
Fraud, involuntary winding up, **Bus Org 11.301 et seq.**
Indebtedness, discharge, **Bus Org 11.053**
Involuntary winding up, **Bus Org 11.301 et seq.**
Judgments and decrees, **Bus Org 11.301 et seq.**
Jurisdiction, involuntary winding up, **Bus Org 11.308, 11.314**
Notice, **Bus Org 11.052**
Involuntary winding up, **Bus Org 11.302, 11.310**
Orders of court, involuntary winding up, **Bus Org 11.314**
Publication, involuntary winding up, **Bus Org 11.310**
Records and recordation, **Bus Org 101.501**
Remand, involuntary winding up, **Bus Org 11.307**
Revocation or suspension, **Bus Org 11.151**
Series limited liability companies, **Bus Org 101.618**
Series limited liability companies, **Bus Org 101.614 et seq.**
Service of process, involuntary winding up, **Bus Org 11.309**
Supersedeas or stay, involuntary winding up, **Bus Org 11.306**
Supervision, **Bus Org 11.054**
Time, **Bus Org 11.056**
Cancellation, **Bus Org 11.152**
Involuntary winding up, **Bus Org 11.305, 11.313**
Venue, involuntary winding up, **Bus Org 11.308**
Withdrawal,
Distribution and distributors, **Bus Org 101.205**
Filing, fines and penalties, **Bus Org 21.802**

LIMITED LIABILITY COMPANIES —Cont'd
Withdrawal—Cont'd
Foreign limited liability companies, ante
Members, **Bus Org 101.107**
Names, reservation, fees, **Bus Org 5.1041**
Witnesses, indemnity, expenses and expenditures, **Bus Org 8.106**
Writings, powers and duties, **Bus Org 2.112**

LIMITED LIABILITY PARTNERSHIPS
Partnerships, this index

LIMITED PARTNERSHIPS
Partnerships, this index

LIQUEFIED PETROLEUM GAS
Gas utilities, application of law, **Util 101.003**
Malodorants, safety, **Util 121.251 et seq.**
Odors, malodorants, safety, **Util 121.251 et seq.**

LIQUIDATION
Corporations, this index
Electric cooperative corporations, assets, dissolution, **Util 161.252**
Limited partnerships. Partnerships, this index
Nonprofit Corporations, this index
Partnerships, this index
Telephone cooperative corporations, dissolution, **Util 162.302**

LIQUIFIED PETROLEUM GAS
Liquefied Petroleum Gas, generally, this index

LITERARY ORGANIZATIONS AND SOCIETIES
Nonprofit Corporations, generally, this index

LOANS
Business Development Corporations, this index
Corporations, this index
Electric cooperative corporations, **Util 161.121**
Electricity, **Util 181.003**
Gas utilities, **Util 181.003**
Shareholders, reports, **Util 102.053**
Mortgages, generally, this index
Nonprofit Corporations, this index
Partnerships, **Bus Org 2.101, 154.201**
Public utilities, shareholders, reports, **Util 14.103**
Telecommunications, this index
Telephone cooperative corporations, **Util 162.121**

LOBBYISTS
Legislature, this index

LOCAL DEVELOPMENT CORPORATIONS
Business development corporations, **Bus Org 23.054**

LOCAL GOVERNMENT CODE
Counties, generally, this index
Municipalities, generally, this index
Political Subdivisions, generally, this index

LODGES
Generally, **Bus Org 1.001 et seq.**
Certificate of formation, **Bus Org 3.001 et seq.**
Definitions, **Bus Org 1.002**
Contributions, definitions, business organizations, **Bus Org 1.002**
Definitions, **Bus Org 1.002**
Incorporation, **Bus Org 23.101 et seq.**

LONG DISTANCE SERVICE
Telecommunications, this index

LOW INCOME ELECTRIC CUSTOMER
Definitions, rates and charges, system benefit fund, **Util 39.903**

LOW OR MODERATE INCOME PERSONS
Electric cooperative corporations, rates and charges, system benefit fund, **Util 39.903**
Electricity, rates and charges, system benefit fund, **Util 39.903**

LOW PRESSURE GATHERING SYSTEM
Definitions, gas utilities, pipes and pipelines, sour gas, **Util 121.451**

LP GAS
Liquefied Petroleum Gas, generally, this index

MACHINERY AND EQUIPMENT
Definitions, cable television, **Util 181.101**
Electric Cooperative Corporations, this index
Electricity, this index
Gas Utilities, this index
Solar energy, ratings, devices, **Util 185.001 et seq.**
Telecommunications, this index

MAIL AND MAILING
Cooperative Associations, this index
Nonprofit corporations, meetings, notice, **Bus Org 6.051**

MANAGERS AND MANAGEMENT
Business development corporations, directors, **Bus Org 23.057 et seq.**
Cooperative Associations, this index
Corporations, this index
Definitions, business organizations, **Bus Org 1.002**
Electric cooperative corporations, executive committees, directors, **Util 161.077**

MANAGERS AND MANAGEMENT —Cont'd
Foreign Corporations, this index
Gas utilities, evaluation, **Util 102.201**
Limited Liability Companies, this index
Nonprofit Corporations, this index
Partnerships, this index
Probate Proceedings, generally, this index
Professional Associations and Societies, this index
Professional Corporations, this index
Public utilities, audits, **Util 14.201, 14.202**
Real Estate Investment Trusts, this index
Telecommunications, this index
Telephone cooperative corporations, executive committees, **Util 162.078**

MANDAMUS
Cooperative associations, reports, filing, **Bus Org 251.354**
Electricity, certificates of convenience and necessity, transmission, applications, **Util 37.057**

MANUFACTURERS AND MANUFACTURING
Monopolies and Unfair Trade, generally, this index
Restraint of trade. Monopolies and Unfair Trade, generally, this index
Trusts and monopolies. Monopolies and Unfair Trade, generally, this index

MAPS AND PLATS
Electricity, certificates of convenience and necessity, **Util 37.157**
Telecommunications, **Util 54.258**

MARKET POWER ABUSES
Definitions, electricity, customer choice, **Util 39.157**

MARKET POWER MITIGATION PLAN
Definitions, electricity, customer choice, installed generation capacity, **Util 39.156**

MARKET VALUE
Definitions, electricity, competition, stranded costs, recovery, **Util 39.251**

MARKETS AND MARKETING
Electric cooperative corporations, wholesalers, **Util 41.102**
Electricity, this index
Telecommunications, this index

MARRIAGE
Dissolution of marriage,
  Limited liability companies, members, **Bus Org 101.1115**
  Partnerships, transfers, **Bus Org 152.406**
Partnerships, dissolution of marriage, transfers, **Bus Org 152.406**

MASONIC SOCIETIES
  Generally, **Bus Org 1.001 et seq.**
Application of law, **Bus Org 23.102**

MASONIC SOCIETIES—Cont'd
Bylaws, powers and duties, **Bus Org 23.107**
Certificate of formation, **Bus Org 23.101**
  Time, **Bus Org 23.103**
Constitutions, powers and duties, **Bus Org 23.107**
Damages, **Bus Org 23.110**
Deeds and conveyances, **Bus Org 23.108**
Directors, elections, **Bus Org 23.105**
Elections, **Bus Org 23.105**
Filing, certificate of formation, **Bus Org 23.101**
Franchises, taxation, **Bus Org 23.106**
Liens and incumbrances, **Bus Org 23.109**
Loans, **Bus Org 23.109**
Mortgages, **Bus Org 23.108**
Powers and duties, **Bus Org 23.107**
Property, **Bus Org 23.108**
Real estate, **Bus Org 23.109**
Revocation or suspension, subordinate lodges, **Bus Org 23.104**
Sales, property, **Bus Org 23.108**
Schools and school districts, **Bus Org 23.108**
Subordinate lodges, **Bus Org 23.104**
  Winding up, **Bus Org 23.110**
Termination, subordinate, **Bus Org 23.110**
Time, certificate of formation, **Bus Org 23.103**
Trusts and trustees, elections, **Bus Org 23.105**
Winding up, subordinate lodges, **Bus Org 23.110**

MECHANIZED EQUIPMENT
Definitions, underground facilities, excavations, **Util 251.001**

MEDIA
Television and Radio, generally, this index

MEDICAL CARE AND TREATMENT
Assisted Living Facilities, generally, this index
Hospices, generally, this index
Hospitals, generally, this index
Nursing and Convalescent Homes, generally, this index
Physicians and Surgeons, generally, this index
Telecommunications,
  Lifeline service, **Util 55.015**
  Private network services, **Util 58.251 et seq., 59.071 et seq.**
  Telemedicine service providers, private network services, **Util 58.251 et seq., 59.071 et seq.**
Telemedicine, generally, this index

MEDICAL PRACTICE ACT
Physicians and Surgeons, generally, this index

MEMBER CITIES
Definitions, municipal power agencies, stranded costs, recovery, customer choice, **Util 40.059**

MEMORANDUM OF UNDERSTANDING
Telecommunications, lifeline service, **Util 55.015**

MERGER AND CONSOLIDATION
Cooperative Associations, this index
Corporations, this index
Electric cooperative corporations, **Util 161.201, 161.202**
Electricity, this index
Foreign Corporations, this index
Gas utilities, reports, investigations, **Util 102.051**
Limited Liability Companies, this index
Limited partnerships. Partnerships, this index
Nonprofit Corporations, this index
Partnerships, this index
Professional Associations and Societies, this index
Professional Corporations, this index
Public Utilities, this index
Real estate investment trusts, **Bus Org 200.402 et seq.**
Shares and shareholders. Corporations, this index
Telecommunications, this index
Telephone cooperative corporations, **Util 162.201 et seq.**
  Conversion, **Util 162.253, 162.254**

METERS
Electricity, this index
Gas Meters, generally, this index
Mobile Homes and Mobile Home Parks, this index

MILITARY BASES AGGREGATORS
Definitions, electricity, **Util 39.3535**

MILITARY FORCES
Bases, electricity,
  Aggregators, **Util 39.3535**
  Energy efficiency, incentives, **Util 39.910**
  Rates and charges, **Util 36.354**
Energy efficiency, bases, electricity, incentives, **Util 39.910**

MILITARY SERVICE
Military Forces, generally, this index

MINES AND MINERALS
Oil and Gas, generally, this index

MINORITIES
Discrimination, generally, this index

MISSIONARY CORPORATIONS
Nonprofit Corporations, generally, this index

MOBILE HOMES AND MOBILE HOME PARKS
Application of law, electricity, recreational vehicle parks, **Util 184.032, 184.033**
Electricity,
Complaints, **Util 15.052**
Metering, **Util 184.001 et seq.**
Recreational vehicle parks, **Util 184.031 et seq.**
Gas meters,
Submetering, **Util 124.001, 124.002**
Termination, **Util 104.258**
Meters,
Electricity, **Util 184.001 et seq.**
Recreational vehicle parks, **Util 184.031 et seq.**
Submetering, generally, post
Rates and charges, electricity sales, recreational vehicle parks, **Util 184.034**
Records and recordation,
Electricity,
Sales, recreational vehicle parks, **Util 184.033**
Submetering, **Util 184.014**
Gas submetering, **Util 124.002**
Refunds, electricity sales, recreational vehicle parks, **Util 184.035**
Sales, electricity, submetering, recreational vehicle parks, **Util 184.032, 184.033**
Submetering,
Electricity, **Util 184.013, 184.014**
Recreational vehicle parks, **Util 184.031 et seq.**
Gas meters, **Util 124.001, 124.002**

MOBILE TELEPHONES
Wireless telecommunications. Telecommunications, this index

MONEY
Cooperative associations, **Bus Org 1.009**
Corporations, **Bus Org 1.009**
Limited liability companies, **Bus Org 1.009**
Nonprofit corporations, **Bus Org 1.009**
Partnerships, **Bus Org 1.009**
Professional associations and societies, **Bus Org 1.009**
Professional corporations, **Bus Org 1.009**

MONOPOLIES AND UNFAIR TRADE
Application of law, **Bus Org 10.901**
Electricity, this index
Foreign Corporations, this index
Gas utilities, pipes and pipelines, jurisdiction, **Util 121.051, 121.052**
Liens and incumbrances, state, **Bus Org 12.201**
State, liens and incumbrances, **Bus Org 12.201**

MORTGAGES
Business Development Corporations, this index
Corporations, this index
Foreign Corporations, this index
Gas Utilities, this index
Limited Liability Companies, this index

MORTGAGES—Cont'd
Limited partnerships. Partnerships, this index
Nonprofit Corporations, this index
Partnerships, this index
Real estate investment trusts, **Bus Org 200.405 et seq.**
Telephone cooperative corporations, **Util 162.005, 162.125, 162.126**

MOTOR CARRIERS
Interurban Railroads, generally, this index

MOTOR FUEL
Motor Vehicle Fuel, generally, this index

MOTOR VEHICLE FUEL
Gas utilities, pipes and pipelines, exemptions, **Util 121.006**
Pipes and pipelines, natural gas, exemptions, **Util 121.006**
Utilities, gas utilities, application of law, **Util 101.003**

MOTOR VEHICLES
Fuel. Motor Vehicle Fuel, generally, this index
Mobile Homes and Mobile Home Parks, generally, this index
Oil and gas. Motor Vehicle Fuel, generally, this index

MULTIPLE DWELLINGS
Apartment Houses, generally, this index
Condominiums, generally, this index

MUNICIPAL CORPORATIONS
Municipalities, generally, this index

MUNICIPAL ELECTIONS
Initiative and referendum, gas utilities, jurisdiction, **Util 103.003**
Notice, municipal power agencies, **Util 163.058**
Public utilities, municipal power agencies, **Util 163.058**

MUNICIPAL POWER AGENCIES
Electricity, this index

MUNICIPALITIES
Actions and proceedings, gas utilities, pipes and pipelines, rates and charges, **Util 121.2025**
Alleys. Streets and Alleys, generally, this index
Annexation, telecommunications, authority to serve, **Util 54.203**
Boulevards. Streets and Alleys, generally, this index
Cable Television, this index
Discrimination, competitors, **Util 104.007**
Elections. Municipal Elections, generally, this index
Electric cooperative corporations, competition, **Util 41.005**
Electricity, this index
Fees, telecommunications, bills and billing, **Util 51.009**

MUNICIPALITIES—Cont'd
Fiber optics, leases, cable facilities, **Util 54.2025**
Gas Utilities, this index
Incorporation, telecommunications, authority to serve, **Util 54.203**
Interurban Railroads, generally, this index
Jurisdiction, gas utilities, **Util 103.001**
Surrender, **Util 103.003**
Leases, fiber optics, cable facilities, **Util 54.2025**
Libraries, generally, this index
Limitation of actions, gas utilities, pipes and pipelines, rates and charges, **Util 121.2025**
Monopolies and Unfair Trade, generally, this index
Municipal Elections, generally, this index
Pipes and pipelines, gas utilities, **Util 121.2025**
Public Utilities, this index
Rates and charges. Telecommunications, post
Schools and School Districts, generally, this index
Sewers and Sewer Systems, generally, this index
Street Railroads, generally, this index
Streets and Alleys, generally, this index
Telecommunications,
Access, **Util 54.205**
Annexation, authority to serve, **Util 54.203**
Appeal and review, orders, **Util 51.008**
Assistance, **Util 51.005**
Certificates and certification, **Util 54.201 et seq.**
Discrimination, **Util 54.204**
Easements, **Util 54.203 et seq.**
Fees, **Util 54.204 et seq.**
Bills and billing, **Util 51.009**
Franchises, discrimination, **Util 54.204**
Incorporation, authority to serve, **Util 54.203**
Ordinances, **Util 181.089**
Rates and charges,
Access, **Util 54.204 et seq.**
Classification, **Util 53.003**
Nonresidents, boundaries, **Util 53.005**
Staff and employees, **Util 51.006**
Right of way, **Util 54.203 et seq.**
Standards, ordinances, **Util 181.089**
Standing, public utility commission proceedings, **Util 51.007**
Telegraph connections, orders, **Util 181.064**
Television and Radio, this index
Utilities. Public Utilities, this index
Water Supply, generally, this index

NAMES
Assumed or Fictitious Names, generally, this index
Banks and Banking, this index
Business development corporations, certificate of formation, **Bus Org 23.056**
Colleges and Universities, this index

NAMES—Cont'd
Cooperative Associations, this index
Corporations, this index
Electric cooperative corporations, **Util 161.004, 161.053**
Fictitious names. Assumed or Fictitious Names, generally, this index
Foreign Corporations, this index
Insurance, this index
Limited Liability Companies, this index
Limited partnerships. Partnerships, this index
Nonprofit Corporations, this index
Partnerships, this index
Professional Associations and Societies, this index
Professional Corporations, this index
Real estate investment trusts, managers and management, **Bus Org 200.302**
Telephone Cooperative Corporations, this index
Trust Companies, this index

NATIONAL BANKS
Banks and Banking, generally, this index

NATIONAL ORIGIN
Discrimination, generally, this index

NATURAL GAS
Oil and Gas, generally, this index

NAVY
Military Forces, generally, this index

NEGOTIABLE INSTRUMENTS
Bonds, generally, this index
Notes, electricity, competition, **Util 39.301 et seq.**

NEGOTIATION
Telecommunications, this index

NETWORK SERVICE
Telecommunications, this index

NEW ON SITE GENERATION
Definitions, stranded costs, electricity, competition, recovery, **Util 39.252**

NEWSPAPERS
Audio newspapers, blind persons, telecommunications, universal service fund, **Util 56.301**
Blind persons, audio newspapers, telecommunications, universal service fund, **Util 56.301**
Telecommunications, this index

NINE HUNDRED (900) INFORMATION SERVICE
Telecommunications, community supervision, rates and charges, **Util 55.252**

NINE ONE ONE (911)
Generally, **Util 186.041 et seq.**
Access, services, **Util 60.210**
Basic local telecommunications service, access, **Util 51.002**

NINE ONE ONE (911)—Cont'd
Caller identification service, application of law, **Util 55.102**
Directories, assistance, access, **Util 60.210**
Fraud, party lines, **Util 186.043**
Imputation, prices, local exchange companies, waiver, **Util 60.065**
Obstruction of calls, crimes and offenses, **Util 186.042**
Pay telephones, charges, **Util 55.174, 55.176**

NONPROFIT ASSOCIATIONS
Unincorporated nonprofit associations. Nonprofit Corporations, this index

NONPROFIT CORPORATIONS
Generally, **Bus Org 1.001 et seq., 22.001 et seq., 301.001 et seq.**
Abandonment,
Conversion, **Bus Org 10.201, 10.202, 10.203**
Exchange of property, **Bus Org 10.201, 10.202, 10.203**
Filing, **Bus Org 4.057**
Merger and consolidation, **Bus Org 10.201, 10.202, 10.203**
Unincorporated nonprofit associations, post
Abatement of actions and proceedings,
Reports, forfeitures, **Bus Org 22.363, 22.364**
State, **Bus Org 12.260**
Termination, involuntary termination, **Bus Org 11.304**
Unincorporated nonprofit associations, post
Winding up, involuntary winding up, **Bus Org 11.304**
Acceptance, certificates and certification, **Bus Org 10.156**
Accounts and accounting, **Bus Org 3.151 et seq.**
Examinations and examiners, **Bus Org 12.151 et seq.**
Acknowledgments,
Certificate of formation, **Bus Org 3.004**
Evidence, **Bus Org 3.001**
Filing, **Bus Org 4.002**
Effective date, delay, **Bus Org 4.059**
Unincorporated nonprofit associations, post
Actions and proceedings, **Bus Org 2.101**
Abatement of actions and proceedings, generally, ante
Business Organizations Code, prior law, **Bus Org 402.014**
Certificate of formation, amendments, **Bus Org 3.056**
Foreign corporations, post
Guaranty, **Bus Org 2.104**
Indemnity, **Bus Org 8.001 et seq.**
Insolvency, **Bus Org 12.253 et seq.**
Meetings, **Bus Org 22.154**
Receivers and receivership, **Bus Org 11.406**

NONPROFIT CORPORATIONS—Cont'd
Actions and proceedings—Cont'd
Records and recordation, inspection and inspectors, **Bus Org 3.152**
Reports, forfeitures, **Bus Org 22.362**
State, liens and incumbrances, **Bus Org 12.201 et seq.**
Termination, involuntary termination, **Bus Org 11.303**
Unincorporated nonprofit associations, post
Winding up, post
Actions without meetings, directors, **Bus Org 22.220**
Address, certificate of formation, **Bus Org 3.005**
Administrative law and procedure, unincorporated nonprofit associations, **Bus Org 252.007**
Adoption, Business Organizations Code, **Bus Org 402.003**
Advancements,
Indemnity, expenses and expenditures, **Bus Org 8.104, 8.105**
Reports, **Bus Org 8.152**
Unincorporated nonprofit associations, post
Agent for service of process, **Bus Org 5.251 et seq.**
Unincorporated nonprofit associations, **Bus Org 252.011**
Agents and agencies,
Changes, filing, fines and penalties, **Bus Org 21.802**
Damages, **Bus Org 301.010**
Licenses and permits, **Bus Org 301.006**
Registered agent, generally, post
Agreements. Contracts, generally, post
Allocations, merger and consolidation, property, **Bus Org 10.003**
Alternatives, service of process, **Bus Org 5.256**
Amendments,
Business Organizations Code, statutes, **Bus Org 1.054**
Bylaws, **Bus Org 22.102**
Certificate of formation, post
Filing, **Bus Org 4.106**
Fees, **Bus Org 4.153**
Unincorporated nonprofit associations, post
Ancillary receiverships, **Bus Org 11.409**
Answer, interrogatories, time, **Bus Org 12.002**
Antitrust, application of law, **Bus Org 10.901**
Appeal and review,
Filing, **Bus Org 12.004**
Termination, involuntary termination, **Bus Org 11.307**
Trusts and trustees, privileges and immunities, **Bus Org 2.106**
Unincorporated nonprofit associations, post
Winding up, involuntary winding up, **Bus Org 11.307**

NONPROFIT CORPORATIONS
—Cont'd
Application of law, **Bus Org 301.001**
Antitrust, **Bus Org 10.901**
Business Organizations Code, **Bus Org 402.001 et seq.**
Foreign countries, foreign states, **Bus Org 1.053**
Certificate of formation, **Bus Org 1.101 et seq.**
Elections, **Bus Org 6.301, 6.302**
Indebtedness, **Bus Org 10.901**
Indemnity, **Bus Org 8.002**
Meetings, **Bus Org 6.301, 6.302**
Monopolies and unfair trade, **Bus Org 10.901**
Reorganization, **Bus Org 10.306**
Special purpose corporations, **Bus Org 23.001 et seq.**
Unincorporated nonprofit associations, post
Appointments, receivers and receivership, **Bus Org 11.401 et seq.**
Appraisals and appraisers, reorganization, **Bus Org 10.304**
Arbitration and award, unincorporated nonprofit associations, **Bus Org 252.007**
Assets,
Certificate of formation, distribution, **Bus Org 3.009**
Disposition, **Bus Org 10.251 et seq.**
Reorganization, **Bus Org 10.301**
Distribution and distributors, damages, **Bus Org 22.226 et seq.**
Liens and incumbrances, state, **Bus Org 12.201**
Sales, **Bus Org 22.252**
Business Organizations Code, mandatory application date, **Bus Org 402.010**
Elections, **Bus Org 22.164**
Meetings, **Bus Org 22.253**
Unincorporated nonprofit associations, post
Winding up, distribution and distributors, **Bus Org 11.053**
Assignments, **Bus Org 10.251 et seq.**
Shares and shareholders, certificates and certification, **Bus Org 3.201**
Assumed or fictitious names, names, **Bus Org 5.051 et seq.**
Attachment, state, **Bus Org 12.259**
Attorney fees,
Filing,
Fines and penalties, **Bus Org 21.802**
Fraud, **Bus Org 4.007**
Records and recordation, inspection and inspectors, **Bus Org 3.152**
Unincorporated nonprofit associations, post
Audits and auditors, state agencies, **Bus Org 22.356**
Bankruptcy, **Bus Org 10.301 et seq.**
Board of directors. Directors, generally, post

NONPROFIT CORPORATIONS
—Cont'd
Bonds, **Bus Org 2.101**
Investments, **Bus Org 22.224**
Reorganization, **Bus Org 10.301**
Bonds (officers and fiduciaries), receivers and receivership, **Bus Org 11.406**
Bonuses, officers and employees, **Bus Org 2.101**
Books and papers, **Bus Org 3.151 et seq.**
Audits and auditors, **Bus Org 22.356**
Confidential or privileged information, **Bus Org 12.154**
Disclosure, **Bus Org 12.154**
Duplicates and copies, **Bus Org 12.151 et seq.**
Examinations and examiners, **Bus Org 3.153, 12.151 et seq.**
Inspection and inspectors, **Bus Org 3.152, 22.351**
Powers and duties, limitations, **Bus Org 2.005**
Reorganization, **Bus Org 10.301**
Signatures, **Bus Org 1.007**
Unincorporated nonprofit associations, post
Business Development Corporations, generally, this index
Bylaws, **Bus Org 2.101, 22.102**
Definitions, **Bus Org 22.001**
Meetings, **Bus Org 22.153**
Notice, **Bus Org 22.157**
Statutes, construction, **Bus Org 22.103**
Cancellation,
Reinstatement, **Bus Org 402.013**
Unincorporated nonprofit associations, post
Winding up, **Bus Org 11.152, 22.301 et seq.**
Certificate of formation, **Bus Org 3.001 et seq.**
Amendments, **Bus Org 3.051 et seq., 22.105 et seq.**
Elections, **Bus Org 22.164**
Numbers and numbering, **Bus Org 22.108**
Application of law, **Bus Org 1.101 et seq.**
Definitions, **Bus Org 1.002**
Dentists and dentistry, health service corporations, **Bus Org 22.052**
Directors, post
Elections, amendments, **Bus Org 22.105 et seq., 22.164**
Filing, fees, **Bus Org 4.153**
Incorporation, **Bus Org 22.101**
Merger and consolidation, **Bus Org 3.005, 3.006, 10.002**
Notice, amendments, **Bus Org 22.105**
Numbers and numbering, amendments, **Bus Org 22.108**
Reinstatement, **Bus Org 402.013**
Reorganization, **Bus Org 10.301 et seq.**
Restatement, **Bus Org 3.057 et seq., 22.109**
Signatures, **Bus Org 3.004**
Amendments, **Bus Org 3.052**

NONPROFIT CORPORATIONS
—Cont'd
Certificate of formation—Cont'd
Signatures—Cont'd
Restatement, **Bus Org 3.058, 3.060**
Statements,
Amendments, **Bus Org 3.053**
Restatement, **Bus Org 3.059**
Statutes, construction, **Bus Org 22.103**
Taxation, statements, **Bus Org 2.107**
Time, **Bus Org 3.001, 3.003**
Amendments, **Bus Org 3.056**
Restatement, **Bus Org 3.063**
Unincorporated nonprofit associations, post
Certificates and certification,
Acceptance, **Bus Org 10.156**
Certificate of formation, generally, ante
Conversion, **Bus Org 10.154 et seq.**
Evidence, existence, **Bus Org 4.005**
Exchange of property, **Bus Org 10.151 et seq.**
Filing, **Bus Org 12.001**
Abandonment, **Bus Org 4.057**
Corrections, **Bus Org 4.101 et seq.**
Fines and penalties, **Bus Org 21.802**
Indebtedness, **Bus Org 2.114**
Merger and consolidation, **Bus Org 10.151 et seq.**
Shares and shareholders, **Bus Org 3.201 et seq.**
Termination, post
Unincorporated nonprofit associations, post
Certified copies,
Filing, **Bus Org 4.005**
Involuntary termination, judgments and decrees, **Bus Org 11.414**
Changes,
Directors, numbers and numbering, **Bus Org 22.103**
Registered agent, post
Registered offices, post
Churches, managers and management, **Bus Org 22.233**
Citizens and citizenship, receivers and receivership, **Bus Org 11.406**
Claims,
Receivers and receivership, filing, **Bus Org 11.407**
Termination, **Bus Org 11.351 et seq.**
Unincorporated nonprofit associations, post
Classification, directors, **Bus Org 22.209**
Colleges and Universities, this index
Committees,
Directors, **Bus Org 22.218 et seq.**
Officers and employees, **Bus Org 22.231**
Compensation and salaries,
Officers and employees, **Bus Org 2.101, 22.054**
Receivers and receivership, **Bus Org 11.408**
Complaints, unincorporated nonprofit associations, **Bus Org 252.013**

NONPROFIT CORPORATIONS
—Cont'd
Conduct,
Business Organizations Code, application of law, **Bus Org 402.006**
Damages, **Bus Org 7.001, 301.010**
Confidential or privileged information, interrogatories, **Bus Org 12.003**
Conflict of interest,
Contracts, officers and employees, **Bus Org 22.230**
Elections, **Bus Org 6.152, 6.153**
Conflict of laws, **Bus Org 301.002**
Consent,
Actions without meetings, directors, **Bus Org 22.220**
Duplicates and copies, meetings, action without meeting, **Bus Org 6.205**
Meetings, telecommunications, **Bus Org 22.002**
Registered agents, **Bus Org 5.2011**
Consolidation. Merger and consolidation, generally, post
Construction of laws, Business Organizations Code, statutes, **Bus Org 1.006, 1.051 et seq.**
Contracts, **Bus Org 2.101**
Business Organizations Code, application of law, **Bus Org 402.006**
Elections, **Bus Org 6.252**
Indebtedness, **Bus Org 2.103**
Officers and employees, conflict of interest, **Bus Org 22.230**
Unincorporated nonprofit associations, post
Winding up, **Bus Org 11.152**
Contributions,
Assets, distribution and distributors, **Bus Org 22.229**
Definitions, business organizations, **Bus Org 1.002**
Conversion, **Bus Org 10.101 et seq., 22.256**
Abandonment, **Bus Org 10.201, 10.202, 10.203**
Acceptance, certificates and certification, **Bus Org 10.156**
Business Organizations Code, mandatory application date, **Bus Org 402.010**
Certificates and certification, **Bus Org 10.154 et seq.**
Dissenting shareholders, **Bus Org 10.351 et seq.**
Effective date, **Bus Org 10.105, 10.106**
Elections, **Bus Org 22.164**
Filing,
Certificates and certification, **Bus Org 10.155**
Fees, **Bus Org 4.151, 4.153**
Names, **Bus Org 10.103**
Notice, **Bus Org 10.101**
Plans and specifications, **Bus Org 10.101 et seq.**
Registration, withdrawal, **Bus Org 9.012**
Reorganization, **Bus Org 10.301 et seq.**

NONPROFIT CORPORATIONS
—Cont'd
Conversion—Cont'd
Unincorporated nonprofit associations, post
Conveyances. Deeds and conveyances, generally, post
Cooperative Associations, generally, this index
Copies. Duplicates and copies, generally, post
Corrections, filing, **Bus Org 4.101 et seq.**
Fees, **Bus Org 4.151**
Costs,
Filing,
Fines and penalties, **Bus Org 21.802**
Fraud, **Bus Org 4.007**
Insolvency, dismissal and nonsuit, **Bus Org 12.257**
Liens and incumbrances, foreclosure, dismissal and nonsuit, **Bus Org 12.257**
Unincorporated nonprofit associations, post
Credit Unions, generally, this index
Crimes and offenses,
Books and papers, examinations and examiners, **Bus Org 12.156**
Damages, **Bus Org 7.001**
Filing, fraud, **Bus Org 4.008**
Fraud, generally, post
Termination, involuntary termination, **Bus Org 11.301 et seq.**
Unincorporated nonprofit associations, post
Winding up, involuntary winding up, **Bus Org 11.301 et seq.**
Cumulative voting, **Bus Org 22.161, 22.162**
Damages, **Bus Org 301.010**
Application of law, **Bus Org 1.104**
Assets, distribution and distributors, **Bus Org 22.226 et seq.**
Directors, post
Filing, **Bus Org 21.802**
Fraud, **Bus Org 4.007**
Guaranty, **Bus Org 2.104**
Indemnity, generally, post
Officers and employees, post
Trusts and trustees, privileges and immunities, **Bus Org 2.106**
Unincorporated nonprofit associations, post
Deception, names, **Bus Org 5.052**
Decrees. Judgments and decrees, generally, post
Deeds and conveyances, **Bus Org 10.251 et seq., 22.255**
Property, **Bus Org 2.101**
Receivers and receivership, **Bus Org 11.413**
Records and recordation, **Bus Org 10.253**
Unincorporated nonprofit associations, post
Deeds of trusts, **Bus Org 22.254**

NONPROFIT CORPORATIONS
—Cont'd
Definitions, **Bus Org 1.002, 22.001, 301.003**
Business organizations, **Bus Org 1.002**
Fundamental actions, elections, **Bus Org 22.164**
Indemnity, **Bus Org 8.001**
Mandatory application date, **Bus Org 401.001**
Prior law, **Bus Org 401.001**
Termination, **Bus Org 11.001**
Winding up, **Bus Org 11.001**
Delay, filing, effective date, **Bus Org 4.052 et seq.**
Delivery,
Filing, **Bus Org 4.001**
Meetings, action without meeting, **Bus Org 6.203**
Shares and shareholders, certificates and certification, **Bus Org 3.204**
Unincorporated nonprofit associations, post
Demand, meetings, **Bus Org 22.154**
Dentists and Dentistry, this index
Deposits, termination, claims, **Bus Org 11.352**
Directors, **Bus Org 22.201 et seq.**
Actions without meetings, **Bus Org 22.220**
Agent for service of process, **Bus Org 5.255**
Certificate of formation, **Bus Org 3.007, 3.009**
Amendments, **Bus Org 22.107**
Restatement, **Bus Org 3.060, 3.061, 22.109**
Changes, numbers and numbering, **Bus Org 22.103**
Churches, **Bus Org 22.233**
Classification, **Bus Org 22.209**
Committees, **Bus Org 22.218 et seq.**
Compensation and salaries, **Bus Org 22.054**
Conflict of interest, contracts, **Bus Org 22.230**
Consent, actions without meetings, **Bus Org 22.220**
Contracts, conflict of interest, **Bus Org 22.230**
Damages, **Bus Org 7.001**
Assets, distribution and distributors, **Bus Org 22.226 et seq.**
Loans, **Bus Org 22.225**
Definitions, **Bus Org 22.001**
Dentists and dentistry, health service corporations, **Bus Org 22.052**
Domicile and residence, **Bus Org 22.203**
Elections, **Bus Org 22.161, 22.206, 22.207**
Ex officio members, **Bus Org 22.210**
Good faith,
Investments, **Bus Org 22.224**
Religious organizations and societies, **Bus Org 22.222**
Standards, **Bus Org 22.221**

NONPROFIT CORPORATIONS—Cont'd
Directors—Cont'd
Indemnity, **Bus Org 7.001**
Investments, **Bus Org 22.224**
Loans, **Bus Org 2.101, 22.225**
Meetings, **Bus Org 22.217**
Actions without meetings, **Bus Org 22.220**
Names, **Bus Org 22.205**
Notice,
Meetings, **Bus Org 22.217**
Resignation, **Bus Org 22.2111**
Numbers and numbering, **Bus Org 22.204**
Changes, **Bus Org 22.103**
Organization, meetings, **Bus Org 22.104**
Powers and duties, trusts and trustees, **Bus Org 22.223**
Privileges and immunities, **Bus Org 22.221**
Proxies, **Bus Org 22.214 et seq.**
Quorum, **Bus Org 22.213**
Religious corporations, **Bus Org 22.222**
Removal, **Bus Org 22.208, 22.211**
Resignation, notice, **Bus Org 22.2111**
Revocation or suspension, proxies, **Bus Org 22.216**
Standards, **Bus Org 22.221**
Terms of office, **Bus Org 22.208**
Trusts and trustees, powers and duties, **Bus Org 22.223**
Unincorporated nonprofit associations, post
Vacancies in office, **Bus Org 22.212**
Waiver, meetings, notice, **Bus Org 22.217**
Discharge,
Receivers and receivership, **Bus Org 11.412**
Termination, claims, **Bus Org 11.353**
Unincorporated nonprofit associations, post
Winding up, indebtedness, **Bus Org 11.053**
Disclosure, interrogatories, **Bus Org 12.003**
Dismissal and nonsuit,
Insolvency, **Bus Org 12.257**
Liens and incumbrances, foreclosure, **Bus Org 12.257**
Unincorporated nonprofit associations, post
Dissenting shareholders. Shares and shareholders, post
Dissolution, **Bus Org 2.101**
Filing, fees, **Bus Org 4.153**
Reinstatement, **Bus Org 402.013**
Distribution and distributors, **Bus Org 22.054**
Assets, ante
Dividends, **Bus Org 22.053**
Receivers and receivership, **Bus Org 11.413**
Record date, **Bus Org 6.101 et seq.**
Unincorporated nonprofit associations, post

NONPROFIT CORPORATIONS—Cont'd
Distribution and distributors—Cont'd
Winding up, post
Dividends, **Bus Org 22.053**
Domicile and residence, directors, **Bus Org 22.203**
Dual office holding, officers and employees, **Bus Org 3.103, 22.231**
Duplicates and copies,
Agent for service of process, **Bus Org 5.252**
Books and papers, **Bus Org 12.151 et seq., 22.351**
Consent, meetings, action without meeting, **Bus Org 6.205**
Filing, **Bus Org 4.003**
Financial statements and reports, **Bus Org 22.353**
Records and recordation, **Bus Org 3.152**
Shares and shareholders, certificates and certification, **Bus Org 3.202**
Unincorporated nonprofit associations, post
Duties. Powers and duties, generally, post
Effective date,
Business Organizations Code, **Bus Org 402.001**
Adoption, **Bus Org 402.005**
Conversion, **Bus Org 10.105, 10.106**
Exchange of property, **Bus Org 10.054, 10.055**
Filing, **Bus Org 4.051 et seq.**
Merger and consolidation, **Bus Org 10.007**
Termination, post
Unincorporated nonprofit associations, post
Elections, **Bus Org 6.151 et seq.**
Application of law, **Bus Org 6.301, 6.302**
Assets, sales, **Bus Org 22.252**
Certificate of formation, amendments, **Bus Org 22.105 et seq.**
Conflict of interest, **Bus Org 6.152, 6.153**
Contracts, **Bus Org 6.252**
Conversion, **Bus Org 22.256**
Cumulative voting, **Bus Org 22.161, 22.162**
Directors, ante
Estates, **Bus Org 6.154**
Exchange of property, **Bus Org 22.257**
Fundamental actions, **Bus Org 22.164**
Indemnity, **Bus Org 8.103**
Members, **Bus Org 22.158 et seq.**
Merger and consolidation, **Bus Org 22.251**
Officers and employees, **Bus Org 2.101, 3.103, 22.232**
Pledges, **Bus Org 6.156**
Probate proceedings, **Bus Org 6.154**
Receivers and receivership, **Bus Org 6.155**

NONPROFIT CORPORATIONS—Cont'd
Elections—Cont'd
Trusts and trustees, **Bus Org 6.154, 6.251**
Unincorporated nonprofit associations, post
Winding up, **Bus Org 22.302**
Electric cooperative corporations, status, **Util 161.059**
Electronic communications, consent, meetings, **Bus Org 6.205**
Electronic communications system, meetings, **Bus Org 22.002**
Electronic filing, **Bus Org 12.001**
Emergencies, governance, **Bus Org 3.251 et seq.**
Employees. Officers and employees, generally, post
Errors,
Damages, **Bus Org 301.010**
Termination, reinstatement, **Bus Org 11.201 et seq.**
Escheat, termination, claims, **Bus Org 11.355**
Estates, elections, **Bus Org 6.154**
Evidence,
Certificate of formation, acknowledgments, **Bus Org 3.001**
Existence, certificates and certification, **Bus Org 4.005**
Filing, **Bus Org 4.001**
Indebtedness, fraud, **Bus Org 2.103**
Shares and shareholders, certificates and certification, **Bus Org 3.201**
Unincorporated nonprofit associations, post
Ex officio members, directors, **Bus Org 22.210**
Examinations and examiners,
Books and papers, **Bus Org 12.151 et seq., 22.351**
Elections, contracts, **Bus Org 6.252**
Records and recordation, **Bus Org 3.153**
Unincorporated nonprofit associations, post
Exchange of property, **Bus Org 2.101, 10.051 et seq., 22.257**
Abandonment, **Bus Org 10.201, 10.202, 10.203**
Acceptance, certificates and certification, **Bus Org 10.156**
Certificates and certification, **Bus Org 10.151 et seq.**
Dissenting shareholders, **Bus Org 10.351 et seq.**
Elections, **Bus Org 22.164**
Filing,
Certificates and certification, **Bus Org 10.153**
Fees, **Bus Org 4.151**
Reorganization, **Bus Org 10.301**
Shares and shareholders, post
Unincorporated nonprofit associations, post
Voluntary, **Bus Org 10.902**

NONPROFIT CORPORATIONS
—Cont'd
Exemptions,
Financial statements and reports, **Bus Org 22.355**
Guaranty, powers and duties, **Bus Org 2.104**
Interrogatories, **Bus Org 12.002**
Securities, sales, **Bus Org 301.011**
Termination, involuntary termination, **Bus Org 11.251**
Unincorporated nonprofit associations, post
Expenses and expenditures,
Financial statements and reports, **Bus Org 22.352 et seq.**
Indemnity, **Bus Org 8.001 et seq.**
Facsimile, **Bus Org 1.007**
Consent, meetings, action without meeting, **Bus Org 6.205**
Filing, **Bus Org 4.003**
Indebtedness, certificates and certification, **Bus Org 2.114**
Meetings, notice, **Bus Org 6.051**
Seals, **Bus Org 2.101**
Shares and shareholders, certificates and certification, **Bus Org 3.203**
Unincorporated nonprofit associations, post
Fax. Facsimile, generally, ante
Fees,
Business Organizations Code, effective date, **Bus Org 402.002**
Filing, **Bus Org 4.151 et seq.**
Financial statements and reports, inspection and inspectors, **Bus Org 22.353**
Names, reservation, **Bus Org 5.101**
Withdrawal, **Bus Org 5.1041**
Reports, forfeitures,
Abatement of actions and proceedings, **Bus Org 22.363**
Reinstatement, **Bus Org 22.365**
Unincorporated nonprofit associations, post
Filing, **Bus Org 4.001 et seq., 12.001 et seq.**
Abandonment, **Bus Org 4.057**
Acknowledgments, **Bus Org 4.002**
Effective date, delay, **Bus Org 4.059**
Amendments, **Bus Org 4.106**
Appeal and review, **Bus Org 12.004**
Assumed or fictitious names, **Bus Org 5.051**
Attorney fees,
Fines and penalties, **Bus Org 21.802**
Fraud, **Bus Org 4.007**
Business Organizations Code, effective date, **Bus Org 402.002**
Certificate of formation, **Bus Org 3.001 et seq.**
Certificates and certification, ante
Certified copies, **Bus Org 4.005**
Conversion, ante
Corrections, **Bus Org 4.101 et seq.**
Fees, **Bus Org 4.151**

NONPROFIT CORPORATIONS
—Cont'd
Filing—Cont'd
Costs,
Fines and penalties, **Bus Org 21.802**
Fraud, **Bus Org 4.007**
Damages, **Bus Org 21.802**
Fraud, **Bus Org 4.007**
Delay, effective date, **Bus Org 4.052 et seq.**
Delivery, **Bus Org 4.001**
Dentists and dentistry, health service corporations, **Bus Org 22.052**
Duplicates and copies, **Bus Org 4.003**
Effective date, **Bus Org 4.051 et seq.**
Electronic filing, **Bus Org 12.001**
Evidence, **Bus Org 4.001**
Facsimile, **Bus Org 4.003**
Fees, **Bus Org 4.151 et seq.**
Fines and penalties, **Bus Org 21.802**
Fraud, **Bus Org 4.008**
Foreign corporations, post
Forms, **Bus Org 4.006**
Fraud, **Bus Org 4.007, 4.008**
Interrogatories, **Bus Org 12.002, 12.003**
Jurisdiction, fines and penalties, **Bus Org 21.802**
Limitations,
Corrections, **Bus Org 4.102**
Effective date, delay, **Bus Org 4.058**
Names, registration, **Bus Org 5.152**
Real estate investment trusts, **Bus Org 4.009**
Receivers and receivership, claims, **Bus Org 11.407**
Registered agents, resignation, **Bus Org 5.204**
Reports, **Bus Org 22.359, 22.360**
Service of process, **Bus Org 21.802**
Signatures, **Bus Org 4.001**
Corrections, certificates and certification, **Bus Org 4.101**
Special purpose corporations, records and recordation, **Bus Org 23.002**
Termination, involuntary termination, **Bus Org 11.315**
Time, **Bus Org 4.004**
Corrections, **Bus Org 4.105**
Effective date, **Bus Org 4.051 et seq.**
Fines and penalties, **Bus Org 21.802**
Unincorporated nonprofit associations, post
Winding up, involuntary winding up, **Bus Org 11.315**
Financial statements and reports, **Bus Org 22.352 et seq.**
Officers and employees, good faith, **Bus Org 3.102, 3.105**
Fines and penalties,
Books and papers, examinations and examiners, **Bus Org 12.156**
Filing, **Bus Org 21.802**
Fraud, **Bus Org 4.008**
Financial statements and reports, **Bus Org 22.354**
Registered agents, consent, **Bus Org 5.207**

NONPROFIT CORPORATIONS
—Cont'd
Fines and penalties—Cont'd
Unincorporated nonprofit associations, post
Foreclosure, liens and incumbrances, **Bus Org 12.252 et seq.**
Foreign corporations,
Abatement of actions and proceedings, reports, forfeitures, **Bus Org 22.363, 22.364**
Acknowledgments, registration, **Bus Org 9.008**
Actions and proceedings,
Registration, **Bus Org 9.051 et seq.**
Reports, forfeitures, **Bus Org 22.362**
Transacting business in Texas, **Bus Org 9.251**
Address, registration, **Bus Org 9.006**
Amendments, registration, **Bus Org 9.009**
Application of law, Business Organizations Code, **Bus Org 9.301**
Banks and banking, transacting business in Texas, **Bus Org 9.251**
Certificates and certification, registration,
Reinstatement, **Bus Org 9.104**
Revocation or suspension, **Bus Org 9.102**
Certified copies, registration, revocation or suspension, **Bus Org 9.161**
Claims, transacting business in Texas, **Bus Org 9.251**
Conflict of laws, registration, **Bus Org 9.055**
Conversion, registration, withdrawal, **Bus Org 9.012**
Dismissal and nonsuit, registration, revocation or suspension, **Bus Org 9.156**
Elections, transacting business in Texas, **Bus Org 9.251**
Evidence, registration, acknowledgments, **Bus Org 9.008**
Exemptions, registration, **Bus Org 9.002**
Fees,
Registration, collection, **Bus Org 9.054**
Reports, forfeitures, abatement of actions and proceedings, **Bus Org 22.363**
Filing,
Fees, **Bus Org 4.153**
Registration, revocation or suspension, **Bus Org 9.161**
Reports, **Bus Org 22.359, 22.360**
Fines and penalties, registration, **Bus Org 9.052**
Forfeitures, reports, filing, **Bus Org 22.360 et seq.**
Indebtedness, transacting business in Texas, **Bus Org 9.251**
Injunctions, registration, **Bus Org 9.051**
Investments, transacting business in Texas, **Bus Org 9.251**

NONPROFIT CORPORATIONS
—Cont'd
Foreign corporations—Cont'd
Judgments and decrees, registration, revocation or suspension, **Bus Org 9.154 et seq.**
Jurisdiction, registration, revocation or suspension, **Bus Org 9.158**
Liens and incumbrances, transacting business in Texas, **Bus Org 9.251**
Lists, transacting business in Texas, **Bus Org 9.251, 9.252**
Loans, transacting business in Texas, **Bus Org 9.251**
Meetings, transacting business in Texas, **Bus Org 9.251**
Mines and minerals, transacting business in Texas, **Bus Org 9.251**
Mortgages, transacting business in Texas, **Bus Org 9.251**
Names, registration, **Bus Org 9.006**
Change of name, **Bus Org 9.010**
Reinstatement, **Bus Org 9.105**
Notice,
Registration,
Revocation or suspension, **Bus Org 9.101, 9.152**
Service of process, revocation or suspension, **Bus Org 9.160**
Reports, **Bus Org 22.358**
Filing, forfeitures, **Bus Org 22.361**
Offices, transacting business in Texas, **Bus Org 9.251**
Probate proceedings, transacting business in Texas, **Bus Org 9.251**
Registration, **Bus Org 9.001 et seq.**
Acknowledgments, **Bus Org 9.008**
Actions and proceedings, **Bus Org 9.051 et seq.**
Address, **Bus Org 9.006**
Amendments, **Bus Org 9.009**
Applications, **Bus Org 9.004**
Certificates and certification,
Reinstatement, **Bus Org 9.104**
Revocation or suspension, **Bus Org 9.102**
Certified copies, revocation or suspension, **Bus Org 9.161**
Conflict of laws, **Bus Org 9.055**
Dismissal and nonsuit, revocation or suspension, **Bus Org 9.156**
Evidence, acknowledgments, **Bus Org 9.008**
Exemptions, **Bus Org 9.002**
Fees, collection, **Bus Org 9.054**
Filing, revocation or suspension, **Bus Org 9.161**
Fines and penalties, **Bus Org 9.052**
Fraud, **Bus Org 9.051 et seq.**
Injunctions, **Bus Org 9.051**
Judgments and decrees, revocation or suspension, **Bus Org 9.154 et seq.**
Jurisdiction, revocation or suspension, **Bus Org 9.158**
Names, **Bus Org 9.006**
Change of name, **Bus Org 9.010**

NONPROFIT CORPORATIONS
—Cont'd
Foreign corporations—Cont'd
Registration—Cont'd
Names—Cont'd
Reinstatement, **Bus Org 9.105**
Notice,
Revocation or suspension, **Bus Org 9.101, 9.152**
Service of process, revocation or suspension, **Bus Org 9.160**
Reinstatement, **Bus Org 9.103 et seq.**
Remand, revocation or suspension, **Bus Org 9.157**
Revocation or suspension, **Bus Org 9.101 et seq., 9.151 et seq.**
Same or similar names, reinstatement, **Bus Org 9.105**
Service of process,
Revocation or suspension, **Bus Org 9.159, 9.160**
Withdrawal, **Bus Org 9.011**
Supersedeas or stay, revocation or suspension, **Bus Org 9.156**
Taxation, forfeitures, reinstatement, **Bus Org 9.106**
Time, amendments, **Bus Org 9.009**
Venue, **Bus Org 9.053**
Revocation or suspension, **Bus Org 9.158**
Withdrawal, **Bus Org 9.011**
Reinstatement, registration, **Bus Org 9.103 et seq.**
Remand, registration, revocation or suspension, **Bus Org 9.157**
Reports, **Bus Org 22.357 et seq.**
Revocation or suspension, registration, **Bus Org 9.101 et seq., 9.151 et seq.**
Sales, transacting business in Texas, **Bus Org 9.251**
Same or similar names, registration, reinstatement, **Bus Org 9.105**
Securities, transacting business in Texas, **Bus Org 9.251**
Service of process, registration,
Revocation or suspension, **Bus Org 9.159, 9.160**
Withdrawal, **Bus Org 9.011**
Supersedeas or stay, registration, revocation or suspension, **Bus Org 9.156**
Taxation, registration, forfeitures, reinstatement, **Bus Org 9.106**
Time,
Registration, amendments, **Bus Org 9.009**
Reports, **Bus Org 22.357**
Transacting business in Texas, **Bus Org 9.201 et seq.**
Lists, **Bus Org 9.251, 9.252**
Trusts and trustees, transacting business in Texas, **Bus Org 9.251**
Venue, registration, **Bus Org 9.053**
Revocation or suspension, **Bus Org 9.158**
Withdrawal, registration, **Bus Org 9.011**

NONPROFIT CORPORATIONS
—Cont'd
Foreign countries,
Business Organizations Code, application of law, **Bus Org 1.053**
Certificate of formation, application of law, **Bus Org 1.102**
Unincorporated nonprofit associations, post
Foreign states,
Business Organizations Code, application of law, **Bus Org 1.053**
Certificate of formation, application of law, **Bus Org 1.102**
Meetings, location, **Bus Org 6.001**
Unincorporated nonprofit associations, post
Forfeitures,
Books and papers, examinations and examiners, **Bus Org 12.155**
Reinstatement, **Bus Org 402.013**
Reports, filing, **Bus Org 22.360 et seq.**
Formation. Certificate of formation, generally, ante
Forms,
Filing, **Bus Org 4.006**
Shares and shareholders, certificates and certification, **Bus Org 3.202**
Unincorporated nonprofit associations, post
Fraud,
Filing, **Bus Org 4.007, 4.008**
Guaranty, **Bus Org 2.104**
Indebtedness, evidence, **Bus Org 2.103**
Names, **Bus Org 5.052**
Receivers and receivership, **Bus Org 11.403**
Termination,
Involuntary termination, **Bus Org 11.301 et seq.**
Revocation or suspension, **Bus Org 11.153**
Unincorporated nonprofit associations, post
Winding up, involuntary winding up, **Bus Org 11.301 et seq.**
Frauds, statute of, powers and duties, **Bus Org 2.112**
Fundamental actions, elections, **Bus Org 22.164**
Fundamental business transactions, **Bus Org 22.251 et seq.**
Garnishment, state, **Bus Org 12.259**
Gifts, **Bus Org 2.101**
Good faith,
Assets, distribution and distributors, damages, **Bus Org 22.226**
Damages, **Bus Org 7.001**
Directors, ante
Officers and employees, **Bus Org 3.102, 3.105**
Unincorporated nonprofit associations, post
Guaranty, **Bus Org 2.101**
Powers and duties, **Bus Org 2.104**
Health organization corporations, **Bus Org 22.056**

NONPROFIT CORPORATIONS
—Cont'd
Health service corporations, dentists and dentistry, **Bus Org 22.052**
Hold harmless. Indemnity, generally, post
Holding companies, merger and consolidation, **Bus Org 10.005**
Housing, officers and employees, loans, **Bus Org 22.055**
Identity and identification, names, same or similar, **Bus Org 5.053**
Immunities. Privileges and immunities, generally, post
Incentives, officers and employees, **Bus Org 2.101**
Income, financial statements and reports, **Bus Org 22.352 et seq.**
Incorporation, **Bus Org 22.101**
Indebtedness, **Bus Org 2.101, 2.103**
Application of law, **Bus Org 10.901**
Certificates and certification, **Bus Org 2.114**
Members, privileges and immunities, **Bus Org 22.152**
Unincorporated nonprofit associations, post
Winding up, discharge, **Bus Org 11.053**
Indemnity,
Business Organizations Code, application of law, **Bus Org 402.007**
Insurance, post
Mandatory, **Bus Org 8.051**
Officers and employees, **Bus Org 2.101, 7.001, 8.001 et seq.**
Orders of court, **Bus Org 8.052**
Permissive indemnification, **Bus Org 8.101 et seq.**
Reports, **Bus Org 8.152**
Unincorporated nonprofit associations, post
Injunctions,
Guaranty, **Bus Org 2.104**
State, **Bus Org 12.259**
Insolvency, actions and proceedings, **Bus Org 12.253 et seq.**
Inspection and inspectors,
Books and papers, **Bus Org 12.151 et seq., 22.351**
Financial statements and reports, **Bus Org 22.353**
Members, elections, lists, **Bus Org 22.158**
Records and recordation, **Bus Org 3.152**
Unincorporated nonprofit associations, post
Insurance, indemnity, **Bus Org 2.101, 8.151**
Internal affairs, **Bus Org 1.105**
Internet, meetings, **Bus Org 6.002, 22.002**
Interrogatories, **Bus Org 12.002, 12.003**
Investigations and investigators, unincorporated nonprofit associations, **Bus Org 252.010**
Investments, **Bus Org 2.101, 22.224**

NONPROFIT CORPORATIONS
—Cont'd
Involuntary termination. Termination, post
Joint practices, **Bus Org 301.012**
Judgments and decrees,
Receivers and receivership, termination, **Bus Org 11.412**
Reorganization, **Bus Org 10.305**
Termination, **Bus Org 11.301 et seq.**
Involuntary termination, certified copies, **Bus Org 11.414**
Trusts and trustees, privileges and immunities, **Bus Org 2.106**
Unincorporated nonprofit associations, post
Winding up, **Bus Org 11.301 et seq.**
Jurisdiction,
Filing, fines and penalties, **Bus Org 21.802**
Insolvency, **Bus Org 12.253**
Liens and incumbrances, foreclosure, **Bus Org 12.253**
Receivers and receivership, **Bus Org 11.402 et seq.**
Reorganization, **Bus Org 10.302**
Termination, involuntary termination, **Bus Org 11.308**
Unincorporated nonprofit associations, post
Winding up, involuntary winding up, **Bus Org 11.308**
Leases, **Bus Org 2.101, 10.251 et seq.**
Reorganization, **Bus Org 10.301**
Unincorporated nonprofit associations, post
Legislature, this index
Licenses and permits, **Bus Org 301.006**
Liens and incumbrances,
Foreclosure, **Bus Org 12.252 et seq.**
State, **Bus Org 12.201**
Unincorporated nonprofit associations, post
Limitation of actions, termination, claims, **Bus Org 11.359**
Limitations,
Filing,
Corrections, **Bus Org 4.102**
Effective date, delay, **Bus Org 4.058**
Indemnity, **Bus Org 8.003, 8.004**
Powers and duties, **Bus Org 2.113**
Purposes, **Bus Org 2.003 et seq.**
Unincorporated nonprofit associations, post
Liquidation, receivers and receivership, **Bus Org 12.258**
Orders of court, **Bus Org 11.405**
Lists, members, elections, **Bus Org 22.158**
Loans, **Bus Org 2.101**
Directors, **Bus Org 22.225**
Officers and employees, **Bus Org 22.055**
Location,
Meetings, **Bus Org 6.001**
Organization, **Bus Org 22.104**
Offices, **Bus Org 2.101**
Lottery, names, **Bus Org 5.061**

NONPROFIT CORPORATIONS
—Cont'd
Mail and mailing, meetings, notice, **Bus Org 6.051**
Managers and management,
Agent for service of process, **Bus Org 5.255**
Certificate of formation, **Bus Org 3.009**
Amendments, **Bus Org 22.106**
Damages, **Bus Org 301.010**
Directors, generally, ante
Licenses and permits, **Bus Org 301.006**
Organization, meetings, **Bus Org 22.104**
Resignation, **Bus Org 301.008**
Winding up, **Bus Org 22.307**
Mandatory application date, Business Organizations Code, **Bus Org 401.001 et seq.**
Mediation, unincorporated nonprofit associations, **Bus Org 252.007**
Meetings, **Bus Org 6.001 et seq., 22.153 et seq.**
Action without meeting, **Bus Org 6.102**
Consent, **Bus Org 6.201 et seq.**
Application of law, **Bus Org 6.301, 6.302**
Assets, sales, **Bus Org 22.253**
Business Organizations Code, mandatory application date, **Bus Org 402.008, 402.009**
Bylaws, ante
Consent,
Action without meeting, **Bus Org 6.102, 6.201 et seq.**
Telecommunications, **Bus Org 22.002**
Conversion, **Bus Org 22.256**
Delivery, action without meeting, **Bus Org 6.203**
Directors, ante
Emergencies, **Bus Org 3.251 et seq.**
Exchange of property, **Bus Org 22.257**
Facsimile, notice, **Bus Org 6.051**
Foreign states, location, **Bus Org 6.001**
Fundamental business transactions, **Bus Org 22.253**
Internet, **Bus Org 6.002**
Location, **Bus Org 6.001**
Mail and mailing, notice, **Bus Org 6.051**
Merger and consolidation, **Bus Org 22.253**
Notice, **Bus Org 6.051 et seq., 22.156**
Action without meeting, **Bus Org 6.204**
Bylaws, **Bus Org 22.157**
Objections and exceptions, **Bus Org 6.003**
Notice, waiver, **Bus Org 6.053**
Organization, **Bus Org 22.104**
Record date, **Bus Org 6.101 et seq., 22.163**
Records and recordation, **Bus Org 6.002**
Shares and shareholders, post
Telecommunications, **Bus Org 6.002, 22.002**
Unincorporated nonprofit associations, post

NONPROFIT CORPORATIONS
—Cont'd
Meetings—Cont'd
Video recordings, **Bus Org 6.002**
Waiver, notice, **Bus Org 6.052**
Objections and exceptions, **Bus Org 6.053**
Winding up, **Bus Org 22.303**
Members, **Bus Org 22.151 et seq.**
Certificate of formation, amendments, **Bus Org 22.105**
Classification, **Bus Org 22.151**
Conflict of interest, contracts, **Bus Org 22.230**
Contracts, conflict of interest, **Bus Org 22.230**
Cumulative voting, **Bus Org 22.161, 22.162**
Elections, **Bus Org 22.158 et seq.**
Indebtedness, privileges and immunities, **Bus Org 22.152**
Inspection and inspectors, elections, lists, **Bus Org 22.158**
Lists, elections, **Bus Org 22.158**
Managers and management, **Bus Org 22.202**
Meetings, **Bus Org 22.153 et seq.**
Numbers and numbering, elections, **Bus Org 22.160**
Privileges and immunities, **Bus Org 22.152**
Proxies, elections, **Bus Org 22.160**
Quorum, **Bus Org 22.159**
Merger and consolidation, **Bus Org 10.001 et seq., 22.251**
Abandonment, **Bus Org 10.201, 10.202, 10.203**
Acceptance, certificates and certification, **Bus Org 10.156**
Allocations, property, **Bus Org 10.003**
Business Organizations Code, mandatory application date, **Bus Org 402.010**
Certificate of formation, **Bus Org 3.005, 3.006, 10.002**
Certificates and certification, **Bus Org 10.151 et seq.**
Dissenting shareholders, **Bus Org 10.351 et seq.**
Effect, **Bus Org 10.008**
Effective date, **Bus Org 10.007**
Elections, **Bus Org 22.164**
Filing,
Certificates and certification, **Bus Org 10.153**
Fees, **Bus Org 4.151, 4.153**
Holding companies, **Bus Org 10.005**
Meetings, **Bus Org 22.253**
Names, **Bus Org 10.002**
Plans and specifications, **Bus Org 10.001 et seq.**
Property, allocations, **Bus Org 10.003**
Reorganization, **Bus Org 10.301 et seq.**
Status, **Bus Org 10.010**
Subsidiaries, **Bus Org 10.006**
Certificates and certification, **Bus Org 10.152**

NONPROFIT CORPORATIONS
—Cont'd
Merger and consolidation—Cont'd
Time, effective date, **Bus Org 10.007**
Unincorporated nonprofit associations, post
Misconduct, damages, **Bus Org 7.001**
Money, **Bus Org 1.009**
Monopolies and unfair trade, application of law, **Bus Org 10.901**
Mortgages, **Bus Org 2.101, 22.254**
Powers and duties, **Bus Org 2.104**
Receivers and receivership, **Bus Org 11.403**
Unincorporated nonprofit associations, post
Motions, trusts and trustees, privileges and immunities, judgments and decrees, **Bus Org 2.106**
Names, **Bus Org 5.001 et seq.**
Assumed or fictitious names, **Bus Org 5.051 et seq.**
Certificate of formation, **Bus Org 3.005**
Amendments, **Bus Org 3.053, 3.056**
Conversion, **Bus Org 10.103**
Deception, **Bus Org 5.052**
Directors, **Bus Org 22.205**
Exchange of property, plans and specifications, **Bus Org 10.052**
Fees, reservation, **Bus Org 5.101**
Withdrawal, **Bus Org 5.1041**
Filing,
Fees, **Bus Org 4.151, 4.153**
Registration, **Bus Org 5.152**
Foreign corporations, ante
Fraud, **Bus Org 5.052**
Identity and identification, same or similar, **Bus Org 5.053**
Lottery, **Bus Org 5.061**
Merger and consolidation, **Bus Org 10.002**
Notice, **Bus Org 5.001**
Registration, **Bus Org 5.151 et seq.**
Renewal,
Registration, **Bus Org 5.155**
Reservation, **Bus Org 5.105**
Reservation, **Bus Org 5.101 et seq.**
Same or similar, **Bus Org 5.053**
Registration, **Bus Org 5.153**
Reservation, **Bus Org 5.102**
Termination, reinstatement, **Bus Org 11.203**
Time,
Registration, **Bus Org 5.154**
Reservation, **Bus Org 5.104**
Trademarks and trade names, **Bus Org 5.001**
Transfers, reservation, **Bus Org 5.106**
Unincorporated nonprofit associations, post
University Cooperative Society, **Bus Org 251.452**
Veterans organizations, **Bus Org 5.062**
Negligence, damages, **Bus Org 301.010**
Nonfiling, certificate of formation, **Bus Org 3.002**

NONPROFIT CORPORATIONS
—Cont'd
Notice,
Agent for service of process, **Bus Org 5.252, 5.253**
Certificate of formation, amendments, **Bus Org 22.105 et seq.**
Conversion, **Bus Org 10.101**
Directors, meetings, **Bus Org 22.217**
Foreign corporations, ante
Fundamental business transactions, meetings, **Bus Org 22.253**
Guaranty, fraud, **Bus Org 2.104**
Indemnity, orders of court, **Bus Org 8.052**
Insolvency, **Bus Org 12.256**
Liens and incumbrances,
Foreclosure, **Bus Org 12.256**
State, **Bus Org 12.201**
Meetings, ante
Names, **Bus Org 5.001**
Organization, meetings, **Bus Org 22.104**
Receivers and receivership, claims, **Bus Org 11.407**
Registered agent, resignation, **Bus Org 5.204**
Reorganization, **Bus Org 10.301**
Reports, **Bus Org 22.358**
Filing, forfeitures, **Bus Org 22.361**
Shares and shareholders, post
Termination, post
Unincorporated nonprofit associations, post
Winding up, post
Numbers and numbering,
Certificate of formation, amendments, **Bus Org 22.108**
Dentists and dentistry, health service corporations, directors, **Bus Org 22.052**
Directors, ante
Members, elections, **Bus Org 22.160**
Oaths and affirmations, interrogatories, answer, **Bus Org 12.002**
Objections and exceptions, meetings, **Bus Org 6.003**
Notice, waiver, **Bus Org 6.053**
Offenses. Crimes and offenses, generally, ante
Officers and employees, **Bus Org 3.101 et seq., 22.231 et seq.**
Agent for service of process, **Bus Org 5.255**
Committees, **Bus Org 22.231**
Compensation and salaries, **Bus Org 2.101, 22.054**
Conflict of interest, contracts, **Bus Org 22.230**
Contracts, conflict of interest, **Bus Org 22.230**
Damages, **Bus Org 7.001, 22.235, 301.010**
Application of law, **Bus Org 1.104**
Dual office holding, **Bus Org 3.103, 22.231**
Elections, **Bus Org 2.101, 3.103, 22.232**
Good faith, **Bus Org 3.105**

NONPROFIT CORPORATIONS —Cont'd
Officers and employees—Cont'd
Indemnity, **Bus Org 2.101, 7.001, 8.001 et seq.**
Licenses and permits, **Bus Org 301.006**
Loans, **Bus Org 2.101, 22.055**
Religious organizations and societies, good faith, **Bus Org 22.234**
Removal, **Bus Org 3.104**
Retirement and pensions, **Bus Org 2.101**
Terms of office, **Bus Org 22.232**
Trusts and trustees, privileges and immunities, **Bus Org 2.106**
Unincorporated nonprofit associations, post
Vice president, agent for service of process, **Bus Org 5.255**
Offices, **Bus Org 2.101**
Changes, filing, fines and penalties, **Bus Org 21.802**
Registered offices, generally, post
Reorganization, **Bus Org 10.301**
Unincorporated nonprofit associations, post
Omissions, certificate of formation, restatement, **Bus Org 3.059**
Open records, interrogatories, **Bus Org 12.003**
Orders of court,
Receivers and receivership, **Bus Org 11.402**
Liquidation, **Bus Org 11.405**
Unincorporated nonprofit associations, post
Organization, meetings, **Bus Org 22.104**
Osteopaths, health organization corporations, **Bus Org 22.056**
Parties, receivers and receivership, **Bus Org 11.411**
Payment,
Dividends, **Bus Org 22.053**
Termination,
Claims, **Bus Org 11.354**
Taxation, **Bus Org 11.101**
Penalties. Fines and penalties, generally, ante
Permissive indemnification, **Bus Org 8.101 et seq.**
Personal property, **Bus Org 2.101**
Disposition, **Bus Org 10.251 et seq.**
Reorganization, **Bus Org 10.301**
Shares and shareholders, **Bus Org 21.801**
Unincorporated nonprofit associations, post
Photography and pictures, consent, meetings, action without meeting, **Bus Org 6.205**
Physician assistants, health organization corporations, **Bus Org 22.0561**
Physicians and surgeons, health organization corporations, **Bus Org 22.056**
Plans and specifications,
Conversion, **Bus Org 10.101 et seq.**

NONPROFIT CORPORATIONS —Cont'd
Plans and specifications—Cont'd
Exchange of property, **Bus Org 10.051 et seq.**
Merger and consolidation, **Bus Org 10.001 et seq.**
Unincorporated nonprofit associations, post
Winding up, distribution and distributors, **Bus Org 22.305**
Pledges, **Bus Org 22.254**
Elections, **Bus Org 6.156**
Podiatrists, health organization corporations, **Bus Org 22.056**
Political subdivisions, service of process, **Bus Org 5.257**
Powers and duties, **Bus Org 2.101 et seq.**
Directors, trusts and trustees, **Bus Org 22.223**
Receivers and receivership, **Bus Org 11.406**
President, **Bus Org 22.231**
Agent for service of process, **Bus Org 5.255**
Prior laws, Business Organizations Code, **Bus Org 401.001 et seq.**
Priorities and preferences,
Business Organizations Code, application of law, **Bus Org 1.106**
Certificate of formation, shares and shareholders, **Bus Org 3.007**
Privileges and immunities,
Assets, distribution and distributors, damages, **Bus Org 22.226, 22.228**
Directors, **Bus Org 22.221**
Members, indebtedness, **Bus Org 22.152**
Property, disposition, **Bus Org 10.254**
Registered agents, **Bus Org 5.208**
Trusts and trustees, **Bus Org 2.106**
Probate proceedings, elections, **Bus Org 6.154**
Proceedings. Actions and proceedings, generally, ante
Process. Service of process, generally, post
Profit sharing, officers and employees, **Bus Org 2.101**
Property, **Bus Org 2.101**
Disposition, **Bus Org 10.251 et seq.**
Reorganization, **Bus Org 10.301**
Exchange of property, generally, ante
Liens and incumbrances,
Foreclosure, **Bus Org 12.252 et seq.**
State, **Bus Org 12.201**
Merger and consolidation, allocations, **Bus Org 10.003**
Personal property, generally, ante
Real estate, generally, post
Unincorporated nonprofit associations, post
Proxies,
Directors, **Bus Org 22.214 et seq.**
Members, elections, **Bus Org 22.160**

NONPROFIT CORPORATIONS —Cont'd
Publication,
Termination, involuntary termination, **Bus Org 11.310**
Winding up, involuntary winding up, **Bus Org 11.310**
Purchases and purchasing,
Indemnity, insurance, **Bus Org 8.151**
Title to property, **Bus Org 301.008**
Purposes, **Bus Org 2.001 et seq., 22.051**
Certificate of formation, **Bus Org 3.005**
Quo warranto, insolvency, **Bus Org 12.253 et seq.**
Quorum,
Directors, **Bus Org 22.213**
Members, **Bus Org 22.159**
Real estate, **Bus Org 2.101**
Disposition, **Bus Org 10.251 et seq.**
Reorganization, **Bus Org 10.301**
Officers and employees, loans, **Bus Org 22.055**
Records and recordation, deeds and conveyances, **Bus Org 10.253**
Unincorporated nonprofit associations, post
Receipts, termination, claims, **Bus Org 11.352**
Receivers and receivership, **Bus Org 11.401 et seq.**
Actions and proceedings, **Bus Org 11.406**
Ancillary receiverships, **Bus Org 11.409**
Appointments, **Bus Org 11.401 et seq.**
Bonds (officers and fiduciaries), **Bus Org 11.406**
Citizens and citizenship, **Bus Org 11.406**
Claims, filing, **Bus Org 11.407**
Compensation and salaries, **Bus Org 11.408**
Discharge, **Bus Org 11.412**
Elections, **Bus Org 6.155**
Filing, claims, **Bus Org 11.407**
Foreign entities, **Bus Org 11.409, 11.410**
Fraud, **Bus Org 11.403**
Judgments and decrees, termination, **Bus Org 11.412**
Jurisdiction, **Bus Org 11.402 et seq.**
Liens and incumbrances, state, **Bus Org 12.201**
Liquidation, ante
Mortgages, **Bus Org 11.403**
Notice, claims, **Bus Org 11.407**
Orders of court, **Bus Org 11.402**
Liquidation, **Bus Org 11.405**
Parties, **Bus Org 11.411**
Powers and duties, **Bus Org 11.406**
Registration, **Bus Org 11.406**
Rehabilitation, **Bus Org 11.404**
State, **Bus Org 12.251**
Termination, **Bus Org 11.403**
Judgments and decrees, **Bus Org 11.412**
Unincorporated nonprofit associations, post

NONPROFIT CORPORATIONS
—Cont'd
Record date, **Bus Org 6.101 et seq.**
Meetings, **Bus Org 22.163**
Records and recordation, **Bus Org 3.151 et seq.**
Audits and auditors, **Bus Org 22.356**
Certified copies, filing, **Bus Org 4.005**
Confidential or privileged information, **Bus Org 12.154**
Disclosure, **Bus Org 12.154**
Examinations and examiners, **Bus Org 3.153, 12.151 et seq.**
Inspection and inspectors, **Bus Org 3.152, 22.351**
Interrogatories, open records, **Bus Org 12.003**
Meetings, **Bus Org 6.002**
Real estate, deeds and conveyances, **Bus Org 10.253**
Record date, **Bus Org 6.101 et seq.**
Reorganization, **Bus Org 10.301**
Service of process, **Bus Org 5.254**
Signatures, **Bus Org 1.007**
Special purpose corporations, filing, **Bus Org 23.002**
Termination, removal, **Bus Org 11.104**
Time, record date, **Bus Org 6.101 et seq.**
Unincorporated nonprofit associations, post
Registered agent, **Bus Org 5.200 et seq.**
Changes, **Bus Org 5.202, 5.203**
Filing, fines and penalties, **Bus Org 21.802**
Reorganization, **Bus Org 10.301**
Resignation, **Bus Org 5.204**
Unincorporated nonprofit associations, post
Registered offices, **Bus Org 5.200 et seq.**
Changes, **Bus Org 5.202**
Filing, fines and penalties, **Bus Org 21.802**
Unincorporated nonprofit associations, post
Registration,
Foreign corporations, ante
Names, **Bus Org 5.151 et seq.**
Receivers and receivership, **Bus Org 11.406**
Revocation or suspension, reports, forfeitures, **Bus Org 22.364**
Unincorporated nonprofit associations, post
Rehabilitation, receivers and receivership, **Bus Org 11.404**
Reinstatement,
Elections, **Bus Org 22.164**
Reports, forfeitures, **Bus Org 22.365**
Termination, post
Winding up, **Bus Org 22.301 et seq.**
Rejection, registered agents, **Bus Org 5.205**
Remand,
Termination, involuntary termination, **Bus Org 11.307**

NONPROFIT CORPORATIONS
—Cont'd
Remand—Cont'd
Winding up, involuntary winding up, **Bus Org 11.307**
Removal from office,
Directors, **Bus Org 22.208, 22.211**
Officers and employees, **Bus Org 3.104**
Renewal, names,
Registration, **Bus Org 5.155**
Reservation, **Bus Org 5.105**
Reorganization, **Bus Org 10.301 et seq.**
Business Organizations Code, mandatory application date, **Bus Org 402.010**
Repeals,
Business Organizations Code, statutes, **Bus Org 1.054**
Bylaws, **Bus Org 22.102**
Reports, **Bus Org 22.357 et seq.**
Filing, fees, **Bus Org 4.153**
Indemnity, **Bus Org 8.152**
Officers and employees, good faith, **Bus Org 3.102, 3.105**
Reservation, names, **Bus Org 5.101 et seq.**
Resignation,
Directors, notice, **Bus Org 22.2111**
Managers and management, **Bus Org 301.008**
Registered agent, **Bus Org 5.204**
Resolutions, indemnity, **Bus Org 8.103**
Restatement, certificate of formation, **Bus Org 3.057 et seq.**
Retirement and pensions, officers and employees, **Bus Org 2.101**
Review. Appeal and review, generally, ante
Revocation or suspension,
Directors, proxies, **Bus Org 22.216**
Reinstatement, **Bus Org 402.013**
Termination, fraud, **Bus Org 11.153**
Winding up, **Bus Org 11.151, 22.301 et seq.**
Salaries. Compensation and salaries, generally, ante
Sales, **Bus Org 10.251 et seq.**
Assets, ante
Property, **Bus Org 2.101**
Receivers and receivership, **Bus Org 11.413**
Reorganization, **Bus Org 10.301**
Securities, exemptions, **Bus Org 301.011**
Unincorporated nonprofit associations, post
Same or similar. Names, ante
Seals, **Bus Org 2.101**
Indebtedness, certificates and certification, **Bus Org 2.114**
Shares and shareholders, certificates and certification, **Bus Org 3.202**
Unincorporated nonprofit associations, post
Secretaries, **Bus Org 22.231**
Secretary of state, agent for service of process, **Bus Org 5.251 et seq.**

NONPROFIT CORPORATIONS
—Cont'd
Securities, **Bus Org 2.101**
Investments, **Bus Org 22.224**
Powers and duties, **Bus Org 2.104**
Sales, exemptions, **Bus Org 301.011**
Sequestration, state, **Bus Org 12.259**
Service of process, **Bus Org 5.251 et seq.**
Foreign corporations, ante
Reorganization, **Bus Org 10.301**
Termination, involuntary termination, **Bus Org 11.309**
Unincorporated nonprofit associations, post
Winding up, involuntary winding up, **Bus Org 11.309**
Shares and shareholders,
Abandonment, exchange of property, **Bus Org 10.201, 10.202, 10.203**
Acceptance, exchange of property, certificates and certification, **Bus Org 10.156**
Appointments, dissenting shareholders, appraisal and appraisers, **Bus Org 10.361**
Appraisals and appraisers, dissenting shareholders, **Bus Org 10.354 et seq.**
Assignments, certificates and certification, **Bus Org 3.201**
Books and papers, dissenting shareholders, fair market value, **Bus Org 10.363**
Certificate of formation, numbers and numbering, **Bus Org 3.007**
Certificates and certification, **Bus Org 3.201 et seq.**
Exchange of property, **Bus Org 10.151 et seq.**
Compensation and salaries, dissenting shareholders, appraisals and appraisers, **Bus Org 10.365**
Computation, dissenting shareholders, fair market value, **Bus Org 10.362**
Contracts, elections, **Bus Org 6.252**
Costs, dissenting shareholders, appraisals and appraisers, **Bus Org 10.365**
Delivery,
Certificates and certification, **Bus Org 3.204**
Meetings, action without meeting, **Bus Org 6.203**
Demand, dissenting shareholders, fair market value, **Bus Org 10.357 et seq.**
Dissenting shareholders, **Bus Org 10.351 et seq.**
Appointments, appraisal and appraisers, **Bus Org 10.361**
Appraisals and appraisers, **Bus Org 10.354 et seq.**
Books and papers, fair market value, **Bus Org 10.363**
Compensation and salaries, appraisals and appraisers, **Bus Org 10.365**

NONPROFIT CORPORATIONS
—Cont'd
Shares and shareholders—Cont'd
Dissenting shareholders—Cont'd
Computation, fair market value, **Bus Org 10.362**
Costs, appraisals and appraisers, **Bus Org 10.365**
Definitions, **Bus Org 10.352**
Demand, fair market value, **Bus Org 10.357 et seq.**
Exclusive remedy, **Bus Org 10.368**
Fair market value, demand, **Bus Org 10.357 et seq.**
Forms, **Bus Org 10.353**
Hearings, fair market value, **Bus Org 10.361**
Investigations and investigators, fair market value, **Bus Org 10.363**
Notice, **Bus Org 10.353, 10.355**
Objections and exceptions, appraisals and appraisers, **Bus Org 10.364**
Perfection, **Bus Org 10.356**
Petitions, fair market value, **Bus Org 10.361**
Records and recordation, fair market value, **Bus Org 10.363**
Demand, **Bus Org 10.359**
Reorganization, **Bus Org 10.304**
Termination, **Bus Org 10.367**
Title to property, **Bus Org 10.366**
Withdrawal, **Bus Org 10.357**
Distribution and distributors, record date, **Bus Org 6.101 et seq.**
Duplicates and copies, certificates and certification, **Bus Org 3.202**
Elections,
Contracts, **Bus Org 6.252**
Trusts and trustees, **Bus Org 6.251**
Evidence, certificates and certification, **Bus Org 3.201**
Examinations and examiners, elections, contracts, **Bus Org 6.252**
Exchange of property, **Bus Org 10.051 et seq.**
Abandonment, **Bus Org 10.201, 10.202, 10.203**
Acceptance, certificates and certification, **Bus Org 10.156**
Certificates and certification, **Bus Org 10.151 et seq.**
Filing, certificates and certification, **Bus Org 10.153**
Exclusive remedy, dissenting shareholders, **Bus Org 10.368**
Facsimile, certificates and certification, **Bus Org 3.203**
Fair market value, dissenting shareholders, demand, **Bus Org 10.357 et seq.**
Filing, exchange of property, certificates and certification, **Bus Org 10.153**
Forms,
Certificates and certification, **Bus Org 3.202**

NONPROFIT CORPORATIONS
—Cont'd
Shares and shareholders—Cont'd
Forms—Cont'd
Dissenting shareholders, **Bus Org 10.353**
Hearings, dissenting shareholders, fair market value, **Bus Org 10.361**
Investigations and investigators, dissenting shareholders, fair market value, **Bus Org 10.363**
Investments, **Bus Org 22.224**
Meetings,
Action without meeting, **Bus Org 6.102**
Consent, **Bus Org 6.201 et seq.**
Consent, action without meeting, **Bus Org 6.102, 6.201 et seq.**
Delivery, action without meeting, **Bus Org 6.203**
Notice, action without meeting, **Bus Org 6.204**
Notice,
Dissenting shareholders, **Bus Org 10.353, 10.355**
Meetings, action without meeting, **Bus Org 6.204**
Uncertificated shares, **Bus Org 3.205**
Objections and exceptions, dissenting shareholders, appraisals and appraisers, **Bus Org 10.364**
Perfection, dissenting shareholders, **Bus Org 10.356**
Personal property, **Bus Org 21.801**
Petitions, dissenting shareholders, fair market value, **Bus Org 10.361**
Record date, **Bus Org 6.101 et seq.**
Records and recordation, dissenting shareholders, fair market value, **Bus Org 10.363**
Demand, **Bus Org 10.359**
Reorganization, dissenting shareholders, **Bus Org 10.304**
Seals, certificates and certification, **Bus Org 3.202**
Signatures, certificates and certification, **Bus Org 3.203**
Termination, dissenting shareholders, **Bus Org 10.367**
Time, record date, **Bus Org 6.101 et seq.**
Title to property, dissenting shareholders, **Bus Org 10.366**
Transfers, certificates and certification, **Bus Org 3.201**
Trusts and trustees, elections, **Bus Org 6.251**
Uncertificated shares, **Bus Org 3.201**
Notice, **Bus Org 3.205**
Unincorporated nonprofit associations, post
Withdrawal, dissenting shareholders, **Bus Org 10.357**
Signatures, **Bus Org 1.007**
Certificate of formation, ante
Filing, **Bus Org 4.001**

NONPROFIT CORPORATIONS
—Cont'd
Signatures—Cont'd
Filing—Cont'd
Corrections, certificates and certification, **Bus Org 4.101**
Indebtedness, certificates and certification, **Bus Org 2.114**
Reorganization, **Bus Org 10.302**
Shares and shareholders, certificates and certification, **Bus Org 3.203**
Unincorporated nonprofit associations, post
Special meetings, **Bus Org 22.155**
Special purpose corporations, **Bus Org 23.001 et seq.**
Specifications. Plans and specifications, generally, ante
Standards, directors, **Bus Org 22.221**
State,
Liens and incumbrances, **Bus Org 12.201**
Receivers and receivership, **Bus Org 12.251**
State agencies, audits and auditors, **Bus Org 22.356**
Statements,
Certificate of formation, ante
Officers and employees, good faith, **Bus Org 3.102, 3.105**
Taxation, certificate of formation, **Bus Org 2.107**
Termination,
Certificate of termination, **Bus Org 11.105**
Claims, **Bus Org 11.352**
Unincorporated nonprofit associations, post
Status, merger and consolidation, **Bus Org 10.010**
Statute of limitations, termination, claims, **Bus Org 11.359**
Statutes, Business Organizations Code, construction of laws, **Bus Org 1.006, 1.051 et seq.**
Subsidiaries, merger and consolidation, **Bus Org 10.006**
Certificates and certification, **Bus Org 10.152**
Summons, unincorporated nonprofit associations, **Bus Org 252.013**
Supersedeas or stay,
Termination, involuntary termination, **Bus Org 11.306**
Winding up, involuntary winding up, **Bus Org 11.306**
Supervision, winding up, **Bus Org 11.054**
Suspension. Revocation or suspension, generally, ante
Taxation,
Certificate of formation, statements, **Bus Org 2.107**
Service of process, **Bus Org 5.257**
Termination,
Forfeitures, reinstatement, **Bus Org 11.254, 402.013**
Payment, **Bus Org 11.101**

NONPROFIT CORPORATIONS —Cont'd
Taxation—Cont'd
Unincorporated nonprofit associations, post
Telecommunications, meetings, **Bus Org 6.002, 22.002**
Telephone cooperative corporations, status, **Util 162.059**
Termination, **Bus Org 11.001 et seq.**
Abatement of actions and proceedings, involuntary termination, **Bus Org 11.304**
Actions and proceedings, involuntary termination, **Bus Org 11.303**
Appeal and review, involuntary termination, **Bus Org 11.307**
Business Organizations Code, mandatory application date, **Bus Org 402.011**
Certificates and certification, **Bus Org 11.101 et seq.**
Involuntary termination, **Bus Org 11.252**
Reinstatement, **Bus Org 11.202**
Certified copies, involuntary termination, judgments and decrees, **Bus Org 11.414**
Claims, **Bus Org 11.351 et seq.**
Crimes and offenses, involuntary termination, **Bus Org 11.301 et seq.**
Deposits, claims, **Bus Org 11.352**
Discharge, claims, **Bus Org 11.353**
Effective date, **Bus Org 11.102, 11.103**
Claims, **Bus Org 11.356 et seq.**
Reinstatement, **Bus Org 11.204 et seq.**
Errors, reinstatement, **Bus Org 11.201 et seq.**
Escheat, claims, **Bus Org 11.355**
Exemptions, involuntary termination, **Bus Org 11.251**
Filing,
Fines and penalties, **Bus Org 21.802**
Involuntary termination, **Bus Org 11.315**
Fraud,
Involuntary termination, **Bus Org 11.301 et seq.**
Revocation or suspension, **Bus Org 11.153**
Involuntary termination, **Bus Org 11.251 et seq., 11.301 et seq.**
Certified copies, judgments and decrees, **Bus Org 11.414**
Judgments and decrees, **Bus Org 11.301 et seq.**
Involuntary termination, certified copies, **Bus Org 11.414**
Jurisdiction, involuntary termination, **Bus Org 11.308**
Limitation of actions, claims, **Bus Org 11.359**
Names, reinstatement, **Bus Org 11.203**
Notice,
Claims, **Bus Org 11.358**
Escheat, claims, **Bus Org 11.355**

NONPROFIT CORPORATIONS —Cont'd
Termination—Cont'd
Notice—Cont'd
Involuntary termination, **Bus Org 11.251, 11.302, 11.310**
Payment,
Claims, **Bus Org 11.354**
Taxation, **Bus Org 11.101**
Publication, involuntary termination, **Bus Org 11.310**
Receipts, claims, **Bus Org 11.352**
Receivers and receivership, **Bus Org 11.403**
Judgments and decrees, **Bus Org 11.412**
Records and recordation, removal, **Bus Org 11.104**
Reinstatement, **Bus Org 11.201 et seq.**
Involuntary termination, **Bus Org 11.253**
Taxation, forfeitures, **Bus Org 11.254**
Remand, involuntary termination, **Bus Org 11.307**
Reports, forfeitures, **Bus Org 22.364**
Revocation or suspension, fraud, **Bus Org 11.153**
Service of process, involuntary termination, **Bus Org 11.309**
Statements,
Certificate of termination, **Bus Org 11.105**
Claims, **Bus Org 11.352**
Supersedeas or stay, involuntary termination, **Bus Org 11.306**
Taxation,
Forfeitures, reinstatement, **Bus Org 11.254**
Payment, **Bus Org 11.101**
Time,
Involuntary termination, **Bus Org 11.305, 11.313**
Reinstatement, **Bus Org 11.202**
Unincorporated nonprofit associations, post
Venue, involuntary termination, **Bus Org 11.308**
Terms of office,
Directors, **Bus Org 22.208**
Officers and employees, **Bus Org 22.232**
Time,
Business Organizations Code, effective date, **Bus Org 402.001**
Adoption, **Bus Org 402.005**
Certificate of formation, ante
Exchange of property, **Bus Org 10.054, 10.055**
Filing, ante
Financial statements and reports, **Bus Org 22.352**
Inspection and inspectors, **Bus Org 22.353**
Interrogatories, answer, **Bus Org 12.002**
Merger and consolidation, effective date, **Bus Org 10.007**
Organization, meetings, **Bus Org 22.104**

NONPROFIT CORPORATIONS —Cont'd
Time—Cont'd
Record date, **Bus Org 6.101 et seq.**
Reports, **Bus Org 22.357**
Service of process, **Bus Org 5.254**
Termination, ante
Unincorporated nonprofit associations, post
Winding up, post
Title to property, **Bus Org 301.007 et seq.**
Purchases and purchasing, **Bus Org 301.008**
Trademarks and trade names, names, **Bus Org 5.001**
Transfers,
Names, reservation, **Bus Org 5.106**
Property, **Bus Org 10.251 et seq.**
Shares and shareholders, certificates and certification, **Bus Org 3.201**
Title to property, **Bus Org 301.009**
Unincorporated nonprofit associations, post
Transition, Business Organizations Code, **Bus Org 402.001 et seq.**
Treasurers, **Bus Org 22.231**
Trusts and trustees, **Bus Org 22.254**
Directors, powers and duties, **Bus Org 22.223**
Elections, **Bus Org 6.154, 6.251**
Powers and duties, **Bus Org 2.106**
Privileges and immunities, **Bus Org 2.106**
Reorganization, **Bus Org 10.301 et seq.**
Unincorporated nonprofit associations, post
Uncertificated shares, **Bus Org 3.201**
Notice, **Bus Org 3.205**
Underground facility notification corporation, **Util 251.052**
Uniform unincorporated nonprofit associations. Unincorporated nonprofit associations, generally, post
Unincorporated nonprofit associations, **Bus Org 1.001 et seq., 252.001 et seq., 301.001 et seq.**
Abandonment,
Conversion, **Bus Org 10.201, 10.202, 10.203**
Exchange of property, **Bus Org 10.201, 10.202, 10.203**
Filing, **Bus Org 4.057**
Merger and consolidation, **Bus Org 10.201, 10.202, 10.203**
Abatement of actions and proceedings, **Bus Org 252.012**
State, **Bus Org 12.260**
Termination, involuntary termination, **Bus Org 11.304**
Winding up, involuntary winding up, **Bus Org 11.304**
Acceptance, certificates and certification, **Bus Org 10.156**
Accounts and accounting, **Bus Org 3.151 et seq.**
Examinations and examiners, **Bus Org 12.151 et seq.**

NONPROFIT CORPORATIONS
—Cont'd
Unincorporated nonprofit associations
—Cont'd
Acknowledgments,
Certificate of formation, **Bus Org 3.004**
Evidence, **Bus Org 3.001**
Filing, **Bus Org 4.002**
Effective date, delay, **Bus Org 4.059**
Actions and proceedings, **Bus Org 2.101, 252.007**
Certificate of formation, amendments, **Bus Org 3.056**
Guaranty, **Bus Org 2.104**
Indemnity, **Bus Org 8.001 et seq.**
Insolvency, **Bus Org 12.253 et seq.**
Receivers and receivership, **Bus Org 11.406**
Records and recordation, inspection and inspectors, **Bus Org 3.152**
State, liens and incumbrances, **Bus Org 12.201 et seq.**
Termination, involuntary termination, **Bus Org 11.303**
Winding up, **Bus Org 11.052, 11.055**
Involuntary winding up, **Bus Org 11.303**
Address,
Agent for service of process, **Bus Org 252.013**
Certificate of formation, **Bus Org 3.005**
Administrative law and procedure, **Bus Org 252.007**
Advancements, indemnity, expenses and expenditures, **Bus Org 8.104, 8.105**
Reports, **Bus Org 8.152**
Agent for service of process, **Bus Org 5.251 et seq., 252.011, 252.013**
Agents and agencies, changes, filing, fines and penalties, **Bus Org 21.802**
Allocations, merger and consolidation, property, **Bus Org 10.003**
Alternatives, service of process, **Bus Org 5.256**
Amendments,
Agent for service of process, statements, **Bus Org 252.011**
Business Organizations Code, statutes, **Bus Org 1.054**
Certificate of formation, **Bus Org 3.051 et seq.**
Filing, **Bus Org 4.106**
Ancillary receiverships, **Bus Org 11.409**
Answer, interrogatories, time, **Bus Org 12.002**
Antitrust, application of law, **Bus Org 10.901**
Appeal and review,
Filing, **Bus Org 12.004**
Termination, involuntary termination, **Bus Org 11.307**

NONPROFIT CORPORATIONS
—Cont'd
Unincorporated nonprofit associations
—Cont'd
Appeal and review—Cont'd
Winding up, involuntary winding up, **Bus Org 11.307**
Application of law, **Bus Org 252.002, 252.014 et seq.**
Antitrust, **Bus Org 10.901**
Business Organizations Code, foreign countries, foreign states, **Bus Org 1.053**
Certificate of formation, **Bus Org 1.101 et seq.**
Elections, **Bus Org 6.301, 6.302**
Indebtedness, **Bus Org 10.901**
Indemnity, **Bus Org 8.002**
Meetings, **Bus Org 6.301, 6.302**
Monopolies and unfair trade, **Bus Org 10.901**
Reorganization, **Bus Org 10.306**
Appointments, receivers and receivership, **Bus Org 11.401 et seq.**
Appraisals and appraisers, reorganization, **Bus Org 10.304**
Arbitration and award, **Bus Org 252.007**
Assets,
Disposition, **Bus Org 10.251 et seq.**
Reorganization, **Bus Org 10.301**
Liens and incumbrances, state, **Bus Org 12.201**
Winding up, distribution and distributors, **Bus Org 11.053**
Assignments, **Bus Org 10.251 et seq.**
Shares and shareholders, certificates and certification, **Bus Org 3.201**
Assumed or fictitious names, names, **Bus Org 5.051 et seq.**
Attachment, state, **Bus Org 12.259**
Attorney fees,
Filing,
Fines and penalties, **Bus Org 21.802**
Fraud, **Bus Org 4.007**
Records and recordation, inspection and inspectors, **Bus Org 3.152**
Bankruptcy, **Bus Org 10.301 et seq.**
Beneficiaries, **Bus Org 252.004**
Bonds, **Bus Org 2.101**
Reorganization, **Bus Org 10.301**
Bonds (officers and fiduciaries), receivers and receivership, **Bus Org 11.406**
Bonuses, officers and employees, **Bus Org 2.101**
Books and papers, **Bus Org 3.151 et seq., 252.010**
Confidential or privileged information, **Bus Org 12.154**
Disclosure, **Bus Org 12.154**
Duplicates and copies, **Bus Org 12.151 et seq.**
Examinations and examiners, **Bus Org 3.153, 12.151 et seq.**

NONPROFIT CORPORATIONS
—Cont'd
Unincorporated nonprofit associations
—Cont'd
Books and papers—Cont'd
Inspection and inspectors, **Bus Org 3.152**
Powers and duties, limitations, **Bus Org 2.005**
Reorganization, **Bus Org 10.301**
Bylaws, **Bus Org 2.101**
Cancellation,
Agent for service of process, **Bus Org 252.011**
Winding up, **Bus Org 11.152**
Certificate of formation, **Bus Org 3.001 et seq.**
Amendments, **Bus Org 3.051 et seq.**
Application of law, **Bus Org 1.101 et seq.**
Definitions, **Bus Org 1.002**
Merger and consolidation, **Bus Org 10.002**
Reorganization, **Bus Org 10.301 et seq.**
Restatement, **Bus Org 3.057 et seq.**
Certificates and certification,
Acceptance, **Bus Org 10.156**
Conversion, **Bus Org 10.154 et seq.**
Exchange of property, **Bus Org 10.151 et seq.**
Filing,
Corrections, **Bus Org 4.101 et seq.**
Fines and penalties, **Bus Org 21.802**
Indebtedness, **Bus Org 2.114**
Merger and consolidation, **Bus Org 10.151 et seq.**
Shares and shareholders, **Bus Org 3.201 et seq.**
Termination, **Bus Org 11.101 et seq.**
Involuntary termination, **Bus Org 11.252**
Reinstatement, **Bus Org 11.202**
Certified copies,
Filing, **Bus Org 4.005**
Involuntary termination, judgments and decrees, **Bus Org 11.414**
Changes, registered offices, registered agent, **Bus Org 5.202, 5.203**
Citizens and citizenship, receivers and receivership, **Bus Org 11.406**
Claims,
Abatement of actions and proceedings, **Bus Org 252.012**
Members, **Bus Org 252.006**
Receivers and receivership, filing, **Bus Org 11.407**
Termination, **Bus Org 11.351 et seq.**
Compensation and salaries,
Officers and employees, **Bus Org 2.101**
Receivers and receivership, **Bus Org 11.408**
Complaints, **Bus Org 252.013**
Conduct, damages, **Bus Org 7.001**

NONPROFIT CORPORATIONS
—Cont'd
Unincorporated nonprofit associations
—Cont'd
Confidential or privileged information, interrogatories, **Bus Org 12.003**
Conflict of interest, elections, **Bus Org 6.152, 6.153**
Conflict of laws, **Bus Org 252.016**
Consent, duplicates and copies, meetings, action without meeting, **Bus Org 6.205**
Construction of laws, Business Organizations Code, statutes, **Bus Org 1.051 et seq.**
Contracts, **Bus Org 2.101**
Beneficiaries, **Bus Org 252.004**
Damages, **Bus Org 252.006**
Elections, **Bus Org 6.252**
Indebtedness, **Bus Org 2.103**
Winding up, **Bus Org 11.152**
Contributions, definitions, business organizations, **Bus Org 1.002**
Conversion, **Bus Org 10.101 et seq.**
Abandonment, **Bus Org 10.201, 10.202, 10.203**
Acceptance, certificates and certification, **Bus Org 10.156**
Certificates and certification, **Bus Org 10.154 et seq.**
Dissenting shareholders, **Bus Org 10.351 et seq.**
Effective date, **Bus Org 10.105, 10.106**
Filing,
Certificates and certification, **Bus Org 10.155**
Fees, **Bus Org 4.151**
Names, **Bus Org 10.103**
Notice, **Bus Org 10.101**
Plans and specifications, **Bus Org 10.101 et seq.**
Reorganization, **Bus Org 10.301 et seq.**
Corrections, filing, **Bus Org 4.101 et seq.**
Fees, **Bus Org 4.151**
Costs,
Filing,
Fines and penalties, **Bus Org 21.802**
Fraud, **Bus Org 4.007**
Insolvency, dismissal and nonsuit, **Bus Org 12.257**
Liens and incumbrances, foreclosure, dismissal and nonsuit, **Bus Org 12.257**
Crimes and offenses,
Books and papers, examinations and examiners, **Bus Org 12.156**
Damages, **Bus Org 7.001**
Filing, fraud, **Bus Org 4.008**
Termination, involuntary termination, **Bus Org 11.301 et seq.**
Winding up, involuntary winding up, **Bus Org 11.301 et seq.**
Damages, **Bus Org 252.006**

NONPROFIT CORPORATIONS
—Cont'd
Unincorporated nonprofit associations
—Cont'd
Damages—Cont'd
Application of law, **Bus Org 1.104**
Filing, **Bus Org 21.802**
Fraud, **Bus Org 4.007**
Guaranty, **Bus Org 2.104**
Officers and employees, **Bus Org 7.001**
Deception, names, **Bus Org 5.052**
Deeds and conveyances, **Bus Org 10.251 et seq.**
Property, **Bus Org 2.101**
Receivers and receivership, **Bus Org 11.413**
Records and recordation, **Bus Org 10.253**
Defenses, **Bus Org 252.007**
Definitions, **Bus Org 1.002, 252.001**
Indemnity, **Bus Org 8.001**
Termination, **Bus Org 11.001**
Winding up, **Bus Org 11.001**
Delay, filing, effective date, **Bus Org 4.052 et seq.**
Delivery,
Filing, **Bus Org 4.001**
Meetings, action without meeting, **Bus Org 6.203**
Shares and shareholders, certificates and certification, **Bus Org 3.204**
Deposits, termination, claims, **Bus Org 11.352**
Directors,
Agent for service of process, **Bus Org 5.255**
Certificate of formation, **Bus Org 3.007**
Restatement, **Bus Org 3.060**
Damages, **Bus Org 7.001**
Indemnity, **Bus Org 7.001**
Loans, **Bus Org 2.101**
Discharge,
Receivers and receivership, **Bus Org 11.412**
Termination, claims, **Bus Org 11.353**
Winding up, indebtedness, **Bus Org 11.053**
Disclosure, interrogatories, **Bus Org 12.003**
Dismissal and nonsuit,
Insolvency, **Bus Org 12.257**
Liens and incumbrances, foreclosure, **Bus Org 12.257**
Dissolution, **Bus Org 2.101**
Distribution and distributors,
Receivers and receivership, **Bus Org 11.413**
Record date, **Bus Org 6.101 et seq.**
Winding up, assets, **Bus Org 11.053**
Dual office holding, officers and employees, **Bus Org 3.103**
Duplicates and copies,
Agent for service of process, **Bus Org 5.252**

NONPROFIT CORPORATIONS
—Cont'd
Unincorporated nonprofit associations
—Cont'd
Duplicates and copies—Cont'd
Books and papers, **Bus Org 12.151 et seq.**
Consent, meetings, action without meeting, **Bus Org 6.205**
Filing, **Bus Org 4.003**
Records and recordation, **Bus Org 3.152, 252.010**
Shares and shareholders, certificates and certification, **Bus Org 3.202**
Effective date,
Conversion, **Bus Org 10.105, 10.106**
Exchange of property, **Bus Org 10.054, 10.055**
Filing, **Bus Org 4.051 et seq.**
Merger and consolidation, **Bus Org 10.007**
Termination, **Bus Org 11.102, 11.103**
Claims, **Bus Org 11.356 et seq.**
Reinstatement, **Bus Org 11.204 et seq.**
Elections, **Bus Org 6.151 et seq.**
Application of law, **Bus Org 6.301, 6.302**
Conflict of interest, **Bus Org 6.152, 6.153**
Contracts, **Bus Org 6.252**
Estates, **Bus Org 6.154**
Indemnity, **Bus Org 8.103**
Officers and employees, **Bus Org 2.101, 3.103**
Pledges, **Bus Org 6.156**
Probate proceedings, **Bus Org 6.154**
Receivers and receivership, **Bus Org 6.155**
Trusts and trustees, **Bus Org 6.154, 6.251**
Electronic filing, **Bus Org 12.001**
Errors, termination, reinstatement, **Bus Org 11.201 et seq.**
Escheat, termination, claims, **Bus Org 11.355**
Estates, elections, **Bus Org 6.154**
Evidence,
Certificate of formation, acknowledgments, **Bus Org 3.001**
Filing, **Bus Org 4.001**
Indebtedness, fraud, **Bus Org 2.103**
Shares and shareholders, certificates and certification, **Bus Org 3.201**
Examinations and examiners,
Books and papers, **Bus Org 12.151 et seq.**
Elections, contracts, **Bus Org 6.252**
Records and recordation, **Bus Org 3.153, 252.010**
Exchange of property, **Bus Org 2.101, 10.051 et seq.**
Abandonment, **Bus Org 10.201, 10.202, 10.203**
Acceptance, certificates and certification, **Bus Org 10.156**

NONPROFIT CORPORATIONS
—Cont'd
Unincorporated nonprofit associations
—Cont'd
Exchange of property—Cont'd
Certificates and certification, **Bus Org 10.151 et seq.**
Dissenting shareholders, **Bus Org 10.351 et seq.**
Filing,
Certificates and certification, **Bus Org 10.153**
Fees, **Bus Org 4.151**
Reorganization, **Bus Org 10.301**
Voluntary, **Bus Org 10.902**
Exemptions,
Guaranty, powers and duties, **Bus Org 2.104**
Interrogatories, **Bus Org 12.002**
Termination, involuntary termination, **Bus Org 11.251**
Expenses and expenditures, indemnity, **Bus Org 8.001 et seq.**
Facsimile,
Consent, meetings, action without meeting, **Bus Org 6.205**
Filing, **Bus Org 4.003**
Indebtedness, certificates and certification, **Bus Org 2.114**
Meetings, notice, **Bus Org 6.051**
Seals, **Bus Org 2.101**
Shares and shareholders, certificates and certification, **Bus Org 3.203**
Fees,
Agent for service of process, statements, **Bus Org 252.011**
Filing, **Bus Org 4.159**
Names, reservation, **Bus Org 5.101**
Withdrawal, **Bus Org 5.1041**
Statements, real estate, transfers, **Bus Org 252.005**
Filing, **Bus Org 4.001 et seq., 12.001 et seq.**
Abandonment, **Bus Org 4.057**
Acknowledgments, **Bus Org 4.002**
Effective date, delay, **Bus Org 4.059**
Agent for service of process, statements, **Bus Org 252.011**
Amendments, **Bus Org 4.106**
Appeal and review, **Bus Org 12.004**
Assumed or fictitious names, **Bus Org 5.051**
Attorney fees,
Fines and penalties, **Bus Org 21.802**
Fraud, **Bus Org 4.007**
Certificate of formation, **Bus Org 3.001 et seq.**
Certificates and certification,
Abandonment, **Bus Org 4.057**
Corrections, **Bus Org 4.101 et seq.**
Certified copies, **Bus Org 4.005**
Conversion, certificates and certification, **Bus Org 10.155**
Corrections, **Bus Org 4.101 et seq.**
Fees, **Bus Org 4.151**

NONPROFIT CORPORATIONS
—Cont'd
Unincorporated nonprofit associations
—Cont'd
Filing—Cont'd
Costs,
Fines and penalties, **Bus Org 21.802**
Fraud, **Bus Org 4.007**
Damages, **Bus Org 21.802**
Fraud, **Bus Org 4.007**
Delay, effective date, **Bus Org 4.052 et seq.**
Delivery, **Bus Org 4.001**
Duplicates and copies, **Bus Org 4.003**
Effective date, **Bus Org 4.051 et seq.**
Electronic filing, **Bus Org 12.001**
Evidence, **Bus Org 4.001**
Facsimile, **Bus Org 4.003**
Fees, **Bus Org 4.159**
Fines and penalties, **Bus Org 21.802**
Fraud, **Bus Org 4.008**
Forms, **Bus Org 4.006**
Fraud, **Bus Org 4.007, 4.008**
Interrogatories, **Bus Org 12.002, 12.003**
Jurisdiction, fines and penalties, **Bus Org 21.802**
Limitations,
Corrections, **Bus Org 4.102**
Effective date, delay, **Bus Org 4.058**
Names, registration, **Bus Org 5.152**
Real estate investment trusts, **Bus Org 4.009**
Receivers and receivership, claims, **Bus Org 11.407**
Registered agent, resignation, **Bus Org 5.204**
Service of process, **Bus Org 21.802**
Signatures, **Bus Org 4.001**
Corrections, certificates and certification, **Bus Org 4.101**
Termination, involuntary termination, **Bus Org 11.315**
Time, **Bus Org 4.004**
Corrections, **Bus Org 4.105**
Effective date, **Bus Org 4.051 et seq.**
Fines and penalties, **Bus Org 21.802**
Winding up, involuntary winding up, **Bus Org 11.315**
Financial statements and reports, officers and employees, good faith, **Bus Org 3.102, 3.105**
Fines and penalties,
Books and papers, examinations and examiners, **Bus Org 12.156**
Filing, **Bus Org 21.802**
Fraud, **Bus Org 4.008**
Foreclosure, liens and incumbrances, **Bus Org 12.252 et seq.**
Foreign associations, registration, exemptions, **Bus Org 9.002**

NONPROFIT CORPORATIONS
—Cont'd
Unincorporated nonprofit associations
—Cont'd
Foreign countries,
Business Organizations Code, application of law, **Bus Org 1.053**
Certificate of formation, application of law, **Bus Org 1.102**
Foreign states,
Business Organizations Code, application of law, **Bus Org 1.053**
Certificate of formation, application of law, **Bus Org 1.102**
Meetings, location, **Bus Org 6.001**
Forfeitures, books and papers, examinations and examiners, **Bus Org 12.155**
Forms,
Agent for service of process, statements, **Bus Org 252.011**
Filing, **Bus Org 4.006**
Shares and shareholders, certificates and certification, **Bus Org 3.202**
Fraud,
Filing, **Bus Org 4.007, 4.008**
Guaranty, **Bus Org 2.104**
Indebtedness, evidence, **Bus Org 2.103**
Names, **Bus Org 5.052**
Receivers and receivership, **Bus Org 11.403**
Termination,
Involuntary termination, **Bus Org 11.301 et seq.**
Revocation or suspension, **Bus Org 11.153**
Winding up, involuntary winding up, **Bus Org 11.301 et seq.**
Frauds, statute of, powers and duties, **Bus Org 2.112**
Garnishment, state, **Bus Org 12.259**
Gifts, **Bus Org 2.101**
Good faith,
Damages, **Bus Org 7.001**
Officers and employees, **Bus Org 3.102, 3.105**
Guaranty, **Bus Org 2.101**
Powers and duties, **Bus Org 2.104**
Holding companies, merger and consolidation, **Bus Org 10.005**
Identity and identification, names, same or similar, **Bus Org 5.053**
Incentives, officers and employees, **Bus Org 2.101**
Indebtedness, **Bus Org 2.101, 2.103**
Application of law, **Bus Org 10.901**
Certificates and certification, **Bus Org 2.114**
Winding up, discharge, **Bus Org 11.053**
Indemnity,
Insurance, **Bus Org 8.151**
Mandatory, **Bus Org 8.051**
Officers and employees, **Bus Org 2.101, 7.001, 8.001 et seq.**
Orders of court, **Bus Org 8.052**

NONPROFIT CORPORATIONS —Cont'd
Unincorporated nonprofit associations —Cont'd
Indemnity—Cont'd
Permissive indemnification, **Bus Org 8.101 et seq.**
Reports, **Bus Org 8.152**
Injunctions,
Guaranty, **Bus Org 2.104**
State, **Bus Org 12.259**
Insolvency, actions and proceedings, **Bus Org 12.253 et seq.**
Inspection and inspectors,
Books and papers, **Bus Org 12.151 et seq.**
Records and recordation, **Bus Org 3.152, 252.010**
Insurance, indemnity, **Bus Org 2.101, 8.151**
Internal affairs, **Bus Org 1.105**
Internet, meetings, **Bus Org 6.002**
Interrogatories, **Bus Org 12.002, 12.003**
Intervention, **Bus Org 252.007**
Investigations and investigators, **Bus Org 252.010**
Investments, **Bus Org 2.101**
Involuntary termination,
Certified copies, judgments and decrees, **Bus Org 11.414**
Termination, **Bus Org 11.251 et seq.**
Judgments and decrees, **Bus Org 252.008**
Receivers and receivership, termination, **Bus Org 11.412**
Reorganization, **Bus Org 10.305**
Termination, **Bus Org 11.301 et seq.**
Involuntary termination, certified copies, **Bus Org 11.414**
Winding up, **Bus Org 11.301 et seq.**
Jurisdiction,
Filing, fines and penalties, **Bus Org 21.802**
Insolvency, **Bus Org 12.253**
Liens and incumbrances, foreclosure, **Bus Org 12.253**
Receivers and receivership, **Bus Org 11.402 et seq.**
Reorganization, **Bus Org 10.302**
Termination, involuntary termination, **Bus Org 11.308**
Winding up, involuntary winding up, **Bus Org 11.308**
Leases, **Bus Org 2.101, 10.251 et seq.**
Reorganization, **Bus Org 10.301**
Liens and incumbrances,
Foreclosure, **Bus Org 12.252 et seq.**
Property, **Bus Org 252.003 et seq.**
State, **Bus Org 12.201**
Limitation of actions, termination, claims, **Bus Org 11.359**
Limitations,
Filing,
Corrections, **Bus Org 4.102**
Effective date, delay, **Bus Org 4.058**
Indemnity, **Bus Org 8.003, 8.004**

NONPROFIT CORPORATIONS —Cont'd
Unincorporated nonprofit associations —Cont'd
Limitations—Cont'd
Powers and duties, **Bus Org 2.113**
Purposes, **Bus Org 2.003 et seq.**
Liquidation, receivers and receivership, **Bus Org 12.258**
Orders of court, **Bus Org 11.405**
Loans, **Bus Org 2.101**
Location,
Meetings, **Bus Org 6.001**
Offices, **Bus Org 2.101**
Lottery, names, **Bus Org 5.061**
Mail and mailing, meetings, notice, **Bus Org 6.051**
Managers and management, agent for service of process, **Bus Org 5.255**
Mediation, **Bus Org 252.007**
Meetings, **Bus Org 6.001 et seq.**
Action without meeting, **Bus Org 6.102**
Consent, **Bus Org 6.201 et seq.**
Application of law, **Bus Org 6.301, 6.302**
Consent, action without meeting, **Bus Org 6.102, 6.201 et seq.**
Delivery, action without meeting, **Bus Org 6.203**
Facsimile, notice, **Bus Org 6.051**
Foreign states, location, **Bus Org 6.001**
Internet, **Bus Org 6.002**
Location, **Bus Org 6.001**
Mail and mailing, notice, **Bus Org 6.051**
Notice, **Bus Org 6.051 et seq.**
Action without meeting, **Bus Org 6.204**
Objections and exceptions, **Bus Org 6.003**
Notice, waiver, **Bus Org 6.053**
Record date, **Bus Org 6.101 et seq.**
Records and recordation, **Bus Org 6.002**
Telecommunications, **Bus Org 6.002**
Video recordings, **Bus Org 6.002**
Waiver, notice, **Bus Org 6.052**
Objections and exceptions, **Bus Org 6.053**
Members, **Bus Org 252.006**
Merger and consolidation, **Bus Org 10.001 et seq.**
Abandonment, **Bus Org 10.201, 10.202, 10.203**
Acceptance, certificates and certification, **Bus Org 10.156**
Allocations, property, **Bus Org 10.003**
Certificate of formation, **Bus Org 3.005, 3.006, 10.002**
Certificates and certification, **Bus Org 10.151 et seq.**
Dissenting shareholders, **Bus Org 10.351 et seq.**
Effect, **Bus Org 10.008**

NONPROFIT CORPORATIONS —Cont'd
Unincorporated nonprofit associations —Cont'd
Merger and consolidation—Cont'd
Effective date, **Bus Org 10.007**
Filing,
Certificates and certification, **Bus Org 10.153**
Fees, **Bus Org 4.151**
Holding companies, **Bus Org 10.005**
Names, **Bus Org 10.002**
Plans and specifications, **Bus Org 10.001 et seq.**
Property, allocations, **Bus Org 10.003**
Reorganization, **Bus Org 10.301 et seq.**
Status, **Bus Org 10.010**
Subsidiaries, **Bus Org 10.006**
Certificates and certification, **Bus Org 10.152**
Time, effective date, **Bus Org 10.007**
Misconduct, damages, **Bus Org 7.001**
Monopolies and unfair trade, application of law, **Bus Org 10.901**
Mortgages, **Bus Org 2.101**
Powers and duties, **Bus Org 2.104**
Receivers and receivership, **Bus Org 11.403**
Names, **Bus Org 5.001 et seq.**
Agent for service of process, **Bus Org 252.013**
Assumed or fictitious names, **Bus Org 5.051 et seq.**
Certificate of formation, **Bus Org 3.005**
Amendments, **Bus Org 3.053, 3.056**
Conversion, **Bus Org 10.103**
Deception, **Bus Org 5.052**
Exchange of property, plans and specifications, **Bus Org 10.052**
Fees, reservation, **Bus Org 5.101**
Withdrawal, **Bus Org 5.1041**
Filing,
Fees, **Bus Org 4.151**
Registration, **Bus Org 5.152**
Fraud, **Bus Org 5.052**
Identity and identification, same or similar, **Bus Org 5.053**
Lottery, **Bus Org 5.061**
Merger and consolidation, **Bus Org 10.002**
Notice, **Bus Org 5.001**
Registration, **Bus Org 5.151 et seq.**
Renewal,
Registration, **Bus Org 5.155**
Reservation, **Bus Org 5.105**
Reservation, **Bus Org 5.101 et seq.**
Same or similar, **Bus Org 5.053**
Registration, **Bus Org 5.153**
Reservation, **Bus Org 5.102**
Termination, reinstatement, **Bus Org 11.203**
Time,
Registration, **Bus Org 5.154**
Reservation, **Bus Org 5.104**

NONPROFIT CORPORATIONS
—Cont'd
Unincorporated nonprofit associations
—Cont'd
Names—Cont'd
Trademarks and trade names, **Bus Org 5.001**
Transfers, reservation, **Bus Org 5.106**
Veterans organizations, **Bus Org 5.062**
Nonfiling, certificate of formation, **Bus Org 3.002**
Notice,
Agent for service of process, **Bus Org 5.252, 5.253**
Cancellation, **Bus Org 252.011**
Conversion, **Bus Org 10.101**
Guaranty, fraud, **Bus Org 2.104**
Indemnity, orders of court, **Bus Org 8.052**
Insolvency, **Bus Org 12.256**
Liens and incumbrances,
Foreclosure, **Bus Org 12.256**
State, **Bus Org 12.201**
Meetings, **Bus Org 6.051 et seq.**
Action without meeting, **Bus Org 6.204**
Names, **Bus Org 5.001**
Receivers and receivership, claims, **Bus Org 11.407**
Registered agent, resignation, **Bus Org 5.204**
Reorganization, **Bus Org 10.301**
Shares and shareholders, uncertificated shares, **Bus Org 3.205**
Termination,
Escheat, claims, **Bus Org 11.355**
Involuntary termination, **Bus Org 11.251, 11.302, 11.310**
Winding up, **Bus Org 11.052**
Involuntary winding up, **Bus Org 11.302, 11.310**
Oaths and affirmations, interrogatories, answer, **Bus Org 12.002**
Objections and exceptions, meetings, **Bus Org 6.003**
Notice, waiver, **Bus Org 6.053**
Officers and employees, **Bus Org 3.101 et seq.**
Agent for service of process, **Bus Org 5.255**
Compensation and salaries, **Bus Org 2.101**
Damages, **Bus Org 7.001**
Application of law, **Bus Org 1.104**
Dual office holding, **Bus Org 3.103**
Elections, **Bus Org 2.101, 3.103**
Good faith, **Bus Org 3.105**
Indemnity, **Bus Org 2.101, 7.001, 8.001 et seq.**
Loans, **Bus Org 2.101**
Removal, **Bus Org 3.104**
Retirement and pensions, **Bus Org 2.101**
Offices, **Bus Org 2.101**
Changes, filing, fines and penalties, **Bus Org 21.802**

NONPROFIT CORPORATIONS
—Cont'd
Unincorporated nonprofit associations
—Cont'd
Offices—Cont'd
Reorganization, **Bus Org 10.301**
Omissions, certificate of formation, restatement, **Bus Org 3.059**
Open records, interrogatories, **Bus Org 12.003**
Orders of court, **Bus Org 252.008**
Receivers and receivership, **Bus Org 11.402**
Liquidation, **Bus Org 11.405**
Parties, receivers and receivership, **Bus Org 11.411**
Payment, termination,
Claims, **Bus Org 11.354**
Taxation, **Bus Org 11.101**
Permissive indemnification, **Bus Org 8.101 et seq.**
Personal property, **Bus Org 2.101, 252.003 et seq.**
Disposition, **Bus Org 10.251 et seq.**
Reorganization, **Bus Org 10.301**
Shares and shareholders, **Bus Org 21.801**
Photography and pictures, consent, meetings, action without meeting, **Bus Org 6.205**
Plans and specifications,
Conversion, **Bus Org 10.101 et seq.**
Exchange of property, **Bus Org 10.051 et seq.**
Merger and consolidation, **Bus Org 10.001 et seq.**
Pledges, elections, **Bus Org 6.156**
Political subdivisions, service of process, **Bus Org 5.257**
Powers and duties, **Bus Org 2.101 et seq.**
Receivers and receivership, **Bus Org 11.406**
President, agent for service of process, **Bus Org 5.255**
Priorities and preferences,
Business Organizations Code, application of law, **Bus Org 1.106**
Certificate of formation, shares and shareholders, **Bus Org 3.007**
Privileges and immunities,
Members, **Bus Org 252.006**
Property, disposition, **Bus Org 10.254**
Probate proceedings, elections, **Bus Org 6.154**
Process, **Bus Org 5.251 et seq.**
Profit sharing, officers and employees, **Bus Org 2.101**
Property, **Bus Org 2.101, 252.003 et seq.**
Disposition, **Bus Org 10.251 et seq.**
Reorganization, **Bus Org 10.301**
Liens and incumbrances,
Foreclosure, **Bus Org 12.252 et seq.**
State, **Bus Org 12.201**

NONPROFIT CORPORATIONS
—Cont'd
Unincorporated nonprofit associations
—Cont'd
Property—Cont'd
Merger and consolidation, allocations, **Bus Org 10.003**
Publication,
Termination, involuntary termination, **Bus Org 11.310**
Winding up, involuntary winding up, **Bus Org 11.310**
Purchases and purchasing, indemnity, insurance, **Bus Org 8.151**
Purposes, **Bus Org 2.001 et seq.**
Certificate of formation, **Bus Org 3.005**
Quo warranto, insolvency, **Bus Org 12.253 et seq.**
Real estate, **Bus Org 2.101, 252.003 et seq.**
Disposition, **Bus Org 10.251 et seq.**
Reorganization, **Bus Org 10.301**
Records and recordation, deeds and conveyances, **Bus Org 10.253**
Real Estate Investment Trusts, generally, this index
Receipts, termination, claims, **Bus Org 11.352**
Receivers and receivership, **Bus Org 11.401 et seq.**
Actions and proceedings, **Bus Org 11.406**
Ancillary receiverships, **Bus Org 11.409**
Appointments, **Bus Org 11.401 et seq.**
Bonds (officers and fiduciaries), **Bus Org 11.406**
Citizens and citizenship, **Bus Org 11.406**
Claims, filing, **Bus Org 11.407**
Compensation and salaries, **Bus Org 11.408**
Discharge, **Bus Org 11.412**
Elections, **Bus Org 6.155**
Filing, claims, **Bus Org 11.407**
Foreign entities, **Bus Org 11.409, 11.410**
Fraud, **Bus Org 11.403**
Judgments and decrees, termination, **Bus Org 11.412**
Jurisdiction, **Bus Org 11.402 et seq.**
Liens and incumbrances, state, **Bus Org 12.201**
Liquidation, **Bus Org 12.258**
Orders of court, **Bus Org 11.405**
Mortgages, **Bus Org 11.403**
Notice, claims, **Bus Org 11.407**
Orders of court, **Bus Org 11.402**
Liquidation, **Bus Org 11.405**
Parties, **Bus Org 11.411**
Powers and duties, **Bus Org 11.406**
Registration, **Bus Org 11.406**
Rehabilitation, **Bus Org 11.404**
State, **Bus Org 12.251**
Termination, **Bus Org 11.403**

NONPROFIT CORPORATIONS
—Cont'd
Unincorporated nonprofit associations
—Cont'd
Receivers and receivership—Cont'd
Termination—Cont'd
Judgments and decrees, **Bus Org 11.412**
Record date, **Bus Org 6.101 et seq.**
Records and recordation, **Bus Org 3.151 et seq., 252.010**
Certified copies, filing, **Bus Org 4.005**
Confidential or privileged information, **Bus Org 12.154**
Disclosure, **Bus Org 12.154**
Examinations and examiners, **Bus Org 3.153, 12.151 et seq.**
Inspection and inspectors, **Bus Org 3.152**
Interrogatories, open records, **Bus Org 12.003**
Meetings, **Bus Org 6.002**
Real estate, deeds and conveyances, **Bus Org 10.253**
Record date, **Bus Org 6.101 et seq.**
Reorganization, **Bus Org 10.301**
Service of process, **Bus Org 5.254**
Statements, real estate, transfers, **Bus Org 252.005**
Termination, removal, **Bus Org 11.104**
Time, record date, **Bus Org 6.101 et seq.**
Registered agent, **Bus Org 5.200 et seq.**
Changes, **Bus Org 5.202**
Filing, fines and penalties, **Bus Org 21.802**
Reorganization, **Bus Org 10.301**
Resignation, **Bus Org 5.204**
Registered offices, **Bus Org 5.200 et seq.**
Changes, **Bus Org 5.202**
Filing, fines and penalties, **Bus Org 21.802**
Registration,
Names, **Bus Org 5.151 et seq.**
Receivers and receivership, **Bus Org 11.406**
Rehabilitation, receivers and receivership, **Bus Org 11.404**
Reinstatement, termination, **Bus Org 11.201 et seq.**
Involuntary termination, **Bus Org 11.253**
Remand,
Termination, involuntary termination, **Bus Org 11.307**
Winding up, involuntary winding up, **Bus Org 11.307**
Removal, officers and employees, **Bus Org 3.104**
Renewal, names,
Registration, **Bus Org 5.155**
Reservation, **Bus Org 5.105**
Reorganization, **Bus Org 10.301 et seq.**

NONPROFIT CORPORATIONS
—Cont'd
Unincorporated nonprofit associations
—Cont'd
Repeals, Business Organizations Code, statutes, **Bus Org 1.054**
Reports,
Indemnity, **Bus Org 8.152**
Officers and employees, good faith, **Bus Org 3.102, 3.105**
Reservation, names, **Bus Org 5.101 et seq.**
Resignation, registered agent, **Bus Org 5.204**
Resolutions, indemnity, **Bus Org 8.103**
Restatement, certificate of formation, **Bus Org 3.057 et seq.**
Retirement and pensions, officers and employees, **Bus Org 2.101**
Revocation or suspension,
Termination, fraud, **Bus Org 11.153**
Winding up, **Bus Org 11.151**
Sales, **Bus Org 10.251 et seq.**
Property, **Bus Org 2.101, 252.003 et seq.**
Receivers and receivership, **Bus Org 11.413**
Reorganization, **Bus Org 10.301**
Same or similar, names, **Bus Org 5.053**
Seals, **Bus Org 2.101**
Indebtedness, certificates and certification, **Bus Org 2.114**
Shares and shareholders, certificates and certification, **Bus Org 3.202**
Secretary of state, agent for service of process, **Bus Org 5.251 et seq.**
Securities, **Bus Org 2.101**
Powers and duties, **Bus Org 2.104**
Sequestration, state, **Bus Org 12.259**
Service of process, **Bus Org 5.251 et seq.**
Agent for service of process, **Bus Org 252.011, 252.013**
Reorganization, **Bus Org 10.301**
Termination, involuntary termination, **Bus Org 11.309**
Winding up, involuntary winding up, **Bus Org 11.309**
Shares and shareholders,
Abandonment, exchange of property, **Bus Org 10.201, 10.202, 10.203**
Acceptance, exchange of property, certificates and certification, **Bus Org 10.156**
Appointments, dissenting shareholders, appraisal and appraisers, **Bus Org 10.361**
Appraisals and appraisers, dissenting shareholders, **Bus Org 10.354 et seq.**
Assignments, certificates and certification, **Bus Org 3.201**
Books and papers, dissenting shareholders, fair market value, **Bus Org 10.363**
Certificate of formation, numbers and numbering, **Bus Org 3.007**

NONPROFIT CORPORATIONS
—Cont'd
Unincorporated nonprofit associations
—Cont'd
Shares and shareholders—Cont'd
Certificates and certification, **Bus Org 3.201 et seq.**
Exchange of property, **Bus Org 10.151 et seq.**
Compensation and salaries, dissenting shareholders, appraisals and appraisers, **Bus Org 10.365**
Computation, dissenting shareholders, fair market value, **Bus Org 10.362**
Contracts, elections, **Bus Org 6.252**
Costs, dissenting shareholders, appraisals and appraisers, **Bus Org 10.365**
Delivery,
Certificates and certification, **Bus Org 3.204**
Meetings, action without meeting, **Bus Org 6.203**
Demand, dissenting shareholders, fair market value, **Bus Org 10.357 et seq.**
Dissenting shareholders, **Bus Org 10.351 et seq.**
Appointments, appraisal and appraisers, **Bus Org 10.361**
Appraisals and appraisers, **Bus Org 10.354 et seq.**
Books and papers, fair market value, **Bus Org 10.363**
Compensation and salaries, appraisals and appraisers, **Bus Org 10.365**
Computation, fair market value, **Bus Org 10.362**
Costs, appraisals and appraisers, **Bus Org 10.365**
Definitions, **Bus Org 10.352**
Demand, fair market value, **Bus Org 10.357 et seq.**
Exclusive remedy, **Bus Org 10.368**
Fair market value, demand, **Bus Org 10.357 et seq.**
Forms, **Bus Org 10.353**
Hearings, fair market value, **Bus Org 10.361**
Investigations and investigators, fair market value, **Bus Org 10.363**
Notice, **Bus Org 10.353, 10.355**
Objections and exceptions, appraisals and appraisers, **Bus Org 10.364**
Perfection, **Bus Org 10.356**
Petitions, fair market value, **Bus Org 10.361**
Records and recordation, fair market value, **Bus Org 10.363**
Demand, **Bus Org 10.359**
Reorganization, **Bus Org 10.304**
Termination, **Bus Org 10.367**
Title to property, **Bus Org 10.366**

NONPROFIT CORPORATIONS
—Cont'd
Unincorporated nonprofit associations
—Cont'd
Shares and shareholders—Cont'd
Dissenting shareholders—Cont'd
Withdrawal, **Bus Org 10.357**
Distribution and distributors, record date, **Bus Org 6.101 et seq.**
Duplicates and copies, certificates and certification, **Bus Org 3.202**
Elections,
Contracts, **Bus Org 6.252**
Trusts and trustees, **Bus Org 6.251**
Evidence, certificates and certification, **Bus Org 3.201**
Examinations and examiners, elections, contracts, **Bus Org 6.252**
Exchange of property, **Bus Org 10.051 et seq.**
Abandonment, **Bus Org 10.201, 10.202, 10.203**
Acceptance, certificates and certification, **Bus Org 10.156**
Certificates and certification, **Bus Org 10.151 et seq.**
Filing, certificates and certification, **Bus Org 10.153**
Exclusive remedy, dissenting shareholders, **Bus Org 10.368**
Facsimile, certificates and certification, **Bus Org 3.203**
Fair market value, dissenting shareholders, demand, **Bus Org 10.357 et seq.**
Filing, exchange of property, certificates and certification, **Bus Org 10.153**
Forms,
Certificates and certification, **Bus Org 3.202**
Dissenting shareholders, **Bus Org 10.353**
Hearings, dissenting shareholders, fair market value, **Bus Org 10.361**
Investigations and investigators, dissenting shareholders, fair market value, **Bus Org 10.363**
Meetings,
Action without meeting, **Bus Org 6.102**
Consent, **Bus Org 6.201 et seq.**
Consent, action without meeting, **Bus Org 6.102, 6.201 et seq.**
Delivery, action without meeting, **Bus Org 6.203**
Notice, action without meeting, **Bus Org 6.204**
Notice,
Dissenting shareholders, **Bus Org 10.353, 10.355**
Meetings, action without meeting, **Bus Org 6.204**
Uncertificated shares, **Bus Org 3.205**

NONPROFIT CORPORATIONS
—Cont'd
Unincorporated nonprofit associations
—Cont'd
Shares and shareholders—Cont'd
Objections and exceptions, dissenting shareholders, appraisals and appraisers, **Bus Org 10.364**
Perfection, dissenting shareholders, **Bus Org 10.356**
Personal property, **Bus Org 21.801**
Petitions, dissenting shareholders, fair market value, **Bus Org 10.361**
Record date, **Bus Org 6.101 et seq.**
Records and recordation, dissenting shareholders, fair market value, **Bus Org 10.363**
Demand, **Bus Org 10.359**
Reorganization, dissenting shareholders, **Bus Org 10.304**
Seals, certificates and certification, **Bus Org 3.202**
Signatures, certificates and certification, **Bus Org 3.203**
Termination, dissenting shareholders, **Bus Org 10.367**
Time, record date, **Bus Org 6.101 et seq.**
Title to property, dissenting shareholders, **Bus Org 10.366**
Transfers, certificates and certification, **Bus Org 3.201**
Trusts and trustees, elections, **Bus Org 6.251**
Uncertificated shares, **Bus Org 3.201**
Notice, **Bus Org 3.205**
Withdrawal, dissenting shareholders, **Bus Org 10.357**
Signatures,
Agent for service of process, statements, **Bus Org 252.011**
Certificate of formation, **Bus Org 3.004**
Amendments, **Bus Org 3.052**
Restatement, **Bus Org 3.058, 3.060**
Filing, **Bus Org 4.001**
Corrections, certificates and certification, **Bus Org 4.101**
Indebtedness, certificates and certification, **Bus Org 2.114**
Reorganization, **Bus Org 10.302**
Shares and shareholders, certificates and certification, **Bus Org 3.203**
State,
Liens and incumbrances, **Bus Org 12.201**
Receivers and receivership, **Bus Org 12.251**
Statements,
Agent for service of process, **Bus Org 252.011**
Certificate of formation,
Amendments, **Bus Org 3.053**
Restatement, **Bus Org 3.059**
Officers and employees, good faith, **Bus Org 3.102, 3.105**

NONPROFIT CORPORATIONS
—Cont'd
Unincorporated nonprofit associations
—Cont'd
Statements—Cont'd
Real estate, transfers, **Bus Org 252.005**
Termination,
Certificate of termination, **Bus Org 11.105**
Claims, **Bus Org 11.352**
Status, merger and consolidation, **Bus Org 10.010**
Statutes, Business Organizations Code, construction of laws, **Bus Org 1.051 et seq.**
Subsidiaries, merger and consolidation, **Bus Org 10.006**
Certificates and certification, **Bus Org 10.152**
Summons, **Bus Org 252.013**
Supersedeas or stay,
Termination, involuntary termination, **Bus Org 11.306**
Winding up, involuntary winding up, **Bus Org 11.306**
Supervision, winding up, **Bus Org 11.054**
Taxation,
Service of process, **Bus Org 5.257**
Termination,
Forfeitures, reinstatement, **Bus Org 11.254**
Payment, **Bus Org 11.101**
Telecommunications,
Agent for service of process, **Bus Org 252.013**
Meetings, **Bus Org 6.002**
Termination, **Bus Org 11.101 et seq.**
Abatement of actions and proceedings, involuntary termination, **Bus Org 11.304**
Actions and proceedings, involuntary termination, **Bus Org 11.303**
Appeal and review, involuntary termination, **Bus Org 11.307**
Certificates and certification, **Bus Org 11.101 et seq.**
Involuntary termination, **Bus Org 11.252**
Reinstatement, **Bus Org 11.202**
Certified copies, involuntary termination, judgments and decrees, **Bus Org 11.414**
Claims, **Bus Org 11.351 et seq.**
Crimes and offenses, involuntary termination, **Bus Org 11.301 et seq.**
Deposits, claims, **Bus Org 11.352**
Discharge, claims, **Bus Org 11.353**
Effective date, **Bus Org 11.102, 11.103**
Claims, **Bus Org 11.356 et seq.**
Reinstatement, **Bus Org 11.204 et seq.**
Errors, reinstatement, **Bus Org 11.201 et seq.**
Escheat, claims, **Bus Org 11.355**

NONPROFIT CORPORATIONS
—Cont'd
Unincorporated nonprofit associations
—Cont'd
Termination—Cont'd
Exemptions, involuntary termination, **Bus Org 11.251**
Filing,
Fines and penalties, **Bus Org 21.802**
Involuntary termination, **Bus Org 11.315**
Fraud,
Involuntary termination, **Bus Org 11.301 et seq.**
Revocation or suspension, **Bus Org 11.153**
Involuntary termination, **Bus Org 11.251 et seq., 11.301 et seq.**
Certified copies, judgments and decrees, **Bus Org 11.414**
Judgments and decrees, **Bus Org 11.301 et seq.**
Involuntary termination, certified copies, **Bus Org 11.414**
Jurisdiction, involuntary termination, **Bus Org 11.308**
Limitation of actions, claims, **Bus Org 11.359**
Names, reinstatement, **Bus Org 11.203**
Notice,
Claims, **Bus Org 11.358**
Escheat, claims, **Bus Org 11.355**
Involuntary termination, **Bus Org 11.251, 11.302, 11.310**
Payment,
Claims, **Bus Org 11.354**
Taxation, **Bus Org 11.101**
Publication, involuntary termination, **Bus Org 11.310**
Receipts, claims, **Bus Org 11.352**
Receivers and receivership, **Bus Org 11.403**
Judgments and decrees, **Bus Org 11.412**
Records and recordation, removal, **Bus Org 11.104**
Reinstatement, **Bus Org 11.201 et seq.**
Involuntary termination, **Bus Org 11.253**
Taxation, forfeitures, **Bus Org 11.254**
Remand, involuntary termination, **Bus Org 11.307**
Revocation or suspension, fraud, **Bus Org 11.153**
Service of process, involuntary termination, **Bus Org 11.309**
Statements,
Certificate of termination, **Bus Org 11.105**
Claims, **Bus Org 11.352**
Supersedeas or stay, involuntary termination, **Bus Org 11.306**

NONPROFIT CORPORATIONS
—Cont'd
Unincorporated nonprofit associations
—Cont'd
Termination—Cont'd
Taxation,
Forfeitures, reinstatement, **Bus Org 11.254**
Payment, **Bus Org 11.101**
Time,
Involuntary termination, **Bus Org 11.305, 11.313**
Reinstatement, **Bus Org 11.202**
Venue, involuntary termination, **Bus Org 11.308**
Time,
Certificate of formation, **Bus Org 3.001, 3.003**
Amendments, **Bus Org 3.056**
Restatement, **Bus Org 3.063**
Exchange of property, **Bus Org 10.054, 10.055**
Filing, **Bus Org 4.004**
Corrections, **Bus Org 4.105**
Effective date, **Bus Org 4.051 et seq.**
Fines and penalties, **Bus Org 21.802**
Interrogatories, answer, **Bus Org 12.002**
Merger and consolidation, effective date, **Bus Org 10.007**
Record date, **Bus Org 6.101 et seq.**
Records and recordation, **Bus Org 252.010**
Service of process, **Bus Org 5.254**
Termination,
Involuntary termination, **Bus Org 11.313**
Reinstatement, **Bus Org 11.202**
Winding up, **Bus Org 11.056**
Cancellation, **Bus Org 11.152**
Involuntary winding up, **Bus Org 11.313**
Torts, damages, **Bus Org 252.006**
Trademarks and trade names, names, **Bus Org 5.001**
Transfers,
Names, reservation, **Bus Org 5.106**
Personal property, **Bus Org 252.009**
Property, **Bus Org 10.251 et seq., 252.003 et seq.**
Shares and shareholders, certificates and certification, **Bus Org 3.201**
Trusts and trustees,
Beneficiaries, **Bus Org 252.004**
Elections, **Bus Org 6.154, 6.251**
Reorganization, **Bus Org 10.301 et seq.**
Uncertificated shares, **Bus Org 3.201**
Notice, **Bus Org 3.205**
Venue,
Termination, involuntary termination, **Bus Org 11.308**
Winding up, involuntary winding up, **Bus Org 11.308**

NONPROFIT CORPORATIONS
—Cont'd
Unincorporated nonprofit associations
—Cont'd
Veterans organizations, names, **Bus Org 5.062**
Vice president, agent for service of process, **Bus Org 5.255**
Video recordings, meetings, **Bus Org 6.002**
Waiver, meetings, notice, **Bus Org 6.052**
Objections and exceptions, **Bus Org 6.053**
Wills, beneficiaries, **Bus Org 252.004**
Winding up, **Bus Org 11.001 et seq., 11.051 et seq.**
Abatement of actions and proceedings, involuntary winding up, **Bus Org 11.304**
Actions and proceedings, **Bus Org 11.052, 11.055**
Involuntary winding up, **Bus Org 11.303**
Appeal and review, involuntary winding up, **Bus Org 11.307**
Assets, distribution and distributors, **Bus Org 11.053**
Cancellation, **Bus Org 11.152**
Contracts, **Bus Org 11.152**
Crimes and offenses, involuntary winding up, **Bus Org 11.301 et seq.**
Discharge, indebtedness, **Bus Org 11.053**
Distribution and distributors, assets, **Bus Org 11.053**
Filing, involuntary winding up, **Bus Org 11.315**
Fraud, involuntary winding up, **Bus Org 11.301 et seq.**
Indebtedness, discharge, **Bus Org 11.053**
Involuntary winding up, **Bus Org 11.301 et seq.**
Judgments and decrees, **Bus Org 11.301 et seq.**
Jurisdiction, involuntary winding up, **Bus Org 11.308**
Notice, **Bus Org 11.052**
Involuntary winding up, **Bus Org 11.302, 11.310**
Publication, involuntary winding up, **Bus Org 11.310**
Remand, involuntary winding up, **Bus Org 11.307**
Revocation or suspension, **Bus Org 11.151**
Service of process, involuntary winding up, **Bus Org 11.309**
Supersedeas or stay, involuntary winding up, **Bus Org 11.306**
Supervision, **Bus Org 11.054**
Time, **Bus Org 11.056**
Cancellation, **Bus Org 11.152**
Involuntary winding up, **Bus Org 11.305, 11.313**

NONPROFIT CORPORATIONS
—Cont'd
Unincorporated nonprofit associations
—Cont'd
Winding up—Cont'd
Venue, involuntary winding up, **Bus Org 11.308**
Withdrawal,
Filing, fines and penalties, **Bus Org 21.802**
Names, reservation, fees, **Bus Org 5.1041**
Witnesses, indemnity, expenses and expenditures, **Bus Org 8.106**
Writings, powers and duties, **Bus Org 2.112**
University Cooperative Society, names, **Bus Org 251.452**
Vacancies in office, directors, **Bus Org 22.212**
Venue,
Termination, involuntary termination, **Bus Org 11.308**
Winding up, involuntary winding up, **Bus Org 11.308**
Veterans organizations, names, **Bus Org 5.062**
Vice president, agent for service of process, **Bus Org 5.255**
Video recordings, meetings, **Bus Org 6.002**
Videoconferencing, meetings, **Bus Org 22.002**
Waiver,
Directors, meetings, notice, **Bus Org 22.217**
Meetings, notice, **Bus Org 6.052**
Objections and exceptions, **Bus Org 6.053**
Winding up, **Bus Org 11.001 et seq., 11.051 et seq., 22.301 et seq.**
Abatement of actions and proceedings, involuntary winding up, **Bus Org 11.304**
Actions and proceedings, **Bus Org 11.052, 11.055**
Involuntary winding up, **Bus Org 11.303**
Appeal and review, involuntary winding up, **Bus Org 11.307**
Assets, distribution and distributors, **Bus Org 11.053**
Business Organizations Code, mandatory application date, **Bus Org 402.011**
Cancellation, **Bus Org 11.152**
Contracts, **Bus Org 11.152**
Crimes and offenses, involuntary winding up, **Bus Org 11.301 et seq.**
Discharge, indebtedness, **Bus Org 11.053**
Distribution and distributors, **Bus Org 22.304**
Assets, **Bus Org 11.053**
Plans and specifications, **Bus Org 22.305**
Elections, **Bus Org 22.164**

NONPROFIT CORPORATIONS
—Cont'd
Winding up—Cont'd
Filing, involuntary winding up, **Bus Org 11.315**
Fraud, involuntary winding up, **Bus Org 11.301 et seq.**
Indebtedness, discharge, **Bus Org 11.053**
Involuntary winding up, **Bus Org 11.301 et seq.**
Judgments and decrees, **Bus Org 11.301 et seq.**
Jurisdiction, involuntary winding up, **Bus Org 11.308**
Notice, **Bus Org 11.052**
Involuntary winding up, **Bus Org 11.302, 11.310**
Publication, involuntary winding up, **Bus Org 11.310**
Remand, involuntary winding up, **Bus Org 11.307**
Revocation or suspension, **Bus Org 11.151**
Service of process, involuntary winding up, **Bus Org 11.309**
Supersedeas or stay, involuntary winding up, **Bus Org 11.306**
Supervision, **Bus Org 11.054**
Time, **Bus Org 11.056**
Cancellation, **Bus Org 11.152**
Involuntary winding up, **Bus Org 11.305, 11.313**
Unincorporated nonprofit associations, post
Venue, involuntary winding up, **Bus Org 11.308**
Withdrawal,
Filing, fines and penalties, **Bus Org 21.802**
Foreign corporations, registration, **Bus Org 9.011**
Names, reservation, fees, **Bus Org 5.1041**
Witnesses, indemnity, expenses and expenditures, **Bus Org 8.106**
Writings,
Powers and duties, **Bus Org 2.112**
Signatures, **Bus Org 1.007**

NONPROFIT LEGAL SERVICES CORPORATIONS
Cooperative associations, limitations, **Bus Org 2.011**

NONPROFIT ORGANIZATIONS
Unincorporated nonprofit associations. Nonprofit Corporations, this index

NONRESIDENTS
Electricity, this index
Foreign States, generally, this index
Gas utilities,
Municipal orders, appeals, **Util 103.053**
Rates, municipalities, **Util 104.006**

NOTARIES PUBLIC
Telephone cooperative corporations, directors, officers and members, **Util 162.081**

NOTES
Negotiable Instruments, this index

NOTICE
Business development corporations, members, withdrawal, **Bus Org 23.063**
Cable Television, this index
Carriers, this index
Cooperative Associations, this index
Corporations, this index
Elections, this index
Electric Cooperative Corporations, this index
Electricity, this index
Foreign Corporations, this index
Gas Utilities, this index
Limited Liability Companies, this index
Limited partnerships. Partnerships, this index
Municipal Elections, this index
Nonprofit Corporations, this index
Partnerships, this index
Professional Associations and Societies, this index
Professional Corporations, this index
Public Utilities, this index
Railroads, this index
Real Estate Investment Trusts, this index
School Buildings and Grounds, this index
Sewers and Sewer Systems, this index
Shares and shareholders. Corporations, this index
Sour gas, pipes and pipelines, licenses and permits, applications, **Util 121.453**
Telecommunications, this index
Telephone Cooperative Corporations, this index
Underground Natural Gas, this index
Water Supply, this index

NUCLEAR DECOMMISSIONING TRUST
Definitions, atomic energy, **Util 39.206**

NUCLEAR GENERATING UNIT
Definitions, atomic energy, decommissioning, **Util 39.206**

NUCLEAR POWER PLANTS
Decommissioning, costs, plans and specifications, **Util 39.206**
Safety, fees, **Util 39.9016**
Self insurance, **Util 36.064**

NURSES AND NURSING
Telemedicine, generally, this index

NURSING AND CONVALESCENT HOMES
Definitions, electricity, priorities and preferences, **Util 38.072**
Electricity, priorities and preferences, **Util 38.072**

NURSING AND CONVALESCENT HOMES—Cont'd
Priorities and preferences, electricity, **Util 38.072**

NURSING HOMES
Nursing and Convalescent Homes, generally, this index

OATHS AND AFFIRMATIONS
Gas utilities,
Examinations, **Util 102.204**
Reports, **Util 102.003**
Public utilities, officers and employees, examinations, **Util 14.205**

OBLIGATIONS
Bonds, generally, this index

OBSTRUCTIONS
Telecommunications, this index

OCCUPATIONAL THERAPISTS
Telemedicine, generally, this index

ODD FELLOWS
Independent Order of Odd Fellows, generally, this index

ODORS
Gas utilities, malodorants, safety, **Util 121.251 et seq.**

OFFICE OF PUBLIC UTILITY COUNSEL
Generally, **Util 13.001 et seq.**
Public Utilities, this index

OFFICIAL BONDS
Bonds (Officers and Fiduciaries), generally, this index

OIL AND GAS
See, also, Gas Utilities, generally, this index
Assessments, underground facilities, notification corporation, excavations, **Util 251.062**
Brands, marks and labels, underground facilities,
Crimes and offenses, excavations, **Util 251.203**
Excavations, **Util 251.157, 251.158**
Call router system, underground facilities, contracts, notification corporation, excavations, **Util 251.061**
Contracts,
Agriculture, natural gas, **Util 123.023**
Underground facilities, toll free numbers, notification corporation, excavations, **Util 251.061**
Crimes and offenses, underground facilities, brands, marks and labels, excavations, **Util 251.203**
Damages, underground facilities, **Util 251.001 et seq.**
Notification corporation, excavations, **Util 251.054**

OIL AND GAS—Cont'd
Deeds and conveyances, state, royalties, in kind, **Util 35.101 et seq.**
Directors, underground facilities, notification corporation, excavations, **Util 251.055 et seq.**
Easements, underground facilities, excavations, **Util 251.006**
Electric cooperative corporations, generation, **Util 39.9044, 39.9048**
Electricity, this index
Emergencies, underground facilities, notice, excavations, **Util 251.155**
Excavations, underground facilities, **Util 251.001 et seq.**
Exemptions, underground facilities, notice, excavations, **Util 251.156**
Expenses and expenditures, underground facilities, notification corporation, excavations, **Util 251.054**
Fines and penalties, underground facilities, excavations, **Util 251.201 et seq.**
Fraud, underground facilities, emergencies, excavations, **Util 251.155**
Fines and penalties, **Util 251.201**
Gas Meters, generally, this index
Gas Utilities, generally, this index
Highways and roads, underground facilities, excavations, **Util 251.007**
Insurance, underground facilities, notification center, excavations, **Util 251.104**
Labels. Brands, marks and labels, generally, ante
Licenses and permits, underground facilities, excavations, **Util 251.006**
Liquefied Petroleum Gas, generally, this index
Marks. Brands, marks and labels, generally, ante
Meters. Gas Meters, generally, this index
Motor Vehicle Fuel, generally, this index
Notification center, underground facilities, excavations, **Util 251.101 et seq.**
Notification corporation, underground facilities, excavations, **Util 251.051 et seq.**
Officers and employees, underground facilities, notification corporation, excavations, **Util 251.058**
Open meetings, underground facilities, notification corporation, excavations, **Util 251.053**
Open records, underground facilities, notification corporation, excavations, **Util 251.053**
Payment, underground facilities, notification center, excavations, **Util 251.106**
Pipes and pipelines. Oil and Gas Pipelines, generally, this index
Public utilities. Gas Utilities, generally, this index
Rates and charges, agriculture, natural gas, **Util 123.023**
Records and recordation,
Agriculture, natural gas, **Util 123.023**

OIL AND GAS—Cont'd
Records and recordation—Cont'd
Underground facilities, notification center, excavations, **Util 251.103**
Remedies, underground facilities, excavations, **Util 251.008**
Repairs, underground facilities, excavations, **Util 251.159**
Reports, underground facilities, damages, excavations, **Util 251.159**
Safety, underground facilities, **Util 251.001 et seq.**
Sales, state, royalties, in kind, **Util 35.101 et seq.**
State, sales, royalties, in kind, **Util 35.101 et seq.**
Toll free numbers, underground facilities, contracts, notification corporation, excavations, **Util 251.061**
Underground facilities,
Fraud, emergencies, excavations, **Util 251.155**
Fines and penalties, **Util 251.201**
Warnings, excavations, **Util 251.2011**
Underground Natural Gas, generally, this index
Utilities. Gas Utilities, generally, this index
Venue, underground facilities, fines and penalties, excavations, **Util 251.201**
Warnings, underground facilities, excavations, **Util 251.201, 251.2011**

OIL AND GAS PIPELINES
Assessments, notification corporation, excavations, **Util 251.062**
Brands, marks and labels,
Crimes and offenses, excavations, **Util 251.203**
Excavations, **Util 251.157, 251.158**
Call router system, contracts, notification corporation, excavations, **Util 251.061**
Contracts, toll free numbers, notification corporation, excavations, **Util 251.061**
Conversion, facilities, **Util 251.005**
Crimes and offenses, brands, marks and labels, excavations, **Util 251.203**
Damages, **Util 251.001 et seq.**
Notification corporation, excavations, **Util 251.054**
Directors, notification corporation, excavations, **Util 251.055 et seq.**
Easements,
Excavations, **Util 251.006**
Railroads, right of way, eminent domain, **Util 186.051 et seq.**
Emergencies, notice, excavations, **Util 251.155**
Eminent domain, railroads, right of way, **Util 186.051 et seq.**
Excavations, **Util 251.001 et seq.**
Exemptions, notice, excavations, **Util 251.156**
Expenses and expenditures, notification corporation, excavations, **Util 251.054**

OIL AND GAS PIPELINES—Cont'd
Fees,
Notification center, excavations, **Util 251.105**
Notification corporation, excavations, **Util 251.062**
Railroads, right of way, use, **Util 186.058**
Safety, **Util 121.211**
Fines and penalties,
Excavations, **Util 251.201 et seq.**
Inspection and inspectors, safety, fees, **Util 121.211**
Fraud, underground facilities, emergencies, excavations, **Util 251.155**
Fines and penalties, **Util 251.201**
Highways and roads, excavations, **Util 251.007**
Inspection and inspectors, fees, safety, **Util 121.211**
Insurance, notification center, excavations, **Util 251.104**
Licenses and permits,
Excavations, **Util 251.006**
Railroads, right of way, use, **Util 186.058**
Notice,
Excavations, **Util 251.009, 251.151 et seq.**
Railroads, right of way, easements, **Util 186.054**
Notification center, excavations, **Util 251.101 et seq.**
Notification corporation, excavations, **Util 251.051 et seq.**
Officers and employees, notification corporation, excavations, **Util 251.058**
Open meetings, notification corporation, excavations, **Util 251.053**
Open records, notification corporation, excavations, **Util 251.053**
Payment, notification center, excavations, **Util 251.106**
Powers and duties,
Notification center, excavations, **Util 251.102**
Notification corporation, excavations, **Util 251.060**
Railroads, right of way, easements, eminent domain, **Util 186.051 et seq.**
Rates and charges,
Notification center, excavations, **Util 251.105**
Notification corporation, excavations, **Util 251.062**
Records and recordation, notification center, excavations, **Util 251.103**
Remedies, excavations, **Util 251.008**
Repairs, excavations, **Util 251.159**
Reports, damages, excavations, **Util 251.159**
Safety, **Util 251.001 et seq.**
Fees, **Util 121.211**
Surcharge, inspection and inspectors, safety, fees, **Util 121.211**
Toll free numbers, contracts, notification corporation, excavations, **Util 251.061**

OIL AND GAS PIPELINES—Cont'd
Underground facilities,
Fraud, emergencies, excavations, **Util 251.155**
Fines and penalties, **Util 251.201**
Warnings, excavations, **Util 251.201, 251.2011**
Venue, fines and penalties, excavations, **Util 251.201**
Warnings, underground facilities, excavations, **Util 251.201, 251.2011**

OLD AGE
Aged Persons, generally, this index

OLDER PERSONS
Aged Persons, generally, this index

OPEN END INVESTMENT COMPANIES
Definitions, shares and shareholders, **Bus Org 21.651**
Directors, terms of office, **Bus Org 21.654**
Meetings, shares and shareholders, **Bus Org 21.655**
Shares and shareholders, **Bus Org 21.651 et seq.**

OPEN MEETINGS
Electric cooperative corporations, joint powers agencies, **Util 163.122 et seq.**
Electricity, joint powers agencies, electric cooperative corporations, **Util 163.122 et seq.**

OPTOMETRISTS AND OPTOMETRY
Associations and societies. Professional Associations and Societies, generally, this index
Professional Associations and Societies, generally, this index
Telemedicine, generally, this index

ORDERS
Court orders. Orders of Court, generally, this index
Definitions,
Gas utilities, **Util 101.003**
Public utilities, **Util 11.003**
Electricity, this index
Gas Utilities, this index
Public Utilities, this index
Telecommunications, this index

ORDERS OF COURT
Cable television, franchises, compliance, **Util 66.015**
Corporations, this index
Limited Liability Companies, this index
Limited partnerships. Partnerships, this index
Nonprofit Corporations, this index
Partnerships, this index
Public utilities,
Enforcement, **Util 15.021 et seq.**
Interruption of service, injunctions, **Util 186.005**

ORDERS OF COURT—Cont'd
Television and radio, franchises, compliance, **Util 66.015**

ORDINANCES
Electricity, municipal power agencies, **Util 163.057**

OSTEOPATHS
Health organization corporations, nonprofit corporations, **Bus Org 22.056**
Nonprofit corporations, health organization corporations, **Bus Org 22.056**
Partnerships, **Bus Org 152.055**
Telemedicine, generally, this index

OTHER STATES
Foreign States, generally, this index

OUTSTANDING SHARES
Corporations, **Bus Org 21.171**

PANELS
Caller ID consumer education panel, **Util 55.109**

PAR VALUE SHARES
Corporations, consideration, **Bus Org 21.161**

PARKS AND PLAYGROUNDS
Permits. Licenses and Permits, generally, this index

PAROLE
Telecommunications, nine hundred (900) information service, charges, **Util 55.252**

PARTIES
Limited Liability Companies, this index
Limited partnerships. Partnerships, this index
Partnerships, this index
Public utilities, contested cases, **Util 14.052**

PARTNERSHIPS
Generally, **Bus Org 1.001 et seq., 151.001 et seq., 152.001 et seq., 301.001 et seq.**
Abandonment,
Conversion, **Bus Org 10.201, 10.202, 10.203**
Exchange of property, **Bus Org 10.201, 10.202, 10.203**
Filing, **Bus Org 4.057**
Limited partnerships, post
Merger and consolidation, **Bus Org 10.201, 10.202, 10.203**
Abatement of actions and proceedings,
Limited partnerships, post
Merger and consolidation, **Bus Org 10.201, 10.202**
State, **Bus Org 12.260**
Termination, involuntary termination, **Bus Org 11.304**
Winding up, involuntary winding up, **Bus Org 11.304**

PARTNERSHIPS—Cont'd
Acceptance, certificates and certification, **Bus Org 10.156**
Accounts and accounting, **Bus Org 3.151 et seq.**
  Actions and proceedings, **Bus Org 152.211**
  Examinations and examiners, **Bus Org 12.151 et seq.**
  Loyalty, **Bus Org 152.205**
  Transfers, disclosure, **Bus Org 152.404**
  Winding up, compromise and settlement, **Bus Org 152.707**
Acknowledgments,
  Certificate of formation, **Bus Org 3.004**
    Evidence, **Bus Org 3.001**
  Filing, **Bus Org 4.002**
    Effective date, delay, **Bus Org 4.059**
  Limited partnerships, post
  Merger and consolidation, **Bus Org 10.201, 10.202**
Actions and proceedings, **Bus Org 2.101**
  Abatement of actions and proceedings, generally, ante
  Breach, **Bus Org 152.211**
  Business Organizations Code, prior law, **Bus Org 402.014**
  Certificate of formation, amendments, **Bus Org 3.056**
  Compromise and settlement, winding up, **Bus Org 152.707**
  Guaranty, **Bus Org 2.104**
  Indemnity, **Bus Org 8.001 et seq.**
  Insolvency, **Bus Org 12.253 et seq.**
  Judgments and decrees, generally, post
  Jurisdiction, generally, post
  Limitation of actions, generally, post
  Limited partnerships, post
  Merger and consolidation, **Bus Org 10.201, 10.202**
  Parties, generally, post
  Receivers and receivership, **Bus Org 11.406**
  Records and recordation, inspection and inspectors, **Bus Org 3.152**
  State, liens and incumbrances, **Bus Org 12.201 et seq.**
  Termination, involuntary termination, **Bus Org 11.303**
  Third parties, generally, post
  Venue, generally, post
  Winding up, post
  Withdrawal, redemption, **Bus Org 152.609**
Actions without meetings, contracts, **Bus Org 154.103**
Address,
  Certificate of formation, **Bus Org 3.005**
  Limited partnerships, post
Admissions,
  Consent, **Bus Org 152.201**
  Limited partnerships, post
Adoption, Business Organizations Code, **Bus Org 402.003**
Advancements, **Bus Org 152.203**
  Indemnity, expenses and expenditures, **Bus Org 8.104, 8.105**

PARTNERSHIPS—Cont'd
Advancements—Cont'd
  Indemnity, expenses and expenditures—Cont'd
    Reports, **Bus Org 8.152**
Agent for service of process, **Bus Org 5.251 et seq.**
Agents and agencies, **Bus Org 152.301**
  Changes, filing, fines and penalties, **Bus Org 21.802**
  Damages, **Bus Org 301.010**
  Foreign limited liability partnerships, **Bus Org 152.904**
    Changes, **Bus Org 152.913**
  Licenses and permits, **Bus Org 301.006**
  Limited partnerships, changes, filing, fines and penalties, **Bus Org 21.802**
  Registered agent, generally, post
Agreements. Contracts, generally, post
Allocations,
  Limited partnerships, post
  Merger and consolidation, property, **Bus Org 10.003**
Alternatives, service of process, **Bus Org 5.256**
Amendments,
  Business Organizations Code, statutes, **Bus Org 1.054**
  Certificate of formation, **Bus Org 3.051 et seq.**
  Contracts, **Bus Org 152.208**
  Filing, **Bus Org 4.106**
    Fees, **Bus Org 4.158**
  Foreign limited liability partnerships, registration, **Bus Org 152.911, 152.912**
  Limited liability partnership, registration, **Bus Org 152.802**
  Limited partnerships, post
Ancillary receiverships, **Bus Org 11.409**
Answer, interrogatories, time, **Bus Org 12.002**
Antitrust, application of law, **Bus Org 10.901**
Appeal and review,
  Filing, **Bus Org 12.004**
  Limited partnerships, post
  Termination, involuntary termination, **Bus Org 11.307**
  Winding up, involuntary winding up, **Bus Org 11.307**
Application of law, **Bus Org 152.003, 301.001**
  Antitrust, **Bus Org 10.901**
  Business Organizations Code, **Bus Org 402.001 et seq.**
    Foreign countries, foreign states, **Bus Org 1.053**
  Certificate of formation, **Bus Org 1.101 et seq.**
  Contracts, **Bus Org 152.002**
  Elections, **Bus Org 6.301**
  Foreign limited liability partnerships, **Bus Org 152.901**
  Indebtedness, **Bus Org 10.901**
  Indemnity, **Bus Org 8.002**

PARTNERSHIPS—Cont'd
Application of law—Cont'd
  Limited liability partnership, **Bus Org 152.805**
  Limited partnerships, post
  Meetings, **Bus Org 6.301**
  Monopolies and unfair trade, **Bus Org 10.901**
  Reorganization, **Bus Org 10.306**
  Withdrawal, **Bus Org 152.502**
Applications, foreign limited liability partnerships, registration, **Bus Org 9.007**
Appointments, receivers and receivership, **Bus Org 11.401 et seq.**
Appraisals and appraisers, reorganization, **Bus Org 10.304**
Approval,
  Conversion, **Bus Org 10.107**
  Exchange of property, **Bus Org 10.056**
Assets,
  Disposition, **Bus Org 10.251 et seq.**
    Reorganization, **Bus Org 10.301**
  Liens and incumbrances, state, **Bus Org 12.201**
  Limited partnerships, post
  Sales, Business Organizations Code, mandatory application date, **Bus Org 402.010**
  Winding up,
    Disposition, **Bus Org 152.706**
    Distribution and distributors, **Bus Org 11.053**
Assignments, **Bus Org 10.251 et seq.**
  Information, disclosure, **Bus Org 152.213**
  Limited partnerships, post
  Shares and shareholders, certificates and certification, **Bus Org 3.201**
Assumed or fictitious names, **Bus & C 71.001 et seq.; Bus Org 5.051 et seq.**
  Names, **Bus Org 5.051 et seq.**
Attachment, state, **Bus Org 12.259**
Attorney fees,
  Filing,
    Fines and penalties, **Bus Org 21.802**
    Fraud, **Bus Org 4.007**
  Limited partnerships, post
  Records and recordation, inspection and inspectors, **Bus Org 3.152**
  Transfers, redemption, **Bus Org 152.612**
Attorneys. Attorney fees, generally, ante
Bankruptcy, **Bus Org 10.301 et seq.**
Bonds, **Bus Org 2.101**
  Reorganization, **Bus Org 10.301**
Bonds (officers and fiduciaries), receivers and receivership, **Bus Org 11.406**
Bonuses, officers and employees, **Bus Org 2.101**
Books and papers, **Bus Org 3.151 et seq., 152.212**
  Confidential or privileged information, **Bus Org 12.154**
  Disclosure, **Bus Org 12.154**
  Duplicates and copies, **Bus Org 12.151 et seq.**

PARTNERSHIPS—Cont'd
Books and papers—Cont'd
Examinations and examiners, **Bus Org 3.153, 12.151 et seq.**
Inspection and inspectors, **Bus Org 3.152**
Limited partnerships, post
Powers and duties, limitations, **Bus Org 2.005**
Reorganization, **Bus Org 10.301**
Signatures, **Bus Org 1.007**
Transfers, inspection and inspectors, **Bus Org 152.404**
Breach,
Actions and proceedings, **Bus Org 152.211**
Withdrawal, **Bus Org 152.501, 152.503**
Bylaws, **Bus Org 2.101**
Cancellation,
Limited partnerships, winding up, **Bus Org 11.152, 153.501**
Reinstatement, **Bus Org 402.013**
Winding up, **Bus Org 11.152, 152.709**
Care, powers and duties, **Bus Org 152.206**
Certificate of formation, **Bus Org 3.001 et seq.**
Amendments, **Bus Org 3.051 et seq.**
Application of law, **Bus Org 1.101 et seq.**
Definitions, **Bus Org 1.002**
Directors, post
Limited partnerships, post
Merger and consolidation, **Bus Org 3.005, 3.006, 10.002**
Names, post
Reinstatement, **Bus Org 402.013**
Reorganization, **Bus Org 10.301 et seq.**
Restatement, **Bus Org 3.057 et seq.**
Signatures, **Bus Org 3.004**
Amendments, **Bus Org 3.052, 3.054**
Restatement, **Bus Org 3.058, 3.060**
Statements,
Amendments, **Bus Org 3.053, 3.054**
Restatement, **Bus Org 3.059**
Time, **Bus Org 3.001, 3.003**
Amendments, **Bus Org 3.056**
Restatement, **Bus Org 3.063**
Certificates and certification,
Acceptance, **Bus Org 10.156**
Certificate of formation, generally, ante
Conversion, **Bus Org 10.154 et seq.**
Evidence, existence, **Bus Org 4.005**
Exchange of property, **Bus Org 10.151 et seq.**
Filing, **Bus Org 12.001**
Abandonment, **Bus Org 4.057**
Corrections, **Bus Org 4.101 et seq.**
Fines and penalties, **Bus Org 21.802**
Formation, **Bus Org 3.001 et seq.**
Foreign limited liability partnerships, registration,
Reinstatement, **Bus Org 152.914**
Withdrawal, **Bus Org 152.907**
Indebtedness, **Bus Org 2.114**
Limited partnerships, post
Merger and consolidation, **Bus Org 10.151 et seq.**

PARTNERSHIPS—Cont'd
Certificates and certification—Cont'd
Shares and shareholders, **Bus Org 3.201 et seq.**
Termination, post
Certified copies,
Filing, **Bus Org 4.005**
Involuntary termination, judgments and decrees, **Bus Org 11.414**
Changes,
Limited partnerships, post
Registered offices, registered agent, **Bus Org 5.202, 5.203**
Relationships, **Bus Org 154.202**
Charges. Rates and charges, generally, post
Charging orders, indebtedness, judgments and decrees, **Bus Org 152.308**
Citizens and citizenship, receivers and receivership, **Bus Org 11.406**
Claims,
Receivers and receivership, filing, **Bus Org 11.407**
Termination, **Bus Org 11.351 et seq.**
Classification,
Contracts, **Bus Org 154.101**
Limited partnerships, contracts, **Bus Org 154.101**
Property, **Bus Org 152.102**
Community property, **Bus Org 152.203, 154.001**
Compensation and salaries, **Bus Org 152.203**
Limited partnerships, post
Officers and employees, **Bus Org 2.101**
Receivers and receivership, **Bus Org 11.408**
Compromise and settlement, winding up, **Bus Org 152.707**
Conduct, **Bus Org 152.302**
Business Organizations Code, application of law, **Bus Org 402.006**
Damages, **Bus Org 7.001, 152.303, 301.010**
Limited partnerships, **Bus Org 153.103, 153.104**
Standards, **Bus Org 152.204**
Withdrawal, **Bus Org 152.501, 152.504**
Confidential or privileged information, interrogatories, **Bus Org 12.003**
Conflict of interest, **Bus Org 152.204**
Loyalty, **Bus Org 152.205**
Conflict of laws, **Bus Org 301.002**
Consent,
Admissions, **Bus Org 152.201**
Contracts, amendments, **Bus Org 152.208**
Limited partnerships, post
Registered agents, **Bus Org 5.2011**
Winding up, cancellation, **Bus Org 152.709**
Consolidation. Merger and consolidation, generally, post
Construction of laws, **Bus Org 152.004**
Business Organizations Code, statutes, **Bus Org 1.006, 1.051 et seq.**

PARTNERSHIPS—Cont'd
Continuation, winding up, **Bus Org 152.709**
Contracts, **Bus Org 2.101, 154.101 et seq.**
Actions and proceedings, **Bus Org 152.211**
Actions without meetings, **Bus Org 154.103**
Amendments, **Bus Org 152.208**
Application of law, **Bus Org 152.002**
Business Organizations Code, application of law, **Bus Org 402.006**
Classification, **Bus Org 154.101**
Elections, **Bus Org 154.102**
Indebtedness, **Bus Org 2.103**
Limited partnerships, post
Meetings, elections, **Bus Org 154.102**
Notice, meetings, **Bus Org 154.102**
Transfers, **Bus Org 152.405**
Winding up, **Bus Org 11.152**
Withdrawal, **Bus Org 152.501**
Contributions,
Definitions, business organizations, **Bus Org 1.002**
Limited partnerships, post
Winding up, **Bus Org 152.708**
Disposition, **Bus Org 152.706**
Withdrawal, **Bus Org 152.603**
Conversion, **Bus Org 10.101 et seq.**
Abandonment, **Bus Org 10.201, 10.202, 10.203**
Acceptance, certificates and certification, **Bus Org 10.156**
Business Organizations Code, mandatory application date, **Bus Org 402.010**
Certificates and certification, **Bus Org 10.154 et seq.**
Dissenting shareholders, **Bus Org 10.351 et seq.**
Effective date, **Bus Org 10.105, 10.106**
Filing,
Certificates and certification, **Bus Org 10.155**
Fees, **Bus Org 4.151**
Limited partnerships, post
Names, **Bus Org 10.103**
Notice, **Bus Org 10.101**
Plans and specifications, **Bus Org 10.101 et seq.**
Registration, withdrawal, **Bus Org 9.012**
Reorganization, **Bus Org 10.301 et seq.**
Withdrawal, **Bus Org 152.501**
Conveyances. Deeds and conveyances, generally, post
Copies. Duplicates and copies, generally, post
Corrections. Errors, generally, post
Costs,
Filing,
Fines and penalties, **Bus Org 21.802**
Fraud, **Bus Org 4.007**
Insolvency, dismissal and nonsuit, **Bus Org 12.257**

PARTNERSHIPS—Cont'd
Costs—Cont'd
Liens and incumbrances, foreclosure, dismissal and nonsuit, **Bus Org 12.257**
Limited partnerships, post
Transfers, redemption, **Bus Org 152.612**
Creation, **Bus Org 152.051 et seq.**
Credit, **Bus Org 152.202**
Fraud, **Bus Org 152.307**
Creditors. Indebtedness, generally, post
Crimes and offenses,
Books and papers, examinations and examiners, **Bus Org 12.156**
Damages, **Bus Org 7.001**
Filing, fraud, **Bus Org 4.008**
Fraud, generally, post
Limited partnerships, post
Termination, involuntary termination, **Bus Org 11.301 et seq.**
Winding up, involuntary winding up, **Bus Org 11.301 et seq.**
Damages, **Bus Org 152.210, 301.010**
Application of law, **Bus Org 1.104**
Conduct, **Bus Org 152.303**
Filing, **Bus Org 21.802**
Fraud, **Bus Org 4.007**
Foreign limited liability partnerships, **Bus Org 152.910**
Guaranty, **Bus Org 2.104**
Indebtedness, **Bus Org 152.304**
Indemnity, generally, post
Limited liability partnership, **Bus Org 152.801**
Limited partnerships, post
Merger and consolidation, **Bus Org 10.009**
Officers and employees, post
Third parties, **Bus Org 152.053**
Transfers, **Bus Org 152.404**
Winding up, **Bus Org 152.704, 152.705**
Withdrawal, **Bus Org 152.503 et seq.**
Redemption, **Bus Org 152.609**
Death,
Information, disclosure, **Bus Org 152.213**
Limited partnerships, post
Transfers, **Bus Org 152.406**
Withdrawal, **Bus Org 152.501**
Debtors and creditors. Indebtedness, generally, post
Debts. Indebtedness, generally, post
Deception, names, **Bus Org 5.052**
Decisions, majority, **Bus Org 152.209**
Decrees. Judgments and decrees, generally, post
Deeds and conveyances, **Bus Org 2.101, 10.251 et seq., 152.302**
Limited partnerships, post
Property, **Bus Org 2.101**
Records and recordation, **Bus Org 10.253**
Definitions, **Bus Org 1.002, 151.001, 152.001, 301.003**
Assumed or fictitious names, **Bus & C 71.002**

PARTNERSHIPS—Cont'd
Definitions—Cont'd
Business organizations, **Bus Org 1.002**
Indemnity, **Bus Org 8.001**
Mandatory application date, **Bus Org 401.001**
Prior law, **Bus Org 401.001**
Termination, **Bus Org 11.001**
Winding up, **Bus Org 11.001**
Delay, filing, effective date, **Bus Org 4.052 et seq.**
Delivery,
Filing, **Bus Org 4.001**
Limited partnerships, post
Shares and shareholders, certificates and certification, **Bus Org 3.204**
Demand, withdrawal, redemption, **Bus Org 152.607**
Deposits, termination, claims, **Bus Org 11.352**
Derivative actions. Limited partnerships, post
Directors,
Agent for service of process, **Bus Org 5.255**
Certificate of formation, **Bus Org 3.007**
Amendments, **Bus Org 3.054**
Restatement, **Bus Org 3.060**
Damages, **Bus Org 7.001**
Indemnity, **Bus Org 7.001**
Limited partnerships, post
Loans, **Bus Org 2.101**
Discharge,
Limited partnerships, post
Receivers and receivership, **Bus Org 11.412**
Termination, claims, **Bus Org 11.353**
Winding up, indebtedness, **Bus Org 11.053**
Withdrawal, damages, **Bus Org 152.505**
Disclosure,
Information, **Bus Org 152.213**
Interrogatories, **Bus Org 12.003**
Transfers, accounts and accounting, **Bus Org 152.404**
Dismissal and nonsuit,
Insolvency, **Bus Org 12.257**
Liens and incumbrances, foreclosure, **Bus Org 12.257**
Limited partnerships, post
Dissenting shareholders. Shares and shareholders, post
Dissolution, **Bus Org 2.101**
Involuntary dissolution, reinstatement, **Bus Org 402.013**
Limited partnerships, post
Dissolution of marriage, transfers, **Bus Org 152.406**
Distribution and distributors,
Charging orders, **Bus Org 152.308**
In kind, **Bus Org 154.203**
Limited partnerships, post
Transfers, **Bus Org 152.404**
Winding up, **Bus Org 152.707**
Assets, **Bus Org 11.053**

PARTNERSHIPS—Cont'd
Dog races, limited partnerships, licenses and permits, transfers, **Bus Org 153.555**
Dual office holding, officers and employees, **Bus Org 3.103**
Duplicates and copies,
Agent for service of process, **Bus Org 5.252**
Books and papers, **Bus Org 12.151 et seq.**
Filing, **Bus Org 4.003**
Limited partnerships, post
Records and recordation, **Bus Org 3.152**
Shares and shareholders, certificates and certification, **Bus Org 3.202**
Duties. Powers and duties, generally, post
Effective date,
Business Organizations Code, **Bus Org 402.001**
Adoption, **Bus Org 402.005**
Conversion, **Bus Org 10.105, 10.106**
Exchange of property, **Bus Org 10.054, 10.055**
Filing, **Bus Org 4.051 et seq.**
Limited partnerships, post
Merger and consolidation, **Bus Org 10.007**
Termination, post
Elections,
Application of law, **Bus Org 6.301**
Contracts, **Bus Org 154.102**
Indemnity, **Bus Org 8.103**
Limited partnerships, post
Officers and employees, **Bus Org 2.101, 3.103**
Electronic filing, **Bus Org 12.001**
Emergencies, governance, **Bus Org 3.251 et seq.**
Employees. Officers and employees, generally, post
Errors,
Damages, **Bus Org 301.010**
Filing, **Bus Org 4.101 et seq.**
Fees, **Bus Org 4.151**
Limited partnerships, post
Termination, reinstatement, **Bus Org 11.201 et seq.**
Escheat, termination, claims, **Bus Org 11.355**
Evidence,
Certificate of formation, acknowledgments, **Bus Org 3.001**
Existence, certificates and certification, **Bus Org 4.005**
Filing, **Bus Org 4.001**
Indebtedness, fraud, **Bus Org 2.103**
Limited partnerships, post
Shares and shareholders, certificates and certification, **Bus Org 3.201**
Examinations and examiners,
Books and papers, **Bus Org 12.151 et seq.**
Limited partnerships, post

PARTNERSHIPS—Cont'd
Examinations and examiners—Cont'd
Records and recordation, **Bus Org 3.153**
Exchange of property, **Bus Org 2.101, 10.051 et seq.**
Abandonment, **Bus Org 10.201, 10.202, 10.203**
Acceptance, certificates and certification, **Bus Org 10.156**
Certificates and certification, **Bus Org 10.151 et seq.**
Dissenting shareholders, **Bus Org 10.351 et seq.**
Filing,
Certificates and certification, **Bus Org 10.153**
Fees, **Bus Org 4.151**
Limited partnerships, post
Reorganization, **Bus Org 10.301**
Shares and shareholders, post
Voluntary, **Bus Org 10.902**
Exemptions,
Guaranty, powers and duties, **Bus Org 2.104**
Interrogatories, **Bus Org 12.002**
Limited partnerships, post
Securities, sales, **Bus Org 301.011**
Termination, involuntary termination, **Bus Org 11.251**
Expenses and expenditures,
Indemnity, **Bus Org 8.001 et seq.**
Limited partnerships, post
Transfers, redemption, **Bus Org 152.612**
Expulsion, withdrawal, **Bus Org 152.501**
Facsimile, **Bus Org 1.007**
Filing, **Bus Org 4.003**
Indebtedness, certificates and certification, **Bus Org 2.114**
Limited partnerships, post
Seals, **Bus Org 2.101**
Shares and shareholders, certificates and certification, **Bus Org 3.203**
Factors, **Bus Org 152.052**
Facts,
Knowledge, **Bus Org 151.002**
Notice, **Bus Org 151.003**
Fees,
Attorney fees, generally, ante
Business Organizations Code, effective date, **Bus Org 402.002**
Filing, **Bus Org 4.151 et seq.**
Limited partnerships, post
Names, reservation, **Bus Org 5.101**
Withdrawal, **Bus Org 5.1041**
Filing, **Bus Org 4.001 et seq., 12.001 et seq.**
Abandonment, **Bus Org 4.057**
Acknowledgments, **Bus Org 4.002**
Effective date, delay, **Bus Org 4.059**
Amendments, **Bus Org 4.106**
Appeal and review, **Bus Org 12.004**
Assumed or fictitious names, **Bus Org 5.051**
Attorney fees,
Fines and penalties, **Bus Org 21.802**

PARTNERSHIPS—Cont'd
Filing—Cont'd
Attorney fees—Cont'd
Fraud, **Bus Org 4.007**
Business Organizations Code, effective date, **Bus Org 402.002**
Certificates and certification, ante
Certified copies, **Bus Org 4.005**
Conversion, certificates and certification, **Bus Org 10.155**
Corrections, **Bus Org 4.101 et seq.**
Fees, **Bus Org 4.151**
Costs,
Fines and penalties, **Bus Org 21.802**
Fraud, **Bus Org 4.007**
Damages, **Bus Org 21.802**
Fraud, **Bus Org 4.007**
Delay, effective date, **Bus Org 4.052 et seq.**
Delivery, **Bus Org 4.001**
Duplicates and copies, **Bus Org 4.003**
Effective date, **Bus Org 4.051 et seq.**
Electronic filing, **Bus Org 12.001**
Evidence, **Bus Org 4.001**
Facsimile, **Bus Org 4.003**
Fees, **Bus Org 4.151 et seq.**
Fines and penalties, **Bus Org 21.802**
Fraud, **Bus Org 4.008**
Foreign limited liability partnerships, registration, **Bus Org 152.905**
Forms, **Bus Org 4.006**
Fraud, **Bus Org 4.007, 4.008**
Interrogatories, **Bus Org 12.002, 12.003**
Jurisdiction, fines and penalties, **Bus Org 21.802**
Limitations,
Corrections, **Bus Org 4.102**
Effective date, delay, **Bus Org 4.058**
Limited liability partnership, registration, **Bus Org 152.802**
Limited partnerships, post
Names, registration, **Bus Org 5.152**
Real estate investment trusts, **Bus Org 4.009**
Receivers and receivership, claims, **Bus Org 11.407**
Registered agent, resignation, **Bus Org 5.204**
Service of process, **Bus Org 21.802**
Signatures, **Bus Org 4.001**
Corrections, certificates and certification, **Bus Org 4.101**
Termination, involuntary termination, **Bus Org 11.315**
Time, **Bus Org 4.004**
Corrections, **Bus Org 4.105**
Effective date, **Bus Org 4.051 et seq.**
Fines and penalties, **Bus Org 21.802**
Winding up, involuntary winding up, **Bus Org 11.315**
Financial statements and reports, officers and employees, good faith, **Bus Org 3.102, 3.105**
Fines and penalties,
Books and papers, examinations and examiners, **Bus Org 12.156**
Filing, **Bus Org 21.802**

PARTNERSHIPS—Cont'd
Fines and penalties—Cont'd
Filing—Cont'd
Fraud, **Bus Org 4.008**
Limited partnerships, post
Registered agents, consent, **Bus Org 5.207**
Foreclosure, liens and incumbrances, **Bus Org 12.252 et seq.**
Foreign countries,
Business Organizations Code, application of law, **Bus Org 1.053**
Certificate of formation, application of law, **Bus Org 1.102**
Foreign limited liability partnerships, **Bus Org 152.901 et seq.**
Amendments, registration, **Bus Org 152.911**
Application of law, Business Organizations Code, **Bus Org 402.001 et seq.**
Certificates and certification, registration,
Reinstatement, **Bus Org 152.914**
Withdrawal, **Bus Org 152.907**
Conversion, registration, withdrawal, **Bus Org 9.012**
Damages, **Bus Org 152.910**
Indebtedness, **Bus Org 152.910**
Registered agent, **Bus Org 152.904**
Registered offices, **Bus Org 152.904**
Registration, **Bus Org 152.905**
Amendments, **Bus Org 152.911**
Applications, **Bus Org 9.007**
Certificates and certification, reinstatement, **Bus Org 152.914**
Reinstatement, **Bus Org 152.914**
Revocation or suspension, **Bus Org 9.151 et seq., 152.914**
Withdrawal, **Bus Org 9.011, 152.906, 152.907**
Reinstatement, registration, **Bus Org 152.914**
Revocation or suspension, registration, **Bus Org 152.914**
Termination, registration, **Bus Org 152.907**
Transacting business in Texas, registration, **Bus Org 152.910**
Withdrawal, registration, **Bus Org 152.906, 152.907**
Foreign limited partnerships,
Acknowledgments, registration, **Bus Org 9.008**
Actions and proceedings,
Registration, **Bus Org 9.051 et seq.**
Transacting business in Texas, **Bus Org 9.251**
Agent for service of process, registration, **Bus Org 9.007**
Amendments, registration, **Bus Org 9.009**
Application of law, Business Organizations Code, **Bus Org 9.301, 402.001 et seq.**
Banks and banking, transacting business in Texas, **Bus Org 9.251**

PARTNERSHIPS—Cont'd
Foreign limited partnerships—Cont'd
Business Organizations Code, application of law, **Bus Org 1.053**
Certificate of formation, application of law, **Bus Org 1.102**
Certificates and certification, registration,
Reinstatement, **Bus Org 9.104**
Revocation or suspension, **Bus Org 9.102**
Certified copies, registration, revocation or suspension, **Bus Org 9.161**
Claims, transacting business in Texas, **Bus Org 9.251**
Conflict of laws, registration, **Bus Org 9.055**
Conversion, registration, withdrawal, **Bus Org 9.012**
Definitions, **Bus Org 151.001, 152.001**
Dismissal and nonsuit, registration, revocation or suspension, **Bus Org 9.156**
Elections, transacting business in Texas, **Bus Org 9.251**
Evidence, registration, acknowledgments, **Bus Org 9.008**
Exemptions, registration, **Bus Org 9.002**
Fees,
Filing, **Bus Org 4.158**
Registration, collection, **Bus Org 9.054**
Filing,
Fees, **Bus Org 4.155**
Registration, revocation or suspension, **Bus Org 9.161**
Fines and penalties, registration, **Bus Org 9.052**
Indebtedness, transacting business in Texas, **Bus Org 9.251**
Injunctions, registration, **Bus Org 9.051**
Investments, transacting business in Texas, **Bus Org 9.251**
Judgments and decrees, registration, revocation or suspension, **Bus Org 9.154 et seq.**
Jurisdiction, registration, revocation or suspension, **Bus Org 9.158**
Liens and incumbrances, transacting business in Texas, **Bus Org 9.251**
Lists, transacting business in Texas, **Bus Org 9.251, 9.252**
Loans, transacting business in Texas, **Bus Org 9.251**
Meetings, transacting business in Texas, **Bus Org 9.251**
Mines and minerals, transacting business in Texas, **Bus Org 9.251**
Mortgages, transacting business in Texas, **Bus Org 9.251**
Names, **Bus Org 5.063**
Registration,
Change of name, **Bus Org 9.010**
Reinstatement, **Bus Org 9.105**
Words and phrases, **Bus Org 5.055**

PARTNERSHIPS—Cont'd
Foreign limited partnerships—Cont'd
Notice, registration,
Revocation or suspension, **Bus Org 9.101, 9.152**
Service of process, revocation or suspension, **Bus Org 9.160**
Offices, transacting business in Texas, **Bus Org 9.251**
Probate proceedings, transacting business in Texas, **Bus Org 9.251**
Registration, **Bus Org 9.001 et seq.**
Acknowledgments, **Bus Org 9.008**
Actions and proceedings, **Bus Org 9.051 et seq.**
Amendments, **Bus Org 9.009**
Applications, **Bus Org 9.004**
Certificates and certification,
Reinstatement, **Bus Org 9.104**
Revocation or suspension, **Bus Org 9.102**
Certified copies, revocation or suspension, **Bus Org 9.161**
Conflict of laws, **Bus Org 9.055**
Dismissal and nonsuit, revocation or suspension, **Bus Org 9.156**
Evidence, acknowledgments, **Bus Org 9.008**
Exemptions, **Bus Org 9.002**
Fees, collection, **Bus Org 9.054**
Filing, revocation or suspension, **Bus Org 9.161**
Fines and penalties, **Bus Org 9.052**
Fraud, **Bus Org 9.051 et seq.**
Injunctions, **Bus Org 9.051**
Judgments and decrees, revocation or suspension, **Bus Org 9.154 et seq.**
Jurisdiction, revocation or suspension, **Bus Org 9.158**
Names,
Change of name, **Bus Org 9.010**
Reinstatement, **Bus Org 9.105**
Notice,
Revocation or suspension, **Bus Org 9.101, 9.152**
Service of process, revocation or suspension, **Bus Org 9.160**
Reinstatement, **Bus Org 9.103 et seq.**
Remand, revocation or suspension, **Bus Org 9.157**
Revocation or suspension, **Bus Org 9.101 et seq., 9.151 et seq.**
Same or similar names, reinstatement, **Bus Org 9.105**
Service of process,
Revocation or suspension, **Bus Org 9.159, 9.160**
Withdrawal, **Bus Org 9.011**
Supersedeas or stay, revocation or suspension, **Bus Org 9.156**
Taxation, forfeitures, reinstatement, **Bus Org 9.106**
Time, amendments, **Bus Org 9.009**
Venue, **Bus Org 9.053**
Revocation or suspension, **Bus Org 9.158**

PARTNERSHIPS—Cont'd
Foreign limited partnerships—Cont'd
Registration—Cont'd
Withdrawal, **Bus Org 9.011**
Reinstatement, registration, **Bus Org 9.103 et seq.**
Remand, registration, revocation or suspension, **Bus Org 9.157**
Reports, **Bus Org 153.301 et seq.**
Revocation or suspension, registration, **Bus Org 9.101 et seq., 9.151 et seq.**
Sales, transacting business in Texas, **Bus Org 9.251**
Same or similar names, registration, reinstatement, **Bus Org 9.105**
Securities, transacting business in Texas, **Bus Org 9.251**
Service of process, registration,
Revocation or suspension, **Bus Org 9.159, 9.160**
Withdrawal, **Bus Org 9.011**
Supersedeas or stay, registration, revocation or suspension, **Bus Org 9.156**
Taxation,
Numbers and numbering, registration, **Bus Org 9.007**
Registration, forfeitures, reinstatement, **Bus Org 9.106**
Time, registration, amendments, **Bus Org 9.009**
Transacting business in Texas, **Bus Org 9.201 et seq.**
Lists, **Bus Org 9.251, 9.252**
Trusts and trustees, transacting business in Texas, **Bus Org 9.251**
Venue, registration, **Bus Org 9.053**
Revocation or suspension, **Bus Org 9.158**
Withdrawal, registration, **Bus Org 9.011**
Foreign states,
Business Organizations Code, application of law, **Bus Org 1.053**
Certificate of formation, application of law, **Bus Org 1.102**
Forfeitures,
Books and papers, examinations and examiners, **Bus Org 12.155**
Limited partnerships, post
Reinstatement, **Bus Org 402.013**
Formation. Certificate of formation, generally, ante
Forms,
Filing, **Bus Org 4.006**
Limited partnerships, post
Shares and shareholders, certificates and certification, **Bus Org 3.202**
Fraud, **Bus Org 152.054**
Credit, **Bus Org 152.307**
Filing, **Bus Org 4.007, 4.008**
Guaranty, **Bus Org 2.104**
Indebtedness, evidence, **Bus Org 2.103**
Limited partnerships, post
Names, **Bus Org 5.052**
Receivers and receivership, **Bus Org 11.403**

PARTNERSHIPS—Cont'd
Fraud—Cont'd
Termination,
Involuntary termination, **Bus Org 11.301 et seq.**
Revocation or suspension, **Bus Org 11.153**
Winding up, involuntary winding up, **Bus Org 11.301 et seq.**
Frauds, statute of, powers and duties, **Bus Org 2.112**
Garnishment, state, **Bus Org 12.259**
General partners,
Definitions, **Bus Org 1.002**
Limited partnerships, post
Gifts, **Bus Org 2.101**
Good faith,
Damages, **Bus Org 7.001**
Limited partnerships, post
Officers and employees, **Bus Org 3.102, 3.105**
Guaranty, **Bus Org 2.101**
Powers and duties, **Bus Org 2.104**
Guardian and Ward, this index
Hold harmless. Indemnity, generally, post
Holding companies, merger and consolidation, **Bus Org 10.005**
Horse racing, limited partnerships, licenses and permits, transfers, **Bus Org 153.555**
Husband and wife,
Property, **Bus Org 152.101**
Transfers, **Bus Org 152.406**
Identity and identification, names, same or similar, **Bus Org 5.053**
Incentives, officers and employees, **Bus Org 2.101**
Incumbrances. Liens and incumbrances, generally, post
Indebtedness, **Bus Org 2.101, 2.103**
Application of law, **Bus Org 10.901**
Certificates and certification, **Bus Org 2.114**
Charging orders, **Bus Org 152.308**
Damages, **Bus Org 152.304**
Foreign limited liability partnerships, **Bus Org 152.910**
Interest, rates and charges, **Bus Org 152.005**
Judgment and decrees, charging orders, **Bus Org 152.308**
Judgments and decrees, **Bus Org 152.306**
Limited liability partnerships, **Bus Org 152.801, 153.353**
Limited partnerships, post
Third parties, **Bus Org 152.214**
Winding up, discharge, **Bus Org 11.053**
Indemnity,
Business Organizations Code, application of law, **Bus Org 402.007**
Insurance, **Bus Org 8.151**
Limited partnerships, post
Mandatory, **Bus Org 8.051**
Officers and employees, post
Orders of court, **Bus Org 8.052**

PARTNERSHIPS—Cont'd
Indemnity—Cont'd
Permissive indemnification, **Bus Org 8.101 et seq.**
Reports, **Bus Org 8.152**
Withdrawal, **Bus Org 152.606**
Information, disclosure, **Bus Org 152.213**
Injunctions,
Guaranty, **Bus Org 2.104**
Limited partnerships, post
State, **Bus Org 12.259**
Insolvency, actions and proceedings, **Bus Org 12.253 et seq.**
Inspection and inspectors,
Books and papers, **Bus Org 12.151 et seq.**
Limited partnerships, post
Records and recordation, **Bus Org 3.152, 152.212**
Transfers, books and papers, **Bus Org 152.404**
Insurance,
Indemnity, **Bus Org 2.101, 8.151**
Limited partnerships, indemnity, **Bus Org 2.101, 8.151**
Intention, **Bus Org 152.052**
Interest,
Indebtedness, rates and charges, **Bus Org 152.005**
Withdrawal, redemption, **Bus Org 152.605, 152.608**
Internal affairs, **Bus Org 1.105**
Interrogatories, **Bus Org 12.002, 12.003**
Investments, **Bus Org 2.101**
Limited partnerships, post
Involuntary termination, **Bus Org 11.251 et seq.**
Certified copies, judgments and decrees, **Bus Org 11.414**
Joint practices, **Bus Org 301.012**
Judgments and decrees, **Bus Org 152.306**
Indebtedness, charging orders, **Bus Org 152.308**
Limited partnerships, post
Receivers and receivership, termination, **Bus Org 11.412**
Reorganization, **Bus Org 10.305**
Termination, **Bus Org 11.301 et seq.**
Involuntary termination, certified copies, **Bus Org 11.414**
Winding up, **Bus Org 11.301 et seq.**
Withdrawal, **Bus Org 152.501**
Jurisdiction,
Filing, fines and penalties, **Bus Org 21.802**
Insolvency, **Bus Org 12.253**
Liens and incumbrances, foreclosure, **Bus Org 12.253**
Limited partnerships, post
Receivers and receivership, **Bus Org 11.402 et seq.**
Reorganization, **Bus Org 10.302**
Termination, involuntary termination, **Bus Org 11.308, 11.314**
Winding up, involuntary winding up, **Bus Org 11.308, 11.314**
Knowledge, facts, **Bus Org 151.002**

PARTNERSHIPS—Cont'd
Leases, **Bus Org 2.101, 10.251 et seq.**
Limited partnerships, post
Reorganization, **Bus Org 10.301**
Liability. Damages, generally, ante
Licenses and permits, **Bus Org 301.006**
Liens and incumbrances,
Charging orders, **Bus Org 152.308**
Foreclosure, **Bus Org 12.252 et seq.**
Limited partnerships, post
State, **Bus Org 12.201**
Limitation of actions, **Bus Org 152.211**
Termination, claims, **Bus Org 11.359**
Withdrawal, redemption, **Bus Org 152.609**
Limitations,
Filing,
Corrections, **Bus Org 4.102**
Effective date, delay, **Bus Org 4.058**
Indemnity, **Bus Org 8.003, 8.004**
Limited partnerships, post
Powers and duties, **Bus Org 2.113**
Purposes, **Bus Org 2.003 et seq.**
Limited Liability Companies, generally, this index
Limited liability partnerships, **Bus Org 153.351 et seq.**
Application of law, Business Organizations Code, **Bus Org 402.001 et seq.**
Assumed or fictitious names, **Bus & C 71.001 et seq.**
Damages, **Bus Org 152.801**
Definitions, **Bus Org 1.002**
Foreign limited liability partnerships, generally, ante
Indebtedness, **Bus Org 152.801**
Registration, **Bus Org 152.802, 153.351**
Limited partnerships, **Bus Org 1.001 et seq., 153.001 et seq., 301.001 et seq.**
Abandonment,
Conversion, **Bus Org 10.201, 10.202, 10.203**
Exchange of property, **Bus Org 10.201, 10.202, 10.203**
Filing, **Bus Org 4.057**
Merger and consolidation, **Bus Org 10.201, 10.202, 10.203**
Abatement of actions and proceedings,
State, **Bus Org 12.260**
Termination, involuntary termination, **Bus Org 11.304**
Transacting business in Texas, **Bus Org 153.310**
Winding up, involuntary winding up, **Bus Org 11.304**
Acceptance, certificates and certification, **Bus Org 10.156**
Accounts and accounting, **Bus Org 3.151 et seq.**
Examinations and examiners, **Bus Org 12.151 et seq.**
Acknowledgments,
Certificate of formation, **Bus Org 3.004**
Evidence, **Bus Org 3.001**
Filing, **Bus Org 4.002**

PARTNERSHIPS—Cont'd
Limited partnerships—Cont'd
  Acknowledgments—Cont'd
    Filing—Cont'd
      Effective date, delay, **Bus Org 4.059**
    Reports, **Bus Org 153.306**
  Actions and proceedings, **Bus Org 2.101**
    Certificate of formation, amendments, **Bus Org 3.056**
    Guaranty, **Bus Org 2.104**
    Indemnity, **Bus Org 8.001 et seq.**
    Insolvency, **Bus Org 12.253 et seq.**
    Receivers and receivership, **Bus Org 11.406**
    Records and recordation, inspection and inspectors, **Bus Org 3.152**
    State, liens and incumbrances, **Bus Org 12.201 et seq.**
    Termination, involuntary termination, **Bus Org 11.303**
    Winding up, **Bus Org 11.052, 11.055**
      Involuntary winding up, **Bus Org 11.303**
  Actions without meetings, contracts, meetings, **Bus Org 154.103**
  Address,
    Certificate of formation, **Bus Org 3.005, 3.011**
      Amendments, **Bus Org 153.052**
    Records and recordation, **Bus Org 153.551**
    Reports, forms, **Bus Org 153.302**
  Admissions, **Bus Org 153.101**
    Certificate of formation, amendments, **Bus Org 153.051**
    Damages, **Bus Org 153.103**
    General partners, **Bus Org 153.151**
  Advancements, indemnity, expenses and expenditures, **Bus Org 8.104, 8.105**
    Reports, **Bus Org 8.152**
  Agent for service of process, **Bus Org 5.251 et seq.**
  Agents and agencies, changes, filing, fines and penalties, **Bus Org 21.802**
  Allocations,
    Distribution and distributors, **Bus Org 153.208**
    Merger and consolidation, property, **Bus Org 10.003**
    Profits, losses, **Bus Org 153.206**
  Alternatives, service of process, **Bus Org 5.256**
  Amendments,
    Business Organizations Code, statutes, **Bus Org 1.054**
    Certificate of formation, **Bus Org 3.051 et seq., 153.051, 153.052**
    Filing, **Bus Org 4.106**
      Fees, **Bus Org 4.155**
  Ancillary receiverships, **Bus Org 11.409**
  Answer, interrogatories, time, **Bus Org 12.002**

PARTNERSHIPS—Cont'd
Limited partnerships—Cont'd
  Antitrust, application of law, **Bus Org 10.901**
  Appeal and review,
    Filing, **Bus Org 12.004**
    Termination, involuntary termination, **Bus Org 11.307**
    Winding up, involuntary winding up, **Bus Org 11.307**
  Application, winding up, **Bus Org 153.502**
  Application of law, **Bus Org 153.002**
    Antitrust, **Bus Org 10.901**
    Business Organizations Code, foreign countries, foreign states, **Bus Org 1.053**
    Certificate of formation, **Bus Org 1.101 et seq.**
    Indebtedness, **Bus Org 10.901**
    Indemnity, **Bus Org 8.002**
    Monopolies and unfair trade, **Bus Org 10.901**
    Reorganization, **Bus Org 10.306**
  Appointments, receivers and receivership, **Bus Org 11.401 et seq.**
  Appraisals and appraisers, reorganization, **Bus Org 10.304**
  Approval,
    Conversion, **Bus Org 10.107**
    Exchange of property, **Bus Org 10.056**
  Assets,
    Disposition, **Bus Org 10.251 et seq.**
      Reorganization, **Bus Org 10.301**
    Liens and incumbrances, state, **Bus Org 12.201**
    Winding up,
      Disposition, **Bus Org 153.504**
      Distribution and distributors, **Bus Org 11.053**
  Assignments, **Bus Org 10.251 et seq., 153.251 et seq.**
    General partners, withdrawal, **Bus Org 153.155**
    Shares and shareholders, certificates and certification, **Bus Org 3.201**
  Assumed or fictitious names, **Bus & C 71.001 et seq.; Bus Org 5.051 et seq.**
  Attachment, state, **Bus Org 12.259**
  Attorney fees,
    Derivative actions, **Bus Org 153.405**
    Filing,
      Fines and penalties, **Bus Org 21.802**
      Fraud, **Bus Org 4.007**
      Orders of court, **Bus Org 153.554**
    Records and recordation, inspection and inspectors, **Bus Org 3.152**
  Bankruptcy, **Bus Org 10.301 et seq.**
    General partners, withdrawal, **Bus Org 153.155**
  Bonds, **Bus Org 2.101**
    Reorganization, **Bus Org 10.301**

PARTNERSHIPS—Cont'd
Limited partnerships—Cont'd
  Bonds (officers and fiduciaries), receivers and receivership, **Bus Org 11.406**
  Bonuses, officers and employees, **Bus Org 2.101**
  Books and papers, **Bus Org 3.151 et seq.**
    Confidential or privileged information, **Bus Org 12.154**
    Disclosure, **Bus Org 12.154**
    Duplicates and copies, **Bus Org 12.151 et seq.**
    Examinations and examiners, **Bus Org 3.153, 12.151 et seq.**
    Inspection and inspectors, **Bus Org 3.152**
    Powers and duties, limitations, **Bus Org 2.005**
    Reorganization, **Bus Org 10.301**
    Signatures, **Bus Org 1.007**
  Breach, general partners, withdrawal, **Bus Org 153.157**
  Bylaws, **Bus Org 2.101**
  Cancellation, winding up, **Bus Org 11.152, 153.501**
  Certificate of formation, **Bus Org 3.001 et seq.**
    Amendments, **Bus Org 3.051 et seq., 153.051, 153.052**
      Reports, **Bus Org 153.306**
    Application of law, **Bus Org 1.101 et seq.**
    Definitions, **Bus Org 1.002**
    Duplicates and copies, **Bus Org 153.552**
    Filing,
      Fees, **Bus Org 4.155**
      Orders of court, **Bus Org 153.554**
    Merger and consolidation, **Bus Org 10.002**
    Orders of court, filings, **Bus Org 153.554**
    Records and recordation, **Bus Org 153.551**
    Reinstatement, **Bus Org 153.312**
    Reorganization, **Bus Org 10.301 et seq.**
    Reports, amendments, **Bus Org 153.306**
    Restatement, **Bus Org 3.057 et seq., 153.053**
    Rights, **Bus Org 153.105**
    Signatures, **Bus Org 153.553**
    Termination, **Bus Org 153.311**
      Filings, orders of court, **Bus Org 153.554**
      Signatures, **Bus Org 153.553**
  Certificates and certification,
    Acceptance, **Bus Org 10.156**
    Conversion, **Bus Org 10.154 et seq.**
    Evidence, existence, **Bus Org 4.005**
    Exchange of property, **Bus Org 10.151 et seq.**
    Filing, **Bus Org 12.001**
      Corrections, **Bus Org 4.101 et seq.**

PARTNERSHIPS—Cont'd
Limited partnerships—Cont'd
Certificates and certification—Cont'd
Filing—Cont'd
Fines and penalties, **Bus Org 21.802**
Orders of court, **Bus Org 153.554**
Indebtedness, **Bus Org 2.114**
Merger and consolidation, **Bus Org 10.151 et seq.**
Oaths and affirmations, **Bus Org 153.553**
Orders of court, filings, **Bus Org 153.554**
Shares and shareholders, **Bus Org 3.201 et seq.**
Signatures, **Bus Org 153.553**
Termination, **Bus Org 11.101 et seq.**
Involuntary termination, **Bus Org 11.252**
Reinstatement, **Bus Org 11.202**
Certified copies,
Filing, **Bus Org 4.005**
Involuntary termination, judgments and decrees, **Bus Org 11.414**
Changes,
Registered offices, registered agent, **Bus Org 5.202, 5.203**
Relationships, **Bus Org 154.202**
Citizens and citizenship, receivers and receivership, **Bus Org 11.406**
Claims,
Receivers and receivership, filing, **Bus Org 11.407**
Termination, **Bus Org 11.351 et seq.**
Classification, contracts, **Bus Org 154.101**
Committees, damages, **Bus Org 153.103**
Community property, **Bus Org 154.001**
Compensation and salaries,
General partners, withdrawal, **Bus Org 153.159**
Officers and employees, **Bus Org 2.101**
Receivers and receivership, **Bus Org 11.408**
Complaints, derivative actions, **Bus Org 153.403**
Compromise and settlement, contributions, **Bus Org 153.203**
Conduct, damages, **Bus Org 7.001, 153.103, 153.104**
Confidential or privileged information, interrogatories, **Bus Org 12.003**
Conflict of interest, damages, **Bus Org 153.103**
Consent,
Admissions, **Bus Org 153.101**
General partners, admissions, **Bus Org 153.151**
Winding up, **Bus Org 11.058**
Conservators and conservatorship, powers and duties, **Bus Org 153.113**
Construction of laws, **Bus Org 1.006, 1.051 et seq., 153.002 et seq.**
Consultants, damages, **Bus Org 153.103**
Contractors, damages, **Bus Org 153.103**

PARTNERSHIPS—Cont'd
Limited partnerships—Cont'd
Contracts, **Bus Org 2.101, 154.101 et seq.**
Actions without meetings, meetings, **Bus Org 154.103**
Business Organizations Code, waiver, **Bus Org 153.004**
Classification, **Bus Org 154.101**
Elections, **Bus Org 154.102**
General partners,
Admissions, **Bus Org 153.151**
Withdrawal, **Bus Org 153.155**
Indebtedness, **Bus Org 2.103**
Meetings, elections, **Bus Org 154.102**
Notice, meetings, **Bus Org 154.102**
Records and recordation, **Bus Org 153.551**
Rights, **Bus Org 153.105**
Third parties, waiver, **Bus Org 153.005**
Winding up, **Bus Org 11.152**
Contributions, **Bus Org 153.201 et seq.**
Compromise and settlement, **Bus Org 153.203**
Defaults, **Bus Org 153.202**
Definitions, business organizations, **Bus Org 1.002**
Enforcement, **Bus Org 153.204, 153.205**
Forfeitures, **Bus Org 153.202**
Forms, **Bus Org 153.201**
Frauds, statute of, **Bus Org 153.202**
General partners, **Bus Org 153.154**
Records and recordation, **Bus Org 153.551**
Release, **Bus Org 153.203**
Signatures, **Bus Org 153.202**
Conversion, **Bus Org 10.101 et seq.**
Abandonment, **Bus Org 10.201, 10.202, 10.203**
Acceptance, certificates and certification, **Bus Org 10.156**
Certificates and certification, **Bus Org 10.154 et seq.**
Dissenting shareholders, **Bus Org 10.351 et seq.**
Effective date, **Bus Org 10.105, 10.106**
Filing,
Certificates and certification, **Bus Org 10.155**
Fees, **Bus Org 4.151**
General partners, withdrawal, **Bus Org 153.158 et seq.**
Names, **Bus Org 10.103**
Notice, **Bus Org 10.101**
Plans and specifications, **Bus Org 10.101 et seq.**
Reorganization, **Bus Org 10.301 et seq.**
Corrections, filing, **Bus Org 4.101 et seq.**
Fees, **Bus Org 4.151**
Costs,
Derivative actions, **Bus Org 153.405**

PARTNERSHIPS—Cont'd
Limited partnerships—Cont'd
Costs—Cont'd
Filing,
Fines and penalties, **Bus Org 21.802**
Fraud, **Bus Org 4.007**
Orders of court, **Bus Org 153.554**
Insolvency, dismissal and nonsuit, **Bus Org 12.257**
Liens and incumbrances, foreclosure, dismissal and nonsuit, **Bus Org 12.257**
Crimes and offenses,
Books and papers, examinations and examiners, **Bus Org 12.156**
Damages, **Bus Org 7.001**
Filing, fraud, **Bus Org 4.008**
Termination, involuntary termination, **Bus Org 11.301 et seq.**
Winding up, involuntary winding up, **Bus Org 11.301 et seq.**
Damages, **Bus Org 153.102 et seq.**
Application of law, **Bus Org 1.104**
Assignments, **Bus Org 153.254, 153.255**
Conduct, **Bus Org 153.103, 153.104**
Errors, contributions, **Bus Org 153.109**
Filing, **Bus Org 21.802**
Fraud, **Bus Org 4.007**
General partners, withdrawal, **Bus Org 153.162**
Guaranty, **Bus Org 2.104**
Merger and consolidation, **Bus Org 10.009**
Officers and employees, **Bus Org 7.001**
Statements, **Bus Org 153.107, 153.108**
Third parties, **Bus Org 153.102**
Death,
General partners, withdrawal, **Bus Org 153.155**
Powers and duties, **Bus Org 153.113**
Deception, names, **Bus Org 5.052**
Deeds and conveyances, **Bus Org 10.251 et seq.**
Property, **Bus Org 2.101**
Records and recordation, **Bus Org 10.253**
Defaults, contributions, **Bus Org 153.202**
Definitions, **Bus Org 1.002, 153.001**
Indemnity, **Bus Org 8.001**
Termination, **Bus Org 11.001**
Winding up, **Bus Org 11.001**
Delay, filing, effective date, **Bus Org 4.052 et seq.**
Delivery,
Filing, **Bus Org 4.001**
Reports, **Bus Org 153.304**
Shares and shareholders, certificates and certification, **Bus Org 3.204**
Deposits, termination, claims, **Bus Org 11.352**

PARTNERSHIPS—Cont'd
Limited partnerships—Cont'd
Derivative actions, **Bus Org 153.401 et seq.**
Attorney fees, **Bus Org 153.405**
Complaints, **Bus Org 153.403**
Costs, **Bus Org 153.405**
Dismissal and nonsuit, security, **Bus Org 153.404**
Expenses and expenditures, **Bus Org 153.405**
Security, **Bus Org 153.404**
Parties, **Bus Org 153.402**
Pleadings, **Bus Org 153.403**
Security, **Bus Org 153.404**
Directors,
Agent for service of process, **Bus Org 5.255**
Certificate of formation, **Bus Org 3.007**
Amendments, **Bus Org 3.054**
Restatement, **Bus Org 3.060**
Damages, **Bus Org 7.001**
Indemnity, **Bus Org 7.001**
Loans, **Bus Org 2.101**
Discharge,
Receivers and receivership, **Bus Org 11.412**
Termination, claims, **Bus Org 11.353**
Winding up, indebtedness, **Bus Org 11.053**
Disclosure, interrogatories, **Bus Org 12.003**
Dismissal and nonsuit,
Derivative actions, security, **Bus Org 153.404**
Insolvency, **Bus Org 12.257**
Liens and incumbrances, foreclosure, **Bus Org 12.257**
Dissolution, **Bus Org 2.101**
Filing, fees, **Bus Org 4.155**
Distribution and distributors, **Bus Org 153.207 et seq.**
Allocations, **Bus Org 153.208**
General partners, **Bus Org 153.154**
In kind, **Bus Org 154.203**
Limitations, **Bus Org 153.210**
Returns, **Bus Org 153.112**
Time, **Bus Org 153.209**
Winding up, assets, **Bus Org 11.053**
Withdrawal, **Bus Org 153.111**
Dog races, licenses and permits, transfers, **Bus Org 153.555**
Dual office holding, officers and employees, **Bus Org 3.103**
Duplicates and copies,
Agent for service of process, **Bus Org 5.252**
Books and papers, **Bus Org 12.151 et seq.**
Filing, **Bus Org 4.003**
Records and recordation, **Bus Org 3.152, 153.552**
Reports, **Bus Org 153.305**
Shares and shareholders, certificates and certification, **Bus Org 3.202**

PARTNERSHIPS—Cont'd
Limited partnerships—Cont'd
Effective date,
Conversion, **Bus Org 10.105, 10.106**
Exchange of property, **Bus Org 10.054, 10.055**
Filing, **Bus Org 4.051 et seq.**
Merger and consolidation, **Bus Org 10.007**
Termination, **Bus Org 11.102, 11.103**
Claims, **Bus Org 11.356 et seq.**
Reinstatement, **Bus Org 11.204 et seq.**
Elections,
Contracts, **Bus Org 154.102**
Indemnity, **Bus Org 8.103**
Officers and employees, **Bus Org 2.101, 3.103**
Electronic filing, **Bus Org 12.001**
Emergencies, governance, **Bus Org 3.251 et seq.**
Enforcement, contributions, **Bus Org 153.204, 153.205**
Errors,
Contributions, damages, **Bus Org 153.109**
Status, **Bus Org 153.106**
Termination, reinstatement, **Bus Org 11.201 et seq.**
Escheat, termination, claims, **Bus Org 11.355**
Evidence,
Certificate of formation, acknowledgments, **Bus Org 3.001**
Existence, certificates and certification, **Bus Org 4.005**
Filing, **Bus Org 4.001**
Indebtedness, fraud, **Bus Org 2.103**
Shares and shareholders, certificates and certification, **Bus Org 3.201**
Examinations and examiners,
Books and papers, **Bus Org 12.151 et seq.**
Records and recordation, **Bus Org 3.153, 153.552**
Exchange of property, **Bus Org 2.101, 10.051 et seq.**
Abandonment, **Bus Org 10.201, 10.202, 10.203**
Acceptance, certificates and certification, **Bus Org 10.156**
Certificates and certification, **Bus Org 10.151 et seq.**
Dissenting shareholders, **Bus Org 10.351 et seq.**
Filing,
Certificates and certification, **Bus Org 10.153**
Fees, **Bus Org 4.151**
Reorganization, **Bus Org 10.301**
Voluntary, **Bus Org 10.902**
Exemptions,
Assignments, **Bus Org 153.257**
Guaranty, powers and duties, **Bus Org 2.104**
Interrogatories, **Bus Org 12.002**

PARTNERSHIPS—Cont'd
Limited partnerships—Cont'd
Exemptions—Cont'd
Termination, involuntary termination, **Bus Org 11.251**
Expenses and expenditures,
Derivative actions, **Bus Org 153.405**
Security, **Bus Org 153.404**
Indemnity, **Bus Org 8.001 et seq.**
Facsimile, **Bus Org 1.007**
Filing, **Bus Org 4.003**
Indebtedness, certificates and certification, **Bus Org 2.114**
Seals, **Bus Org 2.101**
Shares and shareholders, certificates and certification, **Bus Org 3.203**
Fees,
Filing, **Bus Org 4.151 et seq., 4.158**
Names, reservation, **Bus Org 5.101**
Withdrawal, **Bus Org 5.1041**
Reports, filing, **Bus Org 153.303**
Filing, **Bus Org 4.001 et seq., 12.001 et seq.**
Abandonment, **Bus Org 4.057**
Acknowledgments, **Bus Org 4.002**
Effective date, delay, **Bus Org 4.059**
Amendments, **Bus Org 4.106**
Appeal and review, **Bus Org 12.004**
Assumed or fictitious names, **Bus Org 5.051**
Attorney fees,
Fines and penalties, **Bus Org 21.802**
Fraud, **Bus Org 4.007**
Orders of court, **Bus Org 153.554**
Certificate of formation, **Bus Org 3.001 et seq.**
Certificates and certification, **Bus Org 12.001**
Abandonment, **Bus Org 4.057**
Corrections, **Bus Org 4.101 et seq.**
Certified copies, **Bus Org 4.005**
Conversion, certificates and certification, **Bus Org 10.155**
Corrections, **Bus Org 4.101 et seq.**
Fees, **Bus Org 4.151**
Costs,
Fines and penalties, **Bus Org 21.802**
Fraud, **Bus Org 4.007**
Orders of court, **Bus Org 153.554**
Damages, **Bus Org 21.802**
Fraud, **Bus Org 4.007**
Statements, **Bus Org 153.107**
Delay, effective date, **Bus Org 4.052 et seq.**
Delivery, **Bus Org 4.001**
Duplicates and copies, **Bus Org 4.003**
Effective date, **Bus Org 4.051 et seq.**
Electronic filing, **Bus Org 12.001**
Evidence, **Bus Org 4.001**
Facsimile, **Bus Org 4.003**
Fees, **Bus Org 4.151 et seq., 4.158**
Fines and penalties, **Bus Org 21.802**
Fraud, **Bus Org 4.008**
Forms, **Bus Org 4.006**

PARTNERSHIPS—Cont'd
Limited partnerships—Cont'd
Filing—Cont'd
Fraud, **Bus Org 4.007, 4.008**
Interrogatories, **Bus Org 12.002, 12.003**
Jurisdiction, fines and penalties, **Bus Org 21.802**
Limitations,
Corrections, **Bus Org 4.102**
Effective date, delay, **Bus Org 4.058**
Names, registration, **Bus Org 5.152**
Orders of court, **Bus Org 153.554**
Real estate investment trusts, **Bus Org 4.009**
Receivers and receivership, claims, **Bus Org 11.407**
Registered agent, resignation, **Bus Org 5.204**
Reports, **Bus Org 153.301 et seq.**
Service of process, **Bus Org 21.802**
Signatures, **Bus Org 4.001, 153.553**
Corrections, certificates and certification, **Bus Org 4.101**
Termination, involuntary termination, **Bus Org 11.315**
Time, **Bus Org 4.004**
Corrections, **Bus Org 4.105**
Effective date, **Bus Org 4.051 et seq.**
Fines and penalties, **Bus Org 21.802**
Winding up, involuntary winding up, **Bus Org 11.315**
Financial statements and reports, officers and employees, good faith, **Bus Org 3.102, 3.105**
Fines and penalties,
Books and papers, examinations and examiners, **Bus Org 12.156**
Filing, **Bus Org 21.802**
Fraud, **Bus Org 4.008**
Foreclosure, liens and incumbrances, **Bus Org 12.252 et seq.**
Foreign countries,
Business Organizations Code, application of law, **Bus Org 1.053**
Certificate of formation, application of law, **Bus Org 1.102**
Foreign limited partnerships, generally, ante
Foreign states,
Business Organizations Code, application of law, **Bus Org 1.053**
Certificate of formation, application of law, **Bus Org 1.102**
Forfeitures,
Books and papers, examinations and examiners, **Bus Org 12.155**
Contributions, **Bus Org 153.202**
Reports, **Bus Org 153.307 et seq.**
Forms,
Contributions, **Bus Org 153.201**
Filing, **Bus Org 4.006**
Reports, **Bus Org 153.302**

PARTNERSHIPS—Cont'd
Limited partnerships—Cont'd
Forms—Cont'd
Shares and shareholders, certificates and certification, **Bus Org 3.202**
Fraud,
Certificate of formation, amendments, **Bus Org 153.051**
Filing, **Bus Org 4.007, 4.008**
Guaranty, **Bus Org 2.104**
Indebtedness, evidence, **Bus Org 2.103**
Names, **Bus Org 5.052**
Receivers and receivership, **Bus Org 11.403**
Termination,
Involuntary termination, **Bus Org 11.301 et seq.**
Revocation or suspension, **Bus Org 11.153**
Winding up, involuntary winding up, **Bus Org 11.301 et seq.**
Frauds, statute of,
Contributions, **Bus Org 153.202**
Powers and duties, **Bus Org 2.112**
Garnishment, state, **Bus Org 12.259**
General partners, **Bus Org 153.151 et seq.**
Admissions, **Bus Org 153.151**
Assignments, withdrawal, **Bus Org 153.155**
Bankruptcy, withdrawal, **Bus Org 153.155**
Breach, withdrawal, **Bus Org 153.157**
Compensation and salaries, withdrawal, **Bus Org 153.159**
Contracts,
Admissions, **Bus Org 153.151**
Withdrawal, **Bus Org 153.155**
Contributions, **Bus Org 153.154**
Conversion, withdrawal, **Bus Org 153.158 et seq.**
Damages, withdrawal, **Bus Org 153.162**
Death, withdrawal, **Bus Org 153.155**
Definitions, **Bus Org 1.002**
Distribution and distributors, **Bus Org 153.154**
Indebtedness, **Bus Org 153.152, 153.153**
Withdrawal, **Bus Org 153.161**
Liquidation, withdrawal, **Bus Org 153.155**
Mental health, withdrawal, **Bus Org 153.155**
Notice, withdrawal, **Bus Org 153.155**
Payment, withdrawal, **Bus Org 153.158, 153.160**
Powers and duties, **Bus Org 153.152, 153.153**
Probate proceedings, withdrawal, **Bus Org 153.155**
Receivers and receivership, withdrawal, **Bus Org 153.155**
Removal, withdrawal, **Bus Org 153.155**

PARTNERSHIPS—Cont'd
Limited partnerships—Cont'd
General partners—Cont'd
Reorganization, withdrawal, **Bus Org 153.155**
Setoff and counterclaims, withdrawal, **Bus Org 153.162**
Termination, withdrawal, **Bus Org 153.155**
Winding up, withdrawal, **Bus Org 153.155**
Withdrawal, **Bus Org 153.155 et seq.**
Gifts, **Bus Org 2.101**
Good faith,
Damages, **Bus Org 7.001**
Officers and employees, **Bus Org 3.102, 3.105**
Status, errors, **Bus Org 153.106**
Guaranty, **Bus Org 2.101**
Powers and duties, **Bus Org 2.104**
Guardian and ward, powers and duties, **Bus Org 153.113**
Holding companies, merger and consolidation, **Bus Org 10.005**
Horse racing, transfers, licenses and permits, **Bus Org 153.555**
Identity and identification, names, same or similar, **Bus Org 5.053**
Incentives, officers and employees, **Bus Org 2.101**
Indebtedness, **Bus Org 2.101, 2.103**
Application of law, **Bus Org 10.901**
Certificates and certification, **Bus Org 2.114**
Damages, **Bus Org 153.103**
General partners, **Bus Org 153.152, 153.153**
Withdrawal, **Bus Org 153.161**
Winding up, discharge, **Bus Org 11.053**
Indemnity,
Insurance, **Bus Org 8.151**
Mandatory, **Bus Org 8.051**
Officers and employees, **Bus Org 2.101, 7.001, 8.001 et seq.**
Orders of court, **Bus Org 8.052**
Permissive indemnification, **Bus Org 8.101 et seq.**
Reports, **Bus Org 8.152**
Injunctions,
Guaranty, **Bus Org 2.104**
State, **Bus Org 12.259**
Insolvency, actions and proceedings, **Bus Org 12.253 et seq.**
Inspection and inspectors,
Books and papers, **Bus Org 12.151 et seq.**
Records and recordation, **Bus Org 3.152, 153.551, 153.552**
Insurance, indemnity, **Bus Org 2.101, 8.151**
Internal affairs, **Bus Org 1.105**
Interrogatories, **Bus Org 12.002, 12.003**
Investments, **Bus Org 2.101**
Damages, **Bus Org 153.103**
Involuntary termination, **Bus Org 11.251 et seq.**

PARTNERSHIPS—Cont'd
Limited partnerships—Cont'd
Involuntary termination—Cont'd
Certified copies, judgments and decrees, **Bus Org 11.414**
Judgments and decrees,
Assignments, payment, **Bus Org 153.256**
Receivers and receivership, termination, **Bus Org 11.412**
Reorganization, **Bus Org 10.305**
Termination, **Bus Org 11.301 et seq.**
Involuntary termination, certified copies, **Bus Org 11.414**
Winding up, **Bus Org 11.301 et seq.**
Jurisdiction,
Filing, fines and penalties, **Bus Org 21.802**
Insolvency, **Bus Org 12.253**
Liens and incumbrances, foreclosure, **Bus Org 12.253**
Receivers and receivership, **Bus Org 11.402, 11.403**
Reorganization, **Bus Org 10.302**
Termination, involuntary termination, **Bus Org 11.308**
Winding up, involuntary winding up, **Bus Org 11.308**
Leases, **Bus Org 2.101, 10.251 et seq.**
Reorganization, **Bus Org 10.301**
Licenses and permits, racing, transfers, **Bus Org 153.555**
Liens and incumbrances,
Foreclosure, **Bus Org 12.252 et seq.**
Judgments and decrees, **Bus Org 153.256**
State, **Bus Org 12.201**
Limitation of actions, termination, claims, **Bus Org 11.359**
Limitations,
Distribution and distributors, **Bus Org 153.210**
Filing,
Corrections, **Bus Org 4.102**
Effective date, delay, **Bus Org 4.058**
Indemnity, **Bus Org 8.003, 8.004**
Powers and duties, **Bus Org 2.113**
Purposes, **Bus Org 2.003 et seq.**
Liquidation,
General partners, withdrawal, **Bus Org 153.155**
Receivers and receivership, **Bus Org 12.258**
Orders of court, **Bus Org 11.405**
Loans, **Bus Org 2.101, 154.201**
Location, offices, **Bus Org 2.101**
Losses, allocations, **Bus Org 153.206**
Lottery, names, **Bus Org 5.061**
Managers and management, agent for service of process, **Bus Org 5.255**
Meetings,
Actions without meetings, contracts, **Bus Org 154.103**
Contracts, elections, **Bus Org 154.102**
Emergencies, **Bus Org 3.251 et seq.**

PARTNERSHIPS—Cont'd
Limited partnerships—Cont'd
Meetings—Cont'd
Notice, actions without meetings, **Bus Org 154.103**
Members, records and recordation, **Bus Org 153.551**
Mental health,
General partners, withdrawal, **Bus Org 153.155**
Powers and duties, **Bus Org 153.113**
Merger and consolidation, **Bus Org 10.001 et seq.**
Abandonment, **Bus Org 10.201, 10.202, 10.203**
Acceptance, certificates and certification, **Bus Org 10.156**
Allocations, property, **Bus Org 10.003**
Certificate of formation, **Bus Org 3.005, 3.006, 10.002**
Certificates and certification, **Bus Org 10.151 et seq.**
Damages, **Bus Org 10.009, 153.103**
Dissenting shareholders, **Bus Org 10.351 et seq.**
Effect, **Bus Org 10.008**
Effective date, **Bus Org 10.007**
Filing,
Certificates and certification, **Bus Org 10.153**
Fees, **Bus Org 4.151**
Holding companies, **Bus Org 10.005**
Names, **Bus Org 10.002**
Plans and specifications, **Bus Org 10.001 et seq.**
Property, allocations, **Bus Org 10.003**
Reorganization, **Bus Org 10.301 et seq.**
Signatures, **Bus Org 153.553**
Subsidiaries, **Bus Org 10.006**
Certificates and certification, **Bus Org 10.152**
Time, effective date, **Bus Org 10.007**
Misconduct, damages, **Bus Org 7.001**
Money, **Bus Org 1.009**
Monopolies and unfair trade, application of law, **Bus Org 10.901**
Mortgages, **Bus Org 2.101**
Powers and duties, **Bus Org 2.104**
Receivers and receivership, **Bus Org 11.403**
Names, **Bus Org 5.001 et seq., 5.063**
Assumed or fictitious names, **Bus Org 5.051 et seq.**
Certificate of formation, **Bus Org 3.005**
Amendments, **Bus Org 3.053, 3.056, 153.051, 153.052**
Changes, certificate of formation, amendments, **Bus Org 153.051**
Conversion, **Bus Org 10.103**
Deception, **Bus Org 5.052**
Exchange of property, plans and specifications, **Bus Org 10.052**
Fees, reservation, **Bus Org 5.101**
Withdrawal, **Bus Org 5.1041**

PARTNERSHIPS—Cont'd
Limited partnerships—Cont'd
Names—Cont'd
Filing,
Fees, **Bus Org 4.151, 4.155**
Registration, **Bus Org 5.152**
Fraud, **Bus Org 5.052**
Identity and identification, same or similar, **Bus Org 5.053**
Lottery, **Bus Org 5.061**
Merger and consolidation, **Bus Org 10.002**
Notice, **Bus Org 5.001**
Records and recordation, **Bus Org 153.551**
Registration, **Bus Org 5.151 et seq.**
Change of name, **Bus Org 9.010**
Reinstatement, **Bus Org 9.105**
Renewal,
Registration, **Bus Org 5.155**
Reservation, **Bus Org 5.105**
Reports, forms, **Bus Org 153.302**
Reservation, **Bus Org 5.101 et seq.**
Same or similar, **Bus Org 5.053**
Registration, **Bus Org 5.153**
Reservation, **Bus Org 5.102**
Termination, reinstatement, **Bus Org 11.203**
Time,
Registration, **Bus Org 5.154**
Reservation, **Bus Org 5.104**
Trademarks and trade names, **Bus Org 5.001**
Transfers, reservation, **Bus Org 5.106**
Veterans organizations, **Bus Org 5.062**
Words and phrases, **Bus Org 5.055**
Nonfiling, certificate of formation, **Bus Org 3.002**
Notice,
Agent for service of process, **Bus Org 5.252, 5.253**
Certificate of formation, **Bus Org 3.011**
Contracts, meetings, **Bus Org 154.102**
Conversion, **Bus Org 10.101**
General partners, withdrawal, **Bus Org 153.156**
Guaranty, fraud, **Bus Org 2.104**
Indemnity, orders of court, **Bus Org 8.052**
Insolvency, **Bus Org 12.256**
Liens and incumbrances,
Foreclosure, **Bus Org 12.256**
State, **Bus Org 12.201**
Meetings, actions without meetings, **Bus Org 154.103**
Names, **Bus Org 5.001**
Receivers and receivership, claims, **Bus Org 11.407**
Registered agent, resignation, **Bus Org 5.204**
Reorganization, **Bus Org 10.301**
Reports, **Bus Org 153.305**
Forfeitures, **Bus Org 153.308**

PARTNERSHIPS—Cont'd
Limited partnerships—Cont'd
Notice—Cont'd
Shares and shareholders, uncertificated shares, **Bus Org 3.205**
Termination,
Escheat, claims, **Bus Org 11.355**
Involuntary termination, **Bus Org 11.251, 11.302, 11.310**
Winding up, **Bus Org 11.052**
Involuntary winding up, **Bus Org 11.302, 11.310**
Oaths and affirmations,
Certificates and certification, **Bus Org 153.553**
Interrogatories, answer, **Bus Org 12.002**
Officers and employees, **Bus Org 3.101 et seq.**
Agent for service of process, **Bus Org 5.255**
Compensation and salaries, **Bus Org 2.101**
Damages, **Bus Org 7.001**
Application of law, **Bus Org 1.104**
Dual office holding, **Bus Org 3.103**
Elections, **Bus Org 2.101, 3.103**
Good faith, **Bus Org 3.105**
Indemnity, **Bus Org 2.101, 7.001, 8.001 et seq.**
Loans, **Bus Org 2.101**
Removal, **Bus Org 3.104**
Retirement and pensions, **Bus Org 2.101**
Offices, **Bus Org 2.101**
Changes, filing, fines and penalties, **Bus Org 21.802**
Reorganization, **Bus Org 10.301**
Transacting business in Texas, **Bus Org 9.251**
Omissions, certificate of formation, restatement, **Bus Org 3.059**
Open records, interrogatories, **Bus Org 12.003**
Orders of court,
Filings, **Bus Org 153.554**
Receivers and receivership, **Bus Org 11.402**
Liquidation, **Bus Org 11.405**
Parties,
Derivative actions, **Bus Org 153.402**
Receivers and receivership, **Bus Org 11.411**
Payment,
General partners, withdrawal, **Bus Org 153.158, 153.160**
Termination,
Claims, **Bus Org 11.354**
Taxation, **Bus Org 11.101**
Permissive indemnification, **Bus Org 8.101 et seq.**
Personal property, **Bus Org 2.101, 154.001**
Disposition, **Bus Org 10.251 et seq.**
Reorganization, **Bus Org 10.301**
Shares and shareholders, **Bus Org 21.801**

PARTNERSHIPS—Cont'd
Limited partnerships—Cont'd
Plans and specifications,
Conversion, **Bus Org 10.101 et seq.**
Exchange of property, **Bus Org 10.051 et seq.**
Merger and consolidation, **Bus Org 10.001 et seq.**
Pleadings, derivative actions, **Bus Org 153.403**
Political subdivisions, service of process, **Bus Org 5.257**
Power of attorney, records and recordation, **Bus Org 153.551**
Powers and duties, **Bus Org 2.101 et seq.**
Assignments, **Bus Org 153.252, 153.253**
General partners, **Bus Org 153.152, 153.153**
Receivers and receivership, **Bus Org 11.406**
Winding up, **Bus Org 153.503**
President, agent for service of process, **Bus Org 5.255**
Priorities and preferences,
Business Organizations Code, application of law, **Bus Org 1.106**
Certificate of formation, shares and shareholders, **Bus Org 3.007**
Privileges and immunities,
Property, disposition, **Bus Org 10.254**
Status, errors, **Bus Org 153.106**
Probate proceedings,
General partners, withdrawal, **Bus Org 153.155**
Powers and duties, **Bus Org 153.113**
Process, **Bus Org 5.251 et seq.**
Profit sharing, officers and employees, **Bus Org 2.101**
Profits, allocations, **Bus Org 153.206**
Property, **Bus Org 2.101**
Disposition, **Bus Org 10.251 et seq.**
Reorganization, **Bus Org 10.301**
Liens and incumbrances,
Foreclosure, **Bus Org 12.252 et seq.**
State, **Bus Org 12.201**
Merger and consolidation, allocations, **Bus Org 10.003**
Publication,
Termination, involuntary termination, **Bus Org 11.310**
Winding up, involuntary winding up, **Bus Org 11.310**
Purchases and purchasing, indemnity, insurance, **Bus Org 8.151**
Purposes, **Bus Org 2.001 et seq.**
Certificate of formation, **Bus Org 3.005**
Quo warranto, insolvency, **Bus Org 12.253 et seq.**
Racing, licenses and permits, transfers, **Bus Org 153.555**
Real estate, **Bus Org 2.101**
Disposition, **Bus Org 10.251 et seq.**
Reorganization, **Bus Org 10.301**

PARTNERSHIPS—Cont'd
Limited partnerships—Cont'd
Real estate—Cont'd
Records and recordation, deeds and conveyances, **Bus Org 10.253**
Receipts, termination, claims, **Bus Org 11.352**
Receivers and receivership, **Bus Org 11.401 et seq.**
Actions and proceedings, **Bus Org 11.406**
Ancillary receiverships, **Bus Org 11.409**
Appointments, **Bus Org 11.401 et seq.**
Bonds (officers and fiduciaries), **Bus Org 11.406**
Citizens and citizenship, **Bus Org 11.406**
Claims, filing, **Bus Org 11.407**
Compensation and salaries, **Bus Org 11.408**
Discharge, **Bus Org 11.412**
Filing, claims, **Bus Org 11.407**
Foreign entities, **Bus Org 11.409, 11.410**
Fraud, **Bus Org 11.403**
General partners, withdrawal, **Bus Org 153.155**
Judgments and decrees, termination, **Bus Org 11.412**
Jurisdiction, **Bus Org 11.402, 11.403, 11.408**
Liens and incumbrances, state, **Bus Org 12.201**
Liquidation, **Bus Org 12.258**
Orders of court, **Bus Org 11.405**
Mortgages, **Bus Org 11.403**
Notice, claims, **Bus Org 11.407**
Orders of court, **Bus Org 11.402**
Liquidation, **Bus Org 11.405**
Parties, **Bus Org 11.411**
Powers and duties, **Bus Org 11.406**
Registration, **Bus Org 11.406**
Rehabilitation, **Bus Org 11.404**
State, **Bus Org 12.251**
Termination, **Bus Org 11.403**
Judgments and decrees, **Bus Org 11.412**
Records and recordation, **Bus Org 3.151 et seq., 153.551**
Certified copies, filing, **Bus Org 4.005**
Confidential or privileged information, **Bus Org 12.154**
Disclosure, **Bus Org 12.154**
Examinations and examiners, **Bus Org 3.153, 12.151 et seq., 153.552**
Inspection and inspectors, **Bus Org 3.152, 153.551, 153.552**
Interrogatories, open records, **Bus Org 12.003**
Real estate, deeds and conveyances, **Bus Org 10.253**
Reorganization, **Bus Org 10.301**
Service of process, **Bus Org 5.254**

PARTNERSHIPS—Cont'd
Limited partnerships—Cont'd
Records and recordation—Cont'd
Signatures, **Bus Org 1.007**
Termination, removal, **Bus Org 11.104**
Registered agent, **Bus Org 5.200 et seq.**
Changes, **Bus Org 5.202**
Filing, fines and penalties, **Bus Org 21.802**
Reorganization, **Bus Org 10.301**
Resignation, **Bus Org 5.204**
Registered offices, **Bus Org 5.200 et seq.**
Changes, **Bus Org 5.202**
Filing, fines and penalties, **Bus Org 21.802**
Records and recordation, **Bus Org 153.551**
Registration,
Jurisdiction, revocation or suspension, **Bus Org 9.158**
Names, **Bus Org 5.151 et seq.**
Receivers and receivership, **Bus Org 11.406**
Reinstatement, **Bus Org 153.312**
Revocation or suspension, **Bus Org 153.311**
Rehabilitation, receivers and receivership, **Bus Org 11.404**
Reinstatement,
Certificate of formation, **Bus Org 153.312**
Consent, **Bus Org 153.505**
Registration, **Bus Org 153.312**
Termination, **Bus Org 11.201 et seq.**
Involuntary termination, **Bus Org 11.253**
Relationships, changes, **Bus Org 154.202**
Release, contributions, **Bus Org 153.203**
Remand,
Termination, involuntary termination, **Bus Org 11.307**
Winding up, involuntary winding up, **Bus Org 11.307**
Removal,
General partners, withdrawal, **Bus Org 153.155**
Officers and employees, **Bus Org 3.104**
Renewal, names,
Registration, **Bus Org 5.155**
Reservation, **Bus Org 5.105**
Reorganization, **Bus Org 10.301 et seq.**
General partners, withdrawal, **Bus Org 153.155**
Repeals, Business Organizations Code, statutes, **Bus Org 1.054**
Reports, **Bus Org 153.301 et seq.**
Filing, fees, **Bus Org 4.155**
Indemnity, **Bus Org 8.152**
Officers and employees, good faith, **Bus Org 3.102, 3.105**
Reservation, names, **Bus Org 5.101 et seq.**

PARTNERSHIPS—Cont'd
Limited partnerships—Cont'd
Resignation, registered agent, **Bus Org 5.204**
Resolutions, indemnity, **Bus Org 8.103**
Restatement, certificate of formation, **Bus Org 3.057 et seq., 153.053**
Retirement and pensions, officers and employees, **Bus Org 2.101**
Returns, distribution and distributors, **Bus Org 153.112**
Revocation or suspension,
Registration, **Bus Org 153.311**
Termination, fraud, **Bus Org 11.153**
Winding up, **Bus Org 11.151, 153.501**
Rights, **Bus Org 153.105**
Assignments, **Bus Org 153.252, 153.253**
Sales, **Bus Org 10.251 et seq.**
Property, **Bus Org 2.101**
Reorganization, **Bus Org 10.301**
Same or similar, names, **Bus Org 5.053**
Seals, **Bus Org 2.101**
Indebtedness, certificates and certification, **Bus Org 2.114**
Shares and shareholders, certificates and certification, **Bus Org 3.202**
Secretary of state, agent for service of process, **Bus Org 5.251 et seq.**
Securities, **Bus Org 2.101**
Powers and duties, **Bus Org 2.104**
Security, derivative actions, **Bus Org 153.404**
Sequestration, state, **Bus Org 12.259**
Service of process, **Bus Org 5.251 et seq.**
Reorganization, **Bus Org 10.301**
Termination, involuntary termination, **Bus Org 11.309**
Winding up, involuntary winding up, **Bus Org 11.309**
Setoff and counterclaims, general partners, withdrawal, **Bus Org 153.162**
Shares and shareholders,
Abandonment, exchange of property, **Bus Org 10.201, 10.202, 10.203**
Acceptance, exchange of property, certificates and certification, **Bus Org 10.156**
Appointments, dissenting shareholders, appraisal and appraisers, **Bus Org 10.361**
Appraisals and appraisers, dissenting shareholders, **Bus Org 10.354 et seq.**
Assignments, certificates and certification, **Bus Org 3.201**
Books and papers, dissenting shareholders, fair market value, **Bus Org 10.363**
Certificate of formation, numbers and numbering, **Bus Org 3.007**
Certificates and certification, **Bus Org 3.201 et seq.**
Exchange of property, **Bus Org 10.151 et seq.**

PARTNERSHIPS—Cont'd
Limited partnerships—Cont'd
Shares and shareholders—Cont'd
Compensation and salaries, dissenting shareholders, appraisals and appraisers, **Bus Org 10.365**
Computation, dissenting shareholders, fair market value, **Bus Org 10.362**
Costs, dissenting shareholders, appraisals and appraisers, **Bus Org 10.365**
Delivery, certificates and certification, **Bus Org 3.204**
Demand, dissenting shareholders, fair market value, **Bus Org 10.357 et seq.**
Dissenting shareholders, **Bus Org 10.351 et seq.**
Appointments, appraisal and appraisers, **Bus Org 10.361**
Appraisals and appraisers, **Bus Org 10.354 et seq.**
Books and papers, fair market value, **Bus Org 10.363**
Compensation and salaries, appraisals and appraisers, **Bus Org 10.365**
Computation, fair market value, **Bus Org 10.362**
Costs, appraisals and appraisers, **Bus Org 10.365**
Definitions, **Bus Org 10.352**
Demand, fair market value, **Bus Org 10.357 et seq.**
Exclusive remedy, **Bus Org 10.368**
Fair market value, demand, **Bus Org 10.357 et seq.**
Forms, **Bus Org 10.353**
Hearings, fair market value, **Bus Org 10.361**
Investigations and investigators, fair market value, **Bus Org 10.363**
Notice, **Bus Org 10.353, 10.355**
Objections and exceptions, appraisals and appraisers, **Bus Org 10.364**
Perfection, **Bus Org 10.356**
Petitions, fair market value, **Bus Org 10.361**
Records and recordation, fair market value, **Bus Org 10.363**
Demand, **Bus Org 10.359**
Reorganization, **Bus Org 10.304**
Termination, **Bus Org 10.367**
Title to property, **Bus Org 10.366**
Withdrawal, **Bus Org 10.357**
Duplicates and copies, certificates and certification, **Bus Org 3.202**
Evidence, certificates and certification, **Bus Org 3.201**
Exchange of property, **Bus Org 10.051 et seq.**
Abandonment, **Bus Org 10.201, 10.202, 10.203**

PARTNERSHIPS—Cont'd
Limited partnerships—Cont'd
Shares and shareholders—Cont'd
Exchange of property—Cont'd
Acceptance, certificates and certification, **Bus Org 10.156**
Certificates and certification, **Bus Org 10.151 et seq.**
Filing, certificates and certification, **Bus Org 10.153**
Exclusive remedy, dissenting shareholders, **Bus Org 10.368**
Facsimile, certificates and certification, **Bus Org 3.203**
Fair market value, dissenting shareholders, demand, **Bus Org 10.357 et seq.**
Filing, exchange of property, certificates and certification, **Bus Org 10.153**
Forms,
Certificates and certification, **Bus Org 3.202**
Dissenting shareholders, **Bus Org 10.353**
Hearings, dissenting shareholders, fair market value, **Bus Org 10.361**
Investigations and investigators, dissenting shareholders, fair market value, **Bus Org 10.363**
Notice,
Dissenting shareholders, **Bus Org 10.353, 10.355**
Uncertificated shares, **Bus Org 3.205**
Objections and exceptions, dissenting shareholders, appraisals and appraisers, **Bus Org 10.364**
Perfection, dissenting shareholders, **Bus Org 10.356**
Personal property, **Bus Org 21.801**
Petitions, dissenting shareholders, fair market value, **Bus Org 10.361**
Records and recordation, dissenting shareholders, fair market value, **Bus Org 10.363**
Demand, **Bus Org 10.359**
Reorganization, dissenting shareholders, **Bus Org 10.304**
Seals, certificates and certification, **Bus Org 3.202**
Signatures, certificates and certification, **Bus Org 3.203**
Termination, dissenting shareholders, **Bus Org 10.367**
Title to property, dissenting shareholders, **Bus Org 10.366**
Transfers, certificates and certification, **Bus Org 3.201**
Uncertificated shares, **Bus Org 3.201**
Notice, **Bus Org 3.205**
Withdrawal, dissenting shareholders, **Bus Org 10.357**
Signatures, **Bus Org 1.007**

PARTNERSHIPS—Cont'd
Limited partnerships—Cont'd
Signatures—Cont'd
Certificate of formation, **Bus Org 3.004, 153.553**
Amendments, **Bus Org 3.052, 3.054**
Restatement, **Bus Org 3.058, 3.060**
Contributions, **Bus Org 153.202**
Damages, statements, **Bus Org 153.107**
Filing, **Bus Org 4.001**
Corrections, certificates and certification, **Bus Org 4.101**
Indebtedness, certificates and certification, **Bus Org 2.114**
Reorganization, **Bus Org 10.302**
Shares and shareholders, certificates and certification, **Bus Org 3.203**
State,
Liens and incumbrances, **Bus Org 12.201**
Receivers and receivership, **Bus Org 12.251**
Statements,
Certificate of formation,
Amendments, **Bus Org 3.053, 3.054**
Restatement, **Bus Org 3.059**
Damages, **Bus Org 153.107, 153.108**
Officers and employees, good faith, **Bus Org 3.102, 3.105**
Termination, claims, **Bus Org 11.352**
Status, errors, **Bus Org 153.106**
Statutes, construction of laws, **Bus Org 1.006, 1.051 et seq., 153.002 et seq.**
Subsidiaries, merger and consolidation, **Bus Org 10.006**
Certificates and certification, **Bus Org 10.152**
Supersedeas or stay,
Termination, involuntary termination, **Bus Org 11.306**
Winding up, involuntary winding up, **Bus Org 11.306**
Supervision, winding up, **Bus Org 11.054**
Tax returns,
Duplicates and copies, **Bus Org 153.552**
Records and recordation, **Bus Org 153.551**
Taxation,
Service of process, **Bus Org 5.257**
Termination,
Forfeitures, reinstatement, **Bus Org 11.254**
Payment, **Bus Org 11.101**
Termination, **Bus Org 11.001 et seq.**
Abatement of actions and proceedings, involuntary termination, **Bus Org 11.304**
Actions and proceedings, involuntary termination, **Bus Org 11.303**
Appeal and review, involuntary termination, **Bus Org 11.307**

PARTNERSHIPS—Cont'd
Limited partnerships—Cont'd
Termination—Cont'd
Certificates and certification, **Bus Org 11.101 et seq.**
Involuntary termination, **Bus Org 11.252**
Reinstatement, **Bus Org 11.202**
Certified copies, involuntary termination, judgments and decrees, **Bus Org 11.414**
Claims, **Bus Org 11.351 et seq.**
Consent, reinstatement, **Bus Org 153.505**
Crimes and offenses, involuntary termination, **Bus Org 11.301 et seq.**
Deposits, claims, **Bus Org 11.352**
Discharge, claims, **Bus Org 11.353**
Effective date, **Bus Org 11.102, 11.103**
Claims, **Bus Org 11.356 et seq.**
Reinstatement, **Bus Org 11.204 et seq.**
Errors, reinstatement, **Bus Org 11.201 et seq.**
Escheat, claims, **Bus Org 11.355**
Exemptions, involuntary termination, **Bus Org 11.251**
Filing,
Fines and penalties, **Bus Org 21.802**
Involuntary termination, **Bus Org 11.315**
Fraud,
Involuntary termination, **Bus Org 11.301 et seq.**
Revocation or suspension, **Bus Org 11.153**
General partners, withdrawal, **Bus Org 153.155**
Involuntary termination, **Bus Org 11.251 et seq., 11.301 et seq.**
Certified copies, judgments and decrees, **Bus Org 11.414**
Judgments and decrees, **Bus Org 11.301 et seq.**
Involuntary termination, certified copies, **Bus Org 11.414**
Jurisdiction, involuntary termination, **Bus Org 11.308**
Limitation of actions, claims, **Bus Org 11.359**
Names, reinstatement, **Bus Org 11.203**
Notice,
Claims, **Bus Org 11.358**
Escheat, claims, **Bus Org 11.355**
Involuntary termination, **Bus Org 11.251, 11.302, 11.310**
Payment,
Claims, **Bus Org 11.354**
Taxation, **Bus Org 11.101**
Publication, involuntary termination, **Bus Org 11.310**
Receipts, claims, **Bus Org 11.352**
Receivers and receivership, **Bus Org 11.403**

PARTNERSHIPS—Cont'd
Limited partnerships—Cont'd
Termination—Cont'd
Receivers and receivership—Cont'd
Judgments and decrees, **Bus Org 11.412**
Records and recordation, removal, **Bus Org 11.104**
Reinstatement, **Bus Org 11.201 et seq.**
Involuntary termination, **Bus Org 11.253**
Taxation, forfeitures, **Bus Org 11.254**
Remand, involuntary termination, **Bus Org 11.307**
Revocation or suspension, fraud, **Bus Org 11.153**
Service of process, involuntary termination, **Bus Org 11.309**
Statements, claims, **Bus Org 11.352**
Supersedeas or stay, involuntary termination, **Bus Org 11.306**
Taxation,
Forfeitures, reinstatement, **Bus Org 11.254**
Payment, **Bus Org 11.101**
Time,
Involuntary termination, **Bus Org 11.305, 11.313**
Reinstatement, **Bus Org 11.202**
Venue, involuntary termination, **Bus Org 11.308**
Winding up, **Bus Org 153.501**
Third parties,
Contracts, waiver, **Bus Org 153.005**
Damages, **Bus Org 153.102**
Time,
Admissions, **Bus Org 153.101**
Certificate of formation, **Bus Org 3.001, 3.003**
Amendments, **Bus Org 3.056**
Restatement, **Bus Org 3.063**
Damages, statements, **Bus Org 153.107**
Distribution and distributors, **Bus Org 153.209**
Exchange of property, **Bus Org 10.054, 10.055**
Filing, **Bus Org 4.004**
Corrections, **Bus Org 4.105**
Effective date, **Bus Org 4.051 et seq.**
Fines and penalties, **Bus Org 21.802**
Interrogatories, answer, **Bus Org 12.002**
Merger and consolidation, effective date, **Bus Org 10.007**
Reports,
Delivery, **Bus Org 153.304**
Filing, **Bus Org 153.301**
Service of process, **Bus Org 5.254**
Termination,
Involuntary termination, **Bus Org 11.313**
Reinstatement, **Bus Org 11.202**

PARTNERSHIPS—Cont'd
Limited partnerships—Cont'd
Time—Cont'd
Winding up, **Bus Org 11.056**
Cancellation, **Bus Org 11.152**
Involuntary winding up, **Bus Org 11.313**
Withdrawal, **Bus Org 153.110**
Distribution and distributors, **Bus Org 153.111**
Trademarks and trade names, names, **Bus Org 5.001**
Transacting business in Texas,
Abatement of actions and proceedings, **Bus Org 153.310**
Reports, forfeitures, **Bus Org 153.307 et seq.**
Transfers, **Bus Org 154.002**
Names, reservation, **Bus Org 5.106**
Property, **Bus Org 10.251 et seq.**
Racing, licenses and permits, **Bus Org 153.555**
Shares and shareholders, certificates and certification, **Bus Org 3.201**
Trusts and trustees,
Reorganization, **Bus Org 10.301 et seq.**
Transacting business in Texas, **Bus Org 9.251**
Uncertificated shares, **Bus Org 3.201**
Notice, **Bus Org 3.205**
Venue,
Registration, **Bus Org 9.053**
Revocation or suspension, **Bus Org 9.158**
Termination, involuntary termination, **Bus Org 11.308**
Winding up, involuntary winding up, **Bus Org 11.308**
Veterans organizations, names, **Bus Org 5.062**
Vice president, agent for service of process, **Bus Org 5.255**
Waiver,
Business Organizations Code, **Bus Org 153.004**
Third parties, contracts, **Bus Org 153.005**
Winding up, **Bus Org 11.001 et seq., 11.051 et seq., 153.501 et seq.**
Abatement of actions and proceedings, involuntary winding up, **Bus Org 11.304**
Actions and proceedings, **Bus Org 11.052, 11.055**
Involuntary winding up, **Bus Org 11.303**
Appeal and review, involuntary winding up, **Bus Org 11.307**
Assets, distribution and distributors, **Bus Org 11.053**
Cancellation, **Bus Org 11.152**
Certificate of formation, amendments, **Bus Org 153.052**
Consent, **Bus Org 11.058**
Contracts, **Bus Org 11.152**

PARTNERSHIPS—Cont'd
Limited partnerships—Cont'd
Winding up—Cont'd
Crimes and offenses, involuntary winding up, **Bus Org 11.301 et seq.**
Damages, **Bus Org 153.103**
Discharge, indebtedness, **Bus Org 11.053**
Distribution and distributors, assets, **Bus Org 11.053**
Filing, involuntary winding up, **Bus Org 11.315**
Fraud, involuntary winding up, **Bus Org 11.301 et seq.**
General partners, withdrawal, **Bus Org 153.155**
Indebtedness, discharge, **Bus Org 11.053**
Involuntary winding up, **Bus Org 11.301 et seq.**
Judgments and decrees, **Bus Org 11.301 et seq.**
Jurisdiction, involuntary winding up, **Bus Org 11.308**
Notice, **Bus Org 11.052**
Involuntary winding up, **Bus Org 11.302, 11.310**
Publication, involuntary winding up, **Bus Org 11.310**
Records and recordation, **Bus Org 153.551**
Remand, involuntary winding up, **Bus Org 11.307**
Revocation or suspension, **Bus Org 11.058, 11.151**
Service of process, involuntary winding up, **Bus Org 11.309**
Supersedeas or stay, involuntary winding up, **Bus Org 11.306**
Supervision, **Bus Org 11.054**
Time, **Bus Org 11.056**
Cancellation, **Bus Org 11.152**
Involuntary winding up, **Bus Org 11.305, 11.313**
Venue, involuntary winding up, **Bus Org 11.308**
Withdrawal, **Bus Org 153.110**
Certificate of formation, amendments, **Bus Org 153.051, 153.052**
Distribution and distributors, **Bus Org 153.111**
Filing, fines and penalties, **Bus Org 21.802**
General partners, **Bus Org 153.155 et seq.**
Names, reservation, fees, **Bus Org 5.1041**
Registration, **Bus Org 9.011**
Witnesses, indemnity, expenses and expenditures, **Bus Org 8.106**
Writings,
Powers and duties, **Bus Org 2.112**
Signatures, **Bus Org 1.007**
Limited partnerships (Revised Act).
Limited partnerships, generally, ante

PARTNERSHIPS—Cont'd
Liquidation,
Limited partnerships, ante
Receivers and receivership, **Bus Org 12.258**
Orders of court, **Bus Org 11.405**
Loans, **Bus Org 2.101, 154.201**
Lobbyists. Legislature, this index
Location, offices, **Bus Org 2.101**
Losses, credits, **Bus Org 152.202**
Lottery, names, **Bus Org 5.061**
Loyalty, **Bus Org 152.205**
Managers and management, **Bus Org 152.203**
Agent for service of process, **Bus Org 5.255**
Damages, **Bus Org 301.010**
Licenses and permits, **Bus Org 301.006**
Resignation, **Bus Org 301.008**
Transfers, **Bus Org 152.402**
Mandatory application date, Business Organizations Code, **Bus Org 401.001 et seq.**
Marriage, dissolution of marriage, transfers, **Bus Org 152.406**
Meetings,
Actions without meetings, contracts, **Bus Org 154.103**
Application of law, **Bus Org 6.301**
Business Organizations Code, mandatory application date, **Bus Org 402.008, 402.009**
Contracts, elections, **Bus Org 154.102**
Emergencies, **Bus Org 3.251 et seq.**
Limited partnerships, ante
Notice, actions without meetings, **Bus Org 154.103**
Mental health,
Information, disclosure, **Bus Org 152.213**
Withdrawal, **Bus Org 152.501**
Merger and consolidation, **Bus Org 10.001 et seq.**
Abandonment, **Bus Org 10.201, 10.202, 10.203**
Acceptance, certificates and certification, **Bus Org 10.156**
Allocations, property, **Bus Org 10.003**
Business Organizations Code, mandatory application date, **Bus Org 402.010**
Certificate of formation, **Bus Org 3.005, 3.006, 10.002**
Certificates and certification, **Bus Org 10.151 et seq.**
Damages, **Bus Org 10.009**
Definitions, **Bus Org 1.002**
Dissenting shareholders, **Bus Org 10.351 et seq.**
Effective date, **Bus Org 10.007, 10.008**
Filing,
Certificates and certification, **Bus Org 10.153**
Fees, **Bus Org 4.151**
Holding companies, **Bus Org 10.005**
Limited partnerships, ante
Names, **Bus Org 10.002**

PARTNERSHIPS—Cont'd
Merger and consolidation—Cont'd
Plans and specifications, **Bus Org 10.001 et seq.**
Property, allocations, **Bus Org 10.003**
Reorganization, **Bus Org 10.301 et seq.**
Subsidiaries, **Bus Org 10.006**
Certificates and certification, **Bus Org 10.152**
Time, effective date, **Bus Org 10.007**
Misconduct, damages, **Bus Org 7.001**
Money, **Bus Org 1.009**
Monopolies and Unfair Trade, generally, this index
Mortgages, **Bus Org 2.101**
Limited partnerships, ante
Powers and duties, **Bus Org 2.104**
Receivers and receivership, **Bus Org 11.403**
Names, **Bus Org 5.001 et seq.**
Assumed or fictitious names, **Bus Org 5.051 et seq.**
Certificate of formation, **Bus Org 3.005**
Amendments, **Bus Org 3.053, 3.056**
Conversion, **Bus Org 10.103**
Deception, **Bus Org 5.052**
Exchange of property, plans and specifications, **Bus Org 10.052**
Fees, reservation, **Bus Org 5.101**
Withdrawal, **Bus Org 5.1041**
Filing,
Fees, **Bus Org 4.151**
Registration, **Bus Org 5.152**
Foreign limited liability partnerships, **Bus Org 152.902**
Foreign limited partnerships, ante
Fraud, **Bus Org 5.052**
Identity and identification, same or similar, **Bus Org 5.053**
Limited liability partnerships, **Bus Org 152.803**
Limited partnerships, ante
Lottery, **Bus Org 5.061**
Merger and consolidation, **Bus Org 10.002**
Notice, **Bus Org 5.001**
Registration, **Bus Org 5.151 et seq.**
Renewal,
Registration, **Bus Org 5.155**
Reservation, **Bus Org 5.105**
Reservation, **Bus Org 5.101 et seq.**
Same or similar, **Bus Org 5.053**
Registration, **Bus Org 5.153**
Reservation, **Bus Org 5.102**
Termination, reinstatement, **Bus Org 11.203**
Time,
Registration, **Bus Org 5.154**
Reservation, **Bus Org 5.104**
Trademarks and trade names, **Bus Org 5.001**
Transfers, reservation, **Bus Org 5.106**
Veterans organizations, **Bus Org 5.062**
Nature, **Bus Org 152.051 et seq.**
Negligence, damages, **Bus Org 301.010**
Nonfiling, certificate of formation, **Bus Org 3.002**

PARTNERSHIPS—Cont'd
Notice,
Agent for service of process, **Bus Org 5.252, 5.253**
Contracts, meetings, **Bus Org 154.102**
Conversion, **Bus Org 10.101**
Facts, **Bus Org 151.003**
Guaranty, fraud, **Bus Org 2.104**
Indemnity, orders of court, **Bus Org 8.052**
Insolvency, **Bus Org 12.256**
Liens and incumbrances,
Foreclosure, **Bus Org 12.256**
State, **Bus Org 12.201**
Limited liability partnership, registration, withdrawal, **Bus Org 152.802**
Limited partnerships, ante
Meetings, actions without meetings, **Bus Org 154.103**
Names, **Bus Org 5.001**
Receivers and receivership, claims, **Bus Org 11.407**
Registered agent, resignation, **Bus Org 5.204**
Reorganization, **Bus Org 10.301**
Shares and shareholders,
Involuntary termination, **Bus Org 11.251**
Uncertificated shares, **Bus Org 3.205**
Termination, post
Transfers, **Bus Org 152.404**
Winding up, post
Oaths and affirmations, interrogatories, answer, **Bus Org 12.002**
Offenses. Crimes and offenses, generally, ante
Officers and employees, **Bus Org 3.101 et seq., 151.004**
Agent for service of process, **Bus Org 5.255**
Compensation and salaries, **Bus Org 2.101**
Damages, **Bus Org 7.001, 301.010**
Application of law, **Bus Org 1.104**
Dual office holding, **Bus Org 3.103**
Elections, **Bus Org 2.101, 3.103**
Good faith, **Bus Org 3.105**
Indemnity, **Bus Org 2.101, 7.001, 8.001 et seq.**
Licenses and permits, **Bus Org 301.006**
Limited partnerships, ante
Loans, **Bus Org 2.101**
Removal, **Bus Org 3.104**
Retirement and pensions, **Bus Org 2.101**
Offices, **Bus Org 2.101**
Changes, filing, fines and penalties, **Bus Org 21.802**
Foreign limited liability partnerships, **Bus Org 152.904**
Changes, **Bus Org 152.913**
Limited partnerships, ante
Records and recordation, **Bus Org 152.212**
Registered offices, generally, post
Reorganization, **Bus Org 10.301**

PARTNERSHIPS—Cont'd
Omissions, certificate of formation, restatement, **Bus Org 3.059**
Open records, interrogatories, **Bus Org 12.003**
Opinions and decisions, majority, **Bus Org 152.209**
Orders of court,
  Charging orders, indebtedness, judgment and decrees, **Bus Org 152.308**
  Limited partnerships, ante
  Receivers and receivership, **Bus Org 11.402**
    Liquidation, **Bus Org 11.405**
  Termination, involuntary termination, **Bus Org 11.314**
  Winding up, involuntary winding up, **Bus Org 11.314**
Osteopaths, **Bus Org 152.055**
Papers. Books and papers, generally, ante
Parties, **Bus Org 152.305**
  Limited partnerships, ante
  Receivers and receivership, **Bus Org 11.411**
  Third parties, generally, post
  Winding up, **Bus Org 152.702**
Payment, **Bus Org 152.203**
  Limited partnerships, ante
  Termination,
    Claims, **Bus Org 11.354**
    Taxation, **Bus Org 11.101**
  Withdrawal, redemption, **Bus Org 152.607 et seq.**
Penalties. Fines and penalties, generally, ante
Permissive indemnification, **Bus Org 8.101 et seq.**
Personal property, **Bus Org 2.101, 154.001**
  Disposition, **Bus Org 10.251 et seq.**
    Reorganization, **Bus Org 10.301**
  Limited partnerships, ante
  Shares and shareholders, **Bus Org 21.801**
Physician assistants, **Bus Org 152.0551**
Physicians and surgeons, **Bus Org 152.055**
  Physician assistants, **Bus Org 152.0551**
Plans and specifications,
  Conversion, **Bus Org 10.101 et seq.**
  Exchange of property, **Bus Org 10.051 et seq.**
  Limited partnerships, ante
  Merger and consolidation, **Bus Org 10.001 et seq.**
Podiatrists, **Bus Org 152.055**
Political subdivisions, service of process, **Bus Org 5.257**
Powers and duties, **Bus Org 2.101 et seq., 152.203**
  Limited partnerships, ante
  Receivers and receivership, **Bus Org 11.406**
  Transfers, **Bus Org 152.403, 152.404**
  Winding up, **Bus Org 152.703**
President, agent for service of process, **Bus Org 5.255**

PARTNERSHIPS—Cont'd
Presumptions,
  Care, powers and duties, **Bus Org 152.206**
  Property, **Bus Org 152.102**
Prices, withdrawal, redemption, **Bus Org 152.602**
Prior laws, Business Organizations Code, **Bus Org 401.001 et seq.**
Priorities and preferences,
  Business Organizations Code, application of law, **Bus Org 1.106**
  Certificate of formation, shares and shareholders, **Bus Org 3.007**
Privileges and immunities,
  Property, disposition, **Bus Org 10.254**
  Registered agents, **Bus Org 5.208**
Proceedings. Actions and proceedings, generally, ante
Process, **Bus Org 5.251 et seq.**
  Limited partnerships, **Bus Org 5.251 et seq.**
  Service of process, generally, post
Profits,
  Credits, **Bus Org 152.202**
  Loyalty, **Bus Org 152.205**
  Sharing, officers and employees, **Bus Org 2.101**
Property, **Bus Org 2.101, 152.101, 152.102**
  Community property, **Bus Org 152.203**
  Disposition, **Bus Org 10.251 et seq.**
    Reorganization, **Bus Org 10.301**
  Exchange of property, generally, ante
  Liens and incumbrances,
    Foreclosure, **Bus Org 12.252 et seq.**
    State, **Bus Org 12.201**
  Limited partnerships, ante
  Loyalty, **Bus Org 152.205**
  Merger and consolidation, allocations, **Bus Org 10.003**
  Personal property, generally, ante
  Real estate, generally, post
Publication,
  Termination, involuntary termination, **Bus Org 11.310**
  Winding up, involuntary winding up, **Bus Org 11.310**
Purchases and purchasing,
  Indemnity, insurance, **Bus Org 8.151**
  Title to property, **Bus Org 301.008**
Purposes, **Bus Org 2.001 et seq.**
  Certificate of formation, **Bus Org 3.005**
Qualifications, **Bus Org 152.053**
Quo warranto, insolvency, **Bus Org 12.253 et seq.**
Racing, limited partnerships, licenses and permits, transfers, **Bus Org 153.555**
Rates and charges, **Bus Org 152.202**
  Indebtedness, interest, **Bus Org 152.005**
  Records and recordation, inspection and inspectors, **Bus Org 152.212**
Real estate, **Bus Org 2.101**
  Disposition, **Bus Org 10.251 et seq.**
    Reorganization, **Bus Org 10.301**
  Limited partnerships, ante
  Records and recordation, deeds and conveyances, **Bus Org 10.253**

PARTNERSHIPS—Cont'd
Receipts, termination, claims, **Bus Org 11.352**
Receivers and receivership, **Bus Org 11.401 et seq.**
  Actions and proceedings, **Bus Org 11.406**
  Ancillary receiverships, **Bus Org 11.409**
  Appointments, **Bus Org 11.401 et seq.**
  Bonds (officers and fiduciaries), **Bus Org 11.406**
  Citizens and citizenship, **Bus Org 11.406**
  Claims, filing, **Bus Org 11.407**
  Compensation and salaries, **Bus Org 11.408**
  Discharge, **Bus Org 11.412**
  Filing, claims, **Bus Org 11.407**
  Foreign entities, **Bus Org 11.409, 11.410**
  Fraud, **Bus Org 11.403**
  Judgments and decrees, termination, **Bus Org 11.412**
  Jurisdiction, **Bus Org 11.402 et seq.**
  Liens and incumbrances, state, **Bus Org 12.201**
  Limited partnerships, ante
  Liquidation, **Bus Org 12.258**
    Orders of court, **Bus Org 11.405**
  Mortgages, **Bus Org 11.403**
  Notice, claims, **Bus Org 11.407**
  Orders of court, **Bus Org 11.402**
    Liquidation, **Bus Org 11.405**
  Parties, **Bus Org 11.411**
  Powers and duties, **Bus Org 11.406**
  Registration, **Bus Org 11.406**
  Rehabilitation, **Bus Org 11.404**
  State, **Bus Org 12.251**
  Termination, **Bus Org 11.403**
    Judgments and decrees, **Bus Org 11.412**
Records and recordation, **Bus Org 3.151 et seq., 152.212**
  Certified copies, filing, **Bus Org 4.005**
  Confidential or privileged information, **Bus Org 12.154**
  Disclosure, **Bus Org 12.154**
  Examinations and examiners, **Bus Org 3.153, 12.151 et seq.**
  Foreign limited liability partnerships, removal, **Bus Org 152.909**
  Inspection and inspectors, **Bus Org 3.152**
  Interrogatories, open records, **Bus Org 12.003**
  Limited partnerships, ante
  Real estate, deeds and conveyances, **Bus Org 10.253**
  Reorganization, **Bus Org 10.301**
  Service of process, **Bus Org 5.254**
  Signatures, **Bus Org 1.007**
  Termination, removal, **Bus Org 11.104**
Redemption,
  Transfers, **Bus Org 152.611**
    Actions and proceedings, **Bus Org 152.612**
    Death, **Bus Org 152.406**

PARTNERSHIPS—Cont'd
Redemption—Cont'd
Withdrawal, **Bus Org 152.601 et seq.**
Registered agent, **Bus Org 5.200 et seq.**
Changes, **Bus Org 5.202**
Filing, fines and penalties, **Bus Org 21.802**
Foreign limited liability partnerships, **Bus Org 152.904**
Changes, **Bus Org 152.913**
Limited partnerships, ante
Reorganization, **Bus Org 10.301**
Resignation, **Bus Org 5.204**
Registered offices, **Bus Org 5.200 et seq.**
Changes, **Bus Org 5.202**
Filing, fines and penalties, **Bus Org 21.802**
Foreign limited liability partnerships, **Bus Org 152.904**
Changes, **Bus Org 152.913**
Limited partnerships, ante
Registration,
Foreign limited liability partnerships, ante
Foreign limited partnerships, ante
Limited liability partnerships, **Bus Org 152.802, 153.352**
Limited partnerships, ante
Names, **Bus Org 5.151 et seq.**
Receivers and receivership, **Bus Org 11.406**
Rehabilitation, receivers and receivership, **Bus Org 11.404**
Reinstatement,
Foreign limited liability partnerships, registration, **Bus Org 152.914**
Limited partnerships, ante
Termination, post
Winding up, **Bus Org 152.710**
Rejection, registered agents, **Bus Org 5.205**
Relationships, changes, **Bus Org 154.202**
Remand,
Termination, involuntary termination, **Bus Org 11.307**
Winding up, involuntary winding up, **Bus Org 11.307**
Removal,
Foreign limited liability partnerships, records and recordation, **Bus Org 152.909**
Officers and employees, **Bus Org 3.104**
Renewal,
Foreign limited liability partnerships, registration, **Bus Org 152.908**
Names,
Registration, **Bus Org 5.155**
Reservation, **Bus Org 5.105**
Reorganization, **Bus Org 10.301 et seq.**
Business Organizations Code, mandatory application date, **Bus Org 402.010**
Limited partnerships, ante
Repeals, Business Organizations Code, statutes, **Bus Org 1.054**
Reports,
Indemnity, **Bus Org 8.152**

PARTNERSHIPS—Cont'd
Reports—Cont'd
Limited partnerships, ante
Officers and employees, good faith, **Bus Org 3.102, 3.105**
Reservation, names, **Bus Org 5.101 et seq.**
Resignation,
Managers and management, **Bus Org 301.008**
Registered agent, **Bus Org 5.204**
Resolutions, indemnity, **Bus Org 8.103**
Restatement, certificate of formation, **Bus Org 3.057 et seq.**
Restraint of trade. Monopolies and Unfair Trade, generally, this index
Retirement and pensions, officers and employees, **Bus Org 2.101**
Review. Appeal and review, generally, ante
Revised limited partnerships. Limited partnerships, generally, ante
Revocation or suspension,
Foreign limited liability partnerships, registration, **Bus Org 152.914**
Limited partnerships, ante
Reinstatement, **Bus Org 402.013**
Termination, fraud, **Bus Org 11.153**
Winding up, **Bus Org 11.151, 152.709**
Rights. Limited partnerships, ante
Salaries. Compensation and salaries, generally, ante
Sales, **Bus Org 10.251 et seq.**
Limited partnerships, ante
Property, **Bus Org 2.101**
Reorganization, **Bus Org 10.301**
Securities, exemptions, **Bus Org 301.011**
Same or similar. Names, ante
Seals, **Bus Org 2.101**
Indebtedness, certificates and certification, **Bus Org 2.114**
Limited partnerships, ante
Shares and shareholders, certificates and certification, **Bus Org 3.202**
Secretary of state, agent for service of process, **Bus Org 5.251 et seq.**
Securities, **Bus Org 2.101**
Limited partnerships, ante
Powers and duties, **Bus Org 2.104**
Sales, exemptions, **Bus Org 301.011**
Security, withdrawal, redemption, **Bus Org 152.609**
Sequestration, state, **Bus Org 12.259**
Service of process, **Bus Org 5.251 et seq.**
Limited partnerships, ante
Reorganization, **Bus Org 10.301**
Termination, involuntary termination, **Bus Org 11.309**
Winding up, involuntary winding up, **Bus Org 11.309**
Setoff and counterclaim, withdrawal, redemption, **Bus Org 152.604**
Settlement, winding up, **Bus Org 152.707**
Shares and shareholders,
Abandonment, exchange of property, **Bus Org 10.201, 10.202, 10.203**

PARTNERSHIPS—Cont'd
Shares and shareholders—Cont'd
Acceptance, exchange of property, certificates and certification, **Bus Org 10.156**
Appointments, dissenting shareholders, appraisal and appraisers, **Bus Org 10.361**
Appraisals and appraisers, dissenting shareholders, **Bus Org 10.354 et seq.**
Assignments, certificates and certification, **Bus Org 3.201**
Books and papers, dissenting shareholders, fair market value, **Bus Org 10.363**
Certificate of formation, numbers and numbering, **Bus Org 3.007**
Certificates and certification, **Bus Org 3.201 et seq.**
Exchange of property, **Bus Org 10.151 et seq.**
Compensation and salaries, dissenting shareholders, appraisals and appraisers, **Bus Org 10.365**
Computation, dissenting shareholders, fair market value, **Bus Org 10.362**
Costs, dissenting shareholders, appraisals and appraisers, **Bus Org 10.365**
Delivery, certificates and certification, **Bus Org 3.204**
Demand, dissenting shareholders, fair market value, **Bus Org 10.357 et seq.**
Dissenting shareholders, **Bus Org 10.351 et seq.**
Appointments, appraisal and appraisers, **Bus Org 10.361**
Appraisals and appraisers, **Bus Org 10.354 et seq.**
Books and papers, fair market value, **Bus Org 10.363**
Compensation and salaries, appraisals and appraisers, **Bus Org 10.365**
Computation, fair market value, **Bus Org 10.362**
Costs, appraisals and appraisers, **Bus Org 10.365**
Definitions, **Bus Org 10.352**
Demand, fair market value, **Bus Org 10.357 et seq.**
Exclusive remedy, **Bus Org 10.368**
Fair market value, demand, **Bus Org 10.357 et seq.**
Forms, **Bus Org 10.353**
Hearings, fair market value, **Bus Org 10.361**
Investigations and investigators, fair market value, **Bus Org 10.363**
Notice, **Bus Org 10.353, 10.355**
Objections and exceptions, appraisals and appraisers, **Bus Org 10.364**
Perfection, **Bus Org 10.356**
Petitions, fair market value, **Bus Org 10.361**

PARTNERSHIPS—Cont'd
Shares and shareholders—Cont'd
Dissenting shareholders—Cont'd
Records and recordation, fair market value, **Bus Org 10.363**
Demand, **Bus Org 10.359**
Reorganization, **Bus Org 10.304**
Termination, **Bus Org 10.367**
Title to property, **Bus Org 10.366**
Withdrawal, **Bus Org 10.357**
Duplicates and copies, certificates and certification, **Bus Org 3.202**
Evidence, certificates and certification, **Bus Org 3.201**
Exchange of property, **Bus Org 10.051 et seq.**
Abandonment, **Bus Org 10.201, 10.202, 10.203**
Acceptance, certificates and certification, **Bus Org 10.156**
Certificates and certification, **Bus Org 10.151 et seq.**
Filing, certificates and certification, **Bus Org 10.153**
Exclusive remedy, dissenting shareholders, **Bus Org 10.368**
Facsimile, certificates and certification, **Bus Org 3.203**
Fair market value, dissenting shareholders, demand, **Bus Org 10.357 et seq.**
Filing, exchange of property, certificates and certification, **Bus Org 10.153**
Forms,
Certificates and certification, **Bus Org 3.202**
Dissenting shareholders, **Bus Org 10.353**
Hearings, dissenting shareholders, fair market value, **Bus Org 10.361**
Investigations and investigators, dissenting shareholders, fair market value, **Bus Org 10.363**
Limited partnerships, ante
Notice,
Dissenting shareholders, **Bus Org 10.353, 10.355**
Uncertificated shares, **Bus Org 3.205**
Objections and exceptions, dissenting shareholders, appraisals and appraisers, **Bus Org 10.364**
Perfection, dissenting shareholders, **Bus Org 10.356**
Personal property, **Bus Org 21.801**
Petitions, dissenting shareholders, fair market value, **Bus Org 10.361**
Records and recordation, dissenting shareholders, fair market value, **Bus Org 10.363**
Demand, **Bus Org 10.359**
Reorganization, dissenting shareholders, **Bus Org 10.304**
Seals, certificates and certification, **Bus Org 3.202**
Signatures, certificates and certification, **Bus Org 3.203**

PARTNERSHIPS—Cont'd
Shares and shareholders—Cont'd
Termination, dissenting shareholders, **Bus Org 10.367**
Title to property, dissenting shareholders, **Bus Org 10.366**
Transfers, certificates and certification, **Bus Org 3.201**
Uncertificated shares, **Bus Org 3.201**
Notice, **Bus Org 3.205**
Withdrawal, dissenting shareholders, **Bus Org 10.357**
Signatures, **Bus Org 1.007**
Certificate of formation, ante
Filing, **Bus Org 4.001**
Corrections, certificates and certification, **Bus Org 4.101**
Foreign limited liability partnerships, registration, **Bus Org 152.905**
Amendments, **Bus Org 152.912**
Indebtedness, certificates and certification, **Bus Org 2.114**
Limited liability partnerships, registration, **Bus Org 152.802, 153.352**
Limited partnerships, ante
Reorganization, **Bus Org 10.302**
Shares and shareholders, certificates and certification, **Bus Org 3.203**
Standards,
Conduct, **Bus Org 152.204**
Winding up, **Bus Org 152.207**
State,
Liens and incumbrances, **Bus Org 12.201**
Limited partnerships, ante
Receivers and receivership, **Bus Org 12.251**
Statements,
Certificate of formation, ante
Limited partnerships, ante
Officers and employees, good faith, **Bus Org 3.102, 3.105**
Termination, claims, **Bus Org 11.352**
Statute of limitations. Limitation of actions, generally, ante
Statutes,
Business Organizations Code, construction of laws, **Bus Org 1.006, 1.051 et seq.**
Construction, **Bus Org 152.004**
Subsidiaries, merger and consolidation, **Bus Org 10.006**
Certificates and certification, **Bus Org 10.152**
Suits. Actions and proceedings, generally, ante
Supersedeas or stay,
Termination, involuntary termination, **Bus Org 11.306**
Winding up, involuntary winding up, **Bus Org 11.306**
Supervision, winding up, **Bus Org 11.054**
Surplus, winding up, disposition, **Bus Org 152.706**
Suspension. Revocation or suspension, generally, ante

PARTNERSHIPS—Cont'd
Taxation,
Limited partnerships, ante
Service of process, **Bus Org 5.257**
Termination,
Forfeitures, reinstatement, **Bus Org 11.254, 402.013**
Payment, **Bus Org 11.101**
Termination, **Bus Org 11.001 et seq.**
Abatement of actions and proceedings, involuntary termination, **Bus Org 11.304**
Actions and proceedings, involuntary termination, **Bus Org 11.303**
Appeal and review, involuntary termination, **Bus Org 11.307**
Business Organizations Code, mandatory application date, **Bus Org 402.011**
Certificates and certification, **Bus Org 11.101 et seq.**
Involuntary termination, **Bus Org 11.252**
Reinstatement, **Bus Org 11.202**
Certified copies, involuntary termination, judgments and decrees, **Bus Org 11.414**
Claims, **Bus Org 11.351 et seq.**
Crimes and offenses, involuntary termination, **Bus Org 11.301 et seq.**
Deposits, claims, **Bus Org 11.352**
Discharge, claims, **Bus Org 11.353**
Effective date, **Bus Org 11.102, 11.103**
Claims, **Bus Org 11.356 et seq.**
Reinstatement, **Bus Org 11.204 et seq.**
Errors, reinstatement, **Bus Org 11.201 et seq.**
Escheat, claims, **Bus Org 11.355**
Exemptions, involuntary termination, **Bus Org 11.251**
Filing,
Fines and penalties, **Bus Org 21.802**
Involuntary termination, **Bus Org 11.315**
Foreign limited liability partnerships, registration, **Bus Org 152.907**
Fraud,
Involuntary termination, **Bus Org 11.301 et seq.**
Revocation or suspension, **Bus Org 11.153**
Involuntary termination, **Bus Org 11.251 et seq., 11.301 et seq.**
Certified copies, judgments and decrees, **Bus Org 11.414**
Judgments and decrees, **Bus Org 11.301 et seq.**
Involuntary termination, certified copies, **Bus Org 11.414**
Jurisdiction, involuntary termination, **Bus Org 11.308, 11.314**
Limitation of actions, claims, **Bus Org 11.359**
Limited partnerships, ante
Names, reinstatement, **Bus Org 11.203**

PARTNERSHIPS—Cont'd
Termination—Cont'd
Notice,
Claims, **Bus Org 11.358**
Escheat, claims, **Bus Org 11.355**
Involuntary termination, **Bus Org 11.251, 11.302, 11.310**
Orders of court, involuntary termination, **Bus Org 11.314**
Payment,
Claims, **Bus Org 11.354**
Taxation, **Bus Org 11.101**
Publication, involuntary termination, **Bus Org 11.310**
Receipts, claims, **Bus Org 11.352**
Receivers and receivership, **Bus Org 11.403**
Judgments and decrees, **Bus Org 11.412**
Records and recordation, removal, **Bus Org 11.104**
Reinstatement, **Bus Org 11.201 et seq.**
Involuntary termination, **Bus Org 11.253**
Taxation, forfeitures, **Bus Org 11.254**
Remand, involuntary termination, **Bus Org 11.307**
Revocation or suspension, fraud, **Bus Org 11.153**
Service of process, involuntary termination, **Bus Org 11.309**
Statements, claims, **Bus Org 11.352**
Supersedeas or stay, involuntary termination, **Bus Org 11.306**
Taxation,
Forfeitures, reinstatement, **Bus Org 11.254**
Payment, **Bus Org 11.101**
Time,
Involuntary termination, **Bus Org 11.305, 11.313**
Reinstatement, **Bus Org 11.202**
Venue, involuntary termination, **Bus Org 11.308**
Third parties,
Damages, **Bus Org 152.053**
Indebtedness, **Bus Org 152.214**
Limited partnerships, ante
Withdrawal, damages, **Bus Org 152.506**
Time,
Business Organizations Code, effective date, **Bus Org 402.001**
Adoption, **Bus Org 402.005**
Certificate of formation, ante
Effective date, generally, ante
Exchange of property, **Bus Org 10.054, 10.055**
Filing, ante
Interrogatories, answer, **Bus Org 12.002**
Limited liability partnerships, registration, **Bus Org 152.802**
Limited partnerships, ante
Merger and consolidation, effective date, **Bus Org 10.007**
Service of process, **Bus Org 5.254**
Termination, ante
Winding up, post

PARTNERSHIPS—Cont'd
Time—Cont'd
Withdrawal, **Bus Org 152.501**
Title to property, **Bus Org 301.007 et seq.**
Purchases and purchasing, **Bus Org 301.008**
Trademarks and trade names, names, **Bus Org 5.001**
Transacting business in Texas,
Foreign limited liability partnerships, **Bus Org 152.903**
Registration, **Bus Org 152.910**
Limited partnerships, ante
Transfers, **Bus Org 152.401 et seq., 154.002**
Definitions, **Bus Org 152.001**
Names, reservation, **Bus Org 5.106**
Property, **Bus Org 10.251 et seq., 152.102**
Redemption, ante
Shares and shareholders, certificates and certification, **Bus Org 3.201**
Title to property, **Bus Org 301.009**
Withdrawal, **Bus Org 152.501**
Transition, Business Organizations Code, **Bus Org 402.001 et seq.**
Trusts and monopolies. Monopolies and Unfair Trade, generally, this index
Trusts and trustees,
Limited partnerships, ante
Reorganization, **Bus Org 10.301 et seq.**
Uncertificated shares, **Bus Org 3.201**
Notice, **Bus Org 3.205**
Venue,
Limited partnerships, ante
Termination, involuntary termination, **Bus Org 11.308**
Winding up, involuntary winding up, **Bus Org 11.308**
Veterans organizations, names, **Bus Org 5.062**
Vice president, agent for service of process, **Bus Org 5.255**
Wages. Compensation and salaries, generally, ante
Winding up, **Bus Org 11.001 et seq., 11.051 et seq., 152.701 et seq.**
Abatement of actions and proceedings, involuntary winding up, **Bus Org 11.304**
Accounts and accounting, compromise and settlement, **Bus Org 152.707**
Actions and proceedings, **Bus Org 11.052, 11.055**
Involuntary winding up, **Bus Org 11.303**
Appeal and review, involuntary winding up, **Bus Org 11.307**
Assets,
Disposition, **Bus Org 152.706**
Distribution and distributors, **Bus Org 11.053**
Business Organizations Code, mandatory application date, **Bus Org 402.011**
Cancellation, **Bus Org 11.152, 152.709**

PARTNERSHIPS—Cont'd
Winding up—Cont'd
Care, powers and duties, **Bus Org 152.206**
Compromise and settlement, **Bus Org 152.707**
Continuation, **Bus Org 152.709**
Contracts, **Bus Org 11.152**
Contributions, **Bus Org 152.708**
Disposition, **Bus Org 152.706**
Crimes and offenses, involuntary winding up, **Bus Org 11.301 et seq.**
Damages, **Bus Org 152.704, 152.705**
Discharge, indebtedness, **Bus Org 11.053**
Distribution and distributors, **Bus Org 152.707**
Assets, **Bus Org 11.053**
Filing, involuntary winding up, **Bus Org 11.315**
Fraud, involuntary winding up, **Bus Org 11.301 et seq.**
Good faith, **Bus Org 152.204**
Indebtedness, discharge, **Bus Org 11.053**
Involuntary winding up, **Bus Org 11.301 et seq.**
Judgments and decrees, **Bus Org 11.301 et seq.**
Jurisdiction, involuntary winding up, **Bus Org 11.308, 11.314**
Limited partnerships, ante
Loyalty, **Bus Org 152.205**
Notice, **Bus Org 11.052, 11.057**
Involuntary winding up, **Bus Org 11.302, 11.310**
Orders of court, involuntary winding up, **Bus Org 11.314**
Parties, **Bus Org 152.702**
Powers and duties, **Bus Org 152.703**
Publication, involuntary winding up, **Bus Org 11.310**
Redemption, withdrawal, **Bus Org 152.601 et seq.**
Reinstatement, **Bus Org 152.710**
Remand, involuntary winding up, **Bus Org 11.307**
Revocation or suspension, **Bus Org 11.057, 11.151, 152.709**
Service of process, involuntary winding up, **Bus Org 11.309**
Standards, **Bus Org 152.207**
Supersedeas or stay, involuntary winding up, **Bus Org 11.306**
Supervision, **Bus Org 11.054**
Surplus, disposition, **Bus Org 152.706**
Time, **Bus Org 11.056, 11.057, 152.709**
Cancellation, **Bus Org 11.152**
Involuntary winding up, **Bus Org 11.305, 11.313**
Transfers, **Bus Org 152.402, 152.404**
Venue, involuntary winding up, **Bus Org 11.308**
Withdrawal, **Bus Org 152.501**
Redemption, **Bus Org 152.601 et seq.**

PARTNERSHIPS—Cont'd
Withdrawal, **Bus Org 152.501 et seq.**
  Actions and proceedings, **Bus Org 152.211**
  Damages, ante
  Definitions, **Bus Org 152.001**
  Filing, fines and penalties, **Bus Org 21.802**
  Foreign limited liability partnerships, registration, **Bus Org 9.011, 152.906, 152.907**
  Limited liability partnership, registration, **Bus Org 152.802**
  Limited partnerships, ante
  Names, reservation, fees, **Bus Org 5.1041**
  Redemption, **Bus Org 152.601 et seq.**
  Transfers, **Bus Org 152.402**
Witnesses,
  Indemnity, expenses and expenditures, **Bus Org 8.106**
  Limited partnerships, ante
Writings,
  Powers and duties, **Bus Org 2.112**
  Signatures, **Bus Org 1.007**

PARTY LINES
Telecommunications, this index

PATRIOTIC CORPORATIONS
Nonprofit Corporations, generally, this index

PAY
Compensation and Salaries, generally, this index

PAY TELEPHONES
Telecommunications, this index

PAY TELEVISION
Cable Television, generally, this index

PAYMENT
Electricity, this index
Foreign Corporations, this index
Gas Utilities, this index
Limited Liability Companies, this index
Limited partnerships. Partnerships, this index
Nonprofit Corporations, this index
Oil and Gas, this index
Partnerships, this index
Public Utilities, this index
Shares and shareholders. Corporations, this index
Telecommunications, this index
Water Supply, this index

PECUNIARY INTEREST
Conflict of Interest, generally, this index

PERFORMANCE BOND
Bonds (Officers and Fiduciaries), generally, this index

PERMITS
Licenses and Permits, generally, this index

PERSONAL PROPERTY
Carriers, generally, this index
Cooperative Associations, this index
Corporations, this index
Executions, generally, this index
Foreign Corporations, this index
Limited Liability Companies, this index
Limited partnerships. Partnerships, this index
Nonprofit Corporations, this index
Partnerships, this index
Professional Associations and Societies, this index
Professional Corporations, this index
Transportation. Carriers, generally, this index

PERSONS
Definitions,
  Assumed or fictitious names, business and commerce, professions and occupations, **Bus & C 71.002**
  Public utilities, **Util 11.0042**

PETITIONS
Gas utilities, municipal orders, appeals, **Util 103.052 et seq.**
Telecommunications, this index

PETROLEUM AND PETROLEUM PRODUCTS
Oil and Gas, generally, this index

PHARMACISTS
Telemedicine, generally, this index

PHRASES
Words and Phrases, generally, this index

PHYSICAL THERAPISTS
Telemedicine, generally, this index

PHYSICIAN ASSISTANTS
Health organization corporations, nonprofit corporations, **Bus Org 22.0561**
Limited liability companies, professional limited liability companies, **Bus Org 301.012**
Nonprofit corporations, health organization corporations, **Bus Org 22.0561**
Partnerships, **Bus Org 152.0551**
Professional associations and societies, professional limited liability companies, **Bus Org 301.012**

PHYSICIANS AND SURGEONS
  See, also, Medical Care and Treatment, generally, this index
Assistants. Physician Assistants, generally, this index
Drugs and medicine. Telemedicine, generally, this index
Health organization corporations, nonprofit corporations, **Bus Org 22.056**
  Physician assistants, **Bus Org 22.0561**
Limited liability companies, professional limited liability companies, physician assistants, **Bus Org 301.012**

PHYSICIANS AND SURGEONS—Cont'd
Nonprofit corporations, health organization corporations, **Bus Org 22.056**
  Physician assistants, **Bus Org 22.0561**
Partnerships, **Bus Org 152.055**
  Physician assistants, **Bus Org 152.0551**
Physician Assistants, generally, this index
Podiatrists, generally, this index
Professional associations and societies, physician assistants, **Bus Org 301.012**
Professional limited liability companies, physician assistants, **Bus Org 301.012**
Telecommunications. Telemedicine, generally, this index

PICKETING
Labor Disputes, this index

PIPES AND PIPELINES
Carriers, powers and duties, **Bus Org 2.105**
Gas Utilities, this index
Municipalities, this index
Oil and Gas Pipelines, generally, this index
Powers and duties, carriers, **Bus Org 2.105**
Right of way, telecommunications, gas utilities, **Util 121.201**

PLANS AND SPECIFICATIONS
Cooperative Associations, this index
Corporations, this index
Definitions, electricity, customer choice, installed generation capacity, mitigation, **Util 39.156**
Electricity, this index
Emergencies, weather, electricity, reports, **Util 186.007**
Foreign Corporations, this index
Limited Liability Companies, this index
Limited partnerships. Partnerships, this index
Nonprofit Corporations, this index
Partnerships, this index
Professional Associations and Societies, this index
Professional Corporations, this index
Telecommunications, this index
Weather, emergencies, electricity, reports, **Util 186.007**

PLEDGES
Business Development Corporations, this index
Corporations, this index
Real estate investment trusts, **Bus Org 200.405 et seq.**

PODIATRISTS
Health organization corporations, nonprofit corporations, **Bus Org 22.056**
Nonprofit corporations, health organization corporations, **Bus Org 22.056**
Partnerships, **Bus Org 152.055**
Telemedicine, generally, this index

POLES AND WIRES
Broadband over power lines, **Util 43.001 et seq.**
Telecommunications, this index

POLICE
Emergencies, gas utilities, pipes and pipelines, liaison activities, **Util 121.2015**

POLICY
Public Policy, generally, this index

POLITICAL INTEREST GROUPS
Lobbyists. Legislature, this index

POLITICAL SUBDIVISION AGGREGATOR
Definitions, electricity, registration, **Util 39.3545**

POLITICAL SUBDIVISIONS
Counties, generally, this index
Definitions, telecommunications, extended area service, **Util 55.023**
Electricity, aggregators, registration, **Util 39.3545, 39.356**
Municipalities, generally, this index

POLLUTION
Gas utilities, pipes and pipelines, penalties, **Util 121.304 et seq.**

POPULAR NAME LAWS
Agriculture Gas Users Act, **Util 123.021 et seq.**
Assumed Business or Professional Name Act, **Bus & C 71.001 et seq.**
Business Organizations Code, **Bus Org 1.001 et seq.**
Electric Cooperative Corporation Act, **Util 161.001 et seq.**
Gas Utility Regulatory Act, **Util 101.001 et seq.**
Public Utility Regulatory Act, **Util 11.001 et seq.**
Telephone Cooperative Act, **Util 162.001 et seq.**
Underground Facility Damage Prevention and Safety Act, **Util 251.001 et seq.**

POSTSECONDARY EDUCATION
Colleges and Universities, generally, this index

POWER COMPANIES
Electricity, generally, this index

POWER GENERATION COMPANY
Definitions, **Util 31.002**
  Atomic energy, decommissioning, **Util 39.206**

POWER PLANTS
Electricity, generally, this index

POWER REGION
Definitions, electricity, **Util 31.002**

PRACTICE OF LAW
Attorneys, generally, this index

PRACTICE OF MEDICINE
Physicians and Surgeons, generally, this index

PREEMPTION
Real estate investment trusts, shares and shareholders, damages, **Bus Org 200.162**
Telecommunications, code of conduct, **Util 60.202**

PREEMPTIVE RIGHTS
Corporations, shares and shareholders, **Bus Org 21.201 et seq.**

PREFERENCES
Priorities and Preferences, generally, this index

PREPAID CALLING CARD COMPANY
Definitions, telecommunications, **Util 55.253**

PREPAID CALLING SERVICES
Definitions, telecommunications, **Util 55.253**

PRESCRIPTIONS
Telemedicine, generally, this index

PRESIDENT
Business development corporations, **Bus Org 23.060**
Cooperative associations, **Bus Org 251.102**
Corporations, this index
Nonprofit Corporations, this index

PRIMA FACIE EVIDENCE
Evidence, generally, this index

PRINCIPAL AND AGENT
Agents and Agencies, generally, this index

PRIORITIES AND PREFERENCES
Assisted living facilities, electricity, **Util 38.072**
Corporations, this index
Electricity, this index
Foreign Corporations, this index
Gas Utilities, this index
Hospices, electricity, **Util 38.072**
Nursing and convalescent homes, electricity, **Util 38.072**
Telecommunications, this index

PRIVACY
Confidential or Privileged Information, generally, this index

PRIVATE SCHOOLS
Schools and School Districts, this index

PRIVILEGED COMMUNICATIONS
Confidential or Privileged Information, generally, this index

PRIVILEGED INFORMATION
Confidential or Privileged Information, generally, this index

PRIVILEGES AND IMMUNITIES
See, also, Confidential or Privileged Information, generally, this index
Cooperative associations, registered agents, **Bus Org 5.208**
Corporations, this index
Electricity, confidential or privileged information, government operated utilities, **Util 182.055**
Foreign corporations, registered agents, **Bus Org 5.208**
Gas utilities, confidential or privileged information, government operated utilities, **Util 182.055**
Limited Liability Companies, this index
Nonprofit Corporations, this index
Partnerships, registered agents, **Bus Org 5.208**
Professional associations and societies, registered agents, **Bus Org 5.208**
Professional corporations, registered agents, **Bus Org 5.208**
Public Utilities, this index
Real estate investment trusts, managers and management, **Bus Org 200.314**
Telecommunications, this index

PROBATE OF WILL
Probate Proceedings, generally, this index

PROBATE PROCEEDINGS
Children and minors. Guardian and Ward, generally, this index
Corporations,
  Elections, **Bus Org 6.154**
  Shares and shareholders, privileges and immunities, **Bus Org 21.226**
Foreign corporations,
  Shares and shareholders, privileges and immunities, **Bus Org 21.226**
  Transacting business in Texas, **Bus Org 9.251**
Guardian and Ward, generally, this index
Real estate investment trusts, shares and shareholders, privileges and immunities, **Bus Org 200.164**
Shares and shareholders, privileges and immunities, **Bus Org 21.226**

PROCEEDINGS
Actions and Proceedings, generally, this index

PROCESS
Agent for service of process. Partnerships, this index
Injunctions, generally, this index
Limited partnerships, **Bus Org 5.251 et seq.**
Partnerships, this index
Service of process,
  Cooperative Associations, this index
  Corporations, this index
  Foreign Corporations, this index
  Limited Liability Companies, this index
  Partnerships, this index
  Professional Associations and Societies, this index

PROCESS—Cont'd
Service of process—Cont'd
Professional Corporations, this index

PRODUCTION OF BOOKS AND PAPERS
Gas utilities, foreign states, **Util 102.206**
Public Utilities, this index
Public utility commission, **Util 14.051**
Real estate investment trusts, **Bus Org 200.501**

PROFESSIONAL ASSOCIATIONS AND SOCIETIES
Generally, **Bus Org 1.001 et seq., 301.001 et seq., 302.001 et seq.**
Abandonment,
Conversion, **Bus Org 10.201, 10.202, 10.203**
Exchange of property, **Bus Org 10.201, 10.202, 10.203**
Filing, **Bus Org 4.057**
Merger and consolidation, **Bus Org 10.201, 10.202, 10.203**
Abatement of actions and proceedings,
State, **Bus Org 12.260**
Termination, involuntary termination, **Bus Org 11.304**
Winding up, involuntary winding up, **Bus Org 11.304**
Acceptance, certificates and certification, **Bus Org 10.156**
Accounts and accounting, **Bus Org 3.151 et seq.**
Examinations and examiners, **Bus Org 12.151 et seq.**
Acknowledgments, filing, **Bus Org 4.002**
Effective date, delay, **Bus Org 4.059**
Actions and proceedings,
Abatement of actions and proceedings, generally, ante
Business Organizations Code, prior law, **Bus Org 402.014**
Certificate of formation, amendments, **Bus Org 3.056**
Indemnity, **Bus Org 8.001 et seq.**
Insolvency, **Bus Org 12.253 et seq.**
Receivers and receivership, **Bus Org 11.406**
Records and recordation, inspection and inspectors, **Bus Org 3.152**
State, liens and incumbrances, **Bus Org 12.201 et seq.**
Termination, involuntary termination, **Bus Org 11.303**
Winding up, post
Adoption, Business Organizations Code, **Bus Org 402.003**
Advancements, indemnity, expenses and expenditures, **Bus Org 8.104, 8.105**
Reports, **Bus Org 8.152**
Agent for service of process, **Bus Org 5.251 et seq.**
Agents and agencies, **Bus Org 302.009**
Changes, filing, fines and penalties, **Bus Org 21.802**
Damages, **Bus Org 301.010**

PROFESSIONAL ASSOCIATIONS AND SOCIETIES—Cont'd
Agents and agencies—Cont'd
Licenses and permits, **Bus Org 301.006**
Registered agent, generally, post
Agreements. Contracts, generally, post
Allocations, merger and consolidation, property, **Bus Org 10.003**
Alternatives, service of process, **Bus Org 5.256**
Amendments,
Business Organizations Code, statutes, **Bus Org 1.054**
Certificate of formation, **Bus Org 3.051 et seq., 302.003**
Filing, **Bus Org 4.106**
Ancillary receiverships, **Bus Org 11.409**
Answer, interrogatories, time, **Bus Org 12.002**
Antitrust, application of law, **Bus Org 10.901**
Appeal and review,
Filing, **Bus Org 12.004**
Termination, involuntary termination, **Bus Org 11.307**
Winding up, involuntary winding up, **Bus Org 11.307**
Application of law, **Bus Org 301.001, 302.001**
Antitrust, **Bus Org 10.901**
Business Organizations Code, **Bus Org 402.001 et seq.**
Foreign countries, foreign states, **Bus Org 1.053**
Elections, **Bus Org 6.301, 6.302**
Indebtedness, **Bus Org 10.901**
Indemnity, **Bus Org 8.002**
Meetings, **Bus Org 6.301, 6.302**
Monopolies and unfair trade, **Bus Org 10.901**
Reorganization, **Bus Org 10.306**
Appointments, receivers and receivership, **Bus Org 11.401 et seq.**
Appraisals and appraisers, reorganization, **Bus Org 10.304**
Assets,
Disposition, **Bus Org 10.251 et seq.**
Reorganization, **Bus Org 10.301**
Liens and incumbrances, state, **Bus Org 12.201**
Sales, Business Organizations Code, mandatory application date, **Bus Org 402.010**
Winding up, distribution and distributors, **Bus Org 11.053**
Assignments, **Bus Org 10.251 et seq.**
Shares and shareholders, certificates and certification, **Bus Org 3.201**
Assumed or fictitious names, **Bus & C 71.001 et seq.; Bus Org 5.051 et seq.**
Attachment, state, **Bus Org 12.259**
Attorney fees,
Filing,
Fines and penalties, **Bus Org 21.802**
Fraud, **Bus Org 4.007**
Records and recordation, inspection and inspectors, **Bus Org 3.152**

PROFESSIONAL ASSOCIATIONS AND SOCIETIES—Cont'd
Bankruptcy, **Bus Org 10.301 et seq.**
Bonds, reorganization, **Bus Org 10.301**
Bonds (officers and fiduciaries), receivers and receivership, **Bus Org 11.406**
Books and papers, **Bus Org 3.151 et seq.**
Confidential or privileged information, **Bus Org 12.154**
Disclosure, **Bus Org 12.154**
Duplicates and copies, **Bus Org 12.151 et seq.**
Examinations and examiners, **Bus Org 3.153, 12.151 et seq.**
Inspection and inspectors, **Bus Org 3.152**
Powers and duties, limitations, **Bus Org 2.005**
Reorganization, **Bus Org 10.301**
Signatures, **Bus Org 1.007**
Bylaws, **Bus Org 302.004**
Cancellation,
Reinstatement, **Bus Org 402.013**
Winding up, **Bus Org 11.152**
Certificate of formation, **Bus Org 3.015**
Amendments, **Bus Org 3.051 et seq., 302.003**
Definitions, **Bus Org 1.002**
Filing, fees, **Bus Org 4.156**
Merger and consolidation, **Bus Org 10.002**
Reinstatement, **Bus Org 402.013**
Reorganization, **Bus Org 10.301 et seq.**
Restatement, **Bus Org 3.057 et seq.**
Signatures, **Bus Org 3.015**
Amendments, **Bus Org 3.052, 3.054**
Restatement, **Bus Org 3.058, 3.060**
Statements,
Amendments, **Bus Org 3.053, 3.054**
Restatement, **Bus Org 3.059**
Certificates and certification,
Acceptance, **Bus Org 10.156**
Certificate of formation, generally, ante
Conversion, **Bus Org 10.154 et seq.**
Evidence, existence, **Bus Org 4.005**
Exchange of property, **Bus Org 10.151 et seq.**
Filing, **Bus Org 12.001**
Abandonment, **Bus Org 4.057**
Corrections, **Bus Org 4.101 et seq.**
Fines and penalties, **Bus Org 21.802**
Merger and consolidation, **Bus Org 10.151 et seq.**
Shares and shareholders, **Bus Org 3.201 et seq.**
Termination, post
Certified copies,
Filing, **Bus Org 4.005**
Involuntary termination, judgments and decrees, **Bus Org 11.414**
Changes, registered offices, registered agent, **Bus Org 5.202, 5.203**
Citizens and citizenship, receivers and receivership, **Bus Org 11.406**
Claims,
Receivers and receivership, filing, **Bus Org 11.407**

PROFESSIONAL ASSOCIATIONS AND SOCIETIES—Cont'd
Claims—Cont'd
Termination, **Bus Org 11.351 et seq.**
Committees, **Bus Org 302.005**
Compensation and salaries, receivers and receivership, **Bus Org 11.408**
Conduct,
Business Organizations Code, application of law, **Bus Org 402.006**
Damages, **Bus Org 7.001, 301.010**
Confidential or privileged information, interrogatories, **Bus Org 12.003**
Conflict of interest, elections, **Bus Org 6.152, 6.153**
Conflict of laws, **Bus Org 301.002**
Names, **Bus Org 5.060**
Consent,
Duplicates and copies, meetings, action without meeting, **Bus Org 6.205**
Registered agents, **Bus Org 5.2011**
Consolidation. Merger and consolidation, generally, post
Construction of laws, Business Organizations Code, statutes, **Bus Org 1.006, 1.051 et seq.**
Contracts,
Business Organizations Code, application of law, **Bus Org 402.006**
Elections, **Bus Org 6.252**
Winding up, **Bus Org 11.152**
Contributions, definitions, business organizations, **Bus Org 1.002**
Conversion, **Bus Org 10.101 et seq.**
Abandonment, **Bus Org 10.201, 10.202, 10.203**
Acceptance, certificates and certification, **Bus Org 10.156**
Business Organizations Code, mandatory application date, **Bus Org 402.010**
Certificates and certification, **Bus Org 10.154 et seq.**
Dissenting shareholders, **Bus Org 10.351 et seq.**
Effective date, **Bus Org 10.105, 10.106**
Filing,
Certificates and certification, **Bus Org 10.155**
Fees, **Bus Org 4.151**
Names, **Bus Org 10.103**
Notice, **Bus Org 10.101**
Plans and specifications, **Bus Org 10.101 et seq.**
Reorganization, **Bus Org 10.301 et seq.**
Copies. Duplicates and copies, generally, post
Corrections, filing, **Bus Org 4.101 et seq.**
Fees, **Bus Org 4.151**
Costs,
Filing,
Fines and penalties, **Bus Org 21.802**
Fraud, **Bus Org 4.007**
Insolvency, dismissal and nonsuit, **Bus Org 12.257**

PROFESSIONAL ASSOCIATIONS AND SOCIETIES—Cont'd
Costs—Cont'd
Liens and incumbrances, foreclosure, dismissal and nonsuit, **Bus Org 12.257**
Crimes and offenses,
Books and papers, examinations and examiners, **Bus Org 12.156**
Damages, **Bus Org 7.001**
Fraud, generally, post
Termination, involuntary termination, **Bus Org 11.301 et seq.**
Winding up, involuntary winding up, **Bus Org 11.301 et seq.**
Damages, **Bus Org 301.010**
Filing, **Bus Org 21.802**
Fraud, **Bus Org 4.007**
Indemnity, generally, post
Officers and employees, **Bus Org 7.001, 301.010**
Deception, names, **Bus Org 5.052**
Deeds and conveyances, **Bus Org 10.251 et seq.**
Definitions, **Bus Org 1.002, 301.003**
Business organizations, **Bus Org 1.002**
Indemnity, **Bus Org 8.001**
Mandatory application date, **Bus Org 401.001**
Prior law, **Bus Org 401.001**
Termination, **Bus Org 11.001**
Winding up, **Bus Org 11.001**
Delay, filing, effective date, **Bus Org 4.052 et seq.**
Delivery,
Filing, **Bus Org 4.001**
Meetings, action without meeting, **Bus Org 6.203**
Shares and shareholders, certificates and certification, **Bus Org 3.204**
Deposits, termination, claims, **Bus Org 11.352**
Directors, **Bus Org 302.005**
Agent for service of process, **Bus Org 5.255**
Certificate of formation,
Amendments, **Bus Org 3.054**
Restatement, **Bus Org 3.060**
Damages, **Bus Org 7.001**
Indemnity, **Bus Org 7.001**
Discharge,
Receivers and receivership, **Bus Org 11.412**
Termination, claims, **Bus Org 11.353**
Winding up, indebtedness, **Bus Org 11.053**
Disclosure, interrogatories, **Bus Org 12.003**
Dismissal and nonsuit,
Insolvency, **Bus Org 12.257**
Liens and incumbrances, foreclosure, **Bus Org 12.257**
Dissenting shareholders. Shares and shareholders, post
Dissolution, involuntary dissolution, reinstatement, **Bus Org 402.013**

PROFESSIONAL ASSOCIATIONS AND SOCIETIES—Cont'd
Distribution and distributors,
Record date, **Bus Org 6.101 et seq.**
Winding up, assets, **Bus Org 11.053**
Division, profits, **Bus Org 302.011**
Dual office holding, officers and employees, **Bus Org 3.103**
Duplicates and copies,
Agent for service of process, **Bus Org 5.252**
Books and papers, **Bus Org 12.151 et seq.**
Consent, meetings, action without meeting, **Bus Org 6.205**
Filing, **Bus Org 4.003**
Records and recordation, **Bus Org 3.152**
Shares and shareholders, certificates and certification, **Bus Org 3.202**
Duties. Powers and duties, generally, post
Effective date,
Business Organizations Code, **Bus Org 402.001**
Adoption, **Bus Org 402.005**
Conversion, **Bus Org 10.105, 10.106**
Exchange of property, **Bus Org 10.054, 10.055**
Filing, **Bus Org 4.051 et seq.**
Merger and consolidation, **Bus Org 10.007**
Termination, post
Elections, **Bus Org 6.151 et seq., 302.005 et seq.**
Application of law, **Bus Org 6.301, 6.302**
Conflict of interest, **Bus Org 6.152, 6.153**
Contracts, **Bus Org 6.252**
Estates, **Bus Org 6.154**
Indemnity, **Bus Org 8.103**
Officers and employees, **Bus Org 3.103, 302.007**
Pledges, **Bus Org 6.156**
Probate proceedings, **Bus Org 6.154**
Receivers and receivership, **Bus Org 6.155**
Trusts and trustees, **Bus Org 6.154, 6.251**
Electronic communications, consent, meetings, **Bus Org 6.205**
Electronic filing, **Bus Org 12.001**
Emergencies, governance, **Bus Org 3.251 et seq.**
Employees. Officers and employees, generally, post
Errors,
Damages, **Bus Org 301.010**
Termination, reinstatement, **Bus Org 11.201 et seq.**
Escheat, termination, claims, **Bus Org 11.355**
Estates, elections, **Bus Org 6.154**
Ethics, names, **Bus Org 5.060**

PROFESSIONAL ASSOCIATIONS AND SOCIETIES—Cont'd
Evidence,
  Existence, certificates and certification, **Bus Org 4.005**
  Filing, **Bus Org 4.001**
  Shares and shareholders, certificates and certification, **Bus Org 3.201**
Examinations and examiners,
  Books and papers, **Bus Org 12.151 et seq.**
  Elections, contracts, **Bus Org 6.252**
  Records and recordation, **Bus Org 3.153**
Exchange of property, **Bus Org 10.051 et seq.**
  Abandonment, **Bus Org 10.201, 10.202, 10.203**
  Acceptance, certificates and certification, **Bus Org 10.156**
  Certificates and certification, **Bus Org 10.151 et seq.**
  Dissenting shareholders, **Bus Org 10.351 et seq.**
  Filing,
    Certificates and certification, **Bus Org 10.153**
    Fees, **Bus Org 4.151**
  Reorganization, **Bus Org 10.301**
  Shares and shareholders, post
  Voluntary, **Bus Org 10.902**
Exemptions,
  Interrogatories, **Bus Org 12.002**
  Securities, sales, **Bus Org 301.011**
  Termination, involuntary termination, **Bus Org 11.251**
Expenses and expenditures, indemnity, **Bus Org 8.001 et seq.**
Facsimile, **Bus Org 1.007**
  Consent, meetings, action without meeting, **Bus Org 6.205**
  Filing, **Bus Org 4.003**
  Meetings, notice, **Bus Org 6.051**
  Shares and shareholders, certificates and certification, **Bus Org 3.203**
Fees,
  Business Organizations Code, effective date, **Bus Org 402.002**
  Filing, **Bus Org 4.151 et seq.**
  Names, reservation, **Bus Org 5.101**
    Withdrawal, **Bus Org 5.1041**
Filing, **Bus Org 4.001 et seq., 12.001 et seq.**
  Abandonment, **Bus Org 4.057**
  Acknowledgments, **Bus Org 4.002**
    Effective date, delay, **Bus Org 4.059**
  Amendments, **Bus Org 4.106**
  Appeal and review, **Bus Org 12.004**
  Assumed or fictitious names, **Bus Org 5.051**
  Attorney fees,
    Fines and penalties, **Bus Org 21.802**
    Fraud, **Bus Org 4.007**
  Business Organizations Code, effective date, **Bus Org 402.002**
  Certificates and certification, ante
  Certified copies, **Bus Org 4.005**

PROFESSIONAL ASSOCIATIONS AND SOCIETIES—Cont'd
Filing—Cont'd
  Conversion, certificates and certification, **Bus Org 10.155**
  Corrections, **Bus Org 4.101 et seq.**
    Fees, **Bus Org 4.151**
  Costs,
    Fines and penalties, **Bus Org 21.802**
    Fraud, **Bus Org 4.007**
  Damages, **Bus Org 21.802**
    Fraud, **Bus Org 4.007**
  Delay, effective date, **Bus Org 4.052 et seq.**
  Delivery, **Bus Org 4.001**
  Duplicates and copies, **Bus Org 4.003**
  Effective date, **Bus Org 4.051 et seq.**
  Electronic filing, **Bus Org 12.001**
  Evidence, **Bus Org 4.001**
  Facsimile, **Bus Org 4.003**
  Fees, **Bus Org 4.151 et seq.**
  Financial statements and reports, **Bus Org 302.012**
  Fines and penalties, **Bus Org 21.802**
    Fraud, **Bus Org 4.008**
  Foreign associations and societies, registration, **Bus Org 301.005**
  Forms, **Bus Org 4.006**
  Fraud, **Bus Org 4.007, 4.008**
  Interrogatories, **Bus Org 12.002, 12.003**
  Jurisdiction, fines and penalties, **Bus Org 21.802**
  Limitations,
    Corrections, **Bus Org 4.102**
    Effective date, delay, **Bus Org 4.058**
  Names, registration, **Bus Org 5.152**
  Real estate investment trusts, **Bus Org 4.009**
  Receivers and receivership, claims, **Bus Org 11.407**
  Registered agent, resignation, **Bus Org 5.204**
  Service of process, **Bus Org 21.802**
  Signatures, **Bus Org 4.001**
    Corrections, certificates and certification, **Bus Org 4.101**
  Termination, involuntary termination, **Bus Org 11.315**
  Time, **Bus Org 4.004**
    Corrections, **Bus Org 4.105**
    Effective date, **Bus Org 4.051 et seq.**
    Fines and penalties, **Bus Org 21.802**
  Winding up, involuntary winding up, **Bus Org 11.315**
Financial statements and reports, **Bus Org 302.012**
  Officers and employees, good faith, **Bus Org 3.102, 3.105**
Fines and penalties,
  Books and papers, examinations and examiners, **Bus Org 12.156**
  Filing, **Bus Org 21.802**
    Fraud, **Bus Org 4.008**
  Registered agents, consent, **Bus Org 5.207**
Foreclosure, liens and incumbrances, **Bus Org 12.252 et seq.**

PROFESSIONAL ASSOCIATIONS AND SOCIETIES—Cont'd
Foreign associations, **Bus Org 301.001 et seq.**
  Adoption, Business Organizations Code, **Bus Org 402.003**
  Names, **Bus Org 5.058**
    Conflict of laws, **Bus Org 5.060**
  Registration, **Bus Org 301.005**
    Business Organizations Code,
      Adoption, **Bus Org 402.004**
      Mandatory application date, **Bus Org 402.012**
Foreign countries, Business Organizations Code, application of law, **Bus Org 1.053**
Foreign states,
  Business Organizations Code, application of law, **Bus Org 1.053**
  Meetings, location, **Bus Org 6.001**
Forfeitures,
  Books and papers, examinations and examiners, **Bus Org 12.155**
  Reinstatement, **Bus Org 402.013**
Forms,
  Filing, **Bus Org 4.006**
  Shares and shareholders, certificates and certification, **Bus Org 3.202**
Fraud,
  Filing, **Bus Org 4.007, 4.008**
  Names, **Bus Org 5.052**
  Receivers and receivership, **Bus Org 11.403**
  Termination,
    Involuntary termination, **Bus Org 11.301 et seq.**
    Revocation or suspension, **Bus Org 11.153**
  Winding up, involuntary winding up, **Bus Org 11.301 et seq.**
Garnishment, state, **Bus Org 12.259**
Good faith,
  Damages, **Bus Org 7.001**
  Officers and employees, **Bus Org 3.102, 3.105**
Hold harmless. Indemnity, generally, post
Holding companies, merger and consolidation, **Bus Org 10.005**
Identity and identification, names, same or similar, **Bus Org 5.053**
Indebtedness,
  Application of law, **Bus Org 10.901**
  Winding up, discharge, **Bus Org 11.053**
Indemnity,
  Business Organizations Code, application of law, **Bus Org 402.007**
  Insurance, **Bus Org 8.151**
  Mandatory, **Bus Org 8.051**
  Officers and employees, **Bus Org 7.001, 8.001 et seq.**
  Orders of court, **Bus Org 8.052**
  Permissive indemnification, **Bus Org 8.101 et seq.**
  Reports, **Bus Org 8.152**
Injunctions, state, **Bus Org 12.259**

PROFESSIONAL ASSOCIATIONS AND SOCIETIES—Cont'd
Insolvency, actions and proceedings, **Bus Org 12.253 et seq.**
Inspection and inspectors,
  Books and papers, **Bus Org 12.151 et seq.**
  Records and recordation, **Bus Org 3.152**
Insurance, indemnity, **Bus Org 8.151**
Internet, meetings, **Bus Org 6.002**
Interrogatories, **Bus Org 12.002, 12.003**
Involuntary termination, **Bus Org 11.251 et seq.**
  Certified copies, judgments and decrees, **Bus Org 11.414**
Joint practices, **Bus Org 301.012**
Judgments and decrees,
  Receivers and receivership, termination, **Bus Org 11.412**
  Reorganization, **Bus Org 10.305**
  Termination, **Bus Org 11.301 et seq.**
    Involuntary termination, certified copies, **Bus Org 11.414**
  Winding up, **Bus Org 11.301 et seq.**
Jurisdiction,
  Filing, fines and penalties, **Bus Org 21.802**
  Insolvency, **Bus Org 12.253**
  Liens and incumbrances, foreclosure, **Bus Org 12.253**
  Receivers and receivership, **Bus Org 11.402 et seq.**
  Reorganization, **Bus Org 10.302**
  Termination, involuntary termination, **Bus Org 11.308**
  Winding up, involuntary winding up, **Bus Org 11.308**
Leases, **Bus Org 10.251 et seq.**
  Reorganization, **Bus Org 10.301**
Licenses and permits, **Bus Org 301.006**
Liens and incumbrances,
  Foreclosure, **Bus Org 12.252 et seq.**
  State, **Bus Org 12.201**
Limitation of actions, termination, claims, **Bus Org 11.359**
Limitations,
  Filing,
    Corrections, **Bus Org 4.102**
    Effective date, delay, **Bus Org 4.058**
  Indemnity, **Bus Org 8.003, 8.004**
  Purposes, **Bus Org 2.003 et seq.**
Liquidation, receivers and receivership, **Bus Org 12.258**
  Orders of court, **Bus Org 11.405**
Location, meetings, **Bus Org 6.001**
Lottery, names, **Bus Org 5.061**
Mail and mailing, meetings, notice, **Bus Org 6.051**
Managers and management,
  Agent for service of process, **Bus Org 5.255**
  Damages, **Bus Org 301.010**
  Licenses and permits, **Bus Org 301.006**
  Resignation, **Bus Org 301.008**

PROFESSIONAL ASSOCIATIONS AND SOCIETIES—Cont'd
Mandatory application date, Business Organizations Code, **Bus Org 401.001 et seq.**
Meetings, **Bus Org 6.001 et seq.**
  Action without meeting, **Bus Org 6.102**
    Consent, **Bus Org 6.201 et seq.**
  Application of law, **Bus Org 6.301, 6.302**
  Business Organizations Code, mandatory application date, **Bus Org 402.008, 402.009**
  Consent, action without meeting, **Bus Org 6.102, 6.201 et seq.**
  Delivery, action without meeting, **Bus Org 6.203**
  Emergencies, **Bus Org 3.251 et seq.**
  Facsimile, notice, **Bus Org 6.051**
  Foreign states, location, **Bus Org 6.001**
  Internet, **Bus Org 6.002**
  Location, **Bus Org 6.001**
  Mail and mailing, notice, **Bus Org 6.051**
  Notice, **Bus Org 6.051 et seq.**
    Action without meeting, **Bus Org 6.204**
  Objections and exceptions, **Bus Org 6.003**
    Notice, waiver, **Bus Org 6.053**
  Record date, **Bus Org 6.101 et seq.**
  Records and recordation, **Bus Org 6.002**
  Shares and shareholders, post
  Telecommunications, **Bus Org 6.002**
  Video recordings, **Bus Org 6.002**
  Waiver, notice, **Bus Org 6.052**
    Objections and exceptions, **Bus Org 6.053**
Members,
  Elections, **Bus Org 302.006**
  Powers and duties, limitations, **Bus Org 302.010**
Merger and consolidation, **Bus Org 10.001 et seq.**
  Abandonment, **Bus Org 10.201, 10.202, 10.203**
  Acceptance, certificates and certification, **Bus Org 10.156**
  Allocations, property, **Bus Org 10.003**
  Business Organizations Code, mandatory application date, **Bus Org 402.010**
  Certificate of formation, **Bus Org 10.002**
  Certificates and certification, **Bus Org 10.151 et seq.**
  Dissenting shareholders, **Bus Org 10.351 et seq.**
  Effect, **Bus Org 10.008**
  Effective date, **Bus Org 10.007**
  Filing,
    Certificates and certification, **Bus Org 10.153**
    Fees, **Bus Org 4.151**
  Holding companies, **Bus Org 10.005**
  Names, **Bus Org 10.002**

PROFESSIONAL ASSOCIATIONS AND SOCIETIES—Cont'd
Merger and consolidation—Cont'd
  Plans and specifications, **Bus Org 10.001 et seq.**
  Property, allocations, **Bus Org 10.003**
  Reorganization, **Bus Org 10.301 et seq.**
  Subsidiaries, **Bus Org 10.006**
    Certificates and certification, **Bus Org 10.152**
  Time, effective date, **Bus Org 10.007**
Misconduct, damages, **Bus Org 7.001**
Money, **Bus Org 1.009**
Monopolies and unfair trade, application of law, **Bus Org 10.901**
Mortgages, receivers and receivership, **Bus Org 11.403**
Names, **Bus Org 5.001 et seq.**
  Assumed or fictitious names, **Bus Org 5.051 et seq.**
  Certificate of formation, amendments, **Bus Org 3.053, 3.056**
  Conflict of laws, **Bus Org 5.060**
  Conversion, **Bus Org 10.103**
  Deception, **Bus Org 5.052**
  Ethics, **Bus Org 5.060**
  Exchange of property, plans and specifications, **Bus Org 10.052**
  Fees, reservation, **Bus Org 5.101**
    Withdrawal, **Bus Org 5.1041**
  Filing,
    Fees, **Bus Org 4.151**
    Registration, **Bus Org 5.152**
  Fraud, **Bus Org 5.052**
  Identity and identification, same or similar, **Bus Org 5.053**
  Lottery, **Bus Org 5.061**
  Merger and consolidation, **Bus Org 10.002**
  Notice, **Bus Org 5.001**
  Registration, **Bus Org 5.151 et seq.**
  Renewal,
    Registration, **Bus Org 5.155**
    Reservation, **Bus Org 5.105**
  Reservation, **Bus Org 5.101 et seq.**
  Same or similar, **Bus Org 5.053**
    Registration, **Bus Org 5.153**
    Reservation, **Bus Org 5.102**
  Termination, reinstatement, **Bus Org 11.203**
  Time,
    Registration, **Bus Org 5.154**
    Reservation, **Bus Org 5.104**
  Trademarks and trade names, **Bus Org 5.001**
  Transfers, reservation, **Bus Org 5.106**
  Veterans organizations, **Bus Org 5.062**
  Words and phrases, **Bus Org 5.058**
Negligence, damages, **Bus Org 301.010**
Notice,
  Agent for service of process, **Bus Org 5.252, 5.253**
  Conversion, **Bus Org 10.101**
  Indemnity, orders of court, **Bus Org 8.052**
  Insolvency, **Bus Org 12.256**

PROFESSIONAL ASSOCIATIONS AND SOCIETIES—Cont'd
Notice—Cont'd
Liens and incumbrances,
Foreclosure, **Bus Org 12.256**
State, **Bus Org 12.201**
Meetings, **Bus Org 6.051 et seq.**
Action without meeting, **Bus Org 6.204**
Names, **Bus Org 5.001**
Receivers and receivership, claims, **Bus Org 11.407**
Registered agent, resignation, **Bus Org 5.204**
Reorganization, **Bus Org 10.301**
Shares and shareholders, post
Termination, post
Winding up, **Bus Org 11.052**
Involuntary winding up, **Bus Org 11.302, 11.310**
Oaths and affirmations, interrogatories, answer, **Bus Org 12.002**
Objections and exceptions, meetings, **Bus Org 6.003**
Notice, waiver, **Bus Org 6.053**
Offenses. Crimes and offenses, generally, ante
Officers and employees, **Bus Org 3.101 et seq.**
Agent for service of process, **Bus Org 5.255**
Damages, **Bus Org 7.001, 301.010**
Directors, generally, ante
Dual office holding, **Bus Org 3.103**
Elections, **Bus Org 3.103, 302.007**
Good faith, **Bus Org 3.105**
Indemnity, **Bus Org 7.001, 8.001 et seq.**
Licenses and permits, **Bus Org 301.006**
Qualifications, **Bus Org 302.008**
Removal, **Bus Org 3.104**
Offices,
Changes, filing, fines and penalties, **Bus Org 21.802**
Registered offices, generally, post
Reorganization, **Bus Org 10.301**
Omissions, certificate of formation, restatement, **Bus Org 3.059**
Open records, interrogatories, **Bus Org 12.003**
Orders of court, receivers and receivership, **Bus Org 11.402**
Liquidation, **Bus Org 11.405**
Parties, receivers and receivership, **Bus Org 11.411**
Payment, termination,
Claims, **Bus Org 11.354**
Taxation, **Bus Org 11.101**
Penalties. Fines and penalties, generally, ante
Permissive indemnification, **Bus Org 8.101 et seq.**
Personal property,
Disposition, **Bus Org 10.251 et seq.**
Reorganization, **Bus Org 10.301**
Shares and shareholders, **Bus Org 21.801**

PROFESSIONAL ASSOCIATIONS AND SOCIETIES—Cont'd
Photography and pictures, consent, meetings, action without meeting, **Bus Org 6.205**
Physicians and surgeons, physician assistants, **Bus Org 301.012**
Plans and specifications,
Conversion, **Bus Org 10.101 et seq.**
Exchange of property, **Bus Org 10.051 et seq.**
Merger and consolidation, **Bus Org 10.001 et seq.**
Pledges, elections, **Bus Org 6.156**
Political subdivisions, service of process, **Bus Org 5.257**
Powers and duties, **Bus Org 2.108**
Members, limitations, **Bus Org 302.010**
Receivers and receivership, **Bus Org 11.406**
President, agent for service of process, **Bus Org 5.255**
Prior laws, Business Organizations Code, **Bus Org 401.001 et seq.**
Privileges and immunities,
Property, disposition, **Bus Org 10.254**
Registered agents, **Bus Org 5.208**
Probate proceedings, elections, **Bus Org 6.154**
Proceedings. Actions and proceedings, generally, ante
Process. Service of process, generally, post
Profits, division, **Bus Org 302.011**
Property,
Disposition, **Bus Org 10.251 et seq.**
Reorganization, **Bus Org 10.301**
Exchange of property, generally, ante
Liens and incumbrances,
Foreclosure, **Bus Org 12.252 et seq.**
State, **Bus Org 12.201**
Merger and consolidation, allocations, **Bus Org 10.003**
Publication,
Termination, involuntary termination, **Bus Org 11.310**
Winding up, involuntary winding up, **Bus Org 11.310**
Purchases and purchasing,
Indemnity, insurance, **Bus Org 8.151**
Title to property, **Bus Org 301.008**
Purposes, **Bus Org 2.001 et seq.**
Quo warranto, insolvency, **Bus Org 12.253 et seq.**
Real estate,
Disposition, **Bus Org 10.251 et seq.**
Reorganization, **Bus Org 10.301**
Records and recordation, deeds and conveyances, **Bus Org 10.253**
Receipts, termination, claims, **Bus Org 11.352**
Receivers and receivership, **Bus Org 11.401 et seq.**
Actions and proceedings, **Bus Org 11.406**
Ancillary receiverships, **Bus Org 11.409**
Appointments, **Bus Org 11.401 et seq.**

PROFESSIONAL ASSOCIATIONS AND SOCIETIES—Cont'd
Receivers and receivership—Cont'd
Bonds (officers and fiduciaries), **Bus Org 11.406**
Citizens and citizenship, **Bus Org 11.406**
Claims, filing, **Bus Org 11.407**
Compensation and salaries, **Bus Org 11.408**
Discharge, **Bus Org 11.412**
Elections, **Bus Org 6.155**
Filing, claims, **Bus Org 11.407**
Foreign entities, **Bus Org 11.409, 11.410**
Fraud, **Bus Org 11.403**
Judgments and decrees, termination, **Bus Org 11.412**
Jurisdiction, **Bus Org 11.402 et seq.**
Liens and incumbrances, state, **Bus Org 12.201**
Liquidation, **Bus Org 12.258**
Orders of court, **Bus Org 11.405**
Mortgages, **Bus Org 11.403**
Notice, claims, **Bus Org 11.407**
Orders of court, **Bus Org 11.402**
Liquidation, **Bus Org 11.405**
Parties, **Bus Org 11.411**
Powers and duties, **Bus Org 11.406**
Registration, **Bus Org 11.406**
Rehabilitation, **Bus Org 11.404**
State, **Bus Org 12.251**
Termination, **Bus Org 11.403**
Judgments and decrees, **Bus Org 11.412**
Record date, **Bus Org 6.101 et seq.**
Records and recordation, **Bus Org 3.151 et seq.**
Certified copies, filing, **Bus Org 4.005**
Confidential or privileged information, **Bus Org 12.154**
Disclosure, **Bus Org 12.154**
Examinations and examiners, **Bus Org 3.153, 12.151 et seq.**
Inspection and inspectors, **Bus Org 3.152**
Interrogatories, open records, **Bus Org 12.003**
Meetings, **Bus Org 6.002**
Real estate, deeds and conveyances, **Bus Org 10.253**
Record date, **Bus Org 6.101 et seq.**
Reorganization, **Bus Org 10.301**
Service of process, **Bus Org 5.254**
Signatures, **Bus Org 1.007**
Termination, removal, **Bus Org 11.104**
Time, record date, **Bus Org 6.101 et seq.**
Registered agent, **Bus Org 5.200 et seq.**
Changes, **Bus Org 5.202**
Filing, fines and penalties, **Bus Org 21.802**
Reorganization, **Bus Org 10.301**
Resignation, **Bus Org 5.204**
Registered offices, **Bus Org 5.200 et seq.**
Changes, **Bus Org 5.202**

PROFESSIONAL ASSOCIATIONS AND SOCIETIES—Cont'd
Registered offices—Cont'd
Changes—Cont'd
Filing, fines and penalties, **Bus Org 21.802**
Registration,
Foreign associations, ante
Names, **Bus Org 5.151 et seq.**
Receivers and receivership, **Bus Org 11.406**
Rehabilitation, receivers and receivership, **Bus Org 11.404**
Reinstatement. Termination, post
Rejection, registered agents, **Bus Org 5.205**
Remand,
Termination, involuntary termination, **Bus Org 11.307**
Winding up, involuntary winding up, **Bus Org 11.307**
Removal, officers and employees, **Bus Org 3.104**
Renewal, names,
Registration, **Bus Org 5.155**
Reservation, **Bus Org 5.105**
Reorganization, **Bus Org 10.301 et seq.**
Business Organizations Code, mandatory application date, **Bus Org 402.010**
Repeals, Business Organizations Code, statutes, **Bus Org 1.054**
Reports,
Indemnity, **Bus Org 8.152**
Officers and employees, good faith, **Bus Org 3.102, 3.105**
Reservation, names, **Bus Org 5.101 et seq.**
Resignation,
Managers and management, **Bus Org 301.008**
Registered agent, **Bus Org 5.204**
Resolutions, indemnity, **Bus Org 8.103**
Restatement, certificate of formation, **Bus Org 3.057 et seq.**
Review. Appeal and review, generally, ante
Revocation or suspension,
Reinstatement, **Bus Org 402.013**
Termination, fraud, **Bus Org 11.153**
Winding up, **Bus Org 11.151**
Sales, **Bus Org 10.251 et seq.**
Reorganization, **Bus Org 10.301**
Securities, exemptions, **Bus Org 301.011**
Same or similar. Names, ante
Seals, shares and shareholders, certificates and certification, **Bus Org 3.202**
Secretary of state, agent for service of process, **Bus Org 5.251 et seq.**
Securities, sales, exemptions, **Bus Org 301.011**
Sequestration, state, **Bus Org 12.259**
Service of process, **Bus Org 5.251 et seq.**
Reorganization, **Bus Org 10.301**
Termination, involuntary termination, **Bus Org 11.309**

PROFESSIONAL ASSOCIATIONS AND SOCIETIES—Cont'd
Service of process—Cont'd
Winding up, involuntary winding up, **Bus Org 11.309**
Services, certificate of formation, **Bus Org 3.014**
Shares and shareholders,
Abandonment, exchange of property, **Bus Org 10.201, 10.202, 10.203**
Acceptance, exchange of property, certificates and certification, **Bus Org 10.156**
Appointments, dissenting shareholders, appraisal and appraisers, **Bus Org 10.361**
Appraisals and appraisers, dissenting shareholders, **Bus Org 10.354 et seq.**
Assignments, certificates and certification, **Bus Org 3.201**
Books and papers, dissenting shareholders, fair market value, **Bus Org 10.363**
Certificates and certification, **Bus Org 3.201 et seq.**
Exchange of property, **Bus Org 10.151 et seq.**
Compensation and salaries, dissenting shareholders, appraisals and appraisers, **Bus Org 10.365**
Computation, dissenting shareholders, fair market value, **Bus Org 10.362**
Contracts, elections, **Bus Org 6.252**
Costs, dissenting shareholders, appraisals and appraisers, **Bus Org 10.365**
Delivery,
Certificates and certification, **Bus Org 3.204**
Meetings, action without meeting, **Bus Org 6.203**
Demand, dissenting shareholders, fair market value, **Bus Org 10.357 et seq.**
Dissenting shareholders, **Bus Org 10.351 et seq.**
Appointments, appraisal and appraisers, **Bus Org 10.361**
Appraisals and appraisers, **Bus Org 10.354 et seq.**
Books and papers, fair market value, **Bus Org 10.363**
Compensation and salaries, appraisals and appraisers, **Bus Org 10.365**
Computation, fair market value, **Bus Org 10.362**
Costs, appraisals and appraisers, **Bus Org 10.365**
Definitions, **Bus Org 10.352**
Demand, fair market value, **Bus Org 10.357 et seq.**
Exclusive remedy, **Bus Org 10.368**
Fair market value, demand, **Bus Org 10.357 et seq.**
Forms, **Bus Org 10.353**

PROFESSIONAL ASSOCIATIONS AND SOCIETIES—Cont'd
Shares and shareholders—Cont'd
Dissenting shareholders—Cont'd
Hearings, fair market value, **Bus Org 10.361**
Investigations and investigators, fair market value, **Bus Org 10.363**
Notice, **Bus Org 10.353, 10.355**
Objections and exceptions, appraisals and appraisers, **Bus Org 10.364**
Perfection, **Bus Org 10.356**
Petitions, fair market value, **Bus Org 10.361**
Records and recordation, fair market value, **Bus Org 10.363**
Demand, **Bus Org 10.359**
Reorganization, **Bus Org 10.304**
Termination, **Bus Org 10.367**
Title to property, **Bus Org 10.366**
Withdrawal, **Bus Org 10.357**
Distribution and distributors, record date, **Bus Org 6.101 et seq.**
Duplicates and copies, certificates and certification, **Bus Org 3.202**
Elections,
Contracts, **Bus Org 6.252**
Trusts and trustees, **Bus Org 6.251**
Evidence, certificates and certification, **Bus Org 3.201**
Examinations and examiners, elections, contracts, **Bus Org 6.252**
Exchange of property, **Bus Org 10.051 et seq.**
Abandonment, **Bus Org 10.201, 10.202, 10.203**
Acceptance, certificates and certification, **Bus Org 10.156**
Certificates and certification, **Bus Org 10.151 et seq.**
Filing, certificates and certification, **Bus Org 10.153**
Exclusive remedy, dissenting shareholders, **Bus Org 10.368**
Facsimile, certificates and certification, **Bus Org 3.203**
Fair market value, dissenting shareholders, demand, **Bus Org 10.357 et seq.**
Filing, exchange of property, certificates and certification, **Bus Org 10.153**
Forms,
Certificates and certification, **Bus Org 3.202**
Dissenting shareholders, **Bus Org 10.353**
Hearings, dissenting shareholders, fair market value, **Bus Org 10.361**
Investigations and investigators, dissenting shareholders, fair market value, **Bus Org 10.363**
Meetings,
Action without meeting, **Bus Org 6.102**
Consent, **Bus Org 6.201 et seq.**

PROFESSIONAL ASSOCIATIONS AND SOCIETIES—Cont'd
Shares and shareholders—Cont'd
Meetings—Cont'd
Consent, action without meeting, **Bus Org 6.102, 6.201 et seq.**
Delivery, action without meeting, **Bus Org 6.203**
Notice, action without meeting, **Bus Org 6.204**
Notice,
Dissenting shareholders, **Bus Org 10.353, 10.355**
Meetings, action without meeting, **Bus Org 6.204**
Uncertificated shares, **Bus Org 3.205**
Objections and exceptions, dissenting shareholders, appraisals and appraisers, **Bus Org 10.364**
Perfection, dissenting shareholders, **Bus Org 10.356**
Personal property, **Bus Org 21.801**
Petitions, dissenting shareholders, fair market value, **Bus Org 10.361**
Record date, **Bus Org 6.101 et seq.**
Records and recordation, dissenting shareholders, fair market value, **Bus Org 10.363**
Demand, **Bus Org 10.359**
Reorganization, dissenting shareholders, **Bus Org 10.304**
Seals, certificates and certification, **Bus Org 3.202**
Signatures, certificates and certification, **Bus Org 3.203**
Termination, dissenting shareholders, **Bus Org 10.367**
Time, record date, **Bus Org 6.101 et seq.**
Title to property, dissenting shareholders, **Bus Org 10.366**
Transfers, certificates and certification, **Bus Org 3.201**
Trusts and trustees, elections, **Bus Org 6.251**
Uncertificated shares, **Bus Org 3.201**
Notice, **Bus Org 3.205**
Withdrawal, dissenting shareholders, **Bus Org 10.357**
Signatures, **Bus Org 1.007**
Certificate of formation, ante
Filing, **Bus Org 4.001**
Corrections, certificates and certification, **Bus Org 4.101**
Reorganization, **Bus Org 10.302**
Shares and shareholders, certificates and certification, **Bus Org 3.203**
Termination, **Bus Org 302.013**
Specifications. Plans and specifications, generally, ante
State,
Liens and incumbrances, **Bus Org 12.201**
Receivers and receivership, **Bus Org 12.251**
Statements,
Certificate of formation, ante

PROFESSIONAL ASSOCIATIONS AND SOCIETIES—Cont'd
Statements—Cont'd
Filing, fees, **Bus Org 4.156**
Officers and employees, good faith, **Bus Org 3.102, 3.105**
Termination, claims, **Bus Org 11.352**
Statutes, Business Organizations Code, construction of laws, **Bus Org 1.006, 1.051 et seq.**
Subsidiaries, merger and consolidation, **Bus Org 10.006**
Certificates and certification, **Bus Org 10.152**
Supersedeas or stay,
Termination, involuntary termination, **Bus Org 11.306**
Winding up, involuntary winding up, **Bus Org 11.306**
Supervision, winding up, **Bus Org 11.054**
Suspension. Revocation or suspension, generally, ante
Taxation,
Service of process, **Bus Org 5.257**
Termination,
Forfeitures, reinstatement, **Bus Org 11.254, 402.013**
Payment, **Bus Org 11.101**
Telecommunications, meetings, **Bus Org 6.002**
Termination, **Bus Org 11.001 et seq., 302.013**
Abatement of actions and proceedings, involuntary termination, **Bus Org 11.304**
Actions and proceedings, involuntary termination, **Bus Org 11.303**
Appeal and review, involuntary termination, **Bus Org 11.307**
Business Organizations Code, mandatory application date, **Bus Org 402.011**
Certificates and certification, **Bus Org 11.101 et seq.**
Involuntary termination, **Bus Org 11.252**
Reinstatement, **Bus Org 11.202**
Certified copies, involuntary termination, judgments and decrees, **Bus Org 11.414**
Claims, **Bus Org 11.351 et seq.**
Crimes and offenses, involuntary termination, **Bus Org 11.301 et seq.**
Deposits, claims, **Bus Org 11.352**
Discharge, claims, **Bus Org 11.353**
Effective date, **Bus Org 11.102, 11.103**
Claims, **Bus Org 11.356 et seq.**
Reinstatement, **Bus Org 11.204 et seq.**
Errors, reinstatement, **Bus Org 11.201 et seq.**
Escheat, claims, **Bus Org 11.355**
Exemptions, involuntary termination, **Bus Org 11.251**
Filing,
Fines and penalties, **Bus Org 21.802**

PROFESSIONAL ASSOCIATIONS AND SOCIETIES—Cont'd
Termination—Cont'd
Filing—Cont'd
Involuntary termination, **Bus Org 11.315**
Fraud,
Involuntary termination, **Bus Org 11.301 et seq.**
Revocation or suspension, **Bus Org 11.153**
Involuntary termination, **Bus Org 11.251 et seq., 11.301 et seq.**
Certified copies, judgments and decrees, **Bus Org 11.414**
Judgments and decrees, **Bus Org 11.301 et seq.**
Involuntary termination, certified copies, **Bus Org 11.414**
Jurisdiction, involuntary termination, **Bus Org 11.308**
Limitation of actions, claims, **Bus Org 11.359**
Names, reinstatement, **Bus Org 11.203**
Notice,
Claims, **Bus Org 11.358**
Escheat, claims, **Bus Org 11.355**
Involuntary termination, **Bus Org 11.251, 11.302, 11.310**
Payment,
Claims, **Bus Org 11.354**
Taxation, **Bus Org 11.101**
Publication, involuntary termination, **Bus Org 11.310**
Receipts, claims, **Bus Org 11.352**
Receivers and receivership, **Bus Org 11.403**
Judgments and decrees, **Bus Org 11.412**
Records and recordation, removal, **Bus Org 11.104**
Reinstatement, **Bus Org 11.201 et seq.**
Involuntary termination, **Bus Org 11.253**
Taxation, forfeitures, **Bus Org 11.254**
Remand, involuntary termination, **Bus Org 11.307**
Revocation or suspension, fraud, **Bus Org 11.153**
Service of process, involuntary termination, **Bus Org 11.309**
Statements, claims, **Bus Org 11.352**
Supersedeas or stay, involuntary termination, **Bus Org 11.306**
Taxation,
Forfeitures, reinstatement, **Bus Org 11.254**
Payment, **Bus Org 11.101**
Time,
Involuntary termination, **Bus Org 11.305, 11.313**
Reinstatement, **Bus Org 11.202**
Venue, involuntary termination, **Bus Org 11.308**
Time, **Bus Org 302.002**
Business Organizations Code, effective date, **Bus Org 402.001**

PROFESSIONAL ASSOCIATIONS AND SOCIETIES—Cont'd
Time—Cont'd
Business Organizations Code, effective date—Cont'd
Adoption, **Bus Org 402.005**
Certificate of formation,
Amendments, **Bus Org 3.056**
Restatement, **Bus Org 3.063**
Effective date, generally, ante
Exchange of property, **Bus Org 10.054, 10.055**
Filing, ante
Interrogatories, answer, **Bus Org 12.002**
Merger and consolidation, effective date, **Bus Org 10.007**
Record date, **Bus Org 6.101 et seq.**
Service of process, **Bus Org 5.254**
Termination, ante
Winding up, post
Title to property, **Bus Org 301.007 et seq.**
Trademarks and trade names, names, **Bus Org 5.001**
Transfers,
Names, reservation, **Bus Org 5.106**
Property, **Bus Org 10.251 et seq.**
Shares and shareholders, certificates and certification, **Bus Org 3.201**
Title to property, **Bus Org 301.009**
Transition, Business Organizations Code, **Bus Org 402.001 et seq.**
Trusts and trustees,
Elections, **Bus Org 6.154, 6.251**
Reorganization, **Bus Org 10.301 et seq.**
Uncertificated shares, **Bus Org 3.201**
Notice, **Bus Org 3.205**
Venue,
Termination, involuntary termination, **Bus Org 11.308**
Winding up, involuntary winding up, **Bus Org 11.308**
Veterans organizations, names, **Bus Org 5.062**
Vice president, agent for service of process, **Bus Org 5.255**
Video recordings, meetings, **Bus Org 6.002**
Waiver, meetings, notice, **Bus Org 6.052**
Objections and exceptions, **Bus Org 6.053**
Winding up, **Bus Org 11.001 et seq., 11.051 et seq., 302.013**
Abatement of actions and proceedings, involuntary winding up, **Bus Org 11.304**
Actions and proceedings, **Bus Org 11.052, 11.055**
Involuntary winding up, **Bus Org 11.303**
Appeal and review, involuntary winding up, **Bus Org 11.307**
Assets, distribution and distributors, **Bus Org 11.053**
Business Organizations Code, mandatory application date, **Bus Org 402.011**
Cancellation, **Bus Org 11.152**

PROFESSIONAL ASSOCIATIONS AND SOCIETIES—Cont'd
Winding up—Cont'd
Contracts, **Bus Org 11.152**
Crimes and offenses, involuntary winding up, **Bus Org 11.301 et seq.**
Discharge, indebtedness, **Bus Org 11.053**
Distribution and distributors, assets, **Bus Org 11.053**
Filing, involuntary winding up, **Bus Org 11.315**
Fraud, involuntary winding up, **Bus Org 11.301 et seq.**
Indebtedness, discharge, **Bus Org 11.053**
Involuntary winding up, **Bus Org 11.301 et seq.**
Judgments and decrees, **Bus Org 11.301 et seq.**
Jurisdiction, involuntary winding up, **Bus Org 11.308**
Notice, **Bus Org 11.052**
Involuntary winding up, **Bus Org 11.302, 11.310**
Publication, involuntary winding up, **Bus Org 11.310**
Remand, involuntary winding up, **Bus Org 11.307**
Revocation or suspension, **Bus Org 11.151**
Service of process, involuntary winding up, **Bus Org 11.309**
Supersedeas or stay, involuntary winding up, **Bus Org 11.306**
Supervision, **Bus Org 11.054**
Time, **Bus Org 11.056**
Cancellation, **Bus Org 11.152**
Involuntary winding up, **Bus Org 11.305, 11.313**
Venue, involuntary winding up, **Bus Org 11.308**
Withdrawal,
Filing, fines and penalties, **Bus Org 21.802**
Names, reservation, fees, **Bus Org 5.1041**
Witnesses, indemnity, expenses and expenditures, **Bus Org 8.106**
Writings, signatures, **Bus Org 1.007**

PROFESSIONAL CORPORATIONS
Generally, **Bus Org 1.001 et seq., 301.001 et seq., 303.001 et seq.**
Abandonment,
Conversion, **Bus Org 10.201, 10.202, 10.203**
Exchange of property, **Bus Org 10.201, 10.202, 10.203**
Filing, **Bus Org 4.057**
Merger and consolidation, **Bus Org 10.201, 10.202, 10.203**
Abatement of actions and proceedings,
State, **Bus Org 12.260**
Termination, involuntary termination, **Bus Org 11.304**

PROFESSIONAL CORPORATIONS—Cont'd
Abatement of actions and proceedings—Cont'd
Winding up, involuntary winding up, **Bus Org 11.304**
Acceptance, certificates and certification, **Bus Org 10.156**
Accounts and accounting, **Bus Org 3.151 et seq.**
Examinations and examiners, **Bus Org 12.151 et seq.**
Acknowledgments,
Certificate of formation, **Bus Org 3.004**
Evidence, **Bus Org 3.001**
Filing, **Bus Org 4.002**
Effective date, delay, **Bus Org 4.059**
Actions and proceedings,
Abatement of actions and proceedings, generally, ante
Certificate of formation, amendments, **Bus Org 3.056**
Indemnity, **Bus Org 8.001 et seq.**
Insolvency, **Bus Org 12.253 et seq.**
Receivers and receivership, **Bus Org 11.406**
Records and recordation, inspection and inspectors, **Bus Org 3.152**
State, liens and incumbrances, **Bus Org 12.201 et seq.**
Termination, involuntary termination, **Bus Org 11.303**
Winding up, post
Address, certificate of formation, **Bus Org 3.005**
Advancements, indemnity, expenses and expenditures, **Bus Org 8.104, 8.105**
Reports, **Bus Org 8.152**
Agent for service of process, **Bus Org 5.251 et seq.**
Agents and agencies,
Changes, filing, fines and penalties, **Bus Org 21.802**
Damages, **Bus Org 301.010**
Licenses and permits, **Bus Org 301.006**
Registered agent, generally, post
Allocations, merger and consolidation, property, **Bus Org 10.003**
Alternatives, service of process, **Bus Org 5.256**
Amendments,
Business Organizations Code, statutes, **Bus Org 1.054**
Certificate of formation, **Bus Org 3.051 et seq.**
Filing, **Bus Org 4.106**
Ancillary receiverships, **Bus Org 11.409**
Answer, interrogatories, time, **Bus Org 12.002**
Antitrust, application of law, **Bus Org 10.901**
Appeal and review,
Filing, **Bus Org 12.004**
Termination, involuntary termination, **Bus Org 11.307**
Winding up, involuntary winding up, **Bus Org 11.307**

PROFESSIONAL CORPORATIONS
—Cont'd
Application of law, **Bus Org 301.001, 303.001**
  Antitrust, **Bus Org 10.901**
  Business Organizations Code, foreign countries, foreign states, **Bus Org 1.053**
  Certificate of formation, **Bus Org 1.101 et seq.**
  Elections, **Bus Org 6.301, 6.302**
  Indebtedness, **Bus Org 10.901**
  Indemnity, **Bus Org 8.002**
  Meetings, **Bus Org 6.301, 6.302**
  Monopolies and unfair trade, **Bus Org 10.901**
  Reorganization, **Bus Org 10.306**
Appointments, receivers and receivership, **Bus Org 11.401 et seq.**
Appraisals and appraisers, reorganization, **Bus Org 10.304**
Assets,
  Disposition, **Bus Org 10.251 et seq.**
    Reorganization, **Bus Org 10.301**
  Liens and incumbrances, state, **Bus Org 12.201**
  Winding up, distribution and distributors, **Bus Org 11.053**
Assignments, **Bus Org 10.251 et seq.**
  Shares and shareholders, certificates and certification, **Bus Org 3.201**
Assumed or fictitious names, **Bus & C 71.001 et seq.; Bus Org 5.051 et seq.**
Attachment, state, **Bus Org 12.259**
Attorney fees,
  Filing,
    Fines and penalties, **Bus Org 21.802**
    Fraud, **Bus Org 4.007**
  Records and recordation, inspection and inspectors, **Bus Org 3.152**
Bankruptcy, **Bus Org 10.301 et seq.**
Bonds, reorganization, **Bus Org 10.301**
Bonds (officers and fiduciaries), receivers and receivership, **Bus Org 11.406**
Books and papers, **Bus Org 3.151 et seq.**
  Confidential or privileged information, **Bus Org 12.154**
  Disclosure, **Bus Org 12.154**
  Duplicates and copies, **Bus Org 12.151 et seq.**
  Examinations and examiners, **Bus Org 3.153, 12.151 et seq.**
  Inspection and inspectors, **Bus Org 3.152**
  Powers and duties, limitations, **Bus Org 2.005**
  Reorganization, **Bus Org 10.301**
  Signatures, **Bus Org 1.007**
Cancellation, winding up, **Bus Org 11.152**
Certificate of formation, **Bus Org 3.001 et seq.**
  Amendments, **Bus Org 3.051 et seq.**
  Application of law, **Bus Org 1.101 et seq.**
  Definitions, **Bus Org 1.002**
  Merger and consolidation, post
  Reorganization, **Bus Org 10.301 et seq.**

PROFESSIONAL CORPORATIONS
—Cont'd
Certificate of formation—Cont'd
  Restatement, **Bus Org 3.057 et seq.**
  Signatures, **Bus Org 3.004**
    Amendments, **Bus Org 3.052, 3.054**
    Restatement, **Bus Org 3.058, 3.060**
  Statements,
    Amendments, **Bus Org 3.053, 3.054**
    Restatement, **Bus Org 3.059**
  Time, **Bus Org 3.001, 3.003**
    Amendments, **Bus Org 3.056**
    Restatement, **Bus Org 3.063**
Certificates and certification,
  Acceptance, **Bus Org 10.156**
  Certificate of formation, generally, ante
  Conversion, **Bus Org 10.154 et seq.**
  Evidence, existence, **Bus Org 4.005**
  Exchange of property, **Bus Org 10.151 et seq.**
  Filing, **Bus Org 12.001**
    Abandonment, **Bus Org 4.057**
    Corrections, **Bus Org 4.101 et seq.**
    Fines and penalties, **Bus Org 21.802**
  Merger and consolidation, **Bus Org 10.151 et seq.**
  Shares and shareholders, **Bus Org 3.201 et seq.**
  Termination, post
Certified copies,
  Filing, **Bus Org 4.005**
  Involuntary termination, judgments and decrees, **Bus Org 11.414**
Changes, registered offices, registered agent, **Bus Org 5.202, 5.203**
Citizens and citizenship, receivers and receivership, **Bus Org 11.406**
Claims,
  Receivers and receivership, filing, **Bus Org 11.407**
  Termination, **Bus Org 11.351 et seq.**
Compensation and salaries, receivers and receivership, **Bus Org 11.408**
Conduct, damages, **Bus Org 7.001, 301.010**
Confidential or privileged information, interrogatories, **Bus Org 12.003**
Conflict of interest, elections, **Bus Org 6.152, 6.153**
Conflict of laws, **Bus Org 301.002**
  Names, **Bus Org 5.060**
Consent,
  Duplicates and copies, meetings, action without meeting, **Bus Org 6.205**
  Registered agents, **Bus Org 5.2011**
Consolidation. Merger and consolidation, generally, post
Construction of laws, Business Organizations Code, statutes, **Bus Org 1.006, 1.051 et seq.**
Contracts,
  Elections, **Bus Org 6.252**
  Winding up, **Bus Org 11.152**
Contributions, definitions, business organizations, **Bus Org 1.002**

PROFESSIONAL CORPORATIONS
—Cont'd
Conversion, **Bus Org 10.101 et seq.**
  Abandonment, **Bus Org 10.201, 10.202, 10.203**
  Acceptance, certificates and certification, **Bus Org 10.156**
  Certificates and certification, **Bus Org 10.154 et seq.**
  Dissenting shareholders, **Bus Org 10.351 et seq.**
  Effective date, **Bus Org 10.105, 10.106**
  Filing,
    Certificates and certification, **Bus Org 10.155**
    Fees, **Bus Org 4.151**
  Names, **Bus Org 10.103**
  Notice, **Bus Org 10.101**
  Plans and specifications, **Bus Org 10.101 et seq.**
  Reorganization, **Bus Org 10.301 et seq.**
Copies. Duplicates and copies, generally, post
Corrections, filing, **Bus Org 4.101 et seq.**
  Fees, **Bus Org 4.151**
Costs,
  Filing,
    Fines and penalties, **Bus Org 21.802**
    Fraud, **Bus Org 4.007**
  Insolvency, dismissal and nonsuit, **Bus Org 12.257**
  Liens and incumbrances, foreclosure, dismissal and nonsuit, **Bus Org 12.257**
Crimes and offenses,
  Books and papers, examinations and examiners, **Bus Org 12.156**
  Damages, **Bus Org 7.001**
  Filing, fraud, **Bus Org 4.008**
  Fraud, generally, post
  Termination, involuntary termination, **Bus Org 11.301 et seq.**
  Winding up, involuntary winding up, **Bus Org 11.301 et seq.**
Damages, **Bus Org 301.010**
  Application of law, **Bus Org 1.104**
  Filing, **Bus Org 21.802**
    Fraud, **Bus Org 4.007**
  Indemnity, generally, post
  Officers and employees, post
  Shares and shareholders, **Bus Org 303.002**
Deception, names, **Bus Org 5.052**
Deeds and conveyances, **Bus Org 10.251 et seq.**
Definitions, **Bus Org 1.002, 301.003**
  Indemnity, **Bus Org 8.001**
  Termination, **Bus Org 11.001**
  Winding up, **Bus Org 11.001**
Delay, filing, effective date, **Bus Org 4.052 et seq.**
Delivery,
  Filing, **Bus Org 4.001**
  Meetings, action without meeting, **Bus Org 6.203**
  Shares and shareholders, certificates and certification, **Bus Org 3.204**

PROFESSIONAL CORPORATIONS —Cont'd
Deposits, termination, claims, **Bus Org 11.352**
Directors,
  Agent for service of process, **Bus Org 5.255**
  Certificate of formation, **Bus Org 3.007**
    Amendments, **Bus Org 3.054**
    Restatement, **Bus Org 3.060**
  Damages, **Bus Org 7.001**
  Indemnity, **Bus Org 7.001**
Discharge,
  Receivers and receivership, **Bus Org 11.412**
  Termination, claims, **Bus Org 11.353**
  Winding up, indebtedness, **Bus Org 11.053**
Disclosure, interrogatories, **Bus Org 12.003**
Dismissal and nonsuit,
  Insolvency, **Bus Org 12.257**
  Liens and incumbrances, foreclosure, **Bus Org 12.257**
Dissenting shareholders. Shares and shareholders, post
Distribution and distributors,
  Record date, **Bus Org 6.101 et seq.**
  Winding up, assets, **Bus Org 11.053**
Dual office holding, officers and employees, **Bus Org 3.103**
Duplicates and copies,
  Agent for service of process, **Bus Org 5.252**
  Books and papers, **Bus Org 12.151 et seq.**
  Consent, meetings, action without meeting, **Bus Org 6.205**
  Filing, **Bus Org 4.003**
  Records and recordation, **Bus Org 3.152**
  Shares and shareholders, certificates and certification, **Bus Org 3.202**
Effective date,
  Conversion, **Bus Org 10.105, 10.106**
  Exchange of property, **Bus Org 10.054, 10.055**
  Filing, **Bus Org 4.051 et seq.**
  Merger and consolidation, **Bus Org 10.007**
  Termination, post
Elections, **Bus Org 6.151 et seq.**
  Application of law, **Bus Org 6.301, 6.302**
  Conflict of interest, **Bus Org 6.152, 6.153**
  Contracts, **Bus Org 6.252**
  Estates, **Bus Org 6.154**
  Indemnity, **Bus Org 8.103**
  Officers and employees, **Bus Org 3.103**
  Pledges, **Bus Org 6.156**
  Probate proceedings, **Bus Org 6.154**
  Receivers and receivership, **Bus Org 6.155**
  Trusts and trustees, **Bus Org 6.154, 6.251**

PROFESSIONAL CORPORATIONS —Cont'd
Electronic communications, consent, meetings, **Bus Org 6.205**
Electronic filing, **Bus Org 12.001**
Emergencies, governance, **Bus Org 3.251 et seq.**
Employees. Officers and employees, generally, post
Errors,
  Damages, **Bus Org 301.010**
  Termination, reinstatement, **Bus Org 11.201 et seq.**
Escheat, termination, claims, **Bus Org 11.355**
Estates, elections, **Bus Org 6.154**
Ethics, names, **Bus Org 5.060**
Evidence,
  Certificate of formation, acknowledgments, **Bus Org 3.001**
  Existence, certificates and certification, **Bus Org 4.005**
  Filing, **Bus Org 4.001**
  Shares and shareholders, certificates and certification, **Bus Org 3.201**
Examinations and examiners,
  Books and papers, **Bus Org 12.151 et seq.**
  Elections, contracts, **Bus Org 6.252**
  Records and recordation, **Bus Org 3.153**
Exchange of property, **Bus Org 10.051 et seq.**
  Abandonment, **Bus Org 10.201, 10.202, 10.203**
  Acceptance, certificates and certification, **Bus Org 10.156**
  Certificates and certification, **Bus Org 10.151 et seq.**
  Dissenting shareholders, **Bus Org 10.351 et seq.**
  Filing,
    Certificates and certification, **Bus Org 10.153**
    Fees, **Bus Org 4.151**
  Reorganization, **Bus Org 10.301**
  Shares and shareholders, post
  Voluntary, **Bus Org 10.902**
Exemptions,
  Interrogatories, **Bus Org 12.002**
  Physicians and surgeons, **Bus Org 301.003**
  Securities, sales, **Bus Org 301.011**
  Termination, involuntary termination, **Bus Org 11.251**
Expenses and expenditures, indemnity, **Bus Org 8.001 et seq.**
Facsimile, **Bus Org 1.007**
  Consent, meetings, action without meeting, **Bus Org 6.205**
  Filing, **Bus Org 4.003**
  Meetings, notice, **Bus Org 6.051**
  Shares and shareholders, certificates and certification, **Bus Org 3.203**
Fees,
  Filing, **Bus Org 4.157**
  Names, reservation, **Bus Org 5.101**

PROFESSIONAL CORPORATIONS —Cont'd
Fees—Cont'd
  Names, reservation—Cont'd
    Withdrawal, **Bus Org 5.1041**
Filing, **Bus Org 4.001 et seq., 12.001 et seq.**
  Abandonment, **Bus Org 4.057**
  Acknowledgments, **Bus Org 4.002**
    Effective date, delay, **Bus Org 4.059**
  Amendments, **Bus Org 4.106**
  Appeal and review, **Bus Org 12.004**
  Assumed or fictitious names, **Bus Org 5.051**
  Attorney fees,
    Fines and penalties, **Bus Org 21.802**
    Fraud, **Bus Org 4.007**
  Certificate of formation, **Bus Org 3.001 et seq.**
  Certificates and certification, ante
  Certified copies, **Bus Org 4.005**
  Conversion, certificates and certification, **Bus Org 10.155**
  Corrections, **Bus Org 4.101 et seq.**
    Fees, **Bus Org 4.151**
  Costs,
    Fines and penalties, **Bus Org 21.802**
    Fraud, **Bus Org 4.007**
  Damages, **Bus Org 21.802**
    Fraud, **Bus Org 4.007**
  Delay, effective date, **Bus Org 4.052 et seq.**
  Delivery, **Bus Org 4.001**
  Duplicates and copies, **Bus Org 4.003**
  Effective date, **Bus Org 4.051 et seq.**
  Electronic filing, **Bus Org 12.001**
  Evidence, **Bus Org 4.001**
  Facsimile, **Bus Org 4.003**
  Fees, **Bus Org 4.157**
  Fines and penalties, **Bus Org 21.802**
    Fraud, **Bus Org 4.008**
  Foreign corporations, registration, **Bus Org 301.005**
  Forms, **Bus Org 4.006**
  Fraud, **Bus Org 4.007, 4.008**
  Interrogatories, **Bus Org 12.002, 12.003**
  Jurisdiction, fines and penalties, **Bus Org 21.802**
  Limitations,
    Corrections, **Bus Org 4.102**
    Effective date, delay, **Bus Org 4.058**
  Names, registration, **Bus Org 5.152**
  Real estate investment trusts, **Bus Org 4.009**
  Receivers and receivership, claims, **Bus Org 11.407**
  Registered agent, resignation, **Bus Org 5.204**
  Service of process, **Bus Org 21.802**
  Signatures, **Bus Org 4.001**
    Corrections, certificates and certification, **Bus Org 4.101**
  Termination, involuntary termination, **Bus Org 11.315**
  Time, **Bus Org 4.004**
    Corrections, **Bus Org 4.105**
    Effective date, **Bus Org 4.051 et seq.**

PROFESSIONAL CORPORATIONS —Cont'd
Filing—Cont'd
Time—Cont'd
Fines and penalties, **Bus Org 21.802**
Winding up, involuntary winding up, **Bus Org 11.315**
Financial statements and reports, officers and employees, good faith, **Bus Org 3.102, 3.105**
Fines and penalties,
Books and papers, examinations and examiners, **Bus Org 12.156**
Filing, **Bus Org 21.802**
Fraud, **Bus Org 4.008**
Registered agents, consent, **Bus Org 5.207**
Foreclosure, liens and incumbrances, **Bus Org 12.252 et seq.**
Foreign corporations, **Bus Org 301.001 et seq.**
Adoption, Business Organizations Code, **Bus Org 402.003**
Names, **Bus Org 5.054**
Conflict of laws, **Bus Org 5.060**
Registration, **Bus Org 301.005**
Business Organizations Code,
Adoption, **Bus Org 402.004**
Mandatory application date, **Bus Org 402.012**
Statements, Business Organizations Code, adoption, **Bus Org 402.004**
Foreign countries,
Business Organizations Code, application of law, **Bus Org 1.053**
Certificate of formation, application of law, **Bus Org 1.102**
Foreign states,
Business Organizations Code, application of law, **Bus Org 1.053**
Certificate of formation, application of law, **Bus Org 1.102**
Meetings, location, **Bus Org 6.001**
Forfeitures, books and papers, examinations and examiners, **Bus Org 12.155**
Formation. Certificate of formation, generally, ante
Forms,
Filing, **Bus Org 4.006**
Shares and shareholders, certificates and certification, **Bus Org 3.202**
Fraud,
Filing, **Bus Org 4.007, 4.008**
Names, **Bus Org 5.052**
Receivers and receivership, **Bus Org 11.403**
Termination,
Involuntary termination, **Bus Org 11.301 et seq.**
Revocation or suspension, **Bus Org 11.153**
Winding up, involuntary winding up, **Bus Org 11.301 et seq.**
Garnishment, state, **Bus Org 12.259**
Good faith,
Damages, **Bus Org 7.001**

PROFESSIONAL CORPORATIONS —Cont'd
Good faith—Cont'd
Officers and employees, **Bus Org 3.102, 3.105**
Hold harmless. Indemnity, generally, post
Holding companies, merger and consolidation, **Bus Org 10.005**
Identity and identification, names, same or similar, **Bus Org 5.053**
Indebtedness,
Application of law, **Bus Org 10.901**
Winding up, discharge, **Bus Org 11.053**
Indemnity,
Insurance, **Bus Org 8.151**
Mandatory, **Bus Org 8.051**
Officers and employees, post
Orders of court, **Bus Org 8.052**
Permissive indemnification, **Bus Org 8.101 et seq.**
Reports, **Bus Org 8.152**
Injunctions, state, **Bus Org 12.259**
Insolvency, actions and proceedings, **Bus Org 12.253 et seq.**
Inspection and inspectors,
Books and papers, **Bus Org 12.151 et seq.**
Records and recordation, **Bus Org 3.152**
Insurance, indemnity, **Bus Org 8.151**
Internal affairs, **Bus Org 1.105**
Internet, meetings, **Bus Org 6.002**
Interrogatories, **Bus Org 12.002, 12.003**
Involuntary termination, **Bus Org 11.251 et seq.**
Certified copies, judgments and decrees, **Bus Org 11.414**
Joint practices, **Bus Org 301.012**
Judgments and decrees,
Receivers and receivership, termination, **Bus Org 11.412**
Reorganization, **Bus Org 10.305**
Termination, **Bus Org 11.301 et seq.**
Involuntary termination, certified copies, **Bus Org 11.414**
Winding up, **Bus Org 11.301 et seq.**
Jurisdiction,
Filing, fines and penalties, **Bus Org 21.802**
Insolvency, **Bus Org 12.253**
Liens and incumbrances, foreclosure, **Bus Org 12.253**
Receivers and receivership, **Bus Org 11.402 et seq.**
Reorganization, **Bus Org 10.302**
Termination, involuntary termination, **Bus Org 11.308**
Winding up, involuntary winding up, **Bus Org 11.308**
Leases, **Bus Org 10.251 et seq.**
Reorganization, **Bus Org 10.301**
Licenses and permits, **Bus Org 301.006**
Liens and incumbrances,
Foreclosure, **Bus Org 12.252 et seq.**
State, **Bus Org 12.201**

PROFESSIONAL CORPORATIONS —Cont'd
Limitation of actions, termination, claims, **Bus Org 11.359**
Limitations,
Filing,
Corrections, **Bus Org 4.102**
Effective date, delay, **Bus Org 4.058**
Indemnity, **Bus Org 8.003, 8.004**
Purposes, **Bus Org 2.003 et seq.**
Liquidation, receivers and receivership, **Bus Org 12.258**
Orders of court, **Bus Org 11.405**
Location, meetings, **Bus Org 6.001**
Lottery, names, **Bus Org 5.061**
Mail and mailing, meetings, notice, **Bus Org 6.051**
Managers and management,
Agent for service of process, **Bus Org 5.255**
Damages, **Bus Org 301.010**
Licenses and permits, **Bus Org 301.006**
Resignation, **Bus Org 301.008**
Meetings, **Bus Org 6.001 et seq.**
Action without meeting, **Bus Org 6.102**
Consent, **Bus Org 6.201 et seq.**
Application of law, **Bus Org 6.301, 6.302**
Consent, action without meeting, **Bus Org 6.102, 6.201 et seq.**
Delivery, action without meeting, **Bus Org 6.203**
Emergencies, **Bus Org 3.251 et seq.**
Facsimile, notice, **Bus Org 6.051**
Foreign states, location, **Bus Org 6.001**
Internet, **Bus Org 6.002**
Location, **Bus Org 6.001**
Mail and mailing, notice, **Bus Org 6.051**
Notice, **Bus Org 6.051 et seq.**
Action without meeting, **Bus Org 6.204**
Objections and exceptions, **Bus Org 6.003**
Notice, waiver, **Bus Org 6.053**
Record date, **Bus Org 6.101 et seq.**
Records and recordation, **Bus Org 6.002**
Shares and shareholders, post
Telecommunications, **Bus Org 6.002**
Video recordings, **Bus Org 6.002**
Waiver, notice, **Bus Org 6.052**
Objections and exceptions, **Bus Org 6.053**
Merger and consolidation, **Bus Org 10.001 et seq.**
Abandonment, **Bus Org 10.201, 10.202, 10.203**
Acceptance, certificates and certification, **Bus Org 10.156**
Allocations, property, **Bus Org 10.003**
Certificate of formation, **Bus Org 3.005, 3.006, 10.002**
Certificates and certification, **Bus Org 10.151 et seq.**
Dissenting shareholders, **Bus Org 10.351 et seq.**
Effect, **Bus Org 10.008**

PROFESSIONAL CORPORATIONS
—Cont'd
Merger and consolidation—Cont'd
Effective date, **Bus Org 10.007**
Filing,
Certificates and certification, **Bus Org 10.153**
Fees, **Bus Org 4.151**
Holding companies, **Bus Org 10.005**
Names, **Bus Org 10.002**
Plans and specifications, **Bus Org 10.001 et seq.**
Property, allocations, **Bus Org 10.003**
Reorganization, **Bus Org 10.301 et seq.**
Subsidiaries, **Bus Org 10.006**
Certificates and certification, **Bus Org 10.152**
Time, effective date, **Bus Org 10.007**
Misconduct, damages, **Bus Org 7.001**
Money, **Bus Org 1.009**
Monopolies and unfair trade, application of law, **Bus Org 10.901**
Mortgages, receivers and receivership, **Bus Org 11.403**
Names, **Bus Org 5.001 et seq.**
Assumed or fictitious names, **Bus Org 5.051 et seq.**
Certificate of formation, **Bus Org 3.005**
Amendments, **Bus Org 3.053, 3.056**
Conflict of laws, **Bus Org 5.060**
Conversion, **Bus Org 10.103**
Deception, **Bus Org 5.052**
Ethics, **Bus Org 5.060**
Exchange of property, plans and specifications, **Bus Org 10.052**
Fees, reservation, **Bus Org 5.101**
Withdrawal, **Bus Org 5.1041**
Filing,
Fees, **Bus Org 4.151**
Registration, **Bus Org 5.152**
Fraud, **Bus Org 5.052**
Identity and identification, same or similar, **Bus Org 5.053**
Lottery, **Bus Org 5.061**
Merger and consolidation, **Bus Org 10.002**
Notice, **Bus Org 5.001**
Registration, **Bus Org 5.151 et seq.**
Renewal,
Registration, **Bus Org 5.155**
Reservation, **Bus Org 5.105**
Reservation, **Bus Org 5.101 et seq.**
Same or similar, **Bus Org 5.053**
Registration, **Bus Org 5.153**
Reservation, **Bus Org 5.102**
Termination, reinstatement, **Bus Org 11.203**
Time,
Registration, **Bus Org 5.154**
Reservation, **Bus Org 5.104**
Trademarks and trade names, **Bus Org 5.001**
Transfers, reservation, **Bus Org 5.106**
Veterans organizations, **Bus Org 5.062**
Words and phrases, **Bus Org 5.054**
Negligence, damages, **Bus Org 301.010**

PROFESSIONAL CORPORATIONS
—Cont'd
Nonfiling, certificate of formation, **Bus Org 3.002**
Notice,
Agent for service of process, **Bus Org 5.252, 5.253**
Conversion, **Bus Org 10.101**
Indemnity, orders of court, **Bus Org 8.052**
Insolvency, **Bus Org 12.256**
Liens and incumbrances,
Foreclosure, **Bus Org 12.256**
State, **Bus Org 12.201**
Meetings, **Bus Org 6.051 et seq.**
Action without meeting, **Bus Org 6.204**
Names, **Bus Org 5.001**
Receivers and receivership, claims, **Bus Org 11.407**
Registered agent, resignation, **Bus Org 5.204**
Reorganization, **Bus Org 10.301**
Shares and shareholders, post
Termination, post
Winding up, **Bus Org 11.052**
Involuntary winding up, **Bus Org 11.302, 11.310**
Oaths and affirmations, interrogatories, answer, **Bus Org 12.002**
Objections and exceptions, meetings, **Bus Org 6.003**
Notice, waiver, **Bus Org 6.053**
Offenses. Crimes and offenses, generally, ante
Officers and employees, **Bus Org 3.101 et seq.**
Agent for service of process, **Bus Org 5.255**
Damages, **Bus Org 7.001, 301.010**
Application of law, **Bus Org 1.104**
Directors, generally, ante
Dual office holding, **Bus Org 3.103**
Elections, **Bus Org 3.103**
Good faith, **Bus Org 3.105**
Indemnity, **Bus Org 7.001, 8.001 et seq.**
Licenses and permits, **Bus Org 301.006**
Removal, **Bus Org 3.104**
Offices,
Changes, filing, fines and penalties, **Bus Org 21.802**
Registered offices, generally, post
Reorganization, **Bus Org 10.301**
Omissions, certificate of formation, restatement, **Bus Org 3.059**
Open records, interrogatories, **Bus Org 12.003**
Orders of court, receivers and receivership, **Bus Org 11.402**
Liquidation, **Bus Org 11.405**
Parties, receivers and receivership, **Bus Org 11.411**
Payment, termination,
Claims, **Bus Org 11.354**
Taxation, **Bus Org 11.101**
Penalties. Fines and penalties, generally, ante

PROFESSIONAL CORPORATIONS
—Cont'd
Permissive indemnification, **Bus Org 8.101 et seq.**
Personal property,
Disposition, **Bus Org 10.251 et seq.**
Reorganization, **Bus Org 10.301**
Shares and shareholders, **Bus Org 21.801**
Photography and pictures, consent, meetings, action without meeting, **Bus Org 6.205**
Plans and specifications,
Conversion, **Bus Org 10.101 et seq.**
Exchange of property, **Bus Org 10.051 et seq.**
Merger and consolidation, **Bus Org 10.001 et seq.**
Pledges, elections, **Bus Org 6.156**
Political subdivisions, service of process, **Bus Org 5.257**
Powers and duties, **Bus Org 2.109**
Receivers and receivership, **Bus Org 11.406**
President, agent for service of process, **Bus Org 5.255**
Prices, shares and shareholders, redemption, **Bus Org 303.004**
Priorities and preferences,
Business Organizations Code, application of law, **Bus Org 1.106**
Certificate of formation, shares and shareholders, **Bus Org 3.007**
Privileges and immunities,
Property, disposition, **Bus Org 10.254**
Registered agents, **Bus Org 5.208**
Probate proceedings, elections, **Bus Org 6.154**
Process. Service of process, generally, post
Property,
Disposition, **Bus Org 10.251 et seq.**
Reorganization, **Bus Org 10.301**
Liens and incumbrances,
Foreclosure, **Bus Org 12.252 et seq.**
State, **Bus Org 12.201**
Merger and consolidation, allocations, **Bus Org 10.003**
Personal property, generally, ante
Publication,
Termination, involuntary termination, **Bus Org 11.310**
Winding up, involuntary winding up, **Bus Org 11.310**
Purchases and purchasing,
Indemnity, insurance, **Bus Org 8.151**
Title to property, **Bus Org 301.008**
Purposes, **Bus Org 2.001 et seq.**
Certificate of formation, **Bus Org 3.005**
Quo warranto, insolvency, **Bus Org 12.253 et seq.**
Real estate,
Disposition, **Bus Org 10.251 et seq.**
Reorganization, **Bus Org 10.301**
Records and recordation, deeds and conveyances, **Bus Org 10.253**

PROFESSIONAL CORPORATIONS
—Cont'd
Receipts, termination, claims, **Bus Org 11.352**
Receivers and receivership, **Bus Org 11.401 et seq.**
Actions and proceedings, **Bus Org 11.406**
Ancillary receiverships, **Bus Org 11.409**
Appointments, **Bus Org 11.401 et seq.**
Bonds (officers and fiduciaries), **Bus Org 11.406**
Citizens and citizenship, **Bus Org 11.406**
Claims, filing, **Bus Org 11.407**
Compensation and salaries, **Bus Org 11.408**
Discharge, **Bus Org 11.412**
Elections, **Bus Org 6.155**
Filing, claims, **Bus Org 11.407**
Foreign entities, **Bus Org 11.409, 11.410**
Fraud, **Bus Org 11.403**
Judgments and decrees, termination, **Bus Org 11.412**
Jurisdiction, **Bus Org 11.402 et seq.**
Liens and incumbrances, state, **Bus Org 12.201**
Liquidation, **Bus Org 12.258**
Orders of court, **Bus Org 11.405**
Mortgages, **Bus Org 11.403**
Notice, claims, **Bus Org 11.407**
Orders of court, **Bus Org 11.402**
Liquidation, **Bus Org 11.405**
Parties, **Bus Org 11.411**
Powers and duties, **Bus Org 11.406**
Registration, **Bus Org 11.406**
Rehabilitation, **Bus Org 11.404**
State, **Bus Org 12.251**
Termination, **Bus Org 11.403**
Judgments and decrees, **Bus Org 11.412**
Record date, **Bus Org 6.101 et seq.**
Records and recordation, **Bus Org 3.151 et seq.**
Certified copies, filing, **Bus Org 4.005**
Confidential or privileged information, **Bus Org 12.154**
Disclosure, **Bus Org 12.154**
Examinations and examiners, **Bus Org 3.153, 12.151 et seq.**
Inspection and inspectors, **Bus Org 3.152**
Interrogatories, open records, **Bus Org 12.003**
Meetings, **Bus Org 6.002**
Real estate, deeds and conveyances, **Bus Org 10.253**
Record date, **Bus Org 6.101 et seq.**
Reorganization, **Bus Org 10.301**
Service of process, **Bus Org 5.254**
Signatures, **Bus Org 1.007**
Termination, removal, **Bus Org 11.104**
Time, record date, **Bus Org 6.101 et seq.**
Redemption, shares and shareholders, **Bus Org 303.004**

PROFESSIONAL CORPORATIONS
—Cont'd
Registered agent, **Bus Org 5.200 et seq.**
Changes, **Bus Org 5.202**
Filing, fines and penalties, **Bus Org 21.802**
Reorganization, **Bus Org 10.301**
Resignation, **Bus Org 5.204**
Registered offices, **Bus Org 5.200 et seq.**
Changes, **Bus Org 5.202**
Filing, fines and penalties, **Bus Org 21.802**
Registration,
Foreign corporations, ante
Names, **Bus Org 5.151 et seq.**
Receivers and receivership, **Bus Org 11.406**
Rehabilitation, receivers and receivership, **Bus Org 11.404**
Reinstatement. Termination, post
Rejection, registered agents, **Bus Org 5.205**
Remand,
Termination, involuntary termination, **Bus Org 11.307**
Winding up, involuntary winding up, **Bus Org 11.307**
Removal, officers and employees, **Bus Org 3.104**
Renewal, names,
Registration, **Bus Org 5.155**
Reservation, **Bus Org 5.105**
Reorganization, **Bus Org 10.301 et seq.**
Repeals, Business Organizations Code, statutes, **Bus Org 1.054**
Reports,
Indemnity, **Bus Org 8.152**
Officers and employees, good faith, **Bus Org 3.102, 3.105**
Reservation, names, **Bus Org 5.101 et seq.**
Resignation,
Managers and management, **Bus Org 301.008**
Registered agent, **Bus Org 5.204**
Resolutions, indemnity, **Bus Org 8.103**
Restatement, certificate of formation, **Bus Org 3.057 et seq.**
Review. Appeal and review, generally, ante
Revocation or suspension,
Termination, fraud, **Bus Org 11.153**
Winding up, **Bus Org 11.151**
Sales, **Bus Org 10.251 et seq.**
Reorganization, **Bus Org 10.301**
Securities, exemptions, **Bus Org 301.011**
Same or similar. Names, ante
Seals, shares and shareholders, certificates and certification, **Bus Org 3.202**
Secretary of state, agent for service of process, **Bus Org 5.251 et seq.**
Securities, sales, exemptions, **Bus Org 301.011**
Sequestration, state, **Bus Org 12.259**
Service of process, **Bus Org 5.251 et seq.**
Reorganization, **Bus Org 10.301**

PROFESSIONAL CORPORATIONS
—Cont'd
Service of process—Cont'd
Termination, involuntary termination, **Bus Org 11.309**
Winding up, involuntary winding up, **Bus Org 11.309**
Services, certificate of formation, **Bus Org 3.014**
Shares and shareholders,
Abandonment, exchange of property, **Bus Org 10.201, 10.202, 10.203**
Acceptance, exchange of property, certificates and certification, **Bus Org 10.156**
Appointments, dissenting shareholders, appraisal and appraisers, **Bus Org 10.361**
Appraisals and appraisers, dissenting shareholders, **Bus Org 10.354 et seq.**
Assignments, certificates and certification, **Bus Org 3.201**
Books and papers, dissenting shareholders, fair market value, **Bus Org 10.363**
Certificate of formation, numbers and numbering, **Bus Org 3.007**
Certificates and certification, **Bus Org 3.201 et seq.**
Exchange of property, **Bus Org 10.151 et seq.**
Compensation and salaries, dissenting shareholders, appraisals and appraisers, **Bus Org 10.365**
Computation, dissenting shareholders, fair market value, **Bus Org 10.362**
Contracts, elections, **Bus Org 6.252**
Costs, dissenting shareholders, appraisals and appraisers, **Bus Org 10.365**
Damages, **Bus Org 303.002**
Delivery,
Certificates and certification, **Bus Org 3.204**
Meetings, action without meeting, **Bus Org 6.203**
Demand, dissenting shareholders, fair market value, **Bus Org 10.357 et seq.**
Dissenting shareholders, **Bus Org 10.351 et seq.**
Appointments, appraisal and appraisers, **Bus Org 10.361**
Appraisals and appraisers, **Bus Org 10.354 et seq.**
Books and papers, fair market value, **Bus Org 10.363**
Compensation and salaries, appraisals and appraisers, **Bus Org 10.365**
Computation, fair market value, **Bus Org 10.362**
Costs, appraisals and appraisers, **Bus Org 10.365**
Definitions, **Bus Org 10.352**
Demand, fair market value, **Bus Org 10.357 et seq.**

PROFESSIONAL CORPORATIONS —Cont'd
Shares and shareholders—Cont'd
Dissenting shareholders—Cont'd
Exclusive remedy, **Bus Org 10.368**
Fair market value, demand, **Bus Org 10.357 et seq.**
Forms, **Bus Org 10.353**
Hearings, fair market value, **Bus Org 10.361**
Investigations and investigators, fair market value, **Bus Org 10.363**
Notice, **Bus Org 10.353, 10.355**
Objections and exceptions, appraisals and appraisers, **Bus Org 10.364**
Perfection, **Bus Org 10.356**
Petitions, fair market value, **Bus Org 10.361**
Records and recordation, fair market value, **Bus Org 10.363**
Demand, **Bus Org 10.359**
Reorganization, **Bus Org 10.304**
Termination, **Bus Org 10.367**
Title to property, **Bus Org 10.366**
Withdrawal, **Bus Org 10.357**
Distribution and distributors, record date, **Bus Org 6.101 et seq.**
Duplicates and copies, certificates and certification, **Bus Org 3.202**
Elections,
Contracts, **Bus Org 6.252**
Trusts and trustees, **Bus Org 6.251**
Evidence, certificates and certification, **Bus Org 3.201**
Examinations and examiners, elections, contracts, **Bus Org 6.252**
Exchange of property, **Bus Org 10.051 et seq.**
Abandonment, **Bus Org 10.201, 10.202, 10.203**
Acceptance, certificates and certification, **Bus Org 10.156**
Certificates and certification, **Bus Org 10.151 et seq.**
Filing, certificates and certification, **Bus Org 10.153**
Exclusive remedy, dissenting shareholders, **Bus Org 10.368**
Facsimile, certificates and certification, **Bus Org 3.203**
Fair market value, dissenting shareholders, demand, **Bus Org 10.357 et seq.**
Filing, exchange of property, certificates and certification, **Bus Org 10.153**
Forms,
Certificates and certification, **Bus Org 3.202**
Dissenting shareholders, **Bus Org 10.353**
Hearings, dissenting shareholders, fair market value, **Bus Org 10.361**
Investigations and investigators, dissenting shareholders, fair market value, **Bus Org 10.363**

PROFESSIONAL CORPORATIONS —Cont'd
Shares and shareholders—Cont'd
Meetings,
Action without meeting, **Bus Org 6.102**
Consent, **Bus Org 6.201 et seq.**
Consent, action without meeting, **Bus Org 6.102, 6.201 et seq.**
Delivery, action without meeting, **Bus Org 6.203**
Notice, action without meeting, **Bus Org 6.204**
Notice,
Dissenting shareholders, **Bus Org 10.353, 10.355**
Meetings, action without meeting, **Bus Org 6.204**
Transfers, **Bus Org 303.003**
Uncertificated shares, **Bus Org 3.205**
Objections and exceptions, dissenting shareholders, appraisals and appraisers, **Bus Org 10.364**
Perfection, dissenting shareholders, **Bus Org 10.356**
Personal property, **Bus Org 21.801**
Petitions, dissenting shareholders, fair market value, **Bus Org 10.361**
Prices, redemption, **Bus Org 303.004**
Record date, **Bus Org 6.101 et seq.**
Records and recordation, dissenting shareholders, fair market value, **Bus Org 10.363**
Demand, **Bus Org 10.359**
Redemption, **Bus Org 303.004**
Reorganization, dissenting shareholders, **Bus Org 10.304**
Seals, certificates and certification, **Bus Org 3.202**
Signatures, certificates and certification, **Bus Org 3.203**
Termination, dissenting shareholders, **Bus Org 10.367**
Time, record date, **Bus Org 6.101 et seq.**
Title to property, dissenting shareholders, **Bus Org 10.366**
Transfers,
Certificates and certification, **Bus Org 3.201**
Notice, **Bus Org 303.003**
Trusts and trustees, elections, **Bus Org 6.251**
Uncertificated shares, **Bus Org 3.201**
Notice, **Bus Org 3.205**
Withdrawal, dissenting shareholders, **Bus Org 10.357**
Signatures, **Bus Org 1.007**
Certificate of formation, ante
Filing, **Bus Org 4.001**
Corrections, certificates and certification, **Bus Org 4.101**
Reorganization, **Bus Org 10.302**
Shares and shareholders, certificates and certification, **Bus Org 3.203**
Specifications. Plans and specifications, generally, ante

PROFESSIONAL CORPORATIONS —Cont'd
State,
Liens and incumbrances, **Bus Org 12.201**
Receivers and receivership, **Bus Org 12.251**
Statements,
Certificate of formation, ante
Officers and employees, good faith, **Bus Org 3.102, 3.105**
Termination, claims, **Bus Org 11.352**
Statutes, Business Organizations Code, construction of laws, **Bus Org 1.006, 1.051 et seq.**
Subsidiaries, merger and consolidation, **Bus Org 10.006**
Certificates and certification, **Bus Org 10.152**
Supersedeas or stay,
Termination, involuntary termination, **Bus Org 11.306**
Winding up, involuntary winding up, **Bus Org 11.306**
Supervision, winding up, **Bus Org 11.054**
Taxation,
Service of process, **Bus Org 5.257**
Termination,
Forfeitures, reinstatement, **Bus Org 11.254**
Payment, **Bus Org 11.101**
Telecommunications, meetings, **Bus Org 6.002**
Termination, **Bus Org 11.001 et seq., 303.005, 303.006**
Abatement of actions and proceedings, involuntary termination, **Bus Org 11.304**
Actions and proceedings, involuntary termination, **Bus Org 11.303**
Appeal and review, involuntary termination, **Bus Org 11.307**
Certificates and certification, **Bus Org 11.101 et seq., 303.006**
Involuntary termination, **Bus Org 11.252**
Reinstatement, **Bus Org 11.202**
Certified copies, involuntary termination, judgments and decrees, **Bus Org 11.414**
Claims, **Bus Org 11.351 et seq.**
Crimes and offenses, involuntary termination, **Bus Org 11.301 et seq.**
Deposits, claims, **Bus Org 11.352**
Discharge, claims, **Bus Org 11.353**
Effective date, **Bus Org 11.102, 11.103**
Claims, **Bus Org 11.356 et seq.**
Reinstatement, **Bus Org 11.204 et seq.**
Errors, reinstatement, **Bus Org 11.201 et seq.**
Escheat, claims, **Bus Org 11.355**
Exemptions, involuntary termination, **Bus Org 11.251**
Filing,
Fines and penalties, **Bus Org 21.802**

PROFESSIONAL CORPORATIONS
—Cont'd
Termination—Cont'd
Filing—Cont'd
Involuntary termination, **Bus Org 11.315**
Fraud,
Involuntary termination, **Bus Org 11.301 et seq.**
Revocation or suspension, **Bus Org 11.153**
Involuntary termination, **Bus Org 11.251 et seq., 11.301 et seq.**
Certified copies, judgments and decrees, **Bus Org 11.414**
Judgments and decrees, **Bus Org 11.301 et seq.**
Involuntary termination, certified copies, **Bus Org 11.414**
Jurisdiction, involuntary termination, **Bus Org 11.308**
Limitation of actions, claims, **Bus Org 11.359**
Names, reinstatement, **Bus Org 11.203**
Notice,
Claims, **Bus Org 11.358**
Escheat, claims, **Bus Org 11.355**
Involuntary termination, **Bus Org 11.251, 11.302, 11.310**
Payment,
Claims, **Bus Org 11.354**
Taxation, **Bus Org 11.101**
Publication, involuntary termination, **Bus Org 11.310**
Receipts, claims, **Bus Org 11.352**
Receivers and receivership, **Bus Org 11.403**
Judgments and decrees, **Bus Org 11.412**
Records and recordation, removal, **Bus Org 11.104**
Reinstatement, **Bus Org 11.201 et seq.**
Involuntary termination, **Bus Org 11.253**
Taxation, forfeitures, **Bus Org 11.254**
Remand, involuntary termination, **Bus Org 11.307**
Revocation or suspension, fraud, **Bus Org 11.153**
Service of process, involuntary termination, **Bus Org 11.309**
Statements, claims, **Bus Org 11.352**
Supersedeas or stay, involuntary termination, **Bus Org 11.306**
Taxation,
Forfeitures, reinstatement, **Bus Org 11.254**
Payment, **Bus Org 11.101**
Time,
Involuntary termination, **Bus Org 11.305, 11.313**
Reinstatement, **Bus Org 11.202**
Venue, involuntary termination, **Bus Org 11.308**
Time,
Certificate of formation, ante

PROFESSIONAL CORPORATIONS
—Cont'd
Time—Cont'd
Exchange of property, **Bus Org 10.054, 10.055**
Filing, ante
Interrogatories, answer, **Bus Org 12.002**
Merger and consolidation, effective date, **Bus Org 10.007**
Record date, **Bus Org 6.101 et seq.**
Service of process, **Bus Org 5.254**
Termination, ante
Winding up, post
Title to property, **Bus Org 301.007 et seq.**
Purchases and purchasing, **Bus Org 301.008**
Trademarks and trade names, names, **Bus Org 5.001**
Transfers,
Names, reservation, **Bus Org 5.106**
Property, **Bus Org 10.251 et seq.**
Shares and shareholders,
Certificates and certification, **Bus Org 3.201**
Notice, **Bus Org 303.003**
Title to property, **Bus Org 301.009**
Trusts and trustees,
Elections, **Bus Org 6.154, 6.251**
Reorganization, **Bus Org 10.301 et seq.**
Uncertificated shares, **Bus Org 3.201**
Notice, **Bus Org 3.205**
Venue,
Termination, involuntary termination, **Bus Org 11.308**
Winding up, involuntary winding up, **Bus Org 11.308**
Veterans organizations, names, **Bus Org 5.062**
Vice president, agent for service of process, **Bus Org 5.255**
Video recordings, meetings, **Bus Org 6.002**
Waiver, meetings, notice, **Bus Org 6.052**
Objections and exceptions, **Bus Org 6.053**
Winding up, **Bus Org 11.001 et seq., 11.051 et seq., 303.005, 303.006**
Abatement of actions and proceedings, involuntary winding up, **Bus Org 11.304**
Actions and proceedings, **Bus Org 11.052, 11.055**
Involuntary winding up, **Bus Org 11.303**
Appeal and review, involuntary winding up, **Bus Org 11.307**
Assets, distribution and distributors, **Bus Org 11.053**
Cancellation, **Bus Org 11.152**
Contracts, **Bus Org 11.152**
Crimes and offenses, involuntary winding up, **Bus Org 11.301 et seq.**
Discharge, indebtedness, **Bus Org 11.053**
Distribution and distributors, assets, **Bus Org 11.053**

PROFESSIONAL CORPORATIONS
—Cont'd
Winding up—Cont'd
Filing, involuntary winding up, **Bus Org 11.315**
Fraud, involuntary winding up, **Bus Org 11.301 et seq.**
Indebtedness, discharge, **Bus Org 11.053**
Involuntary winding up, **Bus Org 11.301 et seq.**
Judgments and decrees, **Bus Org 11.301 et seq.**
Jurisdiction, involuntary winding up, **Bus Org 11.308**
Notice, **Bus Org 11.052**
Involuntary winding up, **Bus Org 11.302, 11.310**
Publication, involuntary winding up, **Bus Org 11.310**
Remand, involuntary winding up, **Bus Org 11.307**
Revocation or suspension, **Bus Org 11.151**
Service of process, involuntary winding up, **Bus Org 11.309**
Supersedeas or stay, involuntary winding up, **Bus Org 11.306**
Supervision, **Bus Org 11.054**
Time, **Bus Org 11.056**
Cancellation, **Bus Org 11.152**
Involuntary winding up, **Bus Org 11.305, 11.313**
Venue, involuntary winding up, **Bus Org 11.308**
Withdrawal,
Filing, fines and penalties, **Bus Org 21.802**
Names, reservation, fees, **Bus Org 5.1041**
Witnesses, indemnity, expenses and expenditures, **Bus Org 8.106**
Writings, signatures, **Bus Org 1.007**

PROFESSIONAL LIMITED LIABILITY COMPANIES
Limited Liability Companies, this index

PROFESSIONS AND OCCUPATIONS
Assumed or fictitious names, **Bus & C 71.001 et seq.**
Chiropodists. Podiatrists, generally, this index
Dentists and Dentistry, generally, this index
Osteopaths, generally, this index
Physician Assistants, generally, this index
Physicians and Surgeons, generally, this index
Podiatrists, generally, this index

PROFITS
Electric cooperative corporations, **Util 161.059**
Electricity, accounts, **Util 32.103**
Limited Liability Companies, this index
Partnerships, this index

PROFITS—Cont'd
Telephone cooperative corporations, **Util 162.059**

PROMOTIONS
Business Development Corporations, generally, this index
Telecommunications, this index

PROOF
Evidence, generally, this index

PROPERTY
Business development corporations, **Bus Org 23.054**
  Sales, **Bus Org 23.054**
Condominiums, generally, this index
Cooperative Associations, this index
Corporations, this index
Electric cooperative corporations, **Util 161.121**
  Eminent domain, **Util 161.125**
Electricity, this index
Eminent Domain, generally, this index
Entry On Property, generally, this index
Foreign Corporations, this index
Garnishment, generally, this index
Gas utilities, **Util 181.007**
Liens and Incumbrances, generally, this index
Limited Liability Companies, this index
Limited partnerships. Partnerships, this index
Nonprofit Corporations, this index
Partnerships, this index
Professional Associations and Societies, this index
Professional Corporations, this index
Telephone Cooperative Corporations, this index

PROVIDERS
Definitions, gas utilities, termination of service, **Util 104.258**

PROXIES
Corporations, elections, **Bus Org 21.367 et seq.**
Electric cooperative corporations, members, **Util 161.070**

PSYCHOLOGISTS
Telemedicine, generally, this index

PUBLIC BUILDINGS AND WORKS
Gas utilities, relocation, surcharge, **Util 104.112**

PUBLIC FUNDS
Funds, generally, this index

PUBLIC HIGHWAYS
Highways and Roads, generally, this index

PUBLIC HOSPITALS
Hospitals, generally, this index

PUBLIC LANDS
Acquisition. Eminent Domain, generally, this index
Condemnation. Eminent Domain, generally, this index
Eminent Domain, generally, this index

PUBLIC LIBRARIES
Libraries, generally, this index

PUBLIC OFFICERS AND EMPLOYEES
Adverse or pecuniary interest. Conflict of Interest, generally, this index
Compensation and Salaries, generally, this index
Conflict of Interest, generally, this index
Elections, generally, this index
Oaths and Affirmations, generally, this index

PUBLIC POLICY
Cogeneration, **Util 35.061**
Electricity, this index
Gas utilities, **Util 101.002**
  Pipes and pipelines, **Util 121.051, 121.052**
Public Utilities, this index
Telecommunications, this index
Telephone cooperative corporations, **Util 162.002**

PUBLIC PROPERTY
Property, generally, this index

PUBLIC RETAIL CUSTOMER
Definitions, electricity, state, sales, royalties, in kind, **Util 35.101**

PUBLIC RIGHT OF WAY
Right of Way, generally, this index

PUBLIC ROADS
Highways and Roads, generally, this index

PUBLIC SCHOOLS
Schools and School Districts, generally, this index

PUBLIC SECURITIES
Securities, generally, this index

PUBLIC SECURITY PROCEDURES ACT
Bonds, generally, this index

PUBLIC USE
Eminent Domain, generally, this index

PUBLIC UTILITIES
  Generally, **Util 1.001 et seq.**
Accounts and accounting, **Util 14.151**
  Audits, **Util 14.203**
  Commission, **Util 16.042**
Actions and proceedings,
  Commission, United States agencies, labor and employment, **Util 39.4525**
  Consumer advocacy, intervention, **Util 13.003**

PUBLIC UTILITIES—Cont'd
Actions and proceedings—Cont'd
  Enforcement, **Util 15.021 et seq.**
  Fines and penalties, officers and employees, **Util 15.029**
  Historically underutilized businesses, liability, **Util 12.255**
  Interruption of service, restraining orders, **Util 186.005**
  Judicial review, commission decisions, **Util 15.001 et seq.**
  Venue, enforcement, **Util 15.031**
Administrative hearings office, contested cases, **Util 14.053**
Administrative law and procedure, **Util 11.007**
  Contested cases, generally, post
  Orders, generally, post
  Rules and regulations, **Util 14.052**
Administrative penalties, **Util 15.023 et seq.**
Adverse or pecuniary interest. Conflict of interest, generally, post
Advocates, consumers, **Util 13.001, 13.003**
Affected entities, jurisdiction, **Util 11.003, 11.005**
Affiliates, **Util 11.003, 11.006**
  Communications, **Util 14.153**
  Definitions, **Util 11.0042**
  Jurisdiction, **Util 14.154**
  Records and recordation, jurisdiction, **Util 14.154**
  Reports, **Util 14.003**
    Adverse or pecuniary interest, **Util 14.004**
Aged persons,
  Payment, delay, **Util 182.001 et seq.**
  Termination of service, **Util 14.005**
Alternative dispute resolution,
  Commission, **Util 14.0025**
  Office of public utility counsel, **Util 13.003, 13.004**
Apartment houses, central heating and cooling, **Util 184.051, 184.052**
Appeal and review, **Util 15.001 et seq.**
  Administrative hearings office, findings, **Util 14.053**
  Administrative penalties, **Util 15.025, 15.026**
  Commission,
    Defendants, **Util 15.002**
    Electricity, municipal orders, **Util 33.051**
  Compromise and settlement, contested cases, **Util 14.054**
  Costs and attorney fees, **Util 15.003**
  Fines and penalties, **Util 15.025, 15.026**
  Rates and charges, costs and attorney fees, **Util 15.003**
  Supersedeas or stay, **Util 15.004**
Application of law,
  Administrative law and procedure, **Util 11.007**
  Fines and penalties, **Util 15.032**
  Revised code, **Util 1.003**
  State funds, reform, commission, **Util 16.041**

PUBLIC UTILITIES—Cont'd
Assessments,
  Funds, **Util 16.001 et seq.**
  Internet, hearings, meetings, **Util 12.204**
  Underground facilities, notification corporation, excavations, **Util 251.062**
Attorney fees, appeal and review, rates, **Util 15.003**
Attorneys, **Util 13.022, 14.056**
  Public utility counselors, **Util 13.022**
  Right to be heard, **Util 14.056**
Audits and auditors, **Util 14.201 et seq.**
  Accounts, **Util 14.203**
  Commission, **Util 16.043**
  Management audits, **Util 14.202**
Boards and commissions. Commission, generally, post
Bonds (officers and fiduciaries),
  Interruption of service, restraining orders, **Util 186.005**
  Judicial review, administrative penalties, **Util 15.025, 15.026**
Brands, marks and labels, underground facilities,
  Crimes and offenses, excavations, **Util 251.203**
  Excavations, **Util 251.157, 251.158**
Budget, commission, **Util 16.044**
Cable Television, generally, this index
Call router system, underground facilities, contracts, notification corporation, excavations, **Util 251.061**
Charges. Rates and charges, generally, post
Cities. Municipalities, generally, post
Codification of law, **Util 1.001**
Cogeneration, generally, this index
Collections,
  Administrative penalties, **Util 15.027**
  Assessments, **Util 16.004**
  Confidential or privileged information, customers, government operated utilities, **Util 182.052**
Collective bargaining, interference, commission, **Util 14.006**
Commission, **Util 12.001 et seq.**
  Absence and absentees, commissioners, removal, **Util 12.054**
  Accounts and accounting, **Util 16.042**
  Actions and proceedings,
    Fines and penalties, **Util 15.029**
    United States agencies, labor and employment, **Util 39.4525**
  Adverse or pecuniary interest, **Util 12.053, 12.054, 12.151 et seq.**
  Affiliates, jurisdiction, **Util 14.154**
  Alternative dispute resolution, **Util 14.0025**
  Appeal and review,
    Defendants, **Util 15.002**
    Electricity, municipal orders, **Util 33.051**
  Application of law, state funds, reform, **Util 16.041**
  Appointments, commissioners, **Util 12.051**

PUBLIC UTILITIES—Cont'd
Commission—Cont'd
  Assessments, **Util 16.001 et seq.**
  Assistance, municipalities, **Util 14.007**
  Attorney general, representation, **Util 12.004**
  Audits and auditors, **Util 16.043**
  Budget, **Util 16.044**
  Career ladder program, employees, **Util 12.105**
  Certificates of operating authority, telecommunications, jurisdiction, **Util 52.152**
  Collective bargaining, utility employees, interference, **Util 14.006**
  Communications, **Util 14.153**
  Compensation and salaries, commissioners, **Util 12.057**
  Complaints, consumers, **Util 12.201**
  Conduct, officers and employees, **Util 12.156**
  Defendants, judicial review, **Util 15.002**
  Dual office holding, commissioners, **Util 12.055**
  Electricity, municipalities, **Util 33.002 et seq.**
  Equal employment opportunity, employees, **Util 12.106**
  Executive directors, **Util 12.101, 12.103**
  Exemptions, electricity, municipal jurisdiction, **Util 33.004, 33.005**
  Federal aid, **Util 16.021**
  Financing, assessments, **Util 16.001 et seq.**
  Fines and penalties, **Util 15.023 et seq.**
    Commissioners and employees, **Util 15.029**
  Funds, **Util 16.041 et seq.**
  Gifts, commissioners and employees, **Util 12.154**
  Hearings, **Util 14.051, 14.052**
    Internet, **Util 12.204**
  Information, **Util 12.201**
  Jurisdiction, **Util 14.001**
    Competition, safeguards, telecommunications, **Util 60.002**
    Electricity, **Util 32.001 et seq.**
    Joint powers agencies, electric cooperative corporations, **Util 163.123**
    Nonresidents, municipally owned electric utilities, review of rates, **Util 33.123**
    Pay telephones, **Util 55.172**
  Labor and employment, United States agencies, actions and proceedings, **Util 39.4525**
  Lobbyists, officers and employees, **Util 12.151**
  Management audits, **Util 14.202**
  Meetings, **Util 12.058**
    Internet, **Util 12.204**
  Municipally owned utilities, electricity, review of rates, **Util 33.121 et seq.**
  Negotiated rulemaking, **Util 14.0025**
  Nondominant carriers, telecommunications, jurisdiction, **Util 52.102**

PUBLIC UTILITIES—Cont'd
Commission—Cont'd
  Notice,
    Adverse or pecuniary interest, commissioners and employees, **Util 12.152**
    Grounds for removal, **Util 12.054**
      Commissioners, **Util 12.054**
  Office, **Util 12.002**
  Officers and employees, **Util 12.101 et seq.**
    Adverse or pecuniary interest, **Util 12.151 et seq.**
    Fines and penalties, **Util 15.029**
    Qualifications and standards, **Util 12.156**
  Orders, **Util 14.051, 14.057**
  Pay telephones, jurisdiction, **Util 55.172**
  Powers and duties, **Util 12.102 et seq., 14.001 et seq.**
    Telecommunications, **Util 52.001 et seq.**
    Universal service fund, telecommunications, **Util 56.023**
  Presiding officers, **Util 12.052**
  Production of books and papers, **Util 14.051**
  Public participation, **Util 12.202**
  Qualifications,
    Commissioners, **Util 12.053**
    Officers and employees, **Util 12.156**
  Removal, commissioners, **Util 12.054**
  Reports, **Util 12.203**
    Electricity, competition, **Util 31.003**
    Utilities, **Util 14.003**
  Rules and regulations, **Util 14.002**
    Negotiated rulemaking, **Util 14.0025**
  Seals, **Util 12.003**
  Securities, adverse or pecuniary interest, commissioners and employees, **Util 12.152, 12.154**
  Solicitations, commissioners and employees, **Util 12.154**
  Subpoenas, **Util 14.051**
  Subsequent employment, commissioners and employees, **Util 12.155**
  Sunset Act, **Util 12.005**
  Supervision, **Util 14.001**
  Telecommunications,
    Jurisdiction, **Util 52.001 et seq.**
    Rates and charges, authority to regulate, **Util 53.001**
  Telephone cooperative corporations, deregulation, **Util 53.358**
  Terms of office, commissioners, **Util 12.051**
  Time, subsequent employment, commissioners and employees, **Util 12.155**
  Trade associations, adverse or pecuniary interest, commissioners and employees, **Util 12.153**
  Training, **Util 12.059**
    Alternative dispute resolution, **Util 14.0025**
  Traveling expenses, training, **Util 12.059**

PUBLIC UTILITIES—Cont'd
Commission—Cont'd
United States agencies, actions and proceedings, labor and employment, **Util 39.4525**
Universal service fund, telecommunications, **Util 56.023**
Vacancies in office, **Util 12.056**
Witnesses, **Util 14.051**
Communications, regulatory authorities, **Util 14.153**
Compensation and salaries,
Collective bargaining, interference, commission, **Util 14.006**
Office of public utility counsel, employees, **Util 13.041**
Complaints, **Util 15.051 et seq.**
Affected persons, **Util 11.003, 15.051**
Consumers, **Util 12.201**
Office of public utility counsel, **Util 13.005**
Records, **Util 15.051**
Recreational vehicle parks, electricity, **Util 15.052**
Compromise and settlement, contested cases, **Util 14.054**
Confidential or privileged information,
Electricity, sales, affiliates, **Util 14.154**
Government operated utilities, customers, **Util 182.051 et seq.**
Conflict of interest,
Commission, **Util 12.053, 12.054, 12.151 et seq.**
Public utility counselors, **Util 13.022 et seq.**
Conflict of laws, federal law, **Util 11.009**
Consolidation. Merger and consolidation, generally, post
Construction of laws, **Util 1.002**
Regulatory Act, **Util 11.008, 11.009**
Consumers, advocacy, **Util 13.001, 13.003**
Contempt, **Util 15.022**
Contested cases, **Util 14.052**
Compromise and settlement, **Util 14.054**
Conducting hearings, **Util 14.053**
Continuity of service, **Util 186.001 et seq.**
Contracts,
Reports, **Util 14.003**
Underground facilities, toll free numbers, notification corporation, excavations, **Util 251.061**
Control, affiliates, **Util 11.006**
Costs, appeal and review, rates, **Util 15.003**
Counsel. Office of public utility counsel, generally, post
Crimes and offenses, **Util 15.030**
Customers deposits, **Util 183.006**
Office of public utility counsel, subsequent employment, **Util 13.043**
Underground facilities, brands, marks and labels, excavations, **Util 251.203**

PUBLIC UTILITIES—Cont'd
Damages, underground facilities, **Util 251.001 et seq.**
Notification corporation, excavations, **Util 251.054**
Definitions, **Util 11.003, 11.004**
Affiliates, **Util 11.0042**
Continuity of service, **Util 186.001**
Customers deposits, **Util 183.001**
Railroad, right of way, **Util 186.051**
Records, **Util 14.151**
Telecommunications, **Util 51.002**
Deposits, customers, **Util 183.001 et seq.**
Directors,
Commission, adverse or pecuniary interest, commissioners and employees, **Util 12.152, 12.154**
Underground facilities, notification corporation, excavations, **Util 251.055 et seq.**
Discrimination, historically underutilized businesses, **Util 12.254**
Disgorgement, **Util 15.023 et seq.**
Disruption, services, prevention, **Util 186.001 et seq.**
Easements,
Railroads, right of way, eminent domain, **Util 186.051 et seq.**
Streets and alleys, municipal franchises, fees, **Util 14.008**
Underground facilities, excavations, **Util 251.006**
Electric light and power companies. Electricity, generally, this index
Electronic access, information, fees, **Util 14.058**
Emergencies, underground facilities, notice, excavations, **Util 251.155**
Eminent domain, railroads, right of way, **Util 186.051 et seq.**
Employees. Officers and employees, generally, post
Enforcement, interruption of service, **Util 186.003**
Entry on property, inspection, **Util 14.206**
Evidence, aged persons, delay in payment, proof of age, **Util 182.004**
Examinations and examiners,
Audits and auditors, generally, ante
Officers and employees, oaths and affirmations, **Util 14.205**
Excavations, underground facilities, **Util 251.001 et seq.**
Executive orders, continuity of service, **Util 186.003**
Exemptions,
Aged persons, delay in payment, **Util 182.005**
Commission, electricity, municipal jurisdiction, **Util 33.004, 33.005**
Confidential or privileged information, government operated utilities, customers, **Util 182.054**
Major transactions, investigations, **Util 14.101**
Underground facilities, notice, excavations, **Util 251.156**

PUBLIC UTILITIES—Cont'd
Expenses and expenditures, underground facilities, notification corporation, excavations, **Util 251.054**
Federal aid, commission, **Util 16.021**
Federal law, conflict of laws, **Util 11.009**
Fees,
Confidential or privileged information, government operated utilities, **Util 182.053**
Electronic access, information, **Util 14.058**
Railroads, right of way, use, **Util 186.058**
Rates and charges, generally, post
Underground facilities, post
Fines and penalties, **Util 15.023 et seq.**
Amounts, **Util 15.023**
Appeal and review, **Util 15.025, 15.026**
Application of law, **Util 15.032**
Assessments, **Util 15.024**
Delinquency, **Util 16.003**
Collection, **Util 15.027**
Commission, commissioners and employees, **Util 15.029**
Cumulative penalties, **Util 15.032**
Customers deposits, **Util 183.006**
Disposition of funds, **Util 15.027, 15.033**
Hearings, **Util 15.024**
Interest, appeals or writs of error, **Util 15.026**
Notice, **Util 15.024**
Orders, **Util 15.024**
Payment, **Util 15.025**
Reductions, judicial review, **Util 15.026**
Time, payment, **Util 15.025**
Underground facilities, excavations, **Util 251.201 et seq.**
Venue, actions, **Util 15.031**
Foreign states, production of books and papers, **Util 14.207**
Forms,
Confidential or privileged information, government operated utilities, **Util 182.052**
Orders, commission, **Util 14.057**
Records, **Util 14.151**
Reports, **Util 14.003**
Fraud, underground facilities, emergencies, excavations, **Util 251.155**
Fines and penalties, **Util 251.201**
Gas Meters, generally, this index
Gas Utilities, generally, this index
Gifts, commission, **Util 12.154**
Grants, commission, federal aid, **Util 16.021**
Grievances. Complaints, generally, ante
Gross receipts, assessments, funds, **Util 16.001**
Handicapped persons, termination of service, **Util 14.005**
Harassment, interruption of service, **Util 186.004**
Hearings, **Util 14.051 et seq.**
Administrative hearings office, powers and duties, **Util 14.053**

PUBLIC UTILITIES—Cont'd
Hearings—Cont'd
Affiliates, determination, **Util 11.006**
Application of law, administrative law and procedure, **Util 11.007**
Attorneys, **Util 14.056**
Commission, **Util 14.051, 14.052**
Compromise and settlement, contested cases, **Util 14.054**
Consumer advocacy, intervention, **Util 13.003**
Fines and penalties, **Util 15.024**
Historically underutilized businesses, assistance, **Util 12.252**
Internet, commission, **Util 12.204**
Major transactions, investigations, **Util 14.101**
Office of public utility counsel, **Util 13.064**
Public participation,
Commission, **Util 12.202**
Office of public utility counsel, **Util 13.062**
Records and recordations, **Util 14.055**
Representation,
Office of public utility counsel, subsequent employment, **Util 13.043**
Subsequent employment, **Util 12.155**
Right to be heard, **Util 14.056**
Rules and regulations, **Util 14.052**
Transcripts, **Util 14.055, 14.057**
Highways and Roads, this index
Historically underutilized businesses, assistance, **Util 12.251 et seq.**
Information, electronic access, fees, **Util 14.058**
Injunctions, **Util 15.021**
Interruption of service, **Util 186.005**
Venue, **Util 15.031**
Inspection and inspectors, **Util 14.204**
Entry on property, **Util 14.206**
Time, **Util 14.204, 14.206**
Insurance, underground facilities, notification center, excavations, **Util 251.104**
Interest,
Customers deposits, **Util 183.002 et seq.**
Fines and penalties, appeals or writs of error, **Util 15.026**
Interference, municipalities, protection, **Util 181.901, 181.902**
Internet, commission, hearings, meetings, **Util 12.204**
Interruption of service, prevention, **Util 186.001 et seq.**
Interurban Railroads, generally, this index
Intimidation, interruption of service, **Util 186.004**
Investigations and investigators, **Util 14.201**
Major transactions, **Util 14.101**
Investments,
Commission, adverse or pecuniary interest, **Util 12.152, 12.154**
Public utility counselors, adverse or pecuniary interest, **Util 13.022**

PUBLIC UTILITIES—Cont'd
Jurisdiction,
Affiliates, **Util 14.154**
Commission, ante
Providers, **Util 11.005**
Labor disputes, interruption of service, **Util 186.004, 186.006**
Landlord and Tenant, this index
Leases, **Util 14.101**
Rates and charges, major transactions, effect, **Util 14.101**
Reports, major transactions, **Util 14.101**
Licenses and permits,
Railroads, right of way, use, **Util 186.058**
Underground facilities, excavations, **Util 251.006**
Loans, shareholders, reports, **Util 14.103**
Lobbyists,
Commission, **Util 12.151**
Office of public utility counsel, conflict of interest, **Util 13.042**
Managers and management, audits, **Util 14.201, 14.202**
Meetings, commission, **Util 12.058**
Internet, **Util 12.204**
Merger and consolidation, **Util 14.101**
Rates and charges, effect, **Util 14.101**
Reports, major transactions, **Util 14.101**
Mitigation, plans and specifications, **Util 15.023**
Municipalities, **Util 181.901, 181.902**
Assistance, commission, **Util 14.007**
Audits and auditors, **Util 14.203**
Confidential or privileged information, customers, **Util 182.051 et seq.**
Definitions, **Util 11.003**
Efficiency, **Util 39.9051**
Electricity, this index
Gas Utilities, this index
Meters, net metering, **Util 39.914**
Reports, efficiency, **Util 39.9051**
Streets and alleys, franchises, fees, **Util 14.008**
Water Supply, generally, this index
Natural gas,
Gas Utilities, generally, this index
Oil and Gas, generally, this index
Negotiated rulemaking, commission, **Util 14.0025**
Notice,
Commission, ante
Confidential or privileged information, government operated utilities, customers, **Util 182.052**
Fines and penalties, **Util 15.024**
Office of public utility counsel, removal, **Util 13.023**
Public utility counselors, adverse or pecuniary interest, **Util 13.022**
Railroads, right of way, easements, **Util 186.054**
Underground facilities, post
Notification center, underground facilities, excavations, **Util 251.101 et seq.**

PUBLIC UTILITIES—Cont'd
Notification corporation, underground facilities, excavations, **Util 251.051 et seq.**
Oaths and affirmations, officers and employees, examinations, **Util 14.205**
Offenses. Crimes and offenses, generally, ante
Office of public utility counsel, **Util 13.001 et seq.**
Alternative dispute resolution, **Util 13.003, 13.004**
Appointments, counsellors, **Util 13.021**
Career ladder program, **Util 13.044**
Compensation and salaries, employees, **Util 13.041**
Complaints, **Util 13.005**
Conduct, standards, employees, **Util 13.046**
Conflict of interest, counselors, **Util 13.022 et seq.**
Crimes and offenses, subsequent employment, **Util 13.043**
Disability, removal from office, counselors, **Util 13.023**
Equal employment opportunity, **Util 13.045**
Gas utilities, **Util 101.051 et seq.**
Hearings, **Util 13.064**
Information, **Util 13.061**
Lobbyists, conflict of interest, **Util 13.042**
Notice,
Counselors, adverse interest, **Util 13.022**
Removal, **Util 13.023**
Officers and employees, **Util 13.041**
Powers and duties, **Util 13.003 et seq.**
Prohibited acts, counselors, **Util 13.024**
Public participation, **Util 13.062**
Qualifications,
Counsellors, **Util 13.022**
Employees, **Util 13.046**
Removal from office, counselors, **Util 13.023**
Reports, **Util 13.063**
Subsequent employment, **Util 13.043**
Sunset Act, **Util 13.002**
Technology, **Util 13.006**
Terms of office, counsellors, **Util 13.021**
Time, subsequent employment, **Util 13.043**
Trade associations, conflict of interest, **Util 13.042**
Violations, counselors, **Util 13.024**
Officers and employees,
Collective bargaining, interference, utilities, **Util 14.006**
Commission, ante
Examinations and examiners, oaths and affirmations, **Util 14.205**
Harassment, interruption of service, **Util 186.004**
Labor disputes, interruption of service, **Util 186.004, 186.006**
Office of public utility counsel, generally, ante

PUBLIC UTILITIES—Cont'd
Officers and employees—Cont'd
Public utilities commission, **Util 12.101 et seq.**
Subsequent employment, commissioners and employees, **Util 12.155**
Underground facilities, notification corporation, excavations, **Util 251.058**
Oil and gas. Gas Utilities, generally, this index
Open meetings, underground facilities, notification corporation, excavations, **Util 251.053**
Open records, underground facilities, notification corporation, excavations, **Util 251.053**
Orders,
Administrative hearings office, **Util 14.053**
Commission, **Util 14.051, 14.057**
Contempt, **Util 15.022**
Continuity of service, executive orders, **Util 186.003**
Definitions, **Util 11.003**
Enforcement, actions, **Util 15.021 et seq.**
Fines and penalties, **Util 15.024**
Forms, commission, **Util 14.057**
Orders of court,
Enforcement, **Util 15.021 et seq.**
Interruption of service, injunctions, **Util 186.005**
Owners and ownership, reports, substantial interest, **Util 14.004**
Parties, contested cases, **Util 14.052**
Payment,
Aged persons, delay, **Util 182.001 et seq.**
Assessments, **Util 16.002**
Customers deposits, interest, **Util 183.004**
Fines and penalties, **Util 15.025**
Underground facilities, notification center, excavations, **Util 251.106**
Penalties. Fines and penalties, generally, ante
Picketing, interruption of service, **Util 186.004**
Plans and specifications, mitigation, **Util 15.023**
Powers and duties. Underground facilities, post
Privileges and immunities,
Confidential or privileged information, government operated utilities, **Util 182.055**
Underground facilities, excavations, **Util 251.157**
Proceedings. Actions and proceedings, generally, ante
Production of books and papers,
Commission, **Util 14.051**
Contempt, **Util 15.022**
Out of state records, **Util 14.207**
Protection, municipalities, **Util 181.901, 181.902**

PUBLIC UTILITIES—Cont'd
Public policy,
Continuity of service, **Util 186.002**
Public Utility Regulatory Act, **Util 11.002**
Purpose of code, **Util 1.001**
Public utility commission. Commission, generally, ante
Public utility counsel office. Office of public utility counsel, generally, ante
Railroads, generally, this index
Rates and charges,
Appeal and review, costs and attorney fees, **Util 15.003**
Communications, regulatory authorities, **Util 14.153**
Definitions, **Util 11.003**
Deposits, customers, interest, **Util 183.003**
Electricity, this index
Leases, major transactions, effect, **Util 14.101**
Merger and consolidation, effect, **Util 14.101**
Payment, aged persons, delay, **Util 182.001 et seq.**
Sales, major transactions, effect, **Util 14.101**
Telecommunications, this index
Underground facilities, post
Records and recordation, **Util 14.151 et seq.**
Administrative law and procedure, **Util 14.055**
Affiliates, jurisdiction, **Util 14.154**
Communications, regulatory authorities, **Util 14.153**
Complaints, **Util 15.051**
Foreign states, production of books and papers, **Util 14.207**
Forms, **Util 14.151**
Inspection and inspectors, **Util 14.204**
Maintenance, **Util 14.152**
Offices, **Util 14.152**
Public information, commission records, **Util 14.057**
Recreational vehicle parks, electricity, complaints, **Util 15.052**
Removal from state, **Util 14.152**
Transcripts, hearings, **Util 14.055, 14.057**
Underground facilities, notification center, excavations, **Util 251.103**
Refunds, customers deposits, **Util 183.005**
Regulatory Act, **Util 11.001 et seq.**
Remedies, underground facilities, excavations, **Util 251.008**
Repairs, underground facilities, excavations, **Util 251.159**
Reports, **Util 14.003**
Administrative penalties, recommendations, **Util 15.024**
Adverse or pecuniary interest, **Util 14.004**
Affiliates, ante
Commission, ante
Forms, **Util 14.003**

PUBLIC UTILITIES—Cont'd
Reports—Cont'd
Historically underutilized businesses, assistance, **Util 12.253**
Leases, major transactions, **Util 14.101**
Merger and consolidation, major transactions, **Util 14.101**
Municipalities, efficiency, **Util 39.9051**
Office of public utility counsel, **Util 13.063**
Sales, major transactions, **Util 14.101**
Shares and shareholders, post
Time, **Util 14.003**
Underground facilities, damages, excavations, **Util 251.159**
Requests,
Aged persons, delay in payment, **Util 182.002, 182.003**
Confidential or privileged information, government operated utilities, **Util 182.052**
Residential consumers, advocacy, **Util 13.001, 13.003**
Restraining orders, interruption of service, **Util 186.005**
Review. Appeal and review, generally, ante
Revised code, application of law, **Util 1.003**
Rules and regulations,
Commission, **Util 14.002**
Negotiated rulemaking, **Util 14.0025**
Communications, regulatory authorities, **Util 14.153**
Compromise and settlement, contested cases, **Util 14.054**
Hearings, **Util 14.052**
Proceedings, **Util 14.052**
Safety,
Continuity of service, **Util 186.001 et seq.**
Underground facilities, **Util 251.001 et seq.**
Sales, **Util 14.101**
Rates and charges, major transactions, effect, **Util 14.101**
Reports, major transactions, **Util 14.101**
Securities,
Commission, adverse or pecuniary interest, commissioners and employees, **Util 12.152, 12.154**
Reports, adverse or pecuniary interest, **Util 14.004**
Settlement and compromise, contested cases, **Util 14.054**
Sewers and Sewer Systems, generally, this index
Shares and shareholders,
Affiliates, generally, ante
Commission, adverse or pecuniary interest, commissioners and employees, **Util 12.152, 12.154**
Public utility counselors, adverse or pecuniary interest, **Util 13.022**
Purchases, voting stock, reports, **Util 14.102**

PUBLIC UTILITIES—Cont'd
Shares and shareholders—Cont'd
Reports,
Adverse or pecuniary interest, **Util 14.004**
Loans to shareholders, **Util 14.103**
Major transactions, **Util 14.101**
Purchases and purchasing, voting stock, **Util 14.102**
Small businesses, consumer advocacy, **Util 13.001, 13.003**
Street railroads, right of way, easements, eminent domain, **Util 186.051 et seq.**
Streets and alleys, municipal franchises, fees, **Util 14.008**
Subpoenas,
Commission, **Util 14.051**
Contempt, **Util 15.022**
Subsequent employment, office of public utility counsel, **Util 13.043**
Supersedeas or stay,
Appeal and review, **Util 15.004**
Fines and penalties, judicial review, **Util 15.025**
Supervision, commission, **Util 14.001**
Tariffs. Rates and charges, generally, ante
Technology, office of public utility counsel, **Util 13.006**
Telecommunications, generally, this index
Termination of service, aged and handicapped persons, **Util 14.005**
Theft, unauthorized use, municipal ordinances, **Util 181.902**
Threats, interruption of service, **Util 186.004**
Time,
Aged persons, payment, **Util 182.002**
Assessments, payment, **Util 16.002**
Commission, subsequent employment, commissioners and employees, **Util 12.155**
Entry on property, inspection, **Util 14.206**
Fines and penalties, payment, **Util 15.025**
Inspection and inspectors, **Util 14.204**
Office of public utility counsel, subsequent employment, **Util 13.043**
Reports, **Util 14.003**
Toll free numbers, underground facilities, contracts, notification corporation, excavations, **Util 251.061**
Trade associations,
Commission, adverse or pecuniary interest, commissioners and employees, **Util 12.153**
Definitions, **Util 11.003**
Office of public utility counsel, conflict of interest, **Util 13.042**
Training, commission, **Util 12.059**
Alternative dispute resolution, **Util 14.0025**
Transcripts, hearings, **Util 14.055, 14.057**
Traveling expenses, commission, training, **Util 12.059**

PUBLIC UTILITIES—Cont'd
Unauthorized use, municipalities, protection, **Util 181.902**
Underground facilities,
Assessments, notification corporation, excavations, **Util 251.062**
Brands, marks and labels,
Crimes and offenses, excavations, **Util 251.203**
Excavations, **Util 251.157, 251.158**
Call router system, contracts, notification corporation, excavations, **Util 251.061**
Contracts, toll free numbers, notification corporation, excavations, **Util 251.061**
Conversion, **Util 251.005**
Crimes and offenses, brands, marks and labels, excavations, **Util 251.203**
Damages, **Util 251.001 et seq.**
Notification corporation, excavations, **Util 251.054**
Directors, notification corporation, excavations, **Util 251.055 et seq.**
Easements, excavations, **Util 251.006**
Emergencies, notice, excavations, **Util 251.155**
Excavations, **Util 251.001 et seq.**
Exemptions, notice, excavations, **Util 251.156**
Expenses and expenditures, notification corporation, excavations, **Util 251.054**
Fees,
Notification center, excavations, **Util 251.105**
Notification corporation, excavations, **Util 251.062**
Fines and penalties, excavations, **Util 251.201 et seq.**
Fraud, emergencies, excavations, **Util 251.155**
Fines and penalties, **Util 251.201**
Highways and roads, excavations, **Util 251.007**
Insurance, notification center, excavations, **Util 251.104**
Licenses and permits, excavations, **Util 251.006**
Notice, excavations, **Util 251.009, 251.151 et seq.**
Notification center, excavations, **Util 251.101 et seq.**
Notification corporation, excavations, **Util 251.051 et seq.**
Officers and employees, notification corporation, excavations, **Util 251.058**
Open meetings, notification corporation, excavations, **Util 251.053**
Open records, notification corporation, excavations, **Util 251.053**
Payment, notification center, excavations, **Util 251.106**
Powers and duties,
Notification center, excavations, **Util 251.102**

PUBLIC UTILITIES—Cont'd
Underground facilities—Cont'd
Powers and duties—Cont'd
Notification corporation, excavations, **Util 251.060**
Rates and charges,
Notification center, excavations, **Util 251.105**
Notification corporation, excavations, **Util 251.062**
Records and recordation, notification center, excavations, **Util 251.103**
Remedies, excavations, **Util 251.008**
Repairs, excavations, **Util 251.159**
Reports, damages, excavations, **Util 251.159**
Safety, **Util 251.001 et seq.**
Toll free numbers, contracts, notification corporation, excavations, **Util 251.061**
Venue, fines and penalties, excavations, **Util 251.201**
Warnings, excavations, **Util 251.201, 251.2011**
Venue,
Enforcement, **Util 15.031**
Interruption of service, restraining orders, **Util 186.005**
Underground facilities, fines and penalties, excavations, **Util 251.201**
Waiver, payment, underground facilities, notification center, excavations, **Util 251.106**
Warnings, underground facilities, excavations, **Util 251.201, 251.2011**
Waste, unauthorized use, municipalities, protection, **Util 181.902**
Water Supply, generally, this index
Witnesses,
Commission, **Util 14.051**
Contempt, **Util 15.022**
Officers and employees, oaths and affirmations, **Util 14.205**

PUBLIC UTILITY ACT
Public Utilities, generally, this index

PUBLIC UTILITY COMMISSION
Generally, **Util 12.001 et seq.**

PUBLIC UTILITY REGULATORY ACT
Generally, **Util 11.001 et seq.**
Public Utilities, generally, this index

PUBLIC WATER SUPPLY
Water Supply, generally, this index

PUBLICATION
Electricity, this index
Gas utilities, notice, rates and charges, **Util 104.103**
Telecommunications, this index

PUPILS
Schools and School Districts, generally, this index

PURCHASED POWER MARKET VALUE
Definitions, electricity, competition, stranded costs, recovery, **Util 39.251**

PURCHASES AND PURCHASING
Electricity, this index
Sales, generally, this index

QUALIFIED COSTS
Definitions, electricity, securities, competition, **Util 39.302**

QUO WARRANTO
Business organizations, insolvency, **Bus Org 12.253 et seq.**

RACE
Discrimination, generally, this index

RACING
Dog Races, generally, this index
Horse Racing, generally, this index

RADIO
Television and Radio, generally, this index

RAILROAD COMMISSION
Administrative law and procedure, contested cases, hearings, **Util 102.006**
Appeal and review, hearings, contested cases, **Util 102.006**
Gas Utilities, this index
Hearings, contested cases, **Util 102.006**
Rates and charges, hearings, contested cases, **Util 102.006**

RAILROADS
See, also,
Carriers, generally, this index
Public Utilities, generally, this index
Boards and commissions. Railroad Commission, generally, this index
Cable television, right of way, easements, eminent domain, **Util 186.051 et seq.**
Costs, public utilities, right of way, eminent domain, **Util 186.056, 186.059**
Damages, public utilities, right of way, eminent domain, **Util 186.056, 186.059**
Definitions, public utilities, right of way, **Util 186.051**
Easements, public utilities, eminent domain, **Util 186.051 et seq.**
Electric cooperative corporations, right of way, easements, eminent domain, **Util 186.051 et seq.**
Electricity,
Easements, standards of construction, **Util 181.045**
Right of way, easements, eminent domain, **Util 186.051 et seq.**
Eminent domain, public utilities, easements, **Util 186.051 et seq.**
Gas utilities,
Easements, **Util 181.005**
Right of way, easements, eminent domain, **Util 186.051 et seq.**

RAILROADS—Cont'd
Interurban Railroads, generally, this index
Licenses and permits, public utilities, right of way, use, **Util 186.058**
Notice,
Public utilities, right of way, easements, **Util 186.054**
Right of way, public utilities, easements, **Util 186.054**
Oil and gas pipelines, right of way, easements, eminent domain, **Util 186.051 et seq.**
Production of books and papers, public utilities, right of way, easements, **Util 186.055**
Real estate, public utilities, right of way, easements, **Util 186.051 et seq.**
Right of way,
Definitions, public utilities, **Util 186.051**
Easements, eminent domain, **Util 186.051 et seq.**
Public utilities, easements, eminent domain, **Util 186.051 et seq.**
Street Railroads, generally, this index
Telecommunications, right of way, easements, eminent domain, **Util 186.051 et seq.**
Title to property, public utilities, right of way, easements, **Util 186.055**
Water supply, right of way, easements, eminent domain, **Util 186.051 et seq.**

RATES AND CHARGES
Agriculture, natural gas, **Util 123.023**
Apartment houses, central heating and cooling, **Util 184.052**
Contested cases. Administrative Law and Procedure, this index
Definitions,
Electric cooperative corporations, competition, **Util 41.002**
Electricity, **Util 31.002**
Gas utilities, **Util 101.003**
Public utilities, **Util 11.003**
Electric Cooperative Corporations, this index
Electricity, this index
Gas Utilities, this index
Internet, **Util 52.002**
Mobile Homes and Mobile Home Parks, this index
Municipalities, this index
Oil and Gas, this index
Partnerships, this index
Public Utilities, this index
Telecommunications, this index
Telephone Cooperative Corporations, this index
Water Supply, this index

REAL ESTATE
Condominiums, generally, this index
Conveyances. Deeds and Conveyances, generally, this index
Cooperative Associations, generally, this index
Corporations, this index

REAL ESTATE—Cont'd
Deeds and Conveyances, generally, this index
Deeds of Trust, generally, this index
Eminent Domain, generally, this index
Entry On Property, generally, this index
Foreign Corporations, this index
Gas utilities, **Util 181.007**
Investment trusts. Real Estate Investment Trusts, generally, this index
Joint Tenants, generally, this index
Landlord and Tenant, generally, this index
Leases, generally, this index
Liens and incumbrances. Mortgages, generally, this index
Limited Liability Companies, this index
Limited partnerships. Partnerships, this index
Loans. Mortgages, generally, this index
Mortgages, generally, this index
Nonprofit Corporations, this index
Partnerships, this index
Professional Associations and Societies, this index
Professional Corporations, this index
Railroads, this index
Real Estate Investment Trusts, generally, this index
Sales. Deeds and Conveyances, generally, this index
Taking. Eminent Domain, generally, this index

REAL ESTATE INVESTMENT TRUSTS
Generally, **Bus Org 1.001 et seq., 200.001 et seq.**
Accounts and accounting, examinations and examiners, **Bus Org 200.501**
Actions and proceedings, ultra vires, **Bus Org 200.004**
Amendments,
Bylaws, **Bus Org 200.058**
Shareholders, **Bus Org 200.059**
Certificate of formation, post
Application of law, **Bus Org 200.002**
Taxation, **Bus Org 200.503**
Appraisal and appraisers, shares and shareholders, fundamental business transactions, **Bus Org 200.410**
Assets,
Sales, **Bus Org 200.405 et seq.**
Value, **Bus Org 200.209**
Assignments, **Bus Org 200.405 et seq.**
Shares and shareholders, consideration, privileges and immunities, **Bus Org 200.109**
Assumed or fictitious names, **Bus & C 71.001 et seq.**
Certificate of formation, **Bus Org 3.012**
Books and papers, examinations and examiners, **Bus Org 200.501**
Bylaws, **Bus Org 200.058**
Proxies, elections, **Bus Org 200.268**
Shares and shareholders, post
Cancellation, winding up, **Bus Org 200.452**

REAL ESTATE INVESTMENT TRUSTS
—Cont'd
Certificate of formation, **Bus Org 3.001 et seq., 200.051 et seq.**
Amendments, **Bus Org 3.055, 200.053 et seq.**
Elections, **Bus Org 200.261**
Elections, amendments, **Bus Org 200.261**
Managers and management, post
Shares and shareholders, post
Certificates and certification, shares and shareholders, **Bus Org 3.201 et seq.**
Classification, shares and shareholders, **Bus Org 200.102, 200.103**
Closing, shares and shareholders, transfers, **Bus Org 200.254**
Commitments, shares and shareholders, **Bus Org 200.112**
Committees, managers and management, **Bus Org 200.311**
Compensation and salaries, managers and management, **Bus Org 200.305**
Conflict of interest, contracts, **Bus Org 200.317**
Conflict of laws, **Bus Org 200.003**
Conservators and conservatorship, shares and shareholders, privileges and immunities, **Bus Org 200.164**
Consideration, shares and shareholders, **Bus Org 200.104 et seq.**
Contracts,
Conflict of interest, **Bus Org 200.317**
Shares and shareholders, transfers, **Bus Org 200.154, 200.156**
Ultra vires, **Bus Org 200.004**
Contributions, managers and management, **Bus Org 200.315**
Conversion, **Bus Org 200.403 et seq.**
Cumulative voting, managers and management, **Bus Org 200.259**
Damages,
Managers and management, **Bus Org 200.312 et seq.**
Shares and shareholders, privileges and immunities, **Bus Org 200.159 et seq.**
Death, shares and shareholders, joint tenants, **Bus Org 200.158**
Declaration of trust. Certificate of formation, generally, ante
Deeds and conveyances, **Bus Org 200.405 et seq.**
Defenses, ultra vires, **Bus Org 200.004**
Definitions, **Bus Org 200.001**
Business organizations, **Bus Org 1.002**
Fundamental actions, elections, **Bus Org 200.261**
Fundamental business transactions, **Bus Org 200.401**
Dissenting shareholders, shares and shareholders, fundamental business transactions, **Bus Org 200.410**
Distribution and distributors, **Bus Org 200.201 et seq.**
Dissenting shareholders, **Bus Org 200.202**

REAL ESTATE INVESTMENT TRUSTS
—Cont'd
Distribution and distributors—Cont'd
Fractional shares, **Bus Org 200.202**
Indebtedness, **Bus Org 200.202**
Limitations, **Bus Org 200.202**
Priorities and preferences, **Bus Org 200.203**
Redemption, **Bus Org 200.202**
Reserves, surplus, **Bus Org 200.204**
Shares and shareholders, joint tenants, **Bus Org 200.158**
Surplus, reserves, **Bus Org 200.204**
Dividends, shares and shareholders, **Bus Org 200.205 et seq.**
Division, shares and shareholders, **Bus Org 200.211**
Domicile and residence, managers and management, **Bus Org 200.303**
Duplicates and copies, records and recordation, **Bus Org 200.501**
Elections,
Fundamental actions, **Bus Org 200.261**
Managers and management, **Bus Org 200.258, 200.259**
Shares and shareholders, post
Winding up, **Bus Org 200.451, 200.452**
Employees. Officers and employees, generally, post
Examinations and examiners, records and recordation, **Bus Org 200.501**
Exchange of property, **Bus Org 200.404 et seq.**
Filing, **Bus Org 4.009**
Shares and shareholders, classification, **Bus Org 200.103**
Signatures, **Bus Org 200.006**
Financial statements and reports, **Bus Org 200.209**
Foreign real estate investment trusts,
Filing, **Bus Org 4.009**
Registration, **Bus Org 9.001 et seq.**
Transacting business in Texas, **Bus Org 9.201 et seq.**
Forfeitures, shares and shareholders, preformation subscription, **Bus Org 200.111**
Formation. Certificate of formation, generally, ante
Fractional shares, distribution and distributors, **Bus Org 200.202**
Fundamental actions, elections, **Bus Org 200.261**
Fundamental business transactions, **Bus Org 200.401 et seq.**
Guardian and ward, shares and shareholders, privileges and immunities, **Bus Org 200.164**
Indebtedness,
Distribution and distributors, **Bus Org 200.202**
Shares and shareholders, privileges and immunities, **Bus Org 200.161**
Injunctions, ultra vires, **Bus Org 200.004**
Insolvency, **Bus Org 200.209, 200.210**
Joinder, shares and shareholders, **Bus Org 200.502**

REAL ESTATE INVESTMENT TRUSTS
—Cont'd
Joint tenants, shares and shareholders, **Bus Org 200.158**
Privileges and immunities, **Bus Org 200.160**
Leases, **Bus Org 200.405 et seq.**
Limitation of actions, managers and management, **Bus Org 200.313**
Limitations,
Distribution and distributors, **Bus Org 200.202**
Shares and shareholders, dividends, **Bus Org 200.206**
Managers and management, **Bus Org 200.301 et seq.**
Certificate of formation,
Amendments, **Bus Org 200.053, 200.054**
Restatement, **Bus Org 3.062**
Committees, **Bus Org 200.311**
Compensation and salaries, **Bus Org 200.305**
Contracts, **Bus Org 200.317**
Contributions, **Bus Org 200.315**
Damages, **Bus Org 200.312 et seq.**
Domicile and residence, **Bus Org 200.303**
Elections, **Bus Org 200.258, 200.259**
Limitation of actions, **Bus Org 200.313**
Meetings, **Bus Org 200.309**
Names, **Bus Org 200.302**
Notice, meetings, **Bus Org 200.309**
Numbers and numbering, **Bus Org 200.304**
Powers and duties, **Bus Org 200.351**
Privileges and immunities, **Bus Org 200.314**
Quorum, **Bus Org 200.310**
Terms of office, **Bus Org 200.306, 200.307**
Vacancies in office, **Bus Org 200.308**
Winding up, **Bus Org 200.453**
Meetings,
Certificate of formation, amendments, **Bus Org 200.056**
Managers and management, **Bus Org 200.309**
Organization, **Bus Org 200.060**
Shares and shareholders, **Bus Org 200.251 et seq.**
Fundamental business transactions, **Bus Org 200.406**
Merger and consolidation, **Bus Org 200.402 et seq.**
Mortgages, **Bus Org 200.405 et seq.**
Names,
Assumed or fictitious names, certificate of formation, **Bus Org 3.012**
Managers and management, **Bus Org 200.302**
Notice,
Certificate of formation, amendments, meetings, **Bus Org 200.056**
Managers and management, meetings, **Bus Org 200.309**
Shares and shareholders, post

REAL ESTATE INVESTMENT TRUSTS
—Cont'd
Numbers and numbering,
Managers and management, **Bus Org 200.304**
Shares and shareholders, post
Objections and exceptions, shares and shareholders, damages, **Bus Org 200.163**
Officers and employees,
Contracts, **Bus Org 200.317**
Managers and management, generally, ante
Powers and duties, **Bus Org 200.316, 200.351**
Offices, records and recordation, shares and shareholders, **Bus Org 200.113**
Organization, meetings, **Bus Org 200.060**
Par value, shares and shareholders, dividends, **Bus Org 200.207**
Payment, shares and shareholders,
Joint tenants, **Bus Org 200.158**
Preformation subscription, **Bus Org 200.111**
Personal property, shares and shareholders, rights, **Bus Org 200.153**
Pledges, **Bus Org 200.405 et seq.**
Shares and shareholders, privileges and immunities, **Bus Org 200.164**
Powers and duties, **Bus Org 200.005, 200.351**
Officers and employees, **Bus Org 200.316**
Preemption, shares and shareholders, damages, **Bus Org 200.162**
Preemptive rights, shares and shareholders, **Bus Org 200.152**
Preformation subscription, shares and shareholders, **Bus Org 200.111**
Priorities and preferences, distribution and distributors, **Bus Org 200.203**
Privileges and immunities,
Managers and management, **Bus Org 200.314**
Shares and shareholders, damages, **Bus Org 200.159 et seq.**
Probate proceedings, shares and shareholders, privileges and immunities, **Bus Org 200.164**
Production of books and papers, **Bus Org 200.501**
Proxies, shares and shareholders, elections, **Bus Org 200.264 et seq.**
Purposes, limitations, **Bus Org 2.012**
Quorum,
Managers and management, **Bus Org 200.310**
Shares and shareholders, meetings, **Bus Org 200.257**
Receivers and receivership, shares and shareholders, privileges and immunities, **Bus Org 200.164**
Record date, shares and shareholders, **Bus Org 200.255, 200.256**
Records and recordation,
Examinations and examiners, **Bus Org 200.501**

REAL ESTATE INVESTMENT TRUSTS
—Cont'd
Records and recordation—Cont'd
Shares and shareholders, numbers and numbering, **Bus Org 200.113**
Redemption, shares and shareholders, **Bus Org 200.102**
Registration, foreign real estate investment trusts, **Bus Org 9.001 et seq.**
Reinstatement,
Elections, **Bus Org 200.261**
Winding up, **Bus Org 200.452**
Repeals, bylaws, **Bus Org 200.058**
Shareholders, **Bus Org 200.059**
Reserves, distribution and distributors, surplus, **Bus Org 200.204**
Restatement, certificate of formation, **Bus Org 200.057**
Revocation or suspension,
Shares and shareholders, proxies, elections, **Bus Org 200.266**
Winding up, **Bus Org 200.452**
Rights, certificate of formation, shares and shareholders, property, **Bus Org 200.052**
Shares and shareholders, **Bus Org 200.101 et seq.**
Appraisal and appraisers, fundamental business transactions, **Bus Org 200.410**
Assignments, consideration, privileges and immunities, **Bus Org 200.109**
Bylaws, **Bus Org 200.059**
Proxies, elections, **Bus Org 200.268**
Transfers, **Bus Org 200.156**
Certificate of formation, **Bus Org 3.012**
Amendments, **Bus Org 200.055, 200.056**
Property, rights, **Bus Org 200.052**
Certificates and certification, **Bus Org 3.201 et seq.**
Changes, elections, **Bus Org 200.262**
Classification, **Bus Org 200.102, 200.103**
Closing, transfers, **Bus Org 200.254**
Commitments, **Bus Org 200.112**
Conservators and conservatorship, privileges and immunities, **Bus Org 200.164**
Consideration, **Bus Org 200.104 et seq.**
Contracts,
Subscriptions, **Bus Org 200.110**
Transfers, **Bus Org 200.154, 200.156**
Damages, privileges and immunities, **Bus Org 200.159 et seq.**
Death, joint tenants, **Bus Org 200.158**
Dissenting shareholders,
Distribution and distributors, **Bus Org 200.202**
Fundamental business transactions, **Bus Org 200.410**
Distribution and distributors, joint tenants, **Bus Org 200.158**
Dividends, **Bus Org 200.205 et seq.**
Division, **Bus Org 200.211**
Elections, **Bus Org 200.258 et seq.**

REAL ESTATE INVESTMENT TRUSTS
—Cont'd
Shares and shareholders—Cont'd
Elections—Cont'd
Fundamental business transactions, **Bus Org 200.407 et seq.**
Winding up, **Bus Org 200.451, 200.452**
Enforcement,
Proxies, elections, **Bus Org 200.267**
Transfers, **Bus Org 200.157**
Filing, classification, **Bus Org 200.103**
Forfeitures, preformation subscription, **Bus Org 200.111**
Fractional shares, distribution and distributors, **Bus Org 200.202**
Fundamental business transactions, **Bus Org 200.401 et seq.**
Guardian and ward, privileges and immunities, **Bus Org 200.164**
Indebtedness, privileges and immunities, **Bus Org 200.161**
Joinder, **Bus Org 200.502**
Joint tenants, **Bus Org 200.158**
Privileges and immunities, **Bus Org 200.160**
Limitations, dividends, **Bus Org 200.206**
Managers and management, elections, **Bus Org 200.258, 200.259**
Meetings, **Bus Org 200.251 et seq.**
Fundamental business transactions, **Bus Org 200.406**
Notice,
Fundamental business transactions, **Bus Org 200.406**
Meetings, **Bus Org 200.253**
Subscriptions, **Bus Org 200.110**
Numbers and numbering, **Bus Org 200.101**
Elections, **Bus Org 200.263**
Records and recordation, **Bus Org 200.113**
Objections and exceptions, damages, **Bus Org 200.163**
Par value, dividends, **Bus Org 200.207**
Payment,
Joint tenants, **Bus Org 200.158**
Preformation subscription, **Bus Org 200.111**
Personal property, rights, **Bus Org 200.153**
Pledges, privileges and immunities, **Bus Org 200.164**
Preemption, damages, **Bus Org 200.162**
Preemptive rights, **Bus Org 200.152**
Preformation subscription, **Bus Org 200.111**
Privileges and immunities,
Consideration, **Bus Org 200.109**
Damages, **Bus Org 200.159 et seq.**
Probate proceedings, privileges and immunities, **Bus Org 200.164**
Proxies, elections, **Bus Org 200.264 et seq.**
Purchases and purchasing, commitments, **Bus Org 200.112**
Quorum, meetings, **Bus Org 200.257**

REAL ESTATE INVESTMENT TRUSTS
—Cont'd
Shares and shareholders—Cont'd
Receivers and receivership, privileges and immunities, **Bus Org 200.164**
Record date, **Bus Org 200.255, 200.256**
Records and recordation, numbers and numbering, **Bus Org 200.113**
Redemption, **Bus Org 200.102**
Distribution and distributors, **Bus Org 200.202**
Revocation or suspension, proxies, elections, **Bus Org 200.266**
Rights, **Bus Org 200.151 et seq.**
Special meetings, **Bus Org 200.252**
Split up, **Bus Org 200.211**
Subscriptions, **Bus Org 200.110**
Preformation subscription, **Bus Org 200.111**
Surplus, dividends, transfers, **Bus Org 200.208**
Time,
Meetings, **Bus Org 200.251**
Proxies, elections, **Bus Org 200.265**
Subscriptions, **Bus Org 200.110**
Title to property, **Bus Org 200.151**
Transfers, **Bus Org 200.154 et seq.**
Closing, **Bus Org 200.254**
Consideration, privileges and immunities, **Bus Org 200.109**
Dividends, surplus, **Bus Org 200.208**
Winding up, elections, **Bus Org 200.451, 200.452**
Signatures,
Certificate of formation, restatement, **Bus Org 200.057**
Filing, **Bus Org 200.006**
Special meetings, shares and shareholders, **Bus Org 200.252**
Split up, shares and shareholders, **Bus Org 200.211**
Stated capital, value, **Bus Org 200.209**
Subscriptions, shares and shareholders, **Bus Org 200.110**
Surplus,
Distribution and distributors, reserves, **Bus Org 200.204**
Shares and shareholders, dividends, transfers, **Bus Org 200.208**
Value, **Bus Org 200.209**
Time, **Bus Org 200.210**
Taxation, application of law, **Bus Org 200.503**
Terms of office, managers and management, **Bus Org 200.306, 200.307**
Time,
Organization, meetings, **Bus Org 200.060**
Shares and shareholders, ante
Surplus, value, **Bus Org 200.210**
Title to property, shares and shareholders, **Bus Org 200.151**
Transacting business in Texas, foreign real estate investment trusts, **Bus Org 9.201 et seq.**
Transfers, **Bus Org 200.405 et seq.**
Shares and shareholders, ante

REAL ESTATE INVESTMENT TRUSTS
—Cont'd
Transfers—Cont'd
Ultra vires, **Bus Org 200.004**
Ultra vires, **Bus Org 200.004**
Vacancies in office, managers and management, **Bus Org 200.308**
Winding up, **Bus Org 200.451 et seq.**
Cancellation, **Bus Org 200.452**
Elections, **Bus Org 200.261**
Managers and management, **Bus Org 200.453**
Reinstatement, **Bus Org 200.452**
Revocation or suspension, **Bus Org 200.452**

RECEIVERS AND RECEIVERSHIP
Cooperative Associations, this index
Corporations, this index
Foreign Corporations, this index
Gas utilities, pipes and pipelines, violations, **Util 121.301**
Limited Liability Companies, this index
Limited partnerships. Partnerships, this index
Nonprofit Corporations, this index
Partnerships, this index
Professional Associations and Societies, this index
Professional Corporations, this index
Real estate investment trusts, shares and shareholders, privileges and immunities, **Bus Org 200.164**

RECORDS AND RECORDATION
Apartment Houses, this index
Boards and Commissions, this index
Colleges and Universities, this index
Confidential or Privileged Information, generally, this index
Cooperative Associations, this index
Corporations, this index
Court of Criminal Appeals, this index
Courts, this index
Courts of Appeals, this index
Electric Cooperative Corporations, this index
Electricity, this index
Foreign Corporations, this index
Gas Utilities, this index
Legislature, this index
Limited Liability Companies, this index
Limited partnerships. Partnerships, this index
Mobile Homes and Mobile Home Parks, this index
Nonprofit Corporations, this index
Oil and Gas, this index
Oil and Gas Pipelines, this index
Partnerships, this index
Professional Associations and Societies, this index
Professional Corporations, this index
Public Utilities, this index
Sewers and Sewer Systems, this index
State, this index
State Agencies, this index

RECORDS AND RECORDATION
—Cont'd
State Departments, this index
State institutions, nonprofit corporations, audits and auditors, **Bus Org 22.356**
Supreme Court, this index
Telecommunications, this index
Telephone Cooperative Corporations, this index
Water Supply, this index

RECREATIONAL VEHICLES
Parks. Mobile Homes and Mobile Home Parks, generally, this index

REDEMPTION
Partnerships, this index

REFERENDUM
Initiative and Referendum, generally, this index

REFUNDS
Electric Cooperative Corporations, this index
Electricity, this index
Gas Utilities, this index
Mobile Homes and Mobile Home Parks, this index
Public utilities, customers deposits, **Util 183.005**
Telecommunications, this index
Telephone cooperative corporations, earnings, **Util 53.004**

REFUSE
Solid Waste, generally, this index

REGISTERED AGENT
Cooperative Associations, this index
Corporations, this index
Foreign Corporations, this index
Nonprofit Corporations, this index
Partnerships, this index
Professional Associations and Societies, this index
Professional Corporations, this index

REGISTERED OFFICES
Cooperative Associations, this index
Corporations, this index
Foreign Corporations, this index
Nonprofit Corporations, this index
Partnerships, this index
Professional Associations and Societies, this index
Professional Corporations, this index

REGISTRATION
Banks and Banking, this index
Cooperative Associations, this index
Corporations, this index
Electricity, this index
Foreign Corporations, this index
Insurance, this index
Limited Liability Companies, this index
Limited partnerships. Partnerships, this index
Nonprofit Corporations, this index

REGISTRATION—Cont'd
Partnerships, this index
Professional Associations and Societies, this index
Professional Corporations, this index
Savings and Loan Associations, this index
Telecommunications, this index
Trust Companies, this index

REITS
Real Estate Investment Trusts, generally, this index

RELIGIOUS ORGANIZATIONS AND SOCIETIES
Agents and agencies, retirement and pensions, **Bus Org 22.404**
Annuities, retirement and pensions, contributions, **Bus Org 22.403**
Application of law, retirement and pensions, insurance, **Bus Org 22.409**
Assignments, retirement and pensions, **Bus Org 22.408**
Attachment, retirement and pensions, **Bus Org 22.407**
Churches, generally, this index
Contributions, retirement and pensions, **Bus Org 22.403**
Damages, retirement and pensions, indemnity, **Bus Org 22.406**
Definitions, officers and employees, retirement and pensions, **Bus Org 22.401**
Directors,
  Good faith, **Bus Org 22.222**
  Retirement and pensions, **Bus Org 22.401 et seq.**
Domestic relations orders, retirement and pensions, **Bus Org 22.407**
Executions, retirement and pensions, **Bus Org 22.407**
Garnishment, retirement and pensions, **Bus Org 22.407**
Good faith,
  Directors, **Bus Org 22.222**
  Officers and employees, **Bus Org 22.234**
Indemnity. Retirement and pensions, post
Insurance, retirement and pensions, application of law, **Bus Org 22.409**
Investments, retirement and pensions, contributions, **Bus Org 22.403**
Nonprofit Corporations, generally, this index
Officers and employees,
  Good faith, **Bus Org 22.234**
  Retirement and pensions, **Bus Org 22.401 et seq.**
Payment, retirement and pensions, contributions, **Bus Org 22.403**
Retirement and pensions,
  Indemnity, **Bus Org 22.405, 22.406**
  Officers and employees, **Bus Org 22.401 et seq.**
  Reserves, contributions, **Bus Org 22.403**

RELIGIOUS ORGANIZATIONS AND SOCIETIES—Cont'd
Schoolteachers, retirement and pensions, **Bus Org 22.401 et seq.**
Teachers, retirement and pensions, **Bus Org 22.401 et seq.**
Transfers, retirement and pensions, **Bus Org 22.408**
Trusts and trustees, retirement and pensions, **Bus Org 22.401 et seq.**

RENEWABLE ENERGY
Energy, this index

RENEWABLE ENERGY TECHNOLOGY
Definitions, electricity, **Util 39.904**

REORGANIZATION
Corporations, this index
Partnerships, this index

REPEALS
Statutes, this index

REPORTS
Business development corporations, **Bus Org 23.071**
Cooperative Associations, this index
Corporations, this index
Electric Cooperative Corporations, this index
Electricity, this index
Energy, this index
Gas Utilities, this index
Heating, electricity, **Util 39.912**
Legislature, this index
Limited Liability Companies, this index
Limited partnerships. Partnerships, this index
Nonprofit Corporations, this index
Oil and Gas, this index
Oil and Gas Pipelines, this index
Partnerships, this index
Public Utilities, this index
Public utility commission, **Util 12.203**
Public utility counsel office, **Util 13.063**
School buildings and grounds, leaks, pipes and pipelines, gas utilities, **Util 121.506**
Sewers and Sewer Systems, this index
Telecommunications, this index
Water Supply, this index
Weather, emergencies, electricity, plans and specifications, **Util 186.007**

RESERVES
Electric cooperative corporations, **Util 161.059**
Electricity, this index

REST HOMES
Nursing and Convalescent Homes, generally, this index

RESTRAINING ORDERS
Injunctions, generally, this index

RESTRAINT OF TRADE
Monopolies and Unfair Trade, generally, this index

RETAIL ELECTRIC CUSTOMERS
Definitions, atomic energy, decommissioning, **Util 39.206**

RETAIL SALES
Sales, generally, this index

RETIREMENT AND PENSIONS
Churches, this index
Electricity, **Util 36.065**
Gas utilities, **Util 104.059**
Religious Organizations and Societies, this index

REVENUE BONDS
Bonds, generally, this index

REWARDS
Electricity, credit reports, payment, **Util 17.008**

RIGHT OF ENTRY
Entry On Property, generally, this index

RIGHT OF WAY
Cable television, franchises, municipalities, **Util 66.010 et seq.**
Gas utilities, pipes and pipelines, telecommunications, **Util 121.201**
Highways and Roads, this index
Pipes and Pipelines, this index
Railroads, this index
Telecommunications, this index
Television and radio, franchises, municipalities, **Util 66.010 et seq.**

RIVER AUTHORITIES
Affiliates, electricity, improvements, **Util 32.053**
Bonds. Electricity, post
Competition, electricity, **Util 40.001 et seq.**
Conflict of laws, electricity, **Util 32.054**
Contracts, electricity, interference, **Util 40.101**
Electricity,
  Bonds, **Util 40.103**
    Affiliates, **Util 32.053**
    Competition, **Util 40.003**
  Competition, **Util 40.001 et seq.**
  Contracts, interference, **Util 40.101**
  Customer choice, installed generation capacity, reports, **Util 39.155**
  Jurisdiction, **Util 32.051 et seq.**
  Securities, competition, **Util 40.003**
  Stranded costs, securities, competition, **Util 40.003**
  Tax exemptions, **Util 40.104**
  Transition bonds, competition, **Util 40.003**
Gas utilities, **Util 101.003**
Improvements, electricity, **Util 32.052 et seq.**
Leases, electricity, nonprofit corporations, **Util 32.053**

RIVER AUTHORITIES—Cont'd
Limitations, electricity, production, **Util 32.054**
Loans, electricity, nonprofit corporations, **Util 32.053**
Sales, electricity, nonprofit corporations, **Util 32.053**
Securities, electricity, competition, **Util 40.003**
Stranded costs, electricity, securities, competition, **Util 40.003**
Tax exemptions, electricity, **Util 40.104**
Taxation, electricity, affiliates, **Util 32.053**
Transfers, electricity, nonprofit corporations, **Util 32.053**
Transition bonds, electricity, competition, **Util 40.003**

RIVERS AND STREAMS
Authorities. River Authorities, generally, this index

ROADS
Highways and Roads, generally, this index

ROUTINE MAINTENANCE
Definitions, underground facilities, exemptions, notice, excavations, **Util 251.156**

RUBBISH
Solid Waste, generally, this index

RURAL AREAS
Electric cooperative corporations, electrification, **Util 161.122**
Telecommunications, advanced services, **Util 55.014**

SAFETY
Electricity, standards, **Util 38.001**
Gas Utilities, this index
Oil and Gas Pipelines, this index
Public Utilities, this index
Underground Natural Gas, this index

SAILORS
Military Forces, generally, this index

SALARIES
Compensation and Salaries, generally, this index

SALES
Agriculture, natural gas, **Util 123.021 et seq.**
Business Development Corporations, this index
Conveyances. Deeds and Conveyances, generally, this index
Cooperative Associations, this index
Corporations, this index
Deeds and Conveyances, generally, this index
Electric cooperative corporations, nonmembers, energy, **Util 161.124**
Electricity, this index
Foreign Corporations, this index
Gas Utilities, this index

SALES—Cont'd
Limited Liability Companies, this index
Limited partnerships. Partnerships, this index
Mobile Homes and Mobile Home Parks, this index
Monopolies and Unfair Trade, generally, this index
Nonprofit Corporations, this index
Oil and Gas, this index
Partnerships, this index
Professional Associations and Societies, this index
Professional Corporations, this index
Public Utilities, this index
Restraint of trade. Monopolies and Unfair Trade, generally, this index
River Authorities, this index
Shares and shareholders, assets, corporations, **Bus Org 21.455**
Solar energy, school buildings and grounds, **Util 39.914**
Telecommunications, this index
Telephone cooperative corporations, authority, **Util 162.125, 162.126**
Trusts and monopolies. Monopolies and Unfair Trade, generally, this index

SATURDAY NOTIFICATION
Definitions, underground facilities, excavations, **Util 251.001**

SAVINGS AND LOAN ASSOCIATIONS
Franchise Taxes, generally, this index
Registration, names, **Bus Org 5.151 et seq.**
Taxation. Franchise Taxes, generally, this index

SCHOOL BUILDINGS AND GROUNDS
Electricity, efficiencies, assistance, **Util 31.004**
Gas utilities, pipes and pipelines, tests, **Util 121.5005 et seq.**
Notice, gas utilities, pipes and pipelines, tests, **Util 121.504**
Pipes and pipelines, gas utilities, tests, **Util 121.5005 et seq.**
Solar energy,
  Information, **Util 31.004**
  Sales, **Util 39.914**
Tests, gas utilities, pipes and pipelines, **Util 121.5005 et seq.**

SCHOOL DISTRICTS
Schools and School Districts, generally, this index

SCHOOLS AND SCHOOL DISTRICTS
Buildings. School Buildings and Grounds, generally, this index
Charters, gas utilities, pipes and pipelines, tests, **Util 121.5005**
Colleges and Universities, generally, this index
Communications. Telecommunications, generally, post

SCHOOLS AND SCHOOL DISTRICTS—Cont'd
Community colleges and districts. Colleges and Universities, this index
Computers, private network services, telecommunications, **Util 58.251 et seq., 59.071 et seq.**
Distance learning, telecommunications, **Util 57.021 et seq.**
Electricity, rates and charges, **Util 36.352**
Electronic data processing. Computers, generally, ante
Facilities. School Buildings and Grounds, generally, this index
Grants. School Funds, this index
Grounds. School Buildings and Grounds, generally, this index
Machinery and equipment. Computers, generally, ante
Private schools, application of law, gas utilities, pipes and pipelines, tests, **Util 121.5005**
Technology. Computers, generally, ante
Telecommunications,
  Distance learning, **Util 57.021 et seq.**
  Private network services, **Util 58.251 et seq., 59.071 et seq.**
  Truancy, automated dial announcing devices, **Util 55.122**
Truancy, telecommunications, automated dial announcing devices, **Util 55.122**

SCHOOLTEACHERS
Churches, retirement and pensions, **Bus Org 22.401 et seq.**
Religious organizations and societies, retirement and pensions, **Bus Org 22.401 et seq.**

SCIENTIFIC ORGANIZATIONS
Nonprofit Corporations, generally, this index

SEALS
Corporations, this index
Electric cooperative corporations, **Util 161.121**
Foreign Corporations, this index
Limited Liability Companies, this index
Limited partnerships. Partnerships, this index
Nonprofit Corporations, this index
Partnerships, this index
Public utility commission, **Util 12.003**
Telephone cooperative corporations, **Util 162.121**

SEARCHES AND SEIZURES
Telecommunications, fraud, machinery and equipment, disposition, **Util 186.033**

SECRETARY OF STATE
Nonprofit corporations, agent for service of process, **Bus Org 5.251 et seq.**

SECRETS AND SECRECY
Confidential or Privileged Information, generally, this index

SECTARIAN SCHOOLS
Private schools. Schools and School Districts, this index

SECURED FACILITIES
Definitions, underground facilities, excavations, **Util 251.001**

SECURED TRANSACTIONS
Electricity, municipal power agencies, nonnegotiable notes, **Util 163.067**

SECURITIES
Bonds, generally, this index
Corporations, this index
Electric cooperative corporations,
  Exemptions, **Util 161.063**
  Stranded costs, competition, **Util 41.003**
Electricity, this index
Foreign Corporations, this index
Limited Liability Companies, this index
Limited partnerships. Partnerships, this index
Nonprofit Corporations, this index
Partnerships, this index
Public Utilities, this index
River authorities, electricity, competition, **Util 40.003**
Telephone cooperative corporations, exemptions, **Util 162.063**

SECURITY
Bonds (Officers and Fiduciaries), generally, this index

SECURITY BONDS
Bonds (Officers and Fiduciaries), generally, this index

SECURITY INTEREST
Electricity, transition property, securities, competition, **Util 39.309**

SELF INSURANCE
Insurance, this index

SENIOR CITIZENS
Aged Persons, generally, this index

SEPARATELY METERED
Definitions, electricity, **Util 31.002**

SERIES LIMITED LIABILITY COMPANIES
Limited Liability Companies, this index

SERVICE PROVIDERS
Definitions,
  Electricity, deceptive trade practices and consumer protection, **Util 17.002**
  Telecommunications, deceptive trade practices and consumer protection, **Util 17.002, 64.002**

SETTLEMENT
Compromise and Settlement, generally, this index

SETTLOR
Trusts and Trustees, generally, this index

SEWAGE
Sewers and Sewer Systems, generally, this index

SEWERS AND SEWER SYSTEMS
  See, also, Public Utilities, generally, this index
Assessments, underground facilities, notification corporation, excavations, **Util 251.062**
Bills and billing, confidential or privileged information, customers, government operated utilities, **Util 182.052**
Brands, marks and labels, underground facilities,
  Crimes and offenses, excavations, **Util 251.203**
  Excavations, **Util 251.157, 251.158**
Call router system, underground facilities, contracts, notification corporation, excavations, **Util 251.061**
Collections, confidential or privileged information, customers, government operated utilities, **Util 182.052**
Confidential or privileged information, customers, **Util 182.051 et seq.**
Contracts, underground facilities, toll free numbers, notification corporation, excavations, **Util 251.061**
Crimes and offenses, underground facilities, brands, marks and labels, excavations, **Util 251.203**
Damages, underground facilities, **Util 251.001 et seq.**
  Notification corporation, excavations, **Util 251.054**
Directors, underground facilities, notification corporation, excavations, **Util 251.055 et seq.**
Easements, underground facilities, excavations, **Util 251.006**
Emergencies, underground facilities, notice, excavations, **Util 251.155**
Excavations, underground facilities, **Util 251.001 et seq.**
Exemptions, underground facilities, notice, excavations, **Util 251.156**
Expenses and expenditures, underground facilities, notification corporation, excavations, **Util 251.054**
Fees. Underground facilities, post
Fraud, underground facilities, emergencies, excavations, **Util 251.155**
  Fines and penalties, **Util 251.201**
Insurance, underground facilities, notification center, excavations, **Util 251.104**
Licenses and permits, underground facilities, excavations, **Util 251.006**

SEWERS AND SEWER SYSTEMS
—Cont'd
Maintenance and repairs, underground facilities, excavations, **Util 251.159**
Notice,
  Confidential or privileged information, customers, **Util 182.052**
  Underground facilities, post
Notification center, underground facilities, excavations, **Util 251.101 et seq.**
Notification corporation, underground facilities, excavations, **Util 251.051 et seq.**
Officers and employees, underground facilities, notification corporation, excavations, **Util 251.058**
Open meetings, underground facilities, notification corporation, excavations, **Util 251.053**
Open records, underground facilities, notification corporation, excavations, **Util 251.053**
Payment, underground facilities, notification center, excavations, **Util 251.106**
Powers and duties. Underground facilities, post
Rates and charges. Underground facilities, post
Records and recordation, underground facilities, notification center, excavations, **Util 251.103**
Remedies, underground facilities, excavations, **Util 251.008**
Reports, underground facilities, damages, excavations, **Util 251.159**
Safety, underground facilities, **Util 251.001 et seq.**
Toll free numbers, underground facilities, contracts, notification corporation, excavations, **Util 251.061**
Underground facilities,
  Assessments, notification corporation, excavations, **Util 251.062**
  Brands, marks and labels,
    Crimes and offenses, excavations, **Util 251.203**
    Excavations, **Util 251.157, 251.158**
  Call router system, contracts, notification corporation, excavations, **Util 251.061**
  Contracts, toll free numbers, notification corporation, excavations, **Util 251.061**
  Conversion, **Util 251.005**
  Crimes and offenses, brands, marks and labels, excavations, **Util 251.203**
  Damages, **Util 251.001 et seq.**
    Notification corporation, excavations, **Util 251.054**
  Directors, notification corporation, excavations, **Util 251.055 et seq.**
  Easements, excavations, **Util 251.006**
  Emergencies, notice, excavations, **Util 251.155**
  Excavations, **Util 251.001 et seq.**
  Exemptions, notice, excavations, **Util 251.156**

SEWERS AND SEWER SYSTEMS —Cont'd
Underground facilities—Cont'd
Expenses and expenditures, notification corporation, excavations, **Util 251.054**
Fees,
Notification center, excavations, **Util 251.105**
Notification corporation, excavations, **Util 251.062**
Fines and penalties, excavations, **Util 251.201 et seq.**
Fraud, emergencies, excavations, **Util 251.155**
Fines and penalties, **Util 251.201**
Highways and roads, excavations, **Util 251.007**
Insurance, notification center, excavations, **Util 251.104**
Licenses and permits, excavations, **Util 251.006**
Notice, excavations, **Util 251.009, 251.151 et seq.**
Notification center, excavations, **Util 251.101 et seq.**
Notification corporation, excavations, **Util 251.051 et seq.**
Officers and employees, notification corporation, excavations, **Util 251.058**
Open meetings, notification corporation, excavations, **Util 251.053**
Open records, notification corporation, excavations, **Util 251.053**
Payment, notification center, excavations, **Util 251.106**
Powers and duties,
Notification center, excavations, **Util 251.102**
Notification corporation, excavations, **Util 251.060**
Rates and charges,
Notification center, excavations, **Util 251.105**
Notification corporation, excavations, **Util 251.062**
Records and recordation, notification center, excavations, **Util 251.103**
Remedies, excavations, **Util 251.008**
Repairs, excavations, **Util 251.159**
Reports, damages, excavations, **Util 251.159**
Safety, **Util 251.001 et seq.**
Toll free numbers, contracts, notification corporation, excavations, **Util 251.061**
Venue, fines and penalties, excavations, **Util 251.201**
Warnings, excavations, **Util 251.201, 251.2011**
Venue, underground facilities, fines and penalties, excavations, **Util 251.201**
Warnings, underground facilities, excavations, **Util 251.201, 251.2011**

SHARES AND SHAREHOLDERS
Close corporations. Corporations, this index
Cooperative Associations, this index
Corporations, this index
Foreign Corporations, this index
Gas Utilities, this index
Guardian and Ward, this index
Limited Liability Companies, this index
Limited partnerships. Partnerships, this index
Nonprofit Corporations, this index
Partnerships, this index
Professional Associations and Societies, this index
Professional Corporations, this index
Public Utilities, this index
Securities, generally, this index

SHORT TITLE
Popular Name Laws, generally, this index

SIGNATURES
Cooperative Associations, this index
Corporations, this index
Foreign Corporations, this index
Limited Liability Companies, this index
Limited partnerships. Partnerships, this index
Nonprofit Corporations, this index
Partnerships, this index
Professional Associations and Societies, this index
Professional Corporations, this index

SINKING FUNDS
Electricity, municipal power agencies, **Util 163.063, 163.064**

SMALL BUSINESSES
Electricity, contracts, **Util 39.909**
Public utilities, consumer advocacy, **Util 13.001, 13.003**
Telecommunications, contracts, **Util 52.256**

SMALL COMMERCIAL CUSTOMERS
Definitions, electricity, competition, rates and charges, **Util 39.202**

SMALL POWER PRODUCERS
Electricity, this index

SOCIAL CORPORATIONS
Nonprofit Corporations, generally, this index

SOLAR ENERGY
Application of law, ratings, devices, **Util 185.002**
Devices, rating, **Util 185.001 et seq.**
Machinery and equipment, ratings, devices, **Util 185.001 et seq.**
National standards, ratings, devices, **Util 185.004**
Review of standards, ratings, devices, **Util 185.005**
Sales, school buildings and grounds, **Util 39.914**

SOLAR ENERGY—Cont'd
School buildings and grounds,
Information, **Util 31.004**
Sales, **Util 39.914**
Standards, ratings, devices, **Util 185.003 et seq.**

SOLDIERS
Military Forces, generally, this index

SOLICITATIONS
Electricity, customer choice, telecommunications, **Util 39.1025**
Public utility commission, commissioners and employees, **Util 12.154**

SOLID WASTE
Bills and billing, confidential or privileged information, customers, government operated utilities, **Util 182.052**
Collections, confidential or privileged information, customers, government operated utilities, **Util 182.052**
Confidential or privileged information, government operated utilities, customers, **Util 182.051 et seq.**

SOUR GAS PIPELINE FACILITIES
Generally, **Util 121.451 et seq.**

SPECIAL PURPOSE CORPORATIONS
Generally, **Bus Org 23.001 et seq.**

SPECIFICATIONS
Plans and Specifications, generally, this index

SPEECH LANGUAGE PATHOLOGISTS AND AUDIOLOGISTS
Advisory committees, telecommunications relay access service, **Util 56.110 et seq.**
Telecommunications, this index

STANDARDS
Cable television, customer service, franchises, **Util 66.008**
Electricity, this index
Gas Utilities, this index
Partnerships, this index
Solar energy, ratings, devices, **Util 185.003 et seq.**
Telecommunications, this index
Telephone cooperative corporations, construction, **Util 162.006**
Television and radio, customer service, franchises, **Util 66.008**

STANDING
Gas utilities, municipalities, rate proceedings, **Util 103.023**

STATE
Agencies. State Agencies, generally, this index
Audits and auditors, nonprofit corporations, **Bus Org 22.356**
Books and papers, nonprofit corporations, audits and auditors, **Bus Org 22.356**

STATE—Cont'd
Cable television,
Franchises, **Util 66.001 et seq.**
Highways and roads, easements, notice, **Util 181.103**
Colleges and Universities, generally, this index
Departments. State Departments, generally, this index
Electricity, this index
Eminent Domain, generally, this index
Foreign States, generally, this index
Franchises, television and radio, **Util 66.001 et seq.**
Gas Utilities, this index
Institutions. State Institutions, generally, this index
Legislature, generally, this index
Limited partnerships. Partnerships, this index
Monopolies and Unfair Trade, this index
Nonprofit corporations, audits and auditors, **Bus Org 22.356**
Oil and Gas, this index
Partnerships, this index
Political Subdivisions, generally, this index
Records and recordation, nonprofit corporations, audits and auditors, **Bus Org 22.356**
Telecommunications,
Delinquency fees, late payments, **Util 55.010**
Late payments, **Util 55.010**
Television and radio, franchises, **Util 66.001 et seq.**

STATE AGENCIES
Audits and auditors, nonprofit corporations, **Bus Org 22.356**
Boards and Commissions, generally, this index
Books and papers, nonprofit corporations, audits and auditors, **Bus Org 22.356**
Definitions,
Gas utilities, **Util 101.003**
Nonprofit corporations, audits and auditors, **Bus Org 22.356**
Departments. State Departments, generally, this index
Electricity, military bases aggregators, **Util 39.3535**
Gas Utilities, this index
Nonprofit corporations, audits and auditors, **Bus Org 22.356**
Records and recordation, nonprofit corporations, audits and auditors, **Bus Org 22.356**
Sunset Act, generally, this index
Telecommunications, directories, **Util 55.203**
Listing, **Util 55.203**

STATE BANKS
Banks and Banking, generally, this index

STATE BAR
Attorneys, this index

STATE BOARDS AND COMMISSIONS
Boards and Commissions, generally, this index

STATE COMMISSIONS
Boards and Commissions, generally, this index

STATE DEPARTMENTS
See, also, State Agencies, generally, this index
Audits and auditors, nonprofit corporations, **Bus Org 22.356**
Books and papers, audits and auditors, nonprofit corporations, **Bus Org 22.356**
Lobbyists. Legislature, this index
Nonprofit corporations, audits and auditors, **Bus Org 22.356**
Records and recordation, nonprofit corporations, audits and auditors, **Bus Org 22.356**

STATE HOUSING LAW
Generally, **Bus Org 1.001 et seq.**

STATE INSTITUTIONS
Audits and auditors, nonprofit corporations, **Bus Org 22.356**
Books and papers, nonprofit corporations, audits and auditors, **Bus Org 22.356**
Nonprofit corporations, audits and auditors, **Bus Org 22.356**
Records and recordation, nonprofit corporations, audits and auditors, **Bus Org 22.356**

STATE OFFICERS AND EMPLOYEES
Governor, generally, this index
Public utility commission, **Util 12.101 et seq.**

STATE TREASURY
General revenue fund, system benefit fund, **Util 39.303**
System benefit fund, **Util 39.903**

STATED CAPITAL
Corporations, this index

STATUTES
Amendments, Business Organizations Code, statutes, **Bus Org 1.054**
Business Organizations Code, construction of laws, **Bus Org 1.006, 1.051 et seq.**
Code construction, Business Organizations Code, **Bus Org 1.051 et seq.**
Construction of laws,
Business Organizations Code, **Bus Org 1.051 et seq.**
Electricity, joint ownership, public entities, **Util 164.006**
Definitions, business organizations, **Bus Org 1.002**
Federal Law, generally, this index
Partnerships, this index
Popular Name Laws, generally, this index

STATUTES—Cont'd
Repeals, Business Organizations Code, statutes, **Bus Org 1.054**

STAY OF PROCEEDINGS
Supersedeas or Stay, generally, this index

STORMS
Electricity, restoration, bonds, **Util 36.401 et seq.**

STRANDED COSTS
Definitions, electricity, competition, recovery, **Util 39.251**

STRANDED INVESTMENT
Definitions, electric cooperative corporations, competition, **Util 41.002**

STREET CARS
Street Railroads, generally, this index

STREET RAILROADS
Easements, public utilities, right of way, eminent domain, **Util 186.051 et seq.**
Eminent domain, public utilities, easements, right of way, **Util 186.051 et seq.**
Public utilities, right of way, easements, eminent domain, **Util 186.051 et seq.**
Right of way, public utilities, easements, eminent domain, **Util 186.051 et seq.**

STREETS AND ALLEYS
See, also, Highways and Roads, generally, this index
Cable television, easements, **Util 181.101 et seq.**
Easements, public utilities, municipal franchises, fees, **Util 14.008**
Electricity, easements, **Util 181.042 et seq.**
Gas utilities,
Casements, **Util 181.006, 181.022 et seq.**
Easements, **Util 181.005**
Municipal franchises, **Util 103.002**
Relocation, surcharge, **Util 104.112**
Public utilities, municipal franchises, fees, **Util 14.008**
Telecommunications, easements, **Util 181.082**

STRIKES
Labor Disputes, generally, this index

STUDENTS
Colleges and Universities, generally, this index
Schools and School Districts, generally, this index

STUDIES
Telecommunications, pricing, cost studies, local exchange companies, **Util 60.102**

SUBDIVISIONS
Political Subdivisions, generally, this index

SUBMETERING
Mobile Homes and Mobile Home Parks, this index

SUBORDINATE LODGES
Independent Order of Odd Fellows, this index

SUBPOENA DUCES TECUM
Production of Books and Papers, generally, this index

SUBPOENAS
Gas utilities, contempt, **Util 105.022**
Public Utilities, this index
Public utility commission, **Util 14.051**

SUBSCRIPTIONS
Shares and shareholders. Corporations, this index

SUBSIDIARIES
Corporations, this index
Foreign Corporations, this index

SUCCESSOR UTILITIES
Definitions, telecommunications, **Util 54.301**

SUFFRAGE
Elections, generally, this index

SUITS
Actions and Proceedings, generally, this index

SUNSET ACT
Electricity, customer choice, independent organizations, **Util 39.151**
Public utility commission, **Util 12.005**
Public utility counsel office, **Util 13.002**

SUPERSEDEAS OR STAY
Corporations, this index
Foreign Corporations, this index
Gas utilities, pending appeals, **Util 105.002**
Limited Liability Companies, this index
Public utilities,
  Appeal and review, **Util 15.004**
  Fines and penalties, judicial review, **Util 15.025**

SUPPLIERS
Definitions, gas utilities, pipes and pipelines, school buildings and grounds, tests, **Util 121.501**

SUPREME COURT
Audits and auditors, nonprofit corporations, **Bus Org 22.356**
Books and papers, nonprofit corporations, audits and auditors, **Bus Org 22.356**
Courts of Appeals, generally, this index
Nonprofit corporations, audits and auditors, **Bus Org 22.356**
Records and recordation, nonprofit corporations, audits and auditors, **Bus Org 22.356**

SURETIES AND SURETYSHIP
Bonds (Officers and Fiduciaries), generally, this index

SURETY BONDS
Bonds (Officers and Fiduciaries), generally, this index

SURGEONS
Physicians and Surgeons, generally, this index

SURPLUS
Business development corporations, **Bus Org 23.069**
Corporations, this index
Foreign Corporations, this index
Real Estate Investment Trusts, this index

SWITCHED ACCESS SERVICE
Telecommunications, this index

TAKING PROPERTY
Eminent Domain, generally, this index

TARIFFS
Electricity, this index

TAX ASSESSMENTS
Electricity, private and public entities, cooperation, **Util 163.015**
Exemptions. Tax Exemptions, generally, this index

TAX EXEMPTIONS
Cooperative associations, **Bus Org 251.451**
Electric Cooperative Corporations, this index
Electricity, this index
River authorities, electricity, **Util 40.104**
Telephone cooperative corporations, **Util 162.062**

TAXATION
Cooperative Associations, this index
Corporations, this index
Electricity, this index
Exemptions. Tax Exemptions, generally, this index
Foreign Corporations, this index
Franchise Taxes, generally, this index
Gas Utilities, this index
Limited Liability Companies, this index
Limited partnerships. Partnerships, this index
Nonprofit Corporations, this index
Partnerships, this index
Pipes and pipelines. Gas Utilities, this index
Professional Associations and Societies, this index
Professional Corporations, this index
Real estate investment trusts, application of law, **Bus Org 200.503**
River Authorities, this index

TECHNOLOGY
Public utilities, office of public utility counsel, **Util 13.006**

TELECOMMUNICATIONS
  See, also,
    Electronic Communications, generally, this index
    Public Utilities, generally, this index
  Generally, **Util 51.001 et seq., 181.061 et seq.**
Abandonment, successor utilities, termination of service, providers of last resort, **Util 54.304**
Access,
  Numbers and numbering, **Util 60.207**
  Right of way, **Util 60.208**
  Services, **Util 60.210**
Access to services, nondominant carriers, **Util 52.102, 52.105**
Accounts and accounting,
  Certificates of operating authority, holders, **Util 52.153**
  Depreciation, rates, **Util 52.252**
  Goods, wares and merchandise, sales, rates, **Util 52.253**
  Rates and charges,
    Examinations, **Util 52.255**
    Separation, computation of rates, **Util 53.055**
Actions and proceedings,
  Pay telephones, fines and penalties, providers, **Util 15.028**
  Providers of last resort, bankruptcy, **Util 54.305**
  Successor utilities, termination of service, providers of last resort, **Util 54.303, 54.304**
  Telegraph connections, recovery of penalties, **Util 181.065**
Adjustments, universal service fund, **Util 56.031**
  Small and rural incumbent local exchange companies, **Util 56.032**
Administration of law,
  Public utility commission, **Util 52.002**
  Universal service fund, **Util 56.023**
Advanced services, **Util 55.014**
  Television and radio, **Util 62.003**
Advertisements,
  Automated dial announcing devices, contents, **Util 55.127**
  Computation of rates, expenses, **Util 53.062**
Advisory committees, statewide relay access service, hearing and speech impaired persons, **Util 56.110 et seq.**
Affidavits, universal service fund, **Util 56.030**
Affiliates,
  Certificates of convenience and necessity, **Util 54.102**
  Certificates of operating authority, **Util 54.102**
  Income tax, consolidated returns, computation of rates, **Util 53.060**

TELECOMMUNICATIONS—Cont'd
Affiliates—Cont'd
Markets and marketing, local exchange service, joint marketing, **Util 60.164**
Rates and charges,
Local exchange service, **Util 60.165**
Payment, **Util 53.058**
Rules and regulations, local exchange service, **Util 60.165**
Aged Persons, this index
Agreements. Contracts, generally, post
Alternative dispute resolution,
Competition, safeguards, **Util 60.003**
Directories, providers, **Util 55.201**
Interconnection, rates, **Util 60.126**
Amortization, computation of rates, **Util 53.056**
Anticompetitive practices. Deceptive trade practices and consumer protection, generally, post
Appeal and review,
Automated dial announcing devices, penalties, **Util 55.137**
Municipalities, orders, **Util 51.008**
Rates and charges, small incumbent local exchange companies, **Util 53.306**
Telegraph connections, penalties, **Util 181.066**
Application of law, **Util 51.003**
Basic network services, incentives, **Util 58.052**
Broadcaster safeguards, **Util 62.001**
Bulletin board systems, competition, safeguards, **Util 60.006**
Caller identification service, **Util 55.102**
Certificates of operating authority, holders, **Util 52.151**
Code of conduct, **Util 60.202**
Competition, safeguards,
Large incumbent local exchange companies, **Util 60.005**
Small incumbent local exchange companies, **Util 60.004**
Incentives, election, **Util 58.022, 59.021**
Incumbent local exchange companies, **Util 52.052**
Interconnection, **Util 60.123**
Nondominant carriers, **Util 52.101**
Operators, **Util 55.082**
Providers of last resort, **Util 54.3015**
Rates and charges, post
Resales, rates, **Util 60.045**
Small incumbent local exchange companies, rates, **Util 53.302, 53.303**
Armed suspects, services, control, **Util 186.021**
Assessments,
Incumbent local exchange companies, administration fees, **Util 52.060**
Public utility commission, **Util 16.001**
Rates and charges, generally, post
Small incumbent local exchange companies, **Util 53.308**

TELECOMMUNICATIONS—Cont'd
Assessments—Cont'd
Statewide relay access service, hearing and speech impaired persons, **Util 56.106**
Underground facilities, notification corporation, excavations, **Util 251.062**
Universal service fund, **Util 56.022, 56.023**
Assignments, transfers of certificates, **Util 54.255**
Attorney fees, mobile telephones, directories, publication, **Util 64.203**
Audio newspapers, blind persons, universal service fund, **Util 56.301**
Audits and auditors, small incumbent local exchange companies, **Util 53.252**
Automated dial announcing devices, **Util 55.121 et seq.**
Appeal and review, penalties, **Util 55.137**
Collections, **Util 55.127**
Time, **Util 55.125**
Complaints, **Util 55.134**
Contents, **Util 55.127**
Crimes and offenses, **Util 55.138**
Disconnection, time, **Util 55.126**
Duration, message, **Util 55.128**
Exemptions, **Util 55.122**
Fees, permits, **Util 55.130, 55.131**
Fines and penalties, **Util 55.137, 55.138**
Forms, permit applications, **Util 55.130**
Hearings, penalties, **Util 55.137**
Identification, message, **Util 55.127**
Investigations, complaints, **Util 55.134**
Licenses and permits, **Util 55.129 et seq.**
Applications, **Util 55.130**
Fees, **Util 55.131**
Revocation, **Util 55.135**
Local exchange service, notice, **Util 55.133**
Notice,
Local exchange companies, **Util 55.133**
Permitholders, changes, **Util 55.132**
Termination of service, violations, **Util 55.136**
Use, **Util 55.123**
Parity, **Util 60.207**
Pay per call information services, solicitations, rates, **Util 55.127**
Random dialing, **Util 55.124**
Sequential dialing, **Util 55.124**
Termination of service, violations, **Util 55.136**
Time, **Util 55.128**
Disconnection, **Util 55.126**
Hours, **Util 55.125**
Permits, expiration, **Util 55.130**
Availability of service, nondominant carriers, **Util 52.109**
Ballots, expanded toll free local calling areas, **Util 55.047**
Bankruptcy, providers of last resort, termination of service, notice, **Util 54.305**

TELECOMMUNICATIONS—Cont'd
Basic local service, **Util 51.002, 54.251**
Allocations, payment, **Util 55.012, 55.013**
Bundling, long distance service, **Util 55.016**
Certificates and certification, **Util 54.001**
Payment, allocations, **Util 55.012, 55.013**
Providers of last resort, termination of service, **Util 54.301 et seq.**
Universal service fund, **Util 56.023, 56.251 et seq.**
Rates and charges, generally, post
Small incumbent local exchange companies, rate changes, **Util 53.301**
Termination of service, generally, post
Toll blocking, **Util 55.013**
Basic network services, incentives, **Util 58.023, 58.024, 58.051 et seq.**
Bids and bidding, statewide relay access service, hearing and speech impaired persons, **Util 56.108**
Billing. Collections, generally, post
Blind persons, audio newspapers, universal service fund, **Util 56.301**
Blocking, caller identification service, **Util 55.105 et seq.**
Reports, failures, **Util 55.110**
Boards and Commissions, this index
Bonds (officers and fiduciaries), rate changes, pending final determination, **Util 53.110**
BPL, broadband over power lines, **Util 43.001 et seq.**
Brands, marks and labels, underground facilities,
Crimes and offenses, excavations, **Util 251.203**
Excavations, **Util 251.157, 251.158**
Broadband digital special access services, private network services, rates and charges, **Util 58.261**
Broadband over power lines, **Util 43.001 et seq.**
Bulletin board systems, competition, safeguards, application of law, **Util 60.006**
Bundling,
Basic local service, long distance service, **Util 55.016**
Competition, safeguards, **Util 60.021 et seq.**
Burden of proof,
Nondominant carriers, violations, **Util 52.110**
Rates and charges, changes, **Util 53.006**
Business purpose, pricing flexibility, **Util 51.004**
Cable Television, generally, this index
Call forwarding, number portability, interim measures, **Util 60.083**
Call router system, underground facilities, contracts, notification corporation, excavations, **Util 251.061**

TELECOMMUNICATIONS—Cont'd
Caller ID consumer education panel, **Util 55.109**
Caller identification service, **Util 55.101 et seq.**
  Application of law, **Util 55.102**
  Authorization, providing service, **Util 55.103**
  Blocking, **Util 55.105 et seq.**
    Reports, failures, **Util 55.110**
  Commercial use, **Util 55.104**
  Education, **Util 55.109**
  Limitations, blocking, **Util 55.107**
  Per call blocking, **Util 55.105**
  Per line blocking, **Util 55.106**
  Reports, failures, **Util 55.110**
  Rural area, **Util 55.014**
  Use of information, commercial purposes, **Util 55.104**
Calling cards. Credit cards, generally, post
Cellular telephones. Wireless telecommunications, generally, post
Certificates and certification, **Util 54.001 et seq.**
  Amendments, **Util 54.008**
  Applications, **Util 54.005**
    Convenience and necessity, **Util 54.053**
  Assignments, transfers of certificates, **Util 54.255**
  Certificates of operating authority, generally, post
  Contracts, **Util 54.256**
  Convenience and necessity, **Util 54.051 et seq.**
  Deceptive trade practices and consumer protection, **Util 17.051 et seq., 64.051 et seq.**
  Denial, convenience and necessity, **Util 54.054**
  Exemptions, **Util 54.002, 54.003**
  Flexibility plans, incumbent local exchange companies, **Util 54.007**
  Hearings, applications, **Util 54.005**
  Interexchange service, exemptions, **Util 54.003**
  Interference, other utilities, **Util 54.257**
  Issuance, convenience and necessity, **Util 54.054**
  Leases, transfers of certificates, **Util 54.255**
  Maps, **Util 54.258**
  Minimum services, **Util 55.007**
  Municipalities, **Util 54.201 et seq.**
  Notice, hearings, applications, **Util 54.005**
  Operating authority. Certificates of operating authority, generally, post
  Orders, preliminary orders, **Util 54.006**
  Preliminary orders, **Util 54.006**
  Refusal of service, prohibited service, **Util 54.254**
  Relinquishment, certificates of authority, **Util 54.004**
  Requirement, convenience and necessity, **Util 54.052**

TELECOMMUNICATIONS—Cont'd
Certificates and certification—Cont'd
  Revocation, **Util 54.008**
    Unauthorized charges, **Util 17.156, 64.156**
  Sales, transfers of certificates, **Util 54.255**
  Standards, convenience and necessity, **Util 54.054**
  Switching carriers, suspension or revocation, **Util 55.306**
  Termination of service, **Util 54.252, 54.253**
  Transfers of certificates, **Util 54.255**
  Types, **Util 54.001**
Certificates of convenience and necessity, **Util 54.051 et seq.**
  Affiliates, **Util 54.102**
  Providers of last resort, relief, **Util 54.302**
  Uncertificated areas, **Util 56.201 et seq.**
Certificates of operating authority, **Util 52.151 et seq., 54.101 et seq.**
  Accounts and accounting, **Util 52.153**
  Affiliates, **Util 54.102**
  Amendments, **Util 54.008**
  Applications, **Util 54.005, 54.102**
    Service providers, **Util 54.154**
  Assignments, **Util 54.255**
  Denial, **Util 54.103**
    Service providers, **Util 54.155**
  Deregulation, **Util 52.201 et seq.**
    Incumbent local exchange companies, **Util 65.101, 65.102**
  Discrimination, **Util 52.154**
  Dual certificates, service providers, **Util 54.152**
  Eligibility, service providers, **Util 54.153**
  Expanded local calling services, service providers, **Util 54.157**
  Extended area service, service providers, **Util 54.157**
  Feature service, service providers, rates, **Util 54.156**
  Fines and penalties, **Util 54.105**
  Flexibility plans, incumbent local exchange companies, **Util 54.007**
  Hearings, applications, **Util 54.005**
  Incumbent local exchange companies, deregulation, **Util 65.101, 65.102**
  Interference, service providers, local exchange services, **Util 54.158**
  IntraLATA service, **Util 55.009**
  Issuance, **Util 54.103**
    Service providers, **Util 54.155**
  Jurisdiction, **Util 52.152**
  Local exchange service, incumbent local exchange companies, deregulation, **Util 65.101, 65.102**
  Municipalities, **Util 54.201 et seq.**
  Notice, hearings, applications, **Util 54.005**
  Orders, preliminary orders, **Util 54.006**
  Preliminary orders, **Util 54.006**
  Records and recordation, **Util 52.153**
  Refusal of service, **Util 54.254**
  Relinquishment, **Util 54.004**

TELECOMMUNICATIONS—Cont'd
Certificates of operating authority —Cont'd
  Requirement, **Util 54.001**
  Resales, service providers, **Util 54.156 et seq.**
  Retention, local exchange service, resales, **Util 54.159**
  Revocation, **Util 54.008, 54.105**
  Service providers, **Util 54.151 et seq.**
  Services, providing, **Util 54.251 et seq.**
  Standards,
    Issuance, **Util 54.103**
    Service providers, **Util 54.154, 54.155**
  Time, service, **Util 54.104**
  Transfers of certificates, **Util 54.255**
Cessation of service. Termination of service, generally, post
Changes,
  Rates and charges, post
  Switching carriers, generally, post
Charges. Rates and charges, generally, post
Classification,
  Incentives, services, **Util 58.023, 58.024**
  Unbundling of services, assignments, **Util 60.023**
Clearance, construction standards, **Util 181.089**
Cocarriage reciprocity, certificates of operating authority, holders, **Util 52.152**
Code of conduct, **Util 60.201 et seq.**
Coin operated telephones. Pay telephones, generally, post
Collect calls, pay telephones, charges, **Util 55.175**
Collections, **Util 55.016**
  Automated dial announcing devices, ante
  Deceptive trade practices and consumer protection, **Util 17.001 et seq., 64.001 et seq.**
  Interexchange service, local exchange service, notice, **Util 55.011**
  Local exchange service, interexchange service, notice, **Util 55.011**
  Statewide relay access service, hearing and speech impaired persons, **Util 56.104**
  Switching carriers, unauthorized changes, **Util 55.304**
  Universal service fund, assessments, **Util 56.023**
Colleges and Universities, this index
Commercial mobile service. Wireless telecommunications, generally, post
Community supervision, nine hundred (900) information service, charges, **Util 55.252**
Compensation and salaries,
  Reciprocal compensation, **Util 60.209**
  Statewide relay access service, hearing and speech impaired persons,
    Advisory committee, **Util 56.113**
    Carriers, **Util 56.109**
  Switching carriers, unauthorized changes, **Util 55.304**

TELECOMMUNICATIONS—Cont'd
Competition,
Deregulation, generally, post
Pricing, **Util 60.101, 60.102**
Public policy, **Util 51.001**
Safeguards, **Util 60.001 et seq.**
Providers of last resort, **Util 54.303**
Complaints,
Automated dial announcing devices, **Util 55.134**
Incentives, **Util 58.025 et seq., 59.026 et seq.**
New services,
Incentive regulation, rates and charges, **Util 59.030**
Rates and charges, local exchange service, **Util 52.0583**
Nonbasic services, incentive regulation, new services, rates and charges, **Util 58.153**
Nondominant carriers, burden of proof, **Util 52.110**
Operators, **Util 55.089**
Private network services, educational and medical entities, **Util 58.264, 59.079**
Rates and charges, post
Small incumbent local exchange companies, review, rates and charges, **Util 53.306**
Condemnation, certificates of operating authority, holders, **Util 52.152**
Conduct, **Util 60.201 et seq.**
Confidential or privileged information,
Deregulation,
Incumbent local exchange companies, **Util 65.004**
Reports, **Util 52.207**
Statewide relay access service, hearing and speech impaired persons, bids, **Util 56.108**
Universal service fund, assessments, **Util 56.024**
Conflict of laws,
Broadband over power lines, **Util 43.002**
Distance learning and advanced services, **Util 57.001**
Universal services, **Util 56.002**
Connections services, telegraph companies, **Util 181.062 et seq.**
Consent, mobile telephones, directories, **Util 64.202**
Consolidation and merger, **Util 181.088**
Construction,
Aid to construction, rates and charges, **Util 56.210**
Standards, municipal ordinances, **Util 181.089**
Works in progress, computation of rates, **Util 53.054**
Consumer protection. Deceptive trade practices and consumer protection, generally, post
Contested cases, successor utilities, termination of service, providers of last resort, **Util 54.303**

TELECOMMUNICATIONS—Cont'd
Contiguous areas, expansion, tollfree calling areas, **Util 55.042**
Contracts,
Certificates and certification, **Util 54.256**
Customer specific contracts, incentive regulation, **Util 58.003**
Easements, exclusive rights, telegraph utilities, **Util 181.085**
Hearing impaired persons, relay access service, special features, **Util 56.1085**
Incentive regulation, customer specific contracts, **Util 58.003**
Incentives, election, **Util 58.021**
Incumbent local exchange companies, customers, contracts, **Util 52.056**
Interconnection, rates, **Util 60.125**
Landlord and tenant, shared tenants, **Util 54.261**
Operators, access, **Util 55.087**
Private network services, educational and medical entities, **Util 58.255, 59.074**
Relay access service, hearing impaired persons, special features, **Util 56.1085**
Shared tenants, **Util 54.261**
Special features, relay access service, hearing impaired persons, **Util 56.1085**
Speech impairment, relay access service, special features, **Util 56.1085**
Statewide relay access service, hearing and speech impaired persons, **Util 56.108**
Underground facilities, toll free numbers, notification corporation, excavations, **Util 251.061**
Convenience and necessity, certificates of, **Util 54.051 et seq.**
Conversion, incentives, elections, **Util 59.023**
Cooperation, incumbent local exchange companies, infrastructure sharing, **Util 60.163**
Cooperative corporations. Telephone Cooperative Corporations, generally, this index
Corrective action, switching carriers, **Util 55.305**
Costs, recovery. Expenses and expenditures, generally, post
Credit cards,
Fraud, **Util 186.032**
Pay telephones, charges, **Util 55.175, 55.177**
Prepaid calling services, **Util 55.253**
Credit reports,
Deceptive trade practices and consumer protection, payment, **Util 17.009**
Unauthorized charges, nonpayment, **Util 17.152, 64.152**
Crimes and offenses,
Automated dial announcing devices, **Util 55.138**

TELECOMMUNICATIONS—Cont'd
Crimes and offenses—Cont'd
Customers deposits, **Util 183.006**
Deceptive trade practices and consumer protection, generally, post
Directories, emergency calls, notice, **Util 186.045**
Emergency calls, obstruction, **Util 186.042**
Fraud, generally, post
Theft, fraud, **Util 186.032**
Underground facilities, brands, marks and labels, excavations, **Util 251.203**
Custom calling service, rural area, **Util 55.014**
Customer choice, **Util 17.101, 17.102, 64.101, 64.102**
Customer protection. Deceptive trade practices and consumer protection, generally, post
Customers, successor utilities, termination of service, providers of last resort, **Util 54.303**
Damages, underground facilities, **Util 251.001 et seq.**
Deceptive trade practices and consumer protection, **Util 17.001 et seq., 64.001 et seq.**
Certificates and certification, **Util 17.051 et seq., 64.051 et seq.**
Consent, new products or services, rates and charges, **Util 64.151 et seq.**
Credit reports,
Payment, **Util 17.009**
Unauthorized charges, nonpayment, **Util 17.152, 64.152**
Customer choice, **Util 17.101, 17.102, 64.101, 64.102**
Discounts, **Util 17.007**
Disputed charges, records and recordation, **Util 17.153, 64.153**
Fines and penalties, unauthorized charges, **Util 17.156, 64.156**
Incumbent local exchange companies, deregulation, **Util 65.005**
New products or services, rates and charges, **Util 17.151 et seq., 64.151 et seq.**
Notice, new products or services, rates and charges, **Util 17.151 et seq., 64.151 et seq.**
Payment, credit reports, **Util 17.009**
Records and recordation,
Disputed charges, **Util 17.153, 64.153**
Unauthorized charges, **Util 17.152, 64.152**
Registration, **Util 17.051 et seq., 64.051 et seq.**
Reports, **Util 17.051 et seq., 64.051 et seq.**
Standards, **Util 17.004, 64.004**
Switching carriers, **Util 17.101, 17.102, 55.307, 64.101, 64.102**

TELECOMMUNICATIONS—Cont'd
Deceptive trade practices and consumer protection—Cont'd
Termination of service, unauthorized charges, nonpayment, **Util 17.152, 64.152**
Unauthorized charges, **Util 17.151 et seq., 64.151 et seq.**
Definitions, **Util 51.002, 181.061, 181.081**
Emergencies, **Util 186.041**
Fraud, **Util 186.031**
Universal services, **Util 56.001**
Delay, incumbent local exchange companies, competition, safeguards, **Util 60.161**
Depletion, computation of rates, **Util 53.056**
Deposits, customers, **Util 183.001 et seq.**
Depreciation,
Accounts, rates, **Util 52.252**
Federal income tax, computation of rates, **Util 53.059**
Rates and charges, post
Small incumbent local exchange companies, **Util 53.252**
Deregulation, **Util 52.201 et seq.**
Incumbent local exchange companies, **Util 65.001 et seq.**
Universal service fund, **Util 56.032**
Transition, **Util 58.001 et seq., 59.001 et seq.**
Designs, statewide relay access service, hearing and speech impaired persons, **Util 56.105**
Determinations, incumbent local exchange companies, deregulation, **Util 65.051 et seq.**
Devices. Machinery and equipment, generally, post
Dialing. Automated dial announcing devices, generally, ante
Digital services,
Incentives, infrastructure, **Util 58.203 et seq., 59.052**
Minimum service, **Util 55.007**
Direct inward dialing, number portability, interim measures, **Util 60.083**
Directories, **Util 55.201 et seq.**
Assistance, **Util 55.201**
Basic local telecommunications service, **Util 51.002**
Pay telephones, charges, **Util 55.174, 55.176**
Crimes and offenses, emergency calls, notice of offenses, **Util 186.045**
Dispute resolution, providers, **Util 55.201**
Emergency calls, crimes and offenses, notice, **Util 186.044, 186.045**
Fines and penalties, emergency calls, notice of offenses, **Util 186.045**
Hearing impaired persons, financial assistance, lists, **Util 55.203**
Internet, listing, **Util 55.203, 55.204**
Legislature, listing, **Util 55.202, 55.203**
Public services, **Util 55.203**
State agencies, **Util 55.203**

TELECOMMUNICATIONS—Cont'd
Directories—Cont'd
State agencies—Cont'd
Listing, **Util 55.203**
Directors, underground facilities, notification corporation, excavations, **Util 251.055 et seq.**
Disbursements, universal service fund, **Util 56.026**
Disclosure, prepaid calling services, **Util 55.253**
Disconnection, automated dial announcing devices, time, **Util 55.126**
Discontinuation of service. Termination of service, generally, post
Discounts, **Util 51.004**
Certificates of authority, resales, local exchange service, **Util 54.156**
Deceptive trade practices and consumer protection, **Util 17.007**
Discrimination, **Util 60.203**
Certificates of operating authority, holders, rules and regulations, **Util 52.154**
Competitors, services provided to, **Util 55.006**
Incumbent local exchange companies, **Util 60.161**
Landlord and tenant, installations, **Util 54.259**
Minimum service, **Util 55.007**
Municipalities, **Util 54.204**
Rates and charges, post
Display,
Operator service, information, **Util 55.084**
Pay telephones,
Charges, **Util 55.176**
Information, **Util 55.179**
Dispute resolution. Alternative dispute resolution, generally, ante
Disputed charges. Rates and charges, post
Disruption of services, emergency calls, **Util 186.042**
Distance learning, **Util 57.021 et seq.**
Dominant carriers,
Definitions, **Util 51.002**
Minimum requirements, **Util 52.005**
Rules and regulations, **Util 52.206**
Easements, **Util 181.082 et seq.**
Eminent domain, **Util 181.083, 181.084**
Entry on property, **Util 181.083**
Identity and identification, **Util 55.017**
Exclusive contracts, telegraph utilities, **Util 181.085**
Municipalities, **Util 54.203 et seq.**
Railroads, right of way, eminent domain, **Util 186.051 et seq.**
Underground facilities, excavations, **Util 251.006**
Economic conditions, rules and regulations, markets and marketing, **Util 52.202**
Education, distance learning, **Util 57.021 et seq.**

TELECOMMUNICATIONS—Cont'd
Efficiency, return on investments, rates, **Util 53.052**
Eight hundred (800) numbers, pay telephones, charges, **Util 55.176**
Elections, this index
Electricity, customer choice, solicitations, **Util 39.1025**
Emergencies, **Util 186.041 et seq.**
Automated dial announcing devices, exemptions, **Util 55.122**
Crimes and offenses, obstruction of calls, **Util 186.042**
Fraud, party lines, **Util 186.043**
Nine One One (911), generally, this index
Notice, crimes and offenses, **Util 186.044, 186.045**
Services, control, **Util 186.021**
Successor utilities, termination of service, providers of last resort, **Util 54.304**
Underground facilities, notice, excavations, **Util 251.155**
Emergency telephone numbers. Nine One One (911), generally, this index
Eminent domain,
Certificates of operating authority, holders, **Util 52.152**
Easements, **Util 181.083, 181.084**
Railroads, right of way, **Util 186.051 et seq.**
Employees. Officers and employees, generally, post
Enrollment, lifeline service, **Util 55.015**
Entry on property,
Easements, **Util 181.083**
Identity and identification, **Util 55.017**
Landlord and tenant, installations, **Util 54.259, 54.260**
Equipment. Machinery and equipment, generally, post
Evaluation, incentives, reports, **Util 59.054**
Evidence,
Aged persons, delay in payment, proof of age, **Util 182.004**
Competition, safeguards, proceedings, **Util 60.003**
Excavations, underground facilities, **Util 251.001 et seq.**
Exchange service,
IntraLATA service, **Util 55.009**
Local exchange service, generally, post
Splitting, expansion, tollfree calling areas, **Util 55.043**
Telegraph companies, **Util 181.062 et seq.**
Exclusive contracts, easements, telegraph utilities, **Util 181.085**
Exclusive jurisdiction,
Competition, safeguards, **Util 60.002**
Public utility commission, **Util 52.002**
Exemptions,
Aged persons, delay in payment, **Util 182.005**

TELECOMMUNICATIONS—Cont'd
Exemptions—Cont'd
Automated dial announcing devices, **Util 55.122**
Caller identification service, **Util 55.102**
Certificates and certification, **Util 54.002, 54.003**
Expanded toll free calling areas, **Util 55.049**
Local areas, **Util 55.044**
Extended area service, **Util 55.026**
Imputation, prices, local exchange companies, **Util 60.062**
Nondominant carriers, **Util 52.111**
Pay telephone services, registration, **Util 55.173**
Rates and charges, incumbent local exchange companies, deregulation, transitioning companies, **Util 65.154**
Telegraph connections, **Util 181.063**
Underground facilities, notice, excavations, **Util 251.156**
Exiting utilities, providers of last resort, **Util 54.301 et seq.**
Expanded interconnection services, **Util 60.141, 60.162**
Private network services, educational and medical entities, **Util 58.262**
Expanded local calling services, certificates of authority, **Util 54.157**
Expanded toll free local calling areas, **Util 55.041 et seq.**
Expedited proceedings, successor utilities, termination of service, providers of last resort, **Util 54.304**
Expenses and expenditures,
Imputation, prices, cost recovery, **Util 60.064**
Landlord and tenant, installations, **Util 54.260**
Statewide relay access service, hearing and speech impaired persons, **Util 56.105**
Advisory committee, **Util 56.112, 56.113**
Successor utilities, termination of service, providers of last resort, **Util 56.251 et seq.**
Telegraph connections, allocation, **Util 181.064**
Uncertificated areas, recovery, **Util 56.209**
Underground facilities, notification corporation, excavations, **Util 251.054**
Experimental services, incumbent local exchange companies, **Util 52.058**
Extended area service, **Util 55.021 et seq.**
Service providers, certificates of authority, **Util 54.157**
Extensions of service,
Certificates and certification, **Util 54.002**
Expanded toll free calling areas, **Util 55.041 et seq.**
Interference, other utilities, **Util 54.257**

TELECOMMUNICATIONS—Cont'd
Extensions of service—Cont'd
Landlord and tenant, installations, **Util 54.259 et seq.**
Nondominant carriers, **Util 52.109**
Feature service, certificates of authority, local exchange service, **Util 54.156**
Federal law, unbundling of services, **Util 60.021**
Fees,
Automated dial announcing devices, permits, **Util 55.130, 55.131**
Hearing impaired persons, vouchers, machinery and equipment, **Util 56.153**
Incumbent local exchange companies, administration, **Util 52.060**
Municipalities, **Util 54.204 et seq.**
Bills and billing, **Util 51.009**
Railroads, right of way, use, **Util 186.058**
Rates and charges, generally, post
Small incumbent local exchange companies, regulation, **Util 53.308**
Underground facilities, post
Fiber optics,
Infrastructure, incentives, **Util 58.204**
Leases, cable facilities, **Util 54.2025**
Filing,
Rates and charges, post
Rules and regulations, standards of service, **Util 55.003**
Financial assistance, hearing impaired persons, machinery and equipment, **Util 56.151 et seq.**
Fines and penalties,
Automated dial announcing devices, **Util 55.137, 55.138**
Certificates of operating authority, **Util 54.105**
Customers deposits, **Util 183.006**
Directories,
Emergency calls, notice of offenses, **Util 186.045**
Mobile telephones, publication, **Util 64.203**
Emergency calls, obstruction, **Util 186.042**
Fraud, **Util 186.032**
Emergency calls, **Util 186.043**
Mobile telephones, directories, publication, **Util 64.203**
Pay telephones,
Providers, **Util 15.028**
Reception, notice, **Util 55.178**
Prepaid calling services, **Util 55.253**
Rates and charges, post
Switching carriers, **Util 55.305**
Telegraph connections, **Util 181.065**
Unauthorized charges, **Util 17.156, 64.156**
Underground facilities, excavations, **Util 251.201 et seq.**
Flexibility plans,
Incumbent local exchange companies, **Util 54.007**
Rates and charges, post

TELECOMMUNICATIONS—Cont'd
Foreign states,
Cooperation, regulatory authorities, **Util 52.003**
Telegraph lines, **Util 181.086**
Forms,
Automated dial announcing devices,
Permit applications, **Util 55.130**
Solicitations, **Util 55.127**
Expanded toll free local calling areas, petitions, **Util 55.046**
Incentives, basic network services, notice, rates and charges, **Util 58.059**
Notice of intent, rate changes, **Util 53.103, 53.305**
Statements of intent, rate changes, **Util 53.102, 53.304**
Franchises, municipalities, discrimination, **Util 54.204**
Fraud, **Util 186.031 et seq.**
Deceptive trade practices and consumer protection, generally, ante
Emergency calls, party lines, **Util 186.043**
Switching carriers, **Util 55.307**
Underground facilities, emergencies, excavations, **Util 251.155**
Fines and penalties, **Util 251.201**
Fugitives, services, control, **Util 186.021**
Funds,
Statewide relay access service, hearing and speech impaired persons, **Util 56.104, 56.106, 56.107**
Universal service fund, **Util 56.021 et seq.**
Gas utilities, pipes and pipelines, right of way, **Util 121.201**
Geographic markets, deregulation, **Util 52.201 et seq.**
Gifts, computation of rates, expenses, **Util 53.061**
Handicapped persons,
Financial assistance, machinery and equipment, **Util 56.151 et seq.**
Hearing and speech impaired persons, statewide relay access service, **Util 56.101 et seq.**
Lifeline service, **Util 55.015**
Public policy, **Util 51.001**
Termination of service, **Util 14.005**
Hearing impaired persons,
Financial assistance, machinery and equipment, **Util 56.151 et seq.**
Statewide relay access service, **Util 56.101 et seq.**
Hearings,
Automated dial announcing devices, penalties, **Util 55.137**
Burden of proof, nondominant carriers, violations, **Util 52.110**
Certificates and certification, applications, **Util 54.005**
Deregulation, **Util 52.201, 52.205**
Expanded toll free local calling areas, **Util 55.047**
Extended area service, orders, **Util 55.021**

TELECOMMUNICATIONS—Cont'd
Hearings—Cont'd
Improvements, orders, **Util 55.008**
Incentives, complaints, **Util 58.025, 59.026**
Incumbent local exchange companies, competition, **Util 52.055**
Local exchange service, rule changes, **Util 55.004**
Loop resale tariffs, **Util 60.041**
Markets and marketing, **Util 52.004**
Nondominant carriers, **Util 52.107 et seq.**
Investigations, **Util 52.102, 52.104**
Operators, investigations, violations, **Util 55.089**
Rates and charges, post
Rules and regulations, standards, **Util 55.002**
Telegraph connections, **Util 181.064**
Unbundling of services, orders, **Util 60.022**
Uncertificated areas, **Util 56.205**
Universal service fund, adjustments, **Util 56.031**
Highways and Roads, this index
Historically underutilized businesses, contracts, **Util 52.256**
History, credit reports, payment, **Util 17.009**
Hospitals, this index
Hostages, services, control, **Util 186.021**
Hotels and Motels, this index
Hunting services, extended area service, **Util 55.025**
Identity and identification,
Automatic dial announcing devices, contents, **Util 55.127**
Caller identification service, generally, ante
Entry on property, **Util 55.017**
Impairment or interruption, **Util 60.203**
Improvements, orders, **Util 55.008**
Imputation, prices, local exchange companies, **Util 60.061 et seq.**
Incentives, **Util 58.001 et seq., 59.001 et seq.**
Income, computation of rates, **Util 53.057**
Income tax, **Util 53.059**
Rates and charges, consolidated returns, **Util 53.060**
Incumbent local exchange companies, **Util 51.002, 52.051 et seq.**
Deregulation, **Util 52.201 et seq.**
Universal service fund, **Util 56.032**
Local exchange service, generally, post
Rates and charges, post
Information service, operator service, display, **Util 55.084**
Information sharing services, distance learning, **Util 57.021 et seq.**
Infrastructure, investments, incentives, **Util 58.201 et seq., 59.051 et seq.**
Injunctions, mobile telephones, directories, publication, **Util 64.203**
Insurance, this index

TELECOMMUNICATIONS—Cont'd
Interactive multimedia communications, **Util 57.071, 57.072**
Interconnection service, **Util 60.121 et seq., 60.204**
Cooperative corporations, **Util 162.122, 162.123**
Expanded interconnections, **Util 60.141, 60.162**
Incentive regulation, **Util 58.155**
Nonbasic services, incentive regulation, **Util 58.155**
Private network services, educational and medical entities, **Util 58.262, 58.265, 59.080**
Telegraph connections, **Util 181.062 et seq.**
Interest, customers deposits, **Util 183.002 et seq.**
Interexchange service,
Billing, local exchange service, notice, **Util 55.011**
Certificates and certification, exemptions, **Util 54.003**
Collections, local exchange service, notice, **Util 55.011**
Local exchange service, billing, notice, **Util 55.011**
Message services, nondominant carriers, **Util 52.108**
Minimum service, **Util 55.007**
Nondominant carriers,
Predatory practices, **Util 52.107**
Registration, **Util 52.103**
Notice, local exchange service, billing, **Util 55.011**
Rates and charges, incumbent local exchange companies, **Util 53.065**
Switching carriers, generally, post
Interference,
Certificates of authority, resales, local exchange services, **Util 54.158**
Construction, other utilities, **Util 54.257**
Landlord and tenant, installations, **Util 54.259**
Internet, generally, this index
Interruption of service, emergencies, **Util 186.021, 186.042**
Intervention, providers of last resort, bankruptcy, **Util 54.305**
IntraLATA service, **Util 55.009, 58.260**
Private network services, educational and medical entities, rates, **Util 58.259**
Universal service fund, reimbursement, **Util 56.028**
Intrastate switched access rates, **Util 52.112, 52.155**
Investigations and investigators,
Automated dial announcing devices, complaints, **Util 55.134**
Deregulation, competition, **Util 52.205**
Nondominant carriers, **Util 52.102, 52.104**
Operator service, violations, **Util 55.089**
Rates and charges, nonproducing utilities, **Util 53.152**

TELECOMMUNICATIONS—Cont'd
Investments,
Incentives, **Util 58.201 et seq., 59.051 et seq.**
Basic network services, **Util 58.053**
Limitations, incentives, **Util 59.029**
Rates and charges, returns, **Util 53.051 et seq.**
Joint action, telegraph utilities, **Util 181.087**
Joint marketing, local exchange service, affiliates, **Util 60.164**
Jurisdiction,
Certificates of operating authority, holders, **Util 52.152**
Competition, safeguards, **Util 60.002**
Interconnection, **Util 60.122 et seq.**
Nondominant carriers, **Util 52.102**
Public utility commission, **Util 52.001 et seq.**
Labor and employment, diversity, **Util 52.256**
Landlord and tenant, installations, **Util 54.259 et seq.**
Leases,
Certificates and certification, transfers, **Util 54.255**
Fiber optics, cable facilities, **Util 54.2025**
Investigations and investigators, orders, **Util 14.101, 51.010**
Merchandise, computation of rates, **Util 53.063**
Telegraph lines, **Util 181.087**
Legislative advocacy, computation of rates, expenses, **Util 53.061, 53.062**
Legislature, this index
Libraries, this index
Licenses and permits,
Automated dial announcing devices, ante
Railroads, right of way, use, **Util 186.058**
Underground facilities, excavations, **Util 251.006**
Lifeline service, **Util 55.015**
Discounts, deceptive trade practices and consumer protection, **Util 17.007**
Live operators, access, **Util 55.088**
Local access and transport area service. Local exchange service, generally, post
Local exchange service, **Util 51.002**
Adjustments, universal service fund, **Util 56.031**
Automated dial announcing devices, notice, **Util 55.133**
Basic local service, generally, ante
Bills and billing, **Util 55.016**
Interexchange service, notice, **Util 55.011**
Certificates and certification, **Util 54.001**
Flexibility plans, **Util 54.007**
Certificates of authority, resales, **Util 54.156 et seq.**

TELECOMMUNICATIONS—Cont'd
Local exchange service—Cont'd
Certificates of operating authority,
Incumbent local exchange companies, deregulation, **Util 65.101, 65.102**
Standards, issuance, **Util 54.103**
Collections, **Util 55.016**
Interexchange service, notice, **Util 55.011**
Competition, safeguards, **Util 60.161 et seq.**
Incumbent local exchange companies, **Util 60.001 et seq.**
Confidential or privileged information, incumbent local exchange companies, deregulation, **Util 65.004**
Consumer protection, incumbent local exchange companies, deregulation, **Util 65.005**
Deregulation, **Util 52.201 et seq.**
Incumbent local exchange companies, **Util 65.001 et seq.**
Determinations, incumbent local exchange companies, deregulation, **Util 65.051 et seq.**
Directories, **Util 55.201 et seq.**
Elections, incumbent local exchange companies, deregulation, **Util 65.053**
Expanded interconnections, **Util 60.141, 60.162**
Expanded toll free local calling areas, **Util 55.041 et seq.**
Extended area service, **Util 55.021 et seq.**
Feature service, certificates of authority, rates, **Util 54.156**
Hearings, rule changes, **Util 55.004**
Hunting services, extended area service, **Util 55.025**
Imputation, prices, **Util 60.061 et seq.**
Incentives, **Util 58.001 et seq., 59.001 et seq.**
Incumbent local exchange companies, **Util 51.002, 52.051 et seq.**
Deregulation, **Util 65.001 et seq.**
Infrastructure sharing, **Util 60.163**
Interconnection, **Util 60.121**
Interexchange service, billing, notice, **Util 55.011**
Interference, certificates of authority, resales, **Util 54.158**
IntraLATA service, **Util 55.009**
Lifeline service, **Util 55.015**
Markets and marketing, affiliates, joint marketing, **Util 60.164**
Minimum service, **Util 55.007**
New services, **Util 52.058, 52.0583**
Nondominant carriers, **Util 52.102, 52.105, 52.106**
Notice, interexchange service, billing, **Util 55.011**
Operators, access, **Util 55.086, 55.087**
Packaging services, **Util 52.0584**
Promotions, **Util 52.0585**
Pay telephones, charges, **Util 55.175**

TELECOMMUNICATIONS—Cont'd
Local exchange service—Cont'd
Promotions, **Util 52.0585**
Providers of last resort, termination of service, **Util 54.301 et seq.**
Rates and charges, generally, post
Reconnection, fees, **Util 53.007**
Retention, resales, certificates of authority, **Util 54.159**
Rule changes, **Util 55.004**
Rules and regulations,
Affiliates, **Util 60.165**
Changes, **Util 55.004**
Incumbent local exchange companies, deregulation, **Util 65.003**
Small incumbent local exchange companies, **Util 53.251 et seq.**
Incentives, **Util 59.001 et seq.**
Universal service fund, adjustments, **Util 56.032**
Switching carriers, generally, post
Television and radio, **Util 62.003**
Termination of service, generally, post
Transitional incentives, **Util 58.001 et seq., 59.001 et seq.**
Transitioning companies, incumbent local exchange companies, deregulation, **Util 65.151 et seq.**
Universal service fund, **Util 56.021 et seq.**
Long distance service,
Bundling, basic local service, **Util 55.016**
Connections, local exchange service, **Util 51.002**
Distance learning, **Util 57.021 et seq.**
Lifeline service, rates and charges, nonpayment, **Util 55.015**
Nonpayment, rates and charges, basic local service,
Termination, **Util 55.013**
Termination of service, **Util 55.012**
Rates and charges, generally, post
Switching carriers, generally, post
Termination of service, generally, post
Toll blocking, **Util 55.013**
Loop resale tariffs, **Util 60.041**
Lost revenues, universal service fund, adjustments, **Util 56.025**
Machinery and equipment,
Fraud, **Util 186.032, 186.033**
Hearing impaired persons, financial assistance, **Util 56.151 et seq.**
Speech impairment, financial assistance, **Util 56.151 et seq.**
Statewide relay access service, hearing and speech impaired persons, **Util 56.102, 56.103**
Managers and management,
Application of law, **Util 51.003**
Return on investments, rates, **Util 53.052**
Mandatory extended area services, **Util 55.022**
Maps and plats, **Util 54.258**

TELECOMMUNICATIONS—Cont'd
Markets and marketing,
Affiliates, local exchange service, joint marketing, **Util 60.164**
Deregulation, **Util 52.201**
Joint marketing, local exchange service, affiliates, **Util 60.164**
Local exchange service, affiliates, joint marketing, **Util 60.164**
Separation, **Util 52.004**
Medical Care and Treatment, this index
Memorandum of understanding, lifeline service, **Util 55.015**
Merchandise,
Computation of rates, sales and leases, **Util 53.063**
Sales and leases, accounts, rates, **Util 52.253**
Merger and consolidation, **Util 181.088**
Investigations and investigators, orders, **Util 14.101, 51.010**
Minimum service, **Util 60.203**
Certificate holders, **Util 55.007**
Misleading practices. Deceptive trade practices and consumer protection, generally, ante
Mobile telephones. Wireless telecommunications, generally, post
Monitoring, statewide relay access service, hearing and speech impaired persons, advisory committee, **Util 56.111**
Moving,
Number portability, **Util 60.081 et seq.**
Reconnection, fees, **Util 53.007**
Multiple party lines. Party lines, generally, post
Municipalities, this index
Negotiation, **Util 60.206**
Interconnection, rates, **Util 60.125, 60.126**
Network service,
Interconnection, **Util 60.124**
Private network services, **Util 58.251 et seq., 59.071 et seq.**
New services,
Incentive regulation, **Util 59.030**
Incumbent local exchange companies, **Util 52.058, 52.0583**
Nonbasic services, incentive regulation, **Util 58.153**
Rates and charges, post
Newspapers, audio newspapers, blind persons, universal service fund, **Util 56.301**
Nine hundred (900) information service, community supervision, rates and charges, **Util 55.252**
Nine One One (911), generally, this index
Nonbasic services, incentive regulation, **Util 58.023, 58.024, 58.151 et seq.**
Nondominant carriers, **Util 52.101 et seq.**
Deregulation, **Util 52.201 et seq.**
Notice,
Automated dial announcing devices, ante
Bankruptcy, providers of last resort, termination of service, **Util 54.305**

TELECOMMUNICATIONS—Cont'd
Notice—Cont'd
Caller identification service, generally, ante
Certificates and certification, applications, hearings, **Util 54.005**
Emergency calls, crimes and offenses, **Util 186.044, 186.045**
Incentive regulation, elections, **Util 58.021**
New services,
Incentive regulation, **Util 59.030**
Local exchange service, **Util 52.0583**
Nonbasic services, incentive regulation, **Util 58.153**
Operators, information, display, **Util 55.084**
Packaging services, local exchange service, **Util 52.0584**
Pay telephones,
Display, rates and charges, **Util 55.176**
Reception, **Util 55.178**
Prepaid calling services, **Util 55.253**
Railroads, right of way, easements, **Util 186.054**
Rates and charges, post
Switching carriers, rules and regulations, **Util 55.302**
Termination of service, certificates of operating authority, **Util 54.253**
Underground facilities, post
Universal service fund, adjustments, **Util 56.031**
Notification center, underground facilities, excavations, **Util 251.101 et seq.**
Notification corporation, underground facilities, excavations, **Util 251.051 et seq.**
Numbers and numbering,
Access, **Util 60.207**
Fraud, **Util 186.032**
Mobile telephones, publication, **Util 64.201 et seq.**
Nine One One (911), generally, this index
Portability, **Util 60.205**
Changing locations, **Util 60.081 et seq.**
Toll free numbers, generally, post
Obstructions,
Emergency calls, **Util 186.042**
Prevention, **Util 186.001 et seq.**
Offenses. Crimes and offenses, generally, ante
Officers and employees,
Diversity, **Util 52.256**
Operators, generally, post
Small incumbent local exchange companies, reduced rates, **Util 53.307**
Statewide relay access service, hearing and speech impaired persons, advisory committee, **Util 56.112**
Underground facilities, notification corporation, excavations, **Util 251.058**

TELECOMMUNICATIONS—Cont'd
Open meetings, underground facilities, notification corporation, excavations, **Util 251.053**
Open records, underground facilities, notification corporation, excavations, **Util 251.053**
Operating authority. Certificates of operating authority, generally, ante
Operators, **Util 55.081 et seq.**
Basic local telecommunications service, **Util 51.002**
Complaints, **Util 55.089**
Investigations, violations, **Util 55.089**
Live operators, access, **Util 55.088**
Local exchange service, access, **Util 55.086, 55.087**
Pay telephones, charges, **Util 55.175, 55.177**
Rates and charges, quotations, **Util 55.085**
Optical fibers, infrastructure, incentives, **Util 58.204**
Options,
Extended area service, **Util 55.023**
Private network services, educational entities, rates, **Util 58.257, 59.076**
Orders,
Acquisition, investigations, **Util 14.101, 51.010**
Certificates and certification, preliminary orders, **Util 54.006**
Crimes and offenses, services, **Util 186.021**
Extended area service, **Util 55.021 et seq.**
Improvements, **Util 55.008**
Municipalities, judicial review, **Util 51.008**
Nondominant carriers, **Util 52.108**
Investigations, **Util 52.102, 52.104**
Predatory practices, **Util 52.107**
Rates and charges, changes, **Util 53.111, 53.151**
Successor utilities, termination of service, providers of last resort, **Util 54.304**
Telegraph connections, **Util 181.064**
Unbundling of services, **Util 60.022**
Uncertificated areas, **Util 56.207**
Original costs, return on investments, rates, **Util 53.053**
Packaging services,
Basic network service, incentive regulation, **Util 58.063**
Incentive regulation, **Util 58.004, 59.031**
Local exchange service, **Util 52.0584**
Promotions, **Util 52.0585**
Rates and charges, post
Parity, dialing, **Util 60.207**
Parole, nine hundred (900) information service, charges, **Util 55.252**
Party lines,
Emergency calls, obstruction, **Util 186.042**
Fraud, emergency calls, **Util 186.043**

TELECOMMUNICATIONS—Cont'd
Party lines—Cont'd
Notice of offenses, emergency calls, **Util 186.044, 186.045**
Pay per call information services, automated dial announcing devices, solicitations, rates, **Util 55.127**
Pay telephones, **Util 55.171 et seq.**
Access lines, rates and charges, **Util 55.1735**
Deceptive trade practices and consumer protection, **Util 17.001 et seq., 64.001 et seq.**
Expanded toll free local calling areas, exemptions, **Util 55.044**
Fines and penalties, providers, **Util 15.028**
Rates and charges, **Util 55.172 et seq.**
Universal service fund, **Util 56.022**
Payment,
Aged persons, delay, **Util 182.001 et seq.**
Credit reports, deceptive trade practices and consumer protection, **Util 17.009**
Customers, deposits, interest, **Util 183.004**
Fraud, **Util 186.032**
Underground facilities, notification center, excavations, **Util 251.106**
Universal service fund, disbursements, **Util 56.026**
Penalties. Fines and penalties, generally, ante
Petitions,
Expanded toll free local calling areas, **Util 55.045, 55.046**
Incumbent local exchange companies, deregulation, **Util 65.052**
Private network services,
Designated entities, **Util 58.253**
Educational and medical entities, **Util 59.072**
Providers of last resort, **Util 54.304**
Relief, **Util 54.302**
Uncertificated areas, **Util 56.203 et seq.**
Pharmacists, this index
Plans and specifications,
Flexibility plans, incumbent local exchange companies, **Util 54.007**
Historically underutilized businesses, contracts, **Util 52.256**
Officers and employees, diversity, **Util 52.256**
Small businesses, contracts, **Util 52.256**
Poles and wires,
Discrimination, municipalities, **Util 54.204**
Fiber optics, infrastructure, incentives, **Util 58.204**
Right of way, access, **Util 60.208**
Portability, numbers, **Util 60.205**
Changing locations, **Util 60.081 et seq.**
Posting. Display, generally, ante
Powers and duties. Underground facilities, post

TELECOMMUNICATIONS—Cont'd
Predatory prices. Rates and charges, post
Preemption, code of conduct, **Util 60.202**
Preferences. Priorities and preferences, generally, post
Prepaid services, **Util 55.253**
Prerecorded messages. Automated dial announcing devices, generally, ante
Prices. Rates and charges, generally, post
Pricing, cost studies, local exchange companies, **Util 60.102**
Print transmissions, hearing and speech impaired persons, statewide relay access service, **Util 56.102, 56.103**
Priorities and preferences,
Private network services, educational and medical entities, **Util 58.254, 59.073**
Complaints, **Util 58.264**
Rates and charges, post
Service, **Util 55.005**
Universal service fund, assessments, **Util 56.022**
Private network services, educational and medical entities, **Util 58.251 et seq., 59.071 et seq.**
Privileged information. Confidential or privileged information, generally, ante
Privileges and immunities,
Crimes and offenses, services, **Util 186.021**
Weapons, law enforcement officers, **Util 186.021**
Production of books and papers, deregulation, **Util 52.205**
Promotions,
Hearing impaired persons, financial assistance, machinery and equipment, **Util 56.156**
Incentive regulation, **Util 58.004**
Local exchange service, **Util 52.0585**
Rates and charges, deregulation, incumbent local exchange companies, **Util 65.102**
Transitioning companies, **Util 65.153**
Resales, **Util 60.042**
Providers of last resort, termination of service, **Util 54.301 et seq.**
Public policy, **Util 51.001, 52.001**
Fair competition, **Util 60.001**
Hearing and speech impaired persons, statewide relay access service, **Util 56.101**
Incentives, **Util 58.001, 59.001**
Infrastructure, **Util 58.201, 58.202**
Incumbent local exchange companies, **Util 52.051**
Private network services, educational and medical entities, **Util 58.251**
Small incumbent local exchange companies, **Util 53.251**
Standards, service, **Util 55.001**
Public services, directories, **Util 55.203**

TELECOMMUNICATIONS—Cont'd
Publication,
Mobile telephones, numbers and numbering, **Util 64.201 et seq.**
Rates and charges, notice, changes, **Util 53.103**
Railroads, this index
Random dialing, automated dial announcing devices, **Util 55.124**
Rates and charges, **Util 52.251 et seq., 53.001 et seq., 60.101, 60.102**
Access lines,
Incentives, basic network services, adjustments, **Util 58.058**
Pay telephones, **Util 55.1735**
Accounts and accounting,
Examinations, **Util 52.255**
Separation, computation of rates, **Util 53.055**
Adjustments,
Basic network services, incentives, **Util 58.055 et seq.**
Cost recovery, **Util 53.201**
Incentives, **Util 59.055**
Interconnection, **Util 60.128**
Administration of law, public utility commission, **Util 52.002**
Advertisements, computation of rates, expenses, **Util 53.062**
Affiliates,
Local exchange service, **Util 60.165**
Payments to, computation of rates, **Util 53.058**
Amortization, computation of rates, **Util 53.056**
Appeal and review, small incumbent local exchange companies, changes, **Util 53.306**
Application of law, incentives, basic network services, **Util 58.061**
Authority, regulation, **Util 53.001**
Automatic adjustments, cost recovery, **Util 53.201**
Basic network service, incentive regulation, **Util 58.052 et seq.**
Bonds (officers and fiduciaries), changes, pending final determination, **Util 53.110**
Bundling, basic local service, long distance service, **Util 55.016**
Burden of proof, changes, **Util 53.006**
Business purpose, pricing flexibility, **Util 51.004**
Capping,
Incentives, basic network services, **Util 58.054**
Switched access service, **Util 58.302**
Certificates of authority, **Util 54.156**
Changes, **Util 52.007, 53.101 et seq.**
Basic network service, incentive regulation, **Util 58.052 et seq.**
Bonds (officers and fiduciaries), pending final determination, **Util 53.110**
Burden of proof, **Util 53.006**
Complaints, **Util 53.151**

TELECOMMUNICATIONS—Cont'd
Rates and charges—Cont'd
Changes—Cont'd
Cost recovery, adjustments, **Util 53.201**
Distance learning, **Util 57.025**
Early effective dates, **Util 53.104**
Final determination, **Util 53.111**
Hearings, **Util 53.105 et seq., 53.151**
Incentives, **Util 59.024**
Increases, **Util 53.101 et seq.**
Incumbent local exchange companies, promotional rates, **Util 52.058**
Interconnection, **Util 60.128**
Investigations, nonproducing utilities, **Util 53.152**
Major changes, **Util 53.101**
Nonbasic services, incentive regulation, **Util 58.152**
Notice of intent, **Util 53.103, 53.305**
Incentives, basic network services, **Util 58.059**
Orders, **Util 53.111, 53.151**
Preferences, hearings, **Util 53.107**
Private network services, educational and medical entities, **Util 58.258, 58.267, 59.077, 59.082**
Reductions, **Util 53.151, 53.152**
Regional hearings, **Util 53.106**
Small incumbent local exchange companies, **Util 53.301 et seq.**
Statements of intent, **Util 53.102, 53.304**
Suspension, pending final determination, **Util 53.108, 53.112, 53.306**
Switched access service, **Util 53.113**
Temporary rates, pending final determination, **Util 53.109**
Time, **Util 53.102, 53.104**
Universal service fund, **Util 56.025**
Community supervision, nine hundred (900) information service, **Util 55.252**
Competition, pricing, **Util 60.101, 60.102**
Complaints,
Changes, **Util 53.105, 53.151**
Incentive regulation, **Util 59.031**
Incentives, **Util 58.025, 58.026, 59.026, 59.027**
Incumbent local exchange companies, deregulation, transitioning companies, **Util 65.155**
Small incumbent local exchange companies, changes, **Util 53.306**
Compliance, **Util 53.002, 53.004**
Computation, **Util 53.051 et seq.**
Consent, new products or services, **Util 17.151 et seq., 64.151 et seq.**
Construction,
Aid to construction, **Util 56.210**
Works in progress, computation of rates, **Util 53.054**
Contracts, interconnection, **Util 60.125**
Cost method, incumbent local exchange companies, **Util 52.059**

TELECOMMUNICATIONS—Cont'd
Rates and charges—Cont'd
Cost recovery,
Adjustments, **Util 53.201**
Deregulation, **Util 52.204**
Credit reports, unauthorized charges, nonpayment, **Util 17.152, 64.152**
Deceptive trade practices and consumer protection, **Util 17.001 et seq., 64.001 et seq.**
Depletion, computation of rates, **Util 53.056**
Deposits, customers, interest, **Util 183.003**
Depreciation,
Accounts, **Util 52.252**
Computation of rates, **Util 53.056**
Return on investments, **Util 53.053**
Deregulation, generally, ante
Discounts, **Util 51.004**
Certificates of authority, resales, local exchange service, **Util 54.156**
Discrimination, **Util 52.156, 53.003**
Incumbent local exchange companies, **Util 52.053**
Nondominant carriers, **Util 52.108**
Pricing flexibility, **Util 51.004**
Disputed charges, **Util 17.157, 64.157**
Records and recordation, **Util 17.153, 64.153**
Distance learning, **Util 57.022 et seq.**
Eight hundred (800) numbers, pay telephones, **Util 55.176**
Exceeding, **Util 53.004**
Exemptions, incumbent local exchange companies, deregulation, transitioning companies, **Util 65.154**
Existing rate structure, interconnection, adoption, **Util 60.127**
Expanded toll free local calling areas, **Util 55.048**
Expiration, incentives, basic network services, **Util 58.060**
Extended area service, **Util 55.024**
Federal law, separations, basic network systems, incentives, adjustments, **Util 58.056**
Filing, **Util 52.251**
Basic network services, incentives, adjustments, **Util 58.057**
Distance learning, **Util 57.024**
Final determination, changes, **Util 53.111**
Fines and penalties,
Computation of rates, **Util 53.062**
Unauthorized charges, **Util 17.156, 64.156**
Flexibility plans,
Basic network service, incentive regulation, **Util 58.063**
Incumbent local exchange companies, **Util 54.007**
Geographic markets, deregulation, **Util 52.201 et seq.**
Gifts, computation of rates, **Util 53.061**
Hearing impaired persons, statewide relay access service, **Util 56.104**

TELECOMMUNICATIONS—Cont'd
Rates and charges—Cont'd
Hearing impaired persons, statewide relay access service—Cont'd
Compensation and salaries, **Util 56.109**
Hearings,
Changes, **Util 53.105 et seq., 53.151**
Incentives, basic network services, adjustments, **Util 58.059**
Hotels and motels, **Util 55.251**
Hunting services, extended area service, **Util 55.025**
Imputation, local exchange companies, **Util 60.061 et seq.**
Incentives, **Util 58.001 et seq., 59.001 et seq.**
Income, computation of rates, **Util 53.057**
Income tax, computation of rates, **Util 53.059, 53.060**
Increases, **Util 53.101 et seq.**
Incumbent local exchange companies, **Util 52.053, 52.056, 52.058, 52.059**
Transitioning companies, deregulation, **Util 65.153, 65.154**
Complaints, **Util 65.155**
Interactive multimedia communications, **Util 57.072**
Interexchange service, incumbent local exchange companies, **Util 53.065**
Interim numbers, portability, **Util 60.084**
IntraLATA service, universal service fund, reimbursement, **Util 56.028**
Intrastate switched access rates, **Util 52.112, 52.155**
Investigations and investigators, nonproducing utilities, **Util 53.152**
Investments, returns, **Util 53.051 et seq.**
Just and reasonable rates, **Util 53.003**
Legislative advocacy, computation of rates, expenses, **Util 53.061, 53.062**
Lifeline service, termination of service, nonpayment, **Util 55.015**
Major changes, **Util 53.101**
Merchandise, sales and leases,
Computation of rates, **Util 53.063**
Profits and losses, accounts, **Util 52.253**
Minimum rates, deregulation, **Util 52.204**
Minimum service, **Util 55.007**
Minor changes, small incumbent local exchange companies, **Util 53.301 et seq.**
Net income, computation of rates, **Util 53.057**
New services, **Util 17.151 et seq., 64.151 et seq.**
Incentive regulation, **Util 59.030**
Local exchange service, **Util 52.0583**
Nonbasic services, incentive regulation, **Util 58.153**
Small incumbent local exchange companies, **Util 53.303, 53.304**

TELECOMMUNICATIONS—Cont'd
Rates and charges—Cont'd
Nonbasic services, incentive regulation, **Util 58.152**
Nondominant carriers, **Util 52.102 et seq.**
Nonpayment, long distance service, termination of service, basic local service, **Util 55.012**
Notice,
Basic network service, incentive regulation, flexibility, **Util 58.063**
Hearings, changes, **Util 53.105**
Incentive regulation, **Util 59.031**
Intent to change, **Util 53.103, 53.305**
Incentives, basic network services, **Util 58.059**
New products or services, **Util 17.151 et seq., 64.151 et seq.**
Number portability, interim measures, **Util 60.084**
Operators, quotations, **Util 55.085**
Orders,
Changes, **Util 53.111, 53.151**
Incentives, basic network services, adjustments, **Util 58.059**
Original costs, return on investments, **Util 53.053**
Packaging services,
Basic network service, incentive regulation, **Util 58.063**
Incentive regulation, **Util 58.004, 59.031**
Local exchange service, **Util 52.0584**
Parole, nine hundred (900) information service, **Util 55.252**
Pay per call information services, automated dial announcing devices, solicitations, **Util 55.127**
Pay telephones, **Util 55.172 et seq.**
Payment, aged persons, **Util 182.001 et seq.**
Perline blocking, caller identification service, **Util 55.106**
Predatory prices, **Util 52.156**
Discounts, **Util 51.004**
Nondominant carriers, **Util 52.107**
Prejudicial, **Util 52.156**
Prepaid calling services, disclosure, **Util 55.253**
Priorities and preferences, **Util 52.156, 53.003, 60.101**
Changes, hearings, **Util 53.107**
Incumbent local exchange companies, **Util 52.053**
Nondominant carriers, **Util 52.108**
Pricing flexibility, **Util 51.004**
Small incumbent local exchange companies, reduced rates, officers and employees, **Util 53.307**
Private network services, educational and medical entities, **Util 58.256 et seq., 59.075 et seq.**
Promotional rates, incumbent local exchange companies, new services, **Util 52.058**

TELECOMMUNICATIONS—Cont'd
Rates and charges—Cont'd
Promotions, incentive regulation, **Util 58.004, 59.032**
Public policy, **Util 52.001, 52.002**
Public utility commission, authority to regulate, **Util 53.001**
Reasonable and just rates, **Util 53.003**
Reconnection, fees, **Util 53.007**
Records and recordation,
Disputed charges, **Util 17.153, 64.153**
Examinations and examiners, **Util 52.255**
Unauthorized charges, **Util 17.152, 64.152**
Reductions, **Util 53.151, 53.152**
Basic network services, incentives, **Util 58.055**
Refunds,
Bonds (officers and fiduciaries), **Util 53.110**
Cost recovery, **Util 53.062**
Regional hearings, changes, **Util 53.106**
Reimbursement, municipal fees, **Util 54.206**
Reregulation, **Util 52.206**
Resales, **Util 60.041, 60.044**
Service providers, local exchange service, **Util 54.156**
Return on investments, **Util 53.051 et seq.**
Rules and regulations, **Util 53.001**
Filing, **Util 52.251**
Rural local exchange companies, **Util 53.251 et seq.**
Self insurance, computation of rates, **Util 53.064**
Small incumbent local exchange companies, **Util 53.251 et seq.**
State, late payments, **Util 55.010**
Statements of intent, changes, **Util 53.102, 53.304**
Statewide relay access service, hearing and speech impaired persons, **Util 56.104**
Compensation and salaries, **Util 56.109**
Subsidies, **Util 60.101**
Surcharge, generally, post
Suspension, changes, pending final determination, **Util 53.108, 53.112, 53.306**
Switched access service, post
Switching carriers, unauthorized changes, **Util 55.304**
Taxation,
Benefits, **Util 53.059**
Computation of rates, **Util 53.059, 53.060**
Telephone Cooperative Corporations, this index
Temporary rates, changes, pending final determination, **Util 53.109**
Term discounts, incentive regulation, **Util 58.004**
Time,
Changes, effect, **Util 53.102, 53.104**

TELECOMMUNICATIONS—Cont'd
Rates and charges—Cont'd
Time—Cont'd
Early effective dates, changes, **Util 53.104**
Incentives, basic network services, adjustments, **Util 58.059**
Notice of intent, changes, **Util 53.103**
Statements of intent, changes, **Util 53.102**
Toll blocking, **Util 55.013**
Trade associations, computation of rates, expenses, **Util 53.062**
Unauthorized charges, **Util 17.151 et seq., 64.151 et seq.**
Underground facilities, post
Universal service fund,
Assessments, **Util 56.022, 56.023**
Disbursements, **Util 56.026**
IntraLATA service, reimbursement, **Util 56.028**
Volume discounts, incentive regulation, **Util 58.004**
Withdrawal, **Util 52.007**
Reciprocal compensation, **Util 60.209**
Reclassification, incentives, services, **Util 58.024**
Reconnection, fees, **Util 53.007**
Records and recordation,
Certificates of operating authority, holders, **Util 52.153**
Deceptive trade practices and consumer protection, ante
Disputed charges, **Util 17.153, 64.153**
Hearing impaired persons, vouchers, machinery and equipment, **Util 56.153**
Pay telephones, usage, **Util 55.176**
Rates and charges, ante
Unauthorized charges, **Util 17.152, 64.152**
Underground facilities, notification center, excavations, **Util 251.103**
Refunds,
Customers deposits, **Util 183.005**
Rates and charges, ante
Refusal of service, **Util 60.203**
Certificate holders, prohibited service, **Util 54.254**
Registration,
Deceptive trade practices and consumer protection, **Util 17.051 et seq., 64.051 et seq.**
Nondominant carriers, **Util 52.102, 52.103**
Pay telephone services, **Util 55.173**
Revocation or suspension, unauthorized charges, **Util 17.156, 64.156**
Switching carriers, suspension or revocation, **Util 55.306**
Relay access services, hearing and speech impaired persons, **Util 56.101 et seq.**
Remedies, underground facilities, excavations, **Util 251.008**
Repairs, underground facilities, excavations, **Util 251.159**

TELECOMMUNICATIONS—Cont'd
Reports,
Caller identification service, blocking, **Util 55.110**
Competition, **Util 52.006**
Deceptive trade practices and consumer protection, **Util 17.051 et seq., 64.051 et seq.**
Deregulation, **Util 52.207**
Historically underutilized businesses, contracts, **Util 52.256**
Incentives, evaluation, **Util 59.054**
Nondominant carriers, **Util 52.102**
Officers and employees, diversity, **Util 52.256**
Small businesses, contracts, **Util 52.256**
Small incumbent local exchange companies, **Util 53.252**
Underground facilities, damages, excavations, **Util 251.159**
Universal service fund, assessments, **Util 56.024**
Requests, aged persons, delay in payment, **Util 182.002, 182.003**
Reregulation, **Util 52.206**
Resales, **Util 60.041 et seq.**
Application of law, rates, **Util 60.045**
Certificates of authority, **Util 54.156 et seq.**
Classification of service, **Util 60.044**
Imputation, prices, **Util 60.061 et seq.**
Local exchange companies, obligations, **Util 60.043**
Loop resale tariffs, **Util 60.041**
Private network services, educational and medical entities, **Util 58.266, 59.081**
Promotions, **Util 60.042**
Rates and charges, **Util 60.041, 60.044**
Restrictions, **Util 60.042**
Review. Appeal and review, generally, ante
Right of way,
Access, **Util 60.208**
Entry on property, identity and identification, **Util 55.017**
Pipes and pipelines, gas utilities, **Util 121.201**
Rules and regulations,
Affiliates, local exchange service, **Util 60.165**
Distance learning, rates, **Util 57.022**
Expanded interconnections, **Util 60.141**
Filing, standards of service, **Util 55.003**
Incumbent local exchange companies, **Util 52.054**
Deregulation, **Util 65.003**
Infrastructure sharing, local exchange companies, **Util 60.163**
Interconnection, networks, **Util 60.124**
Local exchange service, ante
Municipal ordinances, **Util 181.089**
Numbers, portability, **Util 60.082**
Operators, **Util 55.083**
Prepaid calling services, **Util 55.253**
Rates and charges, **Util 53.001**
Filing, **Util 52.251**

TELECOMMUNICATIONS—Cont'd
Rules and regulations—Cont'd
Standards, service, **Util 55.002 et seq.**
Statewide relay access service, hearing and speech impaired persons, **Util 56.102**
Switching carriers, **Util 55.302**
Universal service fund, **Util 56.023**
Rural area, advanced services, **Util 55.014**
Rural incumbent local exchange companies, **Util 53.251 et seq.**
Universal service fund, adjustments, **Util 56.032**
Safety, underground facilities, **Util 251.001 et seq.**
Salaries. Compensation and salaries, generally, ante
Sales,
Automated dial announcing devices, generally, ante
Certificates and certification, transfers of certificates, **Util 54.255**
Investigations and investigators, orders, **Util 14.101, 51.010**
Merchandise, computation of rates, **Util 53.063**
Resales, generally, ante
Schools and School Districts, this index
Scoring, credit reports, payment, **Util 17.009**
Searches and seizures, fraud, machinery and equipment, **Util 186.033**
Selection. Switching carriers, generally, post
Self insurance, computation of rates, **Util 53.064**
Separation, markets and marketing, **Util 52.004**
Sequential dialing, automated dial announcing devices, **Util 55.124**
Service, uncertificated areas, **Util 56.201 et seq.**
Shares and shareholders, merger and consolidation, approval, **Util 181.088**
Sharing,
Local exchange service, infrastructure sharing, **Util 60.163**
Private network services, educational and medical entities, **Util 58.266, 59.081**
Single party service, minimum service, **Util 55.007**
Small businesses, contracts, **Util 52.256**
Small incumbent local exchange companies. Local exchange service, ante
Solicitations. Automated dial announcing devices, generally, ante
Special features, relay access service, hearing impaired persons, contracts, **Util 56.1085**
Specialized telecommunications assistance program, **Util 56.151 et seq.**
Specifications. Plans and specifications, generally, ante

TELECOMMUNICATIONS—Cont'd
Speech language pathologists and audiologists,
Financial assistance, machinery and equipment, **Util 56.151 et seq.**
Statewide relay access service, **Util 56.101 et seq.**
Splitting exchanges, tollfree calling areas, **Util 55.043**
Standards, **Util 55.001 et seq.**
Certificates of convenience and necessity, **Util 54.054**
Certificates of operating authority, **Util 54.154, 54.155**
Issuance, **Util 54.103**
Conduct, **Util 60.201 et seq.**
Deceptive trade practices and consumer protection, **Util 17.004, 64.004**
Distance learning, service and rates, **Util 57.023**
Incentives, consumer complaints, **Util 58.027, 59.028**
Incumbent local exchange companies, competition, safeguards, **Util 60.161**
Municipal ordinances, **Util 181.089**
Nondominant carriers, services, **Util 52.102, 52.106**
State, this index
State Agencies, this index
Statements of intent, rate changes, **Util 53.102, 53.304**
Statewide relay access service,
Hearing and speech impaired persons, **Util 56.101 et seq.**
Speech impairment, **Util 56.101 et seq.**
Streets and alleys, easements, **Util 181.082 et seq.**
Studies, pricing, cost studies, local exchange companies, **Util 60.102**
Successor utilities, termination of service, providers of last resort, **Util 54.301 et seq.**
Universal service fund, **Util 56.023, 56.251 et seq.**
Surcharge,
Changes, expiration, **Util 53.112**
Hearing impaired persons, vouchers, machinery and equipment, **Util 56.155**
Statewide relay access service, hearing and speech impaired persons, **Util 56.107**
Switched access service,
Certificates and certification, **Util 54.001**
Certificates of authority, eligibility, **Util 54.153**
Imputation, prices, **Util 60.063**
Incentive regulation, **Util 58.301 et seq.**
Incumbent local exchange companies, rates and charges, reduction, deregulation, transitioning companies, **Util 65.201 et seq.**
Infrastructure sharing, local exchange companies, **Util 60.163**

TELECOMMUNICATIONS—Cont'd
Switched access service—Cont'd
Rates and charges, **Util 52.112, 52.155, 58.301 et seq.**
Changes, approval, **Util 53.113**
Incentives, **Util 59.025**
Reduction, incumbent local exchange companies, deregulation, transitioning companies, **Util 65.201 et seq.**
Switching carriers, **Util 17.101, 17.102, 55.301 et seq., 64.101, 64.102**
Authorization, **Util 55.303**
Billing, unauthorized changes, **Util 55.304**
Certificates and certification, suspension or revocation, **Util 55.306**
Collections, unauthorized changes, **Util 55.304**
Compensation and salaries, unauthorized changes, **Util 55.304**
Corrective action, **Util 55.305**
Deceptive trade practices and consumer protection, **Util 55.307**
Fines and penalties, **Util 55.305**
Fraud, **Util 55.307**
Notice, rules and regulations, **Util 55.302**
Rates and charges, unauthorized changes, **Util 55.304**
Registration, suspension or revocation, **Util 55.306**
Reversal, unauthorized changes, **Util 55.304**
Rules and regulations, **Util 55.302**
Unauthorized changes, **Util 55.304**
Tape and sound recordings. Automated dial announcing devices, generally, ante
Tariffs. Rates and charges, generally, ante
Taxation. Rates and charges, ante
Telecommunications provider, definitions, **Util 51.002**
Telemedicine, generally, this index
Telephone Cooperative Corporations, generally, this index
Teletypes, hearing and speech impaired persons, statewide relay access service, **Util 56.102, 56.103**
Television and Radio, generally, this index
Tenant and landlord, installations, **Util 54.259 et seq.**
Term discounts, incentive regulation, **Util 58.004**
Termination of service,
Aged and handicapped persons, **Util 14.005**
Automated dial announcing devices, violations, **Util 55.136**
Certificates of convenience and necessity, grounds, **Util 54.252**
Certificates of operating authority, **Util 54.253**
Crimes and offenses, **Util 186.021**

TELECOMMUNICATIONS—Cont'd
Termination of service—Cont'd
Exiting utilities, providers of last resort, **Util 54.301 et seq.**
Universal service fund, **Util 56.023, 56.251 et seq.**
Lifeline service, rates and charges, nonpayment, **Util 55.015**
Nonpayment, rates and charges, **Util 55.013**
Long distance service, **Util 55.012**
Pay telephones, violations, **Util 55.180**
Providers of last resort, **Util 54.301 et seq.**
Universal service fund, **Util 56.023, 56.251 et seq.**
Successor utilities, providers of last resort, **Util 54.301 et seq.**
Universal service fund, **Util 56.023, 56.251 et seq.**
Unauthorized charges, nonpayment, **Util 17.152, 64.152**
Tests, deregulation, market power tests, **Util 52.203**
Theft, fraud, **Util 186.032**
Time,
Acquisition, orders, **Util 51.010**
Aged persons, payment, **Util 182.002**
Automated dial announcing devices, ante
Certificates of operating authority, service, **Util 54.104**
Delay, incumbent local exchange companies, competition, safeguards, **Util 60.161**
Extensions, infrastructure, incentives, **Util 58.205**
Infrastructure, incentives, **Util 58.203 et seq., 59.052**
Loop resale tariffs, filing, **Util 60.041**
Nondominant carriers, service, **Util 52.109**
Rates and charges, ante
Successor utilities, termination of service, providers of last resort, **Util 54.303**
Uncertificated areas, **Util 56.211**
Toll free numbers,
Internet access, educational institutions, **Util 58.263**
Pay telephones, charges, **Util 55.176**
Underground facilities, contracts, notification corporation, excavations, **Util 251.061**
Tollfree service, lifeline service, blocking, **Util 55.015**
Tone dialing service,
Basic local service, **Util 51.002**
Minimum service, **Util 55.007**
Trade associations, computation of rates, expenses, **Util 53.062**
Transitional incentives, **Util 58.001 et seq., 59.001 et seq.**
Transitioning companies, incumbent local exchange companies, deregulation, **Util 65.151 et seq.**

TELECOMMUNICATIONS—Cont'd
Transmission. Poles and wires, generally, ante
Two way video transmissions, interactive multimedia communications, **Util 57.071, 57.072**
Unauthorized charges, **Util 17.151 et seq., 64.151 et seq.**
Unbundling, competition, safeguards, **Util 60.021 et seq.**
Providers of last resort, **Util 54.303**
Uncertificated areas, **Util 56.201 et seq.**
Underground facilities,
Assessments, notification corporation, excavations, **Util 251.062**
Brands, marks and labels,
Crimes and offenses, excavations, **Util 251.203**
Excavations, **Util 251.157, 251.158**
Call router system, contracts, notification corporation, excavations, **Util 251.061**
Contracts, toll free numbers, notification corporation, excavations, **Util 251.061**
Conversion, **Util 251.005**
Crimes and offenses, brands, marks and labels, excavations, **Util 251.203**
Damages, **Util 251.001 et seq.**
Notification corporation, excavations, **Util 251.054**
Directors, notification corporation, excavations, **Util 251.055 et seq.**
Easements, excavations, **Util 251.006**
Emergencies, notice, excavations, **Util 251.155**
Excavations, **Util 251.001 et seq.**
Exemptions, notice, excavations, **Util 251.156**
Expenses and expenditures, notification corporation, excavations, **Util 251.054**
Fees,
Notification center, excavations, **Util 251.105**
Notification corporation, excavations, **Util 251.062**
Fines and penalties, excavations, **Util 251.201 et seq.**
Fraud, emergencies, excavations, **Util 251.155**
Fines and penalties, **Util 251.201**
Highways and roads, excavations, **Util 251.007**
Insurance, notification center, excavations, **Util 251.104**
Licenses and permits, excavations, **Util 251.006**
Notice, excavations, **Util 251.009, 251.151 et seq.**
Notification center, excavations, **Util 251.101 et seq.**
Notification corporation, excavations, **Util 251.051 et seq.**
Officers and employees, notification corporation, excavations, **Util 251.058**

TELECOMMUNICATIONS—Cont'd
Underground facilities—Cont'd
Open meetings, notification corporation, excavations, **Util 251.053**
Open records, notification corporation, excavations, **Util 251.053**
Payment, notification center, excavations, **Util 251.106**
Powers and duties,
Notification center, excavations, **Util 251.102**
Notification corporation, excavations, **Util 251.060**
Rates and charges,
Notification center, excavations, **Util 251.105**
Notification corporation, excavations, **Util 251.062**
Records and recordation, notification center, excavations, **Util 251.103**
Remedies, excavations, **Util 251.008**
Repairs, excavations, **Util 251.159**
Reports, damages, excavations, **Util 251.159**
Safety, **Util 251.001 et seq.**
Toll free numbers, contracts, notification corporation, excavations, **Util 251.061**
Venue, fines and penalties, excavations, **Util 251.201**
Warnings, excavations, **Util 251.201, 251.2011**
Unfair practices. Deceptive trade practices and consumer protection, generally, ante
Universal service fund, **Util 56.021 et seq.**
Providers of last resort, termination of service, **Util 56.023, 56.251 et seq.**
Rates and charges, ante
Universities. Colleges and Universities, this index
Venue, underground facilities, fines and penalties, excavations, **Util 251.201**
Virtual colocation, private network services, educational and medical entities, **Util 58.262**
Voice over Internet protocol services, rates and charges, **Util 52.002**
Volume discounts, incentive regulation, **Util 58.004**
Vouchers, hearing impaired persons, machinery and equipment, **Util 56.152, 56.153**
Wages. Compensation and salaries, generally, ante
Waiver,
Imputation, prices, local exchange companies, **Util 60.065**
Infrastructure, incentives, **Util 58.205, 59.053**
Warnings, underground facilities, excavations, **Util 251.201, 251.2011**
Wholesale code of conduct, **Util 60.201 et seq.**
Wireless telecommunications,
Directories, **Util 64.201 et seq.**

TELECOMMUNICATIONS—Cont'd
Wireless telecommunications—Cont'd
Interconnection, application of law, **Util 60.123**
Numbers and numbering, publication, **Util 64.201 et seq.**
Publication, numbers and numbering, **Util 64.201 et seq.**
Wires. Poles and wires, generally, ante
Withdrawal, rates and charges, **Util 52.007**

TELECOMMUNICATIONS UTILITIES
Definitions, deceptive trade practices and consumer protection, **Util 17.002, 64.002**

TELEGRAPHS
Telecommunications, generally, this index

TELEHEALTH SERVICES
Telemedicine, generally, this index

TELEMEDICINE
Private network services, **Util 58.251 et seq., 59.071 et seq.**

TELEPHONE COOPERATIVE CORPORATIONS
Generally, **Util 53.251 et seq., 162.001 et seq.**
Actions and proceedings, **Util 162.121**
Affidavits, notice to customers, deregulation, **Util 53.357**
Amendments,
Articles of incorporation, post
Bylaws, **Util 162.064, 162.121**
Appeal and review, deregulation, review, **Util 53.358**
Application of law,
Deregulation, **Util 53.351**
Rates and charges, **Util 53.302**
Securities Act, **Util 162.063**
Articles of amendment, **Util 162.153**
Articles of consolidation, **Util 162.202, 162.254**
Articles of conversion, **Util 162.252**
Articles of incorporation, **Util 162.054**
Amendments, **Util 162.151 et seq.**
Approval, **Util 162.152**
Articles of amendment, **Util 162.153**
Compliance, other corporations, **Util 162.082**
Execution, **Util 162.153, 162.154**
Certificates, **Util 162.055**
Consolidation, **Util 162.205**
Conformity, **Util 162.202**
Conversion, **Util 162.252**
Defective articles, perfecting, **Util 162.058**
Execution, **Util 162.051**
Filing and recording, **Util 162.055**
Forms, **Util 162.054**
Merger, **Util 162.205**
Perfecting, defective articles, **Util 162.058**
Revival, **Util 162.056**
Articles of merger, **Util 162.204**

TELEPHONE COOPERATIVE CORPORATIONS—Cont'd
Ballots, deregulation, **Util 53.352**
Boards and commissions. Directors, generally, post
Boundaries, districts, **Util 162.076**
Bylaws, **Util 162.064, 162.121**
Certificates and certification,
Articles of incorporation, **Util 162.055**
Conversion, **Util 162.252, 162.254**
Dissolution, **Util 162.301, 162.304**
Members and membership, **Util 162.065**
Merger and consolidation, **Util 162.202, 162.204**
Principal offices, changes, **Util 162.080**
Compensation and salaries, directors, **Util 162.073**
Complaints, deregulation, **Util 53.358**
Conflict of laws, amendments of articles, compliance, **Util 162.082**
Connections, service, **Util 162.122, 162.123**
Consolidation and merger, **Util 162.201 et seq.**
Conversion, **Util 162.253, 162.254**
Construction, standards, **Util 162.006**
Contracts, **Util 162.121**
Consolidation, **Util 162.201**
Conversion, **Util 162.251 et seq.**
Deeds of trust, **Util 162.125, 162.126**
Defects, incorporation, dissolution, **Util 162.304**
Definitions, **Util 162.003**
Deregulation, **Util 53.351 et seq.**
Directors, **Util 162.071 et seq.**
Compensation and salaries, **Util 162.073**
Districts, **Util 162.076**
Elections, **Util 162.072, 162.076**
Executive committees, **Util 162.078**
Indemnity, **Util 162.079**
Insurance, **Util 162.074**
Meetings, **Util 162.075**
Notaries public, **Util 162.081**
Officers, **Util 162.077**
Powers and duties, **Util 162.071**
Quorum, **Util 162.075**
Dissolution, **Util 162.301 et seq.**
Distribution of assets, dissolution, **Util 162.303**
Districts, **Util 162.076**
Duration of corporations, **Util 162.052**
Elections,
Deregulation, **Util 53.352, 53.353**
Reversal, **Util 53.359**
Directors, **Util 162.072**
Eligibility, membership, **Util 162.065**
Eminent domain, **Util 162.124**
Employees. Officers and employees, generally, post
Executive committees, directors, **Util 162.078**
Exemptions,
Securities Act, **Util 162.063**
Taxation, **Util 162.062**

TELEPHONE COOPERATIVE CORPORATIONS—Cont'd
Expanded toll free local calling areas, exemptions, **Util 55.044**
Expenses and expenditures, directors, reimbursement, **Util 162.073**
Extensions of service, **Util 162.122, 162.123**
Fees,
Articles of amendment, **Util 162.154**
Articles of consolidation, **Util 162.202**
Articles of conversion and consolidation, **Util 162.252, 162.254**
Articles of incorporation, filing, **Util 162.055**
Articles of merger, **Util 162.204**
Dissolution, **Util 162.301**
Licenses, **Util 162.061**
Principal offices, changes, certificates, **Util 162.080**
Filing. Records and recordation, generally, post
Forms,
Articles of amendment, **Util 162.153**
Articles of consolidation, **Util 162.202, 162.254**
Articles of conversion, **Util 162.202, 162.252**
Articles of incorporation, **Util 162.054**
Articles of merger, **Util 162.204**
Notice, customers, deregulation, **Util 53.356**
Statements of intent, deregulation, **Util 53.355**
Franchise taxes, exemptions, **Util 162.062**
Incorporators, **Util 162.051**
Organizational meetings, **Util 162.057**
Indebtedness, **Util 162.121**
Authority, **Util 162.125, 162.126**
Liability of members, **Util 162.060**
Merger and consolidation, liability, **Util 162.205**
Indemnity, **Util 162.079**
Insurance, directors, **Util 162.074**
Interconnection service, **Util 162.122, 162.123**
Leases, **Util 162.121, 162.125, 162.126**
Licenses and permits, fees, **Util 162.061**
Liens and incumbrances, **Util 162.005, 162.125, 162.126**
Liquidation, dissolution, **Util 162.302**
Loans, **Util 162.121**
Managers and management, executive committees, **Util 162.078**
Meetings,
Directors, **Util 162.075**
Members and membership, **Util 162.067**
Articles of incorporation, amendments, **Util 162.152**
Consolidation, **Util 162.201**
Conversion, approval, **Util 162.251, 162.253**
Dissolution, approval, **Util 162.301, 162.304**
Election of directors, **Util 162.072, 162.076**

TELEPHONE COOPERATIVE CORPORATIONS—Cont'd
Meetings—Cont'd
Members and membership—Cont'd
Merger, approval, **Util 162.203**
Notice, **Util 162.068, 162.069**
Property, liens and encumbrances, **Util 162.126**
Quorum, **Util 162.070**
Voting, **Util 162.070**
Organizational meetings, incorporators, **Util 162.057**
Members and membership, **Util 162.065**
Articles of incorporation, amendments, **Util 162.152**
Certificates, **Util 162.065**
Consolidation, approval, **Util 162.201**
Conversion, approval, **Util 162.251, 162.253**
Dissolution, **Util 162.301 et seq.**
Distribution of assets, dissolution, **Util 162.303**
Eligibility, **Util 162.065**
Indebtedness, liability, **Util 162.060**
Meetings, ante
Merger, approval, **Util 162.203**
Notaries public, **Util 162.081**
Notice, meetings, **Util 162.068, 162.069**
Patrons, **Util 162.003, 162.066**
Voting, **Util 162.070**
Merger and consolidation, **Util 162.201 et seq.**
Conversion, **Util 162.253, 162.254**
Mortgages, **Util 162.005, 162.125, 162.126**
Names, **Util 162.004, 162.053**
Conversion, **Util 162.252**
Merger and consolidation, **Util 162.201, 162.204**
New services, deregulation, **Util 53.354**
Nonprofit corporations, status, **Util 162.059**
Notaries public, directors, officers and members, **Util 162.081**
Notice,
Conversion, approval, voting, **Util 162.251**
Customers, deregulation, **Util 53.356, 53.357**
Meetings, members, **Util 162.068, 162.069**
Merger, approval, members meetings, **Util 162.203**
Organizational meetings, incorporators, **Util 162.057**
Officers and employees, **Util 162.077**
Indemnity, **Util 162.079**
Notaries public, **Util 162.081**
Offices, change of principal office, **Util 162.080**
Partial deregulation, **Util 53.351 et seq.**
Patrons, **Util 162.003, 162.066**
Powers and duties, **Util 162.121 et seq.**
Principal offices, changes, **Util 162.080**
Profits, **Util 162.059**
Property, **Util 162.121**
Authority, liens and encumbrances, **Util 162.125, 162.126**

TELEPHONE COOPERATIVE CORPORATIONS—Cont'd
Property—Cont'd
Dissolution, winding up affairs, **Util 162.302, 162.303**
Eminent domain, **Util 162.124**
Liens and incumbrances, **Util 162.005**
Merger and consolidation, **Util 162.205**
Public policy, **Util 162.002**
Public utility commission, deregulation, **Util 53.358**
Quorum,
Directors, **Util 162.075**
Members, meetings, **Util 162.070**
Rates and charges, **Util 53.251 et seq.**
Deregulation, **Util 53.351 et seq.**
New services, deregulation, **Util 53.354**
Refunds, earnings, **Util 53.004**
Reversal, deregulation, **Util 53.359**
Statements of intent, deregulation, **Util 53.355**
Records and recordation,
Articles of amendment, **Util 162.154**
Articles of consolidation, **Util 162.202, 162.254**
Articles of conversion, **Util 162.252, 162.254**
Articles of incorporation, **Util 162.055**
Articles of merger, **Util 162.204**
Dissolution, **Util 162.301**
Liens and encumbrances, **Util 162.005**
Refunds, earnings, **Util 53.004**
Reversal, deregulation, **Util 53.359**
Revival, articles of incorporation, **Util 162.056**
Right of way, public lands, **Util 162.122**
Sales, authority, **Util 162.125, 162.126**
Seals, **Util 162.121**
Securities Act, exemptions, **Util 162.063**
Shares and shareholders, conversion, approval, **Util 162.253**
To cooperatives, **Util 162.251**
Special meetings, members, **Util 162.067**
Standards, construction, **Util 162.006**
Statements of intent,
Deregulation, **Util 53.355**
Rate changes, **Util 53.304**
Tax exemptions, **Util 162.062**
Time,
Creation of corporations, **Util 162.055**
Duration of corporation, **Util 162.052**
Meetings, members, **Util 162.067**
Notice, deregulation, **Util 53.356**
Vacancies in office, directors, **Util 162.072**
Voting, members, **Util 162.070**
Waiver, members meetings, notice, **Util 162.069**
Winding up affairs, dissolution, **Util 162.302, 162.303**

TELEPHONES
Telecommunications, generally, this index

TELEVISION AND RADIO
Generally, **Util 62.001 et seq.**
Accounts and accounting, franchises, municipalities, fees, **Util 66.006**

TELEVISION AND RADIO—Cont'd
Application of law, **Util 51.003**
Franchises, **Util 66.016**
Applications, franchises, certificate of authority, **Util 66.003 et seq.**
Broadcasters, safeguards, **Util 62.001 et seq.**
Buildout, franchises, exemptions, **Util 66.007**
Cable Television, generally, this index
Certificate of authority, franchises, applications, **Util 66.003 et seq.**
Compliance, orders of court, franchises, **Util 66.015**
Customer service, standards, franchises, **Util 66.008**
Discrimination, franchises, municipalities, **Util 66.010, 66.014**
Educational access channels, franchises, **Util 66.009**
Exemptions, franchises, buildout, **Util 66.007**
Fees, franchises, **Util 66.005**
Municipalities, **Util 66.006**
Franchises,
Municipalities, post
State, **Util 66.001 et seq.**
Governmental access channels, franchises, **Util 66.009**
In kind contributions, franchises, municipalities, **Util 66.006**
Indemnity, franchises, municipalities, **Util 66.012**
Infrastructure, incentives, **Util 58.203, 59.052**
Interactive multimedia communications, **Util 57.071, 57.072**
Local exchange companies, programming, **Util 62.003**
Municipalities, franchises, **Util 66.009 et seq.**
Fees, **Util 66.006**
Termination, **Util 66.004**
Orders of court, compliance, franchises, **Util 66.015**
PEG channels, franchises, municipalities, **Util 66.009**
Private network services, educational and medical entities, **Util 58.251 et seq., 59.071 et seq.**
Programming, local exchange companies, **Util 62.003**
Public access channels, franchises, **Util 66.009**
Right of way, franchises, municipalities, **Util 66.010 et seq.**
Standards, customer service, franchises, **Util 66.008**
State, franchises, **Util 66.001 et seq.**
Termination, franchises, municipalities, **Util 66.004**

TENANTS
Landlord and Tenant, generally, this index

TENEMENTS
Apartment Houses, generally, this index

TESTIMONY
Evidence, generally, this index

TESTS
Definitions, utility meters, **Util 182.101**
Electricity, meters, **Util 38.051, 38.052, 182.101 et seq.**
Gas meters, **Util 104.256, 104.257, 182.101 et seq.**
Gas utilities, pipes and pipelines, school buildings and grounds, **Util 121.5005 et seq.**
Telecommunications, deregulation, market power tests, **Util 52.203**

TEXAS, STATE OF
State, generally, this index

THEFT
Public utilities, unauthorized use, municipal ordinances, **Util 181.902**
Telecommunications, this index

THIRD PARTIES
Limited partnerships. Partnerships, this index
Partnerships, this index

THREATS
Public utilities, interruption of service, **Util 186.004**

TIME PRICE DIFFERENTIAL
Interest, generally, this index

TITLE TO PROPERTY
Corporations, this index
Foreign Corporations, this index
Joint Tenants, generally, this index
Limited Liability Companies, this index
Public utilities, reports, substantial interest, **Util 14.004**

TITLES OF ACTS
Popular Name Laws, generally, this index

TOLL FREE NUMBERS
Telecommunications, this index

TOWNS
Municipalities, generally, this index

TRACKS
Dog Races, generally, this index
Horse Racing, generally, this index

TRADE
Business and Commerce, generally, this index

TRADE ASSOCIATIONS
Definitions, public utilities, **Util 11.003**
Electricity, computation of rates, expenses, **Util 36.062**
Public Utilities, this index

TRADE ASSOCIATIONS—Cont'd
Public utility commission, adverse or pecuniary interest, commissioners and employees, **Util 12.153**
Telecommunications, computation of rates, expenses, **Util 53.062**

TRAFFIC RULES AND REGULATIONS
Mobile Homes and Mobile Home Parks, generally, this index
Street Railroads, generally, this index

TRAINING
Public utilities, underground facilities, excavations, safety, **Util 251.201, 251.2011**
Public utility commission, **Util 12.059**
  Alternative dispute resolution, **Util 14.0025**

TRAINS
Railroads, generally, this index

TRAMS
Street Railroads, generally, this index

TRANSCRIPTS
Public utilities, hearings, **Util 14.055, 14.057**

TRANSPORTATION
Monopolies and Unfair Trade, generally, this index
Railroads, generally, this index

TRANSPORTATION DEPARTMENT
Railroads, generally, this index

TRASH
Solid Waste, generally, this index

TRAVELING EXPENSES
Public utilities, commission, training, **Util 12.059**

TREASURERS
Business development corporations, **Bus Org 23.060**
Cooperative associations, **Bus Org 251.102**
Definitions, business organizations, **Bus Org 1.002**

TREASURY SHARES
Shares and shareholders. Corporations, this index

TREATMENT
Medical Care and Treatment, generally, this index

TRIAL
Evidence, generally, this index
Executions, generally, this index

TROLLEYS
Street Railroads, generally, this index

TROVER
Conversion, generally, this index

TRUANCY
Schools and School Districts, this index

TRUST COMPANIES
  See, also, Banks and Banking, generally, this index
Names, registration, **Bus Org 5.151 et seq.**
Registration, names, **Bus Org 5.151 et seq.**

TRUST DEEDS
Deeds of Trust, generally, this index

TRUST FUNDS
Trusts and Trustees, generally, this index

TRUSTEES
Trusts and Trustees, generally, this index

TRUSTS AND MONOPOLIES
Monopolies and Unfair Trade, generally, this index

TRUSTS AND TRUSTEES
Business trust, foreign business trusts, transacting business in state, **Bus Org 9.201**
Churches, retirement and pensions, **Bus Org 22.401 et seq.**
Corporations, this index
Deeds of Trust, generally, this index
Electricity, this index
Foreign Corporations, this index
Limited partnerships. Partnerships, this index
Nonprofit Corporations, this index
Partnerships, this index
Real Estate Investment Trusts, generally, this index
Religious organizations and societies, retirement and pensions, **Bus Org 22.401 et seq.**

ULTRA VIRES
Corporations, **Bus Org 20.002**
Real estate investment trusts, **Bus Org 200.004**

UNDERGROUND FACILITIES
Cable Television, this index
Electricity, this index
Oil and Gas, this index
Oil and Gas Pipelines, this index
Public Utilities, this index
Water Supply, this index

UNDERGROUND FACILITY DAMAGE PREVENTION AND SAFETY ACT
Generally, **Util 251.001 et seq.**

UNDERGROUND NATURAL GAS
Assessments, notification corporation, excavations, **Util 251.062**
Brands, marks and labels,
  Crimes and offenses, excavations, **Util 251.203**
  Excavations, **Util 251.157, 251.158**
Call router system, contracts, notification corporation, excavations, **Util 251.061**

UNDERGROUND NATURAL GAS
—Cont'd
Contracts, toll free numbers, notification corporation, excavations, **Util 251.061**
Conversion, **Util 251.005**
Crimes and offenses, brands, marks and labels, excavations, **Util 251.203**
Damages, **Util 251.001 et seq.**
Notification corporation, excavations, **Util 251.054**
Directors, notification corporation, excavations, **Util 251.055 et seq.**
Easements, excavations, **Util 251.006**
Emergencies, notice, excavations, **Util 251.155**
Excavations, **Util 251.001 et seq.**
Exemptions, notice, excavations, **Util 251.156**
Expenses and expenditures, notification corporation, excavations, **Util 251.054**
Fees,
Notification center, excavations, **Util 251.105**
Notification corporation, excavations, **Util 251.062**
Fines and penalties, excavations, **Util 251.201 et seq.**
Fraud, emergencies, excavations, **Util 251.155**
Fines and penalties, **Util 251.201**
Highways and roads, excavations, **Util 251.007**
Insurance, notification center, excavations, **Util 251.104**
Licenses and permits, excavations, **Util 251.006**
Notice,
Center, excavations, **Util 251.101 et seq.**
Corporation, excavations, **Util 251.051 et seq.**
Excavations, **Util 251.009, 251.151 et seq.**
Officers and employees, notification corporation, excavations, **Util 251.058**
Open meetings, notification corporation, excavations, **Util 251.053**
Open records, notification corporation, excavations, **Util 251.053**
Payment, notification center, excavations, **Util 251.106**
Powers and duties,
Notification center, excavations, **Util 251.102**
Notification corporation, excavations, **Util 251.060**
Rates and charges,
Notification center, excavations, **Util 251.105**
Notification corporation, excavations, **Util 251.062**
Records and recordation, notification center, excavations, **Util 251.103**
Remedies, excavations, **Util 251.008**
Repairs, excavations, **Util 251.159**
Reports, damages, excavations, **Util 251.159**
Safety, **Util 251.001 et seq.**

UNDERGROUND NATURAL GAS
—Cont'd
Toll free numbers, contracts, notification corporation, excavations, **Util 251.061**
Venue, fines and penalties, excavations, **Util 251.201**
Warnings, excavations, **Util 251.201, 251.2011**

UNDERTAKINGS
Bonds (Officers and Fiduciaries), generally, this index

UNFAIR COMPETITION
Monopolies and Unfair Trade, generally, this index

UNFAIR DISCRIMINATION
Discrimination, generally, this index

UNFAIR TRADE
Monopolies and Unfair Trade, generally, this index

UNINCORPORATED NONPROFIT ASSOCIATIONS
Nonprofit Corporations, this index

UNITED STATES
Federal Law, generally, this index

UNITED STATES AGENCIES
Public utilities, commission, actions and proceedings, labor and employment, **Util 39.4525**

UNIVERSAL SERVICE FUND
Telecommunications, **Util 56.021 et seq.**

UNIVERSITIES
Colleges and Universities, generally, this index

UNIVERSITY COOPERATIVE SOCIETY
Names, **Bus Org 251.452**

UTILITIES
Public Utilities, generally, this index

VALUATION
Electricity, affiliates, transfer of assets, exemptions, wholesale generators and power marketers, **Util 35.035**
Gas utilities, investments, computation of rates, **Util 104.052, 104.053**

VENUE
Corporations, this index
Foreign Corporations, this index
Gas utilities, enforcement actions, **Util 105.025**
Limited partnerships. Partnerships, this index
Nonprofit Corporations, this index
Oil and Gas, this index
Partnerships, this index
Public Utilities, this index
Sewers and Sewer Systems, this index
Telecommunications, this index
Water Supply, this index

VETERINARIANS
Telemedicine, generally, this index

VILLAGES
Municipalities, generally, this index

VISUALLY HANDICAPPED PERSONS
Blind Persons, generally, this index

VOCATIONAL EDUCATION
Community colleges and districts. Colleges and Universities, this index

VOTERS AND VOTING
Elections, generally, this index

VOUCHERS
Telecommunications, hearing impaired persons, machinery and equipment, **Util 56.152, 56.153**

WAGES
Compensation and Salaries, generally, this index

WARD
Guardian and Ward, generally, this index

WAREHOUSE RECEIPTS
Corporations, **Bus Org 1.001 et seq.**

WARNINGS
Public utilities, underground facilities, excavations, **Util 251.201, 251.2011**

WASTE
Public utilities, unauthorized use, municipalities, protection, **Util 181.902**
Sewers and Sewer Systems, generally, this index
Solid Waste, generally, this index

WASTEWATER
Sewers and Sewer Systems, generally, this index

WATER POLLUTION
Gas utilities, pipes and pipelines, penalties, **Util 121.304 et seq.**

WATER SUPPLY
See, also, Public Utilities, generally, this index
Aged persons, payment, delay, **Util 182.001 et seq.**
Aquifers, confidential or privileged information, customers, government operated utilities, **Util 182.052**
Assessments, underground facilities, notification corporation, excavations, **Util 251.062**
Authorities. River Authorities, generally, this index
Brands, marks and labels. Underground facilities, post
Call router system, underground facilities, contracts, notification corporation, excavations, **Util 251.061**
Confidential or privileged information, customers, **Util 182.051 et seq.**

WATER SUPPLY—Cont'd
Continuity of service, **Util 186.001 et seq.**
Contracts, underground facilities, toll free numbers, notification corporation, excavations, **Util 251.061**
Crimes and offenses, underground facilities, brands, marks and labels, excavations, **Util 251.203**
Damages, underground facilities, **Util 251.001 et seq.**
  Notification corporation, excavations, **Util 251.054**
Deposits, customers, **Util 183.001 et seq.**
Directors, underground facilities, notification corporation, excavations, **Util 251.055 et seq.**
Easements,
  Railroads, right of way, eminent domain, **Util 186.051 et seq.**
  Underground facilities, excavations, **Util 251.006**
Emergencies, underground facilities, notice, excavations, **Util 251.155**
Eminent domain, railroads, right of way, **Util 186.051 et seq.**
Excavations, underground facilities, **Util 251.001 et seq.**
Exemptions, underground facilities, notice, excavations, **Util 251.156**
Expenses and expenditures, underground facilities, notification corporation, excavations, **Util 251.054**
Fees,
  Railroads, right of way, use, **Util 186.058**
  Underground facilities, post
Fines and penalties, underground facilities, excavations, **Util 251.201 et seq.**
Fraud, underground facilities, emergencies, excavations, **Util 251.155**
  Fines and penalties, **Util 251.201**
Highways and roads, underground facilities, excavations, **Util 251.007**
Insurance, underground facilities, notification center, excavations, **Util 251.104**
Interest, deposits, **Util 183.002 et seq.**
Interruption of service, prevention, **Util 186.001 et seq.**
Licenses and permits,
  Railroads, right of way, use, **Util 186.058**
  Underground facilities, excavations, **Util 251.006**
Notice,
  Confidential or privileged information, customers, **Util 182.052**
  Railroads, right of way, easements, **Util 186.054**
  Underground facilities, post
Notification center, underground facilities, excavations, **Util 251.101 et seq.**
Notification corporation, underground facilities, excavations, **Util 251.051 et seq.**

WATER SUPPLY—Cont'd
Officers and employees, underground facilities, notification corporation, excavations, **Util 251.058**
Open meetings, underground facilities, notification corporation, excavations, **Util 251.053**
Open records, underground facilities, notification corporation, excavations, **Util 251.053**
Payment,
  Aged persons, delay, **Util 182.001 et seq.**
  Underground facilities, notification center, excavations, **Util 251.106**
Powers and duties. Underground facilities, post
Railroads, this index
Rates and charges,
  Payment, aged persons, delay, **Util 182.001 et seq.**
  Underground facilities, post
Records and recordation, underground facilities, notification center, excavations, **Util 251.103**
Remedies, underground facilities, excavations, **Util 251.008**
Repairs, underground facilities, excavations, **Util 251.159**
Reports, underground facilities, damages, excavations, **Util 251.159**
Requests, aged persons, delay in payment, **Util 182.002, 182.003**
River Authorities, generally, this index
Safety, underground facilities, **Util 251.001 et seq.**
Time, aged persons, payment, **Util 182.002**
Toll free numbers, underground facilities, contracts, notification corporation, excavations, **Util 251.061**
Underground facilities,
  Assessments, notification corporation, excavations, **Util 251.062**
  Brands, marks and labels,
    Crimes and offenses, excavations, **Util 251.203**
    Excavations, **Util 251.157, 251.158**
  Call router system, contracts, notification corporation, excavations, **Util 251.061**
  Contracts, toll free numbers, notification corporation, excavations, **Util 251.061**
  Conversion, **Util 251.005**
  Crimes and offenses, brands, marks and labels, excavations, **Util 251.203**
  Damages, **Util 251.001 et seq.**
    Notification corporation, excavations, **Util 251.054**
  Directors, notification corporation, excavations, **Util 251.055 et seq.**
  Easements, excavations, **Util 251.006**
  Emergencies, notice, excavations, **Util 251.155**
  Excavations, **Util 251.001 et seq.**

WATER SUPPLY—Cont'd
Underground facilities—Cont'd
  Exemptions, notice, excavations, **Util 251.156**
  Expenses and expenditures, notification corporation, excavations, **Util 251.054**
  Fees,
    Notification center, excavations, **Util 251.105**
    Notification corporation, excavations, **Util 251.062**
  Fines and penalties, excavations, **Util 251.201 et seq.**
  Fraud, emergencies, excavations, **Util 251.155**
    Fines and penalties, **Util 251.201**
  Highways and roads, excavations, **Util 251.007**
  Insurance, notification center, excavations, **Util 251.104**
  Licenses and permits, excavations, **Util 251.006**
  Notice, excavations, **Util 251.009, 251.151 et seq.**
  Notification center, excavations, **Util 251.101 et seq.**
  Notification corporation, excavations, **Util 251.051 et seq.**
  Officers and employees, notification corporation, excavations, **Util 251.058**
  Open meetings, notification corporation, excavations, **Util 251.053**
  Open records, notification corporation, excavations, **Util 251.053**
  Payment, notification center, excavations, **Util 251.106**
  Powers and duties,
    Notification center, excavations, **Util 251.102**
    Notification corporation, excavations, **Util 251.060**
  Rates and charges,
    Notification center, excavations, **Util 251.105**
    Notification corporation, excavations, **Util 251.062**
  Records and recordation, notification center, excavations, **Util 251.103**
  Remedies, excavations, **Util 251.008**
  Repairs, excavations, **Util 251.159**
  Reports, damages, excavations, **Util 251.159**
  Safety, **Util 251.001 et seq.**
  Toll free numbers, contracts, notification corporation, excavations, **Util 251.061**
  Venue, fines and penalties, excavations, **Util 251.201**
  Warnings, excavations, **Util 251.201, 251.2011**
Venue, underground facilities, fines and penalties, excavations, **Util 251.201**
Warnings, underground facilities, excavations, **Util 251.201, 251.2011**

WATER SUPPLY OR SEWER SERVICE CORPORATIONS
Generally, **Bus Org 1.001 et seq.**

WATER WELLS
Water Supply, generally, this index

WATERS AND WATERCOURSES
Irrigation, generally, this index
Supply. Water Supply, generally, this index

WATERWORKS AND WATER SUPPLIES
Water Supply, generally, this index

WEATHER
Electricity,
Emergencies, plans and specifications, reports, **Util 186.007**
Termination of service, extreme weather emergencies, **Util 39.101**

WEB (WORLD WIDE)
Internet, generally, this index

WEBSITES
Internet, generally, this index

WEEKENDS
Electricity, termination of service, **Util 39.101**

WEIGHTS AND MEASURES
Gas Meters, generally, this index
Gas Utilities, this index

WHOLESALERS
Electric cooperative corporations, markets and marketing, **Util 41.102**
Electricity, this index

WILLS
Actions and proceedings. Probate Proceedings, generally, this index
Admission to probate. Probate Proceedings, generally, this index
Probate Proceedings, generally, this index

WINDING UP
Cooperative Associations, this index
Corporations, this index
Definitions, business organizations, **Bus Org 11.001**
Foreign Corporations, this index
Limited Liability Companies, this index
Nonprofit Corporations, this index
Partnerships, this index
Professional Associations and Societies, this index
Professional Corporations, this index
Real Estate Investment Trusts, this index

WIRELESS TELECOMMUNICATIONS
Telecommunications, this index

WITHHOLDING
Garnishment, generally, this index

WITNESSES
Partnerships, this index
Public Utilities, this index
Public utility commission, **Util 14.051**

WORDS AND PHRASES
Above market purchased power costs, electricity, competition, stranded costs, recovery, **Util 39.251**
Acquire, electric cooperative corporations, **Util 161.002**
Actual incremental costs, franchises, television and radio, state, **Util 66.002**
Address, assumed or fictitious names, business and commerce, professions and occupations, **Bus & C 71.002**
Advanced service, telecommunications, **Util 55.014**
Affected parties, gas utilities, pipes and pipelines, sour gas, **Util 121.451**
Affected persons,
Gas utilities, **Util 101.003**
Public utilities, **Util 11.003**
Affiliated power generation company, **Util 31.002**
Affiliated retail electric provider, **Util 31.002**
Affiliates,
Business organizations, **Bus Org 1.002**
Gas utilities, **Util 101.003**
Public utilities, **Util 11.003, 11.0042**
Telecommunications, certificates of authority, **Util 54.153**
Television and radio, franchises, state, **Util 66.004**
Agencies, municipal power agencies, **Util 163.051**
Aggregation, electricity, **Util 31.002**
Aggregator, electricity, registration, **Util 39.353**
Agricultural operations, underground facilities, exemptions, notice, excavations, **Util 251.156**
Agriculture energy user, natural gas, **Util 123.022**
Allocation,
Gas utilities, **Util 101.003**
Public utilities, **Util 11.003**
Ancillary services, electricity, transmission, **Util 35.004**
Apartment house owner, heating and cooling, **Util 184.051**
Apartment houses,
Central heating and cooling, **Util 184.051**
Electricity, metering, **Util 184.011**
Gas submetering, **Util 124.001**
Assignees, electricity, securities, competition, **Util 39.302**
Assisted living facilities, electricity, priorities and preferences, **Util 38.072**
Associates, business organizations, **Bus Org 1.002**
Associations,
Business organizations, **Bus Org 1.002**
Partnerships, Revised Partnership Act, **Bus Org 152.051**

WORDS AND PHRASES—Cont'd
Assumed names,
Business and commerce, professions and occupations, **Bus & C 71.002**
Business organizations, **Bus Org 1.002**
Audio programming, telecommunications, broadcaster safeguards, **Util 62.002**
Authorized shares, business organizations, **Bus Org 21.002**
Automated dial announcing devices, **Util 55.121**
Basic local telecommunications service, **Util 51.002**
Beneficial owners, business combinations, **Bus Org 21.603**
Billing agent,
Electricity, deceptive trade practices and consumer protection, **Util 17.002**
Telecommunications, deceptive trade practices and consumer protection, **Util 17.002, 64.002**
Billing utility,
Electricity, deceptive trade practices and consumer protection, **Util 17.002**
Telecommunications, deceptive trade practices and consumer protection, **Util 17.002, 64.002**
Board of directors,
Business organizations, **Bus Org 21.002**
Electric cooperative corporations, competition, **Util 41.002**
Nonprofit corporations, **Bus Org 22.001**
Boards,
Electric cooperative corporations, **Util 161.002**
Telephone cooperative corporations, **Util 162.003**
Body vested with the power to manage and operate a municipally owned utility, electricity, **Util 40.002**
Bonds, municipal power agencies, **Util 163.051**
BPL, broadband over power lines, **Util 43.003**
BPL access, broadband over power lines, **Util 43.003**
BPL electric utility applications, broadband over power lines, **Util 43.003**
BPL Internet service providers, broadband over power lines, **Util 43.003**
BPL operators, broadband over power lines, **Util 43.003**
BPL systems, broadband over power lines, **Util 43.003**
Businesses, organizations, **Bus Org 1.002**
Bylaws, nonprofit corporations, **Bus Org 22.001**
Cable operators, railroads, right of way, **Util 186.051**
Cable service providers, franchises, television and radio, state, **Util 66.002**
Cable services, franchises, television and radio, state, **Util 66.002**
Caller ID service, telecommunications, **Util 55.110**

WORDS AND PHRASES—Cont'd
Caller identification information, telecommunications, **Util 55.101**
Caller identification service, telecommunications, **Util 55.101**
Cancel, business organizations, **Bus Org 21.002**
Capital accounts, partnerships, **Bus Org 151.001**
Central station service, electric cooperative corporations, **Util 161.002**
Central system, utilities, apartment houses, **Util 184.051**
Certificate of formation, business organizations, **Bus Org 1.002**
Certificated ownership interest, business organizations, **Bus Org 1.002**
Certificated telecommunications utility, deceptive trade practices and consumer protection, **Util 17.002, 64.002**
Certificates,
Assumed or fictitious names, business and commerce, professions and occupations, **Bus & C 71.002**
Electricity, convenience and necessity, **Util 37.001**
Telecommunications,
Certificates of authority, **Util 54.151**
Convenience and necessity, **Util 54.051**
Operating authority, **Util 54.101**
Church benefit board, retirement and pensions, **Bus Org 22.401**
Claims, business organizations, termination, winding up, **Bus Org 11.001**
Class A underground facility, excavations, **Util 251.001**
Class B underground facility, excavations, **Util 251.001**
Close corporation provision, business organizations, **Bus Org 21.701**
Close corporations, business organizations, **Bus Org 1.002, 21.701**
Closely held corporation, derivative actions, **Bus Org 21.563**
Closely held limited liability company, limited liability companies, derivative actions, **Bus Org 101.463**
Commercial mobile service providers, telecommunications, directories, **Util 64.201**
Commissioners,
Electricity, state, sales, royalties, in kind, **Util 35.101**
Public utilities, **Util 11.003**
Commissions,
Public utilities, **Util 11.003**
Customers deposits, **Util 183.001**
Meters, **Util 184.001**
Solar energy, ratings, devices, **Util 185.001**
Weather, emergencies, electricity, plans and specifications, reports, **Util 186.007**
Common carriers, railroads, right of way, **Util 186.051**

WORDS AND PHRASES—Cont'd
Common control with a public utility, affiliates, **Util 11.006**
Common control with gas utility, affiliates, **Util 101.004**
Communication service, telephone cooperative corporations, **Util 162.003**
Communications networks, franchises, television and radio, state, **Util 66.002**
Companies,
Assumed or fictitious names, **Bus & C 71.002**
Limited liability, **Bus Org 101.001**
Company agreement, limited liability companies, **Bus Org 101.001**
Competitive affiliate, electricity, customer choice, **Util 39.157**
Concurrent ordinances, municipal power agencies, **Util 163.051**
Confiscation, electricity, municipalities, rate appeals, **Util 33.055**
Conservation commission, electricity, air pollution, emissions, reductions, competition, **Util 39.264**
Construction, gas utilities, pipes and pipelines, sour gas, **Util 121.451**
Consumer price index, telecommunications, small and rural incumbent local exchange companies, universal service fund, **Util 56.032**
Consumer reporting agency, public utilities, confidential or privileged information, **Util 182.051**
Consumers, utility meters, testing, **Util 182.101**
Consuming assets corporation, business organizations, **Bus Org 21.002**
Contributions,
Business organizations, **Bus Org 1.002**
Telecommunications, universal service fund, adjustments, **Util 56.025**
Control, telecommunications, certificates of authority, **Util 54.153**
Conversion, business organizations, **Bus Org 1.002**
Converted entity, business organizations, **Bus Org 1.002**
Converting entities, business organizations, **Bus Org 1.002**
Cooperative associations, business organizations, **Bus Org 1.002**
Cooperative basis, cooperative associations, **Bus Org 251.001**
Cooperative corporation, public utilities, **Util 11.003**
Cooperatives, business organizations, **Bus Org 1.002**
Corporate support services, electricity, customer choice, **Util 39.157**
Corporations,
Agriculture gas users, **Util 123.022**
Assumed or fictitious names, **Bus & C 71.002**
Business development corporations, **Bus Org 23.051**
Business organizations, **Bus Org 21.002**

WORDS AND PHRASES—Cont'd
Corporations—Cont'd
Gas and electrical corporations, **Util 181.001**
Gas utilities, **Util 101.003**
Nonprofit corporations, **Bus Org 22.001**
Public utilities, **Util 11.003, 11.0042**
Underground facilities, excavations, **Util 251.001**
Counselors,
Gas utilities, **Util 101.003**
Public utilities, **Util 11.003**
Courts, close corporations, actions and proceedings, **Bus Org 21.751**
Credit history, public utilities, payment, **Util 17.008**
Credit score, public utilities, payment, **Util 17.008**
Custodians, close corporations, actions and proceedings, **Bus Org 21.751**
Customer choice, electricity, **Util 31.002**
Customers,
Apartment houses, heating and cooling, **Util 184.051**
Electricity, deceptive trade practices and consumer protection, **Util 17.002**
Telecommunications, deceptive trade practices and consumer protection, **Util 17.002, 64.002**
Damages, underground facilities, excavations, **Util 251.001**
Debtor in bankruptcy, business organizations, **Bus Org 1.002**
Decommissioning, atomic energy, costs, **Util 39.206**
Delegate, business organizations, indemnity, **Bus Org 8.001**
Departments, telecommunications, universal services, **Util 56.001**
Deregulated companies, telecommunications, incumbent local exchange companies, **Util 65.001**
Derivative proceedings,
Corporations, shares and shareholders, **Bus Org 21.551**
Limited liability companies, **Bus Org 101.451**
Designated provider, telecommunications, universal services, **Util 56.001**
Direct or indirect wholly owned subsidiary, business organizations, mergers and consolidation, holding companies, **Bus Org 10.005**
Directors, business organizations, **Bus Org 1.002**
Disinterested persons, business organizations, conflict of interest, **Bus Org 1.003**
Dissenting owner, shares and shareholders, **Bus Org 10.352**
Distance learning, **Util 57.021**
Distributed natural gas generation facility, electricity, **Util 31.002**
Distributed renewable generation, electricity, **Util 39.916**

WORDS AND PHRASES—Cont'd
Distributed renewable generation owners, electricity, **Util 39.916**
NonERCOT utilities, **Util 39.554**
Distribution limit, corporations, shares and shareholders, **Bus Org 21.301**
Distribution service, electricity, municipalities, rates and charges, franchises, **Util 33.008**
Distributions,
Business organizations, **Bus Org 21.002**
Partnerships, **Bus Org 151.001**
Domestic, business organizations, **Bus Org 1.002**
Domestic corporation,
Business organizations, **Bus Org 21.002**
Nonprofit corporations, **Bus Org 22.001**
Domestic entity, business organizations, **Bus Org 1.002**
Domestic entity subject to dissenters rights, business organizations, **Bus Org 1.002**
Dominant carrier, telecommunications, **Util 51.002**
Dwelling units,
Central heating and cooling, **Util 184.051**
Electricity, metering, **Util 184.011**
Gas submetering, **Util 124.001**
Educational institutions, distance learning, telecommunications, **Util 57.021**
Effective date of this code, business organizations, **Bus Org 1.002**
Elderly individuals, public utilities, delay in payment, **Util 182.001**
Electing company, telecommunications, incentives, **Util 58.002, 59.002**
Election date, telecommunications, incentives, **Util 59.002**
Electric cooperatives, **Util 11.003, 161.002**
Electric corporation, **Util 181.001**
Electric facility, joint powers agencies, **Util 163.001**
Electric generating facility, air pollution, emissions, reductions, competition, **Util 39.264**
Electric reliability council of Texas, **Util 31.002**
Electric utilities, **Util 31.002, 181.041**
Alternative energy, **Util 35.001**
Broadband over power lines, **Util 43.003**
Certificates of convenience and necessity, **Util 37.001**
Customer choice, auctions and auctioneers, installed generation capacity, entitlements, **Util 39.153**
Deceptive trade practices and consumer protection, **Util 17.002**
Electronic delivery systems, broadband over power lines, **Util 43.003**
Electronic transmissions, business organizations, **Bus Org 1.002**
Emergencies,
Business organizations, governance, **Bus Org 3.251**

WORDS AND PHRASES—Cont'd
Emergencies—Cont'd
Telecommunications, **Util 186.041 et seq.**
Energy transporters, railroads, right of way, **Util 186.051**
Enterprise, business organizations, indemnity, **Bus Org 8.001**
Entities,
Business organizations, **Bus Org 1.002**
Electricity, joint powers agencies, **Util 163.001**
Equipment, cable television, **Util 181.101**
ERCOT, electricity, **Util 31.002**
Event of withdrawal, partnerships, **Bus Org 152.001**
Event requiring a winding up,
Business organizations, winding up, **Bus Org 11.001**
Partnerships, **Bus Org 152.001**
Excavate, underground facilities, **Util 251.001**
Excavator, underground facilities, **Util 251.001**
Excess revenue, public utilities, **Util 15.023**
Exempt wholesale generator, electricity, **Util 31.002**
Existing claims, business organizations, termination, winding up, **Bus Org 11.001**
Existing purchased power contract, electricity, competition, stranded costs, recovery, **Util 39.251**
Exiting utilities, telecommunications, **Util 54.301**
Expenses, business organizations, indemnity, **Bus Org 8.001**
Exploration and production underground facility, excavations, **Util 251.001**
Extended power outages, health care facilities, priorities and preferences, **Util 38.072**
Extreme weather emergencies,
Electricity, termination of service, **Util 39.101**
Gas utilities, termination of service, **Util 104.258**
Facilities,
Gas utilities, **Util 101.003**
Public utilities, **Util 11.003**
Telecommunications, **Util 181.081**
Feature service, telecommunications, certificates of authority, **Util 54.156**
Filing entity, business organizations, **Bus Org 1.002**
Filing instrument, business organizations, **Bus Org 1.002**
Filing officer, business organizations, **Bus Org 1.002**
Financial institutions, business development corporations, **Bus Org 23.051**
Financing orders, electricity,
Hurricanes, reconstruction costs, **Util 39.460**
Restoration, bonds, **Util 36.403**
Securities, competition, **Util 39.302**

WORDS AND PHRASES—Cont'd
Financing party, electricity, securities, competition, **Util 39.302**
Fixed rate products, electricity, **Util 39.112**
For profit corporation, business organizations, **Bus Org 1.002**
For profit entities, **Bus Org 1.002**
Force majeure, electricity, rates and charges, freeze period, **Util 39.055**
Foreign, business organizations, **Bus Org 1.002**
Foreign companies, limited liability companies, **Bus Org 101.001**
Foreign corporations,
Business organizations, **Bus Org 21.002**
Nonprofit corporations, **Bus Org 22.001**
Foreign entity, business organizations, **Bus Org 1.002**
Foreign filing entity, **Bus Org 1.002**
Assumed or fictitious names, **Bus & C 71.002**
Foreign governmental authority, business organizations, **Bus Org 1.002**
Foreign limited liability company, limited liability companies, **Bus Org 101.001**
Foreign limited liability partnerships, partnerships, **Bus Org 152.001**
Foreign limited partnerships, partnerships, **Bus Org 151.001**
Foreign nonfiling entity, business organizations, **Bus Org 1.002**
Former governing person, business organizations, indemnity, **Bus Org 8.001**
Franchises, television and radio, state, **Util 66.002**
Freeze period, electricity, **Util 31.002**
Fundamental actions,
Nonprofit corporations, elections, **Bus Org 22.164**
Real estate investment trusts, elections, **Bus Org 200.261**
Shares and shareholders, elections, **Bus Org 21.364**
Fundamental business transaction, business organizations, **Bus Org 1.002**
Gas, meters, testing, **Util 182.101**
Gas facility, **Util 181.021**
Gas utilities, **Util 101.003, 181.021**
Pipelines, **Util 121.001**
Pipes and pipelines, taxation, **Util 122.001**
Records, **Util 102.101**
General partners, business organizations, **Bus Org 1.002**
General partnerships, business organizations, **Bus Org 1.002**
Generation assets, electricity, competition, stranded costs, recovery, **Util 39.251**
Good cause, telecommunications,
Incentive regulation, elections, withdrawal, **Util 58.021**
Incentives, **Util 59.022**
Governing authority, business organizations, **Bus Org 1.002**

WORDS AND PHRASES—Cont'd
Governing documents, business organizations, **Bus Org 1.002**
Governing person, business organizations, **Bus Org 1.002**
Government operated utility, confidential or privileged information, **Util 182.051**
Governmental bodies, public utilities, confidential or privileged information, **Util 182.051**
Gross income, gas utilities, pipes and pipelines, taxation, **Util 122.001**
Gross revenues, franchises, television and radio, state, **Util 66.002**
Health center, telecommunications, private network services, **Util 58.252**
High speed data transmission, underground facilities, excavations, **Util 251.001**
Historically underutilized businesses, public utilities, **Util 12.251**
Holder of shares, business organizations, **Bus Org 1.002**
Holding companies, business organizations, mergers and consolidation, **Bus Org 10.005**
Hospice services, electricity, priorities and preferences, **Util 38.072**
Housing for older persons, construction, electricity, meters, exemptions, **Util 184.0125**
Hurricane reconstruction costs, electricity, **Util 39.459**
Hurricane Rita, electricity, reconstruction costs, **Util 39.459**
Incumbent cable service providers, franchises, state, **Util 66.002**
Incumbent local exchange company, telecommunications, **Util 51.002**
Independent organizations, electricity, customer choice, **Util 39.151**
Independent persons, business organizations, conflict of interest, **Bus Org 1.004**
Independent system operator, electricity, **Util 31.002**
Individuals, business organizations, **Bus Org 1.002**
Insolvency, business organizations, **Bus Org 1.002**
Insolvent, business organizations, **Bus Org 1.002**
Installed generation capacity, electricity, customer choice, limitation, **Util 39.154**
Institutions of higher education, telecommunications, landlord and tenant, **Util 54.259**
Interactive multimedia communications, telecommunications, **Util 57.071**
Interconnection,
  Electricity, distributed renewable generation, **Util 39.916**
  Telecommunications, **Util 60.121**
Interest exchange, business organizations, **Bus Org 1.002**

WORDS AND PHRASES—Cont'd
Internal Revenue Code, business organizations, **Bus Org 1.002**
Internet protocol enabled services, telecommunications, **Util 51.002**
Invested capital, cooperative associations, **Bus Org 251.001**
Investment companies,
  Corporations, distribution and distributors, **Bus Org 21.301**
  Open end investment companies, shares and shareholders, **Bus Org 21.651**
Investment Company Act, business organizations, **Bus Org 21.002**
Investment dividends, cooperative associations, **Bus Org 251.001**
Issuing public corporation, business combinations, **Bus Org 21.601**
Judgments, business organizations, indemnity, **Bus Org 8.001**
Jurisdiction of formation, business organizations, **Bus Org 1.002**
Laws, business organizations, **Bus Org 1.002**
Legal holiday, underground facilities, excavations, **Util 251.001**
Libraries,
  Distance learning, telecommunications, **Util 57.021**
  Telecommunications, private network services, **Util 58.252, 59.071**
Licensed mental health professional, professional entities, **Bus Org 301.003**
Licenses, business organizations, **Bus Org 1.002**
Lifeline service, telecommunications, **Util 55.015**
Limited liability companies, business organizations, **Bus Org 1.002, 101.001**
Limited liability limited partnerships, business organizations, **Bus Org 1.002**
Limited partners, business organizations, **Bus Org 1.002**
Limited partnerships, business organizations, **Bus Org 1.002**
Loan limit, business development corporations, **Bus Org 23.051**
Local exchange telephone service, **Util 51.002**
Long run incremental cost, telecommunications, **Util 51.002**
Loop resale, telecommunications, **Util 60.041**
Low income electric customer, rates and charges, system benefit fund, **Util 39.903**
Low pressure gathering system, gas utilities, pipes and pipelines, sour gas, **Util 121.451**
Major change,
  Electricity, rates, **Util 36.101**
  Gas utilities, rates, **Util 104.101**
  Telecommunications, rates, **Util 53.101**

WORDS AND PHRASES—Cont'd
Majority in interest,
  Limited partnerships,
    Advancements, expenses and expenditures, **Bus Org 8.104**
    Elections, **Bus Org 8.103**
  Partnerships, **Bus Org 151.001**
    Winding up, **Bus Org 11.057**
Managerial official, business organizations, **Bus Org 1.002**
Managers, business organizations, **Bus Org 1.002**
Mandatory application date, business organizations, **Bus Org 401.001**
Market power abuses, electricity, customer choice, **Util 39.157**
Market power mitigation plan, electricity, customer choice, installed generation capacity, **Util 39.156**
Market value, electricity, competition, stranded costs, recovery, **Util 39.251**
Markets, telecommunications, incumbent local exchange companies, **Util 65.001**
Mechanized equipment, underground facilities, excavations, **Util 251.001**
Member city, municipal power agencies, stranded costs, recovery, customer choice, **Util 40.059**
Members,
  Business development corporations, **Bus Org 23.051**
  Business organizations, **Bus Org 1.002**
  Electric cooperative corporations, **Util 161.002**
  Limited liability companies, derivative actions, **Bus Org 101.451**
  Nonprofit corporations, unincorporated nonprofit associations, **Bus Org 252.001**
  Telephone cooperative corporations, **Util 162.003**
Membership capital, cooperative associations, **Bus Org 251.001**
Membership interest, business organizations, **Bus Org 1.002**
Mergers, business organizations, **Bus Org 1.002**
Merging domestic entities, business organizations, holding companies, merger and consolidation, **Bus Org 10.005**
Meters, utilities, testing, **Util 182.101**
Military bases, electricity, rates and charges, **Util 36.354**
Military bases aggregators, electricity, **Util 39.3535**
Minor change, telecommunication, small local exchange companies, **Util 53.301**
Municipal aggregator, electricity, registration, **Util 39.354**
Municipal electric utility, **Util 181.041**
Municipally owned utility, **Util 11.003**
  Gas utilities, **Util 101.003**
National electric safety code, electricity, **Util 181.045**

WORDS AND PHRASES—Cont'd
National securities exchanges, business organizations, **Bus Org 1.002**
Natural gas technology, electricity, generation, **Util 39.9044**
Net assets, business organizations, **Bus Org 21.002**
Net income, gas utilities, computation of rates, **Util 104.055**
Net savings, cooperative associations, **Bus Org 251.001**
New on site generation, stranded costs, electricity, competition, recovery, **Util 39.252**
Noncode organization, business organizations, **Bus Org 1.002**
Nonfiling entity, business organizations, **Bus Org 1.002**
Nonprofit associations,
  Business organizations, **Bus Org 1.002**
  Unincorporated nonprofit associations, **Bus Org 252.001**
Nonprofit corporations, business organizations, **Bus Org 1.002, 22.001**
Nonprofit entity, business organizations, **Bus Org 1.002**
Nonsubmetered master metered utility services, apartment houses, heating and cooling, **Util 184.051**
NonUnited States entities, business organizations, **Bus Org 1.002**
NonUnited States jurisdictions, business organizations, **Bus Org 1.002**
Nuclear decommissioning trust, atomic energy, **Util 39.206**
Nuclear generating unit, atomic energy, decommissioning, **Util 39.206**
Nursing facilities, electricity, priorities and preferences, **Util 38.072**
Obligations,
  Electric cooperative corporations, **Util 161.002**
  Municipal power agencies, **Util 163.051**
Officers, business organizations, **Bus Org 1.002**
Offices,
  Assumed or fictitious names, **Bus & C 71.002**
  Public utilities, **Util 11.003**
Official capacity, business organizations, indemnity, **Bus Org 8.001**
Operator service, telecommunications, **Util 55.081**
Operators, underground facilities, excavations, **Util 251.001**
Orders,
  Gas utilities, **Util 101.003**
  Public utilities, **Util 11.003**
Ordinary care, nonprofit corporations, **Bus Org 22.001**
Ordinary corporation, close corporations, **Bus Org 21.701**
Organizations, business organizations, **Bus Org 1.002**
Original cost,
  Electricity, computation of rates, **Util 36.053**

WORDS AND PHRASES—Cont'd
Original cost—Cont'd
  Gas utilities, investments, **Util 104.053**
  Telecommunications, return on investments, **Util 53.053**
Other limited partnership provisions, partnerships, limited partnerships (Revised Act), **Bus Org 153.001**
Other partnership provisions, partnerships, **Bus Org 152.001**
Owners, business organizations, **Bus Org 1.002**
Ownership interest, business organizations, **Bus Org 1.002**
Parents, business organizations, **Bus Org 1.002**
Participating shares,
  Corporations, fundamental business transactions, **Bus Org 21.451**
  Real estate investment trusts, fundamental business transactions, **Bus Org 200.401**
Partners, business organizations, **Bus Org 1.002**
Partnership agreements, **Bus Org 151.001**
Partnership interest, business organizations, **Bus Org 1.002**
Partnerships,
  Assumed or fictitious names, **Bus & C 71.002**
  Business organizations, **Bus Org 1.002**
Party line, telecommunications, emergencies, **Util 186.041**
Party to the merger, business organizations, **Bus Org 1.002**
Patron, telephone cooperative corporations, **Util 162.003**
Patronage dividends, cooperative associations, **Bus Org 251.001**
Pay per call information services, telecommunications, automated dial announcing devices, rates, **Util 55.127**
Pecuniary interest, public utility commission, **Util 12.154**
Per call blocking, telecommunications, **Util 55.101**
Per line blocking, telecommunications, **Util 55.101**
Period of duration, business organizations, **Bus Org 1.002**
Permanent residential or business premises, telecommunications, **Util 56.201**
Personal information, public utilities, confidentiality, **Util 182.051**
Persons,
  Agriculture gas users, **Util 123.022**
  Assumed or fictitious names, business and commerce, professions and occupations, **Bus & C 71.002**
  Business combinations, **Bus Org 21.601**
  Business organizations, **Bus Org 1.002**
  Cable television, **Util 181.101**
  Gas utilities, **Util 101.003**
  Natural gas pipelines, **Util 121.001**
  Public utilities, **Util 11.003, 11.0042**

WORDS AND PHRASES—Cont'd
Plans, electricity, customer choice, installed generation capacity, mitigation, **Util 39.156**
Political subdivision aggregator, electricity, registration, **Util 39.3545**
Political subdivisions, telecommunications, extended area service, **Util 55.023**
Power generation company, **Util 31.002**
  Atomic energy, decommissioning, **Util 39.206**
Power marketer, electricity, **Util 31.002**
Power region, electricity, **Util 31.002**
Predecessor enterprise, business organizations, indemnity, **Bus Org 8.001**
Prepaid calling card company, telecommunications, **Util 55.253**
Prepaid calling services, telecommunications, **Util 55.253**
Presidents, business organizations, **Bus Org 1.002**
Pricing flexibility, telecommunications, **Util 51.002**
Prior law, business organizations, **Bus Org 401.001**
Private entities, electricity, joint powers agencies, **Util 163.001**
Private network services, telecommunications,
  Designated entities, **Util 58.252**
  Educational and medical entities, **Util 59.071**
Proceedings,
  Business organizations, indemnity, **Bus Org 8.001**
  Gas utilities, **Util 101.003**
  Public utilities, **Util 11.003**
Professional associations,
  Business organizations, **Bus Org 1.002**
  Professional entities, **Bus Org 301.003**
Professional corporations,
  Business organizations, **Bus Org 1.002**
  Professional entities, **Bus Org 301.003**
Professional entities, business organizations, **Bus Org 1.002, 301.003**
Professional individuals, business organizations, **Bus Org 1.002**
Professional limited liability companies, business organizations, **Bus Org 1.002**
Professional services, business organizations, **Bus Org 1.002, 301.003**
Property, business organizations, **Bus Org 1.002**
Providers,
  Gas utilities, termination of service, **Util 104.258**
  Telecommunications, pay telephones, **Util 55.171**
Providers of last resort, telecommunications, **Util 54.301**
Provisional director, close corporations, actions and proceedings, **Bus Org 21.751**
Public entities, electricity, joint powers agencies, **Util 163.001**

WORDS AND PHRASES—Cont'd
Public retail customer, electricity, state, sales, royalties, in kind, **Util 35.101**
Public right of way, television and radio, franchises, state, **Util 66.002**
Public utilities, **Util 11.004**
  Continuity of service, **Util 186.001**
  Railroad, right of way, **Util 186.051**
  Records, **Util 14.151**
  Telecommunications, **Util 51.002**
Publish, telecommunications, fraud, **Util 186.031**
Purchased power market value, electricity, competition, stranded costs, recovery, **Util 39.251**
Qualified costs, electricity,
  Hurricanes, reconstruction costs, **Util 39.460**
  Restoration, bonds, **Util 36.403**
  Securities, competition, **Util 39.302**
Qualifying cogenerator, electricity, **Util 31.002**
Qualifying facilities, electricity, **Util 31.002**
Railroad right of way, public utilities, **Util 186.051**
Railroads, public utilities, right of way, **Util 186.051**
Ratemaking proceeding, public utilities, **Util 11.003**
Rates,
  Electric cooperative corporations, competition, **Util 41.002**
  Electricity, **Util 31.002**
  Gas utilities, **Util 101.003**
  Public utilities, **Util 11.003**
Real estate investment trusts, business organizations, **Bus Org 1.002, 200.001**
Recreational vehicles, electricity, sales, **Util 184.031**
Registrants, assumed or fictitious names, business and commerce, professions and occupations, **Bus & C 71.002**
Regulated companies, telecommunications, incumbent local exchange companies, **Util 65.001**
Regulatory assets, electricity, securities, competition, **Util 39.302**
Regulatory authorities,
  Gas utilities, **Util 101.003**
  Public utilities, **Util 11.003**
Renewable energy technology, electricity, **Util 39.904**
Representatives,
  Assumed or fictitious names, business and commerce, professions and occupations, **Bus & C 71.002**
  Business organizations, indemnity, **Bus Org 8.001**
Represented domestic entities, registered agents, **Bus Org 5.200**
Represented entities, registered agents, **Bus Org 5.200**
Respondents, business organizations, indemnity, **Bus Org 8.001**
Responsible organization, dissenting shareholders, **Bus Org 10.352**

WORDS AND PHRASES—Cont'd
Retail customer, electricity, **Util 31.002**
Retail electric customers, atomic energy, decommissioning, **Util 39.206**
Retail electric providers, **Util 31.002**
  Deceptive trade practices and consumer protection, **Util 17.002**
Retail electric utility, certificates of convenience and necessity, **Util 37.001**
Retail stranded costs, electricity, competition, recovery, **Util 39.251**
Return of capital, partnerships, limited partnerships (Revised Act), **Bus Org 153.208**
Routine maintenance, underground facilities, exemptions, notice, excavations, **Util 251.156**
Rural areas, electric cooperative corporations, **Util 161.002**
Sale of all or substantially all of the assets,
  Corporations, fundamental business transactions, **Bus Org 21.451**
  Nonprofit corporations, **Bus Org 22.252**
  Real estate investment trusts, fundamental business transactions, **Bus Org 200.401**
Saturday notification, underground facilities, excavations, **Util 251.001**
Savings returns, cooperative associations, **Bus Org 251.001**
Secretaries, business organizations, **Bus Org 1.002**
Secured facility, underground facilities, excavations, **Util 251.001**
Separately metered, electricity, **Util 31.002**
Separation, telecommunications, **Util 51.002**
Service providers,
  Electricity, deceptive trade practices and consumer protection, **Util 17.002**
  Telecommunications, deceptive trade practices and consumer protection, **Util 17.002, 64.002**
Service site, gas utilities, public retail customers, **Util 104.2545**
Services,
  Gas utilities, **Util 101.003**
  Public utilities, **Util 11.003**
Share acquisition date, business combinations, **Bus Org 21.601**
Share dividend, business organizations, **Bus Org 21.002**
Shareholders,
  Business organizations, **Bus Org 1.002**
  Close corporations, actions and proceedings, **Bus Org 21.751**
  Corporations, derivative actions, **Bus Org 21.551**
Shareholders agreement, close corporations, **Bus Org 21.701**
Shares,
  Business organizations, **Bus Org 1.002**

WORDS AND PHRASES—Cont'd
Shares—Cont'd
  Corporations,
    Fundamental business transactions, **Bus Org 21.451**
    Preemptive rights, **Bus Org 21.202**
  Real estate investment trusts, fundamental business transactions, **Bus Org 200.401**
Signatures, business organizations, **Bus Org 1.002**
Small commercial customer, electricity, competition, rates and charges, **Util 39.202**
Solar energy devices, rating, **Util 185.001**
Sour gas pipeline facilities, **Util 121.451**
Stand alone residential local exchange voice service, telecommunications, incumbent local exchange companies, **Util 65.001**
State agencies,
  Gas utilities, **Util 101.003**
  Nonprofit corporations, audits and auditors, **Bus Org 22.356**
Stated capital, business organizations, **Bus Org 21.002**
Stranded cost, electricity, competition, recovery, **Util 39.251**
Stranded investment, electric cooperative corporations, competition, **Util 41.002**
Subscribers, business organizations, **Bus Org 1.002**
Subscriptions, business organizations, **Bus Org 1.002**
Subsidiaries, business organizations, **Bus Org 1.002, 21.601**
Successor entities, television and radio, franchises, state, **Util 66.004**
Successor utilities, telecommunications, **Util 54.301**
Suppliers,
  Agriculture gas users, **Util 123.022**
  Gas utilities, pipes and pipelines, school buildings and grounds, tests, **Util 121.501**
Supplying utility, recreational vehicle parks, electricity, **Util 184.031**
Surplus, business organizations, **Bus Org 21.002**
Surviving entity subsidiaries, business organizations, holding companies, merger and consolidation, **Bus Org 10.005**
System restoration costs, electricity, bonds, **Util 36.402**
Telecommunications number portability, **Util 60.081**
Telecommunications provider, **Util 51.002**
Telecommunications services, fraud, **Util 186.031**
Telecommunications utility, deceptive trade practices and consumer protection, **Util 17.002, 64.002**
Telegraph company, **Util 181.061**
Telegraph corporations, **Util 181.081**

WORDS AND PHRASES—Cont'd
Telemedicine center, telecommunications, private network services, **Util 58.252, 59.071**
Telephone cooperative, **Util 162.003**
Telephone corporation, **Util 181.081**
Tenants, central heating and cooling, **Util 184.051**
Terminated entity, business organizations, **Bus Org 11.001**
Terminated filing entity, business organizations, **Bus Org 11.001**
Test, utility meters, **Util 182.101**
Test year,
  Gas utilities, **Util 101.003**
  Public utilities, **Util 11.003**
Texas trade associations, public utilities, office of public utility counsel, conflict of interest, **Util 13.042**
Tier 1 local exchange company, telecommunications, **Util 51.002**
Trade associations, public utilities, **Util 11.003**
Transfers, partnerships, **Bus Org 152.001**
Transition bonds, electricity,
  Competition, **Util 39.302**
  Hurricanes, reconstruction costs, **Util 39.460**
  Restoration, **Util 36.403**
Transition charges, electricity,
  Hurricanes, reconstruction costs, **Util 39.460**
  Restoration, bonds, **Util 36.403**
  Securities, competition, **Util 39.302**
Transition property, electricity, securities, competition, **Util 39.302**
Transitioning companies, telecommunications, incumbent local exchange companies, **Util 65.001**

WORDS AND PHRASES—Cont'd
Transmission and distribution utility, electricity, **Util 31.002**
Transmission service, electricity, **Util 31.002**
Treasurers, business organizations, **Bus Org 1.002**
Treasury shares, business organizations, **Bus Org 21.002**
Uncertificated ownership interest, business organizations, **Bus Org 1.002**
Underground facility, excavations, **Util 251.001**
Utilities, **Util 11.004**
  Aged persons, delay in payment, **Util 182.001**
  Central heating and cooling, apartment houses, **Util 184.051**
  Deposits, customers, **Util 183.001**
  Meters, testing, **Util 182.101**
  Municipalities, protection, **Util 181.901**
  Telecommunications, **Util 51.002**
Utilities system, joint ownership, public entities, **Util 164.005**
Utility payment date, public utilities, credit reports, payment, **Util 17.008**
Vice presidents, business organizations, **Bus Org 1.002**
Video programming,
  Franchises, state, **Util 66.002**
  Telecommunications, broadcaster safeguards, **Util 62.002**
Video service providers, franchises, state, **Util 66.002**
Video services, franchises, state, **Util 66.002**
Violations, underground facilities, excavations, **Util 251.001**

WORDS AND PHRASES—Cont'd
Voice over Internet protocol services, telecommunications, **Util 51.002**
Voluntary decision to wind up, business organizations, **Bus Org 11.001**
Voluntary winding up, business organizations, **Bus Org 11.001**
Voting shares,
  Business combinations, **Bus Org 21.601**
  Corporations, fundamental business transactions, **Bus Org 21.451**
  Real estate investment trusts, fundamental business transactions, **Bus Org 200.401**
Winding up, business organizations, **Bus Org 11.001**
Withdrawals, partnerships, **Bus Org 152.001**
Withdrawn partner, partnerships, **Bus Org 152.001**
Writings, business organizations, **Bus Org 1.002**
Written, business organizations, **Bus Org 1.002**

WORK STOPPAGES
Labor Disputes, generally, this index

WORLD WIDE WEB
Internet, generally, this index

WRITINGS
Corporations, this index
Foreign Corporations, this index

WRITS
Executions, generally, this index
Garnishment, generally, this index
Injunctions, generally, this index

†